Auditing and Reporting

2019–20

The full text of UK Auditing, Ethical and
Quality Control Standards and related guidance
extant at 30 April 2019

Auditing and Reporting
2019–20

The full text of UK Auditing, Ethical and
Quality Control Standards and related guidance
extant at 30 April 2019

✦ **Croner-i**
HR · Tax · H&S · Audit & Accounting

Disclaimer

This publication is sold with the understanding that neither the publisher nor the authors, with regard to this publication, are engaged in rendering legal or professional services. The material contained in this publication neither purports, nor is intended to be, advice on any particular matter.

Although this publication incorporates a considerable degree of standardisation, subjective judgment by the user, based on individual circumstances, is indispensable. This publication is an aid and cannot be expected to replace such judgment.

Neither the publisher nor the authors can accept any responsibility or liability to any person, whether a purchaser of this publication or not, in respect of anything done or omitted to be done by any such person in reliance, whether sole or partial, upon the whole or any part of the contents of this publication.

© 2019 Croner-i Ltd

Published by Croner-i Ltd
240 Blackfriars Road
London SE1 8NW
Telephone: 0800 231 5199
E-mail: client.experience@croneri.co.uk
Website: croneri.co.uk

ISBN 978-1-78887-284-3

Telephone Helpline Disclaimer Notice

Where purchasers of this publication also have access to any Telephone Helpline Service operated by Croner-i Ltd, then Croner-i's total liability to contract, tort (including negligence, or breach of statutory duty) misrepresentation, restitution or otherwise with respect to any claim arising out of its acts or alleged omissions in the provision of the Helpline Service shall be limited to the yearly subscription fee paid by the Claimant.

No responsibility for loss occasioned to any person acting or refraining from action as a result of any material in this publication can be accepted by the author or publisher.

Material is contained in this publication for which copyright is acknowledged. Permission to reproduce such material cannot be granted by the publisher and application must be made to the copyright holder.

British Library Cataloguing-in-Publication Data

A catalogue record for this book is available from the British Library.

Typeset by Innodata Inc., India.

Printed and bound by L.E.G.O. S.p.A. – Italy

Contents

		Page
Part One	**The Financial Reporting Council**	1
	Professional scepticism – Establishing a common understanding and reaffirming its central role in delivering audit quality	3
	Scope and Authority of Audit and Assurance Pronouncements 2016	19
Part Two	**Ethical Standard**	27
RES	Revised Ethical Standard 2016	29
Part Three	**International Standard on Quality Control (UK)**	141
ISQC 1	ISQC (UK) 1 (Revised June 2016) Quality Control for Firms that Perform Audits and Reviews of Financial Statements, and other Assurance and Related Services Engagements (Updated July 2017)	143
Part Four	**International Standards on Auditing (UK)**	179
ISA 200	Overall Objectives of the Independent Auditor and the Conduct of an Audit in Accordance with International Standards on Auditing (UK) (Revised June 2016)	181
ISA 210	Agreeing the Terms of Audit Engagements (Revised June 2016) (Updated July 2017)	207
ISA 220	Quality Control for an Audit of Financial Statements (Revised June 2016) (Updated July 2017)	229
ISA 230	Audit Documentation (Revised June 2016)	247
ISA 240	The Auditor's Responsibilities Relating to Fraud in an Audit of Financial Statements (Revised June 2016) (Updated July 2017)	259
ISA 250A	Section A – Consideration of Laws and Regulations in an Audit of Financial Statements (Revised December 2017)	299
ISA 250B	Section B – The Auditor's Statutory Right and Duty to Report to Regulators of Public Interest Entities and Regulators of Other Entities in the Financial Sector (Revised June 2016)	345
ISA 260	Communication With Those Charged With Governance (Revised June 2016) (Updated July 2017)	367
ISA 265	Communicating Deficiencies in Internal Control to Those Charged With Governance and Management	401
ISA 300	Planning an Audit of Financial Statements (Revised June 2016)	411

Page

ISA 315	Identifying and Assessing the Risks of Material Misstatement Through Understanding of the Entity and Its Environment (Revised June 2016)	423
ISA 320	Materiality in Planning and Performing an Audit (Revised June 2016)	471
ISA 330	The Auditor's Responses to Assessed Risks (Revised July 2017)	479
ISA 402	Audit Considerations Relating to an Entity Using a Service Organisation	501
ISA 450	Evaluation of Misstatements Identified During the Audit (Revised June 2016) (Updated July 2017)	521
ISA 500	Audit Evidence (Updated July 2017)	533
ISA 501	Audit Evidence – Specific Considerations for Selected Items	549
ISA 505	External Confirmations (Updated July 2017)	559
ISA 510	Initial Audit Engagements – Opening Balances (Revised June 2016)	569
ISA 520	Analytical Procedures	583
ISA 530	Audit Sampling	591
ISA 540	Auditing Accounting Estimates, Including Fair Value Accounting Estimates, and Related Disclosures (Revised June 2016)	607
ISA 540	Auditing Accounting Estimates and Related Disclosures (Revised December 2018)	645
ISA 550	Related Parties	737
ISA 560	Subsequent Events	761
ISA 570	Going Concern (Revised June 2016)	773
ISA 580	Written Representations	805
ISA 600	Special Considerations – Audits of Group Financial Statements (Including the Work of Component Auditors) (Revised June 2016)	819
ISA 610	Using the Work of Internal Auditors (Revised June 2013)	865
ISA 620	Using the Work of an Auditor's Expert (Revised June 2016)	885
ISA 700	Forming an Opinion and Reporting on Financial Statements (Revised June 2016)	903
ISA 701	Communicating Key Audit Matters in the Independent Auditor's Report	959
ISA 705	Modifications to the Opinion in the Independent Auditor's Report (Revised June 2016)	983
ISA 706	Emphasis of Matter Paragraphs and Other Matter Paragraphs in the Independent Auditor's Report (Revised June 2016)	1,009

Page

ISA 710	Comparative Information – Corresponding Figures and Comparative Financial Statements	1,027
ISA 720	The Auditor's Responsibilities Relating to Other Information (Revised June 2016)	1,045
ISA 800	Special Considerations – Audits of Financial Statement prepared in accordance with Special Purpose Frameworks (October 2016)	1,093
ISA 805	Special Considerations – Audits of Single Financial Statements and Specific Elements, Accounts or Items of a Financial Statement (October 2016)	1,113
	Glossary of Terms (auditing and ethics) (2018)	1,137
Part Five	**Practice Notes**	1,169
PN 10	SORP: PN10 Audit of financial statements of public sector bodies in the United Kingdom (now issued by the Public Audit Forum)	1,171
PN 11	The audit of charities in the United Kingdom (Revised) (November 2017)	1,233
PN 14	The audit of housing associations in the United Kingdom	1,301
PN 15	The audit of occupational pension schemes in the United Kingdom (Revised) (November 2017)	1,345
PN 19	The audit of banks and building societies in the United Kingdom (Revised)	1,407
PN 20	The Audit of insurers in the United Kingdom (Revised) (2017)	1,497
PN 23	Special considerations in auditing financial instruments	1,615
Part Six	**Bulletins**	1,677
2006/5	The combined code on corporate governance: requirements of auditors under the Listing Rules of the Financial Services Authority and the Irish Stock Exchange	1,679
2008/1	Audit issues when financial market conditions are difficult and credit facilities may be restricted	1,705
2008/5	Auditor's reports on revised accounts and reports in the United Kingdom	1,715
2008/9	Miscellaneous reports by auditors required by the United Kingdom Companies Act 2006	1,737
2008/10	Going concern issues during the current economic conditions	1,767
2009/4	Developments in corporate governance affecting the responsibilities of auditors of UK companies	1,797
2010/1	XBRL tagging of information in audited financial statements – Guidance for auditors	1,813
Bulletin 2	Guidance for reporting accountants of stakeholder pension schemes in the United Kingdom	1,819

		Page
CAAS	Providing Assurance on Client Assets to the Financial Conduct Authority	1,831
Compendium	Compendium of illustrative auditor's reports on United Kingdom private sector financial statements for periods commencing on or after 17 June 2016	1,903
2017 Bulletin	The Auditor's Association with Preliminary Announcements made in accordance with UK Listing Rules (2017) (December 2017)	1,957
Part Seven	**ICAEW Guidance on Auditing and Reporting**	1,973
TECH 04/02AAF	Management Representation Letters: Explanatory Note (updated March 2018)	1,975
TECH 01/03AAF	The Audit Report and Auditors' Duty of Care to Third Parties (updated May 2018)	1,981
TECH 01/06AAF	Assurance reports on internal controls of service organisations made available to third parties (updated July 2016)	1,993
TECH 02/07AAF	A framework for assurance reports on third party operations	2,051
TECH 01/10AAF	Framework document for accountants' reports on grant claims	2,085
TECH 01/11AAF	Reporting to the Audit Bureau of Circulations Ltd (ABC)	2,145
TECH 10/12AAF	Reporting to Third Parties – (Audit 1/01 Updated)	2,155
TECH 04/13AAF	Assurance Reporting on Relevant Trustees (Relevant Trustee Supplement to ICAEW AAF 02/07)	2,173
TECH 07/13BL	Exemption from Audit by Parent Guarantee	2,195
TECH 09/13AAF	Assurance Review Engagements on Historical Financial Statements (updated March 2019)	2,205
TECH 09/14BL	Accountants' Reports on Commercial Property Service Charge Accounts	2,229
TECH 10/14AAF	Receipt of information in confidence by auditors (supersedes AUDIT 02/99)	2,261
TECH 13/14AAF	Auditing implications of FRS 102 transition (updated November 2017)	2,267
TECH 16/15AAF	Solicitors Regulation Authority (SRA) Accounts Rules: interim guidance for reporting accountants following changes to the accountant's report requirements	2,317
TECH 02/16AAF	Reporting to regulators on regulatory accounts – (update to AUDIT 05/03)	2,357
TECH 07/16AAF	Chartered Accountants' reports on the Compilation of Financial Information of Incorporated Entities (revised update of AAF 02/10)	2,401
TECH 08/16AAF	Chartered Accountants' reports on the Compilation of historical Financial Information of Unincorporated Entities (revised update of AAF 03/10)	2,415

Page

TECH 12/16AAF   Assurance Reporting on Master Trusts
(Master Trusts Supplement to ICAEW AAF 02/07)
(Amended 30 November 2016)   2,427

Part Eight   **Standards for Investment Reporting (SIRs)**   2,445

SIR 1000   Investment Reporting Standards applicable to all
engagements in connection with an investment circular   2,447

SIR 2000   Investment Reporting Standards applicable to public
reporting engagements on historical financial
information (Revised)   2,475

SIR 3000   Investment Reporting Standards applicable to public
reporting engagements on profit forecasts   2,511

SIR 4000   Investment Reporting Standards applicable to public
reporting engagements on pro forma financial
information   2,545

SIR 5000   Investment Reporting Standards applicable to Public
Reporting Engagements on financial information
reconciliations under the Listing Rules   2,569

Part Nine   **Statement of Standards for Reporting Accountants**   2,597

ISRE 2410   ISRE (UK and Ireland) 2410 – Review of interim
financial information performed by the Independent
Auditor of the Entity   2,599

Preface

This book presents, in one convenient bound volume, the UK auditing standards, ethical and quality control standards, FRC Audit Bulletins, Practice Notes and Standards for Investment Reporting, along with key ICAEW guidance, extant at 30 April 2019. Where relevant these have been updated for amendments made since the documents were originally issued.

The selection of documents for inclusion in this volume comes with some challenges, as the body of auditing literature tends to accumulate, with new requirements or pieces of guidance issued more quickly than they are withdrawn. Accordingly, an editorial decision has been taken to include only ISAs and ICAEW guidance issued or revised within the past ten years. All FRC Practice Notes and Bulletins extant at 30 April 2019 have, however, been included. Older and recently withdrawn documents as listed in the table below are available online on *Croner-i Tax and Accounting* along with all the standards and guidance in this book and many other useful auditing tools and resources.

As in previous years, footnotes and editorial notes have been added to refer to any major changes to legal or other references included in standards. However, these are not intended to provide a comprehensive summary.

If you have a comment on the editorial content of Auditing and Reporting 2019–20, please email your views to us at contentqueries@croneri.co.uk or phone 0800 231 5199.

Julia Bowyer ACA

Content Manager, Audit and Accounting

Croner-i Limited

Standards and guidance available online

	Description	Link to Croner-i Tax and Accounting
International Standards on Auditing (UK)		
UK ISAs extant at 30 April 2019 applicable for audits of financial statements commencing before 15 December 2017:		
ISA 250A	Section A – Consideration of Laws and Regulations in an Audit of Financial Statements (Revised June 2016)	https://library.croneri.co.uk/isauk250ar1
ISA 330	The Auditor's Responses to Assessed Risks (Revised June 2016)	https://library.croneri.co.uk/isauk330r1
Practice notes (included in 2018–19 edition and since withdrawn)		
PN 26	Guidance on smaller entity audit documentation	https://library.croneri.co.uk/pn26
ICAEW Guidance on Auditing and Reporting (older than 10 years)		
TECH 02/01AAF	Requests for references on clients' financial status and their ability to service loans	https://library.croneri.co.uk/audit02-01
TECH 04/03AAF	Access to working papers by investigating accountants	https://library.croneri.co.uk/audit04-03
TECH 03/04AAF	Auditing implications of IFRS transition	https://library.croneri.co.uk/audit03-04
TECH 02/06AAF	Identifying and managing certain risks arising from the inclusion of reports from auditors and accountants in prospectuses	https://library.croneri.co.uk/aaf02-06
TECH 04/06AAF	Assurance engagements: management of risk and liability	https://library.croneri.co.uk/aaf04-06

Standards and guidance available online

	Description	Link to Croner-I Tax and Accounting
International Standards on Auditing (UK)		
UK ISAs (2019) as at 30 April 2019 applicable for audits of financial statements commencing before 1 December 2019:		
ISA 250A	Section A – Consideration of Laws and Regulations in an Audit of Financial Statements (Revised June 2016)	https://library.croner-i.co.uk/isaak250a-1
ISA 330	The Auditor's Responses to Assessed Risks (Revised June 2016)	https://library.croner-i.co.uk/isaak330-1
Practice notes (included in 2018-19 edition and since withdrawn)		
PN 26	Guidance on smaller entity audit documentation	https://library.croner-i.co.uk/pn26
ICAEW Guidance on Auditing and Reporting (other than fee levy)		
TECH 02/01AAF	Request for references on clients' financial status and their ability to service loans	https://library.croner-i.co.uk/audit02-01
TECH 02/04AF	Access to working papers by investigating accountants	https://library.croner-i.co.uk/audit04-00
TECH 09/04AF	Auditing implications of IFRS transition	https://library.croner-i.co.uk/audit-01
TECH 02/08AF	Identifying and managing certain risks arising from the inclusion of reports from auditors and accountants in prospectuses	https://library.croner-i.co.uk/audit02-08
TECH 04/06AAF	Assurance engagements on internal control and reliability	https://library.croner-i.co.uk/audit04-06

Part One

The Financial Reporting Council

Professional scepticism – Establishing a common understanding and reaffirming its central role in delivering audit quality

(March 2012)

Contents

Section 1 – Introduction

Section 2 – Exploring the roots of scepticism and identifying lessons for its role in the conduct of an audit

Section 3 – Scientific scepticism and the scientific method

Section 4 – The origins of the modern audit

Section 5 – Conclusions about professional scepticism in the audit

Section 6 – Fostering conditions necessary for auditors to demonstrate the appropriate degree of professional scepticism

Section 7 – Taking these matters forward

Section 1 – Introduction

This paper sets out the APB's considered views on the nature of auditor scepticism and its role in the audit. Given the significance of scepticism to the quality of individual audits, and to the value of audit more generally, we believe that this document is an important point of reference on this topic and one which we hope all auditors will consider with great care.

It is written in an unusual format for an APB document, being much more discursive than is customary and drawing analogies from a diverse group of areas. This is because we believe that what is meant by scepticism needs to be more broadly understood and that drawing these analogies will assist in broadening that understanding. We are also keen to stimulate and provide input to an international debate on the issue of scepticism and believe that this broader and more discursive approach will provide a valuable input to that debate.

This document builds on the APB Discussion Paper published in August 2010 "Auditor Scepticism: Raising the Bar" and the subsequent Feedback Paper published in March 2011, which summarised the comments received and outlined the actions that the APB, and other parts of the FRC, intended to take in light of the responses received.

The Feedback Paper noted the following[1]:

- Responses suggested a wide range of views about what the initial mindset should be and raised concerns for the APB that there is a lack of consensus about the nature of professional scepticism and its role in the conduct of an audit.

- The APB did not accept that the auditor's role is limited to ensuring that management have appropriate evidence to support its assertions if this means accepting the evidence management present without subjecting it to robust challenge and comparison to alternative sources of evidence.

- The APB questioned whether a "neutral mindset", or indeed just an "inquiring mind", is appropriate for an auditor. The auditor's mindset is applied during audit planning to assess the risk of misstatement of the financial statements and such risk assessments determine the nature and extent of audit evidence to be obtained. It is also applied in assessing the validity of accounting estimates that are subject both to significant uncertainties and to considerable management judgment.

The first of the areas in which the APB proposed to undertake further work was ensuring that there is a consistent understanding of the nature of professional scepticism and its role in the conduct of an audit.

Section 2 considers the philosophical origins of scepticism in ancient Greece and how it later influenced scepticism in the scientific method that began to flourish in the 17th Century. The relationship between scepticism and the disposition to believe or disbelieve is explored as well as the influences of evidence and behaviours on that disposition.

Section 3 seeks to provide insight into the mind-set required to develop the audit strategy and plan and to evaluate the audit evidence obtained, by demonstrating how another learning – science – has developed a sceptical approach that now commands respect.

---

[1] See "Auditor scepticism: Raising the bar: Feedback Statement" – March 2011 http://www.frc.org.uk/apb/publications/pub2343.html.

Section 4 seeks to provide further insight into the mindset of the auditor by considering the nature of the agency relationships, and the resultant need for assurance, that gave rise to early auditing traditions in manorial households from the 14th Century.

Section 5 sets out the APB's conclusions from the foregoing analysis as to what a sceptical audit looks like. It suggests that professional scepticism is the cornerstone of audit quality – it defines the quality of each audit judgment and through these the overall effectiveness of the audit in meeting the needs of shareholders and other stakeholders.

Section 6 sets out the APB's views about the conditions that are necessary for auditors to demonstrate the appropriate degree of professional scepticism. It highlights the APB's expectations of individual auditors, engagement teams, audit firms and of the supporting role that can be played by audit committees, management and others.

Finally, Section 7 sets out how the APB proposes to take these matters forward. Professional Scepticism

Section 2 – Exploring the roots of scepticism and identifying lessons for its role in the conduct of an audit

Scepticism is derived from the Greek word "σκέψις" (skepsis), meaning[2]: *examination, inquiry into, hesitation or doubt, especially of the Sceptics or Pyrrhone philosophers.* Greek philosophical Scepticism was a school of thought from the 5th Century BC that doubted the certainty of knowledge. From this developed the philosophical viewpoint that it is not possible to gain certain knowledge (truth) about the natural world.

Scepticism in Greek philosophy

Beyond understanding the etymological basis for the modern term "scepticism", what more can we learn from early Greek philosophical scepticism?

- First, the essence of scepticism is doubt and that doubt stimulates informed challenge and inquiry. The sceptics' doubts arose from the many conflicting views that persisted about fundamental issues. Their doubt stimulated them to challenge conventional wisdom and to inquire after a better understanding of the nature of knowledge.

- Second, in the face of doubt they would suspend their judgment about the truth.

- Third, in its extreme forms scepticism is not pragmatic as it may lead to the conclusion that no judgments about the truth can be made[3].

---

[2] *Liddell & Scott Greek-English Lexicon.*

[3] *Bertrand Russell, in his 1958 book: "The Will to Doubt" illustrates such "heroic" scepticism by retelling the following: "A story is told of Pyrrho, the founder of Pyrrhonism (which was the old name for scepticism). He maintained that we never know enough to be sure that one course of action is wiser than another. In his youth, when he was taking his constitutional one afternoon, he saw his teacher in philosophy (from whom he had imbibed his principles) with his head stuck in a ditch, unable to get out. After contemplating him for some time, he walked on, maintaining that there was no sufficient ground for thinking he would do any good by pulling the man out. Others, less sceptical, effected a rescue, and blamed Pyrrho for his heartlessness. But his teacher, true to his principles, praised him for his consistency."*

The disposition to believe or disbelieve and its conditioning influences

Today, scepticism commonly means "doubt as to the truth of some assertion or supposed fact"[4]. Doubt is unbelief, whose antonyms include belief and trust[5]. Neither doubt nor trust need be absolute. Each has expression in different degrees. Uncertainty lies between them and absolute trust (belief) and absolute distrust (disbelief) are at their extremes. Doubt, trust and uncertainty are passive concepts – states of mind. They describe an individual's disposition to believe or disbelieve an assertion.

The actual level of doubt or trust in the state of mind conditions the individual's response. When the levels of both trust and doubt are low, there is uncertainty which either may result in a passive response – the indefinite suspension of judgment – or may stimulate an active inquiry to pursue the truth or falseness of the assertion. The results of that inquiry will further condition the state of mind and the process may be repeated. Only if and when a state of mind of trust or doubt is sufficiently high will the active response – acceptance or rejection of belief in the assertion – ensue.

The disposition to believe or disbelieve an assertion may be conditioned by many influences. These include not only the results of inquiry but also potentially the biases of the individual (whether conscious or sub-conscious) and the individual's perceptions and assessments of their self-interest. These other conditioning influences must be filtered out if objective truth is to be attained.

In the context of audit judgments, it may be helpful to understand the implications of the behavioural rules ("heuristics") underlying human decision-making and judgment processes. A number of heuristics have been proposed to help explain these processes, especially in the face of complex problems or incomplete information. It is also thought that they may, in some circumstances, introduce systematic errors or biases into these processes.

One illustration of these ideas may be found in a recent academic paper[6], which shows that people are less likely to adjust their beliefs in response to evidence that contradicts their optimistic beliefs than to evidence that contradicts their pessimistic beliefs.

What is needed to counteract this is a mechanism to encourage a structured consideration of the alternative point of view. One example of such a mechanism being applied in a financial services context is "reverse stress testing". In this form of stress testing, the directors consider what it would take to make the entity fail and then assess the evidence as to the likelihood of those circumstances arising.

Evidence based theories of knowledge and scientific scepticism

Later Sceptics were more pragmatic, arguing that there were ways of approaching (even if not quite attaining) the absolute truth. The Empirical school of thought proposed that the only or primary source of knowledge is experience gained through the senses. It therefore emphasised the role of empirical (observed)

---

[4] *The Shorter Oxford English Dictionary.*

[5] *See Roget's Thesaurus of synonyms and antonyms: categories 484 (Belief) and 485 (Unbelief: Doubt).*

[6] *See: How unrealistic optimism is maintained in the face of reality, by Sharot, Korn and Dolan, in Nature Neuroscience, Nov 2011. This and earlier research considering the impact of new evidence on existing beliefs is discussed in a recent Research Paper from Societe Generale: In defence of the doom merchants: when hearing isn't listening, Jan 2012 at: http://www.frc.org.uk/images/uploaded/documents/Societe%20Generale%20Research%20Paper%20January%202012.pdf. The Paper suggests that people have a natural tendency to take note of the evidence which backs their own theories and to ignore evidence which contradicts them. If anything, this tendency is exacerbated when they are exhorted to try harder.*

evidence in inducing knowledge rather than deducing knowledge from innate ideas and traditions.

Empiricism was highly influential in the development of science and the scientific method in the 17th Century. Scientific scepticism doubts the veracity of assertions that are not supported by empirical evidence that is reproducible and therefore seeks to exclude other influences from the scientific search for truth.

Evidence, trust and agency in the audit process

An audit is an evidence-based process to assess and report on the truth and fairness of the financial statements prepared by the directors to whom capital resources are entrusted by the shareholders. The audit is entrusted to another agent of the shareholders – the auditor.

This description refers to two features of an audit which are relevant to scepticism – the evidence-based nature of the audit and the entrustment and agency relationships inherent in the audit. The role of scepticism in relation to each of these is explored further below. The evidence-based nature of the process suggests some parallels with, and is explored in the context of, the scientific method and scientific scepticism in Section 3. In Section 4, lessons about the expression of professional scepticism are also identified by considering the nature of the entrustment and agency relationships and the need for assurance that gave rise to the tradition of auditing servants in the manorial estates of the fourteenth century in the origins of the modern audit in the UK.

Section 3 – Scientific scepticism and the scientific method

The scientific method seeks to understand the causes and effects of natural processes by:

- *Empirical observation* of their behaviours in different conditions;

- Postulating how they work (*constructing theories* of cause and effect that are consistent with the observations) – an approach that relies on inductive logic.

- Predicting effects that would necessarily follow from the truth of a theory in specific conditions (*constructing hypotheses*) – an approach that relies on deductive logic.

- *Testing* those hypotheses by considering not only what evidence would support them but also what evidence would falsify them – accordingly, experiments are designed and performed to find such evidence.

- Each step of the process is *transparent and repeatable*, subject to the critical review of other scientists and capable of being challenged and retested by them.

- In the development of scientific knowledge in a new area, there may be several competing theories, each of which has survived hypothesis testing. The advancement of a theory to the status of accepted scientific knowledge requires a *"critical experiment"*, one capable of providing evidence that will prove the superiority of one theory over all the other competing theories.

This process can disprove a postulated theory but cannot absolutely prove it. If testing falsifies a hypothesis, then theories are reassessed in light of the new observations and if necessary new ones are postulated. A theory that survives rigorous testing remains plausible, for the time being. Scientific knowledge is therefore dynamic and constantly subject to challenge.

Prior to the development of the scientific method, knowledge of the natural world was largely based on accepted ancient wisdom (axiomatic truths) and advanced by developing consequential "knowledge" by logical deduction (the deductive method). A critical development in the evolution of the scientific method was the acceptance that there are no axiomatic truths that can be observed and that there is a continuing need to question and challenge all matters that may appear to be so.

Robert Boyle is widely recognised as the father of modern chemistry and an early proponent of the scientific method. His treatise on the new approach is aptly called "The Sceptical Chymist"[7].

Scepticism in the scientific method can be described as a <u>systematic form of continual informed questioning</u> that requires the scientist:

- To <u>critically appraise</u> existing theories, actively looking for alternative plausible mechanisms of cause and effect that are consistent with their rigorous assessment of the empirical (observed) evidence;

- To undertake experiments that are repeatable and transparent, to look for <u>evidence that contradicts rather than supports</u> the validity of any given theory; and

- To <u>suspend judgment</u> about the validity of any given theory (ie to defer making an active decision to believe or disbelieve it) until it has both survived destructive testing and has been subjected to critical experiments the evidence from which makes it is possible to conclude that one theory is superior to all other current plausible theories.

There are many parallels between the scientific method and the audit and, whilst this analogy should, of course, not be taken too far, at a certain level there is much to learn from a consideration of the nature of scientific scepticism and the role it plays in the conduct of the scientific method. Scientific scepticism is the backbone of the scientific method, influencing every judgment in the process of learning and ultimately supporting the whole body of scientific knowledge.

However, the subject matters of scientific and audit inquiry are different in nature. The subject matter of Science is knowledge of the natural world, which experience shows to ordinarily behave in a systematic way. The subject matter of auditing is the outputs from the business performance and reporting systems of the entity, which though usually intended to operate systematically often do not as they are subject to the vagaries of external influences, as well as human error and fraud.

In science, the potential variables are identified and can be controlled and varied individually under laboratory conditions. In the audit, they cannot and the outputs of the business performance and reporting systems of the entity must be observed in real world (multivariate) conditions.

Notwithstanding these limitations to the analogy between the audit and the scientific method, elements of the scientific method suggest critical audit activities which will underpin appropriate scepticism in the audit:

---

[7] *Robert Boyle, 1661: The Sceptical Chymist: or Chymico-Physical Doubts & Paradoxes Touching the Spagyrist's Principles Commonly call'd Hypostatical As they are wont to be Propos'd and Defended by the Generality of Alchemists.*

- Empirical observation *suggests* developing a good understanding of the business of the audited entity and of the environment;

- Constructing falsifiable hypotheses *suggests* actively considering that material misstatements may exist and designing audit tests to identify them, rather than only considering how well the evidence obtained by management supports their conclusion that there are none; and

- Transparency and repeatability *suggest* the importance of documentation in underpinning transparency and repeatability of the audit work to internal reviewers and to external inspectors.

The comparison says less about how far the auditor should go in pursuing these activities:

- When should the active search for risks of material misstatement stop?

- How far should the auditor's understanding be pursued?

- How much testing and stress testing should the auditor undertake?

- When is the evidence sufficient?

The scientific analogy suggests there is no absolute level to which such matters should be pursued. Scientific scepticism is pursued up to the point where other similarly objective scientists would want to go before they accept or reject a hypothesis. In the scientific field, acceptance of a hypothesis only occurs when the level of trust in that hypothesis is approaching virtual certainty. This may not be the most appropriate point to which professional scepticism should be pursued in the audit. This is considered further in the next section in the context of the historical origins of the modern audit in the UK.

Section 4 – The origins of the modern audit

The origins of the modern audit can be seen in the tradition of auditing household servants in manorial estates that developed from the fourteenth century[8]. The auditor was the most trusted servant in the household and all other servants were required to account to the auditor for the resources entrusted to them.

In its simplest form, an account was required from each household servant of all money and other assets entrusted to them – they were "charged" with the assets when placed in their care and "discharged" when the auditor had heard and accepted their account.

When free incorporation joint stock companies were established in the Joint Stock Companies Act of 1844, there were default provisions for auditors to be appointed, that built on these traditions. Under the default provisions, at least one of the auditors should be appointed by the shareholders, their fees should be paid by the company but set by a government agency (the Commissioners of the Treasury) as they saw fit, and their report should be made publicly available. The auditor was neither required to be a shareholder nor a professional accountant but often was a shareholder and frequently employed professional accountants to assist them.

---

[8] See *Be careful what you wish for: How accountants and Congress created the problem of auditor independence*, 2004, Sean M. O'Connor at: *http://www.bc.edu/dam/files/schools/law/lawreviews/journals/bclawr/45_4/01_FMS.htm*.

The Joint Stock Companies Act of 1856 enhanced the earlier default provisions to specifically allow the auditor to employ accountants to assist them at the company's expense and to prohibit the auditor from being a director or an officer of the company and from having any interest in any transaction of the company other than as a shareholder. The absolute requirement that companies should have an audit (initially just for joint stock banks but later extended to all companies) as opposed to optional default provisions, originated in the 1879 Companies Act following the collapse of the City Bank of Glasgow. In time, the practice of appointing shareholders as auditors fell away and public accountants were employed to undertake the role directly.

Looking back, it would seem that, in its origin, the audit was essentially a check, carried out on behalf of a principal by their trusted associate or agent, on the fidelity of other agents to whom the principal's resources were entrusted. The trust that existed between principal and auditor was a critical ingredient, if not the critical ingredient of the audit. The importance of professional skills only came later. The whole rationale for the audit was that the principal could not assume, and therefore sought assurance about, the fidelity of those to whom their assets were entrusted.

This may suggest how far the auditor should pursue professional scepticism in the audit. The strong bond of trust between the principal and the auditor and the principal's need for assurance about the fidelity of those to whom they had entrusted their assets would have determined the mindset of the auditor. That would have guided the appropriate degree of scepticism in the auditor when holding a hearing to question those entrusted with the principal's assets and to assess whether they had given a proper account of their handling of those assets. They would have asked the questions they would expect their principal to ask, they would have challenged where they would expect their principal to challenge and they would have pursued matters until they were satisfied that the evidence would satisfy their principal.

This is perhaps a fair lens through which to understand the necessary degree of scepticism in the modern audit. What would the shareholders (and other stakeholders) expect the auditor to ask, what matters would they expect them to challenge and what evidence would they need to satisfy those challenges?

Whilst fidelity may have been the issue in the 19th Century and much of the 20th Century (and remains an issue in the 21st Century), the development and increased complexity of business activity, and the increased size and reach of such businesses, combined with the arrival of the technological age mean that there are many other areas in relation to which shareholders (and other users) seek information and reassurance. For example, misalignment of their personal interests may simply lead to misalignment of risk taking appetite between the directors and shareholders.

This suggests that whilst the sceptical mindset is a constant, the degree of action taken by a sceptical auditor (by way of inquiry, challenge and testing) is responsive both to the expectations of shareholders (and other stakeholders) and to what emerges as the audit proceeds. This is the "sliding scale" that was referred to in *Auditor Scepticism: Raising the Bar*.

Because of the need to consider their expectations, the perspective of shareholders and other stakeholders (as users) is embedded in the auditing standards in relation to materiality, and scepticism should embed that perspective in the making of all audit judgments. Against this background, the APB believes that when undertaking a modern audit the following factors accentuate the need for the auditor to be especially vigilant and aware of his or her responsibilities for the exercise of professional scepticism:

- There is potential for auditors not to be sceptical or thought not to be sceptical because they are engaged and paid by the company in a way that is relatively detached from shareholders. In addition, they have little, if any, direct contact with shareholders throughout the audit process; as a result, shareholders have no way of observing, and thereby gaining trust in, the audit process. This emphasises the need for strong governance generally and, in particular, the importance of the responsibility that audit committees have in both assessing and communicating to investors whether the auditors have executed a high quality, sceptical audit;

- Auditors necessarily have strong working relationships with management and audit committees, which may lead them to develop trust that may lead to either a lack of, or reduced, scepticism; and

- The audit firms' business models encourage a culture of building strong relationships with audited entities. This introduces the risk of the auditor putting his or her interests ahead of those of shareholders and could lead the audit firm and the auditor to develop trust or self-interest motivations that may compromise either their objectivity or willingness to challenge management to the extent required.

It is perhaps not surprising that auditors often refer to the audited entity as the "client", given the strength of these relationships and the all but formal appointment of the auditor by the directors and not by the shareholders. However, trust in management may compromise the auditor's exercise of scepticism because that trust may colour his/her judgement as to when and where a sceptical approach is required. It is important to lean against unjustified trust developing, just as it is important to address threats to the auditor's objectivity that may arise from the provision of non-audit services – it is interesting to note in this context that the auditor originally was not permitted to have any interest in any transaction with the company.

The factors described above are widely recognised to pose challenges to the reality and perception of auditors' professional integrity (including their objectivity and independence). The need to address these challenges gives rise to a variety of responses that seek to lean against them, including the responsibilities, liabilities and disclosures relating to the audit and the auditor established in the law and professional standards, including the Ethical Standards. This is also one of the principal reasons for the need for the application and demonstration of appropriate professional scepticism in the audit.

Despite the increasing role of audit committees as independent non-executive directors in monitoring and challenging the entity's financial information and controls (in effect as the representatives of the shareholders), there is also a risk that audit committees' views may be seen too readily by the auditor as a surrogate for those of the shareholders. Just addressing the concerns of the audit committee does not necessarily amount to meeting the expectations of shareholders (and other stakeholders).

For all of these reasons, the rigorous assessment of when, and the degree to which, professional scepticism is required is fundamental to an effective audit.

Section 5 – Conclusions about professional scepticism in the audit

In the growth and development of a living thing, the expression of its DNA in the formation of its cells defines its essence and its effectiveness in meeting the challenges of its environment. In the words of Richard Dawkins[9]:

DNA neither cares nor knows. DNA just is. And we dance to its music.

In the same way, the expression of professional scepticism by the audit team defines the essence of the particular audit. It defines the quality of each audit judgment and, through these, the overall effectiveness of the audit in addressing the challenges it faces in meeting the needs of shareholders (and other stakeholders) who rely on it. The reality and perception of the expression of professional scepticism define and underpin the confidence that others place in the audit and in turn the confidence they place in the audited financial statements.

The preceding analysis suggests that the appropriate application of professional scepticism in the audit requires a mindset which rigorously questions and challenges management's assertions with a degree of doubt that reflects the expectations of shareholders (and other stakeholders) for whose benefit it is performed. All judgments made in the course of the audit should be founded on the perspective of the shareholders (and other stakeholders). That mindset demands the sort of hard evidence – to back each audit judgment and, ultimately, the board's assertion that the financial statements give a true and fair view – that would be convincing and persuasive to shareholders (and other stakeholders), given the auditor's risk assessment.

The analysis suggests that in an appropriately sceptical audit:

- The auditor's risk assessment process should involve a critical appraisal of management's assertions, actively looking for risks of material misstatement.

  These may arise due to fraud or error and may reflect weaknesses in the design or the operation of management's system for controlling and reporting the entity's financial position and performance (such that relevant matters are not identified, or are not adequately controlled or reported, or that the design has not been implemented and operated effectively[10]).

- The auditor develops a high degree of knowledge of the audited entity's business and the environment in which it operates, sufficient to enable it to make its risk assessment through its own fresh and independent eyes rather than through the eyes of management.

- This enables the auditor to make informed challenge of consensus views and to consider the possible incidence of low probability high impact events. The alternative would give rise to the risk of what is known in science as "hypothesis bias" which is an example of "group-think". The challenges in acquiring sufficient knowledge and experience should not be underestimated, especially in relation to complex business models. The traditional pyramid structure of the audit team may not always be

---

[9] *Richard Dawkins: River Out of Eden: A Darwinian View of Life (1995), 133.*

[10] *This is not to suggest that the auditor must always test the operating effectiveness of the financial reporting system, rather than taking a substantive approach and testing the outputs from that system.*

appropriate and different models may need to be explored, such as including experienced business people on the team.

- The auditor designs audit procedures to consider actively if there is any evidence that would contradict management assertions not only to consider the extent to which management has identified evidence that is consistent with them. The opposite of a sceptical audit might be one in which the auditor merely rationalises and documents management's assertions.

- The auditor has strong skills in making evidence-based judgments and suspends judgment about whether the financial statements do or do not give a true and fair view until satisfied that:

  - There has been sufficient inquiry and challenge;
  - Sufficient testing of management's assertions has been undertaken;
  - The quality of the resulting evidence obtained has been critically appraised and judged by the auditor to be sufficiently persuasive; and
  - Where there are plausible alternative treatments of an item in the financial statements (such as different valuation bases), an assessment has been made as to whether one is superior and whether sufficient disclosure of the alternatives has been given, in order to give a true and fair view.

- The auditor approaches and documents audit judgments and audit review processes in a manner that facilitates challenge and demonstrates the rigour of that challenge.

- The auditor's documentation of audit judgments is conclusive rather than conclusionary and therefore always sets out not only the auditor's conclusion but also their rationale for the conclusion, relating it to the nature of the challenges raised in the underlying work and reviews, the strength of the evidence obtained and the perspective of shareholders (and other stakeholders). The auditor needs strong skills in logical argument to do this effectively.

Section 6 – Fostering conditions necessary for auditors to demonstrate the appropriate degree of professional scepticism

The application of an appropriate degree of professional scepticism is a crucial skill for auditors. Unless auditors are prepared to challenge management's assertions they will not be able to confirm with confidence that a company's financial statements present a true and fair view.

The APB believes that in order to demonstrate the value of the audit, the auditor should perform a sceptical audit, evidence the exercise of appropriate scepticism in the audit documentation and convince audit committees and ultimately the shareholders (and other stakeholders) that it has done so.

The challenge for firms is to identify, develop and retain people with the necessary skills and to deploy them appropriately. It also involves nurturing the conditions that allow professional scepticism to flourish.

The prospects for a sceptical audit are likely to be enhanced if the environment in which the auditor operates also recognises and supports the important role that scepticism plays in the audit.

The APB considers that the conditions necessary for auditors to demonstrate the appropriate degree of professional scepticism are likely to include the following.

Individual auditors

● Develop a good understanding of the entity and its business.

● Have a questioning mind and are willing to challenge management assertions.

● Assess critically the information and explanations obtained in the course of their work and corroborate them.

● Seek to understand management motivations for possible misstatement of the financial statements.

● Investigate the nature and cause of deviations or misstatements identified and avoid jumping to conclusions without appropriate audit evidence.

● Are alert for evidence that is inconsistent with other evidence obtained or calls into question the reliability of documents and responses to inquiries.

● Have the confidence to challenge management and the persistence to follow things through to a conclusion – even if predisposed to agree with management's assertion, the auditor should actively consider the alternative views and challenge management to demonstrate that they are not more appropriate.

Engagement teams

● Have good business knowledge and experience.

● Actively consider in what circumstances management numbers may be misstated, whether due to fraud or error, and the possible sources of misstatement, notwithstanding existing knowledge and relationships.

● Develop a good understanding of the entity and its business in order to provide a basis for identifying unusual events or transactions and share information on a regular basis.

● Partners and managers are actively involved in assessing risk and planning the audit procedures to be performed – they think about the changes that are taking place in the entity and its environment and plan audit tests that are responsive to them.

● Partners and managers actively lead and participate in audit team planning meetings to discuss the susceptibility of the entity's financial statements to material misstatement including through fraud and the misuse of related parties.

● Partners and managers are accessible to other staff during the audit and encourage them to consult with them on a timely basis.

● Engagement teams document their key audit judgments and conclusions, especially those reported to the audit committee, in a way that clearly demonstrates that they have exercised an appropriate degree of challenge to management and professional scepticism. In particular, the reasons why the audit team concurs with management's assertions are clearly articulated in a way that, where appropriate, discusses the appropriateness of reasonably credible alternative views and the reasons why they have not been adopted.

- Partners and managers bring additional scepticism to the audit through taking the steps necessary to carry out, face to face where appropriate, a diligent challenge and review of the audit work performed, and the adequacy of the documentation prepared, by other members of the engagement team.

Audit firms

- The culture within the firm emphasises the importance of:
  - understanding and pursuing the perspective of the shareholders (and other stakeholders) of the audited entity in making audit judgments;
  - coaching less experienced staff to foster appropriate scepticism;
  - sharing experiences about difficult audit judgments within the firm;
  - consultation with others about difficult audit judgments; and
  - supporting audit partners when they need to take and communicate difficult audit judgements.

- Scepticism is embedded in the firm's training and competency frameworks used for evaluating and rewarding partner and staff performance.

- The firm requires rigorous engagement quality control reviews that challenge engagement teams' judgments and conclusions.

- Firm methodologies and review processes emphasise the importance of, and provide practical support for auditors in:
  - developing a thorough understanding of the entity's business and its environment, sufficient to enable the auditor to carry out a robust risk assessment through their own fresh eyes;
  - identifying issues early in the planning cycle to allow adequate time for them to be investigated and resolved;
  - rigorously taking such steps as are appropriate to the scale and complexity of the financial reporting systems, to identify unusual transactions;
  - changing risk assessments, materiality and the audit plan in response to audit findings;
  - documenting audit judgments in a conclusive rather than a conclusionary manner and therefore setting out not only the conclusion but also the rationale for the conclusion, relating it to the nature of the challenges raised in the underlying work and reviews, the strength of the evidence obtained and the perspective of shareholders (and other stakeholders);
  - raising matters with the Audit Committee (or those charged with governance) in relation to which the auditor believes the perspective of shareholders (and other stakeholders) about the treatment or disclosure of the matter in the financial statements or related narrative reports could well be different from that adopted by the entity; and
  - ensuring that the disclosures relating to such matters are carefully assessed to ensure that those of relevance to shareholders (and other stakeholders) are sufficient and appropriate in the circumstances, having regard to the auditor's consideration of the true and fair view[11].

---

[11] See the FRC document: True and Fair – July 2011 at: http://www.frc.org.uk/images/uploaded/documents/Paper%20True%20and%20Fair1.pdf.

The role of Audit Committees and management

Whilst it is the responsibility of the auditor to ensure that an appropriate degree of professional scepticism is applied in an audit, the Audit Committee and management can have a significant influencing role.

The Audit Committee's role includes overseeing the integrity of financial reporting and the related processes (including internal financial controls, the independence and objectivity of the external auditor and the effectiveness of the audit process). In this role, the APB believes that Audit Committees should seek to foster appropriate professional scepticism in the external audit, for example, through:

- Promoting the development of a culture within the entity which elicits a constructive response from management and staff to auditor challenge;

- Challenging whether the auditor has developed an adequate understanding of the business and its environment and provided an appropriately informed fresh perspective in making its risk assessment;

- Ensuring that, where management and auditor have resolved either contentious issues or issues that involve significant judgment, these are brought to the audit committee's attention; and

- Seeking to understand in relation to issues brought to their attention (including issues where management and auditor agree the position) whether or not an appropriate degree of challenge was exercised by the auditor – for example, by demanding an explanation of the auditor's rationale for particular conclusions, what alternatives were considered and why the specific judgment was considered to be the most appropriate of the alternatives.

The APB believes that this is consistent with the FRC's *Effective Company Stewardship* proposals[12], under which it is proposed that Audit Committees should produce fuller reports for the Board, in particular setting out their advice on the integrity of the Annual Report and explaining how they discharged their responsibilities for this and other aspects of their remit (such as their oversight of the external audit process and appointment of external auditors). Taken together with the proposal for Boards to discuss these matters in the Annual Report, the effect should be to ensure that the Annual Report demonstrates that the audit addressed those matters of most interest to shareholders and other stakeholders with appropriate challenge and scepticism.

Section 7 – Taking these matters forward

The main purpose of this document is to explain the APB's views on professional scepticism and to encourage auditors to apply its principles in executing high quality sceptical audits and in documenting and demonstrating that they have done so. The APB has also considered the definition of professional scepticism and the extent and manner in which it has been dealt with in the ISAs (UK & I) and in ISQC 1 (UK & I), in light of the conclusions drawn in this Paper.

---

[12] See http://www.frc.org.uk/about/effcompsteward.cfm.

Although these standards contain many elements[13] that support the understanding of professional scepticism developed in this Paper, it is also possible for an auditor to follow the "letter" of the standards without conducting a truly sceptical audit. The APB acknowledges that these standards may well need to be improved further to reflect better some of the conclusions reflected in this Paper and to be clearer about the performance, documentation and communication of professional scepticism.

Accordingly, whilst it has concluded that in taking these matters forward, the immediate emphasis should be on encouraging auditors and others to deliver a step change in behaviours that will achieve consistency in the manner in which professional scepticism is exercised in the conduct of their audits, it also intends to seek to influence the IAASB to enhance the auditing standards in due course.

The APB therefore proposes to:

- Stimulate debate and acceptance by stakeholders of the conclusions set out in this Paper about the nature and role of professional scepticism in the audit;

- Encourage the auditing profession and the audit firms to consider the implications of these conclusions for their business models and culture and for their approach to audits and to implement such changes as are necessary to respond to the challenges they identify – including the need to reflect the perspective of shareholders (and other stakeholders) in exercising their professional judgment;

- Promote these conclusions with Audit Committee members and management to encourage them to recognise and act on the important contribution that they can make to support the appropriate exercise of professional scepticism;

- Promote with those preparing the financial statements and Annual Report the benefits of open communication and consideration of the key judgments involved in doing so and in responding to the challenges raised in the audit; and

- Promote the conclusions set out in this Paper internationally, with a view to identifying ways in which the International Standards on Auditing might be developed to better reflect these conclusions, as part of the post Clarity ISA implementation review.

---

[13] *See IAASB Staff Questions and Answers on "Professional Skepticism in an audit of Financial Statements" at: http://www.ifac.org/sites/default/files/publications/files/IAASB%20Professional%20Skepticism%20QandA-final.pdf.*

Scope and Authority of Audit and Assurance Pronouncements (2016)

(June 2016)

Contents

Paragraphs

Nature and Scope of FRC Audit and Assurance Pronouncements 1 - 10
Standards and Guidance for Audits of Financial Statements 11 - 14
Standards and Guidance for Auditors Acting in Connection With an Engagement
to Report to the Financial Conduct Authority in respect of Client Assets 15
Standards and Guidance for Reporting Accountants Acting in Connection With
an Investment Circular 16
Statements of Standards for Reporting Accountants 17

Authority of FRC Audit and Assurance Pronouncements 18 - 22

Appendix

Editorial note – The FRC issued this scope and authority document which replaces the 2013 version.

Nature and Scope of FRC Audit and Assurance Pronouncements

1   Audit and assurance pronouncements issued by the FRC include:

- Quality control standards for firms that perform audits of financial statements, report in connection with investment circulars, provide assurance on client assets or reviews of interim financial information by the auditor,

- Ethical and engagement standards for audits of financial statements, reports in connection with investment circulars, engagements to provide assurance on client assets and reviews of interim financial information by the auditor, and

- Guidance for auditors of financial statements, reporting accountants and auditors involved in other assurance engagements.

The structure of the audit and assurance pronouncements is shown in the Appendix.

2   Auditors and reporting accountants should not claim compliance with the FRC's audit and assurance or ethical standards unless they have complied fully with all of those standards relevant to an engagement.

3   Quality control standards and engagement standards for audits of financial statements (the International Standards on Quality Control (ISQC) (UK) and the International Standards on Auditing (ISAs) (UK)) and the engagement standard to provide assurance on client assets include objectives for the auditor, together with requirements[1] and related application and other explanatory material. The Ethical Standard contains overarching ethical principles and supporting ethical provisions, the ethical outcomes of which are required to be met, together with requirements[1] and related application and other explanatory material. It is necessary to have an understanding of the entire text of a standard, including its guidance, to understand its objectives, overarching ethical principles or supporting ethical provisions (as applicable) and to apply its requirements properly. Further explanation of the scope, authority and structure of the engagement standards are set out in ISA (UK) 200 (Revised June 2016), *Overall Objectives of the Independent Auditor and the Conduct of an Audit in Accordance with International Standards on Auditing (UK)*.

4   Engagement standards for reporting accountants acting in connection with an investment circular (the Standards for Investment Reporting (SIRs)) and the engagement standard for reviews of interim financial information by the auditor contain requirements, basic principles and essential procedures (identified in bold type lettering[2]) together with related guidance. The requirements, basic principles and essential procedures are to be understood and applied in the context of the explanatory and other material that provide guidance for their application. It is therefore necessary to consider the whole text of a standard to understand and apply the requirements, basic principles and essential procedures properly.

---

[1] *The level of authority of the text in requirements paragraphs is identified by use of the term "shall" (e.g. "the auditor shall ...").*

[2] *The level of authority of the text in these paragraphs is identified by use of the expression "the auditor should ...". in the SIRs and the standard for reviews of interim financial information; and by use of the expression "the auditor shall ..." in the standard for engagements to provide assurance on client assets.*

The ISAs (UK) and ISQC (UK) 1 are based on the corresponding international **5** standards issued by the International Auditing and Assurance Standards Board[3] (IAASB). Where necessary, the international standards have been augmented with additional requirements to address specific UK legal and regulatory requirements; and additional guidance that is appropriate in the UK national legislative, cultural and business context. This additional material is clearly differentiated from the original text of the international standards by the use of grey shading. Requirements derived from the European Audit Regulation[4] and Directive[5] are designated by the letter "R" or "D" respectively[6]. ISAs (UK) are consistent with International Standards on Auditing as issued by the IAASB and the requirements of ISAs (UK) do not conflict with the requirements in ISAs. An audit conducted in accordance with ISAs (UK) does not therefore preclude the auditor from being able to assert compliance with International Standards on Auditing issued by the IAASB.

Requirements in the Audit Regulation contained in the Ethical and Auditing **6** Standards, which are applicable to the audit of Public Interest Entities are applicable to those entities as defined in Article 2 (13) of Directive 2006/43/EC as amended.

For the audit of UK groups, the group auditor needs to be satisfied that the audit of **7** the group financial statements, on which the group auditor gives an audit opinion, is in accordance with the ISAs (UK). Auditors of overseas components are not required to have regard to the additional requirements and guidance material in those standards, although the group auditor may decide to refer to it in their instructions to component auditors[7].

The ISAs and ISQC 1, as issued by the IAASB, require compliance with "relevant **8** ethical requirements" which are described, in the application material, as ordinarily comprising Parts A and B of the International Ethics Standards Board for Accountants (IESBA) *Code of Ethics for Professional Accountants* (the IESBA Code[8]) related to an audit of financial statements together with national requirements that are more restrictive. The ISAs (UK) and ISQC (UK) 1 have supplementary material that makes clear that auditors in the UK are subject to ethical requirements from two sources: the FRC's Ethical Standard, and the ethical pronouncements established by the auditor's relevant professional body.

ISQC (UK) 1 also has supplementary material that makes clear that the Ethical **9** Standard applies to all other public interest assurance engagements that are

---

[3] *IAASB is a committee of the International Federation of Accountants (IFAC). The IAASB's constitution and due process is described in its "Preface to the International Standards on Quality Control, Auditing, Review, Other Assurance and Related Services".*

[4] *Regulation (EU) No 537/2014 of the European Parliament and the Council of 16 April 2014 on specific requirements regarding statutory audit of public-interest entities.*

[5] *Directive 2006/43/EC of the European Parliament and of the Council of 17 May 2006 on statutory audits of annual accounts and consolidated accounts, as amended by Directive 2014/56/EU.*

[6] *The same convention has been used for the numbering of the Ethical Standard.*

[7] *If the auditor of an overseas component is a part of the same firm as the group auditor (i.e. the same legal entity) consideration needs to be given to whether the auditor of the overseas component has the same legal obligations as the group auditor and, therefore, is required to comply with the legal or regulatory requirements of the ISAs (UK). If such obligations exist, consideration needs to be given to the implications for communication between the group auditor and component auditor (for example where necessary to fulfil obligations for reporting money laundering offences or reporting matters to a regulator).*

[8] *The IESBA Code is included in the IFAC "Handbook of the Code of Ethics for Professional Accountants" and can be downloaded free of charge from the publications section of the IAASB website (www.ifac.org/IAASB).*

undertaken in compliance with performance standards issued by the FRC, which comprise:

- Reporting accountants acting in connection with an investment circular (the Standards for Investment Reporting – SIRs),

- Reviews of interim financial information by the independent auditor of the entity (International Standard on Review Engagement (UK and Ireland) 2410), and

- Engagements to provide assurance on client assets to the Financial Conduct Authority (the Client Asset Assurance Standard).

10   The Ethical Standard was developed with the intent that it should adhere to the principles of the IESBA Code.

Standards and Guidance for Audits of Financial Statements

11   The FRC has been designated as the Competent Authority for Audit in the UK[9] and as such has the authority to determine technical standards to be applied for statutory audits of companies in accordance with the Companies Act 2006.

12   Ethical and engagement standards for audits of financial statements, which comprise the Ethical Standard and International Standards on Auditing (ISAs) (UK), apply to auditors carrying out:

- Statutory audits of companies in accordance with the Companies Acts[10];

- Audits of financial statements of entities in accordance with other UK legislation e.g. building societies, credit unions, friendly societies, pension funds, charities and registered social landlords;

- Public sector financial statement audits in the UK, including those carried out either on behalf of the national audit agencies or under contract to those agencies. (The standards governing the conduct and reporting of the audit of financial statements are a matter for the national audit agencies to determine. However, the heads of the national audit agencies[11] in the UK have chosen to adopt the ethical, engagement and quality control standards issued by the FRC for audits as the basis of their approach to the audit of financial statements);

- Other audits performed by audit firms registered with the UK members of the Consultative Committee of Accountancy Bodies (CCAB)[12] unless the nature of the engagement requires the use of other recognised auditing standards and the rules of the relevant CCAB member does not preclude the use of other recognised auditing standards; and

- Other audits where audit firms not registered with members of the CCAB elect, or are required by contract, to perform the work in accordance with UK auditing standards.

---

[9] *By order of SI 2016/649 The Statutory Auditors and Third Country Auditors Regulations 2016.*

[10] *Companies Act 2006.*

[11] *National audit agencies in the UK are the National Audit Office (for the Comptroller and Auditor General), the Wales Audit Office (for the Auditor General for Wales), Audit Scotland (for the Auditor General for Scotland and the Accounts Commission) and the Northern Ireland Audit Office (for the Comptroller and Auditor General for Northern Ireland).*

[12] *The UK members of CCAB are The Institute of Chartered Accountants in England & Wales, The Institute of Chartered Accountants of Scotland, The Association of Chartered Certified Accountants and The Chartered Institute of Public Finance and Accountancy.*

Guidance for auditors of financial statements is also issued in the form of Practice   **13**
Notes and Bulletins. Practice Notes and Bulletins are persuasive rather than
prescriptive and are indicative of good practice. Practice Notes assist auditors in
applying engagement standards to particular circumstances and industries and
Bulletins provide timely guidance on new or emerging issues. Auditors should be
aware of and consider Practice Notes applicable to the engagement. Auditors who
do not consider and apply the guidance included in a relevant Practice Note should
be prepared to explain how the engagement standards have been complied with.

In particular industries or sectors, guidance for auditors may also be issued as   **14**
Statements of Recommended Practice (SORPs) which clarify how engagement
standards may need to be applied in order to be relevant and provide useful
information to users of auditor's reports or other information issued by the auditor
in that industry or sector. SORPS are persuasive rather than prescriptive and are
indicative of good practice. Auditors should be aware of and consider SORPs
applicable to the engagement. Auditors who do not consider and apply the
guidance included in a relevant SORP should be prepared to explain how the
engagement standards have been complied with. SORPs are issued by bodies
recognized for this purpose by the FRC, and developed in accordance with the
FRC's "Policy on Developing Statements of Recommended Practice (SORPs)
(March 2016).

Standards and Guidance for Auditors Acting in Connection With an Engagement to Report to the Financial Conduct Authority in respect of Client Assets

The Client Asset Assurance Standard issued by the FRC applies to auditors when   **15**
carrying out an engagement to report to the Financial Conduct Authority in respect
of client assets.

Standards and Guidance for Reporting Accountants Acting in Connection With an Investment Circular

The Ethical Standard and Standards for Investment Reporting (SIRs) issued by the   **16**
FRC apply to reporting accountants when carrying out engagements involving
investment circulars intended to be issued in connection with a securities
transaction governed wholly or in part by the laws and regulations of the
United Kingdom.

Statements of Standards for Reporting Accountants

The FRC also issues standards and guidance for accountants on assurance   **17**
engagements closely related to an audit of the financial statements. This
includes the International Standard on Reporting Engagements (ISRE) (UK and
Ireland) 2410, *Review of Interim Financial Information Performed by the
Independent Auditor of the Entity*. ISRE (UK and Ireland) 2410 adopts the text
of ISRE 2410 issued by the IAASB and, as with ISAs (UK), a relatively small
amount of additional material (highlighted with grey shading) has been added in
order to clarify certain matters (for example in relation to the rules and regulations
implementing the requirements of the European Transparency Directive
applicable to UK listed companies) and to perpetuate previous guidance that
remains pertinent.

Authority of FRC Audit and Assurance Pronouncements

18   In order to be eligible for appointment in the UK as auditors of companies, or of any of the other entities that require their auditors to be eligible for appointment as auditors under section 1212 of the Companies Act 2006, persons must be registered with a Recognised Supervisory Body (RSB)[13] recognised under that Act and must be eligible for appointment under the rules of that RSB. The Companies Act 2006 requires RSBs to have rules and practices as to the technical standards to be applied in company audit work and the manner in which those standards are to be applied in practice. Those rules must include provision requiring statutory auditors to comply with standards determined by the FRC[14] as the competent authority. Each RSB is also required to have arrangements in place for the effective monitoring and enforcement of compliance with those standards.

19   The members of the CCAB have undertaken to adopt the ethical and engagement standards and guidance issued by the FRC where the application of those standards is not required by law.

20   Apparent failures by auditors to comply with applicable ethical or engagement standards are liable to be investigated by the FRC or the relevant accountancy body. Auditors who do not comply with the applicable ethical or engagement standards when performing company or other audits make themselves liable to regulatory action which may include the withdrawal of registration and hence of eligibility to perform company audits.

21   All relevant FRC pronouncements are likely to be taken into account when the adequacy of the work of auditors is being considered in a court of law or in other contested situations.

22   The nature of the ethical and engagement standards and associated guidance requires professional accountants to exercise professional judgment in applying them. Where, in exceptional circumstances, auditors and reporting accountants judge it necessary to depart from a requirement, basic principle or essential procedure that is relevant in the circumstances of the engagement, the auditor or reporting accountant documents how the alternative procedures performed achieve the objective of the engagement and, unless otherwise clear, the reasons for the departure.

---

[13] *The Institute of Chartered Accountants in England & Wales, The Institute of Chartered Accountants of Scotland, Chartered Accountants Ireland, the Association of Authorised Public Accountants and The Association of Chartered Certified Accountants are Recognised Supervisory Bodies for the purpose of regulating auditors in the UK.*

[14] *Regulation 3(c) of the Statutory Auditors and Third Country Auditors Regulations 2016 (SI 2016/649) places a specific responsibility on the FRC to determine those standards, which must meet requirements set out in Schedule 1.*

Appendix

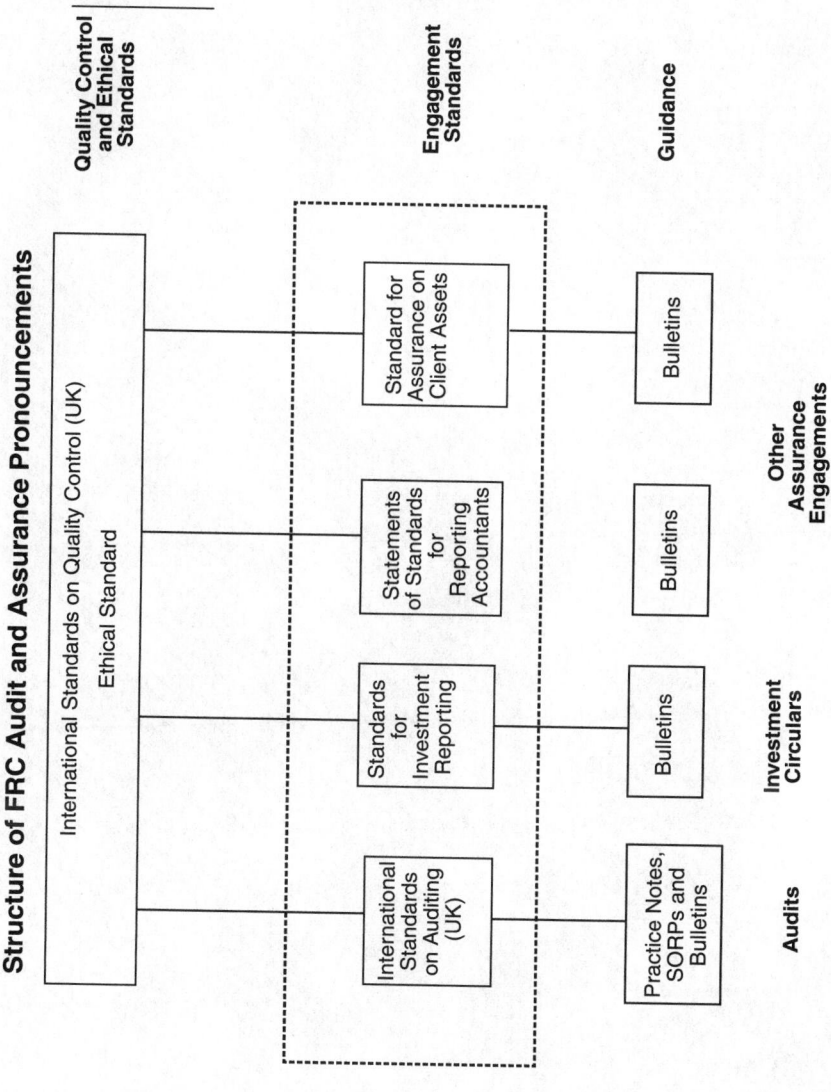

Structure of FRC Audit and Assurance Pronouncements

Quality Control and Ethical Standards

International Standards on Quality Control (UK)

Ethical Standard

Engagement Standards

International Standards on Auditing (UK)

Standards for Investment Reporting

Statements of Standards for Reporting Accountants

Standard for Assurance on Client Assets

Guidance

Practice Notes, SORPs and Bulletins

Bulletins

Bulletins

Bulletins

Audits

Investment Circulars

Other Assurance Engagements

Part Two

Ethical Standard

Revised Ethical Standard 2016

(Effective for audits of financial statements for periods commencing on or after 17 June 2016)

Contents

	Paragraphs
Introduction	I1 - I23
Scope of this Ethical Standard	I1 - I7
Investment Circular Reporting Engagements	I8
Meeting the Ethical Outcomes Established by the Overarching Principles,	
Supporting Ethical Provisions And Specific Requirements	I9 - I19
The 'Third Party Test'	
Threats to Integrity, Objectivity and Independence	
The EU Audit Directive and Regulation	I20 - I22
Definitions	I23

Part A – Overarching Principles and Supporting Ethical Provisions ... 1 - 2.13
Integrity and Objectivity ... 1 - 1.2
    Overarching Principle
    Supporting Ethical Provisions
Independence ... 2 - 2.13
    Overarching Principle
    Supporting Ethical Provisions

Part B ... 1.1D - 6.17

Section 1 – General Requirements and Guidance ... 1.1D - 1.80
Compliance
    Ethics Partner
    Breaches
    Non-involvement in Management Decision-taking
Identification and Assessment of Threats
    Threats to Integrity, Objectivity and Independence
        Investment Circular Reporting Engagements
Identification and Assessment of Safeguards
Other Firms Involved in Engagements
Engagement Quality Control Review
Overall Conclusion
Communication with Those Charged With Governance
Documentation
Effective Date

Section 2 – Financial, Business, Employment and Personal Relationships ... 2.1 - 2.75
Financial Relationships
    General Considerations
    Financial Interests Held as Trustee
    Financial Interests Held by Firm Pension Schemes
    Loans and Guarantees
Business Relationships
Employment Relationships
    Management Role with an Entity Relevant to an Engagement
    Loan Staff Assignments
    Partners and Engagement Team Members Joining an Entity Relevant to an Engagement

Family Members Employed by an Entity Relevant to an Engagement
Governance Role with an Entity Relevant to an Engagement
Employment with the Firm
Family and Other Personal Relationships
External Consultants Involved in an Engagement

**Section 3 – Long Association with Engagements and With Entities Relevant
    To Engagements**   3.1 – 3.23
General Requirements
Public Interest Entities and Other Listed Entities
    Audit Firm Rotation
    Key Audit Partners and Engagement Partners
    Engagement Quality Control Reviewers and Other Key Partners Involved in
        the Engagement
    Other Partners and Staff Involved in the Engagement in
Senior Positions

**Section 4 – Fees, Remuneration and Evaluation Policies, Gifts and
    Hospitality, Litigation**   4.1 – 4.68
Fees
Remuneration and Evaluation Policies
Gifts and Hospitality
Threatened and Actual Litigation

Section 5 – Non-audit/Additional Services   5.1 – 5.173R
General Approach to Non-audit/Additional Services
    Investment Circular Reporting Engagements
    Identification and Assessment of Threats and Safeguards
        Threats to Objectivity and Independence
        Safeguards
    Communication with Those Charged With Governance
    Documentation
Audit Related Services
Evaluation of Specific Non-audit Services and Additional Services
    Internal Audit services
    Information Technology Services
    Valuation Services
    Actuarial Valuation Services
    Tax Services
    Litigation Support Services
    Legal Services
    Recruitment and Remuneration Services
    Corporate Finance Services
    Transaction Related Services
    Restructuring Services
    Accounting Services
Prohibited Non-audit Services for Public Interest Entities

Section 6 – Provisions Available for Audits of Small Entities   6.1 – 6.17
Introduction
Alternative Provisions
    Economic Dependence
    Self-review Threat – Non-audit Services
Exemptions
    Management Threat – Non-audit Services
    Advocacy Threat – Non-audit Services
    Partners and Other Persons Approved as a Statutory Auditor Joining an
        Audited Entity
Disclosure Requirements

**Appendix: Illustrative template for communicating
    information on audit and non-audit services provided to the group**

PREFACE

The FRC's Ethical Standard applies in the audit of financial statements and other *public interest assurance engagements*. It is read in the context of the Statement "The Financial Reporting Council – Scope and Authority of Audit and Assurance Pronouncements" which sets out the application and authority of the FRC's Ethical Standard.

The terms used in the FRC's Ethical Standard are explained in the Glossary on the FRC's website.

The FRC's Ethical Standard applies to audits of financial statements and other *public interest assurance engagements* in both the private and the public sectors.

Editorial note – *For the Glossary of Terms (auditing and ethics) see the end of Part Four International Standards on Auditing (UK)*

Introduction

Scope of this Ethical Standard

I1   This Ethical Standard applies to *audit engagements* and other *public interest assurance engagements*[1]. The term *"engagement"* is used in this Ethical Standard specifically to mean an *audit engagement* or *other public interest assurance engagement*, or both where the context permits, unless stated otherwise. A fundamental objective of any such *engagement* is that the intended users trust and have confidence that the audit or assurance opinion is professionally sound and objective. This in turn should enhance the credibility for users of the information the opinion covers (the *"subject matter information"*[2] – e.g. in the case of an audit engagement, the financial statements). It should also enhance the intended users' understanding of the underlying *"subject matter"* (e.g. in the case of an *audit engagement*, the historical financial position and performance of the entity).

I2   Users are neither responsible for the *subject matter information* nor for the underlying *subject matter* of the *engagement*. Their interest in the *engagement* usually arises because they have an actual or prospective stake in an *entity relevant to the engagement* but do not have direct access to the *subject matter*.

I3   Although auditors and assurance practitioners are reporting to users, they are generally engaged to do so by the entity whose information they are reporting on. Accordingly their contractual "client" (the entity) is different to their beneficial "client" (the users). These principal-agent relationships (where the users are the principals and the directors and auditors of the entity their agents) give rise to the potential for conflicts of interests that need to be addressed if the user is to have trust and confidence in the audit/assurance process, the *subject matter information* and the directors of the entity itself. Regulation and oversight of audit and assurance practitioners, including professional and ethical codes and standards, addresses the need for trust and confidence between users and practitioners. The *engagement* then addresses the need for trust and confidence between the users and the directors of the entity.

I4   In the context of an *engagement*, such conflicts of interest create a potential risk (threat) that the practitioner's judgment or actions in conducting or determining the outcome of the *engagement* may be unduly influenced by interests other than those of the intended user (the beneficial "client" under the *engagement*). Such other interests are potentially wide-ranging and will usually be legitimate in themselves (though they may also not be so). However, they would be objectionable in the circumstances if the practitioner is unduly influenced by

---

[1] *Audits of financial statements(*) undertaken in compliance with International Standards on Auditing (ISAs) (UK) and other engagements undertaken in compliance with performance standards issued by the FRC which, as of 17 June 2016, comprise:*

  (a)   *Reporting accountants acting in connection with an investment circular (the Standards for Investment Reporting – "SIRs");*

  (b)   *Review of interim financial information by the independent auditor of the entity (International Standard on Review Engagements (UK and Ireland) 2410); and*

  (c)   *Engagements to provide assurance on client assets to the Financial Conduct Authority (the CASS Standard).*

  (*) In the public sector the statutory scope of an audit can extend beyond the entity's financial statements to include reporting on an entity's arrangements for the proper conduct of its financial affairs, management of its performance or use of its resources.

[2] *"Subject matter information" is the outcome that results from the evaluation or measurement of "subject matter" against suitable criteria. More full definitions are given in the Glossary of Terms.*

them, because this may prejudice the interests of the intended users, which should be paramount.

Users do not have all the information necessary for judging whether the *firm*, its **I5** partners and *staff* and any other *covered persons* are, in fact, acting with integrity and objectivity. Although the *firm* may be satisfied that the integrity, objectivity and independence of the *firm* or such persons will not in fact be compromised by a particular condition or relationship, an objective, reasonable and informed third party may reach a different conclusion. For example, if such a third party were aware that the *firm*, its partners or *staff* and/or any other covered persons had certain financial, employment, business or personal relationships with an *entity relevant to the engagement*, that third party might reasonably conclude that the *firm* and such persons could be subject to undue influence from the directors of the entity or would not be impartial or unbiased. Public confidence in the integrity, objectivity and independence of the *firm* or such persons could therefore suffer as a result of this perception, irrespective of whether there is any actual impairment.

Other regulators or competent authorities may specify compliance with this **I6** Ethical Standard in relation to other types of work.

Ethical guidance on other matters, together with statements of fundamental ethical **I7** principles governing the work of all professional accountants, are issued by professional accountancy bodies. These also provide a basis for enhancing the trust and confidence of intended users that the *engagement* is professionally sound.

Investment Circular Reporting Engagements

I8 Because investment circulars may relate to transactions that are price sensitive and therefore confidential, the fact that a *firm* has been engaged to undertake an *investment circular reporting engagement* is likely to be known by only a limited number of individuals within the *firm*. For this reason, for such engagements, the supporting ethical provisions and requirements of this Ethical Standard apply only to.

(a)   persons with actual knowledge of the engagement as described in the definition of *covered persons* applicable to an *investment circular reporting engagement*; and

(b)   where required by this Ethical Standard, the *firm*.

Meeting the Ethical Outcomes Established by the Overarching Principles, Supporting Ethical Provisions and Specific Requirements

Part A of this Ethical Standard sets out the overarching principles of integrity, **I9** objectivity and independence, together with supporting ethical provisions. Together, these establish a framework, of ethical outcomes that are required to be met by the auditor or assurance practitioner, to provide a basis for user trust and confidence in the integrity and objectivity of the practitioner in performing the *engagement*.

I10   Part B sets out specific requirements relevant to certain circumstances that may arise in audit and other *public interest assurance engagements*. These specific requirements are designed to assist in meeting the ethical outcomes required by the overarching principles and supporting ethical provisions. However, circumstances relating to *engagements* vary widely and meeting the ethical outcomes required by the overarching principles and supporting ethical provisions is paramount. Compliance with the specific requirements may not always be sufficient to achieve this as Part B does not, nor is it practicable for it to, address all possible circumstances that may exist. Accordingly practitioners need to be alert for, and respond appropriately to, other circumstances that create threats to meeting the ethical outcomes required by the overarching principles and supporting ethical provisions.

I11   The *firm* and persons required to meet the outcomes of the overarching principles and supporting ethical provisions are required to be able to demonstrate that they have, where applicable, identified and addressed relevant conditions and circumstances, including that they have:

- implemented, maintained and/or complied with effective systems and processes to enable them to do so;

- established and operated effective safeguards;

- evaluated the threats and safeguards appropriately; and

- taken any additional steps that are necessary to meet the ethical outcomes required by the overarching principles and supporting ethical provisions.

I12   The FRC believes that stakeholders (users of practitioner's reports issued under *engagements*) expect an equivalent standard of independence for *firms*, their partners and other *covered persons*, whether performing audit or other *public interest assurance engagements*. *Firms*, their partners and *staff*, and other persons where identified, are required to meet the ethical outcomes required by the overarching principles and supporting ethical provisions and to comply with the requirements unless the circumstances to which they apply do not exist.

I13   When a statement or examples are given in this Ethical Standard to help clarify or illustrate a position in relation to particular circumstances, this is not intended to, and should not be interpreted as, indicating that in other circumstances the same position necessarily either is or is not intended. Whether the ethical outcomes required by the overarching principles and supporting ethical provisions are achieved is always paramount and is a matter to be determined exercising professional judgment.

The "Third Party Test"

I14   Importantly, consideration of whether the ethical outcomes required by the overarching principles and supporting ethical provisions have been met should be evaluated by reference to the perspective of an objective, reasonable and informed third party (see the definition of *independence*).

I15   The *firm*, as well as each *covered person*, is required to be independent in the performance (conduct and determination of the outcome) of the *engagement*. Complete freedom from threats to integrity and objectivity, even taking into account safeguards, is not feasible, for example, as a result of the influence that the directors and management of a responsible entity have over the appointment and remuneration of the *firm* where (as in the case of an audit) that entity is the engaging party. Accordingly, independence not being compromised (which is the test to be applied in evaluating the likely consequences of conditions and relationships that may create threats to integrity and objectivity) is not whether the *firm* considers that the integrity and objectivity of the *firm*, its partners and *staff* and any other *covered persons* is impaired, but is whether there is freedom from threats to integrity and objectivity, taking into account safeguards applied, at a level where it is probable (more likely than not) that an objective, reasonable and informed third party would not conclude that integrity or objectivity (and therefore independence) is compromised. This is identified more concisely in Parts A and B of this Ethical Standard as a "level at which independence is not compromised".

Threats to Integrity, Objectivity and Independence

When the threats that exist mean that independence is, or is perceived to be, compromised, an objective, reasonable and informed third party would not have sufficient trust and confidence in the practitioner to perform or continue to perform the *engagement*. Consequently, in those circumstances actions have to be taken: to remove or reduce the threats; or to apply additional safeguards; or, where the threats relate to individuals rather than the *firm*, to exclude those individuals from any role which would put them in a position as a *covered person* to exert influence on the *engagement*. These actions must be taken individually or collectively to such an extent that it is probable that an objective, reasonable and informed third party would no longer conclude that integrity or objectivity (and therefore independence) are compromised. Otherwise, the *firm* is not permitted to accept, or if already engaged is required to withdraw from, the *engagement* unless not permitted to do so by legislation.   **I16**

Conditions and relationships that affect the *firm* or its *network firms* and their partners and *staff* and any other *covered persons* are relevant in the context of identifying conflicts of interest that may give rise to threats to integrity or objectivity in the performance of the *engagement*. Individuals who perform an *engagement* do so in the context of the *firm*'s cultural and ethical values, and its governance and management arrangements (including its quality control systems). In turn, the *firm* operates in the context of its wider network, if any. Accordingly, such conditions and relationships that are relevant in the context of an engagement may arise within the *firm* or its network or externally.   **I17**

Relevant internal conditions would include, for example, the culture, governance and management arrangements within the *firm* and its *network firms*, and their policies and practices with respect to performance, pay and promotion. These internal conditions are expressed, in the context of those responsible for the performance of the *engagement*, through the formal and informal relationships of influence they have with other persons within the *firm*, and potentially within the *firm*'s network, and in turn any such relationships that those other persons may have internally. Such other persons within the *firm* may therefore be *covered persons* in a position to influence the conduct or outcome of the engagement.   **I18**

Relevant external relationships would include, for example: family and personal relationships of *covered persons*; financial, business and employment relationships of the *firm* or such individuals (or closely connected persons) with an *entity relevant to the engagement* and potentially with other entities; and relationships with an entity relevant to the *engagement* that arise in the performance of the *engagement* or other services provided to those entities.   **I19**

Relevant external conditions may include, for example: the culture, governance and management of the entity; long association of those performing the *engagement* with an *entity relevant to the engagement*; and economic dependence on an *entity relevant to the engagement.*

The EU Audit Directive and Regulation

I20   In April 2014 the European Commission published a Directive[3] amending the Statutory Audit Directive[4] and a new Audit Regulation[5]. The Audit Directive establishes specific requirements concerning the *statutory audit* of annual and consolidated financial statements. The Audit Regulation establishes further specific requirements regarding the *statutory audit* of *"public interest entities"* as defined by the Audit Directive (see the definitions below).

I21   The Audit Regulation has the direct effect of law and Member States are required to adopt appropriate provisions to ensure its effective application. The Audit Directive does not have a direct effect in law and Member States are required to adopt and publish the measures necessary to comply with it. Articles in both the Audit Directive and Audit Regulation establish provisions that relate to matters that are the subject of this Ethical Standard. In relation to a number of these provisions there are Member State options that have been implemented in this Ethical Standard.

I22   The overarching principles, supporting ethical provisions and requirements in this Ethical Standard reflect the Audit Directive and Regulation where relevant. These requirements are highlighted with shading and "D" (for the Directive) or "R" (for the Regulation) added to the paragraph number as applicable.

Definitions

I23   Particular terms used in the FRC's Ethical Standard are explained in the Glossary which is available on the FRC website. Defined terms are presented in italicised text.

Integrity, Objectivity and Independence

> *Integrity* – being trustworthy, straightforward, honest, fair and candid; complying with the spirit as well as the letter of applicable ethical principles, laws and regulations; behaving so as to maintain the public's trust in the auditing profession; and respecting confidentiality except where disclosure is in the public interest or is required to adhere to legal and professional responsibilities.

> *Objectivity* – acting and making decisions and judgments impartially, fairly and on merit (having regard to all considerations relevant to the task in hand but no other), without discrimination, bias, or compromise because of commercial or personal self-interest, conflicts of interest or the undue influence of others, and having given due consideration to the best available evidence.

---

[3] *Directive 2014/56/EU*

[4] *Directive 2006/43/EC*

[5] *Regulation 537/2014*

The need for objectivity in performing the engagement arises from, among other things, the fact that many of the important issues involved in the performance of the engagement, including those arising in the preparation of the subject matter information, do not relate to questions of fact but rather to questions of judgment. For example, with regard to financial statements, there are choices to be made by the board of directors in deciding on the accounting policies to be adopted by the entity: the directors have to select the ones that they consider most appropriate and this decision can have a material impact on the financial statements. Furthermore, many items included in the financial statements cannot be measured with absolute precision and certainty. In many cases, estimates have to be made and the directors may have to choose one value from a range of possible outcomes. When exercising discretion in these areas, the directors have regard to the applicable financial reporting framework.

Independence – freedom from conditions and relationships which, in the context of an *engagement*, would compromise the integrity or objectivity of the *firm* or *covered persons*.

Integrity or objectivity (and therefore independence) would be compromised if it is probable (more likely than not) that an objective, reasonable and informed third party would conclude that the threats, arising from any conditions or relationships that exist (taking into account any conflicts of interest that they may cause, or generally be perceived to cause, or otherwise, and having regard to any safeguards implemented), would impair integrity or objectivity to such an extent that it would be inappropriate for the firm to accept or continue to perform the audit or other public interest assurance engagement unless the threats were eliminated or further reduced or unless more, or more effective, safeguards were implemented.

Part A – Overarching Principles and Supporting Ethical Provisions

The overarching principles of integrity, objectivity and independence established by this Ethical Standard are set out below together with the related supporting ethical provisions. Cross references are given to the Sections in Part B of this Ethical Standard that establish related requirements and/or guidance.

Integrity and Objectivity

Overarching Principle

The *firm*, its partners[6] and all *staff*[7] shall behave with integrity and objectivity in all professional and business activities and relationships.   1

---

[6] *The term "partner" includes any individual with authority to bind the firm with respect to the performance of a professional services engagement.*

[7] *The term "staff" includes any natural persons whose services are placed at the disposal or under the control of the firm.*

Supporting Ethical Provisions

1.1   The senior management of the *firm* and those with direct   1.1 – 1.25
responsibility for the management of the *firm*'s audit   Compliance
and other public interest assurance business shall instil
the necessary culture and behaviours respectively
throughout the *firm* and that business, so as to ensure
that meeting the ethical outcomes of the overarching
principles and supporting ethical provisions is
paramount and overrides all commercial interests of
the *firm*.

1.2   The *firm* shall establish and apply confidential whistle-   1.11(h)
blowing policies and procedures across the *firm* which
enable partners and *staff* to report, without fear,
concerns about the *firm*'s commitment to quality work
and professional judgement and values in a way that
properly takes the public interest into consideration.

Independence

Overarching Principle

2   **In relation to each *engagement*, the *firm*, and each
covered person, shall ensure (in the case of a *covered
person*, insofar as they are able to do so) that the *firm*
and each *covered person* is free from conditions and
relationships which would make it probable that an
objective, reasonable and informed third party
would conclude the independence of the *firm* or
any *covered person* is compromised.**

Supporting Ethical Provisions

2.1D   The *firm* and each *covered person*, shall ensure (in
the case of a *covered person*, insofar as they are able
to do so) that the independence of the *firm* and each
covered person is not compromised with respect to
each *entity relevant to the engagement*. This includes
ensuring that the *firm* and each *covered person* is not
involved in the decision-taking of any such entity.
The period during which independence shall not be
compromised is:

(a)   In the case of an audit, at least throughout the
period covered by the financial statements to be
audited and throughout any subsequent period
until the audit has been completed;

(b)   In the case of an other *public interest assurance
engagement*, other than an *investment circular
reporting engagement*, at least throughout any
period over which, or from the time as at which,
the *subject matter* is measured or evaluated in
connection with the engagement and

throughout any subsequent period until the *engagement* has been completed;

(c) In the case of an investment circular reporting engagement, the period during which the engagement is undertaken and any additional period before that but subsequent to the balance sheet date of the most recent audited financial statements of the *entity relevant to the engagement*. [AD 22.1]

The *firm* shall take all reasonable steps to ensure that, when carrying out an *engagement*, the integrity, objectivity and independence of the *firm* and each *covered person* is not affected by any existing or potential conflict of interest or any business or other direct or indirect relationship involving: (i) the *firm*; or where applicable any members of its network; (ii) any of the *firm*'s partners or *staff*; or (iii) the *firm*'s owners, shareholders or any other person directly or indirectly linked to the *firm* by control. [AD 22.1]	1.26 – 1.44 Identification and Assessment of Threats 1.45 – 1.52 Identification and Assessment of Safeguards 1.53 – 1.55 Other Firms	**2.2D**

The *firm* shall not accept, continue or carry out an *engagement*:
 	
(i) if there is any threat of self-review, self-interest, advocacy, familiarity or intimidation created by financial, personal, business, employment or other relationships between:
 	
   (a) the *firm*, any of its *network firms*, or any *covered person*, and
 	
   (b) any *entity* (*relevant to the engagement*; or
 	
(ii) unless required by law or regulation to do so, if any other condition or relationship exists;
 	
which would compromise the independence of the *firm* or any *covered person*. [AD 22.1]
	1.26 – 1.44
	Identification and Assessment of Threats
	
	1.45 – 1.52
	Identification and Assessment of Safeguards
	
	1.53 – 1.55
	Other *Firms*
	
	1.57 – 1.60
	Overall Conclusion
	
	Section 2 – Financial, Business, Employment and Personal Relationships
	
	Section 3 – Long Association with Engagements and with Entities Relevant to Engagements
		2.3D

2.4   For each *engagement*, the *firm* and the *engagement partner* (in the case of the *engagement partner* insofar as they are able to do so) shall ensure that the *firm*'s independence is not compromised as a result of conditions or relationships that would compromise the independence of a *network firm* (whether or not its work is used in the conduct of engagement) or a third party *firm* whose work is used in the conduct of the engagement, having regard to the ethical requirements that are relevant to the engagement as applicable to such other *firm*, which are as follows:

   (a)   For each such other *firm*, the extant version of the IESBA Code[8]; and

   (b)   In the case of a *network firm* whose work is used in the conduct of an *engagement* where any *entity relevant to the engagement* is a *public interest entity*, this Ethical Standard.

1.53 – 1.55
Other Firms

1.61 – 1.71
Communication with Those Charged with Governance

2.5   In evaluating whether or not a condition or relationship would compromise independence, it is the responsibility of (i) the *firm*, and (ii) each *covered person* and any other person with responsibility to behave with integrity and objectivity and to maintain their independence (or to ensure that others do so); to be able to demonstrate that any conditions or relationships that exist, taking account of any safeguards implemented, would not compromise the independence of the *firm* or any covered person.

1.5 – 1.7
Compliance

2.6   All partners and *staff* of the *firm* and all other *covered persons* shall remain alert to conditions or relationships which could compromise the independence of the *firm* or any *covered person*.

1.26 – 1.44
Identification and Assessment of Threats

2.7   All partners and *staff* of the *firm* and all other *covered persons* who become aware of any condition or relationship which could impair the independence of the *firm* or any *covered person* shall report the matter to the *engagement partner* (if known) or (failing that) to the *firm*'s *Ethics Partner*/Function, where applicable, or otherwise to the senior management of the *firm* or those with direct responsibility for the management of the *firm*'s audit and other public interest assurance business, at the earliest opportunity.

2.8   The *firm* shall have policies and procedures designed to ensure that action is taken promptly: to investigate any condition or relationship reported in accordance with supporting ethical provision 2.7, to assess whether the independence of the *firm* or any *covered person* would be compromised and, if so, to eliminate the condition or relationship or apply sufficient safeguards, to reduce

1.45 – 1.52
Identification and Assessment of Safeguards

1.57 – 1.60
Overall Conclusion

---

[8] *The "Code of Ethics for Professional Accountants" issued by the International Ethics Standards Board for Accountants*

threats to a level where the independence of the *firm* and *covered persons* is not compromised, or to withdraw from the *engagement*.

In relation to an *engagement*, a *firm* shall not:		**2.9**
• agree a basis for determining fees, or	Section 4 (4.1 – 4.55)	
• have remuneration and evaluation policies for partners and *staff*,	Section 4 (4.56D – 4.60)	

which would compromise the independence of the *firm* or of any *covered person*.

The *firm*, its partners and *staff* and any other *covered person*, and *persons closely associated* with *covered persons*, shall not provide or accept gifts and hospitality in relation to an *engagement* unless it is probable that an objective, reasonable and informed third party would consider the value thereof to be trivial or inconsequential.	Section 4 (4.61D – 4.65)	**2.10**
The *firm* shall not accept or continue an *engagement* for an entity, unless required by law to do so, where litigation in relation to any *engagement* between the *firm* its partners or any *covered person* and the entity or its *affiliates* is already in progress, or where the *engagement partner* considers such litigation to be probable, and which would compromise the independence of the *firm* or any *covered person*.	Section 4 (4.66 – 4.68)	**2.11**
The *firm* shall not provide any *non-audit/additional services* to an *entity relevant to an engagement*, where such provision would compromise the independence of the *firm* or any *covered person*.	Section 5	**2.12**
Failure to comply with a requirement of this Ethical Standard shall be deemed to compromise independence unless such failure has been addressed in accordance with paragraphs 1.22 and 1.23 of Section 1 of Part B of this Ethical Standard.		**2.13**

Part B

Section 1 – General Requirements and Guidance

Compliance

The *firm* shall establish appropriate policies and procedures to ensure that its owners or shareholders, as well as the members of the administrative, management and supervisory bodies of the *firm*, or of an *affiliate firm*, do not intervene in the carrying-out of an *engagement* in any way which jeopardises the integrity, objectivity or independence of the *firm* or *covered persons*; [AD 24a.1(a)]	**1.1D**

1.2D   The *firm* shall establish appropriate and effective organisational and administrative arrangements:

(a)   that are designed to prevent, identify, eliminate or manage and disclose any threats to its independence; [AD 24a.1(e)]

(b)   for dealing with and recording incidents which have, or may have, serious consequences for the integrity of its audit or other public interest assurance activities; [AD24a.1(i)]

1.3D   The *firm* shall take into consideration the scale and complexity of its activities when complying with the requirements set out in paragraphs 1.1D and 1.2D. [AD 24a.2]

1.4D   The *firm* shall be able to demonstrate to the FRC (or the Recognised Supervisory Body to whom the FRC has delegated regulatory tasks, where applicable) that the policies and procedures designed to achieve such compliance with the requirements in paragraphs 1.1D and 1.2D are appropriate given the scale and complexity of activities of the *firm*. [AD 24a.2]

1.5   The *firm*, its partners and *staff* shall, in so far as they are required to meet the ethical outcomes of the overarching principles and supporting ethical provisions in this Ethical Standard, be able to demonstrate that they have done so. This shall include, in so far as applicable to their roles, being able to demonstrate that they have:

●   implemented and maintained, and/or complied with, effective systems and processes to enable meeting those outcomes;

●   identified and reported relevant conditions and circumstances that threaten meeting those outcomes;

●   established and operated effective safeguards;

●   evaluated the threats and safeguards appropriately;

●   taken any additional steps that are appropriate in the circumstances to meet those outcomes.

1.6   The specific requirements in Sections 1 – 5 of Part B of this Ethical Standard are designed to assist in meeting the ethical outcomes of the overarching principles and supporting ethical provisions. However, circumstances relating to *engagements* vary widely and meeting these ethical outcomes is paramount. Compliance with the specific requirements may not be sufficient to do so as they do not address all possible circumstances.

1.7   When a statement or examples are given in this Ethical Standard to help clarify or illustrate a position in relation to particular circumstances, this is not intended to, and should not be interpreted as, indicating that in other circumstances the same position necessarily either is or is not intended. Whether the ethical outcomes of the overarching principles and supporting ethical provisions are met is always paramount and is a matter to be determined exercising professional judgment.

1.8   Meeting the ethical outcomes of the overarching principles and supporting ethical provisions, and complying with the specific requirements, regarding integrity, objectivity and independence is a responsibility of both the *firm* and of individual partners and *staff*. The *firm* establishes policies and procedures, appropriate to the size and nature of the *firm*, to promote and monitor meeting the ethical outcomes of the overarching principles and supporting ethical provisions, and compliance with the specific requirements, by the *firm*, its partners and its staff.[9],

Supporting ethical provision 1.1 establishes that the senior management of the **1.9** *firm*, and those with direct responsibility for the management of the *firm*'s audit and other public interest assurance business, instil the necessary culture and behaviours throughout the *firm* so as to ensure that meeting the ethical outcomes of the overarching principles and supporting ethical provisions is paramount and supersedes all commercial interests of the *firm*. The senior management of the *firm* influences the internal culture of the *firm* by its actions and by its example ("the tone at the top"). Achieving a robust control environment requires that the senior management give clear, consistent and frequent messages, backed up by appropriate actions, which emphasise the importance of meeting the ethical outcomes of the overarching principles and supporting ethical provisions for *audit* and other *public interest assurance engagements* by all parts of the *firm*, including those parts that are not involved in providing audit and other public interest assurance services.

The senior management of the *firm*, and those with direct responsibility for **1.10** **the management of the *firm*'s audit and other public interest assurance** **business, shall establish appropriate policies, procedures and quality control** **and monitoring systems; dedicate appropriate resources and leadership to** **compliance with supporting ethical provision 1.1; and make appropriate** **arrangements with *network firms* to ensure compliance as necessary across** **the network. The *firm* shall ensure that such appropriate policies, procedures** **and quality control and monitoring systems are implemented and operated** **effectively.**

In order to promote a strong control environment, the *firm* establishes policies and **1.11** procedures that include:

(a)   requirements for its partners and *staff* to report where applicable in relation to an *entity relevant to an engagement* by the *firm*:

- family and other personal relationships involving such an entity;

- financial interests in such an entity;

- decisions to join such an entity.

(b)   monitoring of compliance with the *firm*'s policies and procedures relating to integrity, objectivity and independence. Such monitoring procedures include, on a test basis, periodic review of the *engagement partners'* documentation of the consideration of the integrity, objectivity and independence of the *firm*, its partners and *staff*, addressing, for example:

- financial interests in *entities relevant to an engagement* by the *firm*;

- economic dependence on *entities relevant to an engagement* by the *firm*;

---

[9] *Monitoring of compliance with ethical requirements will often be performed as part of a broader quality control process. ISQC (UK) 1 "Quality Control for Firms that Perform Audits and Reviews of Financial Statements and other Assurance and Related Services Engagements" establishes requirements in relation to a firm's responsibilities for its system of quality control for audits.*

- the performance of *non-audit/additional services*;
- *engagement partner* rotation;

(c)   identification of the entities which partners and *staff*, and, where applicable, *persons closely associated* with them, need to be independent from;

(d)   arrangements for prompt communication of possible or actual breaches of the *firm*'s policies and procedures to the relevant *engagement partners*;

(e)   evaluation by *engagement partners* of the implications of any identified possible or actual breaches of the *firm*'s policies and procedures that are reported to them;

(f)   reporting by *engagement partners* of particular circumstances or relationships as required by this Ethical Standard;

(g)   operation of an enforcement mechanism to promote compliance with policies and procedures;

(h)   empowerment of its *staff* to communicate without fear to senior levels within the *firm* any concerns about the *firm*'s commitment to quality work and professional judgment and values, including issues of integrity, objectivity or independence that concerns them; this includes establishing confidential communication channels open to *staff*, encouraging *staff* to use these channels and ensuring that *staff* who use these channels are not discriminated against and are not subject to disciplinary proceedings as a result.

Ethics Partner

1.12   **The senior management of the *firm* shall designate a partner in the *firm* possessing the necessary seniority, relevant experience, authority and leadership levels (the "*Ethics Partner*") as having responsibility for ensuring the *firm*'s compliance with supporting ethical provision 1.1. The *Ethics Partner* is supported, where appropriate, by other persons with relevant experience in the *firm*, comprising an "Ethics Function". The *Ethics Partner* shall have direct reporting lines to the *firm*'s leadership Board and to the *firm*'s independent non-executives, where applicable.**

1.13   **Save where the circumstances contemplated in paragraph 1.20 apply, the responsibilities of the *Ethics Partner* shall include:**

(a)   **the adequacy of the *firm*'s policies and procedures relating to integrity, objectivity and independence, meeting the ethical outcomes required by the overarching principals and supporting ethical provisions, and compliance with the requirements of this Ethical Standard, and the effectiveness of its communication to its partners and *staff* on these matters within the *firm*; and**

(b)   **providing related guidance to individual partners and *staff* with a view to achieving a consistent approach to the application of this Ethical Standard.**

If differences of opinion arise between the *Ethics Partner* and persons 1.14
consulting him or her, the *firm*'s policies and procedures for dealing with
and resolving differences of opinion shall be followed[10].

The *Ethics Partner* is an individual with seniority and authority at leadership 1.15
levels within the *firm*, possessing relevant experience, and whose decisions and
advice on ethical matters will be respected by persons at all levels within the *firm*,
including by any more senior partners. Experience of audit and/or other *public
interest assurance engagements* would be useful.

The *Ethics Partner* shall not undertake another role within the *firm* which 1.16
conflicts with their responsibilities as Ethics Partner.

Where the *Ethics Partner* undertakes this role together with a role such as 1.17
Compliance or Risk Management he or she ensures that the responsibilities of
the *Ethics Partner* take precedence over the responsibilities of other functions.
Where the *Ethics Partner* is supported by an Ethics Function, the *Ethics Partner*
retains overall responsibility for operation of that function and the decisions made
and advice given by it.

In the case of *firms* that undertake *engagements* for *public interest entities* (PIEs) 1.18
or other *listed entities*, the *Ethics Partner* has direct access to the *firm*'s
independent non-executives where such roles are introduced in the *firm*[11] or,
alternatively, to the *firm*'s most senior governance body.

In assessing the effectiveness of the *firm*'s communication of its policies and 1.19
procedures relating to integrity, objectivity and independence, the *Ethics Partner*
considers whether ethics are covered properly in the *firm*'s induction programmes,
professional training and continuing professional development for all partners and
staff. *Ethics Partners* also provide guidance on matters referred to them and on
matters, which they otherwise become aware of, where a difficult and objective
judgment needs to be made or a consistent position reached. The *Ethics Partner* is
proactive in considering the ethical implications of developments in the business
of the *firm* and the environment in which it operates and in providing advice and
guidance to partners and *staff* where appropriate.

In *firms* with three or fewer partners who are "Responsible Individuals"[12], it may 1.20
not be practicable for an *Ethics Partner* to be designated. In these circumstances
all partners will regularly discuss ethical issues amongst themselves, so ensuring
that they act in a consistent manner and observe the overarching principles and
supporting ethical provisions set out in this Ethical Standard. In the case of a sole
practitioner, advice on matters where a difficult and objective judgment needs to
be made is obtained through the ethics helpline of the practitioner's professional
body, or through discussion with a practitioner from another *firm*. In all cases, it is
important that such discussions are documented.

To be able to discharge his or her responsibilities, the *Ethics Partner* shall be 1.21
provided with sufficient staff support and other resources (the Ethics
Function), commensurate with the size of the *firm*. Alternative
arrangements shall be established to allow for:

---

[10] *ISQC (UK) 1, paragraph 43, requires firms to establish policies and procedures for dealing with and resolving differences of opinion with those consulted.*

[11] *Firms that comply with the Audit Firm Governance Code will have appointed independent non-executives who should have the majority on a body that oversees public interest matters. Other firms may also have independent non-executives.*

[12] *A "Responsible Individual" is a partner or employee of the firm who is responsible for audit work and designated as such under the audit regulations of a Recognised Supervisory Body.*

- the provision of guidance on those audits or other *public interest assurance engagements* where the *Ethics Partner* is the *engagement partner*; and

- situations where the *Ethics Partner* is unavailable, for example due to illness or holidays.

Where such support is shared with other functions such as Compliance or Risk Management, the *Ethics Partner* shall establish policies and procedures to ensure that:

- matters delegated to the Ethics Function by the *Ethics Partner*, whether directly or indirectly through the operation of delegation policies established by the *Ethics Partner*, are clearly identified in internal documentation as relating to the *Ethics Partner* role and are addressed and supervised in a manner consistent with the *Ethics Partner* role, avoiding conflicts with other objectives; and

- all matters required to be communicated to, consulted upon with, or approved by the *Ethics Partner* are communicated to him or her or an authorised delegate personally, on a timely basis.

Breaches

1.22 Whenever a possible or actual breach of this Ethical Standard, or of policies and procedures established pursuant to the overarching principles and supporting ethical provisions and requirements established in it, is identified, the *engagement partner*, in the first instance, and the *Ethics Partner*, where appropriate, assesses the implications of the breach, determines whether there are safeguards that can be put in place or other actions that can be taken to address any potential adverse consequences and considers whether there is a need to resign or withdraw from the *engagement*.

1.23 An inadvertent violation of this Ethical Standard does not necessarily call into question the *firm*'s ability to give an audit or other public interest assurance opinion, provided that:

(a) the *firm* has established policies and procedures that require all partners, *staff* and other *covered persons* to report any breach promptly to the *engagement partner* or to the *Ethics Partner*, as appropriate;

(b) the *engagement partner* or *Ethics Partner* promptly notifies the relevant partner, member of *staff* or other *covered person* that any matter which has given rise to a breach is to be addressed as soon as possible and ensures that such action is taken;

(c) safeguards, where appropriate, are applied, (for example, having another partner review the work done by the relevant partner, member of *staff* or other *covered person* or removing him or her from the *engagement team* or from otherwise being a *covered person*; and

(d) the actions taken and the rationale for them are documented.

Non-involvement in Management Decision-taking

1.24 Supporting ethical provision 2.1D requires that the *firm* and each *covered person* is not involved in the decision-taking of an *entity relevant to the engagement*. Paragraph 5.167R of Section 5 of Part B of this Ethical Standard requires in accordance with the EU Audit Regulation that, in the case of a *statutory audit* of a *public interest entity*, *non-audit services* shall not be provided that involve playing any part in the management or decision-making of an *audited entity*.

It is not possible to specify all types of decision that are the responsibility of management, but they typically involve leading and directing the entity, including making significant judgments and taking decisions regarding the acquisition, deployment and control of human, financial, physical and intangible resources. Examples of judgments and decisions that should not be made by the *firm* or a *covered person* include:

1.25

- Setting policies and strategic direction;

- Directing and taking responsibility for the actions of the entity's employees;

- Authorising transactions;

- Deciding which recommendations of the *firm* or other third parties should be implemented;

- Taking responsibility for the preparation and fair presentation of financial statements in accordance with the applicable financial reporting framework;

- Taking responsibility for the preparation and presentation of *subject matter information* in the case of an other *public interest assurance engagement*; and

- Taking responsibility for designing, implementing and maintaining internal control.

Identification and Assessment of Threats

The *engagement partner* identifies and assesses the circumstances which could adversely affect the integrity or objectivity of the *firm* or of *covered persons* ("threats"), including any that could impair independence, and applies procedures ("safeguards"), which will either:

1.26

(a) eliminate the threat (for example, by eliminating the circumstances, such as removing an individual from the *engagement team* or disposing of a financial interest in the entity); or

(b) reduce the threat to level at which independence is not compromised.

If, during the period covered by the financial statements or by an other *public interest assurance engagement*, an *entity relevant to the engagement* is acquired by, merges with, or acquires another entity, the *firm* and each relevant engagement partner shall identify and evaluate any current or recent interests or relationships, including any *non-audit/additional services* provided to that entity, which, taking into account available safeguards, could compromise the integrity, objectivity or independence of the *firm* or *covered persons* and the ability to continue with the *engagement* after the effective date of the merger or acquisition. As soon as possible, and in any event within three months, the *firm* and each relevant *engagement partner* shall take all such steps as may be necessary to terminate any current interests or relationships that would compromise integrity, objectivity or independence and shall, where possible, adopt safeguards to eliminate or reduce any threat to integrity or objectivity, including any threats that could impair independence, arising from prior and current interests and relationships, to a level where independence is not compromised. [AD 22.6]

1.27D

Threats to Integrity, Objectivity and Independence

1.28   When complying with supporting ethical provisions 2.1D – 2.3D, conditions and relationship that could give rise to threats to the integrity, objectivity or independence of the *firm* or *covered persons* are communicated to the appropriate person, having regard to the nature of the threats and to the part of the *firm* and the identity of any person involved. The consideration of all threats on an individual and cumulative[13] basis and the action taken is documented. If the *engagement partner* is personally involved in the threat, or is unsure about the action to be taken, the matter is resolved through consultation with the *Ethics Partner*/Function who should be provided with all facts relevant to consideration of the issue.

1.29   The principal types of threats to the integrity, objectivity and independence of the *firm* and *covered persons* are:

● **self-interest threat**

  A self-interest threat arises when any of the *firm*, its partners, *staff* or other *covered persons*, has financial or other interests which might cause the *firm* or any *covered person* to be, or perceived to be, reluctant to take actions in connection with the engagement that would be adverse to such interests of the *firm* or any *such person*. For example, such interests may include holding an investment in the entity, seeking to provide additional services to the entity or needing to recover long-outstanding fees from the entity. In relation to *non-audit/additional services*, the main self-interest threats concern fees and economic dependence and these are addressed in Section 4 of this Ethical Standard.

● **self-review threat**

  A self-review threat arises when the results of *non-audit/additional services*, or where the *subject matter* of such services, whether performed by the *firm*, the *engagement team* or others within the *firm*, are addressed in the *engagement* or reflected in the amounts included or disclosed in the financial statements or other *subject matter information* of the *engagement*. For example, a self-review threat may arise where the *firm* has been involved in maintaining the accounting records, or undertaking valuations that are incorporated in financial statements that the *firm* audits or reports on in relation to an initial public offering. In the course of the *engagement*, the persons conducting the *engagement* may need to re-evaluate the work performed in the *non-audit/additional service*. As, by virtue of providing the *non-audit/additional service*, the *firm* is associated with aspects of the preparation of the financial statements or other *subject matter* or *subject matter information* relating to the *non-audit/additional services*, the *firm* or *covered person* may be, or may be perceived to be, unable to take an impartial view of relevant aspects of those financial statements or other *subject matter information*.

  In assessing the significance of the self-review threat, the persons conducting the *engagement* consider the extent to which the *non-audit/additional service* will:

---

[13] *For this purpose, "cumulative" means all current relationships and any past completed relationships that may be expected to have a continuing relevance to the auditor's independence and consideration of the threats that might exist.*

- involve a significant degree of subjective judgment; and
- have a material effect on the preparation and presentation of the financial statements or other *subject matter information* or *subject matter* of the *engagement*. [ES 5.33]

Where a significant degree of judgment is involved in a *non-audit/ additional service* relating to the financial statements, or other *subject matter information*, or to the *subject matter* of an *engagement*, the persons conducting the *engagement* may be inhibited from questioning that judgment in the course of the *engagement*. Whether a significant degree of subjective judgment is involved will depend upon whether the *non-audit/ additional service* involves the application of well-established principles and procedures, and whether reliable information is available. If such circumstances do not exist because the *non-audit/additional service* is based on concepts, methodologies or assumptions that require judgment and are not established by the entity or by authoritative guidance, the integrity and objectivity of the *firm* and *covered persons* and their independence could be compromised. Where the provision of a proposed *non-audit/additional service* would also have a material effect on the financial statements, or other *subject matter information*, or on the *subject matter* of an *engagement*, it is unlikely that any safeguard can eliminate or reduce the self-review threat to a level where independence is not compromised.

In relation to an *investment circular reporting engagement*, there is, for example, a self-review threat where a *firm* prepares an accountant's report on historical financial information which has been included in, or formed part of, financial statements which have already been subject to audit by the same *firm*. In such situations, where the two engagement teams are not independent of each other, the *engagement partner* evaluates the significance of the self-review threat created. If this is other than clearly insignificant, safeguards are applied, such as the appointment of an *engagement quality control reviewer* who has not been involved in the audit.

- ***management threat***

Supporting ethical provision 2.1D requires that the *firm* and each *covered person* is not involved in the decision-taking of an *entity relevant to the engagement*. Paragraph 5.167R of Section 5 of Part B of this Ethical Standard requires in accordance with the EU Audit Regulation that, in the case of a *statutory audit* of a *public interest entity*, *non-audit services* shall not be provided that involve playing any part in the management or decision-making of an *audited entity*. Some activities that may be undertaken by the *firm* or its *staff* may give rise to a threat of being involved in making decisions that are the responsibility of management. A threat to integrity, objectivity and independence also arises where the *firm* provides *non-audit/additional services* and, based on that work, management are required to make judgments and take decisions. The persons conducting the service may become closely aligned with the views and interests of management and this may erode the distinction between the entity and the *firm*, in turn, impairing or calling into question the ability of the persons conducting an *engagement* to apply a proper degree of professional scepticism. The integrity and objectivity of the *firm* and *covered persons could be adversely affected* and their independence could be compromised.

In determining whether a *non-audit/additional service* does or does not give rise to a management threat, the persons conducting the engagement consider whether there is "*informed management*". *Informed management* exists when:

- a member of management (or senior employee of the entity) has been designated by the entity to receive the results of the *non-audit/ additional service* and has been given the authority to make any judgments and decisions of the type set out in paragraphs 1.24 and 1.25 that are needed;

- that member of management has the capability to make independent management judgments and decisions on the basis of the information provided; and

- the results of the *non-audit/additional service* are communicated to the entity and, where judgments or decisions are to be made by management they are supported by an objective analysis of the issues to consider and the entity is given the opportunity to decide between reasonable alternatives.

In the absence of such *informed management* it is unlikely that any other safeguards can eliminate a management threat or reduce it to a level where independence is not compromised.

In relation to an *investment circular reporting engagement*, a management threat arises, for example, when the *firm* undertakes work that involves making judgments and taking decisions, which are the responsibility of the management of the party responsible for issuing the *investment circular* containing the financial information or the party on whose financial information the *firm* is reporting in relation to:

- the transaction (for example, where it has been working closely with a company in developing a divestment strategy); or

- the financial information that is the subject of the *investment circular reporting engagement* (for example, deciding on the assumptions to be used in a profit forecast).

- **advocacy threat**

  An advocacy threat arises when the *firm* undertakes work that involves acting as an advocate for an *entity relevant to an engagement*, and supporting a position taken by management in an adversarial or promotional context (for example, by acting as a legal advocate for the entity in litigation or a regulatory investigation, or undertaking an active responsibility for the marketing of an entity's shares). In order to act in an advocacy role, the *firm* has to adopt a position closely aligned to that of management. This creates both actual and perceived threats to the integrity, objectivity and independence of the *firm* and *covered persons*. For example, where the *firm*, acting as advocate, has supported a particular contention of management, it may be difficult for the persons conducting the *engagement* to take an impartial view of this in the context of an audit of the financial statements.

  Where the provision of a *non-audit/additional service* would require the *firm*, its partners or staff to act as an advocate for the entity in relation to matters that are material to the financial statements or other *subject matter information*, or to the *subject matter* of an *engagement*, it is unlikely that any safeguards can eliminate or reduce the advocacy threat to a level where independence would not be compromised.

- *familiarity (or trust) threat*

    A familiarity (or trust) threat arises when the *firm* or a *covered person* predisposed to accept, or is insufficiently questioning of, the point of view of an *entity relevant to the engagement. Such threats may arise*, for example, where close personal relationships are developed with such an entity's personnel through long association with the entity.

- *intimidation threat*

    An intimidation threat arises when the conduct of the *firm* or a *covered person* is influenced by fear or threats (for example, where the persons conducting the *engagement* encounter an aggressive and/or dominating individual).

    These categories of threat may not be entirely distinct and certain circumstances may give rise to more than one type of threat. For example, where a *firm* wishes to retain the fee income from a large *entity relevant to an engagement*, but encounters an aggressive or dominating individual, there may be a self-interest threat as well as an intimidation threat. Furthermore, relationships with *connected parties* of the entity (such as an *affiliate*) may give rise to similar threats.

Threats to the integrity and objectivity of the *firm* and *covered persons*, including threats that could compromise independence, may, for example, arise where the *firm* is appointed to provide *non-audit/additional services* for an entity not relevant to an *engagement* by the *firm*, but where an entity that is relevant to an *engagement* by the *firm* makes this decision. In such cases, even if the entity not relevant to an *engagement* by the *firm* pays the fee for the *non-audit/additional service* services, the *firm* considers the implication of the threats (especially the self-interest threat) that arise from the appointment. **1.30**

Threats to the integrity or objectivity of the *firm* and *covered persons*, including threats that could compromise independence, may also arise where a *non-audit/additional service* is provided by the *firm* to a third party which is connected (through a relationship) to an *entity relevant to an engagement* by the *firm*, and the outcome of that service has a material impact on the financial statements of the entity or other *subject matter, information*, or on the *subject matter* of the *engagement*. For example, such threats may arise if the *firm* provides actuarial services to the pension scheme of an audited entity, which is in deficit and the *firm* subsequently gives an opinion on financial statements that include judgments given in connection with that service. **1.31**

Similarly threats may arise where the *firm* or any *covered person* has a relationship with any *connected party* of the entity. Where any member of the *engagement team* is aware of such relationships, an assessment is made of whether independence is compromised (see also paragraph 1.37). **1.32**

The *firm* shall establish policies and procedures to require the *engagement partner* to identify and assess the significance of threats to the integrity and objectivity of the *firm* and *covered persons* on an individual and cumulative[10] basis, including any threats that may compromise independence: **1.33**

(a)   when considering whether to accept or retain an *engagement*;

(b)   when planning the *engagement*;

(c)   **when forming an opinion and signing the report on the financial statements or other *subject matter information*;**[14]

(d)   **when considering whether to accept or continue to provide** non-audit/ additional services **to an *engagement* by the *firm*; and**

(e)   **when potential threats are reported to him or her.**

1.34   An initial assessment of the threats to integrity, objectivity and independence is required when the *engagement partner* is considering whether to accept or retain an *engagement*. That assessment is reviewed and updated at the planning stage of each *engagement*. If consideration of whether to accept or retain an *engagement* does not arise, for example where responsibility for the *engagement* is assigned by legislation (e.g. for certain bodies in the public sector), an assessment of the threats to integrity, objectivity and independence is still undertaken. At the end of the *engagement* process, when forming an opinion on the financial statements or other *subject matter information* but before issuing the report, the *engagement partner* draws an overall conclusion as to whether all threats to integrity or objectivity including any that may compromise independence have been properly addressed on an individual and cumulative basis in accordance with this Ethical Standard. If, at any time, the *firm* is invited to provide *non-audit/additional services*, the *engagement partner* considers the impact this may have on the integrity, objectivity and independence of the *firm*, its partners or *staff*.

1.35   **When identifying and assessing threats to the integrity or objectivity of the *firm* or any *covered persons*, including any that may compromise independence, the *engagement partner* shall take into account current relationships with the entity (including *non-audit/additional services* provided and known relationships with *connected parties* of the entity) and with other parties in certain circumstances (see paragraph 1.37), that existed prior to the current *engagement* and any known to be in prospect following the current *engagement*.**

> For an *investment circular reporting engagement*, the *relevant period* for consideration covers the period during which the engagement is undertaken and any additional period before that but subsequent to the balance sheet date of the most recent audited financial statements[15] of the *entity relevant to the engagement*. A *firm*'s procedures will include reference to records of past and current services/*engagements* whenever a new *investment circular reporting engagement* is proposed.

1.36   The requirement in paragraph 1.35 is because those prior and subsequent relationships may be perceived as likely to influence the *firm* or *covered persons* in the performance of the *engagement* or as otherwise compromising the integrity, objectivity or independence of the *firm* or *covered persons*.

1.37   Threats to the integrity or objectivity of the *firm* and *covered persons*, including those that may compromise independence, may arise where a service is provided by the *firm* to a third party which is connected (through a relationship) to an *entity*

---

[14] *In the case of listed entities, the auditor also assesses whether there is any threat to the auditor's integrity, objectivity or independence when discharging responsibilities in relation to preliminary announcements and when reporting on interim results.*

[15] *In the case of newly incorporated clients (not part of an established group of companies), where there has been no financial statement audit, this period is from the date of incorporation.*

relevant to an engagement by the *firm*, and the outcome of that service has a material impact on the financial statements or other *subject matter information* of the entity. For example, if the *firm* provides actuarial services to the pension scheme of an *audited entity*, which is in deficit, and the *firm* subsequently gives an opinion on financial statements that include judgments given in connection with that service.

Where the entity *relevant to an engagement* or a third party calls into question   1.38
the integrity, objectivity or independence of the *firm* in relation to a particular
entity, the *Ethics Partner* shall carry out such investigations as may be
appropriate and determine what action, if any, is needed.

Investment Circular Reporting Engagements

When identifying threats to integrity or objectivity including any that could   1.39
impair independence, *reporting accountants* consider circumstances and
relationships with a number of different parties. For example, the *entities
relevant to the engagement* may constitute one or more parties, dependent on
the circumstances of the transaction which is the subject of the *investment
circular*[16]. Where the party responsible for issuing the *investment circular* is
different from the party whose financial information is included in the
investment circular, the *reporting accountant* makes an assessment of
independence with respect to each of these parties, applying the alternative
procedures set out in paragraph 1.40 as necessary.

Where either: 1.40

- an *investment circular reporting engagement* is undertaken to provide
  a report on the financial information relating to an entity audited by
  the *firm* but the *reporting accountant's* report is to be published in an
  investment circular issued by another entity that is not an entity
  audited by the *firm*; or
- the *reporting accountant's* report is to be published in an *investment
  circular* issued by an entity audited by the *firm* but the *reporting
  accountant's* report is on financial information relating to another
  entity that is not an entity audited by the *firm*,

it may not be practicable in the time available to identify all relationships
and other services or engagements recently undertaken by the *firm* for the
non-audit *entity relevant to the engagement* and its *significant affiliates*. In
such instances the *reporting accountant* undertakes those enquiries[17] that are
practical in the time available into the relationships and other services/
engagements that the *firm* has with the non-audit *entity relevant to the
engagement* and, having regard to its obligations to maintain confidentiality,
addresses any identified threats. Having done so, the *reporting accountant*
discloses to those charged with governance of the issuing *entity relevant to
the engagement* that a consideration of all known threats has been
undertaken and, where appropriate, safeguards applied, but that this does
not constitute a full evaluation of all relationships and other services
provided to the non-audit *entity relevant to the engagement*.

---

[16] *For example, where a report on a target company's financial statements is prepared by that company's auditors
for inclusion in the acquiring company's investment circular.*

[17] *For example, these enquiries are likely to include reviewing the list of engagements recorded in the firm's
accounting systems and an enquiry of individuals within the firm who are responsible for maintaining such systems
as to whether any confidentially coded engagements could be relevant.*

1.41   In addition to considering independence with respect to each *entity relevant to the engagement*, the *reporting accountant* shall also consider relationships with other parties who are connected with the *investment circular*. These parties shall include the sponsor or nominated advisor, other parties from whom, in accordance with the engagement letter, the *reporting accountant* takes instructions and other entities directly involved in the transaction which is the subject of the *investment circular*.[18]

1.42   The *reporting accountant* considers the circumstances involved and uses judgment to assess whether it is probable that an objective, reasonable and informed third party would conclude that the *reporting accountant's* integrity or objectivity is impaired and independence is compromised as a result of relationships held with any of these parties.

1.43   In the case of established financial institutions or advisers, the *reporting accountant* may have extensive relationships with these parties, including for the provision of other services or the purchase of goods and services in the ordinary course of business that are not material to any *entity relevant to the engagement*. These relationships will not generally give rise to a significant threat to the *reporting accountant's* integrity or objectivity.

1.44   Relationships with other parties who are connected with the *investment circular* which are outside the ordinary course of business or which are material to any *entity relevant to the engagement* are more likely to give rise to a significant threat to the *reporting accountant's* integrity or objectivity. Consideration of the threats to the *reporting accountant's* integrity or objectivity in relation to other entities will primarily be concerned with matters that could give rise to self-interest and intimidation threats, for example:

- where there is financial dependence on the relationship with the other party arising from fees (including any contingent element) for *investment circular reporting engagements* undertaken by the *firm* as a result of connections with the other parties;
- joint ventures or similar relationships with the other party or with a senior member of their management;
- significant purchases of goods or services which are not in the ordinary course of business or are not on an arm's length basis;
- personal relationships between *engagement team* members and individuals in senior positions within the other party; or
- large direct financial interests in, or loans made by, the other party.

Identification and Assessment of Safeguards

1.45   If the *engagement partner* identifies threats to the integrity or objectivity of the *firm* or *covered persons*, including any that could compromise independence, he or she shall identify and assess the effectiveness of the available safeguards and apply such safeguards as are sufficient to eliminate the threats or reduce them to a level where independence would not be compromised.

---

[18] *Where such entities are part of a complex group or corporate structure, the reporting accountant considers issues relating to the wider group and not just the entity directly involved in the transaction.*

The nature and extent of safeguards to be applied depend on the significance of the threats. Where a threat is clearly insignificant, no safeguards are needed. **1.46**

Other sections of this Ethical Standard address specific circumstances that can create threats to integrity or objectivity or could impair the independence of the *firm* or *covered persons*. They give examples of safeguards that can, in some circumstances, eliminate the threat or reduce it to level where it would not compromise independence. In some circumstances, the *firm* either does not accept or withdraws from the *engagement* as appropriate or, in the case of threats arising from the provision of *non-audit/additional services*, does not undertake or withdraws from the *non-audit/additional service*. **1.47**

This Ethical Standard contains certain additional requirements or prohibitions that apply only in the case of *engagements* for *public interest entities* (PIEs) or *listed entities or in both cases*: **1.48**

- *Public interest entities* only: paragraphs 1.75R, 2.39(b)(i), 3.10R, 3.18R, 3.19R, 4.34R, 5.167R, 5.168R, 5.170R, 5.171R, 5.172R, 5.173R

- *Listed entities* only (including such entities that are PIEs) other than SME listed entities: paragraphs 5.67(a), 5.74(a), 5.85(a), 5.92, 5.104(a), 5.111, 5.148, 5.155(a)

- *Listed entities* only (including *SME listed entities* and *listed entities* that are PIEs): paragraphs 3.11, 5.47

- *Listed entities* (including *SME listed entities*) and *public interest entities*: paragraphs 1.66, 3.20, 3.21, 4.25, 4.37, 4.42, 4.47

These additional requirements also apply where regulation or legislation requires that the *engagement* for an entity is conducted in accordance with the standards or ethical requirements that are applicable to *engagements* for *public interest entities* or other *listed entities*.

The *firm* shall establish policies and procedures which set out the circumstances in which those additional requirements listed in paragraph 1.48 that apply to *public interest entities* or to *listed entities* or both are applied to other *engagements*. Where such requirements are applied to a *public interest entity* or to a *listed entity* or both, or to an other entity under such policies and procedures, the *engagement partner* shall ensure that fact is communicated to those charged with governance. **1.49**

Such policies and procedures take into consideration any additional criteria set by the *firm*, such as the nature of the entity's business, its size, the number of its employees and the range of its stakeholders. For example, a *firm* may decide to extend the additional requirements to *engagements* for certain large private sector entities. **1.50**

The *engagement partner* shall not accept or shall not continue an *engagement* if he or she concludes that any threats to the integrity or objectivity of the *firm* or *covered persons* cannot be reduced to a level where independence would not be compromised. **1.51**

Where an objective, reasonable and informed third party would regard ceasing to act as the provider of an *engagement* as detrimental to the shareholders of the *audited entity* (or equivalent intended users of the audit or other assurance engagement report) of, or would otherwise be contrary to the public interest, then resignation may not be immediate. However, the *firm* discloses full details of the position to those charged with governance of the entity and, if applicable **1.52** (e.g. for an *investment circular reporting engagement*), other entities and persons the *firm* is instructed to advise, and establishes appropriate safeguards.

Other Firms Involved Engagements

1.53   In order to use the work of another *firm* (including *network firms*) for the purpose of an *engagement*, the lead *firm* for the *engagement* has to be satisfied that such another *firm* is independent of each *entity relevant to the engagement* in accordance with supporting ethical provision 2.4 of this Ethical Standard.

1.54   The *engagement partner* obtains sufficient appropriate evidence[19] as necessary to be satisfied that *network firms* (whether or not involved in the *engagement*), and third party *firms* whose work is used in the conduct of the *engagement*, are independent of each *entity relevant to the engagement* in accordance with supporting ethical provision 2.4. If the *engagement partner* is not able to obtain such evidence, or obtains evidence that the other *firm* does not meet the relevant independence requirements, the *engagement team* cannot use the work of that other *firm* for the purpose of the *engagement*. Work for the purpose of the *engagement* may be undertaken, where possible, by partners and *staff* from the *firm* performing the *engagement* or by another *firm* which is independent of each *entity relevant to the engagement* as required.

1.55   In the case of a *public interest entity* or an other *listed entity*, the *engagement partner* establishes that the *entity relevant to the engagement* has communicated its policy[20] on the use of *firms* to supply *non-audit/additional services* to its *affiliates* and obtains confirmation that the other *firms* involved in the engagement will comply with this policy.

Engagement Quality Control Review

1.56   Requirements for engagement quality control review are established in ISQC (UK) 1.

Overall Conclusion

1.57   **At the end of the *engagement* process, when forming an opinion to be reported, or otherwise reporting on the work undertaken, but before issuing the report, the *engagement partner* shall reach an overall conclusion that any threats to integrity or objectivity including any that could impair independence on an individual and cumulative basis have been properly addressed in accordance with this Ethical Standard. If the *engagement partner* cannot make such a conclusion, he or she shall not report and the *firm* shall resign or otherwise withdraw from the *engagement* unless not permitted to do so by law or regulation.**

1.58   In addition to assessing individual threats to integrity or objectivity including any that could impair independence of the *firm* or *covered persons*, the *engagement partner* assesses the cumulative impact of all the threats identified so as to reach a conclusion that the threats identified, when viewed individually and cumulatively, have been eliminated or reduced to a level where independence would not be compromised.

---

[19] *For an audit, ISA (UK) 600 "Special Considerations – Audits of Group Financial Statements (Including the Work of Component Auditors)" requires that the group engagement team shall obtain an understanding of whether the component auditor understands and will comply with the ethical requirements that are relevant to the group audit and, in particular, is independent.*

[20] *The UK Corporate Governance Code requires audit committees to develop the company's policy on the engagement of the external auditor to supply non-audit services.*

If the *engagement partner* remains unable to conclude that any individual threats **1.59** to integrity or objectivity including any that could impair independence, or that all such threats viewed on a cumulative basis, have been eliminated or reduced to a level where independence would not be compromised, or if there is a disagreement between the *engagement partner* and the *engagement quality control reviewer*, he or she consults the *Ethics Partner*/Function.

In concluding on these matters, the *engagement partner* is entitled to rely on the **1.60** completeness and accuracy of the data developed by the *firm*'s systems relating to independence (for example, in relation to the reporting of financial interests by *staff*), unless informed otherwise by the *firm*. In this context "data" does not include any judgments made about specific matters identified as the responsibility of the *engagement partner* in this Ethical Standard.

Communication with Those Charged With Governance

The *engagement partner* shall ensure that those charged with governance of **1.61** **each *entity relevant to an engagement*, and, in the case of an *investment circular reporting engagement*, any other persons or entities the *firm* is instructed to advise, are appropriately informed on a timely basis of all significant facts and matters that may bear upon the integrity, objectivity and independence of the *firm* or *covered persons*.**

The audit committee, where one exists, is usually responsible for oversight of the **1.62** relationship of an *entity relevant to the engagement* with the *firm* and of the conduct and outcome of the *engagement*. It therefore has a particular interest in being informed about the *firm*'s ability to express an objective opinion on the financial statements or other *subject matter information* or on the *subject matter* of the *engagement*. Where there is no audit committee, or where its responsibilities do not extend to other *public interest assurance engagements*, this role may be undertaken by another body with equivalent responsibilities or by the board of directors.[21].

The aim of these communications is to ensure full and fair disclosure by the *firm* to **1.63** those charged with governance of each *entity relevant to the engagement* on matters in which they have an interest. These matters will generally include the key elements of the *engagement partner's* consideration of integrity, objectivity and independence, such as:

- the principal threats, if any, to integrity or objectivity including any that could impair independence identified by the *firm*, including consideration of all relationships between the entity, its *affiliates* and directors and the *firm*;

- any safeguards adopted and the reasons why they are considered to be effective, including any independent partner review;

- the overall assessment of threats and safeguards;

- information about the general policies and processes within the *firm* for maintaining integrity, objectivity and independence.

---

[21] *Where there is no audit committee or equivalent body, references in this Ethical Standard to communication with the audit committee are to be construed as including communication with the board of directors.*

1.64   For an *investment circular reporting engagement*, if applicable, communications are made also to those from whom, in accordance with the engagement letter, the *firm* takes instructions on matters in which they have an interest. It may be that all of the parties to the engagement letter wish to be informed about all significant facts and matters that bear upon the integrity, objectivity and independence of the *firm* and *covered persons*. In other cases, however, the parties to the engagement letter (other than an *entity relevant to the engagement*) may not wish to be directly involved and may appoint one or more of their number to review these matters on their behalf. At the time of appointment, the *engagement partner* ensures that it is clear in the engagement letter to whom these communications are provided. If no such provision is included in the engagement letter, disclosures will be made to all those from whom, in accordance with the engagement letter, the *firm* takes instructions.

1.65   Communications between the *firm* and those charged with the governance of each *entity relevant to the engagement* and, in the case of an *investment circular reporting engagement*, any other persons the *firm* may be instructed to advise, will be needed at the planning stage and whenever significant judgments are made about threats to integrity, objectivity and independence and the appropriateness of safeguards put in place, for example, when accepting to provide *non-audit/ additional services*.

1.66   **In the case of *public interest entities*, and *listed entities*, relevant to an engagement <u>other than an *investment circular reporting engagement*</u>, the engagement partner shall ensure that the audit committee is provided with:**

(a)   **a written disclosure of relationships (including the provision of *non-audit/additional services*) that may bear on the integrity, objectivity or independence of the *firm* or *covered persons*. This shall have regard to relationships with the entity, its directors and senior management, its *affiliates*, and its *connected parties*, and the threats to integrity or objectivity, including those that could compromise independence, that these create. It shall also detail any safeguards that have been put in place and why they address such threats, together with any other information necessary to enable the integrity, objectivity and independence of the *firm* and each *covered person* to be assessed;**

(b)   **details of *non-audit/additional services* provided and the fees charged in relation thereto;**

(c)   **written confirmation that the *firm* and each *covered person* is independent;**

(d)   **details of any inconsistencies between this Ethical Standard and the policy of the *entity* for the provision of *non-audit/additional services* by the *firm* and any apparent breach of that policy.**

(e)   **an opportunity to discuss independence issues.**

For an *investment circular reporting engagement*, the *engagement partner* shall ensure those charged with governance of each *entity relevant to the engagement*, and any other persons or entities the *firm* is instructed to advise are provided in writing with:

(i)   details of all relationships that the *reporting accountant* considers may reasonably be thought to bear on the integrity, objectivity and independence of the *reporting accountant*, having regard to its relationships with each *entity relevant to the engagement*, its directors and senior management and its *affiliates*. This shall include significant services previously provided by the *firm* and *network firms* involved in the *investment circular reporting engagement* to each *entity relevant to the engagement* and its *significant affiliates*.

(ii)   disclosure of:

- all relationships that give rise to a threat to integrity or objectivity between the *reporting accountant* and:

  - the sponsor and such other parties from whom the *reporting accountant* takes instructions. Where a party to the engagement letter is an established financial institution or adviser, a generic disclosure that the *firm* has extensive relationships entered into in the ordinary course of business with these parties is sufficient with specific disclosure only being made in the case of relationships which are outside the ordinary course of business or which are material to any party;
  - other entities directly involved in the transaction which is the subject of the *investment circular*;

- whether the total amount of fees that the *reporting accountant* is likely to charge an *entity relevant to the engagement* and its *significant affiliates* for the provision of services relating to the transaction which is the subject of the *investment circular* during the *relevant period* is greater than 5% of the fee income of the *firm* in the *relevant period* or the part of the *firm* by reference to which the *engagement partner's* profit share is calculated during the *relevant period*; and

- the related safeguards that are in place and why they are considered effective;

(iii)   confirmation that the *firm* and each *covered person* is independent and, where relevant, the circumstances contemplated in paragraph 1.40 exist and that a consideration of all known threats and safeguards has been undertaken, but this does not constitute a full evaluation of all business relationships and other services provided to the entity.

1.68 The most appropriate time for these final written confirmations of independence is usually at the conclusion of the *engagement*.

1.69 The disclosure in writing of all relationships with the *entity relevant to the engagement*, and its directors and senior management and its *affiliates*, includes all services provided by the *firm* and its network to the entity, its directors and senior management and its *affiliates*, and other services provided to other known *connected parties* that may reasonably be thought to bear on the integrity, objectivity or independence of the *firm* or *covered persons* and the related safeguards that are in place.

1.70 For an *audit engagement*, the *engagement partner* ensures that the total amount of fees that the *firm* and its *network firms* have charged to the *audited entity* and its *affiliates* for the provision of services during the reporting period, analysed into appropriate categories are disclosed. The Appendix to this Ethical Standard contains an illustrative template for the provision of such information to an audit committee[22]. Separately, the auditor provides information on any contingent fee arrangements[23], the amounts of any future services which have been contracted, and details of any written proposal to provide *non-audit services* that has been submitted.

1.71 The written confirmation that the *firm* and each *covered person* is independent indicates that the *firm* considers that it complies with this Ethical Standard and that, in the *engagement partner's* professional judgment, the integrity, objectivity and independence of the *firm* and each *covered person* is not compromised. If it is not possible to make such a confirmation, the communication will include any concerns that the integrity, objectivity or independence of the *firm* or any *covered person* may be compromised (including instances where the *engagement partner* considers that the independence of an other *firm* involved in the *engagement* is compromised) and an explanation of the actions which necessarily follow from this.

Documentation

1.72D **The *firm* shall document in the *engagement* working papers all significant threats to the integrity or objectivity, including any that could impair independence, of the *firm* and all *covered persons* as well as the safeguards applied to mitigate those threats and why they mitigate the threats. [AD 22.3]**

1.73 **The *engagement partner* shall ensure that his or her consideration of the integrity, objectivity and independence of the *firm* and *covered persons* is appropriately documented on a timely basis.**

1.74D **Before accepting or continuing an *engagement*, the *firm* shall assess and document the following:**

- **whether it meets the ethical outcomes of the overarching principles and supporting ethical provisions, and complies with the requirements, of this Ethical Standard;**

---

[22] *When considering how to present this analysis of fees, the auditor takes account of any applicable legislation.*

[23] *Paragraph 4.25 of Section 4 of Part B of this Ethical Standard requires the engagement partner to disclose to the audit committee, in writing, any contingent fee arrangements for non-audit/additional services provided by the firm or its network firms.*

- whether there are threats to its integrity, objectivity or independence and the safeguards applied to mitigate those threats and why they mitigate the threats; [AD 22b.1]

Before accepting or continuing an engagement for a *statutory audit* of a *public interest entity*, ~~a statutory auditor or~~ an *audit firm* shall assess and document, in addition to the provisions of ~~Article 22b of Directive 2006/43/EC~~paragraph 1.74D above, the following:

1.75R

(a) whether ~~he, she or~~ it complies with the requirements of Articles 4[24] and 5[25] of ~~this~~the EU Audit Regulation;

(b) whether the conditions of Article 17[26] of ~~this~~the EU Audit Regulation are complied with;

(c) ~~without prejudice to Directive 2005/60/EC,~~ the integrity of the members of the supervisory, administrative and management bodies of the *public interest entity*. [AR 6.1]

The requirement to document these issues contributes to the clarity and rigour of the *engagement partner's* thinking and the quality of his or her judgments. In addition, such documentation provides evidence that the *engagement partner's* consideration of the integrity, objectivity and independence of the *firm* and *covered person* was properly performed and, for *public interest entities* and other *listed entities* and where otherwise applicable, provides the basis for review by the *engagement quality control reviewer*.

1.76

Matters to be documented[27] include all key elements of the process and any significant judgments concerning:

1.77

- threats identified, other than those which are clearly insignificant, and the process used in identifying them.

  For an *investment circular reporting engagement* this includes threats in relation to each *entity relevant to the engagement*, those from whom, in accordance with the engagement letter, the *reporting accountant* takes instructions and other entities directly involved in the transaction which is the subject of the *investment circular*;

- safeguards adopted and the reasons why they are considered to be effective;

- review by an *engagement quality control reviewer* or an independent partner;

- overall assessment of threats and safeguards on an individual and cumulative basis, and

- communication with those charged with governance and, where applicable, any other persons or entities the *firm* is instructed to advise.

---

[24] *See Section 4, paragraphs 4.6R, 4.7R and 4.34R – 4.36R, of Part B of this Ethical Standard.*

[25] *See Section 5, paragraphs 5.167R – 5.173R, of Part B of this Ethical Standard.*

[26] *See Section 3, paragraphs 3.9, 3.10R, 3.18R, 3.19R, of Part B of this Ethical Standard.*

[27] *The necessary working papers can be combined with those prepared pursuant to paragraph 24 of ISA (UK) 220 "Quality Control for an Audit of Financial Statements", which requires that: "The auditor shall include in the audit documentation conclusions on compliance with independence requirements that apply to the audit engagement, and any relevant discussions with the firm that support these conclusions."*

Effective Date

1.78   This Ethical Standard becomes effective on 17 June 2016.

1.79   *Firms* may complete *engagements* relating to periods commencing before 17 June 2016 in accordance with existing ethical standards, putting in place any necessary changes in the subsequent engagement period.

1.80   Engagements to provide tax services wholly or partly on a *contingent fee basis* to a *listed entity relevant to an engagement* that is not an *SME listed entity* (see paragraph 5.85 of Section 5 of Part B of this Ethical Standard), or a *significant affiliate* of such an entity, entered into before 17 June 2016 may continue until currently active services are completed in accordance with the engagement terms as long as:

- the engagement was permitted under the existing ethical standards; and

- safeguards established continue to be applied

A "currently active service" is one where the entity has already asked the *firm* for advice in relation to a particular matter and the *firm* has commenced work in relation to that matter. It does not include advice on future matters that may, for example, be provided for in an open ended engagement/contract.

Section 2 – Financial, Business, Employment and Personal Relationships

Financial Relationships

General Considerations

2.1   A financial interest in an entity is an interest in a *financial instrument* issued, guaranteed or otherwise supported by an entity, including rights and obligations to acquire such an interest and derivatives directly related to such an interest.

2.2   A financial interest may be:

(a)   a "direct financial interest", held by way of

    (i)   direct ownership of the *financial instrument*; or

    (ii)   a "direct beneficial interest" – i.e. an interest held through an intermediary which is controlled by that person holding the financial interest or where that person has the ability to influence the intermediary's investment policy.

        For example, a direct beneficial interest may exist by virtue of the person being an identified potential beneficiary under a trust, or under a will relating to an estate, where the trust or estate holds an underlying direct financial interest and the person has such control or influence over the trust or estate; or

(b)   an "indirect financial interest", held through an intermediary (other than an intermediary over which the person holding the financial interest has control or influence as described in (a)).

    For example, an indirect financial interest may be held through a diversified collective investment scheme, such as an authorised unit or investment trust, an open ended investment company, managed funds such as pensions or life insurance or other similar investment schemes with diversified investments, diversified investors and independent investment managers.

For an *engagement* other than an *investment circular reporting engagement*, save where otherwise required when the circumstances contemplated in paragraphs 2.7, 2.9, 2.12, 2.18 and 2.20 apply, and always subject to the prohibitions on holding financial interests set out in paragraph 2.4D, the *firm*, each partner in the *firm*, each *covered person* and any *persons closely associated* with any such partner or *covered person*, shall not hold: **2.3D**

(a) any direct financial interest in an *entity relevant to the engagement* or an entity that is an *affiliate* of such an entity; or

(b) any indirect financial interest in an *entity relevant to the engagement* or any entity that is an *affiliate* of such an entity, that is material to the *firm*, or the person or the intermediary; or

(c) any other indirect financial interest in an *entity relevant to the engagement* or an entity that is an *affiliate* of such an entity, where the person holding it has both:

    (i) the ability to influence the investment decisions of the intermediary; and

    (ii) actual knowledge of the existence of the underlying holding of a direct financial interest by the intermediary. [AD22.4]

The *firm*, each of the *firm's key audit partners* and each of the *firm's directly involved covered persons* for any *engagement* other than an *investment circular reporting engagement*, and any *persons closely associated* with the *firm* or any such partner or *covered person*, shall not: **2.4D**

(a) hold any material *financial interest* (other than an indirect financial interest held through a diversified collective investment scheme) in, or engage in any transaction in, any *financial instrument* of any *entity relevant to an engagement* in the *area* of *activity*[28] in which they (or in the case of a *person closely associated*, the *area of activity* in which the *firm*, *key audit partner* or *covered person* with whom they are closely associated) are involved relating to *engagements* other than investment circular reporting engagements; or

(b) hold any financial interest, other than an indirect financial interest held through a diversified collective investment scheme, in:

    (i) any *entity relevant to an engagement* other than an *investment circular reporting engagement* for which they are a *directly involved covered person*; or

    (ii) an entity which is an *affiliate* of such an entity; or

    (iii) any other entity otherwise related to such an entity in circumstances where holding such a financial interest may cause, or may be generally perceived as causing, a conflict of interest;

    or, if a person holds such a financial interest they shall be excluded from any role by virtue of which they would be a *covered person* for any such engagement. [AD 22.2]

---

[28] *In relation to a key audit partner or other covered person, or a person closely associated with such a partner or covered person, any engagements for which the covered person is a directly involved covered person and any other engagements, in relation to which the engagement partner practices in the same office or business unit as the covered person.*

2.5 For an *investment circular reporting engagement*, the *firm* and each *covered person*, and *persons closely associated with them*, shall not hold during the engagement period:

   (a)   a direct financial interest; or

   (b)   an indirect financial interest that is material to the *firm* or to the individual or to the intermediary; or

   (c)   any other indirect financial interest where the person holding it has both (i) the ability to influence the investment decisions of the intermediary, and (ii) actual knowledge of the of the existence of the underlying investment;

in any *entity relevant to the engagement* or in an entity that is an *affiliate* of, or otherwise related to, such an entity.

2.6 The requirements in paragraphs 2.3D to 2.5 have been established because threats to integrity, objectivity and independence in relation to *engagements*, where the *firm* or other persons have direct or indirect financial interests in an *entity relevant to an engagement* in the circumstances referred to in those paragraphs, are such that it is considered that no safeguards can eliminate them or reduce them to a level where they would not compromise independence, and they are therefore precluded.

2.7 Except where prohibited in accordance with paragraph 2.4D, where a *person closely associated* with a partner in the *firm* who is not a *covered person* for an *engagement* of the *firm*, has a financial interest in any *entity relevant to the engagement*, or in any *affiliate* of such an entity, as a consequence of:

- the compensation arrangements of that closely associated person (for example, a share option scheme, where the shares have not vested); or

- a decision made, or a transaction undertaken, by an entity with whom that closely associated person has a contractual business or employment arrangement (for example, a partnership agreement);

such financial interests are not generally considered to threaten integrity or objectivity or to compromise independence in relation to the *engagement*. However, where such interests are significant or the relevant partner or other person referred to in paragraph 2.4D has close working contacts with the *engagement team*, the *Ethics Partner*/Function considers whether any safeguards need to be put in place.

2.8 For the purposes of paragraph 2.3D, where financial interests in a diversified collective investment scheme that is an *entity relevant to an engagement* of the *firm*, or an *affiliate* of such an entity, are held by a partner in the *firm*, or by a *person closely associated* with such a partner and that partner is not a *covered person* for such an *engagement*, such interests are to be treated as indirect financial interests. Such interests can therefore be held as long as:

   (a)   they are not material to the individual; and

   (b)   the individual has no influence over the investment decisions of the entity.

2.9 Except where prohibited in accordance with paragraph 2.4D, for the purposes of paragraph 2.3D, where a person who is a *covered person*, or any *person closely associated* with them, is a member or shareholder of any *entity that is relevant to* *an engagement*, as a result of the entity's membership or equivalent requirements, the *firm* should ensure that no more than the minimum number of shares necessary to comply with the requirement are held and should assess whether this financial interest is material to either the entity or the person holding the interest. Disclosure of such interests should be made to those charged with governance of such an entity, in accordance with paragraph 1.61 of Section 1 of Part B of this Ethical Standard.

Where the *firm*, a partner or a *covered person* holds any financial interests that they would not be permitted to hold, or engages in any transaction in *financial instruments* that they would not be permitted to engage in, in breach of the requirements in paragraphs 2.3D, 2.4D(a) or 2.5 in circumstances other than those contemplated in paragraphs 2.11 or 2.12, either: the entire financial interest is disposed of; or, where only a material holding is not permitted, a sufficient amount of the financial interest is disposed of so that the remaining interest is no longer material. In addition, in the case of a person, they are excluded from any role by virtue of which they would be a *covered person*; and, where the holding or transaction is not permitted in accordance with paragraph 2.4D(a) they are excluded from any role by virtue of which they would be operating in their area of *activity relating to engagements* other than *investment circular reporting engagements*that encompasses any *engagements* for entities in which the financial interests were held, or in whose *financial instruments* the person engaged in transactions. In addition, in the case of a *firm*, the *firm* does not accept (or withdraws from) the *engagement*.   **2.10**

> In relation to an *investment circular reporting engagement*, if the existence of the transaction which is connected with the *investment circular* is price sensitive information then disposal of any financial interest in accordance with paragraph 2.10 may not be possible and the *firm* either does not accept the *engagement* or the relevant individuals are not included in the *engagement team*. Where a person holding the financial interests specified would otherwise be a *covered person*, that person is excluded from any role by virtue of which they would be a *covered person* for the purposes of the particular *investment circular reporting engagement*.   **2.11**

Where a person who is joining the *firm* as a partner or *staff* member, or any *person closely associated* with them, has any financial interests acquired before the person joined the *firm* that they would not be permitted to hold in accordance with the requirements in paragraphs 2.3D or 2.4D, they should: **2.12**

(i)   Where they would not be permitted to hold the financial interests in accordance with paragraph 2.4D, dispose of those financial interests prior to the person joining the *firm*;

(ii)   Where they would not be permitted to hold the financial interests in accordance with paragraph 2.3D, disposed of those financial interests prior to, or immediately when, the person joins the *firm*, unless:

    (a)   the person joining the *firm* is not able to influence the affairs of any *entity relevant to an engagement* in which the interests are held; and

    (b)   either there is no market for such interests, or the individual does not have the power to sell or to direct the sale of the interest; and

(c)   the financial interests are not held in an *entity relevant to an engagement* in relation to which the person joining the *firm*:

- is a *covered person*; or
- works in the same part of the *firm* as the *engagement partner* for any such *engagement*; or
- is involved in the provision of a *non-audit/additional service* to any such entity or in an entity that is an *affiliate* of such an entity;

(d)   Where not disposed of prior to, or immediately when, the person joins the *firm*, financial interests that the person would not be permitted to hold in accordance with paragraph 2.3D must be disposed of as soon as possible after the individual holding them becomes able to make a disposal. The *firm* ensures that:

(a)   the deferral of the disposal of such financial interests is approved by the *Ethics Partner*/Function;

(b)   a record is maintained of such individuals and interests, including a description of the circumstances; and

(c)   this information is communicated to the relevant *engagement partner*.

2.13   Where any financial interest specified in paragraph 2.3D is acquired unintentionally, as a result of an external event (for example, inheritance, gift, or merger of *firms* or companies), the disposal of the financial interest is required immediately, or as soon as possible after the relevant person has actual knowledge of, and the right to dispose of, the interest. More specific requirements are set out in paragraph 1.27D of Section 1 of Part B of this Ethical Standard, that apply in circumstances where during the period covered by the financial statements an *audited entity* is acquired by, merges with, or acquires another entity.

2.14   Where the disposal of a financial interest in accordance with paragraphs 2.4D(b), 2.10, 2.11, 2.12 or 2.13 does not take place immediately, the *firm* should adopt safeguards to preserve integrity, objectivity and independence until the financial interest is disposed of. These may include the temporary exclusion of a *covered person* from any role by virtue of which they would be a *covered person* for the *engagement*, or (where continued participation in the *engagement* is not otherwise precluded in accordance with paragraphs 2.3D or 2.4D) a review of the relevant person's work by a partner having sufficient experience and authority to fulfil the role who is not involved in the *engagement*.

2.15   Where the *firm* or one of the individuals specified in paragraph 2.3D or 2.5 holds an indirect financial interest but does not have both:

(a)   the ability to influence the investment decisions of the intermediary; and

(b)   actual knowledge of the existence of the underlying investment in the *entity relevant to the engagement*;

there may not be a significant threat to integrity or objectivity and independence. For example, where the indirect financial interest takes the form of an investment in a pension fund, the composition of the funds and the size and nature of any underlying investment in the entity may be known but there is unlikely to be any influence on investment decisions, as the fund will generally be managed independently on a discretionary basis. In the case of an "index tracker" fund, the investment in the entity is determined by the composition of the relevant index and there may be no threat to integrity or objectivity. As long as the person holding the indirect interest is not directly involved in an *engagement* involving the intermediary, nor able to influence the individual investment decisions of the intermediary, any threat to integrity or objectivity and any impairment of independence may be regarded as clearly insignificant.

Where the *firm* or one of the individuals specified in paragraph 2.4D or 2.5 holds a **2.16** beneficial interest in a properly operated 'blind' trust, they are (by definition) completely unaware of the identity of the underlying investments. If these include an investment in the entity, this means that they are unaware of the existence of an indirect financial interest. In these circumstances, any threat to integrity or objectivity and any impairment of independence may be regarded as clearly insignificant.

Where a partner in the *firm* or a *covered person* becomes aware that a *close* 2.17 **family member holds any financial interest specified in paragraphs 2.3D,** **2.4D or 2.5, that person shall report the matter to the *engagement partner* to** **take appropriate action. If it is a *close family* member of the *engagement*** **partner, or if the *engagement partner* is in doubt as to the action to be taken,** **the *engagement partner* shall resolve the matter through consultation with the** ***Ethics Partner/*Function.**

Financial Interests Held as Trustee

Where a direct or an indirect financial interest in an *entity relevant to the* **2.18** *engagement* or in any *affiliate* of such an entity is held in a trustee capacity by a *covered person*, or by a *person closely associated* with them, a self-interest threat may be created because either the existence of the trustee interest may influence the conduct or outcome of the *engagement* or the trust may influence the actions of the entity. Accordingly, such a trustee interest is not held when:

● the relevant person is an identified potential beneficiary of the trust; or

● the financial interest held by the trust in the entity is material to the trust; or

● the trust is able to exercise significant influence over the entity or an *affiliate* of the entity; or

● the relevant person has significant influence over the investment decisions made by the trust, in so far as they relate to the financial interest in the entity; or

● such a holding is otherwise precluded by the requirements in paragraph 2.4D.

Where it is not clear whether the financial interest in the entity held by the trust is **2.19** material to the trust or whether the trust is able to exercise significant influence over the entity, the financial interest is reported to the *Ethics Partner/*Function, so that a decision can be made as to the steps that need to be taken.

A direct or an indirect financial interest in the entity or its *affiliates* held in a trustee **2.20** capacity by the *firm* or by a partner in the *firm* who is not a *covered person* or a *person closely associated* with them, cannot be held when the *firm* or relevant person is an identified potential beneficiary of the trust.

Financial Interests Held by Firm Pension Schemes

Where the pension scheme of a *firm* has a financial interest in an *entity relevant to* **2.21** *an engagement*, or in the entity's *affiliates*, and the *firm* has any influence over the trustees' investment decisions (other than indirect strategic and policy decisions), the self-interest threat created is such that no safeguards can eliminate it or reduce it to a level where independence is not compromised. In other cases (for example, where the pension scheme invests through a collective investment scheme and the *firm*'s influence is limited to investment policy decisions, such as the allocation between different categories of investment), the *Ethics Partner* considers the acceptability of the position, having regard to the materiality of the financial interest to the pension scheme.

Loans and Guarantees

2.22 Where *firms, covered persons* or *persons closely associated* with them:

(a)   accept a loan[29] or a guarantee of their borrowings from an *entity relevant to the engagement*; or

(b)   make a loan to or guarantee the borrowings of an *entity relevant to the engagement*,

a self-interest threat and an intimidation threat to integrity or objectivity can be created and independence may be compromised. In a number of situations, as in the case of those addressed in paragraphs 2.23, 2.24 and 2.25, it is considered that no safeguards can eliminate these threats or reduce them to a level where independence is not compromised and accepting and making loans in those circumstances is therefore precluded.

2.23   *Firms, covered persons* **and** *persons closely associated* **with them shall not make a loan to, or guarantee the borrowings of, an** *entity relevant to the engagement,* **or the** *affiliates* **of such an entity, unless this represents a deposit made with a bank or similar deposit taking institution in the ordinary course of business and on normal business terms.**

2.24   *Firms* **shall not accept a loan from, or have their borrowings guaranteed by an** *entity relevant to an engagement,* **or the** *affiliates* **of such an entity, unless:**

(a)   **the entity is a bank or similar deposit taking institution; and**

(b)   **the loan or guarantee is made in the ordinary course of business on normal business terms; and**

(c)   **the loan or guarantee is not material to both the** *firm* **and the entity.**

2.25   *Covered persons* **and** *persons closely associated* **with them shall not accept a loan from, or have their borrowings guaranteed by, the** *entity relevant to the engagement,* **or the** *affiliates* **of such an entity, unless:**

(a)   **the entity is a bank or similar deposit taking institution; and**

(b)   **the loan or guarantee is made in the ordinary course of business on normal business terms; and**

(c)   **the loan or guarantee is not material to the entity.**

2.26   Loans by an *entity relevant to an engagement* that is a bank or similar institution to a *covered person*, or to *persons closely associated* with them (for example, home mortgages, bank overdrafts or car loans), do not create an unacceptable threat to integrity or objectivity that compromises independence, provided that normal business terms apply. However, where such loans are in arrears by a significant amount, this creates an intimidation threat that compromises independence. Where such a situation arises, the *covered person* reports the matter to the *engagement partner* or to the *Ethics Partner*/Function, as appropriate and ceases to have any involvement with the *engagement*. The *engagement partner* or, where

---

[29] *For the purpose of this Ethical Standard, the term "loan" does not include ordinary trade credit arrangements or deposits placed for goods or services, unless they are material to either party (see paragraph 2.29).*

appropriate, the *Ethics Partner*/Function considers whether any *engagement* work is to be reperformed.

Business Relationships

A business relationship between:　　　　　　　　　　　　　　　　　　**2.27**

(a)　the *firm* or a *covered person*, or *persons closely associated* with them; and

(b)　any *entity relevant to the engagement*, or the entity's *affiliates* or its management;

involves the two parties having a common commercial interest. Business relationships may create self-interest, advocacy or intimidation threats to integrity or objectivity and independence may be compromised. Examples include:

- joint ventures with the entity or with a director, officer or other individual who performs a management role for the entity;

- arrangements to combine one or more services or products of the *firm* with one or more services or products of the entity and to market the package with reference to both parties;

- distribution or marketing arrangements under which the *firm* acts as a distributor or marketer of any of the entity's products or services, or the entity acts as the distributor or marketer of any of the products or services of the *firm*;

- other commercial transactions, such as the *firm* leasing its office space from or to the entity.

Subject to the alternative procedures outlined in paragraph 1.40 of Section 1 of Part B of this Ethical standard that may be relevant to an *investment circular reporting engagement*, a *firm* will identify all business relationships entered into by the *firm, covered persons*, or *persons closely associated* with them.

Persons or *firms* referred to in paragraph 2.4D shall not have a business or **2.28D** other relationship with any *entity relevant to an engagement* within the period referred in supporting ethical provision 2.1D that would compromise independence; or, if a person has such a business or other relationship they shall be excluded from any role by virtue of which they would be a *covered person* for such an *engagement*. [AD 22.4]

Firms, covered persons and *persons closely associated* with them shall not **2.29** enter into business relationships with any *entity relevant to the engagement*, or its management or its *affiliates* except where those relationships:

- involve the purchase of goods or services from the *firm* or the entity in the ordinary course of business and on an arm's length basis and which are not material to either party; or

- would be inconsequential to either party in the view of an objective, reasonable and informed third party.

> For an *investment circular reporting engagement*, the requirement in
> paragraph 2.29 shall apply during the *relevant period* – the engagement
> period and any additional period before the engagement period but
> subsequent to the balance sheet date of the most recent audited financial
> statements of the entity.

2.30 Where there are doubts about whether a relationship would be inconsequential to either party in the view of and objective, reasonable and informed third party, then the relationship is not regarded as inconsequential.

2.31 Where a business relationship exists, that is not permitted under paragraph 2.29, and has been entered into by:

(a) *the firm:* either the relationship is terminated or the *firm* does not accept (or withdraws from) the *engagement*;

(b) *a covered person:* either the relationship is terminated or that person is excluded from any role in which they would be a *covered person*;

(c) *a person closely associated* with a *covered person:* either the relationship is terminated or the *covered person* is excluded from any role in which they would be a *covered person*.

> In the case of an *investment circular reporting engagement*, where
> termination of the relationship is necessary it is undertaken before the
> start of the *relevant period*. If the existence of the transaction which is
> connected with the *investment circular* is price sensitive information then
> termination of the business relationship may not be possible and the *firm*
> either does not accept the *engagement* or the relevant individuals are not
> included in the *engagement team*. Where a partner with one of the business
> relationships specified normally has direct supervisory or management
> responsibility over the *engagement team*, he or she is excluded from this
> responsibility for the purposes of the particular *investment circular
> reporting engagement*.

For an *engagement* other than an *investment circular reporting engagement*, where there is an unavoidable delay in the termination of a business relationship, the *firm* adopts safeguards to preserve integrity and objectivity in relation to any relevant *engagements* until the relationship is terminated. These may include a review of the relevant person's *engagement* work or a temporary exclusion of the relevant person from any role in which they would be a *covered person*.

2.32 Compliance with paragraph 2.29 is not intended to prevent a *firm* giving advice in accordance with regulatory requirements[30] to a third party in relation to investment products or services, including those supplied by an *entity relevant to an engagement*. In such circumstances, the *firm* considers the advocacy and self-interest threats that might be created by the provision of this advice where it gives rise to commission or similar payments by the entity to the *firm* and assesses whether any safeguards are required.

---

[30] *Firms providing such services will be authorised either by the Financial Conduct Authority or by their professional accountancy body acting as a Designated Professional Body.*

Where a *covered person* becomes aware that a *close family* member has **2.33** entered into one of the business relationships specified in paragraph 2.27, or any other business relationship that could impair independence, that person shall report the matter to the *engagement partner* to take appropriate action. If it is a *close family* member of the *engagement partner* or if the *engagement partner* is in doubt as to the action to be taken, the *engagement partner* shall resolve the matter through consultation with the *Ethics Partner*/Function.

Where there are doubts as to whether a transaction or series of transactions are **2.34** either in the ordinary course of business and on an arm's length basis or of such materiality that they constitute a threat to the integrity, objectivity or independence of the *firm* or *covered persons*, the *engagement partner* reports the issue:

• to the *Ethics Partner*/Function, so that a decision can be made as to the appropriate action that needs to be taken to ensure that the matter is resolved; and

• in the case of an *engagement* other than an *investment circular reporting engagement*, to those charged with governance of the entity, together with other significant facts and matters that bear upon the integrity, objectivity or independence of the *firm* and *covered persons*, to obtain their views on the matter.

A *firm* shall not provide an *engagement* to any entity or person where that **2.35** entity or person is in a position to influence the affairs of the *firm* or the performance of any *engagement* of the *firm*.

This prohibition applies to: **2.36**

(a)   any entity that owns any significant part of the *firm*, or is an *affiliate* of such an entity; or

(b)   any shareholder, director or other person in a position to direct the affairs of such an entity or its *affiliate*.

A significant ownership is one that carries the ability to influence materially the policy of an entity.[31]

Employment Relationships

Persons or *firms* referred to in paragraph 2.4D shall not have an employment **2.37D**
relationship with an *entity relevant to the engagement*, or an *affiliate* of such
an entity, within the period referred in supporting ethical provision 2.1D that
would compromise independence; or, if a person has such an employment
relationship they shall be excluded from any role by virtue of which they
would be a *covered person* for such an *engagement*. [AD 22.4]

Management Role with an Entity Relevant to an Engagement

A *firm* shall not admit to the partnership, or employ a person in a position as a **2.38** *covered person*, if that person is also employed by any *entity relevant to the engagement*, or by any *affiliate* of such an entity ("dual employment").

Loan Staff Assignments

A *firm* shall not enter into an agreement with an *entity relevant to an* **2.39** *engagement* other than an *investment circular reporting engagement*, or

---

[31] *For companies, competition authorities have generally treated a 15% shareholding as sufficient to provide a material ability to influence policy.*

with the *affiliates* of such an entity, or otherwise, to provide any partner or employee ("loan staff") to work for a temporary period as if that individual were an employee of any such entity or its *affiliates* (a "loan staff assignment") unless:

(a)   the agreement is for a short period of time and does not involve employees or partners performing *non-audit/additional services* that would not be permitted under this Ethical Standard; and

(b)   the entity:

   (i)   agrees that any individual loan staff concerned will not hold a management position, will not be involved in the decision-taking of the entity and, in the case of an *audited entity* that is a *public interest entity*, will not play any part in the management of the entity; and

   (ii)   acknowledges its responsibility for directing and supervising the work to be performed, which will not include such matters as:

   • making management decisions; or
   • exercising discretionary authority to commit the entity to a particular position or accounting treatment.

2.40   A *firm* shall not enter into an agreement with an *entity relevant to an investment circular reporting engagement* to provide any partner or employee ("loan staff") to work for a temporary period as if that individual were an employee of any such entity or its *affiliates* (a "loan staff assignment") during the *relevant period* or for a period of one year before it unless:

(a)   the agreement is for a short period of time and does not involve employees or partners performing *additional services* that would not be permitted under this Ethical Standard; and

(b)   the entity:

   (i)   agrees that any individual loan staff concerned will not hold a management position in relation to the transaction or the financial information that is the subject of the *investment circular reporting engagement*,; and

   (ii)   acknowledges its responsibility for directing and supervising the work to be performed, which will not include such matters as:

   • making management decisions; or
   • exercising discretionary authority to commit the entity to a particular position or accounting treatment.

2.41   Where a *firm* agrees to assist an *entity relevant to an engagement* by providing loan staff, threats to objectivity and independence may be created. A management threat may arise if the employee undertakes work that involves making judgments and taking decisions that are properly the responsibility of management. In the context of applying the requirement in paragraph 2.39(a) and 2.40(a), a short period of time is generally expected to be no more than a small number of months.

A self-review threat may also arise if the individual, during the loan staff **2.42** assignment, is in a position to influence the preparation of the entity's financial statements or other *subject matter information* or *subject matter* of an *engagement*, and then, on completion of that assignment, is assigned to the *engagement team* for that entity, with responsibility to report on matters for which he or she was responsible whilst on that loan staff assignment.

Where a partner or employee returns to the *firm* on completion of a loan staff **2.43** **assignment, that individual shall not be given any role on any *engagement*** **involving any function or activity that he or she performed or supervised** **during that assignment.**

In considering for how long this restriction is to be observed, the need to realise **2.44** the potential value to the effectiveness of the *engagement* of the increased knowledge of the entity's business gained through the assignment has to be weighed against the potential threats to integrity or objectivity and the potential for independence to be compromised. Those threats increase with the length of the assignment and with the intended level of responsibility of the individual within the *engagement team*. As a minimum, this restriction will apply to at least the period until the first *engagement* has been completed following the completion of the loan staff assignment.

Partners and Engagement Team Members Joining an Entity Relevant to an Engagement

Where a former partner in the *firm* joins an *entity relevant to an engagement*, **2.45** **the *firm* shall take action as quickly as possible – and, in any event, before any** **further work is done by the *firm* in connection with any such *engagement* – to** **ensure that no significant connections remain between the *firm* and the** **individual, or to withdraw from the *engagement*.**

Ensuring that no significant connections remain between the *firm* and the **2.46** individual requires that:

- all capital balances and similar financial interests be fully settled (including retirement benefits) unless these are made in accordance with pre-determined arrangements that cannot be influenced by any remaining connections between the individual and the *firm*; and

- the individual does not participate or appear to participate in the *firm's* business or professional activities by way of employment, consultancy or other contractual arrangement, or in any other way.

***Firms* shall establish policies and procedures that require in relation to any** **2.47** ***entity relevant to an engagement* in which an individual is, or was at any time** **over the previous year (two years in the case of a partner), directly involved:**

(a) for all such *engagements*:

  (i) senior members of the *engagement team* to notify the *firm* of any **situation involving their potential employment with any such** **entity; and**

  (ii) other members of the *engagement team* to notify the *firm* of any **situation involving their probable employment with any such** **entity;**

(b)   for an *engagement* other than an *investment circular reporting engagement*:

   (i)   all partners in the *firm* to notify the *firm* of any situation involving their potential employment with any such entity; and

   (ii)   any other employee of the *firm* and any other natural person whose services are placed at the disposal of or under the control of the *firm*, where such employee or other person is personally approved as a *statutory auditor* under relevant legislation within the European Union, to notify the *firm* of any situation involving their probable employment with any such entity;

(c)   anyone who has given such notice to be removed from the *engagement team*; and

(d)   a review of the *engagement* work performed by any resigning or former *engagement team* member in the current and, where appropriate, the most recent *engagement*.

2.48   Integrity, objectivity and independence may be threatened where a director, an officer or an employee of any *entity relevant to an engagement* who is in a position to exert direct and significant influence over the preparation of the financial statements or other *subject matter information* or *subject matter* of an *engagement*, has recently been a partner in the *firm*, a member of the *engagement team* or another employee or person whose services are at the disposal or under the control of the *firm*, where such employee or person is personally approved as a *statutory auditor* within the European Union. Such circumstances may create self-interest, familiarity and intimidation threats, particularly when significant connections remain between the individual and the *firm*. Similarly, integrity or objectivity may be threatened and independence compromised when an individual knows, or has reason to believe, that he or she will or may be joining the entity at some time in the future.

2.49   Where a partner in the *firm* or a member of an *engagement team* for an *entity relevant to an engagement* or another person who is personally approved as a *statutory auditor* as described in paragraph 2.48 has left the *firm* and taken up employment with such an entity, the significance of the self-interest, familiarity and intimidation threats is assessed and normally depends on such factors as:

   ●   the position that individual had in the *engagement team* or *firm*;

   ●   the position that individual has taken at the entity;

   ●   the amount of involvement that individual will have with the *engagement team* (especially where it includes former colleagues with whom he or she worked);

   ●   the length of time since that individual was a member of the *engagement team* or employed by the *firm*.

Following the assessment of any such threats, appropriate safeguards are applied where necessary to reduce such threats to a level where the independence of the *firm* or *covered persons* would not be compromised.

2.50   Any review of *engagement* work is performed by a more senior *engagement* professional. If the individual joining the entity is a partner, the review is performed by a partner who is not involved in the *engagement*. Where, due to its size, the *firm* does not have a partner who was not involved in the *engagement*, it seeks either a review by another *firm* or advice from its professional body.

As required by legislation[32], a natural person appointed as a *statutory auditor*   **2.51**
or *key audit partner* for an entity subject to a *statutory audit* shall not take up:

(a)   any *key management position*;

(b)   membership of the entity's audit committee;

(c)   membership of any body performing equivalent functions to an audit
      committee in relation to the entity;

(d)   any other position as director of the entity or, where the entity's affairs
      are managed by a management body or other committee, membership
      of that management body or committee;

before the end of:

(a)   in the case of a *public interest entity*, two years; and

(b)   in any other case, one year;

beginning with the day on which the person ceased to be the entity's *statutory
auditor* or *key audit partner* in connection with the *statutory audit* of the entity.

The requirements set out in paragraph 2.51 above reflect legal restrictions imposed   **2.52**
on particular individuals who may wish to join an entity subject to a *statutory
audit*. Should a partner or other *covered person* join an *entity relevant to an
engagement*, threats to integrity, objectivity and independence may arise that a
firm will need to address. Such threats may also exist where a former partner or
other *covered person* is employed by an entity that the *firm* is considering
accepting an *engagement* for.

Where a partner[33], or another person (including a person whose services are   **2.53**
at the disposal or under the control of the *firm*) who is personally approved as
a *statutory auditor* as described in paragraph 2.48, is appointed as a director
(including as a non-executive director), a member of the audit committee or
body performing equivalent functions, or to a *key management position* with
an *entity relevant to an engagement*, having previously been a covered person:

(a)   in the case of a partner, at any time during the two years prior to such
      appointment; or

(b)   in the case of another person, at any time during the year prior to such
      appointment;

the *firm* shall resign from the *engagement* where possible under applicable
law or regulation.[34] The *firm* shall not accept an other engagement for the
entity until:

(i)   in the case of a partner, a two-year period; or

(ii)   in the case of another person, a one year period;

commencing when the person ceased to be a *covered person*, has elapsed or
until the person ceases employment with the entity, whichever is the sooner.

---

[32]   *SI 2016/649 The Statutory Auditors and Third Country Auditors Regulations 2016, Schedule 1, paragraph 7.*

[33]   *"Partner" includes any individual with authority to bind the firm with respect to the performance of a
professional services engagement.*

[34]   *The timing of the audit firm's resignation as auditor is determined in accordance with paragraph 1.52 of Section
1 of Part B of this Ethical Standard.*

2.54   In the circumstances covered by paragraph 2.53, where the responsibility for the *engagement* is assigned by legislation or regulation and the auditor cannot resign from the *engagement* (e.g. in the case of certain public sector bodies) the *firm* shall consider alternative safeguards that can be put in place to reduce threats to integrity or objectivity to a level where independence would not be compromised.

2.55   Where a person who is either a partner or another person (including a person whose services are at the disposal or under the control of the *firm*) who is personally approved as a *statutory auditor* as described in paragraph 2.48 (other than someone covered by paragraph 2.53) or was a former member of an *engagement team*, joins the entity as a director (including as a non-executive director), a member of the audit committee or body performing equivalent functions, or in a *key management position*, within two years of ceasing to be a *covered person* for the entity, the *firm* shall ensure that no significant connections remain between the *firm* and the individual and consider whether the composition of the *engagement team* is appropriate (paragraph 2.45 also applies in the case of a former partner).

2.56   The *firm* evaluates the appropriateness of the composition of the *engagement team* by reference to the factors listed in paragraph 2.49 and alters or strengthens the *engagement team* to address any threat to the integrity, objectivity or independence of the *firm* or *covered persons* that may be identified.

2.57   If a former partner of the *firm*, or another person personally approved as a *statutory auditor* as described in paragraph 2.48 formerly employed by or otherwise at the disposal of or under the control of the *firm*, has joined an entity as a director (including as a non-executive director), a member of the audit committee or body performing equivalent functions, or in a *key management position*, the *firm* shall not accept an *engagement* for the entity where the person had, prior to leaving the *firm* and:

   (a)   in the case of a partner, within two years before acceptance of the *engagement*; or

   (b)   in the case of another person, within one year before acceptance of the *engagement*;

been a *covered person* for any *engagement* involving any partner of the *firm* who would be a member of the *engagement team*, or would be the *engagement quality control reviewer*, for the *engagement* were it to be accepted.

2.58   Where a former partner, or person (including a person whose services are at the disposal or under the control of the *firm*) personally approved as a *statutory auditor* as described in paragraph 2.48, left, or ceased to be at the disposal or under the control of, the *firm* earlier than the beginning of the periods specified in paragraph 2.57(a) or (b), the *firm* shall evaluate the significance of any threats to integrity or objectivity and whether independence would be compromised before accepting such an *engagement* for the entity. The *firm* shall not accept the *engagement* unless any threats identified can be reduced to a level where independence would not be compromised.

Family Members Employed by an Entity Relevant to an Engagement

Where a *covered person*, or any partner in the *firm*, becomes aware that a **2.59** person *closely associated* with them, or a *close family* member who is not a person *closely associated* with them, is employed by an *entity relevant to the engagement* and that person is in a position to exercise influence on the accounting records or financial statements or other *subject matter information* or *subject matter* of such an *engagement*, that *covered person* or that partner shall either:

(a)   in the case of a *person closely associated* with them being employed by the entity in such a position, be excluded from any role in which they would be a *covered person*; or

(b)   in the case of a *close family* member of a *covered person* who is not a person *closely associated with them*, or, for an engagement other than an investment circular reporting engagement, any *close family* member of any partner in the *firm* who is not a *person closely associated* with them, report the matter to the *engagement partner* to take appropriate action. If it is a *close family* member of the *engagement partner* or if the *engagement partner* is in doubt as to the action to be taken, the *engagement partner* shall resolve the matter in consultation with the *Ethics Partner*/Function.

Governance Role with an Entity Relevant to an Engagement

Paragraphs 2.61 to 2.63 are supplementary to certain statutory or regulatory **2.60** provisions that prohibit directors of entities from being appointed as their auditor.[35]

The *firm* or a partner or member of *staff* of the *firm* shall not accept **2.61** appointment or perform a role:

(a)   as an officer[36] or member of the board of directors of an *entity relevant to an engagement* of the *firm*;

(b)   as a member of any subcommittee of that board; or

(c)   in such a position in an entity which holds directly or indirectly more than 20% of the voting rights in the *entity relevant to an engagement*, or in an entity in which the *entity relevant to such an engagement* holds directly or indirectly more than 20% of the voting rights.

Where the *firm* is undertaking an *investment circular reporting engagement*, the requirements in this paragraph shall apply during the period of the *engagement*.

---

[35] *For example, in the case of limited companies and certain other organisations, section 1214 of the Companies Act 2006 contains detailed provisions. Amongst other things, these state that:*

   "...A person may not act as statutory auditor of an audited person if [he] is (a) an officer or employee of the audited person, or (b) a partner or employee of such a person, or a partnership of which such a person is a partner."

[36] *As defined in Section 1173 of the Companies Act 2006 as including a director, manager or secretary.*

2.62   Where a *covered person* becomes aware that a *person closely associated* with them, or a *close family* member who is not a *person closely associated* with them, holds a position described in paragraph 2.61, the *firm* shall take appropriate steps to ensure that the relevant person is excluded from any role in which they would be a *covered person*.

2.63   Where a partner or member of *staff* of the *firm*, but who is not a *covered person*, becomes aware that a *person closely associated* with them, or a *close family* member who is not a *person closely associated* with them, holds a position described in paragraph 2.61, that individual shall report that fact to the *engagement partner*, who shall evaluate whether the relationship would compromise independence. If the *engagement partner* concludes that independence may be compromised, they shall consult with the *Ethics Partner*/Function to determine whether appropriate safeguards exist. If no such safeguards exist, the *firm* shall withdraw from the *engagement*.

Employment with the Firm

2.64   Integrity and objectivity may be threatened and independence may be compromised where a former director or employee of an *entity relevant to an engagement* of the *firm* becomes a member of the *engagement team* or is otherwise a *covered person*. Self-interest, self-review and familiarity threats may be created where a member of the *engagement team* has to report on, for example, financial statements which he or she prepared, or other information for which he or she had responsibility, while with the entity.

2.65   Where a former director or a former employee of an *entity relevant to an engagement*, who was in a position to exert significant influence over the preparation of the financial statements or other *subject matter information* or *subject matter* of such an *engagement*, joins the *firm*, that individual shall be excluded from any role in which they would be a *covered person* relevant to that entity or its *affiliates* for a period of two years following the date of leaving the entity.

2.66   Recusal from responsibilities of any particular role with respect to influencing particular matters cannot remove the individual from being in a position to do so. In certain circumstances, a longer period of exclusion from being a *covered person* may be appropriate. For example, threats to integrity, objectivity and independence may exist in relation to an *engagement* for any period where the financial statements or other *subject matter information* or other *subject matter* of such an *engagement*, are materially affected by the work of that person whilst occupying his or her former position of influence with the entity. The significance of these threats depends on factors such as:

- the position the individual held with the entity;

- the length of time since the individual left the entity;

- the position the individual holds in the *engagement team* or the *firm*.

Family and Other Personal Relationships

2.67   A relationship between a *covered person* and a party other than those referred to elsewhere in this Section does not generally affect the consideration of integrity and objectivity and the evaluation of whether independence is compromised. However, if it is a relationship with a family member, and if the family member also has a financial, business or employment relationship with any *entity relevant to the engagement*, then this may create self-interest, familiarity or intimidation threats to integrity and objectivity and may impair independence. The significance of any such threats depends on such factors as:

- the relevant person's involvement in the *engagement*;
- the nature of the relationship between the relevant person and his or her family member;
- the family member's relationship with the entity.

A distinction is made between relationships with *"persons closely associated"* (which include *immediate family* members – a spouse or equivalent and dependents), and other *close family* relationships (which additionally comprise any other parents, non-dependent children and siblings who are not *"persons closely associated"*). While an individual can usually be presumed to be aware of matters concerning *persons closely associated* with them and to be able to influence their behaviour, it is generally recognised that the same levels of knowledge and influence do not exist in the case of *close family* members who are not a *person closely associated* with them.   **2.68**

When considering family relationships, it needs to be acknowledged that the concept of what constitutes a family is evolving and relationships between individuals which have no status formally recognised by law may nevertheless be considered as significant as those which do. It may therefore be appropriate to regard certain other personal relationships, particularly those that would be considered close personal relationships, as if they are family relationships.   **2.69**

The *firm* shall establish policies and procedures that require: **2.70**

(a)   partners and professional *staff* members to report to the *firm* any *persons closely associated* with them, any *close family* who are not a *person closely associated with them*, and other personal relationships, where any of those persons is involved with an *entity relevant to an engagement* of the *firm*, where the partner or professional *staff* member considers that the relationship might create a threat to integrity or objectivity or may compromise independence;

(b)   the relevant *engagement partners* to be notified promptly of any information reported by partners and other professional *staff* members as required by paragraph (a).

The *engagement partner* shall: **2.71**

(a)   assess the threats to integrity and objectivity and evaluate whether independence would be compromised, on the basis of the information reported to the *firm* by partners and other professional *staff* members as required by paragraph 2.70;

(b)   apply appropriate safeguards to eliminate any threats or to reduce them to a level where independence would not be compromised; and

(c)   where there are unresolved matters or the need for clarification, consult with the *Ethics Partner*/Function.

Where such matters are identified or reported, the *engagement partner* or the *Ethics Partner*/Function assesses the information available and the potential for there to be a threat to integrity or objectivity and for independence to be compromised, treating any personal relationship as if it were a family relationship.   **2.72**

External Consultants Involved in an Engagement

2.73   *Firms* may employ external consultants as experts as part of their *engagement*, for example, in an *audit engagement*, in order to obtain sufficient appropriate audit evidence regarding certain financial statement assertions.[37] There may be threats to an expert's integrity or objectivity and their independence may be compromised if the expert is related to any *entity relevant to the engagement*, for example by being financially dependent upon or having an investment in, the entity.

2.74   **The *engagement partner* shall be satisfied that any external consultant involved in the *engagement* will act with integrity and objectivity with respect to the *engagement* and shall document the rationale for that conclusion.**

2.75   The *engagement partner* obtains information from the external consultant as to the existence of any connections that they have with the entity including:

- financial interests;

- business relationships;

- employment (past, present and future);

- family and other personal relationships.

Section 3 – Long Association with Engagements and With Entities Relevant to Engagements

General Requirements

3.1   **The *firm* shall establish policies and procedures to monitor the length of time and extent of involvement that partners and *staff* in senior positions, including those from other disciplines, serve as members of the *engagement team(s)* for recurring *engagements* for particular entities.**

3.2   **Where partners and *staff* in senior positions have a long association or extensive involvement with an *entity relevant to the engagement*, the *firm* shall assess the threats to integrity, objectivity and independence of the *firm* and *covered persons* and shall:**

- **apply safeguards to reduce the threats to a level where independence would not be compromised; and**

- **disclose the *engagements* previously undertaken by the *firm* for an *entity relevant to the engagement* to those charged with governance and, where applicable, any other persons or entities the *firm* is instructed to advise.**

Where appropriate safeguards cannot be applied, the *firm* shall not accept the *engagement*, shall resign from the *engagement* or not stand for reappointment, as appropriate. Where the responsibility for the *engagement* is assigned by legislation or regulation and the *firm* cannot resign from the *engagement* (e.g. in the case of certain public sector bodies) the *firm* shall consider alternative safeguards that can be put in place.

3.3   Where partners and *staff* in senior positions have a long association or extensive involvement with an *entity relevant to the engagement*, self-interest, self-review and familiarity threats to the integrity or objectivity of any person performing the

---

[37] *ISA (UK) 620"Using the Work of an Auditor's Expert" requires that the auditor shall evaluate whether the expert has the necessary objectivity.*

engagement may arise. Similarly, such circumstances may impair, and could compromise, independence. The significance of such threats depends upon factors such as:

- the role of the individual in the *engagement team(s)*;

- the proportion of time that the entity contributes to the individual's annual billable hours;

- the length of time that the individual has been associated with an *entity relevant to the engagement*;

- whether the individual is employed exclusively or principally on an *engagement* that extends for a significant period of time;

- whether the individual is remunerated on the basis of the performance of a part of the *firm* which is substantially dependent on fees from that entity.

For an *investment circular reporting engagement*, the *firm* gives careful consideration to which individual is appointed as the *engagement partner* on such an *engagement*. This consideration will reflect the need for relevant expertise[38] as well as factors such as:

- the nature of the *investment circular reporting engagement* and whether it will involve the reappraisal of previously audited financial information;
- the length of time that the *engagement partner* for the *audit engagement* has been associated with the *audit engagement*;
- the length of time that other partners have acted for the entity on corporate finance and other transaction related engagements;
- whether the objectivity of the *engagement partner* on a subsequent *engagement* could be adversely affected by an opinion on a profit forecast included in the investment circular; and
- the scope of the engagement quality control review.

3.4

In order to address threats that are identified, *firms* apply safeguards. Appropriate safeguards may include:

3.5

- appointing a partner who has no previous involvement with the entity as the *engagement partner*;

- removing ("rotating") the partners and the other senior members of the *engagement team* after a pre-determined number of years;

- involving an additional partner, who is not and has not recently been a member of the *engagement team*, to review the work done by the partners and the other senior members of the *engagement team* and to advise as necessary;

- arranging an engagement quality control review of the *engagement* in question.

Where applicable, once an *engagement partner* has held this role for a continuous period of ten years, careful consideration is given as to whether it is probable that an objective, reasonable and informed third party would conclude the integrity,

3.6

---

[38] *Paragraph 25 of SIR 1000 requires that a partner with appropriate experience should be involved in the conduct of the work.*

objectivity or independence of the *firm* or *covered persons* are compromised. Where the individual concerned is not rotated after ten years, it is important that:

(a)   safeguards other than rotation, such as those noted in paragraph 3.5, are applied; or

(b)   (i)   the reasoning as to why the individual continues to participate in the *engagement* without any safeguards is documented; and

         (ii)   the facts are communicated to those charged with governance of the entity in accordance with paragraphs 1.61 – 1.71 of Section 1 of Part B of this Ethical Standard.

3.7   The *firm's* policies and procedures set out whether there are circumstances in which the *engagement partners, engagement quality control reviewers* and other key partners involved in recurring *engagements* for non-listed entities that are not *public interest entities* are subject to accelerated rotation requirements, such as those set out in paragraph 3.11, as described in paragraph 1.49 of Section 1 of Part B of this Ethical Standard.

3.8   Any scheme of rotation of partners and other senior members of the *engagement team* needs to take into account the factors which affect the quality of the *engagement work*, including the experience and continuity of members of the *engagement team* and the need to ensure appropriate succession planning.

Public Interest Entities and Other Listed Entities

> The requirements and guidance in paragraphs 3.9 – 3.23 are relevant to recurring *engagements* that are undertaken for an entity over periods of five or more years.

Audit Firm Rotation

3.9   **The requirements for *audit firm* rotation, implementing the relevant provisions of Article 17 of the EU Audit Regulation, are set out in legislation[39]. The *firm* shall ensure that it does not accept or continue an *audit engagement* that would cause those requirements to not be complied with.**

Key Audit Partners and Engagement Partners[40]

3.10R   Save where the circumstances in paragraphs 3.14 and 3.15 apply, the *key audit partners* responsible for carrying out a *statutory audit* of a *public interest entity* shall cease their participation in the *statutory audit* of the *audited entity* not later than ~~seven~~five[41] years from the date of their appointment. They shall not participate again in the *statutory audit* of the *audited entity* before ~~three~~five years have elapsed following that cessation. [AR 17.7]

---

[39] *Sections 487 and 489 of the Companies Act 2006.*

[40] *For an audit, the engagement partner is a key audit partner.*

[41] *The FRC has exercised the Member State option in the second sub-paragraph of Article 17.7 to set a shorter period than the default seven year period.*

In the case of *listed entities*, save where the circumstances contemplated in paragraph 3.14 and 3.15 apply, the *firm* shall establish policies and procedures to ensure in respect of a recurring *engagement* that: **3.11**

(a) no one shall act as *engagement partner* for more than five years; and

(b) anyone who has acted as the *engagement partner* for a particular entity for a period of five years, shall not subsequently participate in the *engagement* until a further period of five years has elapsed.

The roles that constitute participating in an *engagement* for the purposes of paragraph 3.11(b), include providing quality control for the *engagement*, advising or consulting with the *engagement team* or the entity regarding technical or industry specific issues, transactions or events, or otherwise directly influencing the conduct or outcome of the *engagement*. This does not include responding to queries in relation to any completed *engagement*. This is not intended to preclude partners whose primary responsibility within a *firm* is to be consulted on technical or industry specific issues from providing such consultation to the *engagement team* or entity after a period of two years has elapsed from their ceasing to act as *engagement partner*, provided that such consultation is in respect of new issues or new types of transactions or events that were not previously required to be considered by that individual in the course of acting as *engagement partner*. **3.12**

Where an *engagement partner* continues in a non-engagement role having been rotated off the *engagement team*, the new *engagement partner* and the individual concerned ensure that that person, while acting in this new role, does not exert any influence on the *engagement*. Positions in which an individual is responsible for the *firm's* client relationship with the particular entity would not be an acceptable non-engagement role. **3.13**

When an entity becomes a *public interest entity* or an other *listed entity*, the length of time the *engagement partner* has served the entity in that capacity is taken into account in calculating the period before the *engagement partner* is rotated off the *engagement team*. However, where the *engagement partner* has already served for four or more years, that individual may continue to serve as the *engagement partner* for not more than two years after the entity becomes such a *public interest entity* or an other *listed entity*. **3.14**

In circumstances where the audit committee (or equivalent) of an entity that is a *public interest entity* or an other *listed entity* decide that a degree of flexibility over the timing of rotation is necessary to safeguard the quality of the *engagement* and the *firm* agrees, the *engagement partner* may continue in this position for an additional period of up to two years, so that no longer than seven years in total is spent in the position of *engagement partner*. An audit committee and the *firm* may consider that such flexibility safeguards the quality of the *engagement*, for example, where: **3.15**

• substantial change has recently been made or will soon be made to the nature or structure of the entity's business; or

• there are unexpected changes in the senior management of the entity; or

• the *firm*, having taken all reasonable succession planning steps, has no other partners with the necessary knowledge and experience who are able to take over as *engagement partner*.

In these circumstances alternative safeguards are applied to reduce any threats to a level where it is not probable that an objective, reasonable and informed third party would conclude the integrity, objectivity or independence of the *firm* or *covered persons* are compromised. Such safeguards may include ensuring that an expanded review of the *engagement* work is undertaken by the *engagement quality control reviewer* or a partner with relevant expertise, who is not involved in the *engagement*.

3.16   For an *audit engagement*, where it has been determined that the *engagement partner* may act for a further period (not to exceed two years) in the interests of audit quality, this fact and the reasons for it, are to be disclosed to the *audited entity's* shareholders as early as practicable and in each of the additional years. If the *audited entity* is not prepared to make such a disclosure, the *audit firm* does not permit the *engagement partner* to continue in this role.

3.17   In the case of joint audit arrangements for *public interest entities* and for other *listed entities, audit firms* will make arrangements for changes of *engagement partners* over a five-year period so that the familiarity threat is avoided, whilst also taking into consideration factors that affect the quality of the audit work.

Engagement Quality Control Reviewers and Other Key Partners Involved in the Engagement

3.18R   **For an audit of a *public interest entity*, the ~~statutory auditor or the~~ *audit firm* shall establish an appropriate gradual rotation mechanism with regard to the most senior personnel involved in the *statutory audit*, including at least the persons who are registered as *statutory auditors*. The gradual rotation mechanism shall be applied in phases on the basis of individuals rather than of the entire *engagement team*. It shall be proportionate in view of the scale and the complexity of the activity of the ~~statutory auditor or the~~ *audit firm*. [AR 17.7]**

3.19R   **For an audit of a *public interest entity*, the ~~statutory auditor or the~~ *audit firm* shall be able to demonstrate to the competent authority[42] that such mechanism is effectively applied and adapted to the scale and the complexity of the activity of the ~~statutory auditor or the~~ *audit firm*. [AR 17.7]**

3.20   In the case of *public interest entities* and other *listed entities*, the *firm* shall establish policies and procedures to ensure in respect of a recurring *engagement* that:

(a)   no one shall act as the *engagement quality control reviewer* or a *key partner involved in the engagement* for a period longer than seven years;

(b)   where an *engagement quality control reviewer* or a *key partner involved in the engagement* becomes the *engagement partner*, the combined period of service in these positions shall not exceed seven years; and

(c)   anyone who has acted:

(i)   as an *engagement quality control reviewer* for a particular entity for a period of seven years, whether continuously or in aggregate, shall not participate in the *engagement* until a further period of five years has elapsed;

(ii)   as a *key partner involved in the engagement* for a particular entity for a period of seven years, whether continuously or in aggregate,

---

[42]   *The FRC or the Recognised Supervisory Body to whom the FRC has delegated regulatory tasks, as applicable.*

shall not participate in the *engagement* until a further period of two years has elapsed;

(iii) in a combination of roles as:

- the *engagement quality control reviewer,*
- a *key partner involved in the engagement,* or
- the *engagement partner*

for a particular entity for a period of seven years, whether continuously or in aggregate, shall not participate in the *engagement* until a further period of five years has elapsed.

Other Partners and Staff Involved in the Engagement in Senior Positions

In the case of *public interest entities* and other *listed entities,* the *engagement*   **3.21**
partner shall review the safeguards put in place to address the threats to the objectivity and independence of the person or persons conducting the *engagement* arising where partners and *staff* have been involved in the *engagement* in senior positions for a continuous period longer than seven years and shall discuss those situations with the *engagement quality control reviewer.* Any unresolved problems or issues shall be referred to the Ethics Function/Partner.

The significance of the threats arising where partners and *staff* have been involved   **3.22**
in the *engagement* in senior positions for a continuous period longer than seven years will depend on:

- the total period of time that the individual has been involved in the *engagement*;
- changes in the nature of the work and the role performed by the individual during that period; and

the portion of time the individual has spent on any engagements with the entity during that period.

Following the assessment of any such threats, appropriate safeguards are applied   **3.23**
where necessary. Safeguards that address these threats might include:

- changes in the roles within the *engagement team*;
- an additional review of the work done by the individual by the *engagement partner* or other partners in the *engagement team*;
- additional procedures carried out as part of the engagement quality control review.

If such safeguards do not reduce the threats to a level where independence is not compromised, the partner or member of *staff* is removed from the *engagement team*.

Section 4 – Fees, Remuneration and Evaluation Policies, Gifts and Hospitality, Litigation

Fees

The *engagement partner* shall be satisfied and able to demonstrate that the   **4.1**
***engagement* has assigned to it sufficient partners and *staff* with appropriate time and skill to perform the *engagement* in accordance with all applicable Engagement and Ethical Standards, irrespective of the *engagement* fee to be charged.**

4.2   Paragraph 4.1 is not intended to prescribe the approach to be taken by *firms* to the setting of *engagement* fees, but rather to emphasise that there are no circumstances where the amount of the *engagement* fee can justify any lack of appropriate resource or time taken to perform a proper engagement in accordance with applicable Engagement and Ethical Standards.

4.3D   **Fees for *engagements* shall not be influenced or determined by the provision of *non-audit/additional services* to an *entity relevant to the engagement*. [AD 25, ES 4.7]**

4.4   The *engagement* fee ordinarily reflects the time spent, the skills and experience of the personnel performing the *engagement* in accordance with all the relevant requirements, and the competitive situation in the market. Paragraph 4.3D is intended to prevent any relationship between the appropriate cost of the *engagement* and the actual or potential provision of *non-audit/additional services*.

4.5   Paragraph 4.3D is not intended to prohibit proper cost savings that can be achieved as a result of providing *non-audit/additional services* in accordance with Section 5 of this Ethical Standard to the entity, for example, where information gained through undertaking a *non-audit service* is referred to by audit staff when carrying out the audit of the financial statements.

4.6R   **Fees for the provision of ~~statutory audits~~*engagements*~~to public-interest entities~~ shall not be contingent fees. [AR 4.1]**

4.7R   ~~Without prejudice to Article 25 of Directive 2006/43/EC, for the purposes of the first subparagraph, c~~Contingent fees means fees ~~for audit engagements~~ calculated on a predetermined basis relating to the outcome or result of a transaction, <u>or other event,</u> or the result of the work performed. Fees shall not be regarded as being contingent if a court, ~~or a~~ competent authority, <u>or other public authority</u> has established them. [AR 4.1]

4.8   A *contingent fee basis* includes any arrangement made at the outset of an *engagement* under which a specified commission on or percentage of any consideration or saving is payable to the *firm* upon the happening of a specified event or the achievement of an outcome (or alternative outcomes). Differential hourly fee rates, or arrangements under which the fee payable will be negotiated after the completion of the *engagement*, or increased to cover additional work identified as necessary during the *engagement*, do not constitute contingent fee arrangements.

4.9   Contingent fee arrangements in respect of *engagements* create self-interest threats to the integrity and objectivity of the *firm* and *covered persons* that are so significant that they cannot be eliminated or reduced to a level where independence would not be compromised.

4.10   The fee for an *engagement* does not depend on whether the *firm's* report on the financial statements, or on *subject matter information* or other *subject matter* of such an *engagement*, is qualified or unqualified. The basis for the calculation of the fee is agreed with the entity before significant *engagement* work is undertaken and ordinarily reflects the time spent and the skills and experience of the personnel performing the *engagement* in accordance with all the relevant requirements. For recurring *engagements*, such as an audit, the fee is agreed before each recurrence. Arrangements under which estimated fees are agreed with the entity on terms where the fees may be varied based on the level of *engagement* work required do not constitute contingent fee arrangements.

Investigations into possible acquisitions or disposals ("due diligence engagements"), particularly those performed in relation to a prospective transaction, typically involve a high level of risk and responsibility. A *firm* carrying out a due diligence engagement may charge a higher fee for work relating to a completed transaction than for the same transaction if it is not completed, for whatever reason, provided that the difference is related to such additional risk and responsibility and not the outcome of the due diligence engagement.

4.11

In relation to *investment circular reporting engagements*, where the *firm* is aware that an *entity relevant to the engagement* has a record of seeking substantial discounts to the fee payable where a transaction is unsuccessful or abortive, the *engagement partner* discusses the position with the *Ethics Partner*. An appropriate safeguard may involve arranging an engagement quality control review of the *investment circular reporting engagement*.

Contingent fee arrangements in respect of *non-audit/additional services* provided by the *firm* in respect of an entity can create significant self-interest threats to the integrity, objectivity and independence of the *firm* and *covered persons*, as they may have, or may appear to have, an interest in the outcome of the *non-audit/additional service*.

4.13

The *firm* shall not provide *non-audit/additional services*, in respect of an *entity relevant to an engagement*, wholly or partly on a *contingent fee basis* where:

4.14

(a)   **the contingent fee is material to the *firm*, or that part of the *firm* by reference to which the *engagement partner's* profit share is calculated; or**

(b)   **the amount of the fee is dependent on an outcome or result of those *non-audit/additional services* that is relevant to a future or contemporary judgment relating to a material matter in the financial statements or other *subject matter information* or *subject matter* of the *engagement*.**

In relation to tax services, the requirements of paragraph 5.85 of Section 5 of Part B of this Ethical Standard also apply.

Where *non-audit/additional services* are provided on a *contingent fee basis*, there may be a perception that the *firm's* interests are so closely aligned with the entity that the integrity, objectivity and independence of the *firm* and *covered persons* could be, or be seen to be, compromised.

4.15

The significance of the self-interest threat is likely to be, or be seen to be, influenced by the materiality of the contingent fee to the *firm* or to the part of the *firm* by reference to which the *engagement partner's* profit share is calculated – any contingent fee that is material to the *firm*, or that part of the *firm* by reference to which the *engagement partner's* profit share is calculated, will create a self-interest threat that cannot be eliminated or reduced to a level where independence is not compromised and the *firm* does not undertake such a service at the same time as an *audit engagement* or other *public interest assurance engagement*.

4.16

In addition, where the contingent fee is dependent on an outcome or result of the *non-audit/additional service* that is relevant to a future or contemporary audit or assurance judgment relating to a material matter that is included in the audited financial

4.17

statements, in the case of an *entity relevant to an engagement*, the self-interest threat cannot be eliminated or reduced to a level where independence is not compromised.

4.18   Paragraph 4.14 is not intended to prohibit a *firm* from charging a lower fee where the service relates to a transaction or engagement that was either aborted or prematurely terminated for whatever reason and where the rationale for the lower fee is to take account of either the reduced risk and responsibility involved or the fact that less work was undertaken than had been anticipated.

4.19   For *non-audit/additional services* provided on a *contingent fee basis*, other than those prohibited under paragraph 4.14, the *engagement partner* assesses the significance of the self-interest threat and considers whether there are safeguards that could be applied which would be effective to eliminate the threat or reduce it to a level where independence is not compromised. The significance of the self-interest threat will depend on factors such as:

- the range of possible fee amounts;

- the nature of the *non-audit/additional service*;

- for an audit, the effect of the outcome of the additional *non-audit service* on the financial statements of the *audited entity*;

- for an other *public interest assurance engagement*, the effect of the outcome of the additional service on the *subject matter information* or *subject matter* of the *engagement*.

4.20   Examples of safeguards that might be applied to reduce any self-interest threats arising from the provision of *non-audit/additional services* on a *contingent fee basis* (other than those set out in paragraph 4.14 above) to a level where independence is not compromised include:

- the provision of such *non-audit/additional services* by partners and *staff* who have no involvement in the *engagement*;

- review of the *engagement* by a partner with relevant expertise who is not involved in the *engagement* to ensure that the *subject matter* of the *non-audit/additional service* has been properly and effectively addressed in the context of the *engagement*.

4.21   For an *investment circular reporting engagement*, in situations where a *reporting accountant* can see at the outset of the *investment circular reporting engagement* that there is likely to be a judgment that will be made in relation to a material aspect of the *investment circular reporting engagement* which could adversely affect the successful completion of the transaction to which the investment circular relates, the *firm* will not agree to undertake any corporate finance services in relation to the transaction on a *contingent fee basis*, or will not accept the *investment circular reporting engagement*. Where corporate finance services are entered into on a *contingent fee basis* and a judgment needs to be made in relation to a material aspect of the *investment circular reporting engagement* during the course of an *investment circular reporting engagement*, then the *firm* changes the terms of the corporate finance service so that it no longer involves a contingent fee or withdraws from either the relevant corporate finance service or the *investment circular reporting engagement*.

Where the *firm* provides a range of corporate finance services to an *entity* **4.22** *relevant to the engagement*, including acting as a Sponsor or Nominated Advisor, on terms that involve a contingent fee, and that *firm* also undertakes a public reporting engagement for an *entity relevant to the engagement*, the self-interest threat caused by contingent fee arrangements may be reduced to a level where independence is not compromised by the application of safeguards, such as the corporate finance services being provided by partners and *staff* who have no involvement in the *investment circular reporting engagement*. In such circumstances the *reporting accountant* ensures that the situation is fully disclosed to the Financial Conduct Authority (FCA), or the London Stock Exchange and any related regulatory requirements have been complied with.

The *firm* shall establish policies and procedures to ensure that the *engagement* **4.23** **partner and the *Ethics Partner*/Function are notified where others within the** **firm propose to adopt contingent fee arrangements in relation to the provision** **of *non-audit/additional services* to the *entity relevant to the engagement* or its** **affiliates.**

Contingent fee arrangements in respect of *non-audit/additional services* provided **4.24** by the *firm* may create a threat to the integrity, objectivity or independence of the *firm* and *covered persons*. The circumstances in which such fee arrangements are not permitted for *non-audit/additional services* are dealt with in paragraph 4.14 of this Section.

In the case of *public interest entities* and of other *listed entities relevant to an* **4.25** **engagement, the *engagement partner* shall disclose to the audit committee, in** **writing, any contingent fee arrangements for *non-audit/additional services*** **provided by the *firm* or its *network firms*.**

In the case of a group *engagement* of a *public interest entity* or of an other *listed* **4.26** *entity*, which involves other *firms*, the letter of instruction sent by the group *engagement partner* to the other *firms* requests disclosure of any contingent fees for *non-audit/additional services* charged or proposed to be charged by the other *firms*.

For a recurring *engagement*, the actual amount of the *engagement* fee for the **4.27** **previous *engagement* and the arrangements for its payment shall be agreed** **with the entity before the *firm* formally accepts appointment for the** **engagement in respect of the following period.**

Ordinarily, any outstanding fees for the previous engagement period are paid **4.28** before the *firm* commences any new *engagement* work. Where they are not, it is important for the *engagement partner* to understand the nature of any disagreement or other issue.

Where fees for professional services from an entity are overdue and the **4.29** **amount cannot be regarded as trivial, the *engagement partner*, in consultation** **with the *Ethics Partner*/Function, shall consider whether the *firm* can accept** **or continue an *engagement* for the entity or whether it is necessary to resign.**

Where fees due from an entity, whether for *an audit engagement, other public* **4.30** *interest assurance engagements*, or for other professional services, remain unpaid for a long time – and, in particular, where a significant part is not paid before the *firm's* audit report on the financial statements for the following year, or report on other *subject matter information* or *subject matter* in the case of an other *public* *interest assurance engagement* for a subsequent *engagement*, is due to be issued – a self-interest threat to the integrity, objectivity and independence of the *firm* and *covered persons* is created because the issue of an unqualified report may enhance the *firm's* prospects of securing payment of such overdue fees.

4.31 Where the outstanding fees are in dispute and the amount involved is significant, the threats to the integrity and objectivity of the *firm* and *covered persons* may be such that they cannot be reduced to a level where independence would not be compromised. The *engagement partner* therefore considers whether the *firm* can continue with the *engagement*.

4.32 Where the outstanding fees are unpaid because of exceptional circumstances (including financial distress), the *engagement partner* considers whether the entity will be able to resolve its difficulties. In deciding what action to take, the *engagement partner* weighs the threats to the integrity, objectivity and independence of the *firm* and *covered persons*, if the *firm* were to remain appointed to provide the *engagement*, against the difficulties the entity would be likely to face in finding a successor, and therefore the public interest considerations, if the *firm* were to resign or withdraw from the *engagement*.

4.33 In any case where the *firm* does not resign from the *engagement*, the *engagement partner* applies appropriate safeguards (such as a review by a partner with relevant expertise who is not involved in the *engagement*) and notifies the *Ethics Partner* of the facts concerning the overdue fees.

4.34R When the ~~statutory auditor or the~~ *audit firm, or a member of its network,* provides to ~~the audited~~ a *public interest* entity that it audits, its parent undertaking or its controlled undertakings, ~~for a period of three or more consecutive financial years,~~ non-audit services other than those referred to in Article 5(1)[43] of ~~this~~ the EU Audit Regulation:

 (a) the total fees for such services provided to the audited entity and its controlled undertakings shall be limited to no more than 70% of the average of the fees paid in the last three consecutive financial years[44] for the ~~statutory~~ audit(s) of the audited entity and ~~of its parent undertaking,~~ of its controlled undertakings and of the consolidated financial statements of that group of undertakings; and

 (b) the total fees for such services provided by the *audit firm* shall be limited to no more than 70% of the average of the fees paid to the *audit firm* in the last three consecutive financial years[44] for the ~~statutory~~ audit(s) of the audited entity and, where applicable, of its parent undertaking, of its controlled undertakings and of the consolidated financial statements of that group of undertakings. [AR 4.2]

4.35R For the purposes of the limits specified in ~~the first subparagraph~~ paragraph 4.34R, non-audit services, other than those referred to in Article 5(1) of the EU Audit Regulation, required by Union or national legislation shall be excluded. [AR 4.2]

---

[43] See paragraph 5.167R of Section 5 of Part B of this Ethical Standard.

[44] This requirement does not apply retrospectively. The cap is based on average audit fees for the three consecutive financial periods commencing on or after 17 June 2016. Following the appointment of a new auditor after that date the cap will apply from the fourth financial period of that engagement.

Upon a request by the ~~statutory auditor or the~~*audit firm*, on an exceptional basis, the competent authority[45] may allow that ~~statutory auditor or~~ *audit firm* to be exempt from the requirements in ~~the first sub-paragraph~~paragraph 4.34R in respect of an *audited entity* for a period not exceeding two financial years. [AR 4.2]   **4.36R**

In the case of *public interest entities* and of other *listed entities*, where: **4.37**

(a)   the fees charged by the *firm* and members of its *network* in aggregate: or

(b)   the fees charged by the *firm* or by any member of its *network* whose work is used in the conduct of the *engagement*;

for *non-audit/additional services*, and for services provided to *connected parties* that may bear on independence, for a financial year are expected to be greater than the aggregate (or the individual firm's) annual fees for the *engagement*, the *engagement partner* shall provide details of the circumstances to the *Ethics Partner*/Function and discuss them with him or her. The *engagement partner* shall determine whether the threats to independence of the *firm* or any such member of its network are at a level where independence is not compromised or, if necessary, put in place appropriate safeguards such that independence is not compromised, which may include the *firm* or member of its network not providing the *non-audit/additional* service.

Where the *firm* and/or members of its network provide services to a group, the requirement in paragraph 4.37 shall apply on a group basis for all services provided by the *firm* and its *network firms* to all entities in the group and to their *connected parties*.   **4.38**

Where substantial fees are regularly generated from the provision of *non-audit/additional services* and the fees for *non-audit/additional services* are greater than the annual fees for recurring *engagements* for an entity, the *engagement partner* has regard to the possibility that there may be perceived to be a loss of independence resulting from the expected or actual level of fees for *non-audit/additional services*. The *engagement partner* determines whether there is any risk that there will be an actual loss of integrity, objectivity or independence by the *firm* or *covered persons*. In making that assessment, the *engagement partner* considers matters such as whether the *non-audit/additional services* were: **4.39**

•   audit related services;

•   provided on a *contingent fee basis*;

•   consistent with the services undertaken and fees received on a consistent basis in previous years;

•   in the case of a group, disproportionate in relation to any individual group entity;

•   unusual in size but unlikely to recur; and/or

•   of such a size and nature that an objective, reasonable and informed third party would be concerned at the effect that such services would have on the integrity, objectivity and independence of the *firm* or *covered persons*.

Having made that assessment, the *engagement partner* determines whether the threats to independence from the level of fees for *non-audit/additional services* are at a level where independence is not compromised (or can be reduced to such a

---

[45] *The competent authority for this purpose is the Financial Reporting Council.*

level by putting in place appropriate safeguards) and appropriately informs the audit committee or those charged with governance of the position on a timely basis in accordance with paragraphs 1.61, 1.66 and 1.67 of Section 1 of Part B of this Ethical Standard.

4.40   Discussing the level of fees for *non-audit/additional services* with the *Ethics Partner*/Function ensures that appropriate attention is paid to the issue by the *firm*. The *firm's* policies and procedures will set out whether there are circumstances in which the *engagement partner* responsible for the *engagement* discusses the level of *non-audit/additional service* fees with the *Ethics Partner*/Function for non-listed entities, that are not *public interest entities*, as described in paragraph 1.49 of Section 1 of Part B of this Ethical Standard.

4.41   Paragraphs 4.42 to 4.52 below do not apply to *engagements* of entities where the responsibility for the *engagement* is assigned by legislation and the *firm* cannot resign from the *engagement*, irrespective of considerations of economic dependence (e.g. for certain public sector bodies).

4.42   **Where it is expected that the total fees for services receivable from a *public interest entity* or other *listed entity* and its subsidiaries relevant to a recurring *engagement* by the *firm*[46] will regularly exceed 10% of the annual fee income of the *firm*[47] or, where profits are not shared on a *firm*-wide basis, of the part of the *firm* by reference to which the *engagement partner's* profit share is calculated, the *firm* shall not act as the provider of the *engagement* for that entity and shall either resign or not stand for reappointment, as appropriate.**

4.43   The requirements in paragraph 4.42 are applied in place of the less stringent requirements in Article 4.3 of the EU Audit Regulation, as permitted by Article 4.4 of the EU Audit regulation.

4.44   **Where it is expected that the total fees for services receivable from a non-listed entity that is not a *public interest entity* and its subsidiaries relevant to a recurring *engagement* by the *firm* will regularly exceed 15% of the annual fee income of the *firm* or, where profits are not shared on a *firm*-wide basis, of the part of the *firm* by reference to which the *engagement partner's* profit share is calculated, the *firm* shall not act as the provider of the *engagement* for that entity and shall either resign or not stand for reappointment, as appropriate.**

4.45   Where it is expected that the total fees for services receivable from an entity and its subsidiaries relevant to a recurring *engagement* by the *firm* will regularly exceed 10%, in the case of *public interest entities* or other *listed entities*, and 15%, in the case of non-listed entities that are not *public interest entities*, of the annual fee income of the part of the *firm* by reference to which the *engagement partner's* profit share is calculated, it may be possible to assign the *engagement* to another part of the *firm*.

4.46   Paragraphs 4.42 and 4.44 are not intended to require the *firm* to resign as provider of a recurring *engagement*, or not stand for reappointment, as a result of an individual event or *engagement*, the nature or size of which was unpredictable and where an objective, reasonable and informed third party would regard ceasing to act as detrimental to the shareholders (or equivalent) of the entity or otherwise contrary to the public interest. However, in such circumstances, the *engagement*

---

[46]   *Total fees will include those billed by others where the firm is entitled to the fees, but will not include fees billed by the firm where it is acting as agent for another party.*

[47]   *In the case of a sole practitioner, annual fee income of the firm includes all earned income received by the individual.*

partner discloses full details of the position to the *Ethics Partner*/Function and to those charged with governance of the entity, including the audit committee where there is one, and discusses with both the threats to the integrity, objectivity and independence of the *firm* and *covered persons* and the safeguards applied to eliminate or reduce those threats to a level where independence would not be compromised.

Where it is expected that the total fees services receivable from a *public*   **4.47**
***interest entity* or other *listed entity* and its subsidiaries relevant to a recurring *engagement* by the *firm* will regularly exceed 5% of the annual fee income of the *firm* or the part of the *firm* by reference to which the *engagement partner's* profit share is calculated, but will not regularly exceed 10%, the *engagement partner* shall disclose that expectation to the *Ethics Partner*/Function and to those charged with governance of the entity, including the audit committee where there is one, and discusses with both the threat to integrity, objectivity and independence of the *firm* and *covered persons* and whether safeguards need to be applied to eliminate or reduce the threat to a level where independence would not be compromised.**

It is fundamental to the integrity and objectivity of the *firm* and *covered persons*   **4.48**
that they be willing and able, if necessary, to disagree with the directors and management, regardless of the consequences to the *firm's* own position. Where the *firm* is, to any significant extent, economically dependent on the entity, this may inhibit the willingness or constrain the *firm*'s ability to express a qualified opinion on the financial statements or other *subject matter information* or *subject matter* of an *engagement*, since this could be viewed as likely to lead to the *firm* losing the *engagement* and the entity as a client.

A *firm* is deemed to be economically dependent on a *public interest entity* or other   **4.49**
listed entity if the total fees for all other services from that entity and its subsidiaries relevant to a recurring *engagement* represent 10% of the total fees of the *firm* or the part of the *firm* by reference to which the *engagement partner's* profit share is calculated. Where such fees are between 5% and 10%, the *engagement partner* and the *Ethics Partner*/Function consider the significance of the threat and the need for appropriate safeguards.

Such safeguards might include: **4.50**

- taking steps to reduce the other work to be undertaken and therefore the fees earned from the entity;
- applying independent internal quality control reviews.

Where it is expected that the total fees for services receivable from a non-   **4.51**
listed entity, that is not a *public interest entity*, and its subsidiaries relevant to a recurring *engagement* will regularly exceed 10% of the annual fee income of the *firm* or the part of the *firm* by reference to which the *engagement partner's* profit share is calculated, but will not regularly exceed 15%, the *engagement partner* shall disclose that expectation to the *Ethics Partner*/Function and to those charged with governance of the entity and the *firm* shall arrange an external independent quality control review of the *engagement* to be undertaken before the *firm's* report is finalised.

A quality control review involves discussion with the *engagement partner*, a   **4.52**
review of the financial statements or other *subject matter information* or *subject matter* of an *engagement* and the *firm's* report thereon, and consideration of whether the report is appropriate. It also involves a review of selected working papers relating to the significant judgments the *engagement team* has made and

the conclusions they have reached. The extent of the review depends on the complexity of the *engagement* and the risk that the report might not be appropriate in the circumstances. The review includes considering the following:

- Significant risks identified during the *engagement* and the responses to those risks.

- Judgments made, particularly with respect to materiality and significant risks.

- The *engagement team's* consideration of the entity's compliance with applicable laws and regulations.

- Whether appropriate consultation has taken place on matters involving differences of opinion or other difficult or contentious matters, and the conclusions arising from those consultations.

- The significance and disposition of corrected and uncorrected misstatements identified during the *engagement*.

- The appropriateness of the report to be issued.

Where the quality control reviewer makes recommendations that the *engagement partner* does not accept and the matter is not resolved to the reviewer's satisfaction, the report is not issued until the matter is resolved by following the *firm's* procedures for dealing with differences of opinion.

4.53 A new *firm* seeking to establish itself may find the requirements relating to economic dependence difficult to comply with in the short term. In these circumstances, such *firms* would:

(a) not undertake any *engagements* of *public interest entities* or other *listed entities*, where fees from such an entity would represent 10% or more of the annual fee income of the *firm*; and

(b) for a period not exceeding two years, require external independent quality control reviews of those of non-listed entities, that are not *public interest entities*, that represent more than 15% of the annual fee income before the *engagement* report/opinion is issued.

The *firm* might also develop its practice by accepting work from entities not relevant to an *engagement* by the *firm* so as to bring the fees payable by each entity which is relevant to an *engagement* below 15%.

4.54 A self-interest threat may also be created where a partner in the *engagement team*:

- is employed exclusively or principally on that *engagement*; and

- is remunerated on the basis of the performance of part of the *firm* which is substantially dependent on fees from that entity.

4.55 Where the circumstances described in paragraph 4.54 arise, the *firm* assesses the significance of the threat and applies safeguards to reduce the threat to a level where independence would not be compromised. Such safeguards might include:

- reducing the dependence of the office, partner or other *covered person* by reallocating the work within the practice;

- a review by an *engagement partner* with relevant expertise who is not involved with the *engagement* to ensure that the integrity, objectivity or independence of the *firm* and *covered persons* is not affected by the self-interest threat.

Remuneration and Evaluation Policies

> A *firm* shall have in place adequate remuneration policies, including profit-sharing policies, providing sufficient performance incentives to secure *engagement* quality. In particular, the amount of revenue that the *firm* derives from providing *non-audit/additional services* to the entity shall not form part of the performance evaluation and remuneration of any *covered person* involved in, or able to influence the carrying out of, an *engagement*. [AD 24a.1(j)]
>
> **4.56D**

The *firm* shall establish policies and procedures to ensure that each of the following is true in relation to each *entity relevant to an engagement* by the *firm*: **4.57**

(a) a primary criterion for evaluating the performance or promotion of members of the *engagement team* is how they have contributed to the quality of *engagements* undertaken;

(b) the objectives of the members of the *engagement team* do not include selling *non-audit/additional services* to the entity;

(c) the criteria for evaluating the performance or promotion of members of the *engagement team* do not include success in selling *non-audit/additional services* to the entity; and

(d) no specific element of the remuneration of a member of the *engagement team* is based on his or her success in selling *non-audit/additional services* to the entity.

This requirement does not apply to those members of the *engagement team* from specialist practice areas where the nature and extent of their involvement in the *engagement* is clearly insignificant.

Where the *firm*, its partners or *staff* identify areas for possible improvement in an *entity relevant to an engagement*, they may provide general business advice, which might include suggested solutions to problems. Before discussing any *non-audit/additional service* that might be provided by the *firm* or effecting any introductions to colleagues from outside the *engagement team*, the *engagement partner* considers the threats that such a service would have on the *engagement*, in line with the requirements in Section 5 of this Ethical Standard, and whether it is probable that an objective, reasonable and informed third party would conclude the integrity, objectivity or independence of the *firm* or *covered persons* are compromised. **4.58**

The last sentence of paragraph 4.57 recognises the fact that an *engagement team* may include personnel from specialist practice areas and that it would be inappropriate to limit the business development activities of such persons where their involvement in the *engagement* is clearly insignificant. **4.59**

The policies and procedures required for compliance with paragraph 4.57 are not intended to inhibit normal profit-sharing arrangements. However, such policies and procedures are central to the ability of a *firm* that provides *engagement* services to demonstrate the integrity, objectivity and independence of the *firm* and *covered persons*, and to rebut any suggestion that an *engagement* that it has undertaken and the report/opinion that it has given are influenced by the nature and extent of any *non-audit/additional services* that it has provided to that entity. The *Ethics Partner*/Function pays particular attention to the actual implementation of those policies and procedures and is available for consultation when needed. **4.60**

Gifts and Hospitality

4.61D | A *firm*, its partners and any *covered person*, and *persons closely associated* with them, shall not solicit or accept pecuniary and non-pecuniary gifts or favours, including hospitality, from an *entity relevant to the engagement*, or any other entity related to that entity, unless an objective, reasonable and informed third party would consider the value thereof as trivial or inconsequential. [AD 22.5]

4.62   Where gifts, favours or hospitality are accepted from an *entity relevant to an engagement*, or from other entities related to that entity, self-interest and familiarity threats to the integrity, objectivity and independence of the *firm*, its partners and any other *covered person* are created. Familiarity threats also arise where gifts, favours or hospitality are offered to an *entity relevant to an engagement*, its partners or any other *covered person*.

4.63   **The *firm* shall establish policies on the nature and value of gifts, favours and hospitality that may be accepted from and offered to an *entity relevant to an engagement*, or any other entity related to that entity, their directors, officers and employees, and shall issue guidance to assist partners and *staff* to comply with such policies.**

4.64   Where gifts, favours and hospitality are accepted or offered more than once, the view of an objective, reasonable and informed third party of the cumulative effect is considered.

4.65   Where there is any doubt as to the acceptability of gifts, favours or hospitality offered by the entity, members of the *engagement team* discuss the position with the *engagement partner*. If there is any doubt as to the acceptability of gifts, favours or hospitality offered to the *engagement partner*, or if the *engagement partner* has any residual doubt about the acceptability of gifts, favours or hospitality to other individuals, the *engagement partner* reports the facts to the *Ethics Partner*/Function, for further consideration regarding any action to be taken.

Threatened and Actual Litigation

4.66   Paragraphs 4.67 and 4.68 below, which support Supporting Ethical Provision 2.11, do not apply to the *engagements* of those entities where the responsibility for the *engagement* is assigned by legislation and the *firm* cannot resign from the *engagement*. In these circumstances the *firm* reports significant litigation to the relevant legislative authority.

4.67   Where litigation (in relation to any services) actually takes place between the *firm*, its partners, or any *covered person*, and the entity or its *affiliates*, or where such litigation is considered probable, self-interest, advocacy and intimidation threats to the integrity, objectivity and independence of the *firm* and *covered persons* are created because the *firm's* interest will be the achievement of an outcome to the dispute or litigation that is favourable to itself. In addition, an effective *engagement* process requires complete candour and full disclosure between the entity's management and the *engagement team*: such disputes or litigation may place the two parties in opposing adversarial positions and may affect management's willingness to make complete disclosure of relevant information. Where the *firm* can foresee that such a threat may arise and independence compromised, the *firm* informs the audit committee of its intention to resign or, where there is no audit committee, the board of directors. Where applicable, the *firm* also informs any other persons or entities the *firm* is instructed to advise of its intention to withdraw from the *engagement*.

The *firm* is not required to resign immediately in circumstances where an **4.68** objective, reasonable and informed third party would not regard it as being in the interests of the shareholders (or equivalent) or otherwise contrary to the public interest. Such circumstances might arise, for example, where:

- the litigation was commenced as the *engagement* was about to be completed, and shareholder (or other stakeholder) interests would be adversely affected by a delay in the *engagement*;

- on appropriate legal advice, the *firm* deems that the threatened or actual litigation is vexatious or designed solely to bring pressure to bear on the opinion to be expressed by the *firm*.

Section 5 – *Non-audit/Additional Services*

General Approach to Non-audit/Additional Services

Investment Circular Reporting Engagements

In relation to an *investment circular reporting engagement*, this Section **5.1** applies only to those *additional services* provided by the *firm* to an *entity relevant to the engagement* during the "*relevant period*". The *relevant period* covers the period during which the *investment circular reporting engagement* is undertaken and any additional period subsequent to the date of the most recent audited financial statements. Other services provided prior to that date are unlikely to create threats to integrity or objectivity because:

- where the *reporting accountant* undertook the last audit of the financial statements of an *entity relevant to the engagement* and complied with the FRC's Ethical Standard, the requirements applicable to the provision of other services will have been observed; or
- where the last audit of the financial statements of an *entity relevant to the engagement* was undertaken by a different *firm*, the work done by the *reporting accountant* in providing other services will have been the subject of independent review in the course of the audit.

Paragraphs 5.3 to 5.39 of this Section set out the general approach to be adopted **5.2** by *firms* in relation to the provision of *non-audit services* to entities audited by them and *additional services* to entities which they may not audit but for which they undertake other public interest assurance services. This approach is applicable irrespective of the nature of the *non-audit/additional services*, which may be in question in a given case. (Paragraphs 5.44 to 5.164 of this Section illustrate the application of the general approach to a number of common *non-audit/additional services*.)

5.3   ISAs (UK) require that auditors exercise professional judgment and maintain professional scepticism throughout the planning and performance of the audit and, among other things:

- Identify and assess risks of material misstatement, whether due to fraud or error, based on an understanding of the entity and its environment, including the entity's internal control.

- Obtain sufficient appropriate audit evidence about whether material misstatements exist, through designing and implementing appropriate responses to the assessed risks.

- Form an opinion on the financial statements based on conclusions drawn from the audit evidence obtained[48].

5.4   Judgments regarding the nature and extent of evidence necessary to support an audit opinion or opinion given in respect of an other *public interest assurance engagement* are a matter for the *firm* but will include:

- Identifying, evaluating and testing, where appropriate, those internal control systems the effectiveness of which is necessary for the *engagement* and where, if any control weaknesses are identified, extended testing will be required; and

- additional work undertaken to respond to risks identified by management or the audit committee that the *firm* considers could impact the *firm's* opinion on financial statements or on other *subject matter information* or *subject matter* of the *engagement*.

5.5   Other work undertaken by the *engagement team* at the request of management or those charged with governance will not be categorised as part of the *engagement* irrespective of whether it forms part of the *engagement* proposal or *engagement*, unless it is clear that the predominant rationale for the performance of the work in question is to enable a soundly based opinion on the financial statements, or on other *subject matter information* or *subject matter* of the *engagement*, to be expressed. Therefore, an *engagement* does not include work where:

- The objective of that work is not to gather evidence to support the *firm's* opinion on the financial statements or on other *subject matter information* or *subject matter* of the *engagement*; or

- The nature and extent of testing is not determined by the *firm*, or in the case of a group, the work of other *firms* in relation to group components, in the context of expressing an opinion on the financial statements or on other *subject matter information* or *subject matter* of the *engagement*; or

- The principal terms and conditions for the work differ from that of the *engagement*.

5.6   In the context of an *audit engagement*, if additional work on financial information[49] and/or financial controls is authorised by those charged with governance, but the objective of that work is not to enable the auditor to provide an audit opinion on the entity's financial statements, it will be considered as an "audit related service" (see paragraph 5.40) for the purpose of this Ethical Standard provided that it:

---

[48] *ISA (UK) 200 "Overall Objectives of the Independent Auditor and the Conduct of an Audit in Accordance with International Standards on Auditing (UK)" paragraph 7.*

[49] *This does not include accounting services.*

- is integrated with the work performed in the audit and performed largely by the existing *audit team*; and

- is performed on the same principal terms and conditions as the audit.

As a consequence of these factors, any threats to auditor independence arising from the performance of such additional work are considered to be clearly insignificant.

For entities audited by the *firm*, other additional work that: **5.7**

- does not relate to financial information and/or financial controls; or

- is not integrated with the work performed in the audit, or is not performed largely by the existing *audit team*, or

- is not on the same principal terms and conditions as the audit;

will be regarded as an "other *non-audit service*" for the purpose of this Ethical Standard.

"*Non-audit services*" comprise any engagement in which a *firm*, or a member of   **5.8** its network, provides professional services to:

- an *audited entity*;

- an *audited entity's affiliates*; or

- another entity where the subject matter of the *engagement* includes the *audited entity*[50] and/or its *significant affiliates*;

other than the audit of financial statements of the *audited entity*.

For a *public interest assurance engagement* other than an audit, "*additional*   **5.9** *services*" comprise any engagement in which a *firm*, or a member of its *network*, provides professional services to an *entity relevant to the engagement* other than pursuant to:

(a) any other *public interest assurance engagement*;

(b) the audit of financial statements; and

(c) those other roles which legislation or regulation specify can be performed by the auditor of the entity (for example, considering the preliminary announcements of listed companies, complying with the procedural and reporting requirements of regulators, such as requirements relating to the audit of the client's internal controls and reports in accordance with Section 714 of the Companies Act 2006).

Where the *entity relevant to the engagement* is a member of a group, *additional services* for the purposes of this Ethical Standard include:

- services provided by the *firm* to the parent entity or to any of its *significant affiliates*; and

- services provided by a *network firm* which is involved in the *engagement* to the *entity relevant to the engagement* or any of its *significant affiliates*.

There may be circumstances where the *firm* is engaged to provide a *non-audit/*   **5.10** *additional service* and where that service and its scope are determined by an entity which is not audited or relevant to an other *public interest assurance engagement* by the *firm*. However, it might be contemplated that an entity relevant to an

---

[50] *For example, where an engagement is undertaken to assist in the preparation of listing particulars for a company acquiring the audited entity*

engagement, may gain some benefit from that *non-audit/additional service*[51]. In some circumstances, there may be no threat to the integrity, objectivity and independence of the *firm* and *covered persons* at the time of appointment. However, the *firm* considers how the *non-audit/additional service* may be expected to develop, whether there are any threats that the *firm* may be subject to if additional relevant parties which are *entities relevant to an engagement*, are identified, and whether any safeguards need to be put in place. For example, when the results of such a *non-audit/additional service* performed by the *firm* are reflected in the financial statements or other *subject matter information* or *subject matter* of an *engagement*; or where the fees earned from such a *non-audit/additional service* performed by the *firm* could be perceived as compromising independence for an *engagement* by the *firm*.

5.11   The *firm* **shall establish policies and procedures that require others within the firm, when considering whether to provide a *non-audit/additional service* to an entity relevant to an engagement, <u>other than an *investment circular reporting engagement*</u>, or to any of its *affiliates*, to communicate details of the proposed *non-audit/additional service* to the *engagement partner*.**

5.12   The *firm* establishes appropriate channels of internal communication to ensure that, in relation to an *entity relevant to an engagement*, the *engagement partner* (or their delegate) is informed about any proposed *non-audit/additional service* to the entity or any of its *affiliates* and that he or she considers the implications for the integrity, objectivity and independence of the *firm* and *covered persons* before provision of the *non-audit/additional service* is accepted. Additionally, when addressing services provided to another entity in respect of an *entity relevant to an engagement*, the procedures address any requirement to preserve client confidentiality.

5.13   In the case of a group audit of a *public interest entity* or an other *listed entity* the group *engagement partner* establishes that the entity has communicated its policy on the engagement of the external auditor to supply *non-audit services* to its *affiliates* and obtains confirmation that the auditors of the *affiliates* will comply with this policy.[52] The group *engagement partner* also requires that relevant information on *non-audit services* provided by *network firms* is communicated on a timely basis.

5.14   **In relation to *investment circular reporting engagements*, the *firm* should establish policies and procedures, including the alternative procedures outlined in paragraph 1.40 of Section 1 of Part B of this Ethical Standard, that enable it to identify circumstances where others within the *firm* and *network firms* involved in the *investment circular reporting engagement* have undertaken to provide during the *relevant period*, an *additional service* to an *entity relevant to the engagement* or any of that entity's *significant affiliates*.**

5.15   The *firm* establishes appropriate policies and procedures to ensure that, in relation to an *entity relevant to an investment circular reporting*

---

[51] *For example, in a vendor due diligence engagement, the engagement is initiated and scoped by the vendor before the purchaser is identified. If an entity audited by the firm undertaking the due diligence engagement is the purchaser, that audited entity may gain the benefit of the report issued by its auditor, it may be a party to the engagement letter and it may pay an element of the fee.*

[52] *The UK Corporate Governance Code requires audit committees to develop the company's policy on the engagement of the external auditor to supply non-audit services.*

engagement, any undertaking to provide an *additional service* to the entity, or any of its *significant affiliates*, during the *relevant period* is identified, so that the *engagement partner* can consider the implications for integrity, objectivity and independence of the *firm* and *covered persons* before the *investment circular reporting engagement* is accepted. Such policies and procedures are likely to involve:

(i) enquiries of each *entity relevant to the engagement*;

(ii) reference to records of past and current *additional services* provided by the *firm*;

(iii) enquiries of *network firms* involved in the *investment circular reporting engagement* as to whether they have provided any *additional services* to an *entity relevant to the engagement* or any of its *significant affiliates* during the *relevant period*.

Such enquiries are undertaken in a manner which seeks to protect confidentiality.

Identification and Assessment of Threats and Safeguards

For an *engagement* <u>other than an *investment circular reporting engagement*</u>, before the *firm* accepts to provide a *non-audit/additional service* to an *entity relevant to the engagement*, the *engagement partner* shall: **5.16**

(a) identify and assess the significance of any related threats to the integrity or objectivity of the *firm* and *covered persons*, including whether independence would be compromised; and

(b) identify and assess the effectiveness of the available safeguards to eliminate the threats or reduce them to a level where independence would not be compromised; and

(c) consider whether it is probable that an objective, reasonable and informed third party, having regard to the threats and safeguards, would conclude that that the proposed *non-audit/additional service* would not impair integrity or objectivity and compromise the independence of the *firm* or *covered persons*.

When assessing the significance of threats to the integrity, objectivity and independence of the *firm* and *covered persons*, the *engagement partner* considers the following factors: **5.17**

• The likely relevance and impact of the *non-audit/additional service* on the financial statements, or on *subject matter information* or *subject matter* of the *engagement*;

• The extent to which performance of the proposed *non-audit/additional service* will involve the exercise of professional judgment;

• The size of the *non-audit/additional service* and the associated fee;

• The basis on which the fee is to be calculated;

• The *staff* who would be carrying out the *non-audit/additional service*[53];

---

[53] *For example, where those handling the non-audit service are particularly expert so that the audit team (or persons advising it) may have difficulty in reviewing effectively the advice given or the work undertaken by the non-audit service team in the course of conducting a subsequent audit, with the result that the effectiveness of the audit might be compromised.*

- The staff from the *entity relevant to the engagement* who would be involved in the *non-audit/additional service*[54].

To ensure that this assessment is made with a proper understanding of the nature of the *non-audit/additional service*, it may be necessary to refer to a draft engagement letter in respect of the proposed *non-audit/additional service* or to discuss the service with the partner involved.

5.18   The assessment of the threats to the integrity, objectivity and independence of the *firm* and *covered persons* arising from any particular *non-audit/additional service* is a matter for the *engagement partner* responsible for the *engagement*. The *engagement partner* may decide to delegate some information gathering activities to senior personnel on the *engagement team* and may allow such personnel to make decisions in relation to routine *non-audit/additional services*. If this is the case, the *engagement partner* will:

- provide specific criteria for such decisions that reflect both the requirements of this Ethical Standard and the entity's policy for the purchase of *non-audit/additional services*; and

- monitor the decisions being made on a regular basis.

5.19   Where the *engagement partner* is not able to undertake the assessment of the significance of threats in relation to a proposed *non-audit/additional service* to an *entity relevant to an engagement*, for example due to illness or holidays, alternative arrangements are established (for example, by authorising the *engagement quality control reviewer* to consider the proposed service).

5.20   **For an *engagement* <u>other than an *investment circular reporting engagement*</u>, where it is probable that an objective, reasonable and informed third party would conclude that the proposed *non-audit/additional service* would impair integrity or objectivity and compromise the independence of the *firm* or *covered persons*, the *firm* shall either:**

   (a)   **not undertake the *non-audit/additional service*; or**

   (b)   **not accept or shall withdraw from the *engagement* as appropriate.**

5.21 | For an *investment circular reporting engagement*, where the *engagement partner* considers that it is probable that a reasonable and informed third party would regard the objectives of an additional service[55] undertaken during the *relevant period* as being inconsistent with the objectives of the *investment circular reporting engagement*, the *firm* shall not accept or shall withdraw from the *investment circular reporting engagement* as appropriate.

5.22   The objectives of *non-audit/additional services* vary and depend on the specific terms of the service. In some cases these objectives may be inconsistent with those of an *audit engagement* or other *public interest assurance engagement* provided by the *firm* and, in such cases, this may give rise to a threat to the integrity or objectivity of the *firm* and *covered persons* and to the appearance of their independence.

---

[54] *For example, the safeguards necessary to address any self-review threat will require careful consideration where those involved are particularly senior and can be expected to be actively involved in any audit discussion as this may also create an intimidation threat.*

[55] *This includes consideration of any private reporting engagements associated with the transaction which is the subject of the investment circular that were undertaken before the investment circular was contemplated.*

Similarly, in relation to a possible appointment as provider of an *audit engagement* **5.23**
or other *public interest assurance engagement* to an entity that the *firm* has not
provided such an *engagement* before, consideration needs to be given to recent,
current and potential *non-audit/additional services* provided by the *firm* to the
entity. The *firm* does not accept appointment to undertake such an *engagement*
unless it is probable that an objective, reasonable and informed third party, taking
into account safeguards applied, would conclude that the independence of the *firm*
or *covered persons* are not compromised.

The passage of time since a service was provided, and audit or review of the **5.24**
outcome of the service by another *firm*, may help mitigate actual and perceived
threats to independence. However, it is still necessary for an assessment of the
threats to be undertaken in accordance with paragraph 1.33 of Section 1 of Part B
of this Ethical Standard before an *engagement* is accepted. Such an assessment
takes account of the nature of the service and significance of the outcome provided
to the proposed *engagement* and whether an objective, reasonable and informed
third party, taking into account safeguards applied, would conclude that the
independence of the *firm* or *covered persons* are not compromised.

When tendering for a new *investment circular reporting engagement* or, in the **5.25**
case of *public interest entities* and other *listed entities*, when tendering for a new
audit engagement or other *public interest assurance engagement*, the *firm* ensures
that relevant information on recent *non-audit/additional services* is drawn to the
attention of the audit committee (or those charged with governance if the entity
does not have an audit committee) and, where applicable, any other persons or
entities the *firm* is instructed to advise, including:

- when recent *non-audit/additional services* were provided;

- the materiality of those *non-audit/additional services* to the proposed
  engagement;

- whether those *non-audit/additional services* would have been prohibited if
  the entity had been an *entity relevant to an engagement* by the *firm* at the
  time when they were undertaken; and

- the extent to which the outcomes of *non-audit/additional services* have been
  audited or reviewed by another *firm*.

Threats to Objectivity and Independence

As identified in Section 1, the principal types of threats to the integrity, objectivity **5.26**
and independence of the *firm* and *covered persons* are:

- self-interest threat;

- self-review threat;

- management threat;

- advocacy threat;

- familiarity (or trust) threat; and

- intimidation threat.

The *firm*, its partners and *staff* remain alert to the possibility that any of these
threats may occur in connection with *non-audit/additional services*. However, the
threats most commonly associated with *non-audit/additional services* are self-
interest threat, self-review threat, management threat and advocacy threat (see
paragraph 1.29 of Section 1 of Part B of this Ethical Standard).

Safeguards

5.27   Where any threat to the integrity and objectivity of the *firm* or any *covered person* and the appearance of their independence is identified, the *engagement partner* assesses the significance of that threat and considers whether there are safeguards that could be applied and which would be effective to eliminate the threat or reduce it to a level where independence is not compromised. If such safeguards can be identified and are applied, the *non-audit/additional service* may be provided. However, where no such safeguards are applied, the only course is for the *firm* either not to undertake the *non-audit/additional service* in question or not to accept or to withdraw from the *engagement*.

5.28   When considering what safeguards, if any, would be effective in reducing the threats to integrity, objectivity and independence to a level where independence is not compromised, the *engagement partner* has regard to the following safeguards which, individually or in combination, may be effective, depending on the circumstances:

(a)   The *non-audit/additional services* are provided by a separate team from the *engagement team*, and:

- if circumstances require, to address the threat identified, there is effective physical and electronic segregation of the individuals in each team, and of their documentation, at all times during the provision of the *engagement* and *non-audit/additional services*; and/ or

- the team providing the *non-audit/additional services* avoids taking any action or making any statement that compromises the integrity or objectivity and independence of the *engagement team*, for example, expressing any opinion about the approach that the *engagement team* might take or the conclusion it might reach when considering the appropriateness of accounting or other judgments.

The *Ethics Partner* establishes policies and procedures to ensure that, where safeguards of this nature are considered appropriate, the arrangements put in place are effective at all times. This will involve the *Ethics Partner*/Function being satisfied that there are effective arrangements in place for each member of the *non-audit/additional services* team to acknowledge their responsibilities and for each member of the *engagement team* to notify him or her of any breach of this requirement that the team member becomes aware of. Where notified of a breach, the *Ethics Partner*/Function considers together with the *engagement partner* the significance of the breach and the implications for the integrity, objectivity and independence of the *engagement team*, including whether any further safeguards are necessary and whether the matter should be reported to those charged with governance of the entity;

(b)   The *engagement quality control reviewer*, or another partner of sufficient relevant experience and seniority who is, and is seen to be, an effective challenge to both the *engagement partner* and the partner leading the *non-audit/additional services*, reviews the work and conclusions of the *engagement team*. The review includes consideration of the judgments of the persons conducting the *engagement*, if any, relating to the *subject matter* of the *non-audit/additional service*, having regard to the self-review threat identified, and determines and documents his or her conclusions as to whether the work is sufficient and the conclusions of the *engagement team* are appropriate. Where the review partner has concerns, the *engagement partner* does not sign the engagement opinion/report until those concerns have been subject to full consultation, including escalation through any processes required by the *firm's* policies. Where this safeguard is considered appropriate, the *Ethics Partner*/Function is satisfied that the review partner undertaking this role is appropriate, that the review partner is aware of the circumstances leading to the conclusion that there is a significant self-review threat and that any concerns raised by the review partner have been satisfactorily resolved before signature of the opinion.

For an *engagement* other than an *investment circular reporting engagement*, where the *engagement partner* concludes, with respect to threats to the integrity or objectivity of the *firm* or *covered persons*, including any threats that could compromise independence, related to a proposed *non-audit/ additional service* to an *entity relevant to the engagement*, that no appropriate safeguards are available to eliminate or reduce such threats to a level where independence would not be compromised, he or she shall inform the others concerned within the *firm* of that conclusion and the *firm* shall either: **5.29**

(a)   not undertake the *non-audit/additional service*; or

(b)   not accept or shall withdraw from the *engagement* as appropriate.

If the *engagement partner* is in doubt as to the appropriate action to be taken, he or she shall resolve the matter through consultation with the *Ethics Partner*/Function.

An initial assessment of the threats to integrity, objectivity and independence and the safeguards to be applied is required when the *engagement partner* is considering the acceptance of a *non-audit/additional service*. The assessment of the threats and the safeguards applied is reviewed whenever the scope and objectives of the *non-audit/ additional service* change significantly. If such a review suggests that safeguards cannot reduce the threat to a level where independence would not be compromised, the *firm* withdraws from the *non-audit/additional service*, or does not accept or withdraws from the *engagement* as appropriate.   **5.30**

Where both an *investment circular reporting engagement* and an engagement to undertake other services are provided concurrently, the initial assessment of the threats to objectivity and independence and the safeguards to be applied shall be reviewed whenever the scope and objectives of the other service or the *investment circular reporting engagement* change significantly. If such a review suggests that safeguards cannot reduce the threat to a level where independence is not compromised, the *firm* shall withdraw from the other service, or withdraw from the *investment circular reporting engagement*.   **5.31**

Where there is doubt as to the appropriate action to be taken, consultation with the *Ethics Partner*/Function ensures that an objective judgment is made and the *firm's* position is consistent.   **5.32**

Communication with Those Charged With Governance

Transparency is a key element in addressing the issues raised by the provision of *non-audit/additional services* by *firms* to the entities audited by them or for which other public interest assurance services are provided. Paragraphs 1.61, 1.66 and 1.67 of Section 1 of part B of this Ethical Standard establish requirements to   **5.33** communicate to those charged with governance, and other persons where appropriate, significant facts and matters that may bear upon the integrity, objectivity and independence of the *firm*. These include relevant facts and matters related to the provision of *non-audit/additional services*.

5.34   In the case of *public interest entities* and other *listed entities*, and entities that may be seeking a listing, ensuring that the audit committee is properly informed about the issues associated with the provision of *non-audit services* will assist them to comply with the provisions of the UK Corporate Governance Code relating to reviewing and monitoring the external auditor's independence and objectivity and to developing a policy on the use of the external auditor to supply *non-audit services*. This will include discussion of any inconsistencies between the entity's policy and this Ethical Standard and ensuring that the policy is communicated to *affiliates*.

5.35   Communications with those charged with governance regarding the impact on the integrity, objectivity or independence of the *firm* and *covered persons* of *non-audit/additional services* are likely to be facilitated if disclosure of such *non-audit/additional services* distinguishes between "audit related services" (see paragraphs 5.40 – 5.43) and other *non-audit/additional services* (see paragraphs 5.8 and 5.9).

Documentation

5.36   **For an *engagement* <u>other than an *investment circular reporting engagement*</u>, the *engagement partner* shall ensure that the reasoning for a decision to provide *non-audit/additional services*, and any safeguards adopted and why they are effective, is appropriately documented.**

5.37   Matters to be documented include any significant judgments concerning:

- threats identified;
- safeguards adopted and the reasons why they are considered to be effective; and
- communication with those charged with governance.

5.38   In situations where a management threat is identified in connection with the provision of *non-audit/additional services*, this documentation will include the assessment of the persons conducting the *engagement* of whether there is *informed management*. The documentation of communications with the entity where judgments and decisions are made by management may take a variety of forms, for example an informal meeting note covering the matters discussed.

5.39   For an *investment circular reporting engagement* the *engagement partner*, in accordance with paragraph 1.73 of Section 1 of Part B of this Ethical Standard, ensures that his or her consideration of the integrity, objectivity and independence of the *firm* and *covered persons* is appropriately documented on a timely basis. This includes consideration of non-audit/additional services provided during the *relevant period*.

Audit Related Services

5.40   Audit related services are those *non-audit services* specified in this Ethical Standard that are largely carried out by members of the *audit engagement team*, and where the work involved is closely related to the work performed in the audit and the threats to auditor independence are clearly insignificant and, as a consequence, safeguards need not be applied. However, such services provided to *public interest entities*, other than those required by Union or national legislation, are still subject to the 70% cap (see paragraphs 4.34R and 4.35R of Section 4 of Part B of this Ethical Standard) and still require approval by the audit committee.

Audit related services are: **5.41**

- Reporting required by law or regulation to be provided by the auditor;
- Reviews of interim financial information;
- Reporting on regulatory returns;
- Reporting to a regulator on client assets:
- Reporting on government grants;
- Reporting on internal financial controls when required by law or regulation;
- Extended audit work that is authorised by those charged with governance performed on financial information[56] and/or financial controls where this work is integrated with the audit work and is performed on the same principal terms and conditions.

The *engagement partner* shall ensure that only those *non-audit services* listed   **5.42**
in paragraph 5.41 are described as audit related services in communications
with those charged with governance of the *audited entity*.

In the UK, legislation requires large companies to disclose fees receivable by their   **5.43**
auditors and their auditors' associates (see the Appendix to this Ethical Standard).
The specified categories of disclosure include "audit related assurance services",
which will only include those services which are identified as audit related
services in paragraph 5.41 above.

Evaluation of Specific Non-audit Services and Additional Services

There are services other than "audit related services" (see paragraphs 5.40 – 5.43)   **5.44**
for which it is generally accepted that the auditor of the entity is an appropriate
provider. However the threats to independence arising from such services are not
necessarily clearly insignificant and the *firm* considers whether such services give
rise to threats to independence and, where appropriate, the need to apply
safeguards. Such services include:

- Reports, that are not "audit related services", required by the competent authorities/regulators supervising the *audited entity*, where the authority/ regulator has either specified the auditor to provide the service or identified to the entity that the auditor would be an appropriate choice for service provider. These might include, for example:
  - in relation to entities regulated under the Financial Services and Markets Act 2000 (FSMA), reports under s166 and s340 of FSMA; and
  - other reports provided for under the rules of a competent authority/ regulator.
- Audit and other services provided as auditor of the entity, or as *reporting accountant*, in relation to information of the *audited entity* for which it is probable that an objective, reasonable and informed third party would conclude that the understanding of the entity obtained by the auditor for

---

[56] *This does not include accounting services.*

the audit of the financial statements is relevant to the service, and where the nature of the service would not compromise independence. These might include, for example:

- audit and other services relating to public reporting as *reporting accountant* on financial or other information of the *audited entity* in a prospectus or circular (including reports that may be required by the Prospectus Rules, the Listing Rules and the Take Over Code);

- services, including private reporting, that are customarily performed by the *reporting accountant* to support statements made by the directors, disclosures in a prospectus or circular or, in the case of premium listed issuers, to support confirmations provided by the sponsor to the FCA;

- audit and other assurance services relating to public reporting on other information issued by the entity, such as reports on information in the front of annual reports not covered by the auditor's report on the financial statements.

The above list is not intended to be fully comprehensive and does not preclude other services being provided. Such services provided to *public interest entities*, other than those required by Union or national legislation, are still subject to the 70% cap (see paragraphs 4.34R and 4.35R of Section 4 of Part B of this Ethical Standard) and still require approval by the audit committee.

5.45   In evaluating threats to compliance with the overarching principles of integrity, objectivity and independence arising from the provision of *non-audit/additional services*, the requirements and guidance below apply to all entities as indicated *relevant to an engagement*. This includes for *public interest entities* and their *significant affiliates* where applicable. Where a more stringent requirement for an audited *public interest entity* is established in paragraph 5.167R below, that more stringent requirement must be complied with.

5.46   For example, with regards to valuation services, paragraph 5.67 requires that the *firm* shall not provide such services to a *listed entity* that is not an *SME listed entity*, or a *significant affiliate* of such an entity, where the valuation would have a material effect on the *listed entity's* financial statements being audited, or on other *subject matter information* or *subject matter* of the *engagement* in the case of an other *public interest assurance engagement*, either separately or in aggregate with other valuations provided. Where the listed entity is also a *public interest entity* audited by the *firm*, paragraph 5.167R prohibits the provision of valuation services, subject to the derogation in paragraph 5.168R, including that the service has no direct or, in the view of an objective, reasonable and informed third party, would have an inconsequential effect, separately or in the aggregate on the audited financial statements of the *public interest entity*.

5.47   **For the purpose of the requirements below, an *"SME listed entity"* is:**

(a)   **An entity whose equity *financial instruments* had an average market capitalisation of less than €200m on the basis of year end quotes for the previous three calendar years; or**

(b)   **An entity that issues exclusively non-equity *financial instruments* if:**

(i)   **the total nominal amount of the non-equity *financial instruments* issued and outstanding does not exceed €200m; or**

(ii)   **according to the last annual or consolidated accounts, meets at least two of the following criteria:**

- an average number of employee during the financial year of less than 250;
- a total balance sheet not exceeding €43m;
- an annual net turnover not exceeding €50m.

An entity whose equity *financial instruments* have been admitted to trading for less than three years shall be deemed an SME if its market capitalisation is below €200m based on:

(a) the closing share price of the first day of trading, if its shares have been admitted to trading for less than one year;

(b) the last closing share price of the first year of trading, if its *financial instruments* have been admitted to trading for more than one year but less than two years; or

(c) the average of the last closing share prices of each of the first two years of trading, if its *financial instruments* have been admitted to trading for more than two years but less than three years.

Internal Audit Services

The range of "internal audit services" is wide and they may not be termed as such   **5.48** by an *entity relevant to an engagement*. For example, the *firm* may undertake:

- to outsource the entity's entire internal audit function; or

- to supplement the entity's internal audit function in specific areas (for example, by providing specialised technical services or resources in particular locations); or

- to provide occasional internal audit services to the entity on an ad hoc basis.

All such services would fall within the term "internal audit services".

The nature of possible internal audit services is also wide. While the internal audit   **5.49** remit will vary from entity to entity, it often involves compliance and assurance activities designed to assess the design and operating effectiveness of existing or proposed systems or controls and advisory activities where advice is given to an entity on the design and implementation of risk management, control and governance processes.

The nature and extent of the threats to the *firm's* independence when undertaking   **5.50** internal audit services vary depending on the nature of the services provided. The main threats to the integrity, objectivity and independence of the *firm* and *covered persons* arising from the provision of internal audit services are the self-review threat and the management threat. Generally these will be lower for activities that are primarily designed to provide assurance to those charged with governance, for example that internal controls are operating effectively, than for advisory activities designed to assist the entity in improving the effectiveness of its risk management, control and governance processes.

Internal audit services – other than those prohibited in paragraph 5.53 – may be   **5.51** undertaken, provided that the *firm* is satisfied that there is *informed management* (see paragraph 1.29 of Section 1 of Part B of this Ethical Standard) and appropriate safeguards are applied to reduce the self-review threat to a level where independence is not compromised.

Examples of safeguards that may be appropriate when internal audit services are   **5.52** provided to an *entity relevant to an engagement* include ensuring that:

- internal audit projects undertaken by the *firm* are performed by partners and *staff* who have no involvement in the *engagement*;

- the *engagement* is reviewed by partner with relevant expertise who is not involved in the *engagement*, to ensure that the internal audit work performed by the *firm* has been properly and effectively assessed in the context of the *engagement*.

5.53   The *firm* shall not provide internal audit services to an *entity relevant to an engagement* where it is reasonably foreseeable that:

(a)   for the purposes of the *engagement*, the *firm* would place significant reliance on the internal audit work performed by the *firm*; or

(b)   where the *firm* is undertaking an *engagement* <u>other than an *investment circular reporting engagement*</u>, for the purposes of the internal audit services, the *firm* would undertake part of the role of management; or

(c)   where the *firm* is undertaking an *investment circular reporting engagement*, for the purposes of the internal audit services, the *firm* would undertake part of the role of management in relation to the transaction or the financial information that is the subject of the *investment circular reporting engagement*.

> For audits of *public interest entities* the prohibition established in paragraph 5.167R(h) must also be complied with.

5.54   The self-review threat is unacceptably high where substantially all of the internal audit activity is outsourced to the *firm* and this is significant to the entity or the *firm* cannot perform the *engagement* without placing significant reliance on the work performed for the purposes of the internal audit service. In the case of *listed entities* that are not SME *listed entities*, the provision of internal audit services in relation to the following examples is likely to be unacceptable as the *engagement team* is likely to place significant reliance on the work performed by the internal audit team in relation to the entity's internal financial controls:

- a significant part of the internal controls over financial reporting;

- financial accounting systems which generate information that is significant to the entity's accounting records;

- amounts or disclosures that are material to the financial statements of the entity or to other *subject matter information* or *subject matter* of the *engagement*.

> Where the *firm* is undertaking an *investment circular reporting engagement*, the above examples are relevant where they involve the *firm* taking decisions in relation to the transaction or the financial information that is the *subject matter* of the *investment circular reporting engagement*.

5.55   The management threat is unacceptably high where the *firm* provides internal audit services that involve *firm* personnel taking decisions or making judgments, which are properly the responsibility of management. For example, such situations arise where the internal audit function is outsourced to the *firm* and this is significant to the entity or where the nature of the internal audit work involves:

- Taking decisions on the scope and nature of the internal audit services to be provided to the entity;

- Designing internal controls or implementing changes thereto;

- Taking responsibility for risk management decisions;

- Undertaking work to evaluate the cost effectiveness of activities, systems and controls;

- Undertaking pre-implementation work on non-financial systems.

> Where the *firm* is undertaking an *investment circular reporting engagement*, the above examples are relevant where they involve the *firm* taking decisions in relation to the transaction or the financial information that is the *subject matter* of the *investment circular reporting engagement*.

During the course of the *engagement*, the persons conducting the *engagement* may **5.56** evaluate the design and test the operating effectiveness of some of the entity's internal financial controls, and the operation of any relevant internal audit function, and provide management with observations on matters that have come to their attention, including comments on weaknesses in the internal control systems and/or the internal audit function together with suggestions for addressing them. This work is a by-product of the *engagement* rather than the result of a separate undertaking to provide *non-audit services* and therefore does not constitute internal audit services for the purposes of this Ethical Standard.

In some circumstances, additional work is undertaken to respond to risks **5.57** identified by management or those charged with governance. Where the persons conducting the *engagement* consider that such risks could impact their opinion on the financial statements, or on other *subject matter information* or *subject matter* of the *engagement*, such work is considered to be *engagement* work for the purposes of this Ethical Standard (see paragraphs 5.6 and 5.7). Where the risks do not impact the opinion, whether it is appropriate for such work to be undertaken by the *firm* will depend on the extent to which it gives rise to a threat to the integrity, objectivity or independence of the *firm* and *covered persons*. The *engagement partner* reviews the scope of the objectives of the proposed work and assesses the threats to which it gives rise and the safeguards available.

If extended audit work on financial information and/or financial controls is **5.58** authorised by those charged with governance, it will be considered as an "audit related service" (see paragraphs 5.40 – 5.43) provided that it is integrated with the work performed in the audit and performed largely by the existing *audit team*, and is performed on the same principal terms and conditions as the audit.

Additional work will not be considered an "audit related service" if it: **5.59**

- does not relate to financial information and/or financial controls; or

- is not authorised by those charged with governance; or

- is not integrated with the work performed in the audit, or is not performed largely by the existing *audit team*; or

- is not on the same principal terms and conditions as the audit.

In such circumstances the threats and the safeguards will be communicated to those charged with governance. The *engagement partner* reviews the scope and objectives of the proposed work and assesses the threats to which it gives rise and the safeguards available. Whether it is appropriate for this work to be undertaken by the *audit firm* will depend on the extent to which it gives rise to threats to the auditor's integrity, objectivity or independence.

Information Technology Services

5.60   Design, provision and implementation of information technology (including financial information technology) systems by *firms* for an *entity relevant to an engagement* creates threats to the integrity, objectivity and independence of the *firm* and *covered persons*. The principal threats are the self-review threat and the management threat.

5.61   Design, provision or implementation of information technology systems that are not important to any significant part of the accounting system or to the production of the financial statements audited by the *firm*, or other *subject matter information* or *subject matter* of the *engagement* in the case of an other *public interest assurance engagement*, and do not have significant reliance placed on them by the persons conducting the *engagement*, may be undertaken, provided that there is *informed management* (see paragraph 1.29 of Section 1 of Part B of this Ethical Standard) and appropriate safeguards are applied to reduce the self-review threat to a level where independence is not compromised.

5.62   Examples of safeguards that may be appropriate when information technology services are provided to an *entity relevant to an engagement* include ensuring that:

● information technology projects undertaken by the *firm* are performed by partners and *staff* who have no involvement in the *engagement*;

● the work undertaken in the course of the *engagement* is reviewed by a partner with relevant expertise who is not involved in the *engagement* to ensure that the information technology work performed has been properly and effectively assessed in the context of the *engagement*.

5.63   **The *firm* shall not design, provide or implement information technology systems for an *entity relevant to an engagement* where:**

(a)   **the systems concerned would be important to any significant part of the accounting system or to the production of the financial statements audited by the *firm*, or of other *subject matter information* or *subject matter* of the *engagement* in the case of an other *public interest assurance engagement*, and the persons conducting the *engagement* would place significant reliance upon them as part of the *engagement*; or**

(b)   **where the *firm* is undertaking an *engagement* other than an *investment circular reporting engagement*, for the purposes of the information technology services, the *firm* would undertake part of the role of management; or**

(c)   **where the *firm* is undertaking an *investment circular reporting engagement*, for the purposes of the information technology services, the *firm* would undertake part of the role of management in relation to the transaction or the financial information that is the subject of the *investment circular reporting engagement*.**

> For audits of *public interest entities* the prohibition established in paragraph
> 5.167R(e) must also be complied with.

Where it is reasonably apparent that, having regard to the activities and size of the   **5.64**
entity and the range and complexity of the proposed system, management lacks
the expertise required to take responsibility for the systems concerned, it is
unlikely that any safeguards would be sufficient to eliminate these threats or to
reduce them to a level where independence is not compromised. In particular,
formal acceptance by management of the systems designed and installed by the
firm is unlikely to be an effective safeguard when, in substance, the *firm* has been
retained by management as experts and makes important decisions in relation to
the design or implementation of systems of internal control and financial reporting
that is the subject of the *engagement*.

The provision and installation of information technology services associated with   **5.65**
a standard "off the shelf accounting package" (including basic set-up procedures
to make the package operate on the entity's existing platform and peripherals,
setting up the chart of accounts and the entry of standard data such as the entity's
product names and prices) is unlikely to create a level of threat to the integrity,
objectivity and independence of the *firm* and *covered persons* that cannot be
addressed through applying appropriate safeguards.

Valuation Services

A valuation comprises the making of assumptions with regard to future   **5.66**
developments, the application of appropriate methodologies and techniques, and
the combination of both to compute a certain value, or range of values, for an
asset, a liability or for a business as a whole.

The *firm* shall not provide a valuation service to: **5.67**

(a)   **a *listed entity relevant to an engagement* that is not an *SME listed entity***
      (see paragraph 5.47), or a *significant affiliate* of such an entity, where
      the valuation would have a material effect on the *listed entity's* financial
      statements, or other *subject matter information* or *subject matter* of the
      engagement, either separately or in aggregate with other valuations
      provided; or

(b)   **any other *entity relevant to an engagement*, where the valuation would**
      both involve a significant degree of subjective judgment and have a
      material effect on the financial statements or other *subject matter*
      information or *subject matter* of the *engagement*, either separately or
      in aggregate with other valuations provided.

> For audits of *public interest entities* the prohibition established in paragraph
> 5.167R(f) must also be complied with, subject to the derogation provided
> for in paragraph 5.168R.

The main threats to the integrity, objectivity and independence of the *firm* and   **5.68**
covered persons arising from the provision of valuation services are the
self-review threat and the management threat. In all cases, the self-review threat
is considered too high to allow the provision of valuation services which involve

the valuation of amounts with a significant degree of subjectivity and that may have a material effect on financial statements subject to an *audit engagement*, or on other *subject matter information* or *subject matter* of the *engagement* in the case of an other *public interest assurance engagement*.

5.69   For *listed entities* that are not SME *listed entities*, or *significant affiliates* of such entities, the threats to integrity, objectivity and independence that would be perceived to be created are too high to allow the *firm* to undertake any valuation that has a material effect on the *listed entity's* financial statements being audited, or on other *subject matter information* or *subject matter* of the *engagement* in the case of an other *public interest assurance engagement*.

5.70   The *firm's* policies and procedures will set out whether there are circumstances in which valuation services are not undertaken for non-listed entities as described in paragraph 1.49 of Section 1 of Part B of this Ethical Standard.

5.71   In circumstances where the *firm* is designated by legislation or regulation as being required to carry out a valuation the restrictions in paragraph 5.67 do not apply. In such circumstances, the *engagement partner* applies appropriate safeguards to reduce threats to integrity, objectivity and independence to a level where independence is not compromised.

5.72   It is usual for the persons conducting an *audit engagement* or *investment circular reporting engagement* (and in some cases other *public interest assurance engagements*) to provide management with accounting advice in relation to valuation matters that have come to the attention of persons conducting the *engagement* during the course of the *engagement*. Such matters might typically include:

- comments on valuation assumptions and their appropriateness;
- errors identified in a valuation calculation and suggestions for correcting them;
- advice on accounting policies and any valuation methodologies used in their application.

Advice on such matters does not constitute valuation services for the purpose of this Ethical Standard.

5.73   Where the *firm* is engaged to collect and verify the accuracy of data to be used in a valuation to be performed by others, such engagements do not constitute valuation services under this Ethical Standard.

Actuarial Valuation Services

5.74   **The *firm* shall not provide actuarial valuation services to:**

   (a)   **a *listed entity relevant to an engagement* that is not an *SME listed entity* (see paragraph 5.47), or a *significant affiliate* of such an entity, unless the *firm* is satisfied that the valuation has no material effect on the *listed entity's* financial statements, or other *subject matter information* or *subject matter* of the *engagement*, either separately or in aggregate with other valuations provided; or**

   (b)   **any other *entity relevant to an engagement*, unless the *firm* is satisfied that either all significant judgments, including the assumptions, are made by *informed management* or the valuation has no material effect on the financial statements, or other *subject matter information* or *subject matter* of the *engagement*, either separately or in aggregate with other valuations provided.**

> For audits of *public interest entities* the prohibition established in paragraph 5.167R(f) must also be complied with, subject to the derogation provided for in paragraph 5.168R.

Actuarial valuation services are subject to the same general principles as other valuation services. In all cases, where they involve the *firm* in making a subjective judgment and have a material effect on the financial statements subject to an audit, or other *subject matter information* or *subject matter* of the *engagement* in the case of an other *public interest assurance engagement*, actuarial valuations give rise to an unacceptable level of self-review threat and so may not be performed by *firms* for *entities relevant to an engagement*.   **5.75**

In the case of non-listed entities that are not *public interest entities*, where all significant judgments concerning the assumptions, methodology and data for the actuarial valuation are made by *"informed management"* and the *firm's* role is limited to applying proven methodologies using the given data, for which the management takes responsibility, it may be possible to establish effective safeguards to protect the integrity, objectivity and independence of the *firm* and *covered persons*.   **5.76**

For *listed entities* that are not *SME listed entities*, or *significant affiliates* of such entities, the threats to integrity, objectivity and independence that would be perceived to be created are too high to allow the *firm* to undertake any actuarial valuation unless the *firm* is satisfied that the valuation has no material effect on the *listed entity's* financial statements being audited, or other *subject matter information* or *subject matter* of the *engagement* in the case of an other *public interest assurance engagement*.   **5.77**

The *firm's* policies and procedures will set out whether there are circumstances in which actuarial valuation services are not undertaken for non-listed entities as described in paragraph 1.49 of Section 1 of Part B of this Ethical Standard.   **5.78**

Tax Services

The range of activities encompassed by the term "tax services" is wide. They include where the *firm*:   **5.79**

(a)   provides advice to the entity on one or more specific matters at the request of the entity; or

(b)   undertakes a substantial proportion of the tax planning or compliance work for the entity; or

(c)   promotes tax structures or products to the entity, the effectiveness of which is likely to be influenced by the manner in which they are accounted for in the financial statements, or in other *subject matter information*.

Whilst it is possible to consider tax services under broad headings, such as tax planning or compliance, in practice these services are often interrelated and it is impracticable to analyse services in this way for the purposes of attempting to identify generically the threats to which specific tax services give rise. As a result, *firms* need to identify and assess, on a case-by-case basis, the potential threats to the integrity, objectivity and independence of the *firm* and *covered persons* before deciding whether to provide tax services to an entity *relevant to an engagement*.

5.80   The provision of tax services by *firms* to *entities relevant to an engagement* may give rise to a number of threats to the integrity, objectivity and independence of the *firm* and *covered persons*, including the self-interest threat, the management threat, the advocacy threat and, where the work involves a significant degree of subjective judgment and has a material effect on the financial statements, or on other *subject matter information* or *subject matter* of an *engagement*, the self-review threat.

5.81   Where the *firm* provides advice to an *entity relevant to an engagement* on one or more specific matters at the request of the entity, a self-review threat may be created. This self-review threat is more significant where the *firm* undertakes a substantial proportion of the tax planning and compliance work for the entity. However, the *firm* may be able to provide such services, provided that there is *informed management* and appropriate safeguards are applied to reduce the self-review threat to a level where independence is not compromised.

5.82   Examples of such safeguards that may be appropriate when tax services are provided to an *entity relevant to an engagement* include ensuring that:

- the tax services are provided by partners and *staff* who have no involvement in the *engagement*;
- the tax services are reviewed by an independent tax partner, or other senior tax employee;
- external independent advice is obtained on the tax work;
- tax computations prepared by the *engagement team* are reviewed by a partner or senior *staff* member with relevant expertise who is not a member of the *engagement team*; or
- a partner with relevant expertise not involved in the *engagement* reviews whether the tax work has been properly and effectively addressed in the context of the *engagement*.

5.83   **The *firm* shall not promote tax structures or products or provide tax advice to an *entity relevant to an engagement* where the *engagement partner* has, or ought to have, reasonable doubt as to whether the related accounting treatment involved is based on well-established interpretations or is appropriate, having regard to the relevant financial reporting framework, including, where applicable, the requirement for financial statements to give a true and fair view.**

> For audits of *public interest entities* the prohibition established in paragraph 5.167R(a)(vii) must also be complied with, subject to the derogation provided for in paragraph 5.168R.

5.84   Where the *firm* promotes tax structures or products or provides tax advice to an *entity relevant to an engagement*, it may be necessary to adopt an accounting treatment that is not based on well-established interpretations or may not be appropriate, in order to achieve the desired result. A self-review threat arises in the course of an *engagement* because the *firm* may be unable to form an impartial view of the accounting treatment to be adopted for the purposes of the proposed arrangements. Accordingly, this Ethical Standard does not permit the promotion of tax structures or products by *firms* to an *entity relevant to an engagement* where, in the view of the *engagement partner*, after such consultation as is appropriate, there is reasonable doubt as to whether the effectiveness of the tax structure or product depends on an accounting treatment that is well-established and appropriate.

The *firm* shall not provide tax services wholly or partly on a *contingent fee* **5.85**
basis to:

(a)   a *listed entity relevant to an engagement* that is not an *SME listed entity* (see paragraph 5.47), or a *significant affiliate* of such an entity; or

(b)   or any other *entity relevant to an engagement*, where not otherwise prohibited by paragraph 4.14 of Section 4 of Part B of this Ethical Standard, for which the tax outcome in respect of the services (and, therefore, the amount of the fee) is uncertain, dependent on the proposed application of tax law, and may be material to present or future financial statements or other *subject matter information* or *subject matter* of the *engagement*.

For audits of *public interest entities* the prohibitions established in paragraph 5.167R(a) must also be complied with, subject to the derogations provided for in paragraph 5.168R.

Paragraph 4.14 of Section 4 of Part B of this Ethical Standard establishes   **5.86**
conditions that preclude providing *non-audit/additional services* on a *contingent fee basis*.

Where tax services, such as advising on corporate structures, structuring   **5.87**
transactions to achieve a particular effect, or otherwise with an objective of
reducing tax charges are undertaken on a *contingent fee basis* for an *entity relevant to an engagement*, self-interest threats to the integrity, objectivity and independence of the *firm* or *covered persons* may arise. The *firm* may have, or may appear to have, an interest in the success of the tax services, causing the *firm* to make a judgment about which there is reasonable doubt as to its appropriateness. For an *entity relevant to an engagement* that is a *listed entity* that is not an SME *listed entity*, or a *significant affiliate* of such an entity, the self-interest threat cannot be eliminated or reduced to a level where independence is not compromised by the application of any safeguards.

For other *entities relevant to an engagement*, the self-interest threat cannot be   **5.88**
eliminated or reduced to a level where independence is not compromised by the
application of any safeguards where the outcome in respect of the services (and, therefore, the amount of the contingent fee) is uncertain, dependent on the proposed application of tax law, and where the tax implications are, or may be, material to present or future financial statements or other *subject matter information* or *subject matter* of the *engagement*.

The *firm* shall not provide tax services to an *entity relevant to an engagement* **5.89**
other than an *investment circular reporting engagement* where the service
would involve the *firm* undertaking a management role.

For audits of *public interest entities* the prohibition established in paragraph 5.167R(b) must also be complied with.

5.90   The *firm* shall not provide tax services to an *entity relevant to an investment circular reporting engagement* where the service would involve the *firm* undertaking a management role in relation to the transaction or the financial information that is the subject of the *investment circular reporting engagement*.

5.91   When providing tax services to an *entity relevant to an engagement*, there is a risk that the *firm* undertakes a management role, unless the *firm* is working with "*informed management*".

5.92   Where an *entity relevant to the engagement* is a *listed entity* that is not an *SME listed entity* (see paragraph 5.47), or a *significant affiliate* of such an entity, the *firm* shall not provide a service to prepare current or deferred tax calculations that are or may reasonably be expected to be used by the entity when preparing accounting entries that are material to the financial statements or other *subject matter information* or *subject matter of the engagement*.

For audits of *public interest entities* the prohibition established in paragraph 5.167R(a)(vi) must also be complied with, subject to the derogation provided for in paragraph 5.168R.

5.93   For *listed entities* that are not *SME listed entities*, or *significant affiliates* of such entities, the threats to integrity, objectivity and independence that would be created are too high to allow the *firm* to provide a service to prepare calculations of current or deferred tax liabilities or assets for the purpose of preparing accounting entries that are material to the financial statements or other *subject matter information* or *subject matter* of the *engagement*, together with associated disclosure notes.

5.94   Paragraph 5.92 is not intended to prevent a *firm* preparing tax calculations after the completion of the *engagement* for the purpose of submitting tax returns.

5.95   For entities other than *public interest entities* and other *listed entities* that are not *SME listed entities*, or *significant affiliates* of *listed entities* that are not *SME listed entities*, the *firm* may provide a service to prepare current or deferred tax calculations for the purpose of preparing accounting entries, provided that:

  (a)   such services:

   (i)   do not involve initiating transactions or taking management decisions; and

   (ii)   are of a technical, mechanical or an informative nature; and

  (b)   appropriate safeguards are applied.

5.96   The *firm's* policies and procedures will set out whether there are circumstances in which current or deferred tax calculations for the purpose of preparing accounting entries are not prepared for non-listed entities as described in paragraph 1.49 of Section 1of Part B of this Ethical Standard.

The *firm* shall not provide tax services to an *entity relevant to an engagement* **5.97**
where this would involve acting as an advocate for the entity in the resolution
of an issue:

(a)   that is material to the entity's present or future financial statements, or
      the *subject matter information* or *subject matter* of the *engagement*; or

(b)   where the outcome of the tax issue is dependent on a future or
      contemporary judgment by the *firm* in relation to the financial
      statements, or other *subject matter information* or *subject matter* of the
      engagement.

For audits of *public interest entities* the prohibition established in paragraph
5.167R(a)(v) must also be complied with, subject to the derogation provided
for in paragraph 5.168R.

Supporting ethical provision 2.3D, which embodies legal requirements for   **5.98**
statutory audits, requires, inter alia, that a *firm* does not accept, continue or
carry out an *engagement* if there is any threat of advocacy which would
compromise the independence of the *firm* or *covered persons*. Where the tax
services to be provided by the *firm* include representing the entity in any
negotiations or proceedings involving the tax authorities, advocacy threats to
the integrity, objectivity and independence of the *firm* and *covered persons* may
arise.

The meaning of an "advocacy threat" is described in paragraph 1.29 of Section 1   **5.99**
of Part B of this Ethical Standard. It includes supporting a position taken by
management in an adversarial context, where the *firm* has to adopt a position
closely aligned to that of management.

The *firm* is not acting as an advocate where the tax services involve the provision   **5.100**
of information to the tax authorities (including an explanation of the approach
being taken and the arguments being advanced by the entity). In such
circumstances effective safeguards may exist and the tax authorities will
undertake their own review of the issues.

Where the *firm* has been providing assistance in dealing with tax authorities and   **5.101**
those tax authorities indicate that they are minded to reject the entity's arguments
on a particular issue and the matter is likely to be determined by an appeals
tribunal or court, the *firm* may become so closely identified with management's
arguments that the *firm* is inhibited from forming an impartial view of the
treatment of the issue in the financial statements, or in other *subject matter
information* or *subject matter* of the *engagement* in the case of an other *public
interest assurance engagement*. In such circumstances, if the issue is material to
the financial statements, or other *subject matter information* or *subject matter* of
the *engagement*, or is dependent on a future or contemporary judgment by the *firm*
in relation to the *engagement*, the advocacy threat will be such that no safeguards
can reduce it to a level where independence is not compromised. Accordingly, in
such circumstances, the *firm* discusses the matter with the entity and makes it clear
that it will have to withdraw from providing tax services that require it to act as
advocate for the entity, or resign from the *engagement* from the time when the
matter is formally listed for hearing before the appeals tribunal.

5.102   If the *firm* withdraws from providing tax services for the reasons described in paragraph 5.101, the *firm* is not precluded from having a continuing role (for example, responding to specific requests for information) for the entity in relation to the appeal, providing that the continuing role does not give rise to an advocacy threat that would compromise the independence of the *firm* or *covered persons*. The *firm* also assesses the threat associated with any continuing role in accordance with paragraphs 5.103 to 5.105 of this Section.

Litigation Support Services

5.103   Although management and advocacy threats may arise in litigation support services, such as acting as an expert witness, the primary issue is that a self-review threat will arise in all cases where such services involve a subjective estimation of the likely outcome of a matter that is material to the amounts to be included or the disclosures to be made in the financial statements.

5.104   **The *firm* shall not provide litigation support services to:**

(a)   **a *listed entity relevant to an engagement* that is not an *SME listed entity* (see paragraph 5.47), or a *significant affiliate* of such an entity, where this would involve the estimation by the *firm* of the likely outcome of a pending legal matter that could be material to the amounts to be included or the disclosures to be made in the *listed entity's* financial statements, or in other *subject matter information* or *subject matter* of the *engagement*, either separately or in aggregate with other estimates and valuations provided; or**

(b)   **any other *entity relevant to an engagement*, where this would involve the estimation by the *firm* of the likely outcome of a pending legal matter that could be material to the amounts to be included or the disclosures to be made in the entity's financial statements, or in other *subject matter information* or *subject matter* of the *engagement*, either separately or in aggregate with other estimates and valuations provided and there is a significant degree of subjectivity involved.**

> For audits of *public interest entities* the prohibition established in paragraph 5.167R(f) must also be complied with, subject to the derogation provided for in paragraph 5.168R.

5.105   In the case of non-listed entities, litigation support services that do not involve such subjective estimations are not prohibited, provided that the *firm* has carefully considered the implications of any threats and established safeguards to reduce those threats to a level where independence is not compromised.

5.106   The *firm's* policies and procedures will set out whether there are circumstances in which litigation support services are not undertaken for non-listed entities as described in paragraph 1.49 of Section 1 of Part B of this Ethical Standard.

Legal Services

5.107   **The *firm* shall not provide legal services to an *entity relevant to an engagement*, where this would involve acting as the solicitor formally nominated to represent the entity in the resolution of a dispute or litigation which is**

**material to the amounts to be included or the disclosures to be made in the
financial statements, or in other *subject matter information* or *subject matter* of
the *engagement*.**

> For audits of *public interest entities* the prohibition established in paragraph
> 5.167R(g) must also be complied with.

Although the provision by the *firm* of certain types of legal services to an *entity*   **5.108**
relevant to an engagement may create advocacy, self-review and management
threats, this Ethical Standard does not impose a general prohibition on the
provision of legal services. However, in view of the degree of advocacy
involved in litigation or other types of dispute resolution procedures and the
potential importance of any assessment by the *firm* of the merits of the entity's
position when undertaking an *engagement*, this Ethical Standard prohibits a *firm*
from acting as the formally nominated representative for an *entity relevant to an
engagement* in the resolution of a dispute or litigation which is material to the
amounts recognised or disclosed the financial statements or other *subject matter
information* or *subject matter* of the *engagement*.

Recruitment and Remuneration Services

The *firm* shall not provide recruitment services to an *entity relevant to an*   **5.109**
***engagement*, that would involve the *firm* taking responsibility for the
appointment of any director or:**

**(a)   where the *firm* is undertaking an *engagement* other than an *investment
circular reporting engagement*, any employee of the entity; or**

**(b)   where the *firm* is undertaking an *investment circular reporting
engagement*, any employee of the entity who will be involved in an
area that is directly concerned with the transaction which is the subject
of the *investment circular*.**

> For audits of *public interest entities* the prohibitions established in
> paragraphs 5.167R(b) and (k) must also be complied with.

A management threat arises where *firm* personnel take responsibility for any   **5.110**
decision as to who is appointed by the entity.

For a *listed entity*, that is not an *SME listed entity* (see paragraph 5.47),   **5.111**
***relevant to an engagement*, the *firm* shall not provide recruitment services in
relation to a *key management position* of the entity, or a *significant affiliate* of
such an entity.**

> For audits of *public interest entities* the prohibition established in paragraph
> 5.167R(k) must also be complied with.

5.112   A familiarity threat arises if the *firm* plays a significant role in relation to the identification and recruitment of senior members of management within the entity, as the *engagement team* may be less likely to be critical of the information or explanations provided by such individuals than might otherwise be the case. Accordingly, for a *listed entity relevant to an engagement*, other than an *investment circular reporting engagement*, that is not an *SME listed entity*, and for *significant affiliates* of such entities, the *firm* does not provide services that involve the recruitment of individuals for *key management positions*.

5.113   The *firm's* policies and procedures will set out whether there are circumstances in which recruitment services are not undertaken for non-listed entities as described in paragraph 1.49 of Section 1 of Part B of this Ethical Standard.

5.114   Where the *firm* providing an *investment circular reporting engagement* has played a significant role in relation to the identification and recruitment of a senior member of management within the entity, including all directors, prior to the "*relevant period*", the *engagement partner* considers whether a familiarity threat exists, taking account of factors such as:

- the closeness of personal relationships between the *firm's* partners, *staff* and other *covered persons*, and the entity's personnel;
- the length of time since the recruitment of the individual in question;
- the position held by the individual at the entity;
- the extent of involvement that the individual will have with the transaction that is the subject of the *investment circular*;
- whether the individual is in a position to exercise influence on the accounting records or financial information.

Following the assessment of any such threats, appropriate safeguards are applied where necessary, such as ensuring that the *engagement team* does not include individuals with a close relationship to the senior member of management or who were involved in the recruitment exercise.

5.115   Recruitment services involve a specifically identifiable, and separately remunerated, engagement. *Firms* and *engagement teams* may contribute to an entity's recruitment process in less formal ways. The prohibitions set out in paragraphs 5.109 and 5.111 do not extend to:

- senior members of an *engagement team* interviewing prospective directors or employees of the entity and advising on the candidate's technical financial competence; or
- the entity using information gathered by the *firm*, including that relating to salary surveys.

5.116   **The *firm* shall not provide advice on the quantum of the remuneration package or the measurement criteria on which the quantum is calculated, for a director or *key management position* of an *entity relevant to an engagement*.**

For audits of *public interest entities* the prohibition established in paragraph 5.167R(k) must also be complied with.

The provision of advice on remuneration packages (including bonus **5.117** arrangements, incentive plans and other benefits) to existing or prospective employees of the entity gives rise to familiarity threats. The significance of the familiarity threat is considered too high to allow advice on the overall amounts to be paid or on the quantitative measurement criteria included in remuneration packages for directors and *key management positions*.

For other employees, these threats can be adequately addressed by the application **5.118** of safeguards, such as the advice being provided by partners and *staff* who have no involvement in the *engagement*.

In cases where all significant judgments concerning the assumptions, **5.119** methodology and data for the calculation of remuneration packages for directors and key management are made by "*informed management*" or a third party and the *firm's* role is limited to applying proven methodologies using the given data, for which the management takes responsibility, it may be possible to establish effective safeguards to protect the integrity, objectivity and independence of the *firm* and *covered persons*.

Advice on tax, pensions and interpretation of accounting standards relating to **5.120** remuneration packages for directors and key management can be provided by the *firm*, provided they are not prohibited by the requirements of this Ethical Standard relating to tax, actuarial valuations and *accounting services*. Disclosure of the provision of any such advice would be made to those charged with governance of the entity (see Section 1 of this Ethical Standard, paragraphs 1.61 to 1.71 of Section 1 of part B of this Ethical Standard).

Corporate Finance Services

The range of services encompassed by the term "corporate finance services" is **5.121** wide. For example, the *firm* may undertake:

- to identify possible purchasers for parts of the entity's business and provide advisory services in the course of such sales; or

- to identify possible "targets" for the entity to acquire; or

- to advise the entity on how to fund its financing requirements; or

- to act as sponsor on admission to listing on the London Stock Exchange, as Nominated Advisor on the admission of the entity on the Alternative Investments Market (AIM); or

- to act as financial adviser to entity offerors or offerees in connection with public takeovers.

The potential for the integrity, objectivity and independence of the *firm* and **5.122** *covered persons* to be compromised through the provision of corporate finance services varies considerably depending on the precise nature of the service provided. The main threats to integrity, objectivity and independence arising from the provision of corporate finance services are the self-review, management and advocacy threats. Self-interest threats may also arise, especially in situations where the *firm* is paid on a *contingent fee basis*.

When providing corporate finance services to an *entity relevant to an engagement*, **5.123** there is a risk that the *firm* undertakes a management role, unless the *firm* is working with "*informed management*". In addition, appropriate safeguards are applied to reduce any self-review threat to a level where independence is not compromised.

5.124 Examples of safeguards that may be appropriate when corporate finance services are provided to an *entity relevant to an engagement*, include ensuring that:

- the corporate finance advice is provided by partners and *staff* who have no involvement in the *engagement*;

- any advice provided is reviewed by an independent corporate finance partner within the *firm*;

- external independent advice on the corporate finance work is obtained;

- a partner who is not involved in the engagement reviews the *engagement* work performed in relation to the *subject matter* of the corporate finance services provided to ensure that such *engagement* work has been properly and effectively reviewed and assessed in the context of the *engagement*.

5.125 Where the *firm* provides corporate finance services to an *entity relevant to an engagement* in connection with conducting the sale or purchase of a material part of the entity's business, the *engagement partner* informs the audit committee (or equivalent) and, where applicable, any other person or entity the *firm* is instructed to advise, about the corporate finance service, as set out in paragraphs 1.61 to 1.71 of Section 1 of Part B of this Ethical Standard.

5.126 **The *firm* shall not provide corporate finance services in respect of an *entity relevant to an engagement*, where:**

(a) **the service would involve the *firm* taking responsibility for dealing in, underwriting, or promoting shares; or**

(b) **the *engagement partner* has, or ought to have, reasonable doubt as to whether an accounting treatment that is subject to a contemporary or future judgment by the *firm* relating to a material matter in the financial statements or in other *subject matter information* or *subject matter* of the engagement, and upon which the success of the related transaction depends:**

(i) **is based on well-established interpretations; or**

(ii) **is appropriate;**

having regard to the requirements of the relevant reporting framework, including where applicable for financial statements to give a true and fair view; or

(c) **the *firm* is undertaking an *engagement* _other than an *investment circular reporting engagement*_, and the service would involve undertaking a management role in the entity; or**

(d) **the *firm* is undertaking an *investment circular reporting engagement*, and the service would involve undertaking a management role in the entity in relation to the transaction or the *subject matter information* or *subject matter* of the *investment circular reporting engagement*.**

> For audits of *public interest entities* the prohibitions established in paragraphs 5.167R(b), (i) and (j) must also be complied with.

An unacceptable advocacy threat arises where, in the course of providing a corporate finance service, the *firm* promotes the interests of the entity by taking responsibility for dealing in, underwriting, or promoting shares.   **5.127**

Where the *firm* acts as a sponsor under the Listing Rules[57], or as Nominated Adviser on the admission of the entity to the AIM, the *firm* is required to confirm that the entity has satisfied all applicable conditions for listing and other relevant requirements of the listing (or AIM or ESM) rules. Where there is, or there ought to be, reasonable doubt that the *firm* will be able to give that confirmation, it does not enter into providing such service.   **5.128**

A self-review threat arises where the outcome or consequences of the corporate finance service provided by the *firm* may be material to the financial statements or other *subject matter information* or *subject matter*, which are, or will be, subject to an *engagement* by the same *firm*. Where the *firm* provides corporate finance services, for example advice to the entity on financing arrangements, it may be necessary to adopt an accounting treatment that is not based on well-established interpretations or which may not be appropriate, in order to achieve the desired result. A self-review threat is created because the *firm* may be unable to form an impartial view of the accounting treatment to be adopted for the purposes of the proposed arrangements. Accordingly, this Ethical Standard does not permit the provision of such services by *firms* in respect of an *entity relevant to an engagement* by them where there is or ought to be reasonable doubt as to whether an accounting treatment that is subject to a contemporary or future judgment by the *firm* relating to a material matter in the financial statements, or in other *subject matter information* or *subject matter*, of the entity and on which the success of a transaction depends is well-established and appropriate.   **5.129**

Advice to entities on funding issues and banking arrangements, where there is no reasonable doubt as to the appropriateness of the accounting treatment, is not prohibited provided this does not involve the *firm* in taking decisions or making judgments which are properly the responsibility of management.   **5.130**

These restrictions do not apply in circumstances where the *firm* is designated by legislation or regulation as being required to carry out a particular service. In such circumstances, the *engagement partner* establishes appropriate safeguards.   **5.131**

Transaction Related Services

In addition to corporate finance services, there are other services associated with transactions that a *firm* may undertake for an *entity relevant to an engagement*. For example: **5.132**

- investigations into possible acquisitions or disposals ("due diligence" investigations); or

- investigations into the tax affairs of possible acquisitions or disposals; or

- the provision of information to management or sponsors in relation to prospectuses and other *investment circulars* (for example, long form reports, comfort letters on the adequacy of working capital); or

- agreed-upon procedures or reports provided to management in relation to particular transactions (for example, securitisations).

---

[57] In the United Kingdom, the UK Listing Authority's publication the "Listing Rules".

5.133   When providing transaction related services to an *entity relevant to an engagement*, there is a risk that the *firm* may face a management threat, unless the *firm* is working with *informed management*. In addition, appropriate safeguards are applied to reduce any self-review threat to a level where independence is not compromised.

5.134   Examples of safeguards that may be appropriate when threats are identified in relation to transaction related services provided to an *entity relevant to an engagement* include ensuring that:

- the transaction related advice is provided by partners and *staff* who have no involvement in the *engagement*;

- any advice provided is reviewed by an independent transactions partner within the *firm*;

- external independent advice on the transaction related work is obtained;

- a partner with relevant expertise who is not involved in the *engagement* reviews the *engagement* work performed in relation to the *subject matter* of the transaction related service provided to ensure that such work has been properly and effectively reviewed and assessed in the context of the *engagement*.

5.135   **The *firm* shall not provide transaction related services in respect of an *entity relevant to an engagement*, where:**

(a)   **the *engagement partner* has, or ought to have, reasonable doubt as to whether an accounting treatment that is subject to a contemporary or future judgment by the *firm* relating to a material matter in the financial statements, or other *subject matter information* or *subject matter* of the *engagement*, and upon which the success of the related transaction depends;**

  (i)   **is based on well-established interpretations; or**

  (ii)   **is appropriate;**

  having regard to the requirements of the relevant reporting framework, including where applicable for financial statements to give a true and fair view; or

(b)   **the *firm* is undertaking an *engagement* other than an *investment circular reporting engagement*, and the service would involve undertaking a management role in the entity; or**

(c)   **the *firm* is undertaking an *investment circular reporting engagement*, and the service would involve undertaking a management role in the entity in relation to the transaction or the *subject matter information* or *subject matter* of the *investment circular reporting engagement*.**

For audits of *public interest entities* the prohibition established in paragraphs 5.167R(b) and (i) must also be complied with.

5.136   A self-review threat arises where the outcome of the transaction related services undertaken by the *firm* may be material to the financial statements or other *subject matter information* or *subject matter* of the entity which are, or will be, subject to an *engagement* by the same *firm*. Where the entity proposes to undertake a transaction, it may be necessary to adopt an accounting treatment that is not based on well-established interpretations or may not be appropriate, in order to achieve the desired result of the transaction (for example, to take assets off the balance sheet). A self-review threat is created if the *firm* undertakes transaction related services in connection with such a transaction. Accordingly, this Ethical Standard does not permit the provision of services by *firms* in respect of an *entity relevant to an engagement* by them where there is or ought to be reasonable doubt as to whether an accounting treatment, that is subject to a contemporary or future judgment by the *firm* relating to a material matter in the financial statements, or in other *subject matter information* or *subject matter* of the entity and on which the success of a related transaction depends, is well-established and appropriate.

These restrictions do not apply in circumstances where the *firm* is designated by legislation or regulation as being required to carry out a particular service. In such circumstances, the *engagement* partner establishes appropriate safeguards. **5.137**

Restructuring Services

Restructuring services are any *non-audit services* provided to an entity in connection with the entity's development or implementation of a transaction or package of transactions (a "restructuring plan") designed to change its equity or debt financing structure, its corporate structure, or its operating structure. There are a variety of possible purposes for developing a restructuring plan, for example to address financial or operating difficulties, to support tax planning, to improve operating efficiency, or to improve the cost of capital. The range of *non-audit/ additional services* that may be regarded as "Restructuring Services" is extensive, and the nature of those services may encompass many of the other types of *non-audit/additional services* discussed in this Ethical Standard. Where applicable, the related requirements and guidance covered elsewhere in this Ethical Standard apply to Restructuring Services. **5.138**

The restructuring services that an entity may use a *firm* to provide may vary considerably and may range from the incidental and routine to advice that is fundamental to the efficacy of the restructuring plan. Consequently, where such services are provided by a *firm* that that provides an *engagement* for the entity, the *engagement partner*: **5.139**

* the threats that the restructuring services may present to the *firm's* ability to conduct any contemporary or future *engagement* with integrity, objectivity and independence; and

* the probability that an objective, reasonable and informed third party would conclude that the independence of the *firm* or *covered persons* would be compromised.

The *firm* shall not provide restructuring services in respect of an *entity relevant to an engagement*, where: **5.140**

(a) **the service would involve the firm undertaking a management role in or on behalf of the entity; or**

(b) **the service would require the *firm* to act as an advocate for the entity in relation to matters that are material to the financial statements, or other *subject matter information* or *subject matter* of the *engagement*.**

> For audits of *public interest entities* the prohibition established in paragraphs 5.167R(b) and (i) must also be complied with.

5.141 The potential for the integrity, objectivity and independence of the *firm* or *covered persons* to be compromised through the provision of restructuring services varies depending on the nature of the service provided. Two of the main threats to integrity, objectivity and independence arising from the provision of restructuring services arise where the *firm* undertakes a management or advocacy role:

- A *firm* undertakes a management role if the entity does not have "*informed management*" capable of taking responsibility for the decisions to be made.

- To avoid undertaking an advocacy role on behalf of the entity, the *firm* takes particular care not to assume (or seen to be assuming) responsibility for the entity's proposals or being regarded as negotiating on behalf of the entity or advocating the appropriateness of the proposals such that its independence would be compromised. This is particularly important when the *firm* attends meetings with the entity's bank or other interested parties.

If the *firm* undertakes a management role or acts as advocate for the entity, the threats to integrity, objectivity and independence of the *firm* and *covered persons* are such that no safeguards can reduce the threat to a level where independence is not compromised[58].

5.142 **The *firm* shall not provide restructuring services in respect of an *entity relevant to engagement*, where that service may give rise to a self-review threat in the course of a contemporary or future *engagement* unless it is satisfied that such threats can be reduced by appropriate safeguards to a level where independence is not compromised and that such safeguards have been put in place.**

> For audits of *public interest entities* the prohibition established in paragraph 5.167R(i) must also be complied with.

5.143 The provision of restructuring services gives rise to a self-review threat where the restructuring services to be provided involve advice or judgments which are likely to be material to a contemporary or future judgment of the *firm* in relation to an *engagement*.

5.144 Examples of restructuring services that the *firm* may be requested to undertake and which may give rise to a self-review threat include:

- Providing preliminary general advice on the options and choices available to management or stakeholders of an entity facing urgent financial or other difficulties.

- Undertaking a review of the business of the entity with a view to advising the entity on liquidity management or operational restructuring options.

---

[58] *"ES – Provisions Available for Small Entities (Revised)" provides exemptions relating to informed management and the advocacy threat for auditors of small entities.*

- Advising on the development of forecasts or projections, for presentation to lenders and other stakeholders, including assumptions.

- Advising the entity on how to fund its financing requirements, including equity and debt restructuring programmes.

- Participating in the design or implementation of an overall restructuring plan including, for example, participating in the preparation of cash flow and other forecasts and financial models underpinning the overall restructuring plan.

The self-review threat arising from the provision of such services is particularly significant where, in relation to an *audit engagement*, it has potential to impact the *firm's* assessment of whether it is appropriate to prepare the entity's financial statements on a going concern basis. Where the *firm* has been involved in aspects of the preparation of a cash flow, a forecast or a financial model, it is probable that an objective, reasonable and informed third party would conclude that the *firm* would have a significant self-review threat in considering the going concern assumption.   **5.145**

The self-review threat arising from the provision of such services is also particularly significant where the restructuring services are provided in respect of an *audited entity* and involve developing or implementing a restructuring plan to address the actual or anticipated financial or operational difficulties that threaten the survival of that entity as a going concern (an "*audited entity in distress*").   **5.146**

The *firm* puts in place those safeguards that it regards as appropriate to reduce the threats to the integrity and objectivity of the *firm* and *covered persons* to a level where independence is not compromised. If the *firm* concludes that the threats arising from some or all of the restructuring services involved cannot be addressed by putting appropriate safeguards in place, it declines providing the service, or those parts of the service affected by those threats that cannot be adequately addressed.   **5.147**

Where an *entity in distress relevant to an engagement*, is a listed entity that is not an *SME listed entity* (see paragraph 5.47), or a *significant affiliate* of such a *listed entity*, the restructuring services provided by the *firm* shall be limited to providing: **5.148**

(a)   preliminary general advice to an *entity in distress*;

(b)   assistance with the implementation of elements of an overall restructuring plan, such as the sale of a non-significant component business, provided those elements are not material to the overall restructuring plan;

(c)   challenging, but in no circumstances developing, the projections and assumptions within a financial model that has been produced by the *entity in distress*;

(d)   reporting on a restructuring plan, or aspects of it, in connection with the proposed issue of an *investment circular*; and

(e)   where specifically permitted by a regulatory body with oversight of the *entity in distress*.

For audits of *public interest entities* the prohibition established in paragraph 5.167R(i) must also be complied with.

5.149   Except to the extent identified in paragraph 5.148, the significance of the self-review threat is too high to permit the provision of other restructuring services to an *entity in distress* that is a *listed entity* that is not an *SME listed entity*, or a *significant affiliate* of such a *listed entity*, because there are no safeguards that would be sufficient to reduce the resultant threats to a level where independence is not compromised.

5.150   The *firm's* policies and procedures will set out whether there are circumstances in which restructuring services are not undertaken for non-listed entities in distress as described in paragraph 1.49 of Section 1 of Part B of this Ethical Standard.

Accounting Services

5.151   For the purpose of this Ethical Standard, the term "*accounting services*" is defined as the provision of services that involve the maintenance of accounting records or the preparation of financial statements or other *subject matter information* or *subject matter* that are then subject to audit or an other *public interest assurance engagement*. Advice on the implementation of current and proposed accounting standards is not included in the term *accounting services*.

5.152   The range of activities encompassed by the term *accounting services* is wide. In some cases, the entity may ask the *firm* to provide a complete accounting service including maintaining all of the accounting records and the preparation of the financial statements. Other common situations are:

- the *firm* may take over the provision of a specific accounting function on an outsourced basis (for example, payroll);

- the entity maintains the accounting records, undertakes basic bookkeeping and prepares a year-end trial balance and asks the *firm* to assist with the preparation of the necessary adjustments and the financial statements.

5.153   The provision of *accounting services* by the *firm* to an *entity relevant to an engagement* creates threats to the integrity, objectivity and independence of the *firm* and *covered persons*, principally self-review and management threats, the significance of which depends on the nature and extent of the *accounting services* in question and upon the level of public interest in the entity.

5.154   When providing *accounting services* to an entity relevant to an audit or other *public interest assurance engagement* by the *firm*, unless the *firm* is working with *informed management*, there is a risk that the *firm* undertakes a management role.

5.155   **The *firm* shall not provide *accounting services* to an *entity relevant to an engagement* other than an *investment circular reporting engagement* where:**

(a)   **the entity is a *listed entity* that is not an *SME listed entity* (see paragraph 5.47), *relevant to an engagement* by the *firm*, or a *significant affiliate* of such an entity; or**

(b)   **for any other entity:**

- **those *accounting services* would involve the *firm* undertaking part of the role of management; or**

- **the financial information is the subject of an *investment circular reporting engagement*.**

For audits of *public interest entities* the prohibitions established in paragraphs 5.167R(a)(i)–(a)(iii), (b), (c) and (d) must also be complied with, subject to the derogation provided for in paragraph 5.168R regarding 5.167R(a)(i).

The *firm* shall not provide *accounting services* in relation to the financial information that is the subject of an *investment circular reporting engagement* by the *firm*. **5.156**

Even where there is no undertaking to provide any *accounting services*, it is usual **5.157** for the *firm* to provide the management with accounting advice on matters that have come to its attention during the course of an *engagement*. Such matters might typically include:

● comments on weaknesses in the accounting records and suggestions for addressing them;

● errors identified in the accounting records and in the financial statements, or other *subject matter information* or *subject matter*, and suggestions for correcting them;

● advice on the accounting policies in use and on the application of current and proposed accounting standards.

This advice is a by-product of the *engagement* rather than the result of any undertaking to provide *non-audit/additional services*. Consequently, as it is part of the *engagement*, such advice is not regarded as giving rise to any threat to the integrity, objectivity and independence of the *firm* and *covered persons*.

For *listed entities* that are not *SME listed entities relevant to an engagement* other **5.158** than an *investment circular reporting engagement*, or *significant affiliates* of such entities, the threats to integrity, objectivity and independence that would be created are too high to allow the *firm* to provide any *accounting services*.

5.159 The threats to the *reporting accountant's* integrity, objectivity and **5.159** independence that would be created are too high to allow the *firm* to provide any *accounting services* in relation to the financial information that is the subject of an *investment circular reporting engagement* by the *firm*.

The *firm's* policies and procedures will set out whether there are circumstances in **5.160** which *accounting services* are not undertaken for non-listed entities as described in paragraph 1.49 of Section 1 of Part B of this Ethical Standard.

For entities other than *listed entities* that are not *SME listed entities* relevant to an **5.161** *engagement* other than an *investment circular reporting engagement*, or *significant affiliates* of such *listed entities*, the *firm* may provide *accounting services*, provided that:

(a) such services:

(i) do not involve initiating transactions or taking management decisions; and

(ii) are of a technical, mechanical or an informative nature; and

(b)   appropriate safeguards are applied to reduce the self-review threat to a level where independence is not compromised.

5.162   The maintenance of the accounting records and the preparation of the financial statements are the responsibility of the management of the entity. Accordingly, in any undertaking to provide the entity with *accounting services*, the *firm* does not initiate any transactions or take any decisions or make any judgments, which are properly the responsibility of the management. These include:

- authorising or approving transactions;

- preparing originating data (including valuation assumptions);

- determining or changing journal entries, or the classifications for accounts or transactions, or other accounting records without management approval.

5.163   Examples of *accounting services* of a technical or mechanical nature or of an informative nature include:

- recording transactions for which management has determined the appropriate account classification, posting coded transactions to the general ledger, posting entries approved by management to the trial balance or providing certain data-processing services (for example, payroll);

- assistance with the preparation of the financial statements where management takes all decisions on issues requiring the exercise of judgment and has prepared the underlying accounting records.

5.164   Examples of safeguards that may be appropriate when *accounting services* are provided to an *entity relevant to an engagement*, include:

- *accounting services* provided by the *firm* are performed by partners and staff who have no involvement in the *engagement*;

- the *accounting services* are reviewed by a partner or other senior *staff* member with relevant expertise who is not a member of the *engagement team*;

- the *engagement* is reviewed by a partner with relevant expertise who is not involved in the *engagement* to ensure that the *accounting services* performed have been properly and effectively assessed in the context of the *engagement*.

Prohibited Non-audit Services for Public Interest Entities

5.165   The requirements in paragraph 5.167R below set out prohibited *non-audit services* for *public interest entities*, as established in the EU Audit Regulation. These prohibitions are applied more widely than the EU where necessary to achieve the ethical outcome of independence, having regard to supporting ethical provision 2.4. Where the work of a *network firm* is used in the conduct of an *engagement*, supporting ethical provision 2.4 stipulates that the ethical requirements that are relevant to the *engagement* are:

"(b)   In the case of a *network firm* whose work is used in the conduct of an *engagement* where any *entity relevant to the engagement* is a *public interest entity*, this Ethical Standard."

Accordingly, such *network firms*, whether or not within the Union, are also subject to the prohibitions in paragraph 5.167R for an *audit engagement* where any *entity relevant to the engagement* is a *public interest entity*.

The *audit firm's* policies and procedures will set out whether there are   **5.166**
circumstances in which the services specified in paragraph 5.167R are
undertaken for entities that are not *public interest entities* as described in
paragraph 1.49 of Section 1 of Part B of this Ethical Standard.

A statutory auditor or An *audit firm* carrying out the *statutory audit* of a   **5.167R**
public interest entity, or any member of the network to which the statutory
auditor or the*audit firm* belongs, shall not directly or indirectly provide to
the *audited entity*, to its parent undertaking or to its controlled
undertakings within the Union any prohibited non-audit services in:

(a)   the period between the beginning of the period audited and the
      issuing of the audit report; and

(b)   the financial year immediately preceding the period referred to in
      point (a) in relation to the services listed in point (e) of the second
      subparagraph.

For these purposes of this Article, prohibited non-audit services shall
mean:

(a)   tax services relating to:

      (i)   preparation of tax forms;

      (ii)   payroll tax;

      (iii) customs duties;

      (iv)   identification of public subsidies and tax incentives unless
             support from the statutory auditor or the*audit firm* in respect
             of such services is required by law;

      (v)   support regarding tax inspections by tax authorities unless
             support from the statutory auditor or the*audit firm* in respect of
             such inspections is required by law;

      (vi)   calculation of direct and indirect tax and deferred tax;

      (vii) provision of tax advice;

(b)   services that involve playing any part in the management or
      decision-making of the *audited entity*;

(c)   bookkeeping and preparing accounting records and financial
      statements;

(d)   payroll services;

(e)   designing and implementing internal control or risk management
      procedures related to the preparation and/or control of financial
      information or designing and implementing financial information
      technology systems;

(f)   valuation services, including valuations performed in connection
      with actuarial services or litigation support services;

(g)   legal services, with respect to:

      (i)   the provision of general counsel;

      (ii)   negotiating on behalf of the *audited entity*; and

      (iii) acting in an advocacy role in the resolution of litigation;

(h)   services related to the *audited entity's* internal audit function;

(i)   services linked to the financing, capital structure and allocation, and investment strategy of the *audited entity*, except providing assurance services in relation to the financial statements, such as the issuing of comfort letters in connection with prospectuses issued by the *audited entity*;

(j)   promoting, dealing in, or underwriting shares in the *audited entity*;

(k)   human resources services, with respect to:

    (i)   management in a position to exert significant influence over the preparation of the accounting records or financial statements which are the subject of the *statutory audit*, where such services involve:

        –   searching for or seeking out candidates for such position; or

        –   undertaking reference checks of candidates for such positions;

    (ii)   structuring the organisation design; and

    (iii)   cost control. [AR 5.1]

5.168R   By way of derogation from the second subparagraph of paragraph ~~15.~~167R, the services referred to in points (a)(i), (a)(iv) to (a)(vii) and (f), may be provided if the following requirements are complied with:

(a)   they have no direct or, <u>in the view of an objective, reasonable and informed third party, would</u> have ~~immaterial~~<u>an inconsequential</u> effect, separately or in the aggregate on the audited financial statements;

(b)   the estimation of the effect on the audited financial statements is comprehensively documented and explained in the additional report to the audit committee ~~referred to in Article 11~~; ~~and~~

(c)   the principles of independence laid down in <u>Section 1 of this Ethical Standard</u>~~the EU Audit Directive 2006/43/EC~~ are complied with ~~by the statutory auditor or the audit *firm*~~; <u>and</u> [AR 5.3]

(d)   <u>for the purposes of the *statutory audit* of the financial statements, the audit firm would not place significant reliance on the work performed by the *audit firm* in performing these services.</u>

5.169   Where there are doubts about whether a service would have an inconsequential effect on the audited financial statements in the view of and objective, reasonable and informed third party, then the effect is not regarded as inconsequential.

5.170R   ~~A statutory auditor or~~ An *audit firm* carrying out *statutory audits* of *public interest entities* and, where ~~the statutory auditor or~~ the *audit firm* belongs to a network, any member of such network, may provide to the *audited entity*, to its parent undertaking or to its controlled undertakings non-audit services other than the prohibited non-audit services referred to in paragraph~~s 1 and 2~~5.167R subject to the approval of the audit committee after it has properly assessed threats to independence and the safeguards applied in accordance with <u>this Ethical Standard</u>~~Article 22b of the EU Audit Directive 2006/43/EC~~. <u>The Audit Regulation requires that</u> the audit committee shall, where applicable, issue guidelines with regard to the services referred to in paragraph ~~3~~5.168R. [AR 5.4]

When a member of a network to which ~~the statutory auditor or~~ the *audit firm*   **5.171R**
carrying out a *statutory audit* of a *public interest entity* belongs provides any of
the non-audit services, referred to in paragraph~~s 1 and 2~~5.167R~~of this Article~~,
to an undertaking incorporated in a third country which is controlled by the
audited *public interest entity*, ~~the statutory auditor or~~ the *audit firm* concerned
shall assess whether ~~his, her or~~ its independence would be compromised by
such provision of services by the member of the network. [AR 5.5]

If ~~his, her or~~ its independence is affected, ~~the statutory auditor or~~ the *audit*   **5.172R**
firm shall apply safeguards where applicable in order to mitigate the threats
caused by such provision of services in a third country.~~The statutory~~
~~auditor or~~ The *audit firm* may continue to carry out the *statutory audit* of
the *public interest entity* only if ~~he, she or~~ it can justify, in accordance with
Article 6 of ~~this~~the EU Audit Regulation and Article 22b[59] of the EU Audit
Directive ~~2006/43/EC~~, that such provision of services does not affect ~~his, her~~
~~or~~ its professional judgement and the audit report. [AR 5.5]

For the purposes of ~~this paragraph~~the requirements in paragraph 5.171R   **5.173R**
and 5.172R:

(a)   being involved in the decision-taking of the *audited entity* and the
provision of the services referred to in points (b), (c) and (e) of the
second subparagraph of paragraph ~~1~~5.167R shall be deemed to
affect such independence in all cases and to be incapable of
mitigation by any safeguards.

(b)   provision of the services referred to in the second subparagraph of
paragraph ~~1~~5.167R other than points (b), (c) and (e) thereof shall be
deemed to affect such independence and therefore to require
safeguards to mitigate the threats caused thereby. [AR 5.5]

Section 6 – Provisions Available for Audits of Small Entities

Introduction

> This Section does not apply for the audit of "*public interest entities*".

This Ethical Standard sets out the overarching principles, supporting ethical   **6.1**
provisions and specific requirements, that auditors are required to comply with
in order to discharge their responsibilities in respect of their integrity, objectivity
and independence. It addresses such matters as:

- How *audit firms* set policies and procedures to ensure that, in relation to
  each audit, the *audit firm* and all those who are *covered persons* act with
  integrity, objectivity and independence;

- Financial, business, employment and personal relationships;

- Long association with the *audit engagement*;

---

[59] *See paragraph 1.74D of Section 1 of Part B of this Ethical Standard.*

- Fees, remuneration and evaluation policies, litigation, gifts and hospitality;
- *Non-audit services* provided to audited entities.

This Ethical Standard applies to all *audit firms* and to all audits and must be read in order to understand the alternative provisions and exemptions contained in this Section of it.

6.2   The FRC is aware that a limited number of the requirements in Sections 1 to 5 of the Ethical Standard are difficult for certain *audit firms* to comply with, particularly when auditing a small entity. Whilst the FRC is clear that Sections 1 to 5 are appropriate in the interests of establishing the integrity, objectivity and independence of auditors, it accepts that certain dispensations, as set out in this Section, are appropriate to facilitate the cost effective audit of the financial statements of Small Entities (as defined below) that are not *"public interest entities"*.

6.3   This Section provides alternative provisions for auditors of Small Entities, that are not *"public interest entities"*, to apply in respect of the threats arising from economic dependence and where tax or *accounting services* are provided and allows the option of taking advantage of exemptions from certain of the requirements in Sections 1 to 5 for a Small Entity *audit engagement*. Where an *audit firm* takes advantage of the exemptions within this Section, it is required to:

(a)   take the steps described in this Section; and

(b)   disclose in the audit report the fact that the *firm* has applied the FRC's Ethical Standard – Provisions Available for Audits of Small Entities.

(i)   In this Standard, for the UK a "Small Entity" is:

(a)   any company, which is not a UK listed company or an *affiliate* thereof, that qualifies as a small company under Section 382 of the Companies Act 2006;

(b)   where group accounts are produced, any group that qualifies as small under Section 383 of the Companies Act 2006;

(c)   any charity with an income of less than the turnover threshold applicable to small companies as identified in Section 382 of the Companies Act 2006;

(d)   any pension fund with less than 100 members (including active, deferred and pensioner members)[60];

(e)   any *firm* regulated by the FCA, which is not required to appoint an auditor in accordance with rule SUP 3.3.2R of the FCA Handbook;

(f)   any credit union which is a mutually owned financial co-operative established under the Credit Unions Act 1979 and the Industrial and Provident Societies Act 1965 (or equivalent legislation), which meets the criteria set out in (a) above;

(g)   any entity registered under the Industrial and Provident Societies Act 1965, incorporated under the Friendly Societies Act 1992 or registered under the Friendly Societies Act 1974 (or equivalent legislation), which meets the criteria set out in (a) above;

---

[60] *In cases where a scheme with more than 100 members has been in wind-up over a number of years, such a scheme does not qualify as a Small Entity, even where the remaining number of members falls below 100.*

(h)   any registered social landlord with less than 250 units; and

(i)   any other entity, such as a club, which would be a Small Entity if it were a company.

Where an entity falls into more than one of the above categories, it is only regarded as a "Small Entity" if it meets the criteria of all relevant categories.   **6.4**

Alternative Provisions

Economic Dependence

When auditing the financial statements of a Small Entity, an *audit firm* is not   **6.5**
required to comply with the requirement in paragraph 4.51 of Section 4 of
Part B of this Ethical Standard that an external independent quality control
review is performed.

Although an external independent quality control review is not required,   **6.6**
nevertheless the *engagement partner* discloses the expectation that fees will
amount to between 10% and 15% of the *firm's* annual fee income to the *Ethics
Partner* and to those charged with governance of the *audited entity*.

Self-review Threat – Non-audit Services

When undertaking *non-audit services* for a Small Entity *audited entity*, the   **6.7**
***audit firm* is not required to apply safeguards to address a self-review threat**
provided:

(a)   the *audited entity* has "*informed management*"; and

(b)   the *audit firm* extends the cyclical inspection of completed *audit*
** *engagements* that is performed for quality control purposes.**

The *audit firm* extends the number of *audit engagements* inspected under the   **6.8**
requirements of ISQC (UK) 1"*Quality Control for Firms that Perform Audits and
Reviews of Financial Statements, and other Assurance and Related Services
Engagements*"[61] to include a random selection of audit engagements where *non-
audit services* have been provided. Particular attention is given to ensuring that
there is documentary evidence that "*informed management*" has made such
judgments and decisions that are needed in relation to the presentation and
disclosure of information in the financial statements.

Those inspecting the *audit engagements* are not involved in performing the *audit*   **6.9**
engagement. Small *audit firms* may wish to use a suitably qualified external
person or another *firm* to carry out *audit engagement* inspections.

In addition to the documentation requirements of ISQC (UK) 1, those inspecting   **6.10**
the *audit engagements* document their evaluation of whether the documentary
evidence that "*informed management*" made such judgments and decisions that
were needed in relation to the presentation and disclosure of information in the
financial statements.

---

[61] *ISQC (UK) 1 requires audit firms to establish policies and procedures which include a periodic inspection of a
selection of completed engagements. Engagements selected for inspection include at least one engagement for each
engagement partner over the inspection cycle, which ordinarily spans no more than three years.*

Exemptions

Management Threat – Non-audit Services

6.11 When undertaking *non-audit services* for Small Entity audited entities, the *audit firm* is not required to adhere to the prohibitions in Section 5 of Part B of this Ethical Standard relating to providing *non-audit services* that involve the *audit firm* undertaking part of the role of management, provided that:

(a) it discusses objectivity and independence issues related to the provision of *non-audit services* with those charged with governance, confirming that management accept responsibility for any decisions taken; and

(b) it discloses the fact that it has applied the FRC's Ethical Standard – Provisions Available for Audits of Small Entities, in accordance with paragraph 6.15.

Advocacy Threat – Non-audit Services

6.12 The *audit firm* of a Small Entity is not required to comply with paragraphs 5.97 (tax services that involve acting as an advocate) and 5.140(b) (restructuring services that involve acting as an advocate) of Section 5 of Part B of this Ethical Standard, provided that it discloses the fact that it has applied the FRC's Ethical Standard – Provisions Available for Audits of Small Entities, in accordance with paragraph 6.15.

Partners and Other Persons Approved as a Statutory Auditor Joining an Audited Entity

6.13 The *audit firm* of a Small Entity is not required to comply with paragraphs 2.53 and 2.57 of Section 2 of Part B of this Ethical Standard, provided that:

(a) it takes appropriate steps to determine that there is no significant threat to the *audit team's* integrity, objectivity and independence; and

(b) it discloses the fact that it has applied the FRC's Ethical Standard – Provisions Available for Audits of Small Entities, in accordance with paragraph 6.15.

6.14 An *audit firm* takes appropriate steps to determine that there is no significant threat to the *audit team's* integrity, objectivity and independence as a result of the employment of a former partner, or other person approved as a *statutory auditor*, by an *audited entity* that is a Small Entity by:

(a) assessing the significance of the self-interest, familiarity or intimidation threats, having regard to the following factors:

  • the position the individual has taken at the *audited entity*;

  • the nature and amount of any involvement the individual will have with the *audit team* or the audit process;

  • the length of time that has passed since the individual was a member of the *audit team* or *firm*; and

  • the former position of the individual within the *audit team* or *firm*, and

(b) if the threat is other than clearly insignificant, applying alternative procedures such as:

  • considering the appropriateness or necessity of modifying the audit plan for the *audit engagement*;

- assigning an *audit team* to the subsequent *audit engagement* that is of sufficient experience in relation to the individual who has joined the *audited entity*;

- involving an audit partner or senior *staff* member with appropriate expertise, who, where the *firm* already audits the entity, was not a member of the *audit team*, to review the work done or otherwise advise as necessary; or

- undertaking an engagement quality control review of the *audit engagement*.

Disclosure Requirements

Where the *audit firm* has taken advantage of an exemption provided in paragraphs 6.11, 6.12 or 6.13, the *engagement partner* shall ensure that: 6.15

(a)   the auditors' report discloses this fact, and

(b)   either the financial statements, or the auditors' report, discloses the type of *non-audit services* provided to the *audited entity* or the fact that a former *engagement partner*, or other person personally approved as a *statutory auditor*, has joined the *audited entity*.

The fact that an *audit firm* has taken advantage of an exemption provided by the FRC's Ethical Standard – Provisions Available for Small Entities is set out in a separate paragraph of the audit report. It does not affect the Opinion paragraph.   6.16

The *engagement partner* ensures that within the financial statements reference is made to the type of *non-audit services* provided to the *audited entity* or the fact that a former partner or other person personally approved as a *statutory auditor* has joined the *audited entity*. Where such a disclosure is not made within the financial statements it is included in the auditors' report.   6.17

APPENDIX: Illustrative template for communicating information on audit and non-audit services provided to the group

	Current year £m	Prior year £m
Audit of company	X	X
Audit of subsidiaries	X	X
Total audit	X	X
Audit related assurance services[62]	X	X
Other assurance services[63,64]	X	X
Total assurance services	X	X
Tax compliance services (i.e. related to assistance with corporate tax returns)	X	X
Tax advisory services	X	X
Services relating to taxation	X	X
Internal audit services	X	X
Services related to corporate finance transactions not covered above	X	X
Other non-audit services not covered above	X	X
Total other non-audit services	X	X
Total non-audit services	X	X
Total fees	X	X
Occupational pension scheme audits	X	X
Non-audit services in respect of the audited entity provided to a third party[65].	X	X

Disclosure of contingent fee arrangements under paragraph 4.25 of Section 4 of Part B of this Ethical Standard can also be facilitated through the use of a footnote to this template.

Disclosures required under UK company legislation[66] are indicated by those categories in bold type above. Fuller information can be provided by companies if desired.

---

[62] *This will, and will only, include those services which are identified as audit related services in paragraph 5.41 of Section 5 of Part B of this Ethical Standard.*

[63] *This will not include any tax or internal audit services, all of which should be disclosed under those headings.*

[64] *The definition of an assurance engagement is provided in the Glossary of Terms on the FRC's website. Services provided under such engagements will include assurance engagements such as those which involve reporting on historical financial information which are included in an investment circular in accordance with the Standards for Investment Reporting 2000 (Revised): Investment reporting standards applicable to public reporting engagements on historical financial information.*

[65] *For the purposes of this Ethical Standard, non-audit services include services provided to another entity in respect of the audited entity, for example, where the audit firm provides transaction related services, in respect of an audited entity's financial information, to a prospective acquirer of the audited entity (see paragraph 5.8 of Section 5 of Part B of this Ethical Standard).*

[66] *SI 2011/2198 "The Companies (Disclosure of Auditor Remuneration and Liability Limitation Agreements) (Amendment) Regulations 2011".*

Part Three

*International Standard on
Quality Control (UK)*

ISQC (UK) 1 (Revised June 2016)
Quality Control for Firms that Perform Audits and Reviews of Financial Statements, and other Assurance and Related Services Engagements (Updated July 2017)

(Effective for engagements relating to financial periods commencing on or after 17 June 2016)[0]

Contents

Paragraphs

Introduction   1 - 10
Scope of this ISQC (UK)   1 - 3
Authority of this ISQC (UK)   4 - 9
Effective date   10

Objective   11

Definitions   12

Requirements   13 - 59
Applying, and complying with, relevant requirements   13 - 15D-1
Elements of a system of quality control   16 - 17
Leadership responsibilities for quality within the firm   18 - 19
Relevant ethical requirements   20 - 25
Acceptance and continuance of client relationships and specific engagements   26 - 28D-1
Human resources   29 - 31D-1
Engagement performance   32 - 47
Monitoring   48 - 48D-1
External monitoring of group audits   48D-2 - 56
Documentation of the system of quality control   57 - 59D-2

Application and other explanatory material
Applying, and complying with, relevant requirements   A1 - A1-1
Elements of a system of quality control   A2 - A3
Leadership responsibilities for quality within the firm   A4 - A6
Relevant ethical requirements   A7 - A17
Acceptance and continuance of client relationships and specific engagements   A18 - A22
Statement by auditor on ceasing to hold office   A22-1 - A23
Human resources   A24 - A31
Engagement performance   A32 - A63
Monitoring   A64 - A72
Documentation of the system of quality control   A73 - A75

International Standard on Quality Control (UK) (ISQC (UK)) 1 (Revised June 2016), *Quality Control for Firms that Perform Audits and Reviews of Financial Statements, and Other Assurance and Related Services Engagements*, should be read in conjunction with ISA (UK) 200 (Revised June 2016), *Overall Objectives of the Independent Auditor and the Conduct of an Audit in Accordance with International Standards on Auditing (UK)*.

---

[0] *Conforming amendments to this standard as a result of ISA (UK) 250 (Revised July 2017), Section A— Consideration of Laws and Regulations in an Audit of Financial Statements, are included that are effective for audits of financial statements for periods commencing on or after 15 December 2017. Details of the amendments are given in the Annexure to ISA (UK) 250 (Revised July 2017).*

Introduction

Scope of this ISQC (UK)

1   This International Standard on Quality Control (UK) (ISQC (UK)) deals with a firm's responsibilities for its system of quality control for audits and reviews of financial statements, and other assurance and related services engagements. This ISQC (UK) is to be read in conjunction with relevant ethical requirements.

1-1   In the UK, ISQC (UK) 1 (Revised June 2016) applies to firms that perform audits of financial statements and other public interest assurance engagements.[1a]

2   Other pronouncements of the International Auditing and Assurance Standards Board (IAASB) set out additional standards and guidance on the responsibilities of firm personnel regarding quality control procedures for specific types of engagements. ISA (UK) 220 (Revised June 2016),[1] for example, deals with quality control procedures for audits of financial statements.

3   A system of quality control consists of policies designed to achieve the objective set out in paragraph 11 and the procedures necessary to implement and monitor compliance with those policies.

Authority of this ISQC (UK)

4   This ISQC (UK) applies to all firms of professional accountants in respect of audits and reviews of financial statements, and other assurance and related services engagements. The nature and extent of the policies and procedures developed by an individual firm to comply with this ISQC (UK) will depend on various factors such as the size and operating characteristics of the firm, and whether it is part of a network.

5   This ISQC (UK) contains the objective of the firm in following the ISQC (UK), and requirements designed to enable the firm to meet that stated objective. In addition, it contains related guidance in the form of application and other explanatory material, as discussed further in paragraph 8, and introductory material that provides context relevant to a proper understanding of the ISQC (UK), and definitions.

6   The objective provides the context in which the requirements of this ISQC (UK) are set, and is intended to assist the firm in:

●   Understanding what needs to be accomplished; and

●   Deciding whether more needs to be done to achieve the objective.

[1a]   *Audits of financial statements[(a)] undertaken in compliance with International Standards on Auditing (UK) and other engagements undertaken in compliance with performance standards issued by the FRC which, as of June 2016, comprise:*

●   *Reporting accountants acting in connection with an investment circular (the Standards for Investment Reporting – "SIRs");*

●   *Review of interim financial information by the independent auditor of the entity (International Standard on Review Engagements (UK and Ireland) 2410); and*

●   *Engagements to provide assurance on client assets to the Financial Conduct Authority (the CASS Standard).*

[(a)]   *In the public sector the statutory scope of an audit can extend beyond the entity's financial statements to include reporting on an entity's arrangements for the proper conduct of its financial affairs, management of its performance or use of its resources.*

[1]   *ISA (UK) 220 (Revised June 2016), Quality Control for an Audit of Financial Statements.*

The requirements of this ISQC (UK) are expressed using "shall."   **7**

Where necessary, the application and other explanatory material provides further   **8**
explanation of the requirements and guidance for carrying them out. In particular,
it may:

- Explain more precisely what a requirement means or is intended to cover.
- Include examples of policies and procedures that may be appropriate in the circumstances.

While such guidance does not in itself impose a requirement, it is relevant to the
proper application of the requirements. The application and other explanatory
material may also provide background information on matters addressed in this
ISQC (UK). Where appropriate, additional considerations specific to public sector
audit organizations or smaller firms are included within the application and other
explanatory material. These additional considerations assist in the application of
the requirements in this ISQC (UK). They do not, however, limit or reduce the
responsibility of the firm to apply and comply with the requirements in this ISQC
(UK).

This ISQC (UK) includes, under the heading "Definitions," a description of the   **9**
meanings attributed to certain terms for purposes of this ISQC (UK). These are
provided to assist in the consistent application and interpretation of this ISQC
(UK), and are not intended to override definitions that may be established for other
purposes, whether in law, regulation or otherwise. The Glossary of Terms[1b]
relating to International Standards issued by the IAASB in the *Handbook of
International Quality Control, Auditing, Review, Other Assurance, and Related
Services* published by IFAC includes the terms defined in this ISQC (UK). It also
includes descriptions of other terms found in this ISQC (UK) to assist in common
and consistent interpretation and translation.

Effective Date

Systems of quality control in compliance with this ISQC (UK) are required to be   **10**
established for engagements relating to financial periods commencing on or after
17 June 2016.

Objective

The objective of the firm is to establish and maintain a system of quality control to   **11**
provide it with reasonable assurance that:

(a)   The firm and its personnel comply with professional standards and
applicable legal and regulatory requirements; and

(b)   Reports issued by the firm or engagement partners are appropriate in the
circumstances.

[1b]   *The FRC's Glossary of Terms defines terms used in the ISAs (UK). It is based on the Glossary of Terms issued
by the IAASB supplemented by a small number of additional definitions.*

Definitions

12   In this ISQC (UK), the following terms have the meanings attributed below:

(a)   Date of report – The date selected by the practitioner to date the report.

(b)   Engagement documentation – The record of work performed, results obtained, and conclusions the practitioner reached (terms such as "working papers" or "workpapers" are sometimes used).

> In the UK, engagement documentation shall include all documents, information, records and other data required by this ISQC (UK), ISAs (UK) and applicable legal and regulatory requirements.

(c)   Engagement partner[2] – The partner or other person in the firm who is responsible for the engagement and its performance, and for the report that is issued on behalf of the firm, and who, where required, has the appropriate authority from a professional, legal or regulatory body.

(d)   Engagement quality control review – A process designed to provide an objective evaluation, on or before the date of the report, of the significant judgments the engagement team made and the conclusions it reached in formulating the report. The engagement quality control review process is for audits of financial statements of listed entities, and those other engagements, if any, for which the firm has determined an engagement quality control review is required.

(e)   Engagement quality control reviewer – A partner, other person in the firm, suitably qualified external person, or a team made up of such individuals, none of whom is part of the engagement team, with sufficient and appropriate experience and authority to objectively evaluate the significant judgments the engagement team made and the conclusions it reached in formulating the report.

(f)   Engagement team – All partners and staff performing the engagement, and any individuals engaged by the firm or a network firm who perform procedures on the engagement. This excludes an auditor's external expert engaged by the firm or by a network firm. The term "engagement team" also excludes individuals within the client's internal audit function who provide direct assistance on an audit engagement when the external auditor complies with the requirements of ISA (UK) 610 (Revised June 2013).[3]

(g)   Firm – A sole practitioner, partnership or corporation or other entity of professional accountants.

(h)   Inspection – In relation to completed engagements, procedures designed to provide evidence of compliance by engagement teams with the firm's quality control policies and procedures.

---

[2] *"Engagement partner", "partner", and "firm" should be read as referring to their public sector equivalents where relevant.*

[3] *ISA 610 (Revised June 2013), Using the Work of Internal Auditors, establishes limits on the use of direct assistance. It also acknowledges that the external auditor may be prohibited by law or regulation from obtaining direct assistance from internal auditors. Therefore, the use of direct assistance is restricted to situations where it is permitted.*

The use of internal auditors to provide direct assistance is prohibited in an audit conducted in accordance with ISAs (UK) – see ISA (UK) 610 (Revised June 2013), paragraph 5-1.

(h)-1 Key audit partner – Is defined in UK legislation[3a] as:

   (i)   The statutory auditor designated by an audit firm for a particular audit engagement as being primarily responsible for carrying out the statutory audit on behalf of the audit firm; or

   (ii)   In the case of a group audit, the statutory auditor designated by an audit firm as being primarily responsible for carrying out the statutory audit at the level of the group and the statutory auditor designated at the level of material subsidiaries; or

   (iii) The statutory auditor who signs the audit report.

(i)   Listed entity – An entity whose shares, stock or debt are quoted or listed on a recognized stock exchange, or are marketed under the regulations of a recognized stock exchange or other equivalent body.

In the UK, this includes any company in which the public can trade shares, stock or debt on the open market, such as those listed on the London Stock Exchange (including those admitted to trading on the Alternative Investments Market) and ISDX Markets. It does not include entities whose quoted or listed shares, stock or debt are in substance not freely transferable or cannot be traded freely by the public or the entity.

(j)   Monitoring – A process comprising an ongoing consideration and evaluation of the firm's system of quality control, including a periodic inspection of a selection of completed engagements, designed to provide the firm with reasonable assurance that its system of quality control is operating effectively.

(k)   Network firm – A firm or entity that belongs to a network.

(l)   Network – A larger structure:

   (i)   That is aimed at cooperation, and

   (ii)   That is clearly aimed at profit or cost-sharing or shares common ownership, control or management, common quality control policies and procedures, common business strategy, the use of a common brand name, or a significant part of professional resources.

(m) Partner – Any individual with authority to bind the firm with respect to the performance of a professional services engagement.

(n)   Personnel – Partners and staff.

(o)   Professional standards – IAASB Engagement Standards, as defined in the IAASB's *Preface to the International Standards on Quality Control, Auditing, Review, Other Assurance, and Related Services*, and relevant ethical requirements.

In the UK, professional standards in the context of ISQC (UK) 1 are the performance standards issued by the FRC.[1a]

(o)-1 Public interest entity – Is defined in UK legislation[3b] as:

[3a] *In the UK, Schedule 10 to the Companies Act 2006.*

[3b] *In the UK, Section 494A of the Companies Act 2006.*

(i)   An issuer whose transferable securities are admitted to trading on a regulated market;[3c]

(ii) A credit institution within the meaning given by Article 4(1)(1) of Regulation (EU) No. 575/2013 of the European Parliament and of the Council, other than one listed in Article 2 of Directive 2013/36/EU of the European Parliament and of the Council on access to the activity of credit institutions and investment firms;

(iii) An insurance undertaking within the meaning given by Article 2(1) of Council Directive 1991/674/EEC of the European Parliament and of the Council on the annual accounts and consolidated accounts of insurance undertakings.

(p) Reasonable assurance – In the context of this ISQC (UK), a high, but not absolute, level of assurance.

(q) Relevant ethical requirements – Ethical requirements to which the engagement team and engagement quality control reviewer are subject, which ordinarily comprise Parts A and B of the International Ethics Standards Board for Accountants' *Code of Ethics for Professional Accountants* (IESBA Code) together with national requirements that are more restrictive.

In the UK, the firm and its personnel are subject to ethical requirements from two sources: the FRC's Ethical Standard concerning the integrity, objectivity and independence of the firm and its personnel, and the ethical pronouncements established by the auditor or assurance practitioner's relevant professional body.

(r) Staff – Professionals, other than partners, including any experts the firm employs.

(s) Suitably qualified external person – An individual outside the firm with the competence and capabilities to act as an engagement partner, for example a partner of another firm, or an employee (with appropriate experience) of either a professional accountancy body whose members may perform audits and reviews of historical financial information, or other assurance or related services engagements, or of an organization that provides relevant quality control services.

Requirements

Applying, and Complying with, Relevant Requirements

13   Personnel within the firm responsible for establishing and maintaining the firm's system of quality control shall have an understanding of the entire text of this ISQC (UK), including its application and other explanatory material, to understand its objective and to apply its requirements properly.

14   The firm shall comply with each requirement of this ISQC (UK) unless, in the circumstances of the firm, the requirement is not relevant to the services provided in respect of audits and reviews of financial statements, and other assurance and related services engagements. (Ref: Para. A1–A1-1)

[3c] *In the UK, "issuer" and "regulated market" have the same meaning as in Part 6 of the Financial Services and Markets Act 2000.*

The requirements are designed to enable the firm to achieve the objective stated in this ISQC (UK). The proper application of the requirements is therefore expected to provide a sufficient basis for the achievement of the objective. However, because circumstances vary widely and all such circumstances cannot be anticipated, the firm shall consider whether there are particular matters or circumstances that require the firm to establish policies and procedures in addition to those required by this ISQC (UK) to meet the stated objective.   **15**

The firm shall: **15D-1**

(a)   Take into consideration the scale and complexity of the firm's activities when complying with the requirements set out in paragraphs 16D-1, 16D-2, 20D-1, 21D-1, 29D-1, 29D-2, 32D-1 and 48D-1 of this ISQC (UK); and

(b)   Be able to demonstrate to the competent authority[3d] that the firm's policies and procedures designed to achieve compliance with the applicable requirements of this ISQC (UK) are appropriate given the scale and complexity of the firm's activities.

Elements of a System of Quality Control

The firm shall establish and maintain a system of quality control that includes policies and procedures that address each of the following elements: **16**

(a)   Leadership responsibilities for quality within the firm.

(b)   Relevant ethical requirements.

(c)   Acceptance and continuance of client relationships and specific engagements.

(d)   Human resources.

(e)   Engagement performance.

(f)   Monitoring.

The firm shall establish appropriate policies and procedures to ensure that no partner, director, member or shareholder of the firm, or partner, director, member or shareholder any affiliate of the firm, intervenes in the carrying out of an engagement in any way which jeopardizes the firm's independence and objectivity in carrying out such work.   **16D-1**

The firm shall have: **16D-2**

(a)   Sound administrative and accounting procedures;

(b)   Internal quality control mechanisms which are designed to secure compliance with decisions and procedures at all levels of the firm's working structure;

(c)   Effective procedures for risk assessment; and

(d)   Effective control and safeguard arrangements for information processing systems.

[3d] *In the UK, the competent authority designated by law is the Financial Reporting Council or the Recognised Supervisory Body to whom the FRC has delegated regulatory tasks, as applicable.*

17   The firm shall document its policies and procedures and communicate them to the firm's personnel. (Ref: Para. A2–A3)

Leadership Responsibilities for Quality within the Firm

18   The firm shall establish policies and procedures designed to promote an internal culture recognizing that quality is essential in performing engagements. Such policies and procedures shall require the firm's chief executive officer (or equivalent) or, if appropriate, the firm's managing board of partners (or equivalent) to assume ultimate responsibility for the firm's system of quality control. (Ref: Para. A4–A5)

19   The firm shall establish policies and procedures such that any person or persons assigned operational responsibility for the firm's system of quality control by the firm's chief executive officer or managing board of partners has sufficient and appropriate experience and ability, and the necessary authority, to assume that responsibility. (Ref: Para. A6)

Relevant Ethical Requirements

20   The firm shall establish policies and procedures designed to provide it with reasonable assurance that the firm and its personnel comply with relevant ethical requirements. (Ref: Para. A7–A10)

20D-1   The firm shall establish appropriate and effective organizational and administrative arrangements for dealing with and recording incidents which have, or may have, serious consequences for the integrity of the firm's audit or other public interest assurance activities.

Independence

21   The firm shall establish policies and procedures designed to provide it with reasonable assurance that the firm, its personnel and, where applicable, others subject to independence requirements (including network firm personnel) maintain independence where required by relevant ethical requirements. Such policies and procedures shall enable the firm to: (Ref: Para. A10)

(a)   Communicate its independence requirements to its personnel and, where applicable, others subject to them; and

(b)   Identify and evaluate circumstances and relationships that create threats to independence, and to take appropriate action to eliminate those threats or reduce them to an acceptable level by applying safeguards, or, if considered appropriate, to withdraw from the engagement, where withdrawal is permitted by law or regulation.

21D-1   The firm shall establish appropriate and effective organizational and administrative arrangements to prevent, identify, eliminate or manage and disclose any threats to the firm's independence required by the FRC's Ethical Standard.

22   Such policies and procedures shall require: (Ref: Para. A10)

(a)   Engagement partners to provide the firm with relevant information about client engagements, including the scope of services, to enable the firm to evaluate the overall impact, if any, on independence requirements;

(b)   Personnel to promptly notify the firm of circumstances and relationships that create a threat to independence so that appropriate action can be taken; and

(c)   The accumulation and communication of relevant information to appropriate personnel so that:

   (i)   The firm and its personnel can readily determine whether they satisfy independence requirements;

   (ii)   The firm can maintain and update its records relating to independence; and

   (iii) The firm can take appropriate action regarding identified threats to independence that are not at an acceptable level.

The firm shall establish policies and procedures designed to provide it with reasonable assurance that it is notified of breaches of independence requirements, and to enable it to take appropriate actions to resolve such situations. The policies and procedures shall include requirements for: (Ref: Para. A10)   **23**

(a)   Personnel to promptly notify the firm of independence breaches of which they become aware;

(b)   The firm to promptly communicate identified breaches of these policies and procedures to:

   (i)   The engagement partner who, with the firm, needs to address the breach; and

   (ii)   Other relevant personnel in the firm and, where appropriate, the network, and those subject to the independence requirements who need to take appropriate action; and

(c)   Prompt communication to the firm, if necessary, by the engagement partner and the other individuals referred to in subparagraph (b)(ii) of the actions taken to resolve the matter, so that the firm can determine whether it should take further action.

At least annually, the firm shall obtain written confirmation of compliance with its policies and procedures on independence from all firm personnel required to be independent by relevant ethical requirements. (Ref: Para. A10–A11)   **24**

The firm shall establish policies and procedures: **25**

(a)   Setting out criteria for determining the need for safeguards to reduce the familiarity threat to an acceptable level when using the same senior personnel on an assurance engagement over a long period of time; and

(b)   Requiring, for audits of financial statements of listed entities, the rotation of the engagement partner and the individuals responsible for engagement quality control review, and where applicable, others subject to rotation requirements, after a specified period in compliance with relevant ethical requirements. (Ref: Para. A10, A12–A17)

Acceptance and Continuance of Client Relationships and Specific Engagements

The firm shall establish policies and procedures for the acceptance and continuance of client relationships and specific engagements, designed to provide the firm with reasonable assurance that it will only undertake or continue relationships and engagements where the firm: **26**

(a)   Is competent to perform the engagement and has the capabilities, including time and resources, to do so; (Ref: Para. A18, A23)

(b)   Can comply with relevant ethical requirements; and

(c) Has considered the integrity of the client, and does not have information that would lead it to conclude that the client lacks integrity. (Ref: Para. A19– A20, A23)

27 Such policies and procedures shall require:

(a) The firm to obtain such information as it considers necessary in the circumstances before accepting an engagement with a new client, when deciding whether to continue an existing engagement, and when considering acceptance of a new engagement with an existing client. (Ref: Para. A21, A23)

(b) If a potential conflict of interest is identified in accepting an engagement from a new or an existing client, the firm to determine whether it is appropriate to accept the engagement.

(c) If issues have been identified, and the firm decides to accept or continue the client relationship or a specific engagement, the firm to document how the issues were resolved.

27D-1 Before accepting or continuing an audit engagement, the firm shall assess the following:

(a) Whether the firm complies with relevant independence and objectivity requirements in the FRC's Ethical Standard;

(b) Whether there are threats to the firm's independence, and the safeguards applied to mitigate those threats;

(c) Whether the firm has the competent *personnel*, time and resources needed in order to carry out the audit in an appropriate manner; and

(d) Whether the key audit partner is eligible for appointment as a statutory auditor.[3e]

27R-2 Before accepting or continuing an engagement for an audit engagement of a public interest entity, the firm shall also assess the following:

(a) Whether the firm complies with the audit fees and the prohibition of the provision of non-audit services requirements in the FRC's Ethical Standard;

(b) Whether the conditions for the duration of the audit engagement in accordance with the Audit Regulation[3f] are complied with; and

(c) Without prejudice to UK anti-money laundering requirements,[3g] the integrity of the members of the supervisory, administrative and management bodies of the public interest entity.

28 The firm shall establish policies and procedures on continuing an engagement and the client relationship, addressing the circumstances where the firm obtains information that would have caused it to decline the engagement had that information been available earlier. Such policies and procedures shall include consideration of:

[3e] *In the UK, eligibility for appointment as a statutory auditor is dealt with in sections 1212 to 1225 of the Companies Act 2006.*

[3f] *Regulation (EU) No 537/2014 of the European Parliament and of the Council of 16 April 2014.*

[3g] *Implemented pursuant to Directive 2005/60/EC of the European Parliament and of the Council of 26 October 2005.*

(a)   The professional and legal responsibilities that apply to the circumstances, including whether there is a requirement for the firm to report to the person or persons who made the appointment or, in some cases, to regulatory authorities; and

(b)   The possibility of withdrawing from the engagement or from both the engagement and the client relationship. (Ref: Para. A22–A23)

For audits of financial statements, where the auditor ceases to hold office as statutory auditor, or ceases to be eligible for appointment as a statutory auditor,[3e] the firm shall provide the successor statutory auditor with access to all relevant information concerning the entity, including information concerning the most recent audit.[3h] (Ref: Para. A22-1)   **28D-1**

Human Resources

The firm shall establish policies and procedures designed to provide it with reasonable assurance that it has sufficient personnel with the competence, capabilities, and commitment to ethical principles necessary to: **29**

(a)   Perform engagements in accordance with professional standards and applicable legal and regulatory requirements; and

(b)   Enable the firm or engagement partners to issue reports that are appropriate in the circumstances. (Ref: Para. A24–A29)

For audits of financial statements, the firm shall: **29D-1**

(a)   Establish appropriate policies and procedures to ensure that the firm's personnel and any other individuals whose services are placed at the firm's disposal or under the firm's control, and who are directly involved in audit activities, have appropriate knowledge and experience for the duties assigned; and

(b)   Have in place adequate remuneration policies, including profit-sharing policies, providing sufficient performance incentives to secure audit quality, including provision that the amount of revenue that the firm derives from providing non-audit services to the audited entity shall not form part of the performance evaluation and remuneration of any person involved in, or able to influence the carrying out of, the audit.

Outsourcing

For audits of financial statements, the firm shall establish appropriate policies and procedures to ensure that outsourcing of important audit functions is not undertaken in such a way as to impair the quality of the firm's internal quality control and the ability of the competent authority[3b] to supervise the firm's compliance with professional standards and applicable legal and regulatory requirements.   **29D-2**

Assignment of Engagement Teams

The firm shall assign responsibility for each engagement to an engagement partner and shall establish policies and procedures requiring that: **30**

(a)   The identity and role of the engagement partner are communicated to key members of client management and those charged with governance;

[3h] *In the UK, the relevant guidance on proposed communications with a predecessor auditor is provided by the pronouncements relating to the work of auditors issued by the auditor's relevant professional body.*

(b)   The engagement partner has the appropriate competence, capabilities, and authority to perform the role; and

(c)   The responsibilities of the engagement partner are clearly defined and communicated to that partner. (Ref: Para. A30)

30D-1   For each audit of financial statements, the firm shall:

(a)   Designate at least one key audit partner;[3i]

(b)   Apply as its main criteria in selecting such a key audit partner the need to secure:

(i)   The quality of the audit; and

(ii)   The firm's independence and competence in carrying out the audit;

(c)   Ensure the key audit partner is actively involved in carrying out of the audit.

31   The firm shall also establish policies and procedures to assign appropriate personnel with the necessary competence, and capabilities to:

(a)   Perform engagements in accordance with professional standards and applicable legal and regulatory requirements; and

(b)   Enable the firm or engagement partners to issue reports that are appropriate in the circumstances. (Ref: Para. A31)

31D-1   For audits of financial statements, the firm shall provide the key audit partner(s) with sufficient resources and with personnel that have the necessary competence and capabilities to carry out the firm's duties appropriately.

Engagement Performance

32   The firm shall establish policies and procedures designed to provide it with reasonable assurance that engagements are performed in accordance with professional standards and applicable legal and regulatory requirements, and that the firm or the engagement partner issue reports that are appropriate in the circumstances. Such policies and procedures shall include:

(a)   Matters relevant to promoting consistency in the quality of engagement performance; (Ref: Para. A32–A33)

(b)   Supervision responsibilities; and (Ref: Para. A34)

(c)   Review responsibilities. (Ref: Para. A35)

32D-1   For audits of financial statements, the firm shall:

(a)   Establish an internal quality control system to ensure the quality of the audit which covers at least the policies and procedures required by paragraph 32D-1(c);

(b)   Ensure that responsibility for the internal quality control system lies with a person who is eligible for appointment as a statutory auditor;[3e]

[3i] *Key audit partner includes engagement partner.*

(c) Establish appropriate policies and procedures for carrying out audits, coaching, supervising and reviewing the activities of the firm's personnel and organizing the structure of the audit file;[3j] and

(d) Use appropriate systems, resources and procedures to ensure continuity and regularity in the carrying out of the firm's audit activities.

The firm's review responsibility policies and procedures shall be determined on the basis that work of less experienced team members is reviewed by more experienced engagement team members. **33**

Consultation

The firm shall establish policies and procedures designed to provide it with reasonable assurance that: **34**

(a) Appropriate consultation takes place on difficult or contentious matters;

(b) Sufficient resources are available to enable appropriate consultation to take place;

(c) The nature and scope of, and conclusions resulting from, such consultations are documented and are agreed by both the individual seeking consultation and the individual consulted; and

(d) Conclusions resulting from consultations are implemented. (Ref: Para. A36–A40)

Engagement Quality Control Review

The firm shall establish policies and procedures requiring, for appropriate engagements, an engagement quality control review that provides an objective evaluation of the significant judgments made by the engagement team and the conclusions reached in formulating the report. Such policies and procedures shall: **35**

(a) Require an engagement quality control review for all audits of financial statements of listed entities;

(b) Set out criteria against which all other audits and reviews of historical financial information and other assurance and related services engagements shall be evaluated to determine whether an engagement quality control review should be performed; and (Ref: Para. A41)

(c) Require an engagement quality control review for all engagements, if any, meeting the criteria established in compliance with subparagraph (b).

The firm shall establish policies and procedures setting out the nature, timing and extent of an engagement quality control review. Such policies and procedures shall require that the engagement report not be dated until the completion of the engagement quality control review. (Ref: Para. A42–A43) **36**

For audits of financial statements of public interest entities, before the auditor's report and the additional report to the audit committee are issued,[3k] the firm shall require that an engagement quality control review shall be performed to **36R-1**

[3j] *ISA (UK) 230 (Revised June 2016), Audit Documentation, paragraph 14 sets out the requirement to assemble the audit documentation in an audit file. Paragraph 57D-1 of this ISQC (UK), paragraphs 24D-1(b) and 25R-2 of ISA (UK) 220 (Revised June 2016), Quality Control for an Audit of Financial Statements, paragraphs 8D-1 and 14D-1 of ISA (UK) 230 (Revised June 2016) and paragraph 23D-1 of ISA (UK) 260 (Revised June 2016), Communication with Those Charged with Governance, set out requirements in respect of documentation for audits.*

[3k] *ISA (UK) 260 (Revised June 2016), paragraph 16R-2 deals with the auditor's responsibilities to prepare an additional report to the audit committee.*

assess whether the key audit partner(s) could reasonably have come to the opinion and conclusions expressed in the draft of those reports.

37   The firm shall establish policies and procedures to require the engagement quality control review to include:

(a)   Discussion of significant matters with the engagement partner;

(b)   Review of the financial statements or other subject matter information and the proposed report;

(c)   Review of selected engagement documentation relating to significant judgments the engagement team made and the conclusions it reached; and

(d)   Evaluation of the conclusions reached in formulating the report and consideration of whether the proposed report is appropriate. (Ref: Para. A44)

37-1   The firm shall establish policies and procedures to require the engagement quality control reviewer to: (Ref: Para. A44-1–A44-2)

(a)   Consider the firm's compliance with the FRC's Ethical Standard in relation to the engagement;

(b)   Form an independent opinion as to the appropriateness and adequacy of the safeguards applied; and

(c)   Consider the adequacy of the documentation of the engagement partner's consideration of the objectivity and independence of the firm and its personnel.

38   For audits of financial statements of listed entities, the firm shall establish policies and procedures to require the engagement quality control review to also include consideration of the following:

(a)   The engagement team's evaluation of the firm's independence in relation to the specific engagement;

(b)   Whether appropriate consultation has taken place on matters involving differences of opinion or other difficult or contentious matters, and the conclusions arising from those consultations; and

(c)   Whether documentation selected for review reflects the work performed in relation to the significant judgments and supports the conclusions reached. (Ref: Para. A45–A46)

Criteria for the Eligibility of Engagement Quality Control Reviewers

39   The firm shall establish policies and procedures to address the appointment of engagement quality control reviewers and establish their eligibility through:

(a)   The technical qualifications required to perform the role, including the necessary experience and authority; and (Ref: Para. A47)

(b)   The degree to which an engagement quality control reviewer can be consulted on the engagement without compromising the reviewer's objectivity. (Ref: Para. A48)

39R-1   For audits of financial statements of public interest entities, the engagement quality control review shall be performed by an engagement quality control reviewer who shall:

(a)   Be eligible for appointment as a statutory auditor;[3e] and

(b) Not be involved in the performance of the audit to which the engagement quality control review relates.

Where the audit is carried out by a firm and all the statutory auditors of that firm were involved in the carrying out of the audit, the firm shall arrange for another firm to perform an engagement quality control review. Documents or information disclosed to the engagement quality control reviewer for this purpose shall be subject to professional secrecy.

The firm shall establish policies and procedures designed to maintain the objectivity of the engagement quality control reviewer. (Ref: Para. A49–A51) **40**

The firm's policies and procedures shall provide for the replacement of the engagement quality control reviewer where the reviewer's ability to perform an objective review may be impaired. **41**

Documentation of the Engagement Quality Control Review

The firm shall establish policies and procedures on documentation of the engagement quality control review which require documentation that: **42**

(a) The procedures required by the firm's policies on engagement quality control review have been performed;

(b) The engagement quality control review has been completed on or before the date of the report; and

(c) The reviewer is not aware of any unresolved matters that would cause the reviewer to believe that the significant judgments the engagement team made and the conclusions it reached were not appropriate.

Differences of Opinion

The firm shall establish policies and procedures for dealing with and resolving differences of opinion within the engagement team, with those consulted and, where applicable, between the engagement partner and the engagement quality control reviewer. (Ref: Para. A52–A53) **43**

For statutory audits of financial statements of public interest entities, the firm shall also establish procedures for determining the manner in which any disagreement between the key audit partner(s) and the engagement quality control reviewer are to be resolved. **43R-1**

Such policies and procedures shall require that: **44**

(a) Conclusions reached be documented and implemented; and

(b) The report not be dated until the matter is resolved.

Engagement Documentation

Completion of the Assembly of Final Engagement Files

The firm shall establish policies and procedures for engagement teams to complete the assembly of final engagement files on a timely basis after the engagement reports have been finalized. (Ref: Para. A54–A55) **45**

Confidentiality, Safe Custody, Integrity, Accessibility and Retrievability of Engagement Documentation

46   The firm shall establish policies and procedures designed to maintain the confidentiality, safe custody, integrity, accessibility and retrievability of engagement documentation. (Ref: Para. A56–A59)

46D-1   The firm shall establish policies and procedures designed to:

(a)   Apply adequate provision on confidentiality and professional secrecy in relation to all information and documents to which the firm has access when carrying out an engagement; and

(b)   Ensure that the firm complies with applicable legal and regulatory requirements relating to the confidentiality of information received in the course of the engagement.

Retention of Engagement Documentation

47   The firm shall establish policies and procedures for the retention of engagement documentation for a period sufficient to meet the needs of the firm or as required by law or regulation. (Ref: Para. A60–A63)

Monitoring

Monitoring the Firm's Quality Control Policies and Procedures

48   The firm shall establish a monitoring process designed to provide it with reasonable assurance that the policies and procedures relating to the system of quality control are relevant, adequate, and operating effectively. This process shall:

(a)   Include an ongoing consideration and evaluation of the firm's system of quality control including, on a cyclical basis, inspection of at least one completed engagement for each engagement partner;

(b)   Require responsibility for the monitoring process to be assigned to a partner or partners or other persons with sufficient and appropriate experience and authority in the firm to assume that responsibility; and

(c)   Require that those performing the engagement or the engagement quality control review are not involved in inspecting the engagements. (Ref: Para. A64–A68)

48D-1   For audits of financial statements, the firm shall:

(a)   Monitor and evaluate the adequacy and effectiveness of the firm's systems, internal quality control mechanisms and arrangements established in accordance with this ISQC (UK) and take appropriate measures to address any deficiencies;

(b)   Carry out an annual evaluation of the internal quality control system, referred to in paragraph 32D-1(a); and

(c)   Keep records of the findings of the evaluation required by paragraph 48D-1(b) and any proposed measure to modify the internal quality control system.

External Monitoring of Group Audits

Where the firm is subject to a quality assurance review or an investigation   **48D-2**
concerning a group audit, the firm shall be responsible for complying with, and
shall establish policies and procedures which require the group engagement
team to comply with, any request by the competent authority:[3d]

(a)   For relevant audit documentation retained by the group engagement team
      concerning the work performed by any component auditor for the
      purposes of the group audit (including any relevant component
      auditor's working papers relevant to the group audit);

(b)   To deliver any additional documentation of the work performed by any
      component auditor from a non-EEA member state for the purposes of the
      group audit, including that component auditor's working papers relevant
      to the group audit, where the competent authority is unable to obtain
      audit documentation of the work carried out by that component auditor.

The firm shall establish policies and procedures, which require that, in order to   **48D-3**
comply with any request under paragraph 48D-2(b), the group engagement
team shall either:

(a)   Retain copies of the documentation of the work carried out by the
      relevant component auditor for the purpose of the group audit (including
      the component auditor's working papers relevant to the group audit); or

(b)   Obtain the agreement of the relevant component auditor that the group
      engagement team shall have unrestricted access to such documentation
      on request; or

(c)   Retain documentation to show that the group engagement team has
      undertaken the appropriate procedures in order to gain access to the audit
      documentation, together with evidence supporting the existence of any
      impediments to such access; or

(d)   Take any other appropriate action.

Evaluating, Communicating and Remedying Identified Deficiencies

The firm shall evaluate the effect of deficiencies noted as a result of the monitoring   **49**
process and determine whether they are either:

(a)   Instances that do not necessarily indicate that the firm's system of quality
      control is insufficient to provide it with reasonable assurance that it complies
      with professional standards and applicable legal and regulatory
      requirements, and that the reports issued by the firm or engagement
      partners are appropriate in the circumstances; or

(b)   Systemic, repetitive or other significant deficiencies that require prompt
      corrective action.

The firm shall communicate to relevant engagement partners and other   **50**
appropriate personnel deficiencies noted as a result of the monitoring process
and recommendations for appropriate remedial action. (Ref: Para. A69)

Recommendations for appropriate remedial actions for deficiencies noted shall   **51**
include one or more of the following:

(a)   Taking appropriate remedial action in relation to an individual engagement
      or member of personnel;

(b)   The communication of the findings to those responsible for training and professional development;

(c)   Changes to the quality control policies and procedures; and

(d)   Disciplinary action against those who fail to comply with the policies and procedures of the firm, especially those who do so repeatedly.

52   The firm shall establish policies and procedures to address cases where the results of the monitoring procedures indicate that a report may be inappropriate or that procedures were omitted during the performance of the engagement. Such policies and procedures shall require the firm to determine what further action is appropriate to comply with relevant professional standards and legal and regulatory requirements and to consider whether to obtain legal advice.

53   The firm shall communicate at least annually the results of the monitoring of its system of quality control to engagement partners and other appropriate individuals within the firm, including the firm's chief executive officer or, if appropriate, its managing board of partners. This communication shall be sufficient to enable the firm and these individuals to take prompt and appropriate action where necessary in accordance with their defined roles and responsibilities. Information communicated shall include the following:

(a)   A description of the monitoring procedures performed.

(b)   The conclusions drawn from the monitoring procedures.

(c)   Where relevant, a description of systemic, repetitive or other significant deficiencies and of the actions taken to resolve or amend those deficiencies.

54   Some firms operate as part of a network and, for consistency, may implement some of their monitoring procedures on a network basis. Where firms within a network operate under common monitoring policies and procedures designed to comply with this ISQC (UK), and these firms place reliance on such a monitoring system, the firm's policies and procedures shall require that:

(a)   At least annually, the network communicate the overall scope, extent and results of the monitoring process to appropriate individuals within the network firms; and

(b)   The network communicate promptly any identified deficiencies in the system of quality control to appropriate individuals within the relevant network firm or firms so that the necessary action can be taken,

in order that engagement partners in the network firms can rely on the results of the monitoring process implemented within the network, unless the firms or the network advise otherwise.

Complaints and Allegations

55   The firm shall establish policies and procedures designed to provide it with reasonable assurance that it deals appropriately with:

(a)   Complaints and allegations that the work performed by the firm fails to comply with professional standards and applicable legal and regulatory requirements; and

(b)   Allegations of non-compliance with the firm's system of quality control.

As part of this process, the firm shall establish clearly defined channels for firm personnel to raise any concerns in a manner that enables them to come forward without fear of reprisals. (Ref: Para. A70)

For audits of financial statements, the firm shall keep records of any complaints 55D-1
made in writing about the performance of the audit engagements carried out.

If during the investigations into complaints and allegations, deficiencies in the 56
design or operation of the firm's quality control policies and procedures or non-
compliance with the firm's system of quality control by an individual or
individuals are identified, the firm shall take appropriate actions as set out in
paragraph 51. (Ref: Para. A71–A72)

Documentation of the System of Quality Control

The firm shall establish policies and procedures requiring appropriate 57
documentation to provide evidence of the operation of each element of its
system of quality control. (Ref: Para. A73–A75)

For audits of financial statements, the firm shall retain engagement 57D-1
documentation that is important for monitoring compliance with this ISQC
(UK) and other applicable legal requirements.

For audits of financial statements, the firm shall also document: 57D-2

(a) Whether the firm complies with the independence and objectivity
requirements in the FRC's Ethical Standard;

(b) Whether there are any threats to the firm's independence, and the
safeguards applied to mitigate those threats;

(c) Whether the firm has the competent personnel, time and resources
needed in order to carry out the audit in an appropriate manner; and

(d) Whether the key audit partner(s) is eligible to be appointed as a statutory
auditor.[3e]

The firm shall establish policies and procedures that require retention of 58
documentation for a period of time sufficient to permit those performing
monitoring procedures to evaluate the firm's compliance with its system of
quality control, or for a longer period if required by law or regulation.

For audits of financial statements, the firm shall establish policies and 58R-1
procedures that require retention of audit documentation for a period that is
not less than any period necessary to satisfy the requirements of any applicable
laws or regulation relating to data protection and to meet the requirements for
any applicable administrative and judicial proceedings, and that is in any case
not less than six years from the date of the auditor's report.

The firm shall establish policies and procedures requiring documentation of 59
complaints and allegations and the responses to them.

For audits of financial statements, the firm shall: 59D-1

(a) Keep records of any breaches (other than breaches which the firm
reasonably considers to be minor breaches) of professional standards
and applicable legal and regulatory requirements;

(b) Keep records of any consequences of any breach recorded in accordance
with paragraph 59D-1(a), the measures taken to address such a breach
and to modify the firm's internal quality control system; and

(c) Prepare an annual report containing an overview of any measures taken
under paragraph 59D-1(b) and communicate that report internally.

59D-2   For audits of financial statements, the firm shall maintain a client account record which includes in respect of every audit:

(a)   The audited entity's name, address and place of business;

(b)   The name of the key audit partner or, where there is more than one key audit partner, the names of all the key audit partners; and

(c)   The fees charged for carrying out the audit and for other services in any financial year.

***

Application and Other Explanatory Material

Applying, and Complying with, Relevant Requirements

Considerations Specific to Smaller Firms
(Ref: Para. 14)

A1   This ISQC (UK) does not call for compliance with requirements that are not relevant, for example, in the circumstances of a sole practitioner with no staff. Requirements in this ISQC (UK) such as those for policies and procedures for the assignment of appropriate personnel to the engagement team (see paragraph 31), for review responsibilities (see paragraph 33), and for the annual communication of the results of monitoring to engagement partners within the firm (see paragraph 53) are not relevant in the absence of staff.

A1-1   Requirements for audits of financial statements that derive from the Audit Directive or the Audit Regulation are required by legislation to be complied with.[31]

Elements of a System of Quality Control
(Ref: Para. 17)

A2   In general, communication of quality control policies and procedures to firm personnel includes a description of the quality control policies and procedures and the objectives they are designed to achieve, and the message that each individual has a personal responsibility for quality and is expected to comply with these policies and procedures. Encouraging firm personnel to communicate their views or concerns on quality control matters recognizes the importance of obtaining feedback on the firm's system of quality control.

Considerations Specific to Smaller Firms

A3   Documentation and communication of policies and procedures for smaller firms may be less formal and extensive than for larger firms.

---

[31] *Directive 2006/43/EC of the European Parliament and of the Council of 17 May 2006 and Regulation (EU) No 537/2014 of the European Parliament and of the Council of 16 April 2014.*

Leadership Responsibilities for Quality within the Firm

Promoting an Internal Culture of Quality
(Ref: Para. 18)

The firm's leadership and the examples it sets significantly influence the internal **A4** culture of the firm. The promotion of a quality-oriented internal culture depends on clear, consistent and frequent actions and messages from all levels of the firm's management that emphasize the firm's quality control policies and procedures, and the requirement to:

(a)   Perform work that complies with professional standards and applicable legal and regulatory requirements; and

(b)   Issue reports that are appropriate in the circumstances.

Such actions and messages encourage a culture that recognizes and rewards high quality work. These actions and messages may be communicated by, but are not limited to, training seminars, meetings, formal or informal dialogue, mission statements, newsletters, or briefing memoranda. They may be incorporated in the firm's internal documentation and training materials, and in partner and staff appraisal procedures such that they will support and reinforce the firm's view on the importance of quality and how, practically, it is to be achieved.

Of particular importance in promoting an internal culture based on quality is the **A5** need for the firm's leadership to recognize that the firm's business strategy is subject to the overriding requirement for the firm to achieve quality in all the engagements that the firm performs. Promoting such an internal culture includes:

(a)   Establishment of policies and procedures that address performance evaluation, compensation, and promotion (including incentive systems) with regard to its personnel, in order to demonstrate the firm's overriding commitment to quality;

(b)   Assignment of management responsibilities so that commercial considerations do not override the quality of work performed; and

(c)   Provision of sufficient resources for the development, documentation and support of its quality control policies and procedures.

Assigning Operational Responsibility for the Firm's System of Quality Control
(Ref: Para. 19)

Sufficient and appropriate experience and ability enables the person or persons **A6** responsible for the firm's system of quality control to identify and understand quality control issues and to develop appropriate policies and procedures. Necessary authority enables the person or persons to implement those policies and procedures.

Relevant Ethical Requirements

Compliance with Relevant Ethical Requirements
(Ref: Para. 20)

The IESBA Code[3m] establishes the fundamental principles of professional ethics, **A7** which include:

(a)   Integrity;

[3m] *See paragraph 12(q). Auditors and assurance practitioners in the UK are subject to ethical requirements from two sources: the FRC's Ethical Standard and the ethical pronouncements established by the auditor's relevant professional body.*

(b)   Objectivity;

(c)   Professional competence and due care;

(d)   Confidentiality; and

(e)   Professional behavior.

A8   Part B of the IESBA Code[3m] illustrates how the conceptual framework is to be applied in specific situations. It provides examples of safeguards that may be appropriate to address threats to compliance with the fundamental principles and also provides examples of situations where safeguards are not available to address the threats.

A9   The fundamental principles are reinforced in particular by:

- The leadership of the firm;

- Education and training;

- Monitoring; and

- A process for dealing with non-compliance.

Definition of "Firm," "Network" and "Network Firm"
(Ref: Para. 20–25)

A10   The definitions of "firm," "network" or "network firm" in relevant ethical requirements may differ from those set out in this ISQC (UK). For example, the IESBA Code defines the "firm" as:

(i)   A sole practitioner, partnership or corporation of professional accountants;

(ii)   An entity that controls such parties through ownership, management or other means; and

(iii)   An entity controlled by such parties through ownership, management or other means.

The IESBA Code also provides guidance in relation to the terms "network" and "network firm."

In complying with the requirements in paragraphs 20–25, the definitions used in the relevant ethical requirements apply in so far as is necessary to interpret those ethical requirements.

Written Confirmation
(Ref: Para. 24)

A11   Written confirmation may be in paper or electronic form. By obtaining confirmation and taking appropriate action on information indicating non-compliance, the firm demonstrates the importance that it attaches to independence and makes the issue current for, and visible to, its personnel.

Familiarity Threat
(Ref: Para. 25)

A12   The IESBA Code[3m] discusses the familiarity threat that may be created by using the same senior personnel on an assurance engagement over a long period of time and the safeguards that might be appropriate to address such threats.

A13   Determining appropriate criteria to address familiarity threat may include matters such as:

- The nature of the engagement, including the extent to which it involves a matter of public interest; and

- The length of service of the senior personnel on the engagement.

Examples of safeguards include rotating the senior personnel or requiring an engagement quality control review.

The IESBA Code[3m] recognizes that the familiarity threat is particularly relevant in the context of financial statement audits of listed entities. For these audits, the IESBA Code requires the rotation of the key audit partner[4] after a pre-defined period, normally no more than seven years,[4a] and provides related standards and guidance. National requirements may establish shorter rotation periods.   **A14**

Considerations specific to public sector audit organizations

Statutory measures may provide safeguards for the independence of public sector auditors. However, threats to independence may still exist regardless of any statutory measures designed to protect it. Therefore, in establishing the policies and procedures required by paragraphs 20–25, the public sector auditor may have regard to the public sector mandate and address any threats to independence in that context.   **A15**

Listed entities as referred to in paragraphs 25 and A14 are not common in the public sector. However, there may be other public sector entities that are significant due to size, complexity or public interest aspects, and which consequently have a wide range of stakeholders. Therefore, there may be instances when a firm determines, based on its quality control policies and procedures, that a public sector entity is significant for the purposes of expanded quality control procedures.   **A16**

In the public sector, legislation may establish the appointments and terms of office of the auditor with engagement partner responsibility. As a result, it may not be possible to comply strictly with the engagement partner rotation requirements envisaged for listed entities. Nonetheless, for public sector entities considered significant, as noted in paragraph A16, it may be in the public interest for public sector audit organizations to establish policies and procedures to promote compliance with the spirit of rotation of engagement partner responsibility.   **A17**

Acceptance and Continuance of Client Relationships and Specific Engagements

Competence, Capabilities, and Resources
(Ref: Para. 26(a))

Consideration of whether the firm has the competence, capabilities, and resources to undertake a new engagement from a new or an existing client involves reviewing the specific requirements of the engagement and the existing partner and staff profiles at all relevant levels, and including whether: **A18**

- Firm personnel have knowledge of relevant industries or subject matters;

- Firm personnel have experience with relevant regulatory or reporting requirements, or the ability to gain the necessary skills and knowledge effectively;

---

[4] *As defined in the IESBA Code.*

The IESBA definition of "key audit partner" is not the same definition as applied in the FRC's ethical and auditing standards as the FRC's definition is derived from the Audit Directive. See paragraph 12(h)-1.

[4a] *The FRC's Ethical Standard, Section 3 – Long Association With Engagements and Entities Relevant to Engagements, specifies for the audits of public interest entities and listed companies the rotation periods for the audit engagement partner, the engagement quality control reviewer, and other key partners involved in the engagement.*

- The firm has sufficient personnel with the necessary competence and capabilities;
- Experts are available, if needed;
- Individuals meeting the criteria and eligibility requirements to perform engagement quality control review are available, where applicable; and
- The firm is able to complete the engagement within the reporting deadline.

Integrity of Client
(Ref: Para. 26(c))

A19   With regard to the integrity of a client, matters to consider include, for example:

- The identity and business reputation of the client's principal owners, key management, and those charged with its governance.
- The nature of the client's operations, including its business practices.
- Information concerning the attitude of the client's principal owners, key management and those charged with its governance towards such matters as aggressive interpretation of accounting standards and the internal control environment.
- Whether the client is aggressively concerned with maintaining the firm's fees as low as possible.
- Indications of an inappropriate limitation in the scope of work.
- Indications that the client might be involved in money laundering or other criminal activities.
- The reasons for the proposed appointment of the firm and non-reappointment of the previous firm.
- The identity and business reputation of related parties.

The extent of knowledge a firm will have regarding the integrity of a client will generally grow within the context of an ongoing relationship with that client.

A20   Sources of information on such matters obtained by the firm may include the following:

- Communications with existing or previous providers of professional accountancy services to the client in accordance with relevant ethical requirements, and discussions with other third parties.
- Inquiry of other firm personnel or third parties such as bankers, legal counsel and industry peers.
- Background searches of relevant databases.

Continuance of Client Relationship
(Ref: Para. 27(a))

A21   Deciding whether to continue a client relationship includes consideration of significant matters that have arisen during the current or previous engagements, and their implications for continuing the relationship. For example, a client may have started to expand its business operations into an area where the firm does not possess the necessary expertise.

Withdrawal
(Ref: Para. 28)

Policies and procedures on withdrawal from an engagement or from both the   **A22**
engagement and the client relationship address issues that include the following:

- Discussing with the appropriate level of the client's management and those charged with its governance the appropriate action that the firm might take based on the relevant facts and circumstances.

- If the firm determines that it is appropriate to withdraw, discussing with the appropriate level of the client's management and those charged with its governance withdrawal from the engagement or from both the engagement and the client relationship, and the reasons for the withdrawal.

- Considering whether there is a professional, legal or regulatory requirement for the firm to remain in place, or for the firm to report the withdrawal from the engagement, or from both the engagement and the client relationship, together with the reasons for the withdrawal, to regulatory authorities.

- Documenting significant matters, consultations, conclusions and the basis for the conclusions.

Statement by Auditor on Ceasing to Hold Office

The auditor of a company in the UK who ceases to hold office as auditor is   **A22-1**
required to comply with the requirements of sections 519 and 521 of the
Companies Act 2006 regarding the statement to be made by the auditor in
relation to ceasing to hold office. In addition, the auditor may need to notify the
appropriate audit authority in accordance with section 522 of the Companies
Act 2006.

Considerations Specific to Public Sector Audit Organizations
(Ref: Para. 26–28)

In the public sector, auditors may be appointed in accordance with statutory   **A23**
procedures. Accordingly, certain of the requirements and considerations regarding
the acceptance and continuance of client relationships and specific engagements
as set out paragraphs 26–28 and A18–A22 may not be relevant. Nonetheless,
establishing policies and procedures as described may provide valuable
information to public sector auditors in performing risk assessments and in
carrying out reporting responsibilities.

Human Resources
(Ref: Para. 29)

Personnel issues relevant to the firm's policies and procedures related to human   **A24**
resources include, for example:

- Recruitment.
- Performance evaluation.
- Capabilities, including time to perform assignments.
- Competence.
- Career development.
- Promotion.

- Compensation.
- The estimation of personnel needs.

Effective recruitment processes and procedures help the firm select individuals of integrity who have the capacity to develop the competence and capabilities necessary to perform the firm's work and possess the appropriate characteristics to enable them to perform competently.

A25   Competence can be developed through a variety of methods, including the following:

- Professional education.
- Continuing professional development, including training.
- Work experience.
- Coaching by more experienced staff, for example, other members of the engagement team.
- Independence education for personnel who are required to be independent.

A26   The continuing competence of the firm's personnel depends to a significant extent on an appropriate level of continuing professional development so that personnel maintain their knowledge and capabilities. Effective policies and procedures emphasize the need for continuing training for all levels of firm personnel, and provide the necessary training resources and assistance to enable personnel to develop and maintain the required competence and capabilities.

A27   The firm may use a suitably qualified external person, for example, when internal technical and training resources are unavailable.

A28   Performance evaluation, compensation and promotion procedures give due recognition and reward to the development and maintenance of competence and commitment to ethical principles. Steps a firm may take in developing and maintaining competence and commitment to ethical principles include:

- Making personnel aware of the firm's expectations regarding performance and ethical principles;
- Providing personnel with evaluation of, and counseling on, performance, progress and career development; and
- Helping personnel understand that advancement to positions of greater responsibility depends, among other things, upon performance quality and adherence to ethical principles, and that failure to comply with the firm's policies and procedures may result in disciplinary action.

Considerations Specific to Smaller Firms

A29   The size and circumstances of the firm will influence the structure of the firm's performance evaluation process. Smaller firms, in particular, may employ less formal methods of evaluating the performance of their personnel.

Assignment of Engagement Teams

Engagement Partners
(Ref: Para. 30)

A30   Policies and procedures may include systems to monitor the workload and availability of engagement partners so as to enable these individuals to have sufficient time to adequately discharge their responsibilities.

Engagement Teams
(Ref: Para. 31)

The firm's assignment of engagement teams and the determination of the level of supervision required, include for example, consideration of the engagement team's: **A31**

- Understanding of, and practical experience with, engagements of a similar nature and complexity through appropriate training and participation;

- Understanding of professional standards and legal and regulatory requirements;

- Technical knowledge and expertise, including knowledge of relevant information technology;

- Knowledge of relevant industries in which the clients operate;

- Ability to apply professional judgment; and

- Understanding of the firm's quality control policies and procedures.

Engagement Performance

Consistency in the Quality of Engagement Performance
(Ref: Para. 32(a))

The firm promotes consistency in the quality of engagement performance through its policies and procedures. This is often accomplished through written or electronic manuals, software tools or other forms of standardized documentation, and industry or subject matter-specific guidance materials. Matters addressed may include: **A32**

- How engagement teams are briefed on the engagement to obtain an understanding of the objectives of their work.

- Processes for complying with applicable engagement standards.

- Processes of engagement supervision, staff training and coaching.

- Methods of reviewing the work performed, the significant judgments made and the form of report being issued.

- Appropriate documentation of the work performed and of the timing and extent of the review.

- Processes to keep all policies and procedures current.

Appropriate teamwork and training assist less experienced members of the engagement team to clearly understand the objectives of the assigned work.   **A33**

Supervision
(Ref: Para. 32(b))

Engagement supervision includes the following: **A34**

- Tracking the progress of the engagement;

- Considering the competence and capabilities of individual members of the engagement team, whether they have sufficient time to carry out their work, whether they understand their instructions and whether the work is being carried out in accordance with the planned approach to the engagement;

- Addressing significant matters arising during the engagement, considering their significance and modifying the planned approach appropriately; and

- Identifying matters for consultation or consideration by more experienced engagement team members during the engagement.

Review
(Ref: Para. 32(c))

A35   A review consists of consideration of whether:

- The work has been performed in accordance with professional standards and applicable legal and regulatory requirements;

- Significant matters have been raised for further consideration;

- Appropriate consultations have taken place and the resulting conclusions have been documented and implemented;

- There is a need to revise the nature, timing and extent of work performed;

- The work performed supports the conclusions reached and is appropriately documented;

- The evidence obtained is sufficient and appropriate to support the report; and

- The objectives of the engagement procedures have been achieved.

Consultation
(Ref: Para. 34)

A36   Consultation includes discussion at the appropriate professional level, with individuals within or outside the firm who have specialized expertise.

A37   Consultation uses appropriate research resources as well as the collective experience and technical expertise of the firm. Consultation helps to promote quality and improves the application of professional judgment. Appropriate recognition of consultation in the firm's policies and procedures helps to promote a culture in which consultation is recognized as a strength and encourages personnel to consult on difficult or contentious matters.

A38   Effective consultation on significant technical, ethical and other matters within the firm, or where applicable, outside the firm can be achieved when those consulted:

- are given all the relevant facts that will enable them to provide informed advice; and

- have appropriate knowledge, seniority and experience,

and when conclusions resulting from consultations are appropriately documented and implemented.

A39   Documentation of consultations with other professionals that involve difficult or contentious matters that is sufficiently complete and detailed contributes to an understanding of:

- The issue on which consultation was sought; and

- The results of the consultation, including any decisions taken, the basis for those decisions and how they were implemented.

Considerations Specific to Smaller Firms

A firm needing to consult externally, for example, a firm without appropriate **A40**
internal resources, may take advantage of advisory services provided by:

● Other firms;

● Professional and regulatory bodies; or

● Commercial organizations that provide relevant quality control services.

Before contracting for such services, consideration of the competence and
capabilities of the external provider helps the firm to determine whether the
external provider is suitably qualified for that purpose.

Engagement Quality Control Review

Criteria for an Engagement Quality Control Review
(Ref: Para. 35(b))

Criteria for determining which engagements other than audits of financial **A41**
statements of listed entities are to be subject to an engagement quality control
review may include, for example:

● The nature of the engagement, including the extent to which it involves a
matter of public interest.

● The identification of unusual circumstances or risks in an engagement or
class of engagements.

● Whether laws or regulations require an engagement quality control review.

Nature, Timing and Extent of the Engagement Quality Control Review
(Ref: Para. 36–37)

The engagement report is not dated until the completion of the engagement quality **A42**
control review. However, documentation of the engagement quality control review
may be completed after the date of the report.

Conducting the engagement quality control review in a timely manner at **A43**
appropriate stages during the engagement allows significant matters to be
promptly resolved to the engagement quality control reviewer's satisfaction on
or before the date of the report.

The extent of the engagement quality control review may depend, among other **A44**
things, on the complexity of the engagement, whether the entity is a listed entity,
and the risk that the report might not be appropriate in the circumstances. The
performance of an engagement quality control review does not reduce the
responsibilities of the engagement partner.

The firm's policies and procedures set out whether there are circumstances in **A44-1**
which an engagement quality control review is performed for other audit or
public interest assurance engagements as described in paragraph 35(b).

Where the involvement of an engagement quality control reviewer provides a **A44-2**
safeguard to reduce to an acceptable level those threats to independence that have
been identified as potentially arising from the provision of non-audit or additional
services, the engagement quality control review specifically addresses the related
threat by ensuring that the work that was performed in the course of the non-audit
or additional service engagement has been properly and effectively assessed in
the context of the audit of the financial statements or other public interest
assurance engagement.

Engagement Quality Control Review of a Listed Entity
(Ref: Para. 38)

A45   Other matters relevant to evaluating the significant judgments made by the engagement team that may be considered in an engagement quality control review of an audit of financial statements of a listed entity include:

- Significant risks identified during the engagement and the responses to those risks.

- Judgments made, particularly with respect to materiality and significant risks.

- The significance and disposition of corrected and uncorrected misstatements identified during the engagement.

- The matters to be communicated to management and those charged with governance and, where applicable, other parties such as regulatory bodies.

These other matters, depending on the circumstances, may also be applicable for engagement quality control reviews for audits of the financial statements of other entities as well as reviews of financial statements and other assurance and related services engagements.

Considerations specific to public sector audit organizations

A46   Although not referred to as listed entities, as described in paragraph A16, certain public sector entities may be of sufficient significance to warrant performance of an engagement quality control review.

Criteria for the Eligibility of Engagement Quality Control Reviewers

Sufficient and Appropriate Technical Expertise, Experience and Authority
(Ref: Para. 39(a))

A47   What constitutes sufficient and appropriate technical expertise, experience and authority depends on the circumstances of the engagement. For example, the engagement quality control reviewer for an audit of the financial statements of a listed entity is likely to be an individual with sufficient and appropriate experience and authority to act as an audit engagement partner on audits of financial statements of listed entities.

Consultation with the Engagement Quality Control Reviewer
(Ref: Para. 39(b))

A48   The engagement partner may consult the engagement quality control reviewer during the engagement, for example, to establish that a judgment made by the engagement partner will be acceptable to the engagement quality control reviewer. Such consultation avoids identification of differences of opinion at a late stage of the engagement and need not compromise the engagement quality control reviewer's eligibility to perform the role. Where the nature and extent of the consultations become significant the reviewer's objectivity may be compromised unless care is taken by both the engagement team and the reviewer to maintain the reviewer's objectivity. Where this is not possible, another individual within the firm or a suitably qualified external person may be appointed to take on the role of either the engagement quality control reviewer or the person to be consulted on the engagement.

Objectivity of the Engagement Quality Control Reviewer
(Ref: Para. 40)

The firm is required to establish policies and procedures designed to maintain **A49** objectivity of the engagement quality control reviewer. Accordingly, such policies and procedures provide that the engagement quality control reviewer:

- Where practicable, is not selected by the engagement partner;
- Does not otherwise participate in the engagement during the period of review;
- Does not make decisions for the engagement team; and
- Is not subject to other considerations that would threaten the reviewer's objectivity.

Considerations specific to smaller firms

It may not be practicable, in the case of firms with few partners, for the **A50** engagement partner not to be involved in selecting the engagement quality control reviewer. Suitably qualified external persons may be contracted where sole practitioners or small firms identify engagements requiring engagement quality control reviews. Alternatively, some sole practitioners or small firms may wish to use other firms to facilitate engagement quality control reviews. Where the firm contracts suitably qualified external persons, the requirements in paragraphs 39–41 and guidance in paragraphs A47–A48 apply.

Considerations specific to public sector audit organizations

In the public sector, a statutorily appointed auditor (for example, an Auditor **A51** General, or other suitably qualified person appointed on behalf of the Auditor General) may act in a role equivalent to that of engagement partner with overall responsibility for public sector audits. In such circumstances, where applicable, the selection of the engagement quality control reviewer includes consideration of the need for independence from the audited entity and the ability of the engagement quality control reviewer to provide an objective evaluation.

Differences of Opinion
(Ref: Para. 43)

Effective procedures encourage identification of differences of opinion at an early **A52** stage, provide clear guidelines as to the successive steps to be taken thereafter, and require documentation regarding the resolution of the differences and the implementation of the conclusions reached.

Procedures to resolve such differences may include consulting with another **A53** practitioner or firm, or a professional or regulatory body.

Engagement Documentation

Completion of the Assembly of Final Engagement Files
(Ref: Para. 45)

Law or regulation may prescribe the time limits by which the assembly of final **A54** engagement files for specific types of engagement is to be completed. Where no such time limits are prescribed in law or regulation, paragraph 45 requires the firm to establish time limits that reflect the need to complete the assembly of final engagement files on a timely basis. In the case of an audit, for example, such a time limit would ordinarily not be more than 60 days after the date of the auditor's report.

A55   Where two or more different reports are issued in respect of the same subject matter information of an entity, the firm's policies and procedures relating to time limits for the assembly of final engagement files address each report as if it were for a separate engagement. This may, for example, be the case when the firm issues an auditor's report on a component's financial information for group consolidation purposes and, at a subsequent date, an auditor's report on the same financial information for statutory purposes.

Confidentiality, Safe Custody, Integrity, Accessibility and Retrievability of Engagement Documentation
(Ref: Para. 46)

A56   Relevant ethical requirements establish an obligation for the firm's personnel to observe at all times the confidentiality of information contained in engagement documentation, unless specific client authority has been given to disclose information, or there are responsibilities under law, regulation or relevant ethical requirements.[5] Specific laws or regulations may impose additional obligations on the firm's personnel to maintain client confidentiality, particularly where data of a personal nature are concerned.

A57   Whether engagement documentation is in paper, electronic or other media, the integrity, accessibility or retrievability of the underlying data may be compromised if the documentation could be altered, added to or deleted without the firm's knowledge, or if it could be permanently lost or damaged. Accordingly, controls that the firm designs and implements to avoid unauthorized alteration or loss of engagement documentation may include those that:

- Enable the determination of when and by whom engagement documentation was created, changed or reviewed;

- Protect the integrity of the information at all stages of the engagement, especially when the information is shared within the engagement team or transmitted to other parties via the Internet;

- Prevent unauthorized changes to the engagement documentation; and

- Allow access to the engagement documentation by the engagement team and other authorized parties as necessary to properly discharge their responsibilities.

A58   Controls that the firm designs and implements to maintain the confidentiality, safe custody, integrity, accessibility and retrievability of engagement documentation may include the following:

- The use of a password among engagement team members to restrict access to electronic engagement documentation to authorized users.

- Appropriate back-up routines for electronic engagement documentation at appropriate stages during the engagement.

---

[5] *See, for example, Section 140.7 and Section 225.35 of the IESBA Code.*

In the UK, the auditor has regard to paragraph 46D-1 of this ISQC (UK) and any specific requirements of the auditor's relevant professional body.

- Procedures for properly distributing engagement documentation to the team members at the start of the engagement, processing it during engagement, and collating it at the end of engagement.

- Procedures for restricting access to, and enabling proper distribution and confidential storage of, hardcopy engagement documentation.

For practical reasons, original paper documentation may be electronically scanned **A59** for inclusion in engagement files. In such cases, the firm's procedures designed to maintain the integrity, accessibility, and retrievability of the documentation may include requiring the engagement teams to:

- Generate scanned copies that reflect the entire content of the original paper documentation, including manual signatures, cross-references and annotations;

- Integrate the scanned copies into the engagement files, including indexing and signing off on the scanned copies as necessary; and

- Enable the scanned copies to be retrieved and printed as necessary.

There may be legal, regulatory or other reasons for a firm to retain original paper documentation that has been scanned.

Retention of Engagement Documentation
(Ref: Para. 47)

The needs of the firm for retention of engagement documentation, and the period **A60** of such retention, will vary with the nature of the engagement and the firm's circumstances, for example, whether the engagement documentation is needed to provide a record of matters of continuing significance to future engagements. The retention period may also depend on other factors, such as whether local law or regulation prescribes specific retention periods for certain types of engagements, or whether there are generally accepted retention periods in the jurisdiction in the absence of specific legal or regulatory requirements.

In the specific case of audit engagements, the retention period would ordinarily be **A61** no shorter than five years from the date of the auditor's report, or, if later, the date of the group auditor's report.

In the UK, for statutory audits of financial statements, engagement documentation is retained in accordance with paragraph 58R-1. For other audit engagements, this requirement is applied having regard to specific requirements of the auditor's relevant professional body.

Procedures that the firm adopts for retention of engagement documentation **A62** include those that enable the requirements of paragraph 47 to be met during the retention period, for example to:

- Enable the retrieval of, and access to, the engagement documentation during the retention period, particularly in the case of electronic documentation since the underlying technology may be upgraded or changed over time;

- Provide, where necessary, a record of changes made to engagement documentation after the engagement files have been completed; and

- Enable authorized external parties to access and review specific engagement documentation for quality control or other purposes.

Ownership of engagement documentation

A63   Unless otherwise specified by law or regulation, engagement documentation is the property of the firm. The firm may, at its discretion, make portions of, or extracts from, engagement documentation available to clients, provided such disclosure does not undermine the validity of the work performed, or, in the case of assurance engagements, the independence of the firm or its personnel.

Monitoring

Monitoring the Firm's Quality Control Policies and Procedures
(Ref: Para. 48)

A64   The purpose of monitoring compliance with quality control policies and procedures is to provide an evaluation of:

● Adherence to professional standards and legal and regulatory requirements;

● Whether the system of quality control has been appropriately designed and effectively implemented; and

● Whether the firm's quality control policies and procedures have been appropriately applied, so that reports that are issued by the firm or engagement partners are appropriate in the circumstances.

A65   Ongoing consideration and evaluation of the system of quality control include matters such as the following:

● Analysis of:

   ● New developments in professional standards and legal and regulatory requirements, and how they are reflected in the firm's policies and procedures where appropriate;

   ● Written confirmation of compliance with policies and procedures on independence;

   ● Continuing professional development, including training; and

   ● Decisions related to acceptance and continuance of client relationships and specific engagements.

● Determination of corrective actions to be taken and improvements to be made in the system, including the provision of feedback into the firm's policies and procedures relating to education and training.

● Communication to appropriate firm personnel of weaknesses identified in the system, in the level of understanding of the system, or compliance with it.

● Follow-up by appropriate firm personnel so that necessary modifications are promptly made to the quality control policies and procedures.

A66   Inspection cycle policies and procedures may, for example, specify a cycle that spans three years. The manner in which the inspection cycle is organized, including the timing of selection of individual engagements, depends on many factors, such as the following:

● The size of the firm.

● The number and geographical location of offices.

● The results of previous monitoring procedures.

- The degree of authority both personnel and offices have (for example, whether individual offices are authorized to conduct their own inspections or whether only the head office may conduct them).

- The nature and complexity of the firm's practice and organization.

- The risks associated with the firm's clients and specific engagements.

The inspection process includes the selection of individual engagements, some of   **A67**
which may be selected without prior notification to the engagement team. In determining the scope of the inspections, the firm may take into account the scope or conclusions of an independent external inspection program. However, an independent external inspection program does not act as a substitute for the firm's own internal monitoring program.

Considerations Specific to Smaller Firms

In the case of small firms, monitoring procedures may need to be performed by   **A68**
individuals who are responsible for design and implementation of the firm's quality control policies and procedures, or who may be involved in performing the engagement quality control review. A firm with a limited number of persons may choose to use a suitably qualified external person or another firm to carry out engagement inspections and other monitoring procedures. Alternatively, the firm may establish arrangements to share resources with other appropriate organizations to facilitate monitoring activities.

Communicating Deficiencies
(Ref: Para. 50)

The reporting of identified deficiencies to individuals other than the relevant   **A69**
engagement partners need not include an identification of the specific engagements concerned, although there may be cases where such identification may be necessary for the proper discharge of the responsibilities of the individuals other than the engagement partners.

Complaints and Allegations

Source of Complaints and Allegations
(Ref: Para. 55)

Complaints and allegations (which do not include those that are clearly frivolous)   **A70**
may originate from within or outside the firm. They may be made by firm personnel, clients or other third parties. They may be received by engagement team members or other firm personnel.

Investigation Policies and Procedures
(Ref: Para. 56)

Policies and procedures established for the investigation of complaints and   **A71**
allegations may include for example, that the partner supervising the investigation:

- Has sufficient and appropriate experience;

- Has authority within the firm; and

- Is otherwise not involved in the engagement.

The partner supervising the investigation may involve legal counsel as necessary.

Considerations specific to smaller firms

A72   It may not be practicable, in the case of firms with few partners, for the partner supervising the investigation not to be involved in the engagement. These small firms and sole practitioners may use the services of a suitably qualified external person or another firm to carry out the investigation into complaints and allegations.

Documentation of the System of Quality Control
(Ref: Para. 57)

A73   The form and content of documentation evidencing the operation of each of the elements of the system of quality control is a matter of judgment and depends on a number of factors, including the following:

- The size of the firm and the number of offices.

- The nature and complexity of the firm's practice and organization.

For example, large firms may use electronic databases to document matters such as independence confirmations, performance evaluations and the results of monitoring inspections.

A74   Appropriate documentation relating to monitoring includes, for example:

- Monitoring procedures, including the procedure for selecting completed engagements to be inspected.

- A record of the evaluation of:

  - Adherence to professional standards and applicable legal and regulatory requirements;

  - Whether the system of quality control has been appropriately designed and effectively implemented; and

  - Whether the firm's quality control policies and procedures have been appropriately applied, so that reports that are issued by the firm or engagement partners are appropriate in the circumstances.

- Identification of the deficiencies noted, an evaluation of their effect, and the basis for determining whether and what further action is necessary.

Considerations Specific to Smaller Firms

A75   Smaller firms may use more informal methods in the documentation of their systems of quality control such as manual notes, checklists and forms.

Part Four

International Standards on Auditing (UK)

ISA (UK) 200 (Revised June 2016) Overall Objectives of the Independent Auditor and the Conduct of an Audit in Accordance with International Standards on Auditing (UK)

(Effective for audits of financial statements for periods commencing on or after 17 June 2016)

Contents

Paragraphs

Introduction
Scope of this ISA (UK)   1 - 2
An audit of financial statements   3 - 9
Effective date   10

Overall objectives of the auditor   11 - 12

Definitions   13

Requirements
Ethical requirements relating to an audit of financial statements   14
Professional skepticism   15
Professional judgment   16
Sufficient appropriate audit evidence and audit risk   17
Conduct of an audit in accordance with ISAs (UK)   18 - 24

Application and other explanatory material
An audit of financial statements   A1 - A13
Definitions   A14 - A15
Ethical requirements relating to an audit of financial statements   A16 - A19
Professional skepticism   A20 - A24
Professional judgment   A25 - A29
Sufficient appropriate audit evidence and audit risk   A30 - A54
Conduct of an audit in accordance with ISAs (UK)   A55 - A78

Introduction

Scope of this ISA (UK)

1   This International Standard on Auditing (UK) (ISA (UK)) deals with the independent auditor's overall responsibilities when conducting an audit of financial statements in accordance with ISAs (UK). Specifically, it sets out the overall objectives of the independent auditor, and explains the nature and scope of an audit designed to enable the independent auditor to meet those objectives. It also explains the scope, authority and structure of the ISAs (UK), and includes requirements establishing the general responsibilities of the independent auditor applicable in all audits, including the obligation to comply with the ISAs (UK). The independent auditor is referred to as "the auditor" hereafter.

2   ISAs (UK) are written in the context of an audit of financial statements by an auditor. They are to be adapted as necessary in the circumstances when applied to audits of other historical financial information. ISAs (UK) do not address the responsibilities of the auditor that may exist in legislation, regulation or otherwise in connection with, for example, the offering of securities to the public.[1a] Such responsibilities may differ from those established in the ISAs (UK). Accordingly, while the auditor may find aspects of the ISAs (UK) helpful in such circumstances, it is the responsibility of the auditor to ensure compliance with all relevant legal, regulatory or professional obligations.

An Audit of Financial Statements

3   The purpose of an audit is to enhance the degree of confidence of intended users in the financial statements. This is achieved by the expression of an opinion by the auditor on whether the financial statements are prepared, in all material respects, in accordance with an applicable financial reporting framework. In the case of most general purpose frameworks, that opinion is on whether the financial statements are presented fairly, in all material respects, or give a true and fair view in accordance with the framework. An audit conducted in accordance with ISAs (UK) and relevant ethical requirements enables the auditor to form that opinion. (Ref: Para. A1)

> The scope of an audit does not, however, constitute an assurance engagement with respect to the future viability of the audited entity or on the efficiency or effectiveness with which the management or administrative body has conducted or will conduct the affairs of the entity. When conducting an audit, the auditor may identify or be required to consider related matters and, where applicable, may be required to report or to communicate with management or those charged with governance or other parties on such matters in accordance with applicable laws or regulations, the ISAs (UK) or relevant ethical requirements.

4   The financial statements subject to audit are those of the entity, prepared by management of the entity with oversight from those charged with governance.[1b]

[1a] *In the UK, standards and guidance for accountants undertaking engagements in connection with an investment circular are set out in the FRC's Standards for Investment Reporting (SIRS).*

[1b] *In the UK, those charged with governance are responsible for the preparation of the financial statements. For corporate entities, directors have a collective responsibility; those charged with governance of other types of entity may also have a collective responsibility established in applicable law or regulation or under the terms of their appointment.*

ISAs (UK) do not impose responsibilities on management or those charged with governance and do not override laws and regulations that govern their responsibilities. However, an audit in accordance with ISAs (UK) is conducted on the premise that management and, where appropriate, those charged with governance have acknowledged certain responsibilities that are fundamental to the conduct of the audit. The audit of the financial statements does not relieve management or those charged with governance of their responsibilities. (Ref: Para. A2–A11)

As the basis for the auditor's opinion, ISAs (UK) require the auditor to obtain   5
reasonable assurance about whether the financial statements as a whole are free from material misstatement, whether due to fraud or error. Reasonable assurance is a high level of assurance. It is obtained when the auditor has obtained sufficient appropriate audit evidence to reduce audit risk (that is, the risk that the auditor expresses an inappropriate opinion when the financial statements are materially misstated) to an acceptably low level. However, reasonable assurance is not an absolute level of assurance, because there are inherent limitations of an audit which result in most of the audit evidence on which the auditor draws conclusions and bases the auditor's opinion being persuasive rather than conclusive. (Ref: Para. A30–A54)

The concept of materiality is applied by the auditor both in planning and   6
performing the audit, and in evaluating the effect of identified misstatements on the audit and of uncorrected misstatements, if any, on the financial statements.[1] In general, misstatements, including omissions, are considered to be material if, individually or in the aggregate, they could reasonably be expected to influence the economic decisions of users taken on the basis of the financial statements. Judgments about materiality are made in the light of surrounding circumstances, and are affected by the auditor's perception of the financial information needs of users of the financial statements, and by the size or nature of a misstatement, or a combination of both. The auditor's opinion deals with the financial statements as a whole and therefore the auditor is not responsible for the detection of misstatements that are not material to the financial statements as a whole.

The ISAs (UK) contain objectives, requirements and application and other   7
explanatory material that are designed to support the auditor in obtaining reasonable assurance. The ISAs (UK) require that the auditor exercise professional judgment and maintain professional skepticism throughout the planning and performance of the audit and, among other things:

- Identify and assess risks of material misstatement, whether due to fraud or error, based on an understanding of the entity and its environment, including the entity's internal control.

- Obtain sufficient appropriate audit evidence about whether material misstatements exist, through designing and implementing appropriate responses to the assessed risks.

- Form an opinion on the financial statements based on conclusions drawn from the audit evidence obtained.

The form of opinion expressed by the auditor will depend upon the applicable   8
financial reporting framework and any applicable law or regulation. (Ref: Para. A12–A13)

---

[1] *ISA (UK) 320 (Revised June 2016), Materiality in Planning and Performing an Audit and ISA (UK) 450 (Revised June 2016), Evaluation of Misstatements Identified during the Audit.*

9   The auditor may also have certain other communication and reporting responsibilities to users, management, those charged with governance, or parties outside the entity, in relation to matters arising from the audit. These may be established by the ISAs (UK) or by applicable law or regulation.[2]

Effective Date

10   This ISA (UK) is effective for audits of financial statements for periods commencing on or after 17 June 2016. Earlier adoption is permitted.

Overall Objectives of the Auditor

11   In conducting an audit of financial statements, the overall objectives of the auditor are:

(a)   To obtain reasonable assurance about whether the financial statements as a whole are free from material misstatement, whether due to fraud or error, thereby enabling the auditor to express an opinion on whether the financial statements are prepared, in all material respects, in accordance with an applicable financial reporting framework; and

(b)   To report on the financial statements, and communicate as required by the ISAs (UK), in accordance with the auditor's findings.

12   In all cases when reasonable assurance cannot be obtained and a qualified opinion in the auditor's report is insufficient in the circumstances for purposes of reporting to the intended users of the financial statements, the ISAs (UK) require that the auditor disclaim an opinion or withdraw (or resign)[3] from the engagement, where withdrawal is possible under applicable law or regulation.

Definitions

13   For purposes of the ISAs (UK), the following terms have the meanings attributed below:

(a)   Applicable financial reporting framework – The financial reporting framework adopted by management and, where appropriate, those charged with governance in the preparation of the financial statements that is acceptable in view of the nature of the entity and the objective of the financial statements, or that is required by law or regulation.

The term "fair presentation framework" is used to refer to a financial reporting framework that requires compliance with the requirements of the framework and:

(i)   Acknowledges explicitly or implicitly that, to achieve fair presentation of the financial statements, it may be necessary for management to provide disclosures beyond those specifically required by the framework; or

(ii) Acknowledges explicitly that it may be necessary for management to depart from a requirement of the framework to achieve fair

---

[2] *See, for example, ISA (UK) 260 (Revised June 2016), Communication with Those Charged with Governance; and paragraph 43 of ISA (UK) 240 (Revised June 2016), The Auditor's Responsibilities Relating to Fraud in an Audit of Financial Statements.*

[3] *In the ISAs (UK), only the term "withdrawal" is used.*

presentation of the financial statements. Such departures are expected to be necessary only in extremely rare circumstances.

The term "compliance framework" is used to refer to a financial reporting framework that requires compliance with the requirements of the framework, but does not contain the acknowledgements in (i) or (ii) above.

In the UK, the applicable financial reporting framework includes the requirements of applicable law.

(b) Audit evidence – Information used by the auditor in arriving at the conclusions on which the auditor's opinion is based. Audit evidence includes both information contained in the accounting records underlying the financial statements and other information. For purposes of the ISAs (UK):

   (i) Sufficiency of audit evidence is the measure of the quantity of audit evidence. The quantity of the audit evidence needed is affected by the auditor's assessment of the risks of material misstatement and also by the quality of such audit evidence.

   (ii) Appropriateness of audit evidence is the measure of the quality of audit evidence; that is, its relevance and its reliability in providing support for the conclusions on which the auditor's opinion is based.

(c) Audit risk – The risk that the auditor expresses an inappropriate audit opinion when the financial statements are materially misstated. Audit risk is a function of the risks of material misstatement and detection risk.

(d) Auditor – "Auditor" is used to refer to the person or persons conducting the audit, usually the engagement partner or other members of the engagement team,[3a] or, as applicable, the firm. Where an ISA (UK) expressly intends that a requirement or responsibility be fulfilled by the engagement partner, the term "engagement partner" rather than "auditor" is used. "Engagement partner" and "firm" are to be read as referring to their public sector equivalents where relevant.

(e) Detection risk – The risk that the procedures performed by the auditor to reduce audit risk to an acceptably low level will not detect a misstatement that exists and that could be material, either individually or when aggregated with other misstatements.

(f) Financial statements – A structured representation of historical financial information, including disclosures, intended to communicate an entity's economic resources or obligations at a point in time or the changes therein for a period of time in accordance with a financial reporting framework. The term "financial statements" ordinarily refers to a complete set of financial statements as determined by the requirements of the applicable financial reporting framework, but can also refer to a single financial statement. Disclosures comprise explanatory or descriptive information, set out as required, expressly permitted or otherwise allowed by the applicable financial reporting framework, on the face of a financial statement, or in the notes, or incorporated therein by cross-reference. (Ref: Para. A14–A15)

(g) Historical financial information – Information expressed in financial terms in relation to a particular entity, derived primarily from that entity's

---

[3a] *In the UK, this includes the key audit partner as defined in ISA (UK) 220 (Revised June 2016), Quality Control for an Audit of Financial Statements, paragraph 7D-1(d).*

accounting system, about economic events occurring in past time periods or about economic conditions or circumstances at points in time in the past.

(h) Management – The person(s) with executive responsibility for the conduct of the entity's operations. For some entities in some jurisdictions, management includes some or all of those charged with governance, for example, executive members of a governance board, or an owner-manager.

In the UK, management will not normally include non-executive directors.

(i) Misstatement – A difference between the amount, classification, presentation, or disclosure of a reported financial statement item and the amount, classification, presentation, or disclosure that is required for the item to be in accordance with the applicable financial reporting framework. Misstatements can arise from error or fraud.

Where the auditor expresses an opinion on whether the financial statements are presented fairly, in all material respects, or give a true and fair view, misstatements also include those adjustments of amounts, classifications, presentation, or disclosures that, in the auditor's judgment, are necessary for the financial statements to be presented fairly, in all material respects, or to give a true and fair view.

(j) Premise, relating to the responsibilities of management and, where appropriate, those charged with governance, on which an audit is conducted – That management and, where appropriate, those charged with governance have acknowledged and understand that they have the following responsibilities that are fundamental to the conduct of an audit in accordance with ISAs (UK). That is, responsibility:

(i)   For the preparation of the financial statements in accordance with the applicable financial reporting framework, including where relevant their fair presentation;

(ii) For such internal control as management and, where appropriate, those charged with governance determine is necessary to enable the preparation of financial statements that are free from material misstatement, whether due to fraud or error; and

(iii) To provide the auditor with:

(a) Access to all information of which management and, where appropriate, those charged with governance are aware that is relevant to the preparation of the financial statements such as records, documentation and other matters;

(b) Additional information that the auditor may request from management and, where appropriate, those charged with governance for the purpose of the audit; and

(c) Unrestricted access to persons within the entity from whom the auditor determines it necessary to obtain audit evidence.

In the case of a fair presentation framework, (i) above may be restated as "for the preparation and *fair* presentation of the financial statements in accordance with the financial reporting framework," or "for the preparation of financial statements *that give a true and fair view* in accordance with the financial reporting framework."

The "premise, relating to the responsibilities of management and, where appropriate, those charged with governance, on which an audit is conducted" may also be referred to as the "premise."

(k)   Professional judgment – The application of relevant training, knowledge and experience, within the context provided by auditing, accounting and ethical standards, in making informed decisions about the courses of action that are appropriate in the circumstances of the audit engagement.

(l)   Professional skepticism – An attitude that includes a questioning mind, being alert to conditions which may indicate possible misstatement due to error or fraud, and a critical assessment of audit evidence.

(m)   Reasonable assurance – In the context of an audit of financial statements, a high, but not absolute, level of assurance.

(n)   Risk of material misstatement – The risk that the financial statements are materially misstated prior to audit. This consists of two components, described as follows at the assertion level:

   (i)   Inherent risk – The susceptibility of an assertion about a class of transaction, account balance or disclosure to a misstatement that could be material, either individually or when aggregated with other misstatements, before consideration of any related controls.

   (ii)   Control risk – The risk that a misstatement that could occur in an assertion about a class of transaction, account balance or disclosure and that could be material, either individually or when aggregated with other misstatements, will not be prevented, or detected and corrected, on a timely basis by the entity's internal control.

(o)   Those charged with governance – The person(s) or organization(s) (for example, a corporate trustee) with responsibility for overseeing the strategic direction of the entity and obligations related to the accountability of the entity. This includes overseeing the financial reporting process. For some entities in some jurisdictions, those charged with governance may include management personnel, for example, executive members of a governance board of a private or public sector entity, or an owner-manager.

In the UK, those charged with governance include the directors (executive and non-executive) of a company and the members of an audit committee where one exists. For other types of entity it usually includes equivalent persons such as the partners, proprietors, committee of management or trustees.

Requirements

Ethical Requirements Relating to an Audit of Financial Statements

The auditor shall comply with relevant ethical requirements, including those pertaining to independence, relating to financial statement audit engagements. (Ref: Para. A16–A19)

14

Professional Skepticism

15   The auditor shall plan and perform an audit with professional skepticism recognizing that circumstances may exist that cause the financial statements to be materially misstated. (Ref: Para. A20–A24)

> In the UK, the auditor shall maintain professional skepticism throughout the audit, recognising the possibility of a material misstatement due to facts or behaviour indicating irregularities, including fraud, or error, notwithstanding the auditor's past experience of the honesty and integrity of the entity's management and of those charged with governance.

Professional Judgment

16   The auditor shall exercise professional judgment in planning and performing an audit of financial statements. (Ref: Para. A25–A29)

Sufficient Appropriate Audit Evidence and Audit Risk

17   To obtain reasonable assurance, the auditor shall obtain sufficient appropriate audit evidence to reduce audit risk to an acceptably low level and thereby enable the auditor to draw reasonable conclusions on which to base the auditor's opinion. (Ref: Para. A30–A54)

Conduct of an Audit in Accordance with ISAs (UK)

Complying with ISAs (UK) Relevant to the Audit

18   The auditor shall comply with all ISAs (UK) relevant to the audit. An ISA (UK) is relevant to the audit when the ISA (UK) is in effect and the circumstances addressed by the ISA (UK) exist. (Ref: Para. A55–A59)

19   The auditor shall have an understanding of the entire text of an ISA (UK), including its application and other explanatory material, to understand its objectives and to apply its requirements properly. (Ref: Para. A60–A68)

20   The auditor shall not represent compliance with ISAs (UK) in the auditor's report unless the auditor has complied with the requirements of this ISA (UK) and all other ISAs (UK) relevant to the audit.

Objectives Stated in Individual ISAs (UK)

21   To achieve the overall objectives of the auditor, the auditor shall use the objectives stated in relevant ISAs (UK) in planning and performing the audit, having regard to the interrelationships among the ISAs (UK), to: (Ref: Para. A69–A71)

(a)   Determine whether any audit procedures in addition to those required by the ISAs (UK) are necessary in pursuance of the objectives stated in the ISAs (UK); and (Ref: Para. A72)

(b)   Evaluate whether sufficient appropriate audit evidence has been obtained. (Ref: Para. A73)

Complying with Relevant Requirements

22   Subject to paragraph 23, the auditor shall comply with each requirement of an ISA (UK) unless, in the circumstances of the audit:

(a) The entire ISA (UK) is not relevant; or

(b) The requirement is not relevant because it is conditional and the condition does not exist. (Ref: Para. A74–A75)

In exceptional circumstances, the auditor may judge it necessary to depart from a **23** relevant requirement in an ISA (UK). In such circumstances, the auditor shall perform alternative audit procedures to achieve the aim of that requirement. The need for the auditor to depart from a relevant requirement is expected to arise only where the requirement is for a specific procedure to be performed and, in the specific circumstances of the audit, that procedure would be ineffective in achieving the aim of the requirement. (Ref: Para. A76)

Failure to Achieve an Objective

If an objective in a relevant ISA (UK) cannot be achieved, the auditor shall **24** evaluate whether this prevents the auditor from achieving the overall objectives of the auditor and thereby requires the auditor, in accordance with the ISAs (UK), to modify the auditor's opinion or withdraw from the engagement (where withdrawal is possible under applicable law or regulation). Failure to achieve an objective represents a significant matter requiring documentation in accordance with ISA (UK) 230 (Revised June 2016).[4] (Ref: Para. A77–A78)

***

Application and Other Explanatory Material

An Audit of Financial Statements

Scope of the Audit
(Ref: Para. 3)

The auditor's opinion on the financial statements deals with whether the financial **A1** statements are prepared, in all material respects, in accordance with the applicable financial reporting framework. Such an opinion is common to all audits of financial statements. The auditor's opinion therefore does not assure, for example, the future viability of the entity nor the efficiency or effectiveness with which management has conducted the affairs of the entity. In some jurisdictions, however, applicable law or regulation may require auditors to provide opinions on other specific matters, such as the effectiveness of internal control, or the consistency of a separate management report with the financial statements. While the ISAs (UK) include requirements and guidance in relation to such matters to the extent that they are relevant to forming an opinion on the financial statements, the auditor would be required to undertake further work if the auditor had additional responsibilities to provide such opinions.

Preparation of the Financial Statements
(Ref: Para. 4)

Law or regulation may establish the responsibilities of management and, where **A2** appropriate, those charged with governance in relation to financial reporting. However, the extent of these responsibilities, or the way in which they are described, may differ across jurisdictions. Despite these differences, an audit in

---

[4] *ISA (UK) 230 (Revised June 2016), Audit Documentation, paragraph 8(c).*

accordance with ISAs (UK) is conducted on the premise that management and, where appropriate, those charged with governance have acknowledged and understand that they have responsibility:

(a)   For the preparation of the financial statements in accordance with the applicable financial reporting framework, including where relevant their fair presentation;

(b)   For such internal control as management and, where appropriate, those charged with governance determine is necessary to enable the preparation of financial statements that are free from material misstatement, whether due to fraud or error; and

(c)   To provide the auditor with:

    (i)   Access to all information of which management and, where appropriate, those charged with governance are aware that is relevant to the preparation of the financial statements such as records, documentation and other matters;

    (ii)   Additional information that the auditor may request from management and, where appropriate, those charged with governance for the purpose of the audit; and

    (iii) Unrestricted access to persons within the entity from whom the auditor determines it necessary to obtain audit evidence.

A3   The preparation of the financial statements by management and, where appropriate, those charged with governance requires:

●   The identification of the applicable financial reporting framework, in the context of any relevant laws or regulations.

●   The preparation of the financial statements in accordance with that framework.

●   The inclusion of an adequate description of that framework in the financial statements.

The preparation of the financial statements requires management to exercise judgment in making accounting estimates that are reasonable in the circumstances, as well as to select and apply appropriate accounting policies. These judgments are made in the context of the applicable financial reporting framework.

A4   The financial statements may be prepared in accordance with a financial reporting framework designed to meet:

●   The common financial information needs of a wide range of users (that is, "general purpose financial statements"); or

●   The financial information needs of specific users (that is, "special purpose financial statements").

A5   The applicable financial reporting framework often encompasses financial reporting standards established by an authorized or recognized standards setting organization, or legislative or regulatory requirements. In some cases, the financial reporting framework may encompass both financial reporting standards established by an authorized or recognized standards setting organization and legislative or regulatory requirements. Other sources may provide direction on the application of the applicable financial reporting framework. In some cases, the applicable financial reporting framework may encompass such other sources, or may even consist only of such sources. Such other sources may include:

- The legal and ethical environment, including statutes, regulations, court decisions, and professional ethical obligations in relation to accounting matters;

- Published accounting interpretations of varying authority issued by standards setting, professional or regulatory organizations;

- Published views of varying authority on emerging accounting issues issued by standards setting, professional or regulatory organizations;

- General and industry practices widely recognized and prevalent; and

- Accounting literature.

Where conflicts exist between the financial reporting framework and the sources from which direction on its application may be obtained, or among the sources that encompass the financial reporting framework, the source with the highest authority prevails.

The requirements of the applicable financial reporting framework determine the **A6** form and content of the financial statements. Although the framework may not specify how to account for or disclose all transactions or events, it ordinarily embodies sufficient broad principles that can serve as a basis for developing and applying accounting policies that are consistent with the concepts underlying the requirements of the framework.

Some financial reporting frameworks are fair presentation frameworks, while **A7** others are compliance frameworks. Financial reporting frameworks that encompass primarily the financial reporting standards established by an organization that is authorized or recognized to promulgate standards to be used by entities for preparing general purpose financial statements are often designed to achieve fair presentation, for example, International Financial Reporting Standards (IFRSs) issued by the International Accounting Standards Board (IASB).

The requirements of the applicable financial reporting framework also determine **A8** what constitutes a complete set of financial statements. In the case of many frameworks, financial statements are intended to provide information about the financial position, financial performance and cash flows of an entity. For such frameworks, a complete set of financial statements would include a balance sheet; an income statement; a statement of changes in equity; a cash flow statement; and related notes. For some other financial reporting frameworks, a single financial statement and the related notes might constitute a complete set of financial statements:

- For example, the International Public Sector Accounting Standard (IPSAS), "Financial Reporting Under the Cash Basis of Accounting" issued by the International Public Sector Accounting Standards Board states that the primary financial statement is a statement of cash receipts and payments when a public sector entity prepares its financial statements in accordance with that IPSAS.

- Other examples of a single financial statement, each of which would include related notes, are:

  - Balance sheet.

  - Statement of income or statement of operations.

- Statement of retained earnings.
- Statement of cash flows.
- Statement of assets and liabilities that does not include owner's equity.
- Statement of changes in owners' equity.
- Statement of revenue and expenses.
- Statement of operations by product lines.

A9   ISA (UK) 210 (Revised June 2016) establishes requirements and provides guidance on determining the acceptability of the applicable financial reporting framework.[5] ISA 800 deals with special considerations when financial statements are prepared in accordance with a special purpose framework.[6]

A10   Because of the significance of the premise to the conduct of an audit, the auditor is required to obtain the agreement of management and, where appropriate, those charged with governance that they acknowledge and understand that they have the responsibilities set out in paragraph A2 as a precondition for accepting the audit engagement.[7]

Considerations Specific to Audits in the Public Sector

A11   The mandates for audits of the financial statements of public sector entities may be broader than those of other entities. As a result, the premise, relating to management's responsibilities, on which an audit of the financial statements of a public sector entity is conducted may include additional responsibilities, such as the responsibility for the execution of transactions and events in accordance with law, regulation or other authority.[8]

Form of the Auditor's Opinion
(Ref: Para. 8)

A12   The opinion expressed by the auditor is on whether the financial statements are prepared, in all material respects, in accordance with the applicable financial reporting framework. The form of the auditor's opinion, however, will depend upon the applicable financial reporting framework and any applicable law or regulation. Most financial reporting frameworks include requirements relating to the presentation of the financial statements; for such frameworks, *preparation* of the financial statements in accordance with the applicable financial reporting framework includes *presentation*.

A13   Where the financial reporting framework is a fair presentation framework, as is generally the case for general purpose financial statements, the opinion required by the ISAs (UK) is on whether the financial statements are presented fairly, in all material respects, or give a true and fair view. Where the financial reporting framework is a compliance framework, the opinion required is on whether the financial statements are prepared, in all material respects, in accordance with the

---

[5] *ISA (UK) 210 (Revised June 2016), Agreeing the Terms of Audit Engagements, paragraph 6(a).*

[6] *ISA (UK) 800 (Revised), Special Considerations—Audits of Financial Statements Prepared in Accordance with Special Purpose Frameworks, paragraph 8.*

[7] *ISA (UK) 210 (Revised June 2016), paragraph 6(b).*

[8] *See paragraph A59.*

framework. Unless specifically stated otherwise, references in the ISAs (UK) to the auditor's opinion cover both forms of opinion.

Definitions

Financial Statements
(Ref: Para. 13(f))

Some financial reporting frameworks may refer to an entity's economic resources   **A14** or obligations in other terms. For example, these may be referred to as the entity's assets and liabilities, and the residual difference between them may be referred to as equity or equity interests.

Explanatory or descriptive information required to be included in the financial   **A15** statements by the applicable financial reporting framework may be incorporated therein by cross-reference to information in another document, such as a management report or a risk report. "Incorporated therein by cross-reference" means cross-referenced from the financial statements to the other document, but not from the other document to the financial statements, Where the applicable financial reporting framework does not expressly prohibit the cross-referencing of where explanatory or descriptive information may be found, and the information has been appropriately cross-referenced, the information will form part of the financial statements.

Ethical Requirements Relating to an Audit of Financial Statements
(Ref: Para. 14)

The auditor is subject to relevant ethical requirements, including those pertaining   **A16** to independence, relating to financial statement audit engagements. Relevant ethical requirements ordinarily comprise Parts A and B of the International Ethics Standards Board of Accountants' *Code of Ethics for Professional Accountants* (the IESBA Code) related to an audit of financial statements together with national requirements that are more restrictive.

In the UK, auditors are subject to ethical requirements from two sources: the   **A16-1** FRC's Ethical Standard concerning the integrity, objectivity and independence of the auditor, and the ethical pronouncements established by the auditor's relevant professional body.

Part A of the IESBA Code establishes the fundamental principles of professional   **A17** ethics relevant to the auditor when conducting an audit of financial statements and provides a conceptual framework for applying those principles. The fundamental principles with which the auditor is required to comply by the IESBA Code are:

(a) Integrity;

(b) Objectivity;

(c) Professional competence and due care;

(d) Confidentiality; and

(e) Professional behavior.

Part B of the IESBA Code illustrates how the conceptual framework is to be applied in specific situations.

In the case of an audit engagement it is in the public interest and, therefore,   **A18** required by the IESBA Code, that the auditor be independent of the entity subject to the audit. The IESBA Code describes independence as comprising both independence of mind and independence in appearance. The auditor's independence from the entity safeguards the auditor's ability to form an audit opinion without being affected by influences that might compromise that opinion. Independence enhances the auditor's ability to act with integrity, to be objective and to maintain an attitude of professional skepticism.

A19   International Standard on Quality Control (ISQC) (UK) 1 (Revised June 2016)[9]), or national requirements that are at least as demanding,[10] deal with the firm's responsibilities to establish and maintain its system of quality control for audit engagements. ISQC (UK) 1 (Revised June 2016) sets out the responsibilities of the firm for establishing policies and procedures designed to provide it with reasonable assurance that the firm and its personnel comply with relevant ethical requirements, including those pertaining to independence.[11] ISA (UK) 220 (Revised June 2016) sets out the engagement partner's responsibilities with respect to relevant ethical requirements. These include remaining alert, through observation and making inquiries as necessary, for evidence of non-compliance with relevant ethical requirements by members of the engagement team, determining the appropriate action if matters come to the engagement partner's attention that indicate that members of the engagement team have not complied with relevant ethical requirements, and forming a conclusion on compliance with independence requirements that apply to the audit engagement.[12] ISA (UK) 220 (Revised June 2016) recognizes that the engagement team is entitled to rely on a firm's system of quality control in meeting its responsibilities with respect to quality control procedures applicable to the individual audit engagement, unless information provided by the firm or other parties suggests otherwise.

Professional Skepticism
(Ref: Para. 15)

A20   Professional skepticism includes being alert to, for example:

- Audit evidence that contradicts other audit evidence obtained.

- Information that brings into question the reliability of documents and responses to inquiries to be used as audit evidence.

- Conditions that may indicate possible fraud.

- Circumstances that suggest the need for audit procedures in addition to those required by the ISAs (UK).

A21   Maintaining professional skepticism throughout the audit is necessary if the auditor is, for example, to reduce the risks of:

- Overlooking unusual circumstances.

- Over generalizing when drawing conclusions from audit observations.

- Using inappropriate assumptions in determining the nature, timing, and extent of the audit procedures and evaluating the results thereof.

A22   Professional skepticism is necessary to the critical assessment of audit evidence. This includes questioning contradictory audit evidence and the reliability of

---

[9]   *International Standard on Quality Control (ISQC) (UK) 1 (Revised June 2016), Quality Control for Firms that Perform Audits and Reviews of Financial Statements, and Other Assurance and Related Services Engagements.*

[10]   *ISA (UK) 220 (Revised June 2016), Quality Control for an Audit of Financial Statements, paragraph 2.*

[11]   *ISQC (UK) 1 (Revised June 2016), paragraphs 20–25.*

[12]   *ISA (UK) 220 (Revised June 2016), paragraphs 9–12.*

documents and responses to inquiries and other information obtained from management and those charged with governance. It also includes consideration of the sufficiency and appropriateness of audit evidence obtained in the light of the circumstances, for example in the case where fraud risk factors exist and a single document, of a nature that is susceptible to fraud, is the sole supporting evidence for a material financial statement amount.

The auditor may accept records and documents as genuine unless the auditor has **A23** reason to believe the contrary. Nevertheless, the auditor is required to consider the reliability of information to be used as audit evidence.[13] In cases of doubt about the reliability of information or indications of possible fraud (for example, if conditions identified during the audit cause the auditor to believe that a document may not be authentic or that terms in a document may have been falsified), the ISAs (UK) require that the auditor investigate further and determine what modifications or additions to audit procedures are necessary to resolve the matter.[14]

The auditor cannot be expected to disregard past experience of the honesty and **A24** integrity of the entity's management and those charged with governance. Nevertheless, a belief that management and those charged with governance are honest and have integrity does not relieve the auditor of the need to maintain professional skepticism or allow the auditor to be satisfied with less-than-persuasive audit evidence when obtaining reasonable assurance.

Professional Judgment
(Ref: Para. 16)

Professional judgment is essential to the proper conduct of an audit. This is **A25** because interpretation of relevant ethical requirements and the ISAs (UK) and the informed decisions required throughout the audit cannot be made without the application of relevant knowledge and experience to the facts and circumstances. Professional judgment is necessary in particular regarding decisions about:

- Materiality and audit risk.

- The nature, timing, and extent of audit procedures used to meet the requirements of the ISAs (UK) and gather audit evidence.

- Evaluating whether sufficient appropriate audit evidence has been obtained, and whether more needs to be done to achieve the objectives of the ISAs (UK) and thereby, the overall objectives of the auditor.

- The evaluation of management's judgments in applying the entity's applicable financial reporting framework.

- The drawing of conclusions based on the audit evidence obtained, for example, assessing the reasonableness of the estimates made by management in preparing the financial statements.

The distinguishing feature of the professional judgment expected of an auditor is **A26** that it is exercised by an auditor whose training, knowledge and experience have assisted in developing the necessary competencies to achieve reasonable judgments.

---

[13] *ISA (UK) 500, Audit Evidence, paragraphs 7–9.*

[14] *ISA (UK) 240 (Revised June 2016), paragraph 13; ISA (UK) 500, paragraph 11; ISA (UK) 505, External Confirmations, paragraphs 10–11, and 16.*

A27　The exercise of professional judgment in any particular case is based on the facts and circumstances that are known by the auditor. Consultation on difficult or contentious matters during the course of the audit, both within the engagement team and between the engagement team and others at the appropriate level within or outside the firm, such as that required by ISA (UK) 220 (Revised June 2016),[15] assist the auditor in making informed and reasonable judgments.

A28　Professional judgment can be evaluated based on whether the judgment reached reflects a competent application of auditing and accounting principles and is appropriate in the light of, and consistent with, the facts and circumstances that were known to the auditor up to the date of the auditor's report.

A29　Professional judgment needs to be exercised throughout the audit. It also needs to be appropriately documented. In this regard, the auditor is required to prepare audit documentation sufficient to enable an experienced auditor, having no previous connection with the audit, to understand the significant professional judgments made in reaching conclusions on significant matters arising during the audit.[16] Professional judgment is not to be used as the justification for decisions that are not otherwise supported by the facts and circumstances of the engagement or sufficient appropriate audit evidence.

Sufficient Appropriate Audit Evidence and Audit Risk
(Ref: Para. 5 and 17)

Sufficiency and Appropriateness of Audit Evidence

A30　Audit evidence is necessary to support the auditor's opinion and report. It is cumulative in nature and is primarily obtained from audit procedures performed during the course of the audit. It may, however, also include information obtained from other sources such as previous audits (provided the auditor has determined whether changes have occurred since the previous audit that may affect its relevance to the current audit[17]) or a firm's quality control procedures for client acceptance and continuance. In addition to other sources inside and outside the entity, the entity's accounting records are an important source of audit evidence. Also, information that may be used as audit evidence may have been prepared by an expert employed or engaged by the entity. Audit evidence comprises both information that supports and corroborates management's assertions, and any information that contradicts such assertions. In addition, in some cases, the absence of information (for example, management's refusal to provide a requested representation) is used by the auditor, and therefore, also constitutes audit evidence. Most of the auditor's work in forming the auditor's opinion consists of obtaining and evaluating audit evidence.

A31　The sufficiency and appropriateness of audit evidence are interrelated. Sufficiency is the measure of the quantity of audit evidence. The quantity of audit evidence needed is affected by the auditor's assessment of the risks of misstatement (the higher the assessed risks, the more audit evidence is likely to be required) and also by the quality of such audit evidence (the higher the quality, the less may be required). Obtaining more audit evidence, however, may not compensate for its poor quality.

---

[15] ISA (UK) 220 (Revised June 2016), paragraph 18.

[16] ISA (UK) 230 (Revised June 2016), paragraph 8.

[17] ISA (UK) 315 (Revised June 2016), Identifying and Assessing the Risks of Material Misstatement through Understanding the Entity and Its Environment, paragraph 9.

Appropriateness is the measure of the quality of audit evidence; that is, its   **A32**
relevance and its reliability in providing support for the conclusions on which the
auditor's opinion is based. The reliability of evidence is influenced by its source
and by its nature, and is dependent on the individual circumstances under which it
is obtained.

Whether sufficient appropriate audit evidence has been obtained to reduce audit   **A33**
risk to an acceptably low level, and thereby enable the auditor to draw reasonable
conclusions on which to base the auditor's opinion, is a matter of professional
judgment. ISA (UK) 500 and other relevant ISAs (UK) establish additional
requirements and provide further guidance applicable throughout the audit
regarding the auditor's considerations in obtaining sufficient appropriate audit
evidence.

Audit Risk

Audit risk is a function of the risks of material misstatement and detection risk.   **A34**
The assessment of risks is based on audit procedures to obtain information
necessary for that purpose and evidence obtained throughout the audit. The
assessment of risks is a matter of professional judgment, rather than a matter
capable of precise measurement.

For purposes of the ISAs (UK), audit risk does not include the risk that the auditor   **A35**
might express an opinion that the financial statements are materially misstated
when they are not. This risk is ordinarily insignificant. Further, audit risk is a
technical term related to the process of auditing; it does not refer to the auditor's
business risks such as loss from litigation, adverse publicity, or other events
arising in connection with the audit of financial statements.

Risks of Material Misstatement
The risks of material misstatement may exist at two levels: **A36**

- The overall financial statement level; and

- The assertion level for classes of transactions, account balances, and
  disclosures.

Risks of material misstatement at the overall financial statement level refer to risks   **A37**
of material misstatement that relate pervasively to the financial statements as a
whole and potentially affect many assertions.

Risks of material misstatement at the assertion level are assessed in order to   **A38**
determine the nature, timing, and extent of further audit procedures necessary to
obtain sufficient appropriate audit evidence. This evidence enables the auditor to
express an opinion on the financial statements at an acceptably low level of audit
risk. Auditors use various approaches to accomplish the objective of assessing the
risks of material misstatement. For example, the auditor may make use of a model
that expresses the general relationship of the components of audit risk in
mathematical terms to arrive at an acceptable level of detection risk. Some
auditors find such a model to be useful when planning audit procedures.

The risks of material misstatement at the assertion level consist of two   **A39**
components: inherent risk and control risk. Inherent risk and control risk are the
entity's risks; they exist independently of the audit of the financial statements.

Inherent risk is higher for some assertions and related classes of transactions,   **A40**
account balances, and disclosures than for others. For example, it may be higher
for complex calculations or for accounts consisting of amounts derived from

accounting estimates that are subject to significant estimation uncertainty. External circumstances giving rise to business risks may also influence inherent risk. For example, technological developments might make a particular product obsolete, thereby causing inventory to be more susceptible to overstatement. Factors in the entity and its environment that relate to several or all of the classes of transactions, account balances, or disclosures may also influence the inherent risk related to a specific assertion. Such factors may include, for example, a lack of sufficient working capital to continue operations or a declining industry characterized by a large number of business failures.

A41 Control risk is a function of the effectiveness of the design, implementation and maintenance of internal control by management to address identified risks that threaten the achievement of the entity's objectives relevant to preparation of the entity's financial statements. However, internal control, no matter how well designed and operated, can only reduce, but not eliminate, risks of material misstatement in the financial statements, because of the inherent limitations of internal control. These include, for example, the possibility of human errors or mistakes, or of controls being circumvented by collusion or inappropriate management override. Accordingly, some control risk will always exist. The ISAs (UK) provide the conditions under which the auditor is required to, or may choose to, test the operating effectiveness of controls in determining the nature, timing and extent of substantive procedures to be performed.[18]

A42 The ISAs (UK) do not ordinarily refer to inherent risk and control risk separately, but rather to a combined assessment of the "risks of material misstatement." However, the auditor may make separate or combined assessments of inherent and control risk depending on preferred audit techniques or methodologies and practical considerations. The assessment of the risks of material misstatement may be expressed in quantitative terms, such as in percentages, or in non-quantitative terms. In any case, the need for the auditor to make appropriate risk assessments is more important than the different approaches by which they may be made.

A43 ISA (UK) 315 (Revised June 2016) establishes requirements and provides guidance on identifying and assessing the risks of material misstatement at the financial statement and assertion levels.

Detection Risk

A44 For a given level of audit risk, the acceptable level of detection risk bears an inverse relationship to the assessed risks of material misstatement at the assertion level. For example, the greater the risks of material misstatement the auditor believes exists, the less the detection risk that can be accepted and, accordingly, the more persuasive the audit evidence required by the auditor.

A45 Detection risk relates to the nature, timing, and extent of the auditor's procedures that are determined by the auditor to reduce audit risk to an acceptably low level. It is therefore a function of the effectiveness of an audit procedure and of its application by the auditor. Matters such as:

- adequate planning;
- proper assignment of personnel to the engagement team;
- the application of professional scepticism; and

---

[18] *ISA (UK) 330 (Revised July 2017), The Auditor's Reponses to Assessed Risks, paragraphs 7–17.*

- supervision and review of the audit work performed,

assist to enhance the effectiveness of an audit procedure and of its application and reduce the possibility that an auditor might select an inappropriate audit procedure, misapply an appropriate audit procedure, or misinterpret the audit results.

ISA (UK) 300 (Revised June 2016)[19] and ISA (UK) 330 (Revised July 2017) establish requirements and provide guidance on planning an audit of financial statements and the auditor's responses to assessed risks. Detection risk, however, can only be reduced, not eliminated, because of the inherent limitations of an audit. Accordingly, some detection risk will always exist.   **A46**

Inherent Limitations of an Audit

The auditor is not expected to, and cannot, reduce audit risk to zero and cannot therefore obtain absolute assurance that the financial statements are free from material misstatement due to fraud or error. This is because there are inherent limitations of an audit, which result in most of the audit evidence on which the auditor draws conclusions and bases the auditor's opinion being persuasive rather than conclusive. The inherent limitations of an audit arise from: **A47**

- The nature of financial reporting;
- The nature of audit procedures; and
- The need for the audit to be conducted within a reasonable period of time and at a reasonable cost.

The Nature of Financial Reporting

The preparation of financial statements involves judgment by management in applying the requirements of the entity's applicable financial reporting framework to the facts and circumstances of the entity. In addition, many financial statement items involve subjective decisions or assessments or a degree of uncertainty, and there may be a range of acceptable interpretations or judgments that may be made. Consequently, some financial statement items are subject to an inherent level of variability which cannot be eliminated by the application of additional auditing procedures. For example, this is often the case with respect to certain accounting estimates. Nevertheless, the ISAs (UK) require the auditor to give specific consideration to whether accounting estimates are reasonable in the context of the applicable financial reporting framework and related disclosures, and to the qualitative aspects of the entity's accounting practices, including indicators of possible bias in management's judgments.[20]   **A48**

The Nature of Audit Procedures

There are practical and legal limitations on the auditor's ability to obtain audit evidence. For example: **A49**

- There is the possibility that management or others may not provide, intentionally or unintentionally, the complete information that is relevant to the preparation of the financial statements or that has been requested by the auditor. Accordingly, the auditor cannot be certain of the completeness

---

[19] ISA (UK) 300 (Revised June 2016), *Planning an Audit of Financial Statements.*

[20] ISA (UK) 540 (Revised June 2016), *Auditing Accounting Estimates, Including Fair Value Accounting Estimates, and Related Disclosures, and ISA (UK) 700 (Revised June 2016), Forming an Opinion and Reporting on Financial Statements, paragraph 12.*

of information, even though the auditor has performed audit procedures to obtain assurance that all relevant information has been obtained.

• Fraud may involve sophisticated and carefully organized schemes designed to conceal it. Therefore, audit procedures used to gather audit evidence may be ineffective for detecting an intentional misstatement that involves, for example, collusion to falsify documentation which may cause the auditor to believe that audit evidence is valid when it is not. The auditor is neither trained as nor expected to be an expert in the authentication of documents.

• An audit is not an official investigation into alleged wrongdoing. Accordingly, the auditor is not given specific legal powers, such as the power of search, which may be necessary for such an investigation.

Timeliness of Financial Reporting and the Balance between Benefit and Cost

A50 The matter of difficulty, time, or cost involved is not in itself a valid basis for the auditor to omit an audit procedure for which there is no alternative or to be satisfied with audit evidence that is less than persuasive. Appropriate planning assists in making sufficient time and resources available for the conduct of the audit. Notwithstanding this, the relevance of information, and thereby its value, tends to diminish over time, and there is a balance to be struck between the reliability of information and its cost. This is recognized in certain financial reporting frameworks (see, for example, the IASB's "Framework for the Preparation and Presentation of Financial Statements"). Therefore, there is an expectation by users of financial statements that the auditor will form an opinion on the financial statements within a reasonable period of time and at a reasonable cost, recognizing that it is impracticable to address all information that may exist or to pursue every matter exhaustively on the assumption that information is in error or fraudulent until proved otherwise.

A51 Consequently, it is necessary for the auditor to:

• Plan the audit so that it will be performed in an effective manner;

• Direct audit effort to areas most expected to contain risks of material misstatement, whether due to fraud or error, with correspondingly less effort directed at other areas; and

• Use testing and other means of examining populations for misstatements.

A52 In light of the approaches described in paragraph A51, the ISAs (UK) contain requirements for the planning and performance of the audit and require the auditor, among other things, to:

• Have a basis for the identification and assessment of risks of material misstatement at the financial statement and assertion levels by performing risk assessment procedures and related activities;[21] and

• Use testing and other means of examining populations in a manner that provides a reasonable basis for the auditor to draw conclusions about the population.[22]

---

[21] *ISA (UK) 315 (Revised June 2016), paragraphs 5–10.*

[22] *ISA (UK) 330 (Revised July 2017); ISA (UK) 500; ISA (UK) 520, Analytical Procedures; ISA (UK) 530, Audit Sampling.*

Other Matters that Affect the Inherent Limitations of an Audit

In the case of certain assertions or subject matters, the potential effects of the **A53** inherent limitations on the auditor's ability to detect material misstatements are particularly significant. Such assertions or subject matters include:

- Fraud, particularly fraud involving senior management or collusion. See ISA (UK) 240 (Revised June 2016) for further discussion.

- The existence and completeness of related party relationships and transactions. See ISA (UK) 550[23] for further discussion.

- The occurrence of non-compliance with laws and regulations. See ISA (UK) 250 (Revised December 2017)[24] for further discussion.

- Future events or conditions that may cause an entity to cease to continue as a going concern. See ISA (UK) 570 (Revised June 2016)[25] for further discussion.

Relevant ISAs (UK) identify specific audit procedures to assist in mitigating the effect of the inherent limitations.

Because of the inherent limitations of an audit, there is an unavoidable risk that **A54** some material misstatements of the financial statements may not be detected, even though the audit is properly planned and performed in accordance with ISAs (UK). Accordingly, the subsequent discovery of a material misstatement of the financial statements resulting from fraud or error does not by itself indicate a failure to conduct an audit in accordance with ISAs (UK). However, the inherent limitations of an audit are not a justification for the auditor to be satisfied with less-than-persuasive audit evidence. Whether the auditor has performed an audit in accordance with ISAs (UK) is determined by the audit procedures performed in the circumstances, the sufficiency and appropriateness of the audit evidence obtained as a result thereof and the suitability of the auditor's report based on an evaluation of that evidence in light of the overall objectives of the auditor.

Conduct of an Audit in Accordance with ISAs (UK)

Nature of the ISAs (UK)
(Ref: Para. 18)

The ISAs (UK), taken together, provide the standards for the auditor's work in **A55** fulfilling the overall objectives of the auditor. The ISAs (UK) deal with the general responsibilities of the auditor, as well as the auditor's further considerations relevant to the application of those responsibilities to specific topics.

The scope, effective date and any specific limitation of the applicability of a **A56** specific ISA (UK) is made clear in the ISA (UK). Unless otherwise stated in the ISA (UK), the auditor is permitted to apply an ISA (UK) before the effective date specified therein.

In performing an audit, the auditor may be required to comply with legal or **A57** regulatory requirements in addition to the ISAs (UK). The ISAs (UK) do not override law or regulation that governs an audit of financial statements. In the event that such law or regulation differs from the ISAs (UK), an audit conducted

---

[23] *ISA (UK) 550, Related Parties.*

[24] *ISA (UK) 250 (Revised December 2017), Section A – Consideration of Laws and Regulations in an Audit of Financial Statements.*

[25] *ISA (UK) 570 (Revised June 2016), Going Concern.*

only in accordance with law or regulation will not automatically comply with ISAs (UK).

A58   The auditor may also conduct the audit in accordance with both ISAs (UK) and auditing standards of a specific jurisdiction or country. In such cases, in addition to complying with each of the ISAs (UK) relevant to the audit, it may be necessary for the auditor to perform additional audit procedures in order to comply with the relevant standards of that jurisdiction or country.

Considerations Specific to Audits in the Public Sector

A59   The ISAs (UK) are relevant to engagements in the public sector. The public sector auditor's responsibilities, however, may be affected by the audit mandate, or by obligations on public sector entities arising from law, regulation or other authority (such as ministerial directives, government policy requirements, or resolutions of the legislature), which may encompass a broader scope than an audit of financial statements in accordance with the ISAs (UK). These additional responsibilities are not dealt with in the ISAs (UK). They may be dealt with in the pronouncements of the International Organization of Supreme Audit Institutions or national standard setters, or in guidance developed by government audit agencies.

Contents of the ISAs (UK)
(Ref: Para. 19)

A60   In addition to objectives and requirements (requirements are expressed in the ISAs (UK) using "shall"), an ISA (UK) contains related guidance in the form of application and other explanatory material. It may also contain introductory material that provides context relevant to a proper understanding of the ISA (UK), and definitions. The entire text of an ISA (UK), therefore, is relevant to an understanding of the objectives stated in an ISA (UK) and the proper application of the requirements of an ISA (UK).

A61   Where necessary, the application and other explanatory material provides further explanation of the requirements of an ISA (UK) and guidance for carrying them out. In particular, it may:

- Explain more precisely what a requirement means or is intended to cover.

- Include examples of procedures that may be appropriate in the circumstances.

While such guidance does not in itself impose a requirement, it is relevant to the proper application of the requirements of an ISA (UK). The application and other explanatory material may also provide background information on matters addressed in an ISA (UK).

A62   Appendices form part of the application and other explanatory material. The purpose and intended use of an appendix are explained in the body of the related ISA (UK) or within the title and introduction of the appendix itself.

A63   Introductory material may include, as needed, such matters as explanation of:

- The purpose and scope of the ISA (UK), including how the ISA (UK) relates to other ISAs (UK).

- The subject matter of the ISA (UK).

- The respective responsibilities of the auditor and others in relation to the subject matter of the ISA (UK).

- The context in which the ISA (UK) is set.

An ISA (UK) may include, in a separate section under the heading "Definitions," a **A64** description of the meanings attributed to certain terms for purposes of the ISAs (UK). These are provided to assist in the consistent application and interpretation of the ISAs (UK), and are not intended to override definitions that may be established for other purposes, whether in law, regulation or otherwise. Unless otherwise indicated, those terms will carry the same meanings throughout the ISAs (UK). The Glossary of Terms relating to International Standards issued by the International Auditing and Assurance Standards Board in the *Handbook of International Quality Control, Auditing, Review, Other Assurance, and Related Services Pronouncements* published by IFAC contains a complete listing of terms defined in the ISAs (UK). It also includes descriptions of other terms found in ISAs (UK) to assist in common and consistent interpretation and translation.

When appropriate, additional considerations specific to audits of smaller entities **A65** and public sector entities are included within the application and other explanatory material of an ISA (UK). These additional considerations assist in the application of the requirements of the ISA (UK) in the audit of such entities. They do not, however, limit or reduce the responsibility of the auditor to apply and comply with the requirements of the ISAs (UK).

Considerations Specific to Smaller Entities

For purposes of specifying additional considerations to audits of smaller entities, a **A66** "smaller entity" refers to an entity which typically possesses qualitative characteristics such as:

(a) Concentration of ownership and management in a small number of individuals (often a single individual – either a natural person or another enterprise that owns the entity provided the owner exhibits the relevant qualitative characteristics); and

(b) One or more of the following:

    (i) Straightforward or uncomplicated transactions;

    (ii) Simple record-keeping;

    (iii) Few lines of business and few products within business lines;

    (iv) Few internal controls;

    (v) Few levels of management with responsibility for a broad range of controls; or

    (vi) Few personnel, many having a wide range of duties.

These qualitative characteristics are not exhaustive, they are not exclusive to smaller entities, and smaller entities do not necessarily display all of these characteristics.

The considerations specific to smaller entities included in the ISAs (UK) have **A67** been developed primarily with unlisted entities in mind. Some of the considerations, however, may be helpful in audits of smaller listed entities.

The ISAs (UK) refer to the proprietor of a smaller entity who is involved in **A68** running the entity on a day-to-day basis as the "owner-manager."

Objectives Stated in Individual ISAs (UK)
(Ref: Para. 21)

A69   Each ISA (UK) contains one or more objectives which provide a link between the requirements and the overall objectives of the auditor. The objectives in individual ISAs (UK) serve to focus the auditor on the desired outcome of the ISA (UK), while being specific enough to assist the auditor in:

● Understanding what needs to be accomplished and, where necessary, the appropriate means of doing so; and

● Deciding whether more needs to be done to achieve them in the particular circumstances of the audit.

A70   Objectives are to be understood in the context of the overall objectives of the auditor stated in paragraph 11 of this ISA (UK). As with the overall objectives of the auditor, the ability to achieve an individual objective is equally subject to the inherent limitations of an audit.

A71   In using the objectives, the auditor is required to have regard to the interrelationships among the ISAs (UK). This is because, as indicated in paragraph A55, the ISAs (UK) deal in some cases with general responsibilities and in others with the application of those responsibilities to specific topics. For example, this ISA (UK) requires the auditor to adopt an attitude of professional skepticism; this is necessary in all aspects of planning and performing an audit but is not repeated as a requirement of each ISA (UK). At a more detailed level, ISA (UK) 315 (Revised June 2016) and ISA (UK) 330 (Revised July 2017) contain, among other things, objectives and requirements that deal with the auditor's responsibilities to identify and assess the risks of material misstatement and to design and perform further audit procedures to respond to those assessed risks, respectively; these objectives and requirements apply throughout the audit. An ISA (UK) dealing with specific aspects of the audit (for example, ISA (UK) 540 (Revised June 2016)) may expand on how the objectives and requirements of such ISAs (UK) as ISA (UK) 315 (Revised June 2016) and ISA (UK) 330 (Revised July 2017) are to be applied in relation to the subject of the ISA (UK) but does not repeat them. Thus, in achieving the objective stated in ISA (UK) 540 (Revised June 2016), the auditor has regard to the objectives and requirements of other relevant ISAs (UK).

Use of Objectives to Determine Need for Additional Audit Procedures
(Ref: Para. 21(a))

A72   The requirements of the ISAs (UK) are designed to enable the auditor to achieve the objectives specified in the ISAs (UK), and thereby the overall objectives of the auditor. The proper application of the requirements of the ISAs (UK) by the auditor is therefore expected to provide a sufficient basis for the auditor's achievement of the objectives. However, because the circumstances of audit engagements vary widely and all such circumstances cannot be anticipated in the ISAs (UK), the auditor is responsible for determining the audit procedures necessary to fulfill the requirements of the ISAs (UK) and to achieve the objectives. In the circumstances of an engagement, there may be particular matters that require the auditor to perform audit procedures in addition to those required by the ISAs (UK) to meet the objectives specified in the ISAs (UK).

Use of Objectives to Evaluate Whether Sufficient Appropriate Audit Evidence Has Been Obtained
(Ref: Para. 21(b))

The auditor is required to use the objectives to evaluate whether sufficient **A73** appropriate audit evidence has been obtained in the context of the overall objectives of the auditor. If as a result the auditor concludes that the audit evidence is not sufficient and appropriate, then the auditor may follow one or more of the following approaches to meeting the requirement of paragraph 21(b):

• Evaluate whether further relevant audit evidence has been, or will be, obtained as a result of complying with other ISAs (UK);

• Extend the work performed in applying one or more requirements; or

• Perform other procedures judged by the auditor to be necessary in the circumstances.

Where none of the above is expected to be practical or possible in the circumstances, the auditor will not be able to obtain sufficient appropriate audit evidence and is required by the ISAs (UK) to determine the effect on the auditor's report or on the auditor's ability to complete the engagement.

Complying with Relevant Requirements

Relevant Requirements
(Ref: Para. 22)

In some cases, an ISA (UK) (and therefore all of its requirements) may not be **A74** relevant in the circumstances. For example, if an entity does not have an internal audit function, nothing in ISA (UK) 610 (Revised June 2013)[26] is relevant.

Within a relevant ISA (UK), there may be conditional requirements. Such a **A75** requirement is relevant when the circumstances envisioned in the requirement apply and the condition exists. In general, the conditionality of a requirement will either be explicit or implicit, for example:

• The requirement to modify the auditor's opinion if there is a limitation of scope[27] represents an explicit conditional requirement.

• The requirement to communicate significant deficiencies in internal control identified during the audit to those charged with governance,[28] which depends on the existence of such identified significant deficiencies; and the requirement to obtain sufficient appropriate audit evidence regarding the presentation and disclosure of segment information in accordance with the applicable financial reporting framework,[29] which depends on that framework requiring or permitting such disclosure, represent implicit conditional requirements.

In some cases, a requirement may be expressed as being conditional on applicable law or regulation. For example, the auditor may be required to withdraw from the audit engagement, *where withdrawal is possible under applicable law or*

---

[26] *ISA (UK) 610 (Revised June 2013), Using the Work of Internal Auditors, paragraph 2.*

[27] *ISA (UK) 705 (Revised June 2016), Modifications to the Opinion in the Independent Auditor's Report, paragraph 13.*

[28] *ISA (UK) 265, Communicating Deficiencies in Internal Control to Those Charged with Governance and Management, paragraph 9.*

[29] *ISA (UK) 501, Audit Evidence—Specific Considerations for Selected Items, paragraph 13.*

regulation, or the auditor may be required to do something, *unless prohibited by law or regulation*. Depending on the jurisdiction, the legal or regulatory permission or prohibition may be explicit or implicit.

Departure from a Requirement
(Ref: Para. 23)

A76   ISA (UK) 230 (Revised June 2016) establishes documentation requirements in those exceptional circumstances where the auditor departs from a relevant requirement.[30] The ISAs (UK) do not call for compliance with a requirement that is not relevant in the circumstances of the audit.

Failure to Achieve an Objective
(Ref: Para. 24)

A77   Whether an objective has been achieved is a matter for the auditor's professional judgment. That judgment takes account of the results of audit procedures performed in complying with the requirements of the ISAs (UK), and the auditor's evaluation of whether sufficient appropriate audit evidence has been obtained and whether more needs to be done in the particular circumstances of the audit to achieve the objectives stated in the ISAs (UK). Accordingly, circumstances that may give rise to a failure to achieve an objective include those that:

- Prevent the auditor from complying with the relevant requirements of an ISA (UK).

- Result in its not being practicable or possible for the auditor to carry out the additional audit procedures or obtain further audit evidence as determined necessary from the use of the objectives in accordance with paragraph 21, for example due to a limitation in the available audit evidence.

A78   Audit documentation that meets the requirements of ISA (UK) 230 (Revised June 2016) and the specific documentation requirements of other relevant ISAs (UK) provides evidence of the auditor's basis for a conclusion about the achievement of the overall objectives of the auditor. While it is unnecessary for the auditor to document separately (as in a checklist, for example) that individual objectives have been achieved, the documentation of a failure to achieve an objective assists the auditor's evaluation of whether such a failure has prevented the auditor from achieving the overall objectives of the auditor.

---

[30] *ISA (UK) 230 (Revised June 2016), paragraph 12.*

ISA (UK) 210 (Revised June 2016)
Agreeing the Terms of Audit Engagements
(Updated July 2017)

*(Effective for audits of financial statements for periods commencing on
or after 17 June 2016)[0]*

Contents

Paragraphs

Introduction   1 - 2
  Scope of this ISA (UK)   1
  Effective date   2

Objective   3

Definitions   4 - 5

Requirements   6 - 21
  Preconditions for an audit   6 - 8
  Agreement on audit engagement terms   9 - 12
  Recurring audits   13
  Acceptance of a change in the terms of the audit engagement   14 - 17
  Additional considerations in engagement acceptance   18 - 21

Application and other explanatory material   A1 - A37
  Scope of this ISA (UK)   A1
  Preconditions for an audit   A2 - A20
  Agreement on audit engagement terms   A21 - A27
  Recurring audits   A28
  Acceptance of a change in the terms of the audit engagement   A29 - A33-1
  Additional considerations in engagement acceptance   A34 - A37

Appendix 1: Example of an audit engagement letter

Appendix 2: Determining the acceptability of general purpose frameworks

> International Standard on Auditing (UK) (ISA (UK)) 210 (Revised June 2016), *Agreeing the Terms of Audit Engagements* should be read in conjunction with ISA (UK) 200 (Revised June 2016), *Overall Objectives of the Independent Auditor and the Conduct of an Audit in Accordance with International Standards on Auditing (UK).*

---

[0] *Conforming amendments to this standard as a result of ISA (UK) 250 (Revised July 2017), Section A—Consideration of Laws and Regulations in an Audit of Financial Statements, are included that are effective for audits of financial statements for periods commencing on or after 15 December 2017. Details of the amendments are given in the Annexure to ISA (UK) 250 (Revised July 2017).*

Introduction

Scope of this ISA (UK)

1   This International Standard on Auditing (UK) (ISA (UK)) deals with the auditor's responsibilities in agreeing the terms of the audit engagement with management and, where appropriate, those charged with governance. This includes establishing that certain preconditions for an audit, responsibility for which rests with management and, where appropriate, those charged with governance, are present. ISA (UK) 220 (Revised June 2016)[1] deals with those aspects of engagement acceptance that are within the control of the auditor. (Ref: Para. A1)

Effective Date

2   This ISA (UK) is effective for audits of financial statements for periods commencing on or after 17 June 2016. Earlier adoption is permitted.

Objective

3   The objective of the auditor is to accept or continue an audit engagement only when the basis upon which it is to be performed has been agreed, through:

(a)   Establishing whether the preconditions for an audit are present; and

(b)   Confirming that there is a common understanding between the auditor and management and, where appropriate, those charged with governance of the terms of the audit engagement.

Definitions

4   For purposes of the ISAs (UK), the following term has the meaning attributed below:

Preconditions for an audit – The use by management[1a] of an acceptable financial reporting framework in the preparation of the financial statements and the agreement of management and, where appropriate, those charged with governance to the premise[2] on which an audit is conducted.

5   For the purposes of this ISA (UK), references to "management" should be read hereafter as "management and, where appropriate, those charged with governance."

Requirements

Preconditions for an Audit

6   In order to establish whether the preconditions for an audit are present, the auditor shall:

(a)   Determine whether the financial reporting framework to be applied in the preparation of the financial statements is acceptable; and (Ref: Para. A2–A10)

---

[1]   *ISA (UK) 220 (Revised June 2016), Quality Control for an Audit of Financial Statements.*

[1a] *In the UK those charged with governance are responsible for the preparation of the financial statements.*

[2]   *ISA (UK) 200 (Revised June 2016), Overall Objectives of the Independent Auditor and the Conduct of an Audit in Accordance with International Standards on Auditing (UK), paragraph 13.*

(b)   Obtain the agreement of management that it acknowledges and understands its responsibility: (Ref: Para. A11–A14, A21)

    (i)   For the preparation of the financial statements in accordance with the applicable financial reporting framework, including where relevant their fair presentation; (Ref: Para. A15–A15-2)

    (ii)   For such internal control as management determines is necessary to enable the preparation of financial statements that are free from material misstatement, whether due to fraud or error; and (Ref: Para. A16–A19)

    (iii)   To provide the auditor with:[2a]

        (a)   Access to all information of which management is aware that is relevant to the preparation of the financial statements such as records, documentation and other matters;

        (b)   Additional information that the auditor may request from management for the purpose of the audit; and

        (c)   Unrestricted access to persons within the entity from whom the auditor determines it necessary to obtain audit evidence.

Limitation on Scope Prior to Audit Engagement Acceptance

If management or those charged with governance impose a limitation on the scope   **7** of the auditor's work in the terms of a proposed audit engagement such that the auditor believes the limitation will result in the auditor disclaiming an opinion on the financial statements, the auditor shall not accept such a limited engagement as an audit engagement, unless required by law or regulation to do so.

Other Factors Affecting Audit Engagement Acceptance

If the preconditions for an audit are not present, the auditor shall discuss the matter   **8** with management. Unless required by law or regulation to do so, the auditor shall not accept the proposed audit engagement:

(a)   If the auditor has determined that the financial reporting framework to be applied in the preparation of the financial statements is unacceptable, except as provided in paragraph 19; or

(b)   If the agreement referred to in paragraph 6(b) has not been obtained.

Agreement on Audit Engagement Terms

The auditor shall agree the terms of the audit engagement with management or   **9** those charged with governance, as appropriate. (Ref: Para. A22)

Subject to paragraph 11, the agreed terms of the audit engagement shall be   **10** recorded in an audit engagement letter or other suitable form of written agreement and shall include: (Ref: Para. A23–A27)

(a)   The objective and scope of the audit of the financial statements;

(b)   The responsibilities of the auditor;

(c)   The responsibilities of management;[2b]

[2a] *Sections 499 and 500 of the Companies Act 2006 set legal requirements in relation to the auditor's right to obtain information.*

[2b] *In the UK, the engagement letter sets out the responsibilities of those charged with governance.*

(d) Identification of the applicable financial reporting framework for the preparation of the financial statements; and

(e) Reference to the expected form and content of any reports to be issued by the auditor; and (Ref: Para. A24)

(f) A statement that there may be circumstances in which a report may differ from its expected form and content.

11 If law or regulation prescribes in sufficient detail the terms of the audit engagement referred to in paragraph 10, the auditor need not record them in a written agreement, except for the fact that such law or regulation applies and that management acknowledges and understands its responsibilities as set out in paragraph 6(b). (Ref: Para. A23, A28–A29)

12 If law or regulation prescribes responsibilities of management similar to those described in paragraph 6(b), the auditor may determine that the law or regulation includes responsibilities that, in the auditor's judgment, are equivalent in effect to those set out in that paragraph. For such responsibilities that are equivalent, the auditor may use the wording of the law or regulation to describe them in the written agreement. For those responsibilities that are not prescribed by law or regulation such that their effect is equivalent, the written agreement shall use the description in paragraph 6(b). (Ref: Para. A28)

Recurring Audits

13 On recurring audits, the auditor shall assess whether circumstances require the terms of the audit engagement to be revised and whether there is a need to remind the entity of the existing terms of the audit engagement. (Ref: Para. A30)

Acceptance of a Change in the Terms of the Audit Engagement

14 The auditor shall not agree to a change in the terms of the audit engagement where there is no reasonable justification for doing so. (Ref: Para. A31–A33)

15 If, prior to completing the audit engagement, the auditor is requested to change the audit engagement to an engagement that conveys a lower level of assurance, the auditor shall determine whether there is reasonable justification for doing so. (Ref: Para. A34–A35)

16 If the terms of the audit engagement are changed, the auditor and management shall agree on and record the new terms of the engagement in an engagement letter or other suitable form of written agreement.

17 If the auditor is unable to agree to a change of the terms of the audit engagement and is not permitted by management to continue the original audit engagement, the auditor shall:

(a) Withdraw from the audit engagement where possible under applicable law or regulation; and

(b) Determine whether there is any obligation, either contractual or otherwise, to report the circumstances to other parties, such as those charged with governance, owners or regulators. (Ref: Para. A35-1)

Additional Considerations in Engagement Acceptance

Financial Reporting Standards Supplemented by Law or Regulation

If financial reporting standards established by an authorized or recognized **18** standards setting organization are supplemented by law or regulation, the auditor shall determine whether there are any conflicts between the financial reporting standards and the additional requirements. If such conflicts exist, the auditor shall discuss with management the nature of the additional requirements and shall agree whether:

(a)   The additional requirements can be met through additional disclosures in the financial statements; or

(b)   The description of the applicable financial reporting framework in the financial statements can be amended accordingly.

If neither of the above actions is possible, the auditor shall determine whether it will be necessary to modify the auditor's opinion in accordance with ISA (UK) 705 (Revised June 2016).[3] (Ref: Para. A36)

Financial Reporting Framework Prescribed by Law or Regulation—Other Matters Affecting Acceptance

If the auditor has determined that the financial reporting framework prescribed by **19** law or regulation would be unacceptable but for the fact that it is prescribed by law or regulation, the auditor shall accept the audit engagement only if the following conditions are present: (Ref: Para. A37)

(a)   Management agrees to provide additional disclosures in the financial statements required to avoid the financial statements being misleading; and

(b)   It is recognized in the terms of the audit engagement that:

   (i)   The auditor's report on the financial statements will incorporate an Emphasis of Matter paragraph, drawing users' attention to the additional disclosures, in accordance with ISA (UK) 706 (Revised June 2016);[4] and

   (ii)   Unless the auditor is required by law or regulation to express the auditor's opinion on the financial statements by using the phrases "present fairly, in all material respects," or "give a true and fair view" in accordance with the applicable financial reporting framework, the auditor's opinion on the financial statements will not include such phrases.

If the conditions outlined in paragraph 19 are not present and the auditor is **20** required by law or regulation to undertake the audit engagement, the auditor shall:

(a)   Evaluate the effect of the misleading nature of the financial statements on the auditor's report; and

(b)   Include appropriate reference to this matter in the terms of the audit engagement.

---

[3] *ISA (UK) 705 (Revised June 2016), Modifications to the Opinion in the Independent Auditor's Report.*

[4] *ISA (UK) 706 (Revised June 2016), Emphasis of Matter Paragraphs and Other Matter Paragraphs in the Independent Auditor's Report.*

Auditor's Report Prescribed by Law or Regulation

21   In some cases, law or regulation of the relevant jurisdiction prescribes the layout or wording of the auditor's report in a form or in terms that are significantly different from the requirements of ISAs (UK). In these circumstances, the auditor shall evaluate:

(a)   Whether users might misunderstand the assurance obtained from the audit of the financial statements and, if so,

(b)   Whether additional explanation in the auditor's report can mitigate possible misunderstanding.[5]

If the auditor concludes that additional explanation in the auditor's report cannot mitigate possible misunderstanding, the auditor shall not accept the audit engagement, unless required by law or regulation to do so. An audit conducted in accordance with such law or regulation does not comply with ISAs (UK). Accordingly, the auditor shall not include any reference within the auditor's report to the audit having been conducted in accordance with ISAs (UK).[6] (Ref: Para. A38–A39)

***

Application and Other Explanatory Material

Scope of this ISA (UK)
(Ref: Para. 1)

A1   Assurance engagements, which include audit engagements, may only be accepted when the practitioner considers that relevant ethical requirements such as independence and professional competence will be satisfied, and when the engagement exhibits certain characteristics.[7] The auditor's responsibilities in respect of ethical requirements in the context of the acceptance of an audit engagement and in so far as they are within the control of the auditor are dealt with in ISA (UK) 220 (Revised June 2016).[8] This ISA (UK) deals with those matters (or preconditions) that are within the control of the entity and upon which it is necessary for the auditor and the entity's management to agree.

Preconditions for an Audit

The Financial Reporting Framework
(Ref: Para. 6(a))

A2   A condition for acceptance of an assurance engagement is that the criteria referred to in the definition of an assurance engagement are suitable and available to intended users.[9] Criteria are the benchmarks used to evaluate or measure the

---

[5]   *ISA (UK) 706 (Revised June 2016).*

[6]   *See also ISA (UK) 700 (Revised June 2016), Forming an Opinion and Reporting on Financial Statements, paragraph 43.*

[7]   *International Framework for Assurance Engagements, paragraph 17.*

The International Framework for Assurance Engagements has not been promulgated by the FRC for application in the UK.

[8]   *ISA (UK) 220 (Revised June 2016), paragraphs 9–11.*

[9]   *International Framework for Assurance Engagements, paragraph 17(b)(ii).*

The International Framework for Assurance Engagements has not been promulgated by the FRC for application in the UK.

subject matter including, where relevant, benchmarks for presentation and disclosure. Suitable criteria enable reasonably consistent evaluation or measurement of a subject matter within the context of professional judgment. For purposes of the ISAs (UK), the applicable financial reporting framework provides the criteria the auditor uses to audit the financial statements, including where relevant their fair presentation.

Without an acceptable financial reporting framework, management does not have **A3** an appropriate basis for the preparation of the financial statements and the auditor does not have suitable criteria for auditing the financial statements. In many cases the auditor may presume that the applicable financial reporting framework is acceptable, as described in paragraphs A8–A9.

Determining the Acceptability of the Financial Reporting Framework

Factors that are relevant to the auditor's determination of the acceptability of the **A4** financial reporting framework to be applied in the preparation of the financial statements include:

- The nature of the entity (for example, whether it is a business enterprise, a public sector entity or a not for profit organization);

- The purpose of the financial statements (for example, whether they are prepared to meet the common financial information needs of a wide range of users or the financial information needs of specific users);

- The nature of the financial statements (for example, whether the financial statements are a complete set of financial statements or a single financial statement); and

- Whether law or regulation prescribes the applicable financial reporting framework.

Many users of financial statements are not in a position to demand financial **A5** statements tailored to meet their specific information needs. While all the information needs of specific users cannot be met, there are financial information needs that are common to a wide range of users. Financial statements prepared in accordance with a financial reporting framework designed to meet the common financial information needs of a wide range of users are referred to as general purpose financial statements.

In some cases, the financial statements will be prepared in accordance with a **A6** financial reporting framework designed to meet the financial information needs of specific users. Such financial statements are referred to as special purpose financial statements. The financial information needs of the intended users will determine the applicable financial reporting framework in these circumstances. ISA 800 discusses the acceptability of financial reporting frameworks designed to meet the financial information needs of specific users.[10]

Deficiencies in the applicable financial reporting framework that indicate that the **A7** framework is not acceptable may be encountered after the audit engagement has been accepted. When use of that framework is prescribed by law or regulation, the requirements of paragraphs 19–20 apply. When use of that framework is not prescribed by law or regulation, management may decide to adopt another framework that is acceptable. When management does so, as required by

---

[10] *ISA 800, Special Considerations—Audits of Financial Statements Prepared in Accordance with Special Purpose Frameworks, paragraph 8.*

ISA 800 has not been promulgated by the FRC for application in the UK.

paragraph 16, new terms of the audit engagement are agreed to reflect the change in the framework as the previously agreed terms will no longer be accurate.

General purpose frameworks

A8   At present, there is no objective and authoritative basis that has been generally recognized globally for judging the acceptability of general purpose frameworks. In the absence of such a basis, financial reporting standards established by organizations that are authorized or recognized to promulgate standards to be used by certain types of entities are presumed to be acceptable for general purpose financial statements prepared by such entities, provided the organizations follow an established and transparent process involving deliberation and consideration of the views of a wide range of stakeholders. Examples of such financial reporting standards include:

- International Financial Reporting Standards (IFRSs) promulgated by the International Accounting Standards Board;

- International Public Sector Accounting Standards (IPSASs) promulgated by the International Public Sector Accounting Standards Board; and

- Accounting principles promulgated by an authorized or recognized standards setting organization in a particular jurisdiction, provided the organization follows an established and transparent process involving deliberation and consideration of the views of a wide range of stakeholders.

These financial reporting standards are often identified as the applicable financial reporting framework in law or regulation governing the preparation of general purpose financial statements.

Financial reporting frameworks prescribed by law or regulation

A9   In accordance with paragraph 6(a), the auditor is required to determine whether the financial reporting framework, to be applied in the preparation of the financial statements, is acceptable. In some jurisdictions, law or regulation may prescribe the financial reporting framework to be used in the preparation of general purpose financial statements for certain types of entities. In the absence of indications to the contrary, such a financial reporting framework is presumed to be acceptable for general purpose financial statements prepared by such entities. In the event that the framework is not considered to be acceptable, paragraphs 19–20 apply.

Jurisdictions that do not have standards setting organizations or prescribed financial reporting frameworks

A10   When an entity is registered or operating in a jurisdiction that does not have an authorized or recognized standards setting organization, or where use of the financial reporting framework is not prescribed by law or regulation, management identifies a financial reporting framework to be applied in the preparation of the financial statements. Appendix 2 contains guidance on determining the acceptability of financial reporting frameworks in such circumstances.

Agreement of the Responsibilities of Management
(Ref: Para. 6(b))

A11   An audit in accordance with ISAs (UK) is conducted on the premise that management has acknowledged and understands that it has the responsibilities set out in paragraph 6(b).[11] In certain jurisdictions, such responsibilities may be

---

[11] *ISA (UK) 200 (Revised June 2016), paragraph A2.*

specified in law or regulation. In others, there may be little or no legal or regulatory definition of such responsibilities. ISAs (UK) do not override law or regulation in such matters. However, the concept of an independent audit requires that the auditor's role does not involve taking responsibility for the preparation of the financial statements or for the entity's related internal control, and that the auditor has a reasonable expectation of obtaining the information necessary for the audit (including information obtained from outside of the general and subsidiary ledgers) in so far as management is able to provide or procure it. Accordingly, the premise is fundamental to the conduct of an independent audit. To avoid misunderstanding, agreement is reached with management that it acknowledges and understands that it has such responsibilities as part of agreeing and recording the terms of the audit engagement in paragraphs 9–12.

The way in which the responsibilities for financial reporting are divided between management and those charged with governance will vary according to the resources and structure of the entity and any relevant law or regulation, and the respective roles of management and those charged with governance within the entity. In most cases, management is responsible for execution while those charged with governance have oversight of management. In some cases, those charged with governance will have, or will assume, responsibility for approving the financial statements or monitoring the entity's internal control related to financial reporting. In larger or public entities, a subgroup of those charged with governance, such as an audit committee, may be charged with certain oversight responsibilities. **A12**

ISA (UK) 580 requires the auditor to request management to provide written representations that it has fulfilled certain of its responsibilities.[12] It may therefore be appropriate to make management aware that receipt of such written representations will be expected, together with written representations required by other ISAs (UK) and, where necessary, written representations to support other audit evidence relevant to the financial statements or one or more specific assertions in the financial statements. **A13**

Where management will not acknowledge its responsibilities, or agree to provide the written representations, the auditor will be unable to obtain sufficient appropriate audit evidence.[13] In such circumstances, it would not be appropriate for the auditor to accept the audit engagement, unless law or regulation requires the auditor to do so. In cases where the auditor is required to accept the audit engagement, the auditor may need to explain to management the importance of these matters, and the implications for the auditor's report. **A14**

Preparation of the Financial Statements
(Ref: Para. 6(b)(i))

Most financial reporting frameworks include requirements relating to the presentation of the financial statements; for such frameworks, *preparation* of the financial statements in accordance with the financial reporting framework includes *presentation*. In the case of a fair presentation framework the importance of the reporting objective of fair presentation is such that the premise agreed with management includes specific reference to fair presentation, or to the responsibility to ensure that the financial statements will "give a true and fair view" in accordance with the financial reporting framework. **A15**

---

[12] *ISA (UK) 580, Written Representations, paragraphs 10–11.*

[13] *ISA (UK) 580, paragraph A26.*

A15-1 In the UK, accounting standards relating to the small companies regime are prohibited by EU law from specifying disclosure requirements in addition to the limited number of disclosures set out in the Accounting Directive, even though the financial statements of those small entities are required by law to give a true and fair view.[13a] Further, it is not sufficient for the auditor to conclude that the financial statements give a true and fair view solely on the basis that the financial statements were prepared in accordance with accounting standards and any other applicable legal requirements.[13b] The auditor therefore considers whether additional disclosures will be necessary in the financial statements when compliance with an accounting standard is insufficient to give a true and fair view.

A15-2 Where the auditor determines that the financial statements do not provide the additional disclosures necessary to achieve fair presentation, ISA (UK) 450 (Revised June 2016)[13c] and ISA (UK) 700 (Revised June 2016)[13d] establish requirements and provide guidance on the evaluation and disposition of misstatements and the effect on the auditor's opinion in the auditor's report.

Internal Control
(Ref: Para. 6(b)(ii))

A16 Management maintains such internal control as it determines is necessary to enable the preparation of financial statements that are free from material misstatement, whether due to fraud or error. Internal control, no matter how effective, can provide an entity with only reasonable assurance about achieving the entity's financial reporting objectives due to the inherent limitations of internal control.[14]

A17 An independent audit conducted in accordance with the ISAs (UK) does not act as a substitute for the maintenance of internal control necessary for the preparation of financial statements by management. Accordingly, the auditor is required to obtain the agreement of management that it acknowledges and understands its responsibility for internal control. However, the agreement required by paragraph 6(b)(ii) does not imply that the auditor will find that internal control maintained by management has achieved its purpose or will be free of deficiencies.

A18 It is for management to determine what internal control is necessary to enable the preparation of the financial statements. The term "internal control" encompasses a wide range of activities within components that may be described as the control environment; the entity's risk assessment process; the information system, including the related business processes relevant to financial reporting, and communication; control activities; and monitoring of controls. This division, however, does not necessarily reflect how a particular entity may design, implement and maintain its internal control, or how it may classify any particular component.[15] An entity's internal control (in particular, its accounting

---

[13a] *In the United Kingdom, the Companies Act 2006 establishes this requirement.*

[13b] *ISA (UK) 700 (Revised June 2016), paragraph 16.*

[13c] *ISA (UK) 450 (Revised June 2016), Evaluation of Misstatements Identified During the Audit.*

[13d] *ISA (UK) 700 (Revised June 2016).*

[14] *ISA (UK) 315 (Revised June 2016), Identifying and Assessing the Risks of Material Misstatement through Understanding the Entity and Its Environment, paragraph A46.*

[15] *ISA (UK) 315 (Revised June 2016), paragraph A51 and Appendix 1.*

books and records, or accounting systems) will reflect the needs of management, the complexity of the business, the nature of the risks to which the entity is subject, and relevant laws or regulation.

In some jurisdictions, law or regulation may refer to the responsibility of **A19** management for the adequacy of accounting books and records, or accounting systems. In some cases, general practice may assume a distinction between accounting books and records or accounting systems on the one hand, and internal control or controls on the other. As accounting books and records, or accounting systems, are an integral part of internal control as referred to in paragraph A18, no specific reference is made to them in paragraph 6(b)(ii) for the description of the responsibility of management. To avoid misunderstanding, it may be appropriate for the auditor to explain to management the scope of this responsibility.

Additional Information
(Ref: Para. 6(b)(iii)b)

Additional information that the auditor may request from management for the purpose **A20** of the audit may include when applicable, matters related to other information in accordance with ISA (UK) 720 (Revised June 2016). When the auditor expects to obtain other information after the date of the auditor's report, the terms of the audit engagement may also acknowledge the auditor's responsibilities relating to such other information including, if applicable, the actions that may be appropriate or necessary if the auditor concludes that a material misstatement of the other information exists in other information obtained after the date of the auditor's report.[15a]

Considerations Relevant to Smaller Entities
(Ref: Para. 6(b))

One of the purposes of agreeing the terms of the audit engagement is to avoid **A21** misunderstanding about the respective responsibilities of management and the auditor. For example, when a third party has assisted with the preparation of the financial statements, it may be useful to remind management that the preparation of the financial statements in accordance with the applicable financial reporting framework remains its responsibility.

Agreement on Audit Engagement Terms

Agreeing the Terms of the Audit Engagement
(Ref: Para. 9)

The roles of management and those charged with governance in agreeing the terms **A22** of the audit engagement for the entity depend on the governance structure of the entity and relevant law or regulation.

Audit Engagement Letter or Other Form of Written Agreement[16]
(Ref: Para. 10–11)

It is in the interests of both the entity and the auditor that the auditor sends an audit **A23** engagement letter before the commencement of the audit to help avoid

---

[15a] *ISA (UK) 700 (Revised June 2016) requires that "The auditor shall not sign, and hence date, the auditor's report earlier than the date on which all the other information contained in the annual report has been approved by those charged with governance and the auditor has considered all necessary available evidence."*

[16] *In the paragraphs that follow, any reference to an audit engagement letter is to be taken as a reference to an audit engagement letter or other suitable form of written agreement.*

misunderstandings with respect to the audit. In some countries, however, the objective and scope of an audit and the responsibilities of management and of the auditor may be sufficiently established by law, that is, they prescribe the matters described in paragraph 10. Although in these circumstances paragraph 11 permits the auditor to include in the engagement letter only reference to the fact that relevant law or regulation applies and that management acknowledges and understands its responsibilities as set out in paragraph 6(b), the auditor may nevertheless consider it appropriate to include the matters described in paragraph 10 in an engagement letter for the information of management.

Form and Content of the Audit Engagement Letter

A24   The form and content of the audit engagement letter may vary for each entity. Information included in the audit engagement letter on the auditor's responsibilities may be based on ISA (UK) 200 (Revised June 2016).[17]Paragraphs 6(b) and 12 of this ISA (UK) deal with the description of the responsibilities of management. In addition to including the matters required by paragraph 10, an audit engagement letter may make reference to, for example:

●   Elaboration of the scope of the audit, including reference to applicable legislation, regulations, ISAs (UK), and ethical and other pronouncements of professional bodies to which the auditor adheres.

●   The form of any other communication of results of the audit engagement.

●   The requirement for the auditor to communicate key audit matters in the auditor's report in accordance with ISA (UK) 701.[18]

●   The fact that because of the inherent limitations of an audit, together with the inherent limitations of internal control, there is an unavoidable risk that some material misstatements may not be detected, even though the audit is properly planned and performed in accordance with ISAs (UK).

●   Arrangements regarding the planning and performance of the audit, including the composition of the audit team.

●   The expectation that management will provide written representations (see also paragraph A13).

●   The expectation that management will provide access to all information of which management is aware that is relevant to the preparation of the financial statements, including an expectation that management will provide access to information relevant to disclosures.

●   The agreement of management to make available to the auditor draft financial statements, including all information relevant to their preparation, whether obtained from within or outside of the general and subsidiary ledgers (including all information relevant to the preparation of disclosures), and the other information,[19] if any, in time to allow the auditor to complete the audit in accordance with the proposed timetable.

●   The agreement of management to inform the auditor of facts that may affect the financial statements, of which management may become aware during the period from the date of the auditor's report to the date the financial statements are issued.

---

[17] *ISA (UK) 200 (Revised June 2016), paragraphs 3–9.*

[18] *ISA (UK) 701, Communicating Key Audit Matters in the Independent Auditor's Report.*

[19] *As defined in ISA (UK) 720 (Revised June 2016), The Auditor's Responsibilities Relating to Other Information.*

- The basis on which fees are computed and any billing arrangements.

- A request for management to acknowledge receipt of the audit engagement letter and to agree to the terms of the engagement outlined therein.

When the auditor is not required to communicate key audit matters, it may be helpful for the auditor to make reference in the terms of the audit engagement to the possibility of communicating key audit matters in the auditor's report and, in certain jurisdictions, it may be necessary for the auditor to include a reference to such possibility in order to retain the ability to do so.   **A25**

When relevant, the following points could also be made in the audit engagement letter: **A26**

- Arrangements concerning the involvement of other auditors and experts in some aspects of the audit.

- Arrangements concerning the involvement of internal auditors and other staff of the entity.

- Arrangements to be made with the predecessor auditor, if any, in the case of an initial audit.

- A reference to, and description of, the auditor's responsibilities under law, regulation or relevant ethical requirements that address reporting identified or suspected non-compliance with laws and regulations to an appropriate authority outside the entity.

- Any restriction of the auditor's liability when such possibility exists.

- A reference to any further agreements between the auditor and the entity.

- Any obligations to provide audit working papers to other parties.

An example of an audit engagement letter is set out in Appendix 1.[19a]

Audits of Components

When the auditor of a parent entity is also the auditor of a component, the factors that may influence the decision whether to send a separate audit engagement letter to the component include the following: **A27**

- Who appoints the component auditor;

- Whether a separate auditor's report is to be issued on the component;

- Legal requirements in relation to audit appointments;

- Degree of ownership by parent; and

- Degree of independence of the component management from the parent entity.

Responsibilities of Management Prescribed by Law or Regulation
(Ref: Para. 11–12)

If, in the circumstances described in paragraphs A23 and A29, the auditor concludes that it is not necessary to record certain terms of the audit engagement in an audit engagement letter, the auditor is still required by paragraph 11 to seek the written agreement from management that it acknowledges and understands that it has the responsibilities set out in paragraph 6(b). However, in accordance with paragraph 12, such written   **A28**

[19a] *The example letter in Appendix 1 has not been tailored for the UK.*

agreement may use the wording of the law or regulation if such law or regulation establishes responsibilities for management that are equivalent in effect to those described in paragraph 6(b). The accounting profession, audit standards setter, or audit regulator in a jurisdiction may have provided guidance as to whether the description in law or regulation is equivalent.

Considerations specific to public sector entities

A29   Law or regulation governing the operations of public sector audits generally mandate the appointment of a public sector auditor and commonly set out the public sector auditor's responsibilities and powers, including the power to access an entity's records and other information. When law or regulation prescribes in sufficient detail the terms of the audit engagement, the public sector auditor may nonetheless consider that there are benefits in issuing a fuller audit engagement letter than permitted by paragraph 11.

Recurring Audits
(Ref: Para. 13)

A30   The auditor may decide not to send a new audit engagement letter or other written agreement each period. However, the following factors may make it appropriate to revise the terms of the audit engagement or to remind the entity of existing terms:

- Any indication that the entity misunderstands the objective and scope of the audit.

- Any revised or special terms of the audit engagement.

- A recent change of senior management.

- A significant change in ownership.

- A significant change in nature or size of the entity's business.

- A change in legal or regulatory requirements.

- A change in the financial reporting framework adopted in the preparation of the financial statements.

- A change in other reporting requirements.

Acceptance of a Change in the Terms of the Audit Engagement

Request to Change the Terms of the Audit Engagement
(Ref: Para. 14)

A31   A request from the entity for the auditor to change the terms of the audit engagement may result from a change in circumstances affecting the need for the service, a misunderstanding as to the nature of an audit as originally requested or a restriction on the scope of the audit engagement, whether imposed by management or caused by other circumstances. The auditor, as required by paragraph 14, considers the justification given for the request, particularly the implications of a restriction on the scope of the audit engagement.

A32   A change in circumstances that affects the entity's requirements or a misunderstanding concerning the nature of the service originally requested may be considered a reasonable basis for requesting a change in the audit engagement.

A33   In contrast, a change may not be considered reasonable if it appears that the change relates to information that is incorrect, incomplete or otherwise unsatisfactory. An example might be where the auditor is unable to obtain sufficient appropriate audit evidence regarding receivables and the entity asks for the audit engagement to be changed to a review engagement to avoid a qualified opinion or a disclaimer of opinion.

Request to Change to a Review or a Related Service
(Ref: Para. 15)

Before agreeing to change an audit engagement to a review or a related service, an auditor who was engaged to perform an audit in accordance with ISAs (UK) may need to assess, in addition to the matters referred to in paragraphs A31–A33 above, any legal or contractual implications of the change.   **A34**

If the auditor concludes that there is reasonable justification to change the audit engagement to a review or a related service, the audit work performed to the date of change may be relevant to the changed engagement; however, the work required to be performed and the report to be issued would be those appropriate to the revised engagement. In order to avoid confusing the reader, the report on the related service would not include reference to: **A35**

(a)   The original audit engagement; or

(b)   Any procedures that may have been performed in the original audit engagement, except where the audit engagement is changed to an engagement to undertake agreed-upon procedures and thus reference to the procedures performed is a normal part of the report.

Statement by Auditor on Ceasing to Hold Office
(Ref: Para. 17)

The auditor of a limited company in the UK who ceases to hold office as auditor is required to comply with the requirements of Sections 519 and 521 of the Companies Act 2006 regarding the statement to be made by the auditor in relation to ceasing to hold office.   **A35-1**

Additional Considerations in Engagement Acceptance

Financial Reporting Standards Supplemented by Law or Regulation
(Ref: Para. 18)

In some jurisdictions, law or regulation may supplement the financial reporting standards established by an authorized or recognized standards setting organization with additional requirements relating to the preparation of financial statements. In those jurisdictions, the applicable financial reporting framework for the purposes of applying the ISAs (UK) encompasses both the identified financial reporting framework and such additional requirements provided they do not conflict with the identified financial reporting framework. This may, for example, be the case when law or regulation prescribes disclosures in addition to those required by the financial reporting standards or when they narrow the range of acceptable choices that can be made within the financial reporting standards.[20]   **A36**

---

[20] *ISA (UK) 700 (Revised June 2016), paragraph 15, includes a requirement regarding the evaluation of whether the financial statements adequately refer to or describe the applicable financial reporting framework.*

Financial Reporting Framework Prescribed by Law or Regulation—Other Matters Affecting Acceptance
(Ref: Para. 19)

A37   Law or regulation may prescribe that the wording of the auditor's opinion use the phrases "present fairly, in all material respects" or "give a true and fair view" in a case where the auditor concludes that the applicable financial reporting framework prescribed by law or regulation would otherwise have been unacceptable. In this case, the terms of the prescribed wording of the auditor's report are significantly different from the requirements of ISAs (UK) (see paragraph 21).

Auditor's Report Prescribed by Law or Regulation
(Ref: Para. 21)

A38   ISAs (UK) require that the auditor shall not represent compliance with ISAs (UK) unless the auditor has complied with all of the ISAs (UK) relevant to the audit.[21] When law or regulation prescribes the layout or wording of the auditor's report in a form or in terms that are significantly different from the requirements of ISAs (UK) and the auditor concludes that additional explanation in the auditor's report cannot mitigate possible misunderstanding, the auditor may consider including a statement in the auditor's report that the audit is not conducted in accordance with ISAs (UK). The auditor is, however, encouraged to apply ISAs (UK), including the ISAs (UK) that address the auditor's report, to the extent practicable, notwithstanding that the auditor is not permitted to refer to the audit being conducted in accordance with ISAs (UK).

A38-1   In the UK, certain small companies are permitted by law to prepare their financial statements in accordance with the micro-entities regime[21a] in which those financial statements are presumed in law to give a true and fair view of the micro-entity's assets, liabilities, financial position and profit or loss. This financial reporting framework is not considered to be a fair presentation framework as defined in ISA (UK) 200 (Revised June 2016)[21b] as it does not explicitly or implicitly acknowledge that to achieve fair presentation of the financial statements it may be necessary for management to either provide additional disclosures beyond those required by the framework or to depart from a requirement of the framework. Accordingly, this financial reporting framework is a compliance framework.

A38-2   Whilst entities eligible to prepare financial statements in accordance with the micro-entities regime are not required by UK legislation to have those financial statements audited, in the rare circumstances that such an audit of financial statements is requested, the auditor is required by law to state whether the financial statements give a true and fair view. In accordance with paragraphs 25 and 26 of ISA (UK) 700 (Revised June 2016) expressing an unmodified opinion in terms of a true and fair view is reserved for financial statements prepared in accordance with a fair presentation framework. Accordingly, there is a risk that the auditor's report may be misunderstood by users as implying that the micro-entities regime is a fair presentation framework. The auditor

---

[21] *ISA (UK) 200 (Revised June 2016), paragraph 20.*

[21a] *The micro-entities regime consists of FRS 105 The Financial Reporting Standard applicable to the Micro-entities Regime and The Small Companies and Groups (Accounts and Directors' Report) Regulations 2008 (SI 2008/409) amended by The Small Companies (Micro-Entities' Accounts) Regulations 2013 (SI 2013/3008) and The Companies, Partnerships and Groups (Accounts and Reports) Regulations 2015 (SI 2015/980).*

[21b] *ISA (UK) 200 (Revised June 2016), paragraph 13(a).*

therefore considers this requirement in light of paragraph 21 of this ISA (UK). It may be possible for the auditor to mitigate the potential misunderstanding through the prominent inclusion of an other matter paragraph addressing this in the auditor's report in accordance with ISA (UK) 706 (Revised June 2016).

Considerations Specific to Public Sector Entities

In the public sector, specific requirements may exist within the legislation governing the audit mandate; for example, the auditor may be required to report directly to a minister, the legislature or the public if the entity attempts to limit the scope of the audit.   **A39**

Appendix 1

(Ref: Para. A24–26)

Example of an Audit Engagement Letter

The example letter in this Appendix has not been tailored for the UK.

The following is an example of an audit engagement letter for an audit of general purpose financial statements prepared in accordance with International Financial Reporting Standards. This letter is not authoritative but is intended only to be a guide that may be used in conjunction with the considerations outlined in this ISA. It will need to be varied according to individual requirements and circumstances. It is drafted to refer to the audit of financial statements for a single reporting period and would require adaptation if intended or expected to apply to recurring audits (see paragraph 13 of this ISA). It may be appropriate to seek legal advice that any proposed letter is suitable.

***

To the appropriate representative of management or those charged with governance of ABC Company:[1-a]

[*The objective and scope of the audit*]

You[2-a] have requested that we audit the financial statements of ABC Company, which comprise the statement of financial position as at December 31, 20X1, and the statement of comprehensive income, statement of changes in equity and statement of cash flows for the year then ended, and notes to the financial statements, including a summary of significant accounting policies. We are pleased to confirm our acceptance and our understanding of this audit engagement by means of this letter.

The objectives of our audit are to obtain reasonable assurance about whether the financial statements as a whole are free from material misstatement, whether due to fraud or error, and to issue an auditor's report that includes our opinion. Reasonable assurance is a high level of assurance, but is not a guarantee that an audit conducted in accordance with International Standards on Auditing (ISAs) will always detect a material misstatement when it exists. Misstatements can arise from fraud or error and are considered material if, individually or in the aggregate, they could reasonably be expected to influence the economic decisions of users taken on the basis of these financial statements.

[*The responsibilities of the auditor*]

We will conduct our audit in accordance with ISAs. Those standards require that we comply with ethical requirements. As part of an audit in accordance with ISAs, we exercise professional judgment and maintain professional skepticism throughout the audit. We also:

● Identify and assess the risks of material misstatement of the financial statements, whether due to fraud or error, design and perform audit procedures responsive to those risks, and obtain audit evidence that is

---

[1-a] *The addressees and references in the letter would be those that are appropriate in the circumstances of the engagement, including the relevant jurisdiction. It is important to refer to the appropriate persons – see paragraph A22.*

[2-a] *Throughout this letter, references to "you," "we," "us," "management," "those charged with governance" and "auditor" would be used or amended as appropriate in the circumstances.*

sufficient and appropriate to provide a basis for our opinion. The risk of not detecting a material misstatement resulting from fraud is higher than for one resulting from error, as fraud may involve collusion, forgery, intentional omissions, misrepresentations, or the override of internal control.

- Obtain an understanding of internal control relevant to the audit in order to design audit procedures that are appropriate in the circumstances, but not for the purpose of expressing an opinion on the effectiveness of the entity's internal control.[3-a] However, we will communicate to you in writing concerning any significant deficiencies in internal control relevant to the audit of the financial statements that we have identified during the audit.

- Evaluate the appropriateness of accounting policies used and the reasonableness of accounting estimates and related disclosures made by management

- Conclude on the appropriateness of management's use of the going concern basis of accounting and, based on the audit evidence obtained, whether a material uncertainty exists related to events or conditions that may cast significant doubt on the Company's ability to continue as a going concern. If we conclude that a material uncertainty exists, we are required to draw attention in our auditor's report to the related disclosures in the financial statements or, if such disclosures are inadequate, to modify our opinion. Our conclusions are based on the audit evidence obtained up to the date of our auditor's report. However, future events or conditions may cause the Company to cease to continue as a going concern.

- Evaluate the overall presentation, structure and content of the financial statements, including the disclosures, and whether the financial statements represent the underlying transactions and events in a manner that achieves fair presentation.

Because of the inherent limitations of an audit, together with the inherent limitations of internal control, there is an unavoidable risk that some material misstatements may not be detected, even though the audit is properly planned and performed in accordance with ISAs.

[The responsibilities of management and identification of the applicable financial reporting framework (for purposes of this example it is assumed that the auditor has not determined that the law or regulation prescribes those responsibilities in appropriate terms; the descriptions in paragraph 6(b) of this ISA are therefore used).]

Our audit will be conducted on the basis that [management and, where appropriate, those charged with governance][4-a] acknowledge and understand that they have responsibility:

(a) For the preparation and fair presentation of the financial statements in accordance with International Financial Reporting Standards;[5-a]

(b) For such internal control as [management] determines is necessary to enable the preparation of financial statements that are free from material misstatement, whether due to fraud or error; and

---

[3-a] *This sentence would be modified, as appropriate, in circumstances when the auditor also has responsibility to issue an opinion on the effectiveness of internal control in conjunction with the audit of the financial statements.*

[4-a] *Use terminology as appropriate in the circumstances.*

[5-a] *Or, if appropriate, "For the preparation of financial statements that give a true and fair view in accordance with International Financial Reporting Standards."*

(c)   To provide us with:[6-a]

   (i)   Access to all information of which [management] is aware that is relevant to the preparation of the financial statements such as records, documentation and other matters;

   (ii)   Additional information that we may request from [management] for the purpose of the audit; and

   (iii)   Unrestricted access to persons within the entity from whom we determine it necessary to obtain audit evidence.

As part of our audit process, we will request from [management and, where appropriate, those charged with governance], written confirmation concerning representations made to us in connection with the audit.

We look forward to full cooperation from your staff during our audit.

[*Other relevant information*]

[*Insert other information, such as fee arrangements, billings and other specific terms, as appropriate.*]

[*Reporting*]

[*Insert appropriate reference to the expected form and content of the auditor's report including, if applicable, the reporting on other information in accordance with ISA 720 (Revised).*]

The form and content of our report may need to be amended in the light of our audit findings.

Please sign and return the attached copy of this letter to indicate your acknowledgement of, and agreement with, the arrangements for our audit of the financial statements including our respective responsibilities.

XYZ & Co.

Acknowledged and agreed on behalf of ABC Company by

(signed)

....

Name and Title

Date

[6-a] *See paragraph A23 for examples of other matters relating to management's responsibilities that may be included.*

Appendix 2

(Ref: Para. A10)

Determining the Acceptability of General Purpose Frameworks

Jurisdictions that Do Not Have Authorized or Recognized Standards Setting Organizations or Financial Reporting Frameworks Prescribed by Law or Regulation

As explained in paragraph A10 of this ISA (UK), when an entity is registered or 1
operating in a jurisdiction that does not have an authorized or recognized standards setting organization, or where use of the financial reporting framework is not prescribed by law or regulation, management identifies an applicable financial reporting framework. Practice in such jurisdictions is often to use the financial reporting standards established by one of the organizations described in paragraph A8 of this ISA (UK).

Alternatively, there may be established accounting conventions in a particular 2
jurisdiction that are generally recognized as the financial reporting framework for general purpose financial statements prepared by certain specified entities operating in that jurisdiction. When such a financial reporting framework is adopted, the auditor is required by paragraph 6(a) of this ISA (UK) to determine whether the accounting conventions collectively can be considered to constitute an acceptable financial reporting framework for general purpose financial statements. When the accounting conventions are widely used in a particular jurisdiction, the accounting profession in that jurisdiction may have considered the acceptability of the financial reporting framework on behalf of the auditors. Alternatively, the auditor may make this determination by considering whether the accounting conventions exhibit attributes normally exhibited by acceptable financial reporting frameworks (see paragraph 3 below), or by comparing the accounting conventions to the requirements of an existing financial reporting framework considered to be acceptable (see paragraph 4 below).

Acceptable financial reporting frameworks normally exhibit the following 3
attributes that result in information provided in financial statements that is useful to the intended users:

(a)   Relevance, in that the information provided in the financial statements is relevant to the nature of the entity and the purpose of the financial statements. For example, in the case of a business enterprise that prepares general purpose financial statements, relevance is assessed in terms of the information necessary to meet the common financial information needs of a wide range of users in making economic decisions. These needs are ordinarily met by presenting the financial position, financial performance and cash flows of the business enterprise.

(b)   Completeness, in that transactions and events, account balances and disclosures that could affect conclusions based on the financial statements are not omitted.

(c)   Reliability, in that the information provided in the financial statements:

    (i)   Where applicable, reflects the economic substance of events and transactions and not merely their legal form; and

    (ii)   Results in reasonably consistent evaluation, measurement, presentation and disclosure, when used in similar circumstances.

(d)   Neutrality, in that it contributes to information in the financial statements that is free from bias.

(e)   Understandability, in that the information in the financial statements is clear and comprehensive and not subject to significantly different interpretation.

4   The auditor may decide to compare the accounting conventions to the requirements of an existing financial reporting framework considered to be acceptable. For example, the auditor may compare the accounting conventions to IFRSs. For an audit of a small entity, the auditor may decide to compare the accounting conventions to a financial reporting framework specifically developed for such entities by an authorized or recognized standards setting organization. When the auditor makes such a comparison and differences are identified, the decision as to whether the accounting conventions adopted in the preparation of the financial statements constitute an acceptable financial reporting framework includes considering the reasons for the differences and whether application of the accounting conventions, or the description of the financial reporting framework in the financial statements, could result in financial statements that are misleading.

5   A conglomeration of accounting conventions devised to suit individual preferences is not an acceptable financial reporting framework for general purpose financial statements. Similarly, a compliance framework will not be an acceptable financial reporting framework, unless it is generally accepted in the particular jurisdictions by preparers and users.

ISA (UK) 220
(Revised June 2016) Quality Control for an Audit of Financial Statements (Updated July 2017)

(Effective for audits of financial statements for periods commencing on or after 17 June 2016)[0]

Contents

	Paragraphs
Introduction	1 - 5
Scope of this ISA (UK)	1
System of quality control and role of engagement teams	2 - 4
Effective date	5
Objective	6
Definitions	7
Requirements	8 - 25R-2
Leadership responsibilities for quality on audits	8
Relevant ethical requirements	9 - 11
Acceptance and continuance of client relationships and audit engagements	12 - 13
Assignment of engagement teams	14
Engagement performance	15 - 22
Monitoring	23
Documentation	24 - 25R-2
Application and other explanatory material	A1 - A35
System of quality control and role of engagement teams	A1 - A2
Leadership responsibilities for quality on audits	A3 - A3-1
Relevant ethical requirements	A4 - A7
Acceptance and continuance of client relationships and audit engagements	A8 - A9
Assignment of engagement teams	A10 - A12
Engagement performance	A13 - A32
Monitoring	A33 - A35
Documentation	A36

International Standard on Auditing (UK) (ISA (UK)) 220 (Revised June 2016), *Quality Control for an Audit of Financial Statements*, should be read in conjunction with ISA (UK) 200 (Revised June 2016), *Overall Objectives of the Independent Auditor and the Conduct of an Audit in Accordance with International Standards on Auditing (UK)*.

---

[0] *Conforming amendments to this standard as a result of ISA (UK) 250 (Revised July 2017), Section A— Consideration of Laws and Regulations in an Audit of Financial Statements, are included that are effective for audits of financial statements for periods commencing on or after 15 December 2017. Details of the amendments are given in the Annexure to ISA (UK) 250 (Revised July 2017).*

Introduction

Scope of this ISA (UK)

1   This International Standard on Auditing (UK) (ISA (UK)) deals with the specific responsibilities of the auditor regarding quality control procedures for an audit of financial statements. It also addresses, where applicable, the responsibilities of the engagement quality control reviewer. This ISA (UK) is to be read in conjunction with relevant ethical requirements.

System of Quality Control and Role of Engagement Teams

2   Quality control systems, policies and procedures are the responsibility of the audit firm. Under ISQC (UK) 1 (Revised June 2016), the firm has an obligation to establish and maintain a system of quality control to provide it with reasonable assurance that:

(a)   The firm and its personnel comply with professional standards and applicable legal and regulatory requirements; and

(b)   The reports issued by the firm or engagement partners are appropriate in the circumstances.[1]

This ISA (UK) is premised on the basis that the firm is subject to ISQC (UK) 1 (Revised June 2016) or to national requirements that are at least as demanding. (Ref: Para. A1)

3   Within the context of the firm's system of quality control, engagement teams have a responsibility to implement quality control procedures that are applicable to the audit engagement and provide the firm with relevant information to enable the functioning of that part of the firm's system of quality control relating to independence.

4   Engagement teams are entitled to rely on the firm's system of quality control, unless information provided by the firm or other parties suggests otherwise. (Ref: Para. A2)

Effective Date

5   This ISA (UK) is effective for audits of financial statements for periods commencing on or after 17 June 2016. Earlier adoption is permitted.

Objective

6   The objective of the auditor is to implement quality control procedures at the engagement level that provide the auditor with reasonable assurance that:

(a)   The audit complies with professional standards and applicable legal and regulatory requirements; and

(b)   The auditor's report issued is appropriate in the circumstances.

---

[1] *ISQC (UK) 1 (Revised June 2016), Quality Control for Firms that Perform Audits and Reviews of Financial Statements, and Other Assurance and Related Services Engagements, paragraph 11.*

Definitions

For purposes of the ISAs (UK), the following terms have the meanings attributed **7** below:

(a) Engagement partner[2] – The partner or other person in the firm who is responsible for the audit engagement and its performance, and for the auditor's report that is issued on behalf of the firm, and who, where required, has the appropriate authority from a professional, legal or regulatory body.

(b) Engagement quality control review – A process designed to provide an objective evaluation, on or before the date of the auditor's report, of the significant judgments the engagement team made and the conclusions it reached in formulating the auditor's report. The engagement quality control review process is only for audits of financial statements of listed entities and those other audit engagements, if any, for which the firm has determined an engagement quality control review is required.

(c) Engagement quality control reviewer – A partner, other person in the firm, suitably qualified external person, or a team made up of such individuals, none of whom is part of the engagement team, with sufficient and appropriate experience and authority to objectively evaluate the significant judgments the engagement team made and the conclusions it reached in formulating the auditor's report.

(d) Engagement team – All partners and staff performing the engagement, and any individuals engaged by the firm or a network firm who perform audit procedures on the engagement. This excludes an auditor's external expert engaged by the firm or by a network firm.[3] The term "engagement team" also excludes individuals within the client's internal audit function who provide direct assistance on an audit engagement when the external auditor complies with the requirements of ISA (UK) 610 (Revised June 2013).[4]

(e) Firm – A sole practitioner, partnership or corporation or other entity of professional accountants.

(f) Inspection – In relation to completed audit engagements, procedures designed to provide evidence of compliance by engagement teams with the firm's quality control policies and procedures.

(f)-1 Key audit partner – Is defined in UK legislation[4a] as:

    (i) The statutory auditor designated by an audit firm for a particular audit engagement as being primarily responsible for carrying out the statutory audit on behalf of the audit firm; or

---

[2] *"Engagement partner," "partner," and "firm" should be read as referring to their public sector equivalents where relevant.*

[3] *ISA (UK) 620 (Revised June 2016), Using the Work of an Auditor's Expert, paragraph 6(a), defines the term "auditor's expert."*

[4] *ISA 610 (Revised June 2013), Using the Work of Internal Auditors, establishes limits on the use of direct assistance. It also acknowledges that the external auditor may be prohibited by law or regulation from obtaining direct assistance from internal auditors. Therefore, the use of direct assistance is restricted to situations where it is permitted.*

The use of internal auditors to provide direct assistance is prohibited in an audit conducted in accordance with ISAs (UK) – see ISA (UK) 610 (Revised June 2013), paragraph 5-1.

[4a] *In the UK, Schedule 10 to the Companies Act 2006.*

(ii)   In the case of a group audit, the statutory auditor designated by an audit firm as being primarily responsible for carrying out the statutory audit at the level of the group and the statutory auditor designated at the level of material subsidiaries; or

(iii)   The statutory auditor who signs the audit report.

(g)   Listed entity – An entity whose shares, stock or debt are quoted or listed on a recognized stock exchange, or are marketed under the regulations of a recognized stock exchange or other equivalent body.

In the UK, this includes any company in which the public can trade shares, stock or debt on the open market, such as those listed on the London Stock Exchange (including those admitted to trading on the Alternative Investments Market) and ISDX Markets. It does not include entities whose quoted or listed shares, stock or debt are in substance not freely transferable or cannot be traded freely by the public or the entity.

(h)   Monitoring – A process comprising an ongoing consideration and evaluation of the firm's system of quality control, including a periodic inspection of a selection of completed engagements, designed to provide the firm with reasonable assurance that its system of quality control is operating effectively.

(i)   Network firm – A firm or entity that belongs to a network.

(j)   Network – A larger structure:

(i)   That is aimed at cooperation, and

(ii)   That is clearly aimed at profit or cost-sharing or shares common ownership, control or management, common quality control policies and procedures, common business strategy, the use of a common brand name, or a significant part of professional resources.

(k)   Partner – Any individual with authority to bind the firm with respect to the performance of a professional services engagement.

(l)   Personnel – Partners and staff.

(m)   Professional standards – International Standards on Auditing (UK) (ISAs (UK)) and relevant ethical requirements.

(m)-1   Public interest entity – Is defined in UK legislation[4b] as:

(i)   An issuer whose transferable securities are admitted to trading on a regulated market;[4c]

(ii)   A credit institution within the meaning given by Article 4(1)(1) of Regulation (EU) No. 575/2013 of the European Parliament and of the Council, other than one listed in Article 2 of Directive 2013/36/ EU of the European Parliament and of the Council on access to the activity of credit institutions and investment firms;

(iii)   An insurance undertaking within the meaning given by Article 2(1) of Council Directive 1991/674/EEC of the European Parliament and of the Council on the annual accounts and consolidated accounts of insurance undertakings.

[4b] *In the UK, Section 494A of the Companies Act 2006.*

[4c] *In the UK, "issuer" and "regulated market" have the same meaning as in Part 6 of the Financial Services and Markets Act 2000.*

(n) Relevant ethical requirements – Ethical requirements to which the engagement team and engagement quality control reviewer are subject, which ordinarily comprise Parts A and B of the International Ethics Standards Board for Accountants' *Code of Ethics for Professional Accountants* (IESBA Code) related to an audit of financial statements together with national requirements that are more restrictive.

> Auditors in the UK are subject to ethical requirements from two sources: the FRC's Ethical Standard concerning the integrity, objectivity and independence of the auditor, and the ethical pronouncements established by the auditor's relevant professional body.

(o) Staff – Professionals, other than partners, including any experts the firm employs.

(p) Suitably qualified external person – An individual outside the firm with the competence and capabilities to act as an engagement partner, for example a partner of another firm, or an employee (with appropriate experience) of either a professional accountancy body whose members may perform audits of historical financial information or of an organization that provides relevant quality control services.

Requirements

Leadership Responsibilities for Quality on Audits

The engagement partner shall take responsibility for the overall quality on each audit engagement to which that partner is assigned. (Ref: Para. A3) **8**

Relevant Ethical Requirements

Throughout the audit engagement, the engagement partner shall remain alert, through observation and making inquiries as necessary, for evidence of non-compliance with relevant ethical requirements by members of the engagement team. (Ref: Para. A4–A5) **9**

If matters come to the engagement partner's attention through the firm's system of quality control or otherwise that indicate that members of the engagement team have not complied with relevant ethical requirements, the engagement partner, in consultation with others in the firm, shall determine the appropriate action. (Ref: Para. A5) **10**

Independence

The engagement partner shall form a conclusion on compliance with independence requirements that apply to the audit engagement. In doing so, the engagement partner shall: (Ref: Para. A5) **11**

(a) Obtain relevant information from the firm and, where applicable, network firms, to identify and evaluate circumstances and relationships that create threats to independence;

(b) Evaluate information on identified breaches, if any, of the firm's independence policies and procedures to determine whether they create a threat to independence for the audit engagement; and

(c) Take appropriate action to eliminate such threats or reduce them to an acceptable level by applying safeguards, or, if considered appropriate, to withdraw from the audit engagement, where withdrawal is possible under applicable law or regulation. The engagement partner shall promptly report to the firm any inability to resolve the matter for appropriate action. (Ref: Para. A6–A7)

Acceptance and Continuance of Client Relationships and Audit Engagements

12   The engagement partner shall be satisfied that appropriate procedures regarding the acceptance and continuance of client relationships and audit engagements have been followed, and shall determine that conclusions reached in this regard are appropriate. (Ref: Para. A8–A9)

13   If the engagement partner obtains information that would have caused the firm to decline the audit engagement had that information been available earlier, the engagement partner shall communicate that information promptly to the firm, so that the firm and the engagement partner can take the necessary action. (Ref: Para. A9)

Assignment of Engagement Teams

14   The engagement partner shall be satisfied that the engagement team, and any auditor's experts who are not part of the engagement team, collectively have the appropriate competence and capabilities to:

(a)   Perform the audit engagement in accordance with professional standards and applicable legal and regulatory requirements; and

(b)   Enable an auditor's report that is appropriate in the circumstances to be issued. (Ref: Para. A10–A12)

Engagement Performance

Direction, Supervision and Performance

15   The engagement partner shall take responsibility for:

(a)   The direction, supervision and performance of the audit engagement in compliance with professional standards and applicable legal and regulatory requirements; and (Ref: Para. A13–A15, A20)

(b)   The auditor's report being appropriate in the circumstances.

Reviews

16   The engagement partner shall take responsibility for reviews being performed in accordance with the firm's review policies and procedures. (Ref: Para. A16–A17, A20)

17   On or before the date of the auditor's report, the engagement partner shall, through a review of the audit documentation and discussion with the engagement team, be satisfied that sufficient appropriate audit evidence has been obtained to support the conclusions reached and for the auditor's report to be issued. (Ref: Para. A18–A20)

Consultation

18   The engagement partner shall:

(a)   Take responsibility for the engagement team undertaking appropriate consultation on difficult or contentious matters;

(b)   Be satisfied that members of the engagement team have undertaken appropriate consultation during the course of the engagement, both within the engagement team and between the engagement team and others at the appropriate level within or outside the firm;

(c)   Be satisfied that the nature and scope of, and conclusions resulting from, such consultations are agreed with the party consulted; and

(d)   Determine that conclusions resulting from such consultations have been implemented. (Ref: Para. A21–A22)

Engagement Quality Control Review

For audits of financial statements of listed entities, and those other audit engagements, if any, for which the firm has determined that an engagement quality control review is required, the engagement partner shall: **19**

(a)   Determine that an engagement quality control reviewer has been appointed;

(b)   Discuss significant matters arising during the audit engagement, including those identified during the engagement quality control review, with the engagement quality control reviewer; and

(c)   Not date the auditor's report until the completion of the engagement quality control review. (Ref: Para. A23–A25)

The engagement quality control reviewer shall perform an objective evaluation of the significant judgments made by the engagement team, and the conclusions reached in formulating the auditor's report. This evaluation shall involve: **20**

(a)   Discussion of significant matters with the engagement partner;

(b)   Review of the financial statements and the proposed auditor's report;

(c)   Review of selected audit documentation relating to the significant judgments the engagement team made and the conclusions it reached; and

(d)   Evaluation of the conclusions reached in formulating the auditor's report and consideration of whether the proposed auditor's report is appropriate. (Ref: Para. A26–A28, A30–A32)

For audits of financial statements of listed entities, the engagement quality control reviewer, on performing an engagement quality control review, shall also consider the following: **21**

(a)   The engagement team's evaluation of the firm's independence in relation to the audit engagement;

(b)   Whether appropriate consultation has taken place on matters involving differences of opinion or other difficult or contentious matters, and the conclusions arising from those consultations; and

(c)   Whether audit documentation selected for review reflects the work performed in relation to the significant judgments and supports the conclusions reached. (Ref: Para. A29–A32)

21R-1   For audits of financial statements of public interest entities, the engagement quality control reviewer, on performing an engagement quality control review,[4d] shall also consider the following elements:

(a)   The independence of the firm from the entity;

(b)   The significant risks which are relevant to the audit and which the key audit partner(s) has identified during the performance of the audit and the measures that the key audit partner(s) has taken to adequately manage those risks;

(c)   The reasoning of the key audit partner(s), in particular with regard to the level of materiality and the significant risks referred to in paragraph 21R-1(b);

(d)   Any request for advice to external experts and the implementation of such advice;

(e)   The nature and scope of the corrected and uncorrected misstatements in the financial statements that were identified during the carrying out of the audit;

(f)   The subjects discussed with the audit committee and management and/or supervisory bodies of the entity;

(g)   The subjects discussed with competent authorities[4e] and, where applicable, with other third parties; and

(h)   Whether the documents and information selected from the file by the engagement quality control reviewer support the opinion of the key audit partner(s) as expressed in the draft of the auditor's report and the additional report to the audit committee.[4f]

21R-2   The engagement quality control reviewer shall discuss the results of the review, including the elements assessed in paragraph 21R-1, with the key audit partner(s).

Differences of Opinion

22   If differences of opinion arise within the engagement team, with those consulted or, where applicable, between the engagement partner and the engagement quality control reviewer, the engagement team shall follow the firm's policies and procedures for dealing with and resolving differences of opinion.

Monitoring

23   An effective system of quality control includes a monitoring process designed to provide the firm with reasonable assurance that its policies and procedures relating to the system of quality control are relevant, adequate, and operating effectively. The engagement partner shall consider the results of the firm's monitoring process as evidenced in the latest information circulated by the firm and, if applicable, other network firms and whether deficiencies noted in that information may affect the audit engagement. (Ref: Para A33–A35)

[4d] *The requirement for an engagement quality control review is established in ISQC (UK) 1 (Revised June 2016), paragraph 36R-1.*

[4e] *In the UK, the competent authority designated by law is the Financial Reporting Council.*

[4f] *The requirements for these reports are set out respectively in ISA (UK) 700 (Revised June 2016), Forming an Opinion and Reporting on Financial Statements and ISA (UK) 260 (Revised June 2016), Communication with Those Charged with Governance.*

Documentation

The auditor shall include in the audit documentation:[5]   **24**

(a)   Issues identified with respect to compliance with relevant ethical requirements and how they were resolved.

(b)   Conclusions on compliance with independence requirements that apply to the audit engagement, and any relevant discussions with the firm that support these conclusions.

(c)   Conclusions reached regarding the acceptance and continuance of client relationships and audit engagements.

(d)   The nature and scope of, and conclusions resulting from, consultations undertaken during the course of the audit engagement. (Ref: Para. A36)

The auditor shall include in the audit documentation: **24D-1**

(a)   All significant threats to the firm's independence as well as the safeguards applied to mitigate those threats; and

(b)   Those matters it is required to assess before accepting or continuing a statutory audit engagement in accordance with ISQC (UK) 1 (Revised June 2016).

The engagement quality control reviewer shall document, for the audit   **25** engagement reviewed, that:

(a)   The procedures required by the firm's policies on engagement quality control review have been performed;

(b)   The engagement quality control review has been completed on or before the date of the auditor's report; and

(c)   The reviewer is not aware of any unresolved matters that would cause the reviewer to believe that the significant judgments the engagement team made and the conclusions it reached were not appropriate.

For audits of financial statements of public interest entities, the engagement   **25R-1** quality control reviewer shall also record:

(a)   The oral and written information provided by the key audit partner(s) to support the significant judgments as well as the main findings of the audit procedures carried out and the conclusions drawn from those findings, whether or not at the request of the engagement quality control reviewer; and

(b)   The opinions of the key audit partner(s), as expressed in the draft of the reports required by ISA (UK) 260 (Revised June 2016) and ISA (UK) 700 (Revised June 2016).

For audits of financial statements of public interest entities, the auditor and the   **25R-2** engagement quality control reviewer shall keep a record of the results of the engagement quality control review, together with the considerations underlying those results, in the audit documentation.

***

---

[5] *ISA (UK) 230 (Revised June 2016), Audit Documentation, paragraphs 8–11, and paragraph A6.*

Application and Other Explanatory Material

System of Quality Control and Role of Engagement Teams
(Ref: Para. 2)

A1   ISQC (UK) 1 (Revised June 2016), or national requirements that are at least as demanding, deals with the firm's responsibilities to establish and maintain its system of quality control for audit engagements. The system of quality control includes policies and procedures that address each of the following elements:

- Leadership responsibilities for quality within the firm;
- Relevant ethical requirements;
- Acceptance and continuance of client relationships and specific engagements;
- Human resources;
- Engagement performance; and
- Monitoring.

National requirements that deal with the firm's responsibilities to establish and maintain a system of quality control are at least as demanding as ISQC (UK) 1 (Revised June 2016) when they address all the elements referred to in this paragraph and impose obligations on the firm that achieve the aims of the requirements set out in ISQC (UK) 1 (Revised June 2016).

Reliance on the Firm's System of Quality Control
(Ref: Para. 4)

A2   Unless information provided by the firm or other parties suggest otherwise, the engagement team may rely on the firm's system of quality control in relation to, for example:

- Competence of personnel through their recruitment and formal training.
- Independence through the accumulation and communication of relevant independence information.
- Maintenance of client relationships through acceptance and continuance systems.
- Adherence to applicable legal and regulatory requirements through the monitoring process.

Leadership Responsibilities for Quality on Audits
(Ref: Para. 8)

A3   The actions of the engagement partner and appropriate messages to the other members of the engagement team, in taking responsibility for the overall quality on each audit engagement, emphasize:

(a)   The importance to audit quality of:

   (i)   Performing work that complies with professional standards and applicable legal and regulatory requirements;

   (ii)   Complying with the firm's quality control policies and procedures as applicable;

   (iii)   Issuing auditor's reports that are appropriate in the circumstances; and

(iv) The engagement team's ability to raise concerns without fear of reprisals; and

(b) The fact that quality is essential in performing audit engagements.

ISQC (UK) 1 (Revised June 2016)[5a] sets out requirements to ensure that securing audit quality, independence and competence are the main criteria used by the firm to select the engagement partner or key audit partner(s).   A3-1

Relevant Ethical Requirements

Compliance with Relevant Ethical Requirements
(Ref: Para. 9)

The IESBA Code[5b] establishes the fundamental principles of professional ethics,   A4
which include:

(a) Integrity;

(b) Objectivity;

(c) Professional competence and due care;

(d) Confidentiality; and

(e) Professional behavior.

Definition of "Firm," "Network" and "Network Firm"
(Ref: Para. 9–11)

The definitions of "firm," "network" or "network firm" in relevant ethical   A5
requirements may differ from those set out in this ISA (UK). For example, the
IESBA Code[5b] defines the "firm" as:

(a) A sole practitioner, partnership or corporation of professional accountants;

(b) An entity that controls such parties through ownership, management or other means; and

(c) An entity controlled by such parties through ownership, management or other means.

The IESBA Code also provides guidance in relation to the terms "network" and "network firm."

In complying with the requirements in paragraphs 9–11, the definitions used in the relevant ethical requirements apply in so far as is necessary to interpret those ethical requirements.

Threats to Independence
(Ref: Para. 11(c))

The engagement partner may identify a threat to independence regarding the audit   A6
engagement that safeguards may not be able to eliminate or reduce to an
acceptable level. In that case, as required by paragraph 11(c), the engagement
partner reports to the relevant person(s) within the firm to determine appropriate

---

[5a] *ISQC (UK) 1 (Revised June 2016), paragraph 30D-1.*

[5b] *In the UK, auditors are subject to ethical requirements from two sources: the FRC's Ethical Standard concerning the integrity, objectivity and independence of the auditor, and the ethical pronouncements established by the auditor's relevant professional body.*

action, which may include eliminating the activity or interest that creates the threat, or withdrawing from the audit engagement, where withdrawal is possible under applicable law or regulation.

Considerations Specific to Public Sector Entities

A7   Statutory measures may provide safeguards for the independence of public sector auditors. However, public sector auditors or audit firms carrying out public sector audits on behalf of the statutory auditor may, depending on the terms of the mandate in a particular jurisdiction, need to adapt their approach in order to promote compliance with the spirit of paragraph 11. This may include, where the public sector auditor's mandate does not permit withdrawal from the engagement, disclosure through a public report, of circumstances that have arisen that would, if they were in the private sector, lead the auditor to withdraw.

Acceptance and Continuance of Client Relationships and Audit Engagements (Ref: Para. 12)

A8   ISQC (UK) 1 (Revised June 2016) requires the firm to obtain information considered necessary in the circumstances before accepting an engagement with a new client, when deciding whether to continue an existing engagement, and when considering acceptance of a new engagement with an existing client.[6] Information such as the following assists the engagement partner in determining whether the conclusions reached regarding the acceptance and continuance of client relationships and audit engagements are appropriate:

- The integrity of the principal owners, key management and those charged with governance of the entity;

- Whether the engagement team is competent to perform the audit engagement and has the necessary capabilities, including time and resources;

- Whether the firm and the engagement team can comply with relevant ethical requirements; and

- Significant matters that have arisen during the current or previous audit engagement, and their implications for continuing the relationship.

A8a   Law, regulation, or relevant ethical requirements[7] may require the auditor to request, prior to accepting the engagement, the predecessor auditor to provide known information regarding any facts or circumstances that, in the predecessor auditor's judgment, the auditor needs to be aware of before deciding whether to accept the engagement. In some circumstances, the predecessor auditor may be required, on request by the proposed successor auditor, to provide information regarding identified or suspected non-compliance with laws and regulations to the proposed successor auditor.[7a] For example, where the predecessor auditor has withdrawn from the engagement as a result of identified or suspected non-

---

[6] *ISQC (UK) 1 (Revised June 2016), paragraph 27(a).*

[7] *See, for example, Sections 210.14 of the IESBA Code.*

In the UK, the relevant guidance on proposed communications with a predecessor auditor is provided by the pronouncements relating to the work of auditors issued by the auditor's relevant professional body.

[7a] *In the UK, the predecessor auditor is required to provide the successor statutory auditor with access to all relevant information concerning the entity, including information concerning the most recent audit. This would include non-compliance with laws and regulations. See ISQC (UK) 1 (Revised June 2016), Quality Control for Firms that Perform Audits and Reviews of Financial Statements, and other Assurance and Related Services Engagements, paragraph 28D-1.*

compliance with laws and regulations, the IESBA Code requires that the predecessor auditor, on request by a proposed successor auditor, provides all such facts and other information concerning such non-compliance that, in the predecessor auditor's opinion, the proposed successor auditor needs to be aware of before deciding whether to accept the audit appointment.[8]

Considerations Specific to Public Sector Entities
(Ref: Para. 12–13)

In the public sector, auditors may be appointed in accordance with statutory **A9** procedures. Accordingly, certain of the requirements and considerations regarding the acceptance and continuance of client relationships and audit engagements as set out in paragraphs 12, 13 and A8 may not be relevant. Nonetheless, information gathered as a result of the process described may be valuable to public sector auditors in performing risk assessments and in carrying out reporting responsibilities.

Assignment of Engagement Teams
(Ref: Para. 14)

An engagement team includes a person using expertise in a specialized area of **A10** accounting or auditing, whether engaged or employed by the firm, if any, who performs audit procedures on the engagement. However, a person with such expertise is not a member of the engagement team if that person's involvement with the engagement is only consultation. Consultations are addressed in paragraph 18, and paragraph A21–A22.

When considering the appropriate competence and capabilities expected of the **A11** engagement team as a whole, the engagement partner may take into consideration such matters as the team's:

- Understanding of, and practical experience with, audit engagements of a similar nature and complexity through appropriate training and participation.

- Understanding of professional standards and applicable legal and regulatory requirements.

- Technical expertise, including expertise with relevant information technology and specialized areas of accounting or auditing.

- Knowledge of relevant industries in which the client operates.

- Ability to apply professional judgment.

- Understanding of the firm's quality control policies and procedures.

Considerations Specific to Public Sector Entities

In the public sector, additional appropriate competence may include skills that are **A12** necessary to discharge the terms of the audit mandate in a particular jurisdiction. Such competence may include an understanding of the applicable reporting arrangements, including reporting to the legislature or other governing body or in the public interest. The wider scope of a public sector audit may include, for example, some aspects of performance auditing or a comprehensive assessment of

---

[8] *See, for example, Sections 225.31 of the IESBA Code.*
In the UK, the auditor has regard to any specific requirements of the auditor's relevant professional body.

compliance with law, regulation or other authority and preventing and detecting fraud and corruption.

Engagement Performance

Direction, Supervision and Performance
(Ref: Para. 15(a))

A13   Direction of the engagement team involves informing the members of the engagement team of matters such as:

- Their responsibilities, including the need to comply with relevant ethical requirements, and to plan and perform an audit with professional skepticism as required by ISA (UK) 200 (Revised June 2016).[9]

- Responsibilities of respective partners where more than one partner is involved in the conduct of an audit engagement.

- The objectives of the work to be performed.

- The nature of the entity's business.

- Risk-related issues.

- Problems that may arise.

- The detailed approach to the performance of the engagement.

Discussion among members of the engagement team allows less experienced team members to raise questions with more experienced team members so that appropriate communication can occur within the engagement team.

A14   Appropriate teamwork and training assist less experienced members of the engagement team to clearly understand the objectives of the assigned work.

A15   Supervision includes matters such as:

- Tracking the progress of the audit engagement.

- Considering the competence and capabilities of individual members of the engagement team, including whether they have sufficient time to carry out their work, whether they understand their instructions, and whether the work is being carried out in accordance with the planned approach to the audit engagement.

- Addressing significant matters arising during the audit engagement, considering their significance and modifying the planned approach appropriately.

- Identifying matters for consultation or consideration by more experienced engagement team members during the audit engagement.

Reviews

Review Responsibilities
(Ref: Para. 16)

A16   Under ISQC (UK) 1 (Revised June 2016), the firm's review responsibility policies and procedures are determined on the basis that work of less experienced team members is reviewed by more experienced team members.[10]

---

[9] *ISA (UK) 200 (Revised June 2016), Overall Objectives of the Independent Auditor and the Conduct of an Audit in Accordance with International Standards on Auditing (UK), paragraph 15.*

[10] *ISQC (UK) 1 (Revised June 2016), paragraph 33.*

A review consists of consideration whether, for example: **A17**

- The work has been performed in accordance with professional standards and applicable legal and regulatory requirements;
- Significant matters have been raised for further consideration;
- Appropriate consultations have taken place and the resulting conclusions have been documented and implemented;
- There is a need to revise the nature, timing and extent of work performed;
- The work performed supports the conclusions reached and is appropriately documented;
- The evidence obtained is sufficient and appropriate to support the auditor's report; and
- The objectives of the engagement procedures have been achieved.

The Engagement Partner's Review of Work Performed
(Ref: Para. 17)

Timely reviews of the following by the engagement partner at appropriate stages   **A18**
during the engagement allow significant matters to be resolved on a timely basis to
the engagement partner's satisfaction on or before the date of the auditor's report:

- Critical areas of judgment, especially those relating to difficult or contentious matters identified during the course of the engagement;
- Significant risks; and
- Other areas the engagement partner considers important.

The engagement partner need not review all audit documentation, but may do so.
However, as required by ISA (UK) 230 (Revised June 2016), the partner
documents the extent and timing of the reviews.[11]

An engagement partner taking over an audit during the engagement may apply the   **A19**
review procedures as described in paragraph A18 to review the work performed to
the date of a change in order to assume the responsibilities of an engagement
partner.

Considerations Relevant Where a Member of the Engagement Team with
Expertise in a Specialized Area of Accounting or Auditing Is Used
(Ref: Para. 15–17)

Where a member of the engagement team with expertise in a specialized area of   **A20**
accounting or auditing is used, direction, supervision and review of that
engagement team member's work may include matters such as:

- Agreeing with that member the nature, scope and objectives of that member's work; and the respective roles of, and the nature, timing and extent of communication between that member and other members of the engagement team.
- Evaluating the adequacy of that member's work including the relevance and reasonableness of that member's findings or conclusions and their consistency with other audit evidence.

---

[11] *ISA (UK) 230 (Revised June 2016), paragraph 9(c).*

Consultation
(Ref: Para. 18)

A21   Effective consultation on significant technical, ethical, and other matters within the firm or, where applicable, outside the firm can be achieved when those consulted:

- Are given all the relevant facts that will enable them to provide informed advice; and
- Have appropriate knowledge, seniority and experience.

A22   It may be appropriate for the engagement team to consult outside the firm, for example, where the firm lacks appropriate internal resources. They may take advantage of advisory services provided by other firms, professional and regulatory bodies, or commercial organizations that provide relevant quality control services.

Engagement Quality Control Review

Completion of the Engagement Quality Control Review before Dating of the Auditor's Report
(Ref: Para. 19(c))

A23   ISA (UK) 700 (Revised June 2016) requires the auditor's report to be dated no earlier than the date on which the auditor has obtained sufficient appropriate evidence on which to base the auditor's opinion on the financial statements.[12] In cases of an audit of financial statements of listed entities or when an engagement meets the criteria for an engagement quality control review, such a review assists the auditor in determining whether sufficient appropriate evidence has been obtained.

A24   Conducting the engagement quality control review in a timely manner at appropriate stages during the engagement allows significant matters to be promptly resolved to the engagement quality control reviewer's satisfaction on or before the date of the auditor's report.

A25   Completion of the engagement quality control review means the completion by the engagement quality control reviewer of the requirements in paragraphs 20–21, and where applicable, compliance with paragraph 22. Documentation of the engagement quality control review may be completed after the date of the auditor's report as part of the assembly of the final audit file. ISA (UK) 230 (Revised June 2016) establishes requirements and provides guidance in this regard.[13]

Nature, Extent and Timing of Engagement Quality Control Review
(Ref: Para. 20)

A26   Remaining alert for changes in circumstances allows the engagement partner to identify situations in which an engagement quality control review is necessary, even though at the start of the engagement, such a review was not required.

A27   The extent of the engagement quality control review may depend, among other things, on the complexity of the audit engagement, whether the entity is a listed entity, and the risk that the auditor's report might not be appropriate in the

---

[12] *ISA (UK) 700 (Revised June 2016), Forming an Opinion and Reporting on Financial Statements, paragraph 41.*

[13] *ISA (UK) 230 (Revised June 2016), paragraphs 14–16.*

circumstances. The performance of an engagement quality control review does not reduce the responsibilities of the engagement partner for the audit engagement and its performance.

When ISA (UK) 701[14] applies, the conclusions reached by the engagement team in formulating the auditor's report include determining: **A28**

- The key audit matters to be included in the auditor's report;

- The key audit matters that will not be communicated in the auditor's report in accordance with paragraph 14 of ISA (UK) 701, if any; and

- If applicable, depending on the facts and circumstances of the entity and the audit, that there are no key audit matters to communicate in the auditor's report.

In addition, the review of the proposed auditor's report in accordance with paragraph 20(b) includes consideration of the proposed wording to be included in the Key Audit Matters section.

Engagement Quality Control Review of Listed Entities
(Ref: Para. 21)

Other matters relevant to evaluating the significant judgments made by the engagement team that may be considered in an engagement quality control review of a listed entity include: **A29**

- Significant risks identified during the engagement in accordance with ISA (UK) 315 (Revised June 2016),[15] and the responses to those risks in accordance with ISA (UK) 330 (Revised July 2017),[16] including the engagement team's assessment of, and response to, the risk of fraud in accordance with ISA (UK) 240 (Revised June 2016).[17]

- Judgments made, particularly with respect to materiality and significant risks.

- The significance and disposition of corrected and uncorrected misstatements identified during the audit.

- The matters to be communicated to management and those charged with governance and, where applicable, other parties such as regulatory bodies.

These other matters, depending on the circumstances, may also be applicable for engagement quality control reviews for audits of financial statements of other entities.

Considerations Specific to Smaller Entities
(Ref: Para. 20–21)

In addition to the audits of financial statements of listed entities, an engagement quality control review is required for audit engagements that meet the criteria established by the firm that subjects engagements to an engagement quality   **A30**

---

[14] *ISA (UK) 701, Communicating Key Audit Matters in the Auditor's Report.*

[15] *ISA (UK) 315 (Revised June 2016), Identifying and Assessing the Risks of Material Misstatement through Understanding the Entity and Its Environment.*

[16] *ISA (UK) 330 (Revised July 2017), The Auditor's Responses to Assessed Risks.*

[17] *ISA (UK) 240 (Revised June 2016), The Auditor's Responsibilities Relating to Fraud in an Audit of Financial Statements.*

control review. In some cases, none of the firm's audit engagements may meet the criteria that would subject them to such a review.

Considerations Specific to Public Sector Entities
(Ref: Para. 20–21)

A31   In the public sector, a statutorily appointed auditor (for example, an Auditor General, or other suitably qualified person appointed on behalf of the Auditor General), may act in a role equivalent to that of engagement partner with overall responsibility for public sector audits. In such circumstances, where applicable, the selection of the engagement quality control reviewer includes consideration of the need for independence from the audited entity and the ability of the engagement quality control reviewer to provide an objective evaluation.

A32   Listed entities as referred to in paragraphs 21 and A29 are not common in the public sector. However, there may be other public sector entities that are significant due to size, complexity or public interest aspects, and which consequently have a wide range of stakeholders. Examples include state owned corporations and public utilities. Ongoing transformations within the public sector may also give rise to new types of significant entities. There are no fixed objective criteria on which the determination of significance is based. Nonetheless, public sector auditors evaluate which entities may be of sufficient significance to warrant performance of an engagement quality control review.

Monitoring
(Ref: Para. 23)

A33   ISQC (UK) 1 (Revised June 2016) requires the firm to establish a monitoring process designed to provide it with reasonable assurance that the policies and procedures relating to the system of quality control are relevant, adequate and operating effectively.[18]

A34   In considering deficiencies that may affect the audit engagement, the engagement partner may have regard to measures the firm took to rectify the situation that the engagement partner considers are sufficient in the context of that audit.

A35   A deficiency in the firm's system of quality control does not necessarily indicate that a particular audit engagement was not performed in accordance with professional standards and applicable legal and regulatory requirements, or that the auditor's report was not appropriate.

Documentation

Documentation of Consultations
(Ref: Para. 24(d))

A36   Documentation of consultations with other professionals that involve difficult or contentious matters that is sufficiently complete and detailed contributes to an understanding of:

● The issue on which consultation was sought; and

● The results of the consultation, including any decisions taken, the basis for those decisions and how they were implemented.

---

[18] *ISQC (UK) 1 (Revised June 2016), paragraph 48.*

ISA (UK) 230 (Revised June 2016)
Audit Documentation

(Effective for audits of financial statements for periods commencing on or after 17 June 2016)

Contents

Paragraphs

Introduction — 1 - 4
Scope of this ISA (UK) — 1
Nature and purposes of audit documentation — 2 - 3
Effective date — 4

Objective — 5

Definitions — 6

Requirements — 7 - 16
Timely preparation of audit documentation — 7
Documentation of the audit procedures performed and audit evidence obtained — 8 - 13
Assembly of the final audit file — 14 - 16

Application and other explanatory material — A1 - A24
Timely preparation of audit documentation — A1
Documentation of the audit procedures performed and audit evidence obtained — A2 - A20
Assembly of the final audit file — A21 - A24

Appendix: Specific audit documentation requirements in other ISAs

International Standard on Auditing (UK) (ISA (UK)) 230 (Revised June 2016), *Audit Documentation*, should be read in conjunction with ISA (UK) 200 (Revised June 2016), *Overall Objectives of the Independent Auditor and the Conduct of an Audit in Accordance with International Standards on Auditing (UK)*.

Introduction

Scope of this ISA (UK)

1   This International Standard on Auditing (UK) (ISA (UK)) deals with the auditor's responsibility to prepare audit documentation for an audit of financial statements. The Appendix lists other ISAs (UK) that contain specific documentation requirements and guidance. The specific documentation requirements of other ISAs (UK) do not limit the application of this ISA (UK). Law or regulation may establish additional documentation requirements.

Nature and Purposes of Audit Documentation

2   Audit documentation that meets the requirements of this ISA (UK) and the specific documentation requirements of other relevant ISAs (UK) provides:

(a)   Evidence of the auditor's basis for a conclusion about the achievement of the overall objectives of the auditor;[1] and

(b)   Evidence that the audit was planned and performed in accordance with ISAs (UK) and applicable legal and regulatory requirements.

3   Audit documentation serves a number of additional purposes, including the following:

●   Assisting the engagement team to plan and perform the audit.

●   Assisting members of the engagement team responsible for supervision to direct and supervise the audit work, and to discharge their review responsibilities in accordance with ISA (UK) 220 (Revised June 2016).[2]

●   Enabling the engagement team to be accountable for its work.

●   Retaining a record of matters of continuing significance to future audits.

●   Enabling the conduct of quality control reviews and inspections in accordance with ISQC (UK) 1 (Revised June 2016)[3] or national requirements that are at least as demanding.[4]

●   Enabling the conduct of external inspections in accordance with applicable legal, regulatory or other requirements.

Effective Date

4   This ISA (UK) is effective for audits of financial statements for periods commencing on or after 17 June 2016. Earlier adoption is permitted.

---

[1] *ISA (UK) 200 (Revised June 2016), Overall Objectives of the Independent Auditor and the Conduct of an Audit in Accordance with International Standards on Auditing (UK), paragraph 11.*

[2] *ISA (UK) 220 (Revised June 2016), Quality Control for an Audit of Financial Statements, paragraphs 15–17.*

[3] *ISQC (UK) 1 (Revised June 2016), Quality Control for Firms that Perform Audits and Reviews of Financial Statements, and Other Assurance and Related Services Engagements, paragraphs 32– 33, 35–38, and 48.*

[4] *ISA (UK) 220 (Revised June 2016), paragraph 2.*

Objective

The objective of the auditor is to prepare documentation that provides: **5**

(a)   A sufficient and appropriate record of the basis for the auditor's report; and

(b)   Evidence that the audit was planned and performed in accordance with ISAs (UK) and applicable legal and regulatory requirements.

Definitions

For purposes of the ISAs (UK), the following terms have the meanings attributed   **6**
below:

(a)   Audit documentation – The record of audit procedures performed, relevant audit evidence obtained, and conclusions the auditor reached (terms such as "working papers" or "workpapers" are also sometimes used).

> In the UK, audit documentation shall include all documents, information, records and other data required by ISQC (UK) 1 (Revised June 2016), ISAs (UK) and applicable legal and regulatory requirements.

(b)   Audit file – One or more folders or other storage media, in physical or electronic form, containing the records that comprise the audit documentation for a specific engagement.

(c)   Experienced auditor – An individual (whether internal or external to the firm) who has practical audit experience, and a reasonable understanding of:

(i)   Audit processes;

(ii)   ISAs (UK) and applicable legal and regulatory requirements;

(iii)   The business environment in which the entity operates; and

(iv)   Auditing and financial reporting issues relevant to the entity's industry.

Requirements

Timely Preparation of Audit Documentation

The auditor shall prepare audit documentation on a timely basis. (Ref: Para. A1)   **7**

Documentation of the Audit Procedures Performed and Audit Evidence Obtained

Form, Content and Extent of Audit Documentation

The auditor shall prepare audit documentation that is sufficient to enable an   **8**
experienced auditor, having no previous connection with the audit, to understand:
(Ref: Para. A2–A5, A16–A17)

(a)   The nature, timing and extent of the audit procedures performed to comply with the ISAs (UK) and applicable legal and regulatory requirements; (Ref: Para. A6–A7)

(b)   The results of the audit procedures performed, and the audit evidence obtained; and

(c)   Significant matters arising during the audit, the conclusions reached thereon, and significant professional judgments made in reaching those conclusions. (Ref: Para. A8–A11)

8D-1   The auditor shall retain any other data and documents that are important in supporting the auditor's report as part of the audit documentation.

9   In documenting the nature, timing and extent of audit procedures performed, the auditor shall record:

(a)   The identifying characteristics of the specific items or matters tested; (Ref: Para. A12)

(b)   Who performed the audit work and the date such work was completed; and

(c)   Who reviewed the audit work performed and the date and extent of such review. (Ref: Para. A13)

10   The auditor shall document discussions of significant matters with management, those charged with governance, and others, including the nature of the significant matters discussed and when and with whom the discussions took place. (Ref: Para. A14)

11   If the auditor identified information that is inconsistent with the auditor's final conclusion regarding a significant matter, the auditor shall document how the auditor addressed the inconsistency. (Ref: Para. A15)

Departure from a Relevant Requirement

12   If, in exceptional circumstances, the auditor judges it necessary to depart from a relevant requirement in an ISA (UK), the auditor shall document how the alternative audit procedures performed achieve the aim of that requirement, and the reasons for the departure. (Ref: Para. A18–A19)

Matters Arising after the Date of the Auditor's Report

13   If, in exceptional circumstances, the auditor performs new or additional audit procedures or draws new conclusions after the date of the auditor's report, the auditor shall document: (Ref: Para. A20)

(a)   The circumstances encountered;

(b)   The new or additional audit procedures performed, audit evidence obtained, and conclusions reached, and their effect on the auditor's report; and

(c)   When and by whom the resulting changes to audit documentation were made and reviewed.

Assembly of the Final Audit File

14   The auditor shall assemble the audit documentation in an audit file and complete the administrative process of assembling the final audit file on a timely basis after the date of the auditor's report. (Ref: Para. A21–A22)

In the UK, the assembly of the final audit file shall be completed no later than 60 days from the date of the auditor's report.

14D-1   The auditor shall retain audit documentation that is important for monitoring compliance with ISAs (UK) and other applicable legal requirements.

15   After the assembly of the final audit file has been completed, the auditor shall not delete or discard audit documentation of any nature before the end of its retention period. (Ref: Para. A23)

In circumstances other than those envisaged in paragraph 13 where the auditor **16** finds it necessary to modify existing audit documentation or add new audit documentation after the assembly of the final audit file has been completed, the auditor shall, regardless of the nature of the modifications or additions, document: (Ref: Para. A24)

(a) The specific reasons for making them; and

(b) When and by whom they were made and reviewed.

***

Application and Other Explanatory Material

Timely Preparation of Audit Documentation
(Ref: Para. 7)

Preparing sufficient and appropriate audit documentation on a timely basis helps **A1** to enhance the quality of the audit and facilitates the effective review and evaluation of the audit evidence obtained and conclusions reached before the auditor's report is finalized. Documentation prepared after the audit work has been performed is likely to be less accurate than documentation prepared at the time such work is performed.

Documentation of the Audit Procedures Performed and Audit Evidence Obtained

Form, Content and Extent of Audit Documentation
(Ref: Para. 8)

The form, content and extent of audit documentation depend on factors such as: **A2**

- The size and complexity of the entity.
- The nature of the audit procedures to be performed.
- The identified risks of material misstatement.
- The significance of the audit evidence obtained.
- The nature and extent of exceptions identified.
- The need to document a conclusion or the basis for a conclusion not readily determinable from the documentation of the work performed or audit evidence obtained.
- The audit methodology and tools used.

Audit documentation may be recorded on paper or on electronic or other media. **A3** Examples of audit documentation include:

- Audit programs.
- Analyses.
- Issues memoranda.
- Summaries of significant matters.
- Letters of confirmation and representation.

- Checklists.

- Correspondence (including e-mail) concerning significant matters.

The auditor may include abstracts or copies of the entity's records (for example, significant and specific contracts and agreements) as part of audit documentation. Audit documentation, however, is not a substitute for the entity's accounting records.

A4 The auditor need not include in audit documentation superseded drafts of working papers and financial statements, notes that reflect incomplete or preliminary thinking, previous copies of documents corrected for typographical or other errors, and duplicates of documents.

A5 Oral explanations by the auditor, on their own, do not represent adequate support for the work the auditor performed or conclusions the auditor reached, but may be used to explain or clarify information contained in the audit documentation.

Documentation of Compliance with ISAs (UK)
(Ref: Para. 8(a))

A6 In principle, compliance with the requirements of this ISA (UK) will result in the audit documentation being sufficient and appropriate in the circumstances. Other ISAs (UK) contain specific documentation requirements that are intended to clarify the application of this ISA (UK) in the particular circumstances of those other ISAs (UK). The specific documentation requirements of other ISAs (UK) do not limit the application of this ISA (UK). Furthermore, the absence of a documentation requirement in any particular ISA (UK) is not intended to suggest that there is no documentation that will be prepared as a result of complying with that ISA (UK).

A7 Audit documentation provides evidence that the audit complies with the ISAs (UK). However, it is neither necessary nor practicable for the auditor to document every matter considered, or professional judgment made, in an audit. Further, it is unnecessary for the auditor to document separately (as in a checklist, for example) compliance with matters for which compliance is demonstrated by documents included within the audit file. For example:

- The existence of an adequately documented audit plan demonstrates that the auditor has planned the audit.

- The existence of a signed engagement letter in the audit file demonstrates that the auditor has agreed the terms of the audit engagement with management or, where appropriate, those charged with governance.

- An auditor's report containing an appropriately qualified opinion on the financial statements demonstrates that the auditor has complied with the requirement to express a qualified opinion under the circumstances specified in the ISAs (UK).

- In relation to requirements that apply generally throughout the audit, there may be a number of ways in which compliance with them may be demonstrated within the audit file:

  - For example, there may be no single way in which the auditor's professional skepticism is documented. But the audit documentation may nevertheless provide evidence of the auditor's exercise of professional skepticism in accordance with the ISAs (UK). Such evidence may include specific procedures performed to corroborate management's responses to the auditor's inquiries.

- Similarly, that the engagement partner has taken responsibility for the direction, supervision and performance of the audit in compliance with the ISAs (UK) may be evidenced in a number of ways within the audit documentation. This may include documentation of the engagement partner's timely involvement in aspects of the audit, such as participation in the team discussions required by ISA (UK) 315 (Revised June 2016).[5]

Documentation of Significant Matters and Related Significant Professional Judgments
(Ref: Para. 8(c))

Judging the significance of a matter requires an objective analysis of the facts and circumstances. Examples of significant matters include: **A8**

- Matters that give rise to significant risks (as defined in ISA (UK) 315 (Revised June 2016)).[6]

- Results of audit procedures indicating (a) that the financial statements could be materially misstated, or (b) a need to revise the auditor's previous assessment of the risks of material misstatement and the auditor's responses to those risks.

- Circumstances that cause the auditor significant difficulty in applying necessary audit procedures.

- Findings that could result in a modification to the audit opinion or the inclusion of an Emphasis of Matter paragraph in the auditor's report.

- **Concerns about the entity's ability to continue as a going concern.**

An important factor in determining the form, content and extent of audit documentation **A9** of significant matters is the extent of professional judgment exercised in performing the work and evaluating the results. Documentation of the professional judgments made, where significant, serves to explain the auditor's conclusions and to reinforce the quality of the judgment. Such matters are of particular interest to those responsible for reviewing audit documentation, including those carrying out subsequent audits when reviewing matters of continuing significance (for example, when performing a retrospective review of accounting estimates).

Some examples of circumstances in which, in accordance with paragraph 8, it is **A10** appropriate to prepare audit documentation relating to the use of professional judgment include, where the matters and judgments are significant:

- The rationale for the auditor's conclusion when a requirement provides that the auditor "shall consider" certain information or factors, and that consideration is significant in the context of the particular engagement.

- The basis for the auditor's conclusion on the reasonableness of areas of subjective judgments (for example, the reasonableness of significant accounting estimates).

- The basis for the auditor's conclusions about the authenticity of a document when further investigation (such as making appropriate use of an expert or of confirmation procedures) is undertaken in response to conditions

---

[5] *ISA (UK) 315 (Revised June 2016), Identifying and Assessing the Risks of Material Misstatement through Understanding the Entity and Its Environment, paragraph 10.*

[6] *ISA (UK) 315 (Revised June 2016), paragraph 4(e).*

identified during the audit that caused the auditor to believe that the document may not be authentic.

- When ISA (UK) 701 applies,[7] the auditor's determination of the key audit matters or the determination that there are no key audit matters to be communicated.

A11   The auditor may consider it helpful to prepare and retain as part of the audit documentation a summary (sometimes known as a completion memorandum) that describes the significant matters identified during the audit and how they were addressed, or that includes cross-references to other relevant supporting audit documentation that provides such information. Such a summary may facilitate effective and efficient reviews and inspections of the audit documentation, particularly for large and complex audits. Further, the preparation of such a summary may assist the auditor's consideration of the significant matters. It may also help the auditor to consider whether, in light of the audit procedures performed and conclusions reached, there is any individual relevant ISA (UK) objective that the auditor cannot achieve that would prevent the auditor from achieving the overall objectives of the auditor.

Identification of Specific Items or Matters Tested, and of the Preparer and Reviewer
(Ref: Para. 9)

A12   Recording the identifying characteristics serves a number of purposes. For example, it enables the engagement team to be accountable for its work and facilitates the investigation of exceptions or inconsistencies. Identifying characteristics will vary with the nature of the audit procedure and the item or matter tested. For example:

- For a detailed test of entity-generated purchase orders, the auditor may identify the documents selected for testing by their dates and unique purchase order numbers.

- For a procedure requiring selection or review of all items over a specific amount from a given population, the auditor may record the scope of the procedure and identify the population (for example, all journal entries over a specified amount from the journal register).

- For a procedure requiring systematic sampling from a population of documents, the auditor may identify the documents selected by recording their source, the starting point and the sampling interval (for example, a systematic sample of shipping reports selected from the shipping log for the period from April 1 to September 30, starting with report number 12345 and selecting every 125th report).

- For a procedure requiring inquiries of specific entity personnel, the auditor may record the dates of the inquiries and the names and job designations of the entity personnel.

- For an observation procedure, the auditor may record the process or matter being observed, the relevant individuals, their respective responsibilities, and where and when the observation was carried out.

---

[7] *ISA (UK) 701, Communicating Key Audit Matters in the Independent Auditor's Report.*

ISA (UK) 220 (Revised June 2016) requires the auditor to review the audit work   **A13**
performed through review of the audit documentation.[8] The requirement to
document who reviewed the audit work performed does not imply a need for
each specific working paper to include evidence of review. The requirement,
however, means documenting what audit work was reviewed, who reviewed such
work, and when it was reviewed.

Documentation of Discussions of Significant Matters with Management, Those
Charged with Governance, and Others
(Ref: Para. 10)

The documentation is not limited to records prepared by the auditor but may   **A14**
include other appropriate records such as minutes of meetings prepared by the
entity's personnel and agreed by the auditor. Others with whom the auditor may
discuss significant matters may include other personnel within the entity, and
external parties, such as persons providing professional advice to the entity.

Documentation of How Inconsistencies have been Addressed
(Ref: Para. 11)

The requirement to document how the auditor addressed inconsistencies in   **A15**
information does not imply that the auditor needs to retain documentation that
is incorrect or superseded.

Considerations Specific to Smaller Entities
(Ref: Para. 8)

The audit documentation for the audit of a smaller entity is generally less extensive   **A16**
than that for the audit of a larger entity. Further, in the case of an audit where the
engagement partner performs all the audit work, the documentation will not include
matters that might have to be documented solely to inform or instruct members of
an engagement team, or to provide evidence of review by other members of the
team (for example, there will be no matters to document relating to team
discussions or supervision). Nevertheless, the engagement partner complies with
the overriding requirement in paragraph 8 to prepare audit documentation that can
be understood by an experienced auditor, as the audit documentation may be
subject to review by external parties for regulatory or other purposes.

When preparing audit documentation, the auditor of a smaller entity may also find   **A17**
it helpful and efficient to record various aspects of the audit together in a single
document, with cross-references to supporting working papers as appropriate.
Examples of matters that may be documented together in the audit of a smaller
entity include the understanding of the entity and its internal control, the overall
audit strategy and audit plan, materiality determined in accordance with ISA (UK)
320 (Revised June 2016),[9] assessed risks, significant matters noted during the
audit, and conclusions reached.

Departure from a Relevant Requirement
(Ref: Para. 12)

The requirements of the ISAs (UK) are designed to enable the auditor to achieve   **A18**
the objectives specified in the ISAs (UK), and thereby the overall objectives of the

---

[8] *ISA (UK) 220 (Revised June 2016), paragraph 17.*

[9] *ISA (UK) 320 (Revised June 2016), Materiality in Planning and Performing an Audit.*

auditor. Accordingly, other than in exceptional circumstances, the ISAs (UK) call for compliance with each requirement that is relevant in the circumstances of the audit.

A19   The documentation requirement applies only to requirements that are relevant in the circumstances. A requirement is not relevant[10] only in the cases where:

(a)   The entire ISA (UK) is not relevant (for example, if an entity does not have an internal audit function, nothing in ISA (UK) 610 (Revised June 2013)[11] is relevant); or

(b)   The requirement is conditional and the condition does not exist (for example, the requirement to modify the auditor's opinion where there is an inability to obtain sufficient appropriate audit evidence, and there is no such inability).

Matters Arising after the Date of the Auditor's Report
(Ref: Para. 13)

A20   Examples of exceptional circumstances include facts which become known to the auditor after the date of the auditor's report but which existed at that date and which, if known at that date, might have caused the financial statements to be amended or the auditor to modify the opinion in the auditor's report.[12] The resulting changes to the audit documentation are reviewed in accordance with the review responsibilities set out in ISA (UK) 220 (Revised June 2016),[13] with the engagement partner taking final responsibility for the changes.

Assembly of the Final Audit File
(Ref: Para. 14–16)

A21   ISQC (UK) 1 (Revised June 2016) (or national requirements that are at least as demanding) requires firms to establish policies and procedures for the timely completion of the assembly of audit files.[14] An appropriate time limit within which to complete the assembly of the final audit file is ordinarily not more than 60 days after the date of the auditor's report.[15]

A22   The completion of the assembly of the final audit file after the date of the auditor's report is an administrative process that does not involve the performance of new audit procedures or the drawing of new conclusions. Changes may, however, be made to the audit documentation during the final assembly process if they are administrative in nature. Examples of such changes include:

● Deleting or discarding superseded documentation.

● Sorting, collating and cross-referencing working papers.

● Signing off on completion checklists relating to the file assembly process.

● Documenting audit evidence that the auditor has obtained, discussed and agreed with the relevant members of the engagement team before the date of the auditor's report.

---

[10] *ISA (UK) 200 (Revised June 2016), paragraph 22.*

[11] *ISA (UK) 610 (Revised June 2013), Using the Work of Internal Auditors, paragraph 2.*

[12] *ISA (UK) 560, Subsequent Events, paragraph 14.*

[13] *ISA (UK) 220 (Revised June 2016), paragraph 16.*

[14] *ISQC (UK) 1 (Revised June 2016), paragraph 45.*

[15] *ISQC (UK) 1 (Revised June 2016), paragraph A54.*

ISQC (UK) 1 (Revised June 2016) (or national requirements that are at least as **A23** demanding) requires firms to establish policies and procedures for the retention of engagement documentation.[16] The retention period for audit engagements ordinarily is no shorter than five years from the date of the auditor's report, or, if later, the date of the group auditor's report.[17]

An example of a circumstance in which the auditor may find it necessary to **A24** modify existing audit documentation or add new audit documentation after file assembly has been completed is the need to clarify existing audit documentation arising from comments received during monitoring inspections performed by internal or external parties.

---

[16] *ISQC (UK) 1 (Revised June 2016), paragraph 47.*

[17] *ISQC (UK) 1 (Revised June 2016), paragraph A61.*
In the UK, the auditor has regard to specific requirements of the auditor's relevant professional body.

Appendix – Specific Audit Documentation Requirements in Other ISAs (UK)

(Ref: Para. 1)

This appendix identifies paragraphs in other ISAs (UK) that contain specific documentation requirements. The list is not a substitute for considering the requirements and related application and other explanatory material in ISAs (UK).

* ISA (UK) 210 (Revised June 2016), *Agreeing the Terms of Audit Engagements* – paragraphs 10–12

* ISA (UK) 220 (Revised June 2016), *Quality Control for an Audit of Financial Statements* – paragraphs 24–25R-2

* ISA (UK) 240 (Revised June 2016), *The Auditor's Responsibilities Relating to Fraud in an Audit of Financial Statements* – paragraphs 44–47

* ISA (UK) 250 (Revised June 2016), Section A—*Consideration of Laws and Regulations in an Audit of Financial Statements* – paragraph 29

* ISA (UK) 260 (Revised June 2016), Communication with Those Charged with Governance – paragraphs 23 and 23D-1

* ISA (UK) 300 (Revised June 2016), *Planning an Audit of Financial Statements* – paragraph 12

* ISA (UK) 315 (Revised June 2016), *Identifying and Assessing the Risks of Material Misstatement through Understanding the Entity and Its Environment* – paragraph 32

* ISA (UK) 320 (Revised June 2016), *Materiality in Planning and Performing an Audit* – paragraph 14

* ISA (UK) 330 (Revised June 2016), *The Auditor's Responses to Assessed Risks* – paragraphs 28–30

* ISA (UK) 450 (Revised June 2016), *Evaluation of Misstatements Identified During the Audit* – paragraph 15

* ISA (UK) 540 (Revised June 2016), *Auditing Accounting Estimates, Including Fair Value Accounting Estimates, and Related Disclosures* – paragraph 23

* ISA (UK) 550, *Related Parties* – paragraph 28

* ISA (UK) 600 (Revised June 2016), *Special Considerations—Audits of Group Financial Statements (Including the Work of Component Auditors)* – paragraphs 50–50D-3

* ISA (UK) 610 (Revised June 2013), *Using the Work of Internal Auditors* – paragraphs 36 and 37

* ISA (UK) 620 (Revised June 2016), *Using the Work of an Auditor's Expert* – paragraph 15D-1

* ISA (UK) 701, *Communicating Key Audit Matters in the Independent Auditor's Report* – paragraph 18

* ISA (UK) 720 (Revised June 2016), *The Auditor's Responsibilities Relating to Other Information* – paragraph 25

ISA (UK) 240 (Revised June 2016) The Auditor's Responsibilities Relating to Fraud in an Audit of Financial Statements (Updated July 2017)

(Effective for audits of financial statements for periods commencing on or after 17 June 2016)[0]

Contents

	Paragraphs
Introduction	1 - 9
Scope of this ISA (UK)	1
Characteristics of fraud	2 - 3
Responsibility for the prevention and detection of fraud	4 - 8
Effective date	9
Objectives	10
Definitions	11
Requirements	12 - 47
Professional skepticism	12 - 14
Discussion among the engagement team	15
Risk assessment procedures and related activities	16 - 24
Identification and assessment of the risks of material misstatement due to fraud	25 - 27
Responses to the assessed risks of material misstatement due to fraud	28 - 33
Evaluation of audit evidence	34 - 37
Auditor unable to continue the engagement	38
Written representations	39
Communications to management and with those charged with governance	40 - 42
Communications to regulatory and enforcement authorities	43 - 43R-1
Documentation	44 - 47
Application and other explanatory material	A1 - A67
Characteristics of fraud	A1 - A5
Responsibility for the prevention and detection of fraud	A5a - A6
Professional skepticism	A7 - A9
Discussion among the engagement team	A10 - A11
Risk assessment procedures and related activities	A12 - A27
Identification and assessment of the risks of material misstatement due to fraud	A28 - A32
Responses to the assessed risks of material misstatement due to fraud	A33 - A48
Evaluation of audit evidence	A49 - A53
Auditor unable to continue the engagement	A54 - A57
Written representations	A58 - A59
Communications to management and with those charged with governance	A59a - A64
Reporting to authorities of public interest entities	A65 - A67

---

[0] *Conforming amendments to this standard as a result of ISA (UK) 250 (Revised July 2017), Section A—Consideration of Laws and Regulations in an Audit of Financial Statements, are included that are effective for audits of financial statements for periods commencing on or after 15 December 2017. Details of the amendments are given in the Annexure to ISA (UK) 250 (Revised July 2017).*

Appendix 1: Examples of fraud risk factors

Appendix 2: Examples of possible audit procedures to address the assessed risks of material misstatement due to fraud

Appendix 3: Examples of circumstances that indicate the possibility of fraud

---

International Standard on Auditing (UK) (ISA (UK)) 240 (Revised June 2016), *The Auditor's Responsibilities Relating to Fraud in an Audit of Financial Statements* should be read in conjunction with ISA (UK) 200 (Revised June 2016), *Overall Objectives of the Independent Auditor and the Conduct of an Audit in Accordance with International Standards on Auditing (UK)*.

Introduction

Scope of this ISA (UK)

This International Standard on Auditing (UK) (ISA (UK)) deals with the auditor's 　1
responsibilities relating to fraud in an audit of financial statements. Specifically, it
expands on how ISA (UK) 315 (Revised June 2016)[1] and ISA (UK) 330 (Revised
July 2017)[2] are to be applied in relation to risks of material misstatement due to
fraud.

Characteristics of Fraud

Misstatements in the financial statements can arise from either fraud or error. The 　2
distinguishing factor between fraud and error is whether the underlying action that
results in the misstatement of the financial statements is intentional or
unintentional.

Although fraud is a broad legal concept, for the purposes of the ISAs (UK), the 　3
auditor is concerned with fraud that causes a material misstatement in the financial
statements. Two types of intentional misstatements are relevant to the auditor –
misstatements resulting from fraudulent financial reporting and misstatements
resulting from misappropriation of assets. Although the auditor may suspect or, in
rare cases, identify the occurrence of fraud, the auditor does not make legal
determinations of whether fraud has actually occurred. (Ref: Para. A1–A6)

Responsibility for the Prevention and Detection of Fraud

The primary responsibility for the prevention and detection of fraud rests with 　4
both those charged with governance of the entity and management. It is
important that management, with the oversight of those charged with
governance, place a strong emphasis on fraud prevention, which may reduce
opportunities for fraud to take place, and fraud deterrence, which could
persuade individuals not to commit fraud because of the likelihood of
detection and punishment. This involves a commitment to creating a culture
of honesty and ethical behavior which can be reinforced by an active oversight
by those charged with governance. Oversight by those charged with
governance includes considering the potential for override of controls or
other inappropriate influence over the financial reporting process, such as
efforts by management to manage earnings in order to influence the
perceptions of analysts as to the entity's performance and profitability.

Responsibilities of the Auditor

An auditor conducting an audit in accordance with ISAs (UK) is responsible 　5
for obtaining reasonable assurance that the financial statements taken as a
whole are free from material misstatement, whether caused by fraud or error.
Owing to the inherent limitations of an audit, there is an unavoidable risk that
some material misstatements of the financial statements may not be detected,

---

[1] *ISA (UK) 315 (Revised June 2016), Identifying and Assessing the Risks of Material Misstatement through
Understanding the Entity and Its Environment.*

[2] *ISA (UK) 330 (Revised July 2017), The Auditor's Responses to Assessed Risks.*

even though the audit is properly planned and performed in accordance with the ISAs (UK).[3]

6   As described in ISA (UK) 200 (Revised June 2016),[4] the potential effects of inherent limitations are particularly significant in the case of misstatement resulting from fraud. The risk of not detecting a material misstatement resulting from fraud is higher than the risk of not detecting one resulting from error. This is because fraud may involve sophisticated and carefully organized schemes designed to conceal it, such as forgery, deliberate failure to record transactions, or intentional misrepresentations being made to the auditor. Such attempts at concealment may be even more difficult to detect when accompanied by collusion. Collusion may cause the auditor to believe that audit evidence is persuasive when it is, in fact, false. The auditor's ability to detect a fraud depends on factors such as the skillfulness of the perpetrator, the frequency and extent of manipulation, the degree of collusion involved, the relative size of individual amounts manipulated, and the seniority of those individuals involved. While the auditor may be able to identify potential opportunities for fraud to be perpetrated, it is difficult for the auditor to determine whether misstatements in judgment areas such as accounting estimates are caused by fraud or error.

7   Furthermore, the risk of the auditor not detecting a material misstatement resulting from management fraud is greater than for employee fraud, because management is frequently in a position to directly or indirectly manipulate accounting records, present fraudulent financial information or override control procedures designed to prevent similar frauds by other employees.

8   When obtaining reasonable assurance, the auditor is responsible for maintaining professional skepticism throughout the audit, considering the potential for management override of controls and recognizing the fact that audit procedures that are effective for detecting error may not be effective in detecting fraud. The requirements in this ISA (UK) are designed to assist the auditor in identifying and assessing the risks of material misstatement due to fraud and in designing procedures to detect such misstatement.

8a   The auditor may have additional responsibilities under law, regulation or relevant ethical requirements regarding an entity's non-compliance with laws and regulations, including fraud, which may differ from or go beyond this and other ISAs (UK), such as: (Ref: Para. A5a)

(a)   Responding to identified or suspected non-compliance with laws and regulations, including requirements in relation to specific communications with management and those charged with governance, assessing the appropriateness of their response to non-compliance and determining whether further action is needed;

(b)   Communicating identified or suspected non-compliance with laws and regulations to other auditors (e.g., in an audit of group financial statements); and

(c)   Documentation requirements regarding identified or suspected non-compliance with laws and regulations.

Complying with any additional responsibilities may provide further information that is relevant to the auditor's work in accordance with this and other ISAs (UK)

---

[3] *ISA (UK) 200 (Revised June 2016), Overall Objectives of the Independent Auditor and the Conduct of an Audit in Accordance with International Standards on Auditing (UK), paragraph A53–A54.*

[4] *ISA (UK) 200 (Revised June 2016), paragraph A53.*

(e.g., regarding the integrity of management or, where appropriate, those charged with governance).

Effective Date

This ISA (UK) is effective for audits of financial statements for periods 9 commencing on or after 17 June 2016. Earlier adoption is permitted.

Objectives

The objectives of the auditor are: 10

(a)   To identify and assess the risks of material misstatement of the financial statements due to fraud;

(b)   To obtain sufficient appropriate audit evidence regarding the assessed risks of material misstatement due to fraud, through designing and implementing appropriate responses; and

(c)   To respond appropriately to fraud or suspected fraud identified during the audit.

Definitions

For purposes of the ISAs (UK), the following terms have the meanings attributed 11 below:

(a)   Fraud – An intentional act by one or more individuals among management, those charged with governance, employees, or third parties, involving the use of deception to obtain an unjust or illegal advantage.

(b)   Fraud risk factors – Events or conditions that indicate an incentive or pressure to commit fraud or provide an opportunity to commit fraud.

Requirements

Professional Skepticism

In accordance with ISA (UK) 200 (Revised June 2016),[5] the auditor shall maintain 12 professional skepticism throughout the audit, recognizing the possibility that a material misstatement due to fraud could exist, notwithstanding the auditor's past experience of the honesty and integrity of the entity's management and those charged with governance. (Ref: Para. A7–A8)

Unless the auditor has reason to believe the contrary, the auditor may accept 13 records and documents as genuine. If conditions identified during the audit cause the auditor to believe that a document may not be authentic or that terms in a document have been modified but not disclosed to the auditor, the auditor shall investigate further. (Ref: Para. A9)

Where responses to inquiries of management or those charged with governance 14 are inconsistent, the auditor shall investigate the inconsistencies.

---

[5] *ISA (UK) 200 (Revised June 2016), paragraph 15.*

Discussion among the Engagement Team

15 ISA (UK) 315 (Revised June 2016) requires a discussion among the engagement team members and a determination by the engagement partner of which matters are to be communicated to those team members not involved in the discussion.[6] This discussion shall place particular emphasis on how and where the entity's financial statements may be susceptible to material misstatement due to fraud, including how fraud might occur. The discussion shall occur setting aside beliefs that the engagement team members may have that management and those charged with governance are honest and have integrity. (Ref: Para. A10–A11)

Risk Assessment Procedures and Related Activities

16 When performing risk assessment procedures and related activities to obtain an understanding of the entity and its environment, including the entity's internal control, required by ISA (UK) 315 (Revised June 2016),[7] the auditor shall perform the procedures in paragraphs 17–24 to obtain information for use in identifying the risks of material misstatement due to fraud.

Management and Others within the Entity

17 The auditor shall make inquiries of management regarding:

(a) Management's assessment of the risk that the financial statements may be materially misstated due to fraud, including the nature, extent and frequency of such assessments; (Ref: Para. A12–A13)

(b) Management's process for identifying and responding to the risks of fraud in the entity, including any specific risks of fraud that management has identified or that have been brought to its attention, or classes of transactions, account balances, or disclosures for which a risk of fraud is likely to exist; (Ref: Para. A14)

(c) Management's communication, if any, to those charged with governance regarding its processes for identifying and responding to the risks of fraud in the entity; and

(d) Management's communication, if any, to employees regarding its views on business practices and ethical behavior.

18 The auditor shall make inquiries of management, and others within the entity as appropriate, to determine whether they have knowledge of any actual, suspected or alleged fraud affecting the entity. (Ref: Para. A15–A17)

19 For those entities that have an internal audit function, the auditor shall make inquiries of appropriate individuals within the function to determine whether they have knowledge of any actual, suspected or alleged fraud affecting the entity, and to obtain its views about the risks of fraud. (Ref: Para. A18)

Those Charged with Governance

20 Unless all of those charged with governance are involved in managing the entity,[8] the auditor shall obtain an understanding of how those charged with governance exercise oversight of management's processes for identifying and responding to

[6] *ISA (UK) 315 (Revised June 2016), paragraph 10.*

[7] *ISA (UK) 315 (Revised June 2016), paragraphs 5–24.*

[8] *ISA (UK) 260 (Revised June 2016), Communication with Those Charged with Governance, paragraph 13.*

the risks of fraud in the entity and the internal control that management has established to mitigate these risks. (Ref: Para. A19–A21)

Unless all of those charged with governance are involved in managing the entity, **21** the auditor shall make inquiries of those charged with governance to determine whether they have knowledge of any actual, suspected or alleged fraud affecting the entity. These inquiries are made in part to corroborate the responses to the inquiries of management.

Unusual or Unexpected Relationships Identified

The auditor shall evaluate whether unusual or unexpected relationships that have **22** been identified in performing analytical procedures, including those related to revenue accounts, may indicate risks of material misstatement due to fraud.

Other Information

The auditor shall consider whether other information obtained by the auditor **23** indicates risks of material misstatement due to fraud. (Ref: Para. A22)

Evaluation of Fraud Risk Factors

The auditor shall evaluate whether the information obtained from the other risk **24** assessment procedures and related activities performed indicates that one or more fraud risk factors are present. While fraud risk factors may not necessarily indicate the existence of fraud, they have often been present in circumstances where frauds have occurred and therefore may indicate risks of material misstatement due to fraud. (Ref: Para. A23–A27)

Identification and Assessment of the Risks of Material Misstatement Due to Fraud

In accordance with ISA (UK) 315 (Revised June 2016), the auditor shall identify **25** and assess the risks of material misstatement due to fraud at the financial statement level, and at the assertion level for classes of transactions, account balances and disclosures.[9]

When identifying and assessing the risks of material misstatement due to fraud, **26** the auditor shall, based on a presumption that there are risks of fraud in revenue recognition, evaluate which types of revenue, revenue transactions or assertions give rise to such risks. Paragraph 47 specifies the documentation required where the auditor concludes that the presumption is not applicable in the circumstances of the engagement and, accordingly, has not identified revenue recognition as a risk of material misstatement due to fraud. (Ref: Para. A28–A30)

The auditor shall treat those assessed risks of material misstatement due to fraud as **27** significant risks and accordingly, to the extent not already done so, the auditor shall obtain an understanding of the entity's related controls, including control activities, relevant to such risks. (Ref: Para. A31–A32)

---

[9] *ISA (UK) 315 (Revised June 2016), paragraph 25.*

Responses to the Assessed Risks of Material Misstatement Due to Fraud

Overall Responses

28   In accordance with ISA (UK) 330 (Revised July 2017), the auditor shall determine overall responses to address the assessed risks of material misstatement due to fraud at the financial statement level.[10] (Ref: Para. A33)

29   In determining overall responses to address the assessed risks of material misstatement due to fraud at the financial statement level, the auditor shall:

(a)   Assign and supervise personnel taking account of the knowledge, skill and ability of the individuals to be given significant engagement responsibilities and the auditor's assessment of the risks of material misstatement due to fraud for the engagement; (Ref: Para. A34–A35)

(b)   Evaluate whether the selection and application of accounting policies by the entity, particularly those related to subjective measurements and complex transactions, may be indicative of fraudulent financial reporting resulting from management's effort to manage earnings; and

(c)   Incorporate an element of unpredictability in the selection of the nature, timing and extent of audit procedures. (Ref: Para. A36)

Audit Procedures Responsive to Assessed Risks of Material Misstatement Due to Fraud at the Assertion Level

30   In accordance with ISA (UK) 330 (Revised July 2017), the auditor shall design and perform further audit procedures whose nature, timing and extent are responsive to the assessed risks of material misstatement due to fraud at the assertion level.[11] (Ref: Para. A37–A40)

Audit Procedures Responsive to Risks Related to Management Override of Controls

31   Management is in a unique position to perpetrate fraud because of management's ability to manipulate accounting records and prepare fraudulent financial statements by overriding controls that otherwise appear to be operating effectively. Although the level of risk of management override of controls will vary from entity to entity, the risk is nevertheless present in all entities. Due to the unpredictable way in which such override could occur, it is a risk of material misstatement due to fraud and thus a significant risk.

32   Irrespective of the auditor's assessment of the risks of management override of controls, the auditor shall design and perform audit procedures to:

(a)   Test the appropriateness of journal entries recorded in the general ledger and other adjustments made in the preparation of the financial statements. In designing and performing audit procedures for such tests, the auditor shall:

(i)   Make inquiries of individuals involved in the financial reporting process about inappropriate or unusual activity relating to the processing of journal entries and other adjustments;

(ii)   Select journal entries and other adjustments made at the end of a reporting period; and

---

[10]   *ISA (UK) 330 (Revised July 2017), paragraph 5.*

[11]   *ISA (UK) 330 (Revised July 2017), paragraph 6.*

(iii) Consider the need to test journal entries and other adjustments throughout the period. (Ref: Para. A41–A44)

(b) Review accounting estimates for biases and evaluate whether the circumstances producing the bias, if any, represent a risk of material misstatement due to fraud. In performing this review, the auditor shall:

(i) Evaluate whether the judgments and decisions made by management in making the accounting estimates included in the financial statements, even if they are individually reasonable, indicate a possible bias on the part of the entity's management that may represent a risk of material misstatement due to fraud. If so, the auditor shall reevaluate the accounting estimates taken as a whole; and

(ii) Perform a retrospective review of management judgments and assumptions related to significant accounting estimates reflected in the financial statements of the prior year. (Ref: Para. A45–A47)

(c) For significant transactions that are outside the normal course of business for the entity, or that otherwise appear to be unusual given the auditor's understanding of the entity and its environment and other information obtained during the audit, the auditor shall evaluate whether the business rationale (or the lack thereof) of the transactions suggests that they may have been entered into to engage in fraudulent financial reporting or to conceal misappropriation of assets. (Ref: Para. A48)

33 The auditor shall determine whether, in order to respond to the identified risks of management override of controls, the auditor needs to perform other audit procedures in addition to those specifically referred to above (that is, where there are specific additional risks of management override that are not covered as part of the procedures performed to address the requirements in paragraph 32).

Evaluation of Audit Evidence
(Ref: Para. A49)

34 The auditor shall evaluate whether analytical procedures that are performed near the end of the audit, when forming an overall conclusion as to whether the financial statements are consistent with the auditor's understanding of the entity, indicate a previously unrecognized risk of material misstatement due to fraud. (Ref: Para. A50)

35 If the auditor identifies a misstatement, the auditor shall evaluate whether such a misstatement is indicative of fraud. If there is such an indication, the auditor shall evaluate the implications of the misstatement in relation to other aspects of the audit, particularly the reliability of management representations, recognizing that an instance of fraud is unlikely to be an isolated occurrence. (Ref: Para. A51)

36 If the auditor identifies a misstatement, whether material or not, and the auditor has reason to believe that it is or may be the result of fraud and that management (in particular, senior management) is involved, the auditor shall reevaluate the assessment of the risks of material misstatement due to fraud and its resulting impact on the nature, timing and extent of audit procedures to respond to the assessed risks. The auditor shall also consider whether circumstances or conditions indicate possible collusion involving employees, management or third parties when reconsidering the reliability of evidence previously obtained. (Ref: Para. A52)

37   If the auditor confirms that, or is unable to conclude whether, the financial statements are materially misstated as a result of fraud the auditor shall evaluate the implications for the audit. (Ref: Para. A53)

Auditor Unable to Continue the Engagement

38   If, as a result of a misstatement resulting from fraud or suspected fraud, the auditor encounters exceptional circumstances that bring into question the auditor's ability to continue performing the audit, the auditor shall:

(a)   Determine the professional and legal responsibilities applicable in the circumstances, including whether there is a requirement for the auditor to report to the person or persons who made the audit appointment or, in some cases, to regulatory authorities;

(b)   Consider whether it is appropriate to withdraw from the engagement, where withdrawal is possible under applicable law or regulation; and

(c)   If the auditor withdraws:

(i)   Discuss with the appropriate level of management and those charged with governance the auditor's withdrawal from the engagement and the reasons for the withdrawal; and

(ii)   Determine whether there is a professional or legal requirement to report to the person or persons who made the audit appointment or, in some cases, to regulatory authorities, the auditor's withdrawal from the engagement and the reasons for the withdrawal. (Ref: Para. A54–A57)

Written Representations

39   The auditor shall obtain written representations from management and, where appropriate, those charged with governance that:

(a)   They acknowledge their responsibility for the design, implementation and maintenance of internal control to prevent and detect fraud;

(b)   They have disclosed to the auditor the results of management's assessment of the risk that the financial statements may be materially misstated as a result of fraud;

(c)   They have disclosed to the auditor their knowledge of fraud or suspected fraud affecting the entity involving:

(i)   Management;

(ii)   Employees who have significant roles in internal control; or

(iii)   Others where the fraud could have a material effect on the financial statements; and

(d)   They have disclosed to the auditor their knowledge of any allegations of fraud, or suspected fraud, affecting the entity's financial statements communicated by employees, former employees, analysts, regulators or others. (Ref: Para. A58–A59)

Communications to Management and with Those Charged with Governance

40   If the auditor has identified a fraud or has obtained information that indicates that a fraud may exist, the auditor shall communicate these matters, unless prohibited by law or regulation, on a timely basis with the appropriate level of management in order to inform those with primary responsibility for the prevention and detection of fraud of matters relevant to their responsibilities. (Ref: Para. A59a–A60)

Unless all of those charged with governance are involved in managing the entity, if **41** the auditor has identified or suspects fraud involving:

(a)   management;

(b)   employees who have significant roles in internal control; or

(c)   others where the fraud results in a material misstatement in the financial statements,

the auditor shall communicate these matters with those charged with governance on a timely basis. If the auditor suspects fraud involving management, the auditor shall communicate these suspicions with those charged with governance and discuss with them the nature, timing and extent of audit procedures necessary to complete the audit. Such communications with those charged with governance are required unless the communication is prohibited by law or regulation. (Ref: Para. A59a, A61–A63)

For audits of financial statements of public interest entities, when an auditor   **41R-1** suspects or has reasonable grounds to suspect that irregularities, including fraud with regard to the financial statements of the entity, may occur or has occurred, the auditor shall, unless prohibited by law or regulation, inform the entity and invite it to investigate the matter and take appropriate measures to deal with such irregularities and to prevent any recurrence of such irregularities in the future. (Ref: Para. A63-1–A63-2)

The auditor shall communicate, unless prohibited by law or regulation, with those   **42** charged with governance any other matters related to fraud that are, in the auditor's judgment, relevant to their responsibilities. (Ref: Para. A59a, A64)

Reporting Fraud to an Appropriate Authority Outside the Entity

If the auditor has identified or suspects a fraud, the auditor shall determine whether   **43** law, regulation or relevant ethical requirements: (Ref: Para. A65–A67)

(a)   Require the auditor to report to an appropriate authority outside the entity.

(b)   Establish responsibilities under which reporting to an appropriate authority outside the entity may be appropriate in the circumstances.

For audits of financial statements of public interest entities, where the entity   **43R-1** does not investigate the matter referred to in paragraph 41R-1, the auditor shall inform the authorities responsible for investigating such irregularities. (Ref: Para. A66-1–A66-2)

Documentation

The auditor shall include the following in the audit documentation[12] of the   **44** auditor's understanding of the entity and its environment and the assessment of the risks of material misstatement required by ISA (UK) 315 (Revised June 2016):[13]

---

[12] *ISA (UK) 230 (Revised June 2016), Audit Documentation, paragraphs 8–11, and paragraph A6.*

[13] *ISA (UK) 315 (Revised June 2016), paragraph 32.*

(a)   The significant decisions reached during the discussion among the engagement team regarding the susceptibility of the entity's financial statements to material misstatement due to fraud; and

(b)   The identified and assessed risks of material misstatement due to fraud at the financial statement level and at the assertion level.

45   The auditor shall include the following in the audit documentation of the auditor's responses to the assessed risks of material misstatement required by ISA (UK) 330 (Revised July 2017):[14]

(a)   The overall responses to the assessed risks of material misstatement due to fraud at the financial statement level and the nature, timing and extent of audit procedures, and the linkage of those procedures with the assessed risks of material misstatement due to fraud at the assertion level; and

(b)   The results of the audit procedures, including those designed to address the risk of management override of controls.

46   The auditor shall include in the audit documentation communications about fraud made to management, those charged with governance, regulators and others.

47   If the auditor has concluded that the presumption that there is a risk of material misstatement due to fraud related to revenue recognition is not applicable in the circumstances of the engagement, the auditor shall include in the audit documentation the reasons for that conclusion.

***

Application and Other Explanatory Material

Characteristics of Fraud
(Ref: Para. 3)

A1   Fraud, whether fraudulent financial reporting or misappropriation of assets, involves incentive or pressure to commit fraud, a perceived opportunity to do so and some rationalization of the act. For example:

- Incentive or pressure to commit fraudulent financial reporting may exist when management is under pressure, from sources outside or inside the entity, to achieve an expected (and perhaps unrealistic) earnings target or financial outcome – particularly since the consequences to management for failing to meet financial goals can be significant. Similarly, individuals may have an incentive to misappropriate assets, for example, because the individuals are living beyond their means.

- A perceived opportunity to commit fraud may exist when an individual believes internal control can be overridden, for example, because the individual is in a position of trust or has knowledge of specific deficiencies in internal control.

- Individuals may be able to rationalize committing a fraudulent act. Some individuals possess an attitude, character or set of ethical values that allow them knowingly and intentionally to commit a dishonest act. However, even otherwise honest individuals can commit fraud in an environment that imposes sufficient pressure on them.

---

[14]   *ISA (UK) 330 (Revised July 2017), paragraph 28.*

Fraudulent financial reporting involves intentional misstatements including **A2** omissions of amounts or disclosures in financial statements to deceive financial statement users. It can be caused by the efforts of management to manage earnings in order to deceive financial statement users by influencing their perceptions as to the entity's performance and profitability. Such earnings management may start out with small actions or inappropriate adjustment of assumptions and changes in judgments by management. Pressures and incentives may lead these actions to increase to the extent that they result in fraudulent financial reporting. Such a situation could occur when, due to pressures to meet market expectations or a desire to maximize compensation based on performance, management intentionally takes positions that lead to fraudulent financial reporting by materially misstating the financial statements. In some entities, management may be motivated to reduce earnings by a material amount to minimize tax or to inflate earnings to secure bank financing.

Fraudulent financial reporting may be accomplished by the following: **A3**

- Manipulation, falsification (including forgery), or alteration of accounting records or supporting documentation from which the financial statements are prepared.

- Misrepresentation in, or intentional omission from, the financial statements of events, transactions or other significant information.

Fraudulent financial reporting often involves management override of controls **A4** that otherwise may appear to be operating effectively. Fraud can be committed by management overriding controls using such techniques as intentionally:

- Recording fictitious journal entries, particularly close to the end of an accounting period, to manipulate operating results or achieve other objectives.

- Inappropriately adjusting assumptions and changing judgments used to estimate account balances.

- Omitting, advancing or delaying recognition in the financial statements of events and transactions that have occurred during the reporting period.

- Omitting, obscuring or misstating disclosures required by the applicable financial reporting framework, or disclosures that are necessary to achieve fair presentation.

- Concealing facts that could affect the amounts recorded in the financial statements.

- Engaging in complex transactions that are structured to misrepresent the financial position or financial performance of the entity.

- Altering records and terms related to significant and unusual transactions.

Misappropriation of assets involves the theft of an entity's assets and is often **A5** perpetrated by employees in relatively small and immaterial amounts. However, it can also involve management who are usually more able to disguise or conceal misappropriations in ways that are difficult to detect. Misappropriation of assets can be accomplished in a variety of ways including:

- Embezzling receipts (for example, misappropriating collections on accounts receivable or diverting receipts in respect of written-off accounts to personal bank accounts).

- Stealing physical assets or intellectual property (for example, stealing inventory for personal use or for sale, stealing scrap for resale, colluding with a competitor by disclosing technological data in return for payment).

- Causing an entity to pay for goods and services not received (for example, payments to fictitious vendors, kickbacks paid by vendors to the entity's purchasing agents in return for inflating prices, payments to fictitious employees).

- Using an entity's assets for personal use (for example, using the entity's assets as collateral for a personal loan or a loan to a related party).

Misappropriation of assets is often accompanied by false or misleading records or documents in order to conceal the fact that the assets are missing or have been pledged without proper authorization.

Responsibility for the Prevention and Detection of Fraud

Responsibilities of the Auditor
(Ref: Para. 8a)

A5a   Law, regulation or relevant ethical requirements may require the auditor to perform additional procedures and take further actions. For example, the Code of Ethics for Professional Accountants issued by the International Ethics Standards Board for Accountants (IESBA Code) requires the auditor to take steps to respond to identified or suspected non-compliance with laws and regulations and determine whether further action is needed. Such steps may include the communication of identified or suspected non-compliance with laws and regulations to other auditors within a group, including a group engagement partner, component auditors or other auditors performing work at components of a group for purposes other than the audit of the group financial statements.[15]

Considerations Specific to Public Sector Entities

A6   The public sector auditor's responsibilities relating to fraud may be a result of law, regulation or other authority applicable to public sector entities or separately covered by the auditor's mandate. Consequently, the public sector auditor's responsibilities may not be limited to consideration of risks of material misstatement of the financial statements, but may also include a broader responsibility to consider risks of fraud.

Professional Skepticism
(Ref: Para. 12–14)

A7   Maintaining professional skepticism requires an ongoing questioning of whether the information and audit evidence obtained suggests that a material misstatement due to fraud may exist. It includes considering the reliability of the information to be used as audit evidence and the controls over its preparation and maintenance where relevant. Due to the characteristics of fraud, the auditor's professional skepticism is particularly important when considering the risks of material misstatement due to fraud.

A8   Although the auditor cannot be expected to disregard past experience of the honesty and integrity of the entity's management and those charged with

---

[15] *See Sections 225.21–225.22 of the IESBA Code.*
In the UK, the auditor has regard to any specific requirements of the auditor's relevant professional body.

governance, the auditor's professional skepticism is particularly important in considering the risks of material misstatement due to fraud because there may have been changes in circumstances.

An audit performed in accordance with ISAs (UK) rarely involves the **A9** authentication of documents, nor is the auditor trained as or expected to be an expert in such authentication.[16] However, when the auditor identifies conditions that cause the auditor to believe that a document may not be authentic or that terms in a document have been modified but not disclosed to the auditor, possible procedures to investigate further may include:

- Confirming directly with the third party.

- Using the work of an expert to assess the document's authenticity.

Discussion among the Engagement Team
(Ref: Para. 15)

Discussing the susceptibility of the entity's financial statements to material **A10** misstatement due to fraud with the engagement team:

- Provides an opportunity for more experienced engagement team members to share their insights about how and where the financial statements may be susceptible to material misstatement due to fraud.

- Enables the auditor to consider an appropriate response to such susceptibility and to determine which members of the engagement team will conduct certain audit procedures.

- Permits the auditor to determine how the results of audit procedures will be shared among the engagement team and how to deal with any allegations of fraud that may come to the auditor's attention.

The discussion may include such matters as: **A11**

- An exchange of ideas among engagement team members about how and where they believe the entity's financial statements (including the individual financial statements and the disclosures) may be susceptible to material misstatement due to fraud, how management could perpetrate and conceal fraudulent financial reporting, and how assets of the entity could be misappropriated.

- A consideration of circumstances that might be indicative of earnings management and the practices that might be followed by management to manage earnings that could lead to fraudulent financial reporting.

- A consideration of the risk that management may attempt to present disclosures in a manner that may obscure a proper understanding of the matters disclosed (for example, by including too much immaterial information or by using unclear or ambiguous language).

- A consideration of the known external and internal factors affecting the entity that may create an incentive or pressure for management or others to commit fraud, provide the opportunity for fraud to be perpetrated, and indicate a culture or environment that enables management or others to rationalize committing fraud.

- A consideration of management's involvement in overseeing employees with access to cash or other assets susceptible to misappropriation.

---

[16] *ISA (UK) 200 (Revised June 2016), paragraph A49.*

- A consideration of any unusual or unexplained changes in behavior or lifestyle of management or employees which have come to the attention of the engagement team.

- An emphasis on the importance of maintaining a proper state of mind throughout the audit regarding the potential for material misstatement due to fraud.

- A consideration of the types of circumstances that, if encountered, might indicate the possibility of fraud.

- A consideration of how an element of unpredictability will be incorporated into the nature, timing and extent of the audit procedures to be performed.

- A consideration of the audit procedures that might be selected to respond to the susceptibility of the entity's financial statement to material misstatement due to fraud and whether certain types of audit procedures are more effective than others.

- A consideration of any allegations of fraud that have come to the auditor's attention.

- A consideration of the risk of management override of controls.

Risk Assessment Procedures and Related Activities

Inquiries of Management

Management's Assessment of the Risk of Material Misstatement Due to Fraud (Ref: Para. 17(a))

A12   Management[16a] accepts responsibility for the entity's internal control and for the preparation of the entity's financial statements. Accordingly, it is appropriate for the auditor to make inquiries of management regarding management's own assessment of the risk of fraud and the controls in place to prevent and detect it. The nature, extent and frequency of management's assessment of such risk and controls may vary from entity to entity. In some entities, management may make detailed assessments on an annual basis or as part of continuous monitoring. In other entities, management's assessment may be less structured and less frequent. The nature, extent and frequency of management's assessment are relevant to the auditor's understanding of the entity's control environment. For example, the fact that management has not made an assessment of the risk of fraud may in some circumstances be indicative of the lack of importance that management places on internal control.

Considerations specific to smaller entities

A13   In some entities, particularly smaller entities, the focus of management's assessment may be on the risks of employee fraud or misappropriation of assets.

Management's Process for Identifying and Responding to the Risks of Fraud (Ref: Para. 17(b))

A14   In the case of entities with multiple locations management's processes may include different levels of monitoring of operating locations, or business

---

[16a] *In the UK, those charged with governance are responsible for the preparation of the financial statements.*

segments. Management may also have identified particular operating locations or business segments for which a risk of fraud may be more likely to exist.

Inquiry of Management and Others within the Entity
(Ref: Para. 18)

The auditor's inquiries of management may provide useful information **A15** concerning the risks of material misstatements in the financial statements resulting from employee fraud. However, such inquiries are unlikely to provide useful information regarding the risks of material misstatement in the financial statements resulting from management fraud. Making inquiries of others within the entity may provide individuals with an opportunity to convey information to the auditor that may not otherwise be communicated.

Examples of others within the entity to whom the auditor may direct inquiries **A16** about the existence or suspicion of fraud include:

- Operating personnel not directly involved in the financial reporting process.

- Employees with different levels of authority.

- Employees involved in initiating, processing or recording complex or unusual transactions and those who supervise or monitor such employees.

- In-house legal counsel.

- Chief ethics officer or equivalent person.

- The person or persons charged with dealing with allegations of fraud.

Management is often in the best position to perpetrate fraud. Accordingly, when **A17** evaluating management's responses to inquiries with an attitude of professional skepticism, the auditor may judge it necessary to corroborate responses to inquiries with other information.

Inquiries of the Internal Audit Function
(Ref: Para. 19)

ISA (UK) 315 (Revised June 2016) and ISA (UK) 610 (Revised June 2013) **A18** establish requirements and provide guidance relevant to audits of those entities that have an internal audit function.[17] In carrying out the requirements of those ISAs (UK) in the context of fraud, the auditor may inquire about specific activities of the function including, for example:

- The procedures performed, if any, by the internal audit function during the year to detect fraud.

- Whether management has satisfactorily responded to any findings resulting from those procedures.

Obtaining an Understanding of Oversight Exercised by Those Charged with Governance
(Ref: Para. 20)

Those charged with governance of an entity oversee the entity's systems for **A19** monitoring risk, financial control and compliance with the law. In many countries, corporate governance practices are well developed and those charged with governance play an active role in oversight of the entity's assessment of the

---

[17] *ISA (UK) 315 (Revised June 2016), paragraphs 6(a) and 23, and ISA (UK) 610 (Revised June 2013), Using the Work of Internal Auditors.*

risks of fraud and of the relevant internal control. Since the responsibilities of those charged with governance and management may vary by entity and by country, it is important that the auditor understands their respective responsibilities to enable the auditor to obtain an understanding of the oversight exercised by the appropriate individuals.[18]

A20   An understanding of the oversight exercised by those charged with governance may provide insights regarding the susceptibility of the entity to management fraud, the adequacy of internal control over risks of fraud, and the competency and integrity of management. The auditor may obtain this understanding in a number of ways, such as by attending meetings where such discussions take place, reading the minutes from such meetings or making inquiries of those charged with governance.

Considerations Specific to Smaller Entities

A21   In some cases, all of those charged with governance are involved in managing the entity. This may be the case in a small entity where a single owner manages the entity and no one else has a governance role. In these cases, there is ordinarily no action on the part of the auditor because there is no oversight separate from management.

Consideration of Other Information
(Ref: Para. 23)

A22   In addition to information obtained from applying analytical procedures, other information obtained about the entity and its environment may be helpful in identifying the risks of material misstatement due to fraud. The discussion among team members may provide information that is helpful in identifying such risks. In addition, information obtained from the auditor's client acceptance and retention processes, and experience gained on other engagements performed for the entity, for example engagements to review interim financial information, may be relevant in the identification of the risks of material misstatement due to fraud.

Evaluation of Fraud Risk Factors
(Ref: Para. 24)

A23   The fact that fraud is usually concealed can make it very difficult to detect. Nevertheless, the auditor may identify events or conditions that indicate an incentive or pressure to commit fraud or provide an opportunity to commit fraud (fraud risk factors). For example:

●   The need to meet expectations of third parties to obtain additional equity financing may create pressure to commit fraud;

●   The granting of significant bonuses if unrealistic profit targets are met may create an incentive to commit fraud; and

●   A control environment that is not effective may create an opportunity to commit fraud.

A24   Fraud risk factors cannot easily be ranked in order of importance. The significance of fraud risk factors varies widely. Some of these factors will be present in entities where the specific conditions do not present risks of material misstatement. Accordingly, the determination of whether a fraud risk factor is present and

---

[18] *ISA (UK) 260 (Revised June 2016), paragraphs A1–A8, discuss with whom the auditor communicates when the entity's governance structure is not well defined.*

whether it is to be considered in assessing the risks of material misstatement of the financial statements due to fraud requires the exercise of professional judgment.

Examples of fraud risk factors related to fraudulent financial reporting and misappropriation of assets are presented in Appendix 1. These illustrative risk factors are classified based on the three conditions that are generally present when fraud exists: **A25**

- An incentive or pressure to commit fraud;
- A perceived opportunity to commit fraud; and
- An ability to rationalize the fraudulent action.

Risk factors reflective of an attitude that permits rationalization of the fraudulent action may not be susceptible to observation by the auditor. Nevertheless, the auditor may become aware of the existence of such information. Although the fraud risk factors described in Appendix 1 cover a broad range of situations that may be faced by auditors, they are only examples and other risk factors may exist.

The size, complexity, and ownership characteristics of the entity have a significant influence on the consideration of relevant fraud risk factors. For example, in the case of a large entity, there may be factors that generally constrain improper conduct by management, such as: **A26**

- Effective oversight by those charged with governance.
- An effective internal audit function.
- The existence and enforcement of a written code of conduct.

Furthermore, fraud risk factors considered at a business segment operating level may provide different insights when compared with those obtained when considered at an entity-wide level.

Considerations Specific to Smaller Entities

In the case of a small entity, some or all of these considerations may be inapplicable or less relevant. For example, a smaller entity may not have a written code of conduct but, instead, may have developed a culture that emphasizes the importance of integrity and ethical behavior through oral communication and by management example. Domination of management by a single individual in a small entity does not generally, in and of itself, indicate a failure by management to display and communicate an appropriate attitude regarding internal control and the financial reporting process. In some entities, the need for management authorization can compensate for otherwise deficient controls and reduce the risk of employee fraud. However, domination of management by a single individual can be a potential deficiency in internal control since there is an opportunity for management override of controls. **A27**

Identification and Assessment of the Risks of Material Misstatement Due to Fraud

Risks of Fraud in Revenue Recognition
(Ref: Para. 26)

Material misstatement due to fraudulent financial reporting relating to revenue recognition often results from an overstatement of revenues through, for example, premature revenue recognition or recording fictitious revenues. It may result also **A28** from an understatement of revenues through, for example, improperly shifting revenues to a later period.

A29   The risks of fraud in revenue recognition may be greater in some entities than others. For example, there may be pressures or incentives on management to commit fraudulent financial reporting through inappropriate revenue recognition in the case of listed entities when, for example, performance is measured in terms of year-over-year revenue growth or profit. Similarly, for example, there may be greater risks of fraud in revenue recognition in the case of entities that generate a substantial portion of revenues through cash sales.

A30   The presumption that there are risks of fraud in revenue recognition may be rebutted. For example, the auditor may conclude that there is no risk of material misstatement due to fraud relating to revenue recognition in the case where a there is a single type of simple revenue transaction, for example, leasehold revenue from a single unit rental property.

Identifying and Assessing the Risks of Material Misstatement Due to Fraud and Understanding the Entity's Related Controls
(Ref: Para. 27)

A31   Management may make judgments on the nature and extent of the controls it chooses to implement, and the nature and extent of the risks it chooses to assume.[19] In determining which controls to implement to prevent and detect fraud, management considers the risks that the financial statements may be materially misstated as a result of fraud. As part of this consideration, management may conclude that it is not cost effective to implement and maintain a particular control in relation to the reduction in the risks of material misstatement due to fraud to be achieved.

A32   It is therefore important for the auditor to obtain an understanding of the controls that management has designed, implemented and maintained to prevent and detect fraud. In doing so, the auditor may learn, for example, that management has consciously chosen to accept the risks associated with a lack of segregation of duties. Information from obtaining this understanding may also be useful in identifying fraud risks factors that may affect the auditor's assessment of the risks that the financial statements may contain material misstatement due to fraud.

Responses to the Assessed Risks of Material Misstatement Due to Fraud

Overall Responses
(Ref: Para. 28)

A33   Determining overall responses to address the assessed risks of material misstatement due to fraud generally includes the consideration of how the overall conduct of the audit can reflect increased professional skepticism, for example, through:

- Increased sensitivity in the selection of the nature and extent of documentation to be examined in support of material transactions.

- Increased recognition of the need to corroborate management explanations or representations concerning material matters.

---

[19] ISA (UK) 315 (Revised June 2016), paragraph A56.

It also involves more general considerations apart from the specific procedures otherwise planned; these considerations include the matters listed in paragraph 29, which are discussed below.

Assignment and Supervision of Personnel
(Ref: Para. 29(a))

The auditor may respond to identified risks of material misstatement due to fraud **A34** by, for example, assigning additional individuals with specialized skill and knowledge, such as forensic and IT experts, or by assigning more experienced individuals to the engagement.

The extent of supervision reflects the auditor's assessment of risks of material **A35** misstatement due to fraud and the competencies of the engagement team members performing the work.

Unpredictability in the Selection of Audit Procedures
(Ref: Para. 29(c))

Incorporating an element of unpredictability in the selection of the nature, timing **A36** and extent of audit procedures to be performed is important as individuals within the entity who are familiar with the audit procedures normally performed on engagements may be more able to conceal fraudulent financial reporting. This can be achieved by, for example:

- Performing substantive procedures on selected account balances and assertions not otherwise tested due to their materiality or risk.

- Adjusting the timing of audit procedures from that otherwise expected.

- Using different sampling methods.

- Performing audit procedures at different locations or at locations on an unannounced basis.

Audit Procedures Responsive to Assessed Risks of Material Misstatement Due to Fraud at the Assertion Level
(Ref: Para. 30)

The auditor's responses to address the assessed risks of material misstatement due **A37** to fraud at the assertion level may include changing the nature, timing and extent of audit procedures in the following ways:

- The nature of audit procedures to be performed may need to be changed to obtain audit evidence that is more reliable and relevant or to obtain additional corroborative information. This may affect both the type of audit procedures to be performed and their combination. For example:

    - Physical observation or inspection of certain assets may become more important or the auditor may choose to use computer-assisted audit techniques to gather more evidence about data contained in significant accounts or electronic transaction files.

    - The auditor may design procedures to obtain additional corroborative information. For example, if the auditor identifies that management is under pressure to meet earnings expectations, there may be a related risk that management is inflating sales by entering into sales agreements that include terms that preclude revenue recognition or by invoicing sales before delivery. In these circumstances, the auditor may, for example, design external confirmations not only to confirm outstanding amounts, but also to confirm the details of the sales agreements, including date, any rights of return and delivery terms. In addition, the auditor might find it effective to supplement such external confirmations with inquiries of non-financial personnel in the entity regarding any changes in sales agreements and delivery terms.

- The timing of substantive procedures may need to be modified. The auditor may conclude that performing substantive testing at or near the period end better addresses an assessed risk of material misstatement due to fraud. The auditor may conclude that, given the assessed risks of intentional misstatement or manipulation, audit procedures to extend audit conclusions from an interim date to the period end would not be effective. In contrast, because an intentional misstatement – for example, a misstatement involving improper revenue recognition – may have been initiated in an interim period, the auditor may elect to apply substantive procedures to transactions occurring earlier in or throughout the reporting period.

- The extent of the procedures applied reflects the assessment of the risks of material misstatement due to fraud. For example, increasing sample sizes or performing analytical procedures at a more detailed level may be appropriate. Also, computer-assisted audit techniques may enable more extensive testing of electronic transactions and account files. Such techniques can be used to select sample transactions from key electronic files, to sort transactions with specific characteristics, or to test an entire population instead of a sample.

A38   If the auditor identifies a risk of material misstatement due to fraud that affects inventory quantities, examining the entity's inventory records may help to identify locations or items that require specific attention during or after the physical inventory count. Such a review may lead to a decision to observe inventory counts at certain locations on an unannounced basis or to conduct inventory counts at all locations on the same date.

A39   The auditor may identify a risk of material misstatement due to fraud affecting a number of accounts and assertions. These may include asset valuation, estimates relating to specific transactions (such as acquisitions, restructurings, or disposals of a segment of the business), and other significant accrued liabilities (such as pension and other post-employment benefit obligations, or environmental remediation liabilities). The risk may also relate to significant changes in assumptions relating to recurring estimates. Information gathered through obtaining an understanding of the entity and its environment may assist the auditor in evaluating the reasonableness of such management estimates and underlying judgments and assumptions. A retrospective review of similar management judgments and assumptions applied in prior periods may also provide insight about the reasonableness of judgments and assumptions supporting management estimates.

A40   Examples of possible audit procedures to address the assessed risks of material misstatement due to fraud, including those that illustrate the incorporation of an element of unpredictability, are presented in Appendix 2. The appendix includes examples of responses to the auditor's assessment of the risks of material misstatement resulting from both fraudulent financial reporting, including fraudulent financial reporting resulting from revenue recognition, and misappropriation of assets.

Audit Procedures Responsive to Risks Related to Management Override of Controls

Journal Entries and Other Adjustments
(Ref: Para. 32(a))

Material misstatement of financial statements due to fraud often involve the manipulation of the financial reporting process by recording inappropriate or unauthorized journal entries. This may occur throughout the year or at period end, or by management making adjustments to amounts reported in the financial statements that are not reflected in journal entries, such as through consolidating adjustments and reclassifications.   **A41**

Further, the auditor's consideration of the risks of material misstatement associated with inappropriate override of controls over journal entries is important since automated processes and controls may reduce the risk of inadvertent error but do not overcome the risk that individuals may inappropriately override such automated processes, for example, by changing the amounts being automatically passed to the general ledger or to the financial reporting system. Furthermore, where IT is used to transfer information automatically, there may be little or no visible evidence of such intervention in the information systems.   **A42**

When identifying and selecting journal entries and other adjustments for testing and determining the appropriate method of examining the underlying support for the items selected, the following matters are of relevance: **A43**

- *The assessment of the risks of material misstatement due to fraud* – the presence of fraud risk factors and other information obtained during the auditor's assessment of the risks of material misstatement due to fraud may assist the auditor to identify specific classes of journal entries and other adjustments for testing.

- *Controls that have been implemented over journal entries and other adjustments* – effective controls over the preparation and posting of journal entries and other adjustments may reduce the extent of substantive testing necessary, provided that the auditor has tested the operating effectiveness of the controls.

- *The entity's financial reporting process and the nature of evidence that can be obtained* – for many entities routine processing of transactions involves a combination of manual and automated steps and procedures. Similarly, the processing of journal entries and other adjustments may involve both manual and automated procedures and controls. Where information technology is used in the financial reporting process, journal entries and other adjustments may exist only in electronic form.

- *The characteristics of fraudulent journal entries or other adjustments* – inappropriate journal entries or other adjustments often have unique identifying characteristics. Such characteristics may include entries (a) made to unrelated, unusual, or seldom-used accounts, (b) made by individuals who typically do not make journal entries, (c) recorded at the end of the period or as post-closing entries that have little or no explanation or description, (d) made either before or during the preparation of the financial statements that do not have account numbers, or (e) containing round numbers or consistent ending numbers.

● *The nature and complexity of the accounts* – inappropriate journal entries or adjustments may be applied to accounts that (a) contain transactions that are complex or unusual in nature, (b) contain significant estimates and period-end adjustments, (c) have been prone to misstatements in the past, (d) have not been reconciled on a timely basis or contain unreconciled differences, (e) contain intercompany transactions, or (f) are otherwise associated with an identified risk of material misstatement due to fraud. In audits of entities that have several locations or components, consideration is given to the need to select journal entries from multiple locations.

● *Journal entries or other adjustments processed outside the normal course of business* – non standard journal entries may not be subject to the same level of internal control as those journal entries used on a recurring basis to record transactions such as monthly sales, purchases and cash disbursements.

A44   The auditor uses professional judgment in determining the nature, timing and extent of testing of journal entries and other adjustments. However, because fraudulent journal entries and other adjustments are often made at the end of a reporting period, paragraph 32(a)(ii) requires the auditor to select the journal entries and other adjustments made at that time. Further, because material misstatements in financial statements due to fraud can occur throughout the period and may involve extensive efforts to conceal how the fraud is accomplished, paragraph 32(a)(iii) requires the auditor to consider whether there is also a need to test journal entries and other adjustments throughout the period.

Accounting Estimates
(Ref: Para. 32(b))

A45   The preparation of the financial statements requires management[14a] to make a number of judgments or assumptions that affect significant accounting estimates and to monitor the reasonableness of such estimates on an ongoing basis. Fraudulent financial reporting is often accomplished through intentional misstatement of accounting estimates. This may be achieved by, for example, understating or overstating all provisions or reserves in the same fashion so as to be designed either to smooth earnings over two or more accounting periods, or to achieve a designated earnings level in order to deceive financial statement users by influencing their perceptions as to the entity's performance and profitability.

A46   The purpose of performing a retrospective review of management judgments and assumptions related to significant accounting estimates reflected in the financial statements of the prior year is to determine whether there is an indication of a possible bias on the part of management. It is not intended to call into question the auditor's professional judgments made in the prior year that were based on information available at the time.

A47   A retrospective review is also required by ISA (UK) 540 (Revised June 2016).[20] That review is conducted as a risk assessment procedure to obtain information regarding the effectiveness of management's prior period estimation process, audit evidence about the outcome, or where applicable, the subsequent re-estimation of prior period accounting estimates that is pertinent to making current period

---

[20] ISA (UK) 540 (Revised June 2016), *Auditing Accounting Estimates, Including Fair Value Accounting Estimates, and Related Disclosures, paragraph 9.*

accounting estimates, and audit evidence of matters, such as estimation uncertainty, that may be required to be disclosed in the financial statements. As a practical matter, the auditor's review of management judgments and assumptions for biases that could represent a risk of material misstatement due to fraud in accordance with this ISA (UK) may be carried out in conjunction with the review required by ISA (UK) 540 (Revised June 2016).

Business Rationale for Significant Transactions
(Ref: Para. 32(c))

Indicators that may suggest that significant transactions that are outside the normal **A48** course of business for the entity, or that otherwise appear to be unusual, may have been entered into to engage in fraudulent financial reporting or to conceal misappropriation of assets include:

- The form of such transactions appears overly complex (for example, the transaction involves multiple entities within a consolidated group or multiple unrelated third parties).

- Management has not discussed the nature of and accounting for such transactions with those charged with governance of the entity, and there is inadequate documentation.

- Management is placing more emphasis on the need for a particular accounting treatment than on the underlying economics of the transaction.

- Transactions that involve non-consolidated related parties, including special purpose entities, have not been properly reviewed or approved by those charged with governance of the entity.

- The transactions involve previously unidentified related parties or parties that do not have the substance or the financial strength to support the transaction without assistance from the entity under audit.

Evaluation of Audit Evidence
(Ref: Para. 34–37)

ISA (UK) 330 (Revised July 2017) requires the auditor, based on the audit **A49** procedures performed and the audit evidence obtained, to evaluate whether the assessments of the risks of material misstatement at the assertion level remain appropriate.[21] This evaluation is primarily a qualitative matter based on the auditor's judgment. Such an evaluation may provide further insight about the risks of material misstatement due to fraud and whether there is a need to perform additional or different audit procedures. Appendix 3 contains examples of circumstances that may indicate the possibility of fraud.

Analytical Procedures Performed Near the End of the Audit in Forming an Overall Conclusion
(Ref: Para. 34)

Determining which particular trends and relationships may indicate a risk of **A50** material misstatement due to fraud requires professional judgment. Unusual relationships involving year-end revenue and income are particularly relevant. These might include, for example: uncharacteristically large amounts of income being reported in the last few weeks of the reporting period or unusual

---

[21] *ISA (UK) 330 (Revised July 2017), paragraph 25.*

transactions; or income that is inconsistent with trends in cash flow from operations.

Consideration of Identified Misstatements
(Ref: Para. 35–37)

A51   Since fraud involves incentive or pressure to commit fraud, a perceived opportunity to do so or some rationalization of the act, an instance of fraud is unlikely to be an isolated occurrence. Accordingly, misstatements, such as numerous misstatements at a specific location even though the cumulative effect is not material, may be indicative of a risk of material misstatement due to fraud.

A52   The implications of identified fraud depend on the circumstances. For example, an otherwise insignificant fraud may be significant if it involves senior management. In such circumstances, the reliability of evidence previously obtained may be called into question, since there may be doubts about the completeness and truthfulness of representations made and about the genuineness of accounting records and documentation. There may also be a possibility of collusion involving employees, management or third parties.

A53   ISA (UK) 450 (Revised June 2016)[22] and ISA (UK) 700 (Revised June 2016)[23] establish requirements and provide guidance on the evaluation and disposition of misstatements and the effect on the auditor's opinion in the auditor's report.

Auditor Unable to Continue the Engagement
(Ref: Para. 38)

A54   Examples of exceptional circumstances that may arise and that may bring into question the auditor's ability to continue performing the audit include:

- The entity does not take the appropriate action regarding fraud that the auditor considers necessary in the circumstances, even where the fraud is not material to the financial statements;

- The auditor's consideration of the risks of material misstatement due to fraud and the results of audit tests indicate a significant risk of material and pervasive fraud; or

- The auditor has significant concern about the competence or integrity of management or those charged with governance.

A55   Because of the variety of the circumstances that may arise, it is not possible to describe definitively when withdrawal from an engagement is appropriate. Factors that affect the auditor's conclusion include the implications of the involvement of a member of management or of those charged with governance (which may affect the reliability of management representations) and the effects on the auditor of a continuing association with the entity.

A56   The auditor has professional and legal responsibilities in such circumstances and these responsibilities may vary by country. In some countries, for example, the auditor may be entitled to, or required to, make a statement or report to the person or persons who made the audit appointment or, in some cases, to regulatory authorities. Given the exceptional nature of the circumstances and the need to consider the legal requirements, the auditor may consider it appropriate to seek legal advice when deciding whether to withdraw from an engagement and in

---

[22] *ISA (UK) 450 (Revised June 2016), Evaluation of Misstatements Identified during the Audit.*

[23] *ISA (UK) 700 (Revised June 2016), Forming an Opinion and Reporting on Financial Statements.*

determining an appropriate course of action, including the possibility of reporting to shareholders, regulators or others.[24]

Considerations Specific to Public Sector Entities

In many cases in the public sector, the option of withdrawing from the engagement may not be available to the auditor due to the nature of the mandate or public interest considerations.   **A57**

Written Representations
(Ref: Para. 39)

ISA (UK) 580[25] establishes requirements and provides guidance on obtaining appropriate representations from management and, where appropriate, those charged with governance in the audit. In addition to acknowledging that they have fulfilled their responsibility for the preparation of the financial statements, it is important that, irrespective of the size of the entity, management and, where appropriate, those charged with governance acknowledge their responsibility for internal control designed, implemented and maintained to prevent and detect fraud.   **A58**

Because of the nature of fraud and the difficulties encountered by auditors in detecting material misstatements in the financial statements resulting from fraud, it is important that the auditor obtain a written representation from management and, where appropriate, those charged with governance confirming that they have disclosed to the auditor: **A59**

(a) The results of management's assessment of the risk that the financial statements may be materially misstated as a result of fraud; and

(b) Their knowledge of actual, suspected or alleged fraud affecting the entity.

Communications to Management and with Those Charged with Governance
(Ref: Para. 40–42)

In some jurisdictions, law or regulation may restrict the auditor's communication of certain matters with management and those charged with governance. Law or regulation may specifically prohibit a communication, or other action, that might prejudice an investigation by an appropriate authority into an actual, or suspected, illegal act, including alerting the entity, for example, when the auditor is required to report the fraud to an appropriate authority pursuant to anti-money laundering legislation. In these circumstances, the issues considered by the auditor may be complex and the auditor may consider it appropriate to obtain legal advice.   **A59a**

Communication to Management
(Ref: Para. 40)

When the auditor has obtained evidence that fraud exists or may exist, it is important that the matter be brought to the attention of the appropriate level of management as soon as practicable. This is so even if the matter might be considered inconsequential (for example, a minor defalcation by an employee at a low level in the entity's organization). The determination of which level of   **A60**

---

[24] *The IESBA Code of Ethics for Professional Accountants provides guidance on communications with an auditor replacing the existing auditor.*

In the UK, the relevant ethical guidance on proposed communications with a successor auditor is provided by the ethical pronouncements relating to the work of auditors issued by the auditor's relevant professional body.

[25] *ISA (UK) 580, Written Representations.*

management is the appropriate one is a matter of professional judgment and is affected by such factors as the likelihood of collusion and the nature and magnitude of the suspected fraud. Ordinarily, the appropriate level of management is at least one level above the persons who appear to be involved with the suspected fraud.

Communication with Those Charged with Governance
(Ref: Para. 41)

A61   The auditor's communication with those charged with governance may be made orally or in writing. ISA (UK) 260 (Revised June 2016) identifies factors the auditor considers in determining whether to communicate orally or in writing.[26] Due to the nature and sensitivity of fraud involving senior management, or fraud that results in a material misstatement in the financial statements, the auditor reports such matters on a timely basis and may consider it necessary to also report such matters in writing.

A62   In some cases, the auditor may consider it appropriate to communicate with those charged with governance when the auditor becomes aware of fraud involving employees other than management that does not result in a material misstatement. Similarly, those charged with governance may wish to be informed of such circumstances. The communication process is assisted if the auditor and those charged with governance agree at an early stage in the audit about the nature and extent of the auditor's communications in this regard.

A63   In the exceptional circumstances where the auditor has doubts about the integrity or honesty of management or those charged with governance, the auditor may consider it appropriate to obtain legal advice to assist in determining the appropriate course of action.

Communication with Those Charged with Governance of Public Interest Entities
(Ref: Para. 41R-1)

A63-1   For audits of financial statements of public interest entities, ISA (UK) 260 (Revised June 2016)[26a] requires the auditor to communicate in the additional report to the audit committee any significant matters involving actual or suspected non-compliance with laws and regulations, including from fraud or suspected fraud, which were identified in the course of the audit.

A63-2   In the UK, laws or regulations may prohibit alerting ("tipping off") the entity when, for example, the auditor is required to report the non-compliance to an appropriate authority pursuant to anti-money laundering legislation.

Other Matters Related to Fraud
(Ref: Para. 42)

A64   Other matters related to fraud to be discussed with those charged with governance of the entity may include, for example:

- Concerns about the nature, extent and frequency of management's assessments of the controls in place to prevent and detect fraud and of the risk that the financial statements may be misstated.

---

[26] *ISA (UK) 260 (Revised June 2016), paragraph A38.*

[26a] *ISA (UK) 260 (Revised June 2016), Communication with Those Charged with Governance, paragraph 16R-2(k).*

- A failure by management to appropriately address identified significant deficiencies in internal control, or to appropriately respond to an identified fraud.

- The auditor's evaluation of the entity's control environment, including questions regarding the competence and integrity of management.

- Actions by management that may be indicative of fraudulent financial reporting, such as management's selection and application of accounting policies that may be indicative of management's effort to manage earnings in order to deceive financial statement users by influencing their perceptions as to the entity's performance and profitability.

- Concerns about the adequacy and completeness of the authorization of transactions that appear to be outside the normal course of business.

Reporting Fraud to an Appropriate Authority outside the Entity
(Ref: Para. 43)

ISA (UK) 250 (Revised July 2017)[27] provides further guidance with respect to the auditor's determination of whether reporting identified or suspected non-compliance with laws or regulations to an appropriate authority outside the entity is required or appropriate in the circumstances, including consideration of the auditor's duty of confidentiality. **A65**

The determination required by paragraph 43 may involve complex considerations and professional judgments. Accordingly, the auditor may consider consulting internally (e.g., within the firm or a network firm) or on a confidential basis with a regulator or professional body (unless doing so is prohibited by law or regulation or would breach the duty of confidentiality). The auditor may also consider obtaining legal advice to understand the auditor's options and the professional or legal implications of taking any particular course of action. **A66**

Reporting to Authorities of Public Interest Entities
(Ref: Para. 43R-1)

The disclosure in good faith to the authorities responsible for investigating such irregularities, by the auditor, of any irregularities referred to in paragraph 43R-1 shall not constitute a breach of any contractual or legal restriction on disclosure of information in accordance with the Audit Regulation.[27a] **A66-1**

The auditor considers whether to take further action when the entity investigates the matter referred to in paragraph 41R-1 but where the measures taken by management or those charged with governance, in the auditor's professional judgement, were not appropriate to deal with the actual or potential risks of fraud identified or would fail to prevent future occurrences of fraud. **A66-2**

Considerations Specific to Public Sector Entities

In the public sector, requirements for reporting fraud, whether or not discovered through the audit process, may be subject to specific provisions of the audit mandate or related law, regulation or other authority. **A67**

---

[27] *ISA (UK) 250 (Revised December 2017), Section A – Consideration of Laws and Regulations in an Audit of Financial Statements, paragraphs A28–A34.*

[27a] *Article 7 of Regulation (EU) No 537/2014 of the European Parliament and of the Council of 16 April 2014.*

Appendix 1

(Ref: Para. A25)

Examples of Fraud Risk Factors

The fraud risk factors identified in this Appendix are examples of such factors that may be faced by auditors in a broad range of situations. Separately presented are examples relating to the two types of fraud relevant to the auditor's consideration – that is, fraudulent financial reporting and misappropriation of assets. For each of these types of fraud, the risk factors are further classified based on the three conditions generally present when material misstatements due to fraud occur: (a) incentives/pressures, (b) opportunities, and (c) attitudes/rationalizations. Although the risk factors cover a broad range of situations, they are only examples and, accordingly, the auditor may identify additional or different risk factors. Not all of these examples are relevant in all circumstances, and some may be of greater or lesser significance in entities of different size or with different ownership characteristics or circumstances. Also, the order of the examples of risk factors provided is not intended to reflect their relative importance or frequency of occurrence.

Risk Factors Relating to Misstatements Arising from Fraudulent Financial Reporting

The following are examples of risk factors relating to misstatements arising from fraudulent financial reporting.

Incentives/Pressures

Financial stability or profitability is threatened by economic, industry, or entity operating conditions, such as (or as indicated by):

- High degree of competition or market saturation, accompanied by declining margins.
- High vulnerability to rapid changes, such as changes in technology, product obsolescence, or interest rates.
- Significant declines in customer demand and increasing business failures in either the industry or overall economy.
- Operating losses making the threat of bankruptcy, foreclosure, or hostile takeover imminent.
- Recurring negative cash flows from operations or an inability to generate cash flows from operations while reporting earnings and earnings growth.
- Rapid growth or unusual profitability especially compared to that of other companies in the same industry.
- New accounting, statutory, or regulatory requirements.

Excessive pressure exists for management to meet the requirements or expectations of third parties due to the following:

- Profitability or trend level expectations of investment analysts, institutional investors, significant creditors, or other external parties (particularly expectations that are unduly aggressive or unrealistic), including expectations created by management in, for example, overly optimistic press releases or annual report messages.

- Need to obtain additional debt or equity financing to stay competitive – including financing of major research and development or capital expenditures.

- Marginal ability to meet exchange listing requirements or debt repayment or other debt covenant requirements.

- Perceived or real adverse effects of reporting poor financial results on significant pending transactions, such as business combinations or contract awards.

Information available indicates that the personal financial situation of management or those charged with governance is threatened by the entity's financial performance arising from the following:

- Significant financial interests in the entity.

- Significant portions of their compensation (for example, bonuses, stock options, and earn-out arrangements) being contingent upon achieving aggressive targets for stock price, operating results, financial position, or cash flow.[1a]

- Personal guarantees of debts of the entity.

There is excessive pressure on management or operating personnel to meet financial targets established by those charged with governance, including sales or profitability incentive goals.

Opportunities

The nature of the industry or the entity's operations provides opportunities to engage in fraudulent financial reporting that can arise from the following:

- Significant related-party transactions not in the ordinary course of business or with related entities not audited or audited by another firm.

- A strong financial presence or ability to dominate a certain industry sector that allows the entity to dictate terms or conditions to suppliers or customers that may result in inappropriate or non-arm's-length transactions.

- Assets, liabilities, revenues, or expenses based on significant estimates that involve subjective judgments or uncertainties that are difficult to corroborate.

- Significant, unusual, or highly complex transactions, especially those close to period end that pose difficult "substance over form" questions.

- Significant operations located or conducted across international borders in jurisdictions where differing business environments and cultures exist.

- Use of business intermediaries for which there appears to be no clear business justification.

- Significant bank accounts or subsidiary or branch operations in tax-haven jurisdictions for which there appears to be no clear business justification.

The monitoring of management is not effective as a result of the following:

[1a] *Management incentive plans may be contingent upon achieving targets relating only to certain accounts or selected activities of the entity, even though the related accounts or activities may not be material to the entity as a whole.*

- Domination of management by a single person or small group (in a non owner-managed business) without compensating controls.

- Oversight by those charged with governance over the financial reporting process and internal control is not effective.

There is a complex or unstable organizational structure, as evidenced by the following:

- Difficulty in determining the organization or individuals that have controlling interest in the entity.

- Overly complex organizational structure involving unusual legal entities or managerial lines of authority.

- High turnover of senior management, legal counsel, or those charged with governance.

Internal control components are deficient as a result of the following:

- Inadequate monitoring of controls, including automated controls and controls over interim financial reporting (where external reporting is required).

- High turnover rates or employment of staff in accounting, information technology, or the internal audit function that are not effective.

- Accounting and information systems that are not effective, including situations involving significant deficiencies in internal control.

Attitudes/Rationalizations

- Communication, implementation, support, or enforcement of the entity's values or ethical standards by management, or the communication of inappropriate values or ethical standards, that are not effective.

- Nonfinancial management's excessive participation in or preoccupation with the selection of accounting policies or the determination of significant estimates.

- Known history of violations of securities laws or other laws and regulations, or claims against the entity, its senior management, or those charged with governance alleging fraud or violations of laws and regulations.

- Excessive interest by management in maintaining or increasing the entity's stock price or earnings trend.

- The practice by management of committing to analysts, creditors, and other third parties to achieve aggressive or unrealistic forecasts.

- Management failing to remedy known significant deficiencies in internal control on a timely basis.

- An interest by management in employing inappropriate means to minimize reported earnings for tax-motivated reasons.

- Low morale among senior management.

- The owner-manager makes no distinction between personal and business transactions.

- Dispute between shareholders in a closely held entity.

- Recurring attempts by management to justify marginal or inappropriate accounting on the basis of materiality.

- The relationship between management and the current or predecessor auditor is strained, as exhibited by the following:
  - Frequent disputes with the current or predecessor auditor on accounting, auditing, or reporting matters.
  - Unreasonable demands on the auditor, such as unrealistic time constraints regarding the completion of the audit or the issuance of the auditor's report.
  - Restrictions on the auditor that inappropriately limit access to people or information or the ability to communicate effectively with those charged with governance.
  - Domineering management behavior in dealing with the auditor, especially involving attempts to influence the scope of the auditor's work or the selection or continuance of personnel assigned to or consulted on the audit engagement.

Risk Factors Arising from Misstatements Arising from Misappropriation of Assets

Risk factors that relate to misstatements arising from misappropriation of assets are also classified according to the three conditions generally present when fraud exists: incentives/pressures, opportunities, and attitudes/rationalization. Some of the risk factors related to misstatements arising from fraudulent financial reporting also may be present when misstatements arising from misappropriation of assets occur. For example, ineffective monitoring of management and other deficiencies in internal control may be present when misstatements due to either fraudulent financial reporting or misappropriation of assets exist. The following are examples of risk factors related to misstatements arising from misappropriation of assets.

Incentives/Pressures

Personal financial obligations may create pressure on management or employees with access to cash or other assets susceptible to theft to misappropriate those assets.

Adverse relationships between the entity and employees with access to cash or other assets susceptible to theft may motivate those employees to misappropriate those assets. For example, adverse relationships may be created by the following:

- Known or anticipated future employee layoffs.
- Recent or anticipated changes to employee compensation or benefit plans.
- Promotions, compensation, or other rewards inconsistent with expectations.

Opportunities

Certain characteristics or circumstances may increase the susceptibility of assets to misappropriation. For example, opportunities to misappropriate assets increase when there are the following:

- Large amounts of cash on hand or processed.
- Inventory items that are small in size, of high value, or in high demand.
- Easily convertible assets, such as bearer bonds, diamonds, or computer chips.

- Fixed assets which are small in size, marketable, or lacking observable identification of ownership.

Inadequate internal control over assets may increase the susceptibility of misappropriation of those assets. For example, misappropriation of assets may occur because there is the following:

- Inadequate segregation of duties or independent checks.
- Inadequate oversight of senior management expenditures, such as travel and other reimbursements.
- Inadequate management oversight of employees responsible for assets, for example, inadequate supervision or monitoring of remote locations.
- Inadequate job applicant screening of employees with access to assets.
- Inadequate record keeping with respect to assets.
- Inadequate system of authorization and approval of transactions (for example, in purchasing).
- Inadequate physical safeguards over cash, investments, inventory, or fixed assets.
- Lack of complete and timely reconciliations of assets.
- Lack of timely and appropriate documentation of transactions, for example, credits for merchandise returns.
- Lack of mandatory vacations for employees performing key control functions.
- Inadequate management understanding of information technology, which enables information technology employees to perpetrate a misappropriation.
- Inadequate access controls over automated records, including controls over and review of computer systems event logs.

Attitudes/Rationalizations

- Disregard for the need for monitoring or reducing risks related to misappropriations of assets.
- Disregard for internal control over misappropriation of assets by overriding existing controls or by failing to take appropriate remedial action on known deficiencies in internal control.
- Behavior indicating displeasure or dissatisfaction with the entity or its treatment of the employee.
- Changes in behavior or lifestyle that may indicate assets have been misappropriated.
- Tolerance of petty theft.

Appendix 2

(Ref: Para. A40)

Examples of Possible Audit Procedures to Address the Assessed Risks of Material Misstatement Due to Fraud

The following are examples of possible audit procedures to address the assessed risks of material misstatement due to fraud resulting from both fraudulent financial reporting and misappropriation of assets. Although these procedures cover a broad range of situations, they are only examples and, accordingly they may not be the most appropriate nor necessary in each circumstance. Also the order of the procedures provided is not intended to reflect their relative importance.

Consideration at the Assertion Level

Specific responses to the auditor's assessment of the risks of material misstatement due to fraud will vary depending upon the types or combinations of fraud risk factors or conditions identified, and the classes of transactions, account balances, disclosures and assertions they may affect.

The following are specific examples of responses:

- Visiting locations or performing certain tests on a surprise or unannounced basis. For example, observing inventory at locations where auditor attendance has not been previously announced or counting cash at a particular date on a surprise basis.

- Requesting that inventories be counted at the end of the reporting period or on a date closer to period end to minimize the risk of manipulation of balances in the period between the date of completion of the count and the end of the reporting period.

- Altering the audit approach in the current year. For example, contacting major customers and suppliers orally in addition to sending written confirmation, sending confirmation requests to a specific party within an organization, or seeking more or different information.

- Performing a detailed review of the entity's quarter-end or year-end adjusting entries and investigating any that appear unusual as to nature or amount.

- For significant and unusual transactions, particularly those occurring at or near year-end, investigating the possibility of related parties and the sources of financial resources supporting the transactions.

- Performing substantive analytical procedures using disaggregated data. For example, comparing sales and cost of sales by location, line of business or month to expectations developed by the auditor.

- Conducting interviews of personnel involved in areas where a risk of material misstatement due to fraud has been identified, to obtain their insights about the risk and whether, or how, controls address the risk.

- When other independent auditors are auditing the financial statements of one or more subsidiaries, divisions or branches, discussing with them the extent of work necessary to be performed to address the assessed risk of material misstatement due to fraud resulting from transactions and activities among these components.

- If the work of an expert becomes particularly significant with respect to a financial statement item for which the assessed risk of misstatement due to fraud is high, performing additional procedures relating to some or all of the expert's assumptions, methods or findings to determine that the findings are not unreasonable, or engaging another expert for that purpose.
- Performing audit procedures to analyze selected opening balance sheet accounts of previously audited financial statements to assess how certain issues involving accounting estimates and judgments, for example, an allowance for sales returns, were resolved with the benefit of hindsight.
- Performing procedures on account or other reconciliations prepared by the entity, including considering reconciliations performed at interim periods.
- Performing computer-assisted techniques, such as data mining to test for anomalies in a population.
- Testing the integrity of computer-produced records and transactions.
- Seeking additional audit evidence from sources outside of the entity being audited.

Specific Responses—Misstatement Resulting from Fraudulent Financial Reporting

Examples of responses to the auditor's assessment of the risks of material misstatement due to fraudulent financial reporting are as follows:

Revenue Recognition
- Performing substantive analytical procedures relating to revenue using disaggregated data, for example, comparing revenue reported by month and by product line or business segment during the current reporting period with comparable prior periods. Computer-assisted audit techniques may be useful in identifying unusual or unexpected revenue relationships or transactions.
- Confirming with customers certain relevant contract terms and the absence of side agreements, because the appropriate accounting often is influenced by such terms or agreements and basis for rebates or the period to which they relate are often poorly documented. For example, acceptance criteria, delivery and payment terms, the absence of future or continuing vendor obligations, the right to return the product, guaranteed resale amounts, and cancellation or refund provisions often are relevant in such circumstances.
- Inquiring of the entity's sales and marketing personnel or in-house legal counsel regarding sales or shipments near the end of the period and their knowledge of any unusual terms or conditions associated with these transactions.
- Being physically present at one or more locations at period end to observe goods being shipped or being readied for shipment (or returns awaiting processing) and performing other appropriate sales and inventory cutoff procedures.
- For those situations for which revenue transactions are electronically initiated, processed, and recorded, testing controls to determine whether

they provide assurance that recorded revenue transactions occurred and are properly recorded.

Inventory Quantities

- Examining the entity's inventory records to identify locations or items that require specific attention during or after the physical inventory count.

- Observing inventory counts at certain locations on an unannounced basis or conducting inventory counts at all locations on the same date.

- Conducting inventory counts at or near the end of the reporting period to minimize the risk of inappropriate manipulation during the period between the count and the end of the reporting period.

- Performing additional procedures during the observation of the count, for example, more rigorously examining the contents of boxed items, the manner in which the goods are stacked (for example, hollow squares) or labeled, and the quality (that is, purity, grade, or concentration) of liquid substances such as perfumes or specialty chemicals. Using the work of an expert may be helpful in this regard.

- Comparing the quantities for the current period with prior periods by class or category of inventory, location or other criteria, or comparison of quantities counted with perpetual records.

- Using computer-assisted audit techniques to further test the compilation of the physical inventory counts – for example, sorting by tag number to test tag controls or by item serial number to test the possibility of item omission or duplication.

Management Estimates

- Using an expert to develop an independent estimate for comparison to management's estimate.

- Extending inquiries to individuals outside of management and the accounting department to corroborate management's ability and intent to carry out plans that are relevant to developing the estimate.

Specific Responses—Misstatements Due to Misappropriation of Assets

Differing circumstances would necessarily dictate different responses. Ordinarily, the audit response to an assessed risk of material misstatement due to fraud relating to misappropriation of assets will be directed toward certain account balances and classes of transactions. Although some of the audit responses noted in the two categories above may apply in such circumstances, the scope of the work is to be linked to the specific information about the misappropriation risk that has been identified.

Examples of responses to the auditor's assessment of the risk of material misstatements due to misappropriation of assets are as follows:

- Counting cash or securities at or near year-end.

- Confirming directly with customers the account activity (including credit memo and sales return activity as well as dates payments were made) for the period under audit.

- Analyzing recoveries of written-off accounts.

- Analyzing inventory shortages by location or product type.
- Comparing key inventory ratios to industry norm.
- Reviewing supporting documentation for reductions to the perpetual inventory records.
- Performing a computerized match of the vendor list with a list of employees to identify matches of addresses or phone numbers.
- Performing a computerized search of payroll records to identify duplicate addresses, employee identification or taxing authority numbers or bank accounts.
- Reviewing personnel files for those that contain little or no evidence of activity, for example, lack of performance evaluations.
- Analyzing sales discounts and returns for unusual patterns or trends.
- Confirming specific terms of contracts with third parties.
- Obtaining evidence that contracts are being carried out in accordance with their terms.
- Reviewing the propriety of large and unusual expenses.
- Reviewing the authorization and carrying value of senior management and related party loans.
- Reviewing the level and propriety of expense reports submitted by senior management.

Appendix 3

(Ref: Para. A49)

Examples of Circumstances that Indicate the Possibility of Fraud

The following are examples of circumstances that may indicate the possibility that the financial statements may contain a material misstatement resulting from fraud.

Discrepancies in the accounting records, including:

- Transactions that are not recorded in a complete or timely manner or are improperly recorded as to amount, accounting period, classification, or entity policy.

- Unsupported or unauthorized balances or transactions.

- Last-minute adjustments that significantly affect financial results.

- Evidence of employees' access to systems and records inconsistent with that necessary to perform their authorized duties.

- Tips or complaints to the auditor about alleged fraud.

Conflicting or missing evidence, including:

- Missing documents.

- Documents that appear to have been altered.

- Unavailability of other than photocopied or electronically transmitted documents when documents in original form are expected to exist.

- Significant unexplained items on reconciliations.

- Unusual balance sheet changes, or changes in trends or important financial statement ratios or relationships – for example, receivables growing faster than revenues.

- Inconsistent, vague, or implausible responses from management or employees arising from inquiries or analytical procedures.

- Unusual discrepancies between the entity's records and confirmation replies.

- Large numbers of credit entries and other adjustments made to accounts receivable records.

- Unexplained or inadequately explained differences between the accounts receivable sub-ledger and the control account, or between the customer statements and the accounts receivable sub-ledger.

- Missing or non-existent cancelled checks in circumstances where cancelled checks are ordinarily returned to the entity with the bank statement.

- Missing inventory or physical assets of significant magnitude.

- Unavailable or missing electronic evidence, inconsistent with the entity's record retention practices or policies.

- Fewer responses to confirmations than anticipated or a greater number of responses than anticipated.

- Inability to produce evidence of key systems development and program change testing and implementation activities for current-year system changes and deployments.

Problematic or unusual relationships between the auditor and management, including:

- Denial of access to records, facilities, certain employees, customers, vendors, or others from whom audit evidence might be sought.

- Undue time pressures imposed by management to resolve complex or contentious issues.

- Complaints by management about the conduct of the audit or management intimidation of engagement team members, particularly in connection with the auditor's critical assessment of audit evidence or in the resolution of potential disagreements with management.

- Unusual delays by the entity in providing requested information.

- Unwillingness to facilitate auditor access to key electronic files for testing through the use of computer-assisted audit techniques.

- Denial of access to key IT operations staff and facilities, including security, operations, and systems development personnel.

- An unwillingness to add or revise disclosures in the financial statements to make them more complete and understandable.

- An unwillingness to address identified deficiencies in internal control on a timely basis.

Other

- Unwillingness by management to permit the auditor to meet privately with those charged with governance.

- Accounting policies that appear to be at variance with industry norms.

- Frequent changes in accounting estimates that do not appear to result from changed circumstances.

- Tolerance of violations of the entity's code of conduct.

ISA (UK) 250 (Revised December 2017) Section A – Consideration of Laws and Regulations in an Audit of Financial Statements

(Effective for audits of financial statements for periods commencing on or after 15 December 2017)

Contents

	Paragraphs
Introduction	1 - 10
Scope of this ISA (UK)	1 - 1-1
Effect of laws and regulations	2
Responsibility for compliance with laws and regulations	3 - 9
Effective date	10
Objectives	11
Definition	12
Requirements	13 - 30
The auditor's consideration of compliance with laws and regulations	13 - 18
Audit procedures when non-compliance is identified or suspected	19 - 22
Communicating and reporting identified or suspected non-compliance	23 - 28
Reporting of identified or suspected non-compliance	29 - 29R-1
Documentation	30
Application and other explanatory material	A1 - A36
Responsibility for compliance with laws and regulations	A1 - A8
Definition	A9 - A10
The auditor's consideration of compliance with laws and regulations	A11 - A16
Audit procedures when non-compliance is identified or suspected	A17 - A25-2
Communicating and reporting identified or suspected non-compliance	A25-3 - A34-3
Documentation	A35 - A36

Appendix: Money Laundering, Terrorist Financing and Proceeds of Crime Legislation in the United Kingdom

Annexure: Conforming Amendments to Other ISAs (UK)

International Standard on Auditing (UK) (ISA (UK)) 250 (Revised December 2017), *Section A – Consideration of Laws and Regulations in an Audit of Financial Statements*, should be read in conjunction with ISA (UK) 200 (Revised June 2016), *Overall Objectives of the Independent Auditor and the Conduct of an Audit in Accordance with International Standards on Auditing (UK)*.

Editor's note: This revised version (issued December 2017) replaces ISA 250A Section A – Consideration of Laws and Regulations in an Audit of Financial Statements (Revised June 2016). This standard is still extant at 30 April 2018 for audits of financial statements commencing before 15/12/17 and is available within Auditing Standards online at Croner-i Tax and Accounting.

Introduction

Scope of this ISA (UK)

1   This International Standard on Auditing (UK) (ISA (UK)) deals with the auditor's responsibility to consider laws and regulations in an audit of financial statements. This ISA (UK) does not apply to other assurance engagements in which the auditor is specifically engaged to test and report separately on compliance with specific laws or regulations.

1-1   Guidance on the auditor's responsibility to report direct to regulators of public interest entities and regulators of other entities in the financial sector is provided in Section B of this ISA (UK).[1a]

Effect of Laws and Regulations

2   The effect on financial statements of laws and regulations varies considerably. Those laws and regulations to which an entity is subject constitute the legal and regulatory framework. The provisions of some laws or regulations have a direct effect on the financial statements in that they determine the reported amounts and disclosures in an entity's financial statements. Other laws or regulations are to be complied with by management or set the provisions under which the entity is allowed to conduct its business but do not have a direct effect on an entity's financial statements. Some entities operate in heavily regulated industries (such as banks and chemical companies). Others are subject only to the many laws and regulations that relate generally to the operating aspects of the business (such as those related to occupational safety and health, and equal employment opportunity). Noncompliance with laws and regulations may result in fines, litigation or other consequences for the entity that may have a material effect on the financial statements.

Responsibility for Compliance with Laws and Regulations
(Ref: Para. A1–A8)

3   It is the responsibility of management, with the oversight of those charged with governance, to ensure that the entity's operations are conducted in accordance with the provisions of laws and regulations, including compliance with the provisions of laws and regulations that determine the reported amounts and disclosures in an entity's financial statements.[1b]

Responsibility of the Auditor

4   The requirements in this ISA (UK) are designed to assist the auditor in identifying material misstatement of the financial statements due to non-compliance with laws and regulations. However, the auditor is not responsible for preventing non-compliance and cannot be expected to detect non-compliance with all laws and regulations.

5   The auditor is responsible for obtaining reasonable assurance that the financial statements, taken as a whole, are free from material misstatement, whether due to fraud or error.[1] In conducting an audit of financial statements, the auditor takes

---

[1a] *ISA (UK) 250 (Revised June 2016), Section B – The Auditor's Statutory Right and Duty to Report to Regulators of Public Interest Entities and Regulators of Other Entities in the Financial Sector.*

[1b] *In the UK, those charged with governance are responsible for the preparation of the financial statements.*

[1] *ISA (UK) 200 (Revised June 2016), Overall Objectives of the Independent Auditor and the Conduct of an Audit in Accordance with International Standards on Auditing (UK), paragraph 5.*

into account the applicable legal and regulatory framework. Owing to the inherent limitations of an audit, there is an unavoidable risk that some material misstatements in the financial statements may not be detected, even though the audit is properly planned and performed in accordance with the ISAs (UK).[2] In the context of laws and regulations, the potential effects of inherent limitations on the auditor's ability to detect material misstatements are greater for such reasons as the following:

- There are many laws and regulations, relating principally to the operating aspects of an entity, that typically do not affect the financial statements and are not captured by the entity's information systems relevant to financial reporting.

- Non-compliance may involve conduct designed to conceal it, such as collusion, forgery, deliberate failure to record transactions, management override of controls or intentional misrepresentations being made to the auditor.

- Whether an act constitutes non-compliance is ultimately a matter to be determined by a court or other appropriate adjudicative body.

Ordinarily, the further removed non-compliance is from the events and transactions reflected in the financial statements, the less likely the auditor is to become aware of it or to recognize the non-compliance.

This ISA (UK) distinguishes the auditor's responsibilities in relation to **6** compliance with two different categories of laws and regulations as follows: (Ref: Para. A6, A12–A13)

(a)   The provisions of those laws and regulations generally recognized to have a direct effect on the determination of material amounts and disclosures in the financial statements such as tax and pension laws and regulations (see paragraph 14) (Ref: Para. A12); and

(b)   Other laws and regulations that do not have a direct effect on the determination of the amounts and disclosures in the financial statements, but compliance with which may be fundamental to the operating aspects of the business, to an entity's ability to continue its business, or to avoid material penalties (e.g., compliance with the terms of an operating license, compliance with regulatory solvency requirements, or compliance with environmental regulations); non-compliance with such laws and regulations may therefore have a material effect on the financial statements (see paragraph 15) (Ref: Para. A13).

In this ISA (UK), differing requirements are specified for each of the above **7** categories of laws and regulations. For the category referred to in paragraph 6(a), the auditor's responsibility is to obtain sufficient appropriate audit evidence regarding compliance with the provisions of those laws and regulations. For the category referred to in paragraph 6(b), the auditor's responsibility is limited to undertaking specified audit procedures to help identify non-compliance with those laws and regulations that may have a material effect on the financial statements.

The auditor is required by this ISA (UK) to remain alert to the possibility that other **8** audit procedures applied for the purpose of forming an opinion on financial statements may bring instances of non-compliance to the auditor's attention. Maintaining professional skepticism throughout the audit, as required by ISA (UK) 200 (Revised June 2016),[3] is important in this context, given the extent of laws and regulations that affect the entity.

---

[2] *ISA (UK) 200 (Revised June 2016), paragraph A51.*

[3] *ISA (UK) 200 (Revised June 2016), paragraph 15.*

9   The auditor may have additional responsibilities under law, regulation or relevant ethical requirements regarding an entity's non-compliance with laws and regulations, which may differ from or go beyond this ISA (UK), such as: (Ref: Para. A8)

    (a)   Responding to identified or suspected non-compliance with laws and regulations, including requirements in relation to specific communications with management and those charged with governance, assessing the appropriateness of their response to non-compliance and determining whether further action is needed;

    (b)   Communicating identified or suspected non-compliance with laws and regulations to other auditors (e.g., in an audit of group financial statements); and

    (c)   Documentation requirements regarding identified or suspected non-compliance with laws and regulations.

Complying with any additional responsibilities may provide further information that is relevant to the auditor's work in accordance with this and other ISAs (UK) (e.g., regarding the integrity of management or, where appropriate, those charged with governance).

Effective Date

10   This ISA (UK) is effective for audits of financial statements for periods commencing on or after 15 December 2017.

Objectives

11   The objectives of the auditor are:

    (a)   To obtain sufficient appropriate audit evidence regarding compliance with the provisions of those laws and regulations generally recognized to have a direct effect on the determination of material amounts and disclosures in the financial statements;

    (b)   To perform specified audit procedures to help identify instances of non-compliance with other laws and regulations that may have a material effect on the financial statements; and

    (c)   To respond appropriately to identified or suspected non-compliance with laws and regulations identified during the audit.

Definition

12   For the purposes of this ISA (UK), the following term has the meaning attributed below:

Non-compliance – Acts of omission or commission intentional or unintentional, committed by the entity, or by those charged with governance, by management or by other individuals working for or under the direction of the entity, which are contrary to the prevailing laws or regulations. Non-compliance does not include personal misconduct unrelated to the business activities of the entity. (Ref: Para. A9–A10)

Requirements

The Auditor's Consideration of Compliance with Laws and Regulations

As part of obtaining an understanding of the entity and its environment in accordance with ISA (UK) 315 (Revised June 2016),[4] the auditor shall obtain a general understanding of: **13**

(a) The legal and regulatory framework applicable to the entity and the industry or sector in which the entity operates; and

(b) How the entity is complying with that framework. (Ref: Para. A11)

The auditor shall obtain sufficient appropriate audit evidence regarding compliance with the provisions of those laws and regulations generally recognized to have a direct effect on the determination of material amounts and disclosures in the financial statements. (Ref: Para. A12–A12-1) **14**

The auditor shall perform the following audit procedures to help identify instances of non-compliance with other laws and regulations that may have a material effect on the financial statements: (Ref: Para. A13–A14-1) **15**

(a) Inquiring of management and, where appropriate, those charged with governance, as to whether the entity is in compliance with such laws and regulations; and

(b) Inspecting correspondence, if any, with the relevant licensing or regulatory authorities.

During the audit, the auditor shall remain alert to the possibility that other audit procedures applied may bring instances of non-compliance or suspected non-compliance with laws and regulations to the auditor's attention. (Ref: Para. A15) **16**

The auditor shall request management and, where appropriate, those charged with governance to provide written representations that all known instances of non-compliance or suspected non-compliance with laws and regulations whose effects should be considered when preparing financial statements have been disclosed to the auditor. (Ref: Para. A16) **17**

In the absence of identified or suspected non-compliance, the auditor is not required to perform audit procedures regarding the entity's compliance with laws and regulations, other than those set out in paragraphs 13–17. **18**

Audit Procedures When Non-Compliance Is Identified or Suspected

If the auditor becomes aware of information concerning an instance of non-compliance or suspected non-compliance with laws and regulations, the auditor shall obtain: (Ref: Para. A17–A18) **19**

(a) An understanding of the nature of the act and the circumstances in which it has occurred; and

(b) Further information to evaluate the possible effect on the financial statements. (Ref: Para. A19)

If the auditor suspects there may be non-compliance, the auditor shall discuss the matter, unless prohibited by law or regulation, with the appropriate level of management and, where appropriate, those charged with governance. If **20**

---

[4] *ISA (UK) 315 (Revised June 2016), Identifying and Assessing the Risks of Material Misstatement through Understanding the Entity and Its Environment, paragraph 11.*

management or, as appropriate, those charged with governance do not provide sufficient information that supports that the entity is in compliance with laws and regulations and, in the auditor's judgment, the effect of the suspected non-compliance may be material to the financial statements, the auditor shall consider the need to obtain legal advice. (Ref: Para. A20–A22)

21   If sufficient information about suspected non-compliance cannot be obtained, the auditor shall evaluate the effect of the lack of sufficient appropriate audit evidence on the auditor's opinion.

22   The auditor shall evaluate the implications of identified or suspected non-compliance in relation to other aspects of the audit, including the auditor's risk assessment and the reliability of written representations, and take appropriate action. (Ref: Para. A23–A25-2)

Communicating and Reporting Identified or Suspected Non-Compliance

Communicating Identified or Suspected Non-Compliance with Those Charged with Governance

23   Unless all of those charged with governance are involved in management of the entity, and therefore are aware of matters involving identified or suspected non-compliance already communicated by the auditor,[5] the auditor shall communicate, unless prohibited by law or regulation, with those charged with governance matters involving non-compliance with laws and regulations that come to the auditor's attention during the course of the audit, other than when the matters are clearly inconsequential.

23R-1   For audits of financial statements of public interest entities, when an auditor suspects or has reasonable grounds to suspect that irregularities, including fraud with regard to the financial statements of the entity, may occur or have occurred, the auditor shall, unless prohibited by law or regulation, inform the entity and invite it to investigate the matter and take appropriate measures to deal with such irregularities and to prevent any recurrence of such irregularities in the future. (Ref: Para. A25-3–A25-4)

24   If, in the auditor's judgment, the non-compliance referred to in paragraph 23 is believed to be intentional and material, the auditor shall communicate the matter with those charged with governance as soon as practicable. (Ref: Para. A25-5)

25   If the auditor suspects that management or those charged with governance are involved in non-compliance, the auditor shall communicate the matter to the next higher level of authority at the entity, if it exists, such as an audit committee or supervisory board. Where no higher authority exists, or if the auditor believes that the communication may not be acted upon or is unsure as to the person to whom to report, the auditor shall consider the need to obtain legal advice. (Ref: Para. A25-6)

Potential Implications of Identified or Suspected Non-Compliance for the Auditor's Report on the Financial Statements
(Ref: Para. A26–27-1)

26   If the auditor concludes that the identified or suspected non-compliance has a material effect on the financial statements, and has not been adequately reflected in the financial statements, the auditor shall, in accordance with ISA (UK) 705

---

[5] *ISA (UK) 260 (Revised June 2016), Communication with Those Charged with Governance, paragraph 13.*

(Revised June 2016), express a qualified opinion or an adverse opinion on the financial statements.[6]

If the auditor is precluded by management or those charged with governance from obtaining sufficient appropriate audit evidence to evaluate whether non-compliance that may be material to the financial statements has, or is likely to have, occurred, the auditor shall express a qualified opinion or disclaim an opinion on the financial statements on the basis of a limitation on the scope of the audit in accordance with ISA (UK) 705 (Revised June 2016).[7]   **27**

If the auditor is unable to determine whether non-compliance has occurred because of limitations imposed by the circumstances rather than by management or those charged with governance, the auditor shall evaluate the effect on the auditor's opinion in accordance with ISA (UK) 705 (Revised June 2016). (Ref: Para. A27-1)   **28**

Reporting Identified or Suspected Non-Compliance to an Appropriate Authority Outside the Entity

If the auditor has identified or suspects non-compliance with laws and regulations, the auditor shall determine whether law, regulation or relevant ethical requirements: (Ref: Para. A28–A34-1)   **29**

(a) Require the auditor to report to an appropriate authority outside the entity.

(b) Establish responsibilities under which reporting to an appropriate authority outside the entity may be appropriate in the circumstances.

For audits of financial statements of public interest entities, where the entity does not investigate the matter referred to in paragraph 23R-1, the auditor shall inform the authorities responsible for investigating such irregularities. (Ref: Para. A34-2–A34-3)   **29R-1**

Documentation

The auditor shall include in the audit documentation[8] identified or suspected non-compliance with laws and regulations and: (Ref: Para. A35–A36)   **30**

(a) The audit procedures performed, the significant professional judgments made and the conclusions reached thereon; and

(b) The discussions of significant matters related to the non-compliance with management, those charged with governance and others, including how management and, where applicable, those charged with governance have responded to the matter.

***

---

[6] *ISA (UK) 705 (Revised June 2016), Modifications to the Opinion in the Independent Auditor's Report, paragraphs 7–8.*

[7] *ISA (UK) 705 (Revised June 2016), paragraphs 7 and 9.*

[8] *ISA (UK) 230 (Revised June 2016), Audit Documentation, paragraphs 8–11, and A6.*

Application and Other Explanatory Material

Responsibility for Compliance with Laws and Regulations
(Ref: Para. 3–9)

A1   It is the responsibility of management, with the oversight of those charged with governance, to ensure that the entity's operations are conducted in accordance with laws and regulations. Laws and regulations may affect an entity's financial statements in different ways: for example, most directly, they may affect specific disclosures required of the entity in the financial statements or they may prescribe the applicable financial reporting framework. They may also establish certain legal rights and obligations of the entity, some of which will be recognized in the entity's financial statements. In addition, laws and regulations may impose penalties in cases of non

A2   The following are examples of the types of policies and procedures an entity may implement to assist in the prevention and detection of non-compliance with laws and regulations:

- Monitoring legal requirements and ensuring that operating procedures are designed to meet these requirements.

- Instituting and operating appropriate systems of internal control.

- Developing, publicizing and following a code of conduct.

- Ensuring employees are properly trained and understand the code of conduct.

- Monitoring compliance with the code of conduct and acting appropriately to discipline employees who fail to comply with it.

- Engaging legal advisors to assist in monitoring legal requirements.

- Maintaining a register of significant laws and regulations with which the entity has to comply within its particular industry and a record of complaints.

In larger entities, these policies and procedures may be supplemented by assigning appropriate responsibilities to the following:

- An internal audit function.

- An audit committee.

- A compliance function.

A2-1   In the UK, in certain sectors or activities (e.g., financial services), there are detailed laws and regulations that specifically require directors to have systems to ensure compliance. Non-compliance with these laws and regulations could have a material effect on the financial statements.

A2-2   In the UK, the directors are responsible for the preparation of financial statements that give a true and fair view. Accordingly it is necessary, where identified or suspected non-compliance with laws and regulations has occurred which may result in a material misstatement in the financial statements, for the directors to ensure that the matter is appropriately reflected and/or disclosed in the financial statements.

In the UK, directors and officers of companies have responsibility to provide information required by the auditor, to which they have a legal right of access.[8a] Such legislation also provides that it is a criminal offence to give to the auditor information or explanations which are misleading, false or deceptive.

A2-3

Responsibility of the Auditor

Non-compliance by the entity with laws and regulations may result in a material misstatement of the financial statements. Detection of non-compliance, regardless of materiality, may affect other aspects of the audit including, for example, the auditor's consideration of the integrity of management, those charged with governance or employees.

A3

Whether an act constitutes non-compliance with laws and regulations is a matter to be determined by a court or other appropriate adjudicative body, which is ordinarily beyond the auditor's professional competence to determine. Nevertheless, the auditor's training, experience and understanding of the entity and its industry or sector may provide a basis to recognize that some acts, coming to the auditor's attention, may constitute non-compliance with laws and regulations.

A4

In accordance with specific statutory requirements, the auditor may be specifically required to report, as part of the audit of the financial statements, on whether the entity complies with certain provisions of laws or regulations. In these circumstances, ISA (UK) 700 (Revised June 2016)[9] or ISA (UK) 800 (Revised)[10] deal with how these audit responsibilities are addressed in the auditor's report. Furthermore, where there are specific statutory reporting requirements, it may be necessary for the audit plan to include appropriate tests for compliance with these provisions of the laws and regulations.

A5

Categories of Laws and Regulations
(Ref: Para. 6)

The nature and circumstances of the entity may impact whether relevant laws and regulations are within the categories of laws and regulations described in paragraphs 6(a) or 6(b). Examples of laws and regulations that may be included in the categories described in paragraph 6 include those that deal with:

A6

- Fraud, corruption and bribery.
- Money laundering,[10a] terrorist financing and proceeds of crime.
- Securities markets and trading.
- Banking and other financial products and services.
- Data protection.
- Tax and pension liabilities and payments.
- Environmental protection.
- Public health and safety.

[8a] *In the UK, under Section 499 of the Companies Act 2006.*

[9] *ISA (UK) 700 (Revised June 2016), Forming an Opinion and Reporting on Financial Statements, paragraph 43.*

[10] *ISA (UK) 800 (Revised) Special Considerations – Audits of Financial Statements Prepared in Accordance with Special Purpose Frameworks, paragraph 11.*

[10a] *"Money laundering" is defined in UK legislation and in general terms involves an act which conceals, disguises, converts, transfers, removes, uses, acquires or possesses property resulting from criminal conduct.*

A6-1   In the UK, legislation relating to money laundering, terrorist financing and proceeds of crime imposes additional responsibilities on the auditor. The Appendix contains further guidance on these responsibilities.

Considerations Specific to Public Sector Entities

A7   In the public sector, there may be additional audit responsibilities with respect to the consideration of laws and regulations which may relate to the audit of financial statements or may extend to other aspects of the entity's operations.

Additional Responsibilities Established by Law, Regulation or Relevant Ethical Requirements
(Ref: Para. 9)

A8   Law, regulation or relevant ethical requirements may require the auditor to perform additional procedures and take further actions. For example, the Code of Ethics for Professional Accountants issued by the International Ethics Standards Board for Accountants (IESBA Code) requires the auditor to take steps to respond to identified or suspected non-compliance with laws and regulations and determine whether further action is needed. Such steps may include the communication of identified or suspected non-compliance with laws and regulations to other auditors within a group, including a group engagement partner, component auditors or other auditors performing work at components of a group for purposes other than the audit of the group financial statements.[11]

Definition
(Ref: Para. 12)

A9   Acts of non-compliance with laws and regulations include transactions entered into by, or in the name of, the entity, or on its behalf, by those charged with governance, by management or by other individuals working for or under the direction of the entity.

A10   Non-compliance also includes personal misconduct related to the business activities of the entity, for example, in circumstances where an individual in a key management position, in a personal capacity, has accepted a bribe from a supplier of the entity and in return secures the appointment of the supplier to provide services or contracts to the entity.

The Auditor's Consideration of Compliance with Laws and Regulations

Obtaining an Understanding of the Legal and Regulatory Framework
(Ref: Para. 13)

A11   To obtain a general understanding of the legal and regulatory framework, and how the entity complies with that framework, the auditor may, for example:

●   Use the auditor's existing understanding of the entity's industry, regulatory and other external factors;

●   Update the understanding of those laws and regulations that directly determine the reported amounts and disclosures in the financial statements;

●   Inquire of management as to other laws or regulations that may be expected to have a fundamental effect on the operations of the entity;

---

[11] *See Sections 225.21–225.22 of the IESBA Code.*
In the UK, the auditor has regard to any specific requirements of the auditor's relevant professional body.

- Inquire of management concerning the entity's policies and procedures regarding compliance with laws and regulations; and

- Inquire of management regarding the policies or procedures adopted for identifying, evaluating and accounting for litigation claims.

Laws and Regulations Generally Recognized to Have a Direct Effect on the Determination of Material Amounts and Disclosures in the Financial Statements (Ref: Para. 6, 14)

Certain laws and regulations are well-established, known to the entity and within the entity's industry or sector, and relevant to the entity's financial statements (as described in paragraph 6(a)). They could include those that relate to, for example: **A12**

- The form and content of financial statements;[11a]

- Industry-specific financial reporting issues;

- Accounting for transactions under government contracts; or

- The accrual or recognition of expenses for income tax or pension costs.

In the UK, these laws and regulations include those which:

- Determine the circumstances under which a company is prohibited from making a distribution except out of profits available for the purpose.[11b]

- Require auditors expressly to report non-compliance, such as the requirements relating to the maintenance of adequate accounting records[11c] or the disclosure of particulars of directors' remuneration in a company's financial statements.[11d]

Some provisions in those laws and regulations may be directly relevant to specific assertions in the financial statements (e.g., the completeness of income tax provisions), while others may be directly relevant to the financial statements as a whole (e.g., the required statements constituting a complete set of financial statements). The aim of the requirement in paragraph 14 is for the auditor to obtain sufficient appropriate audit evidence regarding the determination of amounts and disclosures in the financial statements in compliance with the relevant provisions of those laws and regulations.

Non-compliance with other provisions of such laws and regulations and other laws and regulations may result in fines, litigation or other consequences for the entity, the costs of which may need to be provided for in the financial statements, but are not considered to have a direct effect on the financial statements as described in paragraph 6(a).

In the UK, the auditor's responsibility to express an opinion on an entity's financial statements does not extend to determining whether the entity has complied in every respect with applicable tax legislation. The auditor needs to obtain sufficient appropriate evidence to give reasonable assurance that the amounts included in the financial statements in respect of taxation are not **A12-1**

[11a] *In the UK, under The Small Companies and Groups (Accounts and Directors' Report) Regulations 2008 (SI 2008 No. 409) and The Large and Medium-sized Companies and Groups (Accounts and Reports) Regulations 2008 (SI 2008 No. 410).*

[11b] *In the UK, under Section 830 of the Companies Act 2006.*

[11c] *In the UK, under Section 498 of the Companies Act 2006.*

[11d] *In the UK, under Section 497 of the Companies Act 2006.*

materially misstated. This will usually include making appropriate enquiries of those advising the entity on taxation matters (whether within the firm or elsewhere). If the auditor becomes aware that the entity has failed to comply with the requirements of tax legislation, the auditor considers whether to report the matter to an appropriate authority outside the entity.

Procedures to Identify Instances of Non-Compliance – Other Laws and Regulations
(Ref: Para. 6, 15)

A13 Certain other laws and regulations may need particular attention by the auditor because they have a fundamental effect on the operations of the entity (as described in paragraph 6(b)). Non-compliance with laws and regulations that have a fundamental effect on the operations of the entity may cause the entity to cease operations, or call into question the entity's continuance as a going concern.[12] For example, non-compliance with the requirements of the entity's license or other entitlement to perform its operations could have such an impact (e. g., for a bank, non-compliance with capital or investment requirements).[12a] There are also many laws and regulations relating principally to the operating aspects of the entity that typically do not affect the financial statements and are not captured by the entity's information systems relevant to financial reporting.

A14 As the financial reporting consequences of other laws and regulations can vary depending on the entity's operations, the audit procedures required by paragraph 15 are directed to bringing to the auditor's attention instances of non-compliance with laws and regulations that may have a material effect on the financial statements.

A14-1 When determining the type of procedures necessary in a particular instance the auditor takes account of the particular entity concerned and the complexity of the law and regulations with which it is required to comply. In general, a small entity which does not operate in a regulated area will require few specific procedures compared with a large multinational corporation carrying on complex, regulated business.

Non-Compliance Brought to the Auditor's Attention by Other Audit Procedures
(Ref: Para. 16)

A15 Audit procedures applied to form an opinion on the financial statements may bring instances of non-compliance or suspected non-compliance with laws and regulations to the auditor's attention. For example, such audit procedures may include:

- Reading minutes;

- Inquiring of the entity's management and in-house legal counsel or external legal counsel concerning litigation, claims and assessments; and

- Performing substantive tests of details of classes of transactions, account balances or disclosures.

---

[12] *See ISA (UK) 570 (Revised June 2016), Going Concern.*

[12a] *Such requirements exist in the UK under the Financial Services and Markets Act 2000.*

Written Representations
(Ref: Para. 17)

Because the effect on financial statements of laws and regulations can vary **A16** considerably, written representations provide necessary audit evidence about management's knowledge of identified or suspected non-compliance with laws and regulations, whose effects may have a material effect on the financial statements. However, written representations do not provide sufficient appropriate audit evidence on their own and, accordingly, do not affect the nature and extent of other audit evidence that is to be obtained by the auditor.[13]

Audit Procedures When Non-Compliance Is Identified or Suspected

Indications of Non-Compliance with Laws and Regulations
(Ref: Para. 19)

The auditor may become aware of information concerning an instance of non- **A17** compliance with laws and regulations other than as a result of performing the procedures in paragraphs 13–17 (e.g., when the auditor is alerted to non-compliance by a whistle blower).

The following matters may be an indication of non-compliance with laws and **A18** regulations:

- Investigations by regulatory organizations and government departments or payment of fines or penalties.

- Payments for unspecified services or loans to consultants, related parties, employees or government employees.

- Sales commissions or agent's fees that appear excessive in relation to those ordinarily paid by the entity or in its industry or to the services actually received.

- Purchasing at prices significantly above or below market price.

- Unusual payments in cash, purchases in the form of cashiers' cheques payable to bearer or transfers to numbered bank accounts.

- Unusual transactions with companies registered in tax havens.

- Payments for goods or services made other than to the country from which the goods or services originated.

- Payments without proper exchange control documentation.

- Existence of an information system which fails, whether by design or by accident, to provide an adequate audit trail or sufficient evidence.

- Unauthorized transactions or improperly recorded transactions.

- Adverse media comment.

---

[13] *ISA (UK) 580, Written Representations, paragraph 4.*

Matters Relevant to the Auditor's Evaluation
(Ref: Para. 19(b))

A19 Matters relevant to the auditor's evaluation[13a] of the possible effect on the financial statements include:

- The potential financial consequences of identified or suspected non-compliance with laws and regulations on the financial statements including, for example, the imposition of fines, penalties, damages, threat of expropriation of assets,[13b] enforced discontinuation of operations, and litigation.

- Whether the potential financial consequences require disclosure.

- Whether the potential financial consequences are so serious as to call into question the fair presentation of the financial statements, or otherwise make the financial statements misleading.

Audit Procedures and Communicating Identified or Suspected Non-Compliance with Management and Those Charged with Governance
(Ref: Para. 20)

A20 The auditor is required to discuss the suspected non-compliance with the appropriate level of management and, where appropriate, with those charged with governance, as they may be able to provide additional audit evidence. For example, the auditor may confirm that management and, where appropriate, those charged with governance have the same understanding of the facts and circumstances relevant to transactions or events that have led to the suspected non-compliance with laws and regulations.

A21 However, in some jurisdictions, law or regulation may restrict the auditor's communication of certain matters with management and those charged with governance. Law or regulation may specifically prohibit a communication, or other action, that might prejudice an investigation by an appropriate authority into an actual, or suspected, illegal act, including alerting the entity, for example, when the auditor is required to report the identified or suspected non-compliance to an appropriate authority pursuant to anti-money laundering legislation. In these circumstances, the issues considered by the auditor may be complex and the auditor may consider it appropriate to obtain legal advice.

A21-1 In the UK, the auditor is subject to compliance with legislation relating to "tipping off". "Tipping off" is an offence under Section 333A of the Proceeds of Crime Act 2002 (POCA). It arises when an individual discloses that:

(a) A report (internal or external) has already been made where the disclosure by the individual is likely to prejudice an investigation which might be conducted following the internal or external report that has been made; or

(b) An investigation is being contemplated or is being carried out into allegations that a money laundering offence has been committed and the disclosure by the individual is likely to prejudice that investigation.

[13a] *ISA (UK) 620 (Revised June 2016), Using the Work of an Auditor's Expert applies if the auditor judges it necessary to obtain appropriate expert advice in connection with the evaluation of the possible effect of legal matters on the financial statements.*

[13b] *In the UK, the Proceeds of Crime Act 2002 provides procedures to enable the authorities to confiscate in criminal proceedings or bring an action for civil recovery of assets which represent the benefits of criminal conduct.*

Whilst "tipping off" requires a person to have knowledge or suspicion that a report has been or will be made, a further offence of prejudicing an investigation is included in Section 342 of the POCA. Under this provision, it is an offence to make any disclosure which may prejudice an investigation of which a person has knowledge or suspicion, or to falsify, conceal, destroy or otherwise dispose of, or cause or permit the falsification, concealment, destruction or disposal of, documents relevant to such an investigation.

The disclosure offences under Sections 333A and 342 of the POCA are not committed if the person disclosing does not know or suspect that it is likely to prejudice an investigation.

If management or, as appropriate, those charged with governance do not provide **A22** sufficient information to the auditor that the entity is in fact in compliance with laws and regulations, the auditor may consider it appropriate to consult with the entity's in-house or external legal counsel about the application of the laws and regulations to the circumstances, including the possibility of fraud, and the possible effects on the financial statements. If it is not considered appropriate to consult with the entity's legal counsel or if the auditor is not satisfied with the legal counsel's opinion, the auditor may consider it appropriate to consult on a confidential basis with others within the firm, a network firm, a professional body, or with the auditor's legal counsel as to whether a contravention of a law or regulation is involved, including the possibility of fraud, the possible legal consequences, and what further action, if any, the auditor would take.

Evaluating the Implications of Identified or Suspected Non-Compliance
(Ref: Para. 22)

As required by paragraph 22, the auditor evaluates the implications of identified or **A23** suspected non-compliance in relation to other aspects of the audit, including the auditor's risk assessment and the reliability of written representations. The implications of particular identified or suspected non-compliance will depend on the relationship of the perpetration and concealment, if any, of the act to specific control activities and the level of management or individuals working for, or under the direction of, the entity involved, especially implications arising from the involvement of the highest authority within the entity. As noted in paragraph 9, the auditor's compliance with law, regulation or relevant ethical requirements may provide further information that is relevant to the auditor's responsibilities in accordance with paragraph 22.

Examples of circumstances that may cause the auditor to evaluate the implications **A24** of identified or suspected non-compliance on the reliability of written representations received from management and, where applicable, those charged with governance include when:

● The auditor suspects or has evidence of the involvement or intended involvement of management and, where applicable, those charged with governance in any identified or suspected non-compliance.

● The auditor is aware that management and, where applicable, those charged with governance have knowledge of such non-compliance and, contrary to legal or regulatory requirements, have not reported, or authorized reporting of, the matter to an appropriate authority within a reasonable period.

In certain circumstances, the auditor may consider withdrawing from the **A25** engagement, where permitted by law or regulation, for example when management or those charged with governance do not take the remedial action that the auditor considers appropriate in the circumstances or the identified or suspected non-compliance raises questions regarding the integrity of management or those charged with governance, even when the non-compliance is not material to the financial statements. The auditor may consider it appropriate to obtain legal advice to determine whether withdrawal from the engagement is appropriate. When the auditor determines that withdrawing from the engagement would be appropriate, doing so would not be a substitute for complying with other responsibilities under law, regulation or relevant ethical requirements to respond to identified or suspected non-compliance. Furthermore, paragraph A8a of ISA (UK) 220 (Revised June 2016)[14] indicates that some ethical requirements may require the predecessor auditor, upon request by the proposed successor auditor, to provide information regarding non-compliance with laws and regulations to the successor auditor.

A25-1   Withdrawal from the engagement by the auditor is a step of last resort. It is normally preferable for the auditor to remain in office to fulfil the auditor's statutory duties, particularly where minority interests are involved. However, there are circumstances where there may be no alternative to withdrawal, for example, where the directors of a company refuse to issue its financial statements or the auditor wishes to inform the shareholders or creditors of the company of the auditor's concerns and there is no immediate occasion to do so.

A25-2   If the auditor determines that continued holding of office is untenable or the auditor is removed from office by the entity, the auditor will be mindful of the auditor's reporting duties.[14a]

Communicating and Reporting Identified or Suspected Non-Compliance

Communicating Identified or Suspected Non-Compliance with Those Charged with Governance
(Ref: Para. 23R-1–24)

A25-3   For audits of financial statements of public interest entities, ISA (UK) 260 (Revised June 2016)[14b] requires the auditor to communicate in the additional report to the audit committee any significant matters involving actual or suspected non-compliance with laws and regulations or articles of association which were identified in the course of the audit.

A25-4   In the UK, laws or regulations may prohibit alerting ("tipping off") the entity when, for example, the auditor is required to report the identified or suspected non-compliance with laws and regulations to an appropriate authority outside the entity pursuant to anti-money laundering legislation.

A25-5   If non-compliance with laws and regulations is intentional but not material the auditor considers whether the nature and circumstances make it appropriate to communicate the matter with those charged with governance as soon as practicable.

---

[14] *ISA (UK) 220 (Revised June 2016), Quality Control for an Audit of Financial Statements.*

[14a] *In the UK, under Part 16 of the Companies Act 2006.*

[14b] *ISA (UK) 260 (Revised June 2016), paragraph 16R-2(k).*

Suspicion that Management or Those Charged with Governance are Involved in Non- Compliance
(Ref: Para. 25)

In the case of suspected money laundering it may be appropriate to report the matter direct to an appropriate authority outside the entity (see paragraph A28).   **A25-6**

Potential Implications of Identified or Suspected Non-Compliance for the Auditor's Report
(Ref: Para. 26–28)

Identified or suspected non-compliance with laws and regulation is communicated   **A26**
in the auditor's report when the auditor modifies the opinion in accordance with paragraphs 26–28. In certain other circumstances, the auditor may communicate identified or suspected non-compliance in the auditor's report, for example:

- When the auditor has other reporting responsibilities, in addition to the auditor's responsibilities under the ISAs (UK), as contemplated by paragraph 43 of ISA (UK) 700 (Revised June 2016);

- When the auditor determines that the identified or suspected non-compliance is a key audit matter and accordingly communicates the matter in accordance with ISA (UK) 701,[15] unless paragraph 14 of that ISA (UK) applies; or

- In exceptional cases when management or those charged with governance do not take the remedial action that the auditor considers appropriate in the circumstances and withdrawal from the engagement is not possible (see paragraph A25), the auditor may consider describing the identified or suspected non-compliance in an Other Matter paragraph in accordance with ISA (UK) 706 (Revised June 2016).[16]

In the UK, if the auditor concludes that the view given by the financial   **A26-1**
statements could be affected by a level of uncertainty concerning the consequences of identified or suspected non-compliance with laws and regulations which, in the auditor's professional judgment, is significant, the auditor, subject to a consideration of "tipping off" (see paragraph A21-1), includes an explanatory paragraph referring to the matter in the auditor's report.

Law or regulation may preclude public disclosure by either management, those   **A27**
charged with governance or the auditor about a specific matter. For example, law or regulation may specifically prohibit a communication, or other action, that might prejudice an investigation by an appropriate authority into an actual, or suspected, illegal act, including a prohibition on alerting the entity. When the auditor intends to communicate identified or suspected non-compliance in the auditor's report under the circumstances set out in paragraph A26 or otherwise, such law or regulation may have implications for the auditor's ability to describe the matter in the auditor's report, or in some circumstances to issue the auditor's report. In such cases, the auditor may consider obtaining legal advice to determine the appropriate course of action.

---

[15] *ISA (UK) 701, Communicating Key Audit Matters in the Independent Auditor's Report.*

[16] *ISA (UK) 706 (Revised June 2016), Emphasis of Matter Paragraphs and Other Matter Paragraphs in the Independent Auditor's Report.*

A27-1   In the UK, when considering whether the financial statements reflect the possible consequences of any identified or suspected non-compliance with laws and regulations, the auditor has regard to the requirements of the applicable financial reporting framework. Identified or suspected non-compliance with laws and regulations may require disclosure in the financial statements because, although the immediate financial effect on the entity may not be material,[16a] there could be future material consequences such as fines, litigation or other consequences for the entity. For example, an illegal payment may not itself be material but may result in criminal proceedings against the entity or loss of business which could have a material effect on the true and fair view given by the financial statements.

Reporting Identified or Suspected Non-Compliance to an Appropriate Authority Outside the Entity
(Ref: Para. 29)

A28   Reporting identified or suspected non-compliance with laws and regulations to an appropriate authority outside the entity may be required or appropriate in the circumstances because:

(a)   Law, regulation or relevant ethical requirements require the auditor to report (see paragraph A29–A29-3);

(b)   The auditor has determined reporting is an appropriate action to respond to identified or suspected non-compliance in accordance with relevant ethical requirements (see paragraph A30); or

(c)   Law, regulation or relevant ethical requirements provide the auditor with the right to do so (see paragraph A31).

A29   In some jurisdictions, the auditor may be required by law, regulation or relevant ethical requirements to report identified or suspected non-compliance with laws and regulations to an appropriate authority outside the entity. For example, in some jurisdictions, statutory requirements exist for the auditor of a financial institution to report the occurrence, or suspected occurrence, of non-compliance with laws and regulations to a supervisory authority. Also, misstatements may arise from non-compliance with laws or regulations and, in some jurisdictions, the auditor may be required to report misstatements to an appropriate authority in cases where management or those charged with governance fail to take corrective action.

A29-1   Anti-money laundering legislation in the UK imposes a duty on the auditor to report suspected money laundering activity. There are similar laws and regulations relating to financing terrorist offences.[16b] The impact on the auditor of this legislation can broadly be summarized as follows:

● Partners and staff in the firm are required to report suspicions of conduct which would constitute a criminal offence which gives rise to direct or indirect benefit; and

---

[16a] *As discussed in ISA (UK) 320 (Revised June 2016), Materiality in Planning and Performing an Audit, judgments about materiality are made in light of surrounding circumstances and are affected by the size or nature of a matter or a combination of both.*

[16b] *In the UK, the Terrorism Act 2000 contains reporting requirements for the laundering of terrorist funds which include any funds that are likely to be used for the financing of terrorism.*

- Partners and staff in the firm need to be alert to the dangers of "tipping off" as this will constitute a criminal offence under the anti-money laundering legislation.

The Appendix contains further guidance on the auditor's responsibilities in respect of money laundering, terrorist financing and proceeds of crime legislation in the UK.

For auditors of certain entities subject to statutory regulation,[16c] laws and regulations establish separate responsibilities for the auditor to report certain information direct to an appropriate authority outside the entity. Standards and guidance on these responsibilities is given in Section B of this ISA (UK)[1a] and relevant FRC Practice Notes.

A29-2

The procedures and guidance in Section B of this ISA (UK)[1a] can be adapted to circumstances in which the auditor of other types of entity identifies or suspects non-compliance with laws and regulations which the auditor is under a statutory duty to report.

A29-3

In other cases, the relevant ethical requirements may require the auditor to determine whether reporting identified or suspected non-compliance with laws and regulations to an appropriate authority outside the entity is an appropriate action in the circumstances. For example, the IESBA Code requires the auditor to take steps to respond to identified or suspected non-compliance with laws and regulations and determine whether further action is needed, which may include reporting to an appropriate authority outside the entity.[17] The IESBA Code explains that such reporting would not be considered a breach of the duty of confidentiality under the IESBA Code.[18]

A30

Even if law, regulation or relevant ethical requirements do not include requirements that address reporting identified or suspected non-compliance, they may provide the auditor with the right to report identified or suspected non-compliance to an appropriate authority outside the entity. For example, when auditing the financial statements of financial institutions, the auditor may have the right under law or regulation to discuss matters such as identified or suspected non-compliance with laws and regulations with a supervisory authority.

A31

In other circumstances, the reporting of identified or suspected non-compliance with laws and regulations to an appropriate authority outside the entity may be precluded by the auditor's duty of confidentiality under law, regulation or relevant ethical requirements.

A32

The determination required by paragraph 29 may involve complex considerations and professional judgments. Accordingly the auditor may consider consulting internally (e.g., within the firm or a network firm) or on a confidential basis with a regulator or professional body (unless doing so is prohibited by law or regulation or would breach the duty of confidentiality). The auditor may also consider obtaining legal advice to understand the auditor's options and the professional or legal implications of taking any particular course of action.

A33

[16c] *Auditors of public interest entities and other entities in the financial sector, pension schemes and charities have a statutory responsibility, subject to compliance with legislation relating to "tipping off" (see paragraph A21-1), to report matters that are likely to be of material significance to the regulator.*

[17] *See, for example, Section 225.29 and Sections 225.33–225.36 of the IESBA Code.*
In the UK, the auditor has regard to paragraphs A33-1–A33-8 of this ISA (UK) and any specific requirements of the auditor's relevant professional body.

[18] *See, for example, Section 140.7 and Section 225.35 of the IESBA Code.*
In the UK, the auditor has regard to any specific requirements of the auditor's relevant professional body.

Reporting in the Public Interest

A33-1   Where the auditor has identified or suspects non-compliance with laws and regulations which does not give rise to a responsibility under law, regulation or relevant ethical requirements to report to an appropriate authority outside the entity, the auditor considers whether the matter may be one that ought to be reported in the public interest to an appropriate authority outside the entity and, where this is the case, except in the circumstances covered in paragraph A33-3 below, discusses the matter with those charged with governance, including any audit committee.[18a]

A33-2   If, having considered any views expressed on behalf of the entity and in the light of any legal advice obtained, the auditor concludes that the matter ought to be reported in the public interest to an appropriate authority outside the entity, the auditor notifies those charged with governance in writing of the auditor's conclusion and, if the entity does not voluntarily do so itself or is unable to provide evidence that the matter has been reported, the auditor reports the matter direct to an appropriate authority outside the entity.

A33-3   The auditor reports in the public interest a matter direct to an appropriate authority outside the entity and without discussing the matter with the entity if the auditor concludes that the identified or suspected non-compliance with laws and regulations has caused the auditor no longer to have confidence in the integrity of those charged with governance. Such a conclusion may arise in the circumstances identified in paragraph A24 or as a result of other audit procedures.

A33-4   Determination of where the balance of public interest lies requires careful consideration. An auditor whose suspicions have been aroused uses professional judgment to determine whether the auditor's misgivings justify the auditor in carrying the matter further or are too insubstantial to deserve reporting. The auditor is protected from the risk of liability for breach of confidence or defamation provided that:

- In the case of breach of confidence, disclosure is made in the public interest, and such disclosure is made to an appropriate body or person,[18b] and there is no malice motivating the disclosure; and

---

[18a] *In rare circumstances, according to common law, disclosure might also be justified in the public interest where there is no instance of non-compliance with laws and regulations, e.g. where the public is being misled or their financial interests are being damaged; where a miscarriage of justice has occurred; where the health and safety of members of the public or the environment is being endangered – although such events may well constitute breaches of laws and regulations.*

[18b] *In the UK, appropriate authorities outside the entity could include the Serious Fraud Office, the Crown Prosecution Service, police forces, the Financial Conduct Authority, the Prudential Regulation Authority, the Panel on Takeovers and Mergers, the Society of Lloyd's, local authorities, the Charity Commission for England and Wales, the Office of the Scottish Charity Regulator, the Charity Commission for Northern Ireland, HM Revenue and Customs, the Department of Business, Energy and Industrial Strategy and the Health and Safety Executive.*

- In the case of defamation, disclosure is made in the auditor's capacity as auditor of the entity concerned, and there is no malice motivating the disclosure.

In addition, the auditor is protected from such risks where the auditor is expressly permitted or required by legislation to disclose information.[18c]

"Public interest" is a concept that is not capable of general definition. Each situation must be considered individually. In the UK, legal precedent indicates that matters to be taken into account when considering whether disclosure is justified in the public interest may include:

A33-5

- The extent to which the identified or suspected non-compliance with laws and regulations is likely to affect members of the public.

- Whether those charged with governance have rectified the matter or are taking, or are likely to take, effective corrective action.

- The extent to which non-disclosure is likely to enable the identified or suspected non-compliance with laws and regulations to recur with impunity.

- The gravity of the matter.

- Whether there is a general ethos within the entity of disregarding laws and regulations.

- The weight of evidence and the degree of the auditor's suspicion that there has been non-compliance with laws and regulations.

An auditor who can demonstrate having acted reasonably and in good faith in informing an appropriate authority of non-compliance with laws and regulations which the auditor suspects has been committed would not be held by the court to be in breach of duty to the client even if, an investigation or prosecution having occurred, it were found that there had been no offence.

A33-6

The auditor needs to remember that the auditor's decision as to whether to report, and if so to whom, may be called into question at a future date, for example on the basis of:

A33-7

- What the auditor knew at the time;

- What the auditor ought to have known in the course of the audit;

- What the auditor ought to have concluded; and

- What the auditor ought to have done.

The auditor may also wish to consider the possible consequences if financial loss is occasioned by non-compliance with laws and regulations which the auditor suspects (or ought to suspect) has occurred but decided not to report.

The auditor may need to take legal advice before making a decision on whether identified or suspected non-compliance with laws and regulations needs to be reported to an appropriate authority in the public interest.

A33-8

[18c] *In the UK, the Employments Rights Act 1996 would give similar protection to an individual member of the engagement team who made an appropriate report in the public interest. However, ordinarily a member of the engagement team who believed there was a reportable matter would follow the firm's policies and procedures to address such matters. ISA (UK) 220 (Revised June 2016), Quality Control for an Audit of Financial Statements, paragraph 18(a), requires that the engagement partner shall take responsibility for the engagement team undertaking appropriate consultation on difficult or contentious matters. If differences of opinion arise within the engagement team, ISA (UK) 220 (Revised June 2016) paragraph 22, requires that the engagement team shall follow the firm's policies and procedures for dealing with and resolving differences of opinion.*

Considerations Specific to Public Sector Entities

A34 A public sector auditor may be obliged to report on identified or suspected non-compliance to the legislature or other governing body or to report them in the auditor's report.

Timing of Reports

A34-1 Laws and regulations may stipulate a period within which reports are to be made. If the auditor becomes aware of a suspected or actual non-compliance with laws and regulations which gives rise to a statutory duty to report, the auditor complies with any such stipulated periods for reporting. Ordinarily the auditor makes a report to an appropriate authority outside the entity as soon as practicable.

Reporting to Authorities of Public Interest Entities
(Ref: Para. 29R-1)

A34-2 The disclosure in good faith to the authorities responsible for investigating such irregularities, by the auditor, of any irregularities referred to in paragraph 29R-1 shall not constitute a breach of any contractual or legal restriction on disclosure of information in accordance with the Audit Regulation.[18d]

A34-3 The auditor considers whether to take further action when the entity investigates the matter referred to in paragraph 23R-1 but where the measures taken by management or those charged with governance, in the auditor's professional judgement, were not appropriate to deal with the irregularities identified or would fail to prevent future occurrences.

Documentation
(Ref: Para. 30)

A35 The auditor's documentation of findings regarding identified or suspected non-compliance with laws and regulations may include, for example:

● Copies of records or documents.

● Minutes of discussions held with management, those charged with governance or parties outside the entity.

A36 Law, regulation or relevant ethical requirements may also set out additional documentation requirements regarding identified or suspected non-compliance with laws and regulations.[19]

[18d] *Article 7 of Regulation (EU) No 537/2014 of the European Parliament and of the Council of 16 April 2014.*

[19] *See, for example, Section 225.37 of the IESBA Code.*
In the UK, the auditor has regard to any specific requirements of the auditor's relevant professional body.

Appendix

(Ref: Para. A6-1, A29-1)

Money Laundering, Terrorist Financing and Proceeds of Crime Legislation in the United Kingdom[1]

In the UK, the auditor has additional responsibilities that arise as a result of money laundering, terrorist financing and proceeds of crime legislation, including:[2]

- Proceeds of Crime Act 2002 (POCA) (as subsequently amended by the Serious and Organised Crime and Police Act 2005 (SOCPA)).

- Terrorism Act 2000 (TACT) (as amended).

- Crime and Courts Act 2013.

- Money Laundering, Terrorist Financing and Transfer of Funds (Information on the Payer) Regulations 2017 (SI 692/2017).

- Criminal Finances Act 2017.

Hereafter known collectively as the "Anti-Money Laundering Legislation".

The Anti-Money Laundering Legislation is complex and this Appendix focuses on the impact of the Anti-Money Laundering Legislation on the auditor's responsibilities when auditing and reporting on financial statements, and should be read in conjunction with the more detailed updated guidance, which includes a series of practical examples, issued by the Consultative Committee of Accountancy Bodies (CCAB).[3] To obtain a full understanding of the legal requirements auditors will need to refer to the relevant provisions of the legislation and, if necessary, obtain legal advice.[4]

Changes Under the Money Laundering, Terrorist Financing and Transfer of Funds (Information on the Payer) Regulations 2017

The Money Laundering, Terrorist Financing and Transfer of Funds (Information on the Payer) Regulations 2017 ("2017 Regulations") replace the Money Laundering Regulations 2007. The 2017 Regulations apply to persons acting in the course of business as a statutory auditor within the meaning of Part 42 of the Companies Act 2006, when carrying out statutory audit work within the meaning of Section 1210 of the Companies Act 2006.[5] The 2017 Regulations amend POCA and TACT to make them applicable to those persons carrying out audits in accordance with Section 4(1) of the Local

1

2

3

---

[1] *The revised guidance in this Appendix has been shared with HM Treasury, HM Revenue and Customs and the National Crime Agency (NCA) before being finalised.*

[2] *This Appendix reflects the legislation effective at 26 June 2017. Auditors need to be alert to subsequent changes in legislative requirements.*

[3] *The CCAB has issued revised "Anti-Money Laundering Guidance for the Accountancy Sector" ("CCAB Guidance") which provides detailed guidance on the legislation for all entities providing audit, accountancy, tax advisory or insolvency related services. This is available on the CCAB website at http://www.ccab.org.uk/ documents.php The CCAB Guidance is approved by HM Treasury.*

[4] *Detailed guidance by the NCA is available at: http://www.nationalcrimeagency.gov.uk/publications/725-sar-glossary-code-and-reporting-routes/file*

[5] *Regulation 11(1) of the 2017 Regulations.*

Audit and Accountability Act 2014. Regulation 100(1) also provides an updated list of public bodies and persons who are obliged to report where they know or suspect money laundering has taken place, or have reasonable ground for suspicion thereof, to the National Crime Agency (NCA). For the purposes of this Appendix, "person" is interpreted as referring to a UK firm (or sole practitioner) that is designated as a "Registered Auditor" to which the 2017 Regulations apply. The 2017 Regulations also set out a series of key changes in respect of:

- More prescriptive risk assessments.

- Policies and procedures to mitigate money laundering and terrorist financing risks.

- Enhanced transparency over beneficial owners.

- Customer due diligence.

- Changes to extend the definition of Politically Exposed Persons.

- A person responsible for compliance at Board level.

- Enhanced training requirements.

4   Where a Registered Auditor is not carrying out statutory audit work, the 2017 Regulations will nevertheless often apply as they also cover a firm or sole practitioner who provides accountancy services to, or advice about the tax affairs of, other persons.[6] The 2017 Regulations impose requirements on businesses in the regulated sector relating to systems, procedures and training to prevent money laundering, provide identification procedures for clients, maintaining records, and internal reporting.

To Whom Does the Anti-Money Laundering Legislation Apply?

5   The requirement to make a report under Sections 330 and 331 of POCA applies to information which comes to a person in the course of a business, or a Money Laundering Reporting Officer ("MLRO"), in the regulated sector. That information may relate to money laundering by persons or businesses inside or outside the regulated sector. The offence of failing to report that another person is engaged in money laundering applies to all money laundering, including conduct taking place overseas that would be an offence if it took place in the UK. For that reason, there may be an obligation to report information arising from the audit of non-UK companies or their subsidiaries.

6   Sections 45 and 46 of the Criminal Finances Act 2017 create criminal offences for failing to prevent the facilitation of tax evasion. These offences apply to Companies, Partnerships and Limited Liability Partnerships (LLPs) where:

- Criminal tax evasion takes place under UK or foreign law;

- It is facilitated by the business' employee, agent or those performing services for the business; and

- The business, by virtue of failing to put in place reasonable prevention methods, has failed to prevent that person from enabling the crime.

---

[6] *Regulations 11(3) and 11(4) of the 2017 Regulations.*

When is an Auditor in the UK Regulated Sector?

The regulated sector includes any firm or individual who acts in the course of a   **7**
business carried on in the UK as an auditor. This is set out in more detail in
paragraphs 8–10 of this Appendix.

A person is eligible for appointment as an auditor if the person is a member of a   **8**
Recognised Supervisory Body[7] and is eligible for appointment under the rules
of that Body. A person will fall within the regulated sector in their capacity as
an auditor when carrying out statutory audit work within the meaning of
Section 1210 of the Companies Act 2006. In summary, this comprises the audit
of UK private or public companies, building societies, friendly societies,
Lloyds syndicate aggregate accounts, insurance undertakings, LLPs,
qualifying partnerships, those carrying out audits in accordance with Section
4(1) of the Local Audit and Accountability Act 2014 and any other such bodies
as the Secretary of State may prescribe by Order.

The Anti-Money Laundering Legislation applies to all partners and staff within   **9**
a UK firm who are involved in providing audit services in relation to statutory
audit work in the UK. Where they become involved in audit work in the UK,
such persons may include experts from other disciplines within the UK firm
and employees (both audit partners and staff and experts from other disciplines)
of non-UK firms, including contractors.

Where they are not involved in audit work in the UK such persons may fall   **10**
within other parts of the regulated sector. For example, the provision of
accountancy services to other persons by way of business is within the
regulated sector regardless of whether the person providing the services is or
is not a member of a UK Recognised Supervisory Body.

It is unlikely that it will be practicable or desirable for a UK firm which is   **11**
within the regulated sector to distinguish for reporting purposes between
partners and staff who are providing services in the regulated sector and
those who are not. Accordingly, UK firms may choose to impose procedures
across the firm requiring all partners and staff to report to the firm's MLRO.[8]

The use of the term "auditor" in this Appendix means anyone who is part of the   **12**
engagement team as defined in ISA (UK) 220 (Revised June 2016).[9] For audits
carried out in accordance with the FRC Ethical Standard, the audit team
comprises all persons who are directly involved in the acceptance and
performance of a particular audit. This includes the audit team (including
audit professionals contracted by the firm), professional personnel from other
disciplines involved in the audit engagement, and those who provide quality
control or direct oversight of the audit engagement, but it does not include
experts contracted by the firm.

---

[7] *A Recognised Supervisory Body is a body established in the UK which maintains and enforces rules as to the
eligibility of persons to seek appointment as an auditor and the conduct of audit work, and which is recognised by
the Secretary of State by Order.*

[8] *Persons outside the regulated sector are not obliged to report to their MLRO under Sections 330 and 331 of
POCA (the "failure to report" offence), but can make voluntary reports under Section 337.*

[9] *ISA (UK) 220 (Revised June 2016), Quality Control for an Audit of Financial Statements, paragraph 7(d).*

Key Legal Requirements

13   The Anti-Money Laundering Legislation establishes the following auditor's responsibilities:

- The Anti-Money Laundering Legislation does not extend the scope of the audit, but the auditor is within the regulated sector and is required to report where:

  - The auditor knows or suspects, or has reasonable grounds to know or suspect, that another person is engaged in money laundering; and

  - The auditor can identify the other person or the whereabouts of any of the laundered property, or that the auditor believes, or it is reasonable to expect the auditor to believe, that information that the auditor has obtained will or may assist in identifying that other person or the whereabouts of the laundered property; and

  - The information has come to the auditor in the course of the auditor's "regulated" business.

- POCA defines both the money laundering offences and the auditor's reporting responsibilities. The Anti-Money Laundering Legislation imposes a duty to report money laundering in respect of all criminal property.[10]

- Failure by an auditor to report knowledge or suspicion of, or reasonable grounds to know or suspect, money laundering in relation to the proceeds of any crime is a criminal offence.[11] Auditors (partners and staff) will face criminal penalties[12] if they breach the requirements.

- The requirement to report is not just related to matters that might be considered material to the financial statements; the auditor has to report knowledge or suspicion, or reasonable grounds for knowledge or suspicion, of crimes that potentially have no material financial statement impact. The Anti-Money Laundering Legislation does not contain de minimis concessions.

- A very wide range of offences (e.g., bribery and corruption both in and outside of the UK, and therefore also subject to the provisions of the Bribery Act 2010) may give rise to a responsibility to report money laundering suspicions.

- Where an auditor knows or suspects that the auditor themselves are involved in money laundering, the auditor is required to report this in order that appropriate consent can be obtained.

- The firm must take appropriate measures so that partners and staff are made aware of the provisions of the Anti-Money Laundering Legislation

---

[10] *Property is criminal property if: (i) it constitutes a person's benefit from criminal conduct or it represents such a benefit (in whole or in part and whether directly or indirectly); and (ii) the alleged offender knows or suspects that it constitutes or represents such a benefit.*

[11] *Subject to the provisions of Section 330(6) of POCA relating to information coming to a legal adviser or relevant professional adviser in "privileged circumstances" and Section 330(7A) relating to offences committed overseas.*

[12] *Criminal penalties are covered under Sections 334 and 336(6) of POCA. The maximum penalty for the three principal money laundering offences on conviction on indictment is fourteen years imprisonment. The maximum penalty on conviction on indictment is five years imprisonment. In all cases, an unlimited fine can be imposed.*

and are given training in how to recognise and deal with actual or suspected money laundering activities.

- The firm is required to adopt rigorous client identification procedures and appropriate anti-money laundering procedures.

Money Laundering Offences

There are three principal money laundering offences in POCA which define money laundering to encompass offences relating to:

14

- The concealment (Section 327);
- Becoming involved in arrangements which facilitate the creation (Section 328); and
- Acquisition, use, and possession (Section 329)

of criminal property and involvement in arrangements relating to criminal property. These principal offences apply to all persons and businesses whether or not they are within the regulated sector.

Under Section 330 of POCA, persons working in the regulated sector are required to report knowledge or suspicion, or reasonable grounds for knowledge or suspicion, that another person is engaged in money laundering to a nominated officer where that knowledge or suspicion, or reasonable grounds for knowledge or suspicion, came to those persons in the course of their business or employment in the regulated sector. In a firm, the nominated officer is usually known as a Money Laundering Reporting Officer[13] ("MLRO") and is referred to as such in this Appendix (see paragraphs 22–24 of this Appendix).[14] If, as a result of that report, the MLRO has knowledge or suspicion of, or reasonable grounds to know or suspect money laundering, the MLRO then has a responsibility to report to the Financial Intelligence Unit of the NCA.

15

Auditors who consider that the actions they plan to take, or may be asked to take, will result in themselves committing a principal money laundering offence are required to obtain prior consent to those actions from their MLRO and the MLRO is required to seek appropriate prior consent from the NCA (see paragraphs 49–51 of this Appendix). Auditors could also commit a principal offence through acts of omission.

16

---

[13] *The 2017 legislation creates a new role of "officer responsible for compliance"; however, for the purposes of this guidance the term MLRO should be deemed to cover both roles. More detailed explanation is provided in Section 3 of the CCAB Guidance.*

[14] *Requirements relating to internal reporting procedures do not apply to sole practitioners; however, a sole practitioner is still subject to external reporting obligations under POCA. Where a sole practitioner has knowledge or suspicion of, or reasonable grounds to know or suspect, money laundering they have a responsibility to report to the NCA (see paragraph 23 of this Appendix).*

Firm-wide Practices

17   The Anti-Money Laundering Legislation requires the firm to establish risk-sensitive policies and procedures[15] relating to:

- Customer identification and ongoing monitoring of business relationships.
- Reporting internally and to the NCA.[16]
- Record keeping.
- Internal control, risk assessment and management.
- Training for all relevant employees.
- Monitoring and management of compliance with a firm's policies and procedures.
- The internal communication of such policies and procedures throughout the firm.

In addition, the firm needs to ensure sufficient senior management oversight of the systems used for monitoring compliance with these procedures. It may be helpful for this to be coordinated with the responsibility for the firm's quality control systems under ISQC (UK) 1 (Revised June 2016).[17]

Client Identification and Ongoing Monitoring of Business Relationships

18   Appropriate identification procedures,[18] as required by the Anti-Money Laundering Legislation, are mandatory when accepting appointment as auditor. The extent of information collected about the client and verification of identity undertaken will depend on the client risk assessment.

19   Auditing standards on quality control require the firm to consider the integrity of the client. This involves the firm making appropriate enquiries and may involve discussions with third parties, the obtaining of written references and searches of relevant databases. These procedures may provide some of the relevant client identification information, but may need to be extended to comply with the Anti-Money Laundering Legislation.

20   It may be helpful for the auditor to explain to the client the reason for requiring evidence of identity and this can be achieved by including this matter in pre-engagement letter communications with the potential client. It may also be helpful to inform clients of the auditor's responsibilities under the Anti-Money Laundering Legislation to report knowledge or suspicion, or reasonable grounds to know or suspect, that a money laundering offence has been committed and the restrictions created by the "tipping off" rules on the auditor's ability to discuss such matters with management and those charged with governance. Such wording could be included in the auditor's engagement letter.[19]

---

[15] *Detailed guidance on developing and applying a risk based approach is given in Section 4 of the CCAB Guidance.*

[16] *Whilst a risk based approach is appropriate when devising policies and procedures, the auditor does not adopt a risk based approach to making reports either internally or to the NCA.*

[17] *International Standard on Quality Control (UK) 1 (Revised June 2016), Quality Control for Firms that Perform Audits and Reviews of Financial Statements, and other Assurance and Related Services Engagements.*

[18] *Guidance on identification procedures, including references to financial restrictions regimes (i.e., sanctions), is given in Section 5 of the CCAB Guidance.*

[19] *ISA (UK) 210 (Revised June 2016), Agreeing the Terms of Audit Engagements.*

The activities of and the relationship with the client are monitored by the firm on an ongoing basis. For example, if there has been a change in the client's circumstances, such as changes in beneficial ownership, control or directors, and this information was relied upon originally as part of the client identification procedures, then, depending on the auditor's assessment of risk, the procedures may need to be re-performed and documented. However, annual reappointment as auditor does not, in itself, require the client identification procedures to be re-performed.   **21**

Money Laundering Reporting Officer

The Anti-Money Laundering Legislation requires relevant entities to appoint a nominated officer (usually known as the MLRO[13]). The auditor is required to report to the MLRO where the auditor knows or suspects, or has reasonable grounds to know or suspect, that another person is engaged in money laundering or, for the purposes of obtaining consent, where the auditor knows or suspects that the auditor themselves are involved in money laundering. The Anti-Money Laundering Legislation does not contain de minimis concessions that affect the reporting requirements with the result that reports need to be made irrespective of the quantum of the benefits derived from, or the seriousness of, the offence.   **22**

A sole practitioner is not required to appoint a MLRO; however, the external reporting obligations under the Anti-Money Laundering Legislation remain, and where a sole practitioner has knowledge or suspicion of, or reasonable grounds to know or suspect, money laundering they have a responsibility to report to the NCA. References in this Appendix to reporting matters to the MLRO should be read as making a report directly to the NCA in the case of a sole practitioner.   **23**

Partners and staff in a firm discharge their responsibilities by reporting to the firm's MLRO and, where appropriate, by obtaining consent from the MLRO or the NCA to continue with any prohibited activities. The MLRO is responsible for deciding, on the basis of the information provided by the partners and staff, whether further inquiry is required, whether the matter should be reported to the NCA and for making the report. Partners and staff may seek advice from the MLRO who will often act as the main source of guidance and, if necessary, act as the liaison point for communication with the firm's own legal counsel, the NCA and the relevant law enforcement agency. When a report has been made to the NCA, partners and staff need to be alert to the dangers of disseminating information that is likely to "tip off" a money launderer or prejudice an investigation as this may constitute a criminal offence under the Anti-Money Laundering Legislation.   **24**

Training

Firms are required to take appropriate measures so that partners and staff are made aware of the relevant provisions of the Anti-Money Laundering Legislation and are given training in how to recognise and deal with activities which may be related to money laundering and terrorist financing.[20] The level of training provided to partners and staff needs to be   **25**

---

[20] *Guidance on training is given in Section 3 of the CCAB Guidance and in Regulation 24 of the 2017 Regulations.*

appropriate to both the level of exposure of the individual to money laundering and terrorist financing risk and the individual's role and seniority within the firm. Senior members of the firm whatever their role need to understand the requirements of the Anti-Money Laundering Legislation. Additional training or expertise in criminal law is not required under the Anti-Money Laundering Legislation. However, ISA (UK) 250 (Revised December 2017)[21] requires the auditor to obtain a general understanding of the legal and regulatory framework applicable to the entity and the industry or sector in which the entity operates and how the entity is complying with that framework.

Impact of Anti-Money Laundering Legislation on Audit Procedures

Identification of Knowledge or Suspicions

26 ISA (UK) 250 (Revised December 2017) establishes standards and provides guidance on the auditor's responsibility to consider laws and regulations in an audit of financial statements. The Anti-Money Laundering Legislation does not require the auditor to extend the scope of the audit, save as referred to in paragraph 35 of this Appendix, but during the course of the audit, knowledge or suspicion, or reasonable grounds for knowledge or suspicion, relating to money laundering activities may arise that will need to be reported.

27 ISA (UK) 250 (Revised December 2017) requires the auditor to obtain:

- A general understanding of the legal and regulatory framework applicable to the entity and the industry or sector in which the entity operates and how the entity is complying with that framework;[22] and

- Sufficient appropriate audit evidence regarding compliance with the provisions of those laws and regulations generally recognised to have a direct effect on the determination of material amounts and disclosures in the financial statements.[23]

This may cause the auditor to be suspicious that, for example, breaches of the Companies Act 2006 or tax offences have taken place, which may be criminal offences resulting in criminal property.

28 ISA (UK) 250 (Revised December 2017) also requires the auditor to perform procedures to help identify instances of non-compliance with other laws and regulations which may have a material effect on the financial statements.[24] These procedures may include:

---

[21] *ISA (UK) 250 (Revised December 2017), Section A—Consideration of Laws and Regulations in an Audit of Financial Statements, paragraph 13.*

[22] *ISA (UK) 250 (Revised December 2017) Section A, paragraph 13.*

[23] *ISA (UK) 250 (Revised December 2017) Section A, paragraph 14.*

[24] *ISA (UK) 250 (Revised December 2017) Section A, paragraph 15.*

- Enquiring of management and, where appropriate, those charged with governance as to whether the entity is in compliance with such laws and regulations.

- Inspecting correspondence, if any, with the relevant licensing or regulatory authorities.

These procedures may give the auditor grounds to suspect that criminal offences have been committed.

For entities within the regulated sector[25] or public interest entities, other laws and regulations that may have a material effect on the financial statements will include Anti-Money Laundering Legislation. When auditing the financial statements of entities within the regulated sector, the auditor reviews the steps taken by the entity to comply with the Anti-Money Laundering Legislation, assesses their effectiveness and obtains management representations concerning compliance with that legislation. If the auditor assesses the entity's internal control as ineffective, the auditor considers whether there is a statutory responsibility to report "a matter of material significance" to the regulator in accordance with ISA (UK) 250 (Revised June 2016).[26]   **29**

Where the entity's business is outside the regulated sector, although the auditor's reporting responsibilities under the Anti-Money Laundering Legislation are unchanged, the entity's management is not required to implement the Anti-Money Laundering Legislation. Whilst the principal money laundering offences apply to these entities, the laws relating to money laundering are unlikely to be considered by the auditor to be other laws and regulations that may have a material effect on the financial statements for the purposes of ISA (UK) 250 (Revised December 2017), unless there are other indicators that may lead to a risk of material misstatement of the financial statements.   **30**

ISA (UK) 250 (Revised December 2017) requires the auditor to be alert to the possibility that audit procedures applied for the purpose of forming an opinion on the financial statements may bring instances of possible non-compliance with other laws and regulations to the auditor's attention.[27] This includes non-compliance that might incur obligations for the auditor to report to an appropriate authority outside the entity.   **31**

The auditor also gives consideration to whether any contingent liabilities might arise in this area. For example, there may be regulatory or criminal fines for offences under the Anti-Money Laundering Legislation. Even where no offence under the Anti-Money Laundering Legislation has been committed, civil recovery actions under POCA (Part 5) or other civil claims may give rise to contingent liabilities. The auditor remains alert to the fact that discussions with the entity on such matters may give rise to a risk of "tipping off" (see paragraphs 45–48 of this Appendix).   **32**

---

[25] *For the purposes of this Appendix this includes (but is not restricted to) the following persons acting in the course of business in the UK: credit institutions; financial institutions (including money service operators); auditors, insolvency practitioners, external accountants and tax advisers; independent legal professionals; trust or company service providers; estate agents; high value dealers when dealing in goods of any description which involves accepting a total cash payment of 10,000 or more; and casinos. More detail is provided in Part 2 of the 2017 Regulations.*

[26] *ISA (UK) 250 (Revised June 2016), Section B – The Auditor's Statutory Right and Duty to Report to Regulators of Public interest Entities and Regulators of Other Entities in the Financial Sector.*

[27] *ISA (UK) 250, (Revised December 2017) Section A, paragraph 16.*

33 In some situations the entity may have obtained legal advice to the effect that certain actions or circumstances do not give rise to criminal conduct and therefore cannot give rise to criminal property. Whether an act constitutes non-compliance with laws and regulations may involve consideration of matters beyond the auditor's professional competence to determine. Provided that the auditor considers that the advice has been obtained from a suitably qualified and independent solicitor and that the solicitor was made aware of all relevant circumstances known to the auditor, the auditor may rely on such advice, provided the auditor has complied with the requirements of ISA (UK) 500[28] and ISA (UK) 620 (Revised June 2016).[29]

34 The Anti-Money Laundering Legislation requires the auditor to report the laundering of the proceeds of conduct which takes place overseas if that conduct would constitute an offence in any part of the UK, subject to certain exceptions. The Anti-Money Laundering Legislation does not change the scope of the audit and does not therefore impose any requirement for the group engagement team to change or add to the normal instructions to component auditors of overseas subsidiaries. However, when considering non-UK parts of the group audit, the group engagement team should consider whether information obtained as part of the group audit procedures (e.g., reports made by non-UK component auditors, discussions with non-UK component auditors or discussions with UK and non-UK management and those charged with governance) gives rise to knowledge or suspicion, or reasonable grounds for knowledge or suspicion, such that there is a requirement for the auditor to report to the NCA. The auditor also considers whether such conduct constitutes an offence under Section 6 of the Bribery Act 2010.

Further Inquiry

35 Once the auditor identifies or suspects non-compliance with laws and regulations, the auditor makes further enquiries to assess the implications of this for the audit of the financial statements. ISA (UK) 250 (Revised December 2017) requires that when the auditor becomes aware of information concerning a possible instance of non-compliance, the auditor should obtain an understanding of the nature of the act and the circumstances in which it has occurred, and sufficient other information to evaluate the possible effect on the financial statements.[30] Where the auditor knows or suspects, or has reasonable grounds to know or suspect, that another person is engaged in money laundering, a disclosure must be made to the firm's MLRO. The Anti-Money Laundering Legislation does not require the auditor to undertake any additional enquiries to determine further details of the criminal offence. Where the auditor is uncertain as to whether or not there are grounds to make a disclosure, the engagement partner may wish to seek advice from the firm's MLRO.

36 In performing any further enquiries in the context of the audit of the financial statements, the auditor takes care not to alert a money launderer to the possibility that a report will be or has been made, especially if management and, where applicable, those charged with governance are themselves involved in the suspected criminal activity.

---

[28] *ISA (UK) 500, Audit Evidence.*

[29] *ISA (UK) 620 (Revised June 2016), Using the Work of an Auditor's Expert.*

[30] *ISA (UK) 250 (Revised July 2017) Section A, paragraph 19.*

Reporting to the MLRO and to the NCA

The auditor reports to the firm's MLRO where the auditor knows or suspects, or **37** has reasonable grounds to know or suspect, that another person is engaged in money laundering. Money laundering reports need to be made irrespective of the quantum of the benefits derived from, or the seriousness of, the offence. There is no provision for the auditor not to make a report even where the auditor considers that the matter has already been reported, unless the auditor:

- Does not have the information to identify the money launderer and the whereabouts of any of the laundered property; or

- Does not believe, and it is unreasonable to expect the auditor to believe, that any information held by the auditor will or may assist in identifying the money launderer or the whereabouts of any of the laundered property.

Where suspected money laundering occurs wholly or partially overseas in **38** relation to conduct that is lawful in the country where it occurred the position is more complicated, and the auditor needs to be careful to ensure that the strict requirements of the Anti-Money Laundering Legislation have been satisfied if no report is to be made to the MLRO or to the NCA. In these circumstances, the auditor considers two questions:

- Where the client or third party's money laundering is occurring wholly overseas, is the money laundering lawful there? If it is, a report is not required. However, the auditor needs to be careful to ensure that no consequences of the criminal conduct are, in fact, occurring in the UK;

- Where the client or third party's money laundering is occurring in the UK in relation to underlying conduct which occurred overseas and was lawful there, would the conduct amount to a "serious offence" under UK law[31] if it had occurred here? If it would have amounted to such an offence, a report is required. The auditor should also consider whether such conduct would be an offence under Section 6 of the Bribery Act 2010.

The duties to report on overseas money laundering activity are complex as they rely on knowledge of both overseas and UK law. In practice, the auditor may choose to report all overseas money laundering activity to the firm's MLRO, subject to the auditor having the information set out in paragraph 37 of this Appendix.

During the course of the audit, the auditor may obtain knowledge or form a **39** suspicion about a prohibited act that would be a criminal offence under the Anti-Money Laundering Legislation but has yet to occur. Because attempting or conspiring to commit a money laundering offence is in itself a money laundering offence, a report might need to be made.

---

[31] *A "serious offence" is conduct that would constitute an offence punishable by imprisonment for a maximum term in excess of 12 months if it occurred in any part of the UK, with the exception of an offence under:*

(a)   The Gaming Act 1968;

(b)   The Lotteries and Amusements Act 1976; or

(c)   Section 23 or 25 of the Financial Services and Markets Act 2000.

40   The format of the internal report made to the MLRO is not specified by the Anti-Money Laundering Legislation. MLROs determine the form in which partners and staff report knowledge or suspicion of, or reasonable grounds to know or suspect, money laundering offences. The form and content of these reports will need to provide the MLRO with sufficient information to enable a report to be made to the NCA if necessary, and it may be helpful, therefore, for the reports to use the NCA templates available online for the purposes of gathering information.[32] The auditor follows the firm's internal documentation procedures when considering whether to include documentation relating to money laundering reporting in the audit working papers. In order to prevent "tipping off" where another auditor or professional advisor has access to the audit file, the auditor may wish to exclude from the audit file all details of internal reports held by the MLRO. Reporting as soon as is practicable to the MLRO is the responsibility of the auditor and, although suspicions would normally be discussed within the engagement team before deciding whether or not to make an internal report to the MLRO, this should not delay the report.

41   The MLRO makes the decision as to whether a report is made by the firm to the NCA. Suspicious Activity Reports may be made using one of the NCA's manual or on-line forms.[32]

42   The timing of reporting by the MLRO is governed by the Anti-Money Laundering Legislation which requires the disclosure to be made "as soon as is practicable" after the information or other matter comes to the attention of the MLRO.[33] Where the information includes time sensitive information (e.g., that may allow the recovery of proceeds of crime if communicated immediately) the report will need to be made quickly.

43   Where the auditor has made a report to the MLRO and the MLRO has decided that further inquiry is necessary, the auditor will need to be made aware of the outcome of the inquiry to determine whether there are any implications for the auditor's report or the decision to accept reappointment as auditor.

Legal Privilege

44   Legal privilege can provide a defence for a professional legal adviser to a charge of failing to report knowledge or suspicion of money laundering and is generally available to the legal profession when giving legal advice to a client or acting in relation to litigation.[34] If the auditor is given access to client information over which legal professional privilege may be asserted (e.g., correspondence between clients and solicitors in relation to legal advice or litigation) and that information gives grounds to suspect money laundering, the auditor considers whether the auditor is nevertheless obliged to report to the MLRO. There is some ambiguity about how the issue of legal privilege is interpreted and a prudent approach is to assume that legal privilege does not extend to the auditor. Where the auditor is in possession of client information which is clearly privileged (e.g., a solicitor's advice to an entity), the auditor seeks legal advice.

---

[32] *http://www.nationalcrimeagency.gov.uk/about-us/what-we-do/economic-crime/ukfiu/how-to-report-sars*

[33] *Guidance on the reporting of knowledge and suspicions by the MLRO to the NCA is given in Section 7 of the CCAB Guidance.*

[34] *The Proceeds of Crime Act 2002 and Money Laundering Regulations 2003 (Amendment) Order 2006 (SI 2006/308) extended this defence to accountants, auditors or tax advisers who satisfy certain conditions where the information on which their suspicion of money laundering is based comes to their attention in privileged circumstances. In such circumstances, the auditor may discuss their suspicions with the MLRO without requiring a disclosure to the NCA.*

"Tipping Off" and Prejudicing an Investigation

In the UK, "tipping off" is an offence for individuals in the regulated sector under the Anti-Money Laundering Legislation. This offence arises: **45**

(a)   When an individual discloses that a report (either internal or external) has been made based on information that came to that individual in the course of a business in the regulated sector and the disclosure by the individual is likely to prejudice an investigation which might be conducted; or

(b)   When an individual discloses that an investigation is being contemplated or is being carried out into allegations that a money laundering offence has been committed and the disclosure by the individual is likely to prejudice that investigation and the information on which the report is based came to a person in the course of a business in the regulated sector.

There are a number of exceptions to this offence under the Anti-Money Laundering Legislation, including where disclosures are made: **46**

●   To a fellow auditor employed by a firm that shares common ownership, management or control with the firm;[35]

●   To an auditor in another firm in the EEA (or an equivalent jurisdiction for money laundering purposes, where both are subject to equivalent confidentiality and data protection obligations), in relation to the same entity and a transaction or service involving them both, for the purpose of preventing a money laundering offence;

●   To a supervisory authority for the person making the disclosure;

●   For the purpose of the detection, investigation or prosecution of a criminal offence (whether in the UK or elsewhere);

●   Where the auditor is acting as a relevant professional adviser to the client, for the purpose of dissuading the client from engaging in an offence; or

●   In circumstances where the person making the disclosure does not know or suspect that the disclosure is likely to prejudice an investigation.

A further offence of prejudicing an investigation is included in the Anti-Money Laundering Legislation. Under this provision,[36] it is an offence to make any disclosure which is likely to prejudice an investigation of which a person has knowledge or suspicion, or to falsify, conceal, destroy or otherwise dispose of, or cause or permit the falsification, concealment, destruction or disposal of, documents relevant to such an investigation.   **47**

ISA (UK) 260 (Revised June 2016),[37] requires the auditor to communicate significant findings from the audit with those charged with governance of an entity. The auditor considers whether there is a need to communicate suspicions of money laundering to those charged with governance of an entity. Under the Anti-Money Laundering Legislation a "tipping off" offence is not committed by an auditor where a disclosure is made to the entity in order to dissuade the entity from engaging in a money laundering offence (e.g., where an employee is engaged in money laundering using the entity's financial systems, the auditor may inform management, or, where applicable, those charged with governance   **48**

---

[35] *Some network firms may not meet these criteria.*

[36] *Section 342 of POCA.*

[37] *ISA (UK) 260 (Revised June 2016), Communication with Those Charged with Governance, paragraph 16.*

of the situation in order to prevent the entity from committing a money laundering offence). However, care should be taken as to whom the disclosure is made where management or those charged with governance are, or are suspected to be, involved in the money laundering activity or complicit with it.

Reporting to Obtain Appropriate Consent

49   In addition to the auditor's duty to report knowledge or suspicion of, or reasonable grounds to know or suspect, money laundering under the Anti-Money Laundering Legislation, the auditor may need to obtain appropriate consent to perform an act which could otherwise constitute a principal money laundering offence.[38] For example, if the auditor suspected that the auditor's report was necessary in order for financial statements to be issued in connection with a transaction involving the proceeds of crime, or if the auditor was to issue an auditor's report on financial statements for an entity that was a front for illegal activity, the auditor might be involved in an arrangement which facilitated the acquisition, retention, use or control of criminal property under the Anti-Money Laundering Legislation. In these circumstances, in addition to the normal procedures, the auditor would generally need to obtain appropriate consent from the NCA via the MLRO as soon as is practicable. Consent may be given expressly or may be deemed to have been given following the expiry of certain time limits specified in the Anti-Money Laundering Legislation.[39]

50   The auditor also needs to consider whether continuing to act for the entity could itself constitute money laundering, for example, if it amounted to aiding or abetting the commission of one of the principal money laundering offences, or if it amounted to one of the principal money laundering offences itself, in particular the offence of becoming involved in an arrangement under the Anti-Money Laundering Legislation. In those circumstances, the auditor may want to consider whether to resign, but should firstly contact the MLRO, both to report the suspicions and to seek guidance in respect of "tipping off". If the auditor wishes to continue the engagement the auditor may need to seek NCA consent for such an action to be taken.

51   Appropriate consent from the NCA will protect the auditor from committing a principal money laundering offence but will not relieve the auditor from any civil liability or other professional, legal or ethical obligations. As an alternative to seeking appropriate consent, the auditor may wish to consider resignation from the audit but, in such circumstances, is still required to disclose suspicions to the MLRO. Further guidance on resignation is given in paragraphs 58–62 of this Appendix.

---

[38] *Subject to the SOCPA amendments to Sections 327, 328 and 329 for overseas activities which state that it is not a money laundering offence for a person to deal with the proceeds of conduct which that person knows, or believes on reasonable grounds, occurred in a particular country or territory outside the UK, and which was known to be lawful, at the time it occurred, under the criminal law then applying in that country or territory, and does not constitute a "serious offence" under UK law (see footnote 31).*

[39] *Further guidance on seeking appropriate consent is given in the NCA publication: Requesting a Defence from the NCA under POCA and TACT which can be downloaded from: http://www.nationalcrimeagency.gov.uk/publications/713-requesting-a-defence-under-poca-tact/file*

Reporting to Regulators

Reporting to the NCA does not relieve the auditor from other statutory duties.   **52**
Examples of statutory reporting responsibilities include:

- *Audits of financial statements of public interest entities and other entities in the financial sector*: the auditor has a statutory duty to report matters of "material significance" to the FCA or PRA (or other appropriate authority outside the entity) which come to the auditor's attention in the course of the audit.

- *Audits of financial statements of entities in the public sector*: the auditor of some public sector entities may be required to report on the entity's compliance with requirements to ensure the regularity and propriety of financial transactions. Activity connected with money laundering may be a breach of those requirements.

- *Audits of financial statements of other types of entity*: the auditor of some other entities are also required to report matters of "material significance" to regulators (e.g., charities and occupational pension schemes).

Knowledge or suspicion, or reasonable grounds for knowledge or suspicion, of   **53**
involvement of the entity's management or those charged with governance in
money laundering, or of a failure of a regulated business to comply with the
Anti-Money Laundering Legislation would normally be regarded as being of
material significance to a regulator, and so give rise to a statutory duty to report
to the regulator, in addition to the requirement to report to the NCA. A "tipping
off" offence is not committed when a report is made to that entity's supervisory
authority and where a disclosure is not likely to prejudice an investigation.

The Auditor's Report on Financial Statements

Where money laundering has been identified or is suspected, the auditor   **54**
evaluates the possible effect, both in quantitative and qualitative terms, on the
financial statements, taking into account whether:

- The crime itself has a material effect on the financial statements;

- The consequences of the crime have a material effect on the financial statements; or

- The outcome of any subsequent investigation by the police or other investigatory body may have a material effect on the financial statements.

If it is known that money laundering has occurred and that management or   **55**
those charged with governance were knowingly involved, the auditor needs to
consider whether the auditor's report should:

- Be modified in accordance with ISA (UK) 705 (Revised June 2016);[40] or

- Incorporate an Emphasis of Matter paragraph in accordance with ISA (UK) 706 (Revised June 2016).[41]

---

[40] *ISA (UK) 705 (Revised June 2016), Modifications to the Opinion in the Independent Auditor's Report.*

[41] *ISA (UK) 706 (Revised June 2016), Emphasis of Matter Paragraphs and Other Matter Paragraphs in the Independent Auditor's Report.*

56   However, the auditor also needs to consider whether including information in the auditor's report about any identified or suspected money laundering activities, for example, through modifying the auditor's opinion or communicating key audit matters,[42] could alert a money launderer.

57   Timing may be the crucial factor. Any delay in issuing the auditor's report pending the outcome of an investigation is likely to be impracticable and could in itself alert a money launderer. The auditor seeks advice from the MLRO who acts as the main source of guidance and if necessary is the liaison point for communication with the firm's own legal counsel, the NCA and the relevant law enforcement agency.

Resignation and Communication With Successor Auditors[43]

58   The auditor may wish to resign from the position as auditor if the auditor believes that the entity or an employee of that entity is engaged in money laundering or any other illegal act, particularly where a normal relationship of trust can no longer be maintained. Where the auditor intends to cease to hold office there may be a conflict between the requirements under Section 519 of the Companies Act 2006 for the auditor to deposit a statement at a company's registered office of any circumstances that the auditor believes should be brought to the attention of members or creditors and the risk of "tipping off". This may arise if, for example, the circumstances connected with the resignation of the auditor include knowledge or suspicion of money laundering and an internal or external disclosure being made.

59   Where such disclosure of circumstances may amount to "tipping off", the auditor seeks to agree the wording of the Section 519 statement with the relevant law enforcement agency and, failing that, seeks legal advice. The auditor seeks advice from the MLRO who acts as the main source of guidance, including from the firm's own legal counsel, the NCA and the relevant law enforcement agency. The auditor may as a last resort need to apply to the court for direction as to what is included in the Section 519 statement.

60   The offence of "tipping off" may also cause a conflict with the need to communicate with the prospective successor auditor in accordance with legal and ethical requirements relating to changes in professional appointment. For example, the existing auditor might feel obliged to mention knowledge or suspicion regarding suspected money laundering and any external disclosure made to the NCA. Under the Anti-Money Laundering Legislation this would not constitute "tipping off" if it was done to prevent the successor auditor from committing a money laundering offence.

61   If information about internal and external reports made by the auditor is considered relevant information for the purposes of Paragraph 9 of Schedule 10 of the Companies Act 2006,[44] the auditor considers whether the disclosure of that information would constitute a "tipping off" offence under the Anti-Money

---

[42] *Paragraph A24 of ISA (UK) 260 (Revised June 2016) describes the circumstances in which the auditor is required, or may otherwise consider it necessary, to include additional information in the auditor's report in accordance with the ISAs (UK).*

[43] *Section 9 of the CCAB Guidance provides more general guidance on cessation of work and resignation.*

[44] *The Statutory Auditors and Third Country Auditors Regulations 2016 (SI 2016/649) came into force on 15 June 2016 and amended the Companies Act 2006 requiring auditors to make available all relevant information held in relation to holding the office as auditor to a successor auditor.*

Laundering Legislation as it may prejudice an investigation. If the auditor considers a "tipping off" offence might be committed, the auditor speaks to the NCA to see if they are content that disclosure in those circumstances would not prejudice any investigation. The auditor may, as a last resort, need to apply to the Court for directions as to what is disclosed to the successor auditor.

Where the only information which needs to be disclosed is the underlying **62** circumstances which gave rise to the disclosure, there are two scenarios to consider:

- Where the auditor only wishes to disclose the suspicions about the underlying criminal conduct and the basis for those suspicions, the auditor will not commit an offence under the Anti-Money Laundering Legislation if that information only is disclosed. For example, if audit files are made available to the successor auditor which detail circumstances which have lead the audit team to suspect management of a fraud, this will not constitute a "tipping off" offence.[45]

- If the auditor wishes to disclose any suspicions specifically about money laundering (e.g., if the working papers in the example above indicated that the suspected fraud also constituted a suspicion of money laundering), then as a matter of prudence, the approach adopted follows that described in paragraphs 58–59 of this Appendix in relation to the Section 519 statement.

---

[45] *Where the auditor knows or suspects that a confiscation, civil recovery, detained cash or money laundering investigation is being or is about to be conducted, the auditor also considers Section 342 of POCA. If the auditor suspects that the disclosure of the working papers would be likely to prejudice that investigation, the auditor takes the approach described in paragraphs 56 and 57 of this Appendix in relation to the Section 519 statement.*

Annexure

Conforming amendments to other ISAs (UK)

In July 2017, the FRC issued ISA (UK) 250 (Revised July 2017), *Section A— Consideration of Laws and Regulations in an Audit of Financial Statements*, which reflects the amendments made by the International Auditing and Standards Board (IAASB) to the corresponding international standard.

This Annexure shows the conforming amendments to other ISAs (UK) as a result of ISA (UK) 250 (Revised July 2017). These amendments are effective for audits of financial statements for periods commencing on or after 15 December 2017, and are shown with marked changes from the latest published versions of the ISAs (UK). The footnote numbers within these amendments do not align with the ISAs (UK) that are amended, and reference should be made to those ISAs (UK).

ISQC (UK) 1 (Revised June 2016), Quality Control for Firms that Perform Audits and Reviews of Financial Statements, and Other Assurance and Related Services Engagements

Application and Other Explanatory Material

Confidentiality, Safe Custody, Integrity, Accessibility and Retrievability of Engagement Documentation (Ref: Para. 46)

A56 Relevant ethical requirements establish an obligation for the firm's personnel to observe at all times the confidentiality of information contained in engagement documentation, unless specific client authority has been given to disclose information, or there are responsibilities under law, regulation or relevant ethical requirements~~is a legal or professional duty~~ to do so.[2] Specific laws or regulations may impose additional obligations on the firm's personnel to maintain client confidentiality, particularly where data of a personal nature are concerned.

ISA (UK) 210 (Revised June 2016), Agreeing the Terms of Audit Engagements

Application and Other Explanatory Material

Agreement on Audit Engagement Terms

A24 When relevant, the following points could also be made in the audit engagement letter:

- Arrangements concerning the involvement of other auditors and experts in some aspects of the audit.

- Arrangements concerning the involvement of internal auditors and other staff of the entity.

---

[1] *ISA 250 (Revised), Consideration of Laws and Regulations in an Audit of Financial Statements published in July 2016.*

[2] *See, for example, Section 140.7 and Section 225.35 of the IESBA Code.*

In the UK, the auditor has regard to paragraph 46D-1 of this ISQC (UK) and any specific requirements of the auditor's relevant professional body.

- Arrangements to be made with the predecessor auditor, if any, in the case of an initial audit.

- A reference to, and description of, the auditor's responsibilities under law, regulation or relevant ethical requirements that address reporting identified or suspected non-compliance with laws and regulations to an appropriate authority outside the entity.

- Any restriction of the auditor's liability when such possibility exists.

- A reference to any further agreements between the auditor and the entity.

- Any obligations to provide audit working papers to other parties.

An example of an audit engagement letter is set out in Appendix 1.

ISA (UK) 220 (Revised June 2016), Quality Control for an Audit of Financial Statements

Application and Other Explanatory Material

Acceptance and Continuance of Client Relationships and Audit Engagements (Ref: Para. 12)

Law, regulation, or relevant ethical requirements[3] may require the auditor to request, prior to accepting the engagement, the predecessor auditor to provide known information regarding any facts or circumstances that, in the predecessor auditor's judgment, the auditor needs to be aware of before deciding whether to accept the engagement. In some circumstances, the predecessor auditor may be required, on request by the proposed successor auditor, to provide information regarding identified or suspected non-compliance with laws and regulations to the proposed successor auditor.[3a] For example, where the predecessor auditor has withdrawn from the engagement as a result of identified or suspected non-compliance with laws and regulations, the IESBA Code requires that the predecessor auditor, on request by a proposed successor auditor, provides all such facts and other information concerning such non-compliance that, in the predecessor auditor's opinion, the proposed successor auditor needs to be aware of before deciding whether to accept the audit appointment.[4]

A8a

ISA (UK) 240 (Revised June 2016), The Auditor's Responsibilities Relating to Fraud in an Audit of Financial Statements

Introduction

Responsibility for the Prevention and Detection of Fraud

Responsibilities of the Auditor

---

[3] *See, for example, Sections 210.14 of the IESBA Code.*
In the UK, the relevant guidance on proposed communications with a predecessor auditor is provided by the pronouncements relating to the work of auditors issued by the auditor's relevant professional body.

[3a] *In the UK, the predecessor auditor is required to provide the successor statutory auditor with access to all relevant information concerning the entity, including information concerning the most recent audit. This would include non-compliance with laws and regulations. See ISQC (UK) 1 (Revised June 2016), Quality Control for Firms that Perform Audits and Reviews of Financial Statements, and other Assurance and Related Services Engagements, paragraph 28D-1.*

[4] *See, for example, Sections 225.31 of the IESBA Code.*
In the UK, the auditor has regard to any specific requirements of the auditor's relevant professional body.

8a The auditor may have additional responsibilities under law, regulation or relevant ethical requirements regarding an entity's non-compliance with laws and regulations, including fraud, which may differ from or go beyond this and other ISAs (UK), such as: (Ref: Para. A5a)

(a) Responding to identified or suspected non-compliance with laws and regulations, including requirements in relation to specific communications with management and those charged with governance, assessing the appropriateness of their response to non-compliance and determining whether further action is needed;

(b) Communicating identified or suspected non-compliance with laws and regulations to other auditors (e.g., in an audit of group financial statements); and

(c) Documentation requirements regarding identified or suspected non-compliance with laws and regulations.

Complying with any additional responsibilities may provide further information that is relevant to the auditor's work in accordance with this and other ISAs (UK) (e.g., regarding the integrity of management or, where appropriate, those charged with governance).

Requirements

Communications to Management and with Those Charged with Governance

40 If the auditor has identified a fraud or has obtained information that indicates that a fraud may exist, the auditor shall communicate these matters, unless prohibited by law or regulation, on a timely basis with~~to~~ the appropriate level of management in order to inform those with primary responsibility for the prevention and detection of fraud of matters relevant to their responsibilities. (Ref: Para. A59a–A60)

41 Unless all of those charged with governance are involved in managing the entity, if the auditor has identified or suspects fraud involving:

(a) management;

(b) employees who have significant roles in internal control; or

(c) others where the fraud results in a material misstatement in the financial statements,

the auditor shall communicate these matters with~~to~~ those charged with governance on a timely basis. If the auditor suspects fraud involving management, the auditor shall communicate these suspicions with~~to~~ those charged with governance and discuss with them the nature, timing and extent of audit procedures necessary to complete the audit. Such communications with those charged with governance are required unless the communication is prohibited by law or regulation. (Ref: Para. A59a, A61–A63)

42 The auditor shall communicate, unless prohibited by law or regulation, with those charged with governance any other matters related to fraud that are, in the auditor's judgment, relevant to their responsibilities. (Ref: Para. A59a, A64)

Reporting Fraud to an Appropriate Authority Outside the Entity ~~Communications to Regulatory and Enforcement Authorities~~

43 If the auditor has identified or suspects a fraud, the auditor shall determine whether law, regulation or relevant ethical requirements: ~~there is a responsibility to report~~

~~the occurrence or suspicion to a party outside the entity. Although the auditor's~~ ~~professional duty to maintain the confidentiality of client information may~~ ~~preclude such reporting, the auditor's legal responsibilities may override the~~ ~~duty of confidentiality in some circumstances.~~ (Ref: Para. A65–A67)

(a)   Require the auditor to report to an appropriate authority outside the entity.

(b)   Establish responsibilities under which reporting to an appropriate authority outside the entity may be appropriate in the circumstances.

Application and Other Explanatory Material

Responsibility for the Prevention and Detection of Fraud

Responsibilities of the Auditor (Ref: Para. 8a)

Law, regulation or relevant ethical requirements may require the auditor to   **A5a.** perform additional procedures and take further actions. For example, the *Code of Ethics for Professional Accountants* issued by the International Ethics Standards Board for Accountants (IESBA Code) requires the auditor to take steps to respond to identified or suspected non-compliance with laws and regulations and determine whether further action is needed. Such steps may include the communication of identified or suspected non-compliance with laws and regulations to other auditors within a group, including a group engagement partner, component auditors or other auditors performing work at components of a group for purposes other than the audit of the group financial statements.[5]

Communications to Management and with Those Charged with Governance (Ref: Para. 40–42)

In some jurisdictions, law or regulation may restrict the auditor's communication   **A59a.** of certain matters with management and those charged with governance. Law or regulation may specifically prohibit a communication, or other action, that might prejudice an investigation by an appropriate authority into an actual, or suspected, illegal act, including alerting the entity, for example, when the auditor is required to report the fraud to an appropriate authority pursuant to anti-money laundering legislation. In these circumstances, the issues considered by the auditor may be complex and the auditor may consider it appropriate to obtain legal advice.

Reporting Fraud to an Appropriate Authority outside the Entity ~~Communications~~ ~~to Regulatory and Enforcement Authorities~~ (Ref: Para. 43)

ISA (UK) 250 (Revised June 2016)[6] provides further guidance with respect to the   **A65** auditor's determination of whether reporting identified or suspected non-compliance with laws or regulations to an appropriate authority outside the entity is required or appropriate in the circumstances, including consideration of the auditor's duty of confidentiality. ~~The auditor's professional duty to maintain~~ ~~the confidentiality of client information may preclude reporting fraud to a party~~ ~~outside the client entity. However, the auditor's legal responsibilities vary by~~ ~~country and, in certain circumstances, the duty of confidentiality may be~~ ~~overridden by statute, the law or courts of law. In some countries, the auditor of a~~

---

[5] *See Sections 225.21–225.22 of the IESBA Code.*
In the UK, the auditor has regard to any specific requirements of the auditor's relevant professional body.

[6] *ISA (UK) 250 (Revised July 2017), Consideration of Laws and Regulations in an Audit of Financial Statements,* *paragraphs A28–A34.*

financial institution has a statutory duty to report the occurrence of fraud to supervisory authorities. Also, in some countries the auditor has a duty to report misstatements to authorities in those cases where management and those charged with governance fail to take corrective action.

A66   The determination required by paragraph 43 may involve complex considerations and professional judgments. Accordingly, tThe auditor may consider consulting internally (e.g., within the firm or a network firm) or on a confidential basis with a regulator or professional body (unless doing so is prohibited by law or regulation or would breach the duty of confidentiality). The auditor may also considerit appropriate to obtaining legal advice to understand the auditor's options and the professional or legal implications of taking any particulardetermine the appropriate course of action in the circumstances, the purpose of which is to ascertain the steps necessary in considering the public interest aspects of identified fraud.

ISA (UK) 260 (Revised June 2016), Communication with Those Charged with Governance

Introduction

The Role of Communication

7   In some jurisdictions, Llaw or regulation may restrict the auditor's communication of certain matters with those charged with governance. For example, lLaws or regulations may specifically prohibit a communication, or other action, that might prejudice an investigation by an appropriate authority into an actual, or suspected, illegal act, including alerting the entity, for example, when the auditor is required to report identified or suspected non-compliance with laws and regulations to an appropriate authority pursuant to anti-money laundering legislation. In somethese circumstances, the issues considered by the auditorpotential conflicts between the auditor's obligations of confidentiality and obligations to communicate may be complex. In such cases, and the auditor may consider it appropriate to obtaining legal advice.

ISA (UK) 450 (Revised June 2016), Evaluation of Misstatements Identified During the Audit

Requirements

Communication and Correction of Misstatements

8   The auditor shall communicate, unless prohibited by law or regulation, on a timely basis all misstatements accumulated during the audit with the appropriate level of management, unless prohibited by law or regulation.[7] The auditor shall request management to correct those misstatements. (Ref: Para. A7–A9)

---

[7] *ISA (UK) 260 (Revised June 2016), Communication with Those Charged with Governance, paragraph 7.*

Application and Other Explanatory Material

Communication and Correction of Misstatements (Ref: Para. 8–9)

In some jurisdictions, l~~L~~aw or regulation may restrict the auditor's communication   **A8**
of certain misstatements to management, or others, within the entity. ~~For example,~~
L~~l~~aws or regulations may specifically prohibit a communication, or other action,
that might prejudice an investigation by an appropriate authority into an actual, or
suspected, illegal act, including alerting the entity, for example, when the auditor
is required to report identified or suspected non-compliance with law or regulation
to an appropriate authority pursuant to anti-money laundering legislation. In
some~~t~~hese circumstances, ~~potential conflicts between the auditor's obligations of~~
~~confidentiality and obligations to communicate may be complex. In such cases,~~
the issues considered by the auditor may be complex and the auditor may consider
seeking~~it~~ appropriate to obtain legal advice.

ISA (UK) 500, Audit Evidence

Requirements

Information to Be Used as Audit Evidence

When designing and performing audit procedures, the auditor shall consider the   **7**
relevance and reliability of the information to be used as audit evidence.
(Ref: Para. A26–A33a)

Application and Other Explanatory Material

Information to Be Used as Audit Evidence
Relevance and Reliability
(Ref: Para. 7)

As noted in paragraph A1, while audit evidence is primarily obtained from audit   **A26**
procedures performed during the course of the audit, it may also include
information obtained from other sources such as, for example, previous audits,
in certain circumstances, ~~and a~~ firm's quality control procedures for client
acceptance and continuance and complying with certain additional
responsibilities under law, regulation or relevant ethical requirements
(e.g., regarding an entity's non-compliance with laws and regulations). The
quality of all audit evidence is affected by the relevance and reliability of the
information upon which it is based.

ISA (UK) 250 (Revised July 2017)[8] provides further guidance with respect to the   **A33a**
auditor complying with any additional responsibilities under law, regulation or
relevant ethical requirements regarding an entity's identified or suspected non-
compliance with laws and regulations that may provide further information that is
relevant to the auditor's work in accordance with ISAs (UK) and evaluating the
implications of such non-compliance in relation to other aspects of the audit.

---

[8] *ISA (UK) 250 (Revised July 2017), Consideration of Laws and Regulations in an Audit of Financial Statements,*
paragraph 9.

ISA (UK) 250 (Revised June 2016) Section B – The Auditor's Statutory Right and Duty to Report to Regulators of Public Interest Entities and Regulators of Other Entities in the Financial Sector

(Effective for audits of financial statements for periods commencing on or after 17 June 2016)

Contents

	Paragraphs
Introduction	1 - 7
Scope of this section	1
The auditor's responsibilities	2 - 6
Effective date	7
Objective	8
Definitions	9
Requirements	10 - 17
Conduct of the audit	10 - 12
Reporting	13 - 17
Application and other explanatory material	A1 - A47
The auditor's responsibilities	A1 - A8
Conduct of the audit	A9 - A30
Reporting	A31 - A47

Appendix 1: The regulatory framework

Appendix 2: The application of the statutory duty to report to regulators

Appendix 3: Action by the auditor on discovery of a breach of a regulator's requirements

International Standard on Auditing (UK) (ISA (UK)) 250 (Revised June 2016), *Consideration of Laws and Regulations in an Audit of Financial Statements*, should be read in conjunction with ISA (UK) 200 (Revised June 2016), *Overall Objectives of the Independent Auditor and the Conduct of an Audit in Accordance with International Standards on Auditing (UK)*.

Introduction

Scope of this Section

1   This Section of ISA (UK) 250 deals with the circumstances in which the auditor of an entity subject to statutory regulation (a "regulated entity") is required to report direct to a regulator information which comes to the auditor's attention in the course of the work undertaken in the auditor's capacity as auditor of the regulated entity. This may include work undertaken to express an opinion on the entity's financial statements, other financial information or on other matters specified by legislation or by a regulator.

The Auditor's Responsibilities
(Ref: Para. A1–A8)

2   The auditor of a regulated entity generally has special reporting responsibilities in addition to the responsibility to report on financial statements. These special reporting responsibilities take two forms:

(a)   *A responsibility to provide a report on matters specified in legislation or by a regulator.* This form of report is often made on an annual or other routine basis and does not derive from another set of reporting responsibilities. The auditor is required to carry out appropriate procedures sufficient to form an opinion on the matters concerned. These procedures may be in addition to those carried out to form an opinion on the financial statements; and

(b)   *A statutory duty to report certain information, relevant to the regulators' functions, that come to the auditor's attention in the course of the audit work.* The auditor has no responsibility to carry out procedures to search out the information relevant to the regulator. This form of report is derivative in nature, arising only in the context of another set of reporting responsibilities, and is initiated by the auditor on discovery of a reportable matter.

3   This Section of this ISA (UK) deals with both forms of direct reports. Guidance on the auditor's responsibility to provide special reports on a routine basis on other matters specified in legislation or by a regulator is given in the Practice Notes dealing with regulated business, for example banks, building societies, investment businesses and insurers.

4   The statutory duty to report to a regulator applies to information which comes to the attention of the auditor in the auditor's capacity as auditor. In determining whether information is obtained in that capacity, two criteria in particular need to be considered: first, whether the person who obtained the information also undertook the audit work; and if so, whether it was obtained in the course of or as a result of undertaking the audit work. Appendix 2 to this Section of this ISA (UK) sets out guidance on the application of these criteria.

5   The auditor may have a statutory right to bring information to the attention of the regulator in particular circumstances which lie outside those giving rise to a statutory duty to initiate a direct report. Where this is so, the auditor may use that right to make a direct report relevant to the regulator on a specific matter which comes to the auditor's attention when the auditor concludes that doing so

is necessary to protect the interests of those for whose benefit the regulator is required to act.

The requirements and explanatory material in this section of this ISA (UK) **6** complement but do not replace the legal and regulatory requirements applicable to each regulated entity. Where the application of those legal and regulatory requirements, taking into account any published interpretations, is insufficiently clear for the auditor to determine whether a particular circumstance results in a legal duty to make a report to a regulator, or a right to make such a report, it may be appropriate to take legal advice.

Effective Date

This Section of ISA (UK) 250 (Revised June 2016) is effective for audits of **7** financial statements for periods commencing on or after 17 June 2016. Earlier adoption is permitted.

Objective

The objective of the auditor of a regulated entity is to bring information of **8** which the auditor has become aware in the ordinary course of performing work undertaken to fulfil the auditor's audit responsibilities to the attention of the appropriate regulator as soon as practicable when:

(a)   The auditor concludes that it is relevant to the regulator's functions having regard to such matters as may be specified in statute or any related regulations; and

(b)   In the auditor's opinion there is reasonable cause to believe it is or may be of material significance to the regulator.

Definitions

For purposes of this Section of this ISA (UK), the following terms have the **9** meanings attributed below:

(a)   **The Act(s)** – Means those Acts that give rise to a duty to report to a regulator. For example, in the UK, this includes the Audit Regulation,[1] the Financial Services and Markets Act 2000, the Financial Services Act 2012 and regulations made under those Acts, and any future legislation including provisions relating to the duties of auditors similar to those contained in that statute.

(b)   **Audit** – For the purpose of this Section of this ISA (UK), the term "audit" refers both to an engagement to report on the financial statements of a regulated entity and to an engagement to provide a report on other matters specified by statute or by a regulator undertaken in the capacity of auditor.

(c)   **Auditor** – The term "auditor" should be interpreted in accordance with the requirements of the Acts. Guidance on its interpretation is contained in Practice Notes relating to each area of the financial sector to which the duty applies.

---

[1] *Regulation (EU) No 537/2014 of the European Parliament and of the Council of 16 April 2014.*

(d) **Material significance** – The term "material significance" requires interpretation in the context of the specific legislation applicable to the regulated entity. A matter or group of matters is normally of material significance to a regulator's functions when, due either to its nature or its potential financial impact, it is likely of itself to require investigation by the regulator. Further guidance on the interpretation of the term in the context of specific legislation is contained in Practice Notes dealing with the rights and duties of auditors of regulated entities to report direct to regulators.

(e) **Regulated entity** – An individual, company or other type of entity which is:

(i) Authorized to carry on business in the financial sector which is subject to statutory regulation; or

(ii) A public interest entity.[2]

(f) **Regulator** – Such persons as are empowered by the Act(s) to regulate the entity. The term includes the Financial Conduct Authority, the Prudential Regulation Authority, and such other bodies as may be so empowered in future legislation.

(g) **"Tipping off"** – Involves a disclosure that is likely to prejudice any investigation into suspected money laundering which might arise from a report being made to a regulatory authority.[3] Money laundering involves an act which conceals, disguises, converts, transfers, removes, uses, acquires or possesses property which constitutes or represents a benefit from criminal conduct.

Requirements

Conduct of the Audit

Planning

10   When obtaining an understanding of the business for the purpose of the audit, the auditor of a regulated entity shall obtain an understanding of its current activities, the scope of its authorization and the effectiveness of its control environment. (Ref: Para. A9–A16)

Supervision and Control

11   The auditor shall ensure that all staff involved in the audit of a regulated entity have an understanding of:

(a) The provisions of applicable legislation;

(b) The regulator's rules and any guidance issued by the regulator; and

(c) Any specific requirements which apply to the particular regulated entity,

---

[2] *ISA (UK) 220 (Revised June 2016), Quality Control for an Audit of Financial Statements, paragraph 7(m)-1 defines public interest entity.*

[3] *More detail is provided in the definition contained in Section A of ISA (UK) 250 (Revised June 2016).*

appropriate to their role in the audit and sufficient (in the context of that role) to enable them to identify situations which may give reasonable cause to believe that a matter should be reported to the regulator. (Ref: Para. A17–A23)

Identifying Matters Requiring a Report Direct to Regulators

Where an apparent breach of statutory or regulatory requirements comes to the auditor's attention, the auditor shall:

12

(a)   Obtain such evidence as is available to assess its implications for the auditor's reporting responsibilities;

(b)   Determine whether, in the auditor's opinion, there is reasonable cause to believe that the breach is of material significance to the regulator; and

(c)   Consider whether the apparent breach is criminal conduct that gives rise to criminal property and, as such, should be reported to the specified authorities. (Ref: Para. A24–A30)

Reporting
(Ref: Para. A31–A46)

The Auditor's Statutory Duty to Report Direct to Regulators

When the auditor concludes, after appropriate discussion and investigations, that a matter which has come to the auditor's attention gives rise to a statutory duty to make a report the auditor shall[4] bring the matter to the attention of the regulator as soon as practicable in a form and manner which will facilitate appropriate action by the regulator. When the initial report is made orally, the auditor shall make a contemporaneous written record of the oral report and shall confirm the matter in writing to the regulator. (Ref: Para. A31–A35)

13

For audits of financial statements of public interest entities, the auditor shall:

13R-1

(a)   Report promptly to the regulator any information concerning that public interest entity of which the auditor has become aware while carrying out the audit and which may bring about any of the following:

(i)   A material breach of the laws, regulations or administrative provisions which lay down, where appropriate, the conditions governing authorization or which specifically govern pursuit of the activities of such public interest entity; or

(ii)   A material threat or doubt concerning the continuous functioning of the public interest entity; or

(iii)   A refusal to issue an audit opinion on the financial statements or the issuing of an adverse or qualified opinion.

Report any information referred to in paragraph 13R-1(a)(i)–(iii) of which the auditor becomes aware in the course of carrying out the audit of an undertaking having close links[5] with the public interest entity for which they are also carrying out the audit.

---

[4] *In the UK, subject to compliance with legislation relating to "tipping off".*

[5] *"Close links" is defined in point (38) of Article 4(1) of Regulation (EU) No 575/2013 of the European Parliament and of the Council of 26 June 2013.*

14 When the matter giving rise to a statutory duty to make a report direct to a regulator casts doubt on the integrity of those charged with governance or their competence to conduct the business of the regulated entity, the auditor shall[4] make the report to the regulator as soon as practicable and without informing those charged with governance in advance. (Ref: Para. A35)

The Auditor's Right to Report Direct to Regulators

15 When a matter comes to the auditor's attention which the auditor concludes does not give rise to a statutory duty to report but nevertheless may be relevant to the regulator's exercise of its functions, the auditor shall[2]:

(a)   Consider whether the matter should be brought to the attention of the regulator under the terms of the appropriate legal provisions enabling the auditor to report direct to the regulator; and, if so

(b)   Advise those charged with governance that in the auditor's opinion the matter should be drawn to the regulators' attention.

Where the auditor is unable to obtain, within a reasonable period, adequate evidence that those charged with governance have properly informed the regulator of the matter, the auditor shall[4] make a report direct to the regulator as soon as practicable. (Ref: Para. A36–A37)

Contents of a Report Initiated by the Auditor

16 When making or confirming in writing a report direct to a regulator, the auditor shall:

(a)   State the name of the regulated entity concerned;

(b)   State the statutory power under which the report is made;

(c)   State that the report has been prepared in accordance with ISA (UK) 250, *Section B—The Auditor's Statutory Right and Duty to Report to Regulators of Public Interest Entities and Regulators of Other Entities in the Financial Sector*;

(d)   Describe the context in which the report is given;

(e)   Describe the matter giving rise to the report;

(f)   Request the regulator to confirm that the report has been received; and

(g)   State the name of the auditor, the date of the written report and, where appropriate, the date on which an oral report was made to the regulator and the name and title of the individual to whom the oral report was made. (Ref: Para. A38–A39)

Relationship With Other Reporting Responsibilities

17 When issuing a report expressing an opinion on a regulated entity's financial statements or on other matters specified by legislation or a regulator, the auditor:

(a)   Shall consider whether there are consequential reporting issues affecting the auditor's opinion which arise from any report previously made direct to the regulator in the course of the auditor's appointment; and

(b)   Shall assess whether any matters encountered in the course of the audit indicate a need for a further direct report. (Ref: Para. A40–A43)

***

Application and Other Explanatory Material

The Auditor's Responsibilities
(Ref: Para. 2–6)

Before accepting appointment, the auditor follows the procedures identified in **A1**
the FRC's Ethical Standard and the ethical pronouncements and Audit
Regulations issued by the auditor's relevant professional body.

In the case of regulated entities, the auditor would in particular obtain an **A2**
understanding of the appropriate statutory and regulatory requirements and a
preliminary knowledge of the management and operations of the entity, so as to
enable the auditor to determine whether a level of knowledge of the business
adequate to perform the audit can be obtained. The procedures carried out by the
auditor in seeking to obtain this preliminary understanding may include discussion
with the previous auditor and, in some circumstances, with the regulator.

On ceasing to hold office, the auditor may be required by statute or by **A3**
regulation to make specific reports concerning the circumstances relating to
that event, and would also follow the procedures identified in the ethical
guidance issued by the relevant professional body.

In addition, the auditor of a regulated entity would assess whether it is appropriate **A4**
to bring any matters of which the auditor is then aware to the notice of the
regulator. Under legislation in the UK, this may be done either before or after
ceasing to hold office, as the auditor's statutory right to disclose to a regulator
information obtained in the course of the auditor's appointment is not affected by
the auditor's removal, resignation or otherwise ceasing to hold office.

The duty to make a report direct to a regulator does not impose upon the auditor **A5**
a duty to carry out specific work: it arises solely in the context of work carried
out to fulfil other reporting responsibilities. Accordingly, no auditing
procedures in addition to those carried out in the normal course of auditing
the financial statements, or for the purpose of making any other specified
report, are necessary for the fulfilment of the auditor's responsibilities.

It will, however, be necessary for the auditor to take additional time in carrying out **A6**
a financial statement audit or other engagement to assess whether matters which
come to the auditor's attention should be included in a direct report and, where
appropriate, to prepare and submit the report. These additional planning and
follow-up procedures do not constitute an extension of the scope of the financial
statement audit or of other work undertaken to provide a specified report relating
to a regulated entity. They are necessary solely in order to understand and clarify
the reporting responsibility and, where appropriate, to make a report.

The circumstances in which the auditor is required by statute to make a report **A7**
direct to a regulator include matters which are not considered as part of the
audit of financial statements or of work undertaken to discharge other routine
responsibilities. For example, the duty to report would apply to information of
which the auditor became aware in the course of the auditor's work which is
relevant to the Financial Conduct Authority's criteria for approved persons,

although the auditor is not otherwise required to express an opinion on such matters. However, legislation imposing a duty to make reports direct to regulators does not require the auditor to change the scope of the audit work, nor does it place on the auditor an obligation to conduct the audit work in such a way that there is reasonable certainty that the auditor will discover all matters which regulators might consider as being of material significance. Therefore, whilst the auditor of a regulated entity is required to be alert to matters which may require a report, the auditor is not expected to be aware of all circumstances which, had the auditor known of them, would have led the auditor to make such a report. It is only when the auditor becomes aware of such a matter during the conduct of the normal audit work that the auditor has an obligation to determine whether a report to the regulator is required by statute or appropriate for other reasons.

A8   Similarly, the auditor is not responsible for reporting on a regulated entity's overall compliance with rules with which it is required to comply nor is the auditor required to conduct the audit work in such a way that there is reasonable certainty that the auditor will discover breaches. Nevertheless, breaches of rules with which a regulated entity is required to comply may have implications for the financial statements and, accordingly, the auditor of a regulated entity needs to consider whether any actual or contingent liabilities may have arisen from breaches of regulatory requirements. Breaches of a regulator's requirements may also have consequences for other matters on which the auditor of a regulated entity is required to express an opinion and, if such breaches represent criminal conduct, could give rise to the need to report to specified authorities.

Conduct of the Audit

Planning
(Ref: Para. 10)

A9   ISAs (UK) require the auditor to obtain an understanding of the entity and its environment.[6]

A10   In the context of a regulated entity, the auditor's understanding of its environment needs to extend to the applicable statutory provisions, the rules of the regulator concerned and any guidance issued by the regulator on the interpretation of those rules, together with other guidance issued by relevant authorities, including the FRC.

A11   The auditor is also required to identify and assess the risks of material misstatements to provide a basis for designing and performing further audit procedures.[7] In making such an assessment the auditor takes into account the control environment, including the entity's higher level procedures for complying with the requirements of its regulator. Such a review gives an indication of the extent to which the general atmosphere and controls in the regulated entity are conducive to compliance, for example through consideration of *inter alia:*

- The adequacy of procedures and training to inform staff of the requirements of relevant legislation and the rules or other regulations of the regulator.

- The adequacy of procedures for authorization of transactions.

---

[6] *ISA (UK) 315 (Revised June 2016), Identifying and Assessing the Risks of Material Misstatement through Understanding the Entity and Its Environment, paragraph 11.*

[7] *ISA (UK) 315 (Revised June 2016), paragraph 25.*

- Procedures for internal review of the entity's compliance with regulatory or other requirements.

- The authority of, and any resources available to, the compliance officer/ Money Laundering Reporting Officer (MLRO).

- Procedures to ensure that possible breaches of requirements are investigated by an appropriate person and are brought to the attention of senior management.

In some areas of the financial sector, conducting business outside the scope of the entity's authorization is a serious regulatory breach, and therefore of material significance to the regulator. In addition, it may result in fines, suspension or loss of authorization.   **A12**

Where the auditor's review of the reporting entity's activities indicates that published guidance by the regulator may not be sufficiently precise to enable the auditor to identify circumstances in which it is necessary to initiate a report, the auditor would consider whether it is necessary to discuss the matters specified in legislation with the appropriate regulator with a view to reaching agreement on its interpretation.   **A13**

Similarly, where a group includes two or more companies separately regulated by different regulators, there may be a need to clarify the regulators' requirements in any overlapping areas of activity. However, the statutory duty to make a report as presently defined arises only in respect of the legal entity subject to regulation. Therefore the auditor of an unregulated company in a group that includes one or more other companies which are authorized by regulators would not have a duty to report matters to the regulators of those companies.   **A14**

When a regulated entity is subject to provisions of two or more regulators, the auditor needs to take account of the separate reporting requirements in planning and conducting the audit work. Arrangements may exist for one regulatory body to rely on financial monitoring being carried out by another body (the "lead regulator") and where this is the case, routine reports by the regulated entity's auditor may be made to the lead regulator alone.   **A15**

However, the auditor's statutory duty to report cannot be discharged by reliance on the lead regulator informing others. Therefore, where the auditor concludes that a matter is of material significance to one regulator, the auditor needs to assess the need for separate reports informing each regulator of matters which the auditor concludes are or may be of material significance to it.   **A16**

Supervision and Control
(Ref: Para. 11)

ISAs (UK) require the engagement partner to take responsibility for the direction, supervision and performance of the audit engagement in compliance with professional standards and applicable legal and regulatory requirements.[8] Consequently, in planning and conducting the audit of a regulated entity the auditor needs to ensure that staff are alert to the possibility that a report to its regulator may be required.   **A17**

---

[8] *ISA (UK) 220 (Revised June 2016), Quality Control for an Audit of Financial Statements, paragraph 15.*

A18   Auditing firms also need to establish adequate procedures to ensure that any matters which are discovered in the course of or as a result of audit work and may give rise to a duty to report are brought to the attention of the engagement partner responsible for the audit on a timely basis.

A19   The right and duty to report to a regulator applies to information of which the auditor becomes aware in the auditor's capacity as such. They do not extend automatically to any information obtained by a firm regardless of its source. Consequently partners and staff undertaking work in another capacity are not required to have detailed knowledge of the regulator's requirements (unless necessary for that other work) nor to bring information to the attention of the engagement partner responsible for the audit on a routine basis.

A20   However, as discussed further in Appendix 2, firms need to establish lines of communications, commensurate with their size and complexity, sufficient to ensure that non-audit work undertaken for a regulated entity which is likely to have an effect on the audit is brought to the attention of the engagement partner responsible for the audit, who will need to determine whether the results of non-audit work undertaken for a regulated entity ought to be assessed as part of the audit process.

Use of the Work of Other Auditors

A21   An auditor with responsibilities for reporting on financial statements including financial information of one or more components audited by other auditors is required to obtain sufficient appropriate audit evidence that the work of the other auditors is adequate for the purposes of the audit. The same principle applies to using the work of another auditor in a different type of engagement. The auditor of a regulated entity who uses the work undertaken by other auditors needs to establish reporting arrangements such that the other auditors bring to the attention of the auditor of the regulated entity matters arising from their work which may give rise to a duty to report to a regulator.

A22   The nature of the reporting arrangements will depend on the nature of the work undertaken by the other auditors. For example, the statutory duty to make a report relates to the legal entity subject to regulation rather than to the entire group to which that entity may belong. Consequently, the auditor of a holding company authorized by one regulator would not be expected to have knowledge of all matters which come to the attention of a component auditor. The auditor of the regulated entity would, however, have a duty to report, where appropriate, matters which arise from the audit of the regulated entity's own financial statements and of the consolidated group figures.

A23   Where the audit of a regulated entity is undertaken by joint auditors, knowledge obtained by one firm is likely to be deemed to be known by the other. Care will therefore be needed in agreeing and implementing arrangements to exchange information relating to matters which may give rise to a duty to report to a regulator.

Identifying Matters Requiring a Report Direct to Regulators
(Ref: Para. 12)

The precise matters which give rise to a statutory duty on auditors to make a report to a regulator derive from the relevant Acts. Broadly, such matters fall into three general categories:

(a)   The financial position of the regulated entity;

(b)   Its compliance with requirements for the management of its business; and

(c)   The status of those charged with governance as fit and proper persons.

Further detailed guidance on the interpretation of these matters in the context of specific legislation applicable to each type of regulated entity is contained in Practice Notes dealing with the rights and duties of auditors of regulated entities to report direct to regulators.

In assessing the effect of an apparent breach, the auditor takes into account the quantity and type of evidence concerning such a matter which may reasonably be expected to be available. If the auditor concludes that the auditor has been prevented from obtaining all such evidence concerning a matter which may give rise to a duty to report, the auditor would normally make a report direct to the regulator as soon as practicable.

An apparent breach of statutory or regulatory requirements may not of itself give rise to a statutory duty to make a report to a regulator. There will normally be a need for some further investigation and discussion of the circumstances surrounding the apparent breach with the directors in order to obtain sufficient information to determine whether it points to a matter which is or may be of material significance to the regulator. For example, a minor breach which has been corrected by the regulated entity and reported (if appropriate) to the regulator, and which from the evidence available to the auditor appears to be an isolated occurrence, would not normally give the auditor reasonable cause to believe that it is or may be of material significance to the regulator. However, a minor breach that results in a criminal offence that gave rise to the criminal property would be reportable to the specified authorities under the anti-money laundering legislation.

When determining whether a breach of statutory or regulatory requirements gives rise to a statutory duty to make a report direct to a regulator, the auditor considers factors such as:

- Whether the breach, though minor, is indicative of a general lack of compliance with the regulator's requirements or otherwise casts doubt on the status of those charged with governance as fit and proper persons.

- Whether a breach which occurred before the auditor's visit to the regulated entity was reported by the entity itself and has since been corrected, such that, at the date of the auditor's discovery, no breach exists.

- Whether the circumstances giving rise to a breach which occurred before the auditors visit to the regulated entity continue to exist, or those charged with governance have not taken corrective action, or the breach has re-occurred.

A24

A25

A26

A27

- Whether the circumstances suggest that an immediate report to the regulator is necessary in order to protect the interests of depositors, investors, policyholders, clients of the entity or others in whose interests the regulator is required to act.

A28   The auditor would normally seek evidence to assess the implications of a suspected breach before reporting a matter to the regulator. However, the auditor's responsibility to make a report does not require the auditor to determine the full implications of a matter before reporting: the auditor is required to exercise professional judgment as to whether or not there is reasonable cause to believe that a matter is or may be of material significance to the regulator. In forming that judgment, the auditor undertakes appropriate investigations to determine the circumstances but does not require the degree of evidence which would be a normal part of forming an opinion on financial statements. Such investigations would normally include:

- Enquiry of appropriate level of staff;

- Review of correspondence and documents relating to the transaction or event concerned; and

- Discussion with those charged with governance, or other senior management where appropriate.

In the case of a life company, it would also be appropriate to consult with the appointed actuary, who also has various statutory duties under insurance companies legislation.

A29   The potential gravity of some apparent breaches may be such that an immediate report to the regulator is essential in order to enable the regulator to take appropriate action: in particular, prompt reporting of a loss of client assets may be necessary to avoid further loss to investors or others in whose interests the regulator is required to act. The auditor is therefore required to balance the need for further investigation of the matter with the need for prompt reporting.

A30   On completion of the auditor's investigations, the auditor needs to ensure that the facts and the basis for the auditor's decision (whether to report or not) is adequately documented such that the reasons for that decision may be clearly demonstrated should the need to do so arise in future.

Reporting

The Auditor's Statutory Duty to Report Direct to Regulators
(Ref: Para. 13–14)

A31   Except in the circumstances referred to in paragraph 14 the auditor seeks to reach agreement with those charged with governance on the circumstances giving rise to a report direct to the regulator. However, where a statutory duty to report arises, the auditor is required to make such a report regardless of:

(a)   Whether the matter has been referred to the regulator by other parties (including the company, whether by those charged with governance or otherwise); and

(b)   Any duty owed to other parties, including those charged with governance of the regulated entity and its shareholders (or equivalent persons).

Except in the circumstances set out in paragraph 14, the auditor sends a copy of the auditor's written report to those charged with governance and (where appropriate) audit committee of the regulated entity.   **A32**

In normal circumstances, the auditor would wish to communicate with the regulator with the knowledge and agreement of those charged with governance of the regulated entity. However, in some circumstances immediate notification of the discovery of a matter giving reasonable grounds to believe that a reportable matter exists will be necessary – for example, a phone call to alert the regulator followed by a meeting to discuss the circumstances.   **A33**

Speed of reporting is essential where the circumstances cause the auditor no longer to have confidence in the integrity of those charged with governance. In such circumstances, there may be a serious and immediate threat to the interests of depositors or other persons for whose protection the regulator is required to act; for example where the auditor believes that a fraud or other irregularity may have been committed by, or with the knowledge of, those charged with governance, or have evidence of the intention of those charged with governance to commit or condone a suspected fraud or other irregularity.   **A34**

In circumstances where the auditor no longer has confidence in the integrity of those charged with governance, it is not appropriate to provide those charged with governance with copies of the auditor's report. Since such circumstances will be exceptional and extreme, the auditor may wish to seek legal advice as to the auditor's responsibilities and the appropriate course of action.   **A35**

The Auditor's Right to Report Direct to Regulators
(Ref: Para. 15)

The auditor may become aware of matters which the auditor concludes are relevant to the exercise of the regulator's functions even though they fall outside the statutory definition of matters which must be reported to a regulator. In such circumstances, the Acts in the UK provide the auditor with protection for making disclosure of the matter to the appropriate regulator.   **A36**

Where the auditor considers that a matter which does not give rise to a statutory duty to report is nevertheless, in the auditor's professional judgment, such that it should be brought to the attention of the regulator, it is normally appropriate for the auditor to request those charged with governance of the regulated entity in writing to draw it to the attention of the regulator.   **A37**

Contents of a Report Initiated by the Auditor
(Ref: Para. 16)

Such a report is a by-product of other work undertaken by the auditor. As a result it is not possible for the auditor or the regulator to conclude that all matters relevant to the regulator were encountered in the course of the auditor's work. The auditor's report therefore sets out the context in which the information reported was identified and indicates the extent to which the matter has been investigated and discussed with those charged with governance.   **A38**

A39   Matters to which the auditor may wish to refer when describing the context in which a report is made direct to a regulator include:

- The nature of the appointment from which the report derives. For example, it may be appropriate to distinguish between a report made in the course of an audit of financial statements and one which arises in the course of a more limited engagement, such as an appointment to report on specified matters by the Financial Conduct Authority;

- The applicable legislative requirements and interpretations of those requirements which have informed the auditor's judgment;

- The extent to which the auditor has investigated the circumstances giving rise to the matter reported;

- Whether the matter reported has been discussed with those charged with governance;

- Whether steps to rectify the matter have been taken.

Relationship With Other Reporting Responsibilities
(Ref: Para. 17)

A40   The circumstances which give rise to a report direct to a regulator may involve an uncertainty or other matter which requires disclosure in the financial statements. The auditor will therefore need to consider whether the disclosures made in the financial statements are adequate for the purposes of giving a true and fair view of the regulated entity's state of affairs and profit or loss. Where the auditor considers it necessary to draw users' attention to a matter presented or disclosed in the financial statements that, in the auditor's judgment, is of such importance that it is fundamental to users' understanding of the financial statements, the auditor is required to include an Emphasis of Matter paragraph in the auditor's report.[9]

A41   Similarly, circumstances giving rise to a report direct to a regulator may also require reflection in the auditor's reports on other matters required by legislation or another regulator.

A42   In fulfilling the responsibility to report direct to a regulator, it is important that the auditor not only assess the significance of individual transactions or events but also consider whether a combination of such items over the course of the work undertaken for the auditor's primary reporting responsibilities may give the auditor reasonable grounds to believe that they constitute a matter of material significance to the regulator, and so give rise to a statutory duty to make a report.

A43   As there is no requirement for the auditor to extend the scope of the audit work to search for matters which may give rise to a statutory duty to report, such an assessment of the cumulative effect of evidence obtained in the course of an audit would be made when reviewing the evidence in support of the opinions to be expressed in the reports the auditor has been appointed to make. Where such a review leads to the conclusion that the cumulative effect of matters noted in the course of the audit is of material significance to the regulator, it will be appropriate for a report to be made as set out in paragraph 16. However, reports indicating a "nil return" are not appropriate.

---

[9] *ISA (UK) 706 (Revised June 2016), Emphasis of Matter Paragraphs and Other Matter Paragraphs in the Independent Auditor's Report, paragraph 6.*

Communication of Information by the Regulator

The Acts provide that, in certain exceptional circumstances, regulators may pass confidential information to another party. The precise circumstances in which regulators may disclose information varies, but in general they may do so if considered necessary to fulfil their own obligations under the appropriate Act, or, in some cases, to enable the auditor to fulfil the auditor's duties either to the regulated entity or, in other cases, to the regulator. Confidential information remains confidential in the hands of the recipient.   **A44**

In so far as the law permits, regulators have confirmed that they will consider taking the initiative in bringing a matter to the attention of the auditor of a regulated entity in circumstances where: **A45**

(a)   They believe the matter is of such importance that the auditor's knowledge of it could significantly affect the form of the auditor's report on the entity's financial statements or other matters on which the auditor is required to report, or the way in which the auditor discharges the auditor's reporting responsibilities; and

(b)   The disclosure is for the purpose of enabling or assisting the regulator to discharge its functions under the Acts.

The auditor needs to be aware that there may be circumstances in which the regulators are unable to disclose such information. Where the auditor of a regulated entity is not informed by the regulator of any matter, therefore, the auditor cannot assume that there are no matters known to the regulator which could affect the auditor's judgment as to whether information is of material significance. However, in the absence of disclosure by the regulator, the auditor can only form a judgment in the light of evidence to which the auditor has access.   **A46**

For audits of public interest entities, the Audit Regulation[10] requires an effective dialogue to be established between the supervising credit institutions and insurance undertakings, on the one hand, and the auditor carrying out the audit of those institutions and undertakings, on the other hand. The responsibility for compliance with this requirement of the Audit Regulation rests with both parties to the dialogue.   **A47**

---

[10] *Regulation (EU) No 537/2014 of the European Parliament and of the Council of 16 April 2014.*

Appendix 1

The Regulatory Framework in the Financial Sector

1   In the UK, legislation exists in the principal areas of financial services to protect the interests of investors, depositors in banks and other users of financial services. Regulated entities operating in the financial sector are required to comply with legal and regulatory requirements concerning the way their business is conducted. Compliance with those rules is monitored in four principal ways:

- Internal monitoring by those charged with governance of the regulated entity;

- Submission of regular returns by the regulated entity to the regulator;

- Monitoring and, in some cases, inspection of the entity by the regulator;

- Reports[4] by the reporting entity's auditor on its financial statements and other specified matters required by legislation or by the regulator.

Responsibility for Ensuring Compliance

2   Ensuring compliance with the requirements with which a regulated entity is required to comply in carrying out its business is the responsibility of those charged with governance of a regulated entity. It requires adequate organization and systems of controls. The regulatory framework provides that adequate procedures for compliance must be established and maintained. Those charged with governance of a regulated entity are also normally required to undertake regular reviews of compliance and to inform the regulator of any breach of the rules and regulations applicable to its regulated business. In addition, regulators may undertake compliance visits.

3   The auditor of a regulated entity normally has responsibilities for reporting[4] on particular aspects of its compliance with the regulator's requirements. However, the auditor has no direct responsibility for expressing an opinion on an entity's overall compliance with the requirements for the conduct of its business, nor does an audit provide any assurance that breaches of requirements which are not the subject of regular auditors' reports will be detected.

The Role of Auditors

4   Those charged with governance of regulated entities have primary responsibility for ensuring that all appropriate information is made available to regulators. Normal reporting procedures (including auditor's reports on records, systems and returns, and regular meetings with those charged with governance and/or management and auditors) supplemented by any inspection visits considered necessary by the regulators should provide the regulators with all the information they need to carry out their responsibilities under the relevant Act.

Routine Reporting by Auditors

5   Regulators' requirements for reports by auditors vary. In general terms, however, such reports may include opinions on:

- The regulated entity's annual financial statements;
- The regulated entity's compliance with requirements for financial resources; and
- The adequacy of the regulated entity's system of controls over its transactions and in particular over its clients' money and other property.

As a result of performing the work necessary to discharge their routine reporting responsibilities, or those arising from an appointment to provide a special report required by the regulator, the auditor of a regulated entity may become aware of matters which the auditor considers need to be brought to the regulator's attention sooner than would be achieved by routine reports by the entity or its auditor.   **6**

The auditor of a regulated entity normally has a right to communicate in good faith[4] information the auditor considers is relevant to the regulators' functions.   **7**

The Auditor's Statutory Duty to Report to the Regulator

In addition, the auditor is required by law to report[4] direct to a regulator when the auditor concludes that there is reasonable cause to believe that a matter is or may be of material significance to the regulator. The precise matters which result in a statutory duty to make such a report vary, depending upon the specific requirements of relevant legislation and the regulator's rules. In general, however, a duty to report to a regulator arises when the auditor becomes aware that: **8**

- The regulated entity is in serious breach of:
  - Requirements to maintain adequate financial resources; or
  - Requirements for those charged with governance to conduct its business in a sound and prudent manner (including the maintenance of systems of control over transactions and over any clients' assets held by the business); or
- There are circumstances which give reason to doubt the status of those charged with governance or senior management as fit and proper persons.

Confidentiality

Confidentiality is an implied term of the auditor's contracts with client entities. However, in the circumstances leading to a right or duty to report,[4] the auditor is entitled to communicate to regulators in good faith information or opinions relating to the business or affairs of the entity or any associated body without contravening the duty of confidence owed to the entity and, in the case of a bank, building society and friendly society, its associated bodies.   **9**

The statutory provisions permitting the auditor to communicate information to regulators relate to information obtained in the auditor's capacity as auditor of the regulated entity concerned. Auditors and regulators therefore should be aware that confidential information obtained in other capacities may not normally be disclosed to another party.   **10**

Appendix 2

(Ref: Para. 4)

The Application of the Statutory Duty to Report to Regulators

Introduction

1   The statutory duty to report to a regulator[4] applies to information which comes to the attention of the auditor in the auditor's capacity as auditor. However, neither the term "auditor" nor the phrase "in the capacity of auditor" are defined in the legislation, nor has the court determined how these expressions should be construed.

2   As a result, it is not always clearly apparent when a firm should regard itself as having a duty to report to a regulator. For example, information about a regulated entity may be obtained when partners or staff of the firm which is appointed as its auditor carry out work for another client entity; or when the firm undertakes other work for the regulated entity. Auditors, regulated entities and regulators need to be clear as to when the normal duty of confidentiality will be overridden by the auditor's statutory duty to report to the regulator.

3   In order to clarify whether or not a firm should regard itself as bound by the duty, the FRC developed, in conjunction with HM Treasury and the regulators, guidance on the interpretation of the key conditions for the existence of that duty, namely that the firm is to be regarded as auditor of a regulated entity and that information is obtained in the capacity of auditor.

4   Guidance on the interpretation of the term "auditor" in the context of each Act is contained in the separate Practice Notes dealing with each area affected by the legislation.

5   This appendix sets out guidance on the interpretation of the phrase "in the capacity of auditor". The Board nevertheless continues to hold the view that the meaning of the phrase should be clarified in legislation in the longer term.

In the Capacity of Auditor

6   In determining whether information is obtained in the capacity of auditor, two criteria in particular should be considered:

    (a)   Whether the person who obtained the information also undertook the audit work; and if so

    (b)   Whether it was obtained in the course of or as a result of undertaking the audit work.

7   It is then necessary to apply these criteria to information about a regulated entity which may become known from a number of sources, and by a number of different individuals within a firm. Within a large firm, for example, information may come to the attention of the partner responsible for the audit of a regulated entity, a partner in another office who undertakes a different type of work, or members of the firm's staff at any level. In the case of a sole practitioner who is the auditor of a regulated entity, information about a

regulated entity may also be obtained by the practitioner in the course of work other than its audit.

Non-Audit Work Carried out in Relation to a Regulated Entity

Where partners or staff involved in the audit of a regulated entity carry out work other than its audit (non-audit work) information about the regulated entity will be known to them as individuals. In circumstances which suggest that a matter would otherwise give rise to a statutory duty to report[4] if obtained in the capacity of auditor, it will be prudent for them to make enquiries in the course of their audit work in order to establish whether this is the case from information obtained in that capacity.   **8**

However, where non-audit work is carried out by other partners or staff, neither of the criteria set out in paragraph 6 is met in respect of information which becomes known to them. Nevertheless the firm should take proper account of such information when it could affect the audit so that it is treated in a responsible manner, particularly since in partnership law the knowledge obtained by one partner in the course of the partnership business may be imputed to the entire partnership. In doing so, two types of work may be distinguished: first, work which could affect the firm's work as auditor and, secondly, work which is undertaken purely in an advisory capacity.   **9**

A firm appointed as auditor of a regulated entity needs to have in place appropriate procedures to ensure that the partner responsible for the audit function is made aware of any other relationship which exists between any department of the firm and the regulated entity when that relationship could affect the firm's work as auditor. Common examples of such work include accounting work, particularly for smaller entities, and provision of tax services to the regulated entity.   **10**

Prima facie, information obtained in the course of non-audit work is not covered by either the right or the duty to report to a regulator. However, the firm appointed as auditor needs to consider whether the results of other work undertaken for a regulated entity need to be assessed as part of the audit process. In principle, this is no different to seeking to review a report prepared by outside consultants on, say, the entity's accounting systems so as to ensure that the auditor makes a proper assessment of the risks of misstatement in the financial statements and of the work needed to form an opinion. Consequently, the partner responsible for the audit needs to make appropriate enquiries in the process of planning and completing the audit (see paragraph 17 above). Such enquiries would be directed to those aspects of the non-audit work which might reasonably be expected to be relevant to the audit. When, as a result of such enquiries, those involved in the audit become aware of issues which may be of material significance to a regulator such issues should be considered, and if appropriate reported[4] following the requirements set out in this Section of this ISA (UK).   **11**

Work which is undertaken in an advisory capacity, for example to assist the directors of a regulated entity to determine effective and efficient methods of discharging their duties, would not normally affect the work undertaken for the audit. Nevertheless, in rare instances, the partner responsible for such advisory work may conclude that steps considered necessary in order to comply with the regulator's requirements have not been taken by the directors or that the directors intend in some respect not to comply with the regulator's requirements. Such circumstances would require consideration in the course   **12** of work undertaken for the audit, both to consider the effect on the auditor's routine reports and to determine whether the possible non-compliance is or is likely to be of material significance to the regulator.

Work Relating to a Separate Entity

13   Information obtained in the course of work relating to another entity audited by the same firm (or the same practitioner) is confidential to that other entity. The auditor is not required, and has no right, to report to a regulator confidential information which arises from work undertaken by the same auditing firm for another client. However, as a matter of sound practice, individuals involved in the audit of a regulated entity who become aware (in a capacity other than that of auditor of a regulated entity) of a matter which could otherwise give rise to a statutory duty to report would normally make enquiries in the course of their audit of the regulated entity to establish whether the information concerned is substantiated.

14   In carrying out the audit work, the auditor is required to have due regard to whether disclosure of non-compliance with laws and regulations to a proper authority is appropriate in the public interest. standards and guidance on this general professional obligation is set out in Section A of this ISA (UK).

Conclusion

15   The phrase "in his capacity as auditor" limits information subject to the duty to report to matters of which the auditor becomes aware in the auditor's capacity as such. Consequently, it is unlikely that a partnership can be said to be acting in its capacity as auditor of a particular regulated entity whenever any apparently unrelated material comes to the attention of a partner or member of staff not engaged in that audit, particularly if that material is confidential to another client.

16   The statutory duty to report to a regulator[4] therefore does not extend automatically to any information obtained by a firm regardless of its source. Firms undertaking audits of regulated entities need, however, to establish lines of communication, commensurate with their size and organizational structure, sufficient to ensure that non-audit work undertaken for a regulated entity which is likely to have an effect on the audit is brought to the attention of the partner responsible for the audit and to establish procedures for the partner responsible for the audit to make appropriate enquiries of those conducting such other work as part of the process of planning and completing the audit.

Appendix 3

Action by the Auditor on Discovery of a Breach of a Regulator's Requirements

This appendix sets out in the form of a flowchart the steps involved in assessing whether a report to a regulator is required when a breach of the regulator's requirements comes to the attention of the auditor.

1

The flowchart is intended to provide guidance to readers in understanding this Section of this ISA (UK). It does not form part of the auditing standards contained in the ISA (UK).

2

Action by the Auditor on Discovery of a Breach of a Regulator's Requirement

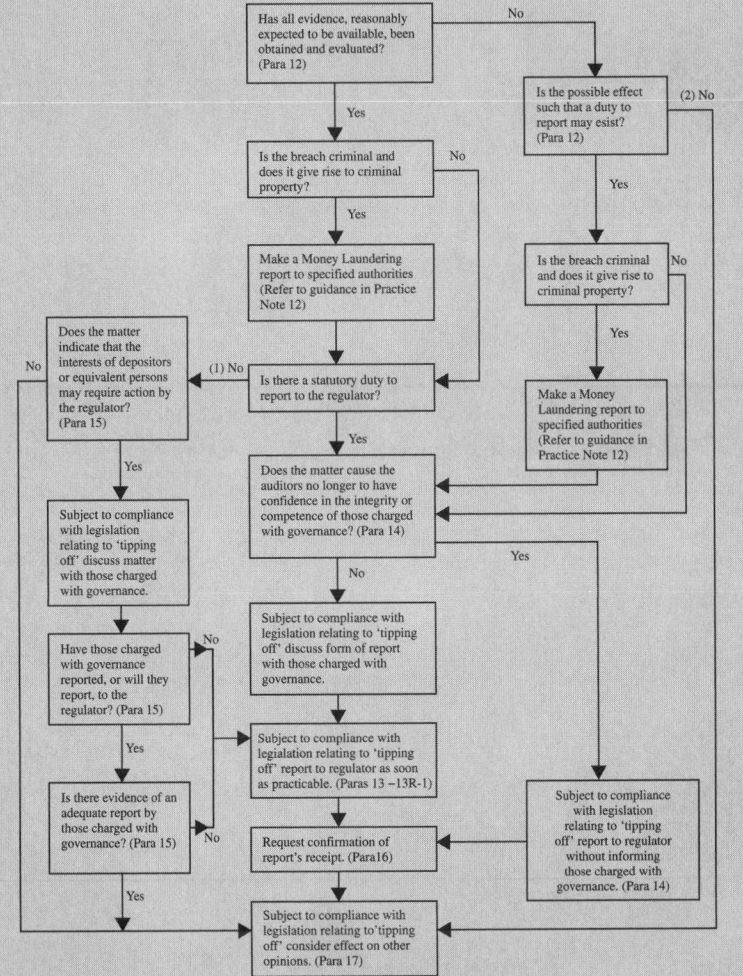

(1) This route would be only followed when a distinct right to report to the regulator exists. Otherwise, where no duty to report exists, the auditor would next consider the effect on other opinions.

(2) Where the auditor considers that a distinct right to report to the regulator exists, the auditor would next consider the question marked (1).

ISA (UK) 260 (Revised June 2016) Communication With Those Charged With Governance (Updated July 2017)

(Effective for audits of financial statements for periods commencing on or after 17 June 2016)[0]

Contents

	Paragraphs
Introduction	1 - 8
Scope of this ISA (UK)	1 - 3
The role of communication	4 - 7
Effective date	8
Objectives	9
Definitions	10
Requirements	11 - 23
Those charged with governance	11 - 13
Matters to be communicated	14 - 16
Entities that report on application of the UK Corporate Governance Code	16-1 - 17R-1
The communication process	18 - 22
Documentation	23 - 23D-1
Application and other explanatory material	A1 - A54
Those charged with governance	A1 - A8
Matters to be communicated	A9 - A28
Entities that report on application of the UK Corporate Governance Code	A28-1 - A32
Auditor independence for public interest entities	A32-1 - A36
The communication process	A37 - A53
Documentation	A54

Appendix 1: Specific requirements in ISQC (UK) 1 and Other ISAs (UK) that refer to communications with those charged with governance

Appendix 2: Qualitative aspects of accounting practices

> International Standard on Auditing (UK) (ISA (UK)) 260 (Revised June 2016), *Communication with Those Charged with Governance*, should be read in conjunction with ISA (UK) 200 (Revised June 2016), *Overall Objectives of the Independent Auditor and the Conduct of an Audit in Accordance with International Standards on Auditing (UK)*.

---

[0] *Conforming amendments to this standard as a result of ISA (UK) 250 (Revised July 2017), Section A— Consideration of Laws and Regulations in an Audit of Financial Statements, are included that are effective for audits of financial statements for periods commencing on or after 15 December 2017. Details of the amendments are given in the Annexure to ISA (UK) 250 (Revised July 2017).*

Introduction

Scope of this ISA (UK)

1   This International Standard on Auditing (UK) (ISA (UK)) deals with the auditor's responsibility to communicate with those charged with governance in an audit of financial statements. Although this ISA (UK) applies irrespective of an entity's governance structure or size, particular considerations apply where all of those charged with governance are involved in managing an entity, and for listed entities. This ISA (UK) does not establish requirements regarding the auditor's communication with an entity's management or owners unless they are also charged with a governance role.

2   This ISA (UK) is written in the context of an audit of financial statements, but may also be applicable, adapted as necessary in the circumstances, to audits of other historical financial information when those charged with governance have a responsibility to oversee the preparation of the other historical financial information.

3   Recognizing the importance of effective two-way communication in an audit of financial statements, this ISA (UK) provides an overarching framework for the auditor's communication with those charged with governance, and identifies some specific matters to be communicated with them. Additional matters to be communicated, which complement the requirements of this ISA (UK), are identified in other ISAs (UK) (see Appendix 1). In addition, ISA (UK) 265[1] establishes specific requirements regarding the communication of significant deficiencies in internal control the auditor has identified during the audit to those charged with governance. Further matters, not required by this or other ISAs (UK), may be required to be communicated by law or regulation, by agreement with the entity, or by additional requirements applicable to the engagement, for example, the standards of a national professional accountancy body. Nothing in this ISA (UK) precludes the auditor from communicating any other matters to those charged with governance. (Ref: Para. A33–A36)

The Role of Communication

4   This ISA (UK) focuses primarily on communications from the auditor to those charged with governance. Nevertheless, effective two-way communication is important in assisting:

(a)   The auditor and those charged with governance in understanding matters related to the audit in context, and in developing a constructive working relationship. This relationship is developed while maintaining the auditor's independence and objectivity;

(b)   The auditor in obtaining from those charged with governance information relevant to the audit.[1a] For example, those charged with governance may assist the auditor in understanding the entity and its environment, in identifying appropriate sources of audit evidence, and in providing information about specific transactions or events; and

---

[1] *ISA (UK) 265, Communicating Deficiencies in Internal Control to Those Charged with Governance and Management.*

[1a] *In the UK, Sections 499 and 500 of the Companies Act 2006 set legal requirements in relation to the auditor's right to obtain information.*

(c)   Those charged with governance in fulfilling their responsibility to oversee the financial reporting process, thereby reducing the risks of material misstatement of the financial statements.

Although the auditor is responsible for communicating matters required by this   5
ISA (UK), management also has a responsibility to communicate matters of governance interest to those charged with governance. Communication by the auditor does not relieve management of this responsibility. Similarly, communication by management with those charged with governance of matters that the auditor is required to communicate does not relieve the auditor of the responsibility to also communicate them. Communication of these matters by management may, however, affect the form or timing of the auditor's communication with those charged with governance.

Clear communication of specific matters required to be communicated by ISAs   6
(UK) is an integral part of every audit. ISAs (UK) do not, however, require the auditor to perform procedures specifically to identify any other matters to communicate with those charged with governance.

In some jurisdictions, law or regulation may restrict the auditor's communication   7
of certain matters with those charged with governance. Law or regulation may specifically prohibit a communication, or other action, that might prejudice an investigation by an appropriate authority into an actual, or suspected, illegal act, including alerting the entity, for example, when the auditor is required to report identified or suspected non-compliance with law or regulation to an appropriate authority pursuant to anti-money laundering legislation. In these circumstances, the issues considered by the auditor may be complex and the auditor may consider it appropriate to obtain legal advice.

Effective Date

This ISA (UK) is effective for audits of financial statements for periods   8
commencing on or after 17 June 2016. Earlier adoption is permitted.

Objectives

The objectives of the auditor are: 9

(a)   To communicate clearly with those charged with governance the responsibilities of the auditor in relation to the financial statement audit, and an overview of the planned scope and timing of the audit;

(b)   To obtain from those charged with governance information relevant to the audit;

(c)   To provide those charged with governance with timely observations arising from the audit that are significant and relevant to their responsibility to oversee the financial reporting process; and

(d)   To promote effective two-way communication between the auditor and those charged with governance.

Definitions

For purposes of the ISAs (UK), the following terms have the meanings attributed   10
below:

(a) Those charged with governance – The person(s) or organization(s) (e.g., a corporate trustee) with responsibility for overseeing the strategic direction of the entity and obligations related to the accountability of the entity. This includes overseeing the financial reporting process. For some entities in some jurisdictions, those charged with governance may include management personnel, for example, executive members of a governance board of a private or public sector entity, or an owner-manager. For discussion of the diversity of governance structures, see paragraphs A1–A8.

> In the UK, those charged with governance include the directors (executive and non-executive) of a company and the members of an audit committee where one exists. For other types of entity it usually includes equivalent persons such as the partners, proprietors, committee of management or trustees.

(b) Management – The person(s) with executive responsibility for the conduct of the entity's operations. For some entities in some jurisdictions, management includes some or all of those charged with governance, for example, executive members of a governance board, or an owner-manager.

> In the UK, management will not normally include non-executive directors.

Requirements

Those Charged with Governance

11   The auditor shall determine the appropriate person(s) within the entity's governance structure with whom to communicate. (Ref: Para. A1–A4-1)

11R-1   For audits of financial statements of public interest entities, if the entity does not have an audit committee, the additional report to the audit committee required by paragraph 16R-2 shall be submitted to the body performing equivalent functions within the entity.

Communication with a Subgroup of Those Charged with Governance

12   If the auditor communicates with a subgroup of those charged with governance, for example, an audit committee, or an individual, the auditor shall determine whether the auditor also needs to communicate with the governing body. (Ref: Para. A5–A7)

When All of Those Charged with Governance Are Involved in Managing the Entity

13   In some cases, all of those charged with governance are involved in managing the entity, for example, a small business where a single owner manages the entity and no one else has a governance role. In these cases, if matters required by this ISA (UK) are communicated with person(s) with management responsibilities, and those person(s) also have governance responsibilities, the matters need not be communicated again with those same person(s) in their governance role. These matters are noted in paragraph 16(c). The auditor shall nonetheless be satisfied that communication with person(s) with management responsibilities adequately informs all of those with whom the auditor would otherwise communicate in their governance capacity. (Ref: Para. A8)

Matters to Be Communicated

The Auditor's Responsibilities in Relation to the Financial Statement Audit

The auditor shall communicate with those charged with governance the **14** responsibilities of the auditor in relation to the financial statement audit, including that:

(a)   The auditor is responsible for forming and expressing an opinion on the financial statements that have been prepared by management[1b] with the oversight of those charged with governance; and

(b)   The audit of the financial statements does not relieve management or those charged with governance of their responsibilities. (Ref: Para. A9–A10)

Planned Scope and Timing of the Audit

The auditor shall communicate with those charged with governance an overview **15** of the planned scope and timing of the audit, which includes communicating about the significant risks identified by the auditor. (Ref: Para. A11–A16)

When the auditor is required or decides to communicate key audit matters in accordance with ISA (UK) 701,[1c] the overview of the planned scope and timing of the audit shall also include communicating about the most significant assessed risks of material misstatement (whether or not due to fraud) identified by the auditor, including those that had the greatest effect on: the overall audit strategy; the allocation of resources in the audit; and directing the efforts of the engagement team.

Significant Findings from the Audit

The auditor shall communicate with those charged with governance: (Ref: Para. **16** A17–A18)

(a)   The auditor's views about significant qualitative aspects of the entity's accounting practices, including accounting policies, accounting estimates and financial statement disclosures. When applicable, the auditor shall explain to those charged with governance why the auditor considers a significant accounting practice, that is acceptable under the applicable financial reporting framework, not to be most appropriate to the particular circumstances of the entity; (Ref: Para. A19–A20)

(b)   Significant difficulties, if any, encountered during the audit; (Ref: Para. A21)

(c)   Unless all of those charged with governance are involved in managing the entity:

    (i)   Significant matters arising during the audit that were discussed, or subject to correspondence, with management; and (Ref: Para. A22)

    (ii)   Written representations the auditor is requesting;

(d)   Circumstances that affect the form and content of the auditor's report, if any; and (Ref: Para. A23–A25)

[1b] *In the UK, those charged with governance are responsible for the preparation of the financial statements.*

[1c] *Paragraphs 30–31 of ISA (UK) 700 (Revised June 2016), Forming an Opinion and Reporting on Financial Statements, set out the requirements to apply ISA (UK) 701, Communicating Key Audit Matters in the Independent Auditor's Report.*

(e)   Any other significant matters arising during the audit that, in the auditor's professional judgment, are relevant to the oversight of the financial reporting process. (Ref: Para. A26–A28)

Entities that Report on Application of the UK Corporate Governance Code

16-1   In the case of entities that are required,[1d] and those that choose voluntarily, to report on how they have applied the UK Corporate Governance Code, or to explain why they have not, the auditor shall communicate to the audit committee the information that the auditor believes will be relevant to: (Ref: Para. A28-1)

- The board (in the context of fulfilling its responsibilities under Code provisions C.1.1, C.1.3, C.2.1, C.2.2 and C.2.3) and, where applicable, the audit committee (in the context of fulfilling its responsibilities under Code provision C.3.4); and

- The audit committee (in the context of fulfilling its responsibilities under Code provision C.3.2) in order to understand the rationale and the supporting evidence the auditor has relied on when making significant professional judgments in the course of the audit and in reaching an opinion on the financial statements.

If not already covered by communications under paragraphs 15, 16 and 16R-2 of this ISA (UK) and paragraph 25 of ISA (UK) 570 (Revised June 2016), this information shall include the auditor's views: (Ref: Para. A28-2–A28-5)

(a)   About business risks relevant to financial reporting objectives, the application of materiality and the implications of their judgments in relation to these for the overall audit strategy, the audit plan and the evaluation of misstatements identified;

(b)   On the significant accounting policies (both individually and in aggregate);

(c)   On management's valuations of the entity's material assets and liabilities and the related disclosures provided by management;

(d)   Without expressing an opinion on the effectiveness of the entity's system of internal control as a whole, and based solely on the audit procedures performed in the audit of the financial statements, about:

    (i)   The effectiveness of the entity's system of internal control relevant to risks that may affect financial reporting; and

    (ii)   Other risks arising from the entity's business model and the effectiveness of related internal controls to the extent, if any, the auditor has obtained an understanding of these matters;

[1d] *In the UK, these include companies with a premium listing of equity shares regardless of whether they are incorporated in the UK or elsewhere.*

(e) About the robustness of the directors' assessment of the principal risks facing the entity, including those that would threaten its business model, future performance, solvency or liquidity and its outcome, including the related disclosures in the annual report confirming that they have carried out such an assessment and describing those risks and explaining how they are being managed or mitigated (in accordance with Code provision C.2.1);

(f) About the directors' explanation in the annual report as to how they have assessed the prospects of the entity, over what period they have done so and why they consider that period to be appropriate (in accordance with Code provision C.2.2), and their statements:

    (i) in the financial statements, as to whether they considered it appropriate to adopt the going concern basis of accounting in preparing them, including any related disclosures identifying any material uncertainties to the entity's ability to continue to do so over a period of at least twelve months from the date of approval of the financial statements (in accordance with Code provision C.1.3); and

    (ii) in the annual report as to whether they have a reasonable expectation that the entity will be able to continue in operation and meet its liabilities as they fall due over the period of their assessment, including any related disclosures drawing attention to any necessary qualifications or assumptions (in accordance with Code provision C.2.2); and

(g) On any other matters identified in the course of the audit that the auditor believes will be relevant to the board or the audit committee in the context of fulfilling their responsibilities referred to above.

The auditor shall include with this communication sufficient explanation to enable the audit committee to understand the context within which the auditor's views relating to the matters in paragraph (d) above are expressed, including the extent to which the auditor has developed an understanding of these matters in the course of the audit and, if not already communicated to the audit committee, that the audit included consideration of internal control relevant to the preparation of the financial statements only in order to design audit procedures that are appropriate in the circumstances, and not for the purpose of expressing an opinion on the effectiveness of internal control.

Public Interest Entities

For audits of financial statements of public interest entities, the auditor shall submit an additional report to the audit committee of the entity explaining the results of the audit carried out and shall at least:

16R-2

(a) Include the declaration of independence required by paragraph 17R-1(a);

(b)   Identify each key audit partner(s)[1e] involved in the audit;

(c)   Where the auditor has made arrangements for any of the auditor's activities to be conducted by another firm[1f] that is not a member of the same network, or has used the work of external experts, the report shall indicate that fact and shall confirm that the auditor received a confirmation from the other firm and/or the external expert regarding their independence;

(d)   Describe the nature, frequency and extent of communication with the audit committee or the body performing equivalent functions within the entity, the management body and the administrative or supervisory body of the entity, including the dates of meetings with those bodies;

(e)   Include a description of the scope and timing of the audit;

(f)   Where more than one auditor has been appointed, describe the distribution of tasks among the auditors;

(g)   Describe the methodology used, including which categories of the balance sheet have been directly verified and which categories have been verified based on system and compliance testing, including an explanation of any substantial variation in the weighting of system and compliance testing when compared to the previous year, even if the previous year's audit was carried out by another firm;

(h)   Disclose the quantitative level of materiality applied to perform the audit for the financial statements as a whole and where applicable the materiality level or levels for particular classes of transactions, account balances or disclosures, and disclose the qualitative factors which were considered when setting the level of materiality;

(i)   Report and explain judgments about events or conditions identified in the course of the audit that may cast significant doubt on the entity's ability to continue as a going concern and whether they constitute a material uncertainty, and provide a summary of all guarantees, comfort letters, undertakings of public intervention and other support measures that have been taken into account when making a going concern assessment;

(j)   Report on any significant deficiencies in the entity's or, in the case of consolidated financial statements, the parent undertaking's internal financial control system, and/or in the accounting system. For each such significant deficiency, the additional report shall state whether or not the deficiency in question has been resolved by management;

(k)   Report any significant matters involving actual or suspected non-compliance with laws and regulations or articles of association which were identified in the course of the audit, in so far as they are considered to be relevant in order to enable the audit committee to fulfil its tasks;

[1e] *"Key audit partner" is defined in paragraph 7(f)-1 of ISA (UK) 220 (Revised June 2016), Quality Control for an Audit of Financial Statements.*

[1f] *"Firm" is defined in ISA (UK) 220 (Revised June 2016) as a sole practitioner, partnership or corporation or other entity of professional accountants.*

(l)   Report the valuation methods[1g] applied to the various items in the annual or consolidated financial statements including any impact of changes of such methods;

(m)   In the case of an audit of consolidated financial statements, explain the scope of consolidation and the exclusion criteria applied by the entity to the non-consolidated entities, if any, and whether those criteria applied are in accordance with the financial reporting framework;

(n)   Where applicable, identify any audit work performed by component auditors in relation to an audit of consolidated financial statements other than by members of the same network to which the auditor of the consolidated financial statements belongs;

(o)   Indicate whether all requested explanations and documents were provided by the entity;

(p)   Report:

     (i)   Any significant difficulties encountered in the course of the audit;

     (ii)   Any significant matters arising from the audit that were discussed or were the subject of correspondence with management; and

     (iii)   Any other matters arising from the audit that in the auditor's professional judgment, are significant to the oversight of the financial reporting process.

Where more than one auditor has been engaged simultaneously, and any disagreement has arisen between them on auditing procedures, accounting rules or any other issue regarding the conduct of the audit, the reasons for such disagreement shall be explained in the additional report to the audit committee.

Auditor Independence

17   In the case of listed entities, the auditor shall communicate with those charged with governance:

(a)   A statement that the engagement team and others in the firm as appropriate, the firm and, when applicable, network firms have complied with relevant ethical requirements regarding independence;[1h] and

(b)   (i)   All relationships and other matters between the firm, network firms, and the entity that, in the auditor's professional judgment, may reasonably be thought to bear on independence. This shall include total fees charged during the period covered by the financial statements for audit and non-audit services provided by the firm and network firms to the entity and components controlled by the entity. These fees shall be allocated to categories that are appropriate to assist those charged with governance in assessing the effect of services on the independence of the auditor; and

---

[1g] *ISA (UK) 330 (Revised July 2017), The Auditor's Responses to Assessed Risks, paragraph 19R-1 deals with the auditor's responsibility to assess the valuation methods applied, including any impact of changes of such methods.*

[1h] *In the UK, auditors are subject to ethical requirements from two sources: the FRC's Ethical Standard concerning the integrity, objectivity and independence of the auditor and the ethical pronouncements established by the auditor's relevant professional body. In the case of listed companies, the FRC's Ethical Standard, Part B, Section 1 – General Requirements and Guidance, paragraphs 1.61 to 1.71 address communication with those charged with governance.*

    (ii)   The related safeguards that have been applied to eliminate identified threats to independence or reduce them to an acceptable level. (Ref: Para. A29–A32)

17R-1   For audits of financial statements of public interest entities, the auditor shall: (Ref: Para. A32-1)

    (a)   Confirm annually in writing to the audit committee that the firm and partners, senior managers and managers, conducting the audit are independent from the audited entity; and

    (b)   Discuss with the audit committee the threats to the auditor's independence and the safeguards applied to mitigate those threats.[1i]

The Communication Process

Establishing the Communication Process

18   The auditor shall communicate with those charged with governance the form, timing and expected general content of communications. (Ref: Para. A37–A45)

Forms of Communication

19   The auditor shall communicate in writing with those charged with governance regarding significant findings from the audit if, in the auditor's professional judgment, oral communication would not be adequate. Written communications need not include all matters that arose during the course of the audit. (Ref: Para. A46–A48)

20   The auditor shall communicate in writing with those charged with governance regarding auditor independence when required by paragraph 17 and 17R-1.

20R-1   For audits of financial statements of public interest entities:

    (a)   The additional report to the audit committee[1j] shall be in writing.

    (b)   The additional report to the audit committee shall be signed and dated by the engagement partner.

    (c)   Upon request by either the auditor or the audit committee, the auditor shall discuss key matters arising from the audit, referred to in the additional report to the audit committee, and in particular deficiencies communicated in accordance with paragraph 16R-2(j).

Timing of Communications

21   The auditor shall communicate with those charged with governance on a timely basis. (Ref: Para. A49–A50-1)

21R-1   For audits of financial statements of public interest entities, the auditor shall submit the additional report to the audit committee not later than the date of submission of the auditor's report.[1k] (Ref: Para. A50-2)

[1i] *Paragraph 27R-2 of ISQC (UK) 1 (Revised June 2016), Quality Control for Firms that Perform Audits and Reviews of Financial Statements, and Other Assurance and Related Services Engagements, deals with the auditor's responsibility to assess such matters.*

[1j] *Paragraph 16R-2 deals with the auditor's responsibilities to prepare an additional report to the audit committee.*

[1k] *ISA (UK) 700 (Revised June 2016), Forming an Opinion and Reporting on Financial Statements.*

Adequacy of the Communication Process

The auditor shall evaluate whether the two-way communication between the **22** auditor and those charged with governance has been adequate for the purpose of the audit. If it has not, the auditor shall evaluate the effect, if any, on the auditor's assessment of the risks of material misstatement and ability to obtain sufficient appropriate audit evidence, and shall take appropriate action. (Ref: Para. A51–A53)

Documentation

Where matters required by this ISA (UK) to be communicated are communicated **23** orally, the auditor shall include them in the audit documentation, and when and to whom they were communicated. Where matters have been communicated in writing, the auditor shall retain a copy of the communication as part of the audit documentation.[2] (Ref: Para. A54)

For audits of financial statements of public interest entities, the auditor shall **23D-1** retain any other data and documents that are important in supporting the additional report to the audit committee[2a] as part of the audit documentation.

***

Application and Other Explanatory Material

Those Charged with Governance
(Ref: Para. 11)

Governance structures vary by jurisdiction and by entity, reflecting influences **A1** such as different cultural and legal backgrounds, and size and ownership characteristics. For example:

● In some jurisdictions a supervisory (wholly or mainly non-executive) board exists that is legally separate from an executive (management) board (a "two-tier board" structure). In other jurisdictions, both the supervisory and executive functions are the legal responsibility of a single, or unitary, board (a "one-tier board" structure).

● In some entities, those charged with governance hold positions that are an integral part of the entity's legal structure, for example, company directors. In others, for example, some government entities, a body that is not part of the entity is charged with governance.

● In some cases, some or all of those charged with governance are involved in managing the entity. In others, those charged with governance and management comprise different persons.

● In some cases, those charged with governance are responsible for approving[3] the entity's financial statements (in other cases management has this responsibility).

---

[2] *ISA (UK) 230 (Revised June 2016), Audit Documentation, paragraphs 8–11, and A6.*

[2a] *Paragraph 16R-2 deals with the auditor's responsibilities to prepare an additional report to the audit committee.*

[3] *As described in paragraph A68 of ISA (UK) 700 (Revised June 2016), Forming an Opinion and Reporting on Financial Statements, having responsibility for approving in this context means having the authority to conclude that all the statements that comprise the financial statements, including the related notes, have been prepared.*

In the UK, those charged with governance are responsible for the approval of the financial statements.

A2   In most entities, governance is the collective responsibility of a governing body, such as a board of directors, a supervisory board, partners, proprietors, a committee of management, a council of governors, trustees, or equivalent persons. In some smaller entities, however, one person may be charged with governance, for example, the owner-manager where there are no other owners, or a sole trustee. When governance is a collective responsibility, a subgroup such as an audit committee or even an individual, may be charged with specific tasks to assist the governing body in meeting its responsibilities. Alternatively, a subgroup or individual may have specific, legally identified responsibilities that differ from those of the governing body.

A3   Such diversity means that it is not possible for this ISA (UK) to specify for all audits the person(s) with whom the auditor is to communicate particular matters. Also, in some cases the appropriate person(s) with whom to communicate may not be clearly identifiable from the applicable legal framework or other engagement circumstances, for example, entities where the governance structure is not formally defined, such as some family-owned entities, some not-for-profit organizations, and some government entities. In such cases, the auditor may need to discuss and agree with the engaging party the relevant person(s) with whom to communicate. In deciding with whom to communicate, the auditor's understanding of an entity's governance structure and processes obtained in accordance with ISA (UK) 315 (Revised June 2016)[4] is relevant. The appropriate person(s) with whom to communicate may vary depending on the matter to be communicated.

A4   ISA (UK) 600 (Revised June 2016) includes specific matters to be communicated by group auditors with those charged with governance.[5] When the entity is a component of a group, the appropriate person(s) with whom the component auditor communicates depends on the engagement circumstances and the matter to be communicated. In some cases, a number of components may be conducting the same businesses within the same system of internal control and using the same accounting practices. Where those charged with governance of those components are the same (e.g., common board of directors), duplication may be avoided by dealing with these components concurrently for the purpose of communication.

A4-1   In the UK, there are statutory obligations on corporate subsidiary undertakings, and their auditors and other parties, to provide the auditor of a corporate parent undertaking with such information and explanations as that auditor may reasonably require for the purposes of the audit.[5a] Where there is no such statutory obligation (e.g., for non corporate entities), permission may be needed by the auditors of the subsidiary undertakings, from those charged with governance of the subsidiary undertakings, to disclose the contents of any

---

[4] ISA (UK) 315 (Revised June 2016), *Identifying and Assessing the Risks of Material Misstatement through Understanding the Entity and Its Environment.*

[5] ISA (UK) 600 (Revised June 2016), *Special Considerations—Audits of Group Financial Statements (Including the Work of Component Auditors), paragraph 49.*

[5a] *In the UK, Section 499 of the Companies Act 2006 specifies that the auditor of a company may require any subsidiary undertaking of the company which is a body corporate incorporated in the UK, and any officer, employee or auditor of any such subsidiary undertaking or any person holding or accountable for any books, accounts or vouchers of any such subsidiary undertaking, to provide him with such information or explanations as he thinks necessary for the performance of his duties as auditor. If a parent company has a subsidiary undertaking that is not a body corporate incorporated in the UK, Section 500 of the Companies Act 2006 specifies that the auditor of the parent company may require it to take all such steps as are reasonably open to it to obtain from the subsidiary undertaking, any officer, employee or auditor of the undertaking, or any person holding or accountable for any of the undertaking's books, accounts or vouchers, such information and explanations as he may reasonably require for the purposes of his duties as auditor.*

communication to them to the auditor of the parent undertaking and also for the auditor of the parent undertaking to pass those disclosures onto those charged with governance of the parent undertaking. The auditor of the parent undertaking seeks to ensure that appropriate arrangements are made at the planning stage for these disclosures. Normally, such arrangements for groups are recorded in the instructions to the auditors of subsidiary undertakings and relevant engagement letters.

Communication with a Subgroup of Those Charged with Governance
(Ref: Para. 12)

When considering communicating with a subgroup of those charged with governance, the auditor may take into account such matters as: **A5**

- The respective responsibilities of the subgroup and the governing body.

- The nature of the matter to be communicated.

- Relevant legal or regulatory requirements.

- Whether the subgroup has the authority to take action in relation to the information communicated, and can provide further information and explanations the auditor may need.

When deciding whether there is also a need to communicate information, in full or in summary form, with the governing body, the auditor may be influenced by the auditor's assessment of how effectively and appropriately the subgroup communicates relevant information with the governing body. The auditor may make explicit in agreeing the terms of engagement that, unless prohibited by law or regulation, the auditor retains the right to communicate directly with the governing body.   **A6**

Audit committees report to the board on various matters related to the discharge of their responsibilities, including those related to the financial statements, the annual report and the audit process (see paragraph A28-1 below). The auditor, when assessing whether there is a need to communicate with the full board regarding matters communicated by the auditor to the audit committee, takes into consideration the adequacy of the communications between the audit committee and the board, including whether they appropriately address relevant matters communicated to the audit committee by the auditor. This may be achieved in one or more ways including: where judged appropriate attending the relevant part of a board meeting where the audit committee reports to the board, holding discussions with individual board members, or reviewing any written reports from the audit committee to the board.   **A6-1**

Audit committees (or similar subgroups with different names) exist in many jurisdictions. Although their specific authority and functions may differ, communication with the audit committee, where one exists, has become a key element in the auditor's communication with those charged with governance. Good governance principles suggest that: **A7**

- The auditor will be invited to regularly attend meetings of the audit committee.

- The chair of the audit committee and, when relevant, the other members of the audit committee, will liaise with the auditor periodically.

- The audit committee will meet the auditor without management present at least annually.

When All of Those Charged with Governance Are Involved in Managing the Entity
(Ref: Para.13)

A8   In some cases, all of those charged with governance are involved in managing the entity, and the application of communication requirements is modified to recognize this position. In such cases, communication with person(s) with management responsibilities may not adequately inform all of those with whom the auditor would otherwise communicate in their governance capacity. For example, in a company where all directors are involved in managing the entity, some of those directors (e.g., one responsible for marketing) may be unaware of significant matters discussed with another director (e.g., one responsible for the preparation of the financial statements).

Matters to Be Communicated

The Auditor's Responsibilities in Relation to the Financial Statement Audit
(Ref: Para. 14)

A9   The auditor's responsibilities in relation to the financial statement audit are often included in the engagement letter or other suitable form of written agreement that records the agreed terms of the engagement.[6] Law, regulation or the governance structure of the entity may require those charged with governance to agree the terms of the engagement with the auditor. When this is not the case, providing those charged with governance with a copy of that engagement letter or other suitable form of written agreement may be an appropriate way to communicate with them regarding such matters as:

●   The auditor's responsibility for performing the audit in accordance with ISAs (UK), which is directed towards the expression of an opinion on the financial statements. The matters that ISAs (UK) require to be communicated, therefore, include significant matters arising during the audit of the financial statements that are relevant to those charged with governance in overseeing the financial reporting process.

●   The fact that ISAs (UK) do not require the auditor to design procedures for the purpose of identifying supplementary matters to communicate with those charged with governance.

●   When ISA (UK) 701[7] applies, the auditor's responsibilities to determine and communicate key audit matters in the auditor's report.

●   When applicable, the auditor's responsibility for communicating particular matters required by law or regulation, by agreement with the entity or by additional requirements applicable to the engagement, for example, the standards of a national professional accountancy body.

A9-1   The provision of copies of the audit engagement letter to the audit committees of listed companies facilitates their review and agreement of the audit engagement letter as recommended by the FRC Guidance on Audit Committees. As part of their review, the guidance further recommends the audit committee to consider whether the audit engagement letter has been updated to reflect changes in circumstances since the previous year.

---

[6] See paragraph 10 of ISA (UK) 210 (Revised June 2016), *Agreeing the Terms of Audit Engagements.*

[7] ISA (UK) 701, *Communicating Key Audit Matters in the Independent Auditor's Report.*

Law or regulation, an agreement with the entity or additional requirements   **A10**
applicable to the engagement may provide for broader communication with
those charged with governance. For example, (a) an agreement with the entity
may provide for particular matters to be communicated when they arise from
services provided by a firm or network firm other than the financial statement
audit; or (b) the mandate of a public sector auditor may provide for matters to be
communicated that come to the auditor's attention as a result of other work, such
as performance audits.

Planned Scope and Timing of the Audit
(Ref: Para. 15)

Communication regarding the planned scope and timing of the audit may: **A11**

(a)   Assist those charged with governance to understand better the consequences
       of the auditor's work, to discuss issues of risk and the concept of materiality
       with the auditor, and to identify any areas in which they may request the
       auditor to undertake additional procedures;[7a] and

(b)   Assist the auditor to understand better the entity and its environment.

The communication of the planned scope of the audit includes, where relevant,   **A11-1**
any limitations on the work the auditor proposes to undertake (e.g., if
limitations are imposed by management).[7b]

Communicating significant risks identified by the auditor helps those charged with   **A12**
governance understand those matters and why they require special audit
consideration. The communication about significant risks may assist those
charged with governance in fulfilling their responsibility to oversee the
financial reporting process.

Matters communicated may include: **A13**

●   How the auditor plans to address the significant risks of material
   misstatement, whether due to fraud or error.

●   How the auditor plans to address areas of higher assessed risks of material
   misstatement.

●   The auditor's approach to internal control relevant to the audit.

●   The application of the concept of materiality in the context of an audit.[8]

●   The nature and extent of specialized skill or knowledge needed to perform
   the planned audit procedures or evaluate the audit results, including the use
   of an auditor's expert.[9]

●   When ISA (UK) 701 applies, the auditor's preliminary views about matters
   that may be areas of significant auditor attention in the audit and therefore
   may be key audit matters.

[7a] *The UK Corporate Governance Code and the FRC Guidance on Audit Committees contain, inter alia, recommendations about the audit committee's relationship with the auditor.*

[7b] *ISA (UK) 210 (Revised June 2016), paragraph 7 requires that if management or those charged with governance impose a limitation on the scope of the auditor's work in the terms of a proposed audit engagement such that the auditor believes the limitation will result in the auditor disclaiming an opinion on the financial statements, the auditor shall not accept such a limited engagement as an audit engagement, unless required by law or regulation to do so.*

[8] *ISA (UK) 320 (Revised June 2016), Materiality in Planning and Performing an Audit.*

[9] *See ISA (UK) 620 (Revised June 2016), Using the Work of an Auditor's Expert.*

- The auditor's planned approach to addressing the implications on the individual statements and the disclosures of any significant changes within the applicable financial reporting framework or in the entity's environment, financial condition or activities.

A13-1   The nature and detail of the planning information communicated will reflect the size and nature of the entity and the manner in which those charged with governance operate.

A13-2   In any particular year, the auditor may decide that there are no significant changes in the planned scope and timing of the audit that have been communicated previously and judge that it is unnecessary to remind those charged with governance of all or part of that information. In these circumstances, the auditor need only make those charged with governance aware that the auditor has no new matters to communicate concerning the planned scope and timing of the audit. Matters that are included in the audit engagement letter need not be repeated.

A14   Other planning matters that it may be appropriate to discuss with those charged with governance include:

- Where the entity has an internal audit function, how the external and internal auditors can work together in a constructive and complementary manner, including any planned use of the work of the internal audit function, and the nature and extent of any planned use of internal auditors to provide direct assistance.[10]

- The views of those charged with governance about:

    - The appropriate person(s) in the entity's governance structure with whom to communicate.

    - The allocation of responsibilities between those charged with governance and management.

    - The entity's objectives and strategies, and the related business risks that may result in material misstatements.

    - Matters those charged with governance consider warrant particular attention during the audit, and any areas where they request additional procedures to be undertaken.

    - Significant communications between the entity and regulators.

    - Other matters those charged with governance consider may influence the audit of the financial statements.

- The attitudes, awareness, and actions of those charged with governance concerning (a) the entity's internal control and its importance in the entity, including how those charged with governance oversee the effectiveness of internal control, and (b) the detection or possibility of fraud.

- The actions of those charged with governance in response to developments in accounting standards, corporate governance practices, exchange listing rules, and related matters, and the effect of such developments on, for example, the overall presentation, structure and content of the financial statements, including:

---

[10] *ISA 610 (Revised June 2013), Using the Work of Internal Auditors, paragraph 31.*

The use of internal auditors to provide direct assistance is prohibited in an audit in accordance with ISAs (UK) – see ISA (UK) 610 (Revised June 2013), paragraph 5-1.

- The relevance, reliability, comparability and understandability of the information presented in the financial statements; and

- Considering whether the financial statements are undermined by the inclusion of information that is not relevant or that obscures a proper understanding of the matters disclosed.

- The responses of those charged with governance to previous communications with the auditor.The documents comprising the other information (as defined in ISA (UK) 720 (Revised June 2016)) and the planned manner and timing of the issuance of such documents. When the auditor expects to obtain other information after the date of the auditor's report, the discussions with those charged with governance may also include the actions that may be appropriate or necessary if the auditor concludes that a material misstatement of the other information exists in other information obtained after the date of the auditor's report.[10a]

While communication with those charged with governance may assist the auditor   **A15**
to plan the scope and timing of the audit, it does not change the auditor's sole responsibility to establish the overall audit strategy and the audit plan, including the nature, timing and extent of procedures necessary to obtain sufficient appropriate audit evidence.

Care is necessary when communicating with those charged with governance about   **A16**
the planned scope and timing of the audit so as not to compromise the effectiveness of the audit, particularly where some or all of those charged with governance are involved in managing the entity. For example, communicating the nature and timing of detailed audit procedures may reduce the effectiveness of those procedures by making them too predictable.

Significant Findings from the Audit
(Ref: Para. 16–16R-2)

The communication of findings from the audit may include requesting further   **A17**
information from those charged with governance in order to complete the audit evidence obtained. For example, the auditor may confirm that those charged with governance have the same understanding of the facts and circumstances relevant to specific transactions or events.

When ISA (UK) 701 applies, the communications with those charged with   **A18**
governance required by paragraph 16, 16-1 and 16R-2, as well as the communication about the significant risks identified by the auditor required by paragraph 15, are particularly relevant to the auditor's determination of matters that required significant auditor attention and which therefore may be key audit matters.[11]

Significant Qualitative Aspects of Accounting Practices
(Ref: Para. 16(a))

Financial reporting frameworks ordinarily allow for the entity to make accounting   **A19**
estimates, and judgments about accounting policies and financial statement disclosures for example, in relation to the use of key assumptions in the

---

[10a] *ISA (UK) 700 (Revised June 2016) requires that "The auditor shall not sign, and hence date, the auditor's report earlier than the date on which all the other information in the annual report has been approved by those charged with governance and the auditor has considered all necessary available evidence."*

[11] *ISA (UK) 701, paragraphs 9–10.*

development of accounting estimates for which there is significant measurement uncertainty. In addition, law, regulation or financial reporting frameworks may require disclosure of a summary of significant accounting policies or make reference to "critical accounting estimates" or "critical accounting policies and practices" to identify and provide additional information to users about the most difficult, subjective or complex judgments made by management in preparing the financial statements.

A20   As a result, the auditor's views on the subjective aspects of the financial statements may be particularly relevant to those charged with governance in discharging their responsibilities for oversight of the financial reporting process. For example, in relation to the matters described in paragraph A19, those charged with governance may be interested in the auditor's evaluation of the adequacy of disclosures of the estimation uncertainty relating to accounting estimates that give rise to significant risks. Open and constructive communication about significant qualitative aspects of the entity's accounting practices also may include comment on the acceptability of significant accounting practices, and the quality of the disclosures. Appendix 2 identifies matters that may be included in this communication.

Significant Difficulties Encountered during the Audit
(Ref: Para. 16(b))

A21   Significant difficulties encountered during the audit may include such matters as:

- Significant delays by management, the unavailability of entity personnel, or an unwillingness by management to provide information necessary for the auditor to perform the auditor's procedures.

- An unreasonably brief time within which to complete the audit.

- Extensive unexpected effort required to obtain sufficient appropriate audit evidence.

- The unavailability of expected information.

- Restrictions imposed on the auditor by management.

- Management's unwillingness to make or extend its assessment of the entity's ability to continue as a going concern when requested.

In some circumstances, such difficulties may constitute a scope limitation that leads to a modification of the auditor's opinion.[12]

Significant Matters Discussed, or Subject to Correspondence with Management
(Ref: Para. 16(c)(i))

A22   Significant matters discussed, or subject to correspondence with management may include such matters as:

- Significant events or transactions that occurred during the year.

- Business conditions affecting the entity, and business plans and strategies that may affect the risks of material misstatement.

- Concerns about management's consultations with other accountants on accounting or auditing matters.

---

[12] *ISA (UK) 705 (Revised June 2016), Modifications to the Opinion in the Independent Auditor's Report.*

- Discussions or correspondence in connection with the initial or recurring appointment of the auditor regarding accounting practices, the application of auditing standards, or fees for audit or other services.

- Significant matters on which there was disagreement with management, except for initial differences of opinion because of incomplete facts or preliminary information that are later resolved by the auditor obtaining additional relevant facts or information.

Circumstances that Affect the Form and Content of the Auditor's Report
(Ref: Para 16(d))

ISA (UK) 210 (Revised June 2016) requires the auditor to agree the terms of   **A23** the audit engagement with management or those charged with governance, as appropriate.[13] The agreed terms of the audit engagement are required to be recorded in an audit engagement letter or other suitable form of written agreement and include, among other things, reference to the expected form and content of the auditor's report.[14] As explained in paragraph A9, if the terms of engagement are not agreed with those charged with governance, the auditor may provide those charged with governance with a copy of the engagement letter to communicate about matters relevant to the audit. The communication required by paragraph 16(d) is intended to inform those charged with governance about circumstances in which the auditor's report may differ from its expected form and content or may include additional information about the audit that was performed.

Circumstances in which the auditor is required or may otherwise consider it   **A24** necessary to include additional information in the auditor's report in accordance with the ISAs (UK), and for which communication with those charged with governance is required, include when:

- The auditor expects to modify the opinion in the auditor's report in accordance with ISA (UK) 705 (Revised June 2016).[15]

- A material uncertainty related to going concern is reported in accordance with ISA (UK) 570 (Revised June 2016).[16]

- Key audit matters are communicated in accordance with ISA (UK) 701.[17]

- The auditor considers it necessary to include an Emphasis of Matter paragraph or Other Matters paragraph in accordance with ISA (UK) 706 (Revised June 2016)[18] or is required to do so by other ISAs (UK).

- The auditor has concluded that there is an uncorrected material misstatement of the other information in accordance with ISA (UK) 720 (Revised June 2016).[19]

---

[13] *ISA (UK) 210 (Revised June 2016), paragraph 9.*

[14] *ISA (UK) 210 (Revised June 2016), paragraph 10.*

[15] *ISA (UK) 705 (Revised June 2016), paragraph 30.*

[16] *ISA (UK) 570 (Revised June 2016), Going Concern, paragraph 25(d).*

[17] *ISA (UK) 701, paragraph 17.*

[18] *ISA (UK) 706 (Revised June 2016), Emphasis of Matter Paragraphs and Other Matter Paragraphs in the Independent Auditor's Report, paragraph 12.*

[19] *ISA (UK) 720 (Revised June 2016), The Auditor's Responsibilities Relating to Other Information, paragraph 18(a).*

In such circumstances, the auditor may consider it useful to provide those charged with governance with a draft of the auditor's report to facilitate a discussion of how such matters will be addressed in the auditor's report.

A25   In the rare circumstances that the auditor intends not to include the name of the engagement partner in the auditor's report in accordance with ISA (UK) 700 (Revised June 2016), the auditor is required to discuss this intention with those charged with governance to inform the auditor's assessment of the likelihood and severity of a significant personal security threat.[20] The auditor also may communicate with those charged with governance in circumstances when the auditor elects not to include the description of the auditor's responsibilities in the body of the auditor's report as permitted by ISA (UK) 700 (Revised June 2016).[21]

Other Significant Matters Relevant to the Financial Reporting Process
(Ref: Para. 16(e))

A26   ISA (UK) 300 (Revised June 2016)[22] notes that, as a result of unexpected events, changes in conditions, or the audit evidence obtained from the results of audit procedures, the auditor may need to modify the overall audit strategy and audit plan and thereby the resulting planned nature, timing and extent of further audit procedures, based on the revised consideration of assessed risks. The auditor may communicate with those charged with governance about such matters, for example, as an update to initial discussions about the planned scope and timing of the audit.

A27   Other significant matters arising during the audit that are directly relevant to those charged with governance in overseeing the financial reporting process may include such matters as material misstatements of the other information that have been corrected.

A28   To the extent not already addressed by the requirements in paragraphs 16(a)–(d) and related application material, the auditor may consider communicating about other matters discussed with, or considered by, the engagement quality control reviewer, if one has been appointed, in accordance with ISA (UK) 220 (Revised June 2016).[23]

---

[20] *ISA (UK) 700 (Revised June 2016), paragraphs 46 and A63.*

[21] *ISA (UK) 700 (Revised June 2016), paragraph 41.*

[22] *ISA (UK) 300 (Revised June 2016), Planning an Audit of Financial Statements, paragraph A13.*

[23] *See paragraphs 19–22 and A23–A32 of ISA (UK) 220 (Revised June 2016), Quality Control for an Audit of Financial Statements.*

Entities that Report on Application of the UK Corporate Governance Code (Ref: Para. 16-1)

Under the UK Corporate Governance Code, the responsibilities of the directors under Code provision C.1.1 include making a statement that they consider the annual report and accounts taken as a whole is fair, balanced and understandable and provides the information necessary for shareholders to assess the entity's position and performance, business model and strategy. The responsibilities of the audit committee under Code provision C.3.4 include, where requested by the board, providing advice in relation to that statement.[23a] The responsibilities of the board under Code provision C.2.3 include monitoring the entity's risk management and internal control systems and, at least annually, carrying out a review of their effectiveness and reporting on that review in the annual report.[23b] The responsibilities of the board under Code provisions C.1.3, C.2.1 and C.2.2 are described in paragraphs 16-1 (e) and (f). The responsibilities of the audit committee under Code provision C.3.2 include: monitoring the integrity of the financial statements of the entity and any formal announcements relating to the entity's financial performance, reviewing significant financial reporting judgments contained in them; reviewing the entity's internal financial controls and, unless expressly addressed by a separate board risk committee composed of independent directors or by the board itself, the entity's internal control and risk management systems,[23c] review and monitor the effectiveness of the audit process; and reporting to the board on how it has discharged its responsibilities. The supporting Guidance on Audit Committees indicates that the report to the board should include, inter alia:[23d]

A28-1

● The significant issues that the audit committee considered in relation to the financial statements and how these issues were addressed; and

● The basis for its advice, where requested by the board, that the annual report and accounts taken as a whole is fair, balanced and understandable and provides the information necessary for shareholders to assess the entity's performance, business model and strategy.

In fulfilling these responsibilities, the audit committee and the board will be assisted by an understanding of:

A28-2

(a) Issues that involve significant judgment; and

(b) Other matters communicated to them by the auditor relevant to those responsibilities.

[23a] *Responsibility for ensuring the annual report is fair, balanced and understandable rests with the board as a whole. The board may ask the audit committee to provide advice on this.*

[23b] *In addition, FCA Rule DTR 7.2.5 R requires companies to describe the main features of the internal control and risk management systems in relation to the financial reporting process.*

[23c] *The FRC issues "Guidance on Risk Management and Internal Control and Related Financial and Business Reporting" for directors on their responsibilities under the UK Corporate Governance Code. The guidance indicates that it is for the board to decide what arrangements to put in place to enable it to exercise its responsibilities. The guidance also indicates the nature of the information the board may include in its narrative statement about these matters. Supplementary considerations for the banking sector are provided in Guidance for Directors of Banks on Solvency and Liquidity Risk Management and the Going Concern Basis of Accounting.*

[23d] *The Guidance on Audit Committees also sets out other matters the audit committee should consider in relation to the annual audit cycle, including in relation to the audit plan and the auditor's findings.*

This will include an understanding of the rationale and supporting evidence for the auditor's significant professional judgments made in the course of the audit and in reaching the opinion on the financial statements, and of other matters communicated to the audit committee by the auditor in accordance with the requirements of paragraph 16-1, including relevant information communicated in accordance with the requirements of paragraphs 15 and 16. The auditor's communications include information regarding separate components of a group where relevant. In fulfilling its responsibilities set out above, the board will be assisted by the report from the audit committee on how the audit committee has discharged its responsibilities.

A28-3   The audit procedures that the auditor designs as part of the audit of the financial statements are not designed for the purpose of expressing an opinion on the effectiveness of the entity's system of internal control as a whole and accordingly the auditor does not express such an opinion on the basis of those procedures. However, communication of the auditor's views about the effectiveness of elements of the entity's system of internal control, based on the audit procedures performed in the audit of the financial statements, may help the audit committee and the board fulfil their respective responsibilities with respect to the entity's internal control and risk management systems.

A28-4   The auditor's understanding of the entity includes the entity's objectives and strategies and those related business risks that may result in risks of material misstatement, obtained in compliance with ISA (UK) 315 (Revised June 2016),[23e] and may also include other risks arising from the entity's business model that are relevant to an understanding of that model and the entity's strategy. To the extent that the auditor has obtained an understanding of such risks and the effectiveness of the entity's system of internal control in addressing them, communicating its views on those matters may be helpful to the audit committee and the board in their evaluation of whether the annual report is fair, balanced and understandable and provides the information necessary for users to assess the entity's position and performance, business model and strategy. However, the auditor is not required to design and perform audit procedures expressly for the purpose of forming views about the effectiveness of the entity's internal control in addressing such risks. Accordingly, to the extent applicable, the auditor may communicate that they have not obtained an understanding of, and therefore are not able to express views about, such risks and related aspects of the entity's internal control.

A28-5   The auditor's communication of views about the effectiveness of the entity's internal control may include, or refer to, the communication of significant deficiencies in internal control, if any, that is required by ISA (UK) 265. However, views about effectiveness can go beyond just identifying such deficiencies. For example they may include views about such matters as the entity's strategies for identifying and responding quickly to significant new financial or operational risks; the quality of the reports that the board receives to provide them with information about risks and the operation of internal control; or how the entity's systems compare in general terms with those of other relevant entities of which the auditor has knowledge, such as the impact on internal control effectiveness that may result from different approaches to maintaining an appropriate control environment. The auditor's

---

[23e] *ISA (UK) 315 (Revised June 2016), paragraph 11(d).*

communications include the auditor's views relating to separate components of a group where relevant.

Auditor Independence
(Ref: Para. 17)

A29   The auditor is required to comply with relevant ethical requirements, including those pertaining to independence, relating to financial statement audit engagements.[24]

A29-1   In the UK, auditors are subject to ethical requirements from two sources: the FRC's Ethical Standard concerning the integrity, objectivity and independence of the auditor,[24a] and the ethical pronouncements established by the auditor's relevant professional body.

A30   The relationships and other matters, and safeguards to be communicated, vary with the circumstances of the engagement, but generally address:

(a)   Threats to independence, which may be categorized as: self-interest threats, self-review threats, advocacy threats, familiarity threats, and intimidation threats; and

(b)   Safeguards created by the profession, legislation or regulation, safeguards within the entity, and safeguards within the firm's own systems and procedures.

A31   Relevant ethical requirements or law or regulation may also specify particular communications to those charged with governance in circumstances where breaches of independence requirements have been identified. For example, the International Ethics Standards Board for Accountants' Code of Ethics for Professional Accountants (IESBA Code) requires the auditor to communicate with those charged with governance in writing about any breach and the action the firm has taken or proposes to take.[25]

A32   The communication requirements relating to auditor independence that apply in the case of listed entities and public interest entities[25a] may also be appropriate in the case of some other entities, including those that may be of significant public interest, for example because they have a large number and wide range of stakeholders and considering the nature and size of the business. Examples of such entities may include financial institutions (such as banks, insurance companies, and pension funds), and other entities such as charities. On the other hand, there may be situations where communications regarding independence may not be relevant, for example, where all of those charged

---

[24]   *ISA (UK) 200 (Revised June 2016), Overall Objectives of the Independent Auditor and the Conduct of an Audit in Accordance with International Standards on Auditing (UK), paragraph 14.*

[24a]   *The FRC's Ethical Standard, Part B, Section 1 – General Requirements and Guidance, paragraphs 1.61 to 1.70 address communication with those charged with governance.*

[25]   *See Section 290.39–49 of the IESBA Code, which addresses breaches of independence.*
In the UK, the FRC's Ethical Standard, Part B, Section 1 – General Requirements and Guidance, paragraph 1.61 requires the audit partner to ensure that those charged with governance are "informed on a timely basis of all significant facts and matters that may bear upon the integrity, objectivity and independence of the firm or covered persons."

[25a]   *A public interest entity is defined in ISA (UK) 220 (Revised June 2016), paragraph 7(m)-1 in accordance with Article 2(13) of the Audit Directive. These public interest entities are distinct from entities that may be of significant public interest.*

with governance have been informed of relevant facts through their management activities. This is particularly likely where the entity is owner-managed, and the auditor's firm and network firms have little involvement with the entity beyond a financial statement audit.

Auditor Independence for Public Interest Entities
(Ref: Para. 17R-1)

A32-1   As part of the auditor's annual confirmation to the audit committee, the auditor identifies the ethical requirements relevant to the group audit that are applicable to component auditors in accordance with Supporting Ethical Provision 2.4 of the FRC's Ethical Standard.[25b]

Supplementary Matters
(Ref: Para. 3)

A33   The oversight of management by those charged with governance includes ensuring that the entity designs, implements and maintains appropriate internal control with regard to reliability of financial reporting, effectiveness and efficiency of operations and compliance with applicable laws and regulations.

A34   The auditor may become aware of supplementary matters that do not necessarily relate to the oversight of the financial reporting process but which are, nevertheless, likely to be significant to the responsibilities of those charged with governance in overseeing the strategic direction of the entity or the entity's obligations related to accountability. Such matters may include, for example, significant issues regarding governance structures or processes, and significant decisions or actions by senior management that lack appropriate authorization.

A35   In determining whether to communicate supplementary matters with those charged with governance, the auditor may discuss matters of this kind of which the auditor has become aware with the appropriate level of management, unless it is inappropriate to do so in the circumstances.

A36   If a supplementary matter is communicated, it may be appropriate for the auditor to make those charged with governance aware that:

(a)   Identification and communication of such matters is incidental to the purpose of the audit, which is to form an opinion on the financial statements;

(b)   No procedures were carried out with respect to the matter other than any that were necessary to form an opinion on the financial statements; and

(c)   No procedures were carried out to determine whether other such matters exist.

The Communication Process

Establishing the Communication Process
(Ref: Para. 18)

A37   Clear communication of the auditor's responsibilities, the planned scope and timing of the audit, and the expected general content of communications helps establish the basis for effective two-way communication.

A38   Matters that may also contribute to effective two-way communication include discussion of:

[25b] *FRC's Ethical Standard, Part A – Overarching Principles and Supporting Ethical Provisions, Supporting Ethical Provision 2.4.*

- The purpose of communications. When the purpose is clear, the auditor and those charged with governance are better placed to have a mutual understanding of relevant issues and the expected actions arising from the communication process.

- The form in which communications will be made.

- The person(s) in the engagement team and amongst those charged with governance who will communicate regarding particular matters.

- The auditor's expectation that communication will be two-way, and that those charged with governance will communicate with the auditor matters they consider relevant to the audit, for example, strategic decisions that may significantly affect the nature, timing and extent of audit procedures, the suspicion or the detection of fraud, and concerns with the integrity or competence of senior management.

- The process for taking action and reporting back on matters communicated by the auditor.

- The process for taking action and reporting back on matters communicated by those charged with governance.

The communication process will vary with the circumstances, including the size **A39** and governance structure of the entity, how those charged with governance operate, and the auditor's view of the significance of matters to be communicated. Difficulty in establishing effective two-way communication may indicate that the communication between the auditor and those charged with governance is not adequate for the purpose of the audit (see paragraph A52).

Considerations Specific to Smaller Entities

In the case of audits of smaller entities, the auditor may communicate in a less **A40** structured manner with those charged with governance than in the case of listed or larger entities.

Communication with Management

Many matters may be discussed with management in the ordinary course of an **A41** audit, including matters required by this ISA (UK) to be communicated with those charged with governance. Such discussions recognize management's executive responsibility for the conduct of the entity's operations and, in particular, management's responsibility for the preparation of the financial statements.

Before communicating matters with those charged with governance, the auditor **A42** may discuss them with management, unless that is inappropriate. For example, it may not be appropriate to discuss questions of management's competence or integrity with management. In addition to recognizing management's executive responsibility, these initial discussions may clarify facts and issues, and give management an opportunity to provide further information and explanations. Similarly, when the entity has an internal audit function, the auditor may discuss matters with appropriate individuals within the function before communicating with those charged with governance.

Communication with Third Parties

Those charged with governance may be required by law or regulation, or may **A43** wish to provide third parties, for example, bankers or certain regulatory authorities, with copies of a written communication from the auditor. In some cases, disclosure to third parties may be illegal or otherwise inappropriate. When a written communication prepared for those charged with governance is provided to third parties, it may be important in the circumstances that the third parties be informed that the communication was not prepared with them in mind, for example, by stating in written communications with those charged with governance:

(a)   That the communication has been prepared for the sole use of those charged with governance and, where applicable, the group management and the group auditor, and should not be relied upon by third parties;

(b)   That no responsibility is assumed by the auditor to third parties; and

(c)   Any restrictions on disclosure or distribution to third parties.

A44   In some jurisdictions the auditor may be required by law or regulation to, for example:

- Notify a regulatory or enforcement body of certain matters communicated with those charged with governance. For example, in some countries the auditor has a duty to report misstatements to authorities where management and those charged with governance fail to take corrective action;

- Submit copies of certain reports prepared for those charged with governance to relevant regulatory or funding bodies, or other bodies such as a central authority in the case of some public sector entities; or

- Make reports prepared for those charged with governance publicly available.

A45   Unless required by law or regulation to provide a third party with a copy of the auditor's written communications with those charged with governance, the auditor may need the prior consent of those charged with governance before doing so.

Forms of Communication
(Ref: Para. 19)

A46   Effective communication may involve structured presentations and written reports as well as less structured communications, including discussions. The auditor may communicate matters other than those identified in paragraphs 19–20R-1 either orally or in writing. Written communications may include an engagement letter that is provided to those charged with governance.

A46-1   The auditor discusses issues clearly and unequivocally with those charged with governance so that the implications of those issues are likely to be fully comprehended by them.

A47   In addition to the significance of a particular matter, the form of communication (e.g., whether to communicate orally or in writing, the extent of detail or summarization in the communication, and whether to communicate in a structured or unstructured manner) may be affected by such factors as:

- Whether a discussion of the matter will be included in the auditor's report. For example, when key audit matters are communicated in the auditor's report, the auditor may consider it necessary to communicate in writing about the matters determined to be key audit matters.

- Whether the matter has been satisfactorily resolved.

- Whether management has previously communicated the matter.

- The size, operating structure, control environment, and legal structure of the entity.

- In the case of an audit of special purpose financial statements, whether the auditor also audits the entity's general purpose financial statements.

- Legal requirements. In some jurisdictions, a written communication with those charged with governance is required in a prescribed form by local law.

- The expectations of those charged with governance, including arrangements made for periodic meetings or communications with the auditor.

- The amount of ongoing contact and dialogue the auditor has with those charged with governance.

- Whether there have been significant changes in the membership of a governing body.

The judgment of whether to communicate significant matters orally or in writing may also be affected by the evaluation, required by paragraph 22, of whether the two-way communication between the auditor and those charged with governance has been adequate for the purpose of the audit. The auditor may judge also that for effective communication a written communication is issued even if its content is limited to explaining that there is nothing the auditor wishes to draw to the attention of those charged with governance. To avoid doubt where there are no matters the auditor wishes to communicate in writing, the auditor may communicate that fact in writing to those charged with governance.   **A47-1**

When a significant matter is discussed with an individual member of those charged with governance, for example, the chair of an audit committee, it may be appropriate for the auditor to summarize the matter in later communications so that all of those charged with governance have full and balanced information.   **A48**

Timing of Communications
(Ref: Para. 21)

Timely communication throughout the audit contributes to the achievement of robust two-way dialogue between those charged with governance and the auditor. However, the appropriate timing for communications will vary with the circumstances of the engagement. Relevant circumstances include the significance and nature of the matter, and the action expected to be taken by those charged with governance. For example: **A49**

- Communications regarding planning matters may often be made early in the audit engagement and, for an initial engagement, may be made as part of agreeing the terms of the engagement.

- It may be appropriate to communicate a significant difficulty encountered during the audit as soon as practicable if those charged with governance are able to assist the auditor to overcome the difficulty, or if it is likely to lead to a modified opinion. Similarly, the auditor may communicate orally to those charged with governance as soon as practicable significant deficiencies in internal control that the auditor has identified, prior to communicating these in writing as required by ISA (UK) 265.[26]

---

[26] *ISA (UK) 265, paragraphs 9 and A14.*

- When ISA (UK) 701 applies, the auditor may communicate preliminary views about key audit matters when discussing the planned scope and timing of the audit (see paragraph A13), and the auditor also may have more frequent communications to further discuss such matters when communicating about significant audit findings.

- Communications regarding independence may be appropriate whenever significant judgments are made about threats to independence and related safeguards, for example, when accepting an engagement to provide non-audit services, and at a concluding discussion.

- Communications regarding findings from the audit, including the auditor's views about the qualitative aspects of the entity's accounting practices, may also be made as part of the concluding discussion.

- When auditing both general purpose and special purpose financial statements, it may be appropriate to coordinate the timing of communications.

A50   Other factors that may be relevant to the timing of communications include:

- The size, operating structure, control environment, and legal structure of the entity being audited.

- Any legal obligation to communicate certain matters within a specified timeframe.

- The expectations of those charged with governance, including arrangements made for periodic meetings or communications with the auditor.

- The time at which the auditor identifies certain matters, for example, the auditor may not identify a particular matter (e.g., non-compliance with a law) in time for preventive action to be taken, but communication of the matter may enable remedial action to be taken.

A50-1   Findings from the audit that are relevant to the financial statements, including the auditor's views about the qualitative aspects of the entity's accounting and financial reporting, are ordinarily communicated to those charged with governance before they approve the financial statements.

Public Interest Entities
(Ref: Para. 21R-1)

A50-2   Whilst the auditor is required to submit the additional report to the audit committee no later than the date of submission of the auditor's report, the auditor has regard to the requirement in paragraph 21 to communicate with those charged with governance on a timely basis and the requirement in 20R-1(c) which requires the auditor, where requested, to discuss key matters arising from the audit referred to in the additional report to the audit committee.

Adequacy of the Communication Process
(Ref: Para. 22)

A51   The auditor need not design specific procedures to support the evaluation of the two-way communication between the auditor and those charged with governance; rather, that evaluation may be based on observations resulting from audit procedures performed for other purposes. Such observations may include:

- The appropriateness and timeliness of actions taken by those charged with governance in response to matters raised by the auditor. Where significant matters raised in previous communications have not been dealt with effectively, it may be appropriate for the auditor to inquire as to why appropriate action has not been taken, and to consider raising the point again. This avoids the risk of giving an impression that the auditor is satisfied that the matter has been adequately addressed or is no longer significant.

- The apparent openness of those charged with governance in their communications with the auditor.

- The willingness and capacity of those charged with governance to meet with the auditor without management present.

- The apparent ability of those charged with governance to fully comprehend matters raised by the auditor, for example, the extent to which those charged with governance probe issues, and question recommendations made to them.

- Difficulty in establishing with those charged with governance a mutual understanding of the form, timing and expected general content of communications.

- Where all or some of those charged with governance are involved in managing the entity, their apparent awareness of how matters discussed with the auditor affect their broader governance responsibilities, as well as their management responsibilities.

- Whether the two-way communication between the auditor and those charged with governance meets applicable legal and regulatory requirements.

As noted in paragraph 4, effective two-way communication assists both the auditor and those charged with governance. Further, ISA (UK) 315 (Revised June 2016) identifies participation by those charged with governance, including their interaction with the internal audit function, if any, and external auditors, as an element of the entity's control environment.[27] Inadequate two-way communication may indicate an unsatisfactory control environment and influence the auditor's assessment of the risks of material misstatements. There is also a risk that the auditor may not have obtained sufficient appropriate audit evidence to form an opinion on the financial statements.   **A52**

If the two-way communication between the auditor and those charged with governance is not adequate and the situation cannot be resolved, the auditor may take such actions as: **A53**

- Modifying the auditor's opinion on the basis of a scope limitation.

- Obtaining legal advice about the consequences of different courses of action.

- Communicating with third parties (e.g., a regulator), or a higher authority in the governance structure that is outside the entity, such as the owners of a business (e.g., shareholders in a general meeting), or the responsible government minister or parliament in the public sector.

- Withdrawing from the engagement, where withdrawal is possible under applicable law or regulation.

[27] *ISA (UK) 315 (Revised June 2016), paragraph A77.*

Documentation
(Ref: Para. 23)

A54   Documentation of oral communication may include a copy of minutes prepared by the entity retained as part of the audit documentation where those minutes are an appropriate record of the communication.

Appendix 1

(Ref: Para. 3)

Specific Requirements in ISQC (UK) 1 and Other ISAs (UK) that Refer to Communications with Those Charged With Governance

This appendix identifies paragraphs in ISQC (UK) 1[1] and other ISAs (UK) that require communication of specific matters with those charged with governance. The list is not a substitute for considering the requirements and related application and other explanatory material in ISAs (UK).

- ISQC (UK) 1 (Revised June 2016), *Quality Control for Firms that Perform Audits and Reviews of Financial Statements, and Other Assurance and Related Services Engagements* – paragraph 30(a)

- ISA (UK) 240 (Revised June 2016), *The Auditor's Responsibilities Relating to Fraud in an Audit of Financial Statements* – paragraphs 21, 38(c)(i) and 40–42

- ISA (UK) 250 (Revised July 2017), Section A—*Consideration of Laws and Regulations in an Audit of Financial Statements* – paragraphs 15, 20 and 26–28

- ISA (UK) 265, *Communicating Deficiencies in Internal Control to Those Charged with Governance and Management* – paragraph 9

- ISA (UK) 450 (Revised June 2016), *Evaluation of Misstatements Identified during the Audit* – paragraphs 12–13

- ISA (UK) 505, *External Confirmations* – paragraph 9

- ISA (UK) 510 (Revised June 2016), *Initial Audit Engagements—Opening Balances* – paragraph 7

- ISA (UK) 550, *Related Parties* – paragraph 27

- ISA (UK) 560, *Subsequent Events* – paragraphs 7(b)–(c), 10(a), 13(b), 14(a) and 17

- ISA (UK) 570 (Revised June 2016), *Going Concern* – paragraph 25

- ISA (UK) 600 (Revised June 2016), *Special Considerations — Audits of Group Financial Statements (Including the Work of Component Auditors)* – paragraph 49

- ISA (UK) 610 (Revised June 2013), *Using the Work of Internal Auditors* – paragraphs 20 and 31

- ISA (UK) 700 (Revised June 2016), *Forming an Opinion and Reporting on Financial Statements* – paragraph 46

- ISA (UK) 701, *Communicating Key Audit Matters in the Independent Auditor's Report* – paragraph 17

---

[1] *ISQC (UK) 1 (Revised June 2016), Quality Control for Firms that Perform Audits and Reviews of Financial Statements, and Other Assurance and Related Services Engagements.*

- ISA (UK) 705 (Revised June 2016), *Modifications to the Opinion in the Independent Auditor's Report* – paragraphs 12, 14, 23 and 30

- ISA (UK) 706 (Revised June 2016), *Emphasis of Matter Paragraphs and Other Matter Paragraphs in the Independent Auditor's Report* – paragraph 12

- ISA (UK) 710, *Comparative Information—Corresponding Figures and Comparative Financial Statements* – paragraph 18

- ISA (UK) 720 (Revised June 2016), *The Auditor's Responsibilities Relating to Other Information* – paragraphs 17–19

Appendix 2

(Ref: Para. 16(a), A17)

Qualitative Aspects of Accounting Practices

The communication required by paragraph 16(a), and discussed in paragraph A19–A20, may include such matters as:

Accounting Policies

- The appropriateness of the accounting policies to the particular circumstances of the entity, having regard to the need to balance the cost of providing information with the likely benefit to users of the entity's financial statements. Where acceptable alternative accounting policies exist, the communication may include identification of the financial statement items that are affected by the choice of significant accounting policies as well as information on accounting policies used by similar entities.

- The initial selection of, and changes in significant accounting policies, including the application of new accounting pronouncements. The communication may include: the effect of the timing and method of adoption of a change in accounting policy on the current and future earnings of the entity; and the timing of a change in accounting policies in relation to expected new accounting pronouncements.

- The effect of significant accounting policies in controversial or emerging areas (or those unique to an industry, particularly when there is a lack of authoritative guidance or consensus).

- The effect of the timing of transactions in relation to the period in which they are recorded.

Accounting Estimates

- For items for which estimates are significant, issues discussed in ISA (UK) 540 (Revised June 2016),[1] including, for example:

  - How management identifies those transactions, events and conditions that may give rise to the need for accounting estimates to be recognized or disclosed in the financial statements.

  - Changes in circumstances that may give rise to new, or the need to revise existing, accounting estimates.

  - Whether management's decision to recognize, or to not recognize, the accounting estimates in the financial statements is in accordance with the applicable financial reporting framework.

  - Whether there has been or ought to have been a change from the prior period in the methods for making the accounting estimates and, if so, why, as well as the outcome of accounting estimates in prior periods.

  - Management's process for making accounting estimates (e.g., when management has used a model), including whether the selected measurement basis for the accounting estimate is in accordance with the applicable financial reporting framework.

---

[1] *ISQC (UK) 1 (Revised June 2016), Quality Control for Firms that Perform Audits and Reviews of Financial Statements, and Other Assurance and Related Services Engagements.*

- Whether the significant assumptions used by management in developing the accounting estimate are reasonable.

- Where relevant to the reasonableness of the significant assumptions used by management or the appropriate application of the applicable financial reporting framework, management's intent to carry out specific courses of action and its ability to do so.

- Risks of material misstatement.

- Indicators of possible management bias.

- How management has considered alternative assumptions or outcomes and why it has rejected them, or how management has otherwise addressed estimation uncertainty in making the accounting estimate.

- The adequacy of disclosure of estimation uncertainty in the financial statements.

Financial Statement Disclosures

- The issues involved, and related judgments made, in formulating particularly sensitive financial statement disclosures (e.g., disclosures related to revenue recognition, remuneration, going concern, subsequent events, and contingency issues).

- The overall neutrality, consistency and clarity of the disclosures in the financial statements.

Related Matters

- The potential effect on the financial statements of significant risks, exposures and uncertainties, such as pending litigation, that are disclosed in the financial statements.

- The extent to which the financial statements are affected by significant transactions, that are outside the normal course of business for the entity, or that otherwise appear to be unusual. This communication may highlight:

  - The non-recurring amounts recognized during the period.

  - The extent to which such transactions are separately disclosed in the financial statements.

  - Whether such transactions appear to have been designed to achieve a particular accounting or tax treatment, or a particular legal or regulatory objective.

  - Whether the form of such transactions appears overly complex or where extensive advice regarding the structuring of the transaction has been taken.

  - Where management is placing more emphasis on the need for a particular accounting treatment than on the underlying economics of the transaction.

- The factors affecting asset and liability carrying values, including the entity's bases for determining useful lives assigned to tangible and intangible assets. The communication may explain how factors affecting carrying values were selected and how alternative selections would have affected the financial statements.

- The selective correction of misstatements, for example, correcting misstatements with the effect of increasing reported earnings, but not those that have the effect of decreasing reported earnings.

ISA (UK) 265 Communicating Deficiencies in Internal Control to Those Charged With Governance and Management

(Effective for audits of financial statements for periods ending on or after 15 December 2010)

Contents

Paragraphs

Introduction   1 - 4
  Scope of this ISA (UK)   1 - 3
  Effective date   4

Objective   5

Definitions   6

Requirements   7 - 11

Application and other explanatory material   A1 - A30
  Determination of whether deficiencies in internal control have been identified   A1 - A4
  Significant deficiencies in internal control   A5 - A11
  Communication of deficiencies in internal control   A12 - A30

International Standard on Auditing (UK) (ISA (UK)) 265, *Communicating Deficiencies in Internal Control to Those Charged with Governance and Management*, should be read in conjunction with ISA (UK) 200 (Revised June 2016), *Overall Objectives of the Independent Auditor and the Conduct of an Audit in Accordance with International Standards on Auditing (UK)*.

Introduction

Scope of this ISA (UK)

1   This International Standard on Auditing (UK) (ISA (UK)) deals with the auditor's responsibility to communicate appropriately to those charged with governance and management deficiencies in internal control[1] that the auditor has identified in an audit of financial statements. This ISA (UK) does not impose additional responsibilities on the auditor regarding obtaining an understanding of internal control and designing and performing tests of controls over and above the requirements of ISA (UK) 315 (Revised June 2016) and ISA (UK) 330 (Revised June 2016).[2] ISA (UK) 260 (Revised June 2016)[3] establishes further requirements and provides guidance regarding the auditor's responsibility to communicate with those charged with governance in relation to the audit.

2   The auditor is required to obtain an understanding of internal control relevant to the audit when identifying and assessing the risks of material misstatement.[4] In making those risk assessments, the auditor considers internal control in order to design audit procedures that are appropriate in the circumstances, but not for the purpose of expressing an opinion on the effectiveness of internal control. The auditor may identify deficiencies in internal control not only during this risk assessment process but also at any other stage of the audit. This ISA (UK) specifies which identified deficiencies the auditor is required to communicate to those charged with governance and management.

3   Nothing in this ISA (UK) precludes the auditor from communicating to those charged with governance and management other internal control matters that the auditor has identified during the audit.

Effective Date

4   This ISA (UK) is effective for audits of financial statements for periods ending on or after 15 December 2010.

Objective

5   The objective of the auditor is to communicate appropriately to those charged with governance and management deficiencies in internal control that the auditor has identified during the audit and that, in the auditor's professional judgment, are of sufficient importance to merit their respective attentions.

Definitions

6   For purposes of the ISAs (UK), the following terms have the meanings attributed below:

---

[1] ISA (UK) 315 (Revised June 2016), *Identifying and Assessing the Risks of Material Misstatement through Understanding the Entity and Its Environment*, paragraphs 4 and 12.

[2] ISA (UK) 330 (Revised June 2016), *The Auditor's Responses to Assessed Risks*.

[3] ISA (UK) 260 (Revised June 2016), *Communication with Those Charged with Governance*.

[4] ISA (UK) 315 (Revised June 2016), paragraph 12. Paragraphs A60–A65 provide guidance on controls relevant to the audit.

(a) Deficiency in internal control – This exists when:

    (i) A control is designed, implemented or operated in such a way that it is unable to prevent, or detect and correct, misstatements in the financial statements on a timely basis; or

    (ii) A control necessary to prevent, or detect and correct, misstatements in the financial statements on a timely basis is missing.

(b) Significant deficiency in internal control – A deficiency or combination of deficiencies in internal control that, in the auditor's professional judgment, is of sufficient importance to merit the attention of those charged with governance. (Ref: Para. A5)

Requirements

The auditor shall determine whether, on the basis of the audit work performed, **7** the auditor has identified one or more deficiencies in internal control. (Ref: Para. A1–A4)

If the auditor has identified one or more deficiencies in internal control, the auditor **8** shall determine, on the basis of the audit work performed, whether, individually or in combination, they constitute significant deficiencies. (Ref: Para. A5–A11)

The auditor shall communicate in writing significant deficiencies in internal **9** control identified during the audit to those charged with governance on a timely basis. (Ref: Para. A12–A18, A27)

The auditor shall also communicate to management at an appropriate level of **10** responsibility on a timely basis: (Ref: Para. A19, A27)

(a) In writing, significant deficiencies in internal control that the auditor has communicated or intends to communicate to those charged with governance, unless it would be inappropriate to communicate directly to management in the circumstances; and (Ref: Para. A14, A20–A21)

(b) Other deficiencies in internal control identified during the audit that have not been communicated to management by other parties and that, in the auditor's professional judgment, are of sufficient importance to merit management's attention. (Ref: Para. A22–A26)

The auditor shall include in the written communication of significant deficiencies **11** in internal control:

(a) A description of the deficiencies and an explanation of their potential effects; and (Ref: Para. A28)

(b) Sufficient information to enable those charged with governance and management to understand the context of the communication. In particular, the auditor shall explain that: (Ref: Para. A29–A30)

    (i) The purpose of the audit was for the auditor to express an opinion on the financial statements;

    (ii) The audit included consideration of internal control relevant to the preparation of the financial statements in order to design audit procedures that are appropriate in the circumstances, but not for the purpose of expressing an opinion on the effectiveness of internal control; and

(iii)   The matters being reported are limited to those deficiencies that the auditor has identified during the audit and that the auditor has concluded are of sufficient importance to merit being reported to those charged with governance.

***

Application and Other Explanatory Material

Determination of Whether Deficiencies in Internal Control Have Been Identified (Ref: Para. 7)

A1   In determining whether the auditor has identified one or more deficiencies in internal control, the auditor may discuss the relevant facts and circumstances of the auditor's findings with the appropriate level of management. This discussion provides an opportunity for the auditor to alert management on a timely basis to the existence of deficiencies of which management may not have been previously aware. The level of management with whom it is appropriate to discuss the findings is one that is familiar with the internal control area concerned and that has the authority to take remedial action on any identified deficiencies in internal control. In some circumstances, it may not be appropriate for the auditor to discuss the auditor's findings directly with management, for example, if the findings appear to call management's integrity or competence into question (see paragraph A20).

A2   In discussing the facts and circumstances of the auditor's findings with management, the auditor may obtain other relevant information for further consideration, such as:

- Management's understanding of the actual or suspected causes of the deficiencies.

- Exceptions arising from the deficiencies that management may have noted, for example, misstatements that were not prevented by the relevant information technology (IT) controls.

- A preliminary indication from management of its response to the findings.

Considerations Specific to Smaller Entities

A3   While the concepts underlying control activities in smaller entities are likely to be similar to those in larger entities, the formality with which they operate will vary. Further, smaller entities may find that certain types of control activities are not necessary because of controls applied by management. For example, management's sole authority for granting credit to customers and approving significant purchases can provide effective control over important account balances and transactions, lessening or removing the need for more detailed control activities.

A4   Also, smaller entities often have fewer employees which may limit the extent to which segregation of duties is practicable. However, in a small owner-managed entity, the owner-manager may be able to exercise more effective oversight than in a larger entity. This higher level of management oversight needs to be balanced against the greater potential for management override of controls.

Significant Deficiencies in Internal Control
(Ref: Para. 6(b), 8)

The significance of a deficiency or a combination of deficiencies in internal **A5** control depends not only on whether a misstatement has actually occurred, but also on the likelihood that a misstatement could occur and the potential magnitude of the misstatement. Significant deficiencies may therefore exist even though the auditor has not identified misstatements during the audit.

Examples of matters that the auditor may consider in determining whether a **A6** deficiency or combination of deficiencies in internal control constitutes a significant deficiency include:

- The likelihood of the deficiencies leading to material misstatements in the financial statements in the future.

- The susceptibility to loss or fraud of the related asset or liability.

- The subjectivity and complexity of determining estimated amounts, such as fair value accounting estimates.

- The financial statement amounts exposed to the deficiencies.

- The volume of activity that has occurred or could occur in the account balance or class of transactions exposed to the deficiency or deficiencies.

- The importance of the controls to the financial reporting process; for example:

  - General monitoring controls (such as oversight of management).

  - Controls over the prevention and detection of fraud.

  - Controls over the selection and application of significant accounting policies.

  - Controls over significant transactions with related parties.

  - Controls over significant transactions outside the entity's normal course of business.

  - Controls over the period-end financial reporting process (such as controls over non-recurring journal entries).

- The cause and frequency of the exceptions detected as a result of the deficiencies in the controls.

- The interaction of the deficiency with other deficiencies in internal control.

Indicators of significant deficiencies in internal control include, for example: **A7**

- Evidence of ineffective aspects of the control environment, such as:

  - Indications that significant transactions in which management is financially interested are not being appropriately scrutinized by those charged with governance.

  - Identification of management fraud, whether or not material, that was not prevented by the entity's internal control.

  - Management's failure to implement appropriate remedial action on significant deficiencies previously communicated.

- Absence of a risk assessment process within the entity where such a process would ordinarily be expected to have been established.

- Evidence of an ineffective entity risk assessment process, such as management's failure to identify a risk of material misstatement that the auditor would expect the entity's risk assessment process to have identified.

- Evidence of an ineffective response to identified significant risks (for example, absence of controls over such a risk).

- Misstatements detected by the auditor's procedures that were not prevented, or detected and corrected, by the entity's internal control.

- Restatement of previously issued financial statements to reflect the correction of a material misstatement due to error or fraud.

- Evidence of management's inability to oversee the preparation of the financial statements.

A8   Controls may be designed to operate individually or in combination to effectively prevent, or detect and correct, misstatements.[5] For example, controls over accounts receivable may consist of both automated and manual controls designed to operate together to prevent, or detect and correct, misstatements in the account balance. A deficiency in internal control on its own may not be sufficiently important to constitute a significant deficiency. However, a combination of deficiencies affecting the same account balance or disclosure, relevant assertion, or component of internal control may increase the risks of misstatement to such an extent as to give rise to a significant deficiency.

A9   Law or regulation in some jurisdictions may establish a requirement (particularly for audits of listed entities) for the auditor to communicate to those charged with governance or to other relevant parties (such as regulators) one or more specific types of deficiency in internal control that the auditor has identified during the audit. Where law or regulation has established specific terms and definitions for these types of deficiency and requires the auditor to use these terms and definitions for the purpose of the communication, the auditor uses such terms and definitions when communicating in accordance with the legal or regulatory requirement.

A10   Where the jurisdiction has established specific terms for the types of deficiency in internal control to be communicated but has not defined such terms, it may be necessary for the auditor to use judgment to determine the matters to be communicated further to the legal or regulatory requirement. In doing so, the auditor may consider it appropriate to have regard to the requirements and guidance in this ISA (UK). For example, if the purpose of the legal or regulatory requirement is to bring to the attention of those charged with governance certain internal control matters of which they should be aware, it may be appropriate to regard such matters as being generally equivalent to the significant deficiencies required by this ISA (UK) to be communicated to those charged with governance.

A11   The requirements of this ISA (UK) remain applicable notwithstanding that law or regulation may require the auditor to use specific terms or definitions.

---

[5] *ISA (UK) 315 (Revised June 2016), paragraph A66.*

Communication of Deficiencies in Internal Control

Communication of Significant Deficiencies in Internal Control to Those Charged with Governance
(Ref: Para. 9)

Communicating significant deficiencies in writing to those charged with **A12** governance reflects the importance of these matters, and assists those charged with governance in fulfilling their oversight responsibilities. ISA (UK) 260 (Revised June 2016) establishes relevant considerations regarding communication with those charged with governance when all of them are involved in managing the entity.[6]

In the UK, where applicable, timely communication of significant deficiencies, **A12-1** in writing, to directors of listed entities can assist them to comply with the provisions of the UK Corporate Governance Code relating to internal control and reporting to shareholders.

In determining when to issue the written communication, the auditor may consider **A13** whether receipt of such communication would be an important factor in enabling those charged with governance to discharge their oversight responsibilities. In addition, for listed entities in certain jurisdictions, those charged with governance may need to receive the auditor's written communication before the date of approval of the financial statements in order to discharge specific responsibilities in relation to internal control for regulatory or other purposes. For other entities, the auditor may issue the written communication at a later date. Nevertheless, in the latter case, as the auditor's written communication of significant deficiencies forms part of the final audit file, the written communication is subject to the overriding requirement[7] for the auditor to complete the assembly of the final audit file on a timely basis. ISA (UK) 230 (Revised June 2016) states that an appropriate time limit within which to complete the assembly of the final audit file is ordinarily not more than 60 days after the date of the auditor's report.[8]

For audits of financial statements of public interest entities, ISA (UK) 260 **A13-1** (Revised June 2016)[8a] requires the auditor to communicate in the additional report to the audit committee any significant deficiencies in the entity's internal financial control system or in the accounting system, and whether or not the deficiencies reported have been resolved by management.

Regardless of the timing of the written communication of significant deficiencies, **A14** the auditor may communicate these orally in the first instance to management and, when appropriate, to those charged with governance to assist them in taking timely remedial action to minimize the risks of material misstatement. Doing so, however, does not relieve the auditor of the responsibility to communicate the significant deficiencies in writing, as this ISA (UK) requires.

The level of detail at which to communicate significant deficiencies is a matter of **A15** the auditor's professional judgment in the circumstances. Factors that the auditor may consider in determining an appropriate level of detail for the communication include, for example:

---

[6] *ISA (UK) 260 (Revised June 2016), paragraph 13.*

[7] *ISA (UK) 230 (Revised June 2016), Audit Documentation, paragraph 14.*

[8] *ISA (UK) 230 (Revised June 2016), paragraph A21.*

[8a] *ISA (UK) 260 (Revised June 2016), paragraph 16R-2(j).*

- The nature of the entity. For instance, the communication required for a public interest entity may be different from that for a non-public interest entity.

- The size and complexity of the entity. For instance, the communication required for a complex entity may be different from that for an entity operating a simple business.

- The nature of significant deficiencies that the auditor has identified.

- The entity's governance composition. For instance, more detail may be needed if those charged with governance include members who do not have significant experience in the entity's industry or in the affected areas.

- Legal or regulatory requirements regarding the communication of specific types of deficiency in internal control.

A16   Management and those charged with governance may already be aware of significant deficiencies that the auditor has identified during the audit and may have chosen not to remedy them because of cost or other considerations. The responsibility for evaluating the costs and benefits of implementing remedial action rests with management and those charged with governance. Accordingly, the requirement in paragraph 9 applies regardless of cost or other considerations that management and those charged with governance may consider relevant in determining whether to remedy such deficiencies.

A17   The fact that the auditor communicated a significant deficiency to those charged with governance and management in a previous audit does not eliminate the need for the auditor to repeat the communication if remedial action has not yet been taken. If a previously communicated significant deficiency remains, the current year's communication may repeat the description from the previous communication, or simply reference the previous communication. The auditor may ask management or, where appropriate, those charged with governance, why the significant deficiency has not yet been remedied. A failure to act, in the absence of a rational explanation, may in itself represent a significant deficiency.

Considerations Specific to Smaller Entities

A18   In the case of audits of smaller entities, the auditor may communicate in a less structured manner with those charged with governance than in the case of larger entities.

Communication of Deficiencies in Internal Control to Management
(Ref: Para. 10)

A19   Ordinarily, the appropriate level of management is the one that has responsibility and authority to evaluate the deficiencies in internal control and to take the necessary remedial action. For significant deficiencies, the appropriate level is likely to be the chief executive officer or chief financial officer (or equivalent) as these matters are also required to be communicated to those charged with governance. For other deficiencies in internal control, the appropriate level may be operational management with more direct involvement in the control areas affected and with the authority to take appropriate remedial action.

Communication of Significant Deficiencies in Internal Control to Management
(Ref: Para. 10(a))

Certain identified significant deficiencies in internal control may call into question   **A20**
the integrity or competence of management. For example, there may be evidence
of fraud or intentional non-compliance with laws and regulations by management,
or management may exhibit an inability to oversee the preparation of adequate
financial statements that may raise doubt about management's competence.
Accordingly, it may not be appropriate to communicate such deficiencies
directly to management.

ISA (UK) 250 (Revised June 2016) establishes requirements and provides   **A21**
guidance on the reporting of identified or suspected non-compliance with laws
and regulations, including when those charged with governance are themselves
involved in such noncompliance.[9] ISA (UK) 240 (Revised June 2016) establishes
requirements and provides guidance regarding communication to those charged
with governance when the auditor has identified fraud or suspected fraud
involving management.[10]

Communication of Other Deficiencies in Internal Control to Management
(Ref: Para. 10(b))

During the audit, the auditor may identify other deficiencies in internal control that   **A22**
are not significant deficiencies but that may be of sufficient importance to merit
management's attention. The determination as to which other deficiencies in
internal control merit management's attention is a matter of professional judgment
in the circumstances, taking into account the likelihood and potential magnitude of
misstatements that may arise in the financial statements as a result of those
deficiencies.

The communication of other deficiencies in internal control that merit   **A23**
management's attention need not be in writing but may be oral. Where the
auditor has discussed the facts and circumstances of the auditor's findings with
management, the auditor may consider an oral communication of the other
deficiencies to have been made to management at the time of these discussions.
Accordingly, a formal communication need not be made subsequently.

If the auditor has communicated deficiencies in internal control other than   **A24**
significant deficiencies to management in a prior period and management has
chosen not to remedy them for cost or other reasons, the auditor need not repeat
the communication in the current period. The auditor is also not required to repeat
information about such deficiencies if it has been previously communicated to
management by other parties, such as the internal audit function or regulators. It
may, however, be appropriate for the auditor to re-communicate these other
deficiencies if there has been a change of management, or if new information has
come to the auditor's attention that alters the prior understanding of the auditor and
management regarding the deficiencies. Nevertheless, the failure of management
to remedy other deficiencies in internal control that were previously
communicated may become a significant deficiency requiring communication
with those charged with governance. Whether this is the case depends on the
auditor's judgment in the circumstances.

---

[9] *ISA (UK) 250 (Revised June 2016), Consideration of Laws and Regulations in an Audit of Financial Statements, paragraphs 22–28.*

[10] *ISA (UK) 240 (Revised June 2016), The Auditor's Responsibilities Relating to Fraud in an Audit of Financial Statements, paragraph 41.*

A25   In some circumstances, those charged with governance may wish to be made aware of the details of other deficiencies in internal control the auditor has communicated to management, or be briefly informed of the nature of the other deficiencies. Alternatively, the auditor may consider it appropriate to inform those charged with governance of the communication of the other deficiencies to management. In either case, the auditor may report orally or in writing to those charged with governance as appropriate.

A26   ISA (UK) 260 (Revised June 2016) establishes relevant considerations regarding communication with those charged with governance when all of them are involved in managing the entity.[11]

Considerations Specific to Public Sector Entities
(Ref: Para. 9–10)

A27   Public sector auditors may have additional responsibilities to communicate deficiencies in internal control that the auditor has identified during the audit, in ways, at a level of detail and to parties not envisaged in this ISA (UK). For example, significant deficiencies may have to be communicated to the legislature or other governing body. Law, regulation or other authority may also mandate that public sector auditors report deficiencies in internal control, irrespective of the significance of the potential effects of those deficiencies. Further, legislation may require public sector auditors to report on broader internal control-related matters than the deficiencies in internal control required to be communicated by this ISA (UK), for example, controls related to compliance with legislative authorities, regulations, or provisions of contracts or grant agreements.

Content of Written Communication of Significant Deficiencies in Internal Control
(Ref: Para. 11)

A28   In explaining the potential effects of the significant deficiencies, the auditor need not quantify those effects. The significant deficiencies may be grouped together for reporting purposes where it is appropriate to do so. The auditor may also include in the written communication suggestions for remedial action on the deficiencies, management's actual or proposed responses, and a statement as to whether or not the auditor has undertaken any steps to verify whether management's responses have been implemented.

A29   The auditor may consider it appropriate to include the following information as additional context for the communication:

- An indication that if the auditor had performed more extensive procedures on internal control, the auditor might have identified more deficiencies to be reported, or concluded that some of the reported deficiencies need not, in fact, have been reported.

- An indication that such communication has been provided for the purposes of those charged with governance, and that it may not be suitable for other purposes.

A30   Law or regulation may require the auditor or management to furnish a copy of the auditor's written communication on significant deficiencies to appropriate regulatory authorities. Where this is the case, the auditor's written communication may identify such regulatory authorities.

---

[11] *ISA (UK) 260 (Revised June 2016), paragraph 13.*

ISA (UK) 300 (Revised June 2016) Planning an Audit of Financial Statements

(Effective for audits of financial statements for periods commencing on or after 17 June 2016)

Contents

Paragraphs

Introduction   1 - 3
Scope of this ISA (UK)   1
The role and timing of planning   2
Effective date   3

Objective   4

Requirements   5 - 13
Involvement of key engagement team members   5
Preliminary engagement activities   6
Planning activities   7 - 11
Documentation   12
Additional considerations in initial audit engagements   13

Application and other explanatory material   A1 - A20
The role and timing of planning   A1 - A3
Involvement of key engagement team members   A4
Preliminary engagement activities   A5 - A7
Planning activities   A8 - A15
Documentation   A16 - A19
Additional considerations in initial audit engagements   A20

Appendix: Considerations in establishing the overall audit strategy

International Standard on Auditing (UK) (ISA (UK)) 300 (Revised June 2016), *Planning an Audit of Financial Statements*, should be read in conjunction with ISA (UK) 200 (Revised June 2016), *Overall Objectives of the Independent Auditor and the Conduct of an Audit in Accordance with International Standards on Auditing (UK)*.

Introduction

Scope of this ISA (UK)

1   This International Standard on Auditing (UK) (ISA (UK)) deals with the auditor's responsibility to plan an audit of financial statements. This ISA (UK) is written in the context of recurring audits. Additional considerations in an initial audit engagement are separately identified.

The Role and Timing of Planning

2   Planning an audit involves establishing the overall audit strategy for the engagement and developing an audit plan. Adequate planning benefits the audit of financial statements in several ways, including the following: (Ref: Para. A1–A3)

- Helping the auditor to devote appropriate attention to important areas of the audit.

- Helping the auditor identify and resolve potential problems on a timely basis.

- Helping the auditor properly organize and manage the audit engagement so that it is performed in an effective and efficient manner.

- Assisting in the selection of engagement team members with appropriate levels of capabilities and competence to respond to anticipated risks, and the proper assignment of work to them.

- Facilitating the direction and supervision of engagement team members and the review of their work.

- Assisting, where applicable, in coordination of work done by auditors of components and experts.

Effective Date

3   This ISA (UK) is effective for audits of financial statements for periods commencing on or after 17 June 2016. Earlier adoption is permitted.

Objective

4   The objective of the auditor is to plan the audit so that it will be performed in an effective manner.

Requirements

Involvement of Key Engagement Team Members

5   The engagement partner and other key members of the engagement team shall be involved in planning the audit, including planning and participating in the discussion among engagement team members. (Ref: Para. A4)

Preliminary Engagement Activities

6   The auditor shall undertake the following activities at the beginning of the current audit engagement:

(a) Performing procedures required by ISA (UK) 220 (Revised June 2016) regarding the continuance of the client relationship and the specific audit engagement;[1]

(b) Evaluating compliance with relevant ethical requirements, including independence, in accordance with ISA (UK) 220 (Revised June 2016);[2] and

(c) Establishing an understanding of the terms of the engagement, as required by ISA (UK) 210 (Revised June 2016).[3] (Ref: Para. A5–A7)

Planning Activities

The auditor shall establish an overall audit strategy that sets the scope, timing and direction of the audit, and that guides the development of the audit plan. **7**

In establishing the overall audit strategy, the auditor shall: **8**

(a) Identify the characteristics of the engagement that define its scope;

(b) Ascertain the reporting objectives of the engagement to plan the timing of the audit and the nature of the communications required;

(c) Consider the factors that, in the auditor's professional judgment, are significant in directing the engagement team's efforts;

(d) Consider the results of preliminary engagement activities and, where applicable, whether knowledge gained on other engagements performed by the engagement partner for the entity is relevant; and

(e) Ascertain the nature, timing and extent of resources necessary to perform the engagement. (Ref: Para. A8–A11)

The auditor shall develop an audit plan that shall include a description of: **9**

(a) The nature, timing and extent of planned risk assessment procedures, as determined under ISA (UK) 315 (Revised June 2016).[4]

(b) The nature, timing and extent of planned further audit procedures at the assertion level, as determined under ISA (UK) 330 (Revised June 2016).[5]

(c) Other planned audit procedures that are required to be carried out so that the engagement complies with ISAs (UK). (Ref: Para. A12–A12b)

The auditor shall update and change the overall audit strategy and the audit plan as necessary during the course of the audit. (Ref: Para. A13) **10**

The auditor shall plan the nature, timing and extent of direction and supervision of engagement team members and the review of their work. (Ref: Para. A14–A15) **11**

Documentation

The auditor shall include in the audit documentation:[6] **12**

(a) The overall audit strategy;

(b) The audit plan; and

---

[1] *ISA (UK) 220 (Revised June 2016), Quality Control for an Audit of Financial Statements, paragraphs 12–13.*

[2] *ISA (UK) 220 (Revised June 2016), paragraphs 9–11.*

[3] *ISA (UK) 210 (Revised June 2016), Agreeing the Terms of Audit Engagements, paragraphs 9–13.*

[4] *ISA (UK) 315 (Revised June 2016), Identifying and Assessing the Risks of Material Misstatement through Understanding the Entity and Its Environment.*

[5] *ISA (UK) 330 (Revised June 2016), The Auditor's Responses to Assessed Risks.*

[6] *ISA (UK) 230 (Revised June 2016), Audit Documentation, paragraphs 8–11, and paragraph A6.*

(c)   Any significant changes made during the audit engagement to the overall audit strategy or the audit plan, and the reasons for such changes. (Ref: Para. A16–A19)

Additional Considerations in Initial Audit Engagements

13   The auditor shall undertake the following activities prior to starting an initial audit:

(a)   Performing procedures required by ISA (UK) 220 (Revised June 2016) regarding the acceptance of the client relationship and the specific audit engagement;[7] and

(b)   Communicating with the predecessor auditor, where there has been a change of auditors, in compliance with relevant ethical requirements. (Ref: Para. A20)

***

Application and Other Explanatory Material

The Role and Timing of Planning
(Ref: Para. 2)

A1   The nature and extent of planning activities will vary according to the size and complexity of the entity, the key engagement team members' previous experience with the entity, and changes in circumstances that occur during the audit engagement.

A2   Planning is not a discrete phase of an audit, but rather a continual and iterative process that often begins shortly after (or in connection with) the completion of the previous audit and continues until the completion of the current audit engagement. Planning, however, includes consideration of the timing of certain activities and audit procedures that need to be completed prior to the performance of further audit procedures. For example, planning includes the need to consider, prior to the auditor's identification and assessment of the risks of material misstatement, such matters as:

● The analytical procedures to be applied as risk assessment procedures.

● Obtaining a general understanding of the legal and regulatory framework applicable to the entity and how the entity is complying with that framework.

● The determination of materiality.

● The involvement of experts.

● The performance of other risk assessment procedures.

A3   The auditor may decide to discuss elements of planning with the entity's management to facilitate the conduct and management of the audit engagement (for example, to coordinate some of the planned audit procedures with the work of the entity's personnel). Although these discussions often occur, the overall audit strategy and the audit plan remain the auditor's responsibility. When discussing matters included in the overall audit strategy or audit plan, care is required in order not to compromise the effectiveness of the audit. For example, discussing the

---

[7] *ISA (UK) 220 (Revised June 2016), paragraphs 12–13.*

nature and timing of detailed audit procedures with management may compromise the effectiveness of the audit by making the audit procedures too predictable.

Involvement of Key Engagement Team Members
(Ref: Para. 5)

The involvement of the engagement partner and other key members of the engagement team in planning the audit draws on their experience and insight, thereby enhancing the effectiveness and efficiency of the planning process.[8]   **A4**

Preliminary Engagement Activities
(Ref: Para. 6)

Performing the preliminary engagement activities specified in paragraph 6 at the beginning of the current audit engagement assists the auditor in identifying and evaluating events or circumstances that may adversely affect the auditor's ability to plan and perform the audit engagement.   **A5**

Performing these preliminary engagement activities enables the auditor to plan an audit engagement for which, for example: **A6**

- The auditor maintains the necessary independence and ability to perform the engagement.

- There are no issues with management[8a] integrity that may affect the auditor's willingness to continue the engagement.

- There is no misunderstanding with the client as to the terms of the engagement.

The auditor's consideration of client continuance and relevant ethical requirements, including independence, occurs throughout the audit engagement as conditions and changes in circumstances occur. Performing initial procedures on both client continuance and evaluation of relevant ethical requirements (including independence) at the beginning of the current audit engagement means that they are completed prior to the performance of other significant activities for the current audit engagement. For continuing audit engagements, such initial procedures often occur shortly after (or in connection with) the completion of the previous audit.   **A7**

Planning Activities

The Overall Audit Strategy
(Ref: Para. 7–8)

The process of establishing the overall audit strategy assists the auditor to determine, subject to the completion of the auditor's risk assessment procedures, such matters as: **A8**

---

[8] *ISA (UK) 315 (Revised June 2016), paragraph 10, establishes requirements and provides guidance on the engagement team's discussion of the susceptibility of the entity to material misstatements of the financial statements. ISA (UK) 240 (Revised June 2016), The Auditor's Responsibilities Relating to Fraud in an Audit of Financial Statements, paragraph 15, provides guidance on the emphasis given during this discussion to the susceptibility of the entity's financial statements to material misstatement due to fraud.*

[8a] *In the UK, the auditor is also concerned to establish that there are no issues with the integrity of those charged with governance that may affect the auditor's willingness to continue the engagement.*

- The resources to deploy for specific audit areas, such as the use of appropriately experienced team members for high risk areas or the involvement of experts on complex matters;

- The amount of resources to allocate to specific audit areas, such as the number of team members assigned to observe the inventory count at material locations, the extent of review of other auditors' work in the case of group audits, or the audit budget in hours to allocate to high risk areas;

- When these resources are to be deployed, such as whether at an interim audit stage or at key cutoff dates; and

- How such resources are managed, directed and supervised, such as when team briefing and debriefing meetings are expected to be held, how engagement partner and manager reviews are expected to take place (for example, on-site or off-site), and whether to complete engagement quality control reviews.

A9   The Appendix lists examples of considerations in establishing the overall audit strategy.

A10   Once the overall audit strategy has been established, an audit plan can be developed to address the various matters identified in the overall audit strategy, taking into account the need to achieve the audit objectives through the efficient use of the auditor's resources. The establishment of the overall audit strategy and the detailed audit plan are not necessarily discrete or sequential processes, but are closely inter-related since changes in one may result in consequential changes to the other.

Considerations Specific to Smaller Entities

A11   In audits of small entities, the entire audit may be conducted by a very small audit team. Many audits of small entities involve the engagement partner (who may be a sole practitioner) working with one engagement team member (or without any engagement team members). With a smaller team, coordination of, and communication between, team members are easier. Establishing the overall audit strategy for the audit of a small entity need not be a complex or time-consuming exercise; it varies according to the size of the entity, the complexity of the audit, and the size of the engagement team. For example, a brief memorandum prepared at the completion of the previous audit, based on a review of the working papers and highlighting issues identified in the audit just completed, updated in the current period based on discussions with the owner-manager, can serve as the documented audit strategy for the current audit engagement if it covers the matters noted in paragraph 8.

The Audit Plan
(Ref: Para. 9)

A12   The audit plan is more detailed than the overall audit strategy in that it includes the nature, timing and extent of audit procedures to be performed by engagement team members. Planning for these audit procedures takes place over the course of the audit as the audit plan for the engagement develops. For example, planning of the auditor's risk assessment procedures occurs early in the audit process. However, planning the nature, timing and extent of specific further audit procedures depends on the outcome of those risk assessment procedures. In addition, the auditor may begin the execution of further audit procedures for some classes of transactions, account balances and disclosures before planning all remaining further audit procedures.

Determining the nature, timing and extent of planned risk assessment procedures, and the further audit procedures, as they relate to disclosures is important in light of both the wide range of information and the level of detail that may be encompassed in those disclosures. Further, certain disclosures may contain information that is obtained from outside of the general and subsidiary ledgers, which may also affect the assessed risks and the nature, timing and extent of audit procedures to address them.   **A12a**

Consideration of disclosures early in the audit assists the auditor in giving appropriate attention to, and planning adequate time for, addressing disclosures in the same way as classes of transactions, events and account balances. Early consideration may also help the auditor to determine the effects on the audit of: **A12b**

- Significant new or revised disclosures required as a result of changes in the entity's environment, financial condition or activities (for example, a change in the required identification of segments and reporting of segment information arising from a significant business combination);

- Significant new or revised disclosures arising from changes in the applicable financial reporting framework;

- The need for the involvement of an auditor's expert to assist with audit procedures related to particular disclosures (for example, disclosures related to pension or other retirement benefit obligations); and

- Matters relating to disclosures that the auditor may wish to discuss with those charged with governance.[9]

Changes to Planning Decisions during the Course of the Audit
(Ref: Para. 10)

As a result of unexpected events, changes in conditions, or the audit evidence obtained from the results of audit procedures, the auditor may need to modify the overall audit strategy and audit plan and thereby the resulting planned nature, timing and extent of further audit procedures, based on the revised consideration of assessed risks. This may be the case when information comes to the auditor's attention that differs significantly from the information available when the auditor planned the audit procedures. For example, audit evidence obtained through the performance of substantive procedures may contradict the audit evidence obtained through tests of controls.   **A13**

Direction, Supervision and Review
(Ref: Para. 11)

The nature, timing and extent of the direction and supervision of engagement team members and review of their work vary depending on many factors, including: **A14**

- The size and complexity of the entity.

- The area of the audit.

- The assessed risks of material misstatement (for example, an increase in the assessed risk of material misstatement for a given area of the audit ordinarily requires a corresponding increase in the extent and timeliness of direction

---

[9] ISA (UK) 260 (Revised June 2016), *Communication with Those Charged With Governance*, paragraph A12.

and supervision of engagement team members, and a more detailed review of their work).

- The capabilities and competence of the individual team members performing the audit work.

ISA (UK) 220 (Revised June 2016) contains further guidance on the direction, supervision and review of audit work.[10]

Considerations Specific to Smaller Entities

A15   If an audit is carried out entirely by the engagement partner, questions of direction and supervision of engagement team members and review of their work do not arise. In such cases, the engagement partner, having personally conducted all aspects of the work, will be aware of all material issues. Forming an objective view on the appropriateness of the judgments made in the course of the audit can present practical problems when the same individual also performs the entire audit. If particularly complex or unusual issues are involved, and the audit is performed by a sole practitioner, it may be desirable to consult with other suitably-experienced auditors or the auditor's professional body.

Documentation
(Ref: Para. 12)

A16   The documentation of the overall audit strategy is a record of the key decisions considered necessary to properly plan the audit and to communicate significant matters to the engagement team. For example, the auditor may summarize the overall audit strategy in the form of a memorandum that contains key decisions regarding the overall scope, timing and conduct of the audit.

A17   The documentation of the audit plan is a record of the planned nature, timing and extent of risk assessment procedures and further audit procedures at the assertion level in response to the assessed risks. It also serves as a record of the proper planning of the audit procedures that can be reviewed and approved prior to their performance. The auditor may use standard audit programs or audit completion checklists, tailored as needed to reflect the particular engagement circumstances.

A18   A record of the significant changes to the overall audit strategy and the audit plan, and resulting changes to the planned nature, timing and extent of audit procedures, explains why the significant changes were made, and the overall strategy and audit plan finally adopted for the audit. It also reflects the appropriate response to the significant changes occurring during the audit.

Considerations Specific to Smaller Entities

A19   As discussed in paragraph A11, a suitable, brief memorandum may serve as the documented strategy for the audit of a smaller entity. For the audit plan, standard audit programs or checklists (see paragraph A17) drawn up on the assumption of few relevant control activities, as is likely to be the case in a smaller entity, may be used provided that they are tailored to the circumstances of the engagement, including the auditor's risk assessments.

---

[10] *ISA (UK) 220 (Revised June 2016), paragraphs 15–17.*

Additional Considerations in Initial Audit Engagements
(Ref: Para. 13)

The purpose and objective of planning the audit are the same whether the audit is **A20**
an initial or recurring engagement. However, for an initial audit, the auditor may
need to expand the planning activities because the auditor does not ordinarily have
the previous experience with the entity that is considered when planning recurring
engagements. For an initial audit engagement, additional matters the auditor may
consider in establishing the overall audit strategy and audit plan include the
following:

- Unless prohibited by law or regulation, arrangements to be made with the
  predecessor auditor, for example, to review the predecessor auditor's
  working papers.

- Any major issues (including the application of accounting principles or of
  auditing and reporting standards) discussed with management in connection
  with the initial selection as auditor, the communication of these matters to
  those charged with governance and how these matters affect the overall
  audit strategy and audit plan.

- The audit procedures necessary to obtain sufficient appropriate audit
  evidence regarding opening balances.[11]

- Other procedures required by the firm's system of quality control for initial
  audit engagements (for example, the firm's system of quality control may
  require the involvement of another partner or senior individual to review the
  overall audit strategy prior to commencing significant audit procedures or to
  review reports prior to their issuance).

---

[11] *ISA (UK) 510 (Revised June 2016), Initial Audit Engagements—Opening Balances.*

Appendix

(Ref: Para. 7–8, A8–A11)

Considerations in Establishing the Overall Audit Strategy

This appendix provides examples of matters the auditor may consider in establishing the overall audit strategy. Many of these matters will also influence the auditor's detailed audit plan. The examples provided cover a broad range of matters applicable to many engagements. While some of the matters referred to below may be required by other ISAs (UK), not all matters are relevant to every audit engagement and the list is not necessarily complete.

Characteristics of the Engagement

- The financial reporting framework on which the financial information to be audited has been prepared, including any need for reconciliations to another financial reporting framework.

- Industry-specific reporting requirements such as reports mandated by industry regulators.

- The expected audit coverage, including the number and locations of components to be included.

- The nature of the control relationships between a parent and its components that determine how the group is to be consolidated.

- The extent to which components are audited by other auditors.

- The nature of the business segments to be audited, including the need for specialized knowledge.

- The reporting currency to be used, including any need for currency translation for the financial information audited.

- The need for a statutory audit of standalone financial statements in addition to an audit for consolidation purposes.

- Whether the entity has an internal audit function and if so, whether, in which areas and to what extent, the work of the function can be used, or internal auditors can be used to provide direct assistance,[11a] for purposes of the audit.

- The availability of the work of internal auditors and the extent of the auditor's potential reliance on such work.

- The entity's use of service organizations and how the auditor may obtain evidence concerning the design or operation of controls performed by them.

- The expected use of audit evidence obtained in previous audits, for example, audit evidence related to risk assessment procedures and tests of controls.

- The effect of information technology on the audit procedures, including the availability of data and the expected use of computer-assisted audit techniques.

[11a] *The use of internal auditors to provide direct assistance is prohibited in an audit conducted in accordance with ISAs (UK) – see ISA (UK) 610 (Revised June 2013), Using the Work of Internal Auditors, paragraph 5-1.*

- The coordination of the expected coverage and timing of the audit work with any reviews of interim financial information and the effect on the audit of the information obtained during such reviews.

- The availability of client personnel and data.

Reporting Objectives, Timing of the Audit, and Nature of Communications

- The entity's timetable for reporting, such as at interim and final stages.

- The organization of meetings with management and those charged with governance to discuss the nature, timing and extent of the audit work.

- The discussion with management and those charged with governance regarding the expected type and timing of reports to be issued and other communications, both written and oral, including the auditor's report, management letters and communications to those charged with governance.

- The discussion with management regarding the expected communications on the status of audit work throughout the engagement.

- Communication with auditors of components regarding the expected types and timing of reports to be issued and other communications in connection with the audit of components.

- The expected nature and timing of communications among engagement team members, including the nature and timing of team meetings and timing of the review of work performed.

- Whether there are any other expected communications with third parties, including any statutory or contractual reporting responsibilities arising from the audit.

Significant Factors, Preliminary Engagement Activities, and Knowledge Gained on Other Engagements

- The determination of materiality in accordance with ISA (UK) 320 (Revised June 2016)[1-a] and, where applicable:

  - The determination of materiality for components and communication thereof to component auditors in accordance with ISA (UK) 600 (Revised June 2016).[2-a]

  - The preliminary identification of significant components and material classes of transactions, account balances and disclosures.

- Preliminary identification of areas where there may be a higher risk of material misstatement.

- The impact of the assessed risk of material misstatement at the overall financial statement level on direction, supervision and review.

- The manner in which the auditor emphasizes to engagement team members the need to maintain a questioning mind and to exercise professional skepticism in gathering and evaluating audit evidence.

[1-a] *ISA (UK) 320 (Revised June 2016), Materiality in Planning and Performing an Audit.*

[2-a] *ISA (UK) 600 (Revised June 2016), Special Considerations—Audits of Group Financial Statements (Including the Work of Component Auditors), paragraphs 21–23 and 40(c).*

- Results of previous audits that involved evaluating the operating effectiveness of internal control, including the nature of identified deficiencies and action taken to address them.

- The discussion of matters that may affect the audit with firm personnel responsible for performing other services to the entity.

- Evidence of management's[13a] commitment to the design, implementation and maintenance of sound internal control, including evidence of appropriate documentation of such internal control.

- Changes within the applicable financial reporting framework, such as changes in accounting standards, which may involve significant new or revised disclosures.

- Volume of transactions, which may determine whether it is more efficient for the auditor to rely on internal control.

- Importance attached to internal control throughout the entity to the successful operation of the business.

- The process(es) management uses to identify and prepare the disclosures required by the applicable financial reporting framework, including disclosures containing information that is obtained from outside of the general and subsidiary ledgers.

- Significant business developments affecting the entity, including changes in information technology and business processes, changes in key management, and acquisitions, mergers and divestments.

- Significant industry developments such as changes in industry regulations and new reporting requirements.

- Other significant relevant developments, such as changes in the legal environment affecting the entity.

Nature, Timing and Extent of Resources

- The selection of the engagement team (including, where necessary, the engagement quality control reviewer) and the assignment of audit work to the team members, including the assignment of appropriately experienced team members to areas where there may be higher risks of material misstatement.

- Engagement budgeting, including considering the appropriate amount of time to set aside for areas where there may be higher risks of material misstatement.

[13a] *In the UK the auditor also considers evidence of the commitment of those charged with governance to the design and operation of sound internal control.*

ISA (UK) 315 (Revised June 2016)
Identifying and Assessing the Risks of Material Misstatement Through Understanding of the Entity and Its Environment

(Effective for audits of financial statements for periods commencing on or after 17 June 2016)

Contents

	Paragraphs

Introduction — 1 - 2
  Scope of this ISA (UK) — 1
  Effective date — 2

Objective — 3

Definitions — 4

Requirements — 5 - 32
  Risk assessment procedures and related activities — 5 - 10
  The required understanding of the entity and its environment, including the entity's
    internal control — 11 - 24
  Identifying and assessing the risks of material misstatement — 25 - 31
  Documentation — 32

Application and other explanatory material
  Risk assessment procedures and related activities — A1 - A24
  The required understanding of the entity and its environment, including the
    entity's internal control — A25 - A121
  Identifying and assessing the risks of material misstatement — A122 - A152
  Documentation — A153 - A156

Appendix 1: Internal control components

Appendix 2: Conditions and events that may indicate risks of material misstatement

---

International Standard on Auditing (UK) (ISA (UK)) 315 (Revised June 2016), *Identifying and Assessing the Risks of Material Misstatement through Understanding the Entity and Its Environment*, should be read in conjunction with ISA (UK) 200 (Revised June 2016), *Overall Objectives of the Independent Auditor and the Conduct of an Audit in Accordance with International Standards on Auditing (UK)*.

Introduction

Scope of this ISA (UK)

1   This International Standard on Auditing (UK) (ISA (UK)) deals with the auditor's responsibility to identify and assess the risks of material misstatement in the financial statements, through understanding the entity and its environment, including the entity's internal control.

Effective Date

2   This ISA (UK) is effective for audits of financial statements for periods commencing on or after 17 June 2016. Earlier adoption is permitted.

Objective

3   The objective of the auditor is to identify and assess the risks of material misstatement, whether due to fraud or error, at the financial statement and assertion levels, through understanding the entity and its environment, including the entity's internal control, thereby providing a basis for designing and implementing responses to the assessed risks of material misstatement.

Definitions

4   For purposes of the ISAs (UK), the following terms have the meanings attributed below:

(a)   Assertions – Representations by management,[1a] explicit or otherwise, that are embodied in the financial statements, as used by the auditor to consider the different types of potential misstatements that may occur.

(b)   Business risk – A risk resulting from significant conditions, events, circumstances, actions or inactions that could adversely affect an entity's ability to achieve its objectives and execute its strategies, or from the setting of inappropriate objectives and strategies.

(c)   Internal control – The process designed, implemented and maintained by those charged with governance, management and other personnel to provide reasonable assurance about the achievement of an entity's objectives with regard to reliability of financial reporting, effectiveness and efficiency of operations, and compliance with applicable laws and regulations. The term "controls" refers to any aspects of one or more of the components of internal control.

(d)   Risk assessment procedures – The audit procedures performed to obtain an understanding of the entity and its environment, including the entity's internal control, to identify and assess the risks of material misstatement, whether due to fraud or error, at the financial statement and assertion levels.

(e)   Significant risk – An identified and assessed risk of material misstatement that, in the auditor's judgment, requires special audit consideration.

[1a] *In the UK, those charged with governance are responsible for preparing the financial statements.*

Requirements

Risk Assessment Procedures and Related Activities

The auditor shall perform risk assessment procedures to provide a basis for the   **5**
identification and assessment of risks of material misstatement at the financial
statement and assertion levels. Risk assessment procedures by themselves,
however, do not provide sufficient appropriate audit evidence on which to base
the audit opinion. (Ref: Para. A1–A5)

The risk assessment procedures shall include the following: **6**

(a)   Inquiries of management, of appropriate individuals within the internal audit
function (if the function exists), and of others within the entity who in the
auditor's judgment may have information that is likely to assist in
identifying risks of material misstatement due to fraud or error. (Ref:
Para. A6–A13)

(b)   Analytical procedures. (Ref: Para. A14–A17)

(c)   Observation and inspection. (Ref: Para. A18)

The auditor shall consider whether information obtained from the auditor's client   **7**
acceptance or continuance process is relevant to identifying risks of material
misstatement.

If the engagement partner has performed other engagements for the entity, the   **8**
engagement partner shall consider whether information obtained is relevant to
identifying risks of material misstatement.

Where the auditor intends to use information obtained from the auditor's previous   **9**
experience with the entity and from audit procedures performed in previous audits,
the auditor shall determine whether changes have occurred since the previous
audit that may affect its relevance to the current audit. (Ref: Para. A19–A20)

The engagement partner and other key engagement team members shall discuss   **10**
the susceptibility of the entity's financial statements to material misstatement, and
the application of the applicable financial reporting framework to the entity's facts
and circumstances. The engagement partner shall determine which matters are to
be communicated to engagement team members not involved in the discussion.
(Ref: Para. A21–A24)

The Required Understanding of the Entity and Its Environment, Including the Entity's Internal Control

The Entity and Its Environment

The auditor shall obtain an understanding of the following: **11**

(a)   Relevant industry, regulatory, and other external factors including the
applicable financial reporting framework. (Ref: Para. A25–A30)

(b)   The nature of the entity, including:

(i)   its operations;

(ii)   its ownership and governance structures;

(iii)   the types of investments that the entity is making and plans to make,
including investments in special-purpose entities; and

(iv)   the way that the entity is structured and how it is financed to enable the auditor to understand the classes of transactions, account balances, and disclosures to be expected in the financial statements. (Ref: Para. A30–A35)

(c)   The entity's selection and application of accounting policies, including the reasons for changes thereto. The auditor shall evaluate whether the entity's accounting policies are appropriate for its business and consistent with the applicable financial reporting framework and accounting policies used in the relevant industry. (Ref: Para. A36)

(d)   The entity's objectives and strategies, and those related business risks that may result in risks of material misstatement. (Ref: Para. A37–A43)

(e)   The measurement and review of the entity's financial performance. (Ref: Para. A44–A49)

The Entity's Internal Control

12   The auditor shall obtain an understanding of internal control relevant to the audit. Although most controls relevant to the audit are likely to relate to financial reporting, not all controls that relate to financial reporting are relevant to the audit. It is a matter of the auditor's professional judgment whether a control, individually or in combination with others, is relevant to the audit. (Ref: Para. A50–A73)

Nature and Extent of the Understanding of Relevant Controls

13   When obtaining an understanding of controls that are relevant to the audit, the auditor shall evaluate the design of those controls and determine whether they have been implemented, by performing procedures in addition to inquiry of the entity's personnel. (Ref: Para. A74–A76)

Components of Internal Control

Control environment

14   The auditor shall obtain an understanding of the control environment. As part of obtaining this understanding, the auditor shall evaluate whether:

(a)   Management, with the oversight of those charged with governance, has created and maintained a culture of honesty and ethical behavior; and

(b)   The strengths in the control environment elements collectively provide an appropriate foundation for the other components of internal control, and whether those other components are not undermined by deficiencies in the control environment. (Ref: Para. A77–A87)

The entity's risk assessment process

15   The auditor shall obtain an understanding of whether the entity has a process for:

(a)   Identifying business risks relevant to financial reporting objectives;

(b)   Estimating the significance of the risks;

(c)   Assessing the likelihood of their occurrence; and

(d)   Deciding about actions to address those risks. (Ref: Para. A88)

16   If the entity has established such a process (referred to hereafter as the "entity's risk assessment process"), the auditor shall obtain an understanding of it, and the results thereof. If the auditor identifies risks of material misstatement that management failed to identify, the auditor shall evaluate whether there was an underlying risk of a kind that the auditor expects would have been identified by the

entity's risk assessment process. If there is such a risk, the auditor shall obtain an understanding of why that process failed to identify it, and evaluate whether the process is appropriate to its circumstances or determine if there is a significant deficiency in internal control with regard to the entity's risk assessment process.

If the entity has not established such a process or has an ad hoc process, the auditor **17** shall discuss with management whether business risks relevant to financial reporting objectives have been identified and how they have been addressed. The auditor shall evaluate whether the absence of a documented risk assessment process is appropriate in the circumstances, or determine whether it represents a significant deficiency in internal control. (Ref: Para. A89)

The information system, including the related business processes, relevant to financial reporting, and communication

The auditor shall obtain an understanding of the information system, including the **18** related business processes, relevant to financial reporting, including the following areas: (Ref: Para. A90–A92, A95–A96)

(a)   The classes of transactions in the entity's operations that are significant to the financial statements;

(b)   The procedures, within both information technology (IT) and manual systems, by which those transactions are initiated, recorded, processed, corrected as necessary, transferred to the general ledger and reported in the financial statements;

(c)   The related accounting records, supporting information and specific accounts in the financial statements that are used to initiate, record, process and report transactions; this includes the correction of incorrect information and how information is transferred to the general ledger. The records may be in either manual or electronic form;

(d)   How the information system captures events and conditions, other than transactions, that are significant to the financial statements;

(e)   The financial reporting process used to prepare the entity's financial statements, including significant accounting estimates and disclosures; and

(f)   Controls surrounding journal entries, including non-standard journal entries used to record non-recurring, unusual transactions or adjustments. (Ref: Para. A93–A94)

This understanding of the information system relevant to financial reporting shall include relevant aspects of that system relating to information disclosed in the financial statements that is obtained from within or outside of the general and subsidiary ledgers.

The auditor shall obtain an understanding of how the entity communicates **19** financial reporting roles and responsibilities and significant matters relating to financial reporting, including: (Ref: Para. A97–A98)

(a)   Communications between management and those charged with governance; and

(b)   External communications, such as those with regulatory authorities.

Control activities relevant to the audit

The auditor shall obtain an understanding of control activities relevant to the audit, **20** being those the auditor judges it necessary to understand in order to assess the risks of material misstatement at the assertion level and design further audit procedures responsive to assessed risks. An audit does not require an understanding of all the control activities related to each significant class of transactions, account balance, and disclosure in the financial statements or to every assertion relevant to them. (Ref: Para. A99–A106)

21   In understanding the entity's control activities, the auditor shall obtain an understanding of how the entity has responded to risks arising from IT. (Ref: Para. A107–A109)

Monitoring of controls

22   The auditor shall obtain an understanding of the major activities that the entity uses to monitor internal control relevant to financial reporting, including those related to those control activities relevant to the audit, and how the entity initiates remedial actions to deficiencies in its controls. (Ref: Para. A110–A112)

23   If the entity has an internal audit function,[1] the auditor shall obtain an understanding of the nature of the internal audit function's responsibilities, its organizational status, and the activities performed, or to be performed. (Ref: Para. A113–A120)

24   The auditor shall obtain an understanding of the sources of the information used in the entity's monitoring activities, and the basis upon which management considers the information to be sufficiently reliable for the purpose. (Ref: Para. A121)

Identifying and Assessing the Risks of Material Misstatement

25   The auditor shall identify and assess the risks of material misstatement at:

(a)   the financial statement level; and (Ref: Para. A122–A125)

(b)   the assertion level for classes of transactions, account balances, and disclosures (Ref: Para. A126–A131)

to provide a basis for designing and performing further audit procedures.

26   For this purpose, the auditor shall:

(a)   Identify risks throughout the process of obtaining an understanding of the entity and its environment, including relevant controls that relate to the risks, and by considering the classes of transactions, account balances, and disclosures (including the quantitative or qualitative aspects of such disclosures) in the financial statements; (Ref: Para. A132–A136)

(b)   Assess the identified risks, and evaluate whether they relate more pervasively to the financial statements as a whole and potentially affect many assertions;

(c)   Relate the identified risks to what can go wrong at the assertion level, taking account of relevant controls that the auditor intends to test; and (Ref: Para. A137–A139)

(d)   Consider the likelihood of misstatement, including the possibility of multiple misstatements, and whether the potential misstatement could result in a material misstatement. (Ref: Para. A140)

---

[1]   ISA (UK) 610 (Revised June 2013), *Using the Work of Internal Auditors*, paragraph 14, defines the term *"internal audit function"* for purposes of the ISAs (UK).

Risks That Require Special Audit Consideration

As part of the risk assessment as described in paragraph 25, the auditor shall **27** determine whether any of the risks identified are, in the auditor's judgment, a significant risk. In exercising this judgment, the auditor shall exclude the effects of identified controls related to the risk.

In exercising judgment as to which risks are significant risks, the auditor shall **28** consider at least the following:

(a) Whether the risk is a risk of fraud;

(b) Whether the risk is related to recent significant economic, accounting or other developments and, therefore, requires specific attention;

(c) The complexity of transactions;

(d) Whether the risk involves significant transactions with related parties;

(e) The degree of subjectivity in the measurement of financial information related to the risk, especially those measurements involving a wide range of measurement uncertainty; and

(f) Whether the risk involves significant transactions that are outside the normal course of business for the entity, or that otherwise appear to be unusual. (Ref: Para. A141–A145)

If the auditor has determined that a significant risk exists, the auditor shall obtain **29** an understanding of the entity's controls, including control activities, relevant to that risk. (Ref: Para. A146–A148)

Risks for Which Substantive Procedures Alone Do Not Provide Sufficient Appropriate Audit Evidence

In respect of some risks, the auditor may judge that it is not possible or practicable **30** to obtain sufficient appropriate audit evidence only from substantive procedures. Such risks may relate to the inaccurate or incomplete recording of routine and significant classes of transactions or account balances, the characteristics of which often permit highly automated processing with little or no manual intervention. In such cases, the entity's controls over such risks are relevant to the audit and the auditor shall obtain an understanding of them. (Ref: Para. A149–A151)

Revision of Risk Assessment

The auditor's assessment of the risks of material misstatement at the assertion **31** level may change during the course of the audit as additional audit evidence is obtained. In circumstances where the auditor obtains audit evidence from performing further audit procedures, or if new information is obtained, either of which is inconsistent with the audit evidence on which the auditor originally based the assessment, the auditor shall revise the assessment and modify the further planned audit procedures accordingly. (Ref: Para. A152)

Documentation

The auditor shall include in the audit documentation:[2] **32**

(a) The discussion among the engagement team where required by paragraph 10, and the significant decisions reached;

---

[2] *ISA (UK) 230 (Revised June 2016), Audit Documentation, paragraphs 8–11, and A6.*

(b)   Key elements of the understanding obtained regarding each of the aspects of the entity and its environment specified in paragraph 11 and of each of the internal control components specified in paragraphs 14–24; the sources of information from which the understanding was obtained; and the risk assessment procedures performed;

(c)   The identified and assessed risks of material misstatement at the financial statement level and at the assertion level as required by paragraph 25; and

(d)   The risks identified, and related controls about which the auditor has obtained an understanding, as a result of the requirements in paragraphs 27–30. (Ref: Para. A153–A156)

***

Application and Other Explanatory Material

Risk Assessment Procedures and Related Activities
(Ref: Para. 5)

A1   Obtaining an understanding of the entity and its environment, including the entity's internal control (referred to hereafter as an "understanding of the entity"), is a continuous, dynamic process of gathering, updating and analyzing information throughout the audit. The understanding establishes a frame of reference within which the auditor plans the audit and exercises professional judgment throughout the audit, for example, when:

- Assessing risks of material misstatement of the financial statements;

- Determining materiality in accordance with ISA (UK) 320 (Revised June 2016);[3]

- Considering the appropriateness of the selection and application of accounting policies, and the adequacy of financial statement disclosures;

- Identifying areas relating to amounts or disclosures in the financial statements where special audit consideration may be necessary, for example, related party transactions or management's assessment of the entity's ability to continue as a going concern, or when considering the business purpose of transactions;

- Developing expectations for use when performing analytical procedures;

- Responding to the assessed risks of material misstatement, including designing and performing further audit procedures to obtain sufficient appropriate audit evidence; and

- Evaluating the sufficiency and appropriateness of audit evidence obtained, such as the appropriateness of assumptions and of management's[3a] oral and written representations.

A2   Information obtained by performing risk assessment procedures and related activities may be used by the auditor as audit evidence to support assessments

---

[3] *ISA (UK) 320 (Revised June 2016), Materiality in Planning and Performing an Audit.*

[3a] *In the UK, as explained in paragraph A2-1 of ISA (UK) 580, Written Representations, it is appropriate for written representations that are critical to obtaining sufficient appropriate audit evidence to be provided by those charged with governance, rather than other levels of the entity's management.*

of the risks of material misstatement. In addition, the auditor may obtain audit evidence about classes of transactions, account balances, or disclosures and related assertions and about the operating effectiveness of controls, even though such procedures were not specifically planned as substantive procedures or as tests of controls. The auditor also may choose to perform substantive procedures or tests of controls concurrently with risk assessment procedures because it is efficient to do so.

The auditor uses professional judgment to determine the extent of the **A3** understanding required. The auditor's primary consideration is whether the understanding that has been obtained is sufficient to meet the objective stated in this ISA (UK). The depth of the overall understanding that is required by the auditor is less than that possessed by management in managing the entity.

The risks to be assessed include both those due to error and those due to fraud, and **A4** both are covered by this ISA (UK). However, the significance of fraud is such that further requirements and guidance are included in ISA (UK) 240 (Revised June 2016) in relation to risk assessment procedures and related activities to obtain information that is used to identify the risks of material misstatement due to fraud.[4]

Although the auditor is required to perform all the risk assessment procedures **A5** described in paragraph 6 in the course of obtaining the required understanding of the entity (see paragraphs 11–24), the auditor is not required to perform all of them for each aspect of that understanding. Other procedures may be performed where the information to be obtained therefrom may be helpful in identifying risks of material misstatement. Examples of such procedures include:

- Reviewing information obtained from external sources such as trade and economic journals; reports by analysts, banks, or rating agencies; or regulatory or financial publications.

- Making inquiries of the entity's external legal counsel or of valuation experts that the entity has used.

Inquiries of Management, the Internal Audit Function and Others within the Entity
(Ref: Para. 6(a))

Much of the information obtained by the auditor's inquiries is obtained from **A6** management and those responsible for financial reporting. Information may also be obtained by the auditor through inquiries with the internal audit function, if the entity has such a function, and others within the entity.

The auditor may also obtain information, or a different perspective in identifying **A7** risks of material misstatement, through inquiries of others within the entity and other employees with different levels of authority. For example:

- Inquiries directed towards those charged with governance may help the auditor understand the environment in which the financial statements are prepared. ISA (UK) 260 (Revised June 2016)[5] identifies the importance of effective two-way communication in assisting the auditor to obtain information from those charged with governance in this regard.

---

[4] ISA (UK) 240 (Revised June 2016), *The Auditor's Responsibilities Relating to Fraud in an Audit of Financial Statements, paragraphs 12–24.*

[5] ISA (UK) 260 (Revised June 2016), *Communication with Those Charged with Governance, paragraph 4(b).*

- Inquiries of employees involved in initiating, processing or recording complex or unusual transactions may help the auditor to evaluate the appropriateness of the selection and application of certain accounting policies.

- Inquiries directed toward in-house legal counsel may provide information about such matters as litigation, compliance with laws and regulations, knowledge of fraud or suspected fraud affecting the entity, warranties, post-sales obligations, arrangements (such as joint ventures) with business partners and the meaning of contract terms.

- Inquiries directed towards marketing or sales personnel may provide information about changes in the entity's marketing strategies, sales trends, or contractual arrangements with its customers.

- Inquiries directed to the risk management function (or those performing such roles) may provide information about operational and regulatory risks that may affect financial reporting.

- Inquiries directed to information systems personnel may provide information about system changes, system or control failures, or other information system-related risks.

A8   As obtaining an understanding of the entity and its environment is a continual, dynamic process, the auditor's inquiries may occur throughout the audit engagement.

Inquiries of the Internal Audit Function

A9   If an entity has an internal audit function, inquiries of the appropriate individuals within the function may provide information that is useful to the auditor in obtaining an understanding of the entity and its environment, and in identifying and assessing risks of material misstatement at the financial statement and assertion levels. In performing its work, the internal audit function is likely to have obtained insight into the entity's operations and business risks, and may have findings based on its work, such as identified control deficiencies or risks, that may provide valuable input into the auditor's understanding of the entity, the auditor's risk assessments or other aspects of the audit. The auditor's inquiries are therefore made whether or not the auditor expects to use the work of the internal audit function to modify the nature or timing, or reduce the extent, of audit procedures to be performed.[6] Inquiries of particular relevance may be about matters the internal audit function has raised with those charged with governance and the outcomes of the function's own risk assessment process.

A10   If, based on responses to the auditor's inquiries, it appears that there are findings that may be relevant to the entity's financial reporting and the audit, the auditor may consider it appropriate to read related reports of the internal audit function. Examples of reports of the internal audit function that may be relevant include the function's strategy and planning documents and reports that have been prepared for management or those charged with governance describing the findings of the internal audit function's examinations.

A11   In addition, in accordance with ISA (UK) 240 (Revised June 2016),[7] if the internal audit function provides information to the auditor regarding any actual, suspected

---

[6] *The relevant requirements are contained in ISA (UK) 610 (Revised June 2013).*

[7] *ISA (UK) 240 (Revised June 2016), paragraph 19.*

or alleged fraud, the auditor takes this into account in the auditor's identification of risk of material misstatement due to fraud.

Appropriate individuals within the internal audit function with whom inquiries are made are those who, in the auditor's judgment, have the appropriate knowledge, experience and authority, such as the chief internal audit executive or, depending on the circumstances, other personnel within the function. The auditor may also consider it appropriate to have periodic meetings with these individuals.   A12

Considerations specific to public sector entities
(Ref: Para 6(a))

Auditors of public sector entities often have additional responsibilities with regard to internal control and compliance with applicable laws and regulations. Inquiries of appropriate individuals in the internal audit function can assist the auditors in identifying the risk of material noncompliance with applicable laws and regulations and the risk of deficiencies in internal control over financial reporting.   A13

Analytical Procedures
(Ref: Para. 6(b))

Analytical procedures performed as risk assessment procedures may identify aspects of the entity of which the auditor was unaware and may assist in assessing the risks of material misstatement in order to provide a basis for designing and implementing responses to the assessed risks. Analytical procedures performed as risk assessment procedures may include both financial and non-financial information, for example, the relationship between sales and square footage of selling space or volume of goods sold.   A14

Analytical procedures may help identify the existence of unusual transactions or events, and amounts, ratios, and trends that might indicate matters that have audit implications. Unusual or unexpected relationships that are identified may assist the auditor in identifying risks of material misstatement, especially risks of material misstatement due to fraud.   A15

However, when such analytical procedures use data aggregated at a high level (which may be the situation with analytical procedures performed as risk assessment procedures), the results of those analytical procedures only provide a broad initial indication about whether a material misstatement may exist. Accordingly, in such cases, consideration of other information that has been gathered when identifying the risks of material misstatement together with the results of such analytical procedures may assist the auditor in understanding and evaluating the results of the analytical procedures.   A16

Considerations Specific to Smaller Entities

Some smaller entities may not have interim or monthly financial information that can be used for purposes of analytical procedures. In these circumstances, although the auditor may be able to perform limited analytical procedures for purposes of planning the audit or obtain some information through inquiry, the auditor may need to plan to perform analytical procedures to identify and assess the risks of material misstatement when an early draft of the entity's financial statements is available.   A17

Observation and Inspection
(Ref: Para. 6(c))

A18   Observation and inspection may support inquiries of management and others, and may also provide information about the entity and its environment. Examples of such audit procedures include observation or inspection of the following:

- The entity's operations.

- Documents (such as business plans and strategies), records, and internal control manuals.

- Reports prepared by management (such as quarterly management reports and interim financial statements) and those charged with governance (such as minutes of board of directors' meetings).

- The entity's premises and plant facilities.

Information Obtained in Prior Periods
(Ref: Para. 9)

A19   The auditor's previous experience with the entity and audit procedures performed in previous audits may provide the auditor with information about such matters as:

- Past misstatements and whether they were corrected on a timely basis.

- The nature of the entity and its environment, and the entity's internal control (including deficiencies in internal control).

- Significant changes that the entity or its operations may have undergone since the prior financial period, which may assist the auditor in gaining a sufficient understanding of the entity to identify and assess risks of material misstatement.

- Those particular types of transactions and other events or account balances (and related disclosures) where the auditor experienced difficulty in performing the necessary audit procedures, for example due to their complexity.

A20   The auditor is required to determine whether information obtained in prior periods remains relevant, if the auditor intends to use that information for the purposes of the current audit. This is because changes in the control environment, for example, may affect the relevance of information obtained in the prior year. To determine whether changes have occurred that may affect the relevance of such information, the auditor may make inquiries and perform other appropriate audit procedures, such as walk-throughs of relevant systems.

Discussion among the Engagement Team
(Ref: Para. 10)

A21   The discussion among the engagement team about the susceptibility of the entity's financial statements to material misstatement:

- Provides an opportunity for more experienced engagement team members, including the engagement partner, to share their insights based on their knowledge of the entity.

- Allows the engagement team members to exchange information about the business risks to which the entity is subject and about how and where the financial statements might be susceptible to material misstatement due to fraud or error.

- Assists the engagement team members to gain a better understanding of the potential for material misstatement of the financial statements in the specific areas assigned to them, and to understand how the results of the audit procedures that they perform may affect other aspects of the audit including the decisions about the nature, timing, and extent of further audit procedures.

- Provides a basis upon which engagement team members communicate and share new information obtained throughout the audit that may affect the assessment of risks of material misstatement or the audit procedures performed to address these risks.

ISA (UK) 240 (Revised June 2016) provides further requirements and guidance in relation to the discussion among the engagement team about the risks of fraud.[8]

As part of the discussion among the engagement team required by paragraph 10, **A22** consideration of the disclosure requirements of the applicable financial reporting framework assists in identifying early in the audit where there may be risks of material misstatement in relation to disclosures. Examples of matters the engagement team may discuss include:

- Changes in financial reporting requirements that may result in significant new or revised disclosures;

- Changes in the entity's environment, financial condition or activities that may result in significant new or revised disclosures, for example, a significant business combination in the period under audit;

- Disclosures for which obtaining sufficient appropriate audit evidence may have been difficult in the past; and

- Disclosures about complex matters, including those involving significant management judgment as to what information to disclose.

It is not always necessary or practical for the discussion to include all members in **A23** a single discussion (as, for example, in a multi-location audit), nor is it necessary for all of the members of the engagement team to be informed of all of the decisions reached in the discussion. The engagement partner may discuss matters with key members of the engagement team including, if considered appropriate, those with specific skills or knowledge, and those responsible for the audits of components, while delegating discussion with others, taking account of the extent of communication considered necessary throughout the engagement team. A communications plan, agreed by the engagement partner, may be useful.

Considerations Specific to Smaller Entities

Many small audits are carried out entirely by the engagement partner (who may be **A24** a sole practitioner). In such situations, it is the engagement partner who, having personally conducted the planning of the audit, would be responsible for considering the susceptibility of the entity's financial statements to material misstatement due to fraud or error.

---

[8] *ISA (UK) 240 (Revised June 2016), paragraph 15.*

The Required Understanding of the Entity and Its Environment, Including the Entity's Internal Control

The Entity and Its Environment

Industry, Regulatory and Other External Factors
(Ref: Para. 11(a))

Industry Factors

A25   Relevant industry factors include industry conditions such as the competitive environment, supplier and customer relationships, and technological developments. Examples of matters the auditor may consider include:

●   The market and competition, including demand, capacity, and price competition.

●   Cyclical or seasonal activity.

●   Product technology relating to the entity's products.

●   Energy supply and cost.

A26   The industry in which the entity operates may give rise to specific risks of material misstatement arising from the nature of the business or the degree of regulation. For example, long-term contracts may involve significant estimates of revenues and expenses that give rise to risks of material misstatement. In such cases, it is important that the engagement team include members with sufficient relevant knowledge and experience.[9]

Regulatory Factors

A27   Relevant regulatory factors include the regulatory environment. The regulatory environment encompasses, among other matters, the applicable financial reporting framework and the legal and political environment. Examples of matters the auditor may consider include:

●   Accounting principles and industry specific practices.

●   Regulatory framework for a regulated industry, including requirements for disclosures.

●   Legislation and regulation that significantly affect the entity's operations, including direct supervisory activities.

●   Taxation (corporate and other).

●   Government policies currently affecting the conduct of the entity's business, such as monetary, including foreign exchange controls, fiscal, financial incentives (for example, government aid programs), and tariffs or trade restrictions policies.

●   Environmental requirements affecting the industry and the entity's business.

A28   ISA (UK) 250 (Revised December 2017) includes some specific requirements related to the legal and regulatory framework applicable to the entity and the industry or sector in which the entity operates.[10]

---

[9] *ISA (UK) 220 (Revised December 2017), Section A – Quality Control for an Audit of Financial Statements, paragraph 14.*

[10] *ISA (UK) 250 (Revised June 2016), Consideration of Laws and Regulations in an Audit of Financial Statements, paragraph 12.*

Considerations specific to public sector entities

For the audits of public sector entities, law, regulation or other authority may affect   **A29**
the entity's operations. Such elements are essential to consider when obtaining an
understanding of the entity and its environment.

Other External Factors

Examples of other external factors affecting the entity that the auditor may   **A30**
consider include the general economic conditions, interest rates and availability
of financing, and inflation or currency revaluation.

Nature of the Entity
(Ref: Para. 11(b))

An understanding of the nature of an entity enables the auditor to understand such   **A31**
matters as:

- Whether the entity has a complex structure, for example with subsidiaries or
  other components in multiple locations. Complex structures often introduce
  issues that may give rise to risks of material misstatement. Such issues may
  include whether goodwill, joint ventures, investments, or special-purpose
  entities are accounted for appropriately and whether adequate disclosure of
  such issues in the financial statements has been made.

- The ownership, and relationships between owners and other people or
  entities. This understanding assists in determining whether related party
  transactions have been appropriately identified, accounted for, and
  adequately disclosed in the financial statements. ISA (UK) 550[11]
  establishes requirements and provides guidance on the auditor's
  considerations relevant to related parties.

Examples of matters that the auditor may consider when obtaining an   **A32**
understanding of the nature of the entity include:

- Business operations such as:
  - Nature of revenue sources, products or services, and markets,
    including involvement in electronic commerce such as Internet sales
    and marketing activities.
  - Conduct of operations (for example, stages and methods of
    production, or activities exposed to environmental risks).
  - Alliances, joint ventures, and outsourcing activities.
  - Geographic dispersion and industry segmentation.
  - Location of production facilities, warehouses, and offices, and
    location and quantities of inventories.
  - Key customers and important suppliers of goods and services,
    employment arrangements (including the existence of union
    contracts, pension and other post employment benefits, stock option
    or incentive bonus arrangements, and government regulation related to
    employment matters).
  - Research and development activities and expenditures.
  - Transactions with related parties.

---

[11] *ISA (UK) 550, Related Parties.*

- Investments and investment activities such as:
  - Planned or recently executed acquisitions or divestitures.
  - Investments and dispositions of securities and loans.
  - Capital investment activities.
  - Investments in non-consolidated entities, including partnerships, joint ventures and special-purpose entities.
- Financing and financing activities such as:
  - Major subsidiaries and associated entities, including consolidated and non-consolidated structures.
  - Debt structure and related terms, including off-balance-sheet financing arrangements and leasing arrangements.
  - Beneficial owners (local, foreign, business reputation and experience) and related parties.
  - Use of derivative financial instruments.
- Financial reporting practices such as:
  - Accounting principles and industry specific practices, including for industry-specific significant classes of transactions, account balances and related disclosures in the financial statements (for example, loans and investments for banks, or research and development for pharmaceuticals).
  - Revenue recognition.
  - Accounting for fair values.
  - Foreign currency assets, liabilities and transactions.
  - Accounting for unusual or complex transactions including those in controversial or emerging areas (for example, accounting for stock-based compensation).

A33   Significant changes in the entity from prior periods may give rise to, or change, risks of material misstatement.

Nature of Special-Purpose Entities

A34   A special-purpose entity (sometimes referred to as a special-purpose vehicle) is an entity that is generally established for a narrow and well-defined purpose, such as to effect a lease or a securitization of financial assets, or to carry out research and development activities. It may take the form of a corporation, trust, partnership or unincorporated entity. The entity on behalf of which the special-purpose entity has been created may often transfer assets to the latter (for example, as part of a derecognition transaction involving financial assets), obtain the right to use the latter's assets, or perform services for the latter, while other parties may provide the funding to the latter. As ISA (UK) 550 indicates, in some circumstances, a special-purpose entity may be a related party of the entity.[12]

A35   Financial reporting frameworks often specify detailed conditions that are deemed to amount to control, or circumstances under which the special-purpose entity

---

[12] *ISA (UK) 550, paragraph A7.*

should be considered for consolidation. The interpretation of the requirements of such frameworks often demands a detailed knowledge of the relevant agreements involving the special-purpose entity.

The Entity's Selection and Application of Accounting Policies
(Ref: Para. 11(c))

An understanding of the entity's selection and application of accounting policies **A36**
may encompass such matters as:

- The methods the entity uses to account for significant and unusual transactions.

- The effect of significant accounting policies in controversial or emerging areas for which there is a lack of authoritative guidance or consensus.

- Changes in the entity's accounting policies.

- Financial reporting standards and laws and regulations that are new to the entity and when and how the entity will adopt such requirements.

Objectives and Strategies and Related Business Risks
(Ref: Para. 11(d))

The entity conducts its business in the context of industry, regulatory and other **A37**
internal and external factors. To respond to these factors, the entity's management or those charged with governance define objectives, which are the overall plans for the entity. Strategies are the approaches by which management intends to achieve its objectives. The entity's objectives and strategies may change over time.

Business risk is broader than the risk of material misstatement of the financial **A38**
statements, though it includes the latter. Business risk may arise from change or complexity. A failure to recognize the need for change may also give rise to business risk. Business risk may arise, for example, from:

- The development of new products or services that may fail;

- A market which, even if successfully developed, is inadequate to support a product or service; or

- Flaws in a product or service that may result in liabilities and reputational risk.

An understanding of the business risks facing the entity increases the likelihood of **A39**
identifying risks of material misstatement, since most business risks will eventually have financial consequences and, therefore, an effect on the financial statements. However, the auditor does not have a responsibility to identify or assess all business risks because not all business risks give rise to risks of material misstatement.

Examples of matters that the auditor may consider when obtaining an **A40**
understanding of the entity's objectives, strategies and related business risks that may result in a risk of material misstatement of the financial statements include:

- Industry developments (a potential related business risk might be, for example, that the entity does not have the personnel or expertise to deal with the changes in the industry).

- New products and services (a potential related business risk might be, for example, that there is increased product liability).

- Expansion of the business (a potential related business risk might be, for example, that the demand has not been accurately estimated).

- New accounting requirements (a potential related business risk might be, for example, incomplete or improper implementation, or increased costs).

- Regulatory requirements (a potential related business risk might be, for example, that there is increased legal exposure).

- Current and prospective financing requirements (a potential related business risk might be, for example, the loss of financing due to the entity's inability to meet requirements).

- Use of IT (a potential related business risk might be, for example, that systems and processes are incompatible).

- The effects of implementing a strategy, particularly any effects that will lead to new accounting requirements (a potential related business risk might be, for example, incomplete or improper implementation).

A41   A business risk may have an immediate consequence for the risk of material misstatement for classes of transactions, account balances, and disclosures at the assertion level or the financial statement level. For example, the business risk arising from a contracting customer base may increase the risk of material misstatement associated with the valuation of receivables. However, the same risk, particularly in combination with a contracting economy, may also have a longer-term consequence, which the auditor considers when assessing the appropriateness of the going concern assumption. Whether a business risk may result in a risk of material misstatement is, therefore, considered in light of the entity's circumstances. Examples of conditions and events that may indicate risks of material misstatement are indicated in Appendix 2.

A42   Usually, management identifies business risks and develops approaches to address them. Such a risk assessment process is part of internal control and is discussed in paragraph 15 and paragraphs A88–A89.

Considerations Specific to Public Sector Entities

A43   For the audits of public sector entities, "management objectives" may be influenced by concerns regarding public accountability and may include objectives which have their source in law, regulation or other authority.

Measurement and Review of the Entity's Financial Performance
(Ref: Para.11(e))

A44   Management and others will measure and review those things they regard as important. Performance measures, whether external or internal, create pressures on the entity. These pressures, in turn, may motivate management to take action to improve the business performance or to misstate the financial statements. Accordingly, an understanding of the entity's performance measures assists the auditor in considering whether pressures to achieve performance targets may result in management actions that increase the risks of material misstatement, including those due to fraud. See ISA (UK) 240 (Revised June 2016) for requirements and guidance in relation to the risks of fraud.

A45   The measurement and review of financial performance is not the same as the monitoring of controls (discussed as a component of internal control in paragraphs A110–A121), though their purposes may overlap:

- The measurement and review of performance is directed at whether business performance is meeting the objectives set by management (or third parties).

- Monitoring of controls is specifically concerned with the effective operation of internal control.

In some cases, however, performance indicators also provide information that enables management to identify deficiencies in internal control.

Examples of internally-generated information used by management for measuring **A46** and reviewing financial performance, and which the auditor may consider, include:

- Key performance indicators (financial and non-financial) and key ratios, trends and operating statistics.

- Period-on-period financial performance analyses.

- Budgets, forecasts, variance analyses, segment information and divisional, departmental or other level performance reports.

- Employee performance measures and incentive compensation policies.

- Comparisons of an entity's performance with that of competitors.

External parties may also measure and review the entity's financial performance. **A47** For example, external information such as analysts' reports and credit rating agency reports may represent useful information for the auditor. Such reports can often be obtained from the entity being audited.

Internal measures may highlight unexpected results or trends requiring **A48** management to determine their cause and take corrective action (including, in some cases, the detection and correction of misstatements on a timely basis). Performance measures may also indicate to the auditor that risks of misstatement of related financial statement information do exist. For example, performance measures may indicate that the entity has unusually rapid growth or profitability when compared to that of other entities in the same industry. Such information, particularly if combined with other factors such as performance-based bonus or incentive remuneration, may indicate the potential risk of management bias in the preparation of the financial statements.

Considerations Specific to Smaller Entities

Smaller entities often do not have processes to measure and review financial **A49** performance. Inquiry of management may reveal that it relies on certain key indicators for evaluating financial performance and taking appropriate action. If such inquiry indicates an absence of performance measurement or review, there may be an increased risk of misstatements not being detected and corrected.

The Entity's Internal Control
(Ref: Para. 12)

An understanding of internal control assists the auditor in identifying types of **A50** potential misstatements and factors that affect the risks of material misstatement, and in designing the nature, timing, and extent of further audit procedures.

The following application material on internal control is presented in four **A51** sections, as follows:

- General Nature and Characteristics of Internal Control.

- Controls Relevant to the Audit.

- Nature and Extent of the Understanding of Relevant Controls.

- Components of Internal Control.

General Nature and Characteristics of Internal Control

Purpose of Internal Control

A52 Internal control is designed, implemented and maintained to address identified business risks that threaten the achievement of any of the entity's objectives that concern:

- The reliability of the entity's financial reporting;
- The effectiveness and efficiency of its operations; and
- Its compliance with applicable laws and regulations.

The way in which internal control is designed, implemented and maintained varies with an entity's size and complexity.

Considerations specific to smaller entities

A53 Smaller entities may use less structured means and simpler processes and procedures to achieve their objectives.

Limitations of Internal Control

A54 Internal control, no matter how effective, can provide an entity with only reasonable assurance about achieving the entity's financial reporting objectives. The likelihood of their achievement is affected by the inherent limitations of internal control. These include the realities that human judgment in decision-making can be faulty and that breakdowns in internal control can occur because of human error. For example, there may be an error in the design of, or in the change to, a control. Equally, the operation of a control may not be effective, such as where information produced for the purposes of internal control (for example, an exception report) is not effectively used because the individual responsible for reviewing the information does not understand its purpose or fails to take appropriate action.

A55 Additionally, controls can be circumvented by the collusion of two or more people or inappropriate management override of internal control. For example, management may enter into side agreements with customers that alter the terms and conditions of the entity's standard sales contracts, which may result in improper revenue recognition. Also, edit checks in a software program that are designed to identify and report transactions that exceed specified credit limits may be overridden or disabled.

A56 Further, in designing and implementing controls, management may make judgments on the nature and extent of the controls it chooses to implement, and the nature and extent of the risks it chooses to assume.

Considerations specific to smaller entities

A57 Smaller entities often have fewer employees which may limit the extent to which segregation of duties is practicable. However, in a small owner-managed entity, the owner-manager may be able to exercise more effective oversight than in a larger entity. This oversight may compensate for the generally more limited opportunities for segregation of duties.

A58 On the other hand, the owner-manager may be more able to override controls because the system of internal control is less structured. This is taken into account by the auditor when identifying the risks of material misstatement due to fraud.

Division of Internal Control into Components

The division of internal control into the following five components, for purposes **A59** of the ISAs (UK), provides a useful framework for auditors to consider how different aspects of an entity's internal control may affect the audit:

(a) The control environment;

(b) The entity's risk assessment process;

(c) The information system, including the related business processes, relevant to financial reporting, and communication;

(d) Control activities; and

(e) Monitoring of controls.

The division does not necessarily reflect how an entity designs, implements and maintains internal control, or how it may classify any particular component. Auditors may use different terminology or frameworks to describe the various aspects of internal control, and their effect on the audit than those used in this ISA (UK), provided all the components described in this ISA (UK) are addressed.

Application material relating to the five components of internal control as they **A60** relate to a financial statement audit is set out in paragraphs A77–A121 below. Appendix 1 provides further explanation of these components of internal control.

Characteristics of Manual and Automated Elements of Internal Control Relevant to the Auditor's Risk Assessment

An entity's system of internal control contains manual elements and often contains **A61** automated elements. The characteristics of manual or automated elements are relevant to the auditor's risk assessment and further audit procedures based thereon.

The use of manual or automated elements in internal control also affects the **A62** manner in which transactions are initiated, recorded, processed, and reported:

- Controls in a manual system may include such procedures as approvals and reviews of transactions, and reconciliations and follow-up of reconciling items. Alternatively, an entity may use automated procedures to initiate, record, process, and report transactions, in which case records in electronic format replace paper documents.

- Controls in IT systems consist of a combination of automated controls (for example, controls embedded in computer programs) and manual controls. Further, manual controls may be independent of IT, may use information produced by IT, or may be limited to monitoring the effective functioning of IT and of automated controls, and to handling exceptions. When IT is used to initiate, record, process or report transactions, or other financial data for inclusion in financial statements, the systems and programs may include controls related to the corresponding assertions for material accounts or may be critical to the effective functioning of manual controls that depend on IT.

An entity's mix of manual and automated elements in internal control varies with the nature and complexity of the entity's use of IT.

Generally, IT benefits an entity's internal control by enabling an entity to: **A63**

- Consistently apply predefined business rules and perform complex calculations in processing large volumes of transactions or data;

- Enhance the timeliness, availability, and accuracy of information;

- Facilitate the additional analysis of information;

- Enhance the ability to monitor the performance of the entity's activities and its policies and procedures;

- Reduce the risk that controls will be circumvented; and

- Enhance the ability to achieve effective segregation of duties by implementing security controls in applications, databases, and operating systems.

A64   IT also poses specific risks to an entity's internal control, including, for example:

- Reliance on systems or programs that are inaccurately processing data, processing inaccurate data, or both.

- Unauthorized access to data that may result in destruction of data or improper changes to data, including the recording of unauthorized or non-existent transactions, or inaccurate recording of transactions. Particular risks may arise where multiple users access a common database.

- The possibility of IT personnel gaining access privileges beyond those necessary to perform their assigned duties thereby breaking down segregation of duties.

- Unauthorized changes to data in master files.

- Unauthorized changes to systems or programs.

- Failure to make necessary changes to systems or programs.

- Inappropriate manual intervention.

- Potential loss of data or inability to access data as required.

A65   Manual elements in internal control may be more suitable where judgment and discretion are required such as for the following circumstances:

- Large, unusual or non-recurring transactions.

- Circumstances where errors are difficult to define, anticipate or predict.

- In changing circumstances that require a control response outside the scope of an existing automated control.

- In monitoring the effectiveness of automated controls.

A66   Manual elements in internal control may be less reliable than automated elements because they can be more easily bypassed, ignored, or overridden and they are also more prone to simple errors and mistakes. Consistency of application of a manual control element cannot therefore be assumed. Manual control elements may be less suitable for the following circumstances:

- High volume or recurring transactions, or in situations where errors that can be anticipated or predicted can be prevented, or detected and corrected, by control parameters that are automated.

- Control activities where the specific ways to perform the control can be adequately designed and automated.

A67   The extent and nature of the risks to internal control vary depending on the nature and characteristics of the entity's information system. The entity responds to the risks arising from the use of IT or from use of manual elements in internal control by establishing effective controls in light of the characteristics of the entity's information system.

Controls Relevant to the Audit

There is a direct relationship between an entity's objectives and the controls it   **A68**
implements to provide reasonable assurance about their achievement. The entity's
objectives, and therefore controls, relate to financial reporting, operations and
compliance; however, not all of these objectives and controls are relevant to the
auditor's risk assessment.

Factors relevant to the auditor's judgment about whether a control, individually or   **A69**
in combination with others, is relevant to the audit may include such matters as the
following:

- Materiality.

- The significance of the related risk.

- The size of the entity.

- The nature of the entity's business, including its organization and ownership
  characteristics.

- The diversity and complexity of the entity's operations.

- Applicable legal and regulatory requirements.

- The circumstances and the applicable component of internal control.

- The nature and complexity of the systems that are part of the entity's internal
  control, including the use of service organizations.

- Whether, and how, a specific control, individually or in combination with
  others, prevents, or detects and corrects, material misstatement.

Controls over the completeness and accuracy of information produced by the   **A70**
entity may be relevant to the audit if the auditor intends to make use of the
information in designing and performing further procedures. Controls relating to
operations and compliance objectives may also be relevant to an audit if they
relate to data the auditor evaluates or uses in applying audit procedures.

Internal control over safeguarding of assets against unauthorized acquisition, use,   **A71**
or disposition may include controls relating to both financial reporting and
operations objectives. The auditor's consideration of such controls is generally
limited to those relevant to the reliability of financial reporting.

An entity generally has controls relating to objectives that are not relevant to an   **A72**
audit and therefore need not be considered. For example, an entity may rely on a
sophisticated system of automated controls to provide efficient and effective
operations (such as an airline's system of automated controls to maintain flight
schedules), but these controls ordinarily would not be relevant to the audit.
Further, although internal control applies to the entire entity or to any of its
operating units or business processes, an understanding of internal control relating
to each of the entity's operating units and business processes may not be relevant
to the audit.

Considerations Specific to Public Sector Entities

Public sector auditors often have additional responsibilities with respect to internal   **A73**
control, for example to report on compliance with an established code of practice.
Public sector auditors can also have responsibilities to report on compliance with
law, regulation or other authority. As a result, their review of internal control may
be broader and more detailed.

Nature and Extent of the Understanding of Relevant Controls
(Ref: Para. 13)

A74   Evaluating the design of a control involves considering whether the control, individually or in combination with other controls, is capable of effectively preventing, or detecting and correcting, material misstatements. Implementation of a control means that the control exists and that the entity is using it. There is little point in assessing the implementation of a control that is not effective, and so the design of a control is considered first. An improperly designed control may represent a significant deficiency in internal control.

A75   Risk assessment procedures to obtain audit evidence about the design and implementation of relevant controls may include:

- Inquiring of entity personnel.

- Observing the application of specific controls.

- Inspecting documents and reports.

- Tracing transactions through the information system relevant to financial reporting.

Inquiry alone, however, is not sufficient for such purposes.

A76   Obtaining an understanding of an entity's controls is not sufficient to test their operating effectiveness, unless there is some automation that provides for the consistent operation of the controls. For example, obtaining audit evidence about the implementation of a manual control at a point in time does not provide audit evidence about the operating effectiveness of the control at other times during the period under audit. However, because of the inherent consistency of IT processing (see paragraph A63), performing audit procedures to determine whether an automated control has been implemented may serve as a test of that control's operating effectiveness, depending on the auditor's assessment and testing of controls such as those over program changes. Tests of the operating effectiveness of controls are further described in ISA (UK) 330 (Revised July 2017).[13]

Components of Internal Control—Control Environment
(Ref: Para. 14)

A77   The control environment includes the governance and management functions and the attitudes, awareness, and actions of those charged with governance and management concerning the entity's internal control and its importance in the entity. The control environment sets the tone of an organization, influencing the control consciousness of its people.

A78   Elements of the control environment that may be relevant when obtaining an understanding of the control environment include the following:

(a)   *Communication and enforcement of integrity and ethical values* – These are essential elements that influence the effectiveness of the design, administration and monitoring of controls.

(b)   *Commitment to competence* – Matters such as management's consideration of the competence levels for particular jobs and how those levels translate into requisite skills and knowledge.

---

[13] *ISA (UK) 330 (Revised July 2017), The Auditor's Responses to Assessed Risks.*

(c) *Participation by those charged with governance* – Attributes of those charged with governance such as:

- Their independence from management.

- Their experience and stature.

- The extent of their involvement and the information they receive, and the scrutiny of activities.

- The appropriateness of their actions, including the degree to which difficult questions are raised and pursued with management, and their interaction with internal and external auditors.

(d) *Management's philosophy and operating style* – Characteristics such as management's:

- Approach to taking and managing business risks.

- Attitudes and actions toward financial reporting.

- Attitudes toward information processing and accounting functions and personnel.

(e) *Organizational structure* – The framework within which an entity's activities for achieving its objectives are planned, executed, controlled, and reviewed.

(f) *Assignment of authority and responsibility* – Matters such as how authority and responsibility for operating activities are assigned and how reporting relationships and authorization hierarchies are established.

(g) *Human resource policies and practices* – Policies and practices that relate to, for example, recruitment, orientation, training, evaluation, counselling, promotion, compensation, and remedial actions.

Audit Evidence for Elements of the Control Environment

Relevant audit evidence may be obtained through a combination of inquiries and other risk assessment procedures such as corroborating inquiries through observation or inspection of documents. For example, through inquiries of management and employees, the auditor may obtain an understanding of how management communicates to employees its views on business practices and ethical behavior. The auditor may then determine whether relevant controls have been implemented by considering, for example, whether management has a written code of conduct and whether it acts in a manner that supports the code. **A79**

The auditor may also consider how management has responded to the findings and recommendations of the internal audit function regarding identified deficiencies in internal control relevant to the audit, including whether and how such responses have been implemented, and whether they have been subsequently evaluated by the internal audit function. **A80**

Effect of the Control Environment on the Assessment of the Risks of Material Misstatement

Some elements of an entity's control environment have a pervasive effect on assessing the risks of material misstatement. For example, an entity's control consciousness is influenced significantly by those charged with governance, because one of their roles is to counterbalance pressures on management in relation to financial reporting that may arise from market demands or **A81** remuneration schemes. The effectiveness of the design of the control environment in relation to participation by those charged with governance is therefore influenced by such matters as:

- Their independence from management and their ability to evaluate the actions of management.

- Whether they understand the entity's business transactions.

- The extent to which they evaluate whether the financial statements are prepared in accordance with the applicable financial reporting framework, including whether the financial statements include adequate disclosures.

A82   An active and independent board of directors may influence the philosophy and operating style of senior management. However, other elements may be more limited in their effect. For example, although human resource policies and practices directed toward hiring competent financial, accounting, and IT personnel may reduce the risk of errors in processing financial information, they may not mitigate a strong bias by top management to overstate earnings.

A83   The existence of a satisfactory control environment can be a positive factor when the auditor assesses the risks of material misstatement. However, although it may help reduce the risk of fraud, a satisfactory control environment is not an absolute deterrent to fraud. Conversely, deficiencies in the control environment may undermine the effectiveness of controls, in particular in relation to fraud. For example, management's failure to commit sufficient resources to address IT security risks may adversely affect internal control by allowing improper changes to be made to computer programs or to data, or unauthorized transactions to be processed. As explained in ISA (UK) 330 (Revised July 2017), the control environment also influences the nature, timing, and extent of the auditor's further procedures.[14]

A84   The control environment in itself does not prevent, or detect and correct, a material misstatement. It may, however, influence the auditor's evaluation of the effectiveness of other controls (for example, the monitoring of controls and the operation of specific control activities) and thereby, the auditor's assessment of the risks of material misstatement.

Considerations Specific to Smaller Entities

A85   The control environment within small entities is likely to differ from larger entities. For example, those charged with governance in small entities may not include an independent or outside member, and the role of governance may be undertaken directly by the owner-manager where there are no other owners. The nature of the control environment may also influence the significance of other controls, or their absence. For example, the active involvement of an owner-manager may mitigate certain of the risks arising from a lack of segregation of duties in a small entity; it may, however, increase other risks, for example, the risk of override of controls.

A86   In addition, audit evidence for elements of the control environment in smaller entities may not be available in documentary form, in particular where communication between management and other personnel may be informal, yet effective. For example, small entities might not have a written code of conduct but,

---

[14]   *ISA (UK) 330 (Revised July 2017), paragraphs A2–A3.*

instead, develop a culture that emphasizes the importance of integrity and ethical behavior through oral communication and by management example.

Consequently, the attitudes, awareness and actions of management or the owner-manager are of particular importance to the auditor's understanding of a smaller entity's control environment.   **A87**

Components of Internal Control—The Entity's Risk Assessment Process
(Ref: Para. 15)

The entity's risk assessment process forms the basis for how management   **A88**
determines the risks to be managed. If that process is appropriate to the circumstances, including the nature, size and complexity of the entity, it assists the auditor in identifying risks of material misstatement. Whether the entity's risk assessment process is appropriate to the circumstances is a matter of judgment.

Considerations Specific to Smaller Entities
(Ref: Para. 17)

There is unlikely to be an established risk assessment process in a small entity. In   **A89**
such cases, it is likely that management will identify risks through direct personal involvement in the business. Irrespective of the circumstances, however, inquiry about identified risks and how they are addressed by management is still necessary.

Components of Internal Control—The Information System, Including Related Business Processes, Relevant to Financial Reporting, and Communication

The Information System, Including Related Business Processes, Relevant to Financial Reporting
(Ref: Para. 18)

The information system relevant to financial reporting objectives, which includes   **A90**
the accounting system, consists of the procedures and records designed and established to:

● Initiate, record, process, and report entity transactions (as well as events and conditions) and to maintain accountability for the related assets, liabilities, and equity;

● Resolve incorrect processing of transactions, for example, automated suspense files and procedures followed to clear suspense items out on a timely basis;

● Process and account for system overrides or bypasses to controls;

● Transfer information from transaction processing systems to the general ledger;

● Capture information relevant to financial reporting for events and conditions other than transactions, such as the depreciation and amortization of assets and changes in the recoverability of accounts receivables; and

● Ensure information required to be disclosed by the applicable financial reporting framework is accumulated, recorded, processed, summarized and appropriately reported in the financial statements.

Financial statements may contain information that is obtained from outside of the   **A91**
general and subsidiary ledgers. Examples of such information may include:

- Information obtained from lease agreements disclosed in the financial statements, such as renewal options or future lease payments.

- Information disclosed in the financial statements that is produced by an entity's risk management system.

- Fair value information produced by management's experts and disclosed in the financial statements.

- Information disclosed in the financial statements that has been obtained from models, or from other calculations used to develop estimates recognized or disclosed in the financial statements, including information relating to the underlying data and assumptions used in those models, such as:

  - Assumptions developed internally that may affect an asset's useful life; or

  - Data such as interest rates that are affected by factors outside the control of the entity.

- Information disclosed in the financial statements about sensitivity analyses derived from financial models that demonstrates that management has considered alternative assumptions.

- Information recognized or disclosed in the financial statements that has been obtained from an entity's tax returns and records.

- Information disclosed in the financial statements that has been obtained from analyses prepared to support management's assessment of the entity's ability to continue as a going concern, such as disclosures, if any, related to events or conditions that have been identified that may cast significant doubt on the entity's ability to continue as a going concern.[15]

A92   The understanding of the information system relevant to financial reporting required by paragraph 18 of this ISA (UK) (including the understanding of relevant aspects of that system relating to information disclosed in the financial statements that is obtained from within or outside of the general and subsidiary ledgers) is a matter of the auditor's professional judgment. For example, certain amounts or disclosures in the entity's financial statements (such as disclosures about credit risk, liquidity risk, and market risk) may be based on information obtained from the entity's risk management system. However, the auditor is not required to understand all aspects of the risk management system, and uses professional judgment in determining the necessary understanding.

Journal entries

A93   An entity's information system typically includes the use of standard journal entries that are required on a recurring basis to record transactions. Examples might be journal entries to record sales, purchases, and cash disbursements in the general ledger, or to record accounting estimates that are periodically made by management, such as changes in the estimate of uncollectible accounts receivable.

A94   An entity's financial reporting process also includes the use of non-standard journal entries to record non-recurring, unusual transactions or adjustments. Examples of such entries include consolidating adjustments and entries for a business combination or disposal or non-recurring estimates such as the

---

[15] *See paragraphs 19–20 of ISA (UK) 570 (Revised June 2016), Going Concern.*

impairment of an asset. In manual general ledger systems, non-standard journal entries may be identified through inspection of ledgers, journals, and supporting documentation. When automated procedures are used to maintain the general ledger and prepare financial statements, such entries may exist only in electronic form and may therefore be more easily identified through the use of computer-assisted audit techniques.

Related business processes

An entity's business processes are the activities designed to: **A95**

- Develop, purchase, produce, sell and distribute an entity's products and services;

- Ensure compliance with laws and regulations; and

- Record information, including accounting and financial reporting information.

Business processes result in the transactions that are recorded, processed and reported by the information system. Obtaining an understanding of the entity's business processes, which include how transactions are originated, assists the auditor obtain an understanding of the entity's information system relevant to financial reporting in a manner that is appropriate to the entity's circumstances.

Considerations specific to smaller entities

The information system, and related business processes, relevant to financial **A96** reporting in small entities, including relevant aspects of that system relating to information disclosed in the financial statements that is obtained from within or outside of the general and subsidiary ledgers, is likely to be less sophisticated than in larger entities, but its role is just as significant. Small entities with active management involvement may not need extensive descriptions of accounting procedures, sophisticated accounting records, or written policies. Understanding the entity's information system relevant to financial reporting may therefore be easier in an audit of smaller entities, and may be more dependent on inquiry than on review of documentation. The need to obtain an understanding, however, remains important.

Communication
(Ref: Para. 19)

Communication by the entity of the financial reporting roles and responsibilities **A97** and of significant matters relating to financial reporting involves providing an understanding of individual roles and responsibilities pertaining to internal control over financial reporting. It includes such matters as the extent to which personnel understand how their activities in the financial reporting information system relate to the work of others and the means of reporting exceptions to an appropriate higher level within the entity. Communication may take such forms as policy manuals and financial reporting manuals. Open communication channels help ensure that exceptions are reported and acted on.

Considerations specific to smaller entities

Communication may be less structured and easier to achieve in a small entity than **A98** in a larger entity due to fewer levels of responsibility and management's greater visibility and availability.

Components of Internal Control—Control Activities Relevant to the Audit
(Ref: Para. 20)

A99   Control activities are the policies and procedures that help ensure that management directives are carried out. Control activities, whether within IT or manual systems, have various objectives and are applied at various organizational and functional levels. Examples of specific control activities include those relating to the following:

- Authorization.
- Performance reviews.
- Information processing.
- Physical controls.
- Segregation of duties.

A100   Control activities that are relevant to the audit are:

- Those that are required to be treated as such, being control activities that relate to significant risks and those that relate to risks for which substantive procedures alone do not provide sufficient appropriate audit evidence, as required by paragraphs 29 and 30, respectively; or
- Those that are considered to be relevant in the judgment of the auditor.

A101   The auditor's judgment about whether a control activity is relevant to the audit is influenced by the risk that the auditor has identified that may give rise to a material misstatement and whether the auditor thinks it is likely to be appropriate to test the operating effectiveness of the control in determining the extent of substantive testing.

A102   The auditor's emphasis may be on identifying and obtaining an understanding of control activities that address the areas where the auditor considers that risks of material misstatement are likely to be higher. When multiple control activities each achieve the same objective, it is unnecessary to obtain an understanding of each of the control activities related to such objective.

A103   Control activities relevant to the audit may include controls established by management that address risks of material misstatement related to disclosures not being prepared in accordance with the applicable financial reporting framework, in addition to controls that address risks related to account balances and transactions. Such control activities may relate to information included in the financial statements that is obtained from outside of the general and subsidiary ledgers.

A104   The auditor's knowledge about the presence or absence of control activities obtained from the understanding of the other components of internal control assists the auditor in determining whether it is necessary to devote additional attention to obtaining an understanding of control activities.

Considerations Specific to Smaller Entities

A105   The concepts underlying control activities in small entities are likely to be similar to those in larger entities, but the formality with which they operate may vary. Further, small entities may find that certain types of control activities are not relevant because of controls applied by management. For example, management's sole authority for granting credit to customers and approving significant purchases can provide strong control over important account balances and transactions, lessening or removing the need for more detailed control activities.

Control activities relevant to the audit of a smaller entity are likely to relate to the main transaction cycles such as revenues, purchases and employment expenses. **A106**

Risks Arising from IT
(Ref: Para. 21)

The use of IT affects the way that control activities are implemented. From the auditor's perspective, controls over IT systems are effective when they maintain the integrity of information and the security of the data such systems process, and include effective general IT controls and application controls. **A107**

General IT controls are policies and procedures that relate to many applications and support the effective functioning of application controls. They apply to mainframe, miniframe, and end-user environments. General IT controls that maintain the integrity of information and security of data commonly include controls over the following: **A108**

• Data center and network operations.

• System software acquisition, change and maintenance.

• Program change.

• Access security.

• Application system acquisition, development, and maintenance.

They are generally implemented to deal with the risks referred to in paragraph A64 above.

Application controls are manual or automated procedures that typically operate at a business process level and apply to the processing of transactions by individual applications. Application controls can be preventive or detective in nature and are designed to ensure the integrity of the accounting records. Accordingly, application controls relate to procedures used to initiate, record, process and report transactions or other financial data. These controls help ensure that transactions occurred, are authorized, and are completely and accurately recorded and processed. Examples include edit checks of input data, and numerical sequence checks with manual follow-up of exception reports or correction at the point of data entry. **A109**

Components of Internal Control—Monitoring of Controls
(Ref: Para. 22)

Monitoring of controls is a process to assess the effectiveness of internal control performance over time. It involves assessing the effectiveness of controls on a timely basis and taking necessary remedial actions. Management accomplishes monitoring of controls through ongoing activities, separate evaluations, or a combination of the two. Ongoing monitoring activities are often built into the normal recurring activities of an entity and include regular management and supervisory activities. **A110**

Management's monitoring activities may include using information from communications from external parties such as customer complaints and regulator comments that may indicate problems or highlight areas in need of improvement. **A111**

Considerations Specific to Smaller Entities

A112   Management's monitoring of control is often accomplished by management's or the owner-manager's close involvement in operations. This involvement often will identify significant variances from expectations and inaccuracies in financial data leading to remedial action to the control.

The Entity's Internal Audit Function
(Ref: Para. 23)

A113   If the entity has an internal audit function, obtaining an understanding of that function contributes to the auditor's understanding of the entity and its environment, including internal control, in particular the role that the function plays in the entity's monitoring of internal control over financial reporting. This understanding, together with the information obtained from the auditor's inquiries in paragraph 6(a) of this ISA (UK), may also provide information that is directly relevant to the auditor's identification and assessment of the risks of material misstatement.

A114   The objectives and scope of an internal audit function, the nature of its responsibilities and its status within the organization, including the function's authority and accountability, vary widely and depend on the size and structure of the entity and the requirements of management and, where applicable, those charged with governance. These matters may be set out in an internal audit charter or terms of reference.

A115   The responsibilities of an internal audit function may include performing procedures and evaluating the results to provide assurance to management and those charged with governance regarding the design and effectiveness of risk management, internal control and governance processes. If so, the internal audit function may play an important role in the entity's monitoring of internal control over financial reporting. However, the responsibilities of the internal audit function may be focused on evaluating the economy, efficiency and effectiveness of operations and, if so, the work of the function may not directly relate to the entity's financial reporting.

A116   The auditor's inquiries of appropriate individuals within the internal audit function in accordance with paragraph 6(a) of this ISA (UK) help the auditor obtain an understanding of the nature of the internal audit function's responsibilities. If the auditor determines that the function's responsibilities are related to the entity's financial reporting, the auditor may obtain further understanding of the activities performed, or to be performed, by the internal audit function by reviewing the internal audit function's audit plan for the period, if any, and discussing that plan with the appropriate individuals within the function.

A117   If the nature of the internal audit function's responsibilities and assurance activities are related to the entity's financial reporting, the auditor may also be able to use the work of the internal audit function to modify the nature or timing, or reduce the extent, of audit procedures to be performed directly by the auditor in obtaining audit evidence. Auditors may be more likely to be able to use the work of an entity's internal audit function when it appears, for example, based on experience in previous audits or the auditor's risk assessment procedures, that the entity has an internal audit function that is adequately and appropriately resourced relative to the size of the entity and the nature of its operations, and has a direct reporting relationship to those charged with governance.

If, based on the auditor's preliminary understanding of the internal audit function, **A118** the auditor expects to use the work of the internal audit function to modify the nature or timing, or reduce the extent, of audit procedures to be performed, ISA (UK) 610 (Revised June 2013) applies.

As is further discussed in ISA (UK) 610 (Revised June 2013), the activities of an **A119** internal audit function are distinct from other monitoring controls that may be relevant to financial reporting, such as reviews of management accounting information that are designed to contribute to how the entity prevents or detects misstatements.

Establishing communications with the appropriate individuals within an entity's **A120** internal audit function early in the engagement, and maintaining such communications throughout the engagement, can facilitate effective sharing of information. It creates an environment in which the auditor can be informed of significant matters that may come to the attention of the internal audit function when such matters may affect the work of the auditor. ISA (UK) 200 (Revised June 2016) discusses the importance of the auditor planning and performing the audit with professional skepticism, including being alert to information that brings into question the reliability of documents and responses to inquiries to be used as audit evidence. Accordingly, communication with the internal audit function throughout the engagement may provide opportunities for internal auditors to bring such information to the auditor's attention. The auditor is then able to take such information into account in the auditor's identification and assessment of risks of material misstatement.

Sources of Information
(Ref: Para. 24)

Much of the information used in monitoring may be produced by the entity's **A121** information system. If management assumes that data used for monitoring are accurate without having a basis for that assumption, errors that may exist in the information could potentially lead management to incorrect conclusions from its monitoring activities. Accordingly, an understanding of:

● the sources of the information related to the entity's monitoring activities; and

● the basis upon which management considers the information to be sufficiently reliable for the purpose,

is required as part of the auditor's understanding of the entity's monitoring activities as a component of internal control.

Identifying and Assessing the Risks of Material Misstatement

Assessment of Risks of Material Misstatement at the Financial Statement Level (Ref: Para. 25 (a))

Risks of material misstatement at the financial statement level refer to risks that **A122** relate pervasively to the financial statements as a whole and potentially affect many assertions. Risks of this nature are not necessarily risks identifiable with specific assertions at the class of transactions, account balance, or disclosure level. Rather, they represent circumstances that may increase the risks of material misstatement at the assertion level, for example, through management override of internal control. Financial statement level risks may be especially relevant to the auditor's consideration of the risks of material misstatement arising from fraud.

A123 Risks at the financial statement level may derive in particular from a deficient control environment (although these risks may also relate to other factors, such as declining economic conditions). For example, deficiencies such as a lack of management competence or lack of oversight over the preparation of the financial statements may have a more pervasive effect on the financial statements and may require an overall response by the auditor.

A124 The auditor's understanding of internal control may raise doubts about the auditability of an entity's financial statements. For example:

- Concerns about the integrity of the entity's management may be so serious as to cause the auditor to conclude that the risk of management misrepresentation in the financial statements is such that an audit cannot be conducted.

- Concerns about the condition and reliability of an entity's records may cause the auditor to conclude that it is unlikely that sufficient appropriate audit evidence will be available to support an unmodified opinion on the financial statements.

A125 ISA (UK) 705 (Revised June 2016)[16] establishes requirements and provides guidance in determining whether there is a need for the auditor to express a qualified opinion or disclaim an opinion or, as may be required in some cases, to withdraw from the engagement where withdrawal is possible under applicable law or regulation.

Assessment of Risks of Material Misstatement at the Assertion Level (Ref: Para. 25(b))

A126 Risks of material misstatement at the assertion level for classes of transactions, account balances, and disclosures need to be considered because such consideration directly assists in determining the nature, timing, and extent of further audit procedures at the assertion level necessary to obtain sufficient appropriate audit evidence. In identifying and assessing risks of material misstatement at the assertion level, the auditor may conclude that the identified risks relate more pervasively to the financial statements as a whole and potentially affect many assertions.

The Use of Assertions

A127 In representing that the financial statements are in accordance with the applicable financial reporting framework, management implicitly or explicitly makes assertions regarding recognition, measurement and presentation of classes of transactions and events, account balances and disclosures.

A128 The auditor may use the assertions as described in paragraph A129(a)–(b) below or may express them differently provided all aspects described below have been covered. For example, the auditor may choose to combine the assertions about classes of transactions and events, and related disclosures, with the assertions about account balances, and related disclosures.

Assertions about classes of transaction, account balances, and related disclosures

A129 Assertions used by the auditor in considering the different types of potential misstatements that may occur may fall into the following categories:

---

[16] *ISA (UK) 705 (Revised June 2016), Modifications to the Opinion in the Independent Auditor's Report.*

(a) Assertions about classes of transactions and events, and related disclosures, for the period under audit:

    (i) Occurrence—transactions and events that have been recorded or disclosed, have occurred, and such transactions and events pertain to the entity.

    (ii) Completeness—all transactions and events that should have been recorded have been recorded, and all related disclosures that should have been included in the financial statements have been included.

    (iii) Accuracy—amounts and other data relating to recorded transactions and events have been recorded appropriately, and related disclosures have been appropriately measured and described.

    (iv) Cutoff—transactions and events have been recorded in the correct accounting period.

    (v) Classification—transactions and events have been recorded in the proper accounts.

    (vi) Presentation—transactions and events are appropriately aggregated or disaggregated and clearly described, and related disclosures are relevant and understandable in the context of the requirements of the applicable financial reporting framework.

(b) Assertions about account balances, and related disclosures, at the period end:

    (i) Existence—assets, liabilities, and equity interests exist.

    (ii) Rights and obligations—the entity holds or controls the rights to assets, and liabilities are the obligations of the entity.

    (iii) Completeness—all assets, liabilities and equity interests that should have been recorded have been recorded, and all related disclosures that should have been included in the financial statements have been included.

    (iv) Accuracy, valuation and allocation—assets, liabilities, and equity interests have been included in the financial statements at appropriate amounts and any resulting valuation or allocation adjustments have been appropriately recorded, and related disclosures have been appropriately measured and described.

    (v) Classification—assets, liabilities, and equity interests have been recorded in the proper accounts.

    (vi) Presentation—assets, liabilities, and equity interests are appropriately aggregated or disaggregated and clearly described, and related disclosures are relevant and understandable in the context of the requirements of the applicable financial reporting framework.

Assertions about other disclosures

The assertions described in paragraph A129(a)–(b) above, adapted as appropriate, **A130** may also be used by the auditor in considering the different types of potential misstatements that may occur in disclosures not directly related to recorded classes of transactions, events, or account balances. As an example of such a disclosure, the entity may be required to describe its exposure to risks arising from financial instruments, including how the risks arise; the objectives, policies and processes for managing the risks; and the methods used to measure the risks.

Considerations specific to public sector entities

A131   When making assertions about the financial statements of public sector entities, in addition to those assertions set out in paragraph A129(a)–(b), management[1a] may often assert that transactions and events have been carried out in accordance with law, regulation or other authority. Such assertions may fall within the scope of the financial statement audit.

Process of Identifying Risks of Material Misstatement
(Ref: Para. 26(a))

A132   Information gathered by performing risk assessment procedures, including the audit evidence obtained in evaluating the design of controls and determining whether they have been implemented, is used as audit evidence to support the risk assessment. The risk assessment determines the nature, timing, and extent of further audit procedures to be performed. In identifying the risks of material misstatement in the financial statements, the auditor exercise professional skepticism in accordance with ISA (UK) 200 (Revised June 2016).[17]

A133   Appendix 2 provides examples of conditions and events that may indicate the existence of risks of material misstatement, including risks of material misstatement relating to disclosures.

A134   As explained in ISA (UK) 320 (Revised June 2016),[18] materiality and audit risk are considered when identifying and assessing the risks of material misstatement in classes of transactions, account balances and disclosures. The auditor's determination of materiality is a matter of professional judgment, and is affected by the auditor's perception of the financial reporting needs of users of the financial statements.[19]

A135   The auditor's consideration of disclosures in the financial statements when identifying risks includes quantitative and qualitative disclosures, the misstatement of which could be material (i.e., in general, misstatements are considered to be material if they could reasonably be expected to influence the economic decisions of users taken on the basis of the financial statements as a whole). Depending on the circumstances of the entity and the engagement, examples of disclosures that will have qualitative aspects and that may be relevant when assessing the risks of material misstatement include disclosures about:

- Liquidity and debt covenants of an entity in financial distress.

- Events or circumstances that have led to the recognition of an impairment loss.

- Key sources of estimation uncertainty, including assumptions about the future.

- The nature of a change in accounting policy, and other relevant disclosures required by the applicable financial reporting framework, where, for

---

[17] *ISA (UK) 200 (Revised June 2016), Overall Objectives of the Independent Auditor and the Conduct of an Audit in Accordance with International Standards on Auditing (UK), paragraph 15.*

[18] *ISA (UK) 320 (Revised June 2016), Materiality in Planning and Performing an Audit, paragraph A1.*

[19] *ISA (UK) 320 (Revised June 2016), paragraph 4.*

example, new financial reporting requirements are expected to have a significant impact on the financial position and financial performance of the entity.

- Share-based payment arrangements, including information about how any amounts recognized were determined, and other relevant disclosures.

- Related parties, and related party transactions.

- Sensitivity analysis, including the effects of changes in assumptions used in the entity's valuation techniques intended to enable users to understand the underlying measurement uncertainty of a recorded or disclosed amount.

Considerations specific to smaller entities

Disclosures in the financial statements of smaller entities may be less detailed or   **A136** less complex (e.g., some financial reporting frameworks allow smaller entities to provide fewer disclosures in the financial statements). However, this does not relieve the auditor of the responsibility to obtain an understanding of the entity and its environment, including internal control, as it relates to disclosures.

Relating Controls to Assertions
(Ref: Para. 26(c))

In making risk assessments, the auditor may identify the controls that are likely to   **A137** prevent, or detect and correct, material misstatement in specific assertions. Generally, it is useful to obtain an understanding of controls and relate them to assertions in the context of processes and systems in which they exist because individual control activities often do not in themselves address a risk. Often, only multiple control activities, together with other components of internal control, will be sufficient to address a risk.

Conversely, some control activities may have a specific effect on an individual   **A138** assertion embodied in a particular class of transactions or account balance. For example, the control activities that an entity established to ensure that its personnel are properly counting and recording the annual physical inventory relate directly to the existence and completeness assertions for the inventory account balance.

Controls can be either directly or indirectly related to an assertion. The more   **A139** indirect the relationship, the less effective that control may be in preventing, or detecting and correcting, misstatements in that assertion. For example, a sales manager's review of a summary of sales activity for specific stores by region ordinarily is only indirectly related to the completeness assertion for sales revenue. Accordingly, it may be less effective in reducing risk for that assertion than controls more directly related to that assertion, such as matching shipping documents with billing documents.

Material Misstatements

Potential misstatements in individual statements and disclosures may be judged to   **A140** be material due to size, nature or circumstances. (Ref: Para. 26(d))

460 *International Standards on Auditing (UK)*

Significant Risks

Identifying Significant Risks
(Ref: Para. 28)

A141 Significant risks often relate to significant non-routine transactions or judgmental matters. Non-routine transactions are transactions that are unusual, due to either size or nature, and that therefore occur infrequently. Judgmental matters may include the development of accounting estimates for which there is significant measurement uncertainty. Routine, non-complex transactions that are subject to systematic processing are less likely to give rise to significant risks.

A142 Risks of material misstatement may be greater for significant non-routine transactions arising from matters such as the following:

● Greater management intervention to specify the accounting treatment.

● Greater manual intervention for data collection and processing.

● Complex calculations or accounting principles.

● The nature of non-routine transactions, which may make it difficult for the entity to implement effective controls over the risks.

A143 Risks of material misstatement may be greater for significant judgmental matters that require the development of accounting estimates, arising from matters such as the following:

● Accounting principles for accounting estimates or revenue recognition may be subject to differing interpretation.

● Required judgment may be subjective or complex, or require assumptions about the effects of future events, for example, judgment about fair value.

A144 ISA (UK) 330 (Revised July 2017) describes the consequences for further audit procedures of identifying a risk as significant.[20]

Significant risks relating to the risks of material misstatement due to fraud

A145 ISA (UK) 240 (Revised June 2016) provides further requirements and guidance in relation to the identification and assessment of the risks of material misstatement due to fraud.[21]

Understanding Controls Related to Significant Risks
(Ref: Para. 29)

A146 Although risks relating to significant non-routine or judgmental matters are often less likely to be subject to routine controls, management may have other responses intended to deal with such risks. Accordingly, the auditor's understanding of whether the entity has designed and implemented controls for significant risks arising from non-routine or judgmental matters includes whether and how management responds to the risks. Such responses might include:

● Control activities such as a review of assumptions by senior management or experts.

● Documented processes for estimations.

● Approval by those charged with governance.

---

[20] *ISA (UK) 330 (Revised July 2017), paragraphs 15 and 21.*

[21] *ISA (UK) 240 (Revised June 2016), paragraphs 25–27.*

For example, where there are one-off events such as the receipt of notice of a   **A147**
significant lawsuit, consideration of the entity's response may include such
matters as whether it has been referred to appropriate experts (such as internal
or external legal counsel), whether an assessment has been made of the potential
effect, and how it is proposed that the circumstances are to be disclosed in the
financial statements.

In some cases, management may not have appropriately responded to significant   **A148**
risks of material misstatement by implementing controls over these significant
risks. Failure by management to implement such controls is an indicator of a
significant deficiency in internal control.[22]

Risks for Which Substantive Procedures Alone Do Not Provide Sufficient Appropriate Audit Evidence
(Ref: Para. 30)

Risks of material misstatement may relate directly to the recording of routine   **A149**
classes of transactions or account balances, and the preparation of reliable
financial statements. Such risks may include risks of inaccurate or incomplete
processing for routine and significant classes of transactions such as an entity's
revenue, purchases, and cash receipts or cash payments.

Where such routine business transactions are subject to highly automated   **A150**
processing with little or no manual intervention, it may not be possible to
perform only substantive procedures in relation to the risk. For example, the
auditor may consider this to be the case in circumstances where a significant
amount of an entity's information is initiated, recorded, processed, or reported
only in electronic form such as in an integrated system. In such cases:

- Audit evidence may be available only in electronic form, and its sufficiency
  and appropriateness usually depend on the effectiveness of controls over its
  accuracy and completeness.

- The potential for improper initiation or alteration of information to occur
  and not be detected may be greater if appropriate controls are not operating
  effectively.

The consequences for further audit procedures of identifying such risks are   **A151**
described in ISA (UK) 330 (Revised July 2017).[23]

Revision of Risk Assessment
(Ref: Para. 31)

During the audit, information may come to the auditor's attention that differs   **A152**
significantly from the information on which the risk assessment was based. For
example, the risk assessment may be based on an expectation that certain controls
are operating effectively. In performing tests of those controls, the auditor may
obtain audit evidence that they were not operating effectively at relevant times
during the audit. Similarly, in performing substantive procedures the auditor may
detect misstatements in amounts or frequency greater than is consistent with the
auditor's risk assessments. In such circumstances, the risk assessment may not
appropriately reflect the true circumstances of the entity and the further planned

---

[22] *ISA (UK) 265, Communicating Deficiencies in Internal Control to Those Charged with Governance and Management, paragraph A7.*

[23] *ISA (UK) 330 (Revised July 2017), paragraph 8.*

audit procedures may not be effective in detecting material misstatements. See ISA (UK) 330 (Revised July 2017) for further guidance.

Documentation
(Ref: Para. 32)

A153   The manner in which the requirements of paragraph 32 are documented is for the auditor to determine using professional judgment. For example, in audits of small entities the documentation may be incorporated in the auditor's documentation of the overall strategy and audit plan.[24] Similarly, for example, the results of the risk assessment may be documented separately, or may be documented as part of the auditor's documentation of further procedures.[25] The form and extent of the documentation is influenced by the nature, size and complexity of the entity and its internal control, availability of information from the entity and the audit methodology and technology used in the course of the audit.

A154   For entities that have uncomplicated businesses and processes relevant to financial reporting, the documentation may be simple in form and relatively brief. It is not necessary to document the entirety of the auditor's understanding of the entity and matters related to it. Key elements of understanding documented by the auditor include those on which the auditor based the assessment of the risks of material misstatement.

A155   The extent of documentation may also reflect the experience and capabilities of the members of the audit engagement team. Provided the requirements of ISA (UK) 230 (Revised June 2016) are always met, an audit undertaken by an engagement team comprising less experienced individuals may require more detailed documentation to assist them to obtain an appropriate understanding of the entity than one that includes experienced individuals.

A156   For recurring audits, certain documentation may be carried forward, updated as necessary to reflect changes in the entity's business or processes.

---

[24] *ISA (UK) 300 (Revised June 2016), Planning an Audit of Financial Statements, paragraphs 7 and 9.*

[25] *ISA (UK) 330 (Revised July 2017), paragraph 28.*

Appendix 1

(Ref: Para. 4(c), 14–24, A77–A121)

Internal Control Components

This appendix further explains the components of internal control, as set out in   **1**
paragraphs 4(c), 14–24 and A77–A121, as they relate to a financial statement
audit.

Control Environment

The control environment encompasses the following elements: **2**

(a) *Communication and enforcement of integrity and ethical values.* The
    effectiveness of controls cannot rise above the integrity and ethical values
    of the people who create, administer, and monitor them. Integrity and ethical
    behavior are the product of the entity's ethical and behavioral standards,
    how they are communicated, and how they are reinforced in practice. The
    enforcement of integrity and ethical values includes, for example,
    management actions to eliminate or mitigate incentives or temptations
    that might prompt personnel to engage in dishonest, illegal, or unethical
    acts. The communication of entity policies on integrity and ethical values
    may include the communication of behavioral standards to personnel
    through policy statements and codes of conduct and by example.

(b) *Commitment to competence.* Competence is the knowledge and skills
    necessary to accomplish tasks that define the individual's job.

(c) *Participation by those charged with governance.* An entity's control
    consciousness is influenced significantly by those charged with
    governance. The importance of the responsibilities of those charged with
    governance is recognized in codes of practice and other laws and regulations
    or guidance produced for the benefit of those charged with governance.
    Other responsibilities of those charged with governance include oversight of
    the design and effective operation of whistle blower procedures and the
    process for reviewing the effectiveness of the entity's internal control.

(d) *Management's philosophy and operating style.* Management's philosophy
    and operating style encompass a broad range of characteristics. For
    example, management's attitudes and actions toward financial reporting
    may manifest themselves through conservative or aggressive selection from
    available alternative accounting principles, or conscientiousness and
    conservatism with which accounting estimates are developed.

(e) *Organizational structure.* Establishing a relevant organizational structure
    includes considering key areas of authority and responsibility and
    appropriate lines of reporting. The appropriateness of an entity's
    organizational structure depends, in part, on its size and the nature of its
    activities.

(f) *Assignment of authority and responsibility.* The assignment of authority and
    responsibility may include policies relating to appropriate business
    practices, knowledge and experience of key personnel, and resources
    provided for carrying out duties. In addition, it may include policies and
    communications directed at ensuring that all personnel understand the

entity's objectives, know how their individual actions interrelate and contribute to those objectives, and recognize how and for what they will be held accountable.

(g)   *Human resource policies and practices.* Human resource policies and practices often demonstrate important matters in relation to the control consciousness of an entity. For example, standards for recruiting the most qualified individuals – with emphasis on educational background, prior work experience, past accomplishments, and evidence of integrity and ethical behavior – demonstrate an entity's commitment to competent and trustworthy people. Training policies that communicate prospective roles and responsibilities and include practices such as training schools and seminars illustrate expected levels of performance and behavior. Promotions driven by periodic performance appraisals demonstrate the entity's commitment to the advancement of qualified personnel to higher levels of responsibility.

Entity's Risk Assessment Process

3   For financial reporting purposes, the entity's risk assessment process includes how management identifies business risks relevant to the preparation of financial statements in accordance with the entity's applicable financial reporting framework, estimates their significance, assesses the likelihood of their occurrence, and decides upon actions to respond to and manage them and the results thereof. For example, the entity's risk assessment process may address how the entity considers the possibility of unrecorded transactions or identifies and analyzes significant estimates recorded in the financial statements.

4   Risks relevant to reliable financial reporting include external and internal events, transactions or circumstances that may occur and adversely affect an entity's ability to initiate, record, process, and report financial data consistent with the assertions of management[1a] in the financial statements. Management may initiate plans, programs, or actions to address specific risks or it may decide to accept a risk because of cost or other considerations. Risks can arise or change due to circumstances such as the following:

● *Changes in operating environment.* Changes in the regulatory or operating environment can result in changes in competitive pressures and significantly different risks.

● *New personnel.* New personnel may have a different focus on or understanding of internal control.

● *New or revamped information systems.* Significant and rapid changes in information systems can change the risk relating to internal control.

● *Rapid growth.* Significant and rapid expansion of operations can strain controls and increase the risk of a breakdown in controls.

● *New technology.* Incorporating new technologies into production processes or information systems may change the risk associated with internal control.

● *New business models, products, or activities.* Entering into business areas or transactions with which an entity has little experience may introduce new risks associated with internal control.

● *Corporate restructurings.* Restructurings may be accompanied by staff reductions and changes in supervision and segregation of duties that may change the risk associated with internal control.

- *Expanded foreign operations.* The expansion or acquisition of foreign operations carries new and often unique risks that may affect internal control, for example, additional or changed risks from foreign currency transactions.

- *New accounting pronouncements.* Adoption of new accounting principles or changing accounting principles may affect risks in preparing financial statements.

Information System, Including the Related Business Processes, Relevant to Financial Reporting, and Communication

An information system consists of infrastructure (physical and hardware   5
components), software, people, procedures, and data. Many information systems make extensive use of information technology (IT).

The information system relevant to financial reporting objectives, which includes   6
the financial reporting system, encompasses methods and records that:

- Identify and record all valid transactions.

- Describe on a timely basis the transactions in sufficient detail to permit proper classification of transactions for financial reporting.

- Measure the value of transactions in a manner that permits recording their proper monetary value in the financial statements.

- Determine the time period in which transactions occurred to permit recording of transactions in the proper accounting period.

- Present properly the transactions and related disclosures in the financial statements.

The quality of system-generated information affects management's ability to make   7
appropriate decisions in managing and controlling the entity's activities and to prepare reliable financial reports.

Communication, which involves providing an understanding of individual roles   8
and responsibilities pertaining to internal control over financial reporting, may take such forms as policy manuals, accounting and financial reporting manuals, and memoranda. Communication also can be made electronically, orally, and through the actions of management.

Control Activities

Generally, control activities that may be relevant to an audit may be categorized as   9
policies and procedures that pertain to the following:

- *Performance reviews.* These control activities include reviews and analyses of actual performance versus budgets, forecasts, and prior period performance; relating different sets of data – operating or financial – to one another, together with analyses of the relationships and investigative and corrective actions; comparing internal data with external sources of information; and review of functional or activity performance.

- *Information processing.* The two broad groupings of information systems control activities are application controls, which apply to the processing of individual applications, and general IT controls, which are policies and procedures that relate to many applications and support the effective functioning of application controls by helping to ensure the continued proper operation of information systems. Examples of application controls include checking the arithmetical accuracy of records, maintaining and reviewing accounts and trial balances, automated controls such as edit checks of input data and numerical sequence checks, and manual follow-up of exception reports. Examples of general IT controls are program change controls, controls that restrict access to programs or data, controls over the implementation of new releases of packaged software applications, and controls over system software that restrict access to or monitor the use of system utilities that could change financial data or records without leaving an audit trail.

- *Physical controls*. Controls that encompass:

  - The physical security of assets, including adequate safeguards such as secured facilities over access to assets and records.

  - The authorization for access to computer programs and data files.

  - The periodic counting and comparison with amounts shown on control records (for example, comparing the results of cash, security and inventory counts with accounting records).

  The extent to which physical controls intended to prevent theft of assets are relevant to the reliability of financial statement preparation, and therefore the audit, depends on circumstances such as when assets are highly susceptible to misappropriation.

- *Segregation of duties*. Assigning different people the responsibilities of authorizing transactions, recording transactions, and maintaining custody of assets. Segregation of duties is intended to reduce the opportunities to allow any person to be in a position to both perpetrate and conceal errors or fraud in the normal course of the person's duties.

10   Certain control activities may depend on the existence of appropriate higher level policies established by management or those charged with governance. For example, authorization controls may be delegated under established guidelines, such as investment criteria set by those charged with governance; alternatively, non-routine transactions such as major acquisitions or divestments may require specific high level approval, including in some cases that of shareholders.

Monitoring of Controls

11   An important management responsibility is to establish and maintain internal control on an ongoing basis. Management's monitoring of controls includes considering whether they are operating as intended and that they are modified as appropriate for changes in conditions. Monitoring of controls may include activities such as management's review of whether bank reconciliations are being prepared on a timely basis, internal auditors' evaluation of sales personnel's compliance with the entity's policies on terms of sales contracts, and a legal department's oversight of compliance with the entity's ethical or business practice policies. Monitoring is done also to ensure that controls continue to operate effectively over time. For example, if the timeliness and accuracy of bank reconciliations are not monitored, personnel are likely to stop preparing them.

12   Internal auditors or personnel performing similar functions may contribute to the monitoring of an entity's controls through separate evaluations. Ordinarily, they regularly provide information about the functioning of internal control, focusing considerable attention on evaluating the effectiveness of internal control, and

communicate information about strengths and deficiencies in internal control and recommendations for improving internal control.

Monitoring activities may include using information from communications from **13** external parties that may indicate problems or highlight areas in need of improvement. Customers implicitly corroborate billing data by paying their invoices or complaining about their charges. In addition, regulators may communicate with the entity concerning matters that affect the functioning of internal control, for example, communications concerning examinations by bank regulatory agencies. Also, management may consider communications relating to internal control from external auditors in performing monitoring activities.

Appendix 2

(Ref: Para. A41, A133)

Conditions and Events That May Indicate Risks of Material Misstatement

The following are examples of conditions and events that may indicate the existence of risks of material misstatement in the financial statements. The examples provided cover a broad range of conditions and events; however, not all conditions and events are relevant to every audit engagement and the list of examples is not necessarily complete.

- Operations in regions that are economically unstable, for example, countries with significant currency devaluation or highly inflationary economies.

- Operations exposed to volatile markets, for example, futures trading.

- Operations that are subject to a high degree of complex regulation.

- Going concern and liquidity issues including loss of significant customers.

- Constraints on the availability of capital and credit.

- Changes in the industry in which the entity operates.

- Changes in the supply chain.

- Developing or offering new products or services, or moving into new lines of business.

- Expanding into new locations.

- Changes in the entity such as large acquisitions or reorganizations or other unusual events.

- Entities or business segments likely to be sold.

- The existence of complex alliances and joint ventures.

- Use of off balance sheet finance, special-purpose entities, and other complex financing arrangements.

- Significant transactions with related parties.

- Lack of personnel with appropriate accounting and financial reporting skills.

- Changes in key personnel including departure of key executives.

- Deficiencies in internal control, especially those not addressed by management.

- Incentives for management and employees to engage in fraudulent financial reporting.

- Inconsistencies between the entity's IT strategy and its business strategies.

- Changes in the IT environment.

- Installation of significant new IT systems related to financial reporting.

- Inquiries into the entity's operations or financial results by regulatory or government bodies.

- Past misstatements, history of errors or a significant amount of adjustments at period end.

- Significant amount of non-routine or non-systematic transactions including intercompany transactions and large revenue transactions at period end.

- Transactions that are recorded based on management's intent, for example, debt refinancing, assets to be sold and classification of marketable securities.

- Application of new accounting pronouncements.

- Accounting measurements that involve complex processes.

- Events or transactions that involve significant measurement uncertainty, including accounting estimates, and related disclosures.

- Omission, or obscuring, of significant information in disclosures.

- Pending litigation and contingent liabilities, for example, sales warranties, financial guarantees and environmental remediation.

ISA (UK) 320 (Revised June 2016)
Materiality in Planning and
Performing an Audit

*(Effective for audits of financial statements for periods commencing on
or after 17 June 2016)*

Contents

	Paragraphs
Introduction	1 - 7
Scope of this ISA (UK)	1
Materiality in the context of an audit	2 - 6
Effective date	7
Objective	8
Definition	9
Requirements	10 - 14
Determining materiality and performance materiality when planning the audit	10 - 11
Revision as the audit progresses	12 - 13
Documentation	14
Application and other explanatory material	A1 - A13
Materiality and audit risk	A1
Materiality in the context of an audit	A1a
Determining materiality and performance materiality when planning the audit	A2 - A12
Revision as the audit progresses	A13

International Standard on Auditing (UK) (ISA (UK)) 320 (Revised June 2016), *Materiality in Planning and Performing an Audit*, should be read in the context of ISA (UK) 200 (Revised June 2016), *Overall Objectives of the Independent Auditor and the Conduct of an Audit in Accordance with International Standards on Auditing (UK)*.

Introduction

Scope of this ISA (UK)

1   This International Standard on Auditing (UK) (ISA (UK)) deals with the auditor's responsibility to apply the concept of materiality in planning and performing an audit of financial statements. ISA (UK) 450 (Revised June 2016)[1] explains how materiality is applied in evaluating the effect of identified misstatements on the audit and of uncorrected misstatements, if any, on the financial statements.

Materiality in the Context of an Audit

2   Financial reporting frameworks often discuss the concept of materiality in the context of the preparation and presentation of financial statements. Although financial reporting frameworks may discuss materiality in different terms, they generally explain that:

- Misstatements, including omissions, are considered to be material if they, individually or in the aggregate, could reasonably be expected to influence the economic decisions of users taken on the basis of the financial statements;

- Judgments about materiality are made in light of surrounding circumstances, and are affected by the size or nature of a misstatement, or a combination of both; and

- Judgments about matters that are material to users of the financial statements are based on a consideration of the common financial information needs of users as a group.[2] The possible effect of misstatements on specific individual users, whose needs may vary widely, is not considered.

3   Such a discussion, if present in the applicable financial reporting framework, provides a frame of reference to the auditor in determining materiality for the audit. If the applicable financial reporting framework does not include a discussion of the concept of materiality, the characteristics referred to in paragraph 2 provide the auditor with such a frame of reference.

4   The auditor's determination of materiality is a matter of professional judgment, and is affected by the auditor's perception of the financial information needs of users of the financial statements. In this context, it is reasonable for the auditor to assume that users:

(a)   Have a reasonable knowledge of business and economic activities and accounting and a willingness to study the information in the financial statements with reasonable diligence;

(b)   Understand that financial statements are prepared, presented and audited to levels of materiality;

---

[1]   *ISA (UK) 450 (Revised June 2016), Evaluation of Misstatements Identified during the Audit.*

[2]   *For example, the Framework for the Preparation and Presentation of Financial Statements, adopted by the International Accounting Standards Board in April 2001, indicates that, for a profit-oriented entity, as investors are providers of risk capital to the enterprise, the provision of financial statements that meet their needs will also meet most of the needs of other users that financial statements can satisfy.*

The Framework for the Preparation and Presentation of Financial Statements, has not been promulgated by the FRC for application in the UK.

(c)   Recognize the uncertainties inherent in the measurement of amounts based on the use of estimates, judgment and the consideration of future events; and

(d)   Make reasonable economic decisions on the basis of the information in the financial statements.

The concept of materiality is applied by the auditor both in planning and   **5** performing the audit, and in evaluating the effect of identified misstatements on the audit and of uncorrected misstatements, if any, on the financial statements and in forming the opinion in the auditor's report. (Ref: Para. A1)

In planning the audit, the auditor makes judgments about misstatements that will   **6** be considered material. These judgments provide a basis for:

(a)   Determining the nature, timing and extent of risk assessment procedures;

(b)   Identifying and assessing the risks of material misstatement; and

(c)   Determining the nature, timing and extent of further audit procedures.

The materiality determined when planning the audit does not necessarily establish an amount below which uncorrected misstatements, individually or in the aggregate, will always be evaluated as immaterial. The circumstances related to some misstatements may cause the auditor to evaluate them as material even if they are below materiality. It is not practicable to design audit procedures to detect all misstatements that could be material solely because of their nature. However consideration of the nature of potential misstatements in disclosures is relevant to the design of audit procedures to address risks of material misstatement.[3] In addition, when evaluating the effect on the financial statements of all uncorrected misstatements, the auditor considers not only the size but also the nature of uncorrected misstatements, and the particular circumstances of their occurrence.[4] (Ref: Para. A1a)

Effective Date

This ISA (UK) is effective for audits of financial statements for periods   **7** commencing on or after 17 June 2016. Earlier adoption is permitted.

Objective

The objective of the auditor is to apply the concept of materiality appropriately in   **8** planning and performing the audit.

Definition

For purposes of the ISAs (UK), performance materiality means the amount or   **9** amounts set by the auditor at less than materiality for the financial statements as a whole to reduce to an appropriately low level the probability that the aggregate of uncorrected and undetected misstatements exceeds materiality for the financial statements as a whole. If applicable, performance materiality also refers to the amount or amounts set by the auditor at less than the materiality level or levels for particular classes of transactions, account balances or disclosures.

---

[3] See ISA (UK) 315 (Revised June 2016), *Identifying and Assessing the Risks of Material Misstatement through Understanding the Entity and its Environment*, paragraphs A128a–A128b.

[4] *ISA (UK) 450 (Revised June 2016), paragraph A16.*

Requirements

Determining Materiality and Performance Materiality When Planning the Audit

10   When establishing the overall audit strategy, the auditor shall determine materiality for the financial statements as a whole. If, in the specific circumstances of the entity, there is one or more particular classes of transactions, account balances or disclosures for which misstatements of lesser amounts than materiality for the financial statements as a whole could reasonably be expected to influence the economic decisions of users taken on the basis of the financial statements, the auditor shall also determine the materiality level or levels to be applied to those particular classes of transactions, account balances or disclosures. (Ref: Para. A2–A11)

11   The auditor shall determine performance materiality for purposes of assessing the risks of material misstatement and determining the nature, timing and extent of further audit procedures. (Ref: Para. A12)

Revision as the Audit Progresses

12   The auditor shall revise materiality for the financial statements as a whole (and, if applicable, the materiality level or levels for particular classes of transactions, account balances or disclosures) in the event of becoming aware of information during the audit that would have caused the auditor to have determined a different amount (or amounts) initially. (Ref: Para. A13)

13   If the auditor concludes that a lower materiality for the financial statements as a whole (and, if applicable, materiality level or levels for particular classes of transactions, account balances or disclosures) than that initially determined is appropriate, the auditor shall determine whether it is necessary to revise performance materiality, and whether the nature, timing and extent of the further audit procedures remain appropriate.

Documentation

14   The auditor shall include in the audit documentation the following amounts and the factors considered in their determination:[5]

(a)   Materiality for the financial statements as a whole (see paragraph 10);

(b)   If applicable, the materiality level or levels for particular classes of transactions, account balances or disclosures (see paragraph 10);

(c)   Performance materiality (see paragraph 11); and

(d)   Any revision of (a)–(c) as the audit progressed (see paragraphs 12–13).

---

[5] *ISA (UK) 230 (Revised June 2016), Audit Documentation, paragraphs 8–11, and paragraph A6.*

Application and Other Explanatory Material

Materiality and Audit Risk
(Ref: Para. 5)

In conducting an audit of financial statements, the overall objectives of the auditor   **A1**
are to obtain reasonable assurance about whether the financial statements as a
whole are free from material misstatement, whether due to fraud or error, thereby
enabling the auditor to express an opinion on whether the financial statements are
prepared, in all material respects, in accordance with an applicable financial
reporting framework; and to report on the financial statements, and communicate
as required by the ISAs (UK), in accordance with the auditor's findings.[6] The
auditor obtains reasonable assurance by obtaining sufficient appropriate audit
evidence to reduce audit risk to an acceptably low level.[7] Audit risk is the risk that
the auditor expresses an inappropriate audit opinion when the financial statements
are materially misstated. Audit risk is a function of the risks of material
misstatement and detection risk.[8] Materiality and audit risk are considered
throughout the audit, in particular, when:

(a)   Identifying and assessing the risks of material misstatement;[9]

(b)   Determining the nature, timing and extent of further audit procedures;[10] and

(c)   Evaluating the effect of uncorrected misstatements, if any, on the financial
statements[11] and in forming the opinion in the auditor's report.[12]

Materiality in the Context of an Audit
(Ref: Para. 6)

Identifying and assessing the risks of material misstatement[13] involves the use of   **A1a**
professional judgment to identify those classes of transactions, account balances
and disclosures, including qualitative disclosures, the misstatement of which
could be material (i.e., in general, misstatements are considered to be material if
they could reasonably be expected to influence the economic decisions of users
taken on the basis of the financial statements as a whole). When considering
whether misstatements in qualitative disclosures could be material, the auditor
may identify relevant factors such as:

- The circumstances of the entity for the period (for example, the entity may
have undertaken a significant business combination during the period).

- The applicable financial reporting framework, including changes therein
(for example, a new financial reporting standard may require new qualitative
disclosures that are significant to the entity).

---

[6] *ISA (UK) 200 (Revised June 2016), Overall Objectives of the Independent Auditor and the Conduct of an Audit in
Accordance with International Standards on Auditing (UK), paragraph 11.*

[7] *ISA (UK) 200 (Revised June 2016), paragraph 17.*

[8] *ISA (UK) 200 (Revised June 2016), paragraph 13(c).*

[9] *ISA (UK) 315 (Revised June 2016), Identifying and Assessing the Risks of Material Misstatements through
Understanding the Entity and Its Environment.*

[10] *ISA (UK) 330 (Revised June 2016), The Auditor's Responses to Assessed Risks.*

[11] *ISA (UK) 450 (Revised June 2016).*

[12] *ISA (UK) 700 (Revised June 2016), Forming an Opinion and Reporting on Financial Statements.*

[13] *ISA (UK) 315 (Revised June 2016), paragraph 25, requires the auditor to identify and assess the risk of material
misstatement at the financial statement and assertion level.*

- Qualitative disclosures that are important to users of the financial statements because of the nature of an entity (for example, liquidity risk disclosures may be important to users of the financial statements for a financial institution).

Determining Materiality and Performance Materiality When Planning the Audit

Considerations Specific to Public Sector Entities
(Ref: Para. 10)

A2   In the case of a public sector entity, legislators and regulators are often the primary users of its financial statements. Furthermore, the financial statements may be used to make decisions other than economic decisions. The determination of materiality for the financial statements as a whole (and, if applicable, materiality level or levels for particular classes of transactions, account balances or disclosures) in an audit of the financial statements of a public sector entity is therefore influenced by law, regulation or other authority, and by the financial information needs of legislators and the public in relation to public sector programs.

Use of Benchmarks in Determining Materiality for the Financial Statements as a Whole
(Ref: Para. 10)

A3   Determining materiality involves the exercise of professional judgment. A percentage is often applied to a chosen benchmark as a starting point in determining materiality for the financial statements as a whole. Factors that may affect the identification of an appropriate benchmark include the following:

- The elements of the financial statements (for example, assets, liabilities, equity, revenue, expenses);

- Whether there are items on which the attention of the users of the particular entity's financial statements tends to be focused (for example, for the purpose of evaluating financial performance users may tend to focus on profit, revenue or net assets);

- The nature of the entity, where the entity is in its life cycle, and the industry and economic environment in which the entity operates;

- The entity's ownership structure and the way it is financed (for example, if an entity is financed solely by debt rather than equity, users may put more emphasis on assets, and claims on them, than on the entity's earnings); and

- The relative volatility of the benchmark.

A4   Examples of benchmarks that may be appropriate, depending on the circumstances of the entity, include categories of reported income such as profit before tax, total revenue, gross profit and total expenses, total equity or net asset value. Profit before tax from continuing operations is often used for profit-oriented entities. When profit before tax from continuing operations is volatile, other benchmarks may be more appropriate, such as gross profit or total revenues.

A5   In relation to the chosen benchmark, relevant financial data ordinarily includes prior periods' financial results and financial positions, the period-to-date financial results and financial position, and budgets or forecasts for the current period, adjusted for significant changes in the circumstances of the entity (for example, a significant business acquisition) and relevant changes of conditions in the industry or economic environment in which the entity operates. For example, when, as a starting point, materiality for the financial statements as a whole is determined for a particular entity based on a percentage of profit before tax from continuing operations, circumstances that give rise to an exceptional decrease or increase in such profit may lead the auditor to conclude that materiality for the financial statements as a whole is more appropriately determined using a normalized profit before tax from continuing operations figure based on past results.

Materiality relates to the financial statements on which the auditor is reporting. **A6** Where the financial statements are prepared for a financial reporting period of more or less than twelve months, such as may be the case for a new entity or a change in the financial reporting period, materiality relates to the financial statements prepared for that financial reporting period.

Determining a percentage to be applied to a chosen benchmark involves the **A7** exercise of professional judgment. There is a relationship between the percentage and the chosen benchmark, such that a percentage applied to profit before tax from continuing operations will normally be higher than a percentage applied to total revenue. For example, the auditor may consider five percent of profit before tax from continuing operations to be appropriate for a profit-oriented entity in a manufacturing industry, while the auditor may consider one percent of total revenue or total expenses to be appropriate for a not-for-profit entity. Higher or lower percentages, however, may be deemed appropriate in the circumstances.

Considerations Specific to Small Entities

When an entity's profit before tax from continuing operations is consistently **A8** nominal, as might be the case for an owner-managed business where the owner takes much of the profit before tax in the form of remuneration, a benchmark such as profit before remuneration and tax may be more relevant.

Considerations Specific to Public Sector Entities

In an audit of a public sector entity, total cost or net cost (expenses less revenues or **A9** expenditure less receipts) may be appropriate benchmarks for program activities. Where a public sector entity has custody of public assets, assets may be an appropriate benchmark.

Materiality Level or Levels for Particular Classes of Transactions, Account Balances or Disclosures
(Ref: Para. 10)

Factors that may indicate the existence of one or more particular classes of **A10** transactions, account balances or disclosures for which misstatements of lesser amounts than materiality for the financial statements as a whole could reasonably be expected to influence the economic decisions of users taken on the basis of the financial statements include the following:

- Whether law, regulation or the applicable financial reporting framework affect users' expectations regarding the measurement or disclosure of certain items (for example, related party transactions, and the remuneration of management and those charged with governance, and sensitivity analysis for fair value accounting estimates with high estimation uncertainty).

- The key disclosures in relation to the industry in which the entity operates (for example, research and development costs for a pharmaceutical company).

- Whether attention is focused on a particular aspect of the entity's business that is separately disclosed in the financial statements (for example, disclosures about segments or a significant business combination).

A11   In considering whether, in the specific circumstances of the entity, such classes of transactions, account balances or disclosures exist, the auditor may find it useful to obtain an understanding of the views and expectations of those charged with governance and management.

Performance Materiality
(Ref: Para. 11)

A12   Planning the audit solely to detect individually material misstatements overlooks the fact that the aggregate of individually immaterial misstatements may cause the financial statements to be materially misstated, and leaves no margin for possible undetected misstatements. Performance materiality (which, as defined, is one or more amounts) is set to reduce to an appropriately low level the probability that the aggregate of uncorrected and undetected misstatements in the financial statements exceeds materiality for the financial statements as a whole. Similarly, performance materiality relating to a materiality level determined for a particular class of transactions, account balance or disclosure is set to reduce to an appropriately low level the probability that the aggregate of uncorrected and undetected misstatements in that particular class of transactions, account balance or disclosure exceeds the materiality level for that particular class of transactions, account balance or disclosure. The determination of performance materiality is not a simple mechanical calculation and involves the exercise of professional judgment. It is affected by the auditor's understanding of the entity, updated during the performance of the risk assessment procedures; and the nature and extent of misstatements identified in previous audits and thereby the auditor's expectations in relation to misstatements in the current period.

Revision as the Audit Progresses
(Ref: Para. 12)

A13   Materiality for the financial statements as a whole (and, if applicable, the materiality level or levels for particular classes of transactions, account balances or disclosures) may need to be revised as a result of a change in circumstances that occurred during the audit (for example, a decision to dispose of a major part of the entity's business), new information, or a change in the auditor's understanding of the entity and its operations as a result of performing further audit procedures. For example, if during the audit it appears as though actual financial results are likely to be substantially different from the anticipated period end financial results that were used initially to determine materiality for the financial statements as a whole, the auditor revises that materiality.

ISA (UK) 330 (Revised July 2017) The Auditor's Responses to Assessed Risks (2017)

(Effective for audits of financial statements for periods commencing on or after 15 December 2017)

Contents

Paragraphs

Introduction
Scope of this ISA (UK)   1
Effective date   2

Objective   3

Definitions   4

Requirements
Overall responses   5
Audit procedures responsive to the assessed risks of material misstatement
at the assertion level   6 - 23
Adequacy of presentation of the financial statements   24
Evaluating the sufficiency and appropriateness of audit evidence   25 - 27
Documentation   28 - 30

Application and other explanatory material
Overall responses   A1 - A3
Audit procedures responsive to the assessed risks of material misstatement
at the assertion level   A4 - A58
Adequacy of presentation of the financial statements   A59
Evaluating the sufficiency and appropriateness of audit evidence   A60 - A62
Documentation   A63

Annexure: Conforming Amendments to Other ISAs (UK)

International Standard on Auditing (UK) (ISA (UK)) 330 (Revised July 2017), *The Auditor's Responses to Assessed Risks*, should be read in conjunction with ISA (UK) 200 (Revised June 2016), *Overall Objectives of the Independent Auditor and the Conduct of an Audit in Accordance with International Standards on Auditing (UK)*.

Editorial Note: This revised version (issued in July 2017) replaces ISA 330 The Auditor's Responses to Assessed Risks. This standard is still extant at 30 April 2018 for audits of financial statements commencing before 15/12/17, and is available at https://library.croneri.co.uk/isauk330r2

Introduction

Scope of this ISA (UK)

1   This International Standard on Auditing (UK) (ISA (UK)) deals with the auditor's responsibility to design and implement responses to the risks of material misstatement identified and assessed by the auditor in accordance with ISA (UK) 315 (Revised June 2016)[1] in an audit of financial statements.

Effective Date

2   This ISA (UK) is effective for audits of financial statements for periods commencing on or after 15 December 2017.

Objective

3   The objective of the auditor is to obtain sufficient appropriate audit evidence regarding the assessed risks of material misstatement, through designing and implementing appropriate responses to those risks.

Definitions

4   For purposes of the ISAs (UK), the following terms have the meanings attributed below:

(a)   Substantive procedure – An audit procedure designed to detect material misstatements at the assertion level. Substantive procedures comprise:

(i)   Tests of details (of classes of transactions, account balances, and disclosures); and

(ii)   Substantive analytical procedures.

(b)   Test of controls – An audit procedure designed to evaluate the operating effectiveness of controls in preventing, or detecting and correcting, material misstatements at the assertion level.

Requirements

Overall Responses

5   The auditor shall design and implement overall responses to address the assessed risks of material misstatement at the financial statement level. (Ref: Para. A1–A3)

Audit Procedures Responsive to the Assessed Risks of Material Misstatement at the Assertion Level

6   The auditor shall design and perform further audit procedures whose nature, timing, and extent are based on and are responsive to the assessed risks of material misstatement at the assertion level. (Ref: Para. A4–A8)

---

[1] ISA (UK) 315 (Revised June 2016), *Identifying and Assessing the Risks of Material Misstatement through Understanding the Entity and Its Environment.*

In designing the further audit procedures to be performed, the auditor shall: **7**

(a) Consider the reasons for the assessment given to the risk of material misstatement at the assertion level for each class of transactions, account balance, and disclosure, including:

    (i) The likelihood of material misstatement due to the particular characteristics of the relevant class of transactions, account balance, or disclosure (that is, the inherent risk); and

    (ii) Whether the risk assessment takes account of relevant controls (that is, the control risk), thereby requiring the auditor to obtain audit evidence to determine whether the controls are operating effectively (that is, the auditor intends to rely on the operating effectiveness of controls in determining the nature, timing and extent of substantive procedures); and (Ref: Para. A9–A18)

(b) Obtain more persuasive audit evidence the higher the auditor's assessment of risk. (Ref: Para. A19)

Tests of Controls

The auditor shall design and perform tests of controls to obtain sufficient   **8** appropriate audit evidence as to the operating effectiveness of relevant controls if:

(a) The auditor's assessment of risks of material misstatement at the assertion level includes an expectation that the controls are operating effectively (that is, the auditor intends to rely on the operating effectiveness of controls in determining the nature, timing and extent of substantive procedures); or

(b) Substantive procedures alone cannot provide sufficient appropriate audit evidence at the assertion level. (Ref: Para. A20–A24)

In designing and performing tests of controls, the auditor shall obtain more   **9** persuasive audit evidence the greater the reliance the auditor places on the effectiveness of a control. (Ref: Para. A25)

Nature and Extent of Tests of Controls

In designing and performing tests of controls, the auditor shall: **10**

(a) Perform other audit procedures in combination with inquiry to obtain audit evidence about the operating effectiveness of the controls, including:

    (i) How the controls were applied at relevant times during the period under audit;

    (ii) The consistency with which they were applied; and

    (iii) By whom or by what means they were applied. (Ref: Para. A26–29)

(b) Determine whether the controls to be tested depend upon other controls (indirect controls) and, if so, whether it is necessary to obtain audit evidence supporting the effective operation of those indirect controls. (Ref: Para. A30–A31)

Timing of Tests of Controls

The auditor shall test controls for the particular time, or throughout the period, for   **11** which the auditor intends to rely on those controls, subject to paragraphs 12 and 15 below, in order to provide an appropriate basis for the auditor's intended reliance. (Ref: Para. A32)

Using audit evidence obtained during an interim period

12   If the auditor obtains audit evidence about the operating effectiveness of controls during an interim period, the auditor shall:

(a)   Obtain audit evidence about significant changes to those controls subsequent to the interim period; and

(b)   Determine the additional audit evidence to be obtained for the remaining period. (Ref: Para. A33–A34)

Using audit evidence obtained in previous audits

13   In determining whether it is appropriate to use audit evidence about the operating effectiveness of controls obtained in previous audits, and, if so, the length of the time period that may elapse before retesting a control, the auditor shall consider the following:

(a)   The effectiveness of other elements of internal control, including the control environment, the entity's monitoring of controls, and the entity's risk assessment process;

(b)   The risks arising from the characteristics of the control, including whether it is manual or automated;

(c)   The effectiveness of general IT controls;

(d)   The effectiveness of the control and its application by the entity, including the nature and extent of deviations in the application of the control noted in previous audits, and whether there have been personnel changes that significantly affect the application of the control;

(e)   Whether the lack of a change in a particular control poses a risk due to changing circumstances; and

(f)   The risks of material misstatement and the extent of reliance on the control. (Ref: Para. A35)

14   If the auditor plans to use audit evidence from a previous audit about the operating effectiveness of specific controls, the auditor shall establish the continuing relevance of that evidence by obtaining audit evidence about whether significant changes in those controls have occurred subsequent to the previous audit. The auditor shall obtain this evidence by performing inquiry combined with observation or inspection, to confirm the understanding of those specific controls, and:

(a)   If there have been changes that affect the continuing relevance of the audit evidence from the previous audit, the auditor shall test the controls in the current audit. (Ref: Para. A36)

(b)   If there have not been such changes, the auditor shall test the controls at least once in every third audit, and shall test some controls each audit to avoid the possibility of testing all the controls on which the auditor intends to rely in a single audit period with no testing of controls in the subsequent two audit periods. (Ref: Para. A37–A39)

Controls over significant risks

15   If the auditor plans to rely on controls over a risk the auditor has determined to be a significant risk, the auditor shall test those controls in the current period.

Evaluating the Operating Effectiveness of Controls

When evaluating the operating effectiveness of relevant controls, the auditor shall   **16**
evaluate whether misstatements that have been detected by substantive procedures
indicate that controls are not operating effectively. The absence of misstatements
detected by substantive procedures, however, does not provide audit evidence that
controls related to the assertion being tested are effective. (Ref: Para. A40)

If deviations from controls upon which the auditor intends to rely are detected, the   **17**
auditor shall make specific inquiries to understand these matters and their potential
consequences, and shall determine whether: (Ref: Para. A41)

(a)   The tests of controls that have been performed provide an appropriate basis
       for reliance on the controls;

(b)   Additional tests of controls are necessary; or

(c)   The potential risks of misstatement need to be addressed using substantive
       procedures.

Substantive Procedures

Irrespective of the assessed risks of material misstatement, the auditor shall design   **18**
and perform substantive procedures for each material class of transactions,
account balance, and disclosure. (Ref: Para. A42–A47)

The auditor shall consider whether external confirmation procedures are to be   **19**
performed as substantive audit procedures. (Ref: Para. A48–A51)

For audits of financial statements of public interest entities, the auditor shall   **19R-1**
assess the valuation methods applied to the various items in the financial
statements including any impact of changes of such methods. (Ref: Para. A51-1)

Substantive Procedures Related to the Financial Statement Closing Process

The auditor's substantive procedures shall include the following audit procedures   **20**
related to the financial statement closing process:

(a)   Agreeing or reconciling information in the financial statements with the
       underlying accounting records, including agreeing or reconciling
       information in disclosures, whether such information is obtained from
       within or outside of the general and subsidiary ledgers; and

(b)   Examining material journal entries and other adjustments made during the
       course of preparing the financial statements. (Ref: Para. A52)

Substantive Procedures Responsive to Significant Risks

If the auditor has determined that an assessed risk of material misstatement at the   **21**
assertion level is a significant risk, the auditor shall perform substantive
procedures that are specifically responsive to that risk. When the approach to a
significant risk consists only of substantive procedures, those procedures shall
include tests of details. (Ref: Para. A53)

Timing of Substantive Procedures

If substantive procedures are performed at an interim date, the auditor shall cover   **22**
the remaining period by performing:

(a)   substantive procedures, combined with tests of controls for the intervening
       period; or

(b)   if the auditor determines that it is sufficient, further substantive procedures only

that provide a reasonable basis for extending the audit conclusions from the interim date to the period end. (Ref: Para. A54–A57)

23   If misstatements that the auditor did not expect when assessing the risks of material misstatement are detected at an interim date, the auditor shall evaluate whether the related assessment of risk and the planned nature, timing, or extent of substantive procedures covering the remaining period need to be modified. (Ref: Para. A58)

Adequacy of Presentation of the Financial Statements

24   The auditor shall perform audit procedures to evaluate whether the overall presentation of the financial statements is in accordance with the applicable financial reporting framework. In making this evaluation, the auditor shall consider whether the financial statements are presented in a manner that reflects the appropriate:

- Classification and description of financial information and the underlying transactions, events and conditions; and
- Presentation, structure and content of the financial statements. (Ref: Para. A59)

Evaluating the Sufficiency and Appropriateness of Audit Evidence

25   Based on the audit procedures performed and the audit evidence obtained, the auditor shall evaluate before the conclusion of the audit whether the assessments of the risks of material misstatement at the assertion level remain appropriate. (Ref: Para. A60–A61)

26   The auditor shall conclude whether sufficient appropriate audit evidence has been obtained. In forming an opinion, the auditor shall consider all relevant audit evidence, regardless of whether it appears to corroborate or to contradict the assertions in the financial statements. (Ref: Para. A62)

27   If the auditor has not obtained sufficient appropriate audit evidence as to a material financial statement assertion, the auditor shall attempt to obtain further audit evidence. If the auditor is unable to obtain sufficient appropriate audit evidence, the auditor shall express a qualified opinion or disclaim an opinion on the financial statements.

Documentation

28   The auditor shall include in the audit documentation:[2]

(a)   The overall responses to address the assessed risks of material misstatement at the financial statement level, and the nature, timing, and extent of the further audit procedures performed;

(b)   The linkage of those procedures with the assessed risks at the assertion level; and

(c)   The results of the audit procedures, including the conclusions where these are not otherwise clear. (Ref: Para. A63)

---

[2] *ISA (UK) 230 (Revised June 2016), Audit Documentation, paragraphs 8–11, and paragraph A6.*

If the auditor plans to use audit evidence about the operating effectiveness of controls obtained in previous audits, the auditor shall include in the audit documentation the conclusions reached about relying on such controls that were tested in a previous audit. **29**

The auditor's documentation shall demonstrate that information in the financial statements agrees or reconciles with the underlying accounting records, including agreeing or reconciling disclosures, whether such information is obtained from within or outside of the general and subsidiary ledgers. **30**

***

Application and Other Explanatory Material

Overall Responses
(Ref: Para. 5)

Overall responses to address the assessed risks of material misstatement at the financial statement level may include: **A1**

- Emphasizing to the audit team the need to maintain professional skepticism.

- Assigning more experienced staff or those with special skills or using experts.

- Providing more supervision.

- Incorporating additional elements of unpredictability in the selection of further audit procedures to be performed.

- Making general changes to the nature, timing, or extent of audit procedures, for example: performing substantive procedures at the period end instead of at an interim date; or modifying the nature of audit procedures to obtain more persuasive audit evidence.

The assessment of the risks of material misstatement at the financial statement level, and thereby the auditor's overall responses, is affected by the auditor's understanding of the control environment. An effective control environment may allow the auditor to have more confidence in internal control and the reliability of audit evidence generated internally within the entity and thus, for example, allow the auditor to conduct some audit procedures at an interim date rather than at the period end. Deficiencies in the control environment, however, have the opposite effect; for example, the auditor may respond to an ineffective control environment by: **A2**

- Conducting more audit procedures as of the period end rather than at an interim date.

- Obtaining more extensive audit evidence from substantive procedures.

- Increasing the number of locations to be included in the audit scope.

Such considerations, therefore, have a significant bearing on the auditor's general approach, for example, an emphasis on substantive procedures (substantive approach), or an approach that uses tests of controls as well as substantive procedures (combined approach). **A3**

Audit Procedures Responsive to the Assessed Risks of Material Misstatement at the Assertion Level

The Nature, Timing, and Extent of Further Audit Procedures
(Ref: Para. 6)

A4 The auditor's assessment of the identified risks at the assertion level provides a basis for considering the appropriate audit approach for designing and performing further audit procedures. For example, the auditor may determine that:

(a) Only by performing tests of controls may the auditor achieve an effective response to the assessed risk of material misstatement for a particular assertion;

(b) Performing only substantive procedures is appropriate for particular assertions and, therefore, the auditor excludes the effect of controls from the relevant risk assessment. This may be because the auditor's risk assessment procedures have not identified any effective controls relevant to the assertion, or because testing controls would be inefficient and therefore the auditor does not intend to rely on the operating effectiveness of controls in determining the nature, timing and extent of substantive procedures; or

(c) A combined approach using both tests of controls and substantive procedures is an effective approach.

However, as required by paragraph 18, irrespective of the approach selected, the auditor designs and performs substantive procedures for each material class of transactions, account balance, and disclosure.

A5 The nature of an audit procedure refers to its purpose (i.e., test of controls or substantive procedure) and its type (that is, inspection, observation, inquiry, confirmation, recalculation, reperformance, or analytical procedure). The nature of the audit procedures is of most importance in responding to the assessed risks.

A6 Timing of an audit procedure refers to when it is performed, or the period or date to which the audit evidence applies.

A7 Extent of an audit procedure refers to the quantity to be performed, for example, a sample size or the number of observations of a control activity.

A8 Designing and performing further audit procedures whose nature, timing, and extent are based on and are responsive to the assessed risks of material misstatement at the assertion level provides a clear linkage between the auditor's further audit procedures and the risk assessment.

Responding to the Assessed Risks at the Assertion Level
(Ref: Para. 7(a))

Nature

A9 The auditor's assessed risks may affect both the types of audit procedures to be performed and their combination. For example, when an assessed risk is high, the auditor may confirm the completeness of the terms of a contract with the counterparty, in addition to inspecting the document. Further, certain audit procedures may be more appropriate for some assertions than others. For example, in relation to revenue, tests of controls may be most responsive to the assessed risk of misstatement of the completeness assertion, whereas substantive procedures may be most responsive to the assessed risk of misstatement of the occurrence assertion.

The reasons for the assessment given to a risk are relevant in determining the   **A10** nature of audit procedures. For example, if an assessed risk is lower because of the particular characteristics of a class of transactions without consideration of the related controls, then the auditor may determine that substantive analytical procedures alone provide sufficient appropriate audit evidence. On the other hand, if the assessed risk is lower because of internal controls, and the auditor intends to base the substantive procedures on that low assessment, then the auditor performs tests of those controls, as required by paragraph 8(a). This may be the case, for example, for a class of transactions of reasonably uniform, non-complex characteristics that are routinely processed and controlled by the entity's information system.

Timing

The auditor may perform tests of controls or substantive procedures at an interim   **A11** date or at the period end. The higher the risk of material misstatement, the more likely it is that the auditor may decide it is more effective to perform substantive procedures nearer to, or at, the period end rather than at an earlier date, or to perform audit procedures unannounced or at unpredictable times (for example, performing audit procedures at selected locations on an unannounced basis). This is particularly relevant when considering the response to the risks of fraud. For example, the auditor may conclude that, when the risks of intentional misstatement or manipulation have been identified, audit procedures to extend audit conclusions from interim date to the period end would not be effective.

On the other hand, performing audit procedures before the period end may assist   **A12** the auditor in identifying significant matters at an early stage of the audit, and consequently resolving them with the assistance of management or developing an effective audit approach to address such matters.

In addition, certain audit procedures can be performed only at or after the period   **A13** end, for example:

- Agreeing or reconciling information in the financial statements with the underlying accounting records, including agreeing or reconciling disclosures, whether such information is obtained from within or outside of the general and subsidiary ledgers;

- Examining adjustments made during the course of preparing the financial statements; and

- Procedures to respond to a risk that, at the period end, the entity may have entered into improper sales contracts, or transactions may not have been finalized.

Further relevant factors that influence the auditor's consideration of when to   **A14** perform audit procedures include the following:

- The control environment.

- When relevant information is available (for example, electronic files may subsequently be overwritten, or procedures to be observed may occur only at certain times).

- The nature of the risk (for example, if there is a risk of inflated revenues to meet earnings expectations by subsequent creation of false sales agreements, the auditor may wish to examine contracts available on the date of the period end).

- The period or date to which the audit evidence relates.

- The timing of the preparation of the financial statements, particularly for those disclosures that provide further explanation about amounts recorded in the statement of financial position, the statement of comprehensive income, the statement of changes in equity or the statement of cash flows.

Extent

A15   The extent of an audit procedure judged necessary is determined after considering the materiality, the assessed risk, and the degree of assurance the auditor plans to obtain. When a single purpose is met by a combination of procedures, the extent of each procedure is considered separately. In general, the extent of audit procedures increases as the risk of material misstatement increases. For example, in response to the assessed risk of material misstatement due to fraud, increasing sample sizes or performing substantive analytical procedures at a more detailed level may be appropriate. However, increasing the extent of an audit procedure is effective only if the audit procedure itself is relevant to the specific risk.

A16   The use of computer-assisted audit techniques (CAATs) may enable more extensive testing of electronic transactions and account files, which may be useful when the auditor decides to modify the extent of testing, for example, in responding to the risks of material misstatement due to fraud. Such techniques can be used to select sample transactions from key electronic files, to sort transactions with specific characteristics, or to test an entire population instead of a sample.

Considerations specific to public sector entities

A17   For the audits of public sector entities, the audit mandate and any other special auditing requirements may affect the auditor's consideration of the nature, timing and extent of further audit procedures.

Considerations specific to smaller entities

A18   In the case of very small entities, there may not be many control activities that could be identified by the auditor, or the extent to which their existence or operation have been documented by the entity may be limited. In such cases, it may be more efficient for the auditor to perform further audit procedures that are primarily substantive procedures. In some rare cases, however, the absence of control activities or of other components of control may make it impossible to obtain sufficient appropriate audit evidence.

Higher Assessments of Risk
(Ref: Para 7(b))

A19   When obtaining more persuasive audit evidence because of a higher assessment of risk, the auditor may increase the quantity of the evidence, or obtain evidence that is more relevant or reliable, for example, by placing more emphasis on obtaining third party evidence or by obtaining corroborating evidence from a number of independent sources.

Tests of Controls

Designing and Performing Tests of Controls
(Ref: Para. 8)

A20   Tests of controls are performed only on those controls that the auditor has determined are suitably designed to prevent, or detect and correct, a material misstatement in an assertion. If substantially different controls were used at different times during the period under audit, each is considered separately.

Testing the operating effectiveness of controls is different from obtaining an **A21** understanding of and evaluating the design and implementation of controls. However, the same types of audit procedures are used. The auditor may, therefore, decide it is efficient to test the operating effectiveness of controls at the same time as evaluating their design and determining that they have been implemented.

Further, although some risk assessment procedures may not have been specifically **A22** designed as tests of controls, they may nevertheless provide audit evidence about the operating effectiveness of the controls and, consequently, serve as tests of controls. For example, the auditor's risk assessment procedures may have included:

- Inquiring about management's use of budgets.

- Observing management's comparison of monthly budgeted and actual expenses.

- Inspecting reports pertaining to the investigation of variances between budgeted and actual amounts.

These audit procedures provide knowledge about the design of the entity's budgeting policies and whether they have been implemented, but may also provide audit evidence about the effectiveness of the operation of budgeting policies in preventing or detecting material misstatements in the classification of expenses.

In addition, the auditor may design a test of controls to be performed concurrently **A23** with a test of details on the same transaction. Although the purpose of a test of controls is different from the purpose of a test of details, both may be accomplished concurrently by performing a test of controls and a test of details on the same transaction, also known as a dual-purpose test. For example, the auditor may design, and evaluate the results of, a test to examine an invoice to determine whether it has been approved and to provide substantive audit evidence of a transaction. A dual-purpose test is designed and evaluated by considering each purpose of the test separately.

In some cases, the auditor may find it impossible to design effective substantive **A24** procedures that by themselves provide sufficient appropriate audit evidence at the assertion level.[3] This may occur when an entity conducts its business using IT and no documentation of transactions is produced or maintained, other than through the IT system. In such cases, paragraph 8(b) requires the auditor to perform tests of relevant controls.

Audit Evidence and Intended Reliance
(Ref: Para. 9)

A higher level of assurance may be sought about the operating effectiveness of **A25** controls when the approach adopted consists primarily of tests of controls, in particular where it is not possible or practicable to obtain sufficient appropriate audit evidence only from substantive procedures.

---

[3] *ISA (UK) 315 (Revised June 2016), paragraph 30.*

Nature and Extent of Tests of Controls

Other audit procedures in combination with inquiry
(Ref: Para. 10(a))

A26   Inquiry alone is not sufficient to test the operating effectiveness of controls. Accordingly, other audit procedures are performed in combination with inquiry. In this regard, inquiry combined with inspection or reperformance may provide more assurance than inquiry and observation, since an observation is pertinent only at the point in time at which it is made.

A27   The nature of the particular control influences the type of procedure required to obtain audit evidence about whether the control was operating effectively. For example, if operating effectiveness is evidenced by documentation, the auditor may decide to inspect it to obtain audit evidence about operating effectiveness. For other controls, however, documentation may not be available or relevant. For example, documentation of operation may not exist for some factors in the control environment, such as assignment of authority and responsibility, or for some types of control activities, such as control activities performed by a computer. In such circumstances, audit evidence about operating effectiveness may be obtained through inquiry in combination with other audit procedures such as observation or the use of CAATs.

Extent of tests of controls

A28   When more persuasive audit evidence is needed regarding the effectiveness of a control, it may be appropriate to increase the extent of testing of the control. As well as the degree of reliance on controls, matters the auditor may consider in determining the extent of tests of controls include the following:

●   The frequency of the performance of the control by the entity during the period.

●   The length of time during the audit period that the auditor is relying on the operating effectiveness of the control.

●   The expected rate of deviation from a control.

●   The relevance and reliability of the audit evidence to be obtained regarding the operating effectiveness of the control at the assertion level.

●   The extent to which audit evidence is obtained from tests of other controls related to the assertion.

ISA (UK) 530[4] contains further guidance on the extent of testing.

A29   Because of the inherent consistency of IT processing, it may not be necessary to increase the extent of testing of an automated control. An automated control can be expected to function consistently unless the program (including the tables, files, or other permanent data used by the program) is changed. Once the auditor determines that an automated control is functioning as intended (which could be done at the time the control is initially implemented or at some other date), the auditor may consider performing tests to determine that the control continues to function effectively. Such tests might include determining that:

●   Changes to the program are not made without being subject to the appropriate program change controls;

---

[4]   *ISA (UK) 530, Audit Sampling.*

- The authorized version of the program is used for processing transactions; and

- Other relevant general controls are effective.

Such tests also might include determining that changes to the programs have not been made, as may be the case when the entity uses packaged software applications without modifying or maintaining them. For example, the auditor may inspect the record of the administration of IT security to obtain audit evidence that unauthorized access has not occurred during the period.

Testing of indirect controls
(Ref: Para. 10(b))

In some circumstances, it may be necessary to obtain audit evidence supporting   **A30**
the effective operation of indirect controls. For example, when the auditor decides
to test the effectiveness of a user review of exception reports detailing sales in
excess of authorized credit limits, the user review and related follow up is the
control that is directly of relevance to the auditor. Controls over the accuracy of the
information in the reports (for example, the general IT controls) are described as
"indirect" controls.

Because of the inherent consistency of IT processing, audit evidence about the   **A31**
implementation of an automated application control, when considered in
combination with audit evidence about the operating effectiveness of the
entity's general controls (in particular, change controls), may also provide
substantial audit evidence about its operating effectiveness.

Timing of Tests of Controls

Intended period of reliance
(Ref: Para. 11)

Audit evidence pertaining only to a point in time may be sufficient for the   **A32**
auditor's purpose, for example, when testing controls over the entity's physical
inventory counting at the period end. If, on the other hand, the auditor intends to
rely on a control over a period, tests that are capable of providing audit evidence
that the control operated effectively at relevant times during that period are
appropriate. Such tests may include tests of the entity's monitoring of controls.

Using audit evidence obtained during an interim period
(Ref: Para. 12b)

Relevant factors in determining what additional audit evidence to obtain about   **A33**
controls that were operating during the period remaining after an interim period,
include:

- The significance of the assessed risks of material misstatement at the assertion level.

- The specific controls that were tested during the interim period, and significant changes to them since they were tested, including changes in the information system, processes, and personnel.

- The degree to which audit evidence about the operating effectiveness of those controls was obtained.

- The length of the remaining period.

- The extent to which the auditor intends to reduce further substantive procedures based on the reliance of controls.

- The control environment.

A34   Additional audit evidence may be obtained, for example, by extending tests of controls over the remaining period or testing the entity's monitoring of controls.

Using audit evidence obtained in previous audits
(Ref: Para. 13)

A35   In certain circumstances, audit evidence obtained from previous audits may provide audit evidence where the auditor performs audit procedures to establish its continuing relevance. For example, in performing a previous audit, the auditor may have determined that an automated control was functioning as intended. The auditor may obtain audit evidence to determine whether changes to the automated control have been made that affect its continued effective functioning through, for example, inquiries of management and the inspection of logs to indicate what controls have been changed. Consideration of audit evidence about these changes may support either increasing or decreasing the expected audit evidence to be obtained in the current period about the operating effectiveness of the controls.

Controls that have changed from previous audits
(Ref: Para. 14(a))

A36   Changes may affect the relevance of the audit evidence obtained in previous audits such that there may no longer be a basis for continued reliance. For example, changes in a system that enable an entity to receive a new report from the system probably do not affect the relevance of audit evidence from a previous audit; however, a change that causes data to be accumulated or calculated differently does affect it.

Controls that have not changed from previous audits
(Ref: Para. 14(b))

A37   The auditor's decision on whether to rely on audit evidence obtained in previous audits for controls that:

(a)   have not changed since they were last tested; and

(b)   are not controls that mitigate a significant risk,

is a matter of professional judgment. In addition, the length of time between retesting such controls is also a matter of professional judgment, but is required by paragraph 14(b) to be at least once in every third year.

A38   In general, the higher the risk of material misstatement, or the greater the reliance on controls, the shorter the time period elapsed, if any, is likely to be. Factors that may decrease the period for retesting a control, or result in not relying on audit evidence obtained in previous audits at all, include the following:

- A deficient control environment.

- Deficient monitoring of controls.

- A significant manual element to the relevant controls.

- Personnel changes that significantly affect the application of the control.

- Changing circumstances that indicate the need for changes in the control.

- Deficient general IT controls.

When there are a number of controls for which the auditor intends to rely on audit   **A39**
evidence obtained in previous audits, testing some of those controls in each audit
provides corroborating information about the continuing effectiveness of the
control environment. This contributes to the auditor's decision about whether it
is appropriate to rely on audit evidence obtained in previous audits.

Evaluating the Operating Effectiveness of Controls
(Ref: Para. 16–17)

A material misstatement detected by the auditor's procedures is a strong indicator   **A40**
of the existence of a significant deficiency in internal control.

The concept of effectiveness of the operation of controls recognizes that some   **A41**
deviations in the way controls are applied by the entity may occur. Deviations
from prescribed controls may be caused by such factors as changes in key
personnel, significant seasonal fluctuations in volume of transactions and
human error. The detected rate of deviation, in particular in comparison with
the expected rate, may indicate that the control cannot be relied on to reduce risk at
the assertion level to that assessed by the auditor.

Substantive Procedures
(Ref: Para. 18)

Paragraph 18 requires the auditor to design and perform substantive procedures   **A42**
for each material class of transactions, account balance, and disclosure,
irrespective of the assessed risks of material misstatement. This requirement
reflects the facts that:

(a)   the auditor's assessment of risk is judgmental and so may not identify all
      risks of material misstatement; and

(b)   there are inherent limitations to internal control, including management
      override.

Nature and Extent of Substantive Procedures

Depending on the circumstances, the auditor may determine that: **A43**

●   Performing only substantive analytical procedures will be sufficient to
    reduce audit risk to an acceptably low level. For example, where the
    auditor's assessment of risk is supported by audit evidence from tests of
    controls.

●   Only tests of details are appropriate.

●   A combination of substantive analytical procedures and tests of details are
    most responsive to the assessed risks.

Substantive analytical procedures are generally more applicable to large volumes   **A44**
of transactions that tend to be predictable over time. ISA (UK) 520[5] establishes
requirements and provides guidance on the application of analytical procedures
during an audit.

The nature of the risk and assertion is relevant to the design of tests of details. For   **A45**
example, tests of details related to the existence or occurrence assertion may
involve selecting from items contained in a financial statement amount and
obtaining the relevant audit evidence. On the other hand, tests of details related

---

[5] *ISA (UK) 520, Analytical Procedures.*

to the completeness assertion may involve selecting from items that are expected to be included in the relevant financial statement amount and investigating whether they are included.

A46   Because the assessment of the risk of material misstatement takes account of internal control, the extent of substantive procedures may need to be increased when the results from tests of controls are unsatisfactory. However, increasing the extent of an audit procedure is appropriate only if the audit procedure itself is relevant to the specific risk.

A47   In designing tests of details, the extent of testing is ordinarily thought of in terms of the sample size. However, other matters are also relevant, including whether it is more effective to use other selective means of testing. See ISA (UK) 500.[6]

Considering Whether External Confirmation Procedures Are to Be Performed (Ref: Para. 19)

A48   External confirmation procedures frequently are relevant when addressing assertions associated with account balances and their elements, but need not be restricted to these items. For example, the auditor may request external confirmation of the terms of agreements, contracts, or transactions between an entity and other parties. External confirmation procedures also may be performed to obtain audit evidence about the absence of certain conditions. For example, a request may specifically seek confirmation that no "side agreement" exists that may be relevant to an entity's revenue cutoff assertion. Other situations where external confirmation procedures may provide relevant audit evidence in responding to assessed risks of material misstatement include:

● Bank balances and other information relevant to banking relationships.

● Accounts receivable balances and terms.

● Inventories held by third parties at bonded warehouses for processing or on consignment.

● Property title deeds held by lawyers or financiers for safe custody or as security.

● Investments held for safekeeping by third parties, or purchased from stockbrokers but not delivered at the balance sheet date.

● Amounts due to lenders, including relevant terms of repayment and restrictive covenants.

● Accounts payable balances and terms.

A49   Although external confirmations may provide relevant audit evidence relating to certain assertions, there are some assertions for which external confirmations provide less relevant audit evidence. For example, external confirmations provide less relevant audit evidence relating to the recoverability of accounts receivable balances, than they do of their existence.

A50   The auditor may determine that external confirmation procedures performed for one purpose provide an opportunity to obtain audit evidence about other matters. For example, confirmation requests for bank balances often include requests for information relevant to other financial statement assertions. Such considerations may influence the auditor's decision about whether to perform external confirmation procedures.

---

[6] *ISA (UK) 500, Audit Evidence, paragraph 10.*

In the UK, depending on the auditor's risk assessment, the auditor considers whether confirmation is needed in relation to additional information such as trade finance transactions and balances or information about guarantees and other third party securities, in addition to the confirmation of balances and other banking arrangements usually provided in such a request.

Factors that may assist the auditor in determining whether external confirmation   **A51**
procedures are to be performed as substantive audit procedures include:

- The confirming party's knowledge of the subject matter – responses may be more reliable if provided by a person at the confirming party who has the requisite knowledge about the information being confirmed.

- The ability or willingness of the intended confirming party to respond – for example, the confirming party:

    - May not accept responsibility for responding to a confirmation request;

    - May consider responding too costly or time consuming;

    - May have concerns about the potential legal liability resulting from responding;

    - May account for transactions in different currencies; or

    - May operate in an environment where responding to confirmation requests is not a significant aspect of day-to-day operations.

    In such situations, confirming parties may not respond, may respond in a casual manner or may attempt to restrict the reliance placed on the response.

- The objectivity of the intended confirming party – if the confirming party is a related party of the entity, responses to confirmation requests may be less reliable.

Valuation Methods
(Ref: Para. 19R-1)

For audits of financial statements of public interest entities, ISA (UK) 260   **A51-1**
(Revised June 2016)[6a] requires the auditor to communicate in the additional report to the audit committee the auditor's assessment of the valuation methods applied to the various items in the annual or consolidated financial statements including any impact of changes of such methods.

Substantive Procedures Related to the Financial Statement Closing Process
(Ref: Para. 20(b))

The nature, and also the extent, of the auditor's substantive procedures related to   **A52**
the financial statement closing process depends on the nature and complexity of the entity's financial reporting process and the related risks of material misstatement.

[6a] *ISA (UK) 260 (Revised June 2016), Communication with Those Charged With Governance, paragraph 16R-2(l).*

Substantive Procedures Responsive to Significant Risks
(Ref: Para. 21)

A53   Paragraph 21 of this ISA (UK) requires the auditor to perform substantive procedures that are specifically responsive to risks the auditor has determined to be significant risks. Audit evidence in the form of external confirmations received directly by the auditor from appropriate confirming parties may assist the auditor in obtaining audit evidence with the high level of reliability that the auditor requires to respond to significant risks of material misstatement, whether due to fraud or error. For example, if the auditor identifies that management is under pressure to meet earnings expectations, there may be a risk that management is inflating sales by improperly recognizing revenue related to sales agreements with terms that preclude revenue recognition or by invoicing sales before shipment. In these circumstances, the auditor may, for example, design external confirmation procedures not only to confirm outstanding amounts, but also to confirm the details of the sales agreements, including date, any rights of return and delivery terms. In addition, the auditor may find it effective to supplement such external confirmation procedures with inquiries of non-financial personnel in the entity regarding any changes in sales agreements and delivery terms.

Timing of Substantive Procedures
(Ref: Para. 22–23)

A54   In most cases, audit evidence from a previous audit's substantive procedures provides little or no audit evidence for the current period. There are, however, exceptions, for example, a legal opinion obtained in a previous audit related to the structure of a securitization to which no changes have occurred, may be relevant in the current period. In such cases, it may be appropriate to use audit evidence from a previous audit's substantive procedures if that evidence and the related subject matter have not fundamentally changed, and audit procedures have been performed during the current period to establish its continuing relevance.

Using audit evidence obtained during an interim period
(Ref: Para. 22)

A55   In some circumstances, the auditor may determine that it is effective to perform substantive procedures at an interim date, and to compare and reconcile information concerning the balance at the period end with the comparable information at the interim date to:

(a)   Identify amounts that appear unusual;

(b)   Investigate any such amounts; and

(c)   Perform substantive analytical procedures or tests of details to test the intervening period.

A56   Performing substantive procedures at an interim date without undertaking additional procedures at a later date increases the risk that the auditor will not detect misstatements that may exist at the period end. This risk increases as the remaining period is lengthened. Factors such as the following may influence whether to perform substantive procedures at an interim date:

●   The control environment and other relevant controls.

●   The availability at a later date of information necessary for the auditor's procedures.

●   The purpose of the substantive procedure.

- The assessed risk of material misstatement.

- The nature of the class of transactions or account balance and related assertions.

- The ability of the auditor to perform appropriate substantive procedures or substantive procedures combined with tests of controls to cover the remaining period in order to reduce the risk that misstatements that may exist at the period end will not be detected.

Factors such as the following may influence whether to perform substantive **A57** analytical procedures with respect to the period between the interim date and the period end:

- Whether the period end balances of the particular classes of transactions or account balances are reasonably predictable with respect to amount, relative significance, and composition.

- Whether the entity's procedures for analyzing and adjusting such classes of transactions or account balances at interim dates and for establishing proper accounting cutoffs are appropriate.

- Whether the information system relevant to financial reporting will provide information concerning the balances at the period end and the transactions in the remaining period that is sufficient to permit investigation of:

  (a) Significant unusual transactions or entries (including those at or near the period end);

  (b) Other causes of significant fluctuations, or expected fluctuations that did not occur; and

  (c) Other causes of significant fluctuations, or expected fluctuations that did not occur; and

Misstatements detected at an interim date
(Ref: Para. 23)

When the auditor concludes that the planned nature, timing, or extent of **A58** substantive procedures covering the remaining period need to be modified as a result of unexpected misstatements detected at an interim date, such modification may include extending or repeating the procedures performed at the interim date at the period end.

Adequacy of Presentation of the Financial Statements
(Ref: Para. 24)

Evaluating the appropriate presentation, arrangement and content of the financial **A59** statements, includes, for example, consideration of the terminology used as required by the applicable financial reporting framework, the level of detail provided, the aggregation and disaggregation of amounts, and the bases of amounts set forth.

Evaluating the Sufficiency and Appropriateness of Audit Evidence
(Ref: Para. 25–27)

An audit of financial statements is a cumulative and iterative process. As the **A60** auditor performs planned audit procedures, the audit evidence obtained may cause the auditor to modify the nature, timing or extent of other planned audit procedures. Information may come to the auditor's attention that differs significantly from the information on which the risk assessment was based. For example:

- The extent of misstatements that the auditor detects by performing substantive procedures may alter the auditor's judgment about the risk assessments and may indicate a significant deficiency in internal control.

- The auditor may become aware of discrepancies in accounting records, or conflicting or missing evidence.

- Analytical procedures performed at the overall review stage of the audit may indicate a previously unrecognized risk of material misstatement.

In such circumstances, the auditor may need to reevaluate the planned audit procedures, based on the revised consideration of assessed risks for all or some of the classes of transactions, account balances, or disclosures and related assertions. ISA (UK) 315 (Revised June 2016) contains further guidance on revising the auditor's risk assessment.[7]

A61   The auditor cannot assume that an instance of fraud or error is an isolated occurrence. Therefore, the consideration of how the detection of a misstatement affects the assessed risks of material misstatement is important in determining whether the assessment remains appropriate.

A62   The auditor's judgment as to what constitutes sufficient appropriate audit evidence is influenced by such factors as the following:

- Significance of the potential misstatement in the assertion and the likelihood of its having a material effect, individually or aggregated with other potential misstatements, on the financial statements.

- Effectiveness of management's responses and controls to address the risks.

- Experience gained during previous audits with respect to similar potential misstatements.

- Results of audit procedures performed, including whether such audit procedures identified specific instances of fraud or error.

- Source and reliability of the available information.

- Persuasiveness of the audit evidence.

- Understanding of the entity and its environment, including the entity's internal control.

Documentation
(Ref: Para. 28)

A63   The form and extent of audit documentation is a matter of professional judgment, and is influenced by the nature, size and complexity of the entity and its internal control, availability of information from the entity and the audit methodology and technology used in the audit.

---

[7] *ISA (UK) 315 (Revised June 2016), paragraph 31.*

Annexure

Conforming Amendments to Other ISAs (UK)

This annexure shows the conforming amendments to ISAs (UK) as a result of ISA (UK) 330 (Revised July 2017) *The Auditor's Responses to Assessed Risks*. These amendments are effective for audits of financial statements for periods commencing on or after 15 December 2017.

ISA (UK) 505 External Confirmations

Factors to consider when designing confirmation requests include:[13a]   **A4**

- The assertions being addressed.
- Specific identified risks of material misstatement, including fraud risks.
- The layout and presentation of the confirmation request.
- Prior experience on the audit or similar engagements.
- The method of communication (for example, in paper form, or by electronic or other medium).
- Management's authorization or encouragement to the confirming parties to respond to the auditor. Confirming parties may only be willing to respond to a confirmation request containing management's authorization.
- The ability of the intended confirming party to confirm or provide the requested information (for example, individual invoice amount versus total balance).

[13a] *Pro-forma templates to obtain bank confirmations in the United Kingdom which have been agreed with the British Bankers' Association on behalf of the industry can be found at: https://www.bba.org.uk/policy/financial-and-risk-policy/financial-reporting/audit/instructions-for-using-pn16-templates/*

Annexure

Conforming Amendments to Other ISAs (UK)

> This Annexure sets out conforming amendments to other ISAs (UK) as a result of the issue of this ISA (UK). These amendments will be effective for audits of financial statements for periods ended on or after [date]. The amendments are shown with marked up text to illustrate the new or deleted text (deleted text is struck through and new text is underlined).

ISA (UK) 505 *Shared Considerations*

Factors to consider when designing confirmation requests include:

- The assertions being addressed.
- Specific identified risks of material misstatement, including fraud risks.
- The layout and presentation of the confirmation request.
- Prior experience on the audit of similar engagements.
- The method of communication (for example, in paper form, or by electronic or other medium).
- Management's authorisation to its counterpart to the confirming parties to respond to the auditor. Confirming parties may only be willing to respond to a confirmation request containing management's authorization.
- The ability of the intended confirming party to confirm or provide the requested information (for example, individual invoice amount versus total balance).

ISA (UK) 402 Audit Considerations Relating to an Entity Using a Service Organisation

(Effective for audits of financial statements for periods ending on or after 15 December 2010)

Contents

Paragraphs

Introduction
Scope of this ISA (UK)   1 - 5
Effective date   6

Objectives   7

Definitions   8

Requirements
Obtaining an understanding of the services provided by a service organization,
including internal control   9 - 14
Responding to the assessed risks of material misstatement   15 - 17
Type 1 and type 2 reports that exclude the services of a subservice organization   18
Fraud, non-compliance with laws and regulations and uncorrected misstatements
in relation to activities at the service organization   19
Reporting by the user auditor   20 - 22

Application and other explanatory material
Obtaining an understanding of the services provided by a service organization,
including internal control   A1 - A23
Responding to the assessed risks of material misstatement   A24 - A39
Type 1 and type 2 reports that exclude the services of a subservice organization   A40
Fraud, non-compliance with laws and regulations and uncorrected misstatements
in relation to activities at the service organization   A41
Reporting by the user auditor   A42 - A44

International Standard on Auditing (UK) (ISA (UK)) 402, *Audit Considerations Relating to an Entity Using a Service Organization*, should be read in conjunction with ISA (UK) 200 (Revised June 2016), *Overall Objectives of the Independent Auditor and the Conduct of an Audit in Accordance with International Standards on Auditing (UK)*.

Introduction

Scope of this ISA (UK)

1   This International Standard on Auditing (UK) (ISA (UK)) deals with the user auditor's responsibility to obtain sufficient appropriate audit evidence when a user entity uses the services of one or more service organizations. Specifically, it expands on how the user auditor applies ISA (UK) 315 (Revised June 2016)[1] and ISA (UK) 330 (Revised June 2016)[2] in obtaining an understanding of the user entity, including internal control relevant to the audit, sufficient to identify and assess the risks of material misstatement and in designing and performing further audit procedures responsive to those risks.

2   Many entities outsource aspects of their business to organizations that provide services ranging from performing a specific task under the direction of an entity to replacing an entity's entire business units or functions, such as the tax compliance function. Many of the services provided by such organizations are integral to the entity's business operations; however, not all those services are relevant to the audit.

3   Services provided by a service organization are relevant to the audit of a user entity's financial statements when those services, and the controls over them, are part of the user entity's information system, including related business processes, relevant to financial reporting. Although most controls at the service organization are likely to relate to financial reporting, there may be other controls that may also be relevant to the audit, such as controls over the safeguarding of assets. A service organization's services are part of a user entity's information system, including related business processes, relevant to financial reporting if these services affect any of the following:

(a)   The classes of transactions in the user entity's operations that are significant to the user entity's financial statements;

(b)   The procedures, within both information technology (IT) and manual systems, by which the user entity's transactions are initiated, recorded, processed, corrected as necessary, transferred to the general ledger and reported in the financial statements;

(c)   The related accounting records, either in electronic or manual form, supporting information and specific accounts in the user entity's financial statements that are used to initiate, record, process and report the user entity's transactions; this includes the correction of incorrect information and how information is transferred to the general ledger;

(d)   How the user entity's information system captures events and conditions, other than transactions, that are significant to the financial statements;

(e)   The financial reporting process used to prepare the user entity's financial statements, including significant accounting estimates and disclosures; and

(f)   Controls surrounding journal entries, including non-standard journal entries used to record non-recurring, unusual transactions or adjustments.

---

[1] *ISA (UK) 315 (Revised June 2016), Identifying and Assessing the Risks of Material Misstatement through Understanding the Entity and Its Environment.*

[2] *ISA (UK) 330 (Revised June 2016), The Auditor's Responses to Assessed Risks.*

The nature and extent of work to be performed by the user auditor regarding the   **4**
services provided by a service organization depend on the nature and significance
of those services to the user entity and the relevance of those services to the audit.

This ISA (UK) does not apply to services provided by financial institutions that   **5**
are limited to processing, for an entity's account held at the financial institution,
transactions that are specifically authorized by the entity, such as the processing of
checking account transactions by a bank or the processing of securities
transactions by a broker. In addition, this ISA (UK) does not apply to the audit
of transactions arising from proprietary financial interests in other entities, such as
partnerships, corporations and joint ventures, when proprietary interests are
accounted for and reported to interest holders.

Effective Date

This ISA (UK) is effective for audits of financial statements for periods ending on   **6**
or after 15 December 2010.

Objectives

The objectives of the user auditor, when the user entity uses the services of a   **7**
service organization, are:

(a)   To obtain an understanding of the nature and significance of the services
provided by the service organization and their effect on the user entity's
internal control relevant to the audit, sufficient to identify and assess the
risks of material misstatement; and

(b)   To design and perform audit procedures responsive to those risks.

Definitions

For purposes of the ISAs (UK), the following terms have the meanings attributed   **8**
below:

(a)   Complementary user entity controls – Controls that the service organization
assumes, in the design of its service, will be implemented by user entities,
and which, if necessary to achieve control objectives, are identified in the
description of its system.

(b)   Report on the description and design of controls at a service organization
(referred to in this ISA (UK) as a type 1 report) – A report that comprises:

(i)   A description, prepared by management of the service organization, of
the service organization's system, control objectives and related
controls that have been designed and implemented as at a specified
date; and

(ii)   A report by the service auditor with the objective of conveying
reasonable assurance that includes the service auditor's opinion on
the description of the service organization's system, control objectives
and related controls and the suitability of the design of the controls to
achieve the specified control objectives.

(c)   Report on the description, design, and operating effectiveness of controls at a service organization (referred to in this ISA (UK) as a type 2 report) – A report that comprises:

    (i)   A description, prepared by management of the service organization, of the service organization's system, control objectives and related controls, their design and implementation as at a specified date or throughout a specified period and, in some cases, their operating effectiveness throughout a specified period; and

    (ii)   A report by the service auditor with the objective of conveying reasonable assurance that includes:

        (a)   The service auditor's opinion on the description of the service organization's system, control objectives and related controls, the suitability of the design of the controls to achieve the specified control objectives, and the operating effectiveness of the controls; and

        (b)   A description of the service auditor's tests of the controls and the results thereof.

(d)   Service auditor – An auditor who, at the request of the service organization, provides an assurance report on the controls of a service organization.

(e)   Service organization – A third-party organization (or segment of a third-party organization) that provides services to user entities that are part of those entities' information systems relevant to financial reporting.

(f)   Service organization's system – The policies and procedures designed, implemented and maintained by the service organization to provide user entities with the services covered by the service auditor's report.

(g)   Subservice organization – A service organization used by another service organization to perform some of the services provided to user entities that are part of those user entities' information systems relevant to financial reporting.

(h)   User auditor – An auditor who audits and reports on the financial statements of a user entity.

(i)   User entity – An entity that uses a service organization and whose financial statements are being audited.

Requirements

Obtaining an Understanding of the Services Provided by a Service Organization, Including Internal Control

9   When obtaining an understanding of the user entity in accordance with ISA (UK) 315 (Revised June 2016),[3] the user auditor shall obtain an understanding of how a user entity uses the services of a service organization in the user entity's operations, including: (Ref: Para. A1–A2)

(a)   The nature of the services provided by the service organization and the significance of those services to the user entity, including the effect thereof on the user entity's internal control; (Ref: Para. A3–A5)

---

[3] *ISA (UK) 315 (Revised June 2016), paragraph 11.*

(b)   The nature and materiality of the transactions processed or accounts or financial reporting processes affected by the service organization; (Ref: Para. A6)

(c)   The degree of interaction between the activities of the service organization and those of the user entity; and (Ref: Para. A7)

(d)   The nature of the relationship between the user entity and the service organization, including the relevant contractual terms for the activities undertaken by the service organization. (Ref: Para. A8–A11)

(e)   If the service organization maintains all or part of a user entity's accounting records, whether those arrangements impact the work the auditor performs to fulfil reporting responsibilities in relation to accounting records that are established in law or regulation. (Ref: Para. A11-1–A11-3)

When obtaining an understanding of internal control relevant to the audit in accordance with ISA (UK) 315 (Revised June 2016),[4] the user auditor shall evaluate the design and implementation of relevant controls at the user entity that relate to the services provided by the service organization, including those that are applied to the transactions processed by the service organization. (Ref: Para. A12–A14) **10**

The user auditor shall determine whether a sufficient understanding of the nature and significance of the services provided by the service organization and their effect on the user entity's internal control relevant to the audit has been obtained to provide a basis for the identification and assessment of risks of material misstatement. **11**

If the user auditor is unable to obtain a sufficient understanding from the user entity, the user auditor shall obtain that understanding from one or more of the following procedures: **12**

(a)   Obtaining a type 1 or type 2 report, if available;

(b)   Contacting the service organization, through the user entity, to obtain specific information;

(c)   Visiting the service organization and performing procedures that will provide the necessary information about the relevant controls at the service organization; or

(d)   Using another auditor to perform procedures that will provide the necessary information about the relevant controls at the service organization. (Ref: Para. A15–A20)

Using a Type 1 or Type 2 Report to Support the User Auditor's Understanding of the Service Organization

In determining the sufficiency and appropriateness of the audit evidence provided by a type 1 or type 2 report, the user auditor shall be satisfied as to: **13**

(a)   The service auditor's professional competence and independence from the service organization; and

(b)   The adequacy of the standards under which the type 1 or type 2 report was issued. (Ref: Para. A21)

---

[4] *ISA (UK) 315 (Revised June 2016), paragraph 12.*

14   If the user auditor plans to use a type 1 or type 2 report as audit evidence to support the user auditor's understanding about the design and implementation of controls at the service organization, the user auditor shall:

(a)   Evaluate whether the description and design of controls at the service organization is at a date or for a period that is appropriate for the user auditor's purposes;

(b)   Evaluate the sufficiency and appropriateness of the evidence provided by the report for the understanding of the user entity's internal control relevant to the audit; and

(c)   Determine whether complementary user entity controls identified by the service organization are relevant to the user entity and, if so, obtain an understanding of whether the user entity has designed and implemented such controls. (Ref: Para. A22–A23)

Responding to the Assessed Risks of Material Misstatement

15   In responding to assessed risks in accordance with ISA (UK) 330 (Revised June 2016), the user auditor shall:

(a)   Determine whether sufficient appropriate audit evidence concerning the relevant financial statement assertions is available from records held at the user entity; and, if not,

(b)   Perform further audit procedures to obtain sufficient appropriate audit evidence or use another auditor to perform those procedures at the service organization on the user auditor's behalf. (Ref: Para. A24–A28)

Tests of Controls

16   When the user auditor's risk assessment includes an expectation that controls at the service organization are operating effectively, the user auditor shall obtain audit evidence about the operating effectiveness of those controls from one or more of the following procedures:

(a)   Obtaining a type 2 report, if available;

(b)   Performing appropriate tests of controls at the service organization; or

(c)   Using another auditor to perform tests of controls at the service organization on behalf of the user auditor. (Ref: Para. A29–A30)

Using a Type 2 Report as Audit Evidence that Controls at the Service Organization Are Operating Effectively

17   If, in accordance with paragraph 16(a), the user auditor plans to use a type 2 report as audit evidence that controls at the service organization are operating effectively, the user auditor shall determine whether the service auditor's report provides sufficient appropriate audit evidence about the effectiveness of the controls to support the user auditor's risk assessment by:

(a)   Evaluating whether the description, design and operating effectiveness of controls at the service organization is at a date or for a period that is appropriate for the user auditor's purposes;

(b)   Determining whether complementary user entity controls identified by the service organization are relevant to the user entity and, if so, obtaining an understanding of whether the user entity has designed and implemented such controls and, if so, testing their operating effectiveness;

(c)   Evaluating the adequacy of the time period covered by the tests of controls and the time elapsed since the performance of the tests of controls; and

(d)   Evaluating whether the tests of controls performed by the service auditor and the results thereof, as described in the service auditor's report, are relevant to the assertions in the user entity's financial statements and provide sufficient appropriate audit evidence to support the user auditor's risk assessment. (Ref: Para. A31–A39)

Type 1 and Type 2 Reports that Exclude the Services of a Subservice Organization

If the user auditor plans to use a type 1 or a type 2 report that excludes the services provided by a subservice organization and those services are relevant to the audit of the user entity's financial statements, the user auditor shall apply the requirements of this ISA (UK) with respect to the services provided by the subservice organization. (Ref: Para. A40)   **18**

Fraud, Non-Compliance with Laws and Regulations and Uncorrected Misstatements in Relation to Activities at the Service Organization

The user auditor shall inquire of management of the user entity whether the service organization has reported to the user entity, or whether the user entity is otherwise aware of, any fraud, non-compliance with laws and regulations or uncorrected misstatements affecting the financial statements of the user entity. The user auditor shall evaluate how such matters affect the nature, timing and extent of the user auditor's further audit procedures, including the effect on the user auditor's conclusions and user auditor's report. (Ref: Para. A41)   **19**

Reporting by the User Auditor

The user auditor shall modify the opinion in the user auditor's report in accordance with ISA (UK) 705 (Revised June 2016)[5] if the user auditor is unable to obtain sufficient appropriate audit evidence regarding the services provided by the service organization relevant to the audit of the user entity's financial statements. (Ref: Para. A42)   **20**

The user auditor shall not refer to the work of a service auditor in the user auditor's report containing an unmodified opinion unless required by law or regulation to do so. If such reference is required by law or regulation, the user auditor's report shall indicate that the reference does not diminish the user auditor's responsibility for the audit opinion. (Ref: Para. A43)   **21**

If reference to the work of a service auditor is relevant to an understanding of a modification to the user auditor's opinion, the user auditor's report shall indicate that such reference does not diminish the user auditor's responsibility for that opinion. (Ref: Para. A44)   **22**

---

[5] *ISA (UK) 705 (Revised June 2016), Modifications to the Opinion in the Independent Auditor's Report, paragraph 6.*

Application and Other Explanatory Material

Obtaining an Understanding of the Services Provided by a Service Organization, Including Internal Control

Sources of Information
(Ref: Para. 9)

A1 Information on the nature of the services provided by a service organization may be available from a wide variety of sources, such as:

- User manuals.
- System overviews.
- Technical manuals.
- The contract or service level agreement between the user entity and the service organization.
- Reports by service organizations, the internal audit function or regulatory authorities on controls at the service organization.
- Reports by the service auditor, including management letters, if available.

A2 Knowledge obtained through the user auditor's experience with the service organization, for example through experience with other audit engagements, may also be helpful in obtaining an understanding of the nature of the services provided by the service organization. This may be particularly helpful if the services and controls at the service organization over those services are highly standardized.

Nature of the Services Provided by the Service Organization
(Ref: Para. 9(a))

A3 A user entity may use a service organization such as one that processes transactions and maintains related accountability, or records transactions and processes related data. Service organizations that provide such services include, for example, bank trust departments that invest and service assets for employee benefit plans or for others; mortgage bankers that service mortgages for others; and application service providers that provide packaged software applications and a technology environment that enables customers to process financial and operational transactions.

A4 Examples of service organization services that are relevant to the audit include:

- Maintenance of the user entity's accounting records.
- Management of assets.
- Initiating, recording or processing transactions as agent of the user entity.

Compliance with Law and Regulations

A4-1 The user auditor considers whether the activities undertaken by the service organization are in an area in which the user entity is required to comply with requirements of law and regulations (for example, there are legal requirements relating to the maintenance of accounting records by companies – see paragraphs A11-1– A11-3). In such circumstances, non-compliance may have a significant effect on the financial statements. The user auditor therefore determines whether the law and regulations concerned are to be regarded as relevant to the audit[5a] in order to meet the requirements of ISA (UK) 250 (Revised June 2016) Section A"Consideration of Laws and Regulations in an Audit of Financial Statements" and undertake procedures to assess the risk of a misstatement arising from non-compliance as set out in that ISA (UK).

Considerations Specific to Smaller Entities

Smaller entities may use external bookkeeping services ranging from the **A5** processing of certain transactions (for example, payment of payroll taxes) and maintenance of their accounting records to the preparation of their financial statements. The use of such a service organization for the preparation of its financial statements does not relieve management of the smaller entity and, where appropriate, those charged with governance of their responsibilities for the financial statements.[6]

Nature and Materiality of Transactions Processed by the Service Organization
(Ref: Para. 9(b))

A service organization may establish policies and procedures that affect the user **A6** entity's internal control. These policies and procedures are at least in part physically and operationally separate from the user entity. The significance of the controls of the service organization to those of the user entity depends on the nature of the services provided by the service organization, including the nature and materiality of the transactions it processes for the user entity. In certain situations, the transactions processed and the accounts affected by the service organization may not appear to be material to the user entity's financial statements, but the nature of the transactions processed may be significant and the user auditor may determine that an understanding of those controls is necessary in the circumstances.

The Degree of Interaction between the Activities of the Service Organization and the User Entity
(Ref: Para. 9(c))

The significance of the controls of the service organization to those of the user **A7** entity also depends on the degree of interaction between its activities and those of the user entity. The degree of interaction refers to the extent to which a user entity is able to and elects to implement effective controls over the processing performed by the service organization. For example, a high degree of interaction exists between the activities of the user entity and those at the service organization when the user entity authorizes transactions and the service organization processes and does the accounting for those transactions. In these circumstances, it may be practicable for the user entity to implement effective controls over those transactions. On the other hand, when the service organization initiates or initially records, processes, and does the accounting for the user entity's transactions, there is a lower degree of interaction between the two organizations. In these circumstances, the user entity may be unable to, or may

---

[5a] *Laws and regulations are relevant to the audit when they either relate directly to the preparation of the financial statements of the entity, or are fundamental to the operating aspects of its business (ISA (UK) 250 (Revised June 2016) Section A, Consideration of Laws and Regulations in an Audit of Financial Statements, paragraph 6).*

[6] *ISA (UK) 200 (Revised June 2016), Overall Objectives of the Independent Auditor and the Conduct of an Audit in Accordance with International Standards on Auditing (UK), paragraphs 4 and A2–A3.*

elect not to, implement effective controls over these transactions at the user entity and may rely on controls at the service organization.

Nature of the Relationship between the User Entity and the Service Organization (Ref: Para. 9(d))

A8   The contract or service level agreement between the user entity and the service organization may provide for matters such as:

- The information to be provided to the user entity and responsibilities for initiating transactions relating to the activities undertaken by the service organization;

- The application of requirements of regulatory bodies concerning the form of records to be maintained, or access to them;

- The indemnification, if any, to be provided to the user entity in the event of a performance failure;

- Whether the service organization will provide a report on its controls and, if so, whether such report would be a type 1 or type 2 report;

- Whether the user auditor has rights of access to the accounting records of the user entity maintained by the service organization and other information necessary for the conduct of the audit; and

- Whether the agreement allows for direct communication between the user auditor and the service auditor.

A8-1   Other matters which the auditor may consider include:

- The way that accounting records relating to relevant activities are maintained.

- Whether the entity has rights of access to accounting records prepared by the service organization concerning the activities undertaken, and relevant underlying information held by it, and the conditions in which such access may be sought.

- The nature of relevant performance standards.

- The way in which the entity monitors performance of relevant activities and the extent to which its monitoring process relies on controls operated by the service organization.

A8-2   Agreement by a service organization to provide an indemnity does not provide information directly relevant to the user auditor's assessment of the risk of material misstatements relating to financial statement assertions. However, such agreements may help to inform the user auditor's judgment concerning the effect of performance failure on the user entity's financial statements: this may be relevant in instances of performance failure, when the existence of an indemnity may help to ensure that the user entity's status as a going concern is not threatened. Where the user auditor wishes to rely on the operation of the indemnity for this purpose, the resources available to the service organization also need to be considered.

A8-3   The financial standing of a service organization is relevant to the audit insofar as the user auditor considers it necessary to rely on the operation of an indemnity from the service organization in assessing the entity's status as a going concern (see paragraph A8-2). However, a service organization whose cash and/or capital resources are low in relation to the nature of services provided or the volume of its customers may be susceptible to pressures resulting in errors or deliberate misstatements in reporting to the entity, or fraud. If the user auditor considers that this factor may be relevant to the assessment of risk, the user auditor also takes into account the existence of binding arrangements to provide resources to the service organizations from a holding company or other group company, and the financial strength of the group as a whole.

There is a direct relationship between the service organization and the user entity and between the service organization and the service auditor. These relationships do not necessarily create a direct relationship between the user auditor and the service auditor. When there is no direct relationship between the user auditor and the service auditor, communications between the user auditor and the service auditor are usually conducted through the user entity and the service organization. A direct relationship may also be created between a user auditor and a service auditor, taking into account the relevant ethical and confidentiality considerations. A user auditor, for example, may use a service auditor to perform procedures on the user auditor's behalf, such as: **A9**

(a)   Tests of controls at the service organization; or

(b)   Substantive procedures on the user entity's financial statement transactions and balances maintained by a service organization.

Considerations Specific to Public Sector Entities

Public sector auditors generally have broad rights of access established by legislation. However, there may be situations where such rights of access are not available, for example when the service organization is located in a different jurisdiction. In such cases, a public sector auditor may need to obtain an understanding of the legislation applicable in the different jurisdiction to determine whether appropriate access rights can be obtained. A public sector auditor may also obtain or ask the user entity to incorporate rights of access in any contractual arrangements between the user entity and the service organization. **A10**

Public sector auditors may also use another auditor to perform tests of controls or substantive procedures in relation to compliance with law, regulation or other authority. **A11**

Accounting Records
(Ref: Para. 9(e))

Use of a service organization does not diminish the ultimate responsibility of those charged with governance of a user entity for conducting its business in a manner which meets their legal responsibilities, including those of safeguarding the user entity's assets, maintaining adequate accounting records and preparing financial statements which provide information about its economic activities and financial position. Practical issues, including the way in which accounting records will be kept and the manner in which those charged with governance assess the quality of the service, need to be addressed. **A11-1**

An auditor of an entity incorporated under company law has statutory reporting obligations relating to compliance with requirements for companies to maintain adequate accounting records. Where such an entity outsources the preparation of its accounting records to a service organization, issues relating to whether the arrangements with the service organization are such as to permit the user entity to meet its statutory obligations may require careful consideration, by **A11-2** both those charged with governance and the user auditor. Where there is doubt, the user auditor may wish to encourage those charged with governance to take legal advice before issuing the auditor's report on its financial statements.

A11-3   A particular issue arises in relation to companies incorporated in the UK. The wording of UK company law appears to be prescriptive and to require the company itself to keep accounting records. Consequently, whether a company "keeps" records (as opposed to "causes records to be kept") will depend upon the particular terms of the outsourcing arrangements and, in particular, the extent to which the company retains ownership of, has access to, or holds copies of, those records.

Understanding the Controls Relating to Services Provided by the Service Organization
(Ref: Para. 10)

A12   The user entity may establish controls over the service organization's services that may be tested by the user auditor and that may enable the user auditor to conclude that the user entity's controls are operating effectively for some or all of the related assertions, regardless of the controls in place at the service organization. If a user entity, for example, uses a service organization to process its payroll transactions, the user entity may establish controls over the submission and receipt of payroll information that could prevent or detect material misstatements. These controls may include:

● Comparing the data submitted to the service organization with reports of information received from the service organization after the data has been processed.

● Recomputing a sample of the payroll amounts for clerical accuracy and reviewing the total amount of the payroll for reasonableness.

A13   In this situation, the user auditor may perform tests of the user entity's controls over payroll processing that would provide a basis for the user auditor to conclude that the user entity's controls are operating effectively for the assertions related to payroll transactions.

A14   As noted in ISA (UK) 315 (Revised June 2016),[7] in respect of some risks, the user auditor may judge that it is not possible or practicable to obtain sufficient appropriate audit evidence only from substantive procedures. Such risks may relate to the inaccurate or incomplete recording of routine and significant classes of transactions and account balances, the characteristics of which often permit highly automated processing with little or no manual intervention. Such automated processing characteristics may be particularly present when the user entity uses service organizations. In such cases, the user entity's controls over such risks are relevant to the audit and the user auditor is required to obtain an understanding of, and to evaluate, such controls in accordance with paragraphs 9 and 10 of this ISA (UK).

Further Procedures When a Sufficient Understanding Cannot Be Obtained from the User Entity
(Ref: Para. 12)

A15   The user auditor's decision as to which procedure, individually or in combination, in paragraph 12 to undertake, in order to obtain the information necessary to provide a basis for the identification and assessment of the risks of material

---

[7] *ISA (UK) 315 (Revised June 2016), paragraph 30.*

misstatement in relation to the user entity's use of the service organization, may be influenced by such matters as:

- The size of both the user entity and the service organization;
- The complexity of the transactions at the user entity and the complexity of the services provided by the service organization;
- The location of the service organization (for example, the user auditor may decide to use another auditor to perform procedures at the service organization on the user auditor's behalf if the service organization is in a remote location);
- Whether the procedure(s) is expected to effectively provide the user auditor with sufficient appropriate audit evidence; and
- The nature of the relationship between the user entity and the service organization.

A service organization may engage a service auditor to report on the description **A16** and design of its controls (type 1 report) or on the description and design of its controls and their operating effectiveness (type 2 report). Type 1 or type 2 reports may be issued under International Standard on Assurance Engagements (ISAE) 3402[8] or under standards established by an authorized or recognized standards setting organization (which may identify them by different names, such as Type A or Type B reports).

The availability of a type 1 or type 2 report will generally depend on whether the **A17** contract between a service organization and a user entity includes the provision of such a report by the service organization. A service organization may also elect, for practical reasons, to make a type 1 or type 2 report available to the user entities. However, in some cases, a type 1 or type 2 report may not be available to user entities.

In some circumstances, a user entity may outsource one or more significant **A18** business units or functions, such as its entire tax planning and compliance functions, or finance and accounting or the controllership function to one or more service organizations. As a report on controls at the service organization may not be available in these circumstances, visiting the service organization may be the most effective procedure for the user auditor to gain an understanding of controls at the service organization, as there is likely to be direct interaction of management of the user entity with management at the service organization.

Another auditor may be used to perform procedures that will provide the necessary **A19** information about the relevant controls at the service organization. If a type 1 or type 2 report has been issued, the user auditor may use the service auditor to perform these procedures as the service auditor has an existing relationship with the service organization. The user auditor using the work of another auditor may find the guidance in ISA (UK) 600 (Revised June 2016)[9] useful as it relates to understanding another auditor (including that auditor's independence and professional competence), involvement in the work of another auditor in planning the nature, extent and timing of such work, and in evaluating the sufficiency and appropriateness of the audit evidence obtained.

---

[8] *ISAE 3402, Assurance Reports on Controls at a Third Party Service Organization.*

[9] *ISA (UK) 600 (Revised June 2016), Special Considerations-Audits of Group Financial Statements (Including the Work of Component Auditors), paragraph 2, states: "An auditor may find this ISA (UK), adapted as necessary in the circumstances, useful when that auditor involves other auditors in the audit of financial statements that are not group financial statements..." See also paragraph 19 of ISA (UK) 600 (Revised June 2016).*

A20   A user entity may use a service organization that in turn uses a subservice organization to provide some of the services provided to a user entity that are part of the user entity's information system relevant to financial reporting. The subservice organization may be a separate entity from the service organization or may be related to the service organization. A user auditor may need to consider controls at the subservice organization. In situations where one or more subservice organizations are used, the interaction between the activities of the user entity and those of the service organization is expanded to include the interaction between the user entity, the service organization and the subservice organizations. The degree of this interaction, as well as the nature and materiality of the transactions processed by the service organization and the subservice organizations are the most important factors for the user auditor to consider in determining the significance of the service organization's and subservice organization's controls to the user entity's controls.

Using a Type 1 or Type 2 Report to Support the User Auditor's Understanding of the Service Organization
(Ref: Para. 13–14)

A21   The user auditor may make inquiries about the service auditor to the service auditor's professional organization or other practitioners and inquire whether the service auditor is subject to regulatory oversight. The service auditor may be practicing in a jurisdiction where different standards are followed in respect of reports on controls at a service organization, and the user auditor may obtain information about the standards used by the service auditor from the standard setting organization.

A22   A type 1 or type 2 report, along with information about the user entity, may assist the user auditor in obtaining an understanding of:

(a)   The aspects of controls at the service organization that may affect the processing of the user entity's transactions, including the use of subservice organizations;

(b)   The flow of significant transactions through the service organization to determine the points in the transaction flow where material misstatements in the user entity's financial statements could occur;

(c)   The control objectives at the service organization that are relevant to the user entity's financial statement assertions; and

(d)   Whether controls at the service organization are suitably designed and implemented to prevent or detect processing errors that could result in material misstatements in the user entity's financial statements.

A type 1 or type 2 report may assist the user auditor in obtaining a sufficient understanding to identify and assess the risks of material misstatement. A type 1 report, however, does not provide any evidence of the operating effectiveness of the relevant controls.

A23   A type 1 or type 2 report that is as of a date or for a period that is outside of the reporting period of a user entity may assist the user auditor in obtaining a preliminary understanding of the controls implemented at the service organization if the report is supplemented by additional current information from other sources. If the service organization's description of controls is as of a date or for a period that precedes the beginning of the period under audit, the user auditor may perform procedures to update the information in a type 1 or type 2 report, such as:

- Discussing the changes at the service organization with user entity personnel who would be in a position to know of such changes;

- Reviewing current documentation and correspondence issued by the service organization; or

- Discussing the changes with service organization personnel.

Responding to the Assessed Risks of Material Misstatement
(Ref: Para. 15)

Whether the use of a service organization increases a user entity's risk of material misstatement depends on the nature of the services provided and the controls over these services; in some cases, the use of a service organization may decrease a user entity's risk of material misstatement, particularly if the user entity itself does not possess the expertise necessary to undertake particular activities, such as initiating, processing, and recording transactions, or does not have adequate resources (for example, an IT system).   **A24**

When the service organization maintains material elements of the accounting records of the user entity, direct access to those records may be necessary in order for the user auditor to obtain sufficient appropriate audit evidence relating to the operations of controls over those records or to substantiate transactions and balances recorded in them, or both. Such access may involve either physical inspection of records at the service organization's premises or interrogation of records maintained electronically from the user entity or another location, or both. Where direct access is achieved electronically, the user auditor may thereby obtain evidence as to the adequacy of controls operated by the service organization over the completeness and integrity of the user entity's data for which the service organization is responsible.   **A25**

In determining the nature and extent of audit evidence to be obtained in relation to balances representing assets held or transactions undertaken by a service organization on behalf of the user entity, the following procedures may be considered by the user auditor: **A26**

(a)   Inspecting records and documents held by the user entity: the reliability of this source of evidence is determined by the nature and extent of the accounting records and supporting documentation retained by the user entity. In some cases, the user entity may not maintain independent detailed records or documentation of specific transactions undertaken on its behalf.

(b)   Inspecting records and documents held by the service organization: the user auditor's access to the records of the service organization may be established as part of the contractual arrangements between the user entity and the service organization. The user auditor may also use another auditor, on its behalf, to gain access to the user entity's records maintained by the service organization.

(c)   Obtaining confirmations of balances and transactions from the service organization: where the user entity maintains independent records of balances and transactions, confirmation from the service organization corroborating the user entity's records may constitute reliable audit evidence concerning the existence of the transactions and assets concerned. For example, when multiple service organizations are used, such as an investment manager and a custodian, and these service organizations maintain independent records, the user auditor may confirm balances with these organizations in order to compare this information with the independent records of the user entity.

If the user entity does not maintain independent records, information obtained in confirmations from the service organization is merely a statement of what is reflected in the records maintained by the service organization. Therefore, such confirmations do not, taken alone, constitute reliable audit evidence. In these circumstances, the user auditor may consider whether an alternative source of independent evidence can be identified.

(d)   Performing analytical procedures on the records maintained by the user entity or on the reports received from the service organization: the effectiveness of analytical procedures is likely to vary by assertion and will be affected by the extent and detail of information available.

A27   Another auditor may perform procedures that are substantive in nature for the benefit of user auditors. Such an engagement may involve the performance, by another auditor, of procedures agreed upon by the user entity and its user auditor and by the service organization and its service auditor. The findings resulting from the procedures performed by another auditor are reviewed by the user auditor to determine whether they constitute sufficient appropriate audit evidence. In addition, there may be requirements imposed by governmental authorities or through contractual arrangements whereby a service auditor performs designated procedures that are substantive in nature. The results of the application of the required procedures to balances and transactions processed by the service organization may be used by user auditors as part of the evidence necessary to support their audit opinions. In these circumstances, it may be useful for the user auditor and the service auditor to agree, prior to the performance of the procedures, to the audit documentation or access to audit documentation that will be provided to the user auditor.

A28   In certain circumstances, in particular when a user entity outsources some or all of its finance function to a service organization, the user auditor may face a situation where a significant portion of the audit evidence resides at the service organization. Substantive procedures may need to be performed at the service organization by the user auditor or another auditor on its behalf. A service auditor may provide a type 2 report and, in addition, may perform substantive procedures on behalf of the user auditor. The involvement of another auditor does not alter the user auditor's responsibility to obtain sufficient appropriate audit evidence to afford a reasonable basis to support the user auditor's opinion. Accordingly, the user auditor's consideration of whether sufficient appropriate audit evidence has been obtained and whether the user auditor needs to perform further substantive procedures includes the user auditor's involvement with, or evidence of, the direction, supervision and performance of the substantive procedures performed by another auditor.

Tests of Controls
(Ref: Para. 16)

A29   The user auditor is required by ISA (UK) 330 (Revised June 2016)[10] to design and perform tests of controls to obtain sufficient appropriate audit evidence as to the operating effectiveness of relevant controls in certain circumstances. In the context of a service organization, this requirement applies when:

---

[10]   *ISA (UK) 330 (Revised June 2016), paragraph 8.*

(a)   The user auditor's assessment of risks of material misstatement includes an expectation that the controls at the service organization are operating effectively (that is, the user auditor intends to rely on the operating effectiveness of controls at the service organization in determining the nature, timing and extent of substantive procedures); or

(b)   Substantive procedures alone, or in combination with tests of the operating effectiveness of controls at the user entity, cannot provide sufficient appropriate audit evidence at the assertion level.

If a type 2 report is not available, a user auditor may contact the service   **A30** organization, through the user entity, to request that a service auditor be engaged to provide a type 2 report that includes tests of the operating effectiveness of the relevant controls or the user auditor may use another auditor to perform procedures at the service organization that test the operating effectiveness of those controls. A user auditor may also visit the service organization and perform tests of relevant controls if the service organization agrees to it. The user auditor's risk assessments are based on the combined evidence provided by the work of another auditor and the user auditor's own procedures.

Using a Type 2 Report as Audit Evidence that Controls at the Service
Organization Are Operating Effectively
(Ref: Para. 17)

A type 2 report may be intended to satisfy the needs of several different user   **A31** auditors; therefore tests of controls and results described in the service auditor's report may not be relevant to assertions that are significant in the user entity's financial statements. The relevant tests of controls and results are evaluated to determine that the service auditor's report provides sufficient appropriate audit evidence about the effectiveness of the controls to support the user auditor's risk assessment. In doing so, the user auditor may consider the following factors:

(a)   The time period covered by the tests of controls and the time elapsed since the performance of the tests of controls;

(b)   The scope of the service auditor's work and the services and processes covered, the controls tested and tests that were performed, and the way in which tested controls relate to the user entity's controls; and

(c)   The results of those tests of controls and the service auditor's opinion on the operating effectiveness of the controls.

For certain assertions, the shorter the period covered by a specific test and the   **A32** longer the time elapsed since the performance of the test, the less audit evidence the test may provide. In comparing the period covered by the type 2 report to the user entity's financial reporting period, the user auditor may conclude that the type 2 report offers less audit evidence if there is little overlap between the period covered by the type 2 report and the period for which the user auditor intends to rely on the report. When this is the case, a type 2 report covering a preceding or subsequent period may provide additional audit evidence. In other cases, the user auditor may determine it is necessary to perform, or use another auditor to perform, tests of controls at the service organization in order to obtain sufficient appropriate audit evidence about the operating effectiveness of those controls.

It may also be necessary for the user auditor to obtain additional evidence about   **A33** significant changes to the relevant controls at the service organization outside of the period covered by the type 2 report or determine additional audit procedures to be performed. Relevant factors in determining what additional audit evidence to obtain about controls at the service organization that were operating outside of the period covered by the service auditor's report may include:

- The significance of the assessed risks of material misstatement at the assertion level;

- The specific controls that were tested during the interim period, and significant changes to them since they were tested, including changes in the information system, processes, and personnel;

- The degree to which audit evidence about the operating effectiveness of those controls was obtained;

- The length of the remaining period;

- The extent to which the user auditor intends to reduce further substantive procedures based on the reliance on controls; and

- The effectiveness of the control environment and monitoring of controls at the user entity.

A34   Additional audit evidence may be obtained, for example, by extending tests of controls over the remaining period or testing the user entity's monitoring of controls.

A35   If the service auditor's testing period is completely outside the user entity's financial reporting period, the user auditor will be unable to rely on such tests for the user auditor to conclude that the user entity's controls are operating effectively because they do not provide current audit period evidence of the effectiveness of the controls, unless other procedures are performed.

A36   In certain circumstances, a service provided by the service organization may be designed with the assumption that certain controls will be implemented by the user entity. For example, the service may be designed with the assumption that the user entity will have controls in place for authorizing transactions before they are sent to the service organization for processing. In such a situation, the service organization's description of controls may include a description of those complementary user entity controls. The user auditor considers whether those complementary user entity controls are relevant to the service provided to the user entity.

A37   If the user auditor believes that the service auditor's report may not provide sufficient appropriate audit evidence, for example, if a service auditor's report does not contain a description of the service auditor's tests of controls and results thereon, the user auditor may supplement the understanding of the service auditor's procedures and conclusions by contacting the service organization, through the user entity, to request a discussion with the service auditor about the scope and results of the service auditor's work. Also, if the user auditor believes it is necessary, the user auditor may contact the service organization, through the user entity, to request that the service auditor perform procedures at the service organization. Alternatively, the user auditor, or another auditor at the request of the user auditor, may perform such procedures.

A38   The service auditor's type 2 report identifies results of tests, including exceptions and other information that could affect the user auditor's conclusions. Exceptions noted by the service auditor or a modified opinion in the service auditor's type 2 report do not automatically mean that the service auditor's type 2 report will not be useful for the audit of the user entity's financial statements in assessing the risks of material misstatement. Rather, the exceptions and the matter giving rise to a modified opinion in the service auditor's type 2 report are considered in the user auditor's assessment of the testing of controls performed by the service auditor. In considering the exceptions and matters giving rise to a modified opinion, the user auditor may discuss such matters with the service auditor. Such communication is dependent upon the user entity contacting the service organization, and obtaining the service organization's approval for the communication to take place.

Communication of deficiencies in internal control identified during the audit

The user auditor is required to communicate in writing significant deficiencies identified during the audit to both management and those charged with governance on a timely basis.[11] The user auditor is also required to communicate to management at an appropriate level of responsibility on a timely basis other deficiencies in internal control identified during the audit that, in the user auditor's professional judgment, are of sufficient importance to merit management's attention.[12] Matters that the user auditor may identify during the audit and may communicate to management and those charged with governance of the user entity include:

A39

- Any monitoring of controls that could be implemented by the user entity, including those identified as a result of obtaining a type 1 or type 2 report;

- Instances where complementary user entity controls are noted in the type 1 or type 2 report and are not implemented at the user entity; and

- Controls that may be needed at the service organization that do not appear to have been implemented or that are not specifically covered by a type 2 report.

Type 1 and Type 2 Reports that Exclude the Services of a Subservice Organization
(Ref: Para. 18)

If a service organization uses a subservice organization, the service auditor's report may either include or exclude the subservice organization's relevant control objectives and related controls in the service organization's description of its system and in the scope of the service auditor's engagement. These two methods of reporting are known as the inclusive method and the carve-out method, respectively. If the type 1 or type 2 report excludes the controls at a subservice organization, and the services provided by the subservice organization are relevant to the audit of the user entity's financial statements, the user auditor is required to apply the requirements of this ISA (UK) in respect of the subservice organization. The nature and extent of work to be performed by the user auditor regarding the services provided by a subservice organization depend on the nature and significance of those services to the user entity and the relevance of those services to the audit. The application of the requirement in paragraph 9 assists the user auditor in determining the effect of the subservice organization and the nature and extent of work to be performed.

A40

---

[11] *ISA (UK) 265, Communicating Deficiencies in Internal Control to Those Charged with Governance and Management, paragraphs 9–10.*

[12] *ISA (UK) 265, paragraph 10.*

Fraud, Non-Compliance with Laws and Regulations and Uncorrected Misstatements in Relation to Activities at the Service Organization
(Ref: Para. 19)

A41   A service organization may be required under the terms of the contract with user entities to disclose to affected user entities any fraud, non-compliance with laws and regulations or uncorrected misstatements attributable to the service organization's management or employees. As required by paragraph 19, the user auditor makes inquiries of the user entity management regarding whether the service organization has reported any such matters and evaluates whether any matters reported by the service organization affect the nature, timing and extent of the user auditor's further audit procedures. In certain circumstances, the user auditor may require additional information to perform this evaluation, and may request the user entity to contact the service organization to obtain the necessary information.

Reporting by the User Auditor
(Ref: Para. 20)

A42   When a user auditor is unable to obtain sufficient appropriate audit evidence regarding the services provided by the service organization relevant to the audit of the user entity's financial statements, a limitation on the scope of the audit exists. This may be the case when:

●   The user auditor is unable to obtain a sufficient understanding of the services provided by the service organization and does not have a basis for the identification and assessment of the risks of material misstatement;

●   A user auditor's risk assessment includes an expectation that controls at the service organization are operating effectively and the user auditor is unable to obtain sufficient appropriate audit evidence about the operating effectiveness of these controls; or

●   Sufficient appropriate audit evidence is only available from records held at the service organization, and the user auditor is unable to obtain direct access to these records.

Whether the user auditor expresses a qualified opinion or disclaims an opinion depends on the user auditor's conclusion as to whether the possible effects on the financial statements are material or pervasive.

Reference to the Work of a Service Auditor
(Ref: Para. 21–22)

A43   In some cases, law or regulation may require a reference to the work of a service auditor in the user auditor's report, for example, for the purposes of transparency in the public sector. In such circumstances, the user auditor may need the consent of the service auditor before making such a reference.

A44   The fact that a user entity uses a service organization does not alter the user auditor's responsibility under ISAs (UK) to obtain sufficient appropriate audit evidence to afford a reasonable basis to support the user auditor's opinion. Therefore, the user auditor does not make reference to the service auditor's report as a basis, in part, for the user auditor's opinion on the user entity's financial statements. However, when the user auditor expresses a modified opinion because of a modified opinion in a service auditor's report, the user auditor is not precluded from referring to the service auditor's report if such reference assists in explaining the reason for the user auditor's modified opinion. In such circumstances, the user auditor may need the consent of the service auditor before making such a reference.

ISA (UK) 450 (Revised June 2016) Evaluation of Misstatements Identified During the Audit (Updated July 2017)

(Effective for audits of financial statements for periods commencing on or after 17 June 2016)[0]

Contents

Paragraphs

Introduction   1 - 2
  Scope of this ISA (UK)   1
  Effective date   2

Objective   3

Definitions   4

Requirements
  Accumulation of identified misstatements   5
  Consideration of identified misstatements as the audit progresses   6 - 7
  Communication and correction of misstatements   8 - 9
  Evaluating the effect of uncorrected misstatements   10 - 13
  Written representation   14
  Documentation   15

Application and other explanatory material
  Definition of misstatement   A1
  Accumulation of identified misstatements   A2 - A6
  Consideration of identified misstatements as the audit progresses   A7 - A9
  Communication and correction of misstatements   A10 - A13
  Evaluating the effect of uncorrected misstatements   A14 - A28-1
  Written Representation   A29 - A29-1
  Documentation   A30

International Standard on Auditing (UK) (ISA (UK)) 450 (Revised June 2016), *Evaluation of Misstatements Identified during the Audit*, should be read in the context of ISA (UK) 200 (Revised June 2016), *Overall Objectives of the Independent Auditor and the Conduct of an Audit in Accordance with International Standards on Auditing (UK)*.

---

[0] *Conforming amendments to this standard as a result of ISA (UK) 250 (Revised July 2017), Section A—Consideration of Laws and Regulations in an Audit of Financial Statements, are included that are effective for audits of financial statements for periods commencing on or after 15 December 2017. Details of the amendments are given in the Annexure to ISA (UK) 250 (Revised July 2017).*

Introduction

Scope of this ISA (UK)

1   This International Standard on Auditing (UK) (ISA (UK)) deals with the auditor's responsibility to evaluate the effect of identified misstatements on the audit and of uncorrected misstatements, if any, on the financial statements. ISA (UK) 700 (Revised June 2016) deals with the auditor's responsibility, in forming an opinion on the financial statements, to conclude whether reasonable assurance has been obtained about whether the financial statements as a whole are free from material misstatement. The auditor's conclusion required by ISA (UK) 700 (Revised June 2016) takes into account the auditor's evaluation of uncorrected misstatements, if any, on the financial statements, in accordance with this ISA (UK).[1] ISA (UK) 320 (Revised June 2016)[2] deals with the auditor's responsibility to apply the concept of materiality appropriately in planning and performing an audit of financial statements.

Effective Date

2   This ISA (UK) is effective for audits of financial statements for periods commencing on or after 17 June 2016. Earlier adoption is permitted.

Objective

3   The objective of the auditor is to evaluate:

(a)   The effect of identified misstatements on the audit; and

(b)   The effect of uncorrected misstatements, if any, on the financial statements.

Definitions

4   For purposes of the ISAs (UK), the following terms have the meanings attributed below:

(a)   Misstatement – A difference between the reported amount, classification, presentation, or disclosure of a financial statement item and the amount, classification, presentation, or disclosure that is required for the item to be in accordance with the applicable financial reporting framework. Misstatements can arise from error or fraud. (Ref: Para. A1)

When the auditor expresses an opinion on whether the financial statements are presented fairly, in all material respects, or give a true and fair view, misstatements also include those adjustments of amounts, classifications, presentation, or disclosures that, in the auditor's judgment, are necessary for the financial statements to be presented fairly, in all material respects, or to give a true and fair view.

(b)   Uncorrected misstatements – Misstatements that the auditor has accumulated during the audit and that have not been corrected.

---

[1]   ISA (UK) 700 (Revised June 2016), *Forming an Opinion and Reporting on Financial Statements, paragraphs 10–11.*

[2]   ISA (UK) 320 (Revised June 2016), *Materiality in Planning and Performing an Audit.*

Requirements

Accumulation of Identified Misstatements

The auditor shall accumulate misstatements identified during the audit, other than   **5**
those that are clearly trivial. (Ref: Para. A2–A6)

Consideration of Identified Misstatements as the Audit Progresses

The auditor shall determine whether the overall audit strategy and audit plan need   **6**
to be revised if:

(a)   The nature of identified misstatements and the circumstances of their
occurrence indicate that other misstatements may exist that, when
aggregated with misstatements accumulated during the audit, could be
material; or (Ref: Para. A7)

(b)   The aggregate of misstatements accumulated during the audit approaches
materiality determined in accordance with ISA (UK) 320 (Revised June
2016). (Ref: Para. A8)

If, at the auditor's request, management has examined a class of transactions,   **7**
account balance or disclosure and corrected misstatements that were detected, the
auditor shall perform additional audit procedures to determine whether
misstatements remain. (Ref: Para. A9)

Communication and Correction of Misstatements

The auditor shall communicate, unless prohibited by law or regulation, on a timely   **8**
basis all misstatements accumulated during the audit with the appropriate level of
management.[3] The auditor shall request management to correct those
misstatements. (Ref: Para. A10–A12)

If management refuses to correct some or all of the misstatements communicated   **9**
by the auditor, the auditor shall obtain an understanding of management's reasons
for not making the corrections and shall take that understanding into account when
evaluating whether the financial statements as a whole are free from material
misstatement. (Ref: Para. A13)

Evaluating the Effect of Uncorrected Misstatements

Prior to evaluating the effect of uncorrected misstatements, the auditor shall   **10**
reassess materiality determined in accordance with ISA (UK) 320 (Revised June
2016) to confirm whether it remains appropriate in the context of the entity's
actual financial results. (Ref: Para. A14–A15)

The auditor shall determine whether uncorrected misstatements are material,   **11**
individually or in aggregate. In making this determination, the auditor shall
consider:

(a)   The size and nature of the misstatements, both in relation to particular
classes of transactions, account balances or disclosures and the financial
statements as a whole, and the particular circumstances of their occurrence;
and (Ref: Para. A16–A22, A24–A25)

---

[3] *ISA (UK) 260 (Revised June 2016), Communication with Those Charged with Governance, paragraph 7.*

(b)   The effect of uncorrected misstatements related to prior periods on the relevant classes of transactions, account balances or disclosures, and the financial statements as a whole. (Ref: Para. A23)

Communication with Those Charged with Governance

12   The auditor shall communicate with those charged with governance uncorrected misstatements and the effect that they, individually or in aggregate, may have on the opinion in the auditor's report, unless prohibited by law or regulation.[4] The auditor's communication shall identify material uncorrected misstatements individually. The auditor shall request that uncorrected misstatements be corrected. (Ref: Para. A26–A28-1)

13   The auditor shall also communicate with those charged with governance the effect of uncorrected misstatements related to prior periods on the relevant classes of transactions, account balances or disclosures, and the financial statements as a whole.

Written Representation

14   The auditor shall request a written representation from management and, where appropriate, those charged with governance whether they believe the effects of uncorrected misstatements are immaterial, individually and in aggregate, to the financial statements as a whole. A summary of such items shall be included in or attached to the written representation. (Ref: Para. A29–A29-1)

Documentation

15   The auditor shall include in the audit documentation:[5] (Ref: Para. A30)

(a)   The amount below which misstatements would be regarded as clearly trivial (paragraph 5);

(b)   All misstatements accumulated during the audit and whether they have been corrected (paragraphs 5, 8 and 12); and

(c)   The auditor's conclusion as to whether uncorrected misstatements are material, individually or in aggregate, and the basis for that conclusion (paragraph 11).

***

Application and Other Explanatory Material

Definition of Misstatement
(Ref: Para. 4(a))

A1   Misstatements may result from:

(a)   An inaccuracy in gathering or processing data from which the financial statements are prepared;

---

[4] *See footnote 3.*

[5] *ISA (UK) 230 (Revised June 2016), Audit Documentation, paragraphs 8–11, and paragraph A6.*

(b)   An omission of an amount or disclosure, including inadequate or incomplete disclosures, and those disclosures required to meet disclosure objectives of certain financial reporting frameworks as applicable;[6]

(c)   An incorrect accounting estimate arising from overlooking, or clear misinterpretation of, facts;

(d)   Judgments of management concerning accounting estimates that the auditor considers unreasonable or the selection and application of accounting policies that the auditor considers inappropriate.

(e)   An inappropriate classification, aggregation or disaggregation, of information; and

(f)   For financial statements prepared in accordance with a fair presentation framework, the omission of a disclosure necessary for the financial statements to achieve fair presentation beyond disclosures specifically required by the framework.[7]

Examples of misstatements arising from fraud are provided in ISA (UK) 240 (Revised June 2016).[8]

Accumulation of Identified Misstatements
(Ref: Para. 5)

"Clearly Trivial"

Paragraph 5 of this ISA (UK) requires the auditor to accumulate misstatements   **A2**
identified during the audit other than those that are clearly trivial. "Clearly trivial" is not another expression for "not material." Misstatements that are clearly trivial will be of a wholly different (smaller) order of magnitude, or of a wholly different nature than those that would be determined to be material, and will be misstatements that are clearly inconsequential, whether taken individually or in aggregate and whether judged by any criteria of size, nature or circumstances. When there is any uncertainty about whether one or more items are clearly trivial, the misstatement is considered not to be clearly trivial.

Misstatements in Individual Statements

The auditor may designate an amount below which misstatements of amounts in   **A3**
the individual statements would be clearly trivial, and would not need to be accumulated because the auditor expects that the accumulation of such amounts clearly would not have a material effect on the financial statements. However, misstatements of amounts that are above the designated amount are accumulated as required by paragraph 5 of this ISA (UK). In addition, misstatements relating to amounts may not be clearly trivial when judged on criteria of nature or circumstances, and, if not, are accumulated as required by paragraph 5 of this ISA (UK).

---

[6] *For example, International Financial Reporting Standard 7 (IFRS), Financial Instruments: Disclosures, paragraph 42H states that "an entity shall disclose any additional information that it considers necessary to meet the disclosure objectives in paragraph ..."*

[7] *For example, IFRS requires an entity to provide additional disclosures when compliance with the specific requirements in IFRSs is insufficient to enable users to understand the impact of particular transactions, other events and conditions on the entity's financial position and financial performance (International Accounting Standard 1, Presentation of Financial Statements, paragraph 17(c)).*

[8] *ISA (UK) 240 (Revised June 2016), The Auditor's Responsibilities Relating to Fraud in an Audit of Financial Statements, paragraphs A1–A6.*

Misstatements in Disclosures

A4   Misstatements in disclosures may also be clearly trivial whether taken individually or in aggregate, and whether judged by any criteria of size, nature or circumstances. Misstatements in disclosures that are not clearly trivial are also accumulated to assist the auditor in evaluating the effect of such misstatements on the relevant disclosures and the financial statements as a whole. Paragraph A17 of this ISA (UK) provides examples of where misstatements in qualitative disclosures may be material.

Accumulation of Misstatements

A5   Misstatements by nature or circumstances, accumulated as described in paragraphs A3-A4, cannot be added together as is possible in the case of misstatements of amounts. Nevertheless, the auditor is required by paragraph 11 of this ISA (UK) to evaluate those misstatements individually and in aggregate (i.e., collectively with other misstatements) to determine whether they are material.

A6   To assist the auditor in evaluating the effect of misstatements accumulated during the audit and in communicating misstatements to management and those charged with governance, it may be useful to distinguish between factual misstatements, judgmental misstatements and projected misstatements.

• Factual misstatements are misstatements about which there is no doubt.

• Judgmental misstatements are differences arising from the judgments of management including those concerning recognition, measurement, presentation and disclosure in the financial statements (including the selection or application of accounting policies) that the auditor considers unreasonable or inappropriate.

• Projected misstatements are the auditor's best estimate of misstatements in populations, involving the projection of misstatements identified in audit samples to the entire populations from which the samples were drawn. Guidance on the determination of projected misstatements and evaluation of the results is set out in ISA (UK) 530.[9]

Consideration of Identified Misstatements as the Audit Progresses
(Ref: Para. 6–7)

A7   A misstatement may not be an isolated occurrence. Evidence that other misstatements may exist include, for example, where the auditor identifies that a misstatement arose from a breakdown in internal control or from inappropriate assumptions or valuation methods that have been widely applied by the entity.

A8   If the aggregate of misstatements accumulated during the audit approaches materiality determined in accordance with ISA (UK) 320 (Revised June 2016), there may be a greater than acceptably low level of risk that possible undetected misstatements, when taken with the aggregate of misstatements accumulated during the audit, could exceed materiality. Undetected misstatements could exist because of the presence of sampling risk and non-sampling risk.[10]

A9   The auditor may request management to examine a class of transactions, account balance or disclosure in order for management to understand the cause of a misstatement identified by the auditor, perform procedures to determine the

---

[9] *ISA (UK) 530, Audit Sampling, paragraphs 14–15.*

[10] *ISA (UK) 530, paragraph 5(c)–(d).*

amount of the actual misstatement in the class of transactions, account balance or disclosure, and to make appropriate adjustments to the financial statements. Such a request may be made, for example, based on the auditor's projection of misstatements identified in an audit sample to the entire population from which it was drawn.

Communication and Correction of Misstatements
(Ref: Para. 8–9)

Timely communication of misstatements to the appropriate level of management   **A10** is important as it enables management to evaluate whether the classes of transactions, account balances and disclosures are misstated, inform the auditor if it disagrees, and take action as necessary. Ordinarily, the appropriate level of management is the one that has responsibility and authority to evaluate the misstatements and to take the necessary action.

In some jurisdictions, law or regulation may restrict the auditor's communication   **A11** of certain misstatements to management, or others, within the entity. Law or regulation may specifically prohibit a communication, or other action, that might prejudice an investigation by an appropriate authority into an actual, or suspected, illegal act, including alerting the entity, for example, when the auditor is required to report identified or suspected non-compliance with law or regulation to an appropriate authority pursuant to anti-money laundering legislation. In these circumstances, the issues considered by the auditor may be complex and the auditor may consider it appropriate to obtain legal advice.

The correction by management of all misstatements, including those   **A12** communicated by the auditor, enables management to maintain accurate accounting books and records and reduces the risks of material misstatement of future financial statements because of the cumulative effect of immaterial uncorrected misstatements related to prior periods.

ISA (UK) 700 (Revised June 2016) requires the auditor to evaluate whether the   **A13** financial statements are prepared and presented, in all material respects, in accordance with the requirements of the applicable financial reporting framework. This evaluation includes consideration of the qualitative aspects of the entity's accounting practices, including indicators of possible bias in management's judgments,[11] which may be affected by the auditor's understanding of management's reasons for not making the corrections.

Evaluating the Effect of Uncorrected Misstatements
(Ref: Para. 10–11)

The auditor's determination of materiality in accordance with ISA (UK) 320   **A14** (Revised June 2016) is often based on estimates of the entity's financial results, because the actual financial results may not yet be known. Therefore, prior to the auditor's evaluation of the effect of uncorrected misstatements, it may be necessary to revise materiality determined in accordance with ISA (UK) 320 (Revised June 2016) based on the actual financial results.

ISA (UK) 320 (Revised June 2016) explains that, as the audit progresses,   **A15** materiality for the financial statements as a whole (and, if applicable, the materiality level or levels for particular classes of transactions, account balances or disclosures) is revised in the event of the auditor becoming aware of

---

[11] *ISA (UK) 700 (Revised June 2016), paragraph 12.*

information during the audit that would have caused the auditor to have determined a different amount (or amounts) initially.[12] Thus, any significant revision is likely to have been made before the auditor evaluates the effect of uncorrected misstatements. However, if the auditor's reassessment of materiality determined in accordance with ISA (UK) 320 (Revised June 2016) (see paragraph 10 of this ISA (UK)) gives rise to a lower amount (or amounts), then performance materiality and the appropriateness of the nature, timing and extent of the further audit procedures are reconsidered so as to obtain sufficient appropriate audit evidence on which to base the audit opinion.

A16   Each individual misstatement of an amount is considered to evaluate its effect on the relevant classes of transactions, account balances or disclosures, including whether the materiality level for that particular class of transactions, account balance or disclosure, if any, has been exceeded.

A17   In addition, each individual misstatement of a qualitative disclosure is considered to evaluate its effect on the relevant disclosure(s), as well as its overall effect on the financial statements as a whole. The determination of whether a misstatement(s) in a qualitative disclosure is material, in the context of the applicable financial reporting framework and the specific circumstances of the entity, is a matter that involves the exercise of professional judgment. Examples where such misstatements may be material include:

- Inaccurate or incomplete descriptions of information about the objectives, policies and processes for managing capital for entities with insurance and banking activities.

- The omission of information about the events or circumstances that have led to an impairment loss (e.g., a significant long-term decline in the demand for a metal or commodity) in an entity with mining operations.

- The incorrect description of an accounting policy relating to a significant item in the statement of financial position, the statement of comprehensive income, the statement of changes in equity or the statement of cash flows.

- The inadequate description of the sensitivity of an exchange rate in an entity that undertakes international trading activities.

A18   In determining whether uncorrected misstatements by nature are material as required by paragraph 11 of this ISA (UK), the auditor considers uncorrected misstatements in amounts and disclosures. Such misstatements may be considered material either individually, or when taken in combination with other misstatements. For example, depending on the misstatements identified in disclosures, the auditor may consider whether:

(a)   Identified errors are persistent or pervasive; or

(b)   A number of identified misstatements are relevant to the same matter, and considered collectively may affect the users' understanding of that matter.

This consideration of accumulated misstatements is also helpful when evaluating the financial statements in accordance with paragraph 13(d) of ISA (UK) 700 (Revised June 2016),[13] which requires the auditor to consider whether the overall presentation of the financial statements has been undermined by including information that is not relevant or that obscures a proper understanding of the matters disclosed.

---

[12] ISA (UK) 320 (Revised June 2016), paragraph 12.

[13] ISA (UK) 700 (Revised June 2016), Forming an Opinion and Reporting on Financial Statements.

If an individual misstatement is judged to be material, it is unlikely that it can be **A19** offset by other misstatements. For example, if revenue has been materially overstated, the financial statements as a whole will be materially misstated, even if the effect of the misstatement on earnings is completely offset by an equivalent overstatement of expenses. It may be appropriate to offset misstatements within the same account balance or class of transactions; however, the risk that further undetected misstatements may exist is considered before concluding that offsetting even immaterial misstatements is appropriate.[14]

Determining whether a classification misstatement is material involves the **A20** evaluation of qualitative considerations, such as the effect of the classification misstatement on debt or other contractual covenants, the effect on individual line items or sub-totals, or the effect on key ratios. There may be circumstances where the auditor concludes that a classification misstatement is not material in the context of the financial statements as a whole, even though it may exceed the materiality level or levels applied in evaluating other misstatements. For example, a misclassification between balance sheet line items may not be considered material in the context of the financial statements as a whole when the amount of the misclassification is small in relation to the size of the related balance sheet line items and the misclassification does not affect the income statement or any key ratios.

The circumstances related to some misstatements may cause the auditor to **A21** evaluate them as material, individually or when considered together with other misstatements accumulated during the audit, even if they are lower than materiality for the financial statements as a whole. Circumstances that may affect the evaluation include the extent to which the misstatement:

- Affects compliance with regulatory requirements;

- Affects compliance with debt covenants or other contractual requirements;

- Relates to the incorrect selection or application of an accounting policy that has an immaterial effect on the current period's financial statements but is likely to have a material effect on future periods' financial statements;

- Masks a change in earnings or other trends, especially in the context of general economic and industry conditions;

- Affects ratios used to evaluate the entity's financial position, results of operations or cash flows;

- Affects segment information presented in the financial statements (for example, the significance of the matter to a segment or other portion of the entity's business that has been identified as playing a significant role in the entity's operations or profitability);

- Has the effect of increasing management compensation, for example, by ensuring that the requirements for the award of bonuses or other incentives are satisfied;

- Is significant having regard to the auditor's understanding of known previous communications to users, for example, in relation to forecast earnings;

---

[14] *The identification of a number of immaterial misstatements within the same account balance or class of transactions may require the auditor to reassess the risk of material misstatement for that account balance or class of transactions.*

- Relates to items involving particular parties (for example, whether external parties to the transaction are related to members of the entity's management);

- Is an omission of information not specifically required by the applicable financial reporting framework but which, in the judgment of the auditor, is important to the users' understanding of the financial position, financial performance or cash flows of the entity; or

- Affects other information to be included in the entity's annual report (for example, information to be included in a "Management Discussion and Analysis" or an "Operating and Financial Review") that may reasonably be expected to influence the economic decisions of the users of the financial statements. ISA (UK) 720 (Revised June 2016)[15] deals with the auditor's responsibilities relating to other information.

These circumstances are only examples; not all are likely to be present in all audits nor is the list necessarily complete. The existence of any circumstances such as these does not necessarily lead to a conclusion that the misstatement is material.

A22   ISA (UK) 240 (Revised June 2016)[16] explains how the implications of a misstatement that is, or may be, the result of fraud ought to be considered in relation to other aspects of the audit, even if the size of the misstatement is not material in relation to the financial statements. Depending on the circumstances, misstatements in disclosures could also be indicative of fraud, and, for example, may arise from:

- Misleading disclosures that have resulted from bias in management's judgments; or

- Extensive duplicative or uninformative disclosures that are intended to obscure a proper understanding of matters in the financial statements.

When considering the implications of misstatements in classes of transactions, account balances and disclosures, the auditor exercises professional skepticism in accordance with ISA (UK) 200 (Revised June 2016).[17]

A23   The cumulative effect of immaterial uncorrected misstatements related to prior periods may have a material effect on the current period's financial statements. There are different acceptable approaches to the auditor's evaluation of such uncorrected misstatements on the current period's financial statements. Using the same evaluation approach provides consistency from period to period.

Considerations Specific to Public Sector Entities

A24   In the case of an audit of a public sector entity, the evaluation whether a misstatement is material may also be affected by the auditor's responsibilities established by law, regulation or other authority to report specific matters, including, for example, fraud.

A25   Furthermore, issues such as public interest, accountability, probity and ensuring effective legislative oversight, in particular, may affect the assessment whether an item is material by virtue of its nature. This is particularly so for items that relate to compliance with law, regulation or other authority.

---

[15] *ISA (UK) 720 (Revised June 2016), The Auditor's Responsibilities Relating to Other Information.*

[16] *ISA (UK) 240 (Revised June 2016), paragraph 35.*

[17] *ISA (UK) 200 (Revised June 2016), paragraph 15.*

Communication with Those Charged with Governance
(Ref: Para. 12)

If uncorrected misstatements have been communicated with person(s) with **A26** management responsibilities, and those person(s) also have governance responsibilities, they need not be communicated again with those same person(s) in their governance role. The auditor nonetheless has to be satisfied that communication with person(s) with management responsibilities adequately informs all of those with whom the auditor would otherwise communicate in their governance capacity.[18]

Where there is a large number of individual immaterial uncorrected misstatements, **A27** the auditor may communicate the number and overall monetary effect of the uncorrected misstatements, rather than the details of each individual uncorrected misstatement.

ISA (UK) 260 (Revised June 2016) requires the auditor to communicate with **A28** those charged with governance the written representations the auditor is requesting (see paragraph 14 of this ISA (UK)).[19] The auditor may discuss with those charged with governance the reasons for, and the implications of, a failure to correct misstatements, having regard to the size and nature of the misstatement judged in the surrounding circumstances, and possible implications in relation to future financial statements.

If management have corrected material misstatements, communicating those **A28-1** corrections of which the auditor is aware to those charged with governance may assist them to fulfill their governance responsibilities, including reviewing the effectiveness of the system of internal control.

Written Representation
(Ref: Para. 14)

Because the preparation of the financial statements requires management and, **A29** where appropriate, those charged with governance to adjust the financial statements to correct material misstatements, the auditor is required to request them to provide a written representation about uncorrected misstatements. In some circumstances, management and, where appropriate, those charged with governance may not believe that certain uncorrected misstatements are misstatements. For that reason, they may want to add to their written representation words such as: "We do not agree that items … and … constitute misstatements because [description of reasons]." Obtaining this representation does not, however, relieve the auditor of the need to form a conclusion on the effect of uncorrected misstatements.

Requesting those charged with governance to provide written representations **A29-1** that set out their reasons for not correcting misstatements brought to their attention by the auditor may help focus the attention of those charged with governance on those misstatements and the circumstances giving rise to them.

---

[18] *ISA (UK) 260 (Revised June 2016), paragraph 13.*

[19] *ISA (UK) 260 (Revised June 2016), paragraph 16(c)(ii).*

Documentation

(Ref: Para. 15)

A30   The auditor's documentation of uncorrected misstatements may take into account:

(a)   The consideration of the aggregate effect of uncorrected misstatements;

(b)   The evaluation of whether the materiality level or levels for particular classes of transactions, account balances or disclosures, if any, have been exceeded; and

(c)   The evaluation of the effect of uncorrected misstatements on key ratios or trends, and compliance with legal, regulatory and contractual requirements (for example, debt covenants).

ISA (UK) 500 Audit Evidence
(Updated July 2017)

(Effective for audits of financial statements for periods ending on
or after 15 December 2010)[0]

Contents

	Paragraphs
Introduction	1 - 3
Scope of this ISA (UK)	1 - 2
Effective date	3
Objective	4
Definitions	5
Requirements	
Sufficient appropriate audit evidence	6
Information to be used as audit evidence	7 - 9
Selecting items for testing to obtain audit evidence	10
Inconsistency in, or doubts over reliability of, audit evidence	11
Application and other explanatory material	
Sufficient appropriate audit evidence	A1 - A25
Information to be used as audit evidence	A26 - A51
Selecting items for testing to obtain audit evidence	A52 - A56
Inconsistency in, or doubts over reliability of, audit evidence	A57

International Standard on Auditing (UK) (ISA (UK)) 500, *Audit Evidence*, should be read in conjunction with ISA (UK) 200 (Revised June 2016), *Overall Objectives of the Independent Auditor and the Conduct of an Audit in Accordance with International Standards on Auditing (UK)*.

---

[0] *Conforming amendments to this standard as a result of ISA (UK) 250 (Revised July 2017), Section A— Consideration of Laws and Regulations in an Audit of Financial Statements, are included that are effective for audits of financial statements for periods commencing on or after 15 December 2017. Details of the amendments are given in the Annexure to ISA (UK) 250 (Revised July 2017).*

Introduction

Scope of this ISA (UK)

1   This International Standard on Auditing (UK) (ISA (UK)) explains what constitutes audit evidence in an audit of financial statements, and deals with the auditor's responsibility to design and perform audit procedures to obtain sufficient appropriate audit evidence to be able to draw reasonable conclusions on which to base the auditor's opinion.

2   This ISA (UK) is applicable to all the audit evidence obtained during the course of the audit. Other ISAs (UK) deal with specific aspects of the audit (for example, ISA (UK) 315 (Revised June 2016)[1]), the audit evidence to be obtained in relation to a particular topic (for example, ISA (UK) 570 (Revised June 2016)[2]), specific procedures to obtain audit evidence (for example, ISA (UK) 520[3]), and the evaluation of whether sufficient appropriate audit evidence has been obtained (ISA (UK) 200 (Revised June 2016)[4] and ISA (UK) 330 (Revised July 2017)[5]).

Effective Date

3   This ISA (UK) is effective for audits of financial statements for periods ending on or after 15 December 2010.

Objective

4   The objective of the auditor is to design and perform audit procedures in such a way as to enable the auditor to obtain sufficient appropriate audit evidence to be able to draw reasonable conclusions on which to base the auditor's opinion.

Definitions

5   For purposes of the ISAs (UK), the following terms have the meanings attributed below:

(a)   Accounting records – The records of initial accounting entries and supporting records, such as checks and records of electronic fund transfers; invoices; contracts; the general and subsidiary ledgers, journal entries and other adjustments to the financial statements that are not reflected in journal entries; and records such as work sheets and spreadsheets supporting cost allocations, computations, reconciliations and disclosures.

(b)   Appropriateness (of audit evidence) – The measure of the quality of audit evidence; that is, its relevance and its reliability in providing support for the conclusions on which the auditor's opinion is based.

---

[1] *ISA (UK) 315 (Revised June 2016), Identifying and Assessing the Risks of Material Misstatement through Understanding the Entity and Its Environment.*

[2] *ISA (UK) 570 (Revised June 2016), Going Concern.*

[3] *ISA (UK) 520, Analytical Procedures.*

[4] *ISA (UK) 200 (Revised June 2016), Overall Objectives of the Independent Auditor and the Conduct of an Audit in Accordance with International Standards on Auditing (UK).*

[5] *ISA (UK) 330 (Revised July 2017), The Auditor's Responses to Assessed Risks.*

(c)   Audit evidence – Information used by the auditor in arriving at the conclusions on which the auditor's opinion is based. Audit evidence includes both information contained in the accounting records underlying the financial statements and information obtained from other sources.

(d)   Management's expert – An individual or organization possessing expertise in a field other than accounting or auditing, whose work in that field is used by the entity to assist the entity in preparing the financial statements.

(e)   Sufficiency (of audit evidence) – The measure of the quantity of audit evidence. The quantity of the audit evidence needed is affected by the auditor's assessment of the risks of material misstatement and also by the quality of such audit evidence.

Requirements

Sufficient Appropriate Audit Evidence

The auditor shall design and perform audit procedures that are appropriate in the   **6**
circumstances for the purpose of obtaining sufficient appropriate audit evidence.
(Ref: Para. A1–A25)

Information to Be Used as Audit Evidence

When designing and performing audit procedures, the auditor shall consider the   **7**
relevance and reliability of the information to be used as audit evidence. (Ref:
Para. A26–A33a)

If information to be used as audit evidence has been prepared using the work of a   **8**
management's expert, the auditor shall, to the extent necessary, having regard to
the significance of that expert's work for the auditor's purposes,: (Ref: Para. A34–
A36)

(a)   Evaluate the competence, capabilities and objectivity of that expert; (Ref: Para. A37–A43)

(b)   Obtain an understanding of the work of that expert; and (Ref: Para. A44–A47)

(c)   Evaluate the appropriateness of that expert's work as audit evidence for the relevant assertion. (Ref: Para. A48)

When using information produced by the entity, the auditor shall evaluate whether   **9**
the information is sufficiently reliable for the auditor's purposes, including as
necessary in the circumstances:

(a)   Obtaining audit evidence about the accuracy and completeness of the information; and (Ref: Para. A49–A50)

(b)   Evaluating whether the information is sufficiently precise and detailed for the auditor's purposes. (Ref: Para. A51)

Selecting Items for Testing to Obtain Audit Evidence

When designing tests of controls and tests of details, the auditor shall determine   **10**
means of selecting items for testing that are effective in meeting the purpose of the
audit procedure. (Ref: Para. A52–A56)

Inconsistency in, or Doubts over Reliability of, Audit Evidence

11   If:

(a)   audit evidence obtained from one source is inconsistent with that obtained from another; or

(b)   the auditor has doubts over the reliability of information to be used as audit evidence,

the auditor shall determine what modifications or additions to audit procedures are necessary to resolve the matter, and shall consider the effect of the matter, if any, on other aspects of the audit. (Ref: Para. A57)

***

Application and Other Explanatory Material

Sufficient Appropriate Audit Evidence
(Ref: Para. 6)

A1   Audit evidence is necessary to support the auditor's opinion and report. It is cumulative in nature and is primarily obtained from audit procedures performed during the course of the audit. It may, however, also include information obtained from other sources such as previous audits (provided the auditor has determined whether changes have occurred since the previous audit that may affect its relevance to the current audit[6]) or a firm's quality control procedures for client acceptance and continuance. In addition to other sources inside and outside the entity, the entity's accounting records are an important source of audit evidence. Also, information that may be used as audit evidence may have been prepared using the work of a management's expert. Audit evidence comprises both information that supports and corroborates management's assertions, and any information that contradicts such assertions. In addition, in some cases the absence of information (for example, management's refusal to provide a requested representation) is used by the auditor, and therefore, also constitutes audit evidence.

A2   Most of the auditor's work in forming the auditor's opinion consists of obtaining and evaluating audit evidence. Audit procedures to obtain audit evidence can include inspection, observation, confirmation, recalculation, reperformance and analytical procedures, often in some combination, in addition to inquiry. Although inquiry may provide important audit evidence, and may even produce evidence of a misstatement, inquiry alone ordinarily does not provide sufficient audit evidence of the absence of a material misstatement at the assertion level, nor of the operating effectiveness of controls.

A3   As explained in ISA (UK) 200 (Revised June 2016),[7] reasonable assurance is obtained when the auditor has obtained sufficient appropriate audit evidence to reduce audit risk (that is, the risk that the auditor expresses an inappropriate opinion when the financial statements are materially misstated) to an acceptably low level.

---

[6] *ISA (UK) 315 (Revised June 2016), paragraph 9.*

[7] *ISA (UK) 200 (Revised June 2016), paragraph 5.*

The sufficiency and appropriateness of audit evidence are interrelated. Sufficiency **A4** is the measure of the quantity of audit evidence. The quantity of audit evidence needed is affected by the auditor's assessment of the risks of misstatement (the higher the assessed risks, the more audit evidence is likely to be required) and also by the quality of such audit evidence (the higher the quality, the less may be required). Obtaining more audit evidence, however, may not compensate for its poor quality.

Appropriateness is the measure of the quality of audit evidence; that is, its **A5** relevance and its reliability in providing support for the conclusions on which the auditor's opinion is based. The reliability of evidence is influenced by its source and by its nature, and is dependent on the individual circumstances under which it is obtained.

ISA (UK) 330 (Revised July 2017) requires the auditor to conclude whether **A6** sufficient appropriate audit evidence has been obtained.[8] Whether sufficient appropriate audit evidence has been obtained to reduce audit risk to an acceptably low level, and thereby enable the auditor to draw reasonable conclusions on which to base the auditor's opinion, is a matter of professional judgment. ISA (UK) 200 (Revised June 2016) contains discussion of such matters as the nature of audit procedures, the timeliness of financial reporting, and the balance between benefit and cost, which are relevant factors when the auditor exercises professional judgment regarding whether sufficient appropriate audit evidence has been obtained.

Sources of Audit Evidence

Some audit evidence is obtained by performing audit procedures to test the **A7** accounting records, for example, through analysis and review, reperforming procedures followed in the financial reporting process, and reconciling related types and applications of the same information. Through the performance of such audit procedures, the auditor may determine that the accounting records are internally consistent and agree to the financial statements.

More assurance is ordinarily obtained from consistent audit evidence obtained **A8** from different sources or of a different nature than from items of audit evidence considered individually. For example, corroborating information obtained from a source independent of the entity may increase the assurance the auditor obtains from audit evidence that is generated internally, such as evidence existing within the accounting records, minutes of meetings, or a management representation.

Information from sources independent of the entity that the auditor may use as **A9** audit evidence may include confirmations from third parties, analysts' reports, and comparable data about competitors (benchmarking data).

Audit Procedures for Obtaining Audit Evidence

As required by, and explained further in, ISA (UK) 315 (Revised June 2016) and **A10** ISA (UK) 330 (Revised July 2017), audit evidence to draw reasonable conclusions on which to base the auditor's opinion is obtained by performing:

(a)   Risk assessment procedures; and

(b)   Further audit procedures, which comprise:

---

[8] *ISA (UK) 330 (Revised July 2017), paragraph 26.*

(i)   Tests of controls, when required by the ISAs (UK) or when the auditor has chosen to do so; and

(ii)   Substantive procedures, including tests of details and substantive analytical procedures.

A11   The audit procedures described in paragraphs A14–A25 below may be used as risk assessment procedures, tests of controls or substantive procedures, depending on the context in which they are applied by the auditor. As explained in ISA (UK) 330 (Revised July 2017), audit evidence obtained from previous audits may, in certain circumstances, provide appropriate audit evidence where the auditor performs audit procedures to establish its continuing relevance.[9]

A12   The nature and timing of the audit procedures to be used may be affected by the fact that some of the accounting data and other information may be available only in electronic form or only at certain points or periods in time. For example, source documents, such as purchase orders and invoices, may exist only in electronic form when an entity uses electronic commerce, or may be discarded after scanning when an entity uses image processing systems to facilitate storage and reference.

A13   Certain electronic information may not be retrievable after a specified period of time, for example, if files are changed and if backup files do not exist. Accordingly, the auditor may find it necessary as a result of an entity's data retention policies to request retention of some information for the auditor's review or to perform audit procedures at a time when the information is available.

Inspection

A14   Inspection involves examining records or documents, whether internal or external, in paper form, electronic form, or other media, or a physical examination of an asset. Inspection of records and documents provides audit evidence of varying degrees of reliability, depending on their nature and source and, in the case of internal records and documents, on the effectiveness of the controls over their production. An example of inspection used as a test of controls is inspection of records for evidence of authorization.

A15   Some documents represent direct audit evidence of the existence of an asset, for example, a document constituting a financial instrument such as a stock or bond. Inspection of such documents may not necessarily provide audit evidence about ownership or value. In addition, inspecting an executed contract may provide audit evidence relevant to the entity's application of accounting policies, such as revenue recognition.

A16   Inspection of tangible assets may provide reliable audit evidence with respect to their existence, but not necessarily about the entity's rights and obligations or the valuation of the assets. Inspection of individual inventory items may accompany the observation of inventory counting.

Observation

A17   Observation consists of looking at a process or procedure being performed by others, for example, the auditor's observation of inventory counting by the entity's personnel, or of the performance of control activities. Observation provides audit evidence about the performance of a process or procedure, but is limited to the

---

[9] *ISA (UK) 330 (Revised July 2017), paragraph A35.*

point in time at which the observation takes place, and by the fact that the act of being observed may affect how the process or procedure is performed. See ISA (UK) 501 for further guidance on observation of the counting of inventory.[10]

External Confirmation

An external confirmation represents audit evidence obtained by the auditor as a **A18** direct written response to the auditor from a third party (the confirming party), in paper form, or by electronic or other medium. External confirmation procedures frequently are relevant when addressing assertions associated with certain account balances and their elements. However, external confirmations need not be restricted to account balances only. For example, the auditor may request confirmation of the terms of agreements or transactions an entity has with third parties; the confirmation request may be designed to ask if any modifications have been made to the agreement and, if so, what the relevant details are. External confirmation procedures also are used to obtain audit evidence about the absence of certain conditions, for example, the absence of a "side agreement" that may influence revenue recognition. See ISA (UK) 505 for further guidance.[11]

Recalculation

Recalculation consists of checking the mathematical accuracy of documents or **A19** records. Recalculation may be performed manually or electronically.

Reperformance

Reperformance involves the auditor's independent execution of procedures or **A20** controls that were originally performed as part of the entity's internal control.

Analytical Procedures

Analytical procedures consist of evaluations of financial information through **A21** analysis of plausible relationships among both financial and non-financial data. Analytical procedures also encompass such investigation as is necessary of identified fluctuations or relationships that are inconsistent with other relevant information or that differ from expected values by a significant amount. See ISA (UK) 520 for further guidance.

Inquiry

Inquiry consists of seeking information of knowledgeable persons, both financial **A22** and non-financial, within the entity or outside the entity. Inquiry is used extensively throughout the audit in addition to other audit procedures. Inquiries may range from formal written inquiries to informal oral inquiries. Evaluating responses to inquiries is an integral part of the inquiry process.

Responses to inquiries may provide the auditor with information not previously **A23** possessed or with corroborative audit evidence. Alternatively, responses might provide information that differs significantly from other information that the auditor has obtained, for example, information regarding the possibility of management override of controls. In some cases, responses to inquiries provide a basis for the auditor to modify or perform additional audit procedures.

---

[10] *ISA (UK) 501, Audit Evidence—Specific Considerations for Selected Items.*

[11] *ISA (UK) 505, External Confirmations.*

A24   Although corroboration of evidence obtained through inquiry is often of particular importance, in the case of inquiries about management intent, the information available to support management's intent may be limited. In these cases, understanding management's past history of carrying out its stated intentions, management's stated reasons for choosing a particular course of action, and management's ability to pursue a specific course of action may provide relevant information to corroborate the evidence obtained through inquiry.

A25   In respect of some matters, the auditor may consider it necessary to obtain written representations from management and, where appropriate, those charged with governance to confirm responses to oral inquiries. See ISA (UK) 580 for further guidance.[12]

Information to Be Used as Audit Evidence

Relevance and Reliability
(Ref: Para. 7)

A26   As noted in paragraph A1, while audit evidence is primarily obtained from audit procedures performed during the course of the audit, it may also include information obtained from other sources such as, for example, previous audits, in certain circumstances, firm's quality control procedures for client acceptance and continuance and complying with certain additional responsibilities under law, regulation or relevant ethical requirements (e.g., regarding an entity's non-compliance with laws and regulations). The quality of all audit evidence is affected by the relevance and reliability of the information upon which it is based.

Relevance

A27   Relevance deals with the logical connection with, or bearing upon, the purpose of the audit procedure and, where appropriate, the assertion under consideration. The relevance of information to be used as audit evidence may be affected by the direction of testing. For example, if the purpose of an audit procedure is to test for overstatement in the existence or valuation of accounts payable, testing the recorded accounts payable may be a relevant audit procedure. On the other hand, when testing for understatement in the existence or valuation of accounts payable, testing the recorded accounts payable would not be relevant, but testing such information as subsequent disbursements, unpaid invoices, suppliers' statements, and unmatched receiving reports may be relevant.

A28   A given set of audit procedures may provide audit evidence that is relevant to certain assertions, but not others. For example, inspection of documents related to the collection of receivables after the period end may provide audit evidence regarding existence and valuation, but not necessarily cutoff. Similarly, obtaining audit evidence regarding a particular assertion, for example, the existence of inventory, is not a substitute for obtaining audit evidence regarding another assertion, for example, the valuation of that inventory. On the other hand, audit evidence from different sources or of a different nature may often be relevant to the same assertion.

A29   Tests of controls are designed to evaluate the operating effectiveness of controls in preventing, or detecting and correcting, material misstatements at the assertion level. Designing tests of controls to obtain relevant audit evidence includes

---

[12] *ISA (UK) 580, Written Representations.*

identifying conditions (characteristics or attributes) that indicate performance of a control, and deviation conditions which indicate departures from adequate performance. The presence or absence of those conditions can then be tested by the auditor.

Substantive procedures are designed to detect material misstatements at the assertion level. They comprise tests of details and substantive analytical procedures. Designing substantive procedures includes identifying conditions relevant to the purpose of the test that constitute a misstatement in the relevant assertion.   **A30**

Reliability

The reliability of information to be used as audit evidence, and therefore of the audit evidence itself, is influenced by its source and its nature, and the circumstances under which it is obtained, including the controls over its preparation and maintenance where relevant. Therefore, generalizations about the reliability of various kinds of audit evidence are subject to important exceptions. Even when information to be used as audit evidence is obtained from sources external to the entity, circumstances may exist that could affect its reliability. For example, information obtained from an independent external source may not be reliable if the source is not knowledgeable, or a management's expert may lack objectivity. While recognizing that exceptions may exist, the following generalizations about the reliability of audit evidence may be useful: **A31**

- The reliability of audit evidence is increased when it is obtained from independent sources outside the entity.

- The reliability of audit evidence that is generated internally is increased when the related controls, including those over its preparation and maintenance, imposed by the entity are effective.

- Audit evidence obtained directly by the auditor (for example, observation of the application of a control) is more reliable than audit evidence obtained indirectly or by inference (for example, inquiry about the application of a control).

- Audit evidence in documentary form, whether paper, electronic, or other medium, is more reliable than evidence obtained orally (for example, a contemporaneously written record of a meeting is more reliable than a subsequent oral representation of the matters discussed).

- Audit evidence provided by original documents is more reliable than audit evidence provided by photocopies or facsimiles, or documents that have been filmed, digitized or otherwise transformed into electronic form, the reliability of which may depend on the controls over their preparation and maintenance.

ISA (UK) 520 provides further guidance regarding the reliability of data used for purposes of designing analytical procedures as substantive procedures.[13]   **A32**

---

[13] *ISA (UK) 520, paragraph 5(a).*

A33   ISA (UK) 240 (Revised June 2016) deals with circumstances where the auditor has reason to believe that a document may not be authentic, or may have been modified without that modification having been disclosed to the auditor.[14]

A33a   ISA (UK) 250 (Revised July 2017)[15] provides further guidance with respect to the auditor complying with any additional responsibilities under law, regulation or relevant ethical requirements regarding an entity's identified or suspected non-compliance with laws and regulations that may provide further information that is relevant to the auditor's work in accordance with ISAs (UK) and evaluating the implications of such non-compliance in relation to other aspects of the audit.

Reliability of Information Produced by a Management's Expert
(Ref: Para. 8)

A34   The preparation of an entity's financial statements may require expertise in a field other than accounting or auditing, such as actuarial calculations, valuations, or engineering data. The entity may employ or engage experts in these fields to obtain the needed expertise to prepare the financial statements. Failure to do so when such expertise is necessary increases the risks of material misstatement.

A35   When information to be used as audit evidence has been prepared using the work of a management's expert, the requirement in paragraph 8 of this ISA (UK) applies. For example, an individual or organization may possess expertise in the application of models to estimate the fair value of securities for which there is no observable market. If the individual or organization applies that expertise in making an estimate which the entity uses in preparing its financial statements, the individual or organization is a management's expert and paragraph 8 applies. If, on the other hand, that individual or organization merely provides price data regarding private transactions not otherwise available to the entity which the entity uses in its own estimation methods, such information, if used as audit evidence, is subject to paragraph 7 of this ISA (UK), but is not the use of a management's expert by the entity.

A36   The nature, timing and extent of audit procedures in relation to the requirement in paragraph 8 of this ISA (UK), may be affected by such matters as:

- The nature and complexity of the matter to which the management's expert relates.

- The risks of material misstatement in the matter.

- The availability of alternative sources of audit evidence.

- The nature, scope and objectives of the management's expert's work.

- Whether the management's expert is employed by the entity, or is a party engaged by it to provide relevant services.

- The extent to which management can exercise control or influence over the work of the management's expert.

- Whether the management's expert is subject to technical performance standards or other professional or industry requirements.

---

[14] *ISA (UK) 240 (Revised June 2016), The Auditor's Responsibilities Relating to Fraud in an Audit of Financial Statements, paragraph 13.*

[15] *ISA (UK) 250 (Revised July 2017), Section A—Consideration of Laws and Regulations in an Audit of Financial Statements, paragraph 9.*

- The nature and extent of any controls within the entity over the management's expert's work.

- The auditor's knowledge and experience of the management's expert's field of expertise.

- The auditor's previous experience of the work of that expert.

The Competence, Capabilities and Objectivity of a Management's Expert
(Ref: Para. 8(a))

Competence relates to the nature and level of expertise of the management's **A37** expert. Capability relates the ability of the management's expert to exercise that competence in the circumstances. Factors that influence capability may include, for example, geographic location, and the availability of time and resources. Objectivity relates to the possible effects that bias, conflict of interest or the influence of others may have on the professional or business judgment of the management's expert. The competence, capabilities and objectivity of a management's expert, and any controls within the entity over that expert's work, are important factors in relation to the reliability of any information produced by a management's expert.

Information regarding the competence, capabilities and objectivity of a **A38** management's expert may come from a variety of sources, such as:

- Personal experience with previous work of that expert.

- Discussions with that expert.

- Discussions with others who are familiar with that expert's work.

- Knowledge of that expert's qualifications, membership of a professional body or industry association, license to practice, or other forms of external recognition.

- Published papers or books written by that expert.

- An auditor's expert, if any, who assists the auditor in obtaining sufficient appropriate audit evidence with respect to information produced by the management's expert.

Matters relevant to evaluating the competence, capabilities and objectivity of a **A39** management's expert include whether that expert's work is subject to technical performance standards or other professional or industry requirements, for example, ethical standards and other membership requirements of a professional body or industry association, accreditation standards of a licensing body, or requirements imposed by law or regulation.

Other matters that may be relevant include: **A40**

- The relevance of the management's expert's competence to the matter for which that expert's work will be used, including any areas of specialty within that expert's field. For example, a particular actuary may specialize in property and casualty insurance, but have limited expertise regarding pension calculations.

- The management's expert's competence with respect to relevant accounting requirements, for example, knowledge of assumptions and methods, including models where applicable, that are consistent with the applicable financial reporting framework.

- Whether unexpected events, changes in conditions, or the audit evidence obtained from the results of audit procedures indicate that it may be necessary to reconsider the initial evaluation of the competence, capabilities and objectivity of the management's expert as the audit progresses.

A41   A broad range of circumstances may threaten objectivity, for example, self-interest threats, advocacy threats, familiarity threats, self-review threats and intimidation threats. Safeguards may reduce such threats, and may be created either by external structures (for example, the management's expert's profession, legislation or regulation), or by the management's expert's work environment (for example, quality control policies and procedures).

A42   Although safeguards cannot eliminate all threats to a management's expert's objectivity, threats such as intimidation threats may be of less significance to an expert engaged by the entity than to an expert employed by the entity, and the effectiveness of safeguards such as quality control policies and procedures may be greater. Because the threat to objectivity created by being an employee of the entity will always be present, an expert employed by the entity cannot ordinarily be regarded as being more likely to be objective than other employees of the entity.

A43   When evaluating the objectivity of an expert engaged by the entity, it may be relevant to discuss with management and that expert any interests and relationships that may create threats to the expert's objectivity, and any applicable safeguards, including any professional requirements that apply to the expert; and to evaluate whether the safeguards are adequate. Interests and relationships creating threats may include:

- Financial interests.
- Business and personal relationships.
- Provision of other services.

Obtaining an Understanding of the Work of the Management's Expert
(Ref: Para. 8(b))

A44   An understanding of the work of the management's expert includes an understanding of the relevant field of expertise. An understanding of the relevant field of expertise may be obtained in conjunction with the auditor's determination of whether the auditor has the expertise to evaluate the work of the management's expert, or whether the auditor needs an auditor's expert for this purpose.[16]

A45   Aspects of the management's expert's field relevant to the auditor's understanding may include:

- Whether that expert's field has areas of specialty within it that are relevant to the audit.
- Whether any professional or other standards, and regulatory or legal requirements apply.
- What assumptions and methods are used by the management's expert, and whether they are generally accepted within that expert's field and appropriate for financial reporting purposes.

---

[16] ISA (UK) 620 (Revised June 2016), *Using the Work of an Auditor's Expert*, paragraph 7.

● The nature of internal and external data or information the auditor's expert uses.

In the case of a management's expert engaged by the entity, there will ordinarily be **A46** an engagement letter or other written form of agreement between the entity and that expert. Evaluating that agreement when obtaining an understanding of the work of the management's expert may assist the auditor in determining the appropriateness of the following for the auditor's purposes:

● The nature, scope and objectives of that expert's work;

● The respective roles and responsibilities of management and that expert; and

● The nature, timing and extent of communication between management and that expert, including the form of any report to be provided by that expert.

In the case of a management's expert employed by the entity, it is less likely there **A47** will be a written agreement of this kind. Inquiry of the expert and other members of management may be the most appropriate way for the auditor to obtain the necessary understanding.

Evaluating the Appropriateness of the Management's Expert's Work
(Ref: Para. 8(c))

Considerations when evaluating the appropriateness of the management's expert's **A48** work as audit evidence for the relevant assertion may include:

● The relevance and reasonableness of that expert's findings or conclusions, their consistency with other audit evidence, and whether they have been appropriately reflected in the financial statements;

● If that expert's work involves use of significant assumptions and methods, the relevance and reasonableness of those assumptions and methods; and

● If that expert's work involves significant use of source data the relevance, completeness, and accuracy of that source data.

Information Produced by the Entity and Used for the Auditor's Purposes
(Ref: Para. 9(a)–(b))

In order for the auditor to obtain reliable audit evidence, information produced by **A49** the entity that is used for performing audit procedures needs to be sufficiently complete and accurate. For example, the effectiveness of auditing revenue by applying standard prices to records of sales volume is affected by the accuracy of the price information and the completeness and accuracy of the sales volume data. Similarly, if the auditor intends to test a population (for example, payments) for a certain characteristic (for example, authorization), the results of the test will be less reliable if the population from which items are selected for testing is not complete.

Obtaining audit evidence about the accuracy and completeness of such **A50** information may be performed concurrently with the actual audit procedure applied to the information when obtaining such audit evidence is an integral part of the audit procedure itself. In other situations, the auditor may have obtained audit evidence of the accuracy and completeness of such information by testing controls over the preparation and maintenance of the information. In some situations, however, the auditor may determine that additional audit procedures are needed.

A51   In some cases, the auditor may intend to use information produced by the entity for other audit purposes. For example, the auditor may intend to make use of the entity's performance measures for the purpose of analytical procedures, or to make use of the entity's information produced for monitoring activities, such as reports of the internal audit function. In such cases, the appropriateness of the audit evidence obtained is affected by whether the information is sufficiently precise or detailed for the auditor's purposes. For example, performance measures used by management may not be precise enough to detect material misstatements.

Selecting Items for Testing to Obtain Audit Evidence
(Ref: Para. 10)

A52   An effective test provides appropriate audit evidence to an extent that, taken with other audit evidence obtained or to be obtained, will be sufficient for the auditor's purposes. In selecting items for testing, the auditor is required by paragraph 7 to determine the relevance and reliability of information to be used as audit evidence; the other aspect of effectiveness (sufficiency) is an important consideration in selecting items to test. The means available to the auditor for selecting items for testing are:

(a)   Selecting all items (100% examination);

(b)   Selecting specific items; and

(c)   Audit sampling.

The application of any one or combination of these means may be appropriate depending on the particular circumstances, for example, the risks of material misstatement related to the assertion being tested, and the practicality and efficiency of the different means.

Selecting All Items

A53   The auditor may decide that it will be most appropriate to examine the entire population of items that make up a class of transactions or account balance (or a stratum within that population). 100% examination is unlikely in the case of tests of controls; however, it is more common for tests of details. 100% examination may be appropriate when, for example:

●   The population constitutes a small number of large value items;

●   There is a significant risk and other means do not provide sufficient appropriate audit evidence; or

●   The repetitive nature of a calculation or other process performed automatically by an information system makes a 100% examination cost effective.

Selecting Specific Items

A54   The auditor may decide to select specific items from a population. In making this decision, factors that may be relevant include the auditor's understanding of the entity, the assessed risks of material misstatement, and the characteristics of the population being tested. The judgmental selection of specific items is subject to non-sampling risk. Specific items selected may include:

●   *High value or key items.* The auditor may decide to select specific items within a population because they are of high value, or exhibit some other characteristic, for example, items that are suspicious, unusual, particularly risk-prone or that have a history of error.

- *All items over a certain amount.* The auditor may decide to examine items whose recorded values exceed a certain amount so as to verify a large proportion of the total amount of a class of transactions or account balance.

- *Items to obtain information.* The auditor may examine items to obtain information about matters such as the nature of the entity or the nature of transactions.

While selective examination of specific items from a class of transactions or account balance will often be an efficient means of obtaining audit evidence, it does not constitute audit sampling. The results of audit procedures applied to items selected in this way cannot be projected to the entire population; accordingly, selective examination of specific items does not provide audit evidence concerning the remainder of the population. **A55**

Audit Sampling

Audit sampling is designed to enable conclusions to be drawn about an entire population on the basis of testing a sample drawn from it. Audit sampling is discussed in ISA (UK) 530.[17] **A56**

Inconsistency in, or Doubts over Reliability of, Audit Evidence
(Ref: Para. 11)

Obtaining audit evidence from different sources or of a different nature may indicate that an individual item of audit evidence is not reliable, such as when audit evidence obtained from one source is inconsistent with that obtained from another. This may be the case when, for example, responses to inquiries of management, internal auditors, and others are inconsistent, or when responses to inquiries of those charged with governance made to corroborate the responses to inquiries of management are inconsistent with the response by management. ISA (UK) 230 (Revised June 2016) includes a specific documentation requirement if the auditor identified information that is inconsistent with the auditor's final conclusion regarding a significant matter.[18] **A57**

---

[17] *ISA (UK) 530, Audit Sampling.*

[18] *ISA (UK) 230 (Revised June 2016), Audit Documentation, paragraph 11.*

ISA (UK) 501 Audit Evidence – Specific Considerations for Selected Items

(Effective for audits of financial statements for periods ending on or after 15 December 2010)

Contents

Paragraphs

Introduction
Scope of this ISA (UK)   1
Effective Date   2

Objective   3

Requirements
Inventory   4 - 8
Litigation and Claims   9 - 12
Segment Information   13

Application and Other Explanatory Material
Inventory   A1 - A16
Litigation and Claims   A17 - A25
BSegment Information (Ref: Para. 13)   A26 - A27

International Standard on Auditing (UK) (ISA (UK)) 501, *Audit Evidence—Specific Considerations for Selected Items*, should be read in conjunction with ISA (UK) 200 (Revised June 2016), *Overall Objectives of the Independent Auditor and the Conduct of an Audit in Accordance with International Standards on Auditing (UK)*.

Introduction

Scope of this ISA (UK)

1   This International Standard on Auditing (UK) (ISA (UK)) deals with specific considerations by the auditor in obtaining sufficient appropriate audit evidence in accordance with ISA (UK) 330 (Revised June 2016),[1] ISA (UK) 500[2] and other relevant ISAs (UK), with respect to certain aspects of inventory, litigation and claims involving the entity, and segment information in an audit of financial statements.

Effective Date

2   This ISA (UK) is effective for audits of financial statements for periods ending on or after 15 December 2010.

Objective

3   The objective of the auditor is to obtain sufficient appropriate audit evidence regarding the:

(a)   Existence and condition of inventory;

(b)   Completeness of litigation and claims involving the entity; and

(c)   Presentation and disclosure of segment information in accordance with the applicable financial reporting framework.

Requirements

Inventory

4   If inventory is material to the financial statements, the auditor shall obtain sufficient appropriate audit evidence regarding the existence and condition of inventory by:

(a)   Attendance at physical inventory counting, unless impracticable, to: (Ref: Para. A1–A3)

   (i)   Evaluate management's instructions and procedures for recording and controlling the results of the entity's physical inventory counting; (Ref: Para. A4)

   (ii)   Observe the performance of management's count procedures; (Ref: Para. A5)

   (iii)   Inspect the inventory; and (Ref: Para. A6)

   (iv)   Perform test counts; and (Ref: Para. A7–A8)

(b)   Performing audit procedures over the entity's final inventory records to determine whether they accurately reflect actual inventory count results.

5   If physical inventory counting is conducted at a date other than the date of the financial statements, the auditor shall, in addition to the procedures required by paragraph 4, perform audit procedures to obtain audit evidence about whether changes in inventory between the count date and the date of the financial statements are properly recorded. (Ref: Para. A9–A11)

---

[1]   *ISA (UK) 330 (Revised June 2016), The Auditor's Responses to Assessed Risks.*

[2]   *ISA (UK) 500, Audit Evidence.*

If the auditor is unable to attend physical inventory counting due to unforeseen **6** circumstances, the auditor shall make or observe some physical counts on an alternative date, and perform audit procedures on intervening transactions.

If attendance at physical inventory counting is impracticable, the auditor shall **7** perform alternative audit procedures to obtain sufficient appropriate audit evidence regarding the existence and condition of inventory. If it is not possible to do so, the auditor shall modify the opinion in the auditor's report in accordance with ISA (UK) 705 (Revised June 2016).[3] (Ref: Para. A12–A14)

If inventory under the custody and control of a third party is material to the **8** financial statements, the auditor shall obtain sufficient appropriate audit evidence regarding the existence and condition of that inventory by performing one or both of the following:

(a) Request confirmation from the third party as to the quantities and condition of inventory held on behalf of the entity. (Ref: Para. A15)

(b) Perform inspection or other audit procedures appropriate in the circumstances. (Ref: Para. A16)

Litigation and Claims

The auditor shall design and perform audit procedures in order to identify **9** litigation and claims involving the entity which may give rise to a risk of material misstatement, including: (Ref: Para. A17–A19)

(a) Inquiry of management[3a] and, where applicable, others within the entity, including in-house legal counsel;

(b) Reviewing minutes of meetings of those charged with governance and correspondence between the entity and its external legal counsel; and

(c) Reviewing legal expense accounts. (Ref: Para. A20)

If the auditor assesses a risk of material misstatement regarding litigation or claims **10** that have been identified, or when audit procedures performed indicate that other material litigation or claims may exist, the auditor shall, in addition to the procedures required by other ISAs (UK), seek direct communication with the entity's external legal counsel. The auditor shall do so through a letter of inquiry, prepared by management[3b] and sent by the auditor, requesting the entity's external legal counsel to communicate directly with the auditor. If law, regulation or the respective legal professional body prohibits the entity's external legal counsel from communicating directly with the auditor, the auditor shall perform alternative audit procedures. (Ref: Para. A21–A25)

If: **11**

(a) management[3c] refuses to give the auditor permission to communicate or meet with the entity's external legal counsel, or the entity's external legal counsel refuses to respond appropriately to the letter of inquiry, or is prohibited from responding; and

---

[3] *ISA (UK) 705 (Revised June 2016), Modifications to the Opinion in the Independent Auditor's Report.*

[3a] *In the UK the auditor also makes appropriate inquiry of those charged with governance.*

[3b] *In the UK the letter may need to be prepared by those charged with governance.*

[3c] *In the UK permission may be denied by those charged with governance.*

(b)   the auditor is unable to obtain sufficient appropriate audit evidence by performing alternative audit procedures,

the auditor shall modify the opinion in the auditor's report in accordance with ISA (UK) 705 (Revised June 2016).

Written Representations

12   The auditor shall request management and, where appropriate, those charged with governance to provide written representations that all known actual or possible litigation and claims whose effects should be considered when preparing the financial statements have been disclosed to the auditor and accounted for and disclosed in accordance with the applicable financial reporting framework.

Segment Information

13   The auditor shall obtain sufficient appropriate audit evidence regarding the presentation and disclosure of segment information in accordance with the applicable financial reporting framework by: (Ref: Para. A26)

(a)   Obtaining an understanding of the methods used by management in determining segment information, and: (Ref: Para. A27)

    (i)   Evaluating whether such methods are likely to result in disclosure in accordance with the applicable financial reporting framework; and

    (ii)   Where appropriate, testing the application of such methods; and

(b)   Performing analytical procedures or other audit procedures appropriate in the circumstances.

Application and Other Explanatory Material

Inventory[3d]

Attendance at Physical Inventory Counting
(Ref: Para. 4(a))

A1   Management ordinarily establishes procedures under which inventory is physically counted at least once a year to serve as a basis for the preparation of the financial statements and, if applicable, to ascertain the reliability of the entity's perpetual inventory system.

A2   Attendance at physical inventory counting involves:

● Inspecting the inventory to ascertain its existence and evaluate its condition, and performing test counts;

● Observing compliance with management's instructions and the performance of procedures for recording and controlling the results of the physical inventory count; and

● Obtaining audit evidence as to the reliability of management's count procedures.

[3d] *For auditors in the UK further guidance has been promulgated by the FRC in Practice Note 25, Attendance at Stocktaking.*

These procedures may serve as test of controls or substantive procedures depending on the auditor's risk assessment, planned approach and the specific procedures carried out.

Matters relevant in planning attendance at physical inventory counting (or in   **A3** designing and performing audit procedures pursuant to paragraphs 4–8 of this ISA (UK)) include, for example:

- The risks of material misstatement related to inventory.

- The nature of the internal control related to inventory.

- Whether adequate procedures are expected to be established and proper instructions issued for physical inventory counting.

- The timing of physical inventory counting.

- Whether the entity maintains a perpetual inventory system.

- The locations at which inventory is held, including the materiality of the inventory and the risks of material misstatement at different locations, in deciding at which locations attendance is appropriate. ISA (UK) 600 (Revised June 2016)[4] deals with the involvement of other auditors and accordingly may be relevant if such involvement is with regards to attendance of physical inventory counting at a remote location.

- Whether the assistance of an auditor's expert is needed. ISA (UK) 620 (Revised June 2016)[5] deals with the use of an auditor's expert to assist the auditor to obtain sufficient appropriate audit evidence.

Evaluate Management's Instructions and Procedures
(Ref: Para. 4(a)(i))

Matters relevant in evaluating management's instructions and procedures for   **A4** recording and controlling the physical inventory counting include whether they address, for example:

- The application of appropriate control activities, for example, collection of used physical inventory count records, accounting for unused physical inventory count records, and count and re-count procedures.

- The accurate identification of the stage of completion of work in progress, of slow moving, obsolete or damaged items and of inventory owned by a third party, for example, on consignment.

- The procedures used to estimate physical quantities, where applicable, such as may be needed in estimating the physical quantity of a coal pile.

- Control over the movement of inventory between areas and the shipping and receipt of inventory before and after the cutoff date.

Observe the Performance of Management's Count Procedures
(Ref: Para. 4(a)(ii))

Observing the performance of management's count procedures, for example those   **A5** relating to control over the movement of inventory before, during and after the count, assists the auditor in obtaining audit evidence that management's

---

[4] *ISA (UK) 600 (Revised June 2016), Special Considerations—Audits of Group Financial Statements (Including the Work of Component Auditors).*

[5] *ISA (UK) 620 (Revised June 2016), Using the Work of an Auditor's Expert.*

instructions and count procedures are adequately designed and implemented. In addition, the auditor may obtain copies of cutoff information, such as details of the movement of inventory, to assist the auditor in performing audit procedures over the accounting for such movements at a later date.

Inspect the Inventory
(Ref: Para. 4(a)(iii))

A6   Inspecting inventory when attending physical inventory counting assists the auditor in ascertaining the existence of the inventory (though not necessarily its ownership), and in identifying, for example, obsolete, damaged or ageing inventory.

Perform Test Counts
(Ref: Para. 4(a)(iv))

A7   Performing test counts, for example by tracing items selected from management's count records to the physical inventory and tracing items selected from the physical inventory to management's count records, provides audit evidence about the completeness and the accuracy of those records.

A8   In addition to recording the auditor's test counts, obtaining copies of management's completed physical inventory count records assists the auditor in performing subsequent audit procedures to determine whether the entity's final inventory records accurately reflect actual inventory count results.

Physical Inventory Counting Conducted Other than At the Date of the Financial Statements
(Ref: Para. 5)

A9   For practical reasons, the physical inventory counting may be conducted at a date, or dates, other than the date of the financial statements. This may be done irrespective of whether management determines inventory quantities by an annual physical inventory counting or maintains a perpetual inventory system. In either case, the effectiveness of the design, implementation and maintenance of controls over changes in inventory determines whether the conduct of physical inventory counting at a date, or dates, other than the date of the financial statements is appropriate for audit purposes. ISA (UK) 330 (Revised June 2016) establishes requirements and provides guidance on substantive procedures performed at an interim date.[6]

A10   Where a perpetual inventory system is maintained, management may perform physical counts or other tests to ascertain the reliability of inventory quantity information included in the entity's perpetual inventory records. In some cases, management or the auditor may identify differences between the perpetual inventory records and actual physical inventory quantities on hand; this may indicate that the controls over changes in inventory are not operating effectively.

A11   Relevant matters for consideration when designing audit procedures to obtain audit evidence about whether changes in inventory amounts between the count date, or dates, and the final inventory records are properly recorded include:

●   Whether the perpetual inventory records are properly adjusted.

●   Reliability of the entity's perpetual inventory records.

---

[6]   *ISA (UK) 330 (Revised June 2016), paragraphs 22–23.*

- Reasons for significant differences between the information obtained during the physical count and the perpetual inventory records.

Attendance at Physical Inventory Counting Is Impracticable
(Ref: Para. 7)

In some cases, attendance at physical inventory counting may be impracticable.   **A12**
This may be due to factors such as the nature and location of the inventory, for example, where inventory is held in a location that may pose threats to the safety of the auditor. The matter of general inconvenience to the auditor, however, is not sufficient to support a decision by the auditor that attendance is impracticable. Further, as explained in ISA (UK) 200 (Revised June 2016),[7] the matter of difficulty, time, or cost involved is not in itself a valid basis for the auditor to omit an audit procedure for which there is no alternative or to be satisfied with audit evidence that is less than persuasive.

In some cases where attendance is impracticable, alternative audit procedures, for   **A13**
example inspection of documentation of the subsequent sale of specific inventory items acquired or purchased prior to the physical inventory counting, may provide sufficient appropriate audit evidence about the existence and condition of inventory.

In other cases, however, it may not be possible to obtain sufficient appropriate   **A14**
audit evidence regarding the existence and condition of inventory by performing alternative audit procedures. In such cases, ISA (UK) 705 (Revised June 2016) requires the auditor to modify the opinion in the auditor's report as a result of the scope limitation.[8]

Inventory under the Custody and Control of a Third Party

Confirmation
(Ref: Para. 8(a))

ISA (UK) 505[9] establishes requirements and provides guidance for performing   **A15**
external confirmation procedures.

Other Audit Procedures
(Ref: Para. 8(b))

Depending on the circumstances, for example where information is obtained that   **A16**
raises doubt about the integrity and objectivity of the third party, the auditor may consider it appropriate to perform other audit procedures instead of, or in addition to, confirmation with the third party. Examples of other audit procedures include:

- Attending, or arranging for another auditor to attend, the third party's physical counting of inventory, if practicable.
- Obtaining another auditor's report, or a service auditor's report, on the adequacy of the third party's internal control for ensuring that inventory is properly counted and adequately safeguarded.
- Inspecting documentation regarding inventory held by third parties, for example, warehouse receipts.

---

[7] *ISA (UK) 200 (Revised June 2016), Overall Objectives of the Independent Auditor and the Conduct of an Audit in Accordance with International Standards on Auditing (UK), paragraph A48.*

[8] *ISA (UK) 705 (Revised June 2016), paragraph 13.*

[9] *ISA (UK) 505, External Confirmations.*

- Requesting confirmation from other parties when inventory has been pledged as collateral.

Litigation and Claims

Completeness of Litigations and Claims
(Ref: Para. 9)

A17   Litigation and claims involving the entity may have a material effect on the financial statements and thus may be required to be disclosed or accounted for in the financial statements.

A18   In addition to the procedures identified in paragraph 9, other relevant procedures include, for example, using information obtained through risk assessment procedures carried out as part of obtaining an understanding of the entity and its environment to assist the auditor to become aware of litigation and claims involving the entity.

A19   Audit evidence obtained for purposes of identifying litigation and claims that may give rise to a risk of material misstatement also may provide audit evidence regarding other relevant considerations, such as valuation or measurement, regarding litigation and claims. ISA (UK) 540 (Revised June 2016)[10] establishes requirements and provides guidance relevant to the auditor's consideration of litigation and claims requiring accounting estimates or related disclosures in the financial statements.

Reviewing Legal Expense Accounts
(Ref: Para. 9(c))

A20   Depending on the circumstances, the auditor may judge it appropriate to examine related source documents, such as invoices for legal expenses, as part of the auditor's review of legal expense accounts.

Communication with the Entity's External Legal Counsel
(Ref: Para. 10–11)

A21   Direct communication with the entity's external legal counsel assists the auditor in obtaining sufficient appropriate audit evidence as to whether potentially material litigation and claims are known and management's estimates of the financial implications, including costs, are reasonable.

A22   In some cases, the auditor may seek direct communication with the entity's external legal counsel through a letter of general inquiry. For this purpose, a letter of general inquiry requests the entity's external legal counsel to inform the auditor of any litigation and claims that the counsel is aware of, together with an assessment of the outcome of the litigation and claims, and an estimate of the financial implications, including costs involved.

A23   If it is considered unlikely that the entity's external legal counsel will respond appropriately to a letter of general inquiry, for example if the professional body to which the external legal counsel belongs prohibits response to such a letter[10a], the

---

[10] *ISA (UK) 540 (Revised June 2016), Auditing Accounting Estimates, Including Fair Value Accounting Estimates, and Related Disclosures.*

[10a] *In the UK, the Council of the Law Society has advised solicitors that it is unable to recommend them to comply with non-specific requests for information.*

auditor may seek direct communication through a letter of specific inquiry. For this purpose, a letter of specific inquiry includes:

(a)   A list of litigation and claims;

(b)   Where available, management's assessment of the outcome of each of the identified litigation and claims and its estimate of the financial implications, including costs involved; and

(c)   A request that the entity's external legal counsel confirm the reasonableness of management's assessments and provide the auditor with further information if the list is considered by the entity's external legal counsel to be incomplete or incorrect.

In certain circumstances, the auditor also may judge it necessary to meet with the entity's external legal counsel to discuss the likely outcome of the litigation or claims. This may be the case, for example, where: **A24**

●   The auditor determines that the matter is a significant risk.

●   The matter is complex.

●   There is disagreement between management and the entity's external legal counsel.

Ordinarily, such meetings require management's permission[3c] and are held with a representative of management in attendance.

In accordance with ISA (UK) 700 (Revised June 2016),[11] the auditor is required to date the auditor's report no earlier than the date on which the auditor has obtained sufficient appropriate audit evidence on which to base the auditor's opinion on the financial statements. Audit evidence about the status of litigation and claims up to the date of the auditor's report may be obtained by inquiry of management[3a], including in-house legal counsel, responsible for dealing with the relevant matters. In some instances, the auditor may need to obtain updated information from the entity's external legal counsel.   **A25**

BSegment Information
(Ref: Para. 13)

Depending on the applicable financial reporting framework, the entity may be required or permitted to disclose segment information in the financial statements. The auditor's responsibility regarding the presentation and disclosure of segment information is in relation to the financial statements taken as a whole. Accordingly, the auditor is not required to perform audit procedures that would be necessary to express an opinion on the segment information presented on a stand alone basis.   **A26**

Understanding of the Methods Used by Management
(Ref: Para. 13(a))

Depending on the circumstances, example of matters that may be relevant when obtaining an understanding of the methods used by management in determining segment information and whether such methods are likely to result in disclosure in accordance with the applicable financial reporting framework include: **A27**

---

[11] *ISA (UK) 700 (Revise June 2016), Forming an Opinion and Reporting on Financial Statements, paragraph 41.*

- Sales, transfers and charges between segments, and elimination of intersegment amounts.

- Comparisons with budgets and other expected results, for example, operating profits as a percentage of sales.

- The allocation of assets and costs among segments.

- Consistency with prior periods, and the adequacy of the disclosures with respect to inconsistencies.

ISA (UK) 505 External Confirmations (Updated July 2017)

(Effective for audits of financial statements for periods ending on or after 15 December 2010)[0]

Contents

Paragraphs

Introduction
Scope of this ISA (UK) — 1
External Confirmation Procedures to Obtain Audit Evidence — 2 - 3
Effective Date — 4

Objective — 5

Definitions — 6

Requirements
External Confirmation Procedures — 7
Management's Refusal to Allow the Auditor to Send a Confirmation Request — 8 - 9
Results of the External Confirmation Procedures — 10 - 14
Negative Confirmations — 15
Evaluating the Evidence Obtained — 16

Application and Other Explanatory Material
External Confirmation Procedures — A1 - A7
Management's Refusal to Allow the Auditor to Send a Confirmation Request — A8 - A10
Results of the External Confirmation Procedures — A11 - A22
Negative Confirmations (Ref: Para. 15) — A23
Evaluating the Evidence Obtained (Ref: Para. 16) — A24 - A25

International Standard on Auditing (UK) (ISA (UK)) 505, *External Confirmations*, should be read in conjunction with ISA (UK) 200 (Revised June 2016), *Overall Objectives of the Independent Auditor and the Conduct of an Audit in Accordance with International Standards on Auditing (UK)*.

---

[0] *Conforming amendments to this standard as a result of ISA (UK) 330 (Revised July 2017), The Auditor's Responses to Assessed Risks, are included that are effective for audits of financial statements for periods commencing on or after 15 December 2017. Details of the amendments are given in the Annexure to ISA (UK) 330 (Revised July 2017).*

Introduction

Scope of this ISA (UK)

1   This International Standard on Auditing (UK) (ISA (UK)) deals with the auditor's use of external confirmation procedures to obtain audit evidence in accordance with the requirements of ISA (UK) 330 (Revised July 2017)[1] and ISA (UK) 500.[2] It does not address inquiries regarding litigation and claims, which are dealt with in ISA (UK) 501.[3]

External Confirmation Procedures to Obtain Audit Evidence

2   ISA (UK) 500 indicates that the reliability of audit evidence is influenced by its source and by its nature, and is dependent on the individual circumstances under which it is obtained.[4] That ISA (UK) also includes the following generalizations applicable to audit evidence:[5]

- Audit evidence is more reliable when it is obtained from independent sources outside the entity.

- Audit evidence obtained directly by the auditor is more reliable than audit evidence obtained indirectly or by inference.

- Audit evidence is more reliable when it exists in documentary form, whether paper, electronic or other medium.

Accordingly, depending on the circumstances of the audit, audit evidence in the form of external confirmations received directly by the auditor from confirming parties may be more reliable than evidence generated internally by the entity. This ISA (UK) is intended to assist the auditor in designing and performing external confirmation procedures to obtain relevant and reliable audit evidence.

3   Other ISAs (UK) recognize the importance of external confirmations as audit evidence, for example:

- ISA (UK) 330 (Revised July 2017) discusses the auditor's responsibility to design and implement overall responses to address the assessed risks of material misstatement at the financial statement level, and to design and perform further audit procedures whose nature, timing and extent are based on, and are responsive to, the assessed risks of material misstatement at the assertion level.[6] In addition, ISA (UK) 330 (Revised July 2017) requires that, irrespective of the assessed risks of material misstatement, the auditor designs and performs substantive procedures for each material class of transactions, account balance, and disclosure. The auditor is also required to consider whether external confirmation procedures are to be performed as substantive audit procedures.[7]

---

[1]   *ISA (UK) 330 (Revised July 2017), The Auditor's Responses to Assessed Risks.*

[2]   *ISA (UK) 500, Audit Evidence.*

[3]   *ISA (UK) 501, Audit Evidence—Specific Considerations for Selected Items.*

[4]   *ISA (UK) 500, paragraph A5.*

[5]   *ISA (UK) 500, paragraph A31.*

[6]   *ISA (UK) 330 (Revised July 2017), paragraphs 5–6.*

[7]   *ISA (UK) 330 (Revised July 2017), paragraphs 18–19.*

- ISA (UK) 330 (Revised July 2017) requires that the auditor obtain more persuasive audit evidence the higher the auditor's assessment of risk.[8] To do this, the auditor may increase the quantity of the evidence or obtain evidence that is more relevant or reliable, or both. For example, the auditor may place more emphasis on obtaining evidence directly from third parties or obtaining corroborating evidence from a number of independent sources. ISA (UK) 330 (Revised July 2017) also indicates that external confirmation procedures may assist the auditor in obtaining audit evidence with the high level of reliability that the auditor requires to respond to significant risks of material misstatement, whether due to fraud or error.[9]

- ISA (UK) 240 (Revised June 2016) indicates that the auditor may design confirmation requests to obtain additional corroborative information as a response to address the assessed risks of material misstatement due to fraud at the assertion level.[10]

- ISA (UK) 500 indicates that corroborating information obtained from a source independent of the entity, such as external confirmations, may increase the assurance the auditor obtains from evidence existing within the accounting records or from representations made by management.[11]

Effective Date

This ISA (UK) is effective for audits of financial statements for periods ending on or after 15 December 2010.   **4**

Objective

The objective of the auditor, when using external confirmation procedures, is to design and perform such procedures to obtain relevant and reliable audit evidence.   **5**

Definitions

For purposes of the ISAs (UK), the following terms have the meanings attributed below: **6**

(a)   External confirmation – Audit evidence obtained as a direct written response to the auditor from a third party (the confirming party), in paper form, or by electronic or other medium.

(b)   External confirmation – Audit evidence obtained as a direct written response to the auditor from a third party (the confirming party), in paper form, or by electronic or other medium.

(c)   Negative confirmation request – A request that the confirming party respond directly to the auditor only if the confirming party disagrees with the information provided in the request.

---

[8] *ISA (UK) 330 (Revised July 2017), paragraph 7(b).*

[9] *ISA (UK) 330 (Revised July 2017), paragraph A53.*

[10] *ISA (UK) 240 (Revised June 2016), The Auditor's Responsibilities Relating to Fraud in an Audit of Financial Statements, paragraph A37.*

[11] *ISA (UK) 500, paragraph A8–A9.*

(d)   Non-response – A failure of the confirming party to respond, or fully respond, to a positive confirmation request, or a confirmation request returned undelivered.

(e)   Exception – A response that indicates a difference between information requested to be confirmed, or contained in the entity's records, and information provided by the confirming party.

Requirements

External Confirmation Procedures

7   When using external confirmation procedures, the auditor shall maintain control over external confirmation requests, including:

(a)   Determining the information to be confirmed or requested; (Ref: Para. A1)

(b)   Selecting the appropriate confirming party; (Ref: Para. A2)

(c)   Designing the confirmation requests, including determining that requests are properly addressed and contain return information for responses to be sent directly to the auditor; and (Ref: Para. A3–A6)

(d)   Sending the requests, including follow-up requests when applicable, to the confirming party. (Ref: Para. A7)

Management's Refusal to Allow the Auditor to Send a Confirmation Request

8   If management refuses to allow the auditor to send a confirmation request, the auditor shall:

(a)   Inquire as to management's reasons for the refusal, and seek audit evidence as to their validity and reasonableness; (Ref: Para. A8)

(b)   Evaluate the implications of management's refusal on the auditor's assessment of the relevant risks of material misstatement, including the risk of fraud, and on the nature, timing and extent of other audit procedures; and (Ref: Para. A9)

(c)   Perform alternative audit procedures designed to obtain relevant and reliable audit evidence. (Ref: Para. A10)

9   If the auditor concludes that management's refusal to allow the auditor to send a confirmation request is unreasonable, or the auditor is unable to obtain relevant and reliable audit evidence from alternative audit procedures, the auditor shall communicate with those charged with governance in accordance with ISA (UK) 260 (Revised June 2016).[12] The auditor also shall determine the implications for the audit and the auditor's opinion in accordance with ISA (UK) 705 (Revised June 2016).[13]

---

[12] *ISA (UK) 260 (Revised June 2016), Communication with Those Charged with Governance, paragraph 16.*

[13] *ISA (UK) 705 (Revised June 2016), Modifications to the Opinion in the Independent Auditor's Report.*

Results of the External Confirmation Procedures

Reliability of Responses to Confirmation Requests

If the auditor identifies factors that give rise to doubts about the reliability of the **10** response to a confirmation request, the auditor shall obtain further audit evidence to resolve those doubts. (Ref: Para. A11–A16)

If the auditor determines that a response to a confirmation request is not reliable, **11** the auditor shall evaluate the implications on the assessment of the relevant risks of material misstatement, including the risk of fraud, and on the related nature, timing and extent of other audit procedures. (Ref: Para. A17)

Non-Responses

In the case of each non-response, the auditor shall perform alternative audit **12** procedures to obtain relevant and reliable audit evidence. (Ref: Para A18–A19)

When a Response to a Positive Confirmation Request Is Necessary to Obtain Sufficient Appropriate Audit Evidence

If the auditor has determined that a response to a positive confirmation request is **13** necessary to obtain sufficient appropriate audit evidence, alternative audit procedures will not provide the audit evidence the auditor requires. If the auditor does not obtain such confirmation, the auditor shall determine the implications for the audit and the auditor's opinion in accordance with ISA (UK) 705 (Revised June 2016). (Ref: Para A20)

Exceptions

The auditor shall investigate exceptions to determine whether or not they are **14** indicative of misstatements. (Ref: Para. A21–A22)

Negative Confirmations

Negative confirmations provide less persuasive audit evidence than positive **15** confirmations. Accordingly, the auditor shall not use negative confirmation requests as the sole substantive audit procedure to address an assessed risk of material misstatement at the assertion level unless all of the following are present: (Ref: Para. A23)

(a) The auditor has assessed the risk of material misstatement as low and has obtained sufficient appropriate audit evidence regarding the operating effectiveness of controls relevant to the assertion;

(b) The population of items subject to negative confirmation procedures comprises a large number of small, homogeneous, account balances, transactions or conditions;

(c) A very low exception rate is expected; and

(d) The auditor is not aware of circumstances or conditions that would cause recipients of negative confirmation requests to disregard such requests.

Evaluating the Evidence Obtained

The auditor shall evaluate whether the results of the external confirmation **16** procedures provide relevant and reliable audit evidence, or whether further audit evidence is necessary. (Ref: Para A24–A25)

***

Application and Other Explanatory Material

External Confirmation Procedures

Determining the Information to Be Confirmed or Requested
(Ref: Para. 7(a))

A1   External confirmation procedures frequently are performed to confirm or request information regarding account balances and their elements. They may also be used to confirm terms of agreements, contracts, or transactions between an entity and other parties, or to confirm the absence of certain conditions, such as a "side agreement."

Selecting the Appropriate Confirming Party
(Ref: Para. 7(b))

A2   Responses to confirmation requests provide more relevant and reliable audit evidence when confirmation requests are sent to a confirming party the auditor believes is knowledgeable about the information to be confirmed. For example, a financial institution official who is knowledgeable about the transactions or arrangements for which confirmation is requested may be the most appropriate person at the financial institution from whom to request confirmation.

Designing Confirmation Requests
(Ref: Para. 7(c))

A3   The design of a confirmation request may directly affect the confirmation response rate, and the reliability and the nature of the audit evidence obtained from responses.

A4   Factors to consider when designing confirmation requests include:[13a]

- The assertions being addressed.
- Specific identified risks of material misstatement, including fraud risks.
- The layout and presentation of the confirmation request.
- Prior experience on the audit or similar engagements.
- The method of communication (for example, in paper form, or by electronic or other medium).
- Management's authorization or encouragement to the confirming parties to respond to the auditor. Confirming parties may only be willing to respond to a confirmation request containing management's authorization.
- The ability of the intended confirming party to confirm or provide the requested information (for example, individual invoice amount versus total balance).

A5   A positive external confirmation request asks the confirming party to reply to the auditor in all cases, either by indicating the confirming party's agreement with the given information, or by asking the confirming party to provide information. A response to a positive confirmation request ordinarily is expected to provide reliable audit evidence. There is a risk, however, that a confirming party may reply

[13a] *Pro-forma templates to obtain bank confirmations in the United Kingdom which have been agreed with the British Bankers' Association on behalf of the industry can be found at: https://www.bba.org.uk/policy/financial-and-risk-policy/financial-reporting/audit/instructions-for-using-pn16-templates/*

to the confirmation request without verifying that the information is correct. The auditor may reduce this risk by using positive confirmation requests that do not state the amount (or other information) on the confirmation request, and ask the confirming party to fill in the amount or furnish other information. On the other hand, use of this type of "blank" confirmation request may result in lower response rates because additional effort is required of the confirming parties.

Determining that requests are properly addressed includes testing the validity of some or all of the addresses on confirmation requests before they are sent out. **A6**

Follow-Up on Confirmation Requests
(Ref: Para. 7(d))

The auditor may send an additional confirmation request when a reply to a previous request has not been received within a reasonable time. For example, the auditor may, having re-verified the accuracy of the original address, send an additional or follow-up request. **A7**

Management's Refusal to Allow the Auditor to Send a Confirmation Request

Reasonableness of Management's Refusal
(Ref: Para. 8(a))

A refusal by management to allow the auditor to send a confirmation request is a limitation on the audit evidence the auditor may wish to obtain. The auditor is therefore required to inquire as to the reasons for the limitation. A common reason advanced is the existence of a legal dispute or ongoing negotiation with the intended confirming party, the resolution of which may be affected by an untimely confirmation request. The auditor is required to seek audit evidence as to the validity and reasonableness of the reasons because of the risk that management may be attempting to deny the auditor access to audit evidence that may reveal fraud or error. **A8**

Implications for the Assessment of Risks of Material Misstatement
(Ref: Para. 8(b))

The auditor may conclude from the evaluation in paragraph 8(b) that it would be appropriate to revise the assessment of the risks of material misstatement at the assertion level and modify planned audit procedures in accordance with ISA (UK) 315 (Revised June 2016).[14] For example, if management's request to not confirm is unreasonable, this may indicate a fraud risk factor that requires evaluation in accordance with ISA (UK) 240 (Revised June 2016).[15] **A9**

Alternative Audit Procedures
(Ref: Para. 8(c))

The alternative audit procedures performed may be similar to those appropriate for a non-response as set out in paragraphs A18–A19 of this ISA (UK). Such procedures also would take account of the results of the auditor's evaluation in paragraph 8(b) of this ISA (UK). **A10**

---

[14] *ISA (UK) 315 (Revised June 2016), Identifying and Assessing the Risks of Material Misstatement through Understanding the Entity and Its Environment, paragraph 31.*

[15] *ISA (UK) 240 (Revised June 2016), paragraph 24.*

Results of the External Confirmation Procedures

Reliability of Responses to Confirmation Requests
(Ref: Para. 10)

A11   ISA (UK) 500 indicates that even when audit evidence is obtained from sources external to the entity, circumstances may exist that affect its reliability.[16] All responses carry some risk of interception, alteration or fraud. Such risk exists regardless of whether a response is obtained in paper form, or by electronic or other medium. Factors that may indicate doubts about the reliability of a response include that it:

● Was received by the auditor indirectly; or

● Appeared not to come from the originally intended confirming party.

A12   Responses received electronically, for example by facsimile or electronic mail, involve risks as to reliability because proof of origin and authority of the respondent may be difficult to establish, and alterations may be difficult to detect. A process used by the auditor and the respondent that creates a secure environment for responses received electronically may mitigate these risks. If the auditor is satisfied that such a process is secure and properly controlled, the reliability of the related responses is enhanced. An electronic confirmation process might incorporate various techniques for validating the identity of a sender of information in electronic form, for example, through the use of encryption, electronic digital signatures, and procedures to verify web site authenticity.

A13   If a confirming party uses a third party to coordinate and provide responses to confirmation requests, the auditor may perform procedures to address the risks that:

(a)   The response may not be from the proper source;

(b)   A respondent may not be authorized to respond; and

(c)   The integrity of the transmission may have been compromised.

A14   The auditor is required by ISA (UK) 500 to determine whether to modify or add procedures to resolve doubts over the reliability of information to be used as audit evidence.[17] The auditor may choose to verify the source and contents of a response to a confirmation request by contacting the confirming party. For example, when a confirming party responds by electronic mail, the auditor may telephone the confirming party to determine whether the confirming party did, in fact, send the response. When a response has been returned to the auditor indirectly (for example, because the confirming party incorrectly addressed it to the entity rather than to the auditor), the auditor may request the confirming party to respond in writing directly to the auditor.

A15   On its own, an oral response to a confirmation request does not meet the definition of an external confirmation because it is not a direct written response to the auditor. However, upon obtaining an oral response to a confirmation request, the auditor may, depending on the circumstances, request the confirming party to respond in writing directly to the auditor. If no such response is received, in accordance with paragraph 12, the auditor seeks other audit evidence to support the information in the oral response.

---

[16] *ISA (UK) 500, paragraph A31.*

[17] *ISA (UK) 500, paragraph 11.*

A response to a confirmation request may contain restrictive language regarding **A16** its use. Such restrictions do not necessarily invalidate the reliability of the response as audit evidence.

Unreliable Responses
(Ref: Para. 11)

When the auditor concludes that a response is unreliable, the auditor may need to **A17** revise the assessment of the risks of material misstatement at the assertion level and modify planned audit procedures accordingly, in accordance with ISA (UK) 315 (Revised June 2016).[18] For example, an unreliable response may indicate a fraud risk factor that requires evaluation in accordance with ISA (UK) 240 (Revised June 2016).[19]

Non-Responses
(Ref: Para. 12)

Examples of alternative audit procedures the auditor may perform include: **A18**

- For accounts receivable balances – examining specific subsequent cash receipts, shipping documentation, and sales near the period-end.

- For accounts payable balances – examining subsequent cash disbursements or correspondence from third parties, and other records, such as goods received notes.

The nature and extent of alternative audit procedures are affected by the account **A19** and assertion in question. A non-response to a confirmation request may indicate a previously unidentified risk of material misstatement. In such situations, the auditor may need to revise the assessed risk of material misstatement at the assertion level, and modify planned audit procedures, in accordance with ISA (UK) 315 (Revised June 2016).[20] For example, fewer responses to confirmation requests than anticipated, or a greater number of responses than anticipated, may indicate a previously unidentified fraud risk factor that requires evaluation in accordance with ISA (UK) 240 (Revised June 2016).[21]

When a Response to a Positive Confirmation Request Is Necessary to Obtain Sufficient Appropriate Audit Evidence
(Ref: Para. 13)

In certain circumstances, the auditor may identify an assessed risk of material **A20** misstatement at the assertion level for which a response to a positive confirmation request is necessary to obtain sufficient appropriate audit evidence. Such circumstances may include where:

- The information available to corroborate management's assertion(s) is only available outside the entity.

- Specific fraud risk factors, such as the risk of management override of controls, or the risk of collusion which can involve employee(s) and/or management, prevent the auditor from relying on evidence from the entity.

---

[18] *ISA (UK) 315 (Revised June 2016), paragraph 31.*

[19] *ISA (UK) 240 (Revised June 2016), paragraph 24.*

[20] *ISA (UK) 315 (Revised June 2016), paragraph 31.*

[21] *ISA (UK) 240 (Revised June 2016), paragraph 24.*

Exceptions
(Ref: Para. 14)

A21   Exceptions noted in responses to confirmation requests may indicate misstatements or potential misstatements in the financial statements. When a misstatement is identified, the auditor is required by ISA (UK) 240 (Revised June 2016) to evaluate whether such misstatement is indicative of fraud.[22] Exceptions may provide a guide to the quality of responses from similar confirming parties or for similar accounts. Exceptions also may indicate a deficiency, or deficiencies, in the entity's internal control over financial reporting.

A22   Some exceptions do not represent misstatements. For example, the auditor may conclude that differences in responses to confirmation requests are due to timing, measurement, or clerical errors in the external confirmation procedures.

Negative Confirmations
(Ref: Para. 15)

A23   The failure to receive a response to a negative confirmation request does not explicitly indicate receipt by the intended confirming party of the confirmation request or verification of the accuracy of the information contained in the request. Accordingly, a failure of a confirming party to respond to a negative confirmation request provides significantly less persuasive audit evidence than does a response to a positive confirmation request. Confirming parties also may be more likely to respond indicating their disagreement with a confirmation request when the information in the request is not in their favor, and less likely to respond otherwise. For example, holders of bank deposit accounts may be more likely to respond if they believe that the balance in their account is understated in the confirmation request, but may be less likely to respond when they believe the balance is overstated. Therefore, sending negative confirmation requests to holders of bank deposit accounts may be a useful procedure in considering whether such balances may be understated, but is unlikely to be effective if the auditor is seeking evidence regarding overstatement.

Evaluating the Evidence Obtained
(Ref: Para. 16)

A24   When evaluating the results of individual external confirmation requests, the auditor may categorize such results as follows:

(a)   A response by the appropriate confirming party indicating agreement with the information provided in the confirmation request, or providing requested information without exception;

(b)   A response deemed unreliable;

(c)   A non-response; or

(d)   A response indicating an exception.

A25   The auditor's evaluation, when taken into account with other audit procedures the auditor may have performed, may assist the auditor in concluding whether sufficient appropriate audit evidence has been obtained or whether further audit evidence is necessary, as required by ISA (UK) 330 (Revised July 2017).[23]

---

[22] *ISA (UK) 240 (Revised June 2016), paragraph 35.*

[23] *ISA (UK) 330 (Revised July 2017), paragraphs 26–27.*

ISA (UK) 510 (Revised June 2016) Initial Audit Engagements – Opening Balances

(Effective for audits of financial statements for periods commencing on or after 17 June 2016)

Contents

Paragraphs

Introduction
Scope of this ISA (UK)   1
Effective date   2

Objective   3

Definitions   4

Requirements
Audit procedures   5 - 9
Audit conclusions and reporting   10 - 13

Application and other explanatory material
Audit procedures   A1 - A7-1
Audit conclusions and reporting   A8 - A9

Appendix: Illustrations of auditor's reports with modified opinions

International Standard on Auditing (UK) (ISA (UK)) 510 (Revised June 2016), *Initial Audit Engagements—Opening Balances*, should be read in conjunction with ISA (UK) 200 (Revised June 2016), *Overall Objectives of the Independent Auditor and the Conduct of an Audit in Accordance with International Standards on Auditing (UK)*.

Introduction

Scope of this ISA (UK)

1 This International Standard on Auditing (UK) (ISA (UK)) deals with the auditor's responsibilities relating to opening balances in an initial audit engagement. In addition to financial statement amounts, opening balances include matters requiring disclosure that existed at the beginning of the period, such as contingencies and commitments. When the financial statements include comparative financial information, the requirements and guidance in ISA (UK) 710[1] also apply. ISA (UK) 300 (Revised June 2016)[2] includes additional requirements and guidance regarding activities prior to starting an initial audit.

Effective Date

2 This ISA (UK) is effective for audits of financial statements for periods commencing on or after 17 June 2016. Earlier adoption is permitted.

Objective

3 In conducting an initial audit engagement, the objective of the auditor with respect to opening balances is to obtain sufficient appropriate audit evidence about whether:

(a) Opening balances contain misstatements that materially affect the current period's financial statements; and

(b) Appropriate accounting policies reflected in the opening balances have been consistently applied in the current period's financial statements, or changes thereto are appropriately accounted for and adequately presented and disclosed in accordance with the applicable financial reporting framework.

Definitions

4 For the purposes of the ISAs (UK), the following terms have the meanings attributed below:

(a) Initial audit engagement – An engagement in which either:

(i) The financial statements for the prior period were not audited; or

(ii) The financial statements for the prior period were audited by a predecessor auditor.

(b) Opening balances – Those account balances that exist at the beginning of the period. Opening balances are based upon the closing balances of the prior period and reflect the effects of transactions and events of prior periods and accounting policies applied in the prior period. Opening balances also include matters requiring disclosure that existed at the beginning of the period, such as contingencies and commitments.

---

[1] *ISA (UK) 710, Comparative Information—Corresponding Figures and Comparative Financial Statements.*

[2] *ISA (UK) 300 (Revised June 2016), Planning an Audit of Financial Statements.*

(c)   Predecessor auditor – The auditor from a different audit firm, who audited the financial statements of an entity in the prior period and who has been replaced by the current auditor.

Requirements

Audit Procedures

Opening Balances

The auditor shall read the most recent financial statements, if any, and the   **5** predecessor auditor's report thereon, if any, for information relevant to opening balances, including disclosures.

The auditor shall obtain sufficient appropriate audit evidence about whether the   **6** opening balances contain misstatements that materially affect the current period's financial statements by: (Ref: Para. A1–A2)

(a)   Determining whether the prior period's closing balances have been correctly brought forward to the current period or, when appropriate, have been restated;

(b)   Determining whether the opening balances reflect the application of appropriate accounting policies; and

(c)   Performing one or more of the following: (Ref: Para. A3–A7)

    (i)   Where the prior year financial statements were audited, reviewing the predecessor auditor's working papers to obtain evidence regarding the opening balances;

    (ii)   Evaluating whether audit procedures performed in the current period provide evidence relevant to the opening balances; or

    (iii)   Performing specific audit procedures to obtain evidence regarding the opening balances.

If the auditor obtains audit evidence that the opening balances contain   **7** misstatements that could materially affect the current period's financial statements, the auditor shall perform such additional audit procedures as are appropriate in the circumstances to determine the effect on the current period's financial statements. If the auditor concludes that such misstatements exist in the current period's financial statements, the auditor shall communicate the misstatements with the appropriate level of management and those charged with governance in accordance with ISA (UK) 450 (Revised June 2016).[3]

Consistency of Accounting Policies

The auditor shall obtain sufficient appropriate audit evidence about whether the   **8** accounting policies reflected in the opening balances have been consistently applied in the current period's financial statements, and whether changes in the accounting policies have been appropriately accounted for and adequately presented and disclosed in accordance with the applicable financial reporting framework.

---

[3] *ISA (UK) 450 (Revised June 2016), Evaluation of Misstatements Identified during the Audit, paragraphs 8 and 12.*

Required Understanding of Prior Year Responses to Risks

8R-1   For audits of financial statements of public interest entities, the auditor shall obtain an understanding of the predecessor auditor's methodology used to carry out the audit, sufficient to enable the auditor to communicate with those charged with governance those matters required by paragraph 16R-2(g) of ISA (UK) 260 (Revised June 2016).[3a] (Ref: Para. A7-1)

Relevant Information in the Predecessor Auditor's Report

9   If the prior period's financial statements were audited by a predecessor auditor and there was a modification to the opinion, the auditor shall evaluate the effect of the matter giving rise to the modification in assessing the risks of material misstatement in the current period's financial statements in accordance with ISA (UK) 315 (Revised June 2016).[4]

Audit Conclusions and Reporting

Opening Balances

10   If the auditor is unable to obtain sufficient appropriate audit evidence regarding the opening balances, the auditor shall express a qualified opinion or disclaim an opinion on the financial statements, as appropriate, in accordance with ISA (UK) 705 (Revised June 2016).[5] (Ref: Para. A8)

11   If the auditor concludes that the opening balances contain a misstatement that materially affects the current period's financial statements, and the effect of the misstatement is not appropriately accounted for or not adequately presented or disclosed, the auditor shall express a qualified opinion or an adverse opinion, as appropriate, in accordance with ISA (UK) 705 (Revised June 2016).

Consistency of Accounting Policies

12   If the auditor concludes that:

(a)   the current period's accounting policies are not consistently applied in relation to opening balances in accordance with the applicable financial reporting framework; or

(b)   a change in accounting policies is not appropriately accounted for or not adequately presented or disclosed in accordance with the applicable financial reporting framework,

the auditor shall express a qualified opinion or an adverse opinion as appropriate in accordance with ISA (UK) 705 (Revised June 2016).

Modification to the Opinion in the Predecessor Auditor's Report

13   If the predecessor auditor's opinion regarding the prior period's financial statements included a modification to the auditor's opinion that remains relevant and material to the current period's financial statements, the auditor shall modify the auditor's opinion on the current period's financial statements in

---

[3a] *ISA (UK) 260 (Revised June 2016), Communication with Those Charged with Governance.*

[4] *ISA (UK) 315 (Revised June 2016), Identifying and Assessing the Risks of Material Misstatement through Understanding the Entity and Its Environment.*

[5] *ISA (UK) 705 (Revised June 2016), Modifications to the Opinion in the Independent Auditor's Report.*

accordance with ISA (UK) 705 (Revised June 2016) and ISA (UK) 710. (Ref: Para. A9)

Application and Other Explanatory Material

Audit Procedures

Considerations Specific to Public Sector Entities
(Ref: Para. 6)

In the public sector, there may be legal or regulatory limitations on the information **A1** that the current auditor can obtain from a predecessor auditor. For example, if a public sector entity that has previously been audited by a statutorily appointed auditor (for example, an Auditor General, or other suitably qualified person appointed on behalf of the Auditor General) is privatized, the amount of access to working papers or other information that the statutorily appointed auditor can provide a newly-appointed auditor that is in the private sector may be constrained by privacy or secrecy laws or regulations. In situations where such communications are constrained, audit evidence may need to be obtained through other means and, if sufficient appropriate audit evidence cannot be obtained, consideration given to the effect on the auditor's opinion.

If the statutorily appointed auditor outsources an audit of a public sector entity to a **A2** private sector audit firm, and the statutorily appointed auditor appoints an audit firm other than the firm that audited the financial statements of the public sector entity in the prior period, this is not usually regarded as a change in auditors for the statutorily appointed auditor. Depending on the nature of the outsourcing arrangement, however, the audit engagement may be considered an initial audit engagement from the perspective of the private sector auditor in fulfilling their responsibilities, and therefore this ISA (UK) applies.

Opening Balances
(Ref: Para. 6(c))

The nature and extent of audit procedures necessary to obtain sufficient **A3** appropriate audit evidence regarding opening balances depend on such matters as:

- The accounting policies followed by the entity.

- The nature of the account balances, classes of transactions and disclosures and the risks of material misstatement in the current period's financial statements.

- The significance of the opening balances relative to the current period's financial statements.

- Whether the prior period's financial statements were audited and, if so, whether the predecessor auditor's opinion was modified.

If the prior period's financial statements were audited by a predecessor auditor, the **A4** auditor may be able to obtain sufficient appropriate audit evidence regarding the opening balances by reviewing the predecessor auditor's working papers. Whether such a review provides sufficient appropriate audit evidence is influenced by the professional competence and independence of the predecessor auditor.

A4-1   In the UK, where a statutory auditor[5a] is replaced by another statutory auditor, the predecessor auditor is required by ISQC (UK) 1 (Revised June 2016) to provide the auditor with access to all relevant information concerning the entity, including information concerning the most recent audit.[5b]

A5   Relevant ethical and professional requirements guide the current auditor's communications with the predecessor auditor.

A5-1   In the UK, the relevant ethical guidance on proposed communications with a predecessor auditor is provided by the ethical pronouncements relating to the work of auditors issued by the auditor's relevant professional body.

A6   For current assets and liabilities, some audit evidence about opening balances may be obtained as part of the current period's audit procedures. For example, the collection (payment) of opening accounts receivable (accounts payable) during the current period will provide some audit evidence of their existence, rights and obligations, completeness and valuation at the beginning of the period. In the case of inventories, however, the current period's audit procedures on the closing inventory balance provide little audit evidence regarding inventory on hand at the beginning of the period. Therefore, additional audit procedures may be necessary, and one or more of the following may provide sufficient appropriate audit evidence:

- Observing a current physical inventory count and reconciling it to the opening inventory quantities.

- Performing audit procedures on the valuation of the opening inventory items.

- Performing audit procedures on gross profit and cutoff.

A7   For non-current assets and liabilities, such as property plant and equipment, investments and long-term debt, some audit evidence may be obtained by examining the accounting records and other information underlying the opening balances. In certain cases, the auditor may be able to obtain some audit evidence regarding opening balances through confirmation with third parties, for example, for long-term debt and investments. In other cases, the auditor may need to carry out additional audit procedures.

Required Understanding of Prior Year Responses to Risks
(Ref: Para. 8R-1)

A7-1   For audits of financial statements of public interest entities, the Audit Regulation[5c] imposes a requirement on a predecessor auditor to grant the auditor access to the additional report to the audit committee[5d] in respect of previous years.

[5a] *In the UK, eligibility for appointment as a statutory auditor is dealt with in sections 1212 to 1225 of the Companies Act 2006.*

[5b] *ISQC (UK) 1 (Revised June 2016), Quality Control for Firms that Perform Audits and Reviews of Financial Statements, and Other Assurance and Related Services Engagements, paragraph 28D-1.*

[5c] *Regulation (EU) No 537/2014 of the European Parliament and of the Council of 16 April 2014.*

[5d] *ISA (UK) 260 (Revised June 2016), paragraph 16R-2 deals with the auditor's responsibilities to prepare an additional report to the audit committee.*

Audit Conclusions and Reporting

Opening Balances
(Ref: Para. 10)

ISA (UK) 705 (Revised June 2016) establishes requirements and provides **A8**
guidance on circumstances that may result in a modification to the auditor's
opinion on the financial statements, the type of opinion appropriate in the
circumstances, and the content of the auditor's report when the auditor's
opinion is modified. The inability of the auditor to obtain sufficient appropriate
audit evidence regarding opening balances may result in one of the following
modifications to the opinion in the auditor's report:

(a)   A qualified opinion or a disclaimer of opinion, as is appropriate in the
      circumstances; or

(b)   Unless prohibited by law or regulation, an opinion which is qualified or
      disclaimed, as appropriate, regarding the results of operations, and cash
      flows, where relevant, and unmodified regarding financial position.

The Appendix includes illustrative auditors' reports.[5e]

Modification to the Opinion in the Predecessor Auditor's Report
(Ref: Para. 13)

In some situations, a modification to the predecessor auditor's opinion may not be   **A9**
relevant and material to the opinion on the current period's financial statements.
This may be the case where, for example, there was a scope limitation in the prior
period, but the matter giving rise to the scope limitation has been resolved in the
current period.

[5e] *The examples in the Appendix have not been tailored for the UK. Illustrative auditor's reports tailored for use
with audits conducted in accordance with ISAs (UK) are given in the current version of the FRC's Compendium
of Illustrative Auditor's Reports.*

Appendix

(Ref: Para. A8)

Illustrations of Auditor's Reports with Modified Opinions

The examples in the Appendix have not been tailored for the UK. Illustrative auditor's reports tailored for use with audits conducted in accordance with ISAs (UK) are given in the current versions of the FRC's Compendium of Illustrative Auditor's Reports.

Note: Throughout these illustrative auditor's reports, the Opinion section has been positioned first in accordance with ISA (UK) 700 (Revised), and the Basis for Opinion section is positioned immediately after the Opinion section. Also, the first and last sentence that was included in the extant auditor's responsibilities section is now subsumed as part of the new Basis for Opinion section.

Illustration 1:

For purposes of this illustrative auditor's report, the following circumstances are assumed:

- Audit of a complete set of financial statements of an entity other than a listed entity using a fair presentation framework. The audit is not a group audit (i.e., ISA 600[1-a] does not apply).
- The financial statements are prepared by management of the entity in accordance with International Financial Reporting Standards (IFRSs) (a general purpose framework).
- The terms of the audit engagement reflect the description of management's responsibility for the financial statements in ISA 210.[2-a]
- The auditor did not observe the counting of the physical inventory at the beginning of the current period and was unable to obtain sufficient appropriate audit evidence regarding the opening balances of inventory.
- The possible effects of the inability to obtain sufficient appropriate audit evidence regarding opening balances of inventory are deemed to be material but not pervasive to the entity's financial performance and cash flows.[3-a]
- The financial position at year end is fairly presented.
- In this particular jurisdiction, law and regulation prohibit the auditor from giving an opinion which is qualified regarding the financial performance and cash flows and unmodified regarding financial position.

[1-a] *ISA 600, Special Considerations—Audits of Group Financial Statements (Including the Work of Component Auditors).*

[2-a] *ISA 210, Agreeing the Terms of Audit Engagements.*

[3-a] *If the possible effects, in the auditor's judgment, are considered to be material and pervasive to the entity's financial performance and cash flows, the auditor would disclaim an opinion on the financial performance and cash flows.*

- The relevant ethical requirements that apply to the audit are those of the jurisdiction.
- Based on the audit evidence obtained, the auditor has concluded that a material uncertainty does not exist related to events or conditions that may cast significant doubt on the entity's ability to continue as a going concern in accordance with ISA (UK) 570 (Revised).[4-a]The auditor is not required, and has otherwise not decided, to communicate key audit matters in accordance with ISA 701.[5-a]
- The auditor has obtained all of the other information prior to the date of the auditor's report and has not identified a material misstatement of the other information.
- Corresponding figures are presented, and the prior period's financial statements were audited by a predecessor auditor. The auditor is not prohibited by law or regulation from referring to the predecessor auditor's report on the corresponding figures and has decided to do so.
- Those responsible for oversight of the financial statements differ from those responsible for the preparation of the financial statements.
- In addition to the audit of the financial statements, the auditor has other reporting responsibilities required under local law.

INDEPENDENT AUDITOR'S REPORT

To the Shareholders of ABC Company [or Other Appropriate Addressee]

Report on the Audit of the Financial Statements[6-a]

Qualified Opinion

We have audited the financial statements of ABC Company (the Company), which comprise the statement of financial position as at December 31, 20X1, and the statement of comprehensive income, statement of changes in equity and statement of cash flows for the year then ended, and notes to the financial statements, including a summary of significant accounting policies.

In our opinion, except for the possible effects of the matter described in the Basis for Qualified Opinion section of our report, the accompanying financial statements present fairly, in all material respects, (or *give a true and fair view of*) the financial position of the Company as at December 31, 20X1, and (*of*) its financial performance and its cash flows for the year then ended in accordance with International Financial Reporting Standards (IFRSs).

Basis for Qualified Opinion

We were appointed as auditors of the company on June 30, 20X1 and thus did not observe the counting of the physical inventories at the beginning of the year. We were unable to satisfy ourselves by alternative means concerning inventory quantities held at December 31, 20X0. Since opening inventories enter into the determination of the financial performance and cash flows, we were unable to

---

[4-a] *ISA (UK) 570 (Revised), Going Concern.*

[5-a] *ISA 701, Communicating Key Audit Matters in the Independent Auditor's Report.*

[6-a] *The sub-title "Report on the Audit of the Financial Statements" is unnecessary in circumstances when the second sub-title "Report on Other Legal and Regulatory Requirements" is not applicable.*

determine whether adjustments might have been necessary in respect of the profit for the year reported in the statement of comprehensive income and the net cash flows from operating activities reported in the statement of cash flows.

We conducted our audit in accordance with International Standards on Auditing (ISAs). Our responsibilities under those standards are further described in the *Auditor's Responsibilities for the Audit of the Financial Statements* section of our report. We are independent of the Company in accordance with the ethical requirements that are relevant to our audit of the financial statements in [*jurisdiction*], and we have fulfilled our other ethical responsibilities in accordance with these requirements. We believe that the audit evidence we have obtained is sufficient and appropriate to provide a basis for our qualified audit opinion.

Other Matter

The financial statements of the Company for the year ended December 31, 20X0 were audited by another auditor who expressed an unmodified opinion on those statements on March 31, 20X1.

Other Information *[or another title if appropriate such as "Information Other than the Financial Statements and Auditor's Report Thereon"]*

[*Reporting in accordance with the reporting requirements in ISA 720 (Revised) – see Illustration 1 in Appendix 2 of ISA 720 (Revised).*]

Responsibilities of Management and Those Charged with Governance for the Financial Statements[7-a]

[*Reporting in accordance with ISA 700 (Revised)[8-a] – see Illustration 1 in ISA 700 (Revised).*]

Auditor's Responsibilities for the Audit of the Financial Statements

[*Reporting in accordance with ISA 700 (Revised) – see Illustration 1 in ISA 700 (Revised).*]

Report on Other Legal and Regulatory Requirements

[*Reporting in accordance with ISA 700 (Revised) – see Illustration 1 in ISA 700 (Revised).*]

[*Signature in the name of the audit firm, the personal name of the auditor, or both, as appropriate for the particular jurisdiction*]

[*Auditor Address*]

[*Date*]

[7-a] *Throughout these illustrative auditor's reports, the terms management and those charged with governance may need to be replaced by another term that is appropriate in the context of the legal framework in the particular jurisdiction.*

[8-a] *ISA 700 (Revised), Forming an Opinion and Reporting on Financial Statements.*

Illustration 2:

For purposes of this illustrative auditor's report, the following circumstances are assumed:

- Audit of a complete set of financial statements of an entity other than a listed entity using a fair presentation framework. The audit is not a group audit (i.e., ISA 600 does not apply).
- The financial statements are prepared by management of the entity in accordance with IFRSs (a general purpose framework).
- The terms of the audit engagement reflect the description of management's responsibility for the financial statements in ISA 210.
- The auditor did not observe the counting of the physical inventory at the beginning of the current period and was unable to obtain sufficient appropriate audit evidence regarding the opening balances of inventory.
- The possible effects of the inability to obtain sufficient appropriate audit evidence regarding opening balances of inventory are deemed to be material but not pervasive to the entity's financial performance and cash flows.[9-a]
- The financial position at year end is fairly presented.
- An opinion that is qualified regarding the financial performance and cash flows and unmodified regarding financial position is considered appropriate in the circumstances.
- The relevant ethical requirements that apply to the audit are those of the jurisdiction.
- Based on the audit evidence obtained, the auditor has concluded that a material uncertainty does not exist related to events or conditions that may cast significant doubt on the entity's ability to continue as a going concern in accordance with ISA 570 (Revised).
- The auditor is not required, and has otherwise not decided, to communicate key audit matters in accordance with ISA 701.
- The auditor has obtained all of the other information prior to the date of the auditor's report and has not identified a material misstatement of the other information
- Corresponding figures are presented, and the prior period's financial statements were audited by a predecessor auditor. The auditor is not prohibited by law or regulation from referring to the predecessor auditor's report on the corresponding figures and has decided to do so.
- Those responsible for oversight of the financial statements differ from those responsible for the preparation of the financial statements.
- In addition to the audit of the financial statements, the auditor has other reporting responsibilities required under local law.

[9-a] *If the possible effects, in the auditor's judgment, are considered to be material and pervasive to the entity's financial performance and cash flows, the auditor would disclaim the opinion on the financial performance and cash flows.*

INDEPENDENT AUDITOR'S REPORT

To the Shareholders of ABC Company [or Other Appropriate Addressee]

Report on the Audit of the Financial Statements[10-a]

Opinions

We have audited the financial statements of ABC Company (the Company), which comprise the statement of financial position as at December 31, 20X1, and the statement of comprehensive income, statement of changes in equity and statement of cash flows for the year then ended, and notes to the financial statements, including a summary of significant accounting policies.*Qualified Opinion on the Financial Performance and Cash Flows*

In our opinion, except for the possible effects of the matter described in the Basis for Qualified Opinion section of our report, the accompanying statement of Comprehensive Income and Statement of Cash Flows present fairly, in all material respects (or give a true and fair view of) the financial performance and cash flows of the Company for the year ended December 31, 20X1 in accordance with International Financial Reporting Standards (IFRSs).

Opinion on the Financial Position

In our opinion, the accompanying statement of financial position presents fairly, in all material respects (or *gives a true and fair view of*) the financial position of the Company as at December 31, 20X1 in accordance with IFRSs.

Basis for Opinions, including basis for qualified opinion on the Financial Performance and Cash Flows

We were appointed as auditors of the company on June 30, 20X1 and thus did not observe the counting of the physical inventories at the beginning of the year. We were unable to satisfy ourselves by alternative means concerning inventory quantities held at December 31, 20X0. Since opening inventories enter into the determination of the financial performance and cash flows, we were unable to determine whether adjustments might have been necessary in respect of the profit for the year reported in the statement of comprehensive income and the net cash flows from operating activities reported in the statement of cash flows.

We conducted our audit in accordance with International Standards on Auditing (ISAs). Our responsibilities under those standards are further described in the *Auditor's Responsibilities for the Audit of the Financial Statements* section of our report. We are independent of the Company in accordance with the ethical requirements that are relevant to our audit of the financial statements in [*jurisdiction*], and we have fulfilled our other ethical responsibilities in accordance with these requirements. We believe that the audit evidence we have obtained is sufficient and appropriate to provide a basis for our unmodified opinion on the financial position and our qualified audit opinion on the financial performance and cash flows.

[10-a] *The sub-title "Report on the Audit of the Financial Statements" is unnecessary in circumstances when the second sub-title "Report on Other Legal and Regulatory Requirements" is not applicable.*

Other Matter

The financial statements of the Company for the year ended December 31, 20X0 were audited by another auditor who expressed an unmodified opinion on those statements on March 31, 20X1.

Other Information [or another title if appropriate such as "Information Other than the Financial Statements and Auditor's Report Thereon"]

[*Reporting in accordance with the reporting requirements in ISA 720 (Revised) – see Illustration 2 in Appendix 2 of ISA 720 (Revised).*]

Responsibilities of Management and Those Charged With Governance for the Financial Statements[11-a]

[*Reporting in accordance with ISA (Revised) – see Illustration 1 in ISA 700 (Revised).*]

Auditor's Responsibilities for the Audit of the Financial Statements

[*Reporting in accordance with ISA 700 (Revised) – see Illustration 1 in ISA 700 (Revised).*]

Report on Other Legal and Regulatory Requirements

[*Reporting in accordance with ISA 700 (Revised) – see Illustration 1 in ISA 700 (Revised).*]

[*Signature in the name of the audit firm, the personal name of the auditor, or both, as appropriate for the particular jurisdiction*]

[*Auditor Address*]

[*Date*]

[11-a] *Or other terms that are appropriate in the context of the legal framework in the particular jurisdiction.*

ISA (UK) 520
Analytical Procedures

*(Effective for audits of financial statements for periods ending on
or after 15 December 2010)*

Contents

Paragraphs

Introduction   1 - 2
  Scope of this ISA (UK)   1
  Effective date   2

Objectives   3

Definition   4

Requirements   5 - 7
  Substantive analytical procedures   5
  Analytical procedures that assist when forming an overall conclusion   6
  Investigating results of analytical procedures   7

Application and other explanatory material
  Definition of analytical procedures   A1 - A3
  Substantive analytical procedures   A4 - A16
  Analytical procedures that assist when forming an overall conclusion   A17 - A19
  Investigating results of analytical procedures   A20 - A21

International Standard on Auditing (UK) (ISA (UK)) 520, *Analytical Procedures*, should be read in conjunction with ISA (UK) 200 (Revised June 2016), *Overall Objectives of the Independent Auditor and the Conduct of an Audit in Accordance with International Standards on Auditing (UK)*.

Introduction

Scope of this ISA (UK)

1   This International Standard on Auditing (UK) (ISA (UK)) deals with the auditor's use of analytical procedures as substantive procedures ("substantive analytical procedures"). It also deals with the auditor's responsibility to perform analytical procedures near the end of the audit that assist the auditor when forming an overall conclusion on the financial statements. ISA (UK) 315 (Revised June 2016)[1] deals with the use of analytical procedures as risk assessment procedures. ISA (UK) 330 (Revised June 2016) includes requirements and guidance regarding the nature, timing and extent of audit procedures in response to assessed risks; these audit procedures may include substantive analytical procedures.[2]

Effective Date

2   This ISA (UK) is effective for audits of financial statements for periods ending on or after 15 December 2010.

Objectives

3   The objectives of the auditor are:

(a)   To obtain relevant and reliable audit evidence when using substantive analytical procedures; and

(b)   To design and perform analytical procedures near the end of the audit that assist the auditor when forming an overall conclusion as to whether the financial statements are consistent with the auditor's understanding of the entity.

Definition

4   For the purposes of the ISAs (UK), the term "analytical procedures" means evaluations of financial information through analysis of plausible relationships among both financial and non-financial data. Analytical procedures also encompass such investigation as is necessary of identified fluctuations or relationships that are inconsistent with other relevant information or that differ from expected values by a significant amount. (Ref: Para. A1–A3)

Requirements

Substantive Analytical Procedures

5   When designing and performing substantive analytical procedures, either alone or in combination with tests of details, as substantive procedures in accordance with ISA (UK) 330 (Revised June 2016),[3] the auditor shall: (Ref: Para. A4–A5)

---

[1] *ISA (UK) 315 (Revised June 2016), Identifying and Assessing the Risks of Material Misstatement through Understanding the Entity and Its Environment, paragraph 6(b).*

[2] *ISA (UK) 330 (Revised June 2016), The Auditor's Reponses to Assessed Risks, paragraphs 6 and 18.*

[3] *ISA (UK) 330 (Revised June 2016), paragraph 18.*

(a) Determine the suitability of particular substantive analytical procedures for given assertions, taking account of the assessed risks of material misstatement and tests of details, if any, for these assertions; (Ref: Para. A6–A11)

(b) Evaluate the reliability of data from which the auditor's expectation of recorded amounts or ratios is developed, taking account of source, comparability, and nature and relevance of information available, and controls over preparation; (Ref: Para. A12–A14)

(c) Develop an expectation of recorded amounts or ratios and evaluate whether the expectation is sufficiently precise to identify a misstatement that, individually or when aggregated with other misstatements, may cause the financial statements to be materially misstated; and (Ref: Para. A15)

(d) Determine the amount of any difference of recorded amounts from expected values that is acceptable without further investigation as required by paragraph 7. (Ref: Para. A16)

Analytical Procedures that Assist When Forming an Overall Conclusion

The auditor shall design and perform analytical procedures near the end of the audit that assist the auditor when forming an overall conclusion as to whether the financial statements are consistent with the auditor's understanding of the entity. (Ref: Para. A17–A19)   6

Investigating Results of Analytical Procedures

If analytical procedures performed in accordance with this ISA (UK) identify fluctuations or relationships that are inconsistent with other relevant information or that differ from expected values by a significant amount, the auditor shall investigate such differences by: 7

(a) Inquiring of management and obtaining appropriate audit evidence relevant to management's responses; and

(b) Performing other audit procedures as necessary in the circumstances. (Ref: Para. A20–A21)

Application and Other Explanatory Material

Definition of Analytical Procedures
(Ref: Para. 4)

Analytical procedures include the consideration of comparisons of the entity's financial information with, for example: A1

● Comparable information for prior periods.

● Anticipated results of the entity, such as budgets or forecasts, or expectations of the auditor, such as an estimation of depreciation.

● Similar industry information, such as a comparison of the entity's ratio of sales to accounts receivable with industry averages or with other entities of comparable size in the same industry.

Analytical procedures also include consideration of relationships, for example: A2

- Among elements of financial information that would be expected to conform to a predictable pattern based on the entity's experience, such as gross margin percentages.

- Between financial information and relevant non-financial information, such as payroll costs to number of employees.

A3   Various methods may be used to perform analytical procedures. These methods range from performing simple comparisons to performing complex analyses using advanced statistical techniques. Analytical procedures may be applied to consolidated financial statements, components and individual elements of information.

Substantive Analytical Procedures
(Ref: Para. 5)

A4   The auditor's substantive procedures at the assertion level may be tests of details, substantive analytical procedures, or a combination of both. The decision about which audit procedures to perform, including whether to use substantive analytical procedures, is based on the auditor's judgment about the expected effectiveness and efficiency of the available audit procedures to reduce audit risk at the assertion level to an acceptably low level.

A5   The auditor may inquire of management as to the availability and reliability of information needed to apply substantive analytical procedures, and the results of any such analytical procedures performed by the entity. It may be effective to use analytical data prepared by management, provided the auditor is satisfied that such data is properly prepared.

Suitability of Particular Analytical Procedures for Given Assertions
(Ref: Para. 5(a))

A6   Substantive analytical procedures are generally more applicable to large volumes of transactions that tend to be predictable over time. The application of planned analytical procedures is based on the expectation that relationships among data exist and continue in the absence of known conditions to the contrary. However, the suitability of a particular analytical procedure will depend upon the auditor's assessment of how effective it will be in detecting a misstatement that, individually or when aggregated with other misstatements, may cause the financial statements to be materially misstated.

A7   In some cases, even an unsophisticated predictive model may be effective as an analytical procedure. For example, where an entity has a known number of employees at fixed rates of pay throughout the period, it may be possible for the auditor to use this data to estimate the total payroll costs for the period with a high degree of accuracy, thereby providing audit evidence for a significant item in the financial statements and reducing the need to perform tests of details on the payroll. The use of widely recognized trade ratios (such as profit margins for different types of retail entities) can often be used effectively in substantive analytical procedures to provide evidence to support the reasonableness of recorded amounts.

A8   Different types of analytical procedures provide different levels of assurance. Analytical procedures involving, for example, the prediction of total rental income on a building divided into apartments, taking the rental rates, the number of apartments and vacancy rates into consideration, can provide persuasive evidence and may eliminate the need for further verification by means of tests of details, provided the elements are appropriately verified. In contrast, calculation and comparison of gross margin percentages as a means of confirming a revenue figure may provide less persuasive evidence, but may provide useful corroboration if used in combination with other audit procedures.

The determination of the suitability of particular substantive analytical procedures **A9** is influenced by the nature of the assertion and the auditor's assessment of the risk of material misstatement. For example, if controls over sales order processing are deficient, the auditor may place more reliance on tests of details rather than on substantive analytical procedures for assertions related to receivables.

Particular substantive analytical procedures may also be considered suitable when **A10** tests of details are performed on the same assertion. For example, when obtaining audit evidence regarding the valuation assertion for accounts receivable balances, the auditor may apply analytical procedures to an aging of customers' accounts in addition to performing tests of details on subsequent cash receipts to determine the collectability of the receivables.

Considerations Specific to Public Sector Entities

The relationships between individual financial statement items traditionally **A11** considered in the audit of business entities may not always be relevant in the audit of governments or other non-business public sector entities; for example, in many public sector entities there may be little direct relationship between revenue and expenditure. In addition, because expenditure on the acquisition of assets may not be capitalized, there may be no relationship between expenditures on, for example, inventories and fixed assets and the amount of those assets reported in the financial statements. Also, industry data or statistics for comparative purposes may not be available in the public sector. However, other relationships may be relevant, for example, variations in the cost per kilometer of road construction or the number of vehicles acquired compared with vehicles retired.

The Reliability of the Data
(Ref: Para. 5(b))

The reliability of data is influenced by its source and nature and is dependent on **A12** the circumstances under which it is obtained. Accordingly, the following are relevant when determining whether data is reliable for purposes of designing substantive analytical procedures:

(a) Source of the information available. For example, information may be more reliable when it is obtained from independent sources outside the entity;[4]

(b) Comparability of the information available. For example, broad industry data may need to be supplemented to be comparable to that of an entity that produces and sells specialized products;

(c) Nature and relevance of the information available. For example, whether budgets have been established as results to be expected rather than as goals to be achieved; and

(d) Controls over the preparation of the information that are designed to ensure its completeness, accuracy and validity. For example, controls over the preparation, review and maintenance of budgets.

---

[4] *ISA (UK) 500, Audit Evidence, paragraph A31.*

> (e)   Prior year knowledge and understanding. For example, the knowledge gained during previous audits, together with the auditor's understanding of the effectiveness of the accounting and internal control systems and the types of problems that in prior periods have given rise to accounting adjustments.

A13   The auditor may consider testing the operating effectiveness of controls, if any, over the entity's preparation of information used by the auditor in performing substantive analytical procedures in response to assessed risks. When such controls are effective, the auditor generally has greater confidence in the reliability of the information and, therefore, in the results of analytical procedures. The operating effectiveness of controls over non-financial information may often be tested in conjunction with other tests of controls. For example, in establishing controls over the processing of sales invoices, an entity may include controls over the recording of unit sales. In these circumstances, the auditor may test the operating effectiveness of controls over the recording of unit sales in conjunction with tests of the operating effectiveness of controls over the processing of sales invoices. Alternatively, the auditor may consider whether the information was subjected to audit testing. ISA (UK) 500 establishes requirements and provides guidance in determining the audit procedures to be performed on the information to be used for substantive analytical procedures.[5]

A14   The matters discussed in paragraphs A12(a)–A12(d) are relevant irrespective of whether the auditor performs substantive analytical procedures on the entity's period end financial statements, or at an interim date and plans to perform substantive analytical procedures for the remaining period. ISA (UK) 330 (Revised June 2016) establishes requirements and provides guidance on substantive procedures performed at an interim date.[6]

Evaluation Whether the Expectation Is Sufficiently Precise
(Ref: Para. 5(c))

A15   Matters relevant to the auditor's evaluation of whether the expectation can be developed sufficiently precisely to identify a misstatement that, when aggregated with other misstatements, may cause the financial statements to be materially misstated, include:

- The accuracy with which the expected results of substantive analytical procedures can be predicted. For example, the auditor may expect greater consistency in comparing gross profit margins from one period to another than in comparing discretionary expenses, such as research or advertising.

- The degree to which information can be disaggregated. For example, substantive analytical procedures may be more effective when applied to financial information on individual sections of an operation or to financial statements of components of a diversified entity, than when applied to the financial statements of the entity as a whole.

- The availability of the information, both financial and non-financial. For example, the auditor may consider whether financial information, such as budgets or forecasts, and non-financial information, such as the number of units produced or sold, is available to design substantive analytical procedures. If the information is available, the auditor may

---

[5] *ISA (UK) 500, paragraph 10.*

[6] *ISA (UK) 330 (Revised June 2016), paragraphs 22–23.*

also consider the reliability of the information as discussed in paragraphs A12–A13 above.

Amount of Difference of Recorded Amounts from Expected Values that Is Acceptable (Ref: Para. 5(d))

The auditor's determination of the amount of difference from the expectation that can be accepted without further investigation is influenced by materiality [7] and the consistency with the desired level of assurance, taking account of the possibility that a misstatement, individually or when aggregated with other misstatements, may cause the financial statements to be materially misstated. ISA (UK) 330 (Revised June 2016) requires the auditor to obtain more persuasive audit evidence the higher the auditor's assessment of risk.[8] Accordingly, as the assessed risk increases, the amount of difference considered acceptable without investigation decreases in order to achieve the desired level of persuasive evidence.[9]

A16

Analytical Procedures that Assist When Forming an Overall Conclusion (Ref: Para. 6)

The conclusions drawn from the results of analytical procedures designed and performed in accordance with paragraph 6 are intended to corroborate conclusions formed during the audit of individual components or elements of the financial statements. This assists the auditor to draw reasonable conclusions on which to base the auditor's opinion.

A17

Considerations when carrying out such procedures may include:

A17-1

(a) Whether the financial statements adequately reflect the information and explanations previously obtained and conclusions previously reached during the course of the audit;

(b) Whether the procedures reveal any new factors which may affect the presentation of, or disclosures in, the financial statements;

(c) Whether analytical procedures applied when completing the audit, such as comparing the information in the financial statements with other pertinent data, produce results which assist in arriving at the overall conclusion as to whether the financial statements as a whole are consistent with the auditor's knowledge of the entity's business;

(d) Whether the presentation adopted in the financial statements may have been unduly influenced by the desire of those charged with governance to present matters in a favorable or unfavorable light; and

(e) The potential impact on the financial statements of the aggregate of uncorrected misstatements (including those arising from bias in making accounting estimates) identified during the course of the audit and the preceding period's audit, if any.

---

[7] *ISA (UK) 320 (Revised June 2016), Materiality in Planning and Performing an Audit, paragraph A13.*

[8] *ISA (UK) 330 (Revised June 2016), paragraph 7(b).*

[9] *ISA (UK) 330 (Revised June 2016), paragraph A19*

A18   The results of such analytical procedures may identify a previously unrecognized risk of material misstatement. In such circumstances, ISA (UK) 315 (Revised June 2016) requires the auditor to revise the auditor's assessment of the risks of material misstatement and modify the further planned audit procedures accordingly.[10]

A19   The analytical procedures performed in accordance with paragraph 6 may be similar to those that would be used as risk assessment procedures.

Investigating Results of Analytical Procedures
(Ref: Para. 7)

A20   Audit evidence relevant to management's responses may be obtained by evaluating those responses taking into account the auditor's understanding of the entity and its environment, and with other audit evidence obtained during the course of the audit.

A21   The need to perform other audit procedures may arise when, for example, management is unable to provide an explanation, or the explanation, together with the audit evidence obtained relevant to management's response, is not considered adequate.

---

[10]   *ISA (UK) 315 (Revised June 2016), paragraph 31.*

ISA (UK) 530
Audit Sampling

*(Effective for audits of financial statements for periods ending on
or after 15 December 2010)*

Contents

Paragraphs

Introduction 1 - 3
Scope of this ISA (UK) 1 - 2
Effective date 3

Objective 4

Definitions 5

Requirements 6 - 15
Sample design, size and selection of items for testing 6 - 8
Performing audit procedures 9 - 11
Nature and cause of deviations and misstatements 12 - 13
Projecting misstatements 14
Evaluating results of audit sampling 15

Application and other explanatory material
Definitions A1 - A3
Sample design, size and selection of items for testing A4 - A13
Performing audit procedures A14 - A16
Nature and cause of deviations and misstatements A17
Projecting misstatements A18 - A20
Evaluating results of audit sampling A21 - A23

Appendix 1: Stratification and value-weighted selection

Appendix 2: Examples of factors influencing sample size for tests of controls

Appendix 3: Examples of factors influencing sample size for tests of details

Appendix 4: Sample Selection Methods

International Standard on Auditing (UK) (ISA (UK)) 530, *Audit Sampling*, should be read in conjunction with ISA 200 (UK) (Revised June 2016), *Overall Objectives of the Independent Auditor and the Conduct of an Audit in Accordance with International Standards on Auditing (UK).*

Introduction

Scope of this ISA (UK)

1   This International Standard on Auditing (UK) (ISA (UK)) applies when the auditor has decided to use audit sampling in performing audit procedures. It deals with the auditor's use of statistical and non-statistical sampling when designing and selecting the audit sample, performing tests of controls and tests of details, and evaluating the results from the sample.

2   This ISA (UK) complements ISA (UK) 500,[1] which deals with the auditor's responsibility to design and perform audit procedures to obtain sufficient appropriate audit evidence to be able to draw reasonable conclusions on which to base the auditor's opinion. ISA (UK) 500 provides guidance on the means available to the auditor for selecting items for testing, of which audit sampling is one means.

Effective Date

3   This ISA (UK) is effective for audits of financial statements for periods ending on or after 15 December 2010.

Objective

4   The objective of the auditor, when using audit sampling, is to provide a reasonable basis for the auditor to draw conclusions about the population from which the sample is selected.

Definitions

5   For purposes of the ISAs (UK), the following terms have the meanings attributed below:

    (a)   Audit sampling (sampling) – The application of audit procedures to less than 100% of items within a population of audit relevance such that all sampling units have a chance of selection in order to provide the auditor with a reasonable basis on which to draw conclusions about the entire population.

    (b)   Population – The entire set of data from which a sample is selected and about which the auditor wishes to draw conclusions.

    (c)   Sampling risk – The risk that the auditor's conclusion based on a sample may be different from the conclusion if the entire population were subjected to the same audit procedure. Sampling risk can lead to two types of erroneous conclusions:

        (i)   In the case of a test of controls, that controls are more effective than they actually are, or in the case of a test of details, that a material misstatement does not exist when in fact it does. The auditor is primarily concerned with this type of erroneous conclusion because it affects audit effectiveness and is more likely to lead to an inappropriate audit opinion.

---

[1] *ISA (UK) 500, Audit Evidence.*

(ii) In the case of a test of controls, that controls are less effective than they actually are, or in the case of a test of details, that a material misstatement exists when in fact it does not. This type of erroneous conclusion affects audit efficiency as it would usually lead to additional work to establish that initial conclusions were incorrect.

(d) Non-sampling risk – The risk that the auditor reaches an erroneous conclusion for any reason not related to sampling risk. (Ref: Para A1)

(e) Anomaly – A misstatement or deviation that is demonstrably not representative of misstatements or deviations in a population.

(f) Sampling unit – The individual items constituting a population. (Ref: Para A2)

(g) Statistical sampling – An approach to sampling that has the following characteristics:

(i) Random selection of the sample items; and

(ii) The use of probability theory to evaluate sample results, including measurement of sampling risk.

A sampling approach that does not have characteristics (i) and (ii) is considered non-statistical sampling.

(h) Stratification – The process of dividing a population into sub-populations, each of which is a group of sampling units which have similar characteristics (often monetary value).

(i) Tolerable misstatement – A monetary amount set by the auditor in respect of which the auditor seeks to obtain an appropriate level of assurance that the monetary amount set by the auditor is not exceeded by the actual misstatement in the population. (Ref: Para A3)

(j) Tolerable rate of deviation – A rate of deviation from prescribed internal control procedures set by the auditor in respect of which the auditor seeks to obtain an appropriate level of assurance that the rate of deviation set by the auditor is not exceeded by the actual rate of deviation in the population.

Requirements

Sample Design, Size and Selection of Items for Testing

When designing an audit sample, the auditor shall consider the purpose of the audit procedure and the characteristics of the population from which the sample will be drawn. (Ref: Para. A4–A9) **6**

The auditor shall determine a sample size sufficient to reduce sampling risk to an acceptably low level. (Ref: Para. A10–A11) **7**

The auditor shall select items for the sample in such a way that each sampling unit in the population has a chance of selection. (Ref: Para. A12–A13) **8**

Performing Audit Procedures

The auditor shall perform audit procedures, appropriate to the purpose, on each item selected. **9**

If the audit procedure is not applicable to the selected item, the auditor shall perform the procedure on a replacement item. (Ref: Para. A14) **10**

11   If the auditor is unable to apply the designed audit procedures, or suitable alternative procedures, to a selected item, the auditor shall treat that item as a deviation from the prescribed control, in the case of tests of controls, or a misstatement, in the case of tests of details. (Ref: Para. A15–A16)

Nature and Cause of Deviations and Misstatements

12   The auditor shall investigate the nature and cause of any deviations or misstatements identified, and evaluate their possible effect on the purpose of the audit procedure and on other areas of the audit. (Ref: Para. A17)

13   In the extremely rare circumstances when the auditor considers a misstatement or deviation discovered in a sample to be an anomaly, the auditor shall obtain a high degree of certainty that such misstatement or deviation is not representative of the population. The auditor shall obtain this degree of certainty by performing additional audit procedures to obtain sufficient appropriate audit evidence that the misstatement or deviation does not affect the remainder of the population.

Projecting Misstatements

14   For tests of details, the auditor shall project misstatements found in the sample to the population. (Ref: Para. A18–A20)

Evaluating Results of Audit Sampling

15   The auditor shall evaluate:

(a)   The results of the sample; and (Ref: Para. A21–A22)

(b)   Whether the use of audit sampling has provided a reasonable basis for conclusions about the population that has been tested. (Ref: Para. A23)

Application and Other Explanatory Material

Definitions

Non-Sampling Risk
(Ref: Para. 5(d))

A1   Examples of non-sampling risk include use of inappropriate audit procedures, or misinterpretation of audit evidence and failure to recognize a misstatement or deviation.

Sampling Unit
(Ref: Para. 5(f))

A2   The sampling units might be physical items (for example, checks listed on deposit slips, credit entries on bank statements, sales invoices or debtors' balances) or monetary units.

Tolerable Misstatement
(Ref: Para. 5(i))

A3   When designing a sample, the auditor determines tolerable misstatement in order to address the risk that the aggregate of individually immaterial misstatements may cause the financial statements to be materially misstated and provide a margin for possible undetected misstatements. Tolerable misstatement is the application of performance materiality, as defined in ISA (UK) 320 (Revised June 2016),[2] to a particular sampling procedure. Tolerable misstatement may be the same amount or an amount lower than performance materiality.

Sample Design, Size and Selection of Items for Testing

Sample Design
(Ref: Para. 6)

Audit sampling enables the auditor to obtain and evaluate audit evidence about **A4** some characteristic of the items selected in order to form or assist in forming a conclusion concerning the population from which the sample is drawn. Audit sampling can be applied using either non-statistical or statistical sampling approaches.

When designing an audit sample, the auditor's consideration includes the specific **A5** purpose to be achieved and the combination of audit procedures that is likely to best achieve that purpose. Consideration of the nature of the audit evidence sought and possible deviation or misstatement conditions or other characteristics relating to that audit evidence will assist the auditor in defining what constitutes a deviation or misstatement and what population to use for sampling. In fulfilling the requirement of paragraph 10 of ISA (UK) 500, when performing audit sampling, the auditor performs audit procedures to obtain evidence that the population from which the audit sample is drawn is complete.

The auditor's consideration of the purpose of the audit procedure, as required by **A6** paragraph 6, includes a clear understanding of what constitutes a deviation or misstatement so that all, and only, those conditions that are relevant to the purpose of the audit procedure are included in the evaluation of deviations or projection of misstatements. For example, in a test of details relating to the existence of accounts receivable, such as confirmation, payments made by the customer before the confirmation date but received shortly after that date by the client, are not considered a misstatement. Also, a misposting between customer accounts does not affect the total accounts receivable balance. Therefore, it may not be appropriate to consider this a misstatement in evaluating the sample results of this particular audit procedure, even though it may have an important effect on other areas of the audit, such as the assessment of the risk of fraud or the adequacy of the allowance for doubtful accounts.

In considering the characteristics of a population, for tests of controls, the auditor **A7** makes an assessment of the expected rate of deviation based on the auditor's understanding of the relevant controls or on the examination of a small number of items from the population. This assessment is made in order to design an audit sample and to determine sample size. For example, if the expected rate of deviation is unacceptably high, the auditor will normally decide not to perform tests of controls. Similarly, for tests of details, the auditor makes an assessment of the expected misstatement in the population. If the expected misstatement is high, 100% examination or use of a large sample size may be appropriate when performing tests of details.

In considering the characteristics of the population from which the sample will be **A8** drawn, the auditor may determine that stratification or value-weighted selection is

---

[2] *ISA (UK) 320 (Revised June 2016), Materiality in Planning and Performing an Audit, paragraph 9.*

appropriate. Appendix 1 provides further discussion on stratification and value-weighted selection.

A9   The decision whether to use a statistical or non-statistical sampling approach is a matter for the auditor's judgment; however, sample size is not a valid criterion to distinguish between statistical and non-statistical approaches.

Sample Size
(Ref: Para. 7)

A10   The level of sampling risk that the auditor is willing to accept affects the sample size required. The lower the risk the auditor is willing to accept, the greater the sample size will need to be.

A11   The sample size can be determined by the application of a statistically-based formula or through the exercise of professional judgment. Appendices 2 and 3 indicate the influences that various factors typically have on the determination of sample size. When circumstances are similar, the effect on sample size of factors such as those identified in Appendices 2 and 3 will be similar regardless of whether a statistical or non-statistical approach is chosen.

Selection of Items for Testing
(Ref: Para. 8)

A12   With statistical sampling, sample items are selected in a way that each sampling unit has a known probability of being selected. With non-statistical sampling, judgment is used to select sample items. Because the purpose of sampling is to provide a reasonable basis for the auditor to draw conclusions about the population from which the sample is selected, it is important that the auditor selects a representative sample, so that bias is avoided, by choosing sample items which have characteristics typical of the population.

A13   The principal methods of selecting samples are the use of random selection, systematic selection and haphazard selection. Each of these methods is discussed in Appendix 4.

Performing Audit Procedures
(Ref: Para. 10–11)

A14   An example of when it is necessary to perform the procedure on a replacement item is when a voided check is selected while testing for evidence of payment authorization. If the auditor is satisfied that the check has been properly voided such that it does not constitute a deviation, an appropriately chosen replacement is examined.

A15   An example of when the auditor is unable to apply the designed audit procedures to a selected item is when documentation relating to that item has been lost.

A16   An example of a suitable alternative procedure might be the examination of subsequent cash receipts together with evidence of their source and the items they are intended to settle when no reply has been received in response to a positive confirmation request.

Nature and Cause of Deviations and Misstatements
(Ref: Para. 12)

In analyzing the deviations and misstatements identified, the auditor may observe **A17** that many have a common feature, for example, type of transaction, location, product line or period of time. In such circumstances, the auditor may decide to identify all items in the population that possess the common feature, and extend audit procedures to those items. In addition, such deviations or misstatements may be intentional, and may indicate the possibility of fraud.

Projecting Misstatements
(Ref: Para. 14)

The auditor is required to project misstatements for the population to obtain a **A18** broad view of the scale of misstatement but this projection may not be sufficient to determine an amount to be recorded.

When a misstatement has been established as an anomaly, it may be excluded **A19** when projecting misstatements to the population. However, the effect of any such misstatement, if uncorrected, still needs to be considered in addition to the projection of the non-anomalous misstatements.

For tests of controls, no explicit projection of deviations is necessary since the **A20** sample deviation rate is also the projected deviation rate for the population as a whole. ISA (UK) 330 (Revised June 2016)[3] provides guidance when deviations from controls upon which the auditor intends to rely are detected.

Evaluating Results of Audit Sampling
(Ref: Para. 15)

For tests of controls, an unexpectedly high sample deviation rate may lead to an **A21** increase in the assessed risk of material misstatement, unless further audit evidence substantiating the initial assessment is obtained. For tests of details, an unexpectedly high misstatement amount in a sample may cause the auditor to believe that a class of transactions or account balance is materially misstated, in the absence of further audit evidence that no material misstatement exists.

In the case of tests of details, the projected misstatement plus anomalous **A22** misstatement, if any, is the auditor's best estimate of misstatement in the population. When the projected misstatement plus anomalous misstatement, if any, exceeds tolerable misstatement, the sample does not provide a reasonable basis for conclusions about the population that has been tested. The closer the projected misstatement plus anomalous misstatement is to tolerable misstatement, the more likely that actual misstatement in the population may exceed tolerable misstatement. Also if the projected misstatement is greater than the auditor's expectations of misstatement used to determine the sample size, the auditor may conclude that there is an unacceptable sampling risk that the actual misstatement in the population exceeds the tolerable misstatement. Considering the results of other audit procedures helps the auditor to assess the risk that actual misstatement in the population exceeds tolerable misstatement, and the risk may be reduced if additional audit evidence is obtained.

---

[3] *ISA (UK) 330 (Revised June 2016), The Auditor's Responses to Assessed Risks, paragraph 17.*

A23   If the auditor concludes that audit sampling has not provided a reasonable basis for conclusions about the population that has been tested, the auditor may:

- Request management to investigate misstatements that have been identified and the potential for further misstatements and to make any necessary adjustments; or

- Tailor the nature, timing and extent of those further audit procedures to best achieve the required assurance. For example, in the case of tests of controls, the auditor might extend the sample size, test an alternative control or modify related substantive procedures.

Appendix 1

(Ref: Para. A8)

Stratification and Value-Weighted Selection

In considering the characteristics of the population from which the sample will be drawn, the auditor may determine that stratification or value-weighted selection is appropriate. This Appendix provides guidance to the auditor on the use of stratification and value-weighted sampling techniques.*Stratification*

(1)   Audit efficiency may be improved if the auditor stratifies a population by dividing it into discrete sub-populations which have an identifying characteristic. The objective of stratification is to reduce the variability of items within each stratum and therefore allow sample size to be reduced without increasing sampling risk.

(2)   When performing tests of details, the population is often stratified by monetary value. This allows greater audit effort to be directed to the larger value items, as these items may contain the greatest potential misstatement in terms of overstatement. Similarly, a population may be stratified according to a particular characteristic that indicates a higher risk of misstatement, for example, when testing the allowance for doubtful accounts in the valuation of accounts receivable, balances may be stratified by age.

(3)   The results of audit procedures applied to a sample of items within a stratum can only be projected to the items that make up that stratum. To draw a conclusion on the entire population, the auditor will need to consider the risk of material misstatement in relation to whatever other strata make up the entire population. For example, 20% of the items in a population may make up 90% of the value of an account balance. The auditor may decide to examine a sample of these items. The auditor evaluates the results of this sample and reaches a conclusion on the 90% of value separately from the remaining 10% (on which a further sample or other means of gathering audit evidence will be used, or which may be considered immaterial).

(4)   If a class of transactions or account balance has been divided into strata, the misstatement is projected for each stratum separately. Projected misstatements for each stratum are then combined when considering the possible effect of misstatements on the total class of transactions or account balance.

Value-Weighted Selection

(5)   When performing tests of details it may be efficient to identify the sampling unit as the individual monetary units that make up the population. Having selected specific monetary units from within the population, for example, the accounts receivable balance, the auditor may then examine the particular items, for example, individual balances, that contain those monetary units. One benefit of this approach to defining the sampling unit is that audit effort is directed to the larger value items because they have a greater chance of selection, and can result in smaller sample sizes. This approach may be used in conjunction with the systematic method of sample selection (described in Appendix 4) and is most efficient when selecting items using random selection.

Appendix 2

(Ref: Para. A11)

Examples of Factors Influencing Sample Size
for Tests of Controls

The following are factors that the auditor may consider when determining the sample size for tests of controls. These factors, which need to be considered together, assume the auditor does not modify the nature or timing of tests of controls or otherwise modify the approach to substantive procedures in response to assessed risks.

FACTOR	EFFECT ON SAMPLE SIZE	
1. An increase in the extent to which the auditor's risk assessment takes into account relevant controls	Increase	The more assurance the auditor intends to obtain from the operating effectiveness of controls, the lower the auditor's assessment of the risk of material misstatement will be, and the larger the sample size will need to be. When the auditor's assessment of the risk of material misstatement at the assertion level includes an expectation of the operating effectiveness of controls, the auditor is required to perform tests of controls. Other things being equal, the greater the reliance the auditor places on the operating effectiveness of controls in the risk assessment, the greater is the extent of the auditor's tests of controls (and therefore, the sample size is increased).
2. An increase in the tolerable rate of deviation	Decrease	The lower the tolerable rate of deviation, the larger the sample size needs to be.
3. An increase in the expected rate of deviation of the population to be tested	Increase	The higher the expected rate of deviation, the larger the sample size needs to be so that the auditor is in a position to make a reasonable estimate of the actual rate of deviation. Factors relevant to the auditor's consideration of the expected rate of deviation include the auditor's understanding of the business (in particular, risk assessment procedures undertaken to obtain an understanding of internal control), changes in personnel or in internal control, the results of audit procedures applied in prior periods and the results of other audit procedures. High expected control deviation rates ordinarily warrant little, if any, reduction of the assessed risk of material misstatement.

FACTOR	EFFECT ON SAMPLE SIZE
4. An increase in the auditor's desired level of assurance that the tolerable rate of deviation is not exceeded by the actual rate of deviation in the population	Increase
5. An increase in the number of sampling units in the population	Negligible effect

The greater the level of assurance that the auditor desires that the results of the sample are in fact indicative of the actual incidence of deviation in the population, the larger the sample size needs to be.

For large populations, the actual size of the population has little, if any, effect on sample size. For small populations however, audit sampling may not be as efficient as alternative means of obtaining sufficient appropriate audit evidence.

Appendix 3

(Ref: Para. A11)

Examples of Factors Influencing Sample Size
for Tests of Details

The following are factors that the auditor may consider when determining the sample size for tests of details. These factors, which need to be considered together, assume the auditor does not modify the approach to tests of controls or otherwise modify the nature or timing of substantive procedures in response to the assessed risks.

FACTOR	EFFECT ON SAMPLE SIZE	
1. An increase in the auditor's assessment of the risk of material misstatement	Increase	The higher the auditor's assessment of the risk of material misstatement, the larger the sample size needs to be. The auditor's assessment of the risk of material misstatement is affected by inherent risk and control risk. For example, if the auditor does not perform tests of controls, the auditor's risk assessment cannot be reduced for the effective operation of internal controls with respect to the particular assertion. Therefore, in order to reduce audit risk to an acceptably low level, the auditor needs a low detection risk and will rely more on substantive procedures. The more audit evidence that is obtained from tests of details (that is, the lower the detection risk), the larger the sample size will need to be.
2. An increase in the use of other substantive procedures directed at the same assertion	Decrease	The more the auditor is relying on other substantive procedures (tests of details or substantive analytical procedures) to reduce to an acceptable level the detection risk regarding a particular population, the less assurance the auditor will require from sampling and, therefore, the smaller the sample size can be.
3. An increase in the auditor's desired level of assurance that tolerable misstatement is not exceeded by actual misstatement in the population	Increase	The greater the level of assurance that the auditor requires that the results of the sample are in fact indicative of the actual amount of misstatement in the population, the larger the sample size needs to be.
4. An increase in tolerable misstatement	Decrease	The lower the tolerable misstatement, the larger the sample size needs to be.
5. An increase in the amount of misstatement the auditor expects to find in the population	Increase	The greater the amount of misstatement the auditor expects to find in the population, the larger the sample size needs to be in order to make a reasonable estimate of the actual amount of misstatement in the population. Factors relevant to the auditor's consideration of the expected misstatement amount include the extent to which item values are determined subjectively, the results of risk assessment procedures, the results of tests of control, the results of audit procedures applied in prior periods, and the results of other substantive procedures.

FACTOR	EFFECT ON SAMPLE SIZE
6. Stratification of the population when appropriate	Decrease
	When there is a wide range (variability) in the monetary size of items in the population, it may be useful to stratify the population. When a population can be appropriately stratified, the aggregate of the sample sizes from the strata generally will be less than the sample size that would have been required to attain a given level of sampling risk, had one sample been drawn from the whole population.
7. The number of sampling units in the population	Negligible effect
	For large populations, the actual size of the population has little, if any, effect on sample size. Thus, for small populations, audit sampling is often not as efficient as alternative means of obtaining sufficient appropriate audit evidence. (However, when using monetary unit sampling, an increase in the monetary value of the population increases sample size, unless this is offset by a proportional increase in materiality for the financial statements as a whole [and, if applicable, materiality level or levels for particular classes of transactions, account balances or disclosures].)

Appendix 4

(Ref: Para. A13)

Sample Selection Methods

There are many methods of selecting samples. The principal methods are as follows:

(a)   Random selection (applied through random number generators, for example, random number tables).

(b)   Systematic selection, in which the number of sampling units in the population is divided by the sample size to give a sampling interval, for example 50, and having determined a starting point within the first 50, each 50th sampling unit thereafter is selected. Although the starting point may be determined haphazardly, the sample is more likely to be truly random if it is determined by use of a computerized random number generator or random number tables. When using systematic selection, the auditor would need to determine that sampling units within the population are not structured in such a way that the sampling interval corresponds with a particular pattern in the population.

(c)   Monetary Unit Sampling is a type of value-weighted selection (as described in Appendix 1) in which sample size, selection and evaluation results in a conclusion in monetary amounts.

(d)   Haphazard selection, in which the auditor selects the sample without following a structured technique. Although no structured technique is used, the auditor would nonetheless avoid any conscious bias or predictability (for example, avoiding difficult to locate items, or always choosing or avoiding the first or last entries on a page) and thus attempt to ensure that all items in the population have a chance of selection. Haphazard selection is not appropriate when using statistical sampling.

(e)   Block selection involves selection of a block(s) of contiguous items from within the population. Block selection cannot ordinarily be used in audit sampling because most populations are structured such that items in a sequence can be expected to have similar characteristics to each other, but different characteristics from items elsewhere in the population. Although in some circumstances it may be an appropriate audit procedure to examine a block of items, it would rarely be an appropriate sample selection technique when the auditor intends to draw valid inferences about the entire population based on the sample.

ISA (UK) 540 (Revised June 2016) Auditing Accounting Estimates, Including Fair Value Accounting Estimates, and Related Disclosures

(Effective for audits of financial statements for periods commencing on or after 17 June 2016)

Contents

Paragraphs

Introduction
Scope of this ISA (UK)   1
Nature of accounting estimates   2 - 4
Effective date   5

Objective   6

Definitions   7

Requirements
Risk assessment procedures and related activities   8 - 9
Identifying and assessing the risks of material misstatement   10 - 11
Responses to the assessed risks of material misstatement   12 - 14
Further substantive procedures to respond to significant risks   15 - 17
Evaluating the reasonableness of the accounting estimates, and determining misstatements   18
Disclosures related to accounting estimates   19 - 20
Indicators of possible management bias   21 - 21D-1
Written representations   22
Documentation   23

Application and other explanatory material
Nature of accounting estimates   A1 - A11
Risk assessment procedures and related activities   A12 - A44
Identifying and assessing the risks of material misstatement   A45 - A51
Responses to the assessed risks of material misstatement   A52 - A101
Further substantive procedures to respond to significant risks   A102 - A115
Evaluating the reasonableness of the accounting estimates, and determining
misstatements   A116 - A119
Disclosures related to accounting estimates   A120 - A123
Indicators of possible management bias   A124 - A125
Written representations   A126 - A127
Documentation   A128

**Appendix: Fair value measurements and disclosures under different financial
reporting frameworks**

International Standard on Auditing (UK) (ISA (UK)) 540 (Revised June 2016), *Auditing Accounting Estimates, Including Fair Value Accounting Estimates, and Related Disclosures*, should be read in conjunction with ISA (UK) 200 (Revised June 2016), *Overall Objectives of the Independent Auditor and the Conduct of an Audit in Accordance with International Standards on Auditing (UK)*.

Introduction

Scope of this ISA (UK)

1   This International Standard on Auditing (UK) (ISA (UK)) deals with the auditor's responsibilities relating to accounting estimates, including fair value accounting estimates, and related disclosures in an audit of financial statements. Specifically, it expands on how ISA (UK) 315 (Revised June 2016)[1] and ISA (UK) 330 (Revised June 2016)[2] and other relevant ISAs (UK) are to be applied in relation to accounting estimates. It also includes requirements and guidance on misstatements of individual accounting estimates, and indicators of possible management bias.

Nature of Accounting Estimates

2   Some financial statement items cannot be measured precisely, but can only be estimated. For purposes of this ISA (UK), such financial statement items are referred to as accounting estimates. The nature and reliability of information available to management to support the making of an accounting estimate varies widely, which thereby affects the degree of estimation uncertainty associated with accounting estimates. The degree of estimation uncertainty affects, in turn, the risks of material misstatement of accounting estimates, including their susceptibility to unintentional or intentional management bias. (Ref: Para. A1–A11)

3   The measurement objective of accounting estimates can vary depending on the applicable financial reporting framework and the financial item being reported. The measurement objective for some accounting estimates is to forecast the outcome of one or more transactions, events or conditions giving rise to the need for the accounting estimate. For other accounting estimates, including many fair value accounting estimates, the measurement objective is different, and is expressed in terms of the value of a current transaction or financial statement item based on conditions prevalent at the measurement date, such as estimated market price for a particular type of asset or liability. For example, the applicable financial reporting framework may require fair value measurement based on an assumed hypothetical current transaction between knowledgeable, willing parties (sometimes referred to as "marketplace participants" or equivalent) in an arm's length transaction, rather than the settlement of a transaction at some past or future date.[3]

4   A difference between the outcome of an accounting estimate and the amount originally recognized or disclosed in the financial statements does not necessarily represent a misstatement of the financial statements. This is particularly the case for fair value accounting estimates, as any observed outcome is invariably affected by events or conditions subsequent to the date at which the measurement is estimated for purposes of the financial statements.

---

[1] *ISA (UK) 315 (Revised June 2016), Identifying and Assessing the Risks of Material Misstatement through Understanding the Entity and Its Environment.*

[2] *ISA (UK) 330 (Revised June 2016), The Auditor's Responses to Assessed Risks.*

[3] *Different definitions of fair value may exist among financial reporting frameworks.*

Effective Date

This ISA (UK) is effective for audits of financial statements for periods 5
commencing on or after 17 June 2016. Earlier adoption is permitted.

Objective

The objective of the auditor is to obtain sufficient appropriate audit evidence about 6
whether:

(a) accounting estimates, including fair value accounting estimates, in the
financial statements, whether recognized or disclosed, are reasonable; and

(b) related disclosures in the financial statements are adequate,

in the context of the applicable financial reporting framework.

Definitions

For purposes of the ISAs (UK), the following terms have the meanings attributed 7
below:

(a) Accounting estimate – An approximation of a monetary amount in the
absence of a precise means of measurement. This term is used for an amount
measured at fair value where there is estimation uncertainty, as well as for
other amounts that require estimation. Where this ISA (UK) addresses only
accounting estimates involving measurement at fair value, the term "fair
value accounting estimates" is used.

(b) Auditor's point estimate or auditor's range – The amount, or range of
amounts, respectively, derived from audit evidence for use in evaluating
management's point estimate.

(c) Estimation uncertainty – The susceptibility of an accounting estimate and
related disclosures to an inherent lack of precision in its measurement.

(d) Management bias – A lack of neutrality by management in the preparation
of information.

(e) Management's point estimate – The amount selected by management for
recognition or disclosure in the financial statements as an accounting
estimate.

(f) Outcome of an accounting estimate – The actual monetary amount which
results from the resolution of the underlying transaction(s), event(s) or
condition(s) addressed by the accounting estimate.

Requirements

Risk Assessment Procedures and Related Activities

When performing risk assessment procedures and related activities to obtain an 8
understanding of the entity and its environment, including the entity's internal
control, as required by ISA (UK) 315 (Revised June 2016),[4] the auditor shall

---

[4] *ISA (UK) 315 (Revised June 2016), paragraphs 5–6 and 11–12.*

obtain an understanding of the following in order to provide a basis for the identification and assessment of the risks of material misstatement for accounting estimates: (Ref: Para. A12)

(a)   The requirements of the applicable financial reporting framework relevant to accounting estimates, including related disclosures. (Ref: Para. A13–A15)

(b)   How management identifies those transactions, events and conditions that may give rise to the need for accounting estimates to be recognized or disclosed in the financial statements. In obtaining this understanding, the auditor shall make inquiries of management about changes in circumstances that may give rise to new, or the need to revise existing, accounting estimates. (Ref: Para. A16–A21)

(c)   How management makes the accounting estimates, and an understanding of the data on which they are based, including: (Ref: Para. A22–A23)

   (i)   The method, including where applicable the model, used in making the accounting estimate; (Ref: Para. A24–A26-1)

   (ii)   Relevant controls; (Ref: Para. A27–A28)

   (iii)   Whether management has used an expert; (Ref: Para. A29–A30)

   (iv)   The assumptions underlying the accounting estimates; (Ref: Para. A31–A36)

   (v)   Whether there has been or ought to have been a change from the prior period in the methods for making the accounting estimates, and if so, why; and (Ref: Para. A37)

   (vi)   Whether and, if so, how management has assessed the effect of estimation uncertainty. (Ref: Para. A38)

9   The auditor shall review the outcome of accounting estimates included in the prior period financial statements, or, where applicable, their subsequent re-estimation for the purpose of the current period. The nature and extent of the auditor's review takes account of the nature of the accounting estimates, and whether the information obtained from the review would be relevant to identifying and assessing risks of material misstatement of accounting estimates made in the current period financial statements. However, the review is not intended to call into question the judgments made in the prior periods that were based on information available at the time. (Ref: Para. A39–A44)

Identifying and Assessing the Risks of Material Misstatement

10   In identifying and assessing the risks of material misstatement, as required by ISA (UK) 315 (Revised June 2016),[5] the auditor shall evaluate the degree of estimation uncertainty associated with an accounting estimate. (Ref: Para. A45–A46)

11   The auditor shall determine whether, in the auditor's judgment, any of those accounting estimates that have been identified as having high estimation uncertainty give rise to significant risks. (Ref: Para. A47–A51)

---

[5] *ISA (UK) 315 (Revised June 2016), paragraph 25.*

Responses to the Assessed Risks of Material Misstatement

Based on the assessed risks of material misstatement, the auditor shall determine: **12**
(Ref: Para. A52)

(a) Whether management has appropriately applied the requirements of the applicable financial reporting framework relevant to the accounting estimate; and (Ref: Para. A53–A56)

(b) Whether the methods for making the accounting estimates are appropriate and have been applied consistently, and whether changes, if any, in accounting estimates or in the method for making them from the prior period are appropriate in the circumstances. (Ref: Para. A57–A58)

In responding to the assessed risks of material misstatement, as required by **13**
ISA (UK) 330 (Revised June 2016),[6] the auditor shall undertake one or more of the following, taking account of the nature of the accounting estimate: (Ref: Para. A59–A61)

(a) Determine whether events occurring up to the date of the auditor's report provide audit evidence regarding the accounting estimate. (Ref: Para. A62–A67)

(b) Test how management made the accounting estimate and the data on which it is based. In doing so, the auditor shall evaluate whether: (Ref: Para. A68–A70)

    (i) The method of measurement used is appropriate in the circumstances; and (Ref: Para. A71–A76)

    (ii) The assumptions used by management are reasonable in light of the measurement objectives of the applicable financial reporting framework. (Ref: Para. A77–A83)

(c) Test the operating effectiveness of the controls over how management made the accounting estimate, together with appropriate substantive procedures. (Ref: Para. A84–A86)

(d) Develop a point estimate or a range to evaluate management's point estimate. For this purpose: (Ref: Para. A87–A91)

    (i) If the auditor uses assumptions or methods that differ from management's, the auditor shall obtain an understanding of management's assumptions or methods sufficient to establish that the auditor's point estimate or range takes into account relevant variables and to evaluate any significant differences from management's point estimate. (Ref: Para. A92)

    (ii) If the auditor concludes that it is appropriate to use a range, the auditor shall narrow the range, based on audit evidence available, until all outcomes within the range are considered reasonable. (Ref: Para. A93–A95)

In determining the matters identified in paragraph 12 or in responding to the **14**
assessed risks of material misstatement in accordance with paragraph 13, the auditor shall consider whether specialized skills or knowledge in relation to one or

---

[6] *ISA (UK) 330 (Revised June 2016), paragraph 5.*

more aspects of the accounting estimates are required in order to obtain sufficient appropriate audit evidence. (Ref: Para. A96–A101)

Further Substantive Procedures to Respond to Significant Risks

Estimation Uncertainty

15   For accounting estimates that give rise to significant risks, in addition to other substantive procedures performed to meet the requirements of ISA (UK) 330 (Revised June 2016),[7] the auditor shall evaluate the following: (Ref: Para. A102)

(a)   How management has considered alternative assumptions or outcomes, and why it has rejected them, or how management has otherwise addressed estimation uncertainty in making the accounting estimate. (Ref: Para. A103–A106)

(b)   Whether the significant assumptions used by management are reasonable. (Ref: Para. A107–A109)

(c)   Where relevant to the reasonableness of the significant assumptions used by management or the appropriate application of the applicable financial reporting framework, management's intent to carry out specific courses of action and its ability to do so. (Ref: Para. A110)

16   If, in the auditor's judgment, management has not adequately addressed the effects of estimation uncertainty on the accounting estimates that give rise to significant risks, the auditor shall, if considered necessary, develop a range with which to evaluate the reasonableness of the accounting estimate. (Ref: Para. A111–A112)

Recognition and Measurement Criteria

17   For accounting estimates that give rise to significant risks, the auditor shall obtain sufficient appropriate audit evidence about whether:

(a)   management's decision to recognize, or to not recognize, the accounting estimates in the financial statements; and (Ref: Para. A113–A114)

(b)   the selected measurement basis for the accounting estimates, (Ref: Para. A115)

are in accordance with the requirements of the applicable financial reporting framework.

Evaluating the Reasonableness of the Accounting Estimates, and Determining Misstatements

18   The auditor shall evaluate, based on the audit evidence, whether the accounting estimates in the financial statements are either reasonable in the context of the applicable financial reporting framework, or are misstated. (Ref: Para. A116–A119)

Disclosures Related to Accounting Estimates

19   The auditor shall obtain sufficient appropriate audit evidence about whether the disclosures in the financial statements related to accounting estimates are in accordance with the requirements of the applicable financial reporting framework. (Ref: Para. A120–A121)

---

[7] *ISA (UK) 330 (Revised June 2016), paragraph 18.*

For accounting estimates that give rise to significant risks, the auditor shall also **20** evaluate the adequacy of the disclosure of their estimation uncertainty in the financial statements in the context of the applicable financial reporting framework. (Ref: Para. A122–A123)

Indicators of Possible Management Bias

The auditor shall review the judgments and decisions made by management in the **21** making of accounting estimates to identify whether there are indicators of possible management bias. Indicators of possible management bias do not themselves constitute misstatements for the purposes of drawing conclusions on the reasonableness of individual accounting estimates. (Ref: Para. A124–A125)

In accordance with ISA (UK) 200 (Revised June 2016),[7a] the auditor shall **21D-1** maintain professional skepticism throughout the audit and in particular when reviewing management estimates relating to fair values, the impairment of assets and provisions.

Written Representations

The auditor shall obtain written representations from management and, where **22** appropriate, those charged with governance whether they believe significant assumptions used in making accounting estimates are reasonable. (Ref: Para. A126–A127)

Documentation

The auditor shall include in the audit documentation:[8] **23**

(a)   The basis for the auditor's conclusions about the reasonableness of accounting estimates and their disclosure that give rise to significant risks; and

(b)   Indicators of possible management bias, if any. (Ref: Para. A128)

***

Application and Other Explanatory Material

Nature of Accounting Estimates
(Ref: Para. 2)

Because of the uncertainties inherent in business activities, some financial **A1** statement items can only be estimated. Further, the specific characteristics of an asset, liability or component of equity, or the basis of or method of measurement prescribed by the financial reporting framework, may give rise to the need to estimate a financial statement item. Some financial reporting frameworks prescribe specific methods of measurement and the disclosures that are required to be made in the financial statements, while other financial reporting frameworks are less specific. The Appendix to this ISA (UK) discusses fair value measurements and disclosures under different financial reporting frameworks.

[7a] *ISA (UK) 200 (Revised June 2016), Overall Objectives of the Independent Auditor and the Conduct of an Audit in Accordance with International Standards on Auditing (UK), paragraph 15.*

[8] *ISA (UK) 230 (Revised June 2016), Audit Documentation, paragraphs 8–11, and paragraph A6.*

A2   Some accounting estimates involve relatively low estimation uncertainty and may give rise to lower risks of material misstatements, for example:

- Accounting estimates arising in entities that engage in business activities that are not complex.

- Accounting estimates that are frequently made and updated because they relate to routine transactions.

- Accounting estimates derived from data that is readily available, such as published interest rate data or exchange-traded prices of securities. Such data may be referred to as "observable" in the context of a fair value accounting estimate.

- Fair value accounting estimates where the method of measurement prescribed by the applicable financial reporting framework is simple and applied easily to the asset or liability requiring measurement at fair value.

- Fair value accounting estimates where the model used to measure the accounting estimate is well-known or generally accepted, provided that the assumptions or inputs to the model are observable.

A3   For some accounting estimates, however, there may be relatively high estimation uncertainty, particularly where they are based on significant assumptions, for example:

- Accounting estimates relating to the outcome of litigation.

- Fair value accounting estimates for derivative financial instruments not publicly traded.

- Fair value accounting estimates for which a highly specialized entity-developed model is used or for which there are assumptions or inputs that cannot be observed in the marketplace.

A4   The degree of estimation uncertainty varies based on the nature of the accounting estimate, the extent to which there is a generally accepted method or model used to make the accounting estimate, and the subjectivity of the assumptions used to make the accounting estimate. In some cases, estimation uncertainty associated with an accounting estimate may be so great that the recognition criteria in the applicable financial reporting framework are not met and the accounting estimate cannot be made.

A5   Not all financial statement items requiring measurement at fair value, involve estimation uncertainty. For example, this may be the case for some financial statement items where there is an active and open market that provides readily available and reliable information on the prices at which actual exchanges occur, in which case the existence of published price quotations ordinarily is the best audit evidence of fair value. However, estimation uncertainty may exist even when the valuation method and data are well defined. For example, valuation of securities quoted on an active and open market at the listed market price may require adjustment if the holding is significant in relation to the market or is subject to restrictions in marketability. In addition, general economic circumstances prevailing at the time, for example, illiquidity in a particular market, may impact estimation uncertainty.

A6   Additional examples of situations where accounting estimates, other than fair value accounting estimates, may be required include:

- Allowance for doubtful accounts.
- Inventory obsolescence.
- Warranty obligations.
- Depreciation method or asset useful life.
- Provision against the carrying amount of an investment where there is uncertainty regarding its recoverability.
- Outcome of long term contracts.
- Costs arising from litigation settlements and judgments.

Additional examples of situations where fair value accounting estimates may be required include: **A7**

- Complex financial instruments, which are not traded in an active and open market.
- Share-based payments.
- Property or equipment held for disposal.
- Certain assets or liabilities acquired in a business combination, including goodwill and intangible assets.
- Transactions involving the exchange of assets or liabilities between independent parties without monetary consideration, for example, a non-monetary exchange of plant facilities in different lines of business.

Estimation involves judgments based on information available when the financial statements are prepared. For many accounting estimates, these include making assumptions about matters that are uncertain at the time of estimation. The auditor is not responsible for predicting future conditions, transactions or events that, if known at the time of the audit, might have significantly affected management's actions or the assumptions used by management.   **A8**

Management Bias

Financial reporting frameworks often call for neutrality, that is, freedom from bias. Accounting estimates are imprecise, however, and can be influenced by management judgment. Such judgment may involve unintentional or intentional management bias (for example, as a result of motivation to achieve a desired result). The susceptibility of an accounting estimate to management bias increases with the subjectivity involved in making it. Unintentional management bias and the potential for intentional management bias are inherent in subjective decisions that are often required in making an accounting estimate. For continuing audits, indicators of possible management bias identified during the audit of the preceding periods influence the planning and risk identification and assessment activities of the auditor in the current period.   **A9**

Management bias can be difficult to detect at an account level. It may only be identified when considered in the aggregate of groups of accounting estimates or all accounting estimates, or when observed over a number of accounting periods. Although some form of management bias is inherent in subjective decisions, in making such judgments there may be no intention by management to mislead the users of financial statements. Where, however, there is intention to mislead, management bias is fraudulent in nature.   **A10**

Considerations Specific to Public Sector Entities

A11   Public sector entities may have significant holdings of specialized assets for which there are no readily available and reliable sources of information for purposes of measurement at fair value or other current value bases, or a combination of both. Often specialized assets held do not generate cash flows and do not have an active market. Measurement at fair value therefore ordinarily requires estimation and may be complex, and in some rare cases may not be possible at all.

Risk Assessment Procedures and Related Activities
(Ref: Para. 8)

A12   The risk assessment procedures and related activities required by paragraph 8 of this ISA (UK) assist the auditor in developing an expectation of the nature and type of accounting estimates that an entity may have. The auditor's primary consideration is whether the understanding that has been obtained is sufficient to identify and assess the risks of material misstatement in relation to accounting estimates, and to plan the nature, timing and extent of further audit procedures.

Obtaining an Understanding of the Requirements of the Applicable Financial Reporting Framework
(Ref: Para. 8(a))

A13   Obtaining an understanding of the requirements of the applicable financial reporting framework assists the auditor in determining whether it, for example:

● Prescribes certain conditions for the recognition,[9] or methods for the measurement, of accounting estimates.

● Specifies certain conditions that permit or require measurement at a fair value, for example, by referring to management's intentions to carry out certain courses of action with respect to an asset or liability.

● Specifies required or permitted disclosures.

Obtaining this understanding also provides the auditor with a basis for discussion with management about how management has applied those requirements relevant to the accounting estimate, and the auditor's determination of whether they have been applied appropriately.

A14   Financial reporting frameworks may provide guidance for management on determining point estimates where alternatives exist. Some financial reporting frameworks, for example, require that the point estimate selected be the alternative that reflects management's judgment of the most likely outcome.[10] Others may require, for example, use of a discounted probability-weighted expected value. In some cases, management may be able to make a point estimate directly. In other cases, management may be able to make a reliable point estimate only after considering alternative assumptions or outcomes from which it is able to determine a point estimate.

A15   Financial reporting frameworks may require the disclosure of information concerning the significant assumptions to which the accounting estimate is particularly sensitive. Furthermore, where there is a high degree of estimation

---

[9] *Most financial reporting frameworks require incorporation in the balance sheet or income statement of items that satisfy their criteria for recognition. Disclosure of accounting policies or adding notes to the financial statements does not rectify a failure to recognize such items, including accounting estimates.*

[10] *Different financial reporting frameworks may use different terminology to describe point estimates determined in this way.*

uncertainty, some financial reporting frameworks do not permit an accounting estimate to be recognized in the financial statements, but certain disclosures may be required in the notes to the financial statements.

Obtaining an Understanding of How Management Identifies the Need for Accounting Estimates
(Ref: Para. 8(b))

The preparation of the financial statements requires management to determine **A16** whether a transaction, event or condition gives rise to the need to make an accounting estimate, and that all necessary accounting estimates have been recognized, measured and disclosed in the financial statements in accordance with the applicable financial reporting framework.

Management's identification of transactions, events and conditions that give rise **A17** to the need for accounting estimates is likely to be based on:

- Management's knowledge of the entity's business and the industry in which it operates.

- Management's knowledge of the implementation of business strategies in the current period.

- Where applicable, management's cumulative experience of preparing the entity's financial statements in prior periods.

In such cases, the auditor may obtain an understanding of how management identifies the need for accounting estimates primarily through inquiry of management. In other cases, where management's process is more structured, for example, when management has a formal risk management function, the auditor may perform risk assessment procedures directed at the methods and practices followed by management for periodically reviewing the circumstances that give rise to the accounting estimates and re-estimating the accounting estimates as necessary. The completeness of accounting estimates is often an important consideration of the auditor, particularly accounting estimates relating to liabilities.

The auditor's understanding of the entity and its environment obtained during the **A18** performance of risk assessment procedures, together with other audit evidence obtained during the course of the audit, assist the auditor in identifying circumstances, or changes in circumstances, that may give rise to the need for an accounting estimate.

Inquiries of management about changes in circumstances may include, for **A19** example, inquiries about whether:

- The entity has engaged in new types of transactions that may give rise to accounting estimates.

- Terms of transactions that gave rise to accounting estimates have changed.

- Accounting policies relating to accounting estimates have changed, as a result of changes within the requirements of the applicable financial reporting framework or otherwise.

- Regulatory or other changes outside the control of management have occurred that may require management to revise, or make new, accounting estimates.

- New conditions or events have occurred that may give rise to the need for new or revised accounting estimates.

A20   During the audit, the auditor may identify transactions, events and conditions that give rise to the need for accounting estimates that management failed to identify. ISA (UK) 315 (Revised June 2016) deals with circumstances where the auditor identifies risks of material misstatement that management failed to identify, including determining whether there is a significant deficiency in internal control with regard to the entity's risk assessment processes.[11]

Considerations Specific to Smaller Entities

A21   Obtaining this understanding for smaller entities is often less complex as their business activities are often limited and transactions are less complex. Further, often a single person, for example the owner-manager, identifies the need to make an accounting estimate and the auditor may focus inquiries accordingly.

Obtaining an Understanding of How Management Makes the Accounting Estimates
(Ref: Para. 8(c))

A22   The preparation of the financial statements also requires management to establish financial reporting processes for making accounting estimates, including adequate internal control. Such processes include the following:

- Selecting appropriate accounting policies and prescribing estimation processes, including appropriate estimation or valuation methods, including, where applicable, models.

- Developing or identifying relevant data and assumptions that affect accounting estimates.

- Periodically reviewing the circumstances that give rise to the accounting estimates and re-estimating the accounting estimates as necessary.

A23   Matters that the auditor may consider in obtaining an understanding of how management makes the accounting estimates include, for example:

- The types of accounts or transactions to which the accounting estimates relate (for example, whether the accounting estimates arise from the recording of routine and recurring transactions or whether they arise from non-recurring or unusual transactions).

- Whether and, if so, how management has used recognized measurement techniques for making particular accounting estimates.

- Whether the accounting estimates were made based on data available at an interim date and, if so, whether and how management has taken into account the effect of events, transactions and changes in circumstances occurring between that date and the period end.

Method of Measurement, Including the Use of Models
(Ref: Para. 8(c)(i))

A24   In some cases, the applicable financial reporting framework may prescribe the method of measurement for an accounting estimate, for example, a particular model that is to be used in measuring a fair value estimate. In many cases, however, the applicable financial reporting framework does not prescribe the method of measurement, or may specify alternative methods for measurement.

---

[11] *ISA (UK) 315 (Revised June 2016), paragraph 16.*

When the applicable financial reporting framework does not prescribe a particular   **A25**
method to be used in the circumstances, matters that the auditor may consider in
obtaining an understanding of the method or, where applicable the model, used to
make accounting estimates include, for example:

- How management considered the nature of the asset or liability being
  estimated when selecting a particular method.

- Whether the entity operates in a particular business, industry or environment
  in which there are methods commonly used to make the particular type of
  accounting estimate.

There may be greater risks of material misstatement, for example, in cases when   **A26**
management has internally developed a model to be used to make the accounting
estimate or is departing from a method commonly used in a particular industry or
environment.

For audits of financial statements of public interest entities, the auditor's   **A26-1**
obligations for auditing accounting estimates, including fair value accounting
estimates, and related disclosures set out in this ISA (UK) may inform the
auditor's assessment[11a] and communication[11b] in the additional report to the
audit committee of the valuation methods applied to the various items in
the financial statements.

Relevant Controls
(Ref: Para. 8(c)(ii))

Matters that the auditor may consider in obtaining an understanding of relevant   **A27**
controls include, for example, the experience and competence of those who make
the accounting estimates, and controls related to:

- How management determines the completeness, relevance and accuracy of
  the data used to develop accounting estimates.

- The review and approval of accounting estimates, including the assumptions
  or inputs used in their development, by appropriate levels of management
  and, where appropriate, those charged with governance.

- The segregation of duties between those committing the entity to the
  underlying transactions and those responsible for making the accounting
  estimates, including whether the assignment of responsibilities
  appropriately takes account of the nature of the entity and its products or
  services (for example, in the case of a large financial institution, relevant
  segregation of duties may include an independent function responsible for
  estimation and validation of fair value pricing of the entity's proprietary
  financial products staffed by individuals whose remuneration is not tied to
  such products).

Other controls may be relevant to making the accounting estimates depending on   **A28**
the circumstances. For example, if the entity uses specific models for making
accounting estimates, management may put into place specific policies and
procedures around such models. Relevant controls may include, for example,
those established over:

[11a] *ISA (UK) 330 (Revised June 2016), paragraph 19R-1.*

[11b] *ISA (UK) 260 (Revised June 2016), Communication with Those Charged with Governance, paragraph 16R-2(l).*

- The design and development, or selection, of a particular model for a particular purpose.

- The use of the model.

- The maintenance and periodic validation of the integrity of the model.

Management's Use of Experts
(Ref: Para. 8(c)(iii))

A29   Management may have, or the entity may employ individuals with, the experience and competence necessary to make the required point estimates. In some cases, however, management may need to engage an expert to make, or assist in making, them. This need may arise because of, for example:

- The specialized nature of the matter requiring estimation, for example, the measurement of mineral or hydrocarbon reserves in extractive industries.

- The technical nature of the models required to meet the relevant requirements of the applicable financial reporting framework, as may be the case in certain measurements at fair value.

- The unusual or infrequent nature of the condition, transaction or event requiring an accounting estimate.

Considerations specific to smaller entities

A30   In smaller entities, the circumstances requiring an accounting estimate often are such that the owner-manager is capable of making the required point estimate. In some cases, however, an expert will be needed. Discussion with the owner-manager early in the audit process about the nature of any accounting estimates, the completeness of the required accounting estimates, and the adequacy of the estimating process may assist the owner-manager in determining the need to use an expert.

Assumptions
(Ref: Para. 8(c)(iv))

A31   Assumptions are integral components of accounting estimates. Matters that the auditor may consider in obtaining an understanding of the assumptions underlying the accounting estimates include, for example:

- The nature of the assumptions, including which of the assumptions are likely to be significant assumptions.

- How management assesses whether the assumptions are relevant and complete (that is, that all relevant variables have been taken into account).

- Where applicable, how management determines that the assumptions used are internally consistent.

- Whether the assumptions relate to matters within the control of management (for example, assumptions about the maintenance programs that may affect the estimation of an asset's useful life), and how they conform to the entity's business plans and the external environment, or to matters that are outside its control (for example, assumptions about interest rates, mortality rates, potential judicial or regulatory actions, or the variability and the timing of future cash flows).

- The nature and extent of documentation, if any, supporting the assumptions.

Assumptions may be made or identified by an expert to assist management in making the accounting estimates. Such assumptions, when used by management, become management's assumptions.

In some cases, assumptions may be referred to as inputs, for example, where **A32** management uses a model to make an accounting estimate, though the term inputs may also be used to refer to the underlying data to which specific assumptions are applied.

Management may support assumptions with different types of information drawn **A33** from internal and external sources, the relevance and reliability of which will vary. In some cases, an assumption may be reliably based on applicable information from either external sources (for example, published interest rate or other statistical data) or internal sources (for example, historical information or previous conditions experienced by the entity). In other cases, an assumption may be more subjective, for example, where the entity has no experience or external sources from which to draw.

In the case of fair value accounting estimates, assumptions reflect, or are **A34** consistent with, what knowledgeable, willing arm's length parties (sometimes referred to as "marketplace participants" or equivalent) would use in determining fair value when exchanging an asset or settling a liability. Specific assumptions will also vary with the characteristics of the asset or liability being valued, the valuation method used (for example, a market approach, or an income approach) and the requirements of the applicable financial reporting framework.

With respect to fair value accounting estimates, assumptions or inputs vary in **A35** terms of their source and bases, as follows:

(a)   Those that reflect what marketplace participants would use in pricing an asset or liability developed based on market data obtained from sources independent of the reporting entity (sometimes referred to as "observable inputs" or equivalent).

(b)   Those that reflect the entity's own judgments about what assumptions marketplace participants would use in pricing the asset or liability developed based on the best information available in the circumstances (sometimes referred to as "unobservable inputs" or equivalent).

In practice, however, the distinction between (a) and (b) is not always apparent. Further, it may be necessary for management to select from a number of different assumptions used by different marketplace participants.

The extent of subjectivity, such as whether an assumption or input is observable, **A36** influences the degree of estimation uncertainty and thereby the auditor's assessment of the risks of material misstatement for a particular accounting estimate.

Changes in Methods for Making Accounting Estimates
(Ref: Para. 8(c)(v))

In evaluating how management makes the accounting estimates, the auditor is **A37** required to understand whether there has been or ought to have been a change from the prior period in the methods for making the accounting estimates. A specific estimation method may need to be changed in response to changes in the environment or circumstances affecting the entity or in the requirements of the applicable financial reporting framework. If management has changed the method for making an accounting estimate, it is important that management can demonstrate that the new method is more appropriate, or is itself a response to such changes. For example, if management changes the basis of making an accounting estimate from a mark-to-market approach to using a model, the auditor challenges whether management's assumptions about the marketplace are reasonable in light of economic circumstances.

Estimation Uncertainty
(Ref: Para. 8(c)(vi))

A38   Matters that the auditor may consider in obtaining an understanding of whether and, if so, how management has assessed the effect of estimation uncertainty include, for example:

- Whether and, if so, how management has considered alternative assumptions or outcomes by, for example, performing a sensitivity analysis to determine the effect of changes in the assumptions on an accounting estimate.

- How management determines the accounting estimate when analysis indicates a number of outcome scenarios.

- Whether management monitors the outcome of accounting estimates made in the prior period, and whether management has appropriately responded to the outcome of that monitoring procedure.

Reviewing Prior Period Accounting Estimates
(Ref: Para. 9)

A39   The outcome of an accounting estimate will often differ from the accounting estimate recognized in the prior period financial statements. By performing risk assessment procedures to identify and understand the reasons for such differences, the auditor may obtain:

- Information regarding the effectiveness of management's prior period estimation process, from which the auditor can judge the likely effectiveness of management's current process.

- Audit evidence that is pertinent to the re-estimation, in the current period, of prior period accounting estimates.

- Audit evidence of matters, such as estimation uncertainty, that may be required to be disclosed in the financial statements.

A40   The review of prior period accounting estimates may also assist the auditor, in the current period, in identifying circumstances or conditions that increase the susceptibility of accounting estimates to, or indicate the presence of, possible management bias. The auditor's professional skepticism assists in identifying such circumstances or conditions and in determining the nature, timing and extent of further audit procedures.

A41   A retrospective review of management judgments and assumptions related to significant accounting estimates is also required by ISA (UK) 240.[12] That review is conducted as part of the requirement for the auditor to design and perform procedures to review accounting estimates for biases that could represent a risk of material misstatement due to fraud, in response to the risks of management override of controls. As a practical matter, the auditor's review of prior period

---

[12] *ISA (UK) 240 (Revised June 2016), The Auditor's Responsibilities Relating to Fraud in an Audit of Financial Statements, paragraph 32(b)(ii).*

accounting estimates as a risk assessment procedure in accordance with this ISA (UK) may be carried out in conjunction with the review required by ISA (UK) 240.

The auditor may judge that a more detailed review is required for those accounting estimates that were identified during the prior period audit as having high estimation uncertainty, or for those accounting estimates that have changed significantly from the prior period. On the other hand, for example, for accounting estimates that arise from the recording of routine and recurring transactions, the auditor may judge that the application of analytical procedures as risk assessment procedures is sufficient for purposes of the review. **A42**

For fair value accounting estimates and other accounting estimates based on current conditions at the measurement date, more variation may exist between the fair value amount recognized in the prior period financial statements and the outcome or the amount re-estimated for the purpose of the current period. This is because the measurement objective for such accounting estimates deals with perceptions about value at a point in time, which may change significantly and rapidly as the environment in which the entity operates changes. The auditor may therefore focus the review on obtaining information that would be relevant to identifying and assessing risks of material misstatement. For example, in some cases, obtaining an understanding of changes in marketplace participant assumptions which affected the outcome of a prior period fair value accounting estimate may be unlikely to provide relevant information for audit purposes. If so, then the auditor's consideration of the outcome of prior period fair value accounting estimates may be directed more towards understanding the effectiveness of management's prior estimation process, that is, management's track record, from which the auditor can judge the likely effectiveness of management's current process. **A43**

A difference between the outcome of an accounting estimate and the amount recognized in the prior period financial statements does not necessarily represent a misstatement of the prior period financial statements. However, it may do so if, for example, the difference arises from information that was available to management when the prior period's financial statements were finalized, or that could reasonably be expected to have been obtained and taken into account in the preparation of those financial statements. Many financial reporting frameworks contain guidance on distinguishing between changes in accounting estimates that constitute misstatements and changes that do not, and the accounting treatment required to be followed. **A44**

Identifying and Assessing the Risks of Material Misstatement

Estimation Uncertainty
(Ref: Para. 10)

The degree of estimation uncertainty associated with an accounting estimate may be influenced by factors such as: **A45**

- The extent to which the accounting estimate depends on judgment.
- The sensitivity of the accounting estimate to changes in assumptions.
- The existence of recognized measurement techniques that may mitigate the estimation uncertainty (though the subjectivity of the assumptions used as inputs may nevertheless give rise to estimation uncertainty).

- The length of the forecast period, and the relevance of data drawn from past events to forecast future events.

- The availability of reliable data from external sources.

- The extent to which the accounting estimate is based on observable or unobservable inputs.

The degree of estimation uncertainty associated with an accounting estimate may influence the estimate's susceptibility to bias.

A46   Matters that the auditor considers in assessing the risks of material misstatement may also include:

- The actual or expected magnitude of an accounting estimate.

- The recorded amount of the accounting estimate (that is, management's point estimate) in relation to the amount expected by the auditor to be recorded.

- Whether management has used an expert in making the accounting estimate.

- The outcome of the review of prior period accounting estimates.

High Estimation Uncertainty and Significant Risks
(Ref: Para. 11)

A47   Examples of accounting estimates that may have high estimation uncertainty include the following:

- Accounting estimates that are highly dependent upon judgment, for example, judgments about the outcome of pending litigation or the amount and timing of future cash flows dependent on uncertain events many years in the future.

- Accounting estimates that are not calculated using recognized measurement techniques.

- Accounting estimates where the results of the auditor's review of similar accounting estimates made in the prior period financial statements indicate a substantial difference between the original accounting estimate and the actual outcome.

- Fair value accounting estimates for which a highly specialized entity-developed model is used or for which there are no observable inputs.

A48   A seemingly immaterial accounting estimate may have the potential to result in a material misstatement due to the estimation uncertainty associated with the estimation; that is, the size of the amount recognized or disclosed in the financial statements for an accounting estimate may not be an indicator of its estimation uncertainty.

A49   In some circumstances, the estimation uncertainty is so high that a reasonable accounting estimate cannot be made. The applicable financial reporting framework may, therefore, preclude recognition of the item in the financial statements, or its measurement at fair value. In such cases, the significant risks relate not only to whether an accounting estimate should be recognized, or whether it should be measured at fair value, but also to the adequacy of the disclosures. With respect to such accounting estimates, the applicable financial reporting framework may require disclosure of the accounting estimates and the high estimation uncertainty associated with them (see paragraphs A120–A123).

If the auditor determines that an accounting estimate gives rise to a significant risk, **A50** the auditor is required to obtain an understanding of the entity's controls, including control activities.[13]

In some cases, the estimation uncertainty of an accounting estimate may cast **A51** significant doubt about the entity's ability to continue as a going concern. ISA (UK) 570 (Revised June 2016)[14] establishes requirements and provides guidance in such circumstances.

Responses to the Assessed Risks of Material Misstatement
(Ref: Para. 12)

ISA (UK) 330 (Revised June 2016) requires the auditor to design and perform **A52** audit procedures whose nature, timing and extent are responsive to the assessed risks of material misstatement in relation to accounting estimates at both the financial statement and assertion levels.[15] Paragraphs A53–A115 focus on specific responses at the assertion level only.

Application of the Requirements of the Applicable Financial Reporting Framework
(Ref: Para. 12(a))

Many financial reporting frameworks prescribe certain conditions for the **A53** recognition of accounting estimates and specify the methods for making them and required disclosures. Such requirements may be complex and require the application of judgment. Based on the understanding obtained in performing risk assessment procedures, the requirements of the applicable financial reporting framework that may be susceptible to misapplication or differing interpretations become the focus of the auditor's attention.

Determining whether management has appropriately applied the requirements of **A54** the applicable financial reporting framework is based, in part, on the auditor's understanding of the entity and its environment. For example, the measurement of the fair value of some items, such as intangible assets acquired in a business combination, may involve special considerations that are affected by the nature of the entity and its operations.

In some situations, additional audit procedures, such as the inspection by the **A55** auditor of the current physical condition of an asset, may be necessary to determine whether management has appropriately applied the requirements of the applicable financial reporting framework.

The application of the requirements of the applicable financial reporting **A56** framework requires management to consider changes in the environment or circumstances that affect the entity. For example, the introduction of an active market for a particular class of asset or liability may indicate that the use of discounted cash flows to estimate the fair value of such asset or liability is no longer appropriate.

---

[13] *ISA (UK) 315 (Revised June 2016), paragraph 29.*

[14] *ISA (UK) 570 (Revised June 2016), Going Concern.*

[15] *ISA (UK) 330 (Revised June 2016), paragraphs 5–6.*

Consistency in Methods and Basis for Changes
(Ref: Para. 12(b))

A57   The auditor's consideration of a change in an accounting estimate, or in the method for making it from the prior period, is important because a change that is not based on a change in circumstances or new information is considered arbitrary. Arbitrary changes in an accounting estimate result in inconsistent financial statements over time and may give rise to a financial statement misstatement or be an indicator of possible management bias.

A58   Management often is able to demonstrate good reason for a change in an accounting estimate or the method for making an accounting estimate from one period to another based on a change in circumstances. What constitutes a good reason, and the adequacy of support for management's contention that there has been a change in circumstances that warrants a change in an accounting estimate or the method for making an accounting estimate, are matters of judgment.

Responses to the Assessed Risks of Material Misstatements
(Ref: Para. 13)

A59   The auditor's decision as to which response, individually or in combination, in paragraph 13 to undertake to respond to the risks of material misstatement may be influenced by such matters as:

● The nature of the accounting estimate, including whether it arises from routine or non routine transactions.

● Whether the procedure(s) is expected to effectively provide the auditor with sufficient appropriate audit evidence.

● The assessed risk of material misstatement, including whether the assessed risk is a significant risk.

A60   For example, when evaluating the reasonableness of the allowance for doubtful accounts, an effective procedure for the auditor may be to review subsequent cash collections in combination with other procedures. Where the estimation uncertainty associated with an accounting estimate is high, for example, an accounting estimate based on a proprietary model for which there are unobservable inputs, it may be that a combination of the responses to assessed risks in paragraph 13 is necessary in order to obtain sufficient appropriate audit evidence.

A61   Additional guidance explaining the circumstances in which each of the responses may be appropriate is provided in paragraphs A62–A95.

Events Occurring Up to the Date of the Auditor's Report
(Ref: Para. 13(a))

A62   Determining whether events occurring up to the date of the auditor's report provide audit evidence regarding the accounting estimate may be an appropriate response when such events are expected to:

● Occur; and

● Provide audit evidence that confirms or contradicts the accounting estimate.

A63   Events occurring up to the date of the auditor's report may sometimes provide sufficient appropriate audit evidence about an accounting estimate. For example, sale of the complete inventory of a superseded product shortly after the period end may provide audit evidence relating to the estimate of its net realizable value. In such cases, there may be no need to perform additional audit procedures on the accounting estimate, provided that sufficient appropriate evidence about the events is obtained.

For some accounting estimates, events occurring up to the date of the auditor's **A64** report are unlikely to provide audit evidence regarding the accounting estimate. For example, the conditions or events relating to some accounting estimates develop only over an extended period. Also, because of the measurement objective of fair value accounting estimates, information after the period-end may not reflect the events or conditions existing at the balance sheet date and therefore may not be relevant to the measurement of the fair value accounting estimate. Paragraph 13 identifies other responses to the risks of material misstatement that the auditor may undertake.

In some cases, events that contradict the accounting estimate may indicate that **A65** management has ineffective processes for making accounting estimates, or that there is management bias in the making of accounting estimates.

Even though the auditor may decide not to undertake this approach in respect of **A66** specific accounting estimates, the auditor is required to comply with ISA (UK) 560.[16] The auditor is required to perform audit procedures designed to obtain sufficient appropriate audit evidence that all events occurring between the date of the financial statements and the date of the auditor's report that require adjustment of, or disclosure in, the financial statements have been identified[17] and appropriately reflected in the financial statements.[18] Because the measurement of many accounting estimates, other than fair value accounting estimates, usually depends on the outcome of future conditions, transactions or events, the auditor's work under ISA (UK) 560 is particularly relevant.

Considerations specific to smaller entities

When there is a longer period between the balance sheet date and the date of the **A67** auditor's report, the auditor's review of events in this period may be an effective response for accounting estimates other than fair value accounting estimates. This may particularly be the case in some smaller owner-managed entities, especially when management does not have formalized control procedures over accounting estimates.

Testing How Management Made the Accounting Estimate (Ref: Para. 13(b))

Testing how management made the accounting estimate and the data on which it is **A68** based may be an appropriate response when the accounting estimate is a fair value accounting estimate developed on a model that uses observable and unobservable inputs. It may also be appropriate when, for example:

- The accounting estimate is derived from the routine processing of data by the entity's accounting system.

- The auditor's review of similar accounting estimates made in the prior period financial statements suggests that management's current period process is likely to be effective.

---

[16] *ISA (UK) 560, Subsequent Events.*

[17] *ISA (UK) 560, paragraph 6.*

[18] *ISA (UK) 560, paragraph 8.*

- The accounting estimate is based on a large population of items of a similar nature that individually are not significant.

A69 Testing how management made the accounting estimate may involve, for example:

- Testing the extent to which data on which the accounting estimate is based is accurate, complete and relevant, and whether the accounting estimate has been properly determined using such data and management assumptions.

- Considering the source, relevance and reliability of external data or information, including that received from external experts engaged by management to assist in making an accounting estimate.

- Recalculating the accounting estimate, and reviewing information about an accounting estimate for internal consistency.

- Considering management's review and approval processes.

Considerations specific to smaller entities

A70 In smaller entities, the process for making accounting estimates is likely to be less structured than in larger entities. Smaller entities with active management involvement may not have extensive descriptions of accounting procedures, sophisticated accounting records, or written policies. Even if the entity has no formal established process, it does not mean that management is not able to provide a basis upon which the auditor can test the accounting estimate.

Evaluating the method of measurement
(Ref: Para. 13(b)(i))

A71 When the applicable financial reporting framework does not prescribe the method of measurement, evaluating whether the method used, including any applicable model, is appropriate in the circumstances is a matter of professional judgment.

A72 For this purpose, matters that the auditor may consider include, for example, whether:

- Management's rationale for the method selected is reasonable.

- Management has sufficiently evaluated and appropriately applied the criteria, if any, provided in the applicable financial reporting framework to support the selected method.

- The method is appropriate in the circumstances given the nature of the asset or liability being estimated and the requirements of the applicable financial reporting framework relevant to accounting estimates.

- The method is appropriate in relation to the business, industry and environment in which the entity operates.

A73 In some cases, management may have determined that different methods result in a range of significantly different estimates. In such cases, obtaining an understanding of how the entity has investigated the reasons for these differences may assist the auditor in evaluating the appropriateness of the method selected.

Evaluating the use of models

A74 In some cases, particularly when making fair value accounting estimates, management may use a model. Whether the model used is appropriate in the circumstances may depend on a number of factors, such as the nature of the entity and its environment, including the industry in which it operates, and the specific asset or liability being measured.

The extent to which the following considerations are relevant depends on the **A75** circumstances, including whether the model is one that is commercially available for use in a particular sector or industry, or a proprietary model. In some cases, an entity may use an expert to develop and test a model.

Depending on the circumstances, matters that the auditor may also consider in **A76** testing the model include, for example, whether:

- The model is validated prior to usage, with periodic reviews to ensure it is still suitable for its intended use. The entity's validation process may include evaluation of:
    - The model's theoretical soundness and mathematical integrity, including the appropriateness of model parameters.
    - The consistency and completeness of the model's inputs with market practices.
    - The model's output as compared to actual transactions.
- Appropriate change control policies and procedures exist.
- The model is periodically calibrated and tested for validity, particularly when inputs are subjective.
- Adjustments are made to the output of the model, including in the case of fair value accounting estimates, whether such adjustments reflect the assumptions marketplace participants would use in similar circumstances.
- The model is adequately documented, including the model's intended applications and limitations and its key parameters, required inputs, and results of any validation analysis performed.

Assumptions used by management
(Ref: Para. 13(b)(ii))

The auditor's evaluation of the assumptions used by management is based only on **A77** information available to the auditor at the time of the audit. Audit procedures dealing with management assumptions are performed in the context of the audit of the entity's financial statements, and not for the purpose of providing an opinion on assumptions themselves.

Matters that the auditor may consider in evaluating the reasonableness of the **A78** assumptions used by management include, for example:

- Whether individual assumptions appear reasonable.
- Whether the assumptions are interdependent and internally consistent.
- Whether the assumptions appear reasonable when considered collectively or in conjunction with other assumptions, either for that accounting estimate or for other accounting estimates.
- In the case of fair value accounting estimates, whether the assumptions appropriately reflect observable marketplace assumptions.

The assumptions on which accounting estimates are based may reflect what **A79** management expects will be the outcome of specific objectives and strategies. In such cases, the auditor may perform audit procedures to evaluate the reasonableness of such assumptions by considering, for example, whether the assumptions are consistent with:

- The general economic environment and the entity's economic circumstances.

- The plans of the entity.

- Assumptions made in prior periods, if relevant.

- Experience of, or previous conditions experienced by, the entity, to the extent this historical information may be considered representative of future conditions or events.

- Other assumptions used by management relating to the financial statements.

A80   The reasonableness of the assumptions used may depend on management's intent and ability to carry out certain courses of action. Management often documents plans and intentions relevant to specific assets or liabilities and the financial reporting framework may require it to do so. Although the extent of audit evidence to be obtained about management's intent and ability is a matter of professional judgment, the auditor's procedures may include the following:

- Review of management's history of carrying out its stated intentions.

- Review of written plans and other documentation, including, where applicable, formally approved budgets, authorizations or minutes.

- Inquiry of management about its reasons for a particular course of action.

- Review of events occurring subsequent to the date of the financial statements and up to the date of the auditor's report.

- Evaluation of the entity's ability to carry out a particular course of action given the entity's economic circumstances, including the implications of its existing commitments.

Certain financial reporting frameworks, however, may not permit management's intentions or plans to be taken into account when making an accounting estimate. This is often the case for fair value accounting estimates because their measurement objective requires that assumptions reflect those used by marketplace participants.

A81   Matters that the auditor may consider in evaluating the reasonableness of assumptions used by management underlying fair value accounting estimates, in addition to those discussed above where applicable, may include, for example:

- Where relevant, whether and, if so, how management has incorporated market-specific inputs into the development of assumptions.

- Whether the assumptions are consistent with observable market conditions, and the characteristics of the asset or liability being measured at fair value.

- Whether the sources of market-participant assumptions are relevant and reliable, and how management has selected the assumptions to use when a number of different market participant assumptions exist.

- Where appropriate, whether and, if so, how management considered assumptions used in, or information about, comparable transactions, assets or liabilities.

A82   Further, fair value accounting estimates may comprise observable inputs as well as unobservable inputs. Where fair value accounting estimates are based on unobservable inputs, matters that the auditor may consider include, for example, how management supports the following:

● The identification of the characteristics of marketplace participants relevant to the accounting estimate.

● Modifications it has made to its own assumptions to reflect its view of assumptions marketplace participants would use.

● Whether it has incorporated the best information available in the circumstances.

● Where applicable, how its assumptions take account of comparable transactions, assets or liabilities.

If there are unobservable inputs, it is more likely that the auditor's evaluation of the assumptions will need to be combined with other responses to assessed risks in paragraph 13 in order to obtain sufficient appropriate audit evidence. In such cases, it may be necessary for the auditor to perform other audit procedures, for example, examining documentation supporting the review and approval of the accounting estimate by appropriate levels of management and, where appropriate, by those charged with governance.

In evaluating the reasonableness of the assumptions supporting an accounting   **A83**
estimate, the auditor may identify one or more significant assumptions. If so, it may indicate that the accounting estimate has high estimation uncertainty and may, therefore, give rise to a significant risk. Additional responses to significant risks are described in paragraphs A102–A115.

Testing the Operating Effectiveness of Controls (Ref: Para. 13(c))

Testing the operating effectiveness of the controls over how management made the   **A84**
accounting estimate may be an appropriate response when management's process has been well-designed, implemented and maintained, for example:

● Controls exist for the review and approval of the accounting estimates by appropriate levels of management and, where appropriate, by those charged with governance.

● The accounting estimate is derived from the routine processing of data by the entity's accounting system.

Testing the operating effectiveness of the controls is required when: **A85**

(a) The auditor's assessment of risks of material misstatement at the assertion level includes an expectation that controls over the process are operating effectively; or

(b) Substantive procedures alone do not provide sufficient appropriate audit evidence at the assertion level.[19]

Considerations specific to smaller entities

Controls over the process to make an accounting estimate may exist in smaller   **A86**
entities, but the formality with which they operate varies. Further, smaller entities may determine that certain types of controls are not necessary because of active management involvement in the financial reporting process. In the case of very small entities, however, there may not be many controls that the auditor can

---

[19] *ISA (UK) 330 (Revised June 2016), paragraph 8.*

identify. For this reason, the auditor's response to the assessed risks is likely to be substantive in nature, with the auditor performing one or more of the other responses in paragraph 13.

Developing a Point Estimate or Range
(Ref: Para. 13(d))

A87   Developing a point estimate or a range to evaluate management's point estimate may be an appropriate response where, for example:

- An accounting estimate is not derived from the routine processing of data by the accounting system.

- The auditor's review of similar accounting estimates made in the prior period financial statements suggests that management's current period process is unlikely to be effective.

- The entity's controls within and over management's processes for determining accounting estimates are not well designed or properly implemented.

- Events or transactions between the period end and the date of the auditor's report contradict management's point estimate.

- There are alternative sources of relevant data available to the auditor which can be used in making a point estimate or a range.

A88   Even where the entity's controls are well designed and properly implemented, developing a point estimate or a range may be an effective or efficient response to the assessed risks. In other situations, the auditor may consider this approach as part of determining whether further procedures are necessary and, if so, their nature and extent.

A89   The approach taken by the auditor in developing either a point estimate or a range may vary based on what is considered most effective in the circumstances. For example, the auditor may initially develop a preliminary point estimate, and then assess its sensitivity to changes in assumptions to ascertain a range with which to evaluate management's point estimate. Alternatively, the auditor may begin by developing a range for purposes of determining, where possible, a point estimate.

A90   The ability of the auditor to make a point estimate, as opposed to a range, depends on several factors, including the model used, the nature and extent of data available and the estimation uncertainty involved with the accounting estimate. Further, the decision to develop a point estimate or range may be influenced by the applicable financial reporting framework, which may prescribe the point estimate that is to be used after consideration of the alternative outcomes and assumptions, or prescribe a specific measurement method (for example, the use of a discounted probability-weighted expected value).

A91   The auditor may develop a point estimate or a range in a number of ways, for example, by:

- Using a model, for example, one that is commercially available for use in a particular sector or industry, or a proprietary or auditor-developed model.

- Further developing management's consideration of alternative assumptions or outcomes, for example, by introducing a different set of assumptions.

- Employing or engaging a person with specialized expertise to develop or execute the model, or to provide relevant assumptions.

- Making reference to other comparable conditions, transactions or events, or, where relevant, markets for comparable assets or liabilities.

Understanding Management's Assumptions or Method
(Ref: Para. 13(d)(i))

When the auditor makes a point estimate or a range and uses assumptions or a method different from those used by management, paragraph 13(d)(i) requires the auditor to obtain a sufficient understanding of the assumptions or method used by management in making the accounting estimate. This understanding provides the auditor with information that may be relevant to the auditor's development of an appropriate point estimate or range. Further, it assists the auditor to understand and evaluate any significant differences from management's point estimate. For example, a difference may arise because the auditor used different, but equally valid, assumptions as compared with those used by management. This may reveal that the accounting estimate is highly sensitive to certain assumptions and therefore subject to high estimation uncertainty, indicating that the accounting estimate may be a significant risk. Alternatively, a difference may arise as a result of a factual error made by management. Depending on the circumstances, the auditor may find it helpful in drawing conclusions to discuss with management the basis for the assumptions used and their validity, and the difference, if any, in the approach taken to making the accounting estimate. **A92**

Narrowing a Range
(Ref: Para. 13(d)(ii))

When the auditor concludes that it is appropriate to use a range to evaluate the reasonableness of management's point estimate (the auditor's range), paragraph 13(d)(ii) requires that range to encompass all "reasonable outcomes" rather than all possible outcomes. The range cannot be one that comprises all possible outcomes if it is to be useful, as such a range would be too wide to be effective for purposes of the audit. The auditor's range is useful and effective when it is sufficiently narrow to enable the auditor to conclude whether the accounting estimate is misstated. **A93**

Ordinarily, a range that has been narrowed to be equal to or less than performance materiality is adequate for the purposes of evaluating the reasonableness of management's point estimate. However, particularly in certain industries, it may not be possible to narrow the range to below such an amount. This does not necessarily preclude recognition of the accounting estimate. It may indicate, however, that the estimation uncertainty associated with the accounting estimate is such that it gives rise to a significant risk. Additional responses to significant risks are described in paragraphs A102–A115. **A94**

Narrowing the range to a position where all outcomes within the range are considered reasonable may be achieved by: **A95**

(a) Eliminating from the range those outcomes at the extremities of the range judged by the auditor to be unlikely to occur; and

(b) Continuing to narrow the range, based on audit evidence available, until the auditor concludes that all outcomes within the range are considered reasonable. In some rare cases, the auditor may be able to narrow the range until the audit evidence indicates a point estimate.

Considering whether Specialized Skills or Knowledge Are Required
(Ref: Para. 14)

A96   In planning the audit, the auditor is required to ascertain the nature, timing and extent of resources necessary to perform the audit engagement.[20] This may include, as necessary, the involvement of those with specialized skills or knowledge. In addition, ISA (UK) 220 (Revised June 2016) requires the engagement partner to be satisfied that the engagement team, and any auditor's external experts who are not part of the engagement team, collectively have the appropriate competence and capabilities to perform the audit engagement.[21] During the course of the audit of accounting estimates the auditor may identify, in light of the experience of the auditor and the circumstances of the engagement, the need for specialized skills or knowledge to be applied in relation to one or more aspects of the accounting estimates.

A97   Matters that may affect the auditor's consideration of whether specialized skills or knowledge is required include, for example:

● The nature of the underlying asset, liability or component of equity in a particular business or industry (for example, mineral deposits, agricultural assets, complex financial instruments).

● A high degree of estimation uncertainty.

● Complex calculations or specialized models are involved, for example, when estimating fair values when there is no observable market.

● The complexity of the requirements of the applicable financial reporting framework relevant to accounting estimates, including whether there are areas known to be subject to differing interpretation or practice is inconsistent or developing.

● The procedures the auditor intends to undertake in responding to assessed risks.

A98   For the majority of accounting estimates, even when there is estimation uncertainty, it is unlikely that specialized skills or knowledge will be required. For example, it is unlikely that specialized skills or knowledge would be necessary for an auditor to evaluate an allowance for doubtful accounts.

A99   However, the auditor may not possess the specialized skills or knowledge required when the matter involved is in a field other than accounting or auditing and may need to obtain it from an auditor's expert. ISA (UK) 620 (Revised June 2016)[22] establishes requirements and provides guidance in determining the need to employ or engage an auditor's expert and the auditor's responsibilities when using the work of an auditor's expert.

A100   Further, in some cases, the auditor may conclude that it is necessary to obtain specialized skills or knowledge related to specific areas of accounting or auditing. Individuals with such skills or knowledge may be employed by the auditor's firm or engaged from an external organization outside of the auditor's firm. Where such individuals perform audit procedures on the engagement, they are part of the engagement team and accordingly, they are subject to the requirements in ISA (UK) 220 (Revised June 2016).

---

[20] *ISA (UK) 300 (Revised June 2016), Planning an Audit of Financial Statements, paragraph 8(e).*

[21] *ISA (UK) 220 (Revised June 2016), Quality Control for an Audit of Financial Statements, paragraph 14.*

[22] *ISA (UK) 620 (Revised June 2016), Using the Work of an Auditor's Expert.*

Depending on the auditor's understanding and experience of working with the   **A101**
auditor's expert or those other individuals with specialized skills or knowledge,
the auditor may consider it appropriate to discuss matters such as the requirements
of the applicable financial reporting framework with the individuals involved to
establish that their work is relevant for audit purposes.

Further Substantive Procedures to Respond to Significant Risks
(Ref: Para. 15)

In auditing accounting estimates that give rise to significant risks, the auditor's   **A102**
further substantive procedures are focused on the evaluation of:

(a)   How management has assessed the effect of estimation uncertainty on the
accounting estimate, and the effect such uncertainty may have on the
appropriateness of the recognition of the accounting estimate in the
financial statements; and

(b)   The adequacy of related disclosures.

Estimation Uncertainty

Management's Consideration of Estimation Uncertainty
(Ref: Para. 15(a))

Management may evaluate alternative assumptions or outcomes of the accounting   **A103**
estimates through a number of methods, depending on the circumstances. One
possible method used by management is to undertake a sensitivity analysis. This
might involve determining how the monetary amount of an accounting estimate
varies with different assumptions. Even for accounting estimates measured at fair
value there can be variation because different market participants will use different
assumptions. A sensitivity analysis could lead to the development of a number of
outcome scenarios, sometimes characterized as a range of outcomes by
management, such as "pessimistic" and "optimistic" scenarios.

A sensitivity analysis may demonstrate that an accounting estimate is not sensitive   **A104**
to changes in particular assumptions. Alternatively, it may demonstrate that the
accounting estimate is sensitive to one or more assumptions that then become the
focus of the auditor's attention.

This is not intended to suggest that one particular method of addressing estimation   **A105**
uncertainty (such as sensitivity analysis) is more suitable than another, or that
management's consideration of alternative assumptions or outcomes needs to be
conducted through a detailed process supported by extensive documentation.
Rather, it is whether management has assessed how estimation uncertainty may
affect the accounting estimate that is important, not the specific manner in which it
is done. Accordingly, where management has not considered alternative
assumptions or outcomes, it may be necessary for the auditor to discuss with
management, and request support for, how it has addressed the effects of
estimation uncertainty on the accounting estimate.

Considerations specific to smaller entities

Smaller entities may use simple means to assess the estimation uncertainty. In   **A106**
addition to the auditor's review of available documentation, the auditor may
obtain other audit evidence of management consideration of alternative
assumptions or outcomes by inquiry of management. In addition, management
may not have the expertise to consider alternative outcomes or otherwise address

the estimation uncertainty of the accounting estimate. In such cases, the auditor may explain to management the process or the different methods available for doing so, and the documentation thereof. This would not, however, change the responsibilities of management for the preparation of the financial statements.

Significant Assumptions
(Ref: Para. 15(b))

A107 An assumption used in making an accounting estimate may be deemed to be significant if a reasonable variation in the assumption would materially affect the measurement of the accounting estimate.

A108 Support for significant assumptions derived from management's knowledge may be obtained from management's continuing processes of strategic analysis and risk management. Even without formal established processes, such as may be the case in smaller entities, the auditor may be able to evaluate the assumptions through inquiries of and discussions with management, along with other audit procedures in order to obtain sufficient appropriate audit evidence.

A109 The auditor's considerations in evaluating assumptions made by management are described in paragraphs A77–A83.

Management Intent and Ability
(Ref: Para. 15(c))

A110 The auditor's considerations in relation to assumptions made by management and management's intent and ability are described in paragraphs A13 and A80.

Development of a Range
(Ref: Para. 16)

A111 In preparing the financial statements, management may be satisfied that it has adequately addressed the effects of estimation uncertainty on the accounting estimates that give rise to significant risks. In some circumstances, however, the auditor may view the efforts of management as inadequate. This may be the case, for example, where, in the auditor's judgment:

● Sufficient appropriate audit evidence could not be obtained through the auditor's evaluation of how management has addressed the effects of estimation uncertainty.

● It is necessary to explore further the degree of estimation uncertainty associated with an accounting estimate, for example, where the auditor is aware of wide variation in outcomes for similar accounting estimates in similar circumstances.

● It is unlikely that other audit evidence can be obtained, for example, through the review of events occurring up to the date of the auditor's report.

● Indicators of management bias in the making of accounting estimates may exist.

A112 The auditor's considerations in determining a range for this purpose are described in paragraphs A87–A95.

Recognition and Measurement Criteria

Recognition of the Accounting Estimates in the Financial Statements
(Ref: Para. 17(a))

Where management has recognized an accounting estimate in the financial   **A113**
statements, the focus of the auditor's evaluation is on whether the measurement
of the accounting estimate is sufficiently reliable to meet the recognition criteria of
the applicable financial reporting framework.

With respect to accounting estimates that have not been recognized, the focus of   **A114**
the auditor's evaluation is on whether the recognition criteria of the applicable
financial reporting framework have in fact been met. Even where an accounting
estimate has not been recognized, and the auditor concludes that this treatment is
appropriate, there may be a need for disclosure of the circumstances in the notes to
the financial statements. Where applicable, the auditor may also determine that an
accounting estimate that has been identified as having a high estimation
uncertainty is a key audit matter to be communicated in the auditor's report in
accordance with ISA (UK) 701,[23] or may consider it necessary to include an
Emphasis of Matter paragraph in the auditor's report (see ISA (UK) 706 (Revised
June 2016)[24]). If the matter is determined to be a key audit matter, ISA (UK) 706
(Revised June 2016) prohibits the auditor from including an Emphasis of Matter
paragraph in the auditor's report.[25]

Measurement Basis for the Accounting Estimates
(Ref: Para. 17(b))

With respect to fair value accounting estimates, some financial reporting   **A115**
frameworks presume that fair value can be measured reliably as a prerequisite
to either requiring or permitting fair value measurements and disclosures. In some
cases, this presumption may be overcome when, for example, there is no
appropriate method or basis for measurement. In such cases, the focus of the
auditor's evaluation is on whether management's basis for overcoming the
presumption relating to the use of fair value set forth under the applicable
financial reporting framework is appropriate.

**Evaluating the Reasonableness of the Accounting Estimates, and Determining
Misstatements**
(Ref: Para. 18)

Based on the audit evidence obtained, the auditor may conclude that the evidence   **A116**
points to an accounting estimate that differs from management's point estimate.
Where the audit evidence supports a point estimate, the difference between the
auditor's point estimate and management's point estimate constitutes a
misstatement. Where the auditor has concluded that using the auditor's range
provides sufficient appropriate audit evidence, a management point estimate that
lies outside the auditor's range would not be supported by audit evidence. In such
cases, the misstatement is no less than the difference between management's point
estimate and the nearest point of the auditor's range.

---

[23] *ISA (UK) 701, Communicating Key Audit Matters in the Independent Auditor's Report.*

[24] *ISA (UK) 706 (Revised June 2016), Emphasis of Matter Paragraphs and Other Matter Paragraphs in the
Independent Auditor's Report.*

[25] *ISA (UK) 706 (Revised June 2016), paragraph 8(b).*

A117   Where management has changed an accounting estimate, or the method in making it, from the prior period based on a subjective assessment that there has been a change in circumstances, the auditor may conclude based on the audit evidence that the accounting estimate is misstated as a result of an arbitrary change by management, or may regard it as an indicator of possible management bias (see paragraphs A124–A125).

A118   ISA (UK) 450 (Revised June 2016)[26] provides guidance on distinguishing misstatements for purposes of the auditor's evaluation of the effect of uncorrected misstatements on the financial statements. In relation to accounting estimates, a misstatement, whether caused by fraud or error, may arise as a result of:

- Misstatements about which there is no doubt (factual misstatements).

- Differences arising from management's judgments concerning accounting estimates that the auditor considers unreasonable, or the selection or application of accounting policies that the auditor considers inappropriate (judgmental misstatements).

- The auditor's best estimate of misstatements in populations, involving the projection of misstatements identified in audit samples to the entire populations from which the samples were drawn (projected misstatements).

In some cases involving accounting estimates, a misstatement could arise as a result of a combination of these circumstances, making separate identification difficult or impossible.

A119   Evaluating the reasonableness of accounting estimates and related disclosures included in the notes to the financial statements, whether required by the applicable financial reporting framework or disclosed voluntarily, involves essentially the same types of considerations applied when auditing an accounting estimate recognized in the financial statements.

Disclosures Related to Accounting Estimates

Disclosures in Accordance with the Applicable Financial Reporting Framework (Ref: Para. 19)

A120   The presentation of financial statements in accordance with the applicable financial reporting framework includes adequate disclosure of material matters. The applicable financial reporting framework may permit, or prescribe, disclosures related to accounting estimates, and some entities may disclose voluntarily additional information in the notes to the financial statements. These disclosures may include, for example:

- The assumptions used.

- The method of estimation used, including any applicable model.

- The basis for the selection of the method of estimation.

- The effect of any changes to the method of estimation from the prior period.

- The sources and implications of estimation uncertainty.

Such disclosures are relevant to users in understanding the accounting estimates recognized or disclosed in the financial statements, and sufficient appropriate audit evidence needs to be obtained about whether the disclosures are in accordance with the requirements of the applicable financial reporting framework.

---

[26] *ISA (UK) 450 (Revised June 2016), Evaluation of Misstatements Identified during the Audit.*

In some cases, the applicable financial reporting framework may require specific   **A121**
disclosures regarding uncertainties. For example, some financial reporting
frameworks prescribe:

● The disclosure of key assumptions and other sources of estimation
   uncertainty that have a significant risk of causing a material adjustment to
   the carrying amounts of assets and liabilities. Such requirements may be
   described using terms such as "Key Sources of Estimation Uncertainty" or
   "Critical Accounting Estimates."

● The disclosure of the range of possible outcomes, and the assumptions used
   in determining the range.

● The disclosure of information regarding the significance of fair value
   accounting estimates to the entity's financial position and performance.

● Qualitative disclosures such as the exposures to risk and how they arise, the
   entity's objectives, policies and procedures for managing the risk and the
   methods used to measure the risk and any changes from the previous period
   of these qualitative concepts.

● Quantitative disclosures such as the extent to which the entity is exposed to
   risk, based on information provided internally to the entity's key
   management personnel, including credit risk, liquidity risk and market risk.

*Disclosures of Estimation Uncertainty for Accounting Estimates that Give Rise to
Significant Risks*
(Ref: Para. 20)

In relation to accounting estimates having significant risk, even where the   **A122**
disclosures are in accordance with the applicable financial reporting framework,
the auditor may conclude that the disclosure of estimation uncertainty is
inadequate in light of the circumstances and facts involved. The auditor's
evaluation of the adequacy of disclosure of estimation uncertainty increases in
importance the greater the range of possible outcomes of the accounting estimate
is in relation to materiality (see related discussion in paragraph A94).

In some cases, the auditor may consider it appropriate to encourage management   **A123**
to describe, in the notes to the financial statements, the circumstances relating to
the estimation uncertainty. ISA (UK) 705 (Revised June 2016)[27] provides
guidance on the implications for the auditor's opinion when the auditor believes
that management's disclosure of estimation uncertainty in the financial statements
is inadequate or misleading.

Indicators of Possible Management Bias
(Ref: Para. 21)

During the audit, the auditor may become aware of judgments and decisions made   **A124**
by management which give rise to indicators of possible management bias. Such
indicators may affect the auditor's conclusion as to whether the auditor's risk
assessment and related responses remain appropriate, and the auditor may need to
consider the implications for the rest of the audit. Further, they may affect the
auditor's evaluation of whether the financial statements as a whole are free from
material misstatement, as discussed in ISA (UK) 700 (Revised June 2016).[28]

---

[27] *ISA (UK) 705 (Revised June 2016), Modifications to the Opinion in the Independent Auditor's Report.*

[28] *ISA (UK) 700 (Revised June 2016), Forming an Opinion and Reporting on Financial Statements.*

A125   Examples of indicators of possible management bias with respect to accounting estimates include:

- Changes in an accounting estimate, or the method for making it, where management has made a subjective assessment that there has been a change in circumstances.

- Use of an entity's own assumptions for fair value accounting estimates when they are inconsistent with observable marketplace assumptions.

- Selection or construction of significant assumptions that yield a point estimate favorable for management objectives.

- Selection of a point estimate that may indicate a pattern of optimism or pessimism.

Written Representations
(Ref: Para. 22)

A126   ISA (UK) 580[29] discusses the use of written representations. Depending on the nature, materiality and extent of estimation uncertainty, written representations about accounting estimates recognized or disclosed in the financial statements may include representations:

- About the appropriateness of the measurement processes, including related assumptions and models, used by management in determining accounting estimates in the context of the applicable financial reporting framework, and the consistency in application of the processes.

- That the assumptions appropriately reflect management's intent and ability to carry out specific courses of action on behalf of the entity, where relevant to the accounting estimates and disclosures.

- That disclosures related to accounting estimates are complete and appropriate under the applicable financial reporting framework.

- That no subsequent event requires adjustment to the accounting estimates and disclosures included in the financial statements.

A127   For those accounting estimates not recognized or disclosed in the financial statements, written representations may also include representations about:

- The appropriateness of the basis used by management for determining that the recognition or disclosure criteria of the applicable financial reporting framework have not been met (see paragraph A114).

- The appropriateness of the basis used by management to overcome the presumption relating to the use of fair value set forth under the entity's applicable financial reporting framework, for those accounting estimates not measured or disclosed at fair value (see paragraph A115).

Documentation
(Ref: Para. 23)

A128   Documentation of indicators of possible management bias identified during the audit assists the auditor in concluding whether the auditor's risk assessment and related responses remain appropriate, and in evaluating whether the financial statements as a whole are free from material misstatement. See paragraph A125 for examples of indicators of possible management bias.

---

[29] *ISA (UK) 580, Written Representations.*

Appendix

(Ref: Para. A1)

Fair Value Measurements and Disclosures under Different Financial Reporting Frameworks

The purpose of this appendix is only to provide a general discussion of fair value measurements and disclosures under different financial reporting frameworks, for background and context.

(1)   Different financial reporting frameworks require or permit a variety of fair value measurements and disclosures in financial statements. They also vary in the level of guidance that they provide on the basis for measuring assets and liabilities or the related disclosures. Some financial reporting frameworks give prescriptive guidance, others give general guidance, and some give no guidance at all. In addition, certain industry-specific measurement and disclosure practices for fair values also exist.

(2)   Definitions of fair value may differ among financial reporting frameworks, or for different assets, liabilities or disclosures within a particular framework. For example, International Accounting Standard (IAS) 39[1a] defines fair value as "the amount for which an asset could be exchanged, or a liability settled, between knowledgeable, willing parties in an arm's length transaction." The concept of fair value ordinarily assumes a current transaction, rather than settlement at some past or future date. Accordingly, the process of measuring fair value would be a search for the estimated price at which that transaction would occur. Additionally, different financial reporting frameworks may use such terms as "entity-specific value," "value in use," or similar terms, but may still fall within the concept of fair value in this ISA (UK).

(3)   Financial reporting frameworks may treat changes in fair value measurements that occur over time in different ways. For example, a particular financial reporting framework may require that changes in fair value measurements of certain assets or liabilities be reflected directly in equity, while such changes might be reflected in income under another framework. In some frameworks, the determination of whether to use fair value accounting or how it is applied is influenced by management's intent to carry out certain courses of action with respect to the specific asset or liability.

(4)   Different financial reporting frameworks may require certain specific fair value measurements and disclosures in financial statements and prescribe or permit them in varying degrees. The financial reporting frameworks may:

- Prescribe measurement, presentation and disclosure requirements for certain information included in the financial statements or for information disclosed in notes to financial statements or presented as supplementary information;

- Permit certain measurements using fair values at the option of an entity or only when certain criteria have been met;

[1a] *IAS 39, Financial Instruments: Recognition and Measurement.*

- Prescribe a specific method for determining fair value, for example, through the use of an independent appraisal or specified ways of using discounted cash flows;

- Permit a choice of method for determining fair value from among several alternative methods (the criteria for selection may or may not be provided by the financial reporting framework); or

- Provide no guidance on the fair value measurements or disclosures of fair value other than their use being evident through custom or practice, for example, an industry practice.

(5)   Some financial reporting frameworks presume that fair value can be measured reliably for assets or liabilities as a prerequisite to either requiring or permitting fair value measurements or disclosures. In some cases, this presumption may be overcome when an asset or liability does not have a quoted market price in an active market and for which other methods of reasonably estimating fair value are clearly inappropriate or unworkable. Some financial reporting frameworks may specify a fair value hierarchy that distinguishes inputs for use in arriving at fair values ranging from those that involve clearly "observable inputs" based on quoted prices and active markets and those "unobservable inputs" that involve an entity's own judgments about assumptions that marketplace participants would use.

(6)   Some financial reporting frameworks require certain specified adjustments or modifications to valuation information, or other considerations unique to a particular asset or liability. For example, accounting for investment properties may require adjustments to be made to an appraised market value, such as adjustments for estimated closing costs on sale, adjustments related to the property's condition and location, and other matters. Similarly, if the market for a particular asset is not an active market, published price quotations may have to be adjusted or modified to arrive at a more suitable measure of fair value. For example, quoted market prices may not be indicative of fair value if there is infrequent activity in the market, the market is not well established, or small volumes of units are traded relative to the aggregate number of trading units in existence. Accordingly, such market prices may have to be adjusted or modified. Alternative sources of market information may be needed to make such adjustments or modifications. Further, in some cases, collateral assigned (for example, when collateral is assigned for certain types of investment in debt) may need to be considered in determining the fair value or possible impairment of an asset or liability.

(7)   In most financial reporting frameworks, underlying the concept of fair value measurements is a presumption that the entity is a going concern without any intention or need to liquidate, curtail materially the scale of its operations, or undertake a transaction on adverse terms. Therefore, in this case, fair value would not be the amount that an entity would receive or pay in a forced transaction, involuntary liquidation, or distress sale. On the other hand, general economic conditions or economic conditions specific to certain industries may cause illiquidity in the marketplace and require fair values to be predicated upon depressed prices, potentially significantly depressed prices. An entity, however, may need to take its current economic or operating situation into account in determining the fair values of its assets and liabilities if prescribed or permitted to do so by its financial reporting framework and such framework may or may not specify how that is done.

For example, management's plan to dispose of an asset on an accelerated basis to meet specific business objectives may be relevant to the determination of the fair value of that asset.

Prevalence of Fair Value Measurements

(8) Measurements and disclosures based on fair value are becoming increasingly prevalent in financial reporting frameworks. Fair values may occur in, and affect the determination of, financial statements in a number of ways, including the measurement at fair value of the following:

- Specific assets or liabilities, such as marketable securities or liabilities to settle an obligation under a financial instrument, routinely or periodically "marked-to-market."

- Specific components of equity, for example when accounting for the recognition, measurement and presentation of certain financial instruments with equity features, such as a bond convertible by the holder into common shares of the issuer.

- Specific assets or liabilities acquired in a business combination. For example, the initial determination of goodwill arising on the purchase of an entity in a business combination usually is based on the fair value measurement of the identifiable assets and liabilities acquired and the fair value of the consideration given.

- Specific assets or liabilities adjusted to fair value on a one-time basis. Some financial reporting frameworks may require the use of a fair value measurement to quantify an adjustment to an asset or a group of assets as part of an asset impairment determination, for example, a test of impairment of goodwill acquired in a business combination based on the fair value of a defined operating entity or reporting unit, the value of which is then allocated among the entity's or unit's group of assets and liabilities in order to derive an implied goodwill for comparison to the recorded goodwill.

- Aggregations of assets and liabilities. In some circumstances, the measurement of a class or group of assets or liabilities calls for an aggregation of fair values of some of the individual assets or liabilities in such class or group. For example, under an entity's applicable financial reporting framework, the measurement of a diversified loan portfolio might be determined based on the fair value of some categories of loans comprising the portfolio.

- Information disclosed in notes to financial statements or presented as supplementary information, but not recognized in the financial statements.

ISA (UK) 540 (Revised December 2018) Auditing Accounting Estimates and Related Disclosures

(Effective for audits of financial statements for periods beginning on or after 15 December 2019)

Contents

Paragraphs

Introduction
Scope of this ISA (UK) — 1
Nature of accounting estimates — 2 - 3
Key Concepts of This ISA (UK) — 4 - 9
Effective date — 10

Objective — 11

Definitions — 12

Requirements
Risk assessment procedures and related activities — 13 - 15
Identifying and assessing the risks of material misstatement — 16 - 17
Responses to the assessed risks of material misstatement — 18 - 30
Disclosures related to accounting estimates — 31
Indicators of possible management bias — 32 - 32D-1
Overall evaluation based on audit procedures performed — 33 - 36
Written representations — 37
Communication with those charged with governance, management, or other relevant parties — 38
Documentation — 39

Application and other explanatory material
Nature of accounting estimates — A1 - A7
Key concepts of this ISA (UK) — A8 - A13
Definitions — A14 - A18
Risk assessment procedures and related activities — A19 - A63
Identifying and assessing the risks of material misstatement — A64 - A80
Responses to the assessed risks of material misstatement — A81 - A132
Indicators of possible management bias — A133 - A136
Overall evaluation based on audit procedures performed — A137 - A144
Written representations — A145
Communication with those charged with governance, management or other relevant parties — A146 - A148
Documentation — A149 - A152

Appendix 1 – Inherent risk factors

Appendix 2 – Communications with those charged with governance

Annexure – Conforming and consequential amendments to other ISAS (UK)

Editorial note – This standard is effective for audits of financial statements for periods beginning on or after 15 December 2019.

International Standard on Auditing (UK) (ISA (UK)) 540 (Revised December 2018), *Auditing Accounting Estimates and Related Disclosures*, should be read in conjunction with ISA (UK) 200 (Revised June 2016), *Overall Objectives of the Independent Auditor and the Conduct of an Audit in Accordance with International Standards on Auditing (UK).*

Introduction

Scope of this ISA (UK)

This International Standard on Auditing (UK) (ISA (UK)) deals with the auditor's 1
responsibilities relating to accounting estimates and related disclosures in an audit
of financial statements. Specifically, it includes requirements and guidance that
refer to, or expand on, how ISA (UK) 315 (Revised June 2016),[1] ISA (UK) 330
(Revised July 2017),[2] ISA (UK) 450 (Revised June 2016),[3] ISA (UK) 500[4] and
other relevant ISAs (UK) are to be applied in relation to accounting estimates and
related disclosures. It also includes requirements and guidance on the evaluation
of misstatements of accounting estimates and related disclosures, and indicators of
possible management bias.

Nature of Accounting Estimates

Accounting estimates vary widely in nature and are required to be made by 2
management when the monetary amounts cannot be directly observed. The
measurement of these monetary amounts is subject to estimation uncertainty,
which reflects inherent limitations in knowledge or data. These limitations give
rise to inherent subjectivity and variation in the measurement outcomes. The
process of making accounting estimates involves selecting and applying a method
using assumptions and data, which requires judgment by management and can
give rise to complexity in measurement. The effects of complexity, subjectivity or
other inherent risk factors on the measurement of these monetary amounts affects
their susceptibility to misstatement. (Ref: Para. A1–A6, Appendix 1)

Although this ISA (UK) applies to all accounting estimates, the degree to which an 3
accounting estimate is subject to estimation uncertainty will vary substantially.
The nature, timing and extent of the risk assessment and further audit procedures
required by this ISA (UK) will vary in relation to the estimation uncertainty and
the assessment of the related risks of material misstatement. For certain accounting
estimates, estimation uncertainty may be very low, based on their nature, and the
complexity and subjectivity involved in making them may also be very low. For
such accounting estimates, the risk assessment procedures and further audit
procedures required by this ISA (UK) would not be expected to be extensive.
When estimation uncertainty, complexity or subjectivity are very high, such
procedures would be expected to be much more extensive. This ISA (UK)
contains guidance on how the requirements of this ISA (UK) can be scaled.
(Ref: Para. A7)

Key Concepts of This ISA (UK)

This ISA (UK) requires a separate assessment of inherent risk for purposes of 4
assessing the risks of material misstatement at the assertion level for accounting
estimates. Depending on the nature of a particular accounting estimate, the
susceptibility of an assertion to a misstatement that could be material may be
subject to or affected by estimation uncertainty, complexity, subjectivity or other

---

[1] *ISA (UK) 315 (Revised June 2016), Identifying and Assessing the Risks of Material Misstatement through Understanding the Entity and Its Environment.*

[2] *ISA (UK) 330 (Revised July 2017), The Auditor's Responses to Assessed Risks.*

[3] *ISA (UK) 450 (Revised June 2016), Evaluation of Misstatements Identified during the Audit.*

[4] *ISA (UK) 500, Audit Evidence.*

inherent risk factors, and the interrelationship among them. As explained in ISA (UK) 200 (Revised June 2016),[5] inherent risk is higher for some assertions and related classes of transactions, account balances and disclosures than for others. Accordingly, the assessment of inherent risk depends on the degree to which the inherent risk factors affect the likelihood or magnitude of misstatement, and varies on a scale that is referred to in this ISA (UK) as the spectrum of inherent risk. (Ref: Para. A8–A9, A65–A66, Appendix 1)

5   This ISA (UK) refers to relevant requirements in ISA (UK) 315 (Revised June 2016) and ISA (UK) 330 (Revised July 2017), and provides related guidance, to emphasize the importance of the auditor's decisions about controls relating to accounting estimates, including decisions about whether:

- There are controls relevant to the audit, for which the auditor is required to evaluate their design and determine whether they have been implemented.

- To test the operating effectiveness of relevant controls.

6   This ISA (UK) also requires a separate assessment of control risk when assessing the risks of material misstatement at the assertion level for accounting estimates. In assessing control risk, the auditor takes into account whether the auditor's further audit procedures contemplate planned reliance on the operating effectiveness of controls. If the auditor does not perform tests of controls, the auditor's assessment of the risk of material misstatement at the assertion level cannot be reduced for the effective operation of controls with respect to the particular assertion.[6] (Ref: Para. A10)

7   This ISA (UK) emphasizes that the auditor's further audit procedures (including, where appropriate, tests of controls) need to be responsive to the reasons for the assessed risks of material misstatement at the assertion level, taking into account the effect of one or more inherent risk factors and the auditor's assessment of control risk.

8   The exercise of professional skepticism in relation to accounting estimates is affected by the auditor's consideration of inherent risk factors, and its importance increases when accounting estimates are subject to a greater degree of estimation uncertainty or are affected to a greater degree by complexity, subjectivity or other inherent risk factors. Similarly, the exercise of professional skepticism is important when there is greater susceptibility to misstatement due to management bias or fraud. (Ref: Para. A11)

9   This ISA (UK) requires the auditor to evaluate, based on the audit procedures performed and the audit evidence obtained, whether the accounting estimates and related disclosures are reasonable[7] in the context of the applicable financial reporting framework, or are misstated. For purposes of this ISA (UK), reasonable in the context of the applicable financial reporting framework means that the relevant requirements of the applicable financial reporting framework have been applied appropriately, including those that address: (Ref: Para. A12–A13, A139–A144)

---

[5] *ISA (UK) 200 (Revised June 2016), Overall Objectives of the Independent Auditor and the Conduct of an Audit in Accordance with International Standards on Auditing (UK), paragraph A40.*

[6] *ISA (UK) 530, Audit Sampling, Appendix 3.*

[7] *See also ISA (UK) 700 (Revised June 2016), Forming an Opinion and Reporting on Financial Statements, paragraph 13(c).*

- The making of the accounting estimate, including the selection of the method, assumptions and data in view of the nature of the accounting estimate and the facts and circumstances of the entity;
- The selection of management's point estimate; and
- The disclosures about the accounting estimate, including disclosures about how the accounting estimate was developed and that explain the nature, extent, and sources of estimation uncertainty.

Effective Date

This ISA (UK) is effective for audits of financial statements for periods beginning on or after 15 December 2019. Early adoption is permitted.   **10**

Objective

The objective of the auditor is to obtain sufficient appropriate audit evidence about   **11** whether accounting estimates and related disclosures in the financial statements are reasonable in the context of the applicable financial reporting framework.

Definitions

For purposes of the ISAs (UK), the following terms have the meanings attributed   **12** below:

(a) Accounting estimate – A monetary amount for which the measurement, in accordance with the requirements of the applicable financial reporting framework, is subject to estimation uncertainty. (Ref: Para. A14)

(b) Auditor's point estimate or auditor's range – An amount, or range of amounts, respectively, developed by the auditor in evaluating management's point estimate. (Ref: Para. A15)

(c) Estimation uncertainty – Susceptibility to an inherent lack of precision in measurement. (Ref: Para. A16, Appendix 1)

(d) Management bias – A lack of neutrality by management in the preparation of information. (Ref: Para. A17)

(e) Management's point estimate – The amount selected by management for recognition or disclosure in the financial statements as an accounting estimate.

(f) Outcome of an accounting estimate – The actual monetary amount that results from the resolution of the transaction(s), event(s) or condition(s) addressed by an accounting estimate. (Ref: Para. A18)

Requirements

Risk Assessment Procedures and Related Activities

When obtaining an understanding of the entity and its environment, including the   **13** entity's internal control, as required by ISA (UK) 315 (Revised June 2016),[8] the

---

[8] *ISA (UK) 315 (Revised June 2016), paragraphs 3, 5–6, 9, 11–12, 15–17, and 20–21.*

auditor shall obtain an understanding of the following matters related to the entity's accounting estimates. The auditor's procedures to obtain the understanding shall be performed to the extent necessary to provide an appropriate basis for the identification and assessment of risks of material misstatement at the financial statement and assertion levels. (Ref: Para. A19–A22)

The Entity and Its Environment

(a)   The entity's transactions and other events and conditions that may give rise to the need for, or changes in, accounting estimates to be recognized or disclosed in the financial statements. (Ref: Para. A23)

(b)   The requirements of the applicable financial reporting framework related to accounting estimates (including the recognition criteria, measurement bases, and the related presentation and disclosure requirements); and how they apply in the context of the nature and circumstances of the entity and its environment, including how transactions and other events or conditions are subject to, or affected by, inherent risk factors. (Ref: Para. A24–A25)

(c)   Regulatory factors relevant to the entity's accounting estimates, including, when applicable, regulatory frameworks related to prudential supervision. (Ref: Para. A26)

(d)   The nature of the accounting estimates and related disclosures that the auditor expects to be included in the entity's financial statements, based on the auditor's understanding of the matters in 13(a)–(c) above. (Ref: Para. A27)

The Entity's Internal Control

(e)   The nature and extent of oversight and governance that the entity has in place over management's financial reporting process relevant to accounting estimates. (Ref: Para. A28–A30).

(f)   How management identifies the need for, and applies, specialized skills or knowledge related to accounting estimates, including with respect to the use of a management's expert. (Ref: Para. A31)

(g)   How the entity's risk assessment process identifies and addresses risks relating to accounting estimates. (Ref: Para. A32–A33)

(h)   The entity's information system as it relates to accounting estimates, including:

  (i)   The classes of transactions, events and conditions, that are significant to the financial statements and that give rise to the need for, or changes in, accounting estimates and related disclosures; and (Ref: Para. A34–A35)

  (ii)   For such accounting estimates and related disclosures, how management:

    (a)   Identifies the relevant methods, assumptions or sources of data, and the need for changes in them, that are appropriate in the context of the applicable financial reporting framework, including how management: (Ref: Para. A36–A37-1)
      (i)   Selects or designs, and applies, the methods used, including the use of models; (Ref: Para. A38–A39)
      (ii)   Selects the assumptions to be used, including consideration of alternatives, and identifies significant assumptions; and (Ref: Para. A40–A43)
      (iii)   Selects the data to be used; (Ref: Para. A44)

(b) Understands the degree of estimation uncertainty, including through considering the range of possible measurement outcomes; and (Ref: Para. A45)

(c) Addresses the estimation uncertainty, including selecting a point estimate and related disclosures for inclusion in the financial statements. (Ref: Para.A46–A49)

(i) Control activities relevant to the audit over management's process for making accounting estimates as described in paragraph 13(h)(ii). (Ref: Para. A50–A54)

(j) How management reviews the outcome(s) of previous accounting estimates and responds to the results of that review.

The auditor shall review the outcome of previous accounting estimates, or, where **14** applicable, their subsequent re-estimation to assist in identifying and assessing the risks of material misstatement in the current period. The auditor shall take into account the characteristics of the accounting estimates in determining the nature and extent of that review. The review is not intended to call into question judgments about previous period accounting estimates that were appropriate based on the information available at the time they were made. (Ref: Para. A55–A60)

With respect to accounting estimates, the auditor shall determine whether the **15** engagement team requires specialized skills or knowledge to perform the risk assessment procedures, to identify and assess the risks of material misstatement, to design and perform audit procedures to respond to those risks, or to evaluate the audit evidence obtained. (Ref: Para. A61–A63)

Identifying and Assessing the Risks of Material Misstatement

In identifying and assessing the risks of material misstatement relating to an **16** accounting estimate and related disclosures at the assertion level, as required by ISA (UK) 315 (Revised June 2016),[9] the auditor shall separately assess inherent risk and control risk. The auditor shall take the following into account in identifying the risks of material misstatement and in assessing inherent risk: (Ref: Para. A64–A71)

(a) The degree to which the accounting estimate is subject to estimation uncertainty; and (Ref: Para. A72–A75)

(b) The degree to which the following are affected by complexity, subjectivity, or other inherent risk factors: (Ref: Para. A76–A79)

    (i) The selection and application of the method, assumptions and data in making the accounting estimate; or

    (ii) The selection of management's point estimate and related disclosures for inclusion in the financial statements.

The auditor shall determine whether any of the risks of material misstatement **17** identified and assessed in accordance with paragraph 16 are, in the auditor's judgment, a significant risk.[10] If the auditor has determined that a significant risk

---

[9] *ISA (UK) 315 (Revised June 2016), paragraphs 25 and 26.*

[10] *ISA (UK) 315 (Revised June 2016), paragraph 27.*

exists, the auditor shall obtain an understanding of the entity's controls, including control activities, relevant to that risk.[11] (Ref: Para. A80)

Responses to the Assessed Risks of Material Misstatement

18   As required by ISA (UK) 330 (Revised July 2017),[12] the auditor's further audit procedures shall be responsive to the assessed risks of material misstatement at the assertion level,[13] considering the reasons for the assessment given to those risks. The auditor's further audit procedures shall include one or more of the following approaches:

(a)   Obtaining audit evidence from events occurring up to the date of the auditor's report (see paragraph 21);

(b)   Testing how management made the accounting estimate (see paragraphs 22–27); or

(c)   Developing an auditor's point estimate or range (see paragraphs 28–29).

The auditor's further audit procedures shall take into account that the higher the assessed risk of material misstatement, the more persuasive the audit evidence needs to be.[14] The auditor shall design and perform further audit procedures in a manner that is not biased towards obtaining audit evidence that may be corroborative or towards excluding audit evidence that may be contradictory. (Ref: Para. A81–A84)

19   As required by ISA (UK) 330 (Revised July 2017),[15] the auditor shall design and perform tests to obtain sufficient appropriate audit evidence as to the operating effectiveness of relevant controls, if:

(a)   The auditor's assessment of risks of material misstatement at the assertion level includes an expectation that the controls are operating effectively, or

(b)   Substantive procedures alone cannot provide sufficient appropriate audit evidence at the assertion level.

In relation to accounting estimates, the auditor's tests of such controls shall be responsive to the reasons for the assessment given to the risks of material misstatement. In designing and performing tests of controls, the auditor shall obtain more persuasive audit evidence the greater the reliance the auditor places on the effectiveness of a control.[16] (Ref: Para. A85–A89)

20   For a significant risk relating to an accounting estimate, the auditor's further audit procedures shall include tests of controls in the current period if the auditor plans to rely on those controls. When the approach to a significant risk consists only of substantive procedures, those procedures shall include tests of details.[17] (Ref: Para. A90)

---

[11] *ISA (UK) 315 (Revised June 2016), paragraph 29.*

[12] *ISA (UK) 330 (Revised July 2017), paragraphs 6–15 and 18.*

[13] *ISA (UK) 330 (Revised July 2017), paragraphs 6–7 and 21.*

[14] *ISA (UK) 330 (Revised July 2017), paragraph 7(b).*

[15] *ISA (UK) 330 (Revised July 2017), paragraph 8.*

[16] *ISA (UK) 330 (Revised July 2017), paragraph 9.*

[17] *ISA (UK) 330 (Revised July 2017), paragraphs 15 and 21.*

Obtaining Audit Evidence from Events Occurring up to the Date of the Auditor's Report

When the auditor's further audit procedures include obtaining audit evidence from **21** events occurring up to the date of the auditor's report, the auditor shall evaluate whether such audit evidence is sufficient and appropriate to address the risks of material misstatement relating to the accounting estimate, taking into account that changes in circumstances and other relevant conditions between the event and the measurement date may affect the relevance of such audit evidence in the context of the applicable financial reporting framework. (Ref: Para. A91–A93)

Testing How Management Made the Accounting Estimate

When testing how management made the accounting estimate, the auditor's **22** further audit procedures shall include procedures, designed and performed in accordance with paragraphs 23–26, to obtain sufficient appropriate audit evidence regarding the risks of material misstatement relating to: (Ref: Para. A94)

(a)   The selection and application of the methods, significant assumptions and the data used by management in making the accounting estimate; and

(b)   How management selected the point estimate and developed related disclosures about estimation uncertainty.

Methods

In applying the requirements of paragraph 22, with respect to methods, the **23** auditor's further audit procedures shall address:

(a)   Whether the method selected is appropriate in the context of the applicable financial reporting framework, and, if applicable, changes from the method used in prior periods are appropriate; (Ref: Para. A95, A97)

(b)   Whether judgments made in selecting the method give rise to indicators of possible management bias; (Ref: Para. A96)

(c)   Whether the calculations are applied in accordance with the method and are mathematically accurate;

(d)   When management's application of the method involves complex modelling, whether judgments have been applied consistently and whether, when applicable: (Ref: Para. A98–A100)

    (i)   The design of the model meets the measurement objective of the applicable financial reporting framework, is appropriate in the circumstances, and, if applicable, changes from the prior period's model are appropriate in the circumstances; and

    (ii)   Adjustments to the output of the model are consistent with the measurement objective of the applicable financial reporting framework and are appropriate in the circumstances; and

(e)   Whether the integrity of the significant assumptions and the data has been maintained in applying the method. (Ref: Para. A101)

Significant Assumptions

In applying the requirements of paragraph 22, with respect to significant **24** assumptions, the auditor's further audit procedures shall address:

(a)   Whether the significant assumptions are appropriate in the context of the applicable financial reporting framework, and, if applicable, changes from prior periods are appropriate; (Ref: Para. A95, A102–A103)

(b)   Whether judgments made in selecting the significant assumptions give rise to indicators of possible management bias; (Ref: Para. A96)

(c)   Whether the significant assumptions are consistent with each other and with those used in other accounting estimates, or with related assumptions used in other areas of the entity's business activities, based on the auditor's knowledge obtained in the audit; and (Ref: Para. A104)

(d)   When applicable, whether management has the intent to carry out specific courses of action and has the ability to do so. (Ref: Para. A105)

Data

25   In applying the requirements of paragraph 22, with respect to data, the auditor's further audit procedures shall address:

(a)   Whether the data is appropriate in the context of the applicable financial reporting framework, and, if applicable, changes from prior periods are appropriate (Ref: Para. A95, A106);

(b)   Whether judgments made in selecting the data give rise to indicators of possible management bias; (Ref: Para. A96)

(c)   Whether the data is relevant and reliable in the circumstances; and (Ref: Para. A107)

(d)   Whether the data has been appropriately understood or interpreted by management, including with respect to contractual terms. (Ref: Para. A108)

Management's Selection of a Point Estimate and Related Disclosures about Estimation Uncertainty

26   In applying the requirements of paragraph 22, the auditor's further audit procedures shall address whether, in the context of the applicable financial reporting framework, management has taken appropriate steps to:

(a)   Understand estimation uncertainty; and (Ref: Para. A109)

(b)   Address estimation uncertainty by selecting an appropriate point estimate and by developing related disclosures about estimation uncertainty. (Ref: Para. A110–A114)

27   When, in the auditor's judgment based on the audit evidence obtained, management has not taken appropriate steps to understand or address estimation uncertainty, the auditor shall: (Ref: Para. A115–A117)

(a)   Request management to perform additional procedures to understand estimation uncertainty or to address it by reconsidering the selection of management's point estimate or considering providing additional disclosures relating to the estimation uncertainty, and evaluate management's response(s) in accordance with paragraph 26;

(b)   If the auditor determines that management's response to the auditor's request does not sufficiently address estimation uncertainty, to the extent practicable, develop an auditor's point estimate or range in accordance with paragraphs 28–29; and

(c)   Evaluate whether a deficiency in internal control exists and, if so, communicate in accordance with ISA (UK) 265.[18]

Developing an Auditor's Point Estimate or Range

When the auditor develops a point estimate or range to evaluate management's   **28** point estimate and related disclosures about estimation uncertainty, including when required by paragraph 27(b), the auditor's further audit procedures shall include procedures to evaluate whether the methods, assumptions or data used are appropriate in the context of the applicable financial reporting framework. Regardless of whether the auditor uses management's or the auditor's own methods, assumptions or data, these further audit procedures shall be designed and performed to address the matters in paragraphs 23–25. (Ref: Para. A118–A123)

If the auditor develops an auditor's range, the auditor shall: **29**

(a)   Determine that the range includes only amounts that are supported by sufficient appropriate audit evidence and have been evaluated by the auditor to be reasonable in the context of the measurement objectives and other requirements of the applicable financial reporting framework; and (Ref: Para. A124–A125)

(b)   Design and perform further audit procedures to obtain sufficient appropriate audit evidence regarding the assessed risks of material misstatement relating to the disclosures in the financial statements that describe the estimation uncertainty.

Other Considerations Relating to Audit Evidence

In obtaining audit evidence regarding the risks of material misstatement relating to   **30** accounting estimates, irrespective of the sources of information to be used as audit evidence, the auditor shall comply with the relevant requirements in ISA (UK) 500.

When using the work of a management's expert, the requirements in paragraphs 21–29 of this ISA (UK) may assist the auditor in evaluating the appropriateness of the expert's work as audit evidence for a relevant assertion in accordance with paragraph 8(c) of ISA (UK) 500. In evaluating the work of the management's expert, the nature, timing and extent of the further audit procedures are affected by the auditor's evaluation of the expert's competence, capabilities and objectivity, the auditor's understanding of the nature of the work performed by the expert, and the auditor's familiarity with the expert's field of expertise. (Ref: Para. A126–A132)

Disclosures Related to Accounting Estimates

The auditor shall design and perform further audit procedures to obtain sufficient   **31** appropriate audit evidence regarding the assessed risks of material misstatement at the assertion level for disclosures related to an accounting estimate, other than those related to estimation uncertainty addressed in paragraphs 26(b) and 29(b).

---

[18] *ISA (UK) 265, Communicating Deficiencies in Internal Control to Those Charged with Governance and Management.*

Indicators of Possible Management Bias

32 The auditor shall evaluate whether judgments and decisions made by management in making the accounting estimates included in the financial statements, even if they are individually reasonable, are indicators of possible management bias. When indicators of possible management bias are identified, the auditor shall evaluate the implications for the audit. Where there is intention to mislead, management bias is fraudulent in nature. (Ref: Para. A133–A136)

32D-1 In accordance with ISA (UK) 200 (Revised June 2016),[18a] the auditor shall maintain professional skepticism throughout the audit and in particular when reviewing management estimates relating to fair values, the impairment of assets and provisions).

Overall Evaluation Based on Audit Procedures Performed

33 In applying ISA (UK) 330 (Revised July 2017) to accounting estimates,[19] the auditor shall evaluate, based on the audit procedures performed and audit evidence obtained, whether: (Ref: Para. A137–A138)

(a) The assessments of the risks of material misstatement at the assertion level remain appropriate, including when indicators of possible management bias have been identified;

(b) Management's decisions relating to the recognition, measurement, presentation and disclosure of these accounting estimates in the financial statements are in accordance with the applicable financial reporting framework; and

(c) Sufficient appropriate audit evidence has been obtained.

34 In making the evaluation required by paragraph 33(c), the auditor shall take into account all relevant audit evidence obtained, whether corroborative or contradictory.[20] If the auditor is unable to obtain sufficient appropriate audit evidence, the auditor shall evaluate the implications for the audit or the auditor's opinion on the financial statements in accordance with ISA (UK) 705 (Revised June 2016).[21]

Determining Whether the Accounting Estimates are Reasonable or Misstated

35 The auditor shall determine whether the accounting estimates and related disclosures are reasonable in the context of the applicable financial reporting framework, or are misstated. ISA (UK) 450 (Revised June 2016)[22] provides guidance on how the auditor may distinguish misstatements (whether factual, judgmental, or projected) for the auditor's evaluation of the effect of uncorrected misstatements on the financial statements. (Ref: Para. A12–A13, A139–A144)

36 In relation to accounting estimates, the auditor shall evaluate:

(a) In the case of a fair presentation framework, whether management has included disclosures, beyond those specifically required by the framework,

---

[18a] *ISA (UK) 200 (Revised June 2016), paragraph 15.*

[19] *ISA (UK) 330 (Revised July 2017), paragraphs 25–26.*

[20] *ISA (UK) 500, paragraph 11.*

[21] *ISA (UK) 705 (Revised June 2016), Modifications to the Opinion in the Independent Auditor's Report.*

[22] *ISA (UK) 450 (Revised June 2016), paragraph A6.*

that are necessary to achieve the fair presentation of the financial statements as a whole;[23] or

(b)   In the case of a compliance framework, whether the disclosures are those that are necessary for the financial statements not to be misleading.[24]

Written Representations

The auditor shall request written representations from management[25] and, when 37 appropriate, those charged with governance about whether the methods, significant assumptions and the data used in making the accounting estimates and the related disclosures are appropriate to achieve recognition, measurement or disclosure that is in accordance with the applicable financial reporting framework. The auditor shall also consider the need to obtain representations about specific accounting estimates, including in relation to the methods, assumptions, or data used. (Ref: Para. A145)

Communication with Those Charged With Governance, Management, or Other Relevant Parties

In applying ISA (UK) 260 (Revised June 2016)[26] and ISA (UK) 265,[27] the auditor 38 is required to communicate with those charged with governance or management about certain matters, including significant qualitative aspects of the entity's accounting practices and significant deficiencies in internal control, respectively. In doing so, the auditor shall consider the matters, if any, to communicate regarding accounting estimates and take into account whether the reasons given to the risks of material misstatement relate to estimation uncertainty, or the effects of complexity, subjectivity or other inherent risk factors in making accounting estimates and related disclosures. In addition, in certain circumstances, the auditor is required by law or regulation to communicate about certain matters with other relevant parties, such as regulators or prudential supervisors. (Ref: Para. A146–A148)

Documentation

The auditor shall include in the audit documentation:[28] (Ref: Para. A149–A152) 39

(a)   Key elements of the auditor's understanding of the entity and its environment, including the entity's internal control related to the entity's accounting estimates;

(b)   The linkage of the auditor's further audit procedures with the assessed risks of material misstatement at the assertion level,[29] taking into account the reasons (whether related to inherent risk or control risk) given to the assessment of those risks;

---

[23] *See also ISA (UK) 700 (Revised June 2016), Forming an Opinion and Reporting on Financial Statements, paragraph 14.*

[24] *See also ISA (UK) 700 (Revised June 2016), Forming an Opinion and Reporting on Financial Statements, paragraph 19.*

[25] *ISA (UK) 580, Written Representations.*

[26] *ISA (UK) 260 (Revised June 2016), Communication with Those Charged with Governance, paragraph 16(a).*

[27] *ISA (UK) 265, paragraph 9.*

[28] *ISA (UK) 230 (Revised June 2016), Audit Documentation, paragraphs 8–11, A6, A7 and A10.*

[29] *ISA (UK) 330 (Revised July 2017), paragraph 28(b).*

(c)   The auditor's response(s) when management has not taken appropriate steps to understand and address estimation uncertainty;

(d)   Indicators of possible management bias related to accounting estimates, if any, and the auditor's evaluation of the implications for the audit, as required by paragraph 32; and

(e)   Significant judgments relating to the auditor's determination of whether the accounting estimates and related disclosures are reasonable in the context of the applicable financial reporting framework, or are misstated.

***

Application and Other Explanatory Material

Nature of Accounting Estimates
(Ref: Para. 2)

Examples of Accounting Estimates

A1   Examples of accounting estimates related to classes of transactions, account balances and disclosures include:

- Inventory obsolescence.
- Depreciation of property and equipment.
- Valuation of infrastructure assets.
- Valuation of financial instruments.
- Outcome of pending litigation.
- Provision for expected credit losses.
- Valuation of insurance contract liabilities.
- Warranty obligations.
- Employee retirement benefits liabilities.
- Share-based payments.
- Fair value of assets or liabilities acquired in a business combination, including the determination of goodwill and intangible assets.
- Impairment of long-lived assets or property or equipment held for disposal.
- Non-monetary exchanges of assets or liabilities between independent parties.
- Revenue recognized for long-term contracts.

Methods

A2   A method is a measurement technique used by management to make an accounting estimate in accordance with the required measurement basis. For example, one recognized method used to make accounting estimates relating to share-based payment transactions is to determine a theoretical option call price using the Black Scholes option pricing formula. A method is applied using a computational tool or process, sometimes referred to as a model, and involves applying assumptions and data and taking into account a set of relationships between them.

Assumptions and Data

Assumptions involve judgments based on available information about matters   **A3**
such as the choice of an interest rate, a discount rate, or judgments about future
conditions or events. An assumption may be selected by management from a
range of appropriate alternatives. Assumptions that may be made or identified by a
management's expert become management's assumptions when used by
management in making an accounting estimate.

For purposes of this ISA (UK), data is information that can be obtained through   **A4**
direct observation or from a party external to the entity. Information obtained by
applying analytical or interpretive techniques to data is referred to as derived data
when such techniques have a well-established theoretical basis and therefore less
need for management judgment. Otherwise, such information is an assumption.

Examples of data include: **A5**

● Prices agreed in market transactions;

● Operating times or quantities of output from a production machine;

● Historical prices or other terms included in contracts, such as a contracted
interest rate, a payment schedule, and term included in a loan agreement;

● Forward-looking information such as economic or earnings forecasts
obtained from an external information source, or

● A future interest rate determined using interpolation techniques from
forward interest rates (derived data).

Data can come from a wide range of sources. For example, data can be: **A6**

● Generated within the organization or externally;

● Obtained from a system that is either within or outside the general or
subsidiary ledgers;

● Observable in contracts; or

● Observable in legislative or regulatory pronouncements.

Scalability
(Ref: Para. 3)

Examples of paragraphs that include guidance on how the requirements of this   **A7**
ISA (UK) can be scaled include paragraphs A20–A22, A63, A67 and A84.

Key Concepts of This ISA (UK)

Inherent Risk Factors
(Ref: Para. 4)

Inherent risk factors are characteristics of conditions and events that may affect the   **A8**
susceptibility of an assertion to misstatement, before consideration of controls.
Appendix 1 further explains the nature of these inherent risk factors, and their
inter-relationships, in the context of making accounting estimates and their
presentation in the financial statements.

In addition to the inherent risk factors of estimation uncertainty, complexity or   **A9**
subjectivity, other inherent risk factors that the auditor may consider in identifying
and assessing the risks of material misstatement may include the extent to which
the accounting estimate is subject to, or affected by:

- Change in the nature or circumstances of the relevant financial statement items, or requirements of the applicable financial reporting framework which may give rise to the need for changes in the method, assumptions or data used to make the accounting estimate.

- Susceptibility to misstatement due to management bias or fraud in making the accounting estimate.

Control Risk
(Ref: Para. 6)

A10   An important consideration for the auditor in assessing control risk at the assertion level is the effectiveness of the design of the controls that the auditor intends to rely on and the extent to which the controls address the assessed inherent risks at the assertion level. The auditor's evaluation that controls are effectively designed and have been implemented supports an expectation about the operating effectiveness of the controls in determining whether to test them.

Professional Skepticism
(Ref: Para. 8)

A11   Paragraphs A60, A95, A96, A137 and A139 are examples of paragraphs that describe ways in which the auditor can exercise professional skepticism. Paragraph A152 provides guidance on ways in which the auditor's exercise of professional skepticism may be documented, and includes examples of specific paragraphs in this ISA (UK) for which documentation may provide evidence of the exercise of professional skepticism.

Concept of "Reasonable"
(Ref: Para. 9, 35)

A12   Other considerations that may be relevant to the auditor's consideration of whether the accounting estimates and related disclosures are reasonable in the context of the applicable financial reporting framework include whether:

- The data and assumptions used in making the accounting estimate are consistent with each other and with those used in other accounting estimates or areas of the entity's business activities; and

- The accounting estimate takes into account appropriate information as required by the applicable financial reporting framework.

A13   The term "applied appropriately" as used in paragraph 9 means in a manner that not only complies with the requirements of the applicable financial reporting framework but, in doing so, reflects judgments that are consistent with the objective of the measurement basis in that framework.

Definitions

Accounting Estimate
(Ref: Para. 12(a))

A14   Accounting estimates are monetary amounts that may be related to classes of transactions or account balances recognized or disclosed in the financial statements. Accounting estimates also include monetary amounts included in disclosures or used to make judgments about recognition or disclosure relating to a class of transactions or account balance.

Auditor's Point Estimate or Auditor's Range
(Ref: Para. 12(b))

An auditor's point estimate or range may be used to evaluate an accounting **A15** estimate directly (for example, an impairment provision or the fair value of different types of financial instruments), or indirectly (for example, an amount to be used as a significant assumption for an accounting estimate). A similar approach may be taken by the auditor in developing an amount or range of amounts in evaluating a non-monetary item of data or an assumption (for example, an estimated useful life of an asset).

Estimation Uncertainty
(Ref: Para. 12(c))

Not all accounting estimates are subject to a high degree of estimation uncertainty. **A16** For example, some financial statement items may have an active and open market that provides readily available and reliable information on the prices at which actual exchanges occur. However, estimation uncertainty may exist even when the valuation method and data are well defined. For example, valuation of securities quoted on an active and open market at the listed market price may require adjustment if the holding is significant or is subject to restrictions in marketability. In addition, general economic circumstances prevailing at the time, for example, illiquidity in a particular market, may impact estimation uncertainty.

Management Bias
(Ref: Para. 12(d))

Financial reporting frameworks often call for neutrality, that is, freedom from bias. **A17** Estimation uncertainty gives rise to subjectivity in making an accounting estimate. The presence of subjectivity gives rise to the need for judgment by management and the susceptibility to unintentional or intentional management bias (for example, as a result of motivation to achieve a desired profit target or capital ratio). The susceptibility of an accounting estimate to management bias increases with the extent to which there is subjectivity in making the accounting estimate.

Outcome of an Accounting Estimate
(Ref: Para. 12(f))

Some accounting estimates, by their nature, do not have an outcome that is **A18** relevant for the auditor's work performed in accordance with this ISA (UK). For example, an accounting estimate may be based on perceptions of market participants at a point in time. Accordingly, the price realized when an asset is sold or a liability is transferred may differ from the related accounting estimate made at the reporting date because, with the passage of time, the market participants' perceptions of value have changed.

Risk Assessment Procedures and Related Activities

Obtaining an Understanding of the Entity and Its Environment
(Ref: Para. 13)

Paragraphs 11–24 of ISA (UK) 315 (Revised June 2016) require the auditor to **A19** obtain an understanding of certain matters about the entity and its environment, including the entity's internal control. The requirements in paragraph 13 of this

ISA (UK) relate more specifically to accounting estimates and build on the broader requirements in ISA (UK) 315 (Revised June 2016).

Scalability

A20   The nature, timing, and extent of the auditor's procedures to obtain the understanding of the entity and its environment, including the entity's internal control, related to the entity's accounting estimates, may depend, to a greater or lesser degree, on the extent to which the individual matter(s) apply in the circumstances. For example, the entity may have few transactions or other events and conditions that give rise to the need for accounting estimates, the applicable financial reporting requirements may be simple to apply, and there may be no relevant regulatory factors. Further, the accounting estimates may not require significant judgments, and the process for making the accounting estimates may be less complex. In these circumstances, the accounting estimates may be subject to or affected by estimation uncertainty, complexity, subjectivity, or other inherent risk factors to a lesser degree and there may be fewer controls relevant to the audit. If so, the auditor's risk assessment procedures are likely to be less extensive and may be obtained primarily through inquiries of management with appropriate responsibilities for the financial statements and simple walk-throughs of management's process for making the accounting estimate.

A21   By contrast, the accounting estimates may require significant judgments by management, and the process for making the accounting estimates may be complex and involve the use of complex models. In addition, the entity may have a more sophisticated information system, and more extensive controls over accounting estimates. In these circumstances, the accounting estimates may be subject to or affected by estimation uncertainty, subjectivity, complexity or other inherent risk factors to a greater degree. If so, the nature or timing of the auditor's risk assessment procedures are likely to be different, or be more extensive, than in the circumstances in paragraph A20.

A22   The following considerations may be relevant for entities with only simple businesses, which may include many smaller entities:

●   Processes relevant to accounting estimates may be uncomplicated because the business activities are simple or the required estimates may have a lesser degree of estimation uncertainty.

●   Accounting estimates may be generated outside of the general and subsidiary ledgers, controls over their development may be limited, and an owner-manager may have significant influence over their determination. The owner-manager's role in making the accounting estimates may need to be taken into account by the auditor both when identifying the risks of material misstatement and when considering the risk of management bias.

The Entity and Its Environment

The entity's transactions and other events and conditions
(Ref: Para. 13(a))

A23   Changes in circumstances that may give rise to the need for, or changes in, accounting estimates may include, for example, whether:

●   The entity has engaged in new types of transactions;

●   Terms of transactions have changed; or

●   New events or conditions have occurred.

The requirements of the applicable financial reporting framework
(Ref: Para. 13(b))

Obtaining an understanding of the requirements of the applicable financial   **A24**
reporting framework provides the auditor with a basis for discussion with
management and, where applicable, those charged with governance about how
management has applied those requirements relevant to the accounting estimates,
and about the auditor's determination of whether they have been applied
appropriately. This understanding also may assist the auditor in communicating
with those charged with governance when the auditor considers a significant
accounting practice that is acceptable under the applicable financial reporting
framework, not to be the most appropriate in the circumstances of the entity.[30]

In obtaining this understanding, the auditor may seek to understand whether: **A25**

- The applicable financial reporting framework:

    - Prescribes certain criteria for the recognition, or methods for the
      measurement of accounting estimates;

    - Specifies certain criteria that permit or require measurement at a fair
      value, for example, by referring to management's intentions to carry
      out certain courses of action with respect to an asset or liability; or

    - Specifies required or suggested disclosures, including disclosures
      concerning judgments, assumptions, or other sources of estimation
      uncertainty relating to accounting estimates; and

- Changes in the applicable financial reporting framework require changes to
  the entity's accounting policies relating to accounting estimates.

Regulatory factors
(Ref: Para. 13(c))

Obtaining an understanding of regulatory factors, if any, that are relevant to   **A26**
accounting estimates may assist the auditor in identifying applicable regulatory
frameworks (for example, regulatory frameworks established by prudential
supervisors in the banking or insurance industries) and in determining whether
such regulatory framework(s):

- Addresses conditions for the recognition, or methods for the measurement,
  of accounting estimates, or provides related guidance thereon;

- Specifies, or provides guidance about, disclosures in addition to the
  requirements of the applicable financial reporting framework;

- Provides an indication of areas for which there may be a potential for
  management bias to meet regulatory requirements; or

- Contains requirements for regulatory purposes that are not consistent with
  requirements of the applicable financial reporting framework, which may
  indicate potential risks of material misstatement. For example, some
  regulators may seek to influence minimum levels for expected credit loss
  provisions that exceed those required by the applicable financial reporting
  framework.

The nature of the accounting estimates and related disclosures that the auditor
expects to be included in the financial statements
(Ref: Para. 13(d))

---

[30] *ISA (UK) 260 (Revised June 2016), paragraph 16(a).*

A27   Obtaining an understanding of the nature of accounting estimates and related disclosures that the auditor expects to be included in the entity's financial statements assists the auditor in understanding the measurement basis of such accounting estimates and the nature and extent of disclosures that may be relevant. Such an understanding provides the auditor with a basis for discussion with management about how management makes the accounting estimates.

The Entity's Internal Control Relevant to the Audit

The nature and extent of oversight and governance
(Ref: Para. 13(e))

A28   In applying ISA (UK) 315 (Revised June 2016),[31] the auditor's understanding of the nature and extent of oversight and governance that the entity has in place over management's process for making accounting estimates may be important to the auditor's required evaluation as it relates to whether:

- Management, with the oversight of those charged with governance, has created and maintained a culture of honesty and ethical behavior; and

- The strengths in the control environment elements collectively provide an appropriate foundation for the other components of internal control and whether those other components are undermined by deficiencies in the control environment.

A29   The auditor may obtain an understanding of whether those charged with governance:

- Have the skills or knowledge to understand the characteristics of a particular method or model to make accounting estimates, or the risks related to the accounting estimate, for example, risks related to the method or information technology used in making the accounting estimates;

- Have the skills and knowledge to understand whether management made the accounting estimates in accordance with the applicable financial reporting framework;

- Are independent from management, have the information required to evaluate on a timely basis how management made the accounting estimates, and the authority to call into question management's actions when those actions appear to be inadequate or inappropriate;

- Oversee management's process for making the accounting estimates, including the use of models; or

- Oversee the monitoring activities undertaken by management. This may include supervision and review procedures designed to detect and correct any deficiencies in the design or operating effectiveness of controls over the accounting estimates.

A30   Obtaining an understanding of the oversight by those charged with governance may be important when there are accounting estimates that:

- Require significant judgment by management to address subjectivity;

- Have high estimation uncertainty;

- Are complex to make, for example, because of the extensive use of information technology, large volumes of data or the use of multiple data sources or assumptions with complex-interrelationships;

---

[31] *ISA (UK) 315 (Revised June 2016), paragraph 14.*

- Had, or ought to have had, a change in the method, assumptions or data compared to previous periods; or

- Involve significant assumptions.

Management's application of specialized skills or knowledge, including the use of management's experts
(Ref: Para. 13(f))

The auditor may consider whether the following circumstances increase the likelihood that management needs to engage an expert:[32] **A31**

- The specialized nature of the matter requiring estimation, for example, the accounting estimate may involve measurement of mineral or hydrocarbon reserves in extractive industries or the evaluation of the likely outcome of applying complex contractual terms.

- The complex nature of the models required to apply the relevant requirements of the applicable financial reporting framework, as may be the case in certain measurements, such as level 3 fair values.[33]

- The unusual or infrequent nature of the condition, transaction or event requiring an accounting estimate.

The entity's risk assessment process
(Ref: Para. 13(g))

Understanding how the entity's risk assessment process identifies and addresses risks relating to accounting estimates may assist the auditor in considering changes in: **A32**

- The requirements of the applicable financial reporting framework related to the accounting estimates;

- The availability or nature of data sources that are relevant to making the accounting estimates or that may affect the reliability of the data used;

- The entity's information system or IT environment; and

- Key personnel.

Matters that the auditor may consider in obtaining an understanding of how management identified and addresses the susceptibility to misstatement due to management bias or fraud in making accounting estimates, include whether, and if so how, management: **A33**

- Pays particular attention to selecting or applying the methods, assumptions and data used in making accounting estimates.

- Monitors key performance indicators that may indicate unexpected or inconsistent performance compared with historical or budgeted performance or with other known factors.

- Identifies financial or other incentives that may be a motivation for bias.

- Monitors the need for changes in the methods, significant assumptions or the data used in making accounting estimates.

- Establishes appropriate oversight and review of models used in making accounting estimates.

---

[32] *ISA (UK) 500, paragraph 8.*

[33] *See, for example, International Financial Reporting Standard (IFRS) 13, Fair Value Measurement.*

- Requires documentation of the rationale for, or an independent review of, significant judgments made in making accounting estimates.

The entity's information system relating to accounting estimates
(Ref: Para. 13(h)(i))

A34   The classes of transactions, events and conditions within the scope of paragraph 13(h) are the same as the classes of transactions, events and conditions relating to accounting estimates and related disclosures that are subject to paragraphs 18(a) and (d) of ISA (UK) 315 (Revised June 2016). In obtaining the understanding of the entity's information system as it relates to accounting estimates, the auditor may consider:

- Whether the accounting estimates arise from the recording of routine and recurring transactions or whether they arise from non-recurring or unusual transactions.

- How the information system addresses the completeness of accounting estimates and related disclosures, in particular for accounting estimates related to liabilities.

A35   During the audit, the auditor may identify classes of transactions, events and conditions that give rise to the need for accounting estimates and related disclosures that management failed to identify. ISA (UK) 315 (Revised June 2016) deals with circumstances where the auditor identifies risks of material misstatement that management failed to identify, including determining whether there is a significant deficiency in internal control with regard to the entity's risk assessment process.[34]

Management's identification of the relevant methods, assumptions and sources of data
(Ref: Para. 13(h)(ii)(a))

A36   If management has changed the method for making an accounting estimate, considerations may include whether the new method is, for example, more appropriate, is itself a response to changes in the environment or circumstances affecting the entity, or to changes in the requirements of the applicable financial reporting framework or regulatory environment, or whether management has another valid reason.

A37   If management has not changed the method for making an accounting estimate, considerations may include whether the continued use of the previous methods, assumptions and data is appropriate in view of the current environment or circumstances.

A37-1   For audits of financial statements of public interest entities, the auditor's obligations for auditing accounting estimates and related disclosures set out in this ISA (UK) may inform the auditor's assessment[31a] and communication[31b] in the additional report to the audit committee of the valuation methods applied to the various items in the financial statements.

---

[34] *ISA (UK) 315 (Revised June 2016), paragraph 17.*

[31a] *ISA (UK) 330 (Revised July 2017), paragraph 19R-1.*
[31b] *ISA (UK) 260 (Revised June 2016), paragraph 16R-2(l).*

Methods
(Ref: Para. 13(h)(ii)(a)(i))

The applicable financial reporting framework may prescribe the method to be used **A38** in making an accounting estimate. In many cases, however, the applicable financial reporting framework does not prescribe a single method, or the required measurement basis prescribes, or allows, the use of alternative methods.

Models

Management may design and implement specific controls around models used for **A39** making accounting estimates, whether management's own model or an external model. When the model itself has an increased level of complexity or subjectivity, such as an expected credit loss model or a fair value model using level 3 inputs, controls that address such complexity or subjectivity may be more likely to be identified as relevant to the audit. When complexity in relation to models is present, controls over data integrity are also more likely to be relevant to the audit. Factors that may be appropriate for the auditor to consider in obtaining an understanding of the model and of control activities relevant to the audit include the following:

● How management determines the relevance and accuracy of the model;

● The validation or back testing of the model, including whether the model is validated prior to use and revalidated at regular intervals to determine whether it remains suitable for its intended use. The entity's validation of the model may include evaluation of:

   ● The model's theoretical soundness;

   ● The model's mathematical integrity; and

   ● The accuracy and completeness of the data and the appropriateness of data and assumptions used in the model;

● How the model is appropriately changed or adjusted on a timely basis for changes in market or other conditions and whether there are appropriate change control policies over the model;

● Whether adjustments, also referred to as overlays in certain industries, are made to the output of the model and whether such adjustments are appropriate in the circumstances in accordance with the requirements of the applicable financial reporting framework. When the adjustments are not appropriate, such adjustments may be indicators of possible management bias; and

● Whether the model is adequately documented, including its intended applications, limitations, key parameters, required data and assumptions, the results of any validation performed on it and the nature of, and basis for, any adjustments made to its output.

Assumptions
(Ref: Para. 13(h)(ii)(a)(ii))

Matters that the auditor may consider in obtaining an understanding of how **A40** management selected the assumptions used in making the accounting estimates include, for example:

● The basis for management's selection and the documentation supporting the selection of the assumption. The applicable financial reporting framework may provide criteria or guidance to be used in the selection of an assumption.

- How management assesses whether the assumptions are relevant and complete.

- When applicable, how management determines that the assumptions are consistent with each other, with those used in other accounting estimates or areas of the entity's business activities, or with other matters that are:

  - Within the control of management (for example, assumptions about the maintenance programs that may affect the estimation of an asset's useful life), and whether they are consistent with the entity's business plans and the external environment; and

  - Outside the control of management (for example, assumptions about interest rates, mortality rates or potential judicial or regulatory actions).

- The requirements of the applicable financial reporting framework related to the disclosure of assumptions.

A41   With respect to fair value accounting estimates, assumptions vary in terms of the sources of the data and the basis for the judgments to support them, as follows:

(a)   Those that reflect what marketplace participants would use in pricing an asset or liability, developed based on market data obtained from sources independent of the reporting entity.

(b)   Those that reflect the entity's own judgments about what assumptions marketplace participants would use in pricing the asset or liability, developed based on the best data available in the circumstances.

In practice, however, the distinction between (a) and (b) may not always be apparent and distinguishing between them depends on understanding the sources of data and the basis for the judgments that support the assumption. Further, it may be necessary for management to select from a number of different assumptions used by different marketplace participants.

A42   Assumptions used in making an accounting estimate are referred to as significant assumptions in this ISA (UK) if a reasonable variation in the assumption would materially affect the measurement of the accounting estimate. A sensitivity analysis may be useful in demonstrating the degree to which the measurement varies based on one or more assumptions used in making the accounting estimate.

Inactive or illiquid markets

A43   When markets are inactive or illiquid, the auditor's understanding of how management selects assumptions may include understanding whether management has:

- Implemented appropriate policies for adapting the application of the method in such circumstances. Such adaptation may include making model adjustments or developing new models that are appropriate in the circumstances;

- Resources with the necessary skills or knowledge to adapt or develop a model, if necessary on an urgent basis, including selecting the valuation technique that is appropriate in such circumstances;

- The resources to determine the range of outcomes, given the uncertainties involved, for example by performing a sensitivity analysis;

- The means to assess how, when applicable, the deterioration in market conditions has affected the entity's operations, environment and relevant business risks and the implications for the entity's accounting estimates, in such circumstances; and

- An appropriate understanding of how the price data, and the relevance thereof, from particular external information sources may vary in such circumstances.

Data
(Ref: Para. 13(h)(ii)(a)(iii))

Matters that the auditor may consider in obtaining an understanding of how   **A44** management selects the data on which the accounting estimates are based include:

- The nature and source of the data, including information obtained from an external information source.

- How management evaluates whether the data is appropriate.

- The accuracy and completeness of the data.

- The consistency of the data used with data used in previous periods.

- The complexity of the information technology systems used to obtain and process the data, including when this involves handling large volumes of data.

- How the data is obtained, transmitted and processed and how its integrity is maintained.

How management understands and addresses estimation uncertainty
(Ref: Para. 13(h)(ii)(b)–13(h)(ii)(c))

Matters that may be appropriate for the auditor to consider relating to whether and   **A45** how management understands the degree of estimation uncertainty include, for example:

- Whether, and if so, how management identified alternative methods, significant assumptions or sources of data that are appropriate in the context of the applicable financial reporting framework.

- Whether, and if so, how management considered alternative outcomes by, for example, performing a sensitivity analysis to determine the effect of changes in the significant assumptions or the data used in making the accounting estimate.

The requirements of the applicable financial reporting framework may specify the   **A46** approach to selecting management's point estimate from the reasonably possible measurement outcomes. Financial reporting frameworks may recognize that the appropriate amount is one that is appropriately selected from the reasonably possible measurement outcomes and, in some cases, may indicate that the most relevant amount may be in the central part of that range.

For example, with respect to fair value estimates, IFRS 13[35] indicates that, if   **A47** multiple valuation techniques are used to measure fair value, the results (i.e., respective indications of fair value) shall be evaluated considering the reasonableness of the range of values indicated by those results. A fair value measurement is the point within that range that is most representative of fair value in the circumstances. In other cases, the applicable financial reporting framework

---

[35] *IFRS 13, Fair Value Measurement, paragraph 63.*

may specify the use of a probability-weighted average of the reasonably possible measurement outcomes, or of the measurement amount that is most likely or that is more likely than not.

A48   The applicable financial reporting framework may prescribe disclosures or disclosure objectives related to accounting estimates, and some entities may choose to disclose additional information. These disclosures or disclosure objectives may address, for example:

- The method of estimation used, including any applicable model and the basis for its selection.

- Information that has been obtained from models, or from other calculations used to determine estimates recognized or disclosed in the financial statements, including information relating to the underlying data and assumptions used in those models, such as:

  - Assumptions developed internally; or

  - Data, such as interest rates, that are affected by factors outside the control of the entity.

- The effect of any changes to the method of estimation from the prior period.

- The sources of estimation uncertainty.

- Fair value information.

- Information about sensitivity analyses derived from financial models that demonstrates that management has considered alternative assumptions.

A49   In some cases, the applicable financial reporting framework may require specific disclosures regarding estimation uncertainty, for example:

- The disclosure of information about the assumptions made about the future and other major sources of estimation uncertainty that give rise to a higher likelihood or magnitude of material adjustment to the carrying amounts of assets and liabilities after the period end. Such requirements may be described using terms such as "Key Sources of Estimation Uncertainty" or "Critical Accounting Estimates". They may relate to accounting estimates that require management's most difficult, subjective or complex judgments. Such judgments may be more subjective and complex, and accordingly the potential for a consequential material adjustment to the carrying amounts of assets and liabilities may increase, with the number of items of data and assumptions affecting the possible future resolution of the estimation uncertainty. Information that may be disclosed includes:

  - The nature of the assumption or other source of estimation uncertainty;

  - The sensitivity of carrying amounts to the methods and assumptions used, including the reasons for the sensitivity;

  - The expected resolution of an uncertainty and the range of reasonably possible outcomes in respect of the carrying amounts of the assets and liabilities affected; and

  - An explanation of changes made to past assumptions concerning those assets and liabilities, if the uncertainty remains unresolved.

- The disclosure of the range of possible outcomes, and the assumptions used in determining the range.

- The disclosure of specific information, such as:

- Information regarding the significance of fair value accounting estimates to the entity's financial position and performance; and

- Disclosures regarding market inactivity or illiquidity.

- Qualitative disclosures such as the exposures to risk and how they arise, the entity's objectives, policies and procedures for managing the risk and the methods used to measure the risk and any changes from the previous period of these qualitative concepts.

- Quantitative disclosures such as the extent to which the entity is exposed to risk, based on information provided internally to the entity's key management personnel, including credit risk, liquidity risk and market risk.

Control activities relevant to the audit over management's process for making accounting estimates
(Ref: Para. 13(i))

The auditor's judgment in identifying controls relevant to the audit, and therefore **A50** the need to evaluate the design of those controls and determine whether they have been implemented, relates to management's process described in paragraph 13(h)(ii). The auditor may not identify relevant control activities in relation to all the elements of paragraph 13(h)(ii), depending on the complexity associated with the accounting estimate.

As part of obtaining an understanding of the control activities relevant to the audit, **A51** the auditor may consider:

- How management determines the appropriateness of the data used to develop the accounting estimates, including when management uses an external information source or data from outside the general and subsidiary ledgers.

- The review and approval of accounting estimates, including the assumptions or data used in their development, by appropriate levels of management and, where appropriate, those charged with governance.

- The segregation of duties between those responsible for making the accounting estimates and those committing the entity to the related transactions, including whether the assignment of responsibilities appropriately takes account of the nature of the entity and its products or services. For example, in the case of a large financial institution, relevant segregation of duties may consist of an independent function responsible for estimation and validation of fair value pricing of the entity's financial products staffed by individuals whose remuneration is not tied to such products.

- The effectiveness of the design of the control activities. Generally, it may be more difficult for management to design controls that address subjectivity and estimation uncertainty in a manner that effectively prevents, or detects and corrects, material misstatements, than it is to design controls that address complexity. Controls that address subjectivity and estimation uncertainty may need to include more manual elements, which may be less reliable than automated controls as they can be more easily bypassed, ignored or overridden by management. The design effectiveness of controls addressing complexity may vary depending on the reason for, and the nature of, the complexity. For example, it may be easier to design more effective controls related to a method that is routinely used or over the integrity of data.

A52   When management makes extensive use of information technology in making an accounting estimate, controls relevant to the audit are likely to include general IT controls and application controls. Such controls may address risks related to:

- Whether the information technology system has the capability and is appropriately configured to process large volumes of data;

- Complex calculations in applying a method. When diverse systems are required to process complex transactions, regular reconciliations between the systems are made, in particular when the systems do not have automated interfaces or may be subject to manual intervention;

- Whether the design and calibration of models is periodically evaluated;

- The complete and accurate extraction of data regarding accounting estimates from the entity's records or from external information sources;

- Data, including the complete and accurate flow of data through the entity's information system, the appropriateness of any modification to the data used in making accounting estimates, the maintenance of the integrity and security of the data;

- When using external information sources, risks related to processing or recording the data;

- Whether management has controls around access, change and maintenance of individual models to maintain a strong audit trail of the accredited versions of models and to prevent unauthorized access or amendments to those models; and

- Whether there are appropriate controls over the transfer of information relating to accounting estimates into the general ledger, including appropriate controls over journal entries.

A53   In some industries, such as banking or insurance, the term governance may be used to describe activities within the control environment, monitoring of controls, and other components of internal control, as described in ISA (UK) 315 (Revised June 2016).[36]

A54   For entities with an internal audit function, its work may be particularly helpful to the auditor in obtaining an understanding of:

- The nature and extent of management's use of accounting estimates;

- The design and implementation of control activities that address the risks related to the data, assumptions and models used to make the accounting estimates;

- The aspects of the entity's information system that generate the data on which the accounting estimates are based; and

- How new risks relating to accounting estimates are identified, assessed and managed.

Reviewing the Outcome or Re-Estimation of Previous Accounting Estimates
(Ref: Para. 14)

A55   A review of the outcome or re-estimation of previous accounting estimates (retrospective review) assists in identifying and assessing the risks of material misstatement when previous accounting estimates have an outcome through

---

[36] *ISA (UK) 315 (Revised June 2016), paragraph A77.*

transfer or realization of the asset or liability in the current period, or are re-estimated for the purpose of the current period. Through performing a retrospective review, the auditor may obtain:

- Information regarding the effectiveness of management's previous estimation process, from which the auditor can obtain audit evidence about the likely effectiveness of management's current process.

- Audit evidence of matters, such as the reasons for changes that may be required to be disclosed in the financial statements.

- Information regarding the complexity or estimation uncertainty pertaining to the accounting estimates.

- Information regarding the susceptibility of accounting estimates to, or that may be an indicator of, possible management bias. The auditor's professional skepticism assists in identifying such circumstances or conditions and in determining the nature, timing and extent of further audit procedures.

A retrospective review may provide audit evidence that supports the identification **A56** and assessment of the risks of material misstatement in the current period. Such a retrospective review may be performed for accounting estimates made for the prior period's financial statements, or may be performed over several periods or a shorter period (such as half-yearly or quarterly). In some cases, a retrospective review over several periods may be appropriate when the outcome of an accounting estimate is resolved over a longer period.

A retrospective review of management judgments and assumptions related to **A57** significant accounting estimates is required by ISA (UK) 240 (Revised June 2016).[37] As a practical matter, the auditor's review of previous accounting estimates as a risk assessment procedure in accordance with this ISA (UK) may be carried out in conjunction with the review required by ISA (UK) 240 (Revised June 2016).

Based on the auditor's previous assessment of the risks of material misstatement, **A58** for example, if inherent risk is assessed as higher for one or more risks of material misstatement, the auditor may judge that a more detailed retrospective review is required. As part of the detailed retrospective review, the auditor may pay particular attention, when practicable, to the effect of data and significant assumptions used in making the previous accounting estimates. On the other hand, for example, for accounting estimates that arise from the recording of routine and recurring transactions, the auditor may judge that the application of analytical procedures as risk assessment procedures is sufficient for purposes of the review.

The measurement objective for fair value accounting estimates and other **A59** accounting estimates, based on current conditions at the measurement date, deals with perceptions about value at a point in time, which may change significantly and rapidly as the environment in which the entity operates changes. The auditor may therefore focus the review on obtaining information that may be relevant to identifying and assessing risks of material misstatement. For example, in some cases, obtaining an understanding of changes in marketplace participant assumptions that affected the outcome of a previous period's fair value accounting estimates may be unlikely to provide relevant audit evidence. In this

---

[37] *ISA (UK) 240 (Revised June 2016), The Auditor's Responsibilities Relating to Fraud in an Audit of Financial Statements, paragraph 32(b)(ii).*

case, audit evidence may be obtained by understanding the outcomes of assumptions (such as a cash flow projections) and understanding the effectiveness of management's prior estimation process that supports the identification and assessment of the risk of material misstatement in the current period.

A60   A difference between the outcome of an accounting estimate and the amount recognized in the previous period's financial statements does not necessarily represent a misstatement of the previous period's financial statements. However, such a difference may represent a misstatement if, for example, the difference arises from information that was available to management when the previous period's financial statements were finalized, or that could reasonably be expected to have been obtained and taken into account in the context of the applicable financial reporting framework.[38] Such a difference may call into question management's process for taking information into account in making the accounting estimate. As a result, the auditor may reassess control risk and may determine that more persuasive audit evidence needs to be obtained about the matter. Many financial reporting frameworks contain guidance on distinguishing between changes in accounting estimates that constitute misstatements and changes that do not, and the accounting treatment required to be followed in each case.

Specialized Skills or Knowledge
(Ref: Para. 15)

A61   Matters that may affect the auditor's determination of whether the engagement team requires specialized skills or knowledge, include, for example:[39]

- The nature of the accounting estimates for a particular business or industry (for example, mineral deposits, agricultural assets, complex financial instruments, insurance contract liabilities).

- The degree of estimation uncertainty.

- The complexity of the method or model used.

- The complexity of the requirements of the applicable financial reporting framework relevant to accounting estimates, including whether there are areas known to be subject to differing interpretation or practice or areas where there are inconsistencies in how accounting estimates are made.

- The procedures the auditor intends to undertake in responding to assessed risks of material misstatement.

- The need for judgment about matters not specified by the applicable financial reporting framework.

- The degree of judgment needed to select data and assumptions.

- The complexity and extent of the entity's use of information technology in making accounting estimates.

The nature, timing and extent of the involvement of individuals with specialized skills and knowledge may vary throughout the audit.

---

[38] *ISA (UK) 560, Subsequent Events, paragraph 14.*

[39] *ISA (UK) 220 (Revised June 2016), Quality Control for an Audit of Financial Statements, paragraph 14 and ISA (UK) 300 (Revised June 2016), Planning an Audit of Financial Statements, paragraph 8(e).*

The auditor may not possess the specialized skills or knowledge necessary when   **A62**
the matter involved is in a field other than accounting or auditing (for example,
valuation skills) and may need to use an auditor's expert.[40]

Many accounting estimates do not require the application of specialized skills or   **A63**
knowledge. For example, specialized skills or knowledge may not be needed for a
simple inventory obsolescence calculation. However, for example, for expected
credit losses of a banking institution or an insurance contract liability for an
insurance entity, the auditor is likely to conclude that it is necessary to apply
specialized skills or knowledge.

Identifying and Assessing the Risks of Material Misstatement
(Ref: Para. 4, 16)

Identifying and assessing risks of material misstatement at the assertion level   **A64**
relating to accounting estimates is important for all accounting estimates,
including not only those that are recognized in the financial statements, but also
those that are included in the notes to the financial statements.

Paragraph A42 of ISA (UK) 200 (Revised June 2016) states that the ISAs (UK) do   **A65**
not ordinarily refer to inherent risk and control risk separately. However, this ISA
(UK) requires a separate assessment of inherent risk and control risk to provide a
basis for designing and performing further audit procedures to respond to the risks
of material misstatement, including significant risks, at the assertion level for
accounting estimates in accordance with ISA (UK) 330 (Revised July 2017).[41]

In identifying the risks of material misstatement and in assessing inherent risk, the   **A66**
auditor is required to take into account the degree to which the accounting estimate
is subject to, or affected by, estimation uncertainty, complexity, subjectivity, or
other inherent risk factors. The auditor's consideration of the inherent risk factors
may also provide information to be used in determining:

- Where inherent risk is assessed on the spectrum of inherent risk; and

- The reasons for the assessment given to the risks of material misstatement at
  the assertion level, and that the auditor's further audit procedures in
  accordance with paragraph 18 are responsive to those reasons.

The interrelationships between the inherent risk factors are further explained in
Appendix 1.

The reasons for the auditor's assessment of inherent risk at the assertion level may   **A67**
result from one or more of the inherent risk factors of estimation uncertainty,
complexity, subjectivity or other inherent risk factors. For example:

(a)   Accounting estimates of expected credit losses are likely to be complex
      because the expected credit losses cannot be directly observed and may
      require the use of a complex model. The model may use a complex set of
      historical data and assumptions about future developments in a variety of
      entity specific scenarios that may be difficult to predict. Accounting
      estimates for expected credit losses are also likely to be subject to high
      estimation uncertainty and significant subjectivity in making judgments
      about future events or conditions. Similar considerations apply to insurance
      contract liabilities.

---

[40] *ISA (UK) 620 (Revised June 2016), Using the Work of an Auditor's Expert.*

[41] *ISA (UK) 330 (Revised July 2017), paragraph 7(b).*

(b)   An accounting estimate for an obsolescence provision for an entity with a wide range of different inventory types may require complex systems and processes, but may involve little subjectivity and the degree of estimation uncertainty may be low, depending on the nature of the inventory.

(c)   Other accounting estimates may not be complex to make but may have high estimation uncertainty and require significant judgment, for example, an accounting estimate that requires a single critical judgment about a liability, the amount of which is contingent on the outcome of the litigation.

A68   The relevance and significance of inherent risk factors may vary from one estimate to another. Accordingly, the inherent risk factors may, either individually or in combination, affect simple accounting estimates to a lesser degree and the auditor may identify fewer risks or assess inherent risk at the lower end of the spectrum of inherent risk.

A69   Conversely, the inherent risk factors may, either individually or in combination, affect complex accounting estimates to a greater degree, and may lead the auditor to assess inherent risk at the higher end of the spectrum of inherent risk. For these accounting estimates, the auditor's consideration of the effects of the inherent risk factors is likely to directly affect the number and nature of identified risks of material misstatement, the assessment of such risks, and ultimately the persuasiveness of the audit evidence needed in responding to the assessed risks. Also, for these accounting estimates the auditor's application of professional skepticism may be particularly important.

A70   Events occurring after the date of the financial statements may provide additional information relevant to the auditor's assessment of the risks of material misstatement at the assertion level. For example, the outcome of an accounting estimate may become known during the audit. In such cases, the auditor may assess or revise the assessment of the risks of material misstatement at the assertion level,[42] regardless of the degree to which the accounting estimate was subject to, or affected by estimation uncertainty, complexity, subjectivity or other inherent risk factors. Events occurring after the date of the financial statements also may influence the auditor's selection of the approach to testing the accounting estimate in accordance with paragraph 18. For example, for a simple bonus accrual that is based on a straightforward percentage of compensation for selected employees, the auditor may conclude that there is relatively little complexity or subjectivity in making the accounting estimate, and therefore may assess inherent risk at the assertion level at the lower end of the spectrum of inherent risk. The payment of the bonuses subsequent to period end may provide sufficient appropriate audit evidence regarding the assessed risks of material misstatement at the assertion level.

A71   The auditor's assessment of control risk may be done in different ways depending on preferred audit techniques or methodologies. The control risk assessment may be expressed using qualitative categories (for example, control risk assessed as maximum, moderate, minimum) or in terms of the auditor's expectation of how effective the control(s) is in addressing the identified risk, that is, the planned reliance on the effective operation of controls. For example, if control risk is assessed as maximum, the auditor contemplates no reliance on the effective operation of controls. If control risk is assessed at less than maximum, the auditor contemplates reliance on the effective operation of controls.

---

[42]   *ISA (UK) 315 (Revised June 2016), paragraph 31.*

Estimation Uncertainty
(Ref: Para. 16(a))

In taking into account the degree to which the accounting estimate is subject to   **A72**
estimation uncertainty, the auditor may consider:

- Whether the applicable financial reporting framework requires:

  - The use of a method to make the accounting estimate that inherently
    has a high level of estimation uncertainty. For example, the financial
    reporting framework may require the use of unobservable inputs.

  - The use of assumptions that inherently have a high level of estimation
    uncertainty, such as assumptions with a long forecast period,
    assumptions that are based on data that is unobservable and are
    therefore difficult for management to develop, or the use of various
    assumptions that are interrelated.

  - Disclosures about estimation uncertainty.

- The business environment. An entity may be active in a market that
  experiences turmoil or possible disruption (for example, from major
  currency movements or inactive markets) and the accounting estimate
  may therefore be dependent on data that is not readily observable.

- Whether it is possible (or practicable, insofar as permitted by the applicable
  financial reporting framework) for management:

  - To make a precise and reliable prediction about the future realization
    of a past transaction (for example, the amount that will be paid under a
    contingent contractual term), or about the incidence and impact of
    future events or conditions (for example, the amount of a future credit
    loss or the amount at which an insurance claim will be settled and the
    timing of its settlement); or

  - To obtain precise and complete information about a present condition
    (for example, information about valuation attributes that would reflect
    the perspective of market participants at the date of the financial
    statements, to develop a fair value estimate).

The size of the amount recognized or disclosed in the financial statements for an   **A73**
accounting estimate is not, in itself, an indicator of its susceptibility to
misstatement because, for example, the accounting estimate may be understated.

In some circumstances, the estimation uncertainty may be so high that a   **A74**
reasonable accounting estimate cannot be made. The applicable financial
reporting framework may preclude recognition of an item in the financial
statements, or its measurement at fair value. In such cases, there may be risks
of material misstatement that relate not only to whether an accounting estimate
should be recognized, or whether it should be measured at fair value, but also to
the reasonableness of the disclosures. With respect to such accounting estimates,
the applicable financial reporting framework may require disclosure of the
accounting estimates and the estimation uncertainty associated with them (see
paragraphs A112–A113, A143–A144).

A75 In some cases, the estimation uncertainty relating to an accounting estimate may cast significant doubt about the entity's ability to continue as a going concern. ISA (UK) 570 (Revised June 2016)[43] establishes requirements and provides guidance in such circumstances.

Complexity or Subjectivity
(Ref: Para. 16(b))

The Degree to Which Complexity Affects the Selection and Application of the Method

A76 In taking into account the degree to which the selection and application of the method used in making the accounting estimate are affected by complexity, the auditor may consider:

- The need for specialized skills or knowledge by management which may indicate that the method used to make an accounting estimate is inherently complex and therefore the accounting estimate may have a greater susceptibility to material misstatement. There may be a greater susceptibility to material misstatement when management has developed a model internally and has relatively little experience in doing so, or uses a model that applies a method that is not established or commonly used in a particular industry or environment.

- The nature of the measurement basis required by the applicable financial reporting framework, which may result in the need for a complex method that requires multiple sources of historical and forward-looking data or assumptions, with multiple interrelationships between them. For example, an expected credit loss provision may require judgments about future credit repayments and other cash flows, based on consideration of historical experience data and the application of forward looking assumptions. Similarly, the valuation of an insurance contract liability may require judgments about future insurance contract payments to be projected based on historical experience and current and assumed future trends.

The Degree to Which Complexity Affects the Selection and Application of the Data

A77 In taking into account the degree to which the selection and application of the data used in making the accounting estimate are affected by complexity, the auditor may consider:

- The complexity of the process to derive the data, taking into account the relevance and reliability of the data source. Data from certain sources may be more reliable than from others. Also, for confidentiality or proprietary reasons, some external information sources will not (or not fully) disclose information that may be relevant in considering the reliability of the data they provide, such as the sources of the underlying data they used or how it was accumulated and processed.

- The inherent complexity in maintaining the integrity of the data. When there is a high volume of data and multiple sources of data, there may be inherent complexity in maintaining the integrity of data that is used to make an accounting estimate.

---

[43] *ISA (UK) 570, (Revised June 2016), Going Concern.*

- The need to interpret complex contractual terms. For example, the determination of cash inflows or outflows arising from a commercial supplier or customer rebates may depend on very complex contractual terms that require specific experience or competence to understand or interpret.

The Degree to Which Subjectivity Affects the Selection and Application of the Method, Assumptions or Data

In taking into account the degree to which the selection and application of method, assumptions or data are affected by subjectivity, the auditor may consider: **A78**

- The degree to which the applicable financial reporting framework does not specify the valuation approaches, concepts, techniques and factors to use in the estimation method.

- The uncertainty regarding the amount or timing, including the length of the forecast period. The amount and timing are a source of inherent estimation uncertainty, and give rise to the need for management judgment in selecting a point estimate, which in turn creates an opportunity for management bias. For example, an accounting estimate that incorporates forward looking assumptions may have a high degree of subjectivity which may be susceptible to management bias.

Other Inherent Risk Factors
(Ref: Para. 16(b))

The degree of subjectivity associated with an accounting estimate influences the   **A79**
susceptibility of the accounting estimate to misstatement due to management bias or fraud. For example, when an accounting estimate is subject to a high degree of subjectivity, the accounting estimate is likely to be more susceptible to misstatement due to management bias or fraud and this may result in a wide range of possible measurement outcomes. Management may select a point estimate from that range that is inappropriate in the circumstances, or that is inappropriately influenced by unintentional or intentional management bias, and that is therefore misstated. For continuing audits, indicators of possible management bias identified during the audit of preceding periods may influence the planning and risk assessment procedures in the current period.

Significant Risks
(Ref: Para. 17)

The auditor's assessment of inherent risk, which takes into account the degree to   **A80**
which an accounting estimate is subject to, or affected by estimation uncertainty, complexity, subjectivity or other inherent risk factors, assists the auditor in determining whether any of the risks of material misstatement identified and assessed are a significant risk.

Responses to the Assessed Risks of Material Misstatement

The Auditor's Further Audit Procedures
(Ref: Para. 18)

In designing and performing further audit procedures the auditor may use any of   **A81**
the three testing approaches (individually or in combination) listed in paragraph 18. For example, when several assumptions are used to make an accounting

estimate, the auditor may decide to use a different testing approach for each assumption tested.

Obtaining Relevant Audit Evidence Whether Corroborative or Contradictory

A82   Audit evidence comprises both information that supports and corroborates management's assertions, and any information that contradicts such assertions.[44] Obtaining audit evidence in an unbiased manner may involve obtaining evidence from multiple sources within and outside the entity. However, the auditor is not required to perform an exhaustive search to identify all possible sources of audit evidence.

A83   ISA (UK) 330 (Revised July 2017) requires the auditor to obtain more persuasive audit evidence the higher the auditor's assessment of the risk.[45] Therefore, the consideration of the nature or quantity of the audit evidence may be more important when inherent risks relating to an accounting estimate is assessed at the higher end of the spectrum of inherent risk.

Scalability

A84   The nature, timing and extent of the auditor's further audit procedures are affected by, for example:

- The assessed risks of material misstatement, which affect the persuasiveness of the audit evidence needed and influence the approach the auditor selects to audit an accounting estimate. For example, the assessed risks of material misstatement relating to the existence or valuation assertions may be lower for a straightforward accrual for bonuses that are paid to employees shortly after period end. In this situation, it may be more practical for the auditor to obtain sufficient appropriate audit evidence by evaluating events occurring up to the date of the auditor's report, rather than through other testing approaches.

- The reasons for the assessed risks of material misstatement.

When the Auditor Intends to Rely on the Operating Effectiveness of Relevant Controls
(Ref: Para: 19)

A85   Testing the operating effectiveness of relevant controls may be appropriate when inherent risk is assessed as higher on the spectrum of inherent risk, including for significant risks. This may be the case when the accounting estimate is subject to or affected by a high degree of complexity. When the accounting estimate is affected by a high degree of subjectivity, and therefore requires significant judgment by management, inherent limitations in the effectiveness of the design of controls may lead the auditor to focus more on substantive procedures than on testing the operating effectiveness of controls.

A86   In determining the nature, timing and extent of testing of the operating effectiveness of controls relating to accounting estimates, the auditor may consider factors such as:

- The nature, frequency and volume of transactions;

---

[44] *ISA (UK) 500, paragraph A1.*

[45] *ISA (UK) 330 (Revised July 2017), paragraph 7(b), A19.*

- The effectiveness of the design of the controls, including whether controls are appropriately designed to respond to the assessed inherent risk, and the strength of governance;

- The importance of particular controls to the overall control objectives and processes in place at the entity, including the sophistication of the information system to support transactions;

- The monitoring of controls and identified deficiencies in internal control;

- The nature of the risks the controls are intended to address, for example, controls related to the exercise of judgment compared with controls over supporting data;

- The competency of those involved in the control activities;

- The frequency of performance of the control activities; and

- The evidence of performance of control activities.

Substantive Procedures Alone Cannot Provide Sufficient Appropriate Audit Evidence

In some industries, such as the financial services industry, management makes **A87** extensive use of IT to conduct business. It may therefore be more likely that there are risks related to certain accounting estimates for which substantive procedures alone cannot provide sufficient appropriate audit evidence.

Circumstances when risks for which substantive procedures alone cannot provide **A88** sufficient appropriate audit evidence at the assertion level may exist include:

- When controls are necessary to mitigate risks relating to the initiation, recording, processing, or reporting of information obtained from outside of the general and subsidiary ledgers.

- Information supporting one or more assertions is electronically initiated, recorded, processed, or reported. This is likely to be the case when there is a high volume of transactions or data, or a complex model is used, requiring the extensive use of information technology to ensure the accuracy and completeness of the information. A complex expected credit loss provision may be required for a financial institution or utility entity. For example, in the case of a utility entity, the data used in developing the expected credit loss provision may comprise many small balances resulting from a high volume of transactions. In these circumstances, the auditor may conclude that sufficient appropriate audit evidence cannot be obtained without testing controls around the model used to develop the expected credit loss provision.

In such cases, the sufficiency and appropriateness of the audit evidence may depend on the effectiveness of controls over the accuracy and completeness of the information.

As part of the audit of the financial statements for certain entities (such as a bank **A89** or insurer), the auditor also may be required by law or regulation to undertake additional procedures in relation to, or to provide an assurance conclusion on, internal control. In these and other similar circumstances, the auditor may be able to use information obtained in performing such procedures as audit evidence, subject to determining whether subsequent changes have occurred that may affect its relevance to the audit.

Significant Risks
(Ref: Para. 20)

A90 When the auditor's further audit procedures in response to a significant risk consist only of substantive procedures, ISA (UK) 330 (Revised July 2017)[46] requires that those procedures include tests of details. Such tests of details may be designed and performed under each of the approaches described in paragraph 18 of this ISA (UK) based on the auditor's professional judgment in the circumstances. Examples of tests of details for significant risks related to accounting estimates include:

● Examination, for example, examining contracts to corroborate terms or assumptions.

● Recalculation, for example, verifying the mathematical accuracy of a model.

● Agreeing assumptions used to supporting documentation, such as third-party published information.

Obtaining Audit Evidence from Events Occurring up to the Date of the Auditor's Report
(Ref: Para. 21)

A91 In some circumstances, obtaining audit evidence from events occurring up to the date of the auditor's report may provide sufficient appropriate audit evidence to address the risks of material misstatement. For example, sale of the complete inventory of a discontinued product shortly after the period end may provide sufficient appropriate audit evidence relating to the estimate of its net realizable value at the period end. In other cases, it may be necessary to use this testing approach in connection with another approach in paragraph 18.

A92 For some accounting estimates, events occurring up to the date of the auditor's report are unlikely to provide sufficient appropriate audit evidence regarding the accounting estimate. For example, the conditions or events relating to some accounting estimates develop only over an extended period. Also, because of the measurement objective of fair value accounting estimates, information after the period-end may not reflect the events or conditions existing at the balance sheet date and therefore may not be relevant to the measurement of the fair value accounting estimate.

A93 Even if the auditor decides not to undertake this testing approach in respect of specific accounting estimates, the auditor is required to comply with ISA (UK) 560. ISA (UK) 560 requires the auditor to perform audit procedures designed to obtain sufficient appropriate audit evidence that all events occurring between the date of the financial statements and the date of the auditor's report that require adjustment of, or disclosure in, the financial statements have been identified[47] and appropriately reflected in the financial statements.[48] Because the measurement of many accounting estimates, other than fair value accounting estimates, usually depends on the outcome of future conditions, transactions or events, the auditor's work under ISA (UK) 560 is particularly relevant.

---

[46] *ISA (UK) 330 (Revised July 2017), paragraph 21.*

[47] *ISA (UK) 560, paragraph 6.*

[48] *ISA (UK) 560, paragraph 8.*

Testing How Management Made the Accounting Estimate
(Ref: Para. 22)

Testing how management made the accounting estimate may be an appropriate **A94**
approach when, for example:

- The auditor's review of similar accounting estimates made in the prior period financial statements suggests that management's current period process is appropriate.

- The accounting estimate is based on a large population of items of a similar nature that individually are not significant.

- The applicable financial reporting framework specifies how management is expected to make the accounting estimate. For example, this may be the case for an expected credit loss provision.

- The accounting estimate is derived from the routine processing of data.

Testing how management made the accounting estimate may also be an appropriate approach when neither of the other testing approaches is practical to perform, or may be an appropriate approach in combination with one of the other testing approaches.

Changes in Methods, Significant Assumptions and the Data from Prior Periods
(Ref: Para. 23(a), 24(a), 25(a))

When a change from prior periods in a method, significant assumption, or the data **A95**
is not based on new circumstances or new information, or when significant assumptions are inconsistent with each other and with those used in other accounting estimates, or with related assumptions used in other areas of the entity's business activities, the auditor may need to have further discussions with management about the circumstances and, in doing so, challenge management regarding the appropriateness of the assumptions used.

Indicators of Management Bias
(Ref: Para. 23(b), 24(b), 25(b))

When the auditor identifies indicators of possible management bias, the auditor **A96**
may need a further discussion with management and may need to reconsider whether sufficient appropriate audit evidence has been obtained that the method, assumptions and data used were appropriate and supportable in the circumstances. An example of an indicator of management bias for a particular accounting estimate may be when management has developed an appropriate range for several different assumptions, and in each case the assumption used was from the end of the range that resulted in the most favorable measurement outcome.

Methods
The selection of the method
(Ref: Para. 23(a))

Relevant considerations for the auditor regarding the appropriateness of the **A97**
method selected in the context of the applicable financial reporting framework, and, if applicable, the appropriateness of changes from the prior period may include:

- Whether management's rationale for the method selected is appropriate;

- Whether the method is appropriate in the circumstances given the nature of the accounting estimate, the requirements of the applicable financial reporting framework, other available valuation concepts or techniques, regulatory requirements, and the business, industry and environment in which the entity operates;

- When management has determined that different methods result in a range of significantly different estimates, how management has investigated the reasons for these differences; and

- Whether the change is based on new circumstances or new information. When this is not the case, the change may not be reasonable or in compliance with the applicable financial reporting framework. Arbitrary changes result in inconsistent financial statements over time and may give rise to financial statement misstatements or may be an indicator of possible management bias (see also paragraphs A133–A136).

These matters are important when the applicable financial reporting framework does not prescribe the method of measurement or allows multiple methods.

Complex modelling
(Ref: Para. 23(d))

A98   A model, and the related method, is more likely to be complex when:

- Understanding and applying the method, including designing the model and selecting and using appropriate data and assumptions, requires specialized skills or knowledge;

- It is difficult to obtain data needed for use in the model because there are restrictions on the availability or observability of, or access to, data; or

- It is difficult to maintain the integrity (e.g., accuracy, consistency, or completeness) of the data and assumptions in using the model due to multiple valuation attributes, multiple relationships between them, or multiple iterations of the calculation.

A99   Matters that the auditor may consider when management uses a complex model include, for example, whether:

- The model is validated prior to usage or when there has been a change to the model, with periodic reviews to ensure it is still suitable for its intended use. The entity's validation process may include evaluation of:

  - The model's theoretical soundness;

  - The model's mathematical integrity;

  - The accuracy and completeness of the model's data and assumptions; and

  - The model's output as compared to actual transactions.

- Appropriate change control policies and procedures exist.

- Management uses appropriate skills and knowledge in using the model.

These considerations may also be useful for a method that does not involve complex modelling.

A100 Management may make adjustments to the output of the model to meet the requirements of the applicable financial reporting framework. In some industries these adjustments are referred to as overlays. In the case of fair value accounting estimates, it may be relevant to consider whether adjustments to the output of the model, if any, reflect the assumptions marketplace participants would use in similar circumstances.

Maintenance of integrity of significant assumptions and the data used in applying the method
(Ref: Para. 23(e))

Maintaining the integrity of significant assumptions and the data in applying the method refers to the maintenance of the accuracy and completeness of the data and assumptions through all stages of information processing. A failure to maintain such integrity may result in corruption of the data and assumptions and may give rise to misstatements. In this regard, relevant considerations for the auditor may include whether the data and assumptions are subject to all changes intended by management, and not subject to any unintended changes, during activities such as input, storage, retrieval, transmission or processing.   **A101**

Significant Assumptions
(Ref: Para. 24)

Relevant considerations for the auditor regarding the appropriateness of the significant assumptions in the context of the applicable financial reporting framework, and, if applicable, the appropriateness of changes from the prior period may include: **A102**

- Management's rationale for the selection of the assumption;

- Whether the assumption is appropriate in the circumstances given the nature of the accounting estimate, the requirements of the applicable financial reporting framework, and the business, industry and environment in which the entity operates; and

- Whether a change from prior periods in selecting an assumption is based on new circumstances or new information. When it is not, the change may not be reasonable nor in compliance with the applicable financial reporting framework. Arbitrary changes in an accounting estimate may give rise to material misstatements of the financial statements or may be an indicator of possible management bias (see paragraphs A133–A136).

Management may evaluate alternative assumptions or outcomes of accounting estimates, which may be accomplished through a number of approaches depending on the circumstances. One possible approach is a sensitivity analysis. This might involve determining how the monetary amount of an accounting estimate varies with different assumptions. Even for accounting estimates measured at fair value, there may be variation because different market participants will use different assumptions. A sensitivity analysis may lead to the development of a number of outcome scenarios, sometimes characterized as a range of outcomes by management, and including "pessimistic" and "optimistic" scenarios.   **A103**

Through the knowledge obtained in performing the audit, the auditor may become aware of or may have obtained an understanding of assumptions used in other areas of the entity's business. Such matters may include, for example, business prospects, assumptions in strategy documents and future cash flows. Also, if the engagement partner has performed other engagements for the entity, ISA (UK) 315 (Revised June 2016)[49] requires the engagement partner to consider whether information obtained from those other engagements is relevant to identifying risks of material misstatement. This information may also be useful to consider in addressing whether significant assumptions are consistent with each other and with those used in other accounting estimates.   **A104**

---

[49] *ISA (UK) 315 (Revised June 2016), paragraph 8.*

A105   The appropriateness of the significant assumptions in the context of the requirements of the applicable financial reporting framework may depend on management's intent and ability to carry out certain courses of action. Management often documents plans and intentions relevant to specific assets or liabilities and the applicable financial reporting framework may require management to do so. The nature and extent of audit evidence to be obtained about management's intent and ability is a matter of professional judgment. When applicable, the auditor's procedures may include the following:

- Review of management's history of carrying out its stated intentions.

- Inspection of written plans and other documentation, including, when applicable, formally approved budgets, authorizations or minutes.

- Inquiry of management about its reasons for a particular course of action.

- Review of events occurring subsequent to the date of the financial statements and up to the date of the auditor's report.

- Evaluation of the entity's ability to carry out a particular course of action given the entity's economic circumstances, including the implications of its existing commitments and legal, regulatory, or contractual restrictions that could affect the feasibility of management's actions.

- Consideration of whether management has met the applicable documentation requirements, if any, of the applicable financial reporting framework.

Certain financial reporting frameworks, however, may not permit management's intentions or plans to be taken into account when making an accounting estimate. This is often the case for fair value accounting estimates because their measurement objective requires that significant assumptions reflect those used by marketplace participants.

Data
(Ref: Para. 25(a))

A106   Relevant considerations for the auditor regarding the appropriateness of the data selected for use in the context of the applicable financial reporting framework, and, if applicable, the appropriateness of the changes from the prior period may include:

- Management's rationale for the selection of the data;

- Whether the data is appropriate in the circumstances given the nature of the accounting estimate, the requirements of the applicable financial reporting framework, and the business, industry and environment in which the entity operates; and

- Whether the change from prior periods in the sources or items of data selected or data selected, is based on new circumstances or new information. When it is not, it is unlikely to be reasonable nor in compliance with the applicable financial reporting framework. Arbitrary changes in an accounting estimate result in inconsistent financial statements over time and may give rise to financial statement misstatements or may be an indicator of possible management bias (see paragraphs A133–A136).

Relevance and reliability of the data
(Ref: Para. 25(c))

A107   When using information produced by the entity, ISA (UK) 500 requires the auditor to evaluate whether the information is sufficiently reliable for the auditor's purposes, including as necessary in the circumstances, to obtain audit evidence about the accuracy and completeness of the information and evaluating whether the information is sufficiently precise and detailed for the auditor's purposes.[50]

Complex legal or contractual terms
(Ref: Para. 25(d))

Procedures that the auditor may consider when the accounting estimate is based on complex legal or contractual terms include: **A108**

- Considering whether specialized skills or knowledge are needed to understand or interpret the contract;

- Inquiring of the entity's legal counsel regarding the legal or contractual terms; and

- Inspecting the underlying contracts to:

  - Evaluate, the underlying business purpose for the transaction or agreement; and

  - Consider whether the terms of the contracts are consistent with management's explanations.

Management's Selection of a Point Estimate and Related Disclosures about Estimation Uncertainty

Management's steps to understand and address estimation uncertainty
(Ref: Para. 26(a))

Relevant considerations regarding whether management has taken appropriate steps to understand and address estimation uncertainty may include whether management has: **A109**

(a) Understood the estimation uncertainty, through identifying the sources, and assessing the degree of inherent variability in the measurement outcomes and the resulting range of reasonably possible measurement outcomes;

(b) Identified the degree to which, in the measurement process, complexity or subjectivity affect the risk of material misstatement, and addressed the resulting potential for misstatement through applying:

(i) Appropriate skills and knowledge in making accounting estimates; and

(ii) Professional judgment, including by identifying and addressing susceptibility to management bias; and

(c) Addressed estimation uncertainty through appropriately selecting management's point estimate and related disclosures that describe the estimation uncertainty.

The selection of management's point estimate and related disclosures of estimation uncertainty
(Ref: Para. 26(b))

Matters that may be relevant regarding the selection of management's point estimate and the development of related disclosures about estimation uncertainty include whether: **A110**

- The methods and data used were selected appropriately, including when alternative methods for making the accounting estimate and alternative sources of data were available.

---

[50] *ISA (UK) 500, paragraph 9.*

- Valuation attributes used were appropriate and complete.

- The assumptions used were selected from a range of reasonably possible amounts and were supported by appropriate data that is relevant and reliable.

- The data used was appropriate, relevant and reliable, and the integrity of that data was maintained.

- The calculations were applied in accordance with the method and were mathematically accurate.

- Management's point estimate is appropriately chosen from the reasonably possible measurement outcomes.

- The related disclosures appropriately describe the amount as an estimate and explain the nature and limitations of the estimation process, including the variability of the reasonably possible measurement outcomes.

A111   Relevant considerations for the auditor regarding the appropriateness of management's point estimate, may include:

- When the requirements of the applicable financial reporting framework prescribe the point estimate that is to be used after consideration of the alternative outcomes and assumptions, or prescribes a specific measurement method, whether management has followed the requirements of the applicable financial reporting framework.

- When the applicable financial reporting framework has not specified how to select an amount from reasonably possible measurement outcomes, whether management has exercised judgment, taking into account the requirements of the applicable financial reporting framework.

A112   Relevant considerations for the auditor regarding management's disclosures about estimation uncertainty include the requirements of the applicable financial reporting framework, which may require disclosures:

- That describe the amount as an estimate and explain the nature and limitations of the process for making it, including the variability in reasonably possible measurement outcomes. The framework also may require additional disclosures to meet a disclosure objective.[51]

- About significant accounting policies related to accounting estimates. Depending on the circumstances, relevant accounting policies may include matters such as the specific principles, bases, conventions, rules and practices applied in preparing and presenting accounting estimates in the financial statements.

- About significant or critical judgments (for example, those that had the most significant effect on the amounts recognized in the financial statements) as well as significant forward-looking assumptions or other sources of estimation uncertainty.

- In certain circumstances, additional disclosures beyond those explicitly required by the financial reporting framework may be needed in order to achieve fair presentation, or in the case of a compliance framework, for the financial statements not to be misleading.

A113   The greater the degree to which an accounting estimate is subject to estimation uncertainty, the more likely the risks of material misstatement will be assessed as

---

[51] *IFRS 13, Fair Value Measurement, paragraph 92.*

higher and therefore the more persuasive the audit evidence needs to be to determine, in accordance with paragraph 35, whether management's point estimate and related disclosures about estimation uncertainty are reasonable in the context of the applicable financial reporting framework, or are misstated.

If the auditor's consideration of estimation uncertainty associated with an accounting estimate, and its related disclosure, is a matter that required significant auditor attention, then this may constitute a key audit matter.[52]   **A114**

When Management Has Not Taken Appropriate Steps to Understand and Address Estimation Uncertainty
(Ref: Para. 27)

When the auditor determines that management has not taken appropriate steps to understand and address estimation uncertainty, additional procedures that the auditor may request management to perform to understand estimation uncertainty may include, for example, consideration of alternative assumptions or the performance of a sensitivity analysis.   **A115**

In considering whether it is practicable to develop a point estimate or range, matters the auditor may need to take into account include whether the auditor could do so without compromising independence requirements. This may include relevant ethical requirements that address prohibitions on assuming management responsibilities.   **A116**

If, after considering management's response, the auditor determines that it is not practicable to develop an auditor's point estimate or range, the auditor is required to evaluate the implications for the audit or the auditor's opinion on the financial statements in accordance with paragraph 34.   **A117**

Developing an Auditor's Point Estimate or Using an Auditor's Range
(Ref: Para. 28–29)

Developing an auditor's point estimate or range to evaluate management's point estimate and related disclosures about estimation uncertainty may be an appropriate approach when, for example: **A118**

- The auditor's review of similar accounting estimates made in the prior period financial statements suggests that management's current period process is not expected to be effective.

- The entity's controls within and over management's process for making accounting estimates are not well designed or properly implemented.

- Events or transactions between the period end and the date of the auditor's report have not been properly taken into account, when it is appropriate for management to do so, and such events or transactions appear to contradict management's point estimate.

- There are appropriate alternative assumptions or sources of relevant data that can be used in developing an auditor's point estimate or a range.

- Management has not taken appropriate steps to understand or address the estimation uncertainty (see paragraph 27).

The decision to develop a point estimate or range also may be influenced by the applicable financial reporting framework, which may prescribe the point estimate that is to be used after consideration of the alternative outcomes and assumptions,   **A119**

---

[52] ISA (UK) 701, *Communicating Key Audit Matters in the Independent Auditor's Report.*

or prescribe a specific measurement method (for example, the use of a discounted probability-weighted expected value, or the most likely outcome).

A120   The auditor's decision as to whether to develop a point estimate rather than a range may depend on the nature of the estimate and the auditor's judgment in the circumstances. For example, the nature of the estimate may be such that there is expected to be less variability in the reasonably possible outcomes. In these circumstances, developing a point estimate may be an effective approach, particularly when it can be developed with a higher degree of precision.

A121   The auditor may develop a point estimate or a range in a number of ways, for example, by:

- Using a different model than the one used by management, for example, one that is commercially available for use in a particular sector or industry, or a proprietary or auditor-developed model.

- Using management's model but developing alternative assumptions or data sources to those used by management.

- Using the auditor's own method but developing alternative assumptions to those used by management.

- Employing or engaging a person with specialized expertise to develop or execute a model, or to provide relevant assumptions.

- Consideration of other comparable conditions, transactions or events, or, where relevant, markets for comparable assets or liabilities.

A122   The auditor also may develop a point estimate or range for only part of the accounting estimate (for example, for a particular assumption, or when only a certain part of the accounting estimate is giving rise to the risk of material misstatement).

A123   When using the auditor's own methods, assumptions or data to develop a point estimate or range, the auditor may obtain evidence about the appropriateness of management's methods, assumptions or data. For example, if the auditor uses the auditor's own assumptions in developing a range to evaluate the reasonableness of management's point estimate, the auditor may also develop a view about whether management's judgments in selecting the significant assumptions used in making the accounting estimate give rise to indicators of possible management bias.

A124   The requirement in paragraph 29(a) for the auditor to determine that the range includes only amounts that are supported by sufficient appropriate audit evidence does not mean that the auditor is expected to obtain audit evidence to support each possible outcome in the range individually. Rather, the auditor is likely to obtain evidence to determine that the points at both ends of the range are reasonable in the circumstances, thereby supporting that amounts falling between those two points also are reasonable.

A125   The size of the auditor's range may be multiples of materiality for the financial statements as a whole, particularly when materiality is based on operating results (for example, pre-tax income) and this measure is relatively small in relation to assets or other balance sheet measures. This situation is more likely to arise in circumstances when the estimation uncertainty associated with the accounting estimate is itself multiples of materiality, which is more common for certain types of accounting estimates or in certain industries, such as insurance or banking, where a high degree of estimation uncertainty is more typical and there may be specific requirements in the applicable financial reporting framework in that regard. Based on the procedures performed and audit evidence obtained in accordance with the requirements of this ISA (UK), the auditor may conclude that a range that is multiples of materiality is, in the auditor's judgment, appropriate in the circumstances. When this is the case, the auditor's evaluation of the reasonableness of the disclosures about estimation uncertainty becomes increasingly important, particularly whether such disclosures appropriately convey the high degree of estimation uncertainty and the range of possible outcomes. Paragraphs A139–A144 include additional considerations that may be relevant in these circumstances.

Other Considerations Relating to Audit Evidence
(Ref: Para. 30)

Information to be used as audit evidence, regarding risks of material misstatement relating to accounting estimates, may have been produced by the entity, prepared using the work of a management's expert, or provided by an external information source.   **A126**

External Information Sources

As explained in ISA (UK) 500,[53] the reliability of information from an external information source is influenced by its source, its nature, and the circumstances under which it is obtained. Consequently, the nature and extent of the auditor's further audit procedures to consider the reliability of the information used in making an accounting estimate may vary depending on the nature of these factors. For example: **A127**

- When market or industry data, prices, or pricing related data, are obtained from a single external information source, specializing in such information, the auditor may seek a price from an alternative independent source with which to compare.

- When market or industry data, prices, or pricing related data, are obtained from multiple independent external information sources and points to consensus across those sources, the auditor may need to obtain less evidence about the reliability of the data from an individual source.

- When information obtained from multiple information sources points to divergent market views the auditor may seek to understand the reasons for the diversity in views. The diversity may result from the use of different methods, assumptions, or data. For example, one source may be using current prices and another source using future prices. When the diversity relates to estimation uncertainty, the auditor is required by paragraph 26(b) to obtain sufficient appropriate audit evidence about whether, in the context of the applicable financial reporting framework, the disclosures in the financial statements that describe the estimation uncertainty are reasonable. In such cases professional judgment is also important in considering information about the methods, assumptions or data applied.

- When information obtained from an external information source has been developed by that source using its own model(s). Paragraph A33f of ISA (UK) 500 provides relevant guidance.

For fair value accounting estimates, additional considerations of the relevance and reliability of information obtained from external information sources may include: **A128**

(a)   Whether fair values are based on trades of the same instrument or active market quotations;

(b)   When the fair values are based on transactions of comparable assets or liabilities, how those transactions are identified and considered comparable;

(c)   When there are no transactions either for the asset or liability or comparable assets or liabilities, how the information was developed including whether the inputs developed and used represent the assumptions that market participants would use when pricing the asset or liability, if applicable; and

(d)   When the fair value measurement is based on a broker quote, whether the broker quote:

    (i)   Is from a market maker who transacts in the same type of financial instrument;

    (ii)   Is binding or nonbinding, with more weight placed on quotes based on binding offers; and

    (iii)   Reflects market conditions as of the date of the financial statements, when required by the applicable financial reporting framework.

A129   When information from an external information source is used as audit evidence, a relevant consideration for the auditor may be whether information can be obtained, or whether the information is sufficiently detailed to understand the methods, assumptions and other data used by the external information source. This may be limited in some respects and consequently influence the auditor's consideration of the nature, timing and extent of procedures to perform. For example, pricing services often provide information about their methods and assumptions by asset class rather than individual securities. Brokers often provide only limited information about their inputs and assumptions when providing broker indicative quotes for individual securities. Paragraph A33g of ISA (UK) 500 provides guidance with respect to restrictions placed by the external information source on the provision of supporting information.

Management's Expert

A130   Assumptions relating to accounting estimates that are made or identified by a management's expert become management's assumptions when used by management in making an accounting estimate. Accordingly, the auditor applies the relevant requirements in this ISA (UK) to those assumptions.

A131   If the work of a management's expert involves the use of methods or sources of data relating to accounting estimates, or developing or providing findings or conclusions relating to a point estimate or related disclosures for inclusion in the financial statements, the requirements in paragraphs 21–29 of this ISA (UK) may assist the auditor in applying paragraph 8(c) of ISA (UK) 500.

Service Organizations

A132   ISA (UK) 402[54] deals with the auditor's understanding of the services provided by a service organization, including internal control, as well as the auditor's responses to assessed risks of material misstatement. When the entity uses the services of a service organization in making accounting estimates, the requirements and guidance in ISA (UK) 402 may therefore assist the auditor in applying the requirements of this ISA (UK).

---

[54] *ISA (UK) 402, Audit Considerations Relating to an Entity Using a Service Organization.*

Indicators of Possible Management Bias
(Ref: Para. 32)

Management bias may be difficult to detect at an account level and may only be identified by the auditor when considering groups of accounting estimates, all accounting estimates in aggregate, or when observed over a number of accounting periods. For example, if accounting estimates included in the financial statements are considered to be individually reasonable but management's point estimates consistently trend toward one end of the auditor's range of reasonable outcomes that provide a more favorable financial reporting outcome for management, such circumstances may indicate possible bias by management.

A133

Examples of indicators of possible management bias with respect to accounting estimates include:

A134

- Changes in an accounting estimate, or the method for making it, when management has made a subjective assessment that there has been a change in circumstances.

- Selection or development of significant assumptions or the data that yield a point estimate favorable for management objectives.

- Selection of a point estimate that may indicate a pattern of optimism or pessimism.

When such indicators are identified, there may be a risk of material misstatement either at the assertion or financial statement level. Indicators of possible management bias themselves do not constitute misstatements for purposes of drawing conclusions on the reasonableness of individual accounting estimates. However, in some cases the audit evidence may point to a misstatement rather than simply an indicator of management bias.

Indicators of possible management bias may affect the auditor's conclusion as to whether the auditor's risk assessment and related responses remain appropriate. The auditor may also need to consider the implications for other aspects of the audit, including the need to further question the appropriateness of management's judgments in making accounting estimates. Further, indicators of possible management bias may affect the auditor's conclusion as to whether the financial statements as a whole are free from material misstatement, as discussed in ISA (UK) 700 (Revised June 2016).[55]

A135

In addition, in applying ISA (UK) 240 (Revised June 2016), the auditor is required to evaluate whether management's judgments and decisions in making the accounting estimates included in the financial statements indicate a possible bias that may represent a material misstatement due to fraud.[56] Fraudulent financial reporting is often accomplished through intentional misstatement of accounting estimates, which may include intentionally understating or overstating accounting estimates. Indicators of possible management bias that may also be a fraud risk factor, may cause the auditor to reassess whether the auditor's risk assessments, in particular the assessment of fraud risks, and related responses remain appropriate.

A136

---

[55] *ISA (UK) 700 (Revised June 2016), paragraph 11.*

[56] *ISA (UK) 240 (Revised June 2016), paragraph 32(b).*

Overall Evaluation Based on Audit Procedures Performed
(Ref: Para. 33)

A137   As the auditor performs planned audit procedures, the audit evidence obtained may cause the auditor to modify the nature, timing or extent of other planned audit procedures.[57] In relation to accounting estimates, information may come to the auditor's attention through performing procedures to obtain audit evidence that differs significantly from the information on which the risk assessment was based. For example, the auditor may have identified that the only reason for an assessed risk of material misstatement is the subjectivity involved in making the accounting estimate. However, while performing procedures to respond to the assessed risks of material misstatement, the auditor may discover that the accounting estimate is more complex than originally contemplated, which may call into question the assessment of the risk of material misstatement (for example, the inherent risk may need to be re-assessed on the higher end of the spectrum of inherent risk due to the effect of complexity) and therefore the auditor may need to perform additional further audit procedures to obtain sufficient appropriate audit evidence.[58]

A138   With respect to accounting estimates that have not been recognized, a particular focus of the auditor's evaluation may be on whether the recognition criteria of the applicable financial reporting framework have in fact been met. When an accounting estimate has not been recognized, and the auditor concludes that this treatment is appropriate, some financial reporting frameworks may require disclosure of the circumstances in the notes to the financial statements.

Determining Whether the Accounting Estimates are Reasonable or Misstated
(Ref: Para. 9, 35)

A139   In determining whether, based on the audit procedures performed and evidence obtained, management's point estimate and related disclosures are reasonable, or are misstated:

• When the audit evidence supports a range, the size of the range may be wide and, in some circumstances, may be multiples of materiality for the financial statements as a whole (see also paragraph A125). Although a wide range may be appropriate in the circumstances, it may indicate that it is important for the auditor to reconsider whether sufficient appropriate audit evidence has been obtained regarding the reasonableness of the amounts within the range.

• The audit evidence may support a point estimate that differs from management's point estimate. In such circumstances, the difference between the auditor's point estimate and management's point estimate constitutes a misstatement.

• The audit evidence may support a range that does not include management's point estimate. In such circumstances, the misstatement is the difference between management's point estimate and the nearest point of the auditor's range.

A140   Paragraphs A110–A114 provide guidance to assist the auditor in evaluating management's selection of a point estimate and related disclosures to be included in the financial statements.

---

[57] *ISA (UK) 330 (Revised July 2017), paragraph A60.*

[58] *See also ISA (UK) 315 (Revised June 2016), paragraph 31.*

When the auditor's further audit procedures include testing how management **A141** made the accounting estimate or developing an auditor's point estimate or range, the auditor is required to obtain sufficient appropriate audit evidence about disclosures that describe estimation uncertainty in accordance with paragraphs 26(b) and 29(b) and other disclosures in accordance with paragraph 31. The auditor then considers the audit evidence obtained about disclosures as part of the overall evaluation, in accordance with paragraph 35, of whether the accounting estimates and related disclosures are reasonable in the context of the applicable financial reporting framework, or are misstated.

ISA (UK) 450 (Revised June 2016) also provides guidance regarding qualitative **A142** disclosures[59] and when misstatements in disclosures could be indicative of fraud.[60]

When the financial statements are prepared in accordance with a fair presentation **A143** framework, the auditor's evaluation as to whether the financial statements achieve fair presentation[61] includes the consideration of the overall presentation, structure and content of the financial statements, and whether the financial statements, including the related notes, represent the transactions and events in a manner that achieves fair presentation. For example, when an accounting estimate is subject to a higher degree of estimation uncertainty, the auditor may determine that additional disclosures are necessary to achieve fair presentation. If management does not include such additional disclosures, the auditor may conclude that the financial statements are materially misstated.

ISA (UK) 705 (Revised June 2016)[62] provides guidance on the implications for the **A144** auditor's opinion when the auditor believes that management's disclosures in the financial statements are inadequate or misleading, including, for example, with respect to estimation uncertainty.

Written Representations
(Ref: Para. 37)

Written representations about specific accounting estimates may include **A145** representations:

- That the significant judgments made in making the accounting estimates have taken into account all relevant information of which management is aware.

- About the consistency and appropriateness in the selection or application of the methods, assumptions and data used by management in making the accounting estimates.

- That the assumptions appropriately reflect management's intent and ability to carry out specific courses of action on behalf of the entity, when relevant to the accounting estimates and disclosures.

- That disclosures related to accounting estimates, including disclosures describing estimation uncertainty, are complete and are reasonable in the context of the applicable financial reporting framework.

- That appropriate specialized skills or expertise has been applied in making the accounting estimates.

---

[59] *ISA (UK) 450 (Revised June 2016), paragraph A17.*

[60] *ISA (UK) 450 (Revised June 2016), paragraph A22.*

[61] *ISA (UK) 700 (Revised June 2016), paragraph 14.*

[62] *ISA (UK) 705 (Revised June 2016), paragraphs 22–23.*

- That no subsequent event requires adjustment to the accounting estimates and related disclosures included in the financial statements.

- When accounting estimates are not recognized or disclosed in the financial statements, about the appropriateness of management's decision that the recognition or disclosure criteria of the applicable financial reporting framework have not been met.

Communication with Those Charged With Governance, Management or Other Relevant Parties
(Ref: Para. 38)

A146   In applying ISA (UK) 260 (Revised June 2016), the auditor communicates with those charged with governance the auditor's views about significant qualitative aspects of the entity's accounting practices relating to accounting estimates and related disclosures.[63] Appendix 2 includes matters specific to accounting estimates that the auditor may consider communicating to those charged with governance.

A147   ISA (UK) 265 requires the auditor to communicate in writing to those charged with governance significant deficiencies in internal control identified during the audit.[64] Such significant deficiencies may include those related to controls over:

(a)   The selection and application of significant accounting policies, and the selection and application of methods, assumptions and data;

(b)   Risk management and related systems;

(c)   Data integrity, including when data is obtained from an external information source; and

(d)   The use, development and validation of models, including models obtained from an external provider, and any adjustments that may be required.

A148   In addition to communicating with those charged with governance, the auditor may be permitted or required to communicate directly with regulators or prudential supervisors. Such communication may be useful throughout the audit or at particular stages, such as when planning the audit or when finalizing the auditor's report. For example, in some jurisdictions, financial institution regulators seek to cooperate with auditors to share information about the operation and application of controls over financial instrument activities, challenges in valuing financial instruments in inactive markets, expected credit losses, and insurance reserves while other regulators may seek to understand the auditor's views on significant aspects of the entity's operations including the entity's costs estimates. This communication may be helpful to the auditor in identifying, assessing and responding to risks of material misstatement.

Documentation
(Ref: Para. 39)

A149   ISA (UK) 315 (Revised June 2016)[65] and ISA (UK) 330 (Revised July 2017)[66] provide requirements and guidance on documenting the auditor's understanding

---

[63] *ISA (UK) 260 (Revised June 2016), paragraph 16(a).*

[64] *ISA (UK) 265, paragraph 9.*

[65] *ISA (UK) 315 (Revised June 2016), paragraphs 32 and A152–A155.*

[66] *ISA (UK) 330 (Revised July 2017), paragraphs 28 and A63.*

of the entity, risk assessments and responses to assessed risks. This guidance is based on the requirements and guidance in ISA (UK) 230 (Revised June 2016).[67] In the context of auditing accounting estimates, the auditor is required to prepare audit documentation about key elements of the auditor's understanding of the entity and its environment related to accounting estimates. In addition, the auditor's judgments about the assessed risks of material misstatement related to accounting estimates, and the auditor's responses, may likely be further supported by documentation of communications with those charged with governance and management.

In documenting the linkage of the auditor's further audit procedures with the assessed risks of material misstatement at the assertion level, in accordance with ISA (UK) 330 (Revised July 2017), this ISA (UK) requires that the auditor take into account the reasons given to the risks of material misstatement at the assertion level. Those reasons may relate to one or more inherent risk factors or the auditor's assessment of control risk. However, the auditor is not required to document how every inherent risk factor was taken into account in identifying and assessing the risks of material misstatement in relation to each accounting estimate.   **A150**

The auditor also may consider documenting: **A151**

- When management's application of the method involves complex modeling, whether management's judgments have been applied consistently and, when applicable, that the design of the model meets the measurement objective of the applicable financial reporting framework.

- When the selection and application of methods, significant assumptions, or the data is affected by complexity to a higher degree, the auditor's judgments in determining whether specialized skills or knowledge are required to perform the risk assessment procedures, to design and perform procedures responsive to those risks, or to evaluate the audit evidence obtained. In these circumstances, the documentation also may include how the required skills or knowledge were applied.

Paragraph A7 of ISA (UK) 230 (Revised June 2016) notes that, although there may be no single way in which the auditor's exercise of professional skepticism is documented, the audit documentation may nevertheless provide evidence of the auditor's exercise of professional skepticism. For example, in relation to accounting estimates, when the audit evidence obtained includes evidence that both corroborates and contradicts management's assertions, the documentation may include how the auditor evaluated that evidence, including the professional judgments made in forming a conclusion as to the sufficiency and appropriateness of the audit evidence obtained. Examples of other requirements in this ISA (UK) for which documentation may provide evidence of the exercise of professional skepticism by the auditor include: **A152**

- Paragraph 13(d), regarding how the auditor has applied an understanding in developing the auditor's own expectation of the accounting estimates and related disclosures to be included in the entity's financial statements and how that expectation compares with the entity's financial statements prepared by management;

- Paragraph 18, which requires further audit procedures to be designed and performed to obtain sufficient appropriate evidence in a manner that is not

---

[67] *ISA (UK) 230 (Revised June 2016), paragraph 8(c).*

biased toward obtaining audit evidence that may be corroborative or towards excluding audit evidence that may be contradictory;

- Paragraphs 23(b), 24(b), 25(b) and 32, which address indicators of possible management bias; and

- Paragraph 34, which addresses the auditor's consideration of all relevant audit evidence, whether corroborative or contradictory.

Appendix 1 – Inherent Risk Factors

(Ref: Para. 2, 4, 12(c), A8, A66)

Introduction

In identifying, assessing and responding to the risks of material misstatement at   **1**
the assertion level for an accounting estimate and related disclosures, this ISA
(UK) requires the auditor to take into account the degree to which the accounting
estimate is subject to estimation uncertainty, and the degree to which the selection
and application of the methods, assumptions and data used in making the
accounting estimate, and the selection of management's point estimate and
related disclosures for inclusion in the financial statements, are affected by
complexity, subjectivity or other inherent risk factors.

Inherent risk related to an accounting estimate is the susceptibility of an assertion   **2**
about the accounting estimate to material misstatement, before consideration of
controls. Inherent risk results from inherent risk factors, which give rise to
challenges in appropriately making the accounting estimate. This Appendix
provides further explanation about the nature of the inherent risk factors of
estimation uncertainty, subjectivity and complexity, and their inter-relationships,
in the context of making accounting estimates and selecting management's point
estimate and related disclosures for inclusion in the financial statements.

Measurement Basis

The measurement basis and the nature, condition and circumstances of the   **3**
financial statement item give rise to relevant valuation attributes. When the cost
or price of the item cannot be directly observed, an accounting estimate is required
to be made by applying an appropriate method and using appropriate data and
assumptions. The method may be specified by the applicable financial reporting
framework, or is selected by management, to reflect the available knowledge
about how the relevant valuation attributes would be expected to influence the cost
or price of the item on the measurement basis.

Estimation Uncertainty

Susceptibility to a lack of precision in measurement is often referred to in   **4**
accounting frameworks as measurement uncertainty. Estimation uncertainty is
defined in this ISA (UK) as susceptibility to an inherent lack of precision in
measurement. It arises when the required monetary amount for a financial
statement item that is recognized or disclosed in the financial statements cannot
be measured with precision through direct observation of the cost or price. When
direct observation is not possible, the next most precise alternative measurement
strategy is to apply a method that reflects the available knowledge about cost or
price for the item on the relevant measurement basis, using observable data about
relevant valuation attributes.

However, constraints on the availability of such knowledge or data may limit the   **5**
verifiability of such inputs to the measurement process and therefore limit the
precision of measurement outcomes. Furthermore, most accounting frameworks
acknowledge that there are practical constraints on the information that should be

taken into account, such as when the cost of obtaining it would exceed the benefits. The lack of precision in measurement arising from these constraints is inherent because it cannot be eliminated from the measurement process. Accordingly, such constraints are sources of estimation uncertainty. Other sources of measurement uncertainty that may occur in the measurement process are, at least in principle, capable of elimination if the method is applied appropriately and therefore are sources of potential misstatement rather than estimation uncertainty.

6   When estimation uncertainty relates to uncertain future inflows or outflows of economic benefits that will ultimately result from the underlying asset or liability, the outcome of these flows will only be observable after the date of the financial statements. Depending on the nature of the applicable measurement basis and on the nature, condition and circumstances of the financial statement item, this outcome may be directly observable before the financial statements are finalized or may only be directly observable at a later date. For some accounting estimates, there may be no directly observable outcome at all.

7   Some uncertain outcomes may be relatively easy to predict with a high level of precision for an individual item. For example, the useful life of a production machine may be easily predicted if sufficient technical information is available about its average useful life. When it is not possible to predict a future outcome, such as an individual's life expectancy based on actuarial assumptions, with reasonable precision, it may still be possible to predict that outcome for a group of individuals with greater precision. Measurement bases may, in some cases, indicate a portfolio level as the relevant unit of account for measurement purposes, which may reduce inherent estimation uncertainty.

Complexity

8   Complexity (i.e., the complexity inherent in the process of making an accounting estimate, before consideration of controls) gives rise to inherent risk. Inherent complexity may arise when:

- There are many valuation attributes with many or non-linear relationships between them.

- Determining appropriate values for one or more valuation attributes requires multiple data sets.

- More assumptions are required in making the accounting estimate, or when there are correlations between the required assumptions.

- The data used is inherently difficult to identify, capture, access or understand.

9   Complexity may be related to the complexity of the method and of the computational process or model used to apply it. For example, complexity in the model may reflect the need to apply probability-based valuation concepts or techniques, option pricing formulae or simulation techniques to predict uncertain future outcomes or hypothetical behaviors. Similarly, the computational process may require data from multiple sources, or multiple data sets to support the making of an assumption or the application of sophisticated mathematical or statistical concepts.

The greater the complexity, the more likely it is that management will need to apply specialized skills or knowledge in making an accounting estimate or engage a management's expert, for example in relation to: **10**

- Valuation concepts and techniques that could be used in the context of the measurement basis and objectives or other requirements of the applicable financial reporting framework and how to apply those concepts or techniques;

- The underlying valuation attributes that may be relevant given the nature of the measurement basis and the nature, condition and circumstances of the financial statement items for which accounting estimates are being made; or

- Identifying appropriate sources of data from internal sources (including from sources outside the general or subsidiary ledgers) or from external information sources, determining how to address potential difficulties in obtaining data from such sources or in maintaining its integrity in applying the method, or understanding the relevance and reliability of that data.

Complexity relating to data may arise, for example, in the following circumstances: **11**

(a) When data is difficult to obtain or when it relates to transactions that are not generally accessible. Even when such data is accessible, for example through an external information source, it may be difficult to consider the relevance and reliability of the data, unless the external information source discloses adequate information about the underlying data sources it has used and about any data processing that has been performed.

(b) When data reflecting an external information source's views about future conditions or events, which may be relevant in developing support for an assumption, is difficult to understand without transparency about the rationale and information taken into account in developing those views.

(c) When certain types of data are inherently difficult to understand because they require an understanding of technically complex business or legal concepts, such as may be required to properly understand data that comprises the terms of legal agreements about transactions involving complex financial instruments or insurance products.

Subjectivity

Subjectivity (i.e., the subjectivity inherent in the process of making an accounting estimate, before consideration of controls) reflects inherent limitations in the knowledge or data reasonably available about valuation attributes. When such limitations exist, the applicable financial reporting framework may reduce the degree of subjectivity by providing a required basis for making certain judgments. Such requirements may, for example, set explicit or implied objectives relating to measurement, disclosure, the unit of account, or the application of a cost constraint. The applicable financial reporting framework may also highlight the importance of such judgments through requirements for disclosures about those judgments. **12**

Management judgment is generally needed in determining some or all of the following matters, which often involve subjectivity: **13**

- To the extent not specified under the requirements of the applicable financial reporting framework, the appropriate valuation approaches, concepts, techniques and factors to use in the estimation method, having regard to available knowledge;

- To the extent valuation attributes are observable when there are various potential sources of data, the appropriate sources of data to use;

- To the extent valuation attributes are not observable, the appropriate assumptions or range of assumptions to make, having regard to the best available data, including, for example, market views;

- The range of reasonably possible outcomes from which to select management's point estimate, and the relative likelihood that certain points within that range would be consistent with the objectives of the measurement basis required by the applicable financial reporting framework; and

- The selection of management's point estimate, and the related disclosures to be made, in the financial statements.

14   Making assumptions about future events or conditions involves the use of judgment, the difficulty of which varies with the degree to which those events or conditions are uncertain. The precision with which it is possible to predict uncertain future events or conditions depends on the degree to which those events or conditions are determinable based on knowledge, including knowledge of past conditions, events and related outcomes. The lack of precision also contributes to estimation uncertainty, as described above.

15   With respect to future outcomes, assumptions will only need to be made for those features of the outcome that are uncertain. For example, in considering the measurement of a possible impairment of a receivable for a sale of goods at the balance sheet date, the amount of the receivable may be unequivocally established and directly observable in the related transaction documents. What may be uncertain is the amount, if any, for loss due to impairment. In this case, assumptions may only be required about the likelihood of loss and about the amount and timing of any such loss.

16   However, in other cases, the amounts of cash flows embodied in the rights relating to an asset may be uncertain. In those cases, assumptions may have to be made about both the amounts of the underlying rights to cash flows and about potential losses due to impairment.

17   It may be necessary for management to consider information about past conditions and events, together with current trends and expectations about future developments. Past conditions and events provide historical information that may highlight repeating historical patterns that can be extrapolated in evaluating future outcomes. Such historical information may also indicate changing patterns of such behavior over time (cycles or trends). These may suggest that the underlying historical patterns of behavior have been changing in somewhat predictable ways that may also be extrapolated in evaluating future outcomes. Other types of information may also be available that indicate possible changes in historical patterns of such behavior or in related cycles or trends. Difficult judgments may be needed about the predictive value of such information.

18   The extent and nature (including the degree of subjectivity involved) of the judgments taken in making the accounting estimates may create opportunity for management bias in making decisions about the course of action that, according to management, is appropriate in making the accounting estimate. When there is also

a high level of complexity or a high level of estimation uncertainty, or both, the risk of, and opportunity for, management bias or fraud may also be increased.

Relationship of Estimation Uncertainty to Subjectivity and Complexity

Estimation uncertainty gives rise to inherent variation in the possible methods, **19** data sources and assumptions that could be used to make an accounting estimate. This gives rise to subjectivity, and hence, the need for the use of judgment in making the accounting estimate. Such judgments are required in selecting the appropriate methods and data sources, in making the assumptions, and in selecting management's point estimate and related disclosures for inclusion in the financial statements. These judgments are made in the context of the recognition, measurement, presentation and disclosure requirements of the applicable financial reporting framework. However, because there are constraints on the availability and accessibility of knowledge or information to support these judgments, they are subjective in nature.

Subjectivity in such judgments creates the opportunity for unintentional or **20** intentional management bias in making them. Many accounting frameworks require that information prepared for inclusion in the financial statements should be neutral (i.e., that it should not be biased). Given that bias can, at least in principle, be eliminated from the estimation process, sources of potential bias in the judgments made to address subjectivity are sources of potential misstatement rather than sources of estimation uncertainty.

The inherent variation in the possible methods, data sources and assumptions that **21** could be used to make an accounting estimate (see paragraph 19) also gives rise to variation in the possible measurement outcomes. The size of the range of reasonably possible measurement outcomes results from the degree of estimation uncertainty and is often referred to as the sensitivity of the accounting estimate. In addition to determining measurement outcomes, an estimation process also involves analyzing the effect of inherent variations in the possible methods, data sources and assumptions on the range of reasonably possible measurement outcomes (referred to as sensitivity analysis).

Developing a financial statement presentation for an accounting estimate, which, **22** when required by the applicable financial reporting framework, achieves faithful representation (i.e., complete, neutral and free from error) includes making appropriate judgments in selecting a management point estimate that is appropriately chosen from within the range of reasonably possible measurement outcomes and related disclosures that appropriately describe the estimation uncertainty. These judgments may themselves involve subjectivity, depending on the nature of the requirements in the applicable financial reporting framework that address these matters. For example, the applicable financial reporting framework may require a specific basis (such as a probability weighted average or a best estimate) for the selection of the management point estimate. Similarly, it may require specific disclosures or disclosures that meet specified disclosure objectives or additional disclosures that are required to achieve fair presentation in the circumstances.

Although an accounting estimate that is subject to a higher degree of estimation **23** uncertainty may be less precisely measurable than one subject to a lower degree of estimation uncertainty, the accounting estimate may still have sufficient relevance for users of the financial statements to be recognized in the financial statements if, when required by the applicable financial reporting framework, a faithful representation of the item can be achieved. In some cases, estimation uncertainty may be so great that the recognition criteria in the applicable financial reporting framework are not met and the accounting estimate cannot be recognized in the financial statements. Even in these circumstances, there may still be relevant disclosure requirements, for example to disclose the point estimate or range of reasonably possible measurement outcomes and information describing the estimation uncertainty and constraints in recognizing the item. The requirements of the applicable financial reporting framework that apply in these circumstances may be specified to a greater or lesser degree. Accordingly, in these circumstances, there may be additional judgments that involve subjectivity to be made.

Appendix 2 – Communications with Those Charged with Governance

(Ref: Para. A146)

Matters that the auditor may consider communicating with those charged with governance with respect to the auditor's views about significant qualitative aspects of the entity's accounting practices related to accounting estimates and related disclosures include:

(a) How management identifies transactions, other events and conditions that may give rise to the need for, or changes in, accounting estimates and related disclosures.

(b) Risks of material misstatement.

(c) The relative materiality of the accounting estimates to the financial statements as a whole.

(d) Management's understanding (or lack thereof) regarding the nature and extent of, and the risks associated with, accounting estimates.

(e) Whether management has applied appropriate specialized skills or knowledge or engaged appropriate experts.

(f) The auditor's views about differences between the auditor's point estimate or range and management's point estimate.

(g) The auditor's views about the appropriateness of the selection of accounting policies related to accounting estimates and presentation of accounting estimates in the financial statements.

(h) Indicators of possible management bias.

(i) Whether there has been or ought to have been a change from the prior period in the methods for making the accounting estimates.

(j) When there has been a change from the prior period in the methods for making the accounting estimate, why, as well as the outcome of accounting estimates in prior periods.

(k) Whether management's methods for making the accounting estimates, including when management has used a model, are appropriate in the context of the measurement objectives, the nature, conditions and circumstances, and other requirements of the applicable financial reporting framework.

(l) The nature and consequences of significant assumptions used in accounting estimates and the degree of subjectivity involved in the development of the assumptions.

(m) Whether significant assumptions are consistent with each other and with those used in other accounting estimates, or with assumptions used in other areas of the entity's business activities.

(n) When relevant to the appropriateness of the significant assumptions or the appropriate application of the applicable financial reporting framework, whether management has the intent to carry out specific courses of action and has the ability to do so.

(o) How management has considered alternative assumptions or outcomes and why it has rejected them, or how management has otherwise addressed estimation uncertainty in making the accounting estimate.

(p)   Whether the data and significant assumptions used by management in making the accounting estimates are appropriate in the context of the applicable financial reporting framework.

(q)   The relevance and reliability of information obtained from an external information source.

(r)   Significant difficulties encountered when obtaining sufficient appropriate audit evidence relating to data obtained from an external information source or valuations performed by management or a management's expert.

(s)   Significant differences in judgments between the auditor and management or a management's expert regarding valuations.

(t)   The potential effects on the entity's financial statements of material risks and exposures required to be disclosed in the financial statements, including the estimation uncertainty associated with accounting estimates.

(u)   The reasonableness of disclosures about estimation uncertainty in the financial statements.

(v)   Whether management's decisions relating to the recognition, measurement, presentation and disclosure of the accounting estimates and related disclosures in the financial statements are in accordance with the applicable financial reporting framework.

Annexure – Conforming and consequential amendments to other ISAS (UK)

The following are conforming amendments to other ISAs (UK) as a result of the approval of ISA (UK) 540 (Revised December 2018). These amendments will become effective at the same time as ISA (UK) 540 (Revised December 2018) and are shown with marked changes from the latest published versions of the ISAs (UK). The footnote numbers within these amendments as presented here do not align with the ISAs (UK) that are amended, and reference should be made to those ISAs (UK).

ISA (UK) 200 (Revised June 2016), Overall Objectives of the Independent Auditor and the Conduct of an Audit in Accordance With International Standards on Auditing (UK)

Application and Other Explanatory Material

...

Sufficient Appropriate Audit Evidence and Audit Risk
(Ref: Para. 5 and 17)

...

Audit Risk

...

Risks of Material Misstatement

...

The assessment of the risks of material misstatement may be expressed in **A42** quantitative terms, such as in percentages, or in non-quantitative terms. In any case, the need for the auditor to make appropriate risk assessments is more important than the different approaches by which they may be made. The ISAs (UK) do not ordinarily refer to inherent risk and control risk separately, but rather to a combined assessment of the "risks of material misstatement." However, ISA (UK) 540 (Revised December 2018)[68] requires a separate assessment of inherent risk and control risk to provide a basis for designing and performing further audit procedures to respond to the assessed risks of material misstatement, including significant risks, for accounting estimates at the assertion level in accordance with ISA (UK) 330 (Revised July 2017).[69] In identifying and assessing risks of material misstatement for significant classes of transactions, account balances or disclosures other than accounting estimates, the auditor may make separate or combined assessments of inherent and control risk depending on preferred audit

---

[68] *ISA (UK) 540 (Revised December 2018), Auditing Accounting Estimates and Disclosures, paragraph 16.*

[69] *ISA (UK) 330 (Revised July 2017), paragraph 7(b).*

techniques or methodologies and practical considerations. ~~The assessment of the risks of material misstatement may be expressed in quantitative terms, such as in percentages, or in non-quantitative terms. In any case, the need for the auditor to make appropriate risk assessments is more important than the different approaches by which they may be made.~~

***

ISA (UK) 230 (Revised June 2016), Audit Documentation

Requirements

...

Documentation of the Audit Procedures Performed and Audit Evidence Obtained

Form, Content and Extent of Audit Documentation

8   The auditor shall prepare audit documentation that is sufficient to enable an experienced auditor, having no previous connection with the audit, to understand: (Ref: Para. A2–A5, A16–A17)

(a)   The nature, timing and extent of the audit procedures performed to comply with the ISAs (UK) and applicable legal and regulatory requirements; (Ref: Para. A6–A7)

(b)   The results of the audit procedures performed, and the audit evidence obtained; and

(c)   Significant matters arising during the audit, the conclusions reached thereon, and significant professional judgments made in reaching those conclusions. (Ref: Para. A8–A11)

...

Application and Other Explanatory Material

...

Documentation of Compliance with ISAs (UK)
(Ref: Para. 8(a))
...

A7   Audit documentation provides evidence that the audit complies with the ISAs (UK). However, it is neither necessary nor practicable for the auditor to document every matter considered, or professional judgment made, in an audit. Further, it is unnecessary for the auditor to document separately (as in a checklist, for example) compliance with matters for which compliance is demonstrated by documents included within the audit file. For example:

●   The existence of an adequately documented audit plan demonstrates that the auditor has planned the audit.

●   The existence of a signed engagement letter in the audit file demonstrates that the auditor has agreed the terms of the audit engagement with management or, where appropriate, those charged with governance.

- An auditor's report containing an appropriately qualified opinion on the financial statements demonstrates that the auditor has complied with the requirement to express a qualified opinion under the circumstances specified in the ISAs (UK).

- In relation to requirements that apply generally throughout the audit, there may be a number of ways in which compliance with them may be demonstrated within the audit file:

  - For example, there may be no single way in which the auditor's professional skepticism is documented. But the audit documentation may nevertheless provide evidence of the auditor's exercise of professional skepticism in accordance with the ISAs UK). For example, in relation to accounting estimates, when the audit evidence obtained includes evidence that both corroborates and contradicts management's assertions, documenting how the auditor evaluated that evidence, including the professional judgments made in forming a conclusion as to the sufficiency and appropriateness of the audit evidence obtained. Such evidence may include specific procedures performed to corroborate management's responses to the auditor's inquiries.

  - Similarly, that the engagement partner has taken responsibility for the direction, supervision and performance of the audit in compliance with the ISAs (UK) may be evidenced in a number of ways within the audit documentation. This may include documentation of the engagement partner's timely involvement in aspects of the audit, such as participation in the team discussions required by ISA (UK) 315 (Revised June 2016).[70]

...

Documentation of Significant Matters and Related Significant Professional Judgments
(Ref: Para. 8(c))

...

Some examples of circumstances in which, in accordance with paragraph 8, it is **A10** appropriate to prepare audit documentation relating to the use of professional judgment include, where the matters and judgments are significant:

- The rationale for the auditor's conclusion when a requirement provides that the auditor "shall consider" certain information or factors, and that consideration is significant in the context of the particular engagement.

- The basis for the auditor's conclusion on the reasonableness of areas of subjective judgments made by management (for example, the reasonableness of significant accounting estimates).

- The basis for the auditor's evaluation of whether an accounting estimate and related disclosures are reasonable in the context of the applicable financial reporting framework, or are misstated.

---

[70] *ISA (UK) 315 (Revised June 2016), Identifying and Assessing the Risks of Material Misstatement through Understanding the Entity and Its Environment, paragraph 10.*

- The basis for the auditor's conclusions about the authenticity of a document when further investigation (such as making appropriate use of an expert or of confirmation procedures) is undertaken in response to conditions identified during the audit that caused the auditor to believe that the document may not be authentic.

- When ISA (UK) 701 applies,[71] the auditor's determination of the key audit matters or the determination that there are no key audit matters to be communicated.

Appendix – Specific Audit Documentation Requirements in Other ISAs (UK)
(Ref: Para. 1)

...

- ISA (UK) 540 (Revised December 2018), *Auditing Accounting Estimates, Including Fair Value Accounting Estimates, and Related Disclosures –* paragraph 39~~23~~

...

***

ISA (UK) 240 (Revised June 2016), The Auditor's Responsibilities Relating to Fraud in an Audit of Financial Statements Accounting Estimates

Application and Other Explanatory Material

...

A47   A retrospective review is also required by ISA (UK) 540 (Revised December 2018). That review is conducted as a risk assessment procedure to obtain information regarding the effectiveness of management's previous~~prior period estimation process~~ accounting estimates, audit evidence about the outcome, or where applicable, their subsequent re-estimation ~~of prior period accounting estimates that is pertinent to making~~to assist in identifying and assessing the risks of material misstatement in the current period ~~accounting estimates~~, and audit evidence of matters, such as estimation uncertainty, that may be required to be disclosed in the financial statements. As a practical matter, the auditor's review of management judgments and assumptions for biases that could represent a risk of material misstatement due to fraud in accordance with this ISA (UK) may be carried out in conjunction with the review required by ISA (UK) 540 (Revised December 2018).

...

---

[71] *ISA (UK) 701, Communicating Key Audit Matters in the Independent Auditor's Report.*

ISA (UK) 260 (Revised June 2016), Communication with Those Charged with Governance

Requirements

...

Matters to Be Communicated

...

Significant Findings from the Audit

The auditor shall communicate with those charged with governance: (Ref: Para.   **16**
A17–A18)

(a)   The auditor's views about significant qualitative aspects of the entity's accounting practices, including accounting policies, accounting estimates and financial statement disclosures. When applicable, the auditor shall explain to those charged with governance why the auditor considers a significant accounting practice, that is acceptable under the applicable financial reporting framework, not to be most appropriate to the particular circumstances of the entity; (Ref: Para. A19–A20)

(b)   Significant difficulties, if any, encountered during the audit; (Ref: Para. A21)

(c)   Unless all of those charged with governance are involved in managing the entity:

   (i)   Significant matters arising during the audit that were discussed, or subject to correspondence, with management; and (Ref: Para. A22)

   (ii)   Written representations the auditor is requesting;

(d)   Circumstances that affect the form and content of the auditor's report, if any; and (Ref: Para. A23–A25)

(e)   Any other significant matters arising during the audit that, in the auditor's professional judgment, are relevant to the oversight of the financial reporting process. (Ref: Para. A26–A28)

...

Application and Other Explanatory Material

Matters to Be Communicated

...

Significant Findings from the Audit

...

Significant Qualitative Aspects of Accounting Practices
(Ref: Para. 16(a))

Financial reporting frameworks ordinarily allow for the entity to make accounting   **A19**
estimates, and judgments about accounting policies and financial statement disclosures, for example, in relation to the use of ~~key~~ assumptions in the development of accounting estimates ~~for which there is significant measurement~~

~~uncertainty~~. In addition, law, regulation or financial reporting frameworks may require disclosure of a summary of significant accounting policies or make reference to "critical accounting estimates" or "critical accounting policies and practices" to identify and provide additional information to users about the most difficult, subjective or complex judgments made by management in preparing the financial statements.

A20   As a result, the auditor's views on the subjective aspects of the financial statements may be particularly relevant to those charged with governance in discharging their responsibilities for oversight of the financial reporting process. For example, in relation to the matters described in paragraph A19, those charged with governance may be interested in the auditor's ~~evaluation of the adequacy of disclosures of the estimation uncertainty relating to accounting estimates that give rise to significant risks.~~ views on the degree to which complexity, subjectivity or other inherent risk factors affect the selection or application of the methods, assumptions and data used in making a significant accounting estimate, as well as the auditor's evaluation of whether management's point estimate and related disclosures in the financial statements are reasonable in the context of the applicable financial reporting framework. Open and constructive communication about significant qualitative aspects of the entity's accounting practices also may include comment on the acceptability of significant accounting practices and on the quality of the disclosures. When applicable, this may include whether a significant accounting practice of the entity relating to accounting estimates is considered by the auditor not to be most appropriate to the particular circumstances of the entity, for example, when an alternative acceptable method for making an accounting estimate would, in the auditor's judgment, be more appropriate. Appendix 2 identifies matters that may be included in this communication.

...

Appendix 1 – Specific Requirements in ISQC (UK) 1 (Revised June 2016) and Other ISAs (UK) that Refer to Communications with Those Charged with Governance (Ref: Para. 3)

This appendix identifies paragraphs in ISQC (UK) 1 (Revised June 2016)[72] and other ISAs (UK) that require communication of specific matters with those charged with governance. The list is not a substitute for considering the requirements and related application and other explanatory material in ISAs (UK).

- ISQC (UK) 1 (Revised June 2016), *Quality Control for Firms that Perform Audits and Reviews of Financial Statements, and Other Assurance and Related Services Engagements* – paragraph 30(a)

- ISA (UK) 240 (Revised June 2016), *The Auditor's Responsibilities Relating to Fraud in an Audit of Financial Statements* – paragraphs 21, 38(c)(i) and 40–42

---

[72] *ISQC (UK) 1 (Revised June 2016), Quality Control for Firms that Perform Audits and Reviews of Financial Statements, and Other Assurance and Related Services Engagements.*

- ISA (UK) 250 (Revised December 2017), *Section A – Consideration of Laws and Regulations in an Audit of Financial Statements* – paragraphs 14, 19 and 22–24

- ISA (UK) 265, *Communicating Deficiencies in Internal Control to Those Charged with Governance and Management* – paragraph 9

- ISA (UK) 450 (Revised June 2016), *Evaluation of Misstatements Identified during the Audit* – paragraphs 12–13

- ISA (UK) 505, *External Confirmations* – paragraph 9

- ISA (UK) 510, *Initial Audit Engagements – Opening Balances* – paragraph 7

- ISA (UK) 540 (Revised December 2018), *Auditing Accounting Estimates and Related Disclosures* – paragraph 36

- ISA (UK) 550, Related Parties – paragraph 27

- ISA (UK) 560, *Subsequent Events* – paragraphs 7(b)–(c), 10(a), 13(b), 14(a) and 17

- ISA (UK) 570 (Revised June 2016), *Going Concern* – paragraph 25

- ISA (UK) 600 (Revised June 2016), *Special Considerations – Audits of Group Financial Statements (Including the Work of Component Auditors)* – paragraph 49

- ISA (UK) 610 (Revised June 2013), *Using the Work of Internal Auditors* – paragraphs 20 and 31

- ISA (UK) 700 (Revised June 2016), *Forming an Opinion and Reporting on Financial Statements* – paragraph 46

- ISA (UK) 701, *Communicating Key Audit Matters in the Independent Auditor's Report* – paragraph 17

- ISA (UK) 705 (Revised June 2016), *Modifications to the Opinion in the Independent Auditor's Report* – paragraphs 12, 14, 23 and 30

- ISA (UK) 706 (Revised June 2016), *Emphasis of Matter Paragraphs and Other Matter Paragraphs in the Independent Auditor's Report* – paragraph 12

- ISA (UK) 710, *Comparative Information – Corresponding Figures and Comparative Financial Statements* – paragraph 18

- ISA (UK) 720 (Revised June 2016), *The Auditor's Responsibilities Relating to Other Information* – paragraphs 17–19

Appendix 2 – Qualitative Aspects of Accounting Practices (Ref: Para. 16(a), A19–A20)

The communication required by paragraph 16(a), and discussed in paragraphs A19–A20, may include such matters as:

Accounting Policies

...

Accounting Estimates and Related Disclosures

- ~~For items for which estimates are significant, issues discussed in ISA (UK) 540 (Revised June 2016),[73] including, for example:~~Appendix 2 of ISA (UK) 540 (Revised December 2018) includes matters that the auditor may consider communicating with respect to significant qualitative aspects of the entity's accounting practices related to accounting estimates and related disclosures.

  - ~~How management identifies those transactions, events and conditions that may give rise to the need for accounting estimates to be recognized or disclosed in the financial statements.~~

  - ~~Changes in circumstances that may give rise to new, or the need to revise existing, accounting estimates.~~

  - ~~Whether management's decision to recognize, or to not recognize, the accounting estimates in the financial statements is in accordance with the applicable financial reporting framework.~~

  - ~~Whether there has been or ought to have been a change from the prior period in the methods for making the accounting estimates and, if so, why, as well as the outcome of accounting estimates in prior periods.~~

  - ~~Management's process for making accounting estimates (e.g., when management has used a model), including whether the selected measurement basis for the accounting estimate is in accordance with the applicable financial reporting framework.~~

  - ~~Whether the significant assumptions used by management in developing the accounting estimate are reasonable.~~

  - ~~Where relevant to the reasonableness of the significant assumptions used by management or the appropriate application of the applicable financial reporting framework, management's intent to carry out specific courses of action and its ability to do so.~~

  - ~~Risks of material misstatement.~~

  - ~~Indicators of possible management bias.~~

  - ~~How management has considered alternative assumptions or outcomes and why it has rejected them, or how management has otherwise addressed estimation uncertainty in making the accounting estimate.~~

  - ~~The adequacy of disclosure of estimation uncertainty in the financial statements.~~

Financial Statement Disclosures

...

***

---

[73] ~~ISA (UK) 540 (Revised June 2016), Auditing Accounting Estimates, Including Fair Value Accounting Estimates, and Related Disclosures.~~

ISA (UK) 500, Audit Evidence

Introduction

Scope of this ISA (UK)

This International Standard on Auditing (UK) (ISA (UK)) explains what **1** constitutes audit evidence in an audit of financial statements, and deals with the auditor's responsibility to design and perform audit procedures to obtain sufficient appropriate audit evidence to be able to draw reasonable conclusions on which to base the auditor's opinion.

This ISA (UK) is applicable to all the audit evidence obtained during the course of **2** the audit. Other ISAs (UK) deal with specific aspects of the audit (for example, ISA (UK) 315 (Revised June 2016)[74]), the audit evidence to be obtained in relation to a particular topic (for example, ISA (UK) 570 (Revised June 2016)[75]), specific procedures to obtain audit evidence (for example, ISA (UK) 520[76]), and the evaluation of whether sufficient appropriate audit evidence has been obtained (ISA (UK) 200 (Revised June 2016)[77] and ISA (UK) 330 (Revised July 2017)[78]).

Effective Date

This ISA (UK) is effective for audits of financial statements for periods ending on **3** or after 15 December 2010.

Objective

The objective of the auditor is to design and perform audit procedures in such a **4** way as to enable the auditor to obtain sufficient appropriate audit evidence to be able to draw reasonable conclusions on which to base the auditor's opinion.

Definitions

For purposes of ~~the~~this ISA (UK), the following terms have the meanings **5** attributed below:

(a) Accounting records – The records of initial accounting entries and supporting records, such as checks and records of electronic fund transfers; invoices; contracts; the general and subsidiary ledgers, journal entries and other adjustments to the financial statements that are not reflected in journal entries; and records such as work sheets and spreadsheets supporting cost allocations, computations, reconciliations and disclosures.

(b) Appropriateness (of audit evidence) – The measure of the quality of audit evidence; that is, its relevance and its reliability in providing support for the conclusions on which the auditor's opinion is based.

(c) Audit evidence – Information used by the auditor in arriving at the conclusions on which the auditor's opinion is based. Audit evidence

---

[74] *ISA (UK) 315 (Revised June 2016), Identifying and Assessing the Risks of Material Misstatement through Understanding the Entity and Its Environment.*

[75] *ISA (UK) 570 (Revised June 2016), Going Concern.*

[76] *ISA (UK) 520, Analytical Procedures.*

[77] *ISA (UK) 200 (Revised June 2016), Overall Objectives of the Independent Auditor and the Conduct of an Audit in Accordance with International Standards on Auditing (UK).*

[78] *ISA (UK) 330 (Revised July), The Auditor's Responses to Assessed Risks.*

includes both information contained in the accounting records underlying the financial statements and information obtained from other sources.

(cA) External information source – An external individual or organization that provides information that has been used by the entity in preparing the financial statements, or that has been obtained by the auditor as audit evidence, when such information is suitable for use by a broad range of users. When information has been provided by an individual or organization acting in the capacity of a management's expert, service organization[79], or auditor's expert[80] the individual or organization is not considered an external information source with respect to that particular information. (Ref: Para. A1A–A1C)

(d)   Management's expert – An individual or organization possessing expertise in a field other than accounting or auditing, whose work in that field is used by the entity to assist the entity in preparing the financial statements.

(e)   Sufficiency (of audit evidence) – The measure of the quantity of audit evidence. The quantity of the audit evidence needed is affected by the auditor's assessment of the risks of material misstatement and also by the quality of such audit evidence.

Requirements

Sufficient Appropriate Audit Evidence

6   The auditor shall design and perform audit procedures that are appropriate in the circumstances for the purpose of obtaining sufficient appropriate audit evidence. (Ref: Para. A1–A25)

Information to Be Used as Audit Evidence

7   When designing and performing audit procedures, the auditor shall consider the relevance and reliability of the information to be used as audit evidence-, including information obtained from an external information source. (Ref: Para. A26–A33g)

8   If information to be used as audit evidence has been prepared using the work of a management's expert, the auditor shall, to the extent necessary, having regard to the significance of that expert's work for the auditor's purposes: (Ref: Para. A34–A36)

(a)   Evaluate the competence, capabilities and objectivity of that expert; (Ref: Para. A37–A43)

(b)   Obtain an understanding of the work of that expert; and (Ref: Para. A44–A47)

(c)   Evaluate the appropriateness of that expert's work as audit evidence for the relevant assertion. (Ref: Para. A48)

9   When using information produced by the entity, the auditor shall evaluate whether the information is sufficiently reliable for the auditor's purposes, including, as necessary in the circumstances:

---

[79] *ISA (UK) 402, Audit Considerations Relating to an Entity Using a Service Organization, paragraph 8.*

[80] *ISA (UK) 620 (Revised June 2016), Using the Work of an Auditor's Expert, paragraph 6.*

(a)   When using information produced by the entity, the auditor shall evaluate whether the information is sufficiently reliable for the auditor's purposes, including, as necessary in the circumstances:

(b)   Evaluating whether the information is sufficiently precise and detailed for the auditor's purposes. (Ref: Para. A51)

Selecting Items for Testing to Obtain Audit Evidence

When designing tests of controls and tests of details, the auditor shall determine   **10**
means of selecting items for testing that are effective in meeting the purpose of the audit procedure. (Ref: Para. A52–A56)

Inconsistency in, or Doubts over Reliability of, Audit Evidence

If: **11**

(a)   audit evidence obtained from one source is inconsistent with that obtained from another; or

(b)   the auditor has doubts over the reliability of information to be used as audit evidence,

the auditor shall determine what modifications or additions to audit procedures are necessary to resolve the matter, and shall consider the effect of the matter, if any, on other aspects of the audit. (Ref: Para. A57)

***

Application and Other Explanatory Material

External Information Source
(Ref: Para. 5(cA))

External information sources may include pricing services, governmental   **A1a**
organizations, central banks or recognized stock exchanges. Examples of information that may be obtained from external information sources include:

● Prices and pricing related data;

● Macro-economic data, such as historical and forecast unemployment rates and economic growth rates, or census data;

● Credit history data;

● Industry specific data, such as an index of reclamation costs for certain extractive industries, or viewership information or ratings used to determine advertising revenue in the entertainment industry; and

● Mortality tables used to determine liabilities in the life insurance and pension sectors.

A particular set of information is more likely to be suitable for use by a broad   **A1b**
range of users and less likely to be subject to influence by any particular user if the external individual or organization provides it to the public for free, or makes it available to a wide range of users in return for payment of a fee. Judgment may be required in determining whether the information is suitable for use by a broad range of users, taking into account the ability of the entity to influence the external information source.

A1c   An external individual or organization cannot, in respect of any particular set of information, be both an external information source and a management's expert, or service organization or auditor's expert.

A1d   However, an external individual or organization may, for example, be acting as a management's expert when providing a particular set of information, but may be acting as an external information source when providing a different set of information. In some circumstances, professional judgment may be needed to determine whether an external individual or organization is acting as an external information source or as a management's expert with respect to a particular set of information. In other circumstances, the distinction may be clear. For example:

- An external individual or organization may be providing information about real estate prices that is suitable for use by a broad range of users, for example, information made generally available pertaining to a geographical region, and be determined to be an external information source with respect to that set of information. The same external organization may also be acting as a management's or auditor's expert in providing commissioned valuations, with respect to the entity's real estate portfolio specifically tailored for the entity's facts and circumstances.

- Some actuarial organizations publish mortality tables for general use which, when used by an entity, would generally be considered to be information from an external information source. The same actuarial organization may also be a management's expert with respect to different information tailored to the specific circumstances of the entity to help management determine the pension liability for several of the entity's pension plans.

- An external individual or organization may possess expertise in the application of models to estimate the fair value of securities for which there is no observable market. If the external individual or organization applies that expertise in making an estimate specifically for the entity and that work is used by management in preparing its financial statements, the external individual or organization is likely to be a management's expert with respect to that information. If, on the other hand, that external individual or organization merely provides, to the public, prices or pricing-related data regarding private transactions, and the entity uses that information in its own estimation methods, the external individual or organization is likely to be an external information source with respect to such information.

- An external individual or organization may publish information, suitable for a broad range of users, about risks or conditions in an industry. If used by an entity in preparing its risk disclosures (for example in compliance with IFRS 7[81]), such information would ordinarily be considered to be information from an external information source. However, if the same type of information has been specifically commissioned by the entity to use its expertise to develop information about those risks, tailored to the entity's circumstances, the external individual or organization is likely to be acting as a management's expert.

- An external individual or organization may apply its expertise in providing information about current and future market trends, which it makes available to, and is suitable for use by, a broad range of users. If used by the entity to

---

[81] *International Financial Reporting Standards 7 (IFRS). Financial Instruments: Disclosures.*

help make decisions about assumptions to be used in making accounting estimates, such information is likely to be considered to be information from an external information source. If the same type of information has been commissioned by the entity to address current and future trends relevant to the entity's specific facts and circumstances, the external individual or organization is likely to be acting as a management's expert.

Sufficient Appropriate Audit Evidence
(Ref: Para. 6)

Audit evidence is necessary to support the auditor's opinion and report. It is **A1** cumulative in nature and is primarily obtained from audit procedures performed during the course of the audit. It may, however, also include information obtained from other sources such as previous audits (provided the auditor has determined whether changes have occurred since the previous audit that may affect its relevance to the current audit[82]) or a firm's quality control procedures for client acceptance and continuance. In addition to other sources inside and outside the entity, the entity's accounting records and other sources internal to the entity are an important sources of audit evidence. Also, informationInformation that may be used as audit evidence may have been prepared using the work of a management's expert. or be obtained from an external information source. Audit evidence comprises both information that supports and corroborates management's assertions, and any information that contradicts such assertions. In addition, in some cases the absence of information (for example, management's refusal to provide a requested representation) is used by the auditor, and therefore, also constitutes audit evidence.

Most of the auditor's work in forming the auditor's opinion consists of obtaining **A2** and evaluating audit evidence. Audit procedures to obtain audit evidence can include inspection, observation, confirmation, recalculation, reperformance, and analytical procedures, often in some combination, in addition to inquiry. Although inquiry may provide important audit evidence, and may even produce evidence of a misstatement, inquiry alone ordinarily does not provide sufficient audit evidence of the absence of a material misstatement at the assertion level, nor of the operating effectiveness of controls.

As explained in ISA (UK) 200 (Revised June 2016),[83] reasonable assurance is **A3** obtained when the auditor has obtained sufficient appropriate audit evidence to reduce audit risk (that is, the risk that the auditor expresses an inappropriate opinion when the financial statements are materially misstated) to an acceptably low level.

The sufficiency and appropriateness of audit evidence are interrelated. Sufficiency **A4** is the measure of the quantity of audit evidence. The quantity of audit evidence needed is affected by the auditor's assessment of the risks of misstatement (the higher the assessed risks, the more audit evidence is likely to be required) and also by the quality of such audit evidence (the higher the quality, the less may be required). Obtaining more audit evidence, however, may not compensate for its poor quality.

Appropriateness is the measure of the quality of audit evidence; that is, its **A5** relevance and its reliability in providing support for the conclusions on which the

---

[82] *ISA (UK) 315 (Revised June 2016), paragraph 9.*

[83] *ISA (UK) 200 (Revised June 2016), paragraph 5.*

auditor's opinion is based. The reliability of evidence is influenced by its source and by its nature, and is dependent on the individual circumstances under which it is obtained.

A6   ISA (UK) 330 (Revised July 2017) requires the auditor to conclude whether sufficient appropriate audit evidence has been obtained.[84] Whether sufficient appropriate audit evidence has been obtained to reduce audit risk to an acceptably low level, and thereby enable the auditor to draw reasonable conclusions on which to base the auditor's opinion, is a matter of professional judgment. ISA (UK) 200 (Revised June 2016) contains discussion of such matters as the nature of audit procedures, the timeliness of financial reporting, and the balance between benefit and cost, which are relevant factors when the auditor exercises professional judgment regarding whether sufficient appropriate audit evidence has been obtained.

Sources of Audit Evidence

A7   Some audit evidence is obtained by performing audit procedures to test the accounting records, for example, through analysis and review, reperforming procedures followed in the financial reporting process, and reconciling related types and applications of the same information. Through the performance of such audit procedures, the auditor may determine that the accounting records are internally consistent and agree to the financial statements.

A8   More assurance is ordinarily obtained from consistent audit evidence obtained from different sources or of a different nature than from items of audit evidence considered individually. For example, corroborating information obtained from a source independent of the entity may increase the assurance the auditor obtains from audit evidence that is generated internally, such as evidence existing within the accounting records, minutes of meetings, or a management representation.

A9   Information from sources independent of the entity that the auditor may use as audit evidence may include confirmations from third parties, and information from an external information source, including analysts' reports, and comparable data about competitors (benchmarking data).

Audit Procedures for Obtaining Audit Evidence

A10   As required by, and explained further in, ISA (UK) 315 (Revised June 2016) and ISA (UK) 330 (Revised July 2017), audit evidence to draw reasonable conclusions on which to base the auditor's opinion is obtained by performing:

(a)   Risk assessment procedures; and

(b)   Further audit procedures, which comprise:

(i)   Tests of controls, when required by the ISAs (UK) or when the auditor has chosen to do so; and

(ii)   Substantive procedures, including tests of details and substantive analytical procedures.

A11   The audit procedures described in paragraphs A14–A25 below may be used as risk assessment procedures, tests of controls or substantive procedures, depending on the context in which they are applied by the auditor. As explained in ISA (UK) 330

---

[84] *ISA (UK) 330 (Revised July 2017), paragraph 26.*

(Revised July 2017), audit evidence obtained from previous audits may, in certain circumstances, provide appropriate audit evidence where the auditor performs audit procedures to establish its continuing relevance.[85]

The nature and timing of the audit procedures to be used may be affected by the fact that some of the accounting data and other information may be available only in electronic form or only at certain points or periods in time. For example, source documents, such as purchase orders and invoices, may exist only in electronic form when an entity uses electronic commerce, or may be discarded after scanning when an entity uses image processing systems to facilitate storage and reference.   **A12**

Certain electronic information may not be retrievable after a specified period of time, for example, if files are changed and if backup files do not exist. Accordingly, the auditor may find it necessary as a result of an entity's data retention policies to request retention of some information for the auditor's review or to perform audit procedures at a time when the information is available.   **A13**

Inspection

Inspection involves examining records or documents, whether internal or external, in paper form, electronic form, or other media, or a physical examination of an asset. Inspection of records and documents provides audit evidence of varying degrees of reliability, depending on their nature and source and, in the case of internal records and documents, on the effectiveness of the controls over their production. An example of inspection used as a test of controls is inspection of records for evidence of authorization.   **A14**

Some documents represent direct audit evidence of the existence of an asset, for example, a document constituting a financial instrument such as a stock or bond. Inspection of such documents may not necessarily provide audit evidence about ownership or value. In addition, inspecting an executed contract may provide audit evidence relevant to the entity's application of accounting policies, such as revenue recognition.   **A15**

Inspection of tangible assets may provide reliable audit evidence with respect to their existence, but not necessarily about the entity's rights and obligations or the valuation of the assets. Inspection of individual inventory items may accompany the observation of inventory counting.   **A16**

Observation

Observation consists of looking at a process or procedure being performed by others, for example, the auditor's observation of inventory counting by the entity's personnel, or of the performance of control activities. Observation provides audit evidence about the performance of a process or procedure, but is limited to the point in time at which the observation takes place, and by the fact that the act of being observed may affect how the process or procedure is performed. See ISA (UK) 501 for further guidance on observation of the counting of inventory.[86]   **A17**

External Confirmation

An external confirmation represents audit evidence obtained by the auditor as a direct written response to the auditor from a third party (the confirming party), in paper form, or by electronic or other medium. External confirmation procedures frequently are relevant when addressing assertions associated with certain account balances and their elements. However, external confirmations need not be   **A18**

---

[85] *ISA (UK) 330 (Revised July 2017), paragraph A35.*

[86] *ISA (UK) 501, Audit Evidence – Specific Considerations for Selected Items.*

restricted to account balances only. For example, the auditor may request confirmation of the terms of agreements or transactions an entity has with third parties; the confirmation request may be designed to ask if any modifications have been made to the agreement and, if so, what the relevant details are. External confirmation procedures also are used to obtain audit evidence about the absence of certain conditions, for example, the absence of a "side agreement" that may influence revenue recognition. See ISA (UK) 505 for further guidance.[87]

Recalculation

A19   Recalculation consists of checking the mathematical accuracy of documents or records. Recalculation may be performed manually or electronically.

Reperformance

A20   Reperformance involves the auditor's independent execution of procedures or controls that were originally performed as part of the entity's internal control.

Analytical Procedures

A21   Analytical procedures consist of evaluations of financial information through analysis of plausible relationships among both financial and non-financial data. Analytical procedures also encompass such investigation as is necessary of identified fluctuations or relationships that are inconsistent with other relevant information or that differ from expected values by a significant amount. See ISA (UK) 520 for further guidance.

Inquiry

A22   Inquiry consists of seeking information of knowledgeable persons, both financial and non-financial, within the entity or outside the entity. Inquiry is used extensively throughout the audit in addition to other audit procedures. Inquiries may range from formal written inquiries to informal oral inquiries. Evaluating responses to inquiries is an integral part of the inquiry process.

A23   Responses to inquiries may provide the auditor with information not previously possessed or with corroborative audit evidence. Alternatively, responses might provide information that differs significantly from other information that the auditor has obtained, for example, information regarding the possibility of management override of controls. In some cases, responses to inquiries provide a basis for the auditor to modify or perform additional audit procedures.

A24   Although corroboration of evidence obtained through inquiry is often of particular importance, in the case of inquiries about management intent, the information available to support management's intent may be limited. In these cases, understanding management's past history of carrying out its stated intentions, management's stated reasons for choosing a particular course of action, and management's ability to pursue a specific course of action may provide relevant information to corroborate the evidence obtained through inquiry.

A25   In respect of some matters, the auditor may consider it necessary to obtain written representations from management and, where appropriate, those charged with governance to confirm responses to oral inquiries. See ISA (UK) 580 for further guidance.[88]

---

[87] *ISA (UK) 505, External Confirmations.*

[88] *ISA (UK) 580, Written Representations.*

Information to Be Used as Audit Evidence

Relevance and Reliability
(Ref: Para. 7)

As noted in paragraph A1, while audit evidence is primarily obtained from audit **A26** procedures performed during the course of the audit, it may also include information obtained from other sources such as, for example, previous audits, in certain circumstances, a firm's quality control procedures for client acceptance and continuance and complying with certain additional responsibilities under law, regulation or relevant ethical requirements (e.g., regarding an entity's non-compliance with laws and regulations). The quality of all audit evidence is affected by the relevance and reliability of the information upon which it is based.

Relevance

Relevance deals with the logical connection with, or bearing upon, the purpose of **A27** the audit procedure and, where appropriate, the assertion under consideration. The relevance of information to be used as audit evidence may be affected by the direction of testing. For example, if the purpose of an audit procedure is to test for overstatement in the existence or valuation of accounts payable, testing the recorded accounts payable may be a relevant audit procedure. On the other hand, when testing for understatement in the existence or valuation of accounts payable, testing the recorded accounts payable would not be relevant, but testing such information as subsequent disbursements, unpaid invoices, suppliers' statements, and unmatched receiving reports may be relevant.

A given set of audit procedures may provide audit evidence that is relevant to **A28** certain assertions, but not others. For example, inspection of documents related to the collection of receivables after the period end may provide audit evidence regarding existence and valuation, but not necessarily cutoff. Similarly, obtaining audit evidence regarding a particular assertion, for example, the existence of inventory, is not a substitute for obtaining audit evidence regarding another assertion, for example, the valuation of that inventory. On the other hand, audit evidence from different sources or of a different nature may often be relevant to the same assertion.

Tests of controls are designed to evaluate the operating effectiveness of controls in **A29** preventing, or detecting and correcting, material misstatements at the assertion level. Designing tests of controls to obtain relevant audit evidence includes identifying conditions (characteristics or attributes) that indicate performance of a control, and deviation conditions which indicate departures from adequate performance. The presence or absence of those conditions can then be tested by the auditor.

Substantive procedures are designed to detect material misstatements at the **A30** assertion level. They comprise tests of details and substantive analytical procedures. Designing substantive procedures includes identifying conditions relevant to the purpose of the test that constitute a misstatement in the relevant assertion.

Reliability

The reliability of information to be used as audit evidence, and therefore of the **A31** audit evidence itself, is influenced by its source and its nature, and the circumstances under which it is obtained, including the controls over its preparation and maintenance where relevant. Therefore, generalizations about the reliability of various kinds of audit evidence are subject to important exceptions. Even when information to be used as audit evidence is obtained from sources external to the entity, circumstances may exist that could affect its reliability. For example, information obtained from ~~ana source~~ independent ~~external source~~of the entity may not be reliable if the source is not knowledgeable, or a management's expert may lack objectivity. While recognizing that exceptions may exist, the following generalizations about the reliability of audit evidence may be useful:

- The reliability of audit evidence is increased when it is obtained from independent sources outside the entity.

- The reliability of audit evidence that is generated internally is increased when the related controls, including those over its preparation and maintenance, imposed by the entity are effective.

- Audit evidence obtained directly by the auditor (for example, observation of the application of a control) is more reliable than audit evidence obtained indirectly or by inference (for example, inquiry about the application of a control).

- Audit evidence in documentary form, whether paper, electronic, or other medium, is more reliable than evidence obtained orally (for example, a contemporaneously written record of a meeting is more reliable than a subsequent oral representation of the matters discussed).

- Audit evidence provided by original documents is more reliable than audit evidence provided by photocopies or facsimiles, or documents that have been filmed, digitized or otherwise transformed into electronic form, the reliability of which may depend on the controls over their preparation and maintenance.

A32   ISA (UK) 520 provides further guidance regarding the reliability of data used for purposes of designing analytical procedures as substantive procedures.[89]

A33   ISA (UK) 240 (Revised June 2016) deals with circumstances where the auditor has reason to believe that a document may not be authentic, or may have been modified without that modification having been disclosed to the auditor.[90]

A33a   ISA (UK) 250 (Revised December 2017)[91] provides further guidance with respect to the auditor complying with any additional responsibilities under law, regulation or relevant ethical requirements regarding an entity's identified or suspected non-compliance with laws and regulations that may provide further information that is relevant to the auditor's work in accordance with ISAs and evaluating the implications of such noncompliance in relation to other aspects of the audit.

External Information Sources

A33b   The auditor is required by paragraph 7 to consider the relevance and reliability of information obtained from an external information source that is to be used as audit evidence, regardless of whether that information has been used by the entity in preparing the financial statements or obtained by the auditor. For information obtained from an external information source, that consideration may, in certain cases, include audit evidence about the external information source or the

---

[89]   *ISA (UK) 520, paragraph 5(a).*

[90]   *ISA (UK) 240 (Revised June 2016), The Auditor's Responsibilities Relating to Fraud in an Audit of Financial Statements, paragraph 13.*

[91]   *ISA (UK) 250 (Revised December 2017), Section A – Consideration of Laws and Regulations in an Audit of Financial Statements, paragraph 9.*

preparation of the information by the external information source, obtained through designing and performing further audit procedures in accordance with ISA (UK) 330 (Revised July 2017) or, where applicable, ISA (UK) 540 (Revised December 2018).[92]

Obtaining an understanding of why management or, when applicable, a   **A33c**
management's expert uses an external information source, and how the relevance and reliability of the information was considered (including its accuracy and completeness), may help to inform the auditor's consideration of the relevance and reliability of that information.

The following factors may be important when considering the relevance and   **A33d**
reliability of information obtained from an external information source, including its accuracy and completeness, taking into account that some of these factors may only be relevant when the information has been used by management in preparing the financial statements or has been obtained by the auditor:

- The nature and authority of the external information source. For example, a central bank or government statistics office with a legislative mandate to provide industry information to the public is likely to be an authority for certain types of information;

- The ability to influence the information obtained, through relationships between the entity and the information source;

- The competence and reputation of the external information source with respect to the information, including whether, in the auditor's professional judgment, the information is routinely provided by a source with a track record of providing reliable information;

- Past experience of the auditor with the reliability of the information provided by the external information source;

- Evidence of general market acceptance by users of the relevance and/or reliability of information from an external information source for a similar purpose to that for which the information has been used by management or the auditor;

- Whether the entity has in place controls to address the relevance and reliability of the information obtained and used;

- Whether the external information source accumulates overall market information or engages directly in "setting" market transactions;

- Whether the information is suitable for use in the manner in which it is being used and, if applicable, was developed taking into account the applicable financial reporting framework;

- Alternative information that may contradict the information used;

- The nature and extent of disclaimers or other restrictive language relating to the information obtained;

- Information about the methods used in preparing the information, how the methods are being applied including, where applicable, how models have been used in such application, and the controls over the methods; and

---

[92] *ISA (UK) 540 (Revised December 2018), Auditing Accounting Estimates and Disclosures.*

- When available, information relevant to considering the appropriateness of assumptions and other data applied by the external information sources in developing the information obtained.

A33e   The nature and extent of the auditor's consideration takes into account the assessed risks of material misstatement at the assertion level to which the use of the external information is relevant, the degree to which the use of that information is relevant to the reasons for the assessed risks of material misstatement and the possibility that the information from the external information source may not be reliable (for example, whether it is from a credible source). Based on the auditor's consideration of the matters described in paragraph A33b, the auditor may determine that further understanding of the entity and its environment, including its internal control, is needed, in accordance with ISA (UK) 315 (Revised June 2016), or that further audit procedures, in accordance with ISA (UK) 330 (Revised July 2017)[93], and ISA (UK) 540 (Revised December 2018)[94] when applicable, are appropriate in the circumstances, to respond to the assessed risks of material misstatement related to the use of information from an external information source. Such procedures may include:

- Performing a comparison of information obtained from the external information source with information obtained from an alternative independent information source.

- When relevant to considering management's use of an external information source, obtaining an understanding of controls management has in place to consider the reliability of the information from external information sources, and potentially testing the operating effectiveness of such controls.

- Performing procedures to obtain information from the external information source to understand its processes, techniques, and assumptions, for the purposes of identifying, understanding and, when relevant, testing the operating effectiveness of its controls.

A33f   In some situations, there may be only one provider of certain information, for example, information from a central bank or government, such as an inflation rate, or a single recognized industry body. In such cases, the auditor's determination of the nature and extent of audit procedures that may be appropriate in the circumstances is influenced by the nature and credibility of the source of the information, the assessed risks of material misstatement to which that external information is relevant, and the degree to which the use of that information is relevant to the reasons for the assessed risk of material misstatement. For example, when the information is from a credible authoritative source, the extent of the auditor's further audit procedures may be less extensive, such as corroborating the information to the source's website or published information. In other cases, if a source is not assessed as credible, the auditor may determine that more extensive procedures are appropriate and, in the absence of any alternative independent information source against which to compare, may consider whether performing procedures to obtain information from the external information source, when practical, is appropriate in order to obtain sufficient appropriate audit evidence.

A33g   When the auditor does not have a sufficient basis with which to consider the relevance and reliability of information from an external information source, the auditor may have a limitation on scope if sufficient appropriate audit evidence

---

[93]   *ISA (UK) 330 (Revised), paragraph 6.*

[94]   *ISA (UK) 540 (Revised December 2018), paragraph 29.*

cannot be obtained through alternative procedures. Any imposed limitation on scope is evaluated in accordance with the requirements of ISA (UK) 705 (Revised June 2016).[95]

Reliability of Information Produced by a Management's Expert
(Ref: Para. 8)

The preparation of an entity's financial statements may require expertise in a field **A34** other than accounting or auditing, such as actuarial calculations, valuations, or engineering data. The entity may employ or engage experts in these fields to obtain the needed expertise to prepare the financial statements. Failure to do so when such expertise is necessary increases the risks of material misstatement.

When information to be used as audit evidence has been prepared using the work **A35** of a management's expert, the requirement in paragraph 8 of this ISA (UK) applies. For example, an individual or organization may possess expertise in the application of models to estimate the fair value of securities for which there is no observable market. If the individual or organization applies that expertise in making an estimate which the entity uses in preparing its financial statements, the individual or organization is a management's expert and paragraph 8 applies. If, on the other hand, that individual or organization merely provides price data regarding private transactions not otherwise available to the entity which the entity uses in its own estimation methods, such information, if used as audit evidence, is subject to paragraph 7 of this ISA (UK), but is being information from an external information source and not the use of a management's expert by the entity.

The nature, timing and extent of audit procedures in relation to the requirement in **A36** paragraph 8 of this ISA (UK), may be affected by such matters as:

- The nature and complexity of the matter to which the management's expert relates.
- The risks of material misstatement in the matter.
- The availability of alternative sources of audit evidence.
- The nature, scope and objectives of the management's expert's work.
- Whether the management's expert is employed by the entity, or is a party engaged by it to provide relevant services.
- The extent to which management can exercise control or influence over the work of the management's expert.
- Whether the management's expert is subject to technical performance standards or other professional or industry requirements.
- The nature and extent of any controls within the entity over the management's expert's work.
- The auditor's knowledge and experience of the management's expert's field of expertise.
- The auditor's previous experience of the work of that expert.

[95] *ISA (UK) 705 (Revised June 2016), Modifications to the Opinion in the Independent Auditor's Report, paragraph 13.*

The Competence, Capabilities and Objectivity of a Management's Expert
(Ref: Para. 8(a))

A37   Competence relates to the nature and level of expertise of the management's expert. Capability relates the ability of the management's expert to exercise that competence in the circumstances. Factors that influence capability may include, for example, geographic location, and the availability of time and resources. Objectivity relates to the possible effects that bias, conflict of interest or the influence of others may have on the professional or business judgment of the management's expert. The competence, capabilities and objectivity of a management's expert, and any controls within the entity over that expert's work, are important factors in relation to the reliability of any information produced by a management's expert.

A38   Information regarding the competence, capabilities and objectivity of a management's expert may come from a variety of sources, such as:

● Personal experience with previous work of that expert.

● Discussions with that expert.

● Discussions with others who are familiar with that expert's work.

● Knowledge of that expert's qualifications, membership of a professional body or industry association, license to practice, or other forms of external recognition.

● Published papers or books written by that expert.

● An auditor's expert, if any, who assists the auditor in obtaining sufficient appropriate audit evidence with respect to information produced by the management's expert.

A39   Matters relevant to evaluating the competence, capabilities and objectivity of a management's expert include whether that expert's work is subject to technical performance standards or other professional or industry requirements, for example, ethical standards and other membership requirements of a professional body or industry association, accreditation standards of a licensing body, or requirements imposed by law or regulation.

A40   Other matters that may be relevant include:

● The relevance of the management's expert's competence to the matter for which that expert's work will be used, including any areas of specialty within that expert's field. For example, a particular actuary may specialize in property and casualty insurance, but have limited expertise regarding pension calculations.

● The management's expert's competence with respect to relevant accounting requirements, for example, knowledge of assumptions and methods, including models where applicable, that are consistent with the applicable financial reporting framework.

● Whether unexpected events, changes in conditions, or the audit evidence obtained from the results of audit procedures indicate that it may be necessary to reconsider the initial evaluation of the competence, capabilities and objectivity of the management's expert as the audit progresses.

A41   A broad range of circumstances may threaten objectivity, for example, self-interest threats, advocacy threats, familiarity threats, self-review threats and intimidation threats. Safeguards may reduce such threats, and may be created either by external structures (for example, the management's expert's profession, legislation or regulation), or by the management's expert's work environment (for example, quality control policies and procedures).

Although safeguards cannot eliminate all threats to a management's expert's objectivity, threats such as intimidation threats may be of less significance to an expert engaged by the entity than to an expert employed by the entity, and the effectiveness of safeguards such as quality control policies and procedures may be greater. Because the threat to objectivity created by being an employee of the entity will always be present, an expert employed by the entity cannot ordinarily be regarded as being more likely to be objective than other employees of the entity.   **A42**

When evaluating the objectivity of an expert engaged by the entity, it may be relevant to discuss with management and that expert any interests and relationships that may create threats to the expert's objectivity, and any applicable safeguards, including any professional requirements that apply to the expert; and to evaluate whether the safeguards are adequate. Interests and relationships creating threats may include: **A43**

● Financial interests.

● Business and personal relationships.

● Provision of other services.

Obtaining an Understanding of the Work of the Management's Expert
(Ref: Para. 8(b))

An understanding of the work of the management's expert includes an understanding of the relevant field of expertise. An understanding of the relevant field of expertise may be obtained in conjunction with the auditor's determination of whether the auditor has the expertise to evaluate the work of the management's expert, or whether the auditor needs an auditor's expert for this purpose.[96]   **A44**

Aspects of the management's expert's field relevant to the auditor's understanding may include: **A45**

● Whether that expert's field has areas of specialty within it that are relevant to the audit.

● Whether any professional or other standards, and regulatory or legal requirements apply.

● What assumptions and methods are used by the management's expert, and whether they are generally accepted within that expert's field and appropriate for financial reporting purposes.

● The nature of internal and external data or information the management's expert uses.

In the case of a management's expert engaged by the entity, there will ordinarily be an engagement letter or other written form of agreement between the entity and that expert. Evaluating that agreement when obtaining an understanding of the work of the management's expert may assist the auditor in determining the appropriateness of the following for the auditor's purposes: **A46**

---

[96] *ISA (UK) 620 (Revised June 2016),* ~~Using the Work of an Auditor's Expert,~~ *paragraph 7.*

- The nature, scope and objectives of that expert's work;

- The respective roles and responsibilities of management and that expert; and

- The nature, timing and extent of communication between management and that expert, including the form of any report to be provided by that expert.

A47   In the case of a management's expert employed by the entity, it is less likely there will be a written agreement of this kind. Inquiry of the expert and other members of management may be the most appropriate way for the auditor to obtain the necessary understanding.

Evaluating the Appropriateness of the Management's Expert's Work
(Ref: Para. 8(c))

A48   Considerations when evaluating the appropriateness of the management's expert's work as audit evidence for the relevant assertion may include:

- The relevance and reasonableness of that expert's findings or conclusions, their consistency with other audit evidence, and whether they have been appropriately reflected in the financial statements;

- If that expert's work involves use of significant assumptions and methods, the relevance and reasonableness of those assumptions and methods; and

- If that expert's work involves significant use of source data the relevance, completeness, and accuracy of that source data; and

- If that expert's work involves the use of information from an external information source, the relevance and reliability of that information.

Information Produced by the Entity and Used for the Auditor's Purposes
(Ref: Para. 9(a)–(b))

A49   In order for the auditor to obtain reliable audit evidence, information produced by the entity that is used for performing audit procedures needs to be sufficiently complete and accurate. For example, the effectiveness of auditing revenue by applying standard prices to records of sales volume is affected by the accuracy of the price information and the completeness and accuracy of the sales volume data. Similarly, if the auditor intends to test a population (for example, payments) for a certain characteristic (for example, authorization), the results of the test will be less reliable if the population from which items are selected for testing is not complete.

A50   Obtaining audit evidence about the accuracy and completeness of such information may be performed concurrently with the actual audit procedure applied to the information when obtaining such audit evidence is an integral part of the audit procedure itself. In other situations, the auditor may have obtained audit evidence of the accuracy and completeness of such information by testing controls over the preparation and maintenance of the information. In some situations, however, the auditor may determine that additional audit procedures are needed.

A51   In some cases, the auditor may intend to use information produced by the entity for other audit purposes. For example, the auditor may intend to make use of the entity's performance measures for the purpose of analytical procedures, or to make use of the entity's information produced for monitoring activities, such as reports of the internal audit function. In such cases, the appropriateness of the audit evidence obtained is affected by whether the information is sufficiently precise or detailed for the auditor's purposes. For example, performance measures used by management may not be precise enough to detect material misstatements.

Selecting Items for Testing to Obtain Audit Evidence
(Ref: Para. 10)

An effective test provides appropriate audit evidence to an extent that, taken with **A52** other audit evidence obtained or to be obtained, will be sufficient for the auditor's purposes. In selecting items for testing, the auditor is required by paragraph 7 to determine the relevance and reliability of information to be used as audit evidence; the other aspect of effectiveness (sufficiency) is an important consideration in selecting items to test. The means available to the auditor for selecting items for testing are:

(a)   Selecting all items (100% examination);

(b)   Selecting specific items; and

(c)   Audit sampling.

The application of any one or combination of these means may be appropriate depending on the particular circumstances, for example, the risks of material misstatement related to the assertion being tested, and the practicality and efficiency of the different means.

Selecting All Items

The auditor may decide that it will be most appropriate to examine the entire **A53** population of items that make up a class of transactions or account balance (or a stratum within that population). 100% examination is unlikely in the case of tests of controls; however, it is more common for tests of details. 100% examination may be appropriate when, for example:

•   The population constitutes a small number of large value items;

•   There is a significant risk and other means do not provide sufficient appropriate audit evidence; or

•   The repetitive nature of a calculation or other process performed automatically by an information system makes a 100% examination cost effective.

Selecting Specific Items

The auditor may decide to select specific items from a population. In making this **A54** decision, factors that may be relevant include the auditor's understanding of the entity, the assessed risks of material misstatement, and the characteristics of the population being tested. The judgmental selection of specific items is subject to non-sampling risk. Specific items selected may include:

•   *High value or key items*. The auditor may decide to select specific items within a population because they are of high value, or exhibit some other characteristic, for example, items that are suspicious, unusual, particularly risk-prone or that have a history of error.

•   *All items over a certain amount*. The auditor may decide to examine items whose recorded values exceed a certain amount so as to verify a large proportion of the total amount of a class of transactions or account balance.

•   *Items to obtain information*. The auditor may examine items to obtain information about matters such as the nature of the entity, or the nature of transactions.

A55   While selective examination of specific items from a class of transactions or account balance will often be an efficient means of obtaining audit evidence, it does not constitute audit sampling. The results of audit procedures applied to items selected in this way cannot be projected to the entire population; accordingly, selective examination of specific items does not provide audit evidence concerning the remainder of the population.

Audit Sampling

A56   Audit sampling is designed to enable conclusions to be drawn about an entire population on the basis of testing a sample drawn from it. Audit sampling is discussed in ISA (UK) 530.[97]

Inconsistency in, or Doubts over Reliability of, Audit Evidence
(Ref: Para. 11)

A57   Obtaining audit evidence from different sources or of a different nature may indicate that an individual item of audit evidence is not reliable, such as when audit evidence obtained from one source is inconsistent with that obtained from another. This may be the case when, for example, responses to inquiries of management, internal auditors, and others are inconsistent, or when responses to inquiries of those charged with governance made to corroborate the responses to inquiries of management are inconsistent with the response by management. ISA (UK) 230 (Revised June 2016) includes a specific documentation requirement if the auditor identified information that is inconsistent with the auditor's final conclusion regarding a significant matter.[98]

ISA (UK) 580, Written Representations

Appendix 1 – List of ISAs (UK) Containing Requirements for Written Representations
(Ref: Para. 2)

This appendix identifies paragraphs in other ISAs (UK) that require subject-matter specific written representations. The list is not a substitute for considering the requirements and related application and other explanatory material in ISAs (UK).

- ISA (UK) 240 (Revised June 2016), *The Auditor's Responsibilities Relating to Fraud in an Audit of Financial Statements* – paragraph 39

- ISA (UK) 250 (Revised December 2017), *Section A – Consideration of Laws and Regulations in an Audit of Financial Statements* – paragraph 16

- ISA (UK) 450 (Revised June 2016), *Evaluation of Misstatements Identified during the Audit* – paragraph 14

- ISA (UK) 501, *Audit Evidence – Specific Considerations for Selected Items* – paragraph 12

- ISA (UK) 540 (Revised December 2018), *Auditing Accounting Estimates, Including Fair Value Accounting Estimates, and Related Disclosures* – paragraph 2237

---

[97] *ISA (UK) 530, Audit Sampling.*

[98] *ISA (UK) 230 (Revised June 2016), Audit Documentation, paragraph 11.*

- ISA (UK) 550, *Related Parties* – paragraph 26
- ISA (UK) 560, *Subsequent Events* – paragraph 9
- ISA (UK) 570 (Revised June 2016), *Going Concern* – paragraph 16(e)
- ISA (UK) 710, *Comparative Information – Corresponding Figures and Comparative Financial Statements* – paragraph 9
- ISA (UK) 720 (Revised June 2016), *The Auditor's Responsibilities Relating to Other Information* – paragraph 13(c)

Appendix 2 – Illustrative Representation Letter
(Ref: Para. A21)

> This illustrative representation letter has not been tailored for the UK. For example, when describing the responsibilities of management and those charged with governance for the financial statements and providing information to the auditor, the auditor has regard to the manner in which those responsibilities are described in the terms of the audit engagement (see ISA (UK) 210 (Revised June 2016)).

The following illustrative letter includes written representations that are required by this and other ISAs. It is assumed in this illustration that the applicable financial reporting framework is International Financial Reporting Standards; the requirement of ISA 570 (Revised)[99] to obtain a written representation is not relevant; and that there are no exceptions to the requested written representations. If there were exceptions, the representations would need to be modified to reflect the exceptions.

(Entity Letterhead)

(To Auditor)   (Date)

This representation letter is provided in connection with your audit of the financial statements of ABC Company for the year ended December 31, 20XX[100] for the purpose of expressing an opinion as to whether the financial statements are presented fairly, in all material respects, (or *give a true and fair view*) in accordance with International Financial Reporting Standards.

We confirm that (*, to the best of our knowledge and belief, having made such inquiries as we considered necessary for the purpose of appropriately informing ourselves*):

Financial Statements

- We have fulfilled our responsibilities, as set out in the terms of the audit engagement dated [insert date], for the preparation of the financial statements in accordance with International Financial Reporting Standards; in particular the financial statements are fairly presented (or give a true and fair view) in accordance therewith.

---

[99] *ISA 570 (Revised), Going Concern.*

[100] *Where the auditor reports on more than one period, the auditor adjusts the date so that the letter pertains to all periods covered by the auditor's report.*

- ~~Significant~~ The methods, the data, and the significant assumptions used in making accounting estimates, ~~including those measured at fair value,~~ and their related disclosures are appropriate to achieve recognition, measurement or disclosure that is reasonable in the context of the applicable financial reporting framework. (ISA 540 (Revised))

Related party relationships and transactions have been appropriately accounted for and disclosed in accordance with the requirements of International Financial Reporting Standards. (ISA 550)

***

ISA (UK) 700 (Revised June 2016), Forming an Opinion and Reporting on Financial Statements

Requirements

...

Forming an Opinion on the Financial Statements

13   In particular, the auditor shall evaluate whether, in view of the requirements of the applicable financial reporting framework:

(a)   The financial statements appropriately disclose the significant accounting policies selected and applied. In making this evaluation, the auditor shall consider the relevance of the accounting policies to the entity, and whether they have been presented in an understandable manner; (Ref: Para. A4)

(b)   The accounting policies selected and applied are consistent with the applicable financial reporting framework and are appropriate;

(c)   The accounting estimates and related disclosures made by management are reasonable;

(d)   The information presented in the financial statements is relevant, reliable, comparable, and understandable. In making this evaluation, the auditor shall consider whether:

- The information that should have been included has been included, and whether such information is appropriately classified, aggregated or disaggregated, and characterized.

- The overall presentation of the financial statements has been undermined by including information that is not relevant or that obscures a proper understanding of the matters disclosed. (Ref: Para. A5)

(e)   The financial statements provide adequate disclosures to enable the intended users to understand the effect of material transactions and events on the information conveyed in the financial statements; and (Ref: Para. A6)

(f)   The terminology used in the financial statements, including the title of each financial statement, is appropriate.

***

ISA (UK) 701, Communicating Key Audit Matters in the Independent Auditor's Report

Requirements

...

Determining Key Audit Matters

The auditor shall determine, from the matters communicated with those charged   **9**
with governance, those matters that required significant auditor attention in
performing the audit. In making this determination, the auditor shall take into
account the following: (Ref: Para. A9–A18)

(a)   Areas of higher assessed risk of material misstatement, or significant risks
      identified in accordance with ISA (UK) 315 (Revised June 2016). (Ref:
      Para. A19–A22)

(b)   Significant auditor judgments relating to areas in the financial statements
      that involved significant management judgment, including accounting
      estimates that ~~have~~ are subject to ~~been identified as having~~ a high degree
      of estimation uncertainty. (Ref: Para. A23–A24)

(c)   The effect on the audit of significant events or transactions that occurred
      during the period. (Ref: Para. A25–A26)

...

Application and Other Explanatory Material

Significant Auditor Judgments Relating to Areas in the Financial Statements that
Involved Significant Management Judgment, Including Accounting Estimates that
~~Have Been Identified as Having~~Are Subject to a High Degree of Estimation
Uncertainty (Ref: Para. 9(b))

ISA (UK) 260 (Revised June 2016) requires the auditor to communicate with   **A23**
those charged with governance the auditor's views about significant qualitative
aspects of the entity's accounting practices, including accounting policies,
accounting estimates and financial statement disclosures.[101] In many cases, this
relates to critical accounting estimates and related disclosures, which are likely to
be areas of significant auditor attention, and also may be identified as significant
risks.

However, users of the financial statements have highlighted their interest in   **A24**
accounting estimates that ~~have~~ are subject to a ~~been identified as having~~high
degree of estimation uncertainty (~~see~~in accordance withISA (UK) 540 (Revised
December 2018)[102]) that may have not been determined to be significant risks.
Among other things, such estimates are highly dependent on management
judgment and are often the most complex areas of the financial statements, and
may require the involvement of both a management's expert and an auditor's

---

[101] *ISA (UK) 260 (Revised June 2016), paragraph 16(a).*

[102] *See paragraphs* ~~16~~0–17~~1~~ *of ISA (UK) 540 (Revised December 2018), Auditing Accounting Estimates,* ~~Including Fair Value Accounting Estimates,~~ *and Related Disclosures.*

expert. Users have also highlighted that accounting policies that have a significant effect on the financial statements (and significant changes to those policies) are relevant to their understanding of the financial statements, especially in circumstances where an entity's practices are not consistent with others in its industry.

ISA (UK) 550
Related Parties

*(Effective for audits of financial statements for periods ending on
or after 15 December 2010)*

Contents

Paragraphs

Introduction 1 - 8
  Scope of this ISA (UK) 1
  Nature of related party relationships and transactions 2
  Responsibilities of the auditor 3 - 7
  Effective date 8

Objectives 9

Definitions 10

Requirements 11 - 28
  Risk assessment procedures and related activities 11 - 17
  Identification and assessment of the risks of material misstatement associated
  with related party relationships and transactions 18 - 19
  Responses to the risks of material misstatement associated with related
  party relationships and transactions 20 - 24
  Evaluation of the accounting for and disclosure of identified related party
  relationships and transactions 25
  Written representations 26
  Communication with those charged with governance 27
  Documentation 28

Application and other explanatory material
  Responsibilities of the auditor A1 - A3
  Definition of a related party A4 - A7
  Risk assessment procedures and related activities A8 - A28
  Identification and assessment of the risks of material misstatement associated
  with related party relationships and transactions A29 - A30
  Responses to the risks of material misstatement associated with related party
  relationships and transactions A31 - A45
  Evaluation of the accounting for and disclosure of identified related party
  relationships and transactions A46 - A47-1
  Written representations A48 - A49-1
  Communication with those charged with governance A50

International Standard on Auditing (UK) (ISA (UK)) 550, *Related Parties*, should be read in conjunction with ISA (UK) 200 (Revised June 2016), *Overall Objectives of the Independent Auditor and the Conduct of an Audit in Accordance with International Standards on Auditing (UK).*

Introduction

Scope of this ISA (UK)

1   This International Standard on Auditing (UK) (ISA (UK)) deals with the auditor's responsibilities relating to related party relationships and transactions in an audit of financial statements. Specifically, it expands on how ISA (UK) 315 (Revised June 2016),[1] ISA (UK) 330 (Revised June 2016),[2] and ISA (UK) 240 (Revised June 2016)[3] are to be applied in relation to risks of material misstatement associated with related party relationships and transactions.

Nature of Related Party Relationships and Transactions

2   Many related party transactions are in the normal course of business. In such circumstances, they may carry no higher risk of material misstatement of the financial statements than similar transactions with unrelated parties. However, the nature of related party relationships and transactions may, in some circumstances, give rise to higher risks of material misstatement of the financial statements than transactions with unrelated parties. For example:

  ● Related parties may operate through an extensive and complex range of relationships and structures, with a corresponding increase in the complexity of related party transactions.

  ● Information systems may be ineffective at identifying or summarizing transactions and outstanding balances between an entity and its related parties.

  ● Related party transactions may not be conducted under normal market terms and conditions; for example, some related party transactions may be conducted with no exchange of consideration.

Responsibilities of the Auditor

3   Because related parties are not independent of each other, many financial reporting frameworks establish specific accounting and disclosure requirements for related party relationships, transactions and balances to enable users of the financial statements to understand their nature and actual or potential effects on the financial statements. Where the applicable financial reporting framework establishes such requirements[3a], the auditor has a responsibility to perform audit procedures to identify, assess and respond to the risks of material misstatement arising from the entity's failure to appropriately account for or disclose related party relationships, transactions or balances in accordance with the requirements of the framework.

4   Even if the applicable financial reporting framework establishes minimal or no related party requirements, the auditor nevertheless needs to obtain an understanding of the entity's related party relationships and transactions sufficient to be able to conclude whether the financial statements, insofar as they are affected by those relationships and transactions: (Ref: Para. A1)

---

[1] *ISA (UK) 315 (Revised June 2016), Identifying and Assessing the Risks of Material Misstatement through Understanding the Entity and Its Environment.*

[2] *ISA (UK) 330 (Revised June 2016), The Auditor's Responses to Assessed Risks.*

[3] *ISA (UK) 240 (Revised June 2016), The Auditor's Responsibilities Relating to Fraud in an Audit of Financial Statements.*

[3a] *In the UK, specific accounting and disclosure requirements for related party relationships, transactions and balances are established in accounting standards and in law and regulations.*

(a) Achieve fair presentation (for fair presentation frameworks); or (Ref: Para. A2)

(b) Are not misleading (for compliance frameworks). (Ref: Para. A3)

In addition, an understanding of the entity's related party relationships and 5 transactions is relevant to the auditor's evaluation of whether one or more fraud risk factors are present as required by ISA (UK) 240 (Revised June 2016),[4] because fraud may be more easily committed through related parties.

Owing to the inherent limitations of an audit, there is an unavoidable risk that 6 some material misstatements of the financial statements may not be detected, even though the audit is properly planned and performed in accordance with the ISAs (UK).[5] In the context of related parties, the potential effects of inherent limitations on the auditor's ability to detect material misstatements are greater for such reasons as the following:

- Management may be unaware of the existence of all related party relationships and transactions, particularly if the applicable financial reporting framework does not establish related party requirements.

- Related party relationships may present a greater opportunity for collusion, concealment or manipulation by management.

Planning and performing the audit with professional skepticism as required by 7 ISA (UK) 200 (Revised June 2016)[6] is therefore particularly important in this context, given the potential for undisclosed related party relationships and transactions. The requirements in this ISA (UK) are designed to assist the auditor in identifying and assessing the risks of material misstatement associated with related party relationships and transactions, and in designing audit procedures to respond to the assessed risks.

Effective Date

This ISA (UK) is effective for audits of financial statements for periods ending on 8 or after 15 December 2010.

Objectives

The objectives of the auditor are: 9

(a) Irrespective of whether the applicable financial reporting framework establishes related party requirements, to obtain an understanding of related party relationships and transactions sufficient to be able:

   (i) To recognize fraud risk factors, if any, arising from related party relationships and transactions that are relevant to the identification and assessment of the risks of material misstatement due to fraud; and

   (ii) To conclude, based on the audit evidence obtained, whether the financial statements, insofar as they are affected by those relationships and transactions:

---

[4] *ISA (UK) 240 (Revised June 2016), paragraph 24.*

[5] *ISA (UK) 200 (Revised June 2016), Overall Objectives of the Independent Auditor and the Conduct of an Audit in Accordance with International Standards on Auditing (UK), paragraphs A51–A52.*

[6] *ISA (UK) 200 (Revised June 2016), paragraph 15.*

(a)   Achieve fair presentation (for fair presentation frameworks); or

(b)   Are not misleading (for compliance frameworks); and

(b)   In addition, where the applicable financial reporting framework establishes related party requirements, to obtain sufficient appropriate audit evidence about whether related party relationships and transactions have been appropriately identified, accounted for and disclosed in the financial statements in accordance with the framework.

Definitions

10   For purposes of the ISAs (UK), the following terms have the meanings attributed below:

(a)   Arm's length transaction – A transaction conducted on such terms and conditions as between a willing buyer and a willing seller who are unrelated and are acting independently of each other and pursuing their own best interests.

(b)   Related party – A party that is either: (Ref: Para. A4–A7)

   (i)   A related party as defined in the applicable financial reporting framework; or

   (ii)   Where the applicable financial reporting framework establishes minimal or no related party requirements:

      (a)   A person or other entity that has control or significant influence, directly or indirectly through one or more intermediaries, over the reporting entity;

      (b)   Another entity over which the reporting entity has control or significant influence, directly or indirectly through one or more intermediaries; or

      (c)   Another entity that is under common control with the reporting entity through having:
         (i)   Common controlling ownership;
         (ii)   Owners who are close family members; or
         (iii)   Common key management.

However, entities that are under common control by a state (that is, a national, regional or local government) are not considered related unless they engage in significant transactions or share resources to a significant extent with one another.

Requirements

Risk Assessment Procedures and Related Activities

11   As part of the risk assessment procedures and related activities that ISA (UK) 315 (Revised June 2016) and ISA (UK) 240 (Revised June 2016) require the auditor to perform during the audit,[7] the auditor shall perform the audit procedures and related activities set out in paragraphs 12–17 to obtain information relevant to identifying the risks of material misstatement associated with related party relationships and transactions. (Ref: Para. A8)

---

[7]   *ISA (UK) 315 (Revised June 2016), paragraph 5; ISA (UK) 240 (Revised June 2016), paragraph 16.*

Understanding the Entity's Related Party Relationships and Transactions

The engagement team discussion that ISA (UK) 315 (Revised June 2016) and ISA   **12**
(UK) 240 (Revised June 2016) require[8] shall include specific consideration of the
susceptibility of the financial statements to material misstatement due to fraud or
error that could result from the entity's related party relationships and transactions.
(Ref: Para. A9–A10)

The auditor shall inquire of management regarding: **13**

(a)   The identity of the entity's related parties, including changes from the prior
      period; (Ref: Para. A11–A14)

(b)   The nature of the relationships between the entity and these related parties;
      and

(c)   Whether the entity entered into any transactions with these related parties
      during the period and, if so, the type and purpose of the transactions.

The auditor shall inquire of management and others within the entity, and perform   **14**
other risk assessment procedures considered appropriate, to obtain an understanding
of the controls, if any, that management has established to: (Ref: Para. A15–A20)

(a)   Identify, account for, and disclose related party relationships and
      transactions in accordance with the applicable financial reporting
      framework;

(b)   Authorize and approve significant transactions and arrangements with
      related parties; and (Ref: Para. A21)

(c)   Authorize and approve significant transactions and arrangements outside the
      normal course of business.

*Maintaining Alertness for Related Party Information When Reviewing Records or
Documents*

During the audit, the auditor shall remain alert, when inspecting records or   **15**
documents, for arrangements or other information that may indicate the
existence of related party relationships or transactions that management has not
previously identified or disclosed to the auditor. (Ref: Para. A22–A23)

In particular, the auditor shall inspect the following for indications of the existence
of related party relationships or transactions that management has not previously
identified or disclosed to the auditor:

(a)   Bank and legal confirmations obtained as part of the auditor's procedures;

(b)   Minutes of meetings of shareholders and of those charged with governance;
      and

(c)   Such other records or documents as the auditor considers necessary in the
      circumstances of the entity.

If the auditor identifies significant transactions outside the entity's normal course   **16**
of business when performing the audit procedures required by paragraph 15 or
through other audit procedures, the auditor shall inquire of management about:
(Ref: Para. A24–A25)

(a)   The nature of these transactions; and (Ref: Para. A26)

(b)   Whether related parties could be involved. (Ref: Para. A27)

---

[8] *ISA (UK) 315 (Revised June 2016), paragraph 10; ISA (UK) 240 (Revised June 2016), paragraph 15.*

Sharing Related Party Information with the Engagement Team

17 The auditor shall share relevant information obtained about the entity's related parties with the other members of the engagement team. (Ref: Para. A28)

Identification and Assessment of the Risks of Material Misstatement Associated with Related Party Relationships and Transactions

18 In meeting the ISA (UK) 315 (Revised June 2016) requirement to identify and assess the risks of material misstatement,[9] the auditor shall identify and assess the risks of material misstatement associated with related party relationships and transactions and determine whether any of those risks are significant risks. In making this determination, the auditor shall treat identified significant related party transactions outside the entity's normal course of business as giving rise to significant risks.

19 If the auditor identifies fraud risk factors (including circumstances relating to the existence of a related party with dominant influence) when performing the risk assessment procedures and related activities in connection with related parties, the auditor shall consider such information when identifying and assessing the risks of material misstatement due to fraud in accordance with ISA (UK) 240 (Revised June 2016). (Ref: Para. A6 and A29–A30)

Responses to the Risks of Material Misstatement Associated with Related Party Relationships and Transactions

20 As part of the ISA (UK) 330 (Revised June 2016) requirement that the auditor respond to assessed risks,[10] the auditor designs and performs further audit procedures to obtain sufficient appropriate audit evidence about the assessed risks of material misstatement associated with related party relationships and transactions. These audit procedures shall include those required by paragraphs 21–24. (Ref: Para. A31–A34)

Identification of Previously Unidentified or Undisclosed Related Parties or Significant Related Party Transactions

21 If the auditor identifies arrangements or information that suggests the existence of related party relationships or transactions that management has not previously identified or disclosed to the auditor, the auditor shall determine whether the underlying circumstances confirm the existence of those relationships or transactions.

22 If the auditor identifies related parties or significant related party transactions that management has not previously identified or disclosed to the auditor, the auditor shall:

(a) Promptly communicate the relevant information to the other members of the engagement team; (Ref: Para. A35)

(b) Where the applicable financial reporting framework establishes related party requirements:

(i) Request management to identify all transactions with the newly identified related parties for the auditor's further evaluation; and

---

[9] *ISA (UK) 315 (Revised June 2016), paragraph 25.*

[10] *ISA (UK) 330 (Revised June 2016), paragraphs 5–6.*

(ii)   Inquire as to why the entity's controls over related party relationships and transactions failed to enable the identification or disclosure of the related party relationships or transactions;

(c)   Perform appropriate substantive audit procedures relating to such newly identified related parties or significant related party transactions; (Ref: Para. A36)

(d)   Reconsider the risk that other related parties or significant related party transactions may exist that management has not previously identified or disclosed to the auditor, and perform additional audit procedures as necessary; and

(e)   If the non-disclosure by management appears intentional (and therefore indicative of a risk of material misstatement due to fraud), evaluate the implications for the audit. (Ref: Para. A37)

Identified Significant Related Party Transactions outside the Entity's Normal Course of Business

For identified significant related party transactions outside the entity's normal course of business, the auditor shall: **23**

(a)   Inspect the underlying contracts or agreements, if any, and evaluate whether:

(i)   The business rationale (or lack thereof) of the transactions suggests that they may have been entered into to engage in fraudulent financial reporting or to conceal misappropriation of assets;[11] (Ref: Para. A38–A39)

(ii)   The terms of the transactions are consistent with management's explanations; and

(iii)   The transactions have been appropriately accounted for and disclosed in accordance with the applicable financial reporting framework; and

(b)   Obtain audit evidence that the transactions have been appropriately authorized and approved. (Ref: Para. A40–A41)

Assertions That Related Party Transactions Were Conducted on Terms Equivalent to Those Prevailing in an Arm's Length Transaction

If management has made an assertion in the financial statements to the effect that a related party transaction was conducted on terms equivalent to those prevailing in an arm's length transaction, the auditor shall obtain sufficient appropriate audit evidence about the assertion. (Ref: Para. A42–A45)   **24**

Evaluation of the Accounting for and Disclosure of Identified Related Party Relationships and Transactions

In forming an opinion on the financial statements in accordance with ISA (UK) 700 (Revised June 2016),[12] the auditor shall evaluate: (Ref: Para. A46)   **25**

(a)   Whether the identified related party relationships and transactions have been appropriately accounted for and disclosed in accordance with the applicable financial reporting framework; and (Ref: Para. A47–A47-1)

---

[11] *ISA (UK) 240 (Revised June 2016), paragraph 32(c).*

[12] *ISA (UK) 700 (Revised June 2016), Forming an Opinion and Reporting on Financial Statements, paragraphs 10–15.*

(b)   Whether the effects of the related party relationships and transactions:

    (i)   Prevent the financial statements from achieving fair presentation (for fair presentation frameworks); or

    (ii)   Cause the financial statements to be misleading (for compliance frameworks).

Written Representations

26   Where the applicable financial reporting framework establishes related party requirements, the auditor shall obtain written representations from management and, where appropriate, those charged with governance that: (Ref: Para. A48–A49-1)

(a)   They have disclosed to the auditor the identity of the entity's related parties and all the related party relationships and transactions of which they are aware; and

(b)   They have appropriately accounted for and disclosed such relationships and transactions in accordance with the requirements of the framework.

Communication with Those Charged with Governance

27   Unless all of those charged with governance are involved in managing the entity,[13] the auditor shall communicate with those charged with governance significant matters arising during the audit in connection with the entity's related parties. (Ref: Para. A50)

Documentation

28   The auditor shall include in the audit documentation the names of the identified related parties and the nature of the related party relationships.[14]

Application and Other Explanatory Material

Responsibilities of the Auditor

Financial Reporting Frameworks That Establish Minimal Related Party Requirements
(Ref: Para. 4)

A1   An applicable financial reporting framework that establishes minimal related party requirements is one that defines the meaning of a related party but that definition has a substantially narrower scope than the definition set out in paragraph 10(b)(ii) of this ISA (UK), so that a requirement in the framework to disclose related party relationships and transactions would apply to substantially fewer related party relationships and transactions.

---

[13]   *ISA (UK) 260 (Revised June 2016), Communication with Those Charged with Governance, paragraph 13.*

[14]   *ISA (UK) 230 (Revised June 2016), Audit Documentation, paragraphs 8–11, and paragraph A6.*

Fair Presentation Frameworks
(Ref: Para. 4(a))

In the context of a fair presentation framework,[15] related party relationships and **A2** transactions may cause the financial statements to fail to achieve fair presentation if, for example, the economic reality of such relationships and transactions is not appropriately reflected in the financial statements. For instance, fair presentation may not be achieved if the sale of a property by the entity to a controlling shareholder at a price above or below fair market value has been accounted for as a transaction involving a profit or loss for the entity when it may constitute a contribution or return of capital or the payment of a dividend.

Compliance Frameworks
(Ref: Para. 4(b))

In the context of a compliance framework, whether related party relationships and **A3** transactions cause the financial statements to be misleading as discussed in ISA (UK) 700 (Revised June 2016) depends upon the particular circumstances of the engagement. For example, even if non-disclosure of related party transactions in the financial statements is in compliance with the framework and applicable law or regulation, the financial statements could be misleading if the entity derives a very substantial portion of its revenue from transactions with related parties, and that fact is not disclosed. However, it will be extremely rare for the auditor to consider financial statements that are prepared and presented in accordance with a compliance framework to be misleading if in accordance with ISA (UK) 210 (Revised June 2016)[16] the auditor determined that the framework is acceptable.[17]

Definition of a Related Party
(Ref: Para. 10(b))

Many financial reporting frameworks discuss the concepts of control and **A4** significant influence. Although they may discuss these concepts using different terms, they generally explain that:

(a)   Control is the power to govern the financial and operating policies of an entity so as to obtain benefits from its activities; and

(b)   Significant influence (which may be gained by share ownership, statute or agreement) is the power to participate in the financial and operating policy decisions of an entity, but is not control over those policies.

The existence of the following relationships may indicate the presence of control **A5** or significant influence:

(a)   Direct or indirect equity holdings or other financial interests in the entity.

(b)   The entity's holdings of direct or indirect equity or other financial interests in other entities.

(c)   Being part of those charged with governance or key management (that is, those members of management who have the authority and responsibility for planning, directing and controlling the activities of the entity).

---

[15] *ISA (UK) 200 (Revised June 2016), paragraph 13(a), defines the meaning of fair presentation and compliance frameworks.*

[16] *ISA (UK) 210 (Revised June 2016), Agreeing the Terms of Audit Engagements, paragraph 6(a).*

[17] *ISA (UK) 700 (Revised June 2016), paragraph A12.*

(d)   Being a close family member of any person referred to in subparagraph (c).

(e)   Having a significant business relationship with any person referred to in subparagraph (c).

Related Parties with Dominant Influence

A6   Related parties, by virtue of their ability to exert control or significant influence, may be in a position to exert dominant influence over the entity or its management. Consideration of such behavior is relevant when identifying and assessing the risks of material misstatement due to fraud, as further explained in paragraphs A29–A30.

Special-Purpose Entities as Related Parties

A7   In some circumstances, a special-purpose entity[18] may be a related party of the entity because the entity may in substance control it, even if the entity owns little or none of the special-purpose entity's equity.

Risk Assessment Procedures and Related Activities

Risks of Material Misstatement Associated with Related Party Relationships and Transactions
(Ref: Para. 11)

Considerations Specific to Public Sector Entities

A8   The public sector auditor's responsibilities regarding related party relationships and transactions may be affected by the audit mandate, or by obligations on public sector entities arising from law, regulation or other authority. Consequently, the public sector auditor's responsibilities may not be limited to addressing the risks of material misstatement associated with related party relationships and transactions, but may also include a broader responsibility to address the risks of non-compliance with law, regulation and other authority governing public sector bodies that lay down specific requirements in the conduct of business with related parties. Further, the public sector auditor may need to have regard to public sector financial reporting requirements for related party relationships and transactions that may differ from those in the private sector.

Understanding the Entity's Related Party Relationships and Transactions

Discussion among the Engagement Team
(Ref: Para. 12)

A9   Matters that may be addressed in the discussion among the engagement team include:

●   The nature and extent of the entity's relationships and transactions with related parties (using, for example, the auditor's record of identified related parties updated after each audit).

●   An emphasis on the importance of maintaining professional skepticism throughout the audit regarding the potential for material misstatement associated with related party relationships and transactions.

---

[18] *ISA (UK) 315 (Revised June 2016), paragraphs A26–A27, provides guidance regarding the nature of a special-purpose entity.*

- The circumstances or conditions of the entity that may indicate the existence of related party relationships or transactions that management has not identified or disclosed to the auditor for example, a complex organizational structure, use of special-purpose entities for off-balance sheet transactions, or an inadequate information system).

- The records or documents that may indicate the existence of related party relationships or transactions.

- The importance that management and those charged with governance attach to the identification, appropriate accounting for, and disclosure of related party relationships and transactions (if the applicable financial reporting framework establishes related party requirements), and the related risk of management override of relevant controls.

In addition, the discussion in the context of fraud may include specific consideration of how related parties may be involved in fraud. For example: **A10**

- How special-purpose entities controlled by management might be used to facilitate earnings management.

- How transactions between the entity and a known business partner of a key member of management could be arranged to facilitate misappropriation of the entity's assets.

The Identity of the Entity's Related Parties
(Ref: Para. 13(a))

Where the applicable financial reporting framework establishes related party requirements, information regarding the identity of the entity's related parties is likely to be readily available to management because the entity's information systems will need to record, process and summarize related party relationships and transactions to enable the entity to meet the accounting and disclosure requirements of the framework. Management is therefore likely to have a comprehensive list of related parties and changes from the prior period. For recurring engagements, making the inquiries provides a basis for comparing the information supplied by management with the auditor's record of related parties noted in previous audits. **A11**

However, where the framework does not establish related party requirements, the entity may not have such information systems in place. Under such circumstances, it is possible that management may not be aware of the existence of all related parties. Nevertheless, the requirement to make the inquiries specified by paragraph 13 still applies because management may be aware of parties that meet the related party definition set out in this ISA (UK). In such a case, however, the auditor's inquiries regarding the identity of the entity's related parties are likely to form part of the auditor's risk assessment procedures and related activities performed in accordance with ISA (UK) 315 (Revised June 2016) to obtain information regarding: **A12**

- The entity's ownership and governance structures;

- The types of investments that the entity is making and plans to make; and

- The way the entity is structured and how it is financed.

In the particular case of common control relationships, as management is more likely to be aware of such relationships if they have economic significance to the entity, the auditor's inquiries are likely to be more effective if they are focused on whether parties with which the entity engages in significant transactions, or shares resources to a significant degree, are related parties.

A13   In the context of a group audit, ISA (UK) 600 (Revised June 2016) requires the group engagement team to provide each component auditor with a list of related parties prepared by group management and any other related parties of which the group engagement team is aware.[19] Where the entity is a component within a group, this information provides a useful basis for the auditor's inquiries of management regarding the identity of the entity's related parties.

A14   The auditor may also obtain some information regarding the identity of the entity's related parties through inquiries of management during the engagement acceptance or continuance process.

The Entity's Controls over Related Party Relationships and Transactions (Ref: Para. 14)

A15   Others within the entity are those considered likely to have knowledge of the entity's related party relationships and transactions, and the entity's controls over such relationships and transactions. These may include, to the extent that they do not form part of management:

- Those charged with governance;

- Personnel in a position to initiate, process, or record transactions that are both significant and outside the entity's normal course of business, and those who supervise or monitor such personnel;

- The internal audit function;

- In-house legal counsel; and

- The chief ethics officer or equivalent person.

A16   The audit is conducted on the premise that management and, where appropriate, those charged with governance have acknowledged and understand that they have responsibility for the preparation of the financial statements in accordance with the applicable financial reporting framework, including where relevant their fair presentation, and for such internal control as management and, where appropriate, those charged with governance determine is necessary to enable the preparation of financial statements that are free from material misstatement, whether due to fraud or error.[20] Accordingly, where the framework establishes related party requirements, the preparation of the financial statements requires management, with oversight from those charged with governance, to design, implement and maintain adequate controls over related party relationships and transactions so that these are identified and appropriately accounted for and disclosed in accordance with the framework. In their oversight role, those charged with governance monitor how management is discharging its responsibility for such controls. Regardless of any related party requirements the framework may establish, those charged with governance may, in their oversight role, obtain

---

[19] *ISA (UK) 600 (Revised June 2016), Special Considerations—Audits of Group Financial Statements (Including the Work of Component Auditors), paragraph 40(e).*

[20] *ISA (UK) 200 (Revised June 2016), paragraph A2.*

information from management to enable them to understand the nature and business rationale of the entity's related party relationships and transactions.

In meeting the ISA (UK) 315 (Revised) requirement to obtain an understanding of the control environment,[21] the auditor may consider features of the control environment relevant to mitigating the risks of material misstatement associated with related party relationships and transactions, such as: **A17**

- Internal ethical codes, appropriately communicated to the entity's personnel and enforced, governing the circumstances in which the entity may enter into specific types of related party transactions.

- Policies and procedures for open and timely disclosure of the interests that management and those charged with governance have in related party transactions.

- The assignment of responsibilities within the entity for identifying, recording, summarizing, and disclosing related party transactions.

- Timely disclosure and discussion between management and those charged with governance of significant related party transactions outside the entity's normal course of business, including whether those charged with governance have appropriately challenged the business rationale of such transactions (for example, by seeking advice from external professional advisors).

- Clear guidelines for the approval of related party transactions involving actual or perceived conflicts of interest, such as approval by a subcommittee of those charged with governance comprising individuals independent of management.

- Periodic reviews by the internal audit function, where applicable.

- Proactive action taken by management to resolve related party disclosure issues, such as by seeking advice from the auditor or external legal counsel.

- The existence of whistle-blowing policies and procedures, where applicable.

Controls over related party relationships and transactions within some entities may be deficient or non-existent for a number of reasons, such as: **A18**

- The low importance attached by management to identifying and disclosing related party relationships and transactions.

- The lack of appropriate oversight by those charged with governance.

- An intentional disregard for such controls because related party disclosures may reveal information that management considers sensitive, for example, the existence of transactions involving family members of management.

- An insufficient understanding by management of the related party requirements of the applicable financial reporting framework.

- The absence of disclosure requirements under the applicable financial reporting framework.

---

[21] *ISA (UK) 315 (Revised June 2016), paragraph 14.*

Where such controls are ineffective or non-existent, the auditor may be unable to obtain sufficient appropriate audit evidence about related party relationships and transactions. If this were the case, the auditor would, in accordance with ISA (UK) 705 (Revised June 2016),[22] consider the implications for the audit, including the opinion in the auditor's report.

A19   Fraudulent financial reporting often involves management override of controls that otherwise may appear to be operating effectively.[23] The risk of management override of controls is higher if management has relationships that involve control or significant influence with parties with which the entity does business because these relationships may present management with greater incentives and opportunities to perpetrate fraud. For example, management's financial interests in certain related parties may provide incentives for management to override controls by (a) directing the entity, against its interests, to conclude transactions for the benefit of these parties, or (b) colluding with such parties or controlling their actions. Examples of possible fraud include:

● Creating fictitious terms of transactions with related parties designed to misrepresent the business rationale of these transactions.

● Fraudulently organizing the transfer of assets from or to management or others at amounts significantly above or below market value.

● Engaging in complex transactions with related parties, such as special-purpose entities, that are structured to misrepresent the financial position or financial performance of the entity.

Considerations specific to smaller entities

A20   Control activities in smaller entities are likely to be less formal and smaller entities may have no documented processes for dealing with related party relationships and transactions. An owner-manager may mitigate some of the risks arising from related party transactions, or potentially increase those risks, through active involvement in all the main aspects of the transactions. For such entities, the auditor may obtain an understanding of the related party relationships and transactions, and any controls that may exist over these, through inquiry of management combined with other procedures, such as observation of management's oversight and review activities, and inspection of available relevant documentation.

Authorization and approval of significant transactions and arrangements (Ref: Para. 14(b))

A21   Authorization involves the granting of permission by a party or parties with the appropriate authority (whether management, those charged with governance or the entity's shareholders) for the entity to enter into specific transactions in accordance with pre-determined criteria, whether judgmental or not. Approval involves those parties' acceptance of the transactions the entity has entered into as having satisfied the criteria on which authorization was granted. Examples of controls the entity may have established to authorize and approve significant transactions and arrangements with related parties or significant transactions and arrangements outside the normal course of business include:

---

[22] *ISA (UK) 705 (Revised June 2016), Modifications to the Opinion in the Independent Auditor's Report.*

[23] *ISA (UK) 240 (Revised June 2016), paragraphs 31 and A4.*

- Monitoring controls to identify such transactions and arrangements for authorization and approval.

- Approval of the terms and conditions of the transactions and arrangements by management, those charged with governance or, where applicable, shareholders.

Maintaining Alertness for Related Party Information When Reviewing Records or Documents

Records or Documents That the Auditor May Inspect
(Ref: Para. 15)

During the audit, the auditor may inspect records or documents that may provide information about related party relationships and transactions, for example: **A22**

- Third-party confirmations obtained by the auditor (in addition to bank and legal confirmations).

- Entity income tax returns.

- Information supplied by the entity to regulatory authorities.

- Shareholder registers to identify the entity's principal shareholders.

- Statements of conflicts of interest from management and those charged with governance.

- Records of the entity's investments and those of its pension plans.

- Contracts and agreements with key management or those charged with governance.

- Significant contracts and agreements not in the entity's ordinary course of business.

- Specific invoices and correspondence from the entity's professional advisors.

- Life insurance policies acquired by the entity.

- Significant contracts re-negotiated by the entity during the period.

- Reports of the internal audit function.

- Documents associated with the entity's filings with a securities regulator (for example, prospectuses).

Arrangements that may indicate the existence of previously unidentified or undisclosed related party relationships or transactions

An arrangement involves a formal or informal agreement between the entity and one or more other parties for such purposes as: **A23**

- The establishment of a business relationship through appropriate vehicles or structures.

- The conduct of certain types of transactions under specific terms and conditions.

- The provision of designated services or financial support.

Examples of arrangements that may indicate the existence of related party relationships or transactions that management has not previously identified or disclosed to the auditor include:

● Participation in unincorporated partnerships with other parties.

● Agreements for the provision of services to certain parties under terms and conditions that are outside the entity's normal course of business.

● Guarantees and guarantor relationships.

Identification of Significant Transactions outside the Normal Course of Business (Ref: Para. 16)

A24   Obtaining further information on significant transactions outside the entity's normal course of business enables the auditor to evaluate whether fraud risk factors, if any, are present and, where the applicable financial reporting framework establishes related party requirements, to identify the risks of material misstatement.

A25   Examples of transactions outside the entity's normal course of business may include:

● Complex equity transactions, such as corporate restructurings or acquisitions.

● Transactions with offshore entities in jurisdictions with weak corporate laws.

● The leasing of premises or the rendering of management services by the entity to another party if no consideration is exchanged.

● Sales transactions with unusually large discounts or returns.

● Transactions with circular arrangements, for example, sales with a commitment to repurchase.

● Transactions under contracts whose terms are changed before expiry.

Understanding the nature of significant transactions outside the normal course of business
(Ref: Para. 16(a))

A26   Inquiring into the nature of the significant transactions outside the entity's normal course of business involves obtaining an understanding of the business rationale of the transactions, and the terms and conditions under which these have been entered into.

Inquiring into whether related parties could be involved
(Ref: Para. 16(b))

A27   A related party could be involved in a significant transaction outside the entity's normal course of business not only by directly influencing the transaction through being a party to the transaction, but also by indirectly influencing it through an intermediary. Such influence may indicate the presence of a fraud risk factor.

Sharing Related Party Information with the Engagement Team
(Ref: Para. 17)

Relevant related party information that may be shared among the engagement **A28** team members includes, for example:

- The identity of the entity's related parties.

- The nature of the related party relationships and transactions.

- Significant or complex related party relationships or transactions that may require special audit consideration, in particular transactions in which management or those charged with governance are financially involved.

Identification and Assessment of the Risks of Material Misstatement Associated with Related Party Relationships and Transactions

Fraud Risk Factors Associated with a Related Party with Dominant Influence
(Ref: Para. 19)

Domination of management by a single person or small group of persons without **A29** compensating controls is a fraud risk factor.[24] Indicators of dominant influence exerted by a related party include:

- The related party has vetoed significant business decisions taken by management or those charged with governance.

- Significant transactions are referred to the related party for final approval.

- There is little or no debate among management and those charged with governance regarding business proposals initiated by the related party.

- Transactions involving the related party (or a close family member of the related party) are rarely independently reviewed and approved.

Dominant influence may also exist in some cases if the related party has played a leading role in founding the entity and continues to play a leading role in managing the entity.

In the presence of other risk factors, the existence of a related party with dominant **A30** influence may indicate significant risks of material misstatement due to fraud. For example:

- An unusually high turnover of senior management or professional advisors may suggest unethical or fraudulent business practices that serve the related party's purposes.

- The use of business intermediaries for significant transactions for which there appears to be no clear business justification may suggest that the related party could have an interest in such transactions through control of such intermediaries for fraudulent purposes.

- Evidence of the related party's excessive participation in or preoccupation with the selection of accounting policies or the determination of significant estimates may suggest the possibility of fraudulent financial reporting.

---

[24] *ISA (UK) 240 (Revised June 2016), Appendix 1.*

Responses to the Risks of Material Misstatement Associated with Related Party Relationships and Transactions
(Ref: Para. 20)

A31　The nature, timing and extent of the further audit procedures that the auditor may select to respond to the assessed risks of material misstatement associated with related party relationships and transactions depend upon the nature of those risks and the circumstances of the entity.[25]

A32　Examples of substantive audit procedures that the auditor may perform when the auditor has assessed a significant risk that management has not appropriately accounted for or disclosed specific related party transactions in accordance with the applicable financial reporting framework (whether due to fraud or error) include:

- Confirming or discussing specific aspects of the transactions with intermediaries such as banks, law firms, guarantors, or agents, where practicable and not prohibited by law, regulation or ethical rules.

- Confirming the purposes, specific terms or amounts of the transactions with the related parties (this audit procedure may be less effective where the auditor judges that the entity is likely to influence the related parties in their responses to the auditor).

- Where applicable, reading the financial statements or other relevant financial information, if available, of the related parties for evidence of the accounting of the transactions in the related parties' accounting records.

A33　If the auditor has assessed a significant risk of material misstatement due to fraud as a result of the presence of a related party with dominant influence, the auditor may, in addition to the general requirements of ISA (UK) 240 (Revised June 2016), perform audit procedures such as the following to obtain an understanding of the business relationships that such a related party may have established directly or indirectly with the entity and to determine the need for further appropriate substantive audit procedures:

- Inquiries of, and discussion with, management and those charged with governance.

- Inquiries of the related party.

- Inspection of significant contracts with the related party.

- Appropriate background research, such as through the Internet or specific external business information databases.

- Review of employee whistle-blowing reports where these are retained.

A34　Depending upon the results of the auditor's risk assessment procedures, the auditor may consider it appropriate to obtain audit evidence without testing the entity's controls over related party relationships and transactions. In some circumstances, however, it may not be possible to obtain sufficient appropriate audit evidence from substantive audit procedures alone in relation to the risks of material misstatement associated with related party relationships and transactions. For example, where intra-group transactions between the entity and its components are numerous and a significant amount of information regarding

---

[25] *ISA (UK) 330 (Revised June 2016) provides further guidance on considering the nature, timing and extent of further audit procedures. ISA (UK) 240 (Revised June 2016) establishes requirements and provides guidance on appropriate responses to assessed risks of material misstatement due to fraud.*

these transactions is initiated, recorded, processed or reported electronically in an integrated system, the auditor may determine that it is not possible to design effective substantive audit procedures that by themselves would reduce the risks of material misstatement associated with these transactions to an acceptably low level. In such a case, in meeting the ISA (UK) 330 (Revised June 2016) requirement to obtain sufficient appropriate audit evidence as to the operating effectiveness of relevant controls,[26] the auditor is required to test the entity's controls over the completeness and accuracy of the recording of the related party relationships and transactions.

Identification of Previously Unidentified or Undisclosed Related Parties or Significant Related Party Transactions

Communicating Newly Identified Related Party Information to the Engagement Team
(Ref: Para. 22(a))

Communicating promptly any newly identified related parties to the other **A35** members of the engagement team assists them in determining whether this information affects the results of, and conclusions drawn from, risk assessment procedures already performed, including whether the risks of material misstatement need to be reassessed.

Substantive Procedures Relating to Newly Identified Related Parties or Significant Related Party Transactions
(Ref: Para. 22(c))

Examples of substantive audit procedures that the auditor may perform relating to **A36** newly identified related parties or significant related party transactions include:

- Making inquiries regarding the nature of the entity's relationships with the newly identified related parties, including (where appropriate and not prohibited by law, regulation or ethical rules) inquiring of parties outside the entity who are presumed to have significant knowledge of the entity and its business, such as legal counsel, principal agents, major representatives, consultants, guarantors, or other close business partners.

- Conducting an analysis of accounting records for transactions with the newly identified related parties. Such an analysis may be facilitated using computer-assisted audit techniques.

- Verifying the terms and conditions of the newly identified related party transactions, and evaluating whether the transactions have been appropriately accounted for and disclosed in accordance with the applicable financial reporting framework.

Intentional Non-Disclosure by Management
(Ref: Para. 22(e))

The requirements and guidance in ISA (UK) 240 (Revised June 2016) **A37** regarding the auditor's responsibilities relating to fraud in an audit of financial statements are relevant where management appears to have intentionally failed to disclose related parties or significant related party transactions to the auditor. The auditor may also consider whether it is

---

[26] *ISA (UK) 330 (Revised June 2016), paragraph 8(b).*

necessary to re-evaluate the reliability of management's responses to the auditor's inquiries and management's representations to the auditor.

Identified Significant Related Party Transactions outside the Entity's Normal Course of Business

Evaluating the Business Rationale of Significant Related Party Transactions (Ref: Para. 23)

A38   In evaluating the business rationale of a significant related party transaction outside the entity's normal course of business, the auditor may consider the following:

- Whether the transaction:

  - Is overly complex (for example, it may involve multiple related parties within a consolidated group).

  - Has unusual terms of trade, such as unusual prices, interest rates, guarantees and repayment terms.

  - Lacks an apparent logical business reason for its occurrence.

  - Involves previously unidentified related parties.

  - Is processed in an unusual manner.

- Whether management has discussed the nature of, and accounting for, such a transaction with those charged with governance.

- Whether management is placing more emphasis on a particular accounting treatment rather than giving due regard to the underlying economics of the transaction.

If management's explanations are materially inconsistent with the terms of the related party transaction, the auditor is required, in accordance with ISA (UK) 500,[27] to consider the reliability of management's explanations and representations on other significant matters.

A39   The auditor may also seek to understand the business rationale of such a transaction from the related party's perspective, as this may help the auditor to better understand the economic reality of the transaction and why it was carried out. A business rationale from the related party's perspective that appears inconsistent with the nature of its business may represent a fraud risk factor.

Authorization and Approval of Significant Related Party Transactions (Ref: Para. 23(b))

A40   Authorization and approval by management, those charged with governance, or, where applicable, the shareholders of significant related party transactions outside the entity's normal course of business may provide audit evidence that these have been duly considered at the appropriate levels within the entity and that their terms and conditions have been appropriately reflected in the financial statements. The existence of transactions of this nature that were not subject to such authorization and approval, in the absence of rational explanations based on discussion with management or those charged with governance, may indicate risks of material misstatement due to error or fraud. In these circumstances, the auditor may need to be alert for other transactions of a similar nature. Authorization and approval

---

[27] *ISA (UK) 500, Audit Evidence, paragraph 11.*

alone, however, may not be sufficient in concluding whether risks of material misstatement due to fraud are absent because authorization and approval may be ineffective if there has been collusion between the related parties or if the entity is subject to the dominant influence of a related party.

Considerations specific to smaller entities

A smaller entity may not have the same controls provided by different levels of **A41** authority and approval that may exist in a larger entity. Accordingly, when auditing a smaller entity, the auditor may rely to a lesser degree on authorization and approval for audit evidence regarding the validity of significant related party transactions outside the entity's normal course of business. Instead, the auditor may consider performing other audit procedures such as inspecting relevant documents, confirming specific aspects of the transactions with relevant parties, or observing the owner-manager's involvement with the transactions.

Assertions That Related Party Transactions Were Conducted on Terms Equivalent to Those Prevailing in an Arm's Length Transaction
(Ref: Para. 24)

Although audit evidence may be readily available regarding how the price of a **A42** related party transaction compares to that of a similar arm's length transaction, there are ordinarily practical difficulties that limit the auditor's ability to obtain audit evidence that all other aspects of the transaction are equivalent to those of the arm's length transaction. For example, although the auditor may be able to confirm that a related party transaction has been conducted at a market price, it may be impracticable to confirm whether other terms and conditions of the transaction (such as credit terms, contingencies and specific charges) are equivalent to those that would ordinarily be agreed between independent parties. Accordingly, there may be a risk that management's assertion that a related party transaction was conducted on terms equivalent to those prevailing in an arm's length transaction may be materially misstated.

The preparation of the financial statements requires management to substantiate an **A43** assertion that a related party transaction was conducted on terms equivalent to those prevailing in an arm's length transaction. Management's support for the assertion may include:

- Comparing the terms of the related party transaction to those of an identical or similar transaction with one or more unrelated parties.

- Engaging an external expert to determine a market value and to confirm market terms and conditions for the transaction.

- Comparing the terms of the transaction to known market terms for broadly similar transactions on an open market.

Evaluating management's support for this assertion may involve one or more of **A44** the following:

- Considering the appropriateness of management's process for supporting the assertion.

- Verifying the source of the internal or external data supporting the assertion, and testing the data to determine their accuracy, completeness and relevance.

- Evaluating the reasonableness of any significant assumptions on which the assertion is based.

A45   Some financial reporting frameworks require the disclosure of related party transactions not conducted on terms equivalent to those prevailing in arm's length transactions. In these circumstances, if management has not disclosed a related party transaction in the financial statements, there may be an implicit assertion that the transaction was conducted on terms equivalent to those prevailing in an arm's length transaction.

Evaluation of the Accounting for and Disclosure of Identified Related Party Relationships and Transactions

Materiality Considerations in Evaluating Misstatements
(Ref: Para. 25)

A46   ISA (UK) 450 (Revised June 2016) requires the auditor to consider both the size and the nature of a misstatement, and the particular circumstances of its occurrence, when evaluating whether the misstatement is material.[28] The significance of the transaction to the financial statement users may not depend solely on the recorded amount of the transaction but also on other specific relevant factors, such as the nature of the related party relationship.

Evaluation of Related Party Disclosures
(Ref: Para. 25(a))

A47   Evaluating the related party disclosures in the context of the disclosure requirements of the applicable financial reporting framework means considering whether the facts and circumstances of the entity's related party relationships and transactions have been appropriately summarized and presented so that the disclosures are understandable. Disclosures of related party transactions may not be understandable if:

(a)   The business rationale and the effects of the transactions on the financial statements are unclear or misstated; or

(b)   Key terms, conditions, or other important elements of the transactions necessary for understanding them are not appropriately disclosed.

A47-1   Accounting standards and corporate law applicable in the UK include requirements for many entities for disclosures relating to control of the entity. The auditor may only be able to determine the name of the entity's ultimate controlling party through specific inquiry of management or those charged with governance. When the auditor considers it necessary, the auditor obtains corroboration from the ultimate controlling party confirming representations received in this regard.

Written Representations
(Ref: Para. 26)

A48   Circumstances in which it may be appropriate to obtain written representations from those charged with governance include:

*   When they have approved specific related party transactions that (a) materially affect the financial statements, or (b) involve management.

---

[28] *ISA (UK) 450 (Revised June 2016), Evaluation of Misstatements Identified during the Audit, paragraph 11(a). Paragraph A16 of ISA (UK) 450 (Revised June 2016) provides guidance on the circumstances that may affect the evaluation of a misstatement.*

- When they have made specific oral representations to the auditor on details of certain related party transactions.

- When they have financial or other interests in the related parties or the related party transactions.

The auditor may also decide to obtain written representations regarding specific assertions that management may have made, such as a representation that specific related party transactions do not involve undisclosed side agreements. **A49**

An entity may require its management and those charged with governance to sign individual declarations in relation to related party matters. It may be helpful if any such declarations are addressed jointly to a designated official of the entity and also to the auditor. In other cases, the auditor may wish to obtain written representations directly from each of those charged with governance and from members of management. **A49-1**

Communication with Those Charged with Governance
(Ref: Para. 27)

Communicating significant matters arising during the audit[29] in connection with the entity's related parties helps the auditor to establish a common understanding with those charged with governance of the nature and resolution of these matters. Examples of significant related party matters include: **A50**

- Non-disclosure (whether intentional or not) by management to the auditor of related parties or significant related party transactions, which may alert those charged with governance to significant related party relationships and transactions of which they may not have been previously aware.

- The identification of significant related party transactions that have not been appropriately authorized and approved, which may give rise to suspected fraud.

- Disagreement with management regarding the accounting for and disclosure of significant related party transactions in accordance with the applicable financial reporting framework.

- Non-compliance with applicable law or regulations prohibiting or restricting specific types of related party transactions.

- Difficulties in identifying the party that ultimately controls the entity.

---

[29] *ISA (UK) 230 (Revised June 2016), paragraph A8, provides further guidance on the nature of significant matters arising during the audit.*

ISA (UK) 560 Subsequent Events

(Effective for audits of financial statements for periods ending on or after 15 December 2010)

Contents

Paragraphs

Introduction
Scope of this ISA (UK) 1
Subsequent events 2
Effective date 3

Objectives 4

Definitions 5

Requirements
Events occurring between the date of the financial statements and the
date of the auditor's report .... 6 - 9
Facts which become known to the auditor after the date of the auditor's
report but before the date the financial statements are issued .... 10 - 13
Facts which become known to the auditor after the financial statements
have been issued .... 14 - 17

Application and other explanatory material
Scope of this ISA (UK) A1
Definitions .... A2 - A5
Events occurring between the date of the financial statements and the date
of the auditor's report .... A6 - A16
Facts which become known to the auditor after the financial statements
have been issued .... A16a - A18-1

International Standard on Auditing (UK) (ISA (UK)) 560, *Subsequent Events*, should be read in conjunction with ISA (UK) 200 (Revised June 2016), *Overall Objectives of the Independent Auditor and the Conduct of an Audit in Accordance with International Standards on Auditing (UK)*.

Introduction

Scope of this ISA (UK)

1   This International Standard on Auditing (UK) (ISA (UK)) deals with the auditor's responsibilities relating to subsequent events in an audit of financial statements. It does not deal with matters relating to the auditor's responsibilities for other information obtained after the date of the auditor's report, which are addressed in ISA (UK) 720 (Revised June 2016).[1] However, such other information may bring to light a subsequent event that is within the scope of this ISA (UK). (Ref: Para. A1)

Subsequent Events

2   Financial statements may be affected by certain events that occur after the date of the financial statements. Many financial reporting frameworks specifically refer to such events.[2] Such financial reporting frameworks ordinarily identify two types of events:

(a)   Those that provide evidence of conditions that existed at the date of the financial statements; and

(b)   Those that provide evidence of conditions that arose after the date of the financial statements.

ISA (UK) 700 (Revised June 2016) explains that the date of the auditor's report informs the reader that the auditor has considered the effect of events and transactions of which the auditor becomes aware and that occurred up to that date.[3]

Effective Date

3   This ISA (UK) is effective for audits of financial statements for periods ending on or after 15 December 2010.

Objectives

4   The objectives of the auditor are:

(a)   To obtain sufficient appropriate audit evidence about whether events occurring between the date of the financial statements and the date of the auditor's report that require adjustment of, or disclosure in, the financial statements are appropriately reflected in those financial statements in accordance with the applicable financial reporting framework; and

(b)   To respond appropriately to facts that become known to the auditor after the date of the auditor's report, that, had they been known to the auditor at that date, may have caused the auditor to amend the auditor's report.

---

[1]   *ISA (UK) 720 (Revised June 2016), The Auditor's Responsibilities Relating to Other Information.*

[2]   *For example, International Accounting Standard (IAS) 10, Events After the Reporting Period deals with the treatment in financial statements of events, both favorable and unfavorable, that occur between the date of the financial statements (referred to as the "end of the reporting period" in the IAS) and the date when the financial statements are authorized for issue.*

[3]   *ISA (UK) 700 (Revised June 2016), Forming an Opinion and Reporting on Financial Statements, paragraph A61.*

Definitions

For purposes of the ISAs (UK), the following terms have the meanings attributed   **5**
below:

(a)   Date of the financial statements – The date of the end of the latest period
covered by the financial statements.

(b)   Date of approval of the financial statements – The date on which all the
statements that comprise the financial statements, including the related
notes, have been prepared and those with the recognized authority have
asserted that they have taken responsibility for those financial statements.
(Ref: Para. A2)

(c)   Date of the auditor's report – The date the auditor dates the report on the
financial statements in accordance with ISA (UK) 700 (Revised June 2016).
(Ref: Para. A3)

(d)   Date the financial statements are issued – The date that the auditor's report
and audited financial statements are made available to third parties. (Ref:
Para. A4–A5)

(e)   Subsequent events – Events occurring between the date of the financial
statements and the date of the auditor's report, and facts that become known
to the auditor after the date of the auditor's report.

Requirements

Events Occurring between the Date of the Financial Statements and the Date of the Auditor's Report

The auditor shall perform audit procedures designed to obtain sufficient appropriate   **6**
audit evidence that all events occurring between the date of the financial statements
and the date of the auditor's report that require adjustment of, or disclosure in, the
financial statements have been identified. The auditor is not, however, expected to
perform additional audit procedures on matters to which previously applied audit
procedures have provided satisfactory conclusions. (Ref: Para. A6)

The auditor shall perform the procedures required by paragraph 6 so that they   **7**
cover the period from the date of the financial statements to the date of the
auditor's report, or as near as practicable thereto. The auditor shall take into
account the auditor's risk assessment in determining the nature and extent of such
audit procedures, which shall include the following: (Ref: Para. A7–A8)

(a)   Obtaining an understanding of any procedures management has established
to ensure that subsequent events are identified.

(b)   Inquiring of management and, where appropriate, those charged with
governance as to whether any subsequent events have occurred which
might affect the financial statements. (Ref: Para. A9)

(c)   Reading minutes, if any, of the meetings, of the entity's owners,
management and those charged with governance, that have been held
after the date of the financial statements and inquiring about matters
discussed at any such meetings for which minutes are not yet available.
(Ref: Para. A10)

(d)   Reading the entity's latest subsequent interim financial statements, if any.

8   If, as a result of the procedures performed as required by paragraphs 6 and 7, the auditor identifies events that require adjustment of, or disclosure in, the financial statements, the auditor shall determine whether each such event is appropriately reflected in those financial statements in accordance with the applicable financial reporting framework.

Written Representations

9   The auditor shall request management and, where appropriate, those charged with governance, to provide a written representation in accordance with ISA (UK) 580[4] that all events occurring subsequent to the date of the financial statements and for which the applicable financial reporting framework requires adjustment or disclosure have been adjusted or disclosed.

Facts Which Become Known to the Auditor after the Date of the Auditor's Report but before the Date the Financial Statements Are Issued

10   The auditor has no obligation to perform any audit procedures regarding the financial statements after the date of the auditor's report. However, if, after the date of the auditor's report but before the date the financial statements are issued, a fact becomes known to the auditor that, had it been known to the auditor at the date of the auditor's report, may have caused the auditor to amend the auditor's report, the auditor shall: (Ref: Para. A11)

(a)   Discuss the matter with management and, where appropriate, those charged with governance.

(b)   Determine whether the financial statements need amendment and, if so,

(c)   Inquire how management intends to address the matter in the financial statements.

11   If management[4a] amends the financial statements, the auditor shall:

(a)   Carry out the audit procedures necessary in the circumstances on the amendment.

(b)   Unless the circumstances in paragraph 12 apply:

  (i)   Extend the audit procedures referred to in paragraphs 6 and 7 to the date of the new auditor's report; and

  (ii)   Provide a new auditor's report on the amended financial statements. The new auditor's report shall not be dated earlier than the date of approval of the amended financial statements.

12   Where law, regulation or the financial reporting framework does not prohibit management from restricting the amendment of the financial statements to the effects of the subsequent event or events causing that amendment and those responsible for approving the financial statements are not prohibited from restricting their approval to that amendment, the auditor is permitted to restrict the audit procedures on subsequent events required in paragraph 11(b)(i) to that amendment. In such cases, the auditor shall either:

---

[4] *ISA (UK) 580, Written Representations.*

[4a] *In the UK the responsibility for amending the financial statements rests with those charged with governance.*

(a)   Amend the auditor's report to include an additional date restricted to that amendment that thereby indicates that the auditor's procedures on subsequent events are restricted solely to the amendment of the financial statements described in the relevant note to the financial statements; or (Ref: Para. A12)

(b)   Provide a new or amended auditor's report that includes a statement in an Emphasis of Matter paragraph[5] or Other Matter paragraph that conveys that the auditor's procedures on subsequent events are restricted solely to the amendment of the financial statements as described in the relevant note to the financial statements.

In some jurisdictions, management may not be required by law, regulation or the financial reporting framework to issue amended financial statements and, accordingly, the auditor need not provide an amended or new auditor's report. However, if management does not amend the financial statements in circumstances where the auditor believes they need to be amended, then: (Ref: Para. A13–A14)   **13**

(a)   If the auditor's report has not yet been provided to the entity, the auditor shall modify the opinion as required by ISA (UK) 705 (Revised June 2016)[6] and then provide the auditor's report; or

(b)   If the auditor's report has already been provided to the entity, the auditor shall notify management and, unless all of those charged with governance are involved in managing the entity, those charged with governance, not to issue the financial statements to third parties before the necessary amendments have been made. If the financial statements are nevertheless subsequently issued without the necessary amendments, the auditor shall take appropriate action, to seek to prevent reliance on the auditor's report. (Ref. Para: A15–A16)

Facts Which Become Known to the Auditor after the Financial Statements Have Been Issued

After the financial statements have been issued, the auditor has no obligation to perform any audit procedures regarding such financial statements. However, if, after the financial statements have been issued, a fact becomes known to the auditor that, had it been known to the auditor at the date of the auditor's report, may have caused the auditor to amend the auditor's report, the auditor shall: **14**

(a)   Discuss the matter with management and, where appropriate, those charged with governance;

(b)   Determine whether the financial statements need amendment; and, if so,

(c)   Inquire how management intends to address the matter in the financial statements. (Ref: Para. A16-1–A16-3)

If management amends the financial statements,[6a] the auditor shall: (Ref: Para. A17)   **15**

---

[5] *See ISA (UK) 706 (Revised June 2016), Emphasis of Matter Paragraphs and Other Matter Paragraphs in the Independent Auditor's Report.*

[6] *ISA (UK) 705 (Revised June 2016), Modifications to the Opinion in the Independent Auditor's Report.*

[6a] *Detailed regulations governing revised financial statements and directors' reports, where the revision is voluntary, are set out in the UK in section 454 of the Companies Act 2006.*

(a)   Carry out the audit procedures necessary in the circumstances on the amendment.

(b)   Review the steps taken by management to ensure that anyone in receipt of the previously issued financial statements together with the auditor's report thereon is informed of the situation.

(c)   Unless the circumstances in paragraph 12 apply:

(i)   Extend the audit procedures referred to in paragraphs 6 and 7 to the date of the new auditor's report, and date the new auditor's report no earlier than the date of approval of the amended financial statements; and

(ii)   Provide a new auditor's report on the amended financial statements.

(d)   When the circumstances in paragraph 12 apply, amend the auditor's report, or provide a new auditor's report as required by paragraph 12.

16   The auditor shall include in the new or amended auditor's report an Emphasis of Matter paragraph or Other Matter(s) paragraph referring to a note to the financial statements that more extensively discusses the reason for the amendment of the previously issued financial statements and to the earlier report provided by the auditor.

17   If management[6b] does not take the necessary steps to ensure that anyone in receipt of the previously issued financial statements is informed of the situation and does not amend the financial statements in circumstances where the auditor believes they need to be amended, the auditor shall notify management and, unless all of those charged with governance are involved in managing the entity[7], those charged with governance, that the auditor will seek to prevent future reliance on the auditor's report. If, despite such notification, management or those charged with governance do not take these necessary steps, the auditor shall take appropriate action to seek to prevent reliance on the auditor's report. (Ref: Para. A18–A18-1)

Application and Other Explanatory Material

Scope of this ISA (UK)
(Ref: Para. 1)

A1   When the audited financial statements are included in other documents subsequent to the issuance of the financial statements (other than annual reports that would be within the scope of ISA (UK) 720 (Revised June 2016)), the auditor may have additional responsibilities relating to subsequent events that the auditor may need to consider, such as legal or regulatory requirements involving the offering of securities to the public in jurisdictions in which the securities are being offered. For example, the auditor may be required to perform additional audit procedures to the date of the final offering document. These procedures may include those referred to in paragraphs 6 and 7 performed up to a date at or near the effective date of the final offering document, and reading the offering document to assess

---

[6b] *In the UK, those charged with governance have responsibility for taking the steps referred to in paragraph 17.*

[7] *ISA (UK) 260 (Revised June 2016), Communication with Those Charged with Governance, paragraph 13.*

whether the other information in the offering document is consistent with the financial information with which the auditor is associated.[8]

Definitions

Date of Approval of the Financial Statements
(Ref: Para. 5(b))

In some jurisdictions, law or regulation identifies the individuals or bodies (for **A2** example, management or those charged with governance) that are responsible for concluding that all the statements that comprise the financial statements, including the related notes, have been prepared, and specifies the necessary approval process. In other jurisdictions, the approval process is not prescribed in law or regulation and the entity follows its own procedures in preparing and finalizing its financial statements in view of its management and governance structures. In some jurisdictions, final approval of the financial statements by shareholders is required. In these jurisdictions, final approval by shareholders is not necessary for the auditor to conclude that sufficient appropriate audit evidence on which to base the auditor's opinion on the financial statements has been obtained. The date of approval of the financial statements for purposes of the ISAs (UK) is the earlier date on which those with the recognized authority determine that all the statements that comprise the financial statements, including the related notes, have been prepared and that those with the recognized authority have asserted that they have taken responsibility for those financial statements.

Date of the Auditor's Report
(Ref: Para. 5(c))

The auditor's report cannot be dated earlier than the date on which the auditor has **A3** obtained sufficient appropriate audit evidence on which to base the opinion on the financial statements including evidence that all the statements that comprise the financial statements, including the related notes, have been prepared and that those with the recognized authority have asserted that they have taken responsibility for those financial statements.[9] Consequently, the date of the auditor's report cannot be earlier than the date of approval of the financial statements as defined in paragraph 5(b). A time period may elapse due to administrative issues between the date of the auditor's report as defined in paragraph 5(c) and the date the auditor's report is provided to the entity.

Date the Financial Statements Are Issued
(Ref: Para. 5(d))

The date the financial statements are issued generally depends on the regulatory **A4** environment of the entity. In some circumstances, the date the financial statements are issued may be the date that they are filed with a regulatory authority. Since audited financial statements cannot be issued without an auditor's report, the date that the audited financial statements are issued must not only be at or later than the

---

[8] *See ISA (UK) 200 (Revised June 2016), Overall Objectives of the Independent Auditor and the Conduct of an Audit in Accordance with International Standards on Auditing (UK), paragraph 2.*

In the UK, standards and guidance for accountants engaged to prepare a report and/or letter for inclusion in, or in connection with, an investment circular are set out in the FRC's Statements of Investment Circular Reporting Standards (SIRS).

[9] *ISA (UK) 700 (Revised June 2016), paragraph 41. In some cases, law or regulation also identifies the point in the financial statement reporting process at which the audit is expected to be complete.*

date of the auditor's report, but must also be at or later than the date the auditor's report is provided to the entity.

Considerations Specific to Public Sector Entities

A5   In the case of the public sector, the date the financial statements are issued may be the date the audited financial statements and the auditor's report thereon are presented to the legislature or otherwise made public.

Events Occurring between the Date of the Financial Statements and the Date of the Auditor's Report
(Ref: Para. 6–9)

A6   Depending on the auditor's risk assessment, the audit procedures required by paragraph 6 may include procedures, necessary to obtain sufficient appropriate audit evidence, involving the review or testing of accounting records or transactions occurring between the date of the financial statements and the date of the auditor's report. The audit procedures required by paragraphs 6 and 7 are in addition to procedures that the auditor may perform for other purposes that, nevertheless, may provide evidence about subsequent events (for example, to obtain audit evidence for account balances as at the date of the financial statements, such as cut-off procedures or procedures in relation to subsequent receipts of accounts receivable).

A7   Paragraph 7 stipulates certain audit procedures in this context that the auditor is required to perform pursuant to paragraph 6. The subsequent events procedures that the auditor performs may, however, depend on the information that is available and, in particular, the extent to which the accounting records have been prepared since the date of the financial statements. Where the accounting records are not up-to-date, and accordingly no interim financial statements (whether for internal or external purposes) have been prepared, or minutes of meetings of management or those charged with governance have not been prepared, relevant audit procedures may take the form of inspection of available books and records, including bank statements. Paragraph A8 gives examples of some of the additional matters that the auditor may consider in the course of these inquiries.

A8   In addition to the audit procedures required by paragraph 7, the auditor may consider it necessary and appropriate to:

- Read the entity's latest available budgets, cash flow forecasts and other related management reports for periods after the date of the financial statements;

- Inquire, or extend previous oral or written inquiries, of the entity's legal counsel concerning litigation and claims; or

- Consider whether written representations covering particular subsequent events may be necessary to support other audit evidence and thereby obtain sufficient appropriate audit evidence.

Inquiry
(Ref. Para. 7(b))

A9   In inquiring of management and, where appropriate, those charged with governance, as to whether any subsequent events have occurred that might affect the financial statements, the auditor may inquire as to the current status of items that were accounted for on the basis of preliminary or inconclusive data and may make specific inquiries about the following matters:

- Whether new commitments, borrowings or guarantees have been entered into.

- Whether sales or acquisitions of assets have occurred or are planned.

- Whether there have been increases in capital or issuance of debt instruments, such as the issue of new shares or debentures, or an agreement to merge or liquidate has been made or is planned.

- Whether any assets have been appropriated by government or destroyed, for example, by fire or flood.

- Whether there have been any developments regarding contingencies.

- Whether any unusual accounting adjustments have been made or are contemplated.

- Whether any events have occurred or are likely to occur that will bring into question the appropriateness of accounting policies used in the financial statements, as would be the case, for example, if such events call into question the validity of the going concern assumption.

- Whether any events have occurred that are relevant to the measurement of estimates or provisions made in the financial statements.

- Whether any events have occurred that are relevant to the recoverability of assets.

Reading Minutes
(Ref. Para. 7(c))

Considerations Specific to Public Sector Entities

In the public sector, the auditor may read the official records of relevant **A10** proceedings of the legislature and inquire about matters addressed in proceedings for which official records are not yet available.

Implications of Other Information Obtained after the Date of the Auditor's Report
(Ref: Para. 10)

While the auditor has no obligation to perform any audit procedures regarding the **A10a** financial statements after the date of the auditor's report but before the date the financial statements are issued, ISA (UK) 720 (Revised June 2016) contains requirements and guidance with respect to other information obtained after the date of the auditor's report, which might include other information obtained after the date of the auditor's report, but before the date the financial statements are issued.[9a]

[9a] *ISA (UK) 700 (Revised June 2016) requires that "The auditor shall not sign, and hence date, the auditor's report earlier than the date on which all the other information contained in the annual report has been approved by those charged with governance and the auditor has considered all necessary available evidence."*

Facts Which Become Known to the Auditor after the Date of the Auditor's Report but before the Date the Financial Statements Are Issued

Management Responsibility towards Auditor
(Ref: Para. 10)

A11   As explained in ISA (UK) 210 (Revised June 2016), the terms of the audit engagement include the agreement of management[9b] to inform the auditor of facts that may affect the financial statements, of which management may become aware during the period from the date of the auditor's report to the date the financial statements are issued.[10]

Dual Dating
(Ref: Para. 12(a))

A12   When, in the circumstances described in paragraph 12(a), the auditor amends the auditor's report to include an additional date restricted to that amendment, the date of the auditor's report on the financial statements prior to their subsequent amendment by management[3a] remains unchanged because this date informs the reader as to when the audit work on those financial statements was completed. However, an additional date is included in the auditor's report to inform users that the auditor's procedures subsequent to that date were restricted to the subsequent amendment of the financial statements. The following is an illustration of such an additional date:

> "(Date of auditor's report), except as to Note Y, which is as of (date of completion of audit procedures restricted to amendment described in Note Y)."

No Amendment of Financial Statements by Management
(Ref: Para. 13)

A13   In some jurisdictions, management[3a] may not be required by law, regulation or the financial reporting framework to issue amended financial statements. This is often the case when issuance of the financial statements for the following period is imminent, provided appropriate disclosures are made in such statements.

Considerations Specific to Public Sector Entities

A14   In the public sector, the actions taken in accordance with paragraph 13 when management does not amend the financial statements may also include reporting separately to the legislature, or other relevant body in the reporting hierarchy, on the implications of the subsequent event for the financial statements and the auditor's report.

Auditor Action to Seek to Prevent Reliance on Auditor's Report
(Ref: Para. 13(b))

A15   The auditor may need to fulfill additional legal obligations even when the auditor has notified management not to issue the financial statements and management has agreed to this request.

[9b] *In the UK, the responsibility to inform the auditor of facts which may affect the financial statements usually rests with those charged with governance.*

[10] *ISA (UK) 210 (Revised June 2016), Agreeing the Terms of Audit Engagements, paragraph A23.*

Where management has issued the financial statements despite the auditor's **A16** notification not to issue the financial statements to third parties, the auditor's course of action to prevent reliance on the auditor's report on the financial statements depends upon the auditor's legal rights and obligations. Consequently, the auditor may consider it appropriate to seek legal advice.

Facts Which Become Known to the Auditor after the Financial Statements Have Been Issued

Implications of Other Information Received after the Financial Statements Have Been Issued
(Ref: Para. 14)

The auditor's obligations regarding other information received after the date of the **A16a** auditor's report are addressed in ISA (UK) 720 (Revised June 2016). While the auditor has no obligation to perform any audit procedures regarding the financial statements after the financial statements have been issued, ISA (UK) 720 (Revised June 2016) contains requirements and guidance with respect to other information obtained after the date of the auditor's report.[9a]

When issuing a new report the auditor has regard to the regulations relating to **A16-1** reports on revised annual financial statements and directors' reports.[6a]

Where the auditor becomes aware of a fact relevant to the audited financial **A16-2** statements which did not exist at the date of the auditor's report there are no statutory provisions for revising financial statements. The auditor discusses with those charged with governance whether they should withdraw the financial statements and where those charged with governance decide not to do so the auditor may wish to take advice on whether it might be possible to withdraw their report. In both cases, other possible courses of action include the making of a statement by those charged with governance or the auditor at the annual general meeting. In any event legal advice may be helpful.

In the UK, the auditor of a company has a statutory right to attend the Annual **A16-3** General Meeting and be heard on any part of the business of the meeting which concerns them as auditor.[10a] This right could include making a statement about facts discovered after the date of the auditor's report and where subsequent events come to the attention of the auditor, the auditor needs to consider what to do in relation to them.

No Amendment of Financial Statements by Management
(Ref: Para. 15)

Considerations Specific to Public Sector Entities

In some jurisdictions, entities in the public sector may be prohibited from issuing **A17** amended financial statements by law or regulation. In such circumstances, the appropriate course of action for the auditor may be to report to the appropriate statutory body.

[10a] *In the UK, Section 502 of the Companies Act 2006 establishes this right.*

Auditor Action to Seek to Prevent Reliance on Auditor's Report (Ref: Para. 17)

A18   Where the auditor believes that management, or those charged with governance, have failed to take the necessary steps to prevent reliance on the auditor's report on financial statements previously issued by the entity despite the auditor's prior notification that the auditor will take action to seek to prevent such reliance, the auditor's course of action depends upon the auditor's legal rights and obligations. Consequently, the auditor may consider it appropriate to seek legal advice.

A18-1   Where the financial statements of companies are issued but have not yet been laid before the members or equivalent, or if those charged with governance do not intend to make an appropriate statement at the annual general meeting, then the auditor may consider making an appropriate statement at the annual general meeting. The auditor does not have a statutory right to communicate directly in writing with the members although, if the auditor resigns or is removed or is not reappointed, the auditor has, for example, various duties under company law.[10b]

[10b] *The auditor of a limited company in the UK who ceases to hold office as auditor is required to comply with the requirements of section 519 of the Companies Act 2006 regarding the statement to be made by the auditor in relation to ceasing to hold office.*

ISA (UK) 570 (Revised June 2016)
Going Concern

(Effective for audits of financial statements for periods commencing on or after 17 June 2016)

Contents

Paragraphs

Introduction
Scope of this ISA (UK)   1
Going concern basis of accounting   2
Responsibility for assessment of the entity's ability to continue as a going concern   3 - 7
Effective date   8

Objectives   9

Requirements
Risk assessment procedures and related activities   10 - 11
Evaluating management's assessment   12 - 14
Period beyond management's assessment   15
Additional audit procedures when events or conditions are identified   16
Audit or conclusions   17 - 20
Implications for the auditor's report   21
Management unwilling to make or extend its assessment   24
Communication with those charged with governance   25
Significant delay in the approval of financial statements   26

Application and other explanatory material
Scope of this ISA   A1
Going concern basis of accounting   A2
Risk assessment procedures and related activities   A3 - A7
Evaluating management's assessment   A8 - A11-3
Period beyond mnagement's assessment   A14 - A15
Additional audit procedures when events or conditions are identified   A16 - A20
Audit or conclusions   A21 - A27
Management unwilling to make or extend its assessment   A35
Communication with those charged with governance   A35-1

Appendix: Illustrations of auditor's reports relating to going concern

International Standard on Auditing (UK) (ISA (UK)) 570 (Revised June 2016), *Going Concern*, should be read in conjunction with ISA (UK) 200 (Revised June 2016), *Overall Objectives of the Independent Auditor and the Conduct of an Audit in Accordance with International Standards on Auditing (UK)*.

Interpreting the term "going concern" in this ISA (UK)

The financial reporting frameworks applicable in the UK generally require the adoption of the ***going concern basis of accounting*** in financial statements, except in circumstances where management intends to liquidate the entity or to cease trading, or has no realistic alternative to liquidation or cessation of operations. In effect, an entity that does not meet the threshold for that exception is described as a ***going concern***. This requirement applies even when there are uncertainties about events or conditions that may cast significant doubt upon the entity's ability to continue as a going concern in the future. Such uncertainties are required to be disclosed in the financial statements when they are material.

The term ***going concern assumption*** is the defining assumption about the condition of an entity for which adoption of the going concern basis of accounting is appropriate: that the entity is, and will be able to continue as, a going concern. Accordingly, as used in this ISA (UK):

(A)　The term "going concern" applies to any entity unless its management intends to liquidate the entity or to cease trading, or has no realistic alternative to liquidation or cessation of operations; and

(B)　The term "ability to continue as a going concern" is equivalent to the term "ability to continue to adopt the going concern basis of accounting" in the future.

Introduction

Scope of this ISA (UK)

This International Standard on Auditing (UK) (ISA (UK)) deals with the auditor's **1** responsibilities in the audit of financial statements relating to going concern and the implications for the auditor's report. (Ref: Para. A1)

Going Concern Basis of Accounting

Under the going concern basis of accounting, the financial statements are **2** prepared on the assumption that the entity is a going concern and will continue its operations for the foreseeable future. General purpose financial statements are prepared on a going concern basis of accounting, unless management either intends to liquidate the entity or to cease operations, or has no realistic alternative but to do so. Special purpose financial statements may or may not be prepared in accordance with a financial reporting framework for which the going concern basis of accounting is relevant (e.g., the going concern basis is not relevant for some financial statements prepared on a tax basis in particular jurisdictions). When the use of the going concern basis of accounting is appropriate, assets and liabilities are recorded on the basis that the entity will be able to realize its assets and discharge its liabilities in the normal course of business. (Ref: Para. A2)

Responsibility for Assessment of the Entity's Ability to Continue as a Going Concern

Some financial reporting frameworks contain an explicit requirement for **3** management[1a] to make a specific assessment of the entity's ability to continue as a going concern, and standards regarding matters to be considered and disclosures to be made in connection with going concern. For example, International Accounting Standard (IAS) 1 requires management to make an assessment of an entity's ability to continue as a going concern.[1] The detailed requirements regarding management's responsibility to assess the entity's ability to continue as a going concern and related financial statement disclosures may also be set out in law or regulation.

In other financial reporting frameworks, there may be no explicit requirement **4** for management to make a specific assessment of the entity's ability to continue as a going concern. Nevertheless, where the going concern basis of accounting is a fundamental principle in the preparation of financial statements as discussed in paragraph 2, the preparation of the financial statements requires management to assess the entity's ability to continue as a going concern even if the financial reporting framework does not include an explicit requirement to do so.

Management's assessment of the entity's ability to continue as a going concern **5** involves making a judgment, at a particular point in time, about inherently uncertain future outcomes of events or conditions. The following factors are relevant to that judgment:

[1a] *In the UK, those charged with governance are responsible for the preparation of the financial statements and the assessment of the entity's ability to continue as a going concern.*

[1] *IAS 1, Presentation of Financial Statements as at 1 January 2009, paragraphs 25–26.*

- The degree of uncertainty associated with the outcome of an event or condition increases significantly the further into the future an event or condition or the outcome occurs. For that reason, most financial reporting frameworks that require an explicit management assessment specify the period for which management is required to take into account all available information.

- The size and complexity of the entity, the nature and condition of its business and the degree to which it is affected by external factors affect the judgment regarding the outcome of events or conditions.

- Any judgment about the future is based on information available at the time at which the judgment is made. Subsequent events may result in outcomes that are inconsistent with judgments that were reasonable at the time they were made.

Responsibilities of the Auditor

6   The auditor's responsibilities are to obtain sufficient appropriate audit evidence regarding, and conclude on, the appropriateness of management's use of the going concern basis of accounting in the preparation of the financial statements, and to conclude, based on the audit evidence obtained, whether a material uncertainty exists about the entity's ability to continue as a going concern. These responsibilities exist even if the financial reporting framework used in the preparation of the financial statements does not include an explicit requirement for management to make a specific assessment of the entity's ability to continue as a going concern.

7   However, as described in ISA (UK) 200 (Revised June 2016),[2] the potential effects of inherent limitations on the auditor's ability to detect material misstatements are greater for future events or conditions that may cause an entity to cease to continue as a going concern. The auditor cannot predict such future events or conditions. Accordingly, the absence of any reference to a material uncertainty about the entity's ability to continue as a going concern in an auditor's report cannot be viewed as a guarantee as to the entity's ability to continue as a going concern.

Effective Date

8   This ISA (UK) is effective for audits of financial statements for periods commencing on or after 17 June 2016. Earlier adoption is permitted.

Objectives

9   The objectives of the auditor are:

(a)   To obtain sufficient appropriate audit evidence regarding, and conclude on, the appropriateness of management's use of the going concern basis of accounting in the preparation of the financial statements;

(b)   To conclude, based on the audit evidence obtained, whether a material uncertainty exists related to events or conditions that may cast significant doubt on the entity's ability to continue as a going concern; and

(c)   To report in accordance with this ISA (UK).

---

[2] *ISA (UK) 200 (Revised June 2016), Overall Objectives of the Independent Auditor and the Conduct of an Audit in Accordance with International Standards on Auditing (UK).*

Requirements

Risk Assessment Procedures and Related Activities

When performing risk assessment procedures as required by ISA (UK) 315 **10** (Revised June 2016),[3] the auditor shall consider whether events or conditions exist that may cast significant doubt on the entity's ability to continue as a going concern. In so doing, the auditor shall determine whether management has already performed a preliminary assessment of the entity's ability to continue as a going concern, and: (Ref: Para. A2–A6)

(a)   If such an assessment has been performed, the auditor shall discuss the assessment with management and determine whether management has identified events or conditions that, individually or collectively, may cast significant doubt on the entity's ability to continue as a going concern and, if so, management's plans to address them; or

(b)   If such an assessment has not yet been performed, the auditor shall discuss with management the basis for the intended use of the going concern basis of accounting, and inquire of management whether events or conditions exist that, individually or collectively, may cast significant doubt on the entity's ability to continue as a going concern.

The auditor shall remain alert throughout the audit for audit evidence of events or **11** conditions that may cast significant doubt on the entity's ability to continue as a going concern. (Ref: Para. A7)

Evaluating Management's Assessment

The auditor shall evaluate management's assessment of the entity's ability to **12** continue as a going concern. (Ref: Para. A8–A10; A12–A13)

In accordance with ISA (UK) 200 (Revised June 2016),[3a] the auditor shall **12D-1** maintain professional skepticism throughout the audit and in particular when reviewing future cash flow relevant to the entity's ability to continue as a going concern.

In evaluating management's assessment of the entity's ability to continue as a **13** going concern, the auditor shall cover the same period as that used by management to make its assessment as required by the applicable financial reporting framework, or by law or regulation if it specifies a longer period. If management's assessment of the entity's ability to continue as a going concern covers less than twelve months from the date of the financial statements as defined in ISA (UK) 560,[4] the auditor shall request management to extend its assessment period to at least twelve months from that date.[4a] (Ref: Para. A11–A13)

---

[3] *ISA (UK) 315 (Revised June 2016), Identifying and Assessing the Risks of Material Misstatement through Understanding the Entity and Its Environment, paragraph 5.*

[3a] *ISA (UK) 200 (Revised June 2016), paragraph 15.*

[4] *ISA (UK) 560, Subsequent Events, paragraph 5(a).*

[4a] *In the UK, the period used by those charged with governance in making their assessment is usually at least one year from the date of approval of the financial statements.*

14 In evaluating management's assessment, the auditor shall consider whether management's assessment includes all relevant information of which the auditor is aware as a result of the audit.

Period beyond Management's Assessment

15 The auditor shall inquire of management as to its knowledge of events or conditions beyond the period of management's assessment that may cast significant doubt on the entity's ability to continue as a going concern. (Ref: Para. A14–A15)

Additional Audit Procedures When Events or Conditions Are Identified

16 If events or conditions have been identified that may cast significant doubt on the entity's ability to continue as a going concern, the auditor shall obtain sufficient appropriate audit evidence to determine whether or not a material uncertainty exists related to events or conditions that may cast significant doubt on the entity's ability to continue as a going concern (hereinafter referred to as "material uncertainty") through performing additional audit procedures, including consideration of mitigating factors. These procedures shall include: (Ref: Para. A16)

(a)   Where management has not yet performed an assessment of the entity's ability to continue as a going concern, requesting management to make its assessment.

(b)   Evaluating management's plans for future actions in relation to its going concern assessment, whether the outcome of these plans is likely to improve the situation and whether management's plans are feasible in the circumstances. (Ref: Para. A17)

(c)   Where the entity has prepared a cash flow forecast, and analysis of the forecast is a significant factor in considering the future outcome of events or conditions in the evaluation of management's plans for future actions: (Ref: Para. A18–A19)

   (i)   Evaluating the reliability of the underlying data generated to prepare the forecast; and

   (ii)   Determining whether there is adequate support for the assumptions underlying the forecast.

(d)   Considering whether any additional facts or information have become available since the date on which management made its assessment.

(e)   Requesting written representations from management and, where appropriate, those charged with governance, regarding their plans for future actions and the feasibility of these plans. (Ref: Para A20)

Auditor Conclusions

17 The auditor shall evaluate whether sufficient appropriate audit evidence has been obtained regarding, and shall conclude on, the appropriateness of management's use of the going concern basis of accounting in the preparation of the financial statements.

18 Based on the audit evidence obtained, the auditor shall conclude whether, in the auditor's judgment, a material uncertainty exists related to events or conditions that, individually or collectively, may cast significant doubt on the entity's ability to continue as a going concern. A material uncertainty exists when the magnitude of its potential impact and likelihood of occurrence is such that, in the auditor's judgment, appropriate disclosure of the nature and implications of the uncertainty is necessary for: (Ref: Para. A21–A22)

(a)   In the case of a fair presentation financial reporting framework, the fair presentation of the financial statements, or

(b)   In the case of a compliance framework, the financial statements not to be misleading.

18-1

If the period to which those charged with governance have paid particular attention in assessing going concern is less than one year from the date of approval of the financial statements, and those charged with governance have not disclosed that fact, the auditor shall do so within the auditor's report.[4b] (Ref: Para. A21-1–A21-2)

18-2

For entities that are required,[4c] and those that choose voluntarily, to report on how they have applied the UK Corporate Governance Code, or to explain why they have not, the auditor shall read and consider in light of the auditor's knowledge obtained in the audit, including that obtained in the evaluation of management's assessment of the entity's ability to continue as a going concern:

(a)   The directors' confirmation in the annual report that they have carried out a robust assessment of the principal risks facing the entity, including those that would threaten its business model, future performance, solvency or liquidity;

(b)   The disclosures in the annual report that describe those risks and explain how they are being managed or mitigated;

(c)   The directors' statement in the financial statements about whether they considered it appropriate to adopt the going concern basis of accounting in preparing them, and their identification of any material uncertainties to the entity's ability to continue to do so over a period of at least twelve months from the date of approval of the financial statements; and

(d)   The director's explanation in the annual report as to how they have assessed the prospects of the entity, over what period they have done so and why they consider that period to be appropriate, and their statement as to whether they have a reasonable expectation that the entity will be able to continue in operation and meet its liabilities as they fall due over the period of their assessment, including any related disclosures drawing attention to any necessary qualifications or assumptions.

The auditor shall determine whether the auditor has anything material to add or to draw attention to in the auditor's report on the financial statements in relation to these disclosures, and shall report in accordance with the requirements of paragraph 21-2 and ISA (UK) 720 (Revised June 2016).[4d]

[4b] *If the non-disclosure of the fact in the financial statements is a departure from the requirements of the applicable financial reporting framework, the auditor would give a qualified opinion ("except for").*

[4c] *In the UK, these include companies with a premium listing of equity shares regardless of whether they are incorporated in the UK or elsewhere.*

[4d] *ISA (UK) 720 (Revised June 2016), The Auditor's Responsibilities Relating to Other Information, paragraph 22-4.*

18-3 Matters the auditor considers when determining whether there is anything to add or to draw attention to in the auditor's report on the financial statements shall include, based on the auditor's knowledge obtained in the audit, including that obtained in the evaluation of management's assessment of the entity's ability to continue as a going concern:

- Whether the auditor is aware of information that would indicate that the annual report and accounts taken as a whole are not fair, balanced and understandable in relation to the principal risks facing the entity including those that would threaten its business model, future performance, solvency or liquidity; and

- Matters relating to the robustness of the directors' assessment of the principal risks facing the entity and its outcome, including the related disclosures in the annual report and accounts, that the auditor communicated to the audit committee[4e] and that are not appropriately addressed in the section of the annual report that describes the work of the audit committee.

Adequacy of Disclosures When Events or Conditions Have Been Identified and a Material Uncertainty Exists

19 If the auditor concludes that management's use of the going concern basis of accounting is appropriate in the circumstances but a material uncertainty exists, the auditor shall determine whether the financial statements: (Ref: Para. A22–A23)

(a) Adequately disclose the principal events or conditions that may cast significant doubt on the entity's ability to continue as a going concern and management's plans to deal with these events or conditions; and

(b) Disclose clearly that there is a material uncertainty related to events or conditions that may cast significant doubt on the entity's ability to continue as a going concern and, therefore, that it may be unable to realize its assets and discharge its liabilities in the normal course of business.

Adequacy of Disclosures When Events or Conditions Have Been Identified but No Material Uncertainty Exists

20 If events or conditions have been identified that may cast significant doubt on the entity's ability to continue as a going concern but, based on the audit evidence obtained the auditor concludes that no material uncertainty exists, the auditor shall evaluate whether, in view of the requirements of the applicable financial reporting framework, the financial statements provide adequate disclosures about these events or conditions. (Ref: Para. A24–A25)

[4e] *ISA (UK) 260 (Revised June 2016), Communication with Those Charged with Governance, paragraph 16-1 (e).*

Implications for the Auditor's Report

Use of Going Concern Basis of Accounting Is Inappropriate

If the financial statements have been prepared using the going concern basis of **21** accounting but, in the auditor's judgment, management's use of the going concern basis of accounting in the preparation of the financial statements is inappropriate, the auditor shall express an adverse opinion. (Ref: Para. A26–A27)

Use of Going Concern Basis of Accounting is Appropriate and no Material Uncertainty has been Identified

When the auditor is required[4f] or decides to communicate key audit matters in **21-1** accordance with ISA (UK) 701, where the auditor concludes that management's use of the going concern basis of accounting is appropriate in the circumstances and no material uncertainty has been identified, the auditor shall:

(a) Determine in accordance with ISA (UK) 701, in light of the audit evidence obtained and the conclusions reached in the audit and having particular regard to any evaluation the auditor undertakes in accordance with paragraph 20, whether a key audit matter relating to going concern exists that should be communicated in the auditor's report; and

(b) Where a key audit matter exists that should be communicated, communicate the key audit matter in the auditor's report in accordance with ISA (UK) 701.

Where the auditor concludes that management's use of the going concern basis **21-2** of accounting is appropriate in the circumstances and no material uncertainty has been identified, the auditor shall report by exception in accordance with paragraph 43-1 of ISA (UK) 700 (Revised June 2016) in a separate section in the auditor's report with the heading "Conclusions relating to Going Concern", or other appropriate heading, as to whether: (Ref: Para A27-1–A27-2)

(a) For entities that are required, and those that choose voluntarily, to report on how they have applied the UK Corporate Governance Code, or to explain why they have not, the auditor has anything material to add or draw attention to in relation to the directors' statement in the financial statements about whether the directors considered it appropriate to adopt the going concern basis of accounting in preparing the financial statements, and the directors' identification of any material uncertainties to the entity's ability to continue to do so over a period of at least twelve months from the date of approval of the financial statements; or

(b) In other cases, the auditor concludes that:

(i) Management's use of the going concern basis of accounting in the preparation of the entity's financial statements is not appropriate; or

---

[4f] *ISA (UK) 700 (Revised June 2016), Forming an Opinion and Reporting on Financial Statements, paragraphs 30–31 set out the requirements to apply ISA (UK) 701, Communicating Key Audit Matters in the Independent Auditor's Report.*

> (ii)   Management has not disclosed in the entity's financial statements any identified material uncertainties that may cast significant doubt about the entity's ability to continue to adopt the going concern basis of accounting for a period of at least twelve months from when the financial statements are authorized for issue.

Use of Going Concern Basis of Accounting Is Appropriate but a Material Uncertainty Exists

Adequate Disclosure of a Material Uncertainty Is Made in the Financial Statements

22   If adequate disclosure about the material uncertainty is made in the financial statements, the auditor shall express an unmodified opinion and the auditor's report shall include a separate section under the heading "Material Uncertainty Related to Going Concern" to: (Ref: Para. A28–A31, A34–A34-2)

(a)   Draw attention to the note in the financial statements that discloses the matters set out in paragraph 19; and

(b)   State that these events or conditions indicate that a material uncertainty exists that may cast significant doubt on the entity's ability to continue as a going concern and that the auditor's opinion is not modified in respect of the matter.

Adequate Disclosure of a Material Uncertainty Is Not Made in the Financial Statements

23   If adequate disclosure about the material uncertainty is not made in the financial statements, the auditor shall: (Ref: Para. A32–A34-2)

(a)   Express a qualified opinion or adverse opinion, as appropriate, in accordance with ISA (UK) 705 (Revised June 2016)[5]; and

(b)   In the Basis for Qualified (Adverse) Opinion section of the auditor's report, state that a material uncertainty exists that may cast significant doubt on the entity's ability to continue as a going concern and that the financial statements do not adequately disclose this matter.

Management Unwilling to Make or Extend Its Assessment

24   If management is unwilling to make or extend its assessment when requested to do so by the auditor, the auditor shall consider the implications for the auditor's report. (Ref: Para. A35)

Communication with Those Charged with Governance

25   Unless all those charged with governance are involved in managing the entity,[6] the auditor shall communicate with those charged with governance events or conditions identified that may cast significant doubt on the entity's ability to continue as a going concern. Such communication with those charged with governance shall include the following: (Ref: Para. A35-1)

---

[5] *ISA (UK) 705 (Revised June 2016), Modifications to the Opinion in the Independent Auditor's Report.*

[6] *ISA (UK) 260 (Revised June 2016), Communication with Those Charged with Governance, paragraph 13.*

(a)   Whether the events or conditions constitute a material uncertainty;

(b)   Whether management's use of the going concern basis of accounting is appropriate in the preparation of the financial statements;

(c)   The adequacy of related disclosures in the financial statements; and

(d)   Where applicable, the implications for the auditor's report.

Significant Delay in the Approval of Financial Statements

26   If there is significant delay in the approval of the financial statements by management or those charged with governance after the date of the financial statements, the auditor shall inquire as to the reasons for the delay. If the auditor believes that the delay could be related to events or conditions relating to the going concern assessment, the auditor shall perform those additional audit procedures necessary, as described in paragraph 16, as well as consider the effect on the auditor's conclusion regarding the existence of a material uncertainty, as described in paragraph 18.

***

Application and Other Explanatory Material

Scope of this ISA (UK)
(Ref: Para 1)

ISA (UK) 701[7] deals with the auditor's responsibility to communicate key audit   **A1** matters in the auditor's report. That ISA (UK) acknowledges that, when ISA (UK) 701 applies, matters relating to going concern may be determined to be key audit matters, and explains that a material uncertainty related to events or conditions that may cast significant doubt on the entity's ability to continue as a going concern is, by its nature, a key audit matter.[8]

Going Concern Basis of Accounting
(Ref: Para. 2)

Considerations Specific to Public Sector Entities

Management's use of the going concern basis of accounting is also relevant to   **A2** public sector entities. For example, International Public Sector Accounting Standard (IPSAS) 1 addresses the issue of the ability of public sector entities to continue as going concerns.[9] Going concern risks may arise, but are not limited to, situations where public sector entities operate on a for-profit basis, where government support may be reduced or withdrawn, or in the case of privatization. Events or conditions that may cast significant doubt on an entity's ability to continue as a going concern in the public sector may include situations where the public sector entity lacks funding for its continued existence or when policy decisions are made that affect the services provided by the public sector entity.

---

[7] *ISA (UK) 701, Communicating Key Audit Matters in the Independent Auditor's Report.*

[8] *See paragraphs 15 and A41 of ISA (UK) 701.*

[9] *IPSAS 1, Presentation of Financial Statements as at 1 January 2009, paragraphs 38–41.*

Risk Assessment Procedures and Related Activities

Events or Conditions That May Cast Significant Doubt on the Entity's Ability to Continue as a Going Concern
(Ref: Para. 10)

A3   The following are examples of events or conditions that, individually or collectively, may cast significant doubt on the entity's ability to continue as a going concern. This listing is not all-inclusive nor does the existence of one or more of the items always signify that a material uncertainty exists.

Financial

- Net liability or net current liability position.

- Fixed-term borrowings approaching maturity without realistic prospects of renewal or repayment; or excessive reliance on short-term borrowings to finance long-term assets.

- Indications of withdrawal of financial support by creditors.

- Negative operating cash flows indicated by historical or prospective financial statements.

- Adverse key financial ratios.

- Substantial operating losses or significant deterioration in the value of assets used to generate cash flows.

- Arrears or discontinuance of dividends.

- Inability to pay creditors on due dates.

- Inability to comply with the terms of loan agreements.

- Change from credit to cash-on-delivery transactions with suppliers.

- Inability to obtain financing for essential new product development or other essential investments.

Operating

- Management intentions to liquidate the entity or to cease operations.

- Loss of key management without replacement.

- Loss of a major market, key customer(s), franchise, license, or principal supplier(s).

- Labor difficulties.

- Shortages of important supplies.

- Emergence of a highly successful competitor.

Other

- Non-compliance with capital or other statutory or regulatory requirements, such as solvency or liquidity requirements for financial institutions.

- Pending legal or regulatory proceedings against the entity that may, if successful, result in claims that the entity is unlikely to be able to satisfy.

- Changes in law or regulation or government policy expected to adversely affect the entity.

- Uninsured or underinsured catastrophes when they occur.

The significance of such events or conditions often can be mitigated by other factors. For example, the effect of an entity being unable to make its normal debt repayments may be counter-balanced by management's plans to maintain adequate cash flows by alternative means, such as by disposing of assets, rescheduling loan repayments, or obtaining additional capital. Similarly, the loss of a principal supplier may be mitigated by the availability of a suitable alternative source of supply.

The risk assessment procedures required by paragraph 10 help the auditor to **A4** determine whether management's use of the going concern basis of accounting is likely to be an important issue and its impact on planning the audit. These procedures also allow for more timely discussions with management, including a discussion of management's plans and resolution of any identified going concern issues.

Considerations Specific to Smaller Entities
(Ref: Para. 10)

The size of an entity may affect its ability to withstand adverse conditions. Small **A5** entities may be able to respond quickly to exploit opportunities, but may lack reserves to sustain operations.

Conditions of particular relevance to small entities include the risk that banks and **A6** other lenders may cease to support the entity, as well as the possible loss of a principal supplier, major customer, key employee, or the right to operate under a license, franchise or other legal agreement.

Remaining Alert throughout the Audit for Audit Evidence about Events or
Conditions
(Ref: Para. 11)

ISA (UK) 315 (Revised June 2016) requires the auditor to revise the auditor's risk **A7** assessment and modify the further planned audit procedures accordingly when additional audit evidence is obtained during the course of the audit that affects the auditor's assessment of risk.[10] If events or conditions that may cast significant doubt on the entity's ability to continue as a going concern are identified after the auditor's risk assessments are made, in addition to performing the procedures in paragraph 16, the auditor's assessment of the risks of material misstatement may need to be revised. The existence of such events or conditions may also affect the nature, timing and extent of the auditor's further procedures in response to the assessed risks. ISA (UK) 330 (Revised June 2016)[11] establishes requirements and provides guidance on this issue.

---

[10] *ISA (UK) 315 (Revised June 2016), paragraph 31.*

[11] *ISA (UK) 330 (Revised June 2016), The Auditor's Responses to Assessed Risks.*

Evaluating Management's Assessment

Management's Assessment and Supporting Analysis and the Auditor's Evaluation (Ref: Para. 12)

A8   Management's assessment of the entity's ability to continue as a going concern is a key part of the auditor's consideration of management's use of the going concern basis of accounting.

A8-1   In the UK, applicable financial reporting frameworks generally specify that management takes into account all available information about the future.[11a] In evaluating management's assessment of the entity's ability to continue as a going concern, it is likely to be relevant for the auditor: to inquire as to what information is available about the future to management and those charged with governance; and determine whether this has been appropriately considered as part of management's assessment. For example, relevant information may be available to management through business planning activities, risk management processes, and for regulated entities, through regulatory reporting, planning or communications with regulatory, enforcement or supervisory authorities. For entities that are required, and those that choose voluntarily, to report on how they have applied the UK Corporate Governance Code, or to explain why they have not, there may also be information available that has been developed to support reporting about the entity's business model, principal risks and the entity's longer term viability statement.

A9   It is not the auditor's responsibility to rectify the lack of analysis by management. In some circumstances, however, the lack of detailed analysis by management to support its assessment may not prevent the auditor from concluding whether management's use of the going concern basis of accounting is appropriate in the circumstances. For example, when there is a history of profitable operations and a ready access to financial resources, management may make its assessment without detailed analysis. In this case, the auditor's evaluation of the appropriateness of management's assessment may be made without performing detailed evaluation procedures if the auditor's other audit procedures are sufficient to enable the auditor to conclude whether management's use of the going concern basis of accounting in the preparation of the financial statements is appropriate in the circumstances.

A10   In other circumstances, evaluating management's assessment of the entity's ability to continue as a going concern, as required by paragraph 12, may include an evaluation of the process management followed to make its assessment, the assumptions on which the assessment is based and management's plans for future action and whether management's plans are feasible in the circumstances.

[11a] *For example, IAS 1, paragraph 26 and FRS 102, paragraph 3.8 both require that management takes into account all available information about the future.*

The Period of Management's Assessment
(Ref: Para. 13)

Most financial reporting frameworks requiring an explicit management   **A11**
assessment specify the period for which management is required to take into
account all available information.[12]

If the future period to which those charged with governance have paid   **A11-1**
particular attention has been limited, for example, to a period of less than
one year from the date of approval of the financial statements, those charged
with governance will have determined whether, in their opinion, the financial
statements require any additional disclosures to explain adequately the
assumptions that underlie the adoption of the going concern basis of
accounting.

If the future period to which those charged with governance have paid   **A11-2**
particular attention is less than the minimum required by the financial
reporting framework, the auditor considers whether to express a modified
opinion in accordance with ISA (UK) 705 (Revised June 2016).[12a]

The auditor assesses whether to concur with the judgments of those charged   **A11-3**
with governance regarding the need for additional disclosures and their
adequacy. Disclosure, however, does not eliminate the need to make
appropriate judgments about the suitability of the future period as an
adequate basis for assessing the going concern position. Paragraph 18-1
requires the auditor to disclose in the auditor's report if the period to which
those charged with governance have paid particular attention in assessing going
concern is less than one year from the date of approval of the financial
statements, and those charged with governance have not disclosed that fact.
The auditor through discussion with those charged with governance of their
plans and expectations may be able to obtain satisfaction that those charged
with governance have in fact paid particular attention to a period of one year
from the date of approval of the financial statements.

Procedures to Identify Material Matters Indicating Concern

Having regard to the future period to which those charged with governance   **A11-4**
have paid particular attention in assessing going concern, the auditor plans and
performs procedures specifically designed to identify any material matters
which could indicate concern about the entity's ability to continue as a going
concern.

The extent of the auditor's procedures is influenced primarily by the excess of   **A11-5**
the financial resources available to the entity over the financial resources that it
requires. The entity's procedures (and the auditor's procedures) need not
always be elaborate in order to provide sufficient appropriate audit evidence.
A determination of the sufficiency of the evidence supplied to the auditor by

---

[12] *Accounting frameworks do not normally specify a maximum period that should be reviewed as part of the assessment of going concern. However, IAS 1 and FRS 102 The Financial Reporting Standard applicable in the UK and Republic of Ireland both require that management takes into account all available information about the future.*

For example, IAS 1 defines this as a period that should be at least, but is not limited to, twelve months from the end of the reporting period.

FRS 102 requires that in assessing whether the going concern basis of accounting is appropriate, management takes into account all available information about the future, which is at least, but is not limited to, twelve months from the date when the financial statements are authorized for issue.

[12a] *ISA (UK) 705 (Revised June 2016), Modifications to the Opinion in the Independent Auditor's Report.*

those charged with governance will depend on the particular circumstances. For example, to be sufficient the evidence may not require formal cash flow forecasts and budgets to have been prepared for the period ending one year from the date of approval of the financial statements. Although such forecasts and budgets are likely to provide the most persuasive evidence, alternative sources of evidence may also be acceptable. This is particularly likely to be the case in respect of entities with uncomplicated circumstances. Many smaller companies fall into this category.

Considerations Specific to Smaller Entities
(Ref: Para. 12–13)

A12   In many cases, the management of smaller entities may not have prepared a detailed assessment of the entity's ability to continue as a going concern, but instead may rely on in-depth knowledge of the business and anticipated future prospects. Nevertheless, in accordance with the requirements of this ISA (UK), the auditor needs to evaluate management's assessment of the entity's ability to continue as a going concern. For smaller entities, it may be appropriate to discuss the medium and long-term financing of the entity with management, provided that management's contentions can be corroborated by sufficient documentary evidence and are not inconsistent with the auditor's understanding of the entity. Therefore, the requirement in paragraph 13 for the auditor to request management to extend its assessment may, for example, be satisfied by discussion, inquiry and inspection of supporting documentation, for example, orders received for future supply, evaluated as to their feasibility or otherwise substantiated.

A13   Continued support by owner-managers is often important to smaller entities' ability to continue as a going concern. Where a small entity is largely financed by a loan from the owner-manager, it may be important that these funds are not withdrawn. For example, the continuance of a small entity in financial difficulty may be dependent on the owner-manager subordinating a loan to the entity in favor of banks or other creditors, or the owner-manager supporting a loan for the entity by providing a guarantee with his or her personal assets as collateral. In such circumstances, the auditor may obtain appropriate documentary evidence of the subordination of the owner-manager's loan or of the guarantee. Where an entity is dependent on additional support from the owner-manager, the auditor may evaluate the owner-manager's ability to meet the obligation under the support arrangement. In addition, the auditor may request written confirmation of the terms and conditions attaching to such support and the owner-manager's intention or understanding.

Period beyond Management's Assessment
(Ref: Para. 15)

A14   As required by paragraph 11, the auditor remains alert to the possibility that there may be known events, scheduled or otherwise, or conditions that will occur beyond the period of assessment used by management that may bring into question the appropriateness of management's use of the going concern basis of accounting in preparing the financial statements. Since the degree of uncertainty associated with the outcome of an event or condition increases as the event or condition is further into the future, in considering events or conditions further in the future, the indications of going concern issues need to be significant before the auditor needs to consider taking further action. If such events or conditions are identified, the auditor may need to request management to evaluate the potential significance of the event or condition on its assessment of the entity's ability to continue as a going concern. In these circumstances the procedures in paragraph 16 apply.

Other than inquiry of management, the auditor does not have a responsibility to perform any other audit procedures to identify events or conditions that may cast significant doubt on the entity's ability to continue as a going concern beyond the period assessed by management, which, as discussed in paragraph 13, would be at least twelve months from the date of the financial statements.   **A15**

Additional Audit Procedures When Events or Conditions Are Identified
(Ref: Para. 16)

Audit procedures that are relevant to the requirement in paragraph 16 may include the following: **A16**

- Analyzing and discussing cash flow, profit and other relevant forecasts with management.
- Analyzing and discussing the entity's latest available interim financial statements.
- Reading the terms of debentures and loan agreements and determining whether any have been breached.
- Reading minutes of the meetings of shareholders, those charged with governance and relevant committees for reference to financing difficulties.
- Inquiring of the entity's legal counsel regarding the existence of litigation and claims and the reasonableness of management's assessments of their outcome and the estimate of their financial implications.
- Confirming the existence, legality and enforceability of arrangements to provide or maintain financial support with related and third parties and assessing the financial ability of such parties to provide additional funds.
- Evaluating the entity's plans to deal with unfilled customer orders.
- Performing audit procedures regarding subsequent events to identify those that either mitigate or otherwise affect the entity's ability to continue as a going concern.
- Confirming the existence, terms and adequacy of borrowing facilities.
- Obtaining and reviewing reports of regulatory actions.
- Determining the adequacy of support for any planned disposals of assets.

Evaluating Management's Plans for Future Actions
(Ref: Para. 16(b))

Evaluating management's plans for future actions may include inquiries of management as to its plans for future action, including, for example, its plans to liquidate assets, borrow money or restructure debt, reduce or delay expenditures, or increase capital.   **A17**

The Period of Management's Assessment
(Ref: Para. 16(c))

In addition to the procedures required in paragraph 16(c), the auditor may compare: **A18**

- The prospective financial information for recent prior periods with historical results; and

- The prospective financial information for the current period with results achieved to date.

A19   Where management's assumptions include continued support by third parties, whether through the subordination of loans, commitments to maintain or provide additional funding, or guarantees, and such support is important to an entity's ability to continue as a going concern, the auditor may need to consider requesting written confirmation (including of terms and conditions) from those third parties and to obtain evidence of their ability to provide such support.

Written Representations
(Ref: Para. 16(e))

A20   The auditor may consider it appropriate to obtain specific written representations beyond those required in paragraph 16 in support of audit evidence obtained regarding management's plans for future actions in relation to its going concern assessment and the feasibility of those plans.

Auditor Conclusions

Material Uncertainty Related to Events or Conditions that May Cast Significant Doubt on the Entity's Ability to Continue as a Going Concern
(Ref: Para. 18-19)

A21   The phrase "material uncertainty" is used in IAS 1 in discussing the uncertainties related to events or conditions which may cast significant doubt on the entity's ability to continue as a going concern that should be disclosed in the financial statements. In some other financial reporting frameworks the phrase "significant uncertainty" is used in similar circumstances.

A21-1   Where, in forming their opinion, the auditor's assessment of going concern is based on a period to which those charged with governance have paid particular attention which is less than one year from the date of approval of the financial statements, it is appropriate for the auditor to disclose that fact within the basis of the audit opinion, unless it is disclosed in the financial statements or accompanying information (for example, a Corporate Governance Statement). In deciding whether to disclose the fact, the auditor assesses whether the evidence supplied by those charged with governance is sufficient to demonstrate that those charged with governance have, in assessing going concern, paid particular attention to a period of one year from the date of approval of the financial statements (see paragraph A11-3).

A21-2   In complying with the requirements of ISA (UK) 230 (Revised June 2016) to document significant matters arising during the audit,[12b] the auditor documents concerns (if any) about the entity's ability to continue as a going concern.

[12b] *ISA (UK) 230 (Revised June 2016), Audit Documentation, paragraph 8(c).*

Adequacy of Disclosure when Events or Conditions Have Been Identified and a Material Uncertainty Exists

Paragraph 18 explains that a material uncertainty exists when the magnitude of the   **A22** potential impact of the events or conditions and the likelihood of occurrence is such that appropriate disclosure is necessary to achieve fair presentation (for fair presentation frameworks) or for the financial statements not to be misleading (for compliance frameworks). The auditor is required by paragraph 18 to conclude whether such a material uncertainty exists regardless of whether or how the applicable financial reporting framework defines a material uncertainty.

Paragraph 19 requires the auditor to determine whether the financial statement   **A23** disclosures address the matters set forth in that paragraph. This determination is in addition to the auditor determining whether disclosures about a material uncertainty, required by the applicable financial reporting framework, are adequate. Disclosures required by some financial reporting frameworks that are in addition to matters set forth in paragraph 19 may include disclosures about:

- Management's evaluation of the significance of the events or conditions relating to the entity's ability to meet its obligations; or

- Significant judgments made by management as part of its assessment of the entity's ability to continue as a going concern.

Some financial reporting frameworks may provide additional guidance regarding management's consideration of disclosures about the magnitude of the potential impact of the principal events or conditions, and the likelihood and timing of their occurrence.

Adequacy of Disclosures When Events or Conditions Have Been Identified but No Material Uncertainty Exists
(Ref: Para. 20)

Even when no material uncertainty exists, paragraph 20 requires the auditor to   **A24** evaluate whether, in view of the requirements of the applicable financial reporting framework, the financial statements provide adequate disclosure about events or conditions that may cast significant doubt on the entity's ability to continue as a going concern. Some financial reporting frameworks may address disclosures about:

- Principal events or conditions;

- Management's evaluation of the significance of those events or conditions in relation to the entity's ability to meet its obligations;

- Management's plans that mitigate the effect of these events or conditions; or

- Significant judgments made by management as part of its assessment of the entity's ability to continue as a going concern.

When the financial statements are prepared in accordance with a fair presentation   **A25** framework, the auditor's evaluation as to whether the financial statements achieve fair presentation includes the consideration of the overall presentation, structure and content of the financial statements, and whether the financial statements, including the related notes, represent the underlying transactions and events in a manner that achieves fair presentation.[13] Depending on the facts and circumstances, the auditor may determine that additional disclosures are

---

[13] *ISA (UK) 700 (Revised June 2016), Forming an Opinion and Reporting on Financial Statements, paragraph 14.*

necessary to achieve fair presentation. This may be the case, for example, when events or conditions have been identified that may cast significant doubt on the entity's ability to continue as a going concern but, based on the audit evidence obtained, the auditor concludes that no material uncertainty exists, and no disclosures are explicitly required by the applicable financial reporting framework regarding these circumstances.

Implications for the Auditor's Report

Use of Going Concern Basis of Accounting is Inappropriate
(Ref: Para. 21)

A26   If the financial statements have been prepared using the going concern basis of accounting but, in the auditor's judgment, management's use of the going concern basis of accounting in the financial statements is inappropriate, the requirement in paragraph 21 for the auditor to express an adverse opinion applies regardless of whether or not the financial statements include disclosure of the inappropriateness of management's use of the going concern basis of accounting.

A27   When the use of the going concern basis of accounting is not appropriate in the circumstances, management may be required, or may elect, to prepare the financial statements on another basis (e.g., liquidation basis). The auditor may be able to perform an audit of those financial statements provided that the auditor determines that the other basis of accounting is acceptable in the circumstances. The auditor may be able to express an unmodified opinion on those financial statements, provided there is adequate disclosure therein about the basis of accounting on which the financial statements are prepared, but may consider it appropriate or necessary to include an Emphasis of Matter paragraph in accordance with ISA (UK) 706 (Revised June 2016)[14] in the auditor's report to draw the user's attention to that alternative basis and the reasons for its use.

Use of Going Concern Basis of Accounting is Appropriate and no Material Uncertainty has been Identified
(Ref: Para. 21-2)

A27-1   Paragraph 43-1 of ISA (UK) 700 (Revised June 2016) requires that if the auditor is required to report on certain matters by exception the auditor includes a description of the auditor's responsibilities with respect to those matters in the auditor's report. When describing the auditor's responsibilities relating to management's use of the going concern basis of accounting and the disclosure of material uncertainties, the auditor may choose to include this description either:

(a)   in the Conclusions Relating to Going Concern section of the auditor's report; or

(b)   in the Auditor's Responsibilities for the Audit of the Financial Statements section of the auditor's report,

and cross-refer from the respective section as appropriate.

---

[14] *ISA (UK) 706 (Revised June 2016), Emphasis of Matter Paragraphs and Other Matter Paragraphs in the Independent Auditor's Report.*

Auditor's reports which include a description of the auditor's responsibilities **A27-2**
relating to management's use of the going concern basis of accounting and the
disclosure of material uncertainties in the Conclusions Relating to Going
Concern section of the auditor's report will include the minimum elements
of an auditor's report required by paragraph 50(k) of ISA 700 (Revised) and
therefore the auditor is not precluded from being able to assert compliance with
International Standards on Auditing issued by the IAASB.

Use of Going Concern Basis of Accounting Is Appropriate but a Material
Uncertainty Exists
(Ref: Para. 22-23)

The identification of a material uncertainty is a matter that is important to users' **A28**
understanding of the financial statements. The use of a separate section with a
heading that includes reference to the fact that a material uncertainty related to
going concern exists alerts users to this circumstance.

The Appendix[14a] to this ISA (UK) provides illustrations of the statements that are **A29**
required to be included in the auditor's report on the financial statements when
International Financial Reporting Standards (IFRSs) is the applicable financial
reporting framework. If an applicable financial reporting framework other than
IFRSs is used, the illustrative statements presented in the Appendix to this ISA
may need to be adapted to reflect the application of the other financial reporting
framework in the circumstances.

Paragraph 22 establishes the minimum information required to be presented in the **A30**
auditor's report in each of the circumstances described. The auditor may provide
additional information to supplement the required statements, for example to
explain:

- That the existence of a material uncertainty is fundamental to users'
  understanding of the financial statements;[15] or

- How the matter was addressed in the audit. (Ref: Para. A1)

In the UK, the requirement in legislation[15a] to include a statement on any **A30-1**
material uncertainty relating to events or conditions that may cast significant
doubt about the entity's ability to continue as a going concern is met by the
requirements of paragraph 22.

Adequate Disclosure of a Material Uncertainty Is Made in the Financial
Statements
(Ref: Para. 22)

Illustration 1 of the Appendix[15b] to this ISA is an example of an auditor's report **A31**
when the auditor has obtained sufficient appropriate audit evidence regarding the
appropriateness of management's use of the going concern basis of accounting but

---

[14a] *The examples in the Appendix have not been tailored for the UK. Illustrative auditor's reports tailored for use
with audits conducted in accordance with ISAs (UK) are given in the current version of the FRC's Compendium
of Illustrative Auditor's Reports.*

[15] *ISA (UK) 706 (Revised June 2016), paragraph A2.*

[15a] *In the UK, section 495(4) establishes this requirement.*

[15b] *The examples in the Appendix have not been tailored for the UK. Illustrative auditor's reports tailored for use
with audits conducted in accordance with ISAs (UK) are given in the current version of the FRC's Compendium
of Illustrative Auditor's Reports.*

a material uncertainty exists and disclosure is adequate in the financial statements. The Appendix of ISA (UK) 700 (Revised June 2016) also includes illustrative wording to be included in the auditor's report for all entities in relation to going concern to describe the respective responsibilities of those responsible for the financial statements and the auditor in relation to going concern.

Adequate Disclosure of a Material Uncertainty Is Not Made in the Financial Statements
(Ref: Para. 23)

A32   Illustrations 2 and 3 of the Appendix[15b] to this ISA (UK) are examples of auditor's reports containing qualified and adverse opinions, respectively, when the auditor has obtained sufficient appropriate audit evidence regarding the appropriateness of the management's use of the going concern basis of accounting but adequate disclosure of a material uncertainty is not made in the financial statements.

A33   In situations involving multiple uncertainties that are significant to the financial statements as a whole, the auditor may consider it appropriate in extremely rare cases to express a disclaimer of opinion instead of including the statements required by paragraph 22. ISA (UK) 705 (Revised June 2016) provides guidance on this issue.[16]

Communication with Regulators
(Ref: Para. 22–23)

A34   When the auditor of a regulated entity considers that it may be necessary to include a reference to going concern matters in the auditor's report, the auditor may have a duty to communicate with the applicable regulatory, enforcement or supervisory authorities.

> In the UK, in such cases the regulatory, enforcement or supervisory authority might, if it has not already done so, specify corrective action to be taken by the entity.

A34-1   At the time at which the auditor formulates the audit report, the auditor takes account of matters such as:

- Any views expressed by the regulatory, enforcement or supervisory authority.

- Any legal advice obtained by those charged with governance.

- The actual and planned corrective action.

A34-2   For audits of public interest entities, ISA (UK) 250 Section B (Revised June 2016)[16a] requires the auditor to report to the relevant regulatory, enforcement or supervisory authority any information about the public interest entity (or an undertaking having close links with the public interest entity) that may bring about a material threat or doubt concerning the continuous functioning of the entity.

---

[16] *ISA (UK) 705 (Revised June 2016), paragraph 10.*

[16a] *ISA (UK) 250 Section B (Revised June 2016), The Auditor's Statutory Right and Duty to Report to Regulators of Public Interest Entities and Regulators of Other Entities in the Financial Sector, paragraph 13R-1(a)(ii).*

Management Unwilling to Make or Extend Its Assessment
(Ref: Para. 22)

In certain circumstances, the auditor may believe it necessary to request **A35** management to make or extend its assessment. If management is unwilling to do so, a qualified opinion or a disclaimer of opinion in the auditor's report may be appropriate, because it may not be possible for the auditor to obtain sufficient appropriate audit evidence regarding management's use of the going concern basis of accounting in the preparation of the financial statements, such as audit evidence regarding the existence of plans management has put in place or the existence of other mitigating factors.

Communication with Those Charged with Governance
(Ref: Para. 25)

For audits of financial statements of public interest entities, ISA (UK) 260 **A35-1** (Revised June 2016)[16b] requires the auditor to:

- explain the judgments about events or conditions identified in the course of the audit that may cast significant doubt on the entity's ability to continue as a going concern and whether they constitute a material uncertainty; and

- provide a summary of all guarantees, comfort letters, undertakings of public intervention and other support measures that have been taken into account when making a going concern assessment,

in the additional report to the audit committee.

[16b] *ISA (UK) 260 (Revised June 2016), Communication with Those Charged with Governance, paragraph 16R-2 (i).*

Appendix

(Ref: Para. A29, A31–A32)

Illustrations of Auditor's Reports Relating to Going Concern

The examples in the Appendix have not been tailored for the UK. Illustrative auditor's reports tailored for use with audits conducted in accordance with ISAs (UK) are given in the current version of the FRC's Compendium of Illustrative Auditor's Reports.

- Illustration 1: An auditor's report containing an unmodified opinion when the auditor has concluded that a material uncertainty exists and disclosure in the financial statements is adequate.

- Illustration 2: An auditor's report containing a qualified opinion when the auditor has concluded that a material uncertainty exists and that the financial statements are materially misstated due to inadequate disclosure.

- Illustration 3: An auditor's report containing an adverse opinion when the auditor has concluded that a material uncertainty exists and the financial statements omit the required disclosures relating to a material uncertainty.

Illustration 1 – Unmodified Opinion When a Material Uncertainty Exists and Disclosure in the Financial Statements Is Adequate

For purposes of this illustrative auditor's report, the following circumstances are assumed:

- Audit of a complete set of financial statements of a listed entity using a fair presentation framework. The audit is not a group audit (i.e., ISA 600[1-a] does not apply).
- The financial statements are prepared by management of the entity in accordance with IFRSs (a general purpose framework).
- The terms of the audit engagement reflect the description of management's responsibility for the financial statements in ISA 210.[2-a]
- The auditor has concluded an unmodified (i.e., "clean") opinion is appropriate based on the audit evidence obtained.
- The relevant ethical requirements that apply to the audit are those of the jurisdiction.
- Based on the audit evidence obtained, the auditor has concluded that a material uncertainty exists related to events or conditions that may cast significant doubt on the entity's ability to continue as a going concern. The disclosure of the material uncertainty in the financial statements is adequate.
- Key audit matters have been communicated in accordance with ISA 701.

[1-a] *ISA 600, Special Considerations—Audits of Group Financial Statements (Including the Work of Component Auditors.*

[2-a] *ISA 210, Agreeing the Terms of Audit Engagements.*

- The auditor has obtained all of the other information prior to the date of the auditor's report and has not identified a material misstatement of the other information.
- Those responsible for oversight of the financial statements differ from those responsible for the preparation of the financial statements.
- In addition to the audit of the financial statements, the auditor has other reporting responsibilities required under local law.

INDEPENDENT AUDITOR'S REPORT

To the Shareholders of ABC Company [or Other Appropriate Addressee]

Report on the Audit of the Financial Statements[3-a]

Opinion

We have audited the financial statements of ABC Company (the Company), which comprise the statement of financial position as at December 31, 20X1, and the statement of comprehensive income, statement of changes in equity and statement of cash flows for the year then ended, and notes to the financial statements, including a summary of significant accounting policies.

In our opinion, the accompanying financial statements present fairly, in all material respects, (or *give a true and fair view of*) the financial position of the Company as at December 31, 20X1, and (of) its financial performance and its cash flows for the year then ended in accordance with International Financial Reporting Standards (IFRSs).

Basis for Opinion

We conducted our audit in accordance with International Standards on Auditing (ISAs). Our responsibilities under those standards are further described in the *Auditor's Responsibilities for the Audit of the Financial Statements* section of our report. We are independent of the Company in accordance with the ethical requirements that are relevant to our audit of the financial statements in [*jurisdiction*], and we have fulfilled *our* other ethical responsibilities in accordance with these requirements. We believe that the audit evidence we have obtained is sufficient and appropriate to provide a basis for our opinion.

Material Uncertainty Related to Going Concern

We draw attention to Note 6 in the financial statements, which indicates that the Company incurred a net loss of ZZZ *during* the year ended December 31, 20X1 and, as of that date, the Company's current liabilities exceeded its total assets by YYY. As stated in Note 6, these events or conditions, along with other matters as set forth in Note 6, indicate that a material uncertainty exists that may cast significant doubt on the Company's ability to continue as a going concern. Our opinion is not modified in respect of this matter.

[3-a] *The sub-title "Report on the Audit of the Financial Statements" is unnecessary in circumstances when the second sub-title "Report on Other Legal and Regulatory Requirements" is not applicable.*

Key Audit Matters

Key audit matters are those matters that, in our professional judgment, were of most significance in our audit of the financial statements of the current period. These matters were addressed in the context of our audit of the financial statements as a whole, and in forming our opinion thereon, and we do not provide a separate *opinion* on these matters. In addition to the matter described in the *Material Uncertainty Related to Going Concern* section, we have determined the matters described below to be the key audit matters to be communicated in our report.

[Description of each key audit matter in accordance with ISA 701.]

Other Information [or another title if appropriate such as "Information Other than the Financial Statements and Auditor's Report Thereon"]

[Reporting in accordance with the reporting requirements in ISA 720 (Revised) – see Illustration 1 in Appendix 2 of ISA 720 (Revised).]

Responsibilities of Management and Those Charged with Governance for the Financial Statements[4-a]

[Reporting in accordance with ISA 700 (Revised) – see Illustration 1 in ISA 700 (Revised).[5-a]]

Auditor's Responsibilities for the Audit of the Financial Statements

[Reporting in accordance with ISA 700 (Revised) – see Illustration 1 in ISA 700 (Revised).]

Report on Other Legal and Regulatory Requirements

[Reporting in accordance with ISA 700 (Revised) – see Illustration 1 in ISA 700 (Revised).]

The engagement partner on the audit resulting in this independent auditor's report is [*name*].

[Signature in the name of the audit firm, the personal name of the auditor, or both, as appropriate for the particular jurisdiction]

[Auditor Address]

[Date]

[4-a] *Throughout these illustrative auditor's reports, the terms management and those charged with governance may need to be replaced by another term that is appropriate in the context of the legal framework in the particular jurisdiction.*

[5-a] *Paragraphs 34 and 39 of ISA 700 (Revised) require wording to be included in the auditor's report for all entities in relation to going concern to describe the respective responsibilities of those responsible for the financial statements and the auditor in relation to going concern.*

Illustration 2 – Qualified Opinion When a Material Uncertainty Exists and the Financial Statements Are Materially Misstated Due to Inadequate Disclosure

For purposes of this illustrative auditor's report, the following circumstances are assumed:

- Audit of a complete set of financial statements of a listed entity using a fair presentation framework. The audit is not a group audit (i.e., ISA 600 does not apply).
- The financial statements are prepared by management of the entity in accordance with IFRSs (a general purpose framework).
- The terms of the audit engagement reflect the description of management's responsibility for the financial statements in ISA 210.
- The relevant ethical requirements that apply to the audit are those of the jurisdiction.
- Based on the audit evidence obtained, the auditor has concluded that a material uncertainty exists related to events or conditions that may cast significant doubt on the entity's ability to continue as a going concern. Note yy to the financial statements discusses the magnitude of financing arrangements, the expiration and the total financing arrangements; however the financial statements do not include discussion on the impact or the availability of refinancing or characterize this situation as a material uncertainty.
- The financial statements are materially misstated due to the inadequate disclosure of the material uncertainty. A qualified opinion is being expressed because the auditor concluded that the effects on the financial statements of this inadequate disclosure are material but not pervasive to the financial statements.
- Key audit matters have been communicated in accordance with ISA 701.
- The auditor has obtained all of the other information prior to the date of the auditor's report and the matter giving rise to the qualified opinion on the financial statements also affects the other information
- Those responsible for oversight of the financial statements differ from those responsible for the preparation of the financial statements.
- In addition to the audit of the financial statements, the auditor has other reporting responsibilities required under local law.

INDEPENDENT AUDITOR'S REPORT

To the Shareholders of ABC Company [or Other Appropriate Addressee]

Report on the Audit of the Financial Statements[6-a]

Qualified Opinion

We have audited the financial statements of ABC Company (the Company), which comprise the statement of financial position as at December 31, 20X1, and the statement of comprehensive income, statement of changes in equity and statement

---

[6-a] *The sub-title "Report on the Audit of the Financial Statements" is unnecessary in circumstances when the second sub-title "Report on Other Legal and Regulatory Requirements" is not applicable.*

of cash flows for the year then ended, and notes to the financial statements, including a summary of significant accounting policies.

In our opinion, except for the incomplete disclosure of the information referred to in the Basis for Qualified Opinion section of our report, the accompanying financial statements present fairly, in all material respects (or give a true and fair view of), the financial position of the Company as at December 31, 20X1, and (of) its financial performance and its cash flows for the year then ended in accordance with International Financial Reporting Standards (IFRSs).

Basis for Qualified Opinion

As discussed in Note yy, the Company's financing arrangements expire and amounts outstanding are payable on March 19, 20X2. The Company has been unable to conclude renegotiations or obtain replacement financing. This situation indicates that a material uncertainty exists that may cast significant doubt on the Company's ability to continue as a going concern. The financial statements do not adequately disclose this matter.

We conducted our audit in accordance with International Standards on Auditing (ISAs). Our responsibilities under those standards are further described in the *Auditor's Responsibilities for the Audit of the Financial Statements* section of our report. We are independent of the Company in accordance with the ethical requirements that are relevant to our audit of the financial statements in [*jurisdiction*], and we have fulfilled our other ethical responsibilities in accordance with these requirements. We believe that the audit evidence we have obtained is sufficient and appropriate to provide a basis for our qualified opinion.

Other Information [or another title if appropriate such as "Information Other than the Financial Statements and Auditor's Report Thereon"]

[*Reporting in accordance with the reporting requirements in ISA 720 (Revised) – see Illustration 6 in Appendix 2 of ISA 720 (Revised). The last paragraph of the other information section in Illustration 6 would be customized to describe the specific matter giving rise to the qualified opinion that also affects the other information.*]

Key Audit Matters

Key audit matters are those matters that, in our professional judgment, were of most significance in our audit of the financial statements of the current period. These matters were addressed in the context of our audit of the financial statements as a whole, and in forming our opinion thereon, and we do not provide a separate opinion on these matters. In addition to the matter described in the Basis for Qualified Opinion section, we have determined the matters described below to be the key audit matters to be communicated in our report.

[*Descriptions of each key audit matter in accordance with ISA 701.*]

Responsibilities of Management and Those Charged with Governance for the Financial Statements[7-a]

[*Reporting in accordance with ISA 700 (Revised) – see Illustration 1 in ISA 700 (Revised).*[8-a]]

Auditor's Responsibilities for the Audit of the Financial Statements

[*Reporting in accordance with ISA 700 (Revised) – see Illustration 1 in ISA 700 (Revised).*[25]]

Report on Other Legal and Regulatory Requirements

[*Reporting in accordance with ISA 700 (Revised) – see Illustration 1 in ISA 700 (Revised).*]

The engagement partner on the audit resulting in this independent auditor's report is [*name*].

[*Signature in the name of the audit firm, the personal name of the auditor, or both, as appropriate for the particular jurisdiction*]

[*Auditor Address*]

[*Date*]

Illustration 3 – Adverse Opinion When a Material Uncertainty Exists and Is Not Disclosed in the Financial Statements

For purposes of the illustrative auditor's report, the following circumstances are assumed:

- Audit of a complete set of financial statements of an entity other than a listed entity using a fair presentation framework. The audit is not a group audit (i.e., ISA 600 does not apply).
- The financial statements are prepared by management of the entity in accordance with IFRSs (a general purpose framework).
- The terms of the audit engagement reflect the description of management's responsibility for the financial statements in ISA 210.
- The relevant ethical requirements that apply to the audit are those of the jurisdiction.
- Based on the audit evidence obtained, the auditor has concluded that a material uncertainty exists related to events or conditions that may cast significant doubt on the entity's ability to continue as a going concern, and the Company is considering bankruptcy. The financial statements omit the required disclosures relating to the material uncertainty. An adverse opinion is being expressed because the effects on the financial statements of such omission are material and pervasive.
- The auditor is not required, and has otherwise not decided, to communicate key audit matters in accordance with ISA 701.

[7-a] *Or other terms that are appropriate in the context of the legal framework of the particular jurisdiction.*

[8-a] *Paragraphs 34 and 39 of ISA 700 (Revised) require wording to be included in the auditor's report for all entities in relation to going concern to describe the respective responsibilities of those responsible for the financial statements and the auditor in relation to going concern.*

- The auditor has obtained all of the other information prior to the date of the auditor's report and the matter giving rise to the qualified/ adverse opinion on the consolidated financial statements also affects the other information.
- Those responsible for oversight of the financial statements differ from those responsible for the preparation of the financial statements.
- In addition to the audit of the financial statements, the auditor has other reporting responsibilities required under local law.

INDEPENDENT AUDITOR'S REPORT

To the Shareholders of ABC Company [or Other Appropriate Addressee]

Report on the Audit of the Financial Statements[9-a]

Adverse Opinion

We have audited the financial statements of ABC Company (the Company), which comprise the statement of financial position as at December 31, 20X1, and the statement of comprehensive income, statement of changes in equity and statement of cash flows for the year then ended, and notes to the financial statements, including a summary of significant accounting policies.

In our opinion, because of the omission of the information mentioned in the *Basis for Adverse Opinion* section of our report, the accompanying financial statements do not present fairly (or *do not give a true and fair view of*), the financial position of the Company as at December 31, 20X1, and of its financial performance and its cash flows for the year then ended in accordance with International Financial Reporting Standards (IFRSs).

Basis for Adverse Opinion

The Company's financing arrangements expired and the amount outstanding was payable on December 31, 20X1. The Company has been unable to conclude re-negotiations or obtain replacement financing and is considering filing for bankruptcy. This situation indicates that a material uncertainty exists that may cast significant doubt on the Company's ability to continue as a going concern. The financial statements do not adequately disclose this fact.

We conducted our audit in accordance with International Standards on Auditing (ISAs). Our responsibilities under those standards are further described in the *Auditor's Responsibilities for the Audit of the Financial Statements* section of our report. We are independent of the Company in accordance with the ethical requirements that are relevant to our audit of the financial statements in [*jurisdiction*], and we have fulfilled our ethical responsibilities in accordance with these requirements. We believe that the audit evidence we have obtained is sufficient and appropriate to provide a basis for our adverse opinion.

[9-a] *The sub-title "Report on the Audit of the Financial Statements" is unnecessary in circumstances when the second sub-title "Report on Other Legal and Regulatory Requirements" is not applicable.*

Other Information [or another title if appropriate such as "Information Other than the Financial Statements and Auditor's Report Thereon"]

[Reporting in accordance with the reporting requirements in ISA 720 (Revised) – see Illustration 7 in Appendix 2 of ISA 720 (Revised). The last paragraph of the other information section in Illustration 7 would be customized to describe the specific matter giving rise to the qualified opinion that also affects the other information.]

Responsibilities of Management and Those Charged with Governance for the Financial Statements[10-a]

[Reporting in accordance with ISA 700 (Revised) – see Illustration 1 in ISA 700 (Revised).[11-a]]

Auditor's Responsibilities for the Audit of the Financial Statements

[Reporting in accordance with ISA 700 (Revised) – see Illustration 1 in ISA 700 (Revised).[28]]

Report on Other Legal and Regulatory Requirements

[Reporting in accordance with ISA 700 (Revised) – see Illustration 1 in ISA 700 (Revised).]

[Signature in the name of the audit firm, the personal name of the auditor, or both, as appropriate for the particular jurisdiction]

[Auditor Address]

[Date]

[10-a] *Or other terms that are appropriate in the context of the legal framework of the particular jurisdiction.*

[11-a] *Paragraphs 34 and 39 of ISA 700 (Revised) require wording to be included in the auditor's report for all entities in relation to going concern to describe the respective responsibilities of those responsible for the financial statements and the auditor in relation to going concern.*

ISA (UK) 580 Written Representations

(Effective for audits of financial statements for periods ending on or after 15 December 2010)

Contents

Paragraphs

Introduction
Scope of this ISA (UK)   1 - 2
Written representations as audit evidence   3 - 4
Effective date   5

Objectives   6

Definitions   7 - 8

Requirements
Management from whom written representations requested   9
Written representations about management's responsibilities   10 - 12
Other written representations   13
Date of and period(s) covered by written representations   14
Form of written representations   15
Doubt as to the reliability of written representations and requested written
representations not provided   16 - 20

Application and other explanatory material
Written representations as audit evidence   A1
Management from whom written representations requested   A2 - A6
Written representations about management's responsibilities   A7 - A9
Other written representations   A10 - A13
Communicating a threshold amount   A14
Date of and period(s) covered by written representations   A15 - A18
Form of written representations   A19 - A21
Communication with those charged with governance   A22 - A22-2
Doubt as to the reliability of written representations and requested written
representations not provided   A23 - A27

**Appendix 1: List of ISAs (UK) containing requirements for written
representations**

Appendix 2: Illustrative representation letter

International Standard on Auditing (UK) (ISA (UK)) 580, *Written Representations*, should be read in conjunction with ISA (UK) 200 (Revised June 2016), *Overall Objectives of the Independent Auditor and the Conduct of an Audit in Accordance with International Standards on Auditing (UK)*.

Introduction

Scope of this ISA (UK)

1   This International Standard on Auditing (UK) (ISA (UK)) deals with the auditor's responsibility to obtain written representations from management and, where appropriate, those charged with governance in an audit of financial statements.

2   Appendix 1 lists other ISAs (UK) containing subject-matter specific requirements for written representations. The specific requirements for written representations of other ISAs (UK) do not limit the application of this ISA (UK).

Written Representations as Audit Evidence

3   Audit evidence is the information used by the auditor in arriving at the conclusions on which the auditor's opinion is based. [1] Written representations are necessary information that the auditor requires in connection with the audit of the entity's financial statements. Accordingly, similar to responses to inquiries, written representations are audit evidence. (Ref: Para. A1)

4   Although written representations provide necessary audit evidence, they do not provide sufficient appropriate audit evidence on their own about any of the matters with which they deal. Furthermore, the fact that management has provided reliable written representations does not affect the nature or extent of other audit evidence that the auditor obtains about the fulfillment of management's responsibilities, or about specific assertions.

Effective Date

5   This ISA (UK) is effective for audits of financial statements for periods ending on or after 15 December 2010.

Objectives

6   The objectives of the auditor are:

(a)   To obtain written representations from management and, where appropriate, those charged with governance that they believe that they have fulfilled their responsibility for the preparation of the financial statements and for the completeness of the information provided to the auditor;

(b)   To support other audit evidence relevant to the financial statements or specific assertions in the financial statements by means of written representations if determined necessary by the auditor or required by other ISAs (UK); and

(c)   To respond appropriately to written representations provided by management and, where appropriate, those charged with governance, or if management or, where appropriate, those charged with governance do not provide the written representations requested by the auditor.

---

[1] *ISA (UK) 500, Audit Evidence, paragraph 5(c).*

Definitions

For purposes of the ISAs (UK), the following term has the meaning attributed below: **7**

Written representation – A written statement by management provided to the auditor to confirm certain matters or to support other audit evidence. Written representations in this context do not include financial statements, the assertions therein, or supporting books and records.

For purposes of this ISA (UK), references to "management" should be read as "management and, where appropriate, those charged with governance." Furthermore, in the case of a fair presentation framework, management is responsible for the preparation and *fair* presentation of the financial statements in accordance with the applicable financial reporting framework; or the preparation of financial statements *that give a true and fair view* in accordance with the applicable financial reporting framework.   **8**

Requirements

Management from whom Written Representations Requested

The auditor shall request written representations from management with appropriate responsibilities for the financial statements and knowledge of the matters concerned. (Ref: Para. A2–A6)   **9**

Written Representations about Management's Responsibilities

Written Representations about Management's Responsibilities

The auditor shall request management to provide a written representation that it has fulfilled its responsibility for the preparation of the financial statements in accordance with the applicable financial reporting framework, including where relevant their fair presentation, as set out in the terms of the audit engagement.[2] (Ref: Para. A7–A9, A14, A22)   **10**

Information Provided and Completeness of Transactions

The auditor shall request management to provide a written representation that: **11**

(a)   It has provided the auditor with all relevant information and access as agreed in the terms of the audit engagement,[3] and

(b)   All transactions have been recorded and are reflected in the financial statements. (Ref: Para. A7–A9, A14, A22–A22-1)

Management may include in the written representations required by paragraphs 10 and 11 qualifying language to the effect that the representations are made to the best of its knowledge and belief. Such qualifying language does not cause paragraph 20 to apply if, during the audit, the auditor found no evidence that the representations are incorrect. (Ref; Para A5, A8-1)   **11-1**

---

[2] *ISA (UK) 210 (Revised June 2016), Agreeing the Terms of Audit Engagements, paragraph 6(b)(i).*

[3] *ISA (UK) 210 (Revised June 2016), paragraph 6(b)(iii).*

Description of Management's Responsibilities in the Written Representations

12   Management's responsibilities shall be described in the written representations required by paragraphs 10 and 11 in the manner in which these responsibilities are described in the terms of the audit engagement.

Other Written Representations

13   Other ISAs (UK) require the auditor to request written representations. If, in addition to such required representations, the auditor determines that it is necessary to obtain one or more written representations to support other audit evidence relevant to the financial statements or one or more specific assertions in the financial statements, the auditor shall request such other written representations. (Ref: Para. A10–A13, A14, A22–A22-1)

Date of and Period(s) Covered by Written Representations

14   The date of the written representations shall be as near as practicable to, but not after, the date of the auditor's report on the financial statements. The written representations shall be for all financial statements and period(s) referred to in the auditor's report. (Ref: Para. A15–A18)

Form of Written Representations

15   The written representations shall be in the form of a representation letter addressed to the auditor. If law or regulation requires management to make written public statements about its responsibilities, and the auditor determines that such statements provide some or all of the representations required by paragraphs 10 or 11, the relevant matters covered by such statements need not be included in the representation letter. (Ref: Para. A19–A21)

Doubt as to the Reliability of Written Representations and Requested Written Representations Not Provided

Doubt as to the Reliability of Written Representations

16   If the auditor has concerns about the competence, integrity, ethical values or diligence of management, or about its commitment to or enforcement of these, the auditor shall determine the effect that such concerns may have on the reliability of representations (oral or written) and audit evidence in general. (Ref: Para. A24–A25)

17   In particular, if written representations are inconsistent with other audit evidence, the auditor shall perform audit procedures to attempt to resolve the matter. If the matter remains unresolved, the auditor shall reconsider the assessment of the competence, integrity, ethical values or diligence of management, or of its commitment to or enforcement of these, and shall determine the effect that this may have on the reliability of representations (oral or written) and audit evidence in general. (Ref: Para. A23)

18   If the auditor concludes that the written representations are not reliable, the auditor shall take appropriate actions, including determining the possible effect on the opinion in the auditor's report in accordance with ISA (UK) 705 (Revised June 2016),[4] having regard to the requirement in paragraph 20 of this ISA (UK).

---

[4] *ISA (UK) 705 (Revised June 2016), Modifications to the Opinion in the Independent Auditor's Report.*

Requested Written Representations Not Provided

If management does not provide one or more of the requested written **19**
representations, the auditor shall:

(a)   Discuss the matter with management;

(b)   Reevaluate the integrity of management and evaluate the effect that this may
have on the reliability of representations (oral or written) and audit evidence
in general; and

(c)   Take appropriate actions, including determining the possible effect on the
opinion in the auditor's report in accordance with ISA (UK) 705 (Revised
June 2016), having regard to the requirement in paragraph 20 of this ISA
(UK).

Written Representations about Management's Responsibilities

The auditor shall disclaim an opinion on the financial statements in accordance **20**
with ISA (UK) 705 (Revised June 2016) if:

(a)   The auditor concludes that there is sufficient doubt about the integrity of
management such that the written representations required by paragraphs 10
and 11 are not reliable; or

(b)   Management does not provide the written representations required by
paragraphs 10 and 11. (Ref: Para. A26–A27)

Application and Other Explanatory Material

Written Representations as Audit Evidence
(Ref: Para. 3)

Written representations are an important source of audit evidence. If management **A1**
modifies or does not provide the requested written representations, it may alert the
auditor to the possibility that one or more significant issues may exist. Further, a
request for written, rather than oral, representations in many cases may prompt
management to consider such matters more rigorously, thereby enhancing the
quality of the representations.

Management from whom Written Representations Requested
(Ref: Para. 9)

Written representations are requested from those responsible for the preparation of **A2**
the financial statements. Those individuals may vary depending on the governance
structure of the entity, and relevant law or regulation; however, management
(rather than those charged with governance) is often the responsible party. Written
representations may therefore be requested from the entity's chief executive
officer and chief financial officer, or other equivalent persons in entities that do
not use such titles. In some circumstances, however, other parties, such as those
charged with governance, are also responsible for the preparation and presentation
of the financial statements.[4a]

[4a] *In the UK, those charged with governance are responsible for the preparation of the financial statements.*

A2-1   In view of their importance, it is appropriate for written representations that are critical to obtaining sufficient appropriate audit evidence to be provided by those charged with governance rather than the entity's management.

A3   Due to its responsibility for the preparation of the financial statements, and its responsibilities for the conduct of the entity's business, management would be expected to have sufficient knowledge of the process followed by the entity in preparing and presenting the financial statements and the assertions therein on which to base the written representations.

A4   In some cases, however, management may decide to make inquiries of others who participate in preparing and presenting the financial statements and assertions therein, including individuals who have specialized knowledge relating to the matters about which written representations are requested. Such individuals may include:

- An actuary responsible for actuarially determined accounting measurements.

- Staff engineers who may have responsibility for and specialized knowledge about environmental liability measurements.

- Internal counsel who may provide information essential to provisions for legal claims.

A5   In some cases, management may include in the written representations qualifying language to the effect that representations are made to the best of its knowledge and belief. It is reasonable for the auditor to accept such wording if the auditor is satisfied that the representations are being made by those with appropriate responsibilities and knowledge of the matters included in the representations.

A6   To reinforce the need for management to make informed representations, the auditor may request that management include in the written representations confirmation that it has made such inquiries as it considered appropriate to place it in the position to be able to make the requested written representations. It is not expected that such inquiries would usually require a formal internal process beyond those already established by the entity.

Written Representations about Management's Responsibilities
(Ref: Para. 10–11)

A7   Audit evidence obtained during the audit that management has fulfilled the responsibilities referred to in paragraphs 10 and 11 is not sufficient without obtaining confirmation from management that it believes that it has fulfilled those responsibilities. This is because the auditor is not able to judge solely on other audit evidence whether management has prepared and presented the financial statements and provided information to the auditor on the basis of the agreed acknowledgement and understanding of its responsibilities. For example, the auditor could not conclude that management has provided the auditor with all relevant information agreed in the terms of the audit engagement without asking it whether, and receiving confirmation that, such information has been provided.

A7-1   A signed copy of the financial statements for a company may be sufficient evidence of the directors' acknowledgement of their collective responsibility for the preparation of the financial statements where it incorporates a statement to that effect. A signed copy of the financial statements, however, is not, by itself, sufficient appropriate evidence to confirm other representations given to the auditor as it does not, ordinarily, clearly identify and explain the specific separate representations.

The written representations required by paragraphs 10 and 11 draw on the agreed **A8** acknowledgement and understanding of management of its responsibilities in the terms of the audit engagement by requesting confirmation that it has fulfilled them. The auditor may also ask management to reconfirm its acknowledgement and understanding of those responsibilities in written representations. This is common in certain jurisdictions, but in any event may be particularly appropriate when:

● Those who signed the terms of the audit engagement on behalf of the entity no longer have the relevant responsibilities;

● The terms of the audit engagement were prepared in a previous year;

● There is any indication that management misunderstands those responsibilities; or

● Changes in circumstances make it appropriate to do so.

Consistent with the requirement of ISA (UK) 210 (Revised June 2016),[5] such reconfirmation of management's acknowledgement and understanding of its responsibilities is not made subject to the best of management's knowledge and belief (as discussed in paragraph A5 of this ISA (UK)).

Although reconfirmation of management's acknowledgement and **A8-1** understanding of its responsibilities is not made subject to the best of management's knowledge and belief, as discussed in paragraph A8, this does not prevent management from stating that the written representations required by paragraphs 10 and 11 relating to the fulfillment of its responsibilities are given to the best of its knowledge and belief.

Considerations Specific to Public Sector Entities

The mandates for audits of the financial statements of public sector entities may be **A9** broader than those of other entities. As a result, the premise, relating to management's responsibilities, on which an audit of the financial statements of a public sector entity is conducted may give rise to additional written representations. These may include written representations confirming that transactions and events have been carried out in accordance with law, regulation or other authority.

Other Written Representations
(Ref: Para. 13)

Additional Written Representations about the Financial Statements

In addition to the written representation required by paragraph 10, the auditor may **A10** consider it necessary to request other written representations about the financial statements. Such written representations may supplement, but do not form part of, the written representation required by paragraph 10. They may include representations about the following:

● Whether the selection and application of accounting policies are appropriate; and

---

[5] *ISA (UK) 210 (Revised June 2016), paragraph 6(b).*

- Whether matters such as the following, where relevant under the applicable financial reporting framework, have been recognized, measured, presented or disclosed in accordance with that framework:

  - Plans or intentions that may affect the carrying value or classification of assets and liabilities;

  - Liabilities, both actual and contingent;

  - Title to, or control over, assets, the liens or encumbrances on assets, and assets pledged as collateral; and

  - Aspects of laws, regulations and contractual agreements that may affect the financial statements, including non-compliance.

Additional Written Representations about Information Provided to the Auditor

A11   In addition to the written representation required by paragraph 11, the auditor may consider it necessary to request management to provide a written representation that it has communicated to the auditor all deficiencies in internal control of which management is aware.

Written Representations about Specific Assertions

A12   When obtaining evidence about, or evaluating, judgments and intentions, the auditor may consider one or more of the following:

- The entity's past history in carrying out its stated intentions.

- The entity's reasons for choosing a particular course of action.

- The entity's ability to pursue a specific course of action.

- The existence or lack of any other information that might have been obtained during the course of the audit that may be inconsistent with management's judgment or intent.

A13   In addition, the auditor may consider it necessary to request management to provide written representations about specific assertions in the financial statements; in particular, to support an understanding that the auditor has obtained from other audit evidence of management's judgment or intent in relation to, or the completeness of, a specific assertion. For example, if the intent of management is important to the valuation basis for investments, it may not be possible to obtain sufficient appropriate audit evidence without a written representation from management about its intentions. Although such written representations provide necessary audit evidence, they do not provide sufficient appropriate audit evidence on their own for that assertion.

Communicating a Threshold Amount
(Ref: Para. 10–11, 13)

A14   ISA (UK) 450 (Revised June 2016) requires the auditor to accumulate misstatements identified during the audit, other than those that are clearly trivial.[6] The auditor may determine a threshold above which misstatements cannot be regarded as clearly trivial. In the same way, the auditor may consider communicating to management a threshold for purposes of the requested written representations.

---

[6] *ISA (UK) 450 (Revised June 2016), Evaluation of Misstatements Identified during the Audit, paragraph 5.*

Date of and Period(s) Covered by Written Representations
(Ref: Para. 14)

Because written representations are necessary audit evidence, the auditor's **A15** opinion cannot be expressed, and the auditor's report cannot be dated, before the date of the written representations. Furthermore, because the auditor is concerned with events occurring up to the date of the auditor's report that may require adjustment to or disclosure in the financial statements, the written representations are dated as near as practicable to, but not after, the date of the auditor's report on the financial statements.

In some circumstances it may be appropriate for the auditor to obtain a written **A16** representation about a specific assertion in the financial statements during the course of the audit. Where this is the case, it may be necessary to request an updated written representation.

The written representations are for all periods referred to in the auditor's report **A17** because management needs to reaffirm that the written representations it previously made with respect to the prior periods remain appropriate. The auditor and management may agree to a form of written representation that updates written representations relating to the prior periods by addressing whether there are any changes to such written representations and, if so, what they are.

Situations may arise where current management were not present during all **A18** periods referred to in the auditor's report. Such persons may assert that they are not in a position to provide some or all of the written representations because they were not in place during the period. This fact, however, does not diminish such persons' responsibilities for the financial statements as a whole. Accordingly, the requirement for the auditor to request from them written representations that cover the whole of the relevant period(s) still applies.

Form of Written Representations
(Ref: Para. 15)

Written representations are required to be included in a representation letter **A19** addressed to the auditor. In some jurisdictions, however, management may be required by law or regulation to make a written public statement about its responsibilities. Although such statement is a representation to the users of the financial statements, or to relevant authorities, the auditor may determine that it is an appropriate form of written representation in respect of some or all of the representations required by paragraph 10 or 11. Consequently, the relevant matters covered by such statement need not be included in the representation letter. Factors that may affect the auditor's determination include:

- Whether the statement includes confirmation of the fulfillment of the responsibilities referred to in paragraphs 10 and 11.

- Whether the statement has been given or approved by those from whom the auditor requests the relevant written representations.

- Whether a copy of the statement is provided to the auditor as near as practicable to, but not after, the date of the auditor's report on the financial statements (see paragraph 14).

A formal statement of compliance with law or regulation, or of approval of the **A20** financial statements, would not contain sufficient information for the auditor to be satisfied that all necessary representations have been consciously made. The expression of management's responsibilities in law or regulation is also not a substitute for the requested written representations.

A21   Appendix 2[6a] provides an illustrative example of a representation letter.

Communication with Those Charged with Governance
(Ref: Para. 10–11, 13)

A22   ISA (UK) 260 (Revised June 2016) requires the auditor to communicate with those charged with governance the written representations which the auditor has requested from management.[7]

A22-1   In the UK, these communications are made before those charged with governance approve the financial statements, to ensure that they are aware of the representations on which the auditor intends to rely in expressing the auditor's opinion on those financial statements.

A22-2   For audits of financial statements of public interest entities, the written representations requested from those charged with governance are relevant to the auditor's communications in the additional report to the audit committee that all requested explanations and documents were provided by the entity.[7a]

Doubt as to the Reliability of Written Representations and Requested Written Representations Not Provided

Doubt as to the Reliability of Written Representations
(Ref: Para. 16–17)

A23   In the case of identified inconsistencies between one or more written representations and audit evidence obtained from another source, the auditor may consider whether the risk assessment remains appropriate and, if not, revise the risk assessment and determine the nature, timing and extent of further audit procedures to respond to the assessed risks.

A24   Concerns about the competence, integrity, ethical values or diligence of management, or about its commitment to or enforcement of these, may cause the auditor to conclude that the risk of management misrepresentation in the financial statements is such that an audit cannot be conducted. In such a case, the auditor may consider withdrawing from the engagement, where withdrawal is possible under applicable law or regulation, unless those charged with governance put in place appropriate corrective measures. Such measures, however, may not be sufficient to enable the auditor to issue an unmodified audit opinion.

A25   ISA (UK) 230 (Revised June 2016) requires the auditor to document significant matters arising during the audit, the conclusions reached thereon, and significant professional judgments made in reaching those conclusions.[8] The auditor may have identified significant issues relating to the competence, integrity, ethical values or diligence of management, or about its commitment to or enforcement of these, but concluded that the written representations are nevertheless reliable. In such a case, this significant matter is documented in accordance with ISA (UK) 230 (Revised June 2016).

[6a] *The illustrative representation letter in Appendix 2 has not been tailored for the UK.*

[7] *ISA (UK) 260 (Revised June 2016), Communication with Those Charged with Governance, paragraph 16(c)(ii).*

[7a] *ISA (UK) 260 (Revised June 2016), paragraph 16R-2(o).*

[8] *ISA (UK) 230 (Revised June 2016), Audit Documentation, paragraphs 8(c) and 10.*

Written Representations about Management's Responsibilities
(Ref: Para. 20)

As explained in paragraph A7, the auditor is not able to judge solely on other audit   **A26**
evidence whether management has fulfilled the responsibilities referred to in
paragraphs 10 and 11. Therefore, if, as described in paragraph 20(a), the auditor
concludes that the written representations about these matters are unreliable, or if
management does not provide those written representations, the auditor is unable
to obtain sufficient appropriate audit evidence. The possible effects on the
financial statements of such inability are not confined to specific elements,
accounts or items of the financial statements and are hence pervasive. ISA
(UK) 705 (Revised June 2016) requires the auditor to disclaim an opinion on
the financial statements in such circumstances.[9]

A written representation that has been modified from that requested by the auditor   **A27**
does not necessarily mean that management did not provide the written
representation. However, the underlying reason for such modification may
affect the opinion in the auditor's report. For example:

- The written representation about management's fulfillment of its
  responsibility for the preparation of the financial statements may state that
  management believes that, except for material non-compliance with a
  particular requirement of the applicable financial reporting framework, the
  financial statements are prepared in accordance with that framework. The
  requirement in paragraph 20 does not apply because the auditor concluded
  that management has provided reliable written representations. However,
  the auditor is required to consider the effect of the non-compliance on the
  opinion in the auditor's report in accordance with ISA (UK) 705 (Revised
  June 2016).

- The written representation about the responsibility of management to
  provide the auditor with all relevant information agreed in the terms of
  the audit engagement may state that management believes that, except for
  information destroyed in a fire, it has provided the auditor with such
  information. The requirement in paragraph 20 does not apply because the
  auditor concluded that management has provided reliable written
  representations. However, the auditor is required to consider the effects of
  the pervasiveness of the information destroyed in the fire on the financial
  statements and the effect thereof on the opinion in the auditor's report in
  accordance with ISA (UK) 705 (Revised June 2016).

- The written representation that all transactions have been recorded and are
  reflected in the financial statements may be modified, for example to refer
  a threshold amount agreed with the auditor (see paragraph A14) or to state
  that all transactions that may have a material effect on the financial
  statements have been recorded.

---

[9] ISA (UK) 705 (Revised June 2016), paragraph 9.

Appendix 1

(Ref: Para. 2)

List of ISAs (UK) Containing Requirements for Written Representations

This appendix identifies paragraphs in other ISAs (UK) that require subject-matter specific written representations. The list is not a substitute for considering the requirements and related application and other explanatory material in ISAs (UK).

- ISA (UK) 240 (Revised June 2016), *The Auditor's Responsibilities Relating to Fraud in an Audit of Financial Statements* – paragraph 39

- ISA (UK) 250 (Revised June 2016), *Consideration of Laws and Regulations in an Audit of Financial Statements* – paragraph 16

- ISA (UK) 450 (Revised June 2016), *Evaluation of Misstatements Identified during the Audit* – paragraph 14

- ISA (UK) 501, Audit Evidence—*Specific Considerations for Selected Items* – paragraph 12

- ISA (UK) 540 (Revised June 2016), *Auditing Accounting Estimates, Including Fair Value Accounting Estimates, and Related Disclosures* – paragraph 22

- ISA (UK) 550, *Related Parties* – paragraph 26

- ISA (UK) 560, *Subsequent Events* – paragraph 9

- ISA (UK) 570 (Revised June 2016), *Going Concern* – paragraph 16(e)

- ISA (UK) 710, *Comparative Information—Corresponding Figures and Comparative Financial Statements* – paragraph 9

- ISA (UK) 720 (Revised June 2016), *The Auditor's Responsibilities Relating to Other Information* – paragraph 13(c)

Appendix 2

(Ref: Para. A21)

Illustrative Representation Letter

This illustrative representation letter has not been tailored for the UK. For example, when describing the responsibilities of management and those charged with governance for the financial statements and providing information to the auditor, the auditor has regard to the manner in which those responsibilities are described in the terms of the audit engagement (see ISA (UK) 210 (Revised June 2016)).

The following illustrative letter includes written representations that are required by this and other ISAs. It is assumed in this illustration that the applicable financial reporting framework is International Financial Reporting Standards; the requirement of ISA 570 (Revised)[1-a] to obtain a written representation is not relevant; and that there are no exceptions to the requested written representations. If there were exceptions, the representations would need to be modified to reflect the exceptions.

(Entity Letterhead)

(To Auditor)   (Date)

This representation letter is provided in connection with your audit of the financial statements of ABC Company for the year ended December 31, 20XX[2-a] for the purpose of expressing an opinion as to whether the financial statements are presented fairly, in all material respects, (or *give a true and fair view*) in accordance with International Financial Reporting Standards.

We confirm that (, *to the best of our knowledge and belief, having made such inquiries as we considered necessary for the purpose of appropriately informing ourselves*):

Financial Statements

● We have fulfilled our responsibilities, as set out in the terms of the audit engagement dated [insert date], for the preparation of the financial statements in accordance with International Financial Reporting Standards; in particular the financial statements are fairly presented (or *give a true and fair view*) in accordance therewith.

● Significant assumptions used by us in making accounting estimates, including those measured at fair value, are reasonable. (ISA 540)

● Related party relationships and transactions have been appropriately accounted for and disclosed in accordance with the requirements of International Financial Reporting Standards. (ISA 550)

[1-a] *ISA 570 (Revised), Going Concern.*

[2-a] *Where the auditor reports on more than one period, the auditor adjusts the date so that the letter pertains to all periods covered by the auditor's report.*

- All events subsequent to the date of the financial statements and for which International Financial Reporting Standards require adjustment or disclosure have been adjusted or disclosed. (ISA 560)

- The effects of uncorrected misstatements are immaterial, both individually and in the aggregate, to the financial statements as a whole. A list of the uncorrected misstatements is attached to the representation letter. (ISA 450)

- [Any other matters that the auditor may consider appropriate (see paragraph A10 of this ISA).]

Information Provided

- We have provided you with:[3]

  - Access to all information of which we are aware that is relevant to the preparation of the financial statements such as records, documentation and other matters;

  - Additional information that you have requested from us for the purpose of the audit; and

  - Unrestricted access to persons within the entity from whom you determined it necessary to obtain audit evidence.

- All transactions have been recorded in the accounting records and are reflected in the financial statements.

- We have disclosed to you the results of our assessment of the risk that the financial statements may be materially misstated as a result of fraud. (ISA 240)

- We have disclosed to you all information in relation to fraud or suspected fraud that we are aware of and that affects the entity and involves:

  - Management;

  - Employees who have significant roles in internal control; or

  - Others where the fraud could have a material effect on the financial statements. (ISA 240)

- We have disclosed to you all information in relation to allegations of fraud, or suspected fraud, affecting the entity's financial statements communicated by employees, former employees, analysts, regulators or others. (ISA 240)

- We have disclosed to you all known instances of non-compliance or suspected noncompliance with laws and regulations whose effects should be considered when preparing financial statements. (ISA 250)

- We have disclosed to you the identity of the entity's related parties and all the related party relationships and transactions of which we are aware. (ISA 550)

- [Any other matters that the auditor may consider necessary (see paragraph A11 of this ISA).]

---

[3] *ISA (UK) 210 (Revised June 2016), paragraph 6(b)(iii).*

ISA (UK) 600 (Revised June 2016) Special Considerations – Audits of Group Financial Statements (Including the Work of Component Auditors)

(Effective for audits of financial statements for periods commencing on or after 17 June 2016)

Contents

	Paragraphs
Introduction	
Scope of this ISA (UK)	1 - 6
Effective Date	7
Objectives	8
Definitions	9 - 10
Requirements	
Responsibility	11
Acceptance and Continuance	12 - 14
Overall Audit Strategy and Audit Plan	15 - 16
Understanding the Group, Its Components and Their Environments	17 - 18
Understanding the Component Auditor	19 - 20
Materiality	21 - 23
Responding to Assessed Risks	24 - 31
Consolidation Process	32 - 37
Subsequent Events	38 - 39
Communication with the Component Auditor	40 - 41
Evaluating the Sufficiency and Appropriateness of Audit Evidence Obtained	42 - 45
Communication with Group Management and Those Charged with Governance of the Group	46 - 49D-1
Documentation	50 - 50D-3
Application and Other Explanatory Material	
Components Subject to Audit by Statute, Regulation or Other Reason (Ref: Para. 3)	A1 - A1-1
Definitions	A2 - A7
Responsibility (Ref: Para. 11)	A8 - A9
Acceptance and Continuance	A10 - A21
Overall Audit Strategy and Audit Plan (Ref: Para. 16)	A22
Understanding the Group, Its Components and Their Environments	A23 - A31
Understanding the Component Auditor (Ref: Para. 19)	A32 - A41
Materiality (Ref: Para. 21–23)	A42 - A46
Responding to Assessed Risks	A47 - A55
Consolidation Process	A56
Communication with the Component Auditor (Ref: Para. 40–41)	A57 - A60
Evaluating the Sufficiency and Appropriateness of Audit Evidence Obtained	A61 - A63
Communication with Group Management and Those Charged with Governance of the Group	A64 - A66-1

Appendix 1: Illustration of Auditor's Report Where the Group Engagement Team Is Not Able to Obtain Sufficient Appropriate Audit Evidence on Which to Base the Group Audit Opinion

Appendix 2: Examples of Matters about Which the Group Engagement Team Obtains an Understanding

Appendix 3: Examples of Conditions or Events that May Indicate Risks of Material Misstatement of the Group Financial Statements

Appendix 4: Examples of a Component Auditor's Confirmations

Appendix 5: Required and Additional Matters Included in the Group Engagement Team's Letter of Instruction

---

International Standard on Auditing (UK) (ISA (UK)) 600 (Revised June 2016), *Special Considerations — Audits of Group Financial Statements (Including the Work of Component Auditors)*, should be read in conjunction with ISA (UK) 200 (Revised June 2016), *Overall Objectives of the Independent Auditor and the Conduct of an Audit in Accordance with International Standards on Auditing (UK)*.

Introduction

Scope of this ISA (UK)

The International Standards on Auditing (UK) (ISAs (UK)) apply to group audits. **1** This ISA (UK) deals with special considerations that apply to group audits, in particular those that involve component auditors.

An auditor may find this ISA (UK), adapted as necessary in the circumstances, **2** useful when that auditor involves other auditors in the audit of financial statements that are not group financial statements. For example, an auditor may involve another auditor to observe the inventory count or inspect physical fixed assets at a remote location.

A component auditor may be required by statute, regulation or for another **3** reason, to express an audit opinion on the financial statements of a component. The group engagement team may decide to use the audit evidence on which the audit opinion on the financial statements of the component is based to provide audit evidence for the group audit, but the requirements of this ISA (UK) nevertheless apply. (Ref: Para. A1)

In accordance with ISA (UK) 220 (Revised June 2016),[1] the group **4** engagement partner is required to be satisfied that those performing the group audit engagement, including component auditors, collectively have the appropriate competence and capabilities. The group engagement partner is also responsible for the direction, supervision and performance of the group audit engagement.

The group engagement partner applies the requirements of ISA (UK) 220 **5** (Revised June 2016) regardless of whether the group engagement team or a component auditor performs the work on the financial information of a component. This ISA (UK) assists the group engagement partner to meet the requirements of ISA (UK) 220 (Revised June 2016) where component auditors perform work on the financial information of components.

Audit risk is a function of the risk of material misstatement of the financial **6** statements and the risk that the auditor will not detect such misstatements.[2] In a group audit, this includes the risk that the component auditor may not detect a misstatement in the financial information of the component that could cause a material misstatement of the group financial statements, and the risk that the group engagement team may not detect this misstatement. This ISA (UK) explains the matters that the group engagement team considers when determining the nature, timing and extent of its involvement in the risk assessment procedures and further audit procedures performed by the component auditors on the financial information of the components. The purpose of this involvement is to obtain sufficient appropriate audit evidence on which to base the audit opinion on the group financial statements.

---

[1] *ISA (UK) 220 (Revised June 2016), Quality Control for an Audit of Financial Statements, paragraphs 14 and 15.*

[2] *ISA (UK) 200 (Revised June 2016), Overall Objectives of the Independent Auditor and the Conduct of an Audit in Accordance with International Standards on Auditing (UK), paragraph A32.*

Effective Date

7   This ISA (UK) is effective for audits of group financial statements for periods commencing on or after 17 June 2016. Earlier adoption is permitted.

Objectives

8   The objectives of the auditor are:

(a)   To determine whether to act as the auditor of the group financial statements; and

(b)   If acting as the auditor of the group financial statements:

(i)   To communicate clearly with component auditors about the scope and timing of their work on financial information related to components and their findings; and

(ii)   To obtain sufficient appropriate audit evidence regarding the financial information of the components and the consolidation process to express an opinion on whether the group financial statements are prepared, in all material respects, in accordance with the applicable financial reporting framework.

Definitions

9   For purposes of the ISAs (UK), the following terms have the meanings attributed below:

(a)   Component – An entity or business activity for which group or component management prepares financial information that should be included in the group financial statements. (Ref: Para. A2–A4)

(b)   Component auditor – An auditor who, at the request of the group engagement team, performs work on financial information related to a component for the group audit. (Ref: Para. A7)

(c)   Component management – Management responsible for the preparation of the financial information of a component.

(d)   Component materiality – The materiality for a component determined by the group engagement team.

(e)   Group – All the components whose financial information is included in the group financial statements. A group always has more than one component.

(f)   Group audit – The audit of group financial statements.

(g)   Group audit opinion – The audit opinion on the group financial statements.

(h)   Group engagement partner – The partner or other person in the firm who is responsible for the group audit engagement and its performance, and for the auditor's report on the group financial statements that is issued on behalf of the firm. Where joint auditors conduct the group audit, the joint engagement partners and their engagement teams collectively constitute the group engagement partner and the group engagement team. This ISA (UK) does not, however, deal with the relationship between joint auditors or the work that one joint auditor performs in relation to the work of the other joint auditor.

(i)   Group engagement team – Partners, including the group engagement partner, and staff who establish the overall group audit strategy, communicate with component auditors, perform work on the consolidation process, and evaluate the conclusions drawn from the audit evidence as the basis for forming an opinion on the group financial statements.

(j)   Group financial statements – Financial statements that include the financial information of more than one component. The term "group financial statements" also refers to combined financial statements aggregating the financial information prepared by components that have no parent but are under common control. (Ref: Para. A4-1)

(k)   Group management – Management responsible for the preparation of the group financial statements.

(l)   Group-wide controls – Controls designed, implemented and maintained by group management over group financial reporting.

(m)   Significant component – A component identified by the group engagement team (i) that is of individual financial significance to the group, or (ii) that, due to its specific nature or circumstances, is likely to include significant risks of material misstatement of the group financial statements. (Ref: Para. A5–A6)

Reference to "the applicable financial reporting framework" means the financial **10** reporting framework that applies to the group financial statements. Reference to "the consolidation process" includes:

(a)   The recognition, measurement, presentation, and disclosure of the financial information of the components in the group financial statements by way of consolidation, proportionate consolidation, or the equity or cost methods of accounting; and

(b)   The aggregation in combined financial statements of the financial information of components that have no parent but are under common control.

Requirements

Responsibility

The group engagement partner is responsible for the direction, supervision and **11** performance of the group audit engagement in compliance with professional standards and applicable legal and regulatory requirements, and whether the auditor's report that is issued is appropriate in the circumstances.[3] As a result, the auditor's report on the group financial statements shall not refer to a component auditor, unless required by law or regulation to include such reference. If such reference is required by law or regulation, the auditor's report shall indicate that the reference does not diminish the group engagement partner's or the group engagement partner's firm's responsibility for the group audit opinion. (Ref: Para. A8–A9)

---

[3] *ISA (UK) 220 (Revised June 2016), paragraph 15.*

In the UK, the group engagement partner's firm bears the full responsibility for the auditor's report on the group financial statements.

Acceptance and Continuance

12   In applying ISA (UK) 220 (Revised June 2016), the group engagement partner shall determine whether sufficient appropriate audit evidence can reasonably be expected to be obtained in relation to the consolidation process and the financial information of the components on which to base the group audit opinion. For this purpose, the group engagement team shall obtain an understanding of the group, its components, and their environments that is sufficient to identify components that are likely to be significant components. Where component auditors will perform work on the financial information of such components, the group engagement partner shall evaluate whether the group engagement team will be able to be involved in the work of those component auditors to the extent necessary to obtain sufficient appropriate audit evidence. (Ref: Para. A10–A12)

13   If the group engagement partner concludes that:

(a)   it will not be possible for the group engagement team to obtain sufficient appropriate audit evidence due to restrictions imposed by group management; and

(b)   the possible effect of this inability will result in a disclaimer of opinion on the group financial statements),[4]

the group engagement partner shall either:

- in the case of a new engagement, not accept the engagement, or, in the case of a continuing engagement, withdraw from the engagement, where withdrawal is possible under applicable law or regulation; or

- where law or regulation prohibits an auditor from declining an engagement or where withdrawal from an engagement is not otherwise possible, having performed the audit of the group financial statements to the extent possible, disclaim an opinion on the group financial statements. (Ref: Para. A13–A19)

Terms of Engagement

14   The group engagement partner shall agree on the terms of the group audit engagement in accordance with ISA (UK) 210 (Revised June 2016).[5] (Ref: Para. A20–A21)

Overall Audit Strategy and Audit Plan

15   The group engagement team shall establish an overall group audit strategy and shall develop a group audit plan in accordance with ISA (UK) 300 (Revised June 2016).[6]

16   The group engagement partner shall review the overall group audit strategy and group audit plan. (Ref: Para. A22)

---

[4] *ISA (UK) 705 (Revised June 2016), Modifications to the Opinion in the Independent Auditor's Report.*

[5] *ISA (UK) 210 (Revised June 2016), Agreeing the Terms of Audit Engagements.*

[6] *ISA (UK) 300 (Revised June 2016), Planning an Audit of Financial Statements, paragraphs 7–12.*

Understanding the Group, Its Components and Their Environments

The auditor is required to identify and assess the risks of material misstatement   **17**
through obtaining an understanding of the entity and its environment.[7] The group
engagement team shall:

(a)   Enhance its understanding of the group, its components, and their
      environments, including group-wide controls, obtained during the
      acceptance or continuance stage; and

(b)   Obtain an understanding of the consolidation process, including the
      instructions issued by group management to components. (Ref:
      Para. A23–A29)

The group engagement team shall obtain an understanding that is sufficient to: **18**

(a)   Confirm or revise its initial identification of components that are likely to be
      significant; and

(b)   Assess the risks of material misstatement of the group financial statements,
      whether due to fraud or error.[8] (Ref: Para. A30–A31)

Understanding the Component Auditor

If the group engagement team plans to request a component auditor to perform   **19**
work on the financial information of a component, the group engagement team
shall obtain an understanding of the following: (Ref: Para. A32–A35)

(a)   Whether the component auditor understands and will comply with the
      ethical requirements that are relevant to the group audit and, in particular, is
      independent. (Ref: Para. A37–A37-1)

(b)   The component auditor's professional competence. (Ref: Para. A38)

(c)   Whether the group engagement team will be able to be involved in the work
      of the component auditor to the extent necessary to obtain sufficient
      appropriate audit evidence.

(d)   Whether the component auditor operates in a regulatory environment that
      actively oversees auditors. (Ref: Para. A36)

The group engagement team shall request the agreement of the component   **19D-1**
auditor to the transfer of relevant documentation during the conduct of the
group audit, as a condition of the use by the group engagement team of the
work of the component auditor.

If a component auditor does not meet the independence requirements that are   **20**
relevant to the group audit, or the group engagement team has serious
concerns about the other matters listed in paragraph 19(a)–(c), the group
engagement team shall obtain sufficient appropriate audit evidence relating to
the financial information of the component without requesting that component
auditor to perform work on the financial information of that component. (Ref:
Para. A39–A41)

Materiality

The group engagement team shall determine the following: (Ref: Para. A42)   **21**

---

[7] *ISA (UK) 315 (Revised June 2016), Identifying and Assessing the Risks of Material Misstatement through
Understanding the Entity and Its Environment.*

[8] *ISA (UK) 315 (Revised June 2016).*

(a)   Materiality for the group financial statements as a whole when establishing the overall group audit strategy.

(b)   If, in the specific circumstances of the group, there are particular classes of transactions, account balances or disclosures in the group financial statements for which misstatements of lesser amounts than materiality for the group financial statements as a whole could reasonably be expected to influence the economic decisions of users taken on the basis of the group financial statements, the materiality level or levels to be applied to those particular classes of transactions, account balances or disclosures.

(c)   Component materiality for those components where component auditors will perform an audit or a review for purposes of the group audit. To reduce to an appropriately low level the probability that the aggregate of uncorrected and undetected misstatements in the group financial statements exceeds materiality for the group financial statements as a whole, component materiality shall be lower than materiality for the group financial statements as a whole. (Ref: Para. A43–A44)

(d)   The threshold above which misstatements cannot be regarded as clearly trivial to the group financial statements. (Ref: Para. A45)

22   Where component auditors will perform an audit for purposes of the group audit, the group engagement team shall evaluate the appropriateness of performance materiality determined at the component level. (Ref: Para. A46)

23   If a component is subject to audit by statute, regulation or other reason, and the group engagement team decides to use that audit to provide audit evidence for the group audit, the group engagement team shall determine whether:

(a)   materiality for the component financial statements as a whole; and

(b)   performance materiality at the component level

meet the requirements of this ISA (UK).

Responding to Assessed Risks

24   The auditor is required to design and implement appropriate responses to address the assessed risks of material misstatement of the financial statements.[9] The group engagement team shall determine the type of work to be performed by the group engagement team, or the component auditors on its behalf, on the financial information of the components (see paragraphs 26–29). The group engagement team shall also determine the nature, timing and extent of its involvement in the work of the component auditors (see paragraphs 30–31).

25   If the nature, timing and extent of the work to be performed on the consolidation process or the financial information of the components are based on an expectation that group-wide controls are operating effectively, or if substantive procedures alone cannot provide sufficient appropriate audit evidence at the assertion level, the group engagement team shall test, or request a component auditor to test, the operating effectiveness of those controls.

---

[9]   *ISA (UK) 330, The Auditor's Responses to Assessed Risks.*

Determining the Type of Work to Be Performed on the Financial Information of Components
(Ref: Para. A47)

Significant Components

For a component that is significant due to its individual financial significance to **26** the group, the group engagement team, or a component auditor on its behalf, shall perform an audit of the financial information of the component using component materiality.

For a component that is significant because it is likely to include significant risks **27** of material misstatement of the group financial statements due to its specific nature or circumstances, the group engagement team, or a component auditor on its behalf, shall perform one or more of the following:

(a) An audit of the financial information of the component using component materiality.

(b) An audit of one or more account balances, classes of transactions or disclosures relating to the likely significant risks of material misstatement of the group financial statements. (Ref: Para. A48)

(c) Specified audit procedures relating to the likely significant risks of material misstatement of the group financial statements. (Ref: Para. A49)

Components that Are Not Significant Components

For components that are not significant components, the group engagement team **28** shall perform analytical procedures at group level. (Ref: Para. A50)

If the group engagement team does not consider that sufficient appropriate audit **29** evidence on which to base the group audit opinion will be obtained from:

(a) the work performed on the financial information of significant components;

(b) the work performed on group-wide controls and the consolidation process; and

(c) the analytical procedures performed at group level,

the group engagement team shall select components that are not significant components and shall perform, or request a component auditor to perform, one or more of the following on the financial information of the individual components selected: (Ref: Para. A51–A53)

• An audit of the financial information of the component using component materiality.

• An audit of one or more account balances, classes of transactions or disclosures.

• A review of the financial information of the component using component materiality.

• Specified procedures.

The group engagement team shall vary the selection of components over a period of time.

Involvement in the Work Performed by Component Auditors
(Ref: Para. A54–A55)

Significant Components — Risk Assessment

30   If a component auditor performs an audit of the financial information of a significant component, the group engagement team shall be involved in the component auditor's risk assessment to identify significant risks of material misstatement of the group financial statements. The nature, timing and extent of this involvement are affected by the group engagement team's understanding of the component auditor, but at a minimum shall include:

(a)   Discussing with the component auditor or component management those of the component's business activities that are significant to the group;

(b)   Discussing with the component auditor the susceptibility of the component to material misstatement of the financial information due to fraud or error; and

(c)   Reviewing the component auditor's documentation of identified significant risks of material misstatement of the group financial statements. Such documentation may take the form of a memorandum that reflects the component auditor's conclusion with regard to the identified significant risks.

Identified Significant Risks of Material Misstatement of the Group Financial Statements — Further Audit Procedures

31   If significant risks of material misstatement of the group financial statements have been identified in a component on which a component auditor performs the work, the group engagement team shall evaluate the appropriateness of the further audit procedures to be performed to respond to the identified significant risks of material misstatement of the group financial statements. Based on its understanding of the component auditor, the group engagement team shall determine whether it is necessary to be involved in the further audit procedures.

Consolidation Process

32   In accordance with paragraph 17, the group engagement team obtains an understanding of group-wide controls and the consolidation process, including the instructions issued by group management to components. In accordance with paragraph 25, the group engagement team, or component auditor at the request of the group engagement team, tests the operating effectiveness of group-wide controls if the nature, timing and extent of the work to be performed on the consolidation process are based on an expectation that group-wide controls are operating effectively, or if substantive procedures alone cannot provide sufficient appropriate audit evidence at the assertion level.

33   The group engagement team shall design and perform further audit procedures on the consolidation process to respond to the assessed risks of material misstatement of the group financial statements arising from the consolidation process. This shall include evaluating whether all components have been included in the group financial statements.

34   The group engagement team shall evaluate the appropriateness, completeness and accuracy of consolidation adjustments and reclassifications, and shall evaluate whether any fraud risk factors or indicators of possible management bias exist. (Ref: Para. A56)

If the financial information of a component has not been prepared in accordance **35** with the same accounting policies applied to the group financial statements, the group engagement team shall evaluate whether the financial information of that component has been appropriately adjusted for purposes of preparing and presenting the group financial statements.

The group engagement team shall determine whether the financial information **36** identified in the component auditor's communication (see paragraph 41(c)) is the financial information that is incorporated in the group financial statements.

If the group financial statements include the financial statements of a component **37** with a financial reporting period-end that differs from that of the group, the group engagement team shall evaluate whether appropriate adjustments have been made to those financial statements in accordance with the applicable financial reporting framework.

Subsequent Events

Where the group engagement team or component auditors perform audits on the **38** financial information of components, the group engagement team or the component auditors shall perform procedures designed to identify events at those components that occur between the dates of the financial information of the components and the date of the auditor's report on the group financial statements, and that may require adjustment to or disclosure in the group financial statements.

Where component auditors perform work other than audits of the financial **39** information of components, the group engagement team shall request the component auditors to notify the group engagement team if they become aware of subsequent events that may require an adjustment to or disclosure in the group financial statements.

Communication with the Component Auditor

The group engagement team shall communicate its requirements to the component **40** auditor on a timely basis. This communication shall set out the work to be performed, the use to be made of that work, and the form and content of the component auditor's communication with the group engagement team. It shall also include the following: (Ref: Para. A57, A58, A60)

(a)   A request that the component auditor, knowing the context in which the group engagement team will use the work of the component auditor, confirms that the component auditor will cooperate with the group engagement team. (Ref: Para. A59)

(b)   The ethical requirements that are relevant to the group audit and, in particular, the independence requirements.

(c)   In the case of an audit or review of the financial information of the component, component materiality (and, if applicable, the materiality level or levels for particular classes of transactions, account balances or disclosures) and the threshold above which misstatements cannot be regarded as clearly trivial to the group financial statements.

(d)   Identified significant risks of material misstatement of the group financial statements, due to fraud or error, that are relevant to the work of the component auditor. The group engagement team shall request the component auditor to communicate on a timely basis any other identified significant risks of material misstatement of the group financial statements, due to fraud or error, in the component, and the component auditor's responses to such risks.

(e)   A list of related parties prepared by group management, and any other related parties of which the group engagement team is aware. The group engagement team shall request the component auditor to communicate on a timely basis related parties not previously identified by group management or the group engagement team. The group engagement team shall determine whether to identify such additional related parties to other component auditors.

41   The group engagement team shall request the component auditor to communicate matters relevant to the group engagement team's conclusion with regard to the group audit. Such communication shall include: (Ref: Para. A60)

(a)   Whether the component auditor has complied with ethical requirements that are relevant to the group audit, including independence and professional competence;

(b)   Whether the component auditor has complied with the group engagement team's requirements;

(c)   Identification of the financial information of the component on which the component auditor is reporting;

(d)   Information on instances of non-compliance with laws or regulations that could give rise to a material misstatement of the group financial statements;

(e)   A list of uncorrected misstatements of the financial information of the component (the list need not include misstatements that are below the threshold for clearly trivial misstatements communicated by the group engagement team (see paragraph 40(c));

(f)   Indicators of possible management bias;

(g)   Description of any identified significant deficiencies in internal control at the component level;

(h)   Other significant matters that the component auditor communicated or expects to communicate to those charged with governance of the component, including fraud or suspected fraud involving component management, employees who have significant roles in internal control at the component level or others where the fraud resulted in a material misstatement of the financial information of the component;

(i)   Any other matters that may be relevant to the group audit, or that the component auditor wishes to draw to the attention of the group engagement team, including exceptions noted in the written representations that the component auditor requested from component management; and

(j)   The component auditor's overall findings, conclusions or opinion.

Evaluating the Sufficiency and Appropriateness of Audit Evidence Obtained

Evaluating the Component Auditor's Communication and Adequacy of their Work

42   The group engagement team shall evaluate the component auditor's communication (see paragraph 41). The group engagement team shall:

(a)   Discuss significant matters arising from that evaluation with the component auditor, component management or group management, as appropriate; and

(b)   Determine whether it is necessary to review other relevant parts of the component auditor's audit documentation. (Ref: Para. A61)

The group engagement team shall: **42D-1**

(a)   Evaluate and review the work performed by the component auditor for the purpose of the group audit; or

(b)   Where the group engagement team is unable to request or secure the agreement required by paragraph 19D-1, take appropriate measures (including carrying out additional work, either directly or by outsourcing such tasks, in the relevant component) and inform the competent authority.[9a]

If the group engagement team concludes that the work of the component auditor is   **43**
insufficient, the group engagement team shall determine what additional procedures are to be performed, and whether they are to be performed by the component auditor or by the group engagement team.

Sufficiency and Appropriateness of Audit Evidence

The auditor is required to obtain sufficient appropriate audit evidence to reduce   **44**
audit risk to an acceptably low level and thereby enable the auditor to draw reasonable conclusions on which to base the auditor's opinion.[10] The group engagement team shall evaluate whether sufficient appropriate audit evidence has been obtained from the audit procedures performed on the consolidation process and the work performed by the group engagement team and the component auditors on the financial information of the components, on which to base the group audit opinion. (Ref: Para. A62)

The group engagement partner shall evaluate the effect on the group audit opinion   **45**
of any uncorrected misstatements (either identified by the group engagement team or communicated by component auditors) and any instances where there has been an inability to obtain sufficient appropriate audit evidence. (Ref: Para. A63)

Communication with Group Management and Those Charged with Governance of the Group

Communication with Group Management

The group engagement team shall determine which identified deficiencies in   **46**
internal control to communicate to those charged with governance and group management in accordance with ISA (UK) 265.[11] In making this determination, the group engagement team shall consider:

(a)   Deficiencies in group-wide internal control that the group engagement team has identified;

[9a] *In the UK, the competent authority designated by law is the FRC or the Recognised Supervisory Body to whom the FRC has delegated regulatory tasks, as applicable.*

[10] *ISA (UK) 200 (Revised June 2016), paragraph 17.*

[11] *ISA (UK) 265, Communicating Deficiencies in Internal Control to Those Charged with Governance and Management.*

(b)   Deficiencies in internal control that the group engagement team has identified in internal controls at components; and

(c)   Deficiencies in internal control that component auditors have brought to the attention of the group engagement team.

47   If fraud has been identified by the group engagement team or brought to its attention by a component auditor (see paragraph 41(h)), or information indicates that a fraud may exist, the group engagement team shall communicate this on a timely basis to the appropriate level of group management in order to inform those with primary responsibility for the prevention and detection of fraud of matters relevant to their responsibilities. (Ref. Para. A64)

48   A component auditor may be required by statute, regulation or for another reason, to express an audit opinion on the financial statements of a component. In that case, the group engagement team shall request group management to inform component management of any matter of which the group engagement team becomes aware that may be significant to the financial statements of the component, but of which component management may be unaware. If group management refuses to communicate the matter to component management, the group engagement team shall discuss the matter with those charged with governance of the group. If the matter remains unresolved, the group engagement team, subject to legal and professional confidentiality considerations, shall consider whether to advise the component auditor not to issue the auditor's report on the financial statements of the component until the matter is resolved. (Ref: Para. A65)

Communication with Those Charged with Governance of the Group

49   The group engagement team shall communicate the following matters with those charged with governance of the group, in addition to those required by ISA (UK) 260 (Revised June 2016)[12] and other ISAs (UK): (Ref: Para. A66)

(a)   An overview of the type of work to be performed on the financial information of the components.

(b)   An overview of the nature of the group engagement team's planned involvement in the work to be performed by the component auditors on the financial information of significant components.

(c)   Instances where the group engagement team's evaluation of the work of a component auditor gave rise to a concern about the quality of that auditor's work.

(d)   Any limitations on the group audit, for example, where the group engagement team's access to information may have been restricted.

(e)   Fraud or suspected fraud involving group management, component management, employees who have significant roles in group-wide controls or others where the fraud resulted in a material misstatement of the group financial statements.

---

[12]   ISA (UK) 260 (Revised June 2016), *Communication with Those Charged with Governance.*

For audits of group financial statements of public interest entities, the group engagement partner's firm shall bear the full responsibility for the additional report to the audit committee.[12a]   **49D-1**

Documentation

The group engagement team shall include in the audit documentation the following matters:[13]   **50**

(a)   An analysis of components, indicating those that are significant, and the type of work performed on the financial information of the components.

(b)   The nature, timing and extent of the group engagement team's involvement in the work performed by the component auditors on significant components including, where applicable, the group engagement team's review of relevant parts of the component auditors' audit documentation and conclusions thereon. (Ref: Para. A66-1)

(c)   Written communications between the group engagement team and the component auditors about the group engagement team's requirements.

The group engagement team shall include in the audit documentation the nature, timing and extent of the work performed by the component auditor, including, where applicable, the group engagement team's review of relevant parts of the component auditor's audit documentation.   **50D-1**

The group engagement team shall retain sufficient and appropriate audit documentation to enable the competent authority[9a] to review the work of the auditor of the group financial statements.   **50D-2**

Where: **50D-3**

● the group engagement team is subject to a quality assurance review or an investigation concerning the group audit; and

● the competent authority[9a] is unable to obtain audit documentation of the work carried out by any component auditor from a non-EEA member state; and

● the competent authority requests delivery of any additional documentation of the work performed by that component auditor for the purpose of the group audit (including the component auditor's working papers relevant to the group audit),

the group engagement team shall, in order to properly deliver such documentation in accordance with such request, either:

(a)   Retain copies of the documentation of the work carried out by the relevant component auditor for the purpose of the group audit (including the component auditor's working papers relevant to the group audit); or

(b)   Obtain the agreement of the relevant component auditor that the group engagement team shall have unrestricted access to such documentation on request; or

---

[12a] *ISA (UK) 260 (Revised June 2016), paragraph 16R-2 deals with the auditor's responsibilities to prepare an additional report to the audit committee.*

[13] *ISA (UK) 230 (Revised June 2016), Audit Documentation, paragraphs 8–11, and paragraph A6.*

(c)   Retain documentation to show that the group engagement team has undertaken the appropriate procedures in order to gain access to the audit documentation, together with evidence supporting the existence of any impediments to such access; or

(d)   Take any other appropriate action.

***

Application and Other Explanatory Material

Components Subject to Audit by Statute, Regulation or Other Reason
(Ref: Para. 3)

A1   Factors that may affect the group engagement team's decision whether to use an audit required by statute, regulation or for another reason to provide audit evidence for the group audit include the following:

- Differences in the financial reporting framework applied in preparing the financial statements of the component and that applied in preparing the group financial statements.

- Differences in the auditing and other standards applied by the component auditor and those applied in the audit of the group financial statements.

- Whether the audit of the financial statements of the component will be completed in time to meet the group reporting timetable.

Considerations Specific to Public Sector Entities

A1-1   In certain parts of the public sector where the responsibilities of principal and other auditors are governed by statutory provisions, these override the provisions of this ISA (UK).

Definitions

Component
(Ref: Para. 9(a))

A2   The structure of a group affects how components are identified. For example, the group financial reporting system may be based on an organizational structure that provides for financial information to be prepared by a parent and one or more subsidiaries, joint ventures, or investees accounted for by the equity or cost methods of accounting; by a head office and one or more divisions or branches; or by a combination of both. Some groups, however, may organize their financial reporting system by function, process, product or service (or by groups of products or services), or geographical locations. In these cases, the entity or business activity for which group or component management prepares financial information that is included in the group financial statements may be a function, process, product or service (or group of products or services), or geographical location.

A3   Various levels of components may exist within the group financial reporting system, in which case it may be more appropriate to identify components at certain levels of aggregation rather than individually.

A4   Components aggregated at a certain level may constitute a component for purposes of the group audit; however, such a component may also prepare group financial statements that incorporate the financial information of the components it encompasses (that is, a subgroup). This ISA (UK) may therefore be applied by different group engagement partners and teams for different subgroups within a larger group.

Group Financial Statements (Ref: Para 9(j)) In the UK, law or regulation may use other terms to describe the group financial statements including "group accounts", "consolidated accounts" and "consolidated financial statements".	A4-1

Significant Component
(Ref: Para. 9(m))

As the individual financial significance of a component increases, the risks of material misstatement of the group financial statements ordinarily increase. The group engagement team may apply a percentage to a chosen benchmark as an aid to identify components that are of individual financial significance. Identifying a benchmark and determining a percentage to be applied to it involve the exercise of professional judgment. Depending on the nature and circumstances of the group, appropriate benchmarks might include group assets, liabilities, cash flows, profit or turnover. For example, the group engagement team may consider that components exceeding 15% of the chosen benchmark are significant components. A higher or lower percentage may, however, be deemed appropriate in the circumstances.   **A5**

The group engagement team may also identify a component as likely to include significant risks of material misstatement of the group financial statements due to its specific nature or circumstances (that is, risks that require special audit consideration[14]). For example, a component could be responsible for foreign exchange trading and thus expose the group to a significant risk of material misstatement, even though the component is not otherwise of individual financial significance to the group.   **A6**

Component Auditor
(Ref: Para. 9(b))

A member of the group engagement team may perform work on the financial information of a component for the group audit at the request of the group engagement team. Where this is the case, such a member of the engagement team is also a component auditor.   **A7**

Responsibility
(Ref: Para. 11)

Although component auditors may perform work on the financial information of the components for the group audit and as such are responsible for their overall findings, conclusions or opinions, the group engagement partner or the group engagement partner's firm is responsible for the group audit opinion.   **A8**

When the group audit opinion is modified because the group engagement team was unable to obtain sufficient appropriate audit evidence in relation to the financial information of one or more components, the Basis for Modification   **A9**

---

[14] *ISA (UK) 315 (Revised June 2016), paragraphs 27–29.*

paragraph in the auditor's report on the group financial statements describes the reasons for that inability without referring to the component auditor, unless such a reference is necessary for an adequate explanation of the circumstances.[15]

Acceptance and Continuance

Obtaining an Understanding at the Acceptance or Continuance Stage
(Ref: Para. 12)

A10   In the case of a new engagement, the group engagement team's understanding of the group, its components, and their environments may be obtained from:

- Information provided by group management;
- Communication with group management; and
- Where applicable, communication with the previous group engagement team, component management, or component auditors.

A11   The group engagement team's understanding may include matters such as the following:

- The group structure, including both the legal and organizational structure (that is, how the group financial reporting system is organized).
- Components' business activities that are significant to the group, including the industry and regulatory, economic and political environments in which those activities take place.
- The use of service organizations, including shared service centers.
- A description of group-wide controls.
- The complexity of the consolidation process.
- Whether component auditors that are not from the group engagement partner's firm or network will perform work on the financial information of any of the components, and group management's rationale for appointing more than one auditor.
- Whether the group engagement team:
    - Will have unrestricted access to those charged with governance of the group, group management, those charged with governance of the component, component management, component information, and the component auditors (including relevant audit documentation sought by the group engagement team); and
    - Will be able to perform necessary work on the financial information of the components.

A12   In the case of a continuing engagement, the group engagement team's ability to obtain sufficient appropriate audit evidence may be affected by significant changes, for example:

- Changes in the group structure (for example, acquisitions, disposals, reorganizations, or changes in how the group financial reporting system is organized).
- Changes in components' business activities that are significant to the group.

---

[15] *ISA (UK) 705 (Revised June 2016), paragraph 20.*

- Changes in the composition of those charged with governance of the group, group management, or key management of significant components.

- Concerns the group engagement team has with regard to the integrity and competence of group or component management.

- Changes in group-wide controls.

- Changes in the applicable financial reporting framework.

Expectation to Obtain Sufficient Appropriate Audit Evidence
(Ref: Para. 13)

A group may consist only of components not considered significant components. **A13**
In these circumstances, the group engagement partner can reasonably expect to obtain sufficient appropriate audit evidence on which to base the group audit opinion if the group engagement team will be able to:

(a) Perform the work on the financial information of some of these components; and

(b) Be involved in the work performed by component auditors on the financial information of other components to the extent necessary to obtain sufficient appropriate audit evidence.

Access to Information
(Ref: Para. 13)

The group engagement team's access to information may be restricted by **A14**
circumstances that cannot be overcome by group management, for example, laws relating to confidentiality and data privacy, or denial by the component auditor of access to relevant audit documentation sought by the group engagement team. It may also be restricted by group management.

In the UK, there are statutory obligations on corporate subsidiary undertakings, **A14-1**
and their auditors and other parties, to provide the auditor of a corporate parent undertaking with such information and explanations as that auditor may reasonably require for the purposes of the audit.[15a] Where there is no such statutory obligation (e.g. for non corporate entities and overseas subsidiary undertakings), permission may be needed by the auditors of the subsidiary undertakings, from those charged with governance of the subsidiary undertakings, to disclose information to the auditor of the parent undertaking. Permission may also be needed from those charged with governance of the subsidiary undertakings for the auditor of the parent undertaking to pass those disclosures on to those charged with governance of the parent undertaking. The auditor of the parent undertaking seeks to ensure that appropriate arrangements are made at the planning stage for these disclosures. Normally, such arrangements for groups are recorded in the instructions to the auditors of subsidiary undertakings and relevant engagement letters.

[15a] *In the UK, Section 499 of the Companies Act 2006 specifies that the auditor of a company may require any subsidiary undertaking of the company which is a body corporate incorporated in the UK, and any officer, employee or auditor of any such subsidiary undertaking or any person holding or accountable for any books, accounts or vouchers of any such subsidiary undertaking, to provide him with such information or explanations as he thinks necessary for the performance of his duties as auditor. If a parent company has a subsidiary undertaking that is not a body corporate incorporated in the UK, Section 500 of the Companies Act 2006 specifies that the auditor of the parent company may require it to take all such steps as are reasonably open to it to obtain from the subsidiary undertaking, any officer, employee or auditor of the undertaking, or any person holding or accountable for any of the undertaking's books, accounts or vouchers, such information and explanations as he may reasonably require for the purposes of his duties as auditor.*

A15 Where access to information is restricted by circumstances, the group engagement team may still be able to obtain sufficient appropriate audit evidence; however, this is less likely as the significance of the component increases. For example, the group engagement team may not have access to those charged with governance, management, or the auditor (including relevant audit documentation sought by the group engagement team) of a component that is accounted for by the equity method of accounting. If the component is not a significant component, and the group engagement team has a complete set of financial statements of the component, including the auditor's report thereon, and has access to information kept by group management in relation to that component, the group engagement team may conclude that this information constitutes sufficient appropriate audit evidence in relation to that component. If the component is a significant component, however, the group engagement team will not be able to comply with the requirements of this ISA (UK) relevant in the circumstances of the group audit. For example, the group engagement team will not be able to comply with the requirement in paragraphs 30–31 to be involved in the work of the component auditor. The group engagement team will not, therefore, be able to obtain sufficient appropriate audit evidence in relation to that component. The effect of the group engagement team's inability to obtain sufficient appropriate audit evidence is considered in terms of ISA (UK) 705 (Revised June 2016).

A16 The group engagement team will not be able to obtain sufficient appropriate audit evidence if group management restricts the access of the group engagement team or a component auditor to the information of a significant component.

A17 Although the group engagement team may be able to obtain sufficient appropriate audit evidence if such restriction relates to a component considered not a significant component, the reason for the restriction may affect the group audit opinion. For example, it may affect the reliability of group management's responses to the group engagement team's inquiries and group management's representations to the group engagement team.

A18 Law or regulation may prohibit the group engagement partner from declining or withdrawing from an engagement. For example, in some jurisdictions the auditor is appointed for a specified period of time and is prohibited from withdrawing before the end of that period. Also, in the public sector, the option of declining or withdrawing from an engagement may not be available to the auditor due to the nature of the mandate or public interest considerations. In these circumstances, this ISA (UK) still applies to the group audit, and the effect of the group engagement team's inability to obtain sufficient appropriate audit evidence is considered in terms of ISA (UK) 705 (Revised June 2016).

A19 Appendix 1 contains an example of an auditor's report containing a qualified opinion based on the group engagement team's inability to obtain sufficient appropriate audit evidence in relation to a significant component accounted for by the equity method of accounting, but where, in the group engagement team's judgment, the effect is material but not pervasive.[15b]

[15b] *The example in the Appendix has not been tailored for the UK. Illustrative auditor's reports tailored for use with audits conducted in accordance with ISAs (UK) are given in the current version of the FRC's Compendium of Illustrative Auditor's Reports.*

Terms of Engagement
(Ref: Para. 14)

The terms of engagement identify the applicable financial reporting framework.[16] **A20**
Additional matters may be included in the terms of a group audit engagement,
such as the fact that:

- The communication between the group engagement team and the
  component auditors should be unrestricted to the extent possible under
  law or regulation;

- Important communications between the component auditors, those charged
  with governance of the component, and component management, including
  communications on significant deficiencies in internal control, should be
  communicated as well to the group engagement team;

- Important communications between regulatory authorities and components
  related to financial reporting matters should be communicated to the group
  engagement team; and

- To the extent the group engagement team considers necessary, it should be
  permitted:

  - Access to component information, those charged with governance of
    components, component management, and the component auditors
    (including relevant audit documentation sought by the group
    engagement team); and

  - To perform work or request a component auditor to perform work on
    the financial information of the components.

Restrictions imposed on: **A21**

- the group engagement team's access to component information, those
  charged with governance of components, component management, or the
  component auditors (including relevant audit documentation sought by the
  group engagement team); or

- the work to be performed on the financial information of the components

after the group engagement partner's acceptance of the group audit engagement,
constitute an inability to obtain sufficient appropriate audit evidence that may
affect the group audit opinion. In exceptional circumstances it may even lead to
withdrawal from the engagement where withdrawal is possible under applicable
law or regulation.

Overall Audit Strategy and Audit Plan
(Ref: Para. 16)

The group engagement partner's review of the overall group audit strategy and **A22**
group audit plan is an important part of fulfilling the group engagement partner's
responsibility for the direction of the group audit engagement.

---

[16] *ISA (UK) 210 (Revised June 2016), paragraph 8.*

Understanding the Group, Its Components and Their Environments

Matters about Which the Group Engagement Team Obtains an Understanding
(Ref: Para. 17)

A23   ISA (UK) 315 (Revised June 2016) contains guidance on matters the auditor may consider when obtaining an understanding of the industry, regulatory, and other external factors that affect the entity, including the applicable financial reporting framework; the nature of the entity; objectives and strategies and related business risks; and measurement and review of the entity's financial performance.[17]Appendix 2 of this ISA (UK) contains guidance on matters specific to a group, including the consolidation process.

Instructions Issued by Group Management to Components
(Ref: Para. 17)

A24   To achieve uniformity and comparability of financial information, group management ordinarily issues instructions to components. Such instructions specify the requirements for financial information of the components to be included in the group financial statements and often include financial reporting procedures manuals and a reporting package. A reporting package ordinarily consists of standard formats for providing financial information for incorporation in the group financial statements. Reporting packages generally do not, however, take the form of complete financial statements prepared and presented in accordance with the applicable financial reporting framework.

A25   The instructions ordinarily cover:

- The accounting policies to be applied;

- Statutory and other disclosure requirements applicable to the group financial statements, including:

  - The identification and reporting of segments;

  - Related party relationships and transactions;

  - Intra-group transactions and unrealized profits;

  - Intra-group account balances; and

- A reporting timetable.

A26   The group engagement team's understanding of the instructions may include the following:

- The clarity and practicality of the instructions for completing the reporting package.

- Whether the instructions:

  - Adequately describe the characteristics of the applicable financial reporting framework;

  - Provide for disclosures that are sufficient to comply with the requirements of the applicable financial reporting framework, for example, disclosure of related party relationships and transactions, and segment information;

---

[17] *ISA (UK) 315 (Revised June 2016), paragraphs A17–A41.*

- Provide for the identification of consolidation adjustments, for example, intra-group transactions and unrealized profits, and intra-group account balances; and

- Provide for the approval of the financial information by component management.

Fraud
(Ref: Para. 17)

The auditor is required to identify and assess the risks of material misstatement of **A27** the financial statements due to fraud, and to design and implement appropriate responses to the assessed risks.[18] Information used to identify the risks of material misstatement of the group financial statements due to fraud may include the following:

- Group management's assessment of the risks that the group financial statements may be materially misstated as a result of fraud.

- Group management's process for identifying and responding to the risks of fraud in the group, including any specific fraud risks identified by group management, or account balances, classes of transactions, or disclosures for which a risk of fraud is likely.

- Whether there are particular components for which a risk of fraud is likely.

- How those charged with governance of the group monitor group management's processes for identifying and responding to the risks of fraud in the group, and the controls group management has established to mitigate these risks.

- Responses of those charged with governance of the group, group management, appropriate individuals within the internal audit function (and if considered appropriate, component management, the component auditors, and others) to the group engagement team's inquiry whether they have knowledge of any actual, suspected, or alleged fraud affecting a component or the group.

Discussion among Group Engagement Team Members and Component Auditors Regarding the Risks of Material Misstatement of the Group Financial Statements, Including Risks of Fraud
(Ref: Para. 17)

The key members of the engagement team are required to discuss the **A28** susceptibility of an entity to material misstatement of the financial statements due to fraud or error, specifically emphasizing the risks due to fraud. In a group audit, these discussions may also include the component auditors.[19] The group engagement partner's determination of who to include in the discussions, how and when they occur, and their extent, is affected by factors such as prior experience with the group.

The discussions provide an opportunity to: **A29**

- Share knowledge of the components and their environments, including group-wide controls.

---

[18] *ISA (UK) 240 (Revised June 2016), The Auditor's Responsibilities Relating to Fraud in an Audit of Financial Statements.*

[19] *ISA (UK) 240 (Revised June 2016), paragraph 15, and ISA (UK) 315 (Revised June 2016), paragraph 10.*

- Exchange information about the business risks of the components or the group.

- Exchange ideas about how and where the group financial statements may be susceptible to material misstatement due to fraud or error, how group management and component management could perpetrate and conceal fraudulent financial reporting, and how assets of the components could be misappropriated.

- Identify practices followed by group or component management that may be biased or designed to manage earnings that could lead to fraudulent financial reporting, for example, revenue recognition practices that do not comply with the applicable financial reporting framework.

- Consider known external and internal factors affecting the group that may create an incentive or pressure for group management, component management, or others to commit fraud, provide the opportunity for fraud to be perpetrated, or indicate a culture or environment that enables group management, component management, or others to rationalize committing fraud.

- Consider the risk that group or component management may override controls.

- Consider whether uniform accounting policies are used to prepare the financial information of the components for the group financial statements and, where not, how differences in accounting policies are identified and adjusted (where required by the applicable financial reporting framework).

- Discuss fraud that has been identified in components, or information that indicates existence of a fraud in a component.

- Share information that may indicate non-compliance with national laws or regulations, for example, payments of bribes and improper transfer pricing practices.

Risk Factors
(Ref: Para. 18)

A30   Appendix 3 sets out examples of conditions or events that, individually or together, may indicate risks of material misstatement of the group financial statements, including risks due to fraud.

Risk Assessment
(Ref: Para. 18)

A31   The group engagement team's assessment at group level of the risks of material misstatement of the group financial statements is based on information such as the following:

- Information obtained from the understanding of the group, its components, and their environments, and of the consolidation process, including audit evidence obtained in evaluating the design and implementation of group-wide controls and controls that are relevant to the consolidation.

- Information obtained from the component auditors.

Understanding the Component Auditor
(Ref: Para. 19)

The group engagement team obtains an understanding of a component auditor **A32** only when it plans to request the component auditor to perform work on the financial information of a component for the group audit. For example, it will not be necessary to obtain an understanding of the auditors of those components for which the group engagement team plans to perform analytical procedures at group level only.

Group Engagement Team's Procedures to Obtain an Understanding of the Component Auditor and Sources of Audit Evidence
(Ref: Para. 19)

The nature, timing and extent of the group engagement team's procedures to **A33** obtain an understanding of the component auditor are affected by factors such as previous experience with or knowledge of the component auditor, and the degree to which the group engagement team and the component auditor are subject to common policies and procedures, for example:

- Whether the group engagement team and a component auditor share:
  - Common policies and procedures for performing the work (for example, audit methodologies);
  - Common quality control policies and procedures; or
  - Common monitoring policies and procedures.
- The consistency or similarity of:
  - Laws and regulations or legal system;
  - Professional oversight, discipline, and external quality assurance;
  - Education and training;
  - Professional organizations and standards; or
  - Language and culture.

These factors interact and are not mutually exclusive. For example, the extent **A34** of the group engagement team's procedures to obtain an understanding of Component Auditor A, who consistently applies common quality control and monitoring policies and procedures and a common audit methodology or operates in the same jurisdiction as the group engagement partner, may be less than the extent of the group engagement team's procedures to obtain an understanding of Component Auditor B, who is not consistently applying common quality control and monitoring policies and procedures and a common audit methodology or operates in a foreign jurisdiction. The nature of the procedures performed in relation to Component Auditors A and B may also be different.

The group engagement team may obtain an understanding of the component **A35** auditor in a number of ways. In the first year of involving a component auditor, the group engagement team may, for example:

- Evaluate the results of the quality control monitoring system where the group engagement team and component auditor are from a firm or network that operates under and complies with common monitoring policies and procedures;[20]

- Visit the component auditor to discuss the matters in paragraph 19(a)–(c);

- Request the component auditor to confirm the matters referred to in paragraph 19(a)–(c) in writing. Appendix 4 contains an example of written confirmations by a component auditor;

- Request the component auditor to complete questionnaires about the matters in paragraph 19(a)–(c);

- Discuss the component auditor with colleagues in the group engagement partner's firm, or with a reputable third party that has knowledge of the component auditor; or

- Obtain confirmations from the professional body or bodies to which the component auditor belongs, the authorities by which the component auditor is licensed, or other third parties.

In subsequent years, the understanding of the component auditor may be based on the group engagement team's previous experience with the component auditor. The group engagement team may request the component auditor to confirm whether anything in relation to the matters listed in paragraph 19(a)–(c) has changed since the previous year.

A36   Where independent oversight bodies have been established to oversee the auditing profession and monitor the quality of audits, awareness of the regulatory environment may assist the group engagement team in evaluating the independence and competence of the component auditor. Information about the regulatory environment may be obtained from the component auditor or information provided by the independent oversight bodies.

Ethical Requirements that Are Relevant to the Group Audit
(Ref: Para. 19(a))

A37   When performing work on the financial information of a component for a group audit, the component auditor is subject to ethical requirements that are relevant to the group audit. Such requirements may be different or in addition to those applying to the component auditor when performing a statutory audit in the component auditor's jurisdiction. The group engagement team therefore obtains an understanding whether the component auditor understands and will comply with the ethical requirements that are relevant to the group audit, sufficient to fulfill the component auditor's responsibilities in the group audit.

A37-1   As part of obtaining an understanding of whether the component auditor understands and will comply with the ethical requirements that are relevant to the group audit, the group engagement team considers the implications of Supporting Ethical Provision 2.4 of the FRC's Ethical Standard[20a] for the component auditor.

---

[20] *As required by ISQC (UK) 1 (Revised June 2016), Quality Control for Firms that Perform Audits and Reviews of Financial Statements, and Other Assurance and Related Services Engagements, paragraph 54, or national requirements that are at least as demanding.*

[20a] *FRC's Ethical Standard, Part A – Overarching Principles and Supporting Ethical Provisions, Supporting Ethical Provision 2.4.*

The Component Auditor's Professional Competence
(Ref: Para. 19(b))

The group engagement team's understanding of the component auditor's **A38** professional competence may include whether the component auditor:

- Possesses an understanding of auditing and other standards applicable to the group audit that is sufficient to fulfill the component auditor's responsibilities in the group audit;

- Has sufficient resources (e.g. personnel with the necessary capabilities) to perform the work on the financial information of the particular component;

- Possesses the special skills (for example, industry specific knowledge) necessary to perform the work on the financial information of the particular component; and

- Where relevant, possesses an understanding of the applicable financial reporting framework that is sufficient to fulfill the component auditor's responsibilities in the group audit (instructions issued by group management to components often describe the characteristics of the applicable financial reporting framework).

Application of the Group Engagement Team's Understanding of a Component Auditor
(Ref: Para. 20)

The group engagement team cannot overcome the fact that a component auditor is **A39** not independent by being involved in the work of the component auditor or by performing additional risk assessment or further audit procedures on the financial information of the component.

However, the group engagement team may be able to overcome less than serious **A40** concerns about the component auditor's professional competency (for example, lack of industry specific knowledge), or the fact that the component auditor does not operate in an environment that actively oversees auditors, by being involved in the work of the component auditor or by performing additional risk assessment or further audit procedures on the financial information of the component.

Where law or regulation prohibits access to relevant parts of the audit **A41** documentation of the component auditor, the group engagement team may request the component auditor to overcome this by preparing a memorandum that covers the relevant information.

Materiality
(Ref: Para. 21–23)

The auditor is required:[21] **A42**

(a) When establishing the overall audit strategy, to determine:

    (i)   Materiality for the financial statements as a whole; and

    (ii) If, in the specific circumstances of the entity, there are particular classes of transactions, account balances or disclosures for which misstatements of lesser amounts than materiality for the financial statements as a whole could reasonably be expected to influence the

---

[21] *ISA (UK) 320 (Revised June 2016), Materiality in Planning and Performing an Audit, paragraphs 10–11.*

economic decisions of users taken on the basis of the financial statements, the materiality level or levels to be applied to those particular classes of transactions, account balances or disclosures; and

(b)   To determine performance materiality.

In the context of a group audit, materiality is established for both the group financial statements as a whole, and for the financial information of the components. Materiality for the group financial statements as a whole is used when establishing the overall group audit strategy.

A43   To reduce to an appropriately low level the probability that the aggregate of uncorrected and undetected misstatements in the group financial statements exceeds materiality for the group financial statements as a whole, component materiality is set lower than materiality for the group financial statements as a whole. Different component materiality may be established for different components. Component materiality need not be an arithmetical portion of the materiality for the group financial statements as a whole and, consequently, the aggregate of component materiality for the different components may exceed the materiality for the group financial statements as a whole. Component materiality is used when establishing the overall audit strategy for a component.

A44   Component materiality is determined for those components whose financial information will be audited or reviewed as part of the group audit in accordance with paragraphs 26, 27(a) and 29. Component materiality is used by the component auditor to evaluate whether uncorrected detected misstatements are material, individually or in the aggregate.

A45   A threshold for misstatements is determined in addition to component materiality. Misstatements identified in the financial information of the component that are above the threshold for misstatements are communicated to the group engagement team.

A46   In the case of an audit of the financial information of a component, the component auditor (or group engagement team) determines performance materiality at the component level. This is necessary to reduce to an appropriately low level the probability that the aggregate of uncorrected and undetected misstatements in the financial information of the component exceeds component materiality. In practice, the group engagement team may set component materiality at this lower level. Where this is the case, the component auditor uses component materiality for purposes of assessing the risks of material misstatement of the financial information of the component and to design further audit procedures in response to assessed risks as well as for evaluating whether detected misstatements are material individually or in the aggregate.

Responding to Assessed Risks

Determining the Type of Work to Be Performed on the Financial Information of Components
(Ref: Para. 26–27)

A47   The group engagement team's determination of the type of work to be performed on the financial information of a component and its involvement in the work of the component auditor is affected by:

(a)   The significance of the component;

(b)   The identified significant risks of material misstatement of the group financial statements;

(c)   The group engagement team's evaluation of the design of group-wide controls and determination whether they have been implemented; and

(d)   The group engagement team's understanding of the component auditor.

The diagram shows how the significance of the component affects the group engagement team's determination of the type of work to be performed on the financial information of the component.

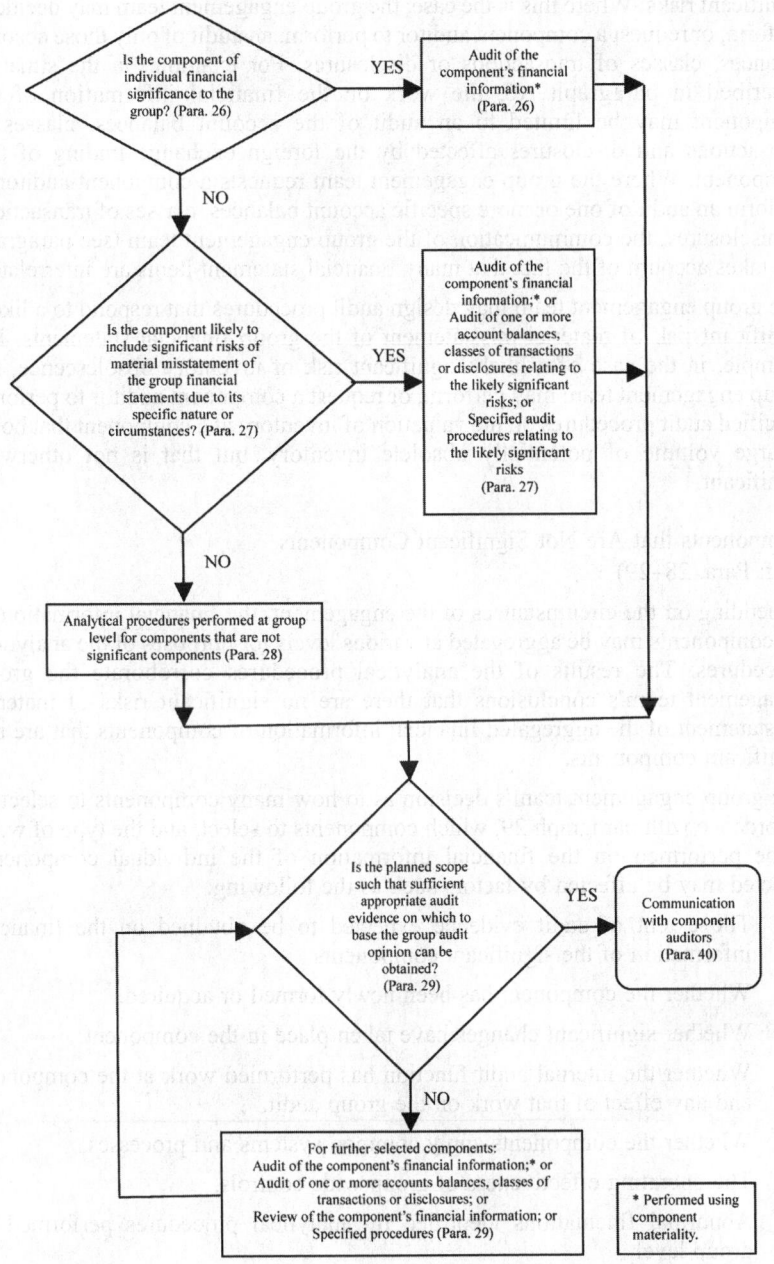

Significant Components
(Ref: Para. 27(b)–(c))

A48   The group engagement team may identify a component as a significant component because that component is likely to include significant risks of material misstatement of the group financial statements due to its specific nature or circumstances. In that case, the group engagement team may be able to identify the account balances, classes of transactions or disclosures affected by the likely significant risks. Where this is the case, the group engagement team may decide to perform, or request a component auditor to perform, an audit of only those account balances, classes of transactions or disclosures. For example, in the situation described in paragraph A6, the work on the financial information of the component may be limited to an audit of the account balances, classes of transactions and disclosures affected by the foreign exchange trading of that component. Where the group engagement team requests a component auditor to perform an audit of one or more specific account balances, classes of transactions or disclosures, the communication of the group engagement team (see paragraph 40) takes account of the fact that many financial statement items are interrelated.

A49   The group engagement team may design audit procedures that respond to a likely significant risk of material misstatement of the group financial statements. For example, in the case of a likely significant risk of inventory obsolescence, the group engagement team may perform, or request a component auditor to perform, specified audit procedures on the valuation of inventory at a component that holds a large volume of potentially obsolete inventory, but that is not otherwise significant.

Components that Are Not Significant Components
(Ref: Para. 28–29)

A50   Depending on the circumstances of the engagement, the financial information of the components may be aggregated at various levels for purposes of the analytical procedures. The results of the analytical procedures corroborate the group engagement team's conclusions that there are no significant risks of material misstatement of the aggregated financial information of components that are not significant components.

A51   The group engagement team's decision as to how many components to select in accordance with paragraph 29, which components to select, and the type of work to be performed on the financial information of the individual components selected may be affected by factors such as the following:

● The extent of audit evidence expected to be obtained on the financial information of the significant components.

● Whether the component has been newly formed or acquired.

● Whether significant changes have taken place in the component.

● Whether the internal audit function has performed work at the component and any effect of that work on the group audit.

● Whether the components apply common systems and processes.

● The operating effectiveness of group-wide controls.

● Abnormal fluctuations identified by analytical procedures performed at group level.

- The individual financial significance of, or the risk posed by, the component in comparison with other components within this category.

- Whether the component is subject to audit required by statute, regulation or for another reason.

Including an element of unpredictability in selecting components in this category may increase the likelihood of identifying material misstatement of the components' financial information. The selection of components is often varied on a cyclical basis.

A review of the financial information of a component may be performed in accordance with International Standard on Review Engagements (ISRE) 2400[22] or ISRE (UK and Ireland) 2410,[23] adapted as necessary in the circumstances. The group engagement team may also specify additional procedures to supplement this work.   **A52**

As explained in paragraph A13, a group may consist only of components that are not significant components. In these circumstances, the group engagement team can obtain sufficient appropriate audit evidence on which to base the group audit opinion by determining the type of work to be performed on the financial information of the components in accordance with paragraph 29. It is unlikely that the group engagement team will obtain sufficient appropriate audit evidence on which to base the group audit opinion if the group engagement team, or a component auditor, only tests group-wide controls and performs analytical procedures on the financial information of the components.   **A53**

Involvement in the Work Performed by Component Auditors
(Ref: Para. 30–31)

Factors that may affect the group engagement team's involvement in the work of the component auditor include: **A54**

(a) The significance of the component;

(b) The identified significant risks of material misstatement of the group financial statements; and

(c) The group engagement team's understanding of the component auditor.

In the case of a significant component or identified significant risks, the group engagement team performs the procedures described in paragraphs 30–31. In the case of a component that is not a significant component, the nature, timing and extent of the group engagement team's involvement in the work of the component auditor will vary based on the group engagement team's understanding of that component auditor. The fact that the component is not a significant component becomes secondary. For example, even though a component is not considered a significant component, the group engagement team nevertheless may decide to be involved in the component auditor's risk assessment, because it has less than serious concerns about the component auditor's professional competency (for example, lack of industry specific knowledge), or the component auditor does not operate in an environment that actively oversees auditors.

---

[22] *ISRE 2400, Engagements to Review Financial Statements.*
ISRE 2400 has not been promulgated by the FRC for application in the UK.

[23] *ISRE (UK and Ireland) 2410, Review of Interim Financial Information Performed by the Independent Auditor of the Entity.*

A55 Forms of involvement in the work of a component auditor other than those described in paragraphs 30–31 and 42 may, based on the group engagement team's understanding of the component auditor, include one or more of the following:

(a) Meeting with component management or the component auditors to obtain an understanding of the component and its environment.

(b) Reviewing the component auditors' overall audit strategy and audit plan.

(c) Performing risk assessment procedures to identify and assess the risks of material misstatement at the component level. These may be performed with the component auditors, or by the group engagement team.

(d) Designing and performing further audit procedures. These may be designed and performed with the component auditors, or by the group engagement team.

(e) Participating in the closing and other key meetings between the component auditors and component management.

(f) Reviewing other relevant parts of the component auditors' audit documentation.

Consolidation Process

Consolidation Adjustments and Reclassifications
(Ref: Para. 34)

A56 The consolidation process may require adjustments to amounts reported in the group financial statements that do not pass through the usual transaction processing systems, and may not be subject to the same internal controls to which other financial information is subject. The group engagement team's evaluation of the appropriateness, completeness and accuracy of the adjustments may include:

● Evaluating whether significant adjustments appropriately reflect the events and transactions underlying them;

● Determining whether significant adjustments have been correctly calculated, processed and authorized by group management and, where applicable, by component management;

● Determining whether significant adjustments are properly supported and sufficiently documented; and

● Checking the reconciliation and elimination of intra-group transactions and unrealized profits, and intra-group account balances.

Communication with the Component Auditor
(Ref: Para. 40–41)

A57 If effective two-way communication between the group engagement team and the component auditors does not exist, there is a risk that the group engagement team may not obtain sufficient appropriate audit evidence on which to base the group audit opinion. Clear and timely communication of the group engagement team's requirements forms the basis of effective two-way communication between the group engagement team and the component auditor.

A58 The group engagement team's requirements are often communicated in a letter of instruction. Appendix 5 contains guidance on required and additional matters that may be included in such a letter of instruction. The component auditor's communication with the group engagement team often takes the form of a memorandum or report of work performed. Communication between the group engagement team and the component auditor, however, may not necessarily be in writing. For example, the group engagement team may visit the component auditor to discuss identified significant risks or review relevant parts of the component auditor's audit documentation. Nevertheless, the documentation requirements of this and other ISAs (UK) apply.

In cooperating with the group engagement team, the component auditor, for example, would provide the group engagement team with access to relevant audit documentation if not prohibited by law or regulation.   **A59**

Where a member of the group engagement team is also a component auditor, the objective for the group engagement team to communicate clearly with the component auditor can often be achieved by means other than specific written communication. For example: **A60**

- Access by the component auditor to the overall audit strategy and audit plan may be sufficient to communicate the group engagement team's requirements set out in paragraph 40; and

- A review of the component auditor's audit documentation by the group engagement team may be sufficient to communicate matters relevant to the group engagement team's conclusion set out in paragraph 41.

Evaluating the Sufficiency and Appropriateness of Audit Evidence Obtained

Reviewing the Component Auditor's Audit Documentation
(Ref: Para. 42(b))

What parts of the audit documentation of the component auditor will be relevant to the group audit may vary depending on the circumstances. Often the focus is on audit documentation that is relevant to the significant risks of material misstatement of the group financial statements. The extent of the review may be affected by the fact that the component auditor's audit documentation has been subjected to the component auditor's firm's review procedures.   **A61**

Sufficiency and Appropriateness of Audit Evidence
(Ref: Para. 44–45)

If the group engagement team concludes that sufficient appropriate audit evidence on which to base the group audit opinion has not been obtained, the group engagement team may request the component auditor to perform additional procedures. If this is not feasible, the group engagement team may perform its own procedures on the financial information of the component.   **A62**

The group engagement partner's evaluation of the aggregate effect of any misstatements (either identified by the group engagement team or communicated by component auditors) allows the group engagement partner to determine whether the group financial statements as a whole are materially misstated.   **A63**

Communication with Group Management and Those Charged with Governance of the Group

Communication with Group Management
(Ref: Para. 46–48)

A64   ISA (UK) 240 (Revised June 2016) contains requirements and guidance on communication of fraud to management and, where management may be involved in the fraud, to those charged with governance.[24]

A65   Group management may need to keep certain material sensitive information confidential. Examples of matters that may be significant to the financial statements of the component of which component management may be unaware include the following:

- Potential litigation.

- Plans for abandonment of material operating assets.

- Subsequent events.

- Significant legal agreements.

A65-1   Information that group management has determined needs to be kept confidential would ordinarily be known to those charged with governance of the group.[24a]

Communication with Those Charged with Governance of the Group
(Ref: Para. 49)

A66   The matters the group engagement team communicates to those charged with governance of the group may include those brought to the attention of the group engagement team by component auditors that the group engagement team judges to be significant to the responsibilities of those charged with governance of the group. Communication with those charged with governance of the group takes place at various times during the group audit. For example, the matters referred to in paragraph 49(a)–(b) may be communicated after the group engagement team has determined the work to be performed on the financial information of the components. On the other hand, the matter referred to in paragraph 49(c) may be communicated at the end of the audit, and the matters referred to in paragraph 49(d)–(e) may be communicated when they occur.

A66-1   For audits of group financial statements of public interest entities, ISA (UK) 260 (Revised June 2016)[24b] requires the group engagement team to:

- confirm that the group engagement team received a confirmation from the component auditor regarding the component auditor's independence;

- report on any significant deficiencies in the parent undertaking's internal financial control system and/or in the accounting system and state whether or not the deficiencies reported have been resolved by management;

---

[24] *ISA (UK) 240 (Revised June 2016), paragraphs 40–42.*

[24a] *ISA (UK) 260 (Revised June 2016), paragraph 16(c), requires that, unless all of those charged with governance are involved in managing the entity, the auditor shall communicate with those charged with governance significant matters, if any, arising from the audit that were discussed, or subject to correspondence with management.*

[24b] *ISA (UK) 260 (Revised June 2016), paragraphs 16R-2 (c), (j), (m) and (n).*

- explain the scope of consolidation and the exclusion criteria applied to non-consolidated entities, and whether those criteria are in accordance with the applicable financial reporting framework; and

- identify any audit work performed by component auditors,

in the additional report to the audit committee.

Appendix 1

(Ref: Para. A19)

Illustration of Auditor's Report Where the Group Engagement Team Is Not Able to Obtain Sufficient Appropriate Audit Evidence on Which to Base the Group Audit Opinion

The example in this Appendix has not been tailored for the UK. Illustrative auditor's reports tailored for use with audits conducted in accordance with ISAs (UK) are given in the current version of the FRC's Compendium of Illustrative Auditor's Reports.

Note: Throughout this illustrative auditor's report, the Opinion section has been positioned first in accordance with ISA 700 (Revised), and the Basis for Opinion section is positioned immediately after the Opinion section. Also, the first and last sentence that was included in the extant auditor's responsibilities section is now subsumed as part of the new Basis for Opinion section.

Illustration – Example of a Qualified Opinion Where the Group Engagement Team Is Not Able to Obtain Sufficient Appropriate Audit Evidence on Which to Base the Group Audit Opinion

For purposes of this illustrative auditor's report, the following circumstances are assumed:

- Audit of a complete set of consolidated financial statements of an entity other than a listed entity using a fair presentation framework. The audit is a group audit (i.e., ISA 600 applies).
- The consolidated financial statements are prepared by management of the entity in accordance with IFRSs (a general purpose framework).
- The terms of the audit engagement reflect the description of management's responsibility for the consolidated financial statements in ISA 210 (Revised).
- The group engagement team is unable to obtain sufficient appropriate audit evidence relating to a significant component accounted for by the equity method (recognized at $15 million in the balance sheet, which reflects total assets of $60 million) because the group engagement team did not have access to the accounting records, management, or auditor of the component.
- The group engagement team has read the audited financial statements of the component as of December 31, 20X1, including the auditor's report thereon, and considered related financial information kept by group management in relation to the component.
- In the group engagement partner's judgment, the effect on the group financial statements of this inability to obtain sufficient appropriate audit evidence is material but not pervasive.[1-a]

[1-a] *If, in the group engagement partner's judgment, the effect on the group financial statements of the inability to obtain sufficient appropriate audit evidence is material and pervasive, the group engagement partner would disclaim an opinion in accordance with ISA 705 (Revised).*

- The International Ethics Standards Board for Accountants' Code of Ethics for Professional Accountants comprises all of the relevant ethical requirements that apply to the audit.
- Based on the audit evidence obtained, the auditor has concluded that a material uncertainty does not exist related to events or conditions that may cast significant doubt on the entity's ability to continue as a going concern in accordance with ISA 570 (Revised).
- The auditor is not required, and has otherwise not decided, to communicate key audit matters in accordance with ISA 701.
- The auditor has obtained all of the other information prior to the date of the auditor's report and the qualified opinion on the consolidated financial statements also affects the other information.
- Those responsible for oversight of the consolidated financial statements differ from those responsible for the preparation of the consolidated financial statements.
- In addition to the audit of the consolidated financial statements, the auditor has other reporting responsibilities required under local law.

INDEPENDENT AUDITOR'S REPORT

To the Shareholders of ABC Company [or Other Appropriate Addressee]

Report on the Audit of the Consolidated Financial Statements[2-a]

Qualified Opinion

We have audited the consolidated financial statements of ABC Company and its subsidiaries (the Group), which comprise the consolidated statement of financial position as at December 31, 20X1, and the consolidated statement of comprehensive income, the statement of changes in equity and the statement of cash flows for the year then ended, and notes to the financial statements, including a summary of significant accounting policies.

In our opinion, except for the possible effects of the matter described in the Basis for Qualified Opinion section of our report, the accompanying consolidated financial statements present fairly, in all material respects, (or *give a true and fair view of*) the financial position of the Group as at December 31, 20X1, and (*of*) their financial performance and cash flows for the year then ended in accordance with International Financial Reporting Standards (IFRSs).

Basis for Qualified Opinion

ABC Company's investment in XYZ Company, a foreign associate acquired during the year and accounted for by the equity method, is carried at $15 million on the consolidated balance sheet as at December 31, 20X1, and ABC's share of XYZ's net income of $1 million is included in the consolidated income statement for the year then ended. We were unable to obtain sufficient appropriate audit evidence about the carrying amount of ABC's investment in XYZ as at December 31, 20X1 and ABC's share of XYZ's net income for the year because we were denied access to the financial information, management, and the auditors of XYZ.

[2-a] *The sub-title, "Report on the Audit of the Consolidated Financial Statements" is unnecessary in circumstances when the second sub-title, "Report on Other Legal and Regulatory Requirements" is not applicable.*

Consequently, we were unable to determine whether any adjustments to these amounts were necessary.

We conducted our audit in accordance with International Standards on Auditing (ISAs). Our responsibilities under those standards are further described in the *Auditor's Responsibilities for the Audit of the Consolidated Financial Statements* section of our report. We are independent of the Group in accordance with the International Ethics Standards Board for Accountants' Code of Ethics for Professional Accountants (IESBA Code), and we have fulfilled our other ethical responsibilities in accordance with the IESBA Code. We believe that the audit evidence we have obtained is sufficient and appropriate to provide a basis for our qualified audit opinion.

Other Information [or another title if appropriate such as "Information Other than the Financial Statements and Auditor's Report Thereon"]

[Reporting in accordance with the reporting requirements in ISA 720 (Revised) – see Illustration 6 in Appendix 2 of ISA 720 (Revised). The last paragraph of the other information section in Illustration 6 would be customized to describe the specific matter giving rise to the qualified opinion that also affects the other information.]

Responsibilities of Management and Those Charged With Governance for the Consolidated Financial Statements[3-a]

[Reporting in accordance with ISA 700 (Revised)[4-a] *– see Illustration 2 in ISA 700 (Revised).]*

Auditor's Responsibilities for the Audit of the Consolidated Financial Statements

[Reporting in accordance with ISA 700 (Revised) – see Illustration 2 in ISA 700 (Revised). The last two paragraphs which are applicable for audits of listed entities only would not be included.]

Report on Other Legal and Regulatory Requirements

[Reporting in accordance with ISA 700 (Revised) – see Illustration 2 in ISA 700 (Revised).]

[Signature in the name of the audit firm, the personal name of the auditor, or both, as appropriate for the particular jurisdiction]

[Auditor Address]

[Date]

[3-a] *Throughout these illustrative auditor's reports, the terms management and those charged with governance may need to be replaced by another term that is appropriate in the context of the legal framework in the particular jurisdiction.*

[4-a] *ISA 700 (Revised), Forming an Opinion and Reporting on Financial Statements.*

Appendix 2

(Ref: Para. A23)

Examples of Matters about Which the Group Engagement Team Obtains an Understanding

The examples provided cover a broad range of matters; however, not all matters are relevant to every group audit engagement and the list of examples is not necessarily complete.

Group-Wide Controls

Group-wide controls may include a combination of the following: **1**

- Regular meetings between group and component management to discuss business developments and to review performance.

- Monitoring of components' operations and their financial results, including regular reporting routines, which enables group management to monitor components' performance against budgets, and to take appropriate action.

- Group management's risk assessment process, that is, the process for identifying, analyzing and managing business risks, including the risk of fraud, that may result in material misstatement of the group financial statements.

- Monitoring, controlling, reconciling, and eliminating intra-group transactions and unrealized profits, and intra-group account balances at group level.

- A process for monitoring the timeliness and assessing the accuracy and completeness of financial information received from components.

- A central IT system controlled by the same general IT controls for all or part of the group.

- Control activities within an IT system that is common for all or some components.

- Monitoring of controls, including activities of internal audit and self-assessment programs.

- Consistent policies and procedures, including a group financial reporting procedures manual.

- Group-wide programs, such as codes of conduct and fraud prevention programs.

- Arrangements for assigning authority and responsibility to component management.

The internal audit function may be regarded as part of group-wide controls, for **2** example, when the function is centralized. ISA (UK) 610 (Revised June 2013)[1-b] deals with the group engagement team's evaluation of whether the internal audit function's organizational status and relevant policies and procedures adequately supports the objectivity of internal auditors, the level of competence of the internal

---

[1-b] *ISA (UK) 610 (Revised June 2013), Using the Work of Internal Auditors, paragraphs 15–16.*

audit function, and whether the function applies a systematic and disciplined approach where the group engagement team expects to use the function's work.

Consolidation Process

3   The group engagement team's understanding of the consolidation process may include matters such as the following:

Matters relating to the applicable financial reporting framework:

- The extent to which component management has an understanding of the applicable financial reporting framework.

- The process for identifying and accounting for components in accordance with the applicable financial reporting framework.

- The process for identifying reportable segments for segment reporting in accordance with the applicable financial reporting framework.

- The process for identifying related party relationships and related party transactions for reporting in accordance with the applicable financial reporting framework.

- The accounting policies applied to the group financial statements, changes from those of the previous financial year, and changes resulting from new or revised standards under the applicable financial reporting framework.

- The procedures for dealing with components with financial year-ends different from the group's year-end.

Matters relating to the consolidation process:

- Group management's process for obtaining an understanding of the accounting policies used by components, and, where applicable, ensuring that uniform accounting policies are used to prepare the financial information of the components for the group financial statements, and that differences in accounting policies are identified, and adjusted where required in terms of the applicable financial reporting framework. Uniform accounting policies are the specific principles, bases, conventions, rules, and practices adopted by the group, based on the applicable financial reporting framework, that the components use to report similar transactions consistently. These policies are ordinarily described in the financial reporting procedures manual and reporting package issued by group management.

- Group management's process for ensuring complete, accurate and timely financial reporting by the components for the consolidation.

- The process for translating the financial information of foreign components into the currency of the group financial statements.

- How IT is organized for the consolidation, including the manual and automated stages of the process, and the manual and programmed controls in place at various stages of the consolidation process.

- Group management's process for obtaining information on subsequent events.

Matters relating to consolidation adjustments:

- The process for recording consolidation adjustments, including the preparation, authorization and processing of related journal entries, and the experience of personnel responsible for the consolidation.

- The consolidation adjustments required by the applicable financial reporting framework.

- Business rationale for the events and transactions that gave rise to the consolidation adjustments.

- Frequency, nature and size of transactions between components.

- Procedures for monitoring, controlling, reconciling and eliminating intra-group transactions and unrealized profits, and intra-group account balances.

- Steps taken to arrive at the fair value of acquired assets and liabilities, procedures for amortizing goodwill (where applicable), and impairment testing of goodwill, in accordance with the applicable financial reporting framework.

- Arrangements with a majority owner or minority interests regarding losses incurred by a component (for example, an obligation of the minority interest to make good such losses).

Appendix 3

(Ref: Para. A30)

Examples of Conditions or Events that May Indicate Risks of Material Misstatement of the Group Financial Statements

The examples provided cover a broad range of conditions or events; however, not all conditions or events are relevant to every group audit engagement and the list of examples is not necessarily complete.

- A complex group structure, especially where there are frequent acquisitions, disposals or reorganizations.

- Poor corporate governance structures, including decision-making processes, that are not transparent.

- Non-existent or ineffective group-wide controls, including inadequate group management information on monitoring of components' operations and their results.

- Components operating in foreign jurisdictions that may be exposed to factors such as unusual government intervention in areas such as trade and fiscal policy, and restrictions on currency and dividend movements; and fluctuations in exchange rates.

- Business activities of components that involve high risk, such as long-term contracts or trading in innovative or complex financial instruments.

- Uncertainties regarding which components' financial information require incorporation in the group financial statements in accordance with the applicable financial reporting framework, for example, whether any special-purpose entities or non-trading entities exist and require incorporation.

- Unusual related party relationships and transactions.

- Prior occurrences of intra-group account balances that did not balance or reconcile on consolidation.

- The existence of complex transactions that are accounted for in more than one component.

- Components' application of accounting policies that differ from those applied to the group financial statements.

- Components with different financial year-ends, which may be utilized to manipulate the timing of transactions.

- Prior occurrences of unauthorized or incomplete consolidation adjustments.

- Aggressive tax planning within the group, or large cash transactions with entities in tax havens.

- Frequent changes of auditors engaged to audit the financial statements of components.

Appendix 4

(Ref: Para. A35)

Examples of a Component Auditor's Confirmations

The following is not intended to be a standard letter. Confirmations may vary from one component auditor to another and from one period to the next.

Confirmations often are obtained before work on the financial information of the component commences.

[Component Auditor Letterhead]

[Date]

[To Group Engagement Partner]

This letter is provided in connection with your audit of the group financial statements of [name of parent] for the year ended [date] for the purpose of expressing an opinion on whether the group financial statements present fairly, in all material respects (give a true and fair view of) the financial position of the group as of [date] and of its financial performance and cash flows for the year then ended in accordance with [indicate applicable financial reporting framework].

We acknowledge receipt of your instructions dated [date], requesting us to perform the specified work on the financial information of [name of component] for the year ended [date].

We confirm that:

(1)   We will be able to comply with the instructions. / We advise you that we will not be able to comply with the following instructions [specify instructions] for the following reasons [specify reasons].

(2)   The instructions are clear and we understand them. / We would appreciate it if you could clarify the following instructions [specify instructions].

(3)   We will cooperate with you and provide you with access to relevant audit documentation.

We acknowledge that:

(1)   The financial information of [name of component] will be included in the group financial statements of [name of parent].

(2)   You may consider it necessary to be involved in the work you have requested us to perform on the financial information of [name of component] for the year ended [date].

(3)   You intend to evaluate and, if considered appropriate, use our work for the audit of the group financial statements of [name of parent].

In connection with the work that we will perform on the financial information of [name of component], a [describe component, for example, wholly-owned subsidiary, subsidiary, joint venture, investee accounted for by the equity or cost methods of accounting] of [name of parent], we confirm the following:

(1)   We have an understanding of [indicate relevant ethical requirements] that is sufficient to fulfill our responsibilities in the audit of the group financial statements, and will comply therewith. In particular, and with respect to [name of parent] and the other components in the group, we are independent within the meaning of [indicate relevant ethical requirements] and comply

with the applicable requirements of [refer to rules] promulgated by [name of regulatory agency].

(2)   We have an understanding of International Standards on Auditing and [indicate other national standards applicable to the audit of the group financial statements] that is sufficient to fulfill our responsibilities in the audit of the group financial statements and will conduct our work on the financial information of [name of component] for the year ended [date] in accordance with those standards.

(3)   We possess the special skills (for example, industry specific knowledge) necessary to perform the work on the financial information of the particular component.

(4)   We have an understanding of [indicate applicable financial reporting framework or group financial reporting procedures manual] that is sufficient to fulfill our responsibilities in the audit of the group financial statements.

We will inform you of any changes in the above representations during the course of our work on the financial information of [name of component].

[Auditor's signature]

[Date]

[Auditor's address]

Appendix 5

(Ref: Para. A58)

Required and Additional Matters Included in the Group Engagement Team's Letter of Instruction

Matters required by this ISA (UK) to be communicated to the component auditor are shown in italicized text.

Matters that are relevant to the planning of the work of the component auditor:

- *A request for the component auditor, knowing the context in which the group engagement team will use the work of the component auditor, to confirm that the component auditor will cooperate with the group engagement team.*

- The timetable for completing the audit.

- Dates of planned visits by group management and the group engagement team, and dates of planned meetings with component management and the component auditor.

- A list of key contacts.

- *The work to be performed by the component auditor, the use to be made of that work*, and arrangements for coordinating efforts at the initial stage of and during the audit, including the group engagement team's planned involvement in the work of the component auditor.

- *The ethical requirements that are relevant to the group audit and, in particular, the independence requirements*, for example, where the group auditor is prohibited by law or regulation from using internal auditors to provide direct assistance, it is relevant for the group auditor to consider whether the prohibition also extends to component auditors and, if so, to address this in the communication to the component auditors.[1-c]

- *In the case of an audit or review of the financial information of the component, component materiality (and, if applicable, the materiality level or levels for particular classes of transactions, account balances or disclosures), and the threshold above which misstatements cannot be regarded as clearly trivial to the group financial statements.*

- *A list of related parties prepared by group management, and any other related parties that the group engagement team is aware of, and a request that the component auditor communicates on a timely basis to the group engagement team related parties not previously identified by group management or the group engagement team.*

- Work to be performed on intra-group transactions and unrealized profits and intra-group account balances.

[1-c] *ISA 610 (Revised June 2013), Using the Work of Internal Auditors, paragraph A31.*
The use of internal auditors to provide direct assistance is prohibited in an audit conducted in accordance with ISAs (UK). For a group audit this prohibition extends to the work of any component auditor which is relied upon by the group auditor, including for overseas components – see ISA (UK) 610 (Revised June 2013), paragraph 5-1.

- Guidance on other statutory reporting responsibilities, for example, reporting on group management's assertion on the effectiveness of internal control.

- Where time lag between completion of the work on the financial information of the components and the group engagement team's conclusion on the group financial statements is likely, specific instructions for a subsequent events review.

Matters that are relevant to the conduct of the work of the component auditor

- The findings of the group engagement team's tests of control activities of a processing system that is common for all or some components, and tests of controls to be performed by the component auditor.

- *Identified significant risks of material misstatement of the group financial statements, due to fraud or error, that are relevant to the work of the component auditor, and a request that the component auditor communicates on a timely basis any other significant risks of material misstatement of the group financial statements, due to fraud or error, identified in the component and the component auditor's response to such risks.*

- The findings of the internal audit function, based on work performed on controls at or relevant to components.

- A request for timely communication of audit evidence obtained from performing work on the financial information of the components that contradicts the audit evidence on which the group engagement team originally based the risk assessment performed at group level.

- A request for a written representation on component management's compliance with the applicable financial reporting framework, or a statement that differences between the accounting policies applied to the financial information of the component and those applied to the group financial statements have been disclosed.

- Matters to be documented by the component auditor.

Other information

- A request that the following be reported to the group engagement team on a timely basis:

  - Significant accounting, financial reporting and auditing matters, including accounting estimates and related judgments.

  - Matters relating to the going concern status of the component.

  - Matters relating to litigation and claims.

  - Significant deficiencies in internal control that the component auditor has identified during the performance of the work on the financial information of the component, and information that indicates the existence of fraud.

- A request that the group engagement team be notified of any significant or unusual events as early as possible.

- *A request that the matters listed in paragraph 41 be communicated to the group engagement team when the work on the financial information of the component is completed.*

ISA (UK) 610 (Revised June 2013)
Using the Work of Internal Auditors
(June 2016)

*(Effective for audits of financial statements for periods ending on
or after 15 June 2014)*

Contents

Paragraphs

Introduction   1 - 12
  Scope of this ISA (UK)   1 - 5-1
  Relationship between ISA (UK) 315 (Revised June 2016) and
    ISA (UK) 610 (Revised June 2013)   6 - 10
  The External Auditor's Responsibility for the Audit   11
  Effective Date   12

Objectives   13

Definitions   14

Requirements   15 - 37
  Determining Whether, in Which Areas, and to What Extent the Work of the
  Internal Audit Function Can Be Used   15 - 20
  Using the Work of the Internal Audit Function   21 - 25
  Determining Whether, in Which Areas, and to What Extent Internal
  Auditors Can Be Used to Provide Direct Assistance   26 - 32
  Using Internal Auditors to Provide Direct Assistance   33 - 35
  Documentation   36 - 37

Application and other explanatory material
  Definition of Internal Audit Function   A1 - A4
  Determining Whether, in Which Areas, and to What Extent the Work of the
  Internal Audit Function Can Be Used   A5 - A23
  Using the Work of the Internal Audit Function   A24 - A30
  Determining Whether, in Which Areas, and to What Extent Internal Auditors
  Can Be Used to Provide Direct Assistance   A31 - A39
  Using Internal Auditors to Provide Direct Assistance   A40 - A41

International Standard on Auditing (UK) (ISA (UK)) 610 (Revised June 2013), *Using the Work of
Internal Auditors*, should be read in conjunction with ISA (UK) 200 (Revised June 2016), *Overall
Objectives of the Independent Auditor and the Conduct of an Audit in Accordance with
International Standards on Auditing (UK).*

Introduction

Scope of this ISA (UK)

1   This International Standard on Auditing (UK) (ISA (UK)) deals with the external auditor's responsibilities if using the work of internal auditors. This includes (a) using the work of the internal audit function in obtaining audit evidence and (b) using internal auditors to provide direct assistance under the direction, supervision and review of the external auditor.

2   This ISA (UK) does not apply if the entity does not have an internal audit function. (Ref: Para. A2)

3   If the entity has an internal audit function, the requirements in this ISA (UK) relating to using the work of that function do not apply if:

   (a)   The responsibilities and activities of the function are not relevant to the audit; or

   (b)   Based on the auditor's preliminary understanding of the function obtained as a result of procedures performed under ISA (UK) 315 (Revised June 2016),[1] the external auditor does not expect to use the work of the function in obtaining audit evidence.

   Nothing in this ISA (UK) requires the external auditor to use the work of the internal audit function to modify the nature or timing, or reduce the extent, of audit procedures to be performed directly by the external auditor; it remains a decision of the external auditor in establishing the overall audit strategy.

4   Furthermore, the requirements in this ISA (UK) relating to direct assistance do not apply if the external auditor does not plan to use internal auditors to provide direct assistance.

5   In some jurisdictions, the external auditor may be prohibited, or restricted to some extent, by law or regulation from using the work of the internal audit function or using internal auditors to provide direct assistance. The ISAs (UK) do not override laws or regulations that govern an audit of financial statements.[2] Such prohibitions or restrictions will therefore not prevent the external auditor from complying with the ISAs (UK). (Ref: Para. A31)

5-1   The use of internal auditors to provide direct assistance is prohibited in an audit conducted in accordance with ISAs (UK). For a group audit this prohibition extends to the work of any component auditor which is relied upon by the group auditor, including for overseas components. Accordingly, the requirements and related application material in this ISA (UK) relating to direct assistance are not applicable.[2a]

Relationship between ISA (UK) 315 (Revised June 2016) and ISA (UK) 610 (Revised June 2013)

6   Many entities establish internal audit functions as part of their internal control and governance structures. The objectives and scope of an internal audit function, the

---

[1] *ISA (UK) 315 (Revised June 2016), Identifying and Assessing the Risks of Material Misstatement through Understanding the Entity and Its Environment.*

[2] *ISA (UK) 200 (Revised June 2016), Overall Objectives of the Independent Auditor and the Conduct of an Audit in Accordance with International Standards on Auditing (UK), paragraph A55.*

[2a] *The non-applicable requirements are those set out in paragraphs 27–35 and 37. The non-applicable application material is that set out in paragraphs A32–A41.*

nature of its responsibilities and its organizational status, including the function's authority and accountability, vary widely and depend on the size and structure of the entity and the requirements of management and, where applicable, those charged with governance.

ISA (UK) 315 (Revised June 2016) addresses how the knowledge and experience **7** of the internal audit function can inform the external auditor's understanding of the entity and its environment and identification and assessment of risks of material misstatement. ISA (UK) 315 (Revised June 2016)[3] also explains how effective communication between the internal and external auditors also creates an environment in which the external auditor can be informed of significant matters that may affect the external auditor's work.

Depending on whether the internal audit function's organizational status and **8** relevant policies and procedures adequately support the objectivity of the internal auditors, the level of competency of the internal audit function, and whether the function applies a systematic and disciplined approach, the external auditor may also be able to use the work of the internal audit function in a constructive and complementary manner. This ISA (UK) addresses the external auditor's responsibilities when, based on the external auditor's preliminary understanding of the internal audit function obtained as a result of procedures performed under ISA (UK) 315 (Revised June 2016), the external auditor expects to use the work of the internal audit function as part of the audit evidence obtained.[4] Such use of that work modifies the nature or timing, or reduces the extent, of audit procedures to be performed directly by the external auditor.

In addition, this ISA (UK) also addresses the external auditor's responsibilities if **9** considering using internal auditors to provide direct assistance under the direction, supervision and review of the external auditor.

There may be individuals in an entity that perform procedures similar to those **10** performed by an internal audit function. However, unless performed by an objective and competent function that applies a systematic and disciplined approach, including quality control, such procedures would be considered internal controls and obtaining evidence regarding the effectiveness of such controls would be part of the auditor's responses to assessed risks in accordance with ISA (UK) 330 (Revised June 2016).[5]

The External Auditor's Responsibility for the Audit

The external auditor has sole responsibility for the audit opinion expressed, and **11** that responsibility is not reduced by the external auditor's use of the work of the internal audit function or internal auditors to provide direct assistance on the engagement. Although they may perform audit procedures similar to those performed by the external auditor, neither the internal audit function nor the internal auditors are independent of the entity as is required of the external auditor in an audit of financial statements in accordance with ISA (UK) 200 (Revised June 2016).[6] This ISA (UK), therefore, defines the conditions that are necessary for the external auditor to be able to use the work of internal auditors. It also defines the necessary work effort to obtain sufficient appropriate evidence that the work of the

---

[3] *ISA (UK) 315 (Revised June 2016), paragraph A116.*

[4] *See paragraphs 15–25.*

[5] *ISA (UK) 330 (Revised June 2016), The Auditor's Responses to Assessed Risks.*

[6] *ISA (UK) 200 (Revised June 2016), paragraph 14.*

internal audit function, or internal auditors providing direct assistance, is adequate for the purposes of the audit. The requirements are designed to provide a framework for the external auditor's judgments regarding the use of the work of internal auditors to prevent over or undue use of such work.

Effective Date

12 This ISA (UK) is effective for audits of financial statements for periods ending on or after 15 June 2014.[6a]

Objectives

13 The objectives of the external auditor, where the entity has an internal audit function and the external auditor expects to use the work of the function to modify the nature or timing, or reduce the extent, of audit procedures to be performed directly by the external auditor, or to use internal auditors to provide direct assistance, are:

(a) To determine whether the work of the internal audit function or direct assistance from internal auditors can be used, and if so, in which areas and to what extent;

and having made that determination:

(b) If using the work of the internal audit function, to determine whether that work is adequate for purposes of the audit; and

(c) If using internal auditors to provide direct assistance, to appropriately direct, supervise and review their work.

Definitions

14 For purposes of the ISAs (UK), the following terms have the meanings attributed below:

(a) Internal audit function – A function of an entity that performs assurance and consulting activities designed to evaluate and improve the effectiveness of the entity's governance, risk management and internal control processes. (Ref: Para. A1–A4)

(b) Direct assistance – The use of internal auditors to perform audit procedures under the direction, supervision and review of the external auditor.

[6a] *For the purpose of audits under ISAs as issued by the IAASB, the material pertaining to the use of direct assistance has an effective date of audits of financial statements for periods ending on or after 15 December 2014. However, as stated in paragraph 5-1, the use of internal auditors to provide direct assistance is prohibited in an audit conducted in accordance with ISAs (UK) – such prohibition being effective from the effective date of this ISA (UK), audits of financial statements for periods ending on or after 15 June 2014.*

Requirements

Determining Whether, in Which Areas, and to What Extent the Work of the Internal Audit Function Can Be Used

Evaluating the Internal Audit Function

The external auditor shall determine whether the work of the internal audit **15** function can be used for purposes of the audit by evaluating the following:

(a) The extent to which the internal audit function's organizational status and relevant policies and procedures support the objectivity of the internal auditors; (Ref: Para. A5–A9)

(b) The level of competence of the internal audit function; and (Ref: Para. A5–A9)

(c) Whether the internal audit function applies a systematic and disciplined approach, including quality control. (Ref: Para. A10–A11)

The external auditor shall not use the work of the internal audit function if the **16** external auditor determines that:

(a) The function's organizational status and relevant policies and procedures do not adequately support the objectivity of internal auditors;

(b) The function lacks sufficient competence; or

(c) The function does not apply a systematic and disciplined approach, including quality control. (Ref: Para. A12–A14)

Determining the Nature and Extent of Work of the Internal Audit Function that Can Be Used

As a basis for determining the areas and the extent to which the work of the **17** internal audit function can be used, the external auditor shall consider the nature and scope of the work that has been performed, or is planned to be performed, by the internal audit function and its relevance to the external auditor's overall audit strategy and audit plan. (Ref: Para. A15–A17)

The external auditor shall make all significant judgments in the audit engagement **18** and, to prevent undue use of the work of the internal audit function, shall plan to use less of the work of the function and perform more of the work directly: (Ref: Para. A15–A17)

(a) The more judgment is involved in:

(i) Planning and performing relevant audit procedures; and

(ii) Evaluating the audit evidence gathered; (Ref: Para. A18–A19)

(b) The higher the assessed risk of material misstatement at the assertion level, with special consideration given to risks identified as significant; (Ref: Para. A20–A22)

(c) The less the internal audit function's organizational status and relevant policies and procedures adequately support the objectivity of the internal auditors; and

(d) The lower the level of competence of the internal audit function.

The external auditor shall also evaluate whether, in aggregate, using the work of **19** the internal audit function to the extent planned would still result in the external auditor being sufficiently involved in the audit, given the external auditor's sole responsibility for the audit opinion expressed. (Ref: Para. A15–A22)

20   The external auditor shall, in communicating with those charged with governance an overview of the planned scope and timing of the audit in accordance with ISA (UK) 260 (Revised June 2016),[7] communicate how the external auditor has planned to use the work of the internal audit function. (Ref: Para. A23)

Using the Work of the Internal Audit Function

21   If the external auditor plans to use the work of the internal audit function, the external auditor shall discuss the planned use of its work with the function as a basis for coordinating their respective activities. (Ref: Para. A24–A26)

22   The external auditor shall read the reports of the internal audit function relating to the work of the function that the external auditor plans to use to obtain an understanding of the nature and extent of audit procedures it performed and the related findings.

23   The external auditor shall perform sufficient audit procedures on the body of work of the internal audit function as a whole that the external auditor plans to use to determine its adequacy for purposes of the audit, including evaluating whether:

(a)   The work of the function had been properly planned, performed, supervised, reviewed and documented;

(b)   Sufficient appropriate evidence had been obtained to enable the function to draw reasonable conclusions; and

(c)   Conclusions reached are appropriate in the circumstances and the reports prepared by the function are consistent with the results of the work performed. (Ref: Para. A27–A30)

24   The nature and extent of the external auditor's audit procedures shall be responsive to the external auditor's evaluation of:

(a)   The amount of judgment involved;

(b)   The assessed risk of material misstatement;

(c)   The extent to which the internal audit function's organizational status and relevant policies and procedures support the objectivity of the internal auditors; and

(d)   The level of competence of the function;[8] (Ref: Para. A27–A29)

and shall include reperformance of some of the work. (Ref: Para. A30)

25   The external auditor shall also evaluate whether the external auditor's conclusions regarding the internal audit function in paragraph 15 of this ISA (UK) and the determination of the nature and extent of use of the work of the function for purposes of the audit in paragraphs 18–19 of this ISA (UK) remain appropriate.

---

[7] *ISA (UK) 260 (Revised June 2016), Communication with Those Charged with Governance, paragraph 15.*
[8] *See paragraph 18.*

Determining Whether, in Which Areas, and to What Extent Internal Auditors Can Be Used to Provide Direct Assistance

Determining Whether Internal Auditors Can Be Used to Provide Direct Assistance for Purposes of the Audit

The external auditor may be prohibited by law or regulation from obtaining direct **26** assistance from internal auditors. If so, paragraphs 27–35 and 37 do not apply.[8a] (Ref: Para. A31)

If using internal auditors to provide direct assistance is not prohibited by law or **27** regulation, and the external auditor plans to use internal auditors to provide direct assistance on the audit, the external auditor shall evaluate the existence and significance of threats to objectivity and the level of competence of the internal auditors who will be providing such assistance. The external auditor's evaluation of the existence and significance of threats to the internal auditors' objectivity shall include inquiry of the internal auditors regarding interests and relationships that may create a threat to their objectivity. (Ref: Para. A32–A34)

The external auditor shall not use an internal auditor to provide direct assistance if: **28**

(a)   There are significant threats to the objectivity of the internal auditor; or

(b)   The internal auditor lacks sufficient competence to perform the proposed work. (Ref: Para. A32–A34)

Determining the Nature and Extent of Work that Can Be Assigned to Internal Auditors Providing Direct Assistance

In determining the nature and extent of work that may be assigned to internal **29** auditors and the nature, timing and extent of direction, supervision and review that is appropriate in the circumstances, the external auditor shall consider:

(a)   The amount of judgment involved in:

    (i)   Planning and performing relevant audit procedures; and

    (ii)   Evaluating the audit evidence gathered;

(b)   The assessed risk of material misstatement; and

(c)   The external auditor's evaluation of the existence and significance of threats to the objectivity and level of competence of the internal auditors who will be providing such assistance. (Ref: Para. A35–A39)

The external auditor shall not use internal auditors to provide direct assistance to **30** perform procedures that:

(a)   Involve making significant judgments in the audit; (Ref: Para. A19)

(b)   Relate to higher assessed risks of material misstatement where the judgment required in performing the relevant audit procedures or evaluating the audit evidence gathered is more than limited; (Ref: Para. A38)

(c)   Relate to work with which the internal auditors have been involved and which has already been, or will be, reported to management or those charged with governance by the internal audit function; or

---

[8a] *The use of internal auditors to provide direct assistance is prohibited in an audit conducted in accordance with ISAs (UK). See paragraph 5-1 above of this ISA (UK).*

(d)   Relate to decisions the external auditor makes in accordance with this ISA (UK) regarding the internal audit function and the use of its work or direct assistance. (Ref: Para. A35–A39)

31   Having appropriately evaluated whether and, if so, to what extent internal auditors can be used to provide direct assistance on the audit, the external auditor shall, in communicating with those charged with governance an overview of the planned scope and timing of the audit in accordance with ISA (UK) 260 (Revised June 2016),[9] communicate the nature and extent of the planned use of internal auditors to provide direct assistance so as to reach a mutual understanding that such use is not excessive in the circumstances of the engagement. (Ref: Para. A39)

32   The external auditor shall evaluate whether, in aggregate, using internal auditors to provide direct assistance to the extent planned, together with the planned use of the work of the internal audit function, would still result in the external auditor being sufficiently involved in the audit, given the external auditor's sole responsibility for the audit opinion expressed.

Using Internal Auditors to Provide Direct Assistance

33   Prior to using internal auditors to provide direct assistance for purposes of the audit, the external auditor shall:

(a)   Obtain written agreement from an authorized representative of the entity that the internal auditors will be allowed to follow the external auditor's instructions, and that the entity will not intervene in the work the internal auditor performs for the external auditor; and

(b)   Obtain written agreement from the internal auditors that they will keep confidential specific matters as instructed by the external auditor and inform the external auditor of any threat to their objectivity.

34   The external auditor shall direct, supervise and review the work performed by internal auditors on the engagement in accordance with ISA (UK) 220 (Revised June 2016).[10] In so doing:

(a)   The nature, timing and extent of direction, supervision, and review shall recognize that the internal auditors are not independent of the entity and be responsive to the outcome of the evaluation of the factors in paragraph 29 of this ISA (UK); and

(b)   The review procedures shall include the external auditor checking back to the underlying audit evidence for some of the work performed by the internal auditors.

The direction, supervision and review by the external auditor of the work performed by the internal auditors shall be sufficient in order for the external auditor to be satisfied that the internal auditors have obtained sufficient appropriate audit evidence to support the conclusions based on that work. (Ref: Para. A40–A41)

35   In directing, supervising and reviewing the work performed by internal auditors, the external auditor shall remain alert for indications that the external auditor's evaluations in paragraph 27 are no longer appropriate.

---

[9] *ISA (UK) 260 (Revised June 2016), paragraph 15.*

[10] *ISA (UK) 220 (Revised June 2016), Quality Control for an Audit of Financial Statements.*

Documentation

If the external auditor uses the work of the internal audit function, the external   **36**
auditor shall include in the audit documentation:

(a)   The evaluation of:

    (i)   Whether the function's organizational status and relevant policies and procedures adequately support the objectivity of the internal auditors;

    (ii)   The level of competence of the function; and

    (iii)   Whether the function applies a systematic and disciplined approach, including quality control;

(b)   The nature and extent of the work used and the basis for that decision; and

(c)   The audit procedures performed by the external auditor to evaluate the adequacy of the work used.

If the external auditor uses internal auditors to provide direct assistance on the   **37**
audit, the external auditor shall include in the audit documentation:

(a)   The evaluation of the existence and significance of threats to the objectivity of the internal auditors, and the level of competence of the internal auditors used to provide direct assistance;

(b)   The basis for the decision regarding the nature and extent of the work performed by the internal auditors;

(c)   Who reviewed the work performed and the date and extent of that review in accordance with ISA (UK) 230 (Revised June 2016);[11]

(d)   The written agreements obtained from an authorized representative of the entity and the internal auditors under paragraph 33 of this ISA (UK); and

(e)   The working papers prepared by the internal auditors who provided direct assistance on the audit engagement.

Application and Other Explanatory Material

Definition of Internal Audit Function
(Ref: Para. 2, 14(a))

The objectives and scope of internal audit functions typically include assurance   **A1**
and consulting activities designed to evaluate and improve the effectiveness of the
entity's governance processes, risk management and internal control such as the
following:

Activities Relating to Governance

- The internal audit function may assess the governance process in its accomplishment of objectives on ethics and values, performance management and accountability, communicating risk and control information to appropriate areas of the organization and effectiveness of communication among those charged with governance, external and internal auditors, and management.

---

[11]   ISA (UK) 230 (Revised June 2016), Audit Documentation.

Activities Relating to Risk Management

- The internal audit function may assist the entity by identifying and evaluating significant exposures to risk and contributing to the improvement of risk management and internal control (including effectiveness of the financial reporting process).

- The internal audit function may perform procedures to assist the entity in the detection of fraud.

Activities Relating to Internal Control

- Evaluation of internal control. The internal audit function may be assigned specific responsibility for reviewing controls, evaluating their operation and recommending improvements thereto. In doing so, the internal audit function provides assurance on the control. For example, the internal audit function might plan and perform tests or other procedures to provide assurance to management and those charged with governance regarding the design, implementation and operating effectiveness of internal control, including those controls that are relevant to the audit.

- Examination of financial and operating information. The internal audit function may be assigned to review the means used to identify, recognize, measure, classify and report financial and operating information, and to make specific inquiry into individual items, including detailed testing of transactions, balances and procedures.

- Review of operating activities. The internal audit function may be assigned to review the economy, efficiency and effectiveness of operating activities, including non-financial activities of an entity.

- Review of compliance with laws and regulations. The internal audit function may be assigned to review compliance with laws, regulations and other external requirements, and with management policies and directives and other internal requirements.

A2 Activities similar to those performed by an internal audit function may be conducted by functions with other titles within an entity. Some or all of the activities of an internal audit function may also be outsourced to a third-party service provider. Neither the title of the function, nor whether it is performed by the entity or a third-party service provider, are sole determinants of whether or not the external auditor can use the work of the function. Rather, it is the nature of the activities; the extent to which the internal audit function's organizational status and relevant policies and procedures support the objectivity of the internal auditors; competence; and systematic and disciplined approach of the function that are relevant. References in this ISA (UK) to the work of the internal audit function include relevant activities of other functions or third-party providers that have these characteristics.

A3 In addition, those in the entity with operational and managerial duties and responsibilities outside of the internal audit function would ordinarily face threats to their objectivity that would preclude them from being treated as part of an internal audit function for the purpose of this ISA (UK), although they may perform control activities that can be tested in accordance with ISA (UK) 330 (Revised June 2016).[12] For this reason, monitoring controls performed by an owner-manager would not be considered equivalent to an internal audit function.

---

[12] *See paragraph 10.*

While the objectives of an entity's internal audit function and the external auditor   **A4**
differ, the function may perform audit procedures similar to those performed by
the external auditor in an audit of financial statements. If so, the external auditor
may make use of the function for purposes of the audit in one or more of the
following ways:

- To obtain information that is relevant to the external auditor's assessments of
  the risks of material misstatement due to error or fraud. In this regard, ISA
  (UK) 315 (Revised June 2016)[13] requires the external auditor to obtain an
  understanding of the nature of the internal audit function's responsibilities,
  its status within the organization, and the activities performed, or to be
  performed, and make inquiries of appropriate individuals within the internal
  audit function (if the entity has such a function); or

- Unless prohibited, or restricted to some extent, by law or regulation, the
  external auditor, after appropriate evaluation, may decide to use work that has
  been performed by the internal audit function during the period in partial
  substitution for audit evidence to be obtained directly by the external auditor.[14]

In addition, unless prohibited, or restricted to some extent, by law or regulation,
the external auditor may use internal auditors to perform audit procedures under
the direction, supervision and review of the external auditor (referred to as "direct
assistance" in this ISA (UK)).[15]

Determining Whether, in Which Areas, and to What Extent the Work of the Internal Audit Function Can Be Used

Evaluating the Internal Audit Function

Objectivity and Competence
(Ref: Para. 15(a)–(b))

The external auditor exercises professional judgment in determining whether the   **A5**
work of the internal audit function can be used for purposes of the audit, and the
nature and extent to which the work of the internal audit function can be used in
the circumstances.

The extent to which the internal audit function's organizational status and relevant   **A6**
policies and procedures support the objectivity of the internal auditors and the
level of competence of the function are particularly important in determining
whether to use and, if so, the nature and extent of the use of the work of the
function that is appropriate in the circumstances.

Objectivity refers to the ability to perform those tasks without allowing bias,   **A7**
conflict of interest or undue influence of others to override professional judgments.
Factors that may affect the external auditor's evaluation include the following:

- Whether the organizational status of the internal audit function, including
  the function's authority and accountability, supports the ability of the
  function to be free from bias, conflict of interest or undue influence of
  others to override professional judgments. For example, whether the internal

---

[13] *ISA (UK) 315 (Revised June 2016), paragraph 6(a).*

[14] *See paragraphs 15–25.*

[15] *See paragraphs 26–35.*

The use of internal auditors to provide direct assistance is prohibited in an audit conducted in accordance with ISAs (UK) – see paragraph 5-1.

audit function reports to those charged with governance or an officer with appropriate authority, or if the function reports to management, whether it has direct access to those charged with governance.

- Whether the internal audit function is free of any conflicting responsibilities, for example, having managerial or operational duties or responsibilities that are outside of the internal audit function.

- Whether those charged with governance oversee employment decisions related to the internal audit function, for example, determining the appropriate remuneration policy.

- Whether there are any constraints or restrictions placed on the internal audit function by management or those charged with governance, for example, in communicating the internal audit function's findings to the external auditor.

- Whether the internal auditors are members of relevant professional bodies and their memberships obligate their compliance with relevant professional standards relating to objectivity, or whether their internal policies achieve the same objectives.

A8   Competence of the internal audit function refers to the attainment and maintenance of knowledge and skills of the function as a whole at the level required to enable assigned tasks to be performed diligently and in accordance with applicable professional standards. Factors that may affect the external auditor's determination include the following:

- Whether the internal audit function is adequately and appropriately resourced relative to the size of the entity and the nature of its operations.

- Whether there are established policies for hiring, training and assigning internal auditors to internal audit engagements.

- Whether the internal auditors have adequate technical training and proficiency in auditing. Relevant criteria that may be considered by the external auditor in making the assessment may include, for example, the internal auditors' possession of a relevant professional designation and experience.

- Whether the internal auditors possess the required knowledge relating to the entity's financial reporting and the applicable financial reporting framework and whether the internal audit function possesses the necessary skills (for example, industry-specific knowledge) to perform work related to the entity's financial statements.

- Whether the internal auditors are members of relevant professional bodies that oblige them to comply with the relevant professional standards including continuing professional development requirements.

A9   Objectivity and competence may be viewed as a continuum. The more the internal audit function's organizational status and relevant policies and procedures adequately support the objectivity of the internal auditors and the higher the level of competence of the function, the more likely the external auditor may make use of the work of the function and in more areas. However, an organizational status and relevant policies and procedures that provide strong support for the objectivity of the internal auditors cannot compensate for the lack of sufficient competence of the internal audit function. Equally, a high level of competence of the internal audit function cannot compensate for an organizational status and policies and procedures that do not adequately support the objectivity of the internal auditors.

Application of a Systematic and Disciplined Approach (Ref: Para. 15(c))

The application of a systematic and disciplined approach to planning, performing, **A10** supervising, reviewing and documenting its activities distinguishes the activities of the internal audit function from other monitoring control activities that may be performed within the entity.

Factors that may affect the external auditor's determination of whether the internal **A11** audit function applies a systematic and disciplined approach include the following:

- The existence, adequacy and use of documented internal audit procedures or guidance covering such areas as risk assessments, work programs, documentation and reporting, the nature and extent of which is commensurate with the size and circumstances of an entity.

- Whether the internal audit function has appropriate quality control policies and procedures, for example, such as those policies and procedures in ISQC (UK) 1 (Revised June 2016)[16] that would be applicable to an internal audit function (such as those relating to leadership, human resources and engagement performance) or quality control requirements in standards set by the relevant professional bodies for internal auditors. Such bodies may also establish other appropriate requirements such as conducting periodic external quality assessments.

Circumstances When Work of the Internal Audit Function Cannot Be Used (Ref: Para. 16)

The external auditor's evaluation of whether the internal audit function's **A12** organizational status and relevant policies and procedures adequately support the objectivity of the internal auditors, the level of competence of the internal audit function, and whether it applies a systematic and disciplined approach may indicate that the risks to the quality of the work of the function are too significant and therefore it is not appropriate to use any of the work of the function as audit evidence.

Consideration of the factors in paragraphs A7, A8 and A11 of this ISA (UK) **A13** individually and in aggregate is important because an individual factor is often not sufficient to conclude that the work of the internal audit function cannot be used for purposes of the audit. For example, the internal audit function's organizational status is particularly important in evaluating threats to the objectivity of the internal auditors. If the internal audit function reports to management, this would be considered a significant threat to the function's objectivity unless other factors such as those described in paragraph A7 of this ISA (UK) collectively provide sufficient safeguards to reduce the threat to an acceptable level.

In addition, the IESBA Code[17] states that a self-review threat is created when the **A14** external auditor accepts an engagement to provide internal audit services to an audit client, and the results of those services will be used in conducting the audit. This is because of the possibility that the engagement team will use the results of the internal audit service without properly evaluating those results or without exercising the same level of professional skepticism as would be exercised when

---

[16] *International Standard on Quality Control (ISQC) (UK) 1 (Revised June 2016), Quality Control for Firms that Perform Audits and Reviews of Financial Statements, and Other Assurance and Related Services Engagements.*

[17] *The International Ethics Standards Board for Accountants' (IESBA) Code of Ethics for Professional Accountants (IESBA Code), Section 290.199.*

the internal audit work is performed by individuals who are not members of the firm. The IESBA Code[18] discusses the prohibitions that apply in certain circumstances and the threats and the safeguards that can be applied to reduce the threats to an acceptable level in other circumstances.

A14-1   Auditors in the UK are subject to ethical requirements from two sources: the FRC's Ethical Standard concerning the integrity, objectivity and independence of the auditor, and the ethical pronouncements established by the auditor's relevant professional body. Requirements and guidance concerning the provision of internal audit services, including to address the self-review threat, are set out in the FRC's Ethical Standard.[18a]

Determining the Nature and Extent of Work of the Internal Audit Function that Can Be Used

Factors Affecting the Determination of the Nature and Extent of the Work of the Internal Audit Function that Can Be Used
(Ref: Para. 17–19)

A15   Once the external auditor has determined that the work of the internal audit function can be used for purposes of the audit, a first consideration is whether the planned nature and scope of the work of the internal audit function that has been performed, or is planned to be performed, is relevant to the overall audit strategy and audit plan that the external auditor has established in accordance with ISA (UK) 300 (Revised June 2016).[19]

A16   Examples of work of the internal audit function that can be used by the external auditor include the following:

- Testing of the operating effectiveness of controls.

- Substantive procedures involving limited judgment.

- Observations of inventory counts.

- Tracing transactions through the information system relevant to financial reporting.

- Testing of compliance with regulatory requirements.

- In some circumstances, audits or reviews of the financial information of subsidiaries that are not significant components to the group (where this does not conflict with the requirements of ISA (UK) 600 (Revised June 2016)).[20]

A17   The external auditor's determination of the planned nature and extent of use of the work of the internal audit function will be influenced by the external auditor's evaluation of the extent to which the internal audit function's organizational status and relevant policies and procedures adequately support the objectivity of the internal auditors and the level of competence of the internal audit function in paragraph 18 of this ISA (UK). In addition, the amount of judgment needed in planning, performing and evaluating such work and the assessed risk of material

---

[18] *IESBA Code, Section 290.195–290.200.*

[18a] *FRC's Ethical Standard, Section 5, Non-audit / Additional Services.*

[19] *ISA (UK) 300 (Revised June 2016), Planning an Audit of Financial Statements.*

[20] *ISA (UK) 600 (Revised June 2016), Special Considerations—Audits of Group Financial Statements (Including the Work of Component Auditors).*

misstatement at the assertion level are inputs to the external auditor's determination. Further, there are circumstances in which the external auditor cannot use the work of the internal audit function for purpose of the audit as described in paragraph 16 of this ISA (UK).

Judgments in planning and performing audit procedures and evaluating results (Ref: Para. 18(a), 30(a))

The greater the judgment needed to be exercised in planning and performing the audit procedures and evaluating the audit evidence, the external auditor will need to perform more procedures directly in accordance with paragraph 18 of this ISA (UK), because using the work of the internal audit function alone will not provide the external auditor with sufficient appropriate audit evidence.   **A18**

Since the external auditor has sole responsibility for the audit opinion expressed, the external auditor needs to make the significant judgments in the audit engagement in accordance with paragraph 18. Significant judgments include the following: **A19**

● Assessing the risks of material misstatement;

● Evaluating the sufficiency of tests performed;

● Evaluating the appropriateness of management's use of the going concern assumption;

● Evaluating significant accounting estimates; and

● Evaluating the adequacy of disclosures in the financial statements, and other matters affecting the auditor's report.

Assessed risk of material misstatement
(Ref: Para. 18(b))

For a particular account balance, class of transaction or disclosure, the higher an assessed risk of material misstatement at the assertion level, the more judgment is often involved in planning and performing the audit procedures and evaluating the results thereof. In such circumstances, the external auditor will need to perform more procedures directly in accordance with paragraph 18 of this ISA (UK), and accordingly, make less use of the work of the internal audit function in obtaining sufficient appropriate audit evidence. Furthermore, as explained in ISA (UK) 200 (Revised June 2016),[21] the higher the assessed risks of material misstatement, the more persuasive the audit evidence required by the external auditor will need to be, and, therefore, the external auditor will need to perform more of the work directly.   **A20**

As explained in ISA (UK) 315 (Revised June 2016),[22] significant risks require special audit consideration and therefore the external auditor's ability to use the work of the internal audit function in relation to significant risks will be restricted to procedures that involve limited judgment. In addition, where the risk of material misstatement is other than low, the use of the work of the internal audit function alone is unlikely to reduce audit risk to an acceptably low level and eliminate the need for the external auditor to perform some tests directly.   **A21**

---

[21] *ISA (UK) 200 (Revised June 2016), paragraph A29.*

[22] *ISA (UK) 315 (Revised June 2016), paragraph 4(e).*

A22 Carrying out procedures in accordance with this ISA (UK) may cause the external auditor to reevaluate the external auditor's assessment of the risks of material misstatement. Consequently, this may affect the external auditor's determination of whether to use the work of the internal audit function and whether further application of this ISA (UK) is necessary.

Communication with Those Charged with Governance
(Ref: Para. 20)

A23 In accordance with ISA (UK) 260 (Revised June 2016),[23] the external auditor is required to communicate with those charged with governance an overview of the planned scope and timing of the audit. The planned use of the work of the internal audit function is an integral part of the external auditor's overall audit strategy and is therefore relevant to those charged with governance for their understanding of the proposed audit approach.

Using the Work of the Internal Audit Function

Discussion and Coordination with the Internal Audit Function
(Ref: Para. 21)

A24 In discussing the planned use of their work with the internal audit function as a basis for coordinating the respective activities, it may be useful to address the following:

- The timing of such work.
- The nature of the work performed.
- The extent of audit coverage.
- Materiality for the financial statements as a whole (and, if applicable, materiality level or levels for particular classes of transactions, account balances or disclosures), and performance materiality.
- Proposed methods of item selection and sample sizes.
- Documentation of the work performed.
- Review and reporting procedures.

A25 Coordination between the external auditor and the internal audit function is effective when, for example:

- Discussions take place at appropriate intervals throughout the period.
- The external auditor informs the internal audit function of significant matters that may affect the function.
- The external auditor is advised of and has access to relevant reports of the internal audit function and is informed of any significant matters that come to the attention of the function when such matters may affect the work of the external auditor so that the external auditor is able to consider the implications of such matters for the audit engagement.

A26 ISA (UK) 200 (Revised June 2016)[24] discusses the importance of the auditor planning and performing the audit with professional skepticism, including being alert to information that brings into question the reliability of documents and

---

[23] *ISA (UK) 260 (Revised June 2016), paragraph 15.*

[24] *ISA (UK) 200 (Revised June 2016), paragraphs 15 and A18.*

responses to inquiries to be used as audit evidence. Accordingly, communication with the internal audit function throughout the engagement may provide opportunities for internal auditors to bring matters that may affect the work of the external auditor to the external auditor's attention.[25] The external auditor is then able to take such information into account in the external auditor's identification and assessment of risks of material misstatement. In addition, if such information may be indicative of a heightened risk of a material misstatement of the financial statements or may be regarding any actual, suspected or alleged fraud, the external auditor can take this into account in the external auditor's identification of risk of material misstatement due to fraud in accordance with ISA (UK) 240 (Revised June 2016).[26]

Procedures to Determine the Adequacy of Work of the Internal Audit Function
(Ref: Para. 23– 24)

The external auditor's audit procedures on the body of work of the internal audit **A27** function as a whole that the external auditor plans to use provide a basis for evaluating the overall quality of the function's work and the objectivity with which it has been performed.

The procedures the external auditor may perform to evaluate the quality of the **A28** work performed and the conclusions reached by the internal audit function, in addition to reperformance in accordance with paragraph 24, include the following:

* Making inquiries of appropriate individuals within the internal audit function.

* Observing procedures performed by the internal audit function.

* Reviewing the internal audit function's work program and working papers.

The more judgment involved, the higher the assessed risk of material **A29** misstatement, the less the internal audit function's organizational status and relevant policies and procedures adequately support the objectivity of the internal auditors, or the lower the level of competence of the internal audit function, the more audit procedures are needed to be performed by the external auditor on the overall body of work of the function to support the decision to use the work of the function in obtaining sufficient appropriate audit evidence on which to base the audit opinion.

Reperformance
(Ref: Para. 24)

For purposes of this ISA (UK), reperformance involves the external auditor's **A30** independent execution of procedures to validate the conclusions reached by the internal audit function. This objective may be accomplished by examining items already examined by the internal audit function, or where it is not possible to do so, the same objective may also be accomplished by examining sufficient other similar items not actually examined by the internal audit function. Reperformance provides more persuasive evidence regarding the adequacy of the work of the internal audit function compared to other procedures the external auditor may perform in paragraph A28. While it is not necessary for the external auditor to do reperformance in each area of work of the internal audit function that is being used, some reperformance is

---

[25] *ISA (UK) 315 (Revised June 2016), paragraph A116.*

[26] *ISA (UK) 315 (Revised June 2016), paragraph A11 in relation to ISA (UK) 240 (Revised June 2016), The Auditor's Responsibilities Relating to Fraud in an Audit of Financial Statements.*

required on the body of work of the internal audit function as a whole that the external auditor plans to use in accordance with paragraph 24. The external auditor is more likely to focus reperformance in those areas where more judgment was exercised by the internal audit function in planning, performing and evaluating the results of the audit procedures and in areas of higher risk of material misstatement.

Determining Whether, in Which Areas and to What Extent Internal Auditors Can Be Used to Provide Direct Assistance

Determining Whether Internal Auditors Can Be Used to Provide Direct Assistance for Purposes of the Audit
(Ref: Para. 5, 26–28)

A31   In jurisdictions where the external auditor is prohibited by law or regulation from using internal auditors to provide direct assistance, it is relevant for the group auditors to consider whether the prohibition also extends to component auditors and, if so, to address this in the communication to the component auditors.[27]

A32   As stated in paragraph A7 of this ISA (UK), objectivity refers to the ability to perform the proposed work without allowing bias, conflict of interest or undue influence of others to override professional judgments. In evaluating the existence and significance of threats to the objectivity of an internal auditor, the following factors may be relevant:

- The extent to which the internal audit function's organizational status and relevant policies and procedures support the objectivity of the internal auditors.[28]

- Family and personal relationships with an individual working in, or responsible for, the aspect of the entity to which the work relates.

- Association with the division or department in the entity to which the work relates.

- Significant financial interests in the entity other than remuneration on terms consistent with those applicable to other employees at a similar level of seniority.

Material issued by relevant professional bodies for internal auditors may provide additional useful guidance.

A33   There may also be some circumstances in which the significance of the threats to the objectivity of an internal auditor is such that there are no safeguards that could reduce them to an acceptable level. For example, because the adequacy of safeguards is influenced by the significance of the work in the context of the audit, paragraph 30 (a) and (b) prohibits the use of internal auditors to provide direct assistance in relation to performing procedures that involve making significant judgments in the audit or that relate to higher assessed risks of material misstatement where the judgment required in performing the relevant audit procedures or evaluating the audit evidence gathered is more than limited. This would also be the case where the work involved creates a self-review threat,

---

[27] *ISA (UK) 600 (Revised June 2016), paragraph 40(b).*

The use of internal auditors to provide direct assistance is prohibited in an audit conducted in accordance with ISAs (UK). For a group audit this prohibition extends to the work of any component auditor which is relied upon by the group auditor, including for overseas components – see paragraph 5-1 above of this ISA (UK).

[28] *See paragraph A7.*

which is why internal auditors are prohibited from performing procedures in the circumstances described in paragraph 30 (c) and (d).

In evaluating the level of competence of an internal auditor, many of the factors in paragraph A8 of this ISA (UK) may also be relevant applied in the context of individual internal auditors and the work to which they may be assigned.   **A34**

Determining the Nature and Extent of Work that Can Be Assigned to Internal Auditors Providing Direct Assistance
(Ref: Para. 29–31)

Paragraphs A15–A22 of this ISA (UK) provide relevant guidance in determining the nature and extent of work that may be assigned to internal auditors.   **A35**

In determining the nature of work that may be assigned to internal auditors, the external auditor is careful to limit such work to those areas that would be appropriate to be assigned. Examples of activities and tasks that would not be appropriate to use internal auditors to provide direct assistance include the following: **A36**

- Discussion of fraud risks. However, the external auditors may make inquiries of internal auditors about fraud risks in the organization in accordance with ISA (UK) 315 (Revised).[29]

- Determination of unannounced audit procedures as addressed in ISA (UK) 240 (Revised June 2016).

Similarly, since in accordance with ISA (UK) 505[30] the external auditor is required to maintain control over external confirmation requests and evaluate the results of external confirmation procedures, it would not be appropriate to assign these responsibilities to internal auditors. However, internal auditors may assist in assembling information necessary for the external auditor to resolve exceptions in confirmation responses.   **A37**

The amount of judgment involved and the risk of material misstatement are also relevant in determining the work that may be assigned to internal auditors providing direct assistance. For example, in circumstances where the valuation of accounts receivable is assessed as an area of higher risk, the external auditor could assign the checking of the accuracy of the aging to an internal auditor providing direct assistance. However, because the evaluation of the adequacy of the provision based on the aging would involve more than limited judgment, it would not be appropriate to assign that latter procedure to an internal auditor providing direct assistance.   **A38**

Notwithstanding the direction, supervision and review by the external auditor, excessive use of internal auditors to provide direct assistance may affect perceptions regarding the independence of the external audit engagement.   **A39**

Using Internal Auditors to Provide Direct Assistance
(Ref: Para. 34)

As individuals in the internal audit function are not independent of the entity as is required of the external auditor when expressing an opinion on financial statements, the external auditor's direction, supervision and review of the work performed by internal auditors providing direct assistance will generally be of a   **A40**

---

[29] *ISA (UK) 315 (Revised June 2016), paragraph 6(a).*

[30] *ISA (UK) 505, External Confirmations, paragraphs 7 and 16.*

different nature and more extensive than if members of the engagement team perform the work.

A41   In directing the internal auditors, the external auditor may for example, remind the internal auditors to bring accounting and auditing issues identified during the audit to the attention of the external auditor. In reviewing the work performed by the internal auditors, the external auditor's considerations include whether the evidence obtained is sufficient and appropriate in the circumstances, and that it supports the conclusions reached.

ISA (UK) 620 (Revised June 2016) Using the Work of an Auditor's Expert

(Effective for audits of financial statements for periods commencing on or after 17 June 2016)

Contents

Paragraphs

Introduction
Scope of this ISA (UK)   1 - 2
The auditor's responsibility for the audit opinion   3
Effective date   4

Objectives   5

Definitions   6

Requirements
Determining the need for an auditor's expert   7
Nature, timing and extent of audit procedures   8
The competence, capabilities and objectivity of the auditor's expert   9 - 9R-1
Obtaining an understanding of the field of expertise of the auditor's expert   10
Agreement with the auditor's expert   11
Evaluating the adequacy of the auditor's expert's work   12 - 13
Reference to the auditor's expert in the auditor's report   14 - 15
Documentation   15D-1

Application and other explanatory material
Definition of an auditor's expert   A1 - A3
Determining the need for an auditor's expert   A4 - A9
Nature, timing and extent of audit procedures   A10 - A13
The competence, capabilities and objectivity of the auditor's expert   A14 - A20
Obtaining an understanding of the field of expertise of the auditor's expert   A21 - A22
Agreement with the auditor's expert   A23 - A31
Evaluating the adequacy of the auditor's expert's work   A32 - A40
Reference to the auditor's expert in the auditor's report   A41 - A42

Appendix: Considerations for agreement between the auditor and an auditor's external expert

International Standard on Auditing (UK) (ISA (UK)) 620 (Revised June 2016), *Using the Work of an Auditor's Expert*, should be read in conjunction with ISA (UK) 200 (Revised June 2016), *Overall Objectives of the Independent Auditor and the Conduct of an Audit in Accordance with International Standards on Auditing (UK).*

Introduction

Scope of this ISA (UK)

1   This International Standard on Auditing (UK) (ISA (UK)) deals with the auditor's responsibilities relating to the work of an individual or organization in a field of expertise other than accounting or auditing, when that work is used to assist the auditor in obtaining sufficient appropriate audit evidence.

2   This ISA (UK) does not deal with:

(a)   Situations where the engagement team includes a member, or consults an individual or organization, with expertise in a specialized area of accounting or auditing, which are dealt with in ISA (UK) 220 (Revised June 2016);[1] or

(b)   The auditor's use of the work of an individual or organization possessing expertise in a field other than accounting or auditing, whose work in that field is used by the entity to assist the entity in preparing the financial statements (a management's expert), which is dealt with in ISA (UK) 500.[2]

The Auditor's Responsibility for the Audit Opinion

3   The auditor has sole responsibility for the audit opinion expressed, and that responsibility is not reduced by the auditor's use of the work of an auditor's expert. Nonetheless, if the auditor using the work of an auditor's expert, having followed this ISA (UK), concludes that the work of that expert is adequate for the auditor's purposes, the auditor may accept that expert's findings or conclusions in the expert's field as appropriate audit evidence.

Effective Date

4   This ISA (UK) is effective for audits of financial statements for periods commencing on or after 17 June 2016. Earlier adoption is permitted.

Objectives

5   The objectives of the auditor are:

(a)   To determine whether to use the work of an auditor's expert; and

(b)   If using the work of an auditor's expert, to determine whether that work is adequate for the auditor's purposes.

Definitions

6   For purposes of the ISAs (UK), the following terms have the meanings attributed below:

(a)   Auditor's expert – An individual or organization possessing expertise in a field other than accounting or auditing, whose work in that field is used by the auditor to assist the auditor in obtaining sufficient appropriate audit

---

[1]   *ISA (UK) 220 (Revised June 2016), Quality Control for an Audit of Financial Statements, paragraphs A10, A20–A22.*

[2]   *ISA (UK) 500, Audit Evidence, paragraphs A34–A48.*

evidence. An auditor's expert may be either an auditor's internal expert (who is a partner[3] or staff, including temporary staff, of the auditor's firm or a network firm), or an auditor's external expert. (Ref: Para. A1–A3)

(b) Expertise – Skills, knowledge and experience in a particular field.

(c) Management's expert – An individual or organization possessing expertise in a field other than accounting or auditing, whose work in that field is used by the entity to assist the entity in preparing the financial statements.

Requirements

Determining the Need for an Auditor's Expert

If expertise in a field other than accounting or auditing is necessary to obtain sufficient appropriate audit evidence, the auditor shall determine whether to use the work of an auditor's expert. (Ref: Para. A4–A9)   **7**

Nature, Timing and Extent of Audit Procedures

The nature, timing and extent of the auditor's procedures with respect to the requirements in paragraphs 9–13 of this ISA (UK) will vary depending on the circumstances. In determining the nature, timing and extent of those procedures, the auditor shall consider matters including: (Ref: Para. A10)   **8**

(a) The nature of the matter to which that expert's work relates;

(b) The risks of material misstatement in the matter to which that expert's work relates;

(c) The significance of that expert's work in the context of the audit;

(d) The auditor's knowledge of and experience with previous work performed by that expert; and

(e) Whether that expert is subject to the auditor's firm's quality control policies and procedures. (Ref: Para. A11–A13)

The Competence, Capabilities and Objectivity of the Auditor's Expert

The auditor shall evaluate whether the auditor's expert has the necessary competence, capabilities and objectivity for the auditor's purposes. In the case of an auditor's external expert, the evaluation of objectivity shall include inquiry regarding interests and relationships that may create a threat to that expert's objectivity. (Ref: Para. A14–A20)   **9**

For audits of financial statements of public interest entities, where the auditor has used the work of an auditor's external expert, the auditor shall obtain a confirmation from the auditor's external expert regarding their independence. (Ref: Para. A20-1)   **9R-1**

Obtaining an Understanding of the Field of Expertise of the Auditor's Expert

The auditor shall obtain a sufficient understanding of the field of expertise of the auditor's expert to enable the auditor to: (Ref: Para. A21–A22)   **10**

---

[3] *"Partner" and "firm" should be read as referring to their public sector equivalents where relevant.*

(a)   Determine the nature, scope and objectives of that expert's work for the auditor's purposes; and

(b)   Evaluate the adequacy of that work for the auditor's purposes.

Agreement with the Auditor's Expert

11   The auditor shall agree, in writing when appropriate, on the following matters with the auditor's expert: (Ref: Para. A23–A26)

(a)   The nature, scope and objectives of that expert's work; (Ref: Para. A27)

(b)   The respective roles and responsibilities of the auditor and that expert; (Ref: Para. A28–A29)

(c)   The nature, timing and extent of communication between the auditor and that expert, including the form of any report to be provided by that expert; and (Ref: Para. A30)

(d)   The need for the auditor's expert to observe confidentiality requirements. (Ref: Para. A31)

Evaluating the Adequacy of the Auditor's Expert's Work

12   The auditor shall evaluate the adequacy of the auditor's expert's work for the auditor's purposes, including: (Ref: Para. A32)

(a)   The relevance and reasonableness of that expert's findings or conclusions, and their consistency with other audit evidence; (Ref: Para. A33–A34)

(b)   If that expert's work involves use of significant assumptions and methods, the relevance and reasonableness of those assumptions and methods in the circumstances; and (Ref: Para. A35–A37)

(c)   If that expert's work involves the use of source data that is significant to that expert's work, the relevance, completeness, and accuracy of that source data. (Ref: Para. A38–A39)

13   If the auditor determines that the work of the auditor's expert is not adequate for the auditor's purposes, the auditor shall: (Ref: Para. A40)

(a)   Agree with that expert on the nature and extent of further work to be performed by that expert; or

(b)   Perform additional audit procedures appropriate to the circumstances.

Reference to the Auditor's Expert in the Auditor's Report

14   The auditor shall not refer to the work of an auditor's expert in an auditor's report containing an unmodified opinion unless required by law or regulation to do so. If such reference is required by law or regulation, the auditor shall indicate in the auditor's report that the reference does not reduce the auditor's responsibility for the auditor's opinion. (Ref: Para. A41)

15   If the auditor makes reference to the work of an auditor's expert in the auditor's report because such reference is relevant to an understanding of a modification to the auditor's opinion, the auditor shall indicate in the auditor's report that such reference does not reduce the auditor's responsibility for that opinion. (Ref: Para. A42)

Documentation

The auditor shall document any request for advice from an auditor's expert,   **15D-1**
together with the advice received.

Application and Other Explanatory Material

Definition of an Auditor's Expert
(Ref: Para. 6(a))

Expertise in a field other than accounting or auditing may include expertise in   **A1**
relation to such matters as:

- The valuation of complex financial instruments, land and buildings, plant and machinery, jewelry, works of art, antiques, intangible assets, assets acquired and liabilities assumed in business combinations and assets that may have been impaired.

- The actuarial calculation of liabilities associated with insurance contracts or employee benefit plans.

- The estimation of oil and gas reserves.

- The valuation of environmental liabilities, and site clean-up costs.

- The interpretation of contracts, laws and regulations.

- The analysis of complex or unusual tax compliance issues.

In many cases, distinguishing between expertise in accounting or auditing, and   **A2**
expertise in another field, will be straightforward, even where this involves a
specialized area of accounting or auditing. For example, an individual with
expertise in applying methods of accounting for deferred income tax can often
be easily distinguished from an expert in taxation law. The former is not an expert
for the purposes of this ISA (UK) as this constitutes accounting expertise; the latter
is an expert for the purposes of this ISA (UK) as this constitutes legal expertise.
Similar distinctions may also be able to be made in other areas, for example,
between expertise in methods of accounting for financial instruments, and
expertise in complex modeling for the purpose of valuing financial instruments.
In some cases, however, particularly those involving an emerging area of
accounting or auditing expertise, distinguishing between specialized areas of
accounting or auditing, and expertise in another field, will be a matter of
professional judgment. Applicable professional rules and standards regarding
education and competency requirements for accountants and auditors may assist
the auditor in exercising that judgment.[4]

It is necessary to apply judgment when considering how the requirements of this   **A3**
ISA (UK) are affected by the fact that an auditor's expert may be either an
individual or an organization. For example, when evaluating the competence,
capabilities and objectivity of an auditor's expert, it may be that the expert is an
organization the auditor has previously used, but the auditor has no prior
experience of the individual expert assigned by the organization for the
particular engagement; or it may be the reverse, that is, the auditor may be
familiar with the work of an individual expert but not with the organization that

---

[4] *For example, International Education Standard 8, Competence Requirements for Audit Professionals may be of
assistance.*

expert has joined. In either case, both the personal attributes of the individual and the managerial attributes of the organization (such as systems of quality control the organization implements) may be relevant to the auditor's evaluation.

Determining the Need for an Auditor's Expert
(Ref: Para. 7)

A4   An auditor's expert may be needed to assist the auditor in one or more of the following:

- Obtaining an understanding of the entity and its environment, including its internal control.

- Identifying and assessing the risks of material misstatement.

- Determining and implementing overall responses to assessed risks at the financial statement level.

- Designing and performing further audit procedures to respond to assessed risks at the assertion level, comprising tests of controls or substantive procedures.

- Evaluating the sufficiency and appropriateness of audit evidence obtained in forming an opinion on the financial statements.

A5   The risks of material misstatement may increase when expertise in a field other than accounting is needed for management[4a] to prepare the financial statements, for example, because this may indicate some complexity, or because management may not possess knowledge of the field of expertise. If in preparing the financial statements management does not possess the necessary expertise, a management's expert may be used in addressing those risks. Relevant controls, including controls that relate to the work of a management's expert, if any, may also reduce the risks of material misstatement.

A6   If the preparation of the financial statements involves the use of expertise in a field other than accounting, the auditor, who is skilled in accounting and auditing, may not possess the necessary expertise to audit those financial statements. The engagement partner is required to be satisfied that the engagement team, and any auditor's experts who are not part of the engagement team, collectively have the appropriate competence and capabilities to perform the audit engagement.[5] Further, the auditor is required to ascertain the nature, timing and extent of resources necessary to perform the engagement.[6] The auditor's determination of whether to use the work of an auditor's expert, and if so when and to what extent, assists the auditor in meeting these requirements. As the audit progresses, or as circumstances change, the auditor may need to revise earlier decisions about using the work of an auditor's expert.

A7   An auditor who is not an expert in a relevant field other than accounting or auditing may nevertheless be able to obtain a sufficient understanding of that field to perform the audit without an auditor's expert. This understanding may be obtained through, for example:

- Experience in auditing entities that require such expertise in the preparation of their financial statements.

[4a] *In the UK, those charged with governance are responsible for the preparation of the financial statements.*

[5] *ISA (UK) 220 (Revised June 2016), paragraph 14.*

[6] *ISA (UK) 300 (Revised June 2016), Planning an Audit of Financial Statements, paragraph 8(e).*

- Education or professional development in the particular field. This may include formal courses, or discussion with individuals possessing expertise in the relevant field for the purpose of enhancing the auditor's own capacity to deal with matters in that field. Such discussion differs from consultation with an auditor's expert regarding a specific set of circumstances encountered on the engagement where that expert is given all the relevant facts that will enable the expert to provide informed advice about the particular matter.[7]

- Discussion with auditors who have performed similar engagements.

In other cases, however, the auditor may determine that it is necessary, or may choose, to use an auditor's expert to assist in obtaining sufficient appropriate audit evidence. Considerations when deciding whether to use an auditor's expert may include: **A8**

- Whether management[4a] has used a management's expert in preparing the financial statements (see paragraph A9).

- The nature and significance of the matter, including its complexity.

- The risks of material misstatement in the matter.

- The expected nature of procedures to respond to identified risks, including: the auditor's knowledge of and experience with the work of experts in relation to such matters; and the availability of alternative sources of audit evidence.

When management has used a management's expert in preparing the financial statements, the auditor's decision on whether to use an auditor's expert may also be influenced by such factors as: **A9**

- The nature, scope and objectives of the management's expert's work.

- Whether the management's expert is employed by the entity, or is a party engaged by it to provide relevant services.

- The extent to which management can exercise control or influence over the work of the management's expert.

- The management's expert's competence and capabilities.

- Whether the management's expert is subject to technical performance standards or other professional or industry requirements.

- Any controls within the entity over the management's expert's work.

ISA (UK) 500[8] includes requirements and guidance regarding the effect of the competence, capabilities and objectivity of management's experts on the reliability of audit evidence.

Nature, Timing and Extent of Audit Procedures
(Ref: Para. 8)

The nature, timing and extent of audit procedures with respect to the requirements in paragraphs 9–13 of this ISA (UK) will vary depending on the circumstances. For example, the following factors may suggest the need for different or more extensive procedures than would otherwise be the case: **A10**

---

[7] *ISA (UK) 220 (Revised June 2016), paragraph A21.*

[8] *ISA (UK) 500, paragraph 8.*

- The work of the auditor's expert relates to a significant matter that involves subjective and complex judgments.

- The auditor has not previously used the work of the auditor's expert, and has no prior knowledge of that expert's competence, capabilities and objectivity.

- The auditor's expert is performing procedures that are integral to the audit, rather than being consulted to provide advice on an individual matter.

- The expert is an auditor's external expert and is not, therefore, subject to the firm's quality control policies and procedures.

The Auditor's Firm's Quality Control Policies and Procedures
(Ref: Para. 8(e))

A11   An auditor's internal expert may be a partner or staff, including temporary staff, of the auditor's firm, and therefore subject to the quality control policies and procedures of that firm in accordance with ISQC (UK) 1[9] or national requirements that are at least as demanding.[10] Alternatively, an auditor's internal expert may be a partner or staff, including temporary staff, of a network firm, which may share common quality control policies and procedures with the auditor's firm.

A12   An auditor's external expert is not a member of the engagement team and is not subject to quality control policies and procedures in accordance with ISQC (UK) 1.[11] In some jurisdictions, however, law or regulation may require that an auditor's external expert be treated as a member of the engagement team, and may therefore be subject to relevant ethical requirements, including those pertaining to independence, and other professional requirements, as determined by that law or regulation.

A13   Engagement teams are entitled to rely on the firm's system of quality control, unless information provided by the firm or other parties suggests otherwise.[12] The extent of that reliance will vary with the circumstances, and may affect the nature, timing and extent of the auditor's procedures with respect to such matters as:

- Competence and capabilities, through recruitment and training programs.

- Objectivity. Auditor's internal experts are subject to relevant ethical requirements, including those pertaining to independence.

- The auditor's evaluation of the adequacy of the auditor's expert's work. For example, the firm's training programs may provide auditor's internal experts with an appropriate understanding of the interrelationship of their expertise with the audit process. Reliance on such training and other firm processes, such as protocols for scoping the work of auditor's internal experts, may affect the nature, timing and extent of the auditor's procedures to evaluate the adequacy of the auditor's expert's work.

- Adherence to regulatory and legal requirements, through monitoring processes.

- Agreement with the auditor's expert.

---

[9] *ISQC (UK) 1 (Revised June 2016), Quality Control for Firms that Perform Audits and Reviews of Financial Statements, and Other Assurance and Related Services Engagements, paragraph 12(f).*

[10] *ISA (UK) 220 (Revised June 2016), paragraph 2.*

[11] *ISQC (UK) 1 (Revised June 2016), paragraph 12(f).*

[12] *ISA (UK) 220 (Revised June 2016), paragraph 4.*

Such reliance does not reduce the auditor's responsibility to meet the requirements of this ISA (UK).

The Competence, Capabilities and Objectivity of the Auditor's Expert (Ref: Para. 9)

The competence, capabilities and objectivity of an auditor's expert are factors that **A14** significantly affect whether the work of the auditor's expert will be adequate for the auditor's purposes. Competence relates to the nature and level of expertise of the auditor's expert. Capability relates to the ability of the auditor's expert to exercise that competence in the circumstances of the engagement. Factors that influence capability may include, for example, geographic location, and the availability of time and resources. Objectivity relates to the possible effects that bias, conflict of interest, or the influence of others may have on the professional or business judgment of the auditor's expert.

Information regarding the competence, capabilities and objectivity of an auditor's **A15** expert may come from a variety of sources, such as:

- Personal experience with previous work of that expert.

- Discussions with that expert.

- Discussions with other auditors or others who are familiar with that expert's work.

- Knowledge of that expert's qualifications, membership of a professional body or industry association, license to practice, or other forms of external recognition.

- Published papers or books written by that expert.

- The auditor's firm's quality control policies and procedures (see paragraphs A11–A13).

Matters relevant to evaluating the competence, capabilities and objectivity of the **A16** auditor's expert include whether that expert's work is subject to technical performance standards or other professional or industry requirements, for example, ethical standards and other membership requirements of a professional body or industry association, accreditation standards of a licensing body, or requirements imposed by law or regulation.

Other matters that may be relevant include: **A17**

- The relevance of the auditor's expert's competence to the matter for which that expert's work will be used, including any areas of specialty within that expert's field. For example, a particular actuary may specialize in property and casualty insurance, but have limited expertise regarding pension calculations.

- The auditor's expert's competence with respect to relevant accounting and auditing requirements, for example, knowledge of assumptions and methods, including models where applicable, that are consistent with the applicable financial reporting framework.

- Whether unexpected events, changes in conditions, or the audit evidence obtained from the results of audit procedures indicate that it may be necessary to reconsider the initial evaluation of the competence, capabilities and objectivity of the auditor's expert as the audit progresses.

A18   A broad range of circumstances may threaten objectivity, for example, self-interest threats, advocacy threats, familiarity threats, self-review threats, and intimidation threats. Safeguards may eliminate or reduce such threats, and may be created by external structures (for example, the auditor's expert's profession, legislation or regulation), or by the auditor's expert's work environment (for example, quality control policies and procedures). There may also be safeguards specific to the audit engagement.

A19   The evaluation of the significance of threats to objectivity and of whether there is a need for safeguards may depend upon the role of the auditor's expert and the significance of the expert's work in the context of the audit. There may be some circumstances in which safeguards cannot reduce threats to an acceptable level, for example, if a proposed auditor's expert is an individual who has played a significant role in preparing the information that is being audited, that is, if the auditor's expert is a management's expert.

A20   When evaluating the objectivity of an auditor's external expert, it may be relevant to:

(a)   Inquire of the entity about any known interests or relationships that the entity has with the auditor's external expert that may affect that expert's objectivity.

(b)   Discuss with that expert any applicable safeguards, including any professional requirements that apply to that expert; and evaluate whether the safeguards are adequate to reduce threats to an acceptable level. Interests and relationships that it may be relevant to discuss with the auditor's expert include:

●   Financial interests.

●   Business and personal relationships.

●   Provision of other services by the expert, including by the organization in the case of an external expert that is an organization.

In some cases, it may also be appropriate for the auditor to obtain a written representation from the auditor's external expert about any interests or relationships with the entity of which that expert is aware.

Confirmation of Independence of an Auditor's External Expert
(Ref: Para. 9R-1)

A20-1   For statutory audits of financial statements of public interest entities, ISA (UK) 260 (Revised June 2016)[12a] requires the auditor to communicate in the additional report to the audit committee when the auditor has used the work of an external expert and to confirm that the auditor obtained confirmation from the auditor's external expert regarding the external expert's independence.

Obtaining an Understanding of the Field of Expertise of the Auditor's Expert
(Ref: Para. 10)

A21   The auditor may obtain an understanding of the auditor's expert's field of expertise through the means described in paragraph A7, or through discussion with that expert.

[12a] *ISA (UK) 260 (Revised June 2016), Communication with Those Charged with Governance, paragraph 16R-2(c).*

Aspects of the auditor's expert's field relevant to the auditor's understanding may **A22** include:

- Whether that expert's field has areas of specialty within it that are relevant to the audit (see paragraph A17).

- Whether any professional or other standards, and regulatory or legal requirements apply.

- What assumptions and methods, including models where applicable, are used by the auditor's expert, and whether they are generally accepted within that expert's field and appropriate for financial reporting purposes.

- The nature of internal and external data or information the auditor's expert uses.

Agreement with the Auditor's Expert
(Ref: Para. 11)

The nature, scope and objectives of the auditor's expert's work may vary **A23** considerably with the circumstances, as may the respective roles and responsibilities of the auditor and the auditor's expert, and the nature, timing and extent of communication between the auditor and the auditor's expert. It is therefore required that these matters are agreed between the auditor and the auditor's expert regardless of whether the expert is an auditor's external expert or an auditor's internal expert.

The matters noted in paragraph 8 may affect the level of detail and formality of the **A24** agreement between the auditor and the auditor's expert, including whether it is appropriate that the agreement be in writing. For example, the following factors may suggest the need for a more detailed agreement than would otherwise be the case, or for the agreement to be set out in writing:

- The auditor's expert will have access to sensitive or confidential entity information.

- The respective roles or responsibilities of the auditor and the auditor's expert are different from those normally expected.

- Multi-jurisdictional legal or regulatory requirements apply.

- The matter to which the auditor's expert's work relates is highly complex.

- The auditor has not previously used work performed by that expert.

- The greater the extent of the auditor's expert's work, and its significance in the context of the audit.

The agreement between the auditor and an auditor's external expert is often in the **A25** form of an engagement letter. The Appendix lists matters that the auditor may consider for inclusion in such an engagement letter, or in any other form of agreement with an auditor's external expert.

When there is no written agreement between the auditor and the auditor's expert, **A26** evidence of the agreement may be included in, for example:

- Planning memoranda, or related working papers such as the audit program.

- The policies and procedures of the auditor's firm. In the case of an auditor's internal expert, the established policies and procedures to which that expert is subject may include particular policies and procedures in relation to that expert's work. The extent of documentation in the auditor's working papers depends on the nature of such policies and procedures. For example, no documentation may be required in the auditor's working papers if the auditor's firm has detailed protocols covering the circumstances in which the work of such an expert is used.

Nature, Scope and Objectives of Work
(Ref: Para. 11(a))

A27   It may often be relevant when agreeing on the nature, scope and objectives of the auditor's expert's work to include discussion of any relevant technical performance standards or other professional or industry requirements that the expert will follow.

Respective Roles and Responsibilities
(Ref: Para. 11(b))

A28   Agreement on the respective roles and responsibilities of the auditor and the auditor's expert may include:

- Whether the auditor or the auditor's expert will perform detailed testing of source data.

- Consent for the auditor to discuss the auditor's expert's findings or conclusions with the entity and others, and to include details of that expert's findings or conclusions in the basis for a modified opinion in the auditor's report, if necessary (see paragraph A42).

- Any agreement to inform the auditor's expert of the auditor's conclusions concerning that expert's work.

Working Papers

A29   Agreement on the respective roles and responsibilities of the auditor and the auditor's expert may also include agreement about access to, and retention of, each other's working papers. When the auditor's expert is a member of the engagement team, that expert's working papers form part of the audit documentation. Subject to any agreement to the contrary, auditor's external experts' working papers are their own and do not form part of the audit documentation.

Communication
(Ref: Para. 11(c))

A30   Effective two-way communication facilitates the proper integration of the nature, timing and extent of the auditor's expert's procedures with other work on the audit, and appropriate modification of the auditor's expert's objectives during the course of the audit. For example, when the work of the auditor's expert relates to the auditor's conclusions regarding a significant risk, both a formal written report at the conclusion of that expert's work, and oral reports as the work progresses, may be appropriate. Identification of specific partners or staff who will liaise with the auditor's expert, and procedures for communication between that expert and the entity, assists timely and effective communication, particularly on larger engagements.

Confidentiality
(Ref: Para. 11(d))

A31   It is necessary for the confidentiality provisions of relevant ethical requirements that apply to the auditor also to apply to the auditor's expert. Additional requirements may be imposed by law or regulation. The entity may also have requested that specific confidentiality provisions be agreed with auditor's external experts.

Evaluating the Adequacy of the Auditor's Expert's Work
(Ref: Para. 12)

The auditor's evaluation of the auditor's expert's competence, capabilities and   **A32**
objectivity, the auditor's familiarity with the auditor's expert's field of expertise,
and the nature of the work performed by the auditor's expert affect the nature,
timing and extent of audit procedures to evaluate the adequacy of that expert's
work for the auditor's purposes.

The Findings and Conclusions of the Auditor's Expert
(Ref: Para. 12(a))

Specific procedures to evaluate the adequacy of the auditor's expert's work for the   **A33**
auditor's purposes may include:

- Inquiries of the auditor's expert.
- Reviewing the auditor's expert's working papers and reports.
- Corroborative procedures, such as:
  - Observing the auditor's expert's work;
  - Examining published data, such as statistical reports from reputable, authoritative sources;
  - Confirming relevant matters with third parties;
  - Performing detailed analytical procedures; and
  - Reperforming calculations.
- Discussion with another expert with relevant expertise when, for example, the findings or conclusions of the auditor's expert are not consistent with other audit evidence.
- Discussing the auditor's expert's report with management.

Relevant factors when evaluating the relevance and reasonableness of the findings   **A34**
or conclusions of the auditor's expert, whether in a report or other form, may
include whether they are:

- Presented in a manner that is consistent with any standards of the auditor's expert's profession or industry;
- Clearly expressed, including reference to the objectives agreed with the auditor, the scope of the work performed and standards applied;
- Based on an appropriate period and take into account subsequent events, where relevant;
- Subject to any reservation, limitation or restriction on use, and if so, whether this has implications for the auditor; and
- Based on appropriate consideration of errors or deviations encountered by the auditor's expert.

Assumptions, Methods and Source Data

Assumptions and Methods
(Ref: Para. 12(b))

When the auditor's expert's work is to evaluate underlying assumptions and   **A35**
methods, including models where applicable, used by management in developing

an accounting estimate, the auditor's procedures are likely to be primarily directed to evaluating whether the auditor's expert has adequately reviewed those assumptions and methods. When the auditor's expert's work is to develop an auditor's point estimate or an auditor's range for comparison with management's point estimate, the auditor's procedures may be primarily directed to evaluating the assumptions and methods, including models where appropriate, used by the auditor's expert.

A36   ISA (UK) 540 (Revised June 2016)[13] discusses the assumptions and methods used by management in making accounting estimates, including the use in some cases of highly specialized, entity-developed models. Although that discussion is written in the context of the auditor obtaining sufficient appropriate audit evidence regarding management's assumptions and methods, it may also assist the auditor when evaluating an auditor's expert's assumptions and methods.

A37   When an auditor's expert's work involves the use of significant assumptions and methods, factors relevant to the auditor's evaluation of those assumptions and methods include whether they are:

- Generally accepted within the auditor's expert's field;

- Consistent with the requirements of the applicable financial reporting framework;

- Dependent on the use of specialized models; and

- Consistent with those of management, and if not, the reason for, and effects of, the differences.

Source Data Used by the Auditor's Expert
(Ref: Para. 12(c))

A38   When an auditor's expert's work involves the use of source data that is significant to that expert's work, procedures such as the following may be used to test that data:

- Verifying the origin of the data, including obtaining an understanding of, and where applicable testing, the internal controls over the data and, where relevant, its transmission to the expert.

- Reviewing the data for completeness and internal consistency.

A39   In many cases, the auditor may test source data. However, in other cases, when the nature of the source data used by an auditor's expert is highly technical in relation to the expert's field, that expert may test the source data. If the auditor's expert has tested the source data, inquiry of that expert by the auditor, or supervision or review of that expert's tests may be an appropriate way for the auditor to evaluate that data's relevance, completeness, and accuracy.

Inadequate Work
(Ref: Para. 13)

A40   If the auditor concludes that the work of the auditor's expert is not adequate for the auditor's purposes and the auditor cannot resolve the matter through the additional audit procedures required by paragraph 13, which may involve further work being performed by both the expert and the auditor, or include employing or engaging

---

[13] *ISA (UK) 540 (Revised June 2016), Auditing Accounting Estimates, Including Fair Value Accounting Estimates, and Related Disclosures, paragraphs 8, 13 and 15.*

another expert, it may be necessary to express a modified opinion in the auditor's report in accordance with ISA (UK) 705 (Revised June 2016) because the auditor has not obtained sufficient appropriate audit evidence.[14]

Reference to the Auditor's Expert in the Auditor's Report
(Ref: Para. 14–15)

In some cases, law or regulation may require a reference to the work of an   **A41** auditor's expert, for example, for the purposes of transparency in the public sector.

It may be appropriate in some circumstances to refer to the auditor's expert in an   **A42** auditor's report containing a modified opinion, to explain the nature of the modification. In such circumstances, the auditor may need the permission of the auditor's expert before making such a reference.

---

[14] *ISA (UK) 705 (Revised June 2016), Modifications to the Opinion in the Independent Auditor's Report, paragraph 6(b).*

Appendix

(Ref: Para. A25)

Considerations for Agreement between the Auditor and an Auditor's External Expert

This Appendix lists matters that the auditor may consider for inclusion in any agreement with an auditor's external expert. The following list is illustrative and is not exhaustive; it is intended only to be a guide that may be used in conjunction with the considerations outlined in this ISA (UK). Whether to include particular matters in the agreement depends on the circumstances of the engagement. The list may also be of assistance in considering the matters to be included in an agreement with an auditor's internal expert.

Nature, Scope and Objectives of the Auditor's External Expert's Work

- The nature and scope of the procedures to be performed by the auditor's external expert.

- The objectives of the auditor's external expert's work in the context of materiality and risk considerations concerning the matter to which the auditor's external expert's work relates, and, when relevant, the applicable financial reporting framework.

- Any relevant technical performance standards or other professional or industry requirements the auditor's external expert will follow.

- The assumptions and methods, including models where applicable, the auditor's external expert will use, and their authority.

- The effective date of, or when applicable the testing period for, the subject matter of the auditor's external expert's work, and requirements regarding subsequent events.

The Respective Roles and Responsibilities of the Auditor and the Auditor's External Expert

- Relevant auditing and accounting standards, and relevant regulatory or legal requirements.

- The auditor's external expert's consent to the auditor's intended use of that expert's report, including any reference to it, or disclosure of it, to others, for example reference to it in the basis for a modified opinion in the auditor's report, if necessary, or disclosure of it to management or an audit committee.[14a]

- The nature and extent of the auditor's review of the auditor's external expert's work.

- Whether the auditor or the auditor's external expert will test source data.

- The auditor's external expert's access to the entity's records, files, personnel and to experts engaged by the entity.

[14a] *Auditors of public interest entities are required by paragraph 16R-1(c) of ISA (UK) 260 (Revised June 2016) to communicate matters relating to the use of the work of the auditor's external expert in the additional report to the audit committee.*

- Procedures for communication between the auditor's external expert and the entity.

- The auditor's and the auditor's external expert's access to each other's working papers.

- Ownership and control of working papers during and after the engagement, including any file retention requirements.

- The auditor's external expert's responsibility to perform work with due skill and care.

- The auditor's external expert's competence and capability to perform the work.

- The expectation that the auditor's external expert will use all knowledge that expert has that is relevant to the audit or, if not, will inform the auditor.

- Any restriction on the auditor's external expert's association with the auditor's report.

- Any agreement to inform the auditor's external expert of the auditor's conclusions concerning that expert's work

Communications and Reporting

- Methods and frequency of communications, including:

  - How the auditor's external expert's findings or conclusions will be reported (for example, written report, oral report, ongoing input to the engagement team).

  - Identification of specific persons within the engagement team who will liaise with the auditor's external expert.

- When the auditor's external expert will complete the work and report findings or conclusions to the auditor.

- The auditor's external expert's responsibility to communicate promptly any potential delay in completing the work, and any potential reservation or limitation on that expert's findings or conclusions.

- The auditor's external expert's responsibility to communicate promptly instances in which the entity restricts that expert's access to records, files, personnel or experts engaged by the entity.

- The auditor's external expert's responsibility to communicate to the auditor all information that expert believes may be relevant to the audit, including any changes in circumstances previously communicated.

- The auditor's external expert's responsibility to communicate circumstances that may create threats to that expert's objectivity, and any relevant safeguards that may eliminate or reduce such threats to an acceptable level.

Confidentiality

- The need for the auditor's expert to observe confidentiality requirements, including:

  - The confidentiality provisions of relevant ethical requirements that apply to the auditor.

  - Additional requirements that may be imposed by law or regulation, if any.

  - Specific confidentiality provisions requested by the entity, if any.

ISA (UK) 700 (Revised June 2016)
Forming an Opinion and Reporting on Financial Statements

(Effective for audits of financial statements for periods commencing on or after 17 June 2016)

Contents

Paragraphs

Introduction
Scope of this ISA (UK)   1 - 4
Effective Date   5

Objectives   6

Definitions   7 - 9

Requirements
Forming an Opinion on the Financial Statements   10 - 15
Form of Opinion   16 - 19
Auditor's Report   20 - 52
Supplementary Information Presented with the Financial
Statements (Ref: Para. A78– A84)   53 - 54

Application and Other Explanatory Material
Qualitative Aspects of the Entity's Accounting Practices (Ref: Para. 12)   A1 - A3
Accounting Policies Appropriately Disclosed in the Financial
Statements (Ref: Para. 13(a))   A4
Information Presented in the Financial Statements Is Relevant, Reliable,
Comparable and Understandable (Ref: Para. 13(d))   A5
Disclosure of the Effect of Material Transactions and Events on the Information
Conveyed in the Financial Statements (Ref: Para. 13(e))   A6
Evaluating Whether the Financial Statements Achieve Fair
Presentation (Ref: Para. 14)   A7 - A9
Consistency with appropriate industry practice, or whether any departures are
relevant to the entity's circumstances and therefore warranted.   A10 - A15
Form of Opinion (Ref: Para. 16, 18–19)   A15-1 - A17
Auditor's Report (Ref: Para. 20)   A18 - A77-1
Supplementary Information Presented with the Financial
Statements (Ref: Para. 53–54)   A78 - A84

Appendix: Illustrations of Independent Auditor's Reports on Financial Statements   737

International Standard on Auditing (ISA) (UK) 700 (Revised June 2016), *Forming an Opinion and Reporting on Financial Statements*, should be read in conjunction with ISA (UK) 200 (Revised June 2016), *Overall Objectives of the Independent Auditor and the Conduct of an Audit in Accordance with International Standards on Auditing (UK)*.

Introduction

Introduction

1   This International Standard on Auditing (UK) (ISA (UK)) deals with the auditor's responsibility to form an opinion on the financial statements. It also deals with the form and content of the auditor's report issued as a result of an audit of financial statements.

2   ISA (UK) 701[1] deals with the auditor's responsibility to communicate key audit matters in the auditor's report. ISA (UK) 705[2] (Revised June 2016) and ISA (UK) 706[3] (Revised June 2016) deal with how the form and content of the auditor's report are affected when the auditor expresses a modified opinion or includes an Emphasis of Matter paragraph or an Other Matter paragraph in the auditor's report. Other ISAs (UK) also contain reporting requirements that are applicable when issuing an auditor's report.

3   This ISA (UK) applies to an audit of a complete set of general purpose financial statements and is written in that context. ISA 800[4] deals with special considerations when financial statements are prepared in accordance with a special purpose framework. ISA 805[5] deals with special considerations relevant to an audit of a single financial statement or of a specific element, account or item of a financial statement. This ISA (UK) also applies to audits for which ISA 800 or ISA 805 apply.

4   The requirements of this ISA (UK) are aimed at addressing an appropriate balance between the need for consistency and comparability in auditor reporting globally and the need to increase the value of auditor reporting by making the information provided in the auditor's report more relevant to users. This ISA (UK) promotes consistency in the auditor's report, but recognizes the need for flexibility to accommodate particular circumstances of individual jurisdictions. Consistency in the auditor's report, when the audit has been conducted in accordance with ISAs (UK), promotes credibility in the global marketplace by making more readily identifiable those audits that have been conducted in accordance with globally recognized standards. It also helps to promote the user's understanding and to identify unusual circumstances when they occur.

Effective Date

5   This ISA (UK) is effective for audits of financial statements for periods commencing on or after 17 June 2016. Earlier adoption is permitted.

---

[1] *ISA (UK) 701, Communicating Key Audit Matters in the Independent Auditor's Report.*

[2] *ISA (UK) 705 (Revised June 2016), Modifications to the Opinion in the Independent Auditor's Report.*

[3] *ISA (UK) 706 (Revised June 2016), Emphasis of Matter Paragraphs and Other Matter Paragraphs in the Independent Auditor's Report.*

[4] *ISA 800, Special Considerations—Audits of Financial Statements Prepared in Accordance with Special Purpose Frameworks.*
ISA 800 has not been promulgated by the FRC for application in the UK.

[5] *ISA 805, Special Considerations—Audits of Single Financial Statements and Specific Elements, Accounts or Items of a Financial Statement.*
ISA 805 has not been promulgated by the FRC for application in the UK.

Objectives

The objectives of the auditor are: **6**

(a)   To form an opinion on the financial statements based on an evaluation of the conclusions drawn from the audit evidence obtained; and

(b)   To express clearly that opinion through a written report.

Definitions

For purposes of the ISAs (UK), the following terms have the meanings attributed   **7** below:

(a)   General purpose financial statements – Financial statements prepared in accordance with a general purpose framework.

(b)   General purpose framework – A financial reporting framework designed to meet the common financial information needs of a wide range of users. The financial reporting framework may be a fair presentation framework or a compliance framework.

The term "fair presentation framework" is used to refer to a financial reporting framework that requires compliance with the requirements of the framework and:

(i)   Acknowledges explicitly or implicitly that, to achieve fair presentation of the financial statements, it may be necessary for management to provide disclosures beyond those specifically required by the framework;[5a] or

(ii)   Acknowledges explicitly that it may be necessary for management to depart from a requirement of the framework to achieve fair presentation of the financial statements.[5b] Such departures are expected to be necessary only in extremely rare circumstances.

The term "compliance framework" is used to refer to a financial reporting framework that requires compliance with the requirements of the framework, but does not contain the acknowledgements in (i) or (ii) above.[6]

(c)   Unmodified opinion – The opinion expressed by the auditor when the auditor concludes that the financial statements are prepared, in all material respects, in accordance with the applicable financial reporting framework.[7]

Reference to "financial statements" in this ISA (UK) means "a complete set of   **8** general purpose financial statements."[8] The requirements of the applicable

---

[5a] *In the IFRS Framework this is acknowledged in paragraph 17(c) of IAS 1. In UK GAAP this is acknowledged in Sections 396(4) and 404(4) of the Companies Act 2006.*

[5b] *This is sometimes referred to as the "true and fair override". In the IFRS Framework this is acknowledged in paragraph 19 of IAS 1. In UK GAAP this is acknowledged in Sections 396(5) and 404(5) of the Companies Act 2006.*

[6] *ISA (UK) 200 (Revised June 2016), Overall Objectives of the Independent Auditor and the Conduct of an Audit in Accordance with International Standards on Auditing (UK), paragraph 13(a).*

[7] *Paragraphs 25–26 deal with the phrases used to express this opinion in the case of a fair presentation framework and a compliance framework respectively.*

[8] *ISA (UK) 200 (Revised June 2016), Overall Objectives of the Independent Auditor and the Conduct of an Audit in Accordance with International Standards on Auditing (UK), paragraph 13(f) sets out the content of financial statements.*

financial reporting framework determine the presentation, structure and content of the financial statements, and what constitutes a complete set of financial statements.

9   Reference to "International Financial Reporting Standards" in this ISA (UK) means the International Financial Reporting Standards (IFRSs) issued by the International Accounting Standards Board, and reference to "International Public Sector Accounting Standards" means the International Public Sector Accounting Standards (IPSASs) issued by the International Public Sector Accounting Standards Board.

Requirements

Forming an Opinion on the Financial Statements

10   The auditor shall form an opinion on whether the financial statements are prepared, in all material respects, in accordance with the applicable financial reporting framework.[9],[10]

11   In order to form that opinion, the auditor shall conclude as to whether the auditor has obtained reasonable assurance about whether the financial statements as a whole are free from material misstatement, whether due to fraud or error. That conclusion shall take into account:

(a)   The auditor's conclusion, in accordance with ISA (UK) 330 (Revised June 2016), whether sufficient appropriate audit evidence has been obtained;[11]

(b)   The auditor's conclusion, in accordance with ISA (UK) 450 (Revised June 2016), whether uncorrected misstatements are material, individually or in aggregate;[12] and

(c)   The evaluations required by paragraphs 12–15.

12   The auditor shall evaluate whether the financial statements are prepared, in all material respects, in accordance with the requirements of the applicable financial reporting framework. This evaluation shall include consideration of the qualitative aspects of the entity's accounting practices, including indicators of possible bias in management's judgments. (Ref: Para. A1–A3)

13   In particular, the auditor shall evaluate whether, in view of the requirements of the applicable financial reporting framework:

(a)   The financial statements appropriately disclose the significant accounting policies selected and applied. In making this evaluation, the auditor shall consider the relevance of the accounting policies to the entity, and whether they have been presented in an understandable manner; (Ref: Para. A4)

(b)   The accounting policies selected and applied are consistent with the applicable financial reporting framework and are appropriate;

---

[9] *ISA (UK) 200 (Revised June 2016), paragraph 11.*

[10] *Paragraphs 25–26 deal with the phrases used to express this opinion in the case of a fair presentation framework and a compliance framework respectively.*

[11] *ISA (UK) 330 (Revised June 2016), The Auditor's Responses to Assessed Risks, paragraph 26.*

[12] *ISA (UK) 450 (Revised June 2016), Evaluation of Misstatements Identified during the Audit, paragraph 11.*

(c)   The accounting estimates made by management are reasonable;

(d)   The information presented in the financial statements is relevant, reliable, comparable, and understandable. In making this evaluation, the auditor shall consider whether:

- The information that should have been included has been included, and whether such information is appropriately classified, aggregated or disaggregated, and characterized.

- The overall presentation of the financial statements has been undermined by including information that is not relevant or that obscures a proper understanding of the matters disclosed. (Ref: Para. A5)

(e)   The financial statements provide adequate disclosures to enable the intended users to understand the effect of material transactions and events on the information conveyed in the financial statements; and (Ref: Para. A6)

(f)   The terminology used in the financial statements, including the title of each financial statement, is appropriate.

When the financial statements are prepared in accordance with a fair presentation **14** framework, the evaluation required by paragraphs 12–13 shall also include whether the financial statements achieve fair presentation. The auditor's evaluation as to whether the financial statements achieve fair presentation shall include consideration of: (Ref: Para A7–A9)

(a)   The overall presentation, structure and content of the financial statements; and

(b)   Whether the financial statements represent the underlying transactions and events in a manner that achieves fair presentation.

The auditor shall evaluate whether the financial statements adequately refer to or **15** describe the applicable financial reporting framework. (Ref: Para. A10–A15)

Form of Opinion

The auditor shall express an unmodified opinion when the auditor concludes that **16** the financial statements are prepared, in all material respects, in accordance with the applicable financial reporting framework.

In the UK, when expressing an unmodified opinion on financial statements prepared in accordance with a fair presentation framework it is not sufficient for the auditor to conclude that the financial statements give a true and fair view solely on the basis that the financial statements were prepared in accordance with accounting standards and any other applicable legal requirements. (Ref: Para. A15-1–A15-2)

If the auditor: **17**

(a)   concludes that, based on the audit evidence obtained, the financial statements as a whole are not free from material misstatement; or

(b)   is unable to obtain sufficient appropriate audit evidence to conclude that the financial statements as a whole are free from material misstatement,

the auditor shall modify the opinion in the auditor's report in accordance with ISA (UK) 705 (Revised June 2016).

If financial statements prepared in accordance with the requirements of a fair **18** presentation framework do not achieve fair presentation, the auditor shall discuss the matter with management and, depending on the requirements of the applicable financial reporting framework and how the matter is resolved, shall determine whether it is necessary to modify the opinion in the auditor's report in accordance with ISA (UK) 705 (Revised June 2016). (Ref: Para. A16)

19   When the financial statements are prepared in accordance with a compliance framework, the auditor is not required to evaluate whether the financial statements achieve fair presentation. However, if in extremely rare circumstances the auditor concludes that such financial statements are misleading, the auditor shall discuss the matter with management and, depending on how it is resolved, shall determine whether, and how, to communicate it in the auditor's report. (Ref: Para. A17)

Auditor's Report

20   The auditor's report shall be in writing. (Ref: Para. A18–A19)

20-1   The auditor's report shall be in clear and unambiguous language.

Auditor's Report for Audits Conducted in Accordance with International Standards on Auditing (UK)

Title

21   The auditor's report shall have a title that clearly indicates that it is the report of an independent auditor. (Ref: Para. A20)

Addressee

22   The auditor's report shall be addressed, as appropriate, based on the circumstances of the engagement. (Ref: Para. A21–A21-1)

Auditor's Opinion

23   The first section of the auditor's report shall include the auditor's opinion, and shall have the heading "Opinion."

24   The Opinion section of the auditor's report shall also:

(a)   Identify the entity whose financial statements have been audited;

(b)   State that the financial statements have been audited;

(c)   Identify the title of each statement comprising the financial statements;

(d)   Refer to the notes, including the summary of significant accounting policies; and

(e)   Specify the date of, or period covered by, each financial statement comprising the financial statements. (Ref: Para. A22–A23)

25   When expressing an unmodified opinion on financial statements prepared in accordance with a fair presentation framework, the auditor's opinion shall, unless otherwise required by law or regulation, use one of the following phrases, which are regarded as being equivalent:

(a)   In our opinion, the accompanying financial statements present fairly, in all material respects, […] in accordance with [the applicable financial reporting framework]; or

(b)   In our opinion, the accompanying financial statements give a true and fair view of […] in accordance with [the applicable financial reporting framework]. (Ref: Para. A24–A31)

In the UK, when expressing an unmodified opinion on financial statements prepared in accordance with a fair presentation framework the opinion paragraph shall clearly state that the financial statements give a true and fair view. (Ref: Para. A24-1–A24-3)

When expressing an unmodified opinion on financial statements prepared in accordance with a compliance framework, the auditor's opinion shall be that the accompanying financial statements are prepared, in all material respects, in accordance with [the applicable financial reporting framework]. (Ref: Para. A26–A31-1) **26**

If the reference to the applicable financial reporting framework in the auditor's opinion is not to IFRSs issued by the International Accounting Standards Board or IPSASs issued by the International Public Sector Accounting Standards Board, the auditor's opinion shall identify the jurisdiction of origin of the framework. **27**

Basis for Opinion

The auditor's report shall include a section, directly following the Opinion section, with the heading "Basis for Opinion", that: (Ref: Para. A32) **28**

(a) States that the audit was conducted in accordance with International Standards on Auditing (UK) and applicable law; (Ref: Para. A33)

(b) Refers to the section of the auditor's report that describes the auditor's responsibilities under the ISAs (UK);

(c) Includes a statement that the auditor is independent of the entity in accordance with the relevant ethical requirements relating to the audit, and has fulfilled the auditor's other ethical responsibilities in accordance with these requirements. The statement shall identify the jurisdiction of origin of the relevant ethical requirements or refer to the International Ethics Standards Board for Accountants' *Code of Ethics for Professional Accountants* (IESBA Code); and (Ref: Para. A34–A39)

In the UK, auditors are subject to ethical requirements from two sources: the FRC's Ethical Standard concerning the integrity, objectivity and independence of the auditor, and the ethical pronouncements established by the auditor's relevant professional body. When identifying the relevant ethical requirements in the auditor's report, the auditor indicates that these include the FRC's Ethical Standard, applied as required for the types of entity determined to be appropriate in the circumstances.

(d) States whether the auditor believes that the audit evidence the auditor has obtained is sufficient and appropriate to provide a basis for the auditor's opinion.

Going Concern

Where applicable, the auditor shall report in accordance with ISA (UK) 570 (Revised June 2016).[13] **29**

---

[13] *ISA (UK) 570 (Revised June 2016), Going Concern, paragraphs 21–23.*

Key Audit Matters

30　For audits of complete sets of general purpose financial statements of listed entities, the auditor shall communicate key audit matters in the auditor's report in accordance with ISA (UK) 701.

30-1　For audits of complete sets of general purpose financial statements of public interest entities and other entities that are required, and those that choose voluntarily, to report on how they have applied the UK Corporate Governance Code, the auditor shall communicate in the auditor's report in accordance with ISA (UK) 701.

31　When the auditor is otherwise required by law or regulation or decides to communicate key audit matters in the auditor's report, the auditor shall do so in accordance with ISA (UK) 701. (Ref: Para. A40–A42)

Other Information

32　Where applicable, the auditor shall report in accordance with ISA (UK) 720 (Revised June 2016).

Responsibilities for the Financial Statements

33　The auditor's report shall include a section with a heading "Responsibilities of Management for the Financial Statements." The auditor's report shall use the term that is appropriate in the context of the legal framework in the particular jurisdiction and need not refer specifically to "management". In some jurisdictions, the appropriate reference may be to those charged with governance.[13a] (Ref: Para. A44–A44-1)

34　This section of the auditor's report shall describe management's responsibility for: (Ref: Para. A45–A48)

(a)　Preparing the financial statements in accordance with the applicable financial reporting framework, and for such internal control as management determines is necessary to enable the preparation of financial statements that are free from material misstatement, whether due to fraud or error; and

(b)　Assessing the entity's ability to continue as a going concern[14] and whether the use of the going concern basis of accounting is appropriate as well as disclosing, if applicable, matters relating to going concern. The explanation of management's responsibility for this assessment shall include a description of when the use of the going concern basis of accounting is appropriate. (Ref: Para. A48)

35　This section of the auditor's report shall also identify those responsible for the oversight of the financial reporting process, when those responsible for such oversight are different from those who fulfill the responsibilities described in paragraph 33 above. In this case, the heading of this section shall also refer to "Those Charged with Governance" or such term that is appropriate in the context of the legal framework in the particular jurisdiction. (Ref: Para. A49)

36　When the financial statements are prepared in accordance with a fair presentation framework, the description of responsibilities for the financial statements in the

---

[13a] *In the UK, those charged with governance are responsible for the preparation of the financial statements.*

[14] *ISA (UK) 570 (Revised June 2016), paragraph 2.*

auditor's report shall refer to "the preparation and fair presentation of these financial statements" or "the preparation of financial statements that give a true and fair view" as appropriate in the circumstances.

In the UK, the auditor's report shall include a statement that [those charged with governance] are responsible for the preparation of financial statements [that give a true and fair view].

Auditor's Responsibilities for the Audit of the Financial Statements

The auditor's report shall include a section with the heading "Auditor's Responsibilities for the Audit of the Financial Statements." **37**

This section of the auditor's report shall: (Ref: Para. A50) **38**

(a) State that the objectives of the auditor are to:

    (i) Obtain reasonable assurance about whether the financial statements as a whole are free from material misstatement, whether due to fraud or error; and

    (ii) Issue an auditor's report that includes the auditor's opinion. (Ref: Para. A51)

(b) State that reasonable assurance is a high level of assurance, but is not a guarantee that an audit conducted in accordance with ISAs (UK) will always detect a material misstatement when it exists; and

(c) State that misstatements can arise from fraud or error, and either:

    (i) Describe that they are considered material if, individually or in the aggregate, they could reasonably be expected to influence the economic decisions of users taken on the basis of these financial statements; or[15]

    (ii) Provide a definition or description of materiality in accordance with the applicable financial reporting framework. (Ref: Para. A52)

The Auditor's Responsibilities for the Audit of the Financial Statements section of the auditor's report shall further: (Ref: Para. A50) **39**

(a) State that, as part of an audit in accordance with ISAs (UK), the auditor exercises professional judgment and maintains professional skepticism throughout the audit; and

(b) Describe an audit by stating that the auditor's responsibilities are:

    (i) To identify and assess the risks of material misstatement of the financial statements, whether due to fraud or error; to design and perform audit procedures responsive to those risks; and to obtain audit evidence that is sufficient and appropriate to provide a basis for the auditor's opinion. The risk of not detecting a material misstatement resulting from fraud is higher than for one resulting from error, as fraud may involve collusion, forgery, intentional omissions, misrepresentations, or the override of internal control.

    (ii) To obtain an understanding of internal control relevant to the audit in order to design audit procedures that are appropriate in the circumstances, but not for the purpose of expressing an opinion on

---

[15] *ISA (UK) 320 (Revised June 2016), Materiality in Planning and Performing an Audit, paragraph 2.*

the effectiveness of the entity's internal control. In circumstances when the auditor also has a responsibility to express an opinion on the effectiveness of internal control in conjunction with the audit of the financial statements, the auditor shall omit the phrase that the auditor's consideration of internal control is not for the purpose of expressing an opinion on the effectiveness of the entity's internal control.

(iii) To evaluate the appropriateness of accounting policies used and the reasonableness of accounting estimates and related disclosures made by management.

(iv) To conclude on the appropriateness of management's use of the going concern basis of accounting and, based on the audit evidence obtained, whether a material uncertainty exists related to events or conditions that may cast significant doubt on the entity's ability to continue as a going concern. If the auditor concludes that a material uncertainty exists, the auditor is required to draw attention in the auditor's report to the related disclosures in the financial statements or, if such disclosures are inadequate, to modify the opinion. The auditor's conclusions are based on the audit evidence obtained up to the date of the auditor's report. However, future events or conditions may cause an entity to cease to continue as a going concern. (Ref: Para A50-1–A50-2)

(v) When the financial statements are prepared in accordance with a fair presentation framework, to evaluate the overall presentation, structure and content of the financial statements, including the disclosures, and whether the financial statements represent the underlying transactions and events in a manner that achieves fair presentation.

(c) When ISA (UK) 600 (Revised June 2016)[16] applies, further describe the auditor's responsibilities in a group audit engagement by stating that:

(i) The auditor's responsibilities are to obtain sufficient appropriate audit evidence regarding the financial information of the entities or business activities within the group to express an opinion on the group financial statements;

(ii) The auditor is responsible for the direction, supervision and performance of the group audit; and

(iii) The auditor remains solely responsible for the auditor's opinion.

40 The Auditor's Responsibilities for the Audit of the Financial Statements section of the auditor's report also shall: (Ref: Para. A50)

(a) State that the auditor communicates with those charged with governance regarding, among other matters, the planned scope and timing of the audit and significant audit findings, including any significant deficiencies in internal control that the auditor identifies during the audit;

(b) For audits of financial statements of listed entities, state that the auditor provides those charged with governance with a statement that the auditor has complied with relevant ethical requirements regarding independence and communicate with them all relationships and other matters that may

---

[16] *ISA (UK) 600 (Revised June 2016), Special Considerations—Audits of Group Financial Statements (Including the Work of Component Auditors).*

reasonably be thought to bear on the auditor's independence, and where applicable, related safeguards; and

(c) For audits of financial statements of listed entities and any other entities for which key audit matters are communicated in accordance with ISA (UK) 701, state that, from the matters communicated with those charged with governance, the auditor determines those matters that were of most significance in the audit of the financial statements of the current period and are therefore the key audit matters. The auditor describes these matters in the auditor's report unless law or regulation precludes public disclosure about the matter or when, in extremely rare circumstances, the auditor determines that a matter should not be communicated in the auditor's report because the adverse consequences of doing so would reasonably be expected to outweigh the public interest benefits of such communication. (Ref: Para. A53)

Location of the Description of the Auditor's Responsibilities for the Audit of the Financial Statements

41 The description of the auditor's responsibilities for the audit of the financial statements required by paragraphs 39–40 shall be included: (Ref: Para. A54)

(a) Within the body of the auditor's report;

(b) Within an appendix to the auditor's report, in which case the auditor's report shall include a reference to the location of the appendix; or (Ref: Para. A54–A55)

(c) By a specific reference within the auditor's report to the location of such a description on a website of an appropriate authority, where law, regulation or national auditing standards expressly permit the auditor to do so. (Ref: Para. A54, A56–A57-1)

In the UK, the auditor is permitted to cross-refer to the applicable version of a "Description of the Auditor's Responsibilities for the Audit of the Financial Statements" that is maintained on the website of an appropriate authority.

42 When the auditor refers to a description of the auditor's responsibilities on a website of an appropriate authority, the auditor shall determine that such description addresses, and is not inconsistent with, the requirements in paragraphs 39–40 of this ISA (UK). (Ref: Para. A56)

Other Reporting Responsibilities

43 If the auditor addresses other reporting responsibilities in the auditor's report on the financial statements that are in addition to the auditor's responsibilities under the ISAs (UK), these other reporting responsibilities shall be addressed in a separate section in the auditor's report with a heading titled "Report on Other Legal and Regulatory Requirements" or otherwise as appropriate to the content of the section, unless these other reporting responsibilities address the same topics as those presented under the reporting responsibilities required by the ISAs (UK) in which case the other reporting responsibilities may be presented in the same section as the related report elements required by the ISAs (UK). (Ref: Para. A58–A60)

| 43-1 | If the auditor is required to report on certain matters by exception, the auditor shall describe in the auditor's report the auditor's responsibilities for such matters and incorporate a suitable conclusion in respect of such matters. (Ref: Para. A58-1–A58-3) |

44　If other reporting responsibilities are presented in the same section as the related report elements required by the ISAs (UK), the auditor's report shall clearly differentiate the other reporting responsibilities from the reporting that is required by the ISAs (UK). (Ref: Para. A60)

45　If the auditor's report contains a separate section that addresses other reporting responsibilities, the requirements of paragraphs 20–40 of this ISA (UK) shall be included under a section with a heading "Report on the Audit of the Financial Statements." The "Report on Other Legal and Regulatory Requirements" shall follow the "Report on the Audit of the Financial Statements." (Ref: Para. A60–A60-14)

45R-1	For audits of financial statements of public interest entities, the auditor's report shall:
	(a) State by whom or which body the auditor(s) was appointed;
	(b) Indicate the date of the appointment and the period of total uninterrupted engagement including previous renewals and reappointments of the firm;
	(c) Explain to what extent the audit was considered capable of detecting irregularities, including fraud;
	(d) Confirm that the audit opinion is consistent with the additional report to the audit committee.[16a] Except as required by paragraph 45R-1(d), the auditor's report shall not contain any cross-references to the additional report to the audit committee;
	(e) Declare that the non-audit services prohibited by the FRC's Ethical Standard were not provided and that the firm remained independent of the entity in conducting the audit; and
	(f) Indicate any services, in addition to the audit, which were provided by the firm to the entity and its controlled undertaking(s), and which have not been disclosed in the annual report or financial statements.

Name of the Engagement Partner

46　The name of the engagement partner shall be included in the auditor's report on financial statements of listed entities unless, in rare circumstances, such disclosure is reasonably expected to lead to a significant personal security threat. In the rare circumstances that the auditor intends not to include the name of the engagement partner in the auditor's report, the auditor shall discuss this intention with those charged with governance to inform the auditor's assessment of the likelihood and severity of a significant personal security threat. (Ref: Para. A61–A63)

Signature of the Auditor

47　The auditor's report shall be signed. (Ref: Para. A64–A65)

[16a] *ISA (UK) 260 (Revised), Communication with Those Charged with Governance, paragraph 16R-2.*

Auditor's Address

The auditor's report shall name the location in the jurisdiction where the auditor **48** practices. (Ref: Para. A65-1)

Date of the Auditor's Report

The auditor's report shall be dated no earlier than the date on which the auditor has **49** obtained sufficient appropriate audit evidence on which to base the auditor's opinion on the financial statements, including evidence that: (Ref: Para. A66–A69)

(a) All the statements and disclosures that comprise the financial statements have been prepared; and

(b) Those with the recognized authority have asserted that they have taken responsibility for those financial statements.

The date of an auditor's report on an entity's financial statements shall be the **49-1** date on which the auditor signed the report expressing an opinion on those financial statements. (Ref: Para. A66)

The auditor shall not sign, and hence date, the auditor's report earlier than the **49-2** date on which all the other information contained in the annual report has been approved by those charged with governance and the auditor has considered all necessary available evidence. (Ref: Para. A67-1–A67-4)

Auditor's Report Prescribed by Law or Regulation

If the auditor is required by law or regulation of a specific jurisdiction to use a **50** specific layout, or wording of the auditor's report, the auditor's report shall refer to International Standards on Auditing only if the auditor's report includes, at a minimum, each of the following elements: (Ref: Para. A70–A71)

(a) A title.

(b) An addressee, as required by the circumstances of the engagement.

(c) An Opinion section containing an expression of opinion on the financial statements and a reference to the applicable financial reporting framework used to prepare the financial statements (including identifying the jurisdiction of origin of the financial reporting framework that is not International Financial Reporting Standards or International Public Sector Accounting Standards, see paragraph 26).

(d) An identification of the entity's financial statements that have been audited.

(e) A statement that the auditor is independent of the entity in accordance with the relevant ethical requirements relating to the audit, and has fulfilled the auditor's other ethical responsibilities in accordance with these requirements. The statement shall identify the jurisdiction of origin of the relevant ethical requirements or refer to the IESBA Code.

(f) Where applicable, a section that addresses, and is not inconsistent with, the reporting requirements in paragraph 22 of ISA 570 (Revised).

(g) Where applicable, a Basis for Qualified (or Adverse) Opinion section that addresses, and is not inconsistent with, the reporting requirements in paragraph 23 of ISA 570 (Revised)S.

(h) Where applicable, a section that includes the information required by ISA 701, or additional information about the audit that is prescribed by law or regulation and that addresses, and is not inconsistent with, the reporting requirements in that ISA.[17] (Ref: Para. A72–A75)

(i)   Where applicable, a section that addresses the reporting requirements in paragraph 24 of ISA 720 (Revised).

(j)   A description of management's responsibilities for the preparation of the financial statements and an identification of those responsible for the oversight of the financial reporting process that addresses, and is not inconsistent with, the requirements in paragraphs 33–36.

(k)   A reference to International Standards on Auditing and the law or regulation, and a description of the auditor's responsibilities for an audit of the financial statements that addresses, and is not inconsistent with, the requirements in paragraphs 37–40. (Ref: Para. A50–A53)

(l)   For audits of complete sets of general purpose financial statements of listed entities, the name of the engagement partner unless, in rare circumstances, such disclosure is reasonably expected to lead to a significant personal security threat.

(m)   The auditor's signature.

(n)   The auditor's address.

(o)   The date of the auditor's report.

Auditor's Report for Audits Conducted in Accordance with Both Auditing Standards of a Specific Jurisdiction and International Standards on Auditing

51   An auditor may be required to conduct an audit in accordance with the auditing standards of a specific jurisdiction (the "national auditing standards"), and has additionally complied with the ISAs in the conduct of the audit. If this is the case, the auditor's report may refer to International Standards on Auditing in addition to the national auditing standards, but the auditor shall do so only if: (Ref: Para. A76–A77-1)

(a)   There is no conflict between the requirements in the national auditing standards and those in ISAs that would lead the auditor (i) to form a different opinion, or (ii) not to include an Emphasis of Matter paragraph or Other Matter paragraph that, in the particular circumstances, is required by ISAs; and

(b)   The auditor's report includes, at a minimum, each of the elements set out in paragraphs 50(a)–(o) in ISA 700 (Revised) when the auditor uses the layout or wording specified by the national auditing standards. However, reference to "law or regulation" in paragraph 50(k) shall be read as reference to the national auditing standards. The auditor's report shall thereby identify such national auditing standards.

52   When the auditor's report refers to both the national auditing standards and International Standards on Auditing, the auditor's report shall identify the jurisdiction of origin of the national auditing standards.

---

[17] *ISA 701, paragraphs 11–16.*

Supplementary Information Presented with the Financial Statements
(Ref: Para. A78– A84)

If supplementary information that is not required by the applicable financial   **53**
reporting framework is presented with the audited financial statements, the auditor
shall evaluate whether, in the auditor's professional judgment, supplementary
information is nevertheless an integral part of the financial statements due to its
nature or how it is presented. When it is an integral part of the financial statements,
the supplementary information shall be covered by the auditor's opinion.

If supplementary information that is not required by the applicable financial   **54**
reporting framework is not considered an integral part of the audited financial
statements, the auditor shall evaluate whether such supplementary information is
presented in a way that sufficiently and clearly differentiates it from the audited
financial statements. If this is not the case, then the auditor shall ask management
to change how the unaudited supplementary information is presented. If
management refuses to do so, the auditor shall identify the unaudited
supplementary information and explain in the auditor's report that such
supplementary information has not been audited.

***

Application and Other Explanatory Material

Qualitative Aspects of the Entity's Accounting Practices
(Ref: Para. 12)

Management makes a number of judgments about the amounts and disclosures in   **A1**
the financial statements.

ISA (UK) 260 (Revised June 2016) contains a discussion of the qualitative aspects   **A2**
of accounting practices.[18] In considering the qualitative aspects of the entity's
accounting practices, the auditor may become aware of possible bias in
management's judgments. The auditor may conclude that the cumulative effect
of a lack of neutrality, together with the effect of uncorrected misstatements,
causes the financial statements as a whole to be materially misstated. Indicators of
a lack of neutrality that may affect the auditor's evaluation of whether the financial
statements as a whole are materially misstated include the following:

- The selective correction of misstatements brought to management's
  attention during the audit (e.g., correcting misstatements with the effect of
  increasing reported earnings, but not correcting misstatements that have the
  effect of decreasing reported earnings).

- Possible management bias in the making of accounting estimates.

ISA (UK) 540 (Revised June 2016) addresses possible management bias in   **A3**
making accounting estimates.[19] Indicators of possible management bias do not
constitute misstatements for purposes of drawing conclusions on the
reasonableness of individual accounting estimates. They may, however, affect
the auditor's evaluation of whether the financial statements as a whole are free
from material misstatement.

---

[18] *ISA (UK) 260 (Revised June 2016), Communication with Those Charged with Governance, Appendix 2.*

[19] *ISA (UK) 540 (Revised June 2016), Auditing Accounting Estimates, Including Fair Value Accounting Estimates, and Related Disclosures, paragraph 21.*

Accounting Policies Appropriately Disclosed in the Financial Statements
(Ref: Para. 13(a))

A4   In evaluating whether the financial statements appropriately disclose the significant accounting policies selected and applied, the auditor's consideration includes matters such as:

- Whether all disclosures related to the significant accounting policies that are required to be included by the applicable financial reporting framework have been disclosed;

- Whether the information about the significant accounting policies that has been disclosed is relevant and therefore reflects how the recognition, measurement and presentation criteria in the applicable financial reporting framework have been applied to classes of transactions, account balances and disclosures in the financial statements in the particular circumstances of the entity's operations and its environment; and

- The clarity with which the significant accounting policies have been presented.

Information Presented in the Financial Statements Is Relevant, Reliable, Comparable and Understandable
(Ref: Para. 13(d))

A5   Evaluating the understandability of the financial statements includes consideration of such matters as whether:

- The information in the financial statements is presented in a clear and concise manner.

- The placement of significant disclosures gives appropriate prominence to them (e.g., when there is perceived value of entity-specific information to users), and whether the disclosures are appropriately cross-referenced in a manner that would not give rise to significant challenges for users in identifying necessary information.

Disclosure of the Effect of Material Transactions and Events on the Information Conveyed in the Financial Statements
(Ref: Para. 13(e))

A6   It is common for financial statements prepared in accordance with a general purpose framework to present an entity's financial position, financial performance and cash flows. Evaluating whether, in view of the applicable financial reporting framework, the financial statements provide adequate disclosures to enable the intended users to understand the effect of material transactions and events on the entity's financial position, financial performance and cash flows includes consideration of such matters as

- The extent to which the information in the financial statements is relevant and specific to the circumstances of the entity; and

- Whether the disclosures are adequate to assist the intended users to understand:

  - The nature and extent of the entity's potential assets and liabilities arising from transactions or events that do not meet the criteria for recognition (or the criteria for derecognition) established by the applicable financial reporting framework.

  - The nature and extent of risks of material misstatement arising from transactions and events.

- The methods used and the assumptions and judgments made, and changes to them, that affect amounts presented or otherwise disclosed, including relevant sensitivity analyses.

Evaluating Whether the Financial Statements Achieve Fair Presentation (Ref: Para. 14)

Some financial reporting frameworks acknowledge explicitly or implicitly the **A7** concept of fair presentation.[20] As noted in paragraph 7(b) of this ISA (UK), a fair presentation[21] financial reporting framework not only requires compliance with the requirements of the framework, but also acknowledges explicitly or implicitly that it may be necessary for management to provide disclosures beyond those specifically required by the framework.[22]

The auditor's evaluation about whether the financial statements achieve fair **A8** presentation, both in respect of presentation and disclosure, is a matter of professional judgment. This evaluation takes into account such matters as the facts and circumstances of the entity, including changes thereto, based on the auditor's understanding of the entity and the audit evidence obtained during the audit. The evaluation also includes consideration, for example, of the disclosures needed to achieve a fair presentation arising from matters that could be material (i. e., in general, misstatements are considered to be material if they could reasonably be expected to influence the economic decisions of the users taken on the basis of the financial statements as a whole), such as the effect of evolving financial reporting requirements or the changing economic environment.

Evaluating whether the financial statements achieve fair presentation may include, **A9** for example, discussions with management and those charged with governance about their views on why a particular presentation was chosen, as well as alternatives that may have been considered. The discussions may include, for example:

- The degree to which the amounts in the financial statements are aggregated or disaggregated, and whether the presentation of amounts or disclosures obscures useful information, or results in misleading information.

- Consistency with appropriate industry practice, or whether any departures are relevant to the entity's circumstances and therefore warranted.

Consistency with appropriate industry practice, or whether any departures are relevant to the entity's circumstances and therefore warranted.

As explained in ISA (UK) 200 (Revised June 2016), the preparation of the **A10** financial statements by management and, where appropriate, those charged with governance requires the inclusion of an adequate description of the applicable financial reporting framework in the financial statements.[23] That description

---

[20] *For example, International Financial Reporting Standards (IFRSs) note that fair presentation requires the faithful representation of the effects of transactions, other events and conditions in accordance with the definitions and recognition criteria for assets, liabilities, income and expenses.*

[21] *See ISA (UK) 200 (Revised June 2016), paragraph 13(a).*

[22] *For example, IFRSs require an entity to provide additional disclosures when compliance with the specific requirements in IFRSs is insufficient to enable users to understand the impact of particular transactions, other events and conditions on the entity's financial position and financial performance (International Accounting Standard 1, Presentation of Financial Statements, paragraph 17(c)).*

[23] *ISA (UK) 200 (Revised June 2016), paragraphs A2–A3.*

advises users of the financial statements of the framework on which the financial statements are based.

A11   A description that the financial statements are prepared in accordance with a particular applicable financial reporting framework is appropriate only if the financial statements comply with all the requirements of that framework that are effective during the period covered by the financial statements.

A12   A description of the applicable financial reporting framework that contains imprecise qualifying or limiting language (e.g., "the financial statements are in substantial compliance with International Financial Reporting Standards") is not an adequate description of that framework as it may mislead users of the financial statements.

Reference to More than One Financial Reporting Framework

A13   In some cases, the financial statements may represent that they are prepared in accordance with two financial reporting frameworks (e.g., the national framework and IFRSs). This may be because management is required, or has chosen, to prepare the financial statements in accordance with both frameworks, in which case both are applicable financial reporting frameworks. Such description is appropriate only if the financial statements comply with each of the frameworks individually. To be regarded as being prepared in accordance with both frameworks, the financial statements need to comply with both frameworks simultaneously and without any need for reconciling statements. In practice, simultaneous compliance is unlikely unless the jurisdiction has adopted the other framework (e.g., IFRSs) as its own national framework, or has eliminated all barriers to compliance with it.

A14   Financial statements that are prepared in accordance with one financial reporting framework and that contain a note or supplementary statement reconciling the results to those that would be shown under another framework are not prepared in accordance with that other framework. This is because the financial statements do not include all the information in the manner required by that other framework.

A15   The financial statements may, however, be prepared in accordance with one applicable financial reporting framework and, in addition, describe in the notes to the financial statements the extent to which the financial statements comply with another framework (e.g., financial statements prepared in accordance with the national framework that also describe the extent to which they comply with IFRSs). Such description may constitute supplementary financial information as discussed in paragraph 53 and is covered by the auditor's opinion if it cannot be clearly differentiated from the financial statements.

Form of Opinion
(Ref: Para. 16, 18–19)

A15-1   The "true and fair" concept has been part of legislation and central to accounting and auditing practice in the UK for many years. However, there is no statutory definition of "true and fair". In 2008, the FRC published a legal opinion, that it had commissioned, entitled "The true and fair requirement revisited" (The Opinion).[23a] The Opinion confirms the overarching nature of the true and fair requirement to the preparation of financial statements in the

---

[23a] *The opinion can be downloaded from the FRC website at https://www.frc.org.uk/Our-Work/Codes-Standards/Accounting-and-Reporting-Policy/True-and-Fair.aspx.*

UK, whether they are prepared in accordance with international or national accounting standards. The Opinion states that "The preparation of financial statements is not a mechanical process where compliance with relevant accounting standards will automatically ensure that those financial statements show a true and fair view, or a fair presentation. Such compliance may be highly likely to produce such an outcome; but it does not guarantee it."

In addition to preparing the financial statements in accordance with a fair **A15-2** presentation framework, the directors are therefore required to consider whether the individual accounting policies applied and the financial statements as a whole present a true and fair view. Similarly, auditors are required to exercise professional judgment in evaluating such matters before expressing an audit opinion. As a result, The Opinion confirms that it will not be sufficient for either directors or auditors to reach such conclusions solely because the financial statements were prepared in accordance with applicable accounting standards.

There may be cases where the financial statements, although prepared in **A16** accordance with the requirements of a fair presentation framework, do not achieve fair presentation. Where this is the case, it may be possible for management to include additional disclosures in the financial statements beyond those specifically required by the framework or, in extremely rare circumstances, to depart from a requirement in the framework in order to achieve fair presentation of the financial statements. (Ref: Para. 18)

It will be extremely rare for the auditor to consider financial statements that are **A17** prepared in accordance with a compliance framework to be misleading if, in accordance with ISA (UK) 210 (Revised June 2016), the auditor determined that the framework is acceptable.[24] (Ref: Para. 19)

Auditor's Report
(Ref: Para. 20)

A written report encompasses reports issued in hard copy and those using an **A18** electronic medium.

The Appendix to this ISA (UK)[24a] contains illustrations of auditor's reports on **A19** financial statements, incorporating the elements set out in paragraphs 20–49. With the exception of the Opinion and Basis for Opinion sections, this ISA (UK) does not establish requirements for ordering the elements of the auditor's report. However, this ISA (UK) requires the use of specific headings, which are intended to assist in making auditor's reports that refer to audits that have been conducted in accordance with ISAs (UK) more recognizable, particularly in situations where the elements of the auditor's report are presented in an order that differs from the illustrative auditor's reports in the Appendix to this ISA (UK).

---

[24] *ISA (UK) 210 (Revised June 2016), Agreeing the Terms of Audit Engagements, paragraph 6(a).*

[24a] *The examples in the Appendix have not been tailored for the UK. Illustrative auditor's reports tailored for use with audits conducted in accordance with ISAs (UK) are given in the current version of the FRC's Compendium of Illustrative Auditor's Reports.*

Auditor's Report for Audits Conducted in Accordance with International Standards on Auditing (UK)

Title
(Ref: Para. 21)

A20 A title indicating the report is the report of an independent auditor, for example, "Independent Auditor's Report," distinguishes the independent auditor's report from reports issued by others.

Addressee
(Ref: Para. 22)

A21 Law, regulation or the terms of the engagement may specify to whom the auditor's report is to be addressed in that particular jurisdiction. The auditor's report is normally addressed to those for whom the report is prepared, often either to the shareholders or to those charged with governance of the entity whose financial statements are being audited.

A21-1 In the UK, for entities incorporated under the Companies Act,[24b] the auditor is required to report to the company's members because the audit is undertaken on their behalf. Such auditor's reports are, therefore, typically addressed to either the members or the shareholders of the company. The auditor's report on financial statements of other types of reporting entity is addressed to the appropriate person or persons, as defined by statute or by the terms of the individual engagement.

Auditor's Opinion
(Ref. Para. 24–26)

Reference to the financial statements that have been audited

A22 The auditor's report states, for example, that the auditor has audited the financial statements of the entity, which comprise [state the title of each financial statement comprising the complete set of financial statements required by the applicable financial reporting framework, specifying the date or period covered by each financial statement] and notes to the financial statements, including a summary of significant accounting policies.

A23 When the auditor is aware that the audited financial statements will be included in a document that contains other information, such as an annual report, the auditor may consider, if the form of presentation allows, identifying the page numbers on which the audited financial statements are presented. This helps users to identify the financial statements to which the auditor's report relates.

"Present fairly, in all material respects" or "give a true and fair view"

A24 The phrases "present fairly, in all material respects," and "give a true and fair view" are regarded as being equivalent. Whether the phrase "present fairly, in all material respects," or the phrase "give a true and fair view" is used in any particular jurisdiction is determined by the law or regulation governing the audit of financial statements in that jurisdiction, or by generally accepted practice in that jurisdiction. Where law or regulation requires the use of different wording, this does not affect the requirement in paragraph 14 of this ISA (UK) for the auditor to evaluate the fair presentation of financial statements prepared in accordance with a fair presentation framework.

[24b] *In the UK, the Companies Act 2006 establishes this requirement.*

For statutory audits of financial statements, the auditor's report is required by UK legislation[24c] to state clearly whether, in the auditor's opinion, the financial statements: **A24-1**

(a)   Give a true and fair view:

    (i)   In the case of an individual balance sheet, of the state of affairs of the entity as at the end of the financial year;

    (ii)   In the case of an individual profit and loss account, of the profit or loss of the entity for the financial year;

    (iii)   In the case of group accounts, of the state of affairs as at the end of the financial year and of the profit or loss for the financial year of the undertakings included in the consolidation as a whole, so far as concerns members of the entity;

(b)   Have been properly prepared in accordance with the relevant financial reporting framework; and

(c)   Have been prepared in accordance with the requirements of the relevant legislation.

UK auditor's reports prepared in accordance with Section 495(3) of the Companies Act 2006 will meet the requirement in paragraph 25. This is supported by recital 10 of EU Directive 2003/51/EC which states "The fundamental requirement that an audit opinion states whether the annual or consolidated accounts give a true and fair view in accordance with the relevant financial reporting framework does not represent a restriction of the scope of that opinion but clarifies the context in which it is expressed". **A24-2**

In the UK, "relevant financial reporting framework" is used in legislation to refer to the applicable financial reporting framework. **A24-3**

When the auditor expresses an unmodified opinion, it is not appropriate to use phrases such as "with the foregoing explanation" or "subject to" in relation to the opinion, as these suggest a conditional opinion or a weakening or modification of opinion. **A25**

Description of the financial statements and the matters they present

The auditor's opinion covers the complete set of financial statements as defined by the applicable financial reporting framework. For example, in the case of many general purpose frameworks, the financial statements may include: a statement of financial position, a statement of comprehensive income, a statement of changes in equity, a statement of cash flows, and related notes, which ordinarily comprise a summary of significant accounting policies and other explanatory information. In some jurisdictions, additional information may also be considered to be an integral part of the financial statements. **A26**

In the case of financial statements prepared in accordance with a fair presentation framework, the auditor's opinion states that the financial statements present fairly, in all material respects, or give a true and fair view of, the matters that the financial statements are designed to present. For example, in the case of financial statements prepared in accordance with IFRSs, these matters are *the financial position of the entity as at the end of the period and the entity's financial performance and cash flows for the period then ended.* Consequently, the [...] in paragraph 25 and **A27**

[24c] *Section 495(3) of the Companies Act 2006.*

elsewhere in this ISA (UK) is intended to be replaced by the words in italics in the preceding sentence when the applicable financial reporting framework is IFRSs or, in the case of other applicable financial reporting frameworks, be replaced with words that describe the matters that the financial statements are designed to present.

Description of the applicable financial reporting framework and how it may affect the auditor's opinion

A28　The identification of the applicable financial reporting framework in the auditor's opinion is intended to advise users of the auditor's report of the context in which the auditor's opinion is expressed; it is not intended to limit the evaluation required in paragraph 14. The applicable financial reporting framework is identified in such terms as:

"... in accordance with International Financial Reporting Standards" or

"... in accordance with accounting principles generally accepted in Jurisdiction X ..."

A28-1　In the UK, the financial reporting framework is normally one of:

●　International Financial Reporting Standards (IFRSs) as adopted by the European Union, and the national law that is applicable when using IFRSs and, in the case of consolidated financial statements of publicly traded companies,[24d] Article 4 of the IAS Regulation (1606/2002/EC).

●　UK Generally Accepted Accounting Practice, which comprises applicable UK law and UK Accounting Standards as issued by the FRC.

A29　When the applicable financial reporting framework encompasses financial reporting standards and legal or regulatory requirements, the framework is identified in such terms as "... in accordance with International Financial Reporting Standards and the requirements of Jurisdiction X Corporations Act."ISA (UK) 210 (Revised June 2016) deals with circumstances where there are conflicts between the financial reporting standards and the legislative or regulatory requirements.[25]

A29-1　In the UK, certain small companies are permitted by law to prepare their financial statements in accordance with the micro-entities regime which is considered to be a compliance framework. Paragraph 26 sets out the form of opinion for a compliance framework, however, the auditor is required by law to state whether the financial statements give a true and fair view.[25a] ISA (UK) 210 (Revised June 2016) provides guidance to support the auditor's response in these circumstances.[25b]

A30　As indicated in paragraph A13, the financial statements may be prepared in accordance with two financial reporting frameworks, which are therefore both applicable financial reporting frameworks. Accordingly, each framework is considered separately when forming the auditor's opinion on the financial statements, and the auditor's opinion in accordance with paragraphs 25–27 refers to both frameworks as follows:

[24d] *A publicly traded company is one whose securities are admitted to trading on a regulated market in any Member State in the European Union.*

[25] ISA (UK) 210 (Revised June 2016), paragraph 18.

[25a] Section 495(3A) of the Companies Act 2006.

[25b] ISA (UK) 210 (Revised June 2016), paragraphs A36-1–A36-2.

(a)   If the financial statements comply with each of the frameworks individually, two opinions are expressed: that is, that the financial statements are prepared in accordance with one of the applicable financial reporting frameworks (e. g., the national framework) and an opinion that the financial statements are prepared in accordance with the other applicable financial reporting framework (e.g., IFRSs). These opinions may be expressed separately or in a single sentence (e.g., the financial statements are presented fairly, in all material respects [...], in accordance with accounting principles generally accepted in Jurisdiction X and with IFRSs).

(b)   If the financial statements comply with one of the frameworks but fail to comply with the other framework, an unmodified opinion can be given that the financial statements are prepared in accordance with the one framework (e.g., the national framework) but a modified opinion given with regard to the other framework (e.g., IFRSs) in accordance with ISA (UK) 705 (Revised June 2016).

As indicated in paragraph A13, the financial statements may represent compliance with the applicable financial reporting framework and, in addition, disclose the extent of compliance with another financial reporting framework. Such supplementary information is covered by the auditor's opinion if it cannot be clearly differentiated from the financial statements (see paragraphs 53–54 and related application material in paragraphs A78–A86). Accordingly,   **A31**

(a)   If the disclosure as to the compliance with the other framework is misleading, a modified opinion is expressed in accordance with ISA (UK) 705 (Revised June 2016).

(b)   If the disclosure is not misleading, but the auditor judges it to be of such importance that it is fundamental to the users' understanding of the financial statements, an Emphasis of Matter paragraph is added in accordance with ISA (UK) 706 (Revised June 2016), drawing attention to the disclosure.

Joint Audits

The Companies Act 2006 permits companies to appoint a sole auditor or joint   **A31-1** auditors. Where a company appoints joint auditors each firm is required to agree on the results of the audit and submit a joint auditor's report and opinion. In the case of disagreement, each firm is required to submit the auditor's opinion in a separate paragraph of the auditor's report and state the reason for the disagreement.[25c]

Basis for Opinion
(Ref: Para. 28)

The Basis for Opinion section provides important context about the auditor's   **A32** opinion. Accordingly, this ISA (UK) requires the Basis for Opinion section to directly follow the Opinion section in the auditor's report.

The reference to the standards used conveys to the users of the auditor's report that   **A33** the audit has been conducted in accordance with established standards.

[25c] *Section 495(5) of the Companies Act 2006.*

Relevant ethical requirements
(Ref: Para. 28(c))

A34   The identification of the jurisdiction of origin of relevant ethical requirements increases transparency about those requirements relating to the particular audit engagement. ISA (UK) 200 (Revised June 2016) explains that relevant ethical requirements ordinarily comprise Parts A and B of the IESBA Code related to an audit of financial statements together with national requirements that are more restrictive.[26] When the relevant ethical requirements include those of the IESBA Code, the statement may also make reference to the IESBA Code. If the IESBA Code constitutes all of the ethical requirements relevant to the audit, the statement need not identify a jurisdiction of origin.

A35   In some jurisdictions, relevant ethical requirements may exist in several different sources, such as the ethical code(s) and additional rules and requirements within law and regulation. When the independence and other relevant ethical requirements are contained in a limited number of sources, the auditor may choose to name the relevant source(s) (e.g., the name of the code, rule or regulation applicable in the jurisdiction), or may refer to a term that is commonly understood and that appropriately summarizes those sources (e.g., independence requirements for audits of private entities in Jurisdiction X).

A35-1   The FRC's Ethical Standard applies to all audit engagements performed in compliance with ISAs (UK). For audit engagements of certain types of entities (Listed; SME Listed; Public Interest), it includes either additional, or less stringent, requirements that apply in certain circumstances.[26a]

A35-2   The firm is required to establish policies and procedures in accordance with the FRC's Ethical Standard[26b] that set out the circumstances in which the additional requirements, applicable to audit engagements for certain types of entities (Listed; SME Listed; Public Interest), apply to other audit engagements.

A35-3   When identifying the relevant ethical requirements in the auditor's report and indicating that these include the FRC's Ethical Standard, the auditor indicates that they were applied as required for each type of entity (Listed; SME Listed; Public Interest) for which the FRC Ethical Standard includes additional requirements:

   (a)   That is relevant in the case of the audited entity; and

   (b)   Where (having regard to the policies and procedures referred to in paragraph A35-2) the auditor determined it to be appropriate to apply to the audit engagement the additional requirements included in the FRC Ethical Standard applicable for that type of entity.

A35-4   Where the firm has taken advantage of an exemption provided in the FRC's Ethical Standard in relation to audits of small entities, the auditor's report discloses this fact.[26c]

A36   Law or regulation, national auditing standards or the terms of an audit engagement may require the auditor to provide in the auditor's report more specific information

---

[26] *ISA (UK) 200 (Revised June 2016), paragraph A14.*

[26a] *FRC's Ethical Standard, Part B, Section 1 – General Requirements and Guidance, paragraph 1.48.*

[26b] *FRC's Ethical Standard, Part B, Section 1 – General Requirements and Guidance, paragraph 1.49.*

[26c] *FRC's Ethical Standard, Part B, Section 6 – Provisions Available for Audits of Small Entities, paragraph 6.15.*

about the sources of the relevant ethical requirements, including those pertaining to independence, that applied to the audit of the financial statements.

In determining the appropriate amount of information to include in the auditor's **A37** report when there are multiple sources of relevant ethical requirements relating to the audit of the financial statements, an important consideration is balancing transparency against the risk of obscuring other useful information in the auditor's report.

Considerations specific to group audits

In group audits when there are multiple sources of relevant ethical requirements, **A38** including those pertaining to independence, the reference in the auditor's report to the jurisdiction ordinarily relates to the relevant ethical requirements that are applicable to the group engagement team. This is because, in a group audit, component auditors are also subject to ethical requirements that are relevant to the group audit.[27]

The ISAs (UK) do not establish specific independence or ethical requirements for **A39** auditors, including component auditors, and thus do not extend, or otherwise override, the independence requirements of the IESBA Code or other ethical requirements to which the group engagement team is subject, nor do the ISAs (UK) require that the component auditor in all cases to be subject to the same specific independence requirements that are applicable to the group engagement team. As a result, relevant ethical requirements, including those pertaining to independence, in a group audit situation may be complex. ISA (UK) 600 (Revised June 2016)[28] provides guidance for auditors in performing work on the financial information of a component for a group audit, including those situations where the component auditor does not meet the independence requirements that are relevant to the group audit.

Key Audit Matters
(Ref: Para. 31)

Law or regulation may require communication of key audit matters for audits of **A40** entities other than listed entities, for example, entities characterized in such law or regulation as public interest entities.

The auditor may also decide to communicate key audit matters for other entities, **A41** including those that may be of significant public interest, for example because they have a large number and wide range of stakeholders and considering the nature and size of the business. Examples of such entities may include financial institutions (such as banks, insurance companies, and pension funds), and other entities such as charities.

ISA (UK) 210 (Revised June 2016) requires the auditor to agree the terms of the **A42** audit engagement with management and those charged with governance, as appropriate, and explains that the roles of management and those charged with governance in agreeing the terms of the audit engagement for the entity depend on the governance arrangements of the entity and relevant law or regulation.[29] ISA (UK) 210 (Revised June 2016) also requires the audit engagement letter or other suitable form of written agreement to include reference to the expected form and

---

[27] *ISA (UK) 600 (Revised June 2016), paragraph A37.*

[28] *ISA (UK) 600 (Revised June 2016), paragraphs 19–20.*

[29] *ISA (UK) 210 (Revised June 2016), paragraphs 9 and A21.*

content of any reports to be issued by the auditor.[30] When the auditor is not otherwise required to communicate key audit matters, ISA (UK) 210 (Revised June 2016)[31] explains that it may be helpful for the auditor to make reference in the terms of the audit engagement to the possibility of communicating key audit matters in the auditor's report and, in certain jurisdictions, it may be necessary for the auditor to include a reference to such possibility in order to retain the ability to do so.

Considerations specific to public sector entities

A43   Listed entities are not common in the public sector. However, public sector entities may be significant due to size, complexity or public interest aspects. In such cases, an auditor of a public sector entity may be required by law or regulation or may otherwise decide to communicate key audit matters in the auditor's report.

Responsibilities for the Financial Statements
(Ref: Para. 33–35)

A44   ISA (UK) 200 (Revised June 2016) explains the premise, relating to the responsibilities of management and, where appropriate, those charged with governance, on which an audit in accordance with ISAs (UK) is conducted.[32] Management and, where appropriate, those charged with governance accept responsibility for the preparation of the financial statements in accordance with the applicable financial reporting framework, including, where relevant, their fair presentation. Management also accepts responsibility for such internal control as it determines is necessary to enable the preparation of financial statements that are free from material misstatement, whether due to fraud or error. The description of management's responsibilities in the auditor's report includes reference to both responsibilities as it helps to explain to users the premise on which an audit is conducted. ISA (UK) 260 (Revised June 2016) uses the term those charged with governance to describe the person(s) or organization(s) with responsibility for overseeing the entity, and provides a discussion about the diversity of governance structures across jurisdictions and by entity.

A44-1   In the UK, the preparation of financial statements requires those charged with governance to make significant accounting estimates and judgments, as well as to determine the appropriate accounting principles and methods used in preparation of the financial statements. This determination will be made in the context of the financial reporting framework that those charged with governance choose, or are required, to use. In contrast, the auditor's responsibility is to audit the financial statements in order to express an opinion on them.

A45   There may be circumstances when it is appropriate for the auditor to add to the descriptions of the responsibilities of management and those charged with governance in paragraphs 34–35 to reflect additional responsibilities that are relevant to the preparation of the financial statements in the context of the particular jurisdiction or the nature of the entity.

---

[30]   *ISA (UK) 210 (Revised June 2016), paragraph 10.*

[31]   *ISA (UK) 210 (Revised June 2016), paragraph A23a.*

[32]   *ISA (UK) 200 (Revised June 2016), paragraph 13(j).*

ISA (UK) 210 (Revised June 2016) requires the auditor to agree management's   **A46**
responsibilities in an engagement letter or other suitable form of written
agreement.[33] ISA (UK) 210 (Revised June 2016) provides some flexibility in
doing so, by explaining that, if law or regulation prescribes the responsibilities of
management and, where appropriate, those charged with governance in relation to
financial reporting, the auditor may determine that the law or regulation includes
responsibilities that, in the auditor's judgment, are equivalent in effect to those set
out in ISA (UK) 210 (Revised June 2016). For such responsibilities that are
equivalent, the auditor may use the wording of the law or regulation to describe
them in the engagement letter or other suitable form of written agreement. In such
cases, this wording may also be used in the auditor's report to describe the
responsibilities as required by paragraph 34(a) of this ISA (UK). In other
circumstances, including where the auditor decides not to use the wording of
law or regulation as incorporated in the engagement letter, the wording in
paragraph 34(a) of this ISA (UK) is used. In addition to including the
description of management's responsibilities in the auditor's report as required
by paragraph 34, the auditor may refer to a more detailed description of these
responsibilities by including a reference to where such information may be
obtained (e.g., in the annual report of the entity or a website of an appropriate
authority).

In some jurisdictions, law or regulation prescribing management's responsibilities   **A47**
may specifically refer to a responsibility for the adequacy of accounting books and
records, or accounting system. As books, records and systems are an integral part
of internal control (as defined in ISA (UK) 315 (Revised June 2016)[34]), the
descriptions in ISA (UK) 210 (Revised June 2016) and in paragraph 34 do not
make specific reference to them.

The Appendix[34a] to this ISA (UK) provides illustrations of how the requirement in   **A48**
paragraph 34(b) would be applied when IFRSs is the applicable financial reporting
framework. If an applicable financial reporting framework other than IFRSs is
used, the illustrative statements featured in the Appendix to this ISA (UK) may
need to be adapted to reflect the application of the other financial reporting
framework in the circumstances.

Oversight of the financial reporting process
(Ref: Para. 35)

When some, but not all, of the individuals involved in the oversight of the   **A49**
financial reporting process are also involved in preparing the financial statements,
the description as required by paragraph 35 of this ISA (UK) may need to be
modified to appropriately reflect the particular circumstances of the entity. When
individuals responsible for the oversight of the financial reporting process are the
same as those responsible for the preparation of the financial statements, no
reference to oversight responsibilities is required.

---

[33] *ISA (UK) 210 (Revised June 2016), paragraph 6(b)(i)–(ii).*

[34] *ISA (UK) 315 (Revised June 2016), Identifying and Assessing the Risks of Material Misstatement through Understanding the Entity and Its Environment, paragraph 4(c).*

[34a] *The examples in the Appendix have not been tailored for the UK. Illustrative auditor's reports tailored for use with audits conducted in accordance with ISAs (UK) are given in the current version of the FRC's Compendium of Illustrative Auditor's Reports.*

Auditor's Responsibilities for the Audit of the Financial Statements
(Ref: Para. 37–40)

A50   The description of the auditor's responsibilities as required by paragraphs 37–40 of this ISA (UK) may be tailored to reflect the specific nature of the entity, for example, when the auditor's report addresses consolidated financial statements. Illustration 2 in the Appendix[34a] to this ISA (UK) includes an example of how this may be done.

A50-1   Where the auditor is required to report by exception on certain matters relating to going concern, the auditor is required to include a description of the auditor's responsibilities with respect to those matters in the auditor's report. When describing the auditor's responsibilities relating to management's use of the going concern basis of accounting and the disclosure of material uncertainties, the auditor may choose to include this description either:

(a)   in the Auditor's Responsibilities for the Audit of the Financial Statements section of the auditor's report; or

(b)   in the Conclusions Relating to Going Concern section of the auditor's report,[34b]

and cross-refer from the respective section as appropriate.

A50-2   Auditor's reports which include a description of the auditor's responsibilities relating to management's use of the going concern basis of accounting and the disclosure of material uncertainties in the Conclusions Relating to Going Concern section of the auditor's report will include the minimum elements of an auditor's report required by paragraph 50(k) of ISA 700 (Revised) and therefore the auditor is not precluded from being able to assert compliance with International Standards on Auditing issued by the IAASB.

Objectives of the auditor
(Ref: Para. 38(a))

A51   The auditor's report explains that the objectives of the auditor are to obtain reasonable assurance about whether the financial statements as a whole are free from material misstatement, whether due to fraud or error, and to issue an auditor's report that includes the auditor's opinion. These are in contrast to management's responsibilities for the preparation for the financial statements.

Description of materiality
(Ref: Para. 38(c))

A52   The Appendix to this ISA (UK) provides illustrations of how the requirement in paragraph 38(c), to provide a description of materiality, would be applied when IFRSs is the applicable financial reporting framework. If an applicable financial reporting framework other than IFRSs is used, the illustrative statements presented in the Appendix to this ISA (UK) may need to be adapted to reflect the application of the other financial reporting framework in the circumstances.

[34b] *ISA (UK) 570 (Revised June 2016), paragraph 21-2 deals with the auditor's responsibilities to include such a section in the auditor's report.*

Auditor's responsibilities relating to ISA (UK) 701
(Ref: Para. 40(c))

The auditor may also consider it useful to provide additional information in the   **A53**
description of the auditor's responsibilities beyond what is required by paragraph
40(c). For example, the auditor may make reference to the requirement in
paragraph 9 of ISA (UK) 701 to determine the matters that required significant
auditor attention in performing the audit, taking into account areas of higher
assessed risk of material misstatement or significant risks identified in accordance
with ISA (UK) 315 (Revised June 2016); significant auditor judgments relating to
areas in the financial statements that involved significant management judgment,
including accounting estimates that have been identified as having high estimation
uncertainty; and the effects on the audit of significant events or transactions that
occurred during the period.

Location of the description of the auditor's responsibilities for the audit of the
financial statements
(Ref: Para. 41, 50(k))

Including the information required by paragraphs 39–40 of this ISA (UK) in an   **A54**
appendix to the auditor's report or, when law, regulation or national auditing
standards expressly permit, referring to a website of an appropriate authority
containing such information may be a useful way of streamlining the content of
the auditor's report. However, because the description of the auditor's
responsibilities contains information that is necessary to inform users'
expectations of an audit conducted in accordance with ISAs (UK), a reference
is required to be included in the auditor's report indicating where such information
can be accessed.

Location in an appendix
(Ref: Para. 41(b), 50(k))

Paragraph 40 permits the auditor to include the statements required by paragraphs   **A55**
39–40 describing the auditor's responsibilities for the audit of the financial
statements in an appendix to the auditor's report, provided that appropriate
reference is made within the body of the auditor's report to the location of the
appendix. The following is an illustration of how such a reference to an appendix
could be made in the auditor's report:

Auditor's Responsibilities for the Audit of the Financial Statements

Our objectives are to obtain reasonable assurance about whether the financial
statements as a whole are free from material misstatement, whether due to fraud or
error, and to issue an auditor's report that includes our opinion. Reasonable
assurance is a high level of assurance, but is not a guarantee that an audit
conducted in accordance with ISAs (UK) will always detect a material
misstatement when it exists. Misstatements can arise from fraud or error and are
considered material if, individually or in the aggregate, they could reasonably be
expected to influence the economic decisions of users taken on the basis of these
financial statements.

A further description of our responsibilities for the audit of the financial statements
is included in appendix X of this auditor's report. This description, which is
located at [*indicate page number or other specific reference to the location of the
description*], forms part of our auditor's report.

Reference to a website of an appropriate authority
(Ref: Para. 41(c), 42)

A56   Paragraph 41 explains that the auditor may refer to a description of the auditor's responsibilities located on a website of an appropriate authority, only if expressly permitted by law, regulation or national auditing standards. The information on the website that is incorporated in the auditor's report by way of a specific reference to the website location where such information can be found may describe the auditor's work, or the audit in accordance with ISAs (UK) more broadly, but it cannot be inconsistent with the description required in paragraphs 39–40 of this ISA (UK). This means that the wording of the description of the auditor's responsibilities on the website may be more detailed, or may address other matters relating to an audit of financial statements, provided that such wording reflects and does not contradict the matters addressed in paragraphs 39–40.

A57   An appropriate authority could be a national auditing standard setter, regulator, or an audit oversight body. Such organizations are well-placed to ensure the accuracy, completeness and continued availability of the standardized information. It would not be appropriate for the auditor to maintain such a website. The following is an illustration of how such a reference to a website could be made in the auditor's report:

Auditor's Responsibilities for the Audit of the Financial Statements

Our objectives are to obtain reasonable assurance about whether the financial statements as a whole are free from material misstatement, whether due to fraud or error, and to issue an auditor's report that includes our opinion. Reasonable assurance is a high level of assurance, but is not a guarantee that an audit conducted in accordance with ISAs (UK) will always detect a material misstatement when it exists. Misstatements can arise from fraud or error and are considered material if, individually or in the aggregate, they could reasonably be expected to influence the economic decisions of users taken on the basis of these financial statements.

A further description of our responsibilities for the audit of the financial statements is located at [*Organization's*] website at: [*website address*]. This description forms part of our auditor's report.

A57-1   The FRC maintains on its web-site a generic "Description of the Auditor's Responsibilities for the Audit of the Financial Statements" of private sector entities.[34c] These descriptions address the auditor's responsibilities under ISAs (UK).

Other Reporting Responsibilities
(Ref: Para. 43–45)

A58   In some jurisdictions, the auditor may have additional responsibilities to report on other matters that are supplementary to the auditor's responsibilities under the ISAs (UK). For example, the auditor may be asked to report certain matters if they come to the auditor's attention during the course of the audit of the financial statements. Alternatively, the auditor may be asked to perform and report on additional specified procedures, or to express an opinion on specific matters, such as the adequacy of accounting books and records, internal control over financial reporting or other information. Auditing standards in the specific jurisdiction often provide guidance on the auditor's responsibilities with respect to specific additional reporting responsibilities in that jurisdiction.

[34c] *The web-site reference relevant to the UK is www.frc.org.uk/auditscopeukprivate.*

In the UK, other reporting responsibilities may be determined by specific   **A58-1**
statutory requirements applicable to the reporting entity, or, in some
circumstances, by the terms of the auditor's engagement. Such matters may
be required to be dealt with by either:

(a)   A positive statement in the auditor's report; or

(b)   By exception.

An example of (b) arises in the UK where company legislation requires the
auditor of a company to report when a company has not maintained adequate
accounting records.[34d]

Where the auditor is required to report by exception and has discharged the   **A58-2**
auditor's responsibilities and has nothing to report in respect of them, the
conclusion could be expressed in the form of the following phrase: "We have
nothing to report in respect of the following."

Where the auditor expresses a modified conclusion in respect of other reporting   **A58-3**
responsibilities (including those on which they are required to report by
exception), ISA (UK) 705 (Revised June 2016), adapted as necessary in the
circumstances, may assist the auditor in considering the nature and form of the
modification that is appropriate. Such a modification may also give rise to a
modification of the auditor's opinion on the financial statements in accordance
with ISA (UK) 705 (Revised June 2016). For example, if adequate accounting
records have not been maintained and as a result it proves impracticable for the
auditor to obtain sufficient appropriate evidence concerning material matters in
the financial statements, the auditor's report on the financial statements
includes a qualified opinion or disclaimer of opinion arising from that
limitation in accordance with ISA (UK) 705 (Revised June 2016).

In some cases, the relevant law or regulation may require or permit the auditor to   **A59**
report on these other responsibilities as part of their auditor's report on the
financial statements. In other cases, the auditor may be required or permitted to
report on them in a separate report.

In the UK, for the audit of certain public sector entities the audit mandate may   **A59-1**
require the auditor to express an opinion on regularity. Regularity is the
requirement that financial transactions are in accordance with the legislation
authorizing them.

Paragraphs 43–45 of this ISA (UK) permit combined presentation of other reporting   **A60**
responsibilities and the auditor's responsibilities under the ISAs (UK) only when
they address the same topics and the wording of the auditor's report clearly
differentiates the other reporting responsibilities from those under the ISAs (UK).
Such clear differentiation may make it necessary for the auditor's report to refer to
the source of the other reporting responsibilities and to state that such responsibilities
are beyond those required under the ISAs (UK). Otherwise, other reporting
responsibilities are required to be addressed in a separate section in the auditor's
report with a heading "Report on Other Legal and Regulatory Requirements," or
otherwise as appropriate to the content of the section. In such cases, paragraph 45
requires the auditor to include reporting responsibilities under the ISAs (UK) under a
heading titled "Report on the Audit of the Financial Statements."

[34d] *Section 498(2) of the Companies Act 2006.*

Auditor's responsibilities and duties for the directors' remuneration report in the UK

A60-1 Section 420 of the Companies Act 2006 sets out the duty of directors of quoted companies[34e] to prepare a directors' remuneration report for each financial year of a company.

A60-2 Section 497 of the Companies Act 2006 requires in respect of quoted companies that the auditor in the auditor's report on the company's annual accounts for the financial year, must:

(a) Report to the company's members on the auditable part of the directors' remuneration report, and

(b) State whether in the auditor's opinion that part of the directors' remuneration report has been properly prepared in accordance with this Act.

A60-3 Section 498(2) of the Companies Act 2006 also requires the auditor of a quoted company to form an opinion as to whether the auditable part of the company's directors' remuneration report is in agreement with the accounting records and returns. If the auditor is of the opinion that the auditable part of the report is not in agreement with the accounting records and returns the auditor is required to state that fact in the auditor's report.

A60-4 Section 498(4) of the Companies Act 2006 further requires that if the requirements of regulations under Section 421 of the Companies Act 2006 as to information forming the auditable part of the directors' remuneration report are not complied with in that report the auditor is required to include in the auditor's report, so far as the auditor is reasonably able to do so, a statement giving the required particulars.

A60-5 Section 498(4) of the Companies Act 2006 has an identical requirement with respect to the disclosures made under Section 412 of the Companies Act 2006 (disclosure of directors' benefits: remuneration, pensions and compensation for loss of office in the notes to the accounts). These latter requirements are separate from the requirements relating to the directors' remuneration report.

Provisions of the directors' remuneration report which are subject to audit

A60-6 The information contained in the directors' remuneration report which is subject to audit is the information required by paragraphs 4–17 of Part 3 of Schedule 8 of The Large and Medium-sized Companies and Groups (Accounts and Reports) Regulations 2008.

Reporting on the directors' remuneration report

A60-7 As the auditor is not required to audit all of the information contained in the directors' remuneration report the auditor will need, in the auditor's report, to describe accurately which elements of the directors' remuneration report the auditor has audited. The auditor, therefore, makes arrangements with the directors, well in advance of the year end, to ensure that the audited disclosures will be clearly distinguished from those that have not been audited.

[34e] *A quoted company is defined in Section 385 of the Companies Act 2006.*

It would be unsatisfactory for an auditor, in the auditor's report, to describe what the auditor has audited in an uninformative manner such as "the disclosures required by Part 3 of Schedule 8 to The Large and Medium-sized Companies and Groups (Accounts and Reports) Regulations" as this would require readers of the auditor's report to have a detailed knowledge of the requirements.

A60-8

The auditor assesses whether the scope of the audit will be capable of being clearly described. If this cannot be achieved to the auditor's satisfaction by cross-reference, the auditor sets out the particulars that have been audited within the auditor's report.

A60-9

Difference between the disclosures required by Schedule 5 and Schedule 8 of The Large and Medium-sized Companies and Groups (Accounts and Reports) Regulations 2008

Schedule 5 of the Regulations requires a company to provide certain information concerning directors' remuneration by way of the notes to the company's financial statements. The majority of the provisions of Schedule 5 apply only to unquoted companies (as the information required to be disclosed would be duplicated by disclosures in the directors' remuneration report). However, the provisions described as "Total amount of directors' remuneration etc." apply to both quoted and unquoted companies.

A60-10

A consequence of this may be that the financial statements of a quoted company disclose aggregate directors' remuneration that may differ from the aggregate directors' remuneration disclosed in the directors' remuneration report. This may arise because the definition of aggregate remuneration differs between the two Schedules.

A60-11

Both of these disclosures are reported on by the auditor. Where both disclosures have been prepared in accordance with the requirements of the Companies Act 2006 and the various Regulations any difference between the disclosures is, prima facie, an inconsistency. However, this inconsistency arises from complying with the law and it would, therefore, be inappropriate to "correct" the inconsistency. However, as users may think the inconsistency is a mistake the auditor encourages the directors to provide an explanation of any difference within the annual report.

A60-12

Issuing the directors' remuneration report as a separate document

If a quoted company issues its directors' remuneration report as a separate document the scope of the auditor's report included in the annual report will, nevertheless, encompass the auditable part of the directors' remuneration report. For this reason the requirements of ISA (UK) 720 (Revised June 2016)[34f] apply to the content of a separate directors' remuneration report, notwithstanding the fact that the Report is not included in a document containing audited financial statements.

A60-13

When the directors' remuneration report is issued as a separate document, although not required by the Companies Act 2006, the auditor:

A60-14

[34f] *ISA (UK) 720 (Revised June 2016), The Auditor's Responsibilities Relating to Other Information.*

(a)   When the auditor's report is unmodified, encourages the directors to indicate within the directors' remuneration report where the auditor's report, prepared in accordance with Section 495 of the Companies Act 2006, may be found; or

(b)   When the auditor expresses either a qualified or adverse opinion or disclaims an opinion, which is relevant to the directors' remuneration report, requires the directors to reproduce the relevant parts of the auditor's report as part of the directors' remuneration report. In the event that the directors do not agree to do so, the auditor considers whether to resign.

Name of the Engagement Partner
(Ref: Para. 46)

A61   ISQC (UK) 1 (Revised June 2016)[35] requires that the firm establish policies and procedures to provide reasonable assurance that engagements are performed in accordance with professional standards and applicable legal and regulatory requirements. Notwithstanding these ISQC (UK) 1 (Revised June 2016) requirements, naming the engagement partner in the auditor's report is intended to provide further transparency to the users of the auditor's report on financial statements of a listed entity.

A62   Law, regulation or national auditing standards may require that the auditor's report include the name of the engagement partner responsible for audits other than those of financial statements of listed entities. The auditor may also be required by law, regulation or national auditing standards, or may decide to include additional information beyond the engagement partner's name in the auditor's report to further identify the engagement partner, for example, the engagement partner's professional license number that is relevant to the jurisdiction where the auditor practices.

A63   In rare circumstances, the auditor may identify information or be subject to experiences that indicate the likelihood of a personal security threat that, if the identity of the engagement partner is made public, may result in physical harm to the engagement partner, other engagement team members or other closely related individuals. However, such a threat does not include, for example, threats of legal liability or legal, regulatory or professional sanctions. Discussions with those charged with governance about circumstances that may result in physical harm may provide additional information about the likelihood or severity of the significant personal security threat. Law, regulation or national auditing standards may establish further requirements that are relevant to determining whether the disclosure of the name of the engagement partner may be omitted.

Signature of the Auditor
(Ref: Para. 47)

A64   The auditor's signature is either in the name of the audit firm, the personal name of the auditor or both, as appropriate for the particular jurisdiction. In addition to the auditor's signature, in certain jurisdictions, the auditor may be required to declare in the auditor's report the auditor's professional accountancy designation or the fact that the auditor or firm, as appropriate, has been recognized by the appropriate licensing authority in that jurisdiction.

---

[35] *ISQC (UK) 1 (Revised June 2016), Quality Control for Firms that Perform Audits and Reviews of Financial Statements, and Other Assurance and Related Services Engagements, paragraph 32.*

The "Senior Statutory Auditor" under the UK Companies Act 2006[35a]

Section 503(3) of the Companies Act 2006 requires, where the auditor is a firm, that the auditor's report must be signed by the "senior statutory auditor in his or her own name for and on behalf of the auditor".   **A64-1**

Sections 503 and 504 of the Companies Act 2006 address the signature of the auditor's report. The requirement for the senior statutory auditor to sign in his or her own name applies to auditor's reports: **A64-2**

(a) Prepared in accordance with the requirements of Sections 495, 496 and 497 of the Companies Act 2006; and

(b) In respect of voluntary revisions of annual accounts and reports made in accordance with Section 454 of the Companies Act 2006.

The Companies Act 2006 sets out a number of requirements regarding the appointment of auditors. However, other than as described in paragraph A59-4, there are no legal requirements concerning eligibility for appointment as the senior statutory auditor. This is an internal matter for the firm as under Section 504(1) of the Companies Act 2006 it is the firm which is required to identify which individual is the senior statutory auditor.   **A64-3**

Eligibility for appointment as senior statutory auditor in the UK

Section 504(2) of the Companies Act 2006 requires that the person identified as senior statutory auditor of a company must be eligible for appointment as auditor of the company in question. Eligibility for appointment is dealt with in Sections 1212 to 1225 of the Companies Act 2006.   **A64-4**

Meaning of "Senior Statutory Auditor" in the UK

Subject to meeting the Companies Act 2006 requirement described in paragraph A59-4, the term "Senior Statutory Auditor" has the same meaning as the term "Engagement Partner" when used in ISAs (UK).[35b]   **A64-5**

Involvement of more than one partner in an audit engagement

Where more than one partner is involved in the conduct of an audit engagement, it is important that the responsibilities of the respective partners are clearly defined and understood by the engagement team.[35c] In particular, it is necessary for it to be clearly understood which partner is designated as the engagement partner and is, therefore, the senior statutory auditor identified by the firm in accordance with Section 504(1) of the Companies Act 2006.   **A64-6**

Meaning of "Signing" the Auditor's Report

Section 505(1) of the Companies Act 2006 requires that the name of the senior statutory auditor must be stated in copies of the auditor's report published by, or on behalf of, the company.   **A64-7**

[35a] *The Secretary of State has appointed the Auditing Practices Board by virtue of Article 11 of the "Statutory Auditors (Delegation of Functions etc) Order 2008". SI 2008 No. 496 to issue guidance with respect to the meaning of the term "senior statutory auditor". This ISA (UK) constitutes that guidance.*

[35b] *ISA (UK) 220 (Revised June 2016), Quality Control for Audits of Historical Financial Information, paragraph 7(a).*

[35c] *ISA (UK) 220 (Revised June 2016), paragraph A13.*

A64-8   In paragraph A59-7 references to the auditor's report is to the auditor's report provided to the company by the auditor upon completion of the audit. Such references do not refer to the authentication of the copy auditor's reports required to be delivered to the Registrar of Companies.[35d]

A64-9   Paragraphs 6–10 of Schedule 1 of "The Companies Act 2006 (Commencement No.5, Transitional Provisions and Savings) Order 2007"[35e] address the authentication of accounts and reports filed with the Registrar. With effect from 6 April 2008 this order requires the copies of auditor's reports delivered to the Registrar to:

(a)   State the name of the auditor and (where the auditor is a firm) the name of the person who signed it as senior statutory auditor; and

(b)   Be signed by the auditor or (where the auditor is a firm) in the name of the firm by a person authorized to sign on the firm's behalf.

The senior statutory auditor, therefore, does not necessarily need to sign copy auditor's reports that are required to be delivered to the Registrar.

Changing the senior statutory auditor during the reporting period

A64-10   Where the firm changes the senior statutory auditor (ie the engagement partner) during the engagement the new senior statutory auditor reviews the audit work performed to the date of the change. The review procedures are sufficient to satisfy the new senior statutory auditor that the audit work performed to the date of the review had been planned and performed in accordance with professional standards and regulatory and legal requirements.[35f]

Senior statutory auditor unable to be present to sign the auditor's report

A64-11   Under Section 503(3) of the Companies Act 2006, the senior statutory auditor must sign the auditor's report. Another partner, or responsible individual, is not able to sign for and on behalf of the senior statutory auditor.

A64-12   In circumstances where the senior statutory auditor is unable to continue to take responsibility for the direction, supervision and performance of the audit, the firm appoints a replacement senior statutory auditor and the circumstances are treated in the same way as a change of engagement partner described in paragraph A19 of ISA (UK) 220 (Revised June 2016).

A64-13   In circumstances where the senior statutory auditor is absent but is still able to, and does, take responsibility for the direction, supervision and performance of the audit, the senior statutory auditor may sign the auditor's report using electronic means (eg e-mail or fax).

A64-14   In circumstances where the auditor's report needs to be signed by a certain date (eg listed entities and other public interest entities) it would be pragmatic for the firm to have a contingency plan as to who would succeed as senior statutory auditor in the event that the audit is at an advanced stage but the senior statutory

---

[35d] *In the Companies Act 2006, the expressions "the Registrar of Companies" and "the Registrar" mean the registrar of companies for England & Wales, Scotland or Northern Ireland, as the case may require (Section 1060 (3) the Companies Act 2006).*

[35e] *SI 2007 No. 3495.*

[35f] *ISA (UK) 220 (Revised June 2016), Quality Control for Audits of Historical Financial Information, paragraph A19.*

auditor is unable to sign the auditor's report. If another audit partner is actively involved in the audit engagement, a suitable contingency plan may be for that other partner to work in parallel with the senior statutory auditor and be able to take over as senior statutory auditor if the need arises. Any contingency plan would also need to take into account the firm's plans for partner rotation in accordance with the requirements of the FRC's Ethical Standard.

An audit is considered to be at an "advanced stage" when it is complete subject only to the following: **A64-15**

(a)   Clearing outstanding matters which are unlikely to have a material impact on the financial statements;

(b)   Completing audit procedures on the detail of note disclosures on the financial statements that will not have a material impact on the primary financial statements and completing the auditor's reading of "other information" in the annual report, in accordance with ISA (UK) 720 (Revised June 2016);

(c)   Updating the subsequent events review covering the period to the date of the auditor's report on the financial statements; and

(d)   Obtaining final written representations from management and establishing that the financial statements have been reviewed and approved by the directors.

Circumstances may arise where another partner has not worked in parallel with the senior statutory auditor. In such exceptional circumstances it may be permissible for the engagement quality control reviewer[35g] to be appointed as the replacement senior statutory auditor[35h] where: **A64-16**

(a)   the engagement quality control reviewer has completed his or her review; and

(b)   the audit is at an "advanced stage".

However, once an engagement quality reviewer has been appointed as a replacement senior statutory auditor he or she can no longer act as the engagement quality control reviewer because his or her objectivity may have been impaired through assuming the role of senior statutory auditor.

Joint Audits

As indicated in paragraph A31-1, where a company appoints joint auditors each firm appoints a senior statutory auditor both of which are required to sign the auditors' report in accordance with the requirements of Section 503 of the Companies Act 2006.   **A64-17**

In some cases, law or regulation may allow for the use of electronic signatures in the auditor's report.   **A65**

[35g] *This is on the assumption that the engagement quality control reviewer is eligible to be appointed as the senior statutory auditor (see paragraph A59-4 for eligibility criterion).*

[35h] *ISA (UK) 220 (Revised June 2016) Quality Control for an Audit of Financial Statements requires an engagement quality control reviewer to be appointed in respect of all listed entities and public interest entities.*

Auditor's Address
(Ref: Para. 48)

A65-1   In the UK, legislation[35i] requires the auditor's report to identify the auditor's place of establishment in addition to naming the location in the jurisdiction where the auditor practices as required by paragraph 48.

Date of the Auditor's Report
(Ref: Para. 49)

A66   The date of the auditor's report informs the user of the auditor's report that the auditor has considered the effect of events and transactions of which the auditor became aware and that occurred up to that date. The auditor's responsibility for events and transactions after the date of the auditor's report is addressed in ISA (UK) 560.[36]

A67   Since the auditor's opinion is provided on the financial statements and the financial statements are the responsibility of management, the auditor is not in a position to conclude that sufficient appropriate audit evidence has been obtained until evidence is obtained that all the statements and disclosures that comprise the financial statements have been prepared and management has accepted responsibility for them.

A67-1   The auditor, therefore, plans the conduct of the audit to take account of the need to ensure, before expressing an opinion on financial statements, that those charged with governance have approved the financial statements and any accompanying other information and that the auditor has completed a sufficient review of post balance sheet events.

A67-2   The date of the auditor's report is, therefore, the date on which the auditor signs the auditor's report expressing an opinion on the financial statements for distribution with those financial statements, following:

(a)   Receipt of the financial statements and accompanying documents in the form approved by those charged with governance for release;

(b)   Review of all documents which the auditor is required to consider in addition to the financial statements (for example the directors' report, chairman's statement or other review of an entity's affairs which will form part of the annual report): and

(c)   Completion of all procedures necessary to form an opinion on the financial statements (and any other opinions required by law or regulation) including a review of post balance sheet events.

A67-3   The form of the financial statements and other information approved by those charged with governance, and considered by the auditor when signing a report expressing the auditor's opinion, may be in the form of final drafts from which printed documents will be prepared. Subsequent production of printed copies of the financial statements and the auditor's report does not constitute the creation of a new document. Copies of the report produced for circulation to shareholders or others may, therefore, reproduce a printed version of the auditor's signature showing the date of actual signature.

[35i] *Section 495(4) of the Companies Act 2006.*

[36] *ISA (UK) 560, Subsequent Events, paragraphs 10–17.*

If the date on which the auditor signs the report is later than that on which those charged with governance approved the financial statements, the auditor takes such steps as are appropriate:

A67-4

(a) To obtain assurance that those charged with governance would have approved the financial statements on that later date (for example, by obtaining confirmation from specified individual members of the board to whom authority has been delegated for this purpose); and

(b) To ensure that the auditor's procedures for reviewing subsequent events cover the period up to that date.

In some jurisdictions, law or regulation identifies the individuals or bodies (e.g., the directors) that are responsible for concluding that all the statements and disclosures that comprise the financial statements have been prepared, and specifies the necessary approval process. In such cases, evidence is obtained of that approval before dating the report on the financial statements. In other jurisdictions, however, the approval process is not prescribed in law or regulation. In such cases, the procedures the entity follows in preparing and finalizing its financial statements in view of its management and governance structures are considered in order to identify the individuals or body with the authority to conclude that all the statements that comprise the financial statements, including the related notes, have been prepared. In some cases, law or regulation identifies the point in the financial statement reporting process at which the audit is expected to be complete.

A68

In some jurisdictions, final approval of the financial statements by shareholders is required before the financial statements are issued publicly. In these jurisdictions, final approval by shareholders is not necessary for the auditor to conclude that sufficient appropriate audit evidence has been obtained. The date of approval of the financial statements for purposes of ISAs (UK) is the earlier date on which those with the recognized authority determine that all the statements and disclosures that comprise the financial statements have been prepared and that those with the recognized authority have asserted that they have taken responsibility for them.

A69

Auditor's Report Prescribed by Law or Regulation
(Ref: Para. 50)

ISA (UK) 200 (Revised June 2016) explains that the auditor may be required to comply with legal or regulatory requirements in addition to ISAs.[37] When the differences between the legal or regulatory requirements and ISAs relate only to the layout and wording of the auditor's report, the requirements in paragraph 50 (a)–(o) set out the minimum elements to be included in the auditor's report to enable a reference to the International Standards on Auditing. In those circumstances, the requirements in paragraphs 21–49 that are not included in paragraph 50(a)–(o) do not need to be applied including, for example, the required ordering of the Opinion and Basis for Opinion sections.

A70

---

[37] *ISA (UK) 200 (Revised June 2016), paragraph A55.*

A70-1 This ISA (UK) is consistent with ISA 700 (Revised)"Forming an Opinion and Reporting on Financial Statements," as issued by the IAASB. Auditor's reports prepared in compliance with the requirements of this ISA (UK) will include the minimum elements of an auditor's report required by paragraph 50(a)–(o) of ISA 700 (Revised) and does not therefore preclude the auditor from being able to assert compliance with International Standards on Auditing issued by the IAASB.

A71 Where specific requirements in a particular jurisdiction do not conflict with ISAs, the layout and wording required by paragraphs 21–48 of ISA 700 (Revised) assist users of the auditor's report in more readily recognizing the auditor's report as a report of an audit conducted in accordance with ISAs.

Information Required by ISA 701
(Ref: Para. 50(h))

A72 Law or regulation may require the auditor to provide additional information about the audit that was performed, which may include information that is consistent with the objectives of ISA 701, or may prescribe the nature and extent of communication about such matters.

A73 The ISAs do not override law or regulation that governs an audit of financial statements. When ISA 701 is applicable, reference can only be made to ISAs in the auditor's report if, in applying the law or regulation, the section required by paragraph 50(h) of this ISA is not inconsistent with the reporting requirements in ISA 701. In such circumstances, the auditor may need to tailor certain aspects of the communication of key audit matters in the auditor's report required by ISA 701, for example by:

- Modifying the heading "Key Audit Matters", if law or regulation prescribes a specific heading;

- Explaining why the information required by law or regulation is being provided in the auditor's report, for example by making a reference to the relevant law or regulation and describing how that information relates to the key audit matters;

- Where law or regulation prescribes the nature and extent of the description, supplementing the prescribed information to achieve an overall description of each key audit matter that is consistent with the requirement in paragraph 13 of ISA 701.

A74 ISA 210 deals with circumstances where law or regulation of the relevant jurisdiction prescribes the layout or wording of the auditor's report in terms that are significantly different from the requirements of ISAs, which in particular includes the auditor's opinion. In these circumstances, ISA 210 requires the auditor to evaluate:

(a) Whether users might misunderstand the assurance obtained from the audit of the financial statements and, if so,

(b) Whether additional explanation in the auditor's report can mitigate possible misunderstanding.

If the auditor concludes that additional explanation in the auditor's report cannot mitigate possible misunderstanding, ISA 210 requires the auditor not to accept the audit engagement, unless required by law or regulation to do so. In accordance with ISA 210, an audit conducted in accordance with such law or regulation does not comply with ISAs. Accordingly, the auditor does not include any reference in the auditor's report to the audit having been conducted in accordance with International Standards on Auditing.[38]

Considerations specific to public sector entities

Auditors of public sector entities may also have the ability pursuant to law or regulation to report publicly on certain matters, either in the auditor's report or in a supplementary report, which may include information that is consistent with the objectives of ISA 701. In such circumstances, the auditor may need to tailor certain aspects of the communication of key audit matters in the auditor's report required by ISA 701 or include a reference in the auditor's report to a description of the matter in the supplementary report.   **A75**

Auditor's Report for Audits Conducted in Accordance with Both Auditing Standards of a Specific Jurisdiction and International Standards on Auditing (Ref: Para. 51)

The auditor may refer in the auditor's report to the audit having been conducted in accordance with both International Standards on Auditing as well as the national auditing standards when, in addition to complying with the relevant national auditing standards, the auditor complies with each of the ISAs relevant to the audit.[39]   **A76**

A reference to both International Standards on Auditing and the national auditing standards is not appropriate if there is a conflict between the requirements in ISAs and those in the national auditing standards that would lead the auditor to form a different opinion or not to include an Emphasis of Matter or Other Matter paragraph that, in the particular circumstances, is required by ISAs. In such a case, the auditor's report refers only to the auditing standards (either International Standards on Auditing or the national auditing standards) in accordance with which the auditor's report has been prepared.   **A77**

ISAs (UK) are consistent with International Standards on Auditing as issued by the IAASB and the requirements of ISAs (UK) do not conflict with the requirements in ISAs. An audit conducted in accordance with ISAs (UK) does not therefore preclude the auditor from being able to assert compliance with International Standards on Auditing issued by the IAASB.   **A77-1**

Supplementary Information Presented with the Financial Statements (Ref: Para. 53–54)

In some circumstances, the entity may be required by law, regulation or standards, or may voluntarily choose, to present together with the financial statements supplementary information that is not required by the applicable financial reporting framework. For example, supplementary information might be presented to enhance a user's understanding of the applicable financial reporting framework or to provide further explanation of specific financial statement items. Such information is normally presented in either supplementary schedules or as additional notes.   **A78**

Paragraph 53 of this ISA (UK) explains that the auditor's opinion covers supplementary information that is an integral part of the financial statements because of its nature or how it is presented. This evaluation is a matter of professional judgment. To illustrate: **A79**

---

[38] *ISA 210, paragraph 21.*

[39] *ISA 200, paragraph A56.*

- When the notes to the financial statements include an explanation or the reconciliation of the extent to which the financial statements comply with another financial reporting framework, the auditor may consider this to be supplementary information that cannot be clearly differentiated from the financial statements. The auditor's opinion would also cover notes or supplementary schedules that are cross-referenced from the financial statements.

- When an additional profit and loss account that discloses specific items of expenditure is disclosed as a separate schedule included as an Appendix to the financial statements, the auditor may consider this to be supplementary information that can be clearly differentiated from the financial statements.

A80   Supplementary information that is covered by the auditor's opinion does not need to be specifically referred to in the auditor's report when the reference to the notes in the description of the statements that comprise the financial statements in the auditor's report is sufficient.

A81   Law or regulation may not require that the supplementary information be audited, and management may decide to ask the auditor not to include the supplementary information within the scope of the audit of the financial statements.

A82   The auditor's evaluation whether unaudited supplementary information is presented in a manner that could be construed as being covered by the auditor's opinion includes, for example, where that information is presented in relation to the financial statements and any audited supplementary information, and whether it is clearly labeled as "unaudited."

A83   Management could change the presentation of unaudited supplementary information that could be construed as being covered by the auditor's opinion, for example, by:

- Removing any cross-references from the financial statements to unaudited supplementary schedules or unaudited notes so that the demarcation between the audited and unaudited information is sufficiently clear.

- Placing the unaudited supplementary information outside of the financial statements or, if that is not possible in the circumstances, at a minimum placing the unaudited notes together at the end of the required notes to the financial statements and clearly labeling them as unaudited. Unaudited notes that are intermingled with the audited notes can be misinterpreted as being audited.

A84   The fact that supplementary information is unaudited does not relieve the auditor of the responsibilities described in ISA (UK) 720 (Revised June 2016).[40]

---

[40] *ISA (UK) 720 (Revised June 2016), The Auditor's Responsibilities Relating to Other Information.*

Appendix

(Ref: Para. A19)

Illustrations of Independent Auditor's Reports on Financial Statements

The examples in the Appendix have not been tailored for the UK. Illustrative auditor's reports tailored for use with audits conducted in accordance with ISAs (UK) are given in the current version of the FRC's Compendium of Illustrative Auditor's Reports.

- Illustration 1: An auditor's report on financial statements of a listed entity prepared in accordance with a fair presentation framework

- Illustration 2: An auditor's report on consolidated financial statements of a listed entity prepared in accordance with a fair presentation framework

- Illustration 3: An auditor's report on financial statements of an entity other than a listed entity prepared in accordance with a fair presentation framework (where reference is made to material that is located on a website of an appropriate authority)

- Illustration 4: An auditor's report on financial statements of an entity other than a listed entity prepared in accordance with a general purpose compliance framework

---

Illustration 1 – Auditor's Report on Financial Statements of a Listed Entity Prepared in Accordance with a Fair Presentation Framework

For purposes of this illustrative auditor's report, the following circumstances are assumed:

- Audit of a complete set of financial statements of a listed entity using a fair presentation framework. The audit is not a group audit (i.e., ISA 600 does not apply).
- The financial statements are prepared by management of the entity in accordance with IFRSs (a general purpose framework).
- The terms of the audit engagement reflect the description of management's responsibility for the financial statements in ISA 210.
- The auditor has concluded an unmodified (i.e., "clean") opinion is appropriate based on the audit evidence obtained.
- The relevant ethical requirements that apply to the audit comprise the International Ethics Standards Board for Accountants' *Code of Ethics for Professional Accountants* together with the ethical requirements relating to the audit in the jurisdiction, and the auditor refers to both.
- Based on the audit evidence obtained, the auditor has concluded that a material uncertainty does not exist related to events or conditions that may cast significant doubt on the entity's ability to continue as a going concern in accordance with ISA 570 (Revised).
- Key audit matters have been communicated in accordance with ISA 701.
- The auditor has obtained all of the other information prior to the date of the auditor's report and has not identified a material misstatement of the other information.

- Those responsible for oversight of the financial statements differ from those responsible for the preparation of the financial statements.
- In addition to the audit of the financial statements, the auditor has other reporting responsibilities required under local law.

INDEPENDENT AUDITOR'S REPORT

To the Shareholders of ABC Company [or Other Appropriate Addressee]

Report on the Audit of the Financial Statements[1-a]

Opinion

We have audited the financial statements of ABC Company (the Company), which comprise the statement of financial position as at December 31, 20X1, and the statement of comprehensive income, statement of changes in equity and statement of cash flows for the year then ended, and notes to the financial statements, including a summary of significant accounting policies.

In our opinion, the accompanying financial statements present fairly, in all material respects, (or *give a true and fair view of*) the financial position of the Company as at December 31, 20X1, and (*of*) its financial performance and its cash flows for the year then ended in accordance with International Financial Reporting Standards (IFRSs).

Basis for Opinion

We conducted our audit in accordance with International Standards on Auditing (ISAs). Our responsibilities under those standards are further described in the *Auditor's Responsibilities for the Audit of the Financial Statements* section of our report. We are independent of the Company in accordance with the International Ethics Standards Board for Accountants' *Code of Ethics for Professional Accountants (IESBA Code)* together with the ethical requirements that are relevant to our audit of the financial statements in [*jurisdiction*], and we have fulfilled our other ethical responsibilities in accordance with these requirements and the IESBA Code. We believe that the audit evidence we have obtained is sufficient and appropriate to provide a basis for our opinion.

Key Audit Matters

Key audit matters are those matters that, in our professional judgment, were of most significance in our audit of the financial statements of the current period. These matters were addressed in the context of our audit of the financial statements as a whole, and in forming our opinion thereon, and we do not provide a separate opinion on these matters.

[*Description of each key audit matter in accordance with ISA 701.*]

Other Information [or another title if appropriate such as "Information Other than the Financial Statements and Auditor's Report Thereon"]

[*Reporting in accordance with the reporting requirements in ISA 720 (Revised) – see Illustration 1 in Appendix 2 of ISA 720 (Revised).*]

[1-a] *The sub-title "Report on the Audit of the Financial Statements" is unnecessary in circumstances when the second sub-title "Report on Other Legal and Regulatory Requirements" is not applicable.*

Responsibilities of Management and Those Charged with Governance for the Financial Statements[2-a]

Management is responsible for the preparation and fair presentation of the financial statements in accordance with IFRSs,[3-a] and for such internal control as management determines is necessary to enable the preparation of financial statements that are free from material misstatement, whether due to fraud or error.

In preparing the financial statements, management is responsible for assessing the Company's ability to continue as a going concern, disclosing, as applicable, matters related to going concern and using the going concern basis of accounting unless management either intends to liquidate the Company or to cease operations, or has no realistic alternative but to do so.

Those charged with governance are responsible for overseeing the Company's financial reporting process.

Auditor's Responsibilities for the Audit of the Financial Statements

Our objectives are to obtain reasonable assurance about whether the financial statements as a whole are free from material misstatement, whether due to fraud or error, and to issue an auditor's report that includes our opinion. Reasonable assurance is a high level of assurance, but is not a guarantee that an audit conducted in accordance with ISAs will always detect a material misstatement when it exists. Misstatements can arise from fraud or error and are considered material if, individually or in the aggregate, they could reasonably be expected to influence the economic decisions of users taken on the basis of these financial statements.

Paragraph 41(b) of this ISA explains that the shaded material below can be located in an Appendix to the auditor's report. Paragraph 41(c) explains that when law, regulation or national auditing standards expressly permit, reference can be made to a website of an appropriate authority that contains the description of the auditor's responsibilities, rather than including this material in the auditor's report, provided that the description on the website addresses, and is not inconsistent with, the description of the auditor's responsibilities below.

As part of an audit in accordance with ISAs, we exercise professional judgment and maintain professional skepticism throughout the audit. We also:

- Identify and assess the risks of material misstatement of the financial statements, whether due to fraud or error, design and perform audit procedures responsive to those risks, and obtain audit evidence that is sufficient and appropriate to provide a basis for our opinion. The risk of not detecting a material misstatement resulting from fraud is higher than for one resulting from error, as fraud may involve collusion, forgery, intentional omissions, misrepresentations, or the override of internal control.

[2-a] *Throughout these illustrative auditor's reports, the terms management and those charged with governance may need to be replaced by another term that is appropriate in the context of the legal framework in the particular jurisdiction.*

[3-a] *Where management's responsibility is to prepare financial statements that give a true and fair view, this may read: "Management is responsible for the preparation of financial statements that give a true and fair view in accordance with International Financial Reporting Standards, and for such ..."*

- Obtain an understanding of internal control relevant to the audit in order to design audit procedures that are appropriate in the circumstances, but not for the purpose of expressing an opinion on the effectiveness of the Company's internal control.[4-a]

- Evaluate the appropriateness of accounting policies used and the reasonableness of accounting estimates and related disclosures made by management.

- Conclude on the appropriateness of management's use of the going concern basis of accounting and, based on the audit evidence obtained, whether a material uncertainty exists related to events or conditions that may cast significant doubt on the Company's ability to continue as a going concern. If we conclude that a material uncertainty exists, we are required to draw attention in our auditor's report to the related disclosures in the financial statements or, if such disclosures are inadequate, to modify our opinion. Our conclusions are based on the audit evidence obtained up to the date of our auditor's report. However, future events or conditions may cause the Company to cease to continue as a going concern.

- Evaluate the overall presentation, structure and content of the financial statements, including the disclosures, and whether the financial statements represent the underlying transactions and events in a manner that achieves fair presentation.

We communicate with those charged with governance regarding, among other matters, the planned scope and timing of the audit and significant audit findings, including any significant deficiencies in internal control that we identify during our audit.

We also provide those charged with governance with a statement that we have complied with relevant ethical requirements regarding independence, and to communicate with them all relationships and other matters that may reasonably be thought to bear on our independence, and where applicable, related safeguards.

From the matters communicated with those charged with governance, we determine those matters that were of most significance in the audit of the financial statements of the current period and are therefore the key audit matters. We describe these matters in our auditor's report unless law or regulation precludes public disclosure about the matter or when, in extremely rare circumstances, we determine that a matter should not be communicated in our report because the adverse consequences of doing so would reasonably be expected to outweigh the public interest benefits of such communication.

Report on Other Legal and Regulatory Requirements

[The form and content of this section of the auditor's report would vary depending on the nature of the auditor's other reporting responsibilities prescribed by local law, regulation, or national auditing standards. The matters addressed by other law, regulation or national auditing standards (referred to as "other reporting responsibilities") shall be addressed within this section unless the other reporting

---

[4-a] *This sentence would be modified, as appropriate, in circumstances when the auditor also has a responsibility to issue an opinion on the effectiveness of internal control in conjunction with the audit of the financial statements.*

responsibilities address the same topics as those presented under the reporting responsibilities required by the ISAs as part of the Report on the Audit of the Financial Statements section. The reporting of other reporting responsibilities that address the same topics as those required by the ISAs may be combined (i.e., included in the Report on the Audit of the Financial Statements section under the appropriate subheadings) provided that the wording in the auditor's report clearly differentiates the other reporting responsibilities from the reporting that is required by the ISAs where such a difference exists.

The engagement partner on the audit resulting in this independent auditor's report is [name].

[Signature in the name of the audit firm, the personal name of the auditor, or both, as appropriate for the particular jurisdiction]

[Auditor Address]

[Date]

Illustration 2 – Auditor's Report on Consolidated Financial Statements of a Listed Entity Prepared in Accordance with a Fair Presentation Framework

For purposes of this illustrative auditor's report, the following circumstances are assumed:

- Audit of a complete set of consolidated financial statements of a listed entity using a fair presentation framework. The audit is a group audit of an entity with subsidiaries (i.e., ISA 600 applies).
- The consolidated financial statements are prepared by management of the entity in accordance with IFRSs (a general purpose framework).
- The terms of the audit engagement reflect the description of management's responsibility for the consolidated financial statements in ISA 210.
- The auditor has concluded an unmodified (i.e., "clean") opinion is appropriate based on the audit evidence obtained.
- The International Ethics Standards Board for Accountants' *Code of Ethics for Professional Accountants* comprises all of the relevant ethical requirements that apply to the audit.
- Based on the audit evidence obtained, the auditor has concluded that a material uncertainty does not exist related to events or conditions that may cast significant doubt on the entity's ability to continue as a going concern in accordance with ISA 570 (Revised).
- Key audit matters have been communicated in accordance with ISA 701.
- The auditor has obtained all of the other information prior to the date of the auditor's report and has not identified a material misstatement of the other information.
- Those responsible for oversight of the consolidated financial statements differ from those responsible for the preparation of the consolidated financial statements.
- In addition to the audit of the consolidated financial statements, the auditor has other reporting responsibilities required under local law.

INDEPENDENT AUDITOR'S REPORT

To the Shareholders of ABC Company [or Other Appropriate Addressee]

Report on the Audit of the Consolidated Financial Statements[5-a]

Opinion

We have audited the consolidated financial statements of ABC Company and its subsidiaries (the Group), which comprise the consolidated statement of financial position as at December 31, 20X1, and the consolidated statement of comprehensive income, consolidated statement of changes in equity and consolidated statement of cash flows for the year then ended, and notes to the consolidated financial statements, including a summary of significant accounting policies.

In our opinion, the accompanying consolidated financial statements present fairly, in all material respects, (or *give a true and fair view of*) the consolidated financial position of the Group as at December 31, 20X1, and (*of*) its consolidated financial performance and its consolidated cash flows for the year then ended in accordance with International Financial Reporting Standards (IFRSs).

Basis for Opinion

We conducted our audit in accordance with International Standards on Auditing (ISAs). Our responsibilities under those standards are further described in the *Auditor's Responsibilities for the Audit of the Consolidated Financial Statements* section of our report. We are independent of the Group in accordance with the International Ethics Standards Board for Accountants' *Code of Ethics for Professional Accountants* (IESBA Code), and we have fulfilled our other ethical responsibilities in accordance with the IESBA Code. We believe that the audit evidence we have obtained is sufficient and appropriate to provide a basis for our opinion.

Key Audit Matters

Key audit matters are those matters that, in our professional judgment, were of most significance in our audit of the consolidated financial statements of the current period. These matters were addressed in the context of our audit of the consolidated financial statements as a whole, and in forming our opinion thereon, and we do not provide a separate opinion on these matters.

[*Description of each key audit matter in accordance with ISA 701.*]

Other Information [or another title if appropriate such as "Information Other than the Financial Statements and Auditor's Report Thereon"]

[*Reporting in accordance with the reporting requirements in ISA 720 (Revised) – see Illustration 1 in Appendix 2 of ISA 720 (Revised).*]

[5-a] *The sub-title "Report on the Audit of the Consolidated Financial Statements" is unnecessary in circumstances when the second sub-title "Report on Other Legal and Regulatory Requirements" is not applicable.*

Responsibilities of Management and Those Charged with Governance for the Consolidated Financial Statements[6-a]

Management is responsible for the preparation and fair presentation of the consolidated financial statements in accordance with IFRSs,[7-a] and for such internal control as management determines is necessary to enable the preparation of consolidated financial statements that are free from material misstatement, whether due to fraud or error.

In preparing the consolidated financial statements, management is responsible for assessing the Group's ability to continue as a going concern, disclosing, as applicable, matters related to going concern and using the going concern basis of accounting unless management either intends to liquidate the Group or to cease operations, or has no realistic alternative but to do so.

Those charged with governance are responsible for overseeing the Group's financial reporting process.

Auditor's Responsibilities for the Audit of the Consolidated Financial Statements

Our objectives are to obtain reasonable assurance about whether the consolidated financial statements as a whole are free from material misstatement, whether due to fraud or error, and to issue an auditor's report that includes our opinion. Reasonable assurance is a high level of assurance, but is not a guarantee that an audit conducted in accordance with ISAs will always detect a material misstatement when it exists. Misstatements can arise from fraud or error and are considered material if, individually or in the aggregate, they could reasonably be expected to influence the economic decisions of users taken on the basis of these consolidated financial statements.

Paragraph 41(b) of this ISA explains that the shaded material below can be located in an Appendix to the auditor's report. Paragraph 41(c) explains that when law, regulation or national auditing standards expressly permit, reference can be made to a website of an appropriate authority that contains the description of the auditor's responsibilities, rather than including this material in the auditor's report, provided that the description on the website addresses, and is not inconsistent with, the description of the auditor's responsibilities below.

As part of an audit in accordance with ISAs, we exercise professional judgment and maintain professional skepticism throughout the audit. We also:

- Identify and assess the risks of material misstatement of the consolidated financial statements, whether due to fraud or error, design and perform audit procedures responsive to those risks, and obtain audit evidence that is sufficient and appropriate to provide a basis for our opinion. The risk of not detecting a material misstatement resulting from fraud is higher than for one resulting from error, as fraud may involve collusion, forgery, intentional omissions, misrepresentations, or the override of internal control.

[6-a] *Or other terms that are appropriate in the context of the legal framework of the particular jurisdiction.*

[7-a] *Where management's responsibility is to prepare financial statements that give a true and fair view, this may read: "Management is responsible for the preparation of financial statements that give a true and fair view in accordance with International Financial Reporting Standards, and for such ..."*

- Obtain an understanding of internal control relevant to the audit in order to design audit procedures that are appropriate in the circumstances, but not for the purpose of expressing an opinion on the effectiveness of the Group's internal control.[8-a]

- Evaluate the appropriateness of accounting policies used and the reasonableness of accounting estimates and related disclosures made by management.

- Conclude on the appropriateness of management's use of the going concern basis of accounting and, based on the audit evidence obtained, whether a material uncertainty exists related to events or conditions that may cast significant doubt on the Group's ability to continue as a going concern. If we conclude that a material uncertainty exists, we are required to draw attention in our auditor's report to the related disclosures in the consolidated financial statements or, if such disclosures are inadequate, to modify our opinion. Our conclusions are based on the audit evidence obtained up to the date of our auditor's report. However, future events or conditions may cause the Group to cease to continue as a going concern.

- Evaluate the overall presentation, structure and content of the consolidated financial statements, including the disclosures, and whether the consolidated financial statements represent the underlying transactions and events in a manner that achieves fair presentation.

- Obtain sufficient appropriate audit evidence regarding the financial information of the entities or business activities within the Group to express an opinion on the consolidated financial statements. We are responsible for the direction, supervision and performance of the group audit. We remain solely responsible for our audit opinion.

We communicate with those charged with governance regarding, among other matters, the planned scope and timing of the audit and significant audit findings, including any significant deficiencies in internal control that we identify during our audit.

We also provide those charged with governance with a statement that we have complied with relevant ethical requirements regarding independence, and to communicate with them all relationships and other matters that may reasonably be thought to bear on our independence, and where applicable, related safeguards.

From the matters communicated with those charged with governance, we determine those matters that were of most significance in the audit of the consolidated financial statements of the current period and are therefore the key audit matters. We describe these matters in our auditor's report unless law or regulation precludes public disclosure about the matter or when, in extremely rare circumstances, we determine that a matter should not be communicated in our report because the adverse consequences of doing so would reasonably be expected to outweigh the public interest benefits of such communication.

[8-a] *This sentence would be modified, as appropriate, in circumstances when the auditor also has a responsibility to issue an opinion on the effectiveness of internal control in conjunction with the audit of the consolidated financial statements.*

Report on Other Legal and Regulatory Requirements

[*The form and content of this section of the auditor's report would vary depending on the nature of the auditor's other reporting responsibilities prescribed by local law, regulation, or national auditing standards. The matters addressed by other law, regulation or national auditing standards (referred to as "other reporting responsibilities") shall be addressed within this section unless the other reporting responsibilities address the same topics as those presented under the reporting responsibilities required by the ISAs as part of the Report on the Audit of the Consolidated Financial Statements section. The reporting of other reporting responsibilities that address the same topics as those required by the ISAs may be combined (i.e., included in the Report on the Audit of the Consolidated Financial Statements section under the appropriate subheadings) provided that the wording in the auditor's report clearly differentiates the other reporting responsibilities from the reporting that is required by the ISAs where such a difference exists.*]

The engagement partner on the audit resulting in this independent auditor's report is [*name*].

[*Signature in the name of the audit firm, the personal name of the auditor, or both, as appropriate for the particular jurisdiction*]

[*Auditor Address*]

[*Date*]

Illustration 3 – Auditor's Report on Financial Statements of an Entity Other than a Listed Entity Prepared in Accordance with a Fair Presentation Framework

For purposes of this illustrative auditor's report, the following circumstances are assumed:

- Audit of a complete set of financial statements of an entity other than a listed entity using a fair presentation framework. The audit is not a group audit (i.e., ISA 600 does not apply).
- The financial statements are prepared by management of the entity in accordance with IFRSs (a general purpose framework).
- The terms of the audit engagement reflect the description of management's responsibility for the financial statements in ISA 210.
- The auditor has concluded an unmodified (i.e., "clean") opinion is appropriate based on the audit evidence obtained.
- The relevant ethical requirements that apply to the audit are those of the jurisdiction.
- Based on the audit evidence obtained, the auditor has concluded that a material uncertainty does not exist related to events or conditions that may cast significant doubt on the entity's ability to continue as a going concern in accordance with ISA 570 (Revised).
- The auditor is not required, and has otherwise not decided, to communicate key audit matters in accordance with ISA 701.
- The auditor has obtained all of the other information prior to the date of the auditor's report and has not identified a material misstatement of the other information.
- Those responsible for oversight of the financial statements differ from those responsible for the preparation of the financial statements.

- The auditor has no other reporting responsibilities required under local law.
- The auditor elects to refer to the description of the auditor's responsibility included on a website of an appropriate authority.

INDEPENDENT AUDITOR'S REPORT

To the Shareholders of ABC Company [or Other Appropriate Addressee]

Opinion

We have audited the financial statements of ABC Company (the Company), which comprise the statement of financial position as at December 31, 20X1, and the statement of comprehensive income, statement of changes in equity and statement of cash flows for the year then ended, and notes to the financial statements, including a summary of significant accounting policies.

In our opinion, the accompanying financial statements present fairly, in all material respects, (or *give a true and fair view of*) the financial position of the Company as at December 31, 20X1, and (*of*) its financial performance and its cash flows for the year then ended in accordance with International Financial Reporting Standards (IFRSs).

Basis for Opinion

We conducted our audit in accordance with International Standards on Auditing (ISAs). Our responsibilities under those standards are further described in the *Auditor's Responsibilities for the Audit of the Financial Statements* section of our report. We are independent of the Company in accordance with the ethical requirements that are relevant to our audit of the financial statements in [*jurisdiction*], and we have fulfilled our other ethical responsibilities in accordance with these requirements. We believe that the audit evidence we have obtained is sufficient and appropriate to provide a basis for our opinion.

Other Information [or another title if appropriate such as "Information Other than the Financial Statements and Auditor's Report Thereon"]

[*Reporting in accordance with the reporting requirements in ISA 720 (Revised) – see Illustration 1 in Appendix 2 of ISA 720 (Revised).*]

Responsibilities of Management and Those Charged with Governance for the Financial Statements[9-a]

Management is responsible for the preparation and fair presentation of the financial statements in accordance with IFRSs,[10-a] and for such internal control as management determines is necessary to enable the preparation of financial statements that are free from material misstatement, whether due to fraud or error.

In preparing the financial statements, management is responsible for assessing the Company's ability to continue as a going concern, disclosing, as applicable, matters related to going concern and using the going concern basis of accounting

---

[9-a] *Or other terms that are appropriate in the context of the legal framework of the particular jurisdiction.*

[10-a] *Where management's responsibility is to prepare financial statements that give a true and fair view, this may read: "Management is responsible for the preparation of financial statements that give a true and fair view in accordance with International Financial Reporting Standards, and for such ..."*

unless management either intends to liquidate the Company or to cease operations, or has no realistic alternative but to do so.

Those charged with governance are responsible for overseeing the Company's financial reporting process.

Auditor's Responsibilities for the Audit of the Financial Statements

Our objectives are to obtain reasonable assurance about whether the financial statements as a whole are free from material misstatement, whether due to fraud or error, and to issue an auditor's report that includes our opinion. Reasonable assurance is a high level of assurance, but is not a guarantee that an audit conducted in accordance with ISAs will always detect a material misstatement when it exists. Misstatements can arise from fraud or error and are considered material if, individually or in the aggregate, they could reasonably be expected to influence the economic decisions of users taken on the basis of these financial statements.

A further description of the auditor's responsibilities for the audit of the financial is located at [*Organization's*] website at: [*website link*]. This description forms part of our auditor's report.

[*Signature in the name of the audit firm, the personal name of the auditor, or both, as appropriate for the particular jurisdiction*]

[*Auditor Address*]

[*Date*]

Illustration 4 – Auditor's Report on Financial Statements of an Entity Other than a Listed Entity Prepared in Accordance with a General Purpose Compliance Framework

For purposes of this illustrative auditor's report, the following circumstances are assumed:

- Audit of a complete set of financial statements of an entity other than a listed entity required by law or regulation. The audit is not a group audit (i.e., ISA 600 does not apply).
- The financial statements are prepared by management of the entity in accordance with the Financial Reporting Framework (XYZ Law) of Jurisdiction X (that is, a financial reporting framework, encompassing law or regulation, designed to meet the common financial information needs of a wide range of users, but which is not a fair presentation framework).
- The terms of the audit engagement reflect the description of management's responsibility for the financial statements in ISA 210.
- The auditor has concluded an unmodified (i.e., "clean") opinion is appropriate based on the audit evidence obtained.
- The relevant ethical requirements that apply to the audit are those of the jurisdiction.
- Based on the audit evidence obtained, the auditor has concluded that a material uncertainty does not exist related to events or conditions that may cast significant doubt on the entity's ability to continue as a going concern in accordance with ISA 570 (Revised).

- The auditor is not required, and has otherwise not decided, to communicate key audit matters in accordance with ISA 701.
- The auditor has obtained all of the other information prior to the date of the auditor's report and has not identified a material misstatement of the other information.
- Those responsible for oversight of the financial statements differ from those responsible for the preparation of the financial statements.
- The auditor has no other reporting responsibilities required under local law.

INDEPENDENT AUDITOR'S REPORT

[Appropriate Addressee]

Opinion

We have audited the financial statements of ABC Company (the Company), which comprise the balance sheet as at December 31, 20X1, and the income statement, statement of changes in equity and cash flow statement for the year then ended, and notes to the financial statements, including a summary of significant accounting policies.

In our opinion, the accompanying financial statements of the Company are prepared, in all material respects, in accordance with XYZ Law of Jurisdiction X.

Basis for Opinion

We conducted our audit in accordance with International Standards on Auditing (ISAs). Our responsibilities under those standards are further described in the *Auditor's Responsibilities for the Audit of the Financial Statements* section of our report. We are independent of the Company in accordance with the ethical requirements that are relevant to our audit of the financial statements in [*jurisdiction*], and we have fulfilled our other responsibilities in accordance with these requirements. We believe that the audit evidence we have obtained is sufficient and appropriate to provide a basis for our opinion.

Other Information [or another title if appropriate such as "Information Other than the Financial Statements and Auditor's Report Thereon"]

[*Reporting in accordance with the reporting requirements in ISA 720 (Revised) – see Illustration 1 in Appendix 2 of ISA 720 (Revised).*]

Responsibilities of Management and Those Charged with Governance for the Financial Statements[11-a]

Management is responsible for the preparation of the financial statements in accordance with XYZ Law of Jurisdiction X,[12-a] and for such internal control as management determines is necessary to enable the preparation of financial statements that are free from material misstatement, whether due to fraud or error.

[11-a] *Or other terms that are appropriate in the context of the legal framework of the particular jurisdiction.*

[12-a] *Where management's responsibility is to prepare financial statements that give a true and fair view, this may read: "Management is responsible for the preparation of financial statements that give a true and fair view in accordance with International Financial Reporting Standards, and for such ..."*

In preparing the financial statements, management is responsible for assessing the Company's ability to continue as a going concern, disclosing, as applicable, matters related to going concern and using the going concern basis of accounting unless management either intends to liquidate the Company or to cease operations, or has no realistic alternative but to do so.

Those charged with governance are responsible for overseeing the Company's financial reporting process.

Auditor's Responsibilities for the Audit of the Financial Statements

Our objectives are to obtain reasonable assurance about whether the financial statements as a whole are free from material misstatement, whether due to fraud or error, and to issue an auditor's report that includes our opinion. Reasonable assurance is a high level of assurance, but is not a guarantee that an audit conducted in accordance with ISAs will always detect a material misstatement when it exists. Misstatements can arise from fraud or error and are considered material if, individually or in the aggregate, they could reasonably be expected to influence the economic decisions of users taken on the basis of these financial statements.

Paragraph 41(b) of this ISA explains that the shaded material below can be located in an Appendix to the auditor's report. Paragraph 41(c) explains that when law, regulation or national auditing standards expressly permit, reference can be made to a website of an appropriate authority that contains the description of the auditor's responsibilities, rather than including this material in the auditor's report, provided that the description on the website addresses, and is not inconsistent with, the description of the auditor's responsibilities below.

As part of an audit in accordance with ISAs, we exercise professional judgment and maintain professional skepticism throughout the audit. We also:

- Identify and assess the risks of material misstatement of the financial statements, whether due to fraud or error, design and perform audit procedures responsive to those risks, and obtain audit evidence that is sufficient and appropriate to provide a basis for our opinion. The risk of not detecting a material misstatement resulting from fraud is higher than for one resulting from error, as fraud may involve collusion, forgery, intentional omissions, misrepresentations, or the override of internal control.

- Obtain an understanding of internal control relevant to the audit in order to design audit procedures that are appropriate in the circumstances, but not for the purpose of expressing an opinion on the effectiveness of the Company's internal control.[13-a]

- Evaluate the appropriateness of accounting policies used and the reasonableness of accounting estimates and related disclosures made by management.

- Conclude on the appropriateness of management's use of the going concern basis of accounting and, based on the audit evidence obtained, whether a material uncertainty exists related to events or conditions that

---

[13-a] *This sentence would be modified, as appropriate, in circumstances when the auditor also has responsibility to issue an opinion on the effectiveness of internal control in conjunction with the audit of the financial statements.*

may cast significant doubt on the Company's ability to continue as a going concern. If we conclude that a material uncertainty exists, we are required to draw attention in our auditor's report to the related disclosures in the financial statements or, if such disclosures are inadequate, to modify our opinion. Our conclusions are based on the audit evidence obtained up to the date of our auditor's report. However, future events or conditions may cause the Company to cease to continue as a going concern.

We communicate with those charged with governance regarding, among other matters, the planned scope and timing of the audit and significant audit findings, including any significant deficiencies in internal control that we identify during our audit.

[Signature in the name of the audit firm, the personal name of the auditor, or both, as appropriate for the particular jurisdiction]

[Auditor Address]

[Date]

ISA (UK) 701 Communicating Key Audit Matters in the Independent Auditor's Report

(Effective for audits of financial statements for periods commencing on or after 17 June 2016)

Contents

Paragraphs

Introduction
Scope of this ISA (UK)   1 - 5
Effective Date   6

Objectives   7

Definitions   8

Requirements
Determining Key Audit Matters   9 - 10
Communicating Key Audit Matters   11 - 16
Communicating Other Audit Planning and Scoping Matters   16-1
Communicating Key Audit Matters and Other Audit Planning and Scoping Matters   16-2
Communication with Those Charged with Governance   17
Documentation   18

Application and Other Explanatory Material
Scope of this ISA (UK) (Ref: Para. 2)   A1 - A8
Definition   A8-1
Determining Key Audit Matters (Ref: Para. 9–10)   A9 - A30
Communicating Key Audit Matters   A31 - A59
Communicating Other Audit Planning and Scoping Matters   A59-1 - A59-2
Communication with Those Charged with Governance   A60 - A63
Documentation (Ref: Para. 18)   A64

International Standard on Auditing (UK) (ISA (UK)) 701, *Communicating Key Audit Matters in the Independent Auditor's Report*, should be read in conjunction with ISA (UK) 200 (Revised June 2016), *Overall Objectives of the Independent Auditor and the Conduct of an Audit in Accordance with International Standards on Auditing (UK)*.

Introduction

Scope of this ISA (UK)

1   This International Standard on Auditing (UK) (ISA (UK)) deals with the auditor's responsibility to communicate key audit matters in the auditor's report. It is intended to address both the auditor's judgment as to what to communicate in the auditor's report and the form and content of such communication.

1-1   This ISA (UK) also deals with the auditor's responsibility to communicate other audit planning and scoping matters in the auditor's report.

2   The purpose of communicating key audit matters is to enhance the communicative value of the auditor's report by providing greater transparency about the audit that was performed. Communicating key audit matters provides additional information to intended users of the financial statements ("intended users") to assist them in understanding those matters that, in the auditor's professional judgment, were of most significance in the audit of the financial statements of the current period. Communicating key audit matters may also assist intended users in understanding the entity and areas of significant management judgment in the audited financial statements. (Ref: Para. A1–A4)

3   The communication of key audit matters in the auditor's report may also provide intended users a basis to further engage with management and those charged with governance about certain matters relating to the entity, the audited financial statements, or the audit that was performed.

4   Communicating key audit matters in the auditor's report is in the context of the auditor having formed an opinion on the financial statements as a whole. Communicating key audit matters in the auditor's report is not:

(a)   A substitute for disclosures in the financial statements that the applicable financial reporting framework requires management to make, or that are otherwise necessary to achieve fair presentation;

(b)   A substitute for the auditor expressing a modified opinion when required by the circumstances of a specific audit engagement in accordance with ISA (UK) 705 (Revised June 2016);[1]

(c)   A substitute for reporting in accordance with ISA (UK) 570 (Revised June 2016)[2] when a material uncertainty exists relating to events or conditions that may cast significant doubt on an entity's ability to continue as a going concern; or

(d)   A separate opinion on individual matters. (Ref: Para. A5–A8)

5   This ISA (UK) applies to audits of complete sets of general purpose financial statements of listed entities and circumstances when the auditor otherwise decides to communicate key audit matters in the auditor's report. This ISA (UK) also applies when the auditor is required by law or regulation to communicate key audit matters in the auditor's report.[3] However, ISA (UK) 705 (Revised June 2016) prohibits the auditor from communicating key audit matters when the auditor disclaims an opinion on the financial statements, unless such reporting is required by law or regulation.[4]

---

[1]   *ISA (UK) 705 (Revised June 2016), Modifications to the Opinion in the Independent Auditor's Report.*

[2]   *ISA (UK) 570 (Revised June 2016), Going Concern, paragraphs 22–23.*

[3]   *ISA (UK) 700 (Revised June 2016), Forming an Opinion and Reporting on Financial Statements, paragraphs 30–31.*

[4]   *ISA (UK) 705 (Revised June 2016), paragraph 29.*

This ISA (UK) also applies to audits of complete sets of general purpose financial statements of other public interest entities and entities that are required, and those that choose voluntarily, to report on how they have applied the UK Corporate Governance Code.

Effective Date

This ISA (UK) is effective for audits of financial statements for periods 6 commencing on or after 17 June 2016. Earlier adoption is permitted.

Objectives

The objectives of the auditor are to determine key audit matters and, having 7 formed an opinion on the financial statements, communicate those matters by describing them in the auditor's report.

Definitions

For purposes of the ISAs (UK), the following term has the meaning attributed 8 below:

Key audit matters—Those matters that, in the auditor's professional judgment, were of most significance in the audit of the financial statements of the current period. Key audit matters are selected from matters communicated with those charged with governance. (Ref: Para. A8-1)

Requirements

Determining Key Audit Matters

The auditor shall determine, from the matters communicated with those charged 9 with governance, those matters that required significant auditor attention in performing the audit. In making this determination, the auditor shall take into account the following: (Ref: Para. A9–A18)

(a) Areas of higher assessed risk of material misstatement, or significant risks identified in accordance with ISA (UK) 315 (Revised June 2016).[5] (Ref: Para. A19–A22)

(b) Significant auditor judgments relating to areas in the financial statements that involved significant management judgment, including accounting estimates that have been identified as having high estimation uncertainty. (Ref: Para. A23–A24)

(c) The effect on the audit of significant events or transactions that occurred during the period. (Ref: Para. A25–A26)

The auditor shall determine which of the matters determined in accordance 10 with paragraph 9 were of most significance in the audit of the financial statements of the current period and therefore are the key audit matters. (Ref: Para. A9–A11, A27–A30)

---

[5] *ISA (UK) 315 (Revised June 2016), Identifying and Assessing the Risks of Material Misstatement through Understanding the Entity and Its Environment.*

Communicating Key Audit Matters

11   The auditor shall describe each key audit matter, using an appropriate subheading, in a separate section of the auditor's report under the heading "Key Audit Matters," unless the circumstances in paragraphs 14 or 15 apply. The introductory language in this section of the auditor's report shall state that:

(a)   Key audit matters are those matters that, in the auditor's professional judgment, were of most significance in the audit of the financial statements [of the current period] and include the most significant assessed risks of material misstatement (whether or not due to fraud) identified by the auditor, including those which had the greatest effect on: the overall audit strategy; the allocation of resources in the audit; and directing the efforts of the engagement team; and

(b)   These matters were addressed in the context of the audit of the financial statements as a whole, and in forming the auditor's opinion thereon, and the auditor does not provide a separate opinion on these matters. (Ref: Para. A31–A33)

Key Audit Matters Not a Substitute for Expressing a Modified Opinion

12   The auditor shall not communicate a matter in the Key Audit Matters section of the auditor's report when the auditor would be required to modify the opinion in accordance with ISA (UK) 705 (Revised June 2016) as a result of the matter. (Ref: Para. A5)

Descriptions of Individual Key Audit Matters

13   The description of each key audit matter in the Key Audit Matters section of the auditor's report shall include a reference to the related disclosure(s), if any, in the financial statements and shall address: (Ref: Para. A33-1–A41)

(a)   Why the matter was considered to be one of most significance in the audit and therefore determined to be a key audit matter; and (Ref: Para. A42–A45)

(b)   How the matter was addressed in the audit. (Ref: Para. A46–A51)

13R-1   For audits of financial statements of public interest entities, in describing each of the key audit matters in accordance with paragraph 13, the auditor's report shall provide, in support of the audit opinion:

(a)   A description of the most significant assessed risks of material misstatement, (whether or not due to fraud);

(b)   A summary of the auditor's response to those risks; and

(c)   Where relevant, key observations arising with respect to those risks.

Where relevant to the above information provided in the auditor's report concerning each of the most significant assessed risks of material misstatement (whether or not due to fraud), the auditor's report shall include a clear reference to the relevant disclosures in the financial statements.

13-2   In describing why the matter was determined to be a key audit matter in accordance with paragraph 13(a), the description shall indicate that the matter was one of the most significant assessed risks of material misstatement (whether or not due to fraud) identified by the auditor.

Circumstances in Which a Matter Determined to Be a Key Audit Matter Is Not Communicated in the Auditor's Report

The auditor shall describe each key audit matter in the auditor's report unless: **14**
(Ref: Para. A53–A56)

(a) Law or regulation precludes public disclosure about the matter; or (Ref: Para. A52)

(b) In extremely rare circumstances, the auditor determines that the matter should not be communicated in the auditor's report because the adverse consequences of doing so would reasonably be expected to outweigh the public interest benefits of such communication. This shall not apply if the entity has publicly disclosed information about the matter.

Interaction between Descriptions of Key Audit Matters and Other Elements Required to Be Included in the Auditor's Report

A matter giving rise to a modified opinion in accordance with ISA (UK) 705   **15**
(Revised June 2016), or a material uncertainty related to events or conditions that may cast significant doubt on the entity's ability to continue as a going concern in accordance with ISA (UK) 570 (Revised June 2016), are by their nature key audit matters. However, in such circumstances, these matters shall not be described in the Key Audit Matters section of the auditor's report and the requirements in paragraphs 13–14 do not apply. Rather, the auditor shall:

(a) Report on these matter(s) in accordance with the applicable ISA(s) (UK); and

(b) Include a reference to the Basis for Qualified (Adverse) Opinion or the Material Uncertainty Related to Going Concern section(s) in the Key Audit Matters section. (Ref: Para. A6–A7)

Form and Content of the Key Audit Matters Section in Other Circumstances

If the auditor determines, depending on the facts and circumstances of the entity   **16**
and the audit, that there are no key audit matters to communicate or that the only key audit matters communicated are those matters addressed by paragraph 15, the auditor shall include a statement to this effect in a separate section of the auditor's report under the heading "Key Audit Matters." (Ref: Para. A57–A59)

Communicating Other Audit Planning and Scoping Matters

The auditor's report shall provide: **16-1**

(a) An explanation of how the auditor applied the concept of materiality in planning and performing the audit. Such explanation shall specify the threshold used by the auditor as being materiality for the financial statements as a whole;[5a] and (Ref: Para. A59-1)

(b) An overview of the scope of the audit,[5b] including an explanation of how such scope:

[5a] *As required by paragraph 10 of ISA (UK) 320 (Revised June 2016), Materiality in Planning and Performing an Audit.*

[5b] *See also paragraphs 15 and A11 to A16 of ISA (UK) 260 (Revised June 2016), Communication with Those Charged with Governance and paragraph 49 of ISA (UK) 600 (Revised June 2016), Special considerations – Audits of Group Financial Statements (Including the Work of Component Auditors).*

(i)   Addressed each Key Audit Matter relating to one of the most significant risks of material misstatement disclosed in accordance with paragraph 13(b); and

(ii) Was influenced by the auditor's application of materiality disclosed in accordance with paragraph 16-1(a). (Ref: Para. A59-2)

Communicating Key Audit Matters and Other Audit Planning and Scoping Matters

16-2   In order to be useful to users of the financial statements, the explanations of the matters required to be set out in the auditor's report in paragraphs 13 and 16-1 shall be described:

(a)   So as to enable a user to understand their significance in the context of the audit of the financial statements as a whole and not as discrete opinions on separate elements of the financial statements;

(b)   In a way that enables them to be related directly to the specific circumstances of the entity and are not, therefore, generic or abstract matters expressed in standardized language; and

(c)   In the case of entities that are required, and those that choose voluntarily, to report on how they have applied the UK Corporate Governance Code, or to explain why they have not, in a manner that complements the description of significant issues relating to the financial statements, required to be set out in the separate section of the annual report describing the work of the audit committee in discharging its responsibilities.[5c] The auditor seeks to coordinate descriptions of overlapping topics addressed in these communications, to avoid duplication of reporting about them, whilst having appropriate regard to the separate responsibilities of the auditor and the board for directly communicating information primarily in their respective domains.

Communication with Those Charged with Governance

17   The auditor shall communicate with those charged with governance:

(a)   Those matters the auditor has determined to be the key audit matters; or

(b)   If applicable, depending on the facts and circumstances of the entity and the audit, the auditor's determination that there are no key audit matters to communicate in the auditor's report. (Ref: Para. A60–A63)

Documentation

18   The auditor shall include in the audit documentation:[6] (Ref: Para. A64)

(a)   The matters that required significant auditor attention as determined in accordance with paragraph 9, and the rationale for the auditor's determination as to whether or not each of these matters is a key audit matter in accordance with paragraph 10;

[5c] *In accordance with provision C.3.8 of the UK Corporate Governance Code.*

[6] *ISA (UK) 230 (Revised June 2016), "Audit Documentation,"paragraphs 8–11 and A6.*

(b)   Where applicable, the rationale for the auditor's determination that there are no key audit matters to communicate in the auditor's report or that the only key audit matters to communicate are those matters addressed by paragraph 15; and

(c)   Where applicable, the rationale for the auditor's determination not to communicate in the auditor's report a matter determined to be a key audit matter.

Application and Other Explanatory Material

Scope of this ISA (UK)
(Ref: Para. 2)

Significance can be described as the relative importance of a matter, taken in context. The significance of a matter is judged by the auditor in the context in which it is being considered. Significance can be considered in the context of quantitative and qualitative factors, such as relative magnitude, the nature and effect on the subject matter and the expressed interests of intended users or recipients. This involves an objective analysis of the facts and circumstances, including the nature and extent of communication with those charged with governance.   **A1**

Users of financial statements have expressed an interest in those matters about which the auditor had the most robust dialogue with those charged with governance as part of the two-way communication required by ISA (UK) 260 (Revised June 2016)[7] and have called for additional transparency about those communications. For example, users have expressed particular interest in understanding significant judgments made by the auditor in forming the opinion on the financial statements as a whole, because they are often related to the areas of significant management judgment in preparing the financial statements.   **A2**

Requiring auditors to communicate key audit matters in the auditor's report may also enhance communications between the auditor and those charged with governance about those matters, and may increase attention by management and those charged with governance to the disclosures in the financial statements to which reference is made in the auditor's report.   **A3**

ISA (UK) 320 (Revised June 2016)[8] explains that it is reasonable for the auditor to assume that users of the financial statements: **A4**

(a)   Have a reasonable knowledge of business and economic activities and accounting and a willingness to study the information in the financial statements with reasonable diligence;

(b)   Understand that the financial statements are prepared, presented and audited to levels of materiality;

(c)   Recognize the uncertainties inherent in the measurement of amounts based on the use of estimates, judgment and the consideration of future events; and

(d)   Make reasonable economic decisions on the basis of the information in the financial statements.

---

[7] *ISA (UK) 260 (Revised June 2016), Communication with Those Charged with Governance.*

[8] *ISA (UK) 320 (Revised June 2016), Materiality in Planning and Performing the Audit, paragraph 4.*

Because the auditor's report accompanies the audited financial statements, the users of the auditor's report are considered to be the same as the intended users of the financial statements.

Relationship between Key Audit Matters, the Auditor's Opinion and Other Elements of the Auditor's Report
(Ref: Para. 4, 12, 15)

A5 ISA (UK) 700 (Revised June 2016) establishes requirements and provides guidance on forming an opinion on the financial statements.[9] Communicating key audit matters is not a substitute for disclosures in the financial statements that the applicable financial reporting framework requires management to make, or that are otherwise necessary to achieve fair presentation. ISA (UK) 705 (Revised June 2016) addresses circumstances in which the auditor concludes that there is a material misstatement relating to the appropriateness or adequacy of disclosures in the financial statements.[10]

A6 When the auditor expresses a qualified or adverse opinion in accordance with ISA (UK) 705 (Revised June 2016), presenting the description of a matter giving rise to a modified opinion in the Basis for Qualified (Adverse) Opinion section helps to promote intended users' understanding and to identify such circumstances when they occur. Separating the communication of this matter from other key audit matters described in the Key Audit Matters section therefore gives it the appropriate prominence in the auditor's report (see paragraph 15). The Appendix in ISA (UK) 705 (Revised June 2016) includes illustrative examples of how the introductory language in the Key Audit Matters section is affected when the auditor expresses a qualified or adverse opinion and other key audit matters are communicated in the auditor's report. Paragraph A58 of this ISA (UK) illustrates how the Key Audit Matters section is presented when the auditor has determined that there are no other key audit matters to be communicated in the auditor's report beyond matters addressed in the Basis for Qualified (Adverse) Opinion section or Material Uncertainty Related to Going Concern section of the auditor's report.

A7 When the auditor expresses a qualified or adverse opinion, communicating other key audit matters would still be relevant to enhancing intended users' understanding of the audit, and therefore the requirements to determine key audit matters apply. However, as an adverse opinion is expressed in circumstances when the auditor has concluded that misstatements, individually or in the aggregate, are both material and pervasive to the financial statements:[11]

- Depending on the significance of the matter(s) giving rise to an adverse opinion, the auditor may determine that no other matters are key audit matters. In such circumstances, the requirement in paragraph 15 applies (see paragraph A58).

- If one or more matters other than the matter(s) giving rise to an adverse opinion are determined to be key audit matters, it is particularly important that the descriptions of such other key audit matters do not imply that the financial statements as a whole are more credible in relation to those matters than would be appropriate in the circumstances, in view of the adverse opinion (see paragraph A47).

---

[9] *ISA (UK) 700 (Revised June 2016), paragraphs 10–15 and A1–A10.*

[10] *See paragraph A7 of ISA (UK) 705 (Revised June 2016).*

[11] *ISA (UK) 705 (Revised June 2016), paragraph 8.*

ISA (UK) 706 (Revised June 2016)[12] establishes mechanisms for auditors of **A8**
financial statements of all entities to include additional communication in the
auditor's report through the use of Emphasis of Matter paragraphs and Other
Matter paragraphs when the auditor considers it necessary to do so. In such cases,
these paragraphs are presented separately from the Key Audit Matters section in
the auditor's report. When a matter has been determined to be a key audit matter,
the use of such paragraphs is not a substitute for the description of the individual
key audit matter in accordance with paragraph 13.[13]ISA (UK) 706 (Revised June
2016) provides further guidance on the relationship between key audit matters and
Emphasis of Matter paragraphs in accordance with that ISA (UK).[14]

Definition

Key audit matters
(Ref: Para. 8)

In the UK, those matters that were of most significance in the audit of the **A8-1**
financial statements of the current period include the most significant assessed
risks of material misstatement (whether or not due to fraud) identified by the
auditor, including those that had the greatest effect on: the overall audit
strategy; the allocation of resources in the audit; and directing the efforts of
the engagement team.

Determining Key Audit Matters
(Ref: Para. 9–10)

The auditor's decision-making process in determining key audit matters is **A9**
designed to select a smaller number of matters from the matters communicated
with those charged with governance, based on the auditor's judgment about which
matters were of most significance in the audit of the financial statements of the
current period.

In the UK, ISA (UK) 260 (Revised June 2016)[14a] requires the auditor to **A9-1**
communicate with those charged with governance those matters that were of
most significance in the audit of the financial statements of the current period
include the most significant assessed risks of material misstatement (whether or
not due to fraud) identified by the auditor, including those that had the greatest
effect on: the overall audit strategy; the allocation of resources in the audit; and
directing the efforts of the engagement team. Such matters are key audit matters
as explained in paragraph A8-1.

The auditor's determination of key audit matters is limited to those matters of most **A10**
significance in the audit of the financial statements of the current period, even
when comparative financial statements are presented (i.e., even when the auditor's
opinion refers to each period for which financial statements are presented).[15]

---

[12] *ISA (UK) 706 (Revised June 2016), Emphasis of Matter Paragraphs and Other Matter Paragraphs in the Independent Auditor's Report.*

[13] *See paragraphs 8(b) and 10(b) of ISA (UK) 706 (Revised June 2016).*

[14] *ISA (UK) 706 (Revised June 2016), paragraphs A1–A3.*

[14a] *ISA (UK) 260 (Revised June 2016), Communication with Those Charged with Governance, paragraph 15.*

[15] *See ISA (UK) 710, Comparative Information—Corresponding Figures and Comparative Financial Statements.*

A11   Notwithstanding that the auditor's determination of key audit matters is for the audit of the financial statements of the current period and this ISA (UK) does not require the auditor to update key audit matters included in the prior period's auditor's report, it may nevertheless be useful for the auditor to consider whether a matter that was a key audit matter in the audit of the financial statements of the prior period continues to be a key audit matter in the audit of the financial statements of the current period.

Matters that Required Significant Auditor Attention
(Ref: Para. 9)

A12   The concept of significant auditor attention recognizes that an audit is risk-based and focuses on identifying and assessing the risks of material misstatement of the financial statements, designing and performing audit procedures responsive to those risks, and obtaining audit evidence that is sufficient and appropriate to provide a basis for the auditor's opinion. For a particular account balance, class of transactions or disclosure, the higher an assessed risk of material misstatement at the assertion level, the more judgment is often involved in planning and performing the audit procedures and evaluating the results thereof. In designing further audit procedures, the auditor is required to obtain more persuasive audit evidence the higher the auditor's assessment of risk.[16] When obtaining more persuasive audit evidence because of a higher assessment of risk, the auditor may increase the quantity of the evidence, or obtain evidence that is more relevant or reliable, for example, by placing more emphasis on obtaining third party evidence or by obtaining corroborating evidence from a number of independent sources.[17]

A13   Accordingly, matters that pose challenges to the auditor in obtaining sufficient appropriate audit evidence or pose challenges to the auditor in forming an opinion on the financial statements may be particularly relevant in the auditor's determination of key audit matters.

A14   Areas of significant auditor attention often relate to areas of complexity and significant management judgment in the financial statements, and therefore often involve difficult or complex auditor judgments. In turn, this often affects the auditor's overall audit strategy, the allocation of resources and extent of audit effort in relation to such matters. These effects may include, for example, the extent of involvement of senior personnel on the audit engagement or the involvement of an auditor's expert or individuals with expertise in a specialized area of accounting or auditing, whether engaged or employed by the firm to address these areas.

A15   Various ISAs (UK) require specific communications with those charged with governance and others that may relate to areas of significant auditor attention. For example:

- ISA (UK) 260 (Revised June 2016) requires the auditor to communicate significant difficulties, if any, encountered during the audit with those charged with governance.[18] The ISAs (UK) acknowledge potential difficulties in relation to, for example:

---

[16] *ISA (UK) 330 (Revised June 2016), The Auditor's Responses to Assessed Risks, paragraph 7(b).*

[17] *ISA (UK) 330 (Revised June 2016), paragraph A19.*

[18] *ISA (UK) 260 (Revised June 2016), paragraphs 16(b) and A21.*

- Related party transactions,[19] in particular limitations on the auditor's ability to obtain audit evidence that all other aspects of a related party transaction (other than price) are equivalent to those of a similar arm's length transaction.

- Limitations on the group audit, for example, where the group engagement team's access to information may have been restricted.[20]

- ISA (UK) 220 (Revised June 2016) establishes requirements for the engagement partner in relation to undertaking appropriate consultation on difficult or contentious matters.[21] For example, the auditor may have consulted with others within the firm or outside the firm on a significant technical matter, which may be an indicator that it is a key audit matter. The engagement partner is also required to discuss, among other things, significant matters arising during the audit engagement with the engagement quality control reviewer.[22]

Considerations in Determining Those Matters that Required Significant Auditor Attention
(Ref: Para. 9)

The auditor may develop a preliminary view at the planning stage about matters   A16
that are likely to be areas of significant auditor attention in the audit and therefore
may be key audit matters. The auditor may communicate this with those charged
with governance when discussing the planned scope and timing of the audit in
accordance with ISA (UK) 260 (Revised June 2016). However, the auditor's
determination of key audit matters is based on the results of the audit or evidence
obtained throughout the audit.

Paragraph 9 includes specific required considerations in the auditor's   A17
determination of those matters that required significant auditor attention. These
considerations focus on the nature of matters communicated with those charged
with governance that are often linked to matters disclosed in the financial
statements, and are intended to reflect areas of the audit of the financial
statements that may be of particular interest to intended users. The fact that
these considerations are required is not intended to imply that matters related to
them are always key audit matters; rather, matters related to such specific
considerations are key audit matters only if they are determined to be of most
significance in the audit in accordance with paragraph 10. As the considerations
may be interrelated (e.g., matters relating to the circumstances described in
paragraphs 9(b)–(c) may also be identified as significant risks), the applicability
of more than one of the considerations to a particular matter communicated with
those charged with governance may increase the likelihood of the auditor
identifying that matter as a key audit matter.

In addition to matters that relate to the specific required considerations in   A18
paragraphs 9, there may be other matters communicated with those charged with
governance that required significant auditor attention and that therefore may be
determined to be key audit matters in accordance with paragraph 10. Such matters

---

[19] *ISA (UK) 550, Related Parties, paragraph A42.*

[20] *ISA (UK) 600 (Revised June 2016), Special Considerations—Audits of Group Financial Statements (Including the Work of Component Auditors), paragraph 49(d).*

[21] *ISA (UK) 220 (Revised June 2016), Quality Control for an Audit of Financial Statements, paragraph 18.*

[22] *ISA (UK) 220 (Revised June 2016), paragraph 19.*

may include, for example, matters relevant to the audit that was performed that may not be required to be disclosed in the financial statements. For example, the implementation of a new IT system (or significant changes to an existing IT system) during the period may be an area of significant auditor attention, in particular if such a change had a significant effect on the auditor's overall audit strategy or related to a significant risk (e.g., changes to a system affecting revenue recognition).

Areas of Higher Assessed Risk of Material Misstatement, or Significant Risks Identified in Accordance with ISA (UK) 315 (Revised June 2016)
(Ref: Para. 9(a))

A19   ISA (UK) 260 (Revised June 2016) requires the auditor to communicate with those charged with governance about the significant risks identified by the auditor.[23]Paragraph A13 of ISA (UK) 260 (Revised June 2016) explains that the auditor may also communicate with those charged with governance about how the auditor plans to address areas of higher assessed risks of material misstatement.

A20   ISA (UK) 315 (Revised June 2016) defines a significant risk as an identified and assessed risk of material misstatement that, in the auditor's judgment, requires special audit consideration. Areas of significant management judgment and significant unusual transactions may often be identified as significant risks. Significant risks are therefore often areas that require significant auditor attention.

A21   However, this may not be the case for all significant risks. For example, ISA (UK) 240 (Revised June 2016) presumes that there are risks of fraud in revenue recognition and requires the auditor to treat those assessed risks of material misstatement due to fraud as significant risks.[24] In addition, ISA (UK) 240 (Revised June 2016) indicates that, due to the unpredictable way in which management override of controls could occur, it is a risk of material misstatement due to fraud and thus a significant risk.[25] Depending on their nature, these risks may not require significant auditor attention, and therefore would not be considered in the auditor's determination of key audit matters in accordance with paragraph 10.

A22   ISA (UK) 315 (Revised June 2016) explains that the auditor's assessment of the risks of material misstatement at the assertion level may change during the course of the audit as additional audit evidence is obtained.[26] Revision to the auditor's risk assessment and reevaluation of the planned audit procedures with respect to a particular area of the financial statements (i.e., a significant change in the audit approach, for example, if the auditor's risk assessment was based on an expectation that certain controls were operating effectively and the auditor has obtained audit evidence that they were not operating effectively throughout the audit period, particularly in an area with higher assessed risk of material misstatement) may result in an area being determined as one requiring significant auditor attention.

---

[23] *ISA (UK) 260 (Revised June 2016), paragraph 15.*

[24] *ISA (UK) 240 (Revised June 2016), The Auditor's Responsibilities Relating to Fraud in an Audit of Financial Statements, paragraphs 26–27.*

[25] *ISA (UK) 240 (Revised June 2016), paragraph 31.*

[26] *ISA (UK) 315 (Revised June 2016), paragraph 31.*

Significant Auditor Judgments Relating to Areas in the Financial Statements that Involved Significant Management Judgment, Including Accounting Estimates that Have Been Identified as Having High Estimation Uncertainty
(Ref: Para. 9(b))

ISA (UK) 260 (Revised June 2016) requires the auditor to communicate with those **A23** charged with governance the auditor's views about significant qualitative aspects of the entity's accounting practices, including accounting policies, accounting estimates and financial statement disclosures.[27] In many cases, this relates to critical accounting estimates and related disclosures, which are likely to be areas of significant auditor attention, and also may be identified as significant risks.

However, users of the financial statements have highlighted their interest in **A24** accounting estimates that have been identified as having high estimation uncertainty in accordance with ISA (UK) 540 (Revised June 2016)[28] that may have not been determined to be significant risks. Among other things, such estimates are highly dependent on management judgment and are often the most complex areas of the financial statements, and may require the involvement of both a management's expert and an auditor's expert. Users have also highlighted that accounting policies that have a significant effect on the financial statements (and significant changes to those policies) are relevant to their understanding of the financial statements, especially in circumstances where an entity's practices are not consistent with others in its industry.

The Effect on the Audit of Significant Events or Transactions that Occurred during the Period
(Ref: Para. 9(c))

Events or transactions that had a significant effect on the financial statements or **A25** the audit may be areas of significant auditor attention and may be identified as significant risks. For example, the auditor may have had extensive discussions with management and those charged with governance at various stages throughout the audit about the effect on the financial statements of significant transactions with related parties or significant transactions that are outside the normal course of business for the entity or that otherwise appear to be unusual.[29] Management may have made difficult or complex judgments in relation to recognition, measurement, presentation or disclosure of such transactions, which may have had a significant effect on the auditor's overall strategy.

Significant economic, accounting, regulatory, industry, or other developments that **A26** affected management's assumptions or judgments may also affect the auditor's overall approach to the audit and result in a matter requiring significant auditor attention.

Matters of Most Significance
(Ref: Para. 10)

Matters that required significant auditor attention also may have resulted in **A27** significant interaction with those charged with governance. The nature and extent of communication about such matters with those charged with

---

[27] *ISA (UK) 260 (Revised June 2016), paragraph 16(a).*

[28] *See paragraphs 10–11 of ISA (UK) 540 (Revised June 2016), Auditing Accounting Estimates, Including Fair Value Accounting Estimates, and Related Disclosures.*

[29] *See paragraphs 16(a), 16(c) and A22, and Appendix 2, of ISA (UK) 260 (Revised June 2016).*

governance often provides an indication of which matters are of most significance in the audit. For example, the auditor may have had more in-depth, frequent or robust interactions with those charged with governance on more difficult and complex matters, such as the application of significant accounting policies that were the subject of significant auditor or management judgment.

A28   The concept of matters of most significance is applicable in the context of the entity and the audit that was performed. As such, the auditor's determination and communication of key audit matters is intended to identify matters specific to the audit and to involve making a judgment about their importance relative to other matters in the audit.

A28-1   In the UK, the assessed risks of material misstatement which had the greatest effect on: the overall audit strategy; the allocation of resources in the audit; and directing the efforts of the engagement team are likely to have been identified by the auditor in meeting the requirements of ISA (UK) 315 (Revised June 2016),[29a] including those relating to significant risks. However, the auditor uses its judgment to determine which, if any, of the significant risks and which, if any, of the other identified risks meet the criteria set out in paragraph 10 and are to be described in the auditor's report.

A29   Other considerations that may be relevant to determining the relative significance of a matter communicated with those charged with governance and whether such a matter is a key audit matter include:

- The importance of the matter to intended users' understanding of the financial statements as a whole, in particular, its materiality to the financial statements.

- The nature of the underlying accounting policy relating to the matter or the complexity or subjectivity involved in management's selection of an appropriate policy compared to other entities within its industry.

- The nature and materiality, quantitatively or qualitatively, of corrected and accumulated uncorrected misstatements due to fraud or error related to the matter, if any.

- The nature and extent of audit effort needed to address the matter, including:
  - The extent of specialized skill or knowledge needed to apply audit procedures to address the matter or evaluate the results of those procedures, if any.
  - The nature of consultations outside the engagement team regarding the matter.

- The nature and severity of difficulties in applying audit procedures, evaluating the results of those procedures, and obtaining relevant and reliable evidence on which to base the auditor's opinion, in particular as the auditor's judgments become more subjective.

- The severity of any control deficiencies identified relevant to the matter.

- Whether the matter involved a number of separate, but related, auditing considerations. For example, long-term contracts may involve significant auditor attention with respect to revenue recognition, litigation or other contingencies, and may have an effect on other accounting estimates.

[29a] *ISA (UK) 315 (Revised June 2016), paragraphs 25 to 31.*

Determining which, and how many, of those matters that required significant **A30** auditor attention were of most significance in the audit of the financial statements of the current period is a matter of professional judgment. The number of key audit matters to be included in the auditor's report may be affected by the size and complexity of the entity, the nature of its business and environment, and the facts and circumstances of the audit engagement. In general, the greater the number of matters initially determined to be key audit matters, the more the auditor may need to reconsider whether each of these matters meets the definition of a key audit matter. Lengthy lists of key audit matters may be contrary to the notion of such matters being those of most significance in the audit.

Communicating Key Audit Matters

Separate Key Audit Matters Section in the Auditor's Report
(Ref: Para. 11)

Placing the separate Key Audit Matters section in close proximity to the auditor's **A31** opinion may give prominence to such information and acknowledge the perceived value of engagement-specific information to intended users.

The order of presentation of individual matters within the Key Audit Matters **A32** section is a matter of professional judgment. For example, such information may be organized in order of relative importance, based on the auditor's judgment, or may correspond to the manner in which matters are disclosed in the financial statements. The requirement in paragraph 11 to include subheadings is intended to further differentiate the matters.

When comparative financial information is presented, the introductory language **A33** of the Key Audit Matters section is tailored to draw attention to the fact that the key audit matters described relate to only the audit of the financial statements of the current period, and may include reference to the specific period covered by those financial statements (e.g., "for the year ended December 31, 20X1").

Communicating Key Audit Matters for Group and Parent Company Financial Statements

An auditor's report for a group may include the auditor's report with respect to **A33-1** both the group and the parent company financial statements. This is typically the case where both sets of financial statements are presented in accordance with IFRSs as adopted in the European Union. However, where the financial statements of the group and the parent company are presented in accordance with different financial reporting frameworks, the financial statements might be presented separately within the annual report and in such circumstances separate auditor's reports in respect of the group and the parent company financial statements might be provided within the annual report.

Most of the key audit matters communicated in the audit of the parent company **A33-2** would likely also be key audit matters in the audit of the group financial statements, subject to any differences in quantitative materiality considerations that may apply in those audits. However, there may be key audit matters that only arise in relation to the audit of the parent company financial statements (such as risks relating to investments in subsidiaries that could, for example, have implications for distributable reserves).

A33-3   An understanding of such key audit matters may be of interest to readers of auditor's reports. Readers may find such key audit matters to be of particular interest when their implications are relevant in the context of the parent company's reported distributable reserves. However, readers of the auditor's report(s) on the group and parent company financial statements will be assisted by avoiding unnecessary duplication or disaggregation of key audit matters arising from these audits in such report(s).

Application where there is a single auditor's report

A33-4   Where the auditor's reports on both the group and parent company financial statements are combined within a single report, it may be appropriate for any relevant key audit matters and other information required by ISA (UK) 701 that are unique to the parent company audit to be separately identified but integrated within the disclosures in that report of corresponding matters arising from the audit of the group financial statements.

Application where the auditor reports separately on the group and parent company financial statements

A33-5   Where the auditor provides separate auditor's reports on the group and parent company financial statements, it may also be appropriate for any relevant key audit matters and other audit planning and scoping matters required by this ISA (UK) that are unique to the parent company audit to be separately identified but integrated within the disclosures within the group auditor's report of corresponding matters arising from the group audit. Except where such matters are required by law or regulation to be included in the auditor's report (as is the case, for example, in relation to an auditor's report on any financial statements of a public interest entity), the auditor could make reference in the other matter paragraph in the parent company auditor's report that refers to the separate auditor's report on the group financial statements to the fact that the key audit matters and other audit planning and scoping matters that relate to the parent company audit have been included in the group auditor's report, rather than repeating the information.

Descriptions of Individual Key Audit Matters
(Ref: Para. 13)

A34   The adequacy of the description of a key audit matter is a matter of professional judgment. The description of a key audit matter is intended to provide a succinct and balanced explanation to enable intended users to understand why the matter was one of most significance in the audit and how the matter was addressed in the audit. Limiting the use of highly technical auditing terms also helps to enable intended users who do not have a reasonable knowledge of auditing to understand the basis for the auditor's focus on particular matters during the audit. The nature and extent of information provided by the auditor is intended to be balanced in the context of the responsibilities of the respective parties (i.e., for the auditor to provide useful information in a concise and understandable form, while not inappropriately being the provider of original information about the entity).

A35   Original information is any information about the entity that has not otherwise been made publicly available by the entity (e.g., has not been included in the financial statements or other information available at the date of the auditor's report, or addressed in other oral or written communications by management or those charged with governance, such as a preliminary announcement of financial information or investor briefings). Such information is the responsibility of the entity's management and those charged with governance.

It is appropriate for the auditor to seek to avoid the description of a key audit **A36** matter inappropriately providing original information about the entity. The description of a key audit matter is not usually of itself original information about the entity, as it describes the matter in the context of the audit. However, the auditor may consider it necessary to include additional information to explain why the matter was considered to be one of most significance in the audit and therefore determined to be a key audit matter, and how the matter was addressed in the audit, provided that disclosure of such information is not precluded by law or regulation. When such information is determined to be necessary by the auditor, the auditor may encourage management or those charged with governance to disclose additional information, rather than the auditor providing original information in the auditor's report.

Management or those charged with governance may decide to include new or **A37** enhanced disclosures in the financial statements or elsewhere in the annual report relating to a key audit matter in light of the fact that the matter will be communicated in the auditor's report. Such new or enhanced disclosures, for example, may be included to provide more robust information about the sensitivity of key assumptions used in accounting estimates or the entity's rationale for a particular accounting practice or policy when acceptable alternatives exist under the applicable financial reporting framework.

ISA (UK) 720 (Revised June 2016) defines the term annual report and explains **A38** that documents such as a management report, management commentary, or operating and financial review or similar reports by those charged with governance (e.g., a directors' report); a Chairman's statement; corporate governance statement; or internal control and risk assessment reports may form part of the annual report.[30] ISA (UK) 720 (Revised June 2016) addresses the auditor's responsibilities relating to other information included in the annual report. Although the auditor's opinion on the financial statements does not cover the other information, the auditor may consider this information, as well as other publicly available communications by the entity or other credible sources, in formulating the description of a key audit matter.

Audit documentation prepared during the audit can also be useful to the auditor in **A39** formulating the description of a key audit matter. For example, written communications, or the auditor's documentation of oral communications, with those charged with governance and other audit documentation provides a useful basis for the auditor's communication in the auditor's report. This is because audit documentation in accordance with ISA (UK) 230 (Revised June 2016) is intended to address the significant matters arising during the audit, the conclusions reached thereon, and significant professional judgments made in reaching those conclusions, and serves as a record of the nature, timing and extent of the audit procedures performed, the results of those procedures, and the audit evidence obtained. Such documentation may assist the auditor in developing a description of key audit matters that explains the significance of the matter and also in applying the requirement in paragraph 18.

---

[30] *ISA (UK) 720 (Revised June 2016), The Auditor's Responsibilities Relating to Other Information, paragraphs 12(a) and A1–A3.*

Reference to Where the Matter Is Disclosed in the Financial Statements
(Ref: Para. 13)

A40   Paragraphs 13(a)–(b) requires the description of each key audit matter to address why the auditor considered the matter to be one of most significance in the audit and how the matter was addressed in the audit. Accordingly, the description of key audit matters is not a mere reiteration of what is disclosed in the financial statements. However, a reference to any related disclosures enables intended users to further understand how management has addressed the matter in preparing the financial statements.

A41   In addition to referring to related disclosure(s), the auditor may draw attention to key aspects of them. The extent of disclosure by management about specific aspects or factors in relation to how a particular matter is affecting the financial statements of the current period may help the auditor in pinpointing particular aspects of how the matter was addressed in the audit such that intended users can understand why the matter is a key audit matter. For example:

- When an entity includes robust disclosure about accounting estimates, the auditor may draw attention to the disclosure of key assumptions, the disclosure of the range of possible outcomes, and other qualitative and quantitative disclosures relating to key sources of estimation uncertainty or critical accounting estimates, as part of addressing why the matter was one of most significance in the audit and how the matter was addressed in the audit.

- When the auditor concludes in accordance with ISA (UK) 570 (Revised June 2016) that no material uncertainty exists relating to events or conditions that may cast significant doubt on the entity's ability to continue as a going concern, the auditor may nevertheless determine that one or more matters relating to this conclusion arising from the auditor's work effort under ISA (UK) 570 (Revised June 2016) are key audit matters. In such circumstances, the auditor's description of such key audit matters in the auditor's report could include aspects of the identified events or conditions disclosed in the financial statements, such as substantial operating losses, available borrowing facilities and possible debt refinancing, or non-compliance with loan agreements, and related mitigating factors.[31]

Why the Auditor Considered the Matter to Be One of Most Significance in the Audit
(Ref: Para. 13(a))

A42   The description of a key audit matter in the auditor's report is intended to provide insight as to why the matter was determined to be a key audit matter. Accordingly, the requirements in paragraphs 9–10 and the application material in paragraphs A12–A29 related to determining key audit matters may also be helpful for the auditor in considering how such matters are to be communicated in the auditor's report. For example, explaining the factors that led the auditor to conclude that a particular matter required significant auditor attention and was of most significance in the audit is likely to be of interest to intended users.

---

[31] *See paragraph A3 of ISA (UK) 570 (Revised June 2016).*

As indicated in paragraph A22, where the auditor significantly revises the   **A42-1**
auditor's assessment of the risks of material misstatement during the course of
the audit, the auditor considers whether to disclose that fact and the
circumstances giving rise to the changed assessment.

The relevance of the information for intended users is a consideration for the   **A43**
auditor in determining what to include in the description of a key audit matter. This
may include whether the description would enable a better understanding of the
audit and the auditor's judgments.

Relating a matter directly to the specific circumstances of the entity may also help   **A44**
to minimize the potential that such descriptions become overly standardized and
less useful over time. For example, certain matters may be determined as key audit
matters in a particular industry across a number of entities due to the
circumstances of the industry or the underlying complexity in financial
reporting. In describing why the auditor considered the matter to be one of
most significance, it may be useful for the auditor to highlight aspects specific to
the entity (e.g., circumstances that affected the underlying judgments made in the
financial statements of the current period) in order to make the description more
relevant for intended users. This also may be important in describing a key audit
matter that recurs over periods.

The description may also make reference to the principal considerations that led   **A45**
the auditor, in the circumstances of the audit, to determine the matter to be one of
most significance, for example:

● Economic conditions that affected the auditor's ability to obtain audit
  evidence, for example illiquid markets for certain financial instruments.

● New or emerging accounting policies, for example entity-specific or
  industry-specific matters on which the engagement team consulted within
  the firm.

● Changes in the entity's strategy or business model that had a material effect
  on the financial statements.

How the Matter Was Addressed in the Audit
(Ref: Para. 13(b))

The amount of detail to be provided in the auditor's report to describe how a key   **A46**
audit matter was addressed in the audit is a matter of professional judgment. In
accordance with paragraph 13(b), the auditor may describe:

● Aspects of the auditor's response or approach that were most relevant to the
  matter or specific to the assessed risk of material misstatement;

● A brief overview of procedures performed;

● An indication of the outcome of the auditor's procedures; or

● Key observations with respect to the matter,

or some combination of these elements.

Law or regulation or national auditing standards may prescribe a specific form or
content for the description of a key audit matter, or may specify the inclusion of
one or more of these elements.

A47   In order for intended users to understand the significance of a key audit matter in the context of the audit of the financial statements as a whole, as well as the relationship between key audit matters and other elements of the auditor's report, including the auditor's opinion, care may be necessary so that language used in the description of a key audit matter:

- Does not imply that the matter has not been appropriately resolved by the auditor in forming the opinion on the financial statements.

- Relates the matter directly to the specific circumstances of the entity, while avoiding generic or standardized language.

- Takes into account how the matter is addressed in the related disclosure(s) in the financial statements, if any.

- Does not contain or imply discrete opinions on separate elements of the financial statements.

A48   Describing aspects of the auditor's response or approach to a matter, in particular when the audit approach required significant tailoring to the facts and circumstances of the entity, may assist intended users in understanding unusual circumstances and significant auditor judgment required to address the risk of material misstatement. In addition, the audit approach in a particular period may have been influenced by entity-specific circumstances, economic conditions, or industry developments. It may also be useful for the auditor to make reference to the nature and extent of communications with those charged with governance about the matter.

A49   For example, in describing the auditor's approach to an accounting estimate that has been identified as having high estimation uncertainty, such as the valuation of complex financial instruments, the auditor may wish to highlight that the auditor employed or engaged an auditor's expert. Such a reference to the use of an auditor's expert does not reduce the auditor's responsibility for the opinion on the financial statements and is therefore not inconsistent with paragraphs 14–15 of ISA (UK) 620 (Revised June 2016).[32]

A50   There may be challenges in describing the auditor's procedures, particularly in complex, judgmental areas of the audit. In particular, it may be difficult to summarize the procedures performed in a succinct way that adequately communicates the nature and extent of the auditor's response to the assessed risk of material misstatement, and the significant auditor judgments involved. Nonetheless, the auditor may consider it necessary to describe certain procedures performed to communicate how the matter was addressed in the audit. Such description may typically be at a high level, rather than include a detailed description of procedures.

A51   As noted in paragraph A46, the auditor may also provide an indication of the outcome of the auditor's response in the description of the key audit matter in the auditor's report. However, if this is done, care is needed to avoid the auditor giving the impression that the description is conveying a separate opinion on an individual key audit matter or that in any way may call into question the auditor's opinion on the financial statements as a whole.

---

[32] *ISA (UK) 620 (Revised June 2016), Using the Work of an Auditor's Expert.*

Circumstances in Which a Matter Determined to Be a Key Audit Matter Is Not Communicated in the Auditor's Report
(Ref: Para. 14)

Law or regulation may preclude public disclosure by either management or the auditor about a specific matter determined to be a key audit matter. For example, law or regulation may specifically prohibit any public communication that might prejudice an investigation by an appropriate authority into an actual, or suspected, illegal act (e.g., matters that are or appear to be related to money laundering).   **A52**

As indicated by paragraph 14(b), it will be extremely rare for a matter determined to be a key audit matter not to be communicated in the auditor's report. This is because there is presumed to be a public interest benefit in providing greater transparency about the audit for intended users. Accordingly, the judgment not to communicate a key audit matter is appropriate only in cases when the adverse consequences to the entity or the public as a result of such communication are viewed as so significant that they would reasonably be expected to outweigh the public interest benefits of communicating about the matter.   **A53**

The determination not to communicate a key audit matter takes into account the facts and circumstances related to the matter. Communication with management and those charged with governance helps the auditor understand management's views about the significance of the adverse consequences that may arise as a result of communicating about a matter. In particular, communication with management and those charged with governance helps to inform the auditor's judgment in determining whether to communicate the matter by: **A54**

- Assisting the auditor in understanding why the matter has not been publicly disclosed by the entity (e.g., if law, regulation or certain financial reporting frameworks permit delayed disclosure or non-disclosure of the matter) and management's views as to the adverse consequences, if any, of disclosure. Management may draw attention to certain aspects in law or regulation or other authoritative sources that may be relevant to the consideration of adverse consequences (e.g., such aspects may include harm to the entity's commercial negotiations or competitive position). However, management's views about the adverse consequences alone do not alleviate the need for the auditor to determine whether the adverse consequences would reasonably be expected to outweigh the public interest benefits of communication in accordance with paragraph 14(b).

- Highlighting whether there have been any communications with applicable regulatory, enforcement or supervisory authorities in relation to the matter, in particular whether such discussions would appear to support management's assertion as to why public disclosure about the matter is not appropriate.

- Enabling the auditor, where appropriate, to encourage management and those charged with governance to make public disclosure of relevant information about the matter. In particular, this may be possible if the concerns of management and those charged with governance about communicating are limited to specific aspects relating to the matter, such that certain information about the matter may be less sensitive and could be communicated.

The auditor also may consider it necessary to obtain a written representation from management as to why public disclosure about the matter is not appropriate, including management's view about the significance of the adverse consequences that may arise as a result of such communication.

A55   It may also be necessary for the auditor to consider the implications of communicating about a matter determined to be a key audit matter in light of relevant ethical requirements. In addition, the auditor may be required by law or regulation to communicate with applicable regulatory, enforcement or supervisory authorities in relation to the matter, regardless of whether the matter is communicated in the auditor's report. Such communication may also be useful to inform the auditor's consideration of the adverse consequences that may arise from communicating about the matter.

A56   The issues considered by the auditor regarding a decision to not communicate a matter are complex and involve significant auditor judgment. Accordingly, the auditor may consider it appropriate to obtain legal advice.

Form and Content of the Key Audit Matters Section in Other Circumstances
(Ref: Para. 16)

A57   The requirement in paragraph 16 applies in three circumstances:

(i)   The auditor determines in accordance with paragraph 10 that there are no key audit matters (seeparagraph A59).

(ii)   The auditor determines in accordance with paragraph 14 that a key audit matter will not be communicated in the auditor's report and no other matters have been determined to be key audit matters.

(iii) The only matters determined to be key audit matters are those communicated in accordance with paragraph 15.

A58   The following illustrates the presentation in the auditor's report if the auditor has determined there are no key audit matters to communicate:

Key Audit Matters

[Except for the matter described in the *Basis for Qualified (Adverse) Opinion* section or *Material Uncertainty Related to Going Concern* section,] We have determined that there are no [other] key audit matters to communicate in our report.

A59   The determination of key audit matters involves making a judgment about the relative importance of matters that required significant auditor attention. Therefore, it may be rare that the auditor of a complete set of general purpose financial statements of a listed entity would not determine at least one key audit matter from the matters communicated with those charged with governance to be communicated in the auditor's report. However, in certain limited circumstances (e.g., for a listed entity that has very limited operations), the auditor may determine that there are no key audit matters in accordance with paragraph 10 because there are no matters that required significant auditor attention.

Communicating Other Audit Planning and Scoping Matters
(Ref: Para. 16-1)

The explanation, of how the auditor applied the concept of materiality in   **A59-1**
planning and performing the audit, is tailored to the particular circumstances
and complexity of the audit and, in addition to specifying the threshold used by
the auditor as being materiality for the financial statements as a whole, might
include, for example:

- Materiality level or levels for those classes of transactions, account
  balances or disclosures where such materiality levels are lower than
  materiality for the financial statements as a whole (as described in
  paragraph 10 of ISA (UK) 320 (Revised June 2016)).

- Performance materiality (as described in paragraph 11 of ISA (UK) 320
  (Revised June 2016)).

- Any significant revisions of materiality thresholds that were made as the
  audit progressed.

- The threshold used for reporting unadjusted differences to the audit
  committee.

- Significant qualitative considerations relating to the auditor's evaluation
  of materiality.

The content of the overview of the scope of the audit is tailored to the particular   **A59-2**
circumstances of the audit and how the scope was influenced by the auditor's
application of materiality and addressed the key audit matters described in the
auditor's report. Such a summary might also include, for example:

- The coverage of revenue, total assets and profit before tax achieved.

- The coverage of revenue, total assets and profit before tax of reportable
  segments achieved.

- The number of locations visited by the auditor as a proportion of the total
  number of locations, and the rationale underlying any program of visits.

- The effect of the group structure on the scope. The audit approach to a group
  consisting of autonomous subsidiary companies may differ from that
  applied to one which consists of a number of non-autonomous divisions.

- The nature and extent of the group auditor's involvement in the work of
  component auditors.

Communication with Those Charged with Governance
(Ref: Para. 17)

ISA (UK) 260 (Revised June 2016) requires the auditor to communicate with   **A60**
those charged with governance on a timely basis.[33] The appropriate timing for
communications about key audit matters will vary with the circumstances of the
engagement. However, the auditor may communicate preliminary views about key
audit matters when discussing the planned scope and timing of the audit, and may
further discuss such matters when communicating about audit findings. Doing so
may help to alleviate the practical challenges of attempting to have a robust two-
way dialogue about key audit matters at the time the financial statements are being
finalized for issuance.

---

[33] *ISA (UK) 260 (Revised June 2016), paragraph 21.*

A61   Communication with those charged with governance enables them to be made aware of the key audit matters that the auditor intends to communicate in the auditor's report, and provides them with an opportunity to obtain further clarification where necessary. The auditor may consider it useful to provide those charged with governance with a draft of the auditor's report to facilitate this discussion. Communication with those charged with governance recognizes their important role in overseeing the financial reporting process, and provides the opportunity for those charged with governance to understand the basis for the auditor's decisions in relation to key audit matters and how these matters will be described in the auditor's report. It also enables those charged with governance to consider whether new or enhanced disclosures may be useful in light of the fact that these matters will be communicated in the auditor's report.

A62   The communication with those charged with governance required by paragraph 17(a) also addresses the extremely rare circumstances in which a matter determined to be a key audit matter is not communicated in the auditor's report (see paragraphs 14 and A54).

A63   The requirement in paragraph 17(b) to communicate with those charged with governance when the auditor has determined there are no key audit matters to communicate in the auditor's report may provide an opportunity for the auditor to have further discussion with others who are familiar with the audit and the significant matters that may have arisen (including the engagement quality control reviewer, where one has been appointed). These discussions may cause the auditor to re-evaluate the auditor's determination that there are no key audit matters.

Documentation
(Ref: Para. 18)

A64   Paragraph 8 of ISA (UK) 230 (Revised June 2016) requires the auditor to prepare audit documentation that is sufficient to enable an experienced auditor, having no previous connection with the audit, to understand, among other things, significant professional judgments. In the context of key audit matters, these professional judgments include the determination, from the matters communicated with those charged with governance, of the matters that required significant auditor attention, as well as whether or not each of those matters is a key audit matter. The auditor's judgments in this regard are likely to be supported by the documentation of the auditor's communications with those charged with governance and the audit documentation relating to each individual matter (see paragraph A39), as well as certain other audit documentation of the significant matters arising during the audit (e.g., a completion memorandum). However, this ISA (UK) does not require the auditor to document why other matters communicated with those charged with governance were not matters that required significant auditor attention.

ISA (UK) 705 (Revised June 2016)
Modifications to the Opinion in the Independent Auditor's Report

(Effective for audits of financial statements for periods commencing on or after 17 June 2016)

Contents

Paragraphs

Introduction
Scope of this ISA (UK)   1
Types of modified opinions   2
Effective date   3

Objective   4

Definitions   5

Requirements
Circumstances when a modification to the auditor's opinion is required   6
Determining the type of modification to the auditor's opinion   7 - 15
Form and content of the auditor's report when the opinion is modified   16 - 29
Communication with those charged with governance   30

Application and other explanatory material
Types of modified opinions   A1
Circumstances when a modification to the auditor's opinion is required   A2 - A12
Determining the type of modification to the auditor's opinion   A13 - A16
Form and content of the auditor's report when the opinion is modified   A17 - A26-1
Communication with those charged with governance   A27 - A27-1

Appendix: Illustrations of auditor's reports with modifications to the opinion

International Standard on Auditing (UK) (ISA (UK)) 705 (Revised June 2016), *Modifications to the Opinion in the Independent Auditor's Report*, should be read in conjunction with ISA (UK) 200 (Revised June 2016), *Overall Objectives of the Independent Auditor and the Conduct of an Audit in Accordance with International Standards on Auditing (UK)*.

Introduction

Scope of this ISA (UK)

1   This International Standard on Auditing (UK) (ISA (UK)) deals with the auditor's responsibility to issue an appropriate report in circumstances when, in forming an opinion in accordance with ISA (UK) 700 (Revised June 2016),[1] the auditor concludes that a modification to the auditor's opinion on the financial statements is necessary. This ISA (UK) also deals with how the form and content of the auditor's report is affected when the auditor expresses a modified opinion. In all cases, the reporting requirements in ISA (UK) 700 (Revised June 2016) apply, and are not repeated in this ISA (UK) unless they are explicitly addressed or amended by the requirements of this ISA (UK).

Types of Modified Opinions

2   This ISA (UK) establishes three types of modified opinions, namely, a qualified opinion, an adverse opinion, and a disclaimer of opinion. The decision regarding which type of modified opinion is appropriate depends upon:

(a)   The nature of the matter giving rise to the modification, that is, whether the financial statements are materially misstated or, in the case of an inability to obtain sufficient appropriate audit evidence, may be materially misstated; and

(b)   The auditor's judgment about the pervasiveness of the effects or possible effects of the matter on the financial statements. (Ref: Para. A1)

Effective Date

3   This ISA (UK) is effective for audits of financial statements for periods commencing on or after 17 June 2016. Earlier adoption is permitted.

Objective

4   The objective of the auditor is to express clearly an appropriately modified opinion on the financial statements that is necessary when:

(a)   The auditor concludes, based on the audit evidence obtained, that the financial statements as a whole are not free from material misstatement; or

(b)   The auditor is unable to obtain sufficient appropriate audit evidence to conclude that the financial statements as a whole are free from material misstatement.

Definitions

5   For purposes of the ISAs (UK), the following terms have the meanings attributed below:

(a)   Pervasive – A term used, in the context of misstatements, to describe the effects on the financial statements of misstatements or the possible effects on the financial statements of misstatements, if any, that are undetected due to

---

[1]   *ISA (UK) 700 (Revised June 2016), Forming an Opinion and Reporting on Financial Statements.*

an inability to obtain sufficient appropriate audit evidence. Pervasive effects on the financial statements are those that, in the auditor's judgment:

(i) Are not confined to specific elements, accounts or items of the financial statements;

(ii) If so confined, represent or could represent a substantial proportion of the financial statements; or

(iii) In relation to disclosures, are fundamental to users' understanding of the financial statements.

(b) Modified opinion – A qualified opinion, an adverse opinion or a disclaimer of opinion.

Requirements

Circumstances When a Modification to the Auditor's Opinion Is Required

The auditor shall modify the opinion in the auditor's report when: **6**

(a) The auditor concludes that, based on the audit evidence obtained, the financial statements as a whole are not free from material misstatement; or (Ref: Para. A2–A7)

(b) The auditor is unable to obtain sufficient appropriate audit evidence to conclude that the financial statements as a whole are free from material misstatement. (Ref: Para. A8–A12)

Determining the Type of Modification to the Auditor's Opinion

Qualified Opinion

The auditor shall express a qualified opinion when: **7**

(a) The auditor, having obtained sufficient appropriate audit evidence, concludes that misstatements, individually or in the aggregate, are material, but not pervasive, to the financial statements; or

(b) The auditor is unable to obtain sufficient appropriate audit evidence on which to base the opinion, but the auditor concludes that the possible effects on the financial statements of undetected misstatements, if any, could be material but not pervasive.

Adverse Opinion

The auditor shall express an adverse opinion when the auditor, having obtained **8** sufficient appropriate audit evidence, concludes that misstatements, individually or in the aggregate, are both material and pervasive to the financial statements.

Disclaimer of Opinion

The auditor shall disclaim an opinion when the auditor is unable to obtain **9** sufficient appropriate audit evidence on which to base the opinion, and the auditor concludes that the possible effects on the financial statements of undetected misstatements, if any, could be both material and pervasive.

The auditor shall disclaim an opinion when, in extremely rare circumstances **10** involving multiple uncertainties, the auditor concludes that, notwithstanding having obtained sufficient appropriate audit evidence regarding each of the individual uncertainties, it is not possible to form an opinion on the financial statements due to the potential interaction of the uncertainties and their possible cumulative effect on the financial statements.

Consequence of an Inability to Obtain Sufficient Appropriate Audit Evidence Due to a Management-Imposed Limitation after the Auditor Has Accepted the Engagement

11   If, after accepting the engagement, the auditor becomes aware that management has imposed a limitation on the scope of the audit that the auditor considers likely to result in the need to express a qualified opinion or to disclaim an opinion on the financial statements, the auditor shall request that management remove the limitation.

12   If management refuses to remove the limitation referred to in paragraph 11 of this ISA (UK), the auditor shall communicate the matter to those charged with governance, unless all of those charged with governance are involved in managing the entity,[2] and determine whether it is possible to perform alternative procedures to obtain sufficient appropriate audit evidence.

13   If the auditor is unable to obtain sufficient appropriate audit evidence, the auditor shall determine the implications as follows:

(a)   If the auditor concludes that the possible effects on the financial statements of undetected misstatements, if any, could be material but not pervasive, the auditor shall qualify the opinion; or

(b)   If the auditor concludes that the possible effects on the financial statements of undetected misstatements, if any, could be both material and pervasive so that a qualification of the opinion would be inadequate to communicate the gravity of the situation, the auditor shall:

   (i)   Withdraw from the audit, where practicable and possible under applicable law or regulation; or (Ref: Para. A13)

   (ii)   If withdrawal from the audit before issuing the auditor's report is not practicable or possible, disclaim an opinion on the financial statements (Ref: Para. A14).

14   If the auditor withdraws as contemplated by paragraph 13(b)(i), before withdrawing, the auditor shall communicate to those charged with governance any matters regarding misstatements identified during the audit that would have given rise to a modification of the opinion. (Ref: Para. A15–A15-1)

Other Considerations Relating to an Adverse Opinion or Disclaimer of Opinion

15   When the auditor considers it necessary to express an adverse opinion or disclaim an opinion on the financial statements as a whole, the auditor's report shall not also include an unmodified opinion with respect to the same financial reporting framework on a single financial statement or one or more specific elements, accounts or items of a financial statement. To include such an unmodified opinion in the same report[3] in these

---

[2] *ISA (UK) 260 (Revised June 2016), Communication with Those Charged with Governance, paragraph 13.*

[3] *ISA 805, Special Considerations—Audits of Single Financial Statements and Specific Elements, Accounts or Items of a Financial Statement, deals with circumstances where the auditor is engaged to express a separate opinion on one or more specific elements, accounts or items of a financial statement.*

ISA 805 has not been promulgated by the FRC for application in the UK.

circumstances would contradict the auditor's adverse opinion or disclaimer of opinion on the financial statements as a whole. (Ref: Para. A16)

Form and Content of the Auditor's Report When the Opinion Is Modified

Auditor's Opinion

When the auditor modifies the audit opinion, the auditor shall use the heading **16** "Qualified Opinion," "Adverse Opinion," or "Disclaimer of Opinion," as appropriate, for the Opinion section. (Ref: Para. A17–A19)

Qualified Opinion

When the auditor expresses a qualified opinion due to a material misstatement in **17** the financial statements, the auditor shall state that, in the auditor's opinion, except for the effects of the matter(s) described in the Basis for Qualified Opinion section:

(a)   When reporting in accordance with a fair presentation framework, the accompanying financial statements present fairly, in all material respects (or give a true and fair view of) [...] in accordance with [the applicable financial reporting framework]; or

(b)   When reporting in accordance with a compliance framework, the accompanying financial statements have been prepared, in all material respects, in accordance with [the applicable financial reporting framework].

When the modification arises from an inability to obtain sufficient appropriate audit evidence, the auditor shall use the corresponding phrase "except for the possible effects of the matter(s) ..." for the modified opinion. (Ref: Para. A20)

Adverse Opinion

When the auditor expresses an adverse opinion, the auditor shall state that, in the **18** auditor's opinion, because of the significance of the matter(s) described in the Basis for Adverse Opinion section:

(a)   When reporting in accordance with a fair presentation framework, the accompanying financial statements do not present fairly (or give a true and fair view of) [...] in accordance with [the applicable financial reporting framework]; or

(b)   When reporting in accordance with a compliance framework, the accompanying financial statements have not been prepared, in all material respects, in accordance with [the applicable financial reporting framework].

Disclaimer of Opinion

When the auditor disclaims an opinion due to an inability to obtain sufficient **19** appropriate audit evidence, the auditor shall:

(a)   State that the auditor does not express an opinion on the accompanying financial statements;

(b)   State that, because of the significance of the matter(s) described in the Basis for Disclaimer of Opinion section, the auditor has not been able to obtain sufficient appropriate audit evidence to provide a basis for an audit opinion on the financial statements; and

(c)   Amend the statement required by paragraph 24(b) of ISA (UK) 700 (Revised June 2016), which indicates that the financial statements have been audited, to state that the auditor was engaged to audit the financial statements.

Basis for Opinion

20   When the auditor modifies the opinion on the financial statements, the auditor shall, in addition to the specific elements required by ISA (UK) 700 (Revised June 2016): (Ref: Para. A21)

(a)   Amend the heading "Basis for Opinion" required by paragraph 28 of ISA (UK) 700 (Revised June 2016) to "Basis for Qualified Opinion," "Basis for Adverse Opinion," or "Basis for Disclaimer of Opinion," as appropriate; and

(b)   Within this section, include a description of the matter giving rise to the modification.

21   If there is a material misstatement of the financial statements that relates to specific amounts in the financial statements (including quantitative disclosures), the auditor shall include in the Basis for Opinion section a description and quantification of the financial effects of the misstatement, unless impracticable. If it is not practicable to quantify the financial effects, the auditor shall so state in this section. (Ref: Para. A22)

22   If there is a material misstatement of the financial statements that relates to qualitative disclosures, the auditor shall include in the Basis for Opinion section an explanation of how the disclosures are misstated.

23   If there is a material misstatement of the financial statements that relates to the nondisclosure of information required to be disclosed, the auditor shall:

(a)   Discuss the non-disclosure with those charged with governance;

(b)   Describe in the Basis for Opinion section the nature of the omitted information; and

(c)   Unless prohibited by law or regulation, include the omitted disclosures, provided it is practicable to do so and the auditor has obtained sufficient appropriate audit evidence about the omitted information. (Ref: Para. A23)

24   If the modification results from an inability to obtain sufficient appropriate audit evidence, the auditor shall include in the Basis for Opinion section the reasons for that inability.

25   When the auditor expresses a qualified or adverse opinion, the auditor shall amend the statement about whether the audit evidence obtained is sufficient and appropriate to provide a basis for the auditor's opinion required by paragraph 28(d) of ISA (UK) 700 (Revised June 2016) to include the word "qualified" or "adverse", as appropriate.

26   When the auditor disclaims an opinion on the financial statements, the auditor's report shall not include the elements required by paragraphs 28(b) and 28(d) of ISA (UK) 700 (Revised June 2016). Those elements are:

(a)   A reference to the section of the auditor's report where the auditor's responsibilities are described; and

(b)   A statement about whether the audit evidence obtained is sufficient and appropriate to provide a basis for the auditor's opinion.

Even if the auditor has expressed an adverse opinion or disclaimed an opinion on **27** the financial statements, the auditor shall describe in the Basis for Opinion section the reasons for any other matters of which the auditor is aware that would have required a modification to the opinion, and the effects thereof. (Ref: Para. A24)

Description of Auditor's Responsibilities for the Audit of the Financial Statements When the Auditor Disclaims an Opinion on the Financial Statements

When the auditor disclaims an opinion on the financial statements due to an **28** inability to obtain sufficient appropriate audit evidence, the auditor shall amend the description of the auditor's responsibilities required by paragraphs 39–41 of ISA (UK) 700 (Revised June 2016) to include only the following: (Ref: Para. A25)

(a) A statement that the auditor's responsibility is to conduct an audit of the entity's financial statements in accordance with International Standards on Auditing (UK) and to issue an auditor's report;

(b) A statement that, however, because of the matter(s) described in the Basis for Disclaimer of Opinion section, the auditor was not able to obtain sufficient appropriate audit evidence to provide a basis for an audit opinion on the financial statements; and

(c) The statement about auditor independence and other ethical responsibilities required by paragraph 28(c) of ISA (UK) 700 (Revised June 2016).

Considerations When the Auditor Disclaims an Opinion on the Financial Statements

Unless required by law or regulation, when the auditor disclaims an opinion on the **29** financial statements, the auditor's report shall not include a Key Audit Matters section in accordance with ISA (UK) 701[4] or an Other Information section in accordance with ISA (UK) 720 (Revised June 2016).[5] (Ref: Para. A26–A26-1)

Communication with Those Charged with Governance

When the auditor expects to modify the opinion in the auditor's report, the auditor **30** shall communicate with those charged with governance the circumstances that led to the expected modification and the wording of the modification. (Ref: Para. A27)

---

[4] *ISA (UK) 701, Communicating Key Audit Matters in the Independent Auditor's Report, paragraphs 11–13.*

[5] *ISA (UK) 720 (Revised June 2016), The Auditor's Responsibilities Relating to Other Information, paragraph A54.*

Application and Other Explanatory Material

Types of Modified Opinions
(Ref: Para. 2)

A1   The table below illustrates how the auditor's judgment about the nature of the matter giving rise to the modification, and the pervasiveness of its effects or possible effects on the financial statements, affects the type of opinion to be expressed.

Nature of Matter Giving Rise to the Modification	Auditor's Judgment about the Pervasiveness of the Effects or Possible Effects on the Financial Statements	
	Material but Not Pervasive	*Material and Pervasive*
Financial statements are materially misstated	Qualified opinion	Adverse opinion
Inability to obtain sufficient appropriate audit evidence	Qualified opinion	Disclaimer of opinion

Circumstances When a Modification to the Auditor's Opinion Is Required

Nature of Material Misstatements
(Ref: Para. 6(a))

A2   ISA (UK) 700 (Revised June 2016) requires the auditor, in order to form an opinion on the financial statements, to conclude as to whether reasonable assurance has been obtained about whether the financial statements as a whole are free from material misstatement.[6] This conclusion takes into account the auditor's evaluation of uncorrected misstatements, if any, on the financial statements in accordance with ISA (UK) 450 (Revised June 2016).[7]

A3   ISA (UK) 450 (Revised June 2016) defines a misstatement as a difference between the reported amount, classification, presentation, or disclosure of a financial statement item and the amount, classification, presentation, or disclosure that is required for the item to be in accordance with the applicable financial reporting framework. Accordingly, a material misstatement of the financial statements may arise in relation to:

(a)   The appropriateness of the selected accounting policies;

(b)   The application of the selected accounting policies; or

(c)   The appropriateness or adequacy of disclosures in the financial statements.

Appropriateness of the Selected Accounting Policies

A4   In relation to the appropriateness of the accounting policies management has selected, material misstatements of the financial statements may arise, for example, when:

---

[6] *ISA (UK) 700 (Revised June 2016), paragraph 11.*

[7] *ISA (UK) 450 (Revised June 2016), Evaluation of Misstatements Identified during the Audit, paragraph 11.*

(a)   The selected accounting policies are not consistent with the applicable financial reporting framework;

(b)   The financial statements do not correctly describe an accounting policy relating to a significant item in the statement of financial position, the statement of comprehensive income, the statement of changes in equity or the statement of cash flows; or

(c)   The financial statements do not represent or disclose the underlying transactions and events in a manner that achieves fair presentation.

Financial reporting frameworks often contain requirements for the accounting for, **A5** and disclosure of, changes in accounting policies. Where the entity has changed its selection of significant accounting policies, a material misstatement of the financial statements may arise when the entity has not complied with these requirements.

Application of the Selected Accounting Policies

In relation to the application of the selected accounting policies, material **A6** misstatements of the financial statements may arise:

(a)   When management has not applied the selected accounting policies consistently with the financial reporting framework, including when management has not applied the selected accounting policies consistently between periods or to similar transactions and events (consistency in application); or

(b)   Due to the method of application of the selected accounting policies (such as an unintentional error in application).

Appropriateness or Adequacy of Disclosures in the Financial Statements

In relation to the appropriateness or adequacy of disclosures in the financial **A7** statements, material misstatements of the financial statements may arise when:

(a)   The financial statements do not include all of the disclosures required by the applicable financial reporting framework;

(b)   The disclosures in the financial statements are not presented in accordance with the applicable financial reporting framework; or

(c)   The financial statements do not provide the additional disclosures necessary to achieve fair presentation beyond disclosures specifically required by the applicable financial reporting framework.

Paragraph A13a of ISA (UK) 450 (Revised June 2016) provides further examples of material misstatements in qualitative disclosures that may arise.

Nature of an Inability to Obtain Sufficient Appropriate Audit Evidence
(Ref: Para. 6(b))

The auditor's inability to obtain sufficient appropriate audit evidence (also referred **A8** to as a limitation on the scope of the audit) may arise from:

(a)   Circumstances beyond the control of the entity;

(b)   Circumstances relating to the nature or timing of the auditor's work; or

(c)   Limitations imposed by management.

An inability to perform a specific procedure does not constitute a limitation on the **A9** scope of the audit if the auditor is able to obtain sufficient appropriate audit evidence by performing alternative procedures. If this is not possible, the requirements of paragraphs 7(b) and 9–10 apply as appropriate. Limitations imposed by management may have other implications for the audit, such as for the auditor's assessment of fraud risks and consideration of engagement continuance.

A10 Examples of circumstances beyond the control of the entity include when:

- The entity's accounting records have been destroyed.

- The accounting records of a significant component have been seized indefinitely by governmental authorities.

A11 Examples of circumstances relating to the nature or timing of the auditor's work include when:

- The entity is required to use the equity method of accounting for an associated entity, and the auditor is unable to obtain sufficient appropriate audit evidence about the latter's financial information to evaluate whether the equity method has been appropriately applied.

- The timing of the auditor's appointment is such that the auditor is unable to observe the counting of the physical inventories.

- The auditor determines that performing substantive procedures alone is not sufficient, but the entity's controls are not effective.

A12 Examples of an inability to obtain sufficient appropriate audit evidence arising from a limitation on the scope of the audit imposed by management include when:

- Management prevents the auditor from observing the counting of the physical inventory.

- Management prevents the auditor from requesting external confirmation of specific account balances.

Determining the Type of Modification to the Auditor's Opinion

Consequence of an Inability to Obtain Sufficient Appropriate Audit Evidence Due to a Management-Imposed Limitation after the Auditor Has Accepted the Engagement (Ref: Para. 13(b)(i)–14)

A13 The practicality of withdrawing from the audit may depend on the stage of completion of the engagement at the time that management imposes the scope limitation. If the auditor has substantially completed the audit, the auditor may decide to complete the audit to the extent possible, disclaim an opinion and explain the scope limitation within the Basis for Disclaimer of Opinion section prior to withdrawing.

A14 In certain circumstances, withdrawal from the audit may not be possible if the auditor is required by law or regulation to continue the audit engagement. This may be the case for an auditor that is appointed to audit the financial statements of public sector entities. It may also be the case in jurisdictions where the auditor is appointed to audit the financial statements covering a specific period, or appointed for a specific period and is prohibited from withdrawing before the completion of the audit of those financial statements or before the end of that period, respectively. The auditor may also consider it necessary to include an Other Matter paragraph in the auditor's report.[8]

---

[8] *ISA (UK) 706 (Revised June 2016), Emphasis of Matter Paragraphs and Other Matter Paragraphs in the Independent Auditor's Report, paragraph A5.*

When the auditor concludes that withdrawal from the audit is necessary because of **A15** a scope limitation, there may be a professional, legal or regulatory requirement for the auditor to communicate matters relating to the withdrawal from the engagement to regulators or the entity's owners.

Statement by Auditor on Ceasing to Hold Office

The auditor of a company in the UK who ceases to hold office as auditor is **A15-1** required to comply with the requirements of Sections 519 and 521 of the Companies Act 2006 regarding the statement to be made by the auditor in relation to ceasing to hold office. In addition, the auditor may need to notify the appropriate audit authority in accordance with Section 522 of the Companies Act 2006.

Other Considerations Relating to an Adverse Opinion or Disclaimer of Opinion (Ref: Para. 15)

The following are examples of reporting circumstances that would not contradict **A16** the auditor's adverse opinion or disclaimer of opinion:

- The expression of an unmodified opinion on financial statements prepared under a given financial reporting framework and, within the same report, the expression of an adverse opinion on the same financial statements under a different financial reporting framework.[9]

- The expression of a disclaimer of opinion regarding the results of operations, and cash flows, where relevant, and an unmodified opinion regarding the financial position (see ISA (UK) 510 (Revised June 2016)[10]). In this case, the auditor has not expressed a disclaimer of opinion on the financial statements as a whole.

Form and Content of the Auditor's Report When the Opinion Is Modified

Illustrative Auditors' Reports[10a] (Ref: Para. 16)

Illustrations 1 and 2 in the Appendix contain auditor's reports with qualified and **A17** adverse opinions, respectively, as the financial statements are materially misstated.

Illustration 3 in the Appendix contains an auditor's report with a qualified opinion **A18** as the auditor is unable to obtain sufficient appropriate audit evidence. Illustration 4 contains a disclaimer of opinion due to an inability to obtain sufficient appropriate audit evidence about a single element of the financial statements. Illustration 5 contains a disclaimer of opinion due to an inability to obtain sufficient appropriate audit evidence about multiple elements of the financial statements. In each of the latter two cases, the possible effects on the financial statements of the inability are both material and pervasive. The Appendices to other ISAs (UK) that include reporting requirements, including ISA (UK) 570

---

[9] *See paragraph A31 of ISA (UK) 700 (Revised June 2016) for a description of this circumstance.*

[10] *ISA (UK) 510 (Revised June 2016), Initial Audit Engagements Opening Balances, paragraph 10.*

[10a] *The examples in the Appendix have not been tailored for the UK. Illustrative auditor's reports tailored for use with audits conducted in accordance with ISAs (UK) are given in the current version of the FRC's Compendium of Illustrative Auditor's Reports.*

(Revised June 2016),[11] also include illustrations of auditor's reports with modified opinions.

Auditor's Opinion
(Ref: Para. 16)

A19   Amending this heading makes it clear to the user that the auditor's opinion is modified and indicates the type of modification.

Qualified Opinion
(Ref: Para. 17)

A20   When the auditor expresses a qualified opinion, it would not be appropriate to use phrases such as "with the foregoing explanation" or "subject to" in the Opinion section as these are not sufficiently clear or forceful.

Basis for Opinion
(Ref: Para. 20, 21, 23, 27)

A21   Consistency in the auditor's report helps to promote users' understanding and to identify unusual circumstances when they occur. Accordingly, although uniformity in the wording of a modified opinion and in the description of the reasons for the modification may not be possible, consistency in both the form and content of the auditor's report is desirable.

A22   An example of the financial effects of material misstatements that the auditor may describe in the Basis for Opinion section in the auditor's report is the quantification of the effects on income tax, income before taxes, net income and equity if inventory is overstated.

A23   Disclosing the omitted information within the Basis for Opinion section would not be practicable if:

(a)   The disclosures have not been prepared by management or the disclosures are otherwise not readily available to the auditor; or

(b)   In the auditor's judgment, the disclosures would be unduly voluminous in relation to the auditor's report.

A24   An adverse opinion or a disclaimer of opinion relating to a specific matter described within the Basis for Opinion section does not justify the omission of a description of other identified matters that would have otherwise required a modification of the auditor's opinion. In such cases, the disclosure of such other matters of which the auditor is aware may be relevant to users of the financial statements.

Description of Auditor's Responsibilities for the Audit of the Financial Statements When the Auditor Disclaims an Opinion on the Financial Statements
(Ref: Para. 28)

A25   When the auditor disclaims an opinion on the financial statements, the following statements are better positioned within the Auditor's Responsibilities for the Audit of the Financial Statements section of the auditor's report, as illustrated in Illustrations 4–5 of the Appendix to this ISA (UK):[10a]

---

[11]   *ISA (UK) 570 (Revised June 2016), Going Concern.*

- The statement required by paragraph 28(a) of ISA (UK) 700 (Revised June 2016), amended to state that the auditor's responsibility is to conduct an audit of the entity's financial statements in accordance with ISAs (UK); and

- The statement required by paragraph 28(c) of ISA (UK) 700 (Revised June 2016) about independence and other ethical responsibilities.

Considerations When the Auditor Disclaims an Opinion on the Financial Statements
(Ref: Para. 29)

Providing the reasons for the auditor's inability to obtain sufficient appropriate audit evidence within the Basis for Disclaimer of Opinion section of the auditor's report provides useful information to users in understanding why the auditor has disclaimed an opinion on the financial statements and may further guard against inappropriate reliance on them. However, communication of any key audit matters other than the matter(s) giving rise to the disclaimer of opinion may suggest that the financial statements as a whole are more credible in relation to those matters than would be appropriate in the circumstances, and would be inconsistent with the disclaimer of opinion on the financial statements as a whole. Similarly, it would not be appropriate to include an Other Information section in accordance with ISA (UK) 720 (Revised June 2016) addressing the auditor's consideration of the consistency of the other information with the financial statements. Accordingly, paragraph 29 of this ISA (UK) prohibits a Key Audit Matters section or an Other Information section from being included in the auditor's report when the auditor disclaims an opinion on the financial statements, unless the auditor is otherwise required by law or regulation to communicate key audit matters or to report on other information.

A26

In the UK, the auditor is required by law or regulation to include a Key Audit Matters section or an Other Information section in the auditor's report, even when the auditor disclaims an opinion on the financial statements in the following circumstances:

A26-1

- For audits of financial statements of public interest entities, the auditor is required to communicate certain key audit matters in accordance with ISA (UK) 701.[11a]

- For entities incorporated under the Companies Acts,[11b] the auditor is required to report in an Other Information section on the strategic report, the directors' report and, where one is prepared, the separate corporate governance statement in accordance with ISA (UK) 720 (Revised June 2016).[11c]

- For entities that are required, and those that choose voluntarily, to report on how they have applied the UK Corporate Governance Code, the auditor is required to report in an Other Information section on certain aspects of the entity's compliance with the UK Corporate Governance Code and the Listing Rules in accordance with ISA (UK) 720 (Revised June 2016).[11d]

[11a] *ISA (UK) 701, paragraph 13R-1.*

[11b] *In the UK, the Companies Act 2006 establishes this requirement.*

[11c] *ISA (UK) 720 (Revised June 2016), paragraphs 22D-1 and 22D-2.*

[11d] *ISA (UK) 720 (Revised June 2016), paragraphs 22-3 and 22-4.*

Communication with Those Charged with Governance
(Ref: Para. 30)

A27 Communicating with those charged with governance the circumstances that lead to an expected modification to the auditor's opinion and the proposed wording of the modification enables:

    (a) The auditor to give notice to those charged with governance of the intended modification(s) and the reasons (or circumstances) for the modification(s);

    (b) The auditor to seek the concurrence of those charged with governance regarding the facts of the matter(s) giving rise to the expected modification(s), or to confirm matters of disagreement with management as such; and

    (c) Those charged with governance to have an opportunity, where appropriate, to provide the auditor with further information and explanations in respect of the matter(s) giving rise to the expected modification(s).

A27-1 For audits of financial statements of public interest entities, ISA (UK) 250 (Revised June 2016) Section B[11e] requires the auditor to report to the relevant regulatory, enforcement or supervisory authority any information about the public interest entity (or an undertaking having close links with the public interest entity) that may bring about a refusal to issue an audit opinion on the financial statements or the issuing of an adverse or qualified opinion.

[11e] *ISA (UK) 250 (Revised June 2016), Section B—The Auditor's Statutory Right and Duty to Report to Regulators of Public Interest Entities and Regulators of Other Entities in the Financial Sector, paragraph 13R-1 (a)(iii).*

Appendix

(Ref: Para. A17–A18, A25)

Illustrations of Auditor's Reports with Modifications to the Opinion

The examples in the Appendix have not been tailored for the UK. Illustrative auditor's reports tailored for use with audits conducted in accordance with ISAs (UK) are given in the current version of the FRC's Compendium of Illustrative Auditor's Reports.

- Illustration 1: An auditor's report containing a qualified opinion due to a material misstatement of the financial statements.

- Illustration 2: An auditor's report containing an adverse opinion due to a material misstatement of the consolidated financial statements.

- Illustration 3: An auditor's report containing a qualified opinion due to the auditor's inability to obtain sufficient appropriate audit evidence regarding a foreign associate.

- Illustration 4: An auditor's report containing a disclaimer of opinion due to the auditor's inability to obtain sufficient appropriate audit evidence about a single element of the consolidated financial statements.

- Illustration 5: An auditor's report containing a disclaimer of opinion due to the auditor's inability to obtain sufficient appropriate audit evidence about multiple elements of the financial statements.

Illustration 1 – Qualified Opinion due to a Material Misstatement of the Financial Statements

For purposes of this illustrative auditor's report, the following circumstances are assumed:

- Audit of a complete set of financial statements of a listed entity using a fair presentation framework. The audit is not a group audit (i.e., ISA 600[1-a] does not apply).
- The financial statements are prepared by management of the entity in accordance with IFRSs (a general purpose framework).
- The terms of the audit engagement reflect the description of management's responsibility for the financial statements in ISA 210.[2-a]
- Inventories are misstated. The misstatement is deemed to be material but not pervasive to the financial statements (i.e., a qualified opinion is appropriate).
- The relevant ethical requirements that apply to the audit are those of the jurisdiction.
- Based on the audit evidence obtained, the auditor has concluded that a material uncertainty does not exist related to events or conditions that

---

[1-a] *ISA 600, Special Considerations—Audits of Group Financial Statements (Including the Work of Component Auditors).*

[2-a] *ISA 210, Agreeing the Terms of Audit Engagements.*

> may cast significant doubt on the entity's ability to continue as a going concern in accordance with ISA (UK) 570 (Revised).
> - Key audit matters have been communicated in accordance with ISA 701.
> - The auditor has obtained all of the other information prior to the date of the auditor's report and the matter giving rise to the qualified opinion on the consolidated financial statements also affects the other information.
> - Those responsible for oversight of the financial statements differ from those responsible for the preparation of the financial statements.
> - In addition to the audit of the financial statements, the auditor has other reporting responsibilities required under local law.

INDEPENDENT AUDITOR'S REPORT

To the Shareholders of ABC Company [or Other Appropriate Addressee]

Report on the Audit of the Financial Statements[3-a]

Qualified Opinion

We have audited the financial statements of ABC Company (the Company), which comprise the statement of financial position as at December 31, 20X1, and the statement of comprehensive income, statement of changes in equity and statement of cash flows for the year then ended, and notes to the financial statements, including a summary of significant accounting policies.

In our opinion, except for the effects of the matter described in the *Basis for Qualified Opinion* section of our report, the accompanying financial statements present fairly, in all material respects, (or *give a true and fair view of*) the financial position of the Company as at December 31, 20X1, and (*of*) its financial performance and its cash flows for the year then ended in accordance with International Financial Reporting Standards (IFRSs).

Basis for Qualified Opinion

The Company's inventories are carried in the statement of financial position at xxx. Management has not stated the inventories at the lower of cost and net realizable value but has stated them solely at cost, which constitutes a departure from IFRSs. The Company's records indicate that, had management stated the inventories at the lower of cost and net realizable value, an amount of xxx would have been required to write the inventories down to their net realizable value. Accordingly, cost of sales would have been increased by xxx, and income tax, net income and shareholders' equity would have been reduced by xxx, xxx and xxx, respectively.

We conducted our audit in accordance with International Standards on Auditing (ISAs). Our responsibilities under those standards are further described in the *Auditor's Responsibilities for the Audit of the Financial Statements* section of our report. We are independent of the Company in accordance with the ethical requirements that are relevant to our audit of the financial statements in [jurisdiction], and we have fulfilled our other ethical responsibilities in

---

[3-a] *The sub-title "Report on the Audit of the Financial Statements" is unnecessary in circumstances when the second sub-title "Report on Other Legal and Regulatory Requirements" is not applicable.*

accordance with these requirements. We believe that the audit evidence we have obtained is sufficient and appropriate to provide a basis for our qualified opinion.

Other Information [or another title if appropriate such as "Information Other than the Financial Statements and Auditor's Report Thereon"]

[*Reporting in accordance with the reporting requirements in ISA 720 (Revised) – see Illustration 6 in Appendix 2 of ISA 720 (Revised). The last paragraph of the other information section in Illustration 6 would be customized to describe the specific matter giving rise to the qualified opinion that also affects the other information.*]

Key Audit Matters

Key audit matters are those matters that, in our professional judgment, were of most significance in our audit of the financial statements of the current period. These matters were addressed in the context of our audit of the financial statements as a whole, and in forming our opinion thereon, and we do not provide a separate opinion on these matters. In addition to the matter described in the *Basis for Qualified Opinion* section we have determined the matters described below to be the key audit matters to be communicated in our report.

[*Description of each key audit matter in accordance with ISA 701.*]

Responsibilities of Management and Those Charged with Governance for the Financial Statements[4-a]

[*Reporting in accordance with ISA 700 (Revised) – see Illustration 1 in ISA 700 (Revised).*]

Auditor's Responsibilities for the Audit of the Financial Statements

[*Reporting in accordance with ISA 700 (Revised) – see Illustration 1 in ISA 700 (Revised).*]

Report on Other Legal and Regulatory Requirements

[*Reporting in accordance with ISA 700 (Revised) – see Illustration 1 in ISA 700 (Revised).*]

The engagement partner on the audit resulting in this independent auditor's report is [*name*].

[*Signature in the name of the audit firm, the personal name of the auditor, or both, as appropriate for the particular jurisdiction*]

[*Auditor Address*]

[*Date*]

[4-a] *Throughout the illustrative auditor's reports, the terms management and those charged with governance may need to be replaced by another term that is appropriate in the context of the legal framework in the particular jurisdiction.*

Illustration 2 – Adverse Opinion due to a Material Misstatement of the Consolidated Financial Statements

For purposes of this illustrative auditor's report, the following circumstances are assumed:

- Audit of a complete set of consolidated financial statements of a listed entity using a fair presentation framework. The audit is a group audit of an entity with subsidiaries (i.e., ISA 600 applies).
- The consolidated financial statements are prepared by management of the entity in accordance with IFRSs (a general purpose framework).
- The terms of the audit engagement reflect the description of management's responsibility for the consolidated financial statements in ISA 210.
- The consolidated financial statements are materially misstated due to the non-consolidation of a subsidiary. The material misstatement is deemed to be pervasive to the consolidated financial statements. The effects of the misstatement on the consolidated financial statements have not been determined because it was not practicable to do so (i.e., an adverse opinion is appropriate).
- The relevant ethical requirements that apply to the audit are those of the jurisdiction.
- Based on the audit evidence obtained, the auditor has concluded that a material uncertainty does not exist related to events or conditions that may cast significant doubt on the entity's ability to continue as a going concern in accordance with ISA 570 (Revised).
- ISA 701 applies; however, the auditor has determined that there are no key audit matters other than the matter described in the Basis for Adverse Opinion section.
- The auditor has obtained all of the other information prior to the date of the auditor's report and the matter giving rise to the adverse opinion on the consolidated financial statements also affects the other information.
- Those responsible for oversight of the consolidated financial statements differ from those responsible for the preparation of the consolidated financial statements.
- In addition to the audit of the consolidated financial statements, the auditor has other reporting responsibilities required under local law.

INDEPENDENT AUDITOR'S REPORT

To the Shareholders of ABC Company [or Other Appropriate Addressee]

Report on the Audit of the Consolidated Financial Statements[5-a]

Adverse Opinion

We have audited the consolidated financial statements of ABC Company and its subsidiaries (the Group), which comprise the consolidated statement of financial

---

[5-a] *The sub-title "Report on the Audit of the Consolidated Financial Statements" is unnecessary in circumstances when the second sub-title "Report on Other Legal and Regulatory Requirements" is not applicable.*

position as at December 31, 20X1, and the consolidated statement of comprehensive income, consolidated statement of changes in equity and consolidated statement of cash flows for the year then ended, and notes to the consolidated financial statements, including a summary of significant accounting policies.

In our opinion, because of the significance of the matter discussed in the *Basis for Adverse Opinion* section of our report, the accompanying consolidated financial statements do not present fairly (or *do not give a true and fair view of*) the consolidated financial position of the Group as at December 31, 20X1, and (*of*) its consolidated financial performance and its consolidated cash flows for the year then ended in accordance with International Financial Reporting Standards (IFRSs).

Basis for Adverse Opinion

As explained in Note X, the Group has not consolidated subsidiary XYZ Company that the Group acquired during 20X1 because it has not yet been able to determine the fair values of certain of the subsidiary's material assets and liabilities at the acquisition date. This investment is therefore accounted for on a cost basis. Under IFRSs, the Company should have consolidated this subsidiary and accounted for the acquisition based on provisional amounts. Had XYZ Company been consolidated, many elements in the accompanying consolidated financial statements would have been materially affected. The effects on the consolidated financial statements of the failure to consolidate have not been determined.

We conducted our audit in accordance with International Standards on Auditing (ISAs). Our responsibilities under those standards are further described in the *Auditor's Responsibilities for the Audit of the Consolidated Financial Statements* section of our report. We are independent of the Group in accordance with the ethical requirements that are relevant to our audit of the consolidated financial statements in [*jurisdiction*], and we have fulfilled our other ethical responsibilities in accordance with these requirements. We believe that the audit evidence we have obtained is sufficient and appropriate to provide a basis for our adverse opinion.

Other Information [or another title if appropriate such as "Information Other than the Financial Statements and Auditor's Report Thereon"]

[*Reporting in accordance with the reporting requirements in ISA 720 (Revised) – see Illustration 7 in Appendix 2 of ISA 720 (Revised). The last paragraph of the other information section in Illustration 7 would be customized to describe the specific matter giving rise to the qualified opinion that also affects the other information.*]

Key Audit Matters

Except for the matter described in the *Basis for Adverse Opinion* section, we have determined that there are no other key audit matters to communicate in our report.

Responsibilities of Management and Those Charged with Governance for the Consolidated Financial Statements[6-a]

[*Reporting in accordance with ISA 700 (Revised) – see Illustration 2 in ISA 700 (Revised)*.]

Auditor's Responsibilities for the Audit of the Consolidated Financial Statements

[*Reporting in accordance with ISA 700 (Revised) – see Illustration 2 in ISA 700 (Revised)*.]

Report on Other Legal and Regulatory Requirements

[*Reporting in accordance with ISA 700 (Revised) – see Illustration 2 in ISA 700 (Revised)*.]

The engagement partner on the audit resulting in this independent auditor's report is [*name*].

[*Signature in the name of the audit firm, the personal name of the auditor, or both, as appropriate for the particular jurisdiction*]

[*Auditor Address*]

[*Date*]

Illustration 3 – Qualified Opinion due to the Auditor's Inability to Obtain Sufficient Audit Evidence Regarding a Foreign Associate

For purposes of this illustrative auditor's report, the following circumstances are assumed:

- Audit of a complete set of consolidated financial statements of a listed entity using a fair presentation framework. The audit is a group audit of an entity with subsidiaries (i.e., ISA 600 applies).
- The consolidated financial statements are prepared by management of the entity in accordance with IFRSs (a general purpose framework).
- The terms of the audit engagement reflect the description of management's responsibility for the consolidated financial statements in ISA 210.
- The auditor was unable to obtain sufficient appropriate audit evidence regarding an investment in a foreign associate. The possible effects of the inability to obtain sufficient appropriate audit evidence are deemed to be material but not pervasive to the consolidated financial statements (i.e., a qualified opinion is appropriate).
- The relevant ethical requirements that apply to the audit are those of the jurisdiction.
- Based on the audit evidence obtained, the auditor has concluded that a material uncertainty does not exist related to events or conditions that may cast significant doubt on the entity's ability to continue as a going concern in accordance with ISA 570 (Revised).
- Key audit matters have been communicated in accordance with ISA 701.

[6-a] *Or other terms that are appropriate in the context of the legal framework in the particular jurisdiction.*

> - The auditor has obtained all of the other information prior to the date of the auditor's report and the matter giving rise to the qualified opinion on the consolidated financial statements also affects the other information.
> - Those responsible for oversight of the consolidated financial statements differ from those responsible for the preparation of the consolidated financial statements.
> - In addition to the audit of the consolidated financial statements, the auditor has other reporting responsibilities required under local law.

INDEPENDENT AUDITOR'S REPORT

To the Shareholders of ABC Company [or Other Appropriate Addressee]

Report on the Audit of the Consolidated Financial Statements[7-a]

Qualified Opinion

We have audited the consolidated financial statements of ABC Company and its subsidiaries (the Group), which comprise the consolidated statement of financial position as at December 31, 20X1, and the consolidated statement of comprehensive income, consolidated statement of changes in equity and consolidated statement of cash flows for the year then ended, and notes to the consolidated financial statements, including a summary of significant accounting policies.

In our opinion, except for the possible effects of the matter described in the *Basis for Qualified Opinion* section of our report, the accompanying consolidated financial statements present fairly, in all material respects, (or *give a true and fair view of*) the financial position of the Group as at December 31, 20X1, and (*of*) its consolidated financial performance and its consolidated cash flows for the year then ended in accordance with International Financial Reporting Standards (IFRSs).

Basis for Qualified Opinion

The Group's investment in XYZ Company, a foreign associate acquired during the year and accounted for by the equity method, is carried at xxx on the consolidated statement of financial position as at December 31, 20X1, and ABC's share of XYZ's net income of xxx is included in ABC's income for the year then ended. We were unable to obtain sufficient appropriate audit evidence about the carrying amount of ABC's investment in XYZ as at December 31, 20X1 and ABC's share of XYZ's net income for the year because we were denied access to the financial information, management, and the auditors of XYZ. Consequently, we were unable to determine whether any adjustments to these amounts were necessary.

We conducted our audit in accordance with International Standards on Auditing (ISAs). Our responsibilities under those standards are further described in the *Auditor's Responsibilities for the Audit of the Consolidated Financial Statements*

[7-a] *The sub-title "Report on the Audit of the Consolidated Financial Statements" is unnecessary in circumstances when the second sub-title "Report on Other Legal and Regulatory Requirements" is not applicable.*

section of our report. We are independent of the Group in accordance with the ethical requirements that are relevant to our audit of the consolidated financial statements in [*jurisdiction*], and we have fulfilled our other ethical responsibilities in accordance with these requirements. We believe that the audit evidence we have obtained is sufficient and appropriate to provide a basis for our qualified opinion.

Other Information [or another title if appropriate such as "Information Other than the Financial Statements and Auditor's Report Thereon"]

[*Reporting in accordance with the reporting requirements in ISA 720 (Revised) – see Illustration 6 in Appendix 2 of ISA 720 (Revised). The last paragraph of the other information section in Illustration 6 would be customized to describe the specific matter giving rise to the qualified opinion that also affects the other information.*]

Key Audit Matters

Key audit matters are those matters that, in our professional judgment, were of most significance in our audit of the consolidated financial statements of the current period. These matters were addressed in the context of our audit of the consolidated financial statements as a whole, and in forming our opinion thereon, and we do not provide a separate opinion on these matters. In addition to the matter described in the *Basis for Qualified Opinion* section, we have determined the matters described below to be the key audit matters to be communicated in our report.

[*Description of each key audit matter in accordance with ISA 701.*]

Responsibilities of Management and Those Charged with Governance for the Consolidated Financial Statements[8-a]

[*Reporting in accordance with ISA 700 (Revised) – see Illustration 2 in ISA 700 (Revised).*]

Auditor's Responsibilities for the Audit of the Consolidated Financial Statements

[*Reporting in accordance with ISA 700 (Revised) – see Illustration 2 in ISA 700 (Revised).*]

Report on Other Legal and Regulatory Requirements

[*Reporting in accordance with ISA 700 (Revised) – see Illustration 2 in ISA 700 (Revised).*]

The engagement partner on the audit resulting in this independent auditor's report is [*name*].

[*Signature in the name of the audit firm, the personal name of the auditor, or both, as appropriate for the particular jurisdiction*]

[*Auditor Address*]

[*Date*]

[8-a] *Or other terms that are appropriate in the context of the legal framework in the particular jurisdiction.*

Illustration 4 – Disclaimer of Opinion due to the Auditor's Inability to Obtain Sufficient Appropriate Audit Evidence about a Single Element of the Consolidated Financial Statements

For purposes of this illustrative auditor's report, the following circumstances are assumed:

- Audit of a complete set of consolidated financial statements of an entity other than a listed entity using a fair presentation framework. The audit is a group audit of an entity with subsidiaries (i.e., ISA 600 applies).
- The consolidated financial statements are prepared by management of the entity in accordance with IFRSs (a general purpose framework).
- The terms of the audit engagement reflect the description of management's responsibility for the consolidated financial statements in ISA 210.
- The auditor was unable to obtain sufficient appropriate audit evidence about a single element of the consolidated financial statements. That is, the auditor was also unable to obtain audit evidence about the financial information of a joint venture investment that represents over 90% of the entity's net assets. The possible effects of this inability to obtain sufficient appropriate audit evidence are deemed to be both material and pervasive to the consolidated financial statements (i.e., a disclaimer of opinion is appropriate).
- The relevant ethical requirements that apply to the audit are those of the jurisdiction.
- Those responsible for oversight of the consolidated financial statements differ from those responsible for the preparation of the consolidated financial statements.
- A more limited description of the auditor's responsibilities section is required.
- In addition to the audit of the consolidated financial statements, the auditor has other reporting responsibilities required under local law.

INDEPENDENT AUDITOR'S REPORT

To the Shareholders of ABC Company [or Other Appropriate Addressee]

Report on the Audit of the Consolidated Financial Statements[9-a]

Disclaimer of Opinion

We were engaged to audit the consolidated financial statements of ABC Company and its subsidiaries (the Group), which comprise the consolidated statement of financial position as at December 31, 20X1, and the consolidated statement of comprehensive income, consolidated statement of changes in equity and consolidated statement of cash flows for the year then ended, and notes to the

---

[9-a] *The sub-title "Report on the Audit of the Consolidated Financial Statements" is unnecessary in circumstances when the second sub-title "Report on Other Legal and Regulatory Requirements" is not applicable.*

consolidated financial statements, including a summary of significant accounting policies.

We do not express an opinion on the accompanying consolidated financial statements of the Group. Because of the significance of the matter described in the *Basis for Disclaimer of Opinion* section of our report, we have not been able to obtain sufficient appropriate audit evidence to provide a basis for an audit opinion on these consolidated financial statements.

Basis for Disclaimer of Opinion

The Group's investment in its joint venture XYZ Company is carried at xxx on the Group's consolidated statement of financial position, which represents over 90% of the Group's net assets as at December 31, 20X1. We were not allowed access to the management and the auditors of XYZ Company, including XYZ Company's auditors' audit documentation. As a result, we were unable to determine whether any adjustments were necessary in respect of the Group's proportional share of XYZ Company's assets that it controls jointly, its proportional share of XYZ Company's liabilities for which it is jointly responsible, its proportional share of XYZ's income and expenses for the year, and the elements making up the consolidated statement of changes in equity and the consolidated cash flow statement.

Responsibilities of Management and Those Charged with Governance for the Consolidated Financial Statements[10-a]

[*Reporting in accordance with ISA 700 (Revised) – see Illustration 2 in ISA 700 (Revised).*]

Auditor's Responsibilities for the Audit of the Consolidated Financial Statements

Our responsibility is to conduct an audit of the Group's consolidated financial statements in accordance with International Standards on Auditing and to issue an auditor's report. However, because of the matter described in the *Basis for Disclaimer of Opinion* section of our report, we were not able to obtain sufficient appropriate audit evidence to provide a basis for an audit opinion on these consolidated financial statements.

We are independent of the Group in accordance with the ethical requirements that are relevant to our audit of the financial statements in [*jurisdiction*], and we have fulfilled our other ethical responsibilities in accordance with these requirements.

Report on Other Legal and Regulatory Requirements

[*Reporting in accordance with ISA 700 (Revised) – see Illustration 2 in ISA 700 (Revised).*]

[*Signature in the name of the audit firm, the personal name of the auditor, or both, as appropriate for the particular jurisdiction*]

[*Auditor Address*]

[*Date*]

[10-a]   *Or other terms that are appropriate in the context of the legal framework of the particular jurisdiction.*

Illustration 5 – Disclaimer of Opinion due to the Auditor's Inability to Obtain Sufficient Appropriate Audit Evidence about Multiple Elements of the Financial Statements

For purposes of this illustrative auditor's report, the following circumstances are assumed:

- Audit of a complete set of financial statements of an entity other than a listed entity using a fair presentation framework. The audit is not a group audit (i.e., ISA 600, does not apply).
- The financial statements are prepared by management of the entity in accordance with IFRSs (a general purpose framework).
- The terms of the audit engagement reflect the description of management's responsibility for the financial statements in ISA 210.
- The auditor was unable to obtain sufficient appropriate audit evidence about multiple elements of the financial statements, that is, the auditor was also unable to obtain audit evidence about the entity's inventories and accounts receivable. The possible effects of this inability to obtain sufficient appropriate audit evidence are deemed to be both material and pervasive to the financial statements.
- The relevant ethical requirements that apply to the audit are those of the jurisdiction.
- Those responsible for oversight of the financial statements differ from those responsible for the preparation of the financial statements.
- A more limited description of the auditor's responsibilities section is required.
- In addition to the audit of the financial statements, the auditor has other reporting responsibilities required under local law.

INDEPENDENT AUDITOR'S REPORT

To the Shareholders of ABC Company [or Other Appropriate Addressee]

Report on the Audit of the Financial Statements[11-a]

Disclaimer of Opinion

We were engaged to audit the financial statements of ABC Company (the Company), which comprise the statement of financial position as at December 31, 20X1, and the statement of comprehensive income, statement of changes in equity and statement of cash flows for the year then ended, and notes to the financial statements, including a summary of significant accounting policies.

We do not express an opinion on the accompanying financial statements of the Company. Because of the significance of the matters described in the *Basis for Disclaimer of Opinion* section of our report, we have not been able to obtain sufficient appropriate audit evidence to provide a basis for an audit opinion on these financial statements.

[11-a] *The sub-title "Report on the Audit of the Financial Statements" is unnecessary in circumstances when the second sub-title "Report on Other Legal and Regulatory Requirements" is not applicable.*

Basis for Disclaimer of Opinion

We were not appointed as auditors of the Company until after December 31, 20X1 and thus did not observe the counting of physical inventories at the beginning and end of the year. We were unable to satisfy ourselves by alternative means concerning the inventory quantities held at December 31, 20X0 and 20X1, which are stated in the statements of financial position at xxx and xxx, respectively. In addition, the introduction of a new computerized accounts receivable system in September 20X1 resulted in numerous errors in accounts receivable. As of the date of our report, management was still in the process of rectifying the system deficiencies and correcting the errors. We were unable to confirm or verify by alternative means accounts receivable included in the statement of financial position at a total amount of xxx as at December 31, 20X1. As a result of these matters, we were unable to determine whether any adjustments might have been found necessary in respect of recorded or unrecorded inventories and accounts receivable, and the elements making up the statement of comprehensive income, statement of changes in equity and statement of cash flows.

Responsibilities of Management and Those Charged with Governance for the Financial Statements[12-a]

[*Reporting in accordance with ISA 700 (Revised) – see Illustration 1 in ISA 700 (Revised).*]

Auditor's Responsibilities for the Audit of the Financial Statements

Our responsibility is to conduct an audit of the Company's financial statements in accordance with International Standards on Auditing and to issue an auditor's report. However, because of the matters described in the *Basis for Disclaimer of Opinion* section of our report, we were not able to obtain sufficient appropriate audit evidence to provide a basis for an audit opinion on these financial statements.

We are independent of the Company in accordance with the ethical requirements that are relevant to our audit of the financial statements in [*jurisdiction*], and we have fulfilled our other ethical responsibilities in accordance with these requirements.

Report on Other Legal and Regulatory Requirements

[*Reporting in accordance with ISA 700 (Revised) – see Illustration 1 in ISA 700 (Revised).*]

[*Signature in the name of the audit firm, the personal name of the auditor, or both, as appropriate for the particular jurisdiction*]

[*Auditor Address*]

[*Date*]

[12-a] *Or other terms that are appropriate in the context of the legal framework of the particular jurisdiction.*

ISA (UK) 706 (Revised June 2016) Emphasis of Matter Paragraphs and Other Matter Paragraphs in the Independent Auditor's Report

(Effective for audits of financial statements for periods commencing on or after 17 June 2016)

Contents

Paragraphs

Introduction
Scope of this ISA (UK)   1 - 4
Effective date   5

Objective   6

Definitions   7

Requirements
Emphasis of matter paragraphs in the auditor's report   8 - 9
Other matter paragraphs in the auditor's report   10 - 11
Communication with those charged with governance   12

Application and other explanatory material
The relationship between emphasis of matter paragraphs and key audit
matters in the auditor's report   A1 - A3
Circumstances in which an emphasis of matter paragraph may be necessary   A4 - A6
Including an emphasis of matter paragraph in the auditor's report   A7 - A8
Other matter paragraphs in the auditor's report   A9 - A15
Placement of emphasis of matter paragraphs and other matter paragraphs in the
auditor's report   A16 - A17
Communication with those charged with governance   A18

**Appendix 1: List of ISAs (UK) containing requirements for emphasis of
matter paragraphs**

**Appendix 2: List of ISAs (UK) containing requirements for other
matter paragraphs**

Appendix 3: Illustration of an auditor's report that includes a key audit matters section

**Appendix 4: Illustration of an auditor's report containing a qualified opinion
due to a departure from the applicable financial reporting framework**

International Standard on Auditing (UK) (ISA (UK)) 706 (Revised June 2016), *Emphasis of Matter Paragraphs and Other Matter Paragraphs in the Independent Auditor's Report*, should be read in conjunction with ISA (UK) 200 (Revised June 2016), *Overall Objectives of the Independent Auditor and the Conduct of an Audit in Accordance with International Standards on Auditing (UK)*.

Introduction

Scope of this ISA (UK)

1   This International Standard on Auditing (UK) (ISA (UK)) deals with additional communication in the auditor's report when the auditor considers it necessary to:

(a)   Draw users' attention to a matter or matters presented or disclosed in the financial statements that are of such importance that they are fundamental to users' understanding of the financial statements; or

(b)   Draw users' attention to any matter or matters other than those presented or disclosed in the financial statements that are relevant to users' understanding of the audit, the auditor's responsibilities or the auditor's report.

2   ISA (UK) 701[1] establishes requirements and provides guidance when the auditor determines key audit matters and communicates them in the auditor's report. When the auditor includes a Key Audit Matters section in the auditor's report, this ISA (UK) addresses the relationship between key audit matters and any additional communication in the auditor's report in accordance with this ISA (UK). (Ref: Para. A1–A3)

3   ISA (UK) 570 (Revised June 2016)[2] and ISA (UK) 720 (Revised June 2016)[3] establish requirements and provide guidance about communication in the auditor's report relating to going concern and other information respectively.

4   Appendices 1 and 2 identify ISAs (UK) that contain specific requirements for the auditor to include Emphasis of Matter paragraphs or Other Matter paragraphs in the auditor's report. In those circumstances, the requirements in this ISA (UK) regarding the form and placement of such paragraphs apply. (Ref: Para. A4)

Effective Date

5   This ISA (UK) is effective for audits of financial statements for periods commencing on or after 17 June 2016. Earlier adoption is permitted.

Objective

6   The objective of the auditor, having formed an opinion on the financial statements, is to draw users' attention, when in the auditor's judgment it is necessary to do so, by way of clear additional communication in the auditor's report, to:

(a)   A matter, although appropriately presented or disclosed in the financial statements, that is of such importance that it is fundamental to users' understanding of the financial statements; or

(b)   As appropriate, any other matter that is relevant to users' understanding of the audit, the auditor's responsibilities or the auditor's report.

---

[1]   *ISA (UK) 701, Communicating Key Audit Matters in the Independent Auditor's Report.*

[2]   *ISA (UK) 570 (Revised June 2016), Going Concern.*

[3]   *ISA (UK) 720 (Revised June 2016), The Auditor's Responsibilities Relating to Other Information.*

Definitions

For the purposes of the ISAs (UK), the following terms have the meanings   **7** attributed below:

(a)   Emphasis of Matter paragraph – A paragraph included in the auditor's report that refers to a matter appropriately presented or disclosed in the financial statements that, in the auditor's judgment, is of such importance that it is fundamental to users' understanding of the financial statements.

(b)   Other Matter paragraph – A paragraph included in the auditor's report that refers to a matter other than those presented or disclosed in the financial statements that, in the auditor's judgment, is relevant to users' understanding of the audit, the auditor's responsibilities or the auditor's report.

Requirements

Emphasis of Matter Paragraphs in the Auditor's Report

If the auditor considers it necessary to draw users' attention to a matter presented   **8** or disclosed in the financial statements that, in the auditor's judgment, is of such importance that it is fundamental to users' understanding of the financial statements, the auditor shall include an Emphasis of Matter paragraph in the auditor's report provided: (Ref: Para. A5–A6)

(a)   The auditor would not be required to modify the opinion in accordance with ISA (UK) 705 (Revised June 2016)[4] as a result of the matter; and

(b)   When ISA (UK) 701 applies, the matter has not been determined to be a key audit matter to be communicated in the auditor's report. (Ref: Para. A1–A3)

When the auditor includes an Emphasis of Matter paragraph in the auditor's   **9** report, the auditor shall:

(a)   Include the paragraph within a separate section of the auditor's report with an appropriate heading that includes the term "Emphasis of Matter";

(b)   Include in the paragraph a clear reference to the matter being emphasized and to where relevant disclosures that fully describe the matter can be found in the financial statements. The paragraph shall refer only to information presented or disclosed in the financial statements; and

(c)   Indicate that the auditor's opinion is not modified in respect of the matter emphasized. (Ref: Para. A7–A8, A16–A17)

Other Matter Paragraphs in the Auditor's Report

If the auditor considers it necessary to communicate a matter other than those that   **10** are presented or disclosed in the financial statements that, in the auditor's judgment, is relevant to users' understanding of the audit, the auditor's responsibilities or the auditor's report, the auditor shall include an Other Matter paragraph in the auditor's report, provided:

(a)   This is not prohibited by law or regulation; and

---

[4] *ISA (UK) 705 (Revised June 2016), Modifications to the Opinion in the Independent Auditor's Report.*

(b)   When ISA (UK) 701 applies, the matter has not been determined to be a key audit matter to be communicated in the auditor's report. (Ref: Para. A9–A14)

11   When the auditor includes an Other Matter paragraph in the auditor's report, the auditor shall include the paragraph within a separate section with the heading "Other Matter," or other appropriate heading. (Ref: Para. A15–A17)

Communication with Those Charged with Governance

12   If the auditor expects to include an Emphasis of Matter or an Other Matter paragraph in the auditor's report, the auditor shall communicate with those charged with governance regarding this expectation and the proposed wording of this paragraph. (Ref: Para. A18)

Application and Other Explanatory Material

The Relationship between Emphasis of Matter Paragraphs and Key Audit Matters in the Auditor's Report
(Ref: Para. 2, 8(b))

A1   Key audit matters are defined in ISA (UK) 701 as those matters that, in the auditor's professional judgment, were of most significance in the audit of the financial statements of the current period. Key audit matters are selected from matters communicated with those charged with governance, which include significant findings from the audit of the financial statements of the current period.[5] Communicating key audit matters provides additional information to intended users of the financial statements to assist them in understanding those matters that, in the auditor's professional judgment, were of most significance in the audit and may also assist them in understanding the entity and areas of significant management judgment in the audited financial statements. When ISA (UK) 701 applies, the use of Emphasis of Matter paragraphs is not a substitute for a description of individual key audit matters.

A2   Matters that are determined to be key audit matters in accordance with ISA (UK) 701 may also be, in the auditor's judgment, fundamental to users' understanding of the financial statements. In such cases, in communicating the matter as a key audit matter in accordance with ISA (UK) 701, the auditor may wish to highlight or draw further attention to its relative importance. The auditor may do so by presenting the matter more prominently than other matters in the Key Audit Matters section (e.g., as the first matter) or by including additional information in the description of the key audit matter to indicate the importance of the matter to users' understanding of the financial statements.

A2-1   In the UK, law or regulation may require a matter to be emphasized in the auditor's report in addition to communicating such a matter as a key audit matter in accordance with ISA (UK) 701.

A3   There may be a matter that is not determined to be a key audit matter in accordance with ISA (UK) 701 (i.e., because it did not require significant auditor attention), but which, in the auditor's judgment, is fundamental to users' understanding of the financial statements (e.g., a subsequent event). If the auditor considers it necessary

---

[5] *ISA (UK) 260 (Revised June 2016), Communication with Those Charged with Governance, paragraph 16.*

to draw users' attention to such a matter, the matter is included in an Emphasis of Matter paragraph in the auditor's report in accordance with this ISA (UK).

Circumstances in Which an Emphasis of Matter Paragraph May Be Necessary (Ref: Para. 4, 8)

Appendix 1 identifies ISAs (UK) that contain specific requirements for the auditor to include Emphasis of Matter paragraphs in the auditor's report in certain circumstances. These circumstances include: **A4**

- When a financial reporting framework prescribed by law or regulation would be unacceptable but for the fact that it is prescribed by law or regulation.

- To alert users that the financial statements are prepared in accordance with a special purpose framework.

- When facts become known to the auditor after the date of the auditor's report and the auditor provides a new or amended auditor's report (i.e., subsequent events).[6]

Examples of circumstances where the auditor may consider it necessary to include an Emphasis of Matter paragraph are: **A5**

- An uncertainty relating to the future outcome of exceptional litigation or regulatory action.

- A significant subsequent event that occurs between the date of the financial statements and the date of the auditor's report.[7]

- Early application (where permitted) of a new accounting standard that has a material effect on the financial statements.

- A major catastrophe that has had, or continues to have, a significant effect on the entity's financial position.

In the UK, under legislation[7a] the auditor is required to include a reference to any matters to which the auditor wishes to draw attention by way of emphasis without modifying the audit opinion. Since it would be necessary for the auditor to do so, such a matter would be required to be included in the auditor's report in accordance with paragraph 8 of this ISA (UK).   **A5-1**

However, a widespread use of Emphasis of Matter paragraphs may diminish the effectiveness of the auditor's communication about such matters.   **A6**

Including an Emphasis of Matter Paragraph in the Auditor's Report (Ref: Para. 9)

The inclusion of an Emphasis of Matter paragraph in the auditor's report does not affect the auditor's opinion. An Emphasis of Matter paragraph is not a substitute for either: **A7**

(a) A modified opinion in accordance with ISA (UK) 705 (Revised June 2016) when required by the circumstances of a specific audit engagement;

---

[6] *ISA (UK) 560, paragraph 6.*

[7] *ISA (UK) 560, paragraph 6.*

[7a] *In the UK, Section 495(4) of the Companies Act 2006 establishes this requirement.*

(b)   Disclosures in the financial statements that the applicable financial reporting framework requires management to make, or that are otherwise necessary to achieve fair presentation; or

(c)   Reporting in accordance with ISA (UK) 705 (Revised June 2016)[8] when a material uncertainty exists relating to events or conditions that may cast significant doubt on an entity's ability to continue as a going concern.

A8   Paragraphs A16–A17 provide further guidance on the placement of Emphasis of Matter paragraphs in particular circumstances.

Other Matter Paragraphs in the Auditor's Report
(Ref: Para. 10–11)

Circumstances in Which an Other Matter Paragraph May Be Necessary

Relevant to Users' Understanding of the Audit

A9   ISA (UK) 260 (Revised June 2016) requires the auditor to communicate with those charged with governance about the planned scope and timing of the audit, which includes communication about the significant risks identified by the auditor.[9] Although matters relating to significant risks may be determined to be key audit matters, other planning and scoping matters (e.g., the planned scope of the audit, or the application of materiality in the context of the audit) are unlikely to be key audit matters because of how key audit matters are defined in ISA (UK) 701. However, law or regulation may require the auditor to communicate about planning and scoping matters in the auditor's report, or the auditor may consider it necessary to communicate about such matters in an Other Matter paragraph.

A9-1   In the UK, when the auditor is required or decides to communicate key audit matters in accordance with ISA (UK) 701, the auditor communicates in the auditor's report other planning and scoping matters in accordance with paragraph 16-1 of ISA (UK) 701.

A10   In the rare circumstance where the auditor is unable to withdraw from an engagement even though the possible effect of an inability to obtain sufficient appropriate audit evidence due to a limitation on the scope of the audit imposed by management is pervasive,[10] the auditor may consider it necessary to include an Other Matter paragraph in the auditor's report to explain why it is not possible for the auditor to withdraw from the engagement.

Relevant to Users' Understanding of the Auditor's Responsibilities or the Auditor's Report

A11   Law, regulation or generally accepted practice in a jurisdiction may require or permit the auditor to elaborate on matters that provide further explanation of the auditor's responsibilities in the audit of the financial statements or of the auditor's report thereon. When the Other Matter section includes more than one matter that, in the auditor's judgment, is relevant to users' understanding of the audit, the auditor's responsibilities or the auditor's report, it may be helpful to use different sub-headings for each matter.

---

[8] *ISA (UK) 705 (Revised June 2016), paragraphs 22–23.*

[9] *ISA (UK) 260 (Revised June 2016), paragraph 15.*

[10] *See paragraph 13(b)(ii) of ISA (UK) 705 (Revised June 2016) for a discussion of this circumstance.*

An Other Matter paragraph does not deal with circumstances where the auditor has **A12** other reporting responsibilities that are in addition to the auditor's responsibility under the ISAs (UK) (see "Other Reporting Responsibilities" section in ISA (UK) 700 (Revised June 2016)[11]), or where the auditor has been asked to perform and report on additional specified procedures, or to express an opinion on specific matters.

Reporting on more than one set of financial statements

An entity may prepare one set of financial statements in accordance with a general **A13** purpose framework (e.g., the national framework) and another set of financial statements in accordance with another general purpose framework (e.g., International Financial Reporting Standards), and engage the auditor to report on both sets of financial statements. If the auditor has determined that the frameworks are acceptable in the respective circumstances, the auditor may include an Other Matter paragraph in the auditor's report, referring to the fact that another set of financial statements has been prepared by the same entity in accordance with another general purpose framework and that the auditor has issued a report on those financial statements.

The situation described in paragraph A13 is differentiated from the situation in **A13-1** paragraphs A13 and A30 of ISA (UK) 700 (Revised June 2016) in that, in the latter case, the auditor is engaged to express in the same auditor's report an opinion on the compliance of the financial statements with an additional financial reporting framework. This is only permissible if the auditor is satisfied that there are no differences between the two financial reporting frameworks that affect the financial statements being reported on.

Restriction on distribution or use of the auditor's report

Financial statements prepared for a specific purpose may be prepared in **A14** accordance with a general purpose framework because the intended users have determined that such general purpose financial statements meet their financial information needs. Since the auditor's report is intended for specific users, the auditor may consider it necessary in the circumstances to include an Other Matter paragraph, stating that the auditor's report is intended solely for the intended users, and should not be distributed to or used by other parties.

Including an Other Matter Paragraph in the Auditor's Report

The content of an Other Matter paragraph reflects clearly that such other matter is **A15** not required to be presented and disclosed in the financial statements. An Other Matter paragraph does not include information that the auditor is prohibited from providing by law, regulation or other professional standards, for example, ethical standards relating to confidentiality of information. An Other Matter paragraph also does not include information that is required to be provided by management.

Placement of Emphasis of Matter Paragraphs and Other Matter Paragraphs in the Auditor's Report
(Ref: Para. 9, 11)

The placement of an Emphasis of Matter paragraph or Other Matter paragraph in **A16** the auditor's report depends on the nature of the information to be communicated,

---

[11] *ISA (UK) 700 (Revised June 2016), Forming an Opinion and Reporting on Financial Statements, paragraphs 42–44.*

and the auditor's judgment as to the relative significance of such information to intended users compared to other elements required to be reported in accordance with ISA (UK) 700 (Revised June 2016). For example:

Emphasis of Matter Paragraphs

- When the Emphasis of Matter paragraph relates to the applicable financial reporting framework, including circumstances where the auditor determines that the financial reporting framework prescribed by law or regulation would otherwise be unacceptable,[12] the auditor may consider it necessary to place the paragraph immediately following the Basis of Opinion section to provide appropriate context to the auditor's opinion.

  ISA 800 has not been promulgated by the FRC for application in the UK.

- When a Key Audit Matters section is presented in the auditor's report, an Emphasis of Matter paragraph may be presented either directly before or after the Key Audit Matters section, based on the auditor's judgment as to the relative significance of the information included in the Emphasis of Matter paragraph. The auditor may also add further context to the heading "Emphasis of Matter", such as "Emphasis of Matter – Subsequent Event", to differentiate the Emphasis of Matter paragraph from the individual matters described in the Key Audit Matters section.

Other Matter Paragraphs

- When a Key Audit Matters section is presented in the auditor's report and an Other Matter paragraph is also considered necessary, the auditor may add further context to the heading "Other Matter", such as "Other Matter – Scope of the Audit", to differentiate the Other Matter paragraph from the individual matters described in the Key Audit Matters section.

- When an Other Matter paragraph is included to draw users' attention to a matter relating to Other Reporting Responsibilities addressed in the auditor's report, the paragraph may be included in the Report on Other Legal and Regulatory Requirements section.

- When relevant to all the auditor's responsibilities or users' understanding of the auditor's report, the Other Matter paragraph may be included as a separate section following the Report on the Audit of the Financial Statements and the Report on Other Legal and Regulatory Requirements.

A17   Appendix 3[12a] is an illustration of the interaction between the Key Audit Matters section, an Emphasis of Matter paragraph and an Other Matter paragraph when all are presented in the auditor's report. The illustrative report in Appendix 4[13a] includes an Emphasis of Matter paragraph in an auditor's report for an entity other than a listed entity that contains a qualified opinion and for which key audit matters have not been communicated.

---

[12] *For example, as required by ISA (UK) 210 (Revised June 2016), Agreeing the Terms of Audit Engagements, paragraph 19 and ISA 800, Special Considerations—Audits of Financial Statements Prepared in Accordance with Special Purpose Frameworks, paragraph 14.*

[12a] *The examples in Appendices 3 and 4 have not been tailored for the UK. Illustrative auditor's reports tailored for use with audits conducted in accordance with ISAs (UK) are given in the current version of the FRC's Compendium of Illustrative Auditor's Reports.*

Communication with Those Charged with Governance
(Ref. Para. 12)

The communication required by paragraph 12 enables those charged with   **A18**
governance to be made aware of the nature of any specific matters that the
auditor intends to highlight in the auditor's report, and provides them with an
opportunity to obtain further clarification from the auditor where necessary.
Where the inclusion of an Other Matter paragraph on a particular matter in the
auditor's report recurs on each successive engagement, the auditor may determine
that it is unnecessary to repeat the communication on each engagement, unless
otherwise required to do so by law or regulation.

Appendix 1

(Ref: Para. 4, A4)

List of ISAs (UK) Containing Requirements for Emphasis of Matter Paragraphs

This appendix identifies paragraphs in other ISAs (UK) that require the auditor to include an Emphasis of Matter paragraph in the auditor's report in certain circumstances. The list is not a substitute for considering the requirements and related application and other explanatory material in ISAs (UK).

- ISA (UK) 210 (Revised June 2016), *Agreeing the Terms of Audit Engagements* – paragraph 19(b)

- ISA (UK) 560, *Subsequent Events* – paragraphs 12(b) and 16

- ISA 800,[12b] *Special Considerations—Audits of Financial Statements Prepared in Accordance with Special Purpose Frameworks* – paragraph 14

[12b] *ISA 800 has not been promulgated by the FRC for application in the UK.*

Appendix 2

(Ref: Para. 4)

List of ISAs (UK) Containing Requirements for Other Matter Paragraphs

This appendix identifies paragraphs in other ISAs (UK) that require the auditor to include an Other Matter paragraph in the auditor's report in certain circumstances. The list is not a substitute for considering the requirements and related application and other explanatory material in ISAs (UK).

- ISA (UK) 560, *Subsequent Events* – paragraphs 12(b) and 16
- ISA (UK) 710, *Comparative Information—Corresponding Figures and Comparative Financial Statements* – paragraphs 13–14, 16–17 and 19

Appendix 3

(Ref: Para. A17)

Illustration of an Auditor's Report that Includes a Key Audit Matters Section, an Emphasis of Matter Paragraph, and an Other Matter Paragraph

The example in the Appendix has not been tailored for the UK. Illustrative auditor's reports tailored for use with audits conducted in accordance with ISAs (UK) are given in the current version of the FRC's Compendium of Illustrative Auditor's Reports.

For purposes of this illustrative auditor's report, the following circumstances are assumed:

- Audit of a complete set of financial statements of a listed entity using a fair presentation framework. The audit is not a group audit (i.e., ISA 600[1-a] does not apply).
- The financial statements are prepared by management of the entity in accordance with International Financial Reporting Standards (IFRSs) (a general purpose framework).
- The terms of the audit engagement reflect the description of management's responsibility for the financial statements in ISA 210.
- The auditor has concluded an unmodified (i.e., "clean") opinion is appropriate based on the audit evidence obtained.
- The relevant ethical requirements that apply to the audit are those of the jurisdiction.
- Based on the audit evidence obtained, the auditor has concluded that a material uncertainty does not exist related to events or conditions that may cast significant doubt on the entity's ability to continue as a going concern in accordance with ISA 570 (Revised).
- Between the date of the financial statements and the date of the auditor's report, there was a fire in the entity's production facilities, which was disclosed by the entity as a subsequent event. In the auditor's judgment, the matter is of such importance that it is fundamental to users' understanding of the financial statements. The matter did not require significant auditor attention in the audit of the financial statements in the current period.
- Key audit matters have been communicated in accordance with ISA 701.
- The auditor has obtained all of the other information prior to the date of the auditor's report and has not identified a material misstatement of the other information.
- Corresponding figures are presented, and the prior period's financial statements were audited by a predecessor auditor. The auditor is not prohibited by law or regulation from referring to the predecessor auditor's report on the corresponding figures and has decided to do so.

[1-a] *ISA 600, Special Considerations—Audits of Group Financial Statements (Including the Work of Component Auditors).*

- Those responsible for oversight of the financial statements differ from those responsible for the preparation of the financial statements.
- In addition to the audit of the financial statements, the auditor has other reporting responsibilities required under local law.

INDEPENDENT AUDITOR'S REPORT

To the Shareholders of ABC Company [or Other Appropriate Addressee]

Report on the Audit of the Financial Statements[2-a]

Opinion

We have audited the financial statements of ABC Company (the Company), which comprise the statement of financial position as at December 31, 20X1, and the statement of comprehensive income, statement of changes in equity and statement of cash flows for the year then ended, and notes to the financial statements, including a summary of significant accounting policies.

In our opinion, the accompanying financial statements present fairly, in all material respects, (or *give a true and fair view of*) the financial position of the Company as at December 31, 20X1, and (*of*) its financial performance and its cash flows for the year then ended in accordance with International Financial Reporting Standards (IFRSs).

Basis for Opinion

We conducted our audit in accordance with International Standards on Auditing (ISAs). Our responsibilities under those standards are further described in the *Auditor's Responsibilities for the Audit of the Financial Statements* section of our report. We are independent of the Company in accordance with the ethical requirements that are relevant to our audit of the financial statements in [*jurisdiction*], and we have fulfilled our other ethical responsibilities in accordance with these requirements. We believe that the audit evidence we have obtained is sufficient and appropriate to provide a basis for our opinion.

Emphasis of Matter[3-a]

We draw attention to Note X of the financial statements, which describes the effects of a fire in the Company's production facilities. Our opinion is not modified in respect of this matter.

Key Audit Matters

Key audit matters are those matters that, in our professional judgment, were of most significance in our audit of the financial statements of the current period. These matters were addressed in the context of our audit of the financial

---

[2-a] *The sub-title "Report on the Audit of the Financial Statements" is unnecessary in circumstances when the second sub-title "Report on Other Legal and Regulatory Requirements" is not applicable.*

[3-a] *As noted in paragraph A16, an Emphasis of Matter paragraph may be presented either directly before or after the Key Audit Matters section based on the auditor's judgment as to the relative significance of the information included in the Emphasis of Matter paragraph.*

statements as a whole, and in forming our opinion thereon, and we do not provide a separate opinion on these matters.

[*Description of each key audit matter in accordance with ISA 701.*]

Other Matter

The financial statements of ABC Company for the year ended December 31, 20X0, were audited by another auditor who expressed an unmodified opinion on those statements on March 31, 20X1.

Other Information [or another title if appropriate such as "Information Other than the Financial Statements and Auditor's Report Thereon"]

[*Reporting in accordance with the reporting requirements in ISA 720 (Revised) – see Illustration 1 in Appendix 2 of ISA 720 (Revised).*]

Responsibilities of Management and Those Charged with Governance for the Financial Statements[4-a]

[*Reporting in accordance with ISA 700 (Revised) – see Illustration 1 in ISA 700 (Revised).*]

Auditor's Responsibilities for the Audit of the Financial Statements

[*Reporting in accordance with ISA 700 (Revised) – see Illustration 1 in ISA 700 (Revised).*]

Report on Other Legal and Regulatory Requirements

[*Reporting in accordance with ISA 700 (Revised) – see Illustration 1 in ISA 700 (Revised).*]

The engagement partner on the audit resulting in this independent auditor's report is [*name*].

[*Signature in the name of the audit firm, the personal name of the auditor, or both, as appropriate for the particular jurisdiction*]

[*Auditor Address*]

[*Date*]

[4-a] *Throughout these illustrative auditor's reports, the terms management and those charged with governance may need to be replaced by another term that is appropriate in the context of the legal framework in the particular jurisdiction.*

Appendix 4

(Ref: Para. A8)

Illustration of an Auditor's Report Containing a Qualified Opinion Due to a Departure from the Applicable Financial Reporting Framework and that Includes an Emphasis of Matter Paragraph

The example in the Appendix has not been tailored for the UK. Illustrative auditor's reports tailored for use with audits conducted in accordance with ISAs (UK) are given in the current version of the FRC's Compendium of Illustrative Auditor's Reports.

For purposes of this illustrative auditor's report, the following circumstances are assumed:

- Audit of a complete set of financial statements of an entity other than a listed entity using a fair presentation framework. The audit is not a group audit (i.e., ISA 600 does not apply).
- The financial statements are prepared by management of the entity in accordance with IFRSs (a general purpose framework).
- The terms of the audit engagement reflect the description of management's responsibility for the financial statements in ISA 210.
- A departure from the applicable financial reporting framework resulted in a qualified opinion.
- The relevant ethical requirements that apply to the audit are those of the jurisdiction.
- Based on the audit evidence obtained, the auditor has concluded that a material uncertainty does not exist related to events or conditions that may cast significant doubt on the entity's ability to continue as a going concern in accordance with ISA 570 (Revised).
- Between the date of the financial statements and the date of the auditor's report, there was a fire in the entity's production facilities, which was disclosed by the entity as a subsequent event. In the auditor's judgment, the matter is of such importance that it is fundamental to users' understanding of the financial statements. The matter did not require significant auditor attention in the audit of the financial statements in the current period.
- The auditor is not required, and has otherwise not decided, to communicate key audit matters in accordance with ISA 701.
- The auditor has not obtained any other information prior to the date of the auditor's report.Those responsible for oversight of the financial statements differ from those responsible for the preparation of the financial statements.
- Those responsible for oversight of the financial statements differ from those responsible for the preparation of the financial statements.
- In addition to the audit of the financial statements, the auditor has other reporting responsibilities required under local law.

INDEPENDENT AUDITOR'S REPORT

To the Shareholders of ABC Company [or Other Appropriate Addressee]

Report on the Audit of the Financial Statements[1-b]

Qualified Opinion

We have audited the financial statements of ABC Company (the Company), which comprise the statement of financial position as at December 31, 20X1, and the statement of comprehensive income, statement of changes in equity and statement of cash flows for the year then ended, and notes to the financial statements, including a summary of significant accounting policies.

In our opinion, except for the effects of the matter described in the Basis for Qualified Opinion section of our report, the accompanying financial statements present fairly, in all material respects, (or *give a true and fair view of*) the financial position of the Company as at December 31, 20X1, and (*of*) its financial performance and its cash flows for the year then ended in accordance with International Financial Reporting Standards (IFRSs).

Basis for Qualified Opinion

The Company's short-term marketable securities are carried in the statement of financial position at xxx. Management has not marked these securities to market but has instead stated them at cost, which constitutes a departure from IFRSs. The Company's records indicate that had management marked the marketable securities to market, the Company would have recognized an unrealized loss of xxx in the statement of comprehensive income for the year. The carrying amount of the securities in the statement of financial position would have been reduced by the same amount at December 31, 20X1, and income tax, net income and shareholders' equity would have been reduced by xxx, xxx and xxx, respectively.

We conducted our audit in accordance with International Standards on Auditing (ISAs). Our responsibilities under those standards are further described in the *Auditor's Responsibilities for the Audit of the Financial Statements* section of our report. We are independent of the Company in accordance with the ethical requirements that are relevant to our audit of the financial statements in [*jurisdiction*], and we have fulfilled our other ethical responsibilities in accordance with these requirements. We believe that the audit evidence we have obtained is sufficient and appropriate to provide a basis for our qualified opinion.

Emphasis of Matter – Effects of a Fire

We draw attention to Note X of the financial statements, which describes the effects of a fire in the Company's production facilities. Our opinion is not modified in respect of this matter.

[1-b] *The sub-title "Report on the Audit of the Financial Statements" is unnecessary in circumstances when the second sub-title "Report on Other Legal and Regulatory Requirements" is not applicable.*

***Responsibilities of Management and Those Charged with Governance for the Financial Statements*^{2-b}**

[Reporting in accordance with ISA 700 (Revised) – see Illustration 1 in ISA 700 (Revised).]

Auditor's Responsibilities for the Audit of the Financial Statements

[Reporting in accordance with ISA 700 (Revised) – see Illustration 1 in ISA 700 (Revised).]

Report on Other Legal and Regulatory Requirements

[Reporting in accordance with ISA 700 (Revised) – see Illustration 1 in ISA 700 (Revised).]

[Signature in the name of the audit firm, the personal name of the auditor, or both, as appropriate for the particular jurisdiction]

[Auditor Address]

[Date]

---

^{2-b} *Or other terms that are appropriate in the context of the legal framework of the particular jurisdiction.*

Responsibilities of Management and Those Charged with Governance for the Financial Statements

[Reporting in accordance with ISA 700 (Revised) — see Illustration 1 in ISA 700 (Revised)]

Auditor's Responsibilities for the Audit of the Financial Statements

[Reporting in accordance with ISA 700 (Revised) — see Illustration 1 in ISA 700 (Revised)]

Report on Other Legal and Regulatory Requirements

[Reporting in accordance with ISA 700 (Revised) — see Illustration 1 in ISA 700 (Revised)]

[The engagement partner on the audit resulting in this independent auditor's report is ... name of the engagement partner.]

[Auditor Address]

[Date]

ISA (UK) 710 Comparative Information – Corresponding Figures and Comparative Financial Statements

(Effective for audits of financial statements for periods ending on or after 15 December 2010)

Contents

Paragraphs

Introduction
Scope of this ISA (UK)   1
The nature of comparative information   2 - 3
Effective date   4

Objectives   5

Definitions   6

Requirements
Audit procedures   7 - 9
Audit reporting   10 - 19

Application and other explanatory material
Audit procedures   A1-1 - A1
Audit reporting   A2 - A12

Appendix: Illustrations of auditor's reports

International Standard on Auditing (UK) (ISA (UK)) 710, *Comparative Information— Corresponding Figures and Comparative Financial Statements*, should be read in conjunction with ISA (UK) 200 (Revised June 2016), *Overall Objectives of the Independent Auditor and the Conduct of an Audit in Accordance with International Standards on Auditing (UK)*.

Introduction

Scope of this ISA (UK)

1   This International Standard on Auditing (UK) (ISA (UK)) deals with the auditor's responsibilities relating to comparative information in an audit of financial statements. When the financial statements of the prior period have been audited by a predecessor auditor or were not audited, the requirements and guidance in ISA (UK) 510 (Revised June 2016)[1] regarding opening balances also apply.

The Nature of Comparative Information

2   The nature of the comparative information that is presented in an entity's financial statements depends on the requirements of the applicable financial reporting framework. There are two different broad approaches to the auditor's reporting responsibilities in respect of such comparative information: corresponding figures and comparative financial statements. The approach to be adopted is often specified by law or regulation but may also be specified in the terms of engagement.

2-1   In the UK, the corresponding figures method of presentation is usually required.

3   The essential audit reporting differences between the approaches are:

(a)   For corresponding figures, the auditor's opinion on the financial statements refers to the current period only; whereas

(b)   For comparative financial statements, the auditor's opinion refers to each period for which financial statements are presented.

This ISA (UK) addresses separately the auditor's reporting requirements for each approach.

Effective Date

4   This ISA (UK) is effective for audits of financial statements for periods ending on or after 15 December 2010.

Objectives

5   The objectives of the auditor are:

(a)   To obtain sufficient appropriate audit evidence about whether the comparative information included in the financial statements has been presented, in all material respects, in accordance with the requirements for comparative information in the applicable financial reporting framework; and

(b)   To report in accordance with the auditor's reporting responsibilities.

---

[1]   *ISA (UK) 510 (Revised June 2016), Initial Audit Engagements—Opening Balances.*

Definitions

For purposes of the ISAs (UK), the following terms have the meanings attributed   **6** below:

(a)   Comparative information – The amounts and disclosures included in the financial statements in respect of one or more prior periods in accordance with the applicable financial reporting framework.

(b)   Corresponding figures – Comparative information where amounts and other disclosures for the prior period are included as an integral part of the current period financial statements, and are intended to be read only in relation to the amounts and other disclosures relating to the current period (referred to as "current period figures"). The level of detail presented in the corresponding amounts and disclosures is dictated primarily by its relevance to the current period figures.

(c)   Comparative financial statements – Comparative information where amounts and other disclosures for the prior period are included for comparison with the financial statements of the current period but, if audited, are referred to in the auditor's opinion. The level of information included in those comparative financial statements is comparable with that of the financial statements of the current period.

For purposes of this ISA (UK), references to "prior period" should be read as "prior periods" when the comparative information includes amounts and disclosures for more than one period.

Requirements

Audit Procedures

The auditor shall determine whether the financial statements include the   **7** comparative information required by the applicable financial reporting framework and whether such information is appropriately classified. For this purpose, the auditor shall evaluate whether:

(a)   The comparative information agrees with the amounts and other disclosures presented in the prior period or, when appropriate, have been restated; (Ref: Para. A1-1) and

(b)   The accounting policies reflected in the comparative information are consistent with those applied in the current period or, if there have been changes in accounting policies, whether those changes have been properly accounted for and adequately presented and disclosed.

If the auditor becomes aware of a possible material misstatement in the   **8** comparative information while performing the current period audit, the auditor shall perform such additional audit procedures as are necessary in the circumstances to obtain sufficient appropriate audit evidence to determine whether a material misstatement exists. If the auditor had audited the prior period's financial statements, the auditor shall also follow the relevant requirements of ISA (UK) 560.[2] If the prior period financial statements are

---

[2] *ISA (UK) 560, Subsequent Events, paragraphs 14–17.*

amended, the auditor shall determine that the comparative information agrees with the amended financial statements.

9   As required by ISA (UK) 580,[3] the auditor shall request written representations for all periods referred to in the auditor's opinion. The auditor shall also obtain a specific written representation regarding any restatement made to correct a material misstatement in prior period financial statements that affect the comparative information. (Ref: Para. A1)

Audit Reporting

Corresponding Figures

10   When corresponding figures are presented, the auditor's opinion shall not refer to the corresponding figures except in the circumstances described in paragraphs 11, 12, and 14. (Ref: Para. A2)

11   If the auditor's report on the prior period, as previously issued, included a qualified opinion, a disclaimer of opinion, or an adverse opinion and the matter which gave rise to the modification is unresolved, the auditor shall modify the auditor's opinion on the current period's financial statements. In the Basis for Modification paragraph in the auditor's report, the auditor shall either:

(a)   Refer to both the current period's figures and the corresponding figures in the description of the matter giving rise to the modification when the effects or possible effects of the matter on the current period's figures are material; or

(b)   In other cases, explain that the audit opinion has been modified because of the effects or possible effects of the unresolved matter on the comparability of the current period's figures and the corresponding figures. (Ref: Para. A3–A5)

12   If the auditor obtains audit evidence that a material misstatement exists in the prior period financial statements on which an unmodified opinion has been previously issued, and the corresponding figures have not been properly restated or appropriate disclosures have not been made, the auditor shall express a qualified opinion or an adverse opinion in the auditor's report on the current period financial statements, modified with respect to the corresponding figures included therein. (Ref: Para. A6)

Prior Period Financial Statements Audited by a Predecessor Auditor

13   If the financial statements of the prior period were audited by a predecessor auditor and the auditor is not prohibited by law or regulation from referring to the predecessor auditor's report on the corresponding figures and decides to do so, the auditor shall state in an Other Matter paragraph in the auditor's report:

(a)   That the financial statements of the prior period were audited by the predecessor auditor;

(b)   The type of opinion expressed by the predecessor auditor and, if the opinion was modified, the reasons therefore; and

(c)   date of that report. (Ref: Para. A7–A7-3)

---

[3] *ISA (UK) 580, Written Representations, paragraph 14.*

Prior Period Financial Statements Not Audited

If the prior period financial statements were not audited, the auditor shall state in **14** an Other Matter paragraph in the auditor's report that the corresponding figures are unaudited. Such a statement does not, however, relieve the auditor of the requirement to obtain sufficient appropriate audit evidence that the opening balances do not contain misstatements that materially affect the current period's financial statements.[4] (Ref: Para. A7a)

Comparative Financial Statements

When comparative financial statements are presented, the auditor's opinion shall **15** refer to each period for which financial statements are presented and on which an audit opinion is expressed. (Ref: Para. A8–A9)

When reporting on prior period financial statements in connection with the **16** current period's audit, if the auditor's opinion on such prior period financial statements differs from the opinion the auditor previously expressed, the auditor shall disclose the substantive reasons for the different opinion in an Other Matter paragraph in accordance with ISA (UK) 706 (Revised June 2016).[5] (Ref: Para. A10)

Prior Period Financial Statements Audited by a Predecessor Auditor

If the financial statements of the prior period were audited by a predecessor **17** auditor, in addition to expressing an opinion on the current period's financial statements, the auditor shall state in an Other Matter paragraph:

(a) that the financial statements of the prior period were audited by a predecessor auditor;

(b) the type of opinion expressed by the predecessor auditor and, if the opinion was modified, the reasons therefore; and

(c) the date of that report,

unless the predecessor auditor's report on the prior period's financial statements is reissued with the financial statements.

If the auditor concludes that a material misstatement exists that affects the prior **18** period financial statements on which the predecessor auditor had previously reported without modification, the auditor shall communicate the misstatement with the appropriate level of management and, unless all of those charged with governance are involved in managing the entity,[6] those charged with governance and request that the predecessor auditor be informed. If the prior period financial statements are amended, and the predecessor auditor agrees to issue a new auditor's report on the amended financial statements of the prior period, the auditor shall report only on the current period. (Ref: Para. A11)

Prior Period Financial Statements Not Audited

If the prior period financial statements were not audited, the auditor shall state in **19** an Other Matter paragraph that the comparative financial statements are unaudited. Such a statement does not, however, relieve the auditor of the

---

[4] *ISA (UK) 510 (Revised June 2016), paragraph 6.*

[5] *ISA (UK) 706 (Revised June 2016), Emphasis of Matter Paragraphs and Other Matter Paragraphs in the Independent Auditor's Report, paragraph 8.*

[6] *ISA (UK) 260 (Revised June 2016), Communication with Those Charged with Governance, paragraph 13.*

requirement to obtain sufficient appropriate audit evidence that the opening balances do not contain misstatements that materially affect the current period's financial statements.[7] (Ref: Para. A12)

Application and Other Explanatory Material

Audit Procedures
(Ref: Para. 7(a))

A1-1   When evaluating whether the comparative information agrees with the amounts and other disclosures presented in the prior period or, where appropriate, have been restated, the auditor's procedures include checking whether the related opening balances in the accounting records were appropriately brought forward.

Written Representations
(Ref: Para. 9)

A1   In the case of comparative financial statements, the written representations are requested for all periods referred to in the auditor's opinion because management needs to reaffirm that the written representations it previously made with respect to the prior period remain appropriate. In the case of corresponding figures, the written representations are requested for the financial statements of the current period only because the auditor's opinion is on those financial statements, which include the corresponding figures. However, the auditor requests a specific written representation regarding any restatement made to correct a material misstatement in the prior period financial statements that affect the comparative information.

Audit Reporting

Corresponding Figures

No Reference in Auditor's Opinion
(Ref: Para. 10)

A2   The auditor's opinion does not refer to the corresponding figures because the auditor's opinion is on the current period financial statements as a whole, including the corresponding figures.

Modification in Auditor's Report on the Prior Period Unresolved
(Ref: Para. 11)

A3   When the auditor's report on the prior period, as previously issued, included a qualified opinion, a disclaimer of opinion, or an adverse opinion and the matter which gave rise to the modified opinion is resolved and properly accounted for or disclosed in the financial statements in accordance with the applicable financial reporting framework, the auditor's opinion on the current period need not refer to the previous modification.

---

[7] *ISA (UK) 510 (Revised June 2016), paragraph 6.*

In some circumstances the auditor may consider it appropriate to qualify the **A3-1**
audit opinion on the current period's financial statements. For example, if a
provision which the auditor considered should have been made in the previous
period is made in the current period.

When the auditor's opinion on the prior period, as previously expressed, was **A4**
modified, the unresolved matter that gave rise to the modification may not be
relevant to the current period figures. Nevertheless, a qualified opinion, a
disclaimer of opinion, or an adverse opinion (as applicable) may be required on
the current period's financial statements because of the effects or possible effects
of the unresolved matter on the comparability of the current and corresponding
figures.

Illustrative examples of the auditor's report if the auditor's report on the prior **A5**
period included a modified opinion and the matter giving rise to the modification
is unresolved are contained in Illustrations 1 and 2 of the Appendix.[7a]

Misstatement in Prior Period Financial Statements
(Ref: Para. 12)

When the prior period financial statements that are misstated have not been **A6**
amended and an auditor's report has not been reissued, but the corresponding
figures have been properly restated or appropriate disclosures have been made in
the current period financial statements, the auditor's report may include an
Emphasis of Matter paragraph describing the circumstances and referring to
where relevant disclosures that fully describe the matter can be found in the
financial statements (see ISA (UK) 706 (Revised June 2016)).

Prior Period Financial Statements Audited by a Predecessor Auditor
(Ref: Para. 13)

An illustrative example of the auditor's report if the prior period financial **A7**
statements were audited by a predecessor auditor and the auditor is not
prohibited by law or regulation from referring to the predecessor auditor's
report on the corresponding figures is contained in Illustration 3 of the
Appendix.[7a]

In the UK, the incoming auditor does not refer to the predecessor auditor's **A7-1**
report on the corresponding figures in the incoming auditor's report for the
current period. The incoming auditor assumes audit responsibility for the
corresponding figures only in the context of the financial statements as a whole.
The incoming auditor reads the preceding period's financial statements and,
using the knowledge gained during the current audit, considers whether they
have been properly reflected as corresponding figures in the current period's
financial statements.

Although the incoming auditor is not required to re-audit the financial **A7-2**
statements of the preceding period, if the incoming auditor becomes aware
of a possible material misstatement of corresponding figures, the requirement
and guidance in paragraphs 12 and A6 apply.

[7a] *The examples in the Appendix have not been tailored for the UK. Illustrative auditor's reports tailored for use
with audits conducted in accordance with ISAs (UK) are given in the current version of the FRC's Compendium
of Illustrative Auditor's Reports.*

A7-3   For audits of financial statements of public interest entities, the incoming auditor may become aware of a possible material misstatement of corresponding figures as part of the requirement in ISA (UK) 510 (Revised June 2016) to obtain an understanding of the methodology used to carry out the audit in the preceding period.[7b]

Prior Period Financial Statements Not Audited
(Ref: Para. 14)

A7a   If the auditor is unable to obtain sufficient appropriate audit evidence regarding the opening balances, the auditor is required by ISA (UK) 705 (Revised June 2016)[8] to express a qualified opinion or disclaim an opinion on the financial statements, as appropriate, in accordance with ISA (UK) 705 (Revised June 2016). If the auditor encountered significant difficulty in obtaining sufficient appropriate audit evidence that the opening balances do not contain misstatements that materially affect the current period's financial statements, the auditor may determine this to be a key audit matter in accordance with ISA (UK) 701.[9]

Comparative Financial Statements

Reference in Auditor's Opinion
(Ref: Para. 15)

A8   Because the auditor's report on comparative financial statements applies to the financial statements for each of the periods presented, the auditor may express a qualified opinion or an adverse opinion, disclaim an opinion, or include an Emphasis of Matter paragraph with respect to one or more periods, while expressing a different auditor's opinion on the financial statements of the other period.

A9   An illustrative example of the auditor's report if the auditor is required to report on both the current and the prior period financial statements in connection with the current year's audit and the prior period included a modified opinion and the matter giving rise to the modification is unresolved, is contained in Illustration 4 of the Appendix.[7a]

Opinion on Prior Period Financial Statements Different from Previous Opinion
(Ref: Para. 16)

A10   When reporting on the prior period financial statements in connection with the current period's audit, the opinion expressed on the prior period financial statements may be different from the opinion previously expressed if the auditor becomes aware of circumstances or events that materially affect the financial statements of a prior period during the course of the audit of the current period. In some jurisdictions, the auditor may have additional reporting responsibilities designed to prevent future reliance on the auditor's previously issued report on the prior period financial statements.

[7b] *ISA (UK) 510 (Revised June 2016), Initial Audit Engagements—Opening Balances, paragraph 8R- 1.*

[8] *ISA (UK) 705 (Revised June 2016), Modifications to the Opinion in the Independent Auditor's Report.*

[9] *ISA (UK) 701, Communicating Key Audit Matters in the Independent Auditor's Report.*

Prior Period Financial Statements Audited by a Predecessor Auditor
(Ref: Para. 18)

The predecessor auditor may be unable or unwilling to reissue the auditor's report **A11** on the prior period financial statements. An Other Matter paragraph of the auditor's report may indicate that the predecessor auditor reported on the financial statements of the prior period before amendment. In addition, if the auditor is engaged to audit and obtains sufficient appropriate audit evidence to be satisfied as to the appropriateness of the amendment, the auditor's report may also include the following paragraph:

> "As part of our audit of the 20X2 financial statements, we also audited the adjustments described in Note X that were applied to amend the 20X1 financial statements. In our opinion, such adjustments are appropriate and have been properly applied. We were not engaged to audit, review, or apply any procedures to the 20X1 financial statements of the company other than with respect to the adjustments and, accordingly, we do not express an opinion or any other form of assurance on the 20X1 financial statements taken as a whole."

Prior Period Financial Statements Not Audited
(Ref: Para. 19)

If the auditor is unable to obtain sufficient appropriate audit evidence regarding **A12** the opening balances, the auditor is required by ISA (UK) 705 (Revised June 2016) to express a qualified opinion or disclaim an opinion on the financial statements, as appropriate, in accordance with ISA (UK) 705 (Revised June 2016). If the auditor encountered significant difficulty in obtaining sufficient appropriate audit evidence that the opening balances do not contain misstatements that materially affect the current period's financial statements, the auditor may determine this to be a key audit matter in accordance with ISA (UK) 701.

Appendix

Illustrations of Auditor's Reports

The examples in the Appendix have not been tailored for the UK. Illustrative auditor's reports tailored for use with audits conducted in accordance with ISAs (UK) are given in the current version of the FRC's Compendium of Illustrative Auditor's Reports.

Note: Throughout these illustrative auditor's reports, the Opinion section has been positioned first in accordance with ISA 700 (Revised), and the Basis for Opinion section is positioned immediately after the Opinion section. Also, the first and last sentence that was included in the extant auditor's responsibilities section is now subsumed as part of the new Basis for Opinion section.

Illustration 1 - Corresponding Figures (Ref: Para. A5)

For purposes of this illustrative auditor's report, the following circumstances are assumed:

- Audit of a complete set of financial statements of an entity other than a listed entity using a fair presentation framework. The audit is not a group audit (i.e., ISA 600[1] does not apply).
- The financial statements are prepared by management of the entity in accordance with International Financial Reporting Standards (IFRSs) (a general purpose framework).
- The terms of the audit engagement reflect the description of management's responsibility for the financial statements in ISA 210.[2]
- The auditor's report on the prior period, as previously issued, included a qualified opinion.
- The matter giving rise to the modification is unresolved.
- The effects or possible effects of the matter on the current period's figures are material and require a modification to the auditor's opinion regarding the current period figures.
- The relevant ethical requirements that apply to the audit are those of the jurisdiction.
- Based on the audit evidence obtained, the auditor has concluded that a material uncertainty does not exist related to events or conditions that may cast significant doubt on the entity's ability to continue as a going concern in accordance with ISA 570 (Revised).[3]
- The auditor is not required, and has otherwise not decided, to communicate key audit matters in accordance with ISA 701.[4]
- The auditor has not obtained any other information prior to the date of the auditor's report.

---

[1] ISA (UK) 510 (Revised June 2016), *Initial Audit Engagements—Opening Balances.*

[2] ISA (UK) 560, *Subsequent Events, paragraphs 14–17.*

[3] ISA (UK) 580, *Written Representations, paragraph 14.*

[4] ISA (UK) 510 (Revised June 2016), *paragraph 6.*

- Those responsible for oversight of the financial statements differ from those responsible for the preparation of the financial statements.
- In addition to the audit of the financial statements, the auditor has other reporting responsibilities required under local law.

INDEPENDENT AUDITOR'S REPORT

To the Shareholders of ABC Company [or Other Appropriate Addressee]

Report on the Audit of the Financial Statements[5]

Qualified Opinion

We have audited the financial statements of ABC Company (the Company), which comprise the statement of financial position as at December 31, 20X1, and the statement of comprehensive income, statement of changes in equity and statement of cash flows for the year then ended, and notes to the financial statements, including a summary of significant accounting policies.

In our opinion, except for the effects of the matter described in the Basis for Qualified Opinion section of our report, the accompanying financial statements present fairly, in all material respects, (or give a true and fair view of) the financial position of the Company as at December 31, 20X1, and (of) its financial performance and its cash flows for the year then ended in accordance with International Financial Reporting Standards (IFRSs).

Basis for Qualified Opinion

As discussed in Note X to the financial statements, no depreciation has been provided in the financial statements, which constitutes a departure from IFRSs. This is the result of a decision taken by management at the start of the preceding financial year and caused us to qualify our audit opinion on the financial statements relating to that year. Based on the straight-line method of depreciation and annual rates of 5% for the building and 20% for the equipment, the loss for the year should be increased by xxx in 20X1 and xxx in 20X0, property, plant and equipment should be reduced by accumulated depreciation of xxx in 20X1 and xxx in 20X0, and the accumulated loss should be increased by xxx in 20X1 and xxx in 20X0.

We conducted our audit in accordance with International Standards on Auditing (ISAs). Our responsibilities under those standards are further described in the *Auditor's Responsibilities for the Audit of the Financial Statements* section of our report. We are independent of the Company in accordance with the ethical requirements that are relevant to our audit of the financial statements in [*jurisdiction*], and we have fulfilled our other ethical responsibilities in accordance with these requirements. We believe that the audit evidence we have obtained is sufficient and appropriate to provide a basis for our qualified audit opinion.

---

[5] *ISA (UK) 706 (Revised June 2016), Emphasis of Matter Paragraphs and Other Matter Paragraphs in the Independent Auditor's Report, paragraph 8.*

***Responsibilities of Management and Those Charged With Governance for the Financial Statements*[6]**

[*Reporting in accordance with ISA 700 (Revised) – see Illustration 1 in ISA 700 (Revised).*]

Auditor's Responsibilities for the Audit of the Financial Statements

[*Reporting in accordance with ISA 700 (Revised) – see Illustration 1 in ISA 700 (Revised).*]

Report on Other Legal and Regulatory Requirements

[*Reporting in accordance with ISA 700 (Revised) – see Illustration 1 in ISA 700 (Revised).*]

[*Signature in the name of the audit firm, the personal name of the auditor, or both, as appropriate for the particular jurisdiction*]

[*Auditor Address*]

[*Date*]

Illustration 2 - Corresponding Figures (Ref: Para. A5)

For purposes of this illustrative auditor's report the following circumstances are assumed:

- Audit of a complete set of financial statements of an entity other than a listed entity using a fair presentation framework. The audit is not a group audit (i.e., ISA 600 does not apply).
- The financial statements are prepared by management of the entity in accordance with IFRSs (a general purpose framework).
- The terms of the audit engagement reflect the description of management's responsibility for the financial statements in ISA 210.
- The auditor's report on the prior period, as previously issued, included a qualified opinion.
- The matter giving rise to the modification is unresolved.
- The effects or possible effects of the matter on the current period's figures are immaterial but require a modification to the auditor's opinion because of the effects or possible effects of the unresolved matter on the comparability of the current period's figures and the corresponding figures.
- The relevant ethical requirements that apply to the audit are those of the jurisdiction.
- Based on the audit evidence obtained, the auditor has concluded that a material uncertainty does not exist related to events or conditions that may cast significant doubt on the entity's ability to continue as a going concern in accordance with ISA 570 (Revised).
- The auditor is not required, and has otherwise has not decided, to communicate key audit matters in accordance with ISA 701.
- The auditor has not obtained any other information prior to the date of the auditor's report.

---

[6] *ISA (UK) 260 (Revised June 2016), Communication with Those Charged with Governance, paragraph 13.*

- Those responsible for oversight of the financial statements differ from those responsible for the preparation of the financial statements.
- In addition to the audit of the financial statements, the auditor has other reporting responsibilities required under local law.

INDEPENDENT AUDITOR'S REPORT

To the Shareholders of ABC Company [or Other Appropriate Addressee]

Report on the Audit of the Financial Statements[7]

Qualified Opinion

We have audited the financial statements of ABC Company (the Company), which comprise the statement of financial position as at December 31, 20X1, and the statement of comprehensive income, statement of changes in equity and statement of cash flows for the year then ended, and notes to the financial statements, including a summary of significant accounting policies.

In our opinion, except for the possible effects on the corresponding figures of the matter described in the Basis for Qualified Opinion section of our report, the accompanying financial statements present fairly, in all material respects, (or *give a true and fair view of*) the financial position of the Company as at December 31, 20X1, and (*of*) its financial performance and its cash flows for the year then ended in accordance with International Financial Reporting Standards (IFRSs).

Basis for Qualified Opinion

Because we were appointed auditors of the Company during 20X0, we were not able to observe the counting of the physical inventories at the beginning of that period or satisfy ourselves concerning those inventory quantities by alternative means. Since opening inventories affect the determination of the results of operations, we were unable to determine whether adjustments to the results of operations and opening retained earnings might be necessary for 20X0. Our audit opinion on the financial statements for the period ended December 31, 20X0 was modified accordingly. Our opinion on the current period's financial statements is also modified because of the possible effect of this matter on the comparability of the current period's figures and the corresponding figures.

We conducted our audit in accordance with International Standards on Auditing (ISAs). Our responsibilities under those standards are further described in the *Auditor's Responsibilities for the Audit of the Financial Statements* section of our report. We are independent of the Company in accordance with the ethical requirements that are relevant to our audit of the financial statements in [*jurisdiction*], and we have fulfilled our other ethical responsibilities in accordance with these requirements. We believe that the audit evidence we have obtained is sufficient and appropriate to provide a basis for our qualified audit opinion.

---

[7] *ISA (UK) 510 (Revised June 2016), paragraph 6.*

***Responsibilities of Management and Those Charged With Governance for the Financial Statements*[8]**

[Reporting in accordance with ISA 700 (Revised) – see Illustration 1 in ISA 700 (Revised).]

Auditor's Responsibilities for the Audit of the Financial Statements

[Reporting in accordance with ISA 700 (Revised) – see Illustration 1 in ISA 700 (Revised).]

Report on Other Legal and Regulatory Requirements

[Reporting in accordance with ISA 700 (Revised) – see Illustration 1 in ISA 700 (Revised).]

[Signature in the name of the audit firm, the personal name of the auditor, or both, as appropriate for the particular jurisdiction]

[Auditor Address]

[Date]

Illustration 3 - Corresponding Figures (Ref: Para. A7)

For purposes of this illustrative auditor's report the following circumstances are assumed:

- Audit of a complete set of financial statements of an entity other than a listed entity using a fair presentation framework. The audit is not a group audit (i.e., ISA 600 does not apply).
- The financial statements are prepared by management of the entity in accordance with IFRSs (a general purpose framework).
- The terms of the audit engagement reflect the description of management's responsibility for the financial statements in ISA 210.
- The auditor has concluded an unmodified (i.e., "clean") opinion is appropriate based on the audit evidence obtained.
- The relevant ethical requirements that apply to the audit are those of the jurisdiction.
- Based on the audit evidence obtained, the auditor has concluded that a material uncertainty does not exist related to events or conditions that may cast significant doubt on the entity's ability to continue as a going concern in accordance with ISA 570 (Revised).
- The auditor is not required, and has otherwise has not decided, to communicate key audit matters in accordance with ISA 701.
- The auditor has obtained all of the other information prior to the date of the auditor's report and has not identified a material misstatement of the other information.
- Corresponding figures are presented, and the prior period's financial statements were audited by a predecessor auditor.
- The auditor is not prohibited by law or regulation from referring to the predecessor auditor's report on the corresponding figures and decides to do so.

---

[8] *ISA (UK) 705 (Revised June 2016), Modifications to the Opinion in the Independent Auditor's Report.*

- Those responsible for oversight of the financial statements differ from those responsible for the preparation of the financial statements.
- In addition to the audit of the financial statements, the auditor has other reporting responsibilities required under local law.

INDEPENDENT AUDITOR'S REPORT

To the Shareholders of ABC Company [or Other Appropriate Addressee]

Report on the Audit of the Financial Statements[9]

Opinion

We have audited the financial statements of ABC Company (the Company), which comprise the statement of financial position as at December 31, 20X1, and the statement of comprehensive income, statement of changes in equity and statement of cash flows for the year then ended, and notes to the financial statements, including a summary of significant accounting policies.

In our opinion, the accompanying financial statements present fairly, in all material respects, (or *give a true and fair view of*) the financial position of the Company as at December 31, 20X1, and (*of*) its financial performance and its cash flows for the year then ended in accordance with International Financial Reporting Standards (IFRSs).

Basis for Opinion

We conducted our audit in accordance with International Standards on Auditing (ISAs). Our responsibilities under those standards are further described in the *Auditor's Responsibilities for the Audit of the Financial Statements* section of our report. We are independent of the Company in accordance with the ethical requirements that are relevant to our audit of the financial statements in [*jurisdiction*], and we have fulfilled our other ethical responsibilities in accordance with these requirements. We believe that the audit evidence we have obtained is sufficient and appropriate to provide a basis for our audit opinion.

Other Matter

The financial statements of the Company for the year ended December 31, 20X0, were audited by another auditor who expressed an unmodified opinion on those statements on March 31, 20X1.

Other Information [or another title if appropriate such as "Information Other than the Financial Statements and Auditor's Report Thereon"]

[*Reporting in accordance with the reporting requirements in ISA 720 (Revised) – see Illustration 1 in Appendix 2 of ISA 720 (Revised).*]

---

[9] *ISA (UK) 701, Communicating Key Audit Matters in the Independent Auditor's Report.*

***Responsibilities of Management and Those Charged With Governance for the Financial Statements*[10]**

[Reporting in accordance with ISA 700 (Revised) – see Illustration 1 in ISA 700 (Revised).]

Auditor's Responsibilities for the Audit of the Financial Statements

[Reporting in accordance with ISA 700 (Revised) – see Illustration 1 in ISA 700 (Revised).]

Report on Other Legal and Regulatory Requirements

[Reporting in accordance with ISA 700 (Revised) – see Illustration 1 in ISA 700 (Revised).]

[Signature in the name of the audit firm, the personal name of the auditor, or both, as appropriate for the particular jurisdiction]

[Auditor Address]

[Date]

Illustration 4 - Comparative Financial Statements (Ref: Para. A9)

For purposes of this illustrative auditor's report the following circumstances are assumed:

- Audit of a complete set of financial statements of an entity other than a listed entity using a fair presentation framework. The audit is not a group audit (i.e., ISA 600 does not apply).
- The financial statements are prepared by management of the entity in accordance with IFRSs (a general purpose framework).
- The terms of the audit engagement reflect the description of management's responsibility for the financial statements in ISA 210.
- The auditor is required to report on both the current period financial statements and the prior period financial statements in connection with the current year's audit.
- The auditor's report on the prior period, as previously issued, included a qualified opinion.
- The matter giving rise to the modification is unresolved.
- The effects or possible effects of the matter on the current period's figures are material to both the current period financial statements and prior period financial statements and require a modification to the auditor's opinion.
- The relevant ethical requirements that apply to the audit are those of the jurisdiction.
- Based on the audit evidence obtained, the auditor has concluded that a material uncertainty does not exist related to events or conditions that may cast significant doubt on the entity's ability to continue as a going concern in accordance with ISA 570 (Revised).
- The auditor is not required, and has otherwise has not decided, to communicate key audit matters in accordance with ISA 701.

---

[10] *Or other terms that are appropriate in the context of the legal framework in the particular jurisdiction.*

- The auditor has not obtained any other information prior to the date of the auditor's report.
- Those responsible for oversight of the financial statements differ from those responsible for the preparation of the financial statements.
- In addition to the audit of the financial statements, the auditor has other reporting responsibilities required under local law.

INDEPENDENT AUDITOR'S REPORT

To the Shareholders of ABC Company [or Other Appropriate Addressee]

Report on the Audit of the Financial Statements[11]

Qualified Opinion

We have audited the financial statements of ABC Company (the Company), which comprise the statements of financial position as at December 31, 20X1 and 20X0, and the statements of comprehensive income, statements of changes in equity and statements of cash flows for the years then ended, and notes to the financial statements, including a summary of significant accounting policies.

In our opinion, except for the effects of the matter described in the Basis for Qualified Opinion paragraph, the accompanying financial statements present fairly, in all material respects, (or *give a true and fair view of*) the financial position of ABC Company as at December 31, 20X1 and 20X0 and (*of*) its financial performance and its cash flows for the years then ended in accordance with International Financial Reporting Standards (IFRSs).

Basis for Qualified Opinion

As discussed in Note X to the financial statements, no depreciation has been provided in the financial statements, which constitutes a departure from IFRSs. Based on the straight-line method of depreciation and annual rates of 5% for the building and 20% for the equipment, the loss for the year should be increased by xxx in 20X1 and xxx in 20X0, property, plant and equipment should be reduced by accumulated depreciation of xxx in 20X1 and xxx in 20X0, and the accumulated loss should be increased by xxx in 20X1 and xxx in 20X0.

We conducted our audit in accordance with International Standards on Auditing (ISAs). Our responsibilities under those standards are further described in the *Auditor's Responsibilities for the Audit of the Financial Statements* section of our report. We are independent of the Company in accordance with the ethical requirements that are relevant to our audit of the financial statements in [*jurisdiction*], and we have fulfilled our other ethical responsibilities in accordance with these requirements. We believe that the audit evidence we have obtained is sufficient and appropriate to provide a basis for our qualified audit opinion.

---

[11] *The sub-title "Report on the Audit of the Financial Statements" is unnecessary in circumstances when the second sub-title "Report on Other Legal and Regulatory Requirements" is not applicable.*

Responsibilities of Management and Those Charged with Governance for the Financial Statements[12]

[Reporting in accordance with ISA 700 (Revised) – see Illustration 1 in ISA 700 (Revised).]

Auditor's Responsibilities for the Audit of the Financial Statements

[Reporting in accordance with ISA 700 (Revised) – see Illustration 1 in ISA 700 (Revised).]

Report on Other Legal and Regulatory Requirements

[Reporting in accordance with ISA 700 (Revised) – see Illustration 1 in ISA 700 (Revised).]

[Signature in the name of the audit firm, the personal name of the auditor, or both, as appropriate for the particular jurisdiction]

[Auditor Address]

[Date]

---

[12] *Or other terms that are appropriate in the context of the legal framework in the particular jurisdiction.*

ISA (UK) 720 (Revised June 2016)
The Auditor's Responsibilities Relating to Other Information

*(Effective for audits of financial statements for periods commencing on
or after 17 June 2016)*

Contents

Paragraphs

Introduction
Scope of this ISA (UK)   1 - 9
Effective Date   10

Objectives   11

Definitions   12

Requirements
Obtaining an Understanding of the Entity and its Environment relating to
    Statutory Other Information   12-1
Obtaining the Other Information   13
Reading and Considering the Other Information   14 - 15
Responding When a Material Inconsistency Appears to Exist or Other Information
    Appears to Be Materially Misstated   16
Responding When the Auditor Concludes That a Material Misstatement of the
    Other Information Exists   17 - 19
Responding When a Material Misstatement in the Financial Statements Exists or
    the Auditor's Understanding of the Entity and Its Environment Needs to Be Updated   20
Reporting   21 - 24
Documentation   25

Application and Other Explanatory Material
Definitions   A1 - A10-1
Obtaining the Other Information   A11 - A22
Reading and Considering the Other Information   A23 - A38
Responding When a Material Inconsistency Appears to Exist or Other Information
    Appears to Be Materially Misstated (Ref: Para. 16)   A39 - A43
Responding When the Auditor Concludes That a Material Misstatement of the
    Other Information Exists   A44 - A50
Responding When a Material Misstatement in the Financial Statements
    Exists or the Auditor's Understanding of the Entity and Its Environment
    Needs to Be Updated   A51
Reporting   A52 - A59

**Appendix 1: Examples of Amounts or Other Items that May Be Included in the
        Other Information**

Appendix 2: Illustrations of Auditor's Reports Relating to Other Information

International Standard on Auditing (UK) (ISA (UK)) 720 (Revised June 2016), *The Auditor's Responsibilities Relating to Other Information*, should be read in conjunction with ISA (UK) 200 (Revised June 2016), *Overall Objectives of the Independent Auditor and the Conduct of an Audit in Accordance with International Standards on Auditing (UK).*

Introduction

Scope of this ISA (UK)

This International Standard on Auditing (UK) (ISA (UK)) deals with the auditor's   **1**
responsibilities relating to other information, whether financial or non-financial
information (other than financial statements and the auditor's report thereon),
included in an entity's annual report. An entity's annual report may be a single
document or a combination of documents that serve the same purpose.

This ISA (UK) also deals with certain additional obligations imposed by law or   **1-1**
regulation on the auditor to report on statutory other information, based on the
work undertaken in the course of the audit.

This ISA (UK) is written in the context of an audit of financial statements by an   **2**
independent auditor. Accordingly, the objectives of the auditor in this ISA (UK)
are to be understood in the context of the overall objectives of the auditor as stated
in paragraph 11 of ISA (UK) 200 (Revised June 2016).[1] The requirements in the
ISAs (UK) are designed to enable the auditor to achieve the objectives specified in
the ISAs (UK), and thereby the overall objectives of the auditor. The auditor's
opinion on the financial statements does not cover the other information, nor does
this ISA (UK) require the auditor to obtain audit evidence beyond that required to
form an opinion on the financial statements.

This ISA (UK) requires the auditor to read and consider the other information   **3**
because other information that is materially inconsistent with the financial
statements or the auditor's knowledge obtained in the audit may indicate that
there is a material misstatement of the financial statements or that a material
misstatement of the other information exists, either of which may undermine the
credibility of the financial statements and the auditor's report thereon. Such
material misstatements may also inappropriately influence the economic decisions
of the users for whom the auditor's report is prepared.

This ISA (UK) may also assist the auditor in complying with relevant ethical   **4**
requirements[2] that require the auditor to avoid being knowingly associated with
information that the auditor believes contains a materially false or misleading
statement, statements or information furnished recklessly, or omits or obscures
information required to be included where such omission or obscurity would be
misleading.

Other information may include amounts or other items that are intended to be the   **5**
same as, to summarize, or to provide greater detail, about amounts or other items
in the financial statements, and other amounts or other items about which the
auditor has obtained knowledge in the audit. Other information may also include
other matters.

The auditor's responsibilities relating to other information (other than applicable   **6**
reporting responsibilities) apply regardless of whether the other information is
obtained by the auditor prior to, or after, the date of the auditor's report.

---

[1] *ISA (UK) 200 (Revised June 2016), Overall Objectives of the Independent Auditor and the Conduct of an Audit in
Accordance with International Standards on Auditing (UK).*

[2] *International Ethics Standards Board for Accountants' Code of Ethics for Professional Accountants (IESBA
Code), paragraph 110.2.*

7   This ISA (UK) does not apply to:

(a)   Preliminary announcements of financial information; or

(b)   Securities offering documents, including prospectuses.

8   The auditor's responsibilities under this ISA (UK) do not constitute an assurance engagement on other information or impose an obligation on the auditor to obtain assurance about the other information except in respect of the auditor's responsibilities to report in accordance with paragraphs 22D-1 and 22D-2.

9   Law or regulation may impose additional obligations on the auditor in relation to other information that are beyond the scope of this ISA (UK).

Effective Date

10   This ISA (UK) is effective for audits of financial statements for periods commencing on or after 17 June 2016. Earlier adoption is permitted.

Objectives

11   The objectives of the auditor, having read the other information, are:

(a)   To consider whether there is a material inconsistency between the other information and the financial statements;

(b)   To consider whether there is a material inconsistency between the other information and the auditor's knowledge obtained in the audit;

(c)   To respond appropriately when the auditor identifies that such material inconsistencies appear to exist, or when the auditor otherwise becomes aware that other information appears to be materially misstated;

(c)-1 Where required by law or regulation, to form an opinion on whether the information given in the other information is consistent with the financial statements and the auditor's knowledge obtained in the audit; and

(d)   To report in accordance with this ISA (UK).

Definitions

12   For purposes of the ISAs (UK), the following terms have the meanings attributed below:

(a)   Annual report – A document, or combination of documents, prepared typically on an annual basis by management or those charged with governance in accordance with law, regulation or custom, the purpose of which is to provide owners (or similar stakeholders) with information on the entity's operations and the entity's financial results and financial position as set out in the financial statements. An annual report contains or accompanies the financial statements and the auditor's report thereon and usually includes information about the entity's developments, its future outlook and risks and uncertainties, a statement by the entity's governing body, and reports covering governance matters. (Ref: Para. A1–A5)

> In the UK, an annual report includes at least:
>
> (i)   The statutory other information; and
>
> (ii)   Any other documents that are incorporated by cross-reference in, or distributed to shareholders with, statutory other information either voluntarily or pursuant to law or regulation or the requirements of a stock exchange listing.

(b)   Misstatement of the other information – A misstatement of the other information exists when the other information is incorrectly stated or otherwise misleading (including because it omits or obscures information necessary for a proper understanding of a matter disclosed in the other information). (Ref: Para. A6–A7)

> In the UK, a misstatement of the other information also exists when the statutory other information has not been prepared in accordance with the legal and regulatory requirements applicable to the statutory other information.

(c)   Other information – Financial or non-financial information (other than financial statements and the auditor's report thereon) included in an entity's annual report. (Ref: Para. A8–A10)

(d)   Statutory other information – Those documents or reports that are required to be prepared and issued by the entity (including any reports or documents that are incorporated by cross reference) in relation to which the auditor is required to report publicly in accordance with law or regulation. (Ref: Para. A10-1)

> In the UK, the statutory other information includes, where required to be prepared:
>
> (i)   The directors' report;
>
> (ii)   The strategic report;
>
> (iii)   The separate corporate governance statement.[2a]

Requirements

Obtaining an Understanding of the Entity and its Environment relating to Statutory Other Information

For entities that are required to prepare statutory other information, as part of obtaining an understanding of the entity and its environment in accordance with ISA (UK) 315 (Revised June 2016),[2b] the auditor shall obtain an understanding of: **12-1**

(a)   The legal and regulatory requirements applicable to the statutory other information; and

(b)   How the entity is complying with those legal and regulatory requirements.

[2a] *When the required information is not included within or incorporated by cross reference to the directors' report.*

[2b] *ISA (UK) 315 (Revised June 2016), Identifying and Assessing the Risks of Material Misstatement through Understanding the Entity and its Environment, paragraph 11.*

Obtaining the Other Information

13   The auditor shall: (Ref: Para. A11–A22)

(a)   Determine, through discussion with management, which document(s) comprises the annual report, and the entity's planned manner and timing of the issuance of such document(s);

(b)   Make appropriate arrangements with management to obtain in a timely manner and, if possible, prior to the date of the auditor's report, the final version of the document(s) comprising the annual report; and

(c)   When some or all of the document(s) determined in (a) will not be available until after the date of the auditor's report, request management to provide a written representation that the final version of the document(s) will be provided to the auditor when available, and prior to its issuance by the entity, such that the auditor can complete the procedures required by this ISA (UK). (Ref: Para. A22)

Reading and Considering the Other Information

14   The auditor shall read the other information and, in doing so shall: (Ref: Para. A23–A24)

(a)   Consider whether there is a material inconsistency between the other information and the financial statements. As the basis for this consideration, the auditor shall, to evaluate their consistency, compare selected amounts or other items in the other information (that are intended to be the same as, to summarize, or to provide greater detail about, the amounts or other items in the financial statements) with such amounts or other items in the financial statements; and (Ref: Para. A25–A29)

(b)   Consider whether there is a material inconsistency between the other information and the auditor's knowledge obtained in the audit, in the context of audit evidence obtained and conclusions reached in the audit. (Ref: Para. A30–A36)

14-1   For entities that are required to prepare statutory other information, the auditor shall read the statutory other information and, in doing so shall consider, based on the work undertaken in the course of the audit, whether the statutory other information appears to be materially misstated in the context of the auditor's understanding of the legal and regulatory requirements applicable to the statutory other information. (Ref: Para. A36-1–A36-4)

14-2   For entities that are required to prepare statutory other information, as the basis for the consideration required by paragraphs 14(a), 14(b) and 14-1, the auditor shall perform such procedures as are necessary in the auditor's professional judgment to identify:

(a)   Any material inconsistencies between the other information and the financial statements;

(b)   Any material inconsistencies between the other information and the auditor's knowledge obtained in the audit, in the context of audit evidence obtained and conclusions reached in the audit; and

(c)   Whether the statutory other information appears to be materially misstated in the context of the auditor's understanding of the legal and regulatory requirements applicable to the statutory other information.

While reading the other information in accordance with paragraph 14, the auditor **15** shall remain alert for indications that the other information not related to the financial statements or the auditor's knowledge obtained in the audit appears to be materially misstated. (Ref: Para. A24, A37–A38)

Responding When a Material Inconsistency Appears to Exist or Other Information Appears to Be Materially Misstated

If the auditor identifies that a material inconsistency appears to exist (or becomes **16** aware that the other information appears to be materially misstated), the auditor shall discuss the matter with management and, if necessary, perform other procedures to conclude whether: (Ref: Para. A39–A43)

(a) A material misstatement of the other information exists;

(b) A material misstatement of the financial statements exists; or

(c) The auditor's understanding of the entity and its environment needs to be updated.

Responding When the Auditor Concludes That a Material Misstatement of the Other Information Exists

If the auditor concludes that a material misstatement of the other information **17** exists, the auditor shall request management to correct the other information. If management:

(a) Agrees to make the correction, the auditor shall determine that the correction has been made; or

(b) Refuses to make the correction, the auditor shall communicate the matter with those charged with governance and request that the correction be made.

If the auditor concludes that a material misstatement exists in other information **18** obtained prior to the date of the auditor's report, and the other information is not corrected after communicating with those charged with governance, the auditor shall take appropriate action, including: (Ref: Para. A44–A44-2)

(a) Considering the implications for the auditor's report and communicating with those charged with governance about how the auditor plans to address the material misstatement in the auditor's report (see paragraph 22(e)(ii)); or (Ref: Para. A45)

(b) Withdrawing from the engagement, where withdrawal is possible under applicable law or regulation. (Ref: Para. A46–A47)

If the auditor concludes that a material misstatement exists in other information **19** obtained after the date of the auditor's report, the auditor shall:

(a) If the other information is corrected, perform the procedures necessary in the circumstances; or (Ref: Para. A48)

(b) If the other information is not corrected after communicating with those charged with governance, take appropriate action considering the auditor's legal rights and obligations, to seek to have the uncorrected material misstatement appropriately brought to the attention of users for whom the auditor's report is prepared. (Ref: Para. A49–A50)

Responding When a Material Misstatement in the Financial Statements Exists or the Auditor's Understanding of the Entity and Its Environment Needs to Be Updated

20   If, as a result of performing the procedures in paragraphs 14–15, the auditor concludes that a material misstatement in the financial statements exists or the auditor's understanding of the entity and its environment needs to be updated, the auditor shall respond appropriately in accordance with the other ISAs (UK). (Ref: Para. A51)

Reporting

21   The auditor's report shall include a separate section with a heading "Other Information", or other appropriate heading, when, at the date of the auditor's report:

(a)   For an audit of financial statements of a listed entity, the auditor has obtained, or expects to obtain, the other information; or

(b)   For an audit of financial statements of an entity other than a listed entity, the auditor has obtained some or all of the other information. (Ref: Para. A52)

> In the UK, the auditor's report shall always include a separate section with a heading "Other Information", or other appropriate heading.[2c]

22   When the auditor's report is required to include an Other Information section in accordance with paragraph 21, this section shall include: (Ref: Para. A53)

(a)   A statement that management is responsible for the other information;

(b)   An identification of:

   (i)   Other information, if any, obtained by the auditor prior to the date of the auditor's report; and

   (ii)   For an audit of financial statements of a listed entity, other information, if any, expected to be obtained after the date of the auditor's report;

(c)   A statement that the auditor's opinion does not cover the other information and, accordingly, that the auditor does not express (or will not express) an audit opinion or any form of assurance conclusion thereon;

> In the UK, where the auditor is required to express an opinion on some or all of the other information in accordance with paragraphs 22D-1 or 22D-2 or otherwise in accordance with law or regulation, the statement required by paragraph 22(c) shall be a modified statement that the auditor's opinion on the financial statements does not cover the other information and, accordingly, the auditor does not express an audit opinion or, except to the extent otherwise explicitly stated in the auditor's report, any form of assurance thereon.

(d)   A description of the auditor's responsibilities relating to reading, considering and reporting on other information as required by this ISA (UK); and

---

[2c] *ISA (UK) 700 (Revised June 2016) requires that "The auditor shall not sign, and hence date, the auditor's report earlier than the date on which all the other information has been approved by those charged with governance and the auditor has considered all necessary available evidence."*

In the UK, the description of the auditor's responsibilities in relation to the other information required by paragraph 22(d) shall also include the auditor's responsibilities under paragraph 14-1, 22D-1, 22D-2, 22-3 and 22-4 where applicable.

(e)   When other information has been obtained prior to the date of the auditor's report, either:

    (i)   A statement that the auditor has nothing to report; or

    (ii)   If the auditor has concluded that there is an uncorrected material misstatement of the other information, a statement that describes the uncorrected material misstatement of the other information.

Strategic Report and Directors' Report

For UK entities that are required to prepare statutory other information,[2d] the auditor shall in the auditor's report: **22D-1**

(a)   State whether, in the auditor's opinion, based on the work undertaken in the course of the audit:

    (i)   The information given in the strategic report (if any) and the directors' report for the financial year for which the accounts are prepared is consistent with those accounts; and

    (ii)   Any such strategic report and the directors' report have been prepared in accordance with applicable legal requirements;

(b)   State whether, in the light of the knowledge and understanding of the company and its environment obtained in the course of the audit, the auditor has identified material misstatements in the strategic report (if any) and the directors' report; and

(c)   If applicable, give an indication of the nature of each of the misstatements referred to in paragraph 22D-1(b).

Separate Corporate Governance Statement

For UK entities that are required to prepare statutory other information,[2e] where the entity prepares a separate corporate governance statement in respect of a financial year, the auditor shall in the auditor's report: (Ref: Para. A53-1) **22D-2**

(a)   State whether, in the auditor's opinion, based on the work undertaken in the course of the audit, the information given in the statement in compliance with rules 7.2.5 and 7.2.6 in the Disclosure Rules and Transparency Rules sourcebook made by the Financial Conduct Authority (information about internal control and risk management systems in relation to financial reporting processes and about share capital structures):

    (i)   Is consistent with those accounts; and

    (ii)   Has been prepared in accordance with applicable legal requirements;

[2d] *In the UK, Section 496 of the Companies Act 2006 as amended by The Companies, Partnerships and Groups (Accounts and Reports) Regulations 2015.*

[2e] *In the UK, Section 497A of the Companies Act 2006 as amended by The Companies, Partnerships and Groups (Accounts and Reports) Regulations 2015.*

(b)   State whether, in the light of the knowledge and understanding of the company and its environment obtained in the course of the audit, the auditor has identified material misstatements in the information in the statement referred to in paragraph 22D-2(a);

(c)   If applicable, give an indication of the nature of each of the misstatements referred to in paragraph 22D-2 (b), and

(d)   State whether, in the auditor's opinion, based on the work undertaken in the course of the audit, rules 7.2.2, 7.2.3 and 7.2.7 in the Disclosure Rules and Transparency Rules sourcebook made by the Financial Conduct Authority (information about the company's corporate governance code and practices and about its administrative, management and supervisory bodies and their committees) have been complied with, if applicable.

UK Corporate Governance Code Reporting

22-3   For entities that are required, and those that choose voluntarily, to report on how they have applied the UK Corporate Governance Code or to explain why they have not, in meeting the auditor's responsibilities to report under paragraph 22(e), the auditor shall specifically address each of the following elements of the other information:

(a)   The statement given by the directors that they consider the annual report and accounts taken as a whole is fair, balanced and understandable and provides the information necessary for shareholders to assess the entity's performance, business model and strategy, that is materially inconsistent with the auditor's knowledge obtained in the audit;

(b)   The section describing the work of the audit committee that does not appropriately address matters communicated by the auditor to the audit committee;

(c)   The explanation as to why the annual report does not include such a statement or section that is materially inconsistent with the auditor's knowledge obtained in the audit;

(d)   The parts of the directors' statement required under the Listing Rules relating to the entity's compliance with the UK Corporate Governance Code containing provisions specified for review by the auditor in accordance with Listing Rule 9.8.10R(2) that do not properly disclose a departure from a relevant provision of the UK Corporate Governance Code; and

(e)   The directors' statement relating to Going Concern required under the Listing Rules in accordance with Listing Rule 9.8.6R(3) that is materially inconsistent with the auditor's knowledge obtained in the audit.

In reporting under paragraph 22, the auditor shall describe the specific reporting responsibility relating to these matters in accordance with paragraph 22(d) and shall report on each of these matters by providing a statement in accordance with paragraph 22(e). (Ref: Para. A53-2–A53-3)

UK Corporate Governance Code Reporting – Statement on the Directors'
Assessment of the Principal Risks that Would Threaten the Solvency or
Liquidity of the Entity

For entities that are required, and those that choose voluntarily, to report on   **22-4**
how they have applied the UK Corporate Governance Code or to explain why
they have not, the auditor shall, having particular regard to the work performed
in accordance with paragraph 18-2 of ISA (UK) 570 (Revised June 2016), give
a statement as to whether the auditor has anything material to add or draw
attention to in respect of:

(a)   The directors' confirmation in the annual report that they have carried out
      a robust assessment of the principal risks facing the entity, including
      those that would threaten its business model, future performance,
      solvency or liquidity;

(b)   The disclosures in the annual report that describe those risks and explain
      how they are being managed or mitigated; and

(c)   The directors' explanation in the annual report as to how they have
      assessed the prospects of the entity, over what period they have done so
      and why they consider that period to be appropriate, and their statement
      as to whether they have a reasonable expectation that the entity will be
      able to continue in operation and meet its liabilities as they fall due over
      the period of their assessment, including any related disclosures drawing
      attention to any necessary qualifications or assumptions.

In reporting under paragraph 22, the description of the auditor's responsibilities
in relation to the other information required by paragraph 22(d) shall also
include the auditor's additional responsibilities under paragraph 18-2 of ISA
(UK) 570 (Revised June 2016) and the auditor's responsibility to report
whether the auditor has anything material to add or draw attention to in
relation to each of the above elements of the other information. In addition,
where the auditor has identified anything material to add or draw attention to in
respect of these elements of the other information, the auditor shall include in
the auditor's report a statement that describes any other material information
that the auditor considers it appropriate to add or draw attention to.

When the auditor expresses a qualified or adverse opinion in accordance with   **23**
ISA (UK) 705 (Revised June 2016)[3], the auditor shall consider the implications
of the matter giving rise to the modification of opinion for the statement
required in paragraph 22(e). (Ref: Para. A54–A58)

Reporting Prescribed by Law or Regulation

If the auditor is required by law or regulation of a specific jurisdiction to refer to   **24**
the other information in the auditor's report using a specific layout or wording, the
auditor's report shall refer to International Standards on Auditing only if the
auditor's report includes, at a minimum: (Ref: Para. A59)

(a)   Identification of the other information obtained by the auditor prior to the
      date of the auditor's report;

---

[3] *ISA (UK) 705 (Revised June 2016), Modifications to the Opinion in the Independent Auditor's Report.*

(b)   A description of the auditor's responsibilities with respect to the other information; and

(c)   An explicit statement addressing the outcome of the auditor's work for this purpose.

Documentation

25   In addressing the requirements of ISA (UK) 230 (Revised June 2016)[4] as it applies to this ISA (UK), the auditor shall include in the audit documentation:

(a)   Documentation of the procedures performed under this ISA (UK); and

(b)   The final version of the other information on which the auditor has performed the work required under this ISA (UK).

***

Application and Other Explanatory Material

Definitions

Annual Report
(Ref: Para. 12(a))

A1   Law, regulation or custom may define the content of an annual report, and the name by which it is to be referred, for entities in a particular jurisdiction; however, the content and the name may vary within a jurisdiction and from one jurisdiction to another.

A2   An annual report is typically prepared on an annual basis. However, when the financial statements being audited are prepared for a period less than or more than a year, an annual report may also be prepared that covers the same period as the financial statements.

A3   In some cases, an entity's annual report may be a single document and referred to by the title "annual report" or by some other title. In other cases, law, regulation or custom may require the entity to report to owners (or similar stakeholders) information on the entity's operations and the entity's financial results and financial position as set out in the financial statements (i.e., an annual report) by way of a single document, or by way of two or more separate documents that in combination serve the same purpose. For example, depending on law, regulation or custom in a particular jurisdiction, one or more of the following documents may form part of the annual report:

●   Management report, management commentary, or operating and financial review or similar reports by those charged with governance (for example, a directors' report).

●   Chairman's statement.

●   Corporate governance statement.

●   Internal control and risk assessment reports.

---

[4] *ISA (UK) 230 (Revised June 2016), Audit Documentation, paragraphs 8–11.*

An annual report may be made available to users in printed form, or electronically,   **A4**
including on the entity's website. A document (or combination of documents) may
meet the definition of an annual report, irrespective of the manner in which it is
made available to users.

An annual report is different in nature, purpose and content from other reports,   **A5**
such as a report prepared to meet the information needs of a specific stakeholder
group or a report prepared to comply with a specific regulatory reporting objective
(even when such a report is required to be publicly available). Examples of reports
that, when issued as standalone documents, are not typically part of the
combination of documents that comprise an annual report (subject to law,
regulation or custom), and that, therefore, are not other information within the
scope of this ISA (UK), include:

- Separate industry or regulatory reports (for example, capital adequacy reports),
  such as may be prepared in the banking, insurance, and pension industries.

- Corporate social responsibility reports.

- Sustainability reports.

- Diversity and equal opportunity reports.

- Product responsibility reports.

- Labor practices and working conditions reports.

- Human rights reports.

Misstatement of the Other Information
(Ref: Para. 12(b))

When a particular matter is disclosed in the other information, the other   **A6**
information may omit or obscure information that is necessary for a proper
understanding of that matter. For example, if the other information purports to
address the key performance indicators used by management, then omission of a
key performance indicator used by management could indicate that the other
information is misleading.

The concept of materiality may be discussed in a framework applicable to the   **A7**
other information and, if so, such a framework may provide a frame of reference
for the auditor in making judgments about materiality under this ISA (UK). In
many cases, however, there may be no applicable framework that includes a
discussion of the concept of materiality as it applies to the other information. In
such circumstances, the following characteristics provide the auditor with a frame
of reference in determining if a misstatement of the other information is material:

- Materiality is considered in the context of the common information needs of
  users as a group. The users of the other information are expected to be the
  same as the users of the financial statements as such users may be expected
  to read the other information to provide context to the financial statements.

- Judgments about materiality take into account the specific circumstances of
  the misstatement, considering whether users would be influenced by the
  effect of the uncorrected misstatement. Not all misstatements will influence
  the economic decisions of users.

- Judgments about materiality involve both qualitative and quantitative
  considerations. Accordingly, such judgments may take into account the
  nature or magnitude of the items that the other information addresses in the
  context of the entity's annual report.

Other Information
(Ref: Para. 12(c))

A8   Appendix 1 contains examples of amounts or other items that may be included in the other information.

A9   In some cases, the applicable financial reporting framework may require specific disclosures but permit them to be located outside of the financial statements.[5] As such disclosures are required by the applicable financial reporting framework, they form part of the financial statements. Accordingly, they do not constitute other information for the purpose of this ISA (UK).

A10   eXtensible Business Reporting Language (XBRL) tags do not represent other information as defined in this ISA (UK).

Statutory Other Information
(Ref: Para. 12(d))

A10-1   Information given in the statutory other information includes information that is included by way of cross reference to other information presented separately from the statutory other information. For example, a UK entity may decide to present a voluntary Operating and Financial Review (OFR) which includes some or all of the matters required for the business performance review section of the Strategic Report or the Directors' Report. Rather than duplicate the information, the entity may cross refer from the Strategic Report or the Directors' Report to the relevant information provided in the OFR.

Obtaining the Other Information
(Ref: Para. 13)

A11   Determining the document(s) that is or comprises the annual report is often clear based on law, regulation or custom. In many cases, management or those charged with governance may have customarily issued a package of documents that together comprise the annual report, or may have committed to do so. In some cases, however, it may not be clear which document(s) is or comprises the annual report. In such cases, the timing and purpose of the documents (and for whom they are intended) are matters that may be relevant to the auditor's determination of which document(s) is or comprises the annual report.

A12   When the annual report is translated into other languages pursuant to law or regulation (such as may occur when a jurisdiction has more than one official language), or when multiple "annual reports" are prepared under different legislation (for example, when an entity is listed in more than one jurisdiction), consideration may need to be given as to whether one, or more than one of the "annual reports" form part of the other information. Local law or regulation may provide further guidance in this respect.

A13   Management, or those charged with governance, is responsible for preparing the annual report. The auditor may communicate with management or those charged with governance:

- The auditor's expectations in relation to obtaining the final version of the annual report (including a combination of documents that together comprise

---

[5] *For example, International Financial Reporting Standards (IFRS) 7, "Financial Instruments: Disclosures," permits certain disclosures required by the IFRSs to either be given in the financial statements or incorporated by cross-reference from the financial statements to some other statement, such as a management commentary or risk report, that is available to users of the financial statements on the same terms as the financial statements and at the same time.*

the annual report) in a timely manner prior to the date of the auditor's report such that the auditor can complete the procedures required by this ISA (UK) before the date of the auditor's report, or if that is not possible, as soon as practicable and in any case prior to the entity's issuance of such information.

- The possible implications when the other information is obtained after the date of the auditor's report.

The communications referred to in paragraph A13 may be particularly appropriate for example: **A14**

- In an initial audit engagement.
- When there has been a change in management or those charged with governance.
- When other information is expected to be obtained after the date of the auditor's report.

Where those charged with governance are to approve the other information prior to its issuance by the entity, the final version of such other information is the one that has been approved by those charged with governance for issuance.   **A15**

In some cases, the entity's annual report may be a single document to be released, in accordance with law or regulation or the entity's reporting practice, shortly after the entity's financial reporting period such that it is available to the auditor prior to the date of the auditor's report. In other cases, such a document may not be required to be released until a later time, or at a time of the entity's choosing. There may also be circumstances when the entity's annual report is a combination of documents, each subject to different requirements or reporting practice by the entity with respect to the timing of their release.   **A16**

There may be circumstances when, at the date of the auditor's report, the entity is considering the development of a document that may be part of the entity's annual report (for example, a voluntary report to stakeholders) but management is unable to confirm to the auditor the purpose or timing of such a document. If the auditor is unable to ascertain the purpose or timing of such a document, the document is not considered other information for purposes of this ISA (UK).   **A17**

Obtaining the other information in a timely manner prior to the date of the auditor's report enables any revisions that are found to be necessary to be made to the financial statements, the auditor's report, or the other information prior to their issuance. The audit engagement letter[6] may make reference to an agreement with management to make available to the auditor the other information in a timely manner, and if possible prior to the date of the auditor's report.   **A18**

When other information is only made available to users via the entity's website, the version of the other information obtained from the entity, rather than directly from the entity's website, is the relevant document on which the auditor would perform procedures in accordance with this ISA (UK). The auditor has no responsibility under this ISA (UK) to search for other information, including other information that may be on the entity's website, nor to perform any procedures to confirm that other information is appropriately displayed on the entity's website or otherwise has been appropriately transmitted or displayed electronically.   **A19**

---

[6] *ISA (UK) 210, Agreeing the Terms of Audit Engagements, paragraph A23.*

A20 The auditor is not precluded from dating or issuing the auditor's report if the auditor has not obtained some or all of the other information.[6a]

A21 When the other information is obtained after the date of the auditor's report, the auditor is not required to update the procedures performed in accordance with paragraphs 6 and 7 of ISA (UK) 560.[7]

A22 ISA (UK) 580[8] establishes requirements and provides guidance on the use of written representations. The written representation required to be requested by paragraph 13(c) regarding other information that will be available only after the date of the auditor's report is intended to support the auditor's ability to complete the procedures required by this ISA (UK) with respect to such information. In addition, the auditor may find it useful to request other written representations, for example, that:

- Management has informed the auditor of all the documents that it expects to issue that may comprise other information;

- The financial statements and any other information obtained by the auditor prior to the date of the auditor's report are consistent with one another, and the other information does not contain any material misstatements; and

- With regard to other information that has not been obtained by the auditor prior to the date of the auditor's report, that management intends to prepare and issue such other information and the expected timing of such issuance.

Reading and Considering the Other Information
(Ref: Para. 14–15)

A23 The auditor is required by ISA (UK) 200 (Revised June 2016)[9] to plan and perform the audit with professional skepticism. Maintaining professional skepticism when reading and considering the other information includes, for example, recognizing that management may be overly optimistic about the success of its plans, and being alert to information that may be inconsistent with:

(a) The financial statements; or

(b) The auditor's knowledge obtained in the audit.

A24 In accordance with ISA (UK) 220 (Revised June 2016),[10] the engagement partner is required to take responsibility for the direction, supervision and performance of the audit engagement in compliance with professional standards and applicable legal and regulatory requirements. In the context of this ISA (UK), factors that may be taken into account when determining the appropriate engagement team members to address the requirements of paragraphs 14–15, include:

- The relative experience of engagement team members.

- Whether the engagement team members to be assigned the tasks have the relevant knowledge obtained in the audit to identify inconsistencies between the other information and that knowledge.

[6a] *ISA (UK) 700 (Revised June 2016) requires that "The auditor shall not sign, and hence date, the auditor's report earlier than the date on which all the other information has been approved by those charged with governance and the auditor has considered all necessary available evidence."*

[7] *ISA (UK) 560, Subsequent Events.*

[8] *ISA (UK) 580, Written Representations.*

[9] *ISA (UK) 200 (Revised June 2016), paragraph 15.*

[10] *ISA (UK) 220 (Revised June 2016), Quality Control for an Audit of Financial Statements, paragraph 15(a).*

- The degree of judgment involved in addressing the requirements of paragraph 14–15. For example, performing procedures to evaluate the consistency of amounts in the other information that are intended to be the same as amounts in the financial statements may be carried out by less experienced engagement team members.

- Whether, in the case of a group audit, it is necessary to make inquiries of a component auditor in addressing the other information related to that component.

Considering Whether There is a Material Inconsistency between the Other Information and the Financial Statements
(Ref: Para. 14(a))

Other information may include amounts or other items that are intended to be the same as, to summarize, or to provide greater detail about, the amounts or other items in the financial statements. Examples of such amounts or other items may include: **A25**

- Tables, charts or graphs containing extracts of the financial statements.

- A disclosure providing greater detail about a balance or account shown in the financial statements, such as "Revenue for 20X1 comprised XXX million from product X and YYY million from product Y."

- Descriptions of the financial results, such as "Total research and development expense was XXX in 20X1."

In evaluating the consistency of selected amounts or other items in the other information with the financial statements, the auditor is not required to compare all amounts or other items in the other information that are intended to be the same as, to summarize, or to provide greater detail about, the amounts or other items in the financial statements, with such amounts or other items in the financial statements.   **A26**

Selecting the amounts or other items to compare is a matter of professional judgment. Factors relevant to this judgment include: **A27**

- The significance of the amount or other item in the context in which it is presented, which may affect the importance that users would attach to the amount or other item (for example, a key ratio or amount).

- If quantitative, the relative size of the amount compared with accounts or items in the financial statements or the other information to which they relate.

- The sensitivity of the particular amount or other item in the other information, for example, share based payments for senior management.

Determining the nature and extent of procedures to address the requirement in paragraph 14(a) is a matter of professional judgment, recognizing that the auditor's responsibilities under this ISA (UK) do not constitute an assurance engagement on the other information or impose an obligation to obtain assurance about the other information. Examples of such procedures include: **A28**

- For information that is intended to be the same as information in the financial statements, comparing the information to the financial statements.

- For information intended to convey the same meaning as disclosures in the financial statements, comparing the words used and considering the significance of differences in wording used and whether such differences imply different meanings.

- Obtaining a reconciliation between an amount within the other information and the financial statements from management and:

    - Comparing items in the reconciliation to the financial statements and the other information; and

    - Checking whether the calculations within the reconciliation are arithmetically accurate.

A29   Evaluating the consistency of selected amounts or other items in the other information with the financial statements includes, when relevant given the nature of the other information, the manner of their presentation compared to the financial statements.

Considering Whether There Is a Material Inconsistency between the Other Information and the Auditor's Knowledge Obtained in the Audit (Ref: Para. 14(b))

A30   Other information may include amounts or items that are related to the auditor's knowledge obtained in the audit (other than those in paragraph 14(a)). Examples of such amounts or items may include:

- A disclosure of the units produced, or a table summarizing such production by geographical region.

- A statement that "The company introduced product X and product Y during the year."

- A summary of the locations of the entity's major operations, such as "the entity's major center of operation is in country X, and there are also operations in countries Y and Z."

A31   The auditor's knowledge obtained in the audit includes the auditor's understanding of the entity and its environment, including the entity's internal control, obtained in accordance with ISA (UK) 315 (Revised June 2016).[11] ISA (UK) 315 (Revised June 2016) sets out the auditor's required understanding, which includes such matters as obtaining an understanding of:

(a)   The relevant industry, regulatory, and other external factors;

(b)   The nature of the entity;

(c)   The entity's selection and application of accounting policies;

(d)   The entity's objectives and strategies;

(e)   The measurement and review of the entity's financial performance; and

(f)   The entity's internal control.

A32   The auditor's knowledge obtained in the audit may also include matters that are prospective in nature. Such matters may include, for example, business prospects and future cash flows that the auditor considered when evaluating the assumptions used by management in performing impairment tests on intangible assets such as goodwill, or when evaluating management's assessment of the entity's ability to continue as a going concern.

---

[11] *ISA (UK) 315 (Revised June 2016), Identifying and Assessing the Risks of Material Misstatement through Understanding the Entity and Its Environment, paragraphs 11–12.*

In considering whether there is a material inconsistency between the other **A33** information and the auditor's knowledge obtained in the audit, the auditor may focus on those matters in the other information that are of sufficient importance that a misstatement of the other information in relation to that matter could be material.

In relation to many matters in the other information, the auditor's recollection of **A34** the audit evidence obtained and conclusions reached in the audit may be sufficient to enable the auditor to consider whether there is a material inconsistency between the other information and the auditor's knowledge obtained in the audit. The more experienced and the more familiar with the key aspects of the audit the auditor is, the more likely it is that the auditor's recollection of relevant matters will be sufficient. For example, the auditor may be able to consider whether there is a material inconsistency between the other information and the auditor's knowledge obtained in the audit in light of the auditor's recollection of discussions held with management or those charged with governance or findings from procedures carried out during the audit such as the reading of board minutes, without the need to take further action.

The auditor may determine that referring to relevant audit documentation or **A35** making inquiries of relevant members of the engagement team or relevant component auditors is appropriate as a basis for the auditor's consideration of whether a material inconsistency exists. For example:

- When the other information describes the planned cessation of a major product line and, although the auditor is aware of the planned cessation, the auditor may make inquiries of the relevant engagement team member who performed the audit procedures in this area to support the auditor's consideration of whether the description is materially inconsistent with the auditor's knowledge obtained during the audit.

- When the other information describes important details of a lawsuit addressed in the audit, but the auditor cannot recall them adequately, it may be necessary to refer to the audit documentation where such details are summarized to support the auditor's recollection.

Whether, and if so the extent to which, the auditor refers to relevant audit **A36** documentation, or makes inquiries of relevant members of the engagement team or relevant component auditors is a matter of professional judgment. However, it may not be necessary for the auditor to refer to relevant audit documentation, or to make inquiries of relevant members of the engagement team or relevant component auditors about any matter included in the other information.

Identifying Whether the Statutory Other Information Has Been Prepared in Accordance with the Applicable Legal and Regulatory Requirements (Ref: Para. 14-1)

As explained in paragraph 12(b), a misstatement of the other information also **A36-1** exists when the statutory other information has not been prepared in accordance with the legal and regulatory requirements applicable to the statutory other information.

In considering whether the statutory other information has been prepared in **A36-2** accordance with the legal and regulatory requirements applicable to the statutory other information, the auditor identifies whether information that is required by law or regulation to be included in the statutory other information has been omitted. This includes situations where the required information is presented separately from the statutory other information without appropriate cross reference.

A36-3   If the auditor concludes that the statutory other information has not been prepared in accordance with the legal and regulatory requirements applicable to the statutory other information, the auditor determines whether non-compliance with the applicable legal or regulatory requirement has a material effect on the financial statements.[11a]

A36-4   For statutory audits of financial statements of public interest entities, the auditor considers whether to communicate any non-compliance with the applicable legal or regulatory requirement in the additional report to the audit committee.[11b]

Remaining Alert for Other Indications that the Other Information Appears to Be Materially Misstated
(Ref: Para. 15)

A37   Other information may include discussion of matters that are not related to the financial statements and may also extend beyond the auditor's knowledge obtained in the audit. For example, the other information may include statements about the entity's greenhouse gas emissions.

A38   Remaining alert for other indications that the other information not related to the financial statements or the auditor's knowledge obtained in the audit appears to be materially misstated assists the auditor in complying with relevant ethical requirements that require the auditor to avoid being knowingly associated with other information that the auditor believes contains a materially false or misleading statement, a statement furnished recklessly, or omits or obscures necessary information such that the other information is misleading.[12] Remaining alert for other indications that the other information appears to be materially misstated could potentially result in the auditor identifying such matters as:

- Differences between the other information and the general knowledge, apart from the knowledge obtained in the audit, of the engagement team member reading the other information that lead the auditor to believe that the other information appears to be materially misstated; or

- An internal inconsistency in the other information that leads the auditor to believe that the other information appears to be materially misstated.

Responding When a Material Inconsistency Appears to Exist or Other Information Appears to Be Materially Misstated
(Ref: Para. 16)

A39   The auditor's discussion with management about a material inconsistency (or other information that appears to be materially misstated) may include requesting management to provide support for the basis of management's statements in the other information. Based on management's further information or explanations,

---

[11a] *ISA (UK) 250 (Revised June 2016), Consideration of Laws and Regulations in an Audit of Financial Statements.*

[11b] *ISA (UK) 260 (Revised June 2016), Communication with Those Charged with Governance, paragraph 16R-2(k).*

[12] *IESBA Code, paragraph 110.2.*

In the UK, the relevant ethical guidance on such matters is provided by the ethical pronouncements issued by the auditor's relevant professional body.

the auditor may be satisfied that the other information is not materially misstated. For example, management explanations may indicate reasonable and sufficient grounds for valid differences of judgment.

Conversely, the discussion with management may provide further information that supports the auditor's conclusion that a material misstatement of the other information exists.   **A40**

It may be more difficult for the auditor to challenge management on matters of judgment than on those of a more factual nature. However, there may be circumstances where the auditor concludes that the other information contains a statement that is not consistent with the financial statements or the auditor's knowledge obtained in the audit. These circumstances may raise doubt about the other information, the financial statements, or the auditor's knowledge obtained in the audit.   **A41**

As there is a wide range of possible material misstatements of the other information, the nature and extent of other procedures the auditor may perform to conclude whether a material misstatement of the other information exists are matters of the auditor's professional judgment in the circumstances.   **A42**

When a matter is unrelated to the financial statements or the auditor's knowledge obtained in the audit, the auditor may not be able to fully assess management's responses to the auditor's inquiries. Nevertheless, based on management's further information or explanations, or following changes made by management to the other information, the auditor may be satisfied that a material inconsistency no longer appears to exist or that the other information no longer appears to be materially misstated. When the auditor is unable to conclude that a material inconsistency no longer appears to exist or that the other information no longer appears to be materially misstated, the auditor may request management to consult with a qualified third party (for example, a management's expert or legal counsel). In certain cases, after considering the responses from management's consultation, the auditor may not be able to conclude whether or not a material misstatement of the other information exists. Actions the auditor may then take include one or more of the following: **A43**

- Obtaining advice from the auditor's legal counsel;
- Considering the implications for the auditor's report for example, whether to describe the circumstances when there is a limitation imposed by management; or
- Withdrawing from the audit, where withdrawal is possible under applicable law or regulation.

Responding When the Auditor Concludes That a Material Misstatement of the Other Information Exists

Responding When the Auditor Concludes That a Material Misstatement Exists in Other Information Obtained prior to the Date of the Auditor's Report
(Ref: Para. 18)

The actions the auditor takes if the other information is not corrected after communicating with those charged with governance are a matter of the auditor's professional judgment. The auditor may take into account whether the rationale given by management and those charged with governance for not making the correction raises doubt about the integrity or honesty of management or those   **A44** charged with governance, such as when the auditor suspects an intention to mislead. The auditor may also consider it appropriate to seek legal advice. In some cases, the auditor may be required by law, regulation or other professional standards to communicate the matter to a regulator or relevant professional body.

A44-1   If the auditor concludes that a material misstatement of the other information exists, and the auditor is unable to resolve the matter through discussion with those charged with governance, the auditor considers requesting those charged with governance to consult with a qualified third party, such as the entity's legal counsel and considers the advice received.

Further Actions Available to the Auditor When a Material Inconsistency or Material Misstatement in Other Information is not Corrected

A44-2   In the UK, the auditor of a limited company may use the auditor's right to be heard at any general meeting of the members on any part of the business of the meeting which concerns the auditor as auditor.[12a]

Reporting Implications
(Ref: Para. 18(a))

A45   In rare circumstances, a disclaimer of opinion on the financial statements may be appropriate when the refusal to correct the material misstatement of the other information casts such doubt on the integrity of management and those charged with governance as to call into question the reliability of audit evidence in general.

Withdrawal from the Engagement
(Ref: Para. 18(b))

A46   Withdrawal from the engagement, where withdrawal is possible under applicable law or regulation, may be appropriate when the circumstances surrounding the refusal to correct the material misstatement of the other information cast such doubt on the integrity of management and those charged with governance as to call into question the reliability of representations obtained from them during the audit.

A46-1   In the case of auditors of limited companies in the UK, the requirements for the auditor to make a statement on ceasing to hold office as auditor apply.[12b] In addition, in the UK the auditor may need to notify the relevant audit authority.[12c]

Considerations specific to public sector entities (Ref: Para. 18(b))

A47   In the public sector, withdrawal from the engagement may not be possible. In such cases, the auditor may issue a report to the legislature providing details of the matter or may take other appropriate actions.

[12a] *In the UK, Section 502 of the Companies Act 2006.*
[12b] *In the UK, Section 519 of the Companies Act 2006.*
[12c] *In the UK, Section 522 of the Companies Act 2006.*

Responding When the Auditor Concludes That a Material Misstatement Exists in Other Information Obtained after the Date of the Auditor's Report
(Ref: Para. 19)

If the auditor concludes that a material misstatement exists in other information   **A48** obtained after the date of the auditor's report, and such a material misstatement has been corrected, the auditor's procedures necessary in the circumstances include determining that the correction has been made (in accordance with paragraph 17(a)) and may include reviewing the steps taken by management to communicate with those in receipt of the other information, if previously issued, to inform them of the revision.

If those charged with governance do not agree to revise the other information,   **A49** taking appropriate action to seek to have the uncorrected misstatement appropriately brought to the attention of users for whom the auditor's report is prepared requires the exercise of professional judgment, and may be affected by relevant law or regulation in the jurisdiction. Accordingly, the auditor may consider it appropriate to seek legal advice about the auditor's legal rights and obligations.

When a material misstatement of the other information remains uncorrected,   **A50** appropriate actions that the auditor may take to seek to have the uncorrected material misstatement appropriately brought to the attention of users for whom the auditor's report is prepared, when permitted by law or regulation, include, for example:

● Providing a new or amended auditor's report to management including a modified section in accordance with paragraph 22, and requesting management to provide this new or amended auditor's report to users for whom the auditor's report is prepared. In doing so, the auditor may need to consider the effect, if any, on the date of the new or amended auditor's report, in view of the requirements of the ISAs (UK) or applicable law or regulation. The auditor may also review the steps taken by management to provide the new or amended auditor's report to such users;

● Bringing the material misstatement of the other information to the attention of the users for whom the auditor's report is prepared (for example, by addressing the matter in a general meeting of shareholders);

● Communicating with a regulator or relevant professional body about the uncorrected material misstatement; or

● Considering the implications for engagement continuance (see also paragraph A46).

Responding When a Material Misstatement in the Financial Statements Exists or the Auditor's Understanding of the Entity and Its Environment Needs to Be Updated
(Ref: Para. 20)

In reading the other information, the auditor may become aware of new   **A51** information that has implications for:

● The auditor's understanding of the entity and its environment and, accordingly, may indicate the need to revise the auditor's risk assessment.[13]

---

[13] *ISA (UK) 315 (Revised June 2016), paragraphs 11, 31, and A1.*

- The auditor's responsibility to evaluate the effect of identified misstatements on the audit and of uncorrected misstatements, if any, on the financial statements.[14]

- The auditor's responsibilities relating to subsequent events.[15]

Reporting
(Ref: Para. 21–24)

a52   For an audit of financial statements of an entity other than a listed entity, the auditor may consider that the identification in the auditor's report of other information that the auditor expects to obtain after the date of the auditor's report would be appropriate in order to provide additional transparency about the other information that is subject to the auditor's responsibilities under this ISA (UK). The auditor may consider it appropriate to do so, for example, when management is able to represent to the auditor that such other information will be issued after the date of the auditor's report.

Illustrative Statements
(Ref: Para. 21–22)

A53   Illustrative examples of the "Other Information" section of the auditor's report are included in Appendix 2.[15a]

Other Reporting Responsibilities for Entities Incorporated under the Companies Acts
(Ref: Para. 22D-2)

A53-1   In the UK, under Section 497A of the Companies Act 2006 the auditor is required to consider whether the information given in the separate Corporate Governance Statement in compliance with rules 7.2.5 and 7.2.6 in the Disclosure Rules and Transparency Rules sourcebook made by the Financial Conduct Authority (information about internal control and risk management systems in relation to financial reporting processes and about share capital structures) is consistent with those accounts, and has been prepared in accordance with applicable legal requirements. The auditor is also required to consider whether rules 7.2.2, 7.2.3 and 7.2.7 in the Disclosure Rules and Transparency Rules sourcebook made by the Financial Conduct Authority (information about the company's corporate governance code and practices and about its administrative, management and supervisory bodies and their committees) have been complied with.

Other Reporting Responsibilities for Entities that Apply the UK Corporate Governance Code
(Ref: Para. 22-3)

A53-2   For entities that apply the UK Corporate Governance Code, the directors are required to give a statement in the annual report that they consider the annual

---

[14] *ISA (UK) 450 (Revised June 2016), Evaluation of Misstatements Identified during the Audit.*

[15] *ISA (UK) 560, paragraphs 10 and 14.*

[15a] *The examples in Appendix 2 have not been tailored for the UK. Illustrative auditor's reports tailored for use with audits conducted in accordance with ISAs (UK) are given in the current version of the FRC's Compendium of Illustrative Auditor's Reports.*

report and accounts taken as a whole is fair, balanced and understandable and provides the information necessary for shareholders to assess the entity's performance, business model and strategy. Such entities are also required to include a separate section of the annual report that describes the work of the audit committee in discharging its responsibilities. This should include, inter alia, the significant issues that the audit committee considered in relation to the financial statements, including appropriate matters considered that were communicated to it by the auditor, and how these issues were addressed.

Where applicable, the auditor includes a statements in accordance with paragraph 22(e)(ii) describing why the auditor believes that any such statement, section, or explanation or other information is materially inconsistent with the auditor's knowledge obtained in the audit or otherwise contains a material misstatement of the other information. If a section of the annual report describing the work of the audit committee does not appropriately disclose any matters communicated by the auditor to the audit committee that in the auditor's judgment should have been disclosed, or if the annual report does not contain such a section, the auditor's report shall also include any such information.   **A53-3**

Reporting Implications When the Auditor's Opinion on the Financial Statements Is Qualified or Adverse
(Ref: Para. 23)

A qualified or adverse auditor's opinion on the financial statements may not have   **A54** an impact on the statement required by paragraph 22(e) if the matter in respect of which the auditor's opinion has been modified is not included or otherwise addressed in the other information and the matter does not affect any part of the other information. For example, a qualified opinion on the financial statements because of non-disclosure of directors' remuneration as required by the applicable financial reporting framework may have no implications for the reporting required under this ISA (UK). In other circumstances, there may be implications for such reporting as described in paragraphs A55–A58.

Qualified Opinion Due to a Material Misstatement in the Financial Statements

In circumstances when the auditor's opinion is qualified, consideration may be   **A55** given as to whether the other information is also materially misstated for the same matter as, or a related matter to, the matter giving rise to the qualified opinion on the financial statements.

Qualified Opinion Due to Limitation of Scope

When there is a limitation of scope with respect to a material item in the financial   **A56** statements, the auditor will not have obtained sufficient appropriate audit evidence about that matter. In these circumstances, the auditor may be unable to conclude whether or not the amounts or other items in the other information related to this matter result in a material misstatement of the other information. Accordingly, the auditor may need to modify the statement required by paragraph 22(e) to refer to the auditor's inability to consider management's description of the matter in the other information in respect of which the auditor's opinion on the financial statements has been qualified as explained in the Basis for Qualified Opinion paragraph. The auditor is nevertheless required to report any other uncorrected material misstatements of the other information that have been identified.

Adverse Opinion

A57 An adverse opinion on the financial statements relating to a specific matter(s) described in the Basis for Adverse Opinion paragraph does not justify the omission of reporting of material misstatements of the other information that the auditor has identified in the auditor's report in accordance with paragraph 22(e)(ii). When an adverse opinion has been expressed on the financial statements, the auditor may need to appropriately modify the statement required by paragraph 22(e) for example, to indicate that amounts or items in the other information is materially misstated for the same matter as, or a related matter to, the matter giving rise to the adverse opinion on the financial statements.

Disclaimer of Opinion

A58 When the auditor disclaims an opinion on the financial statements, providing further details about the audit, including a section to address other information may overshadow the disclaimer of opinion on the financial statements as a whole. Accordingly, in those circumstances, as required by ISA (UK) 705 (Revised June 2016), the auditor's report does not include a section addressing the reporting requirements under this ISA (UK).

Reporting Prescribed by Law or Regulation
(Ref: Para. 24)

A59 ISA (UK) 200 (Revised June 2016)[16] explains that the auditor may be required to comply with legal or regulatory requirements in addition to the ISAs (UK). Where this is the case, the auditor may be obliged to use a specific layout or wording in the auditor's report that differs from that described in this ISA (UK). Consistency in the auditor's report, when the audit has been conducted in accordance with ISAs (UK), promotes credibility in the global marketplace by making more readily identifiable those audits that have been conducted in accordance with globally recognized standards. When the differences between the legal or regulatory requirements to report with respect to the other information and this ISA (UK) relate only to the layout and wording in the auditor's report and, at a minimum, each of the elements identified in paragraph 24 is included in the auditor's report, the auditor's report may refer to International Standards on Auditing. Accordingly, in such circumstances the auditor is considered to have complied with the requirements of this ISA (UK), even when the layout and wording used in the auditor's report are specified by legal or regulatory reporting requirements.

---

[16] *ISA (UK) 200 (Revised June 2016), paragraph A55.*

Appendix 1

(Ref: Para. 14, A8)

Examples of Amounts or Other Items that May Be Included in the Other Information

The following are examples of amounts and other items that may be included in other information. This list is not intended to be exhaustive.

Amounts

- Items in a summary of key financial results, such as net income, earnings per share, dividends, sales and other operating revenues, and purchases and operating expenses.

- Selected operating data, such as income from continuing operations by major operating area, or sales by geographical segment or product line.

- Special items, such as asset dispositions, litigation provisions, asset impairments, tax adjustments, environmental remediation provisions, and restructuring and reorganization expenses.

- Liquidity and capital resource information, such as cash, cash equivalents and marketable securities; dividends; and debt, capital lease and minority interest obligations.

- Capital expenditures by segment or division.

- Amounts involved in, and related financial effects of, off-balance sheet arrangements.

- Amounts involved in guarantees, contractual obligations, legal or environmental claims, and other contingencies.

- Financial measures or ratios, such as gross margin, return on average capital employed, return on average shareholders' equity, current ratio, interest coverage ratio and debt ratio. Some of these may be directly reconcilable to the financial statements.

Other Items

- Explanations of critical accounting estimates and related assumptions.

- Identification of related parties and descriptions of transactions with them.

- Articulation of the entity's policies or approach to manage commodity, foreign exchange or interest rate risks, such as through the use of forward contracts, interest rate swaps, or other financial instruments.

- Descriptions of the nature of off-balance sheet arrangements.

- Descriptions of guarantees, indemnifications, contractual obligations, litigation or environmental liability cases, and other contingencies, including management's qualitative assessments of the entity's related exposures.

- Descriptions of changes in legal or regulatory requirements, such as new tax or environmental regulations, that have materially impacted the entity's operations or fiscal position, or will have a material impact on the entity's future financial prospects.

- Management's qualitative assessments of the impacts of new financial reporting standards that have come into effect during the period, or will come into effect in the following period, on the entity's financial results, financial position and cash flows.

- General descriptions of the business environment and outlook.

- Overview of strategy.

- Descriptions of trends in market prices of key commodities or raw materials.

- Contrasts of supply, demand and regulatory circumstances between geographic regions.

- Explanations of specific factors influencing the entity's profitability in specific segments.

Appendix 2

(Ref: Para. 21-22, A53)

Illustrations of Auditor's Reports Relating to Other Information

The examples in the Appendix have not been tailored for the UK. Illustrative auditor's reports tailored for use with audits conducted in accordance with ISAs (UK) are given in the current version of the FRC's Compendium of Illustrative Auditor's Reports.

Illustrations 2, 3 and 4 would not be relevant for audits of financial statements in the UK as the auditor is required to obtain all of the other information prior to the date of the auditor's report.

- Illustration 1: An auditor's report of any entity, whether listed or other than listed, containing an unmodified opinion when the auditor has obtained all of the other information prior to the date of the auditor's report and has not identified a material misstatement of the other information.

- Illustration 2: An auditor's report of a listed entity containing an unmodified opinion when the auditor has obtained part of the other information prior to the date of the auditor's report, has not identified a material misstatement of the other information, and expects to obtain other information after the date of the auditor's report.

- Illustration 3: An auditor's report of an entity other than a listed entity containing an unmodified opinion when the auditor has obtained part of the other information prior to the date of the auditor's report, has not identified a material misstatement of the other information, and expects to obtain other information after the date of the auditor's report.

- Illustration 4: An auditor's report of a listed entity containing an unmodified opinion when the auditor has obtained no other information prior to the date of the auditor's report but expects to obtain other information after the date of the auditor's report.

- Illustration 5: An auditor's report of any entity, whether listed or other than listed, containing an unmodified opinion when the auditor has obtained all of the other information prior to the date of the auditor's report and has concluded that a material misstatement of the other information exists.

- Illustration 6: An auditor's report of any entity, whether listed or other than listed, containing a qualified opinion when the auditor has obtained all of the other information prior to the date of the auditor's report and there is a limitation of scope with respect to a material item in the consolidated financial statements which also affects the other information.

- Illustration 7: An auditor's report of any entity, whether listed or other than listed, containing an adverse opinion when the auditor has obtained all of the other information prior to the date of the auditor's report and the adverse opinion on the consolidated financial statements also affects the other information.

Illustration 1 – An auditor's report of any entity, whether listed or other than listed, containing an unmodified opinion when the auditor has obtained all of the other information prior to the date of the auditor's report and has not identified a material misstatement of the other information.

For purposes of this illustrative auditor's report, the following circumstances are assumed:

- Audit of a complete set of financial statements of any entity, whether listed or other than listed, using a fair presentation framework. The audit is not a group audit (i.e., ISA 600[1-a] does not apply).
- The financial statements are prepared by management of the entity in accordance with IFRSs (a general purpose framework).
- The terms of the audit engagement reflect the description of management's responsibility for the financial statements in ISA 210.
- The auditor has concluded an unmodified (i.e., "clean") opinion is appropriate based on the audit evidence obtained.
- The relevant ethical requirements that apply to the audit are those of the jurisdiction.
- Based on the audit evidence obtained, the auditor has concluded that a material uncertainty does not exist related to events or conditions that may cast significant doubt on the entity's ability to continue as a going concern in accordance with ISA 570 (Revised).[2-a]
- Key audit matters have been communicated in accordance with ISA 701.[3-a]
- The auditor has obtained all of the other information prior to the date of the auditor's report and has not identified a material misstatement of the other information.
- Those responsible for oversight of the financial statements differ from those responsible for the preparation of the financial statements.
- In addition to the audit of the financial statements, the auditor has other reporting responsibilities required under local law.

INDEPENDENT AUDITOR'S REPORT

To the Shareholders of ABC Company [or Other Appropriate Addressee]

Report on the Audit of the Financial Statements[4-a]

Opinion

We have audited the financial statements of ABC Company (the Company), which comprise the statement of financial position as at December 31, 20X1, and the statement of comprehensive income, statement of changes in equity and statement of cash flows for the year then ended, and notes to the financial statements, including a summary of significant accounting policies.

[1-a] *ISA 600, Special Considerations–Audits of Group Financial Statements (Including the Work of Component Auditors).*

[2-a] *ISA 570 (Revised), Going Concern.*

[3-a] *ISA 701, Communicating Key Audit Matters in the Independent Auditor's Report. The Key Audit Matters section is required for listed entities only.*

[4-a] *The sub-title "Report on the Audit of the Financial Statements" is unnecessary in circumstances when the second sub-title "Report on Other Legal and Regulatory Requirements" is not applicable.*

In our opinion, the accompanying financial statements present fairly, in all material respects, (or *give a true and fair view of*) the financial position of the Company as at December 31, 20X1, and (*of*) its financial performance and its cash flows for the year then ended in accordance with International Financial Reporting Standards (IFRSs).

Basis for Opinion

We conducted our audit in accordance with International Standards on Auditing (ISAs). Our responsibilities under those standards are further described in the *Auditor's Responsibilities for the Audit of the Financial Statements* section of our report. We are independent of the Company in accordance with the ethical requirements that are relevant to our audit of the financial statements in [*jurisdiction*], and we have fulfilled our other ethical responsibilities in accordance with these requirements. We believe that the audit evidence we have obtained is sufficient and appropriate to provide a basis for our opinion.

[Key Audit Matters[5-a]

Key audit matters are those matters that, in our professional judgment, were of most significance in our audit of the financial statements of the current period. These matters were addressed in the context of our audit of the financial statements as a whole, and in forming our opinion thereon, and we do not provide a separate opinion on these matters.

[*Description of each key audit matter in accordance with ISA 701.*]]

Other Information [or another title if appropriate, such as "Information Other than the Financial Statements and Auditor's Report Thereon"]

Management[6-a] is responsible for the other information. The other information comprises the [information included in the X report,[7-a] but does not include the financial statements and our auditor's report thereon.]

Our opinion on the financial statements does not cover the other information and we do not express any form of assurance conclusion thereon.

In connection with our audit of the financial statements, our responsibility is to read the other information and, in doing so, consider whether the other information is materially inconsistent with the financial statements or our knowledge obtained in the audit or otherwise appears to be materially misstated. If, based on the work we have performed, we conclude that there is a material misstatement of this other information, we are required to report that fact. We have nothing to report in this regard.

[5-a] *The Key Audit Matters section is required for listed entities only.*

[6-a] *Or other terms that are appropriate in the context of the legal framework of the particular jurisdiction.*

[7-a] *A more specific description of the other information, such as "the management report and chairman's statement," may be used to identify the other information.*

Responsibilities of Management and Those Charged with Governance for the Financial Statements[8-a]

[*Reporting in accordance with ISA 700 (Revised)*[9-a] *– see Illustration 1 in ISA 700 (Revised).*]

Auditor's Responsibilities for the Audit of the Financial Statements

[*Reporting in accordance with ISA 700 (Revised) – see Illustration 1 in ISA 700 (Revised).*]

Report on Other Legal and Regulatory Requirements

[*Reporting in accordance with ISA 700 (Revised) – see Illustration 1 in ISA 700 (Revised).*]

[The engagement partner on the audit resulting in this independent auditor's report is [*name*].[10-a]]

[*Signature in the name of the audit firm, the personal name of the auditor, or both, as appropriate for the particular jurisdiction*]

[*Auditor Address*]

[*Date*]

Illustration 2 – An auditor's report of a listed entity containing an unmodified opinion when the auditor has obtained part of the other information prior to the date of the auditor's report, has not identified a material misstatement of the other information, and expects to obtain other information after the date of the auditor's report.

For purposes of this illustrative auditor's report, the following circumstances are assumed:

- Audit of a complete set of financial statements of a listed entity using a fair presentation framework. The audit is not a group audit (i.e., ISA 600 does not apply).
- The financial statements are prepared by management of the entity in accordance with IFRSs (a general purpose framework).
- The terms of the audit engagement reflect the description of management's responsibility for the financial statements in ISA 210.
- The auditor has concluded an unmodified (i.e., "clean") opinion is appropriate based on the audit evidence obtained.
- The relevant ethical requirements that apply to the audit are those of the jurisdiction.
- Based on the audit evidence obtained, the auditor has concluded that a material uncertainty does not exist related to events or conditions that may cast significant doubt on the entity's ability to continue as a going concern in accordance with ISA 570 (Revised).

[8-a] *Throughout these illustrative auditor's reports, the terms management and those charged with governance may need to be replaced by another term that is appropriate in the context of the legal framework in the particular jurisdiction.*

[9-a] *ISA 700 (Revised), Forming an Opinion and Reporting on Financial Statements.*

[10-a] *The name of the engagement partner is included in the auditor's report for audits of complete sets of general purpose financial statements of listed entities unless, in rare circumstances, such disclosure is reasonably expected to lead to a significant personal security threat (see ISA 700 (Revised), paragraph 46).*

- Key audit matters have been communicated in accordance with ISA 701.
- The auditor has obtained part of the other information prior to the date of the auditor's report, has not identified a material misstatement of the other information, and expects to obtain other information after the date of the auditor's report.
- Those responsible for oversight of the financial statements differ from those responsible for the preparation of the financial statements.
- In addition to the audit of the financial statements, the auditor has other reporting responsibilities required under local law.

INDEPENDENT AUDITOR'S REPORT

To the Shareholders of ABC Company [or Other Appropriate Addressee]

Report on the Audit of the Financial Statements[11-a]

Opinion

We have audited the financial statements of ABC Company (the Company), which comprise the statement of financial position as at December 31, 20X1, and the statement of comprehensive income, statement of changes in equity and statement of cash flows for the year then ended, and notes to the financial statements, including a summary of significant accounting policies.

In our opinion, the accompanying financial statements present fairly, in all material respects, (or *give a true and fair view of*) the financial position of the Company as at December 31, 20X1, and (*of*) its financial performance and its cash flows for the year then ended in accordance with International Financial Reporting Standards (IFRSs).

Basis for Opinion

We conducted our audit in accordance with International Standards on Auditing (ISAs). Our responsibilities under those standards are further described in the *Auditor's Responsibilities for the Audit of the Financial Statements* section of our report. We are independent of the Company in accordance with the ethical requirements that are relevant to our audit of the financial statements in [*jurisdiction*], and we have fulfilled our other ethical responsibilities in accordance with these requirements. We believe that the audit evidence we have obtained is sufficient and appropriate to provide a basis for our opinion.

Key Audit Matters

Key audit matters are those matters that, in our professional judgment, were of most significance in our audit of the financial statements of the current period. These matters were addressed in the context of our audit of the financial statements as a whole, and in forming our opinion thereon, and we do not provide a separate opinion on these matters.

[11-a] *The sub-title "Report on the Audit of the Financial Statements" is unnecessary in circumstances when the second sub-title "Report on Other Legal and Regulatory Requirements" is not applicable.*

[Description of each key audit matter in accordance with ISA 701.]

Other Information [or another title if appropriate, such as "Information Other than the Financial Statements and Auditor's Report Thereon"]

Management[12-a] is responsible for the other information. The other information comprises the X report[13-a] (but does not include the financial statements and our auditor's report thereon), which we obtained prior to the date of this auditor's report, and the Y report, which is expected to be made available to us after that date.

Our opinion on the financial statements does not cover the other information and we do not and will not express any form of assurance conclusion thereon.

In connection with our audit of the financial statements, our responsibility is to read the other information identified above and, in doing so, consider whether the other information is materially inconsistent with the financial statements or our knowledge obtained in the audit, or otherwise appears to be materially misstated.

If, based on the work we have performed on the other information that we obtained prior to the date of this auditor's report, we conclude that there is a material misstatement of this other information, we are required to report that fact. We have nothing to report in this regard.

[When we read the Y report, if we conclude that there is a material misstatement therein, we are required to communicate the matter to those charged with governance and *[describe actions applicable in the jurisdiction]*.][14-a]

Responsibilities of Management and Those Charged with Governance for the Financial Statements[15-a]

[Reporting in accordance with ISA 700 (Revised) – see Illustration 1 in ISA 700 (Revised).]

Auditor's Responsibilities for the Audit of the Financial Statements

[Reporting in accordance with ISA 700 (Revised) – see Illustration 1 in ISA 700 (Revised).]

Report on Other Legal and Regulatory Requirements

[Reporting in accordance with ISA 700 (Revised) – see Illustration 1 in ISA 700 (Revised).]

The engagement partner on the audit resulting in this independent auditor's report is *[name]*.[16-a]

[Signature in the name of the audit firm, the personal name of the auditor, or both, as appropriate for the particular jurisdiction]

[Auditor Address]

[Date]

[12-a] *Or other terms that are appropriate in the context of the legal framework of the particular jurisdiction.*

[13-a] *A more specific description of the other information, such as "the management report and chair's statement," may be used to identify the other information.*

[14-a] *This additional paragraph may be useful when the auditor has identified an uncorrected material misstatement of the other information obtained after the date of the auditor's report and has a legal obligation to take specific action in response.*

[15-a] *Or other terms that are appropriate in the context of the legal framework of the particular jurisdiction.*

[16-a] *The name of the engagement partner is included in the auditor's report for audits of complete sets of general purpose financial statements of listed entities unless, in rare circumstances, such disclosure is reasonably expected to lead to a significant personal security threat (see ISA 700 (Revised), paragraph 46).*

Illustration 3 – An auditor's report of an entity other than a listed entity containing an unmodified opinion when the auditor has obtained part of the other information prior to the date of the auditor's report, has not identified a material misstatement of the other information, and expects to obtain other information after the date of the auditor's report.

For purposes of this illustrative auditor's report, the following circumstances are assumed:

- Audit of a complete set of financial statements of an entity other than a listed entity using a fair presentation framework. The audit is not a group audit (i.e., ISA 600 does not apply).
- The financial statements are prepared by management of the entity in accordance with IFRSs (a general purpose framework).
- The terms of the audit engagement reflect the description of management's responsibility for the financial statements in ISA 210.
- The auditor has concluded an unmodified (i.e., "clean") opinion is appropriate based on the audit evidence obtained.
- The relevant ethical requirements that apply to the audit are those of the jurisdiction.
- Based on the audit evidence obtained, the auditor has concluded that a material uncertainty does not exist related to events or conditions that may cast significant doubt on the entity's ability to continue as a going concern in accordance with ISA 570 (Revised).
- The auditor is not required, and has otherwise not decided, to communicate key audit matters in accordance with ISA 701.
- The auditor has obtained part of the other information prior to the date of the auditor's report, has not identified a material misstatement of the other information, and expects to obtain other information after the date of the auditor's report.
- Those responsible for oversight of the financial statements differ from those responsible for the preparation of the financial statements.
- The auditor has no other reporting responsibilities required under law or regulation.

INDEPENDENT AUDITOR'S REPORT

To the Shareholders of ABC Company [or Other Appropriate Addressee]

Opinion

We have audited the financial statements of ABC Company (the Company), which comprise the statement of financial position as at December 31, 20X1, and the statement of comprehensive income, statement of changes in equity and statement of cash flows for the year then ended, and notes to the financial statements, including a summary of significant accounting policies.

In our opinion, the accompanying financial statements present fairly, in all material respects, (or *give a true and fair view of*) the financial position of the Company as at December 31, 20X1, and (*of*) its financial performance and its cash flows for the year then ended in accordance with International Financial Reporting Standards (IFRSs).

Basis for Opinion

We conducted our audit in accordance with International Standards on Auditing (ISAs). Our responsibilities under those standards are further described in the *Auditor's Responsibilities for the Audit of the Financial Statements* section of our report. We are independent of the Company in accordance with the ethical requirements that are relevant to our audit of the financial statements in [*jurisdiction*], and we have fulfilled our other ethical responsibilities in accordance with these requirements. We believe that the audit evidence we have obtained is sufficient and appropriate to provide a basis for our opinion.

Other Information [or another title if appropriate, such as "Information Other than the Financial Statements and Auditor's Report Thereon"]

Management[17] is responsible for the other information. The other information obtained at the date of this auditor's report is [information included in the X report,[18] but does not include the financial statements and our auditor's report thereon].

Our opinion on the financial statements does not cover the other information and we do not express any form of assurance conclusion thereon.

In connection with our audit of the financial statements, our responsibility is to read the other information and, in doing so, consider whether the other information is materially inconsistent with the financial statements or our knowledge obtained in the audit, or otherwise appears to be materially misstated.

If, based on the work we have performed on the other information obtained prior to the date of this auditor's report, we conclude that there is a material misstatement of this other information, we are required to report that fact. We have nothing to report in this regard.

Responsibilities of Management and Those Charged with Governance for the Financial Statements[19]

[*Reporting in accordance with ISA 700 (Revised) – see Illustration 1 in ISA 700 (Revised).*]

Auditor's Responsibilities for the Audit of the Financial Statements

[*Reporting in accordance with ISA 700 (Revised) – see Illustration 1 in ISA 700 (Revised).*]

[*Signature in the name of the audit firm, the personal name of the auditor, or both, as appropriate for the particular jurisdiction*]

[*Auditor Address*]

[*Date*]

---

[17] *Or other terms that are appropriate in the context of the legal framework of the particular jurisdiction.*

[18] *A more specific description of the other information, such as "the management report and chair's statement," may be used to identify the other information.*

[19] *Or other terms that are appropriate in the context of the legal framework of the particular jurisdiction.*

Illustration 4 – An auditor's report of a listed entity containing an unmodified opinion when the auditor has obtained no other information prior to the date of the auditor's report but expects to obtain other information after the date of the auditor' s report.

For purposes of this illustrative auditor's report, the following circumstances are assumed:

- Audit of a complete set of financial statements of a listed entity using a fair presentation framework. The audit is not a group audit (i.e., ISA 600 does not apply).
- The financial statements are prepared by management of the entity in accordance with IFRSs (a general purpose framework).
- The terms of the audit engagement reflect the description of management's responsibility for the financial statements in ISA 210.
- The auditor has concluded an unmodified (i.e., "clean") opinion is appropriate based on the audit evidence obtained.
- The relevant ethical requirements that apply to the audit are those of the jurisdiction.
- Based on the audit evidence obtained, the auditor has concluded that a material uncertainty does not exist related to events or conditions that may cast significant doubt on the entity's ability to continue as a going concern in accordance with ISA 570 (Revised).
- Key audit matters have been communicated in accordance with ISA 701.
- The auditor has obtained no other information prior to the date of the auditor's report but expects to obtain other information after the date of the auditor's report.
- Those responsible for oversight of the financial statements differ from those responsible for the preparation of the financial statements.
- In addition to the audit of the financial statements, the auditor has other reporting responsibilities required under local law.

INDEPENDENT AUDITOR'S REPORT

To the Shareholders of ABC Company [or Other Appropriate Addressee]

Report on the Audit of the Financial Statements[20]

Opinion

We have audited the financial statements of ABC Company (the Company), which comprise the statement of financial position as at December 31, 20X1, and the statement of comprehensive income, statement of changes in equity and statement of cash flows for the year then ended, and notes to the financial statements, including a summary of significant accounting policies.

In our opinion, the accompanying financial statements present fairly, in all material respects, (or *give a true and fair view of*) the financial position of the Company as at December 31, 20X1, and (*of*) its financial performance and its cash flows for the year then ended in accordance with International Financial Reporting Standards (IFRSs).

---

[20] *The sub-title "Report on the Audit of the Financial Statements" is unnecessary in circumstances when the second sub-title "Report on Other Legal and Regulatory Requirements" is not applicable.*

Basis for Opinion

We conducted our audit in accordance with International Standards on Auditing (ISAs). Our responsibilities under those standards are further described in the *Auditor's Responsibilities for the Audit of the Financial Statements* section of our report. We are independent of the Company in accordance with the ethical requirements that are relevant to our audit of the financial statements in [*jurisdiction*], and we have fulfilled our other ethical responsibilities in accordance with these requirements. We believe that the audit evidence we have obtained is sufficient and appropriate to provide a basis for our opinion.

Key Audit Matters

Key audit matters are those matters that, in our professional judgment, were of most significance in our audit of the financial statements of the current period. These matters were addressed in the context of our audit of the financial statements as a whole, and in forming our opinion thereon, and we do not provide a separate opinion on these matters.

[*Description of each key audit matter in accordance with ISA 701.*]

Other Information [or another title if appropriate, such as "Information Other than the Financial Statements and Auditor's Report Thereon"]

Management[21] is responsible for the other information. The other information comprises the [information included in the X report,[22] but does not include the financial statements and our auditor's report thereon]. The X report is expected to be made available to us after the date of this auditor's report.

Our opinion on the financial statements does not cover the other information and we will not express any form of assurance conclusion thereon.

In connection with our audit of the financial statements, our responsibility is to read the other information identified above when it becomes available and, in doing so, consider whether the other information is materially inconsistent with the financial statements or our knowledge obtained in the audit, or otherwise appears to be materially misstated.

[When we read the X report, if we conclude that there is a material misstatement therein, we are required to communicate the matter to those charged with governance and [*describe actions applicable in the jurisdiction*].][23]

Responsibilities of Management and Those Charged with Governance for the Financial Statements[24]

[*Reporting in accordance with ISA 700 (Revised) – see Illustration 1 in ISA 700 (Revised).*]

---

[21] *Or other terms that are appropriate in the context of the legal framework of the particular jurisdiction.*

[22] *A more specific description of the other information, such as "the management report and chair's statement," may be used to identify the other information.*

[23] *This additional paragraph may be useful when the auditor has identified an uncorrected material misstatement of the other information obtained after the date of the auditor's report and has a legal obligation to take specific action in response.*

[24] *Or other terms that are appropriate in the context of the legal framework of the particular jurisdiction.*

Auditor's Responsibilities for the Audit of the Financial Statements

[Reporting in accordance with ISA 700 (Revised) – see Illustration 1 in ISA 700 (Revised).]

Report on Other Legal and Regulatory Requirements

[Reporting in accordance with ISA 700 (Revised) – see Illustration 1 in ISA 700 (Revised).]

The engagement partner on the audit resulting in this independent auditor's report is *[name]*.

[Signature in the name of the audit firm, the personal name of the auditor, or both, as appropriate for the particular jurisdiction]

[Auditor Address]

[Date]

Illustration 5 – An auditor's report of any entity, whether listed or other than listed, containing an unmodified opinion when the auditor has obtained all of the other information prior to the date of the auditor's report and has concluded that a material misstatement of the other information exists.

For purposes of this illustrative auditor's report, the following circumstances are assumed:

- Audit of a complete set of financial statements of any entity, whether listed or other than listed, using a fair presentation framework. The audit is not a group audit (i.e., ISA 600 does not apply).
- The financial statements are prepared by management of the entity in accordance with IFRSs (a general purpose framework).
- The terms of the audit engagement reflect the description of management's responsibility for the financial statements in ISA 210.
- The auditor has concluded an unmodified (i.e., "clean") opinion is appropriate based on the audit evidence obtained.
- The relevant ethical requirements that apply to the audit are those of the jurisdiction.
- Based on the audit evidence obtained, the auditor has concluded that a material uncertainty does not exist related to events or conditions that may cast significant doubt on the entity's ability to continue as a going concern in accordance with ISA 570 (Revised).
- Key audit matters have been communicated in accordance with ISA 701.
- The auditor has obtained all of the other information prior to the date of the auditor's report and has concluded that a material misstatement of the other information exists
- Those responsible for oversight of the financial statements differ from those responsible for the preparation of the financial statements.
- The auditor has no other reporting responsibilities required under law or regulation.

INDEPENDENT AUDITOR'S REPORT

To the Shareholders of ABC Company [or Other Appropriate Addressee]

Opinion

We have audited the financial statements of ABC Company (the Company), which comprise the statement of financial position as at December 31, 20X1, and the statement of comprehensive income, statement of changes in equity and statement of cash flows for the year then ended, and notes to the financial statements, including a summary of significant accounting policies.

In our opinion, the accompanying financial statements present fairly, in all material respects, (or *give a true and fair view of*) the financial position of the Company as at December 31, 20X1, and (*of*) its financial performance and its cash flows for the year then ended in accordance with International Financial Reporting Standards (IFRSs).

Basis for Opinion

We conducted our audit in accordance with International Standards on Auditing (ISAs). Our responsibilities under those standards are further described in the *Auditor's Responsibilities for the Audit of the Financial Statements* section of our report. We are independent of the Company in accordance with the ethical requirements that are relevant to our audit of the financial statements in [*jurisdiction*], and we have fulfilled our other ethical responsibilities in accordance with these requirements. We believe that the audit evidence we have obtained is sufficient and appropriate to provide a basis for our opinion.

Other Information [or another title if appropriate, such as "Information Other than the Financial Statements and Auditor's Report Thereon"]

Management[25] is responsible for the other information. The other information comprises the [information included in the X report,[26] but does not include the financial statements and our auditor's report thereon.]

Our opinion on the financial statements does not cover the other information and we do not express any form of assurance conclusion thereon.

In connection with our audit of the financial statements, our responsibility is to read the other information and, in doing so, consider whether the other information is materially inconsistent with the financial statements or our knowledge obtained in the audit or otherwise appears to be materially misstated.

If, based on the work we have performed, we conclude that there is a material misstatement of this other information, we are required to report that fact. As described below, we have concluded that such a material misstatement of the other information exists.

[*Description of material misstatement of the other information*]

---

[25] *Or other terms that are appropriate in the context of the legal framework of the particular jurisdiction.*

[26] *A more specific description of the other information, such as "the management report and chairman's statement," may be used to identify the other information.*

[Key Audit Matters[27]

Key audit matters are those matters that, in our professional judgment, were of most significance in our audit of the financial statements of the current period. These matters were addressed in the context of our audit of the financial statements as a whole, and in forming our opinion thereon, and we do not provide a separate opinion on these matters.

[Description of each key audit matter in accordance with ISA 701.]]

Responsibilities of Management and Those Charged with Governance for the Financial Statements[28]

[Reporting in accordance with ISA 700 (Revised) – see Illustration 1 in ISA 700 (Revised).]

Auditor's Responsibilities for the Audit of the Financial Statements

[Reporting in accordance with ISA 700 (Revised) – see Illustration 1 in ISA 700 (Revised).]

[The engagement partner on the audit resulting in this independent auditor's report is [name].[29]]

[Signature in the name of the audit firm, the personal name of the auditor, or both, as appropriate for the particular jurisdiction]

[Auditor Address]

[Date]

Illustration 6 – An auditor's report of any entity, whether listed or other than listed, containing an qualified opinion when the auditor has obtained all of the other information prior to the date of the auditor's report and there is a limitation of scope with respect to a material item in the consolidated financial statements which also affects the other information.

For purposes of this illustrative auditor's report, the following circumstances are assumed:

- Audit of a complete set of consolidated financial statements of any entity, whether listed or other than listed, using a fair presentation framework. The audit is a group audit (i.e., ISA 600 applies).
- The consolidated financial statements are prepared by management of the entity in accordance with IFRSs (a general purpose framework).
- The terms of the audit engagement reflect the description of management's responsibility for the consolidated financial statements in ISA 210.
- The auditor was unable to obtain sufficient appropriate audit evidence regarding an investment in a foreign associate. The possible effects of the inability to obtain sufficient appropriate audit evidence are deemed

---

[27] *The Key Audit Matters section is required for listed entities only.*

[28] *Or other terms that are appropriate in the context of the legal framework of the particular jurisdiction.*

[29] *The name of the engagement partner is included in the auditor's report for audits of complete sets of general purpose financial statements of listed entities unless, in rare circumstances, such disclosure is reasonably expected to lead to a significant personal security threat (see ISA 700 (Revised), paragraph 46).*

to be material but not pervasive to the consolidated financial statements (i.e., a qualified opinion is appropriate).
- The relevant ethical requirements that apply to the audit are those of the jurisdiction.
- Based on the audit evidence obtained, the auditor has concluded that a material uncertainty does not exist related to events or conditions that may cast significant doubt on the entity's ability to continue as a going concern in accordance with ISA 570 (Revised).
- Key audit matters have been communicated in accordance with ISA 701.
- The auditor has obtained all of the other information prior to the date of the auditor's report and the matter giving rise to the qualified opinion on the consolidated financial statements also affects the other information
- Those responsible for oversight of the consolidated financial statements differ from those responsible for the preparation of the consolidated financial statements.
- The auditor has no other reporting responsibilities required under law or regulation.

INDEPENDENT AUDITOR'S REPORT

To the Shareholders of ABC Company [or Other Appropriate Addressee]

Qualified Opinion

We have audited the consolidated financial statements of ABC Company and its subsidiaries (the Group), which comprise the consolidated statement of financial position as at December 31, 20X1, and the consolidated statement of comprehensive income, consolidated statement of changes in equity and consolidated statement of cash flows for the year then ended, and notes to the consolidated financial statements, including a summary of significant accounting policies.

In our opinion, except for the possible effects of the matter described in the *Basis for Qualified Opinion* section of our report, the accompanying consolidated financial statements present fairly, in all material respects, (or *give a true and fair view of*) the financial position of the Group as at December 31, 20X1, and (*of*) its consolidated financial performance and its consolidated cash flows for the year then ended in accordance with International Financial Reporting Standards (IFRSs).

Basis for Qualified Opinion

The Group's investment in XYZ Company, a foreign associate acquired during the year and accounted for by the equity method, is carried at xxx on the consolidated statement of financial position as at December 31, 20X1, and ABC's share of XYZ's net income of xxx is included in ABC's income for the year then ended. We were unable to obtain sufficient appropriate audit evidence about the carrying amount of ABC's investment in XYZ as at December 31, 20X1 and ABC's share of XYZ's net income for the year because we were denied access to the financial information, management, and the auditors of XYZ. Consequently, we were unable to determine whether any adjustments to these amounts were necessary.

We conducted our audit in accordance with International Standards on Auditing (ISAs). Our responsibilities under those standards are further described in the *Auditor's Responsibilities for the Audit of the Consolidated Financial Statements* section of our report. We are independent of the Group in accordance with the ethical requirements that are relevant to our audit of the consolidated financial statements in [*jurisdiction*], and we have fulfilled our other ethical responsibilities in accordance with these requirements. We believe that the audit evidence we have obtained is sufficient and appropriate to provide a basis for our qualified opinion.

Other Information [or another title if appropriate, such as "Information Other than the Financial Statements and Auditor's Report Thereon"]

Management[30] is responsible for the other information. The other information comprises the [information included in the X report,[31] but does not include the consolidated financial statements and our auditor's report thereon.]

Our opinion on the consolidated financial statements does not cover the other information and we do not express any form of assurance conclusion thereon.

In connection with our audit of the consolidated financial statements, our responsibility is to read the other information and, in doing so, consider whether the other information is materially inconsistent with the consolidated financial statements or our knowledge obtained in the audit or otherwise appears to be materially misstated.

If, based on the work we have performed, we conclude that there is a material misstatement of this other information, we are required to report that fact. As described in the *Basis for Qualified Opinion* section above, we were unable to obtain sufficient appropriate evidence about the carrying amount of ABC's investment in XYZ as at December 31, 20X1 and ABC's share of XYZ's net income for the year. Accordingly, we are unable to conclude whether or not the other information is materially misstated with respect to this matter.

[Key Audit Matters[32]

Key audit matters are those matters that, in our professional judgment, were of most significance in our audit of the consolidated financial statements of the current period. These matters were addressed in the context of our audit of the consolidated financial statements as a whole, and in forming our opinion thereon, and we do not provide a separate opinion on these matters. In addition to the matter described in the *Basis for Qualified Opinion* section we have determined the matters described below to be the key audit matters to be communicated in our report.

[*Description of each key audit matter in accordance with ISA 701.*]]

Responsibilities of Management and Those Charged with Governance for the Financial Statements[33]

[*Reporting in accordance with ISA 700 (Revised) – see Illustration 2 in ISA 700 (Revised).*]

---

[30] *Or other terms that are appropriate in the context of the legal framework of the particular jurisdiction.*

[31] *A more specific description of the other information, such as "the management report and chairman's statement," may be used to identify the other information.*

[32] *The Key Audit Matters section is required for listed entities only.*

[33] *Or other terms that are appropriate in the context of the legal framework of the particular jurisdiction.*

Auditor's Responsibilities for the Audit of the Financial Statements

[*Reporting in accordance with ISA 700 (Revised) – see Illustration 2 in ISA 700 (Revised).*]

[The engagement partner on the audit resulting in this independent auditor's report is [*name*].[34]]

[*Signature in the name of the audit firm, the personal name of the auditor, or both, as appropriate for the particular jurisdiction*]

[*Auditor Address*]

[*Date*]

Illustration 7 – An auditor's report of any entity, whether listed or other than listed, containing an adverse opinion when the auditor has obtained all of the other information prior to the date of the auditor's report and the adverse opinion on the consolidated financial statements also affects the other information.

For purposes of this illustrative auditor's report, the following circumstances are assumed:

- Audit of a complete set of consolidated financial statements of any entity, whether listed or other than listed, using a fair presentation framework. The audit is a group audit (i.e., ISA 600 applies).
- The consolidated financial statements are prepared by management of the entity in accordance with IFRSs (a general purpose framework).
- The terms of the audit engagement reflect the description of management's responsibility for the consolidated financial statements in ISA 210.
- The consolidated financial statements are materially misstated due to the non-consolidation of a subsidiary. The material misstatement is deemed to be pervasive to the consolidated financial statements. The effects of the misstatement on the consolidated financial statements have not been determined because it was not practicable to do so (i.e., an adverse opinion is appropriate).
- The relevant ethical requirements that apply to the audit are those of the jurisdiction.
- Based on the audit evidence obtained, the auditor has concluded that a material uncertainty does not exist related to events or conditions that may cast significant doubt on the entity's ability to continue as a going concern in accordance with ISA 570 (Revised).
- Key audit matters have been communicated in accordance with ISA 701.
- The auditor has obtained all of the other information prior to the date of the auditor's report and the matter giving rise to the adverse opinion on the consolidated financial statements also affects the other information

---

[34] *The name of the engagement partner is included in the auditor's report for audits of complete sets of general purpose financial statements of listed entities unless, in rare circumstances, such disclosure is reasonably expected to lead to a significant personal security threat (see ISA 700 (Revised), paragraph 46).*

- Those responsible for oversight of the consolidated financial statements differ from those responsible for the preparation of the consolidated financial statements.
- The auditor has no other reporting responsibilities required under law or regulation.

INDEPENDENT AUDITOR'S REPORT

To the Shareholders of ABC Company [or Other Appropriate Addressee]

Adverse Opinion

We have audited the consolidated financial statements of ABC Company and its subsidiaries (the Group), which comprise the consolidated statement of financial position as at December 31, 20X1, and the consolidated statement of comprehensive income, consolidated statement of changes in equity and consolidated statement of cash flows for the year then ended, and notes to the consolidated financial statements, including a summary of significant accounting policies.

In our opinion, because of the significance of the matter discussed in the *Basis for Adverse Opinion* section of our report, the accompanying consolidated financial statements do not present fairly (or *do not give a true and fair view of*) the consolidated financial position of the Group as at December 31, 20X1, and (*of*) its consolidated financial performance and its consolidated cash flows for the year then ended in accordance with International Financial Reporting Standards (IFRSs).

Basis for Adverse Opinion

As explained in Note X, the Group has not consolidated subsidiary XYZ Company that the Group acquired during 20X1 because it has not yet been able to determine the fair values of certain of the subsidiary's material assets and liabilities at the acquisition date. This investment is therefore accounted for on a cost basis. Under IFRSs, the Group should have consolidated this subsidiary and accounted for the acquisition based on provisional amounts. Had XYZ Company been consolidated, many elements in the accompanying consolidated financial statements would have been materially affected. The effects on the consolidated financial statements of the failure to consolidate have not been determined.

We conducted our audit in accordance with International Standards on Auditing (ISAs). Our responsibilities under those standards are further described in the *Auditor's Responsibilities for the Audit of the Consolidated Financial Statements* section of our report. We are independent of the Group in accordance with the ethical requirements that are relevant to our audit of the consolidated financial statements in [*jurisdiction*], and we have fulfilled our other ethical responsibilities in accordance with these requirements. We believe that the audit evidence we have obtained is sufficient and appropriate to provide a basis for our adverse opinion.

Other Information [or another title if appropriate, such as "Information Other than the Financial Statements and Auditor's Report Thereon"]

Management[35] is responsible for the other information. The other information comprises the [information included in the X report,[36] but does not include the consolidated financial statements and our auditor's report thereon.]

Our opinion on the consolidated financial statements does not cover the other information and we do not express any form of assurance conclusion thereon.

In connection with our audit of the consolidated financial statements, our responsibility is to read the other information and, in doing so, consider whether the other information is materially inconsistent with the consolidated financial statements or our knowledge obtained in the audit or otherwise appears to be materially misstated. If, based on the work we have performed, we conclude that there is a material misstatement of this other information, we are required to report that fact. As described in the *Basis for Adverse Opinion* section above, the Group should have consolidated XYZ Company and accounted for the acquisition based on provisional amounts. We have concluded that the other information is materially misstated for the same reason with respect to the amounts or other items in the X report affected by the failure to consolidate XYZ Company.

[Key Audit Matters[37]

Key audit matters are those matters that, in our professional judgment, were of most significance in our audit of the consolidated financial statements of the current period. These matters were addressed in the context of our audit of the consolidated financial statements as a whole, and in forming our opinion thereon, and we do not provide a separate opinion on these matters. In addition to the matter described in the *Basis for Adverse Opinion* section we have determined the matters described below to be the key audit matters to be communicated in our report.

[*Description of each key audit matter in accordance with ISA 701.*]]

Responsibilities of Management and Those Charged with Governance for the Financial Statements[38]

[*Reporting in accordance with ISA 700 (Revised) – see Illustration 2 in ISA 700 (Revised).*]

---

[35] *Or other terms that are appropriate in the context of the legal framework of the particular jurisdiction.*

[36] *A more specific description of the other information, such as "the management report and chairman's statement," may be used to identify the other information.*

[37] *The Key Audit Matters section is required for listed entities only.*

[38] *Or other terms that are appropriate in the context of the legal framework of the particular jurisdiction.*

Auditor's Responsibilities for the Audit of the Financial Statements

[*Reporting in accordance with ISA 700 (Revised) – see Illustration 2 in ISA 700 (Revised).*]

[The engagement partner on the audit resulting in this independent auditor's report is [*name*].³⁹]

[*Signature in the name of the audit firm, the personal name of the auditor, or both, as appropriate for the particular jurisdiction*]

[*Auditor Address*]

[*Date*]

---

³⁹ *The name of the engagement partner is included in the auditor's report for audits of complete sets of general purpose financial statements of listed entities unless, in rare circumstances, such disclosure is reasonably expected to lead to a significant personal security threat (see ISA 700 (Revised), paragraph 46).*

Auditor's Responsibilities for the Audit of the financial Statements

[Reporting in accordance with ISA 700 (Revised) – see Illustration 2 in ISA 700 ... as illustrated.]

[The engagement partner on the audit resulting in this independent auditor's report is ... [...] name]

[Signature in the name of the audit firm, the personal name of the auditor, or both, as appropriate for the particular jurisdiction.]

[Auditor Address.]

[Date.]

ISA (UK) 800 (Revised)
Special Considerations – Audits of Financial Statements prepared in accordance with Special Purpose Frameworks (October 2016)

(Effective for audits of financial statements for periods commencing on or after 1 January 2017)

Contents

Paragraphs

Introduction
Scope of this ISA (UK)   1 - 3
Effective Date   4

Objective   5

Definitions   6 - 7

Requirements
Considerations When Accepting the Engagement   8
Considerations When Planning and Performing the Audit   9 - 10
Forming an Opinion and Reporting Considerations   11 - 14

Application and Other Explanatory Material
Definition of Special Purpose Framework   A1 - A4
Considerations When Accepting the Engagement   A5 - A8
Considerations When Planning and Performing the Audit   A9 - A12
Forming an Opinion and Reporting Considerations   A13 - A21

Appendix: Illustrations of Independent Auditor's Reports on Special Purpose Financial Statements

Editorial note – This standard applies to engagements concerning financial periods commencing on or after 1 January 2017, with early adoption permitted. The FRC carried out a public consultation exercise and undertook outreach work to obtain stakeholder feedback which has been supportive of the decision to adopt the new standards.

International Standard on Auditing (UK) (ISA (UK)) 800 (Revised), *Special Considerations— Audits of Financial Statements Prepared in Accordance with Special Purpose Frameworks*, should be read in conjunction with ISA (UK) 200 (Revised June 2016), *Overall Objectives of the Independent Auditor and the Conduct of an Audit in Accordance with International Standards on Auditing (UK)*.

Introduction

Scope of this ISA (UK)

1 The International Standards on Auditing (UK) (ISAs (UK)) in the 100–700 series apply to an audit of financial statements. This ISA (UK) deals with special considerations in the application of those ISAs (UK) to an audit of financial statements prepared in accordance with a special purpose framework.

2 This ISA (UK) is written in the context of a complete set of financial statements prepared in accordance with a special purpose framework. ISA (UK) 805 (Revised)[1] deals with special considerations relevant to an audit of a single financial statement or of a specific element, account or item of a financial statement.

3 This ISA (UK) does not override the requirements of the other ISAs (UK); nor does it purport to deal with all special considerations that may be relevant in the circumstances of the engagement.

Effective Date

4 This ISA (UK) is effective for audits of financial statements for periods commencing on or after 1 January 2017. Early adoption is permitted[2].

Objective

5 The objective of the auditor, when applying ISAs (UK) in an audit of financial statements prepared in accordance with a special purpose framework, is to address appropriately the special considerations that are relevant to:

(a) The acceptance of the engagement;

(b) The planning and performance of that engagement; and

(c) Forming an opinion and reporting on the financial statements.

Definitions

6 For purposes of the ISAs (UK), the following terms have the meanings attributed below:

(a) Special purpose financial statements – Financial statements prepared in accordance with a special purpose framework. (Ref: Para. A4)

(b) Special purpose framework – A financial reporting framework designed to meet the financial information needs of specific users. The financial reporting framework may be a fair presentation framework or a compliance framework.[3] (Ref: Para. A1–A4)

---

[1] *ISA (UK) 805 (Revised), Special Considerations—Audits of Single Financial Statements and Specific Elements, Accounts or Items of a Financial Statement*

[2] *Where ISA (UK) 800 (Revised) is adopted early for the audit of Solvency II Regulatory Returns for periods commencing prior to 1 January 2017 it may be used in conjunction with ISAs (UK and Ireland) where the audit of the statutory financial statements for the same period was conducted in accordance with ISAs (UK and Ireland).*

[3] *ISA (UK) 200 (Revised June 2016), Overall Objectives of the Independent Auditor and the Conduct of an Audit in Accordance with International Standards on Auditing (UK), paragraph 13(a)*

Reference to "financial statements" in this ISA (UK) means "a complete set of   **7**
special purpose financial statements". The requirements of the applicable financial
reporting framework determine the presentation, structure, and content of the
financial statements, and what constitutes a complete set of financial statements.
Reference to "special purpose financial statements" includes the related
disclosures.

Requirements

Considerations When Accepting the Engagement

Acceptability of the Financial Reporting Framework

ISA (UK) 210 (Revised June 2016) requires the auditor to determine the   **8**
acceptability of the financial reporting framework applied in the preparation of
the financial statements.[4] In an audit of special purpose financial statements, the
auditor shall obtain an understanding of: (Ref: Para. A5–A8)

(a)   The purpose for which the financial statements are prepared;

(b)   The intended users; and

(c)   The steps taken by management to determine that the applicable financial
       reporting framework is acceptable in the circumstances.

Considerations When Planning and Performing the Audit

ISA (UK) 200 (Revised June 2016) requires the auditor to comply with all ISAs   **9**
(UK) relevant to the audit.[5] In planning and performing an audit of special purpose
financial statements, the auditor shall determine whether application of the ISAs
(UK) requires special consideration in the circumstances of the engagement.
(Ref: Para. A9–A12)

ISA (UK) 315 (Revised June 2016) requires the auditor to obtain an understanding   **10**
of the entity's selection and application of accounting policies.[6] In the case of
financial statements prepared in accordance with the provisions of a contract, the
auditor shall obtain an understanding of any significant interpretations of the
contract that management made in the preparation of those financial statements.
An interpretation is significant when adoption of another reasonable interpretation
would have produced a material difference in the information presented in the
financial statements.

Forming an Opinion and Reporting Considerations

When forming an opinion and reporting on special purpose financial statements,   **11**
the auditor shall apply the requirements in ISA (UK) 700 (Revised June 2016).[7]
(Ref: Para. A13–A19)

---

[4] *ISA (UK) 210 (Revised June 2016), Agreeing the Terms of Audit Engagements, paragraph 6(a)*

[5] *ISA (UK) 200 (Revised June 2016), paragraph 18*

[6] *ISA (UK) 315 (Revised June 2016), Identifying and Assessing the Risks of Material Misstatement through Understanding the Entity and Its Environment, paragraph 11(c)*

[7] *ISA (UK) 700 (Revised June 2016), Forming an Opinion and Reporting on Financial Statements*

Description of the Applicable Financial Reporting Framework

12   ISA (UK) 700 (Revised June 2016) requires the auditor to evaluate whether the financial statements adequately refer to or describe the applicable financial reporting framework.[8] In the case of financial statements prepared in accordance with the provisions of a contract, the auditor shall evaluate whether the financial statements adequately describe any significant interpretations of the contract on which the financial statements are based.

13   ISA (UK) 700 (Revised June 2016) deals with the form and content of the auditor's report, including the specific ordering for certain elements. In the case of an auditor's report on special purpose financial statements:

(a)   The auditor's report shall also describe the purpose for which the financial statements are prepared and, if necessary, the intended users, or refer to a note in the special purpose financial statements that contains that information; and

(b)   If management has a choice of financial reporting frameworks in the preparation of such financial statements, the explanation of management's[9] responsibility for the financial statements shall also make reference to its responsibility for determining that the applicable financial reporting framework is acceptable in the circumstances.

Alerting Readers that the Financial Statements Are Prepared in Accordance with a Special Purpose Framework

14   The auditor's report on special purpose financial statements shall include an Emphasis of Matter paragraph alerting users of the auditor's report that the financial statements are prepared in accordance with a special purpose framework and that, as a result, the financial statements may not be suitable for another purpose. (Ref: Para. A20–A21)

In the UK, the auditor specifically describes the financial reporting framework as a special purpose framework in the auditor's report. The auditor also specifically states that the audit has been carried out in accordance with ISAs (UK), including ISA (UK) 800 and/or ISA (UK) 805.

***

Application and Other Explanatory Material

Definition of Special Purpose Framework
(Ref: Para. 6)

A1   Examples of special purpose frameworks are:

●   A tax basis of accounting for a set of financial statements that accompany an entity's tax return;

●   The cash receipts and disbursements basis of accounting for cash flow information that an entity may be requested to prepare for creditors;

---

[8] *ISA (UK) 700 (Revised June 2016), paragraph 15*

[9] *Or other term that is appropriate in the context of the legal framework in the particular jurisdiction*

- The financial reporting provisions established by a regulator to meet the requirements of that regulator; or

- The financial reporting provisions of a contract, such as a bond indenture, a loan agreement, or a project grant.

There may be circumstances where a special purpose framework is based on a **A2** financial reporting framework established by an authorized or recognized standards setting organization or by law or regulation, but does not comply with all the requirements of that framework. An example is a contract that requires financial statements to be prepared in accordance with most, but not all, of the Financial Reporting Standards of Jurisdiction X. When this is acceptable in the circumstances of the engagement, it is inappropriate for the description of the applicable financial reporting framework in the special purpose financial statements to imply full compliance with the financial reporting framework established by the authorized or recognized standards setting organization or by law or regulation. In the above example of the contract, the description of the applicable financial reporting framework may refer to the financial reporting provisions of the contract, rather than make any reference to the Financial Reporting Standards of Jurisdiction X.

In the circumstances described in paragraph A2, the special purpose framework **A3** may not be a fair presentation framework even if the financial reporting framework on which it is based is a fair presentation framework. This is because the special purpose framework may not comply with all the requirements of the financial reporting framework established by the authorized or recognized standards setting organization or by law or regulation that are necessary to achieve fair presentation of the financial statements.

Financial statements prepared in accordance with a special purpose framework **A4** may be the only financial statements an entity prepares. In such circumstances, those financial statements may be used by users other than those for whom the financial reporting framework is designed. Despite the broad distribution of the financial statements in those circumstances, the financial statements are still considered to be special purpose financial statements for purposes of the ISAs (UK). The requirements in paragraphs 13–14 are designed to avoid misunderstandings about the purpose for which the financial statements are prepared. Disclosures comprise explanatory or descriptive information, set out as required, expressly permitted or otherwise allowed by the applicable financial reporting framework, on the face of financial statements, or in the notes, or incorporated therein by cross-reference.[10]

Considerations When Accepting the Engagement

Acceptability of the Financial Reporting Framework
(Ref: Para. 8)

In the case of special purpose financial statements, the financial information needs **A5** of the intended users are a key factor in determining the acceptability of the financial reporting framework applied in the preparation of the financial statements.

The applicable financial reporting framework may encompass the financial **A6** reporting standards established by an organization that is authorized or

---

[10] *ISA (UK) 200 (Revised June 2016), paragraph 13(f)*

recognized to promulgate standards for special purpose financial statements. In that case, those standards will be presumed acceptable for that purpose if the organization follows an established and transparent process involving deliberation and consideration of the views of relevant stakeholders. In some jurisdictions, law or regulation may prescribe the financial reporting framework to be used by management in the preparation of special purpose financial statements for a certain type of entity. For example, a regulator may establish financial reporting provisions to meet the requirements of that regulator. In the absence of indications to the contrary, such a financial reporting framework is presumed acceptable for special purpose financial statements prepared by such entity.

A7   Where the financial reporting standards referred to in paragraph A6 are supplemented by legislative or regulatory requirements, ISA (UK) 210 (Revised June 2016) requires the auditor to determine whether any conflicts between the financial reporting standards and the additional requirements exist, and prescribes actions to be taken by the auditor if such conflicts exist.[11]

A8   The applicable financial reporting framework may encompass the financial reporting provisions of a contract, or sources other than those described in paragraphs A6 and A7. In that case, the acceptability of the financial reporting framework in the circumstances of the engagement is determined by considering whether the framework exhibits attributes normally exhibited by acceptable financial reporting frameworks as described in Appendix 2 of ISA (UK) 210 (Revised June 2016). In the case of a special purpose framework, the relative importance to a particular engagement of each of the attributes normally exhibited by acceptable financial reporting frameworks is a matter of professional judgment. For example, for purposes of establishing the value of net assets of an entity at the date of its sale, the vendor and the purchaser may have agreed that very prudent estimates of allowances for uncollectible accounts receivable are appropriate for their needs, even though such financial information is not neutral when compared with financial information prepared in accordance with a general purpose framework.

Considerations When Planning and Performing the Audit
(Ref: Para. 9)

A9   ISA (UK) 200 (Revised June 2016) requires the auditor to comply with (a) relevant ethical requirements, including those pertaining to independence, relating to financial statement audit engagements, and (b) all ISAs (UK) relevant to the audit. It also requires the auditor to comply with each requirement of an ISA (UK) unless, in the circumstances of the audit, the entire ISA (UK) is not relevant or the requirement is not relevant because it is conditional and the condition does not exist. In exceptional circumstances, the auditor may judge it necessary to depart from a relevant requirement in an ISA (UK) by performing alternative audit procedures to achieve the aim of that requirement.[12]

A10   Application of some of the requirements of the ISAs (UK) in an audit of special purpose financial statements may require special consideration by the auditor. For example, in ISA (UK) 320 (Revised June 2016), judgments about matters that are material to users of the financial statements are based on a consideration of the common financial information needs of users as a group.[13] In the case of an audit

---

[11]   *ISA (UK) 210 (Revised June 2016), paragraph 18*

[12]   *ISA (UK) 200 (Revised June 2016), paragraphs 14, 18, and 22–23*

[13]   *ISA (UK) 320 (Revised June 2016), Materiality in Planning and Performing an Audit, paragraph 2*

of special purpose financial statements, however, those judgments are based on a consideration of the financial information needs of the intended users.

In the case of special purpose financial statements, such as those prepared in accordance with the requirements of a contract, management may agree with the intended users on a threshold below which misstatements identified during the audit will not be corrected or otherwise adjusted. The existence of such a threshold does not relieve the auditor from the requirement to determine materiality in accordance with ISA (UK) 320 (Revised June 2016) for purposes of planning and performing the audit of the special purpose financial statements.   **A11**

ISA (UK) 260 (Revised June 2016) requires the auditor to determine the appropriate person(s) within the entity's governance structure with whom to communicate.[14] ISA (UK) 260 (Revised June 2016) notes that, in some cases, all of those charged governance are involved in managing the entity, and the application of the communication requirements is modified to recognize this position.[15] When a complete set of general purpose financial statements is also prepared by the entity, those person(s) responsible for the oversight of the preparation of the special purpose financial statements may not be the same as those charged with governance responsible for the oversight of the preparation of those general purpose financial statements.   **A12**

Forming an Opinion and Reporting Considerations
(Ref: Para. 11)

The Appendix to this ISA (UK)[14a] contains illustrations of independent auditor's[2] reports on special purpose financial statements. Other illustrations of auditor's reports may be relevant to reporting on special purpose financial statements (see for example, the Appendices to ISA (UK) 700 (Revised June 2016), ISA (UK) 705 (Revised June 2016),[16] ISA (UK) 570 (Revised June 2016),[17] ISA (UK) 720 (Revised June 2016), and ISA (UK) 706 (Revised June 2016)).[18]   **A13**

Application of ISA (UK) 700 (Revised June 2016) When Reporting on Special Purpose Financial Statements

Paragraph 11 of this ISA (UK) explains that the auditor is required to apply ISA (UK) 700 (Revised June 2016) when forming an opinion and reporting on special purpose financial statements. In doing so, the auditor is also required to apply the reporting requirements in other ISAs (UK) and may find the special considerations addressed in paragraphs A15–A19 below helpful.   **A14**

Going Concern

Special purpose financial statements may or may not be prepared in accordance with a financial reporting framework for which the going concern basis of accounting is relevant (e.g., the going concern basis of accounting is not   **A15**

---

[14] *ISA (UK) 260 (Revised June 2016), Communication with Those Charged with Governance*

[15] *ISA (UK) 260 (Revised June 2016), paragraph A8*

[14a] *The examples in the Appendix have not been tailored for the UK.*

[16] *ISA (UK) 705 (Revised June 2016), Modifications to the Opinion in the Independent Auditor's Report*

[17] *ISA (UK) 570 (Revised June 2016), Going Concern*

[18] *ISA (UK) 706 (Revised June 2016), Emphasis of Matter Paragraphs and Other Matter Paragraphs in the Independent Auditor's Report*

relevant for some financial statements prepared on a tax basis in particular jurisdictions).[19] Depending on the applicable financial reporting framework used in the preparation of the special purpose financial statements, the description in the auditor's report of management's responsibilities[20] relating to going concern may need to be adapted as necessary. The description in the auditor's report of the auditor's responsibilities[21] may also need to be adapted as necessary depending on how ISA (UK) 570 (Revised June 2016) applies in the circumstances of the engagement.

Key Audit Matters

A16   ISA (UK) 700 (Revised June 2016) requires the auditor to communicate key audit matters in accordance with ISA (UK) 701[22] for audits of complete sets of general purpose financial statements of listed entities. For audits of special purpose financial statements, ISA (UK) 701 only applies when communication of key audit matters in the auditor's report on the special purpose financial statements is required by law or regulation or the auditor otherwise decides to communicate key audit matters. When key audit matters are communicated in the auditor's report on special purpose financial statements, ISA (UK) 701 applies in its entirety.[23]

Other Information

A17   ISA (UK) 720 (Revised June 2016)[24] deals with the auditor's responsibilities relating to other information. In the context of this ISA (UK), reports containing or accompanying the special purpose financial statements—the purpose of which is to provide owners (or similar stakeholders) with information on matters presented in the special purpose financial statements—are considered to be annual reports for the purpose of ISA (UK) 720 (Revised June 2016). In the case of financial statements prepared using a special purpose framework, the term "similar stakeholders" includes the specific users whose financial information needs are met by the design of the special purpose framework used to prepare the special purpose financial statements. When the auditor determines that the entity plans to issue such a report, the requirements in ISA (UK) 720 (Revised June 2016) apply to the audit of the special purpose financial statements.

Name of the Engagement Partner

A18   The requirement in ISA (UK) 700 (Revised June 2016) for the auditor to include the name of the engagement partner in the auditor's report also applies to audits of special purpose financial statements of listed entities.[25] The auditor may be required by law or regulation to include the name of the engagement partner in the auditor's report or may otherwise decide to do so when reporting on special purpose financial statements of entities other than listed entities.

---

[19]   *ISA (UK) 570 (Revised June 2016), Going Concern, paragraph 2*

[20]   *See ISA (UK) 700 (Revised June 2016), paragraphs 34(b) and A48.*

[21]   *See ISA (UK) 700 (Revised June 2016), paragraph 39(b)(iv).*

[22]   *ISA (UK) 701, Communicating Key Audit Matters in the Independent Auditor's Report*

[23]   *ISA (UK) 700 (Revised June 2016), paragraph 31*

[24]   *ISA (UK) 720 (Revised June 2016), The Auditor's Responsibilities Relating to Other Information*

[25]   *See ISA (UK) 700 (Revised June 2016), paragraphs 45 and A56–A58*

Inclusion of a Reference to the Auditor's Report on the Complete Set of General Purpose Financial Statements

The auditor may deem it appropriate to refer, in an Other Matter paragraph in the **A19** auditor's report on the special purpose financial statements, to the auditor's report on the complete set of general purpose financial statements or to matter(s) reported therein (see ISA (UK) 706 (Revised June 2016)).[26] For example, the auditor may consider it appropriate to refer in the auditor's report on the special purpose financial statements to a Material Uncertainty Related to Going Concern section included in the auditor's report on the complete set of general purpose financial statements.

Alerting Readers that the Financial Statements Are Prepared in Accordance with a Special Purpose Framework
(Ref: Para. 14)

The special purpose financial statements may be used for purposes other than **A20** those for which they were intended. For example, a regulator may require certain entities to place the special purpose financial statements on public record. To avoid misunderstandings, the auditor alerts users of the auditor's report by including an Emphasis of Matter paragraph explaining that the financial statements are prepared in accordance with a special purpose framework and, therefore, may not be suitable for another purpose. ISA (UK) 706 (Revised June 2016) requires this paragraph to be included within a separate section of the auditor's report with an appropriate heading that includes the term "Emphasis of Matter".[27]

Restriction on Distribution or Use
(Ref: Para. 14)

In addition to the alert required by paragraph 14, the auditor may consider it **A21** appropriate to indicate that the auditor's report is intended solely for the specific users. Depending on the law or regulation of the particular jurisdiction, this may be achieved by restricting the distribution or use of the auditor's report. In these circumstances, the paragraph referred to in paragraph 14 may be expanded to include these other matters, and the heading modified accordingly (see illustrations in the Appendix to this ISA (UK)[26a]).

---

[26] *See ISA (UK) 706 (Revised June 2016), paragraphs 10–11.*

[27] *See paragraph 9(a) of ISA (UK) 706 (Revised June 2016)*

[26a] *The examples in the Appendix have not been tailored for the UK.*

Appendix

(Ref: Para. A14)

Illustrations of Independent Auditor's Reports on Special Purpose Financial Statements

The examples in the Appendix have not been tailored for the UK.

- Illustration 1: An auditor's report on a complete set of financial statements of an entity other than a listed entity prepared in accordance with the financial reporting provisions of a contract (for purposes of this illustration, a compliance framework).

- Illustration 2: An auditor's report on a complete set of financial statements of an entity other than a listed entity prepared in accordance with the tax basis of accounting in Jurisdiction X (for purposes of this illustration, a compliance framework).

- Illustration 3: An auditor's report on a complete set of financial statements of a listed entity prepared in accordance with the financial reporting provisions established by a regulator (for purposes of this illustration, a fair presentation framework).

Illustration 1: An auditor's report on a complete set of financial statements of an entity other than a listed entity prepared in accordance with the financial reporting provisions of a contract (for purposes of this illustration, a compliance framework).

For purposes of this illustrative auditor's report, the following circumstances are assumed:

- The financial statements have been prepared by management of the entity in accordance with the financial reporting provisions of a contract (that is, a special purpose framework). Management does not have a choice of financial reporting frameworks.
- The applicable financial reporting framework is a compliance framework.
- An auditor's report on the complete set of general purpose financial statements was not issued.
- The terms of the audit engagement reflect the description of management's responsibility for the financial statements in ISA 210.
- The auditor has concluded an unmodified (i.e., "clean") opinion is appropriate based on the audit evidence obtained.
- The relevant ethical requirements that apply to the audit are those of the jurisdiction.
- Based on the audit evidence obtained, the auditor has concluded that a material uncertainty does not exist related to events or conditions that may cast significant doubt on the entity's ability to continue as a going concern in accordance with ISA 570 (Revised).
- Distribution and use of the auditor's report are restricted.
- The auditor is not required, and has otherwise not decided, to communicate key audit matters in accordance with ISA 701.

- The auditor has determined that there is no other information (i.e., the requirements of ISA 720 (Revised) do not apply).
- Those responsible for oversight of the financial reporting process differ from those responsible for the preparation of the financial statements.
- The auditor has no other reporting responsibilities required under local law or regulation.

INDEPENDENT AUDITOR'S REPORT

[Appropriate Addressee]

Opinion

We have audited the financial statements of ABC Company (the Company), which comprise the balance sheet as at December 31, 20X1, and the income statement, statement of changes in equity and cash flow statement for the year then ended, and notes to the financial statements, including a summary of significant accounting policies.

In our opinion, the accompanying financial statements of the Company for the year ended December 31, 20X1 are prepared, in all material respects, in accordance with the financial reporting provisions of Section Z of the contract dated January 1, 20X1 between the Company and DEF Company ("the contract").
[Opinion section positioned first as required in ISA 700 (Revised)]

Basis for Opinion

We conducted our audit in accordance with International Standards on Auditing (ISAs). Our responsibilities under those standards are further described in the *Auditor's Responsibilities for the Audit of the Financial Statements* section of our report. We are independent of the Company in accordance with the ethical requirements that are relevant to our audit of the financial statements in [*jurisdiction*], and we have fulfilled our other ethical responsibilities in accordance with these requirements. We believe that the audit evidence we have obtained is sufficient and appropriate to provide a basis for our opinion.
[The first and last sentences in this section used to be in the Auditor's Responsibility section. Also, the Basis for Opinion section is positioned immediately after the Opinion section as required in ISA 700 (Revised).]

Emphasis of Matter – Basis of Accounting and Restriction on Distribution and Use

We draw attention to Note X to the financial statements, which describes the basis of accounting. The financial statements are prepared to assist the Company in complying with the financial reporting provisions of the contract referred to above. As a result, the financial statements may not be suitable for another purpose. Our report is intended solely for the Company and DEF Company and should not be distributed to or used by parties other than the Company or DEF Company. Our opinion is not modified in respect of this matter.

Responsibilities of Management and Those Charged with Governance for the Financial Statements[28]

Management is responsible for the preparation of the financial statements in accordance with the financial reporting provisions of Section Z of the contract and for such internal control as management determines is necessary to enable the preparation of financial statements that are free from material misstatement, whether due to fraud or error.

In preparing the financial statements, management is responsible for assessing the Company's ability to continue as a going concern, disclosing, as applicable, matters relating to going concern and using the going concern basis of accounting unless management either intends to liquidate the Company or to cease operations, or has no realistic alternative but to do so.

Those charged with governance are responsible for overseeing the Company's financial reporting process.

Auditor's Responsibilities for the Audit of the Financial Statements

Our objectives are to obtain reasonable assurance about whether the financial statements as a whole are free from material misstatement, whether due to fraud or error, and to issue an auditor's report that includes our opinion. Reasonable assurance is a high level of assurance, but is not a guarantee that an audit conducted in accordance with ISAs will always detect a material misstatement when it exists. Misstatements can arise from fraud or error and are considered material if, individually or in the aggregate, they could reasonably be expected to influence the economic decisions of users taken on the basis of these financial statements.

Paragraph 41(b) of ISA 700 (Revised) explains that the shaded material below can be located in an Appendix to the auditor's report. Paragraph 41(c) of ISA 700 (Revised) explains that when law, regulation or national auditing standards expressly permit, reference can be made to a website of an appropriate authority that contains the description of the auditor's responsibilities, rather than including this material in the auditor's report, provided that the description on the website addresses, and is not inconsistent with, the description of the auditor's responsibilities below.

As part of an audit in accordance with ISAs, we exercise professional judgment and maintain professional skepticism throughout the audit. We also:

- Identify and assess the risks of material misstatement of the financial statements, whether due to fraud or error, design and perform audit procedures responsive to those risks, and obtain audit evidence that is sufficient and appropriate to provide a basis for our opinion. The risk of not detecting a material misstatement resulting from fraud is higher than for one resulting from error, as fraud may involve collusion, forgery, intentional omissions, misrepresentations, or the override of internal control.

[28] *Throughout these illustrative auditor's reports, the terms management and those charged with governance may need to be replaced by another term that is appropriate in the context of the legal framework in the particular jurisdiction.*

- Obtain an understanding of internal control relevant to the audit in order to design audit procedures that are appropriate in the circumstances, but not for the purpose of expressing an opinion on the effectiveness of the Company's internal control.[29]

- Evaluate the appropriateness of accounting policies used and the reasonableness of accounting estimates and related disclosures made by management.

- Conclude on the appropriateness of management's use of the going concern basis of accounting and, based on the audit evidence obtained, whether a material uncertainty exists related to events or conditions that may cast significant doubt on the Company's ability to continue as a going concern. If we conclude that a material uncertainty exists, we are required to draw attention in our auditor's report to the related disclosures in the financial statements or, if such disclosures are inadequate, to modify our opinion. Our conclusions are based on the audit evidence obtained up to the date of our auditor's report. However, future events or conditions may cause the Company to cease to continue as a going concern.

We communicate with those charged with governance regarding, among other matters, the planned scope and timing of the audit and significant audit findings, including any significant deficiencies in internal control that we identify during our audit.

Signature in the name of the audit firm, the personal name of the auditor, or both, as appropriate for the particular jurisdiction]

[Auditor address] [Placement of date and address reversed)]

[Date]

Illustration 2: An auditor's report on a complete set of financial statements of an entity other than a listed entity prepared in accordance with the tax basis of accounting in Jurisdiction X (for purposes of this illustration, a compliance framework).

For purposes of this illustrative auditor's report, the following circumstances are assumed:

- Audit of a complete set of financial statements that have been prepared by management of a partnership in accordance with the tax basis of accounting in Jurisdiction X (that is, a special purpose framework) to assist the partners in preparing their individual income tax returns. Management does not have a choice of financial reporting frameworks.

- The applicable financial reporting framework is a compliance framework

- The terms of the audit engagement reflect the description of management's responsibility for the financial statements in ISA 210.

- The auditor has concluded an unmodified (i.e., "clean") opinion is appropriate based on the audit evidence obtained.

---

[29] *This sentence would be modified, as appropriate, in circumstances when the auditor also has responsibility to issue an opinion on the effectiveness of internal control in conjunction with the audit of the financial statements.*

- The relevant ethical requirements that apply to the audit are those of the jurisdiction.
- Based on the audit evidence obtained, the auditor has concluded that a material uncertainty does not exist related to events or conditions that may cast significant doubt on the entity's ability to continue as a going concern in accordance with ISA 570 (Revised).
- Distribution of the auditor's report is restricted.
- The auditor is not required, and has otherwise not decided, to communicate key audit matters in accordance with ISA 701.
- The auditor has determined that there is no other information (i.e., the requirements of ISA 720 (Revised) do not apply).
- Those responsible for oversight of the financial statements differ from those responsible for the preparation of the financial statements.
- The auditor has no other reporting responsibilities required under local law or regulation.

INDEPENDENT AUDITOR'S REPORT

[Appropriate Addressee]

Opinion

We have audited the financial statements of ABC Partnership (the Partnership), which comprise the balance sheet as at December 31, 20X1 and the income statement for the year then ended, and notes to the financial statements, including a summary of significant accounting policies.

In our opinion, the accompanying financial statements of the Partnership for the year ended December 31, 20X1 are prepared, in all material respects, in accordance with [*describe the applicable income tax law*] of Jurisdiction X. [Opinion section positioned first as required in ISA 700 (Revised)]

Basis for Opinion

We conducted our audit in accordance with International Standards on Auditing (ISAs). Our responsibilities under those standards are further described in the *Auditor's Responsibilities for the Audit of the Financial Statements* section of our report. We are independent of the Partnership in accordance with the ethical requirements that are relevant to our audit of the financial statements in [*jurisdiction*], and we have fulfilled our other ethical responsibilities in accordance with these requirements. We believe that the audit evidence we have obtained is sufficient and appropriate to provide a basis for our opinion. [The first and last sentences in this section used to be in the Auditor's Responsibility section. Also, the Basis for Opinion section is positioned immediately after the Opinion section as required in ISA 700 (Revised).]

Emphasis of Matter – Basis of Accounting and Restriction on Distribution

We draw attention to Note X to the financial statements, which describes the basis of accounting. The financial statements are prepared to assist the partners of the Partnership in preparing their individual income tax returns. As a result, the financial statements may not be suitable for another purpose. Our report is intended solely for the Partnership and its partners and should not be distributed to parties other than the Partnership or its partners. Our opinion is not modified in respect of this matter.

Responsibilities of Management and Those Charged with Governance for the Financial Statements[30]

Management is responsible for the preparation of the financial statements in accordance with the tax basis of accounting in Jurisdiction X and for such internal control as management determines is necessary to enable the preparation of financial statements that are free from material misstatement, whether due to fraud or error.

In preparing the financial statements, management is responsible for assessing the Company's ability to continue as a going concern, disclosing, as applicable, matters relating to going concern and using the going concern basis of accounting unless management either intends to liquidate the Company or to cease operations, or has no realistic alternative but to do so.

Those charged with governance are responsible for overseeing the Partnership's financial reporting process.

Auditor's Responsibilities for the Audit of the Financial Statements

Our objectives are to obtain reasonable assurance about whether the financial statements as a whole are free from material misstatement, whether due to fraud or error, and to issue an auditor's report that includes our opinion. Reasonable assurance is a high level of assurance, but is not a guarantee that an audit conducted in accordance with International Standards on Auditing (ISAs) will always detect a material misstatement when it exists. Misstatements can arise from fraud or error and are considered material if, individually or in the aggregate, they could reasonably be expected to influence the economic decisions of users taken on the basis of these financial statements.

Paragraph 41(b) of ISA 700 (Revised) explains that the shaded material below can be located in an Appendix to the auditor's report. Paragraph 41(c) of ISA 700 (Revised) explains that when law, regulation or national auditing standards expressly permit, reference can be made to a website of an appropriate authority that contains the description of the auditor's responsibilities, rather than including this material in the auditor's report, provided that the description on the website addresses, and is not inconsistent with, the description of the auditor's responsibilities below.

As part of an audit in accordance with ISAs, we exercise professional judgment and maintain professional skepticism throughout the audit. We also:

- Identify and assess the risks of material misstatement of the financial statements, whether due to fraud or error, design and perform audit procedures responsive to those risks, and obtain audit evidence that is sufficient and appropriate to provide a basis for our opinion. The risk of not detecting a material misstatement resulting from fraud is higher than for one resulting from error, as fraud may involve collusion, forgery, intentional omissions, misrepresentations, or the override of internal control.

- Obtain an understanding of internal control relevant to the audit in order to design audit procedures that are appropriate in the circumstances, but

---

[30] *Or other terms that are appropriate in the context of the legal framework in the particular jurisdiction*

not for the purpose of expressing an opinion on the effectiveness of the Partnership's internal control.[31]

- Conclude on the appropriateness of management's use of the going concern basis of accounting and, based on the audit evidence obtained, whether a material uncertainty exists related to events or conditions that may cast significant doubt on the Company's ability to continue as a going concern. If we conclude that a material uncertainty exists, we are required to draw attention in our auditor's report to the related disclosures in the financial statements or, if such disclosures are inadequate, to modify our opinion. Our conclusions are based on the audit evidence obtained up to the date of our auditor's report. However, future events or conditions may cause the Company to cease to continue as a going concern.

- Evaluate the appropriateness of accounting policies used and the reasonableness of accounting estimates and related disclosures made by management.

We communicate with those charged with governance regarding, among other matters, the planned scope and timing of the audit and significant audit findings, including any significant deficiencies in internal control that we identify during our audit.

[*Signature in the name of the audit firm, the personal name of the auditor, or both, as appropriate for the particular jurisdiction*]

[*Auditor address*] [Placement of date and address reversed)]

[*Date*]

Illustration 3: An auditor's report on a complete set of financial statements of a listed entity prepared in accordance with the financial reporting provisions established by a regulator (for purposes of this illustration, a fair presentation framework).

For purposes of this illustrative auditor's report, the following circumstances are assumed:

- Audit of a complete set of financial statements of a listed entity that have been prepared by management of the entity in accordance with the financial reporting provisions established by a regulator (that is, a special purpose framework) to meet the requirements of that regulator. Management does not have a choice of financial reporting frameworks.
- The applicable financial reporting framework is a fair presentation framework.
- The terms of the audit engagement reflect the description of management's responsibility for the financial statements in ISA 210.
- The auditor has concluded an unmodified (i.e., "clean") opinion is appropriate based on the audit evidence obtained.
- The relevant ethical requirements that apply to the audit are those of the jurisdiction.

---

[31] *This sentence would be modified, as appropriate, in circumstances when the auditor also has responsibility to issue an opinion on the effectiveness of internal control in conjunction with the audit of the financial statements.*

- Based on the audit evidence obtained, the auditor has concluded that a material uncertainty exists related to events or conditions that may cast significant doubt on the entity's ability to continue as a going concern in accordance with ISA 570 (Revised). The disclosure of the material uncertainty in the financial statements is adequate.
- Distribution or use of the auditor's report is not restricted.
- The auditor is required by the regulator to communicate key audit matters in accordance with ISA 701.
- The auditor has determined that there is no other information (i.e., the requirements of ISA 720 (Revised) do not apply).
- Those responsible for oversight of the financial statements differ from those responsible for the preparation of the financial statements.
- The auditor has no other reporting responsibilities required under local law or regulation.

INDEPENDENT AUDITOR'S REPORT

[To the Shareholders of ABC Company or Appropriate Addressee]

Opinion

We have audited the financial statements of ABC Company (the Company), which comprise the balance sheet as at December 31, 20X1, and the income statement, statement of changes in equity and cash flow statement for the year then ended, and notes to the financial statements, including a summary of significant accounting policies.

In our opinion, the accompanying financial statements present fairly, in all material respects, (or *give a true and fair view of*) the financial position of the Company as at December 31, 20X1, and (*of*) its financial performance and its cash flows for the year then ended in accordance with the financial reporting provisions of Section Y of Regulation Z. [Opinion section positioned first as required in ISA 700 (Revised)]

Basis for Opinion

We conducted our audit in accordance with International Standards on Auditing (ISAs). Our responsibilities under those standards are further described in the *Auditor's Responsibilities for the Audit of the Financial Statements* section of our report. We are independent of the Company in accordance with the ethical requirements that are relevant to our audit of the financial statements in [*jurisdiction*], and we have fulfilled our other ethical responsibilities in accordance with these requirements. We believe that the audit evidence we have obtained is sufficient and appropriate to provide a basis for our opinion. [The first and last sentences in this section used to be in the Auditor's Responsibility section. Also, the Basis for Opinion section is positioned immediately after the Opinion section as required in ISA 700 (Revised).]

Emphasis of Matter – Basis of Accounting

We draw attention to Note X to the financial statements, which describes the basis of accounting. The financial statements are prepared to assist the Company to meet the requirements of Regulator DEF. As a result, the financial statements may not be suitable for another purpose. Our opinion is not modified in respect of this matter.

Material Uncertainty Related to Going Concern

We draw attention to Note 6 in the financial statements, which indicates that the Company incurred a net loss of ZZZ during the year ended December 31, 20X1 and, as of that date, the Company's current liabilities exceeded its total assets by YYY. As stated in Note 6, these events or conditions, along with other matters as set forth in Note 6, indicate that a material uncertainty exists that may cast significant doubt on the Company's ability to continue as a going concern. Our opinion is not modified in respect of this matter.

Key Audit Matters

Key audit matters are those matters that, in our professional judgment, were of most significance in our audit of the financial statements of the current period. These matters were addressed in the context of our audit of the financial statements as a whole, and in forming our opinion thereon, and we do not provide a separate opinion on these matters. In addition to the matter described in the Material Uncertainty Related to Going Concern section above, we have determined the matters described below to be key audit matters to be communicated in our report.

[*Description of each key audit matter in accordance with ISA 701 as applied to this audit.*]

Other Matter

The Company has prepared a separate set of financial statements for the year ended December 31, 20X1 in accordance with International Financial Reporting Standards on which we issued a separate auditor's report to the shareholders of the Company dated March 31, 20X2.

Responsibilities of Management and Those Charged with Governance for the Financial Statements[32]

Management is responsible for the preparation and fair presentation of the financial statements in accordance with the financial reporting provisions of Section Y of Regulation Z[33] and for such internal control as management determines is necessary to enable the preparation of financial statements that are free from material misstatement, whether due to fraud or error.

In preparing the financial statements, management is responsible for assessing the Company's ability to continue as a going concern, disclosing, as applicable, matters relating to going concern and using the going concern basis of accounting unless management either intends to liquidate the Company or to cease operations, or has no realistic alternative but to do so.

Those charged with governance are responsible for overseeing the Company's financial reporting process.

Auditor's Responsibilities for the Audit of the Financial Statements

Our objectives are to obtain reasonable assurance about whether the financial statements as a whole are free from material misstatement, whether due to fraud or error, and to issue an auditor's report that includes our opinion. Reasonable

---

[32] *Or other terms that are appropriate in the context of the legal framework in the particular jurisdiction*

[33] *Where management's responsibility is to prepare financial statements that give a true and fair view, this may read: "Management is responsible for the preparation of a financial statements that give a true and fair view in accordance with the financial reporting provisions of section Y of Regulation Z and for such ..."*

assurance is a high level of assurance, but is not a guarantee that an audit conducted in accordance with International Standards on Auditing (ISAs) will always detect a material misstatement when it exists. Misstatements can arise from fraud or error and are considered material if, individually or in the aggregate, they could reasonably be expected to influence the economic decisions of users taken on the basis of these financial statements.

Paragraph 41(b) of ISA 700 (Revised) explains that the shaded material below can be located in an Appendix to the auditor's report. Paragraph 41(c) of ISA 700 (Revised) explains that when law, regulation or national auditing standards expressly permit, reference can be made to a website of an appropriate authority that contains the description of the auditor's responsibilities, rather than including this material in the auditor's report, provided that the description on the website addresses, and is not inconsistent with, the description of the auditor's responsibilities below.

As part of an audit in accordance with ISAs, we exercise professional judgment and maintain professional skepticism throughout the audit. We also:

- Identify and assess the risks of material misstatement of the financial statements, whether due to fraud or error, design and perform audit procedures responsive to those risks, and obtain audit evidence that is sufficient and appropriate to provide a basis for our opinion. The risk of not detecting a material misstatement resulting from fraud is higher than for one resulting from error, as fraud may involve collusion, forgery, intentional omissions, misrepresentations, or the override of internal control.

- Obtain an understanding of internal control relevant to audit in order to design audit procedures that are appropriate in the circumstances, but not for the purpose of expressing an opinion on the effectiveness of the Company's internal control.[34]

- Evaluate the appropriateness of accounting policies used and the reasonableness of accounting estimates and related disclosures made by management.

- Conclude on the appropriateness of management's use of the going concern basis of accounting and, based on the audit evidence obtained, whether a material uncertainty exists related to events or conditions that may cast significant doubt on the Company's ability to continue as a going concern. If we conclude that a material uncertainty exists, we are required to draw attention in our auditor's report to the related disclosures in the financial statements or, if such disclosures are inadequate, to modify our opinion. Our conclusions are based on the audit evidence obtained up to the date of our auditor's report. However, future events or conditions may cause the Company to cease to continue as a going concern.

- Evaluate the overall presentation, structure and content of the financial statements, including the disclosures, and whether the financial statements represent the underlying transactions and events in a manner that achieves fair presentation.

We communicate with those charged with governance regarding, among other matters, the planned scope and timing of the audit and significant audit

---

[34] *This sentence would be modified, as appropriate, in circumstances when the auditor also has responsibility to issue an opinion on the effectiveness of internal control in conjunction with the audit of the financial statements.*

findings, including any significant deficiencies in internal control that we identify during our audit.

We also provide those charged with governance with a statement that we have complied with relevant ethical requirements regarding independence, and to communicate with them all relationships and other matters that may reasonably be thought to bear on our independence, and where applicable, related safeguards.

From the matters communicated with those charged with governance, we determine those matters that were of most significance in the audit of the financial statements of the current period and are therefore the key audit matters. We describe these matters in our auditor's report unless law or regulation precludes public disclosure about the matter or when, in extremely rare circumstances, we determine that a matter should not be communicated in our report because the adverse consequences of doing so would reasonably be expected to outweigh the public interest benefits of such communication.

The engagement partner on the audit resulting in this independent auditor's report is [*name*].

[*Signature in the name of the audit firm, the personal name of the auditor, or both, as appropriate for the particular jurisdiction*]

[*Auditor address*] [Placement of date and address reversed)]

[*Date*]

ISA (UK) 805 (Revised)
Special Considerations – Audits of Single Financial Statements and Specific Elements, Accounts or Items of a Financial Statement (October 2016)

(Effective for audits of financial statements for periods commencing on or after 1 January 2017)

Contents

Paragraphs

Introduction
Scope of this ISA (UK)   1 - 3
Effective Date   4

Objective   5

Definitions   6

Requirements
Considerations When Accepting the Engagement   7 - 9
Considerations When Planning and Performing the Audit   10
Forming an Opinion and Reporting Considerations   11 - 17

Application and Other Explanatory Material   A1 - A28
Scope of this ISA (UK)   A1 - A4
Considerations When Accepting the Engagement   A5 - A9
Considerations When Planning and Performing the Audit   A10 - A15
Forming an Opinion and Reporting Considerations   A16 - A28

Appendix 1: Examples of Specific Elements, Accounts or Items of a Financial Statement

Appendix 2: Illustrations of Independent Auditor's Reports on a Single Financial Statement and on a Specific Element of a Financial Statement

Editorial note – This standard applies to engagements concerning financial periods commencing on or after 1 January 2017, with early adoption permitted. The FRC carried out a public consultation exercise and undertook outreach work to obtain stakeholder feedback which has been supportive of the decision to adopt the new standards.

> International Standard on Auditing (UK) (ISA (UK)) 805 (Revised), *Special Considerations—Audits of Single Financial Statements and Specific Elements, Accounts or Items of a Financial Statement*, should be read in conjunction with ISA (UK) 200 (Revised June 2016), *Overall Objectives of the Independent Auditor and the Conduct of an Audit in Accordance with International Standards on Auditing (UK).*

Introduction

Scope of this ISA (UK)

1   The International Standards on Auditing (UK) (ISAs (UK)) in the 100–700 series apply to an audit of financial statements and are to be adapted as necessary in the circumstances when applied to audits of other historical financial information. This ISA (UK) deals with special considerations in the application of those ISAs (UK) to an audit of a single financial statement or of a specific element, account or item of a financial statement. The single financial statement or the specific element, account or item of a financial statement may be prepared in accordance with a general or special purpose framework. If prepared in accordance with a special purpose framework, ISA (UK) 800 (Revised)[1] also applies to the audit. (Ref: Para. A1–A4)

2   This ISA (UK) does not apply to the report of a component auditor, issued as a result of work performed on the financial information of a component at the request of a group engagement team for purposes of an audit of group financial statements (see ISA (UK) 600 (Revised June 2016)).[2]

3   This ISA (UK) does not override the requirements of the other ISAs (UK); nor does it purport to deal with all special considerations that may be relevant in the circumstances of the engagement.

Effective Date

4   This ISA (UK) is effective for audits of single financial statements or of specific elements, accounts or items for periods commencing on or after 1 January 2017, early adoption is permitted[3]. In the case of audits of single financial statements or of specific elements, accounts or items of a financial statement as at a specific date, this ISA (UK) is effective for audits of such information as at a date on or after 1 January 2017, early adoption is permitted.[3]

Objective

5   The objective of the auditor, when applying ISAs (UK) in an audit of a single financial statement or of a specific element, account or item of a financial statement, is to address appropriately the special considerations that are relevant to:

(a)   The acceptance of the engagement;

(b)   The planning and performance of that engagement; and

(c)   Forming an opinion and reporting on the single financial statement or on the specific element, account or item of a financial statement.

---

[1] *ISA (UK) 800 (Revised), Special Considerations—Audits of Financial Statements Prepared in Accordance with Special Purpose Frameworks*

[2] *ISA (UK) 600 (Revised June 2016), Special Considerations—Audits of Group Financial Statements (Including the Work of Component Auditors)*

[3] *Where ISA 805 (Revised) is adopted early for the audit of Solvency II Regulatory Returns for periods commencing prior to 1 January 2017 it may be used in conjunction with ISAs (UK and Ireland) where the audit of the statutory financial statements for the same period was conducted in accordance with ISAs (UK and Ireland).*

Definitions

For purposes of this ISA (UK), reference to: **6**

(a) "Element of a financial statement" or "element" means an "element, account or item of a financial statement;"

(b) "International Financial Reporting Standards" means the International Financial Reporting Standards (IFRSs) issued by the International Accounting Standards Board; and

(c) A single financial statement or to a specific element of a financial statement includes the related disclosures. (Ref: Para. A2)

Requirements

Considerations When Accepting the Engagement

Application of ISAs (UK)

ISA (UK) 200 (Revised June 2016) requires the auditor to comply with all ISAs **7** (UK) relevant to the audit.[4] In the case of an audit of a single financial statement or of a specific element of a financial statement, this requirement applies irrespective of whether the auditor is also engaged to audit the entity's complete set of financial statements. If the auditor is not also engaged to audit the entity's complete set of financial statements, the auditor shall determine whether the audit of a single financial statement or of a specific element of those financial statements in accordance with ISAs (UK) is practicable. (Ref: Para. A5–A6)

Acceptability of the Financial Reporting Framework

ISA (UK) 210 (Revised June 2016) requires the auditor to determine the **8** acceptability of the financial reporting framework applied in the preparation of the financial statements.[5] In the case of an audit of a single financial statement or of a specific element of a financial statement, this shall include whether application of the financial reporting framework will result in a presentation that provides adequate disclosures to enable the intended users to understand the information conveyed in the financial statement or the element, and the effect of material transactions and events on the information conveyed in the financial statement or the element. (Ref: Para. A7)

Form of Opinion

ISA (UK) 210 (Revised June 2016) requires that the agreed terms of the audit **9** engagement include the expected form of any reports to be issued by the auditor.[6] In the case of an audit of a single financial statement or of a specific element of a financial statement, the auditor shall consider whether the expected form of opinion is appropriate in the circumstances. (Ref: Para. A8–A9)

---

[4] *ISA (UK) 200 (Revised June 2016), Overall Objectives of the Independent Auditor and the Conduct of an Audit in Accordance with International Standards on Auditing (UK), paragraph 18*

[5] *ISA (UK) 210 (Revised June 2016), Agreeing the Terms of Audit Engagements, paragraph 6(a)*

[6] *ISA (UK) 210 (Revised June 2016), paragraph 10(e)*

Considerations When Planning and Performing the Audit

10   ISA (UK) 200 (Revised June 2016) states that ISAs (UK) are written in the context of an audit of financial statements; they are to be adapted as necessary in the circumstances when applied to audits of other historical financial information.[7,8] In planning and performing the audit of a single financial statement or of a specific element of a financial statement, the auditor shall adapt all ISAs (UK) relevant to the audit as necessary in the circumstances of the engagement. (Ref: Para. A10–A15)

Forming an Opinion and Reporting Considerations

11   When forming an opinion and reporting on a single financial statement or on a specific element of a financial statement, the auditor shall apply the requirements in ISA (UK) 700 (Revised June 2016),[9] and, when applicable, ISA (UK) 800 (Revised) adapted as necessary in the circumstances of the engagement. (Ref: Para. A16–A22)

Reporting on the Entity's Complete Set of Financial Statements and on a Single Financial Statement or on a Specific Element of Those Financial Statements

12   If the auditor undertakes an engagement to report on a single financial statement or on a specific element of a financial statement in conjunction with an engagement to audit the entity's complete set of financial statements, the auditor shall express a separate opinion for each engagement.

13   The audited single financial statement or the audited specific element of a financial statement may be published together with the entity's audited complete set of financial statements. If the auditor concludes that the presentation of the single financial statement or of the specific element of a financial statement does not differentiate it sufficiently from the complete set of financial statements, the auditor shall ask management to rectify the situation. Subject to paragraphs 15 and 16, the auditor shall also differentiate the opinion on the single financial statement or on the specific element of a financial statement from the opinion on the complete set of financial statements. The auditor shall not issue the auditor's report containing the opinion on the single financial statement or on the specific element of a financial statement until satisfied with the differentiation.

Considering the Implications of Certain Matters Included in the Auditor's Report on the Entity's Complete Set of Financial Statements for the Audit of the Single Financial Statement or the Specific Element of a Financial Statement and for the Auditor's Report Thereon

14   If the auditor's report on an entity's complete set of financial statements includes:

(a)   A modified opinion in accordance with ISA (UK) 705 (Revised June 2016);[10]

---

[7] *ISA (UK) 200 (Revised June 2016), paragraph 2*

[8] *ISA (UK) 200 (Revised June 2016), paragraph 13(f), explains that the term "financial statements" ordinarily refers to a complete set of financial statements as determined by the requirements of the applicable financial reporting framework.*

[9] *ISA (UK) 700 (Revised June 2016), Forming an Opinion and Reporting on Financial Statements*

[10] *ISA (UK) 705 (Revised June 2016), Modifications to the Opinion in the Independent Auditor's Report*

(b)   An Emphasis of Matter paragraph or an Other Matter paragraph in accordance with ISA (UK) 706 (Revised June 2016),[11]

(c)   A Material Uncertainty Related to Going Concern section in accordance with ISA (UK) 570 (Revised June 2016);[12]

(d)   Communication of key audit matters in accordance with ISA (UK) 701;[13] or

(e)   A statement that describes an uncorrected material misstatement of the other information in accordance with ISA (UK) 720 (Revised June 2016);[14]

the auditor shall consider the implications, if any, that these matters have for the audit of the single financial statement or of the specific element of a financial statement and for the auditor's report thereon. (Ref: Para. A23–A27)

Adverse Opinion or Disclaimer of Opinion in the Auditor's Report on the Entity's Complete Set of Financial Statements

If the auditor concludes that it is necessary to express an adverse opinion or   **15** disclaim an opinion on the entity's complete set of financial statements as a whole, ISA (UK) 705 (Revised June 2016) does not permit the auditor to include in the same auditor's report an unmodified opinion on a single financial statement that forms part of those financial statements or on a specific element of those financial statements.[15] This is because such an unmodified opinion would contradict the adverse opinion or disclaimer of opinion on the entity's complete set of financial statements as a whole. (Ref: Para. A28)

If the auditor concludes that it is necessary to express an adverse opinion or   **16** disclaim an opinion on the entity's complete set of financial statements as a whole but, in the context of a separate audit of a specific element of those financial statements, the auditor nevertheless considers it appropriate to express an unmodified opinion on that element, the auditor shall only do so if:

(a)   The auditor is not prohibited by law or regulation from doing so;

(b)   That opinion is expressed in an auditor's report that is not published together with the auditor's report containing the adverse opinion or disclaimer of opinion; and

(c)   The element does not constitute a major portion of the entity's complete set of financial statements.

The auditor shall not express an unmodified opinion on a single financial   **17** statement of a complete set of financial statements if the auditor has expressed an adverse opinion or disclaimed an opinion on the complete set of financial statements as a whole. This is the case even if the auditor's report on the single financial statement is not published together with the auditor's report containing the adverse opinion or disclaimer of opinion. This is because a single financial statement is deemed to constitute a major portion of those financial statements.

***

---

[11] *ISA (UK) 706 (Revised June 2016), Emphasis of Matter Paragraphs and Other Matter Paragraphs in the Independent Auditor's Report*

[12] *ISA (UK) 570 (Revised June 2016), Going Concern, paragraph 22*

[13] *ISA (UK) 701, Communicating Key Audit Matters in the Independent Auditor's Report, paragraph 13*

[14] *ISA (UK) 720 (Revised June 2016), The Auditor's Responsibilities Relating to Other Information, paragraph 22(e)(ii)*

[15] *ISA (UK) 705 (Revised June 2016), paragraph 15*

Application and Other Explanatory Material

Scope of this ISA (UK)
(Ref: Para. 1, 6(c))

A1   ISA (UK) 200 (Revised June 2016) defines the term "historical financial information" as information expressed in financial terms in relation to a particular entity, derived primarily from that entity's accounting system, about economic events occurring in past time periods or about economic conditions or circumstances at points in time in the past.[16]

A2   ISA (UK) 200 (Revised June 2016) defines the term "financial statements" as a structured representation of historical financial information, including disclosures, intended to communicate an entity's economic resources or obligations at a point in time or the changes therein for a period of time in accordance with a financial reporting framework. The term "financial statements" ordinarily refers to a complete set of financial statements as determined by the requirements of the applicable financial reporting framework, but can also refer to a single financial statement. Disclosures comprise explanatory or descriptive information, set out as required, expressly permitted or otherwise allowed by the applicable financial reporting framework, on the face of a financial statement, or in the notes, or incorporated therein by cross-reference.[17] As noted in paragraph 6(c), reference to a single financial statement or specific element of a financial statement includes the related disclosures.

A3   ISAs (UK) are written in the context of an audit of financial statements;[18] they are to be adapted as necessary in the circumstances when applied to an audit of other historical financial information, such as a single financial statement or a specific element of a financial statement. This ISA (UK) assists in this regard. (Appendix 1 lists examples of such other historical financial information.)

A4   A reasonable assurance engagement other than an audit of historical financial information is performed in accordance with International Standard on Assurance Engagements (ISAE) 3000 (Revised).[19]

Considerations When Accepting the Engagement

Application of ISAs (UK)
(Ref: Para. 7)

A5   ISA (UK) 200 (Revised June 2016) requires the auditor to comply with (a) relevant ethical requirements, including those pertaining to independence, relating to financial statement audit engagements, and (b) all ISAs (UK) relevant to the audit. It also requires the auditor to comply with each requirement of an ISA (UK) unless, in the circumstances of the audit, the entire ISA (UK) is not relevant or the requirement is not relevant because it is conditional and the condition does not exist. In exceptional circumstances, the auditor may judge it

---

[16] *ISA (UK) 200 (Revised June 2016), paragraph 13(g)*

[17] *ISA (UK) 200 (Revised June 2016), paragraph 13(f)*

[18] *ISA (UK) 200 (Revised June 2016), paragraph 2*

[19] *ISAE 3000 (Revised), Assurance Engagements Other than Audits or Reviews of Historical Financial Information*

necessary to depart from a relevant requirement in an ISA (UK) by performing alternative audit procedures to achieve the aim of that requirement.[20]

Compliance with the requirements of ISAs (UK) relevant to the audit of a single   **A6** financial statement or of a specific element of a financial statement may not be practicable when the auditor is not also engaged to audit the entity's complete set of financial statements. In such cases, the auditor often does not have the same understanding of the entity and its environment, including its internal control, as an auditor who also audits the entity's complete set of financial statements. The auditor also does not have the audit evidence about the general quality of the accounting records or other accounting information that would be acquired in an audit of the entity's complete set of financial statements. Accordingly, the auditor may need further evidence to corroborate audit evidence acquired from the accounting records. In the case of an audit of a specific element of a financial statement, certain ISAs (UK) require audit work that may be disproportionate to the element being audited. For example, although the requirements of ISA (UK) 570 (Revised June 2016) are likely to be relevant in the circumstances of an audit of a schedule of accounts receivable, complying with those requirements may not be practicable because of the audit effort required. If the auditor concludes that an audit of a single financial statement or of a specific element of a financial statement in accordance with ISAs (UK) may not be practicable, the auditor may discuss with management whether another type of engagement might be more practicable.

Acceptability of the Financial Reporting Framework
(Ref: Para. 8)

A single financial statement or a specific element of a financial statement may be   **A7** prepared in accordance with an applicable financial reporting framework that is based on a financial reporting framework established by an authorized or recognized standards setting organization for the preparation of a complete set of financial statements (for example IFRSs). If this is the case, determination of the acceptability of the applicable framework may involve considering whether that framework includes all the requirements of the framework on which it is based that are relevant to the presentation of a single financial statement or of a specific element of a financial statement that provides adequate disclosures.

Form of Opinion
(Ref: Para. 9)

The form of opinion to be expressed by the auditor depends on the applicable   **A8** financial reporting framework and any applicable laws or regulations.[21] In accordance with ISA (UK) 700 (Revised June 2016):[22]

(a)   When expressing an unmodified opinion on a complete set of financial statements prepared in accordance with a fair presentation framework, the auditor's opinion, unless otherwise required by law or regulation, uses one of the following phrases:

     (i)   the financial statements present fairly, in all material respects, in accordance with [the applicable financial reporting framework]; or

---

[20] *ISA (UK) 200 (Revised June 2016), paragraphs 14, 18, and 22–23*

[21] *ISA (UK) 200 (Revised June 2016), paragraph 8*

[22] *ISA (UK) 700 (Revised June 2016), paragraphs 25–26*

    (ii)   the financial statements give a true and fair view in accordance with [the applicable financial reporting framework]; and

(b)   When expressing an unmodified opinion on a complete set of financial statements prepared in accordance with a compliance framework, the auditor's opinion states that the financial statements are prepared, in all material respects, in accordance with [the applicable financial reporting framework].

A9   In the case of a single financial statement or of a specific element of a financial statement, the applicable financial reporting framework may not explicitly address the presentation of the financial statement or of the specific element of the financial statement. This may be the case when the applicable financial reporting framework is based on a financial reporting framework established by an authorized or recognized standards setting organization for the preparation of a complete set of financial statements (for example, IFRSs). The auditor therefore considers whether the expected form of opinion is appropriate in the light of the applicable financial reporting framework. Factors that may affect the auditor's consideration as to whether to use the phrases "presents fairly, in all material respects," or "gives a true and fair view" in the auditor's opinion include:

- Whether the applicable financial reporting framework is explicitly or implicitly restricted to the preparation of a complete set of financial statements.

- Whether the single financial statement or the specific element of a financial statement will:

  - Comply fully with each of those requirements of the framework relevant to the particular financial statement or the particular element, and the presentation of the financial statement or the specific element of a financial statement include the related disclosures.

  - If necessary to achieve fair presentation, provide disclosures beyond those specifically required by the framework or, in exceptional circumstances, depart from a requirement of the framework.

The auditor's decision as to the expected form of opinion is a matter of professional judgment. It may be affected by whether use of the phrases "presents fairly, in all material respects," or "gives a true and fair view" in the auditor's opinion on a single financial statement or on a specific element of a financial statement prepared in accordance with a fair presentation framework is generally accepted in the particular jurisdiction.

Considerations When Planning and Performing the Audit
(Ref: Para. 10)

A10   The relevance of each of the ISAs (UK) requires careful consideration. Even when only a specific element of a financial statement is the subject of the audit, ISAs (UK) such as ISA (UK) 240 (Revised June 2016),[23] ISA (UK) 550[24] and ISA (UK) 570 (Revised June 2016) are, in principle, relevant. This is because the element could be misstated as a result of fraud, the effect of related party

---

[23] *ISA (UK) 240 (Revised June 2016), The Auditor's Responsibilities Relating to Fraud in an Audit of Financial Statements*

[24] *ISA (UK) 550, Related Parties*

transactions, or the incorrect application of the going concern basis of accounting under the applicable financial reporting framework.

ISA (UK) 260 (Revised June 2016) requires the auditor to determine the appropriate person(s) within the entity's governance structure with whom to communicate.[25] ISA (UK) 260 (Revised June 2016) notes that, in some cases, all of those charged with governance are involved in managing the entity, and the application of communication requirements is modified to recognize this position.[26] When a complete set of financial statements is also prepared by the entity, those person(s) responsible for the oversight of the preparation of the single financial statement or the element may not be the same as those charged with governance responsible for the oversight of the preparation of the complete set of financial statements. **A11**

Furthermore, ISAs (UK) are written in the context of an audit of financial statements; they are to be adapted as necessary in the circumstances when applied to the audit of a single financial statement[27] or of a specific element of a financial statement.[28] For example, written representations from management about the complete set of financial statements would be replaced by written representations about the presentation of the financial statement or the element in accordance with the applicable financial reporting framework. **A12**

Matters included in the auditor's report on the complete set of financial statements may have implications for the audit of a single financial statement or of an element of a financial statement (see paragraph 14). When planning and performing an audit of a single financial statement or a specific element of a financial statement in conjunction with the audit of the entity's complete set of financial statements, the auditor may be able to use audit evidence obtained as part of the audit of the entity's complete set of financial statements in the audit of the financial statement or the element. ISAs (UK), however, require the auditor to plan and perform the audit of the financial statement or element to obtain sufficient appropriate audit evidence on which to base the opinion on the financial statement or on the element. **A13**

The individual financial statements that comprise a complete set of financial statements, and many of the specific elements of those financial statements, including their related disclosures, are interrelated. Accordingly, when auditing a single financial statement or a specific element of a financial statement, the auditor may not be able to consider the financial statement or the element in isolation. Consequently, the auditor may need to perform procedures in relation to the interrelated items to meet the objective of the audit. **A14**

Furthermore, the materiality determined for a single financial statement or for a specific element of a financial statement may be lower than the materiality determined for the entity's complete set of financial statements; this will affect the nature, timing and extent of the audit procedures and the evaluation of uncorrected misstatements. **A15**

---

[25] *ISA (UK) 260 (Revised June 2016), Communication with Those Charged with Governance, paragraph 11*

[26] *ISA (UK) 260 (Revised June 2016), paragraph 10(b), 13, A1 (third bullet), A2 and A8.*

[27] *ISA (UK) 200 (Revised June 2016), paragraph 2*

Forming an Opinion and Reporting Considerations
(Ref: Para. 11)

A16   ISA (UK) 700 (Revised June 2016) requires the auditor, in forming an opinion, to evaluate whether the financial statements provide adequate disclosures to enable the intended users to understand the effect of material transactions and events on the information conveyed in the financial statements.[29] In the case of a single financial statement or of a specific element of a financial statement, it is important that the financial statement or the element, in view of the requirements of the applicable financial reporting framework, provides adequate disclosures to enable the intended users to understand the information conveyed in the financial statement or the element, and the effect of material transactions and events on the information conveyed in the financial statement or the element.

A17   Appendix 2[29a] contains illustrations of independent auditor's reports on a single financial statement and on a specific element of a financial statement. Other illustrations of auditor's reports may be relevant to reporting on a single financial statement or on a specific element of a financial statement (see, for example, the Appendices to ISA (UK) 700 (Revised June 2016), ISA (UK) 705 (Revised June 2016), ISA (UK) 570 (Revised June 2016), ISA (UK) 720 (Revised June 2016), and ISA (UK) 706 (Revised June 2016)).

Application of ISA (UK) 700 (Revised June 2016) When Reporting on a Single Financial Statement or on a Specific Element of a Financial Statement

A18   Paragraph 11 of this ISA (UK) explains that the auditor is required to apply the requirements in ISA (UK) 700 (Revised June 2016), adapted as necessary in the circumstances of the engagement, when forming an opinion and reporting on a single financial statement or on a specific element of a financial statement. In doing so, the auditor is also required to apply the reporting requirements in other ISAs (UK) adapted as necessary in the circumstances of the engagement, and may find the considerations addressed in paragraphs A19–A21 below helpful.

Going Concern

A19   Depending on the applicable financial reporting framework used in the preparation of the single financial statement or the specific element of a financial statement, the description in the auditor's report of management's responsibilities[30] relating to going concern may need to be adapted as necessary. The description in the auditor's report of the auditor's responsibilities[31] may also need to be adapted as necessary depending on how ISA (UK) 570 (Revised June 2016) applies in the circumstances of the engagement.

Key Audit Matters

A20   ISA (UK) 700 (Revised June 2016) requires the auditor to communicate key audit matters in accordance with ISA (UK) 701 for audits of complete sets of general purpose financial statements of listed entities.[32] For audits of a single financial statement or a specific element of a financial statement, ISA (UK) 701 only

---

[29] *ISA (UK) 700 (Revised June 2016), paragraph 13(e)*

[29a] *The examples in the Appendix have not been tailored for the UK.*

[30] *See ISA (UK) 700 (Revised June 2016), paragraphs 34(b) and A48.*

[31] *See ISA (UK) 700 (Revised June 2016), paragraphs 39(b)(iv).*

[32] *ISA (UK) 700 (Revised June 2016), paragraph 30*

applies when communication of key audit matters in the auditor's report on such financial statements or elements is required by law or regulation, or the auditor otherwise decides to communicate key audit matters. When key audit matters are communicated in the auditor's report on a single financial statement or a specific element of a financial statement, ISA (UK) 701 applies in its entirety.[33]

Other Information

ISA (UK) 720 (Revised June 2016) deals with the auditor's responsibilities relating to other information. In the context of this ISA (UK), reports containing or accompanying the single financial statement or specific element of a financial statement—the purpose of which is to provide owners (or similar stakeholders) with information on matters presented in the single financial statement or the specific element of a financial statement—are considered to be annual reports for purposes of ISA (UK) 720 (Revised June 2016). When the auditor determines that the entity plans to issue such a report, the requirements in ISA (UK) 720 (Revised June 2016) apply to the audit of the single financial statement or the element.   **A21**

Name of the Engagement Partner

The requirement in ISA (UK) 700 (Revised June 2016) for the auditor to include the name of the engagement partner in the auditor's report also applies to audits of single financial statements of listed entities or specific elements of financial statements of listed entities.[34] The auditor may be required by law or regulation to include the name of the engagement partner in the auditor's report or may otherwise decide to do so when reporting on a single financial statement or on an element of a financial statement of entities other than listed entities.   **A22**

Reporting on the Entity's Complete Set of Financial Statements and on a Single Financial Statement or on a Specific Element of a Financial Statement
(Ref: Para. 14)

Considering the Implications of Certain Matters Included in the Auditor's Report on the Entity's Complete Set of Financial Statements for the Audit of the Single Financial Statement or the Specific Element of a Financial Statement and for the Auditor's Report Thereon

Paragraph 14 requires the auditor to consider the implications, if any, of certain matters included in the auditor's report on the complete set of financial statements for the audit of the single financial statement or the specific element of a financial statement and for the auditor's report thereon. Considering whether a matter included in the auditor's report on the complete set of financial statements is relevant in the context of an engagement to report on a single financial statement or a specific element of a financial statement involves professional judgment.   **A23**

Factors that may be relevant in considering those implications include: **A24**

- The nature of the matter(s) being described in the auditor's report on the complete set of financial statements and the extent to which it relates to what is included in the single financial statement or a specific element of a financial statement.

---

[33] *ISA (UK) 700 (Revised June 2016), paragraph 31*

[34] *See ISA (UK) 700 (Revised June 2016), paragraphs 46 and A61–A63.*

- The pervasiveness of the matter(s) described in the auditor's report on the complete set of financial statements.

- The nature and extent of the differences between the applicable financial reporting frameworks.

- The extent of the difference between the period(s) covered by the complete set of the financial statements compared to the period(s) or dates of the single financial statement or the element of a financial statement.

- The time elapsed since the date of the auditor's report on the complete set of the financial statements.

A25   For example, in the case when there is a qualification of the auditor's opinion in relation to accounts receivable in the auditor's report on the complete set of financial statements, and the single financial statement includes accounts receivable, or the specific element of a financial statement relates to accounts receivable, it is likely that there would be implications for the audit. On the other hand, if the qualification of the auditor's opinion on the complete set of financial statements relates to classification of long-term debt, then it is less likely that there would be implications for an audit of the single financial statement that is the income statement, or if the specific element of the financial statement relates to accounts receivable.

A26   Key audit matters that are communicated in the auditor's report on the complete set of financial statements may have implications for an audit of a single financial statement or the specific element of the financial statement. The information included in the Key Audit Matters section about how the matter was addressed in the audit of the complete set of financial statements may be useful to the auditor's determination of how to address the matter when it is relevant to the audit of the single financial statement or the specific element of the financial statement.

Inclusion of a reference to the auditor's report on the complete set of financial statements

A27   Even when certain matters included in the auditor's report on the complete set of financial statements do not have implications for the audit of, or for the auditor's report on, the single financial statement or the specific element of a financial statement, the auditor may deem it appropriate to refer to the matter(s) in an Other Matter paragraph in an auditor's report on the single financial statement or on the specific element of a financial statement (see ISA (UK) 706 Revised June 2016)).[35] For example, the auditor may consider it appropriate to refer in the auditor's report on the single financial statement or a specific element of the financial statement to a Material Uncertainty Related to Going Concern section included in the auditor's report on the complete set of financial statements.

Adverse Opinion or Disclaimer of Opinion in the Auditor's Report on the Entity's Complete Set of Financial Statements
(Ref: Para. 15)

A28   In the auditor's report on an entity's complete set of financial statements, the expression of a disclaimer of opinion regarding the results of operations and cash flows, where relevant, and an unmodified opinion regarding the financial position is permitted since the disclaimer of opinion is being issued in respect of the results of operations and cash flows only and not in respect of the financial statements as a whole.[36]

---

[35] *See ISA (UK) 706 (Revised June 2016), paragraphs 610–11.*

[36] *ISA (UK) 510 (Revised June 2016), Initial Audit Engagements—Opening Balances, paragraph A8, and ISA 705 (Revised), paragraph A16*

Appendix 1

(Ref: Para. A3)

Examples of Specific Elements, Accounts or Items of a Financial Statement

- Accounts receivable, allowance for doubtful accounts receivable, inventory, the liability for accrued benefits of a private pension plan, the recorded value of identified intangible assets, or the liability for "incurred but not reported" claims in an insurance portfolio, including related notes.

- A schedule of externally managed assets and income of a private pension plan, including related notes.

- A schedule of net tangible assets, including related notes.

- A schedule of disbursements in relation to a lease property, including explanatory notes.

- A schedule of profit participation or employee bonuses, including explanatory notes.

Appendix 2

(Ref: Para. A17)

Illustrations of Independent Auditor's[2] Reports on a Single Financial Statement and on a Specific Element of a Financial Statement

The examples in the Appendix have not been tailored for the UK.

- Illustration 1: An auditor's report on a single financial statement of an entity other than a listed entity prepared in accordance with a general purpose framework (for purposes of this illustration, a fair presentation framework).

- Illustration 2: An auditor's report on a single financial statement of an entity other than a listed entity prepared in accordance with a special purpose framework (for purposes of this illustration, a fair presentation framework).

- Illustration 3: An auditor's report on a specific element of a financial statement of a listed entity prepared in accordance with a special purpose framework (for purposes of this illustration, a compliance framework).

Illustration 1: An auditor's report on a single financial statement of an entity other than a listed entity prepared in accordance with a general purpose framework (for purposes of this illustration, a fair presentation framework).

For purposes of this illustrative auditor's report, the following circumstances are assumed:

- Audit of a balance sheet (that is, a single financial statement) of an entity other than a listed entity.
- The balance sheet has been prepared by management of the entity in accordance with the requirements of the Financial Reporting Framework in Jurisdiction X relevant to preparing a balance sheet.
- The terms of the audit engagement reflect the description of management's responsibility for the financial statements in ISA 210.
- The applicable financial reporting framework is a fair presentation framework designed to meet the common financial information needs of a wide range of users.
- The auditor has determined that it is appropriate to use the phrase "presents fairly, in all material respects," in the auditor's opinion.
- The relevant ethical requirements that apply to the audit are those of the jurisdiction.
- Based on the audit evidence obtained, the auditor has concluded that a material uncertainty exists related to events or conditions that may cast significant doubt on the entity's ability to continue as a going concern in accordance with ISA 570 (Revised). The disclosure of the material uncertainty in the single financial statement is adequate.
- The auditor is not required, and has otherwise not decided, to communicate key audit matters in accordance with ISA 701 in the context of the audit of the balance sheet.
- The auditor has determined that there is no other information (i.e., the requirements of ISA 720 (Revised) do not apply).

> - Those responsible for oversight of the financial statement differ from those responsible for the preparation of the financial statement.
> - The auditor has no other reporting responsibilities required under local law or regulation.

INDEPENDENT AUDITOR'S REPORT

[Appropriate Addressee]

Opinion

We have audited the balance sheet of ABC Company (the Company) as at December 31, 20X1 and notes to the financial statement, including a summary of significant accounting policies (together "the financial statement").

In our opinion, the accompanying financial statement presents fairly, in all material respects, the financial position of the Company as at December 31, 20X1 in accordance with those requirements of the Financial Reporting Framework in Jurisdiction X relevant to preparing such a financial statement. [Opinion section positioned first as required in ISA 700 (Revised)]

Basis for Opinion

We conducted our audit in accordance with International Standards on Auditing (ISAs). Our responsibilities under those standards are further described in the *Auditor's Responsibilities for the Audit of the Financial Statement* section of our report. We are independent of the Company in accordance with the ethical requirements that are relevant to our audit of the financial statement in [*jurisdiction*], and we have fulfilled our other ethical responsibilities in accordance with these requirements. We believe that the audit evidence we have obtained is sufficient and appropriate to provide a basis for our opinion. [The first and last sentences in this section used to be in the Auditor's Responsibility section. Also, the Basis for Opinion section is positioned immediately after the Opinion section as required in ISA 700 (Revised).]

Material Uncertainty Related to Going Concern

We draw attention to Note 6 in the financial statement, which indicates that the Company incurred a net loss of ZZZ during the year ended December 31, 20X1 and, as of that date, the Company's current liabilities exceeded its total assets by YYY. As stated in Note 6, these events or conditions, along with other matters as set forth in Note 6, indicate that a material uncertainty exists that may cast significant doubt on the Company's ability to continue as a going concern. Our opinion is not modified in respect of this matter.

Responsibilities of Management and Those Charged with Governance for the Financial Statement[37]

Management is responsible for the preparation and fair presentation of the financial statement in accordance with those requirements of the Financial Reporting Framework in Jurisdiction X relevant to preparing such a financial statement, and for such internal control as management determines is necessary to

---

[37] *Throughout these illustrative auditor's reports, the terms management and those charged with governance may need to be replaced by another term that is appropriate in the context of the legal framework in the particular jurisdiction.*

enable the preparation of a financial statement that is free from material misstatement, whether due to fraud or error.

In preparing the financial statement, management is responsible for assessing the Company's ability to continue as a going concern, disclosing, as applicable, matters relating to going concern and using the going concern basis of accounting unless management either intends to liquidate the Company or to cease operations, or has no realistic alternative but to do so.

Those charged with governance are responsible for overseeing the Company's financial reporting process.

Auditor's Responsibilities for the Audit of the Financial Statement

Our objectives are to obtain reasonable assurance about whether the financial statement as a whole is free from material misstatement, whether due to fraud or error, and to issue an auditor's report that includes our opinion. Reasonable assurance is a high level of assurance, but is not a guarantee that an audit conducted in accordance with ISAs will always detect a material misstatement when it exists. Misstatements can arise from fraud or error and are considered material if, individually or in the aggregate, they could reasonably be expected to influence the economic decisions of users taken on the basis of this financial statement.

Paragraph 41(b) of ISA 700 (Revised) explains that the shaded material below can be located in an Appendix to the auditor's report. Paragraph 41(c) of ISA 700 (Revised) explains that when law, regulation or national auditing standards expressly permit, reference can be made to a website of an appropriate authority that contains the description of the auditor's responsibilities, rather than including this material in the auditor's report, provided that the description on the website addresses, and is not inconsistent with, the description of the auditor's responsibilities below.

As part of an audit in accordance with ISAs, we exercise professional judgment and maintain professional skepticism throughout the audit. We also:

- Identify and assess the risks of material misstatement of the financial statement, whether due to fraud or error, design and perform audit procedures responsive to those risks, and obtain audit evidence that is sufficient and appropriate to provide a basis for our opinion. The risk of not detecting a material misstatement resulting from fraud is higher than for one resulting from error, as fraud may involve collusion, forgery, intentional omissions, misrepresentations, or the override of internal control.

- Obtain an understanding of internal control relevant to the audit in order to design audit procedures that are appropriate in the circumstances, but not for the purpose of expressing an opinion on the effectiveness of the Company's internal control.[38]

- Evaluate the appropriateness of accounting policies used and the reasonableness of accounting estimates, if any, and related disclosures made by management.;

---

[38] *This sentence would be modified, as appropriate, in circumstances when the auditor also has responsibility to issue an opinion on the effectiveness of internal control in conjunction with the audit of the financial statement.*

- Conclude on the appropriateness of management's use of the going concern basis of accounting and, based on the audit evidence obtained, whether a material uncertainty exists related to events or conditions that may cast significant doubt on the Company's ability to continue as a going concern. If we conclude that a material uncertainty exists, we are required to draw attention in our auditor's report to the related disclosures in the financial statements or, if such disclosures are inadequate, to modify our opinion. Our conclusions are based on the audit evidence obtained up to the date of our auditor's report. However, future events or conditions may cause the Company to cease to continue as a going concern.

- Evaluate the overall presentation, structure and content of the financial statement, including the disclosures, and whether the financial statement represents the underlying transactions and events in a manner that achieves fair presentation.

We communicate with those charged with governance regarding, among other matters, the planned scope and timing of the audit and significant audit findings, including any significant deficiencies in internal control that we identify during our audit.

[Signature in the name of the audit firm, the personal name of the auditor, or both, as appropriate for the particular jurisdiction]

[Auditor address] [Placement of date and address reversed)]

[Date]

Illustration 2: An auditor's report on a single financial statement of an entity other than a listed entity prepared in accordance with a special purpose framework.

For purposes of this illustrative auditor's report, the following Circumstances are assumed:

- Audit of a statement of cash receipts and disbursements (that is, a single financial statement) of an entity other than a listed entity.
- An auditor's report on the complete set of financial statements was not issued.
- The financial statement has been prepared by management of the entity in accordance with the cash receipts and disbursements basis of accounting to respond to a request for cash flow information received from a creditor. Management has a choice of financial reporting frameworks.
- The applicable financial reporting framework is a fair presentation framework designed to meet the financial information needs of specific users.[39]
- The auditor has concluded an unmodified (i.e., "clean") opinion is appropriate based on the audit evidence obtained.
- The auditor has determined that it is appropriate to use the phrase "presents fairly, in all material respects," in the auditor's opinion.
- The relevant ethical requirements that apply to the audit are those of the jurisdiction.

---

[39] *ISA 800 (Revised) contains requirements and guidance on the form and content of financial statements prepared in accordance with a special purpose framework.*

- Distribution or use of the auditor's report is not restricted.
- Based on the audit evidence obtained, the auditor has concluded that a material uncertainty does not exist related to events or conditions that may cast significant doubt on the entity's ability to continue as a going concern in accordance with ISA 570 (Revised).
- The auditor is not required, and has otherwise not decided, to communicate key audit matters in accordance with ISA 701 in the context of the audit of the statement of cash receipts and disbursements.
- The auditor has determined that there is no other information (i.e., the requirements of ISA 720 (Revised) do not apply).
- Management is responsible for the preparation of the financial statement and oversight of the financial reporting process to prepare this financial statement.
- The auditor has no other reporting responsibilities required under local law or regulation.

INDEPENDENT AUDITOR'S REPORT

[Appropriate Addressee]

Opinion

We have audited the statement of cash receipts and disbursements of ABC Company (the Company) for the year ended December 31, 20X1 and notes to the statement of cash receipts and disbursements, including a summary of significant accounting policies (together "the financial statement").

In our opinion, the accompanying financial statement presents fairly, in all material respects, the cash receipts and disbursements of the Company for the year ended December 31, 20X1 in accordance with the cash receipts and disbursements basis of accounting described in Note X. [Opinion section positioned first as required in ISA 700 (Revised)]

Basis for Opinion

We conducted our audit in accordance with International Standards on Auditing (ISAs). Our responsibilities under those standards are further described in the *Auditor's Responsibilities for the Audit of the Financial Statement* section of our report. We are independent of the Company in accordance with the ethical requirements that are relevant to our audit of the financial statement in [*jurisdiction*], and we have fulfilled our other ethical responsibilities in accordance with these requirements. We believe that the audit evidence we have obtained is sufficient and appropriate to provide a basis for our opinion. [The first and last sentences in this section used to be in the Auditor's Responsibility section. Also, the Basis for Opinion section is positioned immediately after the Opinion section as required in ISA 700 (Revised).]

Emphasis of Matter – Basis of Accounting

We draw attention to Note X to the financial statement, which describes the basis of accounting. The financial statement is prepared to provide information to XYZ Creditor. As a result, the statement may not be suitable for another purpose. Our opinion is not modified in respect of this matter.

Responsibilities of Management and Those Charged with Governance for the Financial Statement[40]

Management is responsible for preparation and fair presentation of the financial statement in accordance with the cash receipts and disbursements basis of accounting described in Note X; this includes determining that the cash receipts and disbursements basis of accounting is an acceptable basis for the preparation of the financial statement in the circumstances, and for such internal control as management determines is necessary to enable the preparation of a financial statement that is free from material misstatement, whether due to fraud or error.

In preparing the financial statement, management is responsible for assessing the Company's ability to continue as a going concern, disclosing, as applicable, matters relating to going concern and using the going concern basis of accounting unless management either intends to liquidate the Company or to cease operations, or has no realistic alternative but to do so.

Auditor's Responsibilities for the Audit of the Financial Statement

Our objectives are to obtain reasonable assurance about whether the financial statement as a whole is free from material misstatement, whether due to fraud or error, and to issue an auditor's report that includes our opinion. Reasonable assurance is a high level of assurance, but is not a guarantee that an audit conducted in accordance with ISAs will always detect a material misstatement when it exists. Misstatements can arise from fraud or error and are considered material if, individually or in the aggregate, they could reasonably be expected to influence the economic decisions of users taken on the basis of this financial statement.

Paragraph 41(b) of ISA 700 (Revised) explains that the shaded material below can be located in an Appendix to the auditor's report. Paragraph 41(c) of ISA 700 (Revised) explains that when law, regulation or national auditing standards expressly permit, reference can be made to a website of an appropriate authority that contains the description of the auditor's responsibilities, rather than including this material in the auditor's report, provided that the description on the website addresses, and is not inconsistent with, the description of the auditor's responsibilities below.

As part of an audit in accordance with ISAs, we exercise professional judgment and maintain professional skepticism throughout the audit. We also:

- Identify and assess the risks of material misstatement of the financial statement, whether due to fraud or error, design and perform audit procedures responsive to those risks, and obtain audit evidence that is sufficient and appropriate to provide a basis for our opinion. The risk of not detecting a material misstatement resulting from fraud is higher than for one resulting from error, as fraud may involve collusion, forgery, intentional omissions, misrepresentations, or the override of internal control.

- Obtain an understanding of internal control relevant to the audit in order to design audit procedures that are appropriate in the circumstances, but not for the purpose of expressing an opinion on the effectiveness of the Company's internal control.[41]

---

[40] *Or other terms that are appropriate in the context of the legal framework in the particular jurisdiction*

[41] *This sentence would be modified, as appropriate, in circumstances when the auditor also has responsibility to issue an opinion on the effectiveness of internal control in conjunction with the audit of the financial statement.*

- Conclude on the appropriateness of management's use of the going concern basis of accounting and based on the audit evidence obtained, whether a material uncertainty exists related to events or conditions that may cast significant doubt on the Company's ability to continue as a going concern. If we conclude that a material uncertainty exists, we are required to draw attention in our auditor's report to the related disclosures in the financial statement or, if such disclosures are inadequate, to modify our opinion. Our conclusions are based on the audit evidence obtained up to the date of our auditor's report. However, future events or conditions may cause the Company to cease to continue as a going concern.

- Evaluate the appropriateness of accounting policies used and the reasonableness of accounting estimates, if any, and related disclosures made by management.;

- Evaluate the overall presentation, structure and content of the financial statement, including the disclosures, and whether the financial statement represents the underlying transactions and events in a manner that achieves fair presentation.

We communicate with those charged with governance regarding, among other matters, the planned scope and timing of the audit and significant audit findings, including any significant deficiencies in internal control that we identify during our audit.

[Signature in the name of the audit firm, the personal name of the auditor, or both, as appropriate for the particular jurisdiction]

[Auditor address] [Placement of date and address reversed)]

[Date]

Illustration 3: An auditor's report on a specific element of a financial statement of a listed entity prepared in accordance with a special purpose framework.

For purposes of this illustrative auditor's report, the following circumstances are assumed:

- Audit of an accounts receivable schedule (that is, element, account or item of a financial statement).
- The financial information has been prepared by management of the entity in accordance with the financial reporting provisions established by a regulator to meet the requirements of that regulator. Management does not have a choice of financial reporting frameworks.
- The applicable financial reporting framework is a compliance framework designed to meet the financial information needs of specific users.[42]
- The terms of the audit engagement reflect the description of management's responsibility for the financial statements in ISA 210.
- The auditor has concluded an unmodified (i.e., "clean") opinion is appropriate based on the audit evidence obtained.

---

[42] *ISA 800 (Revised) contains requirements and guidance on the form and content of financial statements prepared in accordance with a special purpose framework.*

- The relevant ethical requirements that apply to the audit are those of the jurisdiction.
- Distribution of the auditor's report is restricted.
- Based on the audit evidence obtained, the auditor has concluded that a material uncertainty does not exist related to events or conditions that may cast significant doubt on the entity's ability to continue as a going concern in accordance with ISA 570 (Revised).
- The auditor is not required, and has otherwise not decided to communicate key audit matters in accordance with ISA 701 in the context of the audit of the accounts receivable schedule.
- The auditor has determined that there is no other information (i.e., the requirements of ISA 720 (Revised) do not apply).
- Those responsible for oversight of the financial statement differ from those responsible for the preparation of the financial statement.
- The auditor has no other reporting responsibilities required under local law or regulation.

INDEPENDENT AUDITOR'S REPORT

[To the Shareholders of ABC Company or Other Appropriate Addressee]

Opinion

We have audited the accounts receivable schedule of ABC Company (the Company) as at December 31, 20X1 ("the schedule").

In our opinion, the financial information in the schedule the Company as at December 31, 20X1 is prepared, in all material respects, in accordance with [describe the financial reporting provisions established by the regulator]. [Opinion section positioned first as required ISA 700 (Revised)]

Basis for Opinion

We conducted our audit in accordance with International Standards on Auditing (ISAs). Our responsibilities under those standards are further described in the *Auditor's Responsibilities for the Audit of the Schedule* section of our report. We are independent of the Company in accordance with the ethical requirements that are relevant to our audit of the schedule in [*jurisdiction*], and we have fulfilled our other ethical responsibilities in accordance with these requirements. We believe that the audit evidence we have obtained is sufficient and appropriate to provide a basis for our opinion. [The first and last sentences in this section used to be in the Auditor's Responsibility section. Also, the Basis for Opinion section is positioned immediately after opinion section as required in ISA 700 (Revised).]

Emphasis of Matter – Basis of Accounting and Restriction on Distribution

We draw attention to Note X to the schedule, which describes the basis of accounting. The schedule is prepared to assist the Company to meet the requirements of Regulator DEF. As a result, the schedule may not be suitable for another purpose. Our report is intended solely for the Company and Regulator DEF and should not be distributed to parties other than the Company or Regulator DEF. Our opinion is not modified in respect of this matter.

Responsibilities of Management and Those Charged with Governance for the Schedule[43]

Management is responsible for the preparation of the schedule in accordance with [describe the financial reporting provisions established by the regulator], and for such internal control as management determines is necessary to enable the preparation of the schedule that is free from material misstatement, whether due to fraud or error.

In preparing the schedule, management is responsible for assessing the Company's ability to continue as a going concern, disclosing, as applicable, matters relating to going concern and using the going concern basis of accounting unless management either intends to liquidate the Company or to cease operations, or has no realistic alternative but to do so.

Those charged with governance are responsible for overseeing the Company's financial reporting process.

Auditor's Responsibilities for the Audit of the Schedule

Our objectives are to obtain reasonable assurance about whether the schedule is free from material misstatement, whether due to fraud or error, and to issue an auditor's report that includes our opinion. Reasonable assurance is a high level of assurance, but is not a guarantee that an audit conducted in accordance with ISAs will always detect a material misstatement when it exists. Misstatements can arise from fraud or error and are considered material if, individually or in the aggregate, they could reasonably be expected to influence the economic decisions of users taken on the basis of this schedule.

Paragraph 41(b) of ISA 700 (Revised) explains that the shaded material below can be located in an Appendix to the auditor's report. Paragraph 41(c) of ISA 700 (Revised) explains that when law, regulation or national auditing standards expressly permit, reference can be made to a website of an appropriate authority that contains the description of the auditor's responsibilities, rather than including this material in the auditor's report, provided that the description on the website addresses, and is not inconsistent with, the description of the auditor's responsibilities below.

As part of an audit in accordance with ISAs, we exercise professional judgment and maintain professional skepticism throughout the audit. We also:

- Identify and assess the risks of material misstatement of the schedule, whether due to fraud or error, design and perform audit procedures responsive to those risks, and obtain audit evidence that is sufficient and appropriate to provide a basis for our opinion. The risk of not detecting a material misstatement resulting from fraud is higher than for one resulting from error, as fraud may involve collusion, forgery, intentional omissions, misrepresentations, or the override of internal control.

- Obtain an understanding of internal control relevant to the audit in order to design audit procedures that are appropriate in the circumstances, but not for the purpose of expressing an opinion on the effectiveness of the Company's internal control.[44]

---

[43] *Or other terms that are appropriate in the context of the legal framework in the particular jurisdiction*

[44] *This sentence would be modified, as appropriate, in circumstances when the auditor also has responsibility to issue an opinion on the effectiveness of internal control in conjunction with the audit of the schedule.*

- Conclude on the appropriateness of management's use of the going concern basis of accounting and, based on the audit evidence obtained, whether a material uncertainty exists related to events or conditions that may cast significant doubt on the Company's ability to continue as a going concern. If we conclude that a material uncertainty exists, we are required to draw attention in our auditor's report to the related disclosures in the schedule or, if such disclosures are inadequate, to modify our opinion. Our conclusions are based on the audit evidence obtained up to the date of our auditor's report. However, future events or conditions may cause the Company to cease to continue as a going concern.

- Evaluate the appropriateness of accounting policies used and the reasonableness of accounting estimates, if any, and related disclosures made by management.

We communicate with those charged with governance regarding, among other matters, the planned scope and timing of the audit and significant audit findings, including any significant deficiencies in internal control that we identify during our audit.

We also provide those charged with governance with a statement that we have complied with relevant ethical requirements regarding independence, and to communicate with them all relationships and other matters that may reasonably be thought to bear on our independence, and where applicable, related safeguards.

The engagement partner on the audit resulting in this independent auditor's report is [*name*].

[*Signature in the name of the audit firm, the personal name of the auditor, or both, as appropriate for the particular jurisdiction*]

[*Auditor address*] [Placement of date and address reversed)]

[Date]

Glossary of Terms[1]
(auditing and ethics) (2018)

(January 2018)

This Glossary defines terms used in the ISAs (UK), the ISQC (UK) and the FRC's Ethical Standard. It is based on the International Auditing and Assurance Standards Board (IAASB) glossary of terms, with supplemental definitions used in the FRC standards shown in grey highlighted text.

Access controls – Procedures designed to restrict access to on-line terminal devices, programs and data. Access controls consist of "user authentication" and "user authorization." "User authentication" typically attempts to identify a user through unique logon identifications, passwords, access cards or biometric data. "User authorization" consists of access rules to determine the computer resources each user may access. Specifically, such procedures are designed to prevent or detect:

● Unauthorized access to on-line terminal devices, programs and data;

● Entry of unauthorized transactions;

● Unauthorized changes to data files;

● The use of computer programs by unauthorized personnel; and

● The use of computer programs that have not been authorized.

Accounting estimate – An approximation of a monetary amount in the absence of a precise means of measurement. This term is used for an amount measured at fair value where there is estimation uncertainty, as well as for other amounts that require estimation. Where ISA (UK) 540 (Revised June 2016)[2] addresses only accounting estimates involving measurement at fair value, the term "fair value accounting estimates" is used.

Accounting records – The records of initial accounting entries and supporting records, such as checks and records of electronic fund transfers; invoices; contracts; the general and subsidiary ledgers, journal entries and other adjustments to the financial statements that are not reflected in formal journal entries; and records such as work sheets and spreadsheets supporting cost allocations, computations, reconciliations and disclosures.

Accounting services – The provision of services that involve the maintenance of accounting records or the preparation of financial statements or other subject matter information or subject matter that are then subject to audit or an other public interest assurance engagement.

---

[1] *In the case of public sector engagements, the terms in this glossary should be read as referring to their public sector equivalents.*
Where accounting terms have not been defined in the pronouncements of the International Auditing and Assurance Standards Board, reference should be made to the Glossary of Terms published by the International Accounting Standards Board.

[2] *ISA (UK) 540 (Revised June 2016), Auditing Accounting Estimates, Including Fair Value Accounting Estimates, and Related Disclosures.*

1,138 International Standards on Auditing (UK)

Additional services – For a public interest assurance engagement other than an audit, "additional services" comprise any engagement in which a firm, or a member of its network, provides professional services to an entity relevant to the engagement other than pursuant to:

(a) Any other public interest assurance engagement;

(b) The audit of financial statements; and

(c) Those other roles which legislation or regulation specify can be performed by the auditor of the entity (for example, considering the preliminary announcements of listed companies, complying with the procedural and reporting requirements of regulators, such as requirements relating to the audit of the client's internal controls and reports in accordance with Section 714 of the Companies Act 2006).

Where the entity relevant to the engagement is a member of a group, additional services for the purposes of the FRC's Ethical Standard include:

– Services provided by the *firm* to the parent entity or to any of its significant affiliates; and

– Services provided by a network firm which is involved in the engagement to the entity relevant to the engagement or any of its significant affiliates.

Affiliate firm – Any undertaking, regardless of its legal form, which is connected to a firm by means of common ownership, control or management.

Affiliate (of an entity)–

For investment circular reporting engagement, an affiliate is any undertaking which is connected to another by means of common ownership, control or management.

For a public interest assurance engagement other than an investment circular reporting engagement, an affiliate is an entity that has any of the following relationships with an entity relevant to the engagement:

(a) An entity that has direct or indirect control over the entity relevant to the engagement if the entity relevant to the engagement is material, quantitatively or qualitatively, to such entity;

(b) An entity with a direct financial interest in the entity relevant to the engagement if that entity has significant influence over the entity relevant to the engagement and the interest in the entity relevant to the engagement is material, quantitatively or qualitatively, to such entity;

(c) An entity over which the entity relevant to the engagement has direct or indirect control;

(d) An entity in which the entity relevant to the engagement, or an affiliate of the entity relevant to the engagement under (c) above, has a direct financial interest that gives it significant influence over such entity and the interest is material, quantitatively or qualitatively, to the entity relevant to the engagement and its affiliate in (c); and

(e) An entity which is under common control with the entity relevant to the engagement (a "sister entity") if the sister entity and the entity relevant to the engagement are both material, quantitatively or qualitatively, to the entity that controls both the entity relevant to the engagement and sister entity.

Factors that may be relevant in determining whether an entity or an interest in an entity is material to another entity include:

- The extent and nature of the relationships between the entity relevant to the engagement and the other entity and the impact these have on the relationships of either entity with the firm, and

- The extent and nature of the relationship(s) between the firm and the other entity and the impact that this has on independence.

Agreed-upon procedures engagement – An engagement in which an auditor or reporting accountant is engaged to carry out those procedures of an audit or assurance nature to which the auditor or reporting accountant and the entity and any appropriate third parties have agreed and to report on factual findings. The recipients of the report form their own conclusions from the report by the auditor or reporting accountant. The report is restricted to those parties that have agreed to the procedures to be performed since others, unaware of the reasons for the procedures, may misinterpret the results.

Analytical procedures – Evaluations of financial information through analysis of plausible relationships among both financial and non-financial data. Analytical procedures also encompass such investigation as is necessary of identified fluctuations or relationships that are inconsistent with other relevant information or that differ from expected values by a significant amount.

Annual report – A document, or combination of documents, prepared typically on an annual basis by management or those charged with governance in accordance with law, regulation or custom, the purpose of which is to provide owners (or similar stakeholders) with information on the entity's operations and the entity's financial results and financial position as set out in the financial statements. An annual report contains or accompanies the financial statements and the auditor's report thereon and usually includes information about the entity's developments, its future outlook and risks and uncertainties, a statement by the entity's governing body, and reports covering governance matters.

In the UK an annual report includes at least:

(i)   The statutory other information; and

(ii)   Any other documents that are incorporated by cross-reference in, or distributed to shareholders with, statutory other information either voluntarily or pursuant to law or regulation or the requirements of a stock exchange listing.

Anomaly – A misstatement or deviation that is demonstrably not representative of misstatements or deviations in a population.

Applicable financial reporting framework – The financial reporting framework adopted by management and, where appropriate, those charged with governance in the preparation of the financial statements that is acceptable in view of the nature of the entity and the objective of the financial statements, or that is required by law or regulation.

The term "fair presentation framework" is used to refer to a financial reporting framework that requires compliance with the requirements of the framework and:

(a)   Acknowledges explicitly or implicitly that, to achieve fair presentation of the financial statements, it may be necessary for management to provide disclosures beyond those specifically required by the framework; or

(b)   Acknowledges explicitly that it may be necessary for management to depart from a requirement of the framework to achieve fair presentation of the financial statements. Such departures are expected to be necessary only in extremely rare circumstances.

The term "compliance framework" is used to refer to a financial reporting framework that requires compliance with the requirements of the framework, but does not contain the acknowledgements in (a) or (b) above.

In the UK the applicable financial reporting framework includes the requirements of applicable law.

Application controls in information technology – Manual or automated procedures that typically operate at a business process level. Application controls can be preventative or detective in nature and are designed to ensure the integrity of the accounting records. Accordingly, application controls relate to procedures used to initiate, record, process and report transactions or other financial data.

Appropriateness (of audit evidence) – The measure of the quality of audit evidence; that is, its relevance and its reliability in providing support for the conclusions on which the auditor's opinion is based.

Area of activity (relating to engagements) – In relation to a key audit partner or other covered person, or a person closely associated with such a partner or covered person, any engagements for which the covered person is a directly involved covered person and any other engagements, in relation to which the engagement partner practices in the same office or business unit as the covered person.

Arm's length transaction – A transaction conducted on such terms and conditions as between a willing buyer and a willing seller who are unrelated and are acting independently of each other and pursuing their own best interests.

Assertions – Representations by management, explicit or otherwise, that are embodied in the financial statements, as used by the auditor to consider the different types of potential misstatements that may occur.

Assess – Analyze identified risks of to conclude on their significance. "Assess," by convention, is used only in relation to risk. (also see *Evaluate*)

Association – (see *Auditor association with financial information*)

Assurance – (see *Reasonable assurance*)

Assurance engagement – An engagement in which a practitioner aims to obtain sufficient appropriate audit evidence in order to express a conclusion designed to enhance the degree of confidence of the intended users other than the responsible party about the subject matter information (that is, the outcome of the measurement or evaluation of an underlying subject matter against criteria).

Reasonable assurance engagement – An assurance engagement in which the practitioner reduces engagement risk to an acceptably low level in the circumstances of the engagement as the basis for the practitioner's conclusion. The practitioner's conclusion is expressed in a form that conveys the practitioner's opinion on the outcome of the measurement or evaluation of the underlying subject matter against criteria.

Limited assurance engagement – An assurance engagement in which the practitioner reduces engagement risk to a level that is acceptable in the circumstances of the engagement, but where that risk is greater than for a reasonable assurance engagement, as the basis for expressing a conclusion in a form that conveys whether, based on the procedures performed and evidence obtained, a matter(s) has come to the practitioner's attention to cause the practitioner to believe that the subject matter information is materially misstated. The nature, timing and extent of procedures performed in a limited assurance engagement is limited compared with that necessary in a reasonable assurance engagement but is planned to obtain a level of assurance that is, in the practitioner's professional judgement, meaningful. To be meaningful, the level of assurance obtained by the practitioner is likely to enhance the intended users' confidence about the subject matter information to a degree that is clearly more than inconsequential.

Assurance engagement risk – The risk that the practitioner expresses an inappropriate conclusion when the subject matter information is materially misstated.

Audit documentation – The record of audit procedures performed, relevant audit evidence obtained, and conclusions the auditor reached (terms such as "working papers" or "workpapers" are also sometimes used).

In the UK audit documentation includes all document, information, records and other data required by ISQC (UK) 1, ISAs (UK) and applicable legal and regulatory requirements.

Audit engagement – An engagement to perform an audit in accordance with the ISAs (UK) and, where applicable, relevant legislation. It includes a statutory audit performed pursuant to the EU Audit Directive and Regulation or otherwise designated by national law as a statutory audit.

Audit evidence – Information used by the auditor in arriving at the conclusions on which the auditor's opinion is based. Audit evidence includes both information contained in the accounting records underlying the financial statements and information obtained from other sources. (See *Sufficiency of audit evidence* and *Appropriateness of audit evidence*.)

Audit file – One or more folders or other storage media, in physical or electronic form, containing the records that comprise the audit documentation for a specific engagement.

Audit firm – The sole practitioner, partnership, limited liability partnership or other corporate entity engaged in the provision of audit services. For the purpose of the FRC's Ethical Standard, audit firm includes network firms in the UK which are controlled by the audit firm or its partners.

Audit opinion – (see *Modified opinion and Unmodified opinion*)

Audit risk – The risk that the auditor expresses an inappropriate audit opinion when the financial statements are materially misstated. Audit risk is a function of the risks of material misstatement and detection risk.

Audit sampling (sampling) – The application of audit procedures to less than 100% of items within a population of audit relevance such that all sampling units have a chance of selection in order to provide the auditor with a reasonable basis on which to draw conclusions about the entire population.

Audit team – All audit professionals who, regardless of their legal relationship with the auditor or audit firm, are assigned to a particular audit engagement in order to perform the audit task (e.g. audit partner(s), audit manager(s) and audit staff).

Audited entity – The entity whose financial statements are subject to audit by the audit firm.

Auditor – "Auditor" is used to refer to the person or persons conducting the audit, usually the engagement partner[3] or other members of the engagement team, or, as applicable, the firm. Where an ISA (UK) expressly intends that a requirement or responsibility be fulfilled by the engagement partner, the term "engagement partner" rather than "auditor" is used. "Engagement partner" and "firm" are to be read as referring to their public sector equivalents where relevant.

Auditor association with financial information – An auditor is associated with financial information when the auditor attaches a report to that information or consents to the use of the auditor's name in a professional connection.

Auditor's expert – An individual or organization possessing expertise in a field other than accounting or auditing, whose work in that field is used by the auditor to assist the auditor in obtaining sufficient appropriate audit evidence. An auditor's expert may be either an auditor's internal expert (who is a partner[4] or staff, including temporary staff, of the auditor's firm or a network firm), or an auditor's external expert.

Auditor's point estimate or auditor's range – The amount, or range of amounts, respectively, derived from audit evidence for use in evaluating management's point estimate.

Auditor's range – (see *Auditor's point estimate*)

Business risk – A risk resulting from significant conditions, events, circumstances, actions or inactions that could adversely affect an entity's ability to achieve its objectives and execute its strategies, or from the setting of inappropriate objectives and strategies.

Close family – A non-dependent parent, child or sibling.

Comparative financial statements – Comparative information where amounts and other disclosures for the prior period are included for comparison with the financial statements of the current period but, if audited, are referred to in the auditor's opinion. The level of information included in those comparative financial statements is comparable with that of the financial statements of the current period.

Comparative information – The amounts and disclosures included in the financial statements in respect of one or more prior periods in accordance with the applicable financial reporting framework.

Compilation engagement – An engagement in which accounting expertise, as opposed to auditing expertise, is used to collect, classify and summarize financial information.

Complementary user entity controls – Controls that the service organization assumes, in the design of its service, will be implemented by user entities, and which, if necessary to achieve control objectives, are identified in the description of its system.

Compliance framework – (see *Applicable financial reporting framework* and *General purpose framework*)

Component – An entity or business activity for which group or component management prepares financial information that should be included in the group financial statements.

---

[3] *In the UK, this includes the key audit partner.*

[4] *"Partner" and "firm" should be read as referring to their public sector equivalents where relevant.*

Component auditor – An auditor who, at the request of the group engagement team, performs work on financial information related to a component for the group audit.

Component management – Management responsible for the preparation of the financial information of a component.

Component materiality – The materiality for a component determined by the group engagement team.

Computer-assisted audit techniques – Applications of auditing procedures using the computer as an audit tool (also known as CAATs).

Connected parties – An entity's connected parties are:

(a)   Its affiliates;

(b)   Key members of management (including but not limited to directors and those charged with governance) of the entity and its significant affiliates, individually or collectively; and

(c)   Any person or entity with an ability to influence (other than in the capacity of professional advisors), whether directly or indirectly, key members of management or those charged with governance of the entity and its significant affiliates, individually or collectively, in relation to their responsibility for or approach to any matter or judgment that is material to the entity's financial statements or other subject matter information or subject matter.

Contingent fee basis – Any arrangement made under which a fee is calculated on a predetermined basis relating to the outcome or result of a transaction, or other event, or the result of the work performed. A fee that is established by a court, competent authority or other public authority is not a contingent fee.

Differential hourly fee rates, or arrangements under which the fee payable will be negotiated after the completion of the engagement, or increased to cover additional work identified as necessary during the engagement, do not constitute contingent fee arrangements.

Control activities – Those policies and procedures that help ensure that management directives are carried out. Control activities are a component of internal control.

Control environment – Includes the governance and management functions and the attitudes, awareness and actions of those charged with governance and management concerning the entity's internal control and its importance in the entity. The control environment is a component of internal control.

Control risk – (see *Risk of material misstatement*)

Corporate governance – (see *Governance*)

Corresponding figures – Comparative information where amounts and other disclosures for the prior period are included as an integral part of the current period financial statements, and are intended to be read only in relation to the amounts and other disclosures relating to the current period (referred to as "current period figures"). The level of detail presented in the corresponding amounts and disclosures is dictated primarily by its relevance to the current period figures.

Covered person – A person in a position to influence the conduct or outcome of the engagement.

For an audit engagement and for an other public interest assurance engagement other than an investment circular reporting engagement:

(a)(i) Each member of the engagement team with responsibilities for managing the performance of the engagement (including the person(s) responsible for "day to day" direction and supervision on site at the entity, and all more senior members of the engagement team above them) and persons who provide engagement quality control review for the engagement;

(a)(ii) All other members of the engagement team;

(b) Any other natural person whose services are placed at the disposal or under the control of the firm and who is involved in the audit or other public interest assurance engagement, including for example any individual who is, or whose services are provided by, any external expert of the firm;

(c) Any person in the firm with supervisory, management or other oversight responsibility over:

   (i) The engagement or the engagement partner or other key partners involved in the engagement; or

   (ii) The conduct of audit or other public interest assurance engagements performed by the firm.

   This includes each partner, principal, shareholder and other person in the firm:

   (a) At each level of firm management, supervision or oversight relating to the audit or other public interest assurance engagement, up to and including individuals who have ultimate responsibility for the management or governance of the firm[5]; or

   (b) Who is in a position to prepare or approve the performance appraisal and/or remuneration of any individual defined in (a)(i), (b), (c)(i) and (c)(ii); and

(d) Any other person within the firm or a network firm who, due to any other circumstances, is in a position to influence the conduct or outcome of the audit or other public interest assurance engagement.

It does not include any independent non-executive individuals on a supervisory or equivalent board.

For an investment circular reporting engagement:

(a) Each member of the engagement team and persons who provide engagement quality control review for the engagement;

---

[5] *Senior or managing partner, chief executive or equivalent, and other members of the firm's management and supervisory bodies.*

(b)   Any other natural person whose services are placed at the disposal or under the control of the firm and who is directly involved in the engagement, including for example any individual who is, or whose services are provided by, any external expert of the firm; and

(c)   Any other person within the firm or a network firm, with actual knowledge of the engagement, who, due to any other circumstances, is in a position to influence the conduct or outcome of the engagement, including for example: those with actual knowledge of the engagement who are in such a position as a result of:

(i)   Their professional or personal relationships with the engagement partner or other key members of the engagement team; or

(ii)   The scope and nature of their responsibilities within the firm's network.

It does not include any independent non-executive individuals on a supervisory or equivalent board.

Criteria – The benchmarks use to measure or evaluate the underlying subject matter. The "applicable criteria" are the criteria used for the particular engagement.

Date of approval of the financial statements – The date on which all the statements that comprise the financial statements, including the related notes, have been prepared and those with the recognized authority have asserted that they have taken responsibility for those financial statements.

Date of report (in relation to quality control) – The date selected by the practitioner to date the report.

Date of the auditor's report – The date the auditor dates the report on the financial statements in accordance with ISA (UK) 700[6].

Date of the financial statements – The date of the end of the latest period covered by the financial statements.

Date the financial statements are issued – The date that the auditor's report and audited financial statements are made available to third parties.

Deficiency in internal control – This exists when:

(a)   A control is designed, implemented or operated in such a way that it is unable to prevent, or detect and correct, misstatements in the financial statements on a timely basis; or

(b)   A control necessary to prevent, or detect and correct, misstatements in the financial statements on a timely basis is missing.

Detection risk – The risk that the procedures performed by the auditor to reduce audit risk to an acceptably low level will not detect a misstatement that exists and that could be material, either individually or when aggregated with other misstatements.

Direct assistance – The use of internal auditors to perform audit procedures under the direction, supervisions and review of the external auditor.

---

[6] *ISA (UK) 700 (Revised June 2016), Forming an Opinion and Reporting on Financial Statements.*

The use of internal auditors to provide direct assistance is prohibited in an audit conducted in accordance with ISAs (UK). See paragraph 5-1 of ISA (UK) 610 (Revised June 2013), "Using the Work of Internal Auditors".

Directly involved covered person – In relation to an engagement, a covered person for the engagement that falls within the scope of paragraphs (a) or (b) of the definition of a covered person.

Emphasis of Matter paragraph – A paragraph included in the auditor's report that refers to a matter appropriately presented or disclosed in the financial statements that, in the auditor's judgment, is of such importance that it is fundamental to users' understanding of the financial statements.

Engagement – In the FRC's Ethical Standard, an audit engagement or an other public interest assurance engagement, or both where the context permits.

Engagement documentation – The record of work performed, results obtained, and conclusions the practitioner reached (terms such as "working papers" or "workpapers" are sometimes used).

Engagement letter – Written terms of an engagement in the form of a letter.

Engagement partner[7] – The partner or other person in the firm who is responsible for the engagement and its performance, and for the report that is issued on behalf of the firm, and who, where required, has the appropriate authority from a professional, legal or regulatory body.

For an audit, the engagement partner is a key audit partner.

Engagement period – For an investment circular reporting engagement, the engagement period starts when the firm accepts the investment circular reporting engagement and ends on the date of the report

Engagement quality control review – A process designed to provide an objective evaluation, on or before the date of the report, of the significant judgments the engagement team made and the conclusions it reached in formulating the report. The engagement quality control review process is for audits of financial statements of listed entities and those other engagements, if any, for which the firm has determined an engagement quality control review is required.

Engagement quality control reviewer – A partner, other person in the firm, suitably qualified external person, or a team made up of such individuals, none of whom is part of the engagement team, with sufficient and appropriate experience and authority to objectively evaluate the significant judgments the engagement team made and the conclusions it reached in formulating the report.

Engagement risk – The risk that the practitioner expresses an inappropriate conclusion when the subject matter information is materially misstated.

Engagement team – All partners and staff performing the engagement, and any individuals engaged by the firm or a network firm who perform procedures on the engagement. This excludes external experts engaged by the firm or a network firm.

For the purposes of the FRC's Ethical Standard, engagement team comprises all persons who are directly involved in the acceptance and performance of a particular audit or other public interest assurance engagement. This includes

---

[7] *"Engagement partner," "partner," and "firm" should be read as referring to their public sector equivalents where relevant.*

the audit / assurance team, professional personnel from other disciplines involved in the engagement and those who provide quality control (other than the engagement quality control reviewer) or direct oversight of the audit engagement, but it does not include any external experts contracted by the firm.

Entity in distress – An entity with actual or anticipated financial or operational difficulties that threaten the survival of that entity as a going concern.

Entity relevant to the engagement – An entity with respect to which the firm and covered persons are required to be independent. In the case of an audit engagement, the entity relevant to the engagement is the audited entity which is responsible for the audited financial statements reported on by the firm. In the case of an other public interest assurance engagement, an entity relevant to the engagement is any entity responsible for the subject matter information of the engagement (except when the responsible entity is the assurance practitioner) or the subject matter of the engagement, reported on by the firm, or (where applicable) both.

In relation to an investment circular reporting engagement, entities relevant to the engagement include the entity responsible for issuing the investment circular containing the financial information (the issuing engagement entity) and, if different, the entity on whose financial information the firm is reporting.

Entity's risk assessment process – A component of internal control that is the entity's process for identifying business risks relevant to financial reporting objectives and deciding about actions to address those risks, and the results thereof.

Error – An unintentional misstatement in financial statements, including the omission of an amount or a disclosure.

Estimation uncertainty – The susceptibility of an accounting estimate and related disclosures to an inherent lack of precision in its measurement.

Ethics Partner – The partner in the firm having responsibility for the adequacy of the firm's policies and procedures relating to integrity, objectivity and independence, their compliance with the FRC's Ethical Standard and the effectiveness of their communication to partners and staff within the firm and providing related guidance to individual partners.

Evaluate – Identify and analyze the relevant issues, including performing further procedures as necessary, to come to a specific conclusion on a matter. "Evaluation," by convention, is used only in relation to a range of matters, including evidence, the results of procedures and the effectiveness of management's response to a risk. (also see *Assess*)

Exception – A response that indicates a difference between information requested to be confirmed, or contained in the entity's records, and information provided by the confirming party.

Experienced auditor – An individual (whether internal or external to the firm) who has practical audit experience, and a reasonable understanding of:

(a)   Audit processes;

(b)   ISAs (UK) and applicable legal and regulatory requirements;

(c)   The business environment in which the entity operates; and

(d)   Auditing and financial reporting issues relevant to the entity's industry.

Expert – (see *Auditor's expert* and *Management's expert*)

Expertise – Skills, knowledge and experience in a particular field.

External confirmation – Audit evidence obtained as a direct written response to the auditor from a third party (the confirming party), in paper form, or by electronic or other medium.

Fair presentation framework – (see *Applicable financial reporting framework* and *General purpose framework*)

Financial instruments – These are defined in EU Directive 2014/65/EU, on markets in financial instruments, as:

(1)   Transferable securities;

(2)   Money-market instruments;

(3)   Units in collective investment undertakings;

(4)   Options, futures, swaps, forward rate agreements and any other derivative contracts relating to securities, currencies, interest rates or yields, emission allowances or other derivatives instruments, financial indices or financial measures which may be settled physically or in cash;

(5)   Options, futures, swaps, forwards and any other derivative contracts relating to commodities that must be settled in cash or may be settled in cash at the option of one of the parties other than by reason of default or other termination event;

(6)   Options, futures, swaps, and any other derivative contract relating to commodities that can be physically settled provided that they are traded on a regulated market, a Multilateral Trading Facility (MTF), or an Organised Trading Facility (OTF), except for wholesale energy products traded on an OTF that must be physically settled;

(7)   Options, futures, swaps, forwards and any other derivative contracts relating to commodities, that can be physically settled not otherwise mentioned in point 6 of this Section and not being for commercial purposes, which have the characteristics of other derivative financial instruments;

(8)   Derivative instruments for the transfer of credit risk;

(9)   Financial contracts for differences;

(10) Options, futures, swaps, forward rate agreements and any other derivative contracts relating to climatic variables, freight rates or inflation rates or other official economic statistics that must be settled in cash or may be settled in cash at the option of one of the parties other than by reason of default or other termination event, as well as any other derivative contracts relating to assets, rights, obligations, indices and measures not otherwise mentioned in this Section, which have the characteristics of other derivative financial instruments, having regard to whether, inter alia, they are traded on a regulated market, OTF, or an MTF;

(11) Emission allowances consisting of any units recognised for compliance with the requirements of Directive 2003/87/EC (Emissions Trading Scheme).

Financial statements – A structured representation of historical financial information, including disclosures, intended to communicate an entity's economic resources or obligations at a point in time or the changes therein for a period of time in accordance with a financial reporting framework. The term "financial statements" ordinarily refers to a complete set of financial statements as determined by the requirements of the applicable financial reporting framework, but it can also refer to a single financial statement. Disclosures comprise explanatory or descriptive information, set out as required, expressly permitted or otherwise allowed by the applicable financial reporting framework, on the face of a financial statement, or in the notes, or incorporated therein by cross reference.

Firm – A sole practitioner, partnership, limited liability partnership, or corporation or other entity of professional accountants engaged in the provision of engagements. "Firm" should be read as referring to its public sector equivalents where relevant.

In the case of an audit engagement, this includes a "statutory auditor" who is a natural person; and a legal person or any other entity, regardless of its legal form, with the appropriate approval to carry out statutory audits. For the purpose of the FRC's Ethical Standard, "firm" also includes network firms in the UK and Ireland which are controlled by the firm or its partners.

Forecast – Prospective financial information prepared on the basis of assumptions as to future events which management expects to take place and the actions management expects to take as of the date the information is prepared (best-estimate assumptions).

Fraud – An intentional act by one or more individuals among management, those charged with governance, employees, or third parties, involving the use of deception to obtain an unjust or illegal advantage.

Fraud risk factors – Events or conditions that indicate an incentive or pressure to commit fraud or provide an opportunity to commit fraud.

Fraudulent financial reporting – Involves intentional misstatements, including omissions of amounts or disclosures in financial statements, to deceive financial statement users.

Further procedures – Procedures performed in response to assessed risks of material misstatement, including tests of controls (if any), tests of details and analytical procedures.

General IT-controls – Policies and procedures that relate to many applications and support the effective functioning of application controls by helping to ensure the continued proper operation of information systems. General IT-controls commonly include controls over data center and network operations; system software acquisition, change and maintenance; access security; and application system acquisition, development, and maintenance.

General purpose financial statements – Financial statements prepared in accordance with a general purpose framework.

General purpose framework – A financial reporting framework designed to meet the common financial information needs of a wide range of users. The financial reporting framework may be a fair presentation framework or a compliance framework.

The term "fair presentation framework" is used to refer to a financial reporting framework that requires compliance with the requirements of the framework and:

(a) Acknowledges explicitly or implicitly that, to achieve fair presentation of the financial statements, it may be necessary for management to provide disclosures beyond those specifically required by the framework; or

(b)   Acknowledges explicitly that it may be necessary for management to depart from a requirement of the framework to achieve fair presentation of the financial statements. Such departures are expected to be necessary only in extremely rare circumstances.

The term "compliance framework" is used to refer to a financial reporting framework that requires compliance with the requirements of the framework, but does not contain the acknowledgements in (a) or (b) above.[8]

Governance – Describes the role of person(s) or organization(s) with responsibility for overseeing the strategic direction of the entity and obligations related to the accountability of the entity.

Group – All the components whose financial information is included in the group financial statements. A group always has more than one component.

Group audit – The audit of group financial statements.

Group audit opinion – The audit opinion on the group financial statements.

Group engagement partner – The partner or other person in the firm who is responsible for the group audit engagement and its performance, and for the auditor's report on the group financial statements that is issued on behalf of the firm. Where joint auditors conduct the group audit, the joint engagement partners and their engagement teams collectively constitute the group engagement partner and the group engagement team.

Group engagement team – Partners, including the group engagement partner, and staff who establish the overall group audit strategy, communicate with component auditors, perform work on the consolidation process, and evaluate the conclusions drawn from the audit evidence as the basis for forming an opinion on the group financial statements.

Group financial statements – Financial statements that include the financial information of more than one component. The term "group financial statements" also refers to combined financial statements aggregating the financial information prepared by components that have no parent but are under common control.

Group management – Management responsible for the preparation of the group financial statements.

Group-wide controls – Controls designed, implemented and maintained by group management over group financial reporting.

Historical financial information – Information expressed in financial terms in relation to a particular entity, derived primarily from that entity's accounting system, about economic events occurring in past time periods or about economic conditions or circumstances at points in time in the past.

Immediate family – A spouse (or equivalent) or dependent.

Independence–

Freedom from conditions and relationships which, in the context of an engagement, would compromise the integrity or objectivity of the firm or covered persons.

Integrity or objectivity (and therefore independence) would be compromised if it is probable (more likely than not) that an objective,

---

[8]   *ISA (UK) 200 (Revised June 2016), Overall Objectives of the Independent Auditor and the Conduct of an Audit in Accordance with International Standards on Auditing (UK), paragraph 13(a).*

> reasonable and informed third party would conclude that the threats,
> arising from any conditions or relationships that exist (taking into
> account any conflicts of interest that they may cause, or generally be
> perceived to cause, or otherwise, and having regard to any safeguards
> implemented), would impair integrity or objectivity to such an extent that
> it would be inappropriate for the firm to accept or continue to perform
> the audit or other public interest assurance engagement unless the
> threats were eliminated or further reduced or unless more, or more
> effective, safeguards were implemented.

Information system relevant to financial reporting – A component of internal control that includes the financial reporting system, and consists of the procedures and records established to initiate, record, process and report entity transactions (as well as events and conditions) and to maintain accountability for the related assets, liabilities and equity.

Informed management – Member of management (or senior employee) of the entity relevant to the engagement who has the authority and capability to make independent management judgments and decisions in relation to non-audit / additional services on the basis of information provided by the firm.

Inherent risk – (see *Risk of material misstatement*)

Initial audit engagement – An engagement in which either:

(a)   The financial statements for the prior period were not audited; or

(b)   The financial statements for the prior period were audited by a predecessor auditor.

Inquiry – Inquiry consists of seeking information of knowledgeable persons, both financial and non-financial, within the entity or outside the entity.

Inspection (as an audit procedure) – Examining records or documents, whether internal or external, in paper form, electronic form, or other media, or a physical examination of an asset.

Inspection (in relation to quality control) – In relation to completed engagements, procedures designed to provide evidence of compliance by engagement teams with the firm's quality control policies and procedures.

Integrity – Being trustworthy, straightforward, honest, fair and candid; complying with the spirit as well as the letter of applicable ethical principles, laws and regulations; behaving so as to maintain the public's trust in the auditing profession; and respecting confidentiality except where disclosure is in the public interest or is required to adhere to legal and professional responsibilities.

Interim financial information or statements – Financial information (which may be less than a complete set of financial statements as defined above) issued at interim dates (usually half-yearly or quarterly) in respect of a financial period.

Internal audit function – A function of an entity that performs assurance and consulting activities designed to evaluate and improve the effectiveness of the entity's governance, risk management and internal control processes.

Internal auditors – Those individuals who perform the activities of the internal audit function. Internal auditors may belong to an internal audit department or equivalent function.

Internal control – The process designed, implemented and maintained by those charged with governance, management and other personnel to provide reasonable assurance about the achievement of an entity's objectives with regard to reliability of financial reporting, effectiveness and efficiency of operations, and compliance with applicable laws and regulations. The term "controls" refers to any aspects of one or more of the components of internal control.

International Financial Reporting Standards – The International Financial Reporting Standards issued by the International Accounting Standards Board.

Investigate – Inquire into matters arising from other procedures to resolve them.

Investment circular – An investment circular is a document issued by an entity pursuant to statutory or regulatory requirements relating to securities on which it is intended that a third party should make an investment decision, including a prospectus, listing particulars, a circular to shareholders or similar document.

Investment circular reporting engagement – Any public or private reporting engagement in connection with an investment circular where the engagement is undertaken in accordance with Standards for Investment Reporting (SIRs).

IT environment – The policies and procedures that the entity implements and the IT infrastructure (hardware, operating systems, etc.) and application software that it uses to support business operations and achieve business strategies.

Key audit matters – Those matters that, in the auditor's professional judgment, were of most significance in the audit of the financial statements of the current period. Key audit matters are selected from matters communicated with those charged with governance.

Key audit partner–

(i)   The statutory auditor designated by an audit firm for a particular audit engagement as being primarily responsible for carrying out the statutory audit on behalf of the audit firm; or

(ii)   In the case of a group audit, the statutory auditor designated by an audit firm as being primarily responsible for carrying out the statutory audit at the level of the group and the statutory auditor designated at the level of material subsidiaries; or

(iii)   The statutory auditor who signs the audit report.

Key management position – Any position at an entity relevant to an engagement which involves the responsibility for fundamental management decisions at the entity (e.g. as a CEO or CFO), including an ability to influence the accounting policies and the preparation of the financial statements of the entity. A key management position also arises where there are contractual and factual arrangements which in substance allow an individual to participate in exercising such a management function in a different way (e.g. via a consulting contract).

Key partner involved in the engagement – A partner, or other person in the engagement team (other than the engagement partner or engagement quality control reviewer) who either:

● Is involved at the group level and is responsible for key aspects of the engagement, including decisions or judgments on significant matters or risk factors that relate to the engagement for that entity, or

● Is primarily responsible for the engagement work in respect of a significant affiliate, division or function of the entity.

Limited assurance engagement – (see *Assurance engagement*)

Listed entity – An entity whose shares, stock or debt are quoted or listed on a recognized stock exchange, or are marketed under the regulations of a recognized stock exchange or other equivalent body.

This includes any company in which the public can trade shares, stock or debt on the open market, such as those listed on the London Stock Exchange (including those admitted to trading on the Alternative Investment Market), and ISDX Markets. It does not include entities whose quoted or listed shares, stock or debt are in substance not freely transferable or cannot be traded freely by the public or the entity.

Management – The person(s) with executive responsibility for the conduct of the entity's operations. For some entities in some jurisdictions, management includes some or all of those charged with governance, for example, executive members of a governance board, or an owner-manager.

In the UK, management will not normally include non-executive directors.

Management bias – A lack of neutrality by management in the preparation of information.

Management's expert – An individual or organization possessing expertise in a field other than accounting or auditing, whose work in that field is used by the entity to assist the entity in preparing the financial statements.

Management's point estimate – The amount selected by management for recognition or disclosure in the financial statements as an accounting estimate.

Misappropriation of assets – Involves the theft of an entity's assets and is often perpetrated by employees in relatively small and immaterial amounts. However, it can also involve management who are usually more capable of disguising or concealing misappropriations in ways that are difficult to detect.

Misstatement – A difference between the reported amount, classification, presentation, or disclosure of a financial statement item and the amount, classification, presentation, or disclosure that is required for the item to be in accordance with the applicable financial reporting framework. Misstatements can arise from error or fraud. Where the auditor expresses an opinion on whether the financial statements are presented fairly, in all material respects, or give a true and fair view, misstatements also include those adjustments of amounts, classifications, presentation, or disclosures that, in the auditor's judgment, are necessary for the financial statements to be presented fairly, in all material respects, or to give a true and fair view.

Misstatement of the other information – A misstatement of the other information exists when the other information is incorrectly stated or otherwise misleading (including because it omits or obscures information necessary for a proper understanding of a matter disclosed in the other information).

In the UK, a misstatement of the other information also exists when the statutory other information has not been prepared in accordance with the legal and regulatory requirements applicable to the statutory other information.

Modified opinion – A qualified opinion, an adverse opinion or a disclaimer of opinion.

Monitoring (in relation to quality control) – A process comprising an ongoing consideration and evaluation of the firm's system of quality control, including a periodic inspection of a selection of completed engagements, designed to provide the firm with reasonable assurance that its system of quality control is operating effectively.

Monitoring of controls – A process to assess the effectiveness of internal control performance over time. It includes assessing the design and operation of controls on a timely basis and taking necessary corrective actions modified for changes in conditions. Monitoring of controls is a component of internal control.

Negative confirmation request – A request that the confirming party respond directly to the auditor only if the confirming party disagrees with the information provided in the request.

Network – A larger structure:

(a)   That is aimed at cooperation, and

(b)   That is clearly aimed at profit or cost-sharing or shares common ownership, control or management, common quality control policies and procedures, common business strategy, the use of a common brand name, or a significant part of professional resources.

Network firm – A firm or entity that belongs to a network.

A network firm is any entity which is part of a larger structure that is aimed at co-operation and which is:

(i)   Controlled by the firm; or

(ii)   Under common control, ownership or management; or

(iii) Part of a larger structure that is clearly aimed at profit or cost sharing; or

(iv)   Otherwise affiliated or associated with the audit firm through common quality control policies and procedures, common business strategy, the use of a common name or through the sharing of significant common professional resources.

Non-audit services – Any engagement in which an audit firm provides professional services to an audited entity, its affiliates or another entity where the subject matter of the engagement includes the audited entity and/ or its significant affiliates other than the audit of financial statements of the audited entity.

Non-compliance (in the context of ISA (UK) 250[9]) – Acts of omission or commission by the entity, either intentional or unintentional, which are contrary to the prevailing laws or regulations. Such acts include transactions entered into by, or in the name of, the entity, or on its behalf, by those charged with governance, management or employees. Noncompliance does not include personal misconduct (unrelated to the business activities of the entity) by those charged with governance, management or employees of the entity.

Non-response – A failure of the confirming party to respond, or fully respond, to a positive confirmation request, or a confirmation request returned undelivered.

Non-sampling risk – The risk that the auditor reaches an erroneous conclusion for any reason not related to sampling risk.

Objectivity – Acting and making decisions and judgments impartially, fairly and on merit (having regard to all considerations relevant to the task in hand but no other), without discrimination, bias, or compromise because of commercial or personal self-interest, conflicts of interest or the undue influence of others, and having given due consideration to the best available evidence.

The need for objectivity in performing the engagement arises from, among other things, the fact that many of the important issues involved in the performance of the engagement, including those arising in the preparation of the subject matter information, do not relate to questions of fact but rather to questions of judgment. For example, with regard to financial statements, there are choices to be made by the board of directors in deciding on the accounting policies to be adopted by the entity: the directors have to select the ones that they consider most appropriate and this decision can have a material impact on the financial statements. Furthermore, many items included in the financial statements cannot be measured with absolute precision and certainty. In many cases, estimates have to be made and the directors may have to choose one value from a range of possible outcomes. When exercising discretion in these areas, the directors have regard to the applicable financial reporting framework.

Observation – Consists of looking at a process or procedure being performed by others, for example, the auditor's observation of inventory counting by the entity's personnel, or of the performance of control activities.

Opening balances – Those account balances that exist at the beginning of the period. Opening balances are based upon the closing balances of the prior period and reflect the effects of transactions and events of prior periods and accounting policies applied in the prior period. Opening balances also include matters requiring disclosure that existed at the beginning of the period, such as contingencies and commitments.

Other information – Financial and non-financial information (other than the financial statements and the auditor's report thereon) included in an entity's annual report.

---

[9] *ISA (UK) 250 (Revised December 2017) Section A – Consideration of Laws and Regulations in an Audit of Financial Statements, and ISA (UK) 250 (Revised June 2016), Section B – The Auditor's Statutory Right and Duty to Report to Regulators of Public Interest Entities and Regulators of Other Entities in the Financial Sector.*

Other Matter paragraph – A paragraph included in the auditor's report that refers to a matter other than those presented or disclosed in the financial statements that, in the auditor's judgment, is relevant to users' understanding of the audit, the auditor's responsibilities or the auditor's report.

Outcome of an accounting estimate – The actual monetary amount which results from the resolution of the underlying transaction(s), event(s) or condition(s) addressed by the accounting estimate.

Overall audit strategy – Sets the scope, timing and direction of the audit, and guides the development of the more detailed audit plan.

Partner – Any individual with authority to bind the firm with respect to the performance of a professional services engagement.

Performance materiality – The amount or amounts set by the auditor at less than materiality for the financial statements as a whole to reduce to an appropriately low level the probability that the aggregate of uncorrected and undetected misstatements exceeds materiality for the financial statements as a whole. If applicable, performance materiality also refers to the amount or amounts set by the auditor at less than the materiality level or levels for particular classes of transactions, account balances or disclosures.

Personnel – Partners and staff.

Persons closely associated[10] – A "person closely associated" is:

(a)   A spouse, or a partner considered to be equivalent to a spouse in accordance with national law;

(b)   A dependent child, in accordance with national law;

(c)   A relative who (at any time in the period from the start of the financial period in respect of which the engagement is being conducted to the date on which the engagement report is signed) has lived in the same household as the person with whom they are associated for at least one year;

(d)   A firm whose managerial responsibilities are discharged by, or which is directly or indirectly controlled by, the firm / person with whom they are associated, or by any person mentioned in (a), (b) or (c) or in which the *firm* or any such person has a beneficial or other substantially equivalent economic interest;

(e)   A trust whose managerial responsibilities are discharged by, or which is directly or indirectly controlled by, or which is set up for the benefit of, or whose economic interests are substantially equivalent to, the firm / person with whom they are associated or any person mentioned in (a), (b) or (c).

Pervasive – A term used, in the context of misstatements, to describe the effects on the financial statements of misstatements or the possible effects on the financial statements of misstatements, if any, that are undetected due to an inability to obtain sufficient appropriate audit evidence. Pervasive effects on the financial statements are those that, in the auditor's judgment:

---

[10] *This definition covers that required by the EU Audit Directive, and persons identified in paragraphs 5(i)(a) and 5(2)(b)(c) and (d) of paragraph 5 of Schedule 1 of SI 2016/649, "The Statutory Auditors and Third Country Auditors Regulations 2016". The EU Audit Directive defines a "person closely associated" as within the meaning in Commission Directive 2004/72/EC. However, Regulation 596/2014 on market abuse (market abuse regulation) repeals and replaces, inter alia, Commission Directive 2004/72/EC with effect from 3 July 2016.*

(a) Are not confined to specific elements, accounts or items of the financial statements;

(b) If so confined, represent or could represent a substantial proportion of the financial statements; or

(c) In relation to disclosures, are fundamental to users' understanding of the financial statements.

Population – The entire set of data from which a sample is selected and about which the auditor wishes to draw conclusions.

Positive confirmation request – A request that the confirming party respond directly to the auditor indicating whether the confirming party agrees or disagrees with the information in the request, or providing the requested information.

Practitioner – A professional accountant in public practice.

Preconditions for an audit – The use by management of an acceptable financial reporting framework in the preparation of the financial statements and the agreement of management and, where appropriate, those charged with governance to the premise[11] on which an audit is conducted.

Predecessor auditor – The auditor from a different audit firm, who audited the financial statements of an entity in the prior period and who has been replaced by the current auditor.

Premise, relating to the responsibilities of management and, where appropriate, those charged with governance, on which an audit is conducted – That management and, where appropriate, those charged with governance have acknowledged and understand that they have the following responsibilities that are fundamental to the conduct of an audit in accordance with ISAs (UK). That is, responsibility:

(a) For the preparation of the financial statements in accordance with the applicable financial reporting framework, including where relevant their fair presentation;

(b) For such internal control as management and, where appropriate, those charged with governance determine is necessary to enable the preparation of financial statements that are free from material misstatement, whether due to fraud or error; and

(c) To provide the auditor with:

(i) Access to all information of which management and, where appropriate, those charged with governance are aware that is relevant to the preparation of the financial statements such as records, documentation and other matters;

(ii) Additional information that the auditor may request from management and, where appropriate, those charged with governance for the purpose of the audit; and

(iii) Unrestricted access to persons within the entity from whom the auditor determines it necessary to obtain audit evidence.

---

[11] *ISA (UK) 200 (Revised June 2016), paragraph 13.*

In the case of a fair presentation framework, (a) above may be restated as "for the preparation and fair presentation of the financial statements in accordance with the financial reporting framework," or "for the preparation of financial statements that give a true and fair view in accordance with the financial reporting framework."

The "premise, relating to the responsibilities of management and, where appropriate, those charged with governance, on which an audit is conducted" may also be referred to as the "premise."

Private reporting engagement – An engagement, in connection with an investment circular, in which a reporting accountant does not express a conclusion that is published in an investment circular.

Professional accountant–

For the purpose of the ISAs (UK) and the FRC's Ethical Standard, *Professional accountants* are those persons who are members of a professional accountancy body, whether in public practice (including a sole practitioner, partnership or corporate body), industry, commerce, the public sector or education.

Professional accountant in public practice – A professional accountant, irrespective of functional classification (for example, audit, tax or consulting) in a firm that provides professional services. This term is also used to refer to a firm of professional accountants in public practice.

Professional judgment – The application of relevant training, knowledge and experience, within the context provided by auditing, accounting and ethical standards, in making informed decisions about the courses of action that are appropriate in the circumstances of the audit engagement.

Professional skepticism – An attitude that includes a questioning mind, being alert to conditions which may indicate possible misstatement due to error or fraud, and a critical assessment of evidence.

Professional standards – International Standards on Auditing (ISAs) (UK) and relevant ethical requirements.

In the UK, professional standards in the context of ISQC (UK) 1 (Revised June 2016)[12] are the Ethical and Engagement Standards described in the Statement "The Financial Reporting Council – Scope and Authority of Audit and Assurance Pronouncements."

Projection – Prospective financial information prepared on the basis of:

(a)   Hypothetical assumptions about future events and management actions which are not necessarily expected to take place, such as when some entities are in a startup phase or are considering a major change in the nature of operations; or

(b)   A mixture of best-estimate and hypothetical assumptions.

Prospective financial information – Financial information based on assumptions about events that may occur in the future and possible actions by an entity. Prospective financial information can be in the form of a forecast, a projection or a combination of both. (see *Forecast* and *Projection*)

---

[12] *ISQC (UK) 1 (Revised June 2016), Quality Control for Firms that Perform Audits and Reviews of Financial Statements, and Other Assurance and Related Services Engagements.*

Public interest assurance engagement – Audits of financial statements[13] undertaken in compliance with International Standards on Auditing (ISAs) (UK) and other engagements undertaken in compliance with performance standards issued by the FRC which, as of June 2016, comprise:

(a) Reporting accountants acting in connection with an investment circular (the Standards for Investment Reporting – "SIRs");

(b) Review of interim financial information by the independent auditor of the entity (International Standard on Review Engagements (UK and Ireland) 2410); and

(c) Engagements to provide assurance on client assets to the Financial Conduct Authority (the CASS Standard).

Public interest entity – These are:

(a) An issuer whose transferable securities are admitted to trading on a regulated market[14];

(b) A credit institution within the meaning of Article 4(1)(1) of Regulation (EU) No 575/2013 of the European Parliament and of the Council[15], other than those listed in Article 2 of Directive 2013/36/EU of the European Parliament and of the Council on access to the activity of credit institutions and investment firms;

(c) An insurance undertaking within the meaning given by Article 2(1) of Council Directive 1991/674/EEC of the European Parliament and of the Council on the annual accounts and consolidated accounts of insurance undertaking.

No other entities have been specifically designated in law in the UK as "public interest entities".

Public reporting engagement – An engagement in which a reporting accountant expresses a conclusion that is published in an investment circular and which is designed to enhance the degree of confidence of the intended users of the report about the "outcome" of the directors' evaluation or measurement of "subject matter" (usually financial information) against suitable criteria.

Public sector – National governments, regional (for example, state, provincial, territorial) governments, local (for example, city, town) governments and related governmental entities (for example, agencies, boards, commissions and enterprises).

Reasonable assurance (in the context of assurance engagements and in quality control) – A high, but not absolute, level of assurance.

Reasonable assurance engagement – (see *Assurance engagement*)

---

[13] *In the public sector the statutory scope of an audit can extend beyond the entity's financial statements to include reporting on an entity's arrangements for the proper conduct of its financial affairs, management of its performance or use of its resources.*

[14] *"issuer" and "regulated market" have the same meaning as in Part 6 of Financial Services and Markets Act 2000. "Transferable securities" means anything which is a transferable security for the purposes of Directive 2004/39/EC of the European Parliament and of the Council on markets in financial instruments.*

[15] *Regulation (EU) 575/2013 of the European Parliament and of the Council of 26 June 2013 on prudential requirements for credit institutions and investment firms and amending Regulation (EU) No 648/2012.*

Recalculation – Consists of checking the mathematical accuracy of documents or records.

Related party – A party that is either:

(a)   A related party as defined in the applicable financial reporting framework; or

(b)   Where the applicable financial reporting framework establishes minimal or no related party requirements:

    (i)   A person or other entity that has control or significant influence, directly or indirectly through one or more intermediaries, over the reporting entity;

    (ii)   Another entity over which the reporting entity has control or significant influence, directly or indirectly through one or more intermediaries; or

    (iii)   Another entity that is under common control with the reporting entity through having:

        (a)   Common controlling ownership;
        (b)   Owners who are close family members; or
        (c)   Common key management.

    However, entities that are under common control by a state (that is, a national, regional or local government) are not considered related unless they engage in significant transactions or share resources to a significant extent with one another.

In the UK relevant definitions of "related party" are set out in the applicable financial reporting frameworks (for example, the definitions in International Accounting Standard 24, *Related Party Disclosures*, or FRS 102, *The Financial Reporting Standard applicable in the UK and the Republic of Ireland*).

Related services – Comprise agreed-upon procedures and compilations.

Relevant ethical requirements–

In the UK the firm and its personnel are subject to ethical requirements from two sources: the FRC's Ethical Standard concerning the integrity, objectivity and independence of the firm and its personnel, and the ethical established by the auditor or assurance practitioner's relevant professional.

Relevant period – The engagement period and any additional period before the engagement period but subsequent to the balance sheet date of the most recent audited financial statements of the engagement client.

Reperformance – The auditor's independent execution of procedures or controls that were originally performed as part of the entity's internal controls.

Report on the description and design of controls at a service organization (referred to in ISA (UK) 402[16] as a type 1 report) – A report that comprises:

(a)   A description, prepared by management of the service organization, of the service organization's system, control objectives and related controls that have been designed and implemented as at a specified date; and

---

[16] ISA (UK) 402, *Audit Considerations Relating to an Entity Using a Service Organization.*

(b) A report by the service auditor with the objective of conveying reasonable assurance that includes the service auditor's opinion on the description of the service organization's system, control objectives and related controls and the suitability of the design of the controls to achieve the specified control objectives.

Report on the description, design, and operating effectiveness of controls at a service organization (referred to in ISA (UK) 402 as a type 2 report) – A report that comprises:

(a) A description, prepared by management of the service organization, of the service organization's system, control objectives and related controls, their design and implementation as at a specified date or throughout a specified period and, in some cases, their operating effectiveness throughout a specified period; and

(b) A report by the service auditor with the objective of conveying reasonable assurance that includes:

　　(i) The service auditor's opinion on the description of the service organization's system, control objectives and related controls, the suitability of the design of the controls to achieve the specified control objectives, and the operating effectiveness of the controls; and

　　(ii) A description of the service auditor's tests of the controls and the results thereof.

Reporting accountant – An accountant engaged to prepare a report for inclusion in, or in connection with, an investment circular. The reporting accountant may or may not be the auditor of the entity issuing the investment circular. The term "reporting accountant" is used to describe either the engagement partner or the engagement partner's firm[17]. The reporting accountant could be a limited company or a principal employed by the company.

Review (in relation to quality control) – Appraising the quality of the work performed and conclusions reached by others.

Review engagement – The objective of a review engagement is to enable an auditor to state whether, on the basis of procedures which do not provide all the evidence that would be required in an audit, anything has come to the auditor's attention that causes the auditor to believe that the financial statements are not prepared, in all material respects, in accordance with an applicable financial reporting framework.

Review procedures – The procedures deemed necessary to meet the objective of a review engagement, primarily inquiries of entity personnel and analytical procedures applied to financial data.

Risk assessment procedures – The audit procedures performed to obtain an understanding of the entity and its environment, including the entity's internal control, to identify and assess the risks of material misstatement, whether due to fraud or error, at the financial statement and assertion levels.

---

[17] *Where the term applies to the engagement partner, it describes the responsibilities or obligations of the engagement partner. Such obligations or responsibilities may be fulfilled by either the engagement partner or another member of the engagement team.*

Risk of material misstatement – The risk that the financial statements are materially misstated prior to audit. This consists of two components, described as follows at the assertion level:

(a)   Inherent risk – The susceptibility of an assertion about a class of transaction, account balance or disclosure to a misstatement that could be material, either individually or when aggregated with other misstatements, before consideration of any related controls.

(b)   Control risk – The risk that a misstatement that could occur in an assertion about a class of transaction, account balance or disclosure and that could be material, either individually or when aggregated with other misstatements, will not be prevented, or detected and corrected, on a timely basis by the entity's internal control.

Sampling – (see *Audit sampling*)

Sampling risk – The risk that the auditor's conclusion based on a sample may be different from the conclusion if the entire population were subjected to the same audit procedure. Sampling risk can lead to two types of erroneous conclusions:

(a)   In the case of a test of controls, that controls are more effective than they actually are, or in the case of a test of details, that a material misstatement does not exist when in fact it does. The auditor is primarily concerned with this type of erroneous conclusion because it affects audit effectiveness and is more likely to lead to an inappropriate audit opinion.

(b)   In the case of a test of controls, that controls are less effective than they actually are, or in the case of a test of details, that a material misstatement exists when in fact it does not. This type of erroneous conclusion affects audit efficiency as it would usually lead to additional work to establish that initial conclusions were incorrect.

Sampling unit – The individual items constituting a population.

Scope of a review – The review procedures deemed necessary in the circumstances to achieve the objective of the review.

Service auditor – An auditor who, at the request of the service organization, provides an assurance report on the controls of a service organization.

Service organization – A third-party organization (or segment of a third-party organization) that provides services to user entities that are part of those entities' information systems relevant to financial reporting.

Service organization's system – The policies and procedures designed, implemented and maintained by the service organization to provide user entities with the services covered by the service auditor's report.

Significance – The relative importance of a matter, taken in context. The significance of a matter is judged by the practitioner in the context in which it is being considered. This might include, for example, the reasonable prospect of its changing or influencing the decisions of intended users of the practitioner's report; or, as another example, where the context is a judgment about whether to report a matter to those charged with governance, whether the matter would be regarded as important by them in relation to their duties. Significance can be considered in the context of quantitative and qualitative factors, such as relative magnitude, the nature and effect on the subject matter and the expressed interests of intended users or recipients.

Significant affiliate – An affiliate identified by the group engagement team:

(i)   That is of individual financial significance to the group, or

(ii)   That, due to its specific nature or circumstances, is likely to include significant risks of material misstatement of the group financial statements.

Significant component – A component identified by the group engagement team (i) that is of individual financial significance to the group, or (ii) that, due to its specific nature or circumstances, is likely to include significant risks of material misstatement of the group financial statements.

Significant deficiency in internal control – A deficiency or combination of deficiencies in internal control that, in the auditor's professional judgment, is of sufficient importance to merit the attention of those charged with governance.

Significant risk – An identified and assessed risk of material misstatement that, in the auditor's judgment, requires special audit consideration.

Smaller entity – An entity which typically possesses qualitative characteristics such as:

(a)   Concentration of ownership and management in a small number of individuals (often a single individual – either a natural person or another enterprise that owns the entity provided the owner exhibits the relevant qualitative characteristics); and

(b)   One or more of the following:

(i)   Straightforward or uncomplicated transactions;

(ii)   Simple record-keeping;

(iii)   Few lines of business and few products within business lines;

(iv)   Few internal controls;

(v)   Few levels of management with responsibility for a broad range of controls; or

(vi)   Few personnel, many having a wide range of duties.

These qualitative characteristics are not exhaustive, they are not exclusive to smaller entities, and smaller entities do not necessarily display all of these characteristics.

In the UK, company law provides a lighter reporting regime for companies that are defined, by legislation, as small. A company qualifies as "small" if it meets particular thresholds in respect of turnover, balance sheet total/gross assets and number of employees and certain other criteria. The thresholds and other criteria are subject to change and reference to the relevant legislation should be made to determine what they are in respect of a particular accounting period.

For the purpose of the FRC's Ethical Standard, a small entity is defined in Section 6 of Part B of that standard.

SME listed entity–

(a)   An entity whose equity financial instruments had an average market capitalisation of less than €200m on the basis of year end quotes for the previous three calendar years; or

(b)   An entity that issues exclusively non-equity financial instruments if:

    (i)   The total nominal amount of the non-equity financial instruments issued and outstanding does not exceed €200m; or

    (ii)   According to the last annual or consolidated accounts, meets at least two of the following criteria:

- An average number of employee during the financial year of less than 250;
- A total balance sheet not exceeding €43m;
- An annual net turnover not exceeding €50m.

An entity whose equity financial instruments have been admitted to trading for less than three years shall be deemed an SME if its market capitalisation is below €200m based on:

(a)   The closing share price of the first day of trading, if its shares have been admitted to trading for less than one year;

(b)   The last closing share price of the first year of trading, if its financial instruments have been admitted to trading for more than one year but less than two years; or

(c)   The average of the last closing share prices of each of the first two years of trading, if its financial instruments have been admitted to trading for more than two years but less than three years.

Special purpose financial statements – Financial statements prepared in accordance with a special purpose framework.

Special purpose framework – A financial reporting framework designed to meet the financial information needs of specific users. The financial reporting framework may be a fair presentation framework or a compliance framework.[18]

Staff – Professionals, other than partners, including any experts the firm employs.

For the FRC's Ethical Standard, "staff" are the firm's, managers, auditors, employees and any other natural persons whose services are placed at the disposal or under the control of the firm.

Statistical sampling – An approach to sampling that has the following characteristics:

(a)   Random selection of the sample items; and

(b)   The use of probability theory to evaluate sample results, including measurement of sampling risk.

A sampling approach that does not have characteristics (a) and (b) is considered non-statistical sampling.

Statutory audit – An audit performed pursuant to the EU Audit Directive and Regulation or otherwise designated by national law as a statutory audit.

Statutory auditor[19] – A natural person with the appropriate approval to carry out statutory audits.

---

[18] *ISA (UK) 200 (Revised June 2016), paragraph 13(a).*

[19] *In the EU Audit Directive and Regulation the term "statutory auditor" is used in the context of a natural person. In the UK Companies Act 2006, the term "statutory auditor" is used for both natural and legal persons.*

Statutory other information – For statutory audits of financial statements, Those documents or reports that are required to be prepared and issued by the entity (including any reports or documents that are incorporated by cross reference) in relation to which the auditor is required to report publicly in accordance with law or regulation.

In the UK, the statutory other information includes, where required to be prepared:

(i)   The directors' report;

(ii)   The strategic report;

(iii)   The separate corporate governance statement.[20]

Stratification – The process of dividing a population into sub-populations, each of which is a group of sampling units which have similar characteristics (often monetary value).

Subject matter – The underlying object of the engagement, the outcome of the evaluation or measurement of which against the criteria comprises the subject matter information.

> *Subject matter varies widely in assurance engagements but in public interest assurance engagements is often one or more financial or non-financial aspects of an entity of interest to the intended users of the assurance report. The entity responsible for the subject matter is therefore usually the entity whose underlying subject matter is being addressed in such engagements. In some engagements, there can be more than one entity responsible for the subject matter.*

Subject matter information – The outcome of the evaluation or measurement of the subject matter against the criteria,

> *The entity responsible for the subject matter information is therefore the entity responsible for the measurement or evaluation of the subject matter against the criteria. In many attestation assurance engagements, this is the same as the entity responsible for the subject matter (as is also the case in an audit engagement). However, there may be a separate evaluator or measurer of the subject matter. In direct assurance engagements (such as the CASS audit[21]), the evaluation or measurement is performed by the assurance practitioner. When the entity responsible for the subject matter information is the assurance practitioner, it is not an entity relevant to the engagement. In some engagements, there can be more than one entity responsible for the subject matter information.*

Subsequent events – Events occurring between the date of the financial statements and the date of the auditor's report, and facts that become known to the auditor after the date of the auditor's report.

---

[20] *When the required information is not included within or incorporated by cross reference to the directors' report.*

[21] *Engagements to provide assurance on client assets to the Financial Conduct Authority.*

Subservice organization – A service organization used by another service organization to perform some of the services provided to user entities that are part of those user entities' information systems relevant to financial reporting.

Substantive procedure – An audit procedure designed to detect material misstatements at the assertion level. Substantive procedures comprise:

(a)   Tests of details (of classes of transactions, account balances, and disclosures); and

(b)   Substantive analytical procedures.

Sufficiency (of audit evidence) – The measure of the quantity of audit evidence. The quantity of the audit evidence needed is affected by the auditor's assessment of the risks of material misstatement and also by the quality of such audit evidence.

Suitably qualified external person – An individual outside the firm with the competence and capabilities to act as an engagement partner, for example a partner of another firm, or an employee (with appropriate experience) of either a professional accountancy body whose members may perform audits and reviews of historical financial information, or other Suitably qualified external person – An individual outside the firm with the competence and capabilities to act as an engagement partner, for example a partner of another firm, or an employee (with appropriate experience) of either a professional accountancy body whose members may perform audits and reviews of historical financial information, or other

Supplementary information – Information that is presented together with the financial statements that is not required by the applicable financial reporting framework used to prepare the financial statements, normally presented in either supplementary schedules or as additional notes.

Test – The application of procedures to some or all items in a population.

Tests of controls – An audit procedure designed to evaluate the operating effectiveness of controls in preventing, or detecting and correcting, material misstatements at the assertion level.

Those charged with governance – The person(s) or organization(s) (e.g., a corporate trustee) with responsibility for overseeing the strategic direction of the entity and obligations related to the accountability of the entity. This includes overseeing the financial reporting process. For some entities in some jurisdictions, those charged with governance may include management personnel, for example, executive members of a governance board of a private or public sector entity, or an owner-manager.[22]

In the UK, those charged with governance include the directors (executive and non-executive) of a company and the members of an audit committee where one exists. For other types of entity it usually includes equivalent persons such as the partners, proprietors, committee of management or trustees.

Tolerable misstatement – A monetary amount set by the auditor in respect of which the auditor seeks to obtain an appropriate level of assurance that the monetary amount set by the auditor is not exceeded by the actual misstatement in the population.

---

[22] *For discussion of the diversity of governance structures, see paragraphs A1–A8 of ISA (UK) 260 (Revised June 2016), Communication with Those Charged with Governance.*

Tolerable rate of deviation – A rate of deviation from prescribed internal control procedures set by the auditor in respect of which the auditor seeks to obtain an appropriate level of assurance that the rate of deviation set by the auditor is not exceeded by the actual rate of deviation in the population.

Uncertainty – A matter whose outcome depends on future actions or events not under the direct control of the entity but that may affect the financial statements.

Uncorrected misstatements – Misstatements that the auditor has accumulated during the audit and that have not been corrected.

Unmodified opinion – The opinion expressed by the auditor when the auditor concludes that the financial statements are prepared, in all material respects, in accordance with the applicable financial reporting framework.

User auditor – An auditor who audits and reports on the financial statements of a user entity.

User entity – An entity that uses a service organization and whose financial statements are being audited.

Walk-through test – Involves tracing a few transactions through the financial reporting system.

Written representation – A written statement by management provided to the auditor to confirm certain matters or to support other audit evidence. Written representations in this context do not include financial statements, the assertions therein, or supporting books and records.

Part Five

Practice Notes

SORP: Practice Note 10: Audit of financial statements of public sector bodies in the United Kingdom

(November 2016)

Contents

Paragraphs

Statement of Recommended Practice – Practice Note 10: Audit of financial statements of public sector bodies in the United Kingdom
Preface
Introduction   1 - 7

Part 1: Application of International Standards on Auditing (UK)   1 - 2
International Standard on Quality Control (UK) 1   3 - 24
ISA (UK) 200: Overall objective of the independent auditor and the conduct of an
audit in accordance with International Standards on Auditing (UK)   25 - 28
ISA (UK) 210: Agreeing the terms of audit engagements   29 - 38
ISA (UK) 220: Quality control for an audit of financial statements   39 - 42
ISA (UK) 240: The auditor's responsibilities relating to fraud in an audit of financial
statements   43 - 51
ISA (UK) 250A – Consideration of laws and regulations in an audit of
financial statements   52 - 60
ISA (UK) 260: Communication with those charged with governance   61 - 71
ISA (UK) 265: Communicating deficiencies in internal control to those charged with
governance and management   72 - 73
ISA (UK) 315: Identifying and assessing the risks of material misstatement through
understanding the entity and its environment   74 - 82
ISA (UK) 320: Materiality in planning and performing an audit   83 - 87
ISA (UK) 330: The auditor's responses to assessed risks   88 - 89
ISA (UK) 402: Audit considerations relating to an entity using a service organisation   90 - 96
ISA (UK) 450: Evaluation of misstatements identified during the audit   97 - 99
ISA (UK) 510: Initial audit engagements – opening balances   100 - 110
ISA (UK) 520: Analytical Procedures   111 - 112
ISA (UK) 540: Auditing accounting estimates, including fair value accounting
estimates, and related disclosures   113 - 117
ISA (UK) 550: Related parties   118 - 121
ISA (UK) 560: Subsequent events   122 - 142
ISA (UK) 570: Going concern   143 - 161
ISA (UK) 580: Written representations   162 - 165
ISA (UK) 600: Special considerations – audits of group financial statements
(including the work of component auditors)   166 - 171
ISA (UK) 610: Using the work of internal auditors   172 - 174
ISA (UK) 620: Using the work of an auditor's expert   175 - 177
ISA (UK) 700: Forming an opinion and reporting on financial statements   178 - 190
ISA (UK) 706: Emphasis of matter paragraphs and other matter paragraphs in the
independent auditor's report   191 - 192
ISA (UK) 720: The auditor's responsibilities relating to other information   193 - 199

Part 2: The audit of regularity

Introduction   1 - 3
Understanding the concept of regularity   4 - 7
How regularity relates to other concepts including propriety and compliance
with laws and regulations   8 - 11
The audit of regularity – an overview   12 - 15
Understanding the entity and its environment   16 - 22
Understanding the entity's internal controls   23 - 30
Materiality for the audit of regularity   31 - 35
Assessing the risk of material irregularity   36 - 40
Planning and performing audit procedures   41 - 48
Areas requiring special consideration   49 - 55
Written representations   56 - 57
Using the work of others   58 - 72
Evaluating irregularities   73 - 76
The risk of fraud in the audit of regularity   77 - 80
Regularity opinion on financial statements   81 - 85
Other reporting on regularity   86 - 89

Appendix One – Glossary of terms

Editorial note – This practice note comes into effect from 22 November 2016 and replaces Practice Note 10 revised in October 2010.

The Financial Reporting Council's Statement on the Statement of Recommended Practice – Practice Note 10: Audit of financial statements of public sector Bodies in the United Kingdom

The aim of the Financial Reporting Council (FRC) is to promote high-quality corporate governance and reporting to foster investment. In relation to auditing standards applicable in the UK the FRC's overriding objective is to enable users of financial statements to have confidence that they have been subject to high-quality, robust and independent audit, proportionate to the size and complexity of the entity and users' information needs. In particular industries or sectors, it may be necessary to clarify how those standards are applied to an entity in a manner that is relevant and provides useful information to the users of financial statements in that industry or sector.

Such clarification is issued in the form of guidance developed and issued in accordance with the FRC's Policy on Developing Statements of Recommended Practice, by bodies recognised for this purpose by the FRC. The Public Audit Forum, comprising the four UK National Audit Agencies has confirmed that it shares the FRC's aim of high-quality audit and has been recognised by the FRC for the purpose of issuing the Statement of Recommended Practice: Practice Note 10 – Audit of financial statements of public sector bodies in the United Kingdom.

In accordance with the FRC's Policy on Developing Statements of Recommended Practice, the FRC carried out a limited scope review of the Statement of Recommended Practice focusing on those aspects relevant to the audit of financial statements.

On the basis of its review, the FRC has concluded that the Statement of Recommended Practice has been developed in accordance with the FRC's Policy on Developing Statements of Recommended Practice and does not appear to contain any fundamental points of principle that are unacceptable in the context of present auditing practices or to conflict with International Standards on Auditing (UK).

22 November 2016
Financial Reporting Council

Statement of Recommended Practice – Practice Note 10: Audit of financial statements of public sector bodies in the United Kingdom

This Statement of Recommended Practice, referred to hereafter as a Practice Note replaces Practice Note 10: Audit of financial statements of public sector bodies in the United Kingdom (Revised), which was issued in October 2010.

Preface

This Practice Note contains guidance on the application of quality control and auditing standards issued by the Financial Reporting Council (FRC) to the audit of public sector bodies in the United Kingdom, as classified by the Office for National Statistics.[1]

This Practice Note is supplementary to, and should be read in conjunction with, International Standards on Auditing (ISAs) (UK) and International Standard on Quality Control 1 (ISQC 1) (UK), which apply to all audits undertaken in the United Kingdom. The Practice Note sets out the special considerations relating to the audit of public sector bodies which arise from individual quality control and auditing standards. It is not the intention of the Practice Note to provide step-by-step guidance on the audit of public sector bodies, so where no special considerations arise from a particular ISA or ISQC 1 (UK), no material is included. Where this document is silent on certain aspects of the auditing requirements, users should refer to relevant auditing standards.

This Practice Note has been prepared by the Public Audit Forum (PAF) with advice and assistance from representatives from each of the UK national audit agencies and certain private sector firms who carry out public sector audit work. It is based on auditing standards, legislation and regulations which were in effect at 1 September 2016. This Practice Note is not an exhaustive list of all of the obligations that public sector auditors may have under legislation.

PAF has been designated by the Financial Reporting Council (FRC) as a "SORP-making body" for the purposes of maintaining and updating Practice Note 10: Audit of financial statements of public sector bodies in the United Kingdom (PN 10). Under "SORP-making body" arrangements PAF is responsible for preparing and consulting on revisions to PN 10 prior to seeking the FRC's endorsement that there is nothing within the Practice Note that is inconsistent with auditing standards or the FRC's wider objectives.

Since the previous revision of the Practice Note 10, there have been a number of changes in the legislative and regulatory frameworks within the devolved administrations and in respect of local audit arrangements in England. The Audit Commission has been disbanded and local auditors in England are now appointed under the Local Audit and Accountability Act 2014. Where appropriate, Codes of Audit Practice were issued by the national audit agencies[2] which require public sector auditors to comply with auditing standards in their work on financial statements. Consequently, this Practice Note has been revised to apply to all public sector auditors, whether these are audit agencies or audit firms.

Revised Auditing Standards and a Revised Ethical Standard were issued in June 2016 and are effective for audits of financial statements for periods commencing on or after 17 June 2016. The revised PN 10 refers to the revised auditing standards so that the guidance can remain relevant for the foreseeable future. This will also mean that the revised PN 10 will be relevant if auditors apply the revised standards early. If auditors do not apply the revised standards early, the guidance in the revised PN 10 will still be relevant except that auditors will need to refer to the requirements on reporting material uncertainty in relation to going concern in

---

[1] *Auditors should note that the publication of ONS decisions takes place after consideration of relevant criteria, and it may be appropriate to consider, on a case-by-case basis, evidence for the classification of an entity that may be subject to ongoing ONS consideration. Decisions are published on the ONS website: www.ons.gov.uk/economy/ nationalaccounts/uksectoraccounts/datasets/publicsectorclassificationguide*

[2] *The Codes can be found on the respective websites of the national audit agencies.*

ISA 570 and extended reporting in ISA 700. This is explained in part 1 of the exposure draft. References to an ISA/ISQC (UK) should be taken as meaning the equivalent ISA/ISQC (UK and Ireland) until the revised ISAs (UK) and ISQC 1 (UK) are adopted.

Part 2 of this Practice Note relates to the audit of regularity. This guidance has been revised to reflect current practice across the United Kingdom in relation to auditors' work on regularity and the relevant legislative requirements and frameworks of authorities that apply to this work. In particular, the proposed revisions to PN 10 are clearer about the work needed to support a separate opinion on regularity where one is needed.

Introduction

External auditors in the public sector give an independent opinion on the financial 1
statements and may review and, where appropriate, report on aspects of the arrangements set in place by the audited body to ensure the proper conduct of its financial affairs and to manage its performance and use of resources. As such, external audit is an essential element in the process of accountability and makes an important contribution to the stewardship of public money and the corporate governance of public services.

Public sector auditors act and report in accordance with the mandates that govern 2
their activities and provide the authority for the auditor to carry out and to report the results of the audit work. These mandates are embodied in legislation and, in some circumstances, set out in Codes of Audit Practice which may be established in accordance with legislation and issued by the national audit agencies.

The mandates of public sector auditors vary in accordance with the requirements laid 3
down in the legislation relevant to each jurisdiction within the public sector and within each geographical area. The legislative framework governing the audit of public sector bodies UK wide and in England, Wales, Scotland and Northern Ireland is set out on websites of the Public Audit Forum and individual national audit agencies.

These mandates establish broadly similar responsibilities for each jurisdiction in 4
relation to:

- the financial statements;

- compliance with legislative and other authorities (sometimes referred to as "regularity"); and

- economy, efficiency and effectiveness (sometimes referred to as "performance audit", "value for money" or "use of resources").

In some parts of the UK, English is not the primary language used by public 5
bodies for the conduct of business including preparation of accounts, for example as a result of applying options available under the Welsh Language Act 1993 and Welsh Language (Wales) Measure 2011. Where this occurs, the auditor ensures that the auditor's responsibilities under auditing standards can be properly discharged through, for example, including staff with the appropriate language skills in the engagement team and the use of translation services.

This Practice Note provides auditors with further guidance on the application of 6
ISAs (UK) to the audit of financial statements, including the regularity opinion where appropriate, in the public sector. The heads of the national audit agencies in the UK have chosen to apply ISAs (UK) and follow Practice Note 10. They require auditors conducting work on their behalf to have regard to Practice Note 10 in the application of ISAs (UK) to that work.

7   Public sector auditors may also be required to review and report on other information prepared by public bodies. Such other information may include aspects of corporate governance or arrangements to secure economy, efficiency and effectiveness in the use of resources. Practice Note 10 does not provide guidance to the auditor on conducting these assignments, unless it is directly related to reporting on the audit of financial statements or regularity. The standards governing other reporting assignments in the public sector are a matter for the national audit agencies and certain regulators to determine. These may be included in a separate Code of Audit Practice.

Part 1: Application of International Standards on Auditing (UK)

1   A list of International Standards on Quality Control (ISQC) and International Standards on Auditing (ISAs) (UK) is shown in the table below. This identifies those ISQC and ISAs in respect of which application guidance is included in this Practice Note and, for completeness, also shows those ISAs for which there is no need for further guidance:

International Standard on Auditing (UK)	Further guidance relevant to the public sector context included in this part of PN 10	No further guidance relevant to the public sector context provided
ISQC 1: Quality control for firms that perform audits and reviews of financial statements, and other assurance and related services engagements	✔	
ISA 200: Overall objectives of the independent auditor and the conduct of an audit in accordance with International Standards on Auditing (UK)	✔	
ISA 210: Agreeing the terms of audit engagements	✔	
ISA 220: Quality control for an audit of financial statements	✔	
ISA 230: Audit documentation		✔
ISA 240: The auditor's responsibilities relating to fraud in an audit of financial statements	✔	
ISA 250A: Consideration of laws and regulations in an audit of financial statements	✔	
ISA 250B: The auditor's statutory right and duty to report to regulators of public interest entities and regulators of other entities in the financial sector[1]		✔

International Standard on Auditing (UK)	Further guidance relevant to the public sector context included in this part of PN 10	No further guidance relevant to the public sector context provided
ISA 260: Communication with those charged with governance	✔	
ISA 265: Communicating deficiencies in internal control to those charged with governance and management	✔	
ISA 300: Planning an audit of financial statements		✔
ISA 315 – Identifying and assessing the risks of material misstatement through understanding the entity and its environment	✔	
ISA 320 – Materiality in planning and performing an audit	✔	
ISA 330 – The auditor's responses to assessed risks	✔	
ISA 402 – Audit considerations relating to an entity using a service organisation	✔	
ISA 450 – Evaluation of misstatements identified during the audit	✔	
ISA 500 – Audit evidence		✔
ISA 501 – Audit evidence – specific considerations for selected items		✔
ISA 505 – External confirmations		✔
ISA 510 – Initial audit engagements – opening balances	✔	
ISA 520 – Analytical procedures	✔	
ISA 530 – Audit sampling		✔
ISA 540 – Auditing accounting estimates, including fair value accounting estimates and related disclosures	✔	
ISA 550 – Related parties	✔	
ISA 560 – Subsequent events	✔	
ISA 570 – Going concern	✔	
ISA 580 – Written representations	✔	

International Standard on Auditing (UK)	Further guidance relevant to the public sector context included in this part of PN 10	No further guidance relevant to the public sector context provided
ISA 600 – Special considerations – audits of group financial statements including the work of component auditors	✓	
ISA 610 – Using the work of internal auditors	✓	
ISA 620 – Using the work of an auditor's expert	✓	
ISA 700 – Forming an opinion and reporting on financial statements	✓	
ISA 701 – Communicating key audit matters in the independent auditor's report[2]		✓
ISA 705 – Modifications to the opinion in the independent auditor's report		✓
ISA 706 – Emphasis of matter paragraphs and other matter paragraphs in the independent auditor's report	✓	
ISA 710 – Comparative information – corresponding figures and comparative financial statements		✓
ISA 720 – The auditor's responsibilities relating to other information	✓	

Notes

[1] ISA 250B: The auditor's right and duty to report to regulators in the financial sector was revised in June 2016 and is now referred to as ISA 250B: The auditor's statutory right and duty to report to regulators of public interest entities and regulators of other entities in the financial sector.

[2] This standard is effective for audits of financial statements for periods commencing on or after 17 June 2016. Early application is permitted.

2   The following sections of this part set out the further guidance on the application of the ISQC (UK) 1 and ISAs (UK) for public sector audit. Where there are public sector considerations in the quality control and auditing standards, these have been referenced throughout this document and shown in grey text. References to ISQC and ISAs in this Practice Note are to standards applicable in the UK. Part 2 of this Practice Note sets out guidance on the audit of regularity.

International Standard on Quality Control (UK) 1

3   **The objective of the [audit organisation or] firm is to establish and maintain a system of quality control to provide it with reasonable assurance that:**

(a)   the firm and its personnel comply with professional standards and applicable legal and regulatory requirements; and

(b)   reports issued by the firm or engagement partners are appropriate in the circumstances (ISQC1, 11).

Interpretation of the requirement to withdraw from an engagement where the appointment is made in statute

In the public sector, auditors may be appointed in accordance with statutory   4
procedures. Accordingly, certain of the requirements and considerations
regarding the acceptance and continuance of client relationships and
specific engagements as set out paragraphs 26–28 and A18–A22 [of ISQC 1]
may not be relevant. Nonetheless, establishing policies and procedures as
described may provide valuable information to public sector auditors in
performing risk assessments and in carrying out reporting responsibilities
(ISQC1, A23 which relates to the requirements in ISQC 1, 26–28; ISA 240,
A57 which relates to the requirements in ISA 240, 38).

In most cases, statutory-appointed auditors have the authority to report publicly   5
such matters that may otherwise have caused their withdrawal or resignation from
a statutory engagement. This may be relevant, for example, to a head of one of the
public audit agencies who is appointed by the legislation as an auditor of specific
public sector bodies.

Quality control for contracted-out engagements

A contracted-out engagement is an engagement where, although responsibility for   6
issuing the audit report remains with the statutory auditor, all or some of the audit
assignment is undertaken by another firm or auditor under contract or agreement,
which in turn provides a fully ISA compliant audit report to the statutory auditor.
For example, the Comptroller and Auditor General contracts out audit work on
some of the statutory appointments, but is still responsible for signing the audit
certificate and report.

For contracted-out engagements, responsibility for quality remains with the   7
statutory auditor. This includes:

● ensuring that the contractor auditor has sufficient personnel with the competencies, capabilities and commitment to ethical principles necessary for compliance with relevant standards;

● confirming that the contractor auditor meets the relevant ethical standards, including independence, on appointment and periodically thereafter;

● ensuring that there are policies and procedures in place to identify and resolve potential conflicts;

● considering whether an internal consultation and the appointment of an engagement quality control reviewer is necessary for contracted-out engagements;

● applying the organisation-wide quality control monitoring policies and procedures to contracted-out engagements;

● reporting any deficiencies identified as a result of monitoring a contracted-out engagement to the contractor auditor undertaking the assignment; and

- establishing policies and procedures designed to provide reasonable assurance that complaints and allegations relating to quality are dealt with appropriately.

8   This does not absolve contractor auditors of responsibility for systems of quality control within their organisations in accordance with ISQC (UK) 1. In practice, the statutory auditor may obtain assurance over quality from its contractors or may undertake procedures to confirm that its contractors' systems of quality control are working effectively.

9   If the contractor auditor identifies deficiencies in any of its public sector assignments that fall within the remit of the statutory auditor, these are communicated, along with the action undertaken, to the relevant statutory auditor.

10   The contractor auditor establishes policies and procedures designed to provide reasonable assurance that it deals appropriately with complaints and allegations relating to quality. These policies and procedures allow for escalation of such issues to the statutory auditor, where relevant.

Quality control for engagements on an "appointment by" basis

11   An assignment undertaken on an "appointment by" basis is an engagement where another firm or individual is responsible for the assignment, its performance and the issuing of the audit report. An example of this arrangement is the relationship between the Accounts Commission in Scotland and its appointed auditors.

12   Where an auditor undertakes the engagement on an "appointment by" basis and issues the audit report in its own name, it assumes responsibility for quality. This does not affect any statutory responsibility the national audit agency has for the oversight of, or quality assurance for, those assignments undertaken on its behalf. The responsibilities of the auditor include:

- ensuring that the engagement has sufficient personnel with the competencies, capabilities and commitment to ethical principles necessary for compliance with relevant standards;

- ensuring that the engagement meets the relevant ethical standards, including independence, on appointment and periodically thereafter;

- ensuring that there are policies and procedures in place to identify and resolve potential conflicts;

- considering whether an internal consultation and the appointment of an engagement quality control reviewer is necessary for "appointment by" engagements;

- applying the firm's quality control monitoring policies and procedures to "appointment by" engagements;

- reporting any deficiencies identified as a result of monitoring "appointment by" engagements to the national audit agency, where appropriate; and

- establishing policies and procedures designed to provide reasonable assurance that complaints and allegations relating to quality are dealt with appropriately.

13   Where an engagement is undertaken on an "appointment by" basis, the national audit agency should also:

- ensure that the appointed auditor has sufficient personnel with the competencies, capabilities and commitment to ethical principles necessary for compliance with relevant standards;

- consider whether to apply quality monitoring arrangements to such assignments;

- confirm whether the appointed auditor meets the relevant ethical standards, including independence, on appointment and periodically thereafter; and

- ensure that there are policies and procedures in place to identify and resolve potential conflicts.

Ethics

Auditors in the public sector may need to meet relevant ethical and propriety   **14** requirements in addition to the FRC's Ethical standard, such as restrictions on political activities or requirements established by regulators. The Official Secrets Act also covers some public sector activities. No other requirement should compromise the ability of the firm or individual auditors to comply with relevant ethical requirements required by ISQC (UK) 1 and the FRC Ethical Standard.

Independence

Statutory measures may provide safeguards for the independence of public   **15** **sector auditors. However, threats to independence may exist regardless of any statutory measures designed to protect it. Therefore, in establishing the policies required by paragraphs 21–25 [of ISQC 1], the public sector auditor may have regard to the public sector mandate and address any threats to independence in that context (ISQC 1, A15 which relates to the requirements of ISQC 1, 21–25).**

Listed entities as referred to in paragraphs 25 and A14 are not common in the   **16** **public sector. However, there may be other public sector entities that are significant due to size, complexity or public interest aspects, and which consequently have a wide range of stakeholders. Therefore, there may be instances when [an auditor or] a firm determines, based on its quality control policies and procedures, that a public sector entity is significant for the purposes of expanded quality control procedures (ISQC 1, A16 which relates to the requirements of ISQC1, 25).**

In the public sector, legislation may establish the appointments and terms of   **17** **office of the auditor with engagement partner responsibility. As a result, it may not be possible to comply strictly with the engagement partner rotation requirements envisaged for listed entities. Nonetheless, for public sector entities considered significant, as noted in paragraph A16 [of ISQC 1], it may be in the public interest for public sector organisations to establish policies and procedures to promote compliance with the spirit of rotation of engagement partner responsibility (ISQC 1, A17 which relates to the requirements of ISQC1, 25).**

Confidentiality

In addition to the provisions of ISQC (UK) 1, public sector auditors may have   **18** additional statutory obligations relating to confidentiality, for example under the Official Secrets Act 1989.

19   As well as complying with applicable statutory obligations relating to confidentiality, auditors must also consider whether audit work is potentially disclosable under applicable freedom of information legislation. For example, where the auditor is classified as a public authority under Schedule 1 of the Freedom of Information Act 2000 or Freedom of Information (Scotland) Act 2002, legislation provides a right of access to recorded information held by that auditor.

20   For auditors not classified as public authorities, relevant audit legislation may permit an auditor to disclose information obtained in the course of an audit except where it would prejudice the effective performance of the auditor's functions.

21   The acceptance of some appointments in the public sector requires the auditor to acknowledge that their working papers may be subject to inspection by the national audit agency that appointed the auditor or that is responsible for the audit of a higher tier entity or by review agencies that have statutory rights of access to information relevant to the auditor's duties. If not bound by a specific statutory requirement (for example, freedom of information legislation), ethical considerations normally require that the national audit agency acquires the duty of confidentiality that is held by the auditor.

Engagement quality control review

22   **Although not referred to as listed entities, as described in paragraph A16 [of ISQC 1], certain public sector entities may be of sufficient significance to warrant performance of an engagement quality control review (ISQC 1, A46 which relates to the requirements of ISQC 1, 38).**

23   **In the public sector, a statutorily appointed auditor (for example, an Auditor General, or other suitably qualified person appointed on behalf of the Auditor General) may act in a role equivalent to that of engagement partner with overall responsibility for public sector audits. In such circumstances, where applicable, the selection of the engagement quality control reviewer includes consideration of the need for independence from the audited entity and the ability of the engagement quality control reviewer to provide an objective evaluation (ISQC 1, A51 which relates to the requirements of ISQC 1, 40; ISA 220, A30–31 which relates to the requirements of ISA 220, 20–21).**

24   Auditors may also appoint engagement quality control reviewers at their discretion, where considered necessary.

ISA (UK) 200: Overall objective of the independent auditor and the conduct of an audit in accordance with International Standards on Auditing (UK)

25   **In conducting an audit of financial statements, the overall objectives of the auditor are:**

   (a)   to obtain reasonable assurance about whether the financial statements as a whole are free from material misstatement, whether due to fraud or error, thereby enabling the auditor to express an opinion on whether the financial statements are prepared, in all material respects, in accordance with an applicable financial reporting framework; and

   (b)   to report on the financial statements, and communicate as required by the ISAs (UK), in accordance with the auditor's findings.

In all cases when reasonable assurance cannot be obtained and a qualified   **26**
opinion in the auditor's report is insufficient in the circumstances for
purposes of reporting to the intended users of the financial statements, the
ISAs (UK) require that the auditor disclaim an opinion or withdraw (or
resign) from the engagement, where withdrawal is possible under applicable
law or regulation (ISA 200, 11–12).

Responsibilities of the public sector auditor

The mandates for audits of the financial statements of public sector entities   **27**
may be broader than those of other entities. As a result, the premise, relating
to management's responsibilities, on which an audit of the financial
statements of a public sector entity is conducted may include additional
responsibilities, such as the responsibility for the execution of transactions
and events in accordance with law, regulation or other authority (ISA 200,
A11 which relates to the requirements of ISA 200, 4).

The ISAs (UK) are relevant to engagements in the public sector. The public   **28**
sector auditor's responsibilities, however, may be affected by the audit
mandate, or by obligations on public sector entities arising from law,
regulation or other authority (such as ministerial directives, government
policy requirements, or resolutions of the legislature), which may encompass
a broader scope than an audit of financial statements in accordance with the
ISAs (UK). These additional responsibilities are not dealt with in the ISAs
(UK). They may be dealt with in the pronouncements of the International
Organisation of Supreme Audit Institutions or national standard setters, or
in guidance developed by national audit agencies (ISA 200, A57 which relates
to the requirements of ISA 200, 18).

ISA (UK) 210: Agreeing the terms of audit engagements

The objective of the auditor is to accept or continue an audit engagement only   **29**
when the basis upon which it is to be performed has been agreed, through:

(a)   establishing whether the preconditions for an audit are present; and

(b)   confirming that there is a common understanding between the auditor
and management and, where appropriate, those charged with
governance of the terms of the audit engagement (ISA 210, 3).

Agreeing the terms of public sector audit engagements

In the public sector, specific requirements may exist within the legislation   **30**
governing the audit mandate; for example, the auditor may be required to
report directly to a minister, the legislature or the public if the entity attempts
to limit the scope of the audit (ISA 210, A37 which relates to the requirements
of ISA 210, 21).

Law or regulation governing the operations of public sector audits generally   **31**
mandate the appointment of a public sector auditor and commonly set out the
public sector auditor's responsibilities and powers, including the power to
access an entity's records and other information. When law or regulation
prescribes in sufficient detail the terms of the audit engagement, the public
sector auditor may nonetheless consider that there are benefits in issuing a
fuller audit engagement letter than permitted by paragraph 11 [of ISA 210]
(ISA 210, A27 which relates to the requirements of ISA 210, 10–11).

32   With some exceptions, the statutory framework allows national audit agencies to mandate a substantial part of the scope and objectives of the audit. In other cases, an appointment letter or Code of Audit Practice issued by a national audit agency may determine the nature and scope of the audit engagement. For this reason, formal engagement letters for statutory engagements may not always be necessary. However, for audits of local bodies in England, for example where appointments have been made directly by the audited bodies under the Local Audit and Accountability Act 2014 or for the audit of Foundation Trusts, a letter of engagement is required.

33   Nevertheless, it remains important that management and the auditor formally recognise their respective responsibilities. It may also be necessary, where legislation does not provide sufficient detail on the scope of the audit, to ensure that it is appropriately understood by those charged with governance. A letter of understanding may therefore be necessary.

34   The auditor may find it appropriate to conclude letters of understanding with the audited entity to confirm the auditor's understanding of the roles of the parties with an interest in the engagement, the requirements of the audit, the responsibilities of each party, how the responsibilities will be met, and the expectations that each party can have of the other. Such a document is not intended to be a substitute for the clarification of any uncertainties in the auditing framework that will need to be resolved with the relevant national audit agency.

35   In circumstances where roles, requirements and responsibilities mandated by the national audit agency are not clear or are debatable, the auditor requests that the national audit agency provides greater clarity in the terms of its appointment; auditor and audited entities should not seek to interpret the intentions behind the uncertainties, without the advice of the national audit agency.

36   Where the auditor has not been appointed under statute, an engagement letter is required to set out the responsibilities of the auditor and the audited body. The auditor agrees the terms of engagement with the addressee of the auditor's report.

37   Where financial statements are laid before Parliament, either by statute or command, the auditor also considers whether HM Treasury agreement of these terms may be required.

Areas that may be covered in a letter of engagement or understanding

38   The auditor determines the areas that may be covered by the letter of engagement or understanding. These areas may change over time and the auditor will need to consider developments that may be relevant to the audited body. In preparing the letter of engagement or understanding, the auditor may consider the following:

- responsibilities of the Accounting Officer or Accountable Officer, and, where relevant, those charged with governance;

- responsibilities of the auditor, with reference to the relevant legislative framework;

- the audit framework, distinguishing between statutory and non-statutory requirements. Statutory considerations might include examination in respect of regularity and Whole of Government Accounts. Non-statutory elements might include, if relevant, the involvement of other auditors and the relationship between the national audit agency and the other auditors;

- reporting responsibilities, acknowledging that there may be wider responsibilities to report to other entities, such as Parliament, or those charged with governance;

- wider auditor responsibilities, such as obligations under the Freedom of Information Act or the Proceeds of Crime Act;

- reviewing the Governance Statement;

- electronic publication of financial statements;

- value for money examinations;

- other audit related services, for example limited assurance reports and other assurance products that are closely related to the work carried out on the audit; and

- audit fees.

ISA (UK) 220: Quality control for an audit of financial statements

The objective of the auditor is to implement quality control procedures at the engagement level that provide the auditor with reasonable assurance that: 39

(a) the audit complies with professional standards and applicable legal and regulatory requirements; and

(b) the auditor's report issued is appropriate in the circumstances (ISA 220, 6).

Quality control for an audit of financial statements in the public sector

Statutory measures may provide safeguards for the independence of public sector auditors. However, public sector auditors or audit firms carrying out public sector audits on behalf of the statutory auditor may, depending on the terms of the mandate in a particular jurisdiction, need to adapt their approach in order to promote compliance with the spirit of paragraph 11 [of ISA 220]. This may include, where the public sector auditor's mandate does not permit withdrawal from the engagement, disclosure through a public report, of circumstances that have arisen that would, if they were in the private sector, lead the auditor to withdraw (ISA 220, A7 which relates to the requirements of ISA 220, 11). 40

In the public sector, auditors may be appointed in accordance with statutory procedures. Accordingly, certain of the requirements and considerations regarding the acceptance and continuance of client relationships and audit engagements as set out in paragraphs 12, 13 and A8 [of ISA 220] may not be relevant. Nonetheless, information gathered as a result of the process described may be valuable to public sector auditors in performing risk assessments and in carrying out reporting responsibilities (ISA 220, A9 which relates to the requirements of ISA 220, 12–13). 41

In the public sector, additional appropriate competence may include skills that are necessary to discharge the terms of the audit mandate in a particular jurisdiction. Such competence may include an understanding of the applicable reporting arrangements, including reporting to the legislature or other governing body or in the public interest. The wider scope of a public sector audit may include, for example, some aspects of performance auditing or assessment of compliance with law, regulation or other authority and 42 preventing and detecting fraud and corruption (ISA 220, A12 which relates to the requirements of ISA 220, 14).

ISA (UK) 240: The auditor's responsibilities relating to fraud in an audit of financial statements

43   The objectives of the auditor are:

(a)   to identify and assess the risks of material misstatement of the financial statements due to fraud;

(b)   to obtain sufficient appropriate audit evidence regarding the assessed risks of material misstatement due to fraud, through designing and implementing appropriate responses; and

(c)   to respond appropriately to fraud or suspected fraud identified during the audit (ISA 240, 10).

The public sector auditor's responsibilities relating to fraud

44   The public sector auditor's responsibilities relating to fraud may be a result of law, regulation or other authority applicable to public sector entities or separately covered by the auditor's mandate. Consequently, the public sector auditor's responsibilities may not be limited to consideration of risks of material misstatement of the financial statements, but may also include a broader responsibility to consider risks of fraud (ISA 240, A6 which relates to the requirements of ISA 240, 3).

The auditor's consideration of the risk of fraudulent financial reporting

45   A public sector auditor needs to consider misstatements that may arise from fraudulent financial reporting where the audited body may manipulate its results to meet externally set targets, for example, the achievement of a statutory break-even duty by a health body or where financial results impact on achievement of objectives and/or wider performance reporting.

46   ISA (UK) 240 states that the auditor ordinarily presumes that there are risks of fraud in revenue recognition, as material misstatements due to fraudulent financial reporting often result from a misstatement of revenue. The auditor may rebut this presumption, for example if revenue is considered immaterial or where there is a single type of simple revenue transaction. However, the auditor may need to consider whether there is a risk of material misstatements due to fraud related to revenue recognition where the audited body is required to meet externally set targets. For example, within central government departments, income may be an immaterial transaction stream but could be manipulated in order to ensure that net expenditure is within the resource limits.

47   In the public sector, auditors focus their consideration of the risk of fraud and error on expenditure. As most public bodies are net spending bodies, then the risk of material misstatement due to fraud related to expenditure may be greater than the risk of material misstatements due to fraud related to revenue recognition.

The auditor's consideration of the risk of fraud external to the audited entity

48   As well as misstatements resulting from the misappropriation of assets and misstatements resulting from fraudulent financial reporting, auditors in the public sector also consider the risk of external fraud. The risk of external fraud may be particularly high where there is an increased risk of fraudulent activity by

individuals or groups outside the immediate control of the entity, for example fraudulent benefit or prescription claims.

The auditor's responsibility for reporting suspected or actual fraud

In considering whether to report a suspected or actual instance of fraud to a proper **49** authority, in addition to paragraph 43 of ISA (UK) 240, the public sector auditor has regard to:

- the provisions relevant to the entity that set out the responsibilities of those charged with governance for the reporting of misconduct, fraud or other irregularity; and

- the duties which the auditor may have under the terms of engagement to report to a third party.

In the public sector, requirements for reporting fraud, whether or not **50** **discovered through the audit process, may be subject to specific provisions of the audit mandate or related law, regulation or other authority (ISA 240, A67 which relates to the requirements of ISA 240, 43).**

Where the public sector auditor considers that there is a duty to report instances or **51** suspected or actual fraud to a third party, they determine the proper authority to whom they are initially expected to report. The relevant authority differs for different parts of the public sector, depending upon the terms of the engagement and statutory requirements. This is in addition to responsibilities under Money Laundering Regulations (2007).

ISA (UK) 250A – Consideration of laws and regulations in an audit of financial statements

The objectives of the auditor are: **52**

(a) **to obtain sufficient appropriate audit evidence regarding compliance with the provisions of those laws and regulations generally recognised to have a direct effect on the determination of material amounts and disclosures in the financial statements;**

(b) **to perform specified audit procedures to help identify instances of non-compliance with other laws and regulations that may have a material effect on the financial statements; and**

(c) **to respond appropriately to non-compliance or suspected non-compliance with laws and regulations identified during the audit (ISA 250A, 10).**

The auditor's consideration of laws and regulations

In the public sector, there may be additional audit responsibilities with **53** **respect to the consideration of laws and regulations which may relate to the audit of financial statements or may extend to other aspects of the entity's operations (ISA 250A, A6 which relates to the requirements of ISA 250A, 3–8).**

Auditors of central government and some health bodies have wider regard to laws **54** and regulations as part of their responsibilities in respect of the audit of regularity. ISA (UK) 250A is concerned with ensuring that the auditor considers the risks of material misstatement in the financial statements due to non-compliance with laws and regulations and performs further audit procedures whose nature, timing and extent are responsive to assessed risks.

55   Auditors of other public sector entities, for example those required to follow a Code of Audit Practice, may be required to have a wider regard to laws and regulations than those to which ISA (UK) 250A is directly relevant. These requirements are set out in the relevant Code of Audit Practice and assign particular duties to the auditor in relation to the entity's arrangements to prevent non-compliance and to matters that come to the auditor's attention that may require consideration under ISA 250A. For example, some local auditors who are required to report on arrangements to secure value for money may, in that work, become aware of instances of non-compliance with laws and regulations.

The public sector auditor's consideration of legislation on corruption

56   The public sector auditor considers to whom the auditor may report suspected or actual acts of corruption, irrespective of whether, in the auditor's opinion, the consequences of the corruption could have a material effect on the financial statements. In the first instance, the auditor normally brings the matter to the attention of those charged with governance. It is then the responsibility of those charged with governance to report the matter to the proper authorities. If the auditor of an entity identifies a suspected or actual instance of corruption and if, having reported the matter to those charged with governance the auditor is unable to establish whether those charged with governance have reported the matter to the relevant third party, the auditor takes the steps set out in paragraph 43 of ISA (UK) 240.

Money laundering regulations in the public sector

57   Guidance on the auditor's responsibilities in relation to the UK anti-money laundering legislation when auditing and reporting on financial statements is provided in the FRC's Practice Note 12. This legislation includes the Money Laundering regulations 2007 and the Proceeds of Crime Act 2002.

58   Under regulation 49 of the Money Laundering Regulations 2007, various listed public authorities (including the Comptroller and Auditor General, the Auditors General for Wales and Scotland and the Comptroller and Auditor General for Northern Ireland) must, if they know or suspect or have reasonable grounds for knowing or suspecting that a person is or has engaged in money laundering or terrorist financing, as soon as reasonably practicable, inform the National Crime Agency. This report will normally be made by the audit organisation's nominated Money Laundering Reporting Officer.

59   The auditor considers the offence of tipping off under section 333 of the 2002 Act. There is also an offence under section 342 of the 2002 Act which applies to all persons. This offence occurs where a person knows or suspects that an appropriate officer (such as an officer from the National Crime Agency) is acting (or proposing to act) in connection with a money laundering investigation which is being or about to be conducted, and makes a disclosure which is likely to prejudice the investigation or falsifies, conceals, destroys or otherwise disposes of, or causes or permits the falsification, concealment, destruction or disposal of, documents which are relevant to the investigation.

Reporting non-compliance

The public sector auditor may be obliged to report on instances of non-   **60**
compliance to the legislature or other governing body or to report them in the
auditor's report (ISA 250A, A20 which relates to the requirements of
ISA 250A, 28).

ISA (UK) 260: Communication with those charged with governance

The objectives of the auditor are: **61**

(a)   to communicate clearly with those charged with governance the
responsibilities of the auditor in relation to the financial statement
audit, and an overview of the planned scope and timing of the audit;

(b)   to obtain from those charged with governance information relevant to
the audit;

(c)   to provide those charged with governance with timely observations
arising from the audit that are significant and relevant to their
responsibility to oversee the financial reporting process; and

(d)   to promote effective two-way communication between the auditor and
those charged with governance (ISA 260, 9).

Determining who is charged with governance in the public sector context

At the outset of the audit, the auditor determines who is charged with governance.   **62**
This may include the Accounting/Accountable Officer (or equivalent) and other
individuals responsible for decision-making, for example a board, scrutiny
committee, Council, governing body or another group.

The responsibilities of those charged with governance may include, for example: **63**

●   ensuring that effective management systems appropriate for the
achievement of the organisation's objectives including financial
monitoring and control systems have been put in place;

●   keeping proper accounts;

●   ensuring internal audit is established and organised in accordance with the
Public Sector Internal Audit Standards; and

●   ensuring the regularity and propriety of public finances.

If the two-way communication between the auditor and those charged with   **64**
governance is not adequate and the situation cannot be resolved, the public
sector auditor may communicate the matter to a responsible government
minister or Parliament (ISA 260, A53 which relates to the requirements of
ISA 260, 22).

Communication with sponsoring bodies

Special arrangements may have developed for reporting to those charged with   **65**
governance by auditors of some entities sponsored by government departments. In
such cases the Accounting/Accountable Officer of the sponsor department must
obtain assurance that the financial and other management controls applied by the
sponsored entity are adequate to ensure regularity and propriety. Reports from the
auditor of the lower tier entity may assist the Accounting/Accountable Officer in
obtaining such assurance. Sponsor departments may, therefore, require auditors of
their arm's length bodies to:

- provide the sponsor department with copies of management letters and other relevant correspondence; and

- report significant matters arising out of the audit work to the sponsor department, including:

  - failures of internal control, misconduct, fraud or other irregularity,

  - occasions where the board, Chief Executive or any other official has fallen short of the high standards of financial integrity expected of those responsible for the management of public assets, or

  - occasions where the entity has incurred expenditure of an extravagant or wasteful nature.

66   The auditors of local health bodies in England have specific responsibilities to refer certain matters to the Secretary of State or other relevant national body.

67   These and any other matters on which the auditor may be required to report to management are normally specified in the terms of appointment or engagement letter or Codes of Audit Practice.

Third party interest in reports to those charged with governance

68   In the public sector there may be a requirement to make public communications between the auditor and audited body. Even where this is not the case, third parties may seek to place reliance on a report by a public sector auditor addressed to those charged with governance. As such, auditors may need to state that the report is for use only by the audited entity to ensure that third parties who see the communication understand that it was not prepared with their use in mind.

69   Codes of Audit Practice applicable to local public audit in England, Northern Ireland, Scotland and Wales set out requirements relating to reporting to those charged with governance and considerations relating to defining who those charged with governance are, addressees and any relevant considerations relating to their purpose. Effective reference to relevant Codes of Audit Practice, as appropriate, in any report to those charged with governance achieves the purpose intended in the ISAs (UK).

Matters to be communicated

70   **Law or regulation, or an agreement with the entity or additional requirements applicable to the engagement may provide for broader communication with those charged with governance. In the public sector, the auditor's mandate may provide for matters to be communicated that come to the auditor's attention as a result of other work, such as performance audits (ISA 260, A10 which relates to the requirements of ISA 260, 14).**

71   The communication requirements relating to auditor independence that apply in the case of listed entities may also be relevant to some public sector entities (other that those that are listed, in which case the requirements are mandatory). The auditor of such bodies may consider whether this additional information would be beneficial where the audited entity has a wide range of stakeholders, as a result of their business, their size or their corporate status.

ISA (UK) 265: Communicating deficiencies in internal control to those charged with governance and management

The objective of the auditor is to communicate appropriately to those charged   72
with governance and management deficiencies in internal control that the
auditor has identified during the audit and that, in the auditor's professional
judgement, are of sufficient importance to merit their respective attentions
(ISA 265, 5).

Public sector auditors may have additional responsibilities to communicate   73
deficiencies in internal control that the auditor has identified during the
audit, in ways, at a level of detail and to parties not envisaged in this ISA
(UK). For example, significant deficiencies may have to be communicated to
the legislature or other governing body. Law, regulation or other authority
may also mandate that public sector auditors report deficiencies in internal
control, irrespective of the significance of the potential effects of those
deficiencies. Further, legislation may require public sector auditors to
report on broader internal control-related matters than the deficiencies in
internal control required to be communicated by this ISA (UK), for example,
controls related to compliance with legislative authorities, regulations, or
provisions of contracts or grant agreements (ISA 265, A27 which relates to
the requirements of ISA 265, 9–10).

ISA (UK) 315: Identifying and assessing the risks of material misstatement through understanding the entity and its environment

The objective of the auditor is to identify and assess the risks of material   74
misstatement, whether due to fraud or error, at the financial statement and
assertion levels, through understanding the entity and its environment,
including the entity's internal control, thereby providing a basis for
designing and implementing responses to the assessed risks of material
misstatement (ISA 315, 3).

Auditors of public sector entities often have additional responsibilities with   75
regard to internal control and compliance with applicable laws and
regulations. Inquiries of appropriate individuals in the internal audit
function can assist the auditors in identifying the risk of material non-
compliance with applicable laws and regulations and the risk of
deficiencies in internal control over financial reporting (ISA 315, A13
which relates to the requirements of ISA 315, 6).

For the audits of public sector entities, law, regulation or other authority may   76
affect the entity's operations. Such elements are essential to consider when
obtaining an understanding of the entity and its environment (ISA 315, A28
which relates to the requirements of ISA 315, 11).

For the audits of public sector entities, "management objectives" may be   77
influenced by concerns regarding public accountability and may include
objectives which have their source in law, regulation or other authority
(ISA 315, A42 which relates to the requirements of ISA 315, 11).

Public sector auditors often have additional responsibilities with respect to   78
internal control, for example to report on compliance with an established
code of practice. Public sector auditors can also have responsibilities to report
on compliance with law, regulation or other authority. As a result, their
review of internal control may be broader and more detailed (ISA 315, A72
which relates to the requirements of ISA 315, 12).

79   **When making assertions about the financial statements of public sector entities, in addition to those assertions set out in paragraph A124 [of ISA 315], management may often assert that transactions and events have been carried out in accordance with law, regulation or other authority. Such assertions may fall within the scope of the financial statement audit (ISA 315, A126 which relates to the requirements of ISA 315, 25).**

80   There are a number of additional factors that may be considered by the auditor when assessing business risks for public sector entities. These arise from the particular coincidence in the public sector of a closely regulated regime, a large volume of transactions processed and a public reporting process. These additional factors may arise where:

●   major new legislation or expenditure programmes have been introduced;

●   there is the possibility of manipulation by management to achieve performance or other targets;

●   an entity is likely to be wound up, reorganised, merged, sold or privatised;

●   there is political pressure on an entity to complete transactions quickly; and

●   the final form of account does not reflect the underlying management and accounting processes.

81   Where entities are required to work to annual limits on resources, the risk of transactions being recorded in the wrong accounting period is increased, since there is a temptation for an entity in surplus to bring forward payments and for an entity in deficit to delay them.

82   When considering compliance with the applicable financial reporting framework, the public sector auditor's procedures are performed in the knowledge that entities have their own legislative framework and accounting provisions that prescribe the form and content of financial statements.

ISA (UK) 320: Materiality in planning and performing an audit

83   **The objective of the auditor is to apply the concept of materiality appropriately in planning and performing the audit (ISA 320, 8).**

84   **In the case of a public sector entity, legislators and regulators are often the primary users of its financial statements. Furthermore, the financial statements may be used to make decisions other than economic decisions. The determination of materiality for the financial statements as a whole (and, if applicable, materiality level or levels for particular classes of transactions, account balances or disclosures) in an audit of the financial statements of a public sector entity is therefore influenced by law, regulation or other authority, and by the financial information needs of legislators and the public in relation to public sector programmes (ISA 320, A2 which relates to the requirements of ISA 320, 10).**

85   **In an audit of a public sector entity, total cost or net cost (expenses less revenues or expenditure less receipts) may be appropriate benchmarks for programme activities. Where a public sector entity has custody of public assets, assets may be an appropriate benchmark (ISA 320, A9 which relates to the requirements of ISA 320, 10).**

86   Therefore, gross expenditure or gross assets/liabilities may be more appropriate than profit or revenue as benchmarks for setting materiality for financial statements as a whole, as set out in the illustrative examples in Box 1 below:

Box 1: Illustrative examples of applying different benchmarks for setting materiality

Example 1: the main role of the entity is to provide services and the majority of expenditure relates to staff costs – the auditor considered it appropriate to use gross expenditure as a benchmark for setting materiality.

Example 2: the audited entity is the pension scheme account and majority of expenditure and income relates to the movements of the pension scheme asset – the auditor decided to use the gross assets as a benchmark for setting materiality.

Example 3: the audited entity manages government's long-term significant provisions, and the value of the liability and related movements is more significant than the value of other financial statement items – the auditor used the gross liabilities as a benchmark for setting materiality.

Example 4: the audited entity has significant non-current assets but its main role is to provide services to the public – the auditor decided that it is more appropriate to use gross expenditure as a benchmark for setting materiality to reflect the entity's role and interest of the users of the financial statements.

Auditors may consider setting a lower materiality threshold for certain balances, transactions or disclosures, where appropriate in the context of the audited entity and the expectations of the users of the financial statements. **87**

ISA (UK) 330: The auditor's responses to assessed risks

The objective of the auditor is to obtain sufficient appropriate audit evidence regarding the assessed risks of material misstatement, through designing and implementing appropriate responses to those risks (ISA 330, 3). **88**

In the public sector, the audit mandate and any other special auditing requirements may affect the auditor's consideration of the nature, timing and extent of further audit procedures (ISA 330, A17 which relates to the requirements of ISA 330, 7). **89**

ISA (UK) 402: Audit considerations relating to an entity using a service organisation

The objectives of the user auditor, when the user entity uses the services of a service organisation, are: **90**

(a) to obtain an understanding of the nature and significance of the services provided by the service organisation and their effect on the user entity's internal control relevant to the audit, sufficient to identify and assess the risks of material misstatement; and

(b) to design and perform audit procedures responsive to those risks (ISA 402, 7).

Use of service organisations in the public sector

91   Public sector entities often use shared service providers. For example, transaction processing or payroll services may be outsourced to another entity, which could be private sector, another public sector organisation, or a joint venture between the two sectors.

92   Auditors consider how the audited body oversees the provider's performance and considers whether this raises the risk of misstatement. Where a national audit agency is the auditor of more than one user organisation for a service provider, the agency obtains an understanding of how each user entity is affected by the service organisation and makes individual assessments of risk and impact on the audit approach for each user entity.

Access rights to service organisations

93   **Public sector auditors generally have broad rights of access established by legislation. However, there may be situations where such rights of access are not available, for example when the service organisation is located in a different jurisdiction. In such cases, a public sector auditor may need to obtain an understanding of the legislation applicable in the different jurisdiction to determine whether appropriate access rights can be obtained. A public sector auditor may also obtain or ask the user entity to incorporate rights of access in any contractual arrangements between the user entity and the service organisation (ISA 402, A10 which relates to the requirements of ISA 402, 9).**

94   ISA (UK) 402 in itself is not sufficient to secure access rights to service organisations for the public sector auditor. It is important that where such access rights are required, appropriate arrangements are made by the audited body to provide assurance to the auditor.

95   **Public sector auditors may use another auditor to perform tests of controls or substantive procedures in relation to compliance with law, regulation or other authority (ISA 402, A11 which relates to the requirements of ISA 402, 9).**

96   **In some cases, law or regulation may require a reference to the work of a service auditor in the user auditor's report, for example, for the purposes of transparency in the public sector. In such circumstances, the user auditor may need the consent of the service auditor before making such a reference (ISA 402, A43 which relates to the requirements of ISA 402, 21).**

ISA (UK) 450: Evaluation of misstatements identified during the audit

97   **The objective of the auditor is to evaluate:**

(a)   **the effect of identified misstatements on the audit; and**

(b)   **the effect of uncorrected misstatements, if any, on the financial statements (ISA 450, 3).**

98   **In the case of an audit of a public sector entity, the evaluation whether a misstatement is material may also be affected by the auditor's responsibilities established by law, regulation or other authority to report specific matters, including, for example, fraud (ISA 450, A19 which relates to the requirements of ISA 450, 11).**

99   **Furthermore, issues such as public interest, accountability, probity and ensuring effective legislative oversight, in particular, may affect the assessment whether an item is material by virtue of its nature. This is**

particularly so for items that relate to compliance with law, regulation or other authority (ISA 450, A20 which relates to the requirements of ISA 450, 11).

ISA (UK) 510: Initial audit engagements – opening balances

In conducting an initial audit engagement, the objective of the auditor with respect to opening balances is to obtain sufficient appropriate audit evidence about whether: **100**

(a)   opening balances contain misstatements that materially affect the current period's financial statements; and

(b)   appropriate accounting policies reflected in the opening balances have been consistently applied in the current period's financial statements, or changes thereto are appropriately accounted for and adequately presented and disclosed in accordance with the applicable financial reporting framework (ISA 510, 3).

Opening balances in the context of a machinery of government change

ISA (UK) 510 is concerned with the opening balances for initial engagements. This can occur when the financial statements for the prior period were audited by another auditor, but is also relevant for "machinery of government changes" that transfer functions from one part of the public sector to another as a going concern.   **101**

Where opening balances are clearly identifiable from the preceding period's audited financial statements for the transferring entity the auditor adopts the requirements in paragraphs 6 and 7 of ISA (UK) 510.   **102**

Where opening balances are not clearly identifiable from the preceding period's audited financial statements for the transferring entity, but have been derived from balances contained in those statements, the auditor discusses with the auditor of the predecessor organisation whether information is available that would provide substantive evidence for the opening balances. In the absence of such evidence, the auditor carries out substantive testing on opening balances to confirm they have been brought forward appropriately in accordance with the terms of the transfer, at an appropriate valuation in line with the accounting policies of the receiving body.   **103**

Where opening balances have been calculated as part of a separate disaggregation or merger exercise, subject to a separate specific review and report by an auditor, the auditor considers the scope and outcomes of that separate review, and considers whether the conclusions can be relied on in accordance with ISA (UK) 500. Where the work from the separate specific review cannot be used, the auditor considers carrying out substantive testing on opening balances.   **104**

Where opening balances have been calculated as part of a separate disaggregation/merger exercise, but not subject to separate specific review and report, the auditor considers substantive testing on opening balances. Completeness of assets and liabilities, together with appropriate valuation can be risks in a disaggregation exercise, and engagement with the audited body should be made at an early stage.   **105**

Where, after performing the procedures described above, the auditor is unable to obtain sufficient appropriate audit evidence concerning the opening balances of the entity, the auditor considers the implications for the auditor's report.   **106**

The audit of opening balances by the incoming auditor

107   In the public sector, in the interests of efficiency and reducing the audit burden, the predecessor auditor is expected by the national audit agencies, relevant Codes of Audit Practice or terms of appointment to adopt a cooperative approach in dealing with enquiries and requests for information from the incoming auditor.

108   Arrangements to support a cooperative approach typically include enabling the incoming auditor to perform a review of the prior year audit documentation or have access to particular reports or papers that may be required rather than the transfer of all the relevant papers or data. While there is a clear expectation that auditors cooperate in support of effective handover arrangements, the incoming auditor remains responsible for meeting the requirements of ISA (UK) 510.

109   **In the public sector, there may be legal or regulatory limitations on the information that the current auditor can obtain from a predecessor auditor. For example, if a public sector entity that has previously been audited by a statutorily appointed auditor (for example, an Auditor General, or other suitably qualified person appointed on behalf of the Auditor General) is privatised, the amount of access to working papers or other information that the statutorily appointed auditor can provide a newly-appointed auditor that is in the private sector may be constrained by privacy or secrecy laws or regulations. In situations where such communications are constrained, audit evidence may need to be obtained through other means and, if sufficient appropriate audit evidence cannot be obtained, consideration is given to the effect on the auditor's opinion (ISA 510, A1 which relates to the requirements of ISA 510, 6).**

110   **If the statutorily appointed auditor outsources an audit of a public sector entity to a private sector audit firm, and the statutorily appointed auditor appoints an audit firm other than the firm that audited the financial statements of the public sector entity in the prior period, this is not usually regarded as a change in auditors for the statutorily appointed auditor. Depending on the nature of the outsourcing arrangement, however, the audit engagement may be considered an initial audit engagement from the perspective of the private sector auditor in fulfilling their responsibilities, and therefore this ISA (UK) applies (ISA 510, A2 which relates to the requirements of ISA 510, 6).**

ISA (UK) 520: Analytical Procedures

111   **The objectives of the auditor are:**

(a)   **to obtain relevant and reliable audit evidence when using substantive analytical procedures; and**

(b)   **to design and perform analytical procedures near the end of the audit that assist the auditor when forming an overall conclusion as to whether the financial statements are consistent with the auditor's understanding of the entity (ISA 520, 3).**

112   **The relationships between individual financial statement items traditionally considered in the audit of business entities may not always be relevant in the audit of governments or other non-business public sector entities; for example, in many public sector entities there may be little direct relationship between revenue and expenditure. In addition, because expenditure on the acquisition of assets may not be capitalised, there may be no relationship between expenditures on, for example, inventories and**

fixed [(non-current)] assets and the amount of those assets reported in the financial statements. Also, industry data or statistics for comparative purposes may not be available in the public sector. However, other relationships may be relevant, for example, variations in the cost per kilometre of road construction or the number of vehicles acquired compared with vehicles retired (ISA 520, A11 which relates to the requirements of ISA 520, 5).

ISA (UK) 540: Auditing accounting estimates, including fair value accounting estimates, and related disclosures

The objective of the auditor is to obtain sufficient appropriate audit evidence about whether: 113

(a)   accounting estimates, including fair value accounting estimates, in the financial statements, whether recognised or disclosed, are reasonable; and

(b)   related disclosures in the financial statements are adequate, in the context of the applicable financial reporting framework (ISA 540, 6).

The risk of management bias in accounting estimates in the public sector

In the public sector, factors outside of the scope of the financial reporting framework can have a significant influence on management's estimates. For example, central government departments must adhere to HM Treasury budgetary controls, so estimates in the financial statements can be influenced by the impact they have on departmental expenditure limits or the administration budget. In the health sector, statutory limits or targets can similarly influence management decisions.   114

Auditors need to understand these influences, some of which come from elsewhere within a departmental or sector group, when considering the appropriateness of accounting estimates and the assumptions applied by management.   115

The use of third-party estimates in the financial statements

Some public sector entities are reliant on accounting estimates provided by other entities within the public sector. The auditor understands how these estimates have been derived, and may need to communicate with the auditors of the entities compiling the accounting estimates on which the public sector body relies.   116

Non-current assets in the public sector

Public sector entities may have significant holdings of specialised assets [for example, heritage or infrastructure assets] for which there are no readily available and reliable sources of information for purposes of measurement at fair value or other current value bases, or a combination of both. Often specialised assets held do not generate cash flows and do not have an active market. Measurement at fair value therefore ordinarily requires estimation and may be complex, and in some rare cases may not be possible at all (ISA 540, A11 which relates to the requirements of ISA 540, 2).   117

ISA (UK) 550: Related parties

118   The objectives of the auditor are:

(a)   Irrespective of whether the applicable financial reporting framework establishes related party requirements, to obtain an understanding of related party relationships and transactions sufficient to be able:

(i)   to recognize fraud risk factors, if any, arising from related party relationships and transactions that are relevant to the identification and assessment of the risks of material misstatement due to fraud; and

(ii)   to conclude, based on the audit evidence obtained, whether the financial statements, insofar as they are affected by those relationships and transactions:

- achieve fair presentation (for fair presentation frameworks); or
- are not misleading (for compliance frameworks); and

(b)   in addition, where the applicable financial reporting framework establishes related party requirements, to obtain sufficient appropriate audit evidence about whether related party relationships and transactions have been appropriately identified, accounted for and disclosed in the financial statements in accordance with the framework (ISA 550, 9).

Public sector specific considerations with regard to related party transactions

119   The public sector auditor's responsibilities regarding related party relationships and transactions may be affected by the audit mandate, or by obligations on public sector entities arising from law, regulation or other authority. Consequently, the public sector auditor's responsibilities may not be limited to addressing the risks of material misstatement associated with related party relationships and transactions, but may also include a broader responsibility to address the risks of non-compliance with law, regulation and other authority governing public sector bodies that lay down specific requirements in the conduct of business with related parties. Further, the public sector auditor may need to have regard to public sector financial reporting requirements for related party relationships and transactions that may differ from those in the private sector (ISA 550, A8 which relates to the requirements of ISA 550, 11).

120   Financial reporting frameworks establish specific accounting and disclosure requirements for related party relationships, transactions and balances to enable users of the financial statements to understand their nature and actual or potential effects on the financial statements. In particular, the audited body may need to consider the definition of a related party in respect of public sector bodies. A public sector body is not automatically a related party to another public sector body due to its classification. The related parties of public sector entities are subject to specific restrictions on the nature and scope of the relationships that they can enter into with the entity, which prescribe practices that might be permissible in relationships outside the public sector.

121   The auditor has a responsibility to perform audit procedures to identify, assess and respond to the risks of material misstatement arising from the entity's failure to appropriately account for or disclose related party relationships, transactions or

balances in accordance with the requirements of the financial reporting framework.

ISA (UK) 560: Subsequent events

The objectives of the auditor are: **122**

(a)   **to obtain sufficient appropriate audit evidence about whether events occurring between the date of the financial statements and the date of the auditor's report that require adjustment of, or disclosure in, the financial statements are appropriately reflected in those financial statements in accordance with the applicable financial reporting framework; and**

(b)   **to respond appropriately to facts that become known to the auditor after the date of the auditor's report, that, had they been known to the auditor at that date, may have caused the auditor to amend the auditor's report (ISA 560, 4).**

Additional considerations with regard to subsequent events in the public sector

In the public sector, the auditor may read the official records of relevant   **123**
proceedings of the legislature and inquire about matters addressed in proceedings for which official records are not yet available (ISA 560, A10 which relates to the requirements of ISA 560, 7).

In addition to giving audit opinions on the financial statements, auditors of certain   **124**
local government and health entities may be required to:

●   discharge certain statutory responsibilities and duties; and

●   issue a certificate confirming that the audit and all related responsibilities and duties have been completed in accordance with the legislation.

The issue of the audit completion certificate marks the end of the exercise of the   **125**
auditor's powers and duties in respect of that statutory audit.

Fulfilling the auditor's other statutory responsibilities and duties may lead to a   **126**
significant delay between when the auditor has obtained sufficient appropriate audit evidence to provide the opinion on the financial statements and when the auditor is in a position to issue the audit completion certificate.

In such circumstances, the auditor assesses whether the actions the auditor expects   **127**
to take in discharge of those additional statutory responsibilities and duties could give rise to matters that could have a material effect on the financial statements. If the auditor believes that discharge of those statutory responsibilities and duties are likely to give rise to matters that would have a material effect on the financial statements, the auditor does not provide an opinion on the financial statements until after those additional steps have been completed.

An opinion given on the financial statements of a local government or health entity   **128**
in advance of the issue of the audit completion certificate is:

●   the final opinion on the financial statements for the purposes of compliance with ISAs (UK); and

●   issued to coincide with the proposed date of issue of the financial statements by the audit committee.

After the audited financial statements have been issued an auditor has no   **129**
obligation to perform audit procedures regarding those financial statements.

Accordingly, when subsequently issuing the audit completion certificate, there is no requirement for the auditor to seek out information that may have implications for the audit opinion that has already been given.

130   If, after the financial statements have been issued, a fact becomes known to the auditor that, had it been known to the auditor at the date of the auditor's report on the financial statements, may have caused the auditor to amend the auditor's report:

- ISA (UK) 560, paragraph 14, requires the auditor to perform further procedures; and

- If, after completing such further procedures, the auditor concludes that there is relevant information that would have impacted the opinion on the financial statements, the auditor refers to such matters in the audit completion certificate.

131   If the auditor has not issued an audit completion certificate on the prior year audit then an audit completion certificate is not issued on the current year audit until the audit completion certificate in relation to the prior year has been issued.

Facts which become known to the auditor after the date of the auditor's report but before the financial statements are issued

132   The financial statements of central government entities are considered to be issued on the following dates:

Central government entities where the statutory auditor is responsible for the printing of the document containing the audited financial statements	Date of despatch by the auditor to the Clerk of the House of Commons or House of Lords for laying before Parliament. This is normally the same date as the auditor's certificate and report.
Central government entities where the financial statements are laid before the Houses of Parliament by the Secretary of State of the sponsoring department or by HM Treasury, and where the statements are considered by an intermediate body before being laid before Parliament	Date of despatch by those charged with governance to the Secretary of State of the sponsoring department or HM Treasury, or to the Members of the intermediate body, whichever is the earlier.
Welsh Government and its sponsored and related public bodies, and NHS Wales entities	Date of despatch by the Auditor General to the Table Office of the National Assembly.
Central government entities in Scotland	Date of despatch by the Auditor General for laying by the Scottish Ministers before the Scottish Parliament.
Central government and health entities in Northern Ireland	Date of despatch by the department, body or person specified in the relevant legislation for laying before the Northern Ireland Assembly.

Date financial statements are laid before members or equivalent

In the case of the public sector, the date the financial statements are issued   133
may be the date the audited financial statements and the auditor's report
thereon are presented to the legislature or otherwise made public (ISA 560,
A5 which relates to the requirements of ISA 560, 5).

In central government, the financial statements of most reporting entities are   134
generally laid before: the House of Commons; the House of Lords; both of these
Houses of Parliament; the National Assembly for Wales, the Northern Ireland
Assembly or the Scottish Parliament. However, for certain entities, usually arm's
length public bodies, the financial statements may also be considered by an
intermediate body (often a board, trustees or equivalent) before being formally
laid before Parliament, either by the intermediate body, by the Secretary of State of
the department responsible for the entity, or by HM Treasury. Where such a
reporting hierarchy exists, the auditor considers subsequent events that the auditor
becomes aware of and that occur from the date of the auditor's report until the date
on which the financial statements are laid before the Parliament or the Assembly.

The financial statements of some central government entities are not formally laid   135
before the Houses of Parliament but may be deposited in the libraries of the House
of Commons and House of Lords by the sponsor department. Because the
financial statements of these entities are not formally laid before Parliament, the
auditor only considers subsequent events that occur up to the date on which the
financial statements are issued. Otherwise, the auditor of a central government
entity follows the requirements of ISA (UK) 560 for subsequent events occurring
between the dates of issue and of laying before the Parliament or the Assembly.

If those charged with governance decide not to amend the financial statements,   136
where the auditor believes that they need to be revised, the auditor considers
taking appropriate steps on a timely basis to prevent reliance on the auditor's
report:

- if the financial statements are considered by an intermediate body before
  being despatched to the Secretary of State of the sponsor department and
  before being laid before Parliament, the auditor considers making a
  statement to that body, depending on the auditor's relationship with the
  intermediate body as may be set out in the auditor's terms of engagement,
  and in the light of any legal advice on the auditor's position; and

- if there is no intermediate body, and the entity has despatched the financial
  statements to the Secretary of State of the sponsor department but they have
  yet to be laid before Parliament, then subject to any legal advice on the
  auditor's position, the auditor considers reporting the auditor's concerns to
  the department. If the content of the auditor's letter of appointment is based
  on the guidance issued by HM Treasury, the auditor normally has right of
  access to report to the department any matters of importance arising out of
  the auditor's work.

In the public sector, the actions taken in accordance with paragraph 13 [of   137
ISA 560] when management does not amend the financial statements may
also include reporting separately to the legislature, or other relevant body in
the reporting hierarchy, on the implications of the subsequent event for the
financial statements and the auditor's report (ISA 560, A14 which relates to
the requirements of ISA 560, 13).

Where the financial statements are produced by an entity which is audited by the   138
Comptroller and Auditor General, the auditor has the possibility of reporting

separately to Parliament on the implications of the subsequent event for the financial statements and the auditor's report. Similar arrangements enable the Auditor General for Wales to report separately to the National Assembly for Wales, the Auditor General for Scotland to report to the Scottish Parliament and for the Comptroller and Auditor General for Northern Ireland to the Northern Ireland Assembly. For local government or health entities the issue of the audit completion certificate marks the closure of the audit and the end of the exercise of the auditor's powers.

139   Where the subsequent event occurred after the date of the auditor's report, the auditor may, in addition to seeking legal advice, discuss the matter with the entity's Chief Executive and with the sponsor department to establish whether it might be possible to withdraw the auditor's report before the financial statements are laid before the Parliament or the Assembly.

140   **In some jurisdictions, entities in the public sector may be prohibited from issuing amended financial statements by law or regulation. In such circumstances, the appropriate course of action for the auditor may be to report to the appropriate statutory body (ISA 560, A17 which relates to the requirements of ISA 560, 15).**

Facts which become known after the financial statements have been issued

141   In the public sector, the issue of the auditor's statutory audit opinion marks the end of the audit and once the financial statements have been issued they cannot be revised and the auditor's report cannot be reissued.

142   If a matter that needs to be drawn to the attention of stakeholders arises once the financial statements have been issued, the auditor has other mechanisms available for making a public statement. For example, in the central government sector the relevant Auditor General can report to Parliament/Assembly or local auditors can consider the issue of a public interest report.

ISA (UK) 570: Going concern

143   **The objectives of the auditor are:**

(a)   **to obtain sufficient appropriate audit evidence regarding, and conclude on, the appropriateness of management's use of the going concern basis of accounting in the preparation of the financial statements;**

(b)   **to conclude, based on the audit evidence obtained, whether a material uncertainty exists related to events or conditions that may cast significant doubt on the entity's ability to continue as a going concern; and**

(c)   **to report in accordance with this ISA (UK). (ISA 570, 9).**

Going concern in the public sector

144   **Going concern issues arise in the public sector. They include, but are not limited to, situations where public sector entities operate on a for-profit basis, where government support may be reduced or withdrawn, or in the case of privatisation. Events or conditions that may cast significant doubt on an entity's ability to continue as a going concern in the public sector may include situations where the public sector entity lacks funding for its continued existence or when policy decisions are made that affect the services provided**

by the public sector entity (ISA 570, A2 which relates to the requirements of ISA 570, 10).

Due to the introduction of the revised auditing standards in June 2016, these **145** sections of this guidance have been amended to reflect the change in the auditor's reporting responsibilities in respect of going concern. In particular, auditors should be aware of reporting by exception on the robustness of management's assessment and adequacy of disclosures in respect of the principal risks facing the entity, as well as reporting on material uncertainty in respect of going concern in a separate section of the auditor's report. Auditors should refer to the relevant version of the standard for audit requirements and further application guidance.

The auditor should, in the first instance, review the management's assessment of **146** going concern and the adequacy of disclosures of the basis for preparing the financial statements. In the public sector, entities may have a deficit of income over expenditure or an excess of liabilities over assets. However, the operational existence of a public sector entity will not always cease, or its scale of operations be subject to a forced reduction, as a result of an inability to finance its operations or of net liabilities. The reasons for this are:

● local government entities are statutory bodies that are required to maintain delivery of functions essential to the local communities, are themselves revenue-raising bodies and have the possibility, on application, of recovering losses over a period;

● there is a general assumption that no part of the NHS will be allowed to cease operations other than by deliberate closure by central government, announced in advance. Legislation is in place under which the liabilities of NHS trusts are transferred to another public entity if the trust is closed; and

● government departments can act to avoid financial failures by individual entities in central government and other parts of the public sector and thus secure continuation of the delivery of public services.

Cessation is most likely to result from a legislative change or a decision made by **147** Parliament/Assembly. A decision may be taken to:

● wind-up and dissolve an entity in its entirety, where central government determines that the entity's functions are no longer required;

● wind-up and dissolve all or part of an entity, but transfer some or all of its functions to another entity in the same sector or another sector;

● merge the entity, or some part of it, with another in the same sector; or

● privatise an entity, or some part of it, where the government decides that certain functions would be better delivered by the private sector.

In each of these cases the operational existence of all or part of the entity ceases, **148** but only in the case of dissolution without any continuation of operations would the going concern basis cease clearly to be appropriate. In the other cases the auditor considers the basis on which the activities are transferred, from the viewpoint of the entity that is relinquishing the assets and liabilities at the accounting date.

In the public sector it is not uncommon for statutory bodies to give guarantees **149** which, if called upon, cannot be met by the resources currently available to the organisation. In such circumstances, the auditor considers whether the disclosures made by management in respect of going concern are adequate and whether the matter needs to be referred to in the auditors report.

150   Where a central government entity operates at arm's length from government, particularly in a trading capacity, the auditor may determine that a deficit of income over expenditure or an excess of liabilities over assets undermines the going concern assumption.

Consideration of the foreseeable future

151   ISA (UK) 570 specifies that, in assessing whether the going concern assumption is appropriate, those charged with governance take into account all available information for the foreseeable future, which is at least 12 months from the reporting date. If the period to which those charged with governance have paid particular attention in assessing going concern is less than one year from the date of approval of the financial statements, and those charged with governance have not disclosed this fact, the auditor shall do so within the auditor's report.

152   Decisions to abolish, transfer or privatise the functions of public sector bodies are inherently subject to political uncertainty, for example changes of government or ministerial positions. However, it is rare that the future cannot be predicted with some certainty for the period up to one year from the date of approval of the financial statements. Political decisions, in particular transfers of functions between different entities, can often be as, or even more uncertain than those completely unforeseeable risks faced by all private sector companies, of which neither the directors nor the auditor could be aware.

The auditor's responsibilities for the consideration of the appropriateness of the going concern basis

153   In forming a view on the entity's ability to continue its operations, the public sector auditor's consideration of going concern covers two separate, but sometimes overlapping, factors:

- the risk associated with changes in policy direction; and

- operational or business risk.

154   The auditor ascertains whether the Parliament/Assembly has a known intention to abolish, transfer or privatise the activities of the audited entity.

155   When the auditor becomes aware of information which indicates that the Parliament/Assembly has made, or plans to make, a decision which is likely to impact on the entity's continued operational existence, the auditor first establishes whether the entity's operational activities are likely to be transferred elsewhere in the public sector. If they are, irrespective of whether the entity will continue to operate, the going concern basis of preparation of the financial statements is likely to remain appropriate. If not, then in considering the going concern assumption, the auditor may decide to request that the audited entity secures from the relevant department or executive body a letter of financial support, confirming that the entity continues to have financial backing to utilise its assets and meet liabilities as they fall due. The decision to obtain evidence of support should take into account other results of the management's or the auditor's assessment of going concern, for example the assessment of forecasts, available resources and material uncertainties.

156   Some public sector bodies may have a statutory duty to break even. The existence of such a requirement may influence the scope and nature of audit procedures, for example, it may be appropriate to consider the financial performance of the entity, including the effectiveness of financial recovery plans. Failing to break-even does not in itself indicate a going concern issue.

Given that a key consideration in the public sector is Parliament's/Assembly's   **157**
intention, the public sector auditor may consider requesting that the entity secures
direct confirmation from the department or executive body responsible for
providing financial backing to the entity. In such circumstances, a
representation provided by the Accounting/Accountable Officer or responsible
financial officer of the entity that financial backing will continue to be received
may not be sufficient as meaningful assurance over the future of an entity. This is
because the representation could be based upon presumption of knowledge of
facts about the intentions of the financial backer that might not be possessed by the
entity or judgements about future conditions for support that the entity is not
capable of making.

Where the auditor judges that the going concern basis is appropriate for the   **158**
preparation of a public sector entity's financial statements substantially on the
basis of third-party confirmations received from the department or executive body
responsible for providing financial backing, the auditor considers whether this is a
matter of such significance that the confirmations are referred to in the financial
statements and in the auditor's report as being relevant to a proper understanding
of the basis of the auditor's opinion.

If no appropriate representations or confirmations can be obtained, the auditor   **159**
considers whether there is a material uncertainty that requires a separate section
under the heading "Material Uncertainty Related to Going Concern" in the
auditor's report.

*Going concern where public sector entities prepare financial statements on a
cash basis*

Where central government entities prepare financial statements on a cash basis,   **160**
ISA (UK) 570 does not apply to the audit as the going concern basis is not used in
the preparation of the statements. However, the auditor still considers whether
there are any matters affecting the audited entity's ability to continue as a going
concern. Where the auditor identifies such matters, the auditor considers the need
to report separately to Parliament on those matters or, where there is material
uncertainty over the use of the going concern basis, the auditor draws attention to
the going concern disclosures under the heading "Material Uncertainty Related to
Going Concern" in the auditor's report. The auditor does not, however, modify the
audit opinion on the proper presentation of the financial statements.

*Public sector auditors' responsibilities for reviewing and reporting upon an
entity's arrangements for securing value for money*

Auditing frameworks may require public sector auditors to review and report upon   **161**
the entity's arrangements for securing value for money and in such cases it may be
appropriate for auditors to consider how the entity ensures that it is able to
maintain the sustainability of its services and finances. But, where auditors
identify concerns about an entity's general financial health, or its arrangements
for maintaining the sustainability of its services and finances, this does not
necessarily cast doubt upon the entity's ability to continue to prepare its
financial statements on a going concern basis.

ISA (UK) 580: Written representations

162   **The objectives of the auditor are:**

(a)   **to obtain written representations from management and, where appropriate, those charged with governance that they believe that they have fulfilled their responsibility for the preparation of the financial statements and for the completeness of the information provided to the auditor;**

(b)   **to support other audit evidence relevant to the financial statements or specific assertions in the financial statements by means of written representations if determined necessary by the auditor or required by other ISAs (UK); and**

(c)   **to respond appropriately to written representations provided by management and, where appropriate, those charged with governance, or if management or, where appropriate, those charged with governance do not provide the written representations requested by the auditor. (ISA 580, 6).**

Identifying who is competent to give written representation in the public sector

163   The auditor takes care to ensure that representations are only accepted from those competent to give them, such that:

●   acknowledgement of the responsibilities of "directors" for the financial statements is made by those in whom the responsibilities are vested; and

●   management representations on matters material to the financial statements are made by persons who have knowledge of the facts or who are authorised to make the judgement or express the opinion.

164   In central government and health entities, representations will usually be obtained from the Accounting Officer or the Accountable Officer. At local government bodies, the responsible finance officer has statutory responsibility for the proper administration of the entity's financial affairs. The auditor of a local government entity may therefore obtain representations from the responsible finance officer.

The content on written representations in the public sector

165   **The mandates for audits of the financial statements of public sector entities may be broader than those of other entities. As a result, the premise, relating to management's responsibilities, on which an audit of the financial statements of a public sector entity is conducted may give rise to additional written representations. These may include written representations confirming that transactions and events have been carried out in accordance with law, regulation or other authority (ISA 580, A9 which relates to the requirements of ISA 580, 10–11).**

ISA (UK) 600: Special considerations – audits of group financial statements (including the work of component auditors)

166   **The objectives of the auditor are:**

(a)   **to determine whether to act as the auditor of the group financial statements; and**

(b)   **if acting as the auditor of the group financial statements:**

(i)   to communicate clearly with component auditors about the scope and timing of their work on financial information related to components and their findings; and

(ii) to obtain sufficient appropriate audit evidence regarding the financial information of the components and the consolidation process to express an opinion on whether the group financial statements are prepared, in all material respects, in accordance with the applicable financial reporting framework (ISA 600, 8).

In certain parts of the public sector where the responsibilities of principal and other   **167** auditors are governed by statutory provisions, these may override the provisions of ISA (UK) 600 (ISA 600, A1-1 which relates to the requirements of ISA 600, 3).

In the public sector, the option of declining or withdrawing from an engagement   **168** may not be available to the auditor due to the nature of the mandate or public interest considerations. In these circumstances, ISA (UK) 600 still applies to the group audit, and the effect of the group engagement team's inability to obtain sufficient appropriate audit evidence is considered in terms of ISA (UK) 705.

Where the group auditor uses the work of component auditors, the group auditor   **169** should determine the component materiality. In particular, the group auditor may need to give careful consideration to the implications of auditors of different entities within the group, some of which may be companies, using a different benchmark for setting materiality for their audited body. The group auditor should consider whether the component materiality is appropriate in respect of the group materiality.

Groups are common in certain parts of the public sector. For example, central   **170** government in the United Kingdom issues consolidated financial statements for government departments and Whole of Government Accounts. Individual public sector entities may have shares or ownership in companies.

Auditors should be aware of the specific public sector interpretations in respect of   **171** preparation of the group accounts and a definition of control. These may be included in the applicable financial reporting framework, for example the Government Financial Reporting Manual. Based on that information, the auditor should assess whether the audited entity should produce group financial statements and which entities should be consolidated.

ISA (UK) 610: Using the work of internal auditors

The objectives of the external auditor, where the entity has an internal audit   **172** function and the external auditor expects to use the work of the function to modify the nature or timing, or reduce the extent, of audit procedures to be performed directly by the external auditor, or to use internal auditors to provide direct assistance, are:

(a)   to determine whether the work of the internal audit function or direct assistance from internal auditors can be used, and if so, in which areas and to what extent;

and having made that determination:

(b)   if using the work of the internal audit function, to determine whether that work is adequate for purposes of the audit; and

(c)   **if using internal auditors to provide direct assistance, to appropriately direct, supervise and review their work. (ISA 610, 13).**

Using the work of internal audit in relation to the auditor's other responsibilities.

173   The auditor may have responsibilities to review the systems of internal control, in addition to the audit of financial statements, for example to provide a negative assurance on the Governance Statement. The work of internal audit may be assessed for such purposes, even if the auditor considers that it may not be possible or desirable to use its work in specific areas for the purpose of the external audit of the financial statements.

174   The work of internal audit may also be considered in relation to the auditor's other responsibilities. Where matters come to the auditor's attention relating to the work of internal audit, these findings are properly reviewed in accordance with ISA (UK) 610 for their potential impact on the audit of the financial statements.

ISA (UK) 620: Using the work of an auditor's expert

175   **The objectives of the auditor are:**

(a)   **to determine whether to use the work of an auditor's expert; and**

(b)   **if using the work of an auditor's expert, to determine whether that work is adequate for the auditor's purposes (ISA 620, 5).**

176   In the public sector, there may be circumstances (in addition to those described in ISA (UK) 620), where the auditor is required to use the work of an auditor's expert. For example, for the audit of specialist or complex accounting estimates, the auditor may need to appoint an expert to obtain understanding of the estimation process. Another example is when one auditor appoints an expert to provide assurance to a number of auditors, for example in respect of professional valuation of properties or a pension scheme.

177   **In some cases, law or regulation may require a reference [in the audit report] to the work of an auditor's expert, for example, for the purposes of transparency in the public sector (ISA 620, A41 which relates to the requirements of ISA 620, 14).**

ISA (UK) 700: Forming an opinion and reporting on financial statements

178   **The objectives of the auditor are:**

(a)   **to form an opinion on the financial statements based on an evaluation of the conclusions drawn from the audit evidence obtained; and**

(b)   **to express clearly that opinion through a written report (ISA 700, 6).**

179   Due to the introduction of the revised auditing standards in June 2016, the section of this guidance on extended auditor's reporting has been amended to reflect the fact that some requirements previously included in ISA (UK) 700 are now covered in a separate standard – ISA (UK) 701. Auditors, who have regard to this Practice Note but have not yet adopted the revised standards, should refer to the requirements on extended reporting in the applicable ISA 700: The independent auditor's report on financial statements.

Addressee of the auditor's report in the public sector

180   ISA (UK) 700 requires the title of an auditor's report to identify the person or persons to whom it is addressed. This is normally the person or persons on whose

behalf the audit is undertaken and will vary across the public sector, depending upon the relevant auditing framework.

Reports by contracted-out auditors to national audit agencies

Where an audit is carried out on a "contracted-out" basis then the contract between   **181**
the firm and the audit agency may specify that the firm issues an audit report to the audit agency. Under these circumstances this is outside of the scope of ISA (UK) 700 and the reporting arrangements will be defined by the contract between the firm and the audit agency. The report the firm issues to the audit agency reflects the scope of the engagement under the terms of the contract.

The requirement to certify that the audit has been completed in the public sector

For certain entities there is a requirement to certify that the audit has been carried   **182**
out or to certify that the audit has been completed. The former is a fundamental part of the audit opinion as required by the legislation for specific public bodies and is incorporated into the wording of the introductory paragraph to the auditor's report. The latter is a wider responsibility for auditors of local government in England and Wales and health entities in England and its link with the opinion on the financial statements needs to be understood. Auditors may refer to the separate guidance on this issue that is published by the relevant national audit agency.

Reference to the basis for the audit in the public sector auditor's report

Where the requirement to audit an entity's financial statements is provided for   **183**
under statute, the auditor refers to the relevant Act of Parliament and accounts direction when identifying the financial statements have been audited. The relevant Act of Parliament and accounts direction will vary across the public sector.

Implications of the prescribed wording of the audit opinion on compliance with International Standards on Auditing (UK)

Although most public sector financial statements require an opinion as to whether   **184**
the financial statements give a true and fair view, some auditing frameworks requires an opinion as to whether the financial statements present fairly or properly present the entity's transactions or balances. Whichever wording is used will not have an impact on the extent to which the auditor observes the requirements of auditing standards.

Extended auditor reporting

Listed entities are not common in the public sector. However, public sector   **185**
entities may be significant due to size, complexity or public interest
aspects. In such cases, an auditor of a public sector entity may be
required by law or regulation or may otherwise decide to communicate
key audit matters in the auditor's report (ISA 700, A38 which relates to
the requirements of ISA 700, 31).

Auditors of public sector entities may also have the ability pursuant to law or   **186**
regulation to report publicly on certain matters, either in the auditor's report
or in a supplementary report, which may include information that is
consistent with the objectives of ISA 701. In such circumstances, the
auditor may need to tailor certain aspects of the communication of key
audit matters in the auditor's report required by ISA 701 or include a

reference in the auditor's report to a description of the matter in the supplementary report (ISA 700, A70 which relates to the requirements of ISA 700, 50).

187 Extended auditor's reporting requirements including key audit matters (as determined by ISA 701)[3] apply in the public sector, where the audited body is required by the regulator or voluntarily chooses to adopt the UK Corporate Governance Code. While many public sector bodies do not meet these criteria, the auditor may consider it appropriate to include this information required by ISA 701 in the audit report or issue a separate report for additional openness and transparency or where required by relevant Codes of Audit Practice or equivalent.

188 Some public sector auditors may have additional statutory powers and responsibilities to report on matters of interest to the relevant Parliament, Assembly or regulator. This may include, for example, background information on the basis for the audit opinion, inadequate financial control or propriety issues.

Matters to be reported by exception in the public sector

189 The Companies Act 2006 requires company auditors to report on certain matters by exception, including where:

- adequate accounting records have not been kept, or returns adequate for the audit have not been received from branches not visited during the audit; or

- the financial statements are not in agreement with the accounting records or returns; or

- they have not received all of the information and explanations they require for their audit.

190 Public sector auditors report on these matters by exception, as set out in the terms of the engagement.

ISA (UK) 706: Emphasis of matter paragraphs and other matter paragraphs in the independent auditor's report

191 **The objective of the auditor, having formed an opinion on the financial statements, is to draw users' attention, when in the auditor's judgement it is necessary to do so, by way of clear additional communication in the auditor's report, to:**

(a) **a matter, although appropriately presented or disclosed in the financial statements, that is of such importance that it is fundamental to users' understanding of the financial statements; or**

(b) **as appropriate, any other matter that is relevant to users' understanding of the audit, the auditor's responsibilities or the auditor's report (ISA 706, 6).**

192 In the public sector withdrawal from the audit may not always be possible. Where this option is preferential, but not available, the auditor may also consider it necessary to include an Other Matter paragraph in the auditor's report or to report relevant matters to the appropriate statutory body.

---

[3] *ISA 701 is effective for audits of financial statements for periods commencing on or after 17 June 2016. Early application is permitted.*

ISA (UK) 720: The auditor's responsibilities relating to other information

The objectives of the auditor, having read the other information, are: **193**

(a)   to consider whether there is a material inconsistency between the other information and the financial statements;

(b)   to consider whether there is a material inconsistency between the other information and the auditor's knowledge obtained in the audit;

(c)   to respond appropriately when the auditor identifies that such material inconsistencies appear to exist, or when the auditor otherwise becomes aware that other information appears to be materially misstated;

(d)   where required by law or regulation, to form an opinion on whether the information given in the other information is consistent with the financial statements and the auditor's knowledge obtained in the audit; and

(e)   to report in accordance with this ISA (UK) (ISA 720, 11).

The auditor's responsibilities relating to the annual report

Many public sector entities are required to include an annual report in the same   **194** documents as the financial statements. For the most part, entities are required to incorporate the elements of the Companies Act Strategic and Directors' Report within this additional material. The terms of engagement for the national audit agency also normally require an opinion to be made on the consistency of that material with the financial statements audited. As the material may be dispersed within other surrounding information published with the accounts, it is important for the audit report to identify what is covered by the consistency opinion.

In addition to this consistency opinion, ISA 720 (UK) requires the auditor to read   **195** all information published with the financial statements, which includes all material covered by the consistency opinion. Again, the audit report clarifies what content has been read.

By agreement with the relevant bodies, some public sector auditors report by   **196** exception where the Governance Statement does not reflect compliance with the relevant guidance. The auditor's responsibility in respect of the Governance Statement is to review the statement. This review is not to provide assurance on the statement, but to:

●   consider the completeness of the disclosures in meeting the reporting requirements;

●   identify whether the disclosures are misleading; and

●   identify any inconsistencies between the disclosures and the information that the auditor is aware of from audit work.

Requirements for publishing other information alongside financial statements   **197** varies depending on the nature of the entity's operations and the reporting requirements. Typically, they may include a statement setting out the responsibilities of the Accounting/Accountable Officer or equivalent and a corporate governance statement.

The auditor might be required to provide a separate opinion on consistency of   **198** summary financial information (or equivalent) with financial statements. Where this information is not published alongside the financial statements, the auditor issues a separate report with a consistency opinion to accompany this information.

Reporting to the legislature

199   **In the public sector, withdrawal from the engagement may not be possible. In such cases, the auditor may issue a report to the legislature providing details of the matter or may take other appropriate actions (ISA 720, A47 which relates to the requirements of ISA 720, 18).**

Part 2: The audit of regularity

Introduction

1   This part of the Practice Note sets out guidance on public sector auditors' considerations of regularity and related matters. It covers:

- understanding the concept of regularity:
- how regularity relates to other concepts including propriety and compliance with laws and regulations;
- the audit of regularity – an overview;
- understanding the entity and its environment;
- understanding the entity's internal controls;
- materiality for the audit of regularity;
- assessing the risk of material irregularity;
- planning and performing audit procedures;
- areas requiring special consideration;
- written representations;
- using the work of others;
- evaluating irregularities;
- the risk of fraud in the audit of regularity;
- regularity opinion on financial statements; and
- other reporting on regularity.

2   Public sector auditors may have statutory powers and responsibilities in relation to how audited bodies use public funds. Some of these responsibilities may be discharged through the audit of regularity, where required by legislation. The audit of regularity is related to the audit of financial statements and so it is covered by this Practice Note. Auditors may also be required to report in respect of propriety or the economy, efficiency and effectiveness (value for money) of the use of public funds. These are not covered by this Practice Note and the auditors should refer to the specific legislative framework and other guidance, for example Codes of Audit Practice development by a relevant audit agency.

3   This part of the Practice Note focuses on the audit of regularity to provide a reasonable assurance opinion. Some public sector entities may require limited or other assurance engagements as part of funding obligations or grant conditions set by other public sector bodies. Guidance on such engagements is not included in this Practice Note and the auditors should consult other relevant information on engagements of this type. For example, academy trusts and college corporations in England are required to commission external auditors, as reporting accountants, to perform an annual review of regularity (which, in this case, is a type of a limited

assurance engagement) as part of their funding conditions. The auditors should refer to the relevant framework document (e.g. an accounts direction or a tripartite agreement) and other professional guidance (e.g. the ICAEW technical release on regularity reporting for academies or International Standard on Assurance Engagements (ISAE) 3000) for further information about other assurance engagement in respect of regularity.

Understanding the concept of regularity

Regularity is the concept that transactions that are reflected in the financial   4
statements of an audited entity must be in accordance with the relevant framework of authorities.

Frameworks of authorities are external frameworks, specific to the audited entity,   5
with which the audited entity's transactions must conform. These frameworks are set up by bodies able to issue and/or enforce the authorities for that entity and might include, for example:

* authorising legislation;

* regulations issued under governing legislation;

* parliamentary authorities (including budgetary laws, for example budget estimates voted by the relevant Parliament/Assembly); and

* government or related authorities (for example *Managing Public Money*[4] issued by HM Treasury).

The concept of regularity reflects concerns of the users of the public sector   6
accounts that public money raised is used only for the purposes intended by relevant framework of authorities. The preparation of financial statements by public bodies is an important means by which they are held accountable for the use of public funds.

For the audit of central government (or equivalent) and some health bodies, there   7
is an explicit statutory requirement on the auditor to provide an additional audit opinion on whether, in all material respects, expenditure and income (payments and receipts) have been applied for the purposes intended by Parliament, where applicable and conform with the authorities which govern them. The auditor can adopt an integrated audit approach covering the audit of the financial statements and supplemented by additional testing of regularity, where necessary. To facilitate this approach, the financial statements auditor would normally be appointed as the regularity auditor.

How regularity relates to other concepts including propriety and compliance with laws and regulations

Whereas regularity is concerned with compliance with a relevant framework of   8
authorities, propriety is concerned more with standards of conduct, behaviour and corporate governance. It includes matters such as fairness, integrity, the avoidance of personal profit from public business, even-handedness in the appointment of staff, open competition in the letting of contracts and the avoidance of waste and extravagance.

---

[4] *Managing Public Money provides guidance on how to handle public funds and sets out the regularity framework for central government in the UK. The document can be found on the following website: www.gov.uk/government/publications/managing-public-money*

9   Propriety is not readily susceptible to objective verification and, as such, is not expressly covered in the opinion on financial statements. When issues of propriety come to light in the course of the audit of financial statements, the auditor considers whether and, if so, how they may be reported.

10   Propriety might be part of the wider statutory role of the auditor or might fall within the terms of the audit engagement. For example, in Scotland, the Public Finance and Accountability (Scotland) Act 2000 requires audits of accounts for which the Auditor General is responsible to include auditor's reports that set out findings on whether the expenditure and receipts shown in the account were incurred or applied in accordance with relevant statutory provisions and with any applicable guidance (whether as to propriety or otherwise) issued by Scottish Ministers.

11   As part of the audit of regularity, the auditor assesses the audited body's compliance with relevant laws and regulations. This consideration feeds into work performed by the auditor under ISA (UK) 250A. The guidance on the application of this ISA can be found in Part 1 of this Practice Note.

The audit of regularity – an overview

12   The auditor's approach to the audit of the regularity of transactions in the financial statements of public sector entities is similar to the audit approach set out in ISA 250A (UK) Section A: Consideration of laws and regulations in an audit of financial statements. It can be summarised as:

- obtaining a sufficient understanding of the framework of authorities that are specific to the entity. The auditor obtains a broad understanding that is sufficient to enable identification of transactions or events that may have a significant effect on the regularity of transactions in the financial statements. The auditor also considers the systems and procedures in place to ensure compliance with the framework of authorities. The auditor obtains an understanding of the internal control environment to enable a preliminary assessment of controls which mitigate the risk of material irregularity;

- obtaining sufficient appropriate evidence to obtain assurance over regularity. Taking into account materiality, the auditor performs audit procedures on transactions through a combination of tests of controls and substantive procedures. Audit procedures can be integrated with those relating to the audit of the financial statements; and

- reporting on regularity through a separate and explicit opinion on regularity or separate reports on regularity issues.

13   In certain parts of the public sector, the principles and procedures applied to obtain sufficient appropriate evidence to support an opinion on the regularity are similar to those applied to the audit of the financial statements. Thus, in forming an opinion on regularity, the auditor seeks to provide reasonable assurance that the financial statements are free from material irregularity.

14   There may, however, be particular considerations in respect of the auditor's assessment of materiality, risk and the design of audit procedures in relation to regularity that are set out in this Practice Note. In addition to these considerations, the auditor may have particular regard to the regularity of receipts, the disclosure of transactions in accordance with relevant framework of authorities, and securing management representations.

The auditor, in the audit of regularity, is expected to comply with the Financial   **15**
Reporting Council's ethical, auditing and quality control standards and the
guidance set out in this Practice Note.

Understanding the entity and its environment

An auditor in the public sector has, or obtains an understanding of the framework   **16**
of authorities governing the audited body and its activities which is sufficient to
enable identification of events, transactions and practices which may have a
material effect on the regularity of transactions in the financial statements.

The extent of the auditor's work in relation to obtaining a sufficient understanding   **17**
of the regulatory framework will depend on the complexity of the laws and
regulations. In complex regulatory environments, the auditor considers the
translation of the framework of authorities into relevant rules and procedures
used by the audited entity.

In all regards, the audited entity retains the responsibility for ensuring the regularity   **18**
of its transactions and for disclosing these transactions in the financial statements.
However, the auditor has a responsibility for understanding the framework of
authorities and cannot wholly rely on management representations about the
framework, as the auditor's opinion on regularity must be based on evidence of
compliance with the framework of authorities, rather than on evidence of
compliance with the entity's understanding of the framework.

The auditor can identify the framework of authorities from a number of sources,   **19**
including:

- a framework document or accounts direction, where issued under the
  authorising legislation;

- previous experience with the entity or similar entities;

- review of legislation and regulations governing the audited body;

- discussions with the staff employed by the entity (finance officers, internal
  audit, policy and legal branches); or

- documents produced by the entity (for example: minutes of board and other
  principal committee meetings; correspondence and minutes of meetings
  with relevant authorising bodies; prior years' financial and annual reports;
  budgets; internal management reports; management policy manuals;
  manuals of accounting and internal control; and scheme control plans).

In considering the framework of authorities, the auditor distinguishes between   **20**
those authorities which are specific to the entity and provide specific direct
authority for its financial transactions and those laws and regulations which
provide the general framework within which it conducts its activities.

Laws and regulations that fall within the general framework include, for example,   **21**
those relating to health and safety, environmental protection and employment.
While non-compliance with those laws and regulations that provide the general
legal framework would not affect the auditor's opinion on the regularity of
transactions, some of these may be relevant to the auditor's assessment of
compliance with laws and regulations under ISA (UK) 250 Section A.

Understanding the framework of authorities and using this information   **22**
appropriately will assist the auditor in developing the audit plan and in
identifying potential material irregularity in the financial statements, for
example, from new and complex legislation or from a misinterpretation of
legislation and its scope. The auditor's understanding of the authorities includes

knowledge of the reasons for the legislation and its objectives as this will aid the auditor's understanding of any secondary legislation or subsidiary regulations. The nature and complexity of the relevant legislation and other authorities has an impact on the extent of the auditor's work on regularity.

Understanding the entity's internal controls

23   In planning the audit of regularity, the auditor considers how the entity's management complies with the framework and where relevant, addresses the risk of material irregularity through controls. This involves an assessment of the general control environment at the entity level and control procedures relating to individual transaction streams that are designed to prevent or detect and correct material irregularities.

24   As part of the auditor's review of the control environment, the auditor considers the general control framework for ensuring regularity, including:

- the entity's organisational structure and the extent to which the responsibility for ensuring regularity is delegated;

- methods of ensuring regularity and accountability where the responsibility for it is delegated;

- the results of any relevant internal audit work which covers controls over compliance with laws and regulations or regularity; and

- the entity's corporate governance arrangements, insofar as the arrangements address compliance with regulations, in particular the work carried out by the entity to support the corporate governance statements, and the auditor's own work in reviewing the statements.

25   Controls and procedures which the audited body operates to ensure regularity of individual transaction streams may include, for example:

- application of desk instructions for staff which translate statutory requirements into a set of operating procedures;

- monitoring of compliance with financial memoranda; or

- receipt of reports on compliance from auditors of other entities.

26   It is sometimes necessary for the auditor to consider major or new legislation affecting the financial transactions or to consider whether regulations are appropriately translated into relevant rules and procedures. The auditor's work on legislation or regulations need only focus on those authorities that are relevant to the entity's financial transactions, such as those that govern the powers of the entity to make payments or receive money, or set out the value of such payments or receipts. It is not concerned with administrative rules or regulations that are not directly linked to financial transactions.

27   The auditor's consideration of the translation of framework of authorities may involve reviewing the legislation to identify the provisions that authorise activities and reviewing the process for their translation and interpretation in subsidiary regulations and guidelines. It may also extend to the process for translation of those regulations into working manuals or other key documentation. In conducting this review the auditor pays particular attention to the statutory regulations which govern, for example:

- the powers of relevant bodies to determine the rules and procedures;

- the controls to be operated by the entity responsible for the administration of a scheme;

- the eligibility of beneficiaries to receive grants or other kinds of financial support under a scheme;

- the calculation of grants or any other payments; and

- the setting of fees and charges and other revenues.

In considering relevant rules and procedures relating to schemes, the auditor also **28** identifies those controls that are designed to prevent or detect and correct material irregularities.

Where the volume of laws or regulations is significant, entities may have systems **29** for the design and monitoring of procedures and controls to ensure that they are appropriate and meet legislative requirements.

The auditor should remain alert for significant problems encountered by the **30** audited body relating to the interpretation of new and existing legislation or the application of regulations and the impact on the audit.

Materiality for the audit of regularity

The concept of materiality applies to the audit of regularity. The auditor is required **31** to obtain sufficient appropriate evidence that the audited body has complied with the relevant framework of authorities "in all material respects". This explicitly recognises the fact that the auditor cannot detect all occurrences of irregularity through the audit work. Materiality affects both the way in which the auditor plans the audit work on regularity and evaluates and reports the results of that work.

The auditor follows ISA (UK) 320 when determining the materiality in the context **32** of regularity. However, the materiality threshold for the audit of regularity may be different to the materiality for the financial statements as a whole. The auditor's assessment of what is material is a matter of judgement and includes both quantitative and qualitative considerations. This is because the users might have an interest in breaches of authority even where the sums of money involved may be small in relation to the overall expenditure in the financial statements.

This might mean that certain classes of transactions, account balances or **33** disclosures need to be considered against a threshold lower than the materiality level. For example, in the context of regularity in central government in the United Kingdom, the auditor may consider material any expenditure incurred in excess of the amounts authorised by Parliament.

The auditor remains alert to the nature of irregularities and considers their **34** significance having regard to the interest of the users of the financial statements in the matter.

The determination of materiality in the public sector is influenced by legislative **35** and regulatory requirements, and by the financial information needs of legislators and the public in relation to public sector programmes. The list of matters will vary from audited body to audited body, however considerations may include:

- the need for openness and transparency, for example senior staff or board members' remuneration;

- public expectations and public interest which might deem separate disclosure necessary; and

- the context in which a matter appears, for example if the matter is also subject to compliance with the framework of authorities, legislation or regulations.

Assessing the risk of material irregularity

36   The auditor considers the risks of material irregularity through the process of obtaining an understanding of the entity, its environment and its internal controls.

37   To assess the inherent risk of a material irregularity occurring, the auditor uses judgement and prior experience and knowledge of the entity and its environment to evaluate a range of factors, for example:

- the complexity of the regulations;
- the introduction of major new legislation or regulations changes in existing ones;
- services and programmes delivered through third parties; and
- payments and receipts made on the basis of claims or declarations.

38   The auditor considers the controls which mitigate the risk that a material irregularity could occur in an account balance or class of transactions and would not be prevented, or detected and corrected on a timely basis by the accounting and control systems. Where the auditor expects to be able to rely on the operation of internal controls to reduce the extent of substantive procedures relating to regularity, the auditor assesses the design and implementation of those controls and plans and performs tests of their effectiveness.

39   Examples of areas of risk and possible mitigating controls in relation to regularity are summarised as follows.

Risk	Description	Mitigating Controls
Complexity of regulations	The more complex the regulations the greater the risk of error. This may occur either through a misunderstanding or misinterpretation of the regulation or through an error in application.	Formal procedures for the translation of statutory requirements into operating instructions. Formal control plans prepared and monitored by scheme managers. Review of scheme control plans and operating manuals by internal audit or some other independent audit function.
New legislation	New legislation may require the introduction of new administrative and control procedures. This may result in errors in either the design or operation of controls required to ensure regularity.	The controls identified above involving formal procedures for the translation of statutory requirements into scheme rules. Formal control plans and the independent review of operating instructions and control plans will also apply where schemes are introduced following new legislation.

Risk	Description	Mitigating Controls
Services and programmes delivered through third parties	Where programmes are administered by agents, departments lose a degree of direct control and may have to rely on agents to ensure compliance with authorities.	Formal agreements between the entity and the agent defining control procedures to be applied in the administration of services.
		Management control and monitoring of third-party activities.
		Inspection visits by internal audit to third parties to review systems and procedures, including those relevant to regularity.
		Independent assurance report on, or certification of, payments and receipts by the third parties' reporting accountant or auditor.
		Established criteria for making claims, clearly set out in departmental instructions and guidance to claimants.
Payments and receipts made on the basis of claims or declarations	An entity's ability to confirm compliance with authorities may be restricted where, for example, criteria specified for receipt of grant are not subject to direct verification.	Standard requirements for documentation evidencing entitlement to be submitted in support of claims. (This may be a condition of payment of grant or a requirement once the activity supported by the grant has been completed).
		Physical inspection of claimants' records etc., to confirm eligibility.
		Procedures for assessing the financial standing of claimants before awarding a grant and for monitoring continuing solvency.
		Independent assurance report on, or certification of, the application of grant by reporting accountant or external auditor.

40   The auditor considers the significance of the identified risks of material irregularity in determining the nature, timing and extent of substantive procedures required to reduce audit risk to an acceptable level. As part of the risk assessment, the auditor determines which of the risks identified require special audit consideration.

Planning and performing audit procedures

41   The nature, timing and extent of the audit procedures is dependent on the complexity of the framework of authorities. For example, where an entity pays grants that are subject to specific restrictions in the grant agreement, the auditor plans and performs adequate procedures to obtain assurance that the grant receiving entity complied with these restrictions.

42   Audit procedures designed to obtain assurance over the regularity of transactions are usually based on a combination of tests of controls and substantive procedures. The auditor performs these in line with ISA (UK) 330.

43   For tests of controls, the auditor determines whether the controls are adequately designed and implemented and are operating effectively to prevent or detect and correct material irregularity. If the auditor concludes that the controls are not effective, the auditor will not obtain assurance from them.

44   For substantive procedures, the auditor confirms that financial transactions conforms to framework of authorities, the range and scope being dependent on identified risks of material irregularity and the extent to which evidence from tests of control provides audit assurance.

45   Where the auditor obtains satisfactory evidence as to the operating effectiveness of the entity's controls in relation to regularity, the auditor may seek to reduce the extent of substantive procedures. The auditor may also have regard to work carried out on the auditor's review of the Governance Statement.

46   Evidence in relation to regularity can be gathered as part of an integrated approach with the audit of financial statements. The auditor considers whether the audit evidence available is sufficient and appropriate to obtain assurance over regularity of transactions.

47   Analytical procedures on their own are unlikely to provide the auditor with sufficient appropriate evidence in support of regularity. They may nevertheless, assist the auditor in assessing whether amounts recorded in financial statements are consistent with expectations. For example, where allowances under a scheme are subject to a maximum value and the number of recipients is known the auditor may use analytical procedures to identify whether the permitted maximum may have been breached.

48   The auditor may carry out specific audit procedures to identify activities and transactions that are not in accordance with the framework of authorities. These tests might involve:

- the review of financial statements and any specific legislation;

- the review of the entity's management accounts to identify any unusual transaction streams or account balances or any incorrect analysis of transactions; and

- the substantive testing of transactions and account balances.

Areas requiring special consideration

The auditor may encounter difficulties obtaining audit evidence regarding certain **49** aspects of regularity, for instance eligibility for grants. Ideally, the auditor requires direct evidence to satisfy the objective of the test. Where this is not available, the auditor considers how the entity satisfied itself as to regularity. This may be through the work of a separate inspection function or by receiving advice or assurance from an independent third party.

Rather than pay grants directly to the recipients intended by relevant framework of **50** authorities, public sector bodies may fund other bodies to administer a scheme. Where this is the case, the auditor of the body may assess the arrangements put in place by the body to ensure proper accountability for such grants. This includes consideration of any work undertaken by the auditor of the other body on the regularity of expenditure.

An auditor engaged in the examination of expenditure on schemes funded by the **51** European Union considers the compliance of transactions with the relevant European legislation and the impact of any non-compliance on the audit of regularity. In particular, the auditor obtains an understanding of the consistency of any regulations established in the UK with the provisions in the governing European Council or Commission Regulation and that these provisions are properly translated into instructions and procedures.

The auditor also remains alert to any legal actions that challenge the provisions of **52** national or delegated legislation implementing European legislation by making enquiries of the entity and obtaining representations.

The auditor takes into account particular considerations when auditing the **53** regularity of fees and charges levied by public sector entities, for example:

- reviewing the relevant primary legislation to confirm that it provides appropriate authority for the audited body to levy fees and charges for the services concerned;

- confirming that fee orders and other types of Statutory Instrument issued under the governing legislation are in accordance with those authorities; and

- confirming that the relevant legislation provides the appropriate authority for the receipts to be applied in aid of expenditure and not used to generate surplus (set up on a cost recovery basis).

As well as determining the authorities for levying fees and charges, the auditor **54** also confirms that receipts are properly utilised and disclosed in the financial statements as authorised in the appropriate legislation.

Depending on the financial reporting framework, there may be additional **55** requirements for disclosures in the financial statements in respect of regularity. In particular, the audited body may be required to disclose any non-compliance with frameworks of authorities. Taking into account materiality, the auditor considers the implications of lack of or inadequate disclosure on the audit opinion on regularity and the need to present a separate report on the matter to a relevant authority.

Written representations

Audit evidence on regularity is gathered from the audit procedures. However, the **56** auditor may also seek representations from management (for example, Accounting Officers or Accountable Officers) on the discharge of their responsibility for the regularity of transactions. This is particularly important in areas, such as benefit and grant schemes, where direct evidence may not be available to the auditor.

57   Management is normally expected to provide a formal statement on the discharge of their responsibility each year. Where this statement is included in the financial statements, the auditor makes reference to the statement or discloses, in the responsibilities section of the auditor's report, the fact that the statement is not included or is not comprehensive in setting out management's responsibilities. The length and formality of management representations on regularity do not influence the scope of the auditor's procedures in obtaining evidence to support the regularity opinion.

Using the work of others

58   The auditor may wish to use the work of the internal auditor to obtain sufficient appropriate evidence in support of regularity. Where the auditor considers internal audit work, the auditor applies ISA (UK) 610. In particular, the auditor is prohibited from the direct use of internal audit staff as part of the engagement team.

59   The auditor may seek to use the work of the auditor of another entity. The auditor may encounter the work of another auditor, for example where the entity:

- consolidates or summarises the financial statements of other bodies;
- has paid a grant to another entity; or
- has contracted out services to a service organisation.

60   Where the entity prepares group financial statements, the auditor of a group determines how to obtain sufficient appropriate evidence over regularity of the group's transactions. Where the auditor of a group wishes to use the work of a component auditor in the audit of regularity, the auditor follows the standards and guidance in ISA (UK) 600.

61   Frameworks of authorities are specific to each entity and the fact that an entity is consolidated does not result in that entity having to apply their parent entity's framework of authorities. For example, a public sector body may not have a specific framework of authorities. Therefore, the component may not require the audit of regularity for the purpose of a group regularity opinion, except for fraud considerations. However, where a consolidated entity has a framework of authorities but was not subject to the audit of regularity, the group auditor may carry out audit procedures (or instruct a component auditor to do so) to obtain assurance over regularity of the component's transactions.

62   The group auditor obtains representations from the component auditor as to that auditor's independence from the entity and their compliance with the relevant auditing and ethical requirements. This also applies if the group auditor uses audited financial statements, signed by the component auditor, which contain a specific opinion on regularity.

63   Where a public sector entity has paid a grant to another entity, it will usually establish controls designed to ensure that the recipient complies with the grant conditions. The management might specify in the financial memoranda or grant conditions to receive an auditor's report or certificate on regularity.

64   The auditor may need to examine the application of grants paid to other entities through, for example:

- examination of the evidence available in the principal entity, including reports by their own internal audit function;

- using the work of the other entity's external auditor;

- consideration of the work of the other entity's internal audit function; and

- direct access to the other entity and performance of appropriate audit procedures.

The auditor may use the certificate and reports issued by the auditor of the grant **65** recipient by:

- confirming that the instructions issued to that auditor address the regularity considerations satisfactorily;

- agreeing the scope; and

- reviewing the results of the quality control review.

Where the auditor of a public sector entity does not have a right of access to the **66** other entity or other sources to obtain sufficient appropriate evidence, an auditor considers whether there is a limitation on the scope of the audit in accordance with ISA (UK) 705.

Where another auditor is required to provide a report or certificate on regularity to **67** the principal entity, it is often the case that this is done a considerable time after the financial period being audited. The auditor ensures that only the evidence available to the principal entity relating to the reporting period is used. Where this is not possible, or if the principal and other entities have different year end dates, then the principal auditor may have to perform additional procedures, including the exercise of inspection rights, where appropriate.

Where the public sector entity has contracted-out services to a service **68** organisation, the need to access that organisation and/or their auditor depends on the nature of the services provided, the information available at the principal entity, and the terms of engagement of the other auditor.

Where a public sector auditor is considering the need to obtain legal opinions **69** concerning the interpretation of statutes or regulations the auditor follows the standards and guidance in ISA (UK) 620.

When determining whether to seek legal advice on a matter of regularity, the **70** auditor considers:

- the materiality of the matter in the context of the financial statements;

- the risk of irregularity based on the nature and complexity of the framework of authorities; and

- the availability of other relevant audit evidence, in particular whether the entity has sought its own legal advice.

Usually where there is doubt about the regularity of transactions, management **71** may seek clarification on the legal position. Where the entity is unwilling to seek legal advice or where the auditor has concerns about the legal advice given to the entity, the auditor may wish to seek a separate legal opinion.

Where the auditor is uncertain about the regularity of expenditure in relation to the **72** framework of authorities other than legislation, the auditor first determines whether the entity sought clarification or, where necessary, obtained the appropriate authorisation from the relevant bodies. The auditor may also seek advice directly from the relevant authority. In these circumstances, the auditor follows similar steps to those the auditor would take when seeking legal advice.

Evaluating irregularities

73   Where non-compliance with regulations is suspected or discovered, the auditor considers the wider implications for the audit opinion on regularity. This will also include consideration of the implications for the auditor's assessment of risks and controls in relation to material irregularities and the extent of assurance that the auditor can obtain from the overall control environment and representations from management.

74   The auditor considers the nature and extent of any non-compliance and, in particular, whether it arises from a fundamental misinterpretation of legislation or a misapplication of rules.

75   Cases of non-compliance with regulations may be reported to management of the entity to allow corrective action to be taken, for example, by recovering overpayments of grant. Where it is not possible for the entity to take corrective action, the management may disclose the non-compliance in the financial statements by outlining the circumstances surrounding the breach of regulations and the possible extent of irregular transactions. Even where a breach of regularity is disclosed, the auditor considers the implications for the audit opinion on regularity and the need to present a separate report on the matter to the relevant authority. In doing so, the auditor considers the materiality of the matter at issue.

76   If the entity's management does not accept the auditor's opinion that the relevant transactions are not in compliance with the appropriate authorities, then the auditor may:

- communicate in a report to the appropriate level of management or those charged with governance the findings from the auditor's investigations into the circumstances surrounding the suspected irregularity and the conclusions drawn therefrom;

- consider whether the matter is one which management is required to report to the relevant authority or group management and if so, request in writing that management notify them;

- report directly to the relevant authority or group management if management are required to do so and the auditor is unable to establish whether management have complied with the requirement; and

- consider modifying the opinion on regularity.

The risk of fraud in the audit of regularity

77   A particular transaction can be determined as fraudulent only through the applicable legal framework. However, the auditor often encounters situations where there is suspicion of fraud, identified by management, internal audit, third parties or the auditor. Although the auditor does not have the authority to determine whether or not a fraud has actually occurred, the auditor considers whether, in the auditor's opinion, the transactions concerned are in compliance with the relevant framework of authorities.

78   Fraudulent transactions are always irregular regardless of the manner or extent of disclosure in the financial statements since they are without proper authority. The auditor considers the impact of suspected or proven fraudulent transactions on the audit opinion, taking into account the materiality of the irregularities.

For the purpose of auditing regularity, fraudulent financial reporting is not itself **79**
irregular, although it may disguise underlying irregular transactions. However,
misappropriation of assets is irregular and risk of material misappropriation of
assets due to fraud should be considered for both the risk of management override
and the audit of regularity.

While ISA 240 is not written to address the audit of regularity, in some instances **80**
compliance with its requirements may be used to gain assurance over regularity,
for example by:

● evaluating whether unusual or unexpected relationships that have been
   identified through analytical procedures are indicative of material
   irregularity due to fraud;

● testing the appropriateness of journal entries; and

● considering the rationale for significant transactions undertaken outside the
   normal course of business.

Regularity opinion on financial statements

For the audit of central government (or equivalent) and some health bodies, the **81**
auditor provides an opinion on the regularity of transactions. The opinion would
normally be included within the audit certificate or report. It may be included next
to the true and fair opinion on the financial statements or within a separate section
of the report entitled "The audit of regularity" or as appropriate. The form of words
used in the regularity opinion should relate to the statutory requirements or the
scope of the engagement agreed with the audited body. The wording also needs to
be accompanied by:

● disclosure of management's responsibilities in relation to regularity in the
   statement of responsibilities and a reference to the disclosure in the
   responsibilities section of the auditor's report; or, full disclosure in the
   responsibilities section; and

● inclusion of the overall work performed with regard to regularity in the
   scope of the basis of opinion section of the auditor's report.

If the auditor modifies the audit opinion on regularity, the auditor should apply the **82**
principles of ISA (UK) 705.

Where the auditor concludes that material financial transactions do not comply **83**
with the relevant framework of authorities, the auditor qualifies the regularity
opinion, stating that the audited body complies with a relevant framework of
authorities, except for the non-compliance identified. Where the impact of the
non-compliance on the financial statements is pervasive, the auditor issues an
adverse opinion on regularity.

Where the auditor is unable to obtain sufficient evidence to reach an opinion, the **84**
auditor qualifies the regularity opinion as limitation of scope or if pervasive, the
auditor issues a disclaimer.

A qualified opinion on regularity does not in itself lead to a qualification of the **85**
truth and fairness, fair presentation or proper presentation opinion on the financial
statements. However, the auditor considers whether the matter is properly
disclosed in the financial statements and whether it is so pervasive as to make
the financial statements misleading.

Other reporting on regularity

86   In certain parts of the public sector, the auditor may be required to provide separate reports, other than through audit opinions, on issues of regularity. The auditor may be required to report matters relating to regularity to third parties, for example a component auditor reporting to the group's management or reporting to a regulator such as the Charity Commission. The form and scope of these reports may be determined by the third party as part of a specific condition of the grant or subsidy and will be subject to specific instructions to the auditor. In other entities, the auditor may be required to submit a more general report on the entities' compliance with regulations, determined by the auditor's terms of engagement.

87   The auditor may also have statutory powers to issue a public interest report on any regularity or propriety matter which comes to the auditor's attention in the course of the audit in order that it is considered by the entity concerned or brought to the attention of the public.

88   In certain parts of the public sector, the auditor considers the need for a separate report where the audit opinion is modified as a consequence of material irregularity. The purpose of a separate report is to provide the users of the financial statements with a detailed explanation of the basis for qualification and support the relevant authority in holding the audited entity to account. This is linked to guidance on additional reporting responsibilities in Part 1 of this Practice Note (ISA 700).

89   The auditor may in some cases identify irregularities during the course of the audit which are not material to the financial statements but which need, in the auditor's judgement, to be drawn to the attention of the addressees of the auditor's report. An example of this may be where expenditure in previous years is retrospectively deemed to be irregular by virtue of a legal challenge to the interpretation of legislation.

Appendix One – Glossary of terms

Accountable Officer[1] – members of the staff of the Scottish Administration designated by the Principal Accountable Officer with responsibility for parts of the Administration, bodies or office holders as regards signing the accounts of the entity and ensuring the propriety and regularity of its finances.

Accountable Officer[2] – the officer (directed as the Chief Executive) responsible for the propriety and regularity of the public finances of health entities, and for the keeping of proper records, as set out in the Accountable Officers' Memorandum issued by the Department of Health or Chief Executive, NHS Wales. In Northern Ireland, the Accountable Officers' Memorandum is issued by the Department of Health.

Accounting Officer – usually the permanent head or senior full-time official of a central government entity or an NHS Foundation Trust, appointed or designated as the Accounting Officer for that entity and with a personal responsibility for, among other things, signing of the financial statements, ensuring that proper financial procedures are followed and accounting records maintained, ensuring that public funds and assets are properly managed and safeguarded and all relevant financial considerations, including issues on propriety, regularity or value for money are taken into account.

Accounts Commission – the independent body with statutory responsibilities for securing the audit of local government entities in Scotland, and to assist such entities in achieving best value. In relation to the audit of the financial statements, the Commission is responsible for appointing auditors, setting the required standards for its appointed auditors and regulating the quality of audits.

Accounts Direction – the document issued by HM Treasury or the Secretary of State of a parent or sponsor department, or by Welsh Ministers or Scottish Ministers which sets out the accounting and disclosure requirements to be applied in preparing the entity's financial statements. In Northern Ireland, the Department of Finance is responsible for issuing accounts directions for central government departments and executive agencies while normally the sponsoring department is empowered to direct the form of accounts for non-departmental public bodies and health service entities, with the consent of the Department of Finance.

"Appointment By" Basis Engagement – An engagement where another firm or individual is responsible for the assignment, its performance and the issuing of the audit report.

Assembly – the National Assembly for Wales or the Northern Ireland Assembly.

Audit Scotland – national audit agency which supports both the Accounts Commission and the Auditor General for Scotland in carrying out their work.

Auditor of a public sector body (a public sector auditor) – a person, or persons appointed under statute or agreement; or appointed by, employed by or acting as the agent of a national audit agency, a secretary of state or a government department acting under statute or by agreement; or appointed as auditor to a body regulated by an independent regulator which has determined that this Practice Note applies.

Auditor General for Scotland – the individual responsible for authorising the issue of public funds from the Scottish Consolidated Fund to government departments and other public sector bodies; for examining or ensuring the examination of parliamentary accounts (which includes determining whether sums paid out of the Fund have been paid out and applied in accordance with statute), and certifying and reporting on them; for carrying out or ensuring the carrying out of examinations into the economy, efficiency and effectiveness with which the Scottish Ministers and the Lord Advocate have used their resources in discharging their functions; and for carrying out or ensuring the carrying out of examinations into the economy, efficiency and effectiveness with which other persons determined under Scottish legislation to whom sums are paid out of the Fund have used those sums in discharging their functions.

Auditor General for Wales – the individual responsible for examining and certifying the accounts of the Welsh Government, its sponsored and other related public bodies, Welsh local government bodies and NHS Wales entities. The Auditor General for Wales is responsible for authorising the issue of public funds from the Welsh Consolidated Fund to Welsh Ministers and other public sector bodies. The Auditor General is also responsible for carrying out value for money work at those bodies.

Auditor's report – any auditor's report expressing an opinion on the truth and fairness, fair presentation or proper presentation of financial statements and, in specified cases, on the regularity of the financial transactions included in them and any other legal and regulatory requirements. In central government, the auditor's report may also be referred to as a Certificate.

Central government entities – defined as government departments and their executive agencies, any entity which operates as a trading fund (a government department, part of a department or an executive agency) and arm's length bodies. For the purposes of this Practice Note, central government does not include National Health Service bodies, local authorities, public corporations, academy trusts, college corporations or nationalised industries.

Certificate[1] – the title of an audit report containing the opinion of the Comptroller and Auditor General, the Auditor General for Wales or the Comptroller and Auditor General for Northern Ireland on financial statements audited under statute where there is a statutory requirement for the examination to be certified, usually on the resource and other accounts produced by government departments (and on accounts produced by health entities in Wales and Northern Ireland). Use of the word "certificate" clearly differentiates the audit report from any other report of the Comptroller and Auditor General, Auditor General for Wales and the Comptroller and Auditor General for Northern Ireland.

Certificate[2] – the declaration by auditors under the Local Audit and Accountability Act 2014 that the audit of a local government or health entity has been completed in accordance with the Act. The certificate is normally, but not necessarily, incorporated in the audit report. A similar certificate is issued by local government auditors in Wales under the Public Audit (Wales) Act 2004 and by local government auditors in Northern Ireland under the Local Government (Northern Ireland) Order 2005.

Chief Executive – the title applied to the senior official of a public sector body, accountable for the management and operations of that agency.

Code of Audit Practice – any document identified as such, issued by a national audit agency or the relevant head of that agency, that prescribes the way in which the auditor is to carry out their functions in respect of the audits of specified entities, embodying what the national audit agency considers to be the best professional practice with respect to the standards, procedures and techniques to be adopted by the auditor.

Comptroller and Auditor General (the C&AG) – the head of the National Audit Office. As Comptroller, the C&AG's duties are to authorise the issue by HM Treasury of public funds from the Consolidated Fund and National Loans Fund to government departments and others; as Auditor General, the C&AG certifies the accounts of all central government departments and some other public bodies, and carries out value-for-money examinations.

Comptroller and Auditor General for Northern Ireland – the individual responsible for authorising the issue of public funds to Northern Ireland departments and other public sector bodies, for carrying out the audit of the financial statements of Northern Ireland central government and health entities (which includes satisfying themselves that expenditure and income have been applied in accordance with the Assembly's intentions and conforms to governing authorities) and for examining the economy, efficiency and effectiveness with which Northern Ireland central government entities have discharged their functions.

Contractor auditor – An auditor who has been engaged to undertake all or some of an auditor assignment on behalf of the statutory auditor under a contract or agreement.

Contracted-out engagement – An engagement where, although responsibility for issuing the audit report remains with the statutory auditor, all or some of the audit assignment is undertaken by another firm or auditor under contract or agreement.

Corruption – the offering, giving, soliciting or acceptance of any inducement or reward that may influence the actions taken by an entity, its members or its officers.

Firm – sole practitioner, partnership, limited liability partnership, or corporation or other entity of professional accountants engaged in the provision of engagements. In the public sector context, firm can also mean a national audit agency and local auditors.

Framework of Authorities – external frameworks, specific to the audited entity, with which the audited entity's transactions must conform. These frameworks are set up by bodies able to issue and/or enforce the authorities for that entity and might include, for example: authorising legislation; regulations issued under governing legislation; Parliamentary authorities (including budgetary laws); government or related authorities.

Government Departments – these represent the top tier of central government, or equivalent, in each country. Parliament/Assembly provides money annually to each department to spend for purposes that are specified in Supply Estimates/Budget Act or equivalent. Each government department is headed by an Accounting Officer who is responsible to Parliament for the application and expenditure of the funds provided in the Supply Estimates.

Grant – payments made by departments to outside bodies to reimburse expenditure on agreed items or functions.

Health entities – individual corporate entities that are part of the National Health Service but do not form part of a department or are constituted as executive agencies, arm's length bodies or public corporations. Includes NHS foundation trusts, NHS trusts and clinical commissioning groups. In Wales, health entities are NHS Trusts and Local Health Boards. In Northern Ireland health entities are Health and Social Services Boards, Trusts and Special Agencies.

Legislation – Acts of Parliament and delegated or subordinate legislation including, for example, Welsh Measures, Statutory Instruments, or Rules and Orders issued by Ministers and submitted to Parliament. The term legislation also includes Regulations, Directives and Decisions issued by the European Council of Ministers and the European Commission.

Local auditors – Auditors of local public sector entities in England, such as local government bodies, appointed under the Local Audit and Accountability Act 2014.

National audit agency – one of the United Kingdom public audit agencies responsible for carrying out the audit of the financial statements of public sector bodies (the National Audit Office for the Comptroller and Auditor General, Wales Audit Office for the Auditor General for Wales, Audit Scotland for the Auditor General for Scotland and the Accounts Commission, and the Northern Ireland Audit Office for the Comptroller and Auditor General for Northern Ireland) and/or responsible for the appointment and regulation of auditors of public sector bodies.

National Audit Office (NAO) – national audit agency which supports the Comptroller and Auditor General (the C&AG) in scrutinising public spending for Parliament.

Northern Ireland Audit Office (NIAO) – national audit agency which supports the Comptroller and Auditor General for Northern Ireland in fulfilling their responsibilities.

Other responsibilities – any function, other than the audit of the financial statements and the giving of an opinion on regularity, that public sector auditors take on whether as a result of statutory prescriptions or direction by the relevant national audit agency.

Parliament – the United Kingdom Parliament and the Scottish Parliament, but not the National Assembly for Wales or the Northern Ireland Assembly.

Performance audit – work performed by the auditor in relation to the economy, efficiency and effectiveness of use of public funds. It may be also referred to as "value for money" work.

Public Audit Forum (PAF) – A consultative and advisory forum of the four national audit agencies in the UK designed to provide a focus for developmental thinking about public audit.

Public sector bodies – include bodies designated as public sector by the Office for National Statistics: government departments and their executive agencies; the Scottish Government, Welsh Government, the Northern Ireland Executive and their sponsored and associated bodies; trading funds; arm's length bodies; local authorities and other local government bodies; National Health Service bodies; in Scotland, further education colleges and the water authority. It does not include other public corporations or the nationalised industries.

Regularity – a concept that transactions that are reflected in the financial statements of an audited entity must be in accordance with the relevant framework of authorities.

Responsible financial officer – the officer appointed by a local government entity to be responsible for the proper administration of its financial affairs.

Sponsor department – normally the department through which Parliamentary funding and accountability is conducted for arm's-length bodies.

Statutory auditor – The auditor appointed to perform an engagement by statute. In this Practice Note the term statutory auditor is not used in the sense in which this is used in the Audit Directive and Regulation and related frameworks.

Tier – any level in a series of entities through which a grant is passed down from Parliament to the intended recipients. Top tier entities are usually government departments. Lower tier entities comprise agencies, arm's-length bodies and non-central government sector organisations

Wales Audit Office – national audit agency constituted as a statutory board, which employs staff, secures and utilises other resources, including additional expertise from private sector accountancy firms, to enable the Auditor General for Wales to carry out his functions.

Practice Note 11 (PN 11) (Revised): The audit of charities in the United Kingdom (Revised) (November 2017)

(November 2017)

Contents

	Paragraphs
Legislative and regulatory framework	5 - 14
Charity regulators	3 - 7
Charity governing documents	8 - 10
Accounting and auditing requirements	11 - 14
The audit of financial statements	15 - 266
210 Agreeing the terms of audit engagements	15 - 18
220 Quality control for an audit of financial statements	19 - 25
240 The auditor's responsibilities relating to fraud in an audit of financial statements	26 - 35
250 Section A – Consideration of laws and regulations in an audit of financial statements	36 - 62
260 Communication with those charged with governance	63 - 68
265 Communicating deficiencies in internal control to those charged with governance and management	69 - 99
320 Materiality in planning and performing an audit	100 - 107
330 The auditor's responses to assessed risks	108 - 124
402 Audit considerations relating to an entity using a service organisation	125 - 133
510 Initial engagements – opening balances	134 - 137
540 Auditing accounting estimates, including fair value accounting estimates, and related disclosures	138 - 146
550 Related parties	147 - 157
570 Going concern	158 - 185
580 Written representations	186 - 189
600 Special Considerations – Audits of group financial statements (including the work of component auditors)	190 - 200
700 Forming an opinion and reporting on financial statements	201 - 215
720 The auditor's responsibilities relating to other information	216 - 229
Reporting matters of material significance to charity regulators	230 - 266

Illustrative example (non-statutory summarised financial statements):
Independent auditor's statement to the trustees of XYZ charity

Appendix 1 – Conditions and events that may indicate risks of material misstatement

Appendix 2 – Charity accounting and audit requirements in the United Kingdom

Editorial note – References to ISAs are to previous versions available online on Croner-i Tax and Accounting.

> **This document is a revision of Practice Note 11 (Revised) published in March 2011. It has been updated to reflect legislative changes when the Charities Act 2011 becomes effective on 14 March 2012 as well as other legislative changes for charities in Scotland and Northern Ireland since March 2011.**

Preface

This Practice Note contains guidance on the application of auditing standards issued by the Financial Reporting Council (FRC) to the audit of financial statements of charities in the United Kingdom.

The Practice Note is intended to assist auditors in applying the requirements of, and should be read in conjunction with, International Standards on Auditing (UK) (ISAs (UK)), which apply to audits of financial statements for periods commencing on or after 17 June 2016. This Practice Note sets out the special considerations relating to the audit of charities which arise from individual ISAs (UK).

The Practice Note does not, and is not intended to, provide comprehensive guidance on the audits of charities, so where no special considerations arise from a particular ISA (UK), no material is included. This Practice Note does not contain commentary on all the requirements included in the ISAs (UK) and reading it should not be seen as an alternative to reading the relevant ISAs (UK) in their entirety.

Practice Note 11 applies to the audit of financial statements prepared in accordance with the Charities Statement of Recommended Practice (Financial Reporting Standard 102) (Charities SORP).[1] It does not apply to the audit of charities preparing their financial statements in accordance with other specialist Statements of Recommended Practice (SORPs) (e.g., charities which are registered social housing providers[2] or higher and further education institutions[3]).

Where an audit is being performed on an entity within the Public Sector in the UK this Practice Note complements Statement of Recommended Practice – *Practice Note 10: Audit of financial statements of public sector bodies in the United Kingdom*.

This Practice Note supersedes the guidance included in Practice Note 11 *The Audit of Charities in the United Kingdom (Revised)* issued by the Auditing Practices Board in March 2012, and takes account of significant regulatory and other developments affecting charities since that date.

The legal framework for charities is devolved, complex and different requirements exist depending on the charity's constitution and the type of activity it undertakes. The FRC's intention is not to provide a comprehensive commentary on all aspects of law that may apply to a charity's operations, and the Practice Note should not be used as a substitute for the auditor obtaining an understanding of the legal and regulatory framework applicable to a charity and the sector in which that charity operates.

The Practice Note is based on the legislation and regulations that have been published at 31 October 2017.

---

[1] *Whilst this Practice Note is intended for the audit of financial statements of charities prepared on an accruals basis, some smaller charities that prepare receipts and payments accounts may be required to have an audit by their governing document or another enactment. The guidance in this Practice Note can be adapted for the audit of receipts and payments accounts accordingly.*

[2] *Housing SORP 2014 – Statement of Recommended Practice for registered social housing providers.*

[3] *Statement of Recommended Practice – Accounting for Further and Higher Education.*

Audit exemption thresholds are established in UK legislation and an independent examination will often be permitted instead of an audit. An independent examination is significantly different from an audit and guidance on the conduct of independent examinations has been published by the charity regulators.[4] This Practice Note does not provide guidance on independent examinations.

In addition to the auditor's report on the financial statements, the auditor of a charity may be requested to provide additional reports, for example, in relation to summarised financial statements or summary financial information, obtaining assurance on consistency with the audited financial statements, or in relation to grant-funded projects, obtaining assurance on matters such as the proper use of money and costs to completion. This Practice Note does not cover such additional engagements.

This Practice Note has been prepared with advice and assistance from staff of the Charity Commission for England and Wales (CCEW), the Office of the Scottish Charity Regulator (OSCR), and the Charity Commission for Northern Ireland (CCNI).

Legislative and regulatory framework

1   The legislation relating to accounting and audit applicable to each jurisdiction in the UK is summarised in Appendix 2 of this Practice Note. The legal requirements in relation to accounting and auditing for charities in Scotland and Northern Ireland differ in some respects from those applicable in England and Wales, and it is important for the auditor to understand what legislation applies. Additionally, some charities may also be subject to other regulatory regimes, for example, registered social housing providers (registered social landlords) and higher and further education institutions.

2   The main laws that relate to a charity's accounts and audit are:

- Charities in England and Wales: the Charities Act 2011 ("2011 Act (E&W)") and, with respect to the disclosure of fundraising, the Charities (Protection and Social Investment) Act 2016.

- All charities registered in Scotland with OSCR: the Charities and Trustee Investment (Scotland) Act 2005 ("2005 Act (Scotland)").

- Charities in Northern Ireland: the Charities Act (Northern Ireland) 2008 ("2008 Act (NI)").

- All charitable companies:[5] the Companies Act 2006.

Charity regulators

3   The primary regulators for charities (which are referred to as "the charity regulators" in this Practice Note are:

---

[4] *CCEW's Independent Examination of Charity Accounts: Examiners' Guide (CC32); OSCR's Independent Examinations for Charities and Independent Examiners; and CCNI's Independent examination of charity accounts: examiner's guide (ARR07).*

[5] *A charitable company is a company which is formed and registered under the Companies Act 2006 and is established for exclusively charitable purposes.*

- England and Wales: the Charity Commission for England and Wales (CCEW).[6]
- Scotland: the Office of the Scottish Charity Regulator (OSCR).[7]
- Northern Ireland: the Charity Commission for Northern Ireland (CCNI).[8]

Charities may be required to comply with aspects of charity law in more than one UK charity law jurisdiction. Such charities are known as "cross border" charities.[9]   **4**

Of relevance to a charity's financial statements and audit is UK tax law.   **5**
Organisations in the UK which are awarded charitable status may qualify for specific tax exemptions and reliefs on income and gains, and on profits from some activities. A charity must be registered with HMRC to be recognised as a charity for tax purposes (e.g., for claiming gift aid). This is separate from being registered with CCEW, OSCR or CCNI. Recognition as a charity for tax purposes does not mean that a charity will never pay tax. If a charity receives taxable (non-exempt) income or gains it must inform HMRC and complete a tax return.

Charities also qualify for business rate exemptions and certain Value-Added Tax   **6**
(VAT) tax reliefs and exemptions. However, if a charity has business activities the VAT rules will apply as they do for any other business. In addition, charities are affected by the whole range of national legislation applicable to business entities, such as employment, tax and pensions law and health and safety regulations.

Reporting direct to charity regulators

In addition to the primary objective of reporting on financial statements, the   **7**
auditor of a charity may have an additional statutory duty to report in certain circumstances to the relevant charity regulator.[10] The auditor also considers their discretionary right to report relevant matters to the charity regulators.

Charity governing documents

The governing documents of charities establish the purpose and constitution of   **8**
each charity. They may also require an audit to be undertaken (which may supplement, but not derogate from, a statutory requirement for an audit). There is no such thing as a standard charity; the governing documents of each charity are individual and will need careful consideration to identify matters relevant to the audit such as particular charitable objects and any special powers conferred on the trustees.

The terms of charities' governing documents tend to be narrower than those for   **9**
commercial entities, the objects of which are usually very generally phrased. This means that the auditor is much more likely to be faced with a situation where a charity has acted ultra vires (i.e., beyond the charity's powers) or in breach of trust than would be the case with an entity in the commercial sector.

---

[6] *More information on the role and responsibilities of CCEW can be found here: https://www.gov.uk/ government/ organisations/charity-commission/about*

[7] *More information on the role and responsibilities of OSCR can be found here: https://www.oscr.org.uk/about/ about-oscr*

[8] *More information on the role and responsibilities of CCNI can be found here: http://www.charitycommissionni. org.uk/about-us/*

[9] *Appendix 2 of this Practice Note provides a summary of current requirements.*

[10] *See Sections ISA (UK) 250 and Reporting matters of material significance to charity regulators of this Practice Note.*

10   Any transaction by a charity that is undertaken outside its objects and powers is potentially a breach of trust. Such transactions require consideration during an audit. Non-compliance with the governing documents is also likely to have financial implications for the charity, and thus needs to be considered in determining whether the financial statements give a "true and fair" view. In addition, such transactions may give rise to a duty to report the matter to the charity regulator.

Accounting and auditing requirements

11   The financial statements of a charity which are prepared to give a "true and fair" view under the requirements of the relevant Charities Acts are required to be prepared in accordance with UK Generally Accepted Accounting Practice (UK GAAP).[11] Additionally, charitable companies comply with company legislation which requires financial statements to be prepared in accordance with applicable laws and regulations, and UK accounting standards.

12   UK GAAP comprises law and accounting standards issued by the FRC. Charities cannot apply International Financial Reporting Standards. All charities preparing "true and fair" accounts are required[12] to apply the Financial Reporting Standard applicable in the UK and Republic of Ireland (FRS 102).

13   The Charities SORP is an interpretation of UK accounting standards for the charity sector and is intended to apply to the financial statements of all charities in the UK required to give a "true and fair" view (unless a separate specialist SORP exists for a class of charity). The Charities SORP is issued by CCEW and OSCR as the joint SORP-making body for charities designated by the FRC.

14   Apart from any requirement for audit in the governing document, the statutory requirement for audit depends on the size of the charity, as defined in relevant legislation or regulations.[13] For charitable companies, the interaction between the thresholds established in the Companies Act 2006 and charity law applicable in each jurisdiction needs to be considered.

ISA (UK) 210: AGREEING THE TERMS OF AUDIT ENGAGEMENTS

ISA (UK) 210 (Revised June 2016) deals with the auditor's responsibilities in agreeing the terms of the audit engagement with management and, where appropriate, those charged with governance.

Agreement on audit engagement terms
(Ref: Para. 9–10)

15   Under UK legislation, the trustees are responsible for the preparation of the financial statements and therefore the auditor agrees the terms of the audit engagement with the trustees of the charity and addresses the letter of engagement to the trustees.

---

[11] *Trustees of small non-company charities in England and Wales, Scotland and Northern Ireland which are within the income thresholds defined by legislation may elect to prepare financial statements on a receipts and payments basis. Financial statements prepared on a receipts and payments basis are not required to give a "true and fair" view, but to be properly presented.*

[12] *FRS 100 Application of Financial Reporting Requirements.*

[13] *Audit exemption thresholds are described in Appendix 2 of this Practice Note.*

Matters that will normally be included in an engagement letter for a charity are: **16**

- The legislative framework under which the financial statements are prepared and the audit is conducted.[14]

- The statutory duty to report to the charity regulators any matters of which the auditor becomes aware that may be of material significance to the respective regulators.

- The auditor's right to report relevant matters to the respective regulators.

- Access to information relevant to the preparation of the charity's financial statements, recognising that not all charities are constituted as limited companies (for which the auditor's rights of access are enshrined in company law).

Trustees may issue other reports to stakeholders in addition to the trustees' annual   **17** report required by statute. For example, the charity may provide summary reports and financial statements, and periodic newsletters. Where this is the case, the engagement letter also sets out the auditor's responsibilities, if any, in respect of such other reports.

It is the responsibility of the trustees to identify the need for any additional reports   **18** required by funders and to instruct the auditor accordingly. It will not be practicable for the auditor to check the documentation relating to all funds received by the charity to identify any conditions requiring special reports. However, the auditor may consider it appropriate to enquire of the trustees whether any reports are required in addition to the auditor's report on the charity's financial statements. The auditor issues separate engagement letters for non-audit work undertaken on behalf of the charity or its trustees.

ISA (UK) 220: QUALITY CONTROL FOR AN AUDIT OF FINANCIAL STATEMENTS

ISA (UK) 220 (Revised June 2016) deals with the specific responsibilities of the auditor regarding quality control procedure for an audit of financial statements.

Relevant ethical requirements
(Ref: Para. 9–10)

The auditor of a charity must comply with the requirements of the FRC's Ethical   **19** Standard (Revised 2016). Within the Ethical Standard there are some specific areas that the auditor considers:

- Considering the self-interest risk posed by auditing a charity may need to be broader than a purely financial interest. The auditor needs to take account of any relationships between covered persons[15] in the engagement team, connected persons and close family members and the charity which may pose a threat to independence.

---

[14] *Scottish charity law requires the auditor to consider the Trustees' Annual Report and to state whether or not the report meets the requirements of the regulations and an opinion, where the auditor has formed one, that there is a material inconsistency between the annual report and the rest of the statement of account. Although there is some legal uncertainty, the Scottish Government has given a provisional view that the Annual Report is outside the scope of the "true and fair" view, and have said that they will clarify the legislation on this point when a suitable legislative vehicle is available.*

[15] *The definition of "covered person" is included in the FRC's Glossary of Terms.*

- Considering the self-review risk where a firm has provided a charity with advice or other support (e.g., the provision of bookkeeping and financial statements preparation services), even where such services are provided pro bono, which may then form part of the material covered by the audit of the financial statements.

- Considering whether other relationships exist between a firm and a charity – although the existence of a business relationship is unlikely, if a firm made regular donations or provided material support to a charity, either financially or by allowing a material donation in kind this may be considered to be an other relationship as described in the Ethical Standard,[16] and may impact on the auditor's independence.

- Ensuring that a covered person in the firm, or a person closely associated with them, does not act in a trustee capacity for a charitable trust where:

  - The relevant person is a potential beneficiary of the trust;

  - The trust holds a financial interest in an entity audited by the firm which is material to it;

  - The trust can exercise significant influence over an audited entity of the firm or its affiliates; and

  - The relevant person can influence the investment decisions of the trust.[17]

20   The Ethical Standard includes certain additional requirements or prohibitions that apply to the audits of public interest entities and listed entities.[18] The Ethical Standard establishes that a firm's policies and procedures will set out the circumstances in which these additional requirements or prohibitions apply to the audits of other entities (which may include some charities), taking into consideration the nature of the entity's business, its size, the number of its employees and the range of its stakeholders.

Assignment of engagement teams
(Ref: Para. 14)

21   Audits of charities required by legislation in the UK may only be carried out by a registered auditor, other persons authorised by statute or, in England and Wales, those to whom CCEW may grant dispensation.[19]

22   Before commencing the audit of a charity, the engagement partner ensures that the firm has enough staff who have adequate knowledge and experience of such audits. Staff involved in an audit of a charity will have a broad understanding, commensurate with the individual's roles and responsibilities in the audit process, of:

- The type of charity being audited.

- Key risks affecting the charity.

---

[16] *Ethical Standard, Part B, Section 2 – Financial, Business, Employment and Personal Relationships, paragraphs 2.28D.*

[17] *Ethical Standard, Part B, Section 2 – Financial, Business, Employment and Personal Relationships, paragraphs 2.18–2.20.*

[18] *Ethical Standard, Part B, Section 1 – General Requirements and Guidance, paragraphs 1.48–1.50.*

[19] *The dispensation arises where a charity is audited under another statutory regime which is considered sufficiently similar to the audit requirements of the 2011 Act (E&W) or audited under arrangements which are sufficiently similar. CCEW can also give a dispensation from audit under the 2011 Act (E&W) in exceptional circumstances allowing an independent examination in place of an audit.*

- The applicable legislative framework, including charity accounting and audit regulations.

- The principles of FRS 102 and the Charities SORP.

- The charity's governing documents, which may also include specific reporting requirements.

- The legal responsibilities and duties of charity trustees.

- The regulatory framework within which charities operate to identify situations which may give the auditor reasonable cause to believe that a matter should be reported to a charity regulator. This includes the charity regulators' guidance on reporting matters of material significance[20] and other relevant charity regulators' guidance.

- Awareness of the guidance issued by the charity regulators on the auditor's right to report relevant matters.[21]

The auditor's responsibilities in this respect are not related to the level of fee charged for the audit. For example, the same levels of rigour are required in respect of audits carried out on a pro bono basis as for audits carried out for a commercial fee and the engagement partner has a responsibility for being satisfied and able to demonstrate that the audit engagement has assigned to it sufficient partners and staff with appropriate time and skill to perform the audit in accordance with all applicable Auditing and Ethical Standards.[22]   **23**

Engagement Quality Control Review
(Ref: Para. 19)

International Standard on Quality Control (UK) (ISQC (UK)) 1[23] requires firms to establish policies and procedures which set out criteria to determine whether engagement quality control reviews shall be performed for other entities. ISQC (UK) 1 notes that one of the criteria that a firm considers when determining whether to require completion of an engagement quality control review includes the nature of the engagement, including the extent to which it involves a matter of public interest.[24] What is a matter of public interest can be difficult to define; factors that may apply to a charity include: **24**

- The size and activities of the charity.

- The charity's national or local profile.

- The charity's sources of funds (including the extent to which the charity receives public funds).

Where safeguards include the review by an engagement quality control reviewer, that reviewer will have sufficient knowledge of the charity sector and the applicable regulatory framework to enable a meaningful review to be completed.   **25**

---

[20] *See Matters of Material Significance reportable to UK charity regulators: A guide for auditors and independent examiners.*

[21] *See Reporting of relevant matters of interest to UK charity regulators: A guide for auditors and independent examiners.*

[22] *Ethical Standard, Part B, Section 4 – Fees, Remuneration and Evaluation Policies, Gifts and Hospitality, Litigation, paragraphs 4.1 and 4.2.*

[23] *ISQC (UK) 1 (Revised June 2016) Quality Control for Firms that Perform Audits and Reviews of Financial Statements, and Other Assurance and Related Services Engagements, paragraph 35(b).*

[24] *ISQC (UK) 1 (Revised June 2016), paragraph A41.*

ISA (UK) 240: THE AUDITOR'S RESPONSIBILITIES RELATING TO FRAUD IN AN AUDIT OF FINANCIAL STATEMENTS

ISA (UK) 240 (Revised June 2016) deals with the auditor's responsibilities relating to fraud in an audit of financial statements.

Responsibility for the prevention and detection of fraud
(Ref: Para. 4)

26   The trustees of a charity are responsible for the prevention and detection of fraud in relation to the charity, even if they have delegated some of their executive functions to senior management. The trustees are expected to safeguard charity assets and reserves through the implementation of appropriate systems of control.

27   Many charities receive funds which have restrictions placed upon them. These funds are held on trust and must be applied to the purpose for which they were given. The misappropriation or misapplication of funds constitutes a breach of trust or duty, whether it was intentional or accidental. In planning, performing and evaluating the audit work the auditor considers the risk of material misstatement arising from breaches of trust.

Evaluation of fraud risk factors
(Ref: Para. 24)

28   A list of fraud risk factors is contained in ISA (UK) 240.[25] Additional charity specific factors may include:

- The limited involvement of trustees in key decision making or monitoring transactions, and limited engagement with charity staff.

- Widespread branches or operations, such as those established in response to emergency appeals in countries where there is no effective system of law and order.

- Reliance on volunteers and staff with limited management or supervision and a lack of segregation and rotation of duties.

- Transactions (income and expenditure) often undertaken in cash.

- Unpredictable patterns of giving (in cash, by cheque, and through donations in kind) by members of the public, both in terms of timing and point of donation.

- Informal banking or cash transfer methods used in areas remote from conventional banking systems.

- Inconsistent regulation across international borders.

- International transfer of funds.

- Diversion of grants payable.

29   The auditor is not required to review or conclude on the adequacy of the approach taken by trustees to assess and address risks faced by the charity. However, where the trustees have produced documentation that sets out their assessment of the various risks facing the charity, and how they believe those risks are controlled and managed, the auditor has regard to that documentation (and any fraud register

---

[25] *ISA (UK) 240 (Revised June 2016) The Auditor's Responsibilities Relating to Fraud in an Audit of Financial Statements, Appendix 1.*

where maintained) when performing the auditor's own assessment of the risk of material misstatements to financial reporting resulting from fraud.

Identification and assessment of the risks of material misstatement due to fraud
(Ref: Para. 25–27)

In assessing the risk of misstatement arising from fraud, the auditor also considers **30** the extent of the trustees' involvement in the day-to-day administration of the charity, the trustees' and senior management's access to its resources and their ability, collectively or individually, to override any internal controls. Additionally, the auditor considers the arrangements the trustees have put in place to monitor work undertaken by third parties (e.g., custodianship of investments and fundraising).

The auditor considers the possibility that the charity's records of income to which **31** it is legally entitled may be incomplete as a result of fraud. A common type of fraud against charities is the diversion of donations. Sources of audit evidence as to whether income from appeals and other "non-routine" sources have been fully recorded can involve the assessment and testing of internal controls, and comparison of donations actually received by the charity to past results for similar appeals, to budgets and to statistics for response rates for charities in general. A further example is where a charity recognises income that it may never receive, for instance on the back of an informal pledge for which there is no formal agreement or payment plan, to provide assurance that the pledged monies will be forthcoming.[26]

The auditor remains aware that, although charities are not profit-making entities, **32** there is still a risk of material misstatement due to fraudulent financial reporting relating to income recognition. The presumption that there are risks of fraud in revenue recognition may not always be appropriate for some public sector bodies which are funded from central government directly by grant-in-aid income where reporting on expenditure and outcomes is also required.

Communications to management and with those charged with governance
(Ref: Para. 40–42)

The auditor will communicate fraud related matters to those charged with **33** governance (i.e., the board of trustees) in all situations. Other appropriate levels of management for many charities will include the chief executive officer or equivalent. All such communications are subject to "tipping off" provisions under anti-money laundering legislation.

Reporting fraud to an appropriate authority outside the entity
(Ref: Para. 43)

Where there is a suspected or actual instance suggesting dishonesty or fraud **34** involving a significant loss of or major risk to charitable funds or assets, the auditor makes a report direct to an appropriate authority outside the charity without delay, and without informing the trustees or any officers of the charity in advance if they are suspected of being involved.[27]

---

[26] *Further guidance on the completeness of income can be found in paragraphs 112–116 of this Practice Note.*

[27] *See also Section Reporting matters of material significance to charity regulators of this Practice Note.*

35   In the case of charities, the appropriate authorities include the National Crime Agency (NCA) where there is a suspicion of money laundering and the appropriate charity regulator.[28]

ISA (UK) 250: SECTION A – CONSIDERATION OF LAWS AND REGULATIONS IN AN AUDIT OF FINANCIAL STATEMENTS

ISA (UK) 250 (Revised July 2017) deals with the auditor's responsibility to consider the laws and regulations in an audit of financial statements.

Responsibility for compliance with laws and regulations
(Ref: Para. 3)

36   The trustees of a charity are responsible for ensuring that the necessary controls are in place to ensure compliance with applicable laws and regulations, and to detect and correct any breaches that have occurred, even if they have delegated some of their executive functions to senior management or professional advisers.

The auditor's consideration of compliance with laws and regulations
(Ref: Para. 13)

37   In the case of charities, the legal and regulatory framework includes charity and trust law, and hence specific requirements as to the use of restricted funds and preservation of any permanent endowments (capital funds).

38   The accounting and auditing requirements of the legal and regulatory framework specific to charities is summarised in Appendix 2 of this Practice Note. In addition, charities are affected by the whole range of national legislation applicable to business entities, such as employment, tax and pensions law, anti-money laundering and anti-bribery legislation, and health and safety regulations.

Laws and regulations generally recognised to have a direct effect on the determination of material amounts and disclosures in the financial statements

39   Laws and regulations which have a direct effect on the determination of material amounts and disclosures in the financial statements for unincorporated charities are contained in the relevant legislation and subordinate regulations[29] relating to the particular UK jurisdiction in which the charity operates. Where individual charities are subject to legislation other than specific charity legislation there may be certain additional disclosure requirements (e.g., charitable companies or charitable housing associations).

40   The auditor also checks whether a charity's governing documents contain any special provisions as to the disclosure of information in the financial statements or reporting requirements for the auditor. Users of the financial statements of a charity reasonably expect that the transactions recorded within them are authorised by the governing documents of the charity and in furtherance of the charity's objects. In order to give a "true and fair" view, due regard needs to be given to disclosure of any significant non-compliance with the governing documents. The governing document may, for example, take the form of a trust deed, a will, a constitution, the Articles of Association of a company, or the governing documents of a charitable incorporated organisation (CIO) or a Scottish charitable incorporated organisation (SCIO).

---

[28] *See also paragraphs 56–58 of this Practice Note.*

[29] *See Appendix 2 of this Practice Note.*

The auditor therefore obtains an understanding of the charity's governing **41** documents and in planning and conducting the audit:

- Ensures that the audit procedures cover compliance with the governing documents.

- Considers any changes in the charity's activities to ensure that these comply with the governing documents.

- Is alert to new or unusual transactions which may not be in accordance with the governing documents.

Charities may receive financial assistance from government or other entities (e.g., **42** grants, loans and loan guarantees). By accepting such assistance, charities often become subject to laws and regulations that may have a direct and material effect on the determination of amounts in the charity's financial statements. Such laws and regulations may specifically address:

- The types of goods or services that charities may purchase with the financial assistance.

- The eligibility of those to whom charities may provide benefits.

- Amounts charities must contribute from their own resources toward projects for which financial assistance is provided.

- Principles and standards for determining the direct and indirect costs that are allowable as charges to such financial assistance programmes.

Laws and regulations where instances of non-compliance may have a material effect on the financial statements

Determination of those laws and regulations where instances of non-compliance **43** may have a material effect on the financial statements of a particular charity requires consideration of its governing documents, the activities it undertakes and any laws and regulations specifically applicable to those activities, as well as the requirements of charity law. To assist in identifying possible or actual instances of non-compliance with these laws and regulations, the auditor inspects any recent correspondence between the charity and the relevant charity regulator in accordance with the provisions of the ISA (UK).

As the charity sector is diverse in terms of activities undertaken and hence the **44** requirements of laws and regulations where instances of non-compliance may have a material effect on the financial statements, the auditor also considers the impact of that particular activity on the overall ability of the charity to operate effectively in terms of the charity's current objectives. Where a particular activity, whilst subject to laws and regulations, does not have a material effect on the financial statements of a charity then the auditor has no responsibility for considering whether such laws and regulations have been observed.

Charity tax and trading income

Failure to comply with tax laws and regulations may have either a direct and **45** material effect on the determination of financial statement amounts (e.g., a charity which incorrectly takes advantage of a VAT or other tax relief or expenditure considered non-charitable under tax legislation) or a material indirect effect on the financial statements that would require appropriate disclosures (e.g., a charity's failure to maintain its tax-exempt status could have serious tax consequences and affect both its financial statements and related disclosures).

46   Whilst charities do not enjoy a general exemption from direct taxation, there are significant tax exemptions available to charities both in relation to income and chargeable gains, as well as certain indirect taxes. The auditor needs to have an understanding of these statutory exemptions and extra-statutory concessions in order to identify activities that may fall outside their scope. Especially where income is receivable that does not fall within such reliefs, a charity can be exposed to significant tax liabilities.

47   Gift aid is an important source of income for many charities, and trustees need to ensure that the charity is complying with the strict rules set out by HMRC for its proper operation. In particular, the completeness of documentation and audit trails, and any transactions with, or benefits passing to, the donor or connected persons will need careful consideration. HMRC may consider the implications for gift aid where a charity's activities are not fulfilling the public benefit test, or where the trustees do not meet the "fit and proper persons" test.[30]

48   Charities which make grants or payments overseas run a greater risk of their payments being deemed non-charitable by HMRC and therefore need to pay particular attention to the HMRC guidance on the steps that HMRC expect organisations to take in order to be able to demonstrate that they have undertaken sufficient due diligence on such payments.[31]

49   The existence of trading activities[32] can affect the charity's compliance with laws and regulations, potential tax liabilities and, in some cases, can give rise to matters to be reported to the relevant charity regulator. Trading by charities falls into two main categories:

- Primary purpose trading (also known as charitable trading) which is generally exempt from direct taxation; and

- Trading to raise funds for charitable purposes, which is generally not exempt from direct taxation, unless the trade falls within the exemptions available for small trades or the concessions made for charity fundraising events.

50   Primary purpose trading is the exercise of a trade in the course of the actual carrying out of a primary purpose of a charity (e.g., the charging of fees by a school which is established as a charity for the advancement of education). The tax exemption available on primary purpose trading also extends to trades where the work is mainly carried out by the beneficiaries of the charity and the remedial or educational value of the work to the beneficiaries can be demonstrated.

51   Charitable trading may also extend beyond primary purpose activities to incorporate "ancillary trading". Ancillary trading, which contributes indirectly to the successful furtherance of the purposes of the charity, is treated as part of "primary purpose trading" for both charity law and tax purposes. An example of ancillary trading is the sale of food and drink in a restaurant or bar by a theatre charity to members of an audience.

52   Trading for fundraising purposes and other non-charitable trading activities, where undertaken directly by a charity on a substantial or regular basis, may be contrary to charity law and the profits may be liable to income or corporation tax.

---

[30] *This requirement was introduced by Section 30 and Schedule 6 of Finance Act 2010. HMRC have issued detailed guidance on how HMRC applies this test which can be found here: https://www.gov.uk/government/publications/charities-fit-and-proper-persons-test/guidance-on-the-fit-and-proper-persons-test*

[31] *HMRC's guidance can be found here: https://www.gov.uk/government/publications/charities-detailed-guidance-notes/annex-ii-non-charitable-expenditure#payments-to-overseas-bodies*

[32] *For more guidance see CCEW's Trustees, trading and tax: how charities may lawfully trade (CC35).*

Substantial permanent trading for fundraising purposes would usually be **53** incompatible with charitable status, and generally such trades would be hived off to a wholly-owned subsidiary company which might in turn agree to donate any profits to its charitable parent. A failure to apply such income or gains for charitable purposes only can result in loss of tax relief. The impact of a tax assessment, perhaps going back a number of years, may affect a charity's ability to continue to conduct its activities.

Charities enjoy no general exemption from VAT, which can apply to a range of **54** goods and services supplied in the course of business. Certain primary purpose trading activities as well as trading for fundraising purposes can fall within the meaning of business activity for VAT purposes. Many areas in which charities operate, such as the supply of certain educational, health and welfare services, may be exempt from VAT, and a number of special reliefs also apply specifically to charities.[33] Non-compliance could have adverse financial consequences for the charity.

Data protection

Charities, like other entities, are subject to data protection legislation and these **55** requirements may apply across multiple areas of the charity, for example, fundraising, campaigning, marketing, managing trustees and volunteers, and recording information about service users. The auditor inquires of management and, where appropriate, the trustees, as to whether the charity is complying with the relevant parts of the legislation.

Money laundering[34]

Auditors in the UK have reporting obligations under anti-money laundering **56** legislation to report knowledge or suspicion of money laundering offences, including those arising from fraud and thefts, to the NCA. For auditors of charitable companies, these reporting obligations arise as the auditor falls within the regulated sector in their capacity as an auditor when carrying out statutory audit work within the meaning of Section 1210 of the Companies Act 2006. For auditors of non-company charities, the auditor still needs to consider whether they are required to comply with the anti-money laundering legislation obligations where the auditor provides a regulated accounting service.

Any knowledge or suspicions of involvement of a charity's trustees in money **57** laundering would normally be regarded as being of material significance to the charity regulators and so give rise to a statutory duty to report in addition to making any necessary report required by legislation relating to money laundering offences. Reporting a matter to the NCA does not relieve the auditor of a duty to report that matter to charity regulators where the information is of material significance to the regulator's function.[35]

A "tipping off" offense is not committed under anti-money laundering legislation **58** where the auditor reports a matter of material significance to the charity regulators.

---

[33] *A number of specific exemptions and zero-rating treatments may be available in relation to supplies by and to a charity.*

[34] *Guidance on the auditor's responsibilities regarding the anti-money laundering legislation is set out in Practice Note 12 (Revised) Money laundering – Guidance for Auditors in the United Kingdom.*

[35] *Further guidance is set out in the Annex to Matters of Material Significance reportable to UK charity regulators and Section 6.4.21 of the CCAB's Anti-Money Laundering Guidance For The Accountancy Sector issued in August 2017. The CCAB guidance is draft and subject to Treasury approval later in 2017.*

Communicating identified or suspected non-compliance with those charged with governance
(Ref: Para. 23–25)

59   The auditor is required to communicate the auditor's findings to the appropriate level of those charged with governance (in the case of a charity, the trustees), unless the auditor concludes that the identified or suspected non-compliance ought to be reported to an appropriate authority outside the charity and that it no longer has confidence in the trustees. In this case, the auditor makes a report direct to an appropriate authority, including the respective charity regulator, without delay and without informing the trustees in advance.

60   In those cases where the trustees are not involved in the day-to-day management of the charity, having delegated this function to staff, and it is the latter who are suspected of involvement in the breach of laws or regulations, the auditor may consider that it is appropriate to communicate with the trustees in the first instance.

Potential implications of identified or suspected non-compliance for the auditor's report on the financial statements
(Ref: Para. 26–28)

61   The auditor's report on a non-company charity's financial statements is usually addressed to its trustees. Although identified or suspected non-compliance with laws or regulations may already have been reported to the trustees of the charity, the auditor is nevertheless required to consider the implications of the identified or suspected non-compliance for the auditor's report and issue an auditor's report that is appropriate in the circumstances.

Reporting identified or suspected non-compliance to an appropriate authority outside the charity
(Ref: Para. 29)

62   Where the auditor identifies or suspects non-compliance with laws or regulations, the auditor considers whether such a matter should be reported to an appropriate authority outside the charity, including whether the matter should be reported to the charity regulators.[36]

ISA (UK) 260: COMMUNICATION WITH THOSE CHARGED WITH GOVERNANCE

ISA (UK) 260 (Revised June 2016) deals with the auditor's responsibility to communicate with those charged with governance in an audit of financial statements.

Those charged with governance
(Ref: Para. 11)

63   Those charged with governance are normally the board of trustees (who are also the directors in the case of a charitable company). Where there are subcommittees of the board, (e.g., an audit committee) the sub-committee may fulfil this role. The auditor's understanding of the charity's governance structure and processes

---

[36] See Section *Reporting matters of material significance to charity regulators* of this Practice Note.

obtained in accordance with ISA (UK) 315[37] will be relevant in determining with whom the auditor communicates.

The appropriate person(s) with whom to communicate may also vary depending **64** on the matter to be communicated, for example, it may be appropriate in some circumstances to communicate minor housekeeping matters only to management.

Where the trustees employ staff to whom certain executive functions are **65** delegated, the auditor will still report to those trustees who are charged with governance, since such executive powers are delegated from the trustee body.

Establishing the communication process
(Ref: Para. 18)

The auditor considers whether any of the matters communicated with those **66** charged with governance should also be reported to the charity regulators as required by the auditor's statutory duty in this regard.[38]

The auditor also considers whether there are any matters communicated with those **67** charged with governance that, whilst they do not appear to be of material significance to the charity regulators, the auditor nevertheless believes, in the auditor's professional judgment, that the matter is likely to be relevant, or of interest to the charity regulators (e.g., where trustees have failed repeatedly to take corrective action, without reasonable cause, to address deficiencies in internal control). In such cases, the auditor may exercise its right to report to the appropriate charity regulator.[39]

Adequacy of the communication process
(Ref: Para. 22)

ISA (UK) 260[40] stresses the need for effective two-way communication between **68** the auditor and those charged with governance. Communications from the auditor need to be understandable and clear and written for an audience of volunteer trustees who may have different skills and experience than those found in a commercial board of directors.[41]

ISA (UK) 265: COMMUNICATING DEFICIENCIES IN INTERNAL CONTROL TO THOSE CHARGED WITH GOVERNANCE AND MANAGEMENT

ISA (UK) 265 deals with the auditor's responsibilities to communicate appropriately to those charged with governance and management deficiencies in internal control that the auditor has identified in an audit of financial statements.

---

[37] *ISA (UK) 315 (Revised June 2016) Identifying and Assessing the Risks of Material Misstatement through Understanding the Entity and its Environment.*

[38] *See Section Reporting matters of material significance to charity regulators of this Practice Note.*

[39] *See paragraph 266 of this Practice Note.*

[40] *ISA (UK) 260 (Revised June 2016), paragraph 4.*

[41] *See paragraph 78 of this Practice Note.*

Communication of significant deficiencies in internal control
(Ref: Para. 9–10)

69   Trustees have a legal duty to manage the charity's resources responsibly and the charity regulators issue general guidance for trustees on implementing appropriate financial controls.[42] Such guidance may help the auditor to identify those areas where there may be deficiencies in internal control.

70   Significant deficiencies in internal control may call into question the integrity or competence of management. In these situations, the auditor considers the need to make a report of matters of material significance to the appropriate charity regulators.[43]

ISA (UK) 315: IDENTIFYING AND ASSESSING THE RISKS OF MATERIAL MISSTATEMENT THROUGH UNDERSTANDING THE ENTITY AND ITS ENVIRONMENT

ISA (UK) 315 (Revised June 2016) deals with the auditor's responsibility to identify and assess the risks of material misstatement in the financial statements, through understanding the entity and its environment, including the entity's internal control.

Inquiries of management and others within the entity
(Ref: Para. 6(a))

71   The auditor inquires of management and, where appropriate, those charged with governance as to whether the trustees have made a report to a charity regulator.[44]

The relevant regulatory framework
(Ref: Para. 11(a))

72   The legal framework for charities is complex, and different requirements exist depending on the charity's constitution, the part of the UK in which the charity is established and the type of activity which it undertakes. The auditor needs to obtain an understanding of the applicable laws and regulations of the jurisdiction within which the charity operates. This involves keeping up to date with laws and regulations relating to charities generally, and to the audited charity in particular. The list of such laws and regulations is likely to be extensive and far reaching and needs to be carefully discussed with the charity to ensure that they are identified in full.

73   The accounting requirements under which charities report depend on how they are constituted and the relevant national jurisdiction within the UK.[45] The auditor has an understanding of the Charities SORP, which sits alongside UK Generally Accepted Practice (FRS 102), and the relevant Charities Acts.

74   A charity may also have activities outside of the UK. As such, the auditor also needs to obtain an understanding of the applicable laws and regulations relating to the charity's activities in jurisdictions outside of the UK.

---

[42] For example, CCEW's Internal financial controls for charities (CC8).

[43] See Section Reporting matters of material significance to charity regulators of this Practice Note.

[44] In England and Wales and Northern Ireland, this is known as a serious incident report; in Scotland, there is a non-statutory notifiable events regime.

[45] The principal categories are set out in Appendix 2 of this Practice Note.

The nature of the entity
(Ref: Para. 11(b))

Knowledge of the charity's activities, governance, operating structure, sources of **75** income and the existence of restricted funds is essential for assessing the risk of material misstatement arising from fraud, error, or non-compliance with applicable laws and regulations and in order to plan and carry out the audit effectively and efficiently.

Governance

Although the detail of regulation differs between different jurisdictions in the UK, **76** the general principles governing the duties of trustees are the same regardless of what they are called in the charity's governing documents.[46]

Auditors can find further information regarding the responsibilities of trustees and **77** charity governance from the relevant Charities Acts, or the charity regulators.[47] The charity sector has its own voluntary code of governance in England and Wales.[48]

Charity trustees are usually unpaid[49] and part-time, and governance structures can **78** be very varied. In planning the audit, the auditor needs to understand the nature of the charity's governance and the influence that this has on the control environment of the charity and on reporting to those charged with governance.[50] The auditor also needs to obtain an understanding of any policy for the payment of trustee expenses to ensure it is disclosed correctly in the financial statements in accordance with the Charities SORP.

The auditor also needs to understand the charity's governing documents. There are **79** many different types of governing instrument or constitution which will determine the objects of the charity and the powers of its trustees, and the audit approach needs to be adapted accordingly. Particular issues include:

• Any limitations in objectives placed on the charity by its governing documents.

• Terms and restrictions placed on material gifts or donations received.

Selection and application of accounting policies
(Ref: Para. 11(c))

The auditor reviews accounting policies and considers the application of the **80** Charities SORP. Accounting policies adopted may have a significant effect on the recognition of assets and liabilities or their presentation within financial statements. Policies that may require careful consideration may include those for the classes of transactions, account balances and disclosures included in Appendix 1 of this Practice Note.

---

[46] *Charity trustees are defined in legislation as "the persons having the general control and management of the administration of a charity".*

[47] *For example, see CCEW's The essential trustee: what you need to know, what you need to do (CC3).*

[48] *There are two versions of the Charity Governance Code, depending on whether a charity defines itself as smaller or larger. The Code versions can be found here: www.charitygovernancecode.org*

[49] *A charity trustee may only be paid where this is in the interests of the charity and provides a significant and clear advantage over other options. There is no power in law to make such payments – it would need to be specifically authorised in the governing documents of the charity, or approved by a charity regulator or a court.*

[50] *See Section ISA (UK) 260 of this Practice Note.*

81   For group audits, the auditor also considers the consistency of accounting policies between the charity and other entities.

82   The auditor considers what steps have been taken by trustees and senior management in respect of cost allocations. Policies that affect the allocation of costs may have a significant impact on how costs are presented in the statement of financial activities.

Measurement and review of financial performance
(Ref: Para. 11(e))

83   The auditor also considers the key performance indicators used to monitor the performance of the charity especially those used by the trustees.

Internal control
(Ref: Para. 12–13)

84   There is a wide variation between different charities in terms of size, activity and organisation. Smaller charities may be administered by volunteer staff or by third party administrators. Larger charities may directly employ professionally qualified, full-time staff. However, the responsibilities of trustees for ensuring that the charity has adequate internal controls and therefore is properly administered, and its assets properly safeguarded apply irrespective of a charity's size or administrative arrangements, and the attitude, role and involvement of each charity's trustees are likely to be fundamental in determining the effectiveness of its control environment.

85   The maintenance of an effective system of internal control is at least as important, if not more so, for charities as it is for other entities, since it is a fundamental duty of charity trustees to protect the property of their charity and to secure its application for the objects of the charity. Failure to do so can render the trustees personally liable for any loss occasioned to the charity. The auditor of certain charities may be subject to specific reporting requirements in respect of internal controls (e.g., registered friendly societies, registered social landlords and charitable NDPBs). Where there is such a requirement, the auditor plans the auditor's work bearing in mind the duty to report if a satisfactory system of control over transactions has not been maintained.

Control environment
(Ref: Para. 14)

86   The role, attitude and actions of the trustees are fundamental in shaping the control environment of a charity.

87   As part of the auditor's risk assessment procedures, the auditor assesses the charity's governance structure and associated control environment. This includes consideration of the skills of trustees and management, the extent of trustee involvement in the governance of the charity, and the policies and processes established (e.g., for managing trustee conflicts of interest). For smaller charities this may include understanding how the segregation of duties risk is mitigated.

The charity's risk assessment process
(Ref: Para. 15)

88   The Charities SORP requires larger charities to include in the trustees' annual report a description of the principal risks and uncertainties facing the charity and its subsidiary undertakings, as identified by the charity trustees, together with a

summary of their plans and strategies for managing those risks. As a result of this, charities will often maintain a risk register as part of a wider risk management process. The auditor reviews this register in order to gain an understanding of the risks currently being managed by the charity and whether any of these could lead to a material misstatement risk for financial reporting.

Information systems and related business processes
(Ref: Para. 18)

The auditor considers as part of the auditor's risk assessment procedures those **89** information systems managed by the charity, including those outside of, or interacting with, the central finance system that could lead to a risk of material misstatement. For example, this may include systems holding donor information, legacy records, patient or beneficiary information, and gift aid data.

For charities it is particularly important that the systems in place are able to capture **90** accurately any restrictions placed on income (whether imposed by the donor or as a result of the charity's fundraising initiatives). The charity also needs to ensure the documentation (including deeds of covenant) supporting the restrictions on the income is retained and easily accessible.

As well as considering the risks of material misstatement associated with all **91** systems identified, the auditor considers the disclosure risk where these systems are expected to be used by the charity to support non-financial disclosures within the trustees' annual report.

Where the charity operates outside of the UK, the auditor also considers the **92** information systems in those jurisdictions as they relate to the entity being audited.

Control activities relevant to the audit
(Ref: Para. 20)

In obtaining an understanding of the control activities relevant to the audit, the **93** auditor takes into account any guidance issued by the charity regulators in respect of internal control.[51]

Risks arising from IT
(Ref: Para. 21)

The auditor considers risks arising from IT which impact on the integrity and **94** security of information. For example, smaller charities may have less resource to commit to IT systems and cyber security, or information relevant to the financial statements may be held on personal computers as the charity does not have its own computer equipment.

Many larger charities have websites which provide facilities for online giving. **95** These may support a donation by credit card, sponsorship or legacy making. Charities will often use third party organisations to manage these systems and processes. The auditor needs to consider whether adequate controls exist over the IT supporting these systems including the assessment of any service organisations used by the charity as part of this control environment.[52]

---

[51] *For example, CCEW's Internal financial controls for charities (CC8).*

[52] *See Section ISA (UK) 402 of this Practice Note.*

Identifying and assessing the risks of material misstatement
(Ref: Para. 25)

96   There is a wide variation between different charities in terms of size, activity and organisation, so that there can be no standard approach to internal controls and risk. The auditor assesses risk and the adequacy of controls in relation to the circumstances of each charity.

97   Appendix 1 of this Practice Note includes examples of events or conditions that may be of particular relevance to charities and may indicate the existence of risks of material misstatement in the financial statements. These examples are in addition to the broad range of events and conditions included in the ISAs (UK).[53]

98   Overseas activities may give rise to additional risks. In these circumstances the auditor will need to ensure that the auditor is able to assess the full extent of the activities, and has the necessary understanding of the regulatory environment in which significant activities are carried out (e.g., in relation to taxation and employment law).[54]

Risks that require special audit consideration
(Ref: Para. 27–29)

99   Issues concerning revenue recognition are likely to give rise to significant risks affecting all charity audits.[55]

ISA (UK) 320: MATERIALITY IN PLANNING AND PERFORMING AN AUDIT

ISA (UK) 320 (Revised June 2016) deals with the auditor's responsibility to apply the concept of materiality in planning and performing an audit of financial statements.

Determining materiality when planning the audit
(Ref: Para. 10)

100   Judgments about materiality are affected by the auditor's perception of the common financial information needs of users of the charity's financial statements. In most cases this is the trustees, but it is not limited to the trustees, and the auditor considers other users relevant to the particular circumstances of the charity, such as beneficiaries, donors, staff, other funding bodies (e.g., grant providers or public sector bodies) and regulators.

101   For a charity, materiality for the financial statements as a whole is often assessed as a percentage of income, expenditure, or net assets. Unlike many commercial entities, charities are not profit-driven and therefore it is relatively rare to use net result for the year as a sole benchmark when determining materiality.

102   ISA (UK) 320 indicates that materiality is considered at both the overall financial statement level and, in certain circumstances of the charity, in relation to one or more particular classes of transactions, account balances or disclosures. This can result in different materiality considerations being applied depending on the item

---

[53] *See ISA (UK) 315 (Revised June 2016), Appendix 2; ISA (UK) 570 (Revised June 2016), paragraph A3; and ISA (UK) 600 (Revised June 2016), Appendix 3.*

[54] *CCEW has issued guidance on charities working internationally which can be found here: https://www.gov.uk/guidance/charities-how-to-manage-risks-when-working-internationally*

[55] *Further guidance on the audit procedures in respect of these risks can be found in Section ISA (UK) 330 of this Practice Note.*

of the financial statements being considered, for example, the degree of accuracy expected in the case of certain disclosures (e.g., transactions with trustees are likely to be considered to be material by nature, even if they are not material by size[56]). Also particular disclosures or expenditure categories may be sensitive and warrant extra attention (e.g., costs of raising funds or overseas transactions).

Branches[57]

The auditor clarifies with management which entities will form part of the financial statements being prepared by the charity. Where a charity operates through branches or subsidiaries, their contribution to the results and financial position of the charity may not be known at the time of planning the audit. In this case, the auditor considers how to decide the likely results of branches or subsidiaries by reference to procedures such as: **103**

● Discussion with management.

● Consideration of problems or particular issues encountered in previous years to see whether there is an identifiable pattern suggestive of weak management or fraud.

● Consideration of prior year figures and any budgeted or preliminary results.

The resulting best estimate is incorporated into materiality for the financial statements as a whole.

Restricted funds

Many charities receive funds which are subject to restrictions. In some cases, these must be reported separately in accordance with the Charities SORP. There is no presumption that the auditor will set a different monetary materiality level for such funds. **104**

The ISA (UK) provides guidance[58] on the factors that may indicate that lesser amounts than materiality could reasonably be expected to influence the economic decisions of users and which may result in different materiality considerations being applied to particular classes of transactions, account balances, or disclosures in the financial statements. **105**

Any breaches of the terms of trusts relating to restricted funds which come to the auditor's attention in the course of the audit, regardless of materiality to the financial statements as a whole, need to be considered in terms of their significance to the auditor's report on the financial statements and brought to the attention of trustees, as a failure on the trustees' part to comply with the terms of trusts may place them in breach of their responsibilities. **106**

In this context, the auditor also considers the disclosure of restricted funds which are subject to specific trusts as to their application, paying particular attention to: **107**

● Any funds that are in deficit.

● Any income funds which are held in illiquid assets (including inter-fund loans) thereby preventing application of the fund.

● Any expenditure of the capital of a permanently endowed fund.

---

[56] *Module 9 of the Charities SORP states that transactions with trustees or related parties are always regarded as material regardless of size.*

[57] *For further guidance on group financial statements see Section ISA (UK) 600 of this Practice Note.*

[58] *ISA (UK) 320 (Revised June 2016), paragraph A10.*

ISA (UK) 330: THE AUDITOR'S RESPONSES TO ASSESSED RISKS

ISA (UK) 330 (Revised July 2017) deals with the auditor's responsibility to design and implement responses to the risks of material misstatement identified and assessed by the auditor in an audit of financial statements.

Risks common to charities

108 The auditor performs risk assessment procedures to identify risks of material misstatement arising in the specific context of the charity. Appendix 1 of this Practice Note provides a list of conditions and events that the auditor may consider when identifying and assessing risks of material misstatement in the financial statements.

109 In addition to the guidance in this Section, the auditor may wish to consult other Sections of this Practice Note in relation to the following areas:

- Unusual business models (see Section *ISA (UK) 315*).

- Significant estimates (see Section *ISA (UK) 540*).

- Related parties (see Section *ISA (UK) 550*).

- Going concern (see Section *ISA (UK) 570*).

Completeness of income

110 Whilst it is the trustees' responsibility to safeguard the assets and income of the charity, the voluntary nature of some elements of its income may restrict the methods available to the trustees to ensure that all income to which the charity is entitled is correctly accounted for.

111 The amount of voluntary income cannot, in many cases, be determined in advance, nor can a charity be regarded as necessarily entitled to funds, even when the amounts have been pledged, before the charity is in receipt of them. Trustees of a charity cannot be held responsible for the security of money or other assets which are intended for its use until that money or assets are, or should be, within the control of the charity. Trustees should, however, establish procedures to ensure appropriate recording and safeguarding as soon as such assets come within their control.

112 The auditor considers the following factors when assessing the risks associated with the completeness of income and how to address any identified risks:

- *Tax-effective giving:* donations may be made tax-effectively, through gift aid, payroll giving, and gifts of land and shares. For most tax-effective schemes, and especially for gift aid, there are detailed requirements relating to the procedures to be followed by donors and recipient charities, as well as detailed rules designed to prevent abuse (e.g., the reciprocal benefit limits). The auditor considers the implications of the significance of these income streams and adapts the audit procedures accordingly.

- *Completeness of donation income:* the completeness of recorded donation income can be difficult to substantiate as such income will not always be supported by invoices or equivalent documentation. Where cash donations are received, the trustees need to make arrangements to institute appropriate controls, to the extent practicable, to ensure that all income is properly accounted for. The auditor may consider the effectiveness of such controls when assessing the sufficiency of evidence about the completeness of the income shown in the charity's financial statements.

- *Recognition of income from third party fundraisers:* income recognition can be a complex issue where a charity obtains resources by means of fundraising organisations.[59] The auditor considers the agreement between the charity and the fundraiser and other documents relating to the transaction to see whether all donations received in the charity's name have been transmitted to the charity or otherwise accounted for, and that amounts have been accounted for gross where appropriate instead of having been netted off at source.

- *Recognition of income from branches, associates or subsidiaries:* if charities use branches, associates or subsidiaries to raise funds, the auditor considers the arrangements made by the main charity to determine at what point income is recognised.

- *Recognition of legacy income:* the recognition criteria for legacy income is set out in the Charities SORP and can be subject to uncertainty. For example, the probability and measurability of the receipt may be affected by subsequent events such as valuations and disputes. The auditor therefore reviews information available up to when the financial statements are approved for evidence relating to legacy income receivable at the balance sheet date. Sources of audit evidence as to whether legacy income has been correctly recorded include probate information, estate accounts, correspondence from executors or solicitors, and legacy fundraising agencies. With charities that receive legacy income, it is possible for them to be able to subscribe to agencies that will notify them on any will where probate is granted where the charity is a named beneficiary. Such notifications can help the auditor in relation to testing for legacy completeness. The auditor needs to understand the terms attached to legacies in order to consider the application of the charity's income recognition policies. The auditor also gives consideration to the valuation of donations in kind where appropriate.

- *Informal fundraising groups:* where informal fundraising groups raise money or other resources for charitable purposes on a voluntary basis, without the knowledge of any particular charity, criteria for recognising income are not met until the funds raised are notified to the recipient charity. In general, neither trustees nor the auditor have an obligation to estimate the extent of income from such sources before this point. Even if a legal entitlement on the part of the charity to the resulting income may arise under trust law, it would normally be inappropriate for the charity to account for income from such sources. This is because its ultimate cash realisation cannot be sufficiently determined by the charity.

- *Grants or contractual income:* in the case of grant or contractually funded charities, an examination of the grant applications or contract and correspondence can assist in confirming completeness of income. The auditor considers obtaining direct confirmation of the amounts receivable from the grant provider. The auditor also has an understanding of the terms under which the funding is granted in order to identify the proper accounting treatment. As well as distinguishing whether the income is restricted or not, the nature of the terms and conditions may affect taxation considerations (e.g., VAT treatment).

---

[59] *The Charities Act 1992 Section 59 (as amended by the Charities (Protection and Social Investment) Act 2016) requires there to be an agreement between the charity and the fundraiser in a prescribed form.*

- *Non-cash donations:* charities often receive non-cash donations. The auditor carries out appropriate audit procedures to obtain assurance over the completeness of such items. Such procedures may include internet research to identify relevant material publicising such donations and review of minutes of trustees' meetings.

113   Substantive analytical procedures may be used as a source of audit evidence about the completeness of income. For example, the use of a substantive analytical procedure may be appropriate to gain assurance over a charity's trading income. However, the degree of inherent uncertainty affecting donated income restricts the reliance which can be placed on such techniques in respect of donations.

114   In the case of larger charities with more complex operations, there are specialist publications and sources of information which can be referred to for general information about charities as well as comparative figures and statistics. These sources include "trade" journals, umbrella organisations, and the charity regulators. Available statistics include responses to mail shots (i.e., donations received), and industry norms such as sales per square foot for trading operations in different areas.

Restricted funds

115   Restricted funds are subject to specific trusts, which may be declared by the donor or created through legal process. They may be restricted income funds (which are expendable at the discretion of the trustees in furtherance of some particular aspect of the objects of the charity) or they may be endowments (where the assets are required or permitted to be invested or retained for future use). If restricted funds are used other than in the way specified, the trustees of the charity will have breached their duty.

116   Restricted funds (including endowments) which are subject to specific trusts as to their application may give rise to a risk of material misstatement.

117   The auditor may consider the following factors when assessing the risks associated with restricted funds and how to address any identified risks:

- *Identification and disclosure of restrictions on funds:* the auditor considers whether restrictions are likely to exist as part of the planning process and when assessing the presentation of funds in a charity's balance sheet.[60] The auditor assesses the design and implementation of the internal control procedures put in place by the charity to identify restricted funds (whether imposed by the donor or as a result of the charity's fundraising initiatives).

- *Cost allocation:* grants are often made for specific purposes and are subject to conditions, breach of which can have serious implications for the charity. There is a risk that the charity may inappropriately allocate costs between funds, potentially resulting in the misuse of a restricted fund. The auditor assesses the procedures used by the charity in allocating costs to ensure that expenditure charged to restricted funds is appropriate.

- Consideration of future funding to cover negative balances.

- *Inappropriate transfers between funds:* the auditor determines the validity of any transfers between funds.

- *Use of the capital element of a permanent endowment without express authority:* where such a situation is identified the auditor considers the

---

[60] *The Charities SORP requires restricted funds to be separately disclosed in the charity's financial statements.*

auditor's obligations under ISA (UK) 250 Section A[61] and whether the auditor has a duty to report to the charity regulators.

Overseas operations

Overseas activities can be undertaken through a number of different structures **118** including branches, subsidiaries, joint ventures with other charities, projects managed by local agents or partners through to the grant funding of autonomous local organisations. The auditor of a charity is responsible for forming an opinion on the financial statements reflecting all of the charity's operations, wherever they are situated and however they are constituted.

The auditor may perform the following procedures in respect of a charity with **119** overseas operations:

- Obtain an understanding of how trustees control overseas operations. Management procedures may involve the vetting of applications, reviewing project reports received, setting thresholds for site visits to projects involving significant grant funding, confirmation of grant receipts, reviewing accounts and the local certification of expenditure.

- Obtain evidence from field officers' reports as to work undertaken.

- Comparison of accounting returns of expenditure with field reports and plans for consistency and reasonableness.

- Analytical review of accounting returns received from overseas components.

- Review of any inspection or internal control visit reports undertaken by any internal audit function.

- Review of audit work undertaken by local auditors, and review of any audit reports carried out on behalf of international donors (e.g., government departments).

- Review of evidence from the audit work of another auditor.

Common risks of material misstatement identified in overseas operations **120** associated with charities include:

- *Completeness and disclosure of material assets held or material funds applied by overseas branches or subsidiaries:* the auditor may seek observational evidence by way of site visits. Such visits may provide valuable evidence of the existence of tangible fixed assets and of project work being undertaken by the charity. The auditor needs to be aware of the logistical arrangements which may be needed where site visits to remote areas are considered.

- *Appropriateness of the charity's oversight mechanisms over the use of funds by autonomous overseas organisations:* where a charity makes a significant grant to an overseas organisation that is autonomous from the charity, the auditor seeks evidence to support receipt of funding by that organisation, and assesses whether the charity has exercised reasonable diligence in ensuring application of the funds for the purposes of the charity's objects.

- *Timing of recognition of expenditure within a complex overseas charity structure:* where the overseas operations are part of the charity, the transfer

---

[61] *ISA (UK) 250 (Revised July 2017) Section A – Consideration of Laws and Regulations in an Audit of Financial Statements.*

of funds by itself does not give rise to expenditure as such funds remain under the control of the charity. However, the auditor obtains an understanding of the structure of the charity to determine at what point expenditure is incurred, and obtains audit evidence to support material expenditure in the field.

121   In some cases it may be more cost effective to engage component auditors to undertake audit work on overseas operations. In such situations the requirements of ISA (UK) 600[62] on group financial statements apply.[63]

Heritage assets[64]

122   The auditor may consider the following factors when assessing the risks associated with heritage assets and how to address any identified risks:

- *Sufficiency of information available to the entity to obtain a valuation of the heritage asset:* in forming a judgment on whether sufficient information is available to obtain a valuation of a heritage asset, the auditor may consider the valuation of comparable assets, the availability and cost of experts in the field and the degree of specialisation of the asset. If additional information on valuation becomes available at a later date the auditor reconsiders the appropriateness of the judgment made.[65]

- *Completeness of heritage assets:* the auditor reviews the charity's internal control mechanisms used to manage the heritage asset portfolio and performs searches to identify any high profile donations or purchases made during the period.

- *Existence/Rights and obligations of heritage assets:* The auditor reviews documents which may evidence ownership (e.g., legal contracts, reports from curators, fixed asset register) or physically inspects assets.

Grants payable

123   Many charities carry out their activities through a combination of direct service provision and the grant funding of third parties to undertake work that contributes to the charity's aims or programme of work.

124   Where charities make grant payments to third parties, the auditor may consider the following factors when assessing risks of material misstatement and how to address any identified risks:

- *Oversight of those charged with governance:* the auditor considers how those charged with governance monitor the charity's grants. For example, a list of grants paid and payable may be shared with those charged with governance, and the charity may have specific procedures in place to manage the formal approval process of recipients. The auditor assesses the design and implementation of the internal control procedures put in place by the charity to allocate and oversee its grants.

---

[62] *ISA (UK) 600 (Revised June 2016) Special considerations – Audits of group financial statements (including the work of component auditors).*

[63] *See Section ISA (UK) 600 of this Practice Note.*

[64] *For charities that are public bodies (NDPBs) Chapter 7 of the Government Financial Reporting Manual (FReM) applies.*

[65] *See Section ISA (UK) 540 of this Practice Note where significant accounting estimates are involved in respect of the valuation of heritage assets.*

- *Diversion of grants to inappropriate recipients:* the auditor may choose to circularise the recipients of grants to ensure no funds have been diverted. The auditor may also review any acknowledgement returns or "thank you" letters received by the charity from grant recipients. The auditor applies professional scepticism when considering the validity of such returns as audit evidence.

ISA (UK) 402: AUDIT CONSIDERATIONS RELATING TO AN ENTITY USING A SERVICE ORGANISATION

ISA (UK) 402 deals with the auditor's responsibility to obtain sufficient appropriate audit evidence when a user entity uses the services of one or more service organisations.

Obtaining an understanding of the services provided by service organisations (Ref: Para. 9)

The auditor of a charity needs to consider the nature and extent of activity undertaken by service organisations to determine whether those activities are relevant to the audit, and whether they give rise to a risk of material misstatement. **125**

Use of a service organisation does not diminish the ultimate responsibility of the trustees for conducting the affairs of the charity in a manner which meets their legal responsibilities, including those of safeguarding the assets, maintaining accounting records and preparing financial statements. Similarly, a charity's use of a service organisation does not alter the auditor's responsibilities when reporting on the charity's financial statements. **126**

Common use of service organisations within the charity sector include: **127**

- Maintenance of accounting records.
- Payroll services.
- Fundraising and donor fulfilment.
- Custodianship of assets, and investment management services.

It is not uncommon for charities to share an accounting function. In such cases the auditor considers the control arrangements for allocation of costs between such connected entities. **128**

Some charities choose to partner with commercial fundraising organisations in order to generate income. However, the legal rules that apply to various types of fundraising can be detailed and complex. Guidance on fundraising has been issued by the charity regulators.[66] **129**

Where investment management arrangements exist, the auditor considers how trustees set investment objectives and monitor performance. The auditor also discusses with the trustees how they ensure that the level of delegation is consistent with the charity's powers and that the investment powers are being properly exercised. **130**

Certain arrangements may also involve a service organisation providing facilities and services direct to a charity's beneficiaries. Examples include: **131**

- Management of a recreational facility (e.g., a sports centre).

---

[66] *As well as the websites of the charity regulators, the Fundraising Regulator has issued guidance which can be downloaded from here: https://www.fundraisingregulator.org.uk/code-of-fundraising-practice/code-of-fundraising-practice-v1-4-310717-docx/*

- Provision of services to beneficiaries (e.g., the management of a care facility).

- Provision of ancillary catering facilities (e.g., a museum restaurant).

132   The charity's governing documents may set out powers for the trustees to delegate activities to outside service organisations, who may not be charities themselves. The auditor reviews such documents where practicable, or alternatively holds discussions with the trustees, to determine whether there is authority, or presumed authority, for outsourcing. In doing so, the auditor considers whether any outsourced arrangements provide a risk of a conflict of interest existing between a trustee or senior staff member of a charity and the outsourcing provider, and considers how these are to be addressed by audit procedures.[67]

133   Where the charity's controls in relation to service organisations are poor or absent, the auditor also considers whether the status of the charity's internal control arrangements should be the subject of a report to the relevant charity regulator.

ISA (UK) 510: INITIAL AUDIT ENGAGEMENTS—OPENING BALANCES

ISA (UK) 510 (Revised June 2016) deals with the auditor's responsibilities relating to opening balances in an initial audit engagement.

Nature and extent of audit procedures on opening balances
(Ref: Para. 6)

134   Special considerations will apply where a non-company charity changes its basis of accounting from a receipts and payments to an accruals basis, or where the financial statements become subject to an audit, having previously been subject to a report by an independent examiner.

135   When there has been a change in the basis of accounting, procedures may include checking bank statements, the review of receipts and payments after the year end, and a physical check of any tangible fixed assets. For analytical procedures performed in the current year the auditor is likely to need to adjust the prior year management information prepared on a receipts and payments basis to enable a proper comparison.

136   If the prior year's financial statements were audited by a predecessor auditor, the auditor takes into account the professional competence and independence of the other auditor (e.g., whether the predecessor auditor is a charity specialist) in determining whether reviewing the predecessor auditor's working papers provides sufficient appropriate audit evidence regarding the opening balances.

137   Predecessor auditors of a charitable company have a statutory duty to provide the auditor with access to all relevant information concerning the charitable company,[68] including information concerning the most recent audit. Where there is no such statutory obligation, as is the case for non-company charities, the auditor may nevertheless request access to the predecessor auditor's working papers. In some circumstances, the predecessor auditor may be prepared to consider granting such access. Where such access is refused, the auditor performs alternative procedures in order to obtain sufficient appropriate audit evidence regarding the opening balances.

---

[67] *See also Section ISA (UK) 550 of this Practice Note.*

[68] *ISQC (UK) 1 (Revised June 2016), paragraph 28D-1.*

ISA (UK) 540: AUDITING ACCOUNTING ESTIMATES, INCLUDING FAIR VALUE ACCOUNTING ESTIMATES, AND RELATED DISCLOSURES

ISA (UK) 540 (Revised June 2016) deals with the auditor's responsibilities relating to accounting estimates, including fair value accounting estimates, and related disclosures in an audit of financial statements.

Obtaining an understanding of the requirements of the applicable financial reporting framework
(Ref: Para. 8(a))

Common areas of charity financial statements which are affected by accounting **138** estimates or fair value adjustments are included in Appendix 1 of this Practice Note.

The Charities SORP provides detailed guidance on appropriate accounting **139** policies and measurement bases. In applying these policies and bases the use of estimates and estimation techniques will be necessary to determine the monetary value of assets and liabilities and to determine the allocation of costs within the Statement of Financial Activities (SoFA) – such as support cost allocation. In order to comply with FRS 102 and the Charities SORP, a charity's financial statements discloses a description of the estimation techniques adopted, including underlying principles, that are significant.

Obtaining an understanding of how management makes the accounting estimates
(Ref: Para. 8(c))

The Charities SORP allows certain valuations to be undertaken by trustees or **140** employees of a charity provided that, in the case of property valuations, they have knowledge of the relevant property market. In this situation, the auditor assesses the individual's relevant experience in accordance with the requirements of ISA (UK) 500[69] and the associated guidance in relation to a management's expert.

Certain items in the financial statements are required to be discounted and the **141** Charities SORP gives some guidance on rates that may be used (e.g., for legacies receivable using the interest rate the charity anticipates it would earn on a comparable deposit over a similar period or for provisions it is the rate which reflects the cost of money to the charity). The auditor assesses whether the discount rate applied is appropriate in the circumstances, taking into account the guidance in the Charities SORP and considering other factors, such as the return on investments foregone. For example, a charity which only receives interest may use an interest rate as a discount factor, whereas a charity invested in stocks and shares could use the rate of return on those assets instead – which would mean that these two rates could vary considerably.

Evidence to support accounting estimates may frequently be obtained as part of **142** the auditor's review of the post-balance sheet period, for example, by checking the subsequent expenditure of designated funds, or recoverability of accrued income in respect of, for example, tax claims, grant awards and legacies.

Evidence relating to cost allocations across the cost categories of the SoFA may **143** sometimes be obtained through observation, for example, by observing the key duties of staff and internal departments to determine whether staff costs are

---

[69] *ISA (UK) 500 Audit Evidence, paragraph 8.*

reasonably allocated between the categories of charitable expenditure and the costs of raising funds. Where material estimates are required to allocate joint costs between the expenditure categories of the SoFA, the auditor needs to consider whether the accounting policies adequately explain the estimation techniques adopted.

144   Where expenditure by a charity relates to a project which is of uncertain duration, because it is subject to external circumstances beyond the control of the trustees, it may be difficult to determine matters such as the expected useful economic life of fixed assets used in the project (e.g., vehicles or other capital equipment used to provide emergency aid in a war zone may have an uncertain future, or the trustees may consider that the economic costs of redeploying equipment exceed its book value). The auditor uses its knowledge of the charity's activities and accounting policies to assess whether the periods for write-down of fixed assets are reasonable and in line with any estimate of service potential.

145   On occasion evidence obtained from post-balance sheet review and observation may be insufficiently conclusive. Where such estimates are likely to be material, the auditor reviews the process by which the estimate was arrived at and considers the basis of the calculation in terms of its reasonableness, justifiability and consistency. In so doing, the auditor will draw heavily on its knowledge of the charity in testing the consistency of principles adopted. Estimates of this nature may include:

- The quantification of future charitable commitments and constructive liabilities.

- Valuations of gifts in kind received, particularly property.

- Valuation of assets received for onward distribution.

- Valuation of fixed asset investments where no market price exists, (e.g., unlisted securities and trading subsidiaries of the parent charity).

- Valuation of heritage assets.

- Valuation of intangible income derived from donated services or use of facilities.

- Estimates of ongoing service potential of fixed assets, in the absence of a cash flow, in an impairment review.

- Impairment of programme-related investments made in furtherance of a charity's objects, rather than for financial return.

- Recoverability of loans made to beneficiaries in the furtherance of a charity's objects.

Indicators of possible management bias
(Ref: Para. 21)

146   In the charity sector, management may be biased in their accounting estimates in order to achieve certain results for the year although bonuses based on results are not common. A management bias may arise from:

- A desire to meet trustee expectations on the results for the year.

- A desire to demonstrate growth.

- A need to meet covenant obligations attached to bank loans.

- Wanting to avoid repayments of grant funds if they are not fully utilised.

Management bias may also extend to those charged with governance.

ISA (UK) 550: RELATED PARTIES

ISA (UK) 550 deals with the auditor's responsibilities relating to related party relationships and transactions in an audit of financial statements.

Understanding the charity's related party relationships and transactions
(Ref: Para. 12–14)

ISA (UK) 550[70] notes that many financial reporting frameworks establish specific **147** accounting and disclosure requirements for related party relationships, transactions and balances. The charity sector has such a framework and the Charities SORP has its own definition of "related parties" which combines the requirements of charity law, company law and FRS 102.[71]

In considering a possible related party relationship, a charity assesses the **148** substance of the relationship and not merely its legal form.

A transaction involving a trustee or other related party is always considered **149** material by nature, regardless of its size.

The charity's controls over related party relationships and transactions
(Ref: Para. 14)

The charity regulators issue guidance on the relevant controls they expect **150** management to put in place to authorise and approve significant related party transactions.[72] The auditor has regard to this guidance, and forms an assessment of the controls necessary to arrive at proper disclosure.

In making inquiries of management, the auditor addresses both the trustees and the **151** senior management team where such a team has delegated powers. This team will generally be the same as those disclosed within the trustees' annual report and captured in the aggregate remuneration disclosure.

The charity regulators have identified conflict of interest as a major factor in many **152** of their inquiries and the auditor therefore obtains sufficient appropriate audit evidence relating to the identification, accounting, and disclosures of related party transactions, recognising that charities have a specific definition of the term.

Maintaining alertness for related party information when reviewing records or documents
(Ref: Para. 15)

In addition to those records or documents that normally may indicate the existence **153** of related party relationships or transactions, the auditor inspects whatever documentation the auditor considers necessary for indications of the existence of related parties (e.g., minutes of trustees' meetings).

---

[70] *ISA (UK) 550, paragraph 3.*

[71] *The term "related parties" is defined in Appendix 1: Glossary of terms of the Charities SORP.*

[72] *For example, see CCEW's Conflicts of interest: a guide for charity trustees (CC29); Section 4 of OSCR's Guidance and Good Practice for Charity Trustees; and Section 6 of CCNI's Running your charity: Support for charity trustees on key aspects of running a charity effectively (EG024).*

Assertions that related party transactions were conducted on terms equivalent to those prevailing in an arm's length transaction
(Ref: Para. 24)

154 Possible assertions in charity financial statements relate to:

- Trustees exceptionally taking on paid senior management team roles.

- Services or goods being bought from a related party due to a lack of available suppliers in the general market.

- Loans and gifts either to or from trustees.

155 The auditor obtains comfort on assertions relating to exchange transactions by assessing the rigour of the process the charity has gone through prior to approving these transactions. Such a process may include the following:

- Comparison to market indices.

- Consideration of alternative sources of expertise (e.g., by obtaining alternative quotations).

- Paying due attention to the sections of the relevant Charities Acts which allow trustees to be paid for certain services.

In addition it is a feature of charities that they conduct non exchange transactions and transactions under market value. The auditor considers these for evidence of related party transactions, noting the specific disclosure requirements of the charity regulators.

156 The auditor also considers whether any circumstances relating to conflicts of interest or related party transactions require the auditor to report a matter of material significance to the charity regulator.[73]

Written representations
(Ref: Para. 26)

157 Because the charity financial reporting framework establishes related party requirements, the auditor obtains written representations from management and, where appropriate, those charged with governance, that they have:

- Disclosed to the auditor the identity of the charity's related parties and all the related party relationships and transactions of which they are aware; and

- Appropriately accounted for and disclosed such relationships and transactions in accordance with the requirements of the framework.

ISA (UK) 570: GOING CONCERN

ISA (UK) 570 (Revised June 2016) deals with the auditor's responsibilities in the audit of financial statements relating to going concern and the implications for the auditor's report.

Going concern basis of accounting (Ref: Para. 2)

158 Charity financial statements are usually prepared on a going concern basis of accounting, which assumes that the charity will continue its activities for the foreseeable future, unless the trustees either intend to liquidate or cease operating, or there is no realistic alternative but to liquidate or to cease activities.

---

[73] *See Section Reporting matters of material significance to charity regulators of this Practice Note.*

The Charities SORP reiterates the relevance of this concept in the preparation of **159** charity financial statements which are intended to show a "true and fair" view. Accounting standards require trustees, when preparing financial statements, to make an assessment of the charity's ability to continue as a going concern. Where material uncertainties related to events or conditions cast significant doubt on the charity's ability to continue as a going concern have been identified, FRS 102 and the Charities SORP require disclosure of those uncertainties in the financial statements.

The Charities SORP also requires that where there are no material uncertainties **160** about the charity's ability to continue as a going concern, the financial statements should state this.[74]

Trustees' responsibility for assessment of the charity's ability to continue as a going concern
(Ref: Para. 3–5)

It is essential that the trustees make their own assessment of the charity's ability to **161** continue as a going concern, as required by the Charities SORP,[75] to assure themselves of the validity of the going concern basis of accounting assumption when preparing the financial statements.[76]

Events or conditions that may cast significant doubt in the charity's ability to continue as a going concern (Ref: Para. 10–11)

The examples of indicators contained in the ISA (UK)[77] apply as much to charities **162** as to commercial entities and include pointers such as an excess of current liabilities over current assets. Charity specific indicators include:

- Inability to finance its operations from its own resources or unrestricted funds.

- Transfer to, or takeover by, another entity of the charity's activities.

- Deficits on unrestricted funds.

- Loss of clients (e.g., where a public authority ends a practice or contract to refer (and pay for) clients to the charity).

- Loss of operating licence (e.g., for a residential care home).

- Significant changes in strategy of major funders, and significant decline in donations by the public.

- Investigation by a charity regulator.

- Claw-back of grant received and gift-aid refunds.

- Reliance on major donors.

- Failure to meet reserves policy targets or carrying reserves insufficient for the current scale of activities (after having regard to any guidance on reserves issued by the respective charity regulator).

---

[74] *Paragraph 3.39 of the Charities SORP.*

[75] *Paragraph 3.14 of the Charities SORP.*

[76] *It may be useful for the auditor to ensure that the trustees are aware of any guidance issued by the charity regulators. For example, CCEW's Managing a charity's finances: planning, managing difficulties and insolvency (CC12).*

[77] *ISA (UK) 570 (Revised June 2016), paragraph A3.*

- Persistent failure to meet the requirement for public benefit, leading to withdrawal of funding or tax liabilities.

Where a charity fails to meet the public benefit requirement either in whole or in part, the auditor also considers the implications of actions taken, or likely to be taken, by the regulator, and assesses the implications on the auditor's opinion.

163   The auditor has no duty to assess whether the charity's activities are for the public benefit in order to establish that the charity is a going concern. However, persistent failure by a charity to meet its public benefit requirement may have an implication for the auditor's assessment of going concern.

Evaluating the trustees' assessment
(Ref: Para. 12)

164   The Charities SORP requires the trustees to take into account all available information about the future when making their assessment of the charity's ability to continue as a going concern.[78] When evaluating the trustees' assessment, the auditor inquires as to what information is available about the future to the trustees (e.g., serious incident reporting or response rates for mailings) and considers whether the trustees have appropriately considered such information in making their assessment.

165   In considering factors relating to a charity's status as a going concern, it is necessary to take account of the particular circumstances of that charity which may affect its ability to continue its activities. Charities vary considerably in how they are funded and therefore the auditor considers the availability of future funding and whether uncertainties over that funding exist and the liabilities and costs that the charity is required to meet. Diverse sources of income and a core of secure funding, avoiding overdependence on any one source, or holding significant reserves or endowments, may help reduce the risk of the charity not being a going concern. The charity's purpose may also require consideration: some charitable activities are focused on a specific purpose, and once this is achieved, the charity may cease to operate.

Income

166   Assessment of the going concern basis can be complicated by the uncertainty as to future income streams to which many charities are subject. In considering projections of income the auditor considers the income sources, their regularity and predictability and the degree of risk attaching to such sources.

167   Although the most significant factor ensuring the future viability of many charities is public goodwill, it is difficult, if not impossible, to value and cannot be included in the balance sheet, nor can the auditor rely solely on the existence of goodwill as evidence to support the going concern assumption.

168   Restrictions placed on the use of particular funds held by a charity may be relevant to the consideration of its going concern status. An understanding of unrestricted and restricted income, and capital or permanently endowed funds is relevant both in relation to the consideration of balance sheet funds held at the year end and to the impact that such restrictions may have on the understanding of future cash flows. Factors the auditor considers may include the:

---

[78] *Paragraph 3.14 of the Charities SORP.*

- Nature and impact of the restrictions placed on the use of any material restricted income funds.

- Liquidity of assets held within restricted income funds.

- Nature of the restrictions placed on expenditure of any endowed funds, the impact such restrictions have on the ability to fund planned activities, the nature of any restrictions to be placed on future appeals or other projected income.

- Operational ability to withdraw from projects or activities which have been subject to fund designations or restrictions.

The auditor requests the trustees to analyse the cash flow forecasts between restricted and unrestricted funds in order to demonstrate that the charity is not drawing down on restricted funds. **169**

Charities receiving grants of public funds (including lottery funds) are normally required to meet certain specified conditions. Expenditure outside grant conditions can lead to disallowance and repayment. Many charities rely on public authorities for grant support. Where the financial effect of withdrawal of funding would be fundamental to a particular charity, the auditor assesses whether compliance with grant conditions has been achieved or otherwise obtains evidence about steps taken by the trustees to ensure compliance. **170**

The timing of cash flows may also be relevant for certain categories of charities. Factors that can impact on a charity's cash flows include: **171**

- Reliance on annual votes of monies from governmental or central funding bodies, reliance on grant funding that reimburses expenditure only once incurred, or delays in the approval or payment of such funding.

- Grant funding provided for specific projects but not for central administrative costs, or funding of long-term projects based only on short-term commitments as to funding receivable.

- The cash flow impact of any constructive liabilities accrued in the balance sheet, or on conditions being met for any contingent grants disclosed within contingent liabilities.

- Constructive obligations, such as grants payable or other funding commitments that are recognised as liabilities but are payable over a number of years.

Reserves

By law, charities must spend the income they receive within a reasonable period of time on achieving their charitable purposes. However, this is balanced against the trustees' duties to manage the charity's resources responsibly, in a way that helps to mitigate financial risks the charity may be exposed to. **172**

As part of the auditor's going concern assessment, the auditor considers the charity's reserves policy. The Charities SORP sets out the disclosures that must be made in respect of the charity's reserves policy, including where the trustees have decided that holding reserves is unnecessary,[79] and associated good practice.[80] Guidance for trustees explains that charities should develop a policy on reserves **173**

---

[79] *Paragraph 1.22 of the Charities SORP.*
[80] *Paragraph 1.48 of the Charities SORP.*

which establishes a level of reserves that is right for the charity and clearly explains to its stakeholders why holding those reserves is necessary.[81]

Additional audit procedures when events or conditions are identified (Ref: Para. 16)

175   Where events or conditions have been identified that may cast significant doubt on the charity's ability to continue as a going concern, the auditor performs additional audit procedures to determine whether a material uncertainty exists related to those events or conditions. In addition to the audit procedures included in the ISA (UK),[82] the following procedures may be particularly relevant to the auditor of a charity:

- Analysing and discussing budgets, cash flow forecasts and business plans, based on past experience and the certainty of inflows and outflows.

- Analysing and discussing any shortfall of identifiable future income on forecast expenditure needing to be made up by voluntary donations of cash or other resources.

- Obtaining and reviewing lists of projects supported or awards made in the year and planned for the following year.

- Analysing and discussing the level of uncommitted reserves remaining available to the charity.

- Determining whether there is any reliance on support by the charity's bankers, major donors, or public authorities; concentration on the provision of services to a particular category of beneficiaries or objects for which future funding or demand may be limited.

176   When analysing and discussing budgets and cash flow forecasts, and business plans, the auditor considers these in the context of the auditor's understanding of the governance structure of the charity, particularly the knowledge and skills of the trustees.

177   Where the charity relies for a significant part of its funding on one or more major institutional donors or granting authorities such as local authorities, the auditor determines whether it would be practical to obtain confirmations[83] from such funders as to their future support for the charity. It is not unusual for granting authorities to be reluctant to confirm to a charity or its auditor that future funds will be made available, particularly where their own budgets have yet to be secured. The absence of confirmation does not, of itself, necessarily cast significant doubt upon the ability of the charity to continue as a going concern. The auditor seeks to differentiate between circumstances where the lack of a confirmation reflects the existence of a material uncertainty regarding going concern and caution on behalf of the funder that is not indicative of a material uncertainty.

178   However, if the auditor concludes that a charity's funders may be refusing to confirm funding for reasons that are specific to the charity, the auditor considers the significance of this and, where appropriate, discusses with the trustees whether there are alternative plans or sources of financing that would enable the going concern basis of accounting to continue to be adopted.

---

[81] *For example, see CCEW's* Charity reserves: building resilience (CC19)*.*

[82] *ISA (UK) 570 (Revised June 2016), paragraph A16.*

[83] *ISA (UK) 505* External Confirmations *deals with the auditor's use of external confirmation procedures to obtain audit evidence.*

The events or conditions described in paragraph 162 of this Practice Note may be **179** mitigated by the charity's ability to adopt alternative strategies that mitigate an uncertainty. For example, the effect of a charity being unable to confirm that a new grant will be received from a public authority may be counterbalanced by the trustees' plans to:

- Review the efficiency and effectiveness of operations and services.

- Seek additional sources of funding or launch an emergency appeal.

- Review or renegotiate commitments.

- Review existing borrowing or loan facilities or seek new facilities.

- Communicate with stakeholders or members who may be able to offer additional help.

- Cut or curtail planned expenditure to try and bring the level of expenditure below the expected income.

- Contract some of the charity's activities.

- Sell some of the charity's fixed assets or investments.

- Collaborate or merge with another charity or other entity.

Where the trustees assert that they have alternative strategies to overcome any **180** adverse factors the auditor assesses whether the outcome of these plans are likely to improve the situation and whether they are feasible in the circumstances.

Where the going concern basis within a charity group involves support between **181** entities, the auditor considers the extent to which such support is within the charitable objects and powers.

Auditor conclusions
(Ref: Para. 20)

Where events or conditions have been identified that may cast significant doubt on **182** the charity's ability to continue as a going concern, but, based on the evidence obtained the auditor concludes that no material uncertainty exists, the auditor evaluates whether, in view of the applicable financial reporting framework, the financial statements provide adequate disclosures about these events or conditions. The following disclosures, where made,[84] may be of particular relevance to the auditor:

- The explanation of the material uncertainties related to events or conditions that cast significant doubt on the charity's ability to continue as a going concern or a statement that there are no material uncertainties about the charity's ability to continue as a going concern.

- The judgments that the trustees have made in the process of applying the charity's accounting policies that have the most significant effect on the amounts recognised in the financial statements.

- The key assumptions concerning the future.

- The description of the principal risks and uncertainties facing the charity and a summary of the trustees' plans and strategies for managing those risks.

---

[84] *Paragraphs 3.38–3.40 of the Charities SORP set out the matters that must be included in the financial statements and good practice.*

183   Where the trustees do not include such disclosures in the financial statements, the auditor considers the implications for the auditor's report. The auditor also considers the auditor's duty to report it as a matter of material significance to the respective charity regulator or to exercise their right to report it as a relevant matter.

Duty to report going concern matters to charity regulators
(Ref: Para. A34)

184   The auditor also considers whether any of the circumstances relating to going concern require the auditor to report a matter of material significance to a UK charity regulator.[85] In particular, where the auditor either:

- Includes a separate section in the auditor's report entitled "Material Uncertainty Related to Going Concern"; or

- Expresses an adverse opinion where the use of the going concern basis of accounting is inappropriate in the circumstances; or

- Expresses a qualified or adverse opinion where adequate disclosure of the material uncertainty has not been made in the charity's financial statements; or

- In extremely rare circumstances, expresses a disclaimer of opinion in situations involving multiple material uncertainties that are significant to the charity's financial statements as a whole,

the auditor has a duty to report such matters to the appropriate charity regulator(s).

185   The auditor may also consider making a report to the charity regulator[86] before the auditor's report is issued where the auditor concludes that there is a significant risk of charity failure or a risk to charitable funds resulting from the consideration of going concern, and that swift intervention by a charity regulator may be necessary.

ISA (UK) 580: WRITTEN REPRESENTATIONS

ISA (UK) 580 deals with the auditor's responsibility to obtain written representations from management and, where appropriate, those charged with governance in an audit of financial statements.

Preparation of the financial statements
(Ref: Para. 10)

186   The trustees as a body are responsible for the contents and presentation of the financial statements. Consequently, discussion of the content of any written representation by the trustee body as a whole may be appropriate before it is signed on behalf of the trustees.

187   For charities where there are executive staff members, it is likely that in practice there are some representations that necessitate discussion with those persons. The auditor often finds it useful to attend the meeting at which trustees consider the financial statements and representation letter, to encourage discussion of significant items or matters, including unadjusted errors, arising in the course of the audit.

---

[85] *See Section Reporting matters of material significance to charity regulators of this Practice Note.*

[86] *See paragraph 266 of this Practice Note.*

Other written representations
(Ref: Para. 13)

In addition to representations required by ISAs (UK), the auditor of a charity also considers obtaining written representations that: **188**

● All income has been recorded.

● Restricted funds have been properly applied.

● Constructive obligations for grants have been recognised.

● All correspondence with regulators has been made available to the auditor including, in England and Wales, any serious incident reports.

● The trustees consider there to be appropriate controls in place to ensure overseas payments are applied for charitable purposes.

Timely communication by the auditor with the trustees on significant issues on which representations will be required is important in this sector, which relies primarily on voluntary trustees who are not involved in the day-to-day running of the affairs of the charity.   **189**

ISA (UK) 600: SPECIAL CONSIDERATIONS—AUDITS OF GROUP FINANCIAL STATEMENTS (INCLUDING THE WORK OF COMPONENT AUDITORS)

ISA (UK) 600 (Revised June 2016) deals with special considerations that apply to group audits, in particular those that involve component auditors.

Understanding the group, its component and their environment
(Ref: Para. 17–18)

Charities may operate through a variety of different structures, which are established either formally as branches or associates, or informally, for example, through an informal partnership arrangement. The requirements of this ISA (UK) apply equally to these informal structures as they do to more conventional group structures.   **190**

For example, ISA (UK) 600 applies in both the following circumstances: **191**

● A centrally administered organisation with branches in the UK and/or overseas where financial information prepared by each branch is aggregated into a single set of financial statements, but where statutory group financial statements are not required to be prepared.

● A parent charity with a group structure including subsidiaries, joint ventures and associates.

Branches

A charity may operate through branches to raise funds or carry out particular aspects of its charitable activities. The principles as to whether branches in the charity's wider structure are accounted for as part of the charity are set out in the Charities SORP and these apply whether operations are carried out in the UK or overseas. In England and Wales, separate charities may in certain circumstances account as one entity where a uniting direction has been issued by CCEW.[87]   **192**

---

[87] *These entities will normally be listed as subsidiary registrations by CCEW.*

193   Some charities will use the term "branches" outside of the Charities SORP meaning to describe a network of charities which are administratively autonomous and as such are separate accounting entities. The constitutional provisions in such cases may require careful consideration. Audits of such branches are regarded as separate engagements where a separate opinion is required.

194   The terms on which branches raise funds will also be relevant to determining the accounting policies of a charity. Local appeals may be for specific purposes, and where this is the case such funds will be restricted in the accounts of the main charity.

195   Irrespective of the accounting treatment of branches, the auditor's application of ISA (UK) 600 is driven by whether the branch prepares financial information that is included in the charity's financial statements.

Overseas operations

196   Where charitable groups have overseas components, the group engagement team considers whether the financial information of the components (whose statutory financial statements may not be prepared in accordance with the Charities SORP) are appropriately consolidated into the group financial statements (which are prepared in accordance with the Charities SORP).

197   The group engagement team considers whether the instructions issued by the charity to components adequately describe the applicable requirements of the Charities SORP to that component.

198   The group engagement team may also request the component auditor to perform specified audit procedures that respond to an identified risk of material misstatement (e.g., asking the component auditor to specifically consider if the component has received any restricted funds). Depending on the local financial reporting framework, this may require details of the accounting requirements under the Charities SORP to be explained to the component auditor.

Access to information (Ref: Para. 13)

199   Where the charity is a company, there is a statutory obligation on any subsidiary undertaking which is a company incorporated in Great Britain, and on its auditor, to give to the auditor of the parent company such information and explanations as it may reasonably require for the purposes of its duties.

200   The auditor in England and Wales acting under the 2011 Act (E&W) has, under Section 154(1)(d) of the Act, a right of access to books, documents and records which relate to the charity. This access right extends beyond those records which are in the ownership of the charity and, under the Charities (Accounts and Reports) Regulations 2008 (as amended), includes the records of any UK subsidiaries of the charity. However, this right does not extend to overseas entities with a separate legal constitution. In Northern Ireland, the auditor will have the same right of access under Section 66(1)(d) of the 2008 Act (NI), when commenced. In Scotland, this right applies to all legal forms of charity registered in Scotland and is given under Regulation 13 of the Charities Accounts (Scotland) Regulations 2006 (as amended).

ISA (UK) 700: FORMING AN OPINION AND REPORTING ON FINANCIAL STATEMENTS

ISA (UK) 700 (Revised June 2016) deals with the auditor's responsibility to form an opinion on the financial statements, and the form and content of the auditor's report issued as a result of an audit of financial statements.

Forming an opinion on the financial statements
(Ref: Para. 10–15)

The auditor's opinion on a charity's financial statements is expressed in the context of the particular legislation and accounting requirements applicable to the charity concerned.   **201**

The auditor is also aware that the governing documents and trust deed establishing a charity may establish additional requirements concerning the contents of its financial statements (but cannot derogate from the statutory requirements). The auditor therefore assesses whether any such requirements are met. Where the auditor becomes aware of information which indicates that a transaction or transactions undertaken by the charity may have breached any terms of its trust deed, the auditor considers the implications for the auditor's reporting responsibilities following the requirements of ISA (UK) 250 Section A[88] and the guidance in Section *ISA (UK) 250* of this Practice Note.   **202**

As far as charitable companies[89] in England and Wales, Scotland and Northern Ireland[90] are concerned, care needs to be taken to understand the interaction between the Companies Act 2006 and the relevant Charities Acts. For charitable companies claiming audit exemption under the Companies Act 2006, the legal requirements for audit are provided in the relevant Charities Acts. A small charitable company that is eligible for audit exemption under Companies Act 2006 but does not claim this exemption continues to be audited under Companies Act 2006 and in England and Wales no additional audit requirement arises under the 2011 Act (E&W).   **203**

For charitable companies that do claim audit exemption and comply with Section 475(2) to (4) of the Companies Act 2006, which requires a statement on the face of the balance sheet confirming that the company is entitled to audit exemption, the audit arrangements referred to in the auditor's reports are the 2011 Act (E&W), the 2005 Act (Scotland) and the 2008 Act (NI).   **204**

For charitable companies below the Companies Act 2006 audit threshold and claiming exemption but above the thresholds of the relevant Charities Acts this could be achieved by a statement such as: **205**

---

[88] *ISA (UK) 250 (Revised July 2017) Section A – Consideration of Laws and Regulations in an audit of Financial Statements.*

[89] *This guidance does not apply to groups.*

[90] *In Northern Ireland, the special rules for the audit of small charitable companies provided by the Companies Act 2006 is currently retained.*

For the year ended [date] the company was entitled to exemption from audit under Section 477 of the Companies Act 2006 relating to small companies but as this company is a charity, it is subject to audit under the [Charities Act 2011 / Charities and Trustee Investment (Scotland) Act 2005 / Charities Act (Northern Ireland) 2008].

(a)   The members have not required the company to obtain an audit of its accounts for the year in question in accordance with Section 476 of the Companies Act 2006.

(b)   The directors acknowledge their responsibilities for complying with the requirements of the Companies Act 2006 with respect to accounting records and the preparation of accounts.

These accounts have been prepared in accordance with the provisions applicable to companies subject to the small companies' regime.

206   The form and content of auditor's reports on the financial statements of charities follow the requirements established by ISA (UK) 700. However, because of the complexity of the legal framework, the auditor needs to ensure descriptions of the legislative basis and responsibilities of the auditor and trustees are specific to the circumstances of the charity audited.

Auditor's report

Addressee
(Ref: Para. 22)

207   Audit reports made under company legislation are addressed to members (in Scotland – members and trustees) whilst reports made under charity law are made to the trustees.

Key audit matters
(Ref: Para. 31)

208   The auditor of a charity is not required by this ISA (UK), or otherwise by laws or regulation,[91] to communicate key audit matters in the auditor's report in accordance with ISA (UK) 701.[92] However, the trustees may be keen to demonstrate their commitment to transparent reporting and therefore may request the auditor to communicate key audit matters in the auditor's report, in which case this is done in accordance with ISA (UK) 700.[93]

Responsibilities for the financial statements
(Ref: Para. 33–36)

209   ISA (UK) 700[94] requires the auditor to include a section describing the trustees' responsibility for:

---

[91] *Unless the charity is also a listed entity, a public interest entity, or an other entity that is required, or chooses voluntarily, to report on how they have applied the UK Corporate Governance Code; in which case, paragraphs 30–30-1 of ISA (UK) 700 (Revised June 2016) apply.*

[92] *ISA (UK) 701 Communicating Key Audit Matters in the Independent Auditor's Report.*

[93] *ISA (UK) 700 (Revised June 2016), paragraph 31.*

[94] *ISA (UK) 700 (Revised June 2016), paragraph 34.*

- The preparation of the financial statements in accordance with the applicable financial reporting framework, and for such internal control as the trustees determine is necessary to enable the preparation of financial statements that are free from material misstatement, whether due to fraud or error; and

- Assessing the charity's ability to continue as a going concern and whether the use of the going concern basis of accounting is appropriate, and, where applicable, disclosing matters relating to going concern.

The responsibilities of the trustees will also vary according to the constitution of **210** the particular charity, for example, the duties of trustees of charitable companies derive from both company and charity law.

The auditor needs to be aware that where charities are required to prepare financial **211** statements under more than one UK jurisdiction, both sets of legal requirements must be adhered to.

Other reporting responsibilities
(Ref: Para. 43–45)

The auditor of a charity may have other reporting responsibilities under legislation **212** or regulation, depending on whether the charity is a company or not. A summary of these responsibilities is set out in Appendix 2 of this Practice Note.

Signature of the auditor
(Ref: Para. 47)

For charitable companies who are required, or opt, to be audited under the **213** Companies Act 2006, the auditor's report is signed by the Senior Statutory Auditor in his or her own name for and on behalf of the firm.

For charitable companies audited under the relevant Charities Acts, or for non- **214** corporate charities, the auditor's report is signed in the name of the firm only.

The relevant Charities Acts require that the auditor state in the auditor's report that **215** the firm is eligible to act as an auditor in terms of Section 1212 of the Companies Act 2006, even where the charity is not audited under the Companies Act 2006. This statement is not required where a charitable company is audited solely in accordance with the Companies Act 2006.

ISA (UK) 720: THE AUDITOR'S RESPONSIBILITIES RELATING TO OTHER INFORMATION

ISA (UK) 720 (Revised June 2016) sets out the auditor's responsibilities relating to other information included in the annual report.

Other information
(Ref: Para. 12(c))

A charity's annual report may include the following other information, alongside **216** the financial statements and auditor's report:

- A trustees' annual report (including, for charitable companies, the directors' report and strategic report as required).

- Statements by the patron, president, chair of the trustees and/or chief executive officer of the charity.

- A financial review.

- An investment policy and performance report.
- A statement of grant making policies.
- A statement of reserves policy.
- A statement of achievements against objectives.
- An impact assessment.
- A risk management statement by trustees (based on the Charities SORP or expanded and based on the UK Corporate Governance Code for listed companies).
- A treasurer's report.
- Financial summaries.
- Projections of future expenditure based on planned activity.

217   Charity trustees may request the auditor specifically to review and report on a corporate governance or risk management statement made by them in their annual report or contained in other information presented with the financial statements. Providing guidance on a review of this nature is beyond the scope of this Practice Note.

Statutory other information
(Ref: Para. 12(d))

218   The trustees' annual report meets the definition of statutory other information as the auditor is required to report publicly on these reports in the auditor's report in accordance with law or regulation. For all charities, the auditor is required to report[95] on whether the information given in the trustees' annual report is inconsistent with the financial statements.

Obtaining an understanding of the charity and its environment relating to statutory other information
(Ref: Para. 12-1)

219   The auditor obtains an understanding of the requirements of the applicable legal and regulatory requirements for the trustees' annual report and how the charity is complying with those requirements.

220   Legal and regulatory requirements applicable to the trustees' annual report include:

- Applicable legislative requirements.[96]
- Those requirements of Module 1 *Trustees' annual report* of the Charities SORP that must be followed.[97]

Reading and considering the other information
(Ref: Para. 14-15)

221   The auditor reads all of the other information included in the charity's annual report and considers whether there is a material inconsistency between the other

---

[95] *For charitable companies, the auditor is required to give an opinion on such matters; whereas for non-company charities, the auditor reports by exception.*

[96] *See Appendix 2 of this Practice Note.*

[97] *The terms "must", "should" and "may" are explained in paragraphs 32–35 of the Charities SORP.*

information and both the financial statements or the auditor's knowledge obtained in the audit.

The ISA (UK) does not require the auditor to perform additional procedures to **222** verify other information that either does not relate to amounts or other items in the financial statements or about which the auditor has no knowledge. For example, the trustees may include in the other information:

- A case study illustrating the difference the charity makes.

- A statement that there has been an increase in visitors to a charity's website during the year.

- An impact assessment on either individual or societal beneficiaries.

For such statements included in the other information, if the financial statements contained no similar disclosures and if the auditor, as part of the audit, had not obtained knowledge in respect of such matters, the auditor would not be required to undertake further procedures to determine whether this information was materially misstated. However, if the auditor, as part of the auditor's work on the financial statements, reads information, for example, in the minutes of trustees' meetings that contradicts a statement, then the auditor needs to undertake further procedures to determine whether that statement is materially misstated.

Similarly, whilst the auditor is not expected to verify any risk management **223** statement made by trustees, the auditor is likely to become aware of the steps taken by the trustees to identify and manage identified financial risks through performing risk assessment procedures in accordance with the requirements of ISA (UK) 315.[98] The auditor may also become aware of non-financial risks during the course of the audit.

Where charities report on matters relating to previous years, such as the results of **224** long term research or other interventions, the auditor is not required to perform additional procedures in relation to those years, unless the auditor becomes aware of a material misstatement between that information and the financial statements or the auditor's knowledge of the charity obtained in the audit.

In addition, because the trustees' annual report is statutory other information, the **225** auditor also considers whether the trustees' annual report appears to be materially misstated in the context of the auditor's understanding of the legal and regulatory requirements.[99]

ISA (UK) 720[100] explains that a misstatement of the other information exists when **226** the other information is incorrectly stated, otherwise misleading or omitted, or not prepared in accordance with applicable law and Charities SORP requirements. For example, where the trustees' annual report does not include commentary on the significant events that have affected the financial performance and financial position of the charity during the year, or, in the auditor's professional judgment, the commentary omits a significant event, a misstatement of the other information arises. Similarly, when reporting on performance charities sometimes refer to activities undertaken by third party grant recipients or umbrella groups. Where a claim suggests such achievements are the direct result of the reporting entity's activities, this too, would constitute a misstatement.

---

[98] *ISA (UK) 315 (Revised June 2016) Identifying and Assessing the Risks of Material Misstatement through Understanding the Entity and its Environment.*

[99] *See paragraphs 219–220 of this Practice Note.*

[100] *ISA (UK) 720 (Revised June 2016), paragraph 12(b).*

227   Where the auditor has identified an apparent misstatement of the other information, the auditor discusses the matter with the trustees. The ISA (UK) acknowledges that it may be more difficult for the auditor to challenge the trustees on matters of judgment than on those of a more factual nature;[101] however, the auditor has a unique insight into the charity and there may be circumstances where the auditor concludes that the trustees' annual report contains information that is not consistent with financial statements or the auditor's knowledge obtained in the audit.

228   In concluding on whether there is a material misstatement of the other information, the auditor applies professional judgment, taking into account such matters, where relevant, as:

- Whether the misstatement of the other information is material by size or by nature.[102]

- The information needs of the primary users of the annual report.

- Whether the element in the Charities SORP is a mandatory requirement (a "must") or indicative of best practice ("should").[103]

- Any views expressed by the charity regulators (or other appropriate authority outside the charity).

Reporting
(Ref: Para. 21–23)

229   The auditor of a charity reports in the auditor's report as follows:

- On the trustees' annual report (and any other statutory other information):

  - For charitable companies, in accordance with paragraph 22D-1 of ISA (UK) 720; and

  - For all other charities, in accordance with the relevant law or regulation.

- On all other information, in accordance with paragraph 22 of ISA (UK) 720.

Reporting matters of material significance to charity regulators

Reporting to charity regulators

230   In addition to the primary objective of reporting on financial statements, the auditor of a charity may:

- have an additional statutory duty to report in certain circumstances; or

- exercise the auditor's statutory right to report

to the relevant charity regulator.

231   The statutory duty to report is wider than the requirement in ISA (UK) 250 Section A to report identified or suspected non-compliance with laws and regulations to an

---

[101] *ISA (UK) 720 (Revised June 2016), paragraph A41.*

[102] *ISA (UK) 720 (Revised June 2016), paragraph A7 discusses the concept of materiality as it applies to the other information.*

[103] *See footnote 97 of this Practice Note.*

appropriate authority outside the charity.[104] In the case of registered charities this duty will be to the charity regulators (CCEW, OSCR or CCNI as appropriate), while for exempt charities this will be their principal regulator (e.g., the Higher Education Funding Council for England in the case of English universities).

In order to assist the auditor to comply with the auditor's statutory duty to report such matters, the charity regulators have jointly issued guidance for auditors ("Matters of Material Significance Guidance").[105] The auditor of a charity is expected to have an understanding of this guidance in order to ensure that the auditor complies with the auditor's additional responsibilities arising from legislation.   **232**

ISA (UK) 250 Section B does not apply generally to charities, unless the charity also meets the definition of "regulated entity" included in that ISA (UK).[106]   **233**

The legislative basis for the charity auditor's statutory duty to report is: **234**

- England and Wales: Sections 156 to 159 of the 2011 Act (E&W) require the auditor to communicate to CCEW certain matters of which the auditor becomes aware in their capacity as the auditor of a charity. The statutory duty to report to CCEW extends to charities excepted from registration but does not extend to exempt charities.[107]

- Scotland: Section 46 of the Charities and Trustee Investment (Scotland) Act 2005, which sets out the duty of the auditor of all forms of charity registered in Scotland to report to OSCR. OSCR has similar investigative powers to those of CCEW.

- Northern Ireland: Section 67 of the 2008 Act (NI) requires the auditor to communicate to CCNI certain matters of which the auditor becomes aware in its capacity as the auditor of a charity or a charitable company.

These provisions also establish the right to report a matter to the charity regulator which does not appear to fall within the scope of the duty to report but which the auditor has reasonable cause to believe is likely to be relevant to the charity regulator for the purposes of the exercise of any of its functions. The right to report, like the duty to report, applies to charitable companies and to non-company charities.

The 2011 Act (E&W), the 2005 Act (Scotland) and the 2008 Act (NI) specify the matters which give rise to a duty to make an immediate report to the relevant regulator as those which: **235**

---

[104] *ISA (UK) 250 (Revised July 2017) Section A – Consideration of Laws and Regulations in an Audit of Financial Statements, paragraph 29.*

[105] *See Matters of Material Significance reportable to UK charity regulators: A guide for auditors and independent examiners.*

[106] *ISA (UK) 250 (Revised June 2016) Section B – The Auditor's Statutory Right and Duty to Report to Regulators of Public Interest Entities and Regulators of Other Entities in the Financial Sector, paragraph 9(e).*

[107] *"Exempt" charities are excluded from CCEW's supervision and monitoring, and consequently its auditors are not required to report matters of material significance to CCEW. Instead, the auditor of an exempt charity reports such matters to the charity's principal regulator. There is, however, no disapplication of the reporting duty for exempt company charities.*

(a)   Relate to the activities or affairs of the charity or of any connected institution or body, and

(b)   The auditor has reasonable cause to believe is, or is likely to be, of material significance for the exercise, in relation to the charity, of the relevant regulator's functions.[108]

236   Where a charity is registered in multiple jurisdictions, if there is any doubt as to which regulator the auditor should make a report to, the auditor makes a report to all relevant regulators.

237   The Charities Acts do not require the auditor to perform any additional audit work as a result of the statutory duty, nor is the auditor required specifically to seek out breaches of the requirements applicable to a particular charity. However, in circumstances where the auditor identifies that a reportable matter may exist, the auditor carries out such extra work, as considered necessary, to determine whether the facts and circumstances give it "reasonable cause to believe" that the matter does in fact exist. The auditor's work does not need to prove that the reportable matter exists.

238   Where possible, it is the charity regulators' practice to seek to resolve issues collaboratively with a charity. However, if the charity declines to co-operate or assist, the charity regulator has the power to institute inquiries with regard to charities or a particular charity or class of charities, either generally or for particular purposes. The charity regulator also has powers to obtain information, including the power to call for documents and require persons to give evidence. The charity's auditor may also be required to provide information.[109]

Criteria for determining the existence of a duty to report to the charity regulators

239   Determining whether a matter is reportable to a charity regulator involves consideration both of whether the auditor has a "reasonable cause to believe" and that the matter in question "is, or is likely to be of material significance" to the charity regulators.

240   "Material significance" is not defined in legislation; however, the Matters of Material Significance Guidance explains that it relates to matters which are of material significance to a regulator in carrying out their functions.

241   Matters which the charity regulators have jointly agreed are of material significance are set out in the Matters of Material Significance Guidance.[110] Other sources of useful information relevant to the particular jurisdiction are also available from the charity regulators' individual websites.

242   "Material significance" does not have the same meaning as materiality in the context of the audit of financial statements. Whilst a particular event may be trivial in terms of its possible effect on the financial statements of a charity, it may be of a

---

[108] *For CCEW, this is Sections 46, 47 and 50 (inquiries) and 76 and 79 to 82 (power to act for protection of charities) of the 2011 Act (E&W); for OSCR, this is Sections 28 (inquiries about charities), 30 (removal from the Register of a charity which no longer meets the test) and 31 (powers of OSCR following enquiries) of the 2005 Act (Scotland); for CCNI, it will be Section 22 (general power to institute inquiries) or 33 (power to act for the protection of charities) of the 2008 Act (NI) once commenced.*

[109] *For CCEW, this is Section 46 of the 2011 Act (E&W); for OSCR, this is Sections 28 and 29 of the 2005 Act (Scotland); for CCNI, this is Section 22 of the 2008 Act (NI).*

[110] *See Sections 2 and 3 of the Matters of Material Significance Guidance for a list of the reportable matters of material significance.*

nature or type that is likely to change the perception of the charity regulator. For example, dishonesty by a trustee may not be significant in financial terms in comparison with the income of the charity but would have a significant effect on the relevant charity regulator's consideration of whether the person concerned should be allowed to continue to act as a charity trustee.

The determination of whether a matter is, or is likely to be, of material significance   **243**
to the charity regulators inevitably requires the auditor to exercise professional judgment. In forming such judgments, the auditor needs to consider not simply the facts of the matter but also their implications. In addition, it is possible that a matter, which is not materially significant in isolation, may become so when other possible breaches are considered, together with other reported and unreported breaches of which the auditor is aware.

The auditor of a charity bases a judgment of "material significance" to the charity   **244**
regulator solely on the auditor's understanding of the facts of which it is aware without making any assumptions about the information available to the charity regulator in connection with any particular charity.

Minor breaches of trustees' obligations, or isolated administrative errors that are   **245**
unlikely to jeopardise the charity's assets or amount to misconduct or mismanagement would not normally be of "material significance". However, based on the auditor's knowledge obtained in the audit, the auditor assesses whether the cumulative effect is of "material significance" such as to give rise to a duty to report to the charity regulator.

Where a situation is identified and the auditor, having considered the Matters of   **246**
Material Significance Guidance and the guidance provided in this Section of the Practice Note, remains uncertain as to whether the matter is likely to be of "material significance" the auditor may wish to discuss the circumstances giving rise to their concern with the charity regulators.[111] Whilst such discussions may help inform the auditor in reaching a conclusion as to whether a particular matter is likely to fall within the charity regulator's regulatory function, it is not used as a substitute for the auditor's own professional judgment. Such discussions do not remove the duty to report where the matter is considered to be reportable.

On completion of any investigations, the auditor ensures that the facts and   **247**
circumstances, and the basis for the conclusion that these are, or are likely to be either of "material significance" to or relevant to the work of the charity regulator, are adequately documented such that the reasons for the auditor's decision to report may be clearly demonstrated if the need to do so arises in future.

Whilst confidentiality is an implied term of the auditor's contract with a charity, in   **248**
the circumstances described in the relevant Charities Acts,[112] it does not prevail. Subject to compliance with legislation regarding "tipping off", in the circumstances leading to a right or duty to report the auditor is required to communicate information or opinions on a matter relating to the affairs of the charity or any connected institution or body. The defence afforded to the auditor from any potential breach of duty is given in respect of information obtained in the capacity as auditor.

---

[111] *The Matters of Material Significance Guidance states: The charity regulators' default preferences for auditors is "When in doubt, report it".*

[112] *Sections 156 to 159 of the 2011 Act (E&W); Section 46 of the 2005 Act (Scotland); and Section 67 of the 2008 Act (NI).*

249   In addition, an auditor who ceases to hold office, for any reason, is required by the relevant Charities Acts or Regulations[113] to make a statement as to whether there are any circumstances connected with the auditor ceasing to hold office which should be brought to the attention of the trustees and to send a copy of the auditor's statement, where there are such circumstances, to the charity regulator.

Conduct of the audit

250   The legislation setting out the statutory duty to report does not require the auditor to perform any additional audit work as a result of this duty, nor is the auditor specifically required to seek out reportable matters. However, the auditor includes procedures within the planning process to ensure that members of the engagement team have sufficient understanding (in the context of the individual's role) to enable them to identify situations which may give reasonable cause to believe that a matter should be reported to the regulator. Any situations identified by the engagement team which may give rise to a duty to report are brought to the attention of the engagement partner without delay in order to determine whether a report to the regulator is required.

251   Where a matter comes to light relating to a previous financial year which would give rise to a duty to report, then the auditor still makes a report, unless the auditor is certain that the matter has already been reported by the auditor or the charity's previous auditor.

Connected entities

252   The auditor needs to be aware that the duty to report extends to any institution or body corporate connected with the charity.[114] The auditor decides whether there are any matters to be reported to the charity regulators relating to the affairs of the charity in the light of the information that the auditor receives about a connected entity for the purpose of auditing the financial statements of the charity. If the auditor is aware of possible circumstances that may fall due to be reported, the auditor has a right and duty to do this under the relevant Charities Acts.[115] At the planning stage of the audit, the auditor of the charity considers whether arrangements need to be put in place to allow the auditor to communicate with the management to obtain further information direct from the management or auditor of the connected entity and to enable the auditor to determine whether the matter should be reported. An inability to communicate with the connected entity or its auditor does not preclude the duty to report. In such circumstances the auditor reports the circumstances and the fact that the auditor has been unable to obtain further information, direct to the charity regulator.

Discussing matters of material significance with trustees

253   The trustees are the persons principally responsible for the governance of the charity. In forming a conclusion, provided it would not give rise to any undue delay in reporting the matter or where it is necessary to properly establish the

---

[113] *Paragraph 35 of the Charities (Accounts and Reports) Regulations 2008 (as amended); Regulation 10(6) of the Charities Accounts (Scotland) Regulations 2006 (as amended); and similar powers are included in the 2008 Act (NI).*

[114] *"Connected" includes any institution controlled by the charity or a body corporate in which the charity has a substantial interest (20% or more of the share capital or voting rights) (Sections 157, 351 and 352 of the 2011 Act (E&W) and Section 46(5) of the 2005 Act (Scotland)).*

[115] *Section 156(2) and 156(4) of the 2011 Act (E&W); Section 46 of the 2005 Act (Scotland); and Section 67(3) of the 2008 Act (NI).*

matter, the auditor may seek to reach agreement with the trustees on the circumstances giving rise to a report and to understand whether the trustees intend to make a report.

The trustees should consider reporting the matters identified to the charity **254** regulator themselves and detail the actions taken or to be taken. Whilst such a report from the trustees may provide valuable information, it does not relieve the auditor of the statutory duty to report directly to the charity regulator.

If the auditor suspects that the trustees are involved in non-compliance, or when **255** the matter giving rise to a statutory duty to make a report direct to a regulator casts doubt on the trustees' integrity or their competence to conduct the charity, the auditor makes the report to the charity regulator without informing the trustees. Additionally, in the case of money laundering suspicions, to ensure that "tipping off" does not occur the auditor cannot undertake to inform trustees in advance of every matter which it brings to the regulator's attention.[116]

Contents of a report to the charity regulators

The reporting of a matter of material significance is a separate report from the **256** auditor's report on the financial statements.

The Matters of Material Significance Guidance sets out the required information. **257**

- In England and Wales and Northern Ireland, the report to CCEW or CCNI is required to be in writing. This can include making a report by email. The auditor is not relieved of the duty to make a written report where an oral report has been previously made to a charity regulator or by any informal discussions of the issue with a charity regulator's staff.

- In Scotland, there is no legislative requirement to make the report in writing but OCSR recommends that a written report or record of any verbal report is forwarded to OSCR.

The auditor is not relieved of the duty to report on the basis that the charity itself, **258** or any other party, has provided relevant information (including the trustees reporting a serious incident to CCEW or CCNI or a non-statutory notifiable event to OSCR), whether written or oral, to a charity regulator.

Where trustees wish to make a submission to the charity regulator as to the **259** circumstances and steps being taken to address a reportable matter, the auditor may attach such a memorandum or report prepared by the trustees to the auditor's report to the charity regulator.

Where such additional information is provided the auditor refers to the additional **260** information in the report, and indicates whether or not the auditor has undertaken additional procedures to determine whether any remedial actions described have been taken.

Timing of a report

The relevant Charities Acts require the report to be made immediately the matter **261** comes to the auditor's attention.

The duty to report arises once the auditor has concluded that there is reasonable **262** cause to believe that the matter is or is likely to be of material significance to the relevant charity regulator's regulatory function. In reaching a conclusion the

---

[116] *See also paragraphs 56–58 of this Practice Note.*

auditor may wish to consult with others within the firm, a network firm, a professional body, or with the auditor's legal counsel.

263   The report is made immediately once a conclusion has been reached. Unless the matter casts doubt on the integrity of the trustees, this will not preclude discussion of the matter with trustees and seeking such further advice as is necessary, so that a decision can be made on whether or not a duty to report exists. However, such consultations and discussions are undertaken on a timely basis to enable the auditor to conclude on the matter without undue delay.

Information received in a capacity other than as auditor

264   There may be circumstances where it is not clear whether information about a charity coming to the attention of the auditor is received in the capacity of auditor[117] or in some other capacity, for example, as general adviser to the charity. Appendix 2 to ISA (UK) 250 Section B[118] provides guidance as to how information obtained may be relevant to the auditor in the planning and conduct of the audit and the steps that need to be taken to ensure the communication of information that is relevant to the audit. The auditor considers matters that are potentially of material significance to the charity regulator, and which arise in this context and, if appropriate, reports these.

Failure to fulfil the statutory duty to report

265   Failure to comply with the relevant Charities Acts[119] is regarded as a matter for the professional bodies to deal with pursuant to their own disciplinary procedures. For cases where the charity regulators have decided to make a complaint they have indicated that, within any legal restrictions that may apply, they will make available to those professional bodies any relevant information in their possession.

Auditor's right to report to a charity regulator

266   The auditor also has a separate right to report where there is no statutory duty.[120] The auditor may determine that other matters that are not specified as reportable in the Matters of Material Significance Guidance[121] are, in the auditor's professional judgment, of such a nature that the auditor considers them reportable as a matter of material significance.[122] The auditor may find it helpful to refer to the guidance issued by the charity regulators on the auditor's right to report relevant matters.[123]

---

[117] *In this context, "auditor" refers to the statutory appointment as auditor for the audit of the annual financial statements under the relevant Legislation or Regulations. It does not relate to engagements where an auditor is also engaged to audit other financial information, such as grant claims.*

[118] *Whilst ISA (UK) 250 (Revised June 2016) Section B does not apply to the audits of charities, the procedures and guidance in that ISA (UK) can be adapted to similar circumstances for the auditor of a charity.*

[119] *Sections 156 to 159 of the 2011 Act (E&W); Section 46 of the 2005 Act (Scotland); or Sections 67 and 103 of the 2008 Act (NI).*

[120] *Section 156(4) for non-company charities and Section 159(1) for charitable companies of the 2011 Act (E&W); Section 46 of the 2005 Act (Scotland); and Section 67 of the 2008 Act (NI).*

[121] *See footnote 110 of this Practice Note.*

[122] *For examples of such matters, see paragraphs 67, 174 and 185 of this Practice Note.*

[123] *See Reporting of relevant matters of interest to UK charity regulators: A guide for auditors and independent examiners.*

Appendix 1

Conditions and events that may indicate risks of material misstatement

The following are examples of conditions and events that may indicate the existence of risks of material misstatement in the financial statements. The examples provided may be of particular relevance to charities and are in addition to the broad range of conditions and events included in the ISAs (UK);[124] however, not all conditions and events are relevant to every audit engagement and the list of examples is not necessarily complete.

General

- Evidence of failure to act in accordance with those objects and powers in the charity's governing documents.

- Extent and nature of non-primary purpose trading activities.

- Difficulties of the charity in establishing ownership and timing of voluntary income where funds are raised by non-controlled bodies.

- Overseas operations. In particular:

  - Significant aspects of a charity's business may be conducted in conditions or locations which impede access to the accounting records.

  - Transactions may be in a number of different and volatile currencies.

  - Due to the location of the activities management may have reduced oversight and limited ability to monitor activities and transactions.

  - Governance, responsibility and accountability may be unclear regarding branches, joint ventures and the use of partners in overseas locations.

  - Non-compliance with local laws and regulation.

  - Conduit funding,[125] or informal banking arrangements.

  - The risk of a tax liability arising if HMRC consider that reasonable steps have not been taken to ensure overseas payments are being allocated to charitable purposes only.

Classes of transactions, account balances and disclosures

- Allocation of costs between different expenditure categories in the Statement of Financial Activities (SoFA).

- Restricted funds which require special considerations as to use and accounting, including clawback of restricted grants or contracts.

- Grants payable or receivable.

---

[124] *See ISA (UK) 315 (Revised June 2016), Appendix 2; ISA (UK) 570 (Revised June 2016), paragraph A3; and ISA (UK) 600 (Revised June 2016), Appendix 3.*

[125] *Resources received and distributed by a charity as agent for another entity, usually another charity. The principal in the arrangement is the charity providing the resources who retains the legal responsibility for the charitable application of the funds.*

- Contracts with performance related conditions.
- Donations in kind (i.e., donated goods, facilities and services including goods for resale, use by the charity or distribution to a third party).
- Legacies.
- Heritage assets.
- Events or transactions that involve significant measurement and recognition uncertainty, including accounting estimates, and related disclosures. In particular:
    - Defined benefit pension schemes, including the complexity of allocating pension deficits/assets between funds and the effect of these deficits/assets on their free reserves.
    - Multi-employer defined benefit pension scheme liabilities, including the recognition of an agreed deficit recovery plan.
    - Investments (including social investments) whether financial or programme-related investments.
    - Properties which are partly used for the charity's operations and partly for investment purposes.
    - Loans where there is a material arrangement calculated using the "effective interest method" (i.e., by applying a constant "interest" rate to the outstanding amount).
    - Fair value of assets and liabilities acquired where acquisition accounting is applied (in this situation, the due diligence process may only provide limited information on the fair value of some assets such as land and buildings and heritage assets).
    - Recognition of second hand goods received for resale or goods for distribution and stock (if applicable).
    - Recognition of other donations in kind at a reasonable estimate of their gross value to the charity and donated services and facilities at a reasonable estimate of the value to the charity of the service or facility received.
    - Other arrangements which are offered or received on extended terms of more than twelve months discounted to their present value (using the market interest rate for an equivalent debt instrument, usually investment return to the charity). This can include:
        - Donations and grants.
        - Long term grant commitments.
        - Accrual for legacies receivable.
    at their present value in the balance sheet.
    - Taxation matters including income from gift aid and the gift aid small donations scheme, the identification of tainted donations and the recognition of irrecoverable VAT.
    - Commitments and liabilities, including constructive obligations.
    - Restricted and unrestricted reserves.
    - Departures from the Charities SORP.

Appendix 2

Charity accounting and audit requirements in the United Kingdom

The information in this Appendix gives an overview of the regulatory framework for charities and the legal framework for charity accounts and audit. Requirements change over time and reference should be made to information on the websites of the charity regulators and directly to the relevant legislation and regulations as considered necessary.

Overview

There are three charity law jurisdictions in the UK and three charity regulators: **1**

- In England and Wales, the Charities Act 2011 ("2011 Act (E&W)") provides the primary legislative framework for charity regulation by the Charity Commission for England and Wales (CCEW) supplemented by some provisions of the Charities (Protection and Social Investment) Act 2016.

- In Scotland, the Charities and Trustee Investment (Scotland) Act 2005 ("2005 Act (Scotland)") provides the primary legislative framework for charity regulation by the Office of the Scottish Charity Regulator (OSCR).

- In Northern Ireland, the Charities (Northern Ireland) Act 2008 ("2008 Act (NI)") provides the primary legislative framework for charity regulation by the Charity Commission for Northern Ireland (CCNI).

Charitable status is available to organisations with different legal forms which   **2** means that they may fall within the scope of regulatory regimes governed by other legislation. It is common for charities to also be companies limited by guarantee and all charitable companies must comply with the Companies Act 2006 including the accounting and auditing requirements therein. Within England and Wales those charities that are classified as exempt may fall to be regulated by an alternative principal regulator and are not regulated by CCEW.

Charities may be required to comply with aspects of charity law in more than one   **3** UK charity law jurisdiction. Such charities are known as "cross border" charities:

- A charity which is established in England and Wales or in Northern Ireland with activities in Scotland may need to register with OSCR. Where the extent of the charity's activities requires registration, the charity must comply with the 2005 Act (Scotland) including the related accounting and external scrutiny requirements. Compliance with the 2005 Act (Scotland) is in addition to any requirements placed on the charity by the charity law of its home jurisdiction, including the accounting and external scrutiny requirements, and any other legislation which applies to its legal form, for example, company law.

- A charity which is established in England and Wales or in Scotland with activities in Northern Ireland may in future be required to register with CCNI if it is not a charity under the law of Northern Ireland but operates for charitable purposes in or from Northern Ireland. Such a charity is known as "a Section 167 charity". Also, in future, a Section 167 charity will be required to file with CCNI a financial statement and a statement of activities relating to its operations in or from Northern Ireland. At the date of publication of this Practice Note, the provisions of Section 167 of the 2008 Act (NI) have not been implemented.

The regulatory framework

England and Wales

4   CCEW is responsible for the registration, supervision and regulation of charities that are not exempt. A public register of charities is maintained. All charities must register with CCEW unless:

- The charity's gross income in the financial year is £5,000 or less;[126] or
- The charity is excepted from registration and gross income in the financial year is £100,000 or less; or
- The charity is exempt from registration by order or regulation.

5   Under the 2011 Act (E&W), CCEW may by order require any person to furnish them with any information in their possession which relates to any charity and is relevant to the discharge of their functions. These powers extend to all charities whatever their legal form. Certain types of charity may also be monitored by other bodies, for example, by the Higher Education Funding Council for England in the case of universities in England or the Education and Skills Funding Agency for academy schools.

Excepted charities

6   Excepted charities are regulated by CCEW. They are called excepted charities because they have been excepted from registration with CCEW by order or regulation. Excepted charities by order with a gross income of more than £100,000 in a financial year can no longer retain excepted status and must now register with CCEW.[127]

7   Excepted charities are required to prepare annual accounts and are subject to the same audit or examination requirements as registered charities. If registered, they must also prepare an annual report and annual return and file them and their accounts with CCEW where required by regulation.

Exempt charities

8   Exempt charities in England and Wales are excluded from CCEW's supervision and monitoring. Principal regulators are appointed for different classes of exempt charities. Exempt charities do not register with CCEW, nor do they submit accounts and annual returns. However, they do have the same status and tax benefits as other charities and must comply with general charity law.

9   Where no suitable principal regulator can be identified for a class of exempt charities, that class of charities will lose its exempt status. Such a charity can become excepted provided its gross income is less than £100,000 in a financial year.

10   Many registered charitable societies within the meaning of the Friendly Societies Act 1974 or the Co-operative and Community Benefit Societies Act 2014 are also currently exempt charities in England and Wales pending the full implementation

---

[126] *This exemption does not apply to Charitable Incorporated Organisations (CIOs) (i.e., all CIOs are required to be registered).*

[127] *The £100,000 threshold is in place until 31 March 2021.*

of changes to the exempt status of such charities. However, it is anticipated that this class of charities other than those which are registered providers of social housing (registered social landlords) will cease to be exempt at some point in the future.

The 2011 Act (E&W) requires the accounts of exempt charities to be prepared on a   **11** "true and fair" basis. The accounting, reporting and audit requirements placed on exempt charities will also be dependent on how such charities are constituted and any specific statutes or regulations applying to them. For example, if constituted as companies then company law reporting duties apply.

Scotland

In Scotland, the main primary legislation is the 2005 Act (Scotland). Supervision   **12** of charities registered in Scotland is carried out by OSCR. OSCR's statutory functions are to:

- Determine whether bodies are charities.

- Keep a public register of charities.

- Encourage, facilitate and monitor compliance with the 2005 Act (Scotland).

- Identify and investigate apparent misconduct, following which it has the power to take remedial action.

- Give information, or make proposals, to the Scottish Ministers on matters relating to OSCR's functions.

Under the 2005 Act (Scotland), there are no excepted or exempt charities.

Northern Ireland

CCNI was established under the 2008 Act (NI) and this Act lays down the general   **13** functions of the Commission, which include:

- Determining whether institutions are or are not charities.

- Establishing and maintaining an accurate and up-to-date register of charities.

- Encouraging and facilitating the better administration of charities.

- Identifying and investigating apparent misconduct or mismanagement in the administration of charities and taking remedial or protective action.

Under the 2008 Act (NI), there are no excepted or exempt charities.

Friendly Societies and Registered Societies

There are relatively few remaining friendly societies with charitable status (also   **14** known as benevolent societies); the Financial Conduct Authority regulates those that remain. The primary legislation relating to charitable societies is the Friendly Societies Act 1974, although new registrations under this Act are not permitted. A number of charities, primarily providers of social housing, are registered under the Co-operative and Community Benefit Societies Act 2014, which applies in England and Wales and Scotland, or the Industrial and Provident Societies Act (Northern Ireland) 1969.

In Scotland, charities which are registered under the Friendly Societies Act or the   **15** Cooperative and Community Benefit Societies Act are still subject to the provisions of the 2005 Act (Scotland). Similar arrangements apply in Northern Ireland.

Accounting and reporting requirements

Summary of accounting requirements

Charitable company	Friendly or registered society	Non-company charity, excluding a friendly or registered society		
UK-wide	UK-wide	England and Wales[128]	Scotland	Northern Ireland
Accruals basis; "true and fair" view required		Gross income no more than £250,000, option to prepare receipts and payments accounts	Gross income less than £250,000, option to prepare receipts and payments accounts	Gross income no more than £250,000, option to prepare receipts and payments accounts
		Accruals basis; "true and fair" view required where gross income is £250,001 (or £250,000) or more		

The Charities SORP and UK legal requirements

16   The Charities SORP applies to all charities in the UK required to prepare "true and fair" accounts for reporting periods commencing on or after 1 January 2015, unless a more specialist Statement of Recommended Practice applies. The Charities SORP[129] states that where a separate SORP exists for a particular class of charities, those charities should adhere to that SORP instead. In the charity sector specialist SORPs exist for: registered social housing providers (registered social landlords); higher and further education institutions; and common investment funds.

17   While the Charities SORP is generally compatible with the requirements of UK law, it is recognised that where necessary, its recommendations should be adapted to meet any statutory requirements applying to the form and content of a charity's annual report and accounts, for example, regulations made in a particular charity law jurisdiction, the Companies Act 2006 or the Co-operative and Community Benefits Societies Act 2014. The recommendations of the Charities SORP should also be adapted to meet any special requirements of the charity's own governing document.

Non-company charities with no additional specialist requirements or exemptions

18   For non-company charities, for example, unincorporated associations, charitable trusts, charitable incorporated organisations (CIOs) and Scottish charitable incorporated organisations (SCIOs), charity law applies to the preparation of the trustees' annual report and accounts as follows:

---

[128]   *In England and Wales, registered charities with a gross income of £25,000 or less, and excepted charities which are not registered, are not required to submit a trustees' annual report and accounts to CCEW, unless requested to do so. All registered charities must prepare a trustees' annual report, even if they are not requested to submit it to CCEW.*

[129]   *Paragraph 15 of the Charities SORP, Scope and application.*

- In England and Wales, this is the 2011 Act (E&W) and related regulations, principally the Charities (Accounts and Reports) Regulations 2008 (as amended) ("2008 Regulations (E&W)").

- In Scotland, this is the 2005 Act (Scotland) and the Charities Accounts (Scotland) Regulations 2006 (as amended) ("2006 Regulations (Scotland)").

- In Northern Ireland, this is the 2008 Act (NI) and the Charities (Accounts and Reports) Regulations (Northern Ireland) 2015 ("2015 Regulations (NI)").

Charitable companies

Charitable companies are generally incorporated as companies limited by **19** guarantee and the requirements of the Companies Act 2006 requires directors of companies to prepare accounts which give a "true and fair" view and to follow the reporting requirements therein. The individual accounts of a charitable company must be prepared in accordance with Section 396 of the Companies Act 2006. Regulations made in accordance with Section 396 allow for the adaption of formats enabling Charities SORP compliant accounts to be prepared by charitable companies. Module 15 of the Charities SORP provides guidance for charitable companies on preparing an annual report and accounts which are compliant with both the Companies Act 2006 and the Charities SORP.

The requirement that company accounts give a "true and fair" view means that **20** charitable companies, however small, must prepare their accounts on an accruals basis.

Charitable companies registered in England and Wales are also subject to certain **21** provisions of the 2011 Act (E&W) relating to reports and accounts. For example, a trustees' annual report must be prepared under the 2011 Act (E&W) and group accounts must be prepared where the aggregate income of the group exceeds £1 million. This is a specialist area and reference should be made directly to the 2011 Act (E&W) and relevant regulations to determine how these apply in specific circumstances.

Charitable companies registered in Scotland are subject in full to the requirements **22** of the 2005 Act (Scotland) and the 2006 Regulations (Scotland) relating to the trustees' annual report and accounts. A similar situation exists for charitable companies in Northern Ireland where they must also comply with the requirements of the 2008 Act (NI) and the 2015 Regulations (NI).

Friendly Societies and Registered Societies

The accounting requirements for registered societies in England and Wales and in **23** Scotland are set out in the Co-operative and Community Benefit Societies Act 2014 which requires "true and fair" accounts to be prepared. All registered societies are required to submit an annual return, including the accounts, which are public records. In Northern Ireland, the equivalent legislation is the Industrial and Provident Societies (Northern Ireland) Act 1969, which will be updated by the Credit Unions and Co-operative and Community Benefit Societies Act (Northern Ireland) 2016, once the Act has been implemented. Similar provisions apply to societies with charitable status registered under the Friendly Societies Act 1974.

External scrutiny requirements: audit and independent examination

Summary of external scrutiny requirements

24   The constitution of the charity may impose more demanding requirements but cannot derogate from the statutory requirements below.

Non-company charities – charity law requirements only

England and Wales	Scotland	Northern Ireland
Independent examination where gross income is between £25,000 and £1 million Where gross income is over £250,000, the examiner must be a member of a specified body	Independent examination where gross income is less than £500,000 Where gross income is £250,000 or more (or where "true and fair" accounts are prepared and gross income is lower than £250,000), the examiner must be a member of a specified body	Independent examination where gross income is £500,000 or less, unless dispensation is given by CCNI Where gross income is over £250,000, the examiner must be a member of a specified body
Audit required where: • gross income is over £1 million or • gross assets are over £3.26 million and gross income is over £250,000	Audit required where: • gross income is £500,000 or more or • gross assets are over £3.26 million (where "true and fair" accounts are prepared)	Audit required where gross income is more than £500,000
An audit must be undertaken by a registered auditor unless CCEW gives a dispensation	An audit must be undertaken by a registered auditor or by the Auditor General for Scotland or by an auditor appointed by the Accounts Commission for Scotland	An audit must be undertaken by a registered auditor or the Comptroller and Auditor General for Northern Ireland unless CCNI gives dispensation

Charitable companies

England and Wales	Scotland	Northern Ireland
Independent examination where gross income is between £25,000 and £1 million Where gross income is over £250,000, the examiner must be a member of a specified body	Independent examination required where gross income is less than £500,000 The examiner must be a member of a specified body	Independent examination where gross income £500,000 or less Where gross income is over £250,000, the examiner must be a member of a specified body
Audit required where: • gross income is over £1 million or • gross assets are over £3.26 million <u>and</u> gross income is over £250,000	Audit required where: • gross income is £500,000 or more or • gross assets are over £3.26 million	Audit required where gross income is more than £500,000
An audit must be undertaken by a registered auditor unless CCEW gives a dispensation	An audit must be undertaken by a registered auditor or by the Auditor General for Scotland or by an auditor appointed by the Accounts Commission for Scotland	An audit must be undertaken by a registered auditor or the Comptroller and Auditor General for Northern Ireland unless CCNI gives dispensation

England and Wales

The 2011 Act (E&W) applies charity audit provisions to non-company charities   **25**
and charitable companies that are not being audited under the Companies Act
2006. Any charity not receiving an audit requires an independent examination
unless its gross income is below £25,000.

However, charitable companies will be subject to the audit requirements of the   **26**
Companies Act 2006 if the charitable company exceeds the Companies Act 2006
audit exemption threshold, or it is below the Companies Act 2006 audit exemption
thresholds but no election has been made for audit exemption under that
legislation.

Scotland

The 2005 Act (Scotland) and the 2006 Regulations (Scotland) apply to the audit   **27**
and independent examination of all charities entered on the Scottish Charity
Register including those also registered in other jurisdictions. Any charity on the
Scottish Charity Register which does not receive an audit must receive an
independent examination.

For charitable companies, the audit requirements of the 2005 Act (Scotland) and   **28**
the 2006 Regulations (Scotland) are in addition to the audit requirements of the
Companies Act 2006. As a result, charitable companies on the Scottish Charity
Register will be audited under both sets of legislation unless the charitable
company elects for audit exemption under the Companies Act 2006. Where

such an election is made, the audit is undertaken solely under the 2005 Act (Scotland) and the 2006 Regulations (Scotland).

29   Scottish charity law requires the auditor to consider the trustees' annual report and to state whether or not the report meets the requirements of the regulations and an opinion, where the auditor has formed one, that there is a material inconsistency between the annual report and the rest of the statement of account. Although there is some legal uncertainty, the Scottish Government has given a provisional view that the annual report is outside the scope of the "true and fair" view, and have said that they will clarify the legislation on this point when a suitable legislative vehicle is available.

30   OSCR has confirmed that it will not take any action if a charity files an auditor's report that does not make a specific reference to the inclusion of the trustees' annual report within the scope of the "true and fair" view.

Northern Ireland

31   The 2008 Act (NI) and the 2015 Regulations (NI) apply to the audit and independent examination of all charities entered on the Northern Ireland Charity Register. Any charity on the Northern Ireland Charity Register which does not receive an audit must receive an independent examination.

32   For charitable companies, the audit requirements of the 2008 Act (NI) and the 2015 Regulations (NI) are in addition to the audit requirements of the Companies Act 2006. As a result, charitable companies on the Northern Ireland Charity Register will be audited under both sets of legislation unless the charitable company elects for audit exemption under the Companies Act 2006. Where such an election is made, the audit is undertaken solely under the 2008 Act (NI) and the 2015 Regulations (NI).

Charitable companies

33   Charitable companies which do not exceed the Companies Act 2006 audit threshold may elect to take advantage of the audit exemption conferred by Section 477 of the Companies Act 2006. However, charitable companies which are eligible for audit exemption under the Companies Act 2006 but are above the lower threshold for audit contained within charity law must receive an audit under charity law if they elect not to be audited under the Companies Act 2006.

34   Only companies which qualify as "small" under the Companies Act 2006 can elect for audit exemption. The criteria in Section 382 of the Companies Act 2006 for qualification as "small" is any company which is not otherwise excluded from the small companies' regime by Section 384, and meets two out of the following three qualifying conditions:[130]

●   Annual gross income not more than £10.2 million;

●   Balance sheet total (i.e., gross assets) not more than £5.1 million; and

●   Average number of employees not more than 50.

35   If a charitable company decides to elect for audit exemption under the Companies Act 2006 then a statement to this effect is required on the charity's balance sheet.

36   If a small company claims audit exemption under the Companies Act 2006, the following applies:

---

[130] *Section 382 of the Companies Act 2006 sets out additional criteria for first financial years and subsequent financial years where the company meets or ceases to meet the qualifying conditions.*

- In England and Wales, it will still need an audit or independent examination under the 2011 Act (E&W), if the relevant threshold in England and Wales charity law is exceeded.

- In Scotland, it will require either an audit or independent examination under the 2005 Act (Scotland), as determined by the relevant threshold in Scottish charity law. This includes "cross border" charities.

- In Northern Ireland, it will still need an audit or independent examination under the 2008 Act (NI) as determined by the relevant threshold in Northern Ireland charity law.

There are further complexities for groups with a charitable parent company. In England and Wales, for example: **37**

- If the Companies Act 2006 requires the preparation of group accounts, these must be prepared and audited under that Act and no requirement arises for the group accounts to be prepared and audited under the 2011 Act (E&W). Under company law, group accounts must be prepared by the parent of medium-sized and large groups.

- If the 2011 Act (E&W) requires a charitable company parent to prepare group accounts, these must be prepared under the Companies Act 2006 and prepared and audited under the 2011 Act (E&W). Under the 2011 Act (E&W), group accounts are required where the aggregate gross income of the group for the financial year exceeds £1 million. In this scenario, group accounts would be prepared on a voluntary basis under the Companies Act 2006 and the parent could elect for audit exemption under company law.

Friendly Societies and Registered Societies

This is a specialist area and reference should be made to the requirements of all applicable legislation. However, in Scotland and Northern Ireland friendly societies and registered societies must also comply with the external scrutiny requirements of applicable charity law. **38**

Other aspects of law relevant to auditors

England and Wales

Content of auditor's report

The 2008 Regulations (E&W) set out the matters to be included in the auditor's report. In addition to giving an opinion on the state of affairs and incoming resources and their application and compliance with the regulations, additional statements in the auditor's report are required where the opinion is formed that: **39**

- Proper accounting records have not been kept in accordance with Section 130 of the 2011 Act (E&W);

- The statement of accounts does not accord with those records;

- Any information contained in the statement of accounts is inconsistent in any material respect with any report of the charity trustees prepared under Section 162 of the 2011 Act (E&W) in respect of the financial year in question; or

- Information and explanations considered necessary have not been provided.

Access to information and explanations

40   Auditors have a right of access with respect to books, documents and other records (however and wherever kept) relating to the charity concerned and any subsidiaries. The auditor is entitled to require, in relation to the charity, information and explanations from past or present charity trustees, or from past or present officers or employees of the charity.

Other reporting duties

41   The auditor is required by Sections 156 to 159 of the 2011 Act (E&W) to report to CCEW in writing if, in connection with an audit of a charity, the auditor becomes aware of a matter of material significance to CCEW's regulatory functions under Sections 46, 47 and 50 (inquiries) and 76 and 79 to 82 (power to act for protection of charities) of the 2011 Act (E&W).[131] A similar reporting duty is imposed on independent examiners. For exempt charities, Section 160 of the 2011 Act (E&W) transfers the reporting duty to the principal regulator.

42   Sections 156, 159 and 160 of the 2011 Act (E&W) provide a statutory discretion for the auditor to report any relevant matter to CCEW, or if the charity is exempt to a principal regulator. Where there is no statutory duty to report, the auditor considers if reporting such a matter is in the public interest or could usefully assist CCEW in its activities.

43   In addition, when an auditor ceases for any reason to hold office it must send to the charity trustees a statement of circumstances connected with its ceasing to hold office, which it considers should be brought to the trustees' attention or, if it considers that there are no such circumstances, a statement that there are none. The auditor considers on resignation if there is a duty to report a matter of material significance and, if not, whether to exercise their discretion to report a relevant matter to CCEW.

Scotland

Content of auditor's report

44   The 2006 Regulations (Scotland) set out the matters to be included in the auditor's report. The auditor must give an opinion as follows:

●   Where Regulation 8 of the 2006 Regulations (Scotland) applies, the statement of account complies with the regulatory requirements, gives a "true and fair" view of the state of affairs of the charity at the year end and of the incoming resources and application of resources during the year.

●   Where Regulation 9 applies, the statement of account complies with the regulatory requirements and properly presents the receipts and payments of the charity for the year and its statement of balances at the year end.

In addition, the auditor is required to make a statement where the opinion is formed that:

●   The accounting records have not been kept in accordance with the 2005 Act (Scotland) and 2006 Regulations (Scotland);

●   The statement of account does not accord with those records;

---

[131] *Detailed guidance on the audit implications of this duty is provided in the Section Reporting matters of material significance to charity regulators of this Practice Note.*

- Any information contained in the statement of account is inconsistent in any material respect with any report of the charity trustees prepared under Section 44(1)(b) of the 2005 Act (Scotland) in respect of the financial year; or

- Any information or explanation to which the auditor is entitled under Regulation 13 has not been afforded to them.

Access to information and explanations

The 2006 Regulations (Scotland) provide that the auditor shall have the right of access at all times to the records of the relevant charity and shall be entitled to require such information and explanations from the present or former trustees as the auditor thinks necessary for the performance of the auditor's duties. **45**

Other reporting duties

Where an auditor ceases to hold office for any reason, Regulation 10 of the 2006 Regulations (Scotland) states that the auditor must include in its notice of resignation a statement as to any circumstances connected with its resignation which it considers should be brought to the trustees' attention, or a statement that there are none. If there are circumstances which it considers should be brought to the trustees' attention, the auditor sends a copy of the statement to OSCR. **46**

The auditor is required by Section 46 of the 2005 Act (Scotland) to report to OSCR if, in connection with an audit of a charity, the auditor becomes aware of a matter of material significance to OSCR's regulatory functions under Sections 28, 30 or 31 of the 2005 Act (Scotland).[132] A similar reporting duty is placed on independent examiners. **47**

Northern Ireland

Content of auditor's report

The 2015 Regulations (NI) set out the matters to be included in the auditor's report. The auditor must give an opinion as follows: **48**

- Whether the statement of accounts complies with the requirements of Regulations 8, 9 or 10, as applicable, and in particular whether the balance sheet gives a "true and fair" view of the state of affairs of the charity at the end of the relevant financial year; and

- In the case of a general charity, the statement of financial activities gives a "true and fair" view of the total incoming resources and expenditure of resources of the charity in the relevant financial year.

In addition, the auditor is required to make a statement where the opinion is formed that: **49**

- Accounting records have not been kept in respect of the charity in accordance with Section 63 of the 2008 Act (NI);

- The statement of accounts does not accord with those records;

- Any information contained in the statement of accounts is inconsistent in any material respect with any report of the charity trustees prepared under Section 68 of the 2008 Act (NI) in respect of the relevant financial year; or

---

[132] *Detailed guidance on the audit implications of this duty is provided in the Section Reporting matters of material significance to charity regulators of this Practice Note.*

- Any information or explanation to which the auditor is entitled under Regulation 26 has not been afforded to the auditor.

Access to information and explanations

50   An auditor has a right of access to any books, documents and other records (however kept) which relate to the charity concerned which the auditor considers it necessary to inspect for the purpose of carrying out the audit.

51   The auditor is entitled to require such information and explanations from past or present charity trustees of the charity, or from past or present officers or employees of the charity, as the auditor considers necessary for the purposes of carrying out the audit.

Other reporting duties

52   The auditor is required by Section 67 of the 2008 Act (NI) to immediately make a written report to CCNI, if in the course of acting as auditor, the auditor becomes aware of a matter relating to the activities or affairs of the charity, or of any connected institution or body, which the auditor has reasonable cause to believe is likely to be of material significance for the purposes of the exercise by CCNI of its functions under Section 22 or 33 of the Charities Act 2008.[133]

Charitable companies

53   If an audit is being undertaken solely under company law or under both company law and charity law, the Companies Act 2006 auditor's report requirements must be complied with.

Auditor's report addressees where the charity appoints the auditor

Charitable companies

54   If an audit is undertaken solely under the Companies Act 2006, the auditor's report is addressed solely to the company's members (e.g., if a charitable company in England and Wales is above the company law audit threshold).

55   If an audit is being undertaken solely under charity law, the auditor's report is addressed solely to the company's trustees (e.g., a charitable company is below the company law audit threshold and has elected for exemption under the Companies Act 2006 but is above the charity law audit threshold).

56   If an audit is being undertaken under both charity law and company law, the auditor's report is addressed to both the members and the trustees (e.g., the charitable company is above the charity law audit threshold and below the company law audit threshold but no election for exemption under the Companies Act 2006 has been taken).

Non-company charities

57   The auditor's report for a non-company charity is normally addressed solely to its trustees. However, for example, in Northern Ireland where CCNI appoints the auditor, the auditor's report is addressed solely to CCNI.

---

[133] *Detailed guidance on the audit implications of this duty is provided in the Section Reporting matters of material significance to charity regulators of this Practice Note.*

Practice Note 14 – The audit of housing associations in the United Kingdom

(January 2014)

Contents

Paragraphs

Background to housing associations   1 - 26
  What are housing associations?   1 - 5
  The magnitude and diversity of the housing association sector   6 - 8
  Financing of housing associations   9 - 13
  Governance of housing associations   14 - 15
  Accounting by housing associations   16 - 21
  Risks inherent in the typical business model of a housing association 22 - 26

The regulation of housing associations   27 - 87
  General   27 - 28
  England   29 - 44
  Northern Ireland   45 - 58
  Scotland   59 - 77
  Wales   78 - 87

Business risks affecting housing associations   88 - 119
  Business risks considered   91
  Increasingly complex and risky financing arrangements   92 - 98
  Increasing motivations for the management of housing associations to
  present a biased financial picture   99 - 102
  Decreasing receipts from housing benefit creating a greater risk of bad debts
  and property voids.   103 - 106
  Diversifying into non-social housing activities   107 - 108
  Working in partnerships and joint ventures   109 - 111
  Increasing regulatory requirements for properties to be improved   112 - 114
  Inability to fund pension liabilities   115 - 118
  Corporate governance and management structures challenged by lack
  of management representation on boards and board members having
  links with similar organisations   119

Audit risks affecting housing associations   120 - 188

Appendix 1 – Overview of the regulation of English housing associations

Appendix 2 – Overview of the regulation of Northern Ireland housing associations

Appendix 3 – Overview of the regulation of Scottish housing associations

Appendix 4 – Overview of the regulation of Welsh housing associations

Appendix 5 – Useful websites

Editorial note – References to ISAs are to previous versions available online on Croner-i Tax and Accounting.

The audit of housing associations in the United Kingdom

Preface

This Practice Note contains guidance on the audit of Housing Associations. This is an economically important regulated sector of the UK economy having its own particular business and audit risks which auditors need to be aware of and, where appropriate, respond to when undertaking engagements in the sector.

Over recent years, the devolved regulatory regimes, particularly that of England, have been subject to change and it is important that auditors are familiar with how the regimes operate and, in particular, how the regulator and auditor interface. In this regard the Practice Note may be particularly useful to auditors who are new to the sector.

The Practice Note consists of the following four principal sections:

(a)   Background information about the sector to provide context for the other three sections;

(b)   A description of the four devolved regulatory regimes, focussing on the interface between the regulator and the auditor and the regulators' viability assessments. Four appendices summarise the regulatory background relating to each regulator;

(c)   A description of generic business risks that could adversely affect a Housing Association to achieve its objectives or successfully execute its strategies and which may give rise to a risk of material misstatement in its financial statements; and

(d)   A discussion of audit risks, primarily arising from the generic business risks, which the auditor is likely to need to pay particular attention to. This section is written in the context of special considerations relating to the audit of Housing Associations which arise from those ISAs (UK and Ireland) which are listed in the contents. As it is not the intention of the Practice Note to provide step-by step guidance to the audit of Housing Associations, no material is included where there are no special considerations arising from an ISA (UK and Ireland).

This Practice Note has been prepared with advice and assistance from staff of the:

(a)   (English) Homes and Communities Agency;

(b)   (Northern Ireland) Department for Social Development's Housing Division;

(c)   Scottish Housing Regulator; and

(d)   Welsh Government's Housing Division.

It is based on the legislation and regulations which were in effect at 31 December 2013. This Practice Note does not, however, constitute general guidance given by the above regulators or Industry Guidance, neither is it intended to be an exhaustive list of all the obligations that Housing Associations and their auditors may have with respect to the various regulators.

This Practice Note was written as at December 2013. Readers are cautioned that the information contained in the Practice Note may be superseded by developments over time, particularly if there is a change in Government or in Government policy. It is suggested that auditors are alert to changes in the environment within which Housing Associations operate and are particularly alert to new or changing regulation or Government policy.

Background to housing associations[1]

What are Housing Associations?

Housing Associations, also known as Registered Social Landlords (RSLs) or **1** Private Registered Providers of Social Housing[2], are independent private sector bodies that primarily:

- Provide affordable "general needs" housing at sub-market rents; and

- Offer those of modest means the opportunity to own their own homes.

Until relatively recently Housing Associations were exclusively not for profit bodies. However, some Registered Providers of Social Housing are now permitted to operate on a for profit basis. The audit of "For Profit Providers" is outside the scope of this Practice Note.

Rental receipts from "general needs" housing make up approximately 80% of the **2** aggregate income of Housing Associations. The stability of this income is underpinned by State Housing Benefit (Universal Credit) which contributes around 70% of rents from "general needs" housing.

A number of Government Schemes have been developed to encourage either full **3** or part purchase (known as shared ownership) of homes for owner occupation. Shared ownership has been offered by Housing Associations for many years with over 80,000 such homes currently existing. Shared ownership involves a buyer purchasing 50% or less[3] of a property from a Housing Association with the Association retaining the residual share and renting it to the purchaser at a subsidised rent.

Housing Associations are regulated by the following regulators: **4**

- England: The Homes and Communities Agency.
- Scotland: Scottish Housing Regulator.
- Wales: Welsh Government's Housing Division.
- Northern Ireland: Department for Social Development's Housing Division.

Housing Associations are independent organisations in the private sector which **5** may be constituted in a number of ways:

- The majority of them are Industrial and Provident Societies registered with the Financial Conduct Authority (FCA) under the Industrial and Provident Societies Act 1965;

- Some Housing Associations are established as companies limited by guarantee (this is common in the case of Housing Associations that were established to receive a transfer of former local authority housing stock); and

- Some Housing Associations are charities.

---

[1] *Information and statistics quoted as background information were current as at August 2013. Readers are cautioned that this information may have changed since publication of the Practice Note.*

[2] *In this Practice Note the term "Housing Association" is used unless the context requires otherwise.*

[3] *In Northern Ireland 50% or more must be purchased.*

The magnitude and diversity of the Housing Association Sector

6   Since the late 1980's, local authorities have been restricted in their ability to build new homes and, since that time, the Housing Association Sector has grown steadily both through building new homes and through the transfer to Housing Associations of existing homes from local authorities. Appendix 5 provides details of a number of websites that may be a useful source of up-to-date information about the sector.

7   UK Housing Associations provide some 3 million homes and operate a number of different business models ranging from small local providers of social rented homes to large diversified organisations participating in both social and commercial activities. Examples of commercial activities undertaken by a number of Housing Associations are development of properties for private rental or sale and the operation of care homes for the sick and the elderly.

8   The largest UK Housing Association controls over 50,000 homes whereas the smallest controls less than 10. Fewer than 400 UK Housing Associations own more than 1,000 homes yet the largest 20 own approximately 30% of the housing stock in the sector.

Financing of Housing Associations

9   At the time of writing, Housing Associations had attracted in excess of £62 billion in bank and capital market finance. As Housing Association finance is outside the public income and expenditure regime its borrowings do not contribute to public debt and are regarded as private finance.

10   Much of the finance for Housing Associations has been provided by a relatively small number of UK banks and building societies. Historically, Housing Associations have frequently sought, and obtained, 30 year maturities on the monies they borrow. However, there is a concern in the sector that lenders are, and will continue to be, less able to offer such long maturities in the context of the more stringent prudential requirements that have been in force since the 2008 financial crisis.

11   In response to this concern, Housing Associations are using a wider range of funding sources including: the capital markets through the issuance of bonds; private placements; and direct investment by pension companies. Since 2008, 20 Housing Associations have issued £5.4 billion in bonds which is more than the value of bonds issued by all Housing Associations in the previous 20 years.

12   Potential investors in bonds have historically placed strong reliance on the security that they derive from the fact that housing benefit is paid by the Government directly to the Housing Association. This reduces the risk of rent arrears and the cost of collection. The security has been facilitated by the tenant waiving their rights to receive benefit personally at the time they first claim it.

13   However, under the Welfare Reform Act 2012[4] the payment of Universal Credit replaces Housing Benefit and is intended to replicate, as far as possible, how people are paid if they are in work. The Act, therefore, enables housing costs within Universal Credit to be paid directly to the individual in the social rented sector, rather than directly to the landlord (e.g. Housing Association). The Government also recognises the importance of stable income from rent for

---

[4] *Most provisions of this Act extend to England, Wales and Scotland, but not to Northern Ireland. Northern Ireland has its own social security legislation, but there is a long standing policy of parity in this area.*

social landlords to support the delivery of new homes. Universal Credit, therefore, contains some safeguards to help protect landlords' income.

Governance of Housing Associations

Housing Associations often have governance structures that do not involve the **14** executive management being members of the main Board. Rather, the Board consists of a number of non-executives who are collectively "those charged with governance". However, in some cases they also co-opt members of their executive management team including the Chief Executive and Finance Director as board members. Many Housing Associations have tenant board members and Stock Transfer Associations[5] are typically required to have tenant board representation as well as board members drawn from local authorities whose stock has been acquired.

Although the proportion of Housing Associations paying their board members is **15** increasing, particularly among the larger Associations, the majority of boards still do not pay their members.

Accounting by Housing Associations

A common element of the regulation of each of the Housing Regulators is the **16** establishment of regulatory accounting requirements. Each of the four regulators has accounting requirements which require Housing Associations, among other things, to state in the notes to the accounts whether the accounts have been prepared in accordance with applicable Accounting Standards and Statements of Recommended Practice (SORPs). Further details of these requirements are not set out in this Practice Note; however information concerning these Regulations is set out with respect to each regulator in appendices 1 to 4.

The Financial Reporting Council (FRC) issues accounting standards that are **17** primarily applicable to general purpose company financial statements. Further guidance that may be required to enable particular sectors to implement accounting standards effectively is issued in the form of SORPs, by bodies recognised for the purpose by the FRC. The SORP relating to Housing Associations is regarded as being the applicable statement referred to in the various regulatory accounting requirements.

The latest version of the SORP; "Accounting by registered social housing **18** providers" was issued in 2010. The Recommended Practice and Explanation in Part 2 of the SORP aims to interpret for social landlords how present best accounting practice (as defined by the FRC) can apply to them. The purpose of the SORP is to provide guidance regarding the applicable accounting requirements but is not intended to be a substitute for them.

Housing Associations that follow the SORP are required to apply all extant **19** accounting standards, Urgent Issues Task Force (UITF) Abstracts (within the provisions set out in the Foreword to Accounting Standards) and relevant legislation.

Auditors actively consider the effect of changing accounting requirements (e.g. **20** Accounting Standards, the SORP and disclosures required by the relevant regulator) on their audit. A revised version of the SORP reflecting the

---

[5] *A Stock Transfer Housing Association is one that has received a transfer of housing stock from a local council. Stock Transfer was established in order to increase investment in social housing. This was possible because Housing Associations had greater resources than local councils to invest in housing, community improvements and services.*

requirements of FRS 102 "The Financial Reporting Standard applicable in the UK and Republic of Ireland" is expected to be published in 2014.

21   The SORP on "Accounting by Charities" is generally not to be regarded as an applicable statement where the Housing Association is a charity registered with one of the social housing regulatory bodies. This is because the Charities SORP states that where a more specialised SORP exists for a particular class of charity, the trustees of charities in that class should adhere to that SORP instead. However, where the SORP on "Accounting by Registered Social Housing Providers" is silent on a matter the Charities SORP is relevant.

Risks inherent in the typical business model of a Housing Association

22   The business model of a Housing Association typically envisages financing the cost of the properties they rent out through a combination of long term borrowings, property sales, capital grants and the Housing Association's own resources. In order to fund their growth, Housing Associations have, in the recent past, looked to borrow from banks and building societies for periods of up to 30 years.

23   In order for a Housing Association's current activities to be viable over the long run the Housing Association requires annual rental income that exceeds the aggregate of:

- Its annual interest costs;

- Its running costs including, for example;

   - Bad debts.

   - The cost of maintaining unoccupied properties that yield no rental income (voids).

   - The on-going costs of repairs.

However, if the Housing Association is planning to significantly expand its activities it will need to be able to generate additional income sufficient to meet any additional borrowing obligations that it enters into.

24   The fact that balance sheets of many Housing Associations are substantial may create an impression of financial strength. However, a Housing Association may not be as financially resilient as it initially appears because relatively small changes in either its income or expenditure may have a disproportionate effect on its liquidity and, in extreme cases, its going concern status. For example, over the last few years:

- The revenue of Housing Associations has, as a result of reduced housing benefits and the introduction of the Universal Credit, been stressed giving rise to an increased risk of bad debts and voids. In addition, income for Supporting People from local Councils has reduced as Council's budgets have also been reduced.

- Long term finance is becoming both harder to obtain and more expensive.

- The costs of maintaining properties are increasing as a result of greater societal expectations regarding the quality of accommodation that should be provided.

- Liquidity has been adversely affected by a need to increase the funding of pension liabilities.

Information about the credit ratings of Housing Associations and the reasons for **25** any changes in such ratings are likely to be of relevance to the auditor's risk assessment. In 2013, for example, the credit ratings of all English Housing Associations were downgraded by a major credit rating agency on the grounds of uncertainty regarding the availability of central government support for Housing Associations in financial distress.

Some Housing Associations have become complex organisations undertaking **26** diverse activities such as outright sales, student accommodation, PFI transactions and care and support activities, and also working in partnership with others. This has given rise to the risk of profitable segments of a Housing Association's business being used to subsidise non-profitable segments. The liquidity difficulties described above may expose the risks associated with cross-subsidisation and ultimately threaten the viability of a Housing Association.

The regulation of housing associations

General

As the regulation of Housing Associations is a devolved responsibility there are **27** separate regulatory regimes relating to England, Northern Ireland, Scotland and Wales. Appendices 1 to 4 provide an overview of the four regulatory regimes. In the following paragraphs more detailed information about specific aspects of the regimes is provided. In particular, information is provided about:

- The auditor's right and duty to report to the regulator; and
- Regulatory viability assessments.

The detailed information about the auditor's relationship with the regulator is of **28** particular relevance to the auditor's responsibilities under ISA (UK and Ireland) 250 B "The Auditor's Right and Duty to Report to Regulators". The detailed information about regulatory viability assessments is of relevance to the auditor's responsibilities under ISA (UK and Ireland) 570 "Going Concern".

England

The Homes and Communities Agency (HCA) became the regulator of social **29** housing within England with effect from 1 April 2012. It follows "The Regulatory Framework for Social Housing in England from April 2012" framework).

The framework includes three economic standards that are of relevance to auditors **30** of Housing Associations:

- Governance and financial viability;
- Value for Money; and
- Rent.

There are no requirements for routine reporting by the auditor to the HCA. **31** However, as described below there are requirements for the auditor to report to the HCA in connection with an "extraordinary audit".

Auditor's right to report to HCA

Section 143 of the Housing and Regeneration Act 2008 provides that the auditor **32** of a registered provider or a reporting accountant in relation to a registered provider may disclose information to the HCA for a purpose connected with the HCA's function;

- Despite any duty of confidentiality; and
- Whether or not the HCA requests the information.

(The reference to disclosing information includes expressing an opinion on it. "Reporting Accountant" means a person who is appointed to prepare a report which, by virtue of any enactment has to be prepared in respect of accounts that are not subject to audit.)

Auditor's duty to report to the HCA

33   The auditor has no duty in the normal course to report to the HCA. However, section 210 of the Housing and Regeneration Act 2008 allows, where an inquiry is being held, for the HCA to have an "extraordinary audit" which has to be undertaken by a qualified auditor appointed by the HCA.

34   Under sections 107 and 108 of the Housing and Regeneration Act 2008 an auditor may be required to provide documents to the HCA.

Regulatory governance and viability assessments

35   The HCA publishes a number of documents about the English housing sector. In particular, its assessment of individual providers with more than 1,000 homes regarding their compliance with the economic standards for all private registered providers.

36   Regulatory judgments are one of the key ways in which the HCA communicates its views about the sector and individual Housing Associations to the wider world. In particular, these judgments contain the HCA's view of whether the Association meets its governance and financial viability standards.

37   The HCA issues two types of report in which it expresses its judgments on viability and governance:

- **Regulatory Judgments (RJ)** are public documents, which discuss the Housing Association's performance in the round and contain two judgments on its compliance with the governance and the viability parts of the Governance and Viability Standard. The HCA publishes graded assessments in relation to both viability and governance as these are key areas where lenders, boards and others value assessments. The HCA expects to refresh these every 2-3 years for all Housing Associations with more than 1,000 homes.

- **Viability Reviews (VR)** are confidential documents, seen only by the Housing Association and (under the terms of loan covenants) their lenders. This document summarises the regulator's assessment of a Housing Association's viability and sets out key financial risk exposures mitigations adopted by the provider and any monitoring activity the HCA will undertake to gain further assurance on the management of the exposures.

38   The viability grades of English Housing Associations arising from the RJ are likely to be of particular relevance to the auditor's assessment of the going concern status of a Housing Association. They are as follows:

- V1 The provider (Housing Association) meets the requirements on viability set out in the Governance and Financial Viability Standard and has the capacity to mitigate its exposures effectively.

- V2 The provider (Housing Association) meets the requirements on viability set out in the Governance and Financial Viability Standard but needs to manage material financial exposures to support continued compliance.

- V3 The provider's (Housing Association's) financial viability is of concern and in agreement with the regulator it is working to improve its position.

- V4 The provider's (Housing Association's) financial viability is of serious concern and it is subject to regulatory intervention or enforcement action[6].

The first two of these grades confirm that the Housing Association is meeting the   **39** HCA's expectations, while the last two indicate a failure to meet its standards. A V2 viability grade is considered to meet the HCA standard because there is no immediate threat to the Association's financial viability, but there are business risks which need to be managed actively. The HCA does not seek to eliminate risk from the sector, but rather to concentrate its resources on identification and management of risk by Associations.

The most significant change in the grading of Housing Associations came in 2008   **40** when the number of V2 gradings rose from around 20% of the sector to the current position of approximately 33%. This was not a reflection of a change in approach by the HCA but was a consequence of the more difficult trading environment that providers faced at that time. Receiving a V2 viability grade from the HCA does not mean that it regards the organisation as likely to fail. It means that there are a range of risks that, if not managed successfully, could have a negative impact on the Housing Association's viability.

The auditor is required to obtain sufficient appropriate audit evidence regarding   **41** the Housing Association's use of the going concern assumption in the preparation of its financial statements and to conclude whether a material uncertainty exists that may cast significant doubt on the Association's ability to continue as a going concern. The auditor of an English Housing Association is likely to find the HCA's viability grades a useful source of audit evidence.

The auditor also seeks access to viability reviews communicated by the HCA to   **42** the Housing Association as these will also be a source of evidence concerning the going concern status of the Housing Association.

The HCA's Governance grading may provide early warning of potential   **43** governance problems at a Housing Association. The gradings are as follows:

- G1 The provider (Housing Association) meets the requirements on governance set out in the Governance and Financial Viability standard.

- G2 The provider (Housing Association) meets the requirements on governance set out in the Governance and Financial Viability standards but needs to improve some aspects of its governance arrangements to support continued compliance.

- G3 The provider (Housing Association) does not meet all of the requirements on governance set out in the Governance and Financial Viability standard. There are issues of regulatory concern and in agreement with the regulator the provider is working to improve its position.

- G4 The provider (Housing Association) does not meet the requirements on governance set out in the Governance and Financial Viability standard. There are issues of serious regulatory concern and in agreement with the

---

[6] *Prior to 2012 the ratings were referred to as J1 to J4.*

regulator the provider is subject to regulatory intervention or enforcement action.

44   The HCA maintains and publishes a list of those Housing Associations where its current published assessment of compliance is under review. These are Housing Associations with which the regulator is actively engaging as issues have arisen since the last published judgment that may impact adversely on the HCA's view of the Association's compliance with governance and/or viability regulatory requirements.

Northern Ireland

45   Registered Housing Associations in Northern Ireland first came into being in 1976 and at the date of publication there were 30 such Associations. The Northern Ireland Department for Social Development (DSD) is responsible for the funding, monitoring, regulation and issue of guidance and policy directives to Registered Housing Associations and has a statutory duty to consult with representatives of Housing Associations.

46   The two main external reports for Registered Housing Associations are the:

- Annual Report and Accounts; and

- Annual Regulatory Return (ARR).

47   These reports are required by the DSD to monitor the financial viability of Associations and ensure the proper management of public funds. There are no requirements for routine reporting by the auditor to the DSD. However, as described below there are requirements for the auditor to report to the DSD in connection with an "extraordinary audit".

48   In addition to the requirements set out in legislation the DSD also requires the Board of a Registered Housing Association to carry out an annual review of its system of internal control. A statement relating to this review is to be included in the audited financial statements.

Auditor's right to report to the DSD

49   There are no rights specified in law or regulation whereby the auditor may report directly to the DSD.

Auditor's duty to report to the DSD

50   The auditor has no duty in the normal course to report to the DSD but Article 24 of the Housing (Northern Ireland) Order 1992 provides that when an inquiry under Article 23 (inquiries into affairs of registered housing associations) is being held, the DSD is allowed to have an "extraordinary audit" which has to be undertaken by a qualified auditor appointed by the DSD.

51   The auditor may be required to provide documents to the DSD and on completion of an extraordinary audit the appointed auditor is required to make a report to the DSD on such matters and in such form as the Department may specify.

Regulatory viability assessments

52   The DSD Inspection Team carry out inspections of Housing Associations on a cyclical basis to ensure compliance with procedures laid down in the "Housing Association Guide".

53   The Housing Association Guide is one of the key management tools employed by the DSD to deliver its regulatory responsibilities for Housing Associations. It sets

out the DSD's guidelines for Registered Housing Associations requiring robust policy and procedural standards across all Associations and equitable quality service provision for social housing tenants. It also contains the rules and procedures that Associations must comply with in order to meet the conditions for receipt of capital grant from the Northern Ireland Housing Executive (Development Programme Group).

The DSD uses a four tier Inspection Grading System on which to base an overall   **54** rating and individual ratings for four areas of focus one of which is financial viability. The four tier grading system is as follows:

- **Substantial Assurance:** Where there is a robust system of risk management, control and governance which ensure that objectives are fully achieved. These Housing Associations will have a well-run system of internal control and a risk management programme resulting in all identified risks being addressed and mitigated.

- **Satisfactory Assurance:** Given to Housing Associations who have shown that they have an effective system of control which will ensure the achievement of objectives. There may be some weaknesses but these would not be regarded as impacting significantly on the overall performance of the Association.

- **Limited Assurance:** Given to Housing Associations where there is a considerable risk that the Association will fail to meet its objectives or where an Association has previously received a "No Assurance" rating and it has shown progress in addressing previous shortcomings. Prompt action is required to improve the adequacy and effectiveness of risk management, control and governance.

- **No Assurance:** Given to Housing Associations where internal systems have failed or there is a real and substantial risk of the Association failing to meet its objectives and where they are also failing to provide any of the following: sound corporate and financial governance, quality housing or value for money. Such Housing Associations are considered a high risk to themselves and the public funds which they might receive.

The auditor is required to obtain sufficient appropriate audit evidence regarding   **55** the Housing Association's use of the going concern assumption in the preparation of its financial statements and to conclude whether a material uncertainty exists that may cast significant doubt on the Association's ability to continue as a going concern. The auditor of a Northern Ireland Association is likely to find the DSD's grading a useful source of audit evidence.

The DSD regularly collects and reviews information from the Housing   **56** Association including Board minutes and financial information (quarterly accounts).

The actions taken by the DSD is dictated by what is found in the inspection or   **57** monitoring process. Any queries identified through the latter are followed up with the Housing Association and may lead to an inspection visit where an acceptable response is not provided. If an Association fails the inspection the DSD can impose a series of tiered sanctions such as suspension from the Development Programme or ultimately consideration of de-registration.

Annual Regulatory Return – Registered Housing Associations are required to   **58** complete the returns annually. The information collected is used to assess key performance indicators in relation to Housing Management and Maintenance.

Scotland

59   The Scottish Housing Regulator (SHR) assumed its full regulatory powers on 1 April 2012 under the Housing (Scotland) Act 2010. The SHR is directly accountable to the Scottish Parliament. In Scotland Housing Associations are known as "Registered Social Landlords" or RSLs.

60   The SHR has a statutory objective to "safeguard and promote the interests of current and future tenants of social landlords, people who are or may become homeless and people who use housing services provided by registered social landlords and local authorities".

61   Part 3 of the 2010 Act requires the SHR to publish regulatory standards and guidance. The SHR has published a Regulatory Framework document (Regulation of Social Housing in Scotland – Our Framework) which includes the details of the regulatory standards for financial management and governance. All RSLs were required to comply with these standards from 1 April 2012.

62   The approach is risk based and proportionate which is intended to enable the SHR to:

- Prioritise resources;

- Plan how to engage with a Housing Association; and

- Use the appropriate level of scrutiny, engagement or intervention required to obtain the level of assurance the SHR needs.

63   To achieve these objectives the SHR will use financial information collected from RSLs such as 5 year financial projections audited accounts, auditor management letters and loan portfolio returns as well as information from the Annual Performance Statistical Return and other regulatory intelligence. There are three levels of regulatory engagement, which are:

- Low   have sufficient assurance via the regulatory returns.

- Medium   additional information is required to seek further assurance.

- High   Intensive or continuous relationship required.

The SHR publishes individual regulation plans for all registered social landlords with Medium and High engagement.

64   "Audit Guidance"[7] is provided for Housing Associations that the SHR identify as having systemic importance (see paragraph 73 for further discussion of the meaning of systemic importance). The guidance requires a tailored level of assurance which goes beyond that specified for the generality of Housing Associations. Housing Associations of systemic importance are required to have a clear focus on, and a defined approach to, the management of risk and to have an audit committee as part of its risk management and internal control systems; to carry out internal scrutiny and give necessary assurance to the governing body.

65   The additional audit guidance is at Regulatory Standard 3 (3.8 to 3.12). Housing Associations of systemic importance are required to implement and comply with this additional guidance. Other Housing Associations may also be required to

---

[7] *The term "Audit Guidance" is a term used by the SHR in its Regulatory Framework Document in relation to the SHR's relationship with Housing Associations identified as having systemic importance. The term does not refer to guidance for Housing Association auditors.*

implement the audit guidance. In such cases this is noted in the published regulation plan for the Housing Association.

While compliance with the audit guidance is not mandatory for all Housing   **66** Associations, they are encouraged to consider its merits.

Auditor's right to report to the SHR

An auditor may disclose information to the SHR (and express an opinion on it)   **67** where it has reasonable cause to believe that the information is likely to be relevant to the performance of any of the SHR's functions.

Auditor's duty to report to the SHR

Section 72 of the Housing (Scotland) Act 2010 Act obliges auditors to disclose   **68** information to the SHR which they believe would have a material impact on the performance of the SHR's function to monitor, assess and report regularly on the registered social landlord's financial well-being and standards of governance.

The section 72 reporting obligations work in conjunction with the notifiable   **69** events requirements[8]. While it is the auditor's judgment that ultimately determines what information falls within section 72, the SHR considers, for example, that it may be materially significant if an auditor becomes aware that the notifiable events guidance has not been complied with. The SHR also expects an auditor to be aware of any published regulation plan for the audited body and to use this information to inform their judgment in determining whether something is likely to be of material significance or relevance.

Regulatory viability assessments

When SHR refers to risk, this means the risk to its statutory objective i.e. to protect   **70** the interests of tenants and other service users. The risks to this regulatory objective are likely to be:

- Poor outcomes for tenants and other service users;
- Poor stock quality and investment failures;
- Poor financial performance and management; and
- Poor governance.

Each year, SHR assesses and prioritises the risks each landlord represents to its   **71** statutory objective and determines what the appropriate response should be. The regulatory response is based on what level of assurance is needed and it can change in response to new information or events. The regulatory cycle consists of:

- Risk identification;
- Risk assessment and prioritisation;
- Decision on regulatory response and resources; and
- Regulatory engagement.

For Housing Associations (RSLs), SHR assesses for each risk: **72**

- Impact – assessing the scale and significance e.g. stock size, quality age and number of tenancies, level of private finance being serviced etc.;
- Probability – likelihood of the risk materialising; and

---

[8] *The SHR issues guidance on "notifiable events". These are events that it requires a registered social landlord to notify it about. At the time of writing the latest guidance was dated April 2012.*

- Manageability – ability of the tools at the SHR's disposal to deal with the risk.

73   A small number of Housing Associations may have such a profile across several of the impact factors that they would present the greatest risk to SHR's objective should they experience business failure. These Housing Associations are considered to have systemic importance and, as discussed in paragraphs 64 and 65, the SHR may define additional assurance requirements as a result.

74   In addition, SHR considers the landlords organisational complexity (including its use of subsidiaries and dependence on them), number of employees, legal status and governance arrangements.

75   On completion of the risk assessment, the level of engagement is categorised as Low, Medium or High. Housing Associations in the Medium and High engagement categories will receive a regulation plan which details what action the Housing Association is to carry out, the engagement SHR plans to have with the Association and the timescale involved.

76   Higher levels of engagement cannot be assumed to equate to poor performance e. g. newly registered Housing Associations or those with large development programmes will have relatively high levels of engagement.

77   The auditor is required to obtain sufficient appropriate audit evidence regarding the Housing Association's use of the going concern assumption in the preparation of its financial statements and to conclude whether a material uncertainty exists that may cast significant doubt on the Association's ability to continue as a going concern. The auditor of a Scottish Housing Association is likely to find the SHRs risk assessment categorisation and regulation plan a useful source of audit evidence.

Wales

78   In Wales the Housing Association Regulator is the Welsh Ministers. They have established a Housing Regulation Team to undertake regulation activity on their behalf. The team is part of the Welsh Government's Housing Division (WGHD).

79   The Review of Affordable Housing in Wales (June 2008) recommended the development of a new Regulatory Framework for Housing Associations. This has now been issued as "The Regulatory Framework for Housing Associations Registered in Wales".

80   The ultimate purpose of the Regulatory Framework is to ensure that Housing Associations provide good quality homes and services to tenants and others who use their services. It does this by ensuring that each Association is:

- Well governed – led effectively and well managed by boards, executives, staff, tenants and partners, who work together to make and implement business decisions;

- Financially viable – has the money to meet current and future business commitments and effectively manages its finances; and

- Delivering high quality services.

Regulatory assessment

81   All Welsh Housing Associations are expected to carry out a regular self-assessment which evaluates their performance on service delivery, governance and finance and proposes improvement action. This self-assessment is the core

evidence used by the Welsh Ministers in making their regulatory assessment of each Association.

The annual regulatory assessment is used to determine the level of regulatory **82** contact. There are three levels, "low", "medium" and "high". Medium or high levels of contact are tailored to the needs of the Housing Association and can involve:

- Enhanced regulatory contact.
- Increased scrutiny and testing of the self-assessment.
- Increased scrutiny of financial submissions.
- Inspection of one or more elements of an Association's activities.
- More formal responses or interventions.

The assessment is required to be published on the Housing Association's web-site.

Auditor's right to report to the WGHD

There are no rights specified in law or regulation for an auditor to report to the **83** WGHD.

Auditor's duty to report to the WGHD

There are no duties specified in law or regulation which require the auditor to **84** report to the WGHD.

Financial viability judgments

A financial viability judgment is issued to each Housing Association at the end of **85** March each year. This is based on monitoring information through the year, including management accounts, statutory accounts, private finance returns and 30 year forecasts. The judgment is required to be available on the Housing Association's website on the 10th working day from the date of receipt.

There are three categories of financial judgment: **86**

- Pass;
- Pass with closer regulatory monitoring; or
- Fail.

Where a judgment of "fail" applies, the Welsh Ministers will have already been working closely with the Association to address the underlying issues. Where the judgment is "pass with closer regulatory monitoring", the Welsh Ministers are of the view that additional work and/or scrutiny is required to provide stronger assurance on financial viability.

The auditor is required to obtain sufficient appropriate audit evidence regarding **87** the Housing Association's use of the going concern assumption in the preparation of its financial statements and to conclude whether a material uncertainty exists that may cast significant doubt on the Association's ability to continue as a going concern. The auditor of a Welsh Housing Association is likely to find the Welsh Ministers' Regulatory Assessments a useful source of audit evidence.

Business risks affecting housing associations

88 A business risk is a risk resulting either from significant conditions, events, circumstances, actions or inactions that could adversely affect a Housing Association's ability to achieve its objectives and execute its strategies, or from the setting of inappropriate objectives and strategies.

89 As all Housing Associations have business risks it is important that they have clear strategies for dealing with the risks and policies on how to manage the risks. There is a wide range of risk management strategies that Associations may adopt. It is important that the auditor has an understanding of the way in which the Housing Association seeks to address the business risks that it confronts and in particular assesses whether there are on-going processes embedded within the Association's operations which monitor the effective application of the policies, processes and activities related to risk management.

90 The following discussion of business risks that may result in a risk of material misstatement at a Housing Association is, necessarily, written at a generic level and is intended only to guide auditors as to relevant business risks that they might consider with respect to the Housing Associations that they audit. As each Association is unique auditors consider whether there are other relevant business risks that may be applicable to the Association that they are auditing.

Business risks considered

91 The following list sets out some of the key business risks that may give rise to a risk of material misstatement:

- Housing Associations entering into increasingly complex and risky financing arrangements.

- Increasing motivations for the management of Housing Associations to present a biased financial picture.

- Decreasing receipts from Government housing benefit creating a greater risk of bad debts and property voids.

- As a result of reduction in Government support, diversifying into non-social housing activities that may give rise to increased and unforeseen risks.

- Increasing regulatory requirements for properties to be improved increasing the costs of Housing Associations in an environment where there is pressure on revenues.

- Risks surrounding working in partnerships, joint ventures and non-registered subsidiaries.

- Housing Associations may be unable to fund their pension liabilities.

- The Board may not have the requisite skills and experience.

Increasingly complex and risky financing arrangements
Increasing borrowings from the capital markets

92 Until the recent financial crisis banks had been willing to lend to Housing Associations for long terms and to charge relatively low rates of interest. A key factor in obtaining such lending was the ability of the Housing Association to receive its tenants' housing benefit directly from the Government (rather than via the tenant).

However, these traditional lenders are increasingly looking to lend shorter term   **93** than they have in the past and are also charging higher margins on new debt and on existing debt where they have an opportunity to re-price. Banks typically are now looking to lend for 5 or 10 year terms rather than 30 year terms.

As described in paragraph 11 Housing Associations have increasingly been   **94** looking to the wholesale bond markets to satisfy their financing needs. Larger Housing Associations often access the capital markets directly using a particular arranger whereas smaller Housing Associations are able to access the capital markets through aggregating bodies such as The Housing Finance Corporation which is able to "lend on" funds to Housing Associations on the same terms as it is able to borrow.

Although wholesale bonds are usually relatively straightforward financial   **95** instruments, the terms and conditions associated with an issuance may be complicated and need to be well understood by management, the Board of the Housing Association and the auditor. Bonds, for example, may be issued in overseas markets in currencies other than Sterling and thus give rise to foreign currency risk.

Housing Associations have increasingly been entering into interest rate swaps,   **96** typically to convert variable rate loans into fixed rate loans to enable the Housing Association to build some certainty into its business plan. Although the swaps are usually undertaken with a financial institution there is a growing incidence of swaps being undertaken between Housing Associations. Such swaps are typically less costly than swaps involving a financial institution. However they may be much more risky to the extent that they rely on the counterparty Housing Association continuing in business during the period in which the swap is effective.

When a Housing Association issues a bond such bonds may be listed on the   **97** Official List thus giving rise to the obligations that arise from being listed.

Guarantees

Financings may involve complex guarantees and Housing Associations need to be   **98** aware of the implications of guarantees both that they enter into and also of guarantee obligations that they may have acquired when making a business acquisition. In the latter case the existence of guarantees against loans may not be apparent in the absence of appropriate due diligence activities at the time of the business acquisition. Risks associated with guarantees may be particularly acute where a Housing Association diversifies into non-social housing activities.

Increasing motivations for the management of Housing Associations to present a biased financial picture

Management of Housing Associations may be motivated by many factors to   **99** present a biased financial picture. A perceived risk of damage to the Association's reputation may give rise to motivations to inhibit disclosure of detrimental circumstances or events.

An example of a detrimental circumstance arises from the constraints that arise   **100** from the covenants specified in the funding agreements within which a Housing Association operates. As the impact of non-compliance with covenants could be significant for a Housing Association there is an incentive for the preparers of the financial statements, management of the Housing Association or the Board to alter the financial statements to disguise the fact that a breach has in fact occurred.

101   In addition, some activities of a Housing Association group (for example, its commercial activities or care and support services) may be subject to separate scrutiny by regulators, funders or tax authorities. Since there is some risk of issues arising should these business segments be either particularly profitable or loss making, there is an incentive for a Housing Association to present its financial statements in a manner that avoids such issues being identified by a reader of the financial statements.

102   SORP 2010 at paragraph 164 relating to mixed tenure development requires surpluses generated by an element of the development to be offset against elements having shortfalls. A consequence of this accounting cross-subsidisation of elements may be an incentive to manipulate the accounting for the various elements to enable surpluses to be inappropriately recorded.

Decreasing receipts from Housing Benefit creating a greater risk of bad debts and property voids.

103   The Welfare Reform Act 2012 is likely to have a significant impact on the revenues of Housing Associations. Among other things, the Act:

- Is intended to cut the amount of benefit being received by those tenants that have a spare bedroom; and

- Envisages many more social housing tenants receiving housing benefit (which will now be incorporated into the "The Universal Credit") directly. (Rather than the benefit being paid directly to their landlord.)

104   These changes could adversely affect the cash flows of Housing Associations through, for example:

- Increased arrears.

- New debt collection procedures (including the possible need for additional staff).

- Legal costs.

105   Rent increases are typically tied to the Retail Price Index (RPI). Low annual increases in retail prices affects Housing Associations to the extent that rent increases are lower than expected.

106   In determining the audit evidence that it wishes to obtain with respect to bad debts the auditor may wish to evaluate the Association's stress testing of its business model against these changes.

Diversifying into non-social housing activities

107   A number of Housing Associations have diversified into activities other than core social housing activities. An example of such a non-core activity is care and support activities. Such activities may expose the Housing Association to additional risks, with a key consideration being heightened reputational risk resulting from the vulnerability of the tenants being cared for.

108   Care and support activities can be contracted or subcontracted to or from partner organisations. This may increase the inherent risk as the Housing Association is dependent on the performance of others. If performance targets are not met in line with funding agreements, it can directly impact on the amounts of revenue that can be recognised and result in returns being less than expected. Ultimately this can affect the financial viability of the non-social housing activities and the Association.

Working in partnerships and joint ventures

Joint ventures and other arrangements are now more common in the sector **109** bringing with it a number of additional risks (although in many cases the rationale behind the structures was intended to help in managing risk).

Care needs to be taken to ensure that the Housing Association's obligations are **110** fully understood, including any contractual obligations and/or guarantees. Boards of Housing Associations need to be aware of the full range of risks involved in these arrangements, and whether they have the ability and resources to meet these obligations. Housing Associations also need to understand what returns they have a right to and ensure that any income due is received.

Working in partnership is underpinned by the terms of the agreement between the **111** parties. Both sides need to understand their roles and responsibilities. The Association needs to ensure that it has effective oversight over all activities and the ability to act when concerns arise.

Increasing regulatory requirements for properties to be improved

From 2000 to 2010 the Government, in England, pursued a "decent home for all" **112** policy goal (Beyond Decent Homes). When the policy was established the Government stated "When the decent homes target was set in 2001, the aim was to eliminate a backlog of disrepair and ensure that no one was living in a home that was below a basic minimum level of decency."

A primary issue facing Housing Associations is balancing their spending between **113** the two objectives of building new homes and improving the existing stock. The future of grant funding is uncertain and any reduction in grants for new build homes could result in Housing Associations reducing its investment in improving the existing stock. However, as Housing Associations are required by the Regulator to maintain the standard of their existing stock, the Regulator will take action if a Housing Association is considered to be investing in new homes at the expense of current tenants.

Housing Associations will have to balance these competing demands in the **114** context of the future regulatory environment and in England in the context of any successor programme to "Beyond Decent Homes". In Northern Ireland, the Housing Association is required to have completed a stock condition survey and to have plans in place to deliver the required maintenance investment. In Scotland, the Scottish Housing Quality Standard was introduced in 2004 to be the Scottish Government's principal measure of housing quality in Scotland. The purpose of introducing a minimum housing standard in Scotland is essentially to provide a "floor" below which a property ideally should not fall. The Scottish Government has set a policy target for Housing Associations to bring their stock up to every element of the standard by April 2015. In Wales the Welsh Ministers have implemented the Welsh Housing Quality Standard which it expects all Welsh Housing Associations to adopt and have brought their properties up to date by the end of 2012, or later by agreement with the Ministers.

Inability to fund pension liabilities

Many Housing Associations are members of multi-employer defined benefit **115** pension schemes such as the Social Housing Pension Scheme (SHPS) in England and the Scottish Housing Association Pension Scheme (SHAPS). The SORP 2010 requires Housing Associations to comply with the disclosure requirements for defined benefit schemes in FRS 17, unless:

- The employer has no obligation other than to pay a contribution which reflects the benefits earned in the current period (i.e. it is in effect a defined contribution pension scheme); or

- The employer's contributions are affected by a surplus or deficit in the scheme but the employer is unable to identify its share of the underlying assets and liabilities on a consistent and reasonable basis.

In which case the Association is required to comply with the disclosure requirements for defined contribution schemes

116   The Pension Trust which administers SHPS and SHAPS has indicated that it is unable to provide a breakdown of pension assets and liabilities by Housing Association on a consistent and reasonable basis. Therefore, it is not possible for an asset or liability relating to these pension schemes to be reflected in the financial statements of Housing Associations. Many Associations, therefore, have been unable to properly reflect the defined benefit scheme in their accounts and as a result are only able to reflect pension contributions paid.

117   In recent years due to low asset growth, salary growth rates, a fall in government bond yields and increasing pension scheme liabilities amongst other factors, the funding position of many pension schemes has deteriorated. The Pension Trust has had to implement a recovery plan for the social housing pension schemes in order to reduce past funding deficits and require its members to pay towards the deficit by way of additional contributions.

118   The additional contributions in respect of the past deficit together with a likely rise in future service contributions means that pension contributions are an increasing cost for Housing Associations at a time when budgets are under pressure and funding is more limited.

Corporate governance and management structures challenged by lack of management representation on Boards and Board members having links with similar organisations

119   In line with many other types of "not for profit" organisations, Housing Associations often have governance structures that do not involve members of the executive management team (including the finance director) being members of the Board. Instead, there are a number of non-executive members who are collectively "those charged with governance". As a result there is a risk that the governance of the Housing Association may be divided between the Board and the executive management in a disconnected way. In particular, the Board and executive management may not communicate and share their thinking with each other effectively.

Audit risks affecting housing associations

120   Audit risk is the risk that the auditor expresses an inappropriate audit opinion when the financial statements are materially misstated. Audit risk is a function of the risks of material misstatement and the risk that the procedures performed by the auditor will not detect a misstatement. Examples of business risks that may result in a risk of material misstatement are discussed at paragraphs 91 to 119 above.

121   The discussion in the following paragraphs is to draw attention to aspects of International Standards on Auditing (UK and Ireland) that may be particularly

applicable to audit risk in the context of Housing Associations. Where a specific ISA (UK and Ireland) is not discussed this is not because its requirements are not relevant to the audit of Housing Associations but because there are no significant additional considerations arising as a result of the entity being a Housing Association.

The ISAs (UK and Ireland) discussed in the following paragraphs are: **122**

- 240 The Auditor's Responsibilities relating to Fraud in an Audit of Financial Statements.

- 250 Section A: Consideration of Laws and Regulations in an Audit of Financial Statements.

- 250 Section B: The Auditor's Right and Duty to Report to Regulators in the Financial Sector.

- 260 Communication with Those Charged with Governance.

- 315 Identifying and Assessing the Risk of Material Misstatement Through Understanding of the Entity and its Environment.

- 320 Materiality in Planning and Performing an Audit.

- 520 Analytical Procedures.

- 540 Auditing Accounting Estimates Including Fair Value Accounting Estimates and Related Disclosures.

- 550 Related Parties.

- 570 Going Concern.

The Auditor's Responsibilities Relating to Fraud in an Audit of Financial Statements. ISA (UK and Ireland) 240

> **Applicable Business Risk – Motivations for Housing Association management to present a biased financial picture**

123 Two types of intentional financial statement misstatement are likely to be particularly relevant to the auditor of a Housing Association:

- Misstatements arising from fraudulent financial reporting; and

- Misstatements resulting from misappropriation of assets.

124 Fraudulent financial reporting involving intentional misstatements to deceive financial statement users by influencing their perceptions as to the Housing Association's performance and profitability may be less likely than in some commercial entities due to the absence of trading in shares or significant management bonus arrangements.

125 However, there are a number of other external issues which may motivate the management of Housing Associations to present a biased financial picture. Some of these business risks are discussed in paragraphs 99 to 102. The strategies being adopted by Housing Associations to manage these issues may result in incentives for material misstatement of the financial statements.

126 Housing Associations may have significant borrowings with covenant terms (generally interest cover and gearing covenants). This may create pressures on the Association that, in turn, may motivate management to take action to misstate the reported business performance in the financial statements.

127 With respect to misappropriation, areas where the board might, where relevant, be expected to introduce strong internal controls to avoid the occurrence of misappropriation or error include, where material:

- Purchasing (for development and maintenance).

- The collection of rent in cash.

- Major fund flows (for example the draw down and repayment of loans and grants).

- Recognition of development or maintenance expenditure in the correct period.

Consideration of Laws and Regulations in an Audit of Financial Statements: ISA (UK and Ireland) 250 Section A

128 ISA (UK and Ireland) 250 Section A requires the auditor, among other things, to obtain sufficient appropriate audit evidence regarding compliance with the provisions of those laws and regulations generally recognised to have a direct effect on the determination of material amounts and disclosures in the financial statements. Determination of which laws and regulations have such a direct effect requires consideration of its governing document, the activities it undertakes and those laws and regulations specifically applicable to those activities.

Laws and regulations are likely to have a direct effect on the determination of **129** material amounts and disclosures in the financial statements where breaches would have any of the following consequences:

(a) Intervention by the regulatory body to direct the affairs of the Housing Association, for example non-compliance with the various laws relating to fraud and corruption under which the regulatory body possesses various powers of intervention;

(b) Loss of necessary licenses to continue a major element of the Housing Association's work (primarily law and regulations applicable to building and planning regulations or contaminated land, or health and safety regulations in relation to homes in multiple occupation); or

(c) Financial effects resulting in liabilities which are likely to exceed the available resources of the Housing Association. For example, expenditure or activities outside grant conditions imposed by the regulatory body can lead to disallowance and repayment of grant.

The social housing sector includes a number of diverse activities and hence the **130** requirements of laws and regulations that have a direct effect on the determination of material amounts and disclosures in the financial statements are likely to be derived from the activities undertaken as well as arising from registration with the regulatory body. For example, Housing Associations providing residential care in England and Wales will be subject to the requirements of the Care Standards Act 2000. Significant breaches can result in loss of registration and hence ability to undertake particular activities. Similar legislative requirements can affect social housing operations in different parts of the sector and in different parts of the United Kingdom.

Housing Associations which have charitable status have significant direct tax **131** exemptions in relation to income and chargeable gains. Auditors need to have an understanding of these exemptions and concessions in order to determine if there are any activities which may be incompatible with chartable status. Similarly, auditors need to have an understanding of other tax legislation, such as VAT, as non-compliance or errors could have adverse financial consequences for the Housing Association.

Money laundering

Given the significant cash flows involved in the purchase and development of **132** land, and in particular the fact that some land deals are undertaken at below market value, auditors need to be aware of the potential for money laundering to occur. Auditors, therefore, consider the guidance in Practice Note 12 (Revised): "Money Laundering – Guidance for auditors in UK legislation".

Reporting

Auditors communicate their findings to the appropriate level of management, **133** unless the suspected or actual instance of non-compliance casts doubt on the integrity of the Board. In those cases where the Board is not involved in the day-to-day management of the Housing Association, having delegated this function to staff, and it is the latter who are suspected of involvement in the breach of law or regulations, the auditor may consider that it is appropriate to communicate with the Board in the first instance.

The Auditor's Right and Duty to Report to Regulators in the Financial Sector:
ISA (UK and Ireland) 250 Section B.

134   The auditor's right and duty to report to regulators of Housing Associations is set out in the section of this Practice Note entitled "The Regulation of Housing Associations" and summarised in Appendices 1 to 4.

135   There is a statutory duty for auditors of unincorporated charities in England and Wales to report suspected or actual instances of non-compliance with the law or regulations that are of material significance to the Charity Commission. Guidance on this topic, for auditors of unincorporated charitable Housing Associations, is given in the FRC's Practice Note 11: The Audit of Charities in the United Kingdom (March 2012).

136   Other than as described in paragraph 134, auditors of Housing Associations, which are not unincorporated charities, do not have a statutory duty to report suspected or actual instances of non-compliance with the law or regulations to an appropriate authority. ISA (UK and Ireland) 250, however, requires auditors of all entities to consider whether a suspected instance of non-compliance with law and regulations should be reported to the appropriate authority in the public interest. (For example, a failure to report a significant fraud or misappropriation of grant monies). The auditor may need to take legal advice before making a decision on whether a matter should be reported in the public interest.

137   In respect of Housing Associations the proper authority to which an auditor reports is ordinarily the relevant national regulatory body and, in any part of the United Kingdom, the Police.

Communication with Those Charged with Governance: ISA (UK and Ireland)
260.

> *Applicable Business Risk – Corporate governance and management*
> *structures challenged by lack of management representation on Boards*
> *and Board members having links with similar organisations.*

Those charged with the governance of a Housing Association typically include the   **138**
members (executive and non-executive) of the Board of a Housing Association
and the members of an audit committee where one exists.

They have responsibilities at least as onerous as those of full-time paid directors of   **139**
commercial enterprises in relation to the security of an Association's income,
assets and their proper application.

However, unlike many commercial organisations, Housing Associations often   **140**
have governance structures that do not include members of the executive team
(including the finance director) as members of the Board. Instead there are a
number of non-executive members who are collectively "those charged with
governance".

Auditors of Housing Associations, therefore, need to carefully consider how they   **141**
determine who "those charged with governance" are and establish an appropriate
communication process with both those individuals and members of the executive
team.

The objectives of the auditor in communicating with those charged with   **142**
governance are:

(a)   To communicate clearly with those charged with governance the
      responsibilities of the auditor in relation to the financial statement audit,
      and an overview of the planned scope and timing of the audit;

(b)   To obtain from those charged with governance information relevant to the
      audit;

(c)   To provide those charged with governance with timely observations arising
      from the audit that are significant and relevant to their responsibility to
      oversee the financial reporting process; and

(d)   To promote effective two-way communication between the auditor and
      those charged with governance.

The business risk that the governance of the Housing Association may be divided   **143**
between the Board and the executive management in a disconnected way gives
rise to a risk that the auditor of a Housing Association may not establish
appropriate two-way communication channels with the Board, the audit
committee (where there is one) and the members of the executive management
team. In such circumstances, effective two-way communication is unlikely to be
achieved when the auditor communicates with those charged with governance
solely by means of formal written reports. In such circumstances auditors seek to
attend audit committee and board meetings to discuss their reports and where
appropriate suggest that those charged with governance meet with the auditors
without the executive management team being present.

Identifying and Assessing the Risk of Material Misstatement Through Understanding of the Entity and its Environment: ISA (UK and Ireland) 315

Applicable Business Risks:

- Entering into increasingly complex and risky financing arrangements
- Diversifying into non-social housing activities
- Risks surrounding working in partnerships and joint ventures
- Increasing regulatory requirements for properties to be improved.
- Motivations for Housing Association management to present a biased financial picture

---

144   The auditor seeks to understand the overall structure, activities, finances and governance of the Housing Association. Areas the auditor consider include:

- The overall governance arrangements of the Housing Association which support the systems of internal control including the audit committee, risk management and internal audit arrangements.

- The main business activities of the Housing Association and any significant developments since the previous audit, for example new development activity, acquisitions or disposals and organic growth areas.

- Cross-subsidies between different business activities of the Housing Association.

- Component accounting and the need to determine useful economic lives for separate components of fixed assets.

- Policies on capitalisation of internal costs, interest incurred during development and the capital/revenue split of works to existing properties.

- The financing and funding structure which supports the Housing Association's activities and any significant internal or external developments which may impact on the Association.

- The framework for business planning, financial and performance management.

- The Annual Regulatory Assessment including published regulation plans and/or viability assessments. The nature of regulatory assessments varies between countries and details are set out in the Regulation of Housing Associations section of this Practice Note.

- Changes in accounting treatment of financial statement items following changes in accounting standards.[9]

145   Housing Associations may participate in complex projects such as schemes developed under the Private Finance Initiative (PFI). A Housing Association may, for example, undertake the renovation and management of properties or provide other services, such as residential care, over a defined period without having ownership of the properties. Auditors consider the accounting for such schemes in accordance with Application Note F "Private Finance Initiative and similar contracts" of FRS 5 "Reporting the Substance of Transactions".

---

[9] *In 2014, for example, the implementation of FRS 102 may give rise to significant changes in treatment of certain financial statement items.*

Accounting Policies

Accounting policies that are typically relevant to Housing Associations include: **146**

- Valuation of properties;
- Depreciation;
- Capitalisation of building costs (including component costs);
- Allocation of overhead costs; and
- Impairment.

Under FRS 15 "Tangible fixed assets" Housing Associations are required to   **147** depreciate their housing properties. As a result judgments need to be made on the useful economic lives of properties which depend on matters such as property type, method of construction and location. In addition, the depreciation to properties carried at a valuation, and the need to depreciate only the value of buildings (as distinct from the land on which they are situated) results in additional complexity. The complexity arises from splitting the property into its key components and determining the useful economic lives of these. Accounting for the grants given by Government for new social housing now needs to be split between the land, building structure and possibly components and impacts on the amount carried in the balance sheet.

Under the 2010 update of the SORP depreciation is required to be separately   **148** calculated on discrete components of housing. Roofs, windows and doors, kitchens and bathrooms are the most common components on which separate depreciation calculations are made. The adoption of component accounting/ depreciation requires assumptions and estimates to be made by Associations.

FRS 11 "Impairment of fixed assets and goodwill" requires that impairments   **149** resulting from a major reduction in the service potential of a property which might, for example, result from a reduction in demand in the local community, should be recognised in the Income and Expenditure Account. As a result judgments need to be made regarding the likely future service potential of the property.

Internal control

The responsibility for the establishment and proper operation of a system of   **150** internal control lies with the board of each Housing Association. Relevant factors for the auditor to consider when planning the work that will be performed on internal controls in the audit of Housing Associations, include:

- The expectation (in Scotland and Wales, the requirement) that the auditor's management letter will be passed on to the regulator.
- Any additional procedures that have been agreed with those charged with governance.

Auditors of Housing Associations that are Industrial and Provident Societies are   **151** required to state in the auditor's report if in their opinion the Housing Association has failed to maintain a satisfactory system of control over transactions. ISA (UK and Ireland) 700 requires the auditor to describe such responsibilities to report by exception in the auditor's report and to incorporate a suitable conclusion in respect of such matters[10]. An illustrative example of an Auditor's Report on a Housing Association Registered in England that is an Industrial and Provident Society is provided by example 28 in Bulletin 2010/2.

---

[10] *ISA (UK and Ireland) 700 paragraph 22.*

Materiality in Planning and Performing an Audit of Housing Associations:
ISA (UK and Ireland) 320

Applicable Business Risks:

- **Motivations for Housing Association managements to present a biased financial picture.**

---

152   The principles of assessing materiality in the audit of a housing association are the same as those applying to the audit of any other entity. In particular, the auditor's consideration of materiality is a matter of professional judgment, and is affected by the auditor's perception of the common information needs of users of the financial statements.

153   A percentage is often applied to a chosen benchmark as a starting point in determining materiality for the financial statements as a whole. Examples of benchmarks that may be appropriate include categories of reported income, (such as net income, total revenue and total expenses), or net asset value. Determining a percentage to be applied to the chosen benchmark involves professional judgment based on the circumstances of the Housing Association. There is a relationship between the percentage and the chosen benchmark such that, for example, a percentage applied to net income will normally be higher than a percentage applied to total revenue or net assets. In view of Housing Associations' social objectives and their inability to distribute surpluses, the most relevant bases for materiality are usually gross revenues or net assets.

154   A key difference of a Housing Association from many other entities is that balance sheet balances tend to be much larger compared to the income statement, so that the application of materiality based on income may be too low when auditing some aspects of elements of the balance sheet.

155   To deal with this, the auditor typically uses materiality based on the income statement if a misstatement in a balance sheet item could affect the income statement or accumulated surplus. If, however, a misstatement in a balance sheet item is likely only to lead to a reclassification between line items within assets and liabilities, a higher materiality level can be applied for identifying and evaluating such misstatements only. Although paragraph 10 of ISA (UK and Ireland) 320 indicates that there can only be one overall measure of materiality for the accounts as a whole, paragraph A15 of ISA (UK and Ireland) 450 states that there may be circumstances involving the evaluation of qualitative considerations where the auditor concludes that a classification misstatement is not material in the context of the financial statements as a whole when the amount of the misclassification is small in relation to the size of the related balance sheet items and the misclassification does not affect the income statement.

156   A feature of the business of Housing Associations is uncertainty relating to the ultimate collectability of rents. As a result, whilst quantitative measures of materiality are of assistance in directing the focus of the auditor's work, qualitative factors relating to the extent and nature of disclosures in the financial statements will also be of importance. Where such uncertainty is considered to be significant, Housing Association auditors consider the disclosures made in the financial statements, and the effect upon the auditor's report.

Materiality in the context of tables of housing stock

Financial statements of Housing Associations often include, in the notes to the financial statements, numerical tables of housing stock. Such notes report in numbers of units rather than in monetary amounts. Because such notes form part of the financial statements the auditor is required to audit them in accordance with auditing standards.   **157**

The auditor's evaluation of materiality with respect to such numerical notes would not be based on the quantitative thresholds determined for the financial statements. However, the auditor would be aware in determining how to evaluate the materiality for tables of housing stock that such tables are unlikely to be subject to estimation uncertainty.   **158**

Analytical Procedures: ISA (UK and Ireland) 520

> *Applicable Business Risks:*
> - **Decreasing receipts from Government housing benefit**

Analytical Procedures based on information available about the sector

159   The Housing Association Regulators publish extensive information and numerical data about Housing Associations[11]. The existence of such information and data can greatly assist auditors by providing an indication of trends and current ratios. In particular, consideration of such data will assist the auditor in developing expectations of plausible relationships among both financial and non-financial information.

160   Analytical procedures also encompass such investigation as is necessary of identified fluctuations or relationships that are inconsistent with other relevant information or that differ from expected values by a significant amount.

Analytical Procedures specific to a particular Housing Association

161   Because elements of the income and expenditure of a Housing Association, for example interest payable and rental income receivable are predictable, analytical procedures are suitable for use as substantive procedures.

162   In respect of rental income, for example, the auditor may perform analytical procedures with respect to:

- The relationship between the number of housing units available for occupation, the incidence of empty units (sometimes referred to as voids) and rents receivable;

- Movements, and any unexpected or unusual relationships, between current and prior year budgets for rents received or service charges;

- Movements, and unexpected or unusual relationships, between current year, prior year and budget for voids and bad debts as a percentage of rents; and

- Rents and service charges for each month.

163   Analytical procedures with respect to interest expense might typically include:

- Predicting interest expense for the period by category of borrowing by multiplying the average principal amounts outstanding during the period by the expected average interest rates. At the year-end differences from expectations are investigated; and

- At the year-end calculating average effective interest rates for the period by category of borrowing or by type of debt instrument by dividing recorded interest expense by the average principal amounts outstanding during the period. The actual interest rates so determined are compared to expected interest rates based on debt agreements. Significant differences are investigated.

---

[11] *Examples of such information are described in Appendices 1 to 4.*

Auditing Accounting Estimates, Including Fair Value Accounting Estimates,
and Related Disclosures: ISA (UK and Ireland) 540

Applicable Business Risks:

- **Housing Associations entering into increasingly complex and risky financing arrangements.**
- **Motivations for Housing Association managements to present a biased financial picture.**
- **Inability to fund pension liabilities**

Housing Associations need to make a number of accounting estimates when   **164**
preparing their financial statements. The main areas where estimates are likely to
be required in connection with the core business relate to:

(a)   Fair value of housing properties;

(b)   Depreciation of housing properties and separate components of fixed assets.
Key to the making of these estimates is the determination of their estimated
useful economic life;

(c)   The level of bad and doubtful debt provisions against tenant rent arrears;

(d)   Impairment provisions, including situations where existing use valuations
are below net cost but the Housing Association assesses the net realisable
value of the property, after deducting any grants that would need to be repaid
or recycled, to be higher than net cost. Further judgments may be required in
order to determine whether an alternative measure of service potential may
be more appropriate where assets are held for social purposes;

(e)   Pension liabilities (see paragraphs 115 to 118);

(f)   Overhead allocation especially between different segments of the business;
and

(g)   Assets and liabilities associated with financing arrangements.

Fair value of housing properties

For Housing Associations, the fair value measurements and disclosures in the   **165**
financial statements are derived using the methodologies outlined in the SORP.
The auditor assesses:

- The suitability of the valuer selected by the Housing Association to perform
the valuation; and

- The reasonableness of the assumptions used.

In practice, there are a relatively small number of valuers who regularly provide   **166**
this service within the sector as the skills required to perform valuations of social
housing property are quite distinct from those required to perform more generic
residential property valuations.

An assumption that has particular significance for social housing valuations is the   **167**
discount rate used. The auditor, therefore, considers whether the discount rate used
is reasonable.

Depreciation of housing properties

168 Depreciation charges may be difficult to assess where the useful economic lives of properties are lengthy. In assessing the economic lives of properties the auditor takes into account any special factors affecting the housing stock of the particular Housing Association, such as type of house, location and method of construction. Where no particular special factors have been identified, the auditor may decide to assess the reasonableness of the lives adopted by the Housing Association by comparing them with those prevalent in the sector. If the Housing Association's lives are out of line with lives generally used in the sector the auditor establishes the reasons for the variance and considers whether the reasons are plausible.

Bad and doubtful debt provisions

169 When evaluating whether adequate provision has been made for bad and doubtful debts, an effective approach is likely to involve consideration of applicable ratios and trends together with an evaluation of the effectiveness of the housing management system. Analytical procedures are likely to be an effective technique because of the high volume of relatively small amounts due to a Housing Association. When reliance is placed on analytical procedures the auditor considers whether past ratios and trends continue to be applicable in current economic circumstances. The coming into force of the Welfare Reform Act, which is discussed in paragraphs 103-106, is expected to adversely affect the cash flows of Housing Associations. The use of ratios and trends relating to the period prior to the legislative change may not be relevant following the change. As noted in paragraph 106 the auditor may be able to obtain audit evidence about the adequacy of bad and doubtful debt provisions by evaluating the stress testing of its business model against these changes, that the Housing Association has undertaken.

Impairment provisions

170 The SORP includes a lengthy commentary on impairment judgments for Housing Associations. In particular, it observes that financial matters may not be the only aspects to consider in assessing whether a social housing property is impaired and similarly a social housing property may not be impaired even when its financial value and value in use are both below its net carrying value. This is based on the premise that an intentional shortfall in value is not an impairment provided the social benefit is being delivered. The auditor, therefore, may need to consider the audit evidence supporting impairment judgments with particular care.[12]

Overhead allocation

171 Many Housing Associations undertake a number of diverse activities and the allocation of central overheads between such activities can be an important determinant as to whether such activities appear to be profitable or loss making. Management may be incentivised to bias the allocation of overheads to hide the true financial status of an activity or subsidiary.

172 On a consolidated basis, and assuming there is no intention to dispose of any activities or subsidiaries, inappropriate allocation of overhead may not, of itself, give rise to a misleading outcome in the financial statements. However, when an activity or subsidiary is disposed of the consequences of inappropriate overhead allocation may be to render the retained activities (which may have been considered profitable) as being unprofitable. It is important, therefore, that overhead allocation is based on objective criteria.

---

[12] *As noted in paragraph 20 the SORP is likely to be revised in 2014. This revision is likely to have a significant effect on the guidance that is provided with respect to impairment provisions.*

Assets and liabilities associated with financing arrangements

Arising from their traditional funding sources being less willing to advance funds, **173** some Housing Associations have been entering into more sophisticated financing arrangements such as looking to the wholesale bond markets to satisfy their financing needs and entering into interest rate swaps.

The auditor evaluates whether the Association's treasury function operates within **174** an appropriate framework of defined Board approved policies and procedures including establishing permissible funding and hedging instruments, exposure limits and a system of authorities for approval and execution of transactions.

Where applicable, the valuation techniques used to value or disclose such **175** derivative financial instruments may be complex and rely heavily on accounting estimates made by the Housing Association itself, usually with the advice of external advisors.

Related Parties: ISA (UK and Ireland) 550

Applicable Business Risk:

- **Corporate governance and management structures challenged by lack of management representation on Boards and Board members having links with similar organisations**

---

176   Members of the Board of a Housing Association often have links with other Housing Associations or similar organisations. Consequently the audit of related parties and related party transactions can be particularly challenging to auditors.

177   The management of some Housing Associations maintain registers (or other forms of records) of related parties and may require Board members to declare related party transactions at each meeting including describing the nature of the transactions. Such registers and Board minutes are likely to provide audit evidence with respect to the existence of related parties and the occurrence of related party transactions.

Going Concern: ISA (UK and Ireland) 570

Applicable Business Risks:

- **Entering into increasingly complex and risky financing arrangements**
- **Motivations for Housing Association managements to present a biased financial picture**
- **Decreasing receipts from Government housing benefit creating a greater risk of bad debts and property voids**
- **Increasing regulatory requirements for properties to be improved**
- **Inability to fund pension liabilities**

Periodic regulatory viability assessments

178   The various national regulators make periodic regulatory viability assessments of individual Housing Associations and publish the findings of these assessments on their respective web-sites. The details of the various national regulatory approaches to viability assessments are summarised in "The Regulation of Housing Associations" section of this Practice Note (paragraphs 27 to 87). The latest viability assessment published by the regulator on a particular Housing Association is likely to be the logical starting point of the auditor's consideration of going concern.

Responsibility of the Board

179   The Board of a Housing Association is responsible for assessing the ability of the Housing Association to continue as a going concern. The Board's assessment should be documented and rigorous in nature. The Board's process supporting its assessment should be proportionate in nature and depth depending upon the size, level of financial risk and complexity of the Housing Association and its operations.

In assessing going concern, the Board considers the extent to which there may be **180** adverse variations from expected funding or revenue, or additional unexpected costs, and any uncertainties as to whether or not the Housing Association can continue in operational existence for the foreseeable future.

Auditor's responsibility

Although the regulator's viability assessment and directors' going concern **181** assessment may be helpful to the auditor, the auditor is still required to meet the requirements of ISA (UK and Ireland) 570. In particular, the auditor has to determine whether there are any material uncertainties that may cast significant doubt on the Housing Association's ability to continue as a going concern.

In applying ISA (UK and Ireland) 570 to Housing Associations, auditors consider **182** the circumstances in which Housing Associations may cease to continue in operational existence. Growing Housing Associations may have particular going concern risks arising from any necessity they may have to finance housing developments which may have short term negative cash flows. This issue requires an understanding of

(a)   Commitments and future development intentions;

(b)   The availability of finance through loan facilities etc;

(c)   The amount of available security to underpin a necessary loan facility;

(d)   The ability to repay the loans, which normally means consideration of a long term financial plan; and

(e)   Covenant compliance.

Useful information concerning the assessment of going concern in the current **183** period may be derived from considering the assessment made in the previous period in relation to the actual out-turn.

Some of the particular factors which may indicate a potential going concern **184** problem at a Housing Association are:

(a)   Threatened or actual regulatory intervention by the regulatory body;

(b)   For a transferee Housing Association, transfers of housing stock where the acquisition cost or carrying value is not covered by the long-term projected net rental income;

(c)   Onerous contractual terms; this may be particularly relevant where the Housing Association has entered into Public Finance Initiative or Public Private Partnership contracts which may transfer significant risk to the Housing Association;

(d)   Inability to service interest payments;

(e)   Contracts under "supporting people", joint ventures or outsourcing agreements becoming unsustainable;

(f)   A significant amount of variable interest rate borrowings at a time when interest rates are predicted to rise. From 2008 until the time of writing interest rates were very low and Housing Associations with variable interest rate borrowings would become vulnerable in the event that interest rates increased;

(g)   A significant short-term repair obligation that the Housing Association will have difficulty in meeting from its own resources. Such an obligation might arise from government policy such as the "decent homes for all" policy;

(h)   A fundamental decrease in demand to rent the Housing Association's properties, leading to significant void rates and a substantial fall in income;

(i)   An increase in bad debts because tenant housing benefit is no longer paid directly to the Housing Association (see paragraphs 103 to 106);

(j)   Loan repayments or refinancing (for example balloon payments) which cannot be met from the Housing Association's own resources;

(k)   A deteriorating funding position of its pension scheme (see paragraphs 115 to 118);

(l)   Breaches of loan covenants; and

(m)   Significant loans or guarantees provided to subsidiaries involved in activities such as shared ownership or developments for sale in a housing market where sales prices are falling.

185   Historically, Housing Associations acquired properties with the assistance of grants or long term financing. This method of financing typically led to predictable cash flows in that loan repayments could be predicted and, the Housing Association was able to plan to meet its obligations from available resources.

186   As discussed in paragraphs 92 to 94 the availability of long term bank financing has been reducing and its cost increasing. Consequently, some Housing Associations have been raising funds through the issuance of bonds which may be quite complex financial instruments. It is particularly important that the funding (cash flow) complexities of such financial instruments are fully understood by the Housing Association management and the auditor.

187   Housing Associations have a relatively long business cycle and, in preparing its financial forecasts, the board may consider a longer period of time than for entities with a shorter business cycle. Indeed regulatory viability assessments frequently call for cash flow forecasts 30 years into the future.

188   If there are any indications that a particular source of funds or revenue may need to be renewed or renegotiated, the auditor considers requesting the Housing Association to contact the source of such funds for confirmation that the facility, or grant, will continue to be made available to the Housing Association. Where there continues to be uncertainty, it may be necessary for the Board to disclose the circumstances in the financial statements and for the auditor to draw attention to the matter in an emphasis of matter paragraph in the auditor's report.

Appendix 1 – Overview of the regulation of English housing associations

SUBJECT	ENGLAND	PARAS
Regulator	The Homes and Communities Agency (HCA) http://www.homesandcommunities.co.uk/	
Governing Legislation	• Housing and Regeneration Act 2008 • The Localism Act 2011	
Regulatory Framework	• The Regulatory Framework for Social Housing in England from April 2012. See also the publication "Regulating the Standards". • The HCA's regulatory responsibility is discharged through a Regulation Committee. It publishes a Regulatory Committee Protocol.	
Regulatory accounting requirements	• Accounting Direction for Social Housing in England from April 2012 • SORP 2010	
Regulatory viability judgments	Regulatory Governance and Viability Assessments. These can be accessed via a web page on the Homes and Communities Agency web-site.	35 to 44
Auditor's right to report to HCA	Section 143 of the Housing and Regeneration Act 2008	32
Auditor's duty to report to HCA	• Section 210 of the Housing and Regeneration Act 2008 in relation to an inquiry being held by the HCA. • Sections 107 and 108 of the Housing and Regeneration Act 2008	
Auditor's routine periodic reporting to HCA	No requirements	
Auditor's reporting on internal control	No requirements	
Periodic reports by Housing Association to HCA	There are no specific requirements but a general power on the collection of information and documents in sections 107 and 108 of the Housing and Regeneration Act 2008. This may include information produced by providers for public reporting or for internal management purposes.	
Useful information/data published by HCA	• Register of Social Housing Providers • Sector Risk Profile • Global accounts of housing providers • Quarterly Survey of Private Registered Providers	

Appendix 2 – Overview of the regulation of Northern Ireland housing associations

SUBJECT	NORTHERN IRELAND	PARAS
Regulator	Department for Social Development's Housing Division (DSD) http://www.dsdni.gov.uk/index/hsdiv-housing-link	
Governing Legislation	• Industrial and Provident Societies Act (Northern Ireland) 1969 • The Housing (Northern Ireland) Order 1992 • The Housing (Amendment) (Northern Ireland) Order 2006	
Regulatory Framework	Housing Association Guide • Development Guide • Finance Guide • Governance Guide • Housing Management Guide • Procurement	52-53
Regulatory accounting requirements	• The Registered Housing Associations (Accounting Requirements) Order Northern Ireland 1993 • SORP 2010	
Regulatory viability judgments	Inspection Reports on Housing Associations. These can be accessed via the Department of Social Developments website www.dsdni.gov.uk/index/hsdiv-housing/registered_housing_associations/housingrha_inspection_programme/rha_inspection_reports.htm	52-58
Auditor's right to report to DSD	No rights specified in law or regulation	49
Auditor's duty to report to DSD	Articles 23 and 24 of the Housing (Northern Ireland) Order 1992	50-51
Auditor's routine periodic reporting to DSD	No requirements	

Auditor's reporting on internal control	• Board is required to carry out an annual review of their system of internal control and a statement relating to this review is to be included in the audited financial statements • No direct requirements but Housing Association required to provide auditor's management letter to Regulator. Also ISA (UK and Ireland) 720 applies to the statement included in the audited financial statements.
Periodic reports by Housing Association to DSD	• Annual Report and Accounts • Annual Regulatory Return (ARR) • Board Minutes • Quarterly Accounts • Auditor's report and management letter
Useful information/ data published by DSD or Housing Association	• Performance Indicators • Consultations • Social Housing Development Register • Inspection Team Summary Reports • Housing Association Contact Details

Appendix 3 – Overview of the regulation of Scottish housing associations

SUBJECT	SCOTLAND	PARAS
Regulator	Scottish Housing Regulator (SHR) http://www.scottishhousingregulator.gov.uk/	59-60
Governing Legislation	Housing (Scotland) Act 2010	
Regulatory Framework	Regulation of Social Housing in Scotland – Our Framework	61-66
Regulatory accounting requirements	• The Determination of Accounting Requirements 2012 • SORP 2010 • Financial Statements should make clear disclosures and document a thorough assessment of whether the RSL is a going concern. (Going concern issues are notifiable events)	
Regulatory viability judgments	• Annual information requirements on financial viability • Publish annual Regulation Plans for those RSLs with High or Medium Engagement. • List of Low Engagement RSL's published. • Procurement	70-77
Auditor's right to report to SHR	An auditor of an RSL may disclose information to SHR.	67
Auditor's duty to report to SHR	Section 72 of the Housing Scotland Act	68-69
Auditor's routine periodic reporting to SHR	No requirements	
Auditor's reporting on internal control	No direct requirements but Housing Association required to provide auditor's management letter and the Board's response to that letter to the SHR.	
Periodic reports by Housing Association to SHR	• Five Year Financial Projections • Annual accounts • Auditor's Management Letter • Loan Portfolio Information • Annual Performance and Statistical Return	

| Useful information/ data published by SHR or Housing Association | • Register of Social Landlords
• Benchmarking Tables
• Financial Tables
• Performance Tables
• Regulatory Guidance
• Regulatory Recommended Practice
• Regulatory Advisory Notes
• Regulatory Analysis Reports
• Regulation Plans for specific RSLs | |

Appendix 4 – Overview of the regulation of Welsh housing associations

SUBJECT	WALES	PARAS
Regulator	Welsh Government's Housing Division (WGHD) http://wales.gov.uk/topics/housingandcommunity/housing/?lang=en	78
Governing Legislation	• Housing Associations Act 1985 • Part 1 of the Housing Act 1996 • Housing (Wales) Measure 2011	
Regulatory Framework	Regulatory Framework for Housing Associations Registered in Wales. Annual Regulatory Assessment • The assessment is required to be published on the HA's web-site.	79-82
Regulatory accounting requirements	• SORP 2010	
Regulatory viability judgments	Financial Viability Judgment Required to be published on HA's web-site	85-87
Auditor's right to report to WGHD	No rights specified in law or regulation	
Auditor's duty to report to WGHD	No requirements specified in law or regulation	
Auditor's routine periodic reporting to WGHD	No requirements	
Auditor's reporting on internal control	No direct requirements but Housing Association required to provide auditor's management letter to Housing Division	
Periodic reports by Housing Association to WGHD	• 30 year financial forecasts • Annual data including audited accounts and auditor's management letter. • Loan portfolio information • Half yearly management accounts	
Useful information/data published by WGHD or Housing Association	• Review of 30 year Financial Forecasts of Housing Associations • Self-assessments on governance and finance for each HA to be published	

Appendix 5 – Useful websites

Regulators	
The Homes and Communities Agency (England)	http://www.homesandcommunities.co.uk
Department for Social Development's Housing Division (Northern Ireland)	http://www.dsdni.gov.uk/index/hsdiv-housing-link
Scottish Housing Regulator	http://www.scottishhousingregulator.gov.uk
Welsh Government's Housing Division	http://wales.gov.uk/topics/housingandcommunity/housing/? lang = en http://wales.gov.uk/topics/housingandcommunity/housing/? skip = 1 < = cy (Welsh)
Trade Body	
National Housing Federation	http://www.housing.org.uk
Publications	
Inside Housing	http://www.insidehousing.co.uk
24dash	http://www.24dash.com
Social Housing Magazine	http://www.socialhousing.co.uk

Details of the above websites are provided for the benefit of users of this Practice Note. However, the Financial Reporting Council does not necessarily endorse the content of these websites.

Practice Note 15 (PN 15) (Revised): The audit of occupational pension schemes in the United Kingdom (November 2017)

(November 2017)

Contents

Paragraphs

Introduction   1

ISA (UK) 200: Overall objectives of the independent auditor and the
conduct of an audit in accordance with international standards on auditing (UK)   63 - 66

ISA (UK) 210: Agreeing the terms of audit engagements   67 - 87

ISA (UK) 240: The auditor's responsibilities relating to fraud in an
audit of financial statements   88 - 97

ISA (UK) 250: Section A – Consideration of laws and regulations in an
audit of financial statements   98 - 106

ISA (UK) 260: Communication with those charged with governance   107 - 109

ISA (UK) 265: Communicating deficiencies in internal control to
those charged with governance and management   110 - 113

ISA (UK) 300: Planning an audit of financial statements   114 - 119

ISA (UK) 315: Identifying and assessing the risks of material
Misstatement through Understanding the entity and its environment   120 - 131

ISA (UK) 320: Materiality in planning and performing an audit   132 - 137

ISA (UK) 402: Audit considerations relating to an entity using a
service organisation   138 - 151

ISA (UK) 500: Audit evidence   152 - 154

ISA (UK) 520: Analytical procedures   155 - 157

ISA (UK) 540: Auditing accounting estimates, including fair value
accounting estimates, and related disclosures   158 - 172

ISA (UK) 550: Related parties   173 - 180

ISA (UK) 570: Going concern   181 - 191

ISA (UK) 580: Written representations   192 - 195

ISA (UK) 620: Using the work of an auditor's expert   196 - 199

ISA (UK) 700: Forming an opinion and reporting on financial statements   200 - 212

ISA (UK) 720: The auditor's responsibilities relating to other information   213 - 217

The auditor's statement about contributions (the statement)   218 - 256

Liaison with the scheme actuary   257 - 261

Reporting matters of material significance to the pensions regulator   262 - 289

Appendix 1: Illustrative examples of appointment and resignation letters

Appendix 2: Illustrative extracts from example of representation letter

Appendix 3: Illustrative examples of auditor's statements about contributions

Appendix 4: Illustrative statement of trustees' responsibilities

Appendix 5: Definitions

Preface

This Practice Note contains guidance on the application of auditing standards issued by the Financial Reporting Council (FRC) to the statutory audit of trust based occupational pension schemes established under the Pensions Acts in the United Kingdom. This guidance is also applicable to audits undertaken solely under the terms of a scheme's trust deed or other agreement requiring an auditor to provide a similar report, including requests from trustees where the scheme is otherwise exempt from audit or for financial statements prepared other than at the normal scheme year-end. Similar considerations apply to the audits of Common Investment Funds ("CIFs") which are usually set up under trust and require an audit under their trust deed.

Much of the guidance will also be of assistance to auditors of public sector pension schemes, although these schemes are subject to different financial reporting frameworks and different legislation.

This Practice Note is intended to assist auditors in applying the requirements of, and should be read in conjunction with, International Standards on Auditing (ISAs) (UK), which apply to all audits undertaken in the United Kingdom in respect of accounting periods commencing on or after 17 June 2016. This Practice Note sets out the special considerations relating to the audit of occupational pension schemes which arise from the individual ISAs (UK). **This Practice Note does not and is not intended to provide detailed guidance on the audits of occupational pension schemes, so where no special considerations arise from a particular ISA (UK), no material is included. This Practice Note does not contain commentary on all of the requirements included in the ISAs (UK) and reading it should not be seen as an alternative to reading the relevant ISAs (UK) in their entirety.**

This Practice Note has been prepared with advice and assistance from staff of The Pensions Regulator (TPR) and is based on the legislation and regulations in effect at 1 November 2017.

Introduction

Work-based pensions in the UK may be divided into two main types: contract based personal pension schemes and occupational trust based pension schemes.   **1**

Contract based personal pension schemes are individual arrangements made by individuals with the pension provider and need not have a link with an employer. These arrangements are subject to different legislation from trust based occupational pension schemes and generally are not subject to the pension scheme audit regime. These arrangements are open to all individuals whether or not they also contribute to an occupational pension scheme. They may accept contributions from the employer as well as the employee. Some employers set up group personal pension schemes, which are arrangements for the employees of a particular employer to participate in a personal pension scheme on a grouped basis.   **2**

Occupational trust based pension schemes are those run by employers for the benefit of their employees and, from an employee viewpoint must have a sponsoring employer(s) and are linked with employment. On leaving the service of the employer, active membership ceases, though the employee may leave the benefits accrued to date in the scheme. Most occupational pension schemes in the UK are required to produce annual financial statements and to   **3** appoint a scheme auditor to report on those financial statements and on the payment of contributions to the scheme. There are some exemptions from these requirements although where statutory provisions do not require an audit, a scheme's trust deed and rules may still require its financial statements to be audited.

4   Audits of occupational pension schemes may only be carried out by a registered auditor eligible for appointment as a statutory auditor under Part 42 of the Companies Act 2006 or other person approved by the Secretary of State for Work and Pensions. A registered auditor is required to comply with ISAs (UK) when conducting audits. This principle applies in the context of occupational pension schemes in the same way as to entities in any sector, irrespective of their size, but the way in which ISAs (UK) are applied needs to be adapted to suit the particular characteristics of the entity audited.

Occupational pension schemes – key characteristics

Benefit structures

5   Occupational pension schemes have two main types of benefit structure:

- defined benefit – normally a final salary or career average arrangement. Final salary benefits are calculated by reference to the member's pensionable earnings usually for a period ending at or before normal pension date or leaving service and on pensionable service. Career average benefits are calculated for each year of service based on pensionable earnings for that year. Because of the uncertainties in determining the extent of future liabilities of such schemes, the trustees of such schemes are required to obtain regular actuarial assessments of the schemes' liabilities and estimated future costs; and

- defined contribution (or money purchase) – a pension scheme where the individual member's benefit is determined by reference to contributions paid into the scheme in respect of that member, increased or decreased by an amount reflecting the investment return on those contributions. Because the scheme's commitment to pay future pensions is determined by the extent of funds available, no actuarial valuation is normally required.

6   An occupational pension scheme can have both defined benefit and defined contribution sections, or its benefits may be calculated as the better of two alternatives on a defined benefit and a defined contribution basis. These types of scheme are generally both referred to as hybrid schemes.

Sponsoring, principal, participating and associated employers

7   Most occupational schemes in the UK are established by an employer for their employees. Where this is the case the employer is often referred to as the principal or sponsoring employer and has certain specified responsibilities set out under the scheme documentation. Where the employees of employers other than the sponsoring employer are allowed to be members of the pension scheme these other employers are referred to as participating employers. Associated employers are participating employers who are under common control.

Master trusts

8   Some occupational schemes in the UK are set up as master trusts. Under these arrangements the master trust is typically established by a *founder* and is open,

normally by invitation, to non-associated participating employers and their employees. The Pensions Schemes Act 2017[1] defines a Master Trust as "an occupational pension scheme which:

(a)   provides money purchase benefits (whether alone or in conjunction with other benefits);

(b)   is used, or intended to be used, by two or more employers;

(c)   is not used, or intended to be used, only by employers which are connected with each other; and

(d)   is not a relevant public service pension scheme."

Governance and operational structures

Occupational pension schemes are usually established under trust as a separate legal entity from the employer. The main activities of an occupational pension scheme typically comprise the collection of contributions from the employer and members, the investment of those contributions and the payment of benefits to retiring or leaving members. **9**

The trust is governed by trustees. They may be individual trustees or a corporate trustee with trustee directors. Trustees of occupational pension schemes – who do not necessarily have first-hand actuarial, accounting or other relevant experience – frequently rely on advice or services from experts in order to fulfil their responsibilities to safeguard the interests of scheme members. The Pensions Act 1995 (PA 95) also requires trustees to appoint professional advisers in certain areas (for example, the scheme auditor, scheme actuary and investment managers). Law and regulations applicable to professional advisers includes provisions relating to their appointment and removal or resignation, and also establish a duty to report breaches of the law to The Pensions Regulator (see paragraph 32). **10**

Trustees will normally be supported by scheme management in governing the scheme. The sponsoring employer may provide trustee management and support services or they may be provided by third party providers, or in the case of master trusts, typically by the founder. **11**

The employer will typically be responsible for the collection of contributions from members and remittance of member and employer contributions to a pension scheme. The trustees make arrangements for the receipt of pension contributions by the scheme administrator from the employer. **12**

The scheme administrator will normally receive member and employer contributions, maintain member records and calculate and pay benefits on behalf of the trustees. Trustees of pension schemes may delegate aspects of administration (although not ultimate responsibility) to a third party, possibly the sponsoring employer. **13**

Trustees will normally appoint third party investment managers to undertake the management of the funds available for investment but the trustees retain ultimate responsibility for the proper use of the scheme's funds. The investment policy is set out in the trustees' Statement of Investment Principles. If the scheme invests in direct securities the trustees will also normally appoint a third-party custodian to hold the scheme investments on behalf of the trustees. **14**

---

[1] *The PSA 2017 provides for an authorisation and supervision regime for master trusts to be introduced, so that master trusts would have to demonstrate to The Pensions Regulator that they meet certain key criteria on establishment, and then continue to do so.*

15   When trustees have appointed third party service organisations to undertake work on their behalf, including the employer, the scheme auditor considers the system of controls operated by the trustees over the service organisations (refer to ISA (UK) 402 for further guidance).

16   The Occupational Pension Schemes (Scheme Administration) Regulations 1996 No. 1715 ("the Administration Regulations") require sponsoring employers (and former sponsoring employers), their auditor or actuary to provide trustees with "such information as is reasonably required" for the trustees' professional advisers, including the scheme auditor, to carry out their duties. Trustees must provide similar information to their professional advisers and also make the scheme's books, accounts and records available.

Scheme actuary

17   For the majority of defined benefit schemes, trustees are specifically required by statute to appoint a scheme actuary to provide them with necessary valuations and advice. Further commentary concerning liaison with the scheme actuary is set out in a separate section of this Practice Note (see paragraphs 257 to 261).

18   Trustees or managers of defined contribution schemes are not required by statute to appoint a scheme actuary, although they may take actuarial advice to assess the potential level of benefits available and/or the potential level of contributions required to fund a particular level of benefits.

Legislative and regulatory framework

19   Occupational pension schemes operate within a complex framework involving both trust law and specific statutory provisions, set out primarily in Pension Schemes Act 1993 (PSA 1993), PA 1995 and Pensions Act 2004 (PA 2004) and The Occupational Pension Schemes (Requirement to obtain Audited Accounts and a Statement from the Auditor) Regulations 1996 No.1975 (the "Audited Accounts Regulations") made under those Acts. To the extent necessary to carry out their audits, it is essential for auditors of occupational pension schemes to have a good understanding of current pensions legislation and associated regulations. In addition, the activities of occupational pension schemes are subject to HM Revenue & Customs (HMRC) regulations and financial services legislation. Scheme auditors need to be aware of the accounting and auditing implications of these requirements.

Auditor eligibility

20   The specific requirements for eligibility and ineligibility as scheme auditor are set out in Regulation 4 to the Occupational Pension Schemes (Scheme Administration) Regulations 1996. Audits of occupational pension schemes may only be carried out by a registered auditor eligible for appointment as a statutory auditor under the Part 42 of the Companies Act 2006 or other person approved by the Secretary of State for Work and Pensions.

21   The auditor appointment is that of a firm (or a sole practitioner) and not an individual. No director, partner or employee of the audit firm may act as trustee of a scheme that is an audit client of the firm. Furthermore, a person cannot be appointed as auditor where:

●   that person is a member of the scheme;

●   that person is employed under contract of service by the trustees or managers of the scheme; or

- that person is an employer in relation to the scheme.

In addition, a firm cannot audit a pension scheme if an audit partner of that firm is a director of a participating employer. However, this ineligibility rule does not apply in relation to a scheme which had at least 500 participating employers on the first day of its accounting period.   **22**

Any scheme auditor who acts as trustee of a scheme they audit is guilty of an offence.   **23**

Trust law and trustees

Occupational pension schemes constituted under trusts are subject to trust law. A trust is usually established by a legal document, the trust deed, which places the responsibility for the stewardship and custody of the assets on the trustees. The trustees are required to comply with the general requirements of the trust, the general law and legislation which almost entirely applies to pension scheme trusts, such as PSA 1993, PA 1995 and PA 2004 and related Regulations, some of whose provisions override those of the trust.   **24**

The general duties and powers of pension scheme trustees are essentially the same as those of other trustees. The principal elements of their responsibilities under trust law and statute are the proper management of funds provided by employees and their sponsoring employers during the course of their employment so as to provide pension benefits and, subsequently, the payment of these benefits to those entitled to them.   **25**

Trustees must act in the best interests of beneficiaries of the scheme, and ensure that no one who is not entitled receives any trust property. Where a trustee is also a director or employee of the sponsoring employer, he or she should set aside any other concerns, duties or responsibilities when acting in the capacity as a trustee.   **26**

There is a legal obligation for trustees not to delegate the performance of their duties and powers, however this is qualified in that trustees may be permitted to delegate matters either under statute or, if specifically authorised to do so, under the terms of their trust. As statutory provisions are limited, many trust deeds include wide powers of delegation. Permission to delegate does not release trustees from responsibility. Given they are fiduciaries, trustees must take due care in selecting the delegate, in determining suitable guidelines for the performance of the matter delegated, and in monitoring the delegate's actual performance and compliance with the guidelines set.   **27**

Sections 241 to 243 of PA 2004 require schemes to make arrangements that provide for at least one third of trustees in an occupational pension scheme to be member nominated. If the trustee is a company, the arrangements must provide for at least one third of the directors to be member nominated. Schemes have to go through this process to appoint one third but could have less if there are insufficient nominations. TPR's Code of Practice 08 provides guidance for trustees in this area, including the expected frequency for re-running a nomination process to refill vacancies.   **28**

Master trusts must have at least three trustees. The majority of the trustees, including the chair of the trustees, must be *non-affiliated* i.e. must be independent of any undertaking which provides advisory, administration, investment or other resources to the master trust. Where there is a chair of the trustees at the time any other trustee is appointed, the chair must be consulted on the appointment. Refer to the Administration Regulations for further details.   **29**

30   A trustee may be removed by court order for misconduct or mismanagement. In accordance with the Pensions Act 1995, as amended, The Pensions Regulator (TPR) (see below) may prohibit a person from being a trustee of a particular trust scheme, a particular class of trust schemes or trust schemes in general. TPR may also suspend a trustee pending consideration being given to a prohibition order. Where TPR prohibits a trustee, TPR may appoint a replacement. TPR may also appoint a trustee where they are satisfied that this is reasonable in order to enable the trustees as a whole to have, or to exercise, the necessary knowledge and skill for the proper administration of the scheme, for the number of trustees to be sufficient for the proper administration of the scheme or otherwise to protect the interests of the generality of scheme members.

The Pensions Regulator

31   TPR is the body responsible for the regulation of work-based occupational pension schemes and is able to make use of a wide range of statutory powers. Codes of Practice and other TPR guidance are relevant to auditors of occupational pension schemes and can be found on TPR's website at www.thepensionsregulator.gov.uk.

32   A scheme auditor is required by section 70 of PA 2004 to consider reporting directly to TPR breaches of law which affect the pension scheme. The decision to report will depend whether there is reasonable cause to believe there has been a breach of the law and, if so, whether the breach is likely to be of "material significance" to TPR (see paragraphs 265 to 274). The scheme auditor is not required to put into place arrangements to detect matters to be reported under section 70 as the auditor's obligation is limited to reporting those which come to its attention. Further guidance for scheme auditors on reporting is given in TPR's Code of Practice 01 "Reporting breaches of the law".

33   The statutory duty to report matters of material significance to TPR applies to the scheme actuary, the trustees and all others who are involved in the administration of a scheme, as well as to the scheme auditor.

The Pension Protection Fund

34   The Pension Protection Fund (PPF) was established to pay compensation to members of eligible defined benefit pension schemes, when there is a qualifying insolvency event in relation to the employer and where there are insufficient assets in the pension scheme to cover Pension Protection Fund levels of compensation.

35   The PPF is a statutory fund run by the Board of the PPF, a statutory corporation established under the provisions of the Pensions Act 2004. Further information on the PPF is available on its website (www.pensionprotectionfund.org.uk).

36   When a pension scheme enters a PPF assessment period the trustees continue to govern the scheme and the statutory obligation to obtain audited financial statements remains. This applies through to the point that a scheme is admitted to the PPF.

Tax status

37   All schemes need to register with HMRC to become Registered Pension Schemes and therefore receive certain tax reliefs. However, Registered Pension Schemes remain subject to some taxes, including VAT and withholding taxes. Limitations on untaxed pension scheme benefits include:

- a maximum annual tax allowable contribution or inflow of value into a member's pension fund which is known as the *Annual Allowance*;

- a maximum lifetime fund limit that can be accumulated which is known as the *Lifetime Allowance*;

- a minimum age at which retirement benefits can be taken;

- penalties apply where registered pension schemes make "unauthorised" payments (those that do not meet the conditions specified in the tax rules[2]). If a pension scheme continually makes unauthorised payments it may be deregistered; and

- where benefits exceed tax free limits, tax is payable.

Details of the lifetime allowances and annual allowances and other limitations in place currently are available at the HMRC website (www.hmrc.gov.uk).   **38**

Scheme funding and actuarial matters for defined benefit schemes

PA 2004 sets out the framework for the legislation relating to the role of the actuary in relation to defined benefit schemes. Section 224, PA 2004 and the Occupational Pension Schemes (Scheme Funding) Regulations (SI 2005/3377), hereafter referred to as the Funding Regulations, require ongoing actuarial valuations to be undertaken normally every three years. The Funding Regulations specify the way in which the assets and liabilities of the scheme are to be determined, calculated and verified by the actuary. Asset values are to be those stated in the latest available audited financial statements.   **39**

PA 2004 and the Funding Regulations require the preparation of a schedule of contributions within 15 months after the effective date of an actuarial valuation showing: **40**

- separately the rates of contributions payable towards the scheme by or on behalf of the employer and the active members of the scheme; and

- the dates on or before which the contributions must be paid. Where additional contributions are required in order to give effect to a recovery plan, the rates and dates of those contributions must be shown separately from other contributions.

The schedule must be signed by the trustees or managers of the scheme and make provision for signature by the employer (unless the scheme rules provide otherwise) in order to signify agreement to matters included therein. The schedule must incorporate the actuary's certification, as set out in the Regulations.   **41**

The schedule must be reviewed by the trustees and where necessary revised from time to time in accordance with PA 2004 and the Funding Regulations.   **42**

Section 226 of PA 2004 requires that if an actuarial valuation shows that the scheme does not meet the statutory funding objective, a recovery plan must be put in place by the trustees. The recovery plan sets out how the statutory funding objective is to be met and over what period. When preparing the recovery plan the trustees must obtain the agreement of the employer, unless the rules of the scheme provide otherwise, and take actuarial advice. A copy of the recovery plan must be sent to TPR.   **43**

---

[2] *See www.gov.uk/guidance/pension-schemes-and-unauthorised-payments*

Annual report

44 Trustees of nearly all occupational pension schemes are required by Regulations made under PA 1995[3] to make available to members an annual report within seven months of the scheme year end. The content of the annual report varies with the type of scheme but generally comprises the following:

- trustees' report, giving a review of the management of the scheme, membership statistics, investment performance developments and compliance matters during the period;

- for schemes with defined contribution arrangements, a statutory Chair's governance statement in respect of those arrangements;

- financial statements showing a true and fair view of the financial transactions of the scheme during the period and of the disposition of its assets and liabilities (other than liabilities to pay pensions and benefits after the end of the scheme year) at the end of the period;

- an independent auditor's report on the financial statements;

- for schemes with less than 20 participating employees at the start of the scheme year, an independent auditor's statement about contributions payable to the scheme (it is usual for a trustees' summary of contributions to be included that the auditor can report against);

- for defined benefit schemes a report on actuarial liabilities as required by FRS 102 to be provided alongside the financial statements; and

- for defined benefit schemes, the actuarial certification of the schedule of contributions.

Financial statements, books and records

45 The Audited Accounts Regulations require scheme trustees to obtain financial statements which:

(a)   contain specified information; and

(b)   show a true and fair view of the financial transactions of the scheme during the scheme year and of the amount and disposition as at the end of the scheme year of its assets and of its liabilities, other than liabilities to pay pensions and benefits after the end of the scheme year.

46 The Audited Accounts Regulations require trustees to state whether the financial statements have been prepared in accordance with the relevant financial reporting framework applicable to pension schemes, which is currently FRS 102 The Financial Reporting Standard applicable in the UK and Republic of Ireland, the Statement of Recommended Practice "Financial Reports of Pension Schemes" ("the Pensions SORP")[4], and applicable requirements of the Audited Accounts Regulations, and, if not, an indication of where there are any material departures from this framework.

47 FRS 102 applies to pension scheme financial reporting and in particular sets out specific accounting requirements for occupational pension schemes in its section dealing with Specialised Activities. Under FRS 102 the financial statements include liabilities other than the actuarial present value of promised retirement

---

[3] *The Occupational and Personal Pension Schemes (Disclosure of Information) Regulations SI 2013 No.2734*

[4] *Issued by the Pensions Research Accountants Group (PRAG) in accordance with the Financial Reporting Council's Policy and Code of Practice for SORPs.*

benefits which are required to be disclosed together with other actuarial information in a report alongside the financial statements.

The Pensions SORP provides further guidance on financial reporting for occupational pension schemes. Consequently, it is normally necessary to follow FRS 102 and the guidance in the Pensions SORP in order for pension scheme financial statements to show a true and fair view.   **48**

Section 49 of PA 1995 requires trustees to maintain books and records of the transactions of the scheme. The nature of the accounting books and records to be maintained are set out in the Scheme Administration Regulations and consist of particular items specified in the Regulations[5]. Further requirements relating to records of contributions for defined benefit schemes are set out in Funding Regulations.   **49**

Contents of the auditor's report on pension scheme financial statements

Under the Audited Accounts Regulations and FRS 102, occupational pension scheme financial statements exclude the actuarial present value of promised retirement benefits. Thus, the Audited Accounts Regulations do not require a scheme auditor to express an opinion as to whether the financial statements of a pension scheme show a true and fair view of its state of affairs but whether the financial statements obtained by the trustees show a true and fair view of the scheme's: **50**

(a)   financial transactions and assets; and

(b)   liabilities, other than liabilities to pay pensions and benefits, after the end of the scheme year.

When forming an opinion on the view shown by an occupational pension scheme's financial statements which have been prepared in accordance with FRS 102 and the SORP, the scheme auditor is therefore not required to express an opinion as to the completeness and accuracy of the long-term liabilities to pay benefits as determined by the scheme actuary.   **51**

A scheme auditor's statutory responsibilities under PA 1995 do not require the auditor to undertake work to determine whether the trustees' report or other sections of the scheme's annual report, including the Report on Actuarial Liabilities, are properly prepared[6].   **52**

However, the auditor is subject to the requirements of ISA (UK) 720, including to consider whether other information included in the annual report, which contains or accompanies the financial statements and the auditor's report thereon, is materially inconsistent with the financial statements or the auditor's knowledge obtained in the audit.   **53**

Obtaining audited financial statements for purposes other than the annual report

Trustees may decide to obtain audited financial statements other than at the statutory accounting date for reasons other than the requirement to include them in the annual report, for example for the purposes of an actuarial valuation.   **54**

---

[5] *These requirements are the minimum. Trustees are likely to require more detailed and historic records for the effective management of their scheme than the minimum set down in legislation.*

[6] *However, a breach of requirements relating to the annual report may give rise to a statutory duty to report directly to The Pensions Regulator.*

Reporting on contributions

55   The Audited Accounts Regulations require trustees to obtain from the scheme auditor a statement as to whether or not in the auditor's opinion contributions have in all material respects been paid at least in accordance with the payment schedule for defined contribution schemes or the schedule of contributions, as certified by the scheme actuary, for other schemes unless the scheme had at least 20 participating employers at the start of the scheme year (in such cases there is no requirement to obtain an auditor's statement[7]). The work undertaken by the scheme auditor in respect of contributions takes into account both the auditor's obligation to report its opinion on the financial statements and, separately, to report whether contributions have in all material respects been paid at least in accordance with the schedule of contributions or payment schedule. If a schedule of contributions or payment schedule is not in place the scheme auditor reports whether contributions have been paid in accordance with the scheme rules or contracts under which they were payable, and (where appropriate) recommendations of the scheme actuary.

56   The Occupational and Personal Pension Schemes (Disclosure of Information) Regulations 2013 (the "Disclosure Regulations") require scheme trustees to explain in the annual report the reasons for any qualified or negative auditor's statement and to state how the situation has been or is likely to be resolved.

Earmarked schemes

57   An "earmarked scheme" is a scheme under which all the benefits other than death benefits are money purchase benefits and all are secured by one or more policies of insurance or annuity contracts, and such policies or contracts are specifically allocated to the provision of benefits for individual members or any other person who has a right to benefits under the scheme. The trustees of an earmarked scheme are normally required to appoint an auditor to issue a report about contributions, but the trustees are exempt from having to obtain audited financial statements unless the deed and rules specifically require them.

Audit exemptions

58   Schemes which meet the relevant criteria[8] are exempt from appointing a scheme auditor under PA 1995, including schemes with:

- fewer than 2 members;
- fewer than 12 members where all the members are trustees of the scheme; and either
    - the provisions of the scheme provide that all decisions which fall to be made by the trustees are made by unanimous agreement by the trustees who are members of the scheme; or
    - the scheme has a trustee who is independent in relation to the scheme for the purposes of section 23 of the 1995 Act (power to appoint independent trustees), and is recorded in the register maintained by TPR in accordance with regulations made under subsection (4) of that section.

---

[7] *The Occupational Pension Schemes (Requirement to obtain Audited Accounts and a Statement from the Auditor) Regulations 1996 No.1975 2(c), as amended.*

[8] *Criteria for exemption from the requirements to appoint professional advisers (including an auditor) are set out in the The Occupational Pension Schemes (Scheme Administration) Regulations 1996, as amended.*

This exemption therefore does not apply if, for example, there are deferred members who are not trustees. Even if the exemption applies, the scheme's trust deed and rules may still require an audit and HMRC and the scheme actuary may require scheme financial statements. Schemes which are exempt from the requirement to appoint an auditor are mostly also exempt from the requirement to prepare a payment schedule or schedule of contributions. **59**

Auditing financial instruments

Occupational pension schemes typically invest in a range of investments which include financial instruments such as equities, bonds, derivatives (both exchange traded or over the counter) and pooled investment vehicles. These are reported at fair value under FRS 102 and are typically the most material item in the financial statements. The FRC has issued Practice Note 23"Special considerations in auditing financial instruments" which is relevant to the audit of all entities which use financial instruments, including pension schemes of all sizes. The practice note provides background information to financial instruments and a discussion of audit considerations relating to financial instruments. Auditors of pension schemes should be aware of and consider the guidance in Practice Note 23 where it is applicable to the engagement. **60**

Going concern

The principal liabilities of a defined benefit scheme consist of obligations to pay future pensions, the extent of which are assessed by the scheme actuary rather than the scheme auditor. Such liabilities do not arise in defined contribution schemes, as the benefits payable are determined by the extent of funds available. **61**

The going concern basis is assumed in the preparation of the financial statements of pension schemes unless a decision has been made to wind up the scheme, an event triggering wind up has occurred, e.g. insolvency of the employer, or the scheme has entered the PPF assessment period and there is no realistic alternative to the eventual admission of the scheme and the transfer of its assets and liabilities to the PPF. The auditor's responsibilities in relation to the consideration of going concern are discussed further in the section on ISA (UK) 570 in this Practice Note. **62**

ISA (UK) 200: OVERALL OBJECTIVES OF THE INDEPENDENT AUDITOR AND THE CONDUCT OF AN AUDIT IN ACCORDANCE WITH INTERNATIONAL STANDARDS ON AUDITING (UK)

ISA (UK) 200 deals with the independent auditor's overall responsibilities when conducting an audit of financial statements in accordance with ISAs (UK). **63**

ISAs (UK) include a requirement for the auditor to comply with the FRC's Ethical Standard and relevant ethical guidance issued by the auditor's professional body in the conduct of any audit of financial statements, which apply equally to audits of pension schemes. A fundamental principle is that practitioners should not accept or perform work which they are not competent to undertake. Practitioners should not undertake the audit of occupational pension schemes unless they are satisfied that they have or can attain the necessary level of competence. **64**

Before commencing the audit of an occupational pension scheme, a firm ensures that it has enough staff who have adequate knowledge and experience of such audits. Staff involved in an audit of an occupational pension scheme will have a **65** broad understanding, commensurate with the individual's role and responsibilities in the audit process of:

- the type of scheme being audited (e.g. defined benefit, defined contribution or hybrid);
- the status of the scheme (e.g. open, closed to new members, closed to future accrual);
- key risks affecting the scheme;
- the scheme's trust deed and rules;
- pensions legislation and regulations;
- relevant TPR Codes of Practice and guidance; and
- the principles of FRS 102 and the Pensions SORP.

66   An audit firm must be eligible to act as a scheme auditor – see paragraphs 20 to 23.

ISA (UK) 210: AGREEING THE TERMS OF AUDIT ENGAGEMENTS

67   ISA (UK) 210 sets out the auditor's responsibilities when agreeing the terms of audit engagements. These include establishing that the "preconditions for an audit" are present and that there is a common understanding between the auditor and management and, where appropriate, those charged with governance. For a pension scheme audit the terms of engagement are agreed with the trustees.

68   ISA (UK) 210 requires that an engagement letter be obtained for all audit appointments. This requirement supplements that included in PA 1995 whereby trustees are required to appoint the scheme's auditor.

The appointment of the scheme auditor

69   Section 47(1)(a) of PA 1995 requires the trustees or managers of most occupational pension schemes to appoint a scheme auditor.

70   To be effective, the appointment of a scheme auditor must be made in accordance with the Regulations[9]. The trustees or managers of the scheme forward a Notice of Appointment to the auditor specifying:

- the date the appointment is due to take effect;
- to whom the auditor is to report; and
- from whom the auditor will take instructions.

71   The date the appointment is due to take effect ("the effective date") is at a future date. The date of appointment does not become effective until the auditor has acknowledged receipt of the Notice of Appointment. This being the case, a practical approach may be for the Notice of Appointment to specify the "effective date" as being the date of the auditor's acknowledgement of the appointment.

72   The name of the scheme and the year-end should be clear. If the appointment is in relation to a scheme year which has already ended the engagement terms should specify which scheme year(s) will be subject to audit.

73   In the case of an appointment covering a number of schemes, there should normally be separate Notices of Appointment for each or, if particular circumstances warrant it such as a common trustee body for a number of schemes, a schedule detailing the separate schemes.

---

[9] *The Occupational Pension Schemes (Scheme Administration) Regulations 1996, SI 1996 No. 1715, as amended.*

For the appointment to be effective, PA 1995 and the Scheme Administration **74** Regulations requires the auditor to acknowledge receipt of the Notice of Appointment within one month of its date of receipt. The appointment is not effective unless and until this acknowledgement is sent by the auditor within the one month period. If the auditor does not acknowledge appointment within one month, the Notice of Appointment ceases to be valid. The trustees or managers will then need to provide a new Notice of Appointment.

PA 1995 and the Scheme Administration Regulations also require the auditor to **75** confirm in writing that he will notify the trustees or managers immediately he becomes aware of the existence of any conflict of interest to which the auditor is subject in relation to the scheme.

An example Notice of Appointment and an example letter of Acknowledgement **76** of Appointment are set out in Appendix 1.

If the resignation, removal or death of a scheme auditor occurs, the Scheme **77** Administration Regulations require that a new appointment be made within three months. Failure to appoint a new auditor within the three-month period may be a matter of material significance to TPR. If an auditor is requested to accept appointment after three months from the date when a previous auditor left office, or if there was no previous auditor appointed under PA 1995 and the scheme is not a new one, the breach will need to be noted and may need to be reported to TPR.

There is no legal time limit for the appointment of a scheme auditor for new **78** schemes (or schemes which no longer qualify for an exemption) but from a practical perspective the appointment should be made in sufficient time[10] to enable the trustees' duties relating to obtaining audited financial statements to be met.

Where there is no statutory requirement for a scheme auditor, the trustees may **79** nevertheless appoint an auditor. A non-statutory auditor falls within the definition of the term "professional adviser" used in the Occupational Pension Schemes (Scheme Administration) Regulations, so the provisions relating to the appointment and removal of the scheme auditor (as discussed in paragraphs 69 to 78 above and 86 and 87 below) apply to the appointment of a non-statutory auditor, with the following differences:

- the appointment is as "professional adviser" rather than "scheme auditor";

- the eligibility and ineligibility rules in the Regulations do not apply to "professional adviser" appointments; and

- the three month limit on vacancy in office does not apply.

The letter of engagement

The scheme auditor agrees the terms of the audit engagement with the trustees of **80** the scheme and addresses the letter of engagement to the trustees.

The scheme auditor sets out the nature and scope of its audit obligations under PA **81** 1995 so as to ensure that trustees are aware of the extent of those responsibilities. In particular, the auditor includes reference to its responsibility to report on the contributions payable to the scheme (if applicable) and to the statutory duty to report to TPR in certain circumstances, making it clear that the duty is to report

---

[10] *Normally, appointments will take place as the scheme is established as one of a series of adviser and service provider appointments by the trustees.*

matters if found, and does not involve undertaking additional work to identify reportable matters.

82   Under PA 1995, the scheme auditor does not have a right of access to information held by third parties. Consequently, it is necessary for the scheme auditor to request such information, through the trustees when necessary for the external audit. The scheme auditor therefore includes in the engagement letter a paragraph relating to access to third parties to whom the trustees delegate particular functions, and to their records relating to the pension scheme. The scheme auditor may require information from the:

- administrator;
- investment manager(s);
- custodian(s);
- sponsoring employer – or employers where there is a multi-employer scheme – and the sponsoring employer's auditor; and
- scheme actuary.

83   When a pension scheme uses another organisation or the sponsoring employer to deal with the administration of contributions and benefits and to maintain membership and financial records, the trustees arrange for the scheme auditor to have direct access to the records and personnel of the relevant organisation acting as scheme administrator.

84   In view of the importance of the scheme actuary's work to the information contained in the scheme's annual report, it is normally appropriate for the scheme auditor to obtain the trustees' agreement to direct dealings between the auditor and the scheme actuary, both in terms of ongoing liaison regarding the affairs of the scheme and also in respect of the scheme actuary's and scheme auditor's duty to report matters of material significance directly to TPR, and to document this agreement in the engagement letter.

85   Regulations made under PA 1995 and the Scheme Administration Regulations require the employer to notify the trustees, within one month, of the occurrence of any event relating to the employer which there is reasonable cause to believe will be of material significance to the trustees or the scheme's professional advisers in the exercise of their functions. The scheme auditor may wish to include a term in the engagement letter requiring the trustees to inform the scheme auditor of any matters which come to their attention which may be relevant to the audit.

Resignation or removal of the auditor

86   The Scheme Administration Regulations require a written notice of resignation by the scheme auditor which should contain either:

- a statement specifying the circumstances; or
- a declaration of no circumstances.

87   The statement is made by the outgoing scheme auditor specifying any circumstances connected with their resignation which, in its opinion, significantly affect the interests of the members or prospective members of, or beneficiaries under, the scheme. Under the Disclosure Regulations, the annual report must include a copy of any statement made on resignation or removal in accordance with Regulations made under section 47(6) PA 1995. Where the auditor knows of no such circumstances, and hence makes a declaration to that effect, there is no requirement to include this declaration in the annual report,

although it is often included for the avoidance of doubt. The trustees are required to provide a copy of the statement or declaration to the succeeding scheme auditor and the scheme actuary within 14 days. The scheme auditor reports a statement of circumstances to TPR if it is considered to be a matter of material significance to TPR (see paragraphs 265 to 274).

ISA (UK) 240: THE AUDITOR'S RESPONSIBILITIES RELATING TO FRAUD IN AN AUDIT OF FINANCIAL STATEMENTS

ISA (UK) 240 deals with the auditor's responsibilities relating to fraud in an audit of financial statements. **88**

Auditors of pension schemes are aware that the potential for fraud exists in all schemes. Even if the auditor considers that the nature of pension schemes (not profit-making and not trading) reduces the risk of fraudulent financial reporting, the risk of misappropriation of assets remains. Professional scepticism therefore remains key. **89**

The trustees of a pension scheme are responsible for ensuring that the assets and revenues of the scheme are adequately safeguarded against the effects of fraud through the implementation of appropriate controls. This legal responsibility remains with trustees even if they have delegated some or all of their executive functions to third parties. **90**

Examples of conditions or events which may increase the risk of fraud include: **91**

- failure by the trustees to establish and operate adequate internal control mechanisms, as required by legislation;

- trustees or scheme management displaying a significant disregard for the various regulatory authorities;

- trustees or scheme management having little or no involvement in the day-to-day administration of the scheme;

- trustees or scheme management having ready access to the scheme's assets and an ability to override any internal controls;

- trustees or scheme management failing to put in place arrangements to monitor activities undertaken by third parties, including the employer;

- trustees or scheme management displaying a lack of candour in dealings with members, the scheme actuary or the scheme auditor on significant matters affecting scheme assets;

- the sponsoring employer operating in an industry with increasing business failures, or itself having financial difficulties;

- significant levels, or unusual types, of related party transactions (including employer-related investments) involving unaudited entities or entities audited by other firms; and

- opaque investment arrangements where the flow of information to the trustees is restricted and therefore making it more difficult to control the investment and understand the position.

The audit planning process includes an assessment of the risk of material misstatements arising from fraud. Conditions or events which increase the risk of fraud include previous experience or incidents which call into question the competence or integrity of persons involved in the operation of the scheme. **92**

93   The risk of material misstatements arising from fraud is normally most likely to arise in relation to investments as investment transactions and balances are normally much larger than transactions and balances with members.

94   In practice, investment related frauds are fairly uncommon. Although member related fraud is relatively more common, for example the continuing payment of benefits to a deceased pensioner, amounts involved are unlikely to be material to the pension scheme financial statements.

95   Under the requirements of ISA (UK) 240 (paragraph 47) if the auditor has concluded that the risk of material misstatement due to fraud related to revenue recognition is not applicable in the circumstances of the engagement, the auditor shall include in the audit documentation the reasons for that conclusion.

96   Revenue in a pension scheme generally comprises contributions and investment income. Pension schemes are not profit-making entities and pension scheme financial statements are not publicly available. Additionally, unlike sales revenue of a commercial entity, there is little scope to manipulate revenue of a pension scheme, for example, through false invoicing or misuse of credit notes. Given these facts, there is normally little incentive or opportunity for revenue to be fraudulently misstated and therefore limited risk of material misstatement arising due to fraud. However, the scheme auditor gives consideration to the risks arising in connection with the types of fraud that may occur in the context of an occupational pension scheme (see paragraph 91 above) and documents its conclusion and the reasoning behind it.

97   There has been increasing concerns over "pension scams" whereby pension scheme members transfer out their benefits to unapproved or inappropriate arrangements. Trustees are required under guidance from TPR to put in place controls to check that transfers out are made to authorised pension schemes and in certain circumstances to check that the member has sought advice before making the transfer. If the auditor becomes aware of a possible scam during the course of their audit work they raise the matter with the trustees.

ISA (UK) 250: SECTION A – CONSIDERATION OF LAWS AND REGULATIONS IN AN AUDIT OF FINANCIAL STATEMENTS

98   ISA (UK) 250 Section A deals with the responsibilities of an auditor when considering laws and regulations in an audit of financial statements.

99   All staff involved in a pension scheme audit need a broad understanding of legislation and related Regulations, the trust deed and rules, FRS 102 and in particular the relevant part of FRS 102 relating to financial reporting for pension schemes under "Specialised Activities" and the Pensions SORP. This level of knowledge and understanding needs to be commensurate with roles and responsibilities in the audit.

100   An overview of the legislative and regulatory framework applicable to occupational pension schemes is given in the "Occupational Pension Schemes – key characteristics" section of this Practice Note.

101   Users of the financial statements of a scheme reasonably expect that the transactions recorded within them are authorised by the governing document(s): hence, in order to show a true and fair view, due regard needs to be given to disclosure of any material noncompliance with the governing document(s).

Laws relating to the payment of contributions to the scheme

The trustees are required to obtain from the scheme auditor a statement as to **102** whether the scheme has received contributions in accordance with legislative requirements (except for schemes with at least 20 participating employers at the start of the scheme financial year – see paragraph 55).

Further considerations relating to reporting on contributions are set out in **103** paragraphs 218 to 256 below.

Laws and regulations where instances of non-compliance may have a material effect on the financial statements

In the context of pension schemes, instances of non-compliance with laws and **104** regulations that may have a material effect on the financial statements for a particular scheme would include those where breaches would have consequences, such as:

- action by the HMRC to rescind registered status (for example, as a result of a change to the constitution or the nature and value of benefits provided which do not comply with the legislation);

- the penalty regime for breaches of the Finance Act 2004;

- the penalty regime for breaches of data protection laws and regulations; or

- action by TPR to remove or replace the scheme's trustees. Action to remove trustees can be taken where, in TPR's opinion, a trustee is not a fit and proper person.

The Pensions Ombudsman may also make determinations concerning remedial **105** action necessary in particular cases, which may lead to investigation and action by TPR. The scheme auditor therefore includes a review of correspondence with that body, as well as correspondence with TPR and HMRC, as part of the procedures to assess the risk of noncompliance with laws and regulations which may have a material effect on the financial statements of a pension scheme.

Money laundering

When reporting to TPR, partners and staff in audit firms need to be alert to the **106** dangers of tipping-off under the anti-money laundering legislation. Any knowledge or suspicions of involvement of a pension scheme's trustees in money laundering would normally be regarded as a matter of material significance to TPR and so give rise to a statutory duty to report to TPR in addition to making any necessary report required by legislation relating to money laundering offences. More guidance in relation to this legislation is given in ISA (UK) 250 Section A.

ISA (UK) 260: COMMUNICATION WITH THOSE CHARGED WITH GOVERNANCE

ISA (UK) 260 deals with the responsibilities of the auditor when communicating **107** with those charged with governance.

ISA (UK) 260 stresses that communication should be active, two-way **108** communication between the auditor and those charged with governance. This is unlikely to be achieved if communication is only by way of written reports. Some trustee bodies of occupational pension schemes operate their relationship with the auditor through individuals such as a professional trustee or the secretary to the trustees in these circumstances. There may be a tiered approach to communication, with the detailed matters being communicated to an audit committee (or similar group) and less detailed matters being communicated with the trustee body. It may therefore be difficult to ensure that oral communication is transmitted to all trustees and written communication may also be necessary.

109 The scheme auditor notifies trustees of all breaches, discovered in the course of its work,[11] of duties relevant to the administration of the scheme imposed by any enactment or rule of law on the trustees or managers, the employer, any professional adviser or any prescribed person acting in connection with the scheme, regardless of whether the matter gave rise to a statutory duty to report to TPR. Such notification normally takes place in the course of assessing the consequences of each particular breach. However, the scheme auditor may also summarise such breaches in the auditor's report of audit matters to those charged with governance.

ISA (UK) 265: COMMUNICATING DEFICIENCIES IN INTERNAL CONTROL TO THOSE CHARGED WITH GOVERNANCE AND MANAGEMENT

110 ISA (UK) 265 deals with the responsibilities of the auditor when communicating deficiencies in internal control to those charged with governance and management

111 Section 249A of PA 2004 states that schemes should have adequate internal control mechanisms in place. Therefore, trustees of an occupational pension scheme have a statutory obligation to establish and operate adequate internal controls. TPR's Code of Practice 09 on Internal Controls and supporting guidance provides guidelines on the standards of conduct and practice expected in this regard and sets out the processes and controls that TPR considers to be adequate for the purposes of satisfying the legal requirement.

112 When determining whether individual deficiencies in internal control that are identified during the audit merit the attention of the trustees, the auditor has regard to factors such as the following:

- the significance and nature of the risk(s) to the scheme's activities which are not addressed (adequately or at all) as a result of the deficiency;
- the possible impact of the deficiency on the security of scheme assets;
- the possible impact of the deficiency on the payment of members' benefits;
- the extent to which the operation of controls is informal and undocumented, rather than formal and documented;
- whether detective controls are in operation to compensate for deficiencies in preventative controls; and
- whether aspects of the role of parties such as third-party service organisations compensate for deficiencies in controls operated by the trustees.

113 The auditor considers the impact, individually and in aggregate, of identified control deficiencies (including controls operated by third-party service organisations) when deciding whether to report them to the trustees. Where the effect and wider implications of a scheme not having in place adequate internal

---

[11] *Subject to compliance with legislation relating to "tipping off".*

controls, either individually or in aggregate, are likely to be of material significance to TPR, the auditor makes a report to TPR.

ISA (UK) 300: PLANNING AN AUDIT OF FINANCIAL STATEMENTS

ISA (UK) 300 deals with the responsibilities of auditors in respect of planning an audit of financial statements. **114**

When planning the work to be undertaken in respect of a pension scheme audit, it is important to identify those areas which are key to its operations as reflected in its financial statements. The key areas of most schemes' financial statements could include the following: **115**

- contributions receivable;
- benefits payable;
- investment return; and
- investment assets.

Where relevant, the scheme auditor's plan also takes account of the steps necessary to obtain sufficient appropriate evidence in order to discharge the auditor's statutory obligation to report on the payment of contributions where relevant. **116**

Neither the scope of the audit, nor the scheme auditor's assessment of materiality for planning purposes, is affected by the duty to report matters that are likely to be of material significance to TPR. **117**

When planning the work to be undertaken, the scheme auditor considers the other information available focussing on understanding investment arrangements, administration, scheme governance and the role of third parties. Possible sources of information include: **118**

- discussions with trustees;
- minutes of trustees' meetings;
- membership records;
- actuarial valuations; and
- discussions with scheme management on changes to the scheme, for example in investment strategy, including de-risking initiatives.

When planning the audit of a pension scheme's financial statements, the scheme auditor also takes into account the importance of the work of third parties in the administration, investment and accounting on behalf of the trustees and the extent to which third parties provide these services. Where significant functions have been delegated to third parties, the scheme auditor reviews any such service level agreements with third parties as part of the planning process where they are relevant to the audit. **119**

ISA (UK) 315: IDENTIFYING AND ASSESSING THE RISKS OF MATERIAL MISSTATEMENT THROUGH UNDERSTANDING THE ENTITY AND ITS ENVIRONMENT

ISA (UK) 315 sets out the responsibilities of an auditor in respect of identifying and assessing the risks of material misstatement. **120**

Understanding the Pension Scheme and its environment, including its internal controls

121   This section focuses on the control environment and controls of the entity (i.e. the pension scheme) itself, rather than those service organisations which may be relevant to the audit.

Financial Reporting

122   The auditor obtains an understanding of the accounting framework under which the financial statements are prepared and their impact on the audit. Accounting principles for pension schemes include those set out in:

- specific legislation;
- FRS102 The Financial Reporting Standard applicable in the UK and Republic of Ireland;
- the Pensions SORP; and
- accounting and other recommendations issued by the PPF where relevant.

Legislative and regulatory requirements

123   Pension schemes operate within a framework of law and regulation which is complex and differs in a number of respects from that applicable to commercial enterprises. An overview of this framework is given in the Introduction to this Practice Note.

Financial and other risks

124   The auditor obtains an understanding of the pension scheme's objectives and strategies, and those related business risks that may result in risks of material misstatement. However, it is important to recognise that whilst trustees consider investment risks and other risks associated with the operation of a pension scheme, these are not necessarily the same as financial reporting risks. To avoid misunderstanding and confusion between the auditor and trustees, financial reporting risks are distinguished from other risks.

The nature of the scheme

125   The scheme auditor's understanding of the nature of the scheme usually includes obtaining and reviewing information and documentation in relation to:

(a)   **Scheme nature**
- trust deed and rules and amendments thereto;
- the definition of pensionable earnings/pay, where not covered by the above;
- contribution rates;
- membership profile;
- type of scheme and type of benefits provided;
- scheme booklet; and
- documentation of the scheme's registered pension scheme status and related correspondence with HMRC.

(b)   **Scheme governance:**
- membership of the trustee body and the governance framework;

- statutory chair's statement and supporting documentation (DC schemes);
- outsourcing arrangements and principal terms of contractual agreements with third-party service organisations;
- availability and use of relevant reports on the internal controls of service organisations including investment managers, custodians and administrators;
- correspondence with TPR/ the Pensions Ombudsman/the Pensions Advisory Service (TPAS);
- minutes of meetings of the trustee body and key sub-committees;
- internal dispute resolution procedure and any disputes in progress;
- arrangements for agreeing schedule of contributions or payment schedule with the sponsoring employer and taking actuarial advice where necessary; and
- annual scheme return.

(c) **Information about sponsoring and participating employers:**
- identity of the sponsoring and other participating employer(s);
- relevant covenants and funding arrangements;
- employer and HR payroll arrangements relevant to the remittance of scheme contributions; and
- arrangements for payment of additional voluntary contributions.

(d) **Actuarial documentation (where relevant):**
- letter of appointment;
- valuation reports and details of funding requirements;
- statement of funding principles;
- schedule of contributions;
- recovery plan;
- latest certificates; and
- annual summary funding statement.

(e) **Approach to scheme administration and finance:**
- service level agreements;
- division of administrative and financial responsibilities;
- accounting and membership records;
- stewardship and financial reports provided to the trustees; and
- systems and controls documentation as applicable to the pension scheme.

(f) **Investments:**
- investment strategy and approach to implementation of that strategy;
- statement of investment principles;
- custody arrangements;

- investment management agreements and service agreements with custodians;
- reports provided to the trustees by the investment managers;
- nature of investments and extent of complex and opaque investment structures;
- asset-backed special purpose vehicles;
- common investment fund arrangements;
- employer-related investments;
- subsidiaries; and
- AVC arrangements.

(g) Other advisers:

- services provided by other advisers.

Trustees' financial governance and internal controls

126   There is a wide variation between schemes in terms of size, activity and organisation. Smaller schemes may be administered by the staff of the sponsoring employer or by third-party administrators or a combination of both. Larger schemes may employ their own professionally qualified, staff. However, the legal requirement to operate internal controls[12] and the responsibilities of trustees for ensuring that the scheme has adequate internal controls and therefore is properly administered and its assets properly safeguarded apply irrespective of a scheme's size or administrative arrangements.

127   The attitude, role and involvement of each scheme's trustees are likely to be fundamental in determining the effectiveness of its control environment. TPR's Code of Practice 09 "Internal controls" and supporting guidance provides trustees with guidelines on their duty to establish and operate adequate internal controls.

128   Factors taken into account when considering the governance of the scheme by the trustees include:

- the skills and qualifications of individual trustees;
- training undertaken by trustees;
- the regularity and effectiveness of trustees' meetings;
- the trustees' approach to dealing with matters in between trustees' meetings;
- adequacy of minutes of trustees' meetings;
- arrangements to monitor adherence to the scheme's statements of investment and funding principles;
- compliance with industry guidelines (for example, TPR's Codes of Practice and guidance);
- the policy on dealing with trustees and other conflicts;
- the division of duties between trustees;
- the involvement of trustees in supervision and control procedures, including matters such as banking arrangements;

---

[12] *Section 249A Pensions Act 2004.*

- the trustees' attitude towards third parties to whom they delegate the conduct of scheme activities;

- arrangements for trustees to monitor scheme income and expenditure; and

- the attitude of trustees to previously identified breaches or control deficiencies.

Use of service organisations

Paragraph A68 of ISA (UK) 315 makes it clear that a scheme's use of service **129** organisations is relevant to the auditor's consideration of the controls that are relevant to the audit. The auditor's work at scheme entity level is designed to provide the auditor with a sufficient understanding of risk on which to base its planning of audit procedures (see the section on ISA (UK) 402 in this Practice Note).

Assessing the risks of material misstatement

The scheme auditor assesses risk and the adequacy of controls in relation to the **130** circumstances of each scheme. Factors considered by the auditor in assessing whether there may be an increased level of risk of material misstatement at the financial statement level include:

- complex scheme structures;

- major changes in the scheme or the participating/sponsoring employers;

- inadequacy of general resources;

- informal arrangements for scheme governance; and

- experience from previous years' audits.

Factors considered by the auditor in assessing whether there may be an increased **131** level of risk of material misstatement at the assertion level especially in a year where changes are made include:

- complex contribution arrangements;

- changes in contribution rates;

- complex benefit structures;

- membership profile;

- non-compliance with schedule of contributions or payment schedule; and

- complex, opaque or illiquid investments.

ISA (UK) 320: MATERIALITY IN PLANNING AND PERFORMING AN AUDIT

ISA (UK) 320 deals with the auditor's responsibility to apply the concept of **132** materiality in planning and performing an audit of financial statements.

Financial statement audits

For the financial statement audit opinion, net earnings or level of working capital **133** are not among the prime indicators for a pension scheme and therefore, when considering materiality, the focus is directed at scheme assets (mainly investments), contributions, benefits and / or returns on investments.

Materiality for pension schemes may vary with the nature of the scheme and needs **134** to be assessed for each individual scheme rather than applying any general guidelines. It is also important to distinguish, especially for the benefit of the trustees, that materiality in relation to the audit of the pension scheme's financial statements will not necessarily coincide with the expectations of materiality of an individual member of the scheme in relation to his or her expected benefits. Even in the case of defined contribution arrangements, the scheme auditor's judgments about materiality are made in the context of the financial statements as a whole and the account balances and classes of transactions reported in those statements, rather than in the context of an individual member's designated assets, contributions or benefits.

Auditor's statement about contributions

135   In addition to an independent auditor's report on the financial statements, the scheme auditor may also be required to provide a statement about contributions, which may then require separate considerations about materiality.

136   The scheme auditor's statement about contributions requires assessment of whether specific conditions have been met. This narrower and more factual focus of the report entails close consideration of payment dates and amounts, and hence a different level of materiality to that used in relation to the scheme's financial statements may be appropriate. The auditor documents the approach and factors considered in the determination of the level of materiality for the statement of contributions separately even if it is the same as that used for the audit of the financial statements. Materiality for the purposes of the auditor's statement is typically considered by reference to those contributions which are subject to the requirements of the schedule and not all contributions.

Regulatory reporting

137   The scheme auditor has a duty under PA 1995, if the auditor becomes aware of breaches of law which it has reasonable grounds to believe are "of material significance" to the exercise of the functions of TPR, to report such matters to TPR. The meaning of the term "of material significance" differs from "materiality" in the context of forming an opinion as to whether financial statements show a true and fair view (see paragraphs 265 to 274 which address this in more detail).

ISA (UK) 402: AUDIT CONSIDERATIONS RELATING TO AN ENTITY USING A SERVICE ORGANISATION

138   ISA (UK) 402 deals with the auditor's responsibilities relating to an entity using a service organisation.

Use of service organisations by pension schemes

139   Third party organisations undertake a wide range of activities within the pensions sector. Many of these involve financial transactions and balances and are therefore relevant to the financial statements so may fall for consideration under ISA (UK) 402 as "service organisations". Consequently, the auditor of a pension scheme needs to consider the nature and extent of activity undertaken by service organisations to determine whether those activities are relevant to the audit, and what their effect is on audit risk.

140   Examples of activities that may be undertaken by service organisations include:

- maintenance of the scheme's accounting and/or membership records;
- collection and investment of contributions paid over by the employer;

- custody and management of the scheme's investment assets; and
- calculation and payment of benefits.

Use of a service organisation does not diminish the ultimate responsibility of the **141** trustees for meeting their legal responsibilities, including those of safeguarding the assets, maintaining proper accounting records and preparing financial statements.

Information prepared on behalf of the trustees of a pension scheme by service **142** organisations which is relevant to the audit of the financial statements (which may include investment managers, custodians and scheme administrators) should be considered as being "produced by the entity" and therefore the auditor is required to obtain audit evidence about the accuracy and completeness of that information (see also ISA (UK) 500).

Sources of audit evidence

In determining the nature of work and sources of evidence, there are some issues **143** that apply to all service organisations used by trustees:

(a) The trustees' own procedures for appointment and ongoing monitoring of a third-party service organisation;

(b) The level of supervision that the trustees exercise over any third parties and their activities; and

(c) The availability of internal control reports produced under either AAF 01/06 "Assurance reports on internal controls of service organisations made available to third parties" (a Technical Release issued by the Audit and Assurance Faculty of the ICAEW) or other equivalent guidance.

If the auditor is able to obtain sufficient audit evidence that the trustees operate **144** adequate controls over the service organisation, the auditor will not need to supplement that understanding and assessment by making further enquiries about the control arrangements of relevant service organisations. In gathering audit evidence, the auditor considers what information is supplied to the trustees by the organisation, how the trustees monitor activities and performance of the organisation and whether the trustees carry out reviews of available reports by a service auditor on internal control.

The auditor considers the information available from the trustees over the **145** activities of the service organisation and determines whether that is sufficient based on the auditor's assessment of risk. If not, the auditor considers carrying out audit procedures at the service organisation.

Planning considerations

At the time when the auditor is planning the audit and performing assessments of **146** risk, the latest available report by a service auditor on internal control may not cover all or even any of the period whose financial statements are to be audited. Rather than disregard the service auditor's report on internal control, it may assist the auditor in obtaining a preliminary understanding of the controls implemented at the service organisation, supplemented by considerations such as whether:

- the conclusions reported in the service auditor's reports on internal control in recent years have presented fundamentally the same conclusions as the latest available report;

- the service organisation has changed its systems since the period/date covered by the latest available service auditor's report on internal control; and

- the trustees are aware of any errors affecting the client scheme during the period to be audited that have arisen from the activities of the service organisation, either reported by the service organisation itself or detected by the trustees' own control procedures.

147   The auditor then assesses the impact on the planned audit approach and makes adjustments to the audit work as necessary.

148   Where a report by a service auditor on internal control covers a periods which is not coterminous with the scheme reporting period, the scheme auditor considers alternative procedures to obtain evidence regarding the controls at the service organisation from the date of the service auditor's report on internal control to the end of the scheme reporting period. Such procedures can include, but are not limited to, requesting a bridging letter from the service organisation, discussions with trustees and management on the quality of the services received from the service organisation and/or review of performance reports and other information received from the service organisation.

Administration of contributions by the employer

149   It is the statutory duty of the employer and the employer's auditor to disclose on request to the trustees such information as is reasonably required for the performance of the duties of the trustees or their professional advisers, including their scheme auditor. The trustees in turn have a statutory duty to disclose such information to the scheme auditor as the auditor reasonably requires to perform the auditor's duties. If the scheme auditor requires the assistance of the employer's auditor in providing information or in carrying out certain audit procedures, for example the collection of contributions, it is appropriate for the initial request to be made to the employer through the trustees.

150   The scheme auditor specifies the procedures to be undertaken and provides these to the trustees. The trustees then pass these to the employer and the employer's auditor who is engaged by the employer to undertake the work on the understanding that the results will be passed to the scheme trustees for the purposes of the scheme audit. If the trustees wish to contract directly with the employer's auditor to undertake work on their behalf, the employer's auditor will need to be appointed as a professional adviser to the scheme under the Scheme Administration Regulations in the same way as the scheme auditor.

151   If the foregoing methods of obtaining audit evidence are not available the scheme auditor may need to consider whether this will result in a limitation to the scope of the audit which will affect the audit opinion on the financial statements and the auditor's statement about the payment of contributions where applicable.

ISA (UK) 500: AUDIT EVIDENCE

152   ISA (UK) 500 explains what constitutes audit evidence and deals with the auditor's responsibility to obtain sufficient appropriate evidence.

153   In preparing the financial statements, the trustees may use estimates which have been provided by experts engaged by the trustees or by the employer, e.g. actuaries, investment property valuers. Where the scheme auditor uses information provided by these experts as audit evidence as to the appropriate valuation of these assets held by the scheme, the reliability of such information is

assessed with reference to the competence, capabilities and objectivity of the expert.

As well as being used in providing estimates for the valuation of assets, the scheme actuary will provide an actuarial valuation of the liability to pay pensions after the year-end. However, as this is not within the scope of the financial statements, this valuation will not be used in providing audit evidence in relation to scheme liabilities. Guidance on liaison with the actuary is provided in paragraphs 257 to 261 of this Practice Note. **154**

ISA (UK) 520: ANALYTICAL PROCEDURES

ISA (UK) 520 sets the responsibilities for auditors when using analytical procedures as a basis for the identification and assessment of risks of material misstatement; to obtain relevant and reliable substantive audit evidence; and to assist the auditor when forming an overall conclusion as to whether the financial statements are consistent with the auditor's understanding of the entity. **155**

Analytical review techniques are likely to be particularly useful in the audit of pension schemes, not only at the planning and overall review stages of the audit but also as substantive procedures to supplement other evidence concerning the operation of controls or accuracy of individual balances and transactions. **156**

Although a pension scheme's income, resources and expenditure may fluctuate from year to year, for most transactions there are still ways in which the scheme auditor can establish whether the figures are internally consistent and reflect the pension scheme's operations during the year. Key techniques include comparison of information shown in the financial statements, for example: **157**

- investment income and investment return can be compared with relevant published information;

- monthly and annual patterns of contribution income can be compared to expected amounts using rates set out in the schedule of contributions or payment schedule. However, disaggregation may be required when differing rates of contribution are used for different categories of members;

- monthly and annual patterns of pensions payments can be compared to movements in membership statistics and increases to benefits in payment;

- membership statistics can be reconciled with information from the employer's payroll, and information about active pensioners and deferred members;

- bench-marking reports on investment performance, can be compared to financial information shown in the financial statements to check for correlation;

- non-financial information contained in documents issued by the scheme, such as summary reports, pensions newsletters, or in management information reports concerning scheme membership can be compared to financial information shown in the financial statements;

- actual income and expenditure can be compared to budgets, prior years' figures and trends; and

- actual expenditure can be compared to the scheme auditor's own expectation of expenditure that would be reasonable for the particular transaction under review, for example, average pension payment per pensioner.

Software based tools may be helpful in analysing information.

ISA (UK) 540: AUDITING ACCOUNTING ESTIMATES, INCLUDING FAIR VALUE ACCOUNTING ESTIMATES, AND RELATED DISCLOSURES

158   ISA (UK) 540 deals with the auditor's responsibilities relating to accounting estimates, including fair value accounting estimates, and related disclosures.

159   FRS 102 requires pension schemes to report investments at fair value in accordance with its fair value hierarchy. The fair value of annuities is deemed to be the present value of the related obligation. The Pensions SORP provides further guidance on valuing investments in accordance with FRS 102.

160   Pension schemes may invest in complex financial instruments or illiquid investments for which there may not be an exchange traded price and therefore fair value accounting estimates are made for inclusion in the financial statements.

161   These investments may include:

- non-exchange traded bonds including asset backed securities;
- unquoted securities, including private equity;
- infrastructure;
- investment properties;
- non-exchange traded pooled investment vehicles;
- annuity / buy-ins;
- with-profit insurance policies;
- non-exchange traded derivatives, including options, interest and inflation swaps and forward foreign currency contracts;
- special purpose vehicles such as Scottish Limited Partnerships used for supporting asset backed contribution arrangements;
- longevity swaps; and
- repurchase agreements and reverse repurchase agreements.

Estimation uncertainty

162   Fair value accounting estimates may involve varying degrees of estimation uncertainty. Some fair value accounting estimates involve low estimation uncertainty and may give rise to lower risks of material misstatement, for example, where the data used is readily available and is observable such as published interest rate data or exchange traded prices of securities. For other fair value estimates there may be relatively high estimation uncertainty, particularly where fair values are based on significant assumptions such as for derivative financial instruments not publically traded or where highly specialised entity developed models are used for which assumptions or inputs are not observable in the market place, such as complex over-the-counter derivatives or private equity investments. Where there is a greater degree of uncertainty, there will be an increased risk of valuation misstatement and this will require a greater amount of auditor attention. Sensitivity analysis may be used to demonstrate how estimation uncertainty may affect the fair value accounting estimate.

Significant risks

As part of their risk assessment, the auditor obtains an understanding of the nature **163** of the scheme investments, considers the associated risks and uses judgment to determine whether any accounting estimates identified as having high estimation uncertainty give rise to significant risks. As part of gaining an understanding, the auditor is mindful of the risk of material misstatement in valuation and may consider:

- the nature of the asset (including whether there actually is an asset that can be valued);
- how material is the instrument to the scheme;
- the contractual terms;
- the complexity of the arrangements;
- year on year movements/changes and variation in cash flows;
- the trustees' reasons for investing in this type of asset;
- the basis for valuation;
- the key models and assumptions involved; and
- who is providing the valuation and whether they have the required expertise.

Paragraph 21 of ISA (UK) 330 "The Auditor's Responses to Assessed Risks" **164** requires that if the auditor has determined that an assessed risk of material misstatement at the assertion level is a significant risk, the auditor shall perform substantive procedures that are specifically responsive to that risk. This may apply where significant investments are illiquid and difficult to value and the auditor pays particular attention to the basis adopted by the trustees for obtaining a market valuation. Where the trustees have sought the assistance of specialist valuers, the auditor has regard to the requirements of ISA (UK) 500 "Audit Evidence" when deciding how much direct testing to apply to the values reflected in the scheme's financial statements. Examples of accounting estimates for investment valuations in pension schemes that may have high estimation uncertainty include fair value accounting estimates for which a highly specialised entity-developed model is used or for which there are significant non-observable inputs.

Considerations regarding the assumptions used in accounting estimates are further **165** discussed in paragraphs A31–A36 of ISA (UK) 540.

Management Bias

As part of their risk assessment and understanding of the scheme and the scheme **166** investments, the scheme auditor also considers the degree to which assumptions may be biased by investment managers of the pension scheme. This bias may arise from a desire to meet trustees' expectations on the results for the year or to demonstrate growth in the value of assets. Paragraphs A124–A125 of ISA (UK) 540 include indicators of possible management bias.

Practice Note 23 Financial instruments

Practice Note 23 "Special considerations in auditing financial instruments" **167** provides general guidance to the auditor when planning and performing audit procedures for financial statement assertions related to financial instruments. Financial instruments include equities, bonds, derivatives and pooled investment vehicles. Auditors of pension schemes that hold financial instruments should be familiar with PN 23 and have regard to its guidance when performing their audits.

168   It is the trustees' responsibility to ensure that financial instruments recorded in the financial statements are properly valued and presented. When considering the audit planning, the auditor obtains an understanding of the financial risks to which the use of complex financial instruments exposes the pension scheme and the requirements of the accounting framework and the approach adopted by the trustees.

Pooled investment vehicles

169   Pooled investment vehicles may include the various forms of pooled investments such as unit trusts, unitised or unit linked insurance policies, open-ended investment trusts and open-ended investment companies, shares in limited liability partnerships and hedge funds. Most pooled investment arrangements invested in by pension schemes are not exchange traded. The auditor therefore considers the nature of the pooled vehicle and the underlying investments in determining the risk of material misstatement arising from fair value estimation. Possible factors to consider include:

● whether the investment vehicle is appropriately classified in accordance with the applicable accounting framework;

● the frequency of pricing or determining the net asset value (NAV) of the fund i.e. daily, weekly, monthly or quarterly;

● whether the fund is open-ended or closed-ended;

● whether the fund manager trades at the unit prices or NAVs provided for financial reporting purposes;

● the nature of the investments held by the fund;

● whether the fund is regulated;

● whether the fund is audited;

● whether the fund produces an internal controls report; and

● is the scheme the sole investor in the fund.

170   Based on the auditor's assessment of the risk of material misstatement arising from fair value determination for the pooled vehicle, sources of evidence available to the auditor in respect of fair value accounting estimates may include:

● A report by a service auditor on internal control, such as AAF01/06/ ISAE 3402 reports, where available, which cover controls over the determination of fair values. The auditor reviews the scope and findings of these reports, in accordance with ISA (UK) 402 Audit Considerations Relating to an Entity Using a Service Organisation;

● Evidence of unit prices or NAVs for transactions between investors in the pooled investment vehicle and the pool manager at or around the financial reporting date;

● Audited financial statements for the pooled investment vehicle. The auditor confirms that audited financial statements show that the investments held by the fund are valued at market value or using fair value accounting estimates. It may also be useful to compare the initial unaudited and subsequent audited valuation to assess the robustness of the fair valuation framework. Where the financial year-end of the fund is not coterminous with the scheme year-end, the auditor considers further additional audit work to gain assurance over the movement in valuation from the date of the latest audited accounts to the scheme year-end date, if this movement could potentially be materially misstated. This additional work may include discussions with the pool manager on the approach taken to the valuation of the underlying investments and/or, for example:

(a) analytical review of the fund return compared with published or benchmark indices for the fund strategy; or

(b) obtaining additional more up-to-date supporting substantive evidence for the valuation. This may include reviewing the valuation of the underlying investments where the procedures above are not sufficient to reduce the audit risk to an acceptable level or where other sources of evidence are limited (for example, if the vehicle is unaudited).

Specialist pension investments

Pension schemes may invest in investments that are tailored to defined benefit   **171**
pension schemes and are not generally found in the wider investing community.
These include:

- buy-ins / annuity insurance policies;

- special purpose vehicles normally associated with asset backed contributions; and

- longevity swaps.

These arrangements are typically highly illiquid, valued using mainly non-market   **172**
observable information and use complex valuation methodologies. Typically trustees will use an expert to provide a valuation of these types of investment for financial reporting purposes, for example the scheme actuary. The auditor may therefore require specialist skills or knowledge in order to assess or respond to the risks of material misstatement for estimates related to the fair value of these types of investment. In these circumstances if an auditor's expert is used ISA (UK) 620 "Using the Work of an Auditor's Expert" is applicable. Where the trustees have used an expert to value these types of investments, ISA (UK) 500 "Audit Evidence" covers how the auditor addresses information to be used as audit evidence that has been prepared using the work of a management's expert.

ISA (UK) 550: RELATED PARTIES

ISA (UK) 550 deals with the auditor's responsibility relating to related party   **173**
relationships and transactions.

The related parties of pension schemes fall into two broad categories: **174**

- employer-related; and

- trustee-related.

The Pensions SORP recommends that for financial reporting purposes related   **175**
parties should also be deemed to include other pension schemes for the benefit of employees of companies and businesses related to the employers, or for the benefit of the employees of any entity that is itself a related party of the reporting pension scheme.

The requirements set out in ISA (UK) 550 equally apply to the audit of pension   **176**
schemes. The scheme auditor considers the possibility of related party transactions, for example, where a pension scheme contracts with the employer

or related third parties for the use of a property or for the supply of goods or services to the scheme, even if these result in more favourable terms for the pension scheme than would otherwise be available.

177   The scheme auditor enquires as to the procedures that the trustees have in place to identify related parties and to authorise and record any related party transactions, including transactions with or loans to the sponsoring employer. The Pensions SORP provides guidance on the types of transaction that fall into the categories shown above and the form of disclosure recommended. The scheme auditor considers whether the trustees have made appropriate arrangements for identifying, authorising and recording such transactions in the circumstances of the particular scheme. Such arrangements might include a declaration of interest file and opportunities at trustees' meetings for trustees to declare interests. The scheme auditor also obtains written representations from the trustees concerning the completeness of information provided regarding the related party disclosures in the financial statements.

178   It is a general principle of trust law that trustees do not benefit from their trust. However, some individual trustees may be paid for their services and professional trustee organisations may be paid by a pension scheme. This apart, pension scheme trustees are prohibited from transacting directly with the pension scheme, although transactions between pension schemes and businesses in which any of the trustees have an indirect interest (for example, as a shareholder or a director) are not necessarily prohibited. The pension scheme trustee who is also a scheme member, is not necessarily prohibited from benefiting as a scheme member from decisions taken as a trustee.

179   In addition, employer-related investments are prohibited or restricted by the legislation.

180   Detailed guidance for trustees, employers and advisers on conflicts of interest is provided by TPR and is available on its website[13].

ISA (UK) 570: GOING CONCERN

181   ISA (UK) 570 deals with the auditor's responsibilities relating to going concern and the implications for the auditor's report.

182   FRS 102 requires trustees to prepare a statement of net assets available to meet benefits which excludes the obligations to meet promised pension benefits (for defined benefit schemes). A statement of the actuarial present value of such obligations and related specified disclosures is required to be disclosed in a separate report, which is not required to be audited (but which falls within the scope of ISA (UK) 720), alongside the financial statements.

183   The going concern basis is used in the preparation of the financial statements unless a decision has been made to wind up the scheme, an event triggering wind up has occurred, e.g. insolvency of the employer, or the scheme has entered the PPF assessment period and there is no realistic alternative to the eventual admission of the scheme and the transfer of its assets and liabilities to the PPF. The SORP explains that whilst the pension scheme is in the PPF assessment period and the outcome of the assessment is uncertain, the financial statements

---

[13] *This includes:*
- *www.thepensionsregulator.gov.uk/guidance/guidance-conflicts-of-interest.aspx*
- *www.thepensionsregulator.gov.uk/trustees/db-conflicts-of-interest.aspx*
- *www.thepensionsregulator.gov.uk/conflicts-of-interest.aspx*

continue to be prepared on the going concern basis. Even when the going concern basis is not used, there may not be any impact on the valuation of scheme investments if the timescale of the wind up allows investments to be realised without incurring significant redemption penalties. The SORP states that the basis of preparation of the financial statements does not need to refer to the going concern concept unless the trustees or employer have taken a formal decision to wind up the scheme or there has been a cessation event.

Notwithstanding the considerations above relating to the requirement to use the going concern basis of preparation, the trustees of a pension scheme are required to comply with the requirements of FRS 102 (paragraphs 3.8 and 3.9) regarding the assessment and disclosure of material uncertainties relating to going concern. The Pensions SORP identifies that FRS 102 requires: **184**

- when preparing financial statements, the management of an entity using the FRS shall make an assessment of the entity's ability to continue as a going concern … In assessing whether the going concern basis of accounting is appropriate, management takes into account all available information about the future, which is at least, but is not limited to, twelve months from the date when the financial statements are authorised for issue; and

- when management is aware, in making its assessment, of material uncertainties related to events or conditions that cast significant doubt upon the entity's ability to continue as a going concern, the entity shall disclose those uncertainties.

Events or conditions that may give rise to a winding up of the scheme are likely to be relevant considerations in the trustees' assessment. For example, such events or conditions may give rise to a decision to wind up the scheme (for example, by the sponsoring employer or by the trustees), or may trigger a winding up of the scheme (for example, an event as set out in the trust deed and rules that trigger winding-up) or may otherwise have the potential to make winding up unavoidable. The nature and extent of the trustees' assessment will depend on the circumstances. **185**

In making their assessment of the scheme's ability to continue as a going concern, the trustees of a defined benefit scheme do not necessarily need to prepare and review forecast financial information in order to confirm that their scheme will be able to meet promised benefits in full as they fall due. However, there may be circumstances where it is important to do so. For example, where a scheme is subject to an unexpectedly high number of early retirements, the trustees may need to prepare information (including forecast cash flows) to provide an assessment of whether there are sufficient liquid assets held by the scheme in order to meet pension payments as they fall due. **186**

They may also need to do so as part of the trustees' assessment of the scheme's reliance on the continuation of financial support due under the employer covenant. Trustees also consider whether there are events or conditions that may cast significant doubt on the scheme's ability to continue as a going concern, for example circumstances that indicate that the scheme may be wound up (for example, because the scheme may need to enter a PPF assessment period, or it has and the outcome of the assessment is uncertain). **187**

In applying the requirements of ISA (UK) 570, the scheme auditor's assessment of a scheme's ability to continue as a going concern takes account of the differences between a pension scheme and a commercial entity. **188**

189 In accordance with ISA (UK) 200 (Revised June 2016), the auditor maintains professional scepticism throughout the audit, including when considering the scheme's ability to continue as a going concern. In the case of a pension scheme, the primary area for the attention of the scheme auditor will be whether circumstances have arisen that have triggered the wind up of the scheme or that provide evidence that a winding up of the scheme (either outside the PPF or on transfer of assets into the PPF) may occur. The pension scheme auditor's evaluation of the trustees' assessment of the scheme's ability to continue as a going concern includes making enquiries of the trustees as to whether circumstances have arisen that mean that the scheme must be wound up or that it may be appropriate to wind up the scheme and will include, where appropriate, evaluating the process of assessment followed by the trustees and reviewing the steps that the trustees have taken to confirm the scheme's ability to continue as a going concern. As TPR has the power to order a scheme to be wound up, the scheme auditor also considers the correspondence between the trustees and TPR in relation to considering whether TPR will wind-up the scheme.

190 Where the auditor identifies or is made aware of circumstances which indicate that it is likely that the scheme will be wound up or that it may be appropriate for it to be wound up, the auditor discusses the matter with the trustees and performs procedures as necessary to obtain sufficient appropriate audit evidence to conclude whether the trustees have properly assessed the risk and made appropriate adjustments to asset values (where the going concern basis is not applicable) and / or disclosures in the financial statements and annual report.

191 If events or conditions are identified that may cast significant doubt on the scheme's ability to continue as a going concern but, based on the audit evidence obtained the auditor concludes that no material uncertainty exists, ISA (UK) 570 requires the auditor to evaluate whether, in view of the requirements of the applicable financial reporting framework, including FRS 102, the financial statements provide adequate disclosures about those events or conditions.

ISA (UK) 580: WRITTEN REPRESENTATIONS

192 ISA (UK) 580 deals with the auditor's responsibility to obtain written representations from management and where applicable those charged with governance. Written representations on their own do not provide sufficient appropriate audit evidence about any of the matters with which they deal.

193 The body of trustees as a whole is responsible for the contents and presentation of the financial statements and the representation letter should therefore be approved by the trustee body.

194 Appendix 2 provides extracts of a representation letter which might be different to those included in the example representation letter included in ISA (UK) 580.

195 In most pension schemes, day-to-day management is delegated to a scheme management team or provided by a third-party service organisation. In these circumstances, the trustees may wish scheme management or the third-party service organisation to provide a representation to them in relation to some or all aspects of the preparation of the financial statements. This is a relationship matter for the trustees and should not impact on the nature or strength of the representations made by the trustees to the auditor.

ISA (UK) 620: USING THE WORK OF AN AUDITOR'S EXPERT

ISA (UK) 620 deals with the auditor's responsibilities relating to using the work of **196** an individual or organisation in a field of expertise other than accounting or auditing.

Areas in which the scheme auditor may use the work of its own expert to provide **197** audit evidence include fair value valuations of certain investments, for example, annuities, special purpose vehicles used for asset backed contributions, longevity swaps, unquoted investments, properties, certain derivatives and alternative investment categories. Practice Note 23, *Special considerations in auditing financial instruments*, provides guidance on using experts or specialists in audits involving financial instruments, particularly complex financial instruments.

The nature of the scheme auditor's statutory opinion excludes consideration of **198** liabilities to pay pension and benefits after the end of the scheme year. As a result, the scheme auditor does not ordinarily rely on the work of the scheme actuary to provide audit evidence relating to such liabilities to support the auditor's report on a scheme's financial statements.

ISA (UK) 500 "Audit Evidence" covers how the auditor addresses information **199** prepared using the work of a management's expert. Practice Note 23 also provides guidance on audit considerations in relation to the valuation of financial instruments when a management's expert is used by the audited entity.

ISA (UK) 700: FORMING AN OPINION AND REPORTING ON FINANCIAL STATEMENTS

ISA (UK) 700 deals with the auditor's responsibility to form an opinion on the **200** financial statements and the form and content of the auditor's report.

The form and content of auditor's reports on the financial statements of **201** occupational pension schemes follow the requirements established by ISA (UK) 700, supplemented by the particular detailed requirements of the Audited Accounts Regulations which are explained in the following paragraphs.

Addressee of the report

The Audited Accounts Regulations require trustees to obtain audited financial **202** statements. Hence, the scheme auditor addresses its report on a scheme's financial statements to the trustees of the scheme and to other parties if required by the trust deed and rules.

Responsibilities of trustees for the financial statements

ISA (UK) 700 requires the auditor's report to include a section with a heading **203** "Responsibilities of management for the Financial Statements". However, recognising that "management" may not always be the appropriate term, it requires that the term used is the most appropriate in the context of the relevant legal framework – for pension schemes this will be the trustees.

The responsibilities of the trustees may vary according to the constitution of the **204** particular pension scheme, subject to overarching requirements which apply to all trustees by virtue of statute or the general law.

Requirements of the Pensions Act 1995

205   The Audited Accounts Regulations require the scheme auditor to state whether or not in the auditor's opinion the financial statements contain the information specified in the Regulations.

206   The Audited Accounts Regulations require trustees of a scheme to disclose in its financial statements whether those statements have been prepared following the financial reporting framework current at the end of the year, and, if not, to give details of any material departures. The key aspects of the current financial reporting framework for pension schemes include FRS 102 and the Pensions SORP.

207   FRS 102 contains specific requirements for pension scheme financial statements as set out in its "Specialised Activities" section covering the form, disclosures and accounting policies for pension scheme financial statements. Adherence to FRS 102's requirements is generally considered necessary for pension scheme financial statements to show a true and fair view.

208   The Pensions SORP is issued by PRAG in accordance with the FRC's code of practice for the production and issue of SORPs. The Pensions SORP sets out guidance intended to represent best practice on the form and content of the financial statements of pension schemes prepared in accordance with financial reporting standards current at the time of its issue.

209   Although the Pensions SORP's guidance is not mandatory nor a primary accounting standard, the requirement to disclose non-compliance and the general status of a Pensions SORP issued in accordance with the FRC's code, has the effect of establishing a strong presumption that financial statements which meet the requirement under PA 1995 and the Regulations to show a true and fair view will normally follow the guidance contained in the Pensions SORP. This takes into account any amendment judged to be necessary as a result of changes in financial reporting standards since its issue, as the SORP cannot override accounting standards.

Other considerations

210   The trust deed establishing a scheme may establish additional requirements concerning the contents of its financial statements (but may not derogate from the statutory requirements). The scheme auditor therefore assesses whether any such requirements are met. In addition, where the scheme auditor becomes aware of information which indicates that a transaction or transactions undertaken by the scheme may have breached any terms of its trust deed, the auditor considers the implications for its reporting responsibilities.

Relationship with duty to report to TPR

211   When determining the nature of the auditor's report, the scheme auditor also assesses whether the evidence obtained over the audit as a whole indicates that a statutory duty to report direct to TPR exists in addition to any report already made in respect of particular matters encountered in the course of their work. In making this assessment, the scheme auditor takes into account the accumulated knowledge of the scheme and the attitude of the trustees towards regulatory requirements.

212   In addition, a decision by the scheme auditor either to issue a modified or qualified opinion on the financial statements of the scheme or to qualify the auditor's statement about contributions may be of material significance to TPR and, if so, is reported to TPR by the scheme auditor without waiting for the issue of the annual report and financial statements. The report should take account of the normal reporting guidelines referred to earlier in this Practice Note.

ISA (UK) 720: THE AUDITOR'S RESPONSIBILITIES RELATING TO OTHER INFORMATION

ISA (UK) 720 deals with the auditor's responsibilities relating to "other information" included in the "annual report" that contains or accompanies the financial statements and the auditor's report thereon. **213**

The "other information" which may accompany the financial statements of a pension scheme and examples of areas of potential concern include: **214**

- Trustees' report – membership statistics: are the changes in membership numbers consistent with the financial information?

- Trustees' report – pension increases: is the rate of increase reflected in the benefit payments?

- Trustees' report: is the asset total and investment income/return consistent with the amounts shown in the financial statements?

- FRS 102 requires a Report on Actuarial Liabilities for defined benefit schemes to be reported alongside the financial statements. The SORP recommends this includes the scheme net assets at the date of the actuarial liabilities included in the report. Are the net assets included in the report consistent with the audited net assets at the relevant date?

- Governance statement signed by the Chair for DC arrangements – is it consistent with the auditor's knowledge of the scheme?

There is a legal requirement to include the latest actuary's certificate as to the adequacy of contributions in the annual report which may be different from the certificate applicable to the financial year covered by the annual report. **215**

The actuarial report is not required to be audited. However, if the auditor identifies that a material inconsistency appears to exist with the financial statements or the auditor's knowledge obtained in the audit (or becomes aware the other information appears to be materially misstated), the auditor may wish to liaise with the scheme actuary. Steps to be taken to facilitate necessary liaison with the scheme actuary are discussed in the section of this Practice Note "Liaison with the Scheme Actuary". **216**

The trustees may also distribute other documents together with the financial statements such as personal benefit statements, scheme funding statements, new rules booklets or newsletters. The scheme auditor has no statutory responsibility to consider these documents. They will only be within the scope of ISA (UK) 720 if they are included in the scheme's annual report as defined in ISA (UK) 720. **217**

THE AUDITOR'S STATEMENT ABOUT CONTRIBUTIONS (THE STATEMENT)

Requirement to provide the statement

Under Regulation 2(1)(b) of the Audited Accounts Regulations the trustees of most occupational pension schemes are required to obtain, not more than seven months after the end of the scheme year, an auditor's statement about **218** contributions under the scheme. Regulation 4 (as amended) sets out the form and content of the auditor's statement as follows:

- a statement as to whether or not in its opinion contributions have in all material respects been paid at least in accordance with the schedule of contributions or payment schedule ("the schedule"); and

- if the above statement is negative or qualified, a statement of the reasons.

219 If the trustees have not put in place a schedule the scheme auditor is required to make a statement as to whether or not contributions have been paid in accordance with the scheme rules or the contracts under which they were payable and, if applicable, the recommendations of the scheme actuary. If this statement is negative or qualified, a statement of the reasons must be given.

220 The statement is not an audit opinion. However, it is similar in that it expresses an opinion intended to convey reasonable assurance. It is normal practice for the scheme auditor to provide it at the same time as providing the audit opinion on the financial statements. The work to support the statement will draw on the auditor's work performed in relation to contributions as part of the audit of the scheme's financial statements. Accordingly, guidance to auditors on providing the statement is set out in this Practice Note. The auditor's statement about contributions is presented separately from the opinion on the financial statements.

221 There is no statutory requirement to obtain a statement from the auditor where a scheme has 20 or more participating employers at the start of the year. Such employers only need to be participating, they do not need to be non-associated or contributing to count towards the total.

Schedules of Contributions

222 Under section 227 of PA 2004 the trustees or managers of pension schemes subject to the Act's Scheme Specific Funding requirements must prepare and from time to time review and if necessary revise a schedule of contributions. The required contents of the schedule of contributions are set out in Regulation 10 of the Occupational Pension Schemes (Scheme Funding) Regulations 2005 and include the rates and due dates of all contributions (other than voluntary contributions)

223 The schedule must be signed by the trustees or managers of the scheme and make provision for signature by the employer (unless the scheme rules provide otherwise) in order to signify agreement to matters included therein. The schedule must incorporate the actuary's certification, as set out in the Regulations.

224 A schedule of contributions is only legally effective from the date of certification by the scheme actuary.

Payment Schedules

225 Under section 87 of PA 1995 the trustees of most defined contribution pension schemes must secure that a payment schedule is prepared, maintained and from time to time revised. It is notable that this requirement is worded slightly differently from that for a schedule of contributions. The required contents of a payment schedule include separate entries for the rates and due dates of contributions (other than voluntary contributions) payable towards the scheme by or on behalf of each employer. The content of the payment schedule should be as specified in the scheme documentation or, in the absence of this, as agreed between the trustees and the employer and if agreement cannot be reached with the employer the payment schedule should be prepared and put in place by the trustees without the employer's agreement.

Trustees' regulatory responsibilities

Schedules are part of a regulatory mechanism to make sure that the employer pays **226** the right contributions on time. The relevant TPR Codes of Practice clarify that the trustees are responsible for monitoring that the contributions due to the scheme are in fact paid, taking action to address late or underpaid contributions and reporting to TPR where appropriate. Guidance on the approach to monitoring contributions, taking actions for late or underpaid contributions and reporting late contributions is set out in Code of Practice 03: Funding Defined Benefits (for schedules of contributions), Code of Practice 05: Reporting Late Payment of Contributions to Occupational Schemes (for payment schedules) and Code of Practice 13 Governance and administration of occupational trust-based schemes providing money purchase benefits.

The employer has responsibilities for complying with the schedule and legal **227** requirements for calculation of contributions and for paying them over completely, accurately and on a timely basis.

Scope of schedules and reporting

It is not necessary for schedules to cover all contributions payable to a scheme. **228** The auditor therefore identifies which contributions are covered by the schedule and which are not. It is also important for the readers of the auditor's statement about contributions to understand which contributions are covered by it and which are not. To assist in this the trustees prepare a Summary of Contributions paid to the scheme under the schedule and the scheme auditor refers to this in the auditor's statement. The trustees' Summary of Contributions is included in the annual report and it is helpful for it to include a reconciliation of contributions under the schedule to total contributions reported in the financial statements. Normal reconciling items are, for example, additional voluntary contributions or special employer contributions not included in the schedule.

The schedule should provide sufficient clarity as to the amount and timing of **229** contributions to enable the auditor to form an opinion whether they were paid in accordance with the schedule. The auditor evaluates the disclosure within the Summary of Contributions with particular focus on whether contributions covered by the schedule are clearly distinguished from those which are not covered by the schedule. AVCs and augmentations may not be included in the schedule in which case the auditor does not report on them. However, this is not always the case, and the auditor evaluates the wording of each relevant schedule to ascertain and document reasons why particular classes of contributions are or are not covered by the auditor's statement. As part of this evaluation the auditor considers whether contributions are required by the schedule or are merely referred to in the schedule.

Another potential area of complication is where the recognition point for income **230** in the financial statements differs from the due date for payment, which may be after the year end or even after the deadline for obtaining the auditor's statement. Examples of these are:

- deficit funding contributions which may be recognised on receipt subject to conditions outlined in the SORP, which may be earlier than the strict due date; or

- top-up payments (e.g. for expense contributions or for payroll-related contributions where estimates are paid over monthly with an annual adjustment).

231 Such timing differences may be shown as reconciling items between contributions covered by the schedule and contributions reported in the financial statements. In practice most Summaries of Contributions are prepared by trustees on the same basis of recognition as contributions reported in the financial statements, but it is recognised that a cash basis or due date basis may be more appropriate for some schemes. Where the trustees change basis from one year to the next, the auditor needs to ensure that contributions are not omitted or double-counted as a result of the change.

232 Where a schedule is not in place the auditor reports on whether contributions are paid in accordance with the trust deed and rules and, if applicable, the recommendations of the actuary. These requirements may not be included in the annual report and if so the auditor considers whether it would be useful for them to be included in the Summary of Contributions prepared by the trustees.

Effective date for schedules

233 A schedule of contributions is legally effective from the date of certification by the scheme actuary. Contributions received prior to the certification date need to be considered in relation to the schedule of contributions applicable at that time or, if no schedule of contributions was in place, against the rules of the scheme and, where appropriate, the recommendations of the scheme actuary.

234 Revised schedules of contributions are sometimes drafted so that they are effectively backdated, e.g. to the beginning of the scheme year or the previous valuation date. As the revised schedule is only effective from the date of certification by the scheme actuary, the auditor reports on the schedule of contributions that is legally in force until the revised schedule is certified ignoring any changes to contributions brought about by the subsequent schedule. However, a schedule may specify that a catch-up payment be made by a date after the schedule is effective, for example an extra x % in respect of the previous 12 months payable no later than one month after certification. This catch-up payment is not backdating, and should therefore be considered in scope of the schedule and the auditor's statement thereon, even though it related to periods prior to the effective date and may in practice have been paid before the schedule is certified.

235 Where contributions are increased on a back-dated basis, this will result in additional contributions being classified as "other contributions" in addition to those required by the schedule of contributions. As the statutory requirement is to report whether contributions have in all material respects been paid **at least** in accordance with the schedule, overpayment is not grounds for qualification of the opinion in the auditor's statement.

236 Where contributions are decreased on a back-dated basis, the auditor will need to consider qualifying the statement about contributions if contributions were effectively materially underpaid in the period immediately before the new schedule took legal effect.

237 In relation to payment schedules, there is no equivalent certification requirement to act as a legal trigger to make a payment schedule effective so the picture is not as clear as it is for a schedule of contributions. The law does not require a payment schedule to be physically signed by the trustees or employer, merely agreed between them, or failing agreement, put in place by the trustees. The auditor therefore satisfies itself about the date from which the payment schedule was "in place". In the absence of legal or other guidance the auditor should regard a payment schedule as being effective from the date it is used by the trustees to monitor the receipt of contributions to the scheme from the employer. It therefore follows that a payment schedule is not effective for periods prior to its preparation and use. A payment schedule can be amended by the trustees and the employer to refer to contribution arrangements that were omitted but the omitted arrangements will only be effective from the date they are included in the payment schedule. They cannot have retrospective effect.

Both types of schedule have a legal requirement for periodic review and updating. **238** However, changes may occur in a scheme, such as commencement of auto-enrolment or creation of a new class of members, which may initially not be covered by the schedule. New types of contributions of this nature are therefore in addition to those payable under the schedule and are not covered by the auditor's statement until the schedule is next revised to include them. The law does not allow for the reporting of some contributions against the schedule or schedules and others against the scheme rules (and recommendations of the actuary where relevant) for the same period of time.

Materiality

The scheme auditor provides statements in relation to contributions due under the **239** schedule and therefore plans and carries out its work with a reasonable expectation of detecting errors which are material to contributions due under the schedule as a whole rather than, for example, at an individual member level. Therefore, the scheme auditor needs to consider materiality in relation to the statement about contributions when planning and performing its work.

The auditor provides statements as to whether contributions have in all material **240** respects been paid at least in accordance with the schedule. As a result, the auditor considers whether any breaches of the schedule in relation to the timing and/or amount of contributions that the auditor has detected from its work require the auditor to qualify its statement. This is a matter of professional judgment and it is important that the auditor documents the considerations and conclusions on the identification of breaches of the schedule. In making this judgment, the auditor may consider the effect of late payment on the overall contributions required by the schedule to be paid to the scheme.

Having regard to the reporting requirements in deciding whether or not an **241** exception is material in the context of reporting on contributions, the auditor only takes account of the facts and effects of the exception. The auditor does not take into account the reasons why the exception occurred. The reasons and surrounding circumstances, including action taken to resolve the issue are, however, relevant in deciding whether or not the matter is of significance for reporting to the Pensions Regulator.

In circumstances where a schedule is not in place or a schedule has ceased to have **242** effect, for example, in the case of a schedule of contributions, because the scheme has commenced winding up, or been the subject of a scheme failure notice (triggering commencement of PPF assessment, which causes it to lapse), the Audited Accounts Regulations require the auditor to provide a statement as to whether or not contributions have been paid in accordance with the scheme rules and, if applicable, the recommendations of the scheme actuary. In such circumstances the reporting requirement does not include "in all material respects" which is part of the opinion when reporting against schedule requirements. However, the auditor's statement provides reasonable (not absolute) assurance and the auditor takes this into account when considering, for example, trivial exceptions, as qualifying for trivial breaches of the trust deed and rules may give an unrealistic impression of the precision under which the auditor's work has been performed.

243   Scheme rules do not normally specify the dates on or before which contributions are required to be paid to a scheme. There is a specific legal requirement for contributions deducted from members' pay (which does not include salary sacrifice contributions which are employer contributions) to be paid over by the 19th (or 22nd if paid by electronic means) of the month following deduction. For other types of contributions, in the absence of any specific indications, it may be appropriate to regard the requirements of the scheme rules as having been met if the correct amounts of contributions were paid before the summary of contributions is approved by the trustees.

244   There can be cases where late contributions are not required to be reported to TPR or members by the trustees or the auditor, because they are not judged to be of material significance to TPR (see paragraphs 265 to 274), but do represent a material breach of the schedule of contributions or payment schedule. Therefore, late contributions which are not required to be reported to TPR may nonetheless result in a qualified auditor's statement about contributions.

Work to be performed

245   In order to report on contributions, the scheme auditor obtains either the schedule of contributions or the payment schedule, and undertakes procedures in order to obtain sufficient appropriate evidence to conclude on whether or not contributions payable to the scheme have been paid for the amounts, and at the times, set out in the applicable schedule. In doing this the scheme auditor has regard to both the amount of contributions received and the timing of those contributions.

246   The trustees have responsibility for designing and operating controls to check that the contributions which are due to the scheme are paid in accordance with the schedule or other relevant requirements. Where the auditor considers that effective controls are in place, the auditor may gain evidence to support its opinion by testing those controls. Additional guidance is provided in TPR Code of Practice 03 Funding Defined Benefits, Code of Practice 05 Reporting Late Payment of Contributions to Occupational Money Purchase Schemes and Code of Practice 13 Governance and administration of occupational trust-based schemes providing money purchase benefits.

247   Some issues that may require consideration in assessing whether contributions payable to the scheme have been paid for the amounts, and at the times, set out in the applicable schedule include:

- changes in the rates of contributions payable and the timing of the implementation of the change in the employer payroll and the amendment to the schedules;
- changes in the definition of pensionable pay;
- where calculations of contributions include rates that depend on the identity of the employing company within a group, member age and/or members' employment status. The auditor considers the procedures adopted by the trustees for ensuring the correct allocation of members to age bands, employer groups or senior management/staff membership categories. In

the case of contribution rates that are variable or discretionary, the auditor pays particular attention to the manner in which the trustees exercise their discretion or monitor the discretion of members to change rates as a basis for ensuring that contributions are received in accordance with the requirements of the schedule of contributions or payment schedule (as applicable);

- whether the schedule is sufficiently clear in its drafting to allow the auditor to properly assess whether contributions have been paid in accordance with its requirements;

- the trustees' systems of recording and monitoring contributions;

- any reports to TPR by the trustees of late or inaccurate contributions;

- whether there have been any member complaints about incorrect contributions, for example, in response to annual benefit statements issued to members;

- where contributions are payable on a contingent event, for example profit sharing; and

- where contributions are made with an asset other than cash.

As trustees have responsibility for operating controls and processes to enable them **248** to monitor that contributions required to be paid have in fact been paid, the auditor may be able to gain sufficient evidence of the amount and timing of contributions from the trustees' own records, without the need to visit employer payrolls. However, where sufficient audit evidence is not available from the trustees' records the auditor may need to obtain evidence from employer payrolls. The scheme auditor does not have a legal right of access to the employer (although this can often be arranged by the trustees) but the employer (and its auditor) has a statutory duty to provide information to the trustees which the scheme auditor reasonably requires, and for the trustees to make such information available to the scheme auditor.

Employers may have a significant number of separate payroll sites, and **249** contributions in respect of employees at different sites can rarely be regarded as a homogeneous population for sampling purposes. The auditor therefore needs to consider the nature of employer payroll arrangements when designing and performing procedures to obtain sufficient appropriate evidence.

Reporting

The statement about contributions is not the audit opinion on the financial **250** statements and the work performed by the scheme auditor to provide the statement is different to that of the audit. It is therefore important that the reader of the statement does not confuse it with the audit opinion on the financial statements and, therefore, it is presented separately from the auditor's report on the financial statements.

Trustees are required by the Disclosure Regulations (SI 2013 No 2734) to give **251** additional information in the annual report where contributions have not been paid in accordance with the schedule and the auditor should refer to this disclosure if it is necessary to explain the basis for a modified opinion in the statement.

When reporting, it is important that the auditor identifies which schedule(s) have **252** been used as the basis for testing. For a schedule of contributions this is the date of certification by the actuary. Where payment schedules are dated or sequentially numbered, the date or number can be referred to. Where there is lack of clarity (e.g. the schedule is given a name other than its statutory name, or the schedule is undated/ unnumbered) the trustees should clarify in a footnote to the summary of contributions which documents they regard as the applicable schedule for this purpose, or append the relevant schedule(s) to the summary of contributions, so that the auditor can refer to the trustees' description or appended document.

253 Care is needed when reporting on schemes with multiple concurrent schedules (such as multi-employer or sectionalised schemes). The opinion given by the auditor needs to refer clearly and unambiguously to the relevant schedules. This may be addressed by the trustees by including a table of applicable schedules as part of the summary of contributions.

254 An example auditor's statement about contributions is set out in Appendix 3.

Non-compliance with schedules

255 Legislation requires the scheme auditor to state whether or not contributions have (in all material respects) been paid at least in accordance with the relevant schedule. Therefore, in providing its statement, the scheme auditor considers whether or not contributions have been materially under-paid or paid late at any time during the period covered by the statement. If considered material, the auditor qualifies the auditor's statement although where the impact of the exceptions is considered both material and pervasive an adverse opinion on contributions may be more appropriate.

256 Legislation requires the auditor to report against a schedule if a schedule exists, and if it does not exist, the auditor reports against scheme rules or relevant contracts and, if applicable, recommendations of the actuary. The question arises as to how the auditor should respond in cases where a schedule exists but it is significantly deficient, for example it omits major categories of contributions received by the scheme which would normally be expected to be included in a schedule. Whilst in principle, the absence of expected content would typically lead to a disclaimer of opinion on contributions, the deficiencies may be such that the schedule does not actually meet the legal requirements for a schedule, in which case the auditor would revert to an opinion based on scheme rules. Concluding whether or not a schedule is legally effective is not a matter for the auditor, and trustees would normally be expected to take legal advice in case of doubt in this area. Failure to have a schedule in place where one is required would be a breach of the law and the auditor would also need to consider whether this was of material significance for reporting to TPR.

Liaison with the scheme actuary[14]

257 The ICAEW has issued more general guidance on this subject entitled: TECH 02/08: Actuaries' and Auditors' Inter-professional Communication – Pensions and Other Post-Retirement Benefits.

258 ISA (UK) 720 requires the scheme auditor to consider whether other information included in the annual report, which contains or accompanies the financial statements and the auditor's report thereon, is materially inconsistent with the financial statements or the auditor's knowledge obtained in the audit. If the auditor identifies that a material inconsistency appears to exist (or becomes aware the other information appears to be materially misstated) the auditor is required, inter

---

[14] *The ICAEW has issued more general guidance on this subject entitled: TECH 02/08: Actuaries' and Auditors' Inter-professional Communication – Pensions and Other Post-Retirement Benefits.*

alia, to discuss that matter with management and, if necessary, perform procedures to conclude whether there is a material misstatement of the other information or the financial statements. In performing the procedures required by ISA (UK) 720, the auditor may wish to liaise with the scheme actuary.

The auditor and scheme actuary will ordinarily look to the scheme trustees (rather **259** than each other) as the primary source of information in relation to their professional roles. However, reference to arrangements for direct communication between the scheme auditor and the scheme actuary is normally included in the engagement letters of both the scheme auditor and the actuary. Such access is relevant to a number of areas of the scheme auditor's responsibility not just the application of ISA (UK) 720, including:

(a) in planning the timing of audit procedures in the context of the trustees' timetable for the annual report, the scheme auditor may wish to liaise with the scheme actuary to understand the nature and timing of any planned actuarial statements or certificates;

(b) in relation to the statement about contributions, the scheme auditor may require evidence to confirm that the correct schedule of contributions was being used by the scheme during its financial year, for example, where there is doubt about the effective date of a schedule;

(c) in relation to benefit payments during the scheme year, the scheme auditor may seek to understand the nature and extent of the scheme actuary's involvement in the determination of benefits payable; and

(d) when assessing whether a breach of legal duty discovered by the scheme auditor is likely to be of material significance to TPR, the scheme auditor may if appropriate wish to consult with the scheme actuary in order to assist in forming its opinion, including understanding the content of any report to TPR already submitted by the scheme actuary.

The trustees' annual report must be available within seven months of the end of **260** the scheme year. It should include the latest actuarial certificate of the adequacy of the schedule of contributions.

Further guidance relevant to liaison with the scheme actuary is set out in the **261** section dealing with ISA (UK) 210 "Agreeing the Terms of Audit Engagements".

Reporting matters of material significance to the pensions regulator

The regulatory framework

Section 70(1) of PA 2004 imposes a reporting requirement on the following **262** persons to report breaches of the law to TPR:

● a trustee or manager of an occupational or personal pension scheme;

● a person who "is otherwise involved in" the administration of such a scheme;

● the employer in relation to an occupational pension scheme;

● a professional adviser (including scheme auditor and actuary) in relation to such a scheme; and

- a person who is "otherwise involved" in advising trustees or managers of an occupational or personal pension scheme in relation to the scheme.

263   Section 70(2) requires that a written report must be made to TPR as soon as is practicable where a person has reasonable cause to believe that:

- a duty which is relevant to the administration of the scheme in question, and is imposed by or by virtue of an enactment or rule of law, has not been or is not being complied with; and

- the failure to comply is likely to be of material significance to the TPR in the exercise of any of its functions.

264   The obligation to report under section 70 of PA 2004 does not require the scheme auditor to undertake additional work directed at identifying matters to report over and above that which is necessary to fulfil the auditor's obligations under the Audited Accounts Regulations to report on a scheme's financial statements and on the payment of contributions. The scheme auditor is therefore not required to put into place arrangements to detect matters to be reported under section 70; the auditor's obligation is limited to reporting those which come to its attention. This applies even where, as in the case of certain earmarked schemes, the scheme auditor is reporting only on contributions so that the focus of the auditor's work is very narrow. Although the scope of the auditor's work makes the discovery of reportable items less likely, the auditor of such a scheme may nevertheless find the guidance in this section of the Practice Note helpful in meeting the statutory duty under section 70.

Material significance

265   A scheme auditor conducting activities under PA 1995 needs to assess information of which it becomes aware in the course of its work which indicates that a breach of law may have taken place so as to determine whether, in the auditor's opinion, that information may be relevant to TPR.

266   TPR's Code of Practice 01. "Reporting breaches of the law", contains guidance on determining whether breaches would be of material significance to TPR. The examples are designed to aid the reporter by illustrating situations against which the actual breach can be compared, thus aiding the reporter in reaching an appropriate decision. Additional guidance is also provided in other TPR Codes of Practice, in particular Code of Practice 03 "Funding Defined Benefits" and Code of Practice 05 "Reporting Late Payment of Contributions to Occupational Money Purchase Schemes".

267   The determination of whether a matter is, or is likely to be, of material significance to TPR inevitably requires the scheme auditor to exercise judgment. In forming such judgments, the scheme auditor needs to consider not simply the facts of the matter but also the response by trustees to the breach and the wider implications of the breach. In addition, it is possible that a matter, which is not of material significance in isolation, may become so when other possible breaches are considered, together with other reported and unreported breaches of which the auditor is aware.

268   In forming an opinion as to whether a matter that has been identified is likely to be of material significance, the scheme auditor may wish to liaise with other professional advisers. This procedure helps to ensure that the cumulative effect of all breaches is considered and not only those identified by one professional adviser.

Whilst confidentiality is an implied or explicit term of scheme auditors' and   **269**
actuaries' contracts in respect of pension schemes or other entities, section 70(3)
of PA 2004 states: "No duty to which a person is subject is to be regarded as
contravened merely because of any information or opinion contained in a written
report under this section".

Hence reporting to TPR under section 70 of PA 2004 does not contravene the duty   **270**
of confidentiality, provided that the scheme auditor communicates in good faith
matters which it has reasonable cause to believe amount to a relevant breach, and
which in the auditor's view are likely to be of material significance to TPR in the
exercise of its functions.

All breaches of law require careful assessment, irrespective of their apparent   **271**
individual significance. Breaches which, of themselves, may not be significant,
may be indicative of a general lack of compliance with legal requirements or of a
more significant breach of duty which is likely to be of material significance to
TPR. Where the scheme auditor concludes (after further enquiries, if appropriate)
that this is the case, a duty to report arises. In addition the auditor carries forward a
note of unreported and reported breaches from year to year in order to gauge the
cumulative effect which might suggest a need to report to TPR.

The obligation to report as soon as reasonably practicable does not prevent   **272**
investigation by the auditor taking place as part of the process of forming an
opinion that a duty to report arises. However, the more serious the nature of the
breach, e.g. dishonesty, the more urgently investigation needs to take place.

In certain circumstances, joint reporting (e.g. a shared report between the trustees   **273**
and auditor) of breaches to TPR may be appropriate. A number of difficulties,
however, arise in practice, including:

- delays occurring due to the time taken to agree wording with all the
  signatories of the joint report; and

- the scheme auditor finding it difficult to associate itself with trustees'
  descriptions of action plans to avoid further breaches.

In the light of these practical difficulties, the FRC recommends that the scheme   **274**
auditor does not delay reporting to TPR in order to participate in a joint report;
rather the auditor reports to TPR directly once it has concluded that a breach of
material significance has occurred.

Reporting of late scheme financial statements

One of the civil breaches of PA 1995 and the Scheme Administration Regulations   **275**
is the failure by trustees or managers to obtain audited financial statements within
seven months of the end of the scheme year. Although the obtaining of scheme
financial statements is the responsibility of the trustees (who may decide to
appoint an administrator or other appropriate person to assist them), an auditor
who is aware of persistent or significant failures by trustees or managers to obtain
audited financial statements within seven months of the end of the scheme year
(for example, where the failures are as a result of poorly maintained records or
inadequate administration systems), considers reporting this to TPR where this is
likely to be of material significance to The Regulator.

Matters already reported to TPR

The requirement to report applies to all parties who are subject to the reporting   **276**
duty who become aware of a breach that is likely to be of material significance to

TPR and it is not automatically discharged by another party reporting the breach. Where a breach has already been reported to TPR, the scheme auditor's statutory duty to report should be considered in the light of the nature of the breach, any response by TPR and whether the report fully reflects the auditor's own concerns. TPR Code of Practice 01 indicates that once aware of a particular breach, TPR does not regard that breach as being of material significance for the purpose of making further reports under the requirement to report breaches of the law. An exception is where another reporter has additional or different information about that breach or the circumstances relating to it.

277   In order to document the background to a decision whether to make a report, a scheme auditor should obtain a copy of the report already made to TPR and of TPR's response.

Contents of a report to TPR

278   TPR Code of Practice 01 sets out the information the auditor should give in the report, including the name of the relevant employer.

Describing the context of a report

279   The description of the context in which the report is made sets out information relevant to a proper understanding of its subject matter, primarily concerning the way in which the matter was identified, and the extent to which it has been investigated and discussed with those responsible for stewardship of the scheme. Matters to which the pension scheme auditor may wish to refer include:

- the nature of the engagement from which the report derives. For example, it may be appropriate to distinguish between a report made in the course of the annual audit, and one which arises from the more limited engagement as the auditor of an earmarked scheme who is required to report only about the scheme's contributions;

- the applicable provisions of PA 1995 or PA 2004 and related Regulations and any interpretations of those provisions which have informed the scheme auditor's judgment;

- the extent to which the scheme auditor has investigated the circumstances giving rise to the matter reported, including (in the case of defined benefit schemes) whether the matter has been discussed with the scheme actuary or other third parties;

- whether or not the matter reported has been discussed with the trustees; and

- why the breach is thought to be of material significance.

280   It may be difficult for the auditor to confirm whether or not the trustees have taken steps to rectify a reported matter. In such circumstances, the auditor may decide to encourage the trustees to report the matter and describe their rectification process.

281   Where trustees themselves wish to make a submission to TPR as to the circumstances and steps being taken to address a reportable matter, the auditor may attach such a memorandum or report prepared by the trustees to the auditor's regulatory reports. Where such additional information is provided, the auditor refers to the additional information in the auditor's report to the TPR, and indicates whether or not the auditor has undertaken additional procedures to determine whether any remedial actions described have been taken.

Unreported breaches of legal duty

In circumstances where the auditor is uncertain whether the auditor may be required to make a report or not, the auditor considers taking legal advice. **282**

Information about unreported breaches of legal duties relevant to scheme administration is assessed by a scheme's auditor in order to determine whether the cumulative effect is or is likely to be of material significance to TPR. Where there is evidence of persistent breaches, a duty to report normally arises. **283**

The scheme auditor also takes steps to ensure that the scheme's trustees are made aware of breaches which have come to the auditor's attention in the course of its work, whether or not they have led to a duty to report to TPR, for example, by requesting that copies of any management letters dealing with such breaches are circulated to all the trustees. **284**

Information received in a capacity other than as scheme auditor

Where an audit firm is appointed as scheme auditor and is also engaged to provide services to the scheme's employer, for example, as auditor to the employer, so long as the two engagements are separate (including the staff involved), then the audit firm in its capacity as employer auditor has no duty to consider reporting to TPR. However, if the employer is alerted to a breach by the employer audit engagement team, the employer has a duty to consider reporting it. **285**

Similarly, if the audit firm provides services to other entities that provide services to the pension scheme, for example, investment managers, custodians and pensions administrators, then so long as the pension scheme audit engagement is separate from these other engagements, the audit firm in its capacity as provider of these other services has no duty to consider reporting to TPR. **286**

Failure to fulfil the statutory duty to report matters of material significance

A scheme auditor who fails to report a breach to TPR whilst having reasonable grounds to believe that a breach of law had occurred and that breach was, or was likely to be, of material significance to TPR in the exercise of its functions, is in breach of both the statutory requirement to report and of ISAs (UK) with which registered auditors are required to comply. **287**

Section 70(4) of PA 2004 makes provision for TPR, under section 10 of PA 1995, to impose civil penalties for failure to comply with section 70 of PA 2004, as well as to refer the scheme auditor to its professional body. Within any legal restrictions which may operate, TPR may make available to those bodies all the information in its possession, including copies of correspondence between TPR and the scheme auditor concerned, relevant to such a case. **288**

Non-statutory audit appointments

Certain occupational pension schemes (for example, certain small schemes) may be exempted from the statutory duty to appoint a scheme auditor but may nevertheless appoint an auditor to report on non-statutory financial statements. This may be required by their constitution or be considered prudent or otherwise appropriate by the trustees. In such cases, the auditor would normally still fall to be treated as a "professional adviser" under Section 70(1) of PA 2004 and would have a duty under section 70 to report to TPR. **289**

Appendix 1 – Illustrative examples of appointment and resignation letters

The illustrative examples of letters in this appendix have been drafted to apply to an occupational pension scheme that is subject to the requirement to obtain audited financial statements and a statement about contributions imposed under section 41 of PA 1995 and the Audited Accounts Regulations and to an "earmarked scheme" as defined by those regulations. They are not necessarily comprehensive or appropriate to be used in relation to every pension scheme, and must be tailored to specific circumstances – for example, to any special reporting requirements imposed by regulation on particular types of scheme or by the scheme documentation. Note also that certain categories of occupational pension scheme are exempt from individual provisions of the various regulations made under PA 1995. The provisions of the regulations described in the following letters therefore do not apply to all occupational pension schemes.

Examples

(1)   Example notice of appointment as scheme auditor to an occupational pension scheme under section 47 of PA 1995

(2)   Example acknowledgment of notice of appointment as scheme auditor

(3)   Example resignation letter as scheme auditor

1 Example notice of appointment as Scheme Auditor[15] to an Occupational Pension Scheme under Section 47 of the Pensions Act 1995

This form of notice of appointment has been drafted to apply to an occupational pension scheme that is subject to the requirement to appoint an auditor under section 47 of PA 1995.

(To be typed on the scheme's letterhead)

(Addressed to the auditor)

Date

Dear Sirs,

Notice of appointment as auditor to the (...) Pension Scheme

In accordance with section 47 of the Pensions Act 1995 and the Occupational Pension Schemes (Scheme Administration) Regulations 1996, we hereby give you written notice of your appointment as auditor to the (...) Pension Scheme.

Your appointment by us under the regulations is to take effect from (the date of your letter of acknowledgement). You will take instructions from ... and report to ...[16] Your appointment is initially in respect of the financial statements to be prepared as at ..., the scheme's year-end. (The scheme's previous auditor was ... (name and address, if applicable) A copy of the

---

[15] If the audit appointment is of the "non-statutory" type, then references to "auditor" in the Notice should be changed to "Non-Statutory Auditor".

[16] Auditor's terms of engagement are normally determined by the trustees and the auditor's reports are normally addressed to the trustees although some trust deeds may require otherwise.

previous auditor's statement/declaration on leaving office is attached, and we have authorised them to provide information to you as necessary and appropriate).

We confirm that, under section 27 of the Pensions Act 1995, no trustee of the scheme is connected with, or is an associate of, (firm's name), which would render (firm's name) ineligible to act as auditor to the Scheme.

Regulations require you to acknowledge receipt of this notice and accept appointment within one month.

Yours faithfully,

Signed for and on behalf of the Trustees of the (...) Pension Scheme.

2 Example acknowledgement of notice of appointment as Scheme Auditor to an Occupational Pension Scheme

(To be typed on the firm's letterhead)

The Trustees,

The (...) Pension Scheme

Date

Dear Sirs,

Acknowledgement of Appointment as Auditor of the (...) Pension Scheme

We write to acknowledge receipt of your Notice of Appointment dated ...

Our appointment as auditor of the scheme is effective from (the date of this letter Note this date cannot be retrospective). We understand that our appointment is initially in respect of the financial statements to be prepared as at ..., the scheme's year-end.

We confirm that we will notify you immediately we become aware of the existence of any conflict of interest to which we may become subject in relation to the scheme.

Yours faithfully,

3 Example resignation letter as Scheme Auditor to an Occupational Pension Scheme

(To be typed on the firm's letterhead)

The Trustees

The (...) Pension Scheme

Date

Dear Sirs,

Notice of resignation as Auditor of the () Pension Scheme[17]

We acknowledge receipt of your letter dated ... informing us of your intention to appoint ... as auditor to the scheme.

We hereby give you formal notice of our resignation as auditor of the [NAME] scheme ("the Scheme") with effect from the date of this letter.

There are no circumstances connected with our resignation which we consider significantly affect the interests of the members or prospective members of, or beneficiaries under, the Scheme.

The Trustees are reminded of their responsibility to appoint a replacement auditor within three months from the date of resignation, as required by Regulation 5(8) of the Occupational Pension Schemes (Scheme Administration) Regulations 1996.

Yours faithfully,

---

[17]*A clean notice of resignation cannot be issued if the auditor is aware of matters which are likely to be of material significance to The Pensions Regulator (TPR). In such circumstances, the auditor must report the matter to TPR and refer to them in the notice of resignation. A copy of any statement made on the auditor's resignation or removal which is negative has to be included in the scheme's annual report.*

Appendix 2 – Illustrative extracts from example of representation letter

An illustrative management representation letter is provided in Appendix 2 of ISA (UK) 580 "Written Representations". In the case of a pension scheme, such a representation from the trustees of a scheme to its scheme auditor is normally in the form of a letter, but it is not intended to be a standard letter, nor to imply that management representations must necessarily be in the form of a letter from the trustees. However, the auditor is required to request written representations. Representations by management vary from one entity to another and from one year to the next.

Although seeking representations from the trustees on a variety of matters may serve to focus their attention on those matters, and thus cause them to specifically address those matters in more detail than would otherwise be the case, a scheme auditor is aware of the limitations of management representations as audit evidence as set out in ISA (UK) 580.

The illustrative management representation letter in ISA (UK) 580 is applicable to pension scheme audits, although the auditor will consider the following amendments which may be appropriate:

(1)   The introduction will include the opinion required under the Audited Accounts Regulations and will also refer to the examination of the summary of contributions in addition to the audit of the financial statements.

> This representation letter is provided in connection with your [audit of the Scheme's financial statements/examination of the Scheme's summary of contributions] for the year ended [date] for the purpose of expressing an opinion as to whether the financial statements show a true and fair view of the financial transactions of the scheme during the period from [date] to [date] and of the amount and disposition at the end of the scheme period of its assets and liabilities, other than liabilities to pay pensions and benefits after the end of the period, have been properly prepared in accordance with applicable law and United Kingdom Accounting Standards (United Kingdom Generally Accepted Accounting Practice) and contain the information specified in the Audited Accounts Regulations and making a statement about contributions.

(2)   Other additional paragraphs specific to pension schemes which the auditor may wish to include are:

> We confirm that the scheme is a Registered Pension Scheme. We are not aware of any reason why the tax status of the scheme should change.
>
> We have not made any reports to The Pensions Regulator nor are we aware of any such reports having been made by any of our advisers. We confirm that we are not aware of any late contributions or breaches of the [payment schedule/ schedule of contributions] that have arisen which we considered did not require reporting. We also confirm that we are not aware of any other matters which have arisen that would require a report to The Pensions Regulator.
>
> There have been no other communications with The Pensions Regulator or other regulatory bodies during the scheme year or subsequently concerning matters of noncompliance with any legal duty. [We have drawn to your attention all correspondence and notes of meetings with regulators.]

Except for (give details) we have not commissioned advisory reports which may affect the conduct of your work in relation to the Scheme's financial statements and [schedule of contributions] [payment schedule].

We confirm that, under section 27 of the Pensions Act 1995, no trustee of the scheme is connected with, or is an associate of (Scheme Auditor), which would render (Scheme Auditor) ineligible to act as auditor to the Scheme.

Note

Set out below are some additional issues which, depending on the particular circumstances, the materiality of the amounts concerned to the financial statements and the extent of other audit evidence obtained, may be the subject of representations from management:

- confirmation, if relevant, that the scheme falls within the definition of an earmarked scheme as set out in the Occupational Pension Schemes (Requirement to obtain Audited Accounts and a Statement from the Auditor) Regulations 1996;

- confirmation, if relevant, that the scheme had 20 or more participating employers at the start of the year (and therefore is not required to obtain an auditor's statement about contributions).

The auditor may identify other issues for which they wish to obtain written representations from management.

Appendix 3 – Illustrative examples of auditor's statements about contributions

This appendix includes as example 1 an unmodified Auditor's Statement about Contributions and as example 2 a modified Auditor's Statement about Contributions.

Example 1: Unmodified Auditor's Statement about Contributions

The Statement about Contributions should be tailored to cover all contributions due under the schedule of contributions/payment schedule.

Independent Auditor's Statement about Contributions to the Trustees of the XYZ Pension Scheme

We have examined the summary of contributions to the XYZ Pension Scheme for [or "in respect of"] the scheme year ended […] to which this statement is attached/ which is set out in the Trustees' Report on page x.

In our opinion contributions for the scheme year ended … as reported in the summary of contributions and payable under the [schedule of contributions]/[payment schedule] have in all material respects been paid at least in accordance with the [schedule of contributions certified by the scheme actuary on [ ]/ payment schedule [dated …]].

Scope of work on Statement about Contributions

Our examination involves obtaining evidence sufficient to give reasonable assurance that contributions reported in the attached summary of contributions have in all material respects been paid at least in accordance with the [schedule of contributions/payment schedule]. This includes an examination, on a test basis, of evidence relevant to the amounts of contributions payable to the scheme and the timing of those payments under the [schedule of contributions/payment schedule].

Respective responsibilities of trustees and the auditor

As explained more fully in the Statement of Trustees' Responsibilities, the scheme's trustees are responsible for [preparing, and from time to time reviewing and if necessary revising, a schedule of contributions]/ [securing that a payment schedule is prepared, maintained and from time to time revised and for monitoring whether contributions are made to the scheme by the employer in accordance with the [schedule of contributions/ payment schedule/relevant requirements].

It is our responsibility to provide a Statement about Contributions paid under the [schedule of contributions/payment schedule] and to report our opinion to you.

Statutory Auditor   Address
Date

Example 2: Modified Auditor's Statement about Contributions

Because schedules of contributions and payment schedules are specific in relation to dates and rates, it is sometimes necessary to modify the auditor's statement about contributions under the scheme. An appropriate example for a defined benefit scheme, which may be suitably adapted for a money purchase scheme with a payment schedule, is given below.

Defined benefit (final salary) scheme which has prepared a schedule of contributions. Non-compliance with schedule – Extract from an auditor's statement including a negative statement about contributions

Qualified statement about contributions payable under the [schedule of contributions]/[payment schedule]

In our opinion, except for the effects of the departure from the schedule of contributions, contributions for the scheme year ended ... as reported in the summary of contributions and payable under the [schedule of contributions]/[payment schedule] have in all material respects been paid at least in accordance with the schedule of contributions certified by the actuary on [date].

Basis for qualified statement about contributions

As explained on page [ ], [give brief details of the departure from the schedule including an indication of the frequency of late payments, and quantification of the amounts involved – e.g. "in relation to three months during the year contributions amounting in total to £X were paid [specify timing of payment] later than the due date set out in the schedule of contributions".]

If the reason for the modified statement is both material and pervasive, for example, where no contributions have been paid at all or an incorrect rate has been used, to the auditor makes an "adverse statement about contributions under the scheme" and the wording above will need to be modified accordingly, including changing the heading to refer to an adverse statement.

Appendix 4 – Illustrative statement of trustees' responsibilities

Financial statements

The following illustrative wording may be used as the basis for preparing a statement for inclusion in a scheme's annual report. It should be modified if necessary to reflect specific responsibilities of the trustees.

> The financial statements, which are prepared in accordance with UK Generally Accepted Accounting Practice, including the Financial Reporting Standard applicable in the UK (FRS 102) are the responsibility of the trustees. Pension scheme regulations require, and the trustees are responsible for ensuring, that those financial statements:
>
> - show a true and fair view of the financial transactions of the scheme during the scheme year and of the amount and disposition at the end of the scheme year of its assets and liabilities, other than liabilities to pay pensions and benefits after the end of the scheme year; and
>
> - contain the information specified in Regulation 3A of the Occupational Pension Schemes (Requirement to obtain Audited Accounts and a Statement from the Auditor) Regulations 1996, including making a statement whether the financial statements have been prepared in accordance with the relevant financial reporting framework applicable to occupational pension schemes.
>
> > *The above points summarise the legal requirements and define the applicable financial reporting framework to be applied by those charged with governance. [Regs 3 and 3A of Audited Accounts Regulations]*
> >
> > *Reference to the audited accounts regulations are replaced with: "specified in the Schedule to the Pension Protection Fund (Valuation) Regulations 2005" for audits of relevant accounts.*
>
> In discharging the above responsibilities, the trustees are responsible for selecting suitable accounting policies, to be applied consistently, making any estimates and judgments on a prudent and reasonable basis, and for the preparation of the financial statements on a going concern basis unless it is inappropriate to presume that the scheme will not be wound up.
>
> The trustees are also responsible for making available certain other information about the scheme in the form of an annual report.
>
> The trustees also have a general responsibility for ensuring that adequate accounting records are kept and for taking such steps as are reasonably open to them to safeguard the assets of the scheme and to prevent and detect fraud and other irregularities, including the maintenance of an appropriate system of internal control.

Defined benefit schemes

The trustees are responsible under pensions legislation for preparing, maintaining and from time to time reviewing and if necessary revising a schedule of contributions showing the rates of contributions payable towards the scheme by or on behalf of the employer and the active members of the scheme and the dates on or before which such contributions are to be paid. The trustees are also responsible for keeping records in respect of contributions received in respect of any active member of the scheme and for adopting risk-based processes to monitor whether contributions are made to the scheme by the employer in accordance with the schedule of contributions. Where breaches of the schedule occur, the trustees are required by the Pensions Acts 1995 and 2004 to consider making reports to The Pensions Regulator and the members.

Money purchase schemes

The trustees are responsible under pensions legislation for securing that a payment schedule is prepared, maintained and from time to time revised showing the rates of contributions payable towards the scheme by or on behalf of the employer and the active members of the scheme and the dates on or before which such contributions are to be paid. The trustees are also responsible for keeping records in respect of contributions received in respect of any active member of the scheme and for adopting risk-based processes to monitor whether contributions are made to the Scheme by the employer in accordance with the payment schedule. Where breaches of the schedule occur, the trustees are required by the Pensions Acts 1995 and 2004 to consider making reports to The Pensions Regulator and the members.

Note: further reporting about contributions

In addition to the statutory requirements, the trust deed and rules of many schemes require the auditor to report on whether contributions have been paid to the scheme in accordance with the rules of the scheme and with the recommendations of the actuary, where one is appointed. In such cases, to make it clear that compliance with the rules and recommendations is in the first instance a matter for the trustees, references to the "schedule of contributions" or "payment schedule" in the paragraphs set out above will need to be extended to include "the scheme rules and recommendations of the actuary" (if appointed).

Appendix 5 – Definitions

Terms and abbreviations in this Practice Note for frequently used terms are as follows:

Assurance reports on internal controls of service organisations made available to third parties	*Reports on internal controls, usually those at service organisations, issued in accordance with guidance published by the Institute of Chartered Accountants in England and Wales in Technical Release AAF 01/06*
Audited Accounts Regulations	*The Occupational Pension Schemes (Requirement to obtain Audited Accounts and a Statement from the Auditor) Regulations 1996 (SI 1996/ 1975), as amended*
Disclosure Regulations	*The Occupational and Personal Pension Schemes (Disclosure of Information) Regulations 2013*
Earmarked schemes	*Money purchase schemes under which all benefits are secured by one or more policies of insurance or annuity contracts specifically allocated to individuals or their dependants. Such schemes are not required by statute to obtain audited financial statements.*
FRS	*Financial Reporting Standard issued by the Accounting Standards Board, a part of the Financial Reporting Council*
Funding Regulations	*The Occupational Pension Schemes (Scheme Funding) Regulations 2005 (SI 2005/3377)*
HMRC	*HM Revenue & Customs*
ISAs (UK)	*Auditing standards issued by the Financial Reporting Council that are based on International Standards on Auditing issued by the International Auditing and Assurance Standards Board*
PSA 1993; PA 1995; PA 2004	*The Pension Schemes Act 1993; The Pensions Act 1995; The Pensions Act 2004; Pension Schemes Act 2017*
Pensions SORP	*Financial Reports of Pension Schemes a Statement of Recommended Practice (2015)*
PRAG	*The Pensions Research Accountants Group*

Scheme	*An occupational pension scheme as defined by Part 1 Section 1 of PSA 1993; the activities of occupational pension schemes are defined in s255 of PA 2004*
Scheme Administration Regulations	*The Occupational Pension Schemes (Scheme Administration Regulations 1996 (SI 1996/1715), as amended*
TPR	*The Pensions Regulator*

Practice Note 19: The audit of banks and building societies in the United Kingdom (revised)

(March 2011)

Contents

Paragraphs

Restructuring of the FSA

Introduction   1

Legislative and regulatory framework   6

The audit of financial statements
ISA (UK and Ireland) 200: Overall objectives of the independent auditor and the
conduct of an audit in accordance with international standards on auditing
(UK and Ireland)   34
ISA (UK and Ireland) 210: Agreeing the terms of audit engagements   37
ISA (UK and Ireland) 220: Quality control for an audit of financial statements   39
ISA (UK and Ireland) 240: The auditor's responsibilities relating to fraud in an
audit of financial statements   42
ISA (UK and Ireland) 250: Section A – Consideration of laws and regulations in an
audit of financial statements   50
ISA (UK and Ireland) 250: Section B – The auditor's right and duty to report to regulators
in the financial sector   58
ISA (UK and Ireland) 300: Planning an audit of financial statements   98
ISA (UK and Ireland) 315: Identifying and assessing the risks of material
misstatement through understanding the entity and its environment   100
ISA (UK and Ireland) 320: Materiality in planning and performing an audit   123
ISA (UK and Ireland) 330: The auditor's responses to assessed risks   130
ISA (UK and Ireland) 402: Audit considerations relating to an entity using a service
organisation   148
ISA (UK and Ireland) 505: External confirmations   151
ISA (UK and Ireland) 520: Analytical procedures   156
ISA (UK and Ireland) 540: Auditing accounting estimates, including fair value
accounting estimates, and related disclosures   162
ISA (UK and Ireland) 550: Related parties   187
ISA (UK and Ireland) 560: Subsequent events   193
ISA (UK and Ireland) 570: Going concern   194
ISA (UK and Ireland) 580: Written representations   206
ISA (UK and Ireland) 600: Special considerations – audits of group financial
statements (including the work of component auditors)   208
ISA (UK and Ireland) 620: Using the work of an auditor's expert   224
ISA (UK and Ireland) 700: The auditor's report on financial statements   225
ISA (UK and Ireland) 705: Modifications to opinions in the independent
auditor's report   230
ISA (UK and Ireland) 706: Emphasis of matter paragraphs and other matter paragraphs
in the independent auditor's report   231

Other reports by the auditor   232

Appendix 1: Illustrative examples of auditor's reports

Appendix 2: The main parts of FSMA 2000 relevant to banks and building societies

Appendix 3: FSMA 2000, BS Act 1986 and related statutory instruments: important provisions for auditors

Appendix 4: The FSA handbook

Appendix 5: Possible factors that may indicate going concern issues

Appendix 6: Reporting direct to the FSA – statutory right and protection for disclosure under general law

Appendix 7: The auditors' right and duty to report to the FSA: examples of reportable items

Appendix 8: Definitions

Editorial note – References to ISAs are to previous versions available online on Croner-i Tax and Accounting.

Preface

This Practice Note contains guidance on the application of International Standards on Auditing (ISAs) (UK and Ireland) issued by the Auditing Practices Board ("the APB") to the audit of banks and building societies in the United Kingdom (UK). In addition a number of other entities, for example consumer finance companies, compete with banks in areas of banking business outside of deposit taking and auditors of such entities may find the guidance in this Practice Note helpful. A bank or building society can also be an "authorised firm" in the context of regulation under the Financial Services and Markets Act 2000.

The Practice Note is intended to assist auditors in applying the requirements of, and should be read in conjunction with, ISAs (UK and Ireland), that apply to audits of financial statements for periods ending on or after 15 December 2010. This Practice Note sets out the special considerations relating to the audit of banks and building societies which arise from individual ISAs (UK and Ireland) listed in the contents. It is not the intention of the Practice Note to provide step-by-step guidance to the audit of banks and building societies so where no special considerations arise from a particular ISA (UK and Ireland), no material is included.

Auditors of banks need to be aware of the specific regulatory requirements, including capital adequacy requirements, that apply to banks, some of which impact on the auditor. This Practice Note gives guidance on these. Other particular areas of bank accounts that can necessitate special audit considerations are those that require preparers to exercise significant judgment, particularly the valuation of complex financial instruments and the calculation of impairment provisions for loan portfolios. Many banks have extensive trading portfolios of derivatives and other complex financial instruments and so this Practice Note should be read in conjunction with Practice Note 23 (Revised), "Auditing Complex Financial Instruments – Interim Guidance". The valuation of complex financial instruments is an area where the auditor may need to consider the use of specialist staff.

One further important area where the nature of banking business requires special consideration is in the assessment of going concern and disclosure of related liquidity risks.

The term "Investment Bank" is commonly used to refer to entities that are engaged in primary or secondary trading in the debt, equity and commodity markets or in the provision of corporate finance advice. Many of these entities are banks, i.e. they hold an authorisation to accept deposits but some are not and so the term investment bank can be confusing. This Practice Note together with Practice Note 23 (Revised) considers issues relating to the principal secondary market trading activities of such entities but does not include any special considerations relating to primary market activities or the specialist nature of commodity trading.

This Practice Note has been prepared with advice and assistance from staff of the FSA and is based on the legislation and regulations in effect at 1 February 2011.

Restructuring of the FSA

In June 2010 the UK Government announced that the FSA would be restructured in 2012. In preparation for this the FSA has indicated that it will undertake a reorganization in 2011. The APB intends to update the references to the FSA within Practice Note 19 at the appropriate time. The APB will only consult on this update if there are associated changes in the regulations that have a substantive effect on the audit.

Introduction

1   Banks can operate in the UK as:

- a company incorporated in the UK which is authorised[1] by the Financial Services Authority ("FSA") to accept deposits, which is required to comply with BIPRU[2] and is not a building society ("UK bank");

- a UK branch of an entity incorporated outside the EEA, authorised by the FSA to accept deposits and which is required to comply with BIPRU ("non EEA bank");

- a UK branch of a credit institution incorporated in the EEA which has exercised EEA Passport rights[3] to carry on regulated activities in the UK ("EEA bank").

A building society is a mutual society incorporated under the Building Societies Act 1986 ("BS Act 86") – ("building society").

Auditors of entities that carry out similar business to banks and building societies but do not take deposits may find the guidance in this Practice Note useful.

2   This Practice Note addresses the responsibilities and obligations of the auditor concerning:

- the audit of the financial statements in accordance with the Companies Act 2006[4] ("CA2006") and Large and Medium-sized Companies and Groups (Accounts and Reports) Regulations 2008[5] ("Companies and Groups Accounts Regulations 2008") – applicable to UK banks;

- the audit of the financial statements in accordance with BS Act 1986 and Building Societies (Accounts and Related Provisions) Regulations 1998[6] ("BS Accounts Regulations 1998") and related obligations – applicable to building societies;

- the right and duty to report direct to the FSA[7] in certain circumstances – applicable to UK banks, non EEA banks, building societies and to EEA banks with top-up permissions[8];

---

[1] *Authorised under FSMA 2000 to undertake regulated activities.*

[2] *Prudential sourcebook for Banks, Building Societies and Investment Firms.*

[3] *Exercising passport rights entitles an entity incorporated in one EEA member state ("home country") who is authorised to conduct one or more regulated activities subject to the passport rights in the home country to establish a branch and carry out those regulated activities in another EEA member state ("host country") without the need to be authorised by the host country supervisor, (in the UK the FSA) in respect of activities that are subject to the passport rights.*

[4] *Banks which are incorporated in the United Kingdom are subject to the provisions of the Companies Act 2006.*

[5] *SI 2008/410.*

[6] *SI 1998/504 (as amended).*

[7] *Provided for in s342 and s343 FSMA 2000 and Financial Services and Markets Act 2000 (Communications by Auditors) Regulations 2001 (SI 2001/2587).*

[8] *A Part IV permission granted by the FSA to an EEA bank to enable it to undertake a UK regulated activity in the UK for which authorisation to undertake the activity in the home country is not required by the home country supervisor.*

- reporting on interim net profits for the purposes of their inclusion in capital resources. This is applicable to UK banks and building societies but required only if requested by the entity; and

- reporting on a statement of particulars of transactions and arrangements concerning directors under s78(9) BS Act 86 applicable to building societies.

Non EEA banks and EEA banks are not subject to the audit provisions of the **3** CA2006 and so the terms of engagement are a matter of contract between the auditor and their client who may, for example, be local or head office management or the EEA/non EEA bank's home country auditor. Such engagements take many different forms: the auditor may be asked to report on the financial statements of the UK branch or only on particular aspects thereof, and the form of their opinion will also vary from case to case. The auditor undertaking such an assignment does not have to apply International Standards on Auditing (ISAs) (UK and Ireland) unless required to by the terms of engagement but, if they are not applied, the auditor may find some of the guidance in this Practice Note of assistance.

In addition to accepting deposits, banks and building societies may also undertake **4** other activities regulated under the Financial Services and Markets Act 2000 (FSMA 2000) for which Part IV permissions[9] from the FSA are required. This may include one or more forms of investment business or insurance intermediation. These regulated activities are subject to FSA conduct of business rules and can give rise to auditor reporting responsibilities concerning client assets. This can occur even where the entity is not authorised to hold client assets – a negative assurance report. These reporting responsibilities are addressed in Practice Note 21, "The Audit of Investment Businesses in the United Kingdom (Revised)"[10]. In addition, banks and building societies may also undertake regulated mortgage activity. While this also requires separate Part IV permissions and is also subject to FSA conduct of business rules, no auditor reporting obligations arise in relation to client assets.

The scope of the statutory audit of a UK bank's financial statements is no different **5** from that of the generality of companies incorporated in the UK. Concerning a building society, in addition to the financial statements and the directors' report, the auditor also reports on an annual business statement which accompanies the financial statements. Further, the auditor of a building society is required to report on the summary financial statement that all building societies are obliged to prepare and send to all those members entitled to receive notice of the Annual General Meeting (an option to prepare summary financial statements, rather than a requirement to do so, is available under CA2006 to listed companies including listed UK banks).

Legislative and regulatory framework

The legal and regulatory framework within which banks and building societies **6** operate in the UK is summarised in the following paragraphs.

---

[9] *A permission granted by FSA under Part IV FSMA 2000 permitting an authorised firm to carry on regulated activities as specified in the FSMA 2000 Regulated Activities Order SI 2001/544 as amended.*

[10] *Further guidance is included in ICAEW TECH 1/06: Interim guidance for auditors of insurance intermediaries on client asset reporting requirements.*

Financial statements

7   The form and content of the financial statements of UK banks prepared under UK GAAP is governed by the CA2006, Statements of Standard Accounting Practice ("SSAPs"), Financial Reporting Standards ("FRSs") and Urgent Issues Task Force ("UITF") Abstracts. The prescribed format for a UK banks' financial statements that comply with UK GAAP is set out in the Companies and Groups Accounts Regulations 2008 made under Part 15 CA2006. However, listed UK groups (including listed UK banking groups) must prepare consolidated financial statements in accordance with those International Financial Reporting Standards adopted by the European Union (EU IFRSs)[11] and those parts of CA2006 applicable to companies reporting under EU IFRSs. UK companies or non listed groups, including UK banks and banking groups, are permitted to adopt voluntarily EU IFRSs for their financial statements.

8   The form and content of a building society's financial statements prepared under UK GAAP are prescribed in the BS Accounts Regulations 1998 made under s72C BS Act 1986. These are similar to the Companies and Groups Accounts Regulations 2008 applicable to UK banks. As for UK banks, building societies apply FRSs, SSAPs and UITF abstracts when reporting under UK GAAP. Building societies with listed securities, including permanent interest-bearing shares, are also required to apply EU IFRSs in their consolidated financial statements. Like UK companies, building societies may also voluntarily adopt EU IFRSs for their entity financial statements.

9   In addition to financial statements and a directors' report, building societies are also required, by BS Act 1986, to prepare:

   • an annual business statement – part of the annual report (s74 BS Act 1986); and

   • a summary financial statement (s76 BS Act 1986).

10   The Accounting Standards Board ("ASB") has stated that it intends ultimately to converge UK GAAP with IFRS. Current ASB proposals envisage a differential reporting regime based on public accountability. This will result in all UK banks and building societies having to apply EU IFRS. However these proposals have yet to be finalised and the timetable for this has yet to be determined. In the meantime, UK Accounting Standards covering financial instruments that are consistent with IFRS[12] have been issued but are subject to complex rules as to which entities they apply to and when. As the activities of UK banks and building societies largely comprise financial instruments the auditor considers carefully which of the various accounting standards and BBA SORPs[13] apply to the entity being audited.

11   The British Bankers Association has published a voluntary Code for Financial Reporting Disclosures (the BBA Code). This sets out key principles for disclosure and also establishes a process for banks to consider areas of topical interest that may have an impact on financial reporting disclosures and how to enhance the ability to make comparisons across the banking sector. Each bank subscribing to the BBA Code states as such in its annual report. Auditors need to be alert to any disclosures that will follow from the BBA Code each year.

---

[11] *Article 4 of EC Regulation 1606/2002 as acknowledged in s403 CA2006 – the IAS Regulation.*

[12] *International Financial Reporting Standards.*

[13] *Statements of Recommended Practice issued by the British Bankers' Association and Irish Bankers' Federation.*

Financial Services and Markets Act 2000

FSMA 2000 sets out the high level regulatory framework for the financial sector **12** more generally and does not relate just to banks and building societies. Appendix 2 sets out the main parts of FSMA 2000 relevant to authorised firms which are banks or building societies.

The wide scope of FSMA 2000 reflects the FSA's extensive responsibilities. These **13** are set out in FSMA 2000 as regulatory objectives covering:

- market confidence;
- financial stability;
- the protection of consumers; and
- the reduction of financial crime.

FSMA 2000 covers not only the regulation and supervision of financial sector **14** entities but also other issues such as official listing rules, business transfers, market abuse, compensation and ombudsman schemes, investment exchanges and clearing houses.

FSMA 2000 is also supported by a large number of statutory instruments. **15** Significant components of the definition and scope of the regulatory framework are contained in the main statutory instruments. A list of important provisions of FSMA 2000 and a list of statutory instruments relevant to the auditor is included in Appendix 3.

Under Part X FSMA 2000 the FSA has the power to make "rules". The legal effect **16** of a rule varies depending on the power under which it is made and on the language used in the rule. Rules are mandatory unless a waiver has been agreed with the FSA. If an authorised firm contravenes a rule it may be subject to enforcement action and consequent disciplinary measures under Part XIV FSMA 2000. Furthermore, in certain circumstances an authorised firm may be subject to an action for damages under s150 FSMA 2000. In contrast, guidance is generally issued to throw light on a particular aspect of regulatory requirements, and is not binding. However if an authorised firm acts in accordance with it in the circumstances contemplated by that guidance, the FSA will proceed on the basis that the authorised firm has complied with the rule to which the guidance relates.

Rules made by the FSA and associated guidance are set out in the FSA Handbook **17** of Rules and Guidance ("the FSA Handbook") (see Appendix 4). The main FSA systems and control requirements are set out in the Senior management arrangements, systems and controls element of the high level standards block of the FSA Handbook ("SYSC").

The FSA Handbook is subject to periodic change. The auditor considers carefully **18** which parts of what sourcebook apply to the entity.

It is clearly unrealistic to expect members of an audit engagement team to have **19** detailed knowledge of the entire Handbook; rather ISA (UK and Ireland) 250 Section B requires the level of knowledge to be appropriate to an individual's role in the audit and sufficient (in the context of that role) to enable them to identify situations which may give reasonable cause to believe that the matter should be reported to a regulator. ISA (UK and Ireland) 220 requires the auditor to establish procedures to facilitate consultation and, thereby, to draw on the collective expertise and specialist technical knowledge of those beyond the engagement team of the auditor.

Prudential requirements

20   Banks and building societies are subject to certain prudential requirements which are detailed in GENPRU[14] and BIPRU. These include capital adequacy, liquidity[15], large exposures (concentration risk) and additional related aspects of systems and controls not covered in SYSC. There are also certain specific prudential measures applied by the FSA which entities are required to report to the FSA via prudential returns. The main measures include:

- capital adequacy – ensuring sufficient capital resources in relation to risk requirements to absorb losses;

- liquidity – ensuring sufficient liquid assets or maturing assets to meet liabilities as they fall due; and

- large exposures – avoiding undue credit risk concentrations.

The Building Societies Act 1986

21   In addition to FSMA 2000 which applies to FSA authorised firms generally, BS Act 1986 applies to building societies. It sets out the legal framework applicable to building societies. A list of important provisions of BS Act 1986 and related statutory instruments relevant to the auditor is included in Appendix 3. In addition, further guidance on constitutional matters and compliance with BS Act 1986 is set out in the Building Societies Regulatory Guide ("BSOG") and the Building Societies specialist sourcebook ("BSOCS") which forms part of the FSA Handbook. The BS Act 1986 includes, for example:

- s5 principal purpose (paragraph 22);

- s6 lending limit (paragraphs 23 to 25);

- s7 funding limit (paragraphs 23 to 25); and

- s9A restrictions on treasury activities (paragraph 26).

22   A building society's purpose or principal purpose must be to make loans secured on residential property and funded substantially by its members. The lending and funding limits (see paragraph 23 below) are quantitative criteria which help to determine a building society's compliance with this purpose. However, other factors will also be taken into account by the FSA[16] including:

- whether the society is meeting, and is expected to continue to meet, its lending and funding limits;

- the actual and projected proportion of the society's gross income that is, or is expected to be, derived from activities that are related to the making of loans secured on residential property. (Income from the society's property related insurance and valuation services might be regarded as related to the making of loans secured on residential property, but income from the society's motor insurance business (if any) would not); and

- all other relevant quantitative and qualitative factors.

---

[14]   *General Prudential sourcebook.*

[15]   *The FSA's new prudential liquidity regime is provided in BIPRU 12; transitional arrangements currently govern the transition from the regime contained in IPRU(BANK) to BIPRU 12.*

[16]   *BSOG 1.2.4.*

There are particular quantitative limits specified in BS Act 1986 that are used in **23** the assessment of compliance with this principal purpose criterion – collectively known as "nature limits". The BS Act 1986 limits are as follows:

- at least 75% of business assets must be loans fully secured on residential property-the lending limit (s6 BS Act 1986);

- at least 50% of total funds (i.e. total shareholder funds, wholesale deposits and bills of exchange and debt instruments) must be raised in the form of shares (deposits conferring membership rights) held by individual members-the funding limit (s7 BS Act 1986).

These nature limits are additional to the prudential measures referred to in **24** paragraph 20 above. BSOCS 4 provides more guidance on the application of the funding limit and, in practice, most building societies choose to apply both the funding and the lending limits more restrictively. The funding limit and the lending limit as at the end of the financial year must both be reported to members, together with the statutory limits, in the annual business statement, and are also required to be reported to the FSA. The annual business statement is reported on by the auditor and is attached to the annual accounts of the building society (see paragraphs 226 and 227).

Both these limits must be calculated on a group basis where that is appropriate. **25** With reference to the lending limit, business assets means total assets, plus provisions for bad and doubtful debts, less fixed assets, less liquid assets and less any long-term insurance funds. Business assets, therefore, typically comprise loans, investments in connected undertakings and sundry debtors and prepayments. Building societies preparing their financial statements in accordance with EU IFRS use the appropriate equivalent balance sheet captions. Residential property is defined as being land at least 40% of which is normally used as, or in connection with, one or more dwellings, or which has been, is being, or is to be developed or adapted for such use.

A building society may undertake almost any activity, provided that such activity **26** is included within its Memorandum[17] and provided that the building society or group as a whole continues to comply with the principal purpose and with the nature limits. However s9A BS Act 1986 includes a number of specific prohibitions on a building society's treasury activities, which are that (subject to certain exceptions) a building society is not permitted to:

- act as a market maker in securities, commodities or currencies;

- trade in commodities or currencies; or

- enter into any transaction involving derivative instruments, except in relation to hedging.

Reporting direct to the FSA – statutory right and duty

Under FSMA 2000 (Communications by Auditors) Regulations 2001 (SI 2001/ **27** 2587) the auditor of an authorised firm or the auditor of an entity closely linked to an authorised firm who is also the auditor of that authorised firm has a statutory duty to communicate matters of material significance to the FSA. Under s340 FSMA 2000, "the auditor" is defined as one required to be appointed under FSA

---

[17] *A Memorandum within the meaning of Sch 2 BS Act 1986.*

"rules" or appointed as a result of another enactment. In addition, s342 FSMA 2000 provides that no duty to which the auditor is subject shall be contravened by communicating in good faith to the FSA any information or opinion on a matter that the auditor reasonably believes is relevant to any functions of the FSA. Guidance on the identification of matters to be reported to the regulators is set out in the section dealing with ISA (UK and Ireland) 250 Section B.

28   An EEA bank is not required to appoint an auditor under FSA's rules in respect of its UK branch operations unless it has a top-up permission. Furthermore, a UK branch of a bank incorporated outside the UK is not required to appoint an auditor under CA2006. Consequently, if an EEA bank (without top-up permissions) appoints an auditor to undertake audit procedures at its UK branch this does not fall within the definition of "auditor" for the purposes of s342/3 FSMA 2000 and SI 2001/2587. As a result the auditor undertaking such work has neither a statutory right nor statutory duty to report direct to the FSA and may not have relief from its duty of confidentiality to its client if the auditor decides to do so. In the event that an auditor of an EEA bank identifies a matter that would be likely to be of material significance to the FSA, the auditor considers whether they have a responsibility to report such matters to the "head office" auditors of the EEA bank or to the home country regulator. See Appendix 6 concerning disclosure in the public interest.

29   A non EEA bank is required to appoint an auditor under SUP 3.3.2R in respect of its UK branch operations and therefore an auditor appointed in accordance with this rule has both the right and duty to report. Whilst, in principle, there is a requirement to appoint an auditor, there is no FSA requirement for the auditor to undertake audit procedures and there is no corresponding requirement to report on the results of those procedures. Therefore some non EEA banks with UK operations that are not material to the non EEA bank as a whole may have no need to commission an auditor to undertake audit procedures.

Communication between the FSA and the auditor

30   In February 2011 the FSA published a draft "Code of Practice for the relationship between the external auditor and the supervisor", with a final version expected later in 2011. The code of practice, which is subject to any changes as a result of the consultation, sets out principles that establish, in the context of a particular regulated firm, the nature of the relationship between the supervisor and the auditor, the form and frequency that communication between the two parties should take, and the responsibilities and scope for sharing information between the two parties. The FSA expects supervisors and auditors of banks and building societies to apply the principles set out in the code having regard to the related guidance within it.

31   Within the legal constraints that apply, the FSA may pass on to the auditor any information which it considers relevant to his function. Auditors are bound by the confidentiality provisions set out in Part XXIII of FSMA 2000 (Public record, disclosure of information and co-operation) in respect of confidential information received from the FSA. An auditor may not pass on such confidential information even to the entity being audited without lawful authority (for example if an exception applies under the FSMA 2000 (Disclosure of confidential information) Regulations 2001[18]) or with the consent of the person from whom the information was received and, if different, to whom the information relates. Further guidance

---

[18] *SI 2001/2188.*

in respect of information communicated to the auditor by the FSA is set out in paragraphs 90 – 93 below.

The auditor is required to cooperate with the FSA (SUP3.8.2R). This may involve attending meetings, including routine bilateral meetings, and providing the FSA with information about the authorised firm that the FSA may reasonably request in discharging its functions. For example this can arise in relation to FSA ARROW II risk assessments.   **32**

The auditor must notify the FSA without delay if the auditor is removed from office, resigns before the term of office expires or is not re-appointed by the authorised firm. Notification to the FSA includes communicating any matters connected with this event that the auditor considers ought to be drawn to the FSA's attention or a statement that there are no such matters (s344 FSMA 2000 and SUP3.8.11R and 12R).   **33**

The audit of financial statements

This Practice Note provides guidance for auditors applying those ISAs (UK and Ireland) that are effective for audits of financial statements for periods ending on or after 15 December 2010. The purpose of the following paragraphs is to identify the special considerations arising from the application of the "Requirements" of ISAs (UK and Ireland) to the audit of banks and building societies, and to suggest ways in which these can be addressed (extracts from ISAs (UK and Ireland) are indicated by grey-shaded boxes below). This Practice Note does not contain commentary on all of the requirements included in the ISAs (UK and Ireland) and reading it should not be seen as an alternative to reading the relevant ISAs (UK and Ireland) in their entirety. In addition, where no special considerations arise from a particular ISA (UK and Ireland), no material is included.

ISA (UK AND IRELAND) 200: OVERALL OBJECTIVES OF THE INDEPENDENT AUDITOR AND THE CONDUCT OF AN AUDIT IN ACCORDANCE WITH INTERNATIONAL STANDARDS ON AUDITING (UK AND IRELAND)

Scope of this ISA (UK and Ireland)

This International Standard on Auditing (UK and Ireland) (ISA (UK and Ireland)) deals with the independent auditor's overall responsibilities when conducting an audit of financial statements in accordance with ISAs (UK and Ireland). Specifically, it sets out the overall objectives of the independent auditor, and explains the nature and scope of an audit designed to enable the independent auditor to meet those objectives. It also explains the scope, authority and structure of the ISAs (UK and Ireland), and includes requirements establishing the general responsibilities of the independent auditor applicable in all audits, including the obligation to comply with the ISAs (UK and Ireland). The independent auditor is referred to as "the auditor" hereafter. (Paragraph 1)

Overall objectives of the auditor

In conducting an audit of financial statements, the overall objectives of the auditor are:

(a)   To obtain reasonable assurance about whether the financial statements as a whole are free from material misstatement, whether due to fraud or error, thereby enabling the auditor to express an opinion on whether the financial statements are prepared, in all material respects, in accordance with an applicable financial reporting framework; and

(b)   To report on the financial statements, and communicate as required by the ISAs (UK and Ireland), in accordance with the auditor's findings. (Paragraph 11)

In all cases, when reasonable assurance cannot be obtained and a qualified opinion in the auditor's report is insufficient in the circumstances for purposes of reporting to the intended users of the financial statements, the ISAs (UK and Ireland) require that the auditor disclaim an opinion or withdraw (or resign) from the engagement, where withdrawal is possible under applicable law or regulation. (Paragraph 12)

The auditor shall plan and perform an audit with an attitude of professional scepticism, recognising that circumstances may exist that cause the financial statements to be materially misstated. (Paragraph 15)

34   ISAs (UK and Ireland) include a requirement for the auditor to comply with relevant ethical requirements relating to audit engagements. Auditors in the UK are subject to ethical requirements from two sources: the APB Ethical Standards for Auditors concerning the integrity, objectivity and independence of the auditor, and the ethical pronouncements established by the auditor's relevant professional body. A fundamental principle is that practitioners should not accept or perform work which they are not competent to undertake. The importance of technical competence is also underlined in the Auditors' Code[19], issued by the APB, which states that the necessary degree of professional skill demands an understanding of financial reporting and business. Practitioners should not undertake the audit of a bank or building society unless they are satisfied that they have, or can obtain, the necessary level of competence.

Professional scepticism

35   Professional scepticism is an attitude that includes a questioning mind, being alert to conditions which may indicate possible misstatement due to error or fraud, and a critical assessment of audit evidence. This includes questioning contradictory audit evidence and the reliability of documents and responses to inquiries and other information obtained from management and those charged with governance. It also includes consideration of the sufficiency and appropriateness of audit evidence obtained in the light of the circumstances.

Independence

36   Independence issues can be complex for the auditor of a bank, and to a lesser extent a building society because of banking and other relationships that the auditor and/or its partners and staff may have with the bank. The auditor makes careful reference to the APB's Ethical Standard 2 – Financial, business, employment and personal relationships.

---

[19] *This is appended to the APB's Scope and Authority of Pronouncements.*

ISA (UK AND IRELAND) 210: AGREEING THE TERMS OF AUDIT ENGAGEMENTS

Objective

The objective of the auditor is to accept or continue an audit engagement only when the basis upon which it is to be performed has been agreed, through:

(a) Establishing whether the preconditions for an audit are present; and

(b) Confirming that there is a common understanding between the auditor and management and, where appropriate, those charged with governance of the terms of the audit engagement. (Paragraph 3)

The auditor shall agree the terms of the audit engagement with management or those charged with governance, as appropriate. (Paragraph 9)

Subject to paragraph 11, the agreed terms of the audit engagement shall be recorded in an audit engagement letter or other suitable form of written agreement and shall include:

(a) The objective and scope of the audit of the financial statements;

(b) The responsibilities of the auditor;

(c) The responsibilities of management;

(d) Identification of the applicable financial reporting framework for the preparation of the financial statements; and

(e) Reference to the expected form and content of any reports to be issued by the auditor and a statement that there may be circumstances in which a report may differ from its expected form and content. (Paragraph 10)

If law or regulation prescribes in sufficient detail the terms of the audit engagement referred to in paragraph 10, the auditor need not record them in a written agreement, except for the fact that such law or regulation applies and that management acknowledges and understands its responsibilities as set out in paragraph 6(b). (Paragraph 11)

Matters which the auditor may decide to refer to in the engagement letter are as follows: **37**

- the responsibility of the directors/senior management to comply with applicable FSMA 2000 legislation and FSA Handbook rules and guidance including the need to keep the FSA informed about the affairs of the entity;

- the statutory right and duty of the auditor to report direct to the FSA in certain circumstances (see the section of this Practice Note relating to ISA (UK and Ireland) 250 Section B);

- the requirement to cooperate with the auditor (SUP3.6.1 R). This includes taking steps to ensure that, where applicable, each of its appointed representatives and material outsourcers gives the auditor the same right of access to records, information and explanations as the authorised firm itself is required to provide the auditor (s341 FSMA 2000 and SUP 3.6.2G to 3.6.8G). It is a criminal offence for an authorised firm or its officers, controllers or managers to provide false or misleading information to the auditor (s346 FSMA 2000)[20];

---

[20] *An offence is committed also under s501 CA2006 by a person who knowingly or recklessly makes to an auditor of a company a statement (oral or written) that: (a) conveys or purports to convey any information or explanations which the auditor requires, or is entitled to require, under s 499 CA 2006, and (b) is misleading, false or deceptive in a material particular. An equivalent offence is included under s79(9) of the Building Societies Act 1986.*

- the need for the entity to make the auditor aware when it appoints a third party (including another department or office of the same audit firm) to review, investigate or report on any aspects of its business activities that may be relevant to the audit of the financial statements and to provide the auditor with copies of reports by such a third party promptly after their receipt.

38   In this connection the auditor is aware that:

- the FSA does not need to approve the appointment of an auditor but may seek to satisfy itself that an auditor appointed by a firm is independent and has the necessary skills, resources and experience (SUP 3.4);

- the auditor is required to cooperate with the FSA (SUP3.8.2R); and

- the auditor must notify the FSA if the auditor ceases to be the auditor of an authorised firm.

ISA (UK AND IRELAND) 220: QUALITY CONTROL FOR AN AUDIT OF FINANCIAL STATEMENTS

Objective

The objective of the auditor is to implement quality control procedures at the engagement level that provide the auditor with reasonable assurance that:

(a)   The audit complies with professional standards and applicable legal and regulatory requirements; and

(b)   The auditor's report issued is appropriate in the circumstances. (Paragraph 6)

Reference should also be made to ISQC (UK and Ireland) 1 – *Quality Control for Firms that Perform Audits and Reviews of Financial Statements, and other Assurance and Related Services Engagements.*

The engagement partner shall be satisfied that the engagement team, and any auditor's experts who are not part of the engagement team, collectively have the appropriate competence and capabilities to:

(a)   Perform the audit engagement in accordance with professional standards and applicable legal and regulatory requirements; and

(b)   Enable an auditor's report that is appropriate in the circumstances to be issued. (Paragraph 14)

39   The nature of banking business is one of rapidly changing and evolving markets. Often new products and practices are developed which require specialised auditing and accounting responses. It is therefore important that the auditor is familiar with current practice. Audit firms organise training in these specialist areas where necessary and keep audit staff up to date with knowledge of relevant regulations.

40   As well as ensuring that the engagement team has an appropriate level of knowledge of the industry and its corresponding products, the engagement partner also satisfies himself that the members of the engagement team have sufficient knowledge of the regulatory framework within which the entity operates commensurate with their roles on the engagement.

Under ISQC (UK and Ireland) 1, an audit firm is required to establish a process to **41** monitor the audit firm's quality control policies and procedures[21]. This process is required to include, on a cyclical basis, inspection of at least one completed engagement for each engagement partner. In order to perform an effective review of a completed audit of a bank or building society, those undertaking the review will need an appropriate level of knowledge of the types of banking business undertaken by the entity and the applicable regulatory framework.

ISA (UK AND IRELAND) 240: THE AUDITOR'S RESPONSIBILITIES RELATING TO FRAUD IN AN AUDIT OF FINANCIAL STATEMENTS

Objectives

The objectives of the auditor are:

(a) To identify and assess the risks of material misstatement of the financial statements due to fraud;

(b) To obtain sufficient appropriate audit evidence regarding the assessed risks of material misstatement due to fraud, through designing and implementing appropriate responses; and

(c) To respond appropriately to fraud or suspected fraud identified during the audit. (Paragraph 10)

In accordance with ISA (UK and Ireland) 200, the auditor shall maintain professional scepticism throughout the audit, recognising the possibility that a material misstatement due to fraud could exist, notwithstanding the auditor's past experience of the honesty and integrity of the entity's management and those charged with governance. (Paragraph 12)

When performing risk assessment procedures and related activities to obtain an understanding of the entity and its environment, including the entity's internal control, required by ISA (UK and Ireland) 315, the auditor shall perform the procedures in paragraphs 17-24 [of ISA (UK and Ireland) 240] to obtain information for use in identifying the risks of material misstatement due to fraud. (Paragraph 16)

The auditor shall make inquiries of management and others within the entity as appropriate, to determine whether they have knowledge of any actual, suspected or alleged fraud affecting the entity. (Paragraph 18)

In accordance with ISA (UK and Ireland) 315, the auditor shall identify and assess the risks of material misstatement due to fraud at the financial statement level, and at the assertion level for classes of transactions, account balances and disclosures. (Paragraph 25)

As with other entities, fraud in banks and building societies, either fraudulent **42** financial reporting (for example the manipulation of profits or the concealment of losses) or misappropriation of assets, can occur through a combination of management fraud, employee fraud or fraud perpetrated by third parties. However, various factors make banks and building societies particularly vulnerable to fraud such as:

- They have custody of valuable and fungible assets including money, making them a particular target for fraudsters;

---

[21] *ISQC (UK and Ireland) 1, paragraph 48.*

- They handle very large volumes of transactions and collect and disburse large amounts of money on a daily basis, for example in taking deposits, making loans and providing a payments service to customers. This creates more opportunity for fraud unless properly controlled;

- Certain aspects of their businesses are complex both in terms of the risks taken on and the operational risks the activities entail, which makes their operations more difficult to control; and

- Banks and building societies tend to be very heavily dependent on information technology (IT) to manage their businesses. This represents a significant opportunity for computer based fraud.

As a result, fraud is an increased risk in a banking business.

43 In order to mitigate these fraud risks, it is essential for the entity to have very strong internal controls including:

- The right ethical and cultural framework being set by senior management;

- Appropriate status and authority being given to control functions such as risk and internal audit;

- Clear lines for reporting control deficiencies and suspicions of misdoings;

- Thorough procedures for investigating the background of clients and transactions;

- Strong segregation of duties;

- Clear control policies and requirements that are checked in detail and monitored by management;

- Strong IT controls to prevent fraudulent access and manipulation of data and fraudulent access to assets (e.g. via internet banking); and

- Appropriate measures in place to fight fraudulent activity, both physical and technological.

44 In addition, whilst remuneration policies can create excessive performance pressures in many industries, in certain banks and building societies or divisions of large banks (in particular treasury and investment banking operations) performance related bonuses can be significant, both in absolute terms and in relation to base remuneration. Significant bonus related remuneration often extends beyond senior management to quite junior members of staff and can lead to more pervasive pressures that increase the risks of fraudulent financial reporting as these staff seek to enhance their bonuses or protect their jobs by inflating their reported results. The FSA Remuneration Code (SYSC 19) applies to banks and building societies meeting particular conditions (set out in SYSC 19.1.1) and requires (SYSC 19.2.1) that an authorised firm must establish, implement and maintain remuneration policies, procedures and practices that are consistent with and promote effective risk management.

45 Principle 3 of the FSA Principles for Businesses (PRIN 2.1) requires a firm to take reasonable care to organise and control its affairs responsibly and effectively with adequate risk management systems. SYSC 6.1.1 requires a firm to maintain adequate policies and procedures to ensure compliance with its obligations under the regulatory system and for countering the risk that it might be used to further financial crime[22]. Whilst the inherent risk of fraud may continue to exist, the establishment of accounting

---

[22] *Further, record keeping requirements are set out in SYSC 9.*

and internal control systems sufficient to meet these requirements frequently reduces the likelihood of fraud giving rise to material misstatements in the financial statements. Guidance on the auditor's consideration of accounting systems and internal control is provided in ISA (UK and Ireland) 315 and the section of this Practice Note that covers that standard. Examples of deficiencies in control that could give rise to fraud risk factors are also set out in that section.

In considering how to respond to the threat of misstatement by fraud the auditor considers the following:
46

- A thorough understanding of the nature of the entity's business, and in particular how profits and losses can arise in relation to particular products and transactions, is very important in detecting fraud, because it enables unusual patterns and trends that may indicate fraud to be more easily identified. An auditor considers how to enhance his/her knowledge of the entity's business, for example by:

  - Interviewing a wide range of management, including business as well as financial management;

  - Discussing findings with control functions such as risk, legal, compliance and internal audit together with considering reviews undertaken by third parties such as skilled person's reports prepared under s166 FSMA 2000[23];

  - Using experts to help improve understanding;

  - Comparing the entity to peers in the market where feasible to identify unusual trends.

- Auditors of all entities familiarise themselves with the control environment as a whole and controls designed to prevent fraud that might affect the financial statements. They also assess the robustness of their design. Deficiencies in control are taken into account when planning audit procedures and reported to those in charge of governance. This is a particularly important aspect of the audit of a bank or building society because of the nature of the fraud risks they face and the complexity of the systems and controls required to combat them. The auditor ensures that the engagement team has the appropriate skills available to undertake this task, including the necessary information technology expertise.

- Many basic audit tests also help address audit fraud risk and the auditor considers the implications of the results of such tests for the risk of fraud. In particular, fraud usually has to be concealed through the use of fictitious or misleading balances. These can be revealed through:

  - Comparing balances to external sources, for example through bank and depository reconciliations;

  - Ensuring that suspense and transit accounts (the latter being accounts through which the progress of payments are monitored) are properly reviewed and promptly cleared;

  - Checking that the contents of all balance sheet accounts are properly understood and validated;

  - Verifying valuations to external sources.

---

[23] *Under S166 FSMA 2000 provides the FSA with the power to require a firm to appoint a skilled person to provide a report on any matter that the FSA may reasonably require in connection with the exercise of the functions conferred on it by or under FSMA 2000. The requirements concerning skilled persons are set out in SUP5.*

- Much fraud is brought to the attention of companies through complaints and other more confidential means of reporting. An auditor considers checking the results of whistleblowing and complaints procedures within the entity, including how the entity ensures that these procedures are robust.

- An entity's regulators may also be aware of suspicious activity and the auditor considers maintaining a dialogue with them.

- The expectations of investors and other third parties and management compensation policies can indicate areas of particular pressure for management, which could lead to management fraud. Understanding these areas can help an auditor focus work in particularly vulnerable areas.

Revenue recognition

> When identifying and assessing the risks of material misstatement due to fraud, the auditor shall, based on a presumption that there are risks of fraud in revenue recognition, evaluate which types of revenue, revenue transactions or assertions give rise to such risks.... (Paragraph 26)

47   The auditor considers how revenue recognition can be manipulated:

- Interest and fee income is typically recognized on a systematic basis over the period of a loan or deposit automatically by the bank's IT system. It is likely that the risk of material misstatement due to fraudulent revenue recognition will be reduced where relevant IT controls are strong;

- Trading income is strongly influenced by period-end valuations, so considering how fraudulent misreporting in this area can be prevented is important;

- Many entities generate significant fees, the timing of whose recognition can require considerable judgment. The auditor considers how these judgments are made and whether they are influenced by a desire for a fee to be recorded in a particular period.

Journal entries

> Irrespective of the auditor's assessment of the risks of management override of controls, the auditor shall design and perform audit procedures to:
>
> (a)   Test the appropriateness of journal entries recorded in the general ledger and other adjustments made in the preparation of the financial statements. In designing and performing audit procedures for such tests, the auditor shall:
>
> (i)   Make inquiries of individuals involved in the financial reporting process about inappropriate or unusual activity relating to the processing of journal entries and other adjustments;
>
> (ii)   Select journal entries and other adjustments made at the end of a reporting period; and
>
> (iii)   Consider the need to test journal entries and other adjustments throughout the period. (Paragraph 32)

Banks and building societies will typically have high numbers of journal entries **48** relating to the financial reporting process. When identifying and selecting journal entries for testing, the auditor ensures the complete population is identified and is alert for non-standard and unusual journal entries for further investigation.

Communication

If the auditor has identified a fraud or has obtained information that indicates that a fraud may exist, the auditor shall communicate these matters on a timely basis to the appropriate level of management in order to inform those with primary responsibility for the prevention and detection of fraud of matters relevant to their responsibilities. (Paragraph 40)

Unless all of those charged with governance are involved in managing the entity, if the auditor has identified or suspects fraud involving:

(a)   management;

(b)   employees who have significant roles in internal control; or

(c)   others where the fraud results in a material misstatement in the financial statements,

the auditor shall communicate these matters to those charged with governance on a timely basis. If the auditor suspects fraud involving management, the auditor shall communicate these suspicions to those charged with governance and discuss with them the nature, timing and extent of audit procedures necessary to complete the audit. (Paragraph 41)

If the auditor has identified or suspects a fraud, the auditor shall determine whether there is a responsibility to report the occurrence or suspicion to a party outside the entity. Although the auditor's professional duty to maintain the confidentiality of client information may preclude such reporting, the auditor's legal responsibilities may override the duty of confidentiality in some circumstances. (Paragraph 43)

The auditor shall include in the audit documentation communications about fraud made to management, those charged with governance, regulators and others. (Paragraph 46)

Reduction of financial crime is one of the FSA's statutory objectives. The FSA's **49** rules require authorised firms to report "significant" fraud, errors and other irregularities to the FSA (SUP15.3.17R). The auditor is aware of the auditor's duty to report direct to FSA in certain circumstances (see the section of this Practice Note relating to ISA (UK and Ireland) 250 Section B).

ISA (UK AND IRELAND) 250: SECTION A – CONSIDERATION OF LAWS AND REGULATIONS IN AN AUDIT OF FINANCIAL STATEMENTS

Objectives

The objectives of the auditor are:

(a)   To obtain sufficient appropriate audit evidence regarding compliance with the provisions of those laws and regulations generally recognized to have a direct effect on the determination of material amounts and disclosures in the financial statements;

> (b)   To perform specified audit procedures to help identify instances of non-compliance with other laws and regulations that may have a material effect on the financial statements; and
>
> (c)   To respond appropriately to non-compliance or suspected non-compliance with laws and regulations identified during the audit. (Paragraph 10)
>
> As part of obtaining an understanding of the entity and its environment in accordance with ISA (UK and Ireland) 315, the auditor shall obtain a general understanding of:
>
> (a)   The legal and regulatory framework applicable to the entity and the industry or sector in which the entity operates; and
>
> (b)   How the entity is complying with that framework. (Paragraph 12)

50   FSMA 2000 and related statutory instruments are important elements of the legal and regulatory framework applicable to banks and building societies. Detailed rules and guidance applicable to authorised firms is set out in the FSA Handbook. An overview of this legislation and the FSA Handbook is set out in paragraphs 12 to 19 and 27 to 33 above (and Appendices 2, 3 and 4). In addition to accepting deposits, an entity may also have one or more Part IV permissions from the FSA to undertake one or more types of investment business, insurance intermediation, regulated mortgage activity or other regulated activities. If this is the case, the auditor also considers the laws and regulations (which includes FSMA 2000 and the FSA Handbook) relevant to the entity's ability to conduct these additional regulated activities.

51   The auditor is alert to any indication that the entity is conducting business outside the scope of its Part IV permission or the entity is failing to meet FSMA 2000 Threshold Conditions[24] or contravening any Principles for Businesses[25]. Such action may be a serious regulatory breach, which may result in fines, public censure, suspension or revocation of authorisation. The auditor compares the current activities of the entity with the Scope of Part IV Permission granted by the FSA and considers ISA (UK and Ireland) 250 Section A and where appropriate ISA (UK and Ireland) 250 Section B.

> The auditor shall obtain sufficient appropriate audit evidence regarding compliance with the provisions of those laws and regulations generally recognized to have a direct effect on the determination of material amounts and disclosures in the financial statements. (Paragraph 13)
>
> The auditor shall perform the following audit procedures to help identify instances of non-compliance with other laws and regulations that may have a material effect on the financial statements:
>
> (a)   Inquiring of management and, where appropriate, those charged with governance, as to whether the entity is in compliance with such laws and regulations; and
>
> (b)   Inspecting correspondence, if any, with the relevant licensing or regulatory authorities. (Paragraph 14)

---

[24] *The minimum standards that a firm needs to meet to become and remain authorised by the FSA – see Appendix 4.*

[25] *FSA Handbook defines Principles with which authorised firms must comply – see Appendix 4.*

During the audit, the auditor shall remain alert to the possibility that other audit procedures applied may bring instances of non-compliance or suspected non-compliance with laws and regulations to the auditor's attention. (Paragraph 15)

Specific areas that the auditor's procedures may address include the following: **52**

- obtaining a general understanding of the legal and regulatory framework applicable to the entity and industry, and of the procedures followed to ensure compliance with the framework;

- reviewing the entity's Scope of Part IV Permission (an FSA document which sets out the regulated activities that the firm is permitted to engage in, including any limitations and requirements imposed on those permitted activities);

- reviewing correspondence with the FSA and other regulators (including that relating to any FSA supervisory visits, requests for information by FSA or progress concerning FSA ARROW II risk mitigation programmes);

- holding discussions with the entity's Compliance Officer and other personnel responsible for compliance;

- reviewing compliance reports prepared for the Board, audit committees and other committees; and

- consideration of work on compliance matters performed by internal audit.

Money laundering

As indicated in paragraph A11-1 of ISA (UK and Ireland) 250 Section A, in the **53** UK and Ireland, the auditor is alert for instances of possible or actual non-compliance with laws and regulations including those that might incur obligations for partners and staff in audit firms to report to a regulatory or other enforcement authority. Anti-money laundering legislation in the UK and Ireland imposes a duty on the auditor to report suspected money laundering activity.

Authorised firms are subject to the requirements of the Money Laundering **54** Regulations 2007 and the Proceeds of Crime Act 2002 as well as FSA rules. These laws and regulations require institutions to establish and maintain procedures to identify their customers, establish appropriate reporting and investigation procedures for suspicious transactions, and maintain appropriate records.

Laws and regulations relating to money laundering are integral to the legal and **55** regulatory framework within which banks and building societies conduct their business. By the nature of their business, banks and building societies are ready targets of those engaged in money laundering activities. The effect of this legislation is to make it an offence to provide assistance to those involved in money laundering and makes it an offence not to report suspicions of money laundering to the appropriate authorities, usually the Serious Organised Crime Agency ("SOCA"). FSA requirements are set out in SYSC6. In this context, the FSA has due regard to compliance with the relevant provisions of guidance issued by the Joint Money Laundering Steering Group ("JMLSG") (SYSC 6.3.5).

In addition to considering whether the entity has complied with the money **56** laundering laws and regulations, the auditor has reporting obligations under the Proceeds of Crime Act 2002, and the Money Laundering Regulations 2007, to report knowledge or suspicion of money laundering offences, including those arising from fraud and theft, to SOCA. The auditor is aware of the prohibition on "tipping off" when discussing money laundering matters with the entity. Given the nature of banking business and the likely frequency of needing to report to SOCA, the auditor is aware of the short-form[26] of reporting to SOCA that can be used in appropriate circumstances to report minor and usually numerous items. Further guidance for auditors is provided in Practice Note 12 (Revised), "Money Laundering – Guidance for Auditors on UK Legislation".

57   The auditor, in the context of money laundering, is aware of the auditor's duty to report direct to FSA in certain circumstances (see the section of this Practice Note relating to ISA (UK and Ireland) 250 Section B).

ISA (UK AND IRELAND) 250: SECTION B – THE AUDITOR'S RIGHT AND DUTY TO REPORT TO REGULATORS IN THE FINANCIAL SECTOR

Objective

The objective of the auditor of a regulated entity is to bring information which the auditor has become aware in the ordinary course of performing work undertaken to fulfil the auditor's audit responsibilities to the attention of the appropriate regulator as soon as practicable when:

(a)   The auditor concludes that it is relevant to the regulator's functions having regard to such matters as may be specified in statute or any related regulations; and

(b)   In the auditor's opinion there is reasonable cause to believe it is or may be of material significance to the regulator. (Paragraph 8)

Where an apparent breach of statutory or regulatory requirements comes to the auditor's attention, the auditor shall:

(a)   Obtain such evidence as is available to assess its implications for the auditor's reporting responsibilities;

(b)   Determine whether, in the auditor's opinion, there is reasonable cause to believe that the breach is of material significance to the regulator; and

(c)   Consider whether the apparent breach is criminal conduct that gives rise to criminal property and, as such, should be reported to the specified authorities. (Paragraph 12)

Auditors' duty to report to the FSA

58   Under FSMA 2000 (Communication by Auditors) Regulations 2001 ("the 2001 Regulations"), auditors have duties in certain circumstances to make reports to the FSA. Information and opinions to be communicated are those meeting the criteria set out below which relate to matters of which the auditor[27] of the authorised person (also referred to below as a "regulated entity")[28] has become aware:

(i)   in his capacity as auditor of the authorised person; and

---

[26] *These are termed limited intelligence value reports.*

[27] *An "auditor" is defined for this purpose in the Regulations as a person who is, or has been, an auditor of an authorised person appointed under, or as a result of, a statutory provision including Section 340 of FSMA 2000.*

[28] *In the context of FSA regulation, these terms equate to the term "authorised firm".*

(ii)   if he is also the auditor of a person who has close links with the authorised person, in his capacity as auditor of that person.

The 2001 Regulations do not require auditors to perform any additional audit work as a result of the statutory duty to make a report to the FSA, nor are auditors required specifically to seek out breaches of the requirements applicable to a particular authorised person. However, in circumstances where the auditor identifies that a reportable matter may exist, the auditor carries out such extra work, as the auditor considers necessary, to determine whether the facts and circumstances cause the auditor "reasonably to believe" that the matter does in fact exist. It should be noted that the auditor's work does not need to prove that the reportable matter exists.

The criteria for determining the matters to be reported are as follows: **59**

(i)   the auditor reasonably believes that there is, or has been, or may be, or may have been a contravention of any "relevant requirement" that applies to the person[29] concerned and that contravention may be of material significance to the FSA in determining whether to exercise, in relation to that person, any of its functions under FSMA 2000 (other than in part 6, i.e. rules relating to official listing); or

(ii)   the auditor reasonably believes that the information on, or his opinion on, those matters may be of material significance to the FSA in determining whether the person concerned satisfies and will continue to satisfy the Threshold Conditions;[30] or

(iii)   the auditor reasonably believes that the person concerned is not, may not be, or may cease to be, a going concern; or

(iv)   the auditor is precluded from stating in his report that the annual accounts have been properly prepared in accordance with the CA2006 or, where applicable, give a true and fair view or have been prepared in accordance with relevant rules and legislation[31].

In relation to paragraph 59 (i) above, "relevant requirement" is a requirement by or   **60** under FSMA 2000 which relates to authorisation under FSMA 2000 or to the carrying on of any regulated activity. This includes not only relevant statutory instruments but also the FSA's rules (other than the Listing Rules) including the Principles for Businesses. The duty to report also covers any requirement imposed by or under any other Act[32], the contravention of which constitutes an offence which the FSA has the power to prosecute under FSMA 2000.

In relation to paragraph 59 (ii) above, the duty to report relates to either   **61** information or opinions held by the auditor which may be of significance to the FSA in determining whether the regulated entity satisfies and will continue to satisfy the Threshold Conditions. The duty to report opinions, as well as information, allows for circumstances where adequate information on a matter may not readily be forthcoming from the regulated entity, and where judgments need to be made.

---

[29]   *In this context the person is an "Authorised Person".*

[30]   *The Threshold Conditions are set out in Schedule 6 to FSMA 2000 and represent the minimum conditions that a firm is required to satisfy and continue to satisfy to be given and to retain Part IV permission. The FSA's guidance on compliance with the Threshold Conditions is contained in the COND module of the FSA Handbook.*

[31]   *The relevant rules and legislation are set out in article 2(2)(d) of the 2001 Regulations, and include rules made by the FSA under Section 340 of FSMA 2000, and relevant provisions of, and regulations made under, BS Act 1986.*

[32]   *Examples include The Proceeds of Crime Act 2002 and prescribed regulations relating to money laundering.*

Material significance

62   Determining whether a contravention of a relevant requirement or a Threshold Condition is reportable under the 2001 Regulations involves consideration both of whether the auditor "reasonably believes" and that the matter in question "is, or is likely to be, of material significance" to the regulator.

63   As indicated above, paragraph 12 of ISA (UK and Ireland) 250 Section B requires that, where an apparent breach of statutory or regulatory requirements comes to the auditor's attention, the auditor obtains such evidence as is available to assess its implications for the auditor's reporting responsibilities and determine whether, in the auditor's opinion, there is reasonable cause to believe that the breach is of material significance to the regulator.

64   "Material significance" is described by paragraph 9(d) of ISA (UK and Ireland) 250 Section B as follows:

   'the term "material significance" requires interpretation in the context of the specific legislation applicable to the regulated entity. A matter or group of matters is normally of material significance to a regulator's function when, due either to its nature or its potential financial impact, it is likely of itself to require investigation by the regulator.'

65   "Material significance" does not have the same meaning as materiality in the context of the audit of financial statements. Whilst a particular event may be trivial in terms of its possible effect on the financial statements of an entity, it may be of a nature or type that is likely to change the perception of the regulator. For example, a failure to reconcile client money accounts may not be significant in financial terms but would have a significant effect on the FSA's consideration of whether the regulated entity was satisfactorily controlled and was behaving properly towards its customers.

66   The determination of whether a matter is, or is likely to be, of material significance to the FSA inevitably requires the auditor to exercise judgment. In forming such judgments, the auditor needs to consider not simply the facts of the matter but also their implications. In addition, it is possible that a matter, which is not materially significant in isolation, may become so when other possible breaches are considered.

67   The auditor of a regulated entity bases the judgment of "material significance" to the FSA solely on his understanding of the facts of which the auditor is aware without making any assumptions about the information available to the FSA in connection with any particular regulated entity. Appendix 7 gives examples of areas identified by the FSA where the duty to report might arise.

68   Clearly the concept of material significance means that not every breach or suspected breach, however minor, of relevant requirements needs to be reported. However, in considering whether to report minor matters, the auditor will need to consider (amongst other things):

   ● Whether the breach or suspected breach would relate to the entity's assets or amount to misconduct or mismanagement.

   ● That the cumulative effect of matters which come to the auditor's attention may collectively be of material significance, even if particular matters in isolation might not be regarded as being so.

   ● In circumstances where the auditor concludes that a matter gives rise to a statutory duty to report, the auditor has a duty to report that matter to the FSA even if the entity has already reported it.

On completion of their investigations, the auditor ensures that the facts and **69** circumstances, and the basis for his conclusion as to whether these are, or are likely to be, of "material significance" to the FSA, are adequately documented such that the reasons for his decision to report or not, as the case may be, may be clearly demonstrated.

Section 342 of FSMA 2000 provides that an auditor may communicate matters to **70** the FSA even where this would place the auditor in breach of any duty to which he would ordinarily be subject (such as a duty of confidence to his client). The auditor may communicate information to the FSA which he has become aware of in his capacity as auditor of the regulated entity. He may also communicate his opinion in relation to any such matter. In each case the following conditions must be met: (1) the auditor must be acting in good faith; (2) the auditor must reasonably believe the information or opinion is relevant to any of the functions of the FSA.

Conduct of the audit

The auditor shall ensure that all staff involved in the audit of a regulated entity have an understanding of:

(a)   The provisions of applicable legislation;

(b)   The regulator's rules and any guidance issued by the regulator; and

(c)   Any specific requirements which apply to the particular regulated entity,

appropriate to their role in the audit and sufficient (in the context of that role) to enable them to identify situations which may give reasonable cause to believe that a matter should be reported to the regulator. (Paragraph 11)

Understanding, commensurate with the individual's role and responsibilities in the **71** audit process, is required of:

- the provisions of the 2001 Regulations concerning the auditors' duty to report to the regulator;
- the standards and guidance in ISA (UK and Ireland) 250 Section B, and in this section of this Practice Note; and
- relevant sections of the FSA Handbook including the Principles for Businesses, those provisions relating to the Threshold Conditions, and GENPRU and BIPRU (which contain, amongst other things, the detailed prudential requirements for capital and liquidity).

The auditor includes procedures within his planning process to ensure that **72** members of the audit team have such understanding (in the context of their role) as to enable them to recognise potentially reportable matters, and that such matters are reported to the audit engagement partner without delay so that a decision may be made as to whether a duty to report arises.

An audit firm appointed as auditor of a regulated entity needs to have in place **73** appropriate procedures to ensure that the audit engagement partner is made aware of any other relationship which exists between any department of the firm and the regulated entity when that relationship could affect the firm's work as auditors. (This matter is covered in more detail in Appendix 2 of ISA (UK and Ireland) 250 Section B.) The auditor also requests the regulated entity to advise him when it appoints a third party (including another department or office of the same firm) to review, investigate or report on any aspects of its business activities that may be relevant to the audit of the financial statements and to provide the auditor with copies of reports by such a third party promptly after their receipt. This matter may usefully be referred to in the engagement letter.

Closely linked entities

74   Where the auditor of a regulated entity is also auditor of a closely linked entity[33], a duty to report arises directly in relation to information relevant to the regulated entity of which he becomes aware in the course of his work as auditor of the closely linked entity.

75   The auditor establishes during audit planning whether the regulated entity has one or more closely linked entities of which the audit firm is also the auditor. If there are such entities the auditor considers the significance of the closely linked entities and the nature of the issues that might arise which may be of material significance to the regulator of the regulated entity. Such circumstances may involve:

● activities or uncertainties within the closely linked entity which might significantly impair the financial position of the regulated entity;

● money laundering and, if the closely linked entity is itself regulated;

● matters that the auditor of the closely linked entity is intending to report to its regulator.

76   Following the risk assessment referred to in paragraph 75, the auditor of the regulated entity identifies the closely related entities for which the procedures in this paragraph are necessary. The engagement team of the regulated entity communicates to the engagement team of the selected closely linked entities the audit firm's responsibilities to report to the FSA under the 2001 Regulations and notifies the engagement team of the circumstances that have been identified which, if they exist, might be of material significance to the FSA as regulator of the regulated entity. Prior to completion the auditor of the regulated entity obtains details from the auditor of the closely linked entity of such circumstances or confirmation, usually in writing, that such circumstances do not exist. Where the closely linked entities are part of the inter-auditor group reporting process these steps can be built into that process.

77   Section 343 of FSMA 2000 confers a similar protection on auditors when they report information or opinions to the FSA to that of section 342 (considered above). This enables the auditor to disclose to the FSA information of which he has become aware in his capacity as the auditor of the closely linked entity, or his opinion on such matters. Again two conditions apply: (1) the auditor must be acting in good faith; (2) the auditor must reasonably believe the information or opinion is relevant to any of the functions of the FSA.

78   No duty to report is imposed on the auditor of an entity closely linked to a regulated entity who is not also auditor of the regulated entity.

79   In circumstances where he is not also the auditor of the closely linked entity, the auditor of the regulated entity decides whether there are any matters to be reported to the FSA relating to the affairs of the regulated entity in the light of the information that he receives about a closely linked entity for the purpose of

---

[33] *An entity has close links with an authorised person for this purpose if the entity is a:*

(a)   *parent undertaking of an authorised person;*

(b)   *subsidiary undertaking of an authorised person;*

(c)   *parent undertaking of a subsidiary undertaking of an authorised person; or*

(d)   *subsidiary undertaking of a parent undertaking of an authorised person.*

auditing the financial statements of the regulated entity. If the auditor becomes aware of possible matters that may fall to be reported, he may wish to obtain further information from the management or auditor of the closely linked entity to ascertain whether the matter should be reported. To facilitate such possible discussions, at the planning stage of the audit the auditor of the regulated entity will have considered whether arrangements need to be put in place to allow him to communicate with the management and auditor of the closely linked entity. If the auditor of the regulated entity is unable to communicate with the management and auditor of the closely linked entity to obtain further information concerning the matters he has identified, he reports the matters, and that he has been unable to obtain further information, direct to the FSA.

Information received in a capacity other than as auditor

There may be circumstances where it is not clear whether information about a firm coming to the attention of the auditor is received in the capacity of auditor or in some other capacity, for example as a general adviser to the entity. Appendix 2 to ISA (UK and Ireland) 250 Section B provides guidance as to how information obtained in non-audit work may be relevant to the auditor in the planning and conduct of the audit and the steps that need to be taken to ensure the communication of information that is relevant to the audit.

80

Discussing matters of material significance with the directors

The directors[34] are the persons principally responsible for the management of the regulated entity. The auditor will therefore normally bring a matter of material significance to the attention of the directors subject to compliance with legislation relating to "tipping off" and seek agreement on the facts and circumstances. However, ISA (UK and Ireland) 250 Section B, paragraph 13, emphasises that where the auditor concludes that a duty to report arises, the auditor shall bring the matter to the attention of the regulator as soon as practicable. The directors may wish to report the matters identified to the FSA themselves and detail the actions taken or to be taken. Whilst such a report from the directors may provide valuable information, it does not relieve the auditor of the statutory duty to report directly to the FSA.

81

Timing of a report

The duty to report arises once the auditor has concluded that he reasonably believes that the matter is or is likely to be of material significance to the FSA's regulatory function.

82

The report should be made as soon as is practicable once a conclusion has been reached. Unless the matter casts doubt on the integrity of the directors this should not preclude discussion of the matter with the directors and seeking such further advice as is necessary, so that a decision can be made on whether or not a duty to report exists. Such consultations and discussions are, however, undertaken on a timely basis to enable the auditor to conclude on the matter as soon as practicable.

83

The FSA has set up a dedicated "Auditor's duty to report" mailbox[35] for the storage and logging of these reports. Auditors send any such reports to this mailbox and copy in the supervisor of the firm the report relates to.

84

---

[34] *This term would include the senior management of branches of EEA or non EEA banks.*

[35] *Auditor'sdutytore@fsa.gov.uk.*

Auditors' right to report to the FSA

85   In addition to the duty to report particular information, the auditor has a right to report other information that is relevant to the functions of the FSA. S342 FSMA 2000 provides that no duty to which an auditor of an authorised person is subject shall be contravened by communicating in good faith to the FSA information which he has become aware of in his capacity as auditor of the regulated entity, or his opinion on any such matter. As mentioned above, two conditions apply: (1) the auditor must be acting in good faith; (2) the auditor must reasonably believe the information or opinion is relevant to any of the functions of the FSA.

86   The scope of the duty to report is wide, particularly since, under the FSA's Principle for Businesses 11 (and corresponding application rules and guidance in SUP15.3), an authorised firm must disclose to the FSA appropriately anything relating to the authorised firm of which the FSA would reasonably expect notice. However in circumstances where the auditor concludes that a matter does not give rise to a statutory duty to report but nevertheless should be brought to the attention of the regulator, in the first instance he advises the directors of his opinion. Where the auditor is unable to obtain, within a reasonable period, adequate evidence that the directors have properly informed the FSA of the matter, then the auditor makes a report themselves to the regulator as soon as practicable.

Taking legal advice

87   In considering when to report (or when a report to the FSA benefits from the protection of FSMA, sections 342(3) and 343(3)[36]), an auditor may wish to take legal advice. An auditor may wish to ensure, for example, that only relevant information is disclosed and that the form and content of his report is such as to secure the protection of FSMA 2000. Appendix 6 provides additional guidance on disclosure in the public interest. This is relevant to both the auditor's consideration of the right to report and also where neither the right nor the duty to report exists – as is the case for EEA banks without top up permissions. However, the auditor recognises that legal advice will take time and that speed of reporting is likely to be important in order to protect the interests of customers and/or to enable the FSA to meet its statutory objectives.

Formal bilateral meetings

88   Formal bilateral meetings between the FSA and auditors vary in frequency according to factors such as the FSA's assessment of systemic risk of the bank concerned.

89   The formal bilateral meeting is intended to provide a forum for frank one-to-one discussions on issues of concern to either the FSA or auditor. The FSA does not, however, expect auditors to make supervisory judgments nor, in the normal course of events, does it expect to base its own supervisory judgments and decisions solely on comments provided by auditors.

90   Although there is no requirement to produce an agenda for a formal bilateral meeting, where the FSA has specific matters which it intends to discuss, it will, where possible, communicate these to the auditor in advance. Similarly, the FSA will not, as a matter of course, circulate minutes of the bilateral meeting to the auditor, although they may provide a summary list of the main items covered. Auditors therefore consider taking their own notes of the formal bilateral meeting

---

[36] *Allowing the auditor to report notwithstanding any duty, such as confidentiality, to which the auditor is subject.*

(as explained below, the confidentiality restrictions of FSMA 2000 generally prevent such notes being made available to the bank although they can be shared with the FSA if the auditor considers a particular discussion requires clarification).

The FSA expects auditors to participate fully in the bilateral meeting, and to **91** discuss views and impressions gained within the audit context as well as factual information. Under sections 342 and 343 of FSMA 2000, auditors are protected from breach of their duty of client confidentiality in communicating matters[37] to the FSA provided that they do so "in good faith" and reasonably believe that the information or opinion is relevant to any functions of the FSA. In appropriate cases, the auditor may consider obtaining legal advice on the application of this provision. In general terms, it is not essential that conclusive evidence is available to support an opinion expressed in a bilateral meeting but, in communicating matters "in good faith", the auditor:

(a) reports facts in a balanced manner and without selectivity or bias; and

(b) expresses any opinions in a neutral and responsible manner, making clear that they are opinions and not facts and explaining the basis for them,

and the auditor's actions must be without malice. In addition, general law provides protection in certain circumstances for disclosing certain matters even where a duty of confidence exists to a proper authority in the public interest.[38]

Auditors are bound by the confidentiality regime of FSMA 2000[39] in respect of **92** confidential information[40] communicated to them by the FSA. Under that regime, where confidential information is disclosed to a person by the FSA the information may not be disclosed by that person to any other person unless the requirements of FSMA 2000 are complied with (including to the bank).

In practice, the auditor obtains the express consent of the FSA to any onward **93** disclosure of confidential information. This is because normally the consent of the person who provided the information to the FSA, and, if different, the person to whom the information relates is needed before the information may be disclosed. Some information communicated by the FSA to the auditor will relate only to the bank but many matters discussed may be relevant also to other parties, such as customers or employees. Also, where the FSA has received information which it communicates to auditors and reporting accountants from another regulator or in a capacity other than as banking supervisor, there may be other restrictions on disclosure.

The auditor can, however, disclose to the bank information which the auditor has **94** communicated *to the FSA* during the bilateral meeting (except where to do so would have the effect of disclosing information communicated by the FSA). If the auditor is uncertain about whether particular information can be communicated to the bank, the auditor considers, for the avoidance of doubt, seeking the consent of the FSA.

---

[37] *Specifically, information on a matter which the auditor has or had become aware of in his capacity as auditor of the authorised person, or his opinion on such a matter.*

[38] *Case law provides for when this defence is available, which is not considered in this Practice Note.*

[39] *In Part 23, and in the Financial Services and Markets Act 2000 (Disclosure of Confidential Information) Regulations 2001 (SI 2001/2188).*

[40] *"Confidential information" within the meaning of section 348 of the Act. Note that this is broadly defined (and much broader in scope than information to which a private law duty of confidence would attach), for example, including information relating to the business or affairs of any person or was received by the FSA for the purposes of, or in the discharge of, any of the FSA's functions.*

95 Matters communicated *by the FSA* during the bilateral meeting may be conveyed by those representatives of an accounting firm who were present at the meeting to other partners, directors and employees of the firm who need to know the information in connection with the firm's performance of its duties as auditor without the FSA's express permission.

Other periodic meetings with the FSA

96 In addition to the formal meetings with the FSA outlined above, the auditor may be involved in other discussions with the FSA on either a trilateral or bilateral basis. Examples include:

- meetings with the FSA during the risk assessment phase of the supervisory process (often called the "Arrow visit");

- presentations by the FSA on the results of its risk assessment of a particular bank and the resulting supervisory programme; and

- ad hoc meetings to discuss matters communicated to the FSA by the auditor under the right or duty to report (as discussed above).

97 The normal protections and confidentiality restrictions apply to these meetings in the same way as to formal bilateral meetings.

ISA (UK AND IRELAND) 300: PLANNING AN AUDIT OF FINANCIAL STATEMENTS

Objective

The objective of the auditor is to plan the audit so that it will be performed in an effective manner. (Paragraph 4)

The auditor shall establish an overall audit strategy that sets the scope, timing and direction of the audit, and that guides the development of the audit plan. (Paragraph 7)

The auditor shall develop an audit plan that shall include a description of:

(a) The nature, timing and extent of planned risk assessment procedures, as determined under ISA (UK and Ireland) 315.

(b) The nature, timing and extent of planned further audit procedures at the assertion level, as determined under ISA (UK and Ireland) 330.

(c) Other planned audit procedures that are required to be carried out so that the engagement complies with ISAs (UK and Ireland). (Paragraph 9)

98 Matters the auditor of a bank or building society may consider as part of the planning process for the audit of the financial statements include:

- the nature and scope of the entity's business;

- the extent of head office control over networks of branches;

- the entity's relationships with the FSA and any other regulators;

- changes in applicable laws, regulations and accounting requirements;

- the need to involve specialists in the audit;

- the extent to which controls and procedures are outsourced to a third-party provider; and

- issues relating to the auditor's statutory duty to report.

Guidance on the first four of these matters is set out in the section in this Practice   **99**
Note on ISA (UK and Ireland) 315 "Identifying and assessing the risks of material
misstatement through understanding the entity and its environment".
Considerations in relation to the other matters in planning the audit are:

- the nature and complexity of banking business increases the likelihood that
  the auditor may consider it necessary to involve specialists in the audit
  process. For example, the auditor may wish to utilise the work of an expert
  in the valuation of derivative and other financial instruments not traded in an
  active market. The auditor considers the need to involve such specialists at
  an early stage in planning their work. Where such specialists are to be used,
  they may be involved in the development of the audit plan and may take part
  in discussions with the management and staff, in order to assist in the
  development of knowledge and understanding relating to the business;

- the auditor considers the implications of the outsourcing of functions by the
  entity, and the sources of evidence available to the auditor for transactions
  undertaken by service organizations in planning the audit work. This may
  include the outsourcing of certain functions, such as the IT function; and

- issues relating to the auditor's statutory duty to report include the adequacy
  of the audit team's understanding of the law and the identification of closely
  linked entities.

ISA (UK AND IRELAND) 315: IDENTIFYING AND ASSESSING THE RISKS OF MATERIAL MISSTATEMENT THROUGH UNDERSTANDING THE ENTITY AND ITS ENVIRONMENT

Objective

The objective of the auditor is to identify and assess the risks of material
misstatement, whether due to fraud or error, at the financial statement and
assertion levels, through understanding the entity and its environment,
including the entity's internal control, thereby providing a basis for
designing and implementing responses to the assessed risks of material
misstatement. (Paragraph 3)

Banks and building societies can be complex and the auditor seeks to understand   **100**
the business and the regulatory regime in which they operate. Generally, there is a
close relationship between planning and obtaining an understanding of the entity
and the control environment, which is covered more fully below.

The auditor shall obtain an understanding of the following:

(a)   Relevant industry, regulatory, and other external factors including the
      applicable financial reporting framework.

(b)   The nature of the entity, including:

    (i)   its operations;

    (ii)   its ownership and governance structures;

    (iii) the types of investments that the entity is making and plans to
        make, including investments in special-purpose entities; and

    (iv)   the way that the entity is structured and how it is financed to enable
        the auditor to understand the classes of transactions, account
        balances, and disclosures to be expected in the financial statements.

...

(Paragraph 11)

101   In assessing the nature and scope of the business and its control environment, the auditor may consider:

- The entity's strategy, risk appetite and capital and liquidity resources and how it manages tensions that are likely to exist between them (for example an entity's strategic ambition may require an appetite for risk that those in charge of governance regard as imprudent or strain capital and liquidity too far);

- The products it uses and its strategies for making money from them. An auditor might seek to understand how the entity monitors returns on these products and then check that these are reasonable in the light of returns in the rest of the market;

- How the entity is governed and whether it complies with FSA requirements and best practice;

- The quality of the entity's risk analysis and whether there are risks that are not properly analysed and controlled;

- The views of the regulator about the entity;

- The tone set by senior management and those in charge of governance, the quality of what is reported to them and their consequent ability to run the business;

- The quality of controls and in which locations or functions there may be deficiencies.

In making this assessment the auditor considers gathering information from as wide a range of sources as possible in order to compare one source against another for consistency. In particular it can be important to interview business and front office staff as well as back office and finance staff in order to get a full appreciation of the entity's activities.

102   For the largest institutions, the FSA intends to meet the auditor at an early stage in the financial reporting process and identify areas where there may be concerns over key areas of accounting judgment and perceived areas of risk. These meetings take place at least once a year and could cover areas such as fair value estimates and provisions for impairment.

103   When performing procedures to obtain an understanding of the entity, the auditor considers:

- the relative importance to the entity of each of its business activities[41]. This includes an understanding of the type and extent of specialised activities, for example:

    – derivatives and other complex trading activities (where both documentation, accounting and valuation aspects can be difficult);

    – trade finance, invoice discounting and factoring (where the documentation used can be complex and highly specialised); and

    – leasing (where there are particular accounting issues, especially relating to income recognition);

---

[41] *The auditor of a building society is aware of the BS Act 1986 statutory and the FSA regulatory limitations on funding, lending and treasury activities and considers whether the continuing activities of the society are, for example, within the restrictions of section 9A of the BS Act 1986 and are compliant with the limitations within the society's treasury approach see BSOCS and paragraphs 20-26 of this Practice Note.*

- the introduction of new categories of customers, or products or marketing and distribution channels;
- the relevant aspects of the entity's risk management procedures;
- the complexity of the entity's information systems;
- the legal and operational structure of the entity;
- a change in the market environment (for example, a marked increase in competition);
- the complexity of products;
- the consistency of methods and operations in different departments or locations; and
- the respective roles and responsibilities attributed to the finance, risk control, compliance and internal audit functions.

Many banks and UK banking groups are managed globally on product/business   **104** lines rather than focused around legal structure. Such "matrix management" structures typically involve local reporting (often on a legal entity basis) on operational and compliance matters; and business/product based reporting (often globally) of activities undertaken. In addition, global trading activities may mean that transactions are entered into in one location but are recorded in another; it may even be the case that they are controlled and settled in a third location. Furthermore, parts of a bank's operations may be undertaken through special purpose entities which may have structures and features that can mean they are excluded from financial statement consolidation. Given these factors, the auditor gains an understanding of how and where transactions are undertaken, recorded and controlled, in order to plan the audit. Further guidance on particular matters arising in the audit of banking groups is given in the section on ISA (UK and Ireland) 600 in this Practice Note.

Many banks and building societies operate a network of branches. In such   **105** instances, the auditor determines the degree of head office control over the business and accounting functions at branch level and the scope and effectiveness of the entity's inspection and/or internal audit visits. The extent and impact of visits from regulators is also relevant. Where branches maintain separate accounting records, the extent of audit visits and work on each branch is also dependent on the materiality of, and risks associated with, the operations of each branch and the extent to which controls over branches are exercised centrally. In the case of smaller branches, the degree to which exceptions to the entity's normal control procedures may be caused by minimal staffing levels (the greater difficulty of ensuring adequate segregation of duties, for example) and the consequent need for an increased level of control from outside the branch are relevant to assessing audit risk.

In obtaining an understanding of the regulatory factors the auditor considers: **106**

- any formal communications between the FSA in its capacity as the regulator and the entity, including any new or interim risk assessments issued by the FSA and the results of any other supervisory visits conducted by the FSA;
- the contents of any recent reports prepared by "skilled persons" under s. 166 FSMA 2000 together with any correspondence, minutes or notes of meetings relevant to any recent skilled persons' report;
- any formal communications between the entity and other regulators; and

- discussions with the entity's compliance officer together with others responsible for monitoring regulatory compliance.

> The auditor shall obtain an understanding of...
>
> (c) The entity's selection and application of accounting policies, including the reasons for changes thereto. The auditor shall evaluate whether the entity's accounting policies are appropriate for its business and consistent with the applicable financial reporting framework and accounting policies used in the relevant industry. (Paragraph 11)

107 Accounting policies of particular relevance may include allowances for impairment, hedge accounting, classification of assets and liabilities (and thereby their measurement), embedded derivatives, valuation of complex financial instruments, revenue/expense recognition (including effective interest rates), consolidation of special purpose entities, offsetting and derecognition and debt versus equity classification. The auditor undertakes procedures to consider whether the policies adopted are in compliance with applicable accounting standards and gains an understanding of the procedures, systems and controls applied to maintain compliance with them.

> The auditor shall obtain an understanding of...
>
> (d) The entity's objectives and strategies, and those related business risks that may result in risks of material misstatement. (Paragraph 11)

108 It is important for the auditor to understand the multi-dimensional nature and extent of the financial and business risks which are integral to the environment, and how the entity's systems record and address these risks. Although they may apply to varying degrees, the risks include (but are not limited to):

- credit risk: at its simplest, this is the risk that a borrower or other counterparty will be unable to meet its obligations. However, where credit risk is traded (in the form of secondary market loan trading or credit derivatives, for example), credit risk is often regarded as having two distinct forms:

  - spread risk: the risk arising from day-to-day changes in the price of a credit instrument because of changes in market perceptions about the credit standing of the debtor and the liquidity of the instrument;

  - default risk: the risk that a debtor will default on its obligations; or settlement risk: the risk that a counterparty will be unable to settle its obligations under a transaction (in a securities settlement or payment system, for example) on the due date;

- concentration risk: the risk arising when an entity's exposure is heavily weighted to a particular class or sector of borrower or geographic region and thus runs the risk of disproportionate exposure to problems with that particular class, sector or region;

- liquidity risk: the risk that arises from the possibility that an entity has insufficient liquid funds to meet the demands of depositors or other counterparties;

- interest rate risk: the risk that arises where there is a mismatch between the interest rate reset dates or bases for assets and liabilities;

- currency risk: the risk that arises from the mismatching of assets, liabilities and commitments denominated in different currencies;

- market risk[42]: the risk that changes in the value of assets, liabilities and commitments will occur as a result of movements in relative prices (for example, as a result of changes in the market price of tradable assets or inputs into valuation models for more complex instruments). Market risk is a generic term which, in addition to interest rate and currency risk and, in some environments, spread risk, also includes equity risk and commodity price risk;

- operational risk: the risk of loss, arising from inadequate or failed internal processes, people and systems or from external events including legal risk; and

- regulatory risk: the risk of public censure, fines (together with related compensation payments) and restriction or withdrawal of authorisation to conduct some or all of the entity's activities. In the UK this may arise from enforcement activity by the FSA.

Failure to manage the risks outlined above can also cause serious damage to the entity's reputation, potentially leading to loss of confidence in the entity, withdrawal of deposits or problems in maintaining liquidity (this is sometimes referred to as reputational risk or franchise risk).

The auditor shall obtain an understanding of...

(e) The measurement and review of the entity's financial performance. (Paragraph 11)

The auditor obtains an understanding of the measures used by management to **109** review the entity's performance. Further guidance in respect of key performance indicators is given in the section on ISA (UK and Ireland) 520.

> The auditor shall obtain an understanding of internal control relevant to the audit. Although most controls relevant to the audit are likely to relate to financial reporting, not all controls that relate to financial reporting are relevant to the audit. It is a matter of the auditor's professional judgment whether a control, individually or in combination with others, is relevant to the audit. (Paragraph 12)
>
> When obtaining an understanding of controls that are relevant to the audit, the auditor shall evaluate the design of those controls and determine whether they have been implemented, by performing procedures in addition to inquiry of the entity's personnel. (Paragraph 13)
>
> The auditor shall obtain an understanding of the control environment. As part of obtaining this understanding, the auditor shall evaluate whether:
>
> (a) Management, with the oversight of those charged with governance, has created and maintained a culture of honesty and ethical behaviour; and
>
> (b) The strengths in the control environment elements collectively provide an appropriate foundation for the other components of internal control, and whether those other components are not undermined by deficiencies in the control environment. (Paragraph 14)

---

[42] *Some forms of market risk are "non-linear", i.e. there is not a constant relationship between the profit and loss and the movement in the underlying price. For example, the relationship between an option's price and the price of its underlying instrument is "non-linear"; the "delta" measures the change in the price of an option for a unit change in the price of the underlying instrument whilst the "gamma" indicates the extent of the "non-linearity" (the change in delta for a unit change in the price of the underlying instrument).*

110   The quality of the overall control environment is dependent upon management's attitude towards the operation of controls. A positive attitude may be evidenced by an organizational framework which enables proper segregation of duties and delegation of control functions and which encourages failings to be reported and corrected. Thus, where a lapse in the operation of a control is treated as a matter of concern, the control environment will be stronger and will contribute to effective control systems; whereas a weak control environment will undermine detailed controls, however well designed.

111   In accordance with the requirements of SYSC and PRIN, senior management has a responsibility for establishing and maintaining such systems and controls as are appropriate to the operations of an authorised firm. The FSA can hold senior managers personally accountable for an area or business for which they are responsible. This responsibility extends to personal behaviour not only by senior management but also to other Approved Persons[43]. Statements of Principle and Codes of Practice for Approved Persons (as set out in the FSA Handbook) include acting with integrity, due skill and care and diligence. The fit and proper test applied to Approved Persons includes competence and capability.

112   The FSA requires an authorised firm to maintain systems and controls appropriate for its business[44]. These include (but are not limited to):

- clear and appropriate reporting lines which are communicated within the entity;

- appropriate controls to ensure compliance with laws and regulations (this may mean a separate Compliance function);

- appropriate risk assessment process;

- appropriate management information;

- controls to ensure suitability of staff;

- controls to manage tensions arising out of remuneration policies;

- documented and tested business continuity plans;

- documented business plans or strategies;

- an internal audit function (where appropriate);

- an audit committee (where appropriate); and

- appropriate record keeping arrangements.

113   For large banks and building societies, the volume of transactions can be so great that it may be extremely difficult for the auditor to express an opinion without obtaining considerable assurance from adequate systems of control. Systems of internal control are important in ensuring orderly and prudent operations of the entity and in assisting the directors to prepare financial statements which give a true and fair view. The following features of the business of banks and building societies may be relevant to the auditor's assessment of such internal controls:

- the substantial scale of transactions, both in terms of volume and relative value, makes it important that control systems are in place to ensure that transactions are recorded promptly, accurately and completely and are

---

[43] *Anyone performing a Controlled Function (an FSA defined term that includes roles beyond senior management such as the head of internal audit or the non-executive directors; see SUP10) must be approved by the FSA (an Approved Person).*

[44] *Most FSA systems and control requirements are set out in SYSC, but additional requirements relating to prudential matters also exist in GENPRU and BIPRU.*

checked and approved, and that records are reconciled at appropriate intervals in order to identify and investigate differences promptly;

- processing and accounting for complex transactions or high volumes of less complex transactions will almost inevitably involve the use of sophisticated technology. For example, transactions subject to "straight through processing" involve little or no manual intervention after they have been initiated;

- a bank or building society deals in money or near money instruments. In the case of most commercial organizations, most movements of funds are the result of a related movement of goods and some audit assurance may therefore be obtained by reference to this relationship. This is not available, however, in the case of banks, building societies and similar financial organizations. Management must therefore establish robust systems of control. As the centralised funds transfer departments which exist in larger banks and building societies will often process very high volumes and a high value of transactions each day, the need for strong and effective controls over this area is particularly important. Transactions with customers over the internet are another area requiring strong security controls;

- the fact that banks and building societies deal in money and near money instruments makes proper segregation of duties between and amongst those entering into transactions, those recording the transactions, those settling them and where relevant, those responsible for their physical security particularly important;

- the geographical or organizational dispersal of some entities' operations means that, in order to maintain control over their activities, they need to ensure not only that there are sufficient controls at each location, but also that there are effective communication and control procedures between the various locations and the centre. It is important that there should be clear, comprehensive reporting and responsibility lines, particularly where the business is managed using a "matrix" structure;

- the activities of banks and building societies can typically result in the creation or use of derivatives and other complex transactions. The fact that the resultant cash flows may not take place for a considerable time creates the risk that wrongly recorded or unrecorded positions may exist and that these may not be detected for some time, thereby exposing the entity to risk of misstatement. The valuation of these instruments also poses risks of misstatement, particularly as not all instruments are capable of being valued using observable market prices. Consequently, banks and building societies will normally have developed important operational controls to mitigate such risks of misstatement;

- the provisions of the UK tax legislation require banks and building societies to operate various tax deduction and collection arrangements, such as those relating to paying and collecting agents and lower rate tax deducted from interest paid to individuals. In addition, the VAT position can be particularly complex. These may give rise to significant liabilities if not properly dealt with. Accordingly, an effective control system is essential to ensure that the record-keeping requirements of UK tax legislation are satisfied, and that tax is accounted for promptly and accurately. Similar measures may be needed to address similar provisions arising in any other jurisdictions where the entity operates; and

- the UK regulatory framework is both complex and evolving for banks and building societies. This may give rise to significant liabilities for compensation to clients if not properly dealt with. Accordingly, an effective control system is essential to ensure that the requirements of the UK regulators are satisfied. Measures may also be needed to address regulators in other jurisdictions.

> The auditor shall obtain an understanding of control activities relevant to the audit, being those the auditor judges it necessary to understand in order to assess the risks of material misstatement at the assertion level and to design further audit procedures responsive to assessed risks. An audit does not require an understanding of all the control activities related to each significant class of transactions, account balance, and disclosure in the financial statements or to every assertion relevant to them. (Paragraph 20)

114   There is a wide variation between different banks and building societies in terms of size, activity and organization, so that there can be no standard approach to internal controls and risk. The auditor assesses the adequacy of controls in relation to the circumstances of each entity. Examples of deficiencies that may be relevant to the auditor's assessment of the risk of material misstatement are as follows:

- complex products or processes inadequately understood by management; this includes undue concentration of expertise concerning matters requiring the exercise of significant judgment or capable of manipulation such as valuations of financial instruments or allowances for impairment;
- deficiencies in back office procedures underpinning the completeness and accuracy of accounting records such as:
  - backlogs in key reconciliations, particularly those over correspondent bank accounts, settlement accounts and the custody of assets such as securities (either those held on own account or as collateral);
  - inadequate maintenance of suspense or clearing accounts;
  - deficiencies in controls over completeness and accuracy of data for credit provisioning; and
  - backlogs in confirmation processes relating to financial instrument transactions.
- deficiencies in new product and complex trade approval procedures;
- lack of segregation of duties such as between critical dealing, operational, control, settlement and accounting functions; and
- deficiencies in payments systems such as inadequate controls over access to payment systems and data.

115   Some of the control activities which are usually performed by banks and building societies involve reconciliations of balances and positions with other organizations, testing of which may provide a source of assurance for the auditor as to the accuracy and completeness of the recording of transactions. These include reconciliation of:

- balances payable to or from other banks (sometimes referred to as vostro and nostro balances);
- securities in the course of settlement and the corresponding balances owing to or from the bank with settlement systems such as Euroclear and Crest;

- centrally cleared derivative transactions and margin balances with clearing houses such as the London Clearing House; and
- balances and positions with other group entities.

Controls relating to outsourcing activities are considered in the ISA (UK and Ireland) 402 section of this Practice Note. **116**

> In understanding the entity's control activities, the auditor shall obtain an understanding of how the entity has responded to risks arising from IT. (Paragraph 21)

As a result of the type and complexity of transactions undertaken, and records held, by banks and building societies and the need for swift and accurate information processing and retrieval, many functions are highly automated, including: funds transfer systems, the accounting function, the processing and recording of customer transactions, trading activities, financial instrument valuations, regulatory reporting and the supply of management information. **117**

The auditor assesses the extent, nature and impact of automation within the entity and plans and performs work accordingly. In particular the auditor considers: **118**

- the required level of IT knowledge and skills may be extensive and may require the auditor to obtain advice and assistance from staff with specialist skills;
- the extent of the application of audit software and related audit techniques;
- general controls relating to the environment within which IT based systems are developed, maintained and operated; and
- external interfaces susceptible to breaches of security.

Depending on the size and range of their activities, banks employ a large number of different systems. The auditor identifies and understands the communication between computer systems in order to assess whether appropriate controls are established and maintained to cover all critical systems and the links between them and to identify the most effective audit approach.

Banks also commonly use end user applications (applications that sit on the computer of the end user rather than on a centrally managed server), which can involve the use of complex spreadsheets, to generate important accounting and/or internal control information. Such end user applications are not subject to centrally managed general controls and so the auditor assesses the significance of the use of such applications and plans procedures to test the controls around them as appropriate. **119**

> The auditor shall identify and assess the risks of material misstatement at:
>
> (a) the financial statement level; and
>
> (b) the assertion level for classes of transactions, account balances, and disclosures
>
> to provide a basis for designing and performing further audit procedures. (Paragraph 25)
>
> As part of the risk assessment as described in paragraph 25, the auditor shall determine whether any of the risks identified are, in the auditor's judgment, a significant risk. In exercising this judgment the auditor shall exclude the effects of identified controls related to the risk. (Paragraph 27)

> If the auditor has determined that a significant risk exists, the auditor shall obtain an understanding of the entity's controls, including control activities, relevant to that risk. (Paragraph 29)

120   Significant risks are likely to arise in those areas that are subject to significant judgment by management or are complex and properly understood by comparatively few people within the entity.

121   Examples of significant risks requiring special audit consideration may include:

- allowances for impairment (particularly collective assessments of impairment) (see paragraphs 162 to 170);

- changes to provisions for compensation payable to customers; and

- valuation of certain derivatives and other financial instruments (see paragraphs 172 to 177).

122   The application of complex accounting standards such as IAS 32, IAS 39 and IFRS 7 (for entities using EU IFRS) and FRS 25, 26 and 29 (for entities using UK GAAP) may also give rise to significant risk with respect to hedge accounting, classification of assets/liabilities, revenue/expense recognition (effective interest rates) and over the adequacy of financial statement disclosure.

ISA (UK AND IRELAND) 320: MATERIALITY IN PLANNING AND PERFORMING AN AUDIT

Objective

The objective of the auditor is to apply the concept of materiality appropriately in planning and performing the audit. (Paragraph 8)

When establishing the overall audit strategy, the auditor shall determine materiality for the financial statements as a whole. If, in the specific circumstances of the entity, there is one or more particular classes of transactions, account balances or disclosures for which misstatements of lesser amounts than materiality for the financial statements as a whole could reasonably be expected to influence the economic decisions of users taken on the basis of the financial statements, the auditor shall also determine the materiality level or levels to be applied to those particular classes of transactions, account balances or disclosures. (Paragraph 10)

The auditor shall determine performance materiality for purposes of assessing the risks of material misstatement and determining the nature, timing and extent of further audit procedures. (Paragraph 11)

123   The principles of assessing materiality in the audit of a bank or building society are the same as those applying to the audit of any other entity. In particular the auditor's consideration of materiality is a matter of professional judgment, and is affected by the auditor's perception of the common information needs of users as a group[45].

124   Most banking organizations are profit orientated and a profit based measure, such as a percentage of profit before tax is likely to be used in determining materiality for the financial statements as a whole. However, a key difference of a bank or building society from other entities is that balance sheet balances tend to be much

---

[45] *For example, the "Framework for the Preparation and Presentation of Financial Statements" adopted by the International Accounting Standards Board in April 2001 indicates that, for a profit orientated entity, as investors are providers of risk capital to the enterprise, the provision of financial statements that meets their needs will also meet most of the needs of other users that financial statements can satisfy.*

larger compared to the profit and loss account/income statement, so that the application of materiality based on profit may be too low when auditing elements of the balance sheet.

To deal with this, the auditor typically uses materiality based on the profit and loss **125** account/income statement if a misstatement in a balance sheet item could affect the profit and loss account/income statement or equity and reserves. If, however, a misstatement in a balance sheet item is likely only to lead to a reclassification between line items within assets and liabilities, a higher materiality level can be applied for detecting such misstatements only. Although paragraph 10 of ISA (UK and Ireland) 320 indicates that there can only be one overall measure of materiality for the accounts as a whole, paragraph A15 of ISA (UK and Ireland) 450 states that there may be circumstances involving the evaluation of qualitative considerations where the auditor concludes that a classification misstatement is not material in the context of the financial statements as a whole, even though it may exceed the materiality level or levels applied in evaluating other misstatements. For example, a misclassification between balance sheet line items may not be considered material in the context of the financial statements as a whole when the amount of the misclassification is small in relation to the size of the related balance sheet line items and the misclassification does not affect the income statement or any key ratios. When applying a separate balance sheet materiality level for the purpose of identifying and evaluating the effect of such misclassifications the auditor considers:

- the extent any misstatement of these items would influence the economic decisions of users taken on the basis of the financial statements;

- the extent any misstatement of these items would affect users' expectations regarding the measurement or disclosure of these items;

- the effect of the classification misstatement on debt or other contractual covenants;

- the effect on individual line items or sub-totals; and

- the effect on key ratios.

An example of such an adjustment would be grossing up net counterparty **126** positions into assets and liabilities. The adjustment that is required can only affect the balance sheet; even if wrongly calculated, there will be no case for any write-off or write-back to profit and loss.

ISA (UK and Ireland) 320, paragraph 10, also allows the setting of a lower **127** materiality level for a specific class of transactions, account balance or disclosure, if this class of transactions, account balance or disclosure is of a particular interest to the users of the financial statements. The auditor is alert to the wider constituency of users of the financial statements, when considering this requirement and pays attention to the risk profile of the institution concerned. Factors to be taken into consideration include, for example:

- the concerns of regulators; and

- the attention that may be given to pay and staff and director rewards.

The nature of banks and building societies' exposures means that their value or **128** level of impairment can, at times, be subject to considerable uncertainty. The range of acceptable values or provisions can, as a consequence, be wide and sometimes wider than the materiality set by the auditor. Under such circumstances the auditor needs to assess whether management have determined the most appropriate point in the range for the purposes of the financial statements (which may not be the mid point in the range) and whether the extent of the uncertainty is adequately disclosed.

129   This guidance is not intended to cut across the guidance on the auditor's duty and right to report matters to the FSA, where "material significance" has a different meaning (see ISA (UK and Ireland) 250: Section B and paragraphs 62-70 above).

ISA (UK AND IRELAND) 330: THE AUDITOR'S RESPONSES TO ASSESSED RISKS

Objective

The objective of the auditor is to obtain sufficient appropriate audit evidence regarding the assessed risks of material misstatement, through designing and implementing appropriate responses to those risks. (Paragraph 3)

The auditor shall design and perform tests of controls to obtain sufficient appropriate audit evidence as to the operating effectiveness of relevant controls if:

(a)   The auditor's assessment of risks of material misstatement at the assertion level includes an expectation that the controls are operating effectively (that is, the auditor intends to rely on the operating effectiveness of controls in determining the nature, timing and extent of substantive procedures); or

(b)   Substantive procedures alone cannot provide sufficient appropriate audit evidence at the assertion level. (Paragraph 8)

130   ISA (UK and Ireland) 200, paragraph 17, requires that to obtain reasonable assurance, the auditor shall obtain sufficient appropriate audit evidence to reduce audit risk to an acceptably low level. In practice the nature and high volume of transactions relating to the operations of banks and building societies often means that performing tests of relevant controls is the most effective means of reducing audit risk to an acceptably low level as an approach based on substantive procedures alone is unlikely to be efficient.

131   Whilst some aspects of the income statements and balance sheets of banks and building societies lend themselves to the application of analytical procedures, income and expense resulting from trading activities is unlikely to be susceptible to these methods because of its inherent unpredictability.

The auditor shall perform audit procedures to evaluate whether the overall presentation of the financial statements, including the related disclosures, is in accordance with the applicable financial reporting framework. (Paragraph 24)

132   Specific financial reporting standards can require extensive narrative disclosures in the financial statements of banks and building societies; for example, in relation to the nature and extent of risks arising from financial instruments. In designing and performing procedures to evaluate these disclosures the auditor obtains audit evidence regarding the assertions about presentation and disclosure described in paragraph A111 of ISA (UK and Ireland) 315.

Dual-purpose tests

133   The auditor may design a test of controls to be performed concurrently with a test of details. Although the purpose of a test of controls is different from the purpose of a test of details, both may be accomplished concurrently by performing a test of controls and a test of details on the same transaction, also known as a dual-purpose

test. For example, the auditor may design and evaluate the results of a test to examine the entity's written documentation for a complex financial instrument to determine whether it has been approved and to provide substantive audit evidence of the transaction. A dual-purpose test is designed and evaluated by considering each purpose of the test separately.

In addition some of the controls which are usually performed by banks and   **134** building societies involve reconciling transactions, balances, securities and derivative positions with other banks, settlement systems, clearing houses and group entities. The auditor may design and evaluate the results of tests of such controls, both to obtain assurance as to the effectiveness of those controls and to provide substantive audit evidence.

Disclosure of market risk information under IFRS 7 and FRS 29

IFRS 7/FRS 29 Financial instruments: Disclosures may give rise to particular   **135** issues for the auditor, particularly in relation to market risk sensitivity analysis.

Understanding the risk measurement method adopted by the management

An entity applying IFRS 7/FRS 29, where appropriate, discloses a sensitivity   **136** analysis for each type of market risk to which the entity is exposed. Where an entity uses sensitivity analysis, such as value at risk ("VAR") that reflects interdependencies between risk variables and this is the method used to manage the financial risks of the business, disclosures based on these measures may be used instead of the standard method prescribed by IFRS 7/FRS 29 paragraph 40.

The auditor obtains an understanding of the method adopted by the management   **137** to develop the market price risk information to be disclosed. This may be done in conjunction with obtaining an understanding of the entity's accounting and internal control systems. For example, the auditor considers the independence of the entity's risk management function from the front office in the context of their understanding of the control environment.

Considering the skills needed by the audit team

The audit team is assembled on the basis of the skills needed. The auditor's   **138** approach to the market price risk disclosures is normally based on reviewing and testing the process used by the management to develop the information to be disclosed, rather than on re-performing the calculations (or making or obtaining an independent assessment). However, obtaining an understanding of that process and assumptions used may require technical knowledge of risk measurement methodologies; these can be complex, especially where a VAR model is adopted. Accordingly, when planning the audit, the auditor considers the skills needed in order to obtain and evaluate audit evidence in this part of the engagement.

The nature and extent of any technical knowledge of risk measurement   **139** methodologies that are required depends on the circumstances. The auditor takes into account such factors as the complexity of, and control surrounding, the model used and whether the model has received regulatory recognition. Where appropriate, the auditor may involve an expert in elements of this work (ISA (UK and Ireland) 620 covers using the work of an auditor's expert).

Considering the application of the risk measurement method

The auditor considers whether the risk measurement method adopted has been   **140** applied reasonably by, for example:

- reviewing, and where necessary testing, the internal controls relating to the operation of the entity's risk management system, in order to obtain evidence that the data used in developing the market price risk information are reliable. This may be done in conjunction with the auditor obtaining an understanding of control procedures including those over the data fed into the risk management system, pricing, and independent review of the algorithms. If the entity has applied for regulatory recognition of the method used, the auditor reviews correspondence with the regulator regarding such matters;

- reviewing, and where necessary testing, the internal controls relating to changes in the entity's risk management system (for example, controls over changes to algorithms and assumptions);

- if a VAR model is used, performing analytical review of the model's predictions during the year against actual outcomes (a process commonly referred to as "backtesting"). The auditor normally reviews any comparisons made by the entity as part of its own backtesting procedures (for an entity to receive regulatory recognition of the model used it is required to undertake backtesting procedures);

- agreeing the amount disclosed to the output of the risk management system.

141 If an approach based upon internal controls and backtesting proves to be unsatisfactory, the auditor may wish to consider testing the accuracy of the calculations used to develop the required information. However, this situation may indicate that it would be more appropriate for the entity to make disclosures on the simpler basis described in IFRS 7/FRS 29 paragraph 40.

Considering the adequacy of disclosures

142 Market price risk information is subject to a number of significant limitations which are inherent in the risk measurement methods used. For example:

- there are different VAR models and methods of presenting sensitivity analyses. It is to be expected that, in any particular case, the management of the entity will make an informed choice of the method that it considers to be most suitable. Normally, for the purpose of developing the market price risk information to be disclosed, the management will use the risk measurement method that is used in the entity's risk management system. It would, for example, be reasonable to expect the appropriateness of this method in the past to be supported by the entity's own backtesting procedures, where such procedures are performed. However, in the absence of recognised industry standards on VAR, there is no objective benchmark against which to assess the future appropriateness of management's choice;

- both VAR models and sensitivity analyses involve the management making a number of important assumptions in order to develop the disclosures. These are, by their nature, hypothetical and based on management's judgment (for example, when using a VAR model, assumptions are made concerning the appropriate holding period, confidence level and data set);

- both VAR models and, to a limited extent, sensitivity analyses are based on historical data and cannot take account of the fact that future market price movements, correlations between markets and levels of market liquidity in conditions of market stress may bear no relation to historical patterns; and

- each of the methods permitted for developing market price risk information may lead to the entity reporting significantly different information, depending on the choice made by the management. IFRS 7/FRS 29 paragraph 41 requires the market price risk information disclosed to be supplemented by other disclosures, including explanations of:

  - the method used in preparing such sensitivity analysis and of the main parameters and assumptions underlying the data provided in the disclosures; and

  - the objective of the method used and the limitations that may result in the information not fully reflecting the fair values of assets and liabilities involved.

The auditor considers the overall adequacy of the disclosures made by the entity in response to the requirements of IFRS 7/FRS 29 and whether the market risk information is presented fairly so that its limitations can be understood. In particular, the auditor considers whether it is sufficiently clear that: **143**

- the market price risk information is a relative estimate of risk rather than a precise and accurate number;

- the market price risk information represents a hypothetical outcome and is not intended to be predictive (in the case of probability-based methods, such as VAR, profits and losses are almost certain to exceed the reported amount with a frequency depending on the confidence interval chosen); and

- future market conditions could vary significantly from those experienced in the past.

In many entities and related groups, market price risk is primarily managed at the level of individual business units rather than on a legal entity or group-wide basis. Therefore, the auditor considers the appropriateness of the basis on which the market risk information to be disclosed in the financial statements is to be compiled. It may well be inappropriate simply to aggregate the operating unit information to arrive at the information to be disclosed for the entity or group as a whole.   **144**

Considering the consistency of the risk measurement method adopted

The main purpose of the disclosure of market price risk information is to provide users of an entity's financial statements with a better understanding of the relationship between the entity's profitability and its exposure to risk. For example, an increase in profitability may be achieved by taking on increased risk. IFRS 7/FRS 29 paragraph 40(c) requires disclosure of any changes in the methods and assumptions used and the reasons for the changes. Therefore, the auditor considers the consistency of the method, the main assumptions and parameters with those used in previous years.   **145**

If the method used for developing the market risk information is also used in the entity's risk management system, modifications will be made to the method as the need arises. If the entity performs its own backtesting procedures, this may lead to modification of, for example, the algorithm used, the assumptions and parameters specified or the parts of the trading book covered. Where modifications have been made, the auditor considers their effect on the market risk measures and whether appropriate disclosures about the changes have been made.   **146**

147   In some cases, re-statement may not be possible if the relevant data for the previous year cannot be constructed and in this case the auditor considers whether the disclosures provide sufficient information about the nature and extent of any change in the entity's risk profile. For example, as well as providing the current year figure on the "new" basis, it may be relevant to show both the current year and the previous year figure on the "old" basis. In all such cases, the auditor considers whether the disclosures contain sufficient narrative explanation of the change.

ISA (UK AND IRELAND) 402: AUDIT CONSIDERATIONS RELATING TO AN ENTITY USING A SERVICE ORGANIZATION

Objectives

The objectives of the user auditor, when the user entity uses the services of a service organization, are:

(a)   To obtain an understanding of the nature and significance of the services provided by the service organization and their effect on the user entity's internal control relevant to the audit, sufficient to identify and assess the risks of material misstatement; and

(b)   To design and perform audit procedures responsive to those risks. (Paragraph 7)

When obtaining an understanding of the user entity in accordance with ISA (UK and Ireland) 315, the user auditor shall obtain an understanding of how a user entity uses the services of a service organization in the user entity's operations, including:

(a)   The nature of the services provided by the service organization and the significance of those services to the user entity, including the effect thereof on the user entity's internal control;

(b)   The nature and materiality of the transactions processed or accounts or financial reporting processes affected by the service organization;

(c)   The degree of interaction between the activities of the service organization and those of the user entity;

(d)   The nature of the relationship between the user entity and the service organization, including the relevant contractual terms for the activities undertaken by the service organization; and

(e)   If the service organization maintains all or part of a user entity's accounting records, whether those arrangements impact the work the auditor performs to fulfil reporting responsibilities in relation to accounting records that are established in law or regulation. (Paragraph 9)

In responding to assessed risks in accordance with ISA (UK and Ireland) 330, the user auditor shall:

(a)   Determine whether sufficient appropriate audit evidence concerning the relevant financial statement assertions is available from records held at the user entity; and, if not,

(b)   Perform further audit procedures to obtain sufficient appropriate audit evidence or use another auditor to perform those procedures at the service organization on the user auditor's behalf. (Paragraph 15)

The user auditor shall modify the opinion in the user auditor's report in accordance with ISA (UK and Ireland) 705 if the user auditor is unable to obtain sufficient appropriate audit evidence regarding the services provided by the service organization relevant to the audit of the user entity's financial statements. (Paragraph 20)

In common with other industries the outsourcing of functions to third parties is common for banks and building societies, albeit to a more limited degree for building societies. Some of the more common areas, such as customer call centres, may have no direct impact on the audit, while others such as IT functions may have a direct relevance. The auditor therefore gains an understanding of the extent of outsourced functions and their relevance to the financial statements. The entity is obliged to ensure that the auditor has appropriate access to records, information and explanations from material outsourced operations.   **148**

Whilst an entity may outsource functions to third parties the responsibility for these functions remains that of the entity. The entity should have appropriate controls in place over these arrangements including: **149**

- risk assessment prior to contracting with the service provider, which includes a proper due diligence and periodic review of the appropriateness of the arrangement;

- appropriate contractual agreements or service level agreements;

- contingency plans should the provider fail in delivery of services;

- appropriate management information and reporting from the outsourced provider;

- appropriate controls over customer information; and

- right of access of the entity's internal audit to test the internal controls of the service provider.

If the auditor is unable to obtain sufficient appropriate audit evidence concerning outsourced operations the auditor considers whether it is necessary to report the matter direct to the FSA – see the section of this Practice Note relating to ISA (UK and Ireland) 250 Section B.   **150**

ISA (UK AND IRELAND) 505: EXTERNAL CONFIRMATIONS

Objective

The objective of the auditor, when using external confirmation procedures, is to design and perform such procedures to obtain relevant and reliable audit evidence. (Paragraph 5)

The auditor shall determine whether external confirmation procedures are to be performed as substantive audit procedures. (ISA (UK and Ireland) 330 paragraph 19)

In general, external confirmation procedures may be useful as part of the audit of account balances and classes of transactions such as loans and deposits (including other receivables and payables such as settlement balances and nostro/vostro balances), securities held by third party custodians and derivative transactions. Such procedures are likely to be particularly useful when confirmation can be obtained from settlement systems and clearing counterparties of securities in the course of settlement and centrally cleared derivative and other transactions. As banks and building societies normally have well established control procedures to reconcile such transactions, balances, securities and derivative positions, the   **151** auditor may consider it to be more effective to perform dual purpose tests on these controls as described in paragraph 133.

152   However, external confirmations may not always provide useful audit evidence in relation to:

- retail loans and deposits; and

- certain counterparties of wholesale market balances and transactions such as nostro/vostro balances, interbank loans and deposits and derivative transactions.

153   Retail loans and deposits typically comprise high volumes of comparatively low value amounts. Such third parties do not usually maintain independent records of their balances, largely depending on information already provided to them by the entity. Accordingly the auditor may consider the inherent reliability of such responses is comparatively low.

154   Wholesale counterparties incorporated in some jurisdictions outside the UK have countrywide policies of not responding to confirmation requests by auditors at all. Some counterparties will respond to requests to confirm specified balances and transactions but not open requests for unspecified information.

155   If external confirmations are not used, the auditor seeks sufficient appropriate evidence from tests of control and other substantive procedures. For example, in relation to wholesale market balances and transactions most banks and building societies also have well developed transaction confirmation controls within their trading activities as described in paragraph 115. The auditor may consider it more effective to test these controls, in addition to other substantive procedures, rather than carry out their own confirmation procedures.

ISA (UK AND IRELAND) 520: ANALYTICAL PROCEDURES

Objectives

The objectives of the auditor are:

(a)   To obtain relevant and reliable audit evidence when using substantive analytical procedures; and

(b)   To design and perform analytical procedures near the end of the audit that assist the auditor when forming an overall conclusion as to whether the financial statements are consistent with the auditor's understanding of the entity. (Paragraph 3)

In addition to the objectives and requirements established in ISA (UK and Ireland) 520, requirements for analytical procedures are also established in ISA (UK and Ireland) 315.

The auditor shall perform risk assessment procedures to provide a basis for the identification and assessment of risks of material misstatement at the financial statement and assertion levels. Risk assessment procedures by themselves, however, do not provide sufficient appropriate audit evidence on which to base the audit opinion. (ISA (UK and Ireland) 315 paragraph 5)

The risk assessment procedures shall include the following: ...

(b)   Analytical procedures ... (ISA (UK and Ireland) 315 paragraph 6)

Aspects of the entity's business where there are high volumes of similar **156** transactions or balances, such as interest receivable/payable or interest margins, may lend themselves to analytical procedures to highlight anomalies.

The auditor may wish to consider applying analytical procedures to the following, **157** if the procedures are expected to yield useful audit evidence or where they are considered more efficient or effective than alternative procedures:

- asset quality – e.g. ratio of non-performing loans to total loans and provisions for loan impairment to non-performing loans (overall and by portfolio type);

- earnings/profitability – e.g. cost/income ratio, the ratio of interest income or expense to average interest bearing assets or liabilities and the ratio of net interest income to average interest bearing assets;

- the exposure to and degree of mismatching arising from the market risks below and the comparison of the related risk positions to risk limits set by management. The auditor may find it helpful to consider risk information to be disclosed under IFRS 7/FRS 29:
  - liquidity;
  - interest rates;
  - foreign exchange;
  - other market risks, such as equity and commodity prices;

- the structure of the loan portfolio/credit exposure by industrial, geographic or other category, or by loan impairment provision;

- regulatory compliance – e.g. complaints handling or reporting of suspicious transactions under the Money Laundering regulations; and

- operational risk measures – e.g. failed trade rates, volumes of unreconciled items.

Whilst some aspects of the income statement and balance sheet of a bank or **158** building society lend themselves easily to analytical procedures, income and expense resulting from trading activities is unlikely to be susceptible to these methods because of its inherent unpredictability. Analytical procedures on income and expense items such as interest will be most effective if returns are calculated on the basis of average daily (or at least monthly) balance information.

When performing their review of the financial statements as a whole for **159** consistency with their knowledge of the entity's business and the results of other audit procedures, the auditor considers transactions occurring either side of the year end, including:

- material short-term deposits which are re-lent on broadly similar terms; loan repayments which are received shortly before the year end then re-advanced shortly afterwards; material sale and repurchase transactions or other financing or linked transactions. Experience and judgment are required to identify and assess the implications, if any, of these transactions; they may, for example, be indicative of "window dressing"[46] of the balance sheet over the year end date;

---

[46] *"Window dressing" refers to actions taken or not taken prior to issuing financial statements in order to improve the appearance of the financial statements.*

- other transactions around the year end, apparently at rates which are significantly off market including those that appear to give rise to significant profits or losses;

- the value and nature of transactions between related parties/associated undertakings around the year end; and

- the reclassification of balances and transactions to achieve advantageous income recognition and balance sheet treatment/presentation.

160   The auditor assesses evidence of window dressing and other transactions designed to achieve advantageous income recognition or balance sheet presentation and considers the implications for the financial statements (e.g. whether related disclosure is needed in order for the financial statements to give a true and fair view and, if so, given) and the consequences for the auditor's assessment of risks. If the auditor has concerns about such transactions and their treatment in the financial statements, the auditor communicates those concerns to those charged with governance and considers whether the auditor has a duty to, or should otherwise, make a report direct to the FSA, on which guidance is set out in the section of this Practice Note relating to ISA (UK and Ireland) 250 Section B.

161   Where non financial information or reports produced from systems or processes outside the financial statements accounting system are used in analytical procedures, the auditor considers the reliability of that information or those reports.

ISA (UK AND IRELAND) 540: AUDITING ACCOUNTING ESTIMATES, INCLUDING FAIR VALUE ACCOUNTING ESTIMATES, AND RELATED DISCLOSURES

Objective

The objective of the auditor is to obtain sufficient appropriate audit evidence about whether:

(a)   accounting estimates, including fair value accounting estimates, in the financial statements, whether recognised or disclosed, are reasonable; and

(b)   related disclosures in the financial statements are adequate,

in the context of the applicable financial reporting framework. (Paragraph 6)

When performing risk assessment procedures and related activities to obtain an understanding of the entity and its environment, including the entity's internal control, as required by ISA (UK and Ireland) 315, the auditor shall obtain an understanding of ...:

(b)   How management identifies those transactions, events and conditions that may give rise to the need for accounting estimates to be recognised or disclosed in the financial statements.

(c)   How management makes the accounting estimates, and an understanding of the data on which they are based ... (Paragraph 8)

The auditor shall review the outcome of accounting estimates included in the prior period financial statements, or, where applicable, their subsequent re-estimation for the purpose of the current period. ... (Paragraph 9)

In identifying and assessing the risks of material misstatement, as required by ISA (UK and Ireland) 315, the auditor shall evaluate the degree of estimation uncertainty associated with an accounting estimate. (Paragraph 10)

The auditor shall determine whether, in the auditor's judgment, any of those accounting estimates that have been identified as having high estimation uncertainty give rise to significant risks. (Paragraph 11)

Based on the assessed risks of material misstatement, the auditor shall determine:

(a)   Whether management has appropriately applied the requirements of the applicable financial reporting framework relevant to the accounting estimate; and

(b)   Whether the methods for making the accounting estimates are appropriate and have been applied consistently, and whether changes, if any, in accounting estimates or in the method for making them from the prior period are appropriate in the circumstances. (Paragraph 12)

In responding to the assessed risks of material misstatement, as required by ISA (UK and Ireland) 330, the auditor shall undertake one or more of the following, taking account of the nature of the accounting estimate:

(a)   Determine whether events occurring up to the date of the auditor's report provide audit evidence regarding the accounting estimate.

(b)   Test how management made the accounting estimate and the data on which it is based. In doing so, the auditor shall evaluate whether:

 (i)   The method of measurement used is appropriate in the circumstances; and

 (ii)   The assumptions used by management are reasonable in light of the measurement objectives of the applicable financial reporting framework.

(c)   Test the operating effectiveness of the controls over how management made the accounting estimate, together with appropriate substantive procedures.

(d)   Develop a point estimate or a range to evaluate management's point estimate. For this purpose:

 (i)   If the auditor uses assumptions or methods that differ from management's, the auditor shall obtain an understanding of management's assumptions or methods sufficient to establish that the auditor's point estimate or range takes into account relevant variables and to evaluate any significant differences from management's point estimate.

 (ii)   If the auditor concludes that it is appropriate to use a range, the auditor shall narrow the range, based on audit evidence available, until all outcomes within the range are considered reasonable. (Paragraph 13)

For accounting estimates that give rise to significant risks, in addition to other substantive procedures performed to meet the requirements of ISA (UK and Ireland) 330, the auditor shall evaluate the following:

(a)   How management has considered alternative assumptions or outcomes, and why it has rejected them, or how management has otherwise addressed estimation uncertainty in making the accounting estimate.

(b)   Whether the significant assumptions used by management are reasonable.

(c)   Where relevant to the reasonableness of the significant assumptions used by management or the appropriate application of the applicable financial reporting framework, management's intent to carry out specific courses of action and its ability to do so. (Paragraph 15)

The auditor shall evaluate, based on the audit evidence, whether the accounting estimates in the financial statements are either reasonable in the context of the applicable financial reporting framework, or are misstated. (Paragraph 18)

162   Accounting estimates are used for valuation purposes in a number of areas: the most common examples are impairment calculations, and the fair value measurement of financial instruments where quoted market prices are not available for those instruments, both of which may represent significant risks. Estimates of allowances for impairment or provisions for compensation payable to customers may also represent significant risks.

163   In reviewing the effective interest rate calculations prepared by management the auditor carefully audits the inputs used in the models to determine the estimated cash flows which are then subject to the effective interest rate ("EIR") calculation. The auditor considers the information provided in IAS 39 (and its UK GAAP equivalent FRS 26) Application Guidance as to the reliability of such information being used. When estimating the cash flows management considers all contractual terms of the instrument and includes all reliable estimates of those cash flows. Factors that would be considered include all fees and points paid or received between parties to the contract that are an integral part of the effective interest rate, transaction costs, premiums or discounts, the expectation of timing and amount of the interest cash flows and whether the instrument is a floating or fixed instrument. Generally these will be amortised over the expected life of the instrument, however a shorter period is used if this is the period to which they relate and the auditor would assess the conclusion reached by the entity for reasonableness.

164   IAS 39 (FRS 26) requires all financial assets, with the exception of those measured at fair value through profit and loss to be reviewed for impairment. An impairment loss is only recognised when it is incurred, and it is only incurred if there is objective evidence of impairment as a result of one or more events that occurred after initial recognition and that event has an impact on the estimated future cash flows of the asset or group of assets, that can be reliably measured. The auditor evaluates the policy adopted by the entity to assess for impairment on all financial assets (excluding those measured at fair value through profit and loss) including reviewing what is constituted as a loss event and what events will result in an impairment loss being recognised, as one discrete event may not necessarily imply an impairment loss. Similarly the auditor challenges the entity on those events which have occurred which have not been recognised as a loss event by the entity.

165   IAS 39 (FRS 26) gives guidance on the types of evidence to be considered in identifying whether an event has taken place (a "loss event") which leads to an impairment calculation. Such factors include observable data about the following loss events:

- significant financial difficulties of the issuer or obligor;
- breach of contract;

- a concession (such as a forbearance arrangement) being granted by the lender for economic or legal reasons relating to the borrower's financial difficulty which the lender would not otherwise consider;

- probability that the borrower will enter bankruptcy or financial reorganization;

- disappearance of an active market due to financial difficulties; and

- observable data indicating that there is a measurable decrease in the estimated future cash flows from a group of financial assets since the initial recognition of those assets, although the decrease cannot be observed within individual assets including:

  - adverse changes in the payment status of the borrowers in the group; or

  - national or local economic conditions that correlate with defaults on other assets within the group.

Further factors will apply when considering the impairment of equity investments such as significant changes with an adverse effect that have taken place in the technological, market, economic or legal environment in which the issuer operates or a significant or prolonged decline in the fair value of the equity instrument.

166 If, following the auditor's consideration of the factors outlined in paragraph 165, it is determined that a loss event has taken place, the auditor evaluates the assumptions made by management in arriving at their estimate of likely cash flows to be received from the impaired loans (including, where relevant, assumptions about the values of assets provided by way of security). The auditor assesses whether these assumptions have been made after due consideration and whether they are supported by relevant evidence, including evidence derived from backtesting. In making these assessments, the auditor considers whether an appropriate degree of caution has been exercised by management in judging anticipated future cash flows. In the case of individual loan impairment calculations such evidence will be specific to the borrower but where impairment is estimated for a portfolio of similar loans the auditor considers observable data across the group of assets as a whole such as arrears statistics or national or local economic conditions.

167 Loan impairments are often calculated using extensive and sometimes complex spreadsheet models and the auditor assesses the control over the inputs to the models and the controls that ensure the consistency and integrity of the model. In doing so, the auditor applies the assessments around management assumptions described in paragraph 166 to model inputs. The auditor evaluates models for consistency and accuracy and looks for evidence to support the assumptions being made in the models. These assumptions would include some or all of the following factors: financial guarantees and collateral, the expectation of timing and amount of the cash flows, probabilities of default, loss given default, emergence periods, whether the instrument is a floating or fixed instrument, prepayment speeds and recovery rates.

168 IAS 39 (FRS 26) does permit an entity to assess for impairment on a group of financial assets but only where an entity first considers whether there is objective evidence of an impairment for financial assets that are "individually significant". The auditor evaluates the judgment applied by the entity in assessing what is considered as "individually significant". Where this collective impairment assessment is performed by the entity the auditor evaluates the evidence used in determining the cash flows for reasonableness and grouping of assets with similar risk characteristics. This will involve reviewing historical loss experience for similar assets, peer group experience if none available for specific entity losses and reviewing the methodology and assumptions made by the entity.

169 The auditor considers the mechanics of the models particularly where portfolio calculations are performed in respect of tracking impairment charges and reversals of impairments in order to ensure that the correct accounting has been applied depending on the security involved.

170 Additional complexity has been added to impairment models and effective interest rate models as a result of IAS 39 Reclassification of financial assets, specifically from the Fair Value through Profit and Loss category to the Loans and Receivables category at distressed market prices. The auditor may wish to consult with an expert to assist in the audit of these balances as the calculation of EIR and the need to either record an adjustment to Profit and Loss or revise the EIR can be technical in nature.

171 Based on the audit evidence obtained, the auditor may conclude that the evidence points to an estimate that differs from management's estimate, and that the difference between the auditor's estimate or range and management's estimate constitutes a financial statement misstatement. In such cases, where the auditor has developed a range, a misstatement exists when management's estimate lies outside the auditor's range. The misstatement is measured as the difference between management's estimate and the nearest point of the auditor's range.

172 The valuation of derivative and other financial instruments which are not quoted in an active market and so for which valuation techniques are required is an activity that can give rise to significant audit risk. Such financial instruments are priced using valuation techniques such as discounted cash flow models, options pricing models or by reference to another instrument that is substantially the same as the financial instrument subject to valuation. The auditor reviews the controls, procedures and testing of the valuation techniques used by the entity. Controls and substantive testing could include focusing on:

- valuation technique approval and testing procedures used by the entity;

- the independence of review, sourcing and reasonableness of observable market data and other parameters used in the valuation techniques;

- calibration procedures used by the entity to test the validity of valuation techniques applied by comparing outputs to observable market transactions;

- completeness and appropriate inclusion of all relevant observable market data;

- the observability in practice of data classified by the entity as observable market data;

- the appropriateness and validity of classification of instruments designated as being traded in a non active and in an active market in light of best market practice;

- the appropriateness and validity of the particular valuation technique applied to particular financial instruments;

- the appropriateness and reasonableness of the assumptions used by the entity particularly where these are not supported by observable parameters;

● the appropriateness and validity of the parameters used by the entity to designate an instrument as substantially the same as the financial instrument being valued;

● mathematical integrity of the valuation model; and

● access controls over valuation models.

The auditor performs these procedures in light of their knowledge and experience and of the information readily available to the auditor.

In the more subjective areas of valuation the auditor obtains an understanding of the assumptions used and undertakes a review of the estimates involved for reasonableness, consistency and conformity with generally accepted practices. In some cases, the auditor may use his own valuation techniques to assess the entity's valuations. See paragraphs 135 to 147 above concerning disclosure of market risk information. Given the complexities involved and the subjective nature of the judgments inherent the auditor may involve an expert in elements of this work (see the ISA (UK and Ireland) 620 section of this Practice Note and ISA (UK and Ireland) 220).   173

In addition, the auditor considers whether the valuations overall appear reasonable based on the auditor's industry knowledge, market trends and the auditor's understanding of other entities' valuations (having regard to client confidentiality) and other relevant price indicators. If the valuations appear to be consistently overly aggressive or conservative, this may be evidence of management bias (see paragraphs 182-186). The auditor takes this into consideration when evaluating the audit evidence obtained.   174

Additional guidance is also provided in the IASB Expert Advisory Panel Report issued in October 2008 which deals with measuring and disclosing the fair value of financial instruments in markets that are no longer active.   175

Additional guidance is provided for auditors in Practice Note 23 (Revised), "Auditing Complex Financial Instruments – Interim Guidance", specifically paragraphs 75-80 and 110-142 dealing with the valuation of complex financial instruments. This guidance has not been duplicated in this Practice Note.   176

The auditor may also wish to consider benchmarking the valuation methodologies and assumptions used by management to other comparable companies holding comparable financial instruments to ensure that there is consistency in the market place for such valuation techniques. However, the availability and comparability of data will need to be considered for each case.   177

Disclosure

For accounting estimates that give rise to significant risks, the auditor shall also evaluate the adequacy of the disclosure of their estimation uncertainty in the financial statements in the context of the applicable financial reporting framework. (Paragraph 20)

The auditor assesses the disclosures the entity has made in respect of assumptions they have made about the future and other major sources of estimation uncertainty that have a significant risk of resulting in a material adjustment to the carrying amount of assets and liabilities in the next financial year. This is a requirement of IAS 1, "Presentation of Financial Statements". The auditor considers the difficult, subjective and complex assumptions made by management and assesses whether sufficient information is disclosed to enable the users of the financial statements to understand these uncertainties. The auditor considers factors such as the nature of   178 the assumption, the sensitivity of the carrying amount to that assumption, range of reasonably possible outcomes and any explanations as to changes in these assumptions. Examples of these critical accounting estimates typically include the fair valuation of financial instruments, allowances for loan impairments and other credit risk provisions, goodwill, intangible assets, pensions and retirement benefits and deferred taxation.

179   The requirements of IFRS 7/FRS 29 to disclose information about the financial risks of the entity and how those are managed with reference to how the entity reports internally to key management personnel are a particular focus area for auditors. The auditor evaluates whether the disclosures are complete, appropriate and meet the requirements of the standard.

180   In respect of fair value accounting estimates the auditor may not be able to validate the fair value precisely and should rather determine a range within which there is an expectation that the entity's value would fall within. The auditor also assesses the ranges that are disclosed as part of IFRS 7/FRS 29 where management has made assumptions or judgments in determining the fair value where significant unobservable inputs have been used. The auditor determines whether the entity is disclosing the relevant assumptions and methodologies that have been employed to determine the fair value of their financial instruments in accordance with IFRS 7/FRS 29. For example the entity may disclose information about the assumptions relating to prepayment rates, recovery rates, interest rates, credit spreads, estimated credit losses and other discount rates used.

181   The auditor assesses the reasonableness of the fair value hierarchy that has been prepared by the entity in accordance with IFRS 7/FRS 29 to assess it for accuracy and completeness. The auditor challenges the entity's allocation in the fair value hierarchy by specifically considering the significant inputs used in determining the fair value of the instruments. Where quoted prices in active markets for identical assets or liabilities are used this would be categorised as level 1 (e.g. a corporate bond trading in an active market or a futures contract traded on an exchange). If inputs that are observable for the asset or liability either directly or indirectly are used in the valuation technique this would be regarded as level 2 (e.g. an interest rate swap in a liquid currency for a tenor for which liquid swap curve data is available). Where inputs used in the valuation technique are not based on observable inputs this would imply a level 3 categorisation if these inputs are significant to the fair value measurement in its entirety (e.g. corporate bond trading in an illiquid market where management has had to make an assumption of the implied credit spread to use). The auditor assesses whether there is sufficient evidence supporting the fair value hierarchy and the levels applied and reviews the additional sensitivity analysis required for changing the unobservable inputs in level 3 to reasonably possible changes and the impact on the carrying amount and profit and loss or equity.

Management bias

> The auditor shall review the judgments and decisions made by management in the making of accounting estimates to identify whether there are indicators of possible management bias. Indicators of possible management bias do not themselves constitute misstatements for the purposes of drawing conclusions on the reasonableness of individual accounting estimates. (Paragraph 21)

182   Management bias, whether unintentional or intentional, may be difficult to detect in an individual estimate. ISA (UK and Ireland) 540 indicates that examples of possible management bias with respect to accounting estimates include:

- Changes in an accounting estimate, or the method for making it, where management has made a subjective assessment that there has been a change in circumstances;

- Use of an entity's own assumptions for fair value accounting estimates when they are inconsistent with observable marketplace assumptions;

- Selection or construction of significant assumptions that yield a point estimate favourable for management objectives; and

- Selection of a point estimate that may indicate a pattern of optimism or pessimism.

Management bias may be identified when there has been a change in the method **183** for calculating estimates from the prior period based on a subjective assessment without evidence that there has been a change in circumstances, when considered in the aggregate of groups of estimates or all estimates, or when observed over a number of accounting periods. It may also be identified if management consistently select estimates from the ends of plausible ranges rather than adopting a more neutral approach.

Management may evaluate alternative assumptions or outcomes of the accounting **184** estimates through a number of methods, depending on the circumstances. A sensitivity analysis could lead to the development of a number of outcome scenarios, sometimes characterised as a range of outcomes by management, such as "pessimistic" and "optimistic" scenarios. A sensitivity analysis may demonstrate that an accounting estimate is not sensitive to changes in particular assumptions. Alternatively, it may demonstrate that the accounting estimate is sensitive to one or more assumptions that then become the focus of the auditor's attention.

Although management bias is inherent in subjective decisions, management may **185** have no intention of misleading the users of financial statements. If, however, there is intention to mislead through, for example, the intentional use of unreasonable estimates, management bias is fraudulent in nature. ISA (UK and Ireland) 240, "The Auditor's Responsibilities Relating to Fraud in an Audit of Financial Statements", provides standards and guidance on the auditor's responsibility to consider fraud in an audit of financial statements.

Indicators of management bias are an example of a matter that the auditor may **186** communicate to those charged with governance when fulfilling the requirement in paragraph 16(a) of ISA (UK and Ireland) 260, "Communication With Those Charged With Governance", to communicate the auditor's views about significant qualitative aspects of the entity's accounting practices, including accounting policies, accounting estimates and financial statement disclosures.

ISA (UK AND IRELAND) 550: RELATED PARTIES

Objectives

The objectives of the auditor are:

(a) Irrespective of whether the applicable financial reporting framework establishes related party requirements, to obtain an understanding of related party relationships and transactions sufficient to be able:

   (i) To recognise fraud risk factors, if any, arising from related party relationships and transactions that are relevant to the identification and assessment of the risks of material misstatement due to fraud; and

> (ii)   To conclude, based on the audit evidence obtained, whether the financial statements, insofar as they are affected by those relationships and transactions:
>
>   a.   Achieve fair presentation (for fair presentation frameworks); or
>
>   b.   Are not misleading (for compliance frameworks); and
>
> (b)   In addition, where the applicable financial reporting framework establishes related party requirements, to obtain sufficient appropriate audit evidence about whether related party relationships and transactions have been appropriately identified, accounted for and disclosed in the financial statements in accordance with the framework. (Paragraph 9)
>
> In meeting the ISA (UK and Ireland) 315 requirement to identify and assess the risks of material misstatement, the auditor shall identify and assess the risks of material misstatement associated with related party relationships and transactions and determine whether any of those risks are significant risks. In making this determination, the auditor shall treat identified significant related party transactions outside the entity's normal course of business as giving rise to significant risks. (Paragraph 18)

187   Related party transactions are defined in FRS 8/IAS 24 "Related Party Disclosures". Paragraph 16 of FRS 8 states that the "disclosure provisions do not apply where to comply with them conflicts with the reporting entity's duties of confidentiality arising by operation of law". IAS 24 contains no explicit corresponding exemption. However the potentially overriding impact of law concerning confidentiality in respect of disclosures under IAS 24 still needs to be considered. This is particularly relevant in a banking context: banks and building societies are usually under a strict duty of confidentiality (by operation of statute, contract or common law) regarding the affairs of their clients and, in respect of transactions entered into in certain overseas jurisdictions, this may even preclude a foreign entity from disclosing information to its parent, another group company or their auditor. A provider of finance (in the course of a business in that regard) and its customer are not "related" simply because of that relationship.

188   Both when applying EU IFRS or UK GAAP, under ISA (UK and Ireland) 550, the auditor is required to assess the risk that material undisclosed related party transactions may exist. It is in the nature of banking business that transaction volumes are high but this factor will not, of itself, necessarily lead the auditor to conclude that the inherent risk of material undisclosed related party transactions is high.

189   Authorised firms are required to report to FSA changes in control (in some instances with FSA prior approval), changes in circumstances of existing controlling parties and changes in entities who are closely linked to the authorised firm (SUP 11). In addition, there are annual reporting obligations in respect of controlling parties and entities that are closely linked to the firm (SUP 16). As a result, it will therefore normally be the case that there are controls in place to ensure that this information is properly collated. However, the definition of "controller and closely linked" for regulatory purposes is not congruent with the "related party" definition in FRS 8/IAS 24 and the auditor therefore considers what controls have been put in place by management to capture information on those parties which fall within the accounting definition only.

190   In reviewing related party information for completeness, the auditor may compare the proposed disclosures in the financial statements to information prepared for

regulatory reporting purposes (bearing in mind that the population may be different, as noted in the preceding paragraph).

Whilst related party transactions can arise generally, in the context of UK banks **191** and building societies, they frequently arise in respect of deposits held by directors and/or persons connected with them and in respect of loans and other transactions with directors and/or persons connected with them. They may also arise in respect of the sale or arrangement of insurance products and in respect of the provision of professional and other services. Whilst there are CA2006 provisions relating to transactions by banking companies with directors, there are separate BS Act 1986 requirements for building societies in respect of transactions with directors (s62-69 BS Act 1986). See paragraphs 239 to 241 concerning the related auditor's obligation.

The auditor is aware that BSOG provides additional emphasis for proper approval **192** procedures concerning loans to and transactions with directors (BSOG 1.3.15G and 16G). In addition, the auditor is required to report on the statement that a building society is required to make under s68 BS Act 1986 concerning loans, and certain other transactions with directors, that are subject to s65 BS Act 1986. The auditor is also aware that the Sch10A BS Act 1986 contains specific disclosure requirements applicable to the annual accounts of building societies as regards loans and certain other transactions with directors.

ISA (UK AND IRELAND) 560: SUBSEQUENT EVENTS

Objectives

The objectives of the auditor are:

(a) To obtain sufficient appropriate audit evidence about whether events occurring between the date of the financial statements and the date of the auditor's report that require adjustment of, or disclosure in, the financial statements are appropriately reflected in those financial statements in accordance with the applicable financial reporting framework; and

(b) To respond appropriately to facts that become known to the auditor after the date of the auditor's report, that, had they been known to the auditor at that date, may have caused the auditor to amend the auditor's report. (Paragraph 4)

The auditor shall perform audit procedures designed to obtain sufficient appropriate audit evidence that all events occurring between the date of the financial statements and the date of the auditor's report that require adjustment of, or disclosure in, the financial statements have been identified. The auditor is not, however, expected to perform additional audit procedures on matters to which previously applied audit procedures have provided satisfactory conclusions. (Paragraph 6)

Matters specific to banks and building societies which the auditor may consider in **193** the review of subsequent events include:

- an evaluation of material loans and other receivables identified as being in default or potential default at the period end to provide additional evidence concerning period end loan impairment provisions;

- an assessment of material loans and other receivables identified as (potential) defaults since the period end to consider whether any adjustment to the period end carrying value is required;

- a review of movements in market prices and exchange rates in illiquid markets to consider whether prices or rates used in period end valuations were realistic;

- a review of correspondence with regulators and enquiries of management to determine whether any significant breaches of regulations or other significant regulatory concerns have come to light since the period end; and

- a consideration of post year end liquidity reports for indications of funding difficulties.

ISA (UK AND IRELAND) 570: GOING CONCERN

Objectives

The objectives of the auditor are:

(a)   To obtain sufficient appropriate audit evidence regarding the appropriateness of management's use of the going concern assumption in the preparation of the financial statements;

(b)   To conclude, based on the audit evidence obtained, whether a material uncertainty exists related to events or conditions that may cast significant doubt on the entity's ability to continue as a going concern; and

(c)   To determine the implications for the auditor's report. (Paragraph 9)

When performing risk assessment procedures as required by ISA (UK and Ireland) 315, the auditor shall consider whether there are events or conditions that may cast significant doubt on the entity's ability to continue as a going concern. In so doing, the auditor shall determine whether management has already performed a preliminary assessment of the entity's ability to continue as a going concern, and:

(a)   If such an assessment has been performed, the auditor shall discuss the assessment with management and determine whether management has identified events or conditions that, individually or collectively, may cast significant doubt on the entity's ability to continue as a going concern and, if so, management's plans to address them; or

(b)   If such an assessment has not yet been performed, the auditor shall discuss with management the basis for the intended use of the going concern assumption, and inquire of management whether events or conditions exist that, individually or collectively, may cast significant doubt on the entity's ability to continue as a going concern. (Paragraph 10)

The auditor shall remain alert throughout the audit for audit evidence of events or conditions that may cast significant doubt on the entity's ability to continue as a going concern. (Paragraph 11)

194   The approach for assessing the going concern assumption of a bank or building society is different from that likely to be adopted when making the assessment for a non bank "Corporate" entity. A going concern assessment for a Corporate would typically involve comparing cash requirements at monthly intervals for a future period (e.g. the next 18 months) with available committed borrowing facilities to determine whether the company had sufficient headroom in its banking facilities to accommodate its foreseeable working capital needs.

195   The working capital of a bank or building society is very different in nature. The daily cash flows passing to and from a bank or building society are large. Banks and building societies cannot rely on committed facilities (loans and overdrafts from other banks) as typically they do not have access to facilities in this form. On a contractual basis, banks and building societies have current liabilities, such as on-demand and short-term retail deposits and wholesale unsecured borrowing, which are typically greater than their current assets (loans and other financial assets due within one year) and thus always have funding gaps. Trading activities are typically funded in a different manner (e.g. by repos) to retail/commercial banking and this funding is normally short term.

However, behavioural cash flows impacting a bank or building society are **196** typically very different from that indicated by contractual maturities. Short-term contractual liabilities such as customer demand deposits have much longer behavioural maturities, and certain long-term contractual assets such as mortgages have shorter behavioural maturities (i.e. early redemptions).

At a simple level, banks are likely to face liquidity problems if the incremental **197** demand for new funds across the various divisions of the bank exceed the supply of funding readily available.

Incremental "demand" for funding is created through a number of channels, for **198** example:

- growth in the business (e.g. more lending to customers);
- drawdowns on committed facilities;
- corporate actions (such as acquisitions);
- large losses in trading books;
- significant FX movements; and
- additional collateral requirements on trading positions.

Behavioural factors are also important when assessing funding demand. For **199** instance if the level of early mortgage redemptions falls, less cash will be received and the funding requirement will increase.

The key sources of funding supply on the liability side of the balance sheet are: **200**

- retail and corporate deposits;
- borrowing on wholesale markets/short-term money markets;
- debt securities (typically longer term debt);
- securitisation type arrangements (including covered bonds);
- repos; and
- equity injections from strategic investors (e.g. Sovereign Wealth Funds).

Banks and building societies are required to meet liquidity requirements set by the **201** regulator[47]. A failure to comply with these requirements is likely to prompt action by the regulator.

A further important consideration in a going concern assessment for a bank or **202** building society is the level of its capital ratios. Failure to maintain the required level of regulatory capital is likely to prompt intervention by the regulator. A sharp fall in regulatory capital may also result in a ratings downgrade making funding more expensive and possibly harder to obtain.

---

[47] *For example BIPRU 12 Liquidity Standards.*

203 In reviewing going concern, the auditor may therefore consider the following areas in addition to those set out in ISA (UK and Ireland) 570:

- capital adequacy ratios – e.g. review of management's analysis and rationale for ensuring that the entity is capable of maintaining adequate financial resources in excess of the minimum, this would include a review of stress tests performed by management;

- operations/profitability indicators – e.g. review of the performance of loans in troubled industry sectors in which the entity has a high concentration of exposure;

- funding structure and funding plan – e.g. review of management's funding plans and comparison against recent funding patterns;

- liquidity indicators – e.g. review of the entity's liquidity management process (e.g. maturity mismatch ladders) for signs of undue deterioration, again including a review of stress tests[48] performed by management and including a review of management's analysis of the entity's ability to meet liquidity requirements set by the regulator;

- liquid assets buffer – e.g. review of the results of compliance with the FSA requirement that a firm must periodically realise a proportion of the assets in its liquid assets buffer through repo or outright sale to the market[49];

- customer behaviour indicators – e.g. review of recent deposit withdrawal experience (including, in exceptional circumstances, a run on the bank or building society) and whether there are indicators of changes in behaviour on the asset side of the balance sheet; and

- reputational and other indicators – e.g. review of the financial press and other sources of market intelligence for evidence of deteriorating reputation; review of correspondence with regulators.

Further details of possible factors that may indicate going concern issues in these areas are set out in Appendix 5 to this Practice Note.

204 There may be circumstances where funding for an entity is provided by national governments or central banks and, where applicable, the auditor considers whether such funding is appropriately committed.

205 If the auditor has any doubts as to the ability of the entity to continue as a going concern, the auditor considers whether to make a report direct to the FSA, on which guidance is set out in the section of this Practice Note relating to ISA (UK and Ireland) 250 Section B.

ISA (UK AND IRELAND) 580: WRITTEN REPRESENTATIONS

Objectives

The objectives of the auditor are:

(a) To obtain written representations from management and, where appropriate, those charged with governance that they believe that they have fulfilled their responsibility for the preparation of the financial statements and for the completeness of the information provided to the auditor;

---

[48] *BIPRU 12.4 addresses stress testing and contingency funding.*

[49] *BIPRU 12.7.11.*

(b)   To support other audit evidence relevant to the financial statements or specific assertions in the financial statements by means of written representations if determined necessary by the auditor or required by other ISAs (UK and Ireland); and

(c)   To respond appropriately to written representations provided by management and, where appropriate, those charged with governance, or if management or, where appropriate, those charged with governance do not provide the written representations requested by the auditor. (Paragraph 6)

The auditor shall request written representations from management with appropriate responsibilities for the financial statements and knowledge of the matters concerned. (Paragraph 9)

Other ISAs (UK and Ireland) require the auditor to request written representations. If, in addition to such required representations, the auditor determines that it is necessary to obtain one or more written representations to support other audit evidence relevant to the financial statements or one or more specific assertions in the financial statements, the auditor shall request such other written representations. (Paragraph 13)

ISAs (UK and Ireland) 250 Section A and 550 require the auditor to obtain written confirmation in respect of completeness of disclosure to the auditor of: **206**

- all known instances of non-compliance or suspected non-compliance with laws and regulations whose effects should be considered when preparing financial statements (these include breaches of FSMA 2000, FSA rules, the Money Laundering Regulations, other regulatory requirements or any other circumstance that could jeopardise the authorisation of the firm under FSMA 2000); and

- the completeness of information provided regarding the identification of related parties and the adequacy of related party disclosures in the financial statements.

In addition to the examples of other representations given in ISA (UK and Ireland) 580, the auditor also considers obtaining confirmation: **207**

- as to the adequacy of provisions for loan impairment (including provisions relating to individual loans if material) and the appropriateness of other accounting estimates (such as complex financial instrument valuations or adequate provisions for compensation concerning upheld complaints by customers);

- that all contingent transactions or commitments have been adequately disclosed and/or included in the balance sheet as appropriate; and

- that all correspondence with regulators has been made available to the auditor.

ISA (UK AND IRELAND) 600: SPECIAL CONSIDERATIONS – AUDITS OF GROUP FINANCIAL STATEMENTS (INCLUDING THE WORK OF COMPONENT AUDITORS)

Objectives
The objectives of the auditor are:

(a)   To determine whether to act as the auditor of the group financial statements; and

> (b)   If acting as the auditor of the group financial statements:
>
>   (i)   To communicate clearly with component auditors about the scope and timing of their work on financial information related to components and their findings; and
>
>   (ii) To obtain sufficient appropriate audit evidence regarding the financial information of the components and the consolidation process to express an opinion on whether the group financial statements are prepared, in all material respects, in accordance with the applicable financial reporting framework. (Paragraph 8)

208   Where the entity consists of a group with components, (e.g. subsidiaries, branches or divisions), the requirements and application guidance in ISA (UK and Ireland) 600 are applicable as for groups in other industries. Similar considerations apply, but there are certain aspects that are particularly challenging for the audits of banks and building societies.

Assessment of component risk

> The auditor is required to identify and assess the risks of material misstatement through obtaining an understanding of the entity and its environment. The group engagement team shall:
>
> (a)   Enhance its understanding of the group, its components, and their environments, including group-wide controls, obtained during the acceptance or continuance stage; and
>
> (b)   Obtain an understanding of the consolidation process, including the instructions issued by group management to components. (Paragraph 17)
>
> The group engagement team shall obtain an understanding that is sufficient to:
>
> (a)   Confirm or revise its initial identification of components that are likely to be significant; and
>
> (b)   Assess the risks of material misstatement of the group financial statements, whether due to fraud or error. (Paragraph 18)

209   Generally the significance of components will be assessed based on the size of their balance sheets and profit and loss accounts/income statements. However, it is important also to be alert to the risk of misstatement arising from the nature of the entity's activities. For example a poor control environment in a small remote treasury operation or a small retail bank may lead to errors of a size that are disproportionate to the size of the entity concerned. This risk may be mitigated by testing certain key controls in and over the entity, even if a full scope audit is not conducted.

Special purpose entities

210   One aspect of activities of banks and building societies that can present particular difficulties is their use of special purpose entities ("SPEs"), which are often considerably more numerous than for entities in other industries. The key risks of material misstatement relating to special purpose entities arise from failure:

- to identify all special purpose entities established by the group; and

- to assess appropriately whether the SPEs are required to be consolidated by the group in accordance with the relevant financial reporting framework.

As SPEs tend to have varying legal forms, for example trusts, partnerships or other **211** vehicles, it can sometimes be challenging to ensure that all SPEs established by the group have been accurately identified by management. The auditor considers the process established by management for:

- recording and ongoing monitoring of SPEs; and

- understanding changes to SPE structures that might trigger consolidation accounting for unconsolidated SPEs.

Audit procedures to address this might include: **212**

- inquiries of the senior management and the Board;

- inspection of committee minutes approving the setting up of such entities;

- inspection of approvals from different functions within the group, for example-Compliance, Risk, Legal, Tax, Finance etc.;

- reviewing the list/database of SPEs and changes thereto.

Management of group entities usually perform an assessment of whether SPEs are **213** required to be consolidated or not within the group. This is normally considered as part of the set up process. The assessment is based on whether the group controls the SPE or not and takes into account various factors such as the nature of activities of the SPE, who obtains the majority of the benefits, who bears the majority of the risks and so forth.

The auditor evaluates management's assessment of the accounting treatment of the **214** SPEs in accordance with the applicable reporting framework and challenge the appropriateness of the treatment, where necessary including, for example, if relevant circumstances have changed since management performed its assessment of whether SPEs are required to be consolidated. The auditor also checks the regulatory treatment of SPEs to ascertain whether this provides additional evidence for the accounting treatment and also to ensure that any differences can be rationalised.

For SPEs that are consolidated within the group, the auditor applies the same tests **215** as for other components to identify whether the component is significant from a group perspective and to determine the type of work to be performed on the SPE (either because of its individual financial significance or because it has significant risks).

Offshoring

Another aspect of difficulty in undertaking the group audit of a bank or building **216** society is their use of offshoring. Large banking groups tend to process a huge volume of generally low value transactions on a day-to-day basis. Over the past few years, many banking institutions have increasingly offshored these high volume transaction processing and related control activities to low cost locations around the world to obtain competitive cost advantage.

Offshoring of activities poses a particular risk of breakdown in controls, because **217** processes are broken down into several pieces with different locations potentially looking after each one. If the precise responsibilities of each location are not fully understood and monitored, key aspects of the control process could be omitted or not properly performed.

218   Typical examples of process/control activities that are performed in an offshore location include:

- processing of payments;
- bank and suspense account reconciliations;
- processing of confirmations; and
- processing of settlements.

219   The auditor evaluates the clarity of management's ownership of process and control activities in different locations and where appropriate tests the controls for the end-to-end process.

Overseeing other auditors

If the group engagement team plans to request a component auditor to perform work on the financial information of a component, the group engagement team shall obtain an understanding of the following:

(a)   Whether the component auditor understands and will comply with the ethical requirements that are relevant to the group audit and, in particular, is independent.

(b)   The component auditor's professional competence.

(c)   Whether the group engagement team will be able to be involved in the work of the component auditor to the extent necessary to obtain sufficient appropriate audit evidence.

(d)   Whether the component auditor operates in a regulatory environment that actively oversees auditors. (Paragraph 19)

220   Where the group auditor uses the work of component auditors from another audit firm in testing the design, implementation and operating effectiveness of the controls in offshore locations, the group engagement team provide clear audit instructions to the component audit team so that all significant processes and key controls are appropriately covered in the testing.

221   A group's operations can involve a high degree of reliance being placed by entities within the group upon activities performed by others. For example it would be possible for a trade to be originated in one location, processed in another, valued in a third and booked in a fourth. In addition judgmental decisions around areas such as credit, can be taken in group or other central locations, but affect several entities within the group. Such interdependency requires not just clear allocation of responsibility between the various teams undertaking the audit, but also close ongoing cooperation throughout the work, to ensure that the work undertaken and the judgments made are appropriate for the auditors of all locations affected. The group auditor considers how this can be best achieved.

222   The group auditor considers the competence and capability of the component auditor having regard to the laws, regulation and industry practice relevant to the component and whether the other auditor has access to relevant expertise, for example in the valuation of financial instruments, appropriate to the component's business.

Further procedures may be necessary for a group auditor where the component **223** auditor is not subject to the UK audit regulatory regime. In such a case, the group auditor has due regard to the requirements in the Audit Regulations[50] to ensure all relevant members of the engagement team are and continue to be fit and proper, are and continue to be competent and are aware of and follow the Audit Regulations and any related procedures and requirements established by the audit firm. This includes the auditor's duty to report direct to the FSA in certain circumstances. More detailed consideration of the auditor's duty to report to the FSA is set out in the section of this Practice Note dealing with ISA (UK and Ireland) 250 Section B.

ISA (UK AND IRELAND) 620: USING THE WORK OF AN AUDITOR'S EXPERT

Objectives

The objectives of the auditor are:

(a) To determine whether to use the work of an auditor's expert; and

(b) If using the work of an auditor's expert, to determine whether that work is adequate for the auditor's purposes. (Paragraph 5)

Given the complexity, subjectivity and specialist nature of the activities of banks **224** and building societies the auditor may involve an expert[51] in elements of the audit of these areas, including, for example:

- the valuation of derivative and other financial instruments not traded in an active market;
- VAR (or similarly complex) market risk disclosures;
- commercial property valuations; and
- information technology.

Auditor's experts may assist with the performance of tests of controls and substantive procedures and evaluating disclosures in the financial statements.

ISA (UK AND IRELAND) 700: THE AUDITOR'S REPORT ON FINANCIAL STATEMENTS

Objectives

The objectives of the auditor are to:

(a) Form an opinion on the financial statements based on an evaluation of the conclusions drawn from the audit evidence obtained; and

(b) Express clearly that opinion through a written report that also describes the basis for the opinion. (Paragraph 7)

---

[50] *Audit Regulations and related guidance are issued by the Institute of Chartered Accountants in England and Wales, the Institute of Chartered Accountants in Scotland and the Institute of Chartered Accountants in Ireland.*

[51] *ISA (UK and Ireland) 620 defines an auditor's expert as: "An individual or organization possessing expertise in a field other than accounting or auditing, whose work in that field is used by the auditor to assist the auditor in obtaining sufficient appropriate audit evidence. An auditor's expert may be either an auditor's internal expert (who is a partner or staff, including temporary staff, of the auditor's firm or a network firm), or an auditor's external expert."*
Experts used by the entity to assist in preparing the financial statements are "management's experts". The auditor's considerations in relation to management's experts are addressed in ISA (UK and Ireland) 500.

The auditor's report shall include a statement that those charged with governance are responsible for the preparation of the financial statements and a statement that the responsibility of the auditor is to audit and express an opinion on the financial statements in accordance with applicable legal requirements and International Standards on Auditing (UK and Ireland). The report shall also state that those standards require the auditor to comply with the APB's Ethical Standards for Auditors. (Paragraph 15)

225 The auditor may report on the financial statements of a branch of a bank incorporated outside the UK. ISA (UK and Ireland) 700 (or aspects thereof) may remain applicable in these circumstances. However, in agreeing the form of the opinion for a branch audit, the auditor takes into account matters such as the nature and content of the financial statements to which the report relates, the extent to which transactions recorded in the branch may have been initiated in other locations (and, similarly, whether transactions initiated by the branch may have been recorded elsewhere), the specific terms of the engagement as agreed with the party which has commissioned the work (which may be local and/or head office management or the head office auditor, for example) and whether the report will be public or private.

226 The auditor's reporting responsibilities concerning building societies differ from those applicable to a UK bank. The principal differences are:

- a statutory requirement for the publication of income and expenditure accounts (as opposed to profit and loss account/income statements) separately for both the society and its subsidiary undertakings (group accounts) (s72F BS Act 1986) and the society itself (s72B BS Act 1986) where prepared under UK GAAP. S72H and s72D BS Act 1986 respectively apply where prepared under EU IFRS. This contrasts with the s408(2) CA2006 exemption available to UK companies including UK banks from publishing the profit and loss account of the parent company in group accounts;

- a statutory requirement for an annual business statement to be attached to the annual accounts (s74 BS Act 1986), containing information as prescribed by the BS Accounts Regulations 1998: the prescribed content comprises three sections, being section 1, statutory percentages (the lending and funding limits, see paragraph 21 of this Practice Note), disclosing also the statutory limits and an explanation of the basis for each of these ratios, section 2, other percentages (being five operating ratios with their comparatives and an explanation of each ratio), and section 3, information on the directors and officers of the society. The auditor is required to state whether the annual business statement has been prepared in accordance with BS Act 1986 and regulations made thereunder and whether the information given in the annual business statement (excluding the details of directors and officers) gives a true representation of the matters in respect of which it is given (s78(7)(a) BS Act 1986); and

- a statutory requirement for a directors' report to be produced for each financial year (s75 BS Act 1986), containing information as prescribed in s75 and 75A BS Act 1986 and Sch 8 of the BS Accounts Regulations 1998: in addition to consistency with financial statements the auditor is required to state whether the directors' report has been prepared so as to conform to the requirements of s75 BS Act 1986 and the BS Accounts Regulations 1998 (s78(7) BS Act 1986).

In relation to the annual business statement the term "true representation of the   **227**
matters in respect of which it is given" referred to in paragraph 226 above is the
expression drawn directly from the BS Act 1986. It is not defined in BS Act 1986
nor in any related legislation. The part of the annual business statement covered by
this opinion comprises data and ratios (see paragraphs 22 to 25) that are almost all
derived from audited information within the annual accounts. Procedures
undertaken by the auditor usually involve substantive procedures to ensure that:

- the relevant data has been completely and accurately extracted from audited
  information or from sources that have been subject to audit procedures; and

- the ratios have been accurately calculated in accordance with the statutory
  definitions within the BS Accounts Regulations 1998.

There is also a statutory requirement for a summary financial statement for   **228**
building societies, in a format as prescribed in the BS Accounts Regulations 1998,
which must be sent to all members entitled to receive notice of meetings and which
must be provided on request to all new shareholders (s76 BS Act 1986): the
auditor is required by s76(5) BS Act 1986 to provide an auditor's statement as to
the consistency of the summary financial statement with the accounts, the annual
business statement and the directors' report and its conformity with the
requirements of s76 BS Act 1986 and the BS Accounts Regulations 1998[52].

Illustrative examples of auditors' reports tailored for use with audits conducted in   **229**
accordance with ISAs (UK and Ireland), including reports on the financial
statements of building societies, are provided in various Bulletins issued by the
APB[53]. Examples of other auditor's reports are set out in Appendix 1 of this
Practice Note.

ISA (UK AND IRELAND) 705: MODIFICATIONS TO OPINIONS IN THE INDEPENDENT AUDITOR'S REPORT

Objective

The objective of the auditor is to express clearly an appropriately modified
opinion on the financial statements that is necessary when:

(a) The auditor concludes, based on the audit evidence obtained, that the
financial statements as a whole are not free from material misstatement;
or

(b) The auditor is unable to obtain sufficient appropriate audit evidence to
conclude that the financial statements as a whole are free from material
misstatement. (Paragraph 4)

One of the circumstances in which the FSMA 2000 (Communication by Auditors)   **230**
Regulations 2001 ("the 2001 Regulations"), requires an auditor to report to the
FSA is when "the auditor is precluded from stating in his report that the annual
accounts have been properly prepared in accordance with the CA2006 or, where
applicable, give a true and fair view or have been prepared in accordance with
relevant rules and legislation". Consequently where an auditor is considering

---

[52] *A Listed UK bank may choose to prepare summary financial statements to send to its members, subject to certain
conditions.*

[53] *At the date of publication of this Practice Note, Bulletin 2010/2 (Revised) "Compendium of Illustrative Auditor's
Reports on United Kingdom Private Sector Financial Statements for periods ended on or after 15 December 2010
(Revised)" was the current Compendium Bulletin relating to private sector financial statements. Example reports
23 and 24 therein cover building societies preparing financial statements under UK GAAP and under IFRSs as
adopted in the European Union.*

modifying the auditor's opinion on the financial statements the auditor reports the circumstances requiring the modification to the FSA in advance of issuing the report.

ISA (UK AND IRELAND) 706: EMPHASIS OF MATTER PARAGRAPHS AND OTHER MATTER PARAGRAPHS IN THE INDEPENDENT AUDITOR'S REPORT

Objective

The objective of the auditor, having formed an opinion on the financial statements, is to draw users' attention, when in the auditor's judgment it is necessary to do so, by way of clear additional communication in the auditor's report, to:

(a)   A matter, although appropriately presented or disclosed in the financial statements, that is of such importance that it is fundamental to users' understanding of the financial statements; or

(b)   As appropriate, any other matter that is relevant to users' understanding of the audit, the auditor's responsibilities or the auditor's report. (Paragraph 4)

231   As explained in paragraph 59 the auditor has a duty to report to the FSA if the auditor becomes aware of a matter that could be of material significance to the FSA in determining whether a bank meets the threshold conditions for authorisation. Any matter considered of such importance as to require an emphasis of matter paragraph may well also be of material significance to the FSA and so the auditor considers whether to make a report to the FSA before issuing the auditor's opinion on the financial statements. Similar considerations apply where the auditor is considering including an other matter paragraph.

Other reports by the auditor

Auditor's review reports on interim net profits

232   An authorised firm must maintain at all times capital resources equal to or in excess of its capital resources requirement. An authorised firm may include interim net profits in its capital resources, calculated in accordance with GENPRU2 Annex 2R or 3R, provided those interim net profits have been verified by the external auditor (GENPRU2.2.102R) in accordance with the "relevant Auditing Practices Board's Practice Note" (GENPRU2.2.103G). For this reason the auditor may be asked to report on interim net profits for inclusion in core tier 1 profits for capital adequacy purposes. Authorised firms with a trading book can include net interim trading book profits in lower tier 3 capital without external review (GENPRU2.2.247R).

233   Interim net profits in this context means, net profits of the entity as at a date specified by the entity after the end of its most recently audited financial year end and up to and including its next financial year end, calculated after deductions for tax, foreseeable dividends and other appropriations (GENPRU2.2.102R).

234   GENPRU 2.2.102R does not include specific guidance as to what constitutes an external verification. However, "verification" as used in the context of GENPRU is understood to indicate a degree of assurance which is lower than that given by a full audit. An engagement to "verify" interim profits may therefore be taken to be a

review engagement, and an opinion may be given in terms of negative assurance. The report is normally addressed to the directors of the entity.

As an external "verification" of interim net profits does not require a full scope **235** audit it will be important for the FSA, in considering the adequacy of the "verification" of interim profits, to be informed of the procedures that have been undertaken by the auditor, in support of the auditor's opinion. This is particularly important in the case of entities where no prescribed procedures have been established by the FSA themselves in rules or guidance. Consequently the detailed scope of the work undertaken by the auditor in support of the auditor's opinion is listed in the auditor's report or included in the report by reference to the letter of engagement where the programme of work has been laid down.

In undertaking the review the auditor normally performs the following procedures: **236**

(a) obtains satisfaction that the figures forming the basis of the interim net profits have been properly extracted from the underlying accounting records;

(b) reviews the accounting policies used in calculating the interim net profits for the period under review so as to obtain comfort that they are consistent with those normally adopted by the entity in drawing up its annual financial statements and are in accordance with either UK GAAP or EU IFRS, as appropriate;

(c) performs analytical procedures on the results to date which form the basis of calculating interim net profits, including comparisons of actual performance to date with budget and with the results of the prior period(s);

(d) discusses with management the overall performance and financial position of the entity;

(e) obtains comfort that the implications of current and prospective litigation, all known claims and commitments, changes in business activities, allowances for loan losses and other impairment provisions have been properly taken into account in arriving at interim net profits; and

(f) follows up significant matters of which the auditor is already aware in the course of auditing the entity's most recent financial statements.

The auditor may also consider obtaining appropriate representations from management.

There may be some circumstances in which the auditor considers that additional **237** work is required, for example:

● if the control environment surrounding the preparation of the interim net profits is evaluated as weak;

● if the results of the procedures undertaken in paragraph 236 above are not fully consistent with the interim net profits as reported; or

● if there has been a significant change to the accounting system.

The report is addressed to the directors of the entity. An example auditor's report **238** on interim profits is set out in Appendix 1.3.

Report on directors' transactions – building societies

Under s78(9) BS Act 1986 the auditor is required to report to the members on the **239** annual statement of transactions and arrangements (usually loans falling within s65(1) BS Act 1986) with or to directors and persons connected with them.

240   S78(9) BS Act 1986 requires the auditor to examine the annual statement, as extracted from the Register required to be maintained under s68 BS Act 1986, and that a report from the auditor be annexed to the statement before it is made available to the members and sent to the FSA. Under s78(10) BS Act 1986 the auditor reports whether the statement contains the particulars required by s68 BS Act 1986 and, where that is not the case, the auditor includes such particulars in their report, so far as they are reasonably able to do so.

241   The auditor only reports as to whether the statement contains all the matters contained in the Register in the relevant year. The auditor is not required by s78 BS Act 1986 to confirm whether or not the Register of transactions and arrangements with directors or connected persons is complete. However, if the auditor becomes aware of any transaction, arrangement or loan which should be in the Register and is not, then such an occurrence may indicate a deficiency in the system of control over the complete and accurate compilation of the Register. The results of this work could raise issues of relevance to the statutory duty to report to the FSA. An example of the auditor's report concerning this statement is set out in Appendix 1.2.

Appendix 1

Illustrative examples of auditor's reports

Illustrative examples of auditor's reports tailored for use with audits conducted in accordance with ISAs (UK and Ireland), including reports on the financial statements of building societies, are provided in various Bulletins issued by the APB[54].

This appendix contains the following example auditor's reports:

UK building societies

1.1   Auditor's statement on summary financial statement.

1.2   Auditor's report on the s68 BS Act 1986 statement.

UK banks and building societies

1.3   Auditor's review report on interim net profits.

1.1 – Auditor's statement on summary financial statement (building societies)

Independent auditor's statement to the members and depositors of [XYZ] building society

We have examined the Summary Financial Statement of [XYZ] Building Society [set out/above on pages x to x]*.

Respective responsibilities of directors and auditors

The directors are responsible for preparing the [Summary Financial Statement/ name of document containing summary financial statement]¹*, in accordance with applicable United Kingdom law.

Our responsibility is to report to you our opinion on the consistency of the Summary Financial Statement [within the [name of document containing summary financial statement]]¹* with the [full Annual Accounts]², Annual Business Statement and Directors' Report and its conformity with the relevant requirements of Section 76 of the Building Societies Act 1986 and regulations made under it. [We also read the other information contained in the [name of document containing summary financial statement] and consider the implications

---

[54] *At the date of publication of this Practice Note, Bulletin 2010/2 (Revised) "Compendium of Illustrative Auditor's Reports on United Kingdom Private Sector Financial Statements for periods ended on or after 15 December 2010 (Revised)" was the current Compendium Bulletin relating to private sector financial statements. Example reports 23 and 24 therein cover building societies preparing financial statements under UK GAAP and under IFRSs as adopted in the European Union.*

* *delete/amend as applicable*

¹ *Authorised under FSMA 2000 to undertake regulated activities.*

² *Prudential sourcebook for Banks, Building Societies and Investment Firms.*

for our report if we become aware of any apparent misstatements or material inconsistencies with the Summary Financial Statement.]³*]*. The other information comprises only [the chairman's statement and the corporate governance statement [and the other items listed on the contents page]]³*

Basis of opinion

We conducted our work in accordance with Bulletin 2008/3 "The auditor's statement on the summary financial statement in the United Kingdom" issued by the Auditing Practices Board. Our report on the [Group and Society's]* [full Annual Accounts]² describes the basis of our audit opinion[s] on those [Annual Accounts]².

Opinion on summary financial statement

In our opinion the Summary Financial Statement is consistent with the [full Annual Accounts]², the Annual Business Statement and Directors' Report of [XYZ] Building Society for the year ended [ ] and complies with the applicable requirements of Section 76 of the Building Societies Act 1986 and regulations made under it⁴.

Statutory Auditor

Address

Date

1.2 – Auditor's report on the s68 BS Act 1986 statement (building societies)

Independent auditor's report, under section 78(9) of the Building Societies Act 1986 ("the Act"), to the members of [XYZ] building society on the statement of particulars of transactions and arrangements included in the section 68(1) register at any time during the year ended [ ]

We have examined the foregoing statement of transactions and arrangements with directors and persons connected with them, falling within Section 65(1) of the Act.

Respective responsibilities of directors and auditors

It is the responsibility of the directors, under Section 68(1) of the Act, to maintain a register of every existing transaction and arrangement, as defined in Section 65 (1) of the Act, with directors or persons connected with directors. Section 68(3) of the Act requires the directors to prepare, for each financial year, a statement containing particulars of all information in the register for the last complete financial year. It is our responsibility, under Section 78(9) and (10) of the Act, to form an independent opinion as to whether the statement accurately contains all the particulars in the register from the last financial year and to report our opinion to you.

---

³ *Exercising passport rights entitles an entity incorporated in one EEA member state ("home country") who is authorised to conduct one or more regulated activities subject to the passport rights in the home country to establish a branch and carry out those regulated activities in another EEA member state ("host country") without the need to be authorised by the host country supervisor, (in the UK the FSA) in respect of activities that are subject to the passport rights.*

⁴ *Banks which are incorporated in the United Kingdom are subject to the provisions of the Companies Act 2006.*

Basis of opinion

We planned and performed our work so as to obtain all the information and explanations which we considered necessary in order to provide us with sufficient evidence that the statement gives the particulars required by Section 68 of the Act.

Opinion

In our opinion the statement contains the requisite particulars, as required by Section 68 of the Act, in relation to those transactions recorded by the society in the register of transactions and arrangements maintained under Section 68(1) of the Act.

[Signature]   *Address*

John Smith (Senior Statutory Auditor) for *Date*
and on behalf of ABC LLP Statutory
Auditor

1.3 – Auditor's review report on interim net profits (UK banks and building societies)

Review report by the auditor to the board of directors of [XXXX]

In accordance with our engagement letter dated [ ], we have reviewed the interim net profits of [XXXX] for the period [to] as reported in the reporting statement ("the Statement") for that period, a copy of which is attached as Appendix A.

The preparation of the Statement is the responsibility of the directors. Our review did not constitute an audit performed in accordance with ISAs (UK and Ireland) and accordingly we do not express an audit opinion on the interim net profits reported therein.

Our review has been carried out having regard to GENPRU 2.2.102R and GENPRU 2.2.103G of the FSA Handbook and Practice Note 19 "The audit of banks and building societies in the United Kingdom (Revised)" issued by the Auditing Practices Board.

On the basis of the results of our review, nothing came to our attention to indicate that:

(a)   the interim net profits as reported in the Statement 'have not been calculated on the basis of the accounting policies adopted by [XXXX] in drawing up its annual financial statements for the year ended [ ] [except for][1];

(b)   the accounting policies differ in any material respects from those required by [UK GAAP applicable to [banks/building societies]*[2, 3] /International Financial Reporting Standards adopted by the European Commission in accordance with EC Regulation No 1606/2002]*[except for]; and

(c)   the interim net profits amounting to £ [ ] as so reported are not reasonably stated.

This report has been prepared for the directors of [XXXX] to comply with their regulatory obligations under GENPRU2.2.102R and for no other purpose. We do not, in providing this report, accept or assume responsibility for any other purpose save where expressly agreed by our prior consent in writing.

Statutory Auditor

Address

Date

Appendix 2

The main parts of FSMA 2000 relevant to banks and building societies

Part I (and Sch 1) sets out matters concerning structure and governance of the FSA including its regulatory objectives and the principles to be followed in meeting those objectives.

Part II (and Sch 2) sets out the general prohibition on conducting regulated business unless an entity is either authorised or exempt, including restrictions on financial promotions. Regulated activities are defined in SI 2001/544.

Part III (and Schs 3-5) sets out the requirements to become authorised either by receiving a specific permission from the FSA or through the exercise of EEA passport rights. Exempt persons are listed in SI 2001/1201.

Part IV (and Sch 6) sets out the arrangements for application for a permission to undertake authorised business and the criteria (Threshold Conditions) that must be met. An applicant who is refused can apply to the Financial Services and Markets Tribunal (established under Part IX).

Part V sets out the provisions applying to individuals performing designated functions (controlled functions) in an authorised firm. The FSA can specify controlled functions and authorised firms must take reasonable care to ensure that only persons approved by the FSA can undertake these functions. The FSA can specify qualification, training and competence requirements and approved persons must comply with the FSA's statement of principles and code of conduct for approved persons. Appeals can be made to the Tribunal.

Part VIII gives the FSA powers to impose penalties for market abuse – using information not generally available; creating a false or misleading impression; or, failure to observe normal standards – abuse being judged from the point of view of a regular market user. The FSA's powers extend to all persons – not only authorised firms. The FSA is required to publish a code to provide guidance on behaviours that do and do not constitute market abuse. This forms part of the Market Conduct Sourcebook and is called the Code of Market Conduct.

Part X provides the FSA with general powers to make rules which apply to authorised firms, including rules on specific matters – e.g. client money, money laundering. Rules must be published in draft for consultation. Guidance may be provided individually or generally and may be published. The FSA may modify rules or waive particular rules for particular authorised firms in certain situations.

Part XI allows the FSA to gather information from authorised firms, including use of skilled persons' reports under s166, or to commission investigations into authorised firms.

Part XIV sets out the disciplinary measures available to the FSA which can include public censure, unlimited fines, withdrawal of authorisation.

Part XXII includes provisions relating to auditors and their appointment.

Part XXVI brings together in one place the arrangements applying to warning notices and decision notices concerning possible breaches of various requirements imposed by FSMA 2000 or by FSA rules. A warning notice has to state the reasons for proposed actions and allow reasonable time for representations to be made. This will be followed by a decision notice with a right to appeal to the Tribunal.

Appendix 3

FSMA 2000, BS Act 1986 and related statutory instruments: important provisions for auditors

FSMA 2000 provisions and related statutory instruments relevant for the auditor of a bank or building society are set out below. The legislation can be found on the legislation.gov.uk website – www.legislation.gov.uk (it is published as enacted, i.e. does not take account of subsequent amendments). BS Act 1986 provisions and related statutory instruments relevant only to building societies are also set out below.

FSMA 2000 and statutory instruments as amended

Section/Sch

19	General prohibition from undertaking regulated activity unless authorised
20	Authorised firms acting without permission
21	Restrictions on financial promotion
41	Threshold conditions
59	Approval by FSA of persons undertaking controlled functions
165	FSA's power to require information
166	Reports by skilled persons
167	Appointment of persons to carry out general investigations
168	Appointment of persons to carry out investigations in particular cases
178	Obligation to notify FSA concerning controllers of an authorised firm
340	Appointment of auditor or actuary by FSA
341	Access to books etc (by auditor or actuary)
342	Information given by auditor or actuary to the FSA
343	Information given by auditor or actuary to the FSA: persons with close links
344	Duty of auditor or actuary resigning etc to give notice
345	Disqualification (of auditor or actuary from acting by FSA)
346	Provision of false or misleading information to auditor or actuary
348	Restrictions on disclosure of confidential information by FSA etc
349	Exceptions from s348
351	Competition information (offence relating to the disclosure of competition information)
352	Offences (contravention of s348 to 350(5))
398	Misleading the FSA
Sch 6	
SI 2001	Threshold Conditions
544	Regulated Activities Order

1177	Carrying on Regulated Activities by Way of Business Order
1201	Exemption Order
1857	Disclosure of Information by Prescribed Persons
2188	Disclosure of Confidential Information
2587	Communications by Auditors
1376 and 2511	EEA Passport Rights

BS Act 1986 and statutory instruments as amended

Section/Sch

5	Constitution and powers including principal purpose
6	The lending limit
7	The funding limit
8	Raising funds and borrowing
9A	Restriction on powers including treasury activities
62-69	Dealings with directors and disclosure and record of related businesses of directors
71	Accounting records
72A	Duty to prepare individual accounts
72B	Building Societies Act individual accounts
72C	Form and content of Building Societies Act individual accounts
72D	IAS individual accounts
72E	Duty to prepare group accounts
72F	Building Societies Act group accounts
72G	Form and content of Building Societies Act group accounts
72H	IAS group accounts
72I	Consistency of accounts
72J	Disclosures relating to directors, other officers and employees of societies required in notes to the accounts
72K	Disclosures about related party undertakings required in the notes to the accounts
74	Duty of directors to prepare an annual business statement
75	Directors' report
75A	Business review
76	Summary financial statements for members and depositors
77	Auditors: appointment, tenure, qualifications etc.
78	Auditors' report
78A	Signature of auditors' report
78B	Senior statutory auditor
79	Auditors' duties and powers
80	Signing of balance sheet – documents to be annexed

81	Laying and furnishing accounts, etc to [members and authority]
81A	Requirements in connection with publication of accounts
81B	Interpretation of Part 8
119	Interpretation
Sch 10A	Disclosures about directors, other officers and employees required in notes to the accounts
Sch 10B	Disclosures about related undertakings required in notes to accounts
Sch 10C	Disclosures about auditor remuneration required in notes to accounts
SI 1998/504	BS (Accounts and Related Provisions) Regulations 1998 (as amended)
2001/2617	FSMA 2000 (Mutual Societies) Order 2001

Appendix 4

The FSA Handbook

1   Not all authorised firms are required to comply with all rules contained within the FSA Handbook. This varies with the type of permission-the regulated activity an authorised firm is permitted to undertake is set out in the authorised firms Scope of Permission. The following can be viewed on the FSA website:

- contents of the FSA Handbook – www.fsa.gov.uk/Pages/handbook; and

- FSA register which lists the regulated activities that each authorised firm has permission to undertake – www.fsa.gov.uk/Pages/register.

2   In gaining an understanding of the FSA Handbook the auditor bears in mind the four statutory objectives of the FSA, set out in 13 above, which underpin the content of the FSA Handbook. To facilitate usage the FSA Handbook has been structured into a number of blocks and within each block the material has been subdivided into Sourcebooks, Manuals or Guides. There are Rules, evidential provisions[55] and guidance which are contained within all of the blocks[56]. Contravention of Rules (which includes Principles for Businesses) or evidential provisions can give rise to an obligation on the auditor to report the matter direct to the FSA – see the section of this Practice Note relating to ISA (UK and Ireland) 250 Section B. Details of the high level standards, which are the overarching requirements for all authorised person (firms) and approved persons, are outlined below.

Principles for businesses

3   The eleven Principles for Businesses, which are general statements that set out the fundamental obligations of firms under the regulatory system, are set out in the FSA Handbook. They derive their authority from the FSA's rule-making powers as set out in FSMA 2000 and reflect the regulatory objectives. These Principles are as follows:

- an authorised firm must conduct its business with integrity;

- an authorised firm must conduct its business with due skill, care and diligence;

- an authorised firm must take reasonable care to organise and control its affairs responsibly and effectively with adequate risk management;

- an authorised firm must maintain adequate financial resources;

- an authorised firm must observe proper standards of market conduct;

- an authorised firm must pay due regard to the interests of its customers and treat them fairly;

---

[55] *An evidential provision is not binding in its own right, but will "tend to show" compliance or non-compliance (as the case may be). It is therefore indicative, and establishes a rebuttable presumption of compliance or non-compliance with a rule. Guidance may be used to explain the implications of other provisions, to indicate possible means of compliance, or to recommend a particular course of action or arrangement.*

[56] *Rules are set out in emboldened type and are marked with the icon "R", evidential provisions are marked "E" and guidance "G". Further guidance on the status of the Handbook text is set out in the General Provisions (GEN) Sourcebook Chapter 2.2 and Chapter 6 of the Reader' Guide.*

- an authorised firm must pay due regard to the information needs of its clients, and communicate information to them in a way which is clear, fair and not misleading;

- an authorised firm must manage conflicts of interest fairly, both between itself and its customers and between a customer and another client;

- an authorised firm must take reasonable care to ensure the suitability of its advice and discretionary decisions for any customer who is entitled to rely on its judgment;

- an authorised firm must arrange adequate protection for clients' assets when it is responsible for them; and

- an authorised firm must deal with its regulators in an open and cooperative way, and must disclose to the FSA appropriately anything relating to the authorised firm of which the FSA would reasonably expect notice (see for example SUP15-Notifications to the FSA).

Senior management arrangements, systems and controls

SYSC amplifies Principles for Businesses 3, the requirement for a firm to take **4** reasonable care to organise and control its affairs responsibly and effectively, with adequate risk management systems. The relevant chapters[57] are as follows;

- 3 – systems and controls

- 4 – general organizational requirements

- 5 – employees, agents and other relevant persons

- 6 – compliance, internal audit and financial crime

- 7 – risk control

- 8 – outsourcing

- 9 – record keeping

- 10 – conflicts of interest

- 11 – liquidity risk systems and controls

- 12 – group risk systems and control requirements

- 18 – guidance on Public Interest Disclosure Act – whistle blowing

- 19 – remuneration code

- 20 – reverse stress testing

- 21 – risk control, additional guidance[58].

Threshold conditions

Under s41 and Schedule 6 of FSMA 2000 Threshold Conditions are the minimum **5** requirements that must be met at authorisation and must continue to be met. The five statutory Threshold Conditions are:

- legal status: regulated activities must be conducted through a body corporate or partnership – that is, individuals cannot undertake regulated activities;

---

[57] *Chapters 13-17 apply only to insurers.*
[58] *Effective 1 May 2011.*

- location of offices: the head office of a body corporate must be in the same territory/ member state as the registered office;

- close links: close links must not prevent effective supervision. Entities are regarded as closely linked if there is a group relationship, i.e. parent/ subsidiary/fellow subsidiary (but using the EC 7th Company Law Directive definition of subsidiary). They are also closely linked if one owns or controls 20% or more of the voting rights or capital of the other;

- adequate resources: the authorised firm must have adequate resources (financial and non financial) for the type of business conducted taking into account the impact of other group entities and having regard to provisions made against liabilities (including contingent and future liabilities) and the approach to risk management; and

- suitability: the FSA will consider the fitness and propriety of authorised firms, including whether business is conducted with integrity and in compliance with high standards, and whether there is competent and prudent management and exercise of due skill, care and diligence. This will include consideration of whether those subject to the approved persons regime (i.e. those undertaking controlled functions) are, or will be, approved by the FSA.

Appendix 5

Possible factors that may indicate going concern issues

Capital adequacy ratios

- the entity is operating at or near the limit of its individual capital guidance (excluding capital planning buffer)[59] or limit otherwise set by the FSA, either on a group or solo basis; and

- stress tests indicate that minimum ratios may not be maintained.

Operations/profitability indicators

- marked decline in new lending/dealing volumes during the year or subsequently;

- marked decline in new business margins;

- severe overcapacity in markets leading to low pricing as well as low volumes;

- significant increase in loan defaults or seizure of collateral (e.g. house repossessions);

- excessive exposures to troubled industry sectors;

- unusually aggressive dealing positions and/or regular breaches of dealing or lending limits; and

- redundancies, layoffs or failure to replace natural wastage of personnel.

Liquidity indicators

- unusually large maturity mismatch in the short term (say up to 3 months), either in total or across currencies;

- exceptional levels of medium-term funding due to mature in the near term;

- maturity mismatch ladders prepared on a basis which fail to recognise/use:

    - expected (as opposed to contractual) cash flows;

    - narrow gaps for near maturities;

    - anticipated defaults on loan repayments;

    - a cushion for market value of volatile investments; or

    - off balance sheet commitments;

- dependence on a few large depositors (which may or may not be connected parties);

- withdrawal of (or reduction in) lines of credit by wholesale counterparties;

---

[59] *Individual capital guidance (ICG) is a minimum amount of capital that the FSA requires firms to hold at all times, and it is supplemented by a capital planning buffer (CPB) which firms are required to build up in good times and may release in times of stress. Since CPBs are intended to be released by going concern firms when under stress, such a release does not in itself signify a going concern issue (although the underlying reason for the stress may or may not do so). Similarly, operating near to ICG may be an indicator either of efficient capital management or of financial difficulties, depending on the particular case. Breach of ICG, however, indicates the need for some supervisory action. The action will vary according to the reason for the breach, and a breach does not necessarily mean that a firm will be required to cease trading, but it does trigger this option being actively considered.*

- regularly overdrawn nostro accounts;
- difficulty in meeting liquidity standards set on an individual basis by the FSA;
- uncompetitively low rates of interest offered to depositors (causing outflow of funds);
- very high rates of interest offered to depositors (to prevent outflow of funds, regardless of financial loss);
- special fixed term deposit rate offers which attracted significant funds inflows due to mature; and
- stress tests that indicate that regulatory requirements may not be met.

Reputational and other indicators

- adverse publicity which could lead to loss of confidence or reputation, including fines or public censure by FSA;
- lowering of ratings or issue of negative outlook notices by independent credit agencies;
- urgent attempts to remove assets from the balance sheet, apparently involving material loss of profits or at significant expense; and
- deferral of investment plans or capitalisation of expenditure.

Appendix 6

Reporting direct to the FSA – statutory right and protection for disclosure under general law

When the auditor concludes that a matter does not give rise to a statutory duty to   **1**
report direct to the FSA, the auditor considers the right to report to the FSA. The
right to report is available to the auditor of a UK bank, building society and a non
EEA bank but not to the auditor of an EEA bank which has no top up permissions.

In cases of doubt, general law provides protection for disclosing certain matters to   **2**
a proper authority in the public interest.

Audit firms are protected from the risk of liability from breach of confidence or   **3**
defamation under general law even when carrying out work which is not clearly
undertaken in the capacity of auditor provided that:

- in the case of breach of confidence:

  (i)   disclosure is made in the public interest; and

  (ii)   such disclosure is made to an appropriate body or person; and

  (iii)   there is no malice motivating the disclosure; and

- in the case of defamation:

  (i)   the information disclosed was obtained in a proper capacity; and

  (ii)   there is no malice motivating the disclosure.

The same protection is given even if there is only a reasonable suspicion that non-   **4**
compliance with law or regulations has occurred. Provided that it can be
demonstrated that an audit firm, in disclosing a matter in the public interest, has
acted reasonably and in good faith, it would not be held by the court to be in
breach of duty to the institution even if, an investigation or prosecution having
occurred, it were found that there had been no breach of law or regulation.

When reporting to proper authorities in the public interest, it is important that, in   **5**
order to retain the protection of qualified privilege, the auditor reports only to one
who has a proper interest to receive the information. The FSA is the proper
authority in the case of an authorised institution.

"Public interest" is a concept which is not capable of general definition. Each   **6**
situation must be considered individually. In general circumstances, matters to be
taken into account when considering whether disclosure is justified in the public
interest may include:

- the extent to which the suspected non-compliance with law or regulations is
  likely to affect members of the public;

- whether the directors (or equivalent) have rectified the matter or are taking,
  or are likely to take, effective corrective action;

- the extent to which non-disclosure is likely to enable the suspected non-
  compliance with law or regulations to recur with impunity;

- the gravity of the matter;

- whether there is a general management ethos within the entity of
  disregarding law or regulations; and

- the weight of evidence and the degree of the auditor's suspicion that there has been an instance of non-compliance with law or regulations.

7   Determination of where the balance of public interest lies requires careful consideration. The auditor needs to weigh the public interest in maintaining confidential client relationships against the public interest of disclosure to a proper authority and to use their professional judgment to determine whether their misgivings justify them in carrying the matter further or are too insubstantial to deserve report.

8   In cases where it is uncertain whether the statutory duty requires or s342 or s343 FSMA 2000 permits an auditor to communicate a matter to the FSA, it is possible that the auditor may be able to rely on the defence of disclosure in the public interest if it communicates a matter to the FSA which could properly be regarded as having material significance in conformity with the guidance in ISA (UK and Ireland) 250 Section B and this Practice Note, although the auditor may wish to seek legal advice in such circumstances.

Appendix 7

The auditors' right and duty to report to the FSA: examples of reportable items

This Appendix gives some examples of areas identified by the FSA where **1** particularly close consideration should be given as to whether the duty to report arises (in other words, where a breach of requirements may tend to be more serious). But it is not intended to be comprehensive, and cannot be relied on as a checklist.

Although there are a large number of "relevant requirements" or matters of **2** concern potentially giving rise to a statutory duty to report, these will normally fall within a number of general themes:

- controllers, directors and senior managers who may not be "fit and proper";

- serious breaches of law/regulations;

- potential disciplinary action against the firm or directors;

- undertaking activities outside the scope of their permission;

- failure to comply with limitations or restrictions on permission or individual requirements;

- false or misleading information given to the FSA or matters concealed;

- problems with another "regulator" e.g. Office of Fair Trading (i.e. regards the Consumer Credit Act) or overseas regulators;

- breaches of prudential limits and/or any financial limits;

- significant actual or potential loss by clients e.g. loss of customer assets or breach of client money rules; where there appear to be conflicts of interest; where there appears to be systemic abuse of advice or discretionary decisions; or as identified by complaints or by cases where a customer sues under s150 FSMA;

- failure to clearly allocate responsibilities between senior managers or to implement clear reporting lines;

- major systems and control deficiencies (including major reconciliation failures and backlogs); and

- possible "going-concern" issues.

The above general themes are intended as a guide – any report would need to be **3** made against a specific relevant requirement (see paragraph 60). If an issue has been identified relating to one of the themes (which might be materially significant to the FSA and is in a situation where the auditor is under a duty to report), the auditor should identify the relevant requirement. Even if a specific relevant requirement cannot be established, the auditor should consider whether or not the right to report is appropriate.

Appendix 8

Definitions

Abbreviations and frequently used terms in this Practice Note are set out below.

ARROW II	"Advanced Risk Responsive Operating frameWork". The term used for FSA's risk assessment process – the application of risk based supervision. It is the mechanism through which the FSA evaluates the risk an authorised firm poses to its statutory objectives enabling it to allocate its resources appropriately and respond to the risks identified
Authorised firm	An entity which has been granted one of more Part IV permissions by the FSA and so is authorised under FSMA 2000 to undertake regulated activities – an authorised person
Authorised person	Term used throughout FSMA 2000 and related statutory instruments to refer to an authorised firm – see above
Authorised by FSA	Same as authorised firm or authorised person – see above
BBA SORP	Statements of Recommended Practice issued by the British Bankers Association and the Irish Bankers' Federation
Bank	UK bank, EEA bank and non EEA bank
Banking company	Companies Act 2006 definition s1164
BIPRU	Prudential sourcebook for bank, building societies and investment firms
BS Act 1986	Building Societies Act 1986
BS Accounts Regulations 1998	Building Societies (Accounts and Related Provisions) Regulations 1998
BSOCS	Building Societies specialist sourcebook
BSOG	Building Societies Regulatory Guide
Building society	A society incorporated under the BS Act 1986
CA2006	Companies Act 2006
Closely linked entity	As defined in s343(8) FSMA 2000, an entity has close links with an authorised firm for this purpose if the entity is a:
	(a) Parent undertaking of an authorised firm;
	(b) Subsidiary undertaking of an authorised firm;
	(c) Parent undertaking of a subsidiary undertaking of an authorised firm; or
	(d) Subsidiary undertaking of a parent undertaking of an authorised firm
Companies and Groups Accounts Regulations 2008	Large and Medium-sized Companies and Groups (Accounts and Reports) Regulations 2008 (SI 2008/410)

COND	Threshold Conditions element of the high level standards block of the FSA Handbook
CRD	Capital Requirements Directive
Credit institution	An undertaking whose business is to receive deposits or other repayable funds from the public and to grant credits for its own account and to which the Banking Consolidation Directive applies
Deposit taker	Banks and building societies – authorised firms which under FSMA 2000 have a Part IV permission to accept deposits
EEA	European Economic Area
EEA Bank	A UK branch of a credit institution incorporated in the EEA which has exercised EEA Passport rights to carry on regulated activities in the UK
EEA Passport rights	Exercising passport rights, an entity incorporated in one EEA member state ("home country") which is authorised to conduct one or more regulated activities subject to the passport rights in the home country to establish a branch and carry out those regulated activities in another EEA member state ("host country") without the need to be authorised by the host country supervisor, FSA, in respect of activities that are subject to the passport rights
EIR	Effective interest rate
EU IFRS	International Financial Reporting Standards adopted by the European Union
FRS	Financial Reporting Statements
FSA	The Financial Services Authority
FSMA 2000	Financial Services and Markets Act 2000
FRSSE	Financial Reporting Standard for Smaller Entities
GENPRU	General Prudential Sourcebook
IPRU(BANK)	Interim Prudential Sourcebook for banks
IPRU(BSOC)	Interim Prudential Sourcebook for building societies
JMLSG	Joint Money Laundering Steering Group
MiFID	Markets in Financial Instruments Directive
Material significance	A matter or group of matters is normally of material significance to a regulator's function when, due either to its nature or its potential financial impact, it is likely of itself to require investigation by the regulator
Non EEA Bank	a UK branch of an entity incorporated outside the EEA, authorised by the FSA to accept deposits and which is required to comply with BIPRU
Part IV permission	A permission granted by FSA under Part IV FSMA 2000 permitting an authorised firm to carry on regulated activities as specified in the FSMA 2000 Regulated Activities Order SI 2001/544 as amended

Permission	Part IV permission under FSMA 2000 to undertake one or more regulated activities
Principles for Businesses	FSA Handbook defined principles with which an authorised firm must comply. The 11 principles are included in a stand alone element of the high level Standards block of the FSA Handbook – PRIN
Regulated activities	Activities as defined in the Regulated Activities Order SI 2001/544 as amended
Relevant requirement	In relation to the auditors' duty to report direct to the FSA – requirement by or under FSMA 2000 which relates to authorisation under FSMA 2000 or to the carrying on of any regulated activity. This includes not only relevant statutory instruments but also the FSA's rules (other than the Listing Rules) including the Principles for Businesses. The duty to report also covers any requirement imposed by or under any other Act the contravention of which constitutes an offence which the FSA has the power to prosecute under FSMA 2000
SOCA	Serious and Organised Crime Agency
SUP	Supervision manual of the FSA Handbook
SYSC	Senior management arrangements, systems and controls element of the High Level Standards block of the FSA Handbook
The 2001 Regulations	SI 2001/2587 – FSMA 2000 (Communications by Auditors) Regulations 2001
Those charged with governance	ISAs (UK and Ireland) use the term "those charged with governance" to describe the persons entrusted with the supervision, control and direction of an entity, who will normally be responsible for the quality of financial reporting, and the term "management" to describe those persons who perform senior managerial functions. The FSA Handbook of Rules and Guidance (FSA Handbook) uses the term "governing body" to describe collectively those charged with governance. In the context of this Practice Note, references to those charged with governance include directors of banks and building societies
Threshold Conditions	The minimum standards that an authorised firm needs to meet to become and remain authorised by the FSA. The five conditions are included in a stand alone element of the high level Standards block of the FSA Handbook – COND.
Top up permission	A Part IV permission granted by the FSA to an EEA bank to enable it to undertake a UK regulated activity in the UK for which authorisation to undertake the activity in the home country is not required by the home country supervisor.
UK bank	A company incorporated in the UK which is authorised by the FSA to accept deposits, which is required to comply with BIPRU and is not a building society.

Practice Note 20 (Revised):
The audit of insurers in the United Kingdom

(January 2017)

Contents

Paragraphs

Section 1: Preface

Section 2: Introduction   1 - 3

Section 3: Legislative and Regulatory Framework
Background   1 - 12
Financial Services and Markets Act 2000   13 - 17
Financial Statements   18 - 24
Prudential requirements   25 - 27
Reporting to supervisors, including supervisors of public-interest entities – statutory
right and duty   28 - 45
The Audit Regulation (EU) 537/2014   46 - 51

Section 4: The Audit of Financial Statements
ISA (UK) 210: Agreeing the terms of audit engagements   1 - 3
ISA (UK) 240: The auditor's responsibilities relating to fraud in an audit of
financial statements   4 - 12
ISA (UK) 250: Section A – Consideration of laws and regulations in an audit of
financial statements   13 - 27
ISA (UK) 250: Section B – The auditor's statutory right and duty to report to
regulators of public interest entities and regulators of other entities in the
financial sector   28 - 43
ISA (UK) 265: Communicating deficiencies in internal control to those charged with
governance and management   44 - 46
ISA (UK) 300: Planning an audit of financial statements   47 - 53
ISA (UK) 315: Identifying and assessing the risks of material misstatement through
understanding the entity and its environment   54 - 73
ISA (UK) 320: Materiality in planning and performing an audit   74 - 79
ISA (UK) 330: The auditor's responses to assessed risks   80 - 97
ISA (UK) 402: Audit considerations relating to an entity using a service
organization   98 - 102
ISA (UK) 450: Evaluation of misstatements identified during the audit   103 - 105
ISA (UK) 505: External confirmations   106 - 108
ISA (UK) 520: Analytical procedures   109 - 112
ISA (UK) 540: Auditing accounting estimates, including fair value accounting
estimates, and related disclosures   113 - 131
ISA (UK) 550: Related parties   132 - 141
ISA (UK) 560: Subsequent events   142 - 143
ISA (UK) 570: Going concern   144 - 145
ISA (UK) 580: Written representations   146 - 147
ISA (UK) 700: The auditor's report on financial statements   148 - 152
ISA (UK) 705: Modifications to opinions in the independent auditor's report   153 - 155
ISA (UK) 706: Emphasis of matter paragraphs and other matter paragraphs in the
independent auditor's report   156 - 158
ISA (UK) 720: The auditor's responsibilities relating to other information   159 - 163
Considerations relating to working with specialists and experts   164 - 188

Section 5: The Audit of Financial Statements: Additional Considerations Relating to Lloyd's

ISA (UK) 210: Agreeing the terms of audit engagements   1 - 2

ISA (UK) 240: The auditor's responsibilities relating to fraud in an audit of financial statements   3

ISA (UK) 250: Section A – Consideration of laws and regulations in an audit of financial statements   4 - 7

ISA (UK) 250: Section B – The auditor's statutory right and duty to report to regulators of public interest entities and regulators of other entities in the financial sector   8 - 26

ISA (UK) 300: Planning an audit of financial statements   27

ISA (UK) 315: Identifying and assessing the risks of material misstatement through understanding the entity and its environment   28 - 29

ISA (UK) 402: Audit considerations relating to an entity using a service organization   30

ISA (UK) 540: Auditing accounting estimates, including fair value accounting estimates, and related disclosures   31 - 41

ISA (UK) 560: Subsequent events   42

ISA (UK) 570: Going concern   43 - 44

ISA (UK) 600: Special considerations – audits of group financial statements (including the work of component auditors)   45 - 47

ISA (UK) 700: The auditor's report on financial statements   48 - 53

ISA (UK) 701: Communicating key audit matters in the independent auditor's report   54

Section 6: Reporting on Solvency and Financial Condition Reports for Solvency II ("Directive") Firms   1 - 8

General Principles   9

Audits of Solvency II public reports (SFCRs)   10 - 20

Accepting the Engagement   21 - 32

Planning and Performing the Engagement   33 - 73

Section 7: Illustrative Auditor's Reports – Solvency II ("Directive") Firms

A: An auditor's report on relevant elements of the SFCR: Solo insurer, standard formula

B: An auditor's report on relevant elements of the SFCR: Solo insurer, partial/full internal model

C: An auditor's report on relevant elements of the SFCR: Group, partial/full internal model

Section 8: Reporting on Non Solvency II ("Non-Directive") Firms   1

Authorised insurers   2 - 3

Friendly Societies   4

The form and content of the Regulatory Return   5 - 9

The auditor's responsibilities   10 - 11

Standards to be applied by the auditor   12 - 14

General Principles   15

Key Additional Procedures   16

The Auditor's Procedures on Regulatory Returns Long-term business   17 - 23

Establishing the independence of the suitably qualified independent actuary   24 - 30

Reporting   31 - 33

Subsequent events   34

Modifying the auditor's opinion   35 - 36

Resubmitted returns   37 - 38

Section 9: Illustrative Audit Report – Non-Solvency II Firm

[xx INSURANCE COMPANY LIMITED]

Section 10: Definition of Terms

Editorial note – This revised Practice Note 20 includes illustrative auditor's reports for regulatory engagements, and includes material to support auditors working in the Lloyds market. It is available for immediate use. The FRC has also withdrawn PN 24: The Audit of Friendly Societies in the United Kingdom as this is now superseded by revised material in the revised PN 20.

Section 1: Preface

This Practice Note contains guidance on the application of international standards on auditing UK (ISAs (UK)) issued by the Financial Reporting Council (FRC) to the auditors of insurers and friendly societies carrying on insurance business in the United Kingdom. It also contains guidance on auditor's reports in connection with regulatory reports, including published Solvency and Financial Condition Reports (SFCRs) under Solvency II. Our guidance also covers the auditor's duty to report to regulators and to the Council of Lloyd's. This Practice Note is supplementary to, and should be read in conjunction with, ISAs (UK) that apply to audits of financial statements for periods commencing on or after 17 June 2016. This Practice Note sets out the special considerations relating to the audit of insurers and friendly societies which arise from individual ISAs (UK). It is not the intention of the Practice Note to provide step-by-step guidance to the audit of insurers or friendly societies, so where no special considerations arise from a particular ISA (UK), no material is included.

Audits of Solvency II Pillar 3 public disclosures are conducted in accordance with ISAs (UK), including the requirements of ISA 800 (UK) *Special Considerations – Audits of Financial Statements prepared in accordance with Special Purpose Frameworks* and ISA 805 (UK) *Special Considerations – Audits of Single Financial Statements and Specific Elements, Accounts or Items of a Financial Statement* which are effective for periods commencing on or after 1 January 2017, with early adoption permitted

The guidance in this Practice Note is applicable to auditors of insurance companies and of Lloyd's syndicates and corporate members, as well as of friendly societies carrying on insurance business in the UK. References to insurers throughout this Practice Note also apply to friendly societies, unless specifically excluded. Particular considerations relating to the audit of Lloyd's syndicates are set out in a separate section.

The following Practice Notes issued by the FRC are also relevant to the audit of insurers:

PN 12 (Revised) Money Laundering – Guidance for auditors on UK legislation

PN 23 Special Considerations in Auditing Financial Instruments

Practice Note 24 (Revised) The Audit of Friendly Societies in the United Kingdom has been withdrawn, and relevant guidance incorporated into this Practice Note.

This Practice Note has been prepared with advice and assistance from staff of the PRA (in so far as the obligations of an insurer and its auditor under the PRA Rulebook are concerned). It is based on the legislation, regulations and byelaws which were in effect at 19 January 2017. The Practice Note does not, however, constitute general guidance given by the PRA or Lloyd's or Industry Guidance. It is not an exhaustive summary of all the obligations that an insurer and its auditor may have under the Financial Services and Markets Act 2000 (FSMA 2000), the PRA Rulebook, the FCA Handbook, European regulations or Lloyd's byelaws.

Section 2: Introduction

The term "insurers" in this Practice Note should be taken to refer to the following **1** types of entity (unless specified otherwise in the text):

(a) UK insurance companies authorised by the PRA;

(b) Lloyd's syndicates and corporate members;

(c) Overseas insurers with UK branches;

(d) Friendly societies carrying on insurance business in the UK.

2 This Practice Note applies both to those friendly societies incorporated under the Friendly Societies Act 1992 (the 1992 Act) and those registered under the Friendly Societies Act 1974 (the 1974 Act). It does not apply to other entities registered under the 1974 Act.

3 This Practice Note addresses the responsibilities and obligations of the auditor of an insurer concerning:

- The audit of the insurer's financial statements, as required by sections 495 and 496 of the Companies Act 2006 (CA 2006); sections 72 and 73 of the Friendly Societies Act 1992; Article 10 of the EU Audit Regulation 537/2014 (in respect of public interest entities); and in relation to Lloyd's, the 2008 Regulations[1] and the Syndicate Accounting Byelaw[2].

- Reporting on parts of the insurer's regulatory returns, as required by the PRA Rulebooks for Solvency II directive and non-directive insurers. Guidance on the auditor's work in relation to such returns is set out in the sections of this Practice Note dealing with regulatory returns.

- The right and duty to report direct to the PRA and FCA (and, where appropriate, to Lloyd's) in certain circumstances.[3]

Overseas insurers operating in the UK through branches are not subject to the audit provisions of CA 2006 and so the terms of engagement are a matter of contract between the auditor and its engaging party who may, for example, be local or head office management or the insurer's home country auditor. Such engagements take many different forms: the auditor may be asked to report on the financial statements of the UK branch or only on particular aspects thereof, and the form of its opinion will also vary from case to case. The auditor undertaking such assignments may wish to consider the guidance in this Practice Note where relevant, having regard to the agreed scope of its engagement.

Section 3: Legislative and Regulatory Framework

Background

1 The auditor of an insurer needs to be familiar with relevant legal and regulatory requirements. The extent to which an auditor considers compliance with regulatory requirements in the course of auditing an insurer's financial statements is discussed in the section of this Practice Note that addresses ISA (UK) 250 Section B. Guidance on auditor's responsibilities in relation to

---

[1] *Statutory Instrument SI 2008 No. 1950 "The Insurance Accounts Directive (Lloyd's Syndicate and Aggregate Accounts) Regulations 2008".*

[2] *Auditors of Lloyd's syndicates are required to be "recognised accountants", that is, registered auditors who have been approved by Lloyd's and have given an undertaking to the Council of Lloyd's in a prescribed form.*

[3] *Statutory Instrument SI 2001 No. 2587 "The FSMA 2000 (Communications by Auditors) Regulations 2001 and sections 342 and 343 of FSMA 2000" and the Audit Regulation for auditors of Public Interest Entities. Regulation (EU) 537/2014 of the European Parliament and of the Council of 16 April 2014 on specific requirements regarding statutory audit of public-interest entities and repealing Commission Decision 2005/909/EC.*

regulatory reporting is contained in the "Reporting on regulatory returns" sections 6 and 8 of this Practice Note.

The framework of regulation in the UK involves regulation of insurance activities   2
established by the Financial Services and Markets Act 2000 and European Directive and Regulation, under which insurance regulators have powers to establish specific requirements as well as to institute investigations into insurers and to suspend or remove authorisation to conduct insurance business where appropriate. The relevant insurance regulators are the Financial Conduct Authority (FCA) and the Prudential Regulation Authority (PRA). This Practice Note was written with reference to the framework of law and regulation which existed in January 2017. Practice Note 20 is not intended to provide a complete description of that framework, and nor can it anticipate or reflect changes which have taken place after the date it was written.

For the purpose of this Practice Note, references to the auditor of a regulated entity   3
or an authorised person in the context of FCA conduct supervision, and PRA prudential supervision of insurers, includes the auditor of a Friendly Society, of a Lloyd's syndicate or corporate member, unless otherwise stated.

Insurance business may not be carried on in the United Kingdom without   4
authorisation to do so. Insurance business may be undertaken by:

- Companies holding permission under Part 4A of FSMA 2000 to carry on the regulated activities of effecting and/or carrying out contracts of insurance (companies incorporated under CA 2006 and companies with their head offices outside the EU);

- Members of Lloyd's (see Section 316 of FSMA 2000); and

- Insurers authorised by other EEA member states which may conduct insurance business in the UK on a "freedom to provide services" basis or through the establishment of branches and which qualify automatically for authorisation under FSMA 2000.

In the case of members of Lloyd's, the PRA is the prudential regulator for the   5
Society of Lloyd's, and also of managing agents. The FCA regulates the conduct of the Society of Lloyd's, managing agents and on a prudential and conduct basis, the members' agents and advisors, and Lloyd's brokers.

The Financial Services and Markets Act (FSMA) 2000 gives the PRA the power   6
to discipline external auditors and actuaries of PRA authorised firms if they fail to comply with reporting requirements under FSMA or duties imposed by PRA rules. The range of disciplinary powers that the PRA can use includes fines, public censures or disqualification from working in financial services.

As well as needing permission under Part 4A of FSMA 2000 to effect or carry   7
out contracts of insurance, an insurer is likely to require additional permissions in respect of its activities relating to marketing, arranging or advising on insurance contracts and to dealing in investments as principal where it uses derivatives as part of its investment policy. Life insurers are likely to require further permissions as many life policies are deemed to represent designated investment business.[4]

The principal objective of prudential regulation in the UK is to promote the safety   8
and soundness of firms it supervises and, to contribute to the securing of an

---

[4] *Further guidance in connection with insurance intermediaries is included in the FRC Assurance Standard: Providing Assurance on Client Assets to the Financial Conduct Authority (November 2015).*

appropriate degree of protection for those who are or may become policyholders. Policyholders are protected both by the PRA as prudential regulator and by the FCA as conduct regulator.

Friendly Societies

9   Friendly societies are mutual organisations constituted under specific legislation and are accountable to their members. Friendly societies vary by size and range of activity. Some societies have developed a single product niche. Others offer a range of savings, insurance and banking services. Their focus remains individuals and families (the retail market) rather than commercial customers. They compete with other insurance and banking groups in the financial services market.

10 The directing body of a society or branch is known as the Committee of Management. The Committee carries out equivalent functions to the Board of Directors of a company incorporated under the Companies Acts. ISAs (UK) use the term "those charged with governance" to describe the persons entrusted with the supervision, control and directions of an entity, who will normally be responsible for the quality of financial reporting, and the term "management" to describe those persons who perform senior managerial functions. The PRA Rulebook uses the term "governing body" to describe collectively those charged with governance. In the context of this Practice Note, references to those charged with governance refer to members of the Committee of Management of a friendly society. The members of the Committee are subject to the regulator's "Approved Persons" rules and have to be "fit and proper" to hold office.

11 A summary of the legal forms of friendly society now existing and the main legislation applicable to each type is set out in the table below.

Legal Form	Common designation	Applicable legislation
Established prior to the 1992 Act and re-registered under that Act	"Incorporated"	1992 Act
Established prior to the 1992 Act but not re-registered under it, i.e., remains registered under the 1974 Act	"Registered"/ "Unincorporated"	1992 Act and the 1974 Friendly Societies Act (as amended by Schedule 16 of 1992 Act)
Established after the 1992 Act	"Incorporated"	1992 Act

12 Other legislation with relevance to certain types of mutual organisations such as Industrial and Provident Societies was being revised at the time this guidance was written. Auditors should therefore take steps to ensure that they are aware of the current legislative and regulatory position for each entity.

Financial Services and Markets Act 2000

13 FSMA 2000 sets out the high level regulatory framework for the financial sector more generally and not just insurers and friendly societies.

14 Under Part X FSMA 2000 the PRA and FCA have the power to make "rules" and give guidance. Rules made by the regulators are set out in the PRA rulebook and

FCA handbook. The legal effect of a rule varies depending on the power under which it is made and on the language used in the rule. Rules are mandatory unless a waiver has been agreed. If an authorised firm contravenes a rule it may be subject to enforcement action and consequent disciplinary measures under Part XIV FSMA 2000. In certain circumstances an authorised firm may be subject to an action for damages under section 150 FSMA 2000.

In contrast, guidance is generally issued to provide context relevant to a proper **15** understanding of the regulatory requirements, and is not binding. However if an authorised firm acts in accordance with it in the circumstances contemplated by that guidance, the regulator will proceed on the basis that the authorised firm has complied with the rule to which the guidance relates. ISA (UK) 250 Section B requires the level of knowledge of the members of the audit engagement team of the provisions of the applicable legislation; regulator's rules and guidance; and other specific requirements placed on the audited entity, to be appropriate to the staff member's role in the audit and sufficient (in the context of that role) to enable them to identify situations which may give reasonable cause to believe that a matter should be reported to the regulator.[5] ISA (UK) 220 requires the engagement partner, among other things, to:

- Take responsibility for the engagement team undertaking appropriate consultation on difficult or contentious matters.

- Be satisfied that members of the engagement team have undertaken appropriate consultation during the course of the engagement, both within the engagement team and between the engagement team and others at the appropriate level within or outside the firm.[6]

Lloyd's

Under FSMA 2000, Lloyd's is subject to dual regulation by the PRA and the FCA, **16** with the Council of Lloyd's also having certain statutory regulatory duties. Agreements are in place between Lloyd's and both the PRA and FCA which set out the basis on which they will cooperate in the performance of these duties.[7] Lloyd's is therefore subject to the requirements of the Solvency II Directive, PRA Rulebook and FCA Handbook, including those relating to the "actuarial function". Much of the Lloyd's market rule structure is embedded in a series of byelaws passed by the Council.

Members underwrite insurance business at Lloyd's as a member of one or more **17** syndicates, each syndicate being managed by a managing agent. Syndicates have no legal personality and are merely the vehicle through which the members underwrite insurance risk. Technically, each syndicate is an annual venture. The year during which it writes business is described as an "underwriting year" or a "year of account". Members have no liability for business underwritten by the same syndicate in previous years of account unless they were members in those years or unless they have reinsured the members of that syndicate for the previous years. However, for practical business purposes, syndicates are treated as continuing from one year to the next. Lloyd's maintains central assets, including the Central Fund, which are available to meet a member's underwriting liabilities in the event of any default by the member.

---

[5] *ISA (UK) 250 B para.11.*

[6] *ISA (UK) 220 para. 18.*

[7] *https://www.lloyds.com/lloyds/corporate-governance/regulation-of-lloyds*

Financial Statements

18   The form and content of the financial statements of UK insurers prepared under UK GAAP is governed by CA 2006 and United Kingdom Accounting Standards. (United Kingdom Accounting Standards comprise Financial Reporting Standards ("FRSs")). The prescribed format for a UK insurer's financial statements that comply with UK GAAP is set out in:

(a)   Sections 395 and 396 of CA 2006; and

(b)   Schedules 3 and 6 (part 3) to The Large and Medium-sized Companies and Groups (Accounts and Reports) Regulations 2008 (SI 2008/410) (The 2008 Accounts and Reports Regulations).

19   Listed UK groups (including listed UK insurance groups) must prepare consolidated financial statements in accordance with International Financial Reporting Standards as adopted by the European Union (EU-IFRSs)[8] and those parts of CA 2006 applicable to companies reporting under EU-IFRSs. UK companies or non-listed groups, including friendly societies, UK insurers and insurance groups, are permitted to voluntarily adopt EU-IFRSs for their financial statements.

Friendly Societies

20   The following Regulations and Orders relating to The Friendly Societies Act 1992 have been promulgated. In this Practice Note they are referred to collectively as "the Accounts Regulations". The Accounts Regulations apply to all societies.

Regulation/Order	Statutory Instrument No.	Outline Content
The Friendly Societies (Accounts and Related Provisions) Regulations 1994	SI 1994 No.1983	Regulations which prescribe the format and content of the financial statements and committee of management report
The Friendly Societies Act 1992 (International Accounting Standards and Other Accounting Amendments) Order 2005	SI 2005 No. 2211	Amends the 1992 Act to permit friendly societies to use international financial reporting standards as adopted by the EU. It also inserts into the Committee of Management Report additional disclosure requirements such as a Business Review, Principal Risks and Uncertainties and Key Performance Indicators.
The Friendly Societies Act 1992 (Accounts, Audit and EEA State Amendments) Order 2008	SI 2008 No. 1140	Amends the 1992 Act to implement parts of both the Audit Directive (2006/43/EC) and the Accounts

---

[8]   *Article 4 of EC Regulation 1606/2002 as acknowledged in section 403(1) CA 2006 – the IAS Regulation.*

Regulation/Order	Statutory Instrument No.	Outline Content
		Directive (2006/46/EC). Requires the auditor of an incorporated society to identify a senior statutory auditor. It also inserted a new Schedule 13F into FSA 1992, with audit fee and other services disclosures.
The Friendly Societies (Accounts and Related Provisions) (Amendment) Regulations 2008	SI 2008 No. 1144	Amendments to the 1994 Regulations to reflect certain requirements of the Accounts Directive (2006/46/EC)

Lloyd's

21 The reporting requirements in respect of syndicate activities are set out in "The Insurance Accounts Directive (Lloyd's Syndicate and Aggregate Accounts) Regulations 2008" ("the 2008 Lloyd's Regulations"). The 2008 Lloyd's Regulations require the preparation by managing agents of:

(a) Syndicate annual accounts in accordance with CA 2006 and Schedule 3 to The 2008 Accounts and Reports Regulations showing the performance across all years of account of the syndicate during the calendar year;

(b) Syndicate underwriting year accounts at the closure of a year of account (unless all the relevant members of the syndicate agree otherwise);

and by the Council of Lloyd's

(c) Aggregate accounts for the Lloyd's market as a whole reflecting an accumulation of the syndicate profit and loss accounts and the balance sheets prepared at (a).

(d) In addition, the Syndicate Accounting Byelaw 2005 requires the preparation by managing agents of syndicate underwriting year accounts at 31 December each year in respect of each run-off account (unless all the relevant members of the syndicate agree otherwise).

22 Legally, each year of account of a syndicate is a separate venture established to write insurance business in a specific calendar year. As a consequence of each annual venture being a unique trading entity, a mechanism is necessary to enable each such venture to close, normally at the end of three years. Estimated outstanding liabilities as at the date of closure are reinsured, in consideration for a premium, by a subsequent year of account of the same or another syndicate. This reinsurance arrangement is known as a "reinsurance to close" ("RITC").

23 In certain circumstances, the managing agent may conclude that significant uncertainties (or other factors) exist such that it is not possible to determine an appropriate premium for a RITC at the normal date of closure. When this happens, the relevant year of account is not closed but placed into run-off until such time as the managing agent concludes that this requirement can be satisfied. Technical provisions will be determined for each run-off account and carried forward until the year of account is closed or all its liabilities discharged.

24   Where the Lloyd's corporate member is a UK company it is required to prepare its financial statements in accordance with the requirements of CA 2006 applicable to UK insurance companies whether drawn up in accordance with EU-IFRSs or UK GAAP.

Prudential requirements

Solvency II

25   The Solvency II prudential regime came into force from 1 January 2016. Insurance firms and friendly societies can be either "directive" or "non-directive" firms, with different regulatory reporting requirements as a consequence. A number of criteria determine whether insurance firms are directive or non-directive, relating primarily to the level of gross premium income and amount of gross technical provisions.[9]

Solvency II, and the related PRA rules, establish a comprehensive new prudential regime and require annual public solvency disclosures by directive firms in the form of a Solvency and Financial Condition Report (SFCR) and linked Quantitative Reporting Templates (QRTs), as well as periodic reporting to the competent supervisor. The PRA requires those disclosures to be subject to external audit, and this Practice Note includes a section setting out guidance on the application of the ISAs (UK) to those engagements. Non-directive firms continue to be required to comply with solvency requirements set by the PRA, and with the related reporting regime.

26   The Solvency II Directive, related Implementation Rules, Technical Standards and Guidelines[10], as well as PRA rules, provide the framework for prudential regulation for insurance firms which meet certain criteria ("Directive Firms"), including the level of premiums received and size of technical provisions. That framework is built around "3 pillars":

- Financial Requirements – including Solvency Capital Requirement (SCR) and Minimum Capital Requirement (MCR) thresholds; and detailed rules for the valuation of assets and liabilities;

- Governance and Supervision – including the Own Risk and Solvency Assessment (ORSA); and

- Reporting and Disclosure – including private reporting to the regulator and public SFCRs.

27   Solvency II regulations do not require external audit of Pillar 3 public disclosures. The requirement for an audit of the "relevant elements of the SFCR" is contained within the External Audit chapter of the PRA rulebook which relates to Solvency II firms (**"directive firms"**).[11] There is no formal PRA requirement for the statutory auditor of an insurance entity's financial statements to also carry out the audit of Pillar 3 public disclosures. **"Non-directive firms"** are subject to a separate prudential regime, which is set out in the PRA Rulebook for Non-Solvency II firms. Non-directive friendly societies are subject to different requirements than other insurance entities.

---

[9] *The full criteria are set out in the PRA Rulebook.*

[10] *http://ec.europa.eu/finance/insurance/solvency/solvency2/index_en.htm*

[11] *http://www.prarulebook.co.uk/rulebook/Content/Chapter/321290/22-09-2016*

Reporting to supervisors, including supervisors of public-interest entities – statutory right and duty

Statutory rights and duties to report to supervisors flow from two main sources: **28** the 2001 Regulations under FSMA 2000[12], which apply to the auditors of all authorized insurance entities; and Audit Regulation (EU) 537/2014 in respect of the relationship between auditors and supervisors of "public interest entities", which includes certain insurance undertakings.

These duties do not require the auditor of an insurer to undertake additional work **29** directed at identifying matters to report over and above the work necessary to fulfil its obligations to report on financial statements and regulatory returns.

Duties under the 2001 Regulations

Under the 2001 Regulations the auditor of an authorised firm or the auditor of an **30** entity closely linked to an authorised firm who is also the auditor of that authorised firm has a statutory duty to communicate to the competent supervisor, these and other matters of "material significance". Under section 340 FSMA 2000 "the auditor" is defined as one required to be appointed under "rules" or appointed as a result of another enactment. In addition section 342 FSMA 2000 provides that no duty to which the auditor is subject shall be contravened by communicating in good faith to the regulator any information or opinion on a matter that the auditor reasonably believes is relevant to any functions of the regulator.

There is a similar right and duty of the auditor of a Lloyd's syndicate or corporate **31** member to report direct to Lloyd's by the undertaking required from the auditor of a Lloyd's syndicate or corporate member by the Lloyd's Audit Arrangements Byelaw 1998 and the Lloyd's Membership Byelaw No 5 of 2005.

The 2001 Regulations do not require the auditor to perform any additional audit **32** work as a result of the statutory duty nor is the auditor required specifically to seek out breaches of the requirements applicable to a particular regulated entity. However, in circumstances where the auditor identifies that a reportable matter may exist, it carries out such extra work, as it considers necessary, to determine whether the facts and circumstances cause the auditor "reasonably to believe" that the matter does in fact exist. It should be noted that the auditor's work does not need to prove that the reportable matter exists.

ISA (UK) 250 Section B deals with the statutory right and duty of the auditor of a **33** regulated entity to bring information of which the auditor has become aware in the ordinary course of performing work undertaken to the attention of the appropriate regulator as soon as practicable when:

- The auditor concludes that it is relevant to the regulator's functions having regard to such matters as may be specified in statute or any related regulations; and

- In the auditor's opinion there is reasonable cause to believe it is or may be of material significance to the regulator.[13]

Where an apparent breach of statutory or regulatory requirements comes to the **34** auditor's attention, the auditor shall:

- Obtain such evidence as is available to assess its implications for the auditor's reporting responsibilities;

---

[12] SI 2001 No 2587 "The FSMA 2000 (Communications by Auditors) Regulations 2001".

[13] ISA (UK) 250 Section B – Revised June 2016, para 8.

- Determine whether, in the auditor's opinion, there is reasonable cause to believe that the breach is of material significance to the regulator; and

- Consider whether the apparent breach is criminal conduct that gives rise to criminal property and, as such, should be reported to the specified authorities.[14]

35 The criteria for determining the matters to be reported are as follows:

(a) The auditor reasonably believes that there is, or has been, or may be, or may have been a contravention of any "relevant requirement" that applies to the person[15] concerned and that contravention may be of material significance to the regulator in determining whether to exercise, in relation to that person, any of its functions under FSMA 2000; or

(b) The auditor reasonably believes that the information on, or its opinion on, those matters may be of material significance to the PRA or FCA in determining whether the person concerned satisfies and will continue to satisfy the relevant "Threshold Conditions"[16]; or

(c) The auditor reasonably believes that the person concerned is not, may not be, or may cease to be, a going concern; or

(d) The auditor is precluded from stating in its report that the annual accounts have been properly prepared in accordance with CA 2006 or, where applicable, give a true and fair view or have been prepared in accordance with relevant rules and legislation.

36 In relation to 35(a) above, "relevant requirement" is a requirement by or under FSMA 2000 which relates to authorisation under FSMA 2000 or to the carrying on of any regulated activity. This includes not only relevant statutory instruments but also the FCA/PRA's rules (other than the Listing Rules) including the PRA's Fundamental Rules and the FCA's Principles for Businesses. The duty to report also covers any requirement imposed by or under any other Act the contravention of which constitutes an offence which the PRA or FCA have the power to prosecute under FSMA 2000. In relation to 35(b) above the duty to report relates to either information or opinions held by the auditor which may be of significance to the regulators in determining whether the regulated entity satisfies and will continue to satisfy the Threshold Conditions.

Material significance

37 Determining whether a contravention of a relevant requirement or a Threshold Condition is reportable under the 2001 Regulations involves consideration both of whether the auditor "reasonably believes" and that the matter in question "is, or is likely to be, of material significance" to the regulator.

38 ISA (UK) 250 Section B requires that, where an apparent breach of statutory or regulatory requirements comes to the auditor's attention, it obtains such evidence as is available to assess its implications for the auditor's reporting responsibilities and determines whether, in its opinion, there is reasonable cause to believe that the breach is of material significance to the regulator:

---

[14] *ISA (UK) 250 Section B – Revised June 2016, para 12.*

[15] *In this context the person is an "Authorised Person".*

[16] *The Threshold Conditions are set out in Schedule 6 to FSMA 2000 and represent the minimum conditions that a firm is required to satisfy and continue to satisfy to be given and to retain Part 4A permission. Firms must comply with both PRA specific and FCA specific Threshold Conditions.*

the term "material significance" requires interpretation in the context of the specific legislation applicable to the regulated entity. A matter or group of matters is normally of material significance to a regulator's functions when, due either to its nature or its potential financial impact, it is likely of itself to require investigation by the regulator ...[17]

"Material significance" does not have the same meaning as materiality in the **39** context of the audit of financial statements. Whilst a particular event may be trivial in terms of its possible effect on the financial statements of an entity, it may be of a nature or type that is likely to change the regulator's perception of the entity. The determination of whether a matter is, or is likely to be, of material significance to the PRA and/or FCA inevitably requires the auditor to exercise its judgment. In forming such judgments, the auditor needs to consider not simply the facts of the matter but also their implications. In addition, it is possible that a matter, which is not materially significant in isolation, may become so when other possible breaches are considered.

The auditor of a regulated entity bases its judgment of "material significance" to **40** the regulator solely on its understanding of the facts of which it is aware without making any assumptions about the information available to the PRA in connection with any particular regulated entity.

Minor breaches of the PRA or FCA rules that, for example, are unlikely to **41** jeopardise the entity's assets or amount to misconduct or mismanagement would not normally be of "material significance". ISA (UK) 250 Section B however requires the auditor of regulated entities, when reporting on their financial statements, to review information obtained in the course of the audit and to assess whether the cumulative effect is of "material significance" such as to give rise to a duty to report to the regulator. In circumstances where the auditor is uncertain whether it may be required to make a report or not, it may wish to consider taking legal advice.

On completion of its investigations, the auditor ensures that the facts and **42** circumstances, and the basis for its conclusion as to whether these are, or are likely to be of "material significance" to the regulator, are adequately documented such that the reasons for its decision to report or not, as the case may be, may be clearly demonstrated.

Whilst confidentiality is an implied term of an auditor's contract with a regulated **43** entity, section 342 FSMA 2000 states that an auditor does not contravene that duty if it reports to the regulator information or its opinion, if it is acting in good faith and reasonably believes that the information or opinion is relevant to any function of the PRA and/or FCA. The protection afforded is given in respect of information obtained in its capacity as auditor.

Public Interest Entities

"Public Interest Entities" ("PIEs") are defined[18] as being any one of: **44**

(a) An issuer whose transferable securities are admitted to trading on a regulated market;

(b) A credit institution within the meaning of Article 4(1)(1) of Regulation (EU) No 575/2013 of the European Parliament and of the Council, other than

---

[17] *ISA (UK) 250 Section B, para. 9 (d).*

[18] *ISA (UK) Glossary of Terms (auditing and ethics) 2016.*

those listed in Article 2 of Directive 2013/36/EU of the European Parliament and of the Council on access to the activity of credit institutions and investment firms;

(c)   An insurance undertaking within the meaning given by Article 2(1) of Council Directive 1991/674/EEC of the European Parliament and of the Council on the annual accounts and consolidated accounts of insurance undertaking.

45   An insurance undertaking is a PIE if it meets any of the relevant criteria. In respect of c, which applies specifically to insurance entities, the relevant definition is now set out in the Solvency II Directive 2009/138/EC (which repealed previous relevant Directives). With effect from 17 June 2016 UK insurance and reinsurance undertakings within the scope of the Solvency II Directive are PIEs within the meaning of Audit Directive 2006/43 (as amended by Directive 2014/56). This includes relevant friendly societies and it also includes the Society of Lloyd's (because the society issues securities which are admitted to trading on a regulated market).[19] The auditors of these entities will need to consider the statutory rights and duties set out in both the 2001 Regulations under FSMA 2000 and of the Audit Regulation.

The Audit Regulation (EU) 537/2014

46   The Audit regulation places responsibility for the effectiveness of the dialogue between auditors and supervisors on both parties:

> *An effective dialogue shall be established between competent authorities supervising credit institutions and insurance undertakings, on the one hand, and the statutory auditor (s) and the audit firm (s) carrying out the statutory audit of those institutions and undertakings on the other hand. The responsibility for compliance with this requirement shall rest with both parties to the dialogue.*[20]

47   Article 12 of the Regulation sets out the statutory duty of the auditor or audit firm carrying out the statutory audit of a PIE to report promptly to the competent supervisors[21] any information of which they may have become aware "while carrying out that statutory audit" and which may bring about any of the following (about the PIE or any undertaking having "close links" with the PIE):

● A material breach of the laws, regulations or administrative provisions which lay down, were appropriate, the conditions governing authorization or which specifically govern pursuit of the activities of such public interest entity;

● A material threat or doubt concerning the continuous functioning of the public-interest entity;

● A refusal to issue an audit opinion on the financial statements or the issuing of an adverse or qualified opinion.

---

[19] *The EU requirements on audits of PIEs have not been implemented for participants in the Lloyd's market and the additional requirements in the FRC's Ethical and Auditing Standards applicable to PIEs (paragraphs with the prefix "R") do not apply in to the audit of Lloyd's syndicates.*

[20] *Regulation (EU) 537/2014 of the European Parliament and of the Council of 16 April 2014 on specific requirements regarding statutory audit of public-interest entities and repealing Commission Decision 2005/909/EC, Article 12, p.2.*

[21] *Regulation (EU) 537/2014 of the European Parliament and of the Council of 16 April 2014 on specific requirements regarding statutory audit of public-interest entities and repealing Commission Decision 2005/909/EC.*

The Audit Regulation defines competent supervisors as "the competent authorities **48** supervising that public-interest entity" (in respect of insurance undertakings in the UK this means the PRA and the FCA) or, "where so determined by the Member State concerned, to the competent authority responsible for the oversight of the statutory auditor or audit firm." (which in the UK is the FRC).

A Memorandum of Understanding sets out the relevant relationship between the **49** PRA and FCA, including in respect of firms subject to dual regulation.[22] Further MoUs exist between the PRA and the FRC, and the FCA and the FRC, which explain how they will exercise their respective statutory roles, and the principles which govern information sharing between them.[23]

Dialogue encompasses bodies within the European Union, with the European **50** Systemic Risk Board (ESRB) and the CEAOB being required by the Audit Regulation to organize a meeting "at least once a year … with the statutory auditor (s) and the audit firm (s) carrying out the statutory audit of those institutions and undertakings." EIOPA[24] and the PRA[25] have policies setting out the principles and procedures underpinning the relationship between auditors and supervisors.

The Audit Regulation provides that: **51**

> *The disclosure in good faith to the competent authorities or to ESRB and the CEAOB, by the statutory auditor or the audit firm or network, where applicable, of any information referred to in paragraph 1.* [see paragraph 57 above] … *emerging during the dialogue provided for in paragraph 2 shall not constitute a breach of any contractual or legal restriction on disclosure of information.*[26]

Section 4: The Audit of Financial Statements

This Practice Note contains guidance on the application to the audits of financial statements of insurers (and friendly societies carrying on insurance business in the UK) of those ISAs (UK) that are effective for periods commencing on or after 17 June 2016. In addition, it contains guidance intended to assist the auditors of insurers and friendly societies in reporting on matters specified by regulators, given the auditor's right and duty to report to regulators. This Practice Note does not contain commentary on all of the requirements included in the ISAs (UK) and reading it should not be seen as an alternative to reading the relevant ISAs (UK) in their entirety. In addition, where no special considerations arise from a particular ISA (UK), no material is included.

ISA (UK) 210: AGREEING THE TERMS OF AUDIT ENGAGEMENTS

ISA (UK) 210 sets out the auditor's responsiblities when agreeing the terms of audit engagements. These are to establish whether the "preconditions for an audit"

---

[22] *http://www.fca.org.uk/your-fca/documents/mou/mou-between-the-fca-and-the-pracoordination*

[23] *https://frc.org.uk/Our-Work/Publications/FRC-Board/Memorandum-of-Understanding-PRA-and-FRC.pdf; https://frc.org.uk/Our-Work/Publications/FRC-Board/Memorandum-of-Understanding-PRA-and-FRC.pdf*

[24] *https://eiopa.europa.eu/Pages/News/EIOPA-consults-on-the-Guidelines-facilitating-the-dialogue-between-insurance-supervisors-and-auditors.aspx*

[25] *http://www.bankofengland.co.uk/pra/Pages/publications/ps/2016/ps116.aspx*

[26] *Regulation (EU) 537/2014 of the European Parliament and of the Council of 16 April 2014 on specific requirements regarding statutory audit of public-interest entities and repealing Commission Decision 2005/909/EC, Article 12, p.3.*

are present and that there is a common understanding between the auditor and management and, where appropriate, those charged with governance.

1   Where the auditor is appointed to audit both the statutory financial statements and regulatory reports, the auditor may choose to combine into a single letter the terms of engagement in relation for both engagements. In that case, the auditor should have regard to the requirements of ISA (UK) 210 in respect of each separate engagement, and clearly set out the terms and conditions in respect of each engagement included within the letter of engagement. In respect of the audit of the statutory financial statements, matters which the auditor may decide to refer to in the engagement letter are as follows:

●   The responsibility of the directors/senior management to comply with applicable FSMA 2000 legislation[27], the FCA Handbook[28] and PRA Rules[29] including the need to keep the regulators informed about the affairs of the entity.

●   The statutory right and duty of the auditor to report directly to the FCA and/or PRA in certain circumstances (see the section of this Practice Note relating to ISA (UK) 250 Section B and the section on the regulatory context of the audit of insurers).

●   The requirement on the audited entity to cooperate with the auditor contained within the FCA and PRA rules. This includes taking steps to ensure that, where applicable, each of its appointed representatives, tied agents and material outsourcers gives the auditor the same right of access to records, information and explanations as the authorised firm itself is required to provide the auditor.[30] It is a criminal offence for an insurer or its officers, controllers or managers to provide false or misleading information to the auditor.[31]

●   procedures for the insurer to make the auditor aware when it appoints a third party (including another department or office of the same audit firm) to review, investigate or report on any aspects of its business activities that may be relevant to the audit of the financial statements and to provide the auditor with copies of reports by such a third party promptly after their receipt.

2   In this connection the auditor is aware that:

(a)   The appropriate regulator does not need to approve the appointment of an auditor but may seek to satisfy itself that an auditor appointed by a firm is independent and has the necessary skills, resources and experience[32];

---

[27] *http://www.legislation.gov.uk/ukpga/2000/8/contents*

[28] *https://www.handbook.fca.org.uk/*

[29] *http://www.prarulebook.co.uk/*

[30] *FCA Handbook, Regulatory Processes: SUP Supervision: SUP 3: 3.6.2G–3.6.8G. PRA Solvency II Firms Rulebook: Auditors 5.1–5.2; PRA Non-Solvency Firms Rulebook: Auditors 5.1–5.2.*

[31] *Section 346 FSMA 2000.*

[32] *FCA Handbook, Regulatory Processes: SUP Supervision: SUP 3: 3.4.4G; 3.4.7R; 3.4.8G.*

(b)   *The auditor is required to cooperate with the* regulators[33]*; and*

(c)   *The auditor must notify the appropriate regulator if the auditor ceases to be the auditor of an authorised firm.*[34]

Friendly Societies

The auditor's engagement letter additionally refers to the Friendly Societies   3
Act 1992.

ISA (UK) 240: THE AUDITOR'S RESPONSIBILITIES RELATING TO FRAUD IN AN AUDIT OF FINANCIAL STATEMENTS

ISA (UK) 240 deals with the auditor's responsibilities relating to fraud in an audit of financial statements.

The following are considered to be significant fraud risks which insurers may be   4
subject to:

●   Policyholder fraud.

●   Fraud by directors and employees, or in the case of friendly societies the committee of management and employees.

●   Fraud by agents, brokers, intermediaries or other related parties.

Responsibility for the prevention and detection of fraud and error lies with those   5
charged with governance of an insurer or friendly society, and of the managing
agent of a Lloyd's syndicate, even if they have delegated functions to third parties.
In carrying out their responsibilities, the directors or Committee of Management
have regard to the PRA's Fundamental Rules and the FCA Principles for
Businesses (in particular with regard to the criteria for integrity, skill, care and
diligence and management and control)[35] and to requirements issued by the
Council of Lloyd's. Equivalent provisions apply to directors of managing agents.[36]

The PRA's Fundamental Rule 5 and FCA Principle 3 require an insurer to take   6
reasonable care to organise and control its affairs responsibly and effectively with
adequate risk management systems. The PRA rulebook has specific requirements
for insurers in respect of the processes to be followed to ensure that all persons
who carry out key functions are fit and proper (including being of good repute and
integrity).[37] From 7 March 2016 a new Senior Insurance Managers regime (jointly
introduced by the FCA and PRA) came into force which established new
requirements in respect of the governance arrangements, responsibilities and
individual conduct rules for those working within the authorised insurance
sector.[38] The FCA Handbook SYSC 3.2.20R(1) requires a firm to make and

---

[33] *FCA Handbook, Regulatory Processes: SUP Supervision: SUP 3: 3.8.2R; 3.8.3G; 3.8.4R. PRA Solvency II Firms Rulebook: Auditors 7.1; PRA Non-Solvency Firms Rulebook: Auditors 7.1. For auditors of Public Interest Entities a requirement to report to and to establish an effective dialogue with competent authorities is included in Article 12 of REGULATION (EU) No 537/2014 OF THE EUROPEAN PARLIAMENT AND OF THE COUNCIL of 16 April 2014.*

[34] *FCA Handbook, Regulatory Processes: SUP Supervision: SUP 3: 3.8.11R; 3.8.12R. PRA Solvency II Firms Rulebook: Auditors 7.5 & 7.6; PRA Non-Solvency Firms Rulebook: Auditors 7.5 & 7.6.*

[35] *http://www.bankofengland.co.uk/pra/Documents/authorisations/newfirmauths/fundamentalrulesprinciples.pdf; https://www.handbook.fca.org.uk/handbook/PRIN/2/1.html*

[36] *https://www.lloyds.com/the-market/operating-at-lloyds/lloyds-minimum-standards*

[37] *http://www.prarulebook.co.uk/rulebook/Content/Chapter/212602/14-09-2016-212607; http://www.prarulebook.co.uk/rulebook/Content/Part/318572/14-09-2016; http://www.prarulebook.co.uk/rulebook/Content/Part/302742/14-09-2016*

[38] *https://www.fca.org.uk/firms/senior-insurance-managers-regime*

retain adequate records of matters and dealings (including accounting records) which are the subject of requirements and standards under the regulatory system.[39]

7   Whilst the inherent risk of fraud may continue to exist, the establishment of accounting and internal control systems sufficient to meet these requirements (particularly in the case of insurance companies that accept business involving both a high volume of policies and claims of comparatively low value) reduces the likelihood of fraud giving rise to material misstatements in the financial statements.

8   Fraud against insurers, either fraudulent financial reporting (for example the manipulation of profits or the concealment of losses) or misappropriation of assets, can occur through a combination of management fraud, employee fraud or fraud perpetrated by third parties. However, fraud risk factors particularly relevant to insurers may be due to the following, for example:

- The commission driven nature of many arrangements with business introducers whose interests may be more focused on the volume of business and commission thereon rather than the ultimate profitability and sustainability of the business for the insurer. This may increase the risk of fraud committed by agents and intermediaries.

- The existence of very large estimated liabilities which may not crystallise for many years.

- Complex insurance and reinsurance transactions that may provide an opportunity to conceal inappropriate pricing of the risks transferred and to apply inappropriate accounting treatments which may have a significant impact on the results for a given period and the balance sheet position.

- The transfer of risk under a contract of insurance is not reflected in the passing of any physical asset which may make it difficult for insurers to ensure that all transactions are recorded completely and accurately.

- The nature of delegated underwriting, coupled with large amounts of cash and near liquid assets often held by agents and other intermediaries with delegated authority, may increase the propensity for fraud.

- The practice of insurance contracts incepting before all of the terms are agreed and documented may provide the opportunity for fraudulent manipulation of contract wordings.

9   In smaller insurers, a further risk may arise because segregation of duties may be limited as the processing of receipts and payments vest in a few individuals. There may be only one individual responsible for day to day management. As contributions received from an individual member will often only give rise to benefit payments to that individual over the longer term, there is a risk that amounts may be misappropriated in the interim and escape detection. There is also a risk that related party transactions will be entered into without appropriate review and approval, resulting in non-commercial terms which could be prejudicial to members' interests.

10   ISA (UK) 240 requires that the auditor shall identify and assess risks of material misstatement based on a presumption there are risks of fraud in revenue recognition. In the context of an insurer or friendly society, "revenue" in respect of insurance contracts may take the form of earned premiums. However the auditor also considers the likelihood of fraud in relation to the recognition of

---

[39] *https://www.handbook.fca.org.uk/handbook/SYSC/3/2.html*

income or costs which may have a close relationship to earned premiums, such as reinsurance costs and acquisition costs. Where insurers issue investment contracts that are subject to deposit accounting, "revenue" may be taken as the fees receivable under those contracts. Insurers frequently outsource insurance and accounting functions to service companies. Service companies are considered as agents of the insurance companies and the auditor therefore considers the equivalent risk factors for service companies.

The auditor considers reports or information obtained from the insurer's internal   **11** audit function, compliance department, legal department, and money laundering reporting officer together with reviews undertaken by third parties such as skilled person's reports prepared under section 166 FSMA 2000.[40]

The FCA's rules require authorised firms and friendly societies to report   **12** "significant" fraud, errors and other irregularities to the FCA (SUP 15.3.17R) (and, where applicable, to the Council of Lloyd's).[41]

ISA (UK) 250: SECTION A – CONSIDERATION OF LAWS AND REGULATIONS IN AN AUDIT OF FINANCIAL STATEMENTS

ISA (UK) 250A deals with the responsibilities of an auditor when considering laws and regulations in an audit of financial statements:

> As part of obtaining an understanding of the entity and its environment in accordance with ISA (UK) 315, the auditor shall obtain a general understanding of:
>
> (a)   The legal and regulatory framework applicable to the entity and the industry or sector in which the entity operates; and
>
> (b)   How the entity is complying with that framework.[42]
>
> The auditor shall obtain sufficient appropriate audit evidence regarding compliance with the provisions of those laws and regulations generally recognized to have a direct effect on the determination of material amounts and disclosures in the financial statements.[43]

In the context of insurers and friendly societies, laws and regulations are central to   **13** the conduct of business if breaches would have either of the following consequences:

(a)   Removal of authorisation to carry out insurance business; or

(b)   The imposition of fines or restrictions on business activities whose significance is such that the ability of the insurer to continue as a going concern is threatened.

Non-compliance with laws and regulations that are central to an insurer's activities   **14** is likely to give rise to a statutory duty to report to the FCA, the PRA and/or the Council of Lloyd's. Such reports are made in accordance with the requirements of

---

[40] *Section 166 FSMA 2000 provides the PRA and the FCA with the power to require a firm to appoint a skilled person to provide a report on any matter that the FCA may reasonably require in connection with the exercise of the functions conferred on it by or under FSMA 2000. The requirements concerning skilled persons are set out in the FCA handbook and the PRA rulebook.*

[41] *https://www.handbook.fca.org.uk/handbook/SUP/15/3.html*

[42] *ISA (UK) 250 Section A (Revised June 2016), para. 12.*

[43] *ISA (UK) 250 Section A (Revised June 2016), para. 13.*

ISA (UK) 250 Section B, following the guidance set out in the relevant section of this Practice Note.

15 Insurers are affected by two types of regulation which are central to their activities and of which the auditor needs to obtain a general understanding:

(a) Prudential supervision; and

(b) Market conduct rules.

16 The principal purpose of prudential supervision is to ensure the protection of policyholders because of the promissory nature of transactions between insurers and the public. Many of the rules for prudential supervision are based on European Directives, including the Solvency II framework which became effective from 1 January 2016.

17 Prudential supervision of insurance companies with their head offices in the UK and insurers established outside the EEA with UK branches is carried out by the PRA under rules made by the PRA under FSMA 2000, and in accordance with the Solvency II regime. Ongoing prudential supervision of authorised insurance companies is conducted by means of the regulatory returns submitted by all authorised insurance companies and non-EEA insurers with UK branches. Since 1 January 2016, different reporting rules apply to different categories of insurer:

- Non-directive firms are categorised according to criteria set out in Chapter 2 of the Insurance General Application Part of the PRA Rulebook. In general, they are those with gross premium income below 5 million euro and gross technical provisions of less than 25 million euro. These firms make annual regulatory returns, which are due to the PRA within three months of their balance sheet date for insurers making electronic submissions (otherwise 2 months and 15 days). These returns are subject to audit.

- Solvency II directive firms submit quarterly and annual regulatory returns including a number of quantitative reporting templates depending on the type of business they conduct. These are set out in the reporting section of the PRA rulebook for Solvency II firms. These returns are not subject to audit. Transitional Measures apply during which the deadlines for submission of annual returns are:

  - 20 weeks after the firm's financial year end in relation to its financial year ending on or after 30 June 2016 before 1 January 2017;

  - 18 weeks after the firm's financial year end in relation to its financial year ending on or after 1 January 2017 but before 1 January 2018;

  - 16 weeks after the firm's financial year end in relation to its financial year ending on or after 1 January 2018 but before 1 January 2019;

  - 14 weeks after the firm's financial year end in relation to its financial year ending on or after 1 January 2019 but before 1 January 2020.[44]

- Directive firms are also required to publish annually a SFCR, the required content of which is set out in the reporting section of the PRA rulebook for Solvency II firms, and part of which must be audited. Disclosure of the SFCR is required on the same timetable as set out above in respect of annual regulatory returns.

---

[44] *The 14 week deadline continues to apply after 1 January 2020. The deadline for groups is, in each case, 6 weeks later than for solo firms. PRA Solvency II Rulebook, Transitional Measures section, http://www.prarulebook.co.uk/rulebook/Content/Chapter/213258/14-09-2016-213274*

Market conduct regulation is primarily carried out by the FCA, with rules set out **18** in the FCA Handbook, including general requirements for all regulated entities and specific chapters relating to insurance firms.

There are, in addition, compensation schemes set up to protect individual **19** policyholders for certain classes of business under the Financial Services Compensation Scheme (FSCS) (established under FSMA 2000), and the Motor Insurers' Bureau (established under the Road Traffic Act 1988). Insurers may be required to contribute to levies raised by these guarantee funds depending on the type of insurance business carried on. There are also competition and consumer affairs bodies, such as the Financial Ombudsman Service (which handles consumer complaints) and the Competition and Markets Authority.

ISA (UK) 250A requires the auditor to perform procedures to help identify **20** instances of non-compliance with other laws and regulations that may have a material effect on the financial statements. Specific areas that the auditor's procedures may address include the following:

- Obtaining a general understanding of the legal and regulatory framework applicable to the entity and industry, and of the procedures followed to ensure compliance with the framework.

- The insurer's compliance with prudential capital requirements (including applicable group capital requirements), including reporting to the PRA.

- The insurer's compliance with the scope of its permissions or any limits that may be specified in any Permission Notice issued by the PRA or FCA.

- Reviewing correspondence with the PRA, FCA and other regulators.

- Holding discussions with the insurer's regulatory compliance officer and other personnel responsible for compliance.

- Reviewing compliance reports prepared for the Board, audit committee and other committees.

- Consideration of work on compliance matters performed by internal audit.

- Results of any complaints monitoring procedures of the entity and any trends that may indicate conduct of business issues.

- Where an authorised insurer is a parent company, the impact of breaches of local laws and regulations on the trading status of the parent company, and of the overseas subsidiary/branch if they are likely to have a material effect on the financial statements of the parent company or group. Regard is also had to the powers of intervention exercisable by the relevant regulatory authorities and the potential impact on the group financial statements.

Taxation

The taxation of insurers and friendly societies is a complex area. Some friendly **21** societies are exempt from tax in respect of business other than long-term insurance and others are not. The treatment of long-term insurance business itself follows that for mutual life insurance companies but with a number of added complications. The most important of these is a society may claim to treat part of its business as "tax exempt".

For smaller friendly societies income and gains relating to policies issued may **22** qualify for exemption from tax. For policies taken out since 1995 this applies to life policies with an annual premium of up to £270 or £25 per month, and annuities of up to £156 per annum. The principles of life insurance taxation also require other classes of business to be separated and "ring-fenced". Each category has a different tax treatment. Societies have reporting responsibilities relating to the taxation of their policyholders, with severe penalties for errors. On the occasion of a transfer of engagements, it is important to check the impact on the tax status of the different business categories.

Money Laundering

23   Anti-money laundering legislation in the UK imposes a duty on the auditor to report suspected money laundering activity. There are similar laws and regulations relating to terrorist financing. The detailed legislation can be summarised as follows:

- Partners and staff in audit firms are required to report suspicions of conduct which would constitute a criminal offence which gives rise to direct or indirect benefit.

- Partners and staff in audit firms need to be alert to the dangers of "tipping off", as this will constitute a criminal offence under anti-money laundering legislation.

Further detail is set out in Practice Note 12 (Revised): *Money Laundering – Guidance for auditors on UK legislation.*

24   Authorised firms including insurers are subject to the requirements of the Money Laundering Regulations 2007 (as amended) and the Proceeds of Crime Act 2002 as well as FCA and PRA rules. These laws and regulations require institutions to establish and maintain procedures to identify their customers, establish appropriate reporting and investigation procedures for suspicious transactions, and maintain appropriate records.

25   Laws and regulations relating to money laundering are integral to the legal and regulatory framework within which insurers and friendly societies conduct their business. By the nature of their business, insurers are ready targets of those engaged in money laundering activities. The effect of this legislation is to make it an offence to provide assistance to those involved in money laundering and makes it an offence not to report suspicions of money laundering to the appropriate authorities, usually the National Crime Agency ("NCA"). FCA Handbook requirements[45] have due regard to compliance with the relevant provisions of guidance issued by the Joint Money Laundering Steering Group ("JMLSG").

26   In addition to considering whether an insurer has complied with the money laundering laws and regulations, the auditor has reporting obligations under the Proceeds of Crime Act, 2002 and the Money Laundering Regulations, 2007 (as amended) to report knowledge or suspicion of money laundering offences, including those arising from fraud and theft, to the NCA. The auditor is aware of the prohibition on "tipping off" when discussing money laundering matters with the insurer. Given the nature of insurance business and the likely frequency of needing to report to the NCA the auditor is aware of the guidance issued by the United Kingdom Financial Intelligence Unit (UKFIU) for submitting Suspicious Activity Reports to the NCA.[46]

---

[45] *FCA Handbook, SYSC 3.2.6 (a)–(k)*

[46] *http://www.nationalcrimeagency.gov.uk/publications/517-submitting-a-suspicious-activity-report-sar-within-the-regulated-sector/file*

The auditor, in the context of money laundering, is aware of the auditor's duty to   **27**
report direct to FCA and/or PRA in certain circumstances (see the section of this
Practice Note relating to ISA (UK) 250 Section B).

ISA (UK) 250: SECTION B – THE AUDITOR'S STATUTORY RIGHT AND DUTY TO REPORT TO REGULATORS OF PUBLIC INTEREST ENTITIES AND REGULATORS OF OTHER ENTITIES IN THE FINANCIAL SECTOR

This ISA deals with the statutory right and duty of the auditor of a regulated entity
to bring information of which the auditor has become aware in the ordinary course
of performing work undertaken to the attention of the appropriate regulator as
soon as practicable.

Auditor's duty to report to supervisors

Under the 2001 Regulations[47] and (for auditors of Public Interest Entities) the   **28**
Audit Regulation[48], the auditor has duties in certain circumstances to make reports
to the regulator (supervisor, competent authority)[49]. These responsibilities are set
out in detail in the Regulatory context part of this Practice Note.

Conduct of the audit

The auditor ensures that all staff involved in the audit of a regulated entity have an   **29**
understanding of:

(a)   The provisions of applicable legislation;

(b)   The regulator's rules and any guidance issued by the regulator; and

(c)   Any specific requirements which apply to the regulated entity, appropriate to
      their role in the audit and sufficient (in the context of that role) to enable
      them to identify situations they encounter which may give reasonable cause
      to require that a matter be reported to the regulator.[50]

Understanding, commensurate with the individual's role and responsibilities in the   **30**
audit process, is required of:

(a)   The provisions of the 2001 Regulations concerning the auditor's duty to
      report to the regulator, and the provisions of the Audit Regulation in respect
      of Public Interest Entities;

(b)   The standards and guidance in ISA (UK) 250 Section B, and in this section
      of this Practice Note;

(c)   Relevant sections of the FCA Handbook and the PRA Rulebook, including
      the Principles for Businesses and the Threshold Conditions; and

(d)   In the context of Lloyd's syndicates, the Audit Arrangements Byelaw
      (AAB), the relevant requirements established by the Council of Lloyd's.

The auditor includes procedures within its planning process to ensure that   **31**
members of the audit team have such understanding (in the context of their
role) as to enable them to recognise potentially reportable matters, and that such
matters are reported to the audit engagement partner without delay so that a
decision may be made as to whether a duty to report arises.

---

[47]   SI 2001 No 2587 "The FSMA 2000 (Communications by Auditors) Regulations 2001".

[48]   EU 537/2014.

[49]   Regulation (EU) No 537/2014 of the European Parliament and of the Council of 16 April 2014.

[50]   ISA (UK) 250 Section B (Revised June 2016), para. 11.

32   An audit firm appointed as auditor of a regulated entity needs to have in place appropriate procedures to ensure that the audit engagement partner is made aware of any other relationship which exists between any department of the firm and the regulated entity which could affect the firm's work as auditor. The auditor also requests the regulated entity to advise it when the entity appoints a third party (including another department or office of the same firm) to review, investigate or report on any aspects of its business activities that may be relevant to the audit of the financial statements and to provide the auditor with copies of reports by such a third party promptly after their receipt. This matter may usefully be referred to in the engagement letter.

Closely linked entities

33   Where the auditor of a regulated entity is also auditor of a closely linked entity[51], a duty to report arises directly in relation to information relevant to the regulated entity of which the auditor becomes aware in the course of its work as auditor of the closely linked entity.

34   The auditor establishes during audit planning whether the regulated entity has one or more closely linked entities of which the audit firm is also the auditor. If there are such entities the auditor considers the significance of the closely linked entities and the nature of the issues that might arise which may be of material significance to the regulator of the regulated entity. Such circumstances may involve:

(a)   Activities or uncertainties within the closely linked entity which might significantly impair the financial position of the regulated entity;

(b)   Money laundering; and, if the closely linked entity is itself regulated;

(c)   Matters that the auditor of the closely linked entity is intending to report to its regulator.

35   The auditor of the regulated entity identifies the closely related entities for which the procedures in this paragraph are necessary. The engagement team of the regulated entity communicates to the engagement team of the closely linked entities the audit firm's responsibilities to report to the regulators under applicable law and regulation. The engagement team also explains the circumstances that have been identified which, if they exist, might be of material significance to the regulator of the regulated entity. Prior to completion the auditor of the regulated entity obtains details from the auditor of the closely linked entity of such circumstances or confirmation, usually in writing, that such circumstances do not exist. Where the closely linked entities are part of the inter-auditor group reporting process these steps can be built into that process.

36   In circumstances where it is not the auditor of the closely linked entity, the auditor of the regulated entity decides whether there are any matters to be reported to the regulator relating to the affairs of the regulated entity in the light of the information that it receives about a closely linked entity for the purpose of auditing the financial statements of the regulated entity. If the auditor becomes aware of possible matters to be reported, the auditor may wish to obtain further information from the management or auditor of the closely linked entity to ascertain whether

---

[51] *An entity has close links with an authorised person for this purpose if the entity is a:*

(a)   *Parent undertaking of an authorised person;*

(b)   *Subsidiary undertaking of an authorised person;*

(c)   *Parent undertaking of a subsidiary undertaking of an authorised person; or*

(d)   *Subsidiary undertaking of a parent undertaking of an authorised person.*

the matter should be reported. To facilitate such possible discussions, at the planning stage of the audit, the auditor of the regulated entity will have considered whether arrangements need to be put in place to allow the auditor to communicate with the management and auditor of the closely linked entity. If the auditor of the regulated entity is unable to communicate with the management and auditor of the closely linked entity to obtain further information concerning the matters it has identified the auditor of the regulated entity reports those matters, and that it has been unable to obtain further information, direct to the regulator.

Information received in a capacity other than as auditor

There may be circumstances where it is not clear whether information about a **37** regulated entity coming to the attention of the auditor is received in the capacity of auditor or in some other capacity, for example as a general adviser to the entity. Appendix 2 to ISA (UK) 250 Section B provides guidance as to how information obtained in non-audit work may be relevant to the auditor in the planning and conduct of the audit and the steps that need to be taken to ensure the communication of information that is relevant to the audit.

Discussing matters of material significance with the Directors or Committee of Management

The Directors or (in the case of friendly societies) the Committee of Management, **38** are the persons responsible for the management of the regulated entity. The auditor will, therefore, normally bring a matter of material significance to the attention of the directors, subject to compliance with legislation relating to "tipping off", and seek agreement on the facts and circumstances. However, ISA (UK) 250 Section B emphasises that where the auditor concludes that a duty to report arises it should bring the matter to the attention of the regulator without undue delay. Where the matters identified are reported to the regulator by the directors, it does not relieve the auditor of the statutory duty to report directly to the regulator.

Timing of a report

The duty to report arises once the auditor has concluded that it reasonably believes **39** that the matter is or is likely to be of material significance to the regulator's regulatory function. In reaching its conclusion the auditor may wish to take appropriate legal or other advice and consult with colleagues.

The report should be made without undue delay once a conclusion has been **40** reached. Unless the matter casts doubt on the integrity of the directors this should not preclude discussion of the matter with the directors and seeking such further advice as is necessary, so that a decision can be made on whether or not a duty to report exists. Such consultations and discussions are, however, undertaken on a timely basis to enable the auditor to conclude on the matter without undue delay.

Auditor's right to report to the regulator

Section 342 FSMA 2000 provides that no duty to which an auditor of an **41** authorised person is subject shall be contravened by communicating in good faith to the regulator information or an opinion on a matter that the auditor reasonably believes is relevant to any functions of the regulator. For this purpose, "authorised person" is deemed to include a Lloyd's syndicate.

The scope of the duty to report is wide since, under the PRA's Fundamental Rule 7 **42** and the FCA's Principle for Businesses 11, an authorised firm must disclose to the regulator anything relating to the authorised firm of which the regulator would reasonably expect notice. However, in circumstances where the auditor concludes that a matter does not give rise to a statutory duty to report but nevertheless should be brought to the attention of the regulator it advises the directors of its opinion. Where the auditor is unable to obtain, within a reasonable period, adequate evidence that the directors have properly informed the regulator of the matter, then the auditor makes a report to the regulator without undue delay.

43 The auditor may wish to take legal advice before deciding whether, and in what form, to exercise its right to make a report direct to the regulator in order to ensure, for example, that only relevant information is disclosed and that the form and content of its report is such as to secure the protection of FSMA 2000. However, the auditor recognises that legal advice will take time and that speed of reporting is likely to be important in order to protect the interests of customers and/or to enable the regulator to meet its statutory objectives.

ISA (UK) 265: COMMUNICATING DEFICIENCIES IN INTERNAL CONTROL TO THOSE CHARGED WITH GOVERNANCE AND MANAGEMENT

ISA (UK) 265 deals with the responsibilities of the auditor when communicating deficiencies in internal control to those charged with governance and management.

44 The auditor of a friendly society considers ISA (UK) 265 in the context of

(a) The report on internal control exceptions prepared by management under the FCA's Interim Prudential Sourcebook [IPRU(FSOC) rule 3.1(7) (non-directive societies)]; and

(b) The possibility that the society may wish to provide a written communication to a third party such as the regulator.

45 A non-directive society's responsibility to prepare a Rule 3.1 report will be relevant to the timing of communications to those charged with governance.

46 The auditor has no reporting duty to the regulator in connection with the Rule 3.1 report. However, during the audit the auditor enquires as to the society's progress with identifying and updating matters to be reported and discusses them with management in order to assess their impact, if any, on its audit of the financial statements. The auditor considers whether such weaknesses in internal control that have been identified by management have been communicated to those charged with governance.

ISA (UK) 300: PLANNING AN AUDIT OF FINANCIAL STATEMENTS

47 ISA (UK) 300 deals with the responsibilities of auditors in respect of planning an audit of financial statements. Particular issues likely to require consideration in planning the audit of an insurance entity are:

(a) The need to involve auditor's experts. The nature and complexity of insurance businesses increases the likelihood that the auditor may consider it necessary, in order to obtain sufficient appropriate evidence on which to base its report, to involve auditor's experts in the audit process. For example, the auditor may wish to rely on the work of an actuary or a statistician to assist its consideration of an insurer's technical provisions: that actuary may be engaged as an auditor's expert or as a specialist in accordance with paragraph b depending on the nature of the engagement.

[See "Auditor's internal and external experts" at the end of this section of the Practice Note] Other auditor's experts the auditor may consider involving include regulatory, investment, tax and systems specialists. Consequently, the auditor of an insurer considers the need to involve such auditor's experts at an early stage in planning its work. Where such auditor's experts are to be used, they may take part in discussions with the insurer's management and staff, in order to assist in the development of knowledge and understanding relating to the insurer's business. As part of the planning process the auditor agrees in advance the scope of work of the auditor's actuarial and other experts, including the scope of their reports;

(b)　The need to include in the engagement team persons using expertise in a specialised area of accounting or auditing, whether engaged or employed by the auditing firm who performs audit procedures on the engagement. The application of relevant tax legislation is likely to be complex, and hence the auditor may wish to involve a tax specialist to assist the consideration of provisions for corporation and other taxes included in an insurer's financial statements for the purposes of the audit; and

(c)　The effect of delegated authorities granted by the insurer, and the sources of evidence available to the auditor for transactions undertaken by those to whom such authority has been given. The auditor of an insurer considers the implications of delegated authorities in planning its work, including the existence of delegated underwriting authority by agents or others on behalf of the entity. This may include the outsourcing of certain functions, such as investment management or the delegation of authority to underwrite and/or administer business, and to process and/ or settle claims.

Further guidance in respect of the matters set out at (a) and (b) above are included **48** separately in this Practice Note. Guidance in respect of delegated authorities as set out in (c) above is included in the section dealing with ISA (UK) 402: *Audit Considerations Relating to an Entity Using a Service Organization.*

In view of its responsibility to report on regulatory returns or audit published **49** SFCRs for "directive" firms, the auditor of an authorised insurer or friendly society may plan its work so as to carry out procedures necessary both to form an opinion on the financial statements and to report on matters included in the regulatory returns in an efficient and effective manner. The audits of the statutory financial statements and published SFCRs are nevertheless standalone audits under ISAs (UK), and any procedures carried out to cover both requirements need to be clearly documented to support both audit conclusions.

Actuarial Function

The Solvency II prudential regulation regime came into force from 1 January **50** 2016. The PRA's rulebook reflects the different requirements for Directive and non-Directive firms. This includes relevant rules in respect of the establishment of an actuarial function under Solvency II.

For Directive firms, PRA rules[52] require that: **51**

(1)　A firm must provide for an effective actuarial function to:

(a)　coordinate the calculation of technical provisions;

---

[52] *PRA SII Firms Rulebook, Conditions Governing Business: Actuarial Function: 6.1. http://www.prarulebook.co. uk/rulebook/Content/Chapter/212975/14-09-2016*

(b) ensure the appropriateness of the methodologies and underlying models used, as well as the assumptions made in the calculation of technical provisions;

(c) assess the sufficiency and quality of the data used in the calculation of technical provisions;

(d) compare the best estimate against experience;

(e) inform the governing body of the reliability and adequacy of the calculation of technical provisions;

(f) oversee the calculation of technical provisions;

(g) express an opinion on the overall underwriting policy;

(h) express an opinion on the adequacy of reinsurance arrangements; and

(i) contribute to the effective implementation of the risk-management system ... in particular with respect to the risk modelling underlying the calculation of the SCR and MCR and to the firm's ORSA.

(2) The actuarial function must be carried out by persons who have knowledge of actuarial and financial mathematics, commensurate with the nature, scale and complexity of the risks inherent in the firm's business, and who are able to demonstrate their relevant experience with applicable professional and other standards.

52 There is no identical requirement for the population of non-Directive firms. However, paragraph 52 (3) of Schedule 3 of the Large and Medium-sized Companies and Groups (Accounts and Reports) (SI 2008/410) requires that calculation by (within scope) firms of technical provisions:

> ... *must be made annually by a Fellow of the Institute and Faculty of Actuaries on the basis of recognised actuarial methods.*[53]

53 The auditor discusses elements of its audit plan with the actuary established under the relevant regulation, in order to ensure that its audit procedures have regard to the actuary's work. Where the insurer appoints a separate actuary to fulfil the duties of the actuarial function holder or the with-profits actuary in relation to the insurer's regulatory obligations, the auditor also considers the need for liaison with these individuals.

ISA (UK) 315: IDENTIFYING AND ASSESSING THE RISKS OF MATERIAL MISSTATEMENT THROUGH UNDERSTANDING THE ENTITY AND ITS ENVIRONMENT

ISA (UK) 315 sets out the responsibilities of an auditor in respect of identifying and assessing the risks of material misstatement.

54 Insurers and friendly societies may be complex and the auditor seeks to understand the business environment and the regulatory regime in which they operate.

Business factors

55 It is important for the auditor to understand the multi-dimensional nature and extent of the financial and business risks which are integral to the environment,

---

[53] http://www.legislation.gov.uk/uksi/2008/410/pdfs/uksi_20080410_en.pdf

and how the insurer's systems record and address these risks. Although they may apply to varying degrees, the risks include (but are not limited to):

- Underwriting or insurance risk: which is inherent in any insurance business but will be influenced by, for example, the classes of business underwritten, new products or services introduced and guarantees given.

- Credit risk: at its simplest, this is the risk that a third party will be unable to meet its obligations (for example, recoveries from reinsurers).

- Liquidity risk: the risk that arises from the possibility that an insurer has insufficient liquid funds to meet claims.

- Market risk: the risk that changes in the value of assets, liabilities and commitments will occur as a result of movements in relative prices (for example, as a result of changes in the market price of tradable assets).

- Interest rate risk (a subset of market risk): the risk that arises where there is a mismatch between the interest rate reset dates or bases used for asset and liability measurement.

- Currency risk: the risk that arises from the mismatching of assets, liabilities and commitments denominated in different currencies.

- Pension obligation risk: the risk that the insurer's obligations towards its pension schemes may lead to the insurer not being able to pay its other liabilities as they fall due; and the risk that an increase in the funding requirements results in a significant reduction in the insurer's capital resources.

- Operational risk: the risk of loss, arising from inadequate or failed internal processes, people or systems or from external events, including legal risk and risks associated with the secure management and use of data.

- Regulatory risk: the risk of public censure, fines (together with related compensation payments) and restriction or withdrawal of authorisation to conduct some or all of the insurer's activities.

- Failure to manage the risks outlined above can also cause serious damage to an insurer's reputation, potentially leading to loss of confidence in the insurer's business.

When obtaining an understanding of the insurer's business, the auditor considers, for example: **56**

- The methods by which business is transacted including whether the insurer participates with others in contracts for large commercial risks, and if so whether it transacts business as "leader" in such contracts or as a "follower".

- The characteristics of its insurance products, including those written in previous years where exposure remains.

- The introduction of new categories of products or customers or distribution channels.

- The reinsurance arrangements.

- The complexity of the insurer's information systems.

- The legal and operational structure of the insurer.

- The number and location of branches.

- The regulatory capital position.

- Changes in the market environment (for example, a marked increase in competition).

- Relevant economic developments.

- Developments in relevant legislation and changes resulting from new judicial decisions.

57 Insurance policies written in previous years may continue to have an impact upon insurers' financial statements in subsequent years. For example, for general insurance business the terms of the insurance cover provided and the reinsurance arrangements in force in a previous year are factors involved in the determination of technical provisions not only in the year in which the claims are incurred, but also in subsequent periods if the original estimates of the claims in question change. Similarly for life assurance business guarantees and options and other policyholder promises made on the issue of policies in prior years will be one of the key factors in determining estimates for related technical provisions.

Regulatory Factors

58 In obtaining an understanding of the regulatory factors the auditor considers, for example:

- Any formal communications between the FCA and PRA in their capacity as the regulators and the insurer, including any new or interim risk assessments issued and the results of any other supervisory visits conducted.

- The contents of any recent reports prepared by "skilled persons" under section 166 of FSMA 2000 together with any correspondence, minutes or notes of meetings relevant to any recent skilled persons' report.

- Any formal communications between the insurer and other regulators.

- Discussions with the insurer's regulatory compliance officer together with others responsible for monitoring regulatory compliance [established under the PRA's Senior Insurance Managers Regime and/or the Solvency II Key Functions requirements].

Accounting Policies

59 The application of complex accounting standards such as IAS 32 and 39, IFRS 4, 7 and 9 (for insurers using IFRSs) and FRS 103 (for insurers using UK GAAP) may also give rise to significant risk. This arises from the classification, recognition and measurement of insurance and investment contracts, the classification and measurement of financial assets, hedge accounting, classification of assets/liabilities, revenue/expense recognition. In addition significant risk may arise from the adequacy of financial statement disclosures, notably in respect of insurance and financial risk management. Risks may also arise in relation to regulatory requirements by creating incentives for particularly accounting treatments or classifications to achieve a regulatory outcome.

60 Accounting policies of particular relevance may include those in relation to insurance and investment contracts, embedded derivatives in insurance contracts, deferred acquisition costs, classification of assets and liabilities (and thereby their measurement) and revenue recognition (including investment management service contracts).

Internal Controls

ISA (UK) 315 requires the auditor to obtain an understanding of internal controls **61** relevant to the audit. As part of that understanding, the auditor shall evaluate their design and determine whether they have been implemented.

The PRA's Senor Insurance Managers Regime (SIMR) establishes a requirement **62** for UK insurers to identify key functions and function holders in the business. These requirements are similar but not identical to the "key functions" identified by the Solvency II Framework Directive for Directive firms. Overall the following key functions should be identifiable within the insurance entity:

- the risk management function;

- compliance function;

- internal audit function;

- actuarial function.

- the investment function (accordingly, investment managers would be key function holders);

- the claims management function (especially in general or health insurance firms);

- the IT function; and

- the reinsurance function (where this role is different to other key functions such as risk management).

The quality of the overall control environment is dependent upon management's **63** attitude towards the operation of controls. A positive attitude may be evidenced by an organisational framework which enables proper segregation of duties and delegation of control functions and which encourages failings to be reported and corrected. Thus, where a lapse in the operation of a control is treated as a matter of concern, the control environment will be stronger and will contribute to effective control systems; whereas a weak control environment will undermine detailed controls, however well designed. The systems of control need to have regard to the requirements of the FCA handbook and the PRA rulebook (for both Directive and non-Directive firms). Although the directors are required to certify that they are satisfied that throughout the financial year the insurer has complied in all material respects with these requirements, auditors of insurers do not have responsibility for reporting on whether systems of control meet regulatory requirements.

Systems of internal control of an insurer are important in ensuring orderly and **64** prudent operations of the insurer and in assisting the directors to prepare financial statements which give a true and fair view. The following features of the business of insurers may be relevant to the auditor's assessment of such internal controls:

- The substantial scale of transactions, both in terms of volume and relative value, makes it important that control systems are in place to ensure that transactions are recorded promptly, accurately and completely and are checked and approved, and that records are reconciled at appropriate intervals in order to identify and investigate differences promptly. Processing and accounting for complex transactions or high volumes of less complex transactions will involve the use of information technology. For example, transactions subject to "straight through processing" involve little or no manual intervention after they have been initiated.

- Proper segregation of duties between those writing the risks, those responsible for establishing claims provisions, those responsible for claims handling, those responsible for claims settlement and those recording these transactions, is particularly important.

- Equally as important is the proper segregation of duties between and amongst those responsible for the purchase and sale of investments, those recording these transactions and those responsible for the physical security over the documents of title.

- The geographical location of some insurers' operations means that, in order to maintain control over its activities, insurers need to ensure not only that there are sufficient controls at each location, but also that there are effective communication and control procedures between the various locations and the centre.

- The activities of insurers can result in the use of complex insurance or reinsurance transactions. The assessment as to whether such transactions transfer risk poses risks of misstatement. Consequently, insurers will normally have developed important operational controls to mitigate such risks of misstatement.

- The provisions of UK tax legislation are complex for insurers. Accordingly, an effective control system is essential to ensure that the record-keeping requirements of UK tax legislation are satisfied, and that tax is accounted for promptly and accurately. Similar measures may be needed to address provisions arising in any other jurisdictions where the insurer operates.

- The UK regulatory framework is complex for insurers. This may give rise to significant liabilities for compensation to policyholders if not properly dealt with. Accordingly, an effective control system is essential to ensure that the requirements of the UK regulators are satisfied. Measures may also be needed to address regulators in other jurisdictions.

Insurer Risk Assessments

65   Insurers and friendly societies will normally be required to produce assessments of their capital requirement, including for Solvency II Directive firms an Own Risk and Solvency Assessment (ORSA). These assessments are designed to quantify risks specific to the entity and to generate and quantify an estimated capital requirement for the entity, and include an assessment of operational risk. The auditor will normally review such documentation in assessing the insurer's approach to addressing risks.

Control Activities

66   The ISA requires that auditors:

> ... shall obtain an understanding of control activities relevant to the audit, being those the auditor judges it necessary to understand in order to assess the risks of material misstatement at the assertion level and design further audit procedures responsive to assessed risks. An audit does not require an understanding of all the control activities related to each significant class of transactions, account balance, and disclosure in the financial statements or to every assertion relevant to them.[54]

---

[54] *ISA (UK) 315 (Revised June 2016), para. 20.*

There can be no standard approach to internal controls and risk. The auditor 67
assesses the adequacy of controls in relation to the circumstances of each entity.
Examples of deficiencies in internal control that may be relevant to the auditor's
assessment of the risk of material misstatement are as follows:

- Complex products or processes inadequately understood by management;
  this includes undue concentration of expertise concerning matters requiring
  the exercise of significant judgment or capable of manipulation such as
  valuations of financial instruments, insurance or reinsurance contracts.

- Deficiencies in back office procedures undermining the completeness and
  accuracy of accounting records.

- Deficiencies in new product approval procedures.

- Backlogs in key reconciliations.

- Inadequate maintenance of suspense or clearing accounts.

- Delays in the processing of premiums and claims.

In the case of small insurers the activities and products supplied may be relatively 68
simple or uniform and the segregation of duties may be less sophisticated or less
well developed. The degree to which the auditor decides to test and rely on internal
controls may be limited.

> Controls relating to outsourcing activities are considered in the ISA (UK)
> 402 section of this Practice Note.

> In understanding the entity's control activities, the auditor shall obtain an
> understanding of how the entity has responded to risks arising from IT.[55]

As a result of the type and complexity of transactions undertaken, and records 69
held, by insurers and the need for swift and accurate information processing and
retrieval, many insurers are highly automated, including: the accounting function,
the processing of premiums, reinsurance and claims, regulatory reporting and the
supply of management information.

In addition to providing a basis for preparation of the financial statements and 70
meeting requirements for maintenance of adequate accounting records, a key
feature of the information systems maintained by an insurer is the importance of
reliable historical statistical data to operate the business. Historical statistical data
is important, for example, in calculating technical provisions, and for providing
analyses for regulatory returns.

Characteristics of IT systems in the insurance industry include: 71

(a) High volumes of transactions flowing through IT systems

(b) Complex systems, often with multiple systems for different products or
    transaction cycles (premiums, claims), reinsurance, financial instruments
    etc.

(c) A history of consolidation in the industry yet underlying legacy systems
    have remained.

(d) High degree of reliance on spreadsheets or models, often not managed by IT
    but by business departments.

---

[55] *ISA (UK) 315 (Revised June 2016), para. 21.*

72   An effective control system over the administration of insurance business will therefore seek to ensure the accurate collation, processing and storing of large volumes of data relating, for example, to:

- Acceptance of risk.

- Recording of policy details.

- Collection of premiums.

- Recording, investigation, evaluation and payment of claims.

- Identification of classes of business required to be disclosed in the insurer's regulatory returns.

- Transfer of data from the administration systems to systems used for calculating technical provisions.

73   The auditor assesses the extent, nature and impact of automation within the insurer and plans and performs work accordingly. In particular the auditor considers:

(a)   The required level of IT knowledge and skills – these may be extensive and may require the auditor to obtain advice and assistance from staff with specialist skills;

(b)   The extent of the application of audit software and related audit techniques;

(c)   General controls relating to the environment within which IT based systems are developed, maintained and operated; and

(d)   General controls around data integrity and security.

ISA (UK) 320: MATERIALITY IN PLANNING AND PERFORMING AN AUDIT

74   The principles of assessing materiality in the audit of an insurer or friendly society are the same as those applying to the audit of any other entity. In particular the auditor's consideration of materiality is a matter of professional judgment, and is affected by the auditor's perception of the common information needs of users as a group. ISA (UK) 320 states that:

> When establishing the overall audit strategy, the auditor shall determine materiality for the financial statements as a whole. If, in the specific circumstances of the entity, there is one or more particular classes of transactions, account balances or disclosures for which misstatement of lesser amounts than materiality for the financial statements as a whole could reasonably be expected to influence the economic decisions of users taken on the basis of the financial statements, the auditor shall also determine the materiality level or levels to be applied to those particular classes of transactions, account balances or disclosures.[56]

75   One key difference of an insurer or friendly society from many other entities is that balance sheet balances tend to be much larger compared to the income statement, so that the application of materiality based on income may be too low when auditing some aspects of elements of the balance sheet.

76   The auditor typically uses materiality based on the income statement if a misstatement in a balance sheet item could affect the income statement or equity and reserves. If, however, a misstatement in a balance sheet item is likely only to lead to a reclassification between line items within assets and

---

[56] *ISA (UK) 320 Materiality in Planning and Performing an Audit, (Revised June 2016), para. 10.*

liabilities, a higher materiality level can be applied for identifying and evaluating such misstatements only.

When applying a higher balance sheet materiality level for the purpose of **77** identifying and evaluating the effect of such misclassifications the auditor considers other relevant factors such as:

- The extent any misstatement of these items would influence the economic decisions of users taken on the basis of the financial statements.

- The extent any misstatement of these items would affect users' expectations regarding the measurement or disclosure of these items.

- The effect of the classification misstatement on debt or other contractual covenants.

- The effect on individual line items or sub-totals.

- The effect on key ratios.

Examples of items which may have little or no direct effect on an insurer's income **78** may include:

- Reinsurance arrangements that are entered into to reduce the impact of claims on shareholders' funds. The balance sheet of an insurer is required to include the gross amount of technical provisions within liabilities and any reinsurers' shares of technical provisions within assets. However, a misstatement in the recording of these gross assets and liabilities will have a much lesser effect on the insurer's income statement because the insurer does not bear all of the costs of claims.

- Revenue errors on with-profits business will ordinarily have no impact on income for the year as income is determined by the amount of the bonus distribution.

- Where liabilities of an insurer are determined directly by reference to the value of assets held (e.g. for unit linked business) any misstatement in such liabilities may be offset by a corresponding misstatement in the associated assets (and vice versa).

In the case of many classes of insurance business, uncertainty relating to the **79** ultimate cost of claims is an inherent feature of the business. As a result, whilst quantitative measures of materiality are of assistance in directing the focus of the auditor's work, qualitative factors relating to the extent and nature of disclosures in the financial statements will also be of importance. Where such uncertainty is considered to be significant, insurance entity auditors consider the disclosures made in the financial statements, and the effect upon the auditor's report. This matter is dealt with in the sections in this Practice Note covering ISAs (UK) 450, 540 and 705.

ISA (UK) 330: THE AUDITOR'S RESPONSES TO ASSESSED RISKS

ISA (UK) 330 deals with the auditor's responsibilities to design and implement responses to the assessed risks of material misstatement. The ISA states that:

> The auditor shall design and perform tests of control to obtain sufficient appropriate audit evidence as to the operating effectiveness of relevant controls if:

> (a)　The auditor's assessment of risk of material misstatement at the assertion level includes an expectation that the controls are operating effectively (i.e., the auditor intends to rely on the operating effectiveness of controls in determining the nature, timing and extent of substantive procedures); or
>
> (b)　Substantive procedures alone cannot provide sufficient appropriate audit evidence at the assertion level.[57]

80　In practice the nature and volume of transactions relating to the operations of insurers often means that performing tests of relevant controls is the most efficient means of reducing audit risk to an acceptably low level.

81　Specific accounting standards can require extensive narrative disclosures in the financial statements of insurers; for example, in relation to the nature and extent of risks arising from contracts. In designing and performing procedures to evaluate these disclosures the auditor obtains audit evidence regarding the assertions about presentation and disclosure described in paragraph A124–124a of ISA (UK) 315.[58]

Insurance transactions

82　When considering the completeness and accuracy of processing of insurance transactions, the auditor has regard to the multiple purposes for which an insurer will use data entered into its accounting records. Such data may be used not only for inclusion in the financial statements, but may also be included in the regulatory returns of the insurer and be used as the basis for statistical analysis and extrapolation of past trends and transactions in assessing technical provisions. Errors in the data input may therefore have far reaching impact on the overall reported results. Data input required for such other purposes may therefore require additional detail or higher levels of accuracy of coding and allocation compared with those which might be required solely for the preparation of reliable financial statements.

83　For insurance transactions initiated by the insurer, the auditor considers the controls implemented for each material class of business and location, together with overall controls applied by the accounting function and management. Matters for consideration will include the procedures for the setting of and monitoring of compliance with guidelines for underwriting and product development, and controls over completeness of transactions and risks undertaken. Insurers often transact very large volumes of transactions which are subject to extensive IT controls, so the use of computer-assisted audit techniques may be appropriate.

84　The auditor of an insurer also has regard to the procedures implemented by the insurer to ensure the completeness, accuracy and reliability of information provided by third parties, including intermediaries and agents. The auditor assesses the effectiveness of management's controls implemented to ensure that all risks bound by agents under delegated authorities have been included. Procedures include reviewing the insurer's procedures for the approval of such arrangements and the monitoring of the performance of business introduced through such contracts. These may include inspections by the insurer or third parties of the agent's underwriting activities, records and reports to the insurer.

85　The auditor reviews the contractual terms, and assess the extent to which such agents are reporting transactions on a regular and prompt basis and whether the

---

[57] *ISA (UK) 330, The Auditor's Responses to Assessed Risks, (Revised June 2016), para. 8.*

[58] *ISA (UK) 315, Identifying and Assessing the Risks of Material Misstatement Through Understanding the Entity and its Environment, (Revised June 2016).*

insurer has completely and accurately recorded the reported transactions in the accounting records and statistical databases. Specific consideration will be paid to the terms of the agent's remuneration to ensure for example that all profit commission and expenses recovery entitlements have been recognised.

Where significant insurance risks are underwritten through treaty reinsurance **86** contracts, the nature and complexity of the risks written may differ substantially from those written by the insurer directly. The auditor ascertains the insurer's procedures for approving such contracts, whether relevant transactions are reported regularly and promptly (commonly monthly or quarterly), and whether the insurer has included all such transactions in the accounting records.

Reinsurers maintain records of all treaties and may receive regular statements from **87** the cedant of premiums received, claims paid and other data relating to the treaty. The reinsurer may be reliant upon the cedant's statements to maintain accounting records of the underlying treaty transactions.

Although a reinsurer may have contractual rights to inspect a cedant's books, it is **88** not uncommon for directors to construct the financial records of the reinsurer from cedant statements. The auditor may obtain evidence that controls in relation to treaty reinsurance exist to ensure that:

(a) Statements from the ceding insurer are received and processed on a regular basis;

(b) Statements are reconciled to the reinsurer's accounting records where appropriate; and

(c) A procedure exists for the regular review of major treaty results.

An important aspect of an insurer's controls over completeness and accuracy of **89** processing will often be its procedures for the reconciliation of balances with third parties, the settlement of transactions (including their correction where necessary) and the agreement and clearance of old items. Third parties will include policyholders, brokers, underwriting agents and reinsurers, and procedures may vary for each category. The auditor reviews the insurer's processes and monitoring procedures established to ascertain whether such reconciliations and settlements are up to date. The auditor pays particular attention to the use of suspense or similar accounts, and to whether they are reconciled and cleared regularly and promptly.

A significant issue in the audit of insurers is the assessment of whether or not **90** contracts to which the insurers are party should be accounted for as contracts of insurance (or reinsurance). In forming this assessment accounting conventions may require consideration of the level of insurance risk transferred.

The auditor obtains sufficient, appropriate audit evidence that insurers have **91** properly assessed the level of insurance risk for the purpose of determining whether material contracts or groups of contracts should be accounted for as insurance (or reinsurance), taking into account the applicable accounting requirements.

In evaluating the insurer's mechanism for assessing the level of insurance risk, the **92** auditor may consider the following:

● The process adopted by the insurer.

● The likelihood of loss falling to both insurer and reinsurer under different loss scenarios and the probability of occurrence of the scenarios selected for this exercise.

- The cash flow implications under different loss scenarios.
- Any penalty, default or adjustable clauses in the contract.
- The existence and operation of any experience account.
- The existence and operation of other arrangements, whether or not described as reinsurance, that have the effect of limiting the risk transferred by the reinsurance arrangement under review.

Reinsurance

93 When considering the impact of the insurer's reinsurance arrangements on the financial statements the auditor obtains an understanding of the reinsurance programme, including both facultative and treaty arrangements. The auditor assesses the procedures for the approval of reinsurance contracts, both in overall terms and in detail.

94 Reinsurance contracts can be complex, and a detailed understanding of individual significant contracts and their inter-relationship with others, as well as an understanding of the programme in total, will be necessary for the auditor to conclude whether the accounting treatment is appropriate and consistent with the substance of the transactions.

95 In addition to considering the controls on the purchasing of reinsurance, the auditor considers the controls exercised by the insurer to ensure that all reinsurance recoveries to which it is entitled have been identified, correctly calculated and collected. As with reinsurance cost, the auditor uses its detailed understanding of the relevant reinsurance contracts to assess whether the appropriate accounting treatment has been followed.

96 An important aspect of the uncertainty to which a particular insurer is exposed is the nature and extent of its reinsurance programme. The auditor considers the nature and coverage of any significant reinsurance programmes and, where material, the procedures adopted by the directors or managing agent to determine the financial stability of reinsurers used. The auditor normally considers the operation of significant reinsurance programmes by reviewing whether the risks ceded and the resulting premium and expense information are in accordance with the reinsurance contract. The auditor may also consider the procedures in place for ensuring that material claims or balances, if any, disputed by reinsurers are resolved. Evidence may be obtained by reviewing correspondence with reinsurers or intermediaries and considering the quality and timeliness of reconciliations of reinsurer balances.

97 The auditor also uses its understanding of the insurer's reinsurance protection programme to assess the extent to which it is appropriate to recognise credit for reinsurance recoveries within the technical provisions. In its consideration the auditor tests the matching of reinsurance recoveries against gross claims provisions to ensure consistency of treatment.

ISA (UK) 402: AUDIT CONSIDERATIONS RELATING TO AN ENTITY USING A SERVICE ORGANIZATION

ISA (UK) 402 deals with the auditor's responsibilities relating to an entity using a service organization. The key objectives are to:

> (a) To obtain an understanding of the nature and significance of the services provided by the service organization and their effect on the user entity's internal control relevant to the audit, sufficient to identify and assess the risks of material misstatement; and
>
> (b) To design and perform audit procedures responsive to those risks.[59]

In common with other industries the outsourcing of functions to service organizations by insurers has become common place. Insurers and friendly societies often find this the most economical arrangement, typically involving functions such as investment management, custody of investments and payroll. **98**

The relevant regulatory authorities deal with "outsourcing" or "delegation" arrangements quite extensively, including through the FCA Handbook and Solvency II implementation guidance. The FCA handbook defines outsourcing as "the use of a person to provide customised services to a firm" (other than a member of the firm's governing body or an individual employed by the firm) or "an arrangement of any form between a firm and a service provider by which that service provider performs a process, a service or an activity which would otherwise by undertaken by the firm itself". In the context of insurance entities this means that the "external delegation" of functions such as underwriting or claims handling fall within the definition of "outsourcing", in the same way as more common arrangements such as customer call centres, IT or other back office functions. **99**

The auditing standards define a "service organization" as a "third-party organisation (or segment of a third-party organization) that provides services to user entities that are part of those entities' information systems relevant to financial reporting".[60] The auditor, therefore, gains an understanding of the extent of outsourced functions and their relevance to the financial statements. The insurer is obliged by the FCA Handbook[61] to ensure that the auditor has appropriate access to data related to outsourced activities. **100**

Whilst an insurer or friendly society may outsource functions to service organizations the responsibility for these functions remains that of the insurer, both from the perspective of the financial statement audit and in respect of regulatory requirements. The insurer should have appropriate controls in place over these arrangements including: **101**

- Risk assessment prior to contracting with the service provider, which includes a proper due diligence and periodic review of the appropriateness of the arrangement.

- Appropriate contractual agreements or service level agreements.

- Contingency plans should the provider fail in delivery of services.

- Appropriate management information and reporting from the outsourced provider.

- Appropriate controls over customer information.

If the auditor is unable to obtain sufficient appropriate audit evidence concerning outsourced operations the auditor considers whether it is necessary to report the matter direct to the FCA or PRA. **102**

---

[59] *ISA (UK) 402, para. 7.*

[60] *ISA (UK) 402, para. 8e.*

[61] *FCA Handbook, SYSC 8.1.8 (9).*

ISA (UK) 450: EVALUATION OF MISSTATEMENTS IDENTIFIED DURING THE AUDIT

103   In the course of an audit of the financial statements of an insurance entity or friendly society, there may be circumstances where the auditor concludes that a classification misstatement is not material in the context of the financial statements as a whole. This may be the case even though the misstatement may exceed the materiality level or levels applied in evaluating other misstatements. ISA (UK) 450 states that:

> The auditor shall determine whether uncorrected misstatements are material, individually or in aggregate. In making this determination, the auditor shall consider:
>
> (a)   The size and nature of the misstatements, both in relation to particular classes of transactions, account balances or disclosures and the financial statements as a whole, and the particular circumstances of their occurrence[62]

104   A misclassification between balance sheet line items may not be considered material in the context of the financial statements as a whole when the amount of the misclassification is small in relation to the size of the related balance sheet line items and the misclassification does not affect the income statement or any key ratios. Such qualitative considerations may be relevant when considering certain misstatements in respect of insurers. For example:

- A misstatement of technical provisions may give rise to an offsetting misstatement in reinsurance recoveries to the extent the misstated liabilities have been reinsured.

- A misstatement in respect of revenue from with-profits business may have no direct impact on income where income is determined by the amount of the bonus distribution.

105   Where liabilities of an insurer are determined directly by reference to the value of assets held (e.g. for unit linked business) any misstatement in such liabilities may be offset by a corresponding misstatement in the associated assets (and vice versa).

ISA (UK) 505: EXTERNAL CONFIRMATIONS

ISA (UK) 505 sets out the auditor's responsibilities in respect of external confirmation procedures. ISA (UK) 330 The Auditor's Responses to Assessed Risks specifically requires auditor's to consider whether external confirmation procedures are to be performed as substantive audit procedures.[63]

106   In respect of the audit of insurance entities, including friendly societies, external confirmations may not always provide useful audit evidence in relation to insurance balances due to the relative immateriality of individual policyholder balances or transactions. However, external confirmation procedures may be useful as part of the audit of:

(a)   Amounts receivable from reinsurers in respect of claims paid or payable by the entity; and

(b)   Premiums receivable from intermediaries.

---

[62] *ISA (UK) 450 (Revised June 2016), para. 11a.*

[63] *ISA (UK) 330 (Revised June 2016), para. 19.*

Amounts receivable from reinsurers may comprise an insurer's calculation of **107** amounts that will be recoverable from reinsurers in respect of the insurer's estimate of incurred claims. The relevant reinsurers are unlikely to be in a position to confirm amounts in relation to these claims until such time as the validity of these claims has been assessed, the amounts payable determined, and this has been communicated to and agreed by the relevant reinsurers. Therefore the relevant reinsurers may not be able to provide sufficient appropriate evidence in response to a confirmation request that includes such amounts. The auditor may, however, determine that confirmation would be an effective procedure in respect of individual material reinsurance recoveries where the reinsurer has agreed the amount involved but the balance has not yet been paid.

In deciding to what extent to use external confirmations in respect of premiums **108** receivable from intermediaries, the auditor considers the assessed risk of misstatement together with the characteristics of the environment in which the insurer operates and the practice of potential respondents in dealing with requests for direct confirmation. For example where a captive insurer's premium income comprises solely an annual premium from its parent company and this is due at the year-end then this may be a significant balance and it may be assessed that the parent undertaking is likely to be able to respond to a confirmation request. In these circumstances the auditor may decide to seek positive confirmation from the parent undertaking. Conversely, where premiums receivable comprise a high volume of low value amounts which may be due from individuals or entities that do not have information systems that facilitate external confirmation, the auditor may decide that confirmation may not be an effective audit procedure and may seek to obtain sufficient appropriate evidence from other sources.

ISA (UK) 520: ANALYTICAL PROCEDURES

ISA (UK) 520 sets the responsibilities for auditors when using analytical procedures as a basis for the identification and assessment of risks of material misstatement; to obtain relevant and reliable substantive audit evidence; and to assist the auditor when forming an overall conclusion as to whether the financial statements are consistent with the auditor's understanding of the entity.

There are a number of potential analytical relationships which may be relevant to **109** the audit of an insurance entity or friendly society, and which the auditor may consider when complying with the requirements of this standard. They include, but may not be limited to the following circumstances:

- The deferral and matching principles applied by insurers mean that there are relationships between the movement in balance sheet items and specific items that affect income (for example deferred acquisition costs, claims provisions and unearned premiums provisions);

- There are likely to be expected relationships between a number of income statement items such as written and earned premiums, incurred claims and earned premiums and premiums and claims gross and reinsurers' share thereof.

The nature of the insurance business means that data supporting financial **110** reporting, and which may be critical to the successful completion of analytical procedures, may have been collected over a long period of time, drawn from legacy systems or simply a diverse range of current operational systems. Poor data management may have a significant impact on the operations of insurance businesses. For this reason the auditor considers the procedures necessary to place reliance on data used as part of analytic procedures – including the controls which underpin the integrity of that data.

111   Given the nature of insurance business, nonfinancial data plays a significant part in managing the pricing and reserving processes. The auditor may consider the usefulness of nonfinancial data such as policy numbers, sums assured, retention levels and claim numbers and their interrelation with financial data in designing analytical review procedures. In addition the auditor may consider measures relating to regulatory compliance – e.g. complaints handling and breaches of conduct of business rules, and operational risk measures – e.g. volumes of unreconciled items.

112   Where non-financial information or reports produced from systems or processes outside the financial statements accounting system are used in analytical procedures, the auditor considers the reliability of that information or those reports.

ISA (UK) 540: AUDITING ACCOUNTING ESTIMATES, INCLUDING FAIR VALUE ACCOUNTING ESTIMATES, AND RELATED DISCLOSURES

ISA (UK) 540 is concerned with the audit of accounting estimates, including fair value estimates.

Technical provisions

For most insurers and friendly societies, the estimation of technical provisions will involve relatively high estimation uncertainty because it will involve significant assumptions about future conditions, transactions or events that are uncertain at the time of the estimation. Changes in estimation approach are likely to have a significant effect on the profit or surplus figure in the financial statements.

113   When designing audit procedures to test how management made the technical provisions estimate, the auditor obtains an understanding of:

(a)   The policies for setting such provisions;

(b)   The complexity and nature of the models or measurement techniques used to estimate the technical provisions;

(c)   The source data;

(d)   The assumptions used to develop those provisions; and

(e)   Management's controls over the development of technical provisions.

114   Matters that the auditor may consider in obtaining an understanding of relevant controls over how management makes the technical provisions estimate include, for example, the experience and competence of those who make the estimates of the technical provisions, and controls related to:

●   How management determines the completeness, relevance and accuracy of the data used to estimate technical provisions.

●   The review and approval of technical provisions, including the assumptions or inputs used in their development, by appropriate levels of management and, where appropriate, those charged with governance.

●   The segregation of duties between those committing the insurer to the underlying transactions and those responsible for determining technical provisions, including whether the assignment of responsibilities appropriately takes account of the nature of the entity (for example, in the case of a larger insurer, relevant segregation of duties may include an independent function responsible for estimating technical provisions).

- Where the insurer uses specific models for estimating technical provisions, specific policies and procedures around such models, for example, those established over:

  - The design and development, or selection, of a particular model for a particular purpose.

  - The use of the model, including any relevant testing of outputs.

  - Controls over access to the model.

  - The maintenance of and periodic revalidation of the integrity of the model.

  - Wider developments in the sector, or in the operations of the business, which might indicate that the model is no longer appropriate for the purpose intended.

  - The extent to which the entity retains individuals with the expertise to operate the model effectively.

As part of Pillar 2 of Solvency II, directive firms are required to demonstrate that where internal models are used in the calculation of the SCR that this is widely used in, and plays an important role in their system of governance, risk management system, decision making processes and the Own Risk and Solvency Assessment (ORSA). To the extent that common assumptions about the business underpin the calculation of the SCR, the presentation of the ORSA and technical provisions, auditors consider the consistency of these assumptions when assessing technical provisions in the statutory financial statements. Under Pillar 3, directive firms are also required to disclose in the "Valuation for Solvency Purposes" section of the annual Solvency and Financial Condition Report (SFCR): *separately for each material line of business, a quantitative and qualitative explanation of any material differences between the bases, methods and main assumptions used by that undertaking for the valuation for solvency purposes and those used for their valuation in financial statements.* The auditor considers this disclosure, when available, when assessing technical provisions. **115**

The models used to estimate the technical provisions are dependent upon the accuracy and completeness of financial and non-financial data and accordingly the audit procedures will need to address the effectiveness of management's controls over the integrity, use and reliability of such data. As required by auditing standards the auditor exercises professional scepticism when evaluating and testing management's controls, and the reasonableness of the assumptions being made. **116**

The assumptions made by management are integral components of accounting estimates and are intended to provide a reasonable basis for the setting of the technical provisions. The objective of the audit procedures performed for the purpose of evaluating these assumptions is not to obtain sufficient appropriate audit evidence to provide an opinion on the assumptions themselves. The auditor's consideration of management's assumptions is based only on information available to the auditor at the time of the audit. The auditor is not responsible for predicting future conditions, transactions or events that, if they had been known at the time of the audit, might have significantly affected management's actions or management's assumptions underlying the technical provisions and related disclosures. However, the auditor is required to obtain an understanding of **117** the assumptions made by management. Matters that the auditor may consider in obtaining an understanding of the assumptions underlying the accounting estimates include, for example:

- The nature of the assumptions, including which of the assumptions are likely to be significant assumptions.

- How management assesses whether the assumptions are relevant and complete (that is, that all relevant variables have been taken into account).

- Where applicable, how management determines that the assumptions used are internally consistent.

- Whether the assumptions relate to matters within the control of management (for example, assumptions about loss adjustment expenses), and how they conform to the entity's business plans and the external environment, or to matters that are outside its control (for example, assumptions about interest rates, mortality rates, potential judicial or regulatory actions, or the variability and the timing of future cash flows).

- The nature and extent of the documentation, if any, supporting the assumptions. Assumptions may be made or identified by an expert to assist management in making the technical provisions. Such assumptions, when used by management, become management's assumptions.

118   The auditor applies its understanding of the assumptions made by management to assess their reasonableness, considering for example:

- Whether individual assumptions appear reasonable

- Whether assumptions are interdependent and internally consistent

- Whether the assumptions appear reasonable when considered collectively or in conjunction with other assumptions, either for that accounting estimate or for other accounting estimates.

- In the case of fair value accounting estimates, whether the assumptions appropriately reflect observable marketplace assumptions.[64]

119   For life insurers, the valuation of with-profits liabilities uses a range of estimation techniques. The provision will comprise both historic (most likely asset share based) and projected (option and guarantee) information. Options and guarantees are often valued using stochastic modelling techniques. The auditor assesses whether regulatory requirements have been met and whether sufficient scenarios have been run. Any assertions regarding future management and policyholder actions also require careful consideration, including the extent to which management actions are supported by the Principles and Practices of Financial Management (PPFM)[65] or board resolution. Solvency II directive firms are also required to "establish a comprehensive future management actions plan, approved by the administrative, management or supervisory body of the insurance and reinsurance undertaking."[66]

120   Solvency II Directive firms are required to establish an "actuarial function" in accordance with the Solvency II framework. Non-directive firms are not required

---

[64] *ISA (UK) 540 (Revised June 2016), para. 13b & A78.*

[65] *The requirement for with-profit firms to produce a PPFM, as well as the issues it must cover, can be found in COBS 20.3 of the FCA Handbook, https://www.handbook.fca.org.uk/handbook/COBS/20/.*

[66] *COMMISSION DELEGATED REGULATION (EU) No .../... of XXX supplementing Directive 2009/138/EC of the European Parliament and of the Council on the taking-up and pursuit of the business of Insurance and Reinsurance (Solvency II), Article 236 (3).*

to establish such a function, but are likely to engage an actuary to perform a similar review of technical provisions. If an actuary has prepared a formal report on the technical provisions or on the financial soundness of a general insurance undertaking the auditor reviews the report to gain a better understanding of the scope of the work performed and of any limitations on any opinions expressed. If such a report has not been prepared, it is necessary for the auditor to understand the scope of the work carried out by the insurer's actuary.

Given that the calculation of an insurer's technical provisions is such a significant **121** activity in the preparation of the insurer's financial statements, once management has selected a specific estimation method, it is important that the insurer applies it consistently. If management has changed the method for calculating technical provisions, the auditor considers whether the method to which it has been changed provides a more appropriate basis of measurement, or that the change is supported by a change in the applicable financial reporting framework, or a change in circumstances.

> For accounting estimates that give rise to significant risks, in addition to other substantive procedures performed to meet the requirements of ISA (UK) 330[67], the auditor shall evaluate the following:
>
> (a)   How management has considered alternative assumptions or outcomes, and why it has rejected them, or how management has otherwise addressed estimation uncertainty in making the accounting estimate.
>
> (b)   Whether the significant assumptions used by management are reasonable.
>
> (c)   Where relevant to the reasonableness of the significant assumptions used by management or the appropriate application of the applicable financial reporting framework, management's intent to carry out specific courses of action and its ability to do so.[68]

In obtaining an understanding of whether, and if so how, the insurer has assessed **122** the effect of estimation uncertainty on the technical provisions, the auditor considers matters such as:

- Evaluating how, management has considered alternative assumptions or outcomes and why it has rejected them, or how it has otherwise addressed estimation uncertainty by, for example, performing a sensitivity analysis to determine the effect of changes in the assumptions on the level of technical provisions.

- How management determines the ultimate technical provisions when analysis indicates that there may be a number of outcome scenarios.

- Whether management monitors the outcome of technical provisions made in the prior period, and whether management has appropriately responded to the outcome of that monitoring procedure.

> The auditor shall review the outcome of accounting estimates included in the prior period financial statements, or, where applicable, their subsequent re-estimation for the purpose of the current period. The nature and extent of the auditor's review takes account of the nature of the accounting estimates, and whether the information obtained from the review would be relevant to

---

[67] *ISA (UK) 330 (Revised June 2016), para. 18.*

[68] *ISA (UK) 540 (Revised June 2016), para. 15.*

> identifying and assessing risks of material misstatement of accounting estimates made in the current period financial statement. However, the review is not intended to call into question the judgments made in the prior periods that were based on information available at the time.[69]

123   The review of the outcome or re-estimation of prior period accounting estimates may assist the auditor in identifying circumstances or conditions that could increase the uncertainty of a technical provision.

> The auditor shall review the judgments and decisions made by management in the making of accounting estimates to identify whether there are indicators of possible management bias. Indicators of possible management bias do not themselves constitute misstatements for the purposes of drawing conclusions on the reasonableness of accounting estimates.[70]

124   Management bias, whether unintentional or intentional, can be difficult to detect in a particular technical provision. It may only be identified when there has been a change in the method for calculating technical provisions from the prior period based on a subjective assessment without evidence that there has been a change in circumstances when considered in the aggregate of groups of estimates or all estimates, or when observed over a number of accounting periods. Although some form of management bias is inherent in subjective decisions, management may have no intention of misleading the users of financial statements. However, the intentional use by management of accounting estimates which are known to be unreasonable is fraudulent ISA (UK) 240, provides standards and guidance on the auditor's responsibility to consider fraud in an audit of financial statements.

> The auditor shall obtain sufficient appropriate audit evidence about whether the disclosures in the financial statements related to accounting estimates are in accordance with the requirements of the applicable financial reporting framework.[71]
>
> For accounting estimates that give rise to significant risks, the auditor shall also evaluate the adequacy of the disclosure of their estimation uncertainty in the financial statements in the context of the applicable financial reporting framework.[72]

125   Insurance specific financial reporting standards, which form part of the applicable financial reporting frameworks for insurers, take into account the inherent uncertainty within the insurance industry and the needs of users of financial statements regarding disclosure of estimation uncertainty. The auditor considers the required disclosure of estimation uncertainty by the applicable financial reporting framework and whether the disclosure proposed by management is adequate. In making this determination, the auditor considers whether adequate disclosure is given regarding the sensitivities associated with the significant assumptions underlying the technical provisions, in light of the materiality level established for the engagement.

126   Insurance specific financial reporting standards can require extensive narrative disclosures in the financial statements of insurers; for example, in relation to the

---

[69] *ISA (UK) 540 (Revised June 2016), para. 9.*

[70] *ISA (UK) 540 (Revised June 2016), para. 21.*

[71] *ISA (UK) 540 (Revised June 2016), para. 19.*

[72] *ISA (UK) 540 (Revised June 2016), para. 20.*

nature and extent of risks arising from insurance contracts and the accounting policies applicable to establishing technical provisions in respect of them. In designing and performing procedures to evaluate these disclosures the auditor obtains audit evidence regarding the assertions about presentation and disclosure described in paragraphs A124 and 124a of ISA (UK) 315. Guidance on the types of audit procedures that can be used for obtaining audit evidence can be found in paragraphs A14 to A25 of ISA (UK) 500.

Consideration of the adequacy of disclosure with regard to sensitivities of **127** significant assumptions is of particular importance where the estimation uncertainty of technical provisions may cast significant doubt about the entity's ability to continue as a going concern. ISAs (UK) 570 and 706 establish standards and provide guidance in such circumstances.

> The auditor shall evaluate, based on the audit evidence, whether the accounting estimates in the financial statements are either reasonable in the context of the applicable financial reporting framework, or are misstated.[73]

Based on the audit evidence obtained, the auditor may conclude that the evidence **128** points to an estimate of the required technical provision that differs from management's estimate, and that the difference between the auditor's estimate or range and management's estimate constitutes a financial statement misstatement. In such cases, where the auditor has developed a range, a misstatement exists when management's estimate lies outside the auditor's range. The misstatement is at least the difference between management's point estimate and the nearest point of the auditor's range.

Derivatives and other financial instruments

Further relevant guidance on auditing financial instruments is provided in the **129** FRC's Practice Note 23 *Special Considerations in auditing financial instruments* (PN23). PN23 includes guidance in respect of the requirements of ISA (UK) 540 in obtaining an understanding of the applicable financial reporting framework. In the context of an insurance entity, and the solvency requirements of the prudential regulation regime, the auditor may consider whether an entity's financial instruments "are part of a structured arrangement designed to achieve a particular accounting or regulatory purpose" when obtaining such an understanding.[74] Further, it may be appropriate for the auditor's understanding of relevant industry and regulatory factors in accordance with ISA (UK) 315 to include inquiry of management as to whether there have been discussions with supervisors or other regulators about its policies in respect of financial instruments. It may also be appropriate for the auditor to discuss matters related to the entity's use and disclosure of financial instruments directly with the regulator.[75]

Under Solvency II, directive firms are also required to prepare and disclose **130** significant qualitative and quantitative information to the regulator, and in annually published SFCRs, on significant risk concentrations, including the use and management of derivatives and other financial instruments. Where this

---

[73] *ISA (UK) 540 (Revised June 2016), para. 18.*

[74] *Practice Note 23 Special Considerations in auditing financial instruments (PN23), para. 76.*

[75] *Practice Note 23 Special Considerations in auditing financial instruments (PN23), para. 76-1 and 76-2.*

information is available, the auditor considers it when assessing relevant financial statement disclosures.

131   In respect of insurers the valuation of derivative and other financial instruments which are not traded in an active market and so for which valuation techniques are required is an activity that can give rise to significant audit risk. Such financial instruments are priced using valuation techniques such as discounted cash flow models, options pricing models or by reference to another instrument that is substantially the same as the financial instrument subject to valuation. The auditor reviews the controls, procedures and testing of the valuation techniques used by the insurer. Controls and substantive testing could include focusing on:

- Valuation technique approval and testing procedures used by the insurer.

- The independence of review, sourcing and reasonableness of observable market data and other parameters used in the valuation techniques.

- Calibration procedures used by the insurer to test the validity of valuation techniques applied by comparing outputs to observable market transactions.

- Completeness and appropriate inclusion of all relevant observable market data.

- The observability in practice of data classified by the insurer as observable market data.

- The appropriateness and validity of classification of instruments designated as being traded in a non-active and in an active market.

- The appropriateness and validity of the particular valuation technique applied to particular financial instruments.

- The appropriateness and validity of the parameters used by the insurer to designate an instrument as substantially the same as the financial instrument being valued.

- Mathematical integrity of the valuation models.

- Access controls over valuation models.

ISA (UK) 550: RELATED PARTIES

132   In order to comply with ISA (UK) 550, the auditor is required to assess the risk that material undisclosed related party transactions may exist. It is in the nature of insurance business, including friendly societies conducting insurance business in the UK, that transaction volumes are high but this factor will not, of itself, necessarily lead the auditor to conclude that the inherent risk of material undisclosed related party transactions is high.

133   Insurers are likely to have a particularly wide range of contractual arrangements because the nature of insurance is to spread risk. The directors will, in particular, need to consider how best to obtain information on the interests of related parties in policies issued and in reinsurance arrangements. In capturing this data, insurers may decide to establish criteria for evaluating materiality to the individuals concerned; the policies are, in most cases, unlikely to be material to the insurer. The auditor will need to obtain an understanding of the controls that management has established to identify, account for and disclose such related party transactions.

134   Insurers are required to report to the FCA and PRA changes in control (in some instances with the prior approval of the regulator), changes in circumstances of existing controllers and changes in entities that are closely linked to the firm. In

addition, there are annual reporting obligations in respect of controllers and entities that are closely linked to the firm. As a result, it will normally be the case that there are controls in place to ensure that this information is properly collated. However, the definition of "controller and closely linked" for regulatory purposes is not congruent with the "related party" definition in UK GAAP and IAS 24 and the auditor therefore considers what controls have been put in place by management to capture information on those parties which fall within the accounting definition only.

In reviewing related party information for completeness, the auditor may compare the proposed disclosures in the financial statements to information prepared for regulatory reporting purposes (bearing in mind that the population may be different, as noted in the preceding paragraph). **135**

The auditor inspects, evaluates and obtains audit evidence regarding the authorisation and approval of and significant reinsurance or other funding arrangements with related parties entered into outside the entity's normal course of business. In gaining an understanding of the business rationale of such transactions that auditor makes appropriate enquiries of management. **136**

Additional Considerations in respect of Friendly Societies

Schedule 11 of the 1992 Friendly Societies Act applies sections 62–69 of the Building Societies Act 1986 (the 1986 Act) concerning directors' loans and transactions to friendly societies. In the context of friendly societies, the term "director" is applicable to members of the Committee of Management. **137**

Section 65 of the 1986 Act lists a number of transactions which a friendly society is either not allowed to make or which are subject to strict limitations. Section 68 of the 1986 Act requires the maintenance of a Register by the society recording details of all permitted transactions with directors and connected persons. Extracts from this Register are required to be included in an unaudited annual statement, and to be made available to the members and to the regulator. Friendly societies are also required to disclose in their financial statements certain details of loans outstanding at the year-end to Committee of Management members and connected persons. **138**

In order to comply with statutory requirements, friendly societies should have appropriate systems to ensure that all such loans and transactions are identified, controlled and properly disclosed, both in the Registers and in the financial statements. In order to fulfil these requirements societies normally require each Committee member to confirm, in writing and on an annual basis, the existence and amount of any such matters: negative returns are usually required for completeness. **139**

The auditor considers whether loans and transactions recorded by the society in accordance with the requirements of Sections 65, 68 and 69 of the 1986 Act fall within the related parties criteria under accounting standards and legislation for disclosure in the financial statements. **140**

If the auditor become aware of breaches of the statutory requirements relating to loans and other transactions by individual Committee members, including a failure to notify the society of any relevant matters, such a matter may be considered to trigger the statutory duty to report to the regulator. **141**

ISA (UK) 560: SUBSEQUENT EVENTS

ISA (UK) 560 deals with the auditor's responsibilities in respect of events occurring between the date of the financial statements and the date of the auditor's report. The auditor is required to perform audit procedures designed to obtain sufficient appropriate evidence that:

> ... all events occurring between the date of the financial statements and the date of the auditor's report that require adjustment of, or disclosure in, the financial statements have been identified. The auditor is not, however, expected to perform additional audit procedures on matters to which previously applied audit procedures have provided satisfactory conclusions.[76]

142 Matters specific to insurance companies and friendly societies conducting insurance business in the UK which the auditor may consider in its review of subsequent events include:

- An evaluation of the impact of any material subsequent events on the capital requirements for both Solvency II and non-Directive insurers.

- An assessment of the influence of new information received relevant to claims provisions.

- An assessment of the impact of any developments in doubtful reinsurance recoveries since the balance sheet date.

- An assessment of the impact of any regulatory developments since the balance sheet date.

- A review of relevant correspondence with regulators and enquiries of management to determine whether any significant breaches of regulations or other significant regulatory concerns have come to light since the period end.

143 ISA (UK) 560 establishes requirements for situations when facts become known to the auditor:

(a) After the date of the auditor's report but before the financial statements are issued; and

(b) After the financial statements have been issued

that may have caused the auditor to amend the auditor's report. If the auditor examines the regulatory return of an insurer, or in the case of entities subject to Solvency II requirements the Solvency and Financial Condition Report (SFCR), subsequent to the issuance of its report on the financial statements, the auditor may become aware of subsequent events which, had they occurred or been known of at the date of its report on the financial statements, might have caused the auditor to issue a different report. In such cases the auditor and the directors consider whether the financial statements need to be revised following the statutory provisions relating to the revision of company annual financial statements and directors' reports set out in section 454 of CA 2006 and The Companies (Revision of Defective Accounts and Reports) Regulations 2008.

Where the auditor concludes that this step is appropriate, the matter concerned is likely to be of material significance to the regulator and so gives rise to a duty to report to the regulator.

---

[76] *ISA (UK) 560, para. 6.*

ISA (UK) 570: GOING CONCERN

ISA (UK) 570 was revised in June 2016 to reflect changes arising from the EU Audit Regulation and Directive, and from changes to international standards issued by the International Auditing and Assurance Standards Board (IAASB).

The objectives set out in the revised standard are set out below:

ISA (UK) 570 (Revised June 2016)
Objectives: Paragraph 9
(a) To obtain sufficient appropriate audit evidence regarding, **and conclude on**, the appropriateness of management's use of the going concern basis of accounting in the preparation of the financial statements;
(b) To conclude, based on the audit evidence obtained, whether a material uncertainty exists related to events or conditions that may cast significant doubt on the entity's ability to continue as a going concern; and
(c) **To report** in accordance with this ISA (UK)

With reference to insurance companies or friendly societies, specific audit procedures may include: **144**

- Reviewing the means whereby the board of directors and senior management of an insurer satisfy themselves that the insurer will have capital in excess of its capital resources requirement for the foreseeable future, including a review of the insurer's capital assessments prepared for regulatory purposes (whether under Solvency II or other).

- Considering whether the key assumptions underlying the budgets and/or forecasts appear appropriate in the circumstances. Key assumptions will normally include claims projections (numbers, cost and timing), the profitability of business written, investment performance, the volume of new business and the level of provisions required.

- The auditor may wish to consider differences between the assumptions and data underpinning regulatory "technical provisions" and those provisions included in the financial statements.

- Considering the liquidity of funds to enable the insurer to meet claims and other liabilities as they fall due.

- Reviewing correspondence with the regulators, and considering any actions taken (or likely to be taken) by the regulators.

- Considering the implications of changes in government policy.

- Considering the potential costs of settling claims, (for example uncertainty resulting from judicial decisions) and additional provisions (for example product mis-selling).

- Reviewing any financial condition report produced by the holder of the actuarial function and other actuarial reports.

If the auditor has any doubts as to the ability of an insurer or Friendly Society to   **145** continue to adopt the going concern basis of accounting, the auditor considers whether it ought to make a report direct to the FCA or PRA.

ISA (UK) 580: WRITTEN REPRESENTATIONS

146   ISA (UK) 250 Section A and ISA (UK) 550 require the auditor to obtain written confirmation in respect of:

(a)   The completeness of disclosure to the auditor of all known instances of noncompliance or suspected non-compliance with laws and regulations (including breaches of FSMA 2000, FCA/PRA rules, the Money Laundering Regulations, other regulatory requirements or any other circumstance that could jeopardise the authorisation of the firm under FSMA 2000) whose effects should be considered when preparing financial statements)[77]; and

(b)   The completeness of information provided regarding the identity of related parties, related party relationships and transactions, and the appropriateness of related party disclosures in the financial statements.[78]

147   If, in addition to the requirements in other ISAs (UK) for the auditor to request written representations, the auditor determines that it is necessary to obtain one or more written representations to support other audit evidence relevant to the financial statements or specific assertions this ISA (UK) requires that the auditor request such other written representations. For all insurers and friendly societies, it may be appropriate to obtain a specific representation confirming that full disclosure has been made in respect of any side letters, any multiyear reinsurance contracts or any reinsurance contracts with unusual adjustable features, as well as the adequacy of the claims provision and the IBNR. The auditor may also obtain written representations regarding, for example:

●   The reasonableness of significant assumptions used by the entity in calculating technical provisions.

●   All correspondence with regulators having been made available to the auditor.

ISA (UK) 700: THE AUDITOR'S REPORT ON FINANCIAL STATEMENTS

> *Objectives*
>
> The objectives of the auditor are to:
>
> (a)   Form an opinion on the financial statements based on an evaluation of the conclusions drawn from the audit evidence obtained; and
>
> (b)   Express clearly that opinion through a written report that also describes the basis for the opinion.[79]

Friendly Societies: Reports to Committee of Management

148   Auditor's reports for friendly societies are required by Section 73(4A) of the 1992 Act to include an opinion concerning the consistency of the financial statements with the Report of the Committee of Management and the latter's compliance with the 1992 Act and the regulations made under it.

149   In connection with its opinion on the Report of the Committee of Management, the auditor considers whether all of the information called for by Sections 71 and 71A

---

[77]   *ISA (UK) 250 – Section A (Revised June 2016), para. 16.*

[78]   *ISA (UK) 550, para. 26.*

[79]   *ISA (UK) 700 – (Revised June 2016), para. 6.*

of the Friendly Societies Act 1992 and by Schedule 8 of the Accounts Regulations has been provided. In particular the regulations require the Committee of Management to present a fair review of the activities of the society during the financial year. The Report should give a balanced view of difficulties encountered and issues facing the society as well as achievements and ambitions. The information disclosed includes a Business Review, principal risks and uncertainties and key performance indicators.

As the auditors are required to confirm that the Report has been made in **150** accordance with the regulations they need to consider whether it presents a fair review of the activities, taking into account the information and understanding that they have gained in the course of their work on the financial statements and returns and bearing in mind that these Reports are sometimes used by management as a "marketing tool" for the benefit of the society.

Non-directive Friendly Societies and registered branches

Non-directive societies and registered branches are required to prepare accounts **151** under the abbreviated format of Schedule 7 of The Friendly Societies (Accounts and Related Provisions) Regulations 1994. Unlike the position for directive societies, this format contains no reference to technical provisions. However, this does not preclude the society or branch from providing additional analysis of the benefit funds to show the amount representing technical provisions. Indeed this disclosure will normally be required for the financial statements to show a true and fair view.

Mutual Insurers: Corporate Governance

Many mutual insurers voluntarily adhere to either the UK Corporate Governance **152** Code or the annotated version the code periodically published by the Association of Financial Mutuals (AFM). The AFM recommends that members adhere to this a Code. Although any review responsibility is determined by the terms of the auditor's engagement, rather than by law or regulation, it nevertheless falls within the ambit of the requirements in paragraph 43-1 of ISA (UK) 700. (See paragraph A58-1–A58-3 of that ISA). Applying the Annotated Code is effectively voluntary compliance with the UK Corporate Governance Code, and therefore the relevant requirements of ISA (UK) 701 apply.

ISA (UK) 705: MODIFICATIONS TO OPINIONS IN THE INDEPENDENT AUDITOR'S REPORT

ISA (UK) 705 sets out the auditor's responsibilities in respect of modifications to opinions in the Auditor's Report. The ISA establishes three types of modified opinion – a qualified opinion, an adverse opinion, and a disclaimer of opinion. These requirements are in addition to those set out in ISA (UK) 700.

The basis on which an Insurer's or Friendly Society's financial statements are **153** prepared takes account of the extent of the inherent uncertainty in the types of insurance business it underwrites. Uncertainties arising from insurance contracts may include:

- General uncertainties arising where the outcomes for provisioning are within a range which is not unusual for the nature of the business underwritten.

- Specific uncertainties which are material and subject to a very wide range of outcomes.

- Uncertainties where the financial reporting framework does not require a provision to be established but where disclosure of a contingent liability may be appropriate.

154   If the auditor concludes that the technical provisions are materially misstated or that the disclosures relating to those provisions and the relevant uncertainties are inadequate or misleading and concludes that the effect is material, but not pervasive, to the view given by the financial statements, it is required to express a qualified opinion.

155   If the auditor concludes that the effect is both material and pervasive it is required to express an adverse opinion. If the auditor is unable to obtain sufficient appropriate audit evidence on which to base an opinion, and the auditor concludes that the possible effects on the financial statements of undetected misstatements, if any, could be both material and pervasive the auditor is required to disclaim an opinion.

ISA (UK) 706: EMPHASIS OF MATTER PARAGRAPHS AND OTHER MATTER PARAGRAPHS IN THE INDEPENDENT AUDITOR'S REPORT

ISA (UK) 706 deals with Emphasis of Matter and Other Matter paragraphs in the Independent Auditor's Report:

> The objective of the auditor, having formed an opinion on the financial statements, is to draw users' attention, when in the auditor's judgment it is necessary to do so, by way of clear additional communication in the auditor's report to:
>
> (a)   A matter, although appropriately presented or disclosed in the financial statements, that is of such importance that it is fundamental to users' understanding of the financial statements; or
>
> (b)   As appropriate, any other matter that is relevant to users' understanding of the audit, the auditor's responsibilities or the auditor's report.[80]

156   The standard notes in application material that "widespread use" of such paragraphs "diminishes effectiveness" of the auditor's communication of such matters.[81]

157   Determining technical provisions is subject to a high degree of inherent uncertainty and frequently involves significant assumptions, estimations and statistical techniques. When reporting on an insurer's financial statements, including friendly societies conducting insurance business in the UK, the auditor evaluates whether such uncertainties fall within the category of significant, and so require to be disclosed in its report. In making this evaluation, the auditor takes into account whether the financial statements provide a user with general information about the types of business written such that the overall level of inherent uncertainty likely to apply to those financial statements is apparent.

158   The fact that an auditor of an insurer has identified that the high estimation uncertainty associated with the calculation of technical provisions gives rise to a significant risk does not automatically require the auditor to include an emphasis

---

[80]   *ISA (UK) 706 (Revised June 2016), para. 6. Note that the guidance at paragraphs A1–A3 of ISA (UK) 706 sets out the relationship between additional communications in the auditor's report in accordance with this ISA (UK) and a Key Audit Matters section in accordance with ISA (UK) 701.*

[81]   *ISA (UK) 706 (Revised June 2016), para. A6.*

of matter paragraph in its auditor's report to draw attention to the financial statement note that describes the uncertainties inherent in the technical provisions.

ISA (UK) 720: THE AUDITOR'S RESPONSIBILITIES RELATING TO OTHER INFORMATION

ISA (UK) 720 deals with the auditor's responsibilities in respect of "other information".

Insurance companies undertaking long-term business may include supplementary **159** financial statements prepared on an alternative basis to that used in drawing up the financial statements. Without adequate explanation, such supplementary financial statements may appear inconsistent with the audited financial statements. The requirements and application material in ISA (UK) 720 set out how the auditor discharges its' responsibilities in respect of other information in these circumstances. The auditor also considers whether an adequate explanation of the assumptions and different methodology has been provided in the annual report, and if not, it considers including an "Other matter" paragraph in its report on the financial statements drawing attention to the inadequacy of the explanation.

Supplementary financial statements showing performance arising on long-term **160** business calculated on an alternative basis are prepared using different assumptions and methodologies from those applied in preparing the financial statements. There are many aspects of the supplementary statements not affected by the alternative assumptions and methodologies and where material the auditor considers whether they are treated consistently in both the financial statements and the supplementary financial statements. For those material items where different assumptions and methodologies are applied to the same data to produce the supplementary statements the auditor considers whether consistent data has been used.

The auditor reads the supplementary financial statements in the light of knowledge **161** acquired during the audit and considers whether there are any apparent misstatements therein. The auditor is not expected to verify or audit the information contained in the supplementary financial statements.

The work of the auditor in reporting to the directors on supplementary financial **162** statements prepared on the alternative method of reporting long term business is outside the scope of this Practice Note.

From 1 January 2016, under Solvency II, many insurers will also be required to **163** publish a Solvency and Financial Condition Report (SFCR), elements of which will be subject to a separate external assurance opinion. PRA rules require that where the auditor of the statutory financial statements is also the auditor the SFCR, then they need to consider the consistency of information in "other information" for the SFCR with evidence and knowledge obtained in the course of the audit of the statutory financial statements.

CONSIDERATIONS RELATING TO WORKING WITH SPECIALISTS AND EXPERTS

Introduction

In the course of an audit of an insurance entity, the auditor will consider the need **164** for specialist skills or knowledge in order to obtain sufficient appropriate audit evidence. In the insurance sector this is likely to include the audit of those parts of the financial statements which are derived using actuarial techniques and assumptions (technical provisions for example) or in respect of taxation. The engagement partner remains responsible for the quality of the audit and:

> ... *shall be satisfied that the engagement team, and any auditor's experts who are not part of the of the engagement team, collectively have the appropriate competence and capabilities to:*
>
> (a) *Perform the audit engagement in accordance with professional standards and applicable legal and regulatory requirements, and*
>
> (b) *Enable an auditor's report that is appropriate in the circumstances to be issued.*[82]

165   As well as ensuring that the engagement team has an appropriate level of knowledge of the industry and its corresponding products and business streams, the engagement partner also satisfies themselves that the members of the engagement team have sufficient knowledge of the regulatory framework within which insurers operate commensurate with their roles on the engagement. They also ensure for example that the team includes members with actuarial expertise or has access to external actuarial expertise appropriate to the entity's insurance business.

166   The PRA's Supervisory Statements in respect of the audit of regulatory reporting for Directive and non-Directive firms sets out the expectation in certain cases that auditors will "obtain and pay due regard to" the work of a suitably qualified actuary.

167   The level of involvement of an actuary in the audit process will depend on matters such as the level of expertise of other members of the audit team, the availability of independent actuarial advice to the insurer, and the nature and complexity of the audit issues. They may be used in the initial assessment of the level of risk of each financial statement caption, in assessing the effectiveness of the control environment, in establishing the audit procedures to be adopted and in obtaining and assessing the audit evidence obtained.

168   In some cases a suitably qualified individual or individuals, often employed by the audit firm, may be included within the audit engagement team as either "specialists" or "internal experts". Their work is fully integrated into and documented within the audit file.[83] Where an individual or individuals providing actuarial expertise are treated as "auditor's experts" then the requirements and guidance contained within ISA (UK) 620 (Revised June 2016) *Using the Work of an Auditor's Expert* apply. An "external expert" is not considered to be part of the engagement team, and their working papers are therefore not required to be fully integrated into the audit file. ISA (UK) 620 sets out the documentation requirements in respect of "external experts".

Auditor's internal and external experts

169   ISA (UK) 620 (Revised June 2016) sets out the auditor's responsiblities in respect of using the work of an auditor's expert. An auditor's expert is defined as:

> *An individual or organization possessing expertise in a field other than accounting or auditing, whose work in that field is used by the auditor to assist the auditor in obtaining sufficient appropriate audit evidence. An auditor's expert may be either an auditor's internal expert (who is a partner*

---

[82] *ISA (UK) 220 (Revised June 2016), para. 14.*

[83] *ISA (UK) 220 (Revised June 2016), para. 7d.*

or staff, including temporary staff, of the auditor's firm or a network firm), or an auditor's external expert.[84]

It is a matter of professional judgement whether the actuarial expertise being employed in support of the audit is in a "field other than accounting or auditing", and therefore whether the requirements of ISA (UK) 620 apply. "Expertise in another field" other than accounting or auditing "may" include expertise in relation to, "the actuarial calculation of liabilities associated with insurance contracts or employee benefit plans."[85] The extent to which an individual with actuarial knowledge conducts audit work on the financial statement disclosures, as distinct from providing advice on actuarial methods and assumptions, is important in assessing whether they are an "expert" or a "specialist".   **170**

Where the auditor decides to use an actuary as an auditor's expert in relation to the audit of technical provisions, the auditor assesses the following: **171**

(a)   The professional competence and capabilities of the actuary, taking into consideration its professional qualifications, experience and reputation in the market in which the insurer operates;

(b)   The objectivity of the actuary including whether the actuary is connected in some way to the insurer e.g. being financially dependent on the insurer or having a financial interest in the insurer; and

(c)   The scope of the work to be undertaken and degree of reliance that the auditor can place thereon.

The auditor seeks to ensure that an actuary engaged as an auditor's expert, although guided by its own profession's standards and guidance and by FRC technical standards (TASs), designs and performs its work to provide the auditor with work that fully meets the objectives agreed between the auditor and the actuary.   **172**

Where the actuary is an internal expert (i.e. a partner or staff, including temporary staff, of the auditor's firm or a network firm), the auditor will be able to rely on its firm's quality control systems, recruitment and training to determine the actuary's capabilities and competence, rather than having to evaluate them for each audit engagement (unless information provided to the auditor suggests otherwise).   **173**

Regardless of whether the actuary is an auditor's internal or external expert, ISA (UK) 620 requires the auditor to agree with the actuary: **174**

(a)   The nature, scope and objectives of the actuary's work.

(b)   The respective roles and responsibilities of the auditor and the actuary;

(c)   The nature, timing and extent of communication between the auditor and the actuary, including the form of any report to be provided by the actuary; and

(d)   The need for the actuary to observe confidentiality requirements.

Where appropriate, such agreement is in writing. An agreement between the auditor and an auditor's external actuarial expert will often be in the form of an engagement letter.   **175**

In addition the auditor may wish to arrange to have access to the working papers produced by any actuary who is an auditor's external expert.   **176**

The auditor evaluates the actuary's working papers to determine whether: **177**

---

[84] *ISA (UK) 620 (Revised June 2016), para. 6a.*

[85] *ISA (UK) 620 (Revised June 2016), para. A1.*

(a)   The actuary's findings are relevant and reasonable, based on the auditor's knowledge of the business and the results of other audit procedures;

(b)   The methods and assumptions used by the actuary are relevant and reasonable in the circumstances; and

(c)   The source data used by the actuary is relevant, reasonable, complete and accurate.

178   Although the auditor does not have the same expertise as the actuary this does not preclude the auditor from challenging the actuary's findings.

179   If the actuary's findings are not consistent with other audit evidence, the auditor attempts to resolve the differences by either agreeing with the actuary on the nature and extent of further work to be performed by the actuary or by applying additional audit procedures. If the auditor is not satisfied that it has obtained sufficient appropriate audit evidence to support the audit opinion and there is no satisfactory alternative source of audit evidence, the auditor considers the implications for the auditor's report.

180   Where the auditor uses an auditor's expert, such as an actuary, as part of the audit, the auditor remains solely responsible for the audit of the insurer's financial statements.

Audit documentation

181   If the auditor uses internal actuarial specialists or experts within the engagement team to assist in the audit process, their working papers form part of the audit working papers. (This would also be the case where an actuary is included with the audit engagement team performing the audit of published or private regulatory reports).

182   Where external actuarial "auditor's experts" are engaged by the auditor (in practice usually external actuaries not directly employed by the audit firm), then:

> The auditor shall document any request for advice from an auditor's expert, together with the advice received.[86]

Audit evidence

183   For all insurers, where the work of those with expertise in relation to the actuarial calculation of liabilities is used in the preparation of financial statements then those performing that work are likely to be a management's expert. ISA (UK) 500 states that:

> If information to be used as audit evidence has been prepared using the work of a management's expert, the auditor shall, to the extent necessary, having regard to the significance of that expert's work for the auditor's purposes
>
> (a)   Evaluate the competence, capabilities and objectivity of that expert;
>
> (b)   Obtain an understanding of the work of that expert; and
>
> (c)   Evaluate the appropriateness of that expert's work as audit evidence for the relevant assertion.[87]

---

[86]   *ISA (UK) 620 (Revised June 2016), para. 15D-1.*

[87]   *ISA (UK) 500, para. 8.*

Where the work of management's actuarial expert is to be used as audit evidence **184** by the auditor of an insurer, the auditor performs the procedures set out in ISA (UK) 500 paragraph 8. In performing those procedures the auditor may use an auditor's actuarial expert.

In assessing the competence, capability and objectivity of a management's **185** actuarial expert and the appropriateness of that expert's work as audit evidence the auditor has regard to the relevant standards that apply to the expert and its work. In particular, the auditor evaluates the extent to which data used by management's actuarial expert has been derived from sources that have been the subject of audit testing and whether they are the same sources as used by the insurer in preparing the financial statements. TAS 100 includes the following requirements of actuaries in respect of data:

> *Data used in technical actuarial work shall be appropriate for the purpose of that work so that users can rely on the resulting actuarial information.*

> *Communications shall describe the data used in the technical actuarial work, the source of the data, the rationale for the selection of the data, whether checks and controls have been applied any material uncertainty in the data, and the approach taken to deal with that uncertainty.*

> *Communications shall state any limitations in the actuarial information resulting from the use of insufficient or unreliable data and provide an indication of their impact on the actuarial information.*

Technical actuarial standards

The Institute and Faculty of Actuaries (IFoA) requires compliance with the FRC's **186** Technical Actuarial Standards (TASs). All technical actuarial work done in relation to the UK operations of entities, as well as to any overseas operations which report into the UK, within the context of UK law or regulation fall within the geographical scope of these standards.

In the course of complying with the various requirements of auditing standards **187** when working with actuaries, whether as specialists, auditor's or management's experts, auditors may wish to consider the scope, principles and requirements of the FRC's actuarial standards. TAS 100: Principles for Technical Actuarial Work supports the reliability objective that "the users for whom actuarial information is created should be able to place a high degree of reliance on that information's relevance, transparency of assumptions, completeness and comprehensibility, including the communication of any uncertainty inherent in the information". It does this by setting out key high level principles for actuaries covering:

- Judgement
- Data
- Assumptions
- Models
- Communications
- Documentation

TAS 200: Insurance sets more detailed provisions specifically in respect of **188** actuarial work in the insurance sector, including regulatory reporting related to Solvency II. Specific provisions which relate to the insurance sector are set out to support the principles in TAS 100, including for example work in respect of risk modelling underlying the calculation of regulatory capital requirements and the Own Risk Solvency Assessment (ORSA) Where actuaries are involved with audit and assurance engagements then the TAS sets provisions in respect of:

- Scoping the engagement
- Professional scepticism
- Communications

Section 5: The Audit of Financial Statements: Additional Considerations Relating to Lloyd's

The Society of Lloyd's is a unique institution with its own internal governance and financial reporting arrangements. This section of the Practice Note is concerned with additional considerations for auditors of Lloyd's Syndicates financial statements (other than those required by the Society for regulatory reporting purposes) when conducting an audit in compliance with ISAs (UK). Where no special considerations arise from a particular ISA (UK), no material is included.

Guidance on the audit of regulatory reports is included within the Solvency II directive firms part of this Practice Note.

ISA (UK) 210: AGREEING THE TERMS OF AUDIT ENGAGEMENTS

1   Further matters specific to Lloyd's syndicates and Lloyd's corporate members which may be dealt with in the engagement letter include:

- The responsibilities of the directors of the managing agent or Lloyd's corporate member to keep Lloyd's informed about the affairs of these businesses.

- The auditor's additional duty to report matters to the Council of Lloyd's of which it has become aware in its capacity as auditor which may be of material significance to Lloyd's in its capacity as market supervisor.

- The auditor's duty to provide access to its working papers to the Council of Lloyd's in certain circumstances.

2   The engagement letter for a Lloyd's syndicate also refers to the aspects of the auditor's responsibilities, as set out in the Audit Arrangements Byelaw ("AAB")[88], as the syndicate's "recognised accountant", namely:

(a)   To report on the syndicate's financial statements and related matters;

(b)   To report on any syndicate Annual Return as required by or under the Solvency and Reporting Byelaw; and

(c)   As reporting accountant, if appointed by the Council of Lloyd's to report on other specified matters.

ISA (UK) 240: THE AUDITOR'S RESPONSIBILITIES RELATING TO FRAUD IN AN AUDIT OF FINANCIAL STATEMENTS

3   Examples of fraud by directors or employees of a managing agent include fraudulent recharges of agency expenses to managed syndicates and fraudulent misallocation of transactions to different years of account within those syndicates. Instances of suspected or actual fraud may involve breaches of specific

---

[88]   http://www.lloyds.com/the-market/operating-at-lloyds/regulation/acts-and-byelaws/lloyds-byelaws

requirements relating to syndicates and their managing agents as prescribed by Lloyd's in its capacity as market supervisor, and are likely to be regarded as being of material significance. Syndicate auditors have a duty to consider reporting all such instances to the Council of Lloyd's without delay in accordance with their undertaking given to Lloyd's. Guidance on such reporting is contained in the section on ISA (UK) 250 Section B below.

ISA (UK) 250: SECTION A – CONSIDERATION OF LAWS AND REGULATIONS IN AN AUDIT OF FINANCIAL STATEMENTS

For Lloyd's syndicates, prudential supervision of the Lloyd's market as a whole   4
and of managing agents is carried out by the PRA. Additional supervision of syndicates and managing agents is conducted by Lloyd's. Ongoing prudential supervision of the Lloyd's market is carried out by the PRA on a similar basis to insurance companies including the review of regulatory returns for the market as a whole.

In the context of Lloyd's syndicates, and their management, the principal laws and   5
regulations are those relevant to insurers as set out above and in addition the requirements prescribed by the Council of Lloyd's, non-compliance with which may reasonably be expected to result in Lloyd's exercising its powers of intervention so as to require the syndicate to cease accepting new business and procure the close of existing business on an orderly basis into a third party.

The process for prudential supervision of the market means that Lloyd's centrally   6
has responsibility for reviewing and agreeing with the managing agent for each syndicate an appropriate amount of prudential capital requirements and for determining how those requirements are to be resourced.

In the case of Lloyd's syndicates that undertake business outside the UK, Lloyd's   7
coordinates compliance with the requirements of overseas regulatory authorities, and incorporates relevant provisions as necessary in its own regulatory requirements, thus supporting a global operating licence. The auditor of a Lloyd's syndicate that undertakes business overseas therefore does not need to make a separate assessment of the impact of local laws and regulations over and above those specified by Lloyd's.

ISA (UK) 250: SECTION B – THE AUDITOR'S STATUTORY RIGHT AND DUTY TO REPORT TO REGULATORS OF PUBLIC INTEREST ENTITIES AND REGULATORS OF OTHER ENTITIES IN THE FINANCIAL SECTOR

Lloyd's syndicates

The auditor of a syndicate needs to consider whether it is under a duty or right to   8
report on a particular matter to the regulator, to the Council of Lloyd's or to both.

The duty to report matters of material significance applies to all engagements   9
carried out by recognised accountants. Recognised accountants are not required to carry out procedures to detect matters of material significance. This applies even when the recognised accountant is reporting on specific issues under paragraph 13 of the AAB[88] such that the focus of the work undertaken is very narrow.

The key factor in determining when a duty arises is the existence of circumstances   10
that would either lead to suspension of authorisation to operate in the Lloyd's

market or that warrant use of Lloyd's power of intervention in an individual entity's conduct of business.

11 Under paragraph 6(6) of the AAB, any appointment of a recognised accountant shall include the consent and waiver provisions set out in Schedule 3 to the AAB88.[88] These require the syndicate's managing agent to acknowledge and declare that no duty which the recognised accountant might owe to the syndicate or managing agent concerned would be contravened by the recognised accountant communicating in good faith to the Council any information in relation to a matter of which it has become aware in the ordinary course of work undertaken to fulfil its responsibilities as syndicate auditor or reporting accountant and which it considers is relevant to any function of the Council under the Lloyd's Act 1982 or any byelaws made thereafter.

12 The undertaking given by the recognised accountant as set out in paragraph 4(3) of Schedule 2 of the AAB[88] provides that the recognised accountant undertakes to report to the Council of Lloyd's without delay information of which it becomes aware in the ordinary course of performing either work undertaken to fulfil its audit responsibilities or work undertaken to fulfil its responsibilities as reporting accountant for a syndicate when in its opinion there is reasonable cause to believe that:

(a) The authorisation of the syndicate or managing agent could be withdrawn; or

(b) There is or may be a failure to fulfil relevant criteria of sound and prudent management which is or may be of material significance to Lloyd's in determining whether any of its powers of intervention should be exercised; or

(c) There is or may be breach of the provisions of the Lloyd's Acts 1871 to 1982 (or related byelaws or regulations) which is likely to be of material significance to Lloyd's, such that its powers of intervention should be exercised; or

(d) The continuous functioning of the syndicate or managing agent may be affected; or

(e) The recognised accountant concludes that it cannot issue its report without qualifying its opinion.

13 In accordance with the undertaking given in the form set out in Schedule 2 to the AAB, the recognised accountant agrees to the extent that it may do so lawfully and ethically, to provide the Council with such information, documents and explanations in relation to matters which it has a duty to report of which it has become aware.

14 Taken together, the consent and waiver given by the managing agent of the syndicate and the undertaking given by the recognised accountant provide that a recognised accountant is able to communicate to the Council on any matters which, in the opinion of the recognised accountant, is or may be relevant to any function of Lloyd's as regulator relating to the entity's affairs arising out of the work carried out to fulfil responsibilities as syndicate auditor or reporting accountant. However, the recognised accountant is not protected from any breach of duty if, in making a report to the Council, the reporting accountant does not act in good faith. Accordingly, recognised accountants may wish to take appropriate legal or other professional advice before taking the decision whether, and if so, in what manner, to report to the Council.

Furthermore, the recognised accountant undertakes to report information of which **15** it becomes aware in the ordinary course of performing the work carried out to fulfil responsibilities as syndicate auditor or reporting accountant which relates to any other entity regulated by the Council. This extends to any other entity having close links arising from a control relationship with the entity in relation to which the recognised accountant is performing that work.

If the recognised accountant, after becoming aware of a matter giving rise to a **16** statutory duty to report, fails to report either without delay or at all, the Council can take action under paragraph 5(3) of the AAB[88] to remove them from the list of recognised accountants. Action could also be taken by the recognised accountants' own regulatory body.

The Council accords particular importance to timely notification of matters giving **17** rise to such a report to the Council by recognised accountants. ISA (UK) 250 Section B acknowledges that recognised accountants will normally seek evidence to assess the implications of a suspected breach before reporting a matter. Once they have identified information as being subject to the duty to report, ISA (UK) 250 Section B requires them to bring it to the attention of the regulator without delay. A recognised accountant may fail to discharge its duty to report to the Council if it waits until giving its formal opinion on the financial statements of a syndicate, or (in its capacity as reporting accountant on syndicates appointed under paragraph 13 of the AAB)[88] on other ad hoc reports, or if they agree to delay making a report until management has had the opportunity to take remedial action.

The auditor of a Lloyd's syndicate is required under paragraph 9 of the AAB[88] to **18** give notice to Lloyd's of its resignation, removal or retirement and under paragraph 10 of the AAB[88] such notice shall be accompanied by a statement signed by the auditor to the effect that there are no circumstances connected with its ceasing to hold office which it considers should be brought to the attention of the members of the syndicate or to the managing agent or by a statement by the auditor specifying all such circumstances. In addition the auditor of a Lloyd's syndicate is required to notify the regulator of its resignation, removal or retirement as set out above.

Lloyd's corporate members

Auditors of Lloyd's corporate members are required by the Lloyd's Membership **19** Byelaw to give an undertaking to Lloyd's that includes the following clause: "The auditor undertakes to use its best endeavours, to the extent that it may do so lawfully and ethically, having regard to any relevant guidance on confidentiality to provide to the Council such information or opinions in relation to matters of which it has become aware in its capacity as auditor of the Lloyd's corporate member for the purpose of the exercise by the Council of powers contained in Lloyd's Acts 1871 to 1982 or in byelaws or regulations made thereunder whether or not in respect to a request by or under the authority of the Council. Therefore, the auditor of a Lloyd's corporate member needs to consider whether it has a duty or right to report a particular matter to Lloyd's."

Auditors of Lloyd's corporate members are not required to carry out procedures to **20** detect matters that may be of material significance to Lloyd's.

The key factor in determining whether a duty to report to Lloyd's arises is the **21** existence of circumstances that would either lead to suspension of the Lloyd's corporate member's authorisation to operate in the Lloyd's market or warrant use of Lloyd's power of intervention in the Lloyd's corporate member's conduct of business.

22   The undertaking for a Lloyd's corporate member does not specify the matters described above. However, if the auditor concludes that it cannot issue its report without qualifying the opinion then a duty to report would arise. Reference to an emphasis of matter without qualification of the opinion expressed does not of itself give rise to a duty to report to Lloyd's: however, the factors giving rise to an emphasis of matter may themselves do so.

23   The auditor is not protected from any breach of duty if, in making a report to the Council, the auditor does not act in good faith. Accordingly, the auditor may wish to take appropriate legal or other professional advice before taking the decision whether, and if so, in what manner, to report to the Council.

24   The duty to report to Lloyd's for auditors of Lloyd's corporate members does not extend to any other entity that has close links with the Lloyd's corporate member.

25   The Council accords particular importance to timely notification of matters giving rise to such a report to the Council by auditors of Lloyd's corporate members. ISA (UK) 250 Section B acknowledges that the auditor will normally seek evidence to assess the implications of a suspected breach before reporting a matter. Once it has identified information as being subject to the duty to report, ISA (UK) 250 Section B requires it to bring the matter to the attention of the regulator without delay. An auditor may fail to discharge its duty to report to the Council if it waits until giving its formal opinion on the financial statements of the corporate member or on other ad hoc reports, or if it agrees to delay making a report until management has had the opportunity to take remedial action.

Auditor's right to report to the Regulator

26   Section 342 FSMA 2000 provides that no duty to which an auditor of an authorised person is subject shall be contravened by communicating in good faith to the regulator information or an opinion on a matter that the auditor reasonably believes is relevant to any functions of the regulator. For this purpose, "authorised person" is deemed to include a Lloyd's syndicate.

ISA (UK) 300: PLANNING AN AUDIT OF FINANCIAL STATEMENTS

27   Much of the business conducted in the Lloyd's market uses central services in areas such as policy preparation, claims adjustment and transaction settlement. The service provider's Independent Service Auditor's Report on the operation of systems of control relates to certain of the relevant accounting information systems. As part of audit planning a syndicate auditor considers the extent to which it intends to place reliance on such reports.

ISA (UK) 315: IDENTIFYING AND ASSESSING THE RISKS OF MATERIAL MISSTATEMENT THROUGH UNDERSTANDING THE ENTITY AND ITS ENVIRONMENT

28   Responsibility for the establishment and proper operation of systems of control in a Lloyd's syndicate rests with the board of directors of the managing agent.

29   Responsibility for the establishment and proper operation of systems of control for a Lloyd's corporate member rests with its board of directors. In exercising this responsibility, the directors may conclude that it is appropriate to place reliance on the records maintained, and summaries thereof, prepared by the managing agents

of the underlying syndicates and on other, third party documentation. Such records and summaries may, therefore, be considered by the directors to form part of the accounting records of the corporate member. In addition, the directors of the corporate member and its auditor may conclude that it is appropriate to have regard to the work done by other auditors (including syndicate auditors) and to the reports they may issue. Guidance on this matter is set out in the section on ISA (UK) 600.

ISA (UK) 402: AUDIT CONSIDERATIONS RELATING TO AN ENTITY USING A SERVICE ORGANIZATION

Many syndicates use the centrally operated systems for clearing underwriting   30
transactions. The auditor of those systems provides an Independent Service Auditor's Report on the operation of those systems each calendar year. A syndicate auditor considers the proposed scope of this work as part of its audit planning process and assesses the level of reliance it intends to place on the work performed centrally when determining the extent and nature of procedures to be performed at the syndicate.

ISA (UK) 540: AUDITING ACCOUNTING ESTIMATES, INCLUDING FAIR VALUE ACCOUNTING ESTIMATES, AND RELATED DISCLOSURES

Technical provisions

The Lloyd's Valuation of Liabilities Rules require all Lloyd's syndicates writing   31
general insurance business to provide to the Council of Lloyd's, each year, a Statement of Actuarial Opinion (SAO) on their world-wide reserves, both gross and net of reinsurance.

The SAO should cover all the business of the syndicate for all years of account   32
from 1993 to date. Separate figures are required gross and net of reinsurance for each year of account. The Institute and Faculty of Actuaries published Guidance Note 20 "Actuarial Reporting Under the Lloyd's Valuation of Liabilities Rules". The actuary's report given in the SAO is limited to an opinion as to whether the reserves for solvency purposes established by the agent comply with the Lloyd's valuation of liability rules and are not less than the expected future costs of the liabilities for claims, net of anticipated future premiums, claims handling expenses and bad debts.

In carrying out its work on the syndicate Annual Return, the auditor considers the   33
extent to which it can use the work of the actuary performed on general insurance business. In making this assessment, the auditor reads the entire SAO and, if available, any related reports; it may also, where appropriate, discuss the contents of the SAO and related reports with the actuary. Factors to be taken into account in assessing the extent of reliance that may be placed on the actuary's work include:

Any limitations of scope of opinion expressed in the actuary's report.   34

The reliability of source data used by the actuary and the adequacy of steps taken   35
by the managing agent to ensure the integrity of that data. Care is necessary to avoid inappropriate reliance if management has supplied data to the actuary, on which reliance has been taken, which has not been considered in the course of the audit of the syndicate's financial statements.

The extent of any bias in the actuaries' work as a consequence of the actuarial   36
focus being on sufficiency of reserves.

37   The auditor is also aware that the SAO relates to a particular basis of reserves of the syndicate for each year of account. These may be different to the technical provisions recorded in the annual report of the syndicate or used in determining the closed year profit or loss.

38   In giving its opinion on the syndicate Annual Return, the syndicate auditor has regard to the appropriateness of the allocation of technical provisions between underlying years of account. Such provisions must be determined in accordance with requirements prescribed by Lloyd's.

39   Where a year of account is closed into a subsequent year of account of the same, or another, syndicate, the Syndicate Accounting Byelaw requires technical provisions of the closed year to be shown as a "premium for a reinsurance to close" (RITC) for that account in the underwriting year accounts as at date of closure. This description has the effect, in accounting terms, of enabling the affairs of that year of account to be drawn to a conclusion and the final result for the relevant annual venture determined. Where the year of account has closed by way of a RITC, the syndicate auditor considers whether, in the context of its opinion on the relevant underwriting year accounts, the relationship between the reinsuring and reinsured members of the syndicate gives rise to further materiality considerations.

40   In situations where the annual venture of a syndicate goes into run off provision for any additional costs to be included in a syndicate's annual accounts should be made in the accounting period in which the decision to cease underwriting or not to close a year of account is taken.

41   In order to comply with Lloyd's requirements, technical provisions for life business included in a syndicate Annual Return must be established and certified by an actuary in a prescribed form on a basis set out by Lloyd's.

ISA (UK) 560: SUBSEQUENT EVENTS

42   Currently the syndicate Annual Return is required to be submitted to Lloyd's before the syndicate annual accounts are issued. If there has been an event after the balance sheet date after the syndicate Annual Return has been signed but before the syndicate annual accounts and (where relevant) personal accounts are signed which is of such significance that it materially affects the view shown in these accounts, then they should be amended. Lloyd's rules may require that an amendment is also made to the syndicate Annual Return.

Other matters that the auditor may consider in its review of subsequent events include an evaluation of the impact of any material subsequent events on the syndicate's ability to continue to write business in the current annual venture or annual ventures yet to be established for subsequent years.

ISA (UK) 570: GOING CONCERN

43   The managing agent's responsibility for preparing syndicate annual accounts includes the requirement for the financial statements to be prepared on the basis that the syndicate will continue to write future business unless it is inappropriate to presume the syndicate will do so. Syndicate annual accounts present the collective participations of the members of the syndicate in one or more annual ventures. The ability of a syndicate to meet its obligations as they fall due will reflect the ability of the members of the syndicate to meet their obligations to the syndicate when calls are made. However, irrespective of whether information on a syndicate member's ability to meet its obligations as they fall due is available, the ability of a

syndicate to meet its obligations as they fall due is underpinned by the support provided by Lloyd's solvency process and its chain of security for any syndicate members who are unable to meet their underwriting liabilities.

Unless it is in run-off, at the date the annual accounts are approved the syndicate **44** will have commenced underwriting business through Lloyd's for the new underwriting year, but it will not have established an annual venture for subsequent years. Accordingly an assessment of the available capital resources is not applicable to syndicate annual accounts. However, audit procedures include making enquiries of the managing agent on the plans for the underwriting of business in future annual ventures of the syndicate.

ISA (UK) 600: SPECIAL CONSIDERATIONS – AUDITS OF GROUP FINANCIAL STATEMENTS (INCLUDING THE WORK OF COMPONENT AUDITORS)

Lloyd's syndicates

The auditor of a syndicate frequently experiences situations where audit evidence **45** is derived from information audited by other auditors, for example, where the audit of the managing agent is carried out by a separate firm from the syndicate's auditor. Consequently, the syndicate's auditor may have regard to the work of the agency's auditor, for example, in respect of recharged expenses. Similarly, in the case of certain service company activities on behalf of the syndicate, the syndicate auditor may have regard to the work of the auditor of the service company.

Lloyd's corporate members

Lloyd's has established a central facility to assist corporate members in preparing **46** their statutory financial statements. The facility accumulates information from underlying syndicates and then calculates and aggregates each corporate member's share of that information. The syndicate information is provided to Lloyd's within the syndicate Annual Return together with a syndicate auditor's report thereon.

Where corporate members rely on information provided by way of the central **47** facility, the auditor of corporate members applies the principles of ISA (UK) 600 in considering how the work of syndicate auditors affects its audit. Where the auditor of corporate members relies on the work of syndicate auditors, it considers the professional qualifications, experience and resources of the other auditors in the context of its audit of the corporate member in question. It obtains appropriate evidence that the work of the syndicate auditors is sufficient for the purposes of the audit of the corporate member's financial statements.

ISA (UK) 700: THE AUDITOR'S REPORT ON FINANCIAL STATEMENTS

The auditor of a Lloyd's syndicate's financial statements is required to report its **48** opinion as to whether the annual accounts comply with the requirements of the 2008 Lloyd's Regulations. Where syndicate underwriting year accounts are prepared for a run-off year of account, the auditor is required to report its opinion as to whether those accounts comply with the requirements of the Syndicate Accounting Byelaw.

In addition, its report on the annual accounts includes its opinion on whether they **49** give a true and fair view of the calendar year result and of the state of affairs at the balance sheet date. The report of the auditor on closed year underwriting year accounts includes its opinion on whether they give a true and fair view of the result of the closed year of account.

50   Lloyd's require that the auditor's report on syndicate underwriting year accounts be addressed to the members of the syndicate participating in the year of account to which they relate and not to all members of the syndicate. Different reporting requirements apply to syndicate underwriting year accounts for a closed year of account as apply to syndicate underwriting year accounts for a run-off year of account which is not closing.

51   In preparing underwriting accounts for a closed year of a syndicate, compliance with UK GAAP is normally necessary in order to give a true and fair view of the syndicate's closed year result.

52   ISA (UK) 700 states that:

> *If the auditor is required to report on certain matters by exception, the auditor shall describe in the auditor's report the auditor's responsibilities for such matters and incorporate a suitable conclusion in respect of such matters.*[89]

53   The auditor of a syndicate's annual and underwriting year accounts is required to report by exception if:

(a)   The managing agent has not maintained proper accounting records in respect of the syndicate;

(b)   The underwriting year accounts do not agree with the accounting records; and

(c)   the auditor of the syndicate's annual accounts is additionally required to report by exception if it has not received all the information and explanations that it requires.

ISA (UK) 701: COMMUNICATING KEY AUDIT MATTERS IN THE INDEPENDENT AUDITOR'S REPORT

54   The Society of Lloyd's as a whole is a "public interest entity" within the meaning of the Audit Regulation (EU) No 537/2014, and is within the scope of the Solvency II prudential regulation regime. Lloyd's syndicates are not public interest entities, and therefore the additional reporting requirements contained within ISA (UK) 701 do not apply.

Section 6: Reporting on Solvency and Financial Condition Reports for Solvency II ("Directive") Firms

1   The Solvency II prudential regulation regime came into force for authorised insurance entities, including Friendly Societies in the UK from 1 January 2016. This established different reporting and assurance requirements for "Directive" and "Non-Directive" firms. "Directive" firms must publish audited annual SFCRs, as well as submitting unaudited reports to the PRA as regulator. "Non-directive" firms will continue to submit audited regulatory returns, although some of the requirements have been simplified.

---

[89] *ISA (UK) 700 (Revised June 2016), para. 43-1.*

The PRA Rulebook sets out the full criteria which define which firms are   **2**
"Directive" and which are "Non-Directive".[90] There are multiple criteria relating
predominantly to the size and nature of the insurance (or reinsurance) business
undertaken, and the permissions granted by the FCA or PRA under Part4A of
FSMA 2000. The Society of Lloyd's falls within the scope of the Solvency II
firms' rulebook, and section 3 of the Insurance General Application chapter of the
PRA Rulebook for Solvency II firms explains the application of rules to –
respectively – the Society and managing agents.[91]

This section of PN20 provides guidance for auditors who are providing an opinion   **3**
on published SFCRs under Solvency II. Section 8 provides guidance for the audit
of non-directive firm regulatory reports.

The FRC adopted ISA (UK) 800 *Special Considerations – Audits of Financial*   **4**
Statements Prepared in Accordance with Special Purpose Frameworks and ISA
(UK) 805 *Special Considerations – Audits of Single Financial Statements and
Specific Elements, Accounts or Items of a Financial Statement* in order to support
the PRA's objective of providing reasonable assurance audit opinions on
published SFCRs.[92]

Whereas the ISAs (UK) are generally concerned with the audit of full sets of   **5**
financial statements prepared under general purpose financial reporting
frameworks (such as IFRS or UK GAAP), SFCRs are prepared in accordance
with a special purpose financial reporting framework as defined by ISA (UK) 800:

> For purposes of the ISAs (UK), the following terms have the meanings
> attributed below:
>
> (a) Special purpose financial statements – Financial statements prepared
>   in accordance with a special purpose framework. (Ref: Para. A4)
>
> (b) Special purpose framework – A financial reporting framework
>   designed to meet the financial information needs of specific users.
>   The financial reporting framework may be a fair presentation
>   framework or a compliance framework. (Ref: Para. A1–A4)[93]

ISA (UK) 800 deals with the auditor's considerations when applying ISAs (UK) in   **6**
the series 100–700 to the audit of full sets of financial statements prepared in
accordance with a special purpose financial reporting framework, including the
implications for the auditor's report. ISA (UK) 805 deals with the application of
the ISAs (UK) 100–700 series in the context of the audit of single financial
statements, and specific elements, amounts or items of a financial statement. This
is relevant to the audit of SFCRs because the PRA audit requirement does not
include the complete SFCR or included quantitative reporting templates (QRTs),
and includes additional exclusions from scope for specific disclosures. These
exclusions are described in more detail below.

---

[90] *PRA, SII firms Rulebook, Insurance General Application Rulebook, Chapter 2.*

[91] *PRA, SII firms Rulebook, Insurance General Application Rulebook, Chapter 3.*

[92] *These ISAs became effective for periods commencing on or after 1 January 2017, although early adoption is
allowed. Where these ISAs are adopted early for the audit of Solvency II public disclosures then they are permitted
to be used in conjunction with ISAs (UK and Ireland) where the audit of the statutory financial statements for the
same period was also conducted in accordance with those ISAs (UK and Ireland). In those circumstances, then
references to ISAs (UK) in ISAs (UK) 800 and 805 are deemed to be to the equivalent parts of those ISAs (UK and
Ireland).*

[93] *ISA (UK) 800, para. 6.*

7   The ISAs (UK) provide a framework which allows auditors to provide the required assurance and which can be applied to the Solvency II financial reporting framework. That framework, which is based on directly applicable European regulation and PRA rules, is intended to give the users of those financial statements confidence in the quality of the information being reported on the solvency and financial condition of insurance entities.

8   Audits of SFCRs, in accordance with PRA rules, have the character of a "second audit". This is because a close correlation between the information presented in the SFCR and that presented in the statutory financial statements cannot be assumed. By contrast, when an auditor that reports on a non-directive insurer's regulatory return carries out the audit of its financial statements in accordance with ISAs (UK), the work that the auditor performs on regulatory returns is deemed to be more closely integrated with the statutory audit, and therefore represents a set of additional procedures which enable it to report as required.

General Principles

9   PRA rules require that the auditor's report on the SFCR must be prepared with "due skill, care and diligence". An audit conducted in accordance with ISAs (UK) is intended to meet this requirement.

Audits of Solvency II public reports (SFCRs)

10   Pillar 3 of the Solvency II prudential regulation regime requires extensive public and private reporting of the solvency and financial condition of insurance entities, on a different basis to the previous regime requirements. In addition to the greater complexity of some disclosures, including for example the SCR, Own Funds, Technical Provisions (including risk margin), Solvency II Directive firms and groups are required to publish SFCRs annually. The structure and content of these financial statements are prescribed by the Solvency II Directive (Directive 2009/138/EC), Delegated Act, SFCR Implementing Technical Regulation and PRA rules. PRA rules require an external audit of SFCRs and a "reasonable assurance" audit report in accordance with ISAs (UK).[94]

11   SFCRs have the following prescribed basic structure which includes both financial and narrative content and information:

A   Business and Performance

B   System of Governance

C   Risk Profile

D   Valuation for Solvency Purposes

E   Capital Management

12   SFCRs include a series of QRTs which are also prescribed in regulation and by PRA rules. The scope of the "reasonable assurance" engagement covers sections D "Valuation for Solvency Purposes" and E "Capital Management" of the SFCR; as well as some but not all of the QRTs which are published alongside them. The rules set out the elements of the SFCR which are "relevant" for the purposes of the audit, and the circumstances in which some items are excluded from scope. For example, there are exemptions for elements of the disclosures relating to the SCR when an insurer uses a full or partial internal model, and for group information

---

[94] *See the External Audit Part of the PRA Rulebook pertaining to Solvency II firms, and the related Supervisory Statement SS11/16, Solvency II: external audit of the public disclosure requirement*

prepared and disclosed on a sectoral basis. More guidance on the implication of these "scope exclusions" is provided below.

In respect of group reporting requirements, auditors should refer to the Group   **13** Supervision part of the PRA Rulebook as it applies to Solvency II entities. However, in general participating Solvency II firms, or relevant insurance group undertakings must disclose publically, on an annual basis, a SFCR at group level[95] where:

- a UK Solvency II firm is a participating undertaking in at least one other Solvency II undertaking, third country insurance undertaking or third country reinsurance undertaking; or

- a Solvency II undertaking (other than a UK Solvency II firm) is a participating undertaking in a UK Solvency II firm; or

- the parent undertaking of a UK Solvency II firm is an insurance holding company or a mixed financial holding company which has its head office in an EEA State[96]; or

- the parent undertaking of a UK Solvency II firm is an insurance holding company which has its head office in a third country whose group supervision regime is not deemed "equivalent" and where no "other methods" waiver has been granted[97]

Subject to the agreement of the group supervisor they may provide a single SFCR   **14** which must comprise the following:

-    *... information at the level of the group which must be disclosed ...; and*

-    *... the information for any of the subsidiaries within the group which must be individually identifiable and disclosed ...*[98]

The group SFCR is subject to the same requirement for an external audit as for a   **15** solo SFCR. The information in respect of all subsidiaries is within audit scope. This includes solo level information in respect of EEA insurers outside the UK which would not be subject to the PRA's audit requirements had a single group-wide SFCR not been prepared. When conducting an audit of a single group-wide SFCR the auditor considers the requirements of ISA (UK) 600, including paragraphs 21–23 which relate to materiality.

There is also a separate auditor reporting requirement in respect of information   **16** included within the "relevant elements" of the group SFCR (and associated templates). In respect of the audit of a group SFCR where the "relevant elements" include information which:

- *Pertains to an undertaking that is not a Solvency II undertaking; and*

- *Information has been prepared in accordance with:*

  - *PRA rules other than those implementing the Solvency II Directive; or*

  - *An EU instrument other than the Solvency II Regulations.*[99]

---

[95] PRA, SII firms Rulebook, Group Supervision Chapter, 18.1.1.

[96] PRA, SII firms Rulebook, Group Supervision Chapter, 2.1.1 & 2.1.2.

[97] PRA, SII firms Rulebook, Group Supervision Chapter, 20.1–20.4

[98] PRA, SII firms Rulebook, Group Supervision Chapter, 18.1.2.

[99] PRA Rulebook, SII firms, External Audit Chapter, p. 4.2.1–4.2.2.

The external auditor is required to state in their report that the information has been *"properly compiled in accordance with the relevant PRA rule and EU instrument relating to that undertaking from information provided by members of the group and the relevant insurance group undertaking"*.[100]

17   The information covered by the "properly compiled" statement is not within scope of the reasonable assurance opinion. Further guidance on how the auditor complies with this requirement is set out below in the section on "Forming an opinion and reporting on the engagement".

18   In order to achieve the PRA's required level of (reasonable) assurance these engagements are conducted in accordance with International Standards on Auditing (UK) (ISAs (UK)), including ISA (UK) 800 and ISA (UK) 805.

19   SFCRs are prepared in accordance with a special purpose financial reporting framework (as set out in the Solvency II Directive, Delegated Act, SFCR Implementing Technical Standard and PRA Rules). The PRA audit requirement does not cover all of the elements of the SFCR or the information in related QRTs. The scope of the "reasonable assurance" audit engagement therefore requires the auditor to consider the requirements and guidance contained within ISAs (UK) 800 and 805, including their interactions with other ISAs (UK), when accepting, planning, performing and reporting on engagements of this kind. ISA 805 (UK) is the most appropriate source for requirements and guidance in respect of the PRA's requirement that only relevant elements and templates are included within the scope of the audit. That does not mean the auditor is required to issue a separate opinion on each individual statement or element which is being audited.

20   ISA (UK) 800 and ISA (UK) 805 are designed to help auditors apply the requirements of the ISAs (UK) in the specific context of financial statements prepared in accordance with a special purpose financial reporting framework, and audits of single financial statements and specific elements, accounts or items of a financial statement. They do not override the requirements of the other ISAs (UK), nor do they deal with all special considerations of the engagement.[101] The material in this Practice Note is not intended to represent a complete guide to the application of the ISAs (UK) for engagements of this kind, but focusses on areas where there may be specific relevant considerations.

Accepting the Engagement

21   ISA (UK) 210 (revised) sets out the basic preconditions for an audit. These include (but are not limited to):

- Whether the financial reporting framework is acceptable

- Obtaining the agreement of management that it acknowledges and understands its responsibility for the preparation of the financial statements in accordance with the financial reporting framework[102]

The Solvency II financial reporting framework

22   In order to comply with the ISAs (UK) the auditor must determine the acceptability of the financial reporting framework applied in the preparation of the financial statements and must obtain an understanding of the purpose for

---

[100] *PRA Rulebook, SII firms, External Audit Chapter, p. 4.2.2.*

[101] *ISA (UK) 800, para. 3; ISA (UK) 805, para. 3.*

[102] *ISA (UK) 210 (revised), para. 6.*

which the financial statements are prepared; the intended users; and steps taken by management to determine that the applicable financial reporting framework is acceptable in the circumstances.[103] Paragraphs 37–42 below, which cover the application of materiality to these engagements, goes into more detail about the auditor's considerations of the intended users of SFCRs.

PRA rules, supplemented by a framework of approvals, waivers and supervisory   **23** determinations, implements the requirements of the financial reporting framework required by Directive 2009/138/EC ("the Solvency II Directive"). The UK regulatory framework includes:

- Reporting 3 (and in the case of group reporting, Group Supervision 18 and 20) of the PRA Rulebook applicable to Solvency II firms

- Commission Delegated Regulation (EU) 2015/35 supplementing the Solvency II Directive ("the Delegated Act")

- Commission Implementing Technical Regulation (EU) 2015/2452 ("the SFCR Implementing Technical Standard")

In addition to the formal requirements of the framework, the auditor of a Solvency   **24** II public disclosure might reasonably be expected to have regard to supplementary Guidelines in respect of Solvency II, including public reporting and disclosure, which are published by the European Insurance and Occupational Pensions Authority (EIOPA).[104] The PRA also issues Supervisory Statements which set out additional guidance, including SS11/16 *"Solvency II: external audit of the public disclosure requirement"*.[105]

The principles which are to be followed in presenting information about the   **25** Solvency and Financial Condition of an entity are that:

   (a)   it must reflect the nature, scale and complexity of the business of the undertaking concerned, and in particular the risks inherent in that business;

   (b)   it must be accessible, complete in all material respects, comparable and consistent over time; and

   (c)   it must be relevant, reliable and comprehensible[106]

Paragraph 3.4 of the PRA's Supervisory Statement SS11/16 *"Solvency II: external*   **26** *audit of the public disclosure requirement"* states that the

   ... auditor is not expected to express an opinion on the validity of an approval, waiver or other supervisory determination. Instead approvals, waivers and supervisory determinations provided by the competent authority should be considered as part of the framework against which the audit opinion is being given.[107]

The Solvency II framework sets out those areas where the national supervisor has   **27** the right to grant approvals, waivers and other supervisory determinations in respect of the application of Solvency II. Whilst accepting that these are part of the established framework against which the opinion is given, the auditor may

---

[103]   *ISA (UK) 800, para.8; ISA (UK) 210 (revised), para. 6 (a).*

[104]   *https://eiopa.europa.eu/publications/eiopa-guidelines/guidelines-on-reporting-and-public-disclosure.*

[105]   *http://www.bankofengland.co.uk/pra/Pages/publications/ss/default.aspx*

[106]   *DIRECTIVE 2009/138/EC OF THE EUROPEAN PARLIAMENT AND OF THE COUNCIL of 25 November 2009 on the taking-up and pursuit of the business of Insurance and Reinsurance (Solvency II) (recast) (Text with EEA relevance) Article 35, p.4*

[107]   *PRA Supervisory Statement, SS11/16, "Solvency II: external audit of the public disclosure requirement", p.3.4*

nevertheless need to understand, through discussion and ongoing dialogue with the supervisor, the extent to which any relevant approvals, waivers or supervisory determinations are consistent with the Solvency II framework. Further guidance on the auditor's procedures in respect of approvals, waivers and supervisory determinations is set out below.

28   In determining whether the Solvency II financial reporting framework is acceptable, the auditor considers the guidance in ISA (UK) 800 which discusses financial reporting requirements established by the regulator, and which indicates that they may be presumed to be acceptable:

> *In some jurisdictions, law or regulation may prescribe the financial reporting framework to be used by management in the preparation of special purpose financial statements for a certain type of entity. For example, a regulator may establish financial reporting provisions to meet the requirements of that regulator. In the absence of indications to the contrary, such a financial reporting framework is presumed acceptable for special purpose financial statements prepared by such entity.*[108]

Management responsibilities

29   The written acknowledgement by management of their responsibilities, including for the preparation of the financial statements in accordance with the financial reporting framework is a fundamental precondition for an audit.

30   The PRA's Supervisory Statement SS11/16 states that:

> *... the PRA expects the governing body to take responsibility for ensuring that the SFCR has been properly prepared in all material respects in accordance with the PRA rules and Solvency II regulations. As well as having a written policy in place to ensure the ongoing appropriateness of any information disclosed, the PRA expects that the governing body should be satisfied that:*
>
> (a)   *throughout the financial year in question, the insurer has complied in all material respects with the requirements of the PRA rules and Solvency II regulations as applicable to the insurer; and*
>
> (b)   *it is reasonable to believe that, at the date of the publication of the SFCR, the insurer has continued so to comply, and will continue so to comply in future.*
>
> *The PRA expect the governing body to acknowledge and evidence in writing their responsibility for the SFCR and make this available to potential readers of the SFCR by signing the SFCR and attaching the written acknowledgment to the SFCR.*[109]

31   This acknowledgment is intended to be similar in nature to the Directors Certificate which is required to be prepared by non-directive insurers for their regulatory returns and which are described in the PRA Non SII firms rulebook.[110]

---

[108] *Article 291, Chapter XII Section 1 of the COMMISSION DELEGATED REGULATION (EU) 2015/35 of 10 October 2014, http://eur-lex.europa.eu/legal-content/EN/TXT/PDF/?uri=CELEX:32015R0035&from= ENCOMMISSION DELEGATED REGULATION (EU) 2015/35 of 10 October 2014*

[109] *"Solvency II: external audit of the public disclosure requirement", p.2. Note that in the context of a group SFCR, the statement at (a) does not apply to compliance at the level of components, only to the entity which is preparing the SFCR.*

[110] *PRA Non SII Firms Rulebook 8 Directors Certificate.*

When considering whether the preconditions for an acceptance of an audit exist **32** therefore, auditors may wish to discuss the Supervisory Statement SS11/16 with management, and where relevant, those charged with governance. Auditors may also wish to convey to management the relevant requirements of the ISAs (UK). If management or the governing body will not provide such a written representation then the auditor considers whether the preconditions for accepting the audit have been met.

Planning and Performing the Engagement

ISA 800 provides guidance on the auditor's consideration of whether the **33** application of the ISAs (UK) requires special consideration in the circumstances of the Solvency II engagement.[111] This includes:

(a) Consideration of whether, in the circumstances of the audit, an entire ISA (UK), or requirement of an ISA (UK) is not relevant because it is conditional, and the condition does not exist.[112]

(b) In the audit of a special purpose financial statement such as the SFCR, the auditor considers judgements about materiality based on the needs of the intended users of those financial statements, rather than on a consideration of the common financial information needs of users as a group[113].

(c) Determining the appropriate person(s) within the entity's governance structure with whom to communicate.[114]

Relationship to the audit of statutory financial statements

There is no requirement for an auditor of a SFCR to have conducted the audit of **34** the statutory financial statements. The audit of the SFCR is a separate engagement to the audit of the statutory financial statements.

Where the auditor, or audit firm, conducts the audits of both the statutory financial **35** statements and the SFCR then the auditor considers how the risk assessment, planning, performance and reporting for each engagement could inform the other. The PRA rules do require the auditor to adopt this approach in certain areas of the engagement. For example, the PRA requirements go beyond ISA (UK) 720 (revised) in respect of Other Information by explicitly requiring the auditor of the SFCR to consider information and knowledge obtained in the course of the statutory audit when considering matters of consistency.[115]

There are other areas where there may be scope for the efficient utilization of audit **36** evidence and insight in support of each separate engagement, for example:

(a) Going Concern – where the auditor's review of the Viability Statement in the statutory financial statements, for example, may provide evidence to support the audit of the SFCR;

(b) Review of information systems, data quality and general IT controls;

(c) Review of assumptions and methods underpinning the valuation of assets and liabilities;

---

[111] *ISA (UK) 800, para. 9.*

[112] *ISA (UK) 800, para. A9.*

[113] *ISA (UK) 800, para. A10.*

[114] *ISA (UK) 800, para. A12.*

[115] *The PRA have stated that this additional consistency review should be conducted in accordance with the requirements of ISA 720 (UK).*

(d)   Review of compliance with law and regulation;

(e)   Review of the work of the actuarial function within the entity;

(f)   Review of the work of internal audit.

Materiality

37   The auditor applies the concept of materiality appropriately in planning and performing the audit.[116] ISA (UK) 320 notes that discussion of the concept of materiality within a financial reporting framework provides a frame of reference for the auditor in determining materiality for the audit.[117] Solvency II defines materiality in the context of the SFCR as follows:

> *... the information to be disclosed in the solvency and financial condition report shall be considered as material if its omission or misstatement could influence the decision-making or the judgement of the users of that document, including the supervisory authorities.*[118]

38   The PRA has also made pronouncements which indicate that it should be considered one of the users, rather than the only primary user of the SFCR:

> *The PRA is comfortable that insurers, auditors and users are clear that the PRA is a primary user of the SFCR and audit report without being included as an addressee and has decided to retain existing practice and not be an addressee to the auditor's report.*[119]

39   The intended users of the SFCR are not restricted to the supervisory authorities alone. The objectives of Solvency II are to engender widespread confidence in the systemic health of the insurance sector across the EU, and the effectiveness of prudential regulation. As a consequence, Pillar 3 has introduced mandatory public reporting – in the form of the SFCR – as well as private reporting to supervisory authorities. In determining materiality for the audit of the SFCR, the auditor needs to understand who the other intended users are, and the resulting implications for judgements on materiality. The auditor needs to understand the factors which might influence the decision-making or judgement of the regulator, as well other identified users.

40   The auditor considers how to apply ISA (UK) 320 in the light of the application guidance in ISA (UK) 800. This describes the different judgements about the users of special purpose financial statements, as opposed to those of general purpose financial statements:

> *... in ISA 320, judgements about matters that are material to users of the financial statements are based on a consideration of the common financial information needs of users as a group. In the case of an audit of special purpose financial statements, however, those judgements are based on a consideration of the financial information needs of the intended users.*[120]

---

[116] *ISA (UK) 320 (Revised June 2016), Materiality in Planning and Performing an Audit, para. 8.*

[117] *ISA (UK) 320 (Revised June 2016), Materiality in Planning and Performing an Audit, para. 3.*

[118] *Article 291, Chapter XII Section 1 of the COMMISSION DELEGATED REGULATION (EU) 2015/35 of 10 October 2014, http://eur-lex.europa.eu/legal-content/EN/TXT/PDF/?uri=CELEX:32015R0035&from= ENCOMMISSION DELEGATED REGULATION (EU) 2015/35 of 10 October 2014*

[119] *Consultation Paper | CP23/16 Solvency II: external audit of the public disclosure requirement, July 2016, para.3.1*

[120] *ISA (UK) 800, para. A10.*

The auditor may need to consider whether the materiality judgements made in **41** respect of an audit of the statutory financial statements of an entity, based on the common financial information needs of users as a group, are appropriate to the needs of the intended users of published SFCR's. Many auditors of listed insurance firms in the UK currently use profit or income measures as the benchmark for their materiality calculations for the statutory financial statements *audit*. Others, including some auditors of life insurance entities, use an equity or asset based measure. The primary users of statutory financial statements prepared in accordance with IFRS are generally considered to be *"existing and potential investors, lenders and other creditors"*[121] – although they are also important to other users. The auditor considers whether the benchmark used for the audit of the statutory financial statements – whether profit and income, or asset and equity based – are appropriate for the audit of the published SFCR. In doing so, the auditor considers the needs of the users of these reports in accordance with ISAs (UK).

A further consideration for the auditor when determining materiality for the audit **42** of the SFCR is the scope of the audit. For example when the external audit opinion does not include the SCR because of the use of an internal or partial internal model, this may need to be reflected in the setting of materiality. The PRA requirement for external audit assurance is limited to the "Valuation for solvency purposes" and "Capital management" sections of the SFCR, and some but not all of the included QRTs. The auditor considers the requirements of ISA (UK) 805.[122]

Approvals, modifications and supervisory determinations

In accordance with PRA rules the auditor is not expected to express an opinion on **43** the validity of an approval, modification or other supervisory determination. Instead, they should be considered as being part of the framework against which the audit opinion is being given. The auditor ensures that this framework, including the nature of approvals, modificationss and supervisory determinations is adequately described in the auditor's report.

Subject to considerations of materiality, where approval is given for a specific **44** number or adjustment included within the regulatory report, or used in the calculation of a number included within the report, then the auditor confirms the accuracy of the disclosure to the supervisory approval.

Where approval is given for the use of a specific methodology then (other than **45** those areas where there is a specific limitation on the scope of the audit – SCRs for partial or full internal model firms for example), the auditor confirms that the methodology used is consistent with the approval, and has been applied correctly.

The auditor should consider the adequacy of disclosures in the SFCR which **46** describe the modifications, approvals and determinations which are relevant in each case, and discuss with management any concerns which arise. Where these concerns are not adequately addressed the auditor may consider any implications for the auditor's report.

Modifications, approvals and determinations which might be relevant include: **47**

---

[121] *IASB, The Conceptual Framework for Financial Reporting, OB5, OB10.*

[122] *For example, see application guidance at ISA (UK) 805, para. A15.*

Modifications granted under section 138A of FSMA ("the modifications")

- Permission for non-disclosure of information in SFCR
- Permission to publish a single group-wide SFCR
- Permission to exclude entities from the scope of group supervision
- Permission to use deduction and aggregation method in the calculation of group SCR

Approvals made under The Solvency II Regulations ("the approvals")

- Approval of items of ancillary own funds
- Approval to take credit for "non-standard" items of own funds
- Approval to use the matching adjustment in calculating technical provisions
- Approval to use the volatility adjustment in the calculation of technical provisions
- Approval to use the risk free rate transitional measure in the calculation of technical provisions
- Approval to use the transitional measure on technical provisions
- Approval to use a full or partial internal model
- Approval to use solo or group specific parameters when calculating the SCR

Determinations made in accordance with the PRA Rules and Solvency II regulations on which they are based ("the determinations")

- Determination of any capital add-on to the SCR
- Determination of the extent to which own funds of group members cannot effectively be made available to cover the group SCR.

[note that these are indicative of some of the more common items, and this is not intended to represent a comprehensive list]

Exclusions from the scope of the audit: Partial and Full Internal Model firms.

48   The PRA Solvency II Firms Rulebook excludes from the scope of the external audit certain information in the SFCR, certain quantitative reporting templates and certain information in other templates where it, "… is, or derives from the SCR" and is calculated using a full or partial internal model.[123] A number of disclosures within the "relevant elements of the SFCR" are derived from the SCR. The auditor

---

[123] *PRA, SII firms rulebook, External Audit Chapter, 2.2 (3) & 2.2 (4) & PRA: Supervisory Statement SS11/ 16 "Solvency II: external audit of the public disclosure requirement", Appendix 3.*

therefore considers the implications for the scope of the audit, in accordance with ISA (UK) 805:

> *The individual financial statements that comprise a complete set of financial statements, and many of the specific elements of those financial statements, including their related disclosures, are interrelated. Accordingly, when auditing a single financial statement or a specific element of a financial statement, the auditor may not be able to consider the financial statement or the element in isolation. Consequently, the auditor may need to perform procedures in relation to the interrelated items to meet the objective of the audit.*[124]

Specific examples of items which are related to the SCR, and where an assessment   **49** must be made of whether they are in or out of scope of the audit for partial or full internal model firms include:

Information In Scope

(a)   The Minimum Capital Requirement (MCR) "corridor"

Calculated using a prescribed linear formula, and subject to an absolute floor, the MCR must sit within a "corridor" of 25–45% of the SCR (including any capital addon).[125] The application of the corridor is subject to the MCR not being below its absolute floor (which is a fixed euro amount). MCR QRTs 28.01.01 and 28.02.01, include information about the SCR of the entity and the final MCR which must be calibrated within the 25–45% range.

For composite insurers, the templates also include information about the SCRs which are used to derive separate notional MCRs for the life and non-life components of the business.

In this case the MCR is calculated separately, based on information which is subject to audit. The calibration of the result does not achieve the condition in PRA rules to exclude it from the scope of the audit – namely that it "is, or derives from" the SCR.

Information Out of Scope

(b)   Solvency Capital Ratio for Partial Internal Model firms

The standard formula element of the SCR for a partial internal model firm is out of scope, since the SCR as a whole is outside the scope of the PRA's audit requirement for partial internal model firms.

---

[124] *ISA (UK) 805, para. A14.*

[125] *Article 129 (3), DIRECTIVE 2009/138/EC OF THE EUROPEAN PARLIAMENT AND OF THE COUNCIL of 25 November 2009 on the taking-up and pursuit of the business of Insurance and Reinsurance (Solvency II), Article*

(c)   Risk Margin

The risk margin is dependent on the calculation of current and future SCRs (over the lifetime of relevant obligations). For standard formula firms the risk margin is therefore within the audit scope. For partial and full internal model firms unaudited SCR figures are a key input into the calculation of the risk margin – therefore audit procedures which only cover the arithmetic accuracy of the calculation would not provide the necessary level of assurance to support the auditor's reasonable assurance opinion. The risk margin for partial and full internal model firms would therefore be excluded from the scope of the audit.

(d)   Restricted Own-funds in ring-fenced funds and matching adjustment portfolios

Where these funds and/or portfolios are considered material, then an adjustment is required for any restricted own-funds in excess of the notional SCR which has been calculated for that fund or portfolio. Where these funds and/or portfolios are not considered material, then an adjustment may be made for the total amount of restricted own-funds – in which case there is no need to calculate a notional SCR. This adjustment is a line item in the SFCR reporting template S.23.01.01, and may also be referred to within the main sections of the SFCR.

For standard formula firms, the calculation of any notional SCR and the resulting restricted own-funds adjustment would therefore be within scope of the audit. However, for partial or full internal model firms, the calculation of this adjustment "is, or derives from' the SCR", and is therefore out of scope of the audit.

(e)   Deductions reflecting the non-availability of own-funds items at a group level

A deduction is made for non-available own funds in components to restrict their contribution to the extent of the group component's contribution to the group SCR. As with the examples of the risk margin and restricted own-funds above the deduction, which is included as a line item in the SFCR templates, is calculated using the SCR. This meets the PRA standard of "is, or derives from' the SCR", and is therefore out of scope of the audit for partial or full internal model firms

(f)   Narrative components of the SFCR that relate to or are dependent upon the SCR

There are five sections of the SFCR as well as included QRTs. Two of these five sections are defined by the PRA's audit requirement as being "relevant elements of the SFCR". [Valuation for Solvency Purposes and Capital Management]. These sections include mandatory references to, as well as other quantitative information which relates to or is dependent upon the SCR. In addition, the remaining sections of the SFCR [Business and Performance, System of Governance and Risk Profile] may contain similar information.

This information is not part of the scope of the auditor's reasonable assurance opinion audit, but the auditor applies the requirements and guidance contained within ISA (UK) 720 *The Auditor's Responsibilities Relating to Other Information*.

The transitional measure on technical provisions.

The SFCR and relevant QRTs include information about the effect of adjustments **50** in respect of any transitional measure on technical provisions [not all firms will have sought approval to apply this measure]. This information is included within the "relevant elements" of the SFCR which are subject to audit under PRA rules.

Entities may use the transitional measure, subject to supervisory approval, to **51** spread increases in technical provisions under the Solvency II regime. The adjustment is based on a methodology approved by the supervisor, and which initially calculates the difference between technical provisions as at 31st December 2015, and technical provisions under Solvency II as at 1st January 2016.[126] The PRA Supervisory Statement SS11/16 "Solvency II: external audit of the public disclosure requirement" states that, "For the purposes of transitional measures on technical provisions, Pillar 1 and 2 assets, liabilities and capital calculated in accordance with the previous regime, should be treated as part of the framework against which the audit opinion is being given". This information is therefore to be considered out of scope of the audit requirement. The transitional measure on technical provisions is included within the relevant elements of the Solvency and Financial Condition Report, and is therefore within scope of the audit requirement. However, the calculation of the technical measure, when applied, is materially dependent on Pillar 1 and 2 assets, liabilities and capital calculated in accordance with the previous regime which are not subject to audit.

The PRA's Supervisory Statement SS11/16 also states that supervisory **52** determinations should be considered as part of the framework against which the audit opinion is being given. In respect of the transitional measure on technical provisions supervisory approval provides evidence of the approval of a transitional measure, and of the methodology to be employed in calculating it. It does not provide evidence that the method has been applied correctly and that information disclosed about the transitional measure is free from material error.

The exclusion of the underlying calculations based on the previous regime from **53** the PRA's audit requirement means that the auditor cannot give their opinion on the transitional measure on technical provisions, which is dependent upon them. The auditor therefore considers the implications for the form of their report.

Exclusions from the scope of the audit: Group SFCR.

PRA rules establish a separate reporting requirement in respect of information **54** presented in the "relevant elements" of the group SFCR which is prepared and presented on a sectoral basis. That requirement is in addition to the auditor's requirements under ISAs (UK), and that information is therefore excluded from the scope of the audit. Further guidance on the implications for the auditor's report is provided below.

Use of actuaries

There is no formal requirement for auditors to use the work of an actuary in the **55** course of an audit of the SFCR. However, the PRA's Supervisory Statement SS11/16 makes reference to the requirements of the ISAs (UK) in respect of assessing the need for an auditor's expert to be engaged. Therefore:

---

[126] *PRA Supervisory Statement SS1717/15 para 3.3 states that "Pillar 2 insurance liabilities are the starting point for the transitional deduction. They will capture all relevant features of the liabilities, including those that may not be reflected in a firm's Pillar 1 technical provisions as set out in Chapter 1 of the Prudential Sourcebook for Insurers (INSPRU 1)".*

As a minimum, for firms that write life business, the PRA expects that auditors, in undertaking the external audit, will obtain and pay due regard to the work of a suitably qualified actuary who is independent of the firm.[127]

56 Sections 4 and 8 of this Practice Note set out guidance in respect of the use of actuaries in the context of the audits of both the statutory financial statements and of non-directive regulatory returns. That guidance is also relevant to the use of an actuary in the course of the audit of the SFCR, including agreeing the scope of the work and assessing the independence of the actuary.

Group SFCR

57 The Group SFCR for an insurer may include information derived from third countries where the Solvency II regime does not apply. The Solvency II Directive and the PRA Rulebook sets out the supervisory and reporting arrangements in these circumstances, including the consideration of the equivalence of a third country supervision regime with Solvency II. When conducting an audit of a group SFCR, the auditor considers the requirements and guidance in ISA (UK) 600 *Special Considerations – Audits of Group Financial Statements (including the work of component auditors)*. Circumstances specific to the audit of group SFCRs might include:

- The inclusion of information about a material component on a local rules basis, rather than on a Solvency II basis;

- The inclusion of information about a component where that component has not been subject to audit under the rules which apply in the third country (or in an EEA state where there is no equivalent audit regime);

- Differences in filing deadlines for the submission of regulatory reports in different jurisdictions;

- Other inconsistencies in reported information.

Forming an opinion and reporting on the engagement

58 PRA rules require that the auditor produces *a report that includes an opinion addressed to the governing body confirming that the relevant elements of the SFCR are prepared in all material respects in accordance with the PRA rules and Solvency II regulations on which it is based.*[128]

59 These reports are consistent with those prepared in respect of compliance financial reporting frameworks under the ISAs (UK). Illustrative reports are included in section 7 of this Practice Note. In order to comply with the requirements of ISA (UK) 800 the auditor includes in their report an Emphasis of Matter paragraph alerting users of the auditor's report that the financial statements are prepared in accordance with a special purpose framework and that, as a result, the financial statements may not be suitable for another purpose. The auditor specifically describes the financial reporting framework as a special purpose framework and that the audit has been carried out in accordance with ISAs (UK), including ISA (UK) 800 and/or ISA (UK) 805.[129]

---

[127] *"Supervisory Statement", SS11/16, p.4.3.*

[128] *PRA Rulebook, SII firms, External Audit Chapter, p. 4.1.2.*

[129] *ISA (UK) 800, para. 14. Note that ISAs require the name of the engagement partner to be stated for listed insurers only [ISA 800 (UK) A18].*

Capital Add-Ons

Under section 55M of FSMA, the PRA can apply a capital add-on in circumstances **60** where there has been a risk profile deviation within a firm related to the standard formula, internal model, system of governance, matching adjustment, volatility adjustment or transitional measures[130]. ISA (UK) 700 requires the auditor to evaluate whether, "in view of the requirements of the applicable financial reporting framework ... the financial statements provide adequate disclosures to enable the intended users to understand the effect of material transactions and events on the information conveyed in the financial statements." As part of transitional measures implemented by the PRA, firms have the right to choose not to disclose any such capital add-on in the first years of Solvency II. Preparers are, however, required to disclose whether the UK has made use of the relevant member state option in the SFCR[131]. The auditor therefore considers the adequacy of the disclosure in the SFCR, and considers any implications for their report.

Additional Reporting Requirement: Group SFCRs

In respect of the audit of a group SFCR where the "relevant elements" include **61** information which:

- *Pertains to an undertaking that is not a Solvency II undertaking; and*

- *Information has been prepared in accordance with:*

  - *PRA rules other than those implementing the Solvency II Directive; or*

  - *An EU instrument other than the Solvency II Regulations[132]*

The external auditor is required to state in their report that the information has been *"properly compiled in accordance with the relevant PRA rule and EU instrument relating to that undertaking from information provided by members of the group and the relevant insurance group undertaking".*[133]

The PRA states in the Supervisory Statement SS11/16 for the external audit **62** requirement that:
> *"the group auditor should undertake an assessment of whether that information has been properly extracted in accordance with the relevant sectoral rules, from information provided to the insurer by other undertakings of the insurance group and from the insurer's own records. An external audit of such information is not required".*[134]

This is an separate reporting requirement, other than that required under ISAs **63** (UK). The auditor therefore considers and complies with ISA (UK) 700 by addressing this "requirement under a separate section of the auditor's report with a heading titled "Report on Other Legal and Regulatory Requirements" or otherwise

---

[130] *PRA Supervisory Statement, SS4/15, "Solvency II: the solvency and minimum capital requirements" (March 2015).*

[131] *Article 297 (2) e of the Delegated Regulation 2015/35.*

[132] *PRA Rulebook, SII firms, External Audit Chapter, p. 4.2.1–4.2.2.*

[133] *PRA Rulebook, SII firms, External Audit Chapter, p. 4.2.2.*

[134] *PRA Supervisory Statement, SS11/16, "Solvency II: external audit of the public disclosure requirement". Note that the concepts/terms "properly compiled" or "properly extracted" are not included within ISAs (UK), and that this additional reporting engagement is outside the scope of the SFCR reasonable assurance opinion. However, the auditor may wish to consider other potentially relevant sources of guidance on the process for assessing the "proper compilation" of the sectoral information. SIR 4000 – Investment Reporting Standards Applicable to Public Reporting Engagements on Pro forma Financial Information (2006), for example, includes guidance on aspects of the compilation process for pro forma information which may be helpful in this context.*

as appropriate to the content of the section."[135] The auditor clearly identifies which of the "relevant elements" of the SFCR relate to the "properly compiled" statement, and are therefore out of scope of the audit opinion on the SFCR. An illustrative example of such a report is included as an annex to this Practice Note.

Basis of Preparation

64   ISA (UK) 200 states that, "… an audit in accordance with ISAs (UK) is conducted on the premise that management and, where appropriate, those charged with governance" have acknowledged their responsibility for the preparation of the financial statements in accordance with the applicable financial reporting framework, and for such internal control they determine to be necessary to enable the preparation of financial statements that are free from material misstatement.[136] The preparation of financial statements "requires", "The inclusion of an adequate description of..[the]..framework in the financial statements."[137] ISA (UK) 700 requires that, in forming an opinion on the financial statements, the auditor evaluates whether the, "financial statements appropriately disclose the significant accounting policies selected and applied", and whether the "financial statements adequately refer to or describe the applicable financial reporting framework."[138]

Key Audit Matters, Other Planning and Scoping Matters

65   ISA (UK) 800 states that for audits of special purpose financial statements, the requirements of ISA (UK) 701 only apply when such matters are required to be communicated by law or regulation, or when the auditor otherwise decides to do so. When these matters are communicated in the auditor's report on special purpose financial statements, ISA (UK) 701 applies in its entirety.[139] The PRA rulebook does not require the auditor to communicate key audit matters, or other planning and scoping matters such as materiality in its report.

Other Information

66   For the purposes of the audit of the SFCR and the application of ISA (UK) 720, the auditor considers elements of the SFCR which are published alongside the "relevant elements of the SFCR" to be "statutory other information". This includes information contained within the "relevant elements" which are out of scope of the opinion because they "are or are derived from the SCR".

67   Under PRA rules, where the auditor of the relevant elements of the SFCR is also the auditor of the statutory financial statements, then in addition to the requirements of ISA (UK) 720 it must consider information and knowledge gained in the course of the statutory audit when considering whether the other information is consistent with it.

The Society of Lloyd's and Syndicate reporting

68   The Society of Lloyd's falls within scope of Solvency II, and is therefore subject to Pillar 3 public disclosure requirements. In order to comply with this requirement,

---

[135] *ISA (UK) 700 (Revised June 2016), para. 43.*

[136] *ISA (UK) 200 (revised), para. A2.*

[137] *ISA (UK) 200 (revised), para. A3.*

[138] *ISA (UK) 700 (revised), para. 13(a), 15 & A10–A15.*

[139] *ISA (UK) 800, para. A16.*

the Society has issued instructions to managing agents in respect of syndicate reporting[140], including an audit requirement. The guidance contained within this section of the Practice Note will therefore have relevance for the auditor of syndicate reports to the Society, although they will need to consider the specific circumstances of Lloyd's, including the specified form of the auditor's report.

The Society of Lloyd's collects data from each syndicate to be able to meet its Pillar 3 reporting requirements, using an online data collection system known as Core Market Returns (CMR). **69**

Lloyd's collects a Solvency II balance sheet ("QMC") from syndicates twice a year, at 30 June (subject to a reasonable assurance review), and at 31 December (subject to a full external audit). Syndicates are required to submit the following annual forms: **70**

- ASR Annual Solvency Return

- ASB Annual Solvency Return Part B

- AAD Annual Asset Data

Only certain forms within the ASR fall within the audit scope equivalent to that being applied by PRA to all supervised undertakings. Lloyd's therefore applies an equivalent audit requirement for the following ASR forms: **71**

- ASR002 – Balance Sheet* (EIOPA S.02.01.02)

- ASR220 – Own Funds (EIOPA S.23.01.01)

- ASR240 – Non-Life Technical Provisions Part A* (EIOPA S.17.01.02)

- ASR280 – Life Technical Provisions* (EIOPA S.12.01.01)

- ASR283 – Health SLT Technical Provisions* (EIOPA S.12.01.01)

- ASR510 – Minimum Capital Requirement (Non-Life) (EIOPA S.28.01.01)

- ASR511 – Minimum Capital Requirement (Life) (EIOPA S.28.01.01)

- ASR910 – Managing Agent's Report (sign off by the Board of the managing agent)

The risk margin is not subject to audit where (as in the case of Lloyd's syndicates) it is dependent on an SCR generated by an internal model. **72**

The Society will issue a model auditor's report for use by the external auditors of these regulatory returns. **73**

Section 7: Illustrative Auditor's Reports – Solvency II ("Directive") Firms

A: An auditor's report on relevant elements of the SFCR: Solo insurer, standard formula

For the purpose of this illustrative report the following circumstances are assumed:

- The insurance entity is a solo insurer.

---

[140] *"QMC Return Instructions December 2015 Version 1.0" ("the Instructions"), prepared by the managing agent pursuant to the provisions of the Solvency and Reporting Byelaw (No.5 of 2007) ("the Byelaw") and the requirements referred to by Lloyd's in the Instructions. Auditors should refer to these or any subsequent Llloyd's Solvency II guidance and instructions.*

- The auditor is responsible for the audit of the entity's statutory financial statements as well as of the relevant elements of the Solvency and Financial Condition Report.

- The audited entity has calculated the Solvency Capital Requirement using the standard formula. The applicable financial reporting framework is a compliance framework designed to meet the financial information needs of specific users.

- The terms of the audit engagement reflect the description of management's responsibility for the Solvency and Financial Condition Report in ISA (UK) 210.

- The auditor has concluded an unmodified (i.e. "clean") opinion is appropriate based on the audit evidence obtained.

- The relevant ethical requirements that apply to the audit are the FRC Ethical Standards.

- The auditor's report is published with the Solvency and Financial Condition Report.

- The auditor is not required, and has otherwise decided not to communicate key audit matters in accordance with ISA (UK) 701 in the context of the audit of the relevant elements of the Solvency and Financial Condition Report.

- Those elements of the SFCR, including templates, which are not subject to audit, are treated as "statutory other information" in accordance with the requirements of ISA 720 (UK). The auditor has nothing to report in respect of "other information".

- The auditor has "other reporting responsibilities" as defined by ISA (UK) 700 para. 43. These responsibilities arise from rule 4.1 (3) of the "External Audit" part of the PRA rulebook pertaining to Solvency II firms, and para 3.5 of the PRA "Supervisory Statement SS11/16 "Solvency II: external audit of the public disclosure requirement" September 2016". The auditor is required to: "read and consider all information disclosed by the firm in its SFCR that is not a relevant element of the SFCR to identify material inconsistencies with the relevant elements of the SFCR and any knowledge obtained and other information to which the auditor has had access during the course of the audit of the SFCR engagement *and (where applicable) audit of the financial statements*."

Report of the external independent auditor to the Directors of [Company Name] ("the Company") pursuant to Rule 4.1 (2) of the External Audit Chapter of the PRA Rulebook applicable to Solvency II firms

Report on the Audit of the relevant elements of the Solvency and Financial Condition Report

Opinion

Except as stated below, we have audited the following documents prepared by ABC Company as at [*date*]:

- The "Valuation for solvency purposes" and "Capital Management" sections of the Solvency and Financial Condition Report of ABC Company as at [*date*], ("**the Narrative Disclosures subject to audit**"); and

- Company templates S02.01.02 [S12.01.01, S17.01.02, S22.01.21, S23.01.01, S25.01.21, S28.01.01, S28.02.01[141]] ("**the Templates subject to audit**").

The Narrative Disclosures subject to audit and the Templates subject to audit are collectively referred to as the "relevant elements of the Solvency and Financial Condition Report".

We are not required to audit, nor have we audited, and as a consequence do not express an opinion on the Other Information which comprises:

- The "Business and performance", "System of governance" and "Risk profile" elements of the Solvency and Financial Condition Report;

- Company templates S05.01.02, S05.02.01, S19.01.21;

- Information calculated in accordance with the previous regime used in the calculation of the transitional measure on technical provisions, and as a consequence all information relating to the transitional measures on technical provisions as set out in the Appendix to this report [where disclosed];

- the written acknowledgement by management of their responsibilities, including for the preparation of the solvency and financial condition report ("**the Responsibility Statement**").

In our opinion, the information subject to audit in the relevant elements of the Solvency and Financial Condition Report of ABC Company as at [*date*] is prepared, in all material respects, in accordance with the financial reporting provisions of the PRA Rules and Solvency II regulations on which they are based, as modified by relevant supervisory modifications, and as supplemented by supervisory approvals and determinations.

Basis for opinion

We conducted our audit in accordance with International Standards on Auditing (UK) (ISAs (UK)), including ISA (UK) 800 and ISA (UK) 805. Our responsibilities under those standards are further described in the *Auditor's Responsibilities for the Audit of the relevant elements of the Solvency and Financial Condition Report* section of our report. We are independent of the [Company] in accordance with the ethical requirements that are relevant to our audit of the Solvency and Financial Condition Report in the UK, including the

---

[141] *The templates referred to should be those actually completed by the Company that are within scope of the audit.*

FRC's Ethical Standard as applied to public interest entities, and we have fulfilled our other ethical responsibilities in accordance with these requirements. We believe that the audit evidence we have obtained is sufficient and appropriate to provide a basis for our opinion.

Conclusions relating to going concern

We have nothing to report in respect of the following matters in relation to which the ISAs (UK) require us to report to you where:

- the directors' use of the going concern basis of accounting in the preparation of the SFCR is not appropriate; or

- the directors have not disclosed in the SFCR any identified material uncertainties that may cast significant doubt about the company's ability to continue to adopt the going concern basis of accounting for a period of at least twelve months from the date when the SFCR is authorised for issue.

Emphasis of Matter – Basis of Accounting

We draw attention to the ["Valuation for solvency purposes"] and/or ["Capital Management"] and/or [other relevant disclosures] sections of the Solvency and Financial Condition Report, which describe the basis of accounting. The Solvency and Financial Condition Report is prepared in compliance with the financial reporting provisions of the PRA Rules and Solvency II regulations, and therefore in accordance with a special purpose financial reporting framework. The Solvency and Financial Condition Report is required to be published, and intended users include but are not limited to the Prudential Regulation Authority. As a result, the Solvency and Financial Condition Report may not be suitable for another purpose. Our opinion is not modified in respect of these matters.

Other Information

The [Directors are] [Committee of Management is] responsible for the Other Information.

Our opinion on the relevant elements of the Solvency and Financial Condition Report does not cover the Other Information and, we do not express an audit opinion or any form of assurance conclusion thereon.

In connection with our audit of the Solvency and Financial Condition Report, our responsibility is to read the Other Information and, in doing so, consider whether the Other Information is materially inconsistent with the relevant elements of the Solvency and Financial Condition Report, or our knowledge obtained in the audit, or otherwise appears to be materially misstated. If we identify such material inconsistencies or apparent material misstatements, we are required to determine whether there is a material misstatement in the relevant elements of the Solvency and Financial Condition Report or a material misstatement of the Other Information. If, based on the work we have performed, we conclude that there is a material misstatement of this Other Information, we are required to report that fact. We have nothing to report in this regard.

Responsibilities of [Directors]/[Committee of Management] for the Solvency and Financial Condition Report

The [Directors are] [Committee of Management is] responsible for the preparation of the Solvency and Financial Condition Report in accordance with the financial reporting provisions of the PRA rules and Solvency II regulations. [which have been modified by the modifications, and supplemented by the approvals and determinations made by the PRA under section 138A of FSMA, the PRA Rules and Solvency II regulations on which they are based[142]

The [Directors are] [Committee of Management is] also responsible for such internal control as [they determine]/[it determines] is necessary to enable the preparation of a Solvency and Financial Condition Report that is free from material misstatement, whether due to fraud or error.

Auditor's Responsibilities for the Audit of the relevant elements of the Solvency and Financial Condition Report[143]

It is our responsibility to form an independent opinion as to whether the relevant elements of the Solvency and Financial Condition Report are prepared, in all material respects, with financial reporting provisions of the PRA Rules and Solvency II regulations on which they are based.

Our objectives are to obtain reasonable assurance about whether the relevant elements of the Solvency and Financial Condition Report are free from material misstatement, whether due to fraud or error, and to issue an auditor's report that includes our opinion. Reasonable assurance is a high level of assurance, but it is not a guarantee that an audit conducted in accordance with ISAs (UK) will always detect a material misstatement when it exists. Misstatements can arise from fraud or error and are considered material if, individually or in the aggregate, they could reasonably be expected to influence the decision making or the judgement of the users taken on the basis of the Solvency and Financial Condition Report.

A further description of our responsibilities for the audit of the financial statements is located on the Financial Reporting Council's website at: [*website link*][144]

Report on Other Legal and Regulatory Requirements.

In accordance with Rule 4.1 (3) of the External Audit Chapter of the PRA Rulebook for Solvency II firms we are required to consider whether the Other Information is materially inconsistent with our knowledge obtained in the audit of [ABC Company's] statutory financial statements. If, based on the work we have performed, we conclude that there is a material misstatement of this other information, we are required to report that fact. We have nothing to report in this regard.[145]

Signature in the name of the audit firm, the personal name of the auditor, or both, as appropriate

[*Auditor Address*]

[*Date*]

---

[142] *In accordance with guidance in the PN in section 6 paragraphs 43–47 the auditor should consider the adequacy of disclosures in the SFCR in respect of modifications, approvals and determinations when drafting this section of the auditor's report.*

[143] *Note that the auditor may deem it appropriate to refer, in an Other Matter paragraph, to the auditor's report of the complete set of general purpose financial statements (the statutory financial statements). For example to any Material Uncertainty Related to Going Concern. ISA (UK), A.19.*

[144] *https://www.frc.org.uk/Our-Work/Audit/Audit-and-assurance/Standards-and-guidance/Standards-and-guidance-for-auditors/Auditors-responsibilities-for-audit/Description-of-auditors-responsibilities-for-audit.aspx*

[145] *Relevant where the auditor of the Solvency and Financial Condition Report is also auditor of the Company's statutory financial statements.*

Appendix – relevant elements of the Solvency and Financial Condition Report that are not subject to audit

Solo standard formula

The relevant elements of the Solvency and Financial Condition Report that are not subject to audit comprise:

● The following elements of template S.12.01.02

– Rows R0110 to R0130 – Amount of transitional measure on technical provisions

● The following elements of template S.17.01.02

– Rows R0290 to R0310 – Amount of transitional measure on technical provisions

● The following elements of template S.22.01.21

– Column C0030 – Impact of transitional measure on technical provisions

● Elements of the Narrative Disclosures subject to audit identified as "unaudited".

B: An auditor's report on relevant elements of the SFCR: Solo insurer, partial/ full internal model

For the purpose of this illustrative report the following circumstances are assumed:

● The entity is a solo insurer.

● The auditor is responsible for the audit of the entity's statutory financial statements as well as of the relevant elements of the Solvency and Financial Condition Report.

● The audited entity has calculated the Solvency Capital Requirement using the partial or full internal model method.

● The risk margin; restricted own-funds in ring-fenced funds and matching adjustment portfolios; deductions reflecting the non-availability of own-funds items at a group level; narrative components of the relevant elements of the SFCR that relate to or are derived from the SCR; and the transitional measure for technical provisions are all out of the scope of the audit. The applicable financial reporting framework is a compliance framework designed to meet the financial information needs of specific users.

● The terms of the audit engagement reflect the description of management's responsibility for the Solvency and Financial Condition Report in ISA (UK) 210

● The auditor has concluded an unmodified (i.e. "clean") opinion is appropriate based on the audit evidence obtained.

● The relevant ethical requirements that apply to the audit are the FRC's ethical standards.

● The auditor's report is published with the Solvency and Financial Condition Report.

● The auditor is not required, and has otherwise decided not to communicate key audit matters in accordance with ISA (UK) 701 in the context of the audit of the relevant elements of the Solvency and Financial Condition Report.

- Those elements of the SFCR, including templates, which are not subject to audit, are treated as "statutory other information" in accordance with the requirements of ISA 720 (UK). The auditor has nothing to report in respect of "other information".

- The auditor has "other reporting responsibilities" as defined by ISA (UK) 700 para. 43. These responsibilities arise from rule 4.1 (3) of the "External Audit" part of the PRA rulebook pertaining to Solvency II firms, and para 3.5 of the PRA "Supervisory Statement SS11/16 "Solvency II: external audit of the public disclosure requirement" September 2016". The auditor is required to: "read and consider all information disclosed by the firm in its SFCR that is not a relevant element of the SFCR to identify material inconsistencies with the relevant elements of the SFCR and any knowledge obtained and other information to which the auditor has had access during the course of the audit of the SFCR engagement *and (where applicable) audit of the financial statements.*"

Report of the external independent auditor to the Directors of [Company Name] ("the Company") pursuant to Rule 4.1 (2) of the External Audit Chapter of the PRA Rulebook applicable to Solvency II firms

Report on the Audit of the relevant elements of the Solvency and Financial Condition Report

Opinion

Except as stated below, we have audited the following documents prepared by ABC Company as at [*date*]:

- The "Valuation for solvency purposes" and "Capital Management" sections of the Solvency and Financial Condition Report of ABC Company as at [*date*], ("**the Narrative Disclosures subject to audit**"); and

- Company templates S02.01.02 [S12.01.01, S17.01.02, S22.01.21, S23.01.01, S28.01.01, S28.02.01[146]] ("**the Templates subject to audit**").

The Narrative Disclosures subject to audit and the Templates subject to audit are collectively referred to as the "**relevant elements of the Solvency and Financial Condition Report**".

We are not required to audit, nor have we audited, and as a consequence do not express an opinion on the Other Information which comprises:

- information contained within the relevant elements of the Solvency and Financial Condition Report set out about above which are, or derive from the Solvency Capital Requirement, as identified in the Appendix to this report;

- The "Business and performance", "System of governance" and "Risk profile" elements of the Solvency and Financial Condition Report;

- Company templates S05.01.02, S05.02.01, S19.01.21, S.25.02.21, S.25.03.21;

- Information calculated in accordance with the previous regime used in the calculation of the transitional measure on technical provisions, and as a consequence all information relating to the transitional measures on technical provisions as set out in the Appendix to this report [where disclosed];

- the written acknowledgement by management of their responsibilities, including for the preparation of the solvency and financial condition report ("**the Responsibility Statement**").

To the extent the information subject to audit in the relevant elements of the Solvency and Financial Condition Report includes amounts that are totals, sub-totals or calculations derived from the Other Information, we have relied without verification on the Other Information.

In our opinion, the information subject to audit in the relevant elements of the Solvency and Financial Condition Report of ABC Company as at [*date*] is prepared, in all material respects, in accordance with the financial reporting provisions of the PRA Rules and Solvency II regulations on which they are based, as modified by relevant supervisory modifications, and as supplemented by supervisory approvals and determinations.

---

[146] *The templates referred to should be those actually completed by the Company that are within scope of the audit.*

Basis for opinion

We conducted our audit in accordance with International Standards on Auditing (UK) (ISAs (UK)) including ISA (UK) 800 and ISA (UK) 805, and applicable law. Our responsibilities under those standards are further described in the *Auditor's Responsibilities for the Audit of the relevant elements of the Solvency and Financial Condition Report* section of our report. We are independent of the [Company] in accordance with the ethical requirements that are relevant to our audit of the Solvency and Financial Condition Report in the UK, including the FRC's Ethical Standard as applied to public interest entities, and we have fulfilled our other ethical responsibilities in accordance with these requirements. We believe that the audit evidence we have obtained is sufficient and appropriate to provide a basis for our opinion.

Conclusions relating to going concern

We have nothing to report in respect of the following matters in relation to which the ISAs (UK) require us to report to you where:

- the directors' use of the going concern basis of accounting in the preparation of the SFCR is not appropriate; or

- the directors have not disclosed in the SFCR any identified material uncertainties that may cast significant doubt about the company's ability to continue to adopt the going concern basis of accounting for a period of at least twelve months from the date when the SFCR is authorised for issue.

Emphasis of Matter – Basis of Accounting

We draw attention to the ["Valuation for solvency purposes"] and/or ["Capital Management"] and/or [other relevant disclosures] sections of the Solvency and Financial Condition Report, which describe the basis of accounting. The Solvency and Financial Condition Report is prepared in compliance with the financial reporting provisions of the PRA Rules and Solvency II regulations and Solvency II regulations, and therefore in accordance with a special purpose financial reporting framework. The Solvency and Financial Condition Report is required to be published, and intended users include but are not limited to the Prudential Regulation Authority. As a result, the Solvency and Financial Condition Report may not be suitable for another purpose. Our opinion is not modified in respect of this matter.

Other Information

The [Directors are] [Committee of Management is] responsible for the Other Information.

Our opinion on the relevant elements of the Solvency and Financial Condition Report does not cover the Other Information and, we do not express and audit opinion or any form of assurance conclusion thereon.

In connection with our audit of the Solvency and Financial Condition Report, our responsibility is to read the Other Information and, in doing so, consider whether the Other Information is materially inconsistent with the relevant elements of the Solvency and Financial Condition Report, or our knowledge obtained in the audit, or otherwise appears to be materially misstated. If we identify such material inconsistencies or apparent material misstatements, we are required to determine whether there is a material misstatement in the relevant elements of the Solvency and Financial Condition Report or a material misstatement of the Other Information. If, based on the work we have performed, we conclude that there is a material misstatement of this Other Information, we are required to report that fact. We have nothing to report in this regard.

Responsibilities of [Directors] [Committee of Management] for the Solvency and Financial Condition Report

The [Directors are] [Committee of Management is] responsible for the preparation of the Solvency and Financial Condition Report in accordance with the financial reporting provisions of the PRA rules and Solvency II regulations. [which have been modified by the modifications, and supplemented by the approvals and determinations made by the PRA under section 138A of FSMA, the PRA Rules and Solvency II regulations on which they are based[147]]

The [Directors are] [Committee of Management is] also responsible for such internal control as [they determine]/[it determines] is necessary to enable the preparation of a Solvency and Financial Condition Report that is free from material misstatement, whether due to fraud or error.

Auditor's Responsibilities for the Audit of the relevant elements of the Solvency and Financial Condition Report[148]

It is our responsibility to form an independent opinion as to whether the relevant elements of the Solvency and Financial Condition Report are prepared, in all material respects, with financial reporting provisions of the PRA Rules and Solvency II regulations on whichthey are based.

Our objectives are to obtain reasonable assurance about whether the relevant elements of the Solvency and Financial Condition Report are free from material misstatement, whether due to fraud or error, and to issue an auditor's report that includes our opinion. Reasonable assurance is a high level of assurance, but it is not a guarantee that an audit conducted in accordance with ISAs (UK) will always detect a material misstatement when it exists. Misstatements can arise from fraud or error and are considered material if, individually or in the aggregate, they could reasonably be expected to influence the decision making or the judgement of the users taken on the basis of the Solvency and Financial Condition Report.

A further description of our responsibilities for the audit of the financial statements is located on the Financial Reporting Council's website at: [*website link*].[149]

Other Matter

The Company has authority to calculate its [Group] Solvency Capital Requirement using a [partial] internal model ("the Model") approved by the Prudential Regulation Authority in accordance with the Solvency II Regulations. In forming our opinion (and in accordance with PRA Rules), we are not required to audit the inputs to, design of, operating effectiveness of and outputs from the Model, or whether the Model is being applied in accordance with the Company's application or approval order.

---

[147] *In accordance with guidance in the PN in section 6 paragraphs 43–47 the auditor should consider the adequacy of disclosures in the SFCR in respect of modifications, approvals and determinations when drafting this section of the auditor's report.*

[148] *Note that the auditor may deem it appropriate to refer, in an Other Matter paragraph, to the auditor's report of the complete set of general purpose financial statements (the statutory financial statements). For example to any Material Uncertainty Related to Going Concern. ISA (UK), A.19.*

[149] *https://www.frc.org.uk/Our-Work/Audit/Audit-and-assurance/Standards-and-guidance/Standards-and-guidance-for-auditors/Auditors-responsibilities-for-audit/Description-of-auditors-responsibilities-for-audit.aspx*

Report on Other Legal and Regulatory Requirements.

In accordance with Rule 4.1 (3) of the External Audit Chapter of the PRA Rulebook for Solvency II firms we are also required to consider whether the Other Information is materially inconsistent with our knowledge obtained in the audit of [ABC Company's] statutory financial statements. If, based on the work we have performed, we conclude that there is a material misstatement of this other information, we are required to report that fact. We have nothing to report in this regard.[150]

Signature in the name of the audit firm, the personal name of the auditor, or both, as appropriate

[*Auditor Address*]

[*Date*]

Appendix – relevant elements of the Solvency and Financial Condition Report that are not subject to audit

Solo partial/internal model

The relevant elements of the Solvency and Financial Condition Report that are not subject to audit comprise:

- The following elements of template S.02.01.02:
  - Row R0550: Technical provisions – non-life (excluding health) – risk margin
  - Row R0590: Technical provisions – health (similar to non-life) – risk margin
  - Row R0640: Technical provisions – health (similar to life) – risk margin
  - Row R0680: Technical provisions – life (excluding health and index-linked and unit-linked) – risk margin
  - Row R0720: Technical provisions – Index-linked and unit-linked – risk margin
- The following elements of template S.12.01.02
  - Row R0100: Technical provisions calculated as a sum of BE and RM – Risk margin
  - Rows R0110 to R0130 – Amount of transitional measure on technical provisions
- The following elements of template S.17.01.02
  - Row R0280: Technical provisions calculated as a sum of BE and RM – Risk margin
  - Rows R0290 to R0310 – Amount of transitional measure on technical provisions
- The following elements of template S.22.01.21
  - Column C0030 – Impact of transitional measure on technical provisions

---

[150] *Relevant where the auditor of the Solvency and Financial Condition Report is also auditor of the Company's statutory financial statements.*

- Row R0010 – Technical provisions
- Row R0090 – Solvency Capital Requirement
- The following elements of template S.23.01.01
  - Row R0580: SCR
  - Row R0740: Adjustment for restricted own fund items in respect of matching adjustment portfolios and ring fenced funds
- The following elements of template [S.28.01.01 / S.28.02.01]
  - Row R0310: SCR
- Elements of the Narrative Disclosures subject to audit identified as "unaudited".

C: An auditor's report on relevant elements of the SFCR: Group, partial/full internal model

For the purpose of this illustrative report the following circumstances are assumed:

- The entity is a group insurer and includes information prepared on a sectoral basis which is subject to the "properly compiled" statement required by the PRA.

- The auditor is responsible for the audit of the entity's statutory financial statements as well as of the relevant elements of the Solvency and Financial Condition Report.

- The audited entity has calculated the Solvency Capital Requirement using the partial or full internal model method.

- The risk margin; restricted own-funds in ring-fenced funds and matching adjustment portfolios; deductions reflecting the non-availability of own-funds items at a group level; narrative components of the relevant elements of the SFCR that relate to or are derived from the SCR; the transitional measure for technical provisions; and information prepared on a sectoral basis are all out of the scope of the audit. The applicable financial reporting framework is a compliance framework designed to meet the financial information needs of specific users.

- The terms of the audit engagement reflect the description of management's responsibility for the Solvency and Financial Condition Report in ISA (UK) 210

- The auditor has concluded an unmodified (i.e. "clean") opinion is appropriate based on the audit evidence obtained.

- The relevant ethical requirements that apply to the audit are the FRC's ethical standards.

- The auditor's report is published with the Solvency and Financial Condition Report.

- The auditor is not required, and has otherwise decided not to communicate key audit matters in accordance with ISA (UK) 701 in the context of the audit of the relevant elements of the Solvency and Financial Condition Report.

- Those elements of the SFCR, including templates, which are not subject to audit, are treated as "statutory other information" in accordance with the requirements of ISA 720 (UK). The auditor has nothing to report in respect of "other information".

- The auditor has "other reporting responsibilities" as defined by ISA (UK) 700 para. 43. These responsibilities arise from rule 4.1 (3) of the "External Audit" part of the PRA rulebook pertaining to Solvency II firms, and para 3.5 of the PRA "Supervisory Statement SS11/16 "Solvency II: external audit of the public disclosure requirement" September 2016". The auditor is required to: "read and consider all information disclosed by the firm in its SFCR that is not a relevant element of the SFCR to identify material inconsistencies with the relevant elements of the SFCR and any knowledge obtained and other information to which the auditor has had access during the course of the audit of the SFCR engagement *and (where applicable) audit of the financial statements.*"

Report of the external independent auditor to the Directors of [Company Name] ("the Company") pursuant to Rule 4.1 (2) of the External Audit Chapter of the PRA Rulebook applicable to Solvency II firms

Report on the Audit of the relevant elements of the Group Solvency and Financial Condition Report

Opinion

Except as stated below, we have audited the following documents prepared by ABC Company as at [*date*]:

- The "Valuation for solvency purposes" and "Capital Management" sections of the Group Solvency and Financial Condition Report of ABC Company as at [*date*], (**"the Narrative Disclosures subject to audit"**); and

- Company Group templates S02.01.02 [S22.01.22, S23.01.22, S32.01.22[151]] (**"the Templates subject to audit"**).

The Narrative Disclosures subject to audit and the Templates subject to audit are collectively referred to as the **"relevant elements of the Group Solvency and Financial Condition Report"**.

We are not required to audit, nor have we audited, and as a consequence do not express an opinion on the Other Information which comprises:

- information contained within the relevant elements of the Group Solvency and Financial Condition Report set out about above which are, or derive from the Solvency Capital Requirement, as identified in the Appendix to this report

- The "Business and performance", "System of governance" and "Risk profile" elements of the Group Solvency and Financial Condition Report;

- Group templates S05.01.02, S05.02.01, S.25.02.22, S.25.03.22;

- Information calculated in accordance with the previous regime used in the calculation of the transitional measure on technical provisions, and as a consequence all information relating to the transitional measures on technical provisions as set out in the Appendix to this report [where disclosed]

- the written acknowledgement by management of their responsibilities, including for the preparation of the Group Solvency and Financial Condition Report (**"the Responsibility Statement"**);

- Information which pertains to an undertaking that is not a Solvency II undertaking and has been prepared in accordance with PRA rules other than those implementing the Solvency II Directive or in accordance with an EU instrument other than the Solvency II regulations. [**"the sectoral information"**].[152]

To the extent the information subject to audit in the relevant elements of the Group Solvency and Financial Condition Report includes amounts that are totals, sub-totals or calculations derived from the Other Information, we have relied without verification on the Other Information.

---

[151] *The templates referred to should be those actually completed by the Company that are within scope of the audit.*

[152] *See the separate part of our report, "Other Legal and Regulatory Requirements".*

In our opinion, the information subject to audit in the relevant elements of the Group Solvency and Financial Condition Report of ABC Company as at [*date*] is prepared, in all material respects, in accordance with the financial reporting provisions of the PRA Rules and Solvency II regulations on which they are based, as modified by relevant supervisory modifications, and as supplemented by supervisory approvals and determinations.

Basis for opinion

We conducted our audit in accordance with International Standards on Auditing (UK) (ISAs (UK)) including ISA (UK) 800 and ISA (UK) 805, and applicable law. Our responsibilities under those standards are further described in the *Auditor's Responsibilities for the Audit of the relevant elements of the Group Solvency and Financial Condition Report* section of our report. We are independent of the [Company] in accordance with the ethical requirements that are relevant to our audit of the Group Solvency and Financial Condition Report in the UK, including the FRC's Ethical Standard as applied to public interest entities, and we have fulfilled our other ethical responsibilities in accordance with these requirements. We believe that the audit evidence we have obtained is sufficient and appropriate to provide a basis for our opinion.

Conclusions relating to going concern

We have nothing to report in respect of the following matters in relation to which the ISAs (UK) require us to report to you where:

- the directors' use of the going concern basis of accounting in the preparation of the SFCR is not appropriate; or

- the directors have not disclosed in the SFCR any identified material uncertainties that may cast significant doubt about the company's ability to continue to adopt the going concern basis of accounting for a period of at least twelve months from the date when the SFCR is authorised for issue.

Emphasis of Matter – Basis of Accounting

We draw attention to the ["Valuation for solvency purposes"] and/or ["Capital Management"] and/or [other relevant disclosures] sections of the Group Solvency and Financial Condition Report, which describe the basis of accounting. The Group Solvency and Financial Condition Report is prepared in compliance with the financial reporting provisions of the PRA Rules and Solvency II regulations, and therefore in accordance with a special purpose financial reporting framework. The Solvency and Financial Condition Report is required to be published, and intended users include but are not limited to the Prudential Regulation Authority. As a result, the Group Solvency and Financial Condition Report may not be suitable for another purpose. Our opinion is not modified in respect of this matter.

Other Information

The [Directors are] [Committee of Management is] responsible for the Other Information.

Our opinion on the relevant elements of the Group Solvency and Financial Condition Report does not cover the Other Information and we do not express an audit opinion or any form of assurance conclusion thereon.

In connection with our audit of the Group Solvency and Financial Condition Report, our responsibility is to read the Other Information and, in doing so, consider whether the Other Information is materially inconsistent with the relevant elements of the Group Solvency and Financial Condition Report, or our knowledge obtained in the audit, or otherwise appears to be materially misstated. If we identify such material inconsistencies or apparent material misstatements, we are required to determine whether there is a material misstatement in the relevant elements of the Solvency and Financial Condition Report or a material misstatement of the Other Information. If, based on the work we have performed, we conclude that there is a material misstatement of this Other Information, we are required to report that fact. We have nothing to report in this regard.

Responsibilities of [Directors][Committee of Management] for the Group Solvency and Financial Condition Report

The [Directors are] [Committee of Management is] responsible for the preparation of the Group Solvency and Financial Condition Report in accordance with the financial reporting provisions of the PRA rules and Solvency II regulations. [which have been modified by the modifications, and supplemented by the approvals and determinations made by the PRA under section 138A of FSMA, the PRA Rules and Solvency II regulations on which they are based[153]]

The [Directors are] [Committee of Management is] also responsible for such internal control as [they determine]/[it determines] is necessary to enable the preparation of a Group Solvency and Financial Condition Report that is free from material misstatement, whether due to fraud or error.

Auditor's Responsibilities for the Audit of the relevant elements of the Group Solvency and Financial Condition Report[154]

It is our responsibility to form an independent opinion as to whether the relevant elements of the Group Solvency and Financial Condition Report are prepared, in all material respects, with financial reporting provisions of the PRA Rules and Solvency II regulations on whichthey are based.

Our objectives are to obtain reasonable assurance about whether the relevant elements of the Group Solvency and Financial Condition Report are free from material misstatement, whether due to fraud or error, and to issue an auditor's report that includes our opinion. Reasonable assurance is a high level of assurance, but it is not a guarantee that an audit conducted in accordance with ISAs (UK) will always detect a material misstatement when it exists. Misstatements can arise from fraud or error and are considered material if, individually or in the aggregate, they could reasonably be expected to influence the decision making or the judgement of the users taken on the basis of the Group Solvency and Financial Condition Report.

A further description of our responsibilities for the audit of the financial statements is located on the Financial Reporting Council's website at: [*website link*][155]

Other Matter

The Company has authority to calculate its [Group] Solvency Capital Requirement using a [partial] internal model ("the Model") approved by the

---

[153] *In accordance with guidance in the PN in section 6 paragraphs 43–47 the auditor should consider the adequacy of disclosures in the SFCR in respect of modifications, approvals and determinations when drafting this section of the auditor's report.*

[154] *Note that the auditor may deem it appropriate to refer, in an Other Matter paragraph, to the auditor's report of the complete set of general purpose financial statements (the statutory financial statements). For example to any Material Uncertainty Related to Going Concern. ISA (UK), A.19.*

[155] *https://www.frc.org.uk/Our-Work/Audit/Audit-and-assurance/Standards-and-guidance/Standards-and-guidance-for-auditors/Auditors-responsibilities-for-audit/Description-of-auditors-responsibilities-for-audit.aspx*

Prudential Regulation Authority in accordance with the Solvency II Regulations. In forming our opinion (and in accordance with PRA Rules), we are not required to audit the inputs to, design of, operating effectiveness of and outputs from the Model, or whether the Model is being applied in accordance with the Company's application or approval order.

Report on Other Legal and Regulatory Requirements.

Sectoral Information

In our opinion, in accordance with Rule 4.2 of the External Audit Chapter of the PRA Rulebook, the **sectoral information** has been properly compiled in accordance with the PRA rules and EU instruments relating to that undertaking from information provided by members of the group and the relevant insurance group undertaking.

Other Information

In accordance with Rule 4.1 (3) of the External Audit Chapter of the PRA Rulebook for Solvency II firms we are also required to consider whether the Other Information is materially inconsistent with our knowledge obtained in the audit of [ABC Company's] statutory financial statements. If, based on the work we have performed, we conclude that there is a material misstatement of this other information, we are required to report that fact. We have nothing to report in this regard.[156]

Signature in the name of the audit firm, the personal name of the auditor, or both, as appropriate

[Auditor Address]

[Date]

Appendix – relevant elements of the Group Solvency and Financial Condition Report that are not subject to audit

Group internal model

The relevant elements of the Group Solvency and Financial Condition Report that are not subject to audit comprise:

- The following elements of Group template S.02.01.02:
  - Row R0550: Technical provisions – non-life (excluding health) – risk margin
  - Row R0590: Technical provisions – health (similar to non-life) – risk margin
  - Row R0640: Technical provisions – health (similar to life) – risk margin
  - Row R0680: Technical provisions – life (excluding health and index-linked and unit-linked) – risk margin
  - Row R0720: Technical provisions – Index-linked and unit-linked – risk margin
- The following elements of Group template S.22.01.22

---

[156] *Relevant where the auditor of the Solvency and Financial Condition Report is also auditor of the Company's statutory financial statements.*

- – Column C0030 – Impact of transitional on technical provisions
- – Row R0010 – Technical provisions
- – Row R0090 – Solvency Capital Requirement
- The following elements of Group template S.23.01.22
  - – Row R0020: Non-available called but not paid in ordinary share capital at group level
  - – Row R0060: Non-available subordinated mutual member accounts at group level
  - – Row R0080: Non-available surplus at group level
  - – Row R0100: Non-available preference shares at group level
  - – Row R0120: Non-available share premium account related to preference shares at group level
  - – Row R0150: Non-available subordinated liabilities at group level
  - – Row R0170: The amount equal to the value of net deferred tax assets not available at the group level
  - – Row R0190: Non-available own funds related to other own funds items approved by supervisory authority
  - – Row R0210: Non-available minority interests at group level
  - – Row R0380: Non-available ancillary own funds at group level
  - – Rows R0410 to R0440 – Own funds of other financial sectors
  - – Row R0680: Group SCR
  - – Row R0740: Adjustment for restricted own fund items in respect of matching adjustment portfolios and ring fenced funds
  - – Row R0750: Other non available own funds
- Elements of the Narrative Disclosures subject to audit identified as "unaudited".

Section 8: Reporting on Non Solvency II ("Non-Directive") Firms

1   The PRA Rulebook sets reporting requirements for non-directive firms which applies to:

(1)   all non-directive insurers, other than non-directive friendly societies;

(2)   Swiss general insurers in respect of the activities of the firm carried on from a branch in the UK[157]; and

(3)   ... every firm that is a non-directive friendly society other than:

- *a flat rate benefits business friendly society; and*
- *a partnership pension society.*

There are no reporting requirements for flat rates benefits business friendly societies and partnership pension societies.

---

[157] *PRA Rulebook: Non-Solvency II Firms: Insurance Company – Reporting, paras.1.1–1.2.*

Authorised insurers

An insurer regulated by the PRA is required by rule 9.2 of the Insurance Company   **2**
Reporting section of the non-directive firms rulebook to submit one copy of every
form and document comprising the regulatory return to the PRA within three
months of each financial year-end.[158] The format of this return is prescribed by the
Rulebook.

Rule 2.5 requires the regulatory return to be audited in accordance with Chapter 7   **3**
of the rulebook, by a person qualified in accordance with the Auditors Part of
the PRA Rulebook [with the exception of any directors certificates; form 46;
and form 50].[159]

Friendly Societies

Non-directive friendly societies are not required to have their regulatory reports to   **4**
the PRA audited. The remainder of this section of the PN is therefore not relevant
to the auditors of non-directive friendly societies.[160]

The form and content of the Regulatory Return

The PRA rulebook establishes a requirement for firms to prepare for each   **5**
12 month financial year relevant forms, statements and documents; including a
revenue account for the year, a balance sheet as at the end of the year and a profit
and loss account for the year; or, in the case of an insurer not trading for profit, an
income and expenditure account for the year.[161]

This requirement is separate from the requirement for a UK incorporated insurer to   **6**
prepare financial statements under the Companies Act 2006 (CA 2006). There is,
however, deemed to be a close correlation between the figures included. Except
where over-ridden by the rules in the PRA rule book, words and expressions used
in the 2008 Accounts and Reports Regulations have the same meaning in the
rulebook. The rules are drafted so that insurers can apply the same accounting
policies in both the regulatory return and the financial statements and require that,
except where a rule provides for a different method of recognition or valuation,
then the insurer for the purposes of that rule, recognises the asset, liability, equity
or income statement item and measures it in accordance with UK GAAP or IFRS
as applicable.

The principal differences between the regulatory return and financial statements   **7**
prepared under CA 2006 are as follows:

- The regulatory return is primarily intended to demonstrate the solvency of
  an insurer.

- The balance sheet included in the regulatory return may show items at
  different values from those shown in the financial statements, arising from
  the application of rules in respect of: –

  (a)   Assets that can be treated as admissible; assets that are not admissible
        (for example deferred acquisition costs in respect of long-term
        business) are left out of account;

---

[158] *PRA Rulebook: Non-Solvency II Firms: Insurance Company – Reporting, para. 9.2.*

[159] *PRA Rulebook: Non-Solvency II Firms: Insurance Company – Reporting, para. 2.5.*

[160] *Auditors should refer to the PRA rulebook or the requirements in respect of mutual insurers constituted as companies limited by guarantee or as Industrial and Provident Societies.*

[161] *PRA Rulebook: Non-Solvency II Firms: Insurance Company – Reporting, paras.2.1–2.3.*

(b)   The basic valuation principles to be applied to admissible assets and to liabilities;

(c)   Restrictions on the value of assets where the value arrived at by applying the basic valuation principles exceeds the permitted market risk or counterparty exposure limits; and

(d)   The determination of long-term insurance business liabilities; – the treatment of certain types of hybrid capital; and – a provision for reasonable foreseeable adverse variations where certain commitments are not strictly matched;

● The income statement, particularly for general business, provides a large volume of detailed segmental information including a breakdown into combined categories and further sub-divisions into material risk categories, which are reported by currency and, in some cases, reporting territory. Deposit accounting must not be used in the income statement for long-term insurance contracts even where these contracts are subject to deposit accounting as investment business in the financial statements.

● Additional information is provided in the regulatory return on a variety of topics including:

(a)   The Abstract of the valuation, prepared by the actuarial function holder(s) for an insurer carrying on long-term insurance business;

(b)   General business reinsurance arrangements;

(c)   Financial reinsurance and other financing arrangements;

(d)   Major general business reinsurers and cedants;

(e)   The use of derivatives.

8   The regulatory return is accompanied by a certificate signed by the directors of the firm, which states that:

> *The return has been properly prepared in accordance with the requirements in the Non- Solvency II Firms section of the PRA rule book;*

> *The directors are satisfied that throughout the year in question, the firm has complied in all material respects with the rules in the Non-Solvency II Firms sector of the PRA rule book; and it is reasonable to believe that the firm has continued so to comply subsequently, and will do so in the future.*

9   The directors' certificate, Form 46 and Form 50 are outside the scope of the audit.[162]

The auditor's responsibilities

10   The Insurance Company Reporting part of the PRA's rulebook for Non-Solvency II firms sets out the auditor's responsibilities. These include the required elements of the auditor's report, covering whether, in the auditor's opinion:

(a)   the Forms, statements and documents have been properly prepared in accordance with this Part and the Insurance Company – Overall Resources and Valuation Part and any *specific valuation* rule;

(b)   the methods and assumptions determined by the *firm* and used to perform the *actuarial investigation* (as set out in the valuation reports) appropriately

---

[162] *PRA Rulebook: Non-Solvency II Firms: Insurance Company – Reporting, para. 2.5.*

reflect the requirements of Insurance Company – Mathematical Reserves; and,

(c)   to the extent that any document, form, statement, analysis or report to be audited contains amounts or information abstracted from the *actuarial investigation* performed pursuant to 5.8 and 5.9, the auditor has obtained and paid due regard to advice from a suitably qualified *actuary* who is independent of the *firm*.[163]

Rule 7.5 requires the auditor to report by exception, in accordance with the Companies Act 2006, if they are of the opinion that: **11**

(a)   Adequate accounting records have not been kept, or that returns adequate for its audit have not been received from branches not visited by it;

(b)   The insurer's individual accounts are not in agreement with the accounting records and returns; and

(c)   It has failed to obtain all the information and explanations which, to the best of the auditor's knowledge and belief, are necessary for the purposes of the audit.

Standards to be applied by the auditor

In the case of a UK incorporated insurer, an audit of the financial statements   **12** prepared under CA 2006 will be conducted in accordance with ISAs (UK) issued by the FRC to comply with the requirements of section 495 of CA 2006. If an audit of financial statements in accordance with ISAs (UK) has not been undertaken (as may be the case in relation to the UK branch of an insurer incorporated outside the UK) the regulatory return will need to have been audited in accordance with ISAs UK in order to satisfy the reporting requirement.

Work specific to the auditor's report on an insurer's regulatory return may be   **13** undertaken concurrently with procedures designed to provide evidence for its report on the financial statements or at a later date. In either case, the auditor considers both aspects of the engagement when planning the audit of the financial statements.

Although the PRA rulebook does not require the regulatory return to be drawn up   **14** to show a true and fair view, rule 6.1 says that it "must fairly state the information provided on the basis required by this Part".[164] This is of a similar qualitative standard to the requirement in company law that financial statements give a true and fair view of a company's state of affairs and profit or loss, hence equivalent considerations of materiality apply. In evaluating whether the requirements of rule 6.1 have been met, the auditor applies materiality in relation to the business as a whole. Following this approach, reliance on analytical review techniques may be appropriate in relation to, for example, the segmental information provided within the regulatory return.

General Principles

The auditor: **15**

●   Plans the work to be undertaken so as to perform that work in an effective manner;

---

[163] *PRA Rulebook: Non-Solvency II Firms: Insurance Company – Reporting, para. 7.2.*

[164] *PRA Rulebook: Non-Solvency II Firms: Insurance Company – Reporting, para. 6.1.*

- Familiarises them self with the relevant regulations;
- Complies, where relevant, with FRC Ethical Standards for Auditors and with ethical guidance issued by its relevant professional body.
- Agrees the terms of the engagement with the insurer and records them in writing. The auditor may choose to combine the audit requirements with the financial statement engagement letter. This will include reference, where relevant, to the PRA requirement for the auditor to engage a suitably qualified actuary who is independent of the insurer and pay due regard to advice from that actuary.
- Considers materiality and its relationship with the risk of material misstatement in planning its work and in determining the effect of its findings on its report.
- Undertakes its work with an attitude of professional scepticism and performs procedures designed to obtain sufficient appropriate evidence on which to base its opinion. In particular it:
  - Applies analytical procedures in forming an overall conclusion as to whether the regulatory return as a whole is consistent with its knowledge of the insurer's business; and
  - Obtains written confirmation of appropriate representations from management before its report is issued.
- Records in its working papers:
  - Details of the engagement planning relating to its report;
  - The nature, timing and extent of the procedures performed, and the conclusions drawn; and
  - Its reasoning and conclusions on all significant matters which require the exercise of judgment.
- If reporting on financial information on which a component auditor has reported, obtain sufficient appropriate evidence that the work of the component auditor is adequate for its purposes.
- Issues a report containing a clear expression of its opinion on the regulatory return.
- Considers the matters which have come to its attention while performing the audit and whether they should be included in a report to the governing body of the audited entity.
- Makes a report direct to the PRA if it becomes aware of matters of material significance to the regulator. In addition, when issuing its report, the auditor:
  - Considers whether there are consequential reporting issues affecting its opinion which arise from any report previously made direct to the PRA in the course of the auditor's appointment; and
  - Assesses whether any matters encountered in the course of its work indicate a need for a further direct report.

Key Additional Procedures

16   Key areas in which the auditor needs to undertake procedures additional to those undertaken to report on the financial statements are:

(a)   The application of the prescribed valuation and admissibility rules to assets and liabilities for which existence, title, etc. has already been considered as a part of the audit of the insurer's financial statements;

(b)   The sub-division of general business revenue information into the prescribed categories;

(c)   Presentation of the information in the prescribed forms; and

(d)   The specific additional disclosures that fall within the scope of the auditor's report.

The Auditor's Procedures on Regulatory Returns Long-term business

Rule 7.4 of the Insurance Company – Reporting part of the PRA's rulebook for Non- Solvency II firms requires that where any part of the regulatory return that is subject to audit contains amounts or information abstracted from an actuarial investigation, the auditor is required to obtain and pay due regard to advice from a suitably qualified actuary who is independent of the firm. Chapter 5 of the relevant rulebook sets out the required content of such a report.   **17**

The PRA rulebook does not specify the advice to be obtained from the actuary or provide guidance on the nature or extent of the work to be performed in providing that advice. The responsibility for determining the nature of the advice and, consequently, the scope and extent of the actuary's work lies with the auditor, although the auditor discusses the proposed scope of work with the actuary and considers the views of the actuary before finalising the scope of work.   **18**

The auditor does not have the same expertise as the actuary; however seeks to obtain an understanding of the assumptions and methods used by the firm and to consider whether they are reasonable, based on the auditor's knowledge of the business. If the results of the actuary's work are not consistent with other audit evidence, the auditor attempts to resolve the inconsistency by discussions with the actuary. Applying additional procedures, including possibly engaging another actuary, may also assist in resolving the inconsistency. If the auditor is not satisfied that the work of the actuary provides sufficient appropriate audit evidence to support its opinion on the regulatory returns and there is no satisfactory alternative source of audit evidence, the auditor considers the implications for the auditor's report.   **19**

This Practice Note includes a section on the application of the auditing standards to the audit of statutory financial statements which is also relevant to the procedures carried out in respect of the regulatory return. This includes the need to agree the scope of work, the form of report and compliance with the FRC's Technical Actuarial Standards (TASs).   **20**

In addition to the high level principles set out in TAS 100, TAS 200 includes specific requirements for actuaries who perform technical actuarial work to support the provisions of an auditor's assurance opinion for regulatory reporting. These requirements help the auditor comply with the auditing standards: **21**

(a)   The initial scope of the technical actuarial work and the reasons for any variances from the initial scope shall be documented.

(b)   Technical actuarial work undertaken shall be planned and performed with professional scepticism recognizing the circumstances may exist that cause the financial statements or regulatory information to be materially misstated.

(c)   Communications shall state the nature and extent of any reliance on information prepared by another party and the conclusions of the technical actuarial work including any concerns on material deficiencies or limitations.[165]

22   The auditor obtains advice from the actuary on those elements of an actuarial investigation that the auditor believes, for the purpose of the audit of the annual return, require expert actuarial input to assess. The areas of an actuarial investigation that the auditor will seek advice from an actuary include whether:

(a)   The methods and assumptions used to calculate the mathematical reserves appropriately reflect the requirements of the PRA rulebook ("Mathematical reserves").

(b)   The statement(s) made under on "Valuation reports on long-term insurance business" are made in accordance with the requirements of the PRA rulebook.

23   The auditor obtains advice on all other elements of the actuarial investigation to the extent that they are relevant to the auditable parts of the return. The elements of the actuarial investigation, other than those detailed above, that the auditor may also seek to obtain advice from the actuary on include whether:

(a)   The data underlying the calculation of the mathematical reserves are reliable.

(b)   The models used to apply the methods and assumptions underlying the mathematical reserves are operating appropriate.

(c)   The data contained in Forms 58 and 60 have been correctly abstracted from the actuarial valuation.

(d)   The data contained in lines 51 and 52 of Form 11 have been correctly abstracted from the actuarial valuation.

Establishing the independence of the suitably qualified independent actuary

24   The auditor should be satisfied that any suitably qualified actuary will be independent and document the rationale for that conclusion.

25   When planning the audit of the regulatory return, the engagement partner obtains information from the actuary as to the existence of any connections that the Reviewing Actuary has with the engaging party including:

- Financial interests.

- Business relationships (including the provision of services).

- Employment (past, present and future).

- Family and other personal relationships.

26   The engagement partner assesses the threats to objectivity and independence that arise from any connections disclosed and considers whether the actuary has implemented safeguards to eliminate the threats or reduce them to an acceptable level.

27   When assessing the threats to objectivity and independence which arise from services provided to the engaging party or its affiliates and the effectiveness of safeguards established by the actuarial firm, the engagement partner will consider the following factors:

---

[165] *Technical Actuarial Standard 200: Insurance, paras. 22–24.*

(a)   Whether the actuary was the person responsible for the service provided;

(b)   The materiality and the nature of the services to the actuarial firm; and

(c)   The extent to which the outcomes of services have been reviewed by another actuarial firm.

In certain circumstances, it is unlikely that any safeguards can eliminate the threat to objectivity and independence or reduce it to an acceptable level. The auditor therefore has regard to the requirements of the FRC's ethical standards.   **28**

The engagement partner requires the actuary to notify him or her immediately of changes in the circumstances on which information was obtained at the start of the engagement, or any others that might reasonably be considered a threat to the actuary's objectivity.   **29**

Where the engagement partner identifies a significant threat to objectivity and independence which has not been eliminated or reduced to an acceptable level, he/she discusses with the PRA the circumstances that give rise to the threat and what course of action would be appropriate, including obtaining a rule waiver from the PRA. In circumstances where the matter cannot be resolved satisfactorily, the engagement partner considers making a reference to the independence of the actuary in the report made to the directors.   **30**

Reporting

Auditor's reports on regulatory returns normally include the following matters: **31**

(a)   A title identifying the persons to whom the report is addressed (which will normally be the directors of the insurer);

(b)   An introductory paragraph identifying the documents within the regulatory return which are covered by the report;

(c)   Separate sections, appropriately headed, dealing with:

     (i)   Respective responsibilities of the insurer and the auditor, and

     (ii)   The basis of the auditor's opinion;

(d)   The auditor's opinions on the matters required by the rules;

(e)   The signature of the auditor; and

(f)   The date of the auditor's report.

If the PRA has issued any directions to the insurer, waiving or modifying the application of any rules that affect the audited parts of a regulatory return, the auditor refers to these in the report and expresses the opinions by reference to the rules as modified.   **32**

Section 9 set out illustrative examples of reports on regulatory returns for composite insurers. This illustrative example needs to be tailored to reflect particular circumstances.   **33**

Subsequent events

There may be a gap between the date on which an insurer's statutory financial statements are approved and the date on which it's regulatory return is signed. The auditor undertakes a review of events up to the date of its report on the regulatory return before signing that report.   **34**

Modifying the auditor's opinion

35 When reporting on an insurer's regulatory returns, the auditor modifies its opinion as appropriate, following the principles in ISA (UK) 705 (revised). It is possible for the auditor's opinion on an insurer's financial statements to be modified whilst that on its regulatory return is unmodified, and vice versa. This may occur where the grounds for modification relate to the treatment of a particular item (for example, if an asset is included in the regulatory return at a value which does not take account of the specific requirements of the rules relating to the valuation or admissibility of assets).

36 When the auditor modifies their report, on the regulatory return, by making reference to an uncertainty, the PRA rulebook requires the auditor to state whether, in its opinion, the uncertainty is material to determining whether the insurer has available assets in excess of its capital resources requirement.

Resubmitted returns

37 The PRA may require the insurer to resubmit the regulatory return, or part thereof, where the original regulatory return is considered to be inaccurate or incomplete. The auditor is normally required to express an opinion on the amended or additional material. This can be done by either:

(a)   Withdrawing the original report and issuing a completely new report; or

(b)   Issuing a supplementary report on the amended material only, but including a reference to the original report.

38 The first option is preferable where the nature and volume of changes required gives rise to a resubmission of the complete return. The second option is preferable where the amendments are considered to be relatively minor or are few in number and only the amended forms, supplementary notes and/or statements are resubmitted.

Section 9: Illustrative Audit Report – Non-Solvency II Firm

[xx INSURANCE COMPANY LIMITED]

[Global business/UK branch business] Financial year ended 31 December 201x

Independent auditor's report to the directors pursuant to rules 7.1–7.6 of the Insurance Company – Reporting Part of the Non-Solvency II firms PRA Rulebook.

We have audited the following documents prepared by the insurer pursuant to the Insurance Company – Reporting Part, the Insurance Company – Overall Resource Part and specific valuation rules set out in the Rulebook for non-Solvency II firms ("the Rules"), made by the Prudential Regulation Authority under section 137G of the Financial Services and Markets Act 2000:

- *Forms [xx], (including the supplementary notes) on pages [...] to [...] ("the Forms");*
- *the statements required by Insurance Company – Reporting Part rules xx, xx, xx and xx on pages [...] to [...] ("the statements"); and*
- *the valuation report required by Insurance Company – Reporting Part rules 5.8-5.13 on pages [...] to [...] (the valuation report[s]).*

We are not required to audit and do not express an opinion on:

- the directors' certificate pursuant to rule 2.7 of the Insurance Company – Reporting Part, and
- Forms 46 and 50.

Respective responsibilities of the insurer and its auditor

The insurer is responsible for the preparation of an annual return (including the Forms, the statements and the valuation report[s]) under the provisions of the Rules. **[The requirements of the Rules have been modified by [a] direction[s] issued under section 138A of the Financial Services and Markets Act 2000 on ....200X [and ....200X].** Under the Insurance Company – Reporting Part of the Rulebook for non-Solvency II firms the Forms, the statements, and the valuation report[s] are required to be prepared in the manner specified by the Rules and to state fairly the information provided on the basis required by the Rules. The methods and assumptions determined by the insurer and used to perform the actuarial investigation as set out in the valuation report are required to reflect appropriately the requirements of the Insurance Company – Mathematical Reserves Part of the Rulebook for non-Solvency II firms.

It is our responsibility to form an independent opinion as to whether the Forms, the statements, the valuation report[s] meet these requirements, and to report our opinion to you. We also report to you if, in our opinion:

- adequate accounting records have not been kept, or returns adequate for our audit have not been received from branches not visited by us; or
- the Forms, the statements and the valuation report[s] are not in agreement with the accounting records and returns; or
- we have not received all the information we require for our audit.

Basis of opinion

We conducted our work in accordance with the procedures and guidance set out in Practice Note 20 "The audit of insurers in the United Kingdom (Revised)" issued by the Financial Reporting Council. Our work included examination, on a test basis, of evidence relevant to the amounts and disclosures in the Forms, the statements and the valuation report[s]. The evidence included that previously obtained by us relating to the audit of the financial statements of the insurer for the financial year. It also included an assessment of the significant estimates and judgments made by the insurer in the preparation of the Forms, the statements and the valuation report[s].

We planned and performed our work so as to obtain all the information and explanations which we considered necessary in order to provide us with sufficient evidence to give reasonable assurance that the Forms, the statements and the valuation report[s] are free from material misstatement, whether caused by fraud or other irregularity or error and comply with the Insurance Company – Reporting Part, the Insurance Company – Overall Resource Part and any specific valuation rules in the Rulebook for non-Solvency II firms

In accordance with the Insurance Company – Reporting Part rule 7.2 (2), to the extent that any document, Form, statement, analysis or report to be audited contains amounts or information abstracted from the actuarial investigation performed pursuant to pursuant to the Insurance Company – Reporting Part rules 5.8 and 5.9, we have obtained and paid due regard to advice from a suitably qualified actuary who is independent of the insurer.

Opinion

In our opinion:

- the Forms, the statements and the valuation report[s] fairly state the information provided on the basis required by the Rules [as modified] and have been properly prepared in accordance with the provisions of those Rules; and

- the methods and assumptions determined by the insurer and used to perform the actuarial investigation as set out in the valuation report[s] appropriately reflect the requirements of the Insurance Company – Mathematical Reserves Part of the Rulebook for non-Solvency II firms

Statutory auditor   Address

Date

Section 10: Definition of Terms

AAB	Audit Arrangements Byelaw (applicable to the Lloyd's Insurance Market)
ABI	Association of British Insurers
Association of British Insurers	An Actuary appointed by an insurer carrying on long-term insurance business to perform the actuarial function.
AFM	Association of Financial Mutuals
Auditor's expert	An individual or organization possessing expertise in a field other than accounting or auditing, whose work in that field is used by the auditor to assist the auditor in obtaining sufficient appropriate audit evidence. An auditor's expert may be either an auditor's internal expert (who is a partner or staff, including temporary staff, of the auditor's firm or a network firm), or an auditor's external expert.
Authorised firm	An insurer which has been granted one or more Part 4a permissions by the PRA and so is authorised under FSMA 2000 to undertake regulated activities – an authorised person. Authorised firms include insurers other than Lloyd's corporate members.
Authorised person	Term used throughout FSMA 2000 and related statutory instruments to refer to an authorised firm – see above.
Authorised insurance company	A company registered under CA 2006 that is authorised by the PRA to conduct insurance business, together with UK branches of insurers established outside the EEA.
CA 2006	The Companies Act 2006.
Closely linked entity	As defined in section 343(8) FSMA 2000, an entity has close links with an authorised firm for this purpose if the entity is a: (a) Parent undertaking of an authorised firm; (b) Subsidiary undertaking of an authorised firm; (c) Parent undertaking of a subsidiary undertaking of an authorised firm; or (d) Subsidiary undertaking of a parent undertaking of an authorised firm.
Council of Lloyd's	The Council constituted by section 3 of Lloyd's Act 1982.
EEA	European Economic Area
EU-IFRSs	International Financial Reporting Standards as adopted by the European Union.
FCA	Financial Conduct Authority
Friendly Society	A friendly society is a mutual organisation whose purpose often includes assisting members financially during sickness, unemployment or retirement, and to provide life assurance.
FSMA 2000	The Financial Services and Markets Act 2000.

Fundamental Rules and Principles for Businesses	The PRA have 8 Fundamental Rules.The 11 FCA principles are included in a stand-alone module of the FCA Handbook – High Level Standards PRIN 2.1.
IBNR	Incurred But Not Reported
Insurers	The term "insurers" is used in this Practice Note to refer to insurance companies authorised by the PRA (insurers with their head offices in the UK and, insurers established outside the EEA with UK branches) as well as to Friendly Societies and Lloyd's Syndicates and corporate members.
JMLSG	Joint Money Laundering Steering Group
Lloyd's corporate member	A member of the Society which is a body corporate (including limited liability partnerships) or a Scottish limited partnership.
Management's expert	An individual or organisation possessing expertise in a field other than accounting or auditing, whose work in that field is used by the insurer to assist in preparing the financial statements.
Matching Adjustment	The Matching Adjustment (MA) is a parallel shift applied to the entire basic risk-free term structure and serves the same purpose as the volatility adjustment. It is calculated based on the match between the insurers' assets and the liabilities. Subject to supervisory approval.
Material significance	A matter or group of matters is normally of material significance to a regulator's function when, due either to its nature or its potential financial impact, it is likely of itself to require investigation by the regulator.
Minimum Capital Requirement (MCR)	The MCR is defined in the Solvency II Directive as, "a minimum level of security below which the amount of financial resources should not fall", and corresponds to a minimum amount of basic own funds (or capital) below which policyholders would be exposed to an unacceptable level of risk. The MCR has an absolute floor below which it must not fall, and must also sit within a corridor ("the MCR corridor") of between 25% and 45% of the SCR.
NCA	National Crime Agency
ORSA	Own Risk and Solvency Assessment – a Solvency II requirement.
Part 4A permission	A permission granted by the PRA or FCA under Part 4A FSMA 2000 permitting an authorised firm to carry on regulated activities as specified in the FSMA 2000 Regulated Activities Order SI 2001/544 as amended.
PPFM	Principles and Practices of Financial Management [see COBS 20.3 of the FCA Handbook]
PRA	Prudential Regulation Authority

Public Interest Entity (PIE)	These are: (a) An issuer whose transferable securities are admitted to trading on a regulated market; (b) A credit institution within the meaning of Article 4(1)(1) of Regulation (EU) No 575/2013 of the European Parliament and of the Council, other than those listed in Article 2 of Directive 2013/36/EU of the European Parliament and of the Council on access to the activity of credit institutions and investment firms; (c) An insurance undertaking within the meaning given by Article 2(1) of Council Directive 1991/674/EEC of the European Parliament and of the Council on the annual accounts and consolidated accounts of insurance undertaking. No other entities have been specifically designated in law in the UK as "public interest entities". An insurance undertaking is a PIE if it meets any of the relevant criteria. In respect of c, which applies specifically to insurance entities, the relevant definition is now set out in the Solvency II Directive 2009/138/EC (which repealed previous relevant Directives). With effect from 17 June 2016 UK insurance and reinsurance undertakings within the scope of the Solvency II Directive are PIEs within the meaning of Audit Directive 2006/43 (as amended by Directive 2014/56). This includes relevant friendly societies and it also includes the Society of Lloyd's (because the society issues securities which are admitted to trading on a regulated market).
Recognised Accountant	An accountant included on the Council of Lloyds' list of individuals and firms identified as recognised accountants. Recognised accountants are engaged either by a syndicate to perform the annual solvency audit or annual syndicate audit or by a syndicate or Lloyd's underwriting agent to act as reporting accountant.
Risk Margin	A Solvency II requirement, this is the calculated cost of providing an amount of eligible own funds equal to support the obligations over their lifetime which is included within technical provisions.
RITC	"reinsurance to close"
Run-off account	A Lloyd's syndicate year of account which has not been closed at the normal date of closure and remains open.
2001 Regulations	SI 2001 No 2587 "The FSMA 2000 (Communications by Auditors) Regulations 2001"
2008 Regulations	SI 2008/1950 Insurance Accounts Directive (Lloyd's Syndicate and Aggregate Accounts) Regulations 2008
2008 Accounts and Reports Regulations	SI 2008/410 The Large and Medium-sized Companies and Groups (Accounts and Reports) Regulations 2008
2008 Lloyd's Regulations	SI 2008/1950 Insurance Accounts Directive (Lloyd's Syndicate and Aggregate Accounts) Regulations 2008.

Society	The Society incorporated by the Lloyd's Act 1871 by the names of Lloyd's.
Solvency Capital Requirement (SCR)	The SCR is a risk responsive capital measure calibrated to ensure that the insurer will be able to meet its obligations over the next 12 months with a probability of at least 99.5%. It can be calculated using a standard formula, a combination of the standard formula with an internal model (partial internal model), or a fully bespoke internal model. The expectation is that more complex insurers will use a partial or full internal model approach to reflect the particular circumstances of the risks they are exposed to.
Solvency and Financial Condition Report (SFCR)	Pillar 3 public disclosure under Solvency II. "Relevant elements" of the SFCR are subject to audit in accordance with PRA rules. The "relevant elements" are defined in the PRA's external audit rules pertaining to Solvency II firms.
Solvency II	An EU wide harmonized insurance regulatory regime, which became effective from 1 January 2016, under the Solvency II (Directive 2009/138/EC), Delegated Act and implementing UK legislation.
The Solvency Byelaw	The Solvency and Reporting Byelaw (No 5 of 2007) (applicable to the Lloyd's Insurance Market).
Lloyd's Syndicate	A group of underwriting members underwriting insurance business at Lloyd's through the agency of a managing agent.
TASs	Technical Actuarial Standards issued by the Financial Reporting Council.
Technical Provisions	The current amount an insurer would have to pay for an immediate transfer of obligations to another insurer. Under Solvency II this is the sum of a best estimate and a risk margin. The best estimate is calculated as a probability-weighted average of future cash flows, discounted using the relevant risk-free interest rate.
Those charged with governance	ISAs (UK) use the term "those charged with governance" to describe the persons entrusted with the supervision, control and direction of an entity, who will normally be responsible for the quality of financial reporting, and the term "management" to describe those persons who perform senior managerial functions. The PRA Rulebook uses the term "governing body" to describe collectively those charged with governance. In the context of this Practice Note, references to those charged with governance includes directors of insurance companies, directors of Lloyd's managing agents, and the members of the Council of Lloyd's.
Threshold conditions	The minimum standards that an authorised firm needs to meet to become and remain authorised by the PRA and FCA. The Threshold Conditions are set out in Schedule 6 to FSMA 2000 and represent the minimum conditions that a firm is required to satisfy and continue to satisfy to be given and to retain Part 4A permission. Firms must comply with both PRA specific and FCA specific Threshold Conditions.

Transitional Measures	Specific provisions in place during the implementation period for Solvency II, including for example on reporting deadlines, the risk-free curve and technical provisions. Details are available in the PRA Rulebook for Solvency II Directive firms "Transitional measures" part.
UK GAAP	United Kingdom Generally Accepted Accounting Practice. This consists of applicable law, United Kingdom Accounting Standards including FRS103 Insurance Contracts.
Volatility Adjustment	An adjustment to the relevant risk-free interest rate term structure (in accordance with Regulation 43 of the Solvency 2 Regulations 2015. Subject to supervisory approval.

Practice Note 23 – Special considerations in auditing financial instruments

(July 2013)

This Practice Note is based on International Auditing Practice Note 1000 issued by the International Auditing and Assurance Standards Board. Supplementary FRC guidance is highlighted with grey shading.

Contents

	Paragraphs
Introduction	1 - 10
Section I – Background information about financial instruments	11 - 69
Purpose and risks of using financial instruments	14 - 19
Controls relating to financial instruments	20 - 23
Completeness, accuracy, and existence	24 - 33
Valuation of financial instruments	34 - 64
Presentation and disclosure about financial instruments	65 - 69
Section II – Audit considerations relating to financial instruments	70 - 145
Professional scepticism	71 - 72
Planning considerations	73 - 84
Assessing and responding to the risks of material misstatement	85 - 105
Valuation of financial instruments	106 - 137
Presentation and disclosure of financial instruments	138 - 141
Other relevant audit considerations	142 - 145
Appendix – Examples of controls relating to financial instruments	1 - 33

Editorial note – The FRC issued the updated guidance for audits of entities of all sizes that may be subject to the risks associated with using financial instruments which aims to enhance investor confidence in the depth and reliability of the audit. It follows the consultation paper setting out the Proposed revision of Practice Note 23 (Revised) – Special Considerations in Auditing Financial Instruments on October 2012.

References to ISAs are to previous versions available online on Croner-i Tax and Accounting.

Introduction

1   Financial instruments may be used by financial and non-financial entities of all sizes for a variety of purposes. Some entities have large holdings and transaction volumes while other entities may only engage in a few financial instrument transactions. Some entities may take positions in financial instruments to assume and benefit from risk while other entities may use financial instruments to reduce certain risks by hedging or managing exposures. This ~~International Auditing Practice Note (IAPN)~~ is relevant to all of these situations.

2   The following International Standards on Auditing (ISAs) (UK and Ireland) are particularly relevant to audits of financial instruments:

(a)   ISA (UK and Ireland) 540[1] deals with the auditor's responsibilities relating to auditing accounting estimates, including accounting estimates related to financial instruments measured at fair value;

(b)   ISA (UK and Ireland) 315[2] and ISA (UK and Ireland) 330[3] deal with identifying and assessing risks of material misstatement and responding to those risks; and

(c)   ISA (UK and Ireland) 500[4] explains what constitutes audit evidence and deals with the auditor's responsibility to design and perform audit procedures to obtain sufficient appropriate audit evidence to be able to draw reasonable conclusions on which to base the auditor's opinion.

3   The purpose of this PN is to provide:

(a)   Background information about financial instruments (Section I); and

(b)   Discussion of audit considerations relating to financial instruments (Section II).

~~IAPNs provide practical assistance to auditors. They are intended to be disseminated by those responsible for national standards, or used in developing corresponding national material. They also provide material that firms can use in developing their training programs and internal guidance.~~ PNs are persuasive rather than prescriptive and are indicative of good practice. They are intended to assist auditors in applying ISAs (UK and Ireland) to particular circumstances and industries. Auditors should be aware of and consider PNs applicable to the engagement. Auditors who do not consider and apply the guidance included in a relevant PN should be prepared to explain how the ISAs (UK and Ireland) have been complied with.

4   This PN is relevant to entities of all sizes, as all entities may be subject to risks of material misstatement when using financial instruments.

5   The guidance on valuation[5] in this PN is likely to be more relevant for financial instruments measured or disclosed at fair value, while the guidance on areas other than valuation applies equally to financial instruments either measured at fair

---

[1]   *ISA (UK and Ireland) 540, Auditing Accounting Estimates, Including Fair Value Accounting Estimates, and Related Disclosures.*

[2]   *ISA (UK and Ireland) 315, Identifying and Assessing the Risks of Material Misstatement through Understanding the Entity and Its Environment.*

[3]   *ISA (UK and Ireland) 330, The Auditor's Responses to Assessed Risks.*

[4]   *ISA (UK and Ireland) 500, Audit Evidence.*

[5]   *In this PN, the terms "valuation" and "measurement" are used interchangeably.*

value or amortized cost. This PN is also applicable to both financial assets and financial liabilities. This PN does not deal with instruments such as:

(a)   The simplest financial instruments such as cash, simple loans, trade accounts receivable and trade accounts payable;

(b)   Investments in unlisted equity instruments; or

(c)   Insurance contracts.

Also, this PN does not deal with specific accounting issues relevant to financial   6
instruments, such as hedge accounting, profit or loss on inception (often known as "Day 1" profit or loss), offsetting, risk transfers or impairment, including loan loss provisioning. Although these subject matters can relate to an entity's accounting for financial instruments, a discussion of the auditor's consideration regarding how to address specific accounting requirements is beyond the scope of this PN.

An audit in accordance with ISAs (UK and Ireland) is conducted on the premise   7
that management and, where appropriate, those charged with governance have acknowledged certain responsibilities. Such responsibilities subsume making fair value measurements. This PN does not impose responsibilities on management or those charged with governance nor override laws and regulation that govern their responsibilities.

This PN has been written in the context of general purpose fair presentation   8
financial reporting frameworks, but may also be useful, as appropriate in the circumstance, in other financial reporting frameworks such as special purpose financial reporting frameworks.

This PN focuses on the assertions of valuation, and presentation and disclosure,   9
but also covers, in less detail, completeness, accuracy, existence, and rights and obligations.

Financial instruments are susceptible to estimation uncertainty, which is defined in   10
ISA (UK and Ireland) 540 as "the susceptibility of an accounting estimate and related disclosures to an inherent lack of precision in its measurement."[6] Estimation uncertainty is affected by the complexity of financial instruments, among other factors. The nature and reliability of information available to support the measurement of financial instruments varies widely, which affects the estimation uncertainty associated with their measurement. This PN uses the term "measurement uncertainty" to refer to the estimation uncertainty associated with fair value measurements.

Section I – Background information about financial instruments

Different definitions of financial instruments may exist among financial reporting   11
frameworks. For example, International Financial Reporting Standards (IFRS) define a financial instrument as any contract that gives rise to a financial asset of one entity and a financial liability or equity instrument of another entity.[7] Financial instruments may be cash, the equity of another entity, the contractual right or obligation to receive or deliver cash or exchange financial assets or liabilities, certain contracts settled in an entity's own equity instruments, certain contracts on

---

[6] *ISA (UK and Ireland) 540, paragraph 7(c).*

[7] *International Accounting Standard (IAS) 32, Financial Instruments: Presentation, paragraph 11.*

non-financial items, or certain contracts issued by insurers that do not meet the definition of an insurance contract. This definition encompasses a wide range of financial instruments from simple loans and deposits to complex derivatives, structured products, and some commodity contracts.

12   Financial instruments vary in complexity, though the complexity of the financial instrument can come from difference sources, such as:

- A very high volume of individual cash flows, where a lack of homogeneity requires analysis of each one or a large number of grouped cash flows to evaluate, for example, credit risk (for example, collateralized debt obligations (CDOs)).

- Complex formulae for determining the cash flows.

- Uncertainty or variability of future cash flows, such as that arising from credit risk, option contracts or financial instruments with lengthy contractual terms.

The higher the variability of cash flows to changes in market conditions, the more complex and uncertain the fair value measurement of the financial instrument is likely to be. In addition, sometimes financial instruments that, ordinarily, are relatively easy to value become complex to value because of particular circumstances, for example, instruments for which the market has become inactive or which have lengthy contractual terms. Derivatives and structured products become more complex when they are a combination of individual financial instruments. In addition, the accounting for financial instruments under certain financial reporting frameworks or certain market conditions may be complex.

13   Another source of complexity is the volume of financial instruments held or traded. While a "plain vanilla" interest rate swap may not be complex, an entity holding a large number of them may use a sophisticated information system to identify, value and transact these instruments.

Purpose and risks of using financial instruments

14   Financial instruments are used for:

- Hedging purposes (that is, to change an existing risk profile to which an entity is exposed). This includes:

  - The forward purchase or sale of currency to fix a future exchange rate;

  - Converting future interest rates to fixed rates or floating rates through the use of swaps; and

  - The purchase of option contracts to provide an entity with protection against a particular price movement, including contracts which may contain embedded derivatives;

- Trading purposes (for example, to enable an entity to take a risk position to benefit from short term market movements); and

- Investment purposes (for example, to enable an entity to benefit from long term investment returns).

15   The use of financial instruments can reduce exposures to certain business risks, for example changes in exchange rates, interest rates and commodity prices, or a combination of those risks. On the other hand, the inherent complexities of some financial instruments also may result in increased risk.

Business risk and the risk of material misstatement increase when management **16** and those charged with governance:

● Do not fully understand the risks of using financial instruments and have insufficient skills and experience to manage those risks;

● Do not have the expertise to value them appropriately in accordance with the applicable financial reporting framework;

● Do not have sufficient controls in place over financial instrument activities; or

● Inappropriately hedge risks or speculate.

Management's failure to fully understand the risks inherent in a financial **17** instrument can have a direct effect on management's ability to manage these risks appropriately, and may ultimately threaten the viability of the entity.

The principal types of risk applicable to financial instruments are listed below. **18** This list is not meant to be exhaustive and different terminology may be used to describe these risks or classify the components of individual risks.

(a) Credit (or counterparty) risk is the risk that one party to a financial instrument will cause a financial loss to another party by failing to discharge an obligation and is often associated with default. Credit risk includes settlement risk, which is the risk that one side of a transaction will be settled without consideration being received from the customer or counterparty.

(b) Market risk is the risk that the fair value or future cash flows of a financial instrument will fluctuate because of changes in market prices. Examples of market risk include currency risk, interest rate risk, commodity and equity price risk.

(c) Liquidity risk includes the risk of not being able to buy or sell a financial instrument at an appropriate price in a timely manner due to a lack of marketability for that financial instrument.

(d) Operational risk relates to the specific processing required for financial instruments. Operational risk may increase as the complexity of a financial instrument increases, and poor management of operational risk may increase other types of risk. Operational risk includes:

   (i) The risk that confirmation and reconciliation controls are inadequate resulting in incomplete or inaccurate recording of financial instruments;

   (ii) The risks that there is inappropriate documentation of transactions and insufficient monitoring of these transactions;

   (iii) The risk that transactions are incorrectly recorded, processed or risk managed and, therefore, do not reflect the economics of the overall trade;

   (iv) The risk that undue reliance is placed by staff on the accuracy of valuation techniques, without adequate review, and transactions are therefore incorrectly valued or their risk is improperly measured;

   (v) The risk that the use of financial instruments is not adequately incorporated into the entity's risk management policies and procedures;

(vi)   The risk of loss resulting from inadequate or failed internal processes and systems, or from external events, including the risk of fraud from both internal and external sources;

(vii) The risk that there is inadequate or non-timely maintenance of valuation techniques used to measure financial instruments; and

(viii) Legal risk, which is a component of operational risk, and relates to losses resulting from a legal or regulatory action that invalidates or otherwise precludes performance by the end user or its counterparty under the terms of the contract or related netting arrangements. For example, legal risk could arise from insufficient or incorrect documentation for the contract, an inability to enforce a netting arrangement in bankruptcy, adverse changes in tax laws, or statutes that prohibit entities from investing in certain types of financial instruments.

(e)   Model risk, which is the risk that imperfections and subjectivity of valuation models used to determine the value of certain types of financial instrument are not properly understood and accounted for or adjusted for. This includes the risk that undue reliance is placed by staff on information derived from valuation models, in managing financial instrument positions, with the result that they overlook the fundamentals of risk management and control of market, counterparty and operational risk for these types of transactions.

19   Other considerations relevant to risks of using financial instruments include:

- The risk of fraud that may be increased if, for example, an employee in a position to perpetrate a financial fraud understands both the financial instruments and the processes for accounting for them, but management and those charged with governance have a lesser degree of understanding.

- The risk that master netting arrangements[8] may not be properly reflected in the financial statements.

- The risk that some financial instruments may change between being assets or liabilities during their term and that such change may occur rapidly.

The potential for rapid changes in prices, coupled with the structure of certain financial instruments, also can affect credit risk exposure. For example, highly leveraged financial instruments or financial instruments with longer maturity can result in credit risk exposure increasing quickly after a transaction has been undertaken.

Controls relating to financial instruments

20   The extent of an entity's use of financial instruments and the degree of complexity of the instruments are important determinants of the necessary level of sophistication of the entity's internal control. For example, smaller entities may use less structured products and simple processes and procedures to achieve their objectives.

21   Often, it is the role of those charged with governance to set the tone regarding, and approve and oversee the extent of use of, financial instruments while it is

---

[8] *An entity that undertakes a number of financial instrument transactions with a single counterparty may enter into a master netting arrangement with that counterparty. Such an agreement provides for a single net settlement of all financial instruments covered by the agreement in the event of default of any one contract.*

management's role to manage and monitor the entity's exposures to those risks. Management and, where appropriate, those charged with governance are also responsible for designing and implementing a system of internal control to enable the preparation of financial statements in accordance with the applicable financial reporting framework. An entity's internal control over financial instruments is more likely to be effective when management and those charged with governance have:

(a) Established an appropriate control environment, active participation by those charged with governance in controlling the use of financial instruments, a logical organizational structure with clear assignment of authority and responsibility, and appropriate human resource policies and procedures. In particular, clear rules are needed on the extent to which those responsible for financial instrument activities are permitted to act. Such rules have regard to any legal or regulatory restrictions on using financial instruments. For example, certain public sector entities may not have the power to conduct business using derivatives;

(b) Established a risk management process relative to the size of the entity and the complexity of its financial instruments (for example, in some entities a formal risk management function may exist);

(c) Established information systems that provide those charged with governance with an understanding of the nature of the financial instrument activities and the associated risks, including adequate documentation of transactions;

(d) Designed, implemented and documented a system of internal control to:

- Provide reasonable assurance that the entity's use of financial instruments is within its risk management policies;
- Properly present financial instruments in the financial statements;
- Ensure that the entity is in compliance with applicable laws and regulations; and
- Monitor risk.

The Appendix provides examples of controls that may exist in an entity that deals in a high volume of financial instrument transactions; and

(e) Established appropriate accounting policies, including valuation policies, in accordance with the applicable financial reporting framework.

Key elements of risk management processes and internal control relating to an **22** entity's financial instruments include:

- Setting an approach to define the amount of risk exposure that the entity is willing to accept when engaging in financial instrument transactions (this may be referred to as its "risk appetite"), including policies for investing in financial instruments, and the control framework in which the financial instrument activities are conducted;

- Establishing processes for the documentation and authorization of new types of financial instrument transactions which consider the accounting, regulatory, legal, financial and operational risks that are associated with such instruments;

- Processing financial instrument transactions, including confirmation and reconciliation of cash and asset holdings to external statements, and the payments process;

- Segregation of duties between those investing or trading in the financial instruments and those responsible for processing, valuing and confirming such instruments. For example, a model development function that is involved in assisting in pricing deals is less objective than one that is functionally and organizationally separate from the front office;

- Valuation processes and controls, including controls over data obtained from thirdparty pricing sources; and

- Monitoring of controls.

23 The nature of risks often differs between entities with a high volume and variety of financial instruments and those with only a few financial instrument transactions. This results in different approaches to internal control. For example:

- Typically, an institution with high volumes of financial instruments will have a dealing room type environment in which there are specialist traders and segregation of duties between those traders and the back office (which refers to the operations function that data-checks trades that have been conducted, ensuring that they are not erroneous, and transacting the required transfers). In such environments, the traders will typically initiate contracts verbally over the phone or via an electronic trading platform. Capturing relevant transactions and accurately recording financial instruments in such an environment is significantly more challenging than for an entity with only a few financial instruments, whose existence and completeness often can be confirmed with a bank confirmation to a few banks.

- On the other hand, entities with only a small number of financial instruments often do not have segregation of duties, and access to the market is limited. In such cases, although it may be easier to identify financial instrument transactions, there is a risk that management may rely on a limited number of personnel, which may increase the risk that unauthorized transactions may be initiated or transactions may not be recorded.

Completeness, accuracy, and existence

24 Paragraphs 25-33 describe controls and processes which may be in place in entities with a high volume of financial instrument transactions, including those with trading rooms. By contrast, an entity that does not have a high volume of financial instrument transactions may not have these controls and processes but may instead confirm their transactions with the counterparty or clearing house. Doing so may be relatively straightforward in that the entity may only transact with one or two counterparties.

24-1 Complete and accurate recording of financial instruments is an essential core objective on which many others are built. For example, without a process that completely and accurately records all financial instruments:

- Financial information may be incomplete and/or inaccurate;

- Risks may be improperly managed, because the entity's exposures will be inaccurately recorded;

- The entity may be unable to settle transactions accurately;

- Off-balance sheet instruments and their associated risks may not be appropriately treated.

Trade confirmations and clearing houses

Generally, for transactions undertaken by financial institutions, the terms of **25** financial instruments are documented in confirmations exchanged between counterparties and legal agreements. Clearing houses serve to monitor the exchange of confirmations by matching trades and settling them. A central clearing house is associated with an exchange and entities that clear through clearing houses typically have processes to manage the information delivered to the clearing house.

Not all transactions are settled through such an exchange. In many other markets **26** there is an established practice of agreeing the terms of transactions before settlement begins. To be effective, this process needs to be run separately from those who trade the financial instruments to minimize the risk of fraud. In other markets, transactions are confirmed after settlement has begun and sometimes confirmation backlogs result in settlement beginning before all terms have been fully agreed. This presents additional risk because the transacting entities need to rely on alternative means of agreeing trades. These may include:

● Enforcing rigorous reconciliations between the records of those trading the financial instruments and those settling them (strong segregation of duties between the two are important), combined with strong supervisory controls over those trading the financial instruments to ensure the integrity of the transactions;

● Reviewing summary documentation from counterparties that highlights the key terms even if the full terms have not been agreed; and

● Thorough review of traders' profits and losses to ensure that they reconcile to what the back office has calculated.

Reconciliations with banks and custodians

Some components of financial instruments, such as bonds and shares, may be held **27** in separate depositories. In addition, most financial instruments result in payments of cash at some point and often these cash flows begin early in the contract's life. These cash payments and receipts will pass through an entity's bank account. Regular reconciliation of the entity's records to external banks' and custodians' records enables the entity to ensure transactions are properly recorded.

It should be noted that not all financial instruments result in a cash flow in the early **28** stages of the contract's life or are capable of being recorded with an exchange or custodian. Where this is the case, reconciliation processes will not identify an omitted or inaccurately recorded trade and confirmation controls are more important. Even where such a cash flow is accurately recorded in the early stages of an instrument's life, this does not ensure that all characteristics or terms of the instrument (for example, the maturity or an early termination option) have been recorded accurately.

In addition, cash movements may be quite small in the context of the overall size **29** of the trade or the entity's own balance sheet and may therefore be difficult to identify. The value of reconciliations is enhanced when finance, or other back office staff, review entries in all general ledger accounts to ensure that they are valid and supportable. This process will help identify if the other side to cash entries relating to financial instruments has not been properly recorded. Reviewing suspense and clearing accounts is important regardless of the account balance, as there may be offsetting reconciling items in the account.

30   In entities with a high volume of financial instrument transactions, reconciliation and confirmation controls may be automated and, if so, adequate IT controls need to be in place to support them. In particular, controls are needed to ensure that data is completely and accurately picked up from external sources (such as banks and custodians) and from the entity's records and is not tampered with before or during reconciliation. Controls are also needed to ensure that the criteria on which entries are matched are sufficiently restrictive to prevent inaccurate clearance of reconciling items.

Other controls over completeness, accuracy, and existence

31   The complexity inherent in some financial instruments means that it will not always be obvious how they should be recorded in the entity's systems. In such cases, management may set up control processes to monitor policies that prescribe how particular types of transactions are measured, recorded and accounted for. These policies are typically established and reviewed in advance by suitably qualified personnel who are capable of understanding the full effects of the financial instruments being booked.

32   Some transactions may be cancelled or amended after initial execution. Application of appropriate controls relating to cancellation or amendment can mitigate the risks of material misstatement due to fraud or error. In addition, an entity may have a process in place to reconfirm trades that are cancelled or amended.

33   In financial institutions with a high volume of trading, a senior employee typically reviews daily profits and losses on individual traders' books to evaluate whether they are reasonable based on the employee's knowledge of the market. Doing so may enable management to determine that particular trades were not completely or accurately recorded, or may identify fraud by a particular trader. It is important that there are transaction authorization procedures that support the more senior review.

Valuation of financial instruments

Financial reporting requirements

34   In many financial reporting frameworks, financial instruments, including embedded derivatives, are often measured at fair value for the purpose of balance sheet presentation, calculating profit or loss, and/or disclosure. In general, the objective of fair value measurement is to arrive at the price at which an orderly transaction would take place between market participants at the measurement date under current market conditions; that is, it is not the transaction price for a forced liquidation or distressed sale. In meeting this objective, all relevant available market information is taken into account.

35   Fair value measurements of financial assets and financial liabilities may arise both at the initial recording of transactions and later when there are changes in value. Changes in fair value measurements that occur over time may be treated in different ways under different financial reporting frameworks. For example, such changes may be recorded as profit or loss, or may be recorded in the other comprehensive income. Also, depending on the applicable financial reporting framework, the whole financial instrument or only a component of it (for example, an embedded derivative when it is separately accounted for) may be required to be measured at fair value.

Some financial reporting frameworks establish a fair value hierarchy to develop **36** increased consistency and comparability in fair value measurements and related disclosures. The inputs may be classified into different levels such as:

- Level 1 inputs-Quoted prices (unadjusted) in active markets for identical financial assets or financial liabilities that the entity can access at the measurement date.

- Level 2 inputs-Inputs other than quoted prices included within level 1 that are observable for the financial asset or financial liability, either directly or indirectly. If the financial asset or financial liability has a specified (contractual) term, a level 2 input must be observable for substantially the full term of the financial asset or financial liability. Level 2 inputs include the following:

  - Quoted prices for similar financial assets or financial liabilities in active markets.

  - Quoted prices for identical or similar financial assets or financial liabilities in markets that are not active.

  - Inputs other than quoted prices that are observable for the financial asset or financial liability (for example, interest rates and yield curves observable at commonly quoted intervals, implied volatilities and credit spreads).

  - Inputs that are derived principally from, or corroborated by, observable market data by correlation or other means (market-corroborated inputs).

- Level 3 inputs-Unobservable inputs for the financial asset or financial liability. Unobservable inputs are used to measure fair value to the extent that relevant observable inputs are not available, thereby allowing for situations in which there is little, if any, market activity for the financial asset or financial liability at the measurement date.

In general, measurement uncertainty increases as a financial instrument moves from level 1 to level 2, or level 2 to level 3. Also, within level 2 there may be a wide range of measurement uncertainty depending on the observability of inputs, the complexity of the financial instrument, its valuation, and other factors.

Certain financial reporting frameworks may require or permit the entity to adjust **37** for measurement uncertainties, in order to adjust for risks that a market participant would make in the pricing to take account of the uncertainties of the risks associated with the pricing or cash flows of the financial instrument. For example:

- Model adjustments. Some models may have a known deficiency or the result of calibration may highlight the deficiency for the fair value measurement in accordance with the financial reporting framework.

- Credit-risk adjustments. Some models do not take into account credit risk, including counterparty risk or own credit risk.

- Liquidity adjustments. Some models calculate a mid-market price, even though the financial reporting framework may require use of a liquidity adjusted amount such as a bid/offer spread. Another, more judgmental, liquidity adjustment recognizes that some financial instruments are illiquid which affects the valuation.

- Other risk adjustments. A value measured using a model that does not take into account all other factors that market participants would consider in pricing the financial instrument may not represent fair value on the measurement date, and therefore may need to be adjusted separately to comply with the applicable financial reporting framework.

Adjustments are not appropriate if they adjust the measurement and valuation of the financial instrument away from fair value as defined by the applicable financial reporting framework, for example for conservatism.

Observable and unobservable inputs

38   As mentioned above, financial reporting frameworks often categorize inputs according to the degree of observability. As activity in a market for financial instruments declines and the observability of inputs declines, measurement uncertainty increases. The nature and reliability of information available to support valuation of financial instruments varies depending on the observability of inputs to its measurement, which is influenced by the nature of the market (for example, the level of market activity and whether it is through an exchange or over-the-counter (OTC)). Accordingly, there is a continuum of the nature and reliability of evidence used to support valuation, and it becomes more difficult for management to obtain information to support a valuation when markets become inactive and inputs become less observable.

39   When observable inputs are not available, an entity uses unobservable inputs (level 3 inputs) that reflect the assumption that market participants would use when pricing the financial asset or the financial liability, including assumptions about risk. Unobservable inputs are developed using the best information available in the circumstances. In developing unobservable inputs, an entity may begin with its own data, which is adjusted if reasonably available information indicates that (a) other market participants would use different data or (b) there is something particular to the entity that is not available to other market participants (for example, an entity-specific synergy).

Effects of inactive markets

40   Measurement uncertainty increases and valuation is more complicated when the markets in which financial instruments or their component parts are traded become inactive[8a]. There is no clear point at which an active market becomes inactive, though financial reporting frameworks may provide guidance on this issue. Characteristics of an inactive market include a significant decline in the volume and level of trading activity, available prices vary significantly over time or among market participants or the prices are not current. However, assessing whether a market is inactive requires judgment.

41   When markets are inactive, prices quoted may be stale (that is, out of date), may not represent prices at which market participants may trade or may represent forced transactions (such as when a seller is required to sell an asset to meet regulatory or legal requirements, needs to dispose of an asset immediately to create liquidity or the existence of a single potential buyer as a result of the legal or time restrictions imposed). Accordingly, valuations are developed based on level 2 and level 3 inputs. Under such circumstances, entities may have:

- Protocols for acquiring pricing indicators from as many different sources as possible;

[8a] *Guidance for auditors on issues that may arise in adverse market conditions is provided in Bulletins 2008/1 Audit Issues When Financial Market Conditions are Difficult and Credit Facilities may be Limited and 2008/10 Going Concern Issues During the Current Economic Conditions.*

- A valuation policy that includes a process for determining whether level 1 inputs are available;

- An understanding of how particular prices or inputs from external sources used as inputs to valuation techniques were calculated in order to assess their reliability. For example, in an active market, a broker quote on a financial instrument that has not traded is likely to reflect actual transactions on a similar financial instrument, but, as the market becomes less active, the broker quote may rely more on proprietary valuation techniques to determine prices;

- An understanding of how deteriorating business conditions affect the counterparty, as well as whether deteriorating business conditions in entities similar to the counterparty may indicate that the counterparty may not fulfill its obligations (that is, non-performance risk);

- Policies for adjusting for measurement uncertainties. Such adjustments can include model adjustments, lack of liquidity adjustments, credit risk adjustments, and other risk adjustments;

- The capability to calculate the range of realistic outcomes given the uncertainties involved, for example by performing a sensitivity analysis; and

- Policies for identifying when a fair value measurement input moves to a different level of the fair value hierarchy.

42 Particular difficulties may develop where there is severe curtailment or even cessation of trading in particular financial instruments. In these circumstances, financial instruments that have previously been valued using market prices may need to be valued using a model.

Management's valuation process

43 Techniques that management may use to value their financial instruments include observable prices, recent transactions, and models that use observable or unobservable inputs. Management may also make use of:

(a)   A third-party pricing source, such as a pricing service or broker quote; or

(b)   A valuation expert.

Third-party pricing sources and valuation experts may use one or more of these valuation techniques.

44 In many financial reporting frameworks, the best evidence of a financial instrument's fair value is found in contemporaneous transactions in an active market (that is, level 1 inputs). In such cases, the valuation of a financial instrument may be relatively simple. Quoted prices for financial instruments that are listed on exchanges or traded in liquid over-the-counter markets may be available from sources such as financial publications, the exchanges themselves or third-party pricing sources. When using quoted prices, it is important that management understand the basis on which the quote is given to ensure that the price reflects market conditions at the measurement date. Quoted prices obtained from publications or exchanges may provide sufficient evidence of fair value when, for example:

(a)   The prices are not out of date or "stale" (for example, if the quote is based on the last traded price and the trade occurred some time ago); and

(b)   The quotes are prices at which dealers would actually trade the financial instrument with sufficient frequency and volume.

44-1   The pricing source should be independent and where possible there should be more than one provider of a quote. Prices should not come from quotations provided solely or primarily by the entity being audited.

44-2   It may also be necessary to adjust for factors not present in any market quotations. For example the credit spread of a particular counterparty may not be factored into a general market quote and may need to be adjusted for.

45   Where there is no current observable market price for the financial instrument (that is, a level 1 input), it will be necessary for the entity to gather other price indicators to use in a valuation technique to value the financial instrument. Price indicators may include:

- Recent transactions, including transactions after the date of the financial statements in the same instrument. Consideration is given to whether an adjustment needs to be made for changes in market conditions between the measurement date and the date the transaction was made, as these transactions are not necessarily indicative of the market conditions that existed at the date of the financial statements. In addition it is possible that the transaction represents a forced transaction and is therefore not indicative of a price in an orderly trade.

- Current or recent transactions in similar instruments, often known as "proxy pricing". Adjustments will need to be made to the price of the proxy to reflect the differences between them and the instrument being priced, for example, to take account of differences in liquidity or credit risk between the two instruments.

- Indices for similar instruments. As with transactions in similar instruments, adjustments will need to be made to reflect the difference between the instrument being priced and the instrument(s) from which the index used is derived.

46   It is expected that management will document its valuation policies and model used to value a particular financial instrument, including the rationale for the model(s) used, the selection of assumptions in the valuation methodology, and the entity's consideration of whether adjustments for measurement uncertainty are necessary.

Models

47   Models may be used to value financial instruments when the price cannot be directly observed in the market. Models can be as simple as a commonly used bond pricing formula or involve complex, specifically developed software tools to value financial instruments with level 3 inputs. Many models are based on discounted cash flow calculations.

48   Models comprise a methodology, assumptions and data. The methodology describes rules or principles governing the relationship between the variables in the valuation. Assumptions include estimates of uncertain variables which are used in the model. Data may comprise actual or hypothetical information about the financial instrument, or other inputs to the financial instrument.

49   Depending on the circumstances, matters that the entity may address when establishing or validating a model for a financial instrument include whether:

- The model is validated prior to usage, with periodic reviews to ensure it is still suitable for its intended use. The entity's validation process may include evaluation of:

- • The methodology's theoretical soundness and mathematical integrity, including the appropriateness of parameters and sensitivities.

- • The consistency and completeness of the model's inputs with market practices, and whether the appropriate inputs are available for use in the model.

- There are appropriate change control policies, procedures and security controls over the model.

- The model is appropriately changed or adjusted on a timely basis for changes in market conditions.

- The model is periodically calibrated, reviewed and tested for validity by a separate and objective function. Doing so is a means of ensuring that the model's output is a fair representation of the value that marketplace participants would ascribe to a financial instrument.

- The model maximizes the use of relevant observable inputs and minimizes the use of unobservable inputs.

- Adjustments are made to the output of the model to reflect the assumptions marketplace participants would use in similar circumstances.

- The model is adequately documented, including the model's intended applications and limitations and its key parameters, required data, results of any validation analysis performed and any adjustments made to the output of the model.

- Whether a model used to prepare actuarial information follows the principles in Technical Actuarial Standard M: Modelling[8b].

An example of a common financial instrument

The following describes how models may be applied to value a common financial instrument, known as an asset backed security.[9] Because asset backed securities are often valued based on level 2 or 3 inputs, they are frequently valued using models and involve: **50**

- Understanding the type of security-considering (a) the underlying collateral; and (b) the terms of the security. The underlying collateral is used to estimate the timing and amounts of cash flows such as mortgage or credit card interest and principal payments.

- Understanding the terms of the security-this includes evaluating contractual cash flow rights, such as the order of repayment, and any default events. The order of repayment, often known as seniority, refers to terms which require that some classes of security holders (senior debt) are repaid before others (subordinated debt). The rights of each class of security holder to the cash flows, frequently referred to as the cash flow "waterfall", together with assumptions of the timing and amount of cash flows are used to derive a set of estimated cash flows for each class of security holder. The expected cash flows are then discounted to derive an estimated fair value.

[8b] *Technical Actuarial Standards are issued by the Financial Reporting Council.*

[9] *An asset backed security is a financial instrument which is backed by a pool of underlying assets (known as the collateral, such as credit card receivables or vehicle loans) and derives value and income from those underlying assets.*

51   The cash flows of an asset backed security may be affected by prepayments of the underlying collateral and by potential default risk and resulting estimated loss severities. Prepayment assumptions, if applicable, are generally based on evaluating market interest rates for similar collateral to the rates on the collateral underlying the security. For example, if market interest rates for mortgages have declined then the underlying mortgages in a security may experience higher prepayment rates than originally expected. Estimating potential default and loss severity involves close evaluation of the underlying collateral and borrowers to estimate default rates. For example, when the underlying collateral comprises residential mortgages, loss severities may be affected by estimates of residential housing prices over the term of the security.

Third-party pricing sources

52   Entities may use third-party pricing sources in order to obtain fair value information. The preparation of an entity's financial statements, including the valuation of financial instruments and the preparation of financial statement disclosures relating to these instruments, may require expertise that management does not possess. Entities may not be able to develop appropriate valuation techniques, including models that may be used in a valuation, and may use a third-party pricing source to arrive at a valuation or to provide disclosures for the financial statements. This may particularly be the case in smaller entities or in entities that do not engage in a high volume of financial instruments transactions (for example, non-financial institutions with treasury departments). Even though management has used a third-party pricing source, management is ultimately responsible for the valuation.

53   Third-party pricing sources may also be used because the volume of securities to price over a short timeframe may not be possible by the entity. This is often the case for traded investment funds that must determine a net asset value each day. In other cases, management may have their own pricing process but use third-party pricing sources to corroborate their own valuations.

54   For one or more of these reasons most entities use third-party pricing sources when valuing securities either as a primary source or as a source of corroboration for their own valuations. Third-party pricing sources generally fall into the following categories:

- Pricing services, including consensus pricing services; and
- Brokers providing broker quotes.

Pricing services

55   Pricing services provide entities with prices and price-related data for a variety of financial instruments, often performing daily valuations of large numbers of financial instruments. These valuations may be made by collecting market data and prices from a wide variety of sources, including market makers, and, in certain instances, using internal valuations techniques to derive estimated fair values. Pricing services may combine a number of approaches to arrive at a price. Pricing services are often used as a source of prices based on level 2 inputs. Pricing services may have strong controls around how prices are developed and their customers often include a wide variety of parties, including buy and sell side investors, back and middle office functions, auditors and others.

56   Pricing services often have a formalized process for customers to challenge the prices received from the pricing services. These challenge processes usually require the customer to provide evidence to support an alternative price, with challenges categorized based on the quality of evidence provided. For example, a challenge based on a recent sale of that instrument that the pricing service was not aware of may be upheld, whereas a challenge based on a customer's own valuation technique may be more heavily scrutinized. In this way, a pricing service with a large number of leading participants, both buy and sell side, may be able to constantly correct prices to more fully reflect the information available to market participants.

When considering whether a corrected price gives a suitable basis for valuation in the financial statements, consideration should be given to how long the challenge process has taken and whether the underlying data remains valid or there have been developments, such as market movements, to take account of.

56-1

Consensus pricing services

Some entities may use pricing data from consensus pricing services which differ from other pricing services. Consensus pricing services obtain pricing information about an instrument from several participating entities (subscribers). Each subscriber submits prices to the pricing service. The pricing service treats this information confidentially and returns to each subscriber the consensus price, which is usually an arithmetical average of the data after a data cleansing routine has been employed to eliminate outliers. For some markets, such as for exotic derivatives, consensus prices might constitute the best available data. However, many factors are considered when assessing the representational faithfulness of the consensus prices including, for example:

57

- Whether the prices submitted by the subscribers reflect actual transactions or just indicative prices based on their own valuation techniques.
- The number of sources from which prices have been obtained.
- The quality of the sources used by the consensus pricing service.
- Whether participants include leading market participants.
- Whether the market is one sided, where all the subscribers have positions in the same direction, causing the results to be skewed.

Typically consensus prices are only available to subscribers who have submitted their own prices to the service. Accordingly not all entities will have direct access to consensus prices. Because a subscriber generally cannot know how the prices submitted were estimated, other sources of evidence in addition to information from consensus pricing services may be needed for management to support their valuation. In particular, this may be the case if the sources are providing indicative prices based on their own valuation techniques and management is unable to obtain an understanding of how these sources calculated their prices.

58

Brokers providing broker quotes

As brokers provide quotes only as an incidental service for their clients, quotes they provide differ in many respects from prices obtained in pricing services. Brokers may be unwilling to provide information about the process used to develop their quote, but may have access to information on transactions about which a pricing service may not be aware. Broker quotes may be executable or indicative. Indicative quotes are a broker's best estimate of fair value, whereas an executable quote shows that the broker is willing to transact at this price. Executable quotes are strong evidence of fair value. Indicative quotes are less

59

so because of the lack of transparency into the methods used by the broker to establish the quote. In addition the rigor of controls over the brokers' quote often will differ depending on whether the broker also holds the same security in its own portfolio. Broker quotes are often used for securities with level 3 inputs and sometimes may be the only external information available.

59-1   Where brokers have not observed recent executed transactions the quality of their indicative quotations may be affected. If brokers do not hold positions the quality of their quotes will depend on their interactions with dealers in the specific market.

Further considerations relating to third-party pricing sources

60   Understanding how the pricing sources calculated a price enables management to determine whether such information is suitable for use in its valuation, including as an input to a valuation technique and in what level of inputs the security should be categorized for disclosure purposes. For example, third-party pricing sources may value financial instruments using proprietary models, and it is important that management understands the methodology, assumptions and data used.

61   If fair value measurements obtained from third-party pricing sources are not based on the current prices of an active market, it will be necessary for management to evaluate whether the fair value measurements were derived in a manner that is consistent with the applicable financial reporting framework. Management's understanding of the fair value measurement includes:

- How the fair value measurement was determined-for example, whether the fair value measurement was determined by a valuation technique, in order to assess whether it is consistent with the fair value measurement objective;

- Whether the quotes are indicative prices, indicative spread, or binding offers; and

- How frequently the fair value measurement is estimated by the third-party pricing sources-in order to assess whether it reflects market conditions at the measurement date.

Understanding the bases on which third-party pricing sources have determined their quotes in the context of the particular financial instruments held by the entity assists management in evaluating the relevance and reliability of this evidence to support its valuations.

62   It is possible that there will be disparities between price indicators from different sources. Understanding how the price indicators were derived, and investigating these disparities, assists management in corroborating the evidence used in developing its valuation of financial instruments in order to evaluate whether the valuation is reasonable. Simply taking the average of the quotes provided, without doing further research, may not be appropriate, because one price in the range may be the most representative of fair value and this may not be the average. To evaluate whether its valuations of financial instruments are reasonable, management may:

- Look at the performance of price providers in the past. For example it may be that a price provider consistently over or under prices a particular asset class and that this would reduce the reliance being placed on that provider;

- Consider whether actual transactions represent forced transactions rather than transactions between willing buyers and willing sellers. This may invalidate the price as a comparison;

- Analyze the expected future cash flows of the instrument. This could be performed as an indicator of the most relevant pricing data;

- Depending on the nature of what is unobservable, extrapolate from observed prices to unobserved ones (for example, there may be observed prices for maturities up to ten years but not longer, but the ten year price curve may be capable of being extrapolated beyond ten years as an indicator). Care is needed to ensure that extrapolation is not carried so far beyond the observable curve that its link to observable prices becomes too tenuous to be reliable;

- Compare prices within a portfolio of financial instruments to each other to make sure that they are consistent among similar financial instruments;

- Use more than one model to corroborate the results from each one, having regard to the data and assumptions used in each; or

- Evaluate movements in the prices for related hedging instruments and collateral.

In coming to its judgment as to its valuation, an entity may also consider other factors that may be specific to the entity's circumstances.

Independent Price Verification Function

A feature of some entities' internal control is an independent price verification (IPV) function. This department is responsible for separately verifying the price of some financial instruments and may use alternative data sources, methodologies and assumptions. The IPV function, while not independent of the entity, often provides an objective management challenge to the pricing that has been developed in another part of the entity and is therefore often a key control over management's valuation process. To verify the price of financial instruments independently of management this function may: **62-1**

- Perform revaluation of the entity's financial instruments using independent inputs and assumptions, comparing these values to those developed in another part of the entity.

- Compare the inputs used to develop financial instrument valuations by another part of the entity to independently obtained inputs (parameter based IPV).

- Make recommendations to management around adjustments to books and records to align valuations developed in another part of the entity with fair value.

- Assess the sufficiency and appropriateness of the information used, including evaluating third party pricing services such as consensus pricing services and broker quotes.

- Calculate fair value adjustments or other adjustments required to account for residual uncertainties in the valuation process.

Use of valuation experts

Management may engage a valuation expert from an investment bank, broker, or other valuation firm to value some or all of its securities. Unlike pricing services **63** and broker quotes, generally the methodology and data used are more readily available to management when they have engaged an expert to perform a valuation on their behalf. Even though management has engaged an expert, management is ultimately responsible for the valuation used.

Issues related to financial liabilities

64   Understanding the effect of credit risk is an important aspect of valuing both financial assets and financial liabilities. This valuation reflects the credit quality and financial strength of both the issuer and any credit support providers. In some financial reporting frameworks, the measurement of a financial liability assumes that it is transferred to a market participant at the measurement date. Where there is not an observable market price for a financial liability, its value is typically measured using the same method as a counterparty would use to measure the value of the corresponding asset, unless there are factors specific to the liability (such as third-party credit enhancement). In particular, the entity's own credit risk[10] can often be difficult to measure.

Presentation and disclosure about financial instruments

65   Most financial reporting frameworks require disclosures in the financial statements to enable users of the financial statements to make meaningful assessments of the effects of the entity's financial instrument activities, including the risks and uncertainties associated with financial instruments.

66   Most frameworks require the disclosure of quantitative and qualitative information (including accounting policies) relating to financial instruments. The accounting requirements for fair value measurements in financial statement presentation and disclosures are extensive in most financial reporting frameworks and encompass more than just valuation of the financial instruments. For example, qualitative disclosures about financial instruments provide important contextual information about the characteristics of the financial instruments and their future cash flows that may help inform investors about the risks to which entities are exposed.

Categories of disclosures

67   Disclosure requirements include:

(a)   Quantitative disclosures that are derived from the amounts included in the financial statements-for example, categories of financial assets and liabilities;

(b)   Quantitative disclosures that require significant judgment-for example, sensitivity analysis for each type of market risk to which the entity is exposed; and

(c)   Qualitative disclosures-for example, those that describe the entity's governance over financial instruments; objectives; controls, policies and processes for managing each type of risk arising from financial instruments; and the methods used to measure the risks.

68   The more sensitive the valuation is to movements in a particular variable, the more likely it is that disclosure will be necessary to indicate the uncertainties surrounding the valuation. Certain financial reporting frameworks may also

---

[10] *Own credit risk is the amount of change in fair value that is not attributable to changes in market conditions.*

require disclosure of sensitivity analyses, including the effects of changes in assumptions used in the entity's valuation techniques. For example, the additional disclosures required for financial instruments with fair value measurements that are categorized within level 3 inputs of the fair value hierarchy are aimed at informing users of financial statements about the effects of those fair value measurements that use the most subjective inputs.

Some financial reporting frameworks require disclosure of information that **69** enables users of the financial statements to evaluate the nature and extent of the risks arising from financial instruments to which the entity is exposed at the reporting date. This disclosure may be contained in the notes to the financial statements, or in management's discussion and analysis within its annual report cross-referenced from the audited financial statements. The extent of disclosure depends on the extent of the entity's exposure to risks arising from financial instruments. This includes qualitative disclosures about:

- The exposures to risk and how they arise, including the possible effects on an entity's future liquidity and collateral requirements;

- The entity's objectives, policies and processes for managing the risk and the methods used to measure the risk; and

- Any changes in exposures to risk or objectives, policies or processes for managing risk from the previous period.

Section II – Audit considerations relating to financial instruments

Certain factors may make auditing financial instruments particularly challenging. **70** For example:

- It may be difficult for both management and the auditor to understand the nature of financial instruments and what they are used for, and the risks to which the entity is exposed.

- Market sentiment and liquidity can change quickly, placing pressure on management to manage their exposures effectively.

- Evidence supporting valuation may be difficult to obtain.

- Individual payments associated with certain financial instruments may be significant, which may increase the risk of misappropriation of assets.

- The amounts recorded in the financial statements relating to financial instruments may not be significant, but there may be significant risks and exposures associated with these financial instruments.

- A few employees may exert significant influence on the entity's financial instruments transactions, in particular where their compensation arrangements are tied to revenue from financial instruments, and there may be possible undue reliance on these individuals by others within the entity.

These factors may cause risks and relevant facts to be obscured, which may affect the auditor's assessment of the risks of material misstatement, and latent risks can emerge rapidly, especially in adverse market conditions[10a].

[10a] *Guidance for auditors on issues that may arise in adverse market conditions is provided in Bulletins 2008/1 Audit Issues When Financial Market Conditions are Difficult and Credit Facilities may be Limited and 2008/10 Going Concern Issues During the Current Economic Conditions.*

70-1   The auditor is required to obtain an understanding of the entity's objectives and strategies, the related business risks that may result in risks of material misstatement, and the entity's risk assessment process[10b]. For an entity transacting financial instruments, an understanding of the entity's related risk management processes and risk appetite may identify risks of material misstatement. It is not the job of the auditor to determine the amount of risk an entity should take on or how it should monitor and manage risk. However, obtaining an understanding of the risk management process is important for the auditor because poor risk management processes can affect the audit in a number of indirect ways by, for example:

- Exposing an entity to levels of risk that breach legal or regulatory restrictions. The auditor may have responsibilities in respect of such breaches as set out in ISA (UK and Ireland) 250 Section B, *The auditor's Right and Duty to Report to Regulators in the Financial Sector*;

- Facilitating fraud or error;

- Making it more difficult to obtain an understanding of the impact of financial instruments on the entity as a whole;

- In extreme circumstances, increasing the risk of a going concern problem (for example, if financial instrument assets lose value or become illiquid or liability positions are developed to an extent that results in liquidity and/or solvency risks that threaten the ability of the entity to continue as a going concern).

Professional scepticism[11]

71   Professional scepticism is necessary to the critical assessment of audit evidence and assists the auditor in remaining alert for possible indications of management bias. This includes questioning contradictory audit evidence and the reliability of documents, responses to inquiries and other information obtained from management and those charged with governance. It also includes being alert to conditions that may indicate possible misstatement due to error or fraud and considering the sufficiency and appropriateness of audit evidence obtained in light of the circumstances.

71-1   Maintaining professional scepticism throughout the audit is necessary if the auditor is, for example, to reduce the risks of:

- Overlooking unusual circumstances.

- Over generalizing when drawing conclusions from audit observations.

- Using inappropriate assumptions in determining the nature, timing, and extent of the audit procedures and evaluating the results thereof.

- Not identifying management bias or over-optimism.

71-2   Evaluating audit evidence for assertions about some financial instruments requires considerable judgment because the assertions, especially those about valuation, may be based on highly subjective assumptions or be particularly sensitive to changes in the underlying assumptions. For example, valuation assertions may be based on assumptions about the occurrence of future events

---

[10b] *ISA (UK and Ireland) 315, paragraphs 11(d) and 15-17.*

[11] *ISA (UK and Ireland) 200, paragraph 15.*

for which expectations are difficult to develop or about conditions expected to exist a long time. Accordingly, competent persons could reach different conclusions about valuation estimates or estimates of valuation ranges. Considerable judgment also may be required in evaluating audit evidence for assertions based on features of the financial instrument and applicable accounting principles, including underlying criteria, that are both extremely complex.

Application of professional scepticism is required in all circumstances, and the need for professional scepticism increases with the complexity of financial instruments, for example with regard to: **72**

- Evaluating whether sufficient appropriate audit evidence has been obtained, which can be particularly challenging when models are used or in determining if markets are inactive.

- Evaluating management's judgments, and the potential for management bias, in applying the entity's applicable financial reporting framework, in particular management's choice of valuation techniques, use of assumptions in valuation techniques, and addressing circumstances in which the auditor's judgments and management's judgments differ.

- Drawing conclusions based on the audit evidence obtained, for example assessing the reasonableness of valuations prepared by management's experts and evaluating whether disclosures in the financial statements achieve fair presentation.

Planning considerations[12]

The auditor's focus in planning the audit is particularly on: **73**

- Understanding the accounting and disclosure requirements;
- Understanding the financial instruments to which the entity is exposed, and their purpose and risks;
- Determining whether specialized skills and knowledge are needed in the audit;
- Understanding and evaluating the system of internal control in light of the entity's financial instrument transactions and the information systems that fall within the scope of the audit;
- Understanding the nature, role and activities of the internal audit function;
- Understanding management's process for valuing financial instruments, including whether management has used an expert or a service organization; and
- Assessing and responding to the risk of material misstatement.

---

[12] *ISA (UK and Ireland) 300, Planning an Audit of Financial Statements, deals with the auditor's responsibility to plan an audit of financial statements.*

Materiality

73-1   Determining materiality involves both quantitative and qualitative considerations. When planning the audit, materiality may be difficult to assess for an entity using particular financial instruments given some of their characteristics (e.g. where there is volatility of valuations). In particular, some financial instruments can be assets or liabilities depending on their valuation and this may change over the course of the audit. This factor may be relevant if, for example, materiality is initially determined prior to the period end reflecting estimates of period end valuations which subsequently change as at the actual period end.

Engagement Quality Control Review

73-2   An engagement quality control review is required for all audits of financial statements of listed entities[12a]. Criteria that an audit firm considers when determining which audits other than those of listed entities are to be subject to an engagement quality control review include the identification of unusual circumstances or risks in the engagement[12b]. In this context, the auditor considers whether the attributes of the financial instruments used by the entity or market conditions make the appointment of an engagement quality control reviewer appropriate.

73-3   The engagement quality control reviewer will need an understanding of the financial instruments used by the entity, including their purpose, nature and complexity.

Understanding the accounting and disclosure requirements

74   ISA (UK and Ireland) 540 requires the auditor to obtain an understanding of the requirements of the applicable financial reporting framework relevant to accounting estimates, including related disclosures and any regulatory requirements.[13] The requirements of the applicable financial reporting framework regarding financial instruments may themselves be complex and require extensive disclosures. Reading this PN is not a substitute for a full understanding of all the requirements of the applicable financial reporting framework. Certain financial reporting frameworks require consideration of areas such as:

- Hedge accounting;
- Accounting for "Day 1" profits or losses;
- Recognition and derecognition of financial instrument transactions;
- Own credit risk; and
- Risk transfer and derecognition, in particular where the entity has been involved in the origination and structuring of complex financial instruments.

74-1   An entity's policies for accounting for financial instruments need to take into account the different purposes for which they can be transacted (such as trading, hedging or investment). Relevant accounting standards may be under review and entities need to monitor developments to ensure the correct accounting requirements, including possible transitional arrangements, are

---

[12a] *ISA (UK and Ireland) 220, paragraph 19.*

[12b] *ISQC (UK and Ireland) 1, paragraph A41.*

[13] *ISA (UK and Ireland) 540, paragraph 8(a).*

complied with. Having regard to disclosure requirements is important as they can play a key role in making the levels of holdings of financial instruments, their purpose and the underlying risk profile transparent.

Understanding the financial instruments

The characteristics of financial instruments may obscure certain elements of risk 75 and exposure. Obtaining an understanding of the instruments in which the entity has invested or to which it is exposed, including the characteristics of the instruments, helps the auditor to identify whether:

- Important aspects of a transaction are missing or inaccurately recorded;

- A valuation appears appropriate;

- The risks inherent in them are fully understood and managed by the entity; and

- The financial instruments are appropriately classified into current and non-current assets and liabilities.

Examples of matters that the auditor may consider when obtaining an 76 understanding of the entity's financial instruments include:

- To which types of financial instruments the entity is exposed.

- The use to which they are put.

- Management's and, where appropriate, those charged with governance's understanding of the financial instruments, their use and the accounting requirements.

- Their exact terms and characteristics so that their implications can be fully understood and, in particular where transactions are linked, the overall impact of the financial instrument transactions.

- Whether they are part of a structured arrangement designed to achieve a particular accounting or regulatory purpose. Specialist advice obtained by the entity may be an indicator of this.

- How they fit into the entity's overall risk management strategy.

- Whether there is a possibility of claims, that are material individually or in aggregate, against the entity for mis-selling financial instruments.

Inquiries of the internal audit function, the risk management function, if such functions exist, and discussions with those charged with governance may inform the auditor's understanding.

It may be appropriate for the auditor's understanding of relevant industry and 76-1 regulatory factors in accordance with ISA (UK and Ireland) 315 to include inquiry of management as to whether there have been discussions with supervisors or other regulators during the year about its policies in respect of financial instruments, and whether management has reviewed its processes in the light of those discussions (for example if the regulator has expressed a view that the entity's valuations appear out of line with those of other entities or are not sufficiently prudent). The auditor reviews relevant correspondence, if any, with regulators.

For a regulated entity in the financial sector, it may be appropriate for the 76-2 auditor to discuss matters related to the entity's use and disclosure of financial instruments directly with the regulator in bilateral and/or trilateral meetings (the latter involving representatives of the regulated entity). In July 2013 the FCA published its *Code of Practice for the relationship between the external auditor and the supervisor.* The Code of Practice sets out principles that establish, in the context of a particular regulated firm, the nature of the relationship between the supervisor and the auditor.

77   In some cases, a contract, including a contract for a non-financial instrument may contain a derivative. Some financial reporting frameworks permit or require such "embedded" derivatives to be separated from the host contract in some circumstances. Understanding management's process for identifying, and accounting for, embedded derivatives will assist the auditor in understanding the risks to which the entity is exposed.

77-1   While intended to mitigate risk, inappropriate hedge transactions can cause significant financial loss if the risks are not properly identified or managed. A simple example might be the hedging of baskets of bonds or shares with an index – if the basket does not match the index closely, price movements may not offset each other, therefore increasing risk not reducing it.

Using those with specialised skills and knowledge in the audit[14]

78   A key consideration in audits involving financial instruments, particularly complex financial instruments, is the competence of the auditor. ISA (UK and Ireland) 220[15] requires the engagement partner to be satisfied that the engagement team, and any auditor's experts who are not part of the engagement team, collectively have the appropriate competence and capabilities to perform the audit engagement in accordance with professional standards and applicable legal and regulatory requirements and to enable an auditor's report that is appropriate in the circumstances to be issued. Further, relevant ethical requirements[16] require the auditor to determine whether acceptance of the engagement would create any threats to compliance with the fundamental principles, including the professional competence and due care. Paragraph 79 below provides examples of the types of matters that may be relevant to the auditor's considerations in the context of financial instruments.

79   Accordingly, auditing financial instruments may require the involvement of one or more experts or specialists, for example, in the areas of:

● Understanding the operating characteristics and risk profile of the industry in which the entity operates.

● Understanding the business rationale for the particular financial instruments used by the entity, the related risks and how they are managed.

---

[14] *When such a person's expertise is in auditing and accounting, regardless of whether the person is from within or external to the firm, this person is considered to be part of the engagement team and is subject to the requirements of ISA (UK and Ireland) 220, Quality Control for an Audit of Financial Statements. When such a person's expertise is in a field other than accounting or auditing, such person is considered to be an auditor's expert, and the provisions of ISA (UK and Ireland) 620, Using the Work of an Auditor's Expert, apply. ISA (UK and Ireland) 620 explains that distinguishing between specialized areas of accounting or auditing, and expertise in another field, will be a matter of professional judgment, but notes the distinction may be made between expertise in methods of accounting for financial instruments (accounting and auditing expertise) and expertise in complex valuation techniques for financial instruments (expertise in a field other than accounting or auditing).*

[15] *ISA (UK and Ireland) 220, paragraph 14.*

[16] *IESBA Code of Ethics for Professional Accountants paragraphs 210.1 and 210.6. Auditors in the UK and Ireland are subject to ethical requirements from two sources: the APB Ethical Standards for Auditors, issued by the Financial Reporting Council, concerning the integrity, objectivity and independence of the auditor, and the ethical pronouncements established by the auditor's relevant professional body. The ethical considerations relating to the fundamental principles of professional competence and due care are addressed in the pronouncements established by the professional bodies.*

- Understanding the financial instruments used by the entity and their characteristics, including their level of complexity. Using specialized skills and knowledge may be needed in checking whether all aspects of the financial instrument and related considerations have been captured in the financial statements, and evaluating whether adequate disclosure in accordance with the applicable financial reporting framework has been made where disclosure of risks is required.

- Understanding the applicable financial reporting framework, especially when there are areas known to be subject to differing interpretations, or practice is inconsistent or developing.

- Understanding the legal, regulatory, and tax implications resulting from the financial instruments, including whether the contracts are enforceable by the entity (for example, reviewing the underlying contracts), may require specialized skills and knowledge.

- Understanding the differing regulatory requirements that may apply to group components and the implications for the audit. This may include where regulatory requirements for foreign branches are significantly different than for the entity the auditor is reporting on.

- Assessing the risks inherent in a financial instrument.

- Assisting the engagement team gather evidence to support management's valuations or to develop a point estimate or range, especially when fair value is determined by a complex model; when markets are inactive and data and assumptions are difficult to obtain; when unobservable inputs are used; or when management has used an expert.

- Evaluating information technology controls, especially in entities with a high volume of financial instruments. In such entities information technology may be highly complex, for example when significant information about those financial instruments is transmitted, processed, maintained or accessed electronically. In addition, it may include relevant services provided by a service organization.

The involvement of one or more experts or specialists may be needed especially when:

- The financial instruments are complex;

- Relatively simple financial instruments are combined to produce a more complex product; or

- The entity is engaged in active trading of complex financial instruments.

The nature and use of particular types of financial instruments, the complexities associated with accounting requirements, and market conditions may lead to a need for the engagement team to consult[17] with other accounting and audit professionals, from within or outside the firm, with relevant technical accounting or auditing expertise and experience, taking into account factors such as: **80**

- The capabilities and competence of the engagement team, including the experience of the members of the engagement team.

---

[17] *ISA (UK and Ireland) 220, paragraph 18(b), requires the engagement partner to be satisfied that members of the engagement team have undertaken appropriate consultation during the course of the engagement, both within the engagement team and between the engagement team and others at the appropriate level within or outside the firm.*

- The attributes of the financial instruments used by the entity.

- The identification of unusual circumstances or risks in the engagement, as well as the need for professional judgment, particularly with respect to materiality and significant risks.

- Market conditions.

Understanding internal control

81   ISA (UK and Ireland) 315 establishes requirements for the auditor to understand the entity and its environment, including its internal control. Obtaining an understanding of the entity and its environment, including the entity's internal control, is a continuous, dynamic process of gathering, updating and analyzing information throughout the audit. The understanding obtained enables the auditor to identify and assess the risks of material misstatement at the financial statement and assertion levels, thereby providing a basis for designing and implementing responses to the assessed risks of material misstatement. The volume and variety of the financial instrument transactions of an entity typically determines the nature and extent of controls that may exist at an entity. An understanding of how financial instruments are monitored and controlled assists the auditor in determining the nature, timing and extent of audit procedures. The Appendix describes controls that may exist in an entity that deals in a high volume of financial instrument transactions.

81-1   An understanding of how the entity manages and controls its exposure to financial instruments includes how the entity ensures that:

- All instruments are completely and accurately recorded;

- Payments and receipts are monitored and made on time;

- Financial risks are analysed and monitored;

- Valuations are accurate, reviewed and used for monitoring purposes;

- Only competent and trained staff can enter into transactions;

- Risk limits are applied;

- Segregation of duties between those transacting, settling and accounting for financial instruments are maintained.

Understanding the nature, role and activities of the internal audit function[17a]

82   In many large entities, the internal audit function may perform work that enables senior management and those charged with governance to review and evaluate the entity's controls relating to the use of financial instruments. The internal audit function may assist in identifying the risks of material misstatement due to fraud or error. However, the knowledge and skills required of an internal audit function to understand and perform procedures to provide assurance to management or those charged with governance on the entity's use of financial instruments are generally quite different from those needed for other parts of the business. The extent to which the internal audit function has the knowledge and skill to cover, and has in fact covered, the entity's financial instrument activities, as well as the competence and objectivity of the internal audit function, is a relevant consideration in the

---

[17a] *ISAs (UK and Ireland) 315 and 610 establish requirements regarding the auditor's understanding and use of the work of internal auditors. These include safeguards against inappropriate reliance on or over use of the work of internal auditors.*

external auditor's determination of whether the internal audit function is likely to be relevant to the overall audit strategy and audit plan.

Areas where the work of the internal audit function may be particularly relevant are:[18]   **83**

- Developing a general overview of the nature and extent of use of financial instruments;

- Understanding the control environment;

- Evaluating the appropriateness of policies and procedures and management's compliance with them;

- Evaluating the operating effectiveness of financial instrument control activities;

- Evaluating systems relevant to financial instrument activities; and

- Assessing whether new risks relating to financial instruments are identified, assessed and managed.

Understanding management's methodology for valuing financial instruments

Management's responsibility for the preparation of the financial statements   **84**
includes applying the requirements of the applicable financial reporting framework to the valuation of financial instruments. ISA (UK and Ireland) 540 requires the auditor to obtain an understanding of how management makes accounting estimates and the data on which accounting estimates are based.[19] Management's approach to valuation also takes into account the selection of an appropriate valuation methodology and the level of the evidence expected to be available. To meet the objective of a fair value measurement, an entity develops a valuation methodology to measure the fair value of financial instruments that considers all relevant market information that is available. A thorough understanding of the financial instrument being valued allows an entity to identify and evaluate the relevant market information available about identical or similar instruments that should be incorporated into the valuation methodology.

Assessing and responding to the risks of material misstatement

Overall considerations relating to financial instruments

ISA (UK and Ireland) 540[20] explains that the degree of estimation uncertainty   **85**
affects the risk of material misstatement of accounting estimates. The use of more complex financial instruments, such as those that have a high level of uncertainty and variability of future cash flows, may lead to an increased risk of material misstatement, particularly regarding valuation. Other matters affecting the risk of material misstatement include:

- The volume of financial instruments to which the entity is exposed.

- The terms of the financial instrument, including whether the financial instrument itself includes other financial instruments.

---

[18] *Work performed by functions such as the risk management function, model review functions, and product control, may also be relevant.*

[19] *ISA (UK and Ireland) 540, paragraph 8(c).*

[20] *ISA (UK and Ireland) 540, paragraph 2.*

- The economics and business purpose of the entity's financial instrument activities.

- Whether the instruments are part of a structured arrangement designed to achieve a particular accounting or regulatory purpose.

- An entity's experience with the financial instrument.

- Whether the financial instrument is traded on national exchanges or across borders.

- Whether the financial instrument is traded on an exchange or "over the counter".

- The strength of the entity's control environment.

Fraud risk factors[21]

86   Incentives for fraudulent financial reporting by employees may exist where compensation schemes are dependent on returns made from the use of financial instruments. Understanding how an entity's compensation policies interact with its risk appetite, and the incentives that this may create for its management and traders, may be important in assessing the risk of fraud.

87   Difficult financial market conditions may give rise to increased incentives for management or employees to engage in fraudulent financial reporting: to protect personal bonuses, to hide employee or management fraud or error, to avoid breaching regulatory, liquidity or borrowing limits or to avoid reporting losses. For example, at times of market instability, unexpected losses may arise from extreme fluctuations in market prices, from unanticipated weakness in asset prices, through trading misjudgments, or for other reasons. In addition, financing difficulties create pressures on management concerned about the solvency of the business.

88   Misappropriation of assets and fraudulent financial reporting may often involve override of controls that otherwise may appear to be operating effectively. This may include override of controls over data, assumptions and detailed process controls that allow losses and theft to be hidden. For example, difficult market conditions may increase pressure to conceal or offset trades as they attempt to recover losses.

Assessing the risk of material misstatement

89   The auditor's assessment of the identified risks at the assertion level in accordance with ISA (UK and Ireland) 315 includes evaluating the design and implementation of internal control. It provides a basis for considering the appropriate audit approach for designing and performing further audit procedures in accordance with ISA (UK and Ireland) 330, including both substantive procedures and tests of controls. The approach taken is influenced by the auditor's understanding of internal control relevant to the audit, including the strength of the control environment and any risk management function, the size and complexity of the entity's operations and whether the auditor's assessment of the risks of material misstatement include an expectation that controls are operating effectively.

89-1   An entity may have a control culture that is generally focused on maintaining a high level of internal control. Because of the complexity of some treasury activities, this culture may not pervade the group of personnel responsible for financial instrument activities. Alternatively, because of the risks associated

---

[21] See ISA (UK and Ireland) 240, *The Auditor's Responsibilities Relating to Fraud in an Audit of Financial Statements,* for requirements and guidance dealing with fraud risk factors.

with some financial instrument activities, management may enforce a more strict control environment than it does elsewhere within the entity. In entities without a treasury function, dealing in financial instruments may be rare and management's knowledge and experience limited. Accordingly, the auditor may need to consider in its risk assessment the control environment applicable to those responsible for functions dealing with financial instruments, particularly if the instruments are complex.

In an entity with a complex organisational structure, lack of clarity of lines of responsibility may increase risks – for example, where there is not a clear delineation between front office and middle office control and back office functions in a complex trading environment.   **89-2**

The auditor's assessment of the risk of material misstatement at the assertion level   **90** may change during the course of the audit as additional information is obtained. Remaining alert during the audit, for example, when inspecting records or documents may assist the auditor in identifying arrangements or other information that may indicate the existence of financial instruments that management has not previously identified or disclosed to the auditor. Such records and documents may include, for example:

- Minutes of meetings of those charged with governance; and

- Specific invoices from, and correspondence with, the entity's professional advisors.

Factors to consider in determining whether, and to what extent, to test the operating effectiveness of controls

An expectation that controls are operating effectively may be more common when   **91** dealing with a financial institution with well-established controls, and therefore controls testing may be an effective means of obtaining audit evidence. When an entity has a trading function, substantive tests alone may not provide sufficient appropriate audit evidence due to the volume of contracts and the different systems used. Tests of controls, however, will not be sufficient on their own as the auditor is required by ISA (UK and Ireland) 330 to design and perform substantive procedures for each material class of transactions, account balance and disclosure.[22]

Entities with a high volume of trading and use of financial instruments may have   **92** more sophisticated controls, and an effective risk management function, and therefore the auditor may be more likely to test controls in obtaining evidence about:

- The occurrence, completeness, accuracy, and cutoff of the transactions; and

- The existence, rights and obligations, and completeness of account balances; and

- The valuation of financial instruments where an independent price verification function exists.

In those entities with relatively few financial instrument transactions: **93**

- Management and those charged with governance may have only a limited understanding of financial instruments and how they affect the business;

- The entity may only have a few different types of instruments with little or no interaction between them;

---

[22] *ISA (UK and Ireland) 330, paragraph 18.*

- There is unlikely to be a complex control environment (for example, the controls described in the Appendix may not be in place at the entity);

- Management may use pricing information from third-party pricing sources to value their instruments; and

- Controls over the use of pricing information from third-party pricing sources may be less sophisticated.

94   When an entity has relatively few transactions involving financial instruments, it may be relatively easy for the auditor to obtain an understanding of the entity's objectives for using the financial instruments and the characteristics of the instruments. In such circumstances, much of the audit evidence is likely to be substantive in nature, the auditor may perform the majority of the audit work at year-end, and third-party confirmations are likely to provide evidence in relation to the completeness, accuracy, and existence of the transactions.

95   In reaching a decision on the nature, timing and extent of testing of controls, the auditor may consider factors such as:

- The nature, frequency and volume of financial instrument transactions;

- The strength of controls, including whether controls are appropriately designed to respond to the risks associated with an entity's volume of financial instrument transactions and whether there is a governance framework over the entity's financial instrument activities;

- The importance of particular controls to the overall control objectives and processes in place at the entity, including the sophistication of the information systems to support financial instrument transactions;

- The monitoring of controls and identified deficiencies in control procedures;

- The issues the controls are intended to address, for example, controls related to the exercise of judgments compared with controls over supporting data. Substantive tests are more likely to be effective than relying on controls related to the exercise of judgment;

- The competency of those involved in the control activities, for example whether the entity has adequate capacity, including during periods of stress, and ability to establish and verify valuations for the financial instruments to which it is exposed;

- The frequency of performance of these control activities;

- The level of precision the controls are intended to achieve;

- The evidence of performance of control activities; and

- The timing of key financial instrument transactions, for example, whether they are close to the period end.

95-1   The population from which items are selected for detailed testing is not necessarily limited to the accounting records. Tested items may be drawn from other sources, for example counterparty confirmations and trader tickets, so that the possibility of omission of transactions in the recording procedure can be tested.

Substantive procedures

Designing substantive procedures includes consideration of: **96**

- The use of analytical procedures[23]-While analytical procedures undertaken by the auditor can be effective as risk assessment procedures to provide the auditor with information about an entity's business, they may be less effective as substantive procedures when performed alone. This is because the complex interplay of the drivers of the valuation often mask any unusual trends that might arise.

- Non-routine transactions-Many financial transactions are negotiated contracts between an entity and its counterparty (often known as "over the counter" or OTC). To the extent that financial instrument transactions are not routine and outside an entity's normal activities, a substantive audit approach may be the most effective means of achieving the planned audit objectives. In instances where financial instrument transactions are not undertaken routinely, the auditor's responses to assessed risk, including designing and performing audit procedures, have regard to the entity's possible lack of experience in this area.

- Availability of evidence-For example, when the entity uses a third-party pricing source, evidence concerning the relevant financial statement assertions may not be available from the entity.

- Procedures performed in other audit areas-Procedures performed in other financial statement areas may provide evidence about the completeness of financial instrument transactions. These procedures may include tests of subsequent cash receipts and payments, and the search for unrecorded liabilities.

- Selection of items for testing-In some cases, the financial instrument portfolio will comprise instruments with varying complexity and risk. In such cases, judgmental sampling may be useful.

For example, in the case of an asset-backed security, in responding to the risks of **97** material misstatement for such a security, the auditor may consider performing some of the following audit procedures:

- Examining contractual documentation to understand the terms of the security, the underlying collateral and the rights of each class of security holder.

- Inquiring about management's process of estimating cash flows.

- Evaluating the reasonableness of assumptions, such as prepayment rates, default rates and loss severities.

- Obtaining an understanding of the method used to determine the cash flow waterfall.

- Comparing the results of the fair value measurement with the valuations of other securities with similar underlying collateral and terms.

- Reperforming calculations.

---

[23] *ISA (UK and Ireland) 315, paragraph 6(b), requires the auditor to apply analytical procedures as risk assessment procedures to assist in assessing the risks of material misstatement in order to provide a basis for designing and implementing responses to the assessed risks. ISA (UK and Ireland) 520, Analytical Procedures, paragraph 6, requires the auditor to use analytical procedures in forming an overall conclusion on the financial statements. Analytical procedures may also be applied at other stages of the audit.*

Dual-purpose tests

98   Although the purpose of a test of controls is different from the purpose of a test of details, it may be efficient to perform both at the same time by, for example:

   • Performing a test of controls and a test of details on the same transaction (for example, testing whether a signed contract has been maintained and whether the details of the financial instrument have been appropriately captured in a summary sheet); or

   • Testing controls when testing management's process of making valuation estimates.

Timing of the auditor's procedures[24]

99   After assessing the risks associated with financial instruments, the engagement team determines the timing of planned tests of controls and substantive audit procedures. The timing of planned audit procedures varies depending on a number of factors, including the frequency of the control operation, the significance of the activity being controlled, and the related risk of material misstatement.

100   While it is necessary to undertake most of the audit procedures in relation to valuation and presentation at the period end, audit procedures in relation to other assertions such as completeness and existence can usefully be tested at an interim period. For example tests of controls may be performed at an interim period for more routine controls, such as IT controls and authorizations for new products. Also, it may be effective to test the operating effectiveness of controls over new product approval by gathering evidence of the appropriate level of management sign-off on a new financial instrument for an interim period.

101   Auditors may perform some tests on models as of an interim date, for example, by comparing the output of the model to market transactions. Another possible interim procedure for instruments with observable inputs is to test the reasonableness of the pricing information provided by a third-party pricing source.

102   Areas of more significant judgment are often tested close to, or at, the period end as:

   • Valuations can change significantly in a short period of time, making it difficult to compare and reconcile interim balances with comparable information at the balance sheet date;

   • An entity may engage in an increased volume of financial instrument transactions between an interim period and year-end;

   • Manual journal entries may only be made after the end of the accounting period; and

   • Non-routine or significant transactions may take place late in the accounting period.

---

[24] *Paragraphs 11–12 and 22–23 of ISA (UK and Ireland) 330 establish requirements when the auditor performs procedures at an interim period and explains how such audit evidence can be used.*

Procedures Relating to Completeness, Accuracy, Existence, Occurrence and Rights and Obligations

103 Many of the auditor's procedures can be used to address a number of assertions. For example, procedures to address the existence of an account balance at period end will also address the occurrence of a class of transactions, and may also assist in establishing proper cut-off. This is because financial instruments arise from legal contracts and, by verifying the accuracy of the recording of the transaction, the auditor can also verify its existence, and obtain evidence to support the occurrence and rights and obligations assertions at the same time, and confirm that transactions are recorded in the correct accounting period.

104 Procedures that may provide audit evidence to support the completeness, accuracy, and existence assertions include:

- External confirmation[25] of bank accounts, trades, and custodian statements. This can be done by direct confirmation with the counterparty (including the use of bank confirmations), where a reply is sent to the auditor directly. Alternatively this information may be obtained from the counterparty's systems through a data feed. Where this is done, controls to prevent tampering with the computer systems through which the information is transmitted may be considered by the auditor in evaluating the reliability of the evidence from the confirmation. If confirmations are not received, the auditor may be able to obtain evidence by reviewing contracts and testing relevant controls. External confirmations, however, often do not provide adequate audit evidence with respect to the valuation assertion though they may assist in identifying any side agreements.

- Reviewing reconciliations of statements or data feeds from custodians with the entity's own records. This may necessitate evaluating IT controls around and within automated reconciliation processes and to evaluate whether reconciling items are properly understood and resolved.

- Reviewing operational data, such as reconciliation differences. To do this the auditor will have to obtain sufficient evidence to indicate that this data is reliable.

- Reviewing journal entries and the controls over the recording of such entries. This may assist in, for example:

  - Determining if entries have been made by employees other than those authorized to do so.

  - Identifying unusual or inappropriate end-of-period journal entries, which may be relevant to fraud risk.

- Reading individual contracts and reviewing supporting documentation of the entity's financial instrument transactions, including accounting records, thereby verifying existence and rights and obligations. For example, an auditor may read individual contracts associated with financial instruments and review supporting documentation, including the accounting entries made when the contract was initially recorded, and may also subsequently

---

[25] *ISA (UK and Ireland) 505, External Confirmations, deals with the auditor's use of external confirmation procedures to obtain audit evidence in accordance with the requirements of ISA (UK and Ireland) 330 and ISA (UK and Ireland) 500, Audit Evidence. See also the IAASB Staff Audit Practice Alert, Emerging Practice Issues Regarding the Use of External Confirmations in an Audit of Financial Statements, issued in November 2009. PN 16 (Revised), Bank Reports for Audit Purposes in the United Kingdom, summarises the process agreed between the UK auditing profession and the British Bankers Association regarding the procedures auditors use when requesting confirmation of balances, transactions or arrangements from bankers of an entity being audited.*

review accounting entries made for valuation purposes. Doing so allows the auditor to evaluate whether the complexities inherent in a transaction have been fully identified and reflected in the accounts. Legal arrangements and their associated risks need to be considered by those with suitable expertise to ensure that rights exist

- Testing controls, for example by reperforming controls.

- Reviewing the entity's complaints management systems. Unrecorded transactions may result in the entity's failure to make a cash payment to a counterparty, and may be detected by reviewing complaints received.

- Reviewing master netting arrangements to identify unrecorded instruments.

105   These procedures are particularly important for some financial instruments, such as derivatives or guarantees. This is because they may not have a large initial investment, meaning it may be hard to identify their existence. For example, embedded derivatives are often contained in contracts for non-financial instruments which may not be included in confirmation procedures.

Valuation of financial instruments

Financial reporting requirements

106   Fair presentation financial reporting frameworks often use fair value hierarchies, for example those used in IFRS, and U.S. GAAP and in certain circumstances UK GAAP. This usually means that the volume and detail of the required disclosures increases as the level of measurement uncertainty increases. The distinction between the levels in the hierarchy may require judgment.

107   The auditor may find it useful to obtain an understanding of how the financial instruments relate to the fair value hierarchy. Ordinarily, the risk of material misstatement, and the level of audit procedures to be applied, increases as the level of measurement uncertainty increases. The use of level 3, and some level 2, inputs from the fair value hierarchy may be a useful guide to the level of measurement uncertainty. Level 2 inputs vary from those which are easily obtained to those which are closer to level 3 inputs. The auditor evaluates available evidence and understands both the fair value hierarchy and the risk of management bias in management's categorization of financial instruments in the fair value hierarchy.

108   In accordance with ISA (UK and Ireland) 540,[26] the auditor considers the entity's valuation policies and methodology for data and assumptions used in the valuation methodology. In many cases, the applicable financial reporting framework does not prescribe the valuation methodology. When this is the case, matters that may be relevant to the auditor's understanding of how management values financial instruments include, for example:

- Whether management has a formal valuation policy and, if so, whether the valuation technique used for a financial instrument is appropriately documented in accordance with that policy;

- Which models may give rise to the greatest risk of material misstatement;

- How management considered the complexity of the valuation of the financial instrument when selecting a particular valuation technique;

---

[26] *ISA (UK and Ireland) 540, paragraph 8(c).*

- Whether there is a greater risk of material misstatement because management has internally developed a model to be used to value financial instruments or is departing from a valuation technique commonly used to value the particular financial instrument;

- Whether a model used to prepare actuarial information follows the principles in Technical Actuarial Standard M: Modelling[26a];

- Whether management made use of a third-party pricing source;

- Whether those involved in developing and applying the valuation technique have the appropriate skills and expertise to do so, including whether a management's expert has been used; and

- Whether there are indicators of management bias in selecting the valuation technique to be used.

UK banks and certain other regulated entities in the financial sector are required for regulatory purposes to prepare a Prudent Valuation Return, on a quarterly calendar year basis, to assist the regulator in assessing the capital resources of the entity and gaining a wider understanding of the nature and sources of measurement uncertainty in fair valued instruments. The information within these returns is not required to be included in the financial statements and is not required to be audited or reviewed by the auditor. A return may also not be prepared that coincides with the accounting reference date of the financial statements. However, the auditor of such an entity may find that consideration of the information in the returns assists the understanding of the uncertainties associated with the financial instruments used and disclosed by the entity.   **108-1**

Assessing the risk of material misstatement related to valuation

When evaluating whether the valuation techniques used by an entity are appropriate in the circumstances, and whether controls over valuation techniques are in place, the factors considered by the auditor may include: **109**

- Who developed the valuation techniques and whether design and implementation could have been unduly influenced by traders or others who may not be objective. Where the entity obtains input from traders without independent oversight the auditor considers whether that input is appropriate in the circumstances;

- Whether the valuation techniques are commonly used by other market participants and have been previously demonstrated to provide a reliable estimate of prices obtained from market transactions;

- Whether the valuation techniques operate as intended and there are no flaws in their design, particularly under extreme conditions, and whether they have been objectively validated. Indicators of flaws include inconsistent movements relative to benchmarks;

- Whether the valuation techniques take account of the risks inherent in the financial instrument being valued, including counterparty creditworthiness, and own credit risk in the case of valuation techniques used to measure financial liabilities;

- How the valuation techniques are calibrated to the market, including the sensitivity of the valuation techniques to changes in variables;

[26a] *Technical Actuarial Standards are issued by the Financial Reporting Council.*

- Whether market variables and assumptions are used consistently and whether new conditions justify a change in the valuation techniques, market variables or assumptions used;

- Whether sensitivity analyses indicate that valuations would change significantly with only small or moderate changes in assumptions;

- The organisational structure, such as the existence of an internal department responsible for developing models to value certain instruments, particularly where level 3 inputs are involved. For example, a model development function that is involved in assisting in pricing deals is less objective than one which is functionally and organisationally segregated from the front office; and

- The competence and objectivity of those responsible for the development and application of the valuation techniques, including management's relative experience with particular models that may be newly developed.

The auditor (or auditor's expert) may also independently develop one or more valuation techniques to compare its output with that of the valuation techniques used by management.

Significant Risks

110   The auditor's risk assessment process may lead the auditor to identify one or more significant risks relating to the valuation of financial instruments, when any of the following circumstances exist:

- High measurement uncertainty related to the valuation of financial instruments (for example, those with unobservable inputs).[27]

- Lack of sufficient evidence to support management's valuation of its financial instruments.

- Lack of management understanding of its financial instruments or expertise necessary to value such instruments properly, including the ability to determine whether valuation adjustments are needed.

- Lack of management understanding of complex requirements in the applicable financial reporting framework relating to measurement and disclosure of financial instruments, and inability of management to make the judgments required to properly apply those requirements.

- The significance of valuation adjustments made to valuation technique outputs when the applicable financial reporting framework requires or permits such adjustments.

111   For accounting estimates that give rise to significant risks, in addition to other substantive procedures performed to meet the requirements of ISA (UK and Ireland) 330, ISA (UK and Ireland) 540[28] requires the auditor to evaluate the following:

(a)   How management has considered alternative assumptions or outcomes, and why it has rejected them, or how management has otherwise addressed measurement uncertainty in making the accounting estimate;

---

[27] *Where the auditor determines that the high estimation uncertainty related to the valuation of complex financial instruments gives rise to a significant risk, ISA (UK and Ireland) 540 requires the auditor to perform substantive procedures and evaluate the adequacy of the disclosure of their estimation uncertainty. See ISA (UK and Ireland) 540, paragraphs 11, 15 and 20.*

[28] *ISA (UK and Ireland) 540, paragraph 15(a)-(b).*

(b)   Whether the significant assumptions used by management are reasonable; and

(c)   Where relevant to the reasonableness of the significant assumptions used by management, or the appropriate application of the applicable financial reporting framework, management's intent to carry out specific courses of action and its ability to do so.

As markets become inactive, the change in circumstances may lead to a move **112** from valuation by market price to valuation by model, or may result in a change from one particular model to another. Reacting to changes in market conditions may be difficult if management does not have policies in place prior to their occurrence. Management may also not possess the expertise necessary to develop a model on an urgent basis, or select the valuation technique that may be appropriate in the circumstances. Even where valuation techniques have been consistently used, there is a need for management to examine the continuing appropriateness of the valuation techniques and assumptions used for determining valuation of financial instruments. Further, valuation techniques may have been selected in times where reasonable market information was available, but may not provide reasonable valuations in times of unanticipated stress.

The susceptibility to management bias, whether intentional or unintentional, **113** increases with the subjectivity of the valuation and the degree of measurement uncertainty. For example, management may tend to ignore observable marketplace assumptions or data and instead use their own internally-developed model if the model yields more favourable results. Even without fraudulent intent, there may be a natural temptation to bias judgments towards the most favourable end of what may be a wide spectrum, rather than the point in the spectrum that might be considered to be most consistent with the applicable financial reporting framework. Changing the valuation technique from period to period without a clear and appropriate reason for doing so may also be an indicator of management bias. Although some form of management bias is inherent in subjective decisions relating to the valuation of financial instruments, when there is intention to mislead, management bias is fraudulent in nature.

Developing an Audit Approach

Tests of valuation mainly fall under three headings: **113-1**

*   Verifying the external prices that are used to value financial instruments. External prices may be available directly from markets but it is likely for complex financial instruments that external price information will be used as inputs to valuation models. This is because many complex financial instruments are tailored for particular clients and are not therefore homogenous with each other;

*   Confirming the validity of valuation models. Valuation models are used, where an instrument is not quoted in the market, but prices for its component parts can be derived from instruments that are quoted (where inputs to the model are observable) or from estimates of fair value (where inputs are unobservable);

*   Evaluating the overall result and reserving for residual uncertainties. By their nature complex financial instruments are often not traded in active liquid markets and hence their valuation is often uncertain and requires considerable judgment. Once the detailed evidence has been gathered and valuations have been made on an instrument by instrument basis, it is

important to review the overall result and consider whether there are residual uncertainties not taken into account by the valuation process that require further adjustment.

113-2   The entity being audited should have its own processes to undertake these tasks. The auditor reviews the output from these processes and considers what independent confirmation needs to be undertaken. If there are weaknesses in these processes, the auditor communicates them to those charged with governance. Where there are serious weaknesses, the auditor considers the impact on the audit and whether applicable law and regulations require a report to be made to a regulator.

114   In testing how management values the financial instrument and in responding to the assessed risks of material misstatement in accordance with ISA (UK and Ireland) 540,[29] the auditor undertakes one or more of the following procedures, taking account of the nature of the accounting estimates:

(a)   Test how management made the accounting estimate and the data on which it is based (including valuation techniques used by the entity in its valuations).

(b)   Test the operating effectiveness of the controls over how management made the accounting estimate, together with appropriate substantive procedures.

(c)   Develop a point estimate or a range to evaluate management's point estimate.

(d)   Determine whether events occurring up to the date of the auditor's report provide audit evidence regarding the accounting estimate.

Many auditors find that a combination of testing how management valued the financial instrument, and the data on which it is based, and testing the operating effectiveness of controls, will be an effective and efficient audit approach. While subsequent events may provide some evidence about the valuation of financial instruments, other factors may need to be taken into account to address any changes in market conditions subsequent to the balance sheet date.[30] If the auditor is unable to test how management made the estimate, the auditor may choose to develop a point estimate or range.

115   As described in Section I, to estimate the fair value of financial instruments management may:

•   Utilize information from third-party pricing sources;

•   Gather data to develop their own estimate using various techniques including models; and

•   Engage an expert to develop an estimate.

Management often may use a combination of these approaches. For example, management may have their own pricing process but use third-party pricing sources to corroborate their own values.

---

[29]   *ISA (UK and Ireland) 540, paragraphs 12–14.*

[30]   *Paragraphs A63-A66 of ISA (UK and Ireland) 540 provide examples of some of the factors that may be relevant.*

Audit considerations when management uses a third-party pricing source

Management may make use of a third-party pricing source, such as a pricing **116** service or broker, in valuing the entity's financial instruments. Understanding how management uses the information and how the pricing service operates assists the auditor in determining the nature and extent of audit procedures needed.

The following matters may be relevant where management uses a third-party **117** pricing source:

- *The type of third-party pricing source* – Some third-party pricing sources make more information available about their process. For example, a pricing service often provides information about their methodology, assumptions and data in valuing financial instruments at the asset class level. By contrast, brokers often provide no, or only limited, information about the inputs and assumptions used in developing the quote.

- *The nature of inputs used and the complexity of the valuation technique* – The reliability of prices from third-party pricing sources varies depending on the observability of inputs (and accordingly, the level of inputs in the fair value hierarchy), and the complexity of the methodology for valuing a specific security or asset class. For example, the reliability of a price for an equity investment actively traded in a liquid market is higher than that of a corporate bond traded in a liquid market that has not traded on the measurement date, which, in turn, is more reliable than that of an asset-backed security that is valued using a discounted cash flow model.

- *The reputation and experience of the third-party pricing source* – For example, a third-party pricing source may be experienced in a certain type of financial instrument, and be recognized as such, but may not be similarly experienced in other types of financial instruments. The auditor's past experience with the thirdparty pricing source may also be relevant in this regard.

- *The objectivity of the third-party pricing source* – For example, if a price obtained by management comes from a counterparty such as the broker who sold the financial instrument to the entity, or an entity with a close relationship with the entity being audited, the price may not be reliable.

- *The entity's controls over the use of third-party pricing sources* – The degree to which management has controls in place to assess the reliability of information from third-party pricing sources affects the reliability of the fair value measurement. For example, management may have controls in place to:

  - Review and approve the use of the third-party pricing source, including consideration of the reputation, experience and objectivity of the third-party pricing source.

  - Determine the completeness, relevance and accuracy of the prices and pricing-related data.

- *The third-party pricing source's controls* – The controls and processes over valuations for the asset classes of interest to the auditor. For example, a third-party pricing source may have strong controls around how prices are developed, including the use of a formalized process for customers, both buy and sell side, to challenge the prices received from the pricing service, when supported by appropriate evidence, which may enable the third-party pricing source to constantly correct prices to more fully reflect the information available to market participants.

118 Possible approaches to gathering evidence regarding information from third-party pricing sources may include the following:

- For level 1 inputs, comparing the information from third-party pricing sources with observable market prices.

- Reviewing disclosures provided by third-party pricing sources about their controls and processes, valuation techniques, inputs and assumptions.

- Testing the controls management has in place to assess the reliability of information from third-party pricing sources.

- Performing procedures at the third-party pricing source to understand and test the controls and processes, valuation techniques, inputs and assumptions used for asset classes or specific financial instruments of interest.

- Evaluating whether the prices obtained from third-party pricing sources are reasonable in relation to prices from other third-party pricing sources, the entity's estimate or the auditor's own estimate.

- Evaluating the reasonableness of valuation techniques, assumptions and inputs.

- Developing a point estimate or a range for some financial instruments priced by the third-party pricing source and evaluating whether the results are within a reasonable range of each other.

- Obtaining a service auditor's report that covers the controls over validation of the prices.[31]

119 Obtaining prices from multiple third-party pricing sources may also provide useful information about measurement uncertainty. A wide range of prices may indicate higher measurement uncertainty and may suggest that the financial instrument is sensitive to small changes in data and assumptions. A narrow range may indicate lower measurement uncertainty and may suggest less sensitivity to changes in data and assumptions. Although obtaining prices from multiple sources may be useful, when considering financial instruments that have inputs categorized at levels 2 or 3 of the fair value hierarchy, in particular, obtaining prices from multiple sources is unlikely to provide sufficient appropriate audit evidence on its own. This is because:

(a) What appear to be multiple sources of pricing information may be utilizing the same underlying pricing source; and

(b) Understanding the inputs used by the third-party pricing source in determining the price may be necessary in order to categorize the financial instrument in the fair value hierarchy.

120 In some situations, the auditor may be unable to gain an understanding of the process used to generate the price, including any controls over the process of how reliably the price is determined, or may not have access to the model, including the assumptions and other inputs used. In such cases, the auditor may decide to

---

[31] *Some pricing services may provide reports for users of its data to explain their controls over pricing data, that is, a report prepared in accordance with International Standard on Assurance Engagements (ISAE) 3402, Assurance Reports on Controls at a Service Organization. Management may request, and the auditor may consider obtaining, such a report to develop an understanding of how the pricing data is prepared and evaluate whether the controls at the pricing service can be relied upon.*

undertake to develop a point estimate or a range to evaluate management's point estimate in responding to the assessed risk.

Audit Considerations When the Entity has an Independent Price Verification Function

Where the entity has an independent price verification function in place (see paragraph 62-1), understanding the processes and controls performed by the function with respect to financial instrument valuations may assist the auditor in determining the nature and extent of procedures needed. **120-1**

Audit procedures to test the entity's independent price verification function controls, may include: **120-2**

- Testing the completeness of the price testing population.

- Testing the completeness, accuracy and existence of full revaluation or parameter based pricing differences.

- Testing the calculation of fair value adjustments in accordance with approved policies / methods.

- Testing controls for the reporting of pricing differences and adjustment to the entity's books and records.

Audit considerations when management estimates fair values using a model

Paragraph 13(b) of ISA (UK and Ireland) 540 requires the auditor, if testing management's process of making the accounting estimate, to evaluate whether the method of measurement used is appropriate in the circumstances and the assumptions used by management are reasonable in light of the measurement objectives of the applicable financial reporting framework. **121**

Whether management has used a third-party pricing source, or is undertaking its own valuation, models are often used to value financial instruments, particularly when using inputs at levels 2 and 3 of the fair value hierarchy. In determining the nature, timing and extent of audit procedures on models, the auditor may consider the methodology, assumptions and data used in the model. When considering more complex financial instruments such as those using level 3 inputs, testing all three may be a useful source of audit evidence. However, when the model is both simple and generally accepted, such as some bond price calculations, audit evidence obtained from focusing on the assumptions and data used in the model may be a more useful source of evidence. **122**

Testing a model can be accomplished by two main approaches: **123**

(a) The auditor can test management's model, by considering the appropriateness of the model used by management, the reasonableness of the assumptions and data used, and the mathematical accuracy; or

(b) The auditor can develop their own estimate, and then compare the auditor's valuation with that of the entity.

Where valuation of financial instruments is based on unobservable inputs (that is, level 3 inputs), matters that the auditor may consider include, for example, how management supports the following: **124**

- The identification and characteristics of marketplace participants relevant to the financial instrument.

- How unobservable inputs are determined on initial recognition.

- Modifications it has made to its own assumptions to reflect its view of assumptions marketplace participants would use.

- Whether it has incorporated the best input information available in the circumstances.

- Where applicable, how its assumptions take account of comparable transactions.

- Sensitivity analysis of models when unobservable inputs are used and whether adjustments have been made to address measurement uncertainty.

125   In addition, the auditor's industry knowledge, knowledge of market trends, understanding of other entities' valuations (having regard to confidentiality) and other relevant price indicators informs the auditor's testing of the valuations and the consideration of whether the valuations appear reasonable overall. If the valuations appear to be consistently overly aggressive or conservative, this may be an indicator of possible management bias.

126   Where there is a lack of observable external evidence, it is particularly important that those charged with governance have been appropriately engaged to understand the subjectivity of management's valuations and the evidence that has been obtained to support these valuations. In such cases, it may be necessary for the auditor to evaluate whether there has been a thorough review and consideration of the issues, including any documentation, at all appropriate management levels within the entity, including with those charged with governance.

127   When markets become inactive or dislocated, or inputs are unobservable, management's valuations may be more judgmental and less verifiable and, as a result, may be less reliable. In such circumstances, the auditor may test the model by a combination of testing controls operated by the entity, evaluating the design and operation of the model, testing the assumptions and data used in the model, and comparing its output to a point estimate or range developed by the auditor or to other third-party valuation techniques.[32]

128   It is likely that in testing the inputs used in an entity's valuation methodology,[33] for example, where such inputs are categorized in the fair value hierarchy, the auditor will also be obtaining evidence to support the disclosures required by the applicable financial reporting framework. For example, the auditor's substantive procedures to evaluate whether the inputs used in an entity's valuation technique (that is, level 1, level 2 and level 3 inputs) are appropriate, and tests of an entity's sensitivity analysis, will be relevant to the auditor's evaluation of whether the disclosures achieve fair presentation.

Evaluating whether the assumptions used by management are reasonable

129   An assumption used in a model may be deemed to be significant if a reasonable variation in the assumption would materially affect the measurement of the financial instrument.[34] Management may have considered alternative

---

[32] *ISA (UK and Ireland) 540, paragraph 13(d) describes requirements when the auditor develops a range to evaluate management's point estimate. Valuation techniques developed by third parties and used by the auditor may, in some circumstances be considered the work of an auditor's expert and subject to the requirements in ISA (UK and Ireland) 620.*

[33] *See, for example, paragraph 15 of ISA (UK and Ireland) 540 for requirements relative to the auditor's evaluation of management's assumption regarding significant risks.*

[34] *See ISA (UK and Ireland) 540, paragraph A107.*

assumptions or outcomes by performing a sensitivity analysis. The extent of subjectivity associated with assumptions influences the degree of measurement uncertainty and may lead the auditor to conclude there is a significant risk, for example in the case of level 3 inputs.

Audit procedures to test the assumptions used by management, including those   **130** used as inputs to models, may include evaluating:

- Whether, and if so, how, management has incorporated market inputs into the development of assumptions, as it is generally preferable to seek to maximize the use of relevant observable inputs and minimize unobservable inputs;

- Whether the assumptions are consistent with observable market conditions, and the characteristics of the financial asset or financial liability;

- Whether the sources of market-participant assumptions are relevant and reliable, and how management has selected the assumptions to use when a number of different marketplace assumptions exist; and

- Whether sensitivity analyses indicate that valuations would change significantly with only small or moderate changes in assumptions.

See paragraphs A77 to A83 of ISA (UK and Ireland) 540 for further considerations relative to evaluating the assumptions used by management.

The auditor's consideration of judgments about the future is based on information   **131** available at the time at which the judgment is made. Subsequent events may result in outcomes that are inconsistent with judgments that were reasonable at the time they were made.

In some cases, the discount rate in a present value calculation may be adjusted to   **132** account for the uncertainties in the valuation, rather than adjusting each assumption. In such cases, an auditor's procedures may focus on the discount rate, by looking at an observable trade on a similar security to compare the discount rates used or developing an independent model to calculate the discount rate and compare with that used by management.

Audit considerations when a management's expert is used by the entity

As discussed in Section I, management may engage a valuation expert to value   **133** some or all of their securities. Such experts may be brokers, investment bankers, pricing services that also provide expert valuation services, or other specialized valuation firms.

If the third party applies particular expertise, for example in the use of models,   **133-1** in making an estimate which the entity uses in preparing its financial statements, the third party is considered a management's expert. If, on the other hand, the third party merely provides price data regarding private transactions not otherwise available to the entity which the entity uses in its own estimation methods, such information, if used as audit evidence, is not considered to be evidence produced by a management's expert.

Paragraph 8 of ISA (UK and Ireland) 500 contains requirements for the auditor   **134** when evaluating evidence from an expert engaged by management. The extent of the auditor's procedures in relation to a management's expert and that expert's work depend on the significance of the expert's work for the auditor's purposes. Evaluating the appropriateness of management's expert's work assists the auditor in assessing whether the prices or valuations supplied by a management's expert provide sufficient appropriate audit evidence to support the valuations. Examples of procedures the auditor may perform include:

- Evaluating the competence, capabilities and objectivity of management's expert for example: their relationship with the entity; their reputation and standing in the market; their experience with the particular types of instruments; and their understanding of the relevant financial reporting framework applicable to the valuations;

- Obtaining an understanding of the work of the management's expert, for example by assessing the appropriateness of the valuation technique(s) used and the key market variables and assumptions used in the valuation technique(s);

- Evaluating the appropriateness of that expert's work as audit evidence. At this point, the focus is on the appropriateness of the expert's work at the level of the individual financial instrument. For a sample of the relevant instruments, it may be appropriate to develop an estimate independently (see paragraphs 136 to 137 on developing a point estimate or range), using different data and assumptions, then compare that estimate to that of the management's expert; and

- Other procedures may include:

  - Modeling different assumptions to derive assumptions in another model, then considering the reasonableness of those derived assumptions.

  - Comparing management's point estimates with the auditor's point estimates to determine if management's estimates are consistently higher or lower.

134-1   The auditor considers whether management has given proper consideration to the models used and, if not, the possible impacts on the risks related to these items and others and the implications for the audit. In such cases, the auditor's considerations may include whether:

- It is necessary and possible to obtain information directly, with management's authority, from the third party.

- A report on the third party's internal controls by their auditors is available covering control objectives applicable to the valuations.

135   Assumptions may be made or identified by a management's expert to assist management in valuing its financial instruments. Such assumptions, when used by management, become management's assumptions that the auditor needs to consider in the same manner as management's other assumptions.

Developing a point estimate or range

136   An auditor may develop a valuation technique and adjust the inputs and assumptions used in the valuation technique to develop a range for use in evaluating the reasonableness of management's valuation. Paragraphs 106 to 135 of this PN may assist the auditor in developing a point estimate or range. In accordance with ISA (UK and Ireland) 540,[35] if the auditor uses assumptions, or methodologies that differ from management's, the auditor shall obtain an

---

[35] *ISA (UK and Ireland) 540, paragraph 13(c).*

understanding of management's assumptions or methodologies sufficient to establish that the auditor's range takes into account relevant variables and to evaluate any significant differences from management's valuation. The auditor may find it useful to use the work of an auditor's expert to evaluate the reasonableness of management's valuation.

In some cases, the auditor may conclude that sufficient evidence cannot be obtained from the auditor's attempts to obtain an understanding of management's assumptions or methodology, for example when a third-party pricing source uses internally developed models and software and does not allow access to relevant information. In such cases, the auditor may not be able to obtain sufficient appropriate audit evidence about the valuation if the auditor is unable to perform other procedures to respond to the risks of material misstatement, such as developing a point estimate or a range to evaluate management's point estimate.[36] ISA (UK and Ireland) 705[37] describes the implications of the auditor's inability to obtain sufficient appropriate audit evidence.   **137**

Evaluating the Overall Result and Adjusting for Valuation Uncertainties

Valuing complex financial instruments is not a precise science. Uncertainties over the reliability of market quotes, the validity of models and the accuracy of their calibration to actual market activity will exist, particularly for very complicated instruments that are not actively traded. If such instruments were sold, a buyer might reduce their price to reflect these uncertainties and the risks that (s)he was thereby assuming. Estimating the valuation adjustment required for such factors is very judgmental and will be specific to each entity. The auditor considers all the factors taken into account in the valuation process and uses experience and judgment to evaluate the amount of any adjustment required. The auditor may need to draw on expert help to assist in doing this.   **137-1**

One important factor in evaluating the overall result is to consider whether counterparty risk (the risk that a counterparty to a transaction will not perform their side of the bargain) has been properly taken into account in valuing the instrument. It is inherent in mark to market pricing that counterparty risk is taken into account in arriving at the market price and an entity's pricing process should therefore have already dealt with counterparty risk. However, the auditor considers whether there are any other aspects of counterparty risk that have not properly been addressed, such as the possible need for an impairment provision in respect of an accrual accounted component of a financial instrument (e.g. an interest accrual).   **137-2**

Hedge Accounting

Where hedge accounting techniques are used, the auditor gathers audit evidence to determine whether management's designation of a financial instrument as a hedge is appropriate and the accounting entries are consistent with the relevant accounting standards. The nature and extent of the evidence obtained by the auditor will vary depending on the nature of the hedged items and the hedging instruments. Generally, the auditor obtains evidence as to: **137-3**

(a)   Whether the financial instrument was designated as a hedge at the inception of the transaction;

---

[36] *ISA (UK and Ireland) 540, paragraph 13(d).*

[37] *ISA (UK and Ireland) 705, Modifications to the Opinion in the Independent Auditor's Report.*

(b)   The nature of the hedging relationship;

(c)   The entity's risk management objective and strategy for undertaking the hedge;

(d)   The entity's assessment of the effectiveness of the hedge;

(e)   Where the financial instrument is hedging a future transaction, the entity's assessment of the certainty of that future transaction; and

(f)   Whether the hedging instrument, hedged item and hedging relationship are permitted under the relevant accounting standards.

If there is disagreement with management's use of hedge accounting the auditor considers whether to qualify the audit opinion on the financial statements.

137-4   The auditor gathers audit evidence to determine whether management complied with the applicable hedge accounting requirements of the financial reporting framework, including designation and documentation requirements. In addition, the auditor gathers audit evidence as to whether there is support for management's assessment that the hedging transaction has met the relevant effectiveness tests in accordance with the applicable accounting standards[37a]. The nature and extent of the documentation prepared by the entity will vary depending on the nature of the hedged items and the hedging instruments. If sufficient audit evidence to support management's use of hedge accounting is not available, or there is disagreement with management's use of hedge accounting, the auditor considers the implications for the auditor's report.

Presentation and disclosure of financial instruments

138   Management's responsibilities include the preparation of the financial statements in accordance with the applicable financial reporting framework.[38] Financial reporting frameworks often require disclosures in the financial statements to enable users of the financial statements to make meaningful assessments of the effects of the entity's financial instrument activities, including the risks and uncertainties associated with these financial instruments[38a]. The importance of disclosures regarding the basis of measurement increases as the measurement

---

[37a]   *If the hedging relationship is no longer effective, the hedging instrument ceases to qualify for treatment as a hedge.*

[38]   *See paragraphs 4 and A2 of ISA (UK and Ireland) 200.*

[38a]   *For example, IAS 1, Presentation of Financial Statements, includes requirements to disclose:*

●   *The judgments made in applying the entity's accounting policies that have the most significant effect on the amounts recognised in the financial statements;*

●   *Information about the assumptions concerning the future; and*

●   *Other major sources of estimation uncertainty at the end of the reporting period that have a significant risk of resulting in a material adjustment in the carrying amount of assets and liabilities within the next financial year.*

Further, under UK and Irish company law, in relation to the use of financial instruments by the company, the directors' report is required to give an indication of:

(a)   the financial risk management objectives and policies of the company, including the policy for hedging each major type of forecasted transaction for which hedge accounting is used, and

(b)   the exposure of the company to price risk, credit risk, liquidity risk and cash flow risk,

unless such information is not material for the assessment of the assets, liabilities, financial position and profit or loss of the company. (In the UK: SI 2008/410 – The Large and Medium-sized Companies and Groups (Accounts and Reports) Regulations 2008, Schedule 7.6; in Ireland: Companies (Amendment) Act 1986, s13(1)(f).)

uncertainty of the financial instruments increases and is also affected by the level of the fair value hierarchy.

When evaluating compliance with presentation and disclosure requirements of the applicable financial reporting framework, the auditor determines whether management has had regard to related guidance and recommendations that may have been produced by relevant bodies (e.g. The European Securities and Markets Authority (ESMA), the Financial Stability Board and national regulators of entities providing financial services). The auditor considers whether related disclosures are needed and given for the financial statements as a whole to provide a true and fair view and enable users to obtain an understanding of the entity's position. **138-1**

In representing that the financial statements are in accordance with the applicable financial reporting framework, management implicitly or explicitly makes assertions regarding the presentation and disclosure of the various elements of financial statements and related disclosures. Assertions about presentation and disclosure encompass: **139**

(a) Occurrence and rights and obligations-disclosed events, transactions, and other matters have occurred and pertain to the entity.

(b) Completeness-all disclosures that should have been included in the financial statements have been included.

(c) Classification and understandability-financial information is appropriately presented and described, and disclosures are clearly expressed.

(d) Accuracy and valuation-financial and other information are disclosed fairly and at appropriate amounts.

The auditor's procedures around auditing disclosures are designed in consideration of these assertions.

Procedures relating to the presentation and disclosure of financial instruments

In relation to the presentation and disclosures of financial instruments, areas of particular importance include: **140**

- Financial reporting frameworks generally require additional disclosures regarding estimates, and related risks and uncertainties, to supplement and explain assets, liabilities, income, and expenses. The auditor's focus may need to be on the disclosures relating to risks and sensitivity analysis. Information obtained during the auditor's risk assessment procedures and testing of control activities may provide evidence in order for the auditor to conclude about whether the disclosures in the financial statements are in accordance with the requirements of the applicable financial reporting framework, for example about:

  - The entity's objectives and strategies for using financial instruments, including the entity's stated accounting policies;

  - The entity's control framework for managing its risks associated with financial instruments; and

  - The risks and uncertainties associated with the financial instruments.

- Information may come from systems outside traditional financial reporting systems, such as risk systems. Examples of procedures that the auditor may choose to perform in responding to assessed risks relative to disclosures include testing:

- The process used to derive the disclosed information; and

- The operating effectiveness of the controls over the data used in the preparation of disclosures.

- In relation to financial instruments having significant risk,[39] even where the disclosures are in accordance with the applicable financial reporting framework, the auditor may conclude that the disclosure of estimation uncertainty is inadequate in light of the circumstances and facts involved and, accordingly, the financial statements may not achieve fair presentation. ISA (UK and Ireland) 705 provides guidance on the implications for the auditor's opinion when the auditor believes that management's disclosures in the financial statements are inadequate or misleading.

- Auditors may also consider whether the disclosures are complete and understandable, for example, all relevant information may be included in the financial statements (or accompanying reports) but it may be insufficiently drawn together to enable users of the financial statements to obtain an understanding of the position or there may not be enough qualitative disclosure to give context to the amounts recorded in the financial statements. For example, even when an entity has included sensitivity analysis disclosures, the disclosure may not fully describe the risks and uncertainties that may arise because of changes in valuation, possible effects on debt covenants, collateral requirements, and the entity's liquidity. ISA (UK and Ireland) 260[40] contains requirements and guidance about communicating with those charged with governance, including the auditor's views about significant qualitative aspects of the entity's accounting practices, including accounting policies, accounting estimates and financial statement disclosures.

140-1 The extent and nature of audit procedures has regard to whether the financial instrument disclosures are considered material to the users and the assessed risks of material misstatement. Disclosures are not deemed less significant simply by virtue of being disclosed in a note rather than on the face of the primary statements – for example, disclosures that measure the value of financial instruments on a different basis to the financial statement line item. If information subject to audit is considered to be material, the auditor plans and performs the audit to obtain reasonable assurance that it is not materially misstated on a consistent basis, whether the information is presented on the face of the primary statements or in the related notes.

141 Consideration of the appropriateness of presentation, for example on short-term and long-term classification, in substantive testing of financial instruments is relevant to the auditor's evaluation of the presentation and disclosure.

141-1 Practice Note 19 provides guidance on auditing disclosures of market risk information. It was written specifically for the audit of deposit takers, such as banks and building societies, but may also be helpful for auditors of other businesses that have significant financial instrument activity.

---

[39] *ISA (UK and Ireland) 540, paragraph 20, requires the auditor to perform further procedures on disclosures relating to accounting estimates that give rise to significant risks to evaluate the adequacy of the disclosure of their estimation uncertainty in the financial statements in the context of the applicable financial reporting framework.*

[40] *ISA (UK and Ireland) 260, Communication with Those Charged with Governance.*

141-2

The auditor's conclusion as to whether the financial instruments are presented in conformity with relevant legislation, regulations and applicable financial reporting framework is based on the auditor's judgment as to whether:

- The accounting policies selected and applied are in conformity with the relevant financial reporting framework;

- Management's assumptions are reasonable and are used consistently and whether new conditions that may justify a change have been taken into account appropriately;

- Disclosure is adequate to ensure that the entity is in full compliance with the current disclosure requirements of relevant legislation, regulations and applicable financial reporting framework under which the financial statements are being reported;

- The information presented in the financial statements is classified and summarised in an appropriate and meaningful manner; and

- The financial statements show a true and fair view.

Other relevant audit considerations

Written representations

ISA (UK and Ireland) 540 requires the auditor to obtain written representations   **142**
from management and, where appropriate, those charged with governance whether they believe significant assumptions used in making accounting estimates are reasonable.[41] ISA (UK and Ireland) 580[42] requires that if, in addition to such required representations, the auditor determines that it is necessary to obtain one or more written representations to support other audit evidence relevant to the financial statements or one or more specific assertions in the financial statements, the auditor shall request such other written representations. Depending on the volume and degree of complexity of financial instrument activities, written representations to support other evidence obtained about financial instruments may also include:

- Management's objectives with respect to financial instruments, for example, whether they are used for hedging, asset/liability management or investment purposes;

- Representations about the appropriateness of presentation of the financial statements, for example the recording of financial instrument transactions as sales or financing transactions;

- Representations about the financial statement disclosures concerning financial instruments, for example that:

  - The records reflect all financial instrument transactions; and

  - All embedded derivative instruments have been identified;

---

[41] *ISA (UK and Ireland) 540, paragraph 22. Paragraph 4 of ISA (UK and Ireland) 580, Written Representations, states that written representations from management do not provide sufficient appropriate audit evidence on their own about any of the matters with which they deal. If the auditor is otherwise unable to obtain sufficient appropriate audit evidence, this may constitute a limitation on the scope of the audit that may have implications for the auditor's report (see ISA (UK and Ireland) 705, Modification to the Opinion in the Independent Auditor's Report).*

[42] *ISA (UK and Ireland) 580, paragraph 13.*

- Whether all transactions have been conducted at arm's length and at market value;

- The terms of transactions;

- The appropriateness of the valuations of financial instruments;

- Whether there are any side agreements associated with any financial instruments;

- Whether the entity has entered into any written options;

- Management's intent and ability to carry out certain actions;[43] and

- Whether subsequent events require adjustment to the valuations and disclosures included in the financial statements.

Communication with those charged with governance and others

143 Because of the uncertainties associated with the valuation of financial instruments, the potential effects on the financial statements of any significant risks are likely to be of governance interest. The auditor may communicate the nature and consequences of significant assumptions used in fair value measurements, the degree of subjectivity involved in the development of the assumptions, and the relative materiality of the items being measured at fair value to the financial statements as a whole. In addition, the need for appropriate controls over commitments to enter into financial instrument contracts and over the subsequent measurement processes are matters that may give rise to the need for communication with those charged with governance.

144 ISA (UK and Ireland) 260 deals with the auditor's responsibility to communicate with those charged with governance in an audit of financial statements. With respect to financial instruments, matters to be communicated to those charged with governance may include:

- A lack of management understanding of the nature or extent of the financial instrument activities or the risks associated with such activities;

- Significant deficiencies in the design or operation of the systems of internal control or risk management relating to the entity's financial instrument activities that the auditor has identified during the audit, including a lack of segregation of duties;[44]

- Significant difficulties encountered when obtaining sufficient appropriate audit evidence relating to valuations performed by management or a management's expert, for example, where management is unable to obtain an understanding of the valuation methodology, assumptions and data used by the management's experts, and such information is not made available to the auditor by management's expert;

- Significant differences in judgments between the auditor and management or a management's expert regarding valuations;

---

[43] *Paragraph A80 of ISA (UK and Ireland) 540 provides examples of procedures that may be appropriate in the circumstances.*

[44] *ISA (UK and Ireland) 265, Communicating Deficiencies in Internal Control to Those Charged with Governance and Management, establishes requirements and provides guidance on communicating deficiencies in internal control to management, and communicating significant deficiencies in internal control to those charged with governance. It explains that deficiencies in internal control may be identified during the auditor's risk assessment procedures in accordance with ISA (UK and Ireland) 315 or at any other stage of the audit.*

- The potential effects on the entity's financial statements of material risks and exposures required to be disclosed in the financial statements, including the measurement uncertainty associated with financial instruments;

- The auditor's views about the appropriateness of the selection of accounting policies and presentation of financial instrument transactions in the financial statements;

- The auditor's views about the qualitative aspects of the entity's accounting practices and financial reporting for financial instruments; or

- A lack of comprehensive and clearly stated policies for the purchase, sale and holding of financial instruments, including operational controls, procedures for designating financial instruments as hedges, and monitoring exposures.

The appropriate timing for communications will vary with the circumstances of the engagement; however, it may be appropriate to communicate significant difficulties encountered during the audit as soon as practicable if those charged with governance are able to assist the auditor to overcome the difficulty, or if it is likely to lead to a modified opinion.

Communications with regulators and others

In some cases, auditors may be required,[45] or may consider it appropriate, to communicate directly with regulators or prudential supervisors, in addition to those charged with governance, regarding matters relating to financial instruments. Such communication may be useful throughout the audit. For example, in some jurisdictions, banking regulators seek to cooperate with auditors to share information about the operation and application of controls over financial instrument activities, challenges in valuing financial instruments in inactive markets, and compliance with regulations. This coordination may be helpful to the auditor in identifying risks of material misstatement.

145

---

[45] *For example, ISA (UK and Ireland) 250 Section A, Consideration of Laws and Regulations in an Audit of Financial Statements, requires auditors to determine whether there is a responsibility to report identified or suspected non-compliance with laws and regulations to parties outside the entity. In addition, requirements concerning the auditor's communication to banking supervisors and others may be established in many countries either by law, by supervisory requirement or by formal agreement or protocol.*

Appendix – Examples of controls relating to financial instruments

1   The following provides background information and examples of controls that may exist in an entity that deals in a high volume of financial instrument transactions, whether for trading or investing purposes. The examples are not meant to be exhaustive and entities may establish different control environments and processes depending on their size, the industry in which they operate, and the extent of their financial instrument transactions. Further information on the use of trade confirmations and clearing houses is contained in paragraphs 25–26.

2   As in any control system, it is sometimes necessary to duplicate controls at different control levels (for example, preventative, detective and monitoring) to avoid the risk of material misstatement.

The entity's control environment

Commitment to competent use of financial instruments

3   The degree of complexity of some financial instrument activities may mean that only a few individuals within the entity fully understand those activities or have the expertise necessary to value the instruments on an ongoing basis. Use of financial instruments without relevant expertise within the entity increases the risk of material misstatement.

Participation by those charged with governance

4   Those charged with governance oversee and concur with management's establishment of the entity's overall risk appetite and provide oversight over the entity's financial instrument activities. An entity's policies for the purchase, sale and holding of financial instruments are aligned with its attitude toward risk and the expertise of those involved in financial instrument activities. In addition, an entity may establish governance structures and control processes aimed at:

(a)   Communicating investment decisions and assessments of all material measurement uncertainty to those charged with governance; and

(b)   Evaluating the entity's overall risk appetite when engaging in financial instrument transactions.

Organisational structure

5   Financial instrument activities may be run on either a centralized or a decentralized basis. Such activities and related decision making depend heavily on the flow of accurate, reliable, and timely management information. The difficulty of collecting and aggregating such information increases with the number of locations and businesses in which an entity is involved. The risks of material misstatement associated with financial instrument activities may increase with greater decentralization of control activities. This may especially be true where an entity is based in different locations, some perhaps in other countries.

Assignment of authority and responsibility

Investment and valuation policies

Providing direction, through clearly stated policies approved by those charged **6** with governance for the purchase, sale, and holding of financial instruments enables management to establish an effective approach to taking and managing business risks. These policies are most clear when they state the entity's objectives with regard to its risk management activities, and the investment and hedging alternatives available to meet these objectives, and reflect the:

(a) Level of management's expertise;

(b) Sophistication of the entity's internal control and monitoring systems;

(c) Entity's asset/liability structure;

(d) Entity's capacity to maintain liquidity and absorb losses of capital;

(e) Types of financial instruments that management believes will meet its objectives; and

(f) Uses of financial instruments that management believes will meet its objectives, for example, whether derivatives may be used for speculative purposes or only for hedging purposes.

Management may design policies aligned with its valuation capabilities and may **7** establish controls to ensure that these policies are adhered to by those employees responsible for the entity's valuation. These may include:

(a) Processes for the design and validation of methodologies used to produce valuations, including how measurement uncertainty is addressed; and

(b) Policies regarding maximizing the use of observable inputs and the types of information to be gathered to support valuations of financial instruments.

In smaller entities, dealing in financial instruments may be rare and management's **8** knowledge and experience limited. Nevertheless, establishing policies over financial instruments helps an entity to determine its risk appetite and consider whether investing in particular financial instruments achieves a stated objective.

Human resource policies and practices

Entities may establish policies requiring key employees, both front office and back **9** office, to take mandatory time off from their duties. This type of control is used as a means of preventing and detecting fraud, in particular if those engaged in trading activities are creating false trades or inaccurately recording transactions.

Use of service organisations

Entities may also use service organizations (for example asset managers) to initiate **10** the purchase or sale of financial instruments, to maintain records of transactions for the entity or to value financial instruments. Some entities may be dependent on these service organizations to provide the basis of reporting for the financial instruments held. However, if management does not have an understanding about the controls in place at a service organization, the auditor may not be able to obtain sufficient appropriate audit evidence to rely on controls at that service organization. See ISA (UK and Ireland) 402[46], which establishes requirements

---

[46] *ISA (UK and Ireland) 402, Audit Considerations Relating to an Entity Using a Service Organization.*

for the auditor to obtain sufficient appropriate audit evidence when an entity uses the services of one or more service organizations.

11 The use of service organizations may strengthen or weaken the control environment for financial instruments. For example, a service organization's personnel may have more experience with financial instruments than the entity's management or may have more robust internal control over financial reporting. The use of the service organization also may allow for greater segregation of duties. On the other hand, the service organization may have a poor control environment.

The entity's risk assessment process

12 An entity's risk assessment process exists to establish how management identifies business risks that derive from its use of financial instruments, including how management estimates the significance of the risks, assesses the likelihood of their occurrence and decides upon actions to manage them.

13 The entity's risk assessment process forms the basis for how management determines the risks to be managed. Risk assessment processes exist with the objective of ensuring that management:

(a) Understands the risks inherent in a financial instrument before management enters into it, including the objective of entering into the transaction and its structure (for example, the economics and business purpose of the entity's financial instrument activities);

(b) Performs adequate due diligence commensurate with the risks associated with particular financial instruments;

(c) Monitors the entity's outstanding positions to understand how market conditions are affecting their exposures;

(d) Has procedures in place to reduce or change risk exposure if necessary and for managing reputational risk; and

(e) Subjects these processes to rigorous supervision and review.

14 The structure implemented to monitor and manage exposure to risks should:

(a) Be appropriate and consistent with the entity's attitude toward risk as determined by those charged with governance;

(b) Specify the approval levels for the authorization of different types of financial instruments and transactions that may be entered into and for what purposes. The permitted instruments and approval levels should reflect the expertise of those involved in financial instrument activities, demonstrating management's commitment to competence;

(c) Set appropriate limits for the maximum allowable exposure to each type of risk (including approved counterparties). Levels of allowable exposure may vary depending on the type of risk, or counterparty;

(d) Provide for the objective and timely monitoring of the financial risks and control activities;

(e) Provide for the objective and timely reporting of exposures, risks and the results of financial instrument activities in managing risk; and

(f) Evaluate management's track record for assessing the risks of particular financial instruments.

The types and levels of risks an entity faces are directly related to the types of financial instruments with which it deals, including the complexity of these instruments and the volume of financial instruments transacted. **15**

Risk management function

Some entities, for example large financial institutions with a high volume of financial instrument transactions, may be required by law or regulation, or may choose, to establish a formal risk management function. This function is separated from those responsible for undertaking and managing financial instrument transactions. The function is responsible for reporting on and monitoring financial instrument activities, and may include a formal risk committee established by those charged with governance. Examples of key responsibilities in this area may include: **16**

(a) Implementing the risk management policy set by those charged with governance (including analyses of the risks to which an entity may be exposed);

(b) Designing risk limit structures and ensuring these risk limits are implemented in practice;

(c) Developing stress scenarios and subjecting open position portfolios to sensitivity analysis, including reviews of unusual movements in positions; and

(d) Reviewing and analysing new financial instrument products. and

(e) Independent price verification.

Financial instruments may have the associated risk that a loss might exceed the amount, if any, of the value of the financial instrument recognized on the balance sheet. For example, a sudden fall in the market price of a commodity may force an entity to realize losses to close a forward position in that commodity due to collateral, or margin, requirements. In some cases, the potential losses may be enough to cast significant doubt on the entity's ability to continue as a going concern. The entity may perform sensitivity analyses or value-at-risk analyses to assess the future hypothetical effects on financial instruments subject to market risks. However, value-at-risk analysis does not fully reflect the extent of the risks that may affect the entity; sensitivity and scenario analyses also may be subject to limitations. **17**

The volume and sophistication of financial instrument activity and relevant regulatory requirements will influence the entity's consideration whether to establish a formal risk management function and how the function may be structured. In entities that have not established a separate risk management function, for example entities with relatively few financial instruments or financial instruments that are less complex, reporting on and monitoring financial instrument activities may be a component of the accounting or finance function's responsibility or management's overall responsibility, and may include a formal risk committee established by those charged with governance. **18**

To be effective, a risk management function needs to have sufficient resources and capabilities and status in the entity to control how risk is taken on and managed. **18-1**

The entity's information systems

19   The key objective of an entity's information system is that it is capable of capturing and recording all the transactions accurately, settling them, valuing them, and producing information to enable the financial instruments to be risk managed and for controls to be monitored. Difficulties can arise in entities that engage in a high volume of financial instruments, in particular if there is a multiplicity of systems that are poorly integrated and have manual interfaces without adequate controls.

19-1   The financial risks and exposures inherent in complex financial instruments cannot always be effectively captured in a balance sheet and profit and loss account. For example significant derivative contracts often have zero value at the outset since they are priced at prevailing market rates. The provision of additional information is often required by the financial reporting framework. Entities therefore need to have processes and controls to gather the information required by the applicable financial reporting framework so that it is complete and accurate.

20   Certain financial instruments may require a large number of accounting entries. As the sophistication or level of the financial instrument activities increases, it is necessary for the sophistication of the information system to also increase. Specific issues which can arise with respect to financial instruments include:

(a)   Information systems, in particular for smaller entities, not having the capability or not being appropriately configured to process financial instrument transactions, especially when the entity does not have any prior experience in dealing with financial instruments. This may result in an increased number of manual transactions which may further increase the risk of error;

(b)   The potential diversity of systems required to process more complex transactions, and the need for regular reconciliations between them, in particular when the systems are not interfaced or may be subject to manual intervention;

(c)   The potential that more complex transactions, if they are only traded by a small number of individuals, may be valued or risk managed on spreadsheets rather than on main processing systems, and for the physical and logical password security around those spreadsheets to be more easily compromised;

(d)   A lack of review of systems exception logs, external confirmations and broker quotes, where available, to validate the entries generated by the systems;

(e)   Difficulties in controlling and evaluating the key inputs to systems for valuation of financial instruments, particularly where those systems are maintained by the group of traders known as the front office or a third-party service provider and/or the transactions in question are non-routine or thinly traded;

(f)   Failure to evaluate the design and calibration of complex models used to process these transactions initially and on a periodic basis;

(g)   The potential that management has not set up a library of models, with controls around access, change and maintenance of individual models, in order to maintain a strong audit trail of the accredited versions of models and in order to prevent unauthorized access or amendments to those models;

(h)   The disproportionate investment that may be required in risk management and control systems, where an entity only undertakes a limited number of financial instrument transactions, and the potential for misunderstanding of the output by management if they are not used to these types of transactions;

(i)   The potential requirement for third-party systems provision, for example from a service organization, to record, process, account for or risk manage appropriately financial instrument transactions, and the need to reconcile appropriately and challenge the output from those providers; and

(j)   Additional security and control considerations relevant to the use of an electronic network when an entity uses electronic commerce for financial instrument transactions; and

(k)   Difficulties in recruiting and retaining expert individuals to represent the accounting, processing and risk management of transactions correctly initially on systems and to validate periodically that they continue to be correctly recorded.

Information systems relevant to financial reporting serve as an important source of information for the quantitative disclosures in the financial statements. However, entities may also develop and maintain non-financial systems used for internal reporting and to generate information included in qualitative disclosures, for example regarding risks and uncertainties or sensitivity analyses.   **21**

The entity's control activities

Control activities over financial instrument transactions are designed to prevent or detect problems that hinder an entity from achieving its objectives. These objectives may be either operational, financial reporting, or compliance in nature. Control activities over financial instruments are designed relative to the complexity and volume of transactions of financial instruments and will generally include an appropriate authorization process, adequate segregation of duties, and other policies and procedures designed to ensure that the entity's control objectives are met. Process flow charts may assist in identifying an entity's controls and lack of controls. This PN focuses on control activities related to completeness, accuracy and existence, valuation, and presentation and disclosure.   **22**

Authorisation

Authorization can affect the financial statement assertions both directly and indirectly. For example, even if a transaction is executed outside an entity's policies, it nonetheless may be recorded and accounted for accurately. However, unauthorised transactions could significantly increase risk to the entity, thereby significantly increasing the risk of material misstatement since they would be undertaken outside the system of internal control. To mitigate this risk, an entity will often establish a clear policy as to what transactions can be traded by whom and adherence to this policy will then be monitored by an entity's back office. Monitoring trading activities of individuals, for example by reviewing unusually high volumes or significant gains or losses incurred, will assist management in ensuring compliance with the entity's policies, including the authorization of new types of transactions, and evaluating whether fraud has occurred.   **23**

The function of an entity's deal initiation records is to identify clearly the nature and purpose of individual transactions and the rights and obligations arising under each financial instrument contract, including the enforceability of the contracts. In   **24** addition to the basic financial information, such as a notional amount, complete and accurate records at a minimum typically include:

(a)   The identity of the dealer;

(b)   The identity of the person recording the transaction (if not the dealer), when the transaction was initiated (including the date and time of the transaction), and how it was recorded in the entity's information systems; and

(c)   The nature and purpose of the transaction, including whether or not it is intended to hedge an underlying commercial exposure; and

(d)   Information on compliance with accounting requirements related to hedging, such as:

  –   designation at inception as a hedge; and

  –   identification of the hedged item in a hedging relationship.

Segregation of duties

25   Segregation of duties and the assignment of personnel is an important control activity, particularly when exposed to financial instruments. Financial instrument activities may be segregated into a number of functions, including:

(a)   Executing the transaction (dealing). In entities with a high volume of financial instrument transactions, this may be done by the front office;

(b)   Initiating cash payments and accepting cash receipts (settlements);

(c)   Sending out trade confirmations and reconciling the differences between the entity's records and replies from counterparties, if any;

(d)   Recording of all transactions correctly in the accounting records;

(e)   Monitoring risk limits. In entities with a high volume of financial instrument transactions, this may be performed by the risk management function; and

(f)   Monitoring positions and valuing financial instruments.

26   Many organizations choose to segregate the duties of those investing in financial instruments, those valuing financial instruments, those settling financial instruments and those accounting/recording financial instruments.

27   Where an entity is too small to achieve proper segregation of duties, the role of management and those charged with governance in monitoring financial instrument activities is of particular importance.

28   A feature of some entities' internal control is an independent price verification (IPV) function. This department is responsible for separately verifying the price of some financial instruments, and may use alternative data sources, methodologies and assumptions. The IPV provides an objective look at the pricing that has been developed in another part of the entity.

29   Ordinarily, the middle or back office is responsible for establishing policies on valuation and ensuring adherence to the policy. Entities with a greater use of financial instruments may perform daily valuations of their financial instrument portfolio and examine the contribution to profit or loss of individual financial instrument valuations as a test of the reasonableness of valuations.

Completeness, accuracy, and existence

30   Regular reconciliation of the entity's records to external banks' and custodians' records enables the entity to ensure transactions are properly recorded.

Appropriate segregation of duties between those transacting the trades and those reconciling them is important, as is a rigorous process for reviewing reconciliations and clearing reconciling items.

Controls may also be established that require traders to identify whether a complex   **31** financial instrument may have unique features, for example embedded derivatives. In such circumstances, there may be a separate function that evaluates complex financial instrument transactions at their initiation (which may be known as a product control group), working in connection with an accounting policy group to ensure the transaction is accurately recorded. While smaller entities may not have product control groups, an entity may have a process in place relating to the review of complex financial instrument contracts at the point of origination in order to ensure they are accounted for appropriately in accordance with the applicable financial reporting framework.

Monitoring of controls

The entity's ongoing monitoring activities are designed to detect and correct any   **32** deficiencies in the effectiveness of controls over transactions for financial instruments and their valuation. It is important that there is adequate supervision and review of financial instrument activity within the entity. This includes:

(a)   All controls being subject to review, for example, the monitoring of operational statistics such as the number of reconciling items or the difference between internal pricing and external pricing sources;

(b)   The need for robust information technology (IT) controls and monitoring and validating their application; and

(c)   The need to ensure that information resulting from different processes and systems is adequately reconciled. For example, there is little benefit in a valuation process if the output from it is not reconciled properly into the general ledger.

In larger entities, sophisticated computer information systems generally keep track   **33** of financial instrument activities, and are designed to ensure that settlements occur when due. More complex computer systems may generate automatic postings to clearing accounts to monitor cash movements, and controls over processing are put in place with the objective of ensuring that financial instrument activities are correctly reflected in the entity's records. Computer systems may be designed to produce exception reports to alert management to situations where financial instruments have not been used within authorized limits or where transactions undertaken were not within the limits established for the chosen counterparties. However, even a sophisticated computer system may not ensure the completeness of the recording of financial instrument transactions. Accordingly, management frequently puts additional procedures in place to increase the likelihood that all transactions will be recorded.

Part Six

Bulletins

Bulletin 2006/5 The combined code on corporate governance: requirements of auditors under the Listing Rules of the Financial Services Authority and the Irish Stock Exchange

(September 2006)

Contents

	Paragraphs
Introduction	1 - 4
Requirements of the Listing Rules relating to corporate governance matters	
Requirement for companies to "comply or explain"	5 - 10
The auditor's review of the statement of compliance	11 - 13
Combined Code provisions that the auditor is required to Review	14
General procedures	15 - 17
Non-compliance with provisions of the Combined Code	18 - 20
Auditor's association with company's corporate governance disclosures	21 - 22
Specific procedures	
Responsibilities of the directors and the auditor	23 - 29
Internal control	30 - 55
An audit committee of independent non-executive directors	56 - 59
Role and responsibilities of the audit committee	60
Terms of reference of the audit committee	61
Arrangements by which company's staff may raise concerns	62
Monitoring and review of the effectiveness of the internal audit activities	63
Appointment, reappointment and removal of the external auditor	64
Non-audit activities	65 - 67
Directors' statement on going concern	
Auditor's review of compliance	68 - 72
Reporting requirements derived from other auditing standards	73
Appendix 1 – Extracts from the FSA Listing Rules	
Appendix 2 – Equivalent Irish Stock Exchange Listing Rules	
Appendix 3 – Example terms of engagement paragraphs	

Bulletin 2003/5 The combined code on corporate governance: requirements of auditors under the Listing Rules of the Financial Services Authority and the Irish Stock Exchange

(September 2003)

Contents

	Paragraph
Introduction	
Requirements of the Listing Rules relating to corporate governance matters	
Requirements on companies to report on compliance	5–10
The auditor's review of the statement of compliance	11–13
Combined Code provisions that the auditor is required to review	14
General procedure	15–17
The compliance with provisions of the Code itself	18
Auditor's assessment where appropriate, disclosure and disclosure	19–23
Specific procedures	
Responsibilities of the directors of listed companies	24
Internal control	25–33
The audit committee or the directors' compliance statement	34–59
Terms and conditions of the audit committee	60
Scope of work of the audit committee	61
Arrangements by which employees may raise any concerns	62
Monitoring of review of the effectiveness of internal audit function	63–65
Appointment, reappointment and removal of the external auditors	66
Audit fees	67
Directors' statement on going concern	68
Auditor's review of going concern	
Reporting requirements derived from other auditing standards	69
Appendix 1 Extract from the FSA Listing Rules	
Appendix 2 Extract from the Irish Stock Exchange Listing Rules	
Appendix 3 Example terms of engagement paragraphs	

Introduction

This Bulletin provides guidance for auditors when reviewing a company's   **1**
statement made in relation to "The Combined Code on Corporate Governance"
("Combined Code") in accordance with Listing Rule ("LR") 9.8.10R of the
Financial Services Authority ("FSA") or LR 6.8.9 of the Irish Stock Exchange
("ISE"). It replaces the guidance in:

- APB Bulletin 2004/3, "The Combined Code on Corporate Governance:
  Requirements of Auditors under the Listing Rules of the Financial Services
  Authority" published in November 2004; and

- APB Bulletin 2004/4 "The Combined Code on Corporate Governance:
  Requirements of Auditors under the Listing Rules of the Irish Stock
  Exchange" published in December 2004.

This Bulletin reflects the following: **2**

(a)   The issuance of "Internal Control: Revised Guidance for Directors on the
      Combined Code" ("Turnbull Guidance") by the Financial Reporting
      Council in October 2005. The Turnbull Review Group made only a small
      number of changes to the Turnbull Guidance as first issued in 1999. One of
      these changes is that the board's statement on internal control should
      confirm that necessary actions have been, or are being, taken to remedy
      any significant failings or weaknesses identified from its review of the
      effectiveness of the system of internal control. This development is set out in
      paragraph 36 of the revised Turnbull Guidance and is discussed in
      paragraphs 40 to 44 in this Bulletin.

(b)   The issuance of revised Listing Rules in July 2005. Although there has been
      no change to the substance of the requirements of the Listing Rules in this
      regard the text of the rules differs from the previous rules.

This Bulletin provides guidance for auditors of both: **3**

(a)   companies listed on the Official List maintained by the FSA that are
      incorporated in the United Kingdom; and

(b)   companies listed on the Official List maintained by the ISE that are
      incorporated in Ireland.

The text of the applicable revised Listing Rules issued by the FSA is set out in
Appendix 1. Appendix 2 sets out the references to the equivalent Listing Rules of
the ISE. In the remainder of this Bulletin reference is made to the "Listing Rules"
and footnotes provide the specific references to the Listing Rules issued by the
FSA and the ISE.

This Bulletin does not address the report to shareholders on executive directors'   **4**
remuneration that is required by the Listing Rules[1].

---

[1]   *FSA LR 9.8.6R(7) and LR 9.8.8R; ISE LR 6.8.6(8) and LR 6.8.8.*

Requirements of the Listing Rules relating to corporate governance matters

Requirement for companies to "comply or explain"

5   The FSA Listing Rules require listed companies[2] that are incorporated in the United Kingdom to include in their annual report and accounts a two-part disclosure statement in relation to the Combined Code. The Listing Rules of the ISE have a similar requirement with respect to listed companies that are incorporated in the Republic of Ireland. The first part of the disclosure statement is to explain how the company has applied the principles set out in Section 1 of the Combined Code, in a manner that would enable shareholders to evaluate how the principles have been applied[3].

6   The second part of the disclosure statement requires the company to either[4]:

(a)   Comply – include *"a statement as to whether the listed company has complied throughout the accounting period with all relevant provisions set out in Section 1 of the Combined Code"*; or

(b)   Explain – include *"a statement as to whether the listed company has not complied throughout the accounting period with all relevant provisions set out in Section 1 of the Combined Code and if so, setting out:*

(i)   *those provisions, if any, it has not complied with;*

(ii)   *in the case of provisions whose requirements are of a continuing nature, the period within which, if any, it did not comply with some or all of those provisions; and*

(iii)   *the company's reasons for non-compliance."*

7   It is expected that listed companies will comply with the provisions of the Combined Code most of the time. However, it is recognised that departures from the provisions of the Code may be justified in particular circumstances. The auditor has no responsibility to review or otherwise assess and comment upon a company's decision to depart from the provisions of the Code. It is for shareholders and others to evaluate any such departure and the company's explanation for it.

8   The Listing Rules[5] requires an overseas company with a primary listing to disclose in its annual report and accounts certain matters relating to its corporate governance. There are no requirements relating to auditors in respect of these Listing Rules.

Review of the company's disclosure statement by the auditor

9   The Listing Rules[6] require that *"A listed company must ensure that the auditors review the parts of the statement that relate to the following provisions of the*

---

[2] *A listed company is defined by the FSA and the Irish Stock Exchange as "a company that has any class of its securities listed".*

[3] *FSA LR 9.8.6R(5); ISE LR 6.8.6(6)*

[4] *FSA LR 9.8.6R(6); ISE LR 6.8.6(7)*

[5] *FSA LR 9.8.7R; ISE LR 6.8.7*

[6] *FSA LR 9.8.10R(2); ISE LR 6.8.9(2)*

Combined Code C1.1, C2.1, and C3.1 to C3.7." They require the auditor to review nine of the ten objectively verifiable Combined Code provisions relating to accountability and audit.

The tenth accountability and audit Combined Code provision (C.1.2 on going   **10** concern) is addressed by different Listing Rules[7]. These Listing Rules require the directors to make a statement that the business is a going concern, together with supporting assumptions or qualifications as necessary. This statement is required to be included in the annual report and accounts and to be reviewed by the auditor before publication.

The auditor's review of the statement of compliance

The scope of the auditor's review required by the Listing Rules[8], in comparison to   **11** the totality of the Combined Code, is narrow. The auditor is not required to review the directors' narrative statement of how they have applied the Code principles and is required only to review the directors' compliance statement in relation to nine of the forty-eight Code provisions applicable to companies. Nevertheless, because the directors' narrative statement comprises other information included in a document containing audited financial statements there is a broader requirement under Auditing Standards[9] for the auditor to read such "other information" and if the auditor becomes aware of any apparent misstatements therein, or identifies any material inconsistencies with the audited financial statements, to seek to resolve them.

The Listing Rules are silent as to whether the auditor should report on the auditor's   **12** review of the directors' compliance statement and whether any such report should be published or referred to in the annual report. The APB is of the view that if the auditor's report itself contains a description of the auditor's responsibilities (including the auditor's responsibilities under the Listing Rules), as discussed in paragraphs 24 to 29, there is no necessity for a separate auditor's report dealing with the auditor's review of corporate governance matters.

Because of the limited nature of the auditor's review and in order to avoid the   **13** possibility of misunderstandings arising the APB recommends that:

(a)   the auditor's engagement letter explains the scope of the auditor's review. Example paragraphs are set out in Appendix 3; and

(b)   prior to the release of the annual report and accounts the auditor communicates, and discusses, with those charged with governance the factual findings of the auditor's review.

---

[7] *FSA LR 9.8.6R(3) and LR 9.8.10R(1); ISE LR 6.8.6(3) and LR 6.8.9(1)*

[8] *FSA LR 9.8.10R; ISE LR 6.8.9*

[9] *ISA (UK and Ireland) 720 (Revised) Section A, Other information in documents containing audited financial statements.*

Combined Code provisions that the auditor is required to review

14 The provisions of the Combined Code that the auditor is required to review are set out below, together with a reference to the specific procedures recommended by the APB:

Provision	Detailed recommendation	Specific procedures
C.1.1	The directors should explain in the annual report their responsibility for preparing the accounts and there should be a statement by the auditors about their reporting responsibilities.	23-29
C.2.1	The board should, at least annually, conduct a review of the effectiveness of the group's system of internal controls and should report to shareholders that they have done so. The review should cover all material controls, including financial, operational and compliance controls and risk management systems.	30-55
C.3.1	The board should establish an audit committee of at least three, or in the case of smaller companies[10] two, members, who should all be independent non-executive directors. The board should satisfy itself that at least one member of the audit committee has recent and relevant financial experience.	56-59
C.3.2	The main role and responsibilities of the audit committee should be set out in written terms of reference and should include: • to monitor the integrity of the financial statements of the company, and any formal announcements relating to the company's financial performance, reviewing significant financial reporting judgements contained in them; • to review the company's internal financial controls and, unless expressly addressed by a separate board risk committee composed of independent directors, or by the board itself, to review the company's internal control and risk management systems; • to monitor and review the effectiveness of the company's internal audit function; • to make recommendations to the board, for it to put to the shareholders for their approval in general meeting, in relation to the appointment, re-appointment and removal of the external auditor and to approve the remuneration and terms of engagement of the external auditor; • to review and monitor the external auditor's independence and objectivity and the effectiveness of the audit process, taking into consideration relevant UK professional and regulatory requirements;	60

---

[10] *In the UK, a smaller company is one that is below the FTSE 350 throughout the year immediately prior to the reporting year. The Irish Stock Exchange considers a smaller company to be one that included in the ISEQ Small Cap Index throughout the year immediately prior to the reporting year..*

	• to develop and implement policy on the engagement of the external auditor to supply non-audit services, taking into account relevant ethical guidance regarding the provision of non-audit services by the external audit firm; and to report to the board, identifying any matters in respect of which it considers that action or improvement is needed and making recommendations as to the steps to be taken.	
C.3.3	The terms of reference of the audit committee, including its role and the authority delegated to it by the board, should be made available. A separate section of the annual report should describe the work of the committee in discharging those responsibilities.	61
C.3.4	The audit committee should review arrangements by which staff of the company may, in confidence, raise concerns about possible improprieties in matters of financial reporting or other matters. The audit committee's objective should be to ensure that arrangements are in place for the proportionate and independent investigation of such matters and for appropriate follow-up action.	62
C.3.5	The audit committee should monitor and review the effectiveness of the internal audit activities. Where there is no internal audit function, the audit committee should consider annually whether there is a need for an internal audit function and make a recommendation to the board, and the reasons for the absence of such a function should be explained in the relevant section of the annual report.	63
C.3.6	The audit committee should have primary responsibility for making a recommendation on the appointment, reappointment and removal of the external auditors. If the board does not accept the audit committee's recommendation, it should include in the annual report, and in any papers recommending appointment or reappointment, a statement from the audit committee explaining the recommendation and should set out reasons why the board has taken a different position.	64
C.3.7	The annual report should explain to shareholders how, if the auditor provides non-audit services, auditor objectivity and independence is safeguarded.	65-67

General procedures

Paragraphs 16 to 22 set out general procedures relating to the auditor's review of the statement of compliance. These general procedures are applicable to all of the nine provisions of the Combined Code that the auditor is required to review.   **15**

In relation to all elements of the corporate governance disclosures relating to the provisions of the Combined Code that are within the scope of the auditor's review, the auditor obtains appropriate evidence to support the compliance statement made by the company. The type of procedures usually performed include: **16**

(a)   reviewing the minutes of the meetings of the board of directors, and of relevant board committees;

(b)   reviewing supporting documents prepared for the board of directors or board committees that are relevant to those matters specified for review by the auditor;

(c)   making enquiries of certain directors (such as the chairman of the board of directors and the chairmen of relevant board committees) and the company secretary to satisfy themselves on matters relevant to those provisions of the Combined Code specified for review by the auditor; and

(d)   attending meetings of the audit committee (or the full board if there is no audit committee) at which the annual report and accounts, including the statement of compliance, are considered and approved for submission to the board of directors.

17   The auditor may request the directors to provide written confirmation of oral representations made during the course of the review.

Non-compliance with provisions of the Combined Code

18   Where the auditor becomes aware of any provision of the Combined Code that is within the scope of the auditor's review and with which the company has not complied, the auditor establishes that the departure is described in the directors' statement of compliance. However, the auditor is not required to, and does not, perform additional procedures to investigate the appropriateness of reasons given for non-compliance with the provision.

19   Where there is a departure from a provision specified for the auditor's review but there is proper disclosure of this fact and of the reasons for the departure, as envisaged by the Listing Rules[11], the auditor does not refer to this in its report on the financial statements.

20   However, where the auditor considers that there is not proper disclosure of a departure from a provision of the Combined Code specified for the auditor's review the auditor reports this in the auditor's report on the financial statements. Paragraph 55 describes the way in which such a matter (which does not give rise to a qualified opinion on the financial statements) is reported and provides an example of such an opinion.

Auditor's association with company's corporate governance disclosures

21   The auditor would not wish to be associated with either the statement of compliance or the company's narrative statement of how it has applied the Code principles if the auditor has reason to believe that they may be misleading. The auditor, therefore, reads both of these statements and considers whether any information in either of them is apparently misstated or materially inconsistent with other information of which the auditor has become aware in the course of either the review of the company's compliance statement (insofar as it relates to the nine provisions of the Combined Code that the auditor is required to review under the Listing Rules) or the audit of the financial statements.

22   The auditor is not expected actively to search for misstatements or inconsistencies. However, if the auditor becomes aware of such a matter the auditor discusses it with the directors in order to establish the significance of the lack of proper

---

[11]   *FSA LR 9.8.10R; ISE LR 6.8.9*

disclosure. If such lack of proper disclosure is considered significant by the auditor and the directors cannot be persuaded to amend the disclosure to the auditor's satisfaction, the auditor considers the implications for the auditor's reporting responsibilities and the auditor may need to take legal advice.

Specific procedures

Responsibilities of the directors and the auditor

> **C.1.1 The directors should explain in the annual report their responsibility for preparing the accounts and there should be a statement by the auditors about their reporting responsibilities.**

Directors' responsibilities

While the content of the statement of the directors' responsibilities is determined   **23**
by the directors, the auditor establishes that the directors' responsibility for preparing the accounts is explained in the annual report.

Auditor's responsibilities

The auditor has different responsibilities with respect to the various component   **24**
parts of the annual report. For example, the auditor is required to "audit" the financial statements, "review" the company's compliance with certain aspects of the Combined Code and "read" all information in the annual report that is not subject to any other requirement. The auditor reads such "other information" because the credibility of the financial statements and the related auditor's report may be undermined by material inconsistencies between the financial statements and the "other information", or by apparent misstatements within the other information.

In some instances the auditor has to report positively the results of the work   **25**
whereas in other instances the auditor only has to report by exception. The APB is of the view that users of annual reports will find it difficult to understand the scope of the auditor's involvement in the absence of a clear statement of the auditor's responsibilities towards the whole annual report.

The key elements of a statement of the auditor's responsibilities relate to the   **26**
requirements of:

(a)   statute and Auditing Standards with respect to the audit of the financial statements;

(b)   statute with respect to the auditor's opinion as to whether the information given in the directors report for the financial year for which the financial statements are prepared is consistent with those financial statements;

(c)   statute and the Listing Rules where the auditor is only required to report by exception;

(d)   the Listing Rules for the auditor to review the statement concerning the company's compliance with certain provisions of the Combined Code; and

(e)   Auditing Standards to read the "other information" in the annual report.

27 A description of the auditor's responsibilities may either be included as a separate section of the auditor's report on the financial statements or set out as a separate statement within the annual report. The APB encourages auditors to include a description of the auditor's responsibilities within the auditor's report on the financial statements. Illustrative examples of auditor's reports containing descriptions of the auditor's responsibilities are given in the most recent version of the APB Bulletin *Auditor's Reports on Financial Statements*[12].

28 The content of the statement of the auditor's responsibilities ought to be determined by the auditor regardless of whether it is published as a separate statement, or incorporated into the auditor's report on the financial statements.

29 Appendix 3 to this Bulletin includes illustrative paragraphs that may be included in the auditor's engagement letter to describe the auditor's responsibilities with respect to the company's compliance with the Listing Rules[13]. In practice the auditor tailors the engagement letter to the specific circumstances of the engagement.

Internal control

> **C.2.1 The board should, at least annually, conduct a review of the effectiveness of the group's system of internal controls and should report to shareholders that they have done so. The review should cover all material controls, including financial, operational and compliance controls and risk management systems.**

The auditor's responsibilities with respect to the directors' narrative statement

30 The annual report will contain a narrative statement of how the company has applied Code principle C.2. The Turnbull Guidance recommends that, "In its narrative statement of how the company has applied Code Principle C.2, the board should, as a minimum, disclose that there is an ongoing process for identifying, evaluating and managing the significant risks faced by the company, that it has been in place for the year under review and up to the date of approval of the annual report and accounts, that is regularly reviewed by the board…".[14] The Turnbull Guidance also states that "The annual report and accounts should include such meaningful, high-level information as the board considers necessary to assist shareholders' understanding of the main features of the company's risk management processes and system of internal control, and should not give a misleading impression"[15]. The content of such narrative statements is likely, therefore, to vary widely from company to company.

31 Although the Listing Rules do not require the auditor to review the narrative statement, there are requirements under Auditing Standards for the auditor to read the other information (of which the company's narrative statement forms a part) issued with the audited financial statements and to seek to resolve any apparent misstatements or material inconsistencies with the audited financial statements.

---

[12] *At the date of publication of this Bulletin the most recent version was Bulletin 2005/4*

[13] *FSA LR 9.8.10R; ISE LR 6.8.9*

[14] *Paragraph 34 of the Turnbull Guidance.*

[15] *Paragraph 33 of the Turnbull Guidance*

Auditor's review of compliance

The Turnbull Guidance[16], recommends that the company discloses a summary of **32** the process the board (and where applicable, its committees) has adopted in reviewing the effectiveness of the system of internal control. The Turnbull Guidance[17] describes the directors' process for reviewing effectiveness and in particular states[18]: *"The board should define the process to be adopted for its review of the effectiveness of internal control. This should encompass both the scope and frequency of the reports it receives and reviews during the year, and also the process for its annual assessment, such that it will be provided with sound, appropriately documented, support for its statement on internal control in the company's annual report and accounts".*

The objective of the auditor's review of compliance is to assess whether the **33** company's summary of the process the board (and where applicable its committees) has adopted in reviewing the effectiveness of the system of internal control, is both supported by the documentation prepared by or for the directors and appropriately reflects that process.

To achieve this objective the auditor, in addition to the procedures outlined in **34** paragraph 16;

(a)   obtains an understanding, through enquiry of the directors, of the process defined by the board for its review of the effectiveness of all material internal controls and compares that understanding to the statement made by the board in the annual report and accounts;

(b)   reviews the documentation prepared by or for the directors to support their statement made in connection with Code provision C.2.1 and assesses whether or not it provides sound support for that statement; and

(c)   relates the statement made by the directors to the auditor's knowledge of the company obtained during the audit of the financial statements. As explained in paragraph 36, the scope of the directors' review will be considerably broader in its scope than the knowledge the auditor can be expected to have based on their audit.

The auditor considers whether the directors' statement covers the year under **35** review and the period to the date of approval of the annual report and accounts, as recommended by the Turnbull Guidance[19].

In carrying out the review, the auditor will have regard to the knowledge of the **36** company the auditor has obtained from the audit work. To enable the auditor to perform the audit and express an opinion on the financial statements, the auditor is required by Auditing Standards[20] to obtain an understanding of the entity and its environment, including its internal control, sufficient to identify and assess the risks of material misstatement of the financial statements. Consequently, the auditor's assessment required by Auditing Standards will be considerably narrower in scope than the review performed by the directors for the purpose of reporting on compliance with Code provision C.2.1.

---

[16] *Paragraphs 26-32 and 36 of the Turnbull Guidance.*

[17] *Paragraphs 26-32 of the Turnbull Guidance.*

[18] *Paragraph 27 of the Turnbull Guidance.*

[19] *Paragraph 26 of the Turnbull Guidance.*

[20] *ISA (UK and Ireland) 315, Obtaining an understanding of the entity and its environment and assessing the risks of material misstatement.*

37   The auditor, therefore, is not expected to assess whether all risks and controls have been addressed by the directors or that risks are satisfactorily addressed by internal controls. In order to communicate this fact to users of the annual report, the following sentence is included in the auditor's report on the financial statements.

> "*We are not required to consider whether the board's statements on internal control cover all risks and controls, or form an opinion on the effectiveness of the company's corporate governance procedures or its risk and control procedures.*"

38   However, ISA (UK and Ireland) 260 *Communication of audit matters with those charged with governance* requires, among other things, that the auditor communicates, on a timely basis, to those charged with governance material weaknesses in internal control identified during the audit. A material weakness in internal control is a deficiency in design or operation which could adversely affect the entity's ability to record, process, summarize and report financial and other relevant data so as to result in a material misstatement in the financial statements. A material weakness in control identified by the auditor will be considered by the directors, in the context of the reports they receive and review during the year as part of their overall process for undertaking an annual assessment of the effectiveness of the company's internal control procedures, and it may be considered by them to be a significant failing or weakness as described in the Turnbull Guidance.

39   In view of the obligations placed on directors by the Turnbull Guidance the APB recommends that any material weaknesses in internal control identified by the auditor be reported to those charged with governance as soon as is practicable. The auditor does not wait until the financial statement audit has been completed before reporting such weaknesses. In this way, the directors will be aware of the weaknesses that the auditor has identified and be able to take account of them in making their statements on internal control[21].

Actions taken by the directors to remedy significant failings or weaknesses

40   A revision made to the Turnbull Guidance in October 2005 was to expand the existing recommendation regarding the board's statement on internal control in the annual report in relation to Code provision C2.1. The recommendation was expanded to say that the board should in its statement on internal control, "*confirm that necessary actions have been or are being taken to remedy any significant failings or weaknesses identified from that review*"[22] (The reference to "that review" relates to the board's annual review of the effectiveness of the system of internal control).

41   The auditor's review responsibility with respect to this recommendation includes:

(a)   reviewing the documentation prepared by or for the directors supporting their statement made in connection with Code provision C2.1 that discusses those failings or weaknesses, if any, in internal control that they have

---

[21] *The auditor has a responsibility under ISA (UK and Ireland) 260 to consider whether there is adequate two-way communication between the auditor and those charged with governance, such that an effective audit can take place. As part of this responsibility, amongst other things, the auditor will need to consider the appropriateness and timeliness of actions taken by those charged with governance in response to the recommendations made by the auditor including those regarding material weaknesses in internal control.*

[22] *Paragraph 36 of the Turnbull Guidance*

assessed as "significant" and assessing whether or not it provides sound support for that statement;

(b)   discussing with the directors the actions they have already taken, or consider necessary to take, with respect to the identified significant failings or weaknesses; and

(c)   relating the statement made by the directors to the auditor's knowledge of the company obtained during the audit of the financial statements.

With respect to 41(c) above, the auditor assesses whether the directors, in making their statement, have taken into consideration the material weaknesses in internal control reported to those charged with governance by the auditor in accordance with ISA (UK and Ireland) 260 (See paragraph 38 above). **42**

However, the auditor is not required to assess either the directors' decision as to what constitutes a significant failing or weakness, or whether the actions, taken or to be taken by the directors, will in fact remedy the significant failings or weaknesses identified by the directors. The APB recommends that a statement to this effect be included in the engagement letter (see Appendix 3). **43**

If the auditor: **44**

(a)   considers that the documentation and discussions do not support the directors' confirmation that necessary actions have been, or are being, taken; or

(b)   based on its audit findings is aware of material weaknesses in internal control that have not been considered by the directors

it discusses the position with the directors. If the auditor is not satisfied with the directors' explanations it considers the consequences for its opinion (see paragraph 54).

Internal control aspects of problems disclosed in the annual report

The Turnbull Guidance[23] also recommends that the board discloses *"the process it has applied to deal with material internal control aspects of any significant problems disclosed in the annual report and accounts"*. **45**

This may be a difficult recommendation for directors to satisfy, and for the auditor to review, because what is meant by "significant problems" is not defined and the word "problem" encompasses more than financial matters. A directors' description, for example, of difficulties obtaining raw materials at a remote overseas location may be seen as a significant problem by directors of some companies but not the directors of others. Even when the directors have identified a problem it may not always be clear whether the problem has material internal control aspects. A significant loss-making contract, for example, will necessitate an assessment of whether the problem is attributable to changes in circumstances that could not reasonably have been foreseen as opposed to weaknesses in internal control. **46**

The auditor's review responsibility with respect to this recommendation includes: **47**

(a)   discussing with the directors the steps the directors have taken to determine what "significant problems" are disclosed in the annual report and accounts; and

---

[23] *Paragraph 36 of the Turnbull Guidance.*

(b)   assessing whether disclosures made by the board of the processes it has applied to deal with material internal control aspects of any significant problems disclosed in the annual report and accounts appropriately reflect those processes.

48   The auditor is not required to assess whether the processes described by the directors will, in fact, remedy the problem described in the annual report and accounts.

49   If the auditor is aware of a significant problem that is disclosed in the annual report and accounts for which the board has not disclosed the material internal control aspects it discusses the position with the directors of the company.

50   If the auditor is not able to agree with the directors as to how the matter should be resolved it considers the consequences for its opinion (see paragraph 54).

Failure to conduct a review

51   The Listing Rules[24] require the company to disclose if the board has failed to conduct a review of the effectiveness of internal control. The Turnbull Guidance[25] recommends that where it has not made the required disclosures the board should state that fact and provide an explanation. The auditor considers whether this recommendation is met and whether the explanation is consistent with the auditor's understanding.

Groups of companies

52   The Turnbull Guidance establishes that, for groups of companies, the review of effectiveness should be from the perspective of the group as a whole[26]. Accordingly, the auditor's consideration of the board's description of its process for reviewing the effectiveness of internal control encompasses the group as a whole.

53   Where material joint ventures and associated companies have not been dealt with as part of the group for the purposes of applying the Turnbull Guidance, this fact should be disclosed by the board[27]. The auditor assesses, based on the auditor's knowledge of the group obtained during the audit of the financial statements, whether any material joint ventures or associated companies have not been dealt with and, therefore, if such a disclosure is necessary.

Reporting by exception

54   If the auditor concludes:

(a)   that the board's summary of the process it has applied in reviewing the effectiveness of internal control is either not supported by or does not appropriately reflect the auditor's understanding of the process undertaken (paragraphs 32 to 39);

(b)   that the documentation and discussions do not support the directors' confirmation that necessary actions have been, or are being taken; (paragraphs 40 to 44);

---

[24] *FSA LR 9.8.6R(6)(b); ISE LR 6.8.6(7)(b)*

[25] *Paragraph 37 of the Turnbull Guidance*

[26] *Paragraph 13 of the Turnbull Guidance*

[27] *Paragraph 38 of the Turnbull Guidance*

(c)   that the processes disclosed to deal with material internal control aspects of significant problems disclosed in the annual report and accounts do not appropriately reflect the auditor's understanding of the process undertaken (paragraphs 45 to 50);

(d)   that no disclosure has been made by the board that it has failed to conduct a review of the effectiveness of internal control (paragraph 51);

(e)   where the board discloses that it has not reviewed the effectiveness of internal control, that its explanation is not consistent with the auditor's understanding (paragraph 51); or

(f)   that no disclosure has been made by the board that a material joint venture or associated company has not been dealt with as part of the group (paragraphs 52 to 53),

they report this in their report on the financial statements.

However, as this does not give rise to a qualified audit opinion on the financial   **55** statements the APB recommends that the auditor's comments be included under the heading "Other matter" which would be included in the auditor's report below the auditor's opinion and any emphasis of matter related to the auditor's report on the financial statements as illustrated below:

Opinion

[Standard opinion wording for an auditor's report on group (not including parent company) financial statements of a publicly traded company incorporated in Great Britain[28]]

Emphasis of matter

Where applicable any emphasis of matter paragraph relating to the auditor's report on the financial statements.

Other matter

We have reviewed the board's description of its process for reviewing the effectiveness of internal control set out on page x of the annual report. In our opinion the board's comments concerning ... do not appropriately reflect our understanding of the process undertaken by the board because....

An audit committee of independent non-executive directors

C.3.1 The board should establish an audit committee of at least three, or in the case of smaller companies[29] two, members, who should all be independent non-executive directors. The board should satisfy itself that at least one member of the audit committee has recent and relevant financial experience.

---

[28] *See Example 7 in Bulletin 2005/4*

[29] *In the UK a smaller company is one that is below the FTSE 350 throughout the year immediately prior to the reporting year. The Irish Stock Exchange considers a smaller company to be one that is included in the ISEQ Small Cap Index throughout the year immediately prior to the reporting year.*

Auditor's review of compliance

56   When reviewing the company's compliance with this provision of the Combined Code the APB recommends that the auditor performs the following procedures:

(a)   Checking that the audit committee comprises at least three, or in the case of smaller companies two, members.

(b)   Obtaining an understanding of the process adopted by the board for determining whether:

(i)   the members of the audit committee are all independent non-executive directors (see paragraphs 57 to 58); and

(ii)   at least one member of the audit committee has recent and relevant financial experience (see paragraph 59);

(c)   Reviewing evidence such as minutes and other documentation supporting the board's view that the non-executive directors on the audit committee are independent and, where appropriate, have recent and relevant financial experience.

57   Provision A.3.1 of the Combined Code, requires the board to identify in the annual report each non-executive director it considers to be independent. This provision includes guidance on how independence might be interpreted by listing a number of relationships or circumstances that may indicate that a director is not independent[30]. The Code makes clear, however, that notwithstanding such relationships or circumstances the company is entitled to explain why a director is considered independent.

58   It is not the auditor's responsibility to satisfy itself whether directors are properly described as being "independent" non-executives. Nor does the auditor lay down more precise criteria with respect to the meaning of the term "independent" than those set out in the Combined Code. When reviewing the company's compliance with this provision of the Combined Code the APB recommends that the review procedures be limited to establishing that the audit committee is comprised of non-executive directors who are identified in the annual report as being, in the opinion of the board, independent. However, if the auditor doubts whether the directors are properly described as being "independent" non-executives the auditor communicates those concerns to the audit committee and the board of directors.

59   Similarly, it is not the auditor's responsibility to satisfy itself whether the company is correct in concluding that a particular audit committee member has "recent and relevant financial experience". Nor should the auditor lay down more precise criteria with respect to the meaning of the term "recent and relevant financial experience". When reviewing the company's compliance with this provision of the Combined Code the APB recommends that the review procedures be limited to considering the process adopted by the board for determining that at least one member of the audit committee has "recent and relevant financial experience". However, if the auditor doubts whether the company is correct in concluding that a particular audit committee member has "recent and relevant financial experience"

---

[30] *A footnote to A.3.1 explains "A.2.2 states that the chairman should on appointment meet the independence criteria set out in this provision, but thereafter the test of independence is not appropriate in relation to the chairman".*

the auditor communicates those concerns to the audit committee and the board of directors.[31]

Role and responsibilities of the audit committee[32]

> **C.3.2** **The main role and responsibilities of the audit committee should be set out in written terms of reference and should include:**
>
> - **to monitor the integrity of the financial statements of the company, and any formal announcements relating to the company's financial performance, reviewing significant financial reporting judgements contained in them;**
>
> - **to review the company's internal financial controls and, unless expressly addressed by a separate board risk committee composed of independent directors, or by the board itself, to review the company's internal control and risk management systems;**
>
> - **to monitor and review the effectiveness of the company's internal audit function;**
>
> - **to make recommendations to the board, for it to put to the shareholders for their approval in general meeting, in relation to the appointment, re-appointment and removal of the external auditor and to approve the remuneration and terms of engagement of the external auditor;**
>
> - **to review and monitor the external auditor's independence and objectivity and the effectiveness of the audit process, taking into consideration relevant UK professional and regulatory requirements;**
>
> - **to develop and implement policy on the engagement of the external auditor to supply non-audit services, taking into account relevant ethical guidance regarding the provision of non-audit services by the external audit firm; and to report to the board, identifying any matters in respect of which it considers that action or improvement is needed and making recommendations as to the steps to be taken.**

Auditor's review of compliance

When reviewing the company's compliance with this provision of the Combined Code the APB recommends that the auditor obtains a copy of the terms of reference of the audit committee and reviews whether the roles and responsibilities of the audit committee described in the terms of reference reflect the recommendations of Code provision C.3.2. It is not the auditor's responsibility to consider whether the audit committee has fulfilled its roles and responsibilities.

60

---

[31] *The Combined Code recommends that the board should satisfy itself that at least one member of the audit committee has recent and relevant financial experience. Where this is not the case there is a need for an explanation such as the board has concluded that the audit committee "collectively" has recent and relevant financial experience.*

[32] *In Ireland Section 42(2) of the Companies (Auditing and Accounting) Act 2003 requires the board of directors to establish an audit committee and sets out its responsibilities.*

Terms of reference of the audit committee

> **C.3.3** **The terms of reference of the audit committee, including its role and the authority delegated to it by the board, should be made available[23]. A separate section of the annual report should describe the work of the committee in discharging those responsibilities.**

Auditor's review of compliance

61 When reviewing the company's compliance with this provision of the Combined Code the APB recommends that the auditor performs the following procedures:

(a) Reviewing whether the terms of reference of the audit committee are included on the company's website or that the terms of reference have been reasonably made available or communicated by another method;

(b) Reviewing whether a description of the work performed by the audit committee in discharging its responsibilities, is included in a separate section of the annual report, and is not materially inconsistent with the information that the auditor has obtained in the course of the audit work on the financial statements.

Arrangements by which company's staff may raise concerns

> **C.3.4** **The audit committee should review arrangements by which staff of the company may, in confidence, raise concerns about possible improprieties in matters of financial reporting or other matters. The audit committee's objective should be to ensure that arrangements are in place for the proportionate and independent investigation of such matters and for appropriate follow-up action.**

Auditor's review of compliance

62 When reviewing the company's compliance with this provision of the Combined Code the APB recommends that the auditor performs the following procedures:

(a) Reviewing supporting documentation to determine whether there is evidence that the audit committee has reviewed the arrangements and, if necessary, discussing with members of the audit committee what review procedures they performed;

(b) Reviewing documentation supporting the company's arrangements for the proportionate and independent investigation of concerns raised in confidence by staff relating to possible improprieties in matters of financial reporting or other matters and for appropriate follow-up action. It is not the responsibility of the auditor to consider whether such arrangements will facilitate "proportionate and independent" investigation or "appropriate" follow-up action but the auditor reviews the process by which the audit committee satisfies itself that the recommendation of the Combined Code has been satisfied.

Monitoring and review of the effectiveness of the internal audit activities

> **C.3.5 The audit committee should monitor and review the effectiveness of the internal audit activities. Where there is no internal audit function, the audit committee should consider annually whether there is a need for an internal audit function and make a recommendation to the board, and the reasons for the absence of such a function should be explained in the relevant section of the annual report.**

Auditor's review of compliance

When reviewing the company's compliance with this provision of the Combined **63** Code the APB recommends that the auditor performs the following procedures:

(a) Where there is an internal audit function discussing with the audit committee chairman and reviewing the supporting documentation to establish that the audit committee has monitored and reviewed the effectiveness of the internal audit activities. It is not the auditor's responsibility to consider whether the internal audit activities are effective.

(b) Where there is no internal audit function, reviewing whether:

  (i) the audit committee has considered whether there is a need for an internal audit function;

  (ii) there is documentation that evidences the audit committee's recommendation to the board;

  (iii) the reasons for the absence of such a function are explained in the relevant section of the annual report. It is not the auditor's responsibility to consider whether the reasons given are appropriate.

Appointment, reappointment and removal of the external auditor

> **C.3.6 The audit committee should have primary responsibility for making a recommendation on the appointment, reappointment and removal of the external auditors. If the board does not accept the audit committee's recommendation, it should include in the annual report, and in any papers recommending appointment or re-appointment, a statement from the audit committee explaining the recommendation and should set out reasons why the board has taken a different position.**

Auditor's review of compliance

When reviewing the company's compliance with this provision of the Combined **64** Code the APB recommends that the auditor performs the following procedures:

(a) Reviewing documentation, for example inclusion in the terms of reference of the audit committee, which explains that the audit committee has primary responsibility for making a recommendation on the appointment, reappointment and removal of the external auditors.

(b)   Reviewing documentation that evidences the audit committee's recommendation to the board.

(c)   Where the board has not accepted the audit committee's recommendation, reviewing whether there is included in the annual report and in any papers recommending appointment or re-appointment of the auditors:

   (i)   a statement from the audit committee explaining its recommendation; and

   (ii) a statement from the board setting out reasons why the board has taken a different position from that recommended by the audit committee.

Non-audit activities

> **C.3.7 The annual report should explain to shareholders how, if the auditor provides non-audit services, auditor objectivity and independence is safeguarded.**

Auditor's review of compliance

65   When reviewing the company's compliance with this provision of the Combined Code the APB recommends that the auditor establishes whether the annual report includes a statement explaining to shareholders how, if the auditor provides non-audit services, auditor objectivity and independence is safeguarded.

66   The auditor considers the explanation of how auditor objectivity and independence is safeguarded in the context of the information of which they are aware. While it is not the auditor's responsibility to establish that the audit committee has fulfilled its responsibilities as set out in the terms of reference recommended by the Combined Code (to review and monitor the independence and objectivity of the external auditor and to develop and implement policy on the engagement of the external auditor to supply non-audit services taking into account relevant ethical guidance regarding the provision of non-audit services by the external auditor[24]) the auditor will be aware of whether the audit committee has undertaken these responsibilities and:

(a)   notifies the audit committee and the board of directors if they believe these responsibilities have not been undertaken; and

(b)   considers the requirements of Auditing Standards in relation to other information issued with audited financial statements if they believe the explanation is misleading.

67   APB Ethical Standards ("ESs") 1 to 5 set out the integrity, objectivity and independence requirements for auditors in the audit of financial statements. ES 1[33] requires the audit engagement partner to ensure that those charged with governance of the audit client are appropriately informed on a timely basis of all significant facts and matters that bear upon the auditors "objectivity and independence". In relation to non-audit services, ES 5[34] requires the audit engagement partner to ensure that those charged with governance are informed of any inconsistencies between APB Ethical Standards and the company's policy

---

[33] *Paragraph 49*

[34] *Paragraph 35*

for the supply of non-audit services by the audit firm and any apparent breach of that policy.

Directors' statement on going concern

C.1.3 **The directors should include in the annual report an explanation of the basis on which the company generates or preserves value over the longer term (the business model) and the strategy for delivering the objectives of the company.**

Auditor's review of compliance

The Listing Rules[35] require the directors of certain listed companies[36] to include in the annual report and accounts a statement that: **68**

> *"the business is a going concern, together with supporting assumptions or qualification as necessary, that has been prepared in accordance with "Going Concern and Financial Reporting: Guidance for directors of listed companies registered in the United Kingdom, published in November 1994*[37]*"."*

The Listing Rules[38] require a listed company to ensure that the auditor reviews the   **69** directors' going concern statement. In order for the auditor to meet the review requirements of this rule the auditor:

(a)   assesses the consistency of the directors' going concern statement with the knowledge obtained in the course of the audit of the financial statements. This knowledge will primarily have been obtained in meeting Auditing Standards[39] relating to going concern; and

(b)   assesses whether the directors' statement meets the disclosure requirements of the guidance for directors referred to in the Listing Rules[40]. Illustrative suggested disclosures for directors are set out in paragraphs 47 to 54 of that guidance.

The auditor does not assess or report on whether the directors have complied with   **70** any other detailed requirements of the guidance for directors. In particular, as the auditor does not express an opinion on the ability of the company to continue in operational existence they do not undertake additional procedures that would support such an opinion.

Paragraph 49 of the guidance for directors (dealing with going concern) provides   **71** the following illustrative example of the basic disclosure that directors make when the going concern presumption is appropriate:

---

[35] *FSA LR 9.8.6R(3); ISE LR 6.8.6R(3)*

[36] *In the case of the FSA the Listing Rule applies to companies incorporated in the United Kingdom and in the case of the ISE the Listing Rule applies to companies incorporated in the Republic of Ireland.*

[37] *Going Concern and Financial Reporting: Guidance for directors of listed companies registered in the UK, ICAEW, November 1994. This guidance can be downloaded from the ICAEW web-site.*

[38] *FSA LR 9.8.10R(1); ISE LR 6.8.9(1)*

[39] *ISA (UK and Ireland) 570, The going concern basis in financial statements.*

[40] *FSA 9.8.6R(3); ISE LR 6.8.6(3)*

"*After making enquiries, the directors have a reasonable expectation that the company has adequate resources to continue in operational existence for the foreseeable future. For this reason, they continue to adopt the going concern basis in preparing the accounts.*"

72   It is particularly important that the directors' statement on going concern is not inconsistent with any disclosures regarding going concern in either the financial statements or the auditor's report thereon. Where going concern matters are discussed in the financial statements one method of achieving consistency is for the directors' statement to include a cross reference to the relevant note to the financial statements.

Reporting requirements derived from other auditing standards

73   Auditing Standards set out the auditor's responsibilities in relation to other information in documents containing audited financial statements. These responsibilities extend to the Combined Code disclosures where there is either a material misstatement of fact or a material inconsistency with the audited financial statements. Application of these Standards requires that:

(a)   Where the auditor identifies a material inconsistency between the audited financial statements and the Combined Code disclosures the auditor determines whether the audited financial statements or the Combined Code disclosures need to be amended and seeks to resolve the matter through discussion with those charged with governance:

   (i)   If an amendment is necessary in the audited financial statements and the entity refuses to make the amendment, the auditor expresses a qualified or adverse opinion on the financial statements.

   (ii)   If an amendment is necessary in the Combined Code disclosures and the entity refuses to make the amendment, the auditor considers including in the auditor's report an emphasis of matter paragraph describing the material inconsistency[41] or taking other actions.

(b)   Where the auditor identifies a material misstatement of fact in the Combined Code disclosures the auditor discusses the matter with those charged with governance. Where, after discussion, the auditor still considers that there is an apparent misstatement of fact, the auditor requests those charged with governance to consult with a qualified third party, such as the entity's legal counsel, and considers the advice received.

If the auditor concludes that an amendment is necessary in the Combined Code disclosures, which the entity refuses to correct, the auditor considers taking further appropriate action and considers including in the auditor's report an emphasis of matter paragraph describing the material misstatement.

---

[41] *As explained in paragraph 55, the APB recommends that the auditor's comments be included under the heading "other matter" which would be included in the auditor's report below the auditor's opinion.*

Appendix 1 – Extracts from the FSA Listing Rules[42]

Additional information

LR 9.8.6R

In the case of a *listed company* incorporated in the *United Kingdom*, the following additional items must be included in its annual report and accounts:

(3)   a statement made by the *directors* that the business is a going concern, together with supporting assumptions or qualifications as necessary, that has been prepared in accordance with "Going Concern and Financial Reporting: Guidance for Directors of listed companies registered in the United Kingdom", published in November 1994;

(5)   a statement of how the *listed company* has applied the principles set out in Section 1 of the *Combined Code*, in a manner that would enable shareholders to evaluate how the principles have been applied;

(6)   a statement as to whether the *listed company* has;
    (a)   complied throughout the accounting period with all relevant provisions set out in Section 1 of the *Combined Code*; or
    (b)   not complied throughout the accounting period with all relevant provisions set out in Section 1 of the *Combined Code* and if so, setting out:
        i.   those provisions, if any, it has not complied with;
        ii.   in the case of provisions whose requirements are of a continuing nature, the period within which, if any, it did not comply with some or all of those provisions; and
        iii.   the *company's* reasons for non-compliance; …

LR 9.8.7R

An *overseas company* with a *primary listing* must disclose in its annual report and accounts:

(1)   whether or not it complies with the corporate governance regime of its country or incorporation;
(2)   the significant ways in which its actual corporate governance practices differ from those set out in the *Combined Code*; and
(3)   the unexpired term of the service contract of any *director* proposed for election or re-election at the forthcoming annual general meeting and, if any *director* for election or re-election does not have a service contract, a statement to that effect.

Auditors report

LR 9.8.10R

A *listed company* must ensure that the auditors review each of the following before the annual report is published:

(1)   LR 9.8.6R (3) (statement by the directors that the business is a going concern); and
(2)   the parts of the statement required by LR9.8.6R (6) (corporate governance) that relate to the following provisions of the *Combined Code*:
    a.   C1.1;
    b.   C.2.1; and
    c.   C3.1 to C3.7

---

[42] *See Appendix 2 for references to equivalent Irish Stock Exchange Listing Rules*

Appendix 2 – Equivalent Irish Stock Exchange Listing Rules

FSA Listing Rule	Equivalent Listing Rule of the Irish Stock Exchange
LR 9.8.6R	LR 6.8.6
LR 9.8.6R (3)	LR 6.8.6 (3)
LR 9.8.6R (5)	LR 6.8.6 (6)
LR 9.8.6R (6)	LR 6.8.6 (7)
LR 9.8.6R (7)	LR 6.8.6 (8)
LR 9.8.7R	LR 6.8.7
LR 9.8.8R	LR 6.8.8
LR 9.8.10R	LR 6.8.9
LR 9.8.10R(1)	LR 6.8.9(1)
LR 9.8.10R(2)	LR 6.8.9(2)

Appendix 3 – Example terms of engagement paragraphs

The following is an illustrative example of paragraphs that may be included in the auditor's engagement letter dealing with the auditor's responsibilities with respect to the company's compliance with FSA LR 9.8.10R or ISE LR 6.8.9. In practice the auditor tailors the engagement letter to the specific circumstances of the engagement.

The auditor may wish to include a statement in its engagement letter limiting the auditor's liability in respect of the engagement to review the directors' corporate governance disclosures. The auditor is recommended to take legal advice concerning the wording of such a statement and how it is communicated.

Review of the company's disclosures relating to corporate governance and going concern.

Responsibilities of directors

As directors of the company you are responsible for ensuring that the company complies with the Listing Rules of the [Financial Services Authority including rules LR 9.8.6R (3), (5) and (6) "Additional information" and LR 9.8.10R "Auditors report"] [Irish Stock Exchange including rules LR 6.8.6 (3), (6) and (7) "Additional information" and LR 6.8.9 "Auditors Report"].

Responsibilities of the auditor

Listing Rule [9.8.10R] [6.8.9] states that 'A listed company must ensure that the auditors review each of the following before the annual report is published:

(1)   [LR9.8.6R (3)] [LR 6.8.6 (3)] (statement by the directors that the business is a going concern); and

(2)   the parts of the statement required by [LR 9.8.6R (6)] [LR 6.8.6(7) (corporate governance) that relate to the following provisions of the Combined Code:

    (a)   C1.1;

    (b)   C2.1; and

    (c)   C3.1 to C3.7.

As we have agreed, we will carry out the review required of us by the Listing Rules having regard to the guidance published in APB Bulletin 2006/5. We are not required to form an opinion on the company's corporate governance procedures.

Having finalised our review we expect to communicate and discuss with you the factual findings of our review.

Scope of review

You will provide us with such information and explanations as we consider necessary. We may request you to provide written confirmation of oral representations which you make to us during the course of our review. We shall request sight of all documents or statements which are due to be issued with either the statement of compliance or the going concern statement and all documentation prepared by or for the board in support of the company's statements.

As we have agreed we will attend the meeting of the audit committee [full board] at which the annual report and accounts, including the going concern statement and the statement of compliance, are considered and approved for submission to the board of directors.

Internal control

With respect to Code Provision C.2.1, our work will be restricted to:

(a)   assessing, based on enquiry of the directors, the supporting documentation prepared by or for the directors and our knowledge obtained during the audit of the financial statements, whether the company's summary of the process the board (and where applicable its committees) has adopted in reviewing the effectiveness of internal control appropriately reflects that process; and

(b)   assessing whether the company's disclosures of the processes it has applied to deal with material internal control aspects of any significant problems disclosed in the annual report and accounts appropriately reflects those processes.

As our work is not designed to:

(a)   consider whether the board's statements on internal control cover all risks and controls; or

(b)   form an opinion on the effectiveness of the company's risk and control procedures; or

(c)   assess either the directors' decision as to what constitutes a significant failing or weakness, or whether the actions, taken or to be taken, will in fact remedy the significant failings or weaknesses identified by the directors,

our work on internal control will not be sufficient to enable us to express any assurance as to whether or not your internal controls are effective. In addition our financial statement audit should not be relied upon to draw to your attention matters that may be relevant to your consideration as to whether or not your system of internal control is effective.

Going concern

With respect to the company's going concern statement our work will be restricted to a consideration of whether the statement provides the disclosures required by [LR 9.8.6R (3)] [LR 6.8.6 (3)] and is not inconsistent with the information of which we are aware from our audit work on the financial statements. We will not carry out the additional work necessary to give an opinion that the company has adequate resources to continue in operational existence.

Statement of auditor's responsibilities

Code provision C.1.1 recommends, among other things, that there should be a statement in the annual report about the auditor's reporting responsibilities. As we have agreed we will incorporate a description of our reporting responsibilities in our audit report on the financial statements.

Bulletin 2008/1 Audit issues when financial market conditions are difficult and credit facilities may be restricted

(January 2008)

Contents

	Paragraphs
Introduction	1 - 5
Risk assessment, quality control and communication with those charged with governance	6 - 7
Going concern	8 - 11
Valuation and disclosure of financial instruments	12 - 18
Disclosure of risk in directors' report	19 - 22
Implications for the auditor's report	23 - 25
Ethical issues	26 - 27
Appendix: Risk factors	

Introduction

1 This Bulletin provides guidance on matters that auditors may need to consider when conducting audits in the economic environment following recent developments in the financial markets commonly termed "the credit crunch".

2 In recent months financial market conditions have been characterised by significant trading difficulties compounded by a reduction in liquidity. Although the primary market shock arose due to defaults on sub-prime mortgages in the United States, the effect has been felt globally due to widespread use of structured securities and leveraged funding. Entities with exposure to the financial markets through debt, equity, derivative and leveraged finance activities may experience significant difficulty in trading in and thus valuing certain investments, with a consequential increase in the risk of material misstatement of financial statements. More generally, entities may find it difficult to finance their operations as a result of restricted credit facilities.

3 While the credit crunch is likely to have a particular effect on the audit of financial institutions such as banks, insurance companies and investment businesses, many entities operating outside the financial services sector could also be affected by current market conditions, especially if those entities are dependent on refinancing their operations over the coming months, or may be at risk of having current facilities withdrawn, or have significant investments that have reduced significantly in value or are difficult to value in the absence of an active market.

4 While this Bulletin may be of assistance to the auditors of financial institutions it has been written to apply more generally and focuses on the risks and uncertainties associated with:

- Reduced liquidity in the financial markets and in particular the reduced availability of finance for those who require it. As financing arrangements expire, replacement may prove expensive or impossible, with potentially serious consequences in relation to the "going concern" assumption; and

- Valuation of investments. For some investments there may be a severe curtailment or cessation of market trading, introducing particular difficulties for valuation measurements. Investment in such financial instruments may not be limited to financial institutions. It is possible that other entities, such as those with developed treasury activities and pension funds, may have invested in financial instruments that are currently experiencing severely curtailed/ceased trading which will make their valuation for balance sheet purposes difficult.

5 This Bulletin draws on existing material within APB's standards and guidance and should be read in conjunction with them. It does not establish any new requirements. Not all of the issues addressed will be relevant to all audits, and there may be other issues that auditors need also to consider that are not addressed in this Bulletin.

Risk assessment, quality control and communication with those charged with governance

6 While the credit crunch is most likely to be relevant to the audit of financial institutions, it may also affect audits of entities operating outside the financial services sector. Auditors, as part of their planning and risk assessment process of all entities, consider whether current market conditions could give rise to the risk

of material misstatement of the financial statements and respond accordingly. The appendix to this Bulletin identifies some factors that may increase the risk of material misstatement in financial statements when financial market conditions are difficult and credit facilities may be restricted.

If the audited entity is at risk of material misstatement of the financial statements **7** due to current market conditions, the audit engagement partner will have particular regard to:

- his/her own involvement in the direction, supervision and performance of the audit when complying with the requirements of ISA (UK and Ireland) 220, paragraph 21;

- the capabilities and competence of the engagement team (especially if the audit involves evaluation of the fair value of financial instruments) when complying with the requirements of ISA (UK and Ireland) 220, paragraph 19;

- consultation with other professionals on difficult and contentious matters when complying with the requirements of ISA (UK and Ireland) 220, paragraph 30; and

- the nature and timing of communications with those charged with governance when complying with the requirements of ISA (UK and Ireland) 260.

Going concern

One impact of the "credit crunch" may be to limit finance available to companies **8** and other entities, with, in extreme cases, potentially serious consequences in relation to the "going concern" assumption. Past experience of obtaining necessary financing cannot be relied on alone to provide sufficient evidence of an entity's ability to obtain financing in the future. Lenders may be more risk averse when considering whether to provide or renew finance facilities and may establish new criteria and/or may increase interest rates.

Against that background, auditors will have regard to ISA (UK and Ireland) 570, **9** which establishes standards and provides guidance on the auditor's responsibility with respect to consideration of the going concern assumption used in the preparation of the financial statements. In particular, the guidance on the auditor's examination of borrowing facilities in paragraphs 21-2 and 21-3 may assist.

- Paragraph 21-2 states: "The auditor might be more likely to decide that it is necessary to obtain confirmations of the existence and terms of bank facilities, and to make an independent assessment of the intentions of the bankers relating thereto, in cases where, for example there is a low margin of financial resources available to the entity"; and

- Paragraph 21-3 states: "The auditor considers whether any inability to obtain sufficient appropriate audit evidence regarding the existence and terms of borrowing facilities and the intentions of the lender relating thereto, and/or the factors giving rise to this inability, need to be:

    - Disclosed in the financial statements in order that they give a true and fair view; and/or

— Referred to in the auditor's report (by way of an explanatory paragraph, or a qualified opinion if the auditor believes that the disclosures in the financial statements are not adequate)."

10 Standards and guidance on explanatory paragraphs (e.g. to highlight a material matter that is disclosed in the financial statements regarding a going concern problem) or qualified opinions (e.g. where there is inadequate disclosure in the financial statements of a going concern problem) in the auditor's report are provided in ISAs (UK and Ireland) 570 and 700.

11 Additional considerations apply to the audit of listed companies. Directors of listed companies are required by the Listing Rules[1] to make a statement in the annual financial report that the business is a going concern, together with supporting assumptions or qualifications as necessary, that has been prepared in accordance with *Going Concern and Financial Reporting: Guidance for directors of listed companies registered in the United Kingdom*, published November 1994[2]. APB Bulletin 2006/5[3] emphasises the importance of ensuring that the directors' statement on going concern is not inconsistent with any disclosures regarding going concern in either the financial statements or the auditor's report thereon.

Valuation and disclosure of financial instruments

12 A second impact of the "credit crunch" may be to impair the value of some investments or, especially when they are required to be measured at "fair value", make their valuation for balance sheet purposes difficult (e.g. when trading in a particular investment has been severely curtailed and current market values are difficult to establish). Against this background, auditors will have regard to ISA (UK and Ireland) 545, which establishes standards and provides guidance on auditing fair value measurements and disclosures contained in financial statements. The use of experts with particular knowledge of the valuation of complex financial instruments may be appropriate and, in such cases, the standards and guidance in ISA (UK and Ireland) 620 will be relevant.

13 When the auditor determines there is a significant risk related to fair value, the auditor should evaluate whether the significant assumptions used by management in measuring fair values, taken individually and as a whole, provide a reasonable basis for the fair value measurements and disclosures (ISA (UK and Ireland) 545, paragraph 39). This evaluation includes consideration of whether these assumptions reflect current market conditions and information.

14 Particular difficulties may arise where there is a severe curtailment or even cessation of market trading in certain investments. For example, in these circumstances, investments that have previously been marked to market may need to be valued using a model. If management has changed the valuation method, the auditor considers whether management can adequately demonstrate that the valuation method to which it has changed provides a more appropriate basis of measurement.

---

[1] *Listing Rule 9.8.6R (3)*

[2] *This guidance was a publication of the Cadbury Committee and can be accessed at http://www.icaew.com/index. cfm?route=117590.*

[3] *Bulletin 2006/5 The Combined Code on Corporate Governance: Requirements of Auditors under the Listing Rules of the Financial Services Authority and the Irish Stock Exchange.*

Auditors also need to evaluate whether the disclosures about fair values made by   **15**
the entity are in accordance with the financial reporting framework (ISA (UK and
Ireland) 545, paragraph 56). In the current environment, it will be important that
disclosures of material risks and uncertainties related to fair value measurements
are appropriate to the entity.

For entities applying International Accounting Standards, IAS 1, *Presentation of*   **16**
Financial Statements, disclosure requirements include:

● The judgments, apart from those involving estimations (see the next bullet),
  that management has made in the process of applying the entity's accounting
  policies and that have the most significant effect on the amounts recognised
  in the financial statements;

● Information about the key assumptions concerning the future, and other key
  sources of estimation uncertainty at the balance sheet date, that have a
  significant risk of causing a material adjustment in the carrying amount of
  assets and liabilities within the next financial year.

In addition, recent developments in accounting standards will affect the extent and   **17**
nature of disclosures relating to some financial instruments for audits of financial
statements for periods commencing on or after 1 January 2007[4]. The disclosures
required are extensive and potentially complex including:

● Qualitative disclosures such as the exposures to risk arising from the
  financial instruments;

● Quantitative disclosures such as summary data about the exposures at the
  reporting date; and

● Market risk information such as a sensitivity analysis for each type of
  market risk to which the entity is exposed at the reporting date, showing how
  profit or loss and equity would have been affected by changes in the relevant
  risk variable that were reasonably possible at that date.

APB Practice Note 19 *The Audit of Banks and Building Societies in the United*   **18**
Kingdom provides guidance, in paragraphs 113 to 125, on auditing the disclosure
of market risk information under IFRS 7 and FRS 29, and whether the risk
measurement method adopted has been applied reasonably[5].

Disclosure of risk in Directors' Report

Section 234ZZB of the Companies Act 1985[6] requires that The Directors' Report   **19**
for all companies (except small companies) to contain a business review that
includes:

(a)   a fair review of the business of the company; and

(b)   a description of the principal risks and uncertainties facing the company.

---

[4] *FRS 29 Financial Instruments: Disclosures and IFRS 7 Financial Instruments: Disclosures contain substantially
the same requirements. Reporting entities applying the Financial Reporting Standard for Smaller Entities (FRSSE)
currently applicable are exempt from FRS 29.*

[5] *The same guidance is in the current Exposure Draft of Practice Note 19(I) Banks in the Republic of Ireland
(paragraphs 101 to 113).*

[6] *The requirements of Section 234ZZB have been carried over to section 417 of the Companies Act 2006. Section
417 has some additional requirements for quoted companies and relief when disclosures could be seriously
prejudicial to the interests of the company or certain persons.*

The review is required to be a balanced and comprehensive analysis of the development and performance of the business of the company during the financial year, and the position of the company at the end of that year, consistent with the size and complexity of the business.

20   It is likely that companies affected by the credit crunch will decide to make some reference to the risks and uncertainties facing the company in the business review, such as those relating to the availability of financing and the valuation of financial instruments where relevant. ISA (UK and Ireland) 720, which establishes standards and provides guidance on the auditor's consideration of other information in documents containing audited financial statements, will be particularly relevant in these circumstances.

21   ISA (UK and Ireland) 720 has two sections. Section A applies to all other information in documents containing audited financial statements. Section B contains additional standards and guidance in relation to the auditor's statutory reporting responsibility in relation to Directors' Reports.

22   In the UK and the Republic of Ireland, legislation requires the auditor of a company to state in the auditor's report whether, in the auditor's opinion, the information given in the Directors' Report is consistent with the financial statements. Omission of information from the Directors' Report is not classed as an "inconsistency" in ISA (UK and Ireland) 720 but Section B, paragraph 4, states "The auditor is not required to verify, or report on, the completeness of the information in the directors' report. If, however, the auditor becomes aware that information that is required by law or regulations to be in the directors' report has been omitted the auditor communicates the matter to those charged with governance".

Implications for the auditor's report

23   If the financial statements include a note that discusses a material matter regarding a going concern problem, the auditor is required to highlight that matter by adding an emphasis of matter paragraph to the auditor's report (ISA (UK and Ireland) 700, paragraph 31). If there is a significant uncertainty[7] (other than a going concern problem) disclosed in the financial statement, the resolution of which is dependent upon future events and which may affect the financial statements, the auditor is required to consider adding an emphasis of matter paragraph to highlight that uncertainty (ISA (UK and Ireland) 700, paragraph 32). Significant uncertainties relating to the valuation of financial instruments may be matters that exist and give rise to such an emphasis of matter.

24   In determining whether an uncertainty is significant, the auditor considers:

(a)   the risk that the estimate included in financial statements may be subject to change;

(b)   the range of possible outcomes; and

(c)   the consequences of those outcomes on the view shown in the financial statements.

25   The inclusion of an emphasis of matter paragraph in the auditor's report does not affect the auditor's opinion and is not a substitute for either:

---

[7] *An uncertainty is a matter whose outcome depends upon future actions or events not under the direct control of the entity but that may affect the financial statements.*

(a) a qualified opinion or an adverse opinion, or disclaiming an opinion, when required by the circumstances of a specific audit engagement; or

(b) disclosures in the financial statements that are required by the applicable financial reporting framework.

Ethical issues

The APB's Ethical Standards (ESs) are based on a "threats and safeguards 26 approach" whereby auditors identify and assess the circumstances, which could adversely affect the auditors' objectivity ("threats"), including any perceived loss of independence, and apply procedures ("safeguards"), which will either eliminate the threat or reduce it to an acceptable level, that is a level at which it is not probable that a reasonable and informed third party would conclude that the auditors' objectivity is impaired or is likely to be impaired.

In the current circumstances, where financial market conditions are difficult and 27 credit facilities may be restricted, auditors need to be alert to the possibility of a "management threat" arising that might jeopardise their objectivity and independence. There is a danger that, if asked to provide advice or assistance that could result in them undertaking work that involves making judgments and taking decisions which are the responsibility of the entity's management, the audit firm may become closely aligned with the views and interests of management and the auditor's objectivity and independence may be impaired, or may be perceived to be, impaired (ES 1, paragraph 28[8]).

---

[8] *In October 2007 the APB issued a draft of revised Ethical Standards for Auditors. The intention is that the revised standards will apply to audits for accounting periods commencing on or after 6 April 2008. These include the proposal, to meet the requirements of the Statutory Audit Directive, to add a specific requirement in ES 1 for the audit firm to establish policies and procedures to require partners and employees of the firm to take no decisions taking that is that are the responsibility of management of the audited entity.*

Appendix

Risk Factors

This appendix identifies some factors that may increase the risk of material misstatement in financial statements, especially when financial market conditions are difficult and credit facilities may be restricted. There are many ways in which the current market conditions could impact the financial statements of an entity and its ability to continue as a going concern and other risk factors may exist in the particular circumstances of each entity.

These risk factors may also be relevant in connection with an auditor's review of interim financial information in accordance with ISRE (UK and Ireland) 2410.

Going concern

- Obtaining external financing:
    - Entity has experienced difficulties in the past in obtaining external finance facilities and/or complying with the related terms and covenants;
    - Finance facilities are due for renewal in the next year but have not yet been agreed;
    - Management have no plans for alternative arrangements should current facilities not be extended;
    - Borrowing agreements or executory contracts include clauses relating to debt covenants or subjective clauses (e.g. a "material adverse change clause") that may trigger repayment;
    - Entity has breached some of the terms or covenants giving rise to the risk that the facilities may be withdrawn or not renewed;
    - Terms or covenants of renewed financing are changed and more difficult to comply with (e.g. increased interest rates or charges);
    - Finance facility is secured on assets (e.g. properties) that have decreased in value below the amount of the facility;
    - For financial institutions, reduced deposits from retail customers or reduced availability of funding from wholesale financial markets.
- Management plans to overcome financing difficulties include disposal of assets:
    - Plans developed prior to current market conditions have not been updated;
    - Lack of evidence that management can sell the assets at the values included in the plans.
- Entity provides significant loans or guarantees:
    - Guarantees may be called in;
    - Borrowers may be unable to make payments.
- Entity dependent on guarantees provided by another party:
    - Guarantor no longer able/prepared to provide the guarantee.
- Future cash flows:

- – Uncertain or volatile;
- – Customers taking longer/unable to pay.
- Entity dependent on key suppliers:
  - – Suppliers facing financial difficulties not able to provide essential goods/services;
  - – Entity unable to find alternative suppliers.

Fair values

- Fair values are affected by current market conditions:
  - – Entity needs to change valuation model and/or management's assumptions to reflect current market conditions;
  - – Active market no longer exists, requiring use of a model for valuation purposes;
  - – Inputs to a model are not based on observable market inputs but rather are based on the entity's own data;
  - – Impairment of non-financial assets held at fair value (e.g. properties);
  - – Suspension of external valuation indices triggering a need for alternative valuation approaches;
  - – Entity uses an external pricing service for fair value measurements that needs to change its valuation model and/or assumptions to reflect current market conditions;
  - – Entity does not have necessary expertise to undertake valuations.

Other risk factors

- Impairments of assets other than those held at fair value (e.g. need for increased doubtful debts provisions).
- Impairment of the carrying value of purchased goodwill.
- Pension obligations of an entity increased by reduction in values of assets in a related defined benefits pension scheme.
- Hedging arrangements no longer effective.
- Effects on accounting for Special Purpose Entities and other off balance sheet arrangements.

Bulletin 2008/5 Auditor's reports on revised accounts and reports in the United Kingdom

(April 2008)

Contents

Paragraphs

Introduction 1 - 10
Voluntary revision of accounts or reports 1 - 3
Application to court in respect of defective accounts or reports 4 - 6
Avenues available to an auditor on becoming aware that accounts or reports are defective 7 - 8
Limitation as to extent of revisions permitted by law 9
Applicable requirements and guidance of ISAs (UK and Ireland) 10

Revision by replacement or by supplementary note 11 - 13

Dating the auditor's revised report 14

Auditor's procedures when reporting on revised accounts, directors' reports and directors' remuneration reports 15 - 16

Requirements of the SI 373 Regulations that establish requirements with respect to auditor's reports 17 - 32
Revised annual accounts 18 - 24
Auditor's report where company ceases to be exempt from audit 25
Revised reports 26 - 30
Abbreviated accounts 31
Summary financial statement 32

Appendix 1: Summarisation of requirements of the Companies (Revision of Defective Accounts and Reports) Regulations 2008 (the SI 373 Regulations)

Appendix 2: Illustrative example of an auditor's report on revised annual accounts: revision by replacement

Appendix 3: Illustrative example of an auditor's report on revised annual accounts: revision by supplementary note

Appendix 4: Illustrative auditor's report on revised directors' report: revision by replacement

Appendix 5: Illustrative auditor's report on revised directors' remuneration report: revision by replacement

Appendix 6: Illustrative example of a special report on the revised abbreviated accounts of a small company when full financial statements are revised

Appendix 7: Illustrative auditor's statement on a revised summary financial statement of a quoted company: revision by replacement

Introduction

Voluntary revision of accounts or reports

1   Section 454 of the Companies Act 2006 (CA 2006) grants company directors the authority to revise annual accounts[1], directors' remuneration reports, directors' reports and summary financial statements which do not comply with CA 2006 (or, where applicable, Article 4 of the IAS Regulation).

2   Section 454(3) of CA 2006 enables the Secretary of State to make provision by regulations as to the application of the provisions of CA 2006 in relation to:

(a)   revised annual accounts;

(b)   revised directors' remuneration reports;

(c)   revised directors' reports; and

(d)   revised summary financial statements.

3   Section 454(4) of CA 2006 states that, the regulations may in particular "make provision with respect to the functions of the company's auditor in relation to the revised accounts, report or statement". The regulations referred to in section 454 of CA 2006 are set out in the "Companies (Revision of Defective Accounts and Reports) Regulations 2008"[2] (the SI 373 Regulations).

Application to court in respect of defective accounts or reports

4   Sections 455 and 456 of CA 2006 give the Secretary of State, or a person authorised by him, power to apply to the court for a declaration that the annual accounts of a company do not comply, or a directors' report does not comply, with the requirements of CA 2006 (or, where applicable, Article 4 of the IAS Regulation) and for an order requiring the directors to prepare revised accounts or a revised report.

5   If the court orders the preparation of revised accounts it may give directions as to:

(a)   the auditing of the accounts;

(b)   the revision of any directors' remuneration report, directors' report or summary financial statement;

(c)   the taking of steps by the directors to bring the making of the order to the notice of persons likely to rely on the previous accounts; and

(d)   such other matters as the court thinks fit.

6   Similarly, if the court orders the preparation of a revised directors' report it may give directions as to:

(a)   the review of the report by the auditors;

(b)   the revision of any summary financial statement;

(c)   the taking of steps by the directors to bring the making of the order to the notice of persons likely to rely on the previous report; and

(d)   such other matters as the court thinks fit.

---

[1] *Including abbreviated accounts*

[2] *Statutory Instrument, SI 2008 No.373*

Avenues available to an auditor on becoming aware that accounts or reports are defective

If the auditor becomes aware of a fact relevant to the audited accounts or reports,   **7** of which it was unaware at the date of the auditor's report, which indicates that the annual accounts or reports were defective there are no statutory provisions that require the accounts, or the report, to be revised.

Therefore, in such circumstances, the auditor discusses with those charged with   **8** governance whether they wish to withdraw the accounts or the report and revise them voluntarily in accordance with the provisions of section 454 of CA 2006. If those charged with governance decide not to do so the auditor may wish to take legal advice. Possible courses of action include the making of a statement by those charged with governance, or the auditor, at the annual general meeting[3].

Limitation as to extent of revisions permitted by law

When accounts are revised care needs to be taken that the extent of the revisions   **9** does not exceed those permitted by CA 2006. In particular section 454(2) of CA 2006 requires that

> "the revisions must be confined to:
>
> (a)   the correction of those respects in which the previous accounts or report did not comply with the requirements of this Act (or, where applicable, of Article 4 of the IAS Regulation); and
>
> (b)   the making of any necessary consequential alterations."

Applicable requirements and guidance of ISAs (UK and Ireland)

With respect to revised annual accounts ISA (UK and Ireland) 560 *Subsequent*   **10** *Events* at paragraph 16 requires that "The new auditor's report should include an emphasis of matter paragraph referring to a note to the financial statements[4] that more extensively discusses the reason for the revision of the previously issued financial statements and to the earlier report issued by the auditor". Subsequent guidance in that paragraph states "Local regulations of some countries permit the auditor to restrict the audit procedures regarding the revised financial statements to the effects of the subsequent event that necessitated the revision. In such cases, the new auditor's report would contain a statement to that effect". The application of this requirement and guidance is illustrated in the example auditor's reports set out in Appendices 2 and 3.

Revision by replacement or by supplementary note

Under the SI 373 Regulations annual accounts (including abbreviated accounts),   **11** directors' reports, directors' remuneration reports and summary financial statements may be revised either:

(a)   by replacement; or

(b)   by the issue of a supplementary note.

---

[3] *These paragraphs are derived from paragraph 14-1 of ISA (UK and Ireland) 560 Subsequent events, additional guidance is provided in paragraphs 15 to 18 of that ISA (UK and Ireland).*

[4] *In this Bulletin, other than where necessary in context, the term "annual accounts", which is used in CA 2006, is used rather than "financial statements".*

12   Revision by replacement means revision by the preparation of a replacement set of accounts, directors' report or directors' remuneration report, in substitution for the original defective accounts or reports. Revision by supplementary note means revision by the preparation of a note indicating corrections to be made to the original defective accounts or reports.

13   The SI 373 Regulations contain no conditions which require one form or the other to be used and, therefore, the directors may use whichever approach appears more appropriate to the circumstances. In both instances, the accounts or report are to be prepared as if prepared and approved by the directors as at the date of the original annual accounts or report.

Dating the auditor's revised report

14   The auditor's report on the revised annual accounts (or report) is dated the actual date on which it is signed. From that date it becomes the date of the auditor's report in place of the auditor's report on the original audited accounts (or report). However, this does not imply that the auditor has undertaken a subsequent events review between that date and the previous date.

Auditor's procedures when reporting on revised accounts, directors' reports and directors' remuneration reports

15   The basis of the auditor's opinion on revised annual accounts states: "The audit of revised financial statements includes the performance of procedures to assess whether the revisions made by the directors are appropriate and have been properly made".

16   Therefore, before issuing a report on revised annual accounts, directors' reports or directors' remuneration reports the auditor:

(a)   through discussion with those charged with governance, determines the reasons for the revision and forms a view from available evidence as to whether the reasons are legitimate;

(b)   reviews those working papers relating to the audit of the original accounts or report that will enable the auditor to ascertain whether the issue giving rise to the revision had been considered during the audit and if so how they were resolved. The purpose of this review is to enable the auditor to properly assess the context in which the revision is being made;

(c)   considers the integrity of management and those charged with governance. In particular, the auditor re-assesses earlier representations made by management and those charged with governance;

(d)   obtains sufficient appropriate audit evidence to support the changes being made to the original accounts or report; and

(e)   considers whether the auditor has become aware of events that have occurred since it signed the original auditor's report which are of such significance that the auditor may be unwilling to sign a report on the revised accounts or report.

Requirements of the SI 373 Regulations that establish requirements with respect to auditor's reports

The following paragraphs provide a summary of certain of the requirements of the SI 373 Regulations insofar as they establish requirements with respect to the various auditor's reports set out in Appendices 2 to 7. Appendix 1 provides a summary of those requirements of the SI 373 Regulations that establish requirements with respect to various statements that the directors are required to make with respect to revised accounts and reports. This Bulletin is not intended to be an authoritative guide to all of the requirements of CA 2006 and the SI 373 Regulations with respect to revising annual accounts and reports. For complete and authoritative guidance reference should always be made to CA 2006 and the SI 373 Regulations themselves.   **17**

Revised annual accounts

A company's current auditor is required to make a report to the company's members on any revised annual accounts prepared under section 454 of CA 2006. However, where the auditor's report on the original defective accounts was not made by the company's current auditor, the directors of the company may resolve that the report is to be made by the auditor that made the original report provided that, that auditor agrees to do so and remains qualified for appointment as auditor of the company.   **18**

Where the company requests the current auditor to report to the company's members on revised annual accounts, on which the current auditor has not previously reported, the responsibility of the current auditor is to express its opinion on the revised accounts as a whole. Consequently it informs the company of the need for it to both: **19**

(a)   audit the proposed revisions; and

(b)   obtain sufficient appropriate audit evidence as to the truth and fairness of the annual accounts in question. Such evidence is likely to be obtained from performing a review of the audit working papers of the auditor that made the original report.

An auditor's report on revised annual accounts is required to state whether in the auditor's opinion the revised annual accounts have been properly prepared in accordance with the requirements of CA 2006 and, where applicable, Article 4 of the IAS Regulation, as they have effect under the Regulations. In particular the auditor is required to state whether a true and fair view, seen as at the date the original defective annual accounts were approved, is given by the revised annual accounts with respect to the matters set out in section 495(3)(a) to (c) of CA 2006.   **20**

The report is also required to state whether in the auditor's opinion the original defective annual accounts failed to comply with the requirements of CA 2006 and, where applicable, Article 4 of the IAS Regulation in the respects identified by the directors: **21**

(a)   (in the case of revision by replacement) in the statement required by Regulation 4(2)(a)(iv);

(b)   or (in the case of revision by supplementary note) in the supplementary note.

The auditor is also required to state whether the information contained in the directors' report for the financial year for which the annual accounts are prepared   **22** (or the revised report if the directors' report has been revised under the Regulations) is consistent with those financial statements.

23   Sections 503 (signature of auditor's report)[5] and 505 (names to be stated in published copies of auditor's reports) of CA 2006 apply to an auditor's report made under the SI 373 Regulations as they apply to an auditor's report under section 495(1) of CA 2006, with any necessary modifications.

24   Appendix 2 is an illustrative example of an auditor's report on annual accounts that have been revised by replacement showing changes from a standard auditor's report as shaded text. Appendix 3 is an illustrative example of an auditor's report on annual accounts that have been revised by supplementary note.[6]

Auditor's report where company ceases to be exempt from audit

25   Where, as a result of revisions to the accounts, the company is no longer entitled to exemption from audit, Regulation 8 of the SI 373 Regulations requires the company to cause an auditor's report on the revised accounts to be prepared. The auditor's report is required to be delivered to the Registrar within 28 days after the date of revision of the accounts.

Revised reports

26   A company's current auditor is required to make a report (or further report) to the company's members on any revised directors' report or directors' remuneration report prepared under section 454 of CA 2006 if the relevant annual financial statements have not been revised at the same time. However, where the auditor's report on the annual accounts for the financial year covered by the revised report was not made by the company's current auditor, the directors of the company may resolve that the report is to be made by the auditor that made the original report provided that auditor remains qualified for appointment as auditor of the company.

27   Where the company requests the current auditor to report to the company's members on a revised directors' remuneration report on which the current auditor has not previously reported, the responsibility of the current auditor is to express its opinion on the whole of the auditable part of the directors' remuneration report. Consequently it informs the company of the need for it to both:

(a)   audit the proposed revisions; and

(b)   obtain sufficient appropriate audit evidence as to the proper preparation of the Directors Remuneration Report. Such evidence is likely to be obtained from performing a review of the audit working papers of the auditor that made the original report.

28   Where a revised directors' report is prepared the auditor's report is required to state whether in the auditor's opinion the information given in that revised report is consistent with the annual financial statements for the relevant year.

---

[5] *See Bulletin 2008/6 "The Senior Statutory Auditor" under the United Kingdom Companies Act 2006.*

[6] *The illustrative reports are based on the examples provided in Bulletin 2006/6 Auditor's reports on financial statements in the United Kingdom. Certain aspects of the illustrative reports will likely need to be revised when Bulletin 2006/6 is revised to reflect the requirements of the Companies Act 2006, and any other changes that may arise from the APB's December 2007 Discussion Paper The Auditor's Report: A Time for Change?*

Where a revised directors' remuneration report is prepared the auditor's report is **29** required to state whether in the auditor's opinion any auditable part[7] of that revised report has been properly prepared[8].

Appendix 4 is an illustrative example of an auditor's report on a directors' report **30** revised by replacement. Appendix 5 is an illustrative auditor's report on a directors' remuneration report revised by replacement.

Abbreviated accounts

The SI 373 Regulations require revised abbreviated accounts to be drawn up in **31** accordance with various sections of CA 2006 including sections 444(4) and 445 (4) which are the sections that require the directors to deliver a copy of the special auditor's report required by section 449 of CA 2006. An illustrative example of a special report on the revised abbreviated accounts of a small company is provided in Appendix 6.

Summary financial statement

Regulation 17(2) of the SI 373 Regulations requires a revised summary financial **32** statement to contain the statement from the auditor required by sections 427(d) and 428(d) of CA 2006. (This arises from the fact that the directors are required to prepare a further summary financial statement under section 426 and it in turn requires a summary financial statement to comply with either section 427 or 428). An illustrative example of an auditor's statement on a revised summary financial statement of a quoted company is provided in Appendix 7.

---

[7] *The "auditable part" is defined in Part 3 of Schedule 8 to the Large and Medium-sized Companies and Groups (Accounts and Reports) Regulations 2008 (the SI 410 Regulations).*

[8] *The SI 373 Regulations require the auditor always to report when the directors' remuneration report has been revised. There is no derogation from this requirement for the auditor in those circumstances where the revision affects only the part of the report that is not required to be audited.*

Appendix 1

Summarisation of requirements of the Companies (Revision of Defective Accounts and Reports) Regulations 2008 (the SI 373 Regulations)

1   This Appendix summarises certain of the requirements of the SI 373 Regulations. Neither this Appendix nor the Bulletin is intended to be an authoritative guide to all of the requirements of CA 2006 and the SI 373 Regulations with respect to revising annual accounts and reports. For complete and authoritative guidance reference should always be made to CA 2006 and the SI 373 Regulations themselves.

Directors' statement relating to revised annual accounts: revision by replacement

2   The directors must include a statement concerning the revision in a prominent position in the revised financial statements. In the case of a revision by replacement, Regulation 4(2)(a) requires this to state:

   "(a)   that the revised accounts replace the original annual accounts for the financial year (specifying it);

   (b)   that they are now the statutory accounts of the company for that financial year;

   (c)   that they have been prepared as at the date of the original annual accounts and not as at the date of revision and accordingly do not deal with events between those dates;

   (d)   the respects in which the original annual accounts did not comply with the requirements of CA 2006; and

   (e)   any significant amendments made consequential upon the remedying of those defects."

Directors' statement relating to revised annual accounts: revision by supplementary note

3   When revision is effected by supplementary note, the note itself should provide adequate information concerning the defect in the original financial statements and any consequential amendments, and is required by Regulation 4(2)(b) to include a statement:

   "(a)   that the note revises in certain respects the original annual accounts of the company and is to be treated as forming part of those accounts; and

   (b)   that the annual accounts have been revised as at the date of the original annual accounts and not as at the date of revision and accordingly do not deal with events between those dates."

Directors' statement relating to a revised directors' report or a revised directors' remuneration report: revision by replacement

4   Where a directors' report or a directors' remuneration report is to be revised by replacement the directors are required, before approving the revised report, to

cause statements as to the following matters to be made in a prominent position in the revised directors' report [or directors' remuneration report]:

(a) that the revised directors' report [or directors' remuneration report} replaces the original directors' report [or directors' remuneration report] for the financial year (specifying it);

(b) that it has been prepared as at the date of the original directors' report [or directors' remuneration report] and not as at the date of revision and accordingly does not deal with any events between those dates;

(c) the respects in which the original directors' report [or directors' remuneration report] did not comply with CA 2006; and

(d) any significant amendments made consequential upon the remedying of those defects.

Directors' statement relating to a revised directors' report or a revised directors' remuneration report: revision by supplementary note

Where a directors' report or a directors' remuneration report is to be revised by supplementary note the directors are required, before approving the supplementary note, to cause statements as to the following matters to be made in a prominent position in the supplementary note: **5**

(a) that the note revises in certain respects the original directors' report [or directors' remuneration report] and is to be treated as forming part of that report; and

(b) that the directors' report [or directors' remuneration report] has been revised as at the date of the original report and not as at the date of the revision and accordingly does not deal with events between those dates.

Abbreviated accounts

Regulations 15 and 16 of the SI 373 Regulations apply to abbreviated accounts filed by small and medium sized companies (See Bulletin 2008/4 *The special auditor's report on abbreviated accounts in the United Kingdom*). Regulation 15 addresses the implications for the abbreviated accounts where revised annual financial statements are required to be prepared and the company has, prior to the date of revision, delivered abbreviated accounts to the Registrar. Regulation 16 addresses the revision of abbreviated accounts that may arise in other circumstances. **6**

Regulation 15(2) addresses circumstances where the abbreviated accounts delivered to the registrar would, if they had been prepared by reference to the revised financial statements, not comply with the requirements of CA 2006. This may be because the company would not have qualified as a small or medium-sized company in the light of the revised financial statements or because the financial statements have been revised in a manner which affects the content of the abbreviated accounts. **7**

In such cases the directors of the company are required to cause the company either: **8**

(a) to deliver to the registrar a copy of the revised annual accounts, together with a copy of the directors' report and the auditor's report on the revised annual accounts; or

(b)   if on the basis of the revised annual accounts they are entitled to do so to prepare further abbreviated accounts and to deliver them to the registrar together with a statement as to the effect of the revisions made.

9   Where the abbreviated accounts would, if they had been prepared by reference to the revised annual accounts, remain the same as those originally filed the company is required to deliver to the registrar

(a)   a note stating that the annual accounts of the company have been revised in a respect which has no bearing on the abbreviated accounts delivered for that year, together with;

(b)   a copy of the auditor's report on the revised annual accounts.

10   Where the directors have delivered to the registrar abbreviated accounts which do not comply with the requirements of CA 2006 for reasons other than those specified in Regulation 15(2) the directors of the company shall cause the company:

(a)   to prepare revised abbreviated accounts; and

(b)   to deliver those accounts to the registrar within 28 days after the date of the revision together with a statement as to the effect of the revisions made.

Summary financial statement: revision by replacement

11   Where a summary financial statement does not comply with the requirements of section 426 of CA 2006 or if it had been prepared by reference to revised annual financial statements or a revised report would not have complied with those requirements the directors are required to cause the company to prepare a revised summary financial statement and to send that statement to:

(a)   any person who received a copy of the original summary financial statement; and

(b)   any person to whom the company would be entitled, as at the date the revised summary financial statement is prepared, to send a summary financial statement for the current financial year.

12   Sections 426(1) to (4) (Option to provide summary financial statement), 434(6) (Requirements in connection with publication of statutory accounts) and 435(7) (Requirements in connection with publication of non-statutory accounts) of CA 2006 apply with necessary modifications to a revised summary financial statement.

13   A revised summary financial statement is required to contain a short statement of the revisions made and their effect.

Summary financial statement: revision by supplementary note

14   As an alternative to preparing a revised summary financial statement the company may prepare and send to the persons mentioned in paragraph 11 above a supplementary note indicating the corrections to be made to the original defective summary financial statement. Such a supplementary note is required to contain a statement that it revises the original defective summary financial statement in certain respects and is to be treated as forming part of that statement.

Revision of annual financial statements that has no effect on the summary financial statement

Regulation 17(6) of the Regulations contemplates the situation where the directors   **15**
revise the annual financial statements or reports but that this has no effect on the
summary financial statement as issued. In such circumstances the Regulations
require the directors to cause the company to send to the persons mentioned in
paragraph 11 above a note stating that annual accounts for a specified financial
year or the directors' report or directors' remuneration report for that year have or
has been revised in a respect which has no bearing on the summary financial
statement for that year.

If the auditor's report on the revised annual accounts or report is qualified, a copy   **16**
of that report is required to be attached to the note described in the preceding
paragraph.

Companies that are exempt from audit

Where a company is exempt from audit: **17**

(a)   by virtue of section 477(1) (small companies: conditions for exemption from
audit); or

(b)   by virtue of section 480 (dormant companies: conditions for exemption from
audit);

of CA 2006 the Regulations have effect as if any reference to an auditor's report,
or the making of such a report were omitted. In other words the audit exemptions
apply to the revised accounts and reports.

Modifications of Companies Act 2006

Where the requirements of CA 2006 as to the matters to be included in the annual   **18**
accounts of a company, abbreviated accounts, a directors' report, a directors'
remuneration report or a summary financial statement have been amended after
the date of the original defective accounts, report or statement references in the
Regulations to the requirements of CA 2006 shall be construed as references to the
provisions of CA 2006 as in force as at the date of the original defective accounts,
report or statement.

Appendix 2

Illustrative example of an auditor's report on revised annual accounts: revision by replacement

This example is based on the following assumptions:

- *Non-publicly traded company that does not prepare group accounts.*
- *UK GAAP used for individual company accounts.*
- *Financial statements contain no surround information other than the directors' report.*

REPORT OF THE INDEPENDENT AUDITOR TO THE [MEMBERS] [SHAREHOLDERS] OF XYZ LIMITED

We have audited the revised financial statements of XYZ Limited for the year ended ... which comprise [state the primary financial statements such as the Profit and Loss Account, the Balance Sheet, the Cash Flow Statement, the Statement of Total Recognised Gains and Losses] and the related notes[9]. These revised financial statements have been prepared under the accounting policies set out therein and replace the original financial statements approved by the directors on....

The revised financial statements have been prepared under The Companies (Revision of Defective Accounts and Reports) Regulations 2008 and accordingly do not take account of events which have taken place after the date on which the original financial statements were approved.

Respective responsibilities of directors and auditors

The directors' responsibilities for preparing revised financial statements in accordance with applicable law and United Kingdom Accounting Standards (United Kingdom Generally Accepted Accounting Practice) and for being satisfied that they give a true and fair view are set out in the Statement of Directors' Responsibilities.[10]

Our responsibility is to audit the revised financial statements in accordance with relevant legal and regulatory requirements and International Standards on Auditing (UK and Ireland).

We report to you our opinion as to whether the revised financial statements give a true and fair view, have been properly prepared in accordance with United Kingdom Generally Accepted Accounting Practice and are prepared in accordance with the requirements of the Companies Act 2006 as they have effect under the Companies (Revision of Defective Accounts and Reports) Regulations 2008. We also report to you whether in our opinion the information given in the [revised][11] Directors' Report is consistent with the revised financial statements.

---

[9] *Auditor's reports of entities that do not publish their financial statements on a web site or publish them using "PDF" format may continue to refer to the financial statements by reference to page numbers.*

[10] *If the directors' responsibilities with respect to revised financial statements are not set out in a separate statement, the auditors will include a description in their report.*

[11] *The term "revised" will be needed if the Directors' Report has also been revised.*

In addition we report to you if, in our opinion, the company has not kept adequate accounting records or if we have not received all the information and explanations we require for our audit or if disclosures of directors' benefits, remuneration, pensions and compensation for loss of office specified by law are not made.

We read the [revised][9] Directors' Report and consider the implications for our report if we become aware of any apparent misstatements within it.

We are also required to report whether in our opinion the original financial statements failed to comply with the requirements of the Companies Act 2006 in the respects identified by the directors.

Basis of audit opinion

We conducted our audit in accordance with International Standards on Auditing (UK and Ireland) issued by the Auditing Practices Board. An audit includes examination, on a test basis, of evidence relevant to the amounts and disclosures in the revised financial statements. It also includes an assessment of the significant estimates and judgments made by the directors in the preparation of the revised financial statements, and of whether the accounting policies are appropriate to the company's circumstances, consistently applied and adequately disclosed.

The audit of revised financial statements includes the performance of procedures to assess whether the revisions made by the directors are appropriate and have been properly made.

We planned and performed our audit so as to obtain all the information and explanations which we considered necessary in order to provide us with sufficient evidence to give reasonable assurance that the revised financial statements are free from material misstatement, whether caused by fraud or other irregularity or error. In forming our opinion we also evaluated the overall adequacy of the presentation of information in the revised financial statements.

Opinion

In our opinion:

- the revised financial statements give a true and fair view, seen as at the date the original financial statements were approved, of the state of the company's affairs as at ... and of its profit [loss] for the year then ended;

- the revised financial statements have been properly prepared in accordance with United Kingdom Generally Accepted Accounting Practice seen as at the date the original financial statements were approved;

- the revised financial statements have been properly prepared in accordance with the provisions of the Companies Act 2006 as they have effect under the Companies (Revision of Defective Accounts and Reports) Regulations 2008;

- the original financial statements for the year ended ... failed to comply with the requirements of the Companies Act 2006 in the respects identified by the directors in the statement contained in note [x] to these revised financial statements; and

- the information given in the [revised][9] Directors' Report is consistent with the revised financial statements.

Emphasis of matter – revision of ...

In forming our opinion on the revised financial statements, which is not qualified, we have considered the adequacy of the disclosures made in note [x] to these revised financial statements concerning the need to revise the .... The original financial statements were approved on ...and our previous report was signed on that date. We have not performed a subsequent events review for the period from the date of our previous report to the date of this report.

[Signature]   *Address*

John Smith (senior statutory auditor)   *Date*

for and on behalf of ABC LLP, Statutory auditor

Note: Changes from a standard auditor's report are shown as shaded text.

Appendix 3

Illustrative example of an auditor's report on revised annual accounts: revision by supplementary note

This example is based on the following assumptions:

- *Non-publicly traded company that does not prepare group accounts.*
- *UK GAAP used for individual company accounts.*
- *Financial statements contain no surround information other than the directors' report.*

REPORT OF THE INDEPENDENT AUDITOR TO THE [MEMBERS] [SHAREHOLDERS] OF XYZ LIMITED

We have audited the revised financial statements of XYZ Limited for the year ended.... which comprise [state the primary financial statements such as the Profit and Loss Account, the Balance Sheet, the Cash Flow Statement, the Statement of Total Recognised Gains and Losses] and the related notes.[12] The revised financial statements replace the original financial statements approved by the directors on... and consist of the attached supplementary note together with the original financial statements which were circulated to [members] [shareholders] on....

The revised financial statements have been prepared under The Companies (Revision of Defective Accounts and Reports) Regulations 2008 and accordingly do not take account of events which have taken place after the date on which the original financial statements were approved.

Respective responsibilities of directors and auditors

The directors' responsibilities for preparing revised financial statements in accordance with applicable law and United Kingdom Accounting Standards (United Kingdom Generally Accepted Accounting Practice) and for being satisfied that they give a true and fair view are set out in the Statement of Directors' Responsibilities.[13]

Our responsibility is to audit the revised financial statements in accordance with relevant legal and regulatory requirements and International Standards on Auditing (UK and Ireland).

We report to you our opinion as to whether the revised financial statements give a true and fair view, have been properly prepared in accordance with United Kingdom Generally Accepted Accounting Practice and are prepared in accordance with the requirements of the Companies Act 2006 as they have effect under the Companies (Revision of Defective Accounts and Reports) Regulations 2008. We also report to you whether in our opinion the information given in the [revised][14] Directors' Report is consistent with the financial statements.

---

[12] *Auditor's reports of entities that do not publish their financial statements on a web site or publish them using "PDF" format may continue to refer to the financial statements by reference to page numbers.*

[13] *If the directors' responsibilities with respect to revised financial statements are not set out in a separate statement, the auditors will include a description in their report.*

[14] *The term "revised" will be needed if the Directors' Report has also been revised.*

In addition we report to you if, in our opinion, the company has not kept adequate accounting records or if we have not received all the information and explanations we require for our audit or if disclosures of directors' benefits, remuneration, pensions and compensation for loss of office specified by law are not made.

We read the [revised][12] Directors' Report and consider the implications for our report if we become aware of any apparent misstatements within it.

We are also required to report whether in our opinion the original financial statements failed to comply with the requirements of the Companies Act 2006 in the respects identified by the directors.

Basis of audit opinion

We conducted our audit in accordance with International Standards on Auditing (UK and Ireland) issued by the Auditing Practices Board. An audit includes examination, on a test basis, of evidence relevant to the amounts and disclosures in the revised financial statements. It also includes an assessment of the significant estimates and judgments made by the directors in the preparation of the revised financial statements, and of whether the accounting policies are appropriate to the company's circumstances, consistently applied and adequately disclosed.

The audit of revised financial statements includes the performance of procedures to assess whether the revisions made by the directors are appropriate and have been properly made.

We planned and performed our audit so as to obtain all the information and explanations which we considered necessary in order to provide us with sufficient evidence to give reasonable assurance that the revised financial statements are free from material misstatement, whether caused by fraud or other irregularity or error. In forming our opinion we also evaluated the overall adequacy of the presentation of information in the revised financial statements.

Opinion

In our opinion:

- the revised financial statements give a true and fair view, seen as at the date the original financial statements were approved, of the state of the company's affairs as at ... and of its profit [loss] for the year then ended;

- the revised financial statements have been properly prepared in accordance with United Kingdom Generally Accepted Accounting Practice seen as at the date the original financial statements were approved;

- the revised financial statements have been properly prepared in accordance with the provisions of the Companies Act 2006 as they have effect under the Companies (Revision of Defective Accounts and Reports) Regulations 2008;

- the original financial statements for the year ended ... failed to comply with the requirements of the Companies Act 2006 in the respects identified by the directors in the statement contained in the supplementary note; and

- the information given in the [revised][12] Directors' Report is consistent with the revised financial statements.

Emphasis of matter – revision of ...

In forming our opinion on the revised financial statements, which is not qualified, we have considered the adequacy of the disclosures made in the supplementary note concerning the need to revise the .... The original financial statements were approved on ...and our previous report was signed on that date. We have not performed a subsequent events review for the period from the date of our previous report to the date of this report.

[Signature]   *Address*

John Smith (senior statutory auditor)   *Date*

for and on behalf of ABC LLP, Statutory auditor

Appendix 4

Illustrative auditor's report on revised directors' report: revision by replacement

REPORT OF THE INDEPENDENT AUDITOR TO THE [MEMBERS] [SHAREHOLDERS] OF XYZ LIMITED

We have considered the information given in the revised directors' report for the year ended.... The revised directors' report replaces the original directors' report approved by the directors on... [and consists of the attached supplementary note together with the original report which was circulated to [members] [shareholders] on...][15]. The revised directors' report has been prepared under the Companies (Revision of Defective Accounts and Reports) Regulations 2008 and accordingly does not take account of events which have taken place after the date on which the original directors' report was approved.

Respective responsibilities of directors and auditors

The directors are responsible for the preparation of the revised directors' report.

Our responsibility is to report to you whether the revised directors' report is consistent with the annual financial statements.

Basis of opinion

Our consideration has been directed towards matters of consistency alone and not to whether the revised directors' report complies with the requirements of the Companies Act 2006.

Opinion

In our opinion the information given in the revised directors' report is consistent with the annual financial statements for the year ended... which were circulated to [members] [shareholders] on ....

[Signature]	*Address*
John Smith (senior statutory auditor)	*Date*
for and on behalf of ABC LLP, Statutory auditor	

---

[15] *Omit the words in brackets when the revision is by way of a full replacement.*

Appendix 5

Illustrative auditor's report on revised directors' remuneration report: revision by replacement

REPORT OF THE INDEPENDENT AUDITOR TO THE [MEMBERS] [SHAREHOLDERS] OF XYZ LIMITED

We have considered the revised directors' remuneration report for the year ended.... The revised directors' remuneration report replaces the original directors' remuneration report approved by the directors on... [and consists of the attached supplementary note together with the original report which was circulated to [members] [shareholders] on...][16]. The revised directors' remuneration report has been prepared under the Companies (Revision of Defective Accounts and Reports) Regulations 2008 and accordingly does not take account of events which have taken place after the date on which the original directors' remuneration report was approved.

Respective responsibilities of directors and auditors

The directors are responsible for the preparation of the revised directors' remuneration report.

Our responsibility is to report to you whether the part of the revised directors' remuneration report to be audited has been properly prepared.

Basis of opinion

Our consideration has been directed towards forming an opinion as to whether the part of the revised directors' remuneration report to be audited has been properly prepared in accordance with the requirements of Part 3 of Schedule 8 to the Large and Medium-sized Companies and Groups (Accounts and Reports) Regulations 2008.

Opinion

In our opinion the part of the revised directors' remuneration report to be audited has been properly prepared in accordance with the Companies Act 2006.

[Signature]   *Address*

John Smith (senior statutory auditor)   *Date*

for and on behalf of ABC LLP, Statutory auditor

---

[16] *Omit the words in brackets when the revision is by way of a full replacement.*

Appendix 6

Illustrative example of a special report on the revised abbreviated accounts of a small company when full financial statements are revised

INDEPENDENT AUDITOR'S REPORT TO XYZ LIMITED UNDER SECTION 449 OF THE COMPANIES ACT 2006

We have examined the revised abbreviated accounts set out on pages ... to ..., together with the revised financial statements of XYZ Limited for the year ended...prepared under section 396 of the Companies Act 2006.

Respective responsibilities of directors and auditors

The directors are responsible for preparing the revised abbreviated accounts in accordance with section 444 of the Companies Act 2006. It is our responsibility to form an independent opinion as to whether the company is entitled to deliver abbreviated accounts prepared in accordance with section 444(3) of the Act to the Registrar of Companies and whether the revised abbreviated accounts have been properly prepared in accordance with the regulations made under that section and to report our opinion to you.

We conducted our work in accordance with Bulletin 2008/4 issued by the Auditing Practices Board. In accordance with that Bulletin we have carried out the procedures we consider necessary to confirm, by reference to the revised financial statements, that the company is entitled to deliver abbreviated accounts and that the revised abbreviated accounts to be delivered are properly prepared[17].

Opinion

In our opinion the company is entitled to deliver abbreviated accounts prepared in accordance with section 444(3) of the Companies Act 2006 and the revised abbreviated accounts have been properly prepared in accordance with the regulations made under that section.

[Other information[18]]

[Signature]   Address

John Smith (senior statutory auditor)   Date

for and on behalf of ABC LLP, Statutory Auditor

---

[17] *Add appropriate wording such as "The scope of our work for the purposes of this report does not include examining events occurring after the date of our auditor's report on the full revised financial statements" where special report is dated after the signing of the auditor's report on the full revised financial statements (see paragraph 46 of Bulletin 2008/4).*

[18] *This section is only included in the circumstances described in paragraphs 41 to 44 of Bulletin 2008/4.*

Appendix 7

Illustrative auditor's statement on a revised summary financial statement of a quoted company: revision by replacement

INDEPENDENT AUDITOR'S STATEMENT TO THE [MEMBERS] [SHAREHOLDERS] OF XYZ PLC

We have examined the revised summary financial statement [for the year ended…] [set out on pages…].

Respective responsibilities of the directors and the auditor

The directors are responsible for preparing the [*revised summarised annual report*] in accordance with applicable United Kingdom law.

Our responsibility is to report to you our opinion on the consistency of the revised summary financial statement within the [*revised summarised annual report*] with the revised full annual financial statements[, the [revised][19] Directors' Report][20] and the [revised][21] Directors' Remuneration Report, and its compliance with the relevant requirements of section 428 of the Companies Act 2006 and the regulations made thereunder.

We also read the other information contained in the [*revised summarised annual report*] and consider the implications for our report if we become aware of any apparent misstatements or material inconsistencies with the revised summary financial statement. The other information comprises only [the Chairman's Statement and the Corporate Governance Statement].

We conducted our work in accordance with Bulletin 2008/3 issued by the Auditing Practices Board. Our report on the company's full annual financial statements describes the basis of our opinion[s] on those revised financial statements, the [revised][19] Directors' Report][20] and the [revised][21] Directors' Remuneration Report.

Opinion

In our opinion the revised summary financial statement is consistent with the revised full annual financial statements [, the [revised][19] Directors' Report][20] and the [revised][21] Directors' Remuneration Report of XYZ plc for the year ended … and complies with the applicable requirements of section 428 of the Companies Act 2006, and the regulations made thereunder.

---

[19] *The word "revised" is inserted where the Directors' Report has also been revised*

[20] *There is no requirement for an entity to include a Summary Directors' Report. However, if the directors include information in the summary financial statement that is derived from the Directors' Report the auditor is required to report that such information is consistent with the Directors' Report.*

[21] *The word "revised" is inserted where the Directors' Remuneration Report has also been revised*

[We have not considered the effects of any events between the date on which we signed our report on the revised full annual financial statements and the [revised Directors' Remuneration Report] (insert date) and the date of this statement.][22]

Statutory auditor   *Address*

Date

DIRECTORS' STATEMENT

The auditor has issued unqualified reports on the revised full annual financial statements, the auditable part of the [revised][21] directors' remuneration report and on the consistency of the [revised][19] directors' report with those annual financial statements. Their report on the full annual financial statements and the auditable part of the directors' remuneration report contained no statement under sections 498(2) or 498(3) of the Companies Act 2006.[23]

---

[22] *Include this sentence where the date of this statement is after the date of the auditor's report on the revised full annual financial statements and the [revised] Directors' Remuneration Report.*

[23] *This statement is a requirement of sections 428(4)(e), 428(4)(f) and 428(4)(g) of CA 2006.*

Bulletin 2008/9 Miscellaneous reports by auditors required by the United Kingdom Companies Act 2006

(October 2008)

Contents

Paragraphs

Introduction   1 - 5

Distributions: Justification of distribution by reference to relevant accounts
(Sections 836 to 839 of CA 2006)   6 - 18
   Requirements where the auditor has issued a qualified report on the last annual accounts   9 - 15
   Requirements where interim accounts used   16
   Requirements where initial accounts used   17 - 18

Example 1 – Separate statement on a company's ability to make a distribution where auditor's report was qualified

Example 2 – "Other matter" paragraph included in auditor's report on financial statements on a company's ability to make a distribution where auditor's report was qualified

Example 3 – Report on initial accounts when a public company wishes to make a distribution

Example 4 – Statement by auditor of a company on ceasing to hold office setting out the circumstances connected to the auditor ceasing to hold office

Example 5 – Statement by auditor of an unquoted company on ceasing to hold office where there are no circumstances which need to be brought to the attention of members or creditors

Example 6 – Statement when a private company wishes to re-register as a public company where the auditor's opinion on the balance sheet is unqualified

Example 7 – Statement when a private company wishes to re-register as a public company where the auditor's opinion on the balance sheet is qualified with respect to proper preparation in accordance with the Companies Act 2006, but the qualification is not material

Example 8 – Statement when a private company wishes to re-register as a public company based on a specially prepared balance sheet that is unqualified

Example 9 – Statement when a private company wishes to re-register as a public company based on a specially prepared balance sheet that is qualified with respect to proper preparation in accordance with the Companies Act 2006, but the qualification is not material

Example 10 – Report when a private company wishes to redeem or purchase its own shares out of capital

Example 11 – Report when a public company wishes to allot shares otherwise than for cash

Example 12 – Report when non-cash assets are transferred to a public company by certain of its members

Appendix – Checklist of example reports in Bulletin 2007/1 indicating which Bulletin, or example report in this Bulletin, reflects the requirements of the Companies Act 2006

Introduction

The purpose of this Bulletin is to provide guidance with respect to those reports **1** and statements required to be made by an auditor under the Companies Act 2006 (CA 2006), that are not dealt with in other Bulletins published by the APB.

Other Bulletins published by the APB that address reports and statements required **2** to be made by an auditor under CA 2006 are:

(a)   The auditor's statement on the summary financial statement in the United Kingdom (Bulletin 2008/3);

(b)   The special auditor's report on abbreviated accounts in the United Kingdom (Bulletin 2008/4);

(c)   Auditor's reports on revised accounts and reports, in the United Kingdom (Bulletin 2008/5); and

(d)   Auditor's reports for short accounting periods in compliance with the United Kingdom Companies Act 2006 (Bulletin 2008/8).

The table in the Appendix lists the example reports in Bulletin 2007/1[1] indicating **3** within which APB Bulletin the equivalent example, revised to reflect the requirements of CA 2006, can be found.

The guidance in this Bulletin takes account of the law as at 6 April 2008. Readers **4** are cautioned that the provisions of CA 2006 on which the guidance and examples on pages 21 to 42 are based do not come into effect until 1 October 2009, and may be subject to transitional provisions under the final "Commencement Order" which at the date of this Bulletin is still in draft. Until the provisions of CA 2006 apply, the equivalent illustrative reports in Bulletin 2007/1 *Example reports by auditors under company legislation in Great Britain* remain in effect[2].

Readers are cautioned that the references within CA 2006 may change subsequent **5** to publication of this Bulletin.

Distributions: Justification of distribution by reference to relevant accounts (sections 836 to 839 of CA 2006) *Effective where distribution made on or after 6 April 2008*

Section 830(1) of CA 2006 prohibits companies from making a distribution **6** otherwise than out of profits available for the purpose.

Whether a distribution may be made by a company is determined by reference to **7** the items described in section 836(1) of CA 2006 as stated in the "relevant accounts". The items are:

(a)   profits, losses, assets and liabilities;

(b)   provisions of the following kinds;

    (i)   where the relevant accounts are Companies Act accounts, provisions of a kind specified by paragraph 7 of Schedule 9 to *The Large and Medium-sized Companies and Groups (Accounts and Reports) Regulations 2008*[3] or by paragraph 5 of Schedule 7 to *The Small*

---

[1] *Bulletin 2007/1 updated example reports originally issued by the APB in Practice Note 8.*

[2] *However, see footnote 32 on page 43 for description of transitional provisions.*

[3] *SI 2008 No. 410.*

        Companies and Groups (Accounts and Directors' Report) Regulations 2008[4];

    (ii)   where the relevant accounts are IAS accounts, provisions of any kind;

(c)   share capital and reserves (including undistributable reserves).

8   The relevant accounts are the company's last annual accounts (as defined in section 837 of CA 2006), except that:

(a)   where the distribution would be found to contravene the requirements of Part 23 of CA 2006 by reference to the company's last annual accounts[5], the distribution may be justified by reference to interim accounts; and

(b)   where the distribution is proposed to be declared during the company's first accounting reference period, or before any accounts have been circulated in respect of that period, the distribution may be justified by reference to initial accounts.

Requirements where the auditor has issued a qualified report on the last annual accounts

9   Where the auditor has issued a "qualified report"[6] on the last annual accounts, the company's ability to make a distribution, by reference to those accounts, could be in doubt. In such circumstances, the company may not proceed to make the distribution unless the auditor has made a statement under section 837(4) of CA 2006 as to whether, in the auditor's opinion, the matters in respect of which the auditor's report is qualified are material for determining whether a distribution would contravene the requirements of Part 23 of CA 2006.

10   The auditor's statement under section 837(4) of CA 2006 must be in writing and can be:

(a)   made in a separate statement which would be addressed to the members (see Example 1 on page 7); or

(b)   included as a separate paragraph at the end of the auditor's report to the members on the financial statements (See Example 2 on page 9).

11   The auditor is required to state whether in its opinion the subject matter of the qualification is material for determining whether proposed distributions are permitted[7]. A qualification is not material for this purpose if the financial effect of the matters giving rise to the qualification could not be such as to reduce the distributable profits below the levels required for the purpose of such distributions.

12   The level of the proposed or potential distribution will normally be quantified in the opinion. Where the maximum effect of a qualification cannot be quantified, it would normally be material for distribution purposes unless the auditor can conclude that the qualification either does not impact distributable profits or that its effect could only be favourable.

---

[4] *SI 2008 No. 409.*

[5] *For transitional provisions see paragraph 35 of Schedule 4 of The Companies Act 2006 (Commencement No. 5, Transitional Provisions and Savings) Order 2007(SI 2007 No. 3495 (C. 150). Amongst other things these provisions permit the relevant accounts to be accounts for financial years beginning before 6 April 2008 to which the provisions of the Companies Act 1985 apply.*

[6] *A report that expresses an unqualified opinion but includes an emphasis of matter or "other matter" paragraph is not regarded as being qualified.*

[7] *Section 837(5) of CA 2006 states that "An auditor's statement is sufficient for the purposes of a distribution if it relates to distributions of a description that includes the distribution in question, even if at the time of the statement it had not been proposed."*

A disclaimer of opinion on the financial statements as a whole would be material **13** as the auditor would be unable to form an opinion on the amount at which the company's distributable profits are stated.

If a separate statement is made, the date used is that on which the statement is **14** completed. The statement will need to have been completed by the date of the distribution, at the latest.

On a change of auditor the report under section 837(4) of the Companies Act 2006 **15** can only be made by the statutory auditor who reported on the last annual financial statements.

Requirements where interim accounts used

Section 838 of CA 2006 establishes the requirements for making a distribution **16** where interim accounts are used. In this circumstance there are no requirements made of the company's auditor.

Requirements where initial accounts used

Section 839 of CA 2006 establishes the requirements for making a distribution **17** where initial accounts are used. Where initial accounts are used by a public company to justify a distribution the company's auditor is required to have made a report stating whether, in its opinion, the initial accounts have been "properly prepared".

The "properly prepared report" is discussed in more detail in connection with **18** Example 3, on pages 10 and 11.

Example 1 – Separate statement on a company's ability to make a distribution where auditor's report was qualified

Effective where distribution made on or after 6 April 2008

STATEMENT OF THE INDEPENDENT AUDITOR TO THE [MEMBERS] [SHAREHOLDERS] OF XYZ LIMITED PURSUANT TO SECTION 837 (4)[8] OF THE COMPANIES ACT 2006

We have audited the financial statements of XYZ Limited for the year ended... in accordance with International Standards on Auditing (UK and Ireland) issued by the Auditing Practices Board and have expressed a qualified opinion thereon in our report dated....

Respective responsibilities of directors and auditor

[Summarisation of directors' responsibilities with respect to the financial statements referred to in the introductory paragraph]. They are also responsible for considering whether the company, subsequent to the balance sheet date, has sufficient distributable profits to make a distribution at the time the distribution is made.

---

[8] *Section 837(4) applies where the last annual accounts are used. Where initial accounts are used a similar report is prepared based on the report in Example 3 on page 11.*

Our responsibility is to report whether, in our opinion, the subject matter of our qualification of our auditor's report on the financial statements for the year ended ... is material for determining, by reference to those financial statements, whether the distribution proposed by the company is permitted under section 830⁹ [section 831/832] of the Companies Act 2006. We are not required to form an opinion on whether the company has sufficient distributable reserves to make the distribution proposed at the time it is made.

Opinion

In our opinion the subject matter of the qualification is not material for determining, by reference to those financial statements, whether [the distribution of £...]/[the interim/final dividend for the year ended... of £...] proposed by the company is permitted under section 830⁹ [section 831/832] of the Companies Act 2006.

Statutory auditor   *Address*

Date

Notes:

(1)   *As an alternative the auditor's statement might be expressed in terms of the company's ability to make potential distributions up to a specific level. This may be particularly appropriate where the amount of the dividend has not yet been determined. In such circumstances the opinion paragraph would be worded as follows:*

   "In our opinion the subject matter of the qualification is not material for determining, by reference to those financial statements, whether a distribution of not more than £... by the company is permitted under section 830⁹ [section 831/832] of the Companies Act 2006."

(2)   *As a further alternative the auditor's statement might be expressed in terms of the company's ability to make "any distribution". In such circumstances the opinion paragraph would be worded as follows:*

   "In our opinion the subject matter of the qualification is not material for determining by reference to those financial statements, whether any distribution proposed by the company is permitted under section 830⁹ [section 831/832] of the Companies Act 2006."

(3)   *Where the auditor concludes that the subject matter of the qualification is material to either a specific distribution which is proposed or to any distribution, then an adverse opinion is given. In such circumstances the opinion paragraph would be worded as follows:*

---

⁹ *The reference in all cases to section 830 in this example is extended to cover also section 831 in the case of a public company and also sections 831 and 832 if the public company is also an "investment company".*

"*Adverse opinion*

In our opinion the subject matter of the qualification is material for determining, by reference to those financial statements, whether [the distribution of £...]/[the interim/final dividend for the year ended ... of £...]/[any distribution] proposed by the company is permitted under section 830[9] [section 831/832] of the Companies Act 2006."

Example 2 – "Other matter" paragraph included in auditor's report on financial statements on a company's ability to make a distribution where auditor's report was qualified

Effective where distribution made on or after 6 April 2008

The following statement is added to the end of the auditor's report following either the opinion paragraph or, where there is one, the emphasis of matter paragraph.

"**Statement pursuant to section [837(4)][10]** [839(6)][11] of the Companies Act 2006

Respective responsibilities of directors and the auditor

In addition to their responsibilities described above, the directors are also responsible for considering whether the company, subsequent to the balance sheet date, has sufficient distributable profits to make a distribution at the time the distribution is made.

Our responsibility is to report whether, in our opinion, the subject matter of our qualification of our auditor's report on the financial statements for the year ended ... is material for determining, by reference to those financial statements, whether the distribution proposed by the company is permitted under section 830[12] [section 831/832] of the Companies Act 2006. We are not required to form an opinion on whether the company has sufficient distributable reserves to make the distribution proposed at the time it is made.

Opinion

In our opinion the subject matter of the above qualification is not material for determining whether [the distribution of £...]/[the interim/final dividend for the year ended .... of £....] proposed by the company is permitted under section 830[12] [sections 831/832] of the Companies Act 2006."

Notes:

The notes to Example 1 also apply to this Example.

---

[10] *Section 837(4) applies where the last annual accounts are used.*

[11] *Section 839(6) applies to Example 3 on page 11 where the report on the initial accounts is qualified.*

[12] *The reference in all cases to section 830 in this example is extended to cover also section 831 in the case of a public company and also sections 831 and 832 if the public company is also an "investment company".*

Distributions: The use of initial accounts
(section 839(5) of CA 2006)

Effective where distribution made on or after 6 April 2008

19   A company may wish to make a distribution during its first accounting reference period or after the end of that period but before the accounts for that period have been circulated.

20   In such instances section 839(1) of CA 2006 requires "initial accounts" to be accounts that enable a reasonable judgment to be made as to the amounts of the items mentioned in section 836(1) of CA 2006.

21   Initial accounts of a public company are required to have been "properly prepared" or have been so prepared except for matters that are not material for determining (by reference to the items mentioned in section 836(1) of CA 2006) whether the distribution would contravene Part 23 of CA 2006 (Distributions).

22   "Properly prepared" means prepared in accordance with sections 395 to 397, and the regulations made thereunder, of CA 2006 (requirements for company individual accounts), applying those requirements with such modifications as are necessary because the accounts are prepared otherwise than in respect of an accounting reference period.

23   With respect to a public company, the company's auditor is required, by section 839(5) of CA 2006 to make a report stating whether, in its opinion, the accounts have been properly prepared. (Such a report is illustrated in Example 3 on page 11).

24   If the auditor's opinion is qualified, the auditor must state, in writing (either at the time of the report or subsequently), whether in its opinion the matters giving rise to the qualification are material for determining whether the distribution is permitted. These requirements are discussed further in paragraphs 9 to 15.

25   CA 2006 does not state to whom the report should be addressed. However, it is implicit from CA 2006 that it be addressed to the directors.

26   The same principles apply for the dating of initial accounts as apply to the dating of annual accounts.

Example 3 – Report on initial accounts when a public company wishes to make a distribution

Effective where distribution made on or after 6 April 2008

This example is based on the assumption that the initial accounts have been prepared in accordance with UK GAAP. (Initial accounts may also be prepared in accordance with IFRSs as adopted by the European Union.)

REPORT OF THE INDEPENDENT AUDITOR TO THE DIRECTORS OF XYZ PLC UNDER SECTION 839(5) OF THE COMPANIES ACT 2006

We have examined the initial accounts of XYZ PLC for the period from …. to … which comprise [state the primary financial statements such as the Profit and Loss Account, the Balance Sheet, the Cash Flow Statement, the Statement of Total Recognised Gains and Losses] and the related notes. The initial accounts have been prepared under the accounting policies set out therein.

Respective responsibilities of directors and auditors

As described ... the directors are responsible for the preparation of the initial accounts in accordance with applicable law and United Kingdom Accounting Standards (United Kingdom Generally Accepted Accounting Practice).

Our responsibility is to report to you our opinion as to whether the initial accounts have been properly prepared within the meaning of section 839(4) of the Companies Act 2006.

Opinion

In our opinion the initial accounts for the period from... to... have been properly prepared within the meaning of section 839(4) of the Companies Act 2006.

[Signature]   *Address*

John Smith (Senior Statutory Auditor)   *Date*

for and on behalf of ABC LLP, Statutory Auditor

Statement by auditor on ceasing to hold office (section 519 of CA 2006)

Effective when auditor ceases to hold office on or after 6 April 2008

Unquoted companies

Where an auditor of an unquoted company ceases for any reason to hold office, it must deposit at the company's registered office either: **27**

(a)   a statement of the circumstances connected with it ceasing to hold office (see Example 4 on page 16); or

(b)   where it considers that there are no circumstances in connection with it ceasing to hold office that need to be brought to the attention of members or creditors of the company, a statement to that effect (see Example 5 on page 17).

Quoted companies[13]

Where an auditor of a quoted company ceases for any reason to hold office, it must deposit at the company's registered office a statement of the circumstances connected with its ceasing to hold office. The auditor of a quoted company is not able to deposit a statement stating that there are no circumstances connected with it ceasing to hold office.   **28**

Deadlines for filing the statement

The auditor's statement is required to be deposited: **29**

---

[13] *The definition of "quoted company" set out in sections 385 and 531 of CA 2006 do not strictly apply to the section of CA 2006 that deals with auditor resignation statements. The Institute of Chartered Accountants in England & Wales (ICAEW) suggests, in its note entitled "Auditor cessation statements" (Version 2 July 2008), www.icaew.com/auditnews? that "quoted company" should be taken to mean a company whose equity share capital on the day of the audit cessation:*
(a) has been included in the official list in accordance with the provisions of Part 6 of the Financial Services and Markets Act 2000, or
(b) is officially listed in an EEA State, or
(c) is admitted to dealing on either the New York Stock Exchange or the exchange known as Nasdaq.

(a)   in the case of resignation along with the notice of resignation;

(b)   in the case of failure to seek re-appointment, not less than 14 days before the end of the time allowed for next appointing an auditor;

(c)   in any other case, not later than the end of the period of 14 days beginning with the date on which the auditor ceases to hold office.

Company's duties in relation to statement (section 520 of CA 2006)

30   Where the statement deposited by the auditor sets out the circumstances connected with the auditor ceasing to hold office (ie is not a statement of no circumstances) the company must, within 14 days, either:

(a)   send a copy of it to every person who under section 423 of CA 2006 is entitled to be sent copies of the accounts; or

(b)   apply to the court (in which case it must notify the auditor of the application) to direct that copies need not be sent out where the auditor is using the provisions of section 519 of CA 2006 to secure needless publicity for defamatory matter.

Obligation to send copy of statement to the Registrar of Companies

31   Unless within 21 days beginning with the day on which the auditor deposited the statement under section 519 of CA 2006 the auditor receives notice of an application to the court under section 520 of CA 2006 it must within a further seven days send a copy of the statement to the Registrar of Companies. There are criminal offences for failure to comply with these provisions.

32   If an application to the court has been made under section 520 and the auditor subsequently receives notice that the court is not going to direct that copies of the statement not be sent out, the auditor must within seven days of receiving the notice send a copy of the statement to the Registrar of Companies.

Duty of auditor to notify appropriate audit authority (section 522 of CA 2006)

33   Where in the case of:

(a)   a "major audit" (see paragraph 38), an auditor ceases for any reason to hold office; or

(b)   an audit that is not a major audit, an auditor ceases to hold office before the end of its term of office[14];

the auditor must notify the "appropriate audit authority" (see paragraph 37).

34   The notice must:

(a)   inform the appropriate audit authority that the auditor has ceased to hold office; and

(b)   be accompanied by a copy of the statement deposited by the auditor at the company's registered office in accordance with section 519 of CA 2006.

35   If the statement deposited is to the effect that the auditor considers that there are no circumstances in connection with the auditor ceasing to hold office that need to be brought to the attention of members or creditors of the company, the notice must

---

[14] *The question of when an auditor's term of office ends is more complicated under the provisions of CA 2006 (compared to the provisions of the Companies Act 1985) whereby the auditor of a private company is deemed to be re-appointed automatically. The ICAEW's note referred to in footnote 13 provides helpful guidance in this area.*

also be accompanied by a statement of the reasons for the auditor ceasing to hold office.

The auditor must notify the appropriate audit authority;   36

(a)   in the case of a major audit, at the same time as it deposits a statement at the company's registered office in accordance with section 519 of CA 2006; or

(b)   in the case of an audit that is not a major audit at such time as the appropriate audit authority may require (such time not being earlier than "a").

Meaning of "appropriate audit authority" and "major audit" (section 525 of CA 2006)

In the case of a major audit (other than one conducted by an Auditor General[15]),   37
the term "appropriate audit authority" means the Professional Oversight Board (POB) of the Financial Reporting Council. In the case of an audit (other than one conducted by an Auditor General) that is not a major audit, the term "appropriate audit authority" means the relevant supervisory body as defined in section 1217 of CA 2006.

The term "major audit" means a statutory audit conducted in respect of: 38

(a)   a company any of whose securities have been admitted to the Official List; or

(b)   any other person in whose financial condition there is a major public interest.

The POB has issued guidance (which constitutes statutory guidance) on the   39
circumstances in which the notification should be made to the POB, how it should be sent and what it should cover. This includes guidance on what is a "major audit" for this purpose[16].

Parallel duty of company to notify appropriate audit authority

Where an auditor ceases to hold office before the end of its term of office, the   40
company is also required to notify the appropriate audit authority. The notice provided by the company must:

(a)   inform the appropriate audit authority that the auditor has ceased to hold office; and

(b)   be accompanied by:

    (i)   a statement by the company of the reasons for the auditor ceasing to hold office[17]; or

    (ii)   if the copy of the statement deposited by the auditor at the company's registered office in accordance with section 519 of CA 2006 contains a statement of circumstances in connection with the auditor ceasing to hold office that need to be brought to the attention of members or creditors of the company, a copy of that statement.

---

[15] *See: The Statutory Auditors and Third Country Auditors Regulations 2007 (SI 2007 No. 3494) Regulation 41.*

[16] *This guidance can be found at http://www.frc.org.uk/pob/regulation/auditfirms.cfm.*

[17] *It should be noted that the company is required to provide a statement of the reasons for the auditor ceasing to hold office even in those circumstances where the auditor is permitted to, and has, provided a statement that it considers that there are no circumstances connected with it ceasing to hold office that need to be brought to the attention of the members or creditors of the company.*

41   When the auditor is acting on the basis that the audit is a "major audit" it is helpful if the auditor advises the company of that fact and that the POB, therefore, is the appropriate audit authority that the company should be notifying. Similarly, when the audit is not a major audit it is helpful if the auditor advises the company of the identity of its relevant supervisory body which will be the appropriate audit authority that the company should be notifying.

Example 4 – Statement by auditor of a company on ceasing to hold office setting out the circumstances connected to the auditor ceasing to hold office[18]

Effective when auditor ceases to hold office on or after 6 April 2008

STATEMENT TO XYZ [LIMITED] [PLC] OF CIRCUMSTANCES RELATING TO:

● [THE INTENTION OF PQR NOT TO SEEK RE-APPOINTMENT AS AUDITOR OF XYZ [LIMITED] [PLC] AT THE CONCLUSION OF OUR TERM OF OFFICE]; or

● [THE RESIGNATION OF PQR AS AUDITOR OF XYZ [LIMITED] [PLC]]; or

● [THE REMOVAL OF PQR AS AUDITOR OF XYZ [LIMITED] [PLC]]

In accordance with section 519 of the Companies Act 2006, we consider that the following circumstances connected with our ceasing to hold office should be brought to the attention of the company's members or creditors:

[Set out circumstances]

Statutory auditor   *Address*
Date

Example 5 – Statement by auditor of an unquoted company on ceasing to hold office <u>where there are no circumstances</u> which need to be brought to the attention of members or creditors

Effective when auditor ceases to hold office on or after 6 April 2008

STATEMENT TO XYZ [LIMITED] [PLC] RELATING TO:

● [THE INTENTION OF PQR NOT TO SEEK RE-APPOINTMENT AS AUDITOR OF XYZ [LIMITED] [PLC] AT THE CONCLUSION OF OUR TERM OF OFFICE]; or

● [THE RESIGNATION OF PQR AS AUDITOR OF XYZ [LIMITED] [PLC]]; or

---

[18] *This statement must always be filed in respect of quoted companies. In respect of unquoted companies this statement need only be filed where there are circumstances which the auditor considers should be brought to the attention of members and creditors. See footnote 13 on page 12 for the definition of quoted company to be applied in this respect.*

- **[THE REMOVAL OF PQR AS AUDITOR OF XYZ [LIMITED] [PLC]]**

In accordance with section 519 of the Companies Act 2006, we confirm that there are no circumstances connected with our ceasing to hold office that we consider should be brought to the attention of the company's members or creditors.

Statutory auditor   *Address*

Date

IMPORTANT NOTE:

READERS ARE CAUTIONED THAT THE GUIDANCE (AND THE EXAMPLES) SET OUT ON THE FOLLOWING PAGES DOES NOT COME INTO EFFECT UNTIL 1 OCTOBER 2009 AND MAY BE SUBJECT TO TRANSITIONAL PROVISIONS UNDER THE FINAL "COMMENCEMENT ORDER" WHICH AT THE DATE OF THIS BULLETIN IS STILL IN DRAFT.

Readers should consult the table in the Appendix which sets out where example reports that are effective for the period up to 1 October 2009 may be found.

Auditor's statement with respect to net assets when a private company re-registers as a public company (section 92 of CA 2006)

Effective 1 October 2009

Under CA 2006 a private company may re-register as a public company if, among   **42** other things, it meets certain requirements regarding its net assets. The company's auditor is required to:

(a) make a written statement regarding the net assets; and

(b) to have issued a report on a balance sheet that is prepared at a date no more than seven months before application for re-registration is made to the Registrar of Companies, that is either:

    (i) unqualified; or

    (ii) qualified and the auditor expresses an opinion that the qualification is not material for determining the net assets of the company.

Requirements as to net assets

Section 92 of CA 2006 requires a private company applying to re-register as a   **43** public company to obtain:

(a) a balance sheet of the company prepared as at a date not more than seven months before the date on which the application is delivered to the Registrar of Companies;

(b) an "unqualified report" by the company's auditor on that balance sheet (see paragraph 46 for discussion of the meaning of "unqualified report");

(c) a written statement by the company's auditor that in its opinion at the balance sheet date the amount of the company's net assets was not less than the aggregate of its called-up share capital and undistributable reserves[19]. (The terms "net assets" and "undistributable reserves" have the same meaning as in section 831 of CA 2006).

44   Between the balance sheet date and the date on which the application for re-registration is delivered to the Registrar of Companies, there must be no change in the company's financial position that results in the amount of its net assets becoming less than the aggregate of its called-up share capital and undistributable reserves[20]. As the auditor's statement is required to be made as at the balance sheet date, the auditor has no responsibility for the period between the balance sheet date and the date the application is delivered to the Registrar of Companies by the company.

45   The balance sheet included with the company's latest financial statements is eligible for the purpose of section 92(1)(a) of CA 2006 if:

(a)   it was prepared less than seven months before the company's application to reregister as a public company; and

(b)   at the time it was prepared the balance sheet met the net assets test in section 92(1)(c) of CA 2006.

Meaning of unqualified report

46   In paragraph 43(b) above an unqualified report means[21]:

(a)   if the balance sheet was prepared for a financial year of the company, a report stating without material qualification the auditor's opinion that the balance sheet has been properly prepared in accordance with the requirements of CA 2006;

(b)   if the balance sheet was not prepared for a financial year of the company, a report stating without material qualification the auditor's opinion that the balance sheet has been properly prepared in accordance with the provisions of CA 2006 which would have applied if it had been prepared for a financial year of the company[22].

47   A qualification is material unless the auditor states in its report that the matter giving rise to the qualification is not material for the purpose of determining (by reference to the company's balance sheet) whether at the balance sheet date the amount of the company's net assets was not less than the aggregate of its called up share capital and undistributable reserves[23].

The auditor's statement on net assets

48   Section 92(1) of CA 2006 makes reference to a company applying to re-register as a public company. Therefore, the auditor's statement required by section 92(1)(c) is addressed to the company.

49   With respect to the auditor's responsibility the auditor's statement states that it is limited to an examination of the relationship between the company's net assets and

---

[19]   *Section 92 CA 2006.*

[20]   *Section 92(2) CA 2006.*

[21]   *Section 92(3) CA 2006.*

[22]   *Under section 92(4) of CA 2006 "For the purposes of an auditor's report on a balance sheet that was not prepared for a financial year of the company, the provisions of this Act apply with such modifications as are necessary by reason of that fact".*

[23]   *Section 92(5) CA 2006.*

its called up share capital and undistributable reserves as stated in the audited balance sheet, so that it is clear that no further audit procedures have been carried out.

The statement by the auditor is dated when it is signed, which cannot be earlier than the date of the auditor's report on the balance sheet.   **50**

Auditor's report on the balance sheet

Section 92 of CA 2006 requires that, for it to be "unqualified", the auditor's report   **51**
on the balance sheet must state without material qualification the auditor's opinion that the balance sheet has been properly prepared in accordance with the requirements of CA 2006. For a qualified report to be acceptable, the auditors are required to state in their report that the matter giving rise to the qualification is not material for determining (by reference to the balance sheet) whether at the balance sheet date the amount of the net assets of the company were not less than the aggregate of its called-up share capital and undistributable reserves.

If there has been a change of auditor, the new auditor can accept the balance sheet   **52**
audited by the previous auditor, as a basis for the work referred to in paragraph 49 above, unless the auditor's report thereon contains a material qualification regarding the proper preparation of the balance sheet in accordance with CA 2006. The new auditor indicates in its report by whom the audit of the balance sheet was carried out.

If the balance sheet included with the company's latest financial statements is not   **53**
eligible for use, it will be necessary for the company to prepare a balance sheet. A balance sheet may not be eligible for use if:

(a)   it was prepared more than seven months before the company's application to re-register as a public company; or

(b)   at the time it was prepared it did not meet the net assets test in section 92(1)(c) of CA 2006.

With respect to a balance sheet that has been specially prepared and has not been   **54**
included with the company's annual financial statements the auditor is required to report without material qualification the auditor's opinion that the balance sheet has been properly prepared in accordance with the provisions of CA 2006 which would have applied had it been prepared for a financial year of a company.

Reporting

CA 2006 does not require the auditor's report on the balance sheet and the   **55**
auditor's statement on the net assets to be included within a combined report. However, as a practical matter this will often be the most effective way for the auditor to report on these matters.

The following examples of such combined reports are provided: **56**

(a)   Example 6 Balance Sheet in annual financial statements reported on without qualification (see page 25);

(b)   Example 7 Balance sheet in annual financial statements reported on with a qualification in respect of proper preparation in accordance with CA 2006, but the qualification is not material (see page 26);

(c)   Example 8 Specially prepared balance sheet reported on without qualification (see page 28);

(d)   Example 9 Specially prepared balance sheet reported on with a qualification in respect or proper preparation in accordance with the Companies Act 2006, but the qualification is not material (see page 29).

Example 6 – Statement when a private company wishes to re-register as a public company where the auditor's opinion on the balance sheet is unqualified

Effective 1 October 2009

This example is used when the company's annual financial statements were prepared within seven months before its application to re-register as a public company.

STATEMENT OF THE INDEPENDENT AUDITOR TO XYZ LIMITED FOR THE PURPOSE OF SECTION 92(1)(b) and (c) OF THE COMPANIES ACT 2006

We have examined the balance sheet and related notes of XYZ Limited as at... which formed part of the financial statements for the year then ended which were audited by [us]/[ABC LLP].

Respective responsibilities of directors and auditors

The company's directors are responsible for the preparation of the balance sheet and related notes.

It is our responsibility to:

(a)   report on whether the balance sheet has been properly prepared in accordance with the requirements of the Companies Act 2006; and

(b)   form an independent opinion, based on our examination, concerning the relationship between the company's net assets and its called-up share capital and undistributable reserves at the balance sheet date.

Opinion concerning proper preparation of balance sheet

In our opinion the audited balance sheet at... has been properly prepared in accordance with the requirements of the Companies Act 2006.

Statement on net assets

In our opinion, at ... the amount of the company's net assets (within the meaning given to that expression by section 831(2) of the Companies Act 2006) was not less than the aggregate of its called-up share capital and undistributable reserves.

Statutory auditor   *Address*

Date

Example 7 – Statement when a private company wishes to re-register as a public company where the auditor's opinion on the balance sheet is qualified with respect to proper preparation in accordance with the Companies Act 2006, but the qualification is not material

Effective 1 October 2009

This example is used when the company's annual financial statements were prepared within seven months before its application to re-register as a public company.

STATEMENT OF THE INDEPENDENT AUDITOR TO XYZ LIMITED FOR THE PURPOSE OF SECTION 92(1)(b) AND (c) OF THE COMPANIES ACT 2006

We have examined the balance sheet and related notes of XYZ Limited as at... which formed part of the financial statements for the year then ended which were audited by [us]/[ABC LLP].

Respective responsibilities of directors and auditors

The company's directors are responsible for the preparation of the balance sheet and related notes.

It is our responsibility to:

(a) report on whether the balance sheet has been properly prepared in accordance with the requirements of the Companies Act 2006; and

(b) form an independent opinion, based on our examination, concerning the relationship between the company's net assets and its called-up share capital and undistributable reserves at the balance sheet date.

Qualified opinion concerning proper preparation of balance sheet

[We]/[ABC LLP] audited the financial statements for the year ended ... and expressed a qualified opinion regarding the proper preparation of the balance sheet in accordance with the requirements of the Companies Act 2006.

The matter giving rise to [our]/[the] qualification is not material for determining by reference to the balance sheet at ... whether, at that date, the amount of the company's net assets (within the meaning given to that expression by section 831 (2) of the Companies Act 2006) was not less than the aggregate of its called-up share capital and undistributable reserves.

Statement on net assets

In our opinion at ... the amount of the company's net assets (within the meaning given to that expression by section 831(2) of the Companies Act 2006) was not less than the aggregate of its called-up share capital and undistributable reserves.

Statutory auditor   *Address*

Date

Example 8 – Statement when a private company wishes to re-register as a public company based on a specially prepared balance sheet that is unqualified

Effective 1 October 2009

This example is used when the latest financial statements are not eligible for use as they were prepared more than seven months before the company's application to re-register as a public company, or because at the time they were prepared the balance sheet did not meet the test in section 92(1)(c) of CA 2006. In these circumstances it is necessary for the company to prepare a balance sheet which is required to be audited.

REPORT OF THE INDEPENDENT AUDITOR TO XYZ LIMITED FOR THE PURPOSE OF SECTIONS 92(1)(b) AND (c) OF THE COMPANIES ACT 2006

We have audited the balance sheet and related notes of XYZ Limited as at…set out on pages… to…. which have been prepared under the accounting policies set out therein.

Respective responsibilities of directors and auditors

The company's directors are responsible for the preparation of the balance sheet and related notes.

It is our responsibility to:

(a)   report on whether the balance sheet has been properly prepared in accordance with the provisions of the Companies Act 2006 that would have applied if it had been prepared for a financial year of the company with such modifications as are necessary by reason of that fact; and

(b)   form an independent opinion concerning the relationship between the company's net assets and its called-up share capital and undistributable reserves at the balance sheet date.

Opinion concerning preparation of balance sheet

In our opinion the balance sheet and related notes as at…have been properly prepared in accordance with the provisions of the Companies Act 2006, which would have applied had the balance sheet been prepared for a financial year of the company.

Statement on net assets

In our opinion, at … the amount of the company's net assets (within the meaning given to that expression by section 831(2) of the Companies Act 2006) was not less than the aggregate of its called-up share capital and undistributable reserves.

Statutory auditor   *Address*

Date

Example 9 – Statement when a private company wishes to re-register as a public company based on a specially prepared balance sheet that is qualified with respect to proper preparation in accordance with the Companies Act 2006, but the qualification is not material

Effective 1 October 2009

This example is used when the latest financial statements are not eligible for use as they were prepared more than seven months before the company's application to re-register as a public company, or because at the time they were prepared the balance sheet did not meet the test in section 92(1)(c) of CA 2006. In these circumstances it is necessary for the company to prepare a balance sheet which is required to be audited.

REPORT OF THE INDEPENDENT AUDITOR TO XYZ LIMITED FOR THE PURPOSE OF SECTIONS 92(1)(b) and (c) OF THE COMPANIES ACT 2006

We have audited the balance sheet and related notes of XYZ Limited as at…set out on pages… to…. which have been prepared under the accounting policies set out therein.

Respective responsibilities of directors and auditors

The company's directors are responsible for the preparation of the balance sheet and related notes.

It is our responsibility to:

(a) report on whether the balance sheet has been properly prepared in accordance with the provisions of the Companies Act 2006 that would have applied if it had been prepared for a financial year of the company with such modifications as are necessary by reason of that fact; and

(b) form an independent opinion concerning the relationship between the company's net assets and its called-up share capital and undistributable reserves at the balance sheet date.

Qualified opinion concerning proper preparation of balance sheet

[Except for [describe area of non-compliance with CA 2006] in our opinion the balance sheet and related notes as at… have been properly prepared in accordance with the provisions of the Companies Act 2006, which would have applied had the balance sheet been prepared for a financial year of the company.][24]

[Because ……… [*describe area of non-compliance with CA 2006*] in our opinion the balance sheet and related notes as at…have not been properly prepared in accordance with the provisions of the Companies Act 2006, which would have applied had the balance sheet been prepared for a financial year of the company.][25]

---

[24] *This style of wording is used where the auditor's have expressed a qualified opinion concerning the proper preparation of the balance sheet.*

[25] *This style of wording is used where the auditor's have expressed an adverse opinion concerning the proper preparation of the balance sheet.*

However, in our opinion, this matter is not material for determining by reference to the balance sheet at … whether, at that date, the amount of the company's net assets (within the meaning given to that expression by section 831(2) of the Companies Act 2006) was not less than the aggregate of its called-up share capital and undistributable reserves.

Statement on net assets

In our opinion, at … the amount of the company's net assets (within the meaning given to that expression by section 831(2) of the Companies Act 2006) was not less than the aggregate of its called-up share capital and undistributable reserves.

Statutory auditor   *Address*

Date

Report when a private company wishes to redeem or purchase its own shares out of capital (section 714(6) of CA 2006)
Effective 1 October 2009

57   A payment out of capital by a private company for the redemption or purchase of its own shares is not lawful unless the requirements of sections 714, 716, 719, 720 and 721 of CA 2006 are met. Section 716 of CA 2006 requires that a payment out of capital must be approved by special resolution which must be passed on, or within the week immediately following, the date on which the directors make the statement required by section 714 of CA 2006.

Directors' statement

58   To make a payment out of capital the directors are required by sections 714(1) to (5) of CA 2006 to make a statement specifying the amount of the permissible capital payment for the shares in question. Section 714(3) requires the directors to state that, having made full inquiry into the affairs and prospects of the company, the directors have formed the opinion:

(a)   as regards its initial situation immediately following the date on which the payment out of capital is proposed to be made, that there will be no grounds on which the company could then be found unable to pay its debts, and

(b)   as regards its prospects for the year immediately following that date, that having regard to:

(i)   their intentions with respect to the management of the company's business during that year; and

(ii)   the amount and character of the financial resources that will in their view be available to the company during that year;

(iii)   the company will be able to continue to carry on business as a going concern (and will accordingly be able to pay its debts as they fall due) throughout that year.

In forming their opinion, in respect of paragraph 58(a) above, the directors are **59** required to take into account all of the company's liabilities (including any contingent or prospective liabilities).

The permissible capital payment (section 710 of CA 2006)

The payment that may be made out of capital is described as the "permissible **60** capital payment" and is such amount as, after applying:

(a)   any available profits of the company; and

(b)   the proceeds of any fresh issue of shares made for the purposes of the redemption or purchase

is required to meet the price of redemption or purchase.

Determination of available profits (sections 711 and 712 of CA 2006)

The available profits of the company are determined as follows: **61**

---

1.   First, determine the profits of the company by reference to the following items as stated in the relevant accounts (see paragraph 62):

    (a)   profits, losses, assets and liabilities;

    (b)   provisions of the following kinds:

        (i)   where the relevant accounts are Companies Act accounts, provisions of a kind specified for the purposes of this subsection by paragraph 4 of Schedule 9 to *The Large and Medium-sized Companies and Groups (Accounts and Reports) Regulations 2008*[26] or by paragraph 4 of Schedule 7 to *The Small Companies and Groups (Accounts and Directors' Report) Regulations 2008*[27] by regulations under section 396 of CA 2006;

        (ii)   where the relevant accounts are IAS accounts, provisions of any kind.

    (c)   share capital and reserves (including undistributable reserves).

2.   Second, reduce the amount so determined by the amount of

    (a)   any distribution lawfully made by the company, and

    (b)   any other relevant payment lawfully made[28] by the company out of distributable profits,

after the date of the relevant accounts and before the end of the relevant period (see paragraph 62).

3.   The resulting figure is the amount of available profits.

The "relevant accounts" are any accounts that: **62**

(a)   are prepared as at a date within the relevant period; and

---

[26]   *SI 2008 No. 410.*

[27]   *SI 2008 No. 409.*

[28]   *See section 712(4) of CA 2006 for definition of "other payments lawfully made".*

(b)   are such as to enable a reasonable judgment to be made as to the amounts of the items mentioned under "1" in the above table.

The "relevant period" means the period of three months ending with the date on which the directors' statement is made in accordance with section 714 of CA 2006.

Report by the company's auditor

63   The directors' statement is required by section 714(6) to have annexed to it a report addressed to the directors by the company's auditor (see Example 10 on page 34) stating that:

(a)   it has inquired into the company's state of affairs;

(b)   the amount specified in the statement as the permissible capital payment for the shares in question is in its view properly determined in accordance with sections 710 to 712 of CA 2006;and

(c)   it is not aware of anything to indicate that the opinion expressed by the directors in their statement as to any of the matters mentioned in subsection (3) of section 714 of CA 2006 is unreasonable in all the circumstances.

64   The directors' statement and therefore the annexed auditor's report are required to be made in the week before the resolution is passed specifying the amount of the permissible capital payment for the shares in question. The auditor's report cannot be dated earlier than the date of the director's statement to which it relates. The date of the auditor's report is the date on which the auditor signs its report expressing its opinion.

65   There is no provision for the auditor's report to be other than unqualified. Unless the opinion is unqualified the auditor does not issue a report.

Example 10 – Report when a private company wishes to redeem or purchase its own shares out of capital

Effective 1 October 2009

REPORT OF THE INDEPENDENT AUDITOR TO THE DIRECTORS OF XYZ LIMITED PURSUANT TO SECTION 714(6) OF THE COMPANIES ACT 2006

We report on the attached statement of the directors dated…, prepared pursuant to the Companies Act 2006, in connection with the company's proposed [purchase]/ [redemption] of… (number) [ordinary]/ [preferred] shares by a payment out of capital.

Basis of opinion

We have inquired into the company's state of affairs in order to review the bases for the directors' statement.

Opinion

In our opinion the amount of £… specified in the directors' statement as the permissible capital payment for the shares to be [purchased]/ [redeemed] is properly determined in accordance with sections 710 to 712 of the Companies Act 2006.

We are not aware of anything to indicate that the opinion expressed by the directors in their statement as to any of the matters mentioned in section 714(3) of the Companies Act 2006 is unreasonable in all the circumstances.

Statutory auditor   *Address*

Date

Report when a public company wishes to allot shares otherwise than for cash (section 593 of CA 2006)

Effective 1 October 2009

Section 593 of CA 2006 addresses the valuation of non-cash consideration for **66** shares in a public company. Where a public company proposes to allot shares for such non-cash consideration it must, subject to certain exceptions, obtain during the six months before the date of the allotment a report on the value of the assets to be received in payment for the shares. Sections 594 and 595 of CA 2006 set out exceptions to the valuation requirement with respect to mergers and certain "arrangements" with other companies.

Section 596 of CA 2006 sets out the requirements as to the valuation and the report **67** and in particular provides that the provisions of sections 1150 to 1153 of CA 2006 should apply to the valuation and report required by section 593. Under section 1150 of CA 2006 the valuation and the report must be made by a person who:

(a)   is eligible for appointment as a statutory auditor (see section 1212 of CA 2006); and

(b)   meets the independence requirement in section 1151 of CA 2006.

However, where it appears to the valuer to be reasonable for the valuation of the **68** consideration, or part of it, to be made by another person (an expert) the valuer may arrange for or accept such a valuation, together with a report which will enable him to make his own report.

If the company's own statutory auditor is requested to undertake a valuation in **69** accordance with section 593 of CA 2006 the standards and guidance in APB Ethical Standard 5 (Revised) *Non-audit services provided to audited entities* are applied[29].

Guidance on the work to be carried out when relying on an expert is contained in **70** ISA (UK and Ireland) 620"Using the work of an expert". The expert must report to the valuer so as to enable the valuer to make its report.

The valuer's report will incorporate the following elements (see Example 11 on **71** page 38):

(a)   *Addressee* – the report is made to the company itself and sent to the company secretary for circulation to the proposed allottees;

(b)   *Introductory paragraph/s* – in addition to expressing the opinion set out in (d) below, the report must include the following information:

    (i)   the nominal value of the shares to be wholly or partly paid for by the consideration in question;

---

[29] *Section 1150 of CA 2006 requires the valuation and report required by section 593 to be made by a person who is eligible for appointment as a statutory auditor and meets the independence requirements in Section 1151 of CA 2006. By virtue of section 1151(2) of CA 2006 the auditor of the company meets the independence requirements in section 1151.*

      (ii)   the amount of any premium payable on the shares;

      (iii) a description of the consideration;

      (iv) a description of the part of the consideration valued by the valuer, the method used to value it and the date of the valuation; and

      (v)   the extent to which the nominal value of the shares and any premium are to be treated as paid up:

- by the consideration;
- in cash;

(c)   ***Basis of valuation*** – the report indicates the basis of valuation of the consideration. If the valuation has been made by another person (ie an expert) the expert's name and relevant qualifications are stated in the basis of valuation. The basis of valuation also describes the part of the consideration valued by the expert, the method used to value it and specifies the date of the valuation;

(d)   ***Opinion*** – section 596(3) of CA 2006 requires that the valuer's report must contain, or be accompanied by, a note from the valuer, stating:

      (i)   if the valuation has been made by an expert, it appears to be reasonable to arrange for it to be so made or to accept a valuation so made;

      (ii)   the method of valuation of the consideration was reasonable in all the circumstances;

      (iii) there appears to have been no material change in the value of the consideration since the date at which the valuation was made; and

      (iv) on the basis of the valuation, the value of the consideration, together with any cash by which the nominal value of the shares or any premium payable on them is to be paid up, is not less than so much of the aggregate of the nominal value and the whole of any such premium as is treated as paid up by the consideration and any such cash;

(e)   ***Date*** – the date used is the date on which the report is signed.

72   There is no provision for the report to be qualified. Unless the opinion is unqualified the valuer does not issue a report.

73   In certain circumstances the allotment of shares may represent only a part of the consideration for the transfer of a non-cash asset to the allotting company (e.g. cash may also be paid). In such cases, the valuer's report must cover the proportion of the value of the non-cash assets which apples to the full value of shares issued (ie nominal value and any premium). The report must also state:

(a)   what valuations have been made in order to determine that proportion of the consideration;

(b)   the reason for those valuations;

(c)   the method and date of any such valuation; and

(d)   any other matters which may be relevant to that determination.

74   Before the valuer can make a statement that there appears to have been no material change in the value of the asset since the valuation, it may have to perform additional work. If the period of time between the making of the valuation and the date of the report is such that there may have been a change in the value, the valuer will need to reconsider the valuation. If the auditor made arrangements for an expert to perform the valuation the auditor obtains written confirmation from that expert as to whether there has been a change in value.

Example 11 – Report when a public company wishes to allot shares otherwise than for cash

Effective 1 October 2009

REPORT OF THE INDEPENDENT [VALUER] [AUDITOR] TO XYZ PLC FOR THE PURPOSES OF SECTION 593(1) OF THE COMPANIES ACT 2006

We report on the value of the consideration for the allotment to... [name of allottee] of... [number] shares, having a nominal value of [...] each, to be issued at a premium of... pence per share. The shares and share premium are to be treated as fully paid up.

The consideration for the allotment to [name of allottee] is the [freehold building situated at... address] and... [number] shares, having a nominal value of [...] each, in LMN PLC.

Basis of valuation

The freehold building was valued on the basis of its open market value by [name of expert], a Fellow of the Royal Institution of Chartered Surveyors.

The shares in LMN PLC were valued by us on... on the basis of the price shown in the Stock Exchange Daily Official List at....

Opinion

In our opinion:

- it is reasonable to accept the valuation made by (name of expert);
- the methods of valuation of the freehold building and the shares in LMN PLC were reasonable in all the circumstances; and
- there appears to have been no material change in the value of either part of the consideration since the date(s) at which the valuations were made.

On the basis of the valuations, in our opinion, the value of the total consideration is not less than the aggregate of the nominal value and share premium to be treated as paid up by the consideration.

Qualified independent person   *Address*

Date

Report when non-cash assets are transferred to a public company by certain of its members (section 599 of CA 2006)

Effective 1 October 2009

75   Section 598 of CA 2006 requires, amongst other things, that during the first two years following receipt of its trading certificate[30] a public company may not lawfully acquire from certain of its members a non-cash asset for a consideration worth one tenth or more of the company's issued share capital unless:

(a)   the terms of the transfer have been approved by an ordinary resolution of the company (see section 601 of CA 2006); and

(b)   a valuer's report has been made to the company within six months immediately preceding the date of the agreement to transfer the non-cash assets (see section 599 of CA 2006).

76   Under section 1150 of CA 2006 the valuation and the report must be made by a person who:

(a)   is eligible for appointment as a statutory auditor (see section 1212 of CA 2006); and

(b)   meets the independence requirement in section 1151 of CA 2006.

77   However, where it appears to the valuer to be reasonable for the valuation of the consideration to be made by another person (an expert) the valuer may arrange for or accept such a valuation, together with a report which will enable him to make his own report.

78   If the company's own statutory auditor is requested to undertake a valuation in accordance with section 599 of CA 2006 the standards and guidance in APB Ethical Standard 5 (Revised) *Non-audit services provided to audited entities* are applied[31].

79   Guidance on the work to be carried out when relying on an expert is contained in ISA (UK and Ireland) 620 *Using the work of an expert*. The expert must report to the valuer so as to enable the valuer to make its own report.

80   Section 600(2) of CA 2006 requires that the valuer's report must state:

●   the consideration to be received by the company, describing the asset in question (specifying the amount to be received in cash) and the consideration to be given by the company (specifying the amount to be given in cash); and

●   the method and date of valuation.

81   Section 600(3) further requires that the valuer's report must contain or be accompanied by a note from the valuer stating:

(a)   in the case of a valuation made by an expert that it appeared reasonable to arrange for it to be so made or to accept a valuation so made;

---

[30] *A trading certificate is conclusive evidence that the company is entitled to do business and exercise any borrowing powers.*

[31] *Section 1150 CA 2006 requires the valuation and report required by Section 599 to be made by a person ("the valuer") who is eligible for appointment as a statutory auditor and meets the independence requirements in section 1151 of CA 2006. By virtue of section 1151(2) of CA 2006 the auditor of the company meets the independence requirements in section 1151.*

Miscellaneous reports by auditors Bulletin 2008/9 1,763

(b) that the method of valuation was reasonable in all the circumstances (whoever made the valuation);

(c) that it appears to the valuer that there has been no material change in the value of the consideration since the valuation; and

(d) that, on the basis of the valuation, the value of the consideration to be received by the company is not less than the value of the consideration to be given by it.

Sections 600(4) and (5), of CA 2006, set out the requirements where the **82** consideration is given partly for the transfer of the asset.

Where the consideration, or part of it, is valued by an expert rather than the valuer **83** the valuer's report must state that fact and also:

(a) state the expert's name and what knowledge and experience the expert has to carry out the valuation; and

(b) describe the asset valued by the expert and the method used to value it specifying the date of the valuation.

The report which is illustrated in example 12 on page 42 incorporates the **84** following elements:

(a) *Addressee* – the report is made to the company itself and sent to the company secretary for circulation to the members of the company and to the person selling the asset;

(b) *Introductory Paragraphs* – in addition to expressing the opinion set out in (d) below, the report must contain the following information:

    (i) the consideration to be received by the company, describing the asset in question, and the consideration to be given by the company and specifying any amounts to be received or given in cash; and

    (ii) the method and date of valuation;

(c) *Basis of valuation* – the report indicates the basis of valuation of the consideration. If the valuation has been made by another person (ie an expert) the expert's name is stated in the basis of opinion as well as the knowledge and experience the expert has to carry out the valuation. The basis of opinion also describes the part of the consideration valued by the expert, the method used to value it and specifies the date of the valuation;

(d) *Opinion* – the valuer must state that in its opinion:

    (i) if the valuation has been made by an expert, it appears to be reasonable to accept or arrange for such a valuation;

    (ii) the method of valuation was reasonable in all the circumstances;

    (iii) there appears to have been no material change in the values of the asset in question since the date at which the valuation was made, and

    (iv) on the basis of the valuation used, the value of the consideration to be received by the company is not less than the value of the consideration to be given by the company;

(e) *Date* – the date used is that on which the report is signed.

There is no provision for the report to be qualified. Unless the opinion is **85** unqualified the valuer does not issue a report.

86   Before the valuer can make a statement that there appears to have been no material change in the value of the asset since the valuation, it may have to perform additional work. If the period of time between the making of the valuation and the date of the report is such that there may have been a change in the value, the valuer will need to reconsider the valuation. If the auditor made arrangements for an expert to perform the valuation the auditor obtains written confirmation from that expert as to whether there has been a change in value.

Example 12 – Report when non-cash assets are transferred to a public company by certain of its members

Effective 1 October 2009

REPORT OF THE INDEPENDENT [VALUER] [AUDITOR] TO XYZ PLC FOR THE PURPOSES OF SECTION 599 OF THE COMPANIES ACT 2006

We report on the transfer of non-cash assets to XYZ PLC ('the Company') by subscribers to the Company's memorandum of association.

The consideration to be received by the Company is a [freehold building situated at... address] ('the consideration to be received').

The consideration to be given by the Company is... [number] shares, having a nominal value of £1 each, in LMN PLC ('the consideration to be given').

Basis of valuation

The freehold building was valued on the basis of its open market value by [name of expert], a Fellow of the Royal Institution of Chartered Surveyors.

The shares in LMN PLC were valued by us on... on the basis of the price shown in the Stock Exchange Daily Official List at....

Opinion

In our opinion:

- it is reasonable to accept the valuation made by (name of expert);

- the methods of valuation of the freehold building and the shares in LMN PLC were reasonable in all the circumstances; and

- there appears to have been no material change in the value of the consideration to be received or the consideration to be given since the date(s) at which the valuations were made.

On the basis of the valuations, in our opinion, the value of the consideration to be received by the Company is not less than the value of the consideration to be given by the Company.

Qualified independent person   *Address*

Date

Appendix – Checklist of example reports in Bulletin 2007/1 indicating which Bulletin, or example report in this Bulletin, reflects the requirements of the Companies Act 2006

Example Report in Bulletin 2007/1 (reflecting the requirements of CA 1985)	Location of equivalent example report reflecting the requirements of CA 2006	Commencement date of report under CA 2006
1 Auditor's report on revised financial statements: revision by replacement.	Bulletin 2008/5 (Appendix 2)	Periods beginning on or after 6 April 2008
2 Auditor's report on revised financial statements: revision by supplementary note.	Bulletin 2008/5 (Appendix 3)	Periods beginning on or after 6 April 2008
3 Auditor's report on revised directors' report.	Bulletin 2008/5 (Appendix 4)	Periods beginning on or after 6 April 2008
4 Report on abbreviated accounts.	Bulletin 2008/4	Periods beginning on or after 6 April 2008
5 Auditor's statement on a summary financial statement.	Bulletin 2008/3	Periods beginning on or after 6 April 2008
6 Report on entitlement to exemption from preparing group financial statements.	Requirement withdrawn in 1996	n/a
7 Statement on a company's ability to make a distribution.	Examples 1 and 2 of this Bulletin	6 April 2008
8 Statement when a private company wishes to re-register as a public company[32].	Examples 6, 7, 8 and 9 of this Bulletin	1 October 2009
9 Report on balance sheet prepared other than in respect of an accounting reference period for the purpose of a private company re-registering as a public company.	Now combined with the statement when a private company wishes to reregister as a private company (see Examples 8 and 9)	1 October 2009
10 Report when a private company wishes to redeem or purchase its own shares out of capital	Example 10 of this Bulletin	1 October 2009

---

[32] *For private companies re-registering as public companies after 6 April 2008 but before 1 October 2009, paragraph 58 of Schedule 1 to The Companies Act 2006 (Consequential Amendments etc) Order 2008 (SI No. 2008 No 948) will require references to section 264(2) of the Companies Act 1985, in Example 8 of Bulletin 2007/1, to be replaced by references to section 831 of CA 2006.*

11 Report when a private company wishes to provide financial assistance for the purchase of its own shares or those of its holding company.	Report no longer required under CA 2006. (Provisions under CA 1985 repealed as from 1 October 2008 in relation to financial assistance given on or after that date[33])	n/a
12 Report when a public company wishes to allot shares otherwise than for cash.	Example 11 of this Bulletin	1 October 2009
13 Report when non-cash assets are transferred to a public company by certain of its members.	Example 12 of this Bulletin	1 October 2009
14 Report on initial accounts when a public company wishes to make a distribution.	Example 3 of this Bulletin	6 April 2008
15 Report on ceasing to hold office.	Examples 4 and 5 of this Bulletin	6 April 2008

---

[33] *The Companies Act 2006 (Commencement No. 5, Transitional Provisions and Savings) Order 2007 (SI 2007 No. 3495 (C. 150)), Schedule 4 paragraph 51.*

Bulletin 2008/10 Going concern issues during the current economic conditions

(December 2008)

Contents

	Paragraphs
Introduction	1 - 7
The potential impact of the economic outlook on the directors' approach to assessing going concern	8 - 11
Developments in corporate reporting	12 - 13
Planning	14 - 15
Considering the directors' assessment of going concern	16
Evaluating how the directors have satisfied themselves that it is appropriate to adopt the going concern basis	17 - 22
Concluding whether or not to concur with the directors' view	23 - 25
Adequacy of disclosures	26 - 28
Determining the implications for the auditor's report	29 - 40
Nature and materiality of the events or conditions	33 - 38
Ability to adopt alternative strategies that mitigate an uncertainty	39 - 40
Documentation	41
Preliminary announcements	42 - 45
Reviewing interim financial information	46 - 48
Ethical issues	49 - 54
Appendix 1 – Financial reporting council – an update for directors of listed companies: going concern and liquidity risk	
Appendix 2 – Events or conditions that may affect going concern	
Appendix 3 – Risk factors arising from current economic conditions	
Appendix 4 – Examples of conclusions the auditor might draw	

Introduction

1   Current economic conditions provide particular challenges to all involved with annual reports and accounts. One consequence is expected to be an increase in the disclosures in annual reports and accounts about going concern and liquidity risk. As a result, the current conditions will present challenges for:

(a)   directors – who will need to ensure that they prepare thoroughly for their assessment of going concern and make appropriate disclosures; and

(b)   auditors – who will need to ensure that they fully consider going concern assessments and only refer to going concern in their auditor's reports when appropriate.

2   In January 2008 the Auditing Practices Board (APB) issued Bulletin 2008/1[1] to provide guidance on matters that auditors needed to consider when conducting audits in the economic environment that was, at that time, characterised as the "credit crunch".

3   Since then the economic environment has worsened and the UK and Irish economies are entering a period of recession. This economic environment leads to added uncertainty regarding:

(a)   bank lending intentions and the availability of finance more generally;

(b)   the impact of the recession on a company's own business; and

(c)   the impact of the recession on counterparties, including customers and suppliers.

These conditions will create a number of challenges for the preparers of financial statements and their auditors.

4   The effect of the current market conditions on any particular entity requires careful evaluation. However, the general economic situation at the present time does not, of itself, necessarily mean that a material uncertainty exists about an entity's ability to continue as a going concern or justify auditors modifying their auditor's reports to draw attention to going concern. The auditor makes a judgment on the need, or otherwise, to draw attention to going concern on the basis of the facts and circumstances of the entity at the time of signing the auditor's report. This Bulletin gives guidance on relevant factors to be considered and highlights certain requirements and guidance in the ISAs (UK and Ireland).

5   This Bulletin supplements Bulletin 2008/1and in particular:

(a)   updates the listing of risk factors included in that Bulletin (see appendices 2 and 3); and

(b)   provides guidance on a number of going concern issues that auditors are likely to encounter during the forthcoming reporting cycle.

This guidance draws on ISA (UK and Ireland) 570 *Going concern* and does not establish any new requirements.

6   To assist directors, the Financial Reporting Council (FRC), has published guidance entitled "An update for directors of listed companies: going concern and liquidity risk" (Update for Directors). Its purpose is to bring together existing guidance in the context of recent developments relating to going concern and liquidity risk disclosures to assist directors, audit committees and finance teams of

---

[1] *Bulletin 2008/1 Audit Issues when Financial Market Conditions are Difficult and Credit Facilities may be Restricted.*

listed companies during the forthcoming reporting season. It is expected that this Update for Directors will also be useful to directors of unlisted companies and other entities who have similar responsibilities to assess going concern and make appropriate disclosures. This Update for Directors is attached as Appendix 1to this Bulletin.

As with Bulletin 2008/1, this Bulletin has been written by reference to the 7 challenges arising in relation to audits of all entities. The challenges arising in relation to audits of financial institutions such as banks, insurance companies and investment businesses give rise to additional specialist considerations that are not addressed in this Bulletin.

The potential impact of the economic outlook on the directors' approach to assessing going concern

Accounting standards (both IFRS and UK GAAP) require directors to: 8

(a) make an assessment of a company's ability to continue as a going concern when preparing financial statements; and

(b) disclose the uncertainties that the directors are aware of in making their assessment of going concern where those uncertainties may cast significant doubt on the company's ability to continue as a going concern.

The APB believes that the FRC's publication of the Update for Directors will 9 assist auditors as it emphasises the need for directors to apply an appropriate degree of rigour and formality when making their judgments and suggests that directors will need to plan their assessment of going concern as early as practicable, including deciding on the information that will need to be produced (such as board papers) and the processes and procedures that will be undertaken. The Update for Directors further suggests that the directors should address the evidence to be obtained to support their conclusion and develop, where necessary, any remedial action plan.

To help minimise the risk of last minute surprises, the Update for Directors 10 recommends companies have early discussions with their auditor about their plans. It also suggests that it may be useful for a draft of the relevant disclosures about going concern and liquidity risk to be prepared and discussed with the auditor before the end of the financial year. Such discussions may help the auditor plan its audit procedures and minimise the risk of the auditor qualifying its opinion on the grounds of a scope limitation or of a disagreement due to inadequate disclosure. It may also encourage the directors to develop a realistic remedial action plan where one is needed.

Notwithstanding early discussions between the company and its auditors both 11 directors and auditors need to take account of subsequent developments as final assessments of going concern need to be made at the date that the directors approve the annual report and accounts taking into account the relevant facts and circumstances at that date.

Developments in corporate reporting

The Update for Directors describes recent developments in corporate reporting 12 relating to:

(a) the disclosure of the principal risks and uncertainties facing the company in the Business Review to be included in Director's Reports; and

(b) additional disclosures relating to going concern and liquidity risk arising from changes to IFRS and UK GAAP.

13 The current squeeze on corporate cash-flows means that liquidity risk is likely to be a material risk this year for many more entities. As a consequence a greater number of companies are likely to need to present relevant disclosures concerning liquidity risk[2]. Examining the directors' processes underlying the preparation of these disclosures is likely to provide useful audit evidence for auditors with respect to the validity of the going concern assumption.

Planning

14 Risks arising from current economic circumstances are likely to impact a number of different aspects of the financial statements, for example the economic conditions may impact matters such as inventory obsolescence, goodwill impairments and cash flows, which may in turn affect whether the company is a going concern. It is important that auditor judgments on such matters are based on consistent underlying information and views.

15 Because of the significance and pervasive nature of the current economic circumstances auditors need to take account of them at all stages of forthcoming audits and in particular when:

(a) making risk assessments during the planning process and re-assessing those risks as the audit progresses;

(b) performing audit procedures to respond to assessed risks;

(c) evaluating the results of audit procedures (including as part of any engagement quality control review); and

(d) forming an opinion on the financial statements.

Considering the directors' assessment of going concern

16 ISA (UK and Ireland) 570 requires the auditor to consider the appropriateness of the directors' use of the going concern assumption in the preparation of the financial statements, and consider whether there are material uncertainties about the entity's ability to continue as a going concern that need to be disclosed in the financial statements[3]. In order to meet this requirement the auditor's procedures will comprise:

(a) evaluating the means by which the directors have satisfied themselves it is appropriate for them to adopt the going concern basis in preparing the financial statements, (see paragraphs 17 to 22);

(b) concluding whether or not they concur with the directors' view, (see paragraphs 23 to 25);

(c) assessing whether the financial statements contain adequate disclosures relating to going concern, (see paragraphs 26 to 28);

---

[2] *For IFRS, disclosures concerning liquidity risk are required by IFRS 7, IAS 1 and IAS 7. For UK GAAP, disclosures are required by FRS 18 and, where applicable, FRS 13 and FRS 29.*

[3] *Paragraph 9 of ISA (UK and Ireland) 570.*

(d)   determining the implications for the auditor's report on the financial statements (see paragraphs 29 to 40); and (e) preparing appropriate documentation (see paragraph 41).

Evaluating how the directors have satisfied themselves that it is appropriate to adopt the going concern basis

Audit procedures that are likely to be relevant when evaluating the adequacy of the   **17** means by which the directors have satisfied themselves whether it is appropriate for them to adopt the going concern basis in preparing the financial statements include:

- Analysing and discussing cash flow, profit and other relevant forecasts with management;

- Reviewing the terms of loan agreements and determining whether any may have been breached;

- Reading minutes of the meetings of shareholders, those charged with governance and relevant committees for references to financing difficulties;

- Reviewing events after period end to identify those that may mitigate or otherwise affect the entity's ability to continue as a going concern[4].

When analysis of cash flow is a significant factor in considering the future   **18** outcome of future events or conditions the auditor considers:

(a)   the reliability of the entity's information system for generating such information; and

(b)   whether there is adequate support for the assumptions underlying the forecast[5].

The Update for Directors notes that one impact of current conditions may be to   **19** limit finance available from trading counterparties (including suppliers and customers) and providers of finance. Furthermore, lenders may be more risk averse when considering whether to provide or renew finance facilities and may establish new conditions and these conditions may affect the company and its trading counterparties.

The Update for Directors indicates that directors will need to consider carefully the   **20** position in the light of the information available to them and the assumptions as to the future availability of finance. It:

(a)   notes that in the present economic environment, bankers may be reluctant to provide positive confirmations to the directors that facilities will continue to be available;

(b)   provides a number of examples of understandable reasons for this (see paragraph 37); and

(c)   concludes that the absence of bank confirmation of bank facilities does not, of itself, necessarily cast significant doubt upon the ability of an entity to continue as a going concern.

---

[4] *Additional procedures are described in paragraph 28 of ISA (UK and Ireland) 570;*

[5] *Paragraph 29 of ISA (UK and Ireland) 570.*

21   ISA (UK and Ireland) 570 requires that when events or conditions have been identified which may cast significant doubt on the entity's ability to continue as a going concern, the auditor should:

(a)   review the directors' plans for future action based on their going concern assessment;

(b)   gather sufficient appropriate audit evidence to confirm or dispel whether or not a material uncertainty exists through carrying out audit procedures considered necessary, including considering the effect of any plans of the directors and other mitigating factors; and

(c)   seek written representations from the directors regarding their plans for future action[6].

In general terms, the greater the risks arising from current economic circumstances the more audit evidence will be required.

22   The auditor's procedures necessarily involve a consideration of the entity's ability to continue in operational existence for the foreseeable future. In turn, that necessitates consideration both of the current and the likely future circumstances of the business and the environment in which it operates[7]. The auditor may conclude that it will be appropriate to request from the directors written representations on specific matters relating to their assumptions and plans. Such representations may usefully include confirmation as to the completeness of the information provided to the auditor regarding events and conditions relating to going concern at the date of approval of the financial statements.

Concluding whether or not to concur with the directors' view

23   Assessing the going concern assumption involves making a judgment, at a particular point in time, about the future outcome of events or conditions which are inherently uncertain. Generally, the degree of uncertainty associated with the outcome of an event or condition increases the further into the future a judgment is being made about the outcome of an event or condition. Any judgment about the future is based on available evidence and reasonable assumptions about the outcome of the future events made at the time at which the judgment is made.

24   The basis for the auditor's conclusion is the information upon which the directors have based their assessment and their reasoning[8], including, where applicable, advice obtained from external advisers including lawyers. In evaluating the assessment of the directors, the auditor considers the process they followed to make their assessment, the assumptions on which the assessment is based and their plans for future action. The auditor considers whether the assessment has taken into account all relevant information of which the auditor is aware as a result of the audit[9].

25   Where there are events or conditions that cast significant doubt on the ability of the entity to continue as a going concern, the auditor assesses the directors' plans for

---

[6]   *Paragraph 26 of ISA (UK and Ireland) 570.*

[7]   *Paragraph 9-2 of ISA (UK and Ireland) 570.*

[8]   *Paragraph 18-3 of ISA (UK and Ireland) 570.*

[9]   *Paragraph 20 of ISA (UK and Ireland) 570.*

future action, including plans to liquidate assets, borrow money or restructure debt, reduce or delay expenditures, or increase capital.

Adequacy of disclosures

Developments in accounting standards, including those relating to liquidity risk, together with the current economic conditions can be expected to give rise to a greater number of company annual reports and accounts containing liquidity and going-concern related disclosures. **26**

The Update for Directors emphasises the importance, in the current economic conditions, of appropriate disclosures regarding liquidity risk and uncertainties. In its Appendix[10] it provides three illustrative examples of how directors might explain their going concern conclusion in a manner that would facilitate an understanding by readers of annual reports and accounts. **27**

The IASB Framework notes that an essential quality of the information provided in financial statements is that it is readily understandable by users[11]. In reviewing the presentation of the disclosures the auditor considers whether the notes to the financial statements taken together with the primary financial statements present a true and fair view. The understandability of the disclosures is an important factor in determining whether the financial statements give a true and fair view. **28**

Determining the implications for the auditor's report

ISAs (UK and Ireland) provide for a number of different auditor reports depending upon the specific facts and circumstances[12]. For example, if auditors conclude that the disclosures regarding going concern are not adequate to meet the requirements of accounting standards, including the need for financial statements to give a true and fair view, they are required either to express a qualified or adverse opinion, as appropriate. The report is also required to include specific reference to the fact that there is a material uncertainty that may cast significant doubt about the entity's ability to continue as a going concern[13]. **29**

If the auditor concludes that a material uncertainty exists that leads to significant doubt about the ability of the entity to continue as a going concern, and those uncertainties have been adequately disclosed in the financial statements, it is required to modify its report by including an emphasis of matter paragraph[14]. **30**

The current economic circumstances are likely to increase the level of uncertainty existing when the directors make their judgment about the outcome of future events or conditions. However, whilst the effect of current market conditions on **31**

---

[10] *See page 36 of this Bulletin.*

[11] *In UK GAAP Chapter 1 of the Statement of Principles for financial reporting states that "the objective of financial statements is to provide information about the reporting entity's financial performance and position that is useful to a wide range of users for assessing the stewardship of the entity's management and for making economic decisions".*

[12] *See Appendix 4.*

[13] *ISA (UK and Ireland) 570, paragraph 34.*

[14] *ISA (UK and Ireland) 700, paragraph 31 requires "The auditor should modify the auditor's report by adding a paragraph to highlight a material matter regarding a going concern problem". Whereas, ISA (UK and Ireland) 570 uses the term "material uncertainty relating to the event or condition that may cast significant doubt on the entity's ability to continue as a going concern". The term used in ISA (UK and Ireland) 570 is equivalent to the term "material matter regarding a going concern problem" used in ISA (UK and Ireland) 700.*

individual entities requires careful evaluation, it should not be assumed that the general economic situation at the present time in itself means that a material uncertainty, which casts significant doubt on the ability of the entity to continue as a going concern, exists. Nor are extensive disclosures necessarily indicative of the existence of a significant doubt on the entity's ability to continue as a going concern. Indeed an objective of the disclosures may be to explain why the going concern issues that affect the company do not give rise to a significant doubt.

32   What constitutes a material uncertainty that may cast significant doubt on the entity's ability to continue as a going concern is a judgment involving not only

    (a)   the nature and materiality of the events or conditions giving rise to uncertainty; but also

    (b)   the ability of the entity to adopt strategies that mitigate the uncertainty.

Nature and materiality of the events or conditions

33   Accounting standards do not define what constitutes a "material uncertainty". However, determining whether a "material uncertainty" exists involves assessing:

    (a)   the likelihood of events or conditions occurring; and

    (b)   their impact.

Assessment of these elements may require a high degree of judgment both by the directors and subsequently by the auditors depending upon the individual circumstances of the company and/or group.

34   Examples of possible events or conditions which may give rise to business risks, that individually or collectively may cast significant doubt about the going concern assumption are set out in ISA (UK and Ireland) 570 paragraph 8[15], these include:

- A net liability or current liability position;

- Negative operating cash flows;

- Fixed-term borrowings approaching maturity without realistic prospects of renewal or repayment, or excessive reliance on short-term borrowings to finance long-term assets;

- Major debt repayment falling due where refinancing is necessary to the entity's continued existence;

- Inability to comply with the terms of loan agreements or to pay creditors on due dates;

- Loss of a major market, franchise, license or principal supplier. A list of other possible events and conditions that may affect the auditor's assessment of going concern are set out in Appendix 2.

35   A factor listed in ISA (UK and Ireland) 570 is that necessary borrowing facilities have not been agreed. In examining borrowing facilities the auditor could decide, for example, that it is necessary:

    (a)   to obtain confirmations of the existence and terms of bank facilities; and

    (b)   to make its own assessment of the intentions of the bankers relating thereto.

---

[15] *That paragraph also notes that the existence of one or more of the factors does not always signify that a material uncertainty that casts significant doubt on the entity's ability to continue as a going concern exists.*

This latter assessment could involve the auditor examining written evidence or making notes of meetings which it would hold with the directors and, where appropriate, with the directors and the entity's bankers.

As discussed in paragraph 20(a), in the present economic environment bankers **36** may be reluctant to confirm to entities or their auditors that facilities will be renewed. This reluctance may extend to companies with a profitable business and relatively small borrowing requirements. The lack of a positive confirmation from a bank does not of itself provide evidence of a material uncertainty that casts significant doubt on the entity's ability to continue as a going concern. Auditors seek to differentiate between circumstances where the lack of a confirmation reflects the existence of a material matter regarding going concern (which, therefore, falls to be emphasised in the auditor's report) and increased caution on the part of bankers that is not indicative of a material matter regarding going concern (and which, therefore, do not fall to be emphasised in the auditor's report).

There may be a number of reasons why a bank may be reluctant to confirm that a **37** facility will be available in the future, which would not be a material matter regarding going concern, including:

- The bank responding that in the current economic environment, as a matter of policy, it is not providing such confirmations to its customers or their auditors;
- The entity and its bankers are engaged in negotiations about the terms of a facility (e.g. the interest rate), and where there is no evidence that the bank is reluctant to lend to the company;
- The bank renewed a rolling facility immediately prior to the date of the issuance of the annual report and accounts and is reluctant to go through the administrative burden to confirm that the facility will be renewed on expiry.

However, if the auditor concludes that an entity's bankers may be refusing to **38** confirm facilities for reasons that are specific to the entity the auditor considers the significance of this and, where appropriate, discusses with the directors whether there are alternative strategies or sources of financing that would enable the financial statements to be prepared on the going concern basis.

Ability to adopt alternative strategies that mitigate an uncertainty

The adverse factors described in paragraph 34 may be mitigated by other **39** favourable factors. For example, the effect of an entity being unable to make its debt repayments from operating cash flows may be counterbalanced by management's plans to maintain adequate cash flows by alternative means, such as by disposal of assets, rescheduling of loan repayments, or obtaining additional capital. Similarly the loss of a principal supplier may be mitigated by the availability of another suitable source of supply. Where an entity contends that it has alternative strategies to overcome any adverse factors the auditor assesses the effectiveness of such strategies and the ability of management to execute them.

If the auditor, in assessing the alternative strategies, considers that they: **40**

(a)   are realistic;

(b)   have a reasonable expectation of resolving any problems foreseen; and

(c)   that the directors are likely to put the strategies into place effectively[16],

---

[16] *Paragraph 20-1 of ISA (UK and Ireland) 570.*

the auditor may decide that it is unnecessary to include an emphasis of matter paragraph in the auditor's report[17].

Documentation

41   ISA (UK and Ireland) 230 (Revised) *Audit Documentation* requires the auditor to prepare audit documentation so as to enable an experienced auditor, having no previous connection with the audit, to understand significant matters arising during the audit and the conclusions reached thereon. Significant matters include, amongst other things, findings that could result in a modification to the auditor's report. With respect to going concern, it is important, therefore, that the auditor documents its knowledge of conditions and events at the date of the auditor's report, and its reasoning with respect to the conclusions it has drawn.

Preliminary announcements

42   While preliminary announcements are no longer mandatory for listed companies, where a preliminary announcement is issued the directors are required by the Listing Rules to have agreed it with the auditor prior to publication.

43   The Listing Rules require that preliminary announcements "include any significant additional information necessary for the purposes of assessing the results being announced". An example of such information may be the disclosures that the directors propose to make in the annual report and accounts explaining their rationale for adopting the going concern basis in the annual accounts and setting out the uncertainties that they have considered in making their assessment.

44   Under both the UK and Irish Listing Rules a preliminary announcement is required to give details of the nature of any likely modification that may be contained in the auditor's report on the full financial statements. Under the Listing Rules modified auditor's reports encompass auditor's reports that contain an emphasis of matter paragraph. This would include a paragraph highlighting a material uncertainty relating to an event or condition that may cast significant doubt on the entity's ability to continue as a going concern.

45   Before agreeing to a preliminary announcement, therefore, the auditor assesses

    (a)   whether the directors have given adequate prominence to significant additional information concerning going concern[18]; and

    (b)   the adequacy of the directors' disclosure, within the announcement, of any likely modification relating to going concern that may be contained in the auditor's report.

Reviewing interim financial information

46   International Standard on Review Engagements (ISRE) (UK and Ireland) 2410 "Review of Interim Financial Information Performed by the Independent Auditor of the Entity", establishes standards and provides guidance on the auditor's professional responsibilities when the auditor undertakes an engagement to

---

[17] *Paragraph 26(b) of ISA (UK and Ireland) 570.*

[18] *Guidance for auditors on preliminary announcements is set out in Bulletin 2008/2 The auditor's association with preliminary announcements made in accordance with the requirements of the UK and Irish Listing Rules.*

review interim financial information of an audit client and on the form and content of the report.

If, as a result of enquiries or other review procedures, a material uncertainty   **47**
relating to an event or condition comes to the auditor's attention that may cast significant doubt on the entity's ability to continue as a going concern, and adequate disclosure is made in the interim financial information the auditor modifies its review report by adding an emphasis of matter paragraph.

However, if a material uncertainty that casts significant doubt about the entity's   **48**
ability to continue as a going concern is not adequately disclosed in the interim financial information, the auditor is required by ISRE 2410 to express a qualified or adverse conclusion as appropriate. In such circumstances the report is required to include specific reference to the fact that there is such a material uncertainty.

Ethical issues

The APB's Ethical Standards (ESs) are based on a "threats and safeguards   **49**
approach" whereby auditors identify and assess the circumstances which could adversely affect the auditor's objectivity ("threats"), including any perceived loss of independence, and apply procedures ("safeguards"), which will either eliminate the threat or reduce it to an acceptable level, that is a level at which it is not probable that a reasonable and informed third party would conclude that the auditor's objectivity is impaired or is likely to be impaired.

In the current circumstances, where financial market conditions are difficult and   **50**
credit facilities may be restricted, auditors need to be particularly alert to the possibility of self-review, management or advocacy threats arising from the provision of non-audit services in relation to a refinancing or restructuring that might jeopardise their objectivity and independence.

Examples of engagements that the audit firm may be requested to undertake in the   **51**
current economic environment and which may give rise to threats to the auditor's independence and objectivity include:

- Undertaking a review of the business with a view to advising the audited entity on restructuring options;
- Advising on forecasts or projections, for presentation to lenders and other stakeholders, including assumptions;
- Advising the audited entity on how to fund its financing requirements, including debt restructuring programmes.

When such work is undertaken a threat arises from the risk that the audit team may   **52**
not review objectively the work undertaken in relation to going concern for audit purposes. Accordingly, where audit firms (and, in particular, members of the audit team) do undertake such engagements, consideration should be given to safeguards such as:

- A review of the going concern assessment and the conclusion reached by a partner or other senior staff member with appropriate expertise who is not a member of the audit team;
- Additional procedures undertaken as part of an Engagement Quality Control Review.

ES 5 (Revised) states that it is unlikely that safeguards can eliminate a threat or   **53**
reduce it to an acceptable level:

(a)   in the absence of "informed management" (paragraph 27 of ES 5 (Revised)); and

(b)   when the non-audit service would require the auditors to act as advocates for the entity in relation to matters that are material to the Financial Statements (paragraph 30 of ES 5 (Revised)).

54   Consequently, where an audit firm is engaged to provide advice to assist an entity it audits to demonstrate that it is a going concern, the audit firm ensures that the entity has "informed management"[19] capable of taking responsibility for the decisions to be made, thereby reducing the risk that the audit firm may be regarded as taking management decisions for the entity concerned. If the audit firm attends meetings with the entity's bank or other interested parties it takes particular care to avoid assuming responsibility for the entity's proposals or being regarded as negotiating on behalf of the entity or advocating the appropriateness of the proposals such that its independence is compromised.

APPENDIX 1

FINANCIAL REPORTING COUNCIL

AN UPDATE FOR DIRECTORS OF LISTED COMPANIES: GOING CONCERN AND LIQUIDITY RISK

NOVEMBER 2008

---

[19] *ES – Provisions Available for Small Entities provides exemptions relating to informed management for auditors of small entities.*

Contents

		Page
One	Introduction	19
Two	Accounting requirements with respect to going concern	22
Three	Going concern review period	27
Four	Insolvency	28
Five	Disclosures relevant to going concern and liquidity risk	29
Six	Preliminary announcements	34
Appendix – Examples of going concern disclosures		35

Appendix 1 – Financial reporting council – an update for directors of listed companies: going concern and liquidity risk

November 2008

One – Introduction

1   Current economic conditions provide particular challenges to all involved with annual reports and accounts. One consequence is expected to be an increase in the disclosures in annual reports and accounts about going concern and liquidity risk. As a result the current conditions will present challenges for all of the parties involved:

- directors will need to ensure that they prepare thoroughly for their assessment of going concern and make appropriate disclosures;

- auditors will need to ensure that they fully consider going concern assessments and only refer to going concern in their audit reports when appropriate; and

- investors and lenders will need to be prepared to read all of the relevant information in annual reports and accounts before making decisions.

2   The purpose of this document is to bring together existing guidance in the context of recent developments relating to going concern and liquidity risk disclosures to assist directors, audit committees and finance teams of listed companies during the forthcoming reporting season. It does not establish any new requirements but it does highlight the importance of clear disclosure about going concern and liquidity risk in current economic conditions. This update may also be useful for directors of unlisted companies who have similar responsibilities to assess going concern and make appropriate disclosures.

3   Going concern is a fundamental accounting concept that underlies the preparation of the annual report and accounts of all UK companies. Under both International Financial Reporting Standards (IFRS) and UK Generally Accepted Accounting Principles (UK GAAP) directors are required to satisfy themselves that it is reasonable for them to conclude that it is appropriate to prepare financial statements on a going concern basis. These requirements are not intended to, and do not, guarantee that a company will remain a going concern until the next annual report and accounts is issued.

4   Both IFRS and UK GAAP require disclosure of the uncertainties that the directors are aware of in making their assessment of going concern where those uncertainties may cast significant doubt on the group's and company's ability to continue as a going concern.

5   The economic conditions being faced by many companies will necessitate careful consideration by directors when assessing whether it is reasonable for them to use the going concern basis of accounting, and whether adequate disclosure has been given of going concern risks and other uncertainties. Addressing these challenges well before the preparation of annual reports and accounts may help avoid a last-minute problem that might unsettle investors and lenders unnecessarily.

6   Directors will need to plan their assessment of going concern as early as practicable including deciding on the information and analysis that will need to

be produced (such as board papers) and the processes and procedures that will be undertaken. These plans should also address the evidence to be obtained to support their conclusion and develop, where necessary, any remedial action plan.

Early discussions with company auditors about these plans may help minimise the 7 risk of last minute surprises, and it may be helpful for a draft of the relevant disclosures about going concern and liquidity risk to be prepared and discussed with the auditors before the end of the financial year.

The Financial Reporting Council (FRC) published a consultation document on 8 "Going concern and financial reporting: proposals to revise the guidance for directors of listed companies" (the 2008 Consultation) at the beginning of September 2008. Responses to the 2008 Consultation were due on 24 November 2008. The FRC anticipates that an exposure draft will be issued towards the end of the first quarter next year and will not become effective before mid 2009.

The FRC would welcome further feedback on the practical challenges of applying 9 the existing guidance "Going concern and financial reporting: guidance for directors of listed companies registered in the United Kingdom" (the 1994 Guidance), before the end of February 2009.

In the meantime the FRC believes that the existing guidance contained in the 1994 10 Guidance is fit for purpose even in these times of significant economic stress. This guidance can be found on the FRC website at: *http://www.frc.org.uk/corporate/goingconcern.cfm.*

The 1994 Guidance indicates that directors may seek confirmation from their 11 bankers regarding the existence and status of their finance arrangements. In the present economic environment bankers may be reluctant to provide positive confirmation that facilities will continue to be available. The absence of confirmations of bank facilities does not of itself necessarily cast significant doubt upon the ability of an entity to continue as a going concern nor necessarily require auditors to refer to going concern in their reports.

The effect of current market conditions on individual entities requires careful 12 evaluation. The general economic situation at the present time does not of itself necessarily mean that a material uncertainty exists about a company's ability to continue as a going concern. However, it is important that annual accounts contain appropriate disclosure of liquidity risk and uncertainties such as are necessary in order to give a true and fair view.

Examples illustrating how directors might explain their going concern conclusion 13 taking account of current economic conditions which would facilitate an understanding by readers of annual reports and accounts are included in the appendix to this update.

The FRC has recently conducted a study of going concern and liquidity risk 14 disclosures made by companies applying IFRS 7 (Financial instruments: Disclosures) in December 2007 and March 2008 year end annual reports and accounts. The study concluded that there are significant opportunities for improvement by way of better, rather than more, disclosure. In particular, it noted that there was often a significant lack of clarity about how liquidity risk is managed in practice and that much of the relevant information was distributed amongst different parts of annual reports, making it difficult for users to appreciate the full picture.

Two – Accounting requirements with respect to going concern

15 Going concern is a fundamental accounting concept that underlies the preparation of financial statements of all UK companies.

16 Preparing financial statements on a going concern basis is not compatible with the intention or the necessity of a company:

- entering into a scheme of arrangement with the company's creditors;
- making an application for an administration order; or
- being placed into administrative receivership or liquidation.

Assessment of going concern

17 International Accounting Standard (IAS) 1 (Presentation of financial statements) and UK Financial Reporting Standard (FRS) 18 (Accounting policies) require management/directors to make an assessment of an entity's ability to continue as a going concern when preparing financial statements. IAS 1.25 states:

> "When preparing financial statements, management shall make an assessment of an entity's ability to continue as a going concern. An entity shall prepare financial statements on a going concern basis unless management either intends to liquidate the entity or to cease trading, or has no realistic alternative but to do so. When management is aware, in making its assessment, of material uncertainties related to events or conditions that may cast significant doubt upon the entity's ability to continue as a going concern, the entity shall disclose those uncertainties.[20]"

18 For financial reporting purposes, the assessment of going concern is made at the date that the directors approve the annual report and accounts and takes into account the relevant facts and circumstances at that date. IAS 1.26 also notes that the degree of consideration that may need to be given to the going concern assessment will depend upon the facts of each case.

19 The Listing Rules of the Financial Services Authority also require that the annual reports of listed companies include a statement by the directors that the business is a going concern, together with supporting assumptions or qualifications as necessary, that has been prepared in accordance with the 1994 Guidance.

20 The Directors statement on going concern is required to be prepared in accordance with the 1994 Guidance which outlines procedures that the directors may wish to adopt in making their assessment. The 1994 Guidance addresses both annual and interim accounts. In relation to the latter directors of listed companies will also need to consider the requirements of IAS 34 (Interim financial reporting).

21 The procedures that are necessary for the directors to comply with the requirements of IAS 1 or FRS 18 are likely to be similar to those adopted to meet their obligations under the Listing Rules. The 1994 Guidance places particular emphasis on the importance of the processes and procedures that directors carry out and highlights some major areas in which procedures are likely to be appropriate, including:

- forecasts and budgets;
- borrowing requirements;

---

[20] *Similar provision is made by FRS 18 paragraphs 21-25.*

- liability management;
- contingent liabilities;
- products and markets;
- financial risk management;
- other factors; and
- financial adaptability.

The 1994 Guidance notes that this list is not exhaustive and the significance of **22** factors will vary from company to company. In the current economic climate many of these factors will have increased in significance which will require directors to consider them with more rigour and formality.

In forming their conclusion on going concern directors will need to evaluate which **23** of three potential outcomes is appropriate to the specific circumstances of the group and company. The directors may conclude:

- there are no material uncertainties that lead to significant doubt upon the entity's ability to continue as a going concern;
- there are material uncertainties that lead to significant doubt upon the entity's ability to continue as a going concern; or
- the use of the going concern basis is not appropriate.

In addition to the assessment that must be made by directors, auditors are required **24** by auditing standards to determine if, in the auditors' judgment, a material uncertainty exists that may cast significant doubt on the entity's ability to continue as a going concern.

Auditing standards provide for a number of different audit reports depending upon **25** the specific facts and circumstances. Auditors may conclude that it is necessary to qualify their opinion, disclaim an opinion, issue an adverse opinion or modify their report by including an emphasis of matter paragraph.

Auditors are required to consider the disclosures about going concern and liquidity **26** risk made in the financial statements. If auditors conclude that the disclosures are not adequate to meet the requirements of accounting standards, including the need for financial statements to give a true and fair view, they are required to qualify their opinion and to provide their reasons for doing so. If auditors conclude that a material uncertainty exists that leads to significant doubt about the ability of the entity to continue as a going concern, and those uncertainties have been adequately disclosed in the financial statements, they are required to modify their report by including an emphasis of matter paragraph.

The combination of these requirements will generally result in one of the **27** following three outcomes:

Outcome	Consequence for the directors' statement on going concern	Consequence for the auditors' report
No material uncertainties leading to significant doubt about going concern have been identified by the directors.	Disclosure explaining the conclusion on going concern and how that has been reached. *Examples 1 and 2 in the attached appendix illustrate this outcome.*	Unmodified report (clean) – provided the auditors concur with the directors' assessment and supporting disclosures.
Material uncertainties leading to significant doubt about going concern have been identified by the directors.	Disclosures explaining the specific nature of the material uncertainties and explaining why the going concern basis has still been adopted. *Example 3 in the attached appendix illustrates this outcome.*	Modified report including an emphasis of matter paragraph highlighting the existence of material uncertainties – provided auditors concur with the directors' assessment and supporting disclosures.
The directors conclude that the going concern basis is not appropriate.	Disclosures explaining the basis of the conclusion and the accounting policies applied in drawing up financial statements on a non-going concern basis.	Unmodified report (clean) – provided that the accounts contain the necessary disclosures and the auditors consider the basis to be appropriate to the specific facts and circumstances.

28   The 1994 Guidance also provides for disclosure when directors conclude that the going concern basis should be used despite having identified factors which cast doubt on the ability of the company to continue in existence for the foreseeable future. Significant changes to disclosure requirements about risks and uncertainties in IFRS, UK GAAP and the Companies Act 2006 (the Act) since 1994 may mean that sufficient disclosure of the factors giving rise to the problem will have been provided through these disclosures (see paragraphs 40 to 49).

29   One impact of current conditions may be to limit finance available from trading counterparties including suppliers, customers and providers of finance. Furthermore, lenders may be more risk averse when considering whether to provide or renew finance facilities and may establish new conditions and these conditions may affect the company and the group and their trading counterparties.

30   In relation to bank and other facilities, paragraphs 30 to 32 of the 1994 Guidance may assist:

30. *The facilities available to the company should be reviewed and compared to the detailed cash flow forecasts for the period to the next balance sheet date, as a minimum. Sensitivity analyses on the critical assumptions should also be used in the comparison. The directors should seek to ensure that there are no anticipated:*

- *shortfalls in facilities against requirements;*
- *arrears of interest; or*
- *breaches of covenants.*

31. *The directors have responsibility to manage borrowing requirements actively. Any potential deficits, arrears or breaches should be discussed with the company's bankers in order to determine whether any action is appropriate. This may prevent potential problems crystallising. The onus is on the directors to be satisfied that there are likely to be appropriate and committed financing arrangements in place.*

32. *The directors may seek confirmation from their bankers regarding the existence and status of any finance arrangements which the company has entered into.*

Directors will need to consider carefully the position in the light of the information available to them and the assumptions as to the future availability of finance. Accounting standards do not define what constitutes a "material uncertainty that may cast significant doubt upon the entity's ability to continue as a going concern". This involves assessing both the probability of an event occurring and the impact it will have if it does occur. Assessment of these elements may require a high degree of judgment both by the directors, and subsequently by the auditors depending upon individual company and group circumstances. **31**

In the present economic environment bankers may be reluctant to provide positive confirmations to the directors that facilities will continue to be available. This reluctance may extend to companies with a profitable business and relatively small borrowing requirements. There may be a number of understandable reasons why a bank may be reluctant to confirm that a facility will be available in the future including: **32**

- the bank responding that in the current economic environment, as a matter of policy, it is not providing such confirmations to its customers;
- the entity and its bankers are engaged in negotiations about the terms of a facility (e.g. the interest rate), however there is no evidence that the bank is reluctant to lend to the company; and
- the bank renewed a rolling facility immediately prior to the date of the issuance of the annual report and accounts and is reluctant to go through the administrative burden to confirm that the facility will be renewed again in a year's time.

The absence of confirmations of bank facilities does not of itself necessarily cast significant doubt upon the ability of an entity to continue as a going concern nor require necessarily auditors to refer to going concern in their reports. **33**

Three – Going concern review period

34   IFRS contains specific requirements about the period which directors are required to review when assessing going concern. IAS 1.26 provides that management should take into account all available information about the future, which is at least, but not limited to, twelve months from the end of the reporting period.

35   FRS 18 requires disclosure if the period considered by the directors is less than twelve months from the date of approval of the financial statements.

36   Directors should consider the 1994 Guidance which provides that budgets and forecasts should be prepared to cover the period to the next balance sheet date as a minimum and notes that further periods are generally covered by medium or long-term plans which give an indication in general terms of how the directors expect the company to fare. The guidance also notes that the assessment is based on what is known to the directors at the date on which they approve the annual report and accounts which includes events or circumstances of which they are aware that arise after the end of the review period.

37   Where the period considered by the directors has been limited, for example, to a period of less than twelve months from the date of the approval of the annual report and accounts, the directors need to consider whether additional disclosures are necessary to explain adequately the assumptions that underlie the adoption of the going concern basis.

38   Auditing standards also address going concern and the period of the review by the directors. Auditors have an explicit obligation to include an extra paragraph in their audit report if the period covered by the directors' review is less than twelve months from the date of approval of the annual report and accounts and this fact is not disclosed by the directors.

Four – Insolvency

39   Doubts upon the ability of a company to remain a going concern do not necessarily mean that the company is, or is likely to become, insolvent. The solvency of a company is determined by reference to a comparison of its assets and liabilities and by its ability to meet liabilities as they fall due. Where the directors are unable to state that the going concern basis is appropriate, they should consider taking professional advice.

Five – Disclosures relevant to going concern and liquidity risk

Disclosure requirements of the Listing Rules about going concern

40   The Listing Rules require that the annual reports of listed companies include a statement by the directors that the business is a going concern, together with supporting assumptions or qualifications as necessary.

41   The 1994 Guidance notes that if there are doubts as to the appropriateness of the going concern presumption then the annual accounts may need to reflect any relevant factors in greater detail if they are to show a true and fair view. The guidance also notes that when there are factors which, in the event of an unfavourable outcome, cast doubt on the appropriateness of the going concern presumption, the directors should explain the circumstances so as to identify the factors which give rise to the problems (including any external factors outside their control which may affect the outcome) and an explanation of how they intend to deal with the problem so as to resolve it.

Disclosure requirements of IFRS and UK GAAP about going concern and liquidity risk

IAS 1 and FRS 18 have explicit disclosure requirements in the event that the directors conclude that there are material uncertainties that may cast significant doubt upon the entity's ability to continue as a going concern. In addition, in recent years there have also been significant changes to specific accounting standards that are relevant to disclosures about liquidity risk and other risks and uncertainties including: **42**

Requirement	IFRS Reference (2008)	UK GAAP (2007/8)
Disclosures relating to risks arising from financial instruments, including liquidity risk where it is material.	IFRS 7 paragraphs 31 to 42	FRS 29 paragraphs 31 to 42
Estimating future cash flows (in connection with impairment of intangible assets).	IAS 36 paragraphs 33 to 54	FRS 11 paragraphs 36 to 40
Disclosure of undrawn borrowing facilities and any restrictions such as covenant requirements, where relevant.	IAS 7 paragraph 50 (a)	No explicit requirement
Disclosure of defaults and covenant breaches and potential reclassification of loans in default as current liabilities.	IAS 1 paragraphs 74 to 76	No explicit requirement
Disclosure of key sources of estimation uncertainty about the carrying amounts of assets and liabilities.	IAS 1 paragraphs 125 to 133	FRS 18 paragraphs 50 to 55

IFRS liquidity risk disclosures

Liquidity risk is the risk that an entity will encounter difficulty in meeting its obligations associated with financial liabilities. IFRS 7 (FRS 29) requires an entity to make both qualitative and quantitative disclosures concerning liquidity risk, where it is a material financial risk.   **43**

Where liquidity risk is material, IFRS 7 (FRS 29) requires: **44**

- disclosure of information that enables users to evaluate the nature and extent of the entity's exposure to liquidity risk;

- narrative disclosures explaining how liquidity risk arises in the business and how it is managed in practice;

- summary numerical data about liquidity risk based on the information that is provided to key management personnel, often the Board of Directors; and

- certain mandatory disclosures such as a maturity analysis of financial liabilities.

45   The disclosures required by IFRS 7 are supplemented by disclosures required by other IFRS standards. For example, IAS 7 (Statement of cash flows) requires disclosure of undrawn borrowing facilities where relevant to users understanding of the financial position and liquidity of the entity, whilst IAS 1 requires disclosure of defaults and breaches of loan terms and conditions.

46   The current squeeze on corporate cash flows means that liquidity risk is likely to be a material risk this year for many more entities. As a consequence, a greater number of companies are likely to need to present relevant disclosures as required by IFRS 7 (FRS 29), IAS 1, IAS 7 and FRS 18.

Disclosure requirements of the Companies Act 2006 related to Directors' Reports

47   The Act requires the Directors' Report of all companies (except companies subject to the small companies' regime) to include a Business Review.

48   The Business Review is required to be a balanced and comprehensive analysis of the development and performance of the business of the company during the financial year and the position of the company at the end of that year, consistent with the size and complexity of the business. In particular it should include a description of the principal risks and uncertainties facing the company.

49   In the case of a quoted company, the Business Review is also required to provide information on a number of other matters including:

●   the main trends and factors likely to affect the future development, performance or position of the company's business; and

●   information about persons with whom the company has contractual or other arrangements which are essential to the business of the company.

50   Directors will need to explain in the Business Review the principal risks and uncertainties facing the company arising from the current difficult economic conditions. One of the purposes of the Business Review is to help the members assess how the directors have performed their duties so it is reasonable to expect that it will also contain an account of how the directors intend to respond to these risks and uncertainties. Issues which may require disclosure depend upon individual facts and circumstances and may include:

●   uncertainties about current financing arrangements (whether committed or uncommitted);

●   potential changes in financing arrangements such as critical covenants and any need to increase borrowing levels;

●   risks arising from current credit arrangements (including the availability of insurance where relevant) with either customers or suppliers;

●   a dependency on key suppliers and customers; and

●   uncertainties posed by the potential impact of the economic outlook on business activities.

51   The Act also requires auditors to review the Directors' Report and to state in their report whether the information given in the Directors' Report is consistent with the financial statements. Auditing standards provide guidance for auditors on how they should carry out this work.

FRC review of going concern and liquidity risk disclosures

The FRC has published a study into going concern and liquidity risk disclosures in **52**
the financial statements of listed companies that have adopted IFRS 7. The study
can be obtained from the FRC *http://www.frc.org.uk/corporate/goingconcern.cfm.*
The study notes that information about going concern and liquidity risk was
distributed amongst a number of different parts of the annual report and accounts
reviewed, thus making it difficult for users to determine and evaluate the extent to
which liquidity concerns were relevant to the business and how liquidity risk was
being managed in practice.

The study concluded that it would be particularly helpful if all of these disclosures **53**
could be brought together into a single section of a company's annual reports and
accounts.

If it is not practical to provide the information in a single section, the study **54**
recommends that the key disclosures be brought together by way of a note
including cross references to help readers of annual reports and accounts to find all
of the relevant pieces of information.

It would be useful if such a note included the following components: **55**

- Paragraph 1 explaining cash and borrowing positions and how liquidity risk
  is managed in practice;

- Paragraph 2 explaining whether confirmation of the renewal of banking and
  other facilities has been sought and if so whether those confirmations have
  been obtained[21];

- Paragraph 3 stating that the use of the going concern basis of accounting is
  appropriate and explaining the basis of that conclusion.

Examples illustrating these disclosures are included in the appendix to this update. **56**

The FRC study also concluded that, while in general information about cash **57**
balances, borrowings and facilities was provided on a comprehensive basis, the
level of detail about how liquidity risk was managed in practice and the
information used by key management to monitor liquidity risk varied greatly. In
particular:

- For many companies, the disclosures were generic rather than specific in
  nature. Only a minority of companies provided information that shed light
  on how the business managed its day to day cash flow and borrowing levels;

- A conclusion could not be reached on whether appropriate disclosure had
  been made of summarised data about liquidity risk as provided to key
  management personnel (generally the directors). Reaching such a
  conclusion would have required access to internal company documentation.

Six – Preliminary announcements

Preliminary announcements of annual results form one of the focal points for **58**
investor interest, primarily because they confirm or update market expectations.
Under the Listing Rules such announcements are voluntary, although if made their
contents are subject to minimum requirements. Where a company chooses to
publish a preliminary announcement the directors are required by the Listing

---

[21] *See paragraphs 29 to 33.*

Rules to have agreed the preliminary announcement with their auditor prior to publication.

59   The Listing Rules provide that, if a preliminary announcement is made, it should give details of the nature of any likely modification that may be contained in the auditor's report required to be included with the annual report and accounts. Modified audit reports encompass audit reports that:

- are qualified;
- express an adverse opinion;
- express a disclaimer of opinion; or
- contain an emphasis of matter paragraph (including a paragraph highlighting a material matter regarding a going concern problem).

Appendix – Examples of going concern disclosures

The purpose of this appendix is merely to illustrate the principles in paragraph 55 in bringing together going concern and liquidity risk disclosures. In practice such disclosures should be specific to the individual circumstances of each company.

Example 1 – A group with significant positive bank balances, uncomplicated circumstances and little or no exposure to uncertainties in the current economic environment which may impact the going concern assumption.

The group's business activities, together with the factors likely to affect its future development, performance and position are set out in the Business Review on pages X to Y. The financial position of the group, its cash flows, liquidity position and borrowing facilities are described in the Chief Financial Officer's Review on pages P to Q. In addition note A to the financial statements includes the group's objectives, policies and processes for managing its capital; its financial risk management objectives; details of its financial instruments and hedging activities; and its exposures to credit risk and liquidity risk.

The group has considerable financial resources together with long-term contracts with a number of customers and suppliers across different geographic areas and industries. As a consequence, the directors believe that the group is well placed to manage its business risks successfully despite the current uncertain economic outlook.

After making enquiries, the directors have a reasonable expectation that the company and the group have adequate resources to continue in operational existence for the foreseeable future. Accordingly, they continue to adopt the going concern basis in preparing the annual report and accounts.

Example 2 – A group with uncomplicated circumstances, some exposure to the current economic uncertainties and either a current material bank overdraft or loan and a need to renew this facility in the foreseeable future albeit not imminently.

Paragraph similar to example 1, paragraph 1.

As highlighted in note B to the financial statements, the group meets its day to day working capital requirements through an overdraft facility which is due for renewal on [date]. The current economic conditions create uncertainty particularly over (a) the level of demand for the group's products; (b) the exchange rate between sterling and currency X and thus the consequence for the cost of the group's raw materials; and (c) the availability of bank finance in the foreseeable future.

The group's forecasts and projections, taking account of reasonably possible changes in trading performance, show that the group should be able to operate within the level of its current facility. The group will open renewal negotiations with the bank in due course and has at this stage not sought any written commitment that the facility will be renewed. However, the group has held discussion with its bankers about its future borrowing needs and no matters have been drawn to its attention to suggest that renewal may not be forthcoming on acceptable terms.

Paragraph as per example 1, paragraph 3.

Example 3 – A group with complicated circumstances, considerable exposure to the current economic uncertainties and either a current material bank overdraft or loan which requires renewal and perhaps an increase in the year ahead.

Paragraph as example 1, paragraph 1.

As described in the directors' report on page X the current economic environment is challenging and the group has reported an operating loss for the year. The directors' consider that the outlook presents significant challenges in terms of sales volume and pricing as well as input costs. Whilst the directors have instituted measures to preserve cash and secure additional finance, these circumstances create material uncertainties over future trading results and cash flows.

As explained on page X, the directors are seeking to sell a property to provide additional working capital. The group is in negotiations with a potential purchaser but there can be no certainty that a sale will proceed. Based on negotiations conducted to date the directors have a reasonable expectation that it will proceed successfully, but if not the group will need to secure additional finance facilities.

As explained in the Business Review on Page Y, the group's has commenced discussions with its bankers about an additional facility that may prove to be necessary should the sale of the property not proceed or should material adverse changes in sales volumes or margins occur. It is likely that these discussions will not be completed for some time. The directors are also pursuing alternative sources of funding in case an additional facility is not forthcoming, but have not yet secured a commitment.

The directors have concluded that the combination of these circumstances represent a material uncertainty that casts significant doubt upon the group's and the company's ability to continue as a going concern. Nevertheless after making enquiries, and considering the uncertainties described above, the directors have a reasonable expectation that the group and the company have adequate resources to continue in operational existence for the foreseeable future. For these reasons, they continue to adopt the going concern basis in preparing the annual report and accounts.

Appendix 2 – Events or conditions that may affect going concern

Possible events and conditions that may affect the auditor's assessment of going concern are listed below.

- Obtaining external finance:

    - Entity has experienced difficulties in the past in obtaining external finance facilities and/or complying with the related terms and covenants;

    - Borrowing agreements or executory contracts include clauses relating to debt covenants or subjective clauses (e.g. a "material adverse change clause") that trigger repayment;

    - Entity has breached some of the terms or covenants giving rise to the risk that the facilities may be withdrawn or not renewed;

    - Finance facilities are due for renewal in the next year;

    - Management have no plans for alternative arrangements should current facilities not be extended;

    - Finance facility is secured on assets (e.g. properties) that have decreased in value below the amount of the facility;

    - There are significant doubts about the financial strength of the entity's bankers;

    - Financing is provided by a syndicate of banks and other financial institutions and there are concerns about the viability of one or more of the members of the syndicate.

- Management plans to overcome financing difficulties include disposal of assets or possible rights issues:

    - Plans developed prior to current market conditions have not been updated or stress tested;

    - Lack of evidence that management can realise the assets at the values arising from planned disposals or obtain the support of shareholders in relation to a rights issue.

- Entity provides significant loans or guarantees:

    - Guarantees that may be called in;

    - Borrowers who may be unable to make payments.

- Entity dependent on guarantees provided by another party:

    - Guarantor no longer able/prepared to provide the guarantee.

- Future cash flows:

    - Reduction in cash flows resulting from unfavourable economic conditions;

    - Customers taking longer/unable to pay;

    - Terms or covenants of renewed financing are changed and become more difficult to comply with (e.g. increased interest rates or charges);

    - Entity is subject to margin calls as a result of a decrease in fair market value of financial instruments that it holds;

  – Entities have issued loans (or received borrowings) having an introductory period during which favourable terms are in force which revert to normal market rates in the forthcoming year.

● Entity heavily dependent on counterparties such as suppliers and customers:

  – Suppliers facing financial difficulties provide essential goods/ services;

  – Entity unable to find alternative suppliers.

Appendix 3 – Risk factors arising from current economic conditions

This Appendix identifies some factors that may increase the risk of material misstatement in financial statements during the current economic conditions, other than in relation to going concern.

Fair Values:

- Entity needs to change valuation model and/or management's assumptions to reflect current market conditions.

- Active market no longer exists, requiring use of a model for valuation purposes.

- Inputs to a model are not based on observable market inputs but rather are based on the entity's own data.

- Impairment of non-financial assets held at fair value (e.g. properties).

- Suspension of external valuation indices triggering a need for alternative valuation approaches.

- Entity uses an external pricing service for fair value measurements that needs to change its valuation model and/or assumptions to reflect current market conditions.

- Entity does not have necessary expertise to undertake valuations.

- Recent amendments to GAAP (IAS 39, IFRS 7, FRS 26 and FRS 29) may require or permit the reclassification of certain financial assets.

Impairments:

- Impairments of assets other than those held at fair value (e.g. need for increased doubtful debt provisions because previously reliable customers may not be able to pay their debts when due).

- Stock obsolescence resulting from significant decreases in demand for certain types of product.

- Impairment of the carrying amount of purchased goodwill.

- Increasing discount rates used in impairment calculations because capital has become more expensive.

- Effect on impairment calculations of subsequent events, in particular those relating to counterparties.

- Current credit market conditions may lead to the triggering of acceleration clauses which may lead to the impairment of financial assets.

Current versus non-current classification:

- Current market conditions may bring into question the classification of assets and liabilities as current or non-current. (For example the re-classification of liabilities as a result of a breach of loan covenants).

Revenue recognition:

- Current credit market conditions may make it more difficult to demonstrate that the revenue recognition criteria, in (IAS 18), have been met.

Pensions:

- Pension obligations of an entity increased by reduction in value of assets in a related defined benefits pension scheme.

- Effect of illiquid investments and decreases in expected rates of return on investments.

Hedging:

- Hedging arrangements no longer effective when a derivative counterparty is experiencing financial difficulty or, more generally due to widening credit spreads on the derivative counterparty.

- In current market conditions, hedge effectiveness may have failed for the current period either because it is no longer probable that a derivative counterparty will meet its obligations, or because counterparty credit spreads have increased substantially, or because of the effect of changes in inter-bank lending rates on fair value interest rate hedges.

Insurance:

- The ability of an insurance company providing credit insurance to meet claims.

Deferred income taxes:

- If a company is reporting losses or is exposed to future losses there may be a need for a valuation allowance for deferred tax assets.

Appendix 4 – Examples of conclusions the auditor might draw

Auditor's report	Circumstances	Example modified audit reports[22]
	Auditor agrees with the directors' assessment	
Clean	Preparing the financial statements on the going concern basis is appropriate, the going concern and liquidity disclosures are adequate and there are no material uncertainties that cast significant doubt on the entity's ability to continue as a going concern. (See examples 1 and 2 in the appendix to the Update for Directors)	n/a
Modified by inclusion of emphasis of matter paragraph[23]	Preparing the financial statements on the going concern basis is appropriate but there are material uncertainties described in the financial statements that cast significant doubt on the entity's ability to continue as a going concern. (See example 3 in the appendix to the Update for Directors)	Example 1
	Auditor disagrees with the directors' assessment	
Qualified opinion	Preparing the financial statements on the going concern basis is appropriate but there are material uncertainties that cast significant doubt on the entity's ability to continue as a going concern that are not adequately described in the financial statements	Example 5
Adverse opinion	The financial statements have been prepared on the going concern basis but the auditor has concluded that using the going concern basis is inappropriate.	Example 8
	The directors refuse to undertake, or extend, an assessment of going concern	
Disclaimer of opinion	Where the directors' refusal either to undertake or to extend an assessment of going concern results in the auditor being unable to form an opinion on whether the financial statements give a true and fair view as the scope of the audit has been limited because the directors' consideration of going concern is completely inadequate.	Example 7

In all cases, if the period used by the directors in making their assessment of going concern is less than one year from the date of approval of the financial statements, and they have not disclosed that fact in the financial statements, the auditor is required by paragraph 31-4 of ISA (UK and Ireland) 570 to do so within the auditor's report.

---

[22] *References are to the examples in Appendix 3 to Bulletin 2006/6 Auditor's Reports on Financial Statements in the United Kingdom*

[23] *ISA (UK and Ireland) 700 Paragraph 34 notes that in extreme cases, such as situations involving multiple uncertainties that are significant to the financial statements, the auditor may consider it appropriate to express a disclaimer of opinion.*

Bulletin 2009/4 Developments in corporate governance affecting the responsibilities of auditors of UK companies

(December 2009)

Contents

	Paragraphs
Introduction	1
Directors' statement on going concern required by the listing rules	2 - 12
Auditor's review of compliance	2 - 4
Consistency with auditor's knowledge obtained in the course of the audit	5 - 12
The corporate governance statement required by the "Disclosure rules and transparency rules"	13 - 34
Section 7.2 of the disclosure rules and transparency rules	15 - 18
Consistency of the corporate governance statement with the financial statements	19 - 24
Apparent material misstatement of fact	25
Corporate governance statement included in the directors' report	26 - 28
Separate corporate governance statement	29 - 33
Amending the APB's illustrative auditor's reports when a Separate Corporate governance statement is issued	34
Changes to the structure of the listing regime effective october 2009	35 - 40

Appendix 1: Illustrative auditor's report from bulletin 2009/2 showing the additional wording that is required when a separate corporate governance statement is issued by the company either in its annual report or in a separate document

Appendix 2: Illustrative auditor's report from Bulletin 2009/2 showing the changes necessary for it to apply to a standard listed company

Introduction

1   This Bulletin:

(a)   updates and supersedes the guidance in paragraphs 68 to 72 of Bulletin 2006/5[1] issued by the Auditing Practices Board (APB) relating to the requirement in the Listing Rules for the auditor to review the directors' going concern statement. The need for the update arises from the issuance by the Financial Reporting Council of "Going Concern and Liquidity Risk: Guidance for Directors of UK Companies 2009" (FRC Guidance) which supersedes the guidance for directors to which the relevant guidance for auditors in Bulletin 2006/5 relates. The updated guidance for auditors is set out in paragraphs 2 to 12 of this Bulletin;

(b)   provides guidance for the auditor with respect to its responsibilities under the Companies Act 2006 (CA 2006) regarding Corporate Governance Statements that the Disclosure Rules and Transparency Rules of the Financial Services Authority (FSA) require certain companies to make. This guidance is set out in paragraphs 13 to 34 and Appendix 1 of this Bulletin; and

(c)   provides an illustration of how the example auditor's reports in Bulletin 2009/2 are amended to apply to "standard listed companies"[2] that are incorporated in the UK. The Listing Regime was changed with effect from 6 October 2009 to permit UK companies a choice of being either a "standard listed company" or a "premium listed company". Previously, all UK listed companies were subject to the regime that will apply to "premium listed companies". Guidance is set out in paragraphs 35 to 40 and Appendix 2 of this Bulletin.

Directors' statement on going concern required by the Listing Rules

Auditor's review of compliance

2   The Listing Rules require the directors of certain listed companies[3] to include in the annual financial report a statement that:

> *"the business is a going concern, together with supporting assumptions or qualification as necessary, that has been prepared in accordance with Going Concern and Liquidity Risk: Guidance for directors of UK companies 2009, published by the Financial Reporting Council in October 2009."*

---

[1] *APB Bulletin 2006/5, "The Combined Code on Corporate Governance: Requirements of Auditors under the Listing Rules of the Financial Services Authority and the Irish Stock Exchange" published in September 2006.*

[2] *From 6 October 2009 to 6 April 2010, such companies will be described as "secondary listed companies". The change of name to "standard listed company" will be effective from 6 April 2010.*

[3] *FSA LR 9.8.6R(3); ISE LR 6.8.3(3). These Listing Rules apply to companies that have a primary listing of equity shares, preference shares or securities convertible into equity shares. The FSA's Listing Rule applies to such companies incorporated in the United Kingdom and the ISE's Listing Rule applies to such companies incorporated in the Republic of Ireland. From 6 April 2010, a primary listing will be described as a premium listing.*

The FRC Guidance provides a framework to assist directors in determining   **3**
whether it is appropriate to adopt the going concern basis for preparing financial
statements and in making balanced, proportionate and understandable disclosures.
It encourages directors to focus on the three principles set out in the FRC
Guidance and to apply them in a manner proportionate to the nature of their
businesses.

The Listing Rules[4] also require a listed company to ensure that the auditor reviews   **4**
the directors' going concern statement prior to the publication of the annual
financial report. The auditor's review responsibility with respect to the directors'
going concern statement includes:

(a) reviewing the documentation prepared by or for the directors which explains
     the basis of the directors' conclusion with respect to going concern. If the
     going concern assessment has been prepared for the directors, the FRC
     Guidance recommends that the directors review and approve the
     documented assessment at the Board meeting at which the Board
     approves the financial statements;

> ### *Principle 1 of the FRC Guidance*
>
> ### *Assessing Going Concern*
>
> *Directors should make and document a rigorous assessment of whether the
> company is a going concern when preparing annual and half-yearly
> financial statements. The process carried out by the directors should be
> proportionate in nature and depth depending upon the size, level of
> financial risk and complexity of the company and its operations.*

(b) evaluating the consistency of the directors' going concern statement with the
     auditor's knowledge obtained in the course of the audit of the financial
     statements. This knowledge will primarily have been obtained in meeting the
     requirements of International Standard on Auditing (ISA) (UK and Ireland)
     570 "Going Concern"; and

> ### *Principle 2 of the FRC Guidance*
>
> ### *The Review Period*
>
> *Directors should consider all available information about the future when
> concluding whether the company is a going concern at the date they
> approve the financial statements. Their review should usually cover a
> period of at least twelve months from the date of approval of annual and
> half-yearly financial statements.*

(c) whether the directors' statement meets the disclosure requirements of the
     FRC Guidance.

---

[4] *FSA LR 9.8.10R(1); ISE LR 6.8.6(1).*

> ### Principle 3 of the FRC Guidance
> ### Disclosures
> *Directors should make balanced, proportionate and clear disclosures about going concern for the financial statements to give a true and fair view. Directors should disclose if the period that they have reviewed is less than twelve months from the date of approval of annual and half-yearly financial statements and explain their justification for limiting their review period.*

Consistency with auditor's knowledge obtained in the course of the audit

5   ISA (UK and Ireland) 570 requires the auditor, based on the audit evidence obtained, to determine if, in its judgment, a material uncertainty exists related to events or conditions that alone or in aggregate may cast significant doubt on the company's ability to continue as a going concern[5]. The FRC Guidance requires the directors to make the same assessment.

No material uncertainties

6   If the directors conclude that there are no material uncertainties related to events or conditions that may cast significant doubt about the ability of the company to continue as a going concern, the Listing Rules require that a statement be made by the directors that the business is a going concern together with their supporting assumptions as necessary.

7   If the auditor also determines that there are no material uncertainties related to events or conditions that may cast doubt about the ability of the company to continue as a going concern, the auditor will be able to issue an unmodified opinion on the financial statements (i.e. there is no need for a going concern emphasis of matter paragraph).

8   However if, in the auditor's opinion, the directors' disclosures in their going concern statement are not balanced, proportionate or clear, the auditor considers whether it is necessary to communicate this fact in the auditor's report. If the auditor considers this to be necessary, paragraph 55 of ISA (UK and Ireland) 700 (Revised) requires the auditor to communicate this matter in an "other matter" paragraph in the auditor's report.

Material uncertainties but going concern basis appropriate

9   If the directors conclude that there is a material uncertainty related to events or conditions that may cast significant doubt about the ability of the company to continue as a going concern but that the going concern basis remains appropriate, the Listing Rules require that a statement be made by the directors that the business is a going concern together with supporting assumptions or qualifications as necessary.

10 If the auditor also determines that there is a material uncertainty related to events or conditions that may cast significant doubt about the ability of the company to continue as a going concern, but that the going concern basis remains appropriate, the auditor assesses whether adequate disclosure has been made both in the financial statements and in the directors' going concern statement.

---

[5] *ISA (UK and Ireland) 570 Going concern, paragraph 30.*

If adequate disclosure is made in the financial statements, the auditor should **11** express an unqualified opinion on the financial statements but modify the auditor's report by adding an emphasis of matter paragraph. That paragraph highlights the existence of the material uncertainty, relating to the event or condition that may cast significant doubt on the company's ability to continue as a going concern, and draws attention to the note in the financial statements describing the uncertainty.

If adequate disclosure is made in the financial statements but in the auditor's **12** opinion the directors' disclosures in their going concern statement are not balanced, proportionate or clear, the auditor considers whether it is necessary to communicate this fact in the auditor's report as described in paragraph 8 above.

The Corporate Governance Statement required by the "Disclosure Rules and Transparency Rules"

Directive 2006/46 (the Directive), of the European Parliament and the Council, on **13** Company Reporting requires, among other things, that publicly traded companies[6] include a Corporate Governance Statement in their annual (directors') report. The requirements of the Directive and the responsibilities of the auditor with respect to Corporate Governance Statements have been implemented in the United Kingdom through:

(a)   section 7.2 of the Disclosure Rules and Transparency Rules (DTR) of the FSA[7];

(b)   section 496 of CA 2006; and

(c)   Statutory Instrument 2009, No. 1581, "The Companies Act 2006 (Accounts, Reports and Audit) Regulations 2009" (the Regulations).

The FSA requirements for the preparation of a Corporate Governance Statement **14** came into force on 29 June 2008 for financial years beginning on or after that date. The amendments to CA 2006 made by the Regulations came into force on 27 June 2009 and are effective for financial years beginning on or after 29 June 2008 which had not ended by 27 June 2009.

Section 7.2 of the Disclosure Rules and Transparency Rules

Section 7.2 of the DTR requires disclosure of certain matters in the Corporate **15** Governance Statement[8] many of which have, for some time, been required (by either company law or the Listing Rules) to be disclosed by UK listed companies in their annual reports (typically in the directors' report).

The requirements regarding the content of the Corporate Governance Statement **16** are set out in the following DTRs.

---

[6] *Companies whose securities are admitted to trading on a regulated market within the meaning of Article 4(1), point (14) of Directive 2004/39/EC. This definition includes both standard and premium listed companies (see paragraph 37 of this Bulletin).*

[7] *Section 7.2 was inserted by the Disclosure Rules and Transparency Rules Sourcebook (Corporate Governance Rules) Instrument 2008 (FSA 2008/32).*

[8] *The detailed requirements regarding the content of the Corporate Governance Statement are set out in DTRs 7.2.2R to 7.2.8G and 7.2.10R.*

DTR	Synopsis of requirement and comments
7.2.2R and 7.2.3R	**The Corporate Governance Code to which the issuer is subject**
	Requirements satisfied by compliance with LR 9.8.6R (3) (the "comply or explain" rule in the Combined Code) (see DTR 7.2.4G).
7.2.5R	**Description of the main features of the issuer's internal control and risk management systems in relation to the financial reporting process**
	A new requirement (see paragraph 17 below).
7.2.6R	**Takeover Directive disclosures about share capital**
	Required by paragraph 13(2)(c), (d), (f), (h) and (i) of Schedule 7 to the Large and Medium-sized Companies and Groups (Accounts and Reports) Regulations 2008.[9] These requirements are not new, having been in force for financial years beginning on or after 20 May 2006.
7.2.7R	**Description of the composition and operation of the issuer's administrative, management and supervisory bodies and their committees**
	In the FSA's view, the information specified in provisions A.1.1, A.1. 2, A.4.6, B.2.1 and C.3.3 of the Combined Code satisfy this requirement (see DTR 7.2.8G).

17   Although the requirement in 7.2.5R is new, the Government has stated: "We do not believe that these regulations should add to the costs of audit because the test for consistency should not be onerous, and in a number of companies, the audited financial statements may not contain information on internal control and risk management systems".

18   Section 7.2 of the DTR requires those companies to which it applies to include a Corporate Governance Statement, either:

(a)   as a specific section of the directors' report (DTR 7.2.1R); or

(b)   in a separate report which is either;

    (i)   published together with, and in the same manner as, its annual report (DTR 7.2.9(1)R); or

    (ii)   by means of a cross reference in its directors' report to where such document is publicly available on the company's website (DTR 7.2.9(2)R).

[9] *Statutory Instrument (SI) 2008/410.*

Consistency of the Corporate Governance Statement with the financial statements

The auditor's responsibility with respect to assessing the consistency of the   **19**
Corporate Governance Statement with the financial statements will differ
dependent on whether the Statement:

(a)   is included in the directors' report or is a separate Statement; and

(b)   is included in a document containing audited financial statements (if it does
      so the requirements of ISA (UK and Ireland) 720 Section A are applicable).

The following table sets out, with respect to the various possible locations of the   **20**
Corporate Governance Statement, what the appropriate requirements are and the
relevant paragraphs of this Bulletin that provide guidance.

Location of Corporate Governance Statement	CA 2006			ISA (UK & I) 720	Paragraphs In Bulletin
	S 496	S 497A	S 498A		
In directors' report[10]	✓	n/a	n/a	✓ Sections A and B	21 – 28
Separate: in a document containing audited financial statements	n/a	✓	✓	✓ Section A	21 – 25 29 – 34
Separate: not in a document containing audited financial statements	n/a	✓	✓	n/a	21 – 24 29 – 32
No statement made by directors	n/a	n/a	✓	n/a	31 – 32

Regardless of whether the Corporate Governance Statement is included in the   **21**
directors' report or is a separate Statement, the auditor is required to form an
opinion as to whether the information given in the Statement for the financial year
in relation to the requirements of DTR 7.2.5R and 7.2.6R is consistent with the
financial statements for that year.

An inconsistency arises when information in the Corporate Governance Statement   **22**
contradicts information contained in the financial statements. If the auditor
identifies an inconsistency, the auditor needs to determine whether the audited
financial statements or the Corporate Governance Statement need to be revised.

Where there are no inconsistencies and the Corporate Governance Statement   **23**
forms part of the directors' report, no additional words are required to be included
in the auditor's report (see paragraphs 26 to 28 below). However, with respect to a
Separate Corporate Governance Statement, the auditor is required to report (in the
auditor's report on the financial statements) on the consistency of the information
relating to DTRs 7.2.5R and 7.2.6R in the Statement with the financial statements
(see paragraphs 29 to 30 below and Appendix 1).

In either case, if the auditor considers that revision of the audited financial   **24**
statements is necessary, and the directors refuse to make the revision, the auditor is
required to modify its opinion on the financial statements in accordance with the

requirements of ISA (UK and Ireland) 700 (Revised) "The auditor's report on financial statements".

Apparent material misstatement of fact

25   If the Corporate Governance Statement is included in a document containing audited financial statements, the auditor, in meeting the requirements of ISA (UK and Ireland) 720 (Revised) Section A "Other information in documents containing audited financial statements", may become aware of apparent material misstatements of fact. A material misstatement of fact in the Statement exists when information in the Statement, which is not related to matters appearing in the audited financial statements, is incorrectly stated or presented. A material misstatement of fact would potentially include an inconsistency between information obtained by the auditor during the audit and information included in the Statement.

Corporate Governance Statement included in the directors' report

26   Where the Corporate Governance Statement is included in the directors' report, section 496 of CA 2006 requires:

> ### Section 496 of CA 2006
>
> The auditor must state in his report on the company's annual accounts whether in his opinion the information given in the directors' report for the financial year for which the accounts are prepared is consistent with those accounts.

27   Sections A and B of ISA (UK and Ireland) 720 (Revised) set out standards and guidance with respect to the auditor's statutory reporting responsibility with respect to a Corporate Governance Statement included in a directors' report.

28   Where the Corporate Governance Statement is included in the directors' report and the auditor has not identified any inconsistencies, the illustrative unmodified auditor's reports set out in Appendices 1 to 4 of Bulletin 2009/2 "Auditor's Reports on Financial Statements in the United Kingdom" do not need amendment. If the auditor does identify an inconsistency, Appendix 10 of Bulletin 2009/2 illustrates the way in which this would be done.

Separate Corporate Governance Statement

29   Where a Separate Corporate Governance Statement is issued, the Regulations insert a new section 497A into CA 2006 which requires:

> ### Section 497A of CA 2006
>
> (1) Where the company prepares a separate corporate governance statement in respect of a financial year the auditor must state in his report on the company's annual accounts for that year whether in his opinion the information given in the statement in compliance with rules 7.2.5 and 7.2.6 in the Disclosure Rules and Transparency Rules sourcebook issued by the Financial Service Authority (information about internal control and risk management systems in relation to financial reporting processes and about share capital structures) is consistent with those accounts.

Where there is a Separate Corporate Governance Statement, the auditor is **30** required, therefore, to consider whether the information included in that statement in respect of DTR Rules 7.2.5 and 7.2.6 is consistent with the financial statements and report as required by section 497A of CA 2006.

The Regulations also insert into CA 2006 new section 498A which requires: **31**

Section 498A of CA 2006

Where the company is required to prepare a corporate governance statement in respect of a financial year and no such statement is included in the directors' report:

(a) the company's auditor, in preparing his report on the company's annual accounts for that year, must ascertain whether a corporate governance statement has been prepared; and

(b) if it appears to the auditor that no such statement has been prepared, he must state that fact in his report.

Section 498A of CA 2006 merely requires the auditor to ascertain whether or not a **32** Corporate Governance Statement has been prepared by the directors. It does not require the auditor to take steps additional to the requirements of sections 496 and 497A of CA 2006. In particular, section 498A of CA 2006 does not require the auditor to evaluate whether a Separate Corporate Governance Statement has been properly prepared by the directors in accordance with the Disclosure Rules and Transparency Rules.

However, if the Corporate Governance Statement forms part of a document that **33** includes the audited financial statements, the requirements of ISA (UK and Ireland) 720 (Revised) Section A apply.

Amending the APB's illustrative auditor's reports when a Separate Corporate Governance Statement is issued

Where a company issues a Separate Corporate Governance Statement, the **34** illustrative examples of auditor's reports of publicly traded companies and groups in Bulletin 2009/2 will need to be amended. In to this Bulletin, example 4 from Bulletin 2009/2 is reproduced and marked up to illustrate the necessary changes. The other example auditor's reports in Bulletin 2009/2 relating to publicly traded companies and groups should be similarly amended where a separate corporate governance statement is issued.

Changes to the structure of the Listing Regime effective October 2009

In its Consultation Paper CP 09/24 "Listing Regime Review", the Financial **35** Services Authority announced changes to the Listing Regime (and the detailed Listing Rules) which have the objective of providing more clarity about the Regime for market participants.

36   Most of the changes to the regime are effective from 6 April 2010. However, the Listing Rules have been changed with effect from 6 October 2009 to enable UK companies to join the Standard Listing Segment[11]. Prior to that date, this segment was only available to overseas companies.

37   The principal changes which are effective from 6 April 2010 are:

- re-structuring the regime into two segments, Premium and Standard – the former denoting the more stringent super-equivalent standards (such as those relating to going concern and Corporate Governance Statements) and the latter, European Union minimum standards;

- requiring overseas premium listed companies to "comply or explain" against the UK Combined Code;

- requiring overseas standard listed companies to provide a Corporate Governance Statement which, among other things, describes the main features of their internal control and risk management systems;

38   If a UK company joins the Standard Listing Segment, or migrates to it from the Premium Listing Segment, there are implications for the content of its auditor's report. From 6 October 2009, secondary listed companies[11] incorporated in the UK are no longer required to make either the going concern statement required by Listing Rule 9.8.6(R)(3) or the corporate governance statement required by Listing Rule 9.8.6(R)(6) and, therefore, the auditors of such companies are no longer required to review such statements.

39   Appendix 2 of this Bulletin sets out how the section of the auditor's report relating to "Matters on which we are required to report by exception", as illustrated in the example illustrative auditor's reports in Bulletin 2009/2, is amended.

40   As the APB does not provide guidance for auditors of overseas listed companies, this Bulletin does not address the wording of auditor's reports for such companies.

---

[11] *The Listing Rules have been changed with effect from 6 October 2009 to enable UK companies to be secondary listed companies. With effect from 6 April 2010, the category "secondary listed company" will be known as "standard listed company".*

Appendix 1

Illustrative auditor's report from Bulletin 2009/2 showing the additional wording that is required when a Separate Corporate Governance Statement is issued by the company either in its annual report or in a separate document[12]

- *Illustration based on Example 4 of Appendix 1 of Bulletin 2009/2*

INDEPENDENT AUDITOR'S REPORT TO THE MEMBERS OF XYZ PLC

We have audited the financial statements of (name of entity) for the year ended ... which comprise [specify the titles of the primary statements such as the Statement of Financial Position, the Statement of Comprehensive Income, the Statement of Cash Flow, the Statement of Changes in Equity] and the related notes. The financial reporting framework that has been applied in their preparation is applicable law and International Financial Reporting Standards (IFRSs) as adopted by the European Union.

Respective responsibilities of directors and auditors

As explained more fully in the Directors' Responsibilities Statement [set out [on page ...]], the directors are responsible for the preparation of the financial statements and for being satisfied that they give a true and fair view. Our responsibility is to audit the financial statements in accordance with applicable law and International Standards on Auditing (UK and Ireland). Those standards require us to comply with the Auditing Practices Board's [(APB's)] Ethical Standards for Auditors.

Scope of the audit of the financial statements

Either:

> A description of the scope of an audit of financial statements is [provided on the APB's website at www.frc.org.uk/apb/scope/UKP] / [set out [on page ...] of the Annual Report].

Or:

> An audit involves obtaining evidence about the amounts and disclosures in the financial statements sufficient to give reasonable assurance that the financial statements are free from material misstatement, whether caused by fraud or error. This includes an assessment of: whether the accounting policies are appropriate to the company's circumstances and have been

---

[12] *The additional wording shown in this illustration is not required in an unmodified auditor's report where the Corporate Governance Statement is included in the Directors' Report.*

consistently applied and adequately disclosed; the reasonableness of significant accounting estimates made by the directors; and the overall presentation of the financial statements.

Opinion on financial statements

In our opinion, the financial statements:

- give a true and fair view of the state of the company's affairs as at ... and of its profit [loss] for the year then ended;

- have been properly prepared in accordance with IFRSs as adopted by the European Union; and

- have been prepared in accordance with the requirements of the Companies Act 2006.

[Separate opinion in relation to IFRSs as issued by the IASB

As explained in note [x] to the financial statements, the company in addition to applying IFRSs as adopted by the European Union, has also applied IFRSs as issued by the International Accounting Standards Board (IASB).

In our opinion, the financial statements comply with IFRSs as issued by the IASB.]

Opinion on other matters prescribed by the Companies Act 2006

In our opinion:

- the part of the Directors' Remuneration Report to be audited has been properly prepared in accordance with the Companies Act 2006; and

- the information given in the Directors' Report for the financial year for which the financial statements are prepared is consistent with the financial statements; and

- the information given in the Corporate Governance Statement set out [on pages] [in *describe document*] [at *include web-address*[13]] with respect to internal control and risk management systems in relation to financial reporting processes and about share capital structures is consistent with the financial statements[12].

Matters on which we are required to report by exception

We have nothing to report in respect of the following:

Under the Companies Act 2006, we are required to report to you if, in our opinion:

- adequate accounting records have not been kept, or returns adequate for our audit have not been received from branches not visited by us; or

- the financial statements and the part of the Directors' Remuneration Report to be audited are not in agreement with the accounting records and returns; or

---

[13] *Care should be taken to ensure that the web address is to the page on the website where the Corporate Governance Statement is located. As a website may be difficult to navigate it would be unhelpful if the web address is one, (for example that of the home page of the website), that does not lead directly to the Corporate Governance Statement.*

- certain disclosures of directors' remuneration specified by law are not made; or

- we have not received all the information and explanations we require for our audit; **or**

- a Corporate Governance Statement has not been prepared by the company[12].

Under the Listing Rules, we are required to review:

- the directors' statement, [set out [on page…]], in relation to going concern; and

- the part of the Corporate Governance Statement [on pages] [in *describe document*] [at *include web* address] relating to the company's compliance with the nine provisions of the [2006] [June 2008] Combined Code specified for our review.

[Signature]   *Address*

John Smith (Senior Statutory Auditor)   *Date*

for and on behalf of ABC LLP, Statutory Auditor

Appendix 2

Illustrative auditor's report from Bulletin 2009/2 showing the changes necessary for it to apply to a standard listed company[14]

- *Illustration based on Example 4 of Appendix 1 of Bulletin 2009/2*

...

Opinion on other matters prescribed by the Companies Act 2006

In our opinion:

- the part of the Directors' Remuneration Report to be audited has been properly prepared in accordance with the Companies Act 2006; ~~and~~

- the information given in the Directors' Report for the financial year for which the financial statements are prepared is consistent with the financial statements; and

- [the information given in the Corporate Governance Statement set out [on pages] [in *describe document*] [at *include web-address*[13]] with respect to internal control and risk management systems in relation to financial reporting processes and about share capital structures is consistent with the financial statements[12]].

Matters on which we are required to report by exception

We have nothing to report in respect of the following:

Under the Companies Act 2006, we are required to report to you if, in our opinion:

- adequate accounting records have not been kept, or returns adequate for our audit have not been received from branches not visited by us; or

- the financial statements and the part of the Directors' Remuneration Report to be audited are not in agreement with the accounting records and returns; or

- certain disclosures of directors' remuneration specified by law are not made; or

- we have not received all the information and explanations we require for our audit [; or

- a Corporate Governance Statement has not been prepared by the company[12]].

~~Under the Listing Rules we are required to review:~~

- ~~the directors' statement, [set out [on page...]], in relation to going concern; and~~

---

[14] *The UK Listing Regime changed with effect from 6 October 2009 to permit UK companies to be "secondary listed companies". With effect from 6 April 2010 such companies will be described under the Listing Rules as "standard listed companies".*

- ~~the part of the Corporate Governance Statement relating to the company's compliance with the nine provisions of the [2006] [June 2008] Combined Code specified for our review.~~[15]

[Signature]   *Address*

John Smith (Senior Statutory Auditor)   *Date*

for and on behalf of ABC LLP, Statutory Auditor

---

[15] *The struck out words will continue to be included in the auditor's reports of UK "premium listed companies" (such companies are described as "primary listed companies" until 6 April 2010).*

Bulletin 2010/1 XBRL tagging of information in audited financial statements – Guidance for auditors

(February 2010)

Contents

	Paragraphs
Introduction	1 - 2
HMRC requirement	3 - 6
XBRL	7 - 14
Audit	15 - 18
Non-audit services and possible threats to auditor independence	19 - 21
Management threat	22 - 24
Self-review threat	25 - 28

Introduction

1   XBRL tagging of UK statutory financial statements is required for tax purposes in 2011. This Bulletin:

- Provides background information on the HM Revenue & Customs (HMRC) requirement and XBRL tagging;

- Explains that currently XBRL tagging is not within the scope of an audit performed under ISAs (UK and Ireland); and

- Provides guidance on the application of the APB's Ethical Standards for Auditors to non-audit services relating to XBRL tagging that auditors may be asked to perform. Particular threats to be considered include the "management threat" and the "self-review threat" as discussed below.

2   The use of XBRL is a developing area. Over time it is possible that XBRL will become integrated into accounting systems and will be used to generate the financial statements. The APB intends to keep its use by preparers of financial information, and the role of auditors in relation to it, under review and will issue updated guidance in the future as necessary to reflect changing circumstances.

HMRC requirement

3   In 2006 Lord Carter in his "Review of HMRC Online Services" recommended that all companies should be required to file their company tax returns online, using XBRL.

4   In September 2009, in a joint statement[1] issued with Companies House, HMRC announced that the Company Tax Return, including the supporting statutory accounts and tax computations showing the derivation from those accounts of the entries in the Company Tax Return, must be delivered electronically using the Inline XBRL (iXBRL) format. This will be mandatory when filing a Company Tax Return for accounting periods ending after 31 March 2010 and submitted to HMRC after 31 March 2011[2]

5   The HMRC requirement does not include a requirement for the auditor to provide assurance on the XBRL tagging of the information submitted. Indeed many of the companies that will be required to submit iXBRL financial statements will be below the audit exemption threshold and will not be subject to an audit.

6   In order to reduce potential administrative burdens on business, Companies House has announced that it will accept company accounts in the iXBRL format[3]. In the short term it is not expected that Companies House will make available the data in XBRL form (although the financial statements themselves will be viewable). However, in the longer term Companies House will be disseminating XBRL data to facilitate its use by users of company information.

---

[1] *Copies of the statement dated 1 September 2009 are available on the HMRC website at www.hmrc.gov.uk and the Companies House website at www.companieshouse.gov.uk.*

[2] *The legal requirement for delivering company tax returns electronically in a means approved by HMRC is established in SI 2009/3218, "The Income and Corporation Taxes (Electronic Communications) (Amendment) Regulations 2009."*

[3] *Companies House stated they will add iXBRL software filing for unaudited full accounts to their service by the summer of 2010, and then continue to develop their iXBRL capability for all the main types of accounts they receive by summer 2011.*

XBRL

XBRL, which stands for eXtensible Business Reporting Language, is a computer   7
based language for the electronic communication of business data.

XBRL works through tagging individual items of information with machine-   8
readable codes (e.g. for the individual numbers in a set of financial statements).
The codes are drawn from a library of codes referred to as a "taxonomy";
taxonomies are pre-prepared by various organisations and are freely available[4].

The value of XBRL tagging is that it allows data to become more easily accessible,   9
manipulable and reviewable. XBRL allows users to customise their analysis and
presentation of tagged information using computer software tools.

Aspects of the tagging process may be automated but, in the case of financial   10
statements, it is likely to be necessary for people to exercise judgement over the
tag to be applied to a particular piece of information. Judgement will also be
needed if the taxonomy does not cover all items of information that are disclosed
in a set of financial statements. In such circumstances XBRL permits users to
extend the taxonomy by creating new bespoke tags for data. This is why the word
"extensible" features in the name.

"Inline XBRL" embeds XBRL tags within documents that can still be read by the   11
human eye. When looked at on a computer screen the document looks like a
normal document but the data will have underlying tags that can be revealed, for
example by positioning the mouse cursor over the data.

There are a number of ways for entities to create financial statements using XBRL: 12

- Companies House stated they will add iXBRL software filing for unaudited
  full accounts to their service by the summer of 2010, and then continue to
  develop their iXBRL capability for all the main types of accounts they
  receive by summer 2011.

- The taxonomy for International Financial Reporting Standards (IFRS) is the
  responsibility of the International Accounting Standards Committee
  Foundation (IASCF), the oversight body of the International Accounting
  Standards Board (IASB). In the UK, XBRL UK has issued a "UK IFRS"
  taxonomy, which takes the IASCF taxonomy and adds the extra tags needed
  by UK listed companies (e.g. to cover data that is required by company law
  in addition to the accounting standards) and a "UK GAAP" taxonomy.

- After they have been finalised, financial statements can be mapped into
  XBRL either manually or using "bolt-on" applications which consist of
  software that compiles XBRL data from the traditional financial statements
  into XBRL format.

- XBRL-aware accounting software products are becoming available which
  will support the export of data in XBRL form. These tools allow users to
  map charts of accounts and other structures to XBRL tags.

The route which an individual entity may take will depend on its requirements and   13
the accounting software and systems it currently uses.

---

[4] *The taxonomy for International Financial Reporting Standards (IFRS) is the responsibility of the International
Accounting Standards Committee Foundation (IASCF), the oversight body of the International Accounting
Standards Board (IASB). In the UK, XBRL UK has issued a "UK IFRS" taxonomy, which takes the IASCF
taxonomy and adds the extra tags needed by UK listed companies (e.g. to cover data that is required by company
law in addition to the accounting standards) and a "UK GAAP" taxonomy.*

14   To help with the introduction of mandatory online filing for tax returns, HMRC will initially accept accounts with only some of the data needing to be tagged[5]. HMRC has already published "minimum tagging lists" for the UK GAAP taxonomies and will be doing so for UK IFRS. These lists specify the items that must be tagged if they are present in any given set of accounts. Companies may choose to adopt full tagging immediately.

Audit

15   As described above, HMRC is requiring the financial statements supporting a company's tax return to be transmitted to it using the iXBRL format. There is no requirement for an audit of the data or indeed the XBRL tagging.

16   With respect to the audit of financial statements, the current position is that ISAs (UK and Ireland) do not impose a general requirement on the auditor to check XBRL tagging of the financial statements as part of the audit. Furthermore, because the XBRL tagging is simply a machine-readable rendering of the data within the financial statements, rather than a discrete document, it does not constitute "other information" as defined in ISA (UK and Ireland) 720 Section A. Accordingly the requirement of ISA (UK and Ireland) 720 Section A for the auditor to "read" the other information for the purpose of identifying material inconsistencies or material misstatements of fact is not applicable to XBRL tags.[6]

17   Whether management seeks to increase its confidence concerning the accuracy of its iXBRL tagging for HMRC through a service provided by the company's auditors, or another accountancy firm, is a matter for management to determine. If management does seek such a service, the extent and nature of the engagement to provide it is a matter for agreement between management and the auditor or other accountancy firm.

18   As usage of XBRL evolves in the UK and Ireland the APB will consider the needs of users and the extent to which an audit of financial statements should be expected to provide assurance on the accuracy of the tagging process. It is also possible that regulators may require auditors to provide assurance on XBRL-tagged data at some stage in the future.

Non-audit services and possible threats to auditor independence

19   While auditors do not provide assurance as to the accuracy of the tagging in the context of an audit of financial statements, there may be a demand for non-audit services to be performed by audit/accountancy firms. These may include:

- Performing the tagging exercise;

---

[5] *Guidance on online filing is provided on the HMRC website (www.hmrc.gov. uk/ct/ct-online/file-return). This includes a guidance document "XBRL-when to tag, how to tag, what to tag" (http:// www.hmrc.gov.uk/ct/ct-online/ file-return/online-xbrltag.pdf).*

[6] *This position is consistent with that set out in the Questions and Answers publication "XBRL: The Emerging Landscape," issued by the staff of the International Auditing and Assurance Standards Board (IAASB) in January 2010, clarifying that the IAASB's auditing pronouncements currently do not impose requirements on auditors with respect to XBRL-tagged data or the representation of this data.*

- Providing a service to the directors of the company as to accuracy of the tagging performed by management (e.g. by undertaking an agreed upon procedures engagement);
- Providing advice on the selection of individual tags;
- Supplying accounts preparation software that automates the tagging;
- Training management in XBRL tagging.

Where non-audit services are provided by the company's auditor, the auditor **20** considers possible threats to independence and objectivity and whether it is appropriate to accept the engagement and, if so, whether to apply appropriate safeguards. The differing nature of possible non-audit services means that the associated requirements and guidance fall under different headings in APB's Ethical Standard (ES) 5 including:

- accounting services;
- taxation services; and
- information technology services.

The main threats addressed in these sections of ES5 relate to the management **21** threat and the self-review threat.

Management threat

Unless they apply the provisions of ES – Provisions Available for Small Entities **22** (ES-PASE)[7] the APB Ethical Standards[8] require audit firms to establish policies and procedures which require partners and employees of the firm, including those providing non-audit services to an audited entity, not to take decisions that are the responsibility of the management of the audited entity.

Some non-audit services related to XBRL may give rise to a management threat. **23** In particular performing the XBRL tagging can involve judgements, especially when a transaction or balance is not covered by the taxonomy, or when more than one item within a taxonomy initially appears to be suitable for application to a particular disclosure. In such circumstances the audit firm will need to ensure that management in the audited entity takes responsibility for making the management decisions and that the entity has informed management in place to help it do so.

Under ES – PASE an audit firm can provide non-audit services that involve the **24** firm undertaking part of the role of management to small entities, provided that it discusses these services with those charged with governance, confirms that management accepts responsibility for any decisions taken and discloses the fact that ES – PASE has been applied in the auditor's report.

Self-review threat

Some non-audit services related to XBRL may give rise to a self-review threat. A **25** self-review threat exists when the results of a non-audit service are reflected in the amounts included or disclosed in the financial statements that are subject to audit. If the audit engagement partner identifies threats to the auditor's independence the

---

[7] *ES – Provisions Available for Small Entities allows auditors of Small Entities to take advantage of exemptions from certain of the requirements in APB Ethical Standards 1 to 5 and provides alternative provisions.*

[8] *ES1 paragraph 30.*

APB Ethical Standards[9] require him to identify the effectiveness of the available safeguards and apply such safeguards as are sufficient to eliminate the threats or reduce them to an acceptable level[10].

26   Whether a self-review threat exists in an XBRL tagging engagement depends on whether XBRL tagging is used to generate the financial statements and whether the tagging is covered in the scope of the audit.

27   In the short term, it is likely that the tagging will take place after the financial statements have been generated and the audit has been completed. Accordingly a self-review threat will not arise in relation to the audit of those financial statements. However tagging performed in "year one" may provide the basis for the tagging in future years. If an audit requirement is established at some stage in the future a self-review threat may exist in relation to this initial work. Because of this audit firms may wish to design an XBRL related non-audit service in a way that would avoid a potential future self-review threat.

28   In the longer term, if XBRL becomes integrated into accounting systems it may be difficult to separate XBRL tagging from accounting services. In such circumstances the provisions of ES 5 in relation to accounting services are likely to apply, including the prohibition in paragraph 127 that accounting services are not provided by audit firms to audited entities that are listed companies or significant affiliates of listed companies.

---

[9] *ES1 paragraph 38.*

[10] *Where a small company is audited under ES – PASE the audit firm is not required to apply safeguards to address the self-review threat associated with non-audit services, as long as the audited entity has informed management and the audit firm extends the cyclical inspection of completed engagements that is performed for quality control purposes (ES – PASE, paragraph 7). In the absence of informed management, the firm needs to apply safeguards to address any self-review threat.*

Bulletin 2: Guidance for reporting accountants of stakeholder pension schemes in the United Kingdom

(February 2013)

Contents

	Paragraphs
Introduction	1 - 11
Trustees' or managers' declarations	12
Reporting accountant's procedures	13 - 22
Reporting accountant's reports	23 - 24
Reporting to the regulators	25 - 28
Letters of comment	29 - 32

Appendix 1 – Example report of the reporting accountant to the trustees or managers of a stakeholder pension scheme

Appendix 2 – Regulation 12 of the stakeholder pension schemes regulations 2000

Editorial note – The Financial Reporting Council issued Bulletin 2: Guidance for Reporting Accountants of Stakeholder Pension Schemes in the United Kingdom (February 2012) which replaces Bulletin 2002/3 of the same title, which was withdrawn in March 2012. The changes primarily update a number of references to legislation and regulations, within the original Bulletin, which had become outdated. The opportunity was also taken to update the language of the illustrative reporting accountant's statement to more closely track that of the regulation requiring it.

Introduction

1   Stakeholder pension schemes can be set up by trustees (trust schemes) or can be established by managers (contract schemes). The Pensions Regulator has responsibility for maintaining the register of stakeholder pension schemes, and for the governance of schemes. Under the regulations The Pensions Regulator cannot register, and must de-register, stakeholder schemes if they fail to meet the conditions for being a stakeholder scheme set out in legislation. The Financial Services Authority (FSA) has responsibility for regulating the sales and marketing of stakeholder pensions, and is also responsible for authorising and supervising the firms acting as stakeholder managers as well as firms involved in managing the funds invested in stakeholder schemes.

2   This Bulletin has been issued by the FRC to provide guidance for reporting accountants in relation to the requirements placed upon them in connection with stakeholder pension schemes. It does not constitute guidance from The Pensions Regulator or the FSA.

3   The principal legislation regulating Stakeholder pensions is The Welfare Reform and Pensions Act 1999 ("the Act") and The Stakeholder Pension Schemes Regulations 2000[1] ("the Regulations"). The relevant parts of the Regulations came into force on 1 October 2000 but have been subject to subsequent amending regulations. This Bulletin reflects the version of the Regulations in force as at 5 April 2012.

4   Regulation 12(2)(a) requires the trustees or manager to make an annual declaration[2] containing various statements in accordance with Regulation 12(5). Regulation 12(5)(a) requires a statement that in the opinion of the trustees or manager there are systems and controls in place which provide reasonable assurance that:

   (i)   Regulations 13, 14 and 14B[3] of the regulations have been complied with in relation to the scheme;

   (ii)   transactions for the purposes of the scheme in securities, property or other assets have occurred at a fair market value;

   (iii) the value of members' rights has been determined in accordance with the provisions in the instruments establishing the scheme; and

   (iv)   adequate records have been maintained for the purposes of providing to members the statement required by Regulation 18A(1)[4] of the regulations.

5   Regulation 12(5)(b) requires a statement describing the process that has been undertaken in order to arrive at the opinion expressed in the statement required by Regulation 12(5)(a).

6   Regulations 12(5)(c) and (d) require statements concerning compliance with the conditions in section 1(1) of the Act, and explaining the requirements of Regulations 13, 14, 14B and 18A(1).

---

[1] *SI 2000 no.1403.*

[2] *Regulation 12 of The Stakeholder Pension Schemes Regulations 2000, as amended, is reproduced in full in Appendix 2 of this Bulletin.*

[3] *These regulations impose limits on the amount of charges and deductions which may be made by a stakeholder pension scheme and on the manner in which charges may be made by such a scheme.*

[4] *This regulation requires a stakeholder pension scheme to provide an annual benefit statement to each member.*

Regulation 12(6) requires the trustees or manager to provide the reporting   **7**
accountant with documentation to demonstrate that the process described in the
statement in accordance with Regulation 12(5)(b) has taken place.

Regulation 12(2)(b) requires that the trustees or manager shall obtain from a   **8**
reporting accountant[5] statements made in accordance with Regulation 12(7) that

(i)   the reporting accountant has been provided with documentation as required
      by Regulation 12(6); and

(ii) nothing has come to the attention of the reporting accountant that is
      inconsistent with the statement made in accordance with Regulation
      12(5)(b), or

so far as the reporting accountant is unable to provide such statements, an
explanation as to why he or she is unable to do so. The reporting accountant is
not required to report on the statements made by the trustees or manager in
accordance with Regulations 12(5)(c) or (d).

The trustees or managers are required by the Regulations to annex the reporting   **9**
accountant's report to their declaration, and shall make the whole document
available to members and beneficiaries of the scheme on request.

It is a condition of a scheme being a stakeholder pension scheme that the   **10**
requirements of the Regulations are complied with.

The declarations by the trustees or managers and the reporting accountant's reports   **11**
are due 6 months after the end of the scheme accounting period.

Trustees' or managers' declarations

As described above, the trustees or managers are required to make statements to   **12**
the effect that systems and controls provide reasonable assurance that specified
aspects of the Regulations have been complied with and to describe the process
that has been undertaken to make such statements. Guidance for trustees and
managers to assist them in fulfilling these responsibilities has been issued by the
Pensions Research Accountants Group (PRAG)[6].

Reporting Accountant's procedures

Regulation 11 sets out the processes to be followed for the appointment and   **13**
resignation of the reporting accountant. The Regulation requires, in particular, that
the reporting accountant acknowledge in writing within one month its receipt of
the notice of appointment, and confirm that it will notify the trustees or managers
of any conflict of interest to which the reporting accountant is subject in relation to
the scheme immediately the reporting accountant becomes aware of its existence.
The reporting accountant is also required, on resignation, to serve on the trustees
or managers a written notice containing a statement specifying any circumstances
connected with the resignation which in its opinion significantly affects the

---

[5] *Regulation 11 defines a reporting accountant as follows:*
   *"A person is eligible for appointment as the reporting accountant if the person is eligible under section 1212
   of the Companies Act 2006 for appointment as a company auditor"*

[6] *"Making the Annual Declaration – A Guide for Trustees and Managers of Stakeholder Pension Schemes".
   Copies of this guidance may be obtained from PRAG's website: www.prag.org.uk.*

interests of the members or beneficiaries of the scheme, or a declaration that it knows of no such circumstances.

14   The objective of the reporting accountant's review in accordance with Regulation 12(2)(b) is to obtain evidence to support an assessment of whether the trustees' or managers' description of the process that has been undertaken in order to arrive at the opinion expressed in the statement required by Regulation 12(5)(a) is supported by the documentation provided to the reporting accountant in accordance with Regulation 12(6) and demonstrates that the process described has taken place. Before commencing its review procedures, the reporting accountant:

(a)   plans the work to be undertaken in relation to the declaration by the trustees or managers so as to perform that work in an effective manner;

(b)   familiarises itself with the Stakeholder Pensions Regulations, particularly those sections governing the preparation of the trustees' or managers' declaration;

(c)   obtains an understanding of the structure and management of the scheme and its processing arrangements, including those that are outsourced;

(d)   ensures that it complies with the independence guidance issued by its professional body and discusses, where appropriate, with the trustees or managers any relationships which may affect the reporting accountant's independence or its objectivity and any related safeguards that are in place; and

(e)   agrees the terms of the engagement with the trustees or managers and records them in writing.

15   Appropriate evidence to support the reporting accountant's assessment will usually be obtained by performing the following procedures:

(a)   obtaining through enquiry of appropriate individuals an understanding both of the framework of controls relevant to the legislation referred to in Regulation 12(5)(a), and the process established by the trustees or managers for the review of the effectiveness of those controls, to enable the reporting accountant to arrive at its opinion and sign the declaration;

(b)   enquiring of the trustees or managers whether they are familiar with, and have considered the applicability to their scheme of, relevant guidance issued to trustees and managers by PRAG[7] and The Pensions Regulator and, if necessary, recommending that they should so consider it;

(c)   reviewing relevant minutes of the meetings of the trustees or managers, and of other committees (for example audit and risk management committees) together with supporting papers presented at those meetings;

(d)   enquiring of the trustees or managers whether they are aware of any instances of non-compliance with the legislation referred to in Regulation 12(5)(a);

(e)   reviewing any relevant correspondence with regulators, particularly The Pensions Regulator and the FSA;

---

[7] *In addition to the PRAG guidance referred to in paragraph 12, PRAG has also issued guidance on possible control procedures entitled "Stakeholder pension schemes – a controls checklist". This can also be downloaded from PRAG's website www.prag.org.uk.*

(f)   reviewing the documentation provided to the reporting accountant by the trustees or managers in accordance with Regulation 12(6), including any documentation relating to functions outsourced to a third party, to ascertain that it demonstrates that the process described in the statement made in accordance with Regulation 12(5)(b) has taken place;

(g)   enquiring of the audit engagement partner whether any relevant matters have come to his or her attention during the audit work (see paragraph 18 below); and

(h)   attending meetings at which the declaration made in accordance with Regulation 12(5)(a), including the statement concerning the review process made in accordance with Regulation 12(5)(b), is considered and approved for signature.

The reporting accountant also: **16**

(a)   records in its working papers

   –   details of the engagement planning,

   –   the nature, timing and extent of the procedures performed in relation to its report, and the conclusions drawn; and

   –   its reasoning and conclusions on all significant matters which require the exercise of judgment;

(b)   considers the matters which have come to its attention while performing the procedures on the declaration and whether they should result in a modification to the reporting accountant's statement or be included in a letter of comment to the trustees or managers; and

(c)   takes steps to ensure that any delegated work is directed, supervised and reviewed in a manner which provides reasonable assurance that such work is performed competently.

The reporting accountant may request the trustees or managers to provide written   **17**
confirmation of oral representations made during the course of the review.

The reporting accountant of a stakeholder pension scheme may also be the   **18**
statutory auditor of the managing entity (in the case of contract schemes), or of the schemes managed by the trustees (in the case of trust schemes). Whilst the reporting accountant's assignment is entirely separate from the audit engagement, the partner in charge of the reporting accountant's work nevertheless requests the audit engagement partner to advise him of any breaches of the requirements specified in Regulation 12(5)(a) of which the audit engagement partner has become aware as a result of the audit.

The reporting accountant is not required to consider whether the trustees' or   **19**
managers' description of the process made in accordance with Regulation 12(5)(b) covers all relevant risks and controls, or to reach a conclusion on the adequacy of the process or on the effectiveness of the controls. However the reporting accountant does consider:

●   whether it has been provided with documentation which supports the trustees' or managers' description of the process, and

●   whether it has become aware of matters which are inconsistent with the description of the process,

and, if necessary, the reporting accountant modifies its statement.

20   The reporting accountant is not required to obtain evidence concerning the specific requirements underlying Regulation 12(5)(a) – for example that the value of members' rights has been determined in accordance with the provisions establishing the scheme. However, if during its review of the trustees' or managers' documentation the reporting accountant identifies facts or circumstances which suggest that:

- the trustees or managers may not be justified in their belief that their systems and controls provide reasonable assurance to enable them to make the statement required by Regulation 12(5)(a), or

- because of apparent breaches of the legislation or other matters, the proposed statement required by Regulation 12(5)(a) is not supportable,

the reporting accountant discusses its concerns with the trustees or managers as soon as is practicable.

21   If as a result of the discussion the reporting accountant remains of the view that significant internal control weaknesses or other matters exist which, in its opinion, call into question the credibility of the statement made by the trustees or managers in accordance with Regulation 12(5)(a), they consider modifying the statement in their report in respect of these matters.

22   Under normal circumstances the reporting accountant modifies its report in respect of apparent undisclosed breaches of the legislation, referred to in Regulation 12(5) (a), of which the reporting accountant becomes aware. In deciding whether to modify its report in respect of such breaches, the reporting accountant considers their significance. The materiality of the breach in monetary terms may not be relevant to a consideration of its significance. However, where breaches have occurred which were identified by the scheme's own control systems, which were not indicative of a systemic problem, and which were corrected subsequently such that there was no monetary impact on any member or beneficiary of the scheme, they are unlikely to be significant.

Reporting Accountant's reports

23   The reporting accountant's report on a declaration normally includes the following matters:

- a title identifying the persons to whom the report is addressed (which will normally be the trustees or managers of the scheme);

- an introductory paragraph identifying the Regulations which are covered by the report;

- separate sections, appropriately headed, dealing with

  - respective responsibilities of the trustees or managers and the reporting accountants, and

  - the basis of the reporting accountant's statement, including (where appropriate) a reference to compliance with the guidance in this Bulletin;

- the reporting accountant's statement on the matters required by the Regulations;

- the signature of the reporting accountant; and

- the date of the reporting accountant's report.

Appendix 1 of this Bulletin sets out an illustrative example of a reporting accountant's report on the declaration. This example wording may need to be tailored to reflect particular circumstances.

As indicated in paragraphs 19-22 above, the reporting accountant modifies the statement in its report if the reporting accountant: **24**

–   has not been provided with documentation to demonstrate that the trustees' or managers' description of the process made in accordance with Regulation 12(5)(a) has taken place, or

–   is aware of matters that are inconsistent with the trustees' or managers' description of the process, made in accordance with Regulation 12(5)(b), or

–   is aware of matters which call into question the credibility of the statement made by the trustees or managers in accordance with Regulation 12(5)(a). These matters are likely to be connected with significant internal control weaknesses, or with breaches of the legislation referred to in Regulation 12(5)(a).

Reporting to the regulators

Section 70(1) of The Pensions Act 2004 imposes on "a person who is otherwise involved in advising trustees or managers of an occupational or personal pension scheme in relation to the scheme" a requirement to report to The Pensions Regulator. The Pensions Regulator's Regulatory Code of Practice 01 "Reporting breaches of the law" clarifies that a reporting accountant appointed to a stakeholder scheme is subject to this requirement. **25**

The reporting requirement referred to in paragraph 25 will exist where the reporting accountant has reasonable cause to believe that: **26**

●   a duty which is relevant to the administration of the scheme in question, and is imposed by or by virtue of an enactment or rule of law, has not been or is not being complied with; and

●   the failure to comply is likely to be of material significance to The Pensions Regulator in the exercise of any of its functions[8].

A reporting accountant of a contract scheme who is also the auditor of the managing entity considers whether it has a duty to report matters of material significance, of which it becomes aware in its capacity as auditor of the managing entity, to the FSA[9] under the FSMA[10] 2000 (Communications by Auditors) Regulations 2001. This is because there may be situations where it is not clear whether information coming to the attention of the reporting accountant is received in that capacity or in its role as auditor. Appendix 2 to ISA (UK and Ireland) 250 Section B provides guidance as to how information obtained in non-audit work may be relevant to the auditor in the planning and conduct of the audit and the steps that need to be taken to ensure the communication of information that is relevant to the audit. **27**

---

[8]   *Further guidance on reporting to The Pensions Regulator is set out in Practice Note 15 (Revised) – The audit of occupational schemes in the United Kingdom.*

[9]   *Further guidance on reporting to the FSA is set out in Practice Note 20 (Revised) – The audit of insurers in the United Kingdom.*

[10]   *The Financial Services and Markets Act.*

28 In general, if a reporting accountant is in any doubt as to whether a report should be made to the regulator or not, it considers taking legal advice.

Letters of comment

29 As indicated in paragraph 24 above, if the reporting accountant considers that significant weaknesses in internal control or other matters exist which call into question whether the trustees' or managers' statements made in accordance with Regulations 12(5)(a) and (b) are justified, it modifies the statement in its report.

30 If, however, the reporting accountant is of the opinion that control weaknesses or other matters exist, but these do not affect the credibility of the statement made by the trustees or managers in accordance with Regulation 12(5)(a), it reports them in a letter of comment to the trustees or managers.

31 Where no significant weaknesses in the scheme's internal control systems come to the reporting accountant's attention during its review, the reporting accountant advises the trustees or managers in writing that no letter of comment is to be issued.

32 Trustees or managers will normally wish to have the opportunity of responding in writing to the comments made in letters of comment. The reporting accountant agrees with the trustees or managers the way in which their responses are to be presented. These discussions should not, however, be allowed to cause an unreasonable delay in issuing the letter of comment.

APPENDIX 1 – Example report of the Reporting Accountant to the Trustees or Managers of a stakeholder pension scheme

The Trustees/Managers of the XYZ pension scheme, Address.

XYZ STAKEHOLDER PENSION SCHEME

We report in accordance with the requirements of Regulation 12(7) of the Stakeholder Pension Schemes Regulations 2000 (as amended) (the Regulations), concerning the annual declaration by the trustees/managers of the XYZ pension scheme. The declaration is made in respect of the period of 12 months ended on xxxx.

Respective responsibilities of the trustees/managers and the reporting accountant

In accordance with Regulation 12(2)(a) the trustees/managers are responsible for the preparation of a declaration, which contains a statement describing the process that the trustees/ managers have undertaken, in order to arrive at their opinion as to whether systems and controls are in place which provide reasonable assurance that specified regulations in relation to stakeholder pensions have been complied with.

It is our responsibility to consider whether documentation has been provided to us to demonstrate that the process described by the trustees'/managers' has taken place, and to report if this is not the case and to consider whether anything has come to our attention that is inconsistent with the description of the process and to report if this is the case.

We are not required to consider whether the trustees'/managers' description of the process made in accordance with Regulation 12(5)(b) covers all relevant risks and controls, or to reach a conclusion on the adequacy of the process or on the effectiveness of the controls or to undertake any work in this regard.

Basis of reporting accountant's statement

We conducted our work in accordance with Bulletin 2 "Guidance for reporting accountants of stakeholder pension schemes in the United Kingdom" issued by the Financial Reporting Council. The work performed involved making enquiries of management and staff and examination of the documentary evidence supporting the existence of the process.

Statement

(Other than the Exception set out below)[11] In accordance with Regulation 12(7) we report that in our opinion:

- we have been provided by the trustees/managers with documentation, which is required by Regulation 12(6) to demonstrate that the process described in the trustees'/managers' statement has taken place; and

---

[11] *In cases where there are no exceptions, the wording in italics would be omitted.*

- nothing has come to our attention that is inconsistent with the trustees'/ managers' description of the process.

(Exception

The trustees'/managers' description concerning ... does not appropriately reflect our understanding of the process undertaken by you because.....")

Reporting accountants   Address
Date

APPENDIX 2 – Regulation 12 of The Stakeholder Pension Schemes Regulations 2000

Requirement for declaration by trustees or manager

12.–(1) For the purposes of section 1(1)(b), it shall be a condition of a scheme being a stakeholder pension scheme that the requirements of this regulation are complied with.

(2) Subject to paragraph (11), the trustees or manager of the scheme shall, no later than the end of 6 months beginning with each reporting date–

   (a)   make a declaration in writing signed by the trustees or manager containing the statements set out in paragraph (5) in relation to the reporting period or, in so far as they are unable to make those statements containing a statement explaining why they are unable to do so; and

   (b)   obtain from the reporting accountant appointed by virtue of regulation 11 the statement specified in paragraph (7) or, in so far as the reporting accountant is unable to make that statement, a statement from the reporting accountant explaining why he is unable to do so.

(3) Subject to paragraph (10), in this regulation reporting date means–

   (a)   in the case of the first reporting date, a date chosen by the trustees or manager that is no later than the last day of the period of 12 months beginning with the date on which the scheme is registered under section 2 of the Act; and

   (b)   in the case of each subsequent reporting date, a date chosen by the trustees or manager that is no later than the last day of the period of 12 months beginning with the date immediately following the previous reporting date.

(4) Subject to paragraph (10), in this regulation reporting period means–

   (a)   in the case of the first reporting period, the period beginning with the date of registration of the scheme under section 2 of the Act and ending on and including the first reporting date;

   (b)   in the case of subsequent reporting periods, the period beginning on the date immediately following the previous reporting date and ending on and including the reporting date.

(5) The statements specified in paragraph (2)(a) shall be–

   (a)   a statement that in the opinion of the trustees or manager there are systems and controls in place which provide reasonable assurance that –

      (i)   regulations 13, 14 and 14B have been complied with in relation to the scheme;

      (ii)   transactions for the purposes of the scheme in securities, property or other assets have occurred at a fair market value;

      (iii)   the value of members' rights has been determined in accordance with the provisions in the instruments establishing the scheme; and

      (iv)   adequate records have been maintained for the purposes of providing to members the statement required by regulation 18A(1);

(b)   a statement describing the process that the trustees or manager have or has undertaken in order to arrive at the opinion expressed in the statement described in paragraph (5)(a);

(c)   a statement that in the opinion of the trustees or manager there are systems and controls in place which provide reasonable assurance that the scheme has complied with the conditions in section 1(1) of the Act, apart from those conditions that are covered by the statement in paragraph (5)(a); and

(d)   a statement which explains that–

   (i)   regulations 13, 14 and 14B impose limits on the amount of charges and deductions which may be made by a stakeholder pension scheme and on the manner in which charges may be made by such a scheme; and

   (ii)   regulation 18A(1) requires a stakeholder pension scheme to provide an annual benefit statement to each member.

(6)   The trustees or manager shall provide the reporting accountant with documentation to demonstrate that the process described in the statement in paragraph (5)(b) has taken place.

(7)   The statement specified in paragraph (2)(b) shall be a statement that–

(a)   the reporting accountant has been provided with documentation as required by paragraph (6); and

(b)   nothing has come to the attention of the reporting accountant that is inconsistent with the statement made in paragraph (5)(b).

(8)   The trustees or manager shall make available to members and beneficiaries of the scheme on request the declaration made by the trustees or manager and the statement obtained from the reporting accountant in accordance with paragraph (2).

(9)   If the statement to be obtained by the trustees or manager under paragraph (2)(b) is obtained from the reporting accountant acting as such while ineligible in contravention of regulation 11(7A)(a)–

(a)   the trustees or manager shall not be regarded as having complied with paragraph (2)(b); and

(b)   for the purposes of paragraph (8), the statement from the reporting accountant shall not be regarded as obtained in accordance with paragraph (2)(b).

(10)   Where a scheme is registered under section 2 of the Act on or before 6th April 2001–

(a)   the first reporting date shall be 5th April 2002; and

(b)   the first reporting period shall be the period commencing on and including 6th April 2001 and ending on and including 5th April 2002.

(11)   Where the reporting date is on or before 30th September 2002 the trustees or manager of the scheme shall make the declaration specified in paragraph (2)(a) and obtain the statement specified in paragraph (2)(b) from the reporting accountant–

(a)   on or before 31st December 2002; or

(b)   by the end of 6 months beginning with the reporting date,

whichever is later.

Providing Assurance on Client Assets to the Financial Conduct Authority

(November 2015)

Contents

	Paragraphs
Client asset assurance standard	1 - 10
Preface	
Introduction	1 - 8
Objectives	9
Definitions	10
Requirements applicable to all client asset engagements	11 - 66
Obtaining an understanding of the firm's business model and the permissions it has received from the FCA	11 - 13
The application of this Standard to the specific circumstances of a firm	14 - 19
Conduct of a Client Asset Engagement in accordance with this Standard	20 - 22
Ethical requirements	23 - 24
Engagement acceptance and continuance	25 - 27
The client assets report	28 - 32
Quality control	33 - 37
Professional scepticism, professional judgment, and requisite mind - sets	38 - 42
Documentation	43 - 50
Written representations	51 - 53
Planning and performing the engagement	54 - 57
The CASS auditor's duty to report to the FCA	58 - 63
The CASS auditor's right to report to the FCA	64 - 66
Requirements applicable to the expression of reasonable assurance opinions in a CASS auditor's report	67 - 145
The requirements and guidance in paragraphs 11 to 66 also apply to the expression of reasonable assurance opinions	67 - 71
Assessing CASS assurance engagement risk	72 - 77
Determining the nature and extent of risk assessment procedures	78 - 79
Responding to the assessment of assurance engagement risk	80 - 93
Obtaining evidence to support the opinion as to whether the firm has maintained systems over client assets adequate to enable it to comply with the relevant CASS rules during the period.	94 - 113
Obtaining evidence to support the opinion as to whether the firm was in compliance with relevant CASS rules at the end of the period	114 - 115
Forming the client assets opinion	116 - 128
Content of a reasonable assurance client assets report	129 - 136
Communicating deficiencies in internal control to management and those charged with governance	137 - 140
Engagement quality control review	141 - 145
Requirements applicable to the expression of limited assurance opinions where a firm claims not to hold client assets	146 - 166
Circumstances giving rise to limited assurance opinions	146 - 148
Limited assurance client assets reports where a firm has permission to hold client money and/or custody assets but management claims it does not hold either client money or custody assets	149 - 160

Written representation   161
Forming the limited assurance opinion   162 - 163
Content of a limited assurance client assets report   164 - 166

The expression of hybrid opinions   167

**Requirements applicable to the provision of reasonable assurance with respect
to special reports**   168 - 175

**Requirements applicable to CASS auditor confirmations in connection with
non-statutory client money trusts**   176 - 181

Appendix 1 – Overview of a reasonable assurance process for a legal entity

**Appendix 2 – Illustrative qualified opinion in a reasonable assurance report
on client assets**

**Appendix 3 – Illustrative adverse opinion in a reasonable assurance
report on client assets**

**Appendix 4 – Illustrative unmodified opinion in a reasonable assurance
report on client assets**

**Appendix 5 – Illustrative unmodified opinion in a limited assurance report on
client assets where firm has permission to hold both client
money and custody assets but claims to hold neither**

**Appendix 6 – Illustrative unmodified opinion in a limited assurance report on
client assets where the firm is permitted to hold client money but not
custody assets and claims to hold neither**

**Appendix 7 – Illustrative unmodified opinion in a limited assurance report
on client assets where the firm does not have permission to
hold client money or custody assets and claims to hold neither**

**Appendix 8 – Illustrative modified limited assurance opinion on client assets
where a firm holds client money but does not have permission to do so**

Appendix 9 – The alternative approach to client money segregation

Appendix 10 – The non-standard method of internal client money reconciliation

**Appendix 11 – Illustrative example of a confirmation letter from the
auditor to the firm regarding a non-statutory client money trust**

Appendix 12 – The CASS auditor's duty to report to the FCA

Editorial note – The FRC has published this Client Assets Assurance Standard (CAAS) which aims to improve the quality of client asset (CASS) audits and other CASS assurance engagements and to support auditors when undertaking these type of engagements. This Standard is effective for reports to the FCA with respect to client assets covering periods commencing on or after 1 January 2016, with early adoption permitted. The Standard replaces Bulletin 2011/2: Providing assurance on client assets to the Financial Services Authority and Bulletin 3: Supplement addressing the use of third party administrators.

CLIENT ASSET ASSURANCE STANDARD

Preface

This Client Asset Assurance Standard contains requirements indicated by paragraphs in bold type, with which a CASS auditor is required to comply in the conduct of an engagement to report to the Financial Conduct Authority in respect of Client Assets.

The Client Asset Assurance Standard also includes implementation guidance, including appendices, in the context of which the requirements are to be understood and applied. It is necessary to consider the whole text of the Client Asset Assurance Standard to understand and apply the requirements.

The Client Asset Assurance Standard is the material referred to in SUP 3.10.5B G to which the FCA expects CASS auditors to have regard for reports for periods commencing on or after 1 January 2016.

For the purposes of the Client Asset Assurance Standard the term "client assets" encompasses "client money" and "custody assets" as defined by the FCA's "Glossary". Notwithstanding that the engagement is not an audit, the generally accepted expression CASS auditor is used in the Client Asset Assurance Standard to refer to the persons conducting the CASS assurance engagement.

Attached to the Client Asset Assurance Standard is contextual material which is intended to provide a non-technical introduction to, and overview of, the Client Asset Assurance Standard. This does not form part of the Standard.

Introduction

Scope of this Standard

This Client Asset Assurance Standard (Standard) establishes requirements and provides guidance for CASS auditors reporting to the Financial Conduct Authority (FCA) in accordance with its SUP (Supervision Manual) rules in respect of engagements that involve evaluating and reporting on a regulated firm's (firm) compliance with the FCA's CASS (Client Asset) rules and other rules relevant to the holding of client assets.   **1**

Arising from the nature of insolvency law, client asset protection (including the CASS rules) is structured on the basis of the legal entities that hold client assets rather than in the context of the business structures (e.g. a consolidated group) within which a legal entity operates. This Standard, therefore, is applicable to the CASS audit of each firm that is required to have a CASS audit pursuant to SUP 3.   **2**

If client assets are transferred to another legal entity such as a sub-custodian or third party administrator the CASS auditor will need to have a clear understanding regarding which client assets are within the scope of the CASS rules on which it has a responsibility to provide assurance and to report Breaches of those rules, where appropriate.   **3**

"CASS audit" describes the work performed by a "CASS auditor" in providing a client assets report to the FCA. Strictly, such engagements are assurance engagements rather than audit engagements; however, the terms "CASS audit" and "CASS auditor" are used because they are commonly used and well understood expressions. The use of these expressions is not intended to change the nature of the engagement to that of an audit.   **4**

5   More specifically, the Standard establishes requirements with respect to:

(a)   The process for forming, and the expression of, reasonable assurance opinions;

(b)   The process for forming, and the expression of, limited assurance opinions;

(c)   The provision of reasonable assurance to the FCA with respect to a firm's proposed adoption of:

(i)   The alternative approach to client money segregation; and

(ii)   A non-standard method of client money reconciliation[1]; and

(d)   CASS auditor confirmations in respect of non-statutory client money trusts.

6   This Standard is the material published by the Financial Reporting Council[2] referred to in SUP 3.10.5B G, that deals specifically with the client assets report which the auditor is required to submit to the FCA, to which the FCA would expect CASS auditors to have regard.

7   The Standard contains references to, and extracts from, certain legislation and the CASS, SUP and SYSC rules of the FCA. These references are not intended to provide CASS auditors with the requisite knowledge of that legislation or those Rules. CASS auditors should have the requisite knowledge of those FCA rules that are relevant to the engagement. Readers are cautioned that the legislation and FCA Rules may change subsequent to publication of this Standard such that the references may no longer be accurate. The latest version of extant FCA rules can be found on the FCA website at: https://www.handbook.fca.org.uk/.

Effective Date

8   This Standard is effective for reports to the FCA with respect to Client Assets for periods commencing on or after 1 January 2016. Earlier adoption is permitted.

Objectives

9   The key objectives of the CASS Assurance Standard are to:

(a)   Improve the quality of CASS audits and other CASS assurance engagements;

(b)   Adequately support and challenge CASS auditors when undertaking CASS assurance engagements and, in particular, to define the nature and extent of the work effort required for both reasonable assurance and limited assurance CASS assurance engagements without undermining the importance of the CASS auditor's judgment;

(c)   Support the objectives of the FCA's Client Asset Regime regarding the effective safekeeping of client assets and client monies and in particular to guard against systemic failure of the CASS Regime;

(d)   Manage the expectations of:

(i)   The management of firms that hold client assets; and

(ii)   Third party administrators

---

[1] *In this Standard CASS auditor's reports on adoption of the alternative approach to client money segregation and the non-standard method of client money reconciliation are collectively referred to as "Special Reports".*

[2] *The SUP rules reference is to the Auditing Practices Board. This reference is outdated and should be to the Financial Reporting Council.*

when a CASS auditor is engaged to provide assurance to the FCA on client assets that they handle or account for;

(e) Support the effective training of CASS auditors by both the accounting bodies and other training organisations;

(f) Help to establish realistic expectations regarding the integrity of the UK Client Asset regime with the beneficial owners of client assets; and

(g) Underpin the effectiveness of the FRC's enforcement and disciplinary activities with respect to CASS assurance engagements.

Definitions

For the purposes of the Client Asset Assurance Standard the following terms have the meanings attributed below: **10**

Applicable criteria: *The CASS rules and other applicable rules used, in the context of the particular CASS assurance engagement, to evaluate the status of a firm, in terms specified by the FCA, in connection with subject matter relating to the holding of client assets. Related assertions are the conditions that need to be met, as expressed or implied by the applicable criteria, if the firm's status could be described in the terms specified by the FCA.*

Breaches schedule: *Part 2 of the Client Assets Report: A Breaches Schedule identifying each CASS rule in respect of which a breach has been identified in the course of the CASS assurance engagement for the period covered by the Client Assets Report, whether identified by the CASS auditor or disclosed to it by the firm, or by any third party.*

CASS: *The Client Assets Sourcebook of the FCA.*

CASS assurance engagement: *An engagement in which a CASS auditor expresses an opinion designed to enhance the degree of confidence of the FCA concerning the status of a firm, in terms specified by the FCA, in connection with subject matter relating to the holding of client assets. CASS assurance engagements include CASS audits and certain other engagements to provide assurance to the FCA with respect to special reports or nonstatutory client money trusts.*

CASS assurance engagement risk: *The risk that the CASS auditor expresses an inappropriate opinion when the subject matter information is materially misstated.*

CASS audit: *A client asset assurance engagement that involves providing a Client Assets Report to the FCA.*

CASS auditor: *The person or persons conducting the CASS audit or other CASS assurance engagement, usually the CASS engagement leader or other members of the engagement team, or, as applicable, the auditing firm. Where a requirement expressly intends that it be fulfilled by the CASS engagement leader the term "CASS engagement leader" rather than "CASS auditor" is used. (N.B. A CASS auditor need not be the firm's statutory auditor).*

CASS auditor's report: *The report of the CASS auditor as required in the context of the CASS assurance engagement – in the case of a CASS audit, the Client Assets Report.*

CASS engagement leader: *The individual charged by the CASS auditor to be responsible for signing the CASS auditor's report.*

CASS engagement team: *All partners and staff performing the CASS assurance engagement, and any individuals engaged by the auditing firm who perform procedures on the engagement. This excludes any external experts engaged by the auditing firm.*

CASS records: *The records of accounting entries and other records, both manual and electronic, that comprise or support the information system that accounts for the receipt, segregation, custody, monitoring, reconciliation, transfer and return of client assets, and for the safeguarding of clients' rights relating to such assets while they are held by the firm, in accordance with the CASS rules and other applicable rules.*

CASS rules: *The rules set out in CASS as denoted by the suffix R.*

Client assets: *Generic term encompassing client money, safe custody assets, and mandates and collateral, if applicable.*

Client Assets Report: *The assurance report that the CASS auditor is required to submit to the FCA either to provide reasonable assurance as to whether a firm's systems are adequate to enable it to comply throughout the period, and as to whether it was in compliance at the end of the period, with the CASS rules or to provide limited assurance that the firm did not hold client assets during the period. For insurance intermediaries, the FCA's rules require the report to be submitted to "the firm".*

CMAR: *The Client Money and Asset Return.*

Control risk: *The risk that a breach of the CASS rules that could be significant in the context of the applicable criteria and related assertions will not be prevented, or detected and corrected, on a timely basis by related internal controls.*

Credit risk: *The risk that a borrower will default on a debt by failing to make required payments.*

Detection risk: *The risk that the CASS auditor will not detect, as applicable in the context of the CASS assurance engagement, a deficiency in the design, implementation or operation of the firm's systems that are intended to enable it to comply with the relevant CASS rules, or a breach of the CASS rules that would be significant in the context of its reporting responsibilities.*

Engagement quality control review: *A process designed to provide an objective evaluation, on or before the date of the report, of the significant judgments the CASS engagement team made and the conclusions it reached in formulating the CASS auditor's report.*

Engagement quality control reviewer: *A partner, other person in the accounting firm, suitably qualified external person, or a team made up of such individuals, none of whom is part of the engagement team, with sufficient and appropriate experience and authority to objectively evaluate the significant judgments the CASS engagement team made and the conclusions it reached in formulating the CASS auditor's report.*

Evaluation risk: *The risk that the CASS auditor will fail to evaluate accurately the underlying subject matter against the applicable criteria and related assertions, in the terms specified by the FCA concerning the firm's status relating to the holding of client assets.*

FCA: *Financial Conduct Authority.*

Firm: *The regulated legal entity in respect of which the CASS auditor is reporting.*

FSMA 2000: *The Financial Services and Markets Act 2000*

Hybrid opinions: *Hybrid opinions are opinions that provide reasonable assurance with respect to one aspect of a firm's status relating to the holding of client assets and limited assurance with respect to another. For example, reasonable assurance may be provided with respect to the firm's compliance with the client money rules and limited assurance with respect to the custody asset rules because the firm's permissions do not allow it to hold custody assets.*

Inherent risk: *The risk of the management of the firm not preventing non-compliance with the CASS rules and other applicable rules due to the underlying susceptibility of the behaviour of the regulated firm to non-compliance with all of the applicable criteria and related assertions under those rules, before the application of internal controls.*

Limited assurance Client Assets Report: *A Client Assets Report providing a level of assurance where the engagement risk is reduced to a level that is acceptable in the circumstances of the engagement, but which is obtained when that risk is greater than the level of assurance that would be provided in a reasonable assurance Client Assets Report, as the basis for a negative form of expression of the CASS auditor's conclusion.*

Nominee Company: *A subsidiary of a firm in whose name custody assets of the firm are registered during the period.*

Practitioner: *A professional accountant in public practice.*

Reasonable assurance Client Assets Report: *A Client Assets Report providing a high but not absolute level of assurance, which is obtained when the CASS auditor has obtained sufficient appropriate assurance evidence to reduce assurance engagement risk to an acceptably low level in the circumstances of the engagement as the basis for a positive form of expression of the CASS auditor's conclusion.*

Re-performance: *The CASS auditor's independent execution of procedures or controls that were originally performed as part of the firm's internal controls.*

Reportable breach: *A breach of the FCA's rules of which the CASS auditor becomes aware which it reasonably believes may be of material significance to the FCA (see para 59).*

Significant deficiency in internal control: *A deficiency or combination of deficiencies in internal control relating to a firm's compliance with the CASS rules or other applicable rules that, in the auditor's professional judgment, is of sufficient importance to require the attention of those charged with governance.*

Special Reports: *The reports prepared by an independent auditor, subject to the provision of which, the FCA permits certain firms to use the "alternative approach" to client money segregation and a "non-standard method" of client money reconciliation under the CASS rules. In this Standard, both are referred to as "Special Reports".*

Subject matter information: *The outcome of the evaluation by the CASS auditor of the underlying subject matter against the applicable criteria and related assertions, in the terms specified by the FCA concerning the firm's status relating to the holding of client assets.*

Those charged with governance: *The person(s) or organisation(s) (for example a corporate trustee) with responsibility for overseeing the strategic direction of the entity and obligations related to the accountability of the firm. This includes overseeing the financial reporting process. For some entities in some jurisdictions, those charged with governance may include management personnel, for example, executive members of a governance board of a private firm or public sector entity, or an owner manager[3].*

Underlying subject matter: *The matter(s) relating to the holding of client assets, in connection with which, in the context of the particular CASS assurance engagement, the CASS auditor is required to express an opinion concerning the firm's status, in terms specified by the FCA.*

> *In a CASS audit, the underlying subject matter is:*
>
> - *when a reasonable assurance Client Assets Report is required – the firm's state of compliance with relevant FCA rules (e.g. the CASS rules) and the design, implementation and operation of the firm's systems intended to enable its compliance with such rules;*
>
> - *when a limited assurance Client Assets Report is required – the firm's holding of client assets to which such rules apply.*
>
> *In a CASS assurance engagement relating to special reports or non-statutory client money trusts, the subject matter is the design and/or implementation of the firm's systems intended to enable its compliance with specified FCA rules.*

Walk-through test: *Involves tracing transactions through the firm's systems used to monitor and report on client assets.*

Requirements Applicable to all Client Asset Engagements

Obtaining an understanding of the firm's business model and the permissions it has received from the FCA

11   **The CASS auditor shall obtain an understanding of the firm's business model that is sufficient to enable the CASS auditor to establish expectations about the existence or otherwise of client assets, including:**

- **the nature of the services it provides to clients.**

- **how it is remunerated for those services and other ancillary services.**

- **the nature of any transactions which it undertakes with or on behalf of, or facilitates or advises on, for clients and how those transactions are executed or settled.**

- **the nature of relationships within a group and with other related parties.**

- **the sources and destinations of cash and other asset inflows and outflows in its own accounts and any accounts it holds or controls on behalf of clients and other parties.**

- **the role of sub-custodians and third party administrators.**

---

[3] *For discussion of the diversity of governance structures, see paragraphs A1–A8 of ISA (UK and Ireland) 260, Communication with Those Charged with Governance.*

Establishing the firm's scope of permissions

The CASS auditor shall establish from responsible officials within the firm the scope of the firm's permissions from the FCA with respect to the holding or controlling of client assets.   **12**

The CASS auditor shall also review the permissions, including any limitations and requirements, set out on the on-line register maintained by the FCA for consistency with both its understanding of the firm's business model and the permissions asserted by the responsible officials within the firm.   **13**

The application of this Standard to the specific circumstances of a firm

Opinions in reasonable assurance reports

Firm (within the ambit of SUP 3.10) has relevant permissions and asserts it holds client assets

Where the scope of the firm's permissions includes the holding or controlling of client assets and the firm claims that it holds or controls client assets, the CASS auditor shall provide a reasonable assurance Client Assets Report including a breaches schedule as required by the FCA's Rules. In such cases the CASS auditor shall comply with all the requirements of this Standard set out in paragraphs 11 to 145 and in the case of non-statutory client money trusts also paragraphs 176 to 181. However, the FCA's Rules do not require a reasonable assurance Client Assets Report in relation to certain firms in certain circumstances[4].   **14**

The CASS auditor shall assess, based on its understanding obtained from meeting the requirements in paragraphs 11 to 14, whether the firm effectively identifies all circumstances when client assets may arise, including cases where it is unable to rely on exemptions, treats them as client assets in accordance with the CASS rules and reports them to the FCA (see paragraph 94). If the auditor becomes aware of categories of client assets that are not being treated as client assets, the CASS auditor shall promptly report this fact to both those charged with governance and the FCA, and reflect this in the assurance engagement risk assessment.   **15**

Opinions in limited assurance reports

Firm (within the ambit of SUP 3.10) has relevant permissions but claims it does not hold client money or custody assets

Where the scope of the firm's permissions includes the holding or controlling of client money and/or custody assets but the firm claims not to hold client money and/ or custody assets, the CASS auditor is required by the FCA's rules to provide a limited assurance Client Assets Report. In such cases the CASS auditor shall comply, as applicable, with all the requirements of this Standard set out in paragraphs 11 to 66 and 146 to 166[5]. (N.B. The FCA rules   **16**

---

[4] *For example at the time of writing reasonable assurance opinions are not required in relation to Insurance intermediaries not holding more than £30,000 at any time in the reporting period in a statutory client money trust.*

[5] *Paragraphs 16 and 17 are considered separately with respect to custody assets and client money. A hybrid Client Assets Report providing, for example, reasonable assurance on client money and limited assurance on custody assets is possible where the scope of the firm's permissions includes the holding of client money but not the holding of custody assets or vice versa (see paragraph 167).*

do not require limited assurance opinions in respect of insurance intermediaries and certain other categories of firms).

Firm (within the ambit of SUP 3.10) does not have relevant permissions

17 Where the scope of the firm's permissions does not include the holding or controlling of client money and/or custody assets, the CASS auditor is required by the FCA's Rules to provide a limited assurance client assets report. In such cases the CASS auditor shall comply, as applicable, with the requirements of this Standard set out in paragraphs 11 to 66 and 146 to 166. (N.B. The FCA rules do not require limited assurance opinions in respect of insurance intermediaries and certain other categories of firms).

Special Reports

18 If the CASS auditor has been requested by the firm to provide a reasonable assurance report to the firm with respect to either the adoption of the alternative approach to client money segregation or a non-standard method of internal client money reconciliation, the CASS auditor shall comply with those requirements of this Standard that are applicable to the provision of such reasonable assurance reports as set out in paragraphs 11 to 66. The additional requirements pertaining to special reports are set out in paragraphs 168 to 175.

Non-statutory client money trust under CASS 5

19 If the CASS auditor has been requested by an insurance intermediary firm to provide a confirmation with respect to whether it has, and maintains, adequate systems and controls over non-statutory client money trusts, the CASS auditor shall comply with those requirements of this Standard that are applicable as set out in paragraphs 11 to 66. The additional requirements pertaining to non-statutory client money trusts are set out in paragraphs 176 to 181.

Conduct of a Client Asset Engagement in accordance with this Standard

Complying with Standards that are relevant to the CASS Engagement

20 The CASS auditor shall not have complied with this Client Asset Assurance Standard unless the CASS auditor has complied with all relevant requirements of this Client Asset Assurance Standard or has met the requirement in paragraph 22.

Requirements that are not relevant

21 Subject to the following paragraph, the CASS auditor shall comply with each relevant requirement of this Client Asset Assurance Standard unless the requirement is conditional and the condition does not exist.

Departing from relevant requirements

22 When, in exceptional circumstances, the CASS auditor judges it necessary to depart from a relevant requirement in this Client Asset Assurance Standard, the CASS auditor shall document the reasons for departing from the requirement and perform additional procedures to achieve the aim of that requirement.

Ethical Requirements

The CASS auditor shall comply with relevant ethical requirements, including those pertaining to independence.   23

CASS auditors in the UK and Ireland are subject to ethical requirements from two sources: the relevant FRC Ethical Standards for Auditors concerning the integrity, objectivity and independence of the auditor, and the ethical pronouncements established by the CASS auditor's relevant professional body. In practice, the UK recognised supervisory bodies have adopted, with minor modifications, The Code of Ethics for Professional Accountants issued by the International Ethics Standards Board for Accountants (the IESBA Code). The FRC is not aware of any significant instances where the relevant parts of the IESBA Code of Ethics are more restrictive than the FRC's Ethical Standard for Auditors.   24

Engagement Acceptance and Continuance

The CASS auditor shall accept or continue a Client Asset Engagement only when the CASS auditor: 25

(a)   **Has reason to believe that all relevant ethical requirements, including independence, will be satisfied;**

(b)   **The CASS auditor is satisfied that those who are to perform the engagement, including the CASS engagement leader, have had appropriate training and will have the appropriate competence and capabilities; and**

(c)   **The basis upon which the engagement is to be performed has been agreed between the CASS auditor and the firm, including the CASS auditor's reporting responsibilities to the FCA.**

(See paragraphs 55 to 58 of the Contextual Material).

Agreeing on the Terms of the Engagement

The CASS auditor shall agree the terms of engagement with the firm by means of an engagement letter. The engagement letter shall cover all aspects of the engagement to report on client assets (and collateral and mandates if applicable) and shall be accepted in writing by the firm. In subsequent years of a recurring engagement the CASS auditor shall assess whether circumstances require the terms of the engagement to be revised and whether there is a need to remind the firm of the existing terms of the engagement.   26

Where the CASS auditor and the financial statement auditor are from the same auditing firm, the terms of the engagement may be included in a separate section of a composite engagement letter sent to the firm. Alternatively, the terms may be the subject of a separate engagement letter. This may be appropriate, for example, where the CASS engagement leader is not the same as the audit engagement partner or where the terms of the engagement have to be agreed by an official at the firm other than the official who agrees the terms of the financial statement audit.   27

The Client Assets Report

The content and wording of the Client Assets Report provided by the CASS auditor shall be as prescribed by the Rules of the FCA and follow the templates in SUP 3 Annex 1R. Any deviations in content and wording beyond   28 those provided for either in the FCA's template, or the wording in the illustrative example reports set out in Appendices 2 to 8 of this Standard shall only be used with the prior agreement of the FCA. The latest version of extant FCA rules can be found on the FCA website at: https://www.handbook.fca.org.uk/.

29   SUP 3.10 sets out the FCA's rules and guidance with respect to the duties of CASS auditors to report on client assets. Amongst other things SUP 3.10 establishes rules relating to:

- The period that a Client Assets Report may cover.
- The time period allowed for the Client Assets Report to be delivered to the FCA and the firm.
- The signing of the Client Assets Report.
- Delivering a draft of the report to the firm.

30   The CASS auditor is required by SUP 3.10.8D R to deliver a draft of its Client Assets Report to the firm such that the firm has an adequate period of time (see paragraph 32) to consider its findings and provide the CASS auditor with comments explaining:

(a)   The circumstances that gave rise to each of the breaches identified in the draft Client Assets Report; and

(b)   Any remedial actions that it has undertaken or plans to undertake to correct those breaches.

31   Such comments are required to be submitted to the CASS auditor on a timely basis i.e. before the CASS auditor is required to deliver its report to the FCA or to the firm. The comments are recorded by the CASS auditor in Column E of the Breaches Schedule.

32   **In order to facilitate the processes outlined in the two preceding paragraphs the CASS auditor shall agree with the firm what constitutes "an adequate period of time" and record the agreement with the firm.**

Quality Control

33   **The CASS auditor shall comply with the applicable standards and guidance set out in International Standard on Quality Control (UK and Ireland) 1, and the CASS engagement leader shall have sufficient competence in the provision of assurance on client assets to accept responsibility for the assurance opinions in respect of the Client Assets Report.**

34   **The CASS engagement leader shall be satisfied that the assigned CASS engagement team collectively has the appropriate competence and capabilities to perform the engagement in accordance with this Standard and applicable legal and regulatory requirements.**

35   **The CASS engagement leader shall be satisfied that it will be able to evaluate the objectivity and competence of any other practitioner, not part of the engagement team, where the assurance work of that practitioner is to be used, to an extent that is sufficient to accept responsibility for the CASS auditor's report.**

Training

The CASS engagement leader shall be satisfied that the CASS engagement   **36**
team includes staff with experience in client asset work who, to the extent
relevant to a particular engagement, have received training relevant to the
circumstances of that engagement, for example in the following:

- The FCA's CASS Rules and applicable SUP[6] rules, in particular what
  constitutes a breach of the CASS Rules and the implications of the situations
  where the CASS rules require the CASS auditor to provide a Special Report
  to the firm.

- A firm's business model, such that reasonable expectations can be
  established throughout the CASS audit team as to the nature of client
  assets that the firm is likely to have (see paragraph 11).

- Assessing the design effectiveness of systems of internal control over client
  assets and evaluating whether the systems of internal control were in effect
  throughout the period and operating effectively.

- Practical challenges associated with the performance and review of client
  asset reconciliations.

- How the CASS rules seek to effectively segregate client assets within the
  context of applicable trust and insolvency law.

  (See paragraphs 56 to 58 of the Contextual Material).

Responsibilities of the CASS engagement leader

The CASS engagement leader shall, within the context of his or her firm's   **37**
quality control standards for assurance engagements, take responsibility for
the overall quality of the engagement. This includes responsibility for:

(a) **Appropriate acceptance and continuance procedures being performed;**

(b) **The engagement being planned and performed (including appropriate**
direction and supervision) to comply with this and other applicable
professional standards and applicable legal and regulatory
requirements;

(c) **Assessing whether the engagement team and any other practitioners**
they intend to consult have sufficient knowledge of the specific aspects
of the industry within which the firm operates and its corresponding
products;

(d) **Appropriate documentation of the work performed on the engagement**
being maintained to provide evidence of the achievement of the CASS
auditor's objectives and that the engagement was performed in
accordance with this Standard and applicable legal and regulatory
requirements;

(e) **Appropriate reviews of the work performed on the engagement,**
including reviewing the engagement documentation, before the date
of the Client Assets Report; and

(f) **Appropriate consultation being undertaken by the engagement team on**
difficult or contentious matters.

---

[6] *At the time of writing SUP 3 is the applicable SUP Rule.*

Professional Scepticism, Professional Judgment, and requisite mind-sets

38   The CASS auditor shall exercise professional judgment in planning and performing an assurance engagement, including when determining the nature, timing and extent of procedures to be performed.

39   **The CASS auditor shall plan and perform the engagement with an attitude of professional scepticism.** Such an attitude requires the CASS engagement leader and CASS engagement team to make critical assessments, with a questioning mind, of the validity of assurance evidence obtained and to be alert for evidence that contradicts or brings into question the reliability of documents or representations.

40   **The engagement team shall assess the plausibility of information and explanations provided to it by those charged with governance and management.** Where appropriate the engagement team considers this in the context of their knowledge and their findings derived from other areas of work undertaken with the same firm.

Compliance and insolvency mind-sets

41   **In planning and performing the engagement, the CASS auditor shall adopt a compliance mind-set that acknowledges:**

(a)   the responsibility of the firm to comply with all applicable CASS rules and to actively manage all risks of non-compliance; and

(b)   the responsibility of the CASS auditor to report to the FCA all breaches of the CASS rules that it becomes aware of in the course of performing its work.

42   **In planning and performing the engagement, the CASS auditor shall also adopt an insolvency mind-set which evaluates the firm's client asset processes on the presumption that the firm may become insolvent** (see paragraphs 36 and 56 of the Contextual Material).

Documentation

43   **The CASS auditor shall document:**

(a)   The overall assurance strategy;

(b)   The assurance plan; and

(c)   Any significant changes made during the engagement to either the strategy or the plan and the reasons for making such changes.

44   **In addition to documenting the strategy and the plan, the CASS auditor shall prepare documentation regarding the execution of the engagement that provides a record of the basis for the assurance report that is sufficient and appropriate to enable an experienced CASS auditor, having no previous connection with the engagement, to understand:**

(a)   The nature, timing and extent of the procedures performed to comply with this Standard and applicable legal and regulatory requirements;

(b)   The results of the procedures performed, and the evidence obtained; and

(c)   Significant matters arising during the engagement, the conclusions reached thereon and significant professional judgments made in reaching those conclusions.

In documenting the nature, timing and extent of procedures performed, the 45
CASS auditor shall record:

(a)   The identifying characteristics of the specific items or matters being
      tested;

(b)   Who performed the procedures and the date such procedures were
      completed; and

(c)   Who reviewed the work performed and the date and extent of such
      reviews.

The CASS auditor shall document discussions of significant matters with the 46
firm, the FCA and any other practitioners engaged by the CASS auditor in
connection with the engagement, including when and with whom the
discussions took place.

If the CASS auditor identifies information that is inconsistent with the CASS 47
auditor's final conclusion regarding a significant matter, the CASS auditor
shall document how the inconsistency was addressed.

Before signing the CASS audit report, the CASS engagement leader shall 48
consider whether it is appropriate to make the required report, and the form
of report to give, having regard to the scope of the work performed and the
evidence obtained. The CASS auditor shall document the thought processes
underlying its decisions in this regard.

The CASS auditor shall assemble the engagement documentation in an 49
engagement file and complete the administrative process of assembling the
final engagement file on a timely basis after the date of its report to the FCA.
After the assembly of the final engagement file has been completed, the CASS
auditor shall not delete or discard documentation of any nature before the
end of its retention period (see ISQC 1, paragraph 47).

If the CASS auditor finds it necessary to amend existing engagement 50
documentation or add new engagement documentation after the assembly
of the final engagement file has been completed, the CASS auditor shall,
regardless of the nature of the amendments or additions, document:

(a)   The specific reasons for making the amendments or additions; and

(b)   When, and by whom, they were made and reviewed.

Written Representations

The CASS auditor shall request from appropriate officials of the firm written 51
representations, including representations that the firm:

(a)   acknowledges its responsibility for maintaining CASS records and
      systems of control in accordance with the rules of the FCA;

(b)   has provided the CASS auditor with all information that the officials
      are aware is, or may be, relevant to the CASS auditor's engagement,
      including any correspondence and notes of meetings with the FCA;

(c)   has provided access to all information and persons that the officials
      believe are relevant to the CASS auditor's engagement; and

(d)   has complied, as far as they are aware, with all relevant CASS Rules
      throughout the period and was in compliance with those Rules at the
      period end, other than in respect of those breaches which they have
      notified to the CASS auditor.

52   **The date of the written representations shall be as near as practicable to, but not subsequent to, the date of the Client Assets Report.**

53   Representations from appropriate officials of the firm cannot replace other evidence the CASS auditor could reasonably expect to be available. Although written representations may provide necessary evidence, they do not provide sufficient appropriate evidence on their own about any of the matters with which they deal. Furthermore, the fact that the CASS auditor has received reliable written representations does not affect the nature or extent of other evidence that the CASS auditor should obtain.

Planning and Performing the Engagement

Planning

54   **The CASS auditor shall plan the engagement so that it will be performed in an effective manner, including setting the scope, timing and direction of the engagement, and determining the nature, timing and extent of those risk assessment and other planned procedures that are required to be carried out in order to achieve the objective of the CASS auditor.**

Understanding the Underlying Subject Matter and Other Engagement Circumstances

55   **The CASS engagement leader and senior members of the CASS engagement team shall meet to discuss the susceptibility of the firm's client asset systems to breaches of the CASS Rules. Such discussions shall include among other things:**

   (a)   **The firm's business model and changes in the model from the preceding year.**

   (b)   **New products and services introduced during the period.**

   (c)   **Changes made to IT and other reporting systems during the period.**

   (d)   **Developments in relevant laws and regulations which may impact on the assurance procedures to be undertaken.**

   (e)   **Waivers and modifications of CASS rules received by the firm during the year and any individual guidance received from the FCA.**

   (f)   **The implications of arrangements for third party administration of client assets.**

56   **Relevant matters shall also be communicated to members of the engagement team not involved in the meeting.**

57   **The CASS auditor shall enquire as to whether the firm has an internal audit function, or a separate compliance function, that is required to review the firm's compliance with the CASS Rules. If so, the CASS auditor shall obtain an understanding of its activities with respect to Client Assets and consider the findings of the internal audit function and/or the compliance function. Findings of an internal audit or compliance function in respect of breaches of the CASS rules will inform the CASS auditor's risk assessment.**

The CASS auditor's duty to report to the FCA

58   Under the Financial Services and Markets Act 2000 (FSMA 2000) (Communications by Auditors) Regulations 2001 CASS auditors have duties in

certain circumstances to make reports to the FCA. A CASS auditor has a duty to report breaches of the FCA's Rules of which it becomes aware which it reasonably believes may be of material significance to the FCA. If a CASS auditor becomes aware of such breaches, it does not wait to report them to the FCA by means of the Breaches Schedule that it appends to its routine assurance reports to the FCA. Appendix 12 sets out guidance for CASS auditors with respect to the duty to report to the FCA.

Where a CASS auditor identifies a breach (that it reasonably believes may   **59**
exist) is of material significance to the FCA and, therefore, reportable, it shall
carry out such additional procedures as it considers necessary, to determine
whether the facts and circumstances causes it reasonably to believe that the
matter does in fact exist.

Where the CASS auditor has reason to believe that a matter (such as a breach   **60**
of the CASS rules) does exist it shall obtain such evidence as is available to
assess its implications for the CASS auditor's reporting responsibilities.

A matter or group of matters is likely to be of material significance to the FCA   **61**
when, due either to its nature or its potential financial impact, it is likely of itself to require investigation by the FCA.

The CASS auditor shall report those matters that it believes to be of material   **62**
significance to the FCA as soon as practicable.

The CASS auditor shall document: **63**

(a)   **The facts and circumstances that caused it to believe that the**
    circumstances (such as a breach of the CASS rules) giving rise to the
    matters existed; and

(b)   **The basis for its conclusions as to whether the matters are, or are likely**
    to be, of material significance to the FCA.

The documentation shall clearly demonstrate the CASS auditor's reasoning
for its decision (as the case may be) to report, or not to report, the matter to
the FCA.

The CASS auditor's right to report to the FCA

Section 342 of FSMA 2000 provides that no duty to which an auditor (including   **64**
CASS auditors) of an authorised person (e.g. a firm) is subject shall be contravened by communicating in good faith to the FCA information or an opinion on a matter that the auditor reasonably believes is relevant to any functions of the FCA.

The scope of the duty to report can be quite wide particularly since, under the   **65**
FCA's Principle for Businesses 11, a firm must disclose to the FCA anything related to the firm of which the FCA would reasonably expect notice. However, in circumstances where the CASS auditor concludes that a matter does not give rise to a statutory duty to report but nevertheless should be brought to the attention of the FCA, in the first instance the CASS auditor advises the directors, or equivalent, of the firm of its opinion. Where the CASS auditor is unable to obtain, within a reasonable period of time, adequate evidence that the directors, or equivalent, have properly informed the FCA of the matter, then the CASS auditor makes a report to the regulator without undue delay.

The CASS auditor may wish to take legal advice before deciding whether, and in   **66**
what form, to exercise its right to make a report directly to the FCA in order to ensure, for example, that only relevant information is disclosed and that the form

and content of its report is such as to secure the protection of FSMA 2000. However, the CASS auditor recognises that obtaining legal advice may take time and that speed of reporting is likely to be important in order to protect the interests of customers and/or to enable the FCA to meet its statutory objectives.

Requirements Applicable to the Expression of Reasonable Assurance Opinions in a CASS Auditor's Report

The requirements and guidance in paragraphs 11 to 66 also apply to the expression of reasonable assurance opinions

67   An overview of the process to form the opinion as to whether the firm has maintained systems adequate to enable it to comply with the relevant CASS rules for the period and that it was in compliance with the rules at the end of the period, along with the relevant considerations relating to various stages in the process, is depicted in the diagram in Appendix 1.

68   The nature and extent of the CASS auditor's work will be a matter of professional judgment based, among other things, on its assessment of "assurance engagement risk". That is the risk that the CASS auditor expresses an unmodified opinion that the firm has maintained systems adequate to enable it to comply with the relevant CASS rules during the period or that it was in compliance with the relevant rules at the end of the period, when reporting to the FCA, in circumstances where such opinions are not correct.

69   Assurance engagement risk with respect to engagements to express a reasonable assurance opinion with respect to Client Assets can be represented by the following components:

(a)   Inherent risk: the risk of the management of the firm not preventing non-compliance with the CASS rules and other relevant FCA rules that are applicable to the firm due to the underlying susceptibility of the behaviour of the regulated firm to non-compliance with all of the assertions and related criteria under the applicable rules before the application of internal controls;

(b)   Control risk: the risk that a breach of the CASS rules that could be significant in the context of the assertions (see paragraph 70) will not be prevented, or detected and corrected, on a timely basis by related internal controls;

(c)   Detection risk: the risk that the CASS auditor will not detect a significant breach of the CASS Rules and will, therefore, fail to report the breach to the FCA; and

(d)   Evaluation risk: the risk that the CASS auditor will fail to measure or evaluate accurately, the underlying subject matter against the criteria.

70   The assertions and the related criteria that are applicable to the engagement may comprise a combination of:

(a)   Applicable provisions of the CASS rules;

(b)   Waivers and Modifications granted to the firm by the FCA; and

(c)   Individual guidance from the FCA to a firm.

71   In overview, building on the understanding of the firm's business model, in order to assess assurance engagement risk with respect to each of the above components the CASS auditor:

(a)   Establishes those FCA rules (especially the CASS rules) which are relevant to the firm's circumstances, systems and procedures;

(b)   Establishes any other applicable criteria;

(c)   In respect of each relevant rule and other criterion, establishes what the objectives of the firm's related controls should be (control objectives) in order to ensure compliance by the firm with the relevant rule, waiver, modification or guidance;

(d)   Carries out a risk assessment and establishes appropriate quality control to address detection and evaluation risk; and

(e)   Determines the nature and extent of assurance procedures that will provide sufficient appropriate assurance evidence that the firm has met the relevant control objectives for the assertions and criteria.

Assessing CASS Assurance Engagement Risk

Inherent risk and control risk

To assess the risk of a firm failing to comply with the CASS rules, the CASS auditor shall obtain an understanding of the firm's organisational structure, operating environment, classes of transactions to which the CASS rules apply, cash flows and other engagement circumstances sufficient to: 72

(a)   **Enable the CASS auditor to identify and assess the risk of inappropriately expressing an unmodified opinion that the firm has maintained systems adequate to enable it to comply with the CASS Rules throughout the period;**

(b)   **Enable the CASS auditor to identify and assess the risk of inappropriately expressing an unmodified opinion that the firm was in compliance with the CASS Rules at the end of the period; and**

(c)   **Thereby, provide a basis for designing and performing procedures to respond to the assessed risks and to obtain reasonable assurance to support the CASS auditor's opinion.**

The CASS auditor shall discuss with management the operation of the business, seek to understand what the firm has done to mitigate risk, and read relevant management information, for example: 73

- Operations Manuals.

- The firm's documentation of systems and controls.

In assessing the risk that the control environment may not be sufficient to prevent or detect a significant breach of the rules, the CASS auditor shall meet with senior management, the CASS Compliance Officer and, where applicable, the CF10a to confirm their understanding of the control environment, gained as set out in paragraph 73. The CASS auditor shall also consider other sources of information, for example: 74

- Compliance monitoring and internal audit programmes and results.

- Records maintained by the firm of any rule breaches and notifications to the FCA that may have occurred during the period.

- CMAR submissions made by the firm.

- The results of recent inspection visits made by the FCA.

- The register of client complaints.

- Any Section 166 Skilled Persons Reports or other relevant external/internal reviews that may have been performed.

75   The CMAR is submitted by the firm to the FCA and is intended to give the FCA an overview of firm-specific CASS positions and an overview of CASS holdings. The CASS auditor is not required to evaluate or report on the firm's compliance with the FCA's CMAR requirements.

76   **The CASS auditor shall read the firm's CMAR submissions and assess their consistency with the CASS auditor's knowledge of the firm's business. If the CASS auditor's procedures reveal inconsistencies with CMARs, the CASS auditor seeks to understand the reasons for the inconsistencies.**

77   **The CASS auditor shall consider the firm's own risk assessment and perform risk assessment procedures considered necessary to provide a basis for the identification and assessment of risks that the firm:**

(a)   **Has not maintained systems adequate to enable it to comply with the CASS rules throughout the period; and**

(b)   **Has not complied with the CASS rules that apply to the business of the firm as at the period end date of the Client Assets Report.**

Such risk assessment procedures shall consider each relevant CASS rule that applies to the firm and on which the CASS auditor is required to report.

Determining the nature and extent of risk assessment procedures

78   The CASS auditor does not evaluate and report on monetary amounts but on whether the firm has maintained adequate systems to enable it to comply, and on the firm's compliance, with the CASS rules. However, forming a reasonable assurance opinion requires the CASS auditor to evaluate the risks of the likelihood of rule breaches and the significance of such rule breaches to the validity of the opinions expressed in the client assets reasonable assurance report.

79   **The extent and nature of the CASS auditor's risk assessment procedures shall be driven by the CASS auditor's evaluation of the significance to its opinion of a firm's failure to maintain systems that are adequate to enable it to comply with a CASS rule. Evaluating "significance" involves a combined assessment of the likelihood of a firm failing to manage or mitigate a risk and the impact of that risk on whether client assets have been held and recorded in accordance with the CASS rules. The significance judgment provides part of the basis for:**

(a)   **Determining the nature, timing and extent of risk assessment procedures;**

(b)   **Identifying and assessing the risk of non-compliance with individual CASS rules applicable to the engagement; and**

(c)   **Determining the nature, timing and extent of further CASS audit procedures to test the firm's compliance with the CASS rules.**

When performing these risk assessment procedures, the CASS auditor shall consider each CASS rule that is applicable to the firm on which the CASS auditor is required to report.

Responding to the assessment of Assurance Engagement Risk

Based on the CASS auditor's understanding obtained through its risk **80** assessment procedures, the CASS auditor shall design and perform procedures to respond to the assessed risks and to obtain sufficient appropriate evidence to support the CASS auditor's reasonable assurance opinion.

Evaluating the design of the system of internal control

The CASS auditor shall evaluate whether the design of the system of internal **81** control, if implemented and operated effectively, would provide reasonable assurance of compliance with those CASS rules that are relevant to the firm. Where changes are made to the system of internal control during the period, the auditor shall evaluate the design of the system of internal control both prior to and subsequent to the change.

In this context the "design of the system of internal control" encompasses **82** consideration of:

(a)   The control environment including the firm's risk assessment processes;

(b)   Monitoring controls; and

(c)   Control activities designed to ensure compliance with the CASS rules.

Consideration of the control environment and monitoring controls is particularly important in a CASS engagement because the CASS auditor is required to form an opinion as to whether the firm has maintained systems adequate to enable it to comply with the CASS rules throughout the period.

The Control Environment

The CASS auditor shall obtain an understanding of the control environment **83** relevant to client assets. When obtaining this understanding, the CASS auditor shall evaluate whether:

(a)   **Management, with the oversight of those charged with governance, seeks to maintain a culture of honesty and ethical behaviour towards the beneficial owners of client assets; and**

(b)   **The strengths in the control environment collectively provide an appropriate foundation for the other components of internal control, and whether those other components are not undermined by deficiencies in the control environment.**

Particular elements of the control environment that may be relevant to the **84** auditor's evaluation include the following:

(a)   Participation by those charged with governance;

(b)   Communication and enforcement of integrity and ethical values;

(c)   Management's consideration of the competence levels for particular jobs and how those levels translate into requisite skills and knowledge; and

(d)   Assignment of authority and responsibility.

The CASS auditor shall obtain an understanding of the firm's process for: **85**

(a)   **Identifying risks relevant to client assets and its compliance with the CASS rules applicable in the context of the engagement;**

(b)   **Evaluating the significance of the risks;**

(c)   Assessing the likelihood of their occurrence; and

(d)   Determining actions to address those risks.

86   If the CASS auditor identifies a risk that management has failed to identify, the auditor shall obtain an understanding of why management's process failed to identify it and determine if there is a significant deficiency in internal control with regard to the firm's risk assessment process.

Monitoring activities

87   The CASS auditor shall obtain an understanding of the major activities that the firm uses to monitor[7] internal control relevant to its compliance with the CASS rules and how the firm initiates remedial actions in response to deficiencies in its controls. Where the firm has an internal audit or compliance function, which covers those major activities intended to deliver compliance with the CASS rules, the CASS auditor shall perform or obtain, as appropriate, and document:

- an evaluation of whether the function's organisational status and relevant policies and procedures adequately support the objectivity of the internal auditors, or compliance function;

- an understanding of the nature of the internal audit or compliance function's responsibilities with respect to client assets;

- an assessment of whether the function applies a systematic and disciplined approach, including quality control; and

- the activities the function has performed or intends to perform with respect to client assets.

88   As the CASS auditor has sole responsibility for the CASS audit opinion, the use of internal auditors to provide direct assistance to a CASS auditor is prohibited in a CASS audit performed in accordance with this Standard. In addition, the CASS auditor's responsibility cannot be reduced by the CASS auditor using the work of the internal audit or compliance function. However, the CASS auditor is likely to find the work and findings of the internal audit or compliance function to be useful in making its risk assessment. The CASS auditor shall document its conclusion and the basis for this conclusion on how the work and findings of the internal audit or compliance function have impacted on the risk assessment.

89   The CASS auditor shall obtain an understanding of the sources of the information used in the firm's monitoring activities, and the basis upon which management considers the information to be sufficiently reliable for the purpose.

90   Much of the information used in monitoring may be produced by the firm's information system. If management assumes that data used for monitoring are accurate without having a basis for that assumption, errors that may exist in the information could potentially lead management to incorrect conclusions from its monitoring activities.

---

[7] *Monitoring of controls is a process to assess the effectiveness of internal control performance over time. It includes assessing the design and operation of controls on a timely basis and taking necessary corrective actions modified for changes in conditions.*

Evaluating the design of control activities

The CASS auditor shall consider how the design of control activities: **91**

(a)   **Enables the firm to identify where client assets may arise in the business;**

(b)   **Seeks to ensure that client assets are segregated and safeguarded effectively;**

(c)   **Addresses the performance of internal and external reconciliations[8] as required by the CASS rules; and**

(d)   **Addresses the establishment and acknowledgement of trust status over client assets.**

In the context of the CASS auditor's consideration required by paragraph 91, the CASS auditor shall evaluate: **92**

(a)   **Whether the system design identifies appropriate control activities in respect of those CASS rules that are applicable to the firm;**

(b)   **Whether those control activities are likely to provide reasonable assurance of compliance with the relevant CASS rules;**

(c)   **The implications of different controls for different parts of the business; and**

(d)   **Where appropriate, whether detective controls will be effective within the time periods (if any) permitted by the CASS Rules.**

The CASS auditor shall further evaluate: **93**

(a)   **Whether there is adequate segregation of duties; and**

(b)   **Whether the design of the system incorporates sufficiently robust controls over system changes.**

Obtaining evidence to support the opinion as to whether the firm has maintained systems over client assets adequate to enable it to comply with the relevant CASS rules during the period.

Evaluating whether internal control activities were put into place as designed and whether their operation was effective

The CASS auditor shall evaluate whether internal control activities were put into place to cover all client assets and whether they were designed effectively. Based on the conclusions reached, the CASS auditor shall adopt a suitable approach to test the effectiveness of the operation of these controls during the period. The CASS auditor's procedures to evaluate whether control activities were put into place as designed shall include walk-through tests of internal control activities. Based on these evaluations, the CASS auditor shall adopt a suitable approach to test the effectiveness of operation of these controls during the period.   **94**

The nature and extent of the auditor's evaluation will be a function of the results of its risk assessment and conclusions regarding the design effectiveness of the internal controls. In addition to the performance of walk-through tests, relevant procedures the CASS auditor considers performing include: **95**

---

[8] *Or bank reconciliations for insurance intermediaries.*

(a)   Making enquiries of personnel at the firm, for example the CF10a.

(b)   Observing the application of controls.

(c)   Inspecting documents and reports, for example computer-generated error reports, client agreements, acknowledgement letters and custody agreements.

(d)   Testing internal and external reconciliations.

96   The CASS auditor is required to report on the adequacy of the systems throughout the period under review. This requirement does not mean that the CASS auditor has to perform tests continuously throughout the period, but bases the extent and nature of its procedures to test the effectiveness of operation of control activities on its:

(a)   risk assessment, including its evaluation of the control environment; and

(b)   evaluation of the design of the system of internal control.

Selecting items for testing to obtain evidence of operation of controls

97   **When designing tests of controls the CASS auditor shall determine the means of selecting items for testing that are effective in meeting the purpose of the assurance procedure.**

98   The means available to the CASS auditor for selecting items for testing are:

(a)   Selecting all items (This is likely to be appropriate only when there is a small number of items);

(b)   Selecting specific items; and

(c)   Sampling.

99   **When evaluating the effectiveness of the operation of controls, the auditor shall evaluate whether breaches that have been identified indicate that controls are or were not operating effectively.**

100   A breach may indicate the existence of a significant deficiency in internal control. The concept of effectiveness of the operation of controls recognises that some deviations in the way controls are applied by the firm may occur. Deviations from prescribed controls may be caused by such factors as changes in key personnel, fluctuations in volume of transactions and human error. The detected rate of deviation may indicate that the control cannot be relied on to sufficiently reduce the risk of breaches of the CASS rules.

101   A firm's systems and controls over client assets may be quite different to the systems and controls that it has over its own assets. It would be inappropriate to draw conclusions about the design and operating effectiveness of internal controls over client assets based on evaluations of the firm's systems and controls over its own assets.

102   The CASS rules require such records of client money and custody assets to be kept as are necessary to enable the firm "at any time and without delay" to distinguish client assets held for one client from client assets held for any other client and from its own assets. CASS auditors need to be aware of the risk that firms may have different systems in place at different times of the day (for example overnight deposit arrangements) or that a firm may have transferred client assets to another legal entity. The scope of their testing should address all the systems that may be applicable to client assets at all times.

Use of Third Party Administrators

When a firm enters into an arrangement with a Third Party Administrator (TPA) to **103** outsource the operation of certain functions, such as fund administration, that are relevant to the firm's compliance with CASS rules, whether the firm retains full regulatory responsibility for compliance with CASS rules depends on the nature of the arrangements entered into between the firm, the TPA and the firm's clients. The firm retains full regulatory responsibility where the TPA simply owes contractual obligations to the firm to perform certain specified services and the TPA does not have a direct contractual relationship with the firm's clients.

An example of an arrangement where the firm retains full regulatory responsibility **104** is an agreement entered into by a stockbroker to outsource clearing and settlement activities to another firm, without any change in the firm's arrangements with its clients. As settlement agent, the other firm undertakes an administrative role in the settlement of trades under a service level agreement. However, the stockbroker remains responsible for compliance with the relevant FCA rules, including CASS. In this type of arrangement, the outsourced functions support the firm's compliance with CASS. Such an arrangement is described as a "Model A Arrangement" in some parts of the stockbroking industry. Another common example of such an arrangement is where a fund management firm outsources certain functions related to fund administration to a TPA (which may or may not be an authorised firm) without any change in the firm's arrangements with its clients.

Alternatively, the firm and its TPA may agree to an arrangement in which the TPA **105** takes direct responsibility for compliance with some or all of the provisions in CASS, which is referred to in some parts of the stockbroking industry as a "Model B Arrangement". For example, Model B is where a second firm takes responsibility for the stockbrokers' clearing and settlement activities, often called "give up broking". In such a scenario, the second firm is responsible for compliance with the FCA's rules (including the CASS Rules) insofar as they apply to clearing and settlement processes that are the subject of the arrangement.

The TPA can only assume such responsibility, if it is authorised by the FCA to **106** conduct investment business and has the requisite permission from the FCA to hold or control the client money and/or custody assets in question. Such a transfer of responsibility only occurs if the firm's clients enter into terms of business with the TPA to establish that the TPA will be directly responsible to the client under CASS for protecting the clients' money or assets. In order to do so, the firm, the TPA and the client may enter into a tri-partite agreement that reflects the terms of business between both firms and the client. Alternatively, the firm and the TPA may each enter into separate agreements with the client to achieve this.

Although Model A and Model B arrangements may each be described as **107** involving TPAs, the regulatory obligations of the firm and the TPA are different under each model and so, their impact on the scope of a CASS auditor's procedures is quite different. The actual arrangements entered into by firms can be extremely complex and members of a CASS engagement team need to have a thorough understanding both of the arrangements with the TPA and the firm's clients and of the firm's business model, particularly of the cash and other asset inflows and outflows as they apply both to the firm and to the TPA. This understanding provides a basis for establishing the respective regulatory responsibilities of the firm and (if any) the TPA for client assets and, therefore, expectations about the existence or otherwise of client assets in the context of the engagement.

108   The CASS engagement team shall obtain an understanding of:

(a)   the firm's arrangements with the TPA and its clients; and

(b)   the firm's business model, particularly the cash and other asset inflows and outflows as they apply both to the firm and to the TPA.

Such an understanding provides a basis for establishing the respective regulatory responsibilities of the firm and (if any) the TPA for client assets and, therefore, expectations about the existence or otherwise of client assets in the context of the engagement.

109   When planning assurance procedures for a firm that has outsourced services to a TPA, the CASS auditor shall confirm the relative responsibilities of the firm and the TPA for compliance with CASS through discussions with management and review of relevant documentation including client agreements, the clients' terms of business (if any) with the TPA and the firm's agreement with the TPA. The CASS auditor also establishes whether the scope of the firm's and, where applicable, the TPA's permissions from the FCA include the holding of client money and/or custody assets.

110   Assurance procedures are designed in a way that treats the TPA as, in effect, an integral part of the firm. In support of this approach SUP 3.6.1R and SUP 3.6.7G require the firm to ensure that the auditor has access to books, accounts and vouchers of the firm held by its TPA and has the co-operation of the TPA.

111   The CASS auditor shall plan to perform assurance procedures that cover outsourced functions for which the firm retains responsibility for client assets under the CASS rules.

112   The CASS auditor's engagement letter shall stipulate that the contractual arrangements between the firm and the TPA should provide for the CASS auditor to have rights of access to the TPA's books and records and to employees of the TPA responsible for operating relevant processes on behalf of the firm. The CASS auditor shall consider its position where such provisions are not in force between the firm and the TPA.

113   In considering its position the CASS auditor may wish to discuss the matter with the FCA and determine an appropriate course of action such as agreeing a lesser scope of work.

Obtaining evidence to support the opinion as to whether the firm was in compliance with relevant CASS rules at the end of the period

114   The CASS auditor shall evaluate the firm's compliance with each relevant CASS rule at the period end date.

115   The nature and extent of the CASS auditor's testing procedures will be a function of the conclusions it has formed on the effectiveness of internal control and the specific nature of the applicable CASS rules. Relevant considerations may include:

- Where applicable, examining the contractual terms between the firm and third parties such as administrators (see paragraphs 103 to 113);

- Testing internal and external reconciliations at the period end date and evaluating whether explanations of reconciling items are legitimate;

- Obtaining external confirmation letters, such as bank confirmations and custodian confirmations; and

- Checking whether client bank account acknowledgement letters have been obtained by the firm and are in force as at the period end.

Forming the Client Assets Opinion

The CASS auditor shall evaluate the sufficiency and appropriateness of the 116
evidence obtained in the context of the engagement and, if necessary, perform
procedures to obtain further evidence. The CASS auditor shall consider all
relevant evidence, regardless of whether it appears to corroborate or to
contradict its evaluations of whether the firm:

(a)   has maintained systems adequate to enable it to comply with the
      relevant CASS rules throughout the period; and

(b)   was in compliance with relevant CASS rules at the end of the period.

If the CASS auditor is unable to obtain necessary further evidence, the CASS
auditor considers the implications for its opinions.

The interrelationship between the forming of the opinion and the reporting of breaches

The CASS auditor shall express unmodified opinions in a reasonable 117
assurance report on client assets when as a result of performing its
assurance procedures it has formed the opinion that the firm has both
maintained systems adequate to comply with the relevant CASS rules
throughout the period and was in compliance with relevant CASS rules at
the end of the period. The process for forming these opinions is depicted in
Appendix 1 and an unmodified opinion is illustrated in Appendix 4.

The CASS auditor is required to report all breaches identified by it or 118
identified to it by any other party including the firm. Although a breach may
be of minor significance, this is not a relevant consideration when
determining if a CASS rule has been breached. The reporting of any
breach of a CASS rules shall result in the CASS auditor expressing a
modified opinion regarding the adequacy of systems during the period.
The reporting of breaches may also result in the need for the CASS
auditor to express a modified opinion regarding compliance with the CASS
rules at the period-end date.

The FCA's report template includes a breaches schedule that is required to be 119
completed by the CASS auditor in order to report all identified breaches of
CASS rules by the firm, of which the CASS auditor becomes aware,
occurring during the period subject to the Client Assets Report. The
breaches reported shall include all the breaches the CASS auditor has
become aware of either through its work or through disclosure to it by the
firm or any other party.

The CASS auditor is not engaged to provide absolute assurance that all breaches 120
committed by the firm are included in the breaches schedule. Where no breaches
have been identified by, or disclosed to it, the CASS auditor provides a nil return.
This is illustrated in Appendix 4.

The CASS auditor shall obtain a written representation from management of 121
the firm that to the best of their knowledge and belief, either the list of
breaches is complete or there have been no breaches identified.

If breaches arose during the period and were identified by or reported to the 122
CASS auditor, but all have been rectified by the period end the CASS auditor
shall issue a modified opinion as to the maintenance of adequate systems
throughout the period and an unmodified opinion on compliance with the
CASS Rules at the period end. This is illustrated in Appendix 2.

123 An absence of breaches may not preclude the need for a modified opinion on the adequacy of systems. A firm could have inadequate systems but through a combination of circumstances have avoided any reportable breaches; however, the requirements within CASS 6.2 and CASS 7.12 require firms to have adequate arrangements, organisational arrangements and robust systems in place. Similarly, the reporting of a specific breach does not necessarily mean that the systems are adequate in all other respects.

124 **Where the CASS auditor determines that a modified opinion is required it shall determine whether to issue an "except for" or an "adverse" opinion in accordance with the requirements and guidance in the FCA's SUP rules.**

125 SUP 3.10.9C(2)G provides the following guidance: "For the purpose of determining whether to qualify its opinion or express an adverse opinion, the FCA would expect an auditor to exercise its professional judgment as to the significance of a rule breach, as well as to its context, duration and incidence of repetition. The FCA would expect an auditor to consider the aggregate effect of any breaches when judging whether a firm had failed to comply with the requirements described in SUP 3.10.5R(1) to (4)".

126 The principle underlying the need for an adverse opinion arises from the CASS auditor concluding that identified weaknesses in control and/or breaches of rules are systemic, or pervasive (and therefore likely to give rise to fundamental issues of control), as opposed to isolated incidents.

127 A practical starting point, when deciding between an "except for" or "adverse" opinion, is for the CASS auditor to consider whether the rule breaches indicate that there has been a systemic or pervasive failure to comply with the principle of protecting client assets. If the firm's system design is significantly flawed or repeatedly fails, an adverse opinion is likely to be appropriate. If the system generally works but there have been isolated breaches, an "except for" opinion is likely to be appropriate.

128 Particular areas the CASS auditor considers which might give rise to an adverse opinion include:

- The extent to which clients might have lost their assets/money if the firm had gone into administration while the breach persisted.
- Whether there had been a breach of the requirement to keep proper records of client assets.
- Whether the firm had failed to carry out, or incorrectly carried out to a significant extent, the reconciliations required by the CASS rules.

Content of a Reasonable Assurance Client Assets Report

129 **A reasonable assurance Client Assets Report shall include the following elements:**

(a) A title that;

    (i) clearly indicates the report is an independent reasonable assurance report;

    (ii) addresses the report to the Financial Conduct Authority[9].

    (iii) states the name of the firm and its FCA Reference number.

---

[9] *In the case of Insurance Intermediaries the FCA's rules require the report to be submitted to "the firm".*

(b) Introductory paragraphs that:

    (i)   specify the start and end date of the period being reported on;

    (ii)   state that the report has been prepared as required by SUP 3.10.4R and is addressed to the Financial Conduct Authority in its capacity as regulator of financial services firms under the Financial Services and Markets Act 2000.

(c) A description of the basis of opinion which shall state, where it is the case, that:

    (i)   the CASS auditor has carried out all relevant procedures specified by this Standard;

    (ii)   the opinions relate only to the period, or as at the date, specified;

    (iii) the opinions do not provide assurance in relation to any future period or date as changes to systems or controls subsequent to the date of this report may alter the validity of the opinions.

(d) An expression of opinion as to whether the firm maintained systems adequate to enable it to comply with the custody rules, collateral rules, mandate rules, client money rules, rules relating to nominee companies and secondary pooling events throughout the period since the last date at which a report was made.

(e) An expression of opinion as to whether the firm was in compliance with the custody rules, collateral rules, mandate rules, client money rules, rules relating to nominee companies and secondary pooling events as at the period end date.

(f) Where required by SUP 3.10.5R(3), an expression of an opinion as to whether the firm's nominee companies that are subsidiaries of the firm, and in whose name custody assets are registered, have maintained throughout the period systems for the custody, identification and control of custody assets which a) where adequate; and b) included reconciliations at appropriate intervals between the records maintained (whether by the firm or the nominee company) and statements of confirmations from custodians or from the person who maintained the record of legal entitlement.

(g) Where required by SUP 3.10.5R(4), a statement as to whether the firm has complied with the rules in CASS 5.6 and CASS 7A (client money distribution) and CASS 11.13 (debt management client money distribution rules) in relation to that pooling event.

(h) A statement that the report should be read in conjunction with the Breaches Schedule that the CASS auditor has prepared.

(i) The CASS engagement leader's signature and the name of the CASS auditor's firm.

(j) The date of the Client Assets Report.

(k) The location in the jurisdiction where the CASS auditor practices.

(l) A Breaches Schedule prepared in accordance with paragraphs 130 to 133 of this Standard.

The FCA Handbook at https://www.handbook.fca.org.uk/ contains the extant version of the FCA's rules listing the requirements for the reasonable assurance report, and should be consulted before the report is prepared.

Detailed reporting of Breaches

130   In columns A to D of the breaches schedule the CASS auditor shall set out those breaches of CASS by the firm, of which it has become aware, occurring during the period covered by the Client Assets Report. The sources of the breaches reported shall include:

(a)   Those breaches the CASS auditor has identified through its own work (such as in the testing of reconciliations);

(b)   Those breaches identified by the firm (such as those included in the firm's breaches register); and

(c)   Breaches identified by and disclosed to the CASS auditor by any other party including the FCA.

131   In column D of the Breaches Schedule the CASS auditor must provide any information that it has in respect of the severity and duration of the breach identified and, where relevant, the frequency with which that breach has occurred.

132   Where no CASS rule breaches have been identified the CASS auditor shall provide a nil return.

133   In column E of the breaches schedule the firm is required to set out any remedial actions taken (if any) associated with the breaches cited, together with an explanation of the circumstances that gave rise to the breach in question. The FCA explicitly states in SUP 3 Annex 1R that the CASS auditor has no responsibility for the content of column E. Nevertheless where the CASS auditor is aware that the comments provided by the firm in the CASS auditor's report in relation to the identified breaches are inaccurate or false, the CASS auditor remains subject to FSMA 2000 reporting requirements and its profession's ethical rules and standards.

Expressing a qualified opinion

134   If the CASS auditor expresses a qualified opinion as a result of breaches of the CASS rules (i.e. states "that except for ..., the firm maintained" or "that except for ..., the firm was in compliance ...") it shall do so by reference to items in columns A to D in the Breaches Schedule, and should be cross referenced to the Schedule. This is illustrated in Appendix 2.

Expressing an adverse opinion

135   If the CASS auditor expresses an adverse opinion (i.e. states the firm "did not maintain ..." or "was not in compliance ...") it shall set out the reasons in the Client Assets Report. This can be done by reference to items in columns A to D in the Breaches Schedule appended to the Client Assets Report, and should be cross referenced to that Schedule. This is illustrated in Appendix 3.

Inability to form an opinion

136   If the CASS auditor is unable to obtain sufficient, appropriate assurance evidence to enable it to form an opinion as to whether one or more of the applicable requirements set out in SUP 3.10.5R have been met, the CASS auditor shall specify in its report those requirements and the reasons why the auditor has been unable to form an opinion.

Communicating deficiencies in internal control to management and those charged with governance

During the CASS audit the CASS auditor may identify deficiencies in internal **137** control that whilst not significant may be of sufficient importance to merit management's attention because the deficiencies may give rise to reportable breaches of the CASS Rules in future periods. Communicating deficiencies in internal control to management and those charged with governance does not remove the requirement to report to the FCA, where appropriate, deficiencies affecting the adequacy of the firm's systems, notwithstanding that a rule has not been breached.

The CASS auditor shall communicate to management at an appropriate level **138** **of responsibility, on a timely basis, deficiencies in internal control that, in the CASS auditor's professional judgment, are of sufficient importance to merit management's attention.**

The CASS auditor shall also communicate in writing significant deficiencies **139** **in internal control identified during the CASS audit to those charged with governance on a timely basis.**

Communicating significant deficiencies in writing to those charged with **140** governance reflects the importance of these matters, and assists those charged with governance in fulfilling their oversight responsibilities.

Engagement Quality Control Review

As the effective segregation of client assets is in the public interest, an **141** **accounting firm's system of engagement quality control reviews shall encompass all such firm's engagements that provide reasonable assurance to the FCA on client assets.**

An important feature of a system of quality control is the Engagement Quality **142** Control Review which is "A process designed to provide an objective evaluation, on or before the date of the report, of:

(a)   the significant judgments made by the CASS engagement team; and

(b)   the conclusions reached in formulating the report".

With respect to Engagement Quality Control reviews of all CASS reasonable **143** **assurance engagements:**

(a)   **The CASS engagement leader shall take responsibility for discussing significant matters arising during the engagement with the engagement quality control reviewer, and not issue or date the assurance report until completion of that review; and**

(b)   **The engagement quality control reviewer shall perform an objective evaluation of the significant judgments made by the engagement team, and the conclusions reached in formulating the assurance opinion. This evaluation shall involve:**

(i)   **Discussion of significant matters (including those arising at the planning stage of the engagement) with the engagement leader;**

(ii)   **Reviewing the outcome of the evaluation of the adequacy of the firm's systems during the period and its compliance with applicable CASS rules at the period end date and the proposed assurance opinion, including the breaches schedule;**

(iii)   **Review of selected engagement documentation relating to the significant judgments the engagement team made and the conclusions it reached; and**

(iv)   **Evaluation of the conclusions reached in formulating the assurance opinion and consideration of whether the proposed assurance report is appropriate.**

144   Other matters that may be considered in an engagement quality control review include:

- The CASS engagement team's evaluation of the firm's independence in relation to the engagement.

- Whether appropriate consultation has taken place on matters involving differences of opinion or other difficult or contentious matters, and the conclusions arising from those consultations.

- Whether engagement documentation selected for review reflects the work performed in relation to the significant judgments and supports the conclusions reached.

145   **If differences of opinion arise:**

(a)   **Within the CASS engagement team;**

(b)   **With those consulted; or**

(c)   **Between the CASS engagement leader and the engagement quality control reviewer**

the engagement team shall follow the CASS auditor's firm's policies and procedures for dealing with and resolving differences of opinion.

Requirements Applicable to the Expression of Limited Assurance Opinions where a Firm Claims not to Hold Client Assets

The requirements and guidance in paragraphs 11 to 66 also apply to the expression of limited assurance opinions where a firm has relevant permissions but claims not to hold client assets and where a firm does not have relevant permissions.

Circumstances giving rise to limited assurance opinions

146   The table in SUP 3.1.2R sets out, among other things, those firms to whom SUP 3.10 "Duties of auditors: notification and report on client assets" applies. Under SUP 3.10.4R where a firm "claims" not to hold client money or custody assets its auditor must submit a Client Assets Report stating whether anything has come to the auditor's attention that causes him to believe that the firm held client money or custody assets during the period covered by the report. **(N.B. The FCA rules do not require limited assurance opinions in respect of insurance intermediaries and certain other categories of firms).**

147   For the purposes of this Standard the term "claims" is deemed to apply in two circumstances:

(a)   Where the scope of the firm's permissions does not include the holding of client money and/or custody assets; and

(b) Where the scope of the firm's permissions does include the holding of client money and/or custody assets but the firm claims not to hold them.

SUP 3.1.1R applies Chapter 3 of SUP to external auditors of firms whether **148** specifically appointed under SUP 3.3 or under, or as a result of, a statutory provision other than in FSMA 2000 (an example would be an appointment as auditor under the Companies Act 2006). An auditor appointed under, for example, CA 2006 is, therefore, responsible for submitting a Client Assets Report to the FCA notwithstanding that they may not have been formally appointed as a CASS auditor.

Limited Assurance Client Assets Reports where a firm has permission to hold client money and/or custody assets but management claims it does not hold either client money or custody assets

The CASS auditor shall obtain an understanding from the firm as to the 149 reasons why the firm has the relevant permission but has not actually held client money or custody assets.

The CASS auditor shall review the CASS-related notifications submitted to 150 the FCA that relate to the period under review and ascertain whether they report that no client money or custody assets were held.

The CASS auditor shall review the conclusions reached when performing the 151 procedures set out in paragraph 11 and shall also evaluate whether effective controls exist within the firm to enable it to identify the existence of client money and/or custody assets, and/or whether the firm is entitled to rely on any exemptions from the CASS rules in relation to any money or assets held[10], and if so whether they are appropriately designed and implemented. Such a system might constitute periodic review by internal audit or the compliance function and encompass substantive reviews of bank accounts and client agreements.

Based on this understanding the auditor performs those procedures set out in the **152** following paragraphs which are appropriate in the circumstances.

Where the CASS auditor is also the financial statements auditor and has 153 access to the work of the financial statements auditor, the CASS auditor shall consider the results of audit procedures performed with respect to the firm's financial statements for the period corresponding, or overlapping, with the period of the client asset audit and whether evidence was found of the existence of client money or custody assets held by the firm.

The CASS auditor shall enquire as to what arrangements the firm has in 154 place to ensure that relevant staff members are aware of what constitutes client assets. These arrangements should be adequately documented and the documentation should be readily available to relevant staff. The documentation should outline the procedures to be followed if client assets are identified.

Where a system of internal control exists to ensure that client assets are not 155 controlled or held, the CASS auditor shall discuss the results of its operation with those responsible for it.

---

[10] *The CASS Rules contain various exemptions that dis-apply the CASS Rules. Examples relate to; Delivery versus Payment arrangements (DVP), Title Transfer Collateral Arrangements, risk transfer and the banking exemption.*

156   The CASS auditor shall enquire of management responsible for dealing with client business, and others as appropriate, as to whether they have knowledge of any client money or custody assets held during the period.

157   The CASS auditor shall review the firm's breaches register or equivalent and correspondence between the firm and the FCA for evidence of the existence of client money or custody assets.

158   The CASS auditor shall enquire as to how settlements are effected on behalf of clients (reference shall be made to client documentation and payment instructions on contract notes or statements) and review the firm's client files to see whether they provide any indication that the firm has held client assets in order to undertake a particular transaction.

159   The CASS auditor shall review a sample of client agreements for statements of how custody of assets and monies is to be operated and as a corollary, review the agreements with any custodians used and the counterparty files for correspondence on settlement procedures to ensure that there is no evidence that the firm has offered client money or custody asset protection.

160   The CASS auditor shall enquire as to how dividends, especially unclaimed dividends, and rights issues are dealt with by the firm.

Written Representation

161   In addition to the representations referred to in paragraph 51, the CASS auditor shall request from appropriate officials of the firm a written representation that the firm has not held any custody assets or client money during the period.

Forming the Limited Assurance Opinion

162   If no evidence is found to the contrary, the CASS auditor shall provide limited assurance in the form of a negative opinion that, based on review procedures performed, nothing has come to the attention of the CASS auditor that causes it to believe that the firm held client money or custody assets during the period.

163   If based on these procedures the CASS auditor becomes aware of evidence that the firm held client money or custody assets contrary either:

(a)   To the permissions it held; or

(b)   To a claim that, where it has permissions, it held none,

the CASS auditor encourages the firm to promptly report the matter to the FCA. If the firm does not report the matter promptly to the FCA the CASS auditor shall promptly report the matter directly to the FCA. The CASS auditor is further required to provide a modified limited assurance report as illustrated in Appendix 8.

Content of a Limited Assurance Client Assets Report

164   A limited assurance Client Assets Report shall include the following elements:

(a)   A title that;

(i)   clearly indicates the report is an independent limited assurance report;

(ii)   addresses the report to the Financial Conduct Authority

    (iii)   states the name of the firm and its FCA Reference number.

(b)   Introductory paragraphs that:

    (i)   specify the start and end date of the period being reported on;

    (ii)   state that the report has been prepared as required by SUP 3.10.4R and is addressed to the Financial Conduct Authority in its capacity as regulator of financial services firms under the Financial Services and Markets Act 2000.

(c)   A description of the basis of opinion which shall state, where it is the case, that:

    (i)   the CASS auditor has carried out such procedures set out in this Standard as it considered necessary;

    (ii)   the work performed was designed to provide limited, rather than reasonable assurance;

    (iii)   the opinions relate only to the period, or as at the date, specified;

    (iv)   the opinions do not provide assurance in relation to any future period or date.

(d)   A statement repeating the assertion of the directors of the firm that either:

    (i)   The firm's permissions do not allow it to hold client money and/or custody assets; or

    (ii)   The firm's permissions do allow it to hold client money and/or custody assets but the firm did not hold client money and/or custody assets during the period.

(e)   An opinion that based on review procedures performed nothing has come to the CASS auditor's attention that causes it to believe that the firm held client money or custody assets during the period.

(f)   The CASS auditor's signature and the name of the CASS auditor's firm.

(g)   The date of the Client Assets Report.

(h)   The location in the jurisdiction where the CASS auditor practices.

The FCA Handbook at https://www.handbook.fca.org.uk/ contains the extant version of the FCA's rules listing the requirements for the limited assurance report, and should be consulted before the report is prepared.

165 Appendices to this Standard provide the following illustrative opinions of unmodified limited assurance Client Assets Reports:

(a)   Where a firm has permission to hold both client money and custody assets and claims to hold neither (Appendix 5);

(b)   Where a firm is permitted to hold client money but not custody assets and claims to hold neither (Appendix 6);

(c)   Where a firm does not have permissions to hold client money or custody assets and claims to hold neither (Appendix 7).

166 Appendix 8 to this Standard illustrates a modified limited assurance opinion where a firm holds client money but does not have permission to do so.

The Expression of Hybrid Opinions

167   Where appropriate the CASS auditor may issue hybrid opinions expressing, for example, a limited assurance opinion with respect to client money and a reasonable assurance opinion with respect to custody assets. This is illustrated in Appendix 3.

Requirements Applicable to the Provision of Reasonable Assurance with Respect to Special Reports

168   The CASS rules permit certain firms to use an "alternative approach" to client money segregation and a "non-standard method" of internal client money reconciliation[11]. In both cases the FCA requires the firm to send a written report to the FCA prepared by an independent auditor in line with a reasonable assurance engagement setting out specific matters regarding the use of either the alternative approach or the non-standard method. This is a separate engagement to the CASS audit.

169   **The CASS auditor shall obtain an understanding of the firm's proposed systems, internal controls and with respect to the alternative approach to client money segregation the calculation of the "mandatory prudent segregation amount" relating to a Special Report sufficient for it to be able to evaluate whether the firm's proposed systems and controls are suitably designed to enable the firm to comply with the relevant CASS rules.**

170   **The CASS auditor shall evaluate whether the design of the firm's systems and controls relating to a Special Report will, if implemented and operated effectively, assure compliance with the CASS rules relating to the alternative approach or nonstandard method. As part of this evaluation the auditor shall consider its findings in relation to paragraphs 83 to 86 relating to the firm's control environment and in relation to paragraphs 87 to 90 relating to the firm's monitoring activities.**

171   **If the CASS auditor is able to obtain reasonable assurance on the matters specified by the FCA it shall prepare and submit to the firm a reasonable assurance report setting out such matters specified by the FCA. Illustrative examples of wording for such reports are set out in Appendices 9 and 10.**

172   The FCA has stated "Nothing in these [CASS] rules stipulates what steps an auditor must take to be able to provide firms with the report on the basis of a reasonable assurance engagement. We understand it is likely that many firms will need to have designed their processes and to have built test systems before an auditor feels able to provide the report".

173   **Although the CASS rules do not require a report from the CASS auditor each year the CASS auditor shall, nevertheless, perform such procedures as it considers necessary each year to assess whether a Special Report remains appropriate. Specifically, the CASS auditor shall evaluate whether there have been any changes to the approach or non-standard method or to the underlying subject matter to which the alternative approach or non-standard method is being applied that would invalidate the reasonable assurance report previously provided by the CASS auditor.**

---

[11] *In this Standard these are referred to collectively as "Special Reports".*

In respect of firms that have changed from a standard approach or method to **174** an alternative approach or non-standard method the CASS auditor shall consider whether the firm has changed to the alternative approach or non-standard method without having provided the necessary documentation and obtained the required auditor's report.

The CASS auditor shall inform the FCA if, in its opinion: **175**

(a) Circumstances have changed such that any previous assurance report relating to the adoption of an alternative approach or non-standard method is no longer valid; or

(b) A firm has adopted an alternative approach or non-standard method without first obtaining a reasonable assurance report from the CASS auditor.

In either case there is a breach of the CASS rules which is likely to lead to a modification of the Client Assets Report.

Requirements Applicable to Cass Auditor Confirmations in Connection with Non-Statutory Client Money Trusts

CASS 5.4 permits an insurance intermediary firm, which has adequate resources, **176** systems and controls, to declare a trust on terms which expressly authorise it, in its capacity as trustee, to make advances of credit to the firm's clients. The client money trust extends to such debt obligations which will arise if the insurance intermediary, as trustee, makes credit advances, to enable a client's premium obligations to be met before the premium is remitted to the firm and similarly if it does so to enable claims and premium refunds to be paid to the client before receiving remittance of those monies from the insurance undertaking.

CASS 5.4 does not permit a firm to make advances of credit to itself out of the **177** client money trust.

An insurance intermediary may not handle client money through a non-statutory **178** client money trust unless the firm has and maintains systems and controls which are adequate to ensure that the firm is able to monitor and manage its client money transactions and any credit risk arising from the operation of the trust arrangement. In addition, if the firm complies with both the rules relating to statutory trusts in CASS 5.3 and non-statutory trusts in CASS 5.4 such systems and controls must extend to both arrangements.

A condition of an insurance intermediary using a non-statutory client money trust **179** is that it must obtain, and keep current, written confirmation from its auditor that it has in place systems and controls which are adequate to meet the requirements described in the preceding paragraph.

In order to provide the written confirmation required by CASS rule 5.4.4(2)R **180** the CASS auditor shall evaluate whether the firm has and maintains systems and controls over both statutory and non-statutory trusts which are adequate to ensure that the firm is able to monitor and manage its client money transactions and any credit risk that arises from the operation of such arrangements. Such an evaluation requires the CASS auditor to:

(a) Assess assurance engagement risk relevant to the operation of trust arrangements.

(b)   Evaluate whether the design of the system of internal control will, if implemented and operated effectively, ensure compliance with the CASS rules that are applicable to non-statutory trusts of insurance intermediaries.

(c)   Perform, on a sample basis, walk through procedures as a means of establishing that controls have been put into place as designed.

181   In performing the evaluation described above the CASS auditor shall evaluate the insurance intermediary's compliance with other applicable CASS requirements such as those relating to the requirements for the insurance intermediary to:

(a)   designate a manager to oversee the firm's day to day compliance with the systems and controls and applicable rules. The CASS auditor's procedures shall include meeting with the designated manager and discussing that manager's authority, scope of work and findings;

(b)   maintain the minimum level of capital resources stipulated by the CASS rules;

(c)   obtain the client's informed consent to the firm holding the client's money in a non-statutory trust; and

(d)   take reasonable steps to ensure that its terms of business adequately explain the implications to a client of its money being held in a non-statutory trust.

APPENDIX 1 – Overview of a Reasonable Assurance Process for a Legal Entity

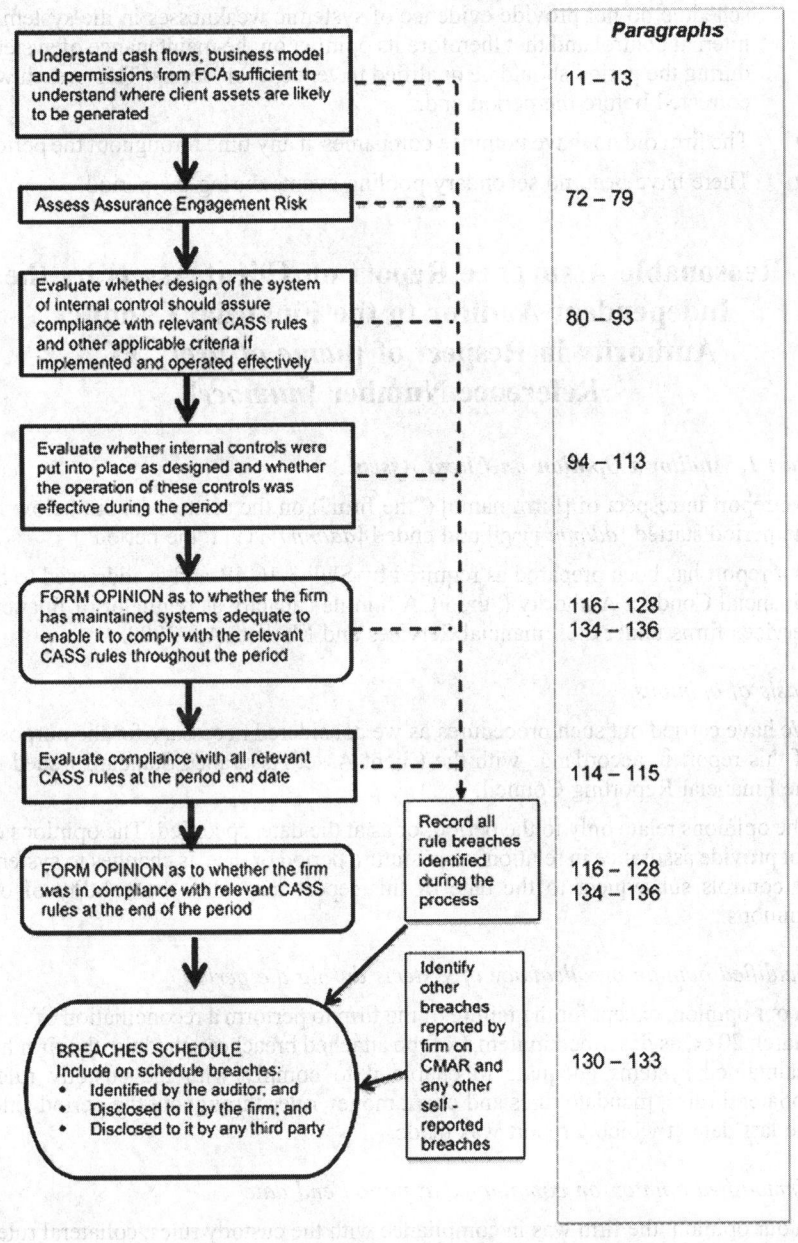

	Paragraphs
Understand cash flows, business model and permissions from FCA sufficient to understand where client assets are likely to be generated	11 – 13
Assess Assurance Engagement Risk	72 – 79
Evaluate whether design of the system of internal control should assure compliance with relevant CASS rules and other applicable criteria if implemented and operated effectively	80 – 93
Evaluate whether internal controls were put into place as designed and whether the operation of these controls was effective during the period	94 – 113
FORM OPINION as to whether the firm has maintained systems adequate to enable it to comply with the relevant CASS rules throughout the period	116 – 128 134 – 136
Evaluate compliance with all relevant CASS rules at the period end date	114 – 115
FORM OPINION as to whether the firm was in compliance with relevant CASS rules at the end of the period	116 – 128 134 – 136
Record all rule breaches identified during the process	
Identify other breaches reported by firm on CMAR and any other self-reported breaches	130 – 133
BREACHES SCHEDULE Include on schedule breaches: • Identified by the auditor; and • Disclosed to it by the firm; and • Disclosed to it by any third party	

APPENDIX 2 – Illustrative Qualified Opinion in a Reasonable Assurance Report on Client Assets

- The CASS auditor has determined that breaches identified on the breaches schedule do not provide evidence of systemic weaknesses in the system of internal control and that therefore its opinion on the maintenance of systems during the period should be qualified in "except for" terms. This breach was corrected before the period end.

- The firm did not have nominee companies at any time throughout the period.

- There have been no secondary pooling events during the period.

Reasonable Assurance Report on Client Assets by the Independent Auditor to the Financial Conduct Authority in Respect of [*name of firm*], FCA Reference Number [*number*]

Part 1: Auditor's Opinion on Client Assets

We report in respect of [Firm name] ("the firm") on the matters set out below for the period started [*dd/mm/yyyy*] and ended [*dd/mm/yyyy*] ("the period").

Our report has been prepared as required by SUP 3.10.4R and is addressed to the Financial Conduct Authority ("the FCA") in its capacity as regulator of financial services firms under the Financial Services and Markets Act 2000.

Basis of opinions

We have carried out such procedures as we considered necessary for the purposes of this report in accordance with the Client Asset Assurance Standard issued by the Financial Reporting Council.

The opinions relate only to the period, or as at the date, specified. The opinions do not provide assurance in relation to any future period or date as changes to systems or controls subsequent to the date of this report may alter the validity of our opinions.

Qualified opinion on adequacy of systems during the period

In our opinion, except for the failure of the firm to perform a reconciliation of ... in March 20xx, as described in item 1 of the attached breaches schedule, the firm has maintained systems adequate to enable it to comply with the custody rules, collateral rules, mandate rules and client money rules throughout the period since the last date at which a report was made.

Unmodified opinion on compliance at period end date

In our opinion, the firm was in compliance with the custody rules, collateral rules, the mandate rules and the client money rules as at the period end date.

Other matters

This report should be read in conjunction with the Breaches Schedule that we have prepared and which is appended.

[Signature]   *Address*

John Smith for and on behalf of   *Date*
[Name of audit firm]

Part 2: Identified CASS Breaches that have occurred during the period

BREACHES SCHEDULE

[Firm name], FCA reference number [number], for the period started *[dd/mm/yyyy]* and ended *[dd/mm/yyyy]*

In accordance with SUP 3.10.9AR, Columns A to D have been completed by and are the responsibility of the auditor. In accordance with SUP 3.11.1G, Column E has been completed by the firm. The auditor has no responsibility for the content of Column E.

Column A	Column B	Column C	Column D	Column E
Item No.	Rule Reference(s)	Identifying Party	Breach identified	Firm's comment
1 *(illustrative details to be inserted)*				
...				

APPENDIX 3 – Illustrative Adverse Opinion in a Reasonable Assurance Report on Client Assets

- The CASS auditor has determined that breaches identified on the breaches schedule taken together indicate systemic weakness in the control systems such that an adverse opinion is warranted in relation to client money.

- The firm claimed not to hold custody assets and the CASS auditor's work has supported this claim.

- The firm did not have nominee companies at any time throughout the period.

- There have been no secondary pooling events during the period.

Assurance Report[12] on Client Assets by the Independent Auditor to the Financial Conduct Authority in Respect of [*name of firm*], FCA Reference Number [*number*]

Part 1: Auditor's Opinion on Client Assets

We report in respect of [Firm name] ("the firm") on the matters set out below for the period started [*dd/mm/yyyy*] and ended [*dd/mm/yyyy*] ("the period").

Our report has been prepared as required by SUP 3.10.4R and is addressed to the Financial Conduct Authority ("the FCA") in its capacity as regulator of financial services firms under the Financial Services and Markets Act 2000.

Basis of opinions

We have carried out such procedures as we considered necessary for the purposes of this report in accordance with the Client Asset Assurance Standard issued by the Financial Reporting Council.

The opinions relate only to the period, or as at the date, specified. The opinions do not provide assurance in relation to any future period or date as changes to systems or controls subsequent to the date of this report may alter the validity of our opinions.

Adverse opinion on adequacy of systems during the period

In our opinion, because of the systemic failure of the firm to carry out reconciliations of … as described in lines 1 to 5 of the attached breaches schedule the firm did not maintain systems adequate to enable it to comply with the client money rules throughout the period since the last date at which a report was made.

Adverse opinion on compliance at period end date

In our opinion, because of the failure to perform the reconciliations described in lines 1 to 5 of the attached breaches schedule the firm was not in compliance with the client money rules as at the period end date.

---

[12] *"Assurance Report" is used as the title because the report is a hybrid containing both a reasonable and a limited assurance opinion.*

Claim not to hold custody assets

The scope of the firm's permissions did not allow it to hold custody assets.

The directors of the firm have stated that the firm did not hold custody assets during the period. Based on review procedures performed, nothing has come to our attention that causes us to believe that the firm held custody assets during the period.

Other matters

This report should be read in conjunction with the Breaches Schedule that we have prepared and which is appended.

[Signature]   *Address*

John Smith for and on behalf of   *Date*
[Name of audit firm]

Breaches Schedule

Part 2: Identified CASS Breaches that have occurred during the period

[*Firm name*], FCA reference number [*number*], for the period started [*dd/mm/yyyy*] and ended [*dd/mm/yyyy*]

In accordance with SUP 3.10.9AR, Columns A to D have been completed by and are the responsibility of the auditor. In accordance with SUP 3.11.1G, Column E has been completed by the firm. The auditor has no responsibility for the content of Column E.

Column A	Column B	Column C	Column D	Column E
Item No.	Rule Reference(s)	Identifying Party	Breach identified	Firm's comment
1 *(illustrative details to be inserted)*				
2				
3				
4				
5				
...				

APPENDIX 4 – Illustrative Unmodified Opinion in a Reasonable Assurance Report on Client Assets

- Neither the CASS auditor nor the firm has identified any breaches; consequently the breaches schedule is a nil return.

- The firm has nominee companies in whose name custody assets of the firm are registered during and at the end of the period.

- A bank, where client money had been placed, failed during the period giving rise to a secondary pooling event.

Reasonable Assurance Report on Client Assets by the Independent Auditor to the Financial Conduct Authority in Respect of [*name of firm*], FCA Reference Number [*number*]

Part 1: Auditor's Opinion on Client Assets

We report in respect of [Firm name] ("the firm") on the matters set out below for the period started [*dd/mm/yyyy*] and ended [*dd/mm/yyyy*] ("the period").

Our report has been prepared as required by SUP 3.10.4R and is addressed to the Financial Conduct Authority ("the FCA") in its capacity as regulator of financial services firms under the Financial Services and Markets Act 2000.

Basis of opinions

We have carried out such procedures as we considered necessary for the purposes of this report in accordance with the Client Asset Assurance Standard issued by the Financial Reporting Council.

The opinions relate only to the period, or as at the date, specified. The opinions do not provide assurance in relation to any future period or date as changes to systems or controls subsequent to the date of this report may alter the validity of our opinions.

Unmodified opinions on adequacy of systems during the period

In our opinion, the firm has maintained systems adequate to enable it to comply with the custody rules, collateral rules, mandate rules and client money rules throughout the period since the last date at which a report was made.

In our opinion [*name of nominee companies*], subsidiaries of the firm which are nominee companies during the period in whose name custody assets are registered, have maintained throughout the period systems for the custody, identification and control of custody assets which:

(a) were adequate; and

(b) included reconciliations at appropriate intervals between the records maintained (whether by the firm or the nominee company) and statements or confirmations from custodians or from the person who maintained the record of legal entitlement.

Unmodified opinion on compliance at period end date

In our opinion, the firm was in compliance with the [custody rules,] [collateral rules,] [the mandate rules] [and] [the client money rules] as at the period end date.

Unmodified opinion on secondary pooling event

In our opinion, in relation to the secondary pooling event during the period, the firm has complied with the rules in [CASS 5.6] [and] [CASS 7A] in relation to that pooling event.

Other matters

Our opinion expressed above does not extend to the appended Breaches Schedule.

[Signature]	*Address*
John Smith for and on behalf of	*Date*
[Name of audit firm]	

Breaches Schedule

Part 2: Identified CASS Breaches that have occurred during the period

[*Firm name*], FCA reference number [*number*], for the period started [*dd/mm/yyyy*] and ended [*dd/mm/yyyy*]

In accordance with SUP 3.10.9AR, Columns A to D have been completed by and are the responsibility of the auditor. In accordance with SUP 3.11.1G, Column E has been completed by the firm. The auditor has no responsibility for the content of Column E.

Column A	Column B	Column C	Column D	Column E
Item No.	Rule Reference(s)	Identifying Party	Breach identified	Firm's comment
			NO BREACHES WERE IDENTIFIED	
...				

APPENDIX 5 – Illustrative Unmodified Opinion in a Limited Assurance Report on Client Assets where firm has Permission to Hold Both Client Money and Custody Assets but Claims to Hold Neither

- The scope of the firm's permissions allows it to hold client money and custody assets but the firm claims not to hold either of them.

Limited Assurance Report on Client Assets by the Independent Auditor to the Financial Conduct Authority in Respect of [*name of firm*], FCA Reference Number [*number*]

We report in respect of [Firm name] ("the firm") on the matters set out below for the period started [*dd/mm/yyyy*] and ended [*dd/mm/yyyy*] ("the period").

Our report has been prepared as required by SUP 3.10.4R and is addressed to the Financial Conduct Authority ("the FCA") in its capacity as regulator of financial services firms under the Financial Services and Markets Act 2000.

Basis of opinion

We have carried out such procedures as we considered necessary for the purposes of this report in accordance with the Client Asset Assurance Standard issued by the Financial Reporting Council.

The opinions relate only to the period, or as at the date, specified. The opinions do not provide assurance in relation to any future period or date.

Unmodified opinion

The directors of the firm have stated that the firm did not hold client money or custody assets during the period. Based on review procedures performed, nothing has come to our attention that causes us to believe that the firm held client money or custody assets during the period.

[*Signature*]   *Address*

John Smith for and on behalf of   *Date*
[*Name of audit firm*]

APPENDIX 6 – Illustrative Unmodified Opinion in a Limited Assurance Report on Client Assets where the Firm is Permitted to Hold Client Money but not Custody Assets and Claims to Hold Neither

- The scope of the firm's permissions allows it to hold client money but not custody assets. The firm claims to hold neither client money nor custody assets.

Limited Assurance Report on Client Assets by the Independent Auditor to the Financial Conduct Authority in Respect of [*name of firm*], FCA Reference Number [*number*]

We report in respect of [Firm name] ("the firm") on the matters set out below for the period started [*dd/mm/yyyy*] and ended [*dd/mm/yyyy*] ("the period").

Our report has been prepared as required by SUP 3.10.4R and is addressed to the Financial Conduct Authority ("the FCA") in its capacity as regulator of financial services firms under the Financial Services and Markets Act 2000.

Basis of opinion

We have carried out such procedures as we considered necessary for the purposes of this report in accordance with the Client Asset Assurance Standard issued by the Financial Reporting Council.

The opinions relate only to the period, or as at the date, specified. The opinions do not provide assurance in relation to any future period or date.

Unmodified opinion

The scope of the firm's permissions did not allow it to hold custody assets.

The directors of the firm have stated that the firm did not hold client money or custody assets during the period. Based on review procedures performed, nothing has come to our attention that causes us to believe that the firm held client money or custody assets during the period.

[Signature]	*Address*
John Smith for and on behalf of	*Date*
[Name of audit firm]	

APPENDIX 7 – Illustrative Unmodified Opinion in a Limited Assurance Report on Client Assets where the Firm does not have Permission to Hold Client Money or Custody Assets and Claims to Hold Neither

- The firm does not have permissions to hold client money or custody assets and the firm claims to hold neither of them.

Limited Assurance Report on Client Assets by the Independent Auditor to the Financial Conduct Authority in Respect of [*name of firm*], FCA Reference Number [*number*]

We report in respect of [Firm name] ("the firm") on the matters set out below for the period started [*dd/mm/yyyy*] and ended [*dd/mm/yyyy*] ("the period").

Our report has been prepared as required by SUP 3.10.4R and is addressed to the Financial Conduct Authority ("the FCA") in its capacity as regulator of financial services firms under the Financial Services and Markets Act 2000.

Basis of opinion

We have carried out such procedures as we considered necessary for the purposes of this report in accordance with the Client Asset Assurance Standard issued by the Financial Reporting Council.

The opinions relate only to the period, or as at the date, specified. The opinions do not provide assurance in relation to any future period or date.

Unmodified opinion

The scope of the firm's permissions did not allow it to hold client money or custody assets.

The directors of the firm have stated that the firm did not hold client money or custody assets during the period. Based on review procedures performed, nothing has come to our attention that causes us to believe that the firm held client money or custody assets during the period.

[Signature]	*Address*
John Smith for and on behalf of	*Date*
[Name of audit firm]	

APPENDIX 8 – Illustrative Modified Limited Assurance Opinion on Client Assets where a Firm Holds Client Money but does not have Permission to do so

- The scope of the firm's permissions allows it to hold custody assets but not client money. The firm claims to hold neither custody assets nor client money.

Limited Assurance Report on Client Assets by the Independent Auditor to the Financial Conduct Authority in Respect of [*name of firm*], FCA Reference Number [*number*]

We report in respect of [Firm name] ("the firm") on the matters set out below for the period started [*dd/mm/yyyy*] and ended [*dd/mm/yyyy*] ("the period").

Our report has been prepared as required by SUP 3.10.4R and is addressed to the Financial Conduct Authority ("the FCA") in its capacity as regulator of financial services firms under the Financial Services and Markets Act 2000.

Basis of opinion

We have carried out such procedures as we considered necessary for the purposes of this report in accordance with the Client Asset Assurance Standard issued by the Financial Reporting Council.

The opinions relate only to the period, or as at the date, specified. The opinions do not provide assurance in relation to any future period or date.

Modified opinion on client money

The scope of the firm's permissions allowed it to hold custody assets but not to hold client money.

The directors (or equivalent corporate officers) of the firm have stated that the firm did not hold client money or custody assets during the period. Arising from the findings of our review procedures it came to our attention that, contrary to its permissions, the firm held client money [include information about how much client money is involved and the circumstances leading to the firm holding such client money] during [specify period during which client money was held].

Unmodified opinion on custody assets

Based on review procedures performed, nothing has come to our attention that causes us to believe that the firm held custody assets during the period.

[*Signature*]	*Address*
John Smith for and on behalf of	*Date*
[*Name of audit firm*]	

APPENDIX 9 – The Alternative Approach to Client Money Segregation

Normal approach to client money segregation

1   Under the so-called normal approach a firm must promptly, and in any event no later than the next business day after receipt, deposit all client money into a segregated client account with a third party bank. This may be either a general client account where client monies are pooled or a designated client account where the client money from one or more clients is deposited to the exclusion of other clients. Notifications are required as a matter of regulation to be made to the third party bank to make it aware that the account is a trust account, and waivers must be obtained from the bank so as to prevent set-off against monies held on behalf of the institution itself.

Alternative approach to client money segregation relating to investment businesses

2   Under the alternative approach, client money is received into and paid out of a firm's own bank account. The firm is then required to carry out end-of-day reconciliations to determine the daily client money requirement (i.e. the total amount of money that constitutes client money required to be segregated). The firm must then immediately reconcile the client money account with the requisite amount. Intra-day the client money account must contain a buffer (now described as a mandatory prudent segregation amount) in an effort to ensure adequate monies are segregated on clients' behalves in case of insolvency.

3   A firm that adopts the alternative approach to segregating client money should (if it follows the standard method of client money reconciliation) carry out an internal client money reconciliation on each business day and calculate how much money it either needs to withdraw from, or place in from its own bank account or its client bank account as a result of any discrepancy arising between its client money requirement and its client money resource as at the close of business on the previous business day.

4   The alternative approach is designed to address the risks that:

(a)   Client money in a firm's own bank account may not be available to be pooled for distribution to clients on the occurrence of a primary pooling event; and

(b)   At the time of a primary pooling event the firm may not have segregated in its client bank account a sufficient amount of client money to meet its client money requirement.

5   Firms that already use the alternative approach to client money segregation and those firms wishing to use it in future will need to establish and document their reasons for using the alternative approach for a particular business line.

6   Before adopting the alternative approach a firm must send a written report to the FCA prepared by an independent auditor of the firm in line with a reasonable assurance engagement stating whether in the auditor's opinion:

(a)   the firm's systems and controls are suitably designed to enable it to comply with CASS 7.13.62R to CASS 7.13.65R; and

(b)   the firm's calculation of its alternative approach mandatory prudent segregation amount (buffer) under CASS 7.13.65R is suitably designed to enable the firm to comply with CASS 7.13.65R.

The FCA in PS14/9 state: 7

> "The report will be prepared on the basis of a reasonable assurance engagement. We understand this is achievable under the FRC's definition of a reasonable assurance engagement. Nothing in these rules stipulates what steps an auditor must take to be able to provide firms with the report on the basis of a reasonable assurance engagement. We understand it is likely that many firms will need to have designed their processes and to have built test systems before an auditor feels able to provide the report. However, the specific steps an auditor may need to follow, and the matters which a firm may need to address before the auditor issues a reasonable assurance report, are matters for the auditor's professional judgment as governed by the requirements and standards imposed on the auditor by its regulator."

An illustrative example of such a report is set out below.   8

Reasonable Assurance Report to xyz plc on its Proposed use of the Alternative Approach to Client Money Segregation

You have informed us that you intend to adopt the alternative approach to client money segregation and send to the Financial Conduct Authority (FCA) a report by an independent auditor in accordance with CASS 7.13.58R. At your request, we have performed a reasonable assurance engagement on the suitability of the design of those systems, controls and calculations that relate to the adoption of the alternative approach.

Respective responsibilities of firm and auditor

The firm is responsible for designing systems, controls and calculations that enable it to comply with the relevant requirements of the CASS rules of the FCA which are applicable to the alternative approach to client money segregation. Our responsibility is to perform a reasonable assurance engagement and express an opinion on the suitability of the design of such systems, controls and calculations that management proposes to establish that will enable the firm to comply with the relevant CASS rules. Our engagement was carried out in accordance with the requirements of the Client Asset Assurance Standard issued by the Financial Reporting Council.

[Inherent limitation in our engagement

As the firm has not yet implemented the systems and controls whose design we have evaluated we are not able to, and do not, provide any assurance as to whether:

(a)   the systems, controls and calculations will be put in place as designed; or

(b)   the systems and controls will operate effectively.]

Opinion

In our opinion:

(a)　the firm's systems and controls are suitably designed to enable it to comply with CASS 7.13.62R to CASS 7.13.65R; and

(b)　the firm's calculation of its alternative approach mandatory prudent segregation amount under CASS 7.13.65R is suitably designed to enable the firm to comply with CASS 7.13.65R.

[Signature]　　　　　　　　　　　　　*Address*

John Smith for and on behalf of　　　*Date*
[Name of audit firm]

APPENDIX 10 – The Non-Standard Method of Internal Client Money Reconciliation

The FCA defines an internal client money reconciliation as "a reconciliation   **1** between a firm's internal records and accounts of the amount of client money held for each client with its internal records and accounts of the client money that the firm should be holding in client bank accounts or have placed in client transaction accounts".

An internal client money reconciliation should: **2**

(a) Be one of the steps a firm takes to arrange adequate protection for client assets when the firm is responsible for them;

(b) Be one of the steps a firm takes to satisfy its obligations under the CASS rules to ensure the accuracy of the firm's records and accounts;

(c) For the normal approach to segregating client money check whether the amount of client money recorded in the firm's records as being segregated in client bank accounts meets the firm's obligations to its clients under the client money rules on a daily basis; and

(d) For the alternative approach to segregating client money calculate the amount of client money to be segregated in client bank accounts which meets the firm's obligations to its clients under the client money rules on a daily basis.

A firm is required to perform an internal client money reconciliation: **3**

(a) Each business day;

(b) Based on the records of the firm as at the close of business on the previous business day.

When performing an internal client money reconciliation a firm must either: **4**

(a) Follow one of the standard methods of internal client money reconciliation set out in the CASS rules; or

(b) Follow a non-standard method of internal client money reconciliation in accordance with the requirements of the CASS rules.

A firm which has adopted the normal approach to segregating client money is   **5** required to use the internal client money reconciliation to check whether its client money resource, as at close of business on the previous business day, was equal to its client money requirement at the close of business on that previous day.

A firm that adopts the alternative approach to segregating client money is required   **6** to use the client money reconciliation to ensure that its client money resource at the close of business on any day it carries out an internal client money reconciliation is equal to its client money requirement at the close of business on the previous day.

Before using a non-standard method of internal client money reconciliation a firm   **7** must send a written report to the FCA prepared by an independent auditor of the firm in line with a reasonable assurance engagement stating whether in the auditor's opinion:

(a) the method of internal client money reconciliation which the firm will use is suitably designed to enable it to (as applicable):

(i)   (for the normal approach to segregating client money) check whether the amount of client money recorded in the firm's records as being segregated in client bank accounts meets the firm's obligation to its clients under the client money rules on a daily basis; or

(ii) (for the alternative approach to segregating client money) calculate the amount of client money to be segregated in client bank accounts which meets the firm's obligations to its clients under the client money rules on a daily basis; and

(b) the firm's systems and controls are suitably designed to enable it to carry out the method of internal client money reconciliation the firm will use.

8   The FCA in PS14/9 state:

"The report will be prepared on the basis of a reasonable assurance engagement. We understand this is achievable under the FRC's definition of a reasonable assurance engagement. Nothing in these rules stipulates what steps an auditor must take to be able to provide firms with the report on the basis of a reasonable assurance engagement. We understand it is likely that many firms will need to have designed their processes and to have built test systems before an auditor feels able to provide the report. However, the specific steps an auditor may need to follow, and the matters which a firm may need to address before the auditor issues a reasonable assurance report, are matters for the auditor's professional judgment as governed by the requirements and standards imposed on the auditor by its regulator."

9   An illustrative example of such a report is set out below.

Reasonable Assurance Report to XYZ plc on its Proposed use of the Non-Standard Method of Internal Client Money Reconciliation

You have informed us that you intend to adopt the non-standard method of internal client money reconciliation and send to the Financial Conduct Authority (FCA) a report by an independent auditor in accordance with CASS 7.15.18R. At your request, we have performed a reasonable assurance engagement on the suitability of the design of those systems and controls that relate to the adoption of the non-standard method.

Respective responsibilities of firm and auditor

The firm is responsible for designing systems and controls that enable it to comply with the relevant requirements of the CASS rules of the FCA which are applicable to the non-standard method of internal client money reconciliation. Our responsibility is to perform a reasonable assurance engagement and express an opinion on the suitability of the design of such systems and controls that management proposes to establish that will enable the firm to comply with the relevant CASS rules. Our engagement will be carried out in accordance with the requirements of the Client Asset Assurance Standard issued by the Financial Reporting Council.

[Inherent limitation in our engagement

As the firm has not yet implemented the systems and controls whose design we have evaluated we are not able to, and do not, provide any assurance as to whether:

(a)   the systems and controls will be put in place as designed; or

(b)   the systems and controls will operate effectively.]

Opinion

In our opinion:

(a)   the method of internal client money reconciliation which the firm will use is suitably designed to enable it to *[as applicable]*:

   (i)   *[for the normal approach to segregating client money]* check whether the amount of client money recorded in the firm's records as being segregated in client bank accounts meets the firm's obligation to its clients under the client money rules on a daily basis; or

   (ii)   *[for the alternative approach to segregating client money]* calculate the amount of client money to be segregated in client bank accounts which meets the firm's obligations to its clients under the client money rules on a daily basis; and

(b)   the firm's systems and controls are suitably designed to enable it to carry out the method of internal client money reconciliation the firm will use.

[Signature]   Address

John Smith for and on behalf of   Date
[Name of audit firm]

APPENDIX 11 – Illustrative Example of a Confirmation Letter from the Auditor to the Firm Regarding a Non-Statutory Client Money Trust

[Name of Firm]

[address]

Dear Sirs:

[*Firm name*] Systems and controls relating to non-statutory client money trusts

In accordance with the requirements of CASS 5.4.4R(2) you have engaged us to confirm that you have in place systems and controls which are adequate to meet the requirements of CASS 5.4.4R(1).

In providing the confirmation set out at the conclusion of this letter, and as previously agreed with you, we have followed the relevant requirements of the Client Asset Assurance Standard issued by the Financial Reporting Council.

Confirmation

We confirm that [insert name of firm] has in place systems and controls which are adequate to meet the requirements of CASS 5.4.4R(1). Specifically we confirm that [insert name of firm] has and maintains systems and controls which are adequate to ensure that [insert name of firm] is able to monitor and manage its client money transactions and any credit risk arising from the operation of the trust arrangement [and such systems and controls extend to both the [insert name of firm] statutory trusts (under CASS 5.3) and non-statutory client money trusts (under CASS 5.4)].[13]

Yours faithfully

[*Name of audit firm*]

---

[13] *The wording in square brackets need only be included where, in accordance with CASS 5.4.2R a firm complies with both the rules in CASS 5.3 and 5.4 as such systems and controls are required to extend to both arrangements.*

APPENDIX 12 – The CASS Auditor's Duty to Report to the FCA

Under The Financial Services and Markets Act 2000 (Communications by **1** Auditors) Regulations 2001 (the 2001 Regulations)[14], CASS auditors have duties in certain circumstances to make reports to the FCA. Information and opinions to be communicated are those meeting the criteria set out below which relate to matters of which the CASS auditor[15] of the firm has become aware:

(i)   in their capacity as CASS auditor of the firm, and

(ii)   if they are also the auditor of a person who has close links with the firm, in their capacity as auditor of that person.

The criteria for determining the matters to be reported are as follows: **2**

(i)   the CASS auditor reasonably believes that there is, or has been, or may be, or may have been a contravention of any "relevant requirement" that applies to the firm concerned and that contravention may be of material significance to the FCA in determining whether to exercise, in relation to that firm, any of its functions under FSMA 2000, or

(ii)   the CASS auditor reasonably believes that the information on, or its opinion on, those matters may be of material significance to the FCA in determining whether the firm concerned satisfies and will continue to satisfy the "threshold conditions".

In relation to 2(i) above, "Relevant requirement" is a requirement by or under **3** FSMA 2000 which relates to authorisation under FSMA 2000 or to the carrying on of any regulated activity. This includes not only relevant statutory instruments but also the FCA's rules (other than the Listing Rules) including the Principles for Businesses. The duty to report also covers any requirement imposed by or under any other Act[16] the contravention of which constitutes an offence which the FCA has the power to prosecute under FSMA 2000.

In relation to 2(ii) above the duty to report relates to either information or opinions **4** held by the CASS auditor which may be of significance to the FCA in determining whether the firm satisfies and will continue to satisfy the "Threshold Conditions". The duty to report opinions, as well as information, allows for circumstances where adequate information on a matter may not readily be forthcoming from the firm, and where judgments need to be made.

Material significance

Determining whether a contravention of a relevant requirement or a Threshold **5** Condition is reportable under the 2001 Regulations involves consideration both of whether the CASS auditor "reasonably believes" and that the matter in question "is, or is likely to be, of material significance" to the regulator.

In circumstances where a CASS auditor identifies that a reportable matter may **6** exist, it carries out such additional procedures, as it considers necessary, to

---

[14] *Statutory Instrument 2001 No. 2587.*

[15] *An "auditor" is defined for this purpose in the Regulations as a person who is, or has been, an auditor of an authorised person appointed under, or as a result of, a statutory provision including Section 340 of FSMA 2000.*

[16] *Examples include Part 5 of the Criminal Justice Act 1993 and prescribed regulations relating to money laundering.*

determine whether the facts and circumstances cause it "reasonably to believe" that the matter does in fact exist. It should be noted that the CASS auditor's work does not need to prove that the reportable matter exists.

7   Where an apparent breach of statutory or regulatory requirements comes to the CASS auditors' attention, it should obtain such evidence as is available to assess its implications for the CASS auditor's reporting responsibilities and determine whether, in its opinion, there is reasonable cause to believe that the breach has occurred and that it relates to a matter that is of material significance to the FCA.

8   "Material significance" is defined as follows:

"*A matter or group of matters is normally of material significance to a regulator's function when, due either to its nature or its potential financial impact, it is likely of itself to require investigation by the regulator.*"

9   The determination of whether a matter is, or is likely to be, of material significance to the FCA inevitably requires the CASS auditor to exercise judgment. In forming such judgments, the auditor needs to consider not simply the facts of the matter but also their implications. In addition, it is possible that a matter, which is not materially significant in isolation, may become so when other possible breaches are considered.

10   The CASS auditor of a firm bases its judgment of "material significance" to the FCA solely on their understanding of the facts of which they are aware without making any assumptions about the information available to the FCA in connection with any particular firm.

11   Minor breaches of the FCA's rules that, for example, are unlikely to: jeopardise the safeguarding of client's assets; or amount to misconduct; or mismanagement would not normally be of "material significance". In circumstances where a CASS auditor is uncertain whether it may be required to make a report or not, it may wish to consider taking legal advice.

12   On completion of its investigations, the CASS auditor ensures that the facts and circumstances, and the basis for its conclusion as to whether these are, or are likely to be of "material significance" to the FCA, are adequately documented such that the reasoning for its decision to report or not, as the case may be, may be clearly demonstrated.

13   Whilst confidentiality is an implied term of CASS auditors' contracts with a firm, section 342 of FSMA 2000 states that an auditor does not contravene that duty if he reports to the FCA information or his opinion, if the auditor is acting in good faith and reasonably believes that the information or opinion is relevant to any function of the FCA. The protection afforded is given in respect of information obtained in his capacity as [CASS] auditor.

Contextual Material to the Client Asset Assurance Standard

Contextual material is part of the FRC's guidance to CASS auditors. Guidance is persuasive not prescriptive and compliance is encouraged. The overall purpose of guidance is to improve the quality of CASS audits. Guidance can be issued for a number of specific purposes, for example to support compliance with Codes or with legislative requirements or regulatory obligations, or for interpretive, explanatory, contextual or educational purposes to support the use of judgment in areas relevant to the FRC's objectives and mission. Adherence to guidance may be promoted by the FRC in order to drive improvements in quality.

Background

The UK has a large number of financial services firms that may hold client money **1** and custody assets (referred to collectively as "**client assets**") belonging to their clients. The Financial Conduct Authority's (FCA's) 10th Principle for Businesses is that "A firm must arrange adequate protection for clients' assets when it is responsible for them".

Rules in respect of the 10th principle are set out in the FCA's Client Assets **2** Sourcebook (CASS rules) which require firms to hold client money and custody assets separately from their own in order to minimise the risk of loss to clients in the event of the firm's insolvency. Such losses may arise, for example, from the claims of its general creditors and from right of set-off by institutions which hold the custody assets or client money. Other FCA rules may also be applicable to CASS auditors. An example of such other FCA rules are the FCA's Supervisory (SUP) rules.

The expression "*CASS auditor*" is used in the Standard to describe the person who **3** is responsible for preparing and submitting a Client Assets Report to the FCA. For insurance intermediaries, the FCA's rules require the report to be submitted to "the firm".

The Financial Services and Markets Act 2000 (FSMA 2000) together with other **4** legislation such as the Companies Act 2006 provide the statutory framework for the obligations of firms and CASS auditors. FSMA 2000 permits the FCA to have rules requiring a firm to appoint an auditor and to impose "other duties" on the auditor of the firm. The duty of an auditor to prepare and submit a Client Assets Report to the FCA is such an "other duty". However, a firm need not appoint its statutory auditor to be its CASS auditor.

Requirement to protect clients' safe custody assets and client money

The fundamental requirement to protect client assets is set out in CASS 6.2.1R **5** with respect to safe custody assets and in CASS 7.12.1R with respect to client money. These CASS rules are as follows[17]:

> **CASS 6.2.1R** A firm must, when holding safe custody assets belonging to clients, make adequate arrangements so as to safeguard clients' ownership rights, especially in the event of the firm's insolvency, and to prevent the use of safe custody assets belonging to a client on the firm's own account except with the client's express consent.

> **CASS 7.12.1R** A firm must, when holding client money, make adequate arrangements to safeguard the client's rights and prevent the use of client money for its own account.

---

[17] *These Explanatory Notes quote certain of the CASS rules in order to illustrate the discussion of the fundamental principles underlying the CASS rules. It is important that a CASS auditor has an understanding of all CASS rules relevant to the engagement it is undertaking and should not rely on reading these notes as a substitute for such knowledge.*

Requirement to have adequate organisational arrangements

6   The provisions of the Market in Financial Instruments Directive (MiFID) and the FCA's rules in the CASS Sourcebook might be taken to imply that client assets and money held by a firm are generally protected, including on the insolvency of the firm. However, this may not always be the case because the interaction between the CASS rules and English law leaves such assets susceptible to various operational risks, such as those arising from inaccurate record-keeping on the part of the firm. There is a consequent risk for clients of the firm who have entrusted their assets or monies to the firm to share resulting losses with other clients of the firm with whom they are not connected.

7   The requirements to protect clients' assets and the operational risks described above give rise to requirements for CASS firms to have adequate organisational arrangements. These fundamental Rules are as follows:

> **CASS 6.2.2R** A firm must introduce adequate organisational arrangements to minimise the risk of the loss or diminution of clients' safe custody assets, or the rights in connection with those safe custody assets, as a result of the misuse of the safe custody assets, fraud, poor administration, inadequate record-keeping or negligence.

> **CASS 7.12.2R** A firm must introduce adequate organisational arrangements to minimise the risk of the loss or diminution of client money, or of rights in connection with client money, as a result of misuse of client money, fraud, poor administration, inadequate record-keeping or negligence.

8   In essence the CASS auditor reports on whether the rules surrounding these requirements have been complied with by the firm during the period and whether the firm was in compliance with those rules at the end of the period.

Four fundamental principles

9   There are perhaps four fundamental principles that underlie the CASS requirements:

Identification:	Has the firm identified where client assets may arise in its business? This can be a far from straightforward matter and requires those responsible for the identification of client assets to have a thorough knowledge of the firm's business model and of its cash inflows and outflows.
Segregation/ Safeguarding	Does the firm segregate client monies and safeguard custody assets in a manner that is likely to be legally effective such that in the event of the insolvency of the firm client assets will be returned on a timely basis to their beneficial owners.

Reconciliation	The firm should perform internal and external reconciliations at the frequency required by the rules. An internal client money reconciliation is between a firm's internal records and accounts of the amount of client money held for each client with its internal records and accounts of the aggregate amount of client money that the firm should be holding in client bank accounts or have placed in client transaction accounts. An external reconciliation is between the firm's internal records and the records of the financial institution with which the monies have been deposited.
Trust/Legal title	The firm should establish and obtain acknowledgement of the trust status over client money and legal title to custody assets.

Other CASS Rules

There are aspects of the Client Asset rules other than the distinction between **10** custody assets (CASS 6) and client money (CASS 7). There are also rules relating to:

Collateral (CASS 3) which provide protection for those assets subject to a "right to use arrangement" under which a client gives a firm certain rights to use an asset and the firm treats the asset as if legal title and associated rights to that asset had been transferred to the firm subject only to an obligation to return equivalent assets to the client upon satisfaction of the client's obligation to the firm.

Insurance Intermediaries (CASS 5) which establish specific requirements for firms (such as insurance brokers) that undertake insurance mediation activity and hold client money. The requirements of CASS 5 are broadly similar to the client money rules in CASS 7 but there are some significant differences.

Mandates (CASS 8) – these rules apply to a firm in respect of any authority from a client under which the firm may control a client's assets or liabilities in the course of, or in connection with, the firm's:

(a)   Investment business; and/or

(b)   Insurance mediation activity.

Debt Management Firms that receive or hold client money (CASS 11) – a debt management firm is a firm which:

(a)   Carries on the activities of debt counselling or debt adjusting, alone or together, with a view to an individual entering into a particular debt solution; or

(b)   Carries on the activity of debt counselling where an associate carries on debt adjusting with the aim in (a) in view; or

(c)   Carries on debt adjusting where an associate carries on debt counselling with the aim of (a) in view; or

(d)   Is a not-for-profit debt advice body

Key Principles underlying the CASS rules

The following table sets out the key principles that the CASS auditor considers **11** with respect to the various CASS rules. It is not exhaustive, and auditors should consider all of the relevant CASS rules and use professional judgment to determine what risks are important to the circumstances of each client.

PRINCIPLE	CASS 3 Collateral	CASS 5 Insurance Intermediaries	CASS 6 Custody Assets	CASS 7 Client Money	CASS 8 Mandates	CASS 11 Debt management firms
1. **Identification:** The firm should identify all sources of client assets and mandates in its business	✓	✓	✓	✓	✓	✓
2. **Protecting client assets:** The firm should make adequate arrangements to safeguard client ownership rights on the insolvency of the firm	✓	✓	✓	✓		✓
3. **Organisational arrangements:** The firm's organisational arrangements should be adequate such that they comply with the CASS Rules	✓	✓	✓	✓	✓	✓
Arrangements in respect of registration and recording of legal titles			✓			
Segregation of client money				✓		
Safe custody assets used only as permitted by the CASS Rules	✓		✓			
4. **Accurate records and accounts:** The firm should have records and accounts that are maintained with sufficient accuracy (and on a timely basis) to enable the firm to comply with the CASS Rules	✓	✓	✓	✓		✓
5. **Reconciliations:** The firm should perform internal and external reconciliations in accordance with the CASS Rules at the requisite frequency in order to rectify discrepancies.						✓

PRINCIPLE	CASS 3 Collateral	CASS 5 Insurance Intermediaries	CASS 6 Custody Assets	CASS 7 Client Money	CASS 8 Mandates	CASS 11 Debt management firms
6	**Rectify discrepancies in reconciliations:** The firm should ensure that discrepancies arising from reconciliations are rectified appropriately.		✓	✓	✓		✓
7	**Trust:** The firm should notify and obtain acknowledgement of trust status over client money.		✓				✓
8	**Non-statutory trust:** The firm should ensure that the conditions for establishing a non-statutory trust are met		✓				
9	**Custody agreements:** The firm should have appropriate custody arrangements setting out the status of client custody accounts and prohibiting inappropriate liens			✓			
10	**Client money distributions:** The firm should ensure that client money distributions are carried out in accordance with the CASS Rules				✓		✓

Status of Standard

12 The Standard contains requirements indicated by paragraphs in bold type with which a CASS auditor is required to comply in the conduct of an engagement to report to the FCA in respect of Client Assets. The Standard also includes implementation guidance, including appendices, in the context of which the basic principles and essential procedures are to be understood and applied. The Standard is the material referred to in SUP 3.10.5B G to which the FCA expects CASS auditors to have regard for reports for periods commencing on or after 1 January 2016.

Reasonable Assurance Client Assets Reports

13 Where the firm holds custody assets and/or client money, the SUP rules require the CASS auditor to provide a Reasonable Assurance Client Assets Report to the FCA. This is a direct reporting assurance engagement whereby the CASS auditor's opinion (subject matter information) is expressed in terms of the "underlying subject matter" and the "applicable criteria" rather than as an opinion on an assertion made by management.

14 The objective of the CASS auditor is to carry out procedures which will provide a high but not absolute level of assurance that reduces "assurance engagement risk" to an acceptably low level as a basis for a positive form of expression of the CASS auditor's opinion.

Underlying Subject Matter

15 The "underlying subject matter" of a reasonable assurance engagement is:

(a) The adequacy of the systems maintained by the firm to enable it to comply with the relevant CASS rules throughout the period since the last date at which a report was made;

(b) The firm's compliance with the relevant CASS rules at the period end date; and

(c) The Breaches Schedule appended to the CASS auditor's report.

Reasonable Assurance Process

16 An overview of the process to form the opinion as to whether the firm was in compliance with the relevant CASS rules throughout and at the end of the period and the relevant considerations relating to various stages in the process is depicted in Appendix 1 of the Client Asset Assurance Standard.

17 Procedures required to form the opinion on the adequacy of systems involve:

(a) evaluating the design of the systems and controls;

(b) evaluating whether those systems and controls had been put into place during the period; and

(c) testing the effectiveness of the operation of the systems and controls during the period.

18 Procedures required to form the opinion on compliance with the CASS rules at the period end date involve evaluating whether or not the firm was in compliance with all relevant CASS rules at that date.

Applicable Criteria

Applicable criteria may comprise a combination of: **19**

(a)   Provisions of the CASS Sourcebook having the suffix "R" (see paragraph 21);

(b)   Waivers and Modifications granted by the FCA (see paragraph 26); and

(c)   Individual guidance from the FCA to a firm (see paragraph 27).

Applicable Criteria – The CASS rules in the CASS Sourcebook

The applicable criteria used to evaluate the subject matter are the relevant CASS   **20**
rules and any other rules of the FCA that are applicable to the firm. For this
purpose a "rule" is a provision of the CASS Sourcebook having the suffix "R" (see
paragraph 21).

The CASS Sourcebook contain different types of provisions whose status is   **21**
indicated by different suffixes:

(a)   "R" – Rule;

(b)   "E" – Evidential Provision (An evidential provision is a rule that is not
binding in its own right. It always relates to another binding rule).

(c)   "G" – Guidance.

A rule is a binding obligation on firms that the FCA regulates and if contravened a   **22**
firm commits a "breach" which renders it subject to potential enforcement action
and in some circumstances an action for damages.

Applicable Criteria – Guidance in the CASS Sourcebook

A number of the provisions in the CASS Sourcebook are guidance (rather than   **23**
rules). CASS guidance can have a number of objectives such as indicating the
implications of other provisions, possible means of compliance to linked rules; or
recommending a particular course of action or arrangement. Guidance is generally
designed to throw light on a particular aspect of regulatory requirements, not to be
an exhaustive description of firm's obligations.

Guidance in the CASS rules are not applicable criteria per se. However, where a   **24**
firm has not followed the guidance, the CASS auditor carefully considers whether
the firm has, nevertheless, remained in compliance with the linked rule. In some
circumstances, if the firm chooses not to apply the guidance it may need to
undertake actions specified in a rule in order to comply with that rule.

References to CASS rules and guidance in the Standard

Members of a CASS engagement team need to have an appropriate knowledge of   **25**
the CASS Sourcebook. Although references to certain CASS rules and guidance
are made in the Standard and accompanying implementation guidance, such
references are not a substitute for an understanding of the CASS Sourcebook as a
whole. Any references to specific CASS rules and guidance in the Standard and
accompanying implementation guidance are not, and should not be construed as
being, interpretations of such rules or guidance.

Applicable Criteria – Waivers and Modifications

A firm can apply to the FCA for a waiver or a modification of provisions in CASS.   **26**
If a waiver or modification is granted by the FCA, the firm must comply with the
waiver or modification in accordance with the formal written direction provided to

that firm by the FCA. If the CASS auditor determines a firm has received any CASS-related waiver or modification notices it must use the provisions set out in the waiver or modification as criteria. A breach of the waiver or modification provision relating to a CASS rule constitutes a breach that is reportable in the breaches schedule.

Applicable Criteria – Individual Guidance

27 The FCA can also provide individual guidance to a firm about how it should interpret a particular provision in the particular circumstances that apply to the firm. Such individual guidance may be requested by the firm or can be provided to a firm on the FCA's initiative. If the guidance has not been provided in writing, the CASS auditor would normally request written confirmation of the guidance. Such individual guidance constitutes "criteria" for the CASS auditor.

Breaches Schedule

28 The CASS auditor is required to provide the FCA with a schedule (appended to its report) which lists each CASS rule in respect of which a breach has been identified. The breaches schedule is required to include every breach of a rule that is within the scope of the Client Assets Report of which the CASS auditor is aware, whether identified by the CASS auditor or disclosed to the CASS auditor by the firm or by any third party.

Limited Assurance Client Assets Reports for investment businesses

29 The need for a Limited Assurance Client Assets Report for an investment business may arise under two general circumstances:

(a)   Firms that have permission to hold either custody assets or client money may claim not to hold them; or

(b)   The scope of the firm's permissions may not include the holding of client money or custody assets.

30 The CASS auditor is required under such circumstances to provide its opinion as to whether "nothing has come to its attention that causes it to believe that the firm held client money or custody assets during the period". In the Standard, requirements in relation to the provision of limited assurance reports are addressed separately from the requirements in relation to the provision of reasonable assurance reports.

Need to understand the firm's business model

31 In order to provide a basis for establishing expectations about the existence or otherwise of client assets, the auditor needs to have a sufficient understanding of the firm's business model to enable it to assess:

(a)   In the case of a firm having permission to hold client assets and actually holding such assets, whether the existence of all categories of client assets are being reported to the FCA; and

(b)   In the case of a firm claiming not to hold client assets, whether the claim is valid based on the CASS auditor's knowledge of the business model.

CASS Operational Oversight

32 It is critical for the firm to understand the interrelationship of its business model and inflows and outflows of cash and assets with the CASS rules. It is important for the CASS auditor to be knowledgeable of the firm's understanding of the interrelationship. Following the crisis, investment firms (but not insurance intermediaries) are now required to appoint an individual to be responsible for oversight of the firm's operational compliance with CASS. Dependent on the quantum of client money or assets held, this individual is either appointed to fulfil a controlled function known as the CF10a or is a director or senior manager approved for another significant influence function.

The Client Money and Asset Return (CMAR), which a firm is required to submit **33** to the FCA periodically, is intended to give the FCA an overview of firm-specific CASS positions and an overview of CASS holdings.

The CASS auditor is not required to report on the firm's compliance with the **34** CMAR requirements. However, reading the CMAR is likely to assist the CASS auditor in understanding the firm's business. The CASS auditor, therefore, should review the firm's CMAR submissions and assess their consistency with its knowledge of the firm's business. If such reviews reveal inconsistencies between the CMARs and the CASS auditor's understanding, it seeks to understand the reasons for the inconsistencies.

Requisite mind-sets

The CASS auditor should have a *compliance mind-set* of seeking to identify the **35** firm's breaches of the CASS rules in order to report those breaches to the FCA to assist it in its risk assessment of the firm's systems and controls.

A key objective of the CASS rules, of keeping client assets separate from the **36** assets of the firm, is to minimise the risk, if the firm becomes insolvent, of legal impediments preventing the ultimate beneficial owners from recovering their assets. Consistent with this objective, CASS auditors need to adopt an *insolvency mind-set*. Such a mind-set, although not requiring the CASS auditor to be an expert in insolvency law, does require the CASS auditor to actively consider the firm's client asset procedures and status against a level of stress which presumes that the firm may become insolvent.

Attitude of professional scepticism

An attitude of professional scepticism is essential to ensure that the CASS **37** engagement leader and CASS engagement team make critical assessments, with a questioning mind, of the validity of assurance evidence obtained and, in particular, are alert for evidence that contradicts or brings into question the reliability of documents or representations.

The CASS engagement team assesses the information and explanations, provided **38** by the directors and management of the firm, critically and, where appropriate, considers them in the context of its knowledge and findings derived from other areas of work undertaken with the same client.

Planning and performing the CASS audit

The concept of materiality as used in financial statement auditing is not applicable **39** to the risk assessment processes of a CASS auditor. This is because the determination of materiality essentially involves the determination of a monetary threshold amount and the CASS auditor does not evaluate and report on monetary amounts but on the adequacy of systems and compliance with the CASS rules.

40 The extent and nature of a CASS auditor's risk assessment procedures is driven by the CASS auditor's evaluation of the "significance" to its opinion of a firm's failure to comply with a CASS rule. Evaluating "significance" involves a combined assessment of the likelihood of a firm failing to adequately manage or mitigate a risk and an assessment of whether client assets have been dealt with in accordance with the CASS rules.

41 The CASS auditor's work should be designed to provide either reasonable or limited assurance. The CASS auditor is not required to provide absolute assurance and, therefore, the concepts of "significance" and sampling may be applied by the CASS auditor both in developing its CASS methodology and when planning and performing individual CASS audits.

42 Significance and sampling are applied as the basis for the CASS auditor's judgments for:

(a) Determining the nature, timing and extent of risk assessment procedures;

(b) Identifying and assessing the risk of non-compliance with individual CASS rules; and

(c) Determining the nature, timing and extent of further CASS audit procedures to test the firm's compliance with the CASS rules, in particular the determination of sample sizes when testing internal controls.

Reporting Breaches to the FCA

43 The FCA requires all breaches identified by both the CASS auditor and disclosed to it by the firm to be reported to it by the CASS auditor. The materiality or significance of a breach of the CASS rules, therefore, are not relevant considerations in determining whether the breach of a CASS rule needs to be reported to the FCA by the CASS auditor. For example, a failure to place client money promptly into a segregated client bank account is a reportable breach of the CASS rules regardless of whether the amount concerned is £5 or £5 million.

Awareness of insolvency and trust law

44 As discussed above, when providing assurance on client assets the CASS auditor is expected to have an understanding of how the CASS rules seek to effectively segregate client assets within the context of applicable trust and insolvency law. The extent of the understanding that the CASS auditor should have is that which enables it to appreciate the likely effectiveness of the firm's procedures in protecting client assets were it to become insolvent.

45 In this regard it is important that CASS auditors appreciate that insolvency law has application to legal entities rather than to businesses within consolidated groups that may encompass a number of legal entities or form only part of a legal entity. As insolvency law may not permit the Courts to see through the "corporate veil" of the limited liability of individual legal entities, client asset protection usually needs to be structured in the context of the legal entity that holds those client assets rather than in the context of the business within which that legal entity operates. If a CASS auditor becomes aware that client assets are being transferred to affiliates such that they may no longer enjoy the same legal protection as if they had not been transferred, the CASS auditor considers taking advice on the implications for either its Client Assets Report or its other responsibilities.

Internal control

A firm's systems and controls over client assets may be quite distinct from the **46** systems and controls that it has over its own assets. Consequently, it would be wholly inappropriate for the CASS auditor to draw conclusions about the design and operating effectiveness of the systems and controls over client assets based on evaluations of the firm's systems and controls over its own assets.

For these reasons the work required to express an opinion on the adequacy of the **47** systems as required by the CASS rules may require a much more detailed evaluation of design and operating effectiveness of internal controls over client assets than that obtained by an auditor in order to express an opinion on the financial statements.

Third party administration of client assets

Firms may enter into arrangements with a "Third Party Administrator" (TPA) to **48** outsource the operation of certain functions that are relevant to the firm's compliance with CASS rules. Such arrangements may be structured such that the firm retains full regulatory responsibility for compliance with CASS rules in respect of the outsourced functions. In simple terms, the firm retains regulatory responsibility where the TPA does not have a contractual relationship with the firm's client and simply has a contractual obligation to the firm to perform certain services on its behalf.

Alternatively, the firm and its TPA may agree to an arrangement in which the TPA **49** takes direct responsibility for compliance with some or all of the provisions in CASS rules. In the stockbroking industry this may arise where a second firm takes responsibility for the stockbrokers' clearing and settlement activities (give up broking). In such a scenario, the second firm is responsible for compliance with the FCA's rules (including the CASS rules) insofar as they apply to clearing and settlement processes that are the subject of the arrangement.

A TPA can only assume such responsibility if it is authorised by the FCA to **50** conduct investment business and has the requisite permission from the FCA to hold or control the client money and/or custody assets in question. Such a transfer of responsibility only occurs if the firm's clients enter into terms of business with the TPA to establish that the TPA will be directly responsible to the client under CASS rules for protecting the clients' money or assets. In order to do so, the firm, the TPA and the client may enter into a tripartite agreement that reflects the terms of business between both firms and the client. Alternatively, the firm and the TPA may each enter into separate agreements with the client to achieve this.

The actual arrangements entered into by firms can be extremely complex and **51** members of a CASS audit engagement team need to have a thorough understanding both of the arrangements with the TPA and the firm's clients and of the firm's business model, particularly of the cash and other asset inflows and outflows as they apply both to the firm and to the TPA. This understanding provides a basis for establishing the respective regulatory responsibilities of the firm and (if any) the TPA for client assets and, therefore, expectations about the existence or otherwise of client assets.

Forming and managing the Client Asset Engagement Team

It is important that careful consideration is given both to the composition of the **52** Client Asset Engagement Team and the manner in which it is managed and organised. As members of the CASS engagement team need to have knowledge and understanding of the CASS and other relevant FCA Rules sufficient to perform the engagement, the CASS engagement should not be considered to be a part of the statutory audit of the financial statements. Reporting on client assets is a distinct specialism requiring, in respect of more complex firms, that the members of the engagement team should include client asset specialists.

53 The nature of many firms' businesses requires them to respond to rapidly changing and evolving markets. New and more sophisticated products and practices may require specialist assurance responses from the CASS engagement team. It is important, therefore, that the CASS engagement team is familiar with current practice.

54 In determining whether the proposed assurance engagement team collectively possess the requisite professional competency, the CASS engagement leader assesses whether they have sufficient knowledge of the specific aspects of the industry within which the firm operates and its corresponding products. The CASS engagement leader also assesses whether the client asset engagement team has sufficient knowledge of the regulatory framework within which the firm operates commensurate with their roles in the engagement.

55 In larger and more complex regulated firms handling client assets, the firm will rely on IT systems, for instance to synchronise and reconcile custody assets and client money, and exchange data with custodians. The use of IT specialists, appropriately trained in the implications of their work for the work of the CASS auditor, should be considered by the CASS engagement leader.

Training

56 The different mind-set required to complete CASS assurance engagement coupled with the FCA's information needs from the CASS auditor have implications for the training of CASS auditors. The CASS engagement team is likely to need training relevant to the circumstances of the engagement, for instance in the following:

(a) The FCA's CASS rules and in particular what constitutes a breach of those Rules;

(b) The firm's business model such that reasonable expectations can be developed by the CASS auditor as to whether a firm is likely to have client assets;

(c) Practical problems associated with the performance and review of internal and external client asset reconciliations;

(d) Assessing the design effectiveness of the systems of internal control over client assets, evaluating whether the systems of internal control were in effect throughout the period and operating effectively; and

(e) Insolvency and trust law in so far as to create an awareness of how the principles of segregation and tracing protect the rights of beneficial owners of client assets in the event of the insolvency of a firm.

57 The CASS auditor is engaged to report on compliance with the CASS Rules. The question of whether or not client assets are effectively ring-fenced is a legal determination and CASS auditors, when reporting on compliance with CASS, are not expected to interpret the general law or predict whether the Courts would determine that assets have been effectively ring-fenced.

58 When providing assurance on client assets the CASS auditor is expected to understand what the CASS Rules are seeking to achieve within the context of trust

and insolvency law. The extent of the understanding that the CASS auditor should have is that which enables it to be sceptical about the likely effectiveness of the firm's procedures in protecting client assets were it to become insolvent.

Special Reports

The CASS rules permit, in certain circumstances, firms to operate:

(a)   An "alternative approach" to client money segregation; and

(b)   A "non-standard method" of internal client money reconciliation.

In both cases the FCA expect the firm to obtain, before carrying out the proposed **59** approach/method, an auditor's report prepared on the basis of a reasonable assurance engagement to the effect that the proposed approach/method will achieve the desired regulatory outcome. The Client Asset Assurance Standard has a separate section of requirements relating to the provision of reasonable assurance with respect to such Special Reports.

Bulletin: Compendium of illustrative auditor's reports on United Kingdom private sector financial statements for periods commencing on or after 17 June 2016

(October 2016)

Contents

	Paragraphs
Introduction	1 - 4
Describing the applicable financial reporting framework	5
Modifications to the auditor's opinion	6 - 8
Opinion in respect of an additional financial reporting framework	9 - 11
Going concern	12 - 14
No material uncertainty identified	15
Material uncertainty identified and adequately disclosed	16
Emphasis of matter and other matter paragraphs	17 - 19
Other information	20 - 22
Strategic report and directors' report	23 - 27
Corporate governance statement	28
Corporate governance statement included as a separate report	29 - 32
Corporate governance statement is included in the directors' report or incorporated in the directors' report by cross reference	33
UK Corporate Governance Code reporting	34
Reporting where the auditor has identified a material misstatement of the other information	35 - 37
Location of the description of the auditor's responsibilities for the audit of the financial statements	38 - 40
Directors' remuneration report	41 - 44
Auditor's reports where consolidated financial statements are prepared	
Omitting the parent company profit and loss account	45 - 46
Alternative presentation options of the financial statements of a group	47 - 52
Appendices	
Appendix 1: Non-publicly traded company preparing financial statements under the small companies regime	
Appendix 2: Non-publicly traded company preparing group and parent company financial statements under UK GAAP	

Appendix 3: Publicly traded AIM listed company preparing financial statements under IFRSs with an emphasis of matter paragraph

Appendix 4: Unlisted public interest entity preparing financial statements under UK GAAP with a material uncertainty related to going concern

Appendix 5: Publicly traded standard listed company preparing group financial statements under IFRSs and parent company financial statements under UK GAAP

Appendix 6: Publicly traded premium listed company preparing group and parent company financial statements under IFRSs

Appendix: Auditor's responsibilities for the audit of the financial statements

Appendix 7A: Publicly traded premium listed company preparing group financial statements under IFRSs (reported on separately from the parent company financial statements)

Appendix 7B: Publicly traded premium listed company preparing parent company financial statements under UK GAAP (reported on separately from the group financial statements)

Editorial note – The FRC published this Compendium which contains examples of auditor's reports illustrating the reporting requirements of the recently revised International Standards on Auditing (UK) (ISAs (UK)) effective for audits of financial statements for periods commencing on or after 17 June 2016.

The FRC has also published a revised description of the auditor's responsibilities for the audit of the financial statements for audits of periods beginning on or after 17 June 2016.

Recent revisions to the ISAs (UK) affect both the auditor's duties and the wording of auditor's reports on the financial statements of companies. This Compendium of illustrative auditor's reports provides a useful reference source for practitioners, and is designed to be persuasive rather than prescriptive as the FRC continues to support profession-led innovation in auditor reporting which promotes audit quality.

Introduction

This Compendium of illustrative auditor's reports is applicable to United   **1**
Kingdom private sector financial statements for periods commencing on or after
17 June 2016. The auditor's reports set out in the Appendices support and
illustrate how the requirements of ISA (UK) 700 (Revised June 2016)[1] and
other reporting requirements of the ISAs (UK) can be applied. They also illustrate
the requirements of the law and regulations applicable to the particular type of
entity to which the illustration applies.

However, other approaches may be adopted provided that the form and content of   **2**
the auditor's report meets the requirements of ISA (UK) 700 (Revised June 2016),
other relevant standards and applicable legal and regulatory requirements. The
FRC supports profession-led innovation in auditor reporting which promotes audit
quality and transparent and accessible auditor's reports for users of the audited
financial statements.

The auditor's report is the key deliverable addressing the output of the audit   **3**
process for users of the audited financial statements. It is therefore important that
the auditor's report is written in clear and unambiguous language.[2]

This Compendium replaces the guidance in: **4**

- Bulletin 2010/2 *Compendium of Illustrative Auditor's Reports on United Kingdom Private Sector Financial Statements for periods ended on or after 15 December 2010 (Revised)* (Updated March 2012); and

- Bulletin 4 *Recent Developments in Company Law, The Listing Rules and Auditing Standards that affect United Kingdom Auditor's Reports (Revised)* (Updated June 2015).

Describing the applicable financial reporting framework

In accordance with ISA (UK) 700 (Revised June 2016), the Opinion section of the   **5**
auditor's report shall make reference to the applicable financial reporting
framework used to prepare the financial statements. In the UK, the applicable
financial reporting framework is usually one of the following:

- International Financial Reporting Standards (IFRSs) as adopted by the European Union, and the national law that is applicable when using IFRSs and, in the case of consolidated financial statements of publicly traded companies,[3] Article 4 of the IAS Regulation (1606/2002/EC).

> The financial reporting framework that has been applied in their preparation is applicable law, and International Financial Reporting Standards (IFRSs) as adopted by the European Union.

- United Kingdom Generally Accepted Accounting Practice (UK GAAP), which comprises applicable UK law including one of the following UK Accounting Standards as issued by the FRC:

---

[1] *ISA (UK) 700 (Revised June 2016) Forming an Opinion and Reporting on Financial Statements.*

[2] *ISA (UK) 700 (Revised June 2016), paragraph 20-1.*

[3] *A publicly traded company is one whose securities are admitted to trading on a regulated market in any Member State in the European Union.*

- Financial Reporting Standard 105,[4] where the financial statements are those of an entity that is eligible to apply FRS 105 and the entity opts to do so;[5]
- Financial Reporting Standard 101,[6] where the financial statements are the individual financial statements of a qualifying entity, and the entity opts to do so;
- Financial Reporting Standard 102.[7]

> The financial reporting framework that has been applied in their preparation is applicable law, and United Kingdom Accounting Standards, including [Financial Reporting Standard 101 *Reduced Disclosure Framework*] [Financial Reporting Standard 102 *The Financial Reporting Standard applicable in the UK and Republic of Ireland*] [Financial Reporting Standard 105 *The Financial Reporting Standard applicable to the Micro-entities Regime*] (United Kingdom Generally Accepted Accounting Practice).

Modifications to the auditor's opinion

6   Where the auditor:

- concludes that, based on the audit evidence obtained, the financial statements as a whole are not free from material misstatement; or
- is unable to obtain sufficient appropriate audit evidence to conclude that the financial statements as a whole are free from material misstatement,

the auditor is required to modify their opinion in the auditor's report in accordance with ISA (UK) 705 (Revised June 2016).[8]

7   The Appendix of ISA (UK) 705 (Revised June 2016) contains illustrations of auditor's reports with modifications to the opinion. Whilst these auditor's reports have not been tailored for the UK, they illustrate the requirements of the ISA (UK) where the auditor is required to modify or disclaim their opinion.

8   The auditor also considers the impact of any modified opinion on the financial statements on the auditor's other reporting responsibilities (including those on which they are required to report by exception). For example, if the auditor has been unable to obtain sufficient appropriate audit evidence to conclude that the financial statements as a whole are free from material misstatement, and issues a qualified or disclaimer of opinion arising from that limitation, the auditor considers whether a modified conclusion should be expressed on whether adequate accounting records have been maintained.[9]

---

[4] *Financial Reporting Standard 105 The Financial Reporting Standard applicable to the Micro-entities Regime (FRS 105).*

[5] *Entities which prepare their annual financial statements in accordance with FRS 105 are not required by UK legislation to have an audit and it is anticipated that the entity will opt to have an audit only in rare circumstances. Further guidance on such matters is included in paragraph A36-1 and A36-2 of ISA (UK) 210 (Revised June 2016) Agreeing the Terms of Audit Engagements.*

[6] *Financial Reporting Standard 101 Reduced Disclosures Framework (FRS 101).*

[7] *Financial Reporting Standard 102 The Financial Reporting Standard applicable in the UK and Republic of Ireland (FRS 102).*

[8] *ISA (UK) 705 (Revised June 2016) Modifications to the Opinion in the Independent Auditor's Report.*

[9] *Similarly, paragraph A58-3 of ISA (UK) 700 (Revised June 2016) sets out the circumstances where a modified conclusion in respect of other reporting responsibilities (including those on which they are required to report by exception) leads to a modification of the auditor's opinion on the financial statements.*

Opinion in respect of an additional financial reporting framework

The financial statements of some companies may be prepared in accordance with 9 two financial reporting frameworks[10] (for example IFRSs as adopted by the European Union and IFRSs as issued by the IASB).

In such circumstances, each framework is considered separately when forming the 10 auditor's opinion on the financial statements and the auditor's opinion refers to both frameworks.

These opinions may be expressed separately or in a single sentence. Appendix 6 11 illustrates where the opinion in respect of an additional financial reporting framework is expressed separately.

Going concern

ISA (UK) 570 (Revised June 2016)[11] sets out the reporting requirements in respect 12 of going concern.

This Compendium includes illustrative examples for the two most common 13 scenarios when reporting on going concern in an auditor's report as follows:

- Where the going concern basis of accounting is appropriate and no material uncertainty has been identified (see paragraph 15); and

- Where the going concern basis of accounting is appropriate and a material uncertainty has been identified and adequately disclosed in the financial statements (see paragraph 16).

For illustrative examples of auditor's reports with modified opinions relating to 14 going concern, see the Appendix in ISA (UK) 570 (Revised June 2016). Whilst these auditor's reports have not been tailored for the UK, they illustrate the requirements of the ISA (UK) where the auditor is required to modify their opinion or report that a material uncertainty exists.

No material uncertainty identified

Where the auditor concludes that management's use of the going concern basis of 15 accounting is appropriate in the circumstances and no material uncertainty has been identified, the auditor is required to report by exception on such matters.[12]

- Appendices 1, 2, 3, 5 and 7B illustrate reporting by exception under the heading Conclusions Relating to Going Concern.

- Appendices 6 and 7A provide alternative illustrations of these reporting requirements using an alternative heading.

---

[10] *ISA (UK) 700 (Revised June 2016), paragraph A13.*

[11] *ISA (UK) 570 (Revised June 2016) Going Concern.*

[12] *ISA (UK) 570 (Revised June 2016), paragraph 21-2.*

Material uncertainty identified and adequately disclosed

16   Where the auditor concludes that a material uncertainty exists and management has appropriately disclosed that fact in the financial statements, the auditor is required to express an unmodified opinion and include a separate section under the heading "Material Uncertainty Related to Going Concern".[13]

●   Appendix 4 illustrates a Material Uncertainty Related to Going Concern section.

Emphasis of matter and other matter paragraphs

17   ISA (UK) 706 (Revised June 2016)[14] deals with additional communication in the auditor's report when the auditor considers it necessary to:

●   Draw users' attention to a matter or matters presented or disclosed in the financial statements that are of such importance that they are fundamental to users' understanding of the financial statements (known as an Emphasis of Matter); or

●   Draw users' attention to any matter or matters other than those presented or disclosed in the financial statements that are relevant to users' understanding of the audit, the auditor's responsibilities or the auditor's report (known as an Other Matter).

18   Appendix 3 illustrates the inclusion of an emphasis of matter paragraph.

19   Appendices 4, 5, 6, 7A and 7B illustrate the inclusion of an other matter paragraph.

Other information

20   For entities that are required to prepare other information, as described in ISA (UK) 720 (Revised June 2016),[15] the auditor is required to report in the auditor's report on that other information in accordance with the ISA (UK). Appendices 1 to 7B include illustrative examples of Other Information sections.

21   The auditor's opinion on the financial statements does not cover the other information, nor is the auditor required to obtain audit evidence beyond that required to form an opinion on the financial statements, except in the circumstances:

●   where the auditor is required to express an opinion, based on the work undertaken in the course of the audit, on the statutory other information[16] and state the nature of the work performed by the auditor; or

●   otherwise in accordance with law or regulation.

---

[13]   *ISA (UK) 570 (Revised June 2016), paragraph 22.*

[14]   *ISA (UK) 706 (Revised June 2016) Emphasis of Matter Paragraphs and Other Matter Paragraphs in the Independent Auditor's Report.*

[15]   *ISA (UK) 720 (Revised June 2016) The Auditor's Responsibilities Relating to Other Information.*

[16]   *Statutory other information is defined in ISA (UK) 720 (Revised June 2016), paragraph 12(d). Where required to be prepared, this would include the directors' report, the strategic report and the separate corporate governance statement.*

Where statutory other information is not prepared, the auditor is required to include a statement that the auditor's opinion on the financial statements does not cover the other information. Where the entity has prepared statutory other information, the statement is amended as follows: **22**

Where statutory other information is not prepared	Where statutory other information is prepared
Other information	**Other information**
Our opinion on the financial statements does not cover the other information and we do not express any form of assurance conclusion thereon.	Our opinion on the financial statements does not cover the other information and, except to the extent otherwise explicitly stated in our report, we do not express any form of assurance conclusion thereon.

Strategic report and directors' report

For entities which are required to prepare a directors' report or a strategic report,[17] the auditor is required to express an opinion on whether the information in the strategic report and the directors' report is consistent with the financial statements and whether those reports have been prepared in accordance with the applicable legal requirements. **23**

The table below sets out the wording to be included in the auditor's report: **24**

Where only a directors' report is prepared	Where both a directors' report and a strategic report are prepared
Opinions on other matters prescribed by the Companies Act 2006	**Opinions on other matters prescribed by the Companies Act 2006**
In our opinion, based on the work undertaken in the course of the audit:	In our opinion, based on the work undertaken in the course of the audit:
• the information given in the directors' report for the financial year for which the financial statements are prepared is consistent with the financial statements; and	• the information given in the strategic report and the directors' report for the financial year for which the financial statements are prepared is consistent with the financial statements; and
• the directors' report has been prepared in accordance with applicable legal requirements.	• the strategic report and the directors' report have been prepared in accordance with applicable legal requirements.
See: Appendix 1	*See: Appendices 2, 3, 4, 5, 6, 7A and 7B*

---

[17] *Section 496 of the Companies Act 2006 as amended by The Companies, Partnerships and Groups (Accounts and Reports) Regulations 2015 sets out this requirement.*

25   Where a directors' report or a strategic report is required to be prepared, the auditor is also required to state whether, in the light of the knowledge and understanding of the entity and its environment obtained in the course of the audit, the auditor has identified any material misstatements in those reports as follows:

Where only a directors' report is prepared	Where both a directors' report and a strategic report are prepared
Matters on which we are required to report by exception	**Matters on which we are required to report by exception**
In the light of the knowledge and understanding of the company and its environment obtained in the course of the audit, we have not identified material misstatements in the directors' report.	In the light of the knowledge and understanding of the company and its environment obtained in the course of the audit, we have not identified material misstatements in the strategic report or the directors' report.
See: Appendix 1	*See: Appendices 2, 3, 4, 5, 6, 7A and 7B*

26   Where the directors of a company have taken advantage of the small companies exemptions in preparing the directors' report and to prepare a strategic report and in the auditor's opinion they were not entitled to do so, the auditor is required[18] to state that fact in the auditor's report.

> **Matters on which we are required to report by exception**
>
> We have nothing to report in respect of the following matters in relation to which the Companies Act 2006 requires us to report to you if, in our opinion:
>
> - ...; or
> - the directors were not entitled to prepare the financial statements in accordance with the small companies regime and take advantage of the small companies' exemptions in preparing the directors' report and from the requirement to prepare a strategic report.

27   Appendix 1 includes an example of the statement to include in the matters to report by exception in respect of this requirement.

Corporate governance statement

28   Publically traded companies are required to include a corporate governance statement in their annual report[19] either:

- As a specific section of the directors' report (DTR 7.2.1R); or
- In a separate report which is either;
  - published together with, and in the same manner as, its annual report (DTR 7.2.9(1)R); or
  - by means of a cross reference in its directors' report to where such document is publicly available on the company's website (DTR 7.2.9(2)R).

---

[18] *Subsection (5)(b) of Section 498 of The Companies Act 2006 sets out this requirement.*

[19] *The requirements relating to the content of the corporate governance statement are set out in Section 7.2 of the Disclosure and Transparency Rules (DTR) of the Financial Conduct Authority.*

Corporate governance statement included as a separate report

If the corporate governance statement is not included in the directors' report, the **29** Companies Act 2006 imposes specific reporting responsibilities on the auditor with respect to the corporate governance statement.[20]

Section 497A of the Companies Act 2006 requires the auditor to report on whether **30** certain information included in the corporate governance statement is consistent with the financial statements and has been prepared in accordance with applicable legal requirements, whether certain of the rules in the Disclosure Rules and Transparency Rules sourcebook made by the Financial Conduct Authority (the FCA Rules) have been complied with and whether the auditor has identified any material misstatements in this information.

The table below sets out illustrative wording to be included in the auditor's report **31** in such circumstances:

Opinion on other matters prescribed by the Companies Act 2006

In our opinion, based on the work undertaken in the course of the audit:

- the information about internal control and risk management systems in relation to financial reporting processes and about share capital structures, given in compliance with rules 7.2.5 and 7.2.6 in the Disclosure Rules and Transparency Rules sourcebook made by the Financial Conduct Authority (the FCA Rules), is consistent with the financial statements and has been prepared in accordance with applicable legal requirements; and

- information about the company's corporate governance code and practices and about its administrative, management and supervisory bodies and their committees complies with rules 7.2.2, 7.2.3 and 7.2.7 of the FCA Rules.

Matters on which we are required to report by exception

In the light of the knowledge and understanding of the company and its environment obtained in the course of the audit, we have not identified material misstatements in:

- the information about internal control and risk management systems in relation to financial reporting processes and about share capital structures, given in compliance with rules 7.2.5 and 7.2.6 of the FCA Rules.

Where the company is required to prepare a corporate governance statement, **32** Section 498A of the Companies Act 2006 also requires the auditor to report on whether or not the company has prepared such a statement. In such cases, the auditor includes the following statement in the auditor's report:

Matters on which we are required to report by exception

We have nothing to report in respect of the following matters in relation to which the Companies Act 2006 requires us to report to you if, in our opinion:

- ...; or

- a corporate governance statement has not been prepared by the company.

---

[20] *Guidance on the auditor's responsibilities in respect of the corporate governance statement is set out more fully in Bulletin 2009/4 Developments in Corporate Governance Affecting the Responsibilities of Auditors of UK Companies.*

Corporate governance statement is included in the directors' report or incorporated in the directors' report by cross reference

33   Where the corporate governance statement is included in the directors' report or incorporated in the directors' report by cross-reference, the reporting required by Sections 497A and 498A, and described in paragraphs 30 and 32, do not apply.

UK Corporate Governance Code reporting

34   For entities that are required, and those that choose voluntarily, to report on how they have applied the UK Corporate Governance Code the auditor also addresses specific elements of the other information in the auditor's report in accordance with paragraphs 22-3 and 22-4 of ISA (UK) 720 (Revised June 2016). These statements are included in Appendices 6 and 7A.

Reporting where the auditor has identified a material misstatement of the other information

35   Where the auditor concludes that there is an uncorrected material misstatement of the other information, the auditor is required to include a statement in the auditor's report that describes the material misstatement. ISA (UK) 720 (Revised June 2016) Appendix 2 includes such a statement in Illustrations 5, 6 and 7. Whilst these auditor's reports have not been tailored for the UK, they illustrate the requirements of the ISA (UK) where there is an uncorrected material misstatement of the other information.

36   Where the auditor concludes that there is an uncorrected material misstatement of the statutory other information, in addition to including the statement noted by paragraph 35, the auditor also considers the reporting implications for the specific opinions, conclusions or statements required by ISAs (UK), law or regulation.

37   The table below sets out example wording that the auditor includes in the auditor's report when a material misstatement of the other information, arising from an inconsistency between the other information and the financial statements, has been identified:

Other information

The other information comprises the information included in the annual report, other than the financial statements and our auditor's report thereon. The directors are responsible for the other information. Our opinion on the financial statements does not cover the other information and, except to the extent otherwise explicitly stated in our report, we do not express any form of assurance conclusion thereon.

In connection with our audit of the financial statements, our responsibility is to read the other information and, in doing so, consider whether the other information is materially inconsistent with the financial statements or our knowledge obtained in the audit or otherwise appears to be materially misstated. If we identify such material inconsistencies or apparent material misstatements, we are required to determine whether there is a material misstatement in the financial statements or a material misstatement of the other information.

If, based on the work we have performed, we conclude that there is a material misstatement of the other information, we are required to report that fact. As described in the Basis for qualified opinion on other matters prescribed by the Companies Act 2006 section of our report we have concluded that a material misstatement of the other information exists.

***

Qualified opinion on other matters prescribed by the Companies Act 2006

Except for the matter described in the Basis for qualified opinion on other matters prescribed by the Companies Act 2006 section of our report, in our opinion, based on the work undertaken in the course of the audit:

● the information given in the strategic report and the directors' report for the financial year for which the financial statements are prepared is consistent with the financial statements; and

● the strategic report and the directors' report have been prepared in accordance with applicable legal requirements.

Basis for qualified opinion on other matters prescribed by the Companies Act 2006

Based on the work undertaken in the course of the audit, the information given in the [*describe location*] of the [strategic / directors'] report is not consistent with the financial statements.

[*Description of material misstatement of statutory other information*]

***

Matters on which we are required to report by exception

Except for the material misstatement described in the Basis for qualified opinion on other matters prescribed by the Companies Act 2006 section of our report, in the light of the knowledge and understanding of the company and its environment obtained in the course of the audit, we have not identified material misstatements in the strategic report or the directors' report.

Location of the description of the auditor's responsibilities for the audit of the financial statements

ISA (UK) 700 (Revised June 2016)[21] permits the description of the auditor's responsibilities for the audit of the financial statements to be included either: **38**

● Within the body of the auditor's report;

● Within an appendix to the auditor's report, in which case the auditor's report includes a reference to the location of the appendix; or

● By a specific reference within the auditor's report to the location of such a description on a website of an appropriate authority.[22]

In the illustrative auditor's reports these alternatives are shown as follows: **39**

● Appendix 2 illustrates where the responsibilities are located within the body of the auditor's report.

● Appendix 6 illustrates where the responsibilities are located within an appendix to the auditor's report.

● Appendices 1, 3, 4, 5, 7A and 7B illustrate where a reference is included in the auditor's report to an appropriate website with a description of the responsibilities.

Further descriptions of the auditor's responsibilities are required to be included (either in the auditor's report, in an appendix or by cross-reference) when they are relevant to the circumstances of the particular audit as follows: **40**

---

[21] *ISA (UK) 700 (Revised June 2016), paragraph 41.*

[22] *The website reference is www.frc.org.uk/auditorsresponsibilities.*

(a)   When the financial statements are prepared in accordance with a fair presentation framework, the description of the auditor's responsibilities includes the responsibility to evaluate the overall presentation, structure and content of the financial statements, including the disclosures, and whether the financial statements represent the underlying transactions and events in a manner that achieves fair presentation. As noted in paragraph 5, the applicable financial reporting frameworks in the UK are either IFRSs as adopted by the EU or UK GAAP, both of which are fair presentation frameworks, hence this paragraph is usually required for audits of financial statements in the UK.

(b)   When ISA (UK) 600 (Revised June 2016)[23] applies the following paragraph is included in the description of the auditor's responsibilities for the audit of the financial statements:

> **Auditor's responsibilities for the audit of the financial statements**
> We also:
> - Obtain sufficient appropriate audit evidence regarding the financial information of the entities or business activities within the group to express an opinion on the [consolidated] financial statements. We are responsible for the direction, supervision and performance of the group audit. We remain solely responsible for our audit opinion.

Appendices 2 and 6 include such a description of the auditor's responsibilities in a group audit engagement.

(c)   When the entity is listed[24] the following statement should be included in the auditor's report:

> **Auditor's responsibilities for the audit of the financial statements**
> We also provide those charged with governance with a statement that we have complied with relevant ethical requirements regarding independence, and to communicate with them all relationships and other matters that may reasonably be thought to bear on our independence, and where applicable, related safeguards.

Appendix 6 illustrates such a description.

(d)   When key audit matters are communicated in accordance with ISA (UK) 701[25] the following statement is included in the auditor's report:

> **Auditor's responsibilities for the audit of the financial statements**
> From the matters communicated with those charged with governance, we determine those matters that were of most significance in the audit of the consolidated financial statements of the current period and are therefore the key audit matters. We describe these matters in our auditor's report unless law or regulation precludes public disclosure about the matter or when, in extremely rare circumstances, we determine that a matter should not be communicated in our report because the adverse consequences of doing so would reasonably be expected to outweigh the public interest benefits of such communication.

Appendix 6 illustrates such a description.

---

[23] *ISA (UK) 600 (Revised June 2016) Special Considerations—Audits of Group Financial Statements (Including the Work of Component Auditors).*

[24] *"Listed entity" is defined in paragraph 7(g) of ISA (UK) 220 (Revised June 2016) Quality Control for an Audit of Financial Statements.*

[25] *ISA (UK) 701 Communicating Key Audit Matters in the Independent Auditor's Report.*

Directors' remuneration report

Quoted companies[26] are required to prepare a directors' remuneration report[27] and   **41**
the auditor has to report on certain aspects of that Report. Companies should
describe clearly within the directors' remuneration report which disclosures have
been audited.

Section 497 of the Companies Act 2006 requires the auditor to report to the   **42**
company's members on whether the auditable part of the directors' remuneration
report has been properly prepared in accordance with the Act. The auditor includes
the following wording in the auditor's report:

Opinion on other matters prescribed by the Companies Act 2006

In our opinion the part of the directors' remuneration report to be audited
has been properly prepared in accordance with the Companies Act 2006.

Section 498 of the Companies Act 2006 also requires the auditor to report on   **43**
whether the auditable part of the directors' remuneration report is not in agreement
with the accounting records and returns. The following underlined text is inserted
into the matters on which the auditor is required to report by exception as follows:

Matters on which we are required to report by exception

We have nothing to report in respect of the following matters in relation to
which the Companies Act 2006 requires us to report to you if, in our opinion:

● ...; or

● the financial statements and the part of the directors' remuneration report to
be audited are not in agreement with the accounting records and returns; or

---

Appendices 5, 6 and 7B illustrate the reporting requirements relating to the   **44**
directors' remuneration report.

Auditor's reports where consolidated financial statements are prepared

Omitting the parent company profit and loss account

Section 408 of the Companies Act 2006 allows a company that prepares group   **45**
accounts to omit the parent company's profit and loss account from the company's
financial statements provided that:

● the notes to the parent company's balance sheet show the parent company's
profit or loss for the financial year determined in accordance with the
Companies Act 2006; and

---

[26] *The definition of "quoted company" for the purposes of the directors' remuneration report is set out in Sections
385(1) and 385(2) of the Companies Act 2006. The definition of a quoted company differs from that of a publicly
traded company. A publicly traded company may not necessarily meet the definition of a quoted company and a
non-publicly traded company may be a quoted company.*

[27] *Part 3 of Schedule 8 to the Large and Medium-sized Companies and Groups (Accounts and Reports)
Regulations 2008 (SI 2008 No. 410) sets out the information in the directors' remuneration report that is
subject to audit.*

- it is disclosed in the parent company's financial statements that the exemption applies.

46   The table below illustrates the difference in the wording that is required to be inserted where the Section 408 exemption has been taken in respect of the parent company's own profit and loss account and where it has not been taken.

Where Section 408 exemption taken	Where Section 408 exemption not taken
Opinion	**Opinion**
We have audited the financial statements of [*name*] for the year ended [*date*] which comprise [*specify the titles of the primary statements*] and notes to the financial statements, including a summary of significant accounting policies. The financial reporting framework that has been applied in their preparation is applicable law and International Financial Reporting Standards (IFRSs) as adopted by the European Union and, as regards the parent company financial statements, as applied in accordance with the provisions of the Companies Act 2006.	We have audited the financial statements of [*name*] for the year ended [*date*] which comprise [*specify the titles of the primary statements*] and notes to the financial statements, including a summary of significant accounting policies. The financial reporting framework that has been applied in their preparation is applicable law and International Financial Reporting Standards (IFRSs) as adopted by the European Union.
In our opinion:	In our opinion the financial statements:
<ul><li>the financial statements give a true and fair view of the state of the group's and of the parent company's affairs as at [*date*] and of the group's [profit / loss] for the year then ended;</li><li>the group financial statements have been properly prepared in accordance with IFRSs as adopted by the European Union;</li><li>the parent company financial statements have been properly prepared in accordance with IFRSs as adopted by the European Union and as applied in accordance with the provisions of the Companies Act 2006; and</li><li>the financial statements have been prepared in accordance with the requirements of the Companies Act 2006 and, as regards the group financial statements, Article 4 of the IAS Regulation.</li></ul>	<ul><li>give a true and fair view of the state of the group's and of the parent company's affairs as at [*date*] and of the group's and the parent company's [profit / loss] for the year then ended;</li><li>have been properly prepared in accordance with IFRSs as adopted by the European Union; and</li><li>have been prepared in accordance with the requirements of the Companies Act 2006 and, as regards the group financial statements, Article 4 of the IAS Regulation.</li></ul>

Alternative presentation options of the financial statements of a group

Group and parent company financial statements may be prepared in accordance **47** with different financial reporting frameworks (for example IFRSs as adopted by the EU used for the group financial statements and UK GAAP used for the parent company financial statements).

Where the financial statements of the group and the parent company are presented **48** in accordance with different financial reporting frameworks the financial statements might be presented separately within the annual report and in such circumstances separate auditor's reports might be provided.[28]

Where separate auditor's reports are provided on the group and parent company **49** financial statements, the requirements of ISA (UK) 701 still apply to each separate auditor's report. Therefore, key audit matters and other audit planning and scoping matters are required to be communicated in respect of both the group and the parent company audits. The auditor may be able to avoid unnecessary duplication in respect of the auditor's reporting responsibilities by incorporating into the auditor's report by cross-reference the location of where such information can be accessed, so long as that cross-referenced material is readily accessible. However, there is certain information required by law or regulation that must be included in the auditor's report to which the financial statements relate.[29]

Appendices 2, 4 and 6 illustrate an auditor's reports where the report on the group **50** financial statements and the report on the parent company financial statements are presented as a single auditor's report.

Appendix 7 illustrates auditor's reports where the group and the parent company **51** financial statements are presented separately. In such cases, the auditor might provide separate auditor's reports on the group financial statements (see Appendix 7A) and on the parent company financial statements (see Appendix 7B).

Where separate auditor's reports are provided on the group and parent company **52** financial statements the illustrative examples assume that:

● The auditor's responsibilities with respect to the corporate governance statement are reported on in the auditor's report on the group financial statements;

● The auditor's responsibilities with respect to the UK Corporate Governance Code are reported on in the auditor's report on the group financial statements; and

● The directors' remuneration report is reported on in the auditor's report on the parent company financial statements.

However, other approaches may be adopted.

---

[28] *The Companies Act 2006 does not require the directors to sign the group balance sheet and thereby evidence their approval of it. Where separate financial statements are presented the auditor obtains evidence of the directors' approval of the group financial statements before signing the auditor's report on those group financial statements.*

[29] *ISA (UK) 701, paragraph A33-5.*

Appendices

- Appendix 1—Non-publicly traded company preparing financial statements under the small companies regime

- Appendix 2—Non-publicly traded company preparing group and parent company financial statements under UK GAAP

- Appendix 3—Publicly traded AIM listed company preparing financial statements under IFRSs with an emphasis of matter paragraph

- Appendix 4—Unlisted public interest entity preparing financial statements under UK GAAP with a material uncertainty related to going concern

- Appendix 5—Publicly traded standard listed company preparing group financial statements under IFRSs and parent company financial statements under UK GAAP

- Appendix 6—Publicly traded premium listed company preparing group and parent company financial statements under IFRSs

- Appendix 7A—Publicly traded premium listed company preparing group financial statements under IFRSs (reported on separately from the parent company financial statements)

- Appendix 7B—Publicly traded premium listed company preparing parent company financial statements under UK GAAP (reported on separately from the group financial statements)

Appendix 1

Non-publicly traded company preparing financial statements under the small companies regime

- Company qualifies as a small company and is not a public interest entity

- Financial statements are prepared in accordance with FRSs 100 and 102 (UK GAAP)

- Directors take advantage of the small companies' exemption in preparing the directors' report and from the requirement to prepare a strategic report

- Company does not prepare group financial statements or ISA (UK) 600 (Revised June 2016) does not otherwise apply

- Description of the auditor's responsibilities for the audit of the financial statements is included by reference to the location of such a description included on the FRC's website

- Auditor is not required, and has otherwise not decided, to communicate key audit matters in accordance with ISA (UK) 701

Independent auditor's report to the members of [XYZ Limited]

Opinion

We have audited the financial statements of [XYZ Limited] (the "company") for the year ended [*date*] which comprise [*specify the titles of the primary statements*][30] and notes to the financial statements, including a summary of significant accounting policies. The financial reporting framework that has been applied in their preparation is applicable law and United Kingdom Accounting Standards, including Financial Reporting Standard 102 *The Financial Reporting Standard applicable in the UK and Republic of Ireland* (United Kingdom Generally Accepted Accounting Practice).

In our opinion, the financial statements:

- give a true and fair view of the state of the company's affairs as at [*date*] and of its [profit/loss] for the year then ended;

- have been properly prepared in accordance with United Kingdom Generally Accepted Accounting Practice;

- have been prepared in accordance with the requirements of the Companies Act 2006.

---

[30] *The terms used to describe the primary financial statements should be the same as those used by the directors.*

Basis for opinion

We conducted our audit in accordance with International Standards on Auditing (UK) (ISAs (UK)) and applicable law. Our responsibilities under those standards are further described in the Auditor's responsibilities for the audit of the financial statements section of our report. We are independent of the company in accordance with the ethical requirements that are relevant to our audit of the financial statements in the UK, including the FRC's Ethical Standard[, and the provisions available for small entities, in the circumstances set out in note [X][31] to the financial statements][32], and we have fulfilled our other ethical responsibilities in accordance with these requirements. We believe that the audit evidence we have obtained is sufficient and appropriate to provide a basis for our opinion.

Conclusions relating to going concern

We have nothing to report in respect of the following matters in relation to which the ISAs (UK) require us to report to you where:

- the directors' use of the going concern basis of accounting in the preparation of the financial statements is not appropriate; or

- the directors have not disclosed in the financial statements any identified material uncertainties that may cast significant doubt about the company's ability to continue to adopt the going concern basis of accounting for a period of at least twelve months from the date when the financial statements are authorised for issue.

Other information

The other information comprises the information included in the annual report,[33] other than the financial statements and our auditor's report thereon. The directors are responsible for the other information. Our opinion on the financial statements does not cover the other information and, except to the extent otherwise explicitly stated in our report, we do not express any form of assurance conclusion thereon. In connection with our audit of the financial statements, our responsibility is to read the other information and, in doing so, consider whether the other information is materially inconsistent with the financial statements or our knowledge obtained in the audit or otherwise appears to be materially misstated. If we identify such material inconsistencies or apparent material misstatements, we are required to determine whether there is a material misstatement in the financial statements or a material misstatement of the other information. If, based on the work we have performed, we conclude that there is a material misstatement of this other information, we are required to report that fact.

We have nothing to report in this regard.

---

[31] *Delete the words in square brackets if the relief and exemptions for audits of small entities provided by the FRC's Ethical Standard are not utilised.*

[32] *As described in paragraph A35-4 of ISA (UK) 700 (Revised June 2016), the FRC's Ethical Standard Section 6 Provisions available for audits of small entities, paragraph 6.15 requires disclosure in the auditor's report where the audit firm has taken advantage of an exemption provided in paragraphs 6.11, 6.12 or 6.13 of the Ethical Standard.*

[33] *The term used to describe the annual report should be the same as that used by the directors.*

Opinions on other matters prescribed by the Companies Act 2006

In our opinion, based on the work undertaken in the course of the audit:

- the information given in the directors' report for the financial year for which the financial statements are prepared is consistent with the financial statements; and

- the directors' report has been prepared in accordance with applicable legal requirements.

Matters on which we are required to report by exception

In the light of the knowledge and understanding of the company and its environment obtained in the course of the audit, we have not identified material misstatements in the directors' report.

We have nothing to report in respect of the following matters in relation to which the Companies Act 2006 requires us to report to you if, in our opinion:

- adequate accounting records have not been kept, or returns adequate for our audit have not been received from branches not visited by us; or

- the financial statements are not in agreement with the accounting records and returns; or

- certain disclosures of directors' remuneration specified by law are not made; or

- we have not received all the information and explanations we require for our audit; or

- the directors were not entitled to prepare the financial statements in accordance with the small companies regime and take advantage of the small companies' exemptions in preparing the directors' report and from the requirement to prepare a strategic report.

Responsibilities of directors

As explained more fully in the directors' responsibilities statement [set out on page ...], the directors are responsible for the preparation of the financial statements and for being satisfied that they give a true and fair view, and for such internal control as the directors determine is necessary to enable the preparation of financial statements that are free from material misstatement, whether due to fraud or error.

In preparing the financial statements, the directors are responsible for assessing the company's ability to continue as a going concern, disclosing, as applicable, matters related to going concern and using the going concern basis of accounting unless the directors either intend to liquidate the company or to cease operations, or have no realistic alternative but to do so.

Auditor's responsibilities for the audit of the financial statements

Our objectives are to obtain reasonable assurance about whether the financial statements as a whole are free from material misstatement, whether due to fraud or error, and to issue an auditor's report that includes our opinion. Reasonable assurance is a high level of assurance, but is not a guarantee that an audit conducted in accordance with ISAs (UK) will always detect a material misstatement when it exists. Misstatements can arise from fraud or error and are considered material if, individually or in the aggregate, they could reasonably be expected to influence the economic decisions of users taken on the basis of these financial statements.

A further description of our responsibilities for the audit of the financial statements is located on the Financial Reporting Council's website at: [*website link*].³⁴ This description forms part of our auditor's report.

[*Signature*]

John Smith (Senior Statutory Auditor)

For and on behalf of ABC LLP, Statutory Auditor

[*Address*]

[*Date*]

---

³⁴ *See paragraph 38 of this Compendium.*

Appendix 2

Non-publicly traded company preparing group and parent company financial statements under UK GAAP

- Company either does not qualify as a small company or qualifies as a small company but chooses not to prepare its financial statements under the small companies regime

- Company is not a public-interest entity

- Financial statements are prepared in accordance with FRSs 100 and 102 (UK GAAP)

- Company prepares group financial statements

- Section 408 exemption taken for parent company's own profit and loss account

- Description of the auditor's responsibilities for the audit of the financial statements is included within the body of the auditor's report

- Auditor is not required, and has otherwise not decided, to communicate key audit matters in accordance with ISA (UK) 701

Independent auditor's report to the members of [XYZ Limited]

Opinion

We have audited the financial statements of [XYZ Limited] (the "parent company") and its subsidiaries (the "group") for the year ended [*date*] which comprise [*specify the titles of the primary statements*][35] and notes to the financial statements, including a summary of significant accounting policies. The financial reporting framework that has been applied in their preparation is applicable law and United Kingdom Accounting Standards, including Financial Reporting Standard 102 *The Financial Reporting Standard applicable in the UK and Republic of Ireland* (United Kingdom Generally Accepted Accounting Practice).

In our opinion, the financial statements:

- give a true and fair view of the state of the group's and of the parent company's affairs as at [*date*] and of the group's [profit/loss] for the year then ended;

- have been properly prepared in accordance with United Kingdom Generally Accepted Accounting Practice;

- have been prepared in accordance with the requirements of the Companies Act 2006.

---

[35] *The terms used to describe the primary financial statements should be the same as those used by the directors.*

Basis for opinion

We conducted our audit in accordance with International Standards on Auditing (UK) (ISAs (UK)) and applicable law. Our responsibilities under those standards are further described in the Auditor's responsibilities for the audit of the financial statements section of our report. We are independent of the group in accordance with the ethical requirements that are relevant to our audit of the financial statements in the UK, including the FRC's Ethical Standard, and we have fulfilled our other ethical responsibilities in accordance with these requirements. We believe that the audit evidence we have obtained is sufficient and appropriate to provide a basis for our opinion.

Conclusions relating to going concern

We have nothing to report in respect of the following matters in relation to which the ISAs (UK) require us to report to you where:

- the directors' use of the going concern basis of accounting in the preparation of the financial statements is not appropriate; or

- the directors have not disclosed in the financial statements any identified material uncertainties that may cast significant doubt about the group's or the parent company's ability to continue to adopt the going concern basis of accounting for a period of at least twelve months from the date when the financial statements are authorised for issue.

Other information

The directors are responsible for the other information. The other information comprises the information included in the annual report,[36] other than the financial statements and our auditor's report thereon. Our opinion on the financial statements does not cover the other information and, except to the extent otherwise explicitly stated in our report, we do not express any form of assurance conclusion thereon.

In connection with our audit of the financial statements, our responsibility is to read the other information and, in doing so, consider whether the other information is materially inconsistent with the financial statements or our knowledge obtained in the audit or otherwise appears to be materially misstated. If we identify such material inconsistencies or apparent material misstatements, we are required to determine whether there is a material misstatement in the financial statements or a material misstatement of the other information. If, based on the work we have performed, we conclude that there is a material misstatement of this other information, we are required to report that fact.

We have nothing to report in this regard.

Opinions on other matters prescribed by the Companies Act 2006

In our opinion, based on the work undertaken in the course of the audit:

- the information given in the strategic report and the directors' report for the financial year for which the financial statements are prepared is consistent with the financial statements; and

- the strategic report and the directors' report have been prepared in accordance with applicable legal requirements.

---

[36] *The term used to describe the annual report should be the same as that used by the directors.*

Matters on which we are required to report by exception

In the light of the knowledge and understanding of the group and the parent company and its environment obtained in the course of the audit, we have not identified material misstatements in the strategic report or the directors' report.

We have nothing to report in respect of the following matters in relation to which the Companies Act 2006 requires us to report to you if, in our opinion:

● adequate accounting records have not been kept by the parent company, or returns adequate for our audit have not been received from branches not visited by us; or

● the parent company financial statements are not in agreement with the accounting records and returns; or

● certain disclosures of directors' remuneration specified by law are not made; or

● we have not received all the information and explanations we require for our audit.

Responsibilities of directors

As explained more fully in the directors' responsibilities statement [set out on page ...], the directors are responsible for the preparation of the financial statements and for being satisfied that they give a true and fair view, and for such internal control as the directors determine is necessary to enable the preparation of financial statements that are free from material misstatement, whether due to fraud or error.

In preparing the financial statements, the directors are responsible for assessing the group's and the parent company's ability to continue as a going concern, disclosing, as applicable, matters related to going concern and using the going concern basis of accounting unless the directors either intend to liquidate the group or the parent company or to cease operations, or have no realistic alternative but to do so.

Auditor's responsibilities for the audit of the financial statements

Our objectives are to obtain reasonable assurance about whether the financial statements as a whole are free from material misstatement, whether due to fraud or error, and to issue an auditor's report that includes our opinion. Reasonable assurance is a high level of assurance, but is not a guarantee that an audit conducted in accordance with ISAs (UK) will always detect a material misstatement when it exists. Misstatements can arise from fraud or error and are considered material if, individually or in the aggregate, they could reasonably be expected to influence the economic decisions of users taken on the basis of these financial statements.

As part of an audit in accordance with ISAs (UK), we exercise professional judgment and maintain professional scepticism throughout the audit. We also:

● Identify and assess the risks of material misstatement of the financial statements, whether due to fraud or error, design and perform audit procedures responsive to those risks, and obtain audit evidence that is sufficient and appropriate to provide a basis for our opinion. The risk of not detecting a material misstatement resulting from fraud is higher than for one resulting from error, as fraud may involve collusion, forgery, intentional omissions, misrepresentations, or the override of internal control.

- Obtain an understanding of internal control relevant to the audit in order to design audit procedures that are appropriate in the circumstances, but not for the purpose of expressing an opinion on the effectiveness of the group's internal control.

- Evaluate the appropriateness of accounting policies used and the reasonableness of accounting estimates and related disclosures made by the directors.

- Conclude on the appropriateness of the directors' use of the going concern basis of accounting and, based on the audit evidence obtained, whether a material uncertainty exists related to events or conditions that may cast significant doubt on the group's or the parent company's ability to continue as a going concern. If we conclude that a material uncertainty exists, we are required to draw attention in our auditor's report to the related disclosures in the financial statements or, if such disclosures are inadequate, to modify our opinion. Our conclusions are based on the audit evidence obtained up to the date of our auditor's report. However, future events or conditions may cause the group or the parent company to cease to continue as a going concern.

- Evaluate the overall presentation, structure and content of the financial statements, including the disclosures, and whether the financial statements represent the underlying transactions and events in a manner that achieves fair presentation.

- Obtain sufficient appropriate audit evidence regarding the financial information of the entities or business activities within the group to express an opinion on the consolidated financial statements. We are responsible for the direction, supervision and performance of the group audit. We remain solely responsible for our audit opinion.[37]

We communicate with those charged with governance regarding, among other matters, the planned scope and timing of the audit and significant audit findings, including any significant deficiencies in internal control that we identify during our audit.

[*Signature*]

John Smith (Senior Statutory Auditor)

For and on behalf of ABC LLP, Statutory Auditor

[*Address*]

[*Date*]

---

[37] *This bullet point is only required where the company prepares group financial statements or ISA (UK) 600 (Revised June 2016) otherwise applies.*

Appendix 3

Publicly traded AIM listed company preparing financial statements under IFRSs with an emphasis of matter paragraph

- Company is an AIM-listed company, an unquoted company and not a public-interest entity

- Financial statements are prepared in accordance with IFRSs as adopted by the EU

- Company does not prepare group financial statements or ISA (UK) 600 (Revised June 2016) does not otherwise apply

- Description of the auditor's responsibilities for the audit of the financial statements is included by reference to the location of such a description included on the FRC's website

- Emphasis of matter paragraph is included in the auditor's report as in the auditor's judgment, the matter is of such importance that it is fundamental to users' understanding of the financial statements

Independent auditor's report to the members of [XYZ Limited]

Opinion

We have audited the financial statements of [XYZ Limited] (the "company") for the year ended [*date*] which comprise [*specify the titles of the primary statements*][38] and notes to the financial statements, including a summary of significant accounting policies. The financial reporting framework that has been applied in their preparation is applicable law and International Financial Reporting Standards (IFRSs) as adopted by the European Union.

In our opinion, the financial statements:

- give a true and fair view of the state of the company's affairs as at [*date*] and of its [profit/loss] for the year then ended;

- have been properly prepared in accordance with IFRSs as adopted by the European Union; and

- have been prepared in accordance with the requirements of the Companies Act 2006.

---

[38] *The terms used to describe the primary financial statements should be the same as those used by the directors.*

Basis for opinion

We conducted our audit in accordance with International Standards on Auditing (UK) (ISAs (UK)) and applicable law. Our responsibilities under those standards are further described in the Auditor's responsibilities for the audit of the financial statements section of our report. We are independent of the company in accordance with the ethical requirements that are relevant to our audit of the financial statements in the UK, including the FRC's Ethical Standard as applied to listed entities,[39] and we have fulfilled our other ethical responsibilities in accordance with these requirements. We believe that the audit evidence we have obtained is sufficient and appropriate to provide a basis for our opinion.

Conclusions relating to going concern

We have nothing to report in respect of the following matters in relation to which the ISAs (UK) require us to report to you where:

- the directors' use of the going concern basis of accounting in the preparation of the financial statements is not appropriate; or

- the directors have not disclosed in the financial statements any identified material uncertainties that may cast significant doubt about the company's ability to continue to adopt the going concern basis of accounting for a period of at least twelve months from the date when the financial statements are authorised for issue.

Emphasis of matter[40]

We draw attention to note [X] of the financial statements, which describes [*brief summary of the matter*]. Our opinion is not modified in this respect.

Key audit matters

Key audit matters are those matters that, in our professional judgment, were of most significance in our audit of the financial statements of the current period and include the most significant assessed risks of material misstatement (whether or not due to fraud) we identified, including those which had the greatest effect on: the overall audit strategy, the allocation of resources in the audit; and directing the efforts of the engagement team. These matters were addressed in the context of our audit of the financial statements as a whole, and in forming our opinion thereon, and we do not provide a separate opinion on these matters.

[*Description of each key audit matter in accordance with ISA (UK) 701.*]

Our application of materiality

[*Explanation of how the auditor applied the concept of materiality in planning and performing the audit. This is required to include the threshold used by the auditor as being materiality for the financial statements as a whole but may include other relevant disclosures.*[41]]

---

[39] *The auditor uses "as applied to SME listed entities" where the relief and exemptions for audits of SME listed entities provided by the FRC's Ethical Standard are utilised. See paragraph A35-3 of ISA (UK) 700 (Revised June 2016).*

[40] *As noted in paragraph A16 of ISA (UK) 706 (Revised June 2016), an emphasis of matter paragraph may be presented either directly before or after the key audit matters section based on the auditor's judgment as to the relative significance of the information included in the emphasis of matter paragraph.*

[41] *ISA (UK) 701, paragraph A59-1 includes other disclosures relevant to an explanation of how the auditor applied the context of materiality in planning and performing the audit.*

An overview of the scope of our audit

[*Overview of the scope of the audit, including an explanation of how the scope addressed each key audit matter and was influenced by the auditor's application of materiality.*]

Other information

The directors are responsible for the other information. The other information comprises the information included in the annual report,[42] other than the financial statements and our auditor's report thereon. Our opinion on the financial statements does not cover the other information and, except to the extent otherwise explicitly stated in our report, we do not express any form of assurance conclusion thereon.

In connection with our audit of the financial statements, our responsibility is to read the other information and, in doing so, consider whether the other information is materially inconsistent with the financial statements or our knowledge obtained in the audit or otherwise appears to be materially misstated. If we identify such material inconsistencies or apparent material misstatements, we are required to determine whether there is a material misstatement in the financial statements or a material misstatement of the other information. If, based on the work we have performed, we conclude that there is a material misstatement of this other information, we are required to report that fact. We have nothing to report in this regard.

Opinions on other matters prescribed by the Companies Act 2006

In our opinion, based on the work undertaken in the course of the audit:

- the information given in the strategic report and the directors' report for the financial year for which the financial statements are prepared is consistent with the financial statements; and

- the strategic report and the directors' report have been prepared in accordance with applicable legal requirements.

Matters on which we are required to report by exception

In the light of the knowledge and understanding of the company and its environment obtained in the course of the audit, we have not identified material misstatements in the strategic report or the directors' report.

We have nothing to report in respect of the following matters in relation to which the Companies Act 2006 requires us to report to you if, in our opinion:

- adequate accounting records have not been kept, or returns adequate for our audit have not been received from branches not visited by us; or

- the financial statements are not in agreement with the accounting records and returns; or

- certain disclosures of directors' remuneration specified by law are not made; or

- we have not received all the information and explanations we require for our audit.

---

[42] *The term used to describe the annual report should be the same as that used by the directors.*

Responsibilities of directors

As explained more fully in the directors' responsibilities statement [set out on page ...], the directors are responsible for the preparation of the financial statements and for being satisfied that they give a true and fair view, and for such internal control as the directors determine is necessary to enable the preparation of financial statements that are free from material misstatement, whether due to fraud or error.

In preparing the financial statements, the directors are responsible for assessing the company's ability to continue as a going concern, disclosing, as applicable, matters related to going concern and using the going concern basis of accounting unless the directors either intend to liquidate the company or to cease operations, or have no realistic alternative but to do so.

Auditor's responsibilities for the audit of the financial statements

Our objectives are to obtain reasonable assurance about whether the financial statements as a whole are free from material misstatement, whether due to fraud or error, and to issue an auditor's report that includes our opinion. Reasonable assurance is a high level of assurance, but is not a guarantee that an audit conducted in accordance with ISAs (UK) will always detect a material misstatement when it exists. Misstatements can arise from fraud or error and are considered material if, individually or in the aggregate, they could reasonably be expected to influence the economic decisions of users taken on the basis of these financial statements.

A further description of our responsibilities for the audit of the financial statements is located on the Financial Reporting Council's website at: [*website link*].[43] This description forms part of our auditor's report.

[*Signature*]

John Smith (Senior Statutory Auditor)

For and on behalf of ABC LLP, Statutory Auditor

[*Address*]

[*Date*]

---

[43] *See paragraph 38 of this Compendium.*

Appendix 4

Unlisted public interest entity preparing financial statements under UK GAAP with a material uncertainty related to going concern

- Company is a public interest entity

- Financial statements are prepared in accordance with FRSs 100 and 102 (UK GAAP)

- Company does not prepare group financial statements or ISA (UK) 600 (Revised June 2016) does not otherwise apply

- Based on the audit evidence obtained, the auditor has concluded that a material uncertainty exists related to events or conditions that may cast significant doubt on the company's ability to continue as a going concern. The disclosure of the material uncertainty in the financial statements is adequate.

- Description of the auditor's responsibilities for the audit of the financial statements is included by reference to the location of such a description included on the FRC's website

Independent auditor's report to the members of [XYZ Limited]

Opinion

We have audited the financial statements of [XYZ Limited] (the "company") for the year ended [*date*] which comprise [*specify the titles of the primary statements*][44] and notes to the financial statements, including a summary of significant accounting policies. The financial reporting framework that has been applied in their preparation is applicable law and United Kingdom Accounting Standards, including Financial Reporting Standard 101 *Reduced Disclosure Framework* (United Kingdom Generally Accepted Accounting Practice).

In our opinion, the financial statements:

- give a true and fair view of the state of the company's affairs as at [*date*] and of its [profit/loss] for the year then ended;

- have been properly prepared in accordance with United Kingdom Generally Accepted Accounting Practice; and

- have been prepared in accordance with the requirements of the Companies Act 2006.

---

[44] *The terms used to describe the primary financial statements should be the same as those used by the directors.*

Basis for opinion

We conducted our audit in accordance with International Standards on Auditing (UK) (ISAs (UK)) and applicable law. Our responsibilities under those standards are further described in the Auditor's responsibilities for the audit of the financial statements section of our report. We are independent of the company in accordance with the ethical requirements that are relevant to our audit of the financial statements in the UK, including the FRC's Ethical Standard as applied to public interest entities, and we have fulfilled our other ethical responsibilities in accordance with these requirements. We believe that the audit evidence we have obtained is sufficient and appropriate to provide a basis for our opinion.

Material uncertainty related to going concern

We draw attention to note [X] in the financial statements, which indicates that [*brief description of events or conditions identified that may cast significant doubt on the entity's ability to continue as a going concern*]. As stated in note [X], these events or conditions, along with the other matters as set forth in note [X], indicate that a material uncertainty exists that may cast significant doubt on the company's ability to continue as a going concern. Our opinion is not modified in respect of this matter.

Key audit matters

Key audit matters are those matters that, in our professional judgment, were of most significance in our audit of the financial statements of the current period and include the most significant assessed risks of material misstatement (whether or not due to fraud) we identified, including those which had the greatest effect on: the overall audit strategy, the allocation of resources in the audit; and directing the efforts of the engagement team. These matters were addressed in the context of our audit of the financial statements as a whole, and in forming our opinion thereon, and we do not provide a separate opinion on these matters.

[*Description of each key audit matter in accordance with ISA (UK) 701.*]

Our application of materiality

[*Explanation of how the auditor applied the concept of materiality in planning and performing the audit. This is required to include the threshold used by the auditor as being materiality for the financial statements as a whole but may include other relevant disclosures.*[45]]

An overview of the scope of our audit

[*Overview of the scope of the audit, including an explanation of how the scope addressed each key audit matter and was influenced by the auditor's application of materiality.*]

Other information

The directors are responsible for the other information. The other information comprises the information included in the annual report,[46] other than the financial statements and our auditor's report thereon. Our opinion on the financial

---

[45] *ISA (UK) 701, paragraph A59-1 includes other disclosures relevant to an explanation of how the auditor applied the context of materiality in planning and performing the audit.*

[46] *The term used to describe the annual report should be the same as that used by the directors.*

statements does not cover the other information and, except to the extent otherwise explicitly stated in our report, we do not express any form of assurance conclusion thereon.

In connection with our audit of the financial statements, our responsibility is to read the other information and, in doing so, consider whether the other information is materially inconsistent with the financial statements or our knowledge obtained in the audit or otherwise appears to be materially misstated. If we identify such material inconsistencies or apparent material misstatements, we are required to determine whether there is a material misstatement in the financial statements or a material misstatement of the other information. If, based on the work we have performed, we conclude that there is a material misstatement of this other information, we are required to report that fact. We have nothing to report in this regard.

Opinions on other matters prescribed by the Companies Act 2006

In our opinion, based on the work undertaken in the course of the audit:

- the information given in the strategic report and the directors' report for the financial year for which the financial statements are prepared is consistent with the financial statements; and

- the strategic report and the directors' report have been prepared in accordance with applicable legal requirements.

Matters on which we are required to report by exception

In the light of the knowledge and understanding of the company and its environment obtained in the course of the audit, we have not identified material misstatements in the strategic report or the directors' report.

We have nothing to report in respect of the following matters in relation to which the Companies Act 2006 requires us to report to you if, in our opinion:

- adequate accounting records have not been kept, or returns adequate for our audit have not been received from branches not visited by us; or

- the financial statements are not in agreement with the accounting records and returns; or

- certain disclosures of directors' remuneration specified by law are not made; or

- we have not received all the information and explanations we require for our audit.

Responsibilities of directors

As explained more fully in the directors' responsibilities statement [set out on page ...], the directors are responsible for the preparation of the financial statements and for being satisfied that they give a true and fair view, and for such internal control as the directors determine is necessary to enable the preparation of financial statements that are free from material misstatement, whether due to fraud or error.

In preparing the financial statements, the directors are responsible for assessing the company's ability to continue as a going concern, disclosing, as applicable, matters related to going concern and using the going concern basis of accounting unless the directors either intend to liquidate the company or to cease operations, or have no realistic alternative but to do so.

Auditor's responsibilities for the audit of the financial statements

Our objectives are to obtain reasonable assurance about whether the financial statements as a whole are free from material misstatement, whether due to fraud or error, and to issue an auditor's report that includes our opinion. Reasonable assurance is a high level of assurance, but is not a guarantee that an audit conducted in accordance with ISAs (UK) will always detect a material misstatement when it exists. Misstatements can arise from fraud or error and are considered material if, individually or in the aggregate, they could reasonably be expected to influence the economic decisions of users taken on the basis of these financial statements.

[*Explanation as to what extent the audit was considered capable of detecting irregularities, including fraud.*]

A further description of our responsibilities for the audit of the financial statements is located on the Financial Reporting Council's website at: [*website link*].[47] This description forms part of our auditor's report.

Other matters which we are required to address

We were appointed by [*state by whom or which body the auditor(s) was appointed*] on [*date*]. The period of total uninterrupted engagement including previous renewals and reappointments of the firm is [X] years.

The non-audit services prohibited by the FRC's Ethical Standard were not provided to the company and we remain independent of the company in conducting our audit.

[*Indicate any services, in addition to the audit, which were provided by the firm to the company that have not been disclosed in the financial statements or elsewhere in the annual report.*]

Our audit opinion is consistent with the additional report to the audit committee.

[*Signature*]

John Smith (Senior Statutory Auditor)

For and on behalf of ABC LLP, Statutory Auditor

[*Address*]

[*Date*]

---

[47] *See paragraph 38 of this Compendium.*

Appendix 5

Publicly traded standard listed company preparing group financial statements under IFRSs and parent company financial statements under UK GAAP

- Company is a standard listed company, a quoted company and a public-interest entity

- Company prepares group financial statements under IFRSs as adopted by the EU and parent company financial statements under UK GAAP (FRSs 100 and 101)

- Section 408 exemption taken in respect of parent company's own profit and loss account

- Corporate governance statement is incorporated into the directors' report either directly or by incorporation by reference

- Description of the auditor's responsibilities for the audit of the financial statements is included by reference to the location of such a description included on the FRC's website

Independent auditor's report to the members of [XYZ Plc]

Opinion

We have audited the financial statements of [XYZ Limited] (the "parent company") and its subsidiaries (the "group") for the year ended [*date*] which comprise [*specify the titles of the primary statements*][48] and notes to the financial statements, including a summary of significant accounting policies. The financial reporting framework that has been applied in the preparation of the group financial statements is applicable law and International Financial Reporting Standards (IFRSs) as adopted by the European Union. The financial reporting framework that has been applied in the preparation of the parent company financial statements is applicable law and United Kingdom Accounting Standards, including Financial Reporting Standard 101 *Reduced Disclosures Framework* (United Kingdom Generally Accepted Accounting Practice).

In our opinion:

- the financial statements give a true and fair view of the state of the group's and of the parent company's affairs as at [*date*] and of the group's [profit/loss] for the year then ended;

- the group financial statements have been properly prepared in accordance with IFRSs as adopted by the European Union;

---

[48] *The terms used to describe the primary financial statements should be the same as those used by the directors.*

- the parent company financial statements have been properly prepared in accordance with United Kingdom Generally Accepted Accounting Practice; and

- the financial statements have been prepared in accordance with the requirements of the Companies Act 2006; and, as regards the group financial statements, Article 4 of the IAS Regulation.

Basis for opinion

We conducted our audit in accordance with International Standards on Auditing (UK) (ISAs (UK)) and applicable law. Our responsibilities under those standards are further described in the Auditor's Responsibilities for the Audit of the Financial Statements section of our report. We are independent of the group and the parent company in accordance with the ethical requirements that are relevant to our audit of the financial statements in the UK, including the FRC's Ethical Standard as applied to listed public interest entities, and we have fulfilled our other ethical responsibilities in accordance with these requirements. We believe that the audit evidence we have obtained is sufficient and appropriate to provide a basis for our opinion.

Conclusions relating to going concern

We have nothing to report in respect of the following matters in relation to which the ISAs (UK) require us to report to you where:

- the directors' use of the going concern basis of accounting in the preparation of the financial statements is not appropriate; or

- the directors have not disclosed in the financial statements any identified material uncertainties that may cast significant doubt about the group's or the parent company's ability to continue to adopt the going concern basis of accounting for a period of at least twelve months from the date when the financial statements are authorised for issue.

Key audit matters

Key audit matters are those matters that, in our professional judgment, were of most significance in our audit of the financial statements of the current period and include the most significant assessed risks of material misstatement (whether or not due to fraud) we identified, including those which had the greatest effect on: the overall audit strategy, the allocation of resources in the audit; and directing the efforts of the engagement team. These matters were addressed in the context of our audit of the financial statements as a whole, and in forming our opinion thereon, and we do not provide a separate opinion on these matters.

[Description of each key audit matter in accordance with ISA (UK) 701.]

Our application of materiality

[Explanation of how the auditor applied the concept of materiality in planning and performing the group and parent company audit. This is required to include the threshold used by the auditor as being materiality for the group and parent company financial statements as a whole but may include other relevant disclosures.[49]]

---

[49] *ISA (UK) 701, paragraph A59-1 includes other disclosures relevant to an explanation of how the auditor applied the context of materiality in planning and performing the audit.*

An overview of the scope of our audit

[*Overview of the scope of the group and parent company audit, including an explanation of how the scope addressed each key audit matter and was influenced by the auditor's application of materiality.*]

Other information

The directors are responsible for the other information. The other information comprises the information included in the annual report,[50] other than the financial statements and our auditor's report thereon. Our opinion on the financial statements does not cover the other information and, except to the extent otherwise explicitly stated in our report, we do not express any form of assurance conclusion thereon. In connection with our audit of the financial statements, our responsibility is to read the other information and, in doing so, consider whether the other information is materially inconsistent with the financial statements or our knowledge obtained in the audit or otherwise appears to be materially misstated. If we identify such material inconsistencies or apparent material misstatements, we are required to determine whether there is a material misstatement in the financial statements or a material misstatement of the other information. If, based on the work we have performed, we conclude that there is a material misstatement of this other information, we are required to report that fact. We have nothing to report in this regard.

Opinions on other matters prescribed by the Companies Act 2006

In our opinion the part of the directors' remuneration report to be audited has been properly prepared in accordance with the Companies Act 2006.

In our opinion, based on the work undertaken in the course of the audit:

- the information given in the strategic report and the directors' report for the financial year for which the financial statements are prepared is consistent with the financial statements; and
- the strategic report and the directors' report have been prepared in accordance with applicable legal requirements.

Matters on which we are required to report by exception

In the light of the knowledge and understanding of the group and the parent company and its environment obtained in the course of the audit, we have not identified material misstatements in the strategic report or the directors' report.

We have nothing to report in respect of the following matters in relation to which the Companies Act 2006 requires us to report to you if, in our opinion:

- adequate accounting records have not been kept by the parent company, or returns adequate for our audit have not been received from branches not visited by us; or
- the parent company financial statements and the part of the directors' remuneration report to be audited are not in agreement with the accounting records and returns; or
- certain disclosures of directors' remuneration specified by law are not made; or
- we have not received all the information and explanations we require for our audit.

---

[50] *The term used to describe the annual report should be the same as that used by the directors.*

Responsibilities of directors

As explained more fully in the directors' responsibilities statement [set out on page ...], the directors are responsible for the preparation of the financial statements and for being satisfied that they give a true and fair view, and for such internal control as the directors determine is necessary to enable the preparation of financial statements that are free from material misstatement, whether due to fraud or error.

In preparing the financial statements, the directors are responsible for assessing the group's and the parent company's ability to continue as a going concern, disclosing, as applicable, matters related to going concern and using the going concern basis of accounting unless the directors either intend to liquidate the group or the parent company or to cease operations, or have no realistic alternative but to do so.

Auditor's responsibilities for the audit of the financial statements

Our objectives are to obtain reasonable assurance about whether the financial statements as a whole are free from material misstatement, whether due to fraud or error, and to issue an auditor's report that includes our opinion. Reasonable assurance is a high level of assurance, but is not a guarantee that an audit conducted in accordance with ISAs (UK) will always detect a material misstatement when it exists. Misstatements can arise from fraud or error and are considered material if, individually or in the aggregate, they could reasonably be expected to influence the economic decisions of users taken on the basis of these financial statements.

[*Explanation as to what extent the audit was considered capable of detecting irregularities, including fraud.*]

A further description of our responsibilities for the audit of the financial statements is located on the Financial Reporting Council's website at: [*website link*].[51] This description forms part of our auditor's report.

Other matters which we are required to address

We were appointed by [*state by whom or which body the auditor was appointed*] on [*date*] to audit the financial statements for the period ending [*date*]. Our total uninterrupted period of engagement is [X] years, covering the periods ending [*date*] to [*date*].

The non-audit services prohibited by the FRC's Ethical Standard were not provided to the group or the parent company and we remain independent of the group and the parent company in conducting our audit.

[*Indicate any services, in addition to the audit, which were provided by the firm to the group that have not been disclosed in the financial statements or elsewhere in the annual report.*]

Our audit opinion is consistent with the additional report to the audit committee.

[*Signature*]

John Smith (Senior Statutory Auditor)

For and on behalf of ABC LLP, Statutory Auditor

[*Address*]

[*Date*]

---

[51] *See paragraph 38 of this Compendium.*

Appendix 6

Publicly traded premium listed company preparing group and parent company financial statements under IFRSs

- Company is a premium listed company, a quoted company and a public interest entity

- Financial statements are prepared in accordance with IFRSs as adopted by the EU and are also prepared in accordance with IFRSs as issued by the IAASB

- Company prepares group financial statements

- Section 408 exemption not taken in respect of parent company's own profit and loss account

- Corporate governance statement not incorporated into the strategic report or the directors' report, either directly or by incorporation by cross-reference

- Description of the auditor's responsibilities for the audit of the financial statements is included within an appendix to the auditor's report

Independent auditor's report to the members of [XYZ Plc]

Opinion

We have audited the financial statements of [XYZ Plc] (the "parent company") and its subsidiaries (the "group") for the year ended [*date*] which comprise [*specify the titles of the primary statements*][52] and notes to the financial statements, including a summary of significant accounting policies. The financial reporting framework that has been applied in their preparation is applicable law and International Financial Reporting Standards (IFRSs) as adopted by the European Union.

In our opinion the financial statements:

- give a true and fair view of the state of the group's and of the parent company's affairs as at [*date*] and of the group's and the parent company's [profit/loss] for the year then ended;

- have been properly prepared in accordance with [IFRSs as adopted by the European Union]; and

- have been prepared in accordance with the requirements of the Companies Act 2006 and, as regards the group financial statements, Article 4 of the IAS Regulation.

---

[52] *The terms used to describe the primary financial statements should be the same as those used by the directors.*

Separate opinion in relation to IFRSs as issued by the IASB

As explained in note [X] to the group financial statements, the group in addition to complying with its legal obligation to apply IFRSs as adopted by the European Union, has also applied IFRSs as issued by the International Accounting Standards Board (IASB).

In our opinion the group financial statements give a true and fair view of the consolidated financial position of the group as at [*date*] and of its consolidated financial performance and its consolidated cash flows for the year then ended in accordance with IFRSs as issued by the IASB.

Basis for opinion

We conducted our audit in accordance with International Standards on Auditing (UK) (ISAs (UK)) and applicable law. Our responsibilities under those standards are further described in the Auditor's responsibilities for the audit of the financial statements section of our report. We are independent of the group in accordance with the ethical requirements that are relevant to our audit of the financial statements in the UK, including the FRC's Ethical Standard as applied to listed public interest entities, and we have fulfilled our other ethical responsibilities in accordance with these requirements. We believe that the audit evidence we have obtained is sufficient and appropriate to provide a basis for our opinion.

Conclusions relating to principal risks, going concern and viability statement

We have nothing to report in respect of the following information in the annual report, in relation to which the ISAs (UK) require us to report to you whether we have anything material to add or draw attention to:

- the disclosures in the annual report[53] [set out on page ...] that describe the principal risks and explain how they are being managed or mitigated;

- the directors' confirmation [set out on page ...] in the annual report that they have carried out a robust assessment of the principal risks facing the group, including those that would threaten its business model, future performance, solvency or liquidity;

- the directors' statement [set out on page ...] in the financial statements about whether the directors considered it appropriate to adopt the going concern basis of accounting in preparing the financial statements and the directors' identification of any material uncertainties to the group and the parent company's ability to continue to do so over a period of at least twelve months from the date of approval of the financial statements;

- whether the directors' statement relating to going concern required under the Listing Rules in accordance with Listing Rule 9.8.6R(3) is materially inconsistent with our knowledge obtained in the audit; or

- the directors' explanation [set out on page ...] in the annual report as to how they have assessed the prospects of the group, over what period they have done so and why they consider that period to be appropriate, and their statement as to whether they have a reasonable expectation that the group will be able to continue in operation and meet its liabilities as they fall due over the period of their assessment, including any related disclosures drawing attention to any necessary qualifications or assumptions.

---

[53] *The term used to describe the annual report should be the same as that used by the directors.*

Key audit matters

Key audit matters are those matters that, in our professional judgment, were of most significance in our audit of the financial statements of the current period and include the most significant assessed risks of material misstatement (whether or not due to fraud) that we identified. These matters included those which had the greatest effect on: the overall audit strategy, the allocation of resources in the audit; and directing the efforts of the engagement team. These matters were addressed in the context of our audit of the financial statements as a whole, and in forming our opinion thereon, and we do not provide a separate opinion on these matters.

[*Description of each key audit matter in accordance with ISA (UK) 701.*]

Our application of materiality

[*Explanation of how the auditor applied the concept of materiality in planning and performing the group and parent company audit. This is required to include the threshold used by the auditor as being materiality for the group and parent company financial statements as a whole but may include other relevant disclosures.*[54]]

An overview of the scope of our audit

[*Overview of the scope of the group and parent company audit, including an explanation of how the scope addressed each key audit matter and was influenced by the auditor's application of materiality.*]

[*Explanation as to what extent the audit was considered capable of detecting irregularities, including fraud.*]

Other information

The other information comprises the information included in the annual report [set out on pages …][,including [specify the titles of the other information][set out on pages …]], other than the financial statements and our auditor's report thereon. The directors are responsible for the other information. Our opinion on the financial statements does not cover the other information and, except to the extent otherwise explicitly stated in our report, we do not express any form of assurance conclusion thereon. In connection with our audit of the financial statements, our responsibility is to read the other information and, in doing so, consider whether the other information is materially inconsistent with the financial statements or our knowledge obtained in the audit or otherwise appears to be materially misstated. If we identify such material inconsistencies or apparent material misstatements, we are required to determine whether there is a material misstatement in the financial statements or a material misstatement of the other information. If, based on the work we have performed, we conclude that there is a material misstatement of the other information, we are required to report that fact.

We have nothing to report in this regard.

In this context, we also have nothing to report in regard to our responsibility to specifically address the following items in the other information and to report as uncorrected material misstatements of the other information where we conclude that those items meet the following conditions:

---

[54] *ISA (UK) 701, paragraph A59-1 includes other disclosures relevant to an explanation of how the auditor applied the context of materiality in planning and performing the audit.*

- **Fair, balanced and understandable [set out on page ...]** – [the statement given / the explanation as to why the annual report does not include a statement] by the directors that they consider the annual report and financial statements taken as a whole is fair, balanced and understandable and provides the information necessary for shareholders to assess the group's performance, business model and strategy, is materially inconsistent with our knowledge obtained in the audit; or

- **Audit committee reporting [set out on page ...]** – [the section describing the work of the audit committee does not appropriately address matters communicated by us to the audit committee / the explanation as to why the annual report does not include a section describing the work of the audit committee is materially inconsistent with our knowledge obtained in the audit]; or

- **Directors' statement of compliance with the UK Corporate Governance Code [set out on page ...]** – the parts of the directors' statement required under the Listing Rules relating to the company's compliance with the UK Corporate Governance Code containing provisions specified for review by the auditor in accordance with Listing Rule 9.8.10R(2) do not properly disclose a departure from a relevant provision of the UK Corporate Governance Code.

Opinions on other matters prescribed by the Companies Act 2006

In our opinion, the part of the directors' remuneration report to be audited has been properly prepared in accordance with the Companies Act 2006.

In our opinion, based on the work undertaken in the course of the audit:

- the information given in the strategic report and the directors' report for the financial year for which the financial statements are prepared is consistent with the financial statements and those reports have been prepared in accordance with applicable legal requirements;

- the information about internal control and risk management systems in relation to financial reporting processes and about share capital structures, given in compliance with rules 7.2.5 and 7.2.6 in the Disclosure Rules and Transparency Rules sourcebook made by the Financial Conduct Authority (the FCA Rules), is consistent with the financial statements and has been prepared in accordance with applicable legal requirements; and

- information about the company's corporate governance code and practices and about its administrative, management and supervisory bodies and their committees complies with rules 7.2.2, 7.2.3 and 7.2.7 of the FCA Rules.

Matters on which we are required to report by exception

In the light of the knowledge and understanding of the group and the parent company and its environment obtained in the course of the audit, we have not identified material misstatements in:

- the strategic report or the directors' report; or

- the information about internal control and risk management systems in relation to financial reporting processes and about share capital structures, given in compliance with rules 7.2.5 and 7.2.6 of the FCA Rules.

We have nothing to report in respect of the following matters in relation to which the Companies Act 2006 requires us to report to you if, in our opinion:

- adequate accounting records have not been kept by the parent company, or returns adequate for our audit have not been received from branches not visited by us; or

- the parent company financial statements and the part of the directors' remuneration report to be audited are not in agreement with the accounting records and returns; or

- certain disclosures of directors' remuneration specified by law are not made; or

- we have not received all the information and explanations we require for our audit; or

- a corporate governance statement has not been prepared by the parent company.

Responsibilities of directors

As explained more fully in the directors' responsibilities statement [set out on page ...], the directors are responsible for the preparation of the financial statements and for being satisfied that they give a true and fair view, and for such internal control as the directors determine is necessary to enable the preparation of financial statements that are free from material misstatement, whether due to fraud or error.

In preparing the financial statements, the directors are responsible for assessing the group's and the parent company's ability to continue as a going concern, disclosing, as applicable, matters related to going concern and using the going concern basis of accounting unless the directors either intend to liquidate the group or the parent company or to cease operations, or have no realistic alternative but to do so.

Auditor's responsibilities for the audit of the financial statements

Our objectives are to obtain reasonable assurance about whether the financial statements as a whole are free from material misstatement, whether due to fraud or error, and to issue an auditor's report that includes our opinion. Reasonable assurance is a high level of assurance, but is not a guarantee that an audit conducted in accordance with ISAs (UK) will always detect a material misstatement when it exists. Misstatements can arise from fraud or error and are considered material if, individually or in the aggregate, they could reasonably be expected to influence the economic decisions of users taken on the basis of these financial statements.

A further description of our responsibilities for the audit of the financial statements is included in appendix [X] of this auditor's report. This description, which is located at [*indicate page number of other specific reference to the location of the description*], forms part of our auditor's report.

Other matters which we are required to address

Following the recommendation of the audit committee, we were appointed by [*state by whom or which body the auditor was appointed*] on [*date*] to audit the financial statements for the year ending [*date*] and subsequent financial periods.

The period of total uninterrupted engagement is [X] years, covering the years ending [*date*] to [*date*].

The non-audit services prohibited by the FRC's Ethical Standard were not provided to the group or the parent company and we remain independent of the group and the parent company in conducting our audit.

[*Indicate any services, in addition to the audit, which were provided by the firm to the group that have not been disclosed in the financial statements or elsewhere in the annual report.*]

Our audit opinion is consistent with the additional report to the audit committee.

[*Signature*]

John Smith (Senior Statutory Auditor)

For and on behalf of ABC LLP, Statutory Auditor

[*Address*]

[*Date*]

Appendix: Auditor's responsibilities for the audit of the financial statements

As part of an audit in accordance with ISAs (UK), we exercise professional judgment and maintain professional scepticism throughout the audit. We also:

- Identify and assess the risks of material misstatement of the financial statements, whether due to fraud or error, design and perform audit procedures responsive to those risks, and obtain audit evidence that is sufficient and appropriate to provide a basis for our opinion. The risk of not detecting a material misstatement resulting from fraud is higher than for one resulting from error, as fraud may involve collusion, forgery, intentional omissions, misrepresentations, or the override of internal control.

- Obtain an understanding of internal control relevant to the audit in order to design audit procedures that are appropriate in the circumstances, but not for the purpose of expressing an opinion on the effectiveness of the group's internal control.

- Evaluate the appropriateness of accounting policies used and the reasonableness of accounting estimates and related disclosures made by the directors.

- Conclude on the appropriateness of the directors' use of the going concern basis of accounting and, based on the audit evidence obtained, whether a material uncertainty exists related to events or conditions that may cast significant doubt on the group's or the parent company's ability to continue as a going concern. If we conclude that a material uncertainty exists, we are required to draw attention in our auditor's report to the related disclosures in the financial statements or, if such disclosures are inadequate, to modify our opinion. Our conclusions are based on the audit evidence obtained up to the date of our auditor's report. However, future events or conditions may cause the group or the parent company to cease to continue as a going concern.

- Evaluate the overall presentation, structure and content of the financial statements, including the disclosures, and whether the financial statements represent the underlying transactions and events in a manner that achieves fair presentation.

- Obtain sufficient appropriate audit evidence regarding the financial information of the entities or business activities within the group to express an opinion on the group financial statements. We are responsible for the direction, supervision and performance of the group audit. We remain solely responsible for our audit opinion.[55]

We communicate with those charged with governance regarding, among other matters, the planned scope and timing of the audit and significant audit findings, including any significant deficiencies in internal control that we identify during our audit.

We also provide those charged with governance with a statement that we have complied with relevant ethical requirements regarding independence, and to communicate with them all relationships and other matters that may reasonably

---

[55] *This bullet point is only required where the entity prepares group financial statements or ISA (UK) 600 (Revised June 2016) otherwise applies. See paragraph 40(b) of this Compendium.*

be thought to bear on our independence, and where applicable, related safeguards.[56]

From the matters communicated with those charged with governance, we determine those matters that were of most significance in the audit of the consolidated financial statements of the current period and are therefore the key audit matters. We describe these matters in our auditor's report unless law or regulation precludes public disclosure about the matter or when, in extremely rare circumstances, we determine that a matter should not be communicated in our report because the adverse consequences of doing so would reasonably be expected to outweigh the public interest benefits of such communication.[57]

---

[56] *This bullet point is only required where the entity is a listed entity. See paragraph 40(c) of this Compendium.*

[57] *This bullet point is only required where the auditor is required, or has otherwise decided, to communicate key audit matters in accordance with ISA (UK) 701. See paragraph 40(d) of this Compendium.*

Appendix 7A

Publicly traded premium listed company preparing group financial statements under IFRSs (reported on separately from the parent company financial statements)

- Company is a premium listed company, a quoted company and a public interest entity

- Company prepares group financial statements

- Corporate governance statement incorporated into the directors' report, either directly or by incorporation by cross-reference and reported on in the auditor's report on the group financial statements

- UK Corporate Governance Code reported on in the auditor's report on the group financial statements

- Directors' Remuneration Report reported on in the auditor's report on the parent company financial statements

- Description of the auditor's responsibilities for the audit of the financial statements is included by reference to the location of such a description included on the FRC's website

Independent auditor's report to the members of [XYZ Plc]

Opinion

We have audited the group financial statements of [XYZ Plc] for the year ended [*date*] which comprise [*specify the titles of the primary statements*][58] and notes to the financial statements, including a summary of significant accounting policies. The financial reporting framework that has been applied in their preparation is applicable law and International Financial Reporting Standards (IFRSs) as adopted by the European Union.

The terms used to describe the primary financial statements should be the same as those used by the directors.

- give a true and fair view of the state of the group's affairs as at [*date*] and of its [profit/loss] for the year then ended;

- have been properly prepared in accordance with IFRSs as adopted by the European Union; and

- have been prepared in accordance with the requirements of the Companies Act 2006 and Article 4 of the IAS Regulation.

Basis for opinion

We conducted our audit in accordance with International Standards on Auditing (UK) (ISAs (UK)) and applicable law. Our responsibilities under those standards

---

[58] *The terms used to describe the primary financial statements should be the same as those used by the directors.*

are further described in the Auditor's Responsibilities for the audit of the group financial statements section of our report. We are independent of the group in accordance with the ethical requirements that are relevant to our audit of the financial statements in the UK, including the FRC's Ethical Standard as applied to listed public interest entities, and we have fulfilled our other ethical responsibilities in accordance with these requirements. We believe that the audit evidence we have obtained is sufficient and appropriate to provide a basis for our opinion.

Conclusions relating to principal risks, going concern and viability statement

We have nothing to report in respect of the following information in the annual report, in relation to which the ISAs (UK) require us to report to you whether we have anything material to add or draw attention to:

- the disclosures in the annual report[59] that describe the principal risks and explain how they are being managed or mitigated;

- the directors' confirmation in the annual report that they have carried out a robust assessment of the principal risks facing the group, including those that would threaten its business model, future performance, solvency or liquidity;

- the directors' statement in the financial statements about whether the directors considered it appropriate to adopt the going concern basis of accounting in preparing the financial statements and the directors' identification of any material uncertainties to the group's ability to continue to do so over a period of at least twelve months from the date of approval of the financial statements;

- whether the directors' statement relating to going concern required under the Listing Rules in accordance with Listing Rule 9.8.6R(3) is materially inconsistent with our knowledge obtained in the audit; or

- the directors' explanation in the annual report as to how they have assessed the prospects of the group, over what period they have done so and why they consider that period to be appropriate, and their statement as to whether they have a reasonable expectation that the group will be able to continue in operation and meet its liabilities as they fall due over the period of their assessment, including any related disclosures drawing attention to any necessary qualifications or assumptions.

Key audit matters

Key audit matters are those matters that, in our professional judgment, were of most significance in our audit of the group financial statements of the current period and include the most significant assessed risks of material misstatement (whether or not due to fraud) we identified, including those which had the greatest effect on: the overall audit strategy, the allocation of resources in the audit; and directing the efforts of the engagement team. These matters were addressed in the context of our audit of the group financial statements as a whole, and in forming our opinion thereon, and we do not provide a separate opinion on these matters.

[Description of each key audit matter in accordance with ISA (UK) 701.]

---

[59] *The term used to describe the annual report should be the same as that used by the directors.*

Our application of materiality

[Explanation of how the auditor applied the concept of materiality in planning and performing the group audit. This is required to include the threshold used by the auditor as being materiality for the group financial statements as a whole but may include other relevant disclosures.[60]*]*

An overview of the scope of our audit

[Overview of the scope of the group audit, including an explanation of how the scope addressed each key audit matter and was influenced by the auditor's application of materiality.]

Other information

The directors are responsible for the other information. The other information comprises the information included in the annual report, other than the financial statements and our auditor's report thereon. Our opinion on the financial statements does not cover the other information and, except to the extent otherwise explicitly stated in our report, we do not express any form of assurance conclusion thereon.

In connection with our audit of the group financial statements, our responsibility is to read the other information and, in doing so, consider whether the other information is materially inconsistent with the group financial statements or our knowledge obtained in the audit or otherwise appears to be materially misstated. If we identify such material inconsistencies or apparent material misstatements, we are required to determine whether there is a material misstatement of the group financial statements or a material misstatement of the other information. If, based on the work we have performed, we conclude that there is a material misstatement of this other information, we are required to report that fact. We have nothing to report in this regard.

In this context, we also have nothing to report in regard to our responsibility to specifically address the following items in the other information and to report as uncorrected material misstatements of the other information where we conclude that those items meet the following conditions:

- **Fair, balanced and understandable** – [the statement given / the explanation as to why the annual report does not include a statement] by the directors that they consider the annual report and financial statements taken as a whole is fair, balanced and understandable and provides the information necessary for shareholders to assess the group's performance, business model and strategy, is materially inconsistent with our knowledge obtained in the audit; or

- **Audit committee reporting** – [the section describing the work of the audit committee does not appropriately address matters communicated by us to the audit committee / the explanation as to why the annual report does not include a section describing the work of the audit committee is materially inconsistent with our knowledge obtained in the audit]; or

- **Directors' statement of compliance with the UK Corporate Governance Code** – the parts of the directors' statement required under the Listing Rules relating to the company's compliance with the UK Corporate Governance

---

[60] *ISA (UK) 701, paragraph A59-1 includes other disclosures relevant to an explanation of how the auditor applied the context of materiality in planning and performing the audit.*

Code containing provisions specified for review by the auditor in accordance with Listing Rule 9.8.10R(2) do not properly disclose a departure from a relevant provision of the UK Corporate Governance Code.

Opinions on other matters prescribed by the Companies Act 2006

In our opinion, based on the work undertaken in the course of the audit:

- the information given in the strategic report and the directors' report for the financial year for which the group financial statements are prepared is consistent with the financial statements; and

- the strategic report and the directors' report have been prepared in accordance with applicable legal requirements.

Matters on which we are required to report by exception

In the light of the knowledge and understanding of the group and its environment obtained in the course of the audit, we have not identified material misstatements in the strategic report or the directors' report.

We have nothing to report in respect of the following matters in relation to which the Companies Act 2006 requires us to report to you if, in our opinion:

- certain disclosures of directors' remuneration specified by law are not made; or

- we have not received all the information and explanations we require for our audit.

Responsibilities of directors

As explained more fully in the directors' responsibilities statement [set out on page ...], the directors are responsible for the preparation of the group financial statements and for being satisfied that they give a true and fair view, and for such internal control as the directors determine is necessary to enable the preparation of group financial statements that are free from material misstatement, whether due to fraud or error.

In preparing the group financial statements, the directors are responsible for assessing the group's ability to continue as a going concern, disclosing, as applicable, matters related to going concern and using the going concern basis of accounting unless the directors either intend to liquidate the group or to cease operations, or have no realistic alternative but to do so.

Auditor's responsibilities for the audit of the group financial statements

Our objectives are to obtain reasonable assurance about whether the group financial statements as a whole are free from material misstatement, whether due to fraud or error, and to issue an auditor's report that includes our opinion. Reasonable assurance is a high level of assurance, but is not a guarantee that an audit conducted in accordance with ISAs (UK) will always detect a material misstatement when it exists. Misstatements can arise from fraud or error and are considered material if, individually or in the aggregate, they could reasonably be expected to influence the economic decisions of users taken on the basis of these group financial statements.

[*Explanation as to what extent the audit was considered capable of detecting irregularities, including fraud.*]

A further description of our responsibilities for the audit of the financial statements is located on the Financial Reporting Council's website at: [*website link*].[61] This description forms part of our auditor's report.

Other matters which we are required to address

We were appointed by [*state by whom or which body the auditor was appointed*] on [*date*]. The period of total uninterrupted engagement including previous renewals and reappointments of the firm is [X] years.

The non-audit services prohibited by the FRC's Ethical Standard were not provided to the group and we remain independent of the group in conducting our audit.

[*Indicate any services, in addition to the audit, which were provided by the firm to the group that have not been disclosed in the financial statements or elsewhere in the annual report.*]

Our audit opinion is consistent with the additional report to the audit committee.

We have reported separately on the parent company financial statements of [XYZ Plc] for the year ended [*date*]. [That report includes details of the parent company key audit matters; how we applied the concept of materiality in planning and performing our audit; and an overview of the scope of our audit.[62]] [That report includes a statement on a material uncertainty related to going concern.] [That report includes an emphasis of matter.] [The opinion in that report is [qualified / an adverse opinion / a disclaimer of opinion].]

[*Signature*]

John Smith (Senior Statutory Auditor)

For and on behalf of ABC LLP, Statutory Auditor

[*Address*]

[*Date*]

---

[61] *See paragraph 38 of this Compendium.*

[62] *See paragraph 49 of this Compendium.*

Appendix 7B

Publicly traded premium listed company preparing parent company financial statements under UK GAAP (reported on separately from the group financial statements)

- Company is a premium listed company, a quoted company and a public-interest entity

- Company prepares group financial statements

- Corporate governance statement incorporated into the directors' report, either directly or by incorporation by cross-reference and reported on in the auditor's report on the group financial statements

- UK Corporate Governance Code reported on in the auditor's report on the group financial statements

- Directors' remuneration report reported on in the auditor's report on the parent company financial statements

- Description of the auditor's responsibilities for the audit of the financial statements is included by reference to the location of such a description included on the FRC's website

Independent auditor's report to the members of [XYZ Plc]

Opinion

We have audited the parent company financial statements of [XYZ Plc] for the year ended [*date*] which comprise [*specify the titles of the primary statements*][63] and notes to the financial statements, including a summary of significant accounting policies. The financial reporting framework that has been applied in their preparation is applicable law and United Kingdom Accounting Standards, including Financial Reporting Standard 102 *The Financial Reporting Standard applicable in the UK and Republic of Ireland* (United Kingdom Generally Accepted Accounting Practice).

In our opinion the parent company financial statements:

- give a true and fair view of the state of the parent company's affairs as at [*date*] [and of its [profit/loss] for the year then ended];[64]

- have been properly prepared in accordance with United Kingdom Generally Accepted Accounting Practice; and

- have been prepared in accordance with the requirements of the Companies Act 2006.

---

[63] *The terms used to describe the primary financial statements should be the same as those used by the directors.*

[64] *The words "and of its profit (or loss) for the year then ended" are included only where Section 408 exemption is not taken in respect of the parent company's own profit and loss account.*

Basis for opinion

We conducted our audit in accordance with International Standards on Auditing (UK) (ISAs (UK)) and applicable law. Our responsibilities under those standards are further described in the Auditor's Responsibilities for the audit of the parent company financial statements section of our report. We are independent of the parent company in accordance with the ethical requirements that are relevant to our audit of the parent company financial statements in the UK, including the FRC's Ethical Standard as applied to listed public interest entities, and we have fulfilled our other ethical responsibilities in accordance with these requirements. We believe that the audit evidence we have obtained is sufficient and appropriate to provide a basis for our opinion.

Conclusions relating to going concern

We have nothing to report in respect of the following matter in relation to which the ISAs (UK) require us to report to you whether we have anything material to add or draw attention to in relation to:

- the directors' statement in the parent company financial statements about whether the directors considered it appropriate to adopt the going concern basis of accounting in preparing the parent company financial statements and the directors' identification of any material uncertainties to the parent company's ability to continue to do so over a period of at least twelve months from the date of approval of the parent company financial statements.

Key audit matters[65]

Key audit matters are those matters that, in our professional judgment, were of most significance in our audit of the parent company financial statements of the current period and include the most significant assessed risks of material misstatement (whether or not due to fraud) we identified, including those which had the greatest effect on: the overall audit strategy, the allocation of resources in the audit; and directing the efforts of the engagement team. These matters were addressed in the context of our audit of the parent company financial statements as a whole, and in forming our opinion thereon, and we do not provide a separate opinion on these matters.

[*Description of each key audit matter in accordance with ISA (UK) 701.*]

Our application of materiality[66]

[*Explanation of how the auditor applied the concept of materiality in planning and performing the parent company audit. This is required to include the threshold used by the auditor as being materiality for the parent company financial statements as a whole but may include other relevant disclosures.[67]*]

---

[65] *Key audit matters that relate solely to the parent company must be included within the auditor's report on the parent company financial statements for public interest entities and cannot be cross-referred to the auditor's report on the group financial statements.*

[66] *As noted in paragraph 49 of this Compendium, the explanation of how the auditor applied the concept of materiality in planning and performing the parent company audit may be presented either in the auditor's report on the parent company financial statements or separately identified in the auditor's report on the group financial statements via a cross-reference from the Other Matter paragraph.*

[67] *ISA (UK) 701, paragraph A59-1 includes other disclosures relevant to an explanation of how the auditor applied the context of materiality in planning and performing the audit.*

An overview of the scope of our audit[68]

[Overview of the scope of the parent company audit, including an explanation of how the scope addressed each key audit matter and was influenced by the auditor's application of materiality for the parent company financial statements as a whole.]

Other information

The directors are responsible for the other information. The other information comprises the information included in the annual report,[69] other than the financial statements and our auditor's report thereon. Our opinion on the financial statements does not cover the other information and, except to the extent otherwise explicitly stated in our report, we do not express any form of assurance conclusion thereon.

In connection with our audit of the parent company financial statements, our responsibility is to read the other information and, in doing so, consider whether the other information is materially inconsistent with the parent company financial statements or our knowledge obtained in the audit or otherwise appears to be materially misstated. If we identify such material inconsistencies or apparent material misstatements, we are required to determine whether there is a material misstatement of the parent company financial statements or a material misstatement of the other information.

If, based on the work we have performed, we conclude that there is a material misstatement of this other information, we are required to report that fact. We have nothing to report in this regard.

Opinion on other matters prescribed by the Companies Act 2006

In our opinion, the part of the directors' remuneration report to be audited has been properly prepared in accordance with the Companies Act 2006.

In our opinion, based on the work undertaken in the course of the audit:

- the information given in the strategic report and the directors' report for the financial year for which the parent company financial statements are prepared is consistent with the financial statements; and

- the strategic report and the directors' report have been prepared in accordance with applicable legal requirements.

In the light of the knowledge and understanding of the parent company and its environment obtained in the course of the audit, we have not identified material misstatements in the strategic report or the directors' report.

Matters on which we are required to report by exception

We have nothing to report in respect of the following matters in relation to which the Companies Act 2006 requires us to report to you if, in our opinion:

- adequate accounting records have not been kept by the parent company, or returns adequate for our audit have not been received from branches not visited by us; or

---

[68] *As noted in paragraph 49 of this Compendium, the overview of the scope of the parent company audit may be presented either in the auditor's report on the parent company financial statements or separately identified in the auditor's report on the group financial statements via a cross-reference from the Other Matter paragraph.*

[69] *The term used to describe the annual report should be the same as that used by the directors.*

- the parent company financial statements and the part of the directors' remuneration report to be audited are not in agreement with the accounting records and returns; or

- certain disclosures of directors' remuneration specified by law are not made; or

- we have not received all the information and explanations we require for our audit.

Responsibilities of directors

As explained more fully in the directors' responsibilities statement [set out on page ...], the directors are responsible for the preparation of the parent company financial statements and for being satisfied that they give a true and fair view, and for such internal control as the directors determine is necessary to enable the preparation of parent company financial statements that are free from material misstatement, whether due to fraud or error.

In preparing the parent company financial statements, the directors are responsible for assessing the parent company's ability to continue as a going concern, disclosing, as applicable, matters related to going concern and using the going concern basis of accounting unless the directors either intend to liquidate the parent company or to cease operations, or have no realistic alternative but to do so.

Auditor's responsibilities for the audit of the parent company financial statements

Our objectives are to obtain reasonable assurance about whether the parent company financial statements as a whole are free from material misstatement, whether due to fraud or error, and to issue an auditor's report that includes our opinion. Reasonable assurance is a high level of assurance, but is not a guarantee that an audit conducted in accordance with ISAs (UK) will always detect a material misstatement when it exists. Misstatements can arise from fraud or error and are considered material if, individually or in the aggregate, they could reasonably be expected to influence the economic decisions of users taken on the basis of these parent company financial statements.

[*Explanation as to what extent the audit was considered capable of detecting irregularities, including fraud.*]

A further description of our responsibilities for the audit of the parent company financial statements is located on the Financial Reporting Council's website at: [*website link*].[70] This description forms part of our auditor's report.

Other matters which we are required to address

We were appointed by [*state by whom or which body the auditor was appointed*] on [*date*]. The period of total uninterrupted engagement including previous renewals and reappointments of the firm is [X] years.

The non-audit services prohibited by the FRC's Ethical Standard were not provided to the parent company and its controlled undertakings and we remain independent of the parent company and its controlled undertakings in conducting our audit.

---

[70] *See paragraph 38 of this Compendium.*

[Indicate any services, in addition to the audit, which were provided by the firm to the parent company and its controlled undertaking(s) that have not been disclosed in the financial statements or elsewhere in the annual report.]

Our audit opinion is consistent with the additional report to the audit committee.

We have reported separately on the group financial statements of [XYZ Plc] for the year ended [*date*]. [That report includes details of the group key audit matters; how we applied the concept of materiality in planning and performing our audit; and an overview of the scope of our audit.[71]] [That report includes a statement on a material uncertainty related to going concern.] [That report includes an emphasis of matter.] [The opinion in that report is [qualified / an adverse opinion / a disclaimer of opinion].]

[Signature]

John Smith (Senior Statutory Auditor)

For and on behalf of ABC LLP, Statutory Auditor

[Address]

[Date]

---

[71] *See paragraph 49 of this Compendium.*

Bulletin: The Auditor's Association with Preliminary Announcements made in accordance with UK Listing Rules (2017)

(December 2017)

Contents

	Paragraphs
Introduction	1
Listing Rule requirements	2 - 4
Companies Act requirements	5 - 6
UK Corporate Governance Code	7
The Role of the Auditor	8 - 14
Terms of engagement	15 - 18
Procedures	19 - 40
Planning	19
Preliminary announcements based on audited financial statements	20
Preliminary announcements based on draft financial statements	21 - 24
All preliminary announcements	25 - 26
Alternative performance measures	27 - 30
Management commentary	31 - 34
Directors' approval of the preliminary announcement	35
Modification of the auditor's report	36 - 37
Communication of agreement	38 - 40

Appendices

Appendix 1 – Illustrative example letter to directors indicating auditor's agreement with preliminary announcement

Appendix 2 – Illustrative example terms of engagement: audit completed

Appendix 3 – Illustrative example terms of engagement: audit not completed

Appendix 4 – Illustrative report on the auditor's agreement to the preliminary announcement and the status of the audit of the statutory financial statements"

Introduction

1   This Bulletin provides guidance for the auditor concerning its responsibilities with regard to preliminary announcements.[1] The updated Bulletin reflects:

(a)   changes in the UK Listing Rules since 2008;

(b)   changes to International Standards on Auditing (ISAs) (UK);

(c)   new guidance from the European Securities and Markets Authority (ESMA) about alternative performance measures[2]; and

(d)   changes to the UK Corporate Governance Code and the principle that the board should present a fair, balanced and understandable assessment of the company's position and prospects.[3]

Listing Rule Requirements

2   There is no requirement for a listed company to publish a preliminary statement of annual results. When a listed company choses to do so, then under UKLA Listing Rule 9.7A.1R:

(1)   the statement must be published as soon as possible after it has been approved by the board;

(2)   the statement must be agreed with the company's auditors prior to publication;

(3)   the statement must show the figures in the form of a table, including the items required for a half-yearly report, consistent with the presentation to be adopted in the annual accounts for that financial year;[4]

(4)   the statement must give details of the nature of any likely modification or emphasis-of-matter paragraph that may be contained in the auditor's report required to be included with the annual financial report; and

(5)   the statement must include any significant additional information necessary for the purpose of assessing the results being announced.

3   There are no formal requirements which relate to the preparation of preliminary announcements by companies listed on other exchanges such as the Alternative Investment Market (AIM). In practice, however, other sectors of the UK listed market tend to follow the practice adopted by FTSE companies.

4   In accordance with UKLA[5] Listing Rule 9.7A.3 the FCA may authorise the omission from any preliminary announcement of information required by UKLA Listing Rule 9.7A.1 R if it considers that disclosure of such information would be contrary to the public interest or seriously detrimental to the listed company, provided that such omission would not be likely to mislead the public with regard

---

[1] In the Listing Rules preliminary announcements are described as "preliminary statements of annual results".

[2] https://www.esma.europa.eu/press-news/esma-news/esma-publishes-final-guidelines-alternative-performance-measures.

[3] https://www.frc.org.uk/getattachment/ca7e94c4-b9a9-49e2-a824-ad76a322873c/UK-Corporate-Governance-Code-April-2016.pdf.

[4] In March 2017 the UKLA clarified that: "We are aware that some issuers have read this requirement in conjunction with the requirement to prepare half-yearly accounts in accordance with International Accounting Standard (IAS) 34 and have concluded that they must comply with IAS 34 for prelims. It is not the intent of either the LRs or the DTRs to require prelims, where prepared, to be in accordance with IAS 34." UKLA / TN / 502.2.

[5] In the UK the term "Listing Authority" refers to the United Kingdom Listing Authority (UKLA) of the Financial Conduct Authority ("FCA") acting in its capacity as the competent authority for the purposes of Part VI of the Financial Services and Markets Act 2000.

to facts and circumstances, knowledge of which is essential for the assessment of the shares.

Companies Act Requirements

In the United Kingdom, preliminary announcements constitute non-statutory accounts under section 435 of the Companies Act 2006 (CA 2006) and must include a statement indicating: **5**

(a)   that they are not the company's statutory accounts;

(b)   whether statutory accounts dealing with any financial year with which the non-statutory accounts purport to deal have been delivered to the registrar;

(c)   whether an auditor's report has been made on the company's statutory accounts for any such financial year; and if so whether the report –

    (i)   was qualified or unqualified, or included a reference to any matters to which the auditor drew attention by way of emphasis without qualifying the report, or

    (ii)   contained a statement under section 498(2) (accounting records or returns inadequate or accounts or directors' remuneration report not agreeing with records and returns), or section 498(3) (failure to obtain necessary information and explanations).

The company must not publish with non-statutory accounts the auditor's report on the company's statutory accounts (section 435(2) CA 2006).   **6**

UK Corporate Governance Code

A main principle of the UK Corporate Governance Code is that the board should present a fair, balanced and understandable assessment of the company's position and prospects. A supporting principle of the Code is that, "The board's responsibility to present a fair, balanced and understandable assessment extends to interim and other price-sensitive public reports and reports to regulators as well as to information required to be presented by statutory requirements. The board should establish arrangements that will enable it to ensure that the information presented is fair, balanced and understandable."[6]   **7**

The Role of the Auditor

If a company decides to make a preliminary announcement it will be the first public communication of that company's full year results and year-end financial position. Preliminary announcements form one of the focal points for investor interest, primarily because they confirm or update market expectations. Because of this the auditor of a listed company has an important role to play in the process leading to the orderly release of preliminary announcements.   **8**

Both the content and the preparation of any preliminary announcement are the responsibility of the company's directors. The directors of companies having equities on the Official List are required by the Listing Rules to have agreed the preliminary announcement with the auditor prior to publication (UKLA Listing Rule 9.7A.1R (2)).   **9**

---

[6]   *C.1, UK Corporate Governance Code (2016), https://www.frc.org.uk/getattachment/ca7e94c4-b9a9-49e2-a824-ad76a322873c/UK-Corporate-Governance-Code-April-2016.pdf*

10   The UK Listing Rules do not indicate what form the agreement with the auditor should take, or the extent of work expected of the auditor before the auditor gives its agreement. This Bulletin provides guidance on the procedures that would normally be carried out by the auditor and on communicating the outcome of such procedures to the directors.

11   Many companies provide more information in their preliminary announcement than the minimum requirements of the Listing Rules. In the opinion of the FRC it is neither practical nor desirable for the auditor to agree to anything less than the entire content of the preliminary announcement.

12   In this Bulletin the term "Preliminary Announcement" encompasses:

(a)   the disclosures required to be made by United Kingdom Listing Authority (UKLA) Listing Rule 9.7A.1R; and

(b)   other additional information (highlights, Chairman's Statement, narrative disclosures, management commentary, press release etc) that is released to a Regulatory Information Service[7] as part of a preliminary announcement.

Any presentation to analysts, trading statement, interim management statement or half-yearly financial report is not included within the definition of preliminary announcement.

13   There is an expectation that the information in a preliminary announcement will be consistent with that in the audited financial statements. There is an unavoidable risk that the company may wish to revise its preliminary announcement in the light of audit findings or other developments arising unless the preliminary announcement is issued at the same time that the full financial statements are approved by the directors and the auditor has signed the auditor's report on them. However, it has also been the accepted practice of some companies to issue the preliminary announcement, with their auditor's agreement, when the audit is at an "advanced stage" but before the auditor's report on the financial statements has been signed. This Bulletin provides guidance on interpreting the expression "advanced stage".

14   There is no requirement for a preliminary announcement to include an auditor's report. However, to avoid possible misunderstanding and to make explicit their agreement to the preliminary announcement the auditor issues a letter to the company signifying its agreement (see Appendix 1). The auditor may also wish to agree to the inclusion of a voluntary report by the auditor within the preliminary announcement, which sets out the respective responsibilities of the directors and the auditors; procedures performed by the auditor to agree to its publication; and, the status of the audit of the related statutory financial statements (see Appendix 4). The auditor could, if the auditor's report has been issued refer to key audit matters and other matters addressed in the report.

Terms of Engagement

15   It is in the interests of both the auditor and the company that the auditor's role in respect of the preliminary announcement is set out in writing; typically by including relevant paragraphs in the audit engagement letter. To avoid misunderstandings the engagement letter describes the auditor's understanding of the process of "agreeing" the preliminary announcement.

---

[7] *Regulatory Information Service is the term used for any organisation through which the Listing Rules require listed companies to disseminate price sensitive information.*

In circumstances where the auditor is to agree to a preliminary announcement **16** based on financial statements on which its audit is not complete the engagement letter includes cautionary language to the effect that there is an unavoidable risk that the company may wish to revise its preliminary announcement in the light of audit findings or other developments occurring before the completion of the audit. (See Appendix 3).

Matters that may be dealt with in the engagement letter include: **17**

(a) the responsibility of the directors for the preparation of any preliminary announcement;

(b) the fact that the auditor will conduct its work in accordance with this Bulletin;

(c) a statement as to whether the auditor believes it is management's intention that the preliminary announcement will be based on audited financial statements or on draft financial statements upon which the auditor has not issued a report;

(d) a statement that the auditor will issue a letter confirming its agreement to the preliminary announcement;

(e) whether a voluntary statement by the auditor on the status of the audit, and the procedures carried out when agreeing to the publication of the preliminary announcement, will be prepared and included;

(f) that the auditor will consider the appropriateness of any details included within the preliminary announcement which relate to any likely or actual modification of the auditor's report, or emphasis of matter paragraph, on the statutory financial statements; and

(g) a statement explaining the inherent limitations of the auditor's work.

Examples of suitable paragraphs for inclusion in a letter of engagement are given **18** in Appendix 2 for circumstances where the preliminary announcement is to be based on audited financial statements and in Appendix 3 for circumstances where the preliminary announcement is to be based on draft financial statements.

Procedures

Planning

Where the preliminary announcement is to be based on draft financial statements **19** the company's timetable should allow the auditor to have completed the audit other than for those matters set out in paragraph 23 below.

Preliminary announcements based on audited financial statements

There is an expectation on the part of users that the information in a preliminary **20** announcement will be consistent with that in the audited financial statements. The only way of achieving absolute certainty of this is for the audit of the financial statements to have been completed and the contents of the preliminary announcement to have been extracted from audited financial statements that had been approved and signed by the directors and upon which the auditor has signed the auditor's report. Current market practice is for the majority of entities who issue preliminary announcements to do so based on audited information.

Preliminary announcements based on draft financial statements

21   Companies may wish to issue their preliminary announcement before the audit is complete. There are additional risks for directors in these circumstances if further information comes to light as a result of the auditor's procedures that the directors decide should be reflected in the financial statements and gives rise to the need for a revised announcement by the company. Before agreeing to the release of the preliminary announcement, therefore, the directors will need to ensure they are satisfied that the information it contains will be consistent with the information that will be contained in the audited financial statements.

22   The auditor will need to be satisfied that any matters outstanding with respect to the audit will be unlikely to result in changes to the information contained in the preliminary announcement. This means that the audit of the financial statements must be at an advanced stage and that, subject only to unforeseen events, the auditor expects to be in a position to issue the auditor's report on the financial statements incorporating the amounts upon which the preliminary announcement is based, and know what that auditor's report will state.

23   This means completing the audit, including the engagement quality control review as described in paragraphs 19 to 22 of ISA (UK) 220 (Revised June 2016) "Quality control for an audit of financial statements", subject only to the following:

    (a)   clearing outstanding audit matters which the auditor is satisfied are unlikely to have a material impact on the financial statements or disclosures insofar as they affect the preliminary announcement;

    (b)   completing audit procedures on the detail of note disclosures to the financial statements that will not have a material impact on the primary financial statements and completing the auditor's work relating to "other information" in the annual report, in accordance with ISA (UK) 720 (Revised June 2016) "The Auditor's Responsibilities Relating to Other Information";

    (c)   updating the subsequent events review to cover the period between the issue of the preliminary announcement and the date of the auditor's report on the financial statements; and

    (d)   obtaining final signed written representations from management and establishing that the financial statements have been reviewed and approved by the directors.

24   In advance of the preliminary announcement the auditor discusses with management the representations that the auditor will be likely to require in order to issue its report on the financial statements. If management expresses reservations about its ability or willingness to make such representations the auditor does not agree to the preliminary announcement.

All preliminary announcements

25   The following procedures will normally be carried out by the auditor in relation to the preliminary announcement itself regardless of whether it is based on draft financial statements or extracted from audited financial statements:

    (a)   checking that the figures in the preliminary announcement covering the full year have been accurately extracted from the audited or draft financial statements; and reflect the presentation to be adopted in the audited financial statements. For example, any summarisation should not change the order in which items are presented where this is specified by law or accounting standards;

(b) considering whether the information (including the management commentary) is consistent with other expected contents of the annual report of which the auditor is aware; and

(c) considering whether the financial information in the preliminary announcement is misstated. A misstatement exists when the information is stated incorrectly or presented in a misleading manner. A misstatement may arise, for example, as a result of an omission of a significant change of accounting policy disclosed or due to be disclosed in the audited financial statements.

The auditor considers whether the preliminary announcement includes a statement **26** by directors as required by section 435 of CA 2006 (see paragraph 5) and whether the preliminary announcement includes the minimum information required by UKLA Listing Rule 9.7A.1 (see paragraph 2).

Alternative performance measures

Regulators recognise that in some circumstances the presentation of alternative **27** performance measures (APMs)[8] and associated narrative explanations with the statutory results may help shareholders understand better the financial performance of a company. The FRC believes that when APMs are presented in an Annual Report, compliance with Guidelines issued by the European Securities and Markets Authority (ESMA), will help ensure that, taken as a whole, it is fair, balanced and understandable.[9]

However, regulators are also concerned that in other instances such APMs have **28** the potential to be misleading and shareholders may sometimes be misinformed by the manner in which APMs are included in preliminary announcements with which the auditor is associated. The Listing Rules require that, "An issuer must take reasonable care to ensure that any information it notifies to a RIS or makes available through the FCA is not misleading, false or deceptive and does not omit anything likely to affect the import of the information."[10] In this context, the ESMA guidelines provide a useful framework which the auditor may draw on in its consideration of the use and presentation of APMs in the preliminary announcement.

In this context where the preliminary announcement includes APMs, before **29** agreeing to its release, the auditor considers whether appropriate prominence is given to statutory financial information and whether:

(a) the use, relevance and reliability of APMs has been explained;

(b) the APMs used have been clearly defined, and have been given meaningful labels reflecting their content and basis of calculation;

(c) the APMs have been reconciled to the most directly reconcilable line item, subtotal or total presented in the financial statements of the corresponding period; and

---

[8] *The European Securities and Markets Authority define an APM as, "a financial measure of historical or future financial performance, financial position or cash flows, other than a financial measure defined or specified in the applicable financial reporting framework." ESMA Guidelines on Alternative Performance Measures, para.17.*

[9] *https://www.frc.org.uk/news/may-2016/faqs-on-esma-apm-guidelines.*

[10] *UKLA Listing Rule 1.3.3R.*

(d)   comparatives have been included, and where the basis of calculation has changed over time this is explained.[11]

30   If the auditor does not believe that the preliminary announcement satisfies these conditions, it seeks to resolve the issues arising with the directors. If it is unable to resolve the issues the auditor considers whether to withhold its consent to the release of the announcement.

Management commentary

31   An important feature of preliminary announcements is a management commentary on the company's performance during the year and its position at the year-end. Such management commentary may include comments on the final interim period in the preliminary announcement and separate presentation of the final interim period figures to the extent this is necessary to support the management commentary. The extent of information on the final interim period will vary from company to company and in some cases this may only consist of a reference to the key figures in the management commentary.

32   The auditor reads the management commentary, any other narrative disclosures and any final interim period figures and considers whether:

(a)   the management commentary is fair, balanced and understandable;

(b)   there is a material inconsistency between the other information and the financial statements. As the basis for this consideration, the auditor shall, to evaluate their consistency, compare selected amounts or other items in the other information (that are intended to be the same as, to summarize, or to provide greater detail about, the amounts or other items in the financial statements) with such amounts or other items in the financial statements; and

(c)   there is a material inconsistency between the other information and the auditor's knowledge obtained in the audit, in the context of audit evidence obtained and conclusions reached in the audit.

Alternative performance measures (APMs) are part of management commentary and (b) above applies to it. The management commentary is taken to mean everything in the preliminary announcement that is not financial information extracted from the audited or draft financial statements. This consideration is based on the consideration required in ISA (UK) 720 and that the application material in that ISA may assist the auditor in performing their work on the management commentary.

33   If the auditor becomes aware of any material inconsistencies with the draft financial statements or with information obtained during the audit, it seeks to resolve them with the directors. If it is unable to resolve the matters the auditor withholds its consent to the publication of the preliminary announcement.

34   In the case of a preliminary announcement based on audited financial statements, the auditor will read the text of any Chairman's Statement, business review or similar document to be included in the annual report from which the management commentary in the preliminary announcement will usually be derived. For a preliminary announcement based on draft financial statements, this will be done on the latest draft of such documents that are available.

---

[11]   *https://www.esma.europa.eu/press-news/esma-news/esma-publishes-final-guidelines-alternative-performancemeasures*

Directors' approval of the preliminary announcement

The auditor does not agree to the preliminary announcement until its entire content **35** has been formally approved by the board or by a duly authorised committee[12] of the board.

Modification of the auditor's report

The Listing Rules require that the preliminary announcement must give details of **36** the nature of any likely modification or emphasis-of-matter paragraph that may be contained in the auditor's report required to be included with the annual financial report.[13]

Where reference is made in a preliminary announcement to an actual or possible **37** qualified opinion or emphasis of matter, the directors should give adequate prominence to that information in the announcement and the auditor should be satisfied in this regard.[14] If the auditor has concerns about the appropriateness of the wording of a statement referring to a modified report it, and cannot resolve these concerns through discussion with management, it should consider what actions to take. These actions may include raising the matter with the UK Listing Authority, communicating with the audit committee, not giving agreement to publication of the preliminary announcement, and/or seeking legal advice.

Communication of agreement

The FRC encourages the auditor to make explicit its agreement to the issue of the **38** preliminary announcement by sending a letter to the directors. An example of such a letter is given in Appendix 1. Similarly, if the auditor is not in agreement with the content of the preliminary announcement, it communicates this to the directors by sending them a letter setting out the reasons for its disagreement, advising the directors that the preliminary announcement should not be published.

The auditor may become aware that a company has released a preliminary **39** announcement without first obtaining its agreement. There may be a number of reasons for this ranging from innocent oversight on the part of the directors to the directors knowingly releasing a preliminary announcement with which the auditor disagrees. The action that the auditor takes depends on the particular circumstances. In circumstances where a preliminary announcement is inadvertently released without the auditor's knowledge, but with which the auditor does in fact agree, the auditor may wish to remind the directors of their obligation under the Listing Rules to have obtained the auditor's agreement.

However, at the other end of the spectrum, where the auditor becomes aware that **40** the directors have released an announcement with which it disagrees, it notifies the UK Listing Authority of the fact that it had not agreed to the announcement, and takes legal advice.

---

[12] *The UK Corporate Governance Code states that one of the main roles and responsibilities of the audit committee is "to monitor the integrity of the financial statements of the company, and any formal announcements relating to the company's financial performance, reviewing significant financial reporting judgements contained in them" (UK Corporate Governance Code provision C.3.2).*

[13] *UKLA Listing Rule 9.7a.1.R.*

[14] *In accordance with UKLA Listing Rule 1.3.3R (see para. 28 above).*

Appendices

- **Appendix 1** – Illustrative Example Letter to Directors Indicating Auditor's Agreement to Preliminary Announcement

- **Appendix 2** – Illustrative Example Terms of Engagement: Audit Completed

- **Appendix 3** – Illustrative Example Terms of Engagement: Audit Not Completed

- **Appendix 4** – Illustrative Report on the Auditor's Agreement to the Preliminary Announcement and the Status of the Audit of the Statutory Financial Statements

Appendix 1 – Illustrative Example Letter To Directors Indicating Auditor's Agreement With Preliminary Announcement

The Directors

XYZ plc: preliminary announcement of results for year ended [...]

In accordance with the terms of our engagement letter dated [ ], we have reviewed the attached proposed preliminary announcement of XYZ plc for the year ended [ ]. Our work was conducted having regard to the Financial Reporting Council's Bulletin "The Auditor's Association with Preliminary Announcements made in accordance with the requirements of the UK Listing Rules". As directors you have accepted responsibility for preparing and issuing the preliminary announcement.

Our responsibility is solely to give our agreement to the preliminary announcement having carried out the procedures specified in the Bulletin as providing a basis for such agreement. In this regard we agree to the preliminary announcement being notified to [a Regulatory Information Service]].

[As you are aware we are not in a position to sign our auditor's report on the annual financial statements as they have not yet been approved by the directors and we have not yet ... [insert significant procedures that are yet to be completed, for example completing the subsequent events review and obtaining final signed written representations from directors ...]. Consequently there can be no absolute certainty that we will be in a position to issue an unmodified audit report on financial statements consistent with the results and financial position reported in the preliminary announcement. However, at the present time, we are not aware of any matters that may give rise to a modification to our report. In the event that such matters do come to our attention we will inform you immediately.]

Yours faithfully

[*Signature*]

John Smith (Senior Statutory Auditor)

For and on behalf of ABC LLP, Statutory Auditor

[*Address*]

[*Date*]

Appendix 2 – Illustrative Example Terms of Engagement: Audit Completed

Extract from Letter of Engagement

The Listing Rules require that "a preliminary statement of annual results … must be agreed with the company's auditor prior to publication". As directors of the company, you have accepted responsibility for preparing and issuing any preliminary announcement and ensuring that we agree to its release.

We undertake to review the preliminary announcement having regard to the Financial Reporting Council's Bulletin "The Auditor's Association with Preliminary Announcements made in accordance with the requirements of the UK Listing Rules". Accordingly, our review will be limited to checking the accuracy of extraction of the financial information in the preliminary announcement from the audited financial statements of the company for that year, considering whether any "alternative performance measures" and associated narrative explanations may be misleading and reading the management commentary, including any comments on or separate presentation of the final interim period figures, and considering whether it is in conflict with the information that we obtained in the course of our audit.

The Listing Rules require that the preliminary announcement must include a statement including details of the nature of any likely modification or emphasis-of-matter paragraph that may be contained in the auditor's report required to be included with the annual financial report.[15] We will also review the appropriateness of the wording of any such statement.

You will provide us with such information and explanations as we consider necessary for the purposes of our work. We shall request sight of the preliminary announcement in sufficient time to enable us to complete our work. The Board/ committee of the Board will formally approve the preliminary announcement before we agree to it.

In the event that we disagree with the release of the preliminary announcement we will send you a letter setting out the reasons why.

---

[15] *UKLA Listing Rule 9.7a.1.R.*

Appendix 3 – Illustrative Example Terms of Engagement: Audit Not Completed

Extract from Letter of Engagement

The Listing Rules require that "a preliminary statement[1] of annual results ... must be agreed with the company's auditor prior to publication". As directors of the company, you have accepted responsibility for preparing and issuing any preliminary announcement and ensuring that we agree to its release.

We undertake to review the preliminary announcement having regard to the Financial Reporting Council's Bulletin "The Auditor's Association with Preliminary Announcements made in accordance with the requirements of the UK Listing Rules". Accordingly, our review will be limited to checking the accuracy of extraction of the financial information in the preliminary announcement from the latest available draft financial statements of the company for that year, considering whether any "alternative performance measures" and associated narrative explanations may be misleading and reading the management commentary, including any comments on or separate presentation of the final interim period figures, and considering whether it is in conflict with the information that we have obtained in the course of our audit.

The Listing Rules require that the preliminary announcement must include a statement including details of the nature of any likely modification or emphasis-of-matter paragraph that may be contained in the auditor's report required to be included with the annual financial report.[16] We will also review the appropriateness of the wording of any such statement.

You will provide us with such information and explanations as we consider necessary for the purposes of our work. We shall request sight of the preliminary announcement in sufficient time to enable us to complete our work. The Board/committee of the Board will formally approve the preliminary announcement before we agree to it. You will also make available to us the proposed text of the company's annual report.

We will not agree to the release of the preliminary announcement until the audit is complete subject only to the following:

(a) clearing outstanding audit matters which we are satisfied are unlikely to have a material impact on the financial statements or disclosures insofar as they affect the preliminary announcement;

(b) completing audit procedures on the detail of note disclosures to the financial statements that will not have a material impact on the primary financial statements and completing our reading of other information in the annual report, in accordance with ISA (UK) 720 (Revised June 2016), "The Auditor's Responsibilities Relating to Other Information";

(c) updating the subsequent events review to cover the period between the date of the preliminary announcement and the date of our auditor's report on the financial statements; and

(d) obtaining final signed written representations from management and establishing that the financial statements have been reviewed and approved by the directors.

---

[16] *UKLA Listing Rule 9.7a.1.R.*

The scope of our work will be necessarily limited in that, we will only be able to check the consistency of the preliminary announcement with draft financial statements on which our audit is incomplete. Accordingly, we shall not, at that stage, know whether further adjustments may be required to those draft financial statements. Consequently, there is an unavoidable risk that the company may wish to revise its preliminary announcement in the light of audit findings or other developments occurring between the preliminary announcement being notified to a Regulatory Information Service and the completion of the audit.

In the event that we disagree with the release of the preliminary announcement we will send you a letter setting out the reasons why.

Appendix 4 – Illustrative Report on the Auditor's Agreement to the Preliminary Announcement and the Status of the Audit of the Statutory Financial Statements

INDEPENDENT AUDITOR'S REPORT TO THE SHAREHOLDERS OF XYZ PLC ON THE PRELIMINARY ANNOUNCEMENT OF XYZ PLC

As the independent auditor of [XYZ PLC] we are required by UK Listing Rule LR 9.7A.1 (2) R[17] to agree to the publication of [XYZ PLC]'s preliminary statement of annual results for the period ended [Date].

The preliminary statement of annual results for the period ended [Date] includes [description of the content of the preliminary announcement which the auditor has agreed to be published, including disclosures required by the Listing rules and any additional content such as highlights/overview, Chairman's Statement, narrative disclosures, management commentary, press release etc.]. We are not required to agree to the publication of [description of additional information published alongside the preliminary statement of annual results, which may include presentations to analysts, trading statement, interim management statement or half-yearly financial report].

The Directors of [XYZ PLC] are responsible for the preparation, presentation and publication of the preliminary statement of annual results in accordance with the UK Listing Rules.

We are responsible for agreeing to the publication of the preliminary statement of annual results, having regard to the Financial Reporting Council's Bulletin "The Auditor's Association with Preliminary Announcements made in accordance with the requirements of the UK Listing Rules".

Status of our audit of the financial statements

[Our audit of the annual financial statements of XYZ PLC is complete and we signed our auditor's report on [Date]. Our auditor's report [is not modified and contains no emphasis of matter paragraph]/[description of modification/emphasis of matter]]

[We are not in a position to sign our auditor's report on the annual financial statements [of XYZ PLC] as they have not yet been approved by the Directors. In accordance with the FRC's Bulletin "The Auditor's Association with Preliminary Announcements made in accordance with the requirements of the UK Listing Rules" our audit is complete to an advanced stage, except for [insert significant procedures that are yet to be completed, for example completing the subsequent events review and obtaining final signed written representations from Directors ...]. Consequently there can be no absolute certainty that we will be in a position to issue an unmodified audit report on financial statements consistent with the results and financial position reported in the preliminary announcement. However, at the present time, we are not aware of any matters that may give rise to a modification to our report and/or and emphasis of matter paragraph.]

---

[17] *Issued by the UK Listing Authority of the Financial Conduct Authority*

Procedures performed to agree to the preliminary announcement of annual results

In order to agree to the publication of the preliminary announcement of annual results [of XYZ PLC] we carried out the following procedures:

[insert description of procedures carried out]

[*Signature*]

John Smith (Senior Statutory Auditor)

For and on behalf of ABC LLP, Statutory Auditor

[*Address*]

[*Date*]

Part Seven

*ICAEW Guidance on
Auditing and Reporting*

Tech 04/02AAF – Management Representation Letters: Explanatory Note (2018)

Contents

ISA (UK) 580 WRITTEN REPRESENTATIONS

INCREASING THE USEFULNESS OF WRITTEN REPRESENTATIONS
AS AUDIT EVIDENCE

REMINDING THE DIRECTORS OF THEIR RESPONSIBILITIES UNDER THE
COMPANIES ACT 2006

This guidance was issued by the Audit and Assurance Faculty of the Institute of Chartered Accountants in England and Wales in November 2002 and updated in March 2018.

The purpose of this guidance is to remind auditors of the need to consider the reliability of written representations as audit evidence. This guidance draws attention to specific application and other explanatory material in International Standard on Auditing (ISA) (UK) 580 *Written Representations*, in order to underline the importance of ensuring that such representations are reliable. The guidance is not intended to be comprehensive and is not a substitute for the procedures or related material contained in ISA (UK) 580, or for specific measures that may be appropriate to particular matters or engagements.

ISBN 978-1-78363-937-3

ISA (UK) 580 WRITTEN REPRESENTATIONS

ISA (UK) 580 requires auditors to request written representations from management with appropriate responsibilities and knowledge of the matters concerned before their report is issued. In the UK, representations are requested from the directors (or, for entities other than companies, representatives of the body charged with governance). In particular, the auditor should obtain evidence that the directors acknowledge that they have fulfilled their collective responsibility for the preparation of the financial statements and that they have approved them. ISA (UK) 580 also requires that the auditor should request representations that the directors have provided the auditor with all relevant information and access as agreed in the terms of the audit engagement, and that all transactions have been recorded and are reflected in the financial statements. The auditor also requests other representations that they determine are necessary to support other audit evidence relevant to the financial statements or one or more specific assertions in the financial statements.

Paragraph 3 of ISA (UK) 580 states that, *Written representations are necessary information that the auditor requires in connection with the audit of the entity's financial statements.* However, as paragraph 4 of ISA (UK) 580 points out, *Although written representations provide necessary audit evidence, they do not provide sufficient appropriate audit evidence on their own about any of the matters with which they deal.* Unsupported representations by management do not normally constitute sufficient audit evidence. The only situations where corroborative evidence may not be available are those where the subject of the representations are management judgment or intentions.

Whatever their function in the body of evidence collected by an auditor to support the audit opinion, written representations are not a mere formality. This is why ISA (UK) 580 requires the auditor to take appropriate actions if the directors do not provide one or more of the requested representations, and specifically requires the auditor to disclaim their opinion if certain representations are not provided or if they conclude that certain representations are not reliable (ISA (UK) 580 paragraph 20).

INCREASING THE USEFULNESS OF WRITTEN REPRESENTATIONS AS AUDIT EVIDENCE

A High Court decision in 2002[1] emphasised the need for auditors to consider whether the directors making representations are sufficiently well-informed to do so. In this legal case, the auditor claimed that the representations by the director were recklessly fraudulent, and therefore gave them an absolute defence of circuity against the claim in damages which they faced. The auditor's claim failed, however, because they did not establish to the judge's satisfaction that the director signed the representation letters:

(i)   knowing that the statements in the letters were untrue, without an honest belief in their truth, or indifferent as to whether or not they were true;

(ii)   knowing that he had no reasonable grounds for making the statements, without an honest belief that he had such grounds, or indifferent as to whether he had or not.

---

[1] *Barings Futures Singapore v Deloitte & Touche.*

The judge did, however, address the issue of the result if the auditor had proved that, in signing the representation letters, the director was reckless of their truth or falsity. He concluded that, had such a case for fraudulent misrepresentation been established, he would have held that the company was vicariously liable for the director's action, and thus the auditor would have succeeded in their claim.

The need to consider the directors' ability to make the representations is reflected in the application guidance in ISA (UK) 580, which makes the following points (paragraphs A3 to A6):

- Due to their responsibilities for the preparation of the financial statements and the conduct of the entity's business, the directors would be expected to have sufficient knowledge of the process followed by the entity in preparing and presenting the financial statements and the assertions therein on which to base their representations

- The directors may decide to make inquiries of others, including individuals with specialised knowledge, such as internal counsel who may provide information essential to provisions for legal claims

- The directors may include qualifying language such as "to the best of our knowledge and belief", and it is normally reasonable for the auditor to accept such wording

- The auditor may request the directors to include in the representations a confirmation that they have made such inquiries as they considered appropriate to place them in the position to be able to make the requested representations.

In order to assist this process, and in particular to focus directors' attention on whether proper inquiries have been made, the auditor may find it helpful to request the directors to add a sentence to the representation letter. The illustrative representation letter in appendix 2 of ISA (UK) 580 includes the following suggestion:

We confirm that (, to the best of our knowledge and belief, having made such inquiries as we considered necessary for the purpose of appropriately informing ourselves):

Alternatively, the auditor might consider some wording along the following lines:

We confirm that the above/following representations are made on the basis of enquiries of management and staff with relevant knowledge and experience (and, where appropriate, of inspection of supporting documentation) sufficient to satisfy ourselves that we can properly make each of the above/following representations to you.

This wording is suggested for illustration only, and is not mandatory. It could help to reduce the impression given to directors that phrases such as *to the best of our knowledge and belief* may enable them not to make proper inquiries.

The auditor would further be well advised to ask the signatory(ies) what steps they took to obtain comfort that such an assertion had substance. In circumstances where the representations are being made by those distanced from the activities involved, for example the use of complex financial instruments, the auditor could suggest that the relevant member of management responsible provide specialised representations to the board. In this case it may be useful for the directors' own letter of representation to attach and refer to the specialist memorandum, to ensure that they retained overall responsibility.

REMINDING THE DIRECTORS OF THEIR RESPONSIBILITIES UNDER THE COMPANIES ACT 2006

Auditors may take the opportunity when discussing representations with the directors (and other staff, if applicable) to remind them of the statutory provisions relating to false or misleading statements. In particular, under section 501 of the Companies Act it is a criminal offence to knowingly or recklessly make to an auditor of a company a statement (oral or written) that conveys, or purports to convey, information or explanations that the auditor requires, or is entitled to require, that is misleading, false or deceptive in a material particular.

Similarly, under section 418 of the Companies Act, the directors' report is required to contain a statement that for each director, so far as they are aware, there is no relevant audit information of which the company's auditor is unaware, and they have taken all the steps that they ought to have taken as a director in order to make themselves aware of any relevant audit information and to establish that the company's auditor is aware of that information. Where this statement is false, every director who knew that it was false, or was reckless as to whether it was false, and failed to take reasonable steps to prevent the directors' report from being approved, is guilty of a criminal offence.

TECH 01/03AAF The Audit Report and Auditors' Duty of Care to Third Parties (Revised May 2018)

(May 2018)

Contents

	Paragraphs
Preface	
Background	1 - 3
Changes to audit reports	4 - 8
Responsibilities of auditors	9
Wording to include in the audit report	10 - 14
Purpose of the recommended wording	15
Wording for the engagement letter	16
Other points to communicate to clients	17
Alternative and/or additional actions	18 - 19
Legal considerations	20
Scope	21
Appendix 1	
Appendix 2	

This guidance was issued by the Audit and Assurance Faculty of the Institute of Chartered Accountants in England and Wales in January 2003, to assist auditors in managing the risk of inadvertently assuming a duty of care to third parties in relation to their audit reports. The guidance does not constitute an auditing standard. Professional judgement should be used in its application. It was updated in May 2018.

Preface

Auditors have been aware of the risk of taking on responsibilities to third parties with regard to their audit reports for a number of years. Sometimes a duty of care to a third party might be assumed inadvertently as a result of action or inaction by the auditors.

As the result of a judgment in the Scottish Court of Session, ICAEW took the advice of Leading Counsel and issued guidance which recommended that auditors who wish to manage the risk of liability to third parties use wording expressing clearly to whom they owe a duty of care (a "disclaimer").

The disclaimer recommended by ICAEW has subsequently been widely used by the profession in the statutory and non-statutory audit and other assurance reports of a range of entities.

Following a more recent judgment, as well as a number of changes to audit reports, ICAEW has again taken the advice of Leading Counsel and updated this guidance.

ICAEW continues to emphasise that the best risk management policy is for firms to take the steps that are necessary to carry out high quality audits. ICAEW's Audit and Assurance Faculty has provided guidance on this in its publications *Quality Control in the Audit Environment* on the International Standard on Quality Control 1 and *Improving Audit Quality Using Root Cause Analysis*, which actively promote audit quality. ICAEW's Audit and Assurance Faculty has also provided thought leadership on extended audit reports and the revolution in auditor communications in its publication *The Start of a Conversation*. Nothing in this guidance in any way detracts from what is said in those publications.

The Questions and Answers in Appendix 2 have been included to assist members in dealing with possible issues and misunderstandings that they might encounter.

Background

A Scottish judgment in *Royal Bank of Scotland plc v Bannerman Johnstone Maclay and others* ("*Bannerman*") highlighted the potential exposure of auditors to parties, other than the members of a company as a body, who assert that they rely on audit reports, in circumstances where the auditors have failed expressly to disclaim responsibility to those third parties. ICAEW issued guidance in 2003 to assist members in managing the risk of inadvertently assuming a duty of care in relation to their audit reports to third parties.   **1**

A more recent judgment of the High Court in England has provided helpful guidance: *Barclays Bank plc v Grant Thornton* ("*Barclays*"). The case concerned non-statutory audit reports prepared by the defendant auditor, which were passed to the claimant bank. There was no contract between the bank and the auditor. The bank alleged that the reports had been prepared negligently; that the auditor must have known that they would be passed to it; and that it had suffered loss as a result of relying on the misleading reports. It further alleged that the auditor owed it a duty of care in tort. The auditor made a summary application for the claim to be struck out on the ground that the presence of a *Bannerman*-type disclaimer in the reports made it impossible for the bank to prove that it was owed a duty of care. The judge, Cooke J., accepted this argument and struck out the claim. His judgment recognised that such disclaimers are commonly incorporated in audit reports. In effect, he held that users of audit reports can be expected to be   **2** commercially sophisticated parties, and that there is no good reason not to give effect to the terms of a clearly expressed disclaimer.

3   ICAEW believes that the *Barclays* decision provides strong support for the approach which it has been recommending to members since 2003.

Changes to audit reports

4   In June 2013, the Financial Reporting Council (FRC) issued a revised International Standard on Auditing (ISA) (UK and Ireland) 700 *The Independent Auditor's Report on Financial statements* which required auditors reporting on companies which complied with the UK Corporate Governance Code to provide significantly increased disclosure around risks, materiality and scope of the audit. The revisions were designed to complement changes to the UK Corporate Governance Code in October 2012 and were effective for the audits of financial statements for periods commencing on or after 1 October 2012.

5   In June 2016, the FRC issued new and revised ISAs (UK) which include the following:

5.1   Impacting all audit reports – ISA (UK) 700 (Revised June 2016) *Forming an Opinion and Reporting on Financial Statements*; and

5.2   Impacting the audit reports of listed, public interest and certain other entities – ISA (UK) 701 *Communicating Key Audit Matters in the Independent Auditor's Report.*

The changes are effective for the audits of financial statements for periods commencing on or after 17 June 2016.

6   Some of the key changes to audit reports for all entities are as follows:

6.1   Changes to the order of the reports, for example the "Opinion" section is the first section of the report; and

6.2   New requirements to report on going concern and other information, together with more detailed descriptions of the responsibilities of the directors and auditor, which increase the length of the reports.

7   There are further new requirements for audit reports of listed entities, public interest entities and other entities that are required, and those that choose voluntarily, to report on how they have applied the UK Corporate Governance Code. These include the requirement to communicate key audit matters, which may increase the length of the reports considerably depending on the number of such matters identified and reported.

8   ICAEW has now updated this guidance to reflect these changes to audit reports.

Responsibilities of auditors

9   Auditors have a responsibility to carry out their audits in accordance with auditing standards. These responsibilities are unchanged as a result of this guidance. The guidance is instead concerned with the question of to whom responsibilities are owed.

Wording to include in the audit report

It is clear that an auditor assumes responsibility for the audit report to the members   **10**
as a body. The *Bannerman* decision, read with earlier case law, indicates that the
absence of a disclaimer **may** (depending on the other circumstances in the
particular case) enable an inference to be drawn that the auditor has assumed
responsibility for the audit report to a third party. Having taken advice from
Leading Counsel, ICAEW continues to recommend that auditors who wish to
manage the risk of liability to third parties use a disclaimer. ICAEW would regard
the following wording as appropriate, and as suitably placed as the final section of
the audit report, directly preceding the auditor's signature:

> "*Use of our report*
>
> *This report is made solely to the company's members, as a body, in
> accordance with Chapter 3 of Part 16 of the Companies Act 2006. Our
> audit work has been undertaken so that we might state to the company's
> members those matters we are required to state to them in an auditor's
> report and for no other purpose. To the fullest extent permitted by law, we do
> not accept or assume responsibility to anyone other than the company and
> the company's members as a body, for our audit work, for this report, or for
> the opinions we have formed.*"

An example of an unqualified audit report for a non-publicly traded company   **11**
(based on the examples in Appendices 1 and 2 of the FRC's Bulletin:
*Compendium of illustrative auditor's reports on United Kingdom private sector
financial statements for periods commencing on or after 17 June 2016*), with this
wording included, is attached as Appendix 1 to this guidance. The wording may
also be included in this place in any of the example audit reports for general
purpose financial statements, including those with the requirement to
communicate key audit matters, in the FRC's Bulletin.

In the event that the text of the audit report differs from these examples, a check   **12**
should be made (with the assistance of legal advice where appropriate) to ensure that
this wording remains suitable without amendment. For entities other than companies,
the reference to the Companies Act will need to be replaced with reference to the
relevant legislation or, for non-statutory audits, the purpose of the report. ICAEW's
Helpsheets Preparing an audit report include appropriate wording for entities other
than companies, for non-statutory audits and for a range of specific situations.

Based on advice from Leading Counsel, ICAEW believes that it is desirable that   **13**
the same wording should appear in the same position in audit reports generally.
Consistency in these respects will promote clarity and certainty as to the scope of
the auditor's responsibility.

A possible exception to the location suggested above is in the example audit   **14**
reports for special purpose financial statements, single financial statements and
specific elements, accounts or items in ISA (UK) 800 (Revised) *Special
Considerations – Audits of Financial Statements prepared in accordance with
Special Purpose Frameworks* and ISA (UK) 805 (Revised) *Special
Considerations – Audits of Single Financial Statements and Specific Elements,
Accounts or Items of a Financial Statement.* ISA (UK) 800 requires that for special
purpose financial statements the auditor's report include an Emphasis of Matter
paragraph alerting users to the fact that the financial statements are for a special
purpose and further suggests that, where there is restriction on distribution or use,

this is included as part of that paragraph. It would seem reasonable to treat this wording in the same manner.

Purpose of the recommended wording

15   Auditors' responsibilities to their clients remain unaltered and as stated in paragraph 9 above, they are still required to carry out the audit in accordance with auditing standards. The purpose of the wording outlined in paragraph 10 above is to reduce the scope for the assumption of responsibilities to third parties.

Wording for the engagement letter

16   The form of an audit report is a matter for the discretion of the auditors (see ISA (UK) 700 (Revised June 2016) *Forming an Opinion and Reporting on Financial Statements*), provided that the opinion meets Companies Act requirements and is in accordance with auditing standards. It is not mandatory to amend engagement letters to make provision for the wording outlined in paragraph 10 above. However, having regard to the desirability of providing full information to the client, members may wish to include the following in the engagement letter:

> *"As noted above, our report will be made solely to the company's members, as a body, in accordance with Chapter 3 of Part 16 of the Companies Act 2006. Our audit work will be undertaken so that we might state to the company's members those matters we are required to state to them in an auditor's report and for no other purpose. In those circumstances, to the fullest extent permitted by law, we will not accept or assume responsibility to anyone other than the company and the company's members as a body, for our audit work, for the audit report, or for the opinions we form."*

Other points to communicate to clients

17   When auditors include the wording outlined in paragraph 10 above, it may be helpful to explain the following important points to their clients:

(a)   The inclusion of this wording does not affect the auditors' obligations to their clients. In fact it clarifies that the audit is for the benefit of the company's members in accordance with Chapter 3 of Part 16 of the Companies Act 2006. Auditors will have the same duties and liabilities to their clients as they have always had.

(b)   This wording does not mean that auditors will never agree to take on responsibilities to third parties such as lenders. All it does is make clear that auditors will only accept duties that are expressly agreed. It must be clear that if third parties want to rely on the audit work then they should approach the auditors to agree expressly the scope and nature of work auditors can do for them that meets their purposes.

Alternative and/or additional actions

18   Auditors may take alternative or additional steps to communicate with third parties which are intended to have the same effect as the recommended wording.

However, ICAEW strongly recommends that the auditor's report should include a disclaimer in the terms set out above.

If the wording outlined in paragraph 10 above is included in the audit report, **19** auditors should nevertheless remain vigilant to avoid the words being overridden by actions (contemporaneous or subsequent) which might be regarded as being inconsistent with the disclaimer. In particular, where auditors are aware of circumstances that might give rise to a duty of care to a third party. Where auditors wish to disclaim responsibility to the third party in these circumstances, as would normally be the case, they state this expressly in writing through the issue of a letter to the particular third party.

Legal considerations

This guidance provides a summary of what ICAEW believes to be the most **20** relevant considerations, based on the law at the time of issue and advice from Leading Counsel, but should not be regarded as a substitute for the specific legal and professional advice which firms may need to take on particular matters or engagements. The need for specific legal advice is particularly acute where auditors find that they are being asked to, or expected to, communicate directly with third parties in connection with the contents of the audit report.

Scope

This guidance applies to all audit reports issued by firms. Auditors should also **21** consider the application of the guidance to other public reporting engagements, such as interim reviews, regulatory reports and reports issued under other statutes, as well as to private reporting engagements.

Appendix 1

Example audit report with an unqualified opinion for a non-publicly traded company (based on the examples in Appendices 1 and 2 of the FRC's Bulletin: *Compendium of illustrative auditor's reports on United Kingdom private sector financial statements for periods commencing on or after 17 June 2016)*[1]

Independent auditor's report to the members of [XYZ Limited]

Opinion

We have audited the financial statements of [XYZ Limited] (the "company") for the year ended [date] which comprise [specify the titles of the primary statements] and notes to the financial statements, including a summary of significant accounting policies. The financial reporting framework that has been applied in their preparation is applicable law and United Kingdom Accounting Standards, including Financial Reporting Standard 102 *The Financial Reporting Standard applicable in the UK and Republic of Ireland (United Kingdom Generally Accepted Accounting Practice).*

In our opinion, the financial statements:

- give a true and fair view of the state of the company's affairs as at [date] and of its [profit/loss] for the year then ended;

- have been properly prepared in accordance with United Kingdom Generally Accepted Accounting Practice; and

- have been prepared in accordance with the requirements of the Companies Act 2006.

Basis for opinion

We conducted our audit in accordance with International Standards on Auditing (UK) (ISAs (UK)) and applicable law. Our responsibilities under those standards are further described in the Auditor's responsibilities for the audit of the financial statements section of our report. We are independent of the company in accordance with the ethical requirements that are relevant to our audit of the financial statements in the UK, including the FRC's Ethical Standard, and we have fulfilled our other ethical responsibilities in accordance with these requirements. We believe that the audit evidence we have obtained is sufficient and appropriate to provide a basis for our opinion.

Conclusions relating to going concern

We have nothing to report in respect of the following matters in relation to which the ISAs (UK) require us to report to you where:

- the directors' use of the going concern basis of accounting in the preparation of the financial statements is not appropriate; or

---

[1] *This example is for a non-publicly traded company. For listed entities, public interest entities and other entities that are required, and those that choose voluntarily, to report on how they have applied the UK Corporate Governance Code additional wording will be required, for example on key audit matters.*

- the directors have not disclosed in the financial statements any identified material uncertainties that may cast significant doubt about the company's ability to continue to adopt the going concern basis of accounting for a period of at least twelve months from the date when the financial statements are authorised for issue.

Other information

The directors are responsible for the other information. The other information comprises the information included in the annual report, other than the financial statements and our auditor's report thereon. Our opinion on the financial statements does not cover the other information and, except to the extent otherwise explicitly stated in our report, we do not express any form of assurance conclusion thereon.

In connection with our audit of the financial statements, our responsibility is to read the other information and, in doing so, consider whether the other information is materially inconsistent with the financial statements or our knowledge obtained in the audit or otherwise appears to be materially misstated. If we identify such material inconsistencies or apparent material misstatements, we are required to determine whether there is a material misstatement in the financial statements or a material misstatement of the other information. If, based on the work we have performed, we conclude that there is a material misstatement of this other information, we are required to report that fact.

We have nothing to report in this regard.

Opinions on other matters prescribed by the Companies Act 2006

In our opinion, based on the work undertaken in the course of the audit:

- the information given in the strategic report and the directors' report for the financial year for which the financial statements are prepared is consistent with the financial statements; and
- the strategic report and the directors' report have been prepared in accordance with applicable legal requirements.

Matters on which we are required to report by exception

In the light of the knowledge and understanding of the company and its environment obtained in the course of the audit, we have not identified material misstatements in the strategic report or the directors' report.

We have nothing to report in respect of the following matters in relation to which the Companies Act 2006 requires us to report to you if, in our opinion:

- adequate accounting records have not been kept, or returns adequate for our audit have not been received from branches not visited by us; or
- the financial statements are not in agreement with the accounting records and returns; or
- certain disclosures of directors' remuneration specified by law are not made; or
- we have not received all the information and explanations we require for our audit.

Responsibilities of directors

As explained more fully in the directors' responsibilities statement [set out on page ...], the directors are responsible for the preparation of the financial statements and for being satisfied that they give a true and fair view, and for such internal control as the directors determine is necessary to enable the preparation of financial statements that are free from material misstatement, whether due to fraud or error.

In preparing the financial statements, the directors are responsible for assessing the company's ability to continue as a going concern, disclosing, as applicable, matters related to going concern and using the going concern basis of accounting unless the directors either intend to liquidate the company or to cease operations, or have no realistic alternative but to do so.

Auditor's responsibilities for the audit of the financial statements

Our objectives are to obtain reasonable assurance about whether the financial statements as a whole are free from material misstatement, whether due to fraud or error, and to issue an auditor's report that includes our opinion. Reasonable assurance is a high level of assurance, but is not a guarantee that an audit conducted in accordance with ISAs (UK) will always detect a material misstatement when it exists. Misstatements can arise from fraud or error and are considered material if, individually or in the aggregate, they could reasonably be expected to influence the economic decisions of users taken on the basis of these financial statements.

[As part of an audit in accordance with ISAs (UK), we exercise professional judgment and maintain professional scepticism throughout the audit. We also:

- Identify and assess the risks of material misstatement of the financial statements, whether due to fraud or error, design and perform audit procedures responsive to those risks, and obtain audit evidence that is sufficient and appropriate to provide a basis for our opinion. The risk of not detecting a material misstatement resulting from fraud is higher than for one resulting from error, as fraud may involve collusion, forgery, intentional omissions, misrepresentations, or the override of internal control.

- Obtain an understanding of internal control relevant to the audit in order to design audit procedures that are appropriate in the circumstances, but not for the purpose of expressing an opinion on the effectiveness of the company's internal control.

- Evaluate the appropriateness of accounting policies used and the reasonableness of accounting estimates and related disclosures made by the directors.

- Conclude on the appropriateness of the directors' use of the going concern basis of accounting and, based on the audit evidence obtained, whether a material uncertainty exists related to events or conditions that may cast significant doubt on the company's ability to continue as a going concern. If we conclude that a material uncertainty exists, we are required to draw attention in our auditor's report to the related disclosures in the financial statements or, if such disclosures are inadequate, to modify our opinion. Our conclusions are based on the audit evidence obtained up to the date of our auditor's report. However, future events or conditions may cause the company to cease to continue as a going concern.

- Evaluate the overall presentation, structure and content of the financial statements, including the disclosures, and whether the financial statements represent the underlying transactions and events in a manner that achieves fair presentation.

We communicate with those charged with governance regarding, among other matters, the planned scope and timing of the audit and significant audit findings, including any significant deficiencies in internal control that we identify during our audit.]

OR

[A further description of our responsibilities for the audit of the financial statements is located on the Financial Reporting Council's website at: www.frc. org.uk/auditorsresponsibilities. This description forms part of our auditor's report.]

Use of our report

This report is made solely to the company's members, as a body, in accordance with Chapter 3 of Part 16 of the Companies Act 2006. Our audit work has been undertaken so that we might state to the company's members those matters we are required to state to them in an auditor's report and for no other purpose. To the fullest extent permitted by law, we do not accept or assume responsibility to anyone other than the company and the company's members as a body, for our audit work, for this report, or for the opinions we have formed.

[Signature]

John Smith (Senior Statutory Auditor)

For and on behalf of ABC LLP, Statutory Auditor

[Address]

[Date]

Appendix 2

Questions and Answers intended to be of practical help for members in applying the guidance and in countering possible issues and misunderstandings about it.

Q1: *Does the inclusion of the recommended wording devalue the audit?*

A1: No, the purpose and value of the audit remains the same. It is still carried out in accordance with auditing standards and firms should be doing all they can to achieve the highest audit quality (see comments about this in the fifth paragraph of the Preface). However, other than the addressees of the audit report, readers of the audit opinion rely on the report entirely at their own risk and the auditors do not accept any duty or responsibility to them. The recommended wording does no more than clarify to whom the auditors owe duties.

Q2: *Aren't auditors paid to take on these risks?*

A2: No, auditors are paid to carry out an audit to provide a report for, and only for, the members of the company as a body in accordance with Chapter 3 of Part 16 of the Companies Act 2006.

Q3: *Is the legal position of auditors altered as a result of this guidance?*

A3: No, the recommended wording simply clarifies to whom auditors owe duties as established by the case *Caparo Industries plc v Dickman*. Auditors are not restricting their liability to the entity which has retained them to carry out the audit. Subject to certain limited exceptions, the Companies Act 2006 makes ineffective any attempt to exclude or limit liability in that respect.

Q4: *If my firm includes the recommended wording in the audit report, does this guarantee that we will not owe any duty of care to third parties?*

A4: No, auditors should remain vigilant and take or avoid any additional actions as appropriate to prevent such duties being created – see paragraph 19 of this guidance.

Q5: *What do we do when a third party seeks our agreement in writing that they can rely on the audited accounts? In these situations there might be some client pressure to comply with this request.*

A5: In these situations auditors clarify the purpose of the audit and their responsibilities with regard to it as set out in the audit report – see Appendix 1. The audit is for a specific purpose and is not carried out with the interests of third parties in mind. If lenders or other third parties seek assurance on certain matters, auditors may discuss the possibility of separate engagements to provide specific assurances to them.

TECH 01/06AAF Assurance reports on internal controls of service organisations made available to third parties

(July 2016)

Contents

Paragraphs

1. Introduction
   1. Importance of outsourcing activities   1-2
   2. Need for new guidance
   3. Scope
   4. Transition from FRAG 21/94 (Revised)

2. Assurance engagements
   5. International developments
   6. The types of assurance
   7. Nature of engagement
   8. Control objectives as criteria

3. Responsibilities of a service organisation
   9. The role of a service organisation
   10. The responsibility of the directors
   11. Significant deficiencies
   12. Complementary control procedures of customers
   13. Other responsibilities of the service organisation
   14. Service organisations that use other service organisations
   15. Other information provided by the service organisation

4. Guidance for reporting accountants
   16. Accepting an engagement
   17. Managing professional liability
   18. Agreeing on the terms of engagement
   19. Planning
   20. Reporting accountants' procedures
   21. Nature, timing and extent of tests
   22. Assurance report
   23. Using the work of internal auditors
   24. Considerations for uncorrected errors, fraud or illegal acts
   25. Management representation letter

Appendices
   1. Control objectives
   2. Example paragraphs from the report by the directors
   3. Pro-forma reporting accountants' assurance reports (i) and (ii) (revised July 2016)
   4. Examples of explanatory paragraphs and qualification wording
   5. Example extracts from an engagement letter
   6. Example sample size table
   7. Illustrative definition of enquiry, inspection, observation and re-performance
   8. International Standard on Assurance Engagements (ISAE) 3402
      Assurance Reports on Controls at a Service Organisation and a pro-forma
      report, revised for assurance reports dated on or after 15 December 2015

Supplement
Assurance reporting on the UK Stewardship Code

1. Introduction

1. Importance of outsourcing activities

Many entities use outside service organisations to accomplish tasks that affect the entity's internal controls. These services range from performing a specific task under the direction of the entity to replacing entire business units as functions of an entity. In recent years, there has been a significant increase in the use of service organisations, and because many of the functions performed are integral to the entity's business operations, the entity's management is concerned to ensure the control procedures at the service organisation complement those operated by their own organisation. In addition, because many of the functions performed by service organisations affect an entity's financial statements, auditors may also seek information about the control procedures surrounding those services.

The provision of outsourced services is particularly prevalent within financial service activities. The service organisations include custodians that hold and service assets, investment managers for securities and property, and organisations that provide software applications and a technology environment for the processing of transactions or accounting for pension schemes and investment funds. Accordingly, reporting accountants may be engaged by a service organisation to issue a report on specific control procedures undertaken by the service organisation which it may wish to make available to its customers ("customers") and the auditors of those customers. Reporting accountants are the accountants that perform an engagement for the service organisation. Customers are the clients of the service organisation using its services.

2. Need for new guidance

Since the original issue of FRAG 21/94, interest in reporting on internal controls among the investment communities has increased as a direct response to changes in the corporate governance environment and specific government initiated projects such as Paul Myners' report on investment practices. In order to provide information to these investment communities, thirdparty reporting using frameworks such as FRAG 21/94 has been widely applied as a means to increase external scrutiny of internal control processes.

Meanwhile, customers of service organisations have begun to focus on the need to replace the existing reporting framework that was last reviewed in 1997. Customers are increasingly seeking assurance on both the design and operating effectiveness of service organisations' control procedures. They are also seeking greater consistency between service organisations as to the scope and contents of their reports and greater transparency as to the extent of testing undertaken by reporting accountants.

These factors and comments on the use made of such reports on internal controls have led the Audit and Assurance Faculty of ICAEW to issue new reporting guidance[1]. This guidance sets out the conditions service organisations meet in providing information on internal controls, control procedures and the framework within which reporting accountants deliver assurance reporting.

1.

2.

---

[1] *In conducting its work, the working group has included representatives from ICAEW, the National Association of Pension Funds, the Investment Management Association and service organisations.*

This guidance is specifically developed for a range of financial service activities, including:

- Custody;
- Investment management;
- Pension administration;
- Property management;
- Fund accounting; and
- Transfer agency.

To apply this guidance to other engagement circumstances involving activities such as payroll processing, additional considerations may be required.

The Audit and Assurance Faculty of ICAEW will keep the guidance under regular review to accommodate industry developments in relation to the control objectives set out in Appendix 1 and the range of activities set out in paragraph 6. Industry groups and other representative bodies or service organisations who wish to propose further service activities for inclusion within the guidance or to comment on the control objectives currently contained within Appendix 1 are encouraged to submit any such proposals in writing to the Audit and Assurance Faculty at tdaf@icaew.com.

Within the financial service activities listed above, it is anticipated that the control objectives include appropriate references to information technology.

It is for the directors of the service organisation to decide whether to prepare a report on their organisation's control procedures and whether to have this reported on by reporting accountants. In certain circumstances, directors may, for example, consider it more appropriate to allow access to customers and their auditors or provide a report on a specific aspect of its operations as this impacts an individual customer. It is not the intention of the guidance to oblige service organisations to report on control procedures in the manner described in this guidance. However, if the directors decide to provide a report other than in accordance with this guidance, they may not make any reference to this guidance in their report.

Where the directors decide to prepare a report on internal controls, it is of greater benefit to customers and their auditors if it covers control procedures in operation throughout a given period. However, a report on control procedures at a single point in time may be an alternative where a service organisation is preparing its report on internal controls for the first time[2]. The guidance that follows generally assumes that the report covers a period.

A service organisation may have more than one type of financial service activity. In such a case, the directors explain to the reporting accountants the types of financial services the service organisation carries out at the outset of the engagement. The directors may prepare either a combined report or a separate report on each area of financial service activity as they deem appropriate. The reporting accountants report accordingly.

---

[2] *Where the directors and reporting accountants are reporting only on controls in place and not on their operating effectiveness during the specified period, this fact is clearly stated in the reports. The accountants modify their conclusions so as not to conclude on the operating effectiveness of control procedures during the specified period.*

3. Scope

This Technical Release provides guidance to reporting accountants on undertaking an assurance engagement and providing a report ("assurance report") in relation to the internal controls of a service organisation.

It is also expected to assist customers in understanding the scope and type of assurance conveyed in the assurance report. The guidance is also aimed at providing assistance to the directors of service organisations who prepare a report on their internal controls by clarifying their expected responsibilities.

This guidance replaces the Institute's guidance AUDIT 4/97 Reports on internal controls of investment custodians made available to third parties, FRAG 21/94 (Revised).

4. Transition from FRAG 21/94 (Revised)

The Technical Release is effective for periods ending on or after 31 March 2007. However, service organisations and reporting accountants are encouraged to apply this guidance before that date as best practice.

2. Assurance engagements

5. International developments

In 2004, the International Auditing and Assurance Standards Board (IAASB) published the International Framework for Assurance Engagements (the Framework) and the first International Standard on Assurance Engagements (ISAE) 3000, Assurance Engagements Other Than Audits or Reviews of Historical Financial Information. This standard was revised for assurance reports signed on or after 15 December 2015, and is now referred to as ISAE 3000 (revised). At the same time, a revised Framework was published. These pronouncements provide high-level principles for assurance engagements other than audits and reviews of historical financial statements.

The Framework defines the elements of assurance engagements and describes objectives for such engagements. ISAE 3000 provides generic guidance on the principal aspects of assurance engagements and refers to an assurance engagement involving three separate parties. Together these two international pronouncements provide the appropriate framework within which to develop specific guidance covering subject areas and topics such as internal control where, hitherto, no specific guidance has existed.

6. The types of assurance

There are two types of assurance engagements and associated objectives specified in the Framework: reasonable assurance engagements and limited assurance engagements.

In a reasonable assurance engagement, reporting accountants seek to obtain sufficient appropriate evidence that enables them to express a positive conclusion on the directors' report prepared for customers. In a limited assurance engagement, reporting accountants seek to gather evidence sufficient to obtain a meaningful level of assurance as the basis for a negative form of expression. This Technical Release is prepared for reporting accountants performing a reasonable assurance engagement.

7. Nature of engagement

The service organisation is responsible for providing information on specific control procedures "control procedures") to meet the control objectives described in this guidance. The reporting accountants perform the engagement in accordance with this guidance. As discussed below the directors' and assurance reports may be made available to others, eg, pension scheme trustees or auditors.

The directors of the service organisation are responsible for preparing a report concerning the control procedures in place. The report is for the information of customers and their auditors and focuses on the operations which are likely to be relevant to them. It is therefore appropriate that any report provided by service organisations has regard to these relevant operations as well as those specified in this guidance.

The reporting package comprises a report by the directors of the service organisation concerning the control procedures of the service organisation and a reasonable assurance report by the reporting accountants, explaining the scope of work carried out and giving their conclusion on relevant parts of the directors' report. The conclusion is in the form of a qualitative judgement. The judgement and the report relate to historic matters.

8. Control objectives as criteria

Assurance engagements require reporting accountants to express an overall conclusion on the information assessed relative to certain criteria. Criteria also help the directors of a service organisation and their customers to understand how the reporting accountants have evaluated internal controls to reach their conclusion. In an assurance report on internal controls, the criteria are the control objectives around which the service organisation has designed its control procedures. The criteria need to be relevant, complete, reliable, neutral and understandable so as to communicate the basis of the evaluation.

The control objectives collectively reflect the level of control over customers' assets[3] and related transactions set by the service organisation.

Appendix 1 sets out detailed control objectives for the financial service activities referred to in paragraph 6. These control objectives are guidance only and not intended to be exhaustive and it remains the responsibility of the directors to ensure that the described control objectives are sufficient to meet the expectations of customers. A service organisation may therefore consider the need to add further objectives and supporting control procedures where appropriate. If certain criteria do not apply to a service organisation, for example because the relevant activities are outsourced, the service organisation explains the omission of the criteria in the directors' report.

Reporting accountants consider the control objectives and observe supporting control procedures specified by the service organisation to form an overall opinion in the specific engagement circumstances at the time the work was undertaken. Reporting accountants also consider the linkage of the control procedures to the stated objectives and obtain sufficient appropriate evidence to reach their opinion. Through tests of control procedures, reporting accountants obtain sufficient appropriate evidence to conclude whether the relevant specified control objectives are met.

---

[3] *Reference may need to be made for liabilities, for instance for pension administration.*

3. Responsibilities of a service organisation

9. The role of a service organisation

The role of a service organisation in relation to the customers is likely to involve some combination of initiation, recording, processing, safeguarding or reporting the customers' assets and related transactions.

10. The responsibility of the directors

To meet the customers' expectations in terms of the level of control over customers' assets and related transactions, the directors of the service organisation identify control objectives together with the control procedures which they consider appropriate to enable these control objectives to be met. The key responsibilities of the directors in relation to these are summarised as:

(a) Acceptance of responsibility for internal controls;

(b) Evaluation of the effectiveness of the service organisation's control procedures using suitable criteria;

(c) Supporting their evaluation with sufficient evidence, including documentation; and

(d) Providing a written report of the effectiveness of the service organisation's control procedures for the relevant period.

(a) Acceptance of responsibility for internal controls

The directors are responsible for the design, implementation and operation of the control procedures of the service organisation. This is acknowledged in their report. It is also the responsibility of the directors to take reasonable steps to prevent and detect fraud.

Suitably designed control procedures, when complied with individually or in combination with other control procedures, are expected to operate so as to prevent or detect errors that could result in the failure to achieve specified control objectives. The directors also evaluate the design and operation of control procedures during the relevant reporting period. In this regard, the reporting accountants' tests are separate from the service organisation's own procedures for evaluating the effectiveness of the control procedures. The work of the reporting accountants cannot be used as part of the basis for the service organisation's assessment of whether control procedures are suitably designed or the operation of the control procedures is effective.

(b) Evaluation of the effectiveness of the service organisation's control procedures using suitable criteria

In order to evaluate the effectiveness of control procedures the directors refer to suitable criteria.

The control objectives in Appendix 1 are considered to be suitable criteria for the financial service activities specified in paragraph 6 of this guidance. The directors make a statement in their report that they have referred to the control objectives in this guidance. Most service organisations depend on computer processing to perform commissioned services and the service organisations' description of control procedures also includes a description of the computer environment and the related general computer control procedures. Suitable criteria relating to such information technology are also provided in Appendix 1.

(c) Supporting their evaluation with sufficient evidence, including documentation

The directors support their assertions with respect to the design, implementation and operating effectiveness of the service organisation's control procedures with sufficient evidence. The nature of the directors' evaluation activities depends largely on the circumstances of the entity and the significance of particular controls but evaluation procedures include review and testing by internal audit, business risk and compliance review, direct testing by others under the direction of management or review by means of a self-assessment process. The directors consider the sufficiency of this evidence and whether any additional evaluation of specific areas or locations may be appropriate to enable them to provide a written assessment of the effectiveness of the internal controls. The process that the directors undertake includes considering:

- evidence available from on-going monitoring of control procedures;

- whether further control procedures are to be tested by them, including consideration of the locations or business units to include in the evaluation for an entity with multiple locations or business units;

- any deficiencies in control procedures that have come to their attention, for example, through management testing, internal audit reports and reports by regulators; and

- evaluation as to the likelihood that the failure of certain control procedures could result in a control objective not being met, the extent to which it might not be met and the degree to which other control procedures, if effective, achieve the same control objective.

Documentation of control procedures in place is in itself evidence of control procedures being identifiable, capable of being monitored and communicable to those responsible for their performance. Inadequate documentation may indicate a deficiency in the service organisation's control procedures and is subject to evaluation by the reporting accountants as to its significance (eg, it could be merely a deficiency, a material weakness or in extreme cases a limitation on the scope of the engagement).

Documentation of control procedures may take various forms depending on the nature and the type of the relevant information. For instance, policy manuals, process models, flowcharts and job descriptions could be used for recording the control procedure design, while documents and forms could be the record of operating and monitoring of control procedures.

The directors evaluate whether the documentation includes:

- the design of control procedures over all relevant control objectives;

- information about how significant transactions are initiated, authorised, recorded, processed and reported; and

- the results of management's testing and evaluation. Where the service organisation has introduced significant changes to its control procedures within the past 12 months, the control procedures before and after the change and the implications are documented. The judgement as to the significance of the change is based on its impact on the risk assessment of the customers and their auditors.

(d) Providing a written report of the effectiveness of the service organisation's control procedures for the relevant period

Through evaluation and documentation, the directors accumulate sufficient information to come to an overall conclusion as to the effectiveness of the service organisation's control procedures during a specified period. Their conclusion is based on the specified criteria, and includes an assessment of the impact of exceptions and deficiencies. The directors communicate the conclusion and the details of significant deficiencies to customers in their report. The following key matters are to be included in the report of the directors:

Contents of the directors' report

(a)   A statement of the directors' responsibilities.

(b)   The service organisation's control objectives, and a reference to the control objectives specified in this guidance, with details of any omitted or additional control objectives considered appropriate by the directors with explanations for such omissions and additions.

(c)   Aspects of the service organisation's control environment, risk assessment, management information, communication and monitoring process that may be relevant to the services provided.

(d)   Details of each of the specific control procedures designed to achieve the control objectives.

(e)   Reference to the use of this guidance.

(f)   Details of any significant changes to the control objectives and procedures during the period.

(g)   Details of any significant deficiencies and exceptions and their impact on the control objectives during the period.

(h)   A statement by the directors that they have assessed the effectiveness of the control procedures and their opinion that:

   i.   their report describes fairly the control procedures that relate to the control objectives referred to in (b) above which were in place as at [date];

   ii.   the control procedures described are suitably designed such that there is reasonable assurance that the specified control objectives would be achieved if the described control procedures were complied with satisfactorily [and customers applied the control procedures contemplated]; and

   iii. the control procedures described were operating with sufficient effectiveness to provide reasonable assurance that the related control objectives were achieved during the specified period.

(i)   The name and signature of the director signing on behalf of the Board of Directors.

(j)   The directors' report date.

Example paragraphs from an illustrative directors' report on matters referred to at (a), (e), (h), and (i) above are set out at Appendix 2.

In applying the framework presented above, it is not necessary to list the control procedures and related control objectives in both the directors' report and in the assurance report.

The directors are responsible for the completeness, accuracy, validity and method of presentation of the description of control objectives and procedures. The description sets out information about the service organisation's control objectives and procedures that may be relevant to the customers. The reporting accountants may assist the service organisation in preparing the description; however, the representations in the description are the responsibility of the service organisation's directors.

The directors, where appropriate, seek to describe control procedures in a manner which permits verification and is understandable to customers. To achieve this and to promote consistency in approach, the directors may find it helpful to differentiate between the different components of the overall system which are being described in their report. The principal components are in general likely to include control objectives, control policies, process descriptions and control procedures. Process and control procedure descriptions in particular are factual and precise wherever possible in order to avoid the possibility of different interpretations being placed on these by different customers.

The description of control objectives and procedures does not necessarily address every service provided by the service organisation but presents a level of detail that provides sufficient information for customers to assess control risk and for the auditors of the customers to plan an audit of the customers' financial statements, as if a service organisation were not used.

11. Significant deficiencies

A control procedure deficiency (or a combination of control procedure deficiencies) is classified as a significant deficiency where, by itself or in combination with other control procedure deficiencies, it results in more than a remote likelihood that a control objective may not be met. Where such significant deficiencies are corrected during the year, customers may find it helpful to be informed of this in the directors' report.

12. Complementary control procedures of customers

The activities of the service organisation may be described with the assumption that customers have control procedures in place, with respect to such general matters as the authorisation of transactions, the written notification of changes, the timely review of reports provided by the service organisation, and appropriate restrictions on access to on-line terminals. If this is the case, the description of the control procedures at the service organisation refers to such required complementary control procedures of the customers.

13. Other responsibilities of the service organisation

Other responsibilities of the service organisation include:

- providing the reporting accountants with access to appropriate service organisation resources, such as service organisation personnel, systems documentation, contracts and minutes of management/audit committee meetings;
- disclosing to the reporting accountants any significant changes in control procedures that have occurred since the service organisation's last examination or within the last 12 months if the service organisation has not previously engaged reporting accountants to issue an assurance report;

- disclosing to the reporting accountants and the affected customers any illegal acts, fraud, or uncorrected errors attributable to the service organisation's management or employees that may affect its customers and the entity's whistle-blowing arrangements;

- disclosing to the reporting accountants any relevant design deficiencies in control procedures of which it is aware, including those for which the directors believe the cost of corrective action may exceed the benefits;

- disclosing to the reporting accountants all significant instances of which it is aware when control procedures have not operated with sufficient effectiveness to achieve the specified control objectives; and

- providing the reporting accountants with a letter of representation.

14. Service organisations that use other service organisations

Additional considerations are required where a service organisation uses another service organisation (a sub-service organisation) to perform certain aspects of the processing performed for the customers.

In addition to describing its control objectives and procedures, a service organisation that uses a sub-service organisation describes the functions and nature of the processing performed by the sub-service organisation in sufficient detail for the customers and their auditors to understand the significance of the sub-service organisation's operations to the processing of the customers' transactions.

The purpose of the description of the functions and nature of the processing performed by the sub-service organisation is to alert the customers and their auditors to the fact that another entity is involved in the processing of the customers' transactions and to summarise the functions the sub-service organisation performs.

The service organisation determines whether its description of control procedures includes the relevant control procedures of the sub-service organisation. The two alternative methods of dealing with sub-service organisations are as follows:

The exclusive method: The sub-service organisation's relevant control objectives and procedures are excluded from the description and from the scope of the reporting accountants' engagement. The service organisation states in the description that the sub-service organisation's control objectives and related procedures are omitted from the description and that the control objectives in the report include only the objectives which the service organisation's control procedures are intended to achieve.

The inclusive method: The sub-service organisation's relevant control procedures are included in the description and in the scope of the engagement. The description clearly differentiates between control procedures of the service organisation and control procedures of the sub-service organisation. The set of control objectives includes all of the control objectives which both the service organisation and the sub-service organisation are expected to achieve. To accomplish this, the service organisation coordinates the preparation and presentation of the description of control procedures with the sub-service organisation.

15. Other information provided by the service organisation

A service organisation may wish to present other information that is not a part of the description of internal controls in its report: for example, background information on the entities involved and the services they provide. Where information of this nature is presented, it is presented in a separate section of the report and made clear that it does not constitute a part of the service organisation's description of control objectives and control procedures.

4. Guidance for reporting accountants

16. Accepting an engagement

It is important that there is a clear understanding and agreement concerning the scope and purpose of the engagement between the reporting accountants and the service organisation and, if applicable, the customers that are party to the engagement (see paragraph 55).

Reporting accountants consider whether the engagement team collectively possesses the necessary professional competencies having regard to the nature of the assignment. As part of the engagement acceptance process reporting accountants also consider relevant ethical requirements.

In carrying out an assurance engagement, chartered accountants are subject to ethical guidance as laid down by the Institute in its ethical code. The requirements in the ethical code include, among other things, adherence to the Fundamental Principles in all of their professional and business activities as set out in the introduction. When conducting an assurance engagement, there are additional requirements in Independence for Assurance Engagements within the code. This applies to all assurance engagements outside the scope of audit and is in compliance with the Code of Ethics established by the International Federation of Accountants (IFAC).

The reporting accountants' adherence to the independence requirements involves an assessment of likely threats to independence and, where necessary, the application of safeguards. For example, the provision of assistance to a service organisation in preparing its report may result in a self-review threat if the impact of the assistance on the matter being reported on is highly subjective and material. The subjectivity of the report proposed to be issued will also be relevant. If other than insignificant threats are identified, safeguards need to be considered. These might include:

the use of independent teams, where appropriate; or

an independent review of the key judgements on the engagement.

The assurance report may be received by a range of persons who are not party to the engagement. Reporting accountants do not intend to assume responsibility to persons who are not party to the engagement, but legal actions from such persons may nonetheless occur. Reporting accountants therefore need to apply appropriate engagement acceptance procedures in order to assess the risks associated with taking on a particular engagement and accordingly whether to do so and, if so, on what terms. Where the reporting accountants do accept such an engagement, suitably rigorous internal risk management policies are applied to manage any increased level of risk. Relevant steps for managing professional liability are covered in the following section[4].

17. Managing professional liability

Depending on the engagement circumstances reporting accountants enter into one or a combination of the following arrangements:

(a)   A tri-partite or multi-partite engagement contract with the service organisation and the customers, accepting that they owe a duty of care not only to the service organisation but also to those customers, including provisions limiting liability if appropriate (recognising that such a contract may not be achievable where the customers are numerous).

(b)   An engagement with the service organisation with the facility for customers to enjoy a duty of care from the reporting accountants if they accept the relevant terms of the engagement letter previously agreed with the service organisation as if they had signed that letter when originally issued, including the same provisions limiting liability[5].

(c)   An engagement with the service organisation alone but before allowing the customers access to the assurance report, require the customers

   i.   to acknowledge in writing that the reporting accountants owe the customers no duty of care and

   ii.   to agree in writing that no claims may be brought against the reporting accountants by the customers in relation to the assurance report[6].

(d)   An engagement with the service organisation alone disclaiming any liability or duty to others (including customers) by notice in the assurance report. Reporting accountants also consider supporting this disclaimer with an indemnity from the service organisation to apply where a third party claim is made (recognising that such an indemnity may not be attractive commercially, may not be effective if the service organisation is not financially stable, and may not operate to prevent a claim: see further paragraph 63 below)[7]. It is also open to reporting accountants to consider with their legal advisers the use of the Contract (Rights of Third Parties) Act 1999 to manage the risk of liability to third parties. The above arrangements do not prevent customers taking legal action against the service organisation.

Reporting accountants will describe carefully in their report the work that they do, including the description of the tests. In the latter context, close definition of what is meant by enquiry, inspection, observation and re-performance is desirable. Some illustrative definitions are set out at Appendix 7.

---

[4] *Further guidance may be found in Statement 1.311, Managing the professional liability of accountants in the Institute's Members' Handbook.*

[5] *This will require the consent of the service organisation/original addressees, ideally in the engagement letter. Also see footnotes 18, page 34 and 21, page 35.*

[6] *Reporting accountants may wish to have regard to the principles outlined in Audit 04/03 Access to working papers by investigating accountants, bearing in mind that Audit 04/03 addresses different circumstances relating to third party issues, when developing a written form of such acknowledgment and agreement.*

[7] *Reporting accountants consider the legal effectiveness of disclaiming liability and of the proposed disclaimer in light of the particular circumstances of their engagement (see for example, the guidance in Statement 1.311 on Managing the professional liability of accountants). Reporting accountants are advised to seek their own independent legal advice.*

Reporting accountants disclaim responsibility and liability to customers' auditors, having regard to the responsibility of customers' auditors for their own audit reports and for determining to what extent (if any) the assurance report amounts to sufficient appropriate audit evidence for the purposes of their audit of a relevant customer's financial statements.

Reporting accountants may become aware of other third parties that are not customers of the service organisation, such as banks and other lenders or prospective purchasers of the service organisation, who may also request the assurance report. The service organisation or the third party may approach the reporting accountants for consent to make the assurance report available to such third parties, as the engagement contract agreed with the service organisation contains disclosure and use restrictions. The assurance report is not prepared for third parties or with their interests or needs in mind, and the reporting accountants may decline this request. The reporting accountants will have set out the purpose of their report in the assurance report, and will have included a disclaimer of liability to third parties in line with paragraph 55(d) above in that report. If the request is not declined, the reporting accountants will advise the third party that the assurance report was not prepared for the third party or the third party's benefit, that consent to their report being made available to a third party will only be given if the third party agrees that the third party should not rely on the report and acknowledges in writing that the reporting accountants owe the third party no duty of care and agrees that no claims may be brought against the reporting accountants by the third party in relation to the report.

Reporting accountants may also receive requests from the service organisation for consent to the release of the assurance report to potential customers with whom the service organisation may be exploring the possibility of a relationship, or reporting accountants may become aware that contrary to disclosure and use restrictions agreed with the service organisation in the engagement contract, such potential customers are gaining access to the assurance report. The reporting accountants may decline any such request. If the request is not declined, the written acknowledgement and agreement described above in relation to other third parties may be a practical solution to the management of risk in relation to potential customers. Where that is not practical, the reporting accountants require the service organisation (as a condition for giving consent, where requested) to send all such potential customers a written statement, to accompany the assurance report, pointing out that the reporting accountants did not undertake the work for potential customers and do not accept any responsibility to potential customers and deny liability to them. Reporting accountants may wish to provide the service organisation with a pro-forma statement and may wish to include reference to this in their engagement letter.

If correspondence between reporting accountants and customers, potential customers or third parties results from a disclaimer notice or otherwise, the reporting accountants decide (with independent legal advice if appropriate) how to bring such correspondence to a satisfactory close before it becomes protracted or undermines the original objective.

18. Agreeing on the terms of engagement

Prior to accepting the engagement, reporting accountants establish that the directors of the service organisation acknowledge in writing their responsibility on behalf of the organisation for the design and operation of effective internal controls over its activities to achieve control objectives.

Reporting accountants agree on the terms of engagement with the parties to the engagement in accordance with the contractual relationship as discussed in paragraph 55. To avoid misunderstandings, the agreed terms are recorded in writing in an engagement letter. Example extracts from an engagement letter for an assurance report on internal controls of a service organisation are given in Appendix 5 for illustrative purposes. Reporting accountants apply their own judgement to develop suitable wording for their engagement letters to reflect the guidance in this Technical Release and their own particular circumstances. Where the engaging parties include customers, the nature and the content of an engagement letter may differ from the example extracts.

The written terms of the reporting accountants' engagement include:

● the agreed use of the report and the extent to which, the context in which, and the basis on which, the report may be made available by the directors to customers and their auditors;

● the directors' and the reporting accountants' respective responsibilities for the different elements of the report;

● the scope of the work to be performed by the reporting accountants;

● a reference to the likely need for management representations;

● an explanation of the inherent limitations of the work, and for whom the work is being undertaken;

● limitations to the liability of the reporting accountants, including an appropriate liability cap; and

● provisions for an indemnity if considered appropriate[8].

In particular, reporting accountants exclude liability in respect of any loss or damage caused by, or arising from fraudulent acts, misrepresentation, concealment of information or deliberate default on the part of the service organisation, its directors, employees or agents.

If, before the completion of the engagement, reporting accountants receive a request from the service organisation, to change an assurance engagement to a non-assurance or limited assurance engagement or to change, for instance, the scope of the engagement, the reporting accountants consider whether this has reasonable justification. Engagement parties' misunderstanding concerning the nature of the engagement or a change in circumstances that affects the customers' requirements is likely to justify such a request from the service organisation. Where accepting a request for a change, the reporting accountants do not disregard evidence that was already obtained prior to the change, and the details of the change should be documented and agreed in writing with the parties to the engagement letter.

19. Planning

Where reports are referred to as being prepared in accordance with the framework for reporting set out in this Technical Release, reporting accountants plan and perform their work so as to provide a reasonable basis for their conclusion.

---

[8] *It may be appropriate to obtain an indemnity from the service organisation in respect of claims from third parties arising from the contents of the assurance report. It must be remembered that an indemnity does not prevent a claim from being brought against the indemnified party. It merely gives him a right to pass on the liability to the indemnifier. It follows, therefore, that if the indemnity is in some way ineffective or the indemnifier does not have adequate resources to meet the liability, the indemnified party may be left unprotected.*

Professional judgement is needed to determine the required nature, timing and extent of the tests to be carried out and the reliance, if applicable, on the service organisation's internal audit department.

The reporting accountants' work is planned so as to have a reasonable expectation of detecting, at the time the work is undertaken, significant deficiencies in respect of the control procedures described by the directors and tested in accordance with the terms of the engagement. However, the work cannot be expected to detect problems which may be considered significant from the point of view of a particular customer and the scope of the work may mean that all control procedures relevant to an individual customer may not have been tested.

Reporting accountants are not expected to assess the adequacy of the evaluation of controls performed by the directors as part of an engagement to report on the entity's control procedures.

20. Reporting accountants' procedures

Fairness of the description

Reporting accountants read the description of control procedures to gain an understanding of the representations made by the directors in the description. After reading the description, the reporting accountants perform procedures to determine whether the description presents fairly, in all material respects, the service organisation's control procedures that relate to the control objectives referred to by the directors which were in place as at the end of the relevant period.

To determine whether the description is fairly presented, the reporting accountants gain an understanding of the services provided by the service organisation. Procedures to gain this understanding may include:

> discussing aspects of the control framework and relevant control procedures with management and other personnel of the service organisation;

> determining who the customers are and how the services provided by the service organisation are likely to affect the customers, for example, the predominant type of customers;

> reviewing standard terms of contracts with the customers to gain an understanding of the service organisation's contractual obligations;

> observing the procedures performed by the service organisation's personnel;

> reviewing the service organisation's policy and procedure manuals and other systems documentation, for example, flowcharts and narratives; and

performing walk-throughs of selected transactions and control procedures.

Reporting accountants compare their understanding of the services provided to the customers by the service organisation with the directors' representations made in their report to determine the fairness of the description. Fairly described control procedures do not omit or distort significant information that may affect the customers' assessments of control risk.

Fairly described control procedures include a complete set of associated control objectives that are developed based on the criteria in Appendix 1. If there are omissions or misstatements with regard to the control objectives, the reporting accountants ask the directors to amend the description. If it is not amended the reporting accountants consider the need to state that fact in their report.

Design of control procedures

As a part of their work, reporting accountants determine whether the control procedures are suitably designed. A control procedure is suitably designed if individually, or in combination with other control procedures, it is likely to prevent or detect errors that could result in the nonachievement of specified control objectives when the described control procedures are complied with satisfactorily.

The reporting accountants' assessment of the suitability of control procedure design may include:

● considering the linkage between the control procedures and the associated control objectives;

● considering the ability of the control procedures to prevent or detect errors related to the control objectives;

● performing walk-throughs of selected transactions and control procedures; and

● performing further procedures, such as enquiry of appropriate entity personnel, inspection of documents and reports and observation of the application of specific control procedures, to determine whether they are suitably designed to achieve the

● specified control objectives and if they are operated as prescribed, by appropriately qualified or experienced persons.

Where certain control procedures of the service organisation are reliant on generic control procedures executed by the customers in order to achieve control objectives, reporting accountants consider whether such complementary control procedures are described in the directors' report. If they are not and the directors fail or refuse to amend the description, the reporting accountants consider adding an explanatory paragraph to describe the required complementary control procedures and consider the implication for the reporting accountants' conclusion on the fairness of the description (see paragraphs 85-90).

Operating effectiveness

Reporting accountants perform tests of the relevant control procedures to obtain evidence about the operating effectiveness of the control procedures during a specified reporting period. Operating effectiveness is concerned with how a control procedure is applied, the consistency with which it is applied, and by whom it is applied. Reporting accountants determine the nature, timing and extent of the tests to be performed to form their conclusion on the operating effectiveness of the control procedures. Reporting accountants may wish to provide the customers with a further explanation of the tests that they have performed in an appendix to their report.

Where reporting accountants are unable to test a described control procedure because, for example, it has not operated during the year, they state the fact that no tests have been carried out and the reason in their description of tests.

21. Nature, timing and extent of tests

Tests of control procedures over operating effectiveness might include a combination of enquiry of the appropriate personnel, observation of the application of the control procedure, inspection of relevant documentation and re-performance of the control procedure. Enquiry alone does not generally provide sufficient evidence to support a conclusion about the operating effectiveness of a specific control procedure.

The period of time over which reporting accountants perform tests of control procedures varies with the nature of the control procedures being tested and with the frequency of specific control procedures. Tests of operating effectiveness provide evidence that enables the reporting accountants to report on the entire period covered by the report. Certain control procedures may not have evidence of their operation that can be tested at a later date and accordingly, reporting accountants test the operating effectiveness of such control procedures at various times throughout the reporting period.

Where the service organisation implemented changes to its control procedures to improve them or to address deficiencies during the period covered, the reporting accountants evaluate the impact which the superseded control procedures had on the control objectives over the period covered. Where a change of control procedures occurs during the period, the reporting accountants agree with the directors whether it is possible for the control procedures to be tested before and after the change. The description of their tests clearly states which control procedures have been tested.

The number of control operations selected as a sample for testing depends on the frequency of performance (for example, quarterly, monthly, daily or multiple times a day), the nature (for example, manual or automated) of control procedures, and the reporting accountants' assessment of the system (including the risk of failure of the control procedure that is being tested). An example table for setting sample sizes is given in Appendix 6.

Describing tests of operating effectiveness and exception reporting

Reporting accountants describe the control procedures that were tested, the control objectives they were intended to achieve, the tests carried out and the results of the tests in the assurance report. This information is typically incorporated within the service organisation's description of control procedures or contained within an attachment to the assurance report. The reporting accountants describe tests of operating effectiveness that provide sufficient information to support their conclusion as to whether the service organisation has achieved the relevant control objectives during the period.

In describing the results of the tests, reporting accountants include details and other information where relevant to the customers and their auditors. Test results are also described whether or not the reporting accountants have concluded that the results constitute an exception (see paragraph 89).

Reporting accountants describe the nature, timing and extent of tests applied. In describing the nature of tests, the reporting accountants define the types of tests performed. Illustrative definitions of tests such as enquiry, inspection, observation and re-performance are provided in Appendix 7. In describing the extent of tests, the reporting accountants indicate whether the items tested represent a sample or all the items in the population. If sampling was used, it may be helpful to provide information on the sample size.

Reporting on description misstatements, design deficiencies or when control procedures are not operating effectively

Reporting accountants discuss with the directors when they become aware that the control objectives are incomplete or inappropriate in light of the criteria in this guidance so that the directors may amend the description to include the recommended control objective(s). If the directors refuse or fail to do so the reporting accountants add an explanation in the criteria and scope paragraph of the assurance report identifying the omitted or inappropriate control objective(s) to draw the attention of the customers and their auditors. In addition, the wording of the conclusion paragraph may also be modified. An example paragraph illustrating an exception to the fair description is provided in Appendix 4 (a).

Although reporting accountants may qualify their conclusion on the fairness of the description of control procedures, this does not necessarily affect the suitability of design or operating effectiveness of the control procedures because the reporting accountants' conclusion relates only to the control objectives that are included in the service organisation's description. Reporting accountants note that it is the responsibility of the directors and not the reporting accountants to ensure the completeness and the reasonableness of control procedures over the activities of the service organisation.

Where control procedures associated with stated control objectives are incomplete or inappropriate, reporting accountants also discuss this with the directors so that the directors may amend the description to include the associated control procedures. If the directors refuse or fail to amend the description, the reporting accountants add an explanatory paragraph preceding the conclusion to the report identifying the omitted or inappropriate control procedures to draw the attention of the customers and their auditors. In addition, the wording of the conclusion paragraph may be modified. An example paragraph illustrating an exception to the fair description is provided in Appendix 4 (a).

Where reporting accountants conclude that a set of control procedures are not suitably designed in relation to a specified control objective, they consider the design deficiencies in their overall assessment of the control procedures. If the reporting accountants determine that control procedures are not suitably designed to achieve a specified control objective, they add an explanatory paragraph preceding the conclusion to the report identifying the design deficiencies and modify the conclusion. An example paragraph illustrating an exception to the suitability of design is provided in Appendix 4 (b).

Where the reporting accountants' tests identify exceptions to the operating effectiveness of the control procedures, the reporting accountants consider whether this exception means that a control objective has not been achieved. In some cases deficiencies may be so pervasive that the reporting accountants modify their conclusion on the achievement of one or more control objective or issue an adverse opinion. An example paragraph illustrating an exception to the operating effectiveness is provided in Appendix 4 (c).

Where significant changes are introduced during the period covered in the report, the directors report this fact. If reporting accountants become aware that the description on changes is missing, they request the directors to amend the description. However, the omission of information related to changes in the service organisation's control procedure does not warrant a qualification of the conclusion on the fairness of the description, provided that the directors' description of control procedures is fair as at the date of the description.

Elements of the service organisation report that are not covered by the assurance report

As discussed in paragraph 49 where the service organisation has included information other than that which constitutes a part of the description of control procedures in its report, this is outside the scope of the assurance report. The reporting accountants read such information for consistency with their understanding of the entity.

Elements of reporting accountants' assurance report

(a)   A title indicating that the report is an assurance report.

(b)   An addressee identifying the engaging parties to whom the assurance report is directed.

(c)   Identification of the applicable engagement letter.

(d)   Use of the report by the directors.

(e)   Restrictions on the use of the assurance report to the directors [and customers party to the engagement] and the replication of the report in whole or in part.

(f)   Limitation of the liability of the reporting accountants to the directors [and customers party to the engagement].

(g)   An identification and description of the subject matter information.

(h)   The identification of the directors as the responsible party and the respective responsibilities of the directors and the reporting accountants.

(i)   Reference to ISAE 3000.

(j)   Criteria against which control procedures were evaluated.

(k)   A summary of the work performed.

(l)   Inherent limitations associated with the evaluation/measurement of the subject matter against the criteria.

(m)   The reporting accountants' conclusion with the description of the reporting accountants' findings including sufficient details of errors and exceptions found.

(n)   The name and signature of the firm/reporting accountants and the location of the office performing the engagement.

(o)   The assurance report date.

22. Assurance report

The reporting accountants' conclusion is expressed in a written report attached to the directors' report. The title of the report includes the term "assurance" to distinguish it from non-assurance engagements, for instance, agreed upon procedures engagements. The report draws the attention of the readers to the basis of the reporting accountants' work, ie, ISAE 3000 and this guidance.

The report by the reporting accountants reflects the agreement set out in the engagement letter. The report makes clear for whom it is prepared and who is entitled to rely upon it and for what purpose as established in paragraphs 55 to 60.

Reporting accountants conclude on the fairness of the description and the design and operating effectiveness of control procedures in relation to a specified reporting period.

Control procedures have inherent limitations and accordingly errors and irregularities may occur and not be detected. Also control procedures cannot guarantee protection against fraudulent collusion especially on the part of those holding positions of authority or trust. Reporting accountants refer to such inherent limitations in their report.

Key elements of the assurance report are shown in the table below. Pro-forma reports on the internal controls over custodial operations are available in Appendix 3 (i) and (ii).

The engagement letter confirms that the assurance report is not to be recited or referred to in whole or in part in any other published document. This may also be stated in the report.

23. Using the work of internal auditors

A service organisation may have an internal audit department that performs tests of control procedures as part of its audit plan. The reporting accountants may determine that it might be effective and efficient to use the results of testing performed by internal auditors to alter the nature, timing or extent of the work they might otherwise have performed in forming their conclusion. Where using the work of internal auditors, however, the reporting accountants perform sufficient testing themselves which provides the principal evidence for their conclusion. The reporting accountants also make reference to the work of internal auditors in their report and attribute the performance of the tests and the results of tests to them where appropriate.

24. Considerations for uncorrected errors, fraud or illegal acts

In the course of performing procedures at a service organisation, reporting accountants may become aware of uncorrected errors, fraud or illegal acts attributable to the service organisation's systems, management or employees that may affect one or more customers.

Unless clearly inconsequential, reporting accountants determine from the directors of the service organisation whether this information has been communicated to the affected customers. If the directors of the service organisation have not communicated this information and are unwilling to do so, the reporting accountants inform the service organisation's audit committee or other group of directors with equivalent authority. If the audit committee does not respond appropriately, the reporting accountants consider whether to resign from the engagement. The reporting accountants are generally not required to confirm with the customers that the service organisation has communicated such information.

25. Management representation letter

In all engagements, reporting accountants obtain written representations signed by the directors of the service organisation who the reporting accountants believe are responsible for and knowledgeable, directly or through others in the service organisation, about the matters covered in the representations. The refusal by the directors of the service organisation to provide the written representations considered necessary by the reporting accountants constitutes a limitation on the scope of the engagement and may be considered in forming the reporting accountants' conclusion.

The representation letter is normally dated on the day the directors' report is dated.

Appendices

1. Control objectives

This section sets out detailed control objectives for the financial service activities referred to in paragraph 6. These control objectives are for guidance only and are not intended to be exhaustive, and it remains the responsibility of the directors to ensure that the described control objectives are sufficient to meet the expectations of customers.

Control objectives (h) – (j) have been added and conforming changes were made to (b) and (e) in June 2009.

(i) Custody

Accepting clients

- Accounts are set up and administered in accordance with client agreements and applicable regulations

- Complete and authorised client agreements are operative prior to initiating custody activity

- Investment holdings transferred from prior custodians are received and recorded completely, accurately and on a timely basis

- Client take-ons are monitored, documented and accurately reported to clients

Authorising and processing transactions

- Investment and related cash and foreign exchange transactions are authorised and recorded completely, accurately and on a timely basis

- Investment and related cash and foreign exchange transactions are settled and failures are resolved in a timely manner

- Corporate actions and voting instructions are identified, processed and recorded on a timely basis

- Cash receipts and payments are authorised, processed and recorded completely, accurately and on a timely basis

- Lender and borrower participation in lending programs is authorised and loan initiation, maintenance and termination are accurate and timely

- Loans are fully collateralised and the collateral together with its related income is recorded completely, accurately and on a timely basis

Maintaining financial and other records

- Investment income and related tax reclaims are collected and recorded accurately and on a timely basis

- Investments are valued using current prices obtained from independent external pricing sources and portfolio valuations are complete and distributed on a timely basis

- Asset positions for securities held by third parties such as sub custodians and depositories are accurately recorded and regularly reconciled

Safeguarding assets

- Physically held securities are safeguarded from loss, misappropriation and unauthorised use

Monitoring compliance

- Sub-custodians are approved and performance standards are monitored on a timely basis
- Outsourced activities are properly managed and monitored
- Transaction errors are rectified promptly and clients treated fairly

Reporting

- Client reporting in respect of client asset holdings is complete and accurate and provided within required timescales
- Asset positions and details of securities lent are reported to interested parties accurately and within the required time scale, including those responsible for initiating voting instructions, accurately and within required timescales

Information technology

See Appendix 1 (g)

(ii) Investment management – illustrative control objectives

Accepting clients

- Accounts are set up and administered in accordance with client agreements and applicable regulations
- Complete and authorised client agreements are operative prior to initiating investment activity
- Client take-ons, including in-specie transfers, are monitored, documented and opening positions are accurately reported to clients
- Investment limits and restrictions are established
- In-house pooled fund unitholder activity is recorded completely, accurately and in a timely manner
- Responsibility for generating proxy voting instructions is clearly established

Authorising and processing transactions

- Investment strategy is set and implemented in a timely manner
- Investment transactions are properly authorised, executed and allocated in a timely and accurate manner
- Transactions are undertaken only with approved counterparties
- Commission levels and transaction costs are monitored
- Investment and related cash transactions are completely and accurately recorded and communicated for settlement in a timely manner
- Corporate actions are processed and recorded accurately and in a timely manner
- Proxy voting instructions are generated and recorded and carried out accurately and in a timely manner
- Client new monies and withdrawals are processed and recorded completely and accurately; withdrawals are appropriately authorised

Maintaining financial and other records

- Investment income and related tax are accurately recorded in the proper period

- Investments are valued using current prices obtained from independent external pricing sources or determined according to approved pricing policies and procedures for fair values in circumstances where independent sources are not available

- Cash and investment positions are completely and accurately recorded and reconciled to third party data

- Investment management fees and other account expenses are accurately calculated and recorded

- Pooled funds are priced and administered accurately and in a timely manner

Cash management and segregation of assets

- Uninvested cash is managed with regard to diversification of risk and security of funds

- Investments are properly registered and client money is segregated

Monitoring compliance

- Client portfolios are managed in accordance with investment objectives, monitored for compliance with investment limits and restrictions and performance is measured

- Outsourced activities are properly managed and monitored and conflicts of interest identified to clients

- Transaction errors (including guideline breaches) are rectified promptly and clients treated fairly

- Counterparty exposures are monitored.

Reporting to clients

- Client reporting in respect of portfolio transactions, holdings and performance, commission and voting is complete and accurate and provided within required timescales

Information technology

See Appendix 1 (g)

(iii) Pension administration

Accepting clients

- Accounts are set up and administered in accordance with client agreements and applicable regulations

- Complete and authorised client agreements are operative prior to initiating administration activity

- Pension schemes taken on are properly established in the system in accordance with the scheme rules and individual elections

Authorising and processing transactions

- Contributions to defined contribution plans, defined benefit schemes, or both, and transfers of members' funds between investment options are processed accurately and in a timely manner

- Benefits payable and transfer values are calculated in accordance with scheme rules and relevant legislation and are paid on a timely basis

Maintaining financial and other records

- Member records consist of up to date and accurate information and are updated and reconciled regularly
- Contributions and benefit payments are completely and accurately recorded in the proper period
- Investment transactions, balances and related income are completely and accurately recorded in the proper period
- Scheme documents (deeds, policies, contracts, booklets etc) are complete, up to date and securely held

Safeguarding assets

- Member and scheme data is appropriately stored to ensure security and protection from unauthorised use
- Cash is safeguarded and payments are suitably authorised and controlled

Monitoring compliance

- Contributions are received in accordance with scheme rules and relevant legislation
- Services provided to pension schemes are in line with service level agreements
- Transaction errors are rectified promptly and clients treated fairly.

Reporting to clients

- Periodic reports to participants and scheme sponsors are accurate and complete and provided within required timescales
- Annual reports and accounts are prepared in accordance with applicable law and regulations
- Regulatory reports are made if necessary

Information technology

See Appendix 1 (g)

(iv) Property management

Accepting clients

- Accounts are set up and administered in accordance with client agreements and applicable regulations
- Complete and authorised client agreements are operative prior to initiating investment activity
- Client take-ons are monitored, documented and accurately reported to clients
- Investment guidelines and restrictions are established
- Pooled fund unitholder activity is recorded completely, accurately and in a timely manner

Authorising and processing transactions

- Investment decisions are properly formulated in accordance with investment guidelines, authorised, implemented and reviewed on a timely basis

- Property developments are only undertaken in accordance with acceptable risk criteria
- Costs associated with buying and selling properties are authorised and recorded accurately
- Tenants' covenants and lease conditions are assessed and authorised on a timely basis
- Property and related cash transactions are completely and accurately recorded and settled in a timely manner
- Rental income and service charges are accurately calculated and recorded on a timely basis
- Client new monies and withdrawals are authorised, processed and recorded completely and accurately

Maintaining financial and other records

- Complete and accurate records of each property are maintained
- Valuations are obtained at regular intervals from independent external valuers
- Income entitlements are received in full, wherever possible, and expenses, both recoverable and irrecoverable, are controlled
- Property management fees and other account expenses are accurately calculated and recorded
- Rents are monitored and rent reviews are recorded promptly and accurately
- Pooled funds are priced and administered accurately and in a timely manner

Safeguarding assets

- Properties purchased are of good and marketable title
- Title deeds are safeguarded from loss, misappropriation and unauthorised use
- Uninvested cash is managed with due regard to diversification of risk and security of funds
- Risks arising from investing in property are insured where this is economic to the interests of owners (for example consider claims etc arising from the public where large shopping malls are owned)

Monitoring compliance

- Client portfolios are managed in accordance with investment objectives, monitored for compliance with investment guidelines and restrictions and performance is measured
- Outsourced activities are properly managed and monitored
- Transaction errors (including guideline breaches) are rectified promptly and clients treated fairly

Reporting to clients

- Client reporting in respect of property transactions, holdings and performance is complete and accurate and provided within required timescales

Information technology

See Appendix 1 (g)

(v) Fund accounting – illustrative control objectives (Revised June 2009)

Accepting clients

- Accounts are set up and administered in accordance with client agreements and applicable regulations
- Complete and authorised client agreements are operative prior to initiating accounting activity
- Client take-ons are monitored, documented and accurately reported to clients

Authorising and processing transactions

- Investment and related cash transactions are completely and accurately recorded in a timely manner
- Corporate actions are processed and recorded accurately and on a timely basis

Maintaining financial and other records

- Investment income and related tax are accurately calculated and recorded on a timely basis
- Investments are valued using current prices obtained from independent external pricing sources or determined according to approved pricing policies and procedures for fair values in circumstances where independent sources are not available
- Cash and investments positions are completely and accurately recorded and reconciled to third party data
- Expenses are accurately calculated and recorded in accordance with the requirements of the fund and on a timely basis
- Distribution rates are accurately calculated and authorised and distribution amounts are recorded in a timely manner
- Issues and cancellations of shares/units are recorded completely and accurately, and positions are regularly reconciled
- Fund pricing is accurate and timely

Monitoring compliance

- Outsourced activities are properly managed and monitored and conflicts of interest identified to clients
- Pricing and distribution rate errors are rectified in a timely manner.

Reporting to clients

- Net asset value is accurately calculated and reported in a timely manner
- Periodic reports to fund sponsors are accurate and complete and distributed on a timely basis
- Annual and interim reports and accounts are prepared having regard to disclosure
- requirements and submitted in accordance with timescales determined by applicable law and regulations

Information technology

See Appendix 1 (g)

(vi) Transfer agency

Accepting clients

- Accounts are set up and administered in accordance with client agreements and applicable regulations
- Adherence to subscription limits is checked and recording of client information required by legislation is accurate
- Complete and authorised client agreements are operative prior to initiating accounting activity
- Client take-ons are monitored, documented and accurately reported to clients

Authorising and processing transactions

- Documents received are checked, sorted and distributed for processing in a timely manner
- Investor transactions and adjustments are authorised, processed accurately, completely and in a timely manner
- Cash receipts are processed accurately and banked promptly
- Cheques and certificates issued are accurately generated, matched and authorised prior to despatch
- Fund distributions and related tax withholdings are accurately calculated and authorised and distributed in a timely manner

Maintaining financial and other records

- Transfer agent records accurately reflect securities and cash held by third parties
- Share/unit activity is recorded completely, accurately and positions are regularly reconciled

Safeguarding assets

- Lost and stolen certificates are recorded in a timely manner

Monitoring compliance

- Transaction errors are rectified promptly and clients treated fairly

Reporting to clients

- Compensation payments are authorised, calculated and reviewed by management
- Client reporting is complete and accurate and processed within required timescales

Information technology

See Appendix 1 (g)

(vii) Information technology

Restricting access to systems and data

- Physical access to computer networks, equipment, storage media and program documentation is restricted to authorised individuals

- Logical access to computer systems, programs, master data, transaction data and parameters, including access by administrators to applications, databases, systems and networks, is restricted to authorised individuals via information security tools and techniques
- Segregation of incompatible duties is defined, implemented and enforced by logical security controls in accordance with job roles

Providing integrity and resilience to the information processing environment, commensurate with the value of the information held, information processing performed and external threats

- IT processing is authorised and scheduled appropriately and exceptions are identified and resolved in a timely manner
- Data transmissions between the service organisation and its counterparties are complete, accurate, timely and secure
- Appropriate measures are implemented to counter the threat from malicious electronic attack (eg, firewalls, anti-virus etc.)
- The physical IT equipment is maintained in a controlled environment

Maintaining and developing systems hardware and software

- Development and implementation of new systems, applications and software, and changes to existing systems, applications and software, are authorised, tested, approved and implemented
- Data migration or modification is authorised, tested and, once performed, reconciled back to the source data

Recovering from processing interruptions

- Data and systems are backed up regularly, retained offsite and regularly tested for recoverability
- IT hardware and software issues are monitored and resolved in a timely manner
- Business and information systems recovery plans are documented, approved, tested and maintained

Monitoring compliance

- Outsourced activities are properly managed and monitored

(viii) Private equity – illustrative control objectives

Accepting clients

- New funds are properly developed and authorised, take account of legal and tax requirements and contain a specified investment strategy
- Prospective investors are assessed for suitability and complete relevant legal documentation prior to investment activity
- Investment guidelines and restrictions are established and updated as required

Authorising and processing investment transactions

- Investment decisions are researched, authorised and implemented in accordance with the investment strategy and due diligence and abort costs are controlled
- Investment transactions and commitments are properly authorised and executed in a timely and accurate manner (this is intended to include acquisitions and exits)

- Investment and related cash transactions are completely and accurately recorded and communicated for settlement in a timely manner

- Rights and obligation arising from an exit are recorded and monitored

- Investment allocations are made in accordance with the terms of the partnership or supporting agreements

Maintaining financial and other records

- Investment income and related tax are accurately recorded in the proper period

- Investments are valued in accordance with relevant industry guidelines

- Investor drawdowns and distributions are authorised, processed and recorded completely and accurately

- Investment management fees, carried interest payments and expenses of the funds are authorised, accurately calculated, recorded and allocated in accordance with the fund's legal documentation

- Cash and investment positions are completely and accurately recorded and reconciled to third party data or documents of title held

Safeguarding assets

- Investments are properly registered and securely held

- Uninvested cash is managed with due regard to diversification of risk and security of funds

Monitoring compliance

- Investment performance is monitored

- Outsourced activities are properly managed and monitored and conflicts of interest identified to clients

Reporting to investors

- Investor reporting is complete and accurate and provided within required timescales

- Reports and accounts are prepared having regard to disclosure requirements and submitted in accordance with timescales determined by applicable law and regulations and are distributed to investors on a timely basis

Information technology

See Appendix 1 (g)

(ix) Investment administration – illustrative control objectives

Accepting clients

- Accounts are set up and administered in accordance with client agreements and applicable regulations

- Complete and authorised client agreements are operative prior to initiating administration activity

- Client take-ons, including in specie transfers, are monitored, documented and opening positions are accurately reported to clients

- In-house pooled fund unit-holder activity is recorded completely, accurately and in a timely manner

Authorising and processing transactions

- Investment and related cash transactions are completely and accurately recorded and communicated for settlement in a timely manner
- Corporate actions are processed and recorded accurately and on a timely basis
- Client new monies and withdrawals are processed and recorded completely and accurately withdrawals are appropriately authorised

Maintaining financial and other records

- Investment income and related tax are accurately recorded in the proper period
- Investments are valued using current prices obtained from independent external pricing sources or determined according to approved pricing policies and procedures for fair values in circumstances where independent sources are not available
- Cash and investment positions are completely and accurately recorded and reconciled to third party data
- Expenses are accurately identified and recorded in accordance with client requirements and on a timely basis
- Pooled funds are priced and administered accurately and in a timely manner

Monitoring compliance

- Outsourced activities are properly managed and monitored and conflicts of interest identified to clients

Reporting to clients

- Periodic reports to clients and customers are accurate and complete and distributed on a timely basis

Information technology

See Appendix 1 (g)

(x) Hedge fund management[9] – illustrative control objectives[10]

Accepting clients

- New funds are properly structured and authorised (where applicable), take account of legal and tax requirements and contain a specified investment strategy
- Funds are set up and administered in accordance with the Fund's constitutional agreements and applicable regulations
- Prospective investors are assessed for suitability and complete relevant legal documentation prior to investment activity
- Investment limits and restrictions are established
- Responsibility for generating proxy voting instructions is clearly established

Authorising and processing transactions

- Investment strategy is set and implemented in a timely manner

---

[9] *Hedge fund managers may also consider relevant industry standards and codes of conduct.*

[10] *Managers of funds of hedge funds may consider which of these control objectives are relevant and consider what additional control objectives are appropriate.*

- Investment transactions are properly authorised, executed and allocated in a timely and accurate manner
- Complete and authorised agreements with counterparties (eg, prime broker, administrator and custodian) are operative prior to initiating investment activity
- Transactions are undertaken only with approved counterparties
- Commission levels and transaction costs are monitored
- Corporate actions are processed and recorded accurately and in a timely manner
- Proxy voting instructions are generated and recorded and carried out accurately and in a timely manner
- Investor subscriptions and redemptions are processed and recorded completely and accurately; redemptions are appropriately authorised
- Where quantitative trading strategies are adopted, the design and review of such strategies models is monitored
- Trading activity is only undertaken within the parameters of the Fund's investment strategy (eg, limits on leverage, concentration risk, counterparty risk, type of investments)

Maintaining financial and other records

- Investment income and related tax are accurately recorded in the proper period
- Investments are valued using current prices obtained from independent external pricing sources or determined according to approved pricing policies and procedures for fair values in circumstances where independent sources are not available
- Where reliable market price data is not available hard-to-value assets are valued using consistent valuation arrangements which mitigate conflicts of interest and are disclosed to investors
- Cash and investment positions are completely and accurately recorded
- Reconciliations are undertaken between the prime broker, the administrator and the custodian for daily trades, investment positions, settlements and cash in a timely and accurate manner
- Lock-up periods, redemption gates and penalties are accurately applied in accordance with the Fund's constitutional agreements
- Where hard-to-value assets are placed in side pockets, they are appropriately identified and recorded in accordance with the Fund's constitutional agreements
- Investment management and performance fees and other account expenses are authorised, accurately calculated and recorded

Safeguarding assets

- Liquidity management is undertaken with due regard to investor subscriptions and redemptions, margin calls, terms and duration of bank borrowing and the payments due to creditors
- Uninvested cash is managed with due regarded to diversification of risk and security of funds

- Investments are properly registered and client money is segregated

Monitoring compliance

- Fund portfolios are managed in accordance with investment objectives, monitored for compliance with investment limits and restrictions and performance is measured

- Outsourced activities, including arrangements with prime brokers, administrators and transfer agents are properly managed and monitored and conflicts of interest identified to clients

- Transaction errors (including guidelines breaches) are rectified promptly and investors treated fairly

- Portfolio liquidity is monitored in accordance with client instruction in order to meet redemption requests in a timely manner

- Levels of leverage, margin calls, counterparty exposures and potential events of default are monitored

Reporting to investors

- Reporting to investors in respect of fund net asset values, portfolio transactions, investment holdings, performance, commission and voting and other information agreed with investors is complete and accurate and provided with required timescales

Information technology

See Appendix 1 (g)

2. Example paragraphs from the report by the directors

As directors we are responsible for the identification of control objectives relating to customers' assets[41] and related transactions in the provision of [financial services[12]] and the design, implementation and operation of the control procedures of [name of entity] to provide reasonable assurance that the control objectives are achieved.

In carrying out those responsibilities we have regard not only to the interests of customers but also to those of the owners of the business and the general effectiveness and efficiency of the relevant operations.

We have evaluated the effectiveness of the [name of entity]'s control procedures having regard to ICAEW Technical Release AAF 01/06 and the criteria for [financial services] set out therein.

We set out in this report a description of the relevant control procedures together with the related control objectives which operated during the period [x] to [y] and confirm that

(i)   the report describes fairly the control procedures that relate to the control objectives referred to above which were in place as at [date];

(ii)   the control procedures described are suitably designed such that there is reasonable assurance that the specified control objectives would be achieved

---

[41] *The reference to "assets" may need to be expanded here and elsewhere in the report: see footnote 3, page 5.*

[12] *Refer to relevant financial services as per paragraph 6, page 2.*

if the described control procedures were complied with satisfactorily [and customers applied the control procedures contemplated[42]]; and

(iii)   the control procedures described were operating with sufficient effectiveness to provide reasonable assurance that the related control objectives were achieved during the specified period.

Director

Date

Signed on behalf of the Board of Directors

3. Pro-forma reporting accountants' assurance reports (i) and (ii) (revised July 2016)

(a) Engagement formed between the reporting accountant and the service organisation and to which customers of the service organisation are party

Reporting accountants' assurance report on internal controls of service organisations[43]

To the directors of [name of entity] and [customers party to the engagement]

Use of report[44]

This report is made solely for the use of the directors, as a body, of [name of entity] and [customers party to the engagement], and solely for the purpose of reporting on the internal controls of [name of entity], in accordance with the terms of our engagement letter dated [date] [and attached[45] as appendix [ ]].

Our work has been undertaken so that we might report to the directors and [customers party to the engagement] those matters that we have agreed to state to them in this report and for no other purpose. Our report must not be recited or referred to in whole or in part in any other document nor made available, copied or recited to any other party, in any circumstances, without our express prior written permission.

To the fullest extent permitted by law, we do not accept or assume responsibility to anyone other than the directors as a body, [name of entity] and [customers party to the engagement] for our work, for this report or for the opinions we have formed.

Subject matter

This report covers solely the internal controls of [name of entity] as described in your report as at [date]. Internal controls are processes designed to provide reasonable assurance regarding the level of control over customers' assets[46] and related transactions achieved by [name of entity] in the provision of [outsourced activities] by [name of entity].

The directors' responsibilities and statement are set out on page [ ]. Our responsibility is to form an independent conclusion, based on the work carried out in relation to the control procedures of [name of **entity]'s** [ ] function carried out at

---

[42]   *This additional wording may be considered appropriate in circumstances described in paragraph 43, page 8.*

[43]   *Reporting accountants consider a suitable form of report in accordance with the specific engagement as described in paragraph 55. This report provides an example for an engagement to which customers of the service organisation are party (see paragraph 55(a)).*

[44]   *The two last paragraphs in "Use of report" provide example wording, disclaiming reporting accountants' liability or duty to the customers that are not party to the engagement. Reporting accountants consider the legal effectiveness of disclaiming liability in the particular circumstances of their engagement.*

[45]   *Reporting accountants that do not attach the engagement letter consider including relevant extracts.*

[46]   *The reference to "assets" may need to be expanded here and elsewhere in the report: see footnote 3, page 5.*

the specified business units of [name of entity] [located at [ ]] **as described in the directors' report and** report this to the directors of [name of entity] and [customers party to the engagement].

Our independence and quality control

We have complied with the independence and other ethical requirements of the ICAEW Code of Ethics, which includes the requirements of the Code of Ethics for Professional Accountants issued by the International Ethics Standards Board for Accountants, which is founded on fundamental principles of integrity, objectivity, professional competence and due care, confidentiality and professional behaviour.

The firm applies International Standard on Quality Control 1 and accordingly maintains a comprehensive system of quality control including documented policies and procedures regarding compliance with ethical requirements, professional standards and applicable legal and regulatory requirements.

Criteria and scope

We conducted our engagement in accordance with International Standard on Assurance Engagements (ISAE) 3000 and ICAEW Technical Release AAF 01/06. The criteria against which the control procedures were evaluated are the internal control objectives developed for service organisations as set out within the Technical Release AAF 01/06 and identified by the directors as relevant control objectives relating to the level of control over customers' assets and related transactions in the provision of [outsourced activities]. Our work was based upon obtaining an understanding of the control procedures as described on page [ ] to [ ] in the report by the directors, and evaluating the directors' statement on page [ ] to [ ] in the same report to obtain reasonable assurance so as to form our conclusion.

Inherent limitations

Control procedures designed to address specified control objectives are subject to inherent limitations and, accordingly, errors or irregularities may occur and not be detected. Such control procedures cannot guarantee protection against (among other things) fraudulent collusion especially on the part of those holding positions of authority or trust. Furthermore, our conclusion is based on historical information and the projection of any information or conclusions in the attached report to any future periods would be inappropriate.

Conclusion

In our opinion, in all material respects:

(i)   the accompanying report by the directors describes fairly the control procedures that relate to the control objectives referred to above which were in place as at [date];

(ii)   the control procedures described on pages [ ] to [ ] were suitably designed such that there is reasonable, but not absolute, assurance that the specified control objectives would have been achieved if the described control procedures were complied with satisfactorily [and customers applied the control procedures contemplated[47]]; and

(iii)   the control procedures that were tested, as set out in the attachment to this report, were operating with sufficient effectiveness for us to obtain reasonable, but not absolute, assurance that the related control objectives were achieved in the period [x] to [y].

---

[47] *See footnote 13, page 37.*

Name of firm Chartered Accountants Location Date

(b) Engagement formed between the reporting accountant and the service organisation only

Reporting accountants' assurance report on internal controls of service organisations[48]

To the directors of [name of entity]

Use of report[20]

This report is made solely for the use of the directors, as a body, of [name of entity], and solely for the purpose of reporting on the internal controls of [name of entity], in accordance with the terms of our engagement letter dated [date] [and attached[49] as appendix [ ]].

Our work has been undertaken so that we might report to the directors those matters that we have agreed to state to them in this report and for no other purpose. Our report must not be recited or referred to in whole or in part in any other document nor made available, copied or recited to any other party, in any circumstances, without our express prior written permission.

We permit the disclosure of this report, in full only, by the directors at their discretion to customers [of [name of entity] using [name of entity]'s [financial services[22]] ("customers"),] and to the auditors of such customers, to enable customers and their auditors to verify that a report by reporting accountants has been commissioned by the directors of [name of entity] and issued in connection with the internal controls of [name of entity], and without assuming or accepting any responsibility or liability to customers or their auditors on our part.

To the fullest extent permitted by law, we do not accept or assume responsibility to anyone other than the directors as a body and [name of entity] for our work, for this report or for the conclusions we have formed[50].

---

[48] *Reporting accountants consider a suitable form of report in accordance with the specific engagement as described in paragraph 55. This report provides an example for an engagement formed between the reporting accountants and the service organisation only, applicable to arrangements (c) and (d) as described in paragraph 55, page 10–11. The sentence beginning "we permit" is adapted where paragraph 55(c) is applied.*

[20] *The three last paragraphs in "Use of report" provide example wording, disclaiming reporting accountants' liability or duty to the customers that are not party to the engagement. Reporting accountants consider the legal effectiveness of disclaiming liability in the particular circumstances of their engagement.*

[49] *Reporting accountants that do not attach the engagement letter consider including relevant extracts.*

[22] *See footnote 12, page 32.*

[50] *If arrangement (b) as described in paragraph 55 is considered appropriate then accountants consider including reference to the facility for customers meeting a firm's client acceptance criteria to enjoy a duty of care from the accountants if they accept the relevant terms of the engagement letter agreed previously with the service organisation. Wording that might be used (in particular in place of the paragraphs shown above and beginning "We permit" and "To the fullest extent" is as follows:*

> *"Subject as follows, we are prepared to extend our assumption of responsibility to those customers who first accept in writing (in a form provided to us and confirmed by us to be acceptable to us) the relevant terms of the engagement letter agreed previously with [name of entity] as if the customer had signed that letter when originally issued, and including the provisions limiting liability contained in that letter. This extension will not apply to a customer where we inform that customer, whether before or after the customer accepts the relevant terms of the engagement letter, that they do not meet our client acceptance criteria.*

> *To the fullest extent permitted by law, we do not accept or assume responsibility to anyone other than the directors as a body, the organisation and any customer to whom the extension does apply, for our work, for this report or for the conclusions we have formed."*

Subject matter

This report covers solely the internal controls of [name of entity] as described in your report as at [date]. Internal controls are processes designed to provide reasonable assurance regarding the level of control over customers' assets[51] and related transactions achieved by [name of entity] in the provision of [outsourced activities] by [name of entity].

The directors' responsibilities and statement are set out on page [ ]. Our responsibility is to form an independent conclusion, based on the work carried out in relation to the control procedures of [name of **entity]'s [ ]** function carried out at the specified business units of [name of entity] [located at [ ]] **as described in the directors' report and** report this to the directors of [name of entity] and [customers party to the engagement].

Our independence and quality control

We have complied with the independence and other ethical requirements of the ICAEW Code of Ethics, which includes the requirements of the Code of Ethics for Professional Accountants issued by the International Ethics Standards Board for Accountants, which is founded on fundamental principles of integrity, objectivity, professional competence and due care, confidentiality and professional behaviour.

The firm applies International Standard on Quality Control 1 and accordingly maintains a comprehensive system of quality control including documented policies and procedures regarding compliance with ethical requirements, professional standards and applicable legal and regulatory requirements.

Criteria and scope

We conducted our engagement in accordance with International Standard on Assurance Engagements (ISAE) 3000 (revised) and ICAEW Technical Release AAF 01/06. The criteria against which the control procedures were evaluated are the internal control objectives developed for service organisations as set out within the Technical Release AAF 01/06 and identified by the directors as relevant control objectives relating to the level of control over customers' assets and related transactions in the provision of [outsourced activities]. Our work was based upon obtaining an understanding of the control procedures as described on page [ ] to [ ] in the report by the directors, and evaluating the directors' statement on page [ ] to [ ] in the same report to obtain reasonable assurance so as to form our conclusion.

Inherent limitations

Control procedures designed to address specified control objectives are subject to inherent limitations and, accordingly, errors or irregularities may occur and not be detected. Such control procedures cannot guarantee protection against (among other things) fraudulent collusion especially on the part of those holding positions of authority or trust. Furthermore, our conclusion is based on historical information and the projection of any information or conclusions in the attached report to any future periods would be inappropriate.

Conclusion

In our opinion, in all material respects:

(i)   the accompanying report by the directors describes fairly the control procedures that relate to the control objectives referred to above which were in place as at [date];

---

[51] *The reference to "assets" may need to be expanded here and elsewhere in the report: see footnote 3, page 5.*

(ii)   the control procedures described on pages [ ] to [ ] were suitably designed such that there is reasonable, but not absolute, assurance that the specified control objectives would have been achieved if the described control procedures were complied with satisfactorily [and customers applied the control procedures contemplated[52]]; and

(iii) the control procedures that were tested, as set out in the attachment to this report, were operating with sufficient effectiveness for us to obtain reasonable, but not absolute, assurance that the related control objectives were achieved in the period [x] to [y].

Name of firm Chartered Accountants Location Date

4. Examples of explanatory paragraphs and qualification wording

(a) Description misstatements

Appendix 1 specifies a minimum set of control objectives for inclusion in the directors' reports. Exceptionally, in the event that the directors decide not to include a particular control objective in their report then their report explains the fact and the reasons for the omission. Where directors fail or refuse to disclose the omission, or the reporting accountants consider the justification being unsatisfactory, the reporting accountants disclose the fact and qualify their opinion. For example:

We draw attention to page [x] of the report by the directors which sets out the control objectives. One of the control objectives, [specify], in Technical Release AAF 01/06, is not included in the directors' report and no reason for the omission is explained.

Except for the matter referred to above concerning the fairness of the description of control procedures, in our opinion, ...

The refusal or failure of the directors to amend incomplete or inappropriate descriptions of control procedures or control objectives, may lead to the description of internal controls being considered not fair. Where the reporting accountants consider that this merits qualification, this might be phrased as follows:

The report by the directors states, on page [x], that cash records are reconciled to bank statements on a daily basis. Our work indicates that whilst this is the procedure for UK bank accounts, reconciliations of overseas accounts are only carried out as and when bank statements are received, which is typically once per month.

Except for the matter referred to above concerning the fairness of the description of control procedures, in our opinion, ...

(b) Design deficiencies

Design deficiencies may, for example, result either from a key control being absent or from control procedures that do not prevent or detect errors as described. The following is an example of wording that may be appropriate where reporting accountants qualify their opinion on the control design due to the absence of a key control.

As explained on page [x] of the report by the directors six monthly reconciliations of physical securities held to the books and records are

---

[52] *See footnote 13, page 37.*

undertaken. The reconciliation procedures did not however include a control for follow up of reconciling items and for independent review and approval of the reconciliations.

Except for the matter referred to above concerning the control design, in our opinion, ...

(c) Exceptions to operating effectiveness

Tests of operating effectiveness carried out by reporting accountants in relation to specific control procedures are detailed either (a) adjacent to the relevant control procedures in the report by the directors or (b) in an appendix to the assurance report. Where the results of the tests identify an exception to the control procedures, this is reported after the test, and the reporting accountants consider whether the exceptions affect the achievement of the control objective. Where the achievement of the control objective deserves qualification the reporting accountants insert an explanatory paragraph with appropriate reference and modify their opinion.

> On page [x] of the report by the directors it is stated that six monthly reconciliations of physical securities held to the books and records are undertaken and that there is a process for following up reconciling items. Our tests of operating effectiveness indicated that there were a significant number of reconciling items that were not being resolved on a timely basis in accordance with the organisation's policy.

> Except for the matter referred to above concerning the operating effectiveness of the control procedures, in our opinion, ...

Where the results of the reporting accountants' tests of operational effectiveness and the deficiency have been integrated and fully explained into the report by the directors the reporting accountants may alternatively consider cross-referring their qualification to where these details may be found. For example:

> Except for the matter explained on page [z] concerning the follow up of reconciling items on physical security reconciliations, the control procedures tested, as set out [on pages [x] to [y] of the report by the directors/in the attachment to this report], in our opinion, ...

5. Example extracts from an engagement letter

These extracts are provided for illustrative purposes only. Reporting accountants apply their own judgement to develop suitable wording for their engagement letters to reflect the guidance in this Technical Release and their own particular circumstances[53].

Responsibilities of directors

The board of directors ("the Directors") of [name of entity] in relation to which the reporting accountants' assurance report is to be provided ("the Organisation") are

---

[53] *The above extracts may be appropriate illustrations only for an engagement formed between the reporting accountants and the service organisation. Where a multi-party engagement is formed in line with paragraph 55(a), wording should be revised and additional clauses should be inserted as appropriate. Where a customer agrees to sign up to the engagement terms at a later date, additional wording maybe inserted in line with paragraph 55(b) to clarify the basis on which the customer signs up and to secure the consent of the service organisation/original addressees. The wording will include adjustment of the section on "Use of Report" and the addition of wording in the section on Liability Provisions to refer to the provisions applying to "the Directors as a body, the Organisation (and customers who are or become, by signature, a party to the engagement letter)" and to losses suffered by, and aggregate liability to, "the Directors as a body, the Organisation (and any customers who are or become, by signature, a party to the engagement letter)".*

and shall be responsible for the design, implementation and operation of control procedures that provide adequate level of control over customers' assets[54] and related transactions. The Directors' responsibilities are and shall include:

- acceptance of responsibility for internal controls;

- evaluation of the effectiveness of the service organisation's control procedures using suitable criteria;

- supporting their evaluation with sufficient evidence, including documentation; and

- providing a written report ("Directors' Report") of the effectiveness of the service organisation's internal controls for the relevant financial period.

In drafting this report the Directors have regard to, as a minimum, the criteria specified within the Technical Release AAF 01/06 issued by ICAEW but they may add to these to the extent that this is considered appropriate in order to meet customers' expectations.

Responsibilities of reporting accountants

It is our responsibility to form an independent conclusion, based on the work carried out in relation to the control procedures of the Organisation's [ ] function carried out at the specified business units of the Organisation [located at [ ]] as described in the Directors' report and report this to the Directors.

Scope of the reporting accountants' work

We conduct our work in accordance with the procedures set out in AAF 01/06, issued by the Institute. Our work will include enquiries of management, together with tests of certain specific control procedures which will be set out in an appendix to our report.

In reaching our conclusion, the criteria against which the control procedures are to be evaluated are the internal control objectives developed for service organisations as set out within the AAF 01/06 issued by ICAEW.

Any work already performed in connection with this engagement before the date of this letter will also be governed by the terms and conditions of this letter.

We may seek written representations from the Directors in relation to matters on which independent corroboration is not available. We shall seek confirmation from the Directors that any significant matters of which we should be aware have been brought to our attention.

Inherent limitations

The Directors acknowledge that control procedures designed to address specified control objectives are subject to inherent limitations and, accordingly, errors or irregularities may occur and not be detected. Such procedures cannot guarantee protection against fraudulent collusion especially on the part of those holding positions of authority or trust. Furthermore, the opinion set out in our report will be based on historical information and the projection of any information or conclusions in our report to any future periods will be inappropriate.

Use of our report

Our report will, subject to the permitted disclosures set out in this letter, be made solely for the use of the Directors of the Organisation, and solely for the purpose of

---

[54] *The reference to "assets" may need to be expanded here and elsewhere in the report: see footnote 3, page 5.*

reporting on the internal controls of the Organisation, in accordance with these terms of our engagement.

Our work will be undertaken so that we might report to the Directors those matters that we have agreed to state to them in our report and for no other purpose.

Our report will be issued on the basis that it must not be recited or referred to or disclosed, in whole or in part, in any other document or to any other party, without the express prior written permission of the reporting accountants. We permit the disclosure of our report, in full only, to customers [of the Organisation using the Organisation's [financial services[55]] ("customers")] [(as defined in appendix [ ] to this letter),] and to the auditors of such customers, to enable customers and their auditors to verify that a report by reporting accountants has been commissioned by the Directors of the Organisation and issued in connection with the internal controls of the Organisation without assuming or accepting any responsibility or liability to them on our part.

To the fullest extent permitted by law, we do not and will not accept or assume responsibility to anyone other than the Directors as a body and the Organisation for our work, for our report or for the opinions we will have formed[56].

Liability provisions[57]

We will perform the engagement with reasonable skill and care and acknowledge that we will be liable to the Directors as a body and the Organisation for losses, damages, costs or expenses ("losses") suffered by the Directors as a body and the Organisation as a result of our breach of contract, negligence, fraud or other deliberate breach of duty. Our liability shall be subject to the following provisions:

- We will not be so liable if such losses are due to the provision of false, misleading or incomplete information or documentation or due to the acts or omissions of any person other than us, except where, on the basis of the enquiries normally undertaken by us within the scope set out in these terms of engagement, it would have been reasonable for us to discover such defects;

- We accept liability without limit for the consequences of our own fraud or other deliberate breach of duty and for any other liability which it is not permitted by law to limit or exclude;

- Subject to the previous provisions of this Liability paragraph, our total aggregate liability whether in contract, tort (including negligence) or otherwise, to the Directors as a body and the Organisation, arising from or in connection with the work which is the subject of these terms (including any addition or variation to the work), shall not exceed the amount of [To be discussed and negotiated];

To the fullest extent permitted by law, the Organisation agrees to indemnify and hold harmless [name of reporting accountants] and its partners and staff against all actions, proceedings and claims brought or threatened against [name of reporting accountants] or against any of its partners and staff by any persons other than the Directors as a body and the Organisation, and all loss, damage and expense

---

[55] *See footnote 12, page 32.*

[56] *See footnote 23, page 35.*

[57] *Reporting accountants may wish to seek independent legal advice on language that addresses both the matters covered in the illustrative wording set out in this Liability section together with any related matters such as provisions indicating that liability does not extend to consequential losses. Accountants may also consider any applicable independence requirements.*

(including legal expenses) relating thereto, where any such action, proceeding or claim in any way relates to or concerns or is connected with any of [name of reporting accountants]'s work under this engagement letter.

The Directors as a body and the Organisation agree that they will not bring any claims or proceedings against any of our individual partners, members, directors or employees. This clause is intended to benefit such partners, members, directors and employees who may enforce this clause pursuant to the Contracts (Rights of Third Parties) Act 1999 ("the Act"). Notwithstanding any benefits or rights conferred by this agreement on such partners, members, directors or employees by virtue of the Act, we and the Directors as a body may together agree in writing to vary or rescind the agreement set out in this letter without the consent of any such partners, members, directors or employees. Other than as expressly provided in this paragraph, the provisions of the Act are excluded;

Any claims, whether in contract, negligence or otherwise, must be formally commenced within [years] after the party bringing the claim becomes aware (or ought reasonably to have become aware) of the facts which give rise to the action and in any event no later than [years] after any alleged breach of contract, negligence or other cause of action. This expressly overrides any statutory provision which would otherwise apply.

This engagement is separate from, and unrelated to, our audit work on the financial statements of the Organisation for the purposes of the Companies Act 1985 (or its successor) or other legislation and nothing herein creates obligations or liabilities regarding our statutory audit work, which would not otherwise exist. [Equivalent paragraphs where the Organisation is other than a Companies Act entity].

[Appendix: The list of customers to whom the assurance report may be made available[58].]

6. Example sample size table

In determining the number of items to be tested the reporting accountants need to consider the factors referred to in paragraph 81. Although the extent of testing is a matter of judgement on the part of the reporting accountants the table set out below illustrates a range of possible sample sizes which may assist in making such judgements.

Frequency of control	Number of items tested
Annual	1
Quarterly	1, 2, 3
Monthly	2, 3, 4, 5
Weekly	5, 10, 15
Daily	15, 20, 30, 40
Multiple times per day	25, 30, 45, 60

---

[58] *A list of customers may not be practical where they are multiple.*

7. Illustrative definition of enquiry, inspection, observation and re-performance

In describing the nature of tests carried out, it is desirable for the reporting accountants to define in their report what is meant by such procedures as enquiry, inspection, observation and re-performance (see paragraph 84). Illustrative definitions which may assist reporting accountants in this regard are set out below.

Enquiry

Enquired of appropriate [name of entity] personnel. Enquiries seeking relevant information or representation from personnel were performed to obtain, among other things:

- knowledge, additional information and affirmation regarding the control of procedures; and

- corroborating evidence of the control procedures.

Inspection

Inspected documents and records indicating performance of the control procedures. This included, among other things:

- inspection of reconciliations and management reports that age and/or quantify reconciling items to assess whether balances and reconciling items appear to be properly monitored, controlled and resolved on a timely basis, as required by the related control;

- examination of source documentation and authorisations related to selected transactions processed;

- examination of documents or records for evidence of performance such as the existence of initials or signatures; and

- inspection of [name of entity]'s systems documentation, such as operations, manuals, flow charts and job descriptions.

Observation

Observed the application or existence of specific control procedures as represented.

Re-performance

Re-performed the control or processing application of the control procedures to check the accuracy of their operation. This included, among other things:

- obtaining evidence of the arithmetical accuracy and correct processing of transactions by performing independent calculations; and

- re-performing the matching of various system records by independently matching the same records and comparing reconciling items to reconciliations prepared by the service organisation.

8. International Standard on Assurance Engagements (ISAE) 3402 Assurance Reports on Controls at a Service Organisation and a pro-forma report, revised for assurance reports dated on or after 15 December 2015

In December 2009, the International Auditing and Assurance Standards Board (IAASB) issued International Standard on Assurance Engagements (ISAE) 3402 *Assurance Reports on Controls at a Service Organization*. Consequential amendments were made to this standard by the IAASB at the same time as they issued ISAE 3000 (revised) which take effect for assurance reports signed on or after 15 December 2015. This ISAE is to be applied in a reasonable assurance engagement to report on financial reporting controls at a service organisation. It addresses reports on the description, design and operating effectiveness of controls relating to the broad range of services provided by service organisations. The standard applies internationally.

This appendix is issued to assist with the implementation of ISAE 3402 as the principal reporting framework for reports on internal controls at service organisations in the United Kingdom. ISAE 3402 is consistent with the existing ICAEW guidance AAF 01/06 which provides sets of control objectives as criteria against which internal controls may be assessed.

This Appendix provides a pro-forma report for reporting using ISAE 3402, ISAE 3000 (revised) and AAF 01/06.

There are two key differences between ISAE 3402 and AAF 01/06 which are relevant to considering the scope of the work of reporting accountants. Firstly ISAE 3402's scope is narrower than AAF 01/06 in that it deals only with assurance engagements to report on internal controls at a service organisation that are likely to be relevant to user organisations' internal controls as they relate to financial reporting. Practitioners performing assurance reporting on internal controls that do not relate to financial reporting follow ISAE 3000 (revised) and AAF 01/06[59]. Secondly, in the context of a report that covers controls in operation for a given period ("a type 2 report"), ISAE 3402 requires reporting accountants to report on the fairness of the description and on the design of control procedures throughout the period rather than as of the date at the end of the period.

The structure of reporting under ISAE 3402 has the same key characteristics of an assurance engagement under AAF 01/06 as both are based on ISAE 3000 (revised). These are:

- A three-party relationship
- Appropriate subject matter
- Suitable criteria
- Sufficient appropriate evidence, and
- A written assurance report

ISAE 3402 sets out details of how practitioners should undertake their assurance engagements. AAF 01/06 continues to provide guidance on the responsibilities of a service organisation, guidance for reporting accountants on managing professional liability, and details of the illustrative control objectives agreed with relevant industry bodies or regulators that are considered suitable criteria and collectively reflect the level of service organisations' control over customers' assets and related transactions. Reporting accountants issuing an ISAE 3402 report need to read and comply with ISAE 3402 as reading AAF 01/06 including this appendix alone does not substitute for reading the international standard.

A pro-forma reporting accountants' assurance report in accordance with ISAE 3402[29]

Reporting accountants issue an assurance report in a form suitable for the specific engagement. The report below is based on one of the pro-forma reporting

---

[59] *For some service organisations there may be controls that are closely related to those for financial reporting. Whether such controls, which are typically in operations or compliance, are likely to be relevant to internal control as it relates to financial reporting will be a matter of professional judgement.*

[29] *ISAE 3402 uses the term "service auditor", which may be substituted for "reporting accountant" throughout this report if preferred.*

accountants' assurance reports (ii) Engagement formed between the reporting accountant and the service organisation only in Appendix 3 of AAF 01/06 and provides an illustrative type 2 report.

Reporting accountants' assurance report on internal controls of service organisation[30]

To the directors of [name of entity]

Use of report[31]

This report is made solely for the use of the directors, as a body, of [name of entity], and solely for the purpose of reporting on the internal controls of [name of entity], in accordance with the terms of our engagement letter dated [date] [and attached[32] as appendix [ ]].

Our work has been undertaken so that we might report to the directors those matters that we have agreed to state to them in this report and for no other purpose. Our report must not be recited or referred to in whole or in part in any other document nor made available, copied or recited to any other party, in any circumstances, without our express prior written permission.

We permit the disclosure of this report, in full only, by the directors at their discretion to customers [of [name of entity] using [name of entity]'s [financial services[33]] ("customers"),] and to the auditors of such customers, to enable customers and their auditors to verify that a report by reporting accountants has been commissioned by the directors of [name of entity] and issued in connection with the internal controls of [name of entity], and without assuming or accepting any responsibility or liability to customers or their auditors on our part.

To the fullest extent permitted by law, we do not accept or assume responsibility to anyone other than the directors as a body and [name of entity] for our work, for this report or for the conclusions we have formed.[34]

Scope

We have been engaged to report on [name of entity]'s description of its [service organisation activities or system] throughout the period [date] to [date] (the

---

[30] *Reporting accountants consider a suitable form of report in accordance with the specific engagement as described in paragraph 55 of AAF 01/06. This report provides an example for an engagement formed between the reporting accountants and the service organisation only, applicable to arrangements (c) and (d) as described in paragraph 55.*

[31] *The three last paragraphs in "Use of Report" provide example wording, disclaiming reporting accountants' liability or duty to the customers that are not party to the engagement. Reporting accountants consider the legal effectiveness of disclaiming liability in the particular circumstances of their engagement.*

[32] *Reporting accountants that do not attach the engagement letter consider including relevant extracts.*

[33] *See footnote 12, page 32.*

[34] *If arrangement (b) as described in paragraph 55 is considered appropriate then reporting accountants consider including reference to the facility for customers meeting a firm's client acceptance criteria to enjoy a duty of care from the reporting accountants if they accept the relevant terms of the engagement letter agreed previously with the service organisation. Wording that might be used (in particular in place of the paragraphs shown above and beginning "We permit" and "To the fullest extent" is as follows: "Subject as follows, we are prepared to extend our assumption of responsibility to those customers who first accept in writing (in a form provided to us and confirmed by us to be acceptable to us) the relevant terms of the engagement letter agreed previously with [name of entity] as if the customer had signed that letter when originally issued, and including the provisions limiting liability contained in that letter. This extension will not apply to a customer where we inform that customer, whether before or after the customer accepts the relevant terms of the engagement letter, that they do not meet our client acceptance criteria. To the fullest extent permitted by law, we do not accept or assume responsibility to anyone other than the directors as a body, the organisation and any customer to whom the extension does apply, for our work, for this report or for the conclusions we have formed."*

description), and on the suitability of the design and operating effectiveness of controls to achieve the related control objectives stated in the description.

Service organisation's responsibilities

[Name of entity] is responsible for: preparing the description and the accompanying statement set out on page [ ], including the completeness, accuracy, and method of presentation of the description and the statement; providing the services covered by the description; specifying the criteria including the control objectives and stating them in the description; identifying the risks that threaten the achievement of the control objectives; and designing, implementing and effectively operating controls to achieve the related control objectives stated in the description.

The control objectives stated in the description include the internal control objectives developed for service organisations as set out in the ICAEW Technical Release AAF 01/06.

Our independence and quality control

We have complied with the independence and other ethical requirements of the ICAEW Code of Ethics, which includes the requirements of the Code of Ethics for Professional Accountants issued by the International Ethics Standards Board for Accountants, which is founded on fundamental principles of integrity, objectivity, professional competence and due care, confidentiality and professional behaviour.

The firm applies International Standard on Quality Control 1 and accordingly maintains a comprehensive system of quality control including documented policies and procedures regarding compliance with ethical requirements, professional standards and applicable legal and regulatory requirements.

Reporting accountants' responsibilities

Our responsibility is to express an opinion on the fairness of the presentation of the description and on the suitability of the design and operating effectiveness of the controls to achieve the related control objectives stated in that description. We conducted our engagement in accordance with International Standard on Assurance Engagements 3402, and ICAEW Technical Release AAF 01/06. That standard and guidance require that we plan and perform our procedures to obtain reasonable assurance about whether, in all material respects, the description is fairly presented and the controls were suitably designed and operating effectively to achieve the related control objectives stated in the description, throughout the period [date] to [date].

Our work involved performing procedures to obtain evidence about the presentation of the description of the [service organisation activities or system] and the design and operating effectiveness of those controls. Our procedures included assessing the risks that the description is not fairly presented and that the controls were not suitably designed or operating effectively to achieve the related control objectives stated in the description. Our procedures also included testing the operating effectiveness of those controls that we consider necessary to provide reasonable assurance that the related control objectives stated in the description were achieved. An assurance engagement of this type also includes evaluating the overall presentation of the description and the suitability of the control objectives stated therein, and the suitability of the criteria specified by the service organisation and described at page [ ].

Inherent limitations

[Name of entity's] description is prepared to meet the common needs of a broad range of customers and their auditors and may not, therefore, include every aspect of the [service organisation activities or system] that each individual customer may consider important in its own particular environment Also, because of their nature, controls at a service organisation may not prevent or detect and correct all errors or omissions in processing or reporting transactions [or identification of the function performed by the service organisation or system.

Our opinion is based on historical information and the projection to future periods of any evaluation of the fairness of the presentation of the description, or opinions about the suitability of the design or operating effectiveness of the controls would be inappropriate.

Opinion

In our opinion, in all material respects, based on the criteria including specified control objectives described in the directors' statement on page [ ]:

(a) the description on pages [ ] to [ ] fairly presents the [service organisation activities or system] that were designed and implemented throughout the period from [date] to [date];

(b) the controls related to the control objectives stated in the description on pages [ ] to [ ] were suitably designed to provide reasonable assurance that the specified control objectives would be achieved if the described controls operated effectively throughout the period from [date] to [date];

(c) the controls that we tested were operating with sufficient effectiveness to provide reasonable assurance that the related control objectives stated in the description were achieved throughout the period [date] to [date].

Description of tests of controls

The specific controls tested and the nature, timing and results of those tests are detailed on Pages [ ] to [ ].

Reporting Accountants

Location

Date

AAF 01/06 STEWARDSHIP SUPPLEMENT

Assurance reporting on the UK Stewardship Code

(Revised AAF 01/06 Stewardship Supplement[35])

The Financial Reporting Council (FRC) consulted in April 2012 on changes to the UK Stewardship Code and issued a revised version (the Code) in September 2012 (effective from 1 October 2012)[36]. As noted in the Code, the latest edition does not change the spirit of the 2010 Code.

The FRC encourages all signatories to review their policy statements with a view to producing an updated statement as soon as practical. Where an organisation has updated its policy statement to accord with the Code, this revised AAF 01/06 Stewardship Supplement should be applied.

Background

The Code intends to enhance the quality of engagement between institutional investors and the companies they invest in to help improve long-term returns to investors and the efficient exercise of governance responsibilities.

The FRC sees the Code as complementary to the UK Corporate Governance Code for listed companies, as it should create a link between governance of companies and the investment process. Public disclosures made by asset managers under the Code are intended to assist companies to understand the approach and expectations of their major investors.[37] They should also assist those issuing mandates to asset managers to make a more informed choice, thereby improving the functioning of the market and facilitating the exercise of responsibility on behalf of clients or beneficiaries.

The Code is directed in the first instance to institutional investors, by which is meant asset owners and asset managers with equity holdings in UK listed companies. The Code also applies, by extension, to service providers, such as proxy advisors and investment consultants to which institutional investors may choose to outsource some of the activities associated with stewardship. However, the Code reminds these institutional investors that their responsibilities for stewardship cannot be delegated. The FRC expects that a statement describing how the Code has been applied should be easily found on the signatories' website or in another accessible form.

The application of the Code is on a "comply or explain" basis. In reporting terms, this entails signatories providing a statement (Policy Statement) that contains:

- a description of how each of the Principles of the Code have been applied and disclosure of the specific information requested in the guidance to the Principles; or

- if one or more of the Principles have not been applied or the specific information requested in the guidance has not been disclosed, an explanation of why the signatory has not complied with those elements of the Code. The statement of how the Code has been applied should be aligned with the signatory's role in the investment chain.

---

[35] *This Supplement is subject to revision to incorporate good practice that is expected to evolve over time.*

[36] *frc.org.uk/Our-Work/Publications/Corporate-Governance/UK-Stewardship-Code-September-2012.aspx*

[37] *See the Stewardship Code, Application of the Code, paragraphs 6-9, pp.2-3.*

Independent assurance reporting

Principle 7 of the Code states that institutional investors should report periodically on their stewardship and voting activities. Related guidance contains the following:

"Asset managers that sign up to this Code should obtain an independent opinion on their engagement and voting processes having regard to an international standard or a UK framework such as AAF 01/06[38]. The existence of such assurance reporting should be publicly disclosed. If requested, clients should be provided access to such assurance reports."

Assurance reporting on the UK Stewardship Code

The Stewardship Supplement (the Supplement) to AAF 01/06 *Assurance reports on internal controls of service organisations made available to third parties*[39] as set out in pages 56-64 has been written to assist asset managers to obtain an independent assurance report. It is based on the following features:

- User-driven independent assurance reporting over a wide range of investment management related activities.

- Use of the framework set out in International Standard on Assurance Engagements (ISAE) 3000[40] which assists global understanding of the nature and extent of the assurance opinion given.

- Reporting accountants' procedures to obtain reasonable assurance on the fairness of the description of how certain Principles have been applied.

- The objective of facilitating asset managers' adoption of the Code and obtaining an assurance report on fairness of description in the first instance and widening the scope of reporting to cover design suitability and process implementation as good practices develop.

- The incorporation of criteria closely based on the Code against which the specified Principles are applied and the disclosure of the specific information listed under these Principles is evaluated for use by the responsible persons within the asset managers and the reporting accountants.

- The involvement of a panel of stakeholders, including users, preparers, reporting accountants and other interested parties (Stakeholder Panel).

As explained in the FRC implementation document[41], this guidance on assurance reporting is focused on those aspects of the Code that are considered "objectively verifiable" at present. The Supplement focuses on the provision of an assurance report covering, as a minimum, those elements of the Policy Statement that deal with the description of how Principles 1, 2, 4 (from October 2012), 6 and 7 of the Code have been applied and the disclosure of the specific information listed in the Code under those principles.

The guidance contained in AAF 01/06 provides a framework within which service organisations, such as asset managers, could provide information on their internal

---

[38] *Assurance reports on internal controls of service organisations made available to third parties.*

[39] *AAF 01/06 is available from icaew.com/en/technical/audit-and-assurance/assurance/technical-releaseaaf01-06.*

[40] *ISAE 3000 Assurance Engagements Other Than Audits or Reviews of Historical Financial Information.*

[41] *Implementation of the UK Stewardship Code, Financial Reporting Council, July 2010. See: frc.org.uk/ FRCDocuments/FRC/Implementation-of-the-UK-Stewardship-Code.aspx*

controls that they have applied to the provision of outsourced services such as investment management, and reporting accountants could provide independent assurance reports on those controls[45].

(a)   AAF 01/06 typically envisages a report which provides an assurance opinion on: The description of the objectives (policies) and processes;

(b)   The design effectiveness of the processes to meet the objectives (policies); and

(c)   The operating effectiveness of the processes.

The Supplement contemplates that assurance reporting on stewardship and voting would as a minimum address the description of the policies and processes but does not extend to design suitability or the effectiveness of the implementation of those policies and processes. The scope of assurance reporting relates to Principles 1, 2, 6, 7 and, from October 2012, Principle 4 of the Code and disclosure of the specific information set out in the guidance and whether it has been fairly described. Principles 3 and 5 of the Code are only covered insofar as they include disclosures for the policy statement; in other respects they are currently not considered objectively "verifiable". However, ICAEW intends to monitor how practice develops in this area and convene the AAF 01/06 Working Group and Stakeholder Panel to consider changes.

Although not specified in the Code, it is envisaged that any assurance reporting would be on an annual basis. Where asset managers choose to combine this with their existing assurance report based on AAF 01/06 or other relevant international standard on internal controls then the assurance opinion on the Code should be in a separate report within the same document because of the different nature of the assurance opinion.

Appendix 1 sets out Principles 1, 2, 4, 6 and 7 and a summary of related guidance in the Code. How stewardship is applied in practice by asset managers and asset owners may vary depending on their circumstances.

Key aspects of the guidance included in the Supplement

Against this background, the guidance in the Supplement highlights the following matters:

●   The scope of the Code covered by the reporting accountants' assurance report: ISAE 3000 requires that the criteria need to be relevant, complete, reliable, neutral and understandable. On that basis, the Stakeholder Panel considered that currently Principles 1, 2, 4, 6 and 7 are relevant to assurance reporting. This is not to imply that the adoption of Principles 1, 2, 4, 6 and 7 should take precedence over the remaining Principles. As stated above, ICAEW, as represented by the Working Group and overseen by the Stakeholder Panel, will monitor evolving practice in relation to remaining Principles and consider including them within the scope of assurance reporting in the future.

●   The scope of the reporting accountants' opinion: To encourage wider adoption of independent assurance reporting, the assurance opinion in this Supplement is based on the assumption that reporting accountants give an opinion on the fairness of the description of how the Principles have been

[45] *For a framework on providing independent assurance reports on aspects of business relationships other than internal controls, see AAF 02/07 A framework for assurance reports on third party operations. See icaew.com/index.cfm/route/154008.*

applied and the disclosure of the specific information listed under the Principles. This should help minimise any incremental cost of the assurance engagement. As above, asset managers and reporting accountants may consider that the assurance report can, and possibly should on a pilot basis, go further than this and wish to cover the design suitability and the effectiveness of the process implementation. Relevant sections of AAF 01/06 may provide guidance for reporting on design suitability and the effectiveness of the policy and process implementation.

- Reporting accountants provide a reasonable assurance opinion based on the work they perform. Further guidance on their work procedures is included in the Supplement under "Guidance for reporting accountants."

The reporting accountants may provide details of work performed as part of their report. It is envisaged that in addition to the reporting accountants' report, the asset manager provides detailed disclosures within the document.

AAF 01/06 STEWARDSHIP SUPPLEMENT

Assurance reporting on the UK Stewardship Code

This Stewardship Supplement (the Supplement) provides guidance on assurance reporting on Principles 1, 2, 4, 6 and 7 of the UK Stewardship Code (the Code) for institutional investors issued by the FRC. The guidance supplements ICAEW Technical Release AAF 01/06 *Assurance reports on internal controls of service organisations made available to third parties*. AAF 01/06 is not affected by the issuance of this Supplement. The development of the guidance is based on discussions between a Stakeholder Panel and the Audit and Assurance Faculty of ICAEW. It is intended that the Panel and the Faculty will keep this Supplement under review to ensure that its content continues to be relevant and appropriate.

The Supplement consists of:

- Guidance for asset managers in relation to their Policy Statement on the application of the Principles and specific disclosures;

- Guidance for reporting accountants;

- Appendix 1: Principles and related guidance of the UK Stewardship Code; and

- Appendix 2: A pro forma reporting accountants' assurance report on the UK Stewardship Code.

Although not specified in the Code, it is envisaged that any assurance reporting would be done on an annual basis. Where asset managers choose to combine this with their existing assurance report based on AAF 01/06 or a relevant international standard on internal controls then the assurance opinion on the Code would be in a separate report within the same document because of the different nature of the assurance opinion being given.

Guidance for asset managers in relation to their Policy Statement on the application of the Principles and specific disclosures

In accordance with the preface to the Code, the Policy Statement should describe how the Principles of the Code have been applied and if one or more of the Principles have not been applied or the specific information requested in the guidance has not been disclosed, an explanation of why the signatory has not complied with those elements of the Code should be provided. The Principles state that investors should:

- publicly disclose their policy on how they will discharge their stewardship responsibilities (Principle 1);

- have a robust policy on managing conflicts of interest in relation to stewardship which should be publicly disclosed (Principle 2);

- monitor their investee companies (Principle 3);

- establish clear guidelines on when and how they will escalate their stewardship activities (Principle 4);

- be willing to act collectively with other investors where appropriate (Principle 5);

- have a clear policy on voting and disclosure of voting activity (Principle 6); and

- report periodically on their stewardship and voting activities (Principle 7).

The guidance to these Principles specifies certain information that should be covered in the Policy Statement, including:

- how the institutional investor applies stewardship with the aim of enhancing and protecting the value for the ultimate beneficiary or client (Principle 1);

- the institutional investor's activities within the investment chain, as well as the responsibilities that arise from those activities (Principle 1);

- how outsourcing of activities are compatible with the proper exercise of the institutional investor's stewardship responsibilities and what steps the institutional investor has taken to ensure that they are carried out in a manner consistent with the approach to stewardship set out in the statement (Principle 1);

- arrangements for integrating stewardship with the wider investment process (Principle 1);

- the policy for identifying and managing conflicts of interest with the aim of taking all reasonable steps to put the interests of the institutional investor's client or beneficiary first, including how matters are handled when the interests of clients or beneficiaries diverge from each other (Principle 2);

- the willingness to become an insider and the mechanism by which this could be done if the institutional investor may be willing to do so (Principle 3);

- circumstances when the institutional investor will actively intervene and regularly assess the outcomes of doing so (Principle 4);

- the policy on collective engagement, indicating the institutional investor's readiness to work with other investors through formal and informal groups when this is necessary to achieve their objectives and ensure companies are aware of concerns (Principle 5);

- the kinds of circumstances in which the institutional investor would consider participating in collective engagement (Principle 5);

- the institutional investor's approach to stock lending and recalling lent stock (Principle 6);

- how asset managers are reporting to their clients or beneficiaries (Principle 7);

- the existence of an assurance report on the institutional investor's engagement and voting processes having regard to an international standard or a UK framework such as AAF 01/06 (Principle 7).

Asset managers should have a Policy Statement describing how the Principles of the Code have been applied, disclosing the specific information listed under Principles 1, 2, 4, 6 and 7, and providing an explanation if any of these elements are not complied with. In preparing the Policy Statement, asset managers may wish to refer to Appendix 1 and also have a regard to paragraphs 37 to 41 of the core technical release AAF 01/06.

This Supplement provides guidance to reporting accountants when providing assurance reports on the specific matters that, in accordance with the guidance to the Principles in the Code, should be addressed in a Policy Statement or otherwise disclosed. Assurance reports do not cover the design suitability, the effectiveness of the process implementation or the outcomes of such policies. The AAF 01/06 Working Group and the Stakeholder Panel, established by the ICAEW Audit and Assurance Faculty will monitor evolving practice and consider whether to extend the scope.

Other information provided by asset managers

Where asset managers include information in their report on the application of Principles other than those Principles that are set out in Appendix 1, they should make it clear that this information is not covered within the scope of assurance reporting unless there is a specific agreement with the reporting accountants in the engagement letter that it should be included.

Guidance for reporting accountants
Reporting accountants' procedures on the fairness of the description

To assess the fairness of the asset manager's description of how the specified Principles are applied and the disclosure of the specific information listed under the Principles, reporting accountants perform the following procedures:

(a)   Obtain an understanding of the specific policies and processes put in place to give effect to the specified Principles

Reporting accountants' work needed to gain this understanding includes:

- reviewing standard terms of contracts with customers to gain an understanding of the contractual stewardship obligations;

- making enquiries of, and discussing with the asset manager the processes in place to implement their stewardship policies;

- reviewing policies and process manuals and board or committee minutes;

- performing walk-throughs of certain of the processes;

- comparing their understanding of the stewardship obligations with the asset manager's description; and

- documenting the understanding gained.

(b)   Substantiate the descriptions by corroborating them with evidence

Reporting accountants' corroborative work involves:

- observing, obtaining and inspecting records of processes in place;

- examining other evidence and performing other procedures that are considered appropriate;

- obtaining written representations from management that the information provided is accurate and complete; and

- documenting the work performed.

By performing these procedures, reporting accountants consider whether the asset manager's description includes a complete set of policies and related processes applied to meet the specified Principles and related guidance set out in Appendix 1. If there are omissions or misstatements with regard to the description, the reporting accountants request that they be amended as appropriate. If they are not amended, the reporting accountants consider the implications for their assurance report.

Reporting accountants may provide details of work performed as part of their report.

APPENDICES

1. Principles and related guidance of the UK Stewardship Code

This appendix is based on the specified Principles (1, 2, 4, 6 and 7) and provides a summary of the related guidance contained in the UK Stewardship Code. These are the subject matter of the Policy Statement and related disclosures that are, as a minimum, subject to assurance reporting. The relevant criteria for the fairness of the description of the specified elements of the statement and related disclosures are relevance, completeness, reliability, neutrality and understandability. Asset managers may meet the criteria for reporting by delivering meaningful explanations for non compliance in accordance with the guidance that accompanies the Code.[46]

The reporting accountants evaluate whether the content of the asset manager's Policy Statement is a fair description measured against these criteria.

If, in addition to the minimum contemplated, further assurance is to be provided on design suitability, the effectiveness of process implementation or both, the Stewardship policies are analogous to the control objectives (criteria) described in paragraphs 23 to 26 of AAF 01/06. The reporting accountant evaluates whether these specific criteria are relevant, complete, reliable, neutral and understandable as required by ISAE 3000.

The ICAEW Working Group and the stakeholder panel will monitor the development of practice in this area with a view to developing good practice criteria as appropriate.

Principle 1 – Institutional investors should publicly disclose their policy on how they will discharge their stewardship responsibilities

Institutional investors' policy on stewardship should disclose how the institutional investor applies with the aim of enhancing and protecting the value for the ultimate beneficiary or client.

The statement should reflect the institutional investor's activities within the investment chain, as well as the responsibilities that arise from those activities. In particular, the stewardship responsibilities of those whose primary activities are related to asset ownership may be different from those whose primary activities are related to asset management or other investmentrelated services.

Where activities are outsourced, the statement should explain how this is compatible with the proper exercise of the institutional investor's stewardship responsibilities and what steps the investor has taken to ensure that they are carried out in a manner consistent with the approach to stewardship set out in the statement.

The disclosure should also describe arrangements for integrating stewardship with the wider investment process.

Principle 2 – Institutional investors should have a robust policy on managing conflicts of interest in relation to stewardship and this policy should be publicly disclosed

Conflicts of interest inevitably arise from time to time, which may include when voting on matters affecting a parent company or client.

---

[46] *The UK Stewardship Code, p. 4.*

Institutional investors should put in place, maintain and publicly disclose a policy for identifying and managing conflicts of interest, with the aim of taking all reasonable steps to put the interests of their client or beneficiary first. The policy should also address how matters are handled when the interests of clients or beneficiaries diverge from each other.

Principle 4 – Institutional investors should establish clear guidelines on when and how they will escalate their stewardship activities.

Institutional investors should set out the circumstances in which they will actively intervene and regularly assess the outcomes of doing so. Intervention should be considered regardless of whether an active or passive investment policy is followed. Instances when institutional investors may want to intervene include when they have concerns about the company's strategy, performance, governance, remuneration or approach to risks, including those that may arise from social and environmental matters.

Principle 6 – Institutional investors should have a clear policy on voting and disclosure of voting activity

A policy covering voting and disclosure of voting activity should be publicly disclosed.

Disclosures should include:

- the use made, if any, of proxy voting or other voting advisory services. They should describe the scope of such services, identify the providers and disclose the extent to which they follow, rely upon or use recommendations made by such services.

- their approach to stock lending and recalling lent stock.

Principle 7 – Institutional investors should report periodically on their stewardship and voting activities

Asset managers should regularly account to their clients or beneficiaries as to how they have discharged their responsibilities, comprising both qualitative and quantitative information in a format agreed between agents and their principals. They are not expected to make disclosures that may be counter-productive as confidentiality in specific situations may well be crucial to achieving a positive outcome.

Asset managers should obtain an independent assurance opinion on their engagement and voting processes, having regard to this Supplement to AAF 01/06. In which instance, they should publicly disclose the existence of such assurance reporting[42].

2. A pro forma reporting accountants' assurance report on the UK Stewardship Code (revised July 2016)

Independent reporting accountants issue an assurance report in a form suitable for the specific engagement. The report below is adapted from a pro forma assurance report (ii) Engagement formed between the reporting accountant and the service organisation only in Appendix 3 of AAF 01/06 for the purpose of reporting in relation to Principles 1, 2, 4, 6 and 7 and related guidance of the UK Stewardship Code.

---

[42] *ICAEW guidance on providing access to assurance reports is available from: icaew.com/en/technical/auditand-assurance/assurance/access-to-controls-reports.*

Independent reporting accountants' assurance report on the [name of entity]'s Statement in relation to Principles 1 2 4 6 and 7 and related guidance of the UK Stewardship Code for institutional investors

To xxxxx (See AAF 01/06 for wording)

Use of report

(Example wordings to describe applicable restrictions on the use of the report, together with supporting guidance on alternative forms of engagement and associated duties of care arising, are set out in AAF 01/06).

Scope

We have been engaged to report on [name of entity]'s statement in relation to Principles 1, 2, 4, 6 and 7 of their policy statement with respect to the UK Stewardship Code for institutional investors published by the Financial Reporting Council ("the Code") as at [date] ("the Policy Statement") as attached to this document in Appendix [...].

Assertion of manager's responsibilities

[Name of entity] is responsible for preparing the description in the Policy Statement of how the Principles of the Code, including Principles 1, 2, 4, 6 and 7 ("the specified Principles") and the specific information requested for disclosure have been applied or an explanation where elements of the Code have not been complied with.

Our independence and quality control

We have complied with the independence and other ethical requirements of the ICAEW Code of Ethics, which includes the requirements of the Code of Ethics for Professional Accountants issued by the International Ethics Standards Board for Accountants, which is founded on fundamental principles of integrity, objectivity, professional competence and due care, confidentiality and professional behaviour.

The firm applies International Standard on Quality Control 1 and accordingly maintains a comprehensive system of quality control including documented policies and procedures regarding compliance with ethical requirements, professional standards and applicable legal and regulatory requirements.

Reporting accountant's responsibilities

Our responsibility is to form an independent opinion, based on the work carried out in relation to the Policy Statement and report this to you as the directors. We conducted our engagement in accordance with International Standard on Assurance Engagements (ISAE) 3000 and with ICAEW Technical Release AAF 01/06 including its Stewardship Supplement. ISAE 3000 and AAF 01/06 require, among other things, that we plan and perform our procedures to obtain reasonable assurance as to whether, in all material respects, the Policy Statement is a fair description of [name of entity]'s policy in relation to the disclosure of specific information listed under the specified Principles. The criteria against which the description of the policy in relation to the specified Principles was evaluated are relevance, completeness, reliability, neutrality and understandability.

Our work involved performing procedures including gaining an understanding of the policies and procedures in place and substantiating the descriptions by obtaining evidence about the presentation of the description required by the specified Principles, and assessing the application of the specified Principles and the disclosure of specific information listed under these Principles. Our work did not include an evaluation of either design suitability or the effectiveness of process implementation described in the Policy Statement. In addition, our work did not involve consideration of the effectiveness of the [name of entity]'s stewardship policies as the outcomes are not under its control.

Inherent limitations

[Name of entity]'s Policy Statement was prepared to meet the common needs of a broad range of users and may not, therefore, include every aspect of [name of entity]'s activities with respect to its engagement with the companies it invests in. Also, because of their nature, [name of entity]'s processes may not prevent or detect and correct all errors or omissions in discharging its stewardship responsibilities.

Our opinion is based on historical information. The projection to future periods of any information or opinions in this report to any future period would be inappropriate.

Opinion

In our opinion, in all material respects, based on the procedures and criteria described above, the Policy Statement describes fairly the policy of [name of entity] in relation to the specified Principles of the Code and the specific information requested in the guidance to these Principles as at [date].

Reporting Accountants

Location

Date

TECH 02/07AAF A framework for assurance reports on third party operations

(November 2007)

Contents

	Paragraphs
Introduction	1 - 10
Preface	1
Assurance on third party operations	2 - 4
Scope	5 - 9
International framework	10
Characteristics of third party operations	11 - 12
Third party operations	13 - 17
Types and elements of assurance engagements over third party operations	
Types of Assurance engagements	18 - 20
Elements of assurance engagements	21 - 45
Guidance for practitioners	46 - 105
Accepting an engagement	46 - 50
Professional ethics and independence	51 - 53
Quality control	54 - 56
Agreeing the terms of engagement	57 - 65
Planning and performing the engagement	66 - 73
Nature, timing and extent of tests	74 - 77
Responsible parties that use other organisations	78 - 82
Considering subsequent events	83
Documentation	84
Assurance reporting	85 - 96
Other reporting responsibilities	97 - 98
Using the work of internal auditors	99
Consideration of uncorrected errors, fraud or illegal acts	100 - 102
Management representation letter	103 - 105

Appendix 1 — Characteristics of third party operations and assurance engagements

Appendix 2 — Assurance report

Appendix 3 — Criteria

Appendix 4 — References

Editorial note – In May 2014 the ICAEW issued a supplement to this document (TECH 07/14AAF *Assurance reporting on Master Trusts*) to assist the development of good practice standards of governance by trustees of occupational defined contribution (DC) Master Trusts.

AAF 02/07 is issued by the Audit and Assurance Faculty of the Institute of Chartered Accountants in England and Wales (ICAEW) in November 2007. AAF 02/07 gives guidance on providing assurance services on different aspects of business relationships between two or more parties. AAF 02/07 does not constitute an auditing or assurance standard. Professional judgement should be used in its application, and where appropriate, professional legal assistance should be sought.

No responsibility for loss occasioned to any person acting or refraining from action as a result of any material in AAF 02/07 can be accepted by the ICAEW.

(c) The Institute of Chartered Accountants in England and Wales, 2007

About AAF 02/07

AAF 02/07 is intended to provide high-level yet practical guidance for practitioners who provide assurance services on operations or arrangements agreed between two or more organisations (third party operations). AAF 02/07 provides an overarching framework for assurance engagements on third party operations where specific guidance (e.g. AAF 01/06 and ITF 01/07) does not exist. Its principles are consistent with AAF 01/06 and ITF 01/07.

Whilst the technical release alerts readers to areas where potential risks of duty of care exist, readers refer to AAF 04/06 for detailed guidance.

Introduction

Preface

AAF 02/07 *A framework for assurance reports on third party operations* sets out a **1**
framework for performing assurance engagements on various aspects of business
relations that are undertaken between organisations[1]. AAF 02/07 provides
definitions and objectives of this type of assurance engagement and sets out
engagement procedures to promote consistency in the performance of an
assurance engagement in line with pronouncements published by the
International Auditing and Assurance Standards Board (IAASB) of which the
ICAEW is a member.

Assurance on third party operations

Many user organisations rely on services provided by, or have relationships with, **2**
other parties (each such third party is referred to as "a responsible party")[2].

User organisations may:

- outsource functions or parts of their business operations;

- contract with suppliers, customers and service providers for specific
  activities, use of intellectual property or other items; or

- undertake joint ventures, licensing or other shared arrangements;

- in often complex arrangements usually governed by contractual
  commitments.

User organisations and responsible parties are increasingly seeking assurance on **3**
various aspects of the operations performed by responsible parties for user
organisations. User organisations may wish to be confident, for example, that
they are receiving the service as agreed or paying the appropriate fee for the rights
received. In contrast, responsible parties may wish to demonstrate that they are
performing tasks as agreed with user organisations. This technical release refers to
the aspects of operations that responsible parties provide and may be subject to
external examinations as third party operations.

Professional accountants in public practice (practitioners) can help increase the **4**
confidence of either responsible party or user organisations in their relationships
by performing a number of professional services; namely assurance engagements,
agreed-upon procedures and investigative work. Agreed-upon procedures and
investigative work generally do not result in an independent conclusion conveying
assurance. Such engagements may bear similarities to assurance engagements, but
their purpose, scope and form of reporting are different: in particular, non-
assurance reports typically provide factual findings rather than an independent
conclusion conveying assurance.

---

[1] *Where reporting on regulated entities, the practitioner may wish to refer to the guidance given in the Audit and
Assurance Faculty AUDIT 05/03 Reporting to Regulators of Regulated Entities.*

[2] *The specific terminology used in AAF 02/07, such as "the responsible party" and "the subject matter", is based
on the pronouncements published by the IAASB: International Framework for Assurance Engagements ("the
IAASB Assurance Framework") and ISAE 3000, Assurance Engagements Other Than Audits or Reviews of
Historical Financial Information. The term "user organisations" is used in place of "intended users" in this
guidance. See paragraph 10 for further information on the IAASB pronouncements.*

Scope

5   AAF 02/07 provides generic guidance to practitioners undertaking an assurance engagement on aspects of third party operations such as transactions, operations, or arrangements (the "subject matter", see also paragraphs 33-36). It is intended to provide high-level guidance for practitioners who provide assurance services on third party operations where other detailed guidance does not exist[3]. It is based on the principles set out in the IAASB's pronouncements on assurance engagements as they relate to third party operations (see paragraph 10).

6   AAF 02/07 is also expected to assist user organisations in understanding the scope and type of assurance conveyed in the assurance report. It is also aimed at providing assistance to the directors of the responsible party (or their equivalent in other types of organisation) who prepare a report on the subject matter by clarifying their expected responsibilities.

7   In an assurance engagement, practitioners express a conclusion designed to enhance the degree of confidence of the intended users of the report (usually other than, but possibly including, the responsible party) over the outcome of the evaluation or measurement of a specific aspect of the operations performed by a responsible party against certain criteria.

8   In an agreed-upon procedures engagement, practitioners carry out specific procedures as agreed with the client and other relevant parties as necessary. The report describes the purpose and the agreed-upon procedures of the engagement in sufficient detail to communicate to the addressees the nature and the extent of the work performed. The report lists the specific procedures performed and describes the practitioners' factual findings including description of errors and exceptions found. The report clearly states that the procedures performed do not constitute an assurance engagement and that the report conveys no assurance.

9   In other investigative work, practitioners typically carry out such procedures as are proposed by the practitioners and agreed with the client with the objective of proving or disproving a hypothesis, obtaining specified information or providing what facts the practitioners have found during their enquiries. The report describes the objective and results of the work. It may have a conclusion but also it clearly states that the procedures performed do not constitute an assurance engagement and that the report conveys no assurance.

International framework

10   This guidance follows the framework for assurance engagements set out in the IAASB Assurance Framework and ISAE 3000, published by the IAASB. The IAASB Assurance Framework defines the elements of assurance engagements and describes objectives for such engagements. ISAE 3000 provides generic guidance on the principal aspects of assurance engagements. Together these pronouncements provide high-level principles for assurance engagements other than audits and reviews of historical financial statements.

---

[3] *Practitioners follow other detailed guidance in relation to the provision of specific third party operations where available. For instance, AAF 01/06 Assurance reports on internal controls of service organisations made available to third parties provides guidance to practitioners undertaking an assurance engagement and providing a report in relation to the internal controls of financial services organisations. Similarly ITF 01/07 Assurance reports on the outsourced provision of information services and information processing services provides guidance to practitioners undertaking an assurance engagement on internal controls of outsourced IT services and IT processing services. Also see Appendix 2 for example reports.*

Characteristics of third party operations

The third party operations discussed in this guidance may take a number of   11
different forms. This section describes how assurance engagements over the
operations performed by third parties may be structured.

Relationships between the responsible party and user organisations are usually   12
contractual, but other non-contractual arrangements may exist. Third party
operations will typically arise from the outsourcing of user organisations' own
activities and the procurement of external services. User organisations may also
rely on contractual arrangements with third parties, for example, for the sale of the
user organisations' products and services. Other circumstances can also exist, such
as joint venture arrangements for the development of a new product for a user
organisation or an investor/investee relationship. The nature of the assurance
engagement varies accordingly.

Third party operations

Assurance engagements over the operations performed by third parties usually   13
take one of two forms (illustrated in figures (a) and (b)).

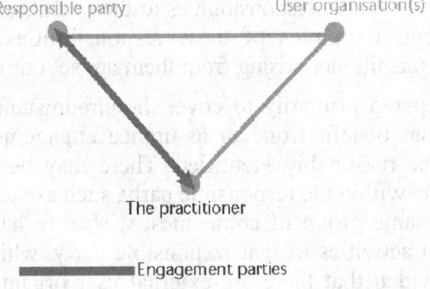

(a) Engagement with the responsible party

Responsible party   User organisation(s)

The practitioner

Engagement parties

Figure (a) illustrates a form of engagement where the responsible party engages   14
the practitioner. The practitioner performs an engagement to provide an assurance
report over the operations performed by the responsible party. This will typically
be with the objective of increasing the confidence of current and possibly
prospective user organisations in the responsible party's activities (see
paragraph 15). The responsible party usually has contractual obligations to
current user organisations and may also be expected to comply with industry or
other standards. It also has responsibilities to the practitioner in relation to the
performance of the assurance engagement. Examples of these responsibilities and
the potential consequences for the practitioner arising from them are set out in
paragraph 58.

In this type of engagement, user organisations may be identified or unidentified,   15
existing or prospective, or combinations of these. Where user organisations are
unidentified, the practitioner accepts an assurance engagement only where a
typical user organisation is identifiable in the context. This is because, without a
reasonably defined user organisation, the practitioner may not be able to specify
suitable criteria against which to assess the subject matter. As discussed in
paragraph 14, the practitioner considers the issues related to the duty of care as
discussed in paragraph and 57.

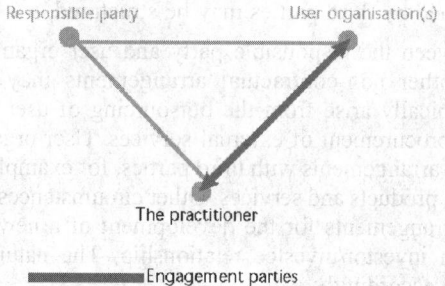

(b) Engagement with user organisations

Responsible party · · · · · · · · · · · User organisation(s)

The practitioner

━━━━━ Engagement parties

16   Figure (b) shows an engagement where one or more user organisations (user organisations) contracts with the practitioner to assess the operations of the responsible party with the objective of increasing the user organisations' confidence over the activities of the responsible party. In this type of engagement, the responsible party has contractual (or other) obligations to the user organisations, and the user organisations have responsibilities to the practitioner in relation to the assurance engagement. Examples of these responsibilities and the potential consequences for the practitioner arising from them are set out in paragraph 63.

17   This guidance is prepared primarily to cover the circumstances where external user organisations that benefit from an assurance engagement on the subject matter exist or can be reasonably identified. There may be circumstances, for instance, where a body within the responsible party, such as the board of directors, or a member of the same group of companies, wishes to have an independent assessment of certain activities of that responsible party, which are in effect its own operations. Provided that there are external user organisations that would benefit from such an engagement, this type of arrangement still conforms with the type of third party operations covered in this guidance, irrespective of whether the assurance report would be made available to the user organisations. Examples on the typical characteristics of assurance engagements on third party operations are available in Appendix 1.

Types and elements of assurance engagements over third party operations

Types of Assurance engagements

18   An assurance engagement is carried out by the practitioner with the objective of conveying assurance either in a positive or negative form. The type of report is agreed at the start of the engagement between the practitioner and the client based on the expected evidence available to form such a conclusion and the requirements of the client.

19   Where the practitioner is able to reduce the assurance engagement risk to an acceptably low level in the specific engagement circumstances to issue a positive conclusion, the engagement is referred to as a reasonable assurance engagement.

Where the practitioner is able to reduce the assurance engagement risk to an **20** acceptably low level but where the risk is nevertheless greater than that of a reasonable assurance engagement, the engagement is referred to as a limited assurance engagement. A limited assurance conclusion is typically expressed in a negative form in contrast to a reasonable assurance conclusion.

Elements of assurance engagements

The IAASB Assurance Framework discusses elements of an assurance **21** engagement. This section expands upon certain aspects of these elements which are likely to require specific consideration where the assurance report is provided on third party operations. These elements are:

(a)   Three party relationship;

(b)   An appropriate subject matter;

(c)   Suitable criteria;

(d)   Sufficient appropriate evidence; and

(e)   A written assurance report in the form appropriate to the type of assurance engagement.

(a) Three party relationship

Assurance engagements envisaged in this technical release involve three parties: **22** the responsible party, user organisations, and the practitioner. The responsible party performs operations or provides information for the benefit of user organisations and hence is responsible for the subject matter over which assurance is sought. User organisations are typically the recipients of services, assets or information of the responsible party, although in some cases the relationship between a user organisation and a responsible party may not be simply one way[4].

Where such a relationship exists, the practitioner may be engaged to perform an **23** assurance engagement in relation to the operations of the responsible party or in relation to the information prepared about those operations. Specific definitions of the responsible party, user organisations and practitioner are given below.

Either the responsible party or user organisations, or in some circumstances both, **24** may become a client.

The responsible party

The responsible party typically performs operations or provides information for **25** user organisations in a manner usually governed by a written contract.

The responsible party may also prepare its own report on the subject matter on **26** which the practitioner performs the assurance engagement.

User organisations

User organisations are the parties that contract with the responsible party to **27** perform specific activities for their benefit. Where appropriate, user organisations may also receive information in relation to the operations of the responsible party.

---

[4] *For third party operations, the responsible party will typically be the party that provides services or assets to user organisations. However, this guidance also refers to a party that performs or shares activities as agreed with a business partner, for instance in a joint venture or as a customer who agrees to comply with certain conditions as a responsible party.*

Depending on the type of the operation performed or information provided by the responsible party, the number of user organisations and type of relevant criteria may vary. The assurance engagement may be performed in relation to all user organisations or may be restricted to specific user organisations. Where an assurance report is intended for specific user organisations, the assurance report clearly indicates that fact.

28   In some cases, there may be user organisations that are unidentified at the start of the engagement. This may happen where the responsible party intends to enable its prospective user organisations to view the report. Where this is the case, the risk of the assurance report being received by those who are not party to the engagement increases. The practitioner's duty of care needs be clearly reflected in the engagement letter, in the assurance report and throughout the conduct of the engagement. See paragraph 56 for further guidance.

The practitioner

29   The practitioner performs the assurance engagement on the operations performed or information provided on such operations by the responsible party. The practitioner is governed by ethical and quality control requirements as set out in paragraphs 51-56.

30   The practitioner agrees with the client the scope of the engagement, the reporting requirements and ensures that there is secure appropriate access to the personnel and information of the responsible party and, if applicable, the user organisation(s).

31   The practitioner's responsibilities will vary depending on the client and their needs. To a large degree, those responsibilities and needs will be driven by whether the client is the responsible party, the user organisations or both. The practitioner considers whether the responsibilities have been defined to an appropriate level for the assignment including the nature of the deliverables when accepting an engagement.

32   In an assurance engagement, the practitioner is responsible for determining the nature, timing and extent of procedures. The practitioner also pursues, to the extent possible, any matter of which the practitioner becomes aware and which leads the practitioner to question whether a material modification should be made by the responsible party to the subject matter where possible or the subject matter information and to consider the effect on the assurance report if no modification is made.

(b) An appropriate subject matter

33   The subject matter includes transactions, operations, or arrangements performed or provided by the responsible party on which the user organisations seek assurance. The responsible party may prepare a written representation about the subject matter (the subject matter information), for instance about its compliance with the agreed contract with the customer. The practitioner may be engaged to report either directly on the subject matter or on the subject matter information.

34   A written contract between the responsible party and the user organisations need to sufficiently describe the aspect of third party operations on which the practitioner performs an assurance engagement. When this does not exist, the practitioner may risk performing an assurance engagement on an inappropriate subject matter, which could lead to the practitioner issuing an inappropriate conclusion or one which is subject to misinterpretation by its recipient. Therefore the practitioner

considers their responsibilities in relation to the assurance engagement and whether the subject matter has been defined to an appropriate level when accepting an engagement.

In assurance engagements over third party operations, the subject matter may take 35 a number of different forms depending on what those operations are. It may comprise:

- Systems and processes (for example, an entity's internal controls or IT system) for which the subject matter information may be an assertion about effectiveness;

- Compliance with agreed contracts or other standards (for example, carrying out certain actions, providing certain information or meeting objective standards; for example, legal and regulatory requirements, ISO standards or industry regulation) for which the subject matter information may be an assertion about compliance therewith;

- Financial performance or conditions (for example, historical or prospective financial position, financial performance and cash flows) for which the subject matter information may be the recognition, measurement, presentation and disclosure in a financial statement or statements;

- Non-financial performance or conditions (for example, performance of a particular function) for which the subject matter information may be key indicators of performance, quantity, condition, efficiency or effectiveness;

- Physical characteristics (for example, capacity of a facility) for which the subject matter information may be a specifications document;

- Behaviour (for example, corporate governance, compliance with regulation, human resource practices) for which the subject matter information may be a statement of compliance or a statement of effectiveness.

The practitioner will consider whether he possesses the relevant skills and competence before agreeing to take on reporting against the subject matter, in particular non-financial performance, physical characteristics and behaviour.

Subject matters have different characteristics, including the degree to which 36 information about them is qualitative versus quantitative, objective versus subjective, historical versus prospective and relates to a point in time or covers a period. Such characteristics affect:

- whether the subject matter is identifiable and capable of being consistently evaluated or measured against criteria; and

- the availability and the persuasiveness of evidence.

The practitioner considers whether the characteristics of the subject matter affect the type of assurance when accepting the engagement as this affects the criteria for assessing the information, evidence gathering and ultimately the assurance report. The assurance report notes any characteristics of particular relevance to the intended users of the report, if appropriate.

(c) Suitable criteria

Assurance engagements require the practitioner to express an overall conclusion 37 on the subject matter assessed in reference to certain criteria. Criteria also help the client and agreed recipients to understand how the practitioner has evaluated the subject matter to reach the conclusion. Criteria are dependent on the subject matter and may be already established or developed for a specific engagement.

38   The practitioner assesses the suitability of criteria for the purpose of a specific assurance engagement. Suitable criteria as set out in the IAASB Assurance Framework exhibit the following characteristics:

- Relevance: relevant criteria contribute to conclusions that assist decision-making by the intended users of the assurance report;

- Completeness: criteria are sufficiently complete when relevant factors that could affect the conclusions in the context of the engagement circumstances are not omitted. Complete criteria include, where relevant, benchmarks for presentation and disclosure;

- Reliability: reliable criteria allow reasonably consistent evaluation or measurement of the subject matter including, where relevant, presentation and disclosure, when used in similar circumstances by similarly qualified practitioners;

- Neutrality: neutral criteria contribute to conclusions that are free from bias;

- Understandability: understandable criteria contribute to conclusions that are clear, comprehensive, and not subject to significantly different interpretations.

39   Established criteria tend to be formal in nature, but the degree of formality depends on the subject matter. Criteria in areas such as compliance with legal or regulatory requirements may be widely recognised, either because they are available to the public or because there is an established standard, for example, BS7799 (information security management) and the COSO framework (internal control). Performance criteria may be set out in contractual arrangements as agreed with the user organisation. The practitioner considers the suitability of the criteria, in particular where established standards are used to ensure their relevance to the needs of the intended users of the assurance report.

40   Criteria may be developed specifically for the engagement where there are no suitable established criteria. Where criteria are developed for a specific engagement, the practitioner considers whether specifically developed criteria are suitable for the purpose of the engagement and considers obtaining a formal acknowledgement from the client and if appropriate also the responsible party or user organisation(s).

41   Criteria need to be available to all the addressees identified in the report. Established criteria are often publicly available and examples are given in Appendix 3. Where criteria are available only to specific parties, for instance in the terms of a contract, the use of the assurance report may need to be restricted to these parties.

(Information related to COSO framework is available from www.coso.org and to BS7799 from www.bsi-global.com.)

(d) Sufficient appropriate evidence

42   The practitioner plans and performs an assurance engagement with an attitude of professional scepticism to obtain sufficient appropriate evidence about whether the subject matter satisfies the criteria or the subject matter information is free of material misstatement. The practitioner considers materiality, assurance engagement risk, and the quantity and quality of available evidence when planning and performing the engagement, in particular when determining the nature, timing and extent of evidence-gathering procedures. Assurance engagement risk is the risk that the practitioner expresses an inappropriate conclusion when the subject matter information is materially misstated.

(e) A written assurance report

The practitioner provides a written report containing a conclusion that conveys the assurance obtained about the subject matter or subject matter information. In the context of assurance engagements over third party operations, ISAE 3000 provides basic elements for assurance reports as included in Appendix 2(i). In addition, the practitioner considers other reporting responsibilities, including communicating with those charged with governance where it is appropriate. **43**

Where the subject matter information is made up of a number of aspects, separate conclusions may be provided on each aspect. While not all such conclusions need to relate to the same extent of evidence-gathering procedures, each conclusion is expressed in the form that is appropriate to either a reasonable assurance or a limited assurance engagement. **44**

The IAASB Assurance Framework states that the practitioner expresses a qualified or adverse conclusion or a disclaimer of conclusion where: **45**

- the practitioner concludes that there is not sufficient appropriate evidence to support an assurance conclusion due to the limitation on the scope of the practitioner's work;

- the responsible party's assertion or the report on the subject matter is materially misstated; or

- after accepting the engagement, the criteria or subject matter turns out to be inappropriate for an assurance engagement;

The practitioner may need to consider withdrawing from the engagement when necessary.

Guidance for practitioners

Accepting an engagement

The practitioner accepts an assurance engagement only where the practitioner's preliminary knowledge of the engagement circumstances indicates that: **46**

- Relevant ethical requirements, such as independence, will be satisfied (see paragraphs 51-53); and

- The engagement exhibits all of the following characteristics:

  - The subject matter is appropriate;

  - The criteria to be used are suitable and will be available to the intended users of the assurance report;

  - The practitioner will have access to sufficient appropriate evidence to support the conclusion;

  - The practitioner's conclusion, in the form appropriate to either a reasonable assurance engagement or a limited assurance engagement, is to be contained in a written report;

  - The practitioner is satisfied that there is a rational purpose for the engagement. If there is a significant limitation on the scope of the practitioner's work, it is unlikely that the engagement has a rational purpose; and

- The practitioner believes that the client has no intention to associate the practitioner's name with the subject matter or subject matter information in an inappropriate manner;

● The engagement team collectively possesses the necessary professional competencies, having regard to the nature of the assignment. Where the required knowledge and skills are so specialised that the fundamental principle of competence is not expected to be met, the practitioner considers whether to accept the engagement.

47 The ability of the practitioner to perform the engagement and to report on the findings depends upon information and access being provided by the responsible party. The nature of the information and access required will be agreed where possible, formally and in writing, between the practitioner, the client, and where appropriate, other parties to the engagement. This requirement for information and access will be referred to in the engagement letter.

48 The practitioner ensures that there is sufficient clarity about the criteria that are to be applied during the engagement and in the assurance report by including appropriate references to the criteria in the engagement letter, particularly where the engagement requires the practitioner to examine the support for management assertions, for example concerning compliance with contractual terms or service standards.

49 The practitioner reads the terms of the contract agreed between the responsible party and the user organisations and consider the impact on the assurance engagement. For instance, unless specifically agreed in writing, the practitioner is not bound by any form of report or the terms of contract agreed between the client and any other party. Where the practitioner becomes aware that there is such an agreement and has identified that the form of report expected from the practitioner is inappropriate because the guidance in this technical release would not be met, the practitioner considers the implications of this for the engagement, which may ultimately result in the practitioner declining the engagement.

50 The assurance report may be received by a range of persons who are not party to the engagement. The practitioner does not normally intend to assume responsibility to persons who are not party to the engagement, but legal actions from such persons may nonetheless occur. The practitioner therefore needs to apply appropriate engagement acceptance procedures in order to assess the risks associated with taking on a particular engagement and accordingly whether to do so and, if so, on what terms. Where the practitioner accepts such an engagement, suitably rigorous internal risk management policies are applied to manage any increased level of risk. Guidance is available in AAF 04/06 *Assurance engagements: Management of risk and liability.*

Professional ethics and independence

(See www.icaew.com/ethics for the ICAEW Code of Ethics. For the IFAC Code of Ethics, see www.ifac.org.)

51 Before accepting any professional engagement, the practitioner considers whether there are any ethical factors which should lead the practitioner to decline the appointment. Chartered accountants are subject to the ethical and other guidance laid down by the Institute, including the Fundamental Principles of the Code of

Ethics, as set out in Statement 1.100 *Introduction and Fundamental Principles in performing any professional services*, to maintain the standard of their conduct. The ICAEW Code of Ethics is in compliance with the Code of Ethics established by the International Federation of Accountants.

When performing non-audit assurance engagements, the practitioner needs to **52** consider applicable independence requirements set out in Statement 1.290 *Independence – Assurance Engagements*. Statement 1.290 is based on a conceptual approach that takes into account threats to independence, accepted safeguards and the public interest. Under this approach, firms and members of assurance teams have an obligation to identify and evaluate circumstances and relationships that create threats to independence and, where necessary, to take appropriate action to eliminate these threats or to reduce them to an acceptable level by the application of safeguards. In particular, appropriate consideration should also be given to independence of mind and in appearance in respect of the responsible party and user organisations. For example, the provision of assistance to a responsible party in preparing its report may result in a self-review threat if the impact of the assistance on the matter being reported on is subjective and material. The subjectivity of the report to be issued will also be relevant. If the practitioner identifies threats other than insignificant, safeguards need to be considered. These might include:

- The use of independent teams where appropriate; and
- An independent review of the key judgements on the engagement.

The practitioner considers the existing relationships between the responsible party **53** and the user organisation in this type of engagement. The practitioner considers the objectivity requirements in Statements 1.280 *Objectivity – all services* which is applicable to all services. Furthermore, a threat to the practitioner's objectivity or confidentiality may also be created when the practitioner performs services for clients whose interests are in conflict or the clients are in dispute with each other in relation to the matter or transaction in question. Statement 1.220 *Conflict of interest* sets out guidance on threats to objectivity or confidentiality when the practitioner provides services to multiple clients whose interests may be in conflict.

Quality control

(To see the ICAEW guide ISQC1 *Quality control in the audit environment*, go to www.icaew.com/aaf and follow the link "publication". ISQC1 is published by the APB and is available from www.frc.org.uk/apb.)

The practitioner performs the assurance engagement in the same professional **54** manner as any other engagement and in accordance with the scope agreed and recorded in the engagement letter. If it is necessary to depart from the terms of the engagement letter, the practitioner agrees an amended scope of work in writing with the client and with the other parties to the engagement. See paragraph 95 for further information on the circumstances where the practitioner is unable to obtain sufficient evidence.

When performing an assurance engagement under ISAE 3000, the practitioner is **55** subject to International Standard on Quality Control (ISQC) 1 *Quality control for firms that perform audits and reviews of historical financial information, other* *assurance and related services engagements[5].* ISQC 1 requires that a firm of professional accountants has an obligation to establish a system of quality control designed to provide it with reasonable assurance that the firm and its personnel comply with relevant professional standards and regulatory and legal requirements and that the assurance reports issued by the firm or engagement partners are appropriate in the circumstances.

56   The elements of such a system of quality control which are relevant to an individual engagement include leadership responsibilities for quality on the engagement, ethical requirements, acceptance and continuance of client relationships and specific engagements, assignment of engagement teams, engagement performance (in particular supervision, consultation, review and documentation) and monitoring.

Agreeing the terms of engagement

(AAF 04/06 is available from www.icaew.com/assurance.)

57   When the practitioner is requested to provide an assurance report on third party operations, it is important that there is a clear understanding and agreement concerning the scope and purpose of the engagement between the practitioner, the client and, where appropriate, other parties that are party to the engagement. To help avoid possible misunderstandings the agreed terms are recorded in writing. AAF 04/06 sets out detailed matters to note in relation to the terms of engagement and how the overall risks of the engagement may be managed by the practitioner. However, these will need to be carefully applied to the particular engagement circumstances because AAF 04/06 primarily focuses on situations where the responsible party is the client (see paragraphs 58-61 below). Paragraphs 62-65 below highlight some of the considerations which arise when the user organisation(s) is the client.

Where the responsible party is the client

58   The responsible party may engage the practitioner to perform an assurance engagement to increase its own and user organisations' comfort over its operations performed in relation to user organisations. Where the responsible party engages the practitioner to perform an assurance engagement, it becomes responsible for enabling the practitioner to perform the necessary procedures to form the assurance conclusion. These include:

● providing sufficient access for the practitioner to allow performance of the necessary procedures. This should include access to personnel within the responsible party, as well as to premises and relevant operational and other records. The responsible party should also be made responsible for the completeness and accuracy of information supplied to the practitioner during the course of the engagement. If the responsible party (or any other party to the engagement) restricts the practitioner from obtaining the evidence required to reach the assurance conclusion, this may be considered a material limitation on the scope of the practitioner's work and may affect the assurance conclusion. See paragraph 77 for further guidance on dealing with circumstances where the responsible party restricts the practitioner's access to obtaining necessary evidence;

---

[5] *In the UK, the Auditing Practices Board has issued ISQC 1 (UK and Ireland) for audits and other engagements where APB standards apply. ISQC 1 (UK and Ireland) is virtually identical to ISQC1 issued by International Federation of Accountants (IFAC).*

- disclosing to the practitioner any significant changes or events that have occurred or are expected to occur that could reasonably be expected to have an effect on the assurance conclusion;

- disclosing to the practitioner, and where appropriate, affected user organisation(s) any illegal acts, fraud, or uncorrected errors attributable to the responsible party's management or employees that may affect the user organisation(s), and the responsible party's whistle-blowing arrangements;

- disclosing to the practitioner at the start of the engagement all other significant matters of which it is aware that affect the operations performed for the user organisation(s) as well as disclosing facts to the practitioner that may significantly impact or change the nature of the report or conclusion to be issued by the practitioner;

- disclosing sufficient information to the practitioner to fully understand the requirements of the assignment. Failure to do so may mean that the requirements are not met by the procedures performed by the practitioner or relevant facts are not disclosed within the report of the practitioner;

- disclosing significant issues within, and with, the user organisations that may have an impact on the scope of the engagement and the practitioner's conclusion; and

- providing the practitioner with a letter of representation that includes the confirmation of the responsible party's responsibilities for the provision of information to the practitioner, and, where appropriate, that the responsible party has complied with the contractual requirements with user organisations and other relevant standards and obligation.

Where the responsible party reports on the subject matter, this may contain **59** descriptions of the operations performed, the evaluation or assessment of the actual performance, any other relevant information (e.g. internal controls exercised over the operations) and any significant matters that the responsible party considers need to be brought to the attention of the user organisations. If the report constitutes the subject matter information, the practitioner assesses whether the responsible party's assertion that it has performed the operations as agreed with the user organisations based on suitable criteria and includes an assessment of the impact of exceptions and deficiencies disclosed in the report.

The responsible party is responsible for the completeness, accuracy, validity and **60** method of presentation of the information within the responsible party's report. The assertions made in the report are also the responsibility of the responsible party and the practitioner obtains representations to that effect.

The practitioner considers the duty of care to its client. AAF 04/06 provides **61** principlesbased best practice guidance on the process that the practitioner undertakes when considering requests from the responsible party for assurance reports.

When the user organisations are the client

User organisations may engage the practitioner to assess aspects of the operations **62** performed, or information provided, by the responsible party with a view to increasing their confidence in these aspects. The practitioner considers the increased assurance engagement risk when accepting an engagement assigned by the user organisations because the responsible party may not be part of the engagement which affects the practitioner's knowledge of the subject matter and evidence gathering process. In this type of engagement, the responsible party has a contractual obligation only to the user organisations and not to the practitioner.

63   Where the user organisations engage the practitioner to perform an assurance engagement, it is expected to fulfil its responsibilities, such as:

- providing sufficient access to the practitioner to perform necessary procedures. This should include access to personnel within the user organisation, as well as premises and relevant operational and other records. The user organisations are also responsible for the completeness and accuracy of information they supply to the practitioner during the course of the engagement;

- arranging access for the practitioner to the responsible party's personnel, information and documentation. The user organisations and the responsible party will need to contract or agree other arrangements that are suitable for the practitioner to obtain sufficient information and evidence to support conclusions. If the responsible party (or any other party to the engagement) restricts the practitioner from obtaining the evidence required to reach the assurance conclusion, this may be considered a material limitation on the scope of the practitioner's work and may affect the assurance conclusion. See paragraph 76 for further guidance on dealing with circumstances when the responsible party restricts the practitioner's access to obtaining the necessary evidence;

- disclosing to the practitioner any significant changes or event that have occurred or are expected to occur that could reasonably be expected to have an effect on the assurance conclusion;

- disclosing sufficient information to enable the practitioner to fully understand the requirements of the assignment. Failure to do so may mean that the needs of the user organisations are not met by the procedures performed by the practitioner or relevant facts are not disclosed within the report of the practitioner;

- disclosing significant issues within, and with, the responsible party, including illegal acts, fraud or uncorrected errors attributable to the responsible party's management or employees that may affect user organisations, and may have an impact on the scope of the engagement and the practitioner's conclusion to the extent that the user organisations are aware of such issues; and

- disclosing to the practitioner all significant matters of which user organisations are aware that affect the operations performed for user organisations as well as disclosing facts to the practitioner that may significantly impact or change the nature of the report prepared by the practitioner, at the start of the engagement.

64   Although a management representation letter from the responsible party may not be obtainable for this type of engagement, the practitioner may find it useful to obtain a written confirmation from the responsible party on the factual findings and its responsibilities in relation to the subject matter (e.g. the terms of the contract) before releasing the draft report to the client. The practitioner may need to contract separately with the responsible party to ensure rights of access and agree information agreement protocols. The practitioner ensures that reporting protocols regarding who has access to draft or final reports and the rights and obligations (for example to confirm factual accuracy of findings) of the responsible party to comment on, or require the practitioner to reflect comments

in, the report, are agreed with the responsible party and where appropriate with the user organisations. The basis of such provision is agreed in writing and does not establish any additional duty of care outside the terms of the engagement.

The practitioner considers the duty of care to its client. While AAF 04/06 provides **65** principles-based best practice guidance on process the practitioner takes when considering requests for assurance reports, it is designed for circumstances where the responsible party is the client. The practitioner may wish to seek independent legal advice where appropriate.

Planning and performing the engagement

The practitioner agrees with the client (and any other party to the engagement **66** letter) the form of report that is appropriate for the purpose of the assurance engagement and the work to be performed. In an assurance engagement, the nature, timing, and extent of evidence-gathering procedures to be performed are planned in accordance with the type of assurance report to be issued.

The practitioner obtains an understanding of the subject matter and other **67** engagement circumstances, sufficient to identify and assess the risks of the subject matter information or the assurance report on the subject matter being materially misstated and sufficient to design and perform evidence-gathering procedures.

Obtaining an understanding of the subject matter and other engagement **68** circumstances such as whether the assurance report is to be made available to specific addressees only or for unidentified recipients is an essential part of planning and performing an assurance engagement. This understanding provides the practitioner with a frame of reference for exercising professional judgement throughout the engagement, for example, when considering the characteristics of the subject matter, assessing the suitability of criteria or determining the nature, timing and extent of procedures for gathering evidence.

As part of the engagement, the practitioner assesses the appropriateness of the **69** subject matter based on the characteristics listed in paragraph 36. The practitioner also assesses the suitability of the criteria to evaluate or measure the subject matter. Suitable criteria have the characteristics listed in paragraph 38. As indicated in paragraph 46, the practitioner does not accept an assurance engagement unless the practitioner's preliminary knowledge of the engagement circumstances indicates that the subject matter is appropriate and criteria are suitable.

The scope and approach to be followed are communicated to the client and **70** documented, normally in the form of an engagement plan or work programme and communicated to the engagement team.

The practitioner considers materiality when planning and performing an assurance **71** engagement. The consideration of materiality is relevant when the practitioner determines the nature, timing and extent of evidence-gathering procedures and when evaluating whether the subject matter information is free of misstatement. Materiality is considered in the context of quantitative and qualitative factors, such as relative magnitude, the nature and extent of the effect of these factors on the evaluation or measurement of the subject matter and the interest of the user organisations. The practitioner uses professional judgement when assessing materiality and the relative importance of quantitative and qualitative factors in a particular engagement.

The practitioner applies procedures to reduce assurance engagement risk to an **72** acceptably low level in the circumstances of the engagement in order to express the agreed type of assurance conclusion which might be either reasonable or limited assurance.

73   After accepting the engagement, if the practitioner concludes that the subject matter or criteria is not appropriate, the practitioner expresses a qualified or adverse conclusion or a disclaimer of conclusion. In some cases, the practitioner may consider withdrawing from the engagement.

Nature, timing and extent of tests

74   The practitioner obtains sufficient and appropriate evidence on which to base the practitioner's conclusion. The nature, timing and extent of work may differ according to the type of assurance engagement. Sufficiency is the measure of the quantity of evidence while appropriateness is the measure of the quality of evidence; that is, its relevance and its reliability. The practitioner uses professional judgement and exercises professional scepticism in evaluating the quantity and quality of evidence, and thus its sufficiency and appropriateness to support the assurance conclusion. The practitioner describes the tests performed to provide sufficient information to support the assurance conclusion.

75   The practitioner therefore plans the nature, timing and extent of work depending on the subject matter and criteria for the specific engagement. Whereas there is no guidance on evidence gathering when performing assurance engagements specifically over the operations performed by third parties, some of the existing standards or guidance on specific subject matters may provide useful information. Such sources are shown in Appendix 3.

76   In particular, depending on the nature of the subject matter, the practitioner may perform tests over a period of time or at a point in time. The decision affects whether the practitioner is able to report on the entire period covered in the assurance report. The practitioner describes the timing of tests and considers the impact on the assurance conclusion.

77   The practitioner may be prevented by the responsible party from access to personnel, premises or operational information during the course of the assignment, in particular when the client is user organisations. Similarly, there may be circumstances beyond the control of the client, regardless of whether the client is the responsible party or the user organisation, where sufficient appropriate evidence may not be available. The practitioner considers whether these restrictions have an impact on the assurance report. Where the practitioner's work is affected by restricted access, the practitioner may need to consider whether to issue a qualified or adverse conclusion, issue a disclaimer of a conclusion, or where appropriate, withdraw from the engagement.

Responsible parties that use other organisations

78   The practitioner may become aware that the responsible party contracts out part of the functions that significantly affect the operations it performs for the user organisation. The responsible party may also have arrangements with another organisation to provide services that significantly affect the overall operations of the responsible party, affecting the functions that the responsible party performs for user organisations. The entity to whom the responsible party contracts out a significant part of its operations is referred to in this guidance as a significant external service provider. For example, a payroll outsourcing organisation may in turn outsource aspects of its information processing to a third party. A pharmaceutical company may have its distribution organised by a service

provider that subcontracts logistics in a particular jurisdiction (where it does not have a suitable presence itself) to another organisation that does.

The practitioner considers the extent to which subject matter is provided by a   **79** significant external service provider to the responsible party and whether the scope of the engagement needs to include consideration of the part of operations provided by the significant external service provider and whether such access is available. If such access is not available and this restricts the practitioner from obtaining the evidence required in reaching the assurance conclusion, the practitioner considers whether this may result in a material limitation on the scope of the practitioner's work the requirement to issue a qualified or adverse conclusion, issue a disclaimer of a conclusion, or where appropriate, withdraw from the engagement.

Where the involvement of a significant external service provider is known prior to   **80** the engagement, the practitioner discusses with the client, regardless of whether it is the responsible party or user organisations, whether the scope of the engagement includes the assessment of functions provided by the significant external service provider. If such involvement is identified during the engagement a similar discussion is undertaken and any amendments to engagement terms and scope are agreed in writing.

Depending on the discussion, the practitioner and the client agree in writing how   **81** the functions performed by the significant external service provider should be dealt with.

- In the case where the practitioner and the client agree that the scope of the practitioner's work excludes externally provided functions, the report on the functions performed by the responsible party describes the functions performed by the significant external service provider in sufficient detail for the user to understand the scope of the practitioner's work and the limitation thereon;

- Where the scope of the engagement includes externally provided functions, the practitioner performs procedures that may include, but are not limited to:

  - describing the functions performed by the significant external service provider, differentiating the role of the responsible party and the significant external service provider. To accomplish this, the practitioner may request the responsible party to co-ordinate with the significant external service provider;

  - reviewing the qualification of the significant external service provider to establish whether any further work would be required;

  - reviewing the contract between the responsible party and the significant external service provider to establish to what extent the practitioner may rely on reports from the significant external service provider, including an assurance report on the services provided by the service provider if available. Where the practitioner plans to use the reports received from the significant external service provider, the practitioner considers the professional competence of the preparer of the report including professional qualifications and experience. The practitioner perform procedures to obtain sufficient appropriate evidence that the externally prepared report is adequate for the practitioners purposes in the context of the engagement covered in this guidance;

> – performing procedures directly on the functions provided by the significant external service provider, if appropriate.

82 If no suitable approach can be determined, the practitioner discusses this limitation with the client and concludes, in the light of the available information, whether to issue a qualified or adverse conclusion, issue a disclaimer of a conclusion, or where appropriate, withdraw from the engagement.

Considering subsequent events

83 The practitioner considers the effect on the subject matter information and on the assurance report of events up to the date of the assurance report. The extent of consideration of subsequent events depends on the extent such events may affect the subject matter information and the appropriateness of the practitioner's conclusion. For example, when the engagement requires a conclusion about the accuracy of historical information at a point in time, events occurring between that point in time and the date of the assurance report may not affect the conclusion or require disclosure.

Documentation

84 The practitioner documents matters that are significant and relevant to support the assurance report and that the engagement was performed as agreed with the client and as set out in the engagement letter. The documentation may include the description of the extent, nature and results of tests, sampling, evidence to support the practitioner's conclusion and a record of the practitioner's reasoning on significant matters that require the exercise of judgement and relevant facts[6].

Assurance reporting

85 The practitioner prepares a written report expressing the assurance conclusion and refers to the key elements of the assurance report shown in the table in Appendix 2 (ii)(a). The practitioner tailors these elements for the specific engagement depending on the subject matter and, where appropriate, adapts for a qualified conclusion. Illustrative assurance reports on third party operations, derived from existing guidance, are available in Appendix 2(ii)(b)[7].

86 The title of the report includes the term "assurance" to distinguish it from non assurance engagements, for instance agreed-upon procedures engagements. The report draws the attention of the addressees to the basis of the practitioner's work, e.g. ISAE 3000 and this technical release.

87 The assurance report reflects the agreement set out in the engagement letter and is supported by the work carried out by the practitioner. The report makes clear for whom it is prepared, who may have access to it, and who is entitled to rely upon it and for what purpose, in accordance with the engagement terms. The practitioner also refers to the guidance in AAF 04/06.

88 Where relevant, the practitioner considers a form of report to be issued by the practitioner, agreed between the responsible party and user organisation but without the practitioner's consent. The form of report requested by the

---

[6] *Additional guidance on documentation can be found in paragraph 42-44 of ISAE 3000 which sets out high level principles. The IAASB is currently drafting ISAE 3402 Assurance reports on a service organization's controls at the time of publication of this technical release and practitioners have regard to further guidance set out in ISAE 3402 as it progresses towards finalisation.*

[7] *The illustrative reports in Appendix 2(ii) are examples of reasonable assurance conclusions. The guidance does not preclude a limited assurance report where the practitioner and the client agree on the form of the report.*

responsible party or user organisation(s) may be inappropriate because the considerations in this guidance are not met. In such circumstances, the practitioner does not agree to issue such a report.

Where the practitioner is also the auditor of the responsible party, the practitioner **89** may include a statement that by delivering the assurance report the practitioner accepts no additional duties in relation to the statutory audit.

The practitioner describes any significant, inherent limitation associated with the **90** evaluation or measurement of the subject matter against the criteria in the assurance report.

Where the responsible party decides the scope of engagement or, in particular, **91** provides the subject matter information, the practitioner communicates the fact, including how the scope of the report is defined and how the criteria have been selected, in the assurance report.

In order for the assurance conclusion not to be misleading, the practitioner needs **92** to consider whether subject matter information provided by the responsible party is complete. The practitioner does not provide an unqualified conclusion where the practitioner becomes aware that the responsible party's set of assertions is incomplete in any material respect.

The assurance report states the restrictions on its replication in whole or in part **93** in other published documents. The practitioner also refers to the guidance in AAF 04/06.

Based on the relevant evidence obtained during the engagement, the practitioner **94** concludes whether the assurance objective has been met. The objective would be for either a positive or negative assurance conclusion to be issued in accordance with the type of assurance as agreed at the start of the engagement.

The practitioner may become aware that the evidence is insufficient to issue the **95** agreed type of assurance conclusion. Insufficient evidence does not however constitute a valid reason for making a change in the agreed type of engagement, for instance, from a reasonable assurance engagement to a limited assurance engagement or from an assurance engagement to non-assurance engagement. The practitioner, however, considers whether to issue a qualified or adverse conclusion, issue a disclaimer of a conclusion, or where appropriate, withdraw from the engagement.

As discussed in paragraph 64, the practitioner may wish, or be required, to provide **96** the draft findings to the responsible party before releasing it to the user organisations for confirmation of the factual accuracy of the details, so that any misunderstandings or unintended limitations of the documentation provided to the practitioner may be addressed or rectified before the report is released to the client where, in particular, it is the user organisations. The basis of such provision is agreed in writing and does not establish any additional duty of care outside the terms of the engagement.

Other reporting responsibilities

The practitioner considers other information supplied by the responsible party or **97** user organisations. If such other information is inconsistent with the assurance conclusion or with other matters that the practitioner is or has become aware of, the practitioner discusses this with the client and may wish to draw attention to the fact in the assurance report.

98   The practitioner only signs the assurance report as agreed in the engagement letter if sufficient and appropriate evidence to support the assurance conclusion is obtained. Where either the responsible party or user organisations subsequently asks the practitioner to provide reports on related matters which are not directly covered by the scope of the engagement, the practitioner is unlikely to be able to issue such reports. The practitioner may, however, be able to issue an alternative form of report which is capable of being supported by work performed as part of the engagement, such as a report of the factual findings of agreed-upon procedures. The practitioner agrees a separate engagement for such assignment with the party that requests an additional report.

Using the work of internal auditors

99   A responsible party may have an internal audit department that as part of its audit plan performs tests of some aspects of the operations which are also the subject of the assurance report. The practitioner may wish to consider whether it might be effective and efficient to use the results of testing performed by internal auditors to alter the nature, timing or extent of the work the practitioner otherwise might have performed in forming the assurance conclusion. Where using the work of internal auditors, the practitioner performs sufficient testing which provides the principal evidence for the assurance conclusion and assesses the independence and competence of the internal auditors where changing the nature, timing or extent of the practitioner's testing. The practitioner also makes reference to the internal auditors in the assurance report and clarifies the extent of use of internal auditors' work.

Consideration of uncorrected errors, fraud or illegal acts

100   While performing procedures on the operations performed by third parties, the practitioner may become aware of uncorrected errors, fraud or illegal acts attributable to the responsible party's systems, management or employees that may affect the functions that interact with the user organisation.

> (Further guidance on anti-money laundering is available in the ICAEW Technical Release TECH 12/04 *Anti-money laundering – 2nd interim guidance*. The ICAEW is currently undertaking a comprehensive revision of the Guidance, which will be available in the autumn of 2007.)

101   Unless clearly inconsequential, the practitioner determines from the responsible party whether this information has been communicated to the affected user organisations. If the responsible party has not communicated this information to the user organisations and is unwilling to do so, then the practitioner considers the implications for the engagement. Where the engagement is with the responsible party, the practitioner informs the responsible party's audit committee or other management with equivalent authority. If the audit committee or equivalent authority does not respond appropriately, the practitioner considers whether to resign from the engagement and whether any other action or reporting is appropriate such as to report in the public interest.

102   The practitioner is generally not required to confirm with the user organisations whether the responsible party has communicated such information. However, if the client is user organisations, the practitioner considers the materiality of the matter and whether the matter has been brought to the attention of the responsible party and promptly corrected. Depending on the outcome, the practitioner may consider communicating the matter to the user organisations.

Management representation letter

The practitioner normally obtains written representations or a form of written **103** confirmation as referred to in paragraph 64 signed by the directors of the responsible party who are responsible for and knowledgeable, directly or through others within the responsible party, about the subject matter. The refusal by the directors of the responsible party to provide written representations considered necessary by the practitioner may constitute a limitation on the scope of the engagement. The representation letter and the assurance report are both dated as of the completion of the engagement.

Management representations cannot replace other evidence that the practitioner **104** could reasonably be able to obtain. Where the practitioner is unable to obtain sufficient appropriate evidence regarding a matter that has, or may have, a material effect on the evaluation or measurement of the subject matter, when such evidence would ordinarily be expected to be available, the practitioner considers if it would constitute a limitation on the scope of the engagement even if management representations are available.

The practitioner is associated with a subject matter when the practitioner reports **105** on information about that subject matter or consents to the use of the practitioner's name in a professional connection with respect to that subject matter. If the practitioner learns that the client (or any other party) is inappropriately using the practitioner's name in association with a subject matter, the practitioner requires the client to cease doing so. The practitioner may also consider what other steps may be needed, such as informing any known parties that may have received the report that inappropriately uses the practitioner's name and seeking legal advice.

Appendix 1

Characteristics of third party operations and assurance engagements

A number of characteristics of the relationship between the responsible party and user organisations may affect the nature of the engagement, as well as the requirements of the clients. The characteristics set out below are often important when considering the risk profile of an engagement. These characteristics are illustrative only and neither mutually exclusive nor exhaustive. Other relevant characteristics also need to be considered for their impact on the specific engagement as appropriate. The characteristics discussed in this appendix are:

(a)   Whether the engagement is initiated by the responsible party or by user organisations;

(b)   Whether outsourced services or functions form part of the user organisations' internal control/operational environment or whether the subject matter relates to a procurement or other business activity which does not; and

(c)   Whether the evaluation of the subject matter against the selected criteria is performed and reported to user organisations by the responsible party or the practitioners.

(a) Engagements initiated by the responsible party or by user organisations

An assurance engagement may be initiated by the responsible party or user organisations, and may be performed to cover overall aspects of performance or to address specific risks or concerns.

An engagement covering wider aspects of a subject matter is typically performed where a responsible party intends to demonstrate to existing and potential user organisations that it performs the relevant services or functions as agreed or to meet a desired standard. The responsible party is likely to be the client and hence defines the scope of the engagement. Some user organisations may be involved in discussions with the responsible party over setting the scope of the engagement. Where user organisations are unidentified or many, it may be difficult to reasonably understand their expectations or needs when identifying suitable criteria. This may affect the practitioner's decision on who may receive the report and to whom the practitioner owes a duty of care.

The responsible party may find the need to defend itself against repeated reviews by user organisations, or respond to the general scrutiny over the provision of particular types of service in the market place. The responsible party, who typically would be the client in this situation, may specify at the start of the engagement which user organisations may have access to the assurance report. The practitioner may wish to refer to AAF 04/06 for guidance in this regard.

User organisations may commission an engagement to have the responsible party's services or functions assessed with specific concerns in mind. This may mean that the practitioner will assess the responsible party's operations to establish if the responsible party's activities for mitigating or managing the user organisation's concerns are appropriate and sufficient.

Alternatively, user organisations may contract with the practitioner to perform an assurance engagement on specific aspects of operations performed by, or reported by, the responsible party; for instance to confirm the accuracy of the fee charged for the service provided by the responsible party. In this case, the practitioner is likely to be engaged to directly report on the operations the responsible party performs as the subject matter and the client may be the only addressee of the report.

(b) Outsourced services or functions that form part of the user organisation's internal control/operational environment

Some organisations outsource parts of their operations. Outsourcing may be regular and continuous, ad-hoc or possibly one-off. The process of outsourcing to a responsible party does not take away a user organisation's need to maintain its oversight, its overall responsibility and, in some cases, a level of management of the outsourced activities and functions. An assurance conclusion from the practitioner may be helpful for the user organisation in demonstrating that it is meeting aspects of its responsibility over the outsourced activity and could form, for instance, part of information requested within the scope of statutory audit of the user organisation.

Typically, the requirement for assurance is over the ongoing performance of the outsourced activities to contractually agreed (and other) standards, which may include reference to specific criteria and service level agreements about, for example, internal control standards or key performance indicators.

In procurement, a user organisation may have pre-requisites for contractual standards that a successful tenderer is expected to meet. In these cases, the practitioner may be engaged by the user organisation to assess whether the tenderer (prospective responsible party) satisfies the requirements or by a tenderer to strengthen its bid.

On an on-going basis, a business may wish to obtain assurance that its suppliers (responsible parties) are continuously compliant with contractually agreed standards. Alternatively, a supplier may wish to be able to demonstrate to its customer (user) organisations that it is in compliance with particular standards.

There are other similar relationships that arise from other business activities. Relationships with agents and distributors, such as sales agents, may give rise to circumstances where one party needs to increase the confidence of the other party about its performance. Similar situations arise under licence agreements. In practice, the form of assurance sought in such cases is likely to be specific to particular risks or concerns and is more likely to originate from the beneficiary (user organisation) rather than the agent or licensee (responsible party). An assurance engagement may be commissioned, for instance, on regularly reported information that forms the basis for the calculation of payments by the beneficiary.

(c) Reporting of subject matter information by the responsible party or the practitioners

Evaluation of the subject matter against the selected criteria may be carried out by the responsible party, the user organisation, or the practitioner.

Where the practitioner gives a conclusion on the outcome of the evaluation or measurement (subject matter information) performed either by the responsible party or by a user organisation, it is referred to as an "assertion-based engagement" as the preparer of the report on the information will make a statement or assertion about its view of the subject matter. Assertions may be about the effectiveness of operations or controls, about the accuracy of performance statistics or about compliance with a contract or with relevant standards. The report may set out facts about the operations of the responsible party and the outcome of its own evaluation and assessment of the operations measured against, for instance, the terms of the contract or relevant standards. The practitioner may be engaged to form a view on the assertions made in the report. In this case, the practitioner is likely to use the criteria used in the report for conducting the engagement, having assessed the suitability of the criteria.

Where the practitioner directly evaluates or measures the subject matter and issues an assurance conclusion, it is referred to as a "direct reporting engagement". The practitioner's report describes the operations of the responsible party, how the practitioner assessed the subject matter and the criteria used to communicate the basis of the conclusion. The criteria used are typically determined by the practitioner for direct reporting engagements, but may be discussed for suitability with the client.

Appendix 2

Assurance report

(i) Illustrative contents of an assurance report

The contents that are consistent with ISAE 3000 are shown in bold below. The remainder are not covered in ISAE 3000 but have been discussed in this guidance.

(a) A title indicating that the report is an assurance report.

(b) An addressee identifying the parties to whom the assurance report is directed.

(c) Identification of the applicable engagement letter.

(d) Restrictions on the use of the assurance report to the client [and other parties to the engagement letter] and on the replication of the report in whole or in part.

(e) Limitation of the liability of the practitioner to the client [and other parties to the engagement letter].

(f) An identification and description of the subject matter information and when appropriate, the subject matter.

(g) The identification of the responsible party, [user organisation(s)] and the respective responsibilities of the client and the practitioner.

(h) Reference to applicable standard and guidance, including this technical release.

(i) Identification of the criteria against which the subject matter is evaluated or measured.

(j) A summary of the work performed including the period covered and frequency of tests, if appropriate.

(k) Inherent limitations associated with the evaluation or measurement of the subject matter against the criteria and any limitations on scope incurred during the work.

(l) Where the criteria used to evaluate or measure the subject matter are available only to specific recipient of the assurance report, or are relevant only to a specific purpose, a statement restricting the use of the assurance report to those intended recipients or that purpose and wording setting out matters related to the practitioner's duty of care.

(m) The practitioner's conclusion in the agreed form (with or without "except for"s), adverse conclusion or disclaimer of a conclusion – with the description of the practitioner's findings including sufficient details of errors and exceptions found. Where appropriate, the conclusion should inform the intended users of the context in which the practitioner's conclusion is to be read.

(n) The name and signature of the firm/practitioner and the location of the office performing the engagement.

(o) The assurance report date.

(ii) Example assurance reports on third party operations

The following extracts are taken from (a) AAF 01/06 *Assurance reports on internal controls of service organisations made available to third parties*[8] and (b) FIT 01/07 *Assurance reports on the outsourced provision of information services and information processing services by service organisations made available to third parties.*

(a) Reporting accountants' assurance report on internal controls of service organisations[9]

To the directors of [name of entity] and [customers party to the engagement]

Use of report[10]

This report is made solely for the use of the directors, as a body, of [name of entity] and [customers party to the engagement], and solely for the purpose of reporting on the internal controls of [name of entity], in accordance with the terms of our engagement letter dated [date] [and attached[11] as appendix [................]].

Our work has been undertaken so that we might report to the directors and [customers party to the engagement] those matters that we have agreed to state to them in this report and for no other purpose. Our report must not be recited or referred to in whole or in part in any other document nor made available, copied or recited to any other party, in any circumstances, without our express prior written permission.

To the fullest extent permitted by law, we do not accept or assume responsibility to anyone other than the directors as a body, [name of entity] and [customers party to the engagement] for our work, for this report or for the opinions we have formed.

Subject matter

This report covers solely the internal controls of [name of entity] as described in your report as at [date]. Internal controls are processes designed to provide reasonable assurance regarding the level of control over customers' assets and related transactions achieved by [name of entity] in the provision of [outsourced activities] by [name of entity].

Respective responsibilities

The directors' responsibilities and assertions are set out on page [................] of your report. Our responsibility is to form an independent conclusion, based on the work carried out in relation to the control procedures of [name of entity]'s [................] function carried out at the specified business units of [name of entity] [located at [................]] as described in the directors' report and report this to the directors of [name of entity] and [customers party to the engagement].

---

[8] *AAF 01/06 was issued by the ICAEW in June 2006 to provide guidance to reporting accountants on undertaking an assurance engagement and providing a report in relation to internal controls of a service organisation. AAF 01/06 does not constitute an auditing standard. Professional judgement should be used in its application, and where appropriate, legal assistance should be sought. No responsibility for loss occasioned to any person acting or refraining from acting as a result of any material in AAF 01/06 can be accepted by the ICAEW. The full report is available to download at www.icaew.co.uk/assurance.*

[9] *Reporting accountants consider a suitable form of report in accordance with the specific engagement. This report provides an example for an engagement to which the service organisation and the customers of the service organisation are party.*

[10] *The two last paragraphs in "Use of report" provide example wording, disclaiming reporting accountants' liability or duty to the customers that are not party to the engagement. Reporting accountants consider the legal effectiveness of disclaiming liability in the particular circumstances of their engagement.*

[11] *Reporting accountants that do not attach the engagement letter consider including relevant extracts.*

Criteria and scope

We conducted our engagement in accordance with International Standard on Assurance Engagements (ISAE) 3000 and the Institute of Chartered Accountants in England and Wales Technical Release AAF 01/06. The criteria against which the control procedures were evaluated are the internal control objectives developed for service organisations as set out within the Technical Release AAF 01/06 and identified by the directors as relevant control objectives relating to the level of control over customers' assets and related transactions in the provision of [outsourced activities].

Our work was based upon obtaining an understanding of the control procedures as described on page [................] to [................] in the report by the directors, and evaluating the directors' assertions as described on page [................] to [................] in the same report to obtain reasonable assurance so as to form our conclusion. Our work also included tests of specific control procedures, to obtain evidence about their effectiveness in meeting the related control objectives. The nature, timing and extent of the tests we applied are detailed on pages [................] to [................].

Our tests are related to [name of entity] as a whole rather than performed to meet the needs of any particular customer.

Inherent limitations

Control procedures designed to address specified control objectives are subject to inherent limitations and, accordingly, errors or irregularities may occur and not be detected. Such control procedures cannot guarantee protection against (among other things) fraudulent collusion especially on the part of those holding positions of authority or trust.

Furthermore, our conclusion is based on historical information and the projection of any information or conclusions in the attached report to any future periods would be inappropriate.

Conclusion

In our opinion, in all material respects:

1. the accompanying report by the directors describes fairly the control procedures that relate to the control objectives referred to above which were in place as at [date];

2. the control procedures described on pages [................] to [................] were suitably designed such that there is reasonable, but not absolute, assurance that the specified control objectives would have been achieved if the described control procedures were complied with satisfactorily [and customers applied the control procedures contemplated]; and

3. the control procedures that were tested, as set out in the attachment to this report, were operating with sufficient effectiveness for us to obtain reasonable, but not absolute, assurance that the related control objectives were achieved in the period [x] to [y].

Name of firm

Chartered Accountants

Location

Date

(b) Assurance reports on the outsourced provision of information services and information processing services[12]

Reporting accountants' assurance report, made available to third parties, on control procedures of service organisations[13] providing information services [/ information processing services]

To the directors of [name of entity] and [customers party to the engagement]

Use of report[14]

This report is made solely for the use of the directors, as a body, of [name of entity] and [customers party to the engagement], and solely for the purpose of reporting on the control procedures of [name of entity], in accordance with the terms of our engagement letter dated [date] [and attached[15] as appendix [...............]].

Our work has been undertaken so that we might report to the directors and [customers party to the engagement] those matters that we have agreed to state to them in this report and for no other purpose. Our report must not be recited or referred to in whole or in part in any other document nor made available, copied or recited to any other party, in any circumstances, without our express prior written permission.

To the fullest extent permitted by law, we do not accept or assume responsibility to anyone other than the directors as a body, [name of entity] and [customers party to the engagement] for our work, for this report or for the conclusions we have formed.

Subject matter

This report covers solely the control procedures of [name of entity] as described in the directors' report as at [date]. Control procedures are designed to provide reasonable assurance regarding the level of control over the information services [/information processing services] provided by [name of entity].

Respective responsibilities

The directors' responsibilities and assertions are set out on page [...............] of the directors' report. Our responsibility is to form an independent conclusion, based on the work carried out in relation to the control procedures of [name of entity]'s information services [/information processing services] carried out at the specified business units of [name of entity] [located at [...............]] as described in the directors' report and report this to the directors of [name of entity] and [customers party to the engagement].

Criteria and scope

We conducted our engagement in accordance with International Standard on Assurance Engagement 3000 and the Institute of Chartered Accountants in England and Wales Technical Release ITF 01/07. The criteria against which the

---

[12] *This guidance is jointly issued by the Information Technology Faculty and Audit and Assurance Faculty of the Institute of Chartered Accountants in England and Wales in April 2007. The technical release does not constitute an auditing standard. Professional judgement should be used in its application, and where appropriate, professional legal assistance should be sought.*

[13] *Reporting accountants consider a suitable form of report in accordance with the specific engagement. This report provides an example for an engagement to which the service organisation and the customers of the service organisation are party.*

[14] *The two last paragraphs in "Use of report" provide example wording, disclaiming reporting accountants' liability or duty to the customers that are not party to the engagement. Reporting accountants consider the legal effectiveness of disclaiming liability in the particular circumstances of their engagement.*

[15] *Reporting accountants that do not attach the engagement letter consider including relevant extracts.*

control procedures were evaluated are the control objectives developed for the service organisation in reference to the control objectives as set out within ITF 01/07 and identified by the directors as relevant control objectives relating to the level of control over the information services [/information processing services] provided by [name of entity] [as outsourced activities]. Our work was based upon obtaining an understanding of the control procedures as described on page [................] to [................] in the report by the directors, and evaluating the directors' assertions as described on page [................] to [................] in the same report to obtain reasonable assurance so as to form our conclusion. [Our work also included tests of specific control procedures, to obtain evidence about their effectiveness in meeting the related control objectives. The nature, timing and extent of the tests we applied are detailed on pages [................] to [................].]

Our tests are related to [name of entity] as a whole rather than performed to meet the needs of any particular user.

Inherent limitations

Control procedures designed to address specified control objectives are subject to inherent limitations and, accordingly, errors or irregularities may occur and not be detected. Such control procedures cannot guarantee protection against (among other things) fraudulent collusion especially on the part of those holding positions of authority or trust. Furthermore, our conclusion is based on historical information and the projection of any information or conclusions in the attached report to any future periods would be inappropriate.

Conclusion

In our opinion, in all material respects:

1. the accompanying report by the directors describes fairly the control procedures that relate to the control objectives referred to above which were in place as at [date];

2. the control procedures described on pages [................] to [................] were suitably designed such that there is reasonable, but not absolute, assurance that the specified control objectives would have been achieved if the described control procedures were complied with satisfactorily [and customers applied the control procedures contemplated]; and

3. [the control procedures that were tested, as set out in the attachment to this report, were operating with sufficient effectiveness for us to obtain reasonable, but not absolute, assurance that the related control objectives were achieved in the period [x] to [y].]

Name of firm

Chartered Accountants

Location

Date

Appendix 3

Criteria

As stated in paragraphs 37 to 41, assurance engagements require the practitioner to express an overall conclusion on the information assessed relative to certain criteria.

While criteria may be specifically developed for an engagement where there are no suitable established criteria, there is a number of standards and guidance that may be relevant to the assurance engagements over different types of third party operations. Such standards and guidance provide a suitable basis for criteria which the responsible party may use to develop its criteria. The directors of responsible party ensure that these criteria meet the characteristics listed in paragraph 39 and consider if these are sufficient to meet the expectations of the user organisation.

These suggestions are set out for guidance only and are not intended to be exhaustive. Directors should describe, as an integral and essential part of their report, a complete set of criteria. It remains the responsibility of the directors to ensure that the described criteria are sufficient to meet the expectations of the user organisation.

Internal controls

- AAF 01/06 *Guidance on Assurance reports on internal controls of service organisations made available to third parties*, published by the Audit and Assurance Faculty in 2006 and replacing FRAG 21/94 (revised) (AUDIT 4/97) *Reports of Internal Controls of Investment Custodians Made Available to Third Parties* provides internal control objectives for financial services;

- The report from the Committee of Sponsoring Organizations of the Treadway Commission (COSO): *Enterprise Risk Management – Integrated Framework* (September 2004). www.coso.org.

IT Risk management

- Guidance from the International Federation of Accountants (IFAC): *E-Business and the Accountant: Risk Management for Accounting Systems in an E-Business Environment*, a discussion paper including comments on E-business assurance and advisory services. www.ifac.org/store

- International Auditing and Assurance Standards Board (IAASB):

  - IAPS 1013 *Electronic Commerce: Effect on the Audit of Financial Statements*

  - IAPS 1008 *Risk Assessments and Internal Control-CIS Characteristics and Considerations*

  - IAPS 1002 *CIS Environments-Online Computer Systems*

  - IAPS 1003 *CIS Environments-Database Systems*.

- British Standards Institution: BS ISO/IEC 27001:2005 (BS 7799-2:2005) BS ISO/IEC 17799:2005: international/British standards on information security management. (Part of ISO 9000:2000 series: international standards on quality management.) www.bsi-global.com

- ISACA (formerly Information Systems Audit & Control Association): *Control Objectives for Information and related Technology* (CobiT). www.isaca.org

- The IT Governance Institute (ITGI; part of ISACA): a reference guide, entitled *IT Control Objectives for Sarbanes-Oxley*, which maps many of the CobiT control objectives to the COSO framework for internal control. www. itgi.org

- *Directive 2006/43/EC of the European Parliament and of the Council of 17 May 2006 on statutory audits of annual accounts and consolidated accounts, amending Council Directives 78/660/EEC and 83/349/EEC and repealing Council Directive 84/253/EEC.*

- The ITIL (*IT Infrastructure Library*), forming the basis of the BS ISO/IEC 20000 (formerly BS 15000) standard. ITIL has been widely adopted across Europe as the standard for best practice in the provision of IT Service. Although the ITIL covers a number of areas, its main focus is on IT Service Management (ITSM). ITSM itself is divided into two main areas: Service Support and Service Delivery. www.itil.org.uk

Appendix 4

References

The ICAEW

AAF 01/06 *Assurance reports on internal controls of service organisations made available to third parties*, 2006

AAF 04/06 *Assurance engagements: Management of risk and liability*, 2006

Code of Ethics (UK and Ireland), 2006

ITF 01/07 *Assurance reports on the outsourced provision of information services and information processing services*, 2007

Other

The Auditing Practices Board

International Standard on Quality Control (ISQC) (UK and Ireland) 1 *Quality control for firms that perform audits and reviews of historical financial information, other assurance and related services engagements*, amended by conforming amendments introduced by ISA (UK and Ireland) 230 (Revised), 2006

The International Auditing and Assurance Standards Board

The International Framework for Assurance Engagements, 2004

ISAE 3000 *Assurance Engagements Other Than Audits or Reviews of Historical Financial Information*, 2004

International Federation of Accountants

International Standard on Quality Control (ISQC) 1 *Quality control for firms that perform audits and reviews of historical financial information, other assurance and related services engagements*, 2006

TECH 01/10AAF Framework document for accountants' reports on grant claims

(March 2010)

Contents

Paragraphs

Section A
Background .... 1 - 8
How this framework can help .... 9 - 18

Section B
Parties to the reporting framework – Their roles and responsibilities ...... 19 - 20
Sponsoring bodies 21
Grant-paying bodies .... 22 - 24
Grant recipients .... 25 - 27
Partnerships and collaborations .... 28 - 29
Independent accountants .... 30 - 32
Statutory audit agencies 33

Section C
Considerations for grant-paying bodies
Design of a new grants scheme 34
Setting of terms and conditions 35
Factors to determine the reporting structure .... 36 - 37
Who is best placed to provide a report? .... 38 - 40
Duty of Care .... 41 - 43
Types of engagement .... 44 - 46
Factors affecting the type of engagement required .... 47 - 52
Scope, nature and extent of work .... 53 - 61
Format and wording of the accountants' report .... 62 - 66
Matters to consider at report stage .... 67 - 68

Section D
Considerations for reporting accountants .... 69 - 72
Engagement terms .... 73 - 76
Agreeing on engagement terms .... 77 - 81
Liability .... 82 - 86
Scope of work .... 87 - 89
Format of report .... 90 - 94
Confidentiality issues .... 95 - 98
Data protection 99
Fraud and illegal acts .... 100 - 101
Freedom of information .... 102 - 103

Section E
Considerations for grant recipient
Application process 104
Grant offer and acceptance .... 105 - 106
Responsibilities and obligations .... 107 - 109

Interim claims   110 - 111
Final returns   112 - 114
Duty of care   115
Types of engagement   116

Appendices

Appendix A: List of terms and conditions that could be usefully included in a grant
                  scheme to provide clarity
Appendix B: Types of engagements - options analysis
Appendix C: Pro forma reports
Appendix D: Examples of types of wording or opinions that may not be acceptable
                  to accountants providing special reports
Appendix E: Example of a model tripartite engagement letter
Appendix F: Example of standardised terms of engagement
Appendix G: Example of clarification language for an accountants' report
Appendix H: Liability caps and proportionality clause

Glossary of terms

Bibliography

Acknowledgments

The ICAEW operates under a Royal Charter, working in the public interest. Its regulation of members, in particular in respect of auditors, is overseen by the Financial Reporting Council. As a world-class professional accountancy body, the ICAEW provides leadership and practical support to over 134,000 members in more than 160 countries, working with governments, regulators and industry to maintain the highest standards. The ICAEW is a founding member of the Global Accounting Alliance with over 775,000 members worldwide.

This guidance is issued by the Audit and Assurance Faculty of the ICAEW to assist reporting accountants when asked to provide reports on grant claims. The guidance does not constitute an auditing standard. Professional judgement should be used in its application.

The guidance also reflects good practice principles for grant-paying bodies and grant recipients. It imposes no mandatory requirements but is intended to be helpful to both those involved in providing special reports on grants and returns and also to those grant-paying bodies that receive and rely on such reports.

Laws and regulations referred to in this consultation paper are stated as of March 2010. No responsibility for any persons acting or refraining to act as a result of any material in this paper can be accepted by the ICAEW or the Audit and Assurance Faculty.

ISBN: 978-1-84152-985-1

Foreword

Grants from government, the European Commission and other organisations can be major sources of finance for many UK public sector bodies, businesses, charities, voluntary groups and academic institutions. Recipients are often required, as a condition of the grant, to ask their auditors (or independent accountants) to report on their grant claims.

This framework document describes the process by which reports are requested from accountants and highlights some common pitfalls that, with proper planning and good communication, can easily be avoided. The objective of the framework document is to help **all parties** involved with the grant reporting process.

- **Accountants** Grants differ widely in nature and complexity, so requests for reports can also be wide-ranging. This framework document outlines the reporting practicalities (from planning to reporting stage) that accountants need to consider when they are asked to take on such an engagement.

- **Grant-paying bodies** Obtaining independent accountants' reports is often an excellent way for grant-paying bodies to gain assurance on how recipients have used their grant funding. This framework document provides some good practice principles that grant-paying bodies may find useful when designing grant schemes and which may help to make these arrangements more practicable and cost-effective for all.

- **Recipients** Acceptance of grant funding comes with an obligation to comply with all of the grant's conditions. It is therefore important that grant recipients have a full understanding of the reporting requirements, and also obtain confirmation that their accountant will be able to provide the required level of assurance. This confirmation should be obtained at the grant acceptance stage, rather than risk encountering problems later when failure to provide assurance can result in claw-back of grant funds.

If all the parties work together and hold discussions early and at the appropriate stages, this will make for a more effective grants process. Grant recipients will be able to access funds quickly and efficiently, while grant-paying bodies will be able to gain the assurance that they require through the most appropriate and cost-effective means. Although this guidance provides separate sections for each party to the grant, we strongly recommend that all parties read the whole document so that they are familiar with the responsibilities of the other parties as well as their own.

John Chastney

Chair of the Public Sector Special Reports of Accountants Panel

Mike Usher

Chair of Public Sector Special Reports of Accountants Stakeholder Forum

Section A

Background

The public sector is responsible for the provision of public services and for the proper use of public funds. An important way in which public sector bodies can achieve their objectives is by funding the activities of other organisations. Grant funding is provided by government departments and other bodies which are 1 ultimately accountable to Parliament and/or the European Commission and which need to make grant payments in accordance with the law and the requirements of propriety, regularity and value for money.

2   Similar considerations apply to grants by or to universities, charities and businesses.

3   Grants have become an essential funding stream for many public, private and not-for-profit organisations and can be a key source of income for:

- charitable and voluntary projects;
- environmental and sustainability projects;
- encouraging innovation;
- helping businesses develop, grow and succeed;
- developing partnerships on social projects;
- developing international trade; and
- increasing the UK's competitiveness and strengthening its economy (subject to state aid rules).

4   On a larger scale, grants are provided to fund capital expenditure in the UK's infrastructure (eg, the building, improvement and maintenance of our highways) or to aid in research and development of new and innovative projects.

5   UK organisations, large and small, across the private, public and not-for-profit sectors receive grant funding (referred to in this document as "grant recipients") and significant amounts of money come from the European Commission. Each year sees a number of new grant schemes set up to help organisations. In some cases, the funding is made available directly from the grant-paying body, while in other cases it is made available through an intermediary. Some of the research grants that are now available seek to promote international collaboration.

6   Where grant funding is made available by central government on an unhypothecated[1] basis to, for example, local government bodies, this does not require independent accountants' reports.

7   Before any grant funding scheme is made available to grant recipients, it is designed and developed in detail by the grant-paying body. Grant schemes can sometimes be complicated and may have complex conditions that grant recipients need to understand and be able to comply with, from the application process to the receiving and spending of the money to the reporting on how it has been used. Often, one of the conditions of the scheme is for the grant recipient to obtain an independent accountant's report on whether the grant monies have been spent for the purpose for which the funding was provided and is in accordance with both the terms and conditions of the scheme and the offer letter attached to that specific grant.

8   Before issuing grants, grant-paying bodies need to decide what sort of evidence they require to confirm that grant monies have been spent only on eligible costs, or that scheme objectives have been achieved. They also need to decide whether to obtain evidence directly from the grant recipient or from independent third parties. Grant-paying bodies often decide to use accountants' reports and incorporate requirements for these into grant schemes. It is worth noting that while accountants may be best placed to report on financial information and other

---

[1] *See Glossary*

measurable outcomes related to financial reporting, accountants' reports may not be capable of providing forms of evidence for all scheme objectives.

EXAMPLE 1: CLARITY IS NEEDED ABOUT WHAT IS REQUIRED

For one major initiative, accountants were required to certify that grant-funded expenditure "was in accord with Parliament's intentions".

Where eligible expenditure is clearly defined in an offer letter or the accompanying terms and conditions, accountants will usually be able to perform suitable tests and report their findings.

However, they cannot be expected to know what was in ministers' minds when initiatives were proposed and what MPs said during debates.

How this framework can help

Accountants and grant-paying bodies share a common desire to achieve greater consistency in the principles adopted in reporting on grants. There needs to be clarity about what accountants are able to provide[2] as well as the statutory, regulatory and propriety requirements that grant-paying bodies have to observe when requiring such reports[3]. Achieving greater consistency among all grant-paying bodies will be difficult. However, this framework document provides good practice guidelines to help grant-paying bodies decide what form of report they need and the best way in which to secure it.   **9**

This document uses as a framework the grants life cycle, from the initial design and development of a grant scheme and the drafting of offer letters through to obtaining independent accountants' reports on the use of the monies at completion of a grant-funded project. It considers the steps that each party needs to go through to make the process economical, efficient and sufficiently effective to enable the grant recipient to access the funding. It also provides grant-paying bodies with some good practice principles to enable them to decide between the types of engagement and forms of report that they can obtain from independent accountants to gain comfort that grant monies have been spent on eligible costs, for the purposes intended and in accordance with the terms and conditions of the scheme.   **10**

In considering the principles within this framework and in determining the type of engagement required of a reporting accountant, grant-paying bodies are encouraged to take a risk-based approach to the processes that they put into place. This should strike an appropriate balance between the size, nature and value of the grant, and take into account the perceived risks associated with the grant and the organisations that are being funded (some of which may be small voluntary organisations or community groups).   **11**

The framework imposes no mandatory requirements but is intended to be helpful to those involved in providing special reports on grants and returns and also to the grant-paying bodies that receive and rely on such reports.   **12**

---

[2] *Accountants reports to third parties are normally governed by international standards (in particular, ISAE 3000, Assurance Engagements other than audits and reviews of historical financial information, and ISRS 4400, Engagements to perform agreed upon procedures regarding financial information.*

[3] *If the grant in question is partly or fully EU-funded, requirements for accountants are set in the relevant EU legislation.*

Scope of this framework

13   There is a wide range of support available to businesses, charities and other voluntary organisations through grants and other funding. This framework document is restricted to instances when grant funding is provided to organisations from government and charities and when the grants require reports from independent accountants. (For other funding that organisations receive which requires a report to third parties, accountants should refer to ICAEW guidance Audit 01/01, *Reporting to Third Parties*.)

14   This framework document does not cover any grants certification regime that has been set up as a result of separate legislation by statutory audit agencies such as the Audit Commission.

15   This framework document is designed to provide good practice principles in relation to reporting on grant claims and returns. It does not consider whether grant recipients have taken reasonable steps to achieve value for money and it does not seek to address whether organisations are achieving efficiency savings.

Effective date

16   The implementation date of this framework for reporting accountants is 1 April 2010, for new grant schemes developed on or after this date. It would be helpful if grant-paying bodies were to consider applying the good practice principles in this framework for new schemes developed from 1 April 2010.

17   The new framework does not apply to existing grant schemes whose terms and conditions are already in place (including those for which the grant may be paid on a phased basis). There is nothing, however, to stop grant-paying bodies considering the good practice principles in this framework for existing grant schemes and using them as a benchmark when the terms and conditions of each scheme are reviewed.

18   Audit 3/03, *Public Sector Special Reporting Engagements – Grant Claims* will remain extant for schemes in operation before 1 April 2010 and continuing after that date where the principles outlined in this new framework have not been adopted.

Section B

Parties To The Reporting Framework – Their Roles And Responsibilities

19   There are a number of parties that may have a direct and relevant interest in the reporting arrangements for a new grant scheme:

- sponsoring bodies;
- grant-paying bodies;
- grant recipients;
- partner organisations that share the work supported by the grant;
- independent accountants; and
- statutory audit agencies.

20   These various parties generally fall into the three main categories that are covered in this document: grant-paying bodies, grant recipients and accountants. Each category will be affected to varying degrees and there may also be different users

within the various categories eg, internal audit departments of some grant-paying bodies may review the reports when they evaluate their own overall internal control frameworks. The chain of responsibility for an awarded grant can sometimes be long with a number of intermediaries. There must be appropriate consideration of the reporting requirements at each level to ensure that the needs and requirements of all parties are met. This will mean that the grant-paying bodies need to ensure that all intermediaries, at each level, have the necessary knowledge about the grant scheme, the processes and the procedures in place to deliver the grant objectives.

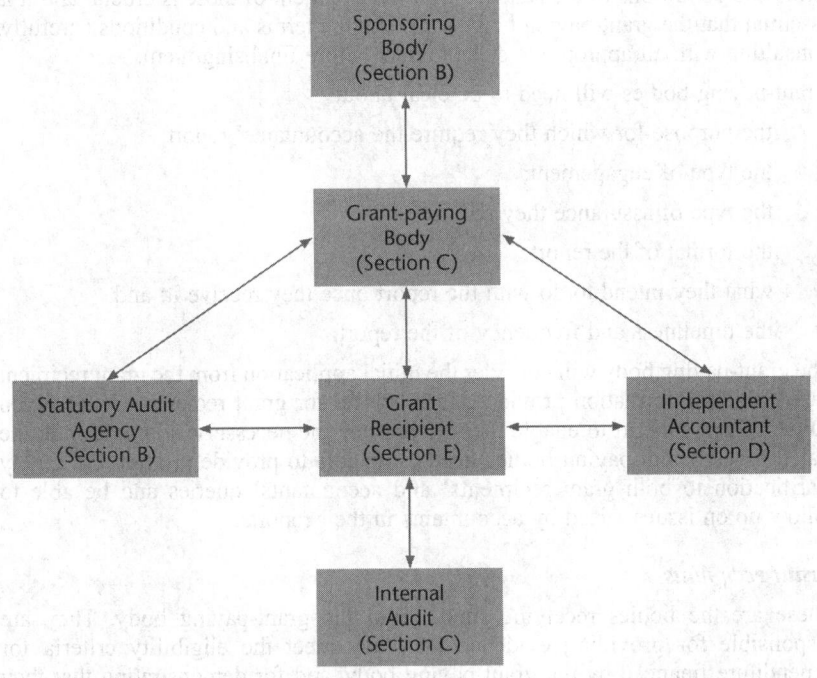

Sponsoring bodies

Sponsoring bodies (such as the European Commission) which are the ultimate   **21**
public-sector funders of an activity may choose to pass the funding through a single grant-paying body or a chain of grant-paying bodies rather than directly to the grant recipient. Sponsoring bodies can sometimes give grants directly. For example in Northern Ireland, the ministerial government departments distribute large quantities of grants. Sponsoring bodies require evidence that all monies paid out in grants to grant recipients are fully accounted for and are used in accordance with the grant conditions. Within UK central government, these sponsoring bodies will each normally have an accounting officer. This is fundamentally important, as the accounting officer is ultimately personally accountable for all funds flowing from the body and it is in part because of this that supporting evidence such as independent accountants' reports are sought. Sometimes the sponsoring body provides grants directly to grant recipients without going through a government department. In this context, these sponsoring bodies are referred to as grant-paying bodies in this framework document.

Grant-paying bodies

22 These are the bodies that provide funding directly to the grant recipient. Grant-paying bodies usually require evidence that the monies paid out in grants are fully accounted for and are used in line with the grant conditions[4]. Where the grant-paying body is acting as an intermediary for a sponsoring body, then it may be responsible to that sponsoring body for providing evidence that it has disbursed the grant according to the sponsoring body's criteria while looking to the grant recipient to provide evidence of eligibility to receive the grant and to confirm that it has been used for the designated purposes. Thus the grant-paying body sets the terms and conditions of the scheme. The development of these is crucial and it is essential that the grant-paying body considers the terms and conditions carefully, consulting with all appropriate stakeholders before finalising them.

23 Grant-paying bodies will need to be clear about:

- the purpose for which they require the accountants' report;
- the type of engagement;
- the type of assurance they require;
- the format of the report;
- what they intend to do with the report once they receive it; and
- the timeliness and frequency of the report.

24 The grant-paying body will consider the initial application from the grant recipient based on the information provided. It is helpful for grant recipients to be given guidance and support to enable them to provide the necessary information at the stated times. Grant-paying bodies need to be able to provide prompt and timely clarification to both grant recipients' and accountants' queries and be able to follow up on issues raised by accountants in their reports.

Grant recipients

25 These are the bodies receiving funds from the grant-paying body. They are responsible for providing evidence that they meet the eligibility criteria for expenditure financed by the grant-paying body, and for demonstrating that they have used the grant for its designated purpose. When making an application they need to understand the terms and conditions of the grant and in particular their responsibilities and obligations in relation to the grant.

26 Grant recipients are ultimately responsible for:

- providing evidence that the grant monies are spent in accordance with the terms and conditions of the grant and for the purposes intended (eg, progress reporting, giving notice of underspends);
- maintaining effective administrative and financial systems to support and record the transactions in relation to the grant scheme;
- keeping supporting documentation and evidence of transactions on both income and expenditure;
- operating effective systems for monitoring delivery (including partners) and internal control;
- preparing interim and final claims and returns accurately for the relevant periods and by the prescribed deadlines;

- ensuring that any requirement to obtain an accountants' report on a grant claim can be met before accepting a grant; and

- where required, engaging independent accountants to report on claims and agreeing the terms which must be consistent with the requirements of the funding conditions. Where possible, this should be a tripartite agreement with the grant-paying body and the independent accountants; otherwise, it should refer to the set of standardised terms published by the grant-paying body.

In the UK, this will typically be in line with HM Treasury's guidance to funders, *Managing Public Money* and the Welsh Assembly Government's *Managing Welsh Public Money*. Where money has come from the EU, grant conditions will be set by the European body responsible for the grant scheme.

If grant recipients are unclear about their responsibilities, they need to discuss   **27** these further with the grant-paying bodies (see paragraph 24 above).

Partnerships and collaborations

Where a grant recipient is part of a partnership (with a number of organisations   **28** receiving the grant) the partnership is usually under obligation to appoint a lead partner who will have the responsibilities outlined under paragraph 25. There should be a signed agreement setting out the roles and responsibilities of each party in relation to the delivery of the scheme. The lead partner, acting as the accountable body, may need to draw all the information together in one place. In some cases, the lead partner may be responsible for the distribution of the grant and for penalties and claw backs and may therefore take on much of the role of the grant-paying body (described under paragraph 22). The partners will need to understand that the accountants will normally have a right of access to all the papers in relation to the use of the grant monies. In some cases, there will not be a designated lead partner which means that all partners could have joint and several liability. With the increase in funding received from Europe, international collaborations are becoming increasingly commonplace: Framework Programme 7 projects, for example, are collaborations.

Each partner must ensure that individually it is eligible to receive the grant money   **29** and that it spends its allocation in accordance with the terms and conditions of the scheme. It must also provide the lead partner with all the necessary information that it will need to confirm this within the dates set. For ease of reference, where organisations within partnerships and collaborations indirectly receive grant funding, they are referred to within this document as grant recipients.

Independent accountants

Accountants are normally engaged to provide an independent report on the grant   **30** recipient's eligibility to claim expenditure and/or use of the grant monies. Although the reports are issued to the grant recipient who will be the client, it is recognised that the reports are also provided for the use of grant-paying bodies and work is usually carried out in the knowledge that the grant-paying body will see the report and may rely on it (see paragraphs 41 to 43).

Accountants will consider the information contained within a claim or return in   **31** accordance with appropriate procedures or an agreed scope of work and will provide an accountants' report. They will need to familiarise themselves with both the terms and conditions of the grant scheme and related offer letter and in particular what information they will need in order to be able to provide the report that the grant-paying body is seeking. Accountants need to ensure that the terms on which they are engaged are consistent with the requirements of the funding conditions and relevant standards on engagements. Where possible, this should be a tripartite engagement with the grant-paying body and the grant recipient; alternatively it should refer to the set of standardised terms published by the grant-paying body. Further information is detailed in paragraph 79.

32   Accountants have a duty to take reasonable care in preparing and providing the report on a timely basis, but they should not be pressured into meeting deadlines if claims are only provided at short notice.

Statutory audit agencies

33   While independent accountants are normally engaged to carry out work and provide an independent report on the grant recipient's eligibility to claim expenditure and/or use of the grant monies, statutory audit agencies can provide similar assurance. Statutory audit agencies (the National Audit Office, Audit Commission, Wales Audit Office, Audit Scotland and the Northern Ireland Audit Office) will often provide reports on grants received by public bodies as well as examine grants given by public bodies. As the statutory auditors of UK public sector accounts, some review the adequacy of management procedures for the control of grant expenditure and consider whether grants comply with legislation and provide value for money. They may also report to third parties, such as the European Commission, on specific engagements. The agencies may also act as the auditor (or appoint auditors) to local government and NHS bodies and have their own arrangements for certification of those claims which fall outside of this guidance. Some of these arrangements may be enshrined in legislation. It is often helpful to consult statutory audit agencies on the documentary evidence justifying grant-funded expenditure that the grant recipient may be required to keep.

Section C – Considerations for grant-paying bodies

Design of a new grants scheme

34   A specific grant scheme may include regulations that a report will be required to confirm that the money has been spent for the purpose intended and in accordance with the terms and conditions of the scheme. For new schemes that are being designed (where an Order or Statutory Instrument or Act is being drafted) or where the requirements for an existing grant scheme are being amended, it is helpful if the grant-paying body (in conjunction with the sponsoring body) considers the terms and conditions and the reporting structure.

Setting of terms and conditions

35   Terms and conditions of any scheme need to be simple, clear and easy to follow and proportionate to the size and nature of the grant and the organisations that are being funded (some of which will be small voluntary organisations and community groups). Appendix A provides a checklist identifying examples of the types of items that a grant-paying body may wish to include when setting the terms and conditions of a grant scheme.

Factors to determine the reporting structure

As part of the terms and conditions, grant-paying bodies will need to consider the **36** purpose for which they need a report, what the report should cover, and the process by which they require the report to be provided.

Relevant factors for grant-paying bodies to consider include the following: **37**

- What is the nature and risk assessment of the grant scheme?

- What are the types of body that will be funded?

- What are the size of grants that will be awarded?

- What is the purpose of the report and is it proportionate to the relative risk, size of grant and type of bodies that will be funded?

- Is there a minimum level of grant below which a report will not be required?

- Are there existing sources of assurance already in place such as spot checks or internal assurance mechanisms, and therefore is a separate report needed?

- What form of report is required (see model reports in Appendix C)?

- What are the contract terms under which the report is required? (see example 3 below)

- Who would be best placed to provide this report and are accountants' reports an effective source for full or partial assurance?

- If so, how will the grant-paying body secure this engagement ie, will it engage directly with the accountants or via the grant recipient and will it expect a duty of care from the accountant?

- Where an independent accountants' report is required, will there need to be clarity about the acceptable qualifications of the accountant?

- What will the grant-paying body do with each report once it is received?

- Who within the grant-paying body will be responsible for analysing the information contained in the accountants' reports and acting upon this information?

- How will the grant-paying body deal with reports that do not provide the confirmation required?

EXAMPLE 2: SETTING THE TERMS AND CONDITIONS

Specifying what is (and is not) eligible for grant and what evidence the grant recipient needs to maintain is very important especially when grants are awarded. This helps avoid misunderstandings and mistakes later. Through lack of clarity, errors can damage both finances and reputations, for example:

- overpayments and a lack of supporting documentary evidence led to the European Commission demanding returns of £31m from north west England and £12m from Wales in 2008; and

- several grant-paying bodies as well as grant recipients have been wound up or reorganised after serious mismanagement of grants.

EXAMPLE 3: STANDARDISED CONTRACT TERMS UNDER WHICH A PARTICULAR TYPE OF ENGAGEMENT IS REQUIRED

It is often the case that the grant-paying body will request a report which contains a wording requiring confirmation such as **"the claim is in accordance with the grant-paying body's offer letter including the schedules thereto"** or **"the service has been rendered in accordance with the grant agreement"**.

Many of these offer letters and grant agreements can be very lengthy and contain conditions relating to a variety of matters. These can include:

● preconditions which must be in place before a claim can be submitted;

● in the case of collaborative grants, the requirement for all participants to enter into a collaboration agreement and provide a copy to the grant-paying body;

● compliance with EU procurement procedures; and

● dates by which the client is required to submit specified claims for the various instalments of grant. There are a number of instances in which the grant-paying body then agrees to accept a late or delayed claim but does not amend the wording of the offer letter/agreement.

In order to confirm that the expenditure on which an accountant is reporting is in accordance with the terms and conditions of the offer letter, it is necessary for the accountants to be satisfied that such terms as outlined in the example above, have been complied with. This can result in:

● extra work for the accountants;

● the associated extra cost for the claimant; and

● additional reservations in a report in relation to matters already known to the grant-paying body particularly in relation to preconditions and late submission of grant claims.

Who is best placed to provide a report?

38   The grant-paying body needs to decide whom it requires to produce a report based on a number of factors which include:

● the risk assessment of the overall grant scheme carried out during the setting of the terms and conditions;

● the monitoring arrangements already in place;

● the amount of grant that each individual grant recipient is likely to receive eg, if the amounts are small, consider the most cost-effective method to obtain the required report; and

● if the report is required for a specialist area, who has the necessary skills and knowledge of that area to provide the required report eg, for capital works a report by either an architect or cost consultant (formerly a quantity surveyor) might be the most appropriate method of getting the necessary assurance.

39   The grant-paying body needs to consider which of the following will be best suited to provide the report that it requires:

(a) **The grant recipient (through self-certification)** – if the value of the amount of grant allocated to a grant recipient or the number of transactions is small, it may be more cost-effective to have the grant recipient self-certify. This relies entirely on the grant recipient providing the required information accurately.

(b) **The grant recipient's internal auditors** – this falls into a similar category to (a) above. The report would be provided by someone other than the officer within the organisation that received the grant. Although the internal auditors may not be independent of the organisation (unless the Internal Audit Service has been outsourced), they do form part of the internal control framework of the organisation and will be independent of the grant-receiving department. The cost would be minimal as they are internal to the organisation but grant-paying bodies would need to provide direction on what needs to be done and by when.

(c) **The internal auditors of the grant-paying body** – some grant-paying bodies have large internal audit departments which may be used to carry out checks on the use of grant monies. If the number of grants was high but the value of each was low, then random spot checks could be carried out. This has the advantage that the grant-paying body can determine its own scope of work and decide whether it wishes to target certain grant recipients or categories of grant recipients. The main disadvantage is that it probably would not be able to carry out checks of all grant recipients each year so a rolling programme of visits may need to be organised. Based on the overall risk assessment and cost-benefit analysis, the grant-paying body would need to decide whether it wanted 100% coverage of bodies over time through the rolling programme. The cost of this type of verification would usually fall to the grant-paying body. This approach could be combined with either (a) or (b).

(d) **Specialists** – sometimes the grant is for a purpose which may need specialist knowledge. It would seem sensible in these cases for either specialists (such as environmental auditors) or a single firm that has knowledge and skills of the specialist area to provide reports for the entire grant scheme. Having a single firm carry out this work could help to reduce the costs of the engagement, as the specialists would build up knowledge of the grant scheme. It may also build the confidence of the grant-paying body in the firm. However, the firm would not necessarily have an in-depth knowledge of each organisation that has received a grant through the scheme.

(e) **Independent accountants who are also the statutory auditors of the organisation** – this would provide grant-paying bodies with an independent report. Using the existing external auditors could be advantageous as they will have an in-depth knowledge of the organisation. However, the work would need to be carried out under a separate engagement. Using independent accountants will also add to the fees that the organisation has to pay and these costs may not always be eligible for grant. If the grant-paying body also requires a report on the organisation's systems and controls, this would be the subject of a separate engagement.

(f) **Independent accountants who are not the statutory auditors of the organisation** – this would provide an independent report. However a new firm of accountants may not have the detailed knowledge of the organisation and may therefore take longer to build that knowledge before completing the work or may even decline to undertake grant claim work for entities that are not their clients. If they do agree to take on the grant claim work, the associated costs may not be eligible for grant.

Where the grant-paying body has carried out its cost-benefit analysis and has determined that, because of the value of the claim and the associated risks, it requires an independent accountants' report, then (e) and (f) above are likely to be the chosen or required options. It would be helpful at this stage to consult this framework document about the purpose of the report, the type of engagement, the scope of work and, finally the reporting requirements before including them in the enabling legislation, Order or Statutory Instrument or into the scheme terms and conditions. The grant-paying body needs to consider the feasibility of its intended requirements and whether what it requires, and what it wants a report on, is achievable.

40

Duty of Care

41   Where a grant-paying body has determined that it does require an independent accountants' report, it then needs to consider whether it also wants a formal "duty of care" from the accountants and then determine the type of engagement that would be best suited to provide it with the comfort that it requires.

42   This decision will affect both how, and the way in which, the grant-paying body sets its requirements for the report. The options are:

(a)   tripartite or multipartite engagement with the grant-paying body(ies), the grant recipient and the independent accountants which allows the three parties to enter into dialogue about the purpose of the report, the type of engagement, the scope of work and the sort of report required. In this case, the accountants' report would be addressed to both the grant-paying body and the grant recipient. Although this would be ideal as the expectations of all parties would be clarified, for large grant-paying bodies where there are numerous grant schemes and a large number of grants are awarded, it may not be practical to have an engagement letter with each individual accountant.

(b)   standardised engagement terms included as part of the terms and conditions and offer letter to the grant recipient. Standardised terms include the terms under which the grant-paying body is willing to contract with accountants at the outset. These do not require the grant-paying body to sign individual engagement letters with accountants. Appendix F provides an example of standardised engagement terms. Accountants would take on the work if they accepted the standard terms set by the grant-paying body implying a duty of care to the grant-paying body. In this case the accountants' report would be addressed to both the grant-paying body and the grant recipient[5].

43   Some grant-paying bodies are clear that they are disclaiming a duty of care from accountants. If this is the case, this needs to be stated in the terms and conditions to the grant recipient so that it is explicit from the outset to all parties involved in the process. Therefore, once the grant-paying body has issued the offer letter, the engagement is between the grant recipient and the accountants, and so the accountants' report should be addressed solely to the grant recipient.

Types of engagement

44   This framework document outlines three main options for an accountants' report:

- **reasonable assurance** – provides a "reasonable assurance" report in the form of a positive worded conclusion;

- **limited assurance** – provides a "limited assurance" report in the form of a negative worded conclusion; and

- **agreed-upon procedures** – does not contain an assurance conclusion, but sets out the agreed scope of work and procedures undertaken, the findings from the procedures, along with details of any exceptions that accountants have identified from their work.

45   The advantages and disadvantages of each of these three options are set out in more detail in Appendix B, with example model reports for each option in Appendix C. The reporting accountants' considerations are outlined in section D

---

[5] *The European Commission has developed such a standardised set of engagement terms as part of its Framework Programme 7.*

of this framework document. It is important to appreciate that it is not possible to combine the three options eg, choosing the "agreed upon procedures" option but expecting a "reasonable assurance" conclusion.

If more help is needed to determine the appropriate type of engagement, grant-   **46**
paying bodies may wish to consult, as appropriate, with the accountants (who will be undertaking the work on the grant claim), the statutory audit agencies and professional bodies. This will help to ensure that the expectations of all parties are met and avoid problems that can arise during the process.

Factors affecting the type of engagement required

Key factors in determining the type of engagement required from accountants   **47**
include:

- the information that the grant-paying body wants from the accountants' report;
- any pre-existing legislative requirements that specify the nature of the accountants' report;
- the level of prescription that the grant-paying body expects regarding the scope, nature and extent of the testing to be completed by the accountants (or conversely, the amount of judgement that accountants are expected to apply when undertaking their work);
- the level of consistency that the grant-paying body expects in the scope, nature and extent of testing to be completed by accountants for any specific range of grants;
- the cost-benefit trade-off that may exist between the different types of engagements that are available;
- any evidence or other assurance that the grant-paying body may obtain from other means (eg, self-certification); and
- the expectations or requirements of other stakeholders that may need to make use of the accountants' report, such as the grant-paying body's own external auditors.

If, for whatever reason, the form and content of the accountants' report is deemed   **48**
to be paramount, or is prescribed by legislation, then this may determine the type of engagement that has to be provided. The form and content of the accountants' report will largely be determined by the type of engagement chosen. It is not possible, for example, to mandate the exact procedures that accountants must undertake (other than as a minimum), with no scope for the accountant to apply their judgement, while expecting accountants to provide a "reasonable assurance" or "limited assurance" conclusion. To provide such an opinion, accountants need the ability to undertake whatever procedures they consider necessary to be able to reach their conclusion.

It is important to note that, while there is some correlation, the type of engagement   **49**
required is not necessarily directly related to the level of work undertaken by accountants. Instead, the type of engagement links directly to who controls the scope of work and the judgement that they are expected to apply in completing their work. This means that there is likely to be consistency in the work carried out among accountants who undertake an "agreed-upon procedures" engagement where the procedures have been agreed with the grant-paying body. However, there is likely to be greater diversity when a "reasonable assurance" or "limited assurance" engagement is required as accountants will each be applying their own

professional judgement in determining the procedures that are necessary to obtain the evidence required for the report. Further guidance can be found in Appendix B, including examples of where different types of engagements may be appropriate.

50   In choosing the type of engagement, grant-paying bodies may wish to note that the cost of each engagement will depend on the size, complexity and value of the scheme and the risk associated with it. But in general terms a "reasonable assurance" engagement may cost more than a "limited assurance" engagement, which may in turn cost more than an "agreed-upon procedures" engagement. The reasons for this relate to the additional procedures that accountants are required to undertake when forming an opinion, which typically involves the judgement of senior members of the engagement team. An "agreed-upon procedures" engagement will therefore usually be the cheapest engagement and a "reasonable assurance" engagement the most expensive.

51   In some cases, the grant-paying body may wish to consider setting a threshold (usually of its quantum of grant) below which involvement of accountants is not required, on the basis that the cost of the accountants' work is likely to outweigh the benefit of obtaining a report from an independent accountant. Whether or not the costs of a report are eligible for grant is a decision for the grant-paying bodies to make on a scheme-by-scheme basis.

52   Where independent accountants are appointed, the grant-paying body (and the grant recipients) should recognise that the accountants will normally want to have a discussion with both the grant-paying body and also the grant recipient to clarify the basis on which they may owe the grant-paying body a duty of care. Further guidance on this can be found in paragraphs 77 to 80.

Scope, nature and extent of work

53   There are a number of factors that will affect the scope, nature and extent of the work that accountants are required to undertake. These include the nature and size of the grant recipient's business, the complexity of the grant scheme, the number of transactions, the nature of the transactions and the level of error or uncertainty that the grant-paying body is prepared to accept, the experience of the grant recipient and any related parties that are involved in the grants process. The type of engagement may, with "reasonable assurance" engagements and some "limited assurance" engagements, require more procedures to be undertaken to form a conclusion on the grant claim.

54   For "agreed-upon procedures" engagements, and possibly "limited assurance" engagements, the scope, nature and extent of the required work should be agreed by the grant-paying body in advance. Accountants will then complete this work and report in the appropriate format. In determining the amount of work (including sample sizes), the grant-paying body will therefore implicitly be determining what level of overall error and/or uncertainty it is prepared to accept when assessing the claim.

55   If 100% of transactions need to be tested then this will have cost implications that will need to be considered; in some cases it may be appropriate (eg, for a grant with a small number of large transactions). The ability to carry out 100% testing will depend on the records maintained by the grant recipient. However, simply checking all transactions to invoices, for example, is not always proof that the payment was eligible for grant. Invoices can be amended or cancelled and prices can be manipulated.

In most cases, it is likely that the grant-paying body will be content for work to be **56** undertaken on a sample basis, although testing of certain key or high value transactions might still be mandated. In this case, the size of the sample tested (whether determined by value or number) will be directly related to the type of engagement and form of report that is being provided. The larger the sample, the more likely the accountants will be able to identify any errors or ineligible expenditure. The grant-paying body may determine that the sample is related to the value of transactions eg, all those over £10,000 or 80% by value.

While it may be appropriate for a grant-paying body to specify minimum **57** procedures for "reasonable assurance" and possibly "limited assurance" engagements, accountants will nevertheless need to apply their professional judgement in undertaking their work. To assist accountants in this, grant-paying bodies may decide to indicate the "materiality" level to which accountants need to have regard. This will help accountants to determine the level of testing and the extent of evidence gathering that is required in order to reach their opinion. The lower the level of materiality, the larger the sample and the greater the extent of testing that accountants will need to undertake in order to provide the required conclusion.

Materiality has both qualitative and quantitative aspects. In addition to setting **58** either a fixed monetary level of materiality or, more commonly, a percentage level of materiality that varies with the size of the grant claim (quantitative), grant-paying bodies may also wish to discuss with accountants certain specific types of transactions that must be tested irrespective of their monetary value (qualitative).

The grant-paying body needs to agree in advance the scope, nature and extent of **59** the testing required by accountants for "agreed-upon procedures" and possibly for "limited assurance" engagements. This can be done in discussion with professional bodies or, if there are only a few firms of accountants carrying out the work, with the accountants themselves. If this is not done, accountants will each need to agree the scope, nature and extent of their testing on a case-by-case basis with the grant-paying body, to mitigate the risk of undertaking a level of work that does not meet the grant-paying body's needs.

EXAMPLE 4: WHAT FIGURES ARE THE ACCOUNTANTS REPORTING UPON?

Reports must be related to claims or accounts in a specified format.

A grant-paying body issued a "certificate" for the recipient's accountant to sign – but did not provide a claim form or specify a format for the associated accounts. The accountant did not know what was required for the "entries" referred to in the certificate.

For "reasonable assurance" and also possibly for "limited assurance" **60** engagements, the grant-paying body should indicate the materiality level that accountants are expected to take note of when undertaking their work. In the absence of any such guidance, accountants may need to agree the level of materiality with the grant-paying body on a case-by-case basis or decline to accept the engagement on the basis that it is unclear what the evaluation criteria for the engagement are in monetary terms. However, both the assessment of materiality and the relative importance of quantitative and qualitative factors in a particular engagement ultimately remain matters for the accountants' own professional judgement.

It is also important to ensure that the scope of work expected of accountants is **61** appropriate and deals with matters that accountants can reasonably be expected to test and on which they form judgements. If suitable criteria for evaluation do not exist and/or cannot be agreed with accountants, it will not be possible for accountants to undertake the work, or specific aspects of the work. This is likely to lead to qualification of the accountants' report or to accountants being unable to accept the engagement.

Format and wording of the accountants' report

62   As already noted in paragraphs 44 to 52, the type of engagement that is being sought by the grant-paying body will determine the form and content of the accountants' report. Model examples of accountants' reports relating to the three types of engagements can be found in Appendix C.

63   Care should be taken when the grant-paying body is required to use terms and/or expressions in the accountants' report which are prescribed by legislation or the grant-paying body intends to specify wording for accountants' reports. Undefined words can lead to misunderstandings. It is therefore important that prescribed terms or expressions are clearly defined at the outset. Accountants should be able to add to any wording prescribed by legislation and modify wording set by the grant-paying body especially if accountants are expected to provide an opinion. Without the ability to add to or amend the wording of the report, accountants may be forced to qualify the report or even resign from the engagement, simply because they are unable to sign up to the prescribed wording which does not reflect their conclusion and opinion on the grant claim.

64   In practice it should be noted that amendments to any template reports are likely to be fairly common and will set out significant issues and/or additional matters that, in the opinion of the accountants, need to be brought to the attention of the grant-paying body and the grant recipient. The ability to amend any standard report wording expected by the grant-paying body may therefore be of direct benefit to the grant-paying body where it provides additional information that is of value when assessing compliance with the grant claim terms and conditions by the grant recipient.

65   Accountants are not bound to sign any form of report (pre-printed or otherwise) that has not been discussed with them or that their professional body has not recommended (nor are they obliged to sign any form even if their professional body has recommended it). If the basic form and content of the report is to be specified, then it would be helpful to discuss this with the professional bodies of the accountants who are likely to be involved in undertaking the work on the grant claim. Often, an early discussion will indicate whether what the grant-paying body is considering is something that accountants will be able to provide a report on. It would also be helpful to discuss the form of report with any other users of the report (eg, the grant-paying body's external auditors) before the start of the engagement. Early discussion will help ensure that expectations of all parties are understood and can be met and avoid problems that can arise during the reporting process.

66   Appendix D includes examples of words that often give rise to problems for reporting accountants. In drafting the specification of accountants' reports it is important to use language that is free from ambiguity. For example, undefined terms such as "review" or "reasonable" are not recommended unless there is a clear definition.

EXAMPLE 5: HAVE "PERFORMANCE AND BUDGETARY INFORMATION" BEEN REPORTED ON BY THE RECIPIENT ALONE?

Sometimes, an investment funded by a grant will generate savings for recipients' revenue budgets. This was the case with a grant for waste minimisation and recycling, as future landfill tax would be less than if tipping continued at previous levels. However, the grant-paying body wanted assurance that recipients would maintain their budgets to safeguard local authorities' expenditure on waste management.

Accountants only needed to report on the expenditure on the new activities as local authority treasurers were left to self-certify that savings were "re-invested" in waste management and not diverted to other activities.

Matters to consider at report stage

The grant-paying body may wish to: 67

- determine a materiality level that supports the level of error and/or risk that it is prepared to accept;
- ensure that it will understand the impact of any errors;
- consider the implications of the various types of reports received;
- be able to interpret the qualifications in accountants' reports or identify issues and make judgements and take appropriate action about whether:
    - to ask accountants to carry out further work (where, for example the accountant has indicated missing records); or
    - not to pay future instalments of grants; or
    - claw back current grants or instalments already paid;
- have a system in place to identify late or missing reports and take appropriate action (either follow up with the grant recipient, suspend payments, impose a greater level of retention or ultimately claw back); and
- have a system in place for accountants to enter into early dialogue with the grant-paying body when they identify significant errors or deficiencies in the grant recipient's records.

Rejection of a report or delays or refusal to pay future grants should not solely be   68
because the report does not reflect a standard form of words. The terms and conditions of both the grant scheme and the offer letter need to identify the trigger that will lead to rejection of a report or delays or refusal to pay future grants. Where accountants' reports are frequently "qualified" for one particular reason, then the grant-paying body could issue guidance to clarify how the particular issue should be considered and dealt with (and update its definitions of eligibility for anything that is not clear).

EXAMPLE 6: CLAW BACK OF GRANT MONIES WHERE THE ACCOUNTANT DID NOT USE THE PRESCRIBED

FORM OF WORDS

A local authority was the lead accountable body for a European-funded Action Plan. The Action Plan sought to address the lack of provision of business advice to SMEs in particularly deprived wards. The actual delivery of the Action Plan was split into a number of sub-projects delivered by third party business advice providers. Each sub-project was required to complete and submit an annual statement of expenditure with an independent report.

The accountants to one of the sub-projects issued a report whose wording was not an exact word for word match to the pro forma issued by the local authority. The local authority rejected the report and sought to commence claw back of the entire monies claimed by the sub-project. The meaning and context of the issued report was the same as the pro forma report.

Section D – Considerations for reporting accountants

69   Before taking on the engagement accountants will need to clarify:

- the purpose of the request for the report;
- the scope of work;
- to whom they will be reporting;
- to whom they will owe a duty of care; and
- what the report will be used for.

70   Accountants will want to understand whether the report is required to confirm the eligibility of expenditure and/or whether the report will be used to confirm that the grant has been spent in accordance with the particular terms and conditions and for the purposes intended. It is important that there is a clear understanding of the scope and purpose of the engagement among all the parties.

71   Accountants will also need to confirm that grant recipients understand their responsibilities in relation to the terms and conditions of the grant and the need to maintain effective systems and documentation to record the transactions in relation to the grant scheme. Accountants may wish to consider whether they need to obtain written confirmation from the grant recipient acknowledging their responsibilities. It will also be useful for accountants to understand at the outset who is paying for the report: the grant-paying body or the grant recipient.

72   It is important that before agreeing to take on the engagement, accountants consider the need to discuss with the grant recipient the form of report that the grant-paying body has requested and whether the accountants will be able to provide this. Accountants should not sign reports until they have been able to perform sufficient work and obtain sufficient evidence to support their findings, opinions and/or conclusions. In all cases, accountants have the right not to accept any engagement if they consider that the required wording is too onerous or where the wording has not been properly defined. Where they do not feel able to accept such responsibility they should decline this work.

Engagement terms

73   In arriving at an understanding about who may have an interest in the accountants' report and for what purpose, accountants need to know who is involved in the engagement, who may wish to rely on it and the parties that may suffer a direct loss.

- Grant recipient – will require the report for the purpose of meeting one of the grant requirements. Failure to obtain an accountants' report could result in the grant-paying body clawing back grant monies that have already been paid to the grant recipient.
- Grant-paying body – may require a report to confirm that the grant recipient's claim is limited to eligible costs and/or that the grant monies have been spent in accordance with both the terms and conditions of the

grant scheme and the offer letter. The grant-paying body may be relying on the report even when the report is not addressed to the grant-paying body.

- Other parties – a sponsoring body or a match funder which has indicated that it will also seek to rely directly on the accountants' report, particularly when it is trying to satisfy itself of the regularity and propriety of grants distributed by the grant-paying body for which it is ultimately accountable.

Any party that will rely on the report and who will suffer a direct loss should consider becoming a party to the engagement (see paragraphs 41 to 43).

There may also be other bodies that are entitled to view the reports and accountants will need to understand which bodies may choose to use their reports, for what purpose and whether they will rely on the report but will not suffer a direct loss. For example: **74**

- sponsoring bodies – that are reviewing the systems and processes in place at the grant-paying body in relation to the administration of the grant scheme rather than reviewing the accountants' report itself may choose to review a sample of accountants' reports as part of their own review of the grant-paying body;

- audit agencies – connected with any of the above parties (including the European Court of Auditors);

- parliament; and

- devolved administrations and legislatures.

There may be other bodies or individuals that wish to have access to the accountants' report or may have a statutory right of access. The extent to which they may place reliance on the report is not always clear.

When taking on this work, accountants may have a responsibility to those that receive the report, rely on it and who suffer a direct loss as a result of that reliance. In such cases, and where all the parties are known, the expectations and/or scope of work should normally be determined with the parties in the engagement. In some cases, this may be difficult to do as the grant-paying body may already have prescribed the scope of work and its expectations as part of its terms and conditions. It would, however, not be reasonable to expect accountants to accept a responsibility to third parties whose interest in the work may not have been known at the time that the work was accepted and performed.   **75**

Accountants will need to consider and apply appropriate engagement acceptance procedures in order to assess the risks associated with taking on any engagement of this nature. They will then determine whether, in the light of their assessment and the risk, it is appropriate to take on the engagement and if so, on what terms.   **76**

Agreeing on engagement terms

If the accountants are not the grant recipient's statutory auditors, then they may wish to include language within their engagement letter which clarifies their responsibilities and liability to the statutory auditor of the financial statements. The two engagements are separate, with the statutory auditors being responsible for their own audit report. The statutory auditors have to determine what reliance, if any, to place on the accountants' work as part of the evidence for their audit. For the same reasons, the accountants should include similar clarifying language within their engagement letters to the auditors of the grant-paying body.   **77**

78   If the accountants are the statutory auditors of the grant recipient, then they will need to carefully manage their relationship for these engagements with the grant recipient and any third parties. Both the grant recipient and the grant-paying body will need clarification that these engagements are separate from the statutory audit engagements. To provide this clarity, accountants may, within the engagement terms, confirm that their responsibilities in relation to the statutory audit engagement are separate and carried out for a different purpose from the engagement to provide a report on the grant funding.

79   Depending on the circumstances, accountants may wish to consider the approach outlined in AAF 04/6, *Assurance Engagements: Management of Risk and Liability*. For the purpose of this work, the most appropriate arrangements for accountants to enter into will be:

(a)   a tripartite or multipartite engagement contract with the grant recipient and the grant-paying body, accepting that they owe a duty of care not only to the grant recipient (who is their client) but also to those grant-paying bodies, including provisions limiting liability if appropriate (recognising that such a contract may not be achievable where there are numerous third parties);

(b)   an engagement with the grant recipient, with the facility available for other third parties to enjoy a duty of care from the accountants if they accept the relevant terms of the engagement which have been previously agreed with the grant recipient as if they had signed that letter when it was issued including the same provisions limiting liability[6].

(c)   if the risks are considered to be high eg, because the engagement itself is considered to be very complex or the accountant is unable to agree acceptable terms with the grant recipient (and/or grant-paying body), then the accountants could consider declining the engagement.

80   Where possible, the terms of engagement need to be agreed by all the parties to the engagement with the agreed terms recorded in writing in the engagement letter. Appendix E provides an example of model terms. In reality, where grant-paying bodies are administering a large scheme, it may not be possible or feasible for the grant-paying body to enter into individual tripartite or multipartite engagements for each and every grant allocated to a grant recipient. However, it may be possible for the grant-paying body to publish standardised engagement terms as part of its terms and conditions, outlining the basis on which they are willing to become a party to an engagement (see example 7 below).

81   Appendix F provides an example of a set of standardised model terms where the grant-paying body is offering to contract, at the outset, through its terms and conditions. Accountants should, however, note that the absence of a tripartite, multipartite engagement letter or a standardised set of terms does not in itself mean that a duty of care is not owed to the grant-paying body. If the purpose for which the grant-paying body has requested the report is clear within the grant terms and conditions and it has clarified that it seeks to rely on the report as a condition of the grant, and if the accountants take on the engagement with this knowledge, then there may be an implied duty of care.

---

[6] *This will require the consent of the grant recipient which should be obtained in the engagement letter;*

EXAMPLE 7: STANDARDISED ENGAGEMENT TERMS

Some grant-paying bodies already provide standardised engagement terms for grant agreements. One example is the Department for Business Innovation and Skills (BIS) with its Grant for Business Investment (GBI) scheme.

Where a grant-paying body provides standardised engagement terms, it does not need to sign an engagement letter as it offers to contract with the accountant on the model engagement terms. Once the offer is accepted by the grant recipient and the accountants upon signature and submission of a report to the grant-paying body, the necessary contract is formed between the grant-paying body, the grant recipient and the accountants.

A separate engagement letter may also be agreed between the grant recipient and the accountants but it should be noted that the terms set out in the separate engagement letter do not bind the grant-paying body, other than those terms set out in the standard terms issued by the grant-paying body.

Liability

Accountants in the UK are advised to address their reports to grant-paying bodies 82 when the basis and extent of their liability to the grant-paying body is clear and agreed within an engagement letter. In deciding and agreeing appropriate engagement terms in England and Wales, accountants should refer to the guidance in the ICAEW's *Members' Handbook Statement 9.1: Managing the professional liability of accountants* and consider the consequences of the Contracts (Rights of Third Parties) Act 1999.

Possible ways of arriving at a liability limit and through separate negotiation are: 83

● to limit the liability to the amount of the grant; and/or

● cap it at a fixed monetary amount.

In most cases, the grant-paying body will seek to recover losses from the grant 84 recipient directly but may seek to recover losses from accountants where it believes that the accountants have been negligent in carrying out their work, or in providing the report.

One option is to limit liability to that proportion of the loss or damage suffered by 85 the grant-paying body for which accountants have contributed to the overall cause agreed between the parties or, in the absence of agreement, it will need to be determined by the courts (subject to an upper limit).

If clarification language is used in the report, accountants will need to consider 86 whether it is reasonable and therefore likely to be effective taking account of the requirements of the Unfair Contract Terms Act 1977. Bear in mind that such wording is not always effective. Accountants are advised to seek their own independent legal advice on the effectiveness of any clarification language that they intend to include within their reports. Example wording for limiting liability and clarification language are provided in Appendices G and H.

Scope of Work

Accountants need to be clear about what the grant-paying body requires a report 87 on. The grant-paying body may want a particular outcome and may also want the work to be carried out in a specific way. Accountants will need to consider whether they can carry out the work requested and, if they are able to, consider what they need to do to provide the form of report requested. If the requirements are not clearly expressed in the terms and conditions of the grant scheme and the offer letter, accountants will want to clarify what is requested of them from the outset, including the type of engagement requested ("reasonable assurance", "limited assurance" or "agreed-upon procedures").

88   Depending on the type of engagement that is required, accountants will determine the procedures that they will need to carry out (including the materiality levels and any sampling methods). Accountants will need to determine whether what they have been requested to report on is actually capable of being reported on.

89   The level of testing carried out depends on the type of engagement required and should, where possible, be agreed with the grant recipient and the grant-paying body at the outset of the engagement. The higher the assurance required, the more detailed the testing is likely to be. The more testing that is carried out, the more likelihood there is of any errors being detected. It is worth noting that, however detailed the testing, not all errors (whether deliberate or otherwise) may be detected.

Format of report

90   The terms and conditions of the grant scheme and the offer letter should make clear the type of report required which will help to determine the type of engagement, the scope of work and form of report.

91   Agreeing the words and form of report at the outset helps to avoid disagreements with the grant recipient or the grant-paying body at a later stage. The accountants' report should reflect the agreement set out in the engagement letter and be supported by the work carried out. The report should make clear:

- for whom it is prepared, who is entitled to rely on it and for what purpose;

- that the engagement was undertaken in accordance with the agreed engagement terms;

- the work performed and the findings; and

- a conclusion or report which can be supported by the work done.

92   Accountants should take care to use clear and precise language to describe specific terms used (such as "enquiry" or "inspection").

93   Accountants and grant-paying bodies need to note that any form of report that has been endorsed as acceptable by the accountants' professional body does not necessarily bind accountants but they may wish carefully to consider the reasons behind the agreement with the professional body before deciding not to agree to the requested form of words. Accountants will also need to bear in mind that some wording included within prescribed forms of reports might be wording that is enshrined in legislation. If this is the case, the grant-paying body will normally have defined the words clearly to avoid any misunderstandings later.

94   Appendix C provides example pro forma reports when either a "reasonable assurance", "limited assurance" or "agreed-upon procedures" engagement is agreed.

Confidentiality issues

95   In carrying out this work, accountants need to be clear about and understand their responsibilities around client confidentiality.

96   Accountants need to understand that there may be statutory rights of access for parties (such as government departments or audit agencies) that need to see their reports (and possibly working papers) for statutory purposes. This may be either to

clarify or confirm the processes that have been put into place by the grant-paying body to allocate and verify the use of grant monies or because they have a statutory duty to report to Parliament matters of significance which may arise out of their reviews.

The accountants' working papers are their legal property and, except where there **97** is a statutory right of access, accountants have a right to restrict or decline access to them. The working papers may contain confidential information about the grant recipient and, by permitting access to them, accountants could be acquiring a significant legal risk. However, refusing access could be unhelpful to the grant recipient and those requiring the access. There are some steps that the accountant might wish to consider taking. Before permitting such access, accountants need to confirm, first whether there is a statutory right of access (complying with these will not breach professional confidentiality). If there is no statutory right of access, the accountants need to establish the reasons for the access and agree a protocol with the body that is making the request on how the access may be obtained so that the interests of all parties can be protected.

Access to the accountants' working papers may be permitted – while managing **98** liability risks – by using client authorisation and release letters. By using client authorisation the grant recipient gives the accountants written authorisation to provide access, information and explanations and agrees that the accountants will not have any liability to the recipient as a result. Release letters entail the body requesting access to agree, among other things, that the accountants do not assume any duty or liabilities to the body as a result of giving such access.

Data protection

Data protection laws apply to the personal data of individuals. Relevant **99** information may contain personal data (for example about employees or about sole traders with whom the client does business). However, the accountant may be obliged to provide access to relevant information by legislation. Therefore, where personal data is disclosed, as long as the information being provided is necessary to discharge that legal obligation, there are no data protection risks for accountants.

Fraud and illegal acts

In the course of performing procedures, accountants may become aware of **100** uncorrected errors, fraud or illegal acts attributable to the grant recipient's system, management or employees which may affect the grant claimed.

Unless clearly inconsequential, accountants determine from the directors of the **101** grant recipient whether this information has been communicated to the grant-paying body. If the directors have not communicated this information and are unwilling to do so, the accountants inform the audit committee, where there is one, or a group of directors with equivalent authority. If the audit committee or equivalent does not respond appropriately, the accountants need to consider whether to resign from the engagement. Accountants generally are not required to confirm with the grant-paying body that the grant recipient has communicated such information. Accountants may, however, wish to consider whether they have other reporting requirements such as one in relation to reporting misconduct by another chartered accountant or requirements under other relevant legislation.

Freedom of information

102 The Freedom of Information Act 2000 aims to increase the transparency and accountability of public bodies and the way in which such bodies carry out their work. Public authorities are listed in the Act. Broadly speaking a public authority is defined by the Act as a UK-wide public authority or a public sector body in England, Wales or Northern Ireland (similar legislation exists in Scotland). The public has a statutory right to access the recorded information held by a public authority from 1 January 2005.

103 In relation to an accountants' report, therefore, unless a valid exemption applies, the public will have a right to see an accountants' report in relation to a grant scheme that falls under information held by a public authority. Obtaining information under the Freedom of Information Act 2000 does not create a duty of care between the accountants and the requestor.

Section E – Considerations for grant recipient

Application process

104 When grant recipients make an application for a grant they will need to understand the terms and conditions of the grant scheme. Grant recipients are responsible for providing evidence to the grant-paying body that they meet the eligibility criteria for receipt of grant funding. This will be at the application stage. The grant-paying body will normally specify what documentation it requires to confirm eligibility and it will be the grant recipient's responsibility to provide the correct documentation directly to the grant-paying body with the application.

Grant offer and acceptance

105 Once a grant-paying body has processed an application, checked and confirmed that the eligibility criteria for a grant have been met and the application for a grant has been approved, it will send a grant offer letter to the grant recipient. The grant offer letter will contain, or refer to, the detailed terms and conditions that the grant recipient must comply with in order to receive the grant.

106 Acceptance of grant funding comes with an obligation to comply with all of the grant's conditions.

It is therefore important that grant recipients have a full understanding of the terms and conditions including their responsibilities, obligations and the reporting requirements. If grant recipients are unclear about their responsibilities and obligations, they will need to clarify these with the grant-paying body and preferably at the acceptance stage.

Responsibilities and obligations

Systems and documentation

107 Grant-paying bodies will provide detailed guidelines to grant recipients so that grant recipients can monitor compliance with the grant conditions. If any aspect of the requirements set by grant-paying bodies is not clear, grant recipients will need to obtain clarification from the grant-paying body and ensure that they fully understand their obligations.

The grant-paying body will set out the documentation that it will require as **108** evidence. It will be the grant recipient's responsibility to set up and maintain sufficient and effective administrative and financial systems which support and record the transactions (both income and expenditure) in relation to the grant scheme and which will provide the relevant supporting documentation to evidence the transactions.

Grant recipients will also need to maintain effective internal control and operating **109** systems which monitor the delivery of the scheme's objectives (including, where appropriate, delivery by partner organisations).

Interim claims

Grant monies may be paid at the start of a scheme and at regular intervals during **110** the course of the financial year or grant period. As part of the terms and conditions of the scheme, the grant-paying body may require the grant recipients periodically to submit evidence that they are spending the grant monies in accordance with the terms and conditions of the grant scheme and in accordance with the purposes intended.

If evidence is required periodically, the grant-paying body will normally require **111** this through the submission of an interim claim or return. The terms and conditions of the scheme will provide details of how interim claims or returns can be submitted. Evidence of expenditure is usually provided through progress reporting at regular intervals during the period of the grant, identifying crucial information such as underspends against profiles. It is the grant recipients' responsibility to ensure that interim claims and progress reports provide relevant and accurate information, reflect the relevant period and are submitted by the prescribed deadlines.

Final returns

At the end of each financial year of the grant scheme and also at the completion **112** stage (if the grant scheme extends over a number of years), grant recipients will be responsible for providing evidence and an independent accountants' report that they have spent the grant monies in accordance with the terms and conditions of the grant scheme and for the purposes intended.

The terms and conditions will provide details of how periodic and final claims and **113** returns should be submitted. It will be for the grant recipient to ensure that the requirements for obtaining and submitting an accountants' report on a grant claim or return can be met before accepting a grant. They should therefore obtain confirmation that their accountants will be able to provide the required report within the time required. This confirmation should be obtained at the grant acceptance stage, rather than risk encountering problems later when failure to provide the report can result in claw-back of grant monies.

Where appropriate, the grant-paying body will, in the terms and conditions, **114** provide details of the reporting structure that it requires to be in place, including:

- the form of report required;

- the contract terms under which the report is required;

- who would be best placed to provide this report;

- how the grant recipient should secure the engagement (ie, does it engage directly with the accountants or will the grant-paying body be a part of the engagement?);

- the qualifications that the accountants will be expected to have;

- the information that the grant recipient will be required to maintain and submit to the accountants in support of the year end or final claim or return;

- where, when and to whom the report is required to be submitted; and

- the process that the grant recipient will need to go through if accountants are unable to provide the confirmation that the grant-paying body requires.

Duty of care

115   Grant-paying bodies will determine whether they want a formal duty of care from accountants and this will determine the type of engagement that they will be willing to enter into with accountants (paragraphs 41 to 43 in section C). The accountants' report will be addressed to the grant recipient. If the grant-paying body agrees to enter into a tripartite or multipartite engagement or provides standardised engagement terms, the accountants' report will also be addressed to the grant-paying body. The terms and conditions should explicitly state all the parties that are involved in the process and thus, to whom the report should be addressed.

Types of engagement

116   It will ultimately be for the grant-paying body to determine the type of engagement it requires. The type of engagement will then determine the scope, nature and extent of work that accountants will carry out and the format and wording of the accountants' report will follow accordingly. The options and relevant factors affecting the type of engagement that the grant-paying body may decide upon are laid out in paragraphs 44 to 52 in section C. The terms of the engagement will partly be determined by the type of engagement chosen. More information on this is provided in paragraphs 73 to 81 in section D.

Appendix A

LIST OF TERMS AND CONDITIONS THAT COULD BE USEFULLY INCLUDED IN A GRANT SCHEME TO PROVIDE CLARITY

Glossary and definitions of terminology used eg, expenditure defrayed.	1
The stages of the application process.	2
What is and isn't eligible eg, cost, location, who can apply?	3
The rate of support.	4
Maximum approved expenditure and maximum amount of grant on offer.	5
Whether the grant is for capital/revenue or both and if the grant is net of any income.	6
Virement between capital and revenue or between various types of capital and revenue.	7
Any restrictions on sourcing equipment or supplies.	8
The systems, procedures and supporting documentary evidence (such as time records) that the grant recipient will be required to maintain, covering the length of the period, for how long and for whom.	9
Clarity about what they require a report on and that what they want a report on can actually be reported on.	10
The accounting policies (including whether the grant return is completed on an accruals or payments "defrayed" basis; and apportionment methods for overheads).	11
Process to be followed when there are instances of double counting/double funding, matched funding, additionality, contributions in kind, expenditure defrayed.	12
Process to be followed when errors occur, how these need to be managed (eg, the method of allocating overheads to the funded activity; the recording of time spent on the project; the treatment of revenue attributable to the funded activity) and intervention options (eg, suspension of payments; re-profiling of future expenditure; holding retention; clawback/termination of grant).	13
Process to be followed when eligible expenditure exceeds the funding limit and what happens if part of the expenditure is disallowed.	14
Cut off points (such as deadline dates for eligibility, timing of interim and annual reports, independent accountants' reports) as there need to be workable periods/deadlines for recipients to compile claims and then for the accountants to do the work necessary for the report.	15
Timeliness of and compliance with the grant-paying bodies reporting requests.	16
If the grant is allocated to a partnership, then clarity around the responsibilities of each partner in relation to the scheme as a whole.	17
Accessibility and availability of the terms and conditions (possibly on a website).	18
Format of the return that the grant recipient will be required to submit (ensuring that it adds up).	19
Format of the accountants' report (bearing in mind the issues highlighted in paragraphs 47 to 66 of this framework document).	20

21   A contact name for queries in relation to the engagement terms and reporting (in the offer letter).

22   For UK grants, a reference to the appropriate UK legislation or regulations that the grant scheme is governed by.

23   For European grants, a reference to the appropriate European Directive or conditions of aid.

The key issue here is that a grant-paying body needs to consider and identify which terms and conditions are relevant for a particular grant scheme, what it is that they want a report on, and who will provide the report. This is, by no means, an exhaustive list. There may be other items that are not included here which may also be relevant to have in a set of terms and conditions. It is often helpful to consult statutory audit agencies on the documentary evidence that the grant recipient may be required to keep to justify the expenditure.

Appendix B

TYPES OF ENGAGEMENT – OPTIONS ANALYSIS

Type of Engagement	Description	Nature of Report	Pros	Cons
Agreed-upon Procedures	The **exact** scope of work (eg, type of test, sample sizes etc) is agreed by the grant-paying body, grant recipient and the accountant. or the reporting accountant follows the exact scope of work set out in the grant claim terms and conditions, or other relevant guidance, that have previously been agreed by the accountant or representative body. The accountant then undertakes these procedures and **reports the results**.	A **detailed report** setting out the work undertaken (or making reference to the scope of work set out in the tripartite engagement letter or making reference to the source of any pre-agreed procedures) and the results of the testing. This is a **factual report and no conclusion is given.**	• Clarity about the scope, nature and extent of the testing agreed at the outset. • Grant-paying body can set out the overall template for the report in the light of its requirements. • Any exceptions that are identified are set out in the report. • The grant-paying body and other potential users of the report (eg, the grant-paying body's external auditors) are able to reach an informed judgement based on the information provided in the report. • Simple engagement from the accountant's perspective and therefore, all other things being equal, cheaper than other options. • Professional guidance in place in the form of International Standard on Related Services (ISRS) 4400, *Engagement to perform agreed-upon procedures regarding financial information*.	• Time needs to be set aside to agree the scope, nature and extent of work upfront. • The accountant will only complete the required work and will not undertake additional procedures even if they identify errors (unless this is required by the scope of work). • No conclusion is given. Therefore the grant-paying body is left to interpret the results and make a judgement. • The grant-paying body may not have the time/skills/ resources to interpret the report/reach a judgement.

Agreed-upon procedures may be the most appropriate type of engagement if the grant-paying body wants to set the procedures to accountants carry out the work:

- obtain the results over compliance with the terms and conditions at the lowest cost (although this can be expensive if the
- ensure consistency in the scope, nature and extent of work undertaken by reporting accountants; and/or
- receive a report setting out details of the work undertaken, the findings and all of the exceptions noted.

Agreed-upon procedures is unlikely to be the most appropriate type of engagement when the grant-paying body:

- wants an assurance "opinion" from a reporting accountant; and/or
- wants accountants to apply their judgement in determining the scope, nature and extent of the work required to provide an assurance opinion on the grant claim.

TYPES OF ENGAGEMENT – OPTIONS ANALYSIS CONT'D

Type of Engagement	Description	Nature of Report	Pros	Cons
Limited Assurance	The scope of work is agreed by the grant-paying body, grant recipient and the accountant or the accountant follows the scope of work set out in the grant claim terms and conditions, or other relevant guidance, that have previously been agreed by the accountant or representative body. The accountant then undertakes these procedures and **provides a 'limited assurance' conclusion** on the grant claim.	A 'limited assurance' **conclusion** on the grant claim in the form of a **negative assurance statement** (eg, 'having carried out the procedures stated (either as set out in the engagement letter or in accordance with an agreed framework), **nothing has come to our attention** to suggest that the grant has not been spent for the intended purpose'.	• Where the exact scope of work has been agreed, everyone is clear as to the scope, nature and extent of the testing that is undertaken as this is agreed at the outset. However, this does not preclude or mitigate the need for the accountants from performing other procedures in order to gather sufficient evidence to reach their conclusion. • The accountant provides a conclusion on the grant claim in the form of a negative assurance statement. There is no need to 'interpret' the results, unless there is a qualified conclusion. • Professional guidance in place in the form of International Standard on Assurance Engagements (ISAE) 3000, *Assurance engagements other than audits or reviews of historical financial information.* • May be cheaper than a 'reasonable assurance' engagement.	• No accepted framework currently in place covering these types of engagements. 'Limited assurance' engagements can therefore take various forms. These can range from being similar to agreed-upon procedures work, through to engagements that are very similar to reasonable assurance. • As a result, such 'limited assurance' engagements can be difficult to agree in practice and agreed-upon procedures or a 'reasonable assurance' engagement may be more appropriate. • Requires 'materiality' to be set or agreed by the grant-paying body, so that reporting accountants can determine the scope, nature and extent of the testing with the expectations of the grant-paying body in mind. • The grant-paying body simply receives a conclusion, rather than a detailed report, unless additional reporting is specified (eg, details of all exceptions identified). • Readers of the report may not know the exact scope, nature or extent of the work undertaken by the accountant, unless the engagement letter is provided or additional reporting is specified. • May be more expensive than an agreed-upon procedures engagement.

The differing nature of "limited assurance" engagements means that it is difficult to comment on them in general terms. In most cases, it is likely that agreed-upon procedures or a "reasonable assurance" engagement will provide the most appropriate type of assurance. Grant-paying bodies are therefore recommended to consider these options before deciding if a "limited assurance" engagement is appropriate.

TYPES OF ENGAGEMENT – OPTIONS ANALYSIS CONT'D

Type of Engagement	Description	Nature of Report	Pros	Cons
Reasonable Assurance	The **overall** scope of work (or a minimum scope of work) is agreed by the grant-paying body, grant recipient and the accountant (**including materiality levels**) or The accountant follows the overall scope of work (or a minimum scope of work) set out in the grant claim terms and conditions, or other relevant guidance, that have previously been agreed by the accountant or representative body, but **the accountant determines the exact scope, nature and extent of the procedures required to support their opinion.** The accountant then undertakes these procedures and provides **a positive conclusion** on the grant claim.	A conclusion on the grant claim in the form of **a positive assurance conclusion** eg, 'in my opinion, the grant claim has been prepared in accordance with the grant instructions and the amounts recorded have been spent for the intended purpose.' While a template wording can be suggested, it should be for the accountant to determine the exact wording of their conclusion which reflects their judgement and is linked to the work actually carried out.	• The grant-paying body is provided with a positive conclusion (or otherwise) on compliance with the grant's key financial terms and conditions. • The accountant is a 'financial expert', and has determined the appropriate scope, nature and extent of testing necessary to reach their conclusion on the grant claim. • Professional guidance in place in the form of International Standard on Assurance Engagements (ISAE) 3000, *Assurance engagements other than audits or reviews of historical financial information.* • No need to 'interpret' the results, unless there is a qualified opinion.	• As each accountant is responsible for determining the exact scope, nature and extent of testing required to support their conclusion (or otherwise) there is likely to be inconsistency between the amount of work undertaken by different accountants. • Requires 'materiality' to be set or agreed by the grant-paying body, so that accountants can determine the scope, nature and extent of the testing with the expectations of the grant-paying body in mind. • The grant-paying body simply receives a conclusion, rather than a detailed report, unless additional reporting is specified (eg, details of all exceptions identified). • Readers of the report may not know the exact scope, nature or extent of the work undertaken by the reporting accountant, unless the engagement letter is attached or additional reporting is specified. • To reach a positive conclusion typically requires additional procedures to be undertaken by the accountant. This type of engagement can therefore be more expensive.

A "reasonable assurance" engagement may be the most appropriate type of engagement when the grant-paying body wants to:

- obtain a conclusion from an accountant; and/or
- allow the accountants to apply their judgement in determining the scope, nature and extent of the work required to provide a conclusion on the grant claim.

A "reasonable assurance" engagement is unlikely to be the most appropriate type of engagement when the grant-paying body wants to:

- ensure that the scope, nature and extent of testing is the same on all grant claims (although it is possible to specify minimum;
- understand exactly what amount of testing has been undertaken by the accountant (although it is possible to request additional;
- be provided with details of all exceptions (although it is possible to request additional disclosures in respect of this);
- avoid being involved in setting a materiality level for the grant claim; and/or
- minimise the costs associated with obtaining the required assurance over the grant claim.

Appendix C

(i) PRO FORMA REPORT – AGREED-UPON PROCEDURES

Report of factual findings in connection with [project]

OFFER LETTER/CONTRACT DATED [DATE][Reference]

To: Directors [and Grant Provider][7] This report is produced in accordance with the terms of our engagement letter dated [XX] for the purpose of reporting to the directors of [client] (the "company") and [grant provider] (the "grant provider")[8] in connection with the grant claim for the monies receivable from the [[grant provider] (the "grant provider")]/[grant provider] under its grant offer letter dated X (the "offer letter") in respect of [project name]/[phase X] for the period ended [date][and in accordance with the terms of our engagement letter dated [date] (attached hereto)].

[Insert appropriate clarifying language from Appendix G]

[Respective responsibilities of the company and [firm of accountants] As directors of the company, you are responsible for ensuring that the company maintains accounting records which disclose with reasonable accuracy, at any time, the financial position of the company, and in respect of grant claims, as the company's directors (the "directors") you are responsible for compiling claims in accordance with grant offer letters, ensuring that only eligible items are included in each grant claim and for ensuring that all terms of such offer letters have been complied with or varied in writing with the provider. It is also the directors' responsibility to extract relevant financial information from the company's accounting records, to make the calculations specified in the offer letter, and to provide relevant financial information to the provider.]

Our approach

For the purpose of the engagement we have been provided by the directors with a schedule (as defined under the offer letter) showing the company's eligible expenditure and the necessary calculations in accordance with the grant offer letter, which is attached as Appendix [X] to this letter (the "schedule"). The directors of the company remain solely responsible for the schedule.

Our engagement was undertaken in accordance with the International Standard on Related Services 4400 applicable to agreed-upon procedures engagements. We were asked to perform the [Y] procedures as detailed in Appendix [X] and our engagement letter.

We confirm that we carried out [X] out of the [Y] procedures. The results of these procedures are as follows:

We were unable to carry out the following procedures: [and state reason]

or

---

[7] *Report will be addressed to grant provider where they have entered into a contract with the accountant.*

[8] *Report will be addressed to grant provider where they have entered into a contract with the accountant.*

We confirm that we carried out the following procedures (except [X] because …)

[List out the findings, with detailed exceptions (including the procedures that could not be performed, where applicable)]

Inherent limitations

Our procedures, [as stated in our engagement letter] do not constitute an examination made in accordance with generally accepted auditing standards, the objective of which would be the expression of assurance on the contents of the schedule. Accordingly, we do not express such assurance. Had we performed additional procedures or had we performed an audit or review of the schedule in accordance with generally accepted auditing or review standards, other matters might have come to our attention that would have been reported to you. This report relates only to the schedule and does not extend to any financial statements of the company, taken as a whole.

[Our audit work on the financial statements of [grant recipient] is carried out in accordance with our statutory obligations and is subject to separate terms and conditions. This engagement will not be treated as having any effect on our separate duties and responsibilities as [grant recipient]'s external auditors. Our audit report on the financial statements is made solely to [grant recipient]'s members, as a body, in accordance with Chapter 3 of Part 16 of the Companies Act 2006. Our audit work has been undertaken so that we might state to [grant recipient]'s members those matters we are required to state to them in an auditor's report and for no other purpose. To the fullest extent permitted by law, we do not accept or assume responsibility to anyone other than [grant recipient] and [grant recipient]'s members as a body, for our audit work, for our audit reports, or for the opinions we have formed.[9]

To the fullest extent permitted by law we do not and will not, by virtue of our reports/confirmations or otherwise, assume or accept any duty of care or liability under this engagement to [grant recipient] or to [grant provider] or to any other party, whether in contract, negligence or otherwise in relation to our audits of [grant recipient]'s financial statements.]

Yours faithfully,

Firm of Accountants Office

Date

(ii) PRO FORMA REPORT – LIMITED ASSURANCE

Independent Limited Assurance Report in connection with [project] OFFER LETTER/CONTRACT DATED [DATE][Reference]

To: Directors [and Grant Provider][10] This report is produced in accordance with the terms of our engagement letter dated [XX] for the purpose of reporting to [the directors of client] (the "company") and [grant provider]

---

[9] *This paragraph is necessary in those situations where the accountants are also the auditors of the grant recipient. Accountants should amend "members" and statutory references and other language as required if the grant recipient is not a company.*

[10] *Report will be addressed to grant provider where they have entered into a contract with the accountant.*

(the "grant provider")[11] in connection with the grant claim for the monies receivable from the [[grant provider] (the "grant provider")]/[grant provider] under its grant offer letter dated X (the "offer letter") in respect of [project name]/[phase X] for the period ended [date] [and in accordance with the terms of our engagement letter dated [date] (attached hereto)].

[Insert appropriate clarifying language from Appendix G]

[Respective responsibilities of the company and [firm of accountants] As directors of the company, you are responsible for ensuring that the company maintains accounting records which disclose with reasonable accuracy, at any time, the financial position of the company, and in respect of grant claims, as the company's directors (the "directors") you are responsible for compiling claims in accordance with grant offer letters, ensuring that only eligible items are included in each grant claim and for ensuring that all terms of such offer letters have been complied with or varied in writing with the provider. It is also the directors' responsibility to extract relevant financial information from the company's accounting records, to make the calculations specified in the grant offer letter, and to provide relevant financial information to the provider.]

Our approach

We conducted our engagement in accordance with [established framework[12]/the procedures set out in our engagement letter dated [date]]. We performed a limited assurance engagement as defined in [the framework/our engagement letter].

For the purpose of the engagement we have been provided by the directors with a schedule (as defined under the offer letter) showing the company's eligible expenditure and the necessary calculations in accordance with the offer letter, which is attached as Appendix [ ] to this letter (the "schedule"). The directors of the company remain solely responsible for the schedule.

The objective of a limited assurance engagement is to perform such procedures as to obtain information and explanations in order to provide us with sufficient appropriate evidence to express a negative conclusion on [the schedule]. [A limited assurance engagement is substantially less in scope than a reasonable assurance engagement and consequently does not enable us to obtain assurance that we would become aware of all significant matters that might be identified in a positive assurance engagement. Accordingly, we do not express a positive opinion.]

Work is performed in accordance with the [applicable framework as laid out in the engagement letter].

[Include summary of work]

---

[11] *Report will be addressed to grant provider where they have entered into a contract with the accountant.*

[12] *The framework will either be the ISAE 3000, Assurance engagements other than audits and reviews of historical financial information or the applicable criteria set by the grant-paying body in its scheme terms and conditions.*

Inherent limitations

[Our audit work on the financial statements of [grant recipient] is carried out in accordance with our statutory obligations and is subject to separate terms and conditions. This engagement will not be treated as having any effect on our separate duties and responsibilities as [grant recipient]'s external auditors. Our audit report on the financial statements is made solely to [grant recipient]'s members, as a body, in accordance with Chapter 3 of Part 16 of the Companies Act 2006. Our audit work has been undertaken so that we might state to [grant recipient]'s members those matters we are required to state to them in an auditor's report and for no other purpose. To the fullest extent permitted by law, we do not accept or assume responsibility to anyone other than [grant recipient] and [grant recipient]'s members as a body, for our audit work, for our audit reports, or for the opinions we have formed.[13]

To the fullest extent permitted by law we do not and will not, by virtue of our reports/confirmations or otherwise, assume or accept any duty of care or liability under this engagement to [grant recipient] or to [grant provider] or to any other party, whether in contract, negligence or otherwise in relation to our audits of [grant recipient]'s financial statements.]

Conclusion

Based on our work described in this report, nothing has come to our attention that causes us to believe that the accompanying [the schedule] has not been prepared in all material respects in accordance with [the framework/our engagement letter].

or

Based on the procedures performed we have identified the following exceptions that [the schedule] has not been prepared in all material respects, in accordance with [the framework/our engagement letter].

[list exceptions]

Firm of Accountants Office

Date

(iii) PRO FORMA REPORT – REASONABLE ASSURANCE

Independent Reasonable Assurance Report in connection with [project]
OFFER LETTER/CONTRACT DATED [DATE][Reference]

---

[13] *This paragraph is necessary in those situations where the accountants are also the auditors of the grant recipient. Accountants should amend "members" and statutory references and other language as required if the grant recipient is not a company.*

To: Directors [and Grant Provider][14] This report is produced in accordance with the terms of our contract dated [XX] for the purpose of reporting to [the directors of client] (the "company") and [grant provider] (the "grant provider")[15] in connection with the grant claim for the monies receivable from the [[grant provider] (the "grant provider'")]/[grant provider] under its grant offer letter dated X (the "offer letter") in respect of [project name]/ [phase X] for the period ended [date] [and in accordance with the terms of our engagement letter dated [date] (attached hereto)].

[Insert appropriate clarifying language from Appendix G]

[Respective responsibilities of the company and [firm of accountants] As directors of the company, you are responsible for ensuring that the company maintains accounting records which disclose with reasonable accuracy, at any time, the financial position of the company, and in respect of grant claims, as the company's directors (the "directors") you are responsible for compiling claims in accordance with grant offer letters, ensuring that only eligible items are included in each grant claim and for ensuring that all terms of such offer letters have been complied with or varied in writing with the provider. It is also the directors' responsibility to extract relevant financial information from the company's accounting records, to make the calculations specified in the grant offer letter, and to provide relevant financial information to the provider.]

Our approach

We conducted our engagement in accordance with [established framework[16]]. We performed a reasonable assurance engagement as defined in [the framework].

For the purpose of the engagement we have been provided by the directors with a schedule (as defined under the offer letter) showing the company's eligible expenditure and the necessary calculations in accordance with the offer letter, which is attached as Appendix [ ] to this letter (the "schedule"). The directors of the company remain solely responsible for the schedule.

The objective of a reasonable assurance engagement is to perform such procedures [on a sample basis] as to obtain information and explanations which we consider necessary in order to provide us with sufficient appropriate evidence to express a positive conclusion on [the schedule].

Inherent limitations

[Our audit work on the financial statements of [grant recipient] is carried out in accordance with our statutory obligations and is subject to separate terms and conditions. This engagement will not be treated as having any effect on our separate duties and responsibilities as [grant recipient]'s external

---

[14] *Report will be addressed to grant provider where they have entered into a contract with the accountant.*

[15] *Report will be addressed to grant provider where they have entered into a contract with the accountant.*

[16] *The framework will either be the ISAE 3000, Assurance engagements other than audits and reviews of historical financial information or the applicable criteria set by the grant-paying body in its scheme terms and conditions.*

auditors. Our audit report on the financial statements is made solely to [grant recipient]'s members, as a body, in accordance with Chapter 3 of Part 16 of the Companies Act 2006. Our audit work has been undertaken so that we might state to [grant recipient]'s members those matters we are required to state to them in an auditor's report and for no other purpose. To the fullest extent permitted by law, we do not accept or assume responsibility to anyone other than [grant recipient] and [grant recipient]'s members as a body, for our audit work, for our audit reports, or for the opinions we have formed.[17]

To the fullest extent permitted by law we do not and will not, by virtue of our reports/confirmations or otherwise, assume or accept any duty of care or liability under this engagement to [grant recipient] or to [grant provider] or to any other party, whether in contract, negligence or otherwise in relation to our audits of [grant recipient]'s financial statements.]

Conclusion

In our opinion, [the schedule] has been prepared, in all material respects, in accordance with [the framework[18]].

or

Except for [detail minor exceptions noted], in our opinion [the schedule] has been prepared, in all material aspects, in accordance with [the framework].

or

In our opinion [the schedule] has not been prepared in all material respects, in accordance with [the framework].

[insert details of issues leading to qualification of opinion]

Firm of Accountants Office

Date

---

[17] *This paragraph is necessary in those situations where the accountants are also the auditors of the grant recipient. Accountants should amend "members" and statutory references and other language as required if the grant recipient is not a company.*

[18] *The framework will either be the ISAE 3000, Assurance engagements other than audits and reviews of historical financial information or the applicable criteria set by the grant-paying body.*

Appendix D

EXAMPLES OF TYPES OF WORDING OR OPINIONS THAT MAY NOT BE ACCEPTABLE TO ACCOUNTANTS PROVIDING SPECIAL REPORTS

1   **Wording giving an opinion on a matter as a statement of fact when that matter, by its nature, is inherently uncertain or a matter of judgement**

Examples include "**we certify**", wording which accountants would not normally (except when required to by legislation) be in a position to use as it implies complete accuracy. Accountants also avoid using words or phrases such as "**correct**" or "**accurate**" or "**we have ensured**" for assertions that can never be made with absolute certainty. However, accountants can certify that they have performed an examination in accordance with agreed criteria.

2   **The use of the term "true and fair" or "presents fairly" when financial information is not prepared applying an acceptable financial reporting framework such as UK Accounting Standards or International Financial Reporting Standards as adopted by the EU**

The use of other phrases such as "**present fairly**" or "**properly prepared**" are avoided unless they are clearly placed in context, for example, "**present fairly in all material respects in the context of reporting upon this grant claim in accordance with…**".

3   **"Fair and reasonable" opinions**

Accountants generally avoid giving "**fair and reasonable**" opinions as they are normally associated with investment banks making recommendations to shareholders in respect of transactions. There is also the risk that they might be construed as valuations, which can give independence problems for accountants.

4   **Wording that might suggest that the grant-paying body is able to rely on the statutory audit of the grant recipient**

Accountants avoid any possibility of a link becoming established between the special report and the statutory audit report. For example, they avoid phrases such as "**we audited the accounts and we…**" or "**during our audit we …**".

5   **Opinions that are open-ended or otherwise cannot be supported by the work carried out by the accountants**

Accountants avoid phrases that are open-ended unless the scope of the work is clear by reference to the engagement letter or relevant standards or guidance, for example phrases such as "**we obtained all the explanations we considered necessary**" or "**we have performed such procedures as we considered necessary**" are not acceptable. Accountants do not give opinions that are not supported by the work carried out, such as assertions about completeness that cannot be supported by a limited amount of work that has been performed. Accountants could use, "**we have performed the tests laid out in the schedule/ work programme which is attached to the engagement letter**". These words would link the report back to the scope of work. Other examples of inappropriate reporting include providing positive opinions on solvency or prospective information which is inherently uncertain. In the same way, it is impossible for accountants to be able positively to state whether receipt of a grant has created or safeguarded a particular number of jobs. In addition, a positive opinion on whether or not the grant recipient has actually obtained **"value for money"** can never be given as VFM is an intangible concept. However, it is reasonable to determine whether a client has sought VFM by reference to specific criteria. A report can only give assurance on the basis of the information available at the time that it is provided.

Opinions which accountants do not have the necessary competence to provide   6

Accountants avoid opinions that are not within their professional competence, such as an opinion of an actuarial nature or a property valuation, where there has been no input from a relevant expert. Another example of this would be the appropriateness of insurance cover.

Opinions on matters beyond the accountants' knowledge and experience   7

Accountants avoid giving any opinion about how **"appropriate"** operational information or records being held or maintained by the grant recipient are, where the information or records relate to matters concerning the specific operational circumstances of the grant recipient which are beyond the scope of the accountants' professional knowledge and experience.

Wording that is open to interpretation   8

Certain words or phrases might be open to interpretation and these are only appropriate to use in clearly defined circumstances where the meaning is well established and understood. The word **"review"** is best avoided as it can be unclear what has been reviewed and the extent of the work. In addition if the term is used it may be misinterpreted that International Standards on Review Engagements as issued by the IAASB or International Standards on Review Engagements (ISRE) (UK and Ireland) 2410, *Review of Interim Financial Information Performed by the Independent Auditor of the Entity* has been applied when in fact, this is not the case.

Words to avoid can also include accounting terms, such as **"net current assets"** in sectors where specific adjusting items might be recognised when assessing liquidity. Accountants always define terms if the meaning might be unclear and do not otherwise use such terms. The word **"material"** is avoided unless this can be referenced to a clear definition.

Reports on internal controls   9

Reports on internal controls are only possible in well-defined and well-established circumstances, where the reporting arrangements have been agreed in a clear manner. Reports on systems and controls are avoided where there are inadequate criteria specified. Reports include an indication of the limitations of a system and are related to a point in time or period.

General guidance is given in the APB Briefing Paper *Providing assurance on the effectiveness of internal control* specifically in relation to certain entities in both AAF 01/06, *Assurance reports on internal controls of service organisations made available to third parties* and ITF 01/07, *Assurance reports on the outsourced provision of information services and information processing services*. It is also useful to clarify in writing the responsibilities of management and in particular, to indicate that they are responsible for identifying, evaluating and managing new and changing risks on an ongoing basis.

Reports without addressees   10

Accountants do not provide reports when it is unclear to whom the report is being provided.

11   Reports on financial information which is not explicitly approved by the grant recipient

The grant recipient has responsibility for the financial information being provided and it is, therefore, not appropriate for the accountants to report on financial information unless it is clear that this has first been approved by the grant recipient.

12   Qualifications in the covering letter only

Accountants provide qualifications in their covering letter only when a pre-printed report (with wording that is acceptable) is requested. In this case, a clear reference to the report and qualification is included in the covering letter and the pre-printed report should be annotated in some way so that it is clear that it should not be read in isolation from the covering letter. Otherwise, such qualifications are included in the main body of the report, so that they cannot be detached. Hence accountants should include any reservations about the claim or qualifications on the claim in the main body of the report. In a similar vein, all explanations of respective responsibilities of the grant recipient, grant-giving body and reporting accountants or limits being placed on circulation of the report or disclaiming of liability by the reporting accountant should be included in the main body of the report. Covering letters should normally be used to explain to the recipients of the letter that a report is being enclosed.

13   Opinions which would impair the auditors' independence

Accountants do not provide opinions that would impair their independence as auditors. For example, where the grant recipient is an SEC registrant, certain forms of valuation opinion are not permitted from auditors.

Appendix E

EXAMPLE OF A MODEL TRIPARTITE ENGAGEMENT LETTER

When a sponsoring body is to be bound into the engagement process, then all references to the grant-paying body should also include references to the sponsoring body.Government Grant Claim/returns – the model tripartite agreement

Addressee details:

(i)   The [grant-paying body]
(ii) Grant recipient

Dear Sirs

Government grant reports/confirmations We are writing to confirm the terms and conditions on which you have engaged [name of firm] to provide reports/confirmations in connection with [description or name of grant] paid by [grant-paying body] to [grant recipient]. These terms and conditions will apply to the reports/confirmations to be supplied for the period [ended/ ending …] and for subsequent periods unless otherwise agreed in writing. We will write separately to the grant recipient regarding practical matters such as the timing of our work, staffing and our charges. Our invoice will be addressed to [grant recipient], who will be solely responsible for payment in full.

Scope of our work

We will complete the relevant work specified below on the schedule (as defined in the offer letter). The schedule is to be prepared by, and is the sole responsibility of [grant recipient]. Our work will comprise the following:

[Set out here details of planned work relevant to the nature of the claim or grant, type of engagement and form and content of report required]

[Having set out the scope above, select one of the following]

[**Reasonable assurance**] On the basis of our work, we will report whether, in our opinion, [the schedule] has been prepared, in all material respects, in accordance with [the framework[19]].

[**Limited assurance**] On the basis of our work, we will report that nothing has come to our attention that causes us to believe that [the schedule] has not been prepared in all material respects in accordance with [the framework/ engagement letter].

[**Agreed-upon procedures**] We will perform the specified procedures set out in Appendix [X] and this engagement letter. Upon completion and on the basis of those procedures, we will provide you with a report with the results of our findings. You have both agreed that the scope of our work, as specified above, is sufficient for your purposes.

---

[19] *The framework will either be the ISAE 3000, Assurance engagements other than audits and reviews of historical financial information or the applicable criteria set by the grant-paying body.*

[Preparation of any document that [grant recipient] may be required to submit to [grant-paying body] in connection with our work will be the responsibility of [grant recipient]'s directors[20], who will also be responsible for ensuring that [grant recipient] maintains adequate accounting records and such other records as may be required by [grant-paying body]. [Grant recipient]'s directors will, on request, supply us with confirmation of matters affecting our work which are dependent on the directors' judgement.]

Save as set out above, we will not seek to establish the accuracy, completeness or reliability of any of the information or documentation made available to us. Our work will not amount to an audit of financial statements and will not give the same level of assurance as an audit.

Our audit work on the financial statements of [grant recipient] is carried out in accordance with our statutory obligations and is subject to separate terms and conditions. This engagement will not be treated as having any effect on our separate duties and responsibilities as [grant recipient]'s external auditors. Our audit reports on the financial statements are made solely to [grant recipient]'s members, as a body, in accordance with

Chapter 3 of Part 16 of the Companies Act 2006. Our audit work is undertaken so that we might state to [grant recipient]'s members those matters we are required to state to them in an auditor's report and for no other purpose. Our audits of [grant recipient]'s financial statements are not planned or conducted to address or reflect matters in which anyone other than such members as a body may be interested for such purpose.[21]

In these circumstances, to the fullest extent permitted by law, we do not accept or assume any responsibility to anyone other than [grant recipient] and [grant recipient]'s members as a body, for our audit work, for our audit reports, or for the opinions we have formed in respect of those audits.

To the fullest extent permitted by law we do not and will not, by virtue of our reports/confirmations or otherwise, assume or accept any duty of care or liability under this engagement to [grant recipient] or to [grant-paying body] or to any other party, whether in contract, negligence or otherwise in relation to our audits of [grant recipient]'s financial statements.

Having carried out our work we will issue reports/confirmations addressed to [grant recipient] and [grant-paying body] in the form set out in the appendix to this engagement letter, if our findings support this. In determining the form of our report we will take into account, (though without being bound by it) any form of reporting that the [grant-paying body] has suggested or agreed with the ICAEW following consultation with them. We will deliver copies to [grant recipient] at the same time. This letter will be identified in our reports/confirmations as the "tripartite agreement" under which our reports/confirmations have been issued. The accountant's reports must not be recited or referred to in whole or in part in any other document (including, without limitation, any publication issued by the [grant-paying body]) without the prior written approval of the accountant except where there is a legal or statutory right of access. If we need to

[20] All references to directors in this model mean either directors, partners, proprietors, board members, trustees, company secretary, or other authorised signatory, as appropriate.

[21] This paragraph is necessary in those situations where the accountants are also the auditors of the grant recipient. Accountants should amend "members" and statutory references and other language as required if the grant recipient is not a company.

qualify our opinion, we will issue a qualified report but will continue to use the agreed form of report for all aspects that are not qualified.

Other matters

Our duties and liabilities in connection with this engagement owed to [grant recipient] and to [grant-paying body] will differ.

[Detail any exclusions and limitations on the firm's liability to both the grant-paying body and the grant recipient and any relevant qualifications required to satisfy statutory reasonableness criteria. Consider the guidance in the ICAEW's technical release AAF 01/10, *Framework document for accountants' reports on grant claims.*

Our duty to [grant-paying body] will be limited to delivery of reports/ confirmations in the agreed form to facilitate the discharge of its statutory obligations. Delivery of such reports/confirmations (or the supply of confirmation that we are unable to do so in the agreed form) at any time will discharge that obligation in full. We will not owe [grant-paying body] any other duty, in contract, negligence or otherwise, in connection with our reports/confirmations or their preparation.

This agreement shall be subject to and governed by [the relevant country and legal system] and all disputes arising from, or under, it shall be subject to the exclusive jurisdiction of the [relevant] courts.

[Detail or append any other terms and conditions to apply to this work.]

Please confirm, by signing below, your agreement to this letter. Once you have done so, this letter will form a tripartite contract between us in respect of the matters covered. If you wish to discuss any aspects of this letter, please contact [name and telephone number].

Yours faithfully

[Name of accountant]

[Grant recipient]

[Grant-paying body]

Appendix F

EXAMPLE OF STANDARDISED TERMS OF ENGAGEMENT

(Agreed as part of the grant conditions instead of a tripartite engagement.)

Where a sponsoring body is to be bound into the engagement process, then all references to the grant-paying body should also include references to the sponsoring body. Example: "In these pre-agreed terms of engagement, references to the [grant-paying body] shall be read as incorporating references to [sponsoring body]."

The following are the pre-agreed terms of engagement on which the [grant-paying body] engages accountants to perform [a reasonable or limited assurance or agreed-upon procedures] engagement and report in connection with the [name of grant claim].

The [grant-paying body] accepts that an agreement between [grant recipient], its reporting accountants and the [grant-paying body] on these terms is formed when the accountants sign and submit to the [grant-paying body] a report as set out in Clause 3 herein. **[NB: The [grant-paying body] will not need to sign anything. By publishing this document the [grant-paying body] confirms that these pre-agreed terms form its agreement with [grant recipient] and the reporting accountants. Once the accountants' report is submitted to the [grant-paying body] in accordance with these terms the [grant-paying body] will accept that an agreement is formed. If the terms of the standardised engagement letter are to**

be revised, the [grant-paying body] will need to confirm its acceptance of the new terms before an agreement is formed.]

In these terms of engagement:

"[grant-paying body]" refers to the body that is providing the grant funding;

"[grant recipient]" refers to the organisation that is required to submit the report to the [grant-paying body];

and

"the accountant" refers to the [grant recipient]'s reporting accountants.

1. Introduction

The [grant recipient] is required to submit to the [grant-paying body] reports as set out in Clause 3 below that are also signed by an accountant to provide independent assurance. These terms of engagement set out the basis on which the accountant will sign the report.

2. The [grant recipient]'s responsibilities

2.1 The [grant recipient] is responsible for producing the [information], maintaining proper records complying with the terms of any legislation or regulatory requirements and the [grant-paying body]'s terms and conditions of grant ("the grant conditions") and providing relevant information to the [grant-paying body] on a basis in accordance with the requirements of the grant conditions. The [grant recipient] is responsible for ensuring that the non-financial records can be reconciled to the financial records.

2.2 The management of the [grant recipient] will make available to the accountant all records, correspondence, information and explanations that the accountant considers necessary to enable the accountant to perform the accountant's work.

2.3 The [grant recipient] and the [grant-paying body] accept that the ability of the accountant to perform its work effectively depends upon the grant recipient providing full and free access to the financial and other records and the [grant recipient] shall procure that any such records held by a third party are made available to the accountant.

2.4 The accountant accepts that, whether or not the [grant recipient] meets its obligations, the accountant remains under an obligation to the [grant-paying body] to perform its work with reasonable care. The failure by the [grant recipient] to meet its obligations may cause the accountant to qualify its report or be unable to provide a report.

3. Scope of the accountant's work

3.1 The [grant recipient] will provide the accountant with such information, explanations and documentation that the accountant considers necessary to carry out its responsibilities. The accountant will seek written representations from management in relation to matters for which independent corroboration is not available. The accountant will also seek confirmation that any significant matters of which the accountant should be aware have been brought to the accountant's attention.

3.2 The accountant will perform the following work in relation to reports required by the [grant-paying body]:

3.2.1 Grant return: The accountant will [carry out a reasonable/limited level of assurance assignment or perform agreed procedures (tests)] [as set out in the terms and conditions of the grant] and subject to any adverse findings will produce a report in the form set out in Appendix X (these should be in line with the ICAEW's technical release AAF 01/10, *Framework document for accountants' reports on grant claims*).

3.2.2 Where a [reasonable/limited] level of assurance is required by the [grant-paying body], the criteria is identified as per the Appendix to this letter.

3.2.3 For an agreed upon procedures engagement, the tests are laid out in the Appendix to this letter.

3.3 The accountant will not subject the information provided by the [grant recipient] to checking or verification except to the extent expressly stated. While the accountant will perform the accountant's work with reasonable skill and care, the accountant's work should not be relied upon to disclose all misstatements, fraud or errors that might exist.

4. Form of the accountant's report

4.1 The accountant's reports are prepared on the following bases:

4.1.1 the accountant's reports are prepared solely for the confidential use of the [grant recipient] and the [grant-paying body] and solely for the purpose of submission to the [grant-paying body] in connection with the [grant-paying body]'s requirements in connection with [name of grant]. They may not be relied upon by the [grant recipient], or the [grant-paying body] for any other purpose;

4.1.2 without imposing on the accountant and without the accountant assuming (or being perceived as assuming) any duty or responsibility and without imposing or accepting any liability to anyone except the [grant recipient] and the [grant-paying body], the [grant-paying body] may disclose the reports to others who demonstrate statutory rights of access to the report;

4.1.3 neither the [grant recipient], the [grant-paying body] [or others] may rely on any oral or draft reports the accountant provides. The accountant accepts responsibility to the [grant recipient], the [grant-paying body] for the accountant's final signed reports only;

4.1.4 the report will be prepared solely for the confidential use of [grant recipient] [and grant-paying body], and solely for the purpose of facilitating the grant claim. The report will be released to [grant recipient] [and grant-paying body] on the basis that it shall not be copied, referred to or disclosed, in whole or in part (save as otherwise permitted by agreed written terms), without our prior written consent, except where there is a legal or statutory right of access. Without assuming or accepting any responsibility or liability in respect of the report to any party other than [grant recipient] [and grant-paying body], we acknowledge that [grant recipient] [and grant-paying body] (or one of them) may be required to disclose this report to parties demonstrating a statutory right to see it, to enable such parties to exercise their statutory rights of access to this report;

4.1.5 to the fullest extent permitted by law, except for the [grant recipient] and the [grant-paying body], the firm of accountants, its partners and staff neither owe nor accept any duty to any person (including, without limitation, any person who may use or refer to any of the [grant-paying body]'s publications) and shall not be liable for any loss, damage or expense of whatsoever nature which is caused by any person's reliance on representations in the accountant's reports.

5. Liability provisions

5.1 The accountant will perform the engagement with reasonable skill and care and accepts responsibility to the [grant recipient], the [grant-paying body] for losses, damages, costs or expenses ("losses") caused by its breach of contract, negligence or wilful default, subject to the following provisions:

5.1.1 The accountant will not be responsible or liable if such losses are due to the provision of false, misleading or incomplete information or documentation or due to the acts or omissions of any person other than the accountant, except where, on the basis of the enquiries normally undertaken by accountants within the scope set out in these terms of engagement, it would have been reasonable for the accountant to discover such defects.

5.1.2 The accountant accepts liability without limit for the consequences of its own fraud and for any other liability which it is not permitted by law to limit or exclude.

5.1.3 Subject to the previous paragraph (5.1.2), the total aggregate liability of the accountant whether in contract, tort (including negligence) or otherwise, to the [grant recipient] and the [grant-paying body], arising from or in connection with the work which is the subject of these terms (including any addition or variation to the work), shall not exceed the amount of [**to be discussed and negotiated**].

5.2 The [grant recipient] and the [grant-paying body] agree that they will not bring any claims or proceedings against any individual partners, members, directors or employees of the accountant. This clause is intended to benefit such partners, members, directors and employees who may enforce this clause pursuant to the Contracts (Rights of Third Parties) Act 1999 ("the Act"). Notwithstanding any benefits or rights conferred by this agreement on any third party by virtue of the Act, the parties to this agreement may agree to vary or rescind this agreement without any third party's consent. Other than as expressly provided in these terms, the Act is excluded.

5.3 Any claims, whether in contract, negligence or otherwise, must be formally commenced within [insert number – eg 4] [years] after the party bringing the claim becomes aware (or ought reasonably to have become aware) of the facts which give rise to the action and in any event no later than [insert number – eg 6] [years] after relevant report was issued (or, if no report was issued, when the accountant accepted the engagement in writing). This expressly overrides any statutory provision which would otherwise apply.

5.4 This engagement is separate from and unrelated to the accountant's audit work on the financial statements of the [grant recipient] for the purposes of any applicable statutory or regulatory or other auditing framework and nothing herein creates obligations or liabilities regarding the accountant's audit work, which would not otherwise exist.

6. Fees

The accountant's fees, together with VAT and out-of-pocket expenses, will be agreed with and billed to the [grant recipient]. The [grant-paying body] is not liable to pay the accountant's fees.

7. Quality of service

The accountant will investigate all complaints. The [grant-paying body] or the [grant recipient] have the right to take any complaint to the ICAEW. The [grant-paying body] or the [grant recipient] may obtain an explanation of the mechanisms that operate in respect of a complaint to the ICAEW at www. icaew.co.uk/complaints or by writing to the ICAEW at the ICAEW Professional Standards Office, Metropolitan House, 321 Avebury Boulevard, Milton Keynes MK9 2FZ UK.

8. Providing services to other parties

The accountant will not be prevented or restricted by virtue of the accountant's relationship with the

[grant recipient] and the [grant-paying body], including anything in these terms of engagement, from providing services to other clients. The accountant's standard internal procedures are designed to ensure that confidential information communicated to the accountant during the course of an assignment will be maintained confidentially.

9. Applicable law and jurisdiction

9.1 This agreement shall be governed by, and interpreted and construed in accordance with, [relevant country] law.

9.2 The [grant recipient], the [grant-paying body] and the accountant irrevocably agree that the courts of [relevant country] shall have exclusive jurisdiction to settle any dispute (including claims for set-off and counterclaims) which may arise on any basis in connection with the validity, effect, interpretation or performance of, or the legal relationship established by this agreement or otherwise arising in connection with this agreement.

10. Alteration to terms

All additions, amendments and variations to these terms of engagement shall be binding only if in writing and signed by the duly authorised representatives of the parties. These terms supersede any previous agreements and representations (unless based on fraud) between the parties in respect of the scope of the accountant's work and the accountant's report or the obligations of any of the parties relating thereto (whether oral or written) and represents the entire agreement and understanding between the parties. These terms do not affect any separate agreement in writing between the [grant recipient] and the accountant.

Appendix G

EXAMPLE OF CLARIFICATION LANGUAGE FOR AN ACCOUNTANTS' REPORT

Where the grant-paying body signs the engagement letter or the pre-agreed terms published by the grant-paying body apply.

Our report is prepared solely for the confidential use of [insert name of grant recipient] [and insert name of grant-paying body], and solely for the purpose of facilitating the grant claim. This report is released to [insert name of grant recipient] [and insert name of grant-paying body] on the basis that it shall not be copied, referred to or disclosed, in whole or in part (save as otherwise permitted by agreed written terms), without our prior written consent except where there is a statutory right of access. Without assuming or accepting any responsibility or liability in respect of this report to any party other than [insert name of grant recipient] [and insert name of grant-paying body], we acknowledge that [insert name of grant recipient] [and insert name of grant-paying body] (or one of them) may be required to disclose this report to parties demonstrating a statutory right to see it, to enable such parties to exercise statutory rights of access to this report.

This report is designed to meet the agreed requirements of [insert name of grant recipient] [and insert name of grant-paying body] and particular features of our engagement determined by their needs at the time. This report should not therefore be regarded as suitable to be used or relied on by any other party wishing to acquire any rights against [name of accountant] for any purpose or in any context. Any party other than [insert name of grant recipient] [and insert name of grant-paying body] which obtains access to this report or a copy and chooses to rely on this report (or any part of it) will do so at its own risk. To the fullest extent permitted by law, [name of accountant] will accept no responsibility or liability in respect of this report to any other party and shall not be liable for any loss, damage or expense of whatsoever nature which is caused by any person's reliance on representations in this report.

[Freedom of Information Act wording – optional] If [insert name of grant-paying body] receives a request for disclosure of this report under the Freedom of Information Act 2000, [insert name of grant-paying body] is asked to consult with [insert name of accountants] and not to make any disclosure in response to any such request without taking into consideration any representations that [insert name of accountants] might make.

Where the grant-paying body does not sign the engagement letter and the pre-agreed terms published by the grant-paying body do not apply.

Our report is prepared solely for the confidential use of [insert name of grant recipient] and solely for the purpose of facilitating the grant claim. This report is released to [insert name of grant recipient] on the basis that it shall not be copied, referred to or disclosed, in whole or in part (save as otherwise permitted by agreed written terms), without our prior written consent. Without assuming or accepting any responsibility or liability in respect of this report to any party other than [insert name of grant recipient], we acknowledge that [insert name of grant recipient] may be required to disclose this report to [insert name of grant-paying body] or other parties demonstrating a statutory right to see it, to enable [insert name of grant-paying body] and such other parties to exercise statutory rights of access to this report.

This report is designed to meet the agreed requirements of [insert name of grant recipient] and particular features of our engagement determined by [insert name of grant recipient]'s needs at the time. This report should not therefore be regarded as suitable to be used or relied on by any other party wishing to acquire any rights against [name of accountant] for any purpose or in any context. Any party other than [insert name of grant recipient] which obtains access to this report or a copy and chooses to rely on this report (or any part of it) will do so at its own risk. To the fullest extent permitted by law, [name of accountant] will accept no responsibility or liability in respect of this report to any other party.

Appendix H

LIABILITY CAPS AND PROPORTIONALITY CLAUSE

Example of a liability cap for the accountants' reporting engagement, where a duty is accepted to the grant recipient and to the grant payer.[22]

To the fullest extent permitted by law, the total aggregate liability, whether to [insert name of grant recipient] or to [insert name of grant-paying body] or both, arising on any basis, whether in contract, tort (including negligence) or otherwise, of [insert name of accountants] for any losses whatsoever and howsoever caused arising from or in any way connected with this engagement shall not exceed [insert amount] (including interest).

Where there is more than one party to whom [the accountant] accepts responsibility, the limit of the liability specified will have to be allocated between those parties. Such allocation will be entirely a matter for those parties, and they will be under no obligation to inform [name of accountants] of it; if (for whatever reason) no such allocation is agreed, the parties will not dispute the validity, enforceability or operation of the limit of liability on the grounds that no such allocation was agreed or that any such allocation is of an unreasonably low sum.

Possible words for a proportionality clause:

Subject to the limitation on [the accountant]'s liability, which (with this paragraph) shall have no application to any liability which cannot lawfully be excluded or limited, [the accountant]'s liability shall in aggregate be limited to that proportion of the total loss or damage, after taking into account contributory negligence (if any), which is just and equitable having regard to the extent of the responsibility of [the accountant] for the loss or damage concerned, and the extent of responsibility of any other person also responsible or potentially responsible ("other person"). In order to calculate the proportionate share of [the accountant]'s liability, no account shall be taken of any matter affecting the possibility of recovering compensation from any other person, including the other person having ceased to exist, having ceased to be liable, having an agreed limit on its liability or being impecunious or for other reasons unable to pay, and full account shall be taken of the responsibility to be attributed to any other person whether or not it is before the competent court as a party to the proceedings or as a witness.

---

[22] *This is an example of a liability cap only, which will be one of a number of provisions relating to the accountants' liability and any limitations thereon. For example, the liability provisions will need to make it clear that the accountants are not seeking to exclude those liabilities (such as liability for their own fraud) which cannot be excluded by law.*

Glossary of terms

Term	Meaning
Accountants	The term **accountants**, refers to an individual accountant, firm of accountants, partner, director, or engagement leader who are responsible for the reporting engagement. The **accountants** provide the requested reports separately from the audit of the annual financial statements of the client. The term **accountants** is therefore also used to differentiate from auditors who audit the annual financial statements.
Additionality	The extra things that happen as a result of the grant, such as new or expanded services, more beneficiaries participating, improved access to widen take-up. Demonstrating additionality is generally a mandatory requirement for projects receiving European funding.
Audit	An audit is usually carried out on an organisation's financial statements in accordance with statutory obligations. An audit will be subject to a separate engagement. The audit report will be provided separately from the accountants' report on grant claims and returns. The term **auditors** is therefore used to differentiate from accountants who will provide other reports on these grants claims and returns.
Audit agencies	Public sector audits in the UK are subject to a variety of audit and related assurance regimes. This work is carried out by five national "audit agencies", which are: * National Audit Office * Audit Commission * Audit Scotland * Wales Audit Office * Northern Ireland Office. Audit and assurance work is also carried out by private sector firms commissioned or engaged by the audit agencies.
Clients	The grant recipients. The organisations that are receiving the money.
Committee of (PAC)	The Committee of Public Accounts is a Select Committee of the House of Commons. Historically, the primary purpose of the PAC's enquiries was to satisfy itself on the accounting for and regularity and propriety of public expenditure. The PAC retains its interest in these matters, but it also explores matters related to economy, efficiency and effectiveness of government business.
Contributions in kind	Non-cash contributions to a project such as equipment, facilities, resources or volunteer time.
Devolved administrations	Public sector bodies which support the elected governments in Scotland, Wales and Northern Ireland.

Engagement letter	These are the terms of the accountants engagement (with the recipient, and sometimes the grant-paying body). This enables all three parties to clarify expectations, the scope of the auditor's work and the agreed form of the accountant's conclusion and report. If a grant-paying body awards many similar grants, it may issue a "standard engagement letter".
Grant	The term "grant" covers a wide range of payments by government bodies for various purposes. In this guidance, reference to grant monies is in relation to payments made by the grant-paying body to an organisation where the grant is to be used for a specific purpose and the grant-paying body seeks to impose specific controls over the expenditure.
Grant in aid	Grant in aid is when a government department or other sponsoring body finances all or part of the costs of an organisation but the body operates at arm's length and the sponsoring body does not seek to impose detailed controls over the expenditure.
Grant-paying bodies	These are the bodies that are providing the funding directly to grant recipients.
Grant recipients	These organisations receive the funding from the grant-paying bodies.
Match funding	Match funding, (or matched funding or partnership funding) arrangements are when the grant recipient is required to make a contribution to the project, either through funding or as a contribution in kind.

Many grants, including those from European Structural Funds, will meet only part of the full project cost. This means that the remaining costs have to be met from other sources, the 'match funds', and it will the recipient's task to secure these. Potential sources of match funds include:

* other government programmes and grants;

* grants from local authorities and other statutory bodies;

* contributions from the voluntary sector, including donations from charities and trusts;

* contributions from the private sector; and

* loans from various organisations.

Match funding can include "contributions in kind" as well as cash – examples would be the use of the recipient's paid staff on the project, volunteers, and accommodation.

NDPB	Non-Departmental Public Body. They are better known as "quangos". These are not part of government departments and are not staffed by civil servants. Examples include regional development agencies and national park authorities.

Objective (of the grant)   The grant's objectives will be the supported activities which will deliver the changes the grant is meant to bring about. The objective needs to be set when the grant is first designed and it should fit in with the grant-paying body's own strategic objectives. This then enables the application forms and bid evaluation scheme to be written.

Offer letter   Letter from the paying body to the recipient which confirms that the bid or application for grant including any delivery plan) is acceptable and that funding is awarded. The offer letter gives full details of the grant, including:

* the name of the recipient (and any wider partnership being funded);

* the eligible activities approved for funding;

* types of eligible expenditure (and anything else which is ineligible);

* the maximum amount of grant to which the recipient will be entitled;

* the nature of the grant (capital, revenue);

* the rate of grant support and the maximum eligible project cost (if grant is less than 100%);

* the period of the grant, showing the project start and end dates and the last date for claims;

* the outputs to be delivered, showing milestones and the final targets;

* the terms and conditions and any other guidance; and

* a claim form (and any out-turn statement).

The letter should include a requirement for the recipient to return a formal letter of "acceptance".

"Offer letters" can also be referred to as "funding agreements".

The Panel   The Public Sector Special Reports of Accountants Panel set up by the Audit and Assurance Faculty of the ICAEW.

Payment (of grant)   Payments to organisations will normally be made on the basis of claim forms submitted by the grant recipient. However, grants to individuals are normally made in full once the application is accepted by the grant-paying body (although the terms and conditions will set out circumstances in which all or part of the grant can be recovered).

Payment of grant is conditional on compliance with the terms and conditions and on satisfactory progress being made against milestones towards the end objectives and targets.

Propriety	Linked to Regularity. Propriety is the concept that patterns of resource consumption should respect Parliament's intentions, conventions and control procedures, including any laid down by the PAC. It is concerned with standards of conduct, behaviour and corporate governance. It includes matters such as fairness, integrity, the avoidance of personal profit from public business, even-handedness in the appointment of staff, open competition in the letting of contracts and the avoidance of waste and extravagance.
Public sector	For the purpose of this guidance only, the public sector is defined as:

* government departments and their executive agencies;

* the National Assembly for Wales and their sponsored bodies;

* trading funds;

* bodies not administered as government departments but which are subject to ministerial and departmental control, for example NDPBs;

* local authorities and other local government bodies; and

* NHS bodies.

This definition does not include public corporations (except where they are NDPBs) or the nationalised industries. The first four parts of the definition are collectively referred to as Central Government.

Additionally, it applies to bodies that receive government grants for specific purposes although they are not public sector bodies:

* charities;

* higher education institutions; and

* further education colleges.

Regularity	Linked to propriety, regularity is the concept that resource consumption should accord with the relevant legislation, the relevant delegated authority and the requirements set down by HM Treasury in *Managing Public Money*.
Retention (of grant)	Grant-paying bodies may choose to protect their position by holding back a small proportion of the grant which the grant recipient would otherwise be entitled to. The retention is then released upon final completion of the project if all is well and, where an accountant's report is required, with the likelihood that the remaining grant will only be paid if the report is received without any qualification.
Special reports	In the context of this guidance, these are specific reports provided by an accountant to grant recipients and/or other parties in relation to work performed on grant claims or returns. The work carried out under these special reports is under a separate arrangement.

Sponsoring bodies   These are the bodies that provide the initial allocation of funding to a grant-paying body to distribute the funds to grant recipients.

Statutory arrangements   Some reports to public sector bodies are put in place through requirements of legislation.

Terms and conditions   Issued with the offer letter (or contained within it), these set out what the paying body requires the recipient to do in return for funding. The terms and conditions need to be specific to the grant being awarded.

Unhypothecated   Grant funding provided for a general purpose and with no specific conditions attached, such as (i) annual Revenue Support Grant from central to local government; or (ii) annual grant-in-aid provided to a Non-Departmental Public Body.

Virement   A transfer of the grant offer from one activity (or expenditure type) to another, giving the grant-paying body and the recipient flexibility to deal with over and underspends. As virements will amend the figures set out in the offer letter, they will normally be agreed in writing by both parties though the terms and conditions may allow small virements (say up to 10% of the grant awarded) to be made by the recipient "as of right" so long as the change is notified to the grant-paying body.

Bibliography

Audit 01/01, Reporting to Third Parties, ICAEW, 2001

Audit 03/03, Public Sector Special Reporting Engagements – Grant Claims, ICAEW, 2003

AAF 04/06, Assurance Engagements: Management of Risk and Liability, ICAEW, 2006

Code of Practice on Guidance on Regulation, Better Regulation Executive, Department for Business, Innovations and Skills, October 2009

Intelligent Monitoring, National Audit Office, June 2009

Managing Public Money, HM Treasury, 2009

Managing Welsh Public Money, Welsh Assembly Government, 2009

Principles of Proportionate Monitoring and Reporting, the Office of the Third Sector of the Cabinet Office, June 2009

The Compact, The Compact Partnership, December 2009

Turning the Tables in England, The Office of the Third Sector and the New Philanthropy Capital, September 2008

Acknowledgments

The Audit and Assurance Faculty of the ICAEW would like to thank the following members of the Public Sector Special Reports of Accountants Panel and Stakeholder Forum for their involvement in the work of the faculty and in particular for their participation in meetings, contributing to discussions and reviewing various drafts of the framework document:

PUBLIC SECTOR SPECIAL REPORTS OF ACCOUNTANTS PANEL

John Chastney (Chair) Independent

Tim Bridle Audit Scotland

Steven Cain CIPFA

Brian Collins Audit Commission

Melanie Crooks RSM Bentley Jennison (now RSM Tenon) Nick Davies Wales Audit Office

Anne-Marie Lavigne Chair of FEE Sub Committee on Certification of Grants Philip Lenton Deloitte LLP

Pauline McGee BDO LLP

Kelly Rosevear PricewaterhouseCoopers LLP

Carol Sayce KPMG LLP

Neil Sayers National Audit Office

Paul Spinks Grant Thornton LLP

Mike Usher Wales Audit Office

David Ward KPMG LLP

PUBLIC SECTOR SPECIAL REPORTS STAKEHOLDER FORUM

Mike Usher (Chair) Wales Audit Office

Andrew Baigent National Audit Office

Adrian Byrne PricewaterhouseCoopers LLP

John Chastney Independent

Ruth Elliot Department for Work and Pensions

Karen Everett Bournemouth University

Sue Gamble HM Treasury

Brian Gray European Commission

Suzanna Orr Home Office

Gavin Paterson Audit Commission

Nick Payne Department for Business Innovation and Skills Nick Sharman Highways Agency

Philippe Taverne European Commission

David Thomson Department of Finance and Personnel Northern Ireland Kerry Twyman Scottish Government

Jim Wager Department for Communities and Local Government Phil Winrow Environment Agency

ICAEW
  Chartered Accountants' Hall
  Moorgate Place
  London
  EC2R 6EA UK
  T +44 (0)20 7920 8493
  F +44 (0)20 7920 8780
  E tdaf@icaew.com
  icaew.com

TECH 01/11AAF Reporting to the Audit Bureau of Circulations Ltd (ABC)

(September 2011)

Contents

Paragraphs

Introduction   1 - 2

Explanation of the reporting arrangements   3 - 5
  (a) The model tripartite agreement   6 - 14
  (b) Reports to ABC   15

The ABC/ICAEW circulation audits forum (ABC forum)   16 - 18

Appendices
I. Audit Bureau of Circulations Limited (ABC) return – The model tripartite agreement
II. Training and communications

This revised guidance is issued by the Audit and Assurance Faculty of ICAEW in September 2011 to update and replace the Technical Release on the topic originally issued in April 2004 (Audit 01/04). It outlines reporting arrangements established with ABC that will become effective for periods ending on or after 1 July 2011. The guidance does not constitute an auditing or assurance standard. Professional judgement should be used in its application and, where appropriate, professional legal assistance should be sought.

This Technical Release does not constitute an audit or other form of professional standard, but provides best practice guidance. No responsibility for any persons acting or refraining to act as a result of any material in this guidance can be accepted by ICAEW or the Audit and Assurance Faculty. Professional judgement should be used in its application.

Introduction

1   Arrangements have been agreed between ICAEW and ABC for reports provided by accountants in respect of returns made to ABC by ABC members (publishers).

2   This Technical Release explains the main elements of these arrangements which were first established in 2004. The new arrangements will become effective for periods ending on or after 1 July 2011.

Explanation of the reporting arrangements

3   The reporting arrangements are based on the reporting framework and principles outlined in Technical Releases Audit 01/01, *Reporting to Third Parties* and AAF 04/06 *Assurance Engagements: Management of Risk and Liability.*

4   ABC has agreed that accountants' reports on ABC returns be provided in accordance with a tripartite agreement between (1) the accountants, (2) ABC and (3) the ABC member (publisher). ABC has agreed a model tripartite agreement for this purpose.

5   This Technical Release provides guidance on the following:–

   (a)   the model tripartite agreement; and

   (b)   reports to ABC.

(a) The model tripartite agreement

6   The model tripartite agreement, reproduced in Appendix I, follows the principles of Audit 1/01 referred to in paragraph 3 above. ABC has agreed that it will contract with accountants on these terms. Once the letter is signed by all relevant parties (ie, the accountants, ABC and the publisher), the necessary contract is formed.

7   The contract will apply to all reports made by the accountants for the publisher in respect of all of that publisher's publications covered by the engagement. From time to time the list of publications (attached as an appendix to the tripartite agreement) may need updating, and the tripartite agreement contains provisions for such updating. Once the tripartite agreement is in place, it will continue until either it is terminated or amended by written agreement between the parties to it.

8   The model tripartite agreement highlights the responsibilities of the publisher. These include responsibility for:

   ●   producing circulation data and maintaining proper records for that purpose;

   ●   preventing and detecting fraud and irregularities;

   ●   preparing the ABC returns for which the member owes a duty of care to ABC; and

   ●   cooperating with the accountants in providing information, documentation and letters of representation to enable the accountants to perform their work.

9   The model tripartite agreement sets out the scope of the work that accountants are required to perform and clarifies the limitations on that work. Accountants interpret the ABC Reporting Standards as necessary for the purpose of their work. ABC recognises that accountants will report on the basis of their (the accountants') understanding of the ABC Reporting Standards, but that accountants are not giving legal advice to ABC or the publisher on that interpretation. If accountants are uncertain as to the interpretation of the ABC

Reporting Standards, they should consider either seeking clarification from ABC, or requesting that the publisher reaches agreement with ABC as to the interpretation. The work performed by accountants is often described as a "circulation audit" but is not an audit and is entirely separate from, and unrelated to, the accountants' statutory audit of the financial statements of the publisher (see paragraph 13 below). The scope of work is limited to that set out in the tripartite agreement.

The tripartite agreement clarifies that the accountants' working papers are the **10** accountants' property and are not made available to ABC. However, communication between ABC and accountants on issues arising from the accountants' work is to be encouraged as this is likely to be helpful to ABC in its work on the circulation data provided by ABC members. This communication will be linked directly to circulation matters and could extend to issues concerning interpretation of the ABC Reporting Standards.

The model tripartite agreement includes provisions relating to accountants' **11** liability to ABC and the publisher for the accountants' reports. ABC has agreed that accountants may cap their liability on an annual basis for all reports provided within each year (running from the date the tripartite agreement is signed). Accountants must agree the amount of any such liability cap with both ABC and the publisher.

Whereas the model tripartite agreement uses the word "circulation", it is also used **12** in connection with publications that are "distributed" ie, given away free.

These reporting engagements to ABC are entirely separate from, and unrelated to, **13** the accountants' audit of the financial statements of the ABC member for the purposes of the Companies Act 2006 and do not create any obligations or liabilities with respect to the statutory audit which would otherwise not exist. They are sometimes referred to as "circulation audits", but it is important to avoid the term "audit" in any public communication so as to avoid any lack of clarity regarding the separation of the engagement from the audit.

Accountants enter into separate agreements with the publisher regarding matters **14** such as fees, timing of the work, and staffing arrangements. ABC is not a party to these separate agreements.

(b) Reports to ABC

Accountants provide their reports on the publisher's circulation return on standard **15** forms that are completed by the publisher. Accountants provide an opinion that the details set out in the circulation return have been properly prepared in accordance with the ABC Reporting Standards. Accountants are required to complete an "audit programme" and submit the completed programme to ABC, together with the forms. The ABC E-return system might be available for the submission of the return electronically. The form may be submitted on paper if necessary where E-returns are not available, and this, the "audit programme" and any changes to the ABC Reporting Standards are available for the accountants and the publisher prior to the end date of each audit period. Additional copies of these documents are available from ABC (contact details on abc.org.uk).

The ABC/ICAEW circulation audits forum (ABC forum)

16 A joint ABC/ICAEW Circulation Audits Forum was set up in 2001 following meetings between senior representatives of ABC and ICAEW. Since its establishment, the ABC Forum has been a vehicle to resolve issues and improve communication between ABC and accountants. The ABC Forum encourages and champions the highest quality of "circulation auditing"[1]. Accountants performing these engagements should comply with the ICAEW Code of Ethics and should have appropriate skills and knowledge of the ABC Reporting Standards and apply sufficient rigour and consistency to their work in relation to ABC.

17 Accountants performing these engagements ensure that their staff receive appropriate training. Information about training offered by ABC is given in Appendix II.

18 Various communication channels exist between ABC and accountants. Further information is also provided in Appendix II.

---

[1] NB: this term is used here as these engagements are commonly referred to as "circulation audits". However, as explained in paragraph 13, they are entirely separate to the audit of financial statements and an audit opinion is not given.

Appendix I – Audit Bureau of Circulations Limited (ABC) return – The model tripartite agreement

(NB: in this model tripartite agreement, the term "Publisher" is used to refer to an ABC member)

The Board of Directors

[Name of Publisher]

[Address]

Audit Bureau of Circulations Limited

[Address]

Ref: [DD/MM/YY]

Dear Sirs

ABC Circulation audits of member publications

1. Introduction

We are writing to confirm the terms on which you have engaged [Name of firm] to provide a report[s] on ABC certificates ("ABC Returns"), which [Name of Publisher] ("the Publisher") is required to submit to the Audit Bureau of Circulations Limited ("ABC") in respect of the publications listed in the attached appendix ("the Publications"). The Publisher may add or remove publications from this list from time to time by giving us and ABC notice in writing of the proposed changes at least 28 days before the ABC Returns are due. **1.1**

These terms will apply to our report(s) to be supplied for the period ending [date] and for subsequent periods unless otherwise agreed in writing by all the parties hereto. We will write separately to the Publisher regarding practical matters such as the timing of our work, staffing and our charges. Our invoice will be addressed to the Publisher, who will be solely responsible for payment of the same in full. **1.2**

2. The Publisher's responsibilities

The Publisher is responsible for producing the circulation data, maintaining proper records and completing the ABC Return in accordance with the Audit Bureau of Circulations Reporting Standards ("the ABC Reporting Standards"). The Publisher is further responsible for ensuring that the non-financial records are reconcilable to the financial records. **2.1**

The Publisher will make available to us all records, correspondence, information and explanations that we consider necessary to enable us to perform our work. **2.2**

The Publisher and ABC accept that any work performed by us under this letter cannot be accepted as being complete, unless we have been given full and free access to the financial and other records in connection with the distribution of the Publications under consideration, and the Publisher shall procure that any such records held by a third party are made available to us. **2.3**

The Publisher will supply to ABC such information as ABC may reasonably require as relevant to the Publications under consideration and other Publications published by the Publisher. **2.4**

2.5   The responsibility for the prevention and detection of fraud and irregularities rests with the management of the Publisher.

2.6   The Publisher owes a duty of care to ABC in relation to the Publisher's obligations to prepare the ABC Return.

3. Scope of our Work

3.1   We will prepare a report in respect of the ABC Return for each of the Publications (each a "Report" and together "our Reports") which will be addressed to ABC. In order to prepare each Report we will perform the following procedures. We will:

> **3.1.1** perform the work set out in the Audit Programme as laid down by ABC in accordance with the instructions contained in the ABC Reporting Standards, as updated and in force at the time our work is conducted;
>
> **3.1.2** subject to the prior consent of the Publisher, answer ABC's reasonable questions arising from our work that relate directly to circulation matters and which could extend to issues concerning interpretation of the ABC Reporting Standards. However, all working papers and documentation generated by us as accountants are our property and are not made available to ABC;
>
> **3.1.3** report to ABC if there have been any limitations or restrictions to the scope of our work and/or the completed ABC Return does not comply with the ABC Reporting Standards and instructions prepared by ABC.

3.2   We will not subject the circulation data or related systems including those systems used by the Publisher for compiling the circulation data and complying with the ABC Reporting Standards to checking or verification procedures, except to the extent expressly stated.

3.3   The nature of the work we will undertake is not designed to detect significant weaknesses in any of the Publisher's systems, including circulation systems, and consequently we (i) may not detect such weaknesses; and (ii) do not accept any liability whatsoever for not detecting any such weaknesses. The responsibility for the Publisher's circulation and other systems rests entirely with the Publisher. However, in the event that we do detect any such weaknesses, we will bring these to the attention of the Publisher.

3.4   The Publisher and ABC accept that our work will be based on internal management information and will be carried out on the assumption that information provided to us by the management of the Publisher is reliable and, in all material respects, accurate and complete. We shall seek written representations from management in relation to matters for which independent corroboration is not available. We shall also seek confirmation that any significant matters of which we should be aware have been brought to our attention.

3.5   This is normal practice when carrying out work of this type, but contrasts significantly with, for example, a statutory audit. Even statutory audit work, with a significant level of detailed testing of transactions and balances, provides no guarantee that fraud will be detected. You will therefore understand that the work we undertake is not designed to and is not likely to reveal fraud or misrepresentation by the Publisher or the Publisher's management. Accordingly, we cannot accept responsibility for detecting fraud (whether by management or by external parties) or for misrepresentation by the Publisher or the Publisher's management. The responsibility for the prevention and detection of fraud, irregularity, error and/or non-compliance with law or regulation therefore rests with the management of the Publisher.

Our work will be based on our understanding of the ABC Reporting Standards. **3.6** We will not give legal advice to the Publisher or ABC on the interpretation of the ABC Reporting Standards and, to the fullest extent permitted by law, we do not accept any liability in contract, tort (including negligence) or otherwise for any loss suffered by the Publisher or ABC or any other person as a result of incorrect interpretation of the ABC Reporting Standards by us or any other person.

4. Form and use of Report

Our Report will be addressed and issued to ABC and, subject to any adverse **4.1** findings, will be in the form determined from time to time by ABC following consultation with ICAEW. The report will include an opinion from us as to whether the details set out in the circulation return have been properly prepared in accordance with the ABC Reporting Standards. So that the Publisher is aware of the contents of our Report, we will deliver copies to the Publisher at the same time. However, our Report is delivered to the Publisher for the Publisher's information only and the Publisher should not use our Report for any other purpose. This letter will be identified in our Reports as the "tripartite agreement" under which our Reports have been issued. Our Reports will be issued to ABC and delivered to the Publisher on the basis that they are not to be copied, referred to or disclosed in whole or in part, to any other person without our prior written consent, which may be conditional.

Neither the Publisher nor ABC may rely on any oral or draft reports we provide. **4.2** We accept responsibility to the Publisher and ABC for our final, signed Reports only.

During the engagement we may wish to communicate electronically with each **4.3** other and ABC may request that we report in electronic form. However, the electronic transmission of information cannot be guaranteed to be secure or virus or error free and consequently such information could be intercepted, corrupted, lost, destroyed, arrive late or incomplete or otherwise be adversely affected or unsafe to use. We each recognise that systems and procedures cannot be a guarantee that transmissions will be unaffected by such hazards, but we each agree to use commercially reasonable procedures to check for the then most commonly known viruses before sending information electronically.

We confirm that we each accept these risks and authorise electronic **4.4** communications between us. We will each be responsible for protecting our own systems and interests in relation to electronic communications and, to the fullest extent permitted by law, neither we, the Publisher, nor ABC (in each case including our respective members, partners, employees, sub-contractors or agents) will have any liability to each other on any basis, whether in contract, tort (including negligence) or otherwise in respect of any error, damage, loss or omission arising from or in connection with the electronic communication of information between us and our reliance on such information.

5. Liability Provisions

We will perform the services set out in this letter with reasonable skill and care. **5.1**

We shall accept liability to ABC and the Publisher to pay damages for losses **5.2** caused by breach of contract or negligence on our part in respect of services provided in connection with or arising out of the engagement set out in this letter (or any variation or addition thereto agreed between the parties in writing) but, to the fullest extent permitted by law, our liability to ABC, the Publisher or any other party (whether in contract, negligence or otherwise) shall in no circumstances exceed [amount] in the aggregate per year (running from the date of this letter and from each anniversary thereafter) in respect of all such services provided in that year.

5.3   This engagement is completely separate from and unrelated to the audit of the Publisher's financial statements for the purposes of the Companies Act 2006 and performed in accordance with separate engagement terms. We do not, and will not, by virtue of providing a report under this letter or otherwise, assume any responsibility whether in contract, negligence or otherwise in relation to the audits of the Publisher's financial statements; we and our partners and employees shall have no liability whether in contract, negligence or otherwise to any other party, including ABC, in relation to the audits of the Publisher's financial statements.

5.4   We do not owe nor accept any duty to any person other than you for the services set out in this letter. We shall not be liable for any losses suffered by any other person caused by that or any other person's use of or reliance on our Reports/ confirmations or our advice. You agree that none of our partners or employees will have any liability to you and you will not bring any claim or proceedings of any nature howsoever arising (whether in contract, tort, breach of statutory duty or otherwise and including, but not limited to, a claim for negligence) in respect of or in connection with this engagement against any of our partners, employees or any subcontractors that we may use to provide the services.

5.5   The foregoing exclusions do not apply to any liability for fraud or other liability that cannot lawfully be excluded under the laws of England and Wales.

5.6   No person who is not a party to this agreement other than us and our subcontractors, if any, shall have any rights under the Contracts (Rights of Third Parties) Act 1999 to enforce any of its terms. This agreement can be varied without any third party's consent.

6. Safeguarding Service

It is our desire to provide you at all times with a professional service to meet your needs. If at any time you would like to discuss with us how our service to you could be improved or if you are dissatisfied with any aspect of our services, please raise the matter immediately with the engagement leader responsible for that aspect of our services to you. If, for any reason, you would prefer to discuss these matters with someone other than the engagement leader, please contact [name]. We undertake to look into any complaint carefully and promptly and to do all we can to explain the position to you. This will not affect your right to complain to ICAEW or other relevant professional body. You may obtain an explanation of the ICAEW complaints process at icaew.com/index.cfm/route/139178

7. Other matters

7.1   Any party may terminate this engagement letter by giving the other parties hereto 30 days notice in writing.

7.2   We may agree additional terms with the Publisher in a separate letter.

7.3   This agreement shall be governed by English law and all disputes arising from or under it shall be subject to the exclusive jurisdiction of the English courts.

8. Acceptance of Terms

Please confirm that you agree to the terms of this letter [including the attached terms of business]² by signing and returning to us the enclosed copy of this letter.

Yours faithfully

[Name of firm]

Countersigned on behalf of the Publisher

....

PRINT NAME

....

Countersigned on behalf of ABC

....

PRINT NAME

....

Attachment:

Appendix – member publications

[publications to be listed]

---

² *Firms may consider whether there are additional terms which would be appropriate to incorporate with the engagement letter by agreement between the three parties. It will be important to ensure that any such additional terms are consistent with those in the model tripartite agreement.*

Appendix II – Training and communications

About ABC

ABC has two roles:

- To manage and uphold standards which reflect media industry needs. These standards determine best practice in how media industry data is prepared and reported.

- To offer audit and compliance services to provide an independent check that data and processes meet these industry agreed standards.

ABC was founded in 1931 in response to advertisers' requests for an independent source of circulation data. Today ABC offers a variety of services for media owners to report their brand performance across print, digital, events and evolving platforms.

ABC is governed by the media industry, for the industry. The ABC Board comprises members from advertisers, media agencies, media owners and trade bodies who make strategic decisions as to how ABC is run. Each media sector has its own Reporting Standards Group drawn from media owners and agencies who work together to agree standards for the sector. Digital media standards are set by JICWEBS (Joint Industry Committee for Web Standards).

ABC has played a leading role in the International Federation of ABCs (IFABC) since its formation in 1967. This group forms a global network of audit bureaux from 36 countries to share knowledge and experience.

For further information, visit abc.org.uk. This website provides access to the latest ABC Reporting Standards.

Training

ABC offers training for external accountancy firms to encourage best practice when carrying out "circulation audits"[3] and to ensure compliance with ABC Reporting Standards. Details of the training are available from ABC, email abcpost@abc.org.uk

Communications

The ABC Forum facilitates two-way communication between ABC and accountants and meets two or three times a year. ICAEW, ABC and accounting firms are represented on the ABC Forum. A list of Forum members can be obtained from the Forum secretary Chris Cantwell, email chris.cantwell@icaew.com. From time to time ABC issues an External Auditor newsletter which covers issues discussed by the Forum. Further information regarding this is available from the ABC website (address above), in the "Newsletters" section.

---

[3] *This term is used here as these engagements are commonly referred to as "circulation audits". However, as explained in paragraph 13, they are entirely separate to the audit of financial statements and an audit opinion is not given.*

TECH 10/12AAF Reporting to Third Parties – (Audit 1/01 Updated)

(November 2012)

Contents

Paragraphs

Foreword

Introduction   1 - 7

Determine who will rely on the professional accountants' work and for
what purpose   8 - 11

Consider the form of report requested by the third party   12 - 14

Agree the work to be performed and the form of report to be given   15 - 24

Agree appropriate terms of engagement   25 - 28

Perform the work   29 - 30

Report   31 - 33

Appendix 1: Flowchart illustrating the process professional accountants follow
in response to requests for reports from third parties

Appendix 2: Examples of types of wording or opinions that are unacceptable to
professional accountants providing special reports

Appendix 3: Example extracts from an engagement letter for an agreed upon
procedures engagement

Appendix 4: Illustrative contents of a report of factual findings for an agreed upon
procedures engagement

Appendix 5: Example of a disclaimer notice for a professional accountants' report

Appendix 6: Example of a liability cap for the professional accountants'
reporting engagement

ABOUT ICAEW

ICAEW is a professional membership organisation, supporting over 138,000 chartered accountants around the world. Through our technical knowledge, skill and expertise, we provide insight and leadership to the global accountancy and finance profession.

Our members provide financial knowledge and guidance based on the highest professional, technical and ethical standards. We develop and support individuals, organisations and communities to help them achieve long-term, sustainable economic value.

The ICAEW Audit and Assurance Faculty is a leading authority on external audit and other assurance activities and is recognised internationally as a source of expertise on audit issues. It is responsible for ICAEW technical audit and assurance leadership and provides a range of information sources to its members which gives practical assurance in key audit and assurance areas.

Foreword

This guidance, ICAEW Technical Release TECH 10/12AAF (Audit 1/01 updated), is issued by the Audit and Assurance Faculty of ICAEW in November 2012 to assist professional accountants when asked to provide reports that have been requested by third parties. ICAEW Technical Release TECH 10/12AAF updates ICAEW Technical Release Audit 1/01, *Reporting to third parties*, originally issued in 2001.

Changes to ICAEW Technical Release Audit 1/01 comprise:

● incorporating, or where appropriate replacing, references and sources that have become available since the original publication of ICAEW Technical Release Audit 1/01 in 2001;

● revising technical terms in line with relevant standards and guidance; and

● adopting the current presentational style for ICAEW Technical Releases.

There is no change to the substance of guidance previously issued as ICAEW Technical Release Audit 1/01. The illustrative wordings in the Appendices remain as set out in 2001 but should be read in the light of subsequent guidance, particularly ICAEW Technical Release TECH 02/11 *Managing the professional liability of accountants*.

Introduction

Professional accountants are often asked by their clients to sign reports that have been requested by trade bodies, regulators and other third parties with whom the client has a relationship ("third parties"). **1**

Professional accountants are not bound by arrangements between clients and third parties to which they were not party and so have no obligation to sign such reports. However, professional accountants wish to assist their clients if possible and endeavour to become familiar with clients' requirements for reporting to third parties at an early stage. They negotiate appropriate engagement terms for providing such reports sufficiently far in advance of the reports becoming due. This helps to avoid any disagreements with the client or the third party regarding the form of the report that is needed. **2**

In the past there has been limited guidance available to assist professional accountants with such requests and accountants often signed reports for third parties without considering the liability to which they were exposed. ICAEW, through the Audit and Assurance Faculty, has developed the practical guidance in this Technical Release to assist professional accountants in deciding whether to accept these engagements and, if they do, the key points they consider when determining the process to follow (see paragraph 7). **3**

This Technical Release provides general guidance for professional accountants seeking to manage their risks effectively. ICAEW's Audit and Assurance Faculty is also active in helping with specific problematic reporting engagements and communicates with a number of third parties in order to agree appropriate forms of report and engagement terms. Where appropriate, specific guidance is issued relating to such reports. **4**

Additional guidance on reporting to third parties can be found in ICAEW Technical Release Audit 4/00 *Firms' reports and duties to lenders in connection with loans and other facilities to clients and related covenants.* **5**

ICAEW Technical Release Audit 4/00 is based on the law governing the duty of care and gives guidance on the matters that should be taken into consideration by professional accountants regarding the extent of their duty of care in respect of audit, review reports and ancillary reporting services.

5a   Further guidance on reporting and third party risks is provided in other ICAEW Technical Releases, including:

- AAF 04/06 *Assurance engagements: management of risks and liability*
- AAF 01/07 *Independent accountants report on packaging waste*
- AAF 02/07 *A framework for assurance reports on third party operations*
- AAF 01/11 *Reporting to the Audit Bureau of Circulations limited (ABC)*
- TECH 02/11 *Managing the professional liability of accountants*
- TECH 07/12AAF *Revised arrangements for accountants reporting to the Civil Aviation Authority*

6   This Technical Release does not cover:-

- corporate finance engagements (but see ICAEW Technical Release AAF 02/06 *Identifying and managing certain risks arising from the inclusion of reports from auditors and accountants in prospectuses (and certain other investment circulars)*;
- reports required under UK company legislation (in this case professional accountants follow the guidance in the Auditing Practices Board's Bulletin 2008/9 *Miscellaneous reports by auditors required by the United Kingdom Companies Act 2006* and ICAEW Technical Release Audit 1/03 *The audit report and the auditors' duty of care to third parties*);
- reports in respect of and/or to public sector[1] entities (ICAEW's Public Sector Reporting Accountants' Panel considers the issues relating to these reports). Relevant guidance has been incorporated into ICAEW Technical Releases Audit 03/03 *Public sector special reporting engagements - grant claims,* Audit 05/03 *Reporting to regulators of regulated entities,* and AAF 01/10 *Framework document for accountants' reports on grant claims*; and
- simple requests for references on clients' financial status and their ability to service loans (guidance on these requests is provided in ICAEW Technical Release Audit 2/01 *Requests for references on clients' financial status and their ability to service loans*).

However, many of the principles of risk management in this Technical Release will still apply.

7   The guidance in this Technical Release is set out under the following headings that describe the process professional accountants follow in response to requests for reports from third parties:

(a)   determine who will rely on the professional accountants' work and for what purpose;

(b)   consider the form of report requested by the third party;

(c)   agree the work to be performed and the form of report to be given;

(d)   agree appropriate terms of engagement;

---

[1] *"Public sector" is defined in the Auditing Practices Board's Practice Note 10 Audit of financial statements of public sector entities in the United Kingdom (Revised).*

(e) perform the work; and

(f) report.

The process is illustrated by the flowchart in Appendix 1.

Determine who will rely on the professional accountants' work and for what purpose

When professional accountants know that their report has been requested by a third party and that the third party will rely on the report, there is a risk, in the absence of an effective disclaimer[2] that the professional accountants owe the third party a duty to take reasonable care in preparing and providing the report. If the professional accountants do owe the third party such a duty, they could be liable to that third party if they were negligent and the third party suffered loss in reliance on the report.
8

It is vital, therefore, for professional accountants to understand who the third party is, why it requires the report and the extent of loss which the third party could suffer in reliance on the report. If, for example, the third party runs a scheme for compensating the client's customers in the event of the client's insolvency, the professional accountants' risk is much greater than if, for example the third party's only role is to perform marketing for a particular service sector.
9

The professional accountants' understanding of the risks involved in providing a report underpins the decisions they make about whether to accept the engagement and on what terms. Depending upon the circumstances professional accountants either:
10

(a) accept that they owe a duty of care to the third party and enter into an engagement contract with the third party, including provisions limiting liability if appropriate; or

(b) proceed with an engagement for their client but before allowing the third party access to their report, require the third party to acknowledge in writing that the professional accountants owe the third party no duty of care; or

(c) proceed with an engagement for their client but disclaim or limit any liability or duty to the third party by notice in their report; or

(d) do not accept the engagement.

If professional accountants regard a report as high risk, they agree to provide the report only if the third party is a party to the engagement contract or the third party has acknowledged in writing that the professional accountants owe no duty of care to the third party. If professional accountants regard a report as low risk, typically because the third party could suffer little or no loss in reliance on the report, then they may decide to provide the report without contracting with the third party. In this case a notice can be included in the report disclaiming or limiting the professional accountants' liability to the third party. In addition to that notice, it may be appropriate for the professional accountants to write to the third party, in advance of the third party receiving the report, notifying the third party of the basis on which the report will be provided. Also, if a third party writes to the professional accountants in an attempt to indicate reliance on a report, the

---

[2] *Professional accountants consider the legal effectiveness of disclaiming liability and of the proposed disclaimer in the particular circumstances of their engagement.*

professional accountants consider whether it is reasonable to accept such reliance. Where it is not, a disclaimer is given in writing.

11   Professional accountants are advised not to allow their reports to be provided to a third party unless the basis and extent of their liability to the third party is clear and agreed. Professional accountants refer to the guidance in ICAEW's Technical Releases AAF 04/06 *Assurance engagements: management of risk and liability* and TECH 02/11 *Managing the professional liability of accountants* and consider the consequences of The Contracts (Rights of Third Parties) Act 1999 - see the guidance in ICAEW Technical Release Audit 4/00.

Consider the form of report requested by the third party

12   As stated in paragraph 2, professional accountants maintain a dialogue with their clients to enable requests for reports to be highlighted at the earliest possible stage, so that difficulties may be addressed. Professional accountants are not bound by any form of report agreed between the client and the third party without the professional accountants' consent. The requested form of report (which can - but might not - take the form of a "standard" report on a pre-printed form), will often be inappropriate because the considerations in this guidance are not met. In such circumstances, professional accountants do not accept third parties' arguments that such reports cannot be changed. If a third party refuses to accept the principles in this guidance, it may be beneficial for the professional accountants to consult ICAEW's Technical Advisory Service. Examples of wording in requested reports that are unacceptable to professional accountants following this guidance are given in Appendix 2 (NB: this is not intended to be an exhaustive list).

13   Professional accountants only sign reports if they have performed sufficient work and obtained sufficient evidence to support the statement they are asked to make in the report. Sometimes third parties ask professional accountants to sign statements concerning such matters as the future solvency or performance of the client, which cannot be supported by any amount of work performed by the professional accountants. By signing such reports misunderstandings may arise that professional accountants may become the equivalent to insurers or guarantors of the clients' obligations to third parties. Professional accountants do not accept this responsibility and refuse to sign such reports, but they may propose alternative forms of report which are capable of being supported by work performed by them. Professional accountants may determine that an agreed upon procedures form of report is the most appropriate (see paragraph 21). If third parties require a guarantee regarding the future solvency of a client, it is usually most appropriate for them to introduce their own procedures to monitor clients' financial solvency, or to require the clients to obtain bank guarantees, or to take out their own separate insurance to cover their potential exposure – a professional accountants' report can never be a substitute for any of these options and it is no part of the professional accountants' function to act as an insurer. Professional accountants refer to ICAEW Technical Release Audit 2/01 *Requests for references on clients' financial status and their ability to service loans* for further guidance.

14   Professional accountants do not agree to forms of report, used by third parties, which place reliance on the statutory audit of the client, for example, wording such as that under the fourth heading in Appendix 2. To avoid the risk of this reliance being established, professional accountants also take into account the guidance in

ICAEW Technical Releases Audit 4/00 and Audit 01/03 on duties of care for the statutory audit. Professional accountants avoid circumstances that may result in a duty of care for the statutory audit report becoming established with a third party. They exercise caution if asked to send audited accounts direct to a third party. For example, they avoid sending the audited accounts direct to the third party unless this is accompanied by an effective disclaimer and they respond in writing to attempts by a third party to establish a duty of care in respect of the statutory audit report by disclaiming all liability to the third party (see Appendix 1 of ICAEW Technical Release Audit 4/00).

Agree the work to be performed and the form of report to be given

Professional accountants make clear to clients and third parties that engagements **15** to provide reports to a third party are separate engagements from the statutory audit engagement. The work performed in order to provide the report for the third party will be separate work and subject to a separate fee from the work performed on the statutory audit, and liability will be limited as appropriate (see paragraph 27).

Professional accountants agree with the client and the third party a form of report **16** that is appropriate taking into account the purpose of the report, the amount of work to be performed and the cost of the work. The timescale for providing the report is agreed at this stage. This timescale should provide sufficient time for the work to be completed and the report to be given - professional accountants do not agree to timescales for providing reports where it is not possible to plan and complete all the necessary work within the timescale requested.

Generally, the higher the level of assurance sought in a report, the more work is **17** necessary and the greater the cost to the client. A common problem is that the third party requests a demanding report but expects the client to pay for the necessary work. If the client is not prepared to pay for the work needed to provide the level of assurance sought then the professional accountants decline to act.

There are no UK auditing standards on the forms of reporting envisaged by this **18** guidance, although there are international and other standards as well as ICAEW Technical Releases which give some guidance[3]. However, it should be noted that the relevant international standards do not apply directly in the UK. In general terms, there are four options for these reporting engagements:

- Reasonable assurance
- Limited assurance
- Agreed upon procedures
- Compilation engagements.

---

[3] *At present, the most relevant international standards are issued by the International Auditing and Assurance Standards Board ("IAASB") and include the International framework for assurance engagements ("the Framework"), ISAE 3000 Assurance engagements other than audits or reviews of historical financial information, ISRS 4400 Engagements to perform agreed-upon procedures regarding financial information and ISRS 4410 Engagements to compile financial statements. ICAEW's guidance includes the Assurance Sourcebook and ICAEW Technical Release AAF 01/06 Assurance reports on internal controls of service organisations made available to third parties. In addition, the FRC has issued standards for engagements to review interim financial information, ISRE (UK and Ireland) 2410, and standards for investment reporting (SIRs).*

19   According to the Framework, issued by the IAASB, an assurance engagement exhibits all of the following elements:

(a)   a three party relationship involving:

- a professional accountant;
- a responsible party; and
- an intended user;

(b)   an appropriate subject matter;

(c)   suitable criteria;

(d)   sufficient appropriate evidence; and

(e)   a written assurance report in the form appropriate to a reasonable assurance engagement or a limited assurance engagement.

The Framework and ISAE 3000 provide guidance on each of these elements and establish basic principles and essential procedures for the performance of assurance engagements.

20   The objective of a reasonable assurance engagement is a reduction in assurance engagement risk to an acceptably low level in the circumstances of the engagement as the basis of the professional accountants' conclusion expressed in positive terms. It is only provided where the subject matter reported on and/or the scope of work are/is such as to enable the professional accountants to issue a reasonable assurance conclusion. An assurance engagement which conveys limited assurance involves performing more limited procedures and may involve providing a negatively formed assurance conclusion in the style of "nothing has come to our attention ….". Further information is available in ICAEW's *Assurance Sourcebook*.

21   An agreed upon procedures engagement involves performing certain specified procedures on factual information and reporting the findings without giving any form of opinion on the implications of the work performed. Example extracts from an engagement letter for an agreed upon procedures engagement are given in Appendix 3 and illustrative contents of a report of factual findings are given in Appendix 4. Professional accountants tailor the engagement letter and report to reflect the specific circumstances of the engagement. They attach to the engagement letter a draft of the type of report of factual findings that will be issued.

22   A compilation engagement involves preparing financial information on behalf of clients. Guidance on such engagements is given in ICAEW Technical Release AAF 02/10 *Chartered accountants' reports on the compilation of financial statements of incorporated entities* or, for unincorporated entities, ICAEW Technical Release AAF 03/10 *Chartered accountants' reports on the compilation of historical financial information of unincorporated entities*. Illustrative extracts from an engagement letter for compilation engagements are available from ICAEW's Technical Advisory Service at icaew.com/practicehelpsheets.

23   In most situations where professional accountants are asked to provide a report to a third party, an agreed upon procedures engagement will best meet the expectations of the third party and the client regarding the work the professional accountants perform and the fees the professional accountants charge. These engagements (see paragraph 21 above) have the advantage that

there is less scope for misunderstanding about the work to be performed and the nature of the results.

When determining the appropriate level of work to perform and the appropriate fee, professional accountants consider risks relating to who the client is and the purpose of the report. In some circumstances, however, the risks, even after appropriate limitation of liability, are so great that they cannot be adequately compensated by any reward and if this is the case, the professional accountants decline to do the work.   **24**

Agree appropriate terms of engagement

When professional accountants are requested by a client to provide a report for the purposes of a third party, professional accountants manage their relationship with not only the client but also with the third party.   **25**

Professional accountants usually manage their relationships by agreeing engagement terms in writing with the client and the third party. If the third party refuses to engage with the professional accountants, then professional accountants either refuse to provide the report or only do so subject to a disclaimer of liability to the third party (see paragraphs 10 and 11). In deciding to issue a disclaimer, professional accountants consider whether the disclaimer will be reasonable and therefore likely to be effective. Professional accountants need to be aware that disclaimers might not always be effective. An example disclaimer notice is provided in Appendix 5.   **26**

Engagement contracts include the following: **27**

- a clear unambiguous description of the scope of work to be performed and the form of report to be provided using defined terms where appropriate to avoid misunderstandings;

- a description of the client's obligations and the client's responsibility for the information on which the professional accountants report;

- clarification that the engagement is separate from the statutory audit and that the professional accountants have no duty of care to the third party in relation to the statutory audit;

- an appropriate liability cap[4], agreed having regard to the nature of the work being performed, the level of fee charged and other relevant factors. Any limitation of liability must be negotiated and agreed with the client, and must be fair and reasonable in compliance with the Unfair Contract Terms Act 1977[5];

- details of the addressee for the report, limitations as to the purpose for which the report is prepared and restrictions on who is entitled to see and rely upon the report and on the distribution of it; and

- a copy of the form of report to be provided.

An example of a liability cap is provided in Appendix 6.

In deciding the appropriate engagement terms, professional accountants also refer to the guidance in ICAEW Technical Releases AAF 04/06 *Assurance*   **28**

---

[4] *Professional accountants consider whether the liability cap is reasonable given the specific circumstances of the engagement.*

[5] *See the guidance in ICAEW Technical Release TECH 02/11 Managing the professional liability of accountants.*

engagements: management of risk and liability, and TECH 02/11 *Managing the professional liability of accountants*, in particular the sections on limiting or excluding liability.

Perform the work

29   The work for a third party report is separate from the work involved in the statutory audit and the professional accountants plan and document the work, retaining separate working papers for each reporting engagement.

30   Professional accountants perform work on a third party reporting engagement in the same professional manner as any other engagement and in accordance with the scope agreed and recorded in the engagement letter. If it is necessary to depart from the terms of the engagement letter, an amended scope of work is agreed, in writing with the client and with the third party.

Report

31   Professional accountants provide a report that reflects the agreement set out in the engagement letter and is supported by the work carried out by them (see paragraph 13). The report makes clear:

- for whom it is prepared and who is entitled to rely upon it and for what purpose;
- that the engagement was undertaken in accordance with the engagement terms; and
- the work performed and the findings.

Where considered appropriate, they also provide a statement that by delivering this report the professional accountants accept no additional duties in relation to the statutory audit.

32   Professional accountants' reports do not include either undefined terms such as "review", without specifying what the terms mean, or open-ended wording, without indicating the scope of the work which has been performed by reference to an engagement letter or relevant standards or guidance. Examples of inappropriate wording are given under the fifth heading in Appendix 2.

33   Professional accountants do not modify the form of their report in response to comments from the client or the third party that it does not meet their needs unless such modification is both appropriate and they have the opportunity to perform the necessary/additional work. If it subsequently transpires that a different form of report is now being requested to that agreed in the engagement terms, the professional accountants either agree a new engagement or decline to issue the requested report, giving the reasons in writing.

Appendix 1: Flowchart illustrating the process professional accountants follow in response to requests for reports from third parties

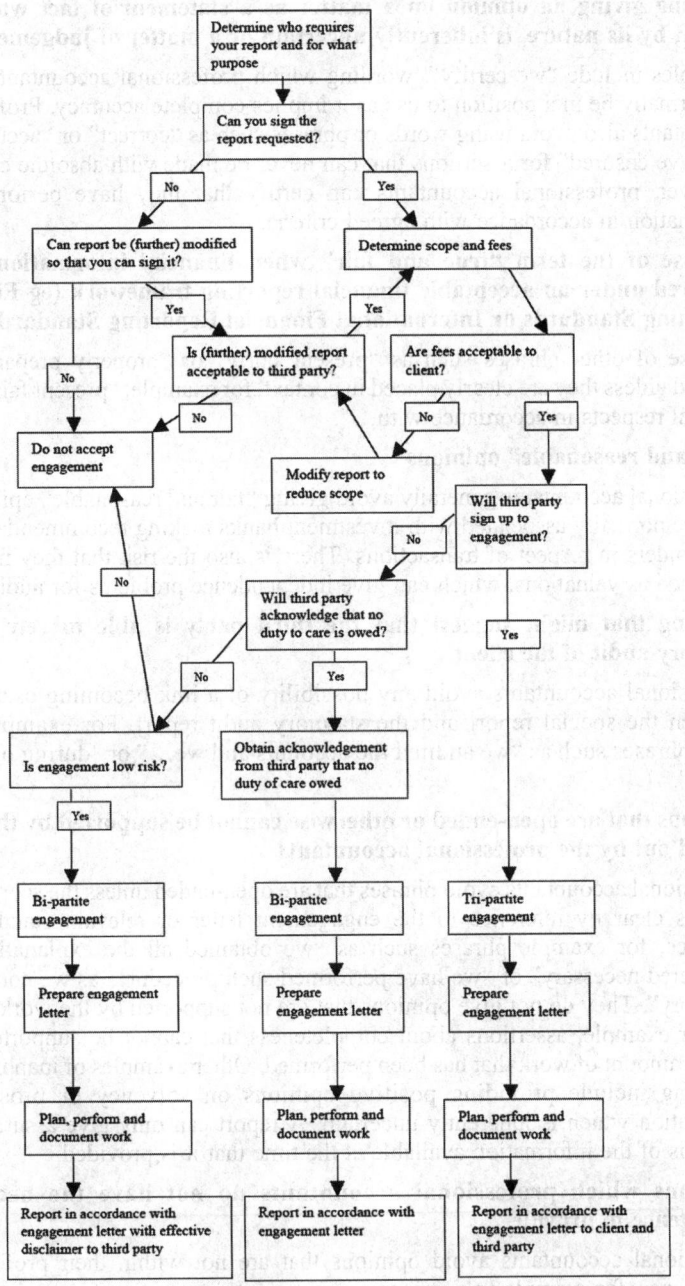

Appendix 2: Examples of types of wording or opinions that are unacceptable to professional accountants providing special reports

1   **Wording giving an opinion on a matter as a statement of fact when that matter, by its nature, is inherently uncertain or a matter of judgement**

Examples include "we certify", wording which professional accountants would not normally be in a position to use as it implies complete accuracy. Professional accountants also avoid using words or phrases such as "correct" or "accurate" or "we have ensured" for assertions that can never be made with absolute certainty. However, professional accountants can certify that they have performed an examination in accordance with agreed criteria.

2   **The use of the term "true and fair" when financial information is not prepared under an acceptable financial reporting framework (eg Financial Reporting Standards or International Financial Reporting Standards)**

The use of other phrases such as "present fairly" or "properly prepared" are avoided unless they are clearly placed in context, for example, "present fairly in all material respects in accordance with…".

3   **"Fair and reasonable" opinions**

Professional accountants generally avoid giving "fair and reasonable" opinions as they are normally associated with investment banks making recommendations to shareholders in respect of transactions. There is also the risk that they might be construed as valuations, which can give independence problems for auditors.

4   **Wording that might suggest that the third party is able to rely on the statutory audit of the client**

Professional accountants avoid any possibility of a link becoming established between the special report and the statutory audit report. For example, they avoid phrases such as "we audited the accounts and we…" or "during our audit we …".

5   **Opinions that are open-ended or otherwise cannot be supported by the work carried out by the professional accountants**

Professional accountants avoid phrases that are open-ended unless the scope of the work is clear by reference to the engagement letter or relevant standards or guidance, for example phrases such as "we obtained all the explanations we considered necessary" or "we have performed such procedures as we considered necessary". They do not give opinions that are not supported by the work carried out, for example, assertions about completeness that cannot be supported by a limited amount of work that has been performed. Other examples of inappropriate reporting include providing positive opinions on solvency or prospective information which is inherently uncertain. A report can only give assurance on the basis of the information available at the time that it is provided.

6   **Opinions which professional accountants do not have the necessary competence to provide**

Professional accountants avoid opinions that are not within their professional competence, for example an opinion of an actuarial nature or a property valuation, where there has been no input from a relevant expert. Another example of this would be the appropriateness of insurance cover.

Opinions on matters beyond the professional accountants' knowledge and experience 7

Professional accountants avoid giving any opinion about how "appropriate" operational information or records being held or maintained by the client are, where the information or records relate to matters concerning the specific operational circumstances of the client which are beyond the scope of the professional accountants' professional knowledge and experience.

Wording that is open to interpretation 8

Certain words or phrases might be open to interpretation and these are only appropriate to use in clearly defined circumstances where the meaning is well established and understood. The words "review" or "verify" are best avoided as it can be unclear what has been reviewed or verified and the extent of the work. Words to avoid can also include accounting terms, for example, "net current assets" in sectors where specific adjusting items might be recognised when assessing liquidity. Professional accountants always define terms if the meaning might be unclear and do not otherwise use such terms. The word "material" is avoided unless this can be referenced to a clear definition.

Reports on internal controls 9

Reports on internal controls are only possible in well-defined and well established circumstances, where the reporting arrangements have been agreed in a clear manner. Reports on systems and controls are avoided where there are inadequate criteria specified. Reports include an indication of the limitations of a system and are related to a point in time or period. Guidance is given in the APB Briefing Paper *Providing assurance on the effectiveness of internal control* and ICAEW Technical Release AAF 01/06 *Assurance reports on internal controls of service organisations made available to third parties*. It is also useful to clarify in writing the responsibilities of management and in particular, to indicate that they are responsible for identifying, evaluating and managing new and changing risks on an on-going basis.

Reports without addressees 10

Professional accountants do not provide reports where it is unclear to whom the report is being provided.

Reports on financial information which is not explicitly approved by the client 11

The client has responsibility for the financial information being provided and it is, therefore, not appropriate for the professional accountants to report on financial information unless it is clear that it has first been approved by the client.

Modifications or qualifications in the covering letter only 12

Professional accountants do not provide modifications or qualifications to the expected form of the report in their covering letter. Such modifications or qualifications are included in the main body of the report, so that they cannot be detached.

Opinions which would impair the auditors' independence 13

Professional accountants do not provide opinions that would impair their independence as auditors. Professional accountants consider the requirements of the APB's Ethical standards or ethical standards promulgated by other standard setters and regulators when audit work is undertaken in accordance with such standards. For example, where the client is an SEC registrant, certain forms of valuation opinion are not permitted from auditors.

Appendix 3: Example extracts from an engagement letter for an agreed upon procedures engagement[6]

Services to be provided

We will complete the specified limited scope procedures set out below:

[Describe the nature, timing and extent of the procedures to be performed, including specific reference, where applicable, to the identity of documents and records to be read, individuals to be contacted and parties from whom confirmations will be obtained.]

The above procedures will be performed solely for your purposes. You are responsible for determining whether the scope of our work specified above is sufficient for your purpose.

Upon completion of the procedures we will provide you with a report of our findings in the form of that attached to this letter, solely for your information [attach pro forma of report]. Our report is not to be used for any other purpose or disclosed to any other person without our consent. [We consent to the report being released to [name of third party] provided that [name of third party] acknowledges in writing that we owe no duty of care to [name of third party] and we will not be liable to [name of third party] for any reliance it chooses to place on the report.]

We have agreed that, under this engagement, we will not perform any verification procedures other than those which are specified in the scope section above. [If we were to perform additional procedures or if we were to perform an audit or any more limited review, other matters might come to our attention that would be reported to you.] Our report will not extend to any financial statements of the Company taken as a whole.

Audit work

Our audit work on the financial statements of the Company is carried out in accordance with our statutory obligations and is subject to a separate engagement letter. Our audit report is intended for the sole benefit of the Company's shareholders as a body, to whom it is addressed, to enable them to exercise their rights in general meeting. Our audits of the Company's financial statements are not planned or conducted to address or reflect matters in which anyone other than such shareholders as a body may be interested.

We do not and will not, by virtue of this report or otherwise, assume any responsibility whether in contract, negligence or otherwise in relation to our audits of the Company's financial statements; we and our employees shall have no liability whether in contract, negligence or otherwise to [name of third party addressee (if applicable), or to] any [other] third parties in relation to our audits of the Company's financial statements.

---

[6] *Refer also to guidance in ICAEW Practice assurance helpsheet PAS2/HS13 Engagement letters and ICAEW Technical Releases AAF 04/06 and TECH 02/11.*

Timetable

We will be able to commence our limited scope procedures on [date] and we expect our work to be completed by [date]. Our work will depend upon receiving without undue delay full co-operation from all relevant officials of the Company and their disclosure to us of all [the accounting records of the Company and all other] records and related information (including certain representations) we may need for the purpose of our work.

Staffing

X will be the partner in charge of the engagement. Y will act as manager.

Scope of our work

The scope of our work and the procedures we shall carry out in preparing our report, together with the limitations inherent therein, are outlined above. If the scope and procedures do not meet your requirements, please tell us so that we can discuss a different scope or additional or alternative procedures. [You should understand that there is no guarantee that these procedures will result in the identification of all matters which may be of interest to you.]

Our work will be based primarily on internal management information and will be carried out on the assumption that information provided to us by the management of the Company is reliable and, in all material respects, accurate and complete. We will not subject the information contained in our reports and letters to checking or verification procedures except to the extent expressly stated. This is normal practice when carrying out such limited scope procedures, but contrasts significantly with, for example, an audit. Even audit work provides no guarantee that fraud will be detected. You will therefore understand that the Services are not designed to and are not likely to reveal fraud or misrepresentation by the management of the Company. Accordingly we cannot accept responsibility for detecting fraud (whether by management or by external parties) or misrepresentation by the management of the Company.

Appendix 4: Illustrative contents of a report of factual findings for an agreed upon procedures engagement[7]

These include:

- Addressee(s);

- Identification of the applicable engagement letter and specific information to which the agreed upon procedures have been applied;

- Statement that the procedures performed were those agreed with the client (and third party, if applicable);

- Identification of the purpose for which the agreed upon procedures were performed;

- Listing of the specific procedures performed (procedures may include: inquiry and analysis; recomputation, comparison and other clerical accuracy checks; observation; inspection; and obtaining confirmations);

- Description of the professional accountants' factual findings, including sufficient details of errors and exceptions found;

- Statement that the procedures performed do not constitute either an audit, ~~or~~ a review;

- Statement that had the professional accountants performed additional procedures, an audit or a review, other matters might have come to light that would have been reported;

- Statement that the report is restricted to those parties that have agreed to the procedures performed;

- Statement that the report relates only to the matters specified and that it does not extend to the entity's financial statements taken as a whole;

- Date of the report;

---

[7] *An illustrative report is available in Appendix 2 to ISRS 4400. Further guidance and other example agreed upon procedures reports are contained in ICAEW Technical Releases AAF 04/10 Guidance for performing agreed-upon procedures engagements that address XBRL-tagged data included within financial statements prepared in iXBRL format, AAF 01/10 Framework document for accountants' reports on grant claims (Appendix C(i)), and TECH 07/12AAF Revised arrangements for accountants reporting to the Civil Aviation Authority.*

Appendix 5: Example of a disclaimer notice for a professional accountants' report

Where the third party signs the engagement letter

Our Report is prepared solely for the confidential use of [insert name of client] [and [insert name of identified third party]], and solely for the purpose of [describe the purpose]. It may not be relied upon by [insert name of client] [or [insert name of identified third party]] for any other purpose whatsoever. Our Report must not be recited or referred to in whole or in part in any other document. Our Report must not be made available, copied or recited to any other party [without our express written permission]. [Insert name of professional accountants] neither owes nor accepts any duty to any other party and shall not be liable for any loss, damage or expense of whatsoever nature which is caused by their reliance on our Report.

Where the third party does not sign the engagement letter

Our Report is prepared solely for the confidential use of [insert name of client] and solely for the purpose of [describe the purpose]. It may not be relied upon by [insert name of client] for any other purpose whatsoever. Our Report must not be recited or referred to in whole or in part in any other document. Our Report must not be made available, copied or recited to any other party [without our express written permission]. [Insert name of professional accountants] neither owes nor accepts any duty to any other party and shall not be liable for any loss, damage or expense of whatsoever nature which is caused by their reliance on our Report.

Appendix 6: Example of a liability cap for the professional accountants' reporting engagement[8]

The aggregate liability, whether to [insert name of client] or [insert name of third party] or any other party, of whatever nature, whether in contract, tort or otherwise, of [insert name of professional accountants] for any losses whatsoever and howsoever caused arising from or in any way connected with this engagement [and this transaction] shall not exceed [insert amount] (including interest).

---

[8] *This is an example of a liability cap only, which will be one of a number of provisions relating to the professional accountants' liability and any limitations thereon. For example, the liability provisions will need to make it clear that the professional accountants are not seeking to exclude those liabilities (such as liability for their own fraud) which cannot be excluded by law. See also ICAEW Technical Releases TECH 02/11 and AAF 04/06 and Practice Assurance helpsheet PAS2/HS03.*

TECH 04/13AAF Assurance Reporting on Relevant Trustees (Relevant Trustee Supplement to ICAEW AAF 02/07)

(February 2013)

Contents

Paragraphs

Foreword

Introduction

Assurance reporting on relevant trustees   1 - 49
  About this Supplement   1 - 5
  Assurance reporting on the control procedures over administrative and
  accounting procedures   6 - 38
  Assurance report   39 - 42
  Reporting on description misstatements, design deficiencies or when control
  procedures are not operating effectively   43 - 49

**Appendix 1 – Principles and related control objectives on "sound
administrative and accounting procedures"**

Appendix 2 – Example paragraphs from the report by the Relevant Trustee

**Appendix 3 – A pro forma practitioner's assurance report on the internal
control procedures of Relevant Trustees**

Glossary

Laws and regulations referred to in this ICAEW Technical Release are stated as at February 2013. Every effort has been made to make sure the information it contains is accurate at the time of creation. ICAEW cannot guarantee the completeness or accuracy of the information in this ICAEW Technical Release and shall not be responsible for errors or inaccuracies. Under no circumstances shall ICAEW be liable for any reliance by you on any information in this ICAEW Technical Release.

ISBN 978-0-85760-911-3

Foreword

This Supplement is intended to assist the development of good practice by "Relevant Trustees." These are trustees, who as part of their business as a trustee, offer pensions trustee services in relation to trust schemes and who either are on the Trustee Register or adopt this framework voluntarily.

The Supplement is effective from 31 March 2013. Assurance reporting on Relevant Trustees will generally cover a period of time, although in certain circumstances may relate to a point in time. See paragraph 4 of the guidance for a discussion of the two subject matter options underlying these two outcomes.

It sets out what is expected from assurance reports provided by independent practitioners on specified control procedures over a Relevant Trustee's administrative and accounting procedures in relation to its own business operations for providing pensions trustee services. The control procedures are assessed in the light of control objectives that are set out in this Supplement.

Introduction

The Occupational Pension Schemes (Independent Trustee) Regulations 2005[1] require the Pensions Regulator (the Regulator) to compile and maintain a register of Relevant Trustees that satisfies certain legislative conditions[2] (the Trustee Register). These conditions are that the applicant:

- has sufficient relevant experience of occupational pension schemes;
- is a fit and proper person to act as a Trustee of an occupational pension scheme;
- operates sound administrative and accounting procedures; and
- has adequate indemnity insurance cover.

The Trustee Register has been in place since 2005 and the Regulator may use it to appoint a trustee to pension schemes "usually, on expedient or protective grounds, to ensure that the scheme is properly administered and the members protected when its employer is insolvent[3]". Both individual and corporate trustees may apply to be on the Trustee Register. To do so is voluntary and being on the Trustee Register does not guarantee appointments[4].

In December 2009, the Regulator consulted and subsequently introduced changes to how it assesses some of the conditions for inclusion on the Trustee Register. These changes were proposed to "reflect the Regulator's experience of the trustee sector and aim to ensure that best practice and standards are increased and maintained by Trustees on the Trustee Register[5]."

Independent assurance reporting

This Supplement relates to one of the conditions mentioned above: to ensure that a trustee operates "sound administrative and accounting procedures." As part of

---

[1] *SI 2005/703.*

[2] *See section 23(4) of the Pensions Act 1995 (the Act) and regulation 3(b)(iii) of SI 2005/703.*

[3] *Consultation on the Pension Regulator's Trustee Register, the Pensions Regulator, December 2009, p. 4.*

[4] *For further information, see http://www.thepensionsRegulator.gov.uk/Trustees/about-the-Trustee-register.aspx.*

[5] *See footnote 5, p. 3.*

demonstrating compliance with this condition to be on the Register, the Regulator requires a Relevant Trustee to:

- prepare an annual report on the trustee's administrative and accounting procedures; and

- obtain an independent assurance report from a practitioner on the trustee's report.

Assurance reports are, therefore, intended to become part of the Regulator's process to assist in its checking that a Relevant Trustee operates sound administrative and accounting procedures, in relation to its own business operations for providing pensions trustee services, when it seeks to be on the Trustee Register. However, it is open to any trustee offering pensions trustee services to adopt this framework regardless of whether it is applying to be on or is on the Trustee Register.

In this Supplement, all these trustees who adopt the framework set out in this Supplement are referred to as "Relevant Trustees"[6].

The Relevant Trustee Supplement to AAF 02/07 *A framework for assurance reports on third party operations* has been written to assist Relevant Trustees to obtain an independent assurance report over their administrative and accounting procedures.[7]

The guidance contained in AAF 02/07 provides a framework within which third party operations provide information on transactions, operations or arrangements that have been applied in the provision of outsourced services and reporting accountants provide independent assurance reports on the third party operations.

The Regulator initially referred in its consultation to the proposed use of AAF 01/06 *Assurance reports on internal controls of service organisations made available to third parties*. In contrast, AAF 02/07 sets out high-level guidance for practitioners who provide assurance reports on services and operations provided by expert third parties.

The subject matter of the assurance reporting consists of the administrative and accounting procedures of Relevant Trustees. These procedures relate to the Relevant Trustee's own business operations for providing pensions trustee services. The subject matter for such reporting needs to be identifiable and capable of consistent measurement or evaluation against the applicable criteria. There needs to be sufficient and appropriate evidence to support an assurance conclusion. Relevant Trustees and practitioners providing assurance reports need to separately examine three aspects of administrative and accounting processes: description, design and operating effectiveness. In the first year of reporting, Relevant Trustees who are included on the Trustee Register may agree with the Regulator to limit the scope of their report to description and design only.

Suitable criteria for use by Relevant Trustees and by practitioners in evaluating the control procedures of a Relevant Trustee's administrative and accounting procedures have been developed by the ICAEW in conjunction with the Regulator in the form of illustrative control objectives which are set out in Appendix 1 of the Supplement.

---

[6] *www.thepensionsregulator.gov.uk/Trustees/assurance-reporting-framework.aspx.*

[7] *AAF 02/07 is available from www.icaew.com/~/media/Files/Technical/Audit-and-assurance/assurance/tech-release-aaf-02-07.pdf.*

The control objectives are accompanied by principles that the Regulator developed to provide the context and to facilitate consistent application of control objectives.

However, ultimate responsibility to ensure the sufficiency of the control objectives remains with Relevant Trustees and they may add further objectives and supporting control procedures where they consider it appropriate. The Relevant Trustee should be able to demonstrate why its control procedures are reasonable and proportionate given both the extent of its trustee service and the size of its overall business operations, and the extent to which their trustee appointment is undertaken alongside other trustees, as trustee appointments vary and sometimes there will be other trustees on the trustee body. The control objectives are, therefore, intended to be considered in each context. Further guidance on this is available in paragraphs 23 to 27.

Assurance reporting on relevant trustees

About this Supplement

This Relevant Trustee Supplement provides guidance on assurance reporting on **1** the Relevant Trustee's internal control procedures (control procedures). When the Relevant Trustee is intending to be included on the Regulator's Trustee Register, the Regulator uses the assurance report to help consider the Relevant Trustee's compliance with its condition that the Relevant Trustee has "sound administrative and accounting procedures in place"[8].

The guidance supplements ICAEW Technical Release AAF 02/07 A framework **2** for assurance reports on third party operations. The development of the guidance reflects discussions held between the Audit and Assurance Faculty of ICAEW and the Regulator. The Audit and Assurance Faculty will keep this Supplement under review.

AAF 02/07 provides a framework for performing assurance engagements on **3** various aspects of business relations that are under taken between organisations including outsourced services. The principles underlying the guidance are broadly applicable to Relevant Trustees. It is the Relevant Trustee who is responsible for putting in place and maintaining control procedures designed to operate "sound administrative and accounting procedures" related to Relevant Trustees' own business operations for providing pensions trustee services[9]. While this Supplement refers to specific sections of AAF 02/07, this does not replace the need to read AAF 02/07 in its entirety and apply it as appropriate.

The subject matter of the assurance reporting envisaged by this guidance may be **4** either: (a) the description and design of control procedures of the Relevant Trustee only at the point in time specified; or (b) the description and design of the control procedures at a point in time, and their operating effectiveness over a period of time. The guidance that follows generally assumes that the report will cover a period of time, but with respect to inclusion on the Trustee Register the Regulator

---

[8] *Section 23(4) of the Pensions Act 1995 and the Occupational Pension Schemes (Independent Trustee) Regulations 2005 (SI 2005/703) (the Regulations).*

[9] *Means "the work as a Trustee carried out by the applicant in relation to trust schemes", regulation 1(2) of the Regulations.*

may agree a report on control procedures at a point in time as an alternative, for example when preparing a report for the first time.

5   The Relevant Trustee Supplement consists of:

- Assurance reporting on the control procedures over administrative and accounting procedures;

- Guidance for practitioners;

- Appendix 1: Principles and related control objectives on "sound administrative and accounting procedures";

- Appendix 2: Example paragraphs from the report by the Relevant Trustee; and

- Appendix 3: Pro forma practitioner's assurance reports on the internal control procedures of the Relevant Trustee.

Assurance reporting on the control procedures over administrative and accounting procedures

The responsibility of Relevant Trustees

6   To be considered for acceptance on, or to remain on, the Trustee Register, the Regulator requires Relevant Trustees to seek an independent assurance report on their control procedures. Relevant Trustees evaluate their control procedures regarding their administrative and accounting procedures by reference to the control objectives set out for each Principle in Appendix 1 to this Supplement[10].

7   Relevant Trustees who voluntarily adopt this framework and who are not seeking to be on the Trustee Register should identify which of the control objectives set in Appendix 1 to this Supplement apply.

Assurance reporting on Relevant Trustee's administrative and accounting procedures

8   The IAASB Assurance Framework, on whose principles ISAE 3000 and AAF 02/07 are based, sets out five elements of an assurance engagement. These five elements are:

- A three party relationship;

- An appropriate subject matter;

- Suitable criteria;

- Sufficient appropriate evidence; and

- A written assurance report in the form appropriate to the type of assurance engagement.

9   Certain aspects of these elements are likely to require specific consideration in the context of this Supplement. These are three party relationship, an appropriate subject matter and suitable criteria and are discussed below.

Three party relationship

10   Assurance engagements involve three parties: a responsible party, intended users, and a practitioner.

---

[10] *Developed in 2011. For further information, see the discussion on p. 11.*

Responsible party

The responsible party performs operations or provides information for the benefit **11** of the intended user and hence is responsible for the subject matter over which assurance is sought. The responsible party is the Relevant Trustee in the context of this Supplement. Relevant Trustees are responsible for their administrative and accounting procedures.

The Relevant Trustee prepares a written report setting out its responsibilities and **12** describing the control procedures in place to support the control objectives set out in this Supplement. The report also includes the Relevant Trustee's conclusion on the description, design and, if applicable, operating effectiveness of those control procedures. When making this statement in their report, the Relevant Trustee states that it is referring to at least all of the control objectives in this guidance and whether their statement is made in connection with the Relevant Trustee's application to be on or to remain on the Trustee Register.

Example paragraphs from an illustrative Relevant Trustee's report are set out in **13** Appendix 2.

Intended users

The intended users of an assurance report are typically the recipients of services, **14** relating to assets or information of the responsible party.

For a Relevant Trustee, who is applying to be or wishes to remain on the Trustee **15** Register, the intended user is the Regulator. Those Relevant Trustees need to be aware that the control objectives and supporting control procedures are designed to assist the Regulator in assessing whether Relevant Trustees have "sound administrative and accounting procedures[11]", in relation to their own business operations for providing pensions trustee services, and communicate the fact to the practitioner. It is for this reason that the Regulator expects that the assurance report, for these purposes, covers all of the control objectives in Appendix 1.

Relevant Trustees might alternatively, or in addition, intend to allow a third party **16** (other than the Regulator) to have sight of the report or might do so at a later date. In these circumstances, the purpose of reporting by the Relevant Trustee on its control objectives and supporting control procedures may be to enhance the confidence of management over their procedures related to administrative and accounting procedures or to increase the confidence of current and possibly prospective users.

The Relevant Trustee communicates to the practitioner the purpose of its report **17** and the associated assurance reporting need.

Practitioner

The practitioner performs the assurance engagement on the Relevant Trustee's **18** reporting on their control procedures. Relevant, generic guidance for the practitioner is set out in AAF 02/07 in the section entitled *(a) Engagement with the responsible party* within *Third party operations* (paragraphs 13 – 15) and *Where the responsible party is the client* in AAF 02/07 (paragraphs 58 - 61). If using this Supplement for different purposes, practitioners consider AAF 04/06 *Assurance engagements: Management of risk and liability* to determine a suitable

---

[11] *See Background of Consultation paper, p.4.*

form of engagement accordingly. Further guidance for the practitioner is set out in the next section.

19   The intended user is the Regulator where the Relevant Trustee is going to submit a copy of the assurance report to the Regulator when it applies to be or seeks to remain on the Trustee Register. The practitioner needs to clarify if there is any additional purpose for which the assurance report is being sought, the potential party (or parties) seeking to benefit from the assurance report, and the use that may be made of the assurance report and refer to considerations set out in paragraph 15.

20   When requested to provide an assurance report to other third parties, the practitioner needs to clarify the purpose for which the assurance report is being sought, the party (or parties) seeking to benefit from the assurance report, and the use that will be made of the assurance report.

Subject matter

21   The subject matter in assurance reporting envisaged in this Supplement is the control procedures related to the Relevant Trustee's administrative and accounting procedures in relation to its own business operations for providing pensions trustee services. The Relevant Trustee prepares a written report describing the control procedures it has designed and implemented to deliver its pension trustee services for a given period (or at a given date, if applicable), having regard to appropriate criteria including the control objectives set out in this Supplement and any other control objectives deemed relevant to administrative and accounting procedures by the Relevant Trustee.

22   Not all of the Relevant Trustee's business needs be considered when evaluating whether the Relevant Trustee's control procedures meet the control objectives. It is sufficient for the control procedures (including those in place across the whole business) to be considered to the extent they are relevant to the control objectives that relate to the Relevant Trustee's own business operations for providing pensions trustee services.

23   The control objectives specified in Appendix 1 are intended to be a minimum set of control objectives for inclusion in the Relevant Trustee's report. Exceptionally, the Relevant Trustee may decide not to include a particular control objective. This could occur when the control objective and all the related control procedures are outsourced, or where administrative services of the Relevant Trustee's own business operations are outsourced. Under these circumstances the Relevant Trustee should seek to obtain an appropriate assurance report from the service organisation to which it has outsourced these services. This assurance report would form part of the evidence of the Relevant Trustee's monitoring of those outsourced activities to demonstrate that it operates "sound administrative and accounting procedures".

Criteria

24   The control objectives in Appendix 1 are considered to be suitable criteria for the evaluation of whether the Relevant Trustees have "sound administrative and accounting procedures". The practitioner will make this evaluation in so far as the procedures are relevant to the control objectives which relate to Relevant Trustee's own business operations for providing pensions trustee services.

25   Control objectives:

- need to be relevant, complete, reliable, neutral and understandable so as to communicate the basis of the evaluation;

- need to collectively reflect the level of control of the Relevant Trustee to satisfy the conditions set out in the relevant regulation for those Relevant Trustees who would like to be admitted on to the Regulator's Trustee Register; and

- are guidance only and not intended to be exhaustive and it remains the responsibility of the Relevant Trustee to ensure that the control objectives that it describes are sufficient to satisfy the conditions and to add further objectives and supporting control procedures where appropriate. If certain criteria do not apply to a Relevant Trustee, for example because the relevant activities are outsourced, the Relevant Trustee explains the omission of the criteria in the Relevant Trustee's report.

The Relevant Trustee describes control procedures for a complete set of associated **26** control objectives that are developed based on the criteria in Appendix 1. If the exceptional circumstances described in paragraphs 22 apply, the Relevant Trustee should explain the nature and reason for any omission in its report, and describe the functions and nature of the activities performed by the service organisations.

Where the Relevant Trustee does not cover all of the control objectives, the **27** practitioner will note this in the assurance report. If there are omissions or misstatements with regard to the control objectives, in particular in the report by the Relevant Trustee who wishes to be on the Trustee Register, the practitioner asks them to amend the description. If it is not amended the practitioner will need to state that fact in the assurance report.

The Relevant Trustee is responsible for providing information on specific control **28** procedures in place to meet the control objectives. Suitable control procedures will vary from Relevant Trustee to Relevant Trustee; therefore, the disclosure of how each objective is addressed by a Relevant Trustee should be unique to the Relevant Trustee.

The Relevant Trustee explains in its report and to the practitioners how its control **29** procedures relate to the control objectives for the provision of its own business operations supporting its provision of pensions trustee services. The Relevant Trustee should be able to demonstrate why its control procedures are reasonable and proportionate given both the extent of its pensions trustee services and the size of its business.

The subject matter of the independent assurance required by the Regulator is the **30** control procedures over administrative and accounting procedures as they apply to the overall business operations of each Relevant Trustee, and not the control procedures applied on a scheme by scheme basis. Furthermore, the Regulator expects that all Relevant Trustees seeking to go on the Trustee Register have procedures designed and documented to address each of the control objectives.

It is possible that in some cases the Relevant Trustee may not have previously **31** documented the procedures to meet certain control objectives because there has never been an occasion to put them into practice. For example, it is easy to see the necessity for procedures to support control objective 6 (a documented policy for identifying, managing and monitoring actual, potential and perceived conflicts of interest for those appointments) where the Relevant Trustee is solely responsible for managing conflicts. However, if the Relevant Trustee is appointed as one of a number of trustees, it is unlikely that they will be acting alone in the management of conflicts. Due to the absence of a need, the Relevant Trustee with no sole appointments, therefore, might never have reason or opportunity to draft its own documented procedures for the management of conflicts. Notwithstanding this, the Regulator requires, for the purposes of being on the Trustee Register, that the Relevant Trustee still design and document procedures to meet all of the control objectives. This applies even in situations where a Relevant Trustee might not have previously needed or currently need to put procedures in place to meet these control objectives.

32   By contrast, if a Relevant Trustee is an individual operating as a sole practitioner it may be necessary to set up mutual support arrangements with others offering pensions trustee services in order to comply with all of the control objectives listed in Appendix 1. Further guidance on the control objectives can be found on the Regulator's website.[12]

Other information provided by Relevant Trustees

33   Relevant Trustees may include in their report information that is not a part of the description of control objectives and procedures that relate to "sound administrative and accounting procedures" and relate to Relevant Trustees' own business operations for providing pensions trustee services. If Relevant Trustees include other information, they should make it clear that this information would be outside the scope of assurance reporting unless there is a specific agreement with the practitioners in the engagement letter that it should be included.

Evidence gathering

34   Where the practitioners are unable to test a described control procedure because, for example, it has not operated during the year, they state the fact that no tests have been carried out and the reason in their description of tests.

35   In some cases (as mentioned above), for example in the first year of implementation, it may be appropriate that the scope of the assurance report by the practitioners may cover only the description and design of the procedures of the Relevant Trustees at the point in time specified. An example of such a report is available in Appendix 3(b).

Guidance for practitioners

36   Practitioners refer to the principles set out in AAF 02/07. The role of practitioners in the assurance reporting framework envisaged in AAF 02/07 is set out in paragraphs 29 to 32.

37   Practitioners refer to the section entitled *Guidance for practitioners* (paragraphs 46 to 105) and apply them as appropriate to the engagement. In particular, practitioners understand and agree the scope and purpose of the assurance engagement between the parties to the engagement as set out in the sub-section entitled *Agreeing the terms of engagement*, and in doing so refer to AAF 04/06 *Assurance engagements: Management of risk and liability* discussed in paragraph 57 of AAF 02/07.

38   Practitioners note that they are governed by ethical and quality control requirements as set out in paragraphs 51 to 56.

Assurance report

39   Practitioners conclude on the fairness of the description and the design and, where applicable, operating effectiveness of control procedures in relation to a specified

---

[12]   *www.thepensionsregulator.gov.uk/trustees/assurance-reporting-framework.aspx*

reporting period. The practitioner's conclusion is expressed in a written assurance report attached to the Relevant Trustee's report.

The assurance report reflects the agreement set out in the engagement letter. The **40** report makes it clear for whom it is prepared and who is entitled to rely upon it and for what purpose as established in accordance with AAF 04/06.

Control procedures have inherent limitations and accordingly errors and **41** irregularities may occur and not be detected. Also control procedures cannot guarantee protection against fraudulent collusion especially on the part of those holding position of authority or trust. Practitioners refer to such inherent limitations in their report.

Pro-forma practitioners' assurance reports on the internal control procedures of **42** Relevant Trustees is available in Appendices 3(a) and (b).

Reporting on description misstatements, design deficiencies or when control procedures are not operating effectively

Practitioners discuss with the Relevant Trustee when they become aware that the **43** control objectives in place are not in accordance with those set out in paragraph 24 so that the Relevant Trustee may amend the description to include the specified control objective(s). If the Relevant Trustee does not to do so the practitioners add an explanation in the assurance report identifying the omitted or inappropriate control objective(s) to draw the attention of the relevant users. In addition, the wording of the conclusion paragraph may also be modified.

Although practitioners may qualify their conclusion on the fairness of the **44** description of control procedures, this does not necessarily affect the suitability of design or, where applicable, operating effectiveness of the control procedures because the practitioners' conclusion relates only to the control objectives that are included in the Relevant Trustee's description. Practitioners note that it is the responsibility of the Relevant Trustee and not the practitioners to ensure the completeness and the reasonableness of control procedures over the "sound administrative and accounting procedures."

Where control procedures associated with stated control objectives are incomplete **45** or inappropriate, practitioners also discuss this with the Relevant Trustee so that the Relevant Trustee may amend the description to include the associated control procedures. If the Relevant Trustee does not amend the description, the practitioners add an explanatory paragraph preceding the conclusion to the report identifying the omitted or inappropriate control procedures to draw the attention of the users of the report. In addition, the wording of the conclusion paragraph may be modified.

Where practitioners conclude that a set of control procedures are not suitably **46** designed in relation to a specified control objective, they consider the design deficiencies in their overall assessment of the control procedures. If the practitioners determine that control procedures are not suitably designed to achieve a specified control objective, they add an explanatory paragraph preceding the conclusion to the report identifying the design deficiencies and modify the conclusion.

Where practitioners' tests identify exceptions to the operating effectiveness of the **47** control procedures, they consider whether this exception means that a control objective has not been achieved. In some cases deficiencies may be so pervasive that the practitioners modify their conclusion on the achievement of one or more control objective or issue an adverse opinion.

48   Where significant changes are introduced during the period covered in the report, the Relevant Trustee reports this fact. If practitioners become aware that the description on changes is missing, they request the Relevant Trustees to amend the description. However, the omission of information related to changes in the Relevant Trustee's control procedure does not warrant a qualification of the conclusion on the fairness of the description, provided that the Relevant Trustee's description of control procedures is fair as at the date of the description.

49   To ensure clarity for readers, when adding an explanation or modifying the assurance conclusion, practitioners should consider the context of the assurance report and the impression given by any additional information provided by the Relevant Trustee in its own report (additional information not covered by the assurance report, as discussed in paragraph 32).

Appendix 1 – Principles and related control objectives on "sound administrative and accounting procedures"

This Appendix sets out detailed control objectives for Relevant Trustees referred to in paragraph 6 which relate to the Relevant Trustees own business operations for providing pension trustee services.

Control objectives are accompanied by principles. These principles were developed by the Regulator for the purpose of providing the context and facilitating the application of control objectives in the light of "sound administrative and accounting procedures" in individual circumstances.

These control objectives are not intended to be exhaustive, and it remains the responsibility of the Relevant Trustee to ensure that the described control objectives (including any additional objectives used) are sufficient to meet the requirement to have "sound administrative and accounting procedures."

The Relevant Trustee's control procedures should be evaluated against the control objectives to the extent that the Relevant Trustee considers that they are relevant to their provision of pension trustee services. The scope of assurance reporting is determined accordingly.

A. ACCEPTING BUSINESS	**(i) Principle:** The Relevant Trustee ensures adequate processes are in place to assess the suitability of new engagements prior to taking on new business. This would include a recorded assessment and evaluation of key risks associated with new engagements including the ability of the Relevant Trustee to competently service this new work and fulfil statutory duties.
Control objective	1. Prior to accepting a new trustee appointment the risks associated with the appointment are identified, recorded, and assessed having regard to the issues facing the pension scheme, which is the subject of the appointment, given its size and complexity.
	(ii) Principle: The Relevant Trustee is able to demonstrate that they have sufficient knowledge and skills to ensure that, upon appointment, the scheme is administered in accordance with the Trust Deed and Rules and other regulatory requirements.
Control objective	2. Trustee appointments are accepted where the Relevant Trustee has identified and concluded that it has the sufficient level of knowledge and skill required for the trustee appointment, and has documented the steps taken in reaching that conclusion. Continuing suitability of all trustee appointments are monitored.
B. KEY INDIVIDUALS	**(iii) Principle:** The Relevant Trustee maintains adequate procedures to ensure that roles, responsibilities and duties of Key Individuals are documented and their ongoing performance is subject to periodic quality reviews.
Control objective	3. Roles, responsibilities and duties of Key Individuals are documented and subject to ongoing performance review.

4. Business decisions are identified, evaluated, managed and monitored. They are recorded, properly authorised and reviewed by someone other than the decision-maker. This review is recorded.

(iv) Principle: The Relevant Trustee maintains adequate procedures for identifying, monitoring and managing conflicts of interest that could affect decision-making or any potential trustee appointments.

Control objective   5. Business conflicts of interest are identified, recorded and addressed in accordance with a defined policy.

6. The Relevant Trustee has a documented procedure for trustee appointments, which includes a documented policy for identifying, managing and monitoring actual, potential and perceived conflicts of interest for those appointments.

(v) Principle: The Relevant Trustee develops and maintains adequate arrangements to minimise disruption in the event that a Key Individual is not able to fulfil his/her role due to periods of absence.

Control objective   7. Documented contingency plans are in place and are implemented should a Key Individual be absent.

(vi) Principle: The Relevant Trustee maintains adequate procedures, including management information systems, for capturing and reporting information which must be notified to the Regulator.

Control objective   8. Notifications to the Regulator, including changes to Key Individuals, and periodic information returns are accurately compiled and submitted on a timely basis.

(vii) Principle: The Relevant Trustee maintains adequate procedures for maintaining pensions knowledge and managing training requirements.

Control objective   9. Training is conducted and training records are maintained for Key Individuals (as well as those providing services with respect to trustee appointments) in accordance with a documented training policy.

C. ADMINISTRA-   **(viii) Principle:** The Relevant Trustee has a formal process for
TIVE AND   selecting and appointing its own legal advisers and other
ACCOUNTING   professional service providers and a suitable set of criteria to
assist the appointment process.

Control objective   10. The appointment of legal advisers and other professional service providers by the Relevant Trustee is subject to a documented approach including selection criteria and an authorisation process.

(ix) Principle: The Relevant Trustee maintains a formal process for monitoring all advisers which must include an ongoing assessment of the quality of legal advice and other professional services provided.

Control objective 11. The Relevant Trustee has a documented procedure for trustee appointments to monitor on an annual basis legal adviser's and other professional service providers' performance and compliance with contractual terms.

12. The Relevant Trustee has a documented procedure with respect to trustee appointments for monitoring investment performance annually, having regard to the Statement of Investment Principles and investment mandates.

(x) Principle: The Relevant Trustee maintains adequate financial management controls which ensure proper books and records are maintained and kept up-to-date.

Control objective 13. Fees charged by legal advisors and other professional service providers to the Relevant Trustee and fees charged by the Relevant Trustee to clients with respect to scheme appointments are accurately calculated in accordance with the terms of appointment, suitably authorised and recorded on a timely basis.

14. The Relevant Trustee has a documented procedure for trustee appointments to obtain scheme accounts (or other forms of summarised financial information) for the pension schemes from service providers on a regular basis in a timely manner.

15. The Relevant Trustee's own records relating to the provision of trustee related services are accurately maintained and kept up-to-date.

(xi) Principle: The Relevant Trustee maintains adequate financial management controls to segregate client assets and assets of Relevant Trustee's own business. All business transactions are subject to authorisation procedures and these are clearly documented.

Control objective 16. Cash and other assets held by, or on behalf of, the Relevant Trustee in respect of trustee appointments are segregated and safeguarded. Payments and receipts are suitably authorised, controlled, and recorded on a timely basis.

(xii) Principle: The Relevant Trustee ensures that arrangements are in place for formally recording minutes of all formal meetings held by the Relevant Trustee.

Control objective 17. Minutes or other written records are maintained for all key business meetings and decisions taken by the Relevant Trustee.

D. RISK MANAGEMENT **(xiii) Principle:** The Relevant Trustee maintains a risk management framework to manage and record business risks and this is subject to ongoing review and assessment (at least annually).

Control objective 18. A review of risks which do or could impact on the Relevant Trustee's own business operations and trustee appointments is undertaken periodically (and at least annually). Risks are identified and evaluated and recorded in a risk register together with internal controls and mitigations identified by the Relevant Trustee.

(xiv) Principle: The Relevant Trustee maintains a documented process for authorising and supervising delegations.

Control objective   19. Delegations (including roles and responsibilities) within the Relevant Trustee's own business are clearly documented, authorised, and monitored.

(xv) Principle: The Relevant Trustee maintains adequate systems and controls to help identify, manage and correct financial and compliance errors on a timely basis.

Control objective   20. Financial and compliance errors in the business are corrected promptly and a formal record and memorandum of the event is retained.

E. INFORMATION TECHNOLOGY   **(xvi) Principle:** The Relevant Trustee maintains adequate controls which help ensure the integrity and security of its computerised information systems and databases.

Control objective   21. Computerised information systems have restricted physical and logical access including appropriate measures to counter the threat from malicious electronic attack (e.g. firewalls, anti-virus etc).

22. Maintenance and development of systems, applications and software is authorised, tested, approved and implemented.

23. Data and systems are backed up regularly and business and information recovery plans are documented, approved and maintained.

Appendix 2 – Example paragraphs from the report by the Relevant Trustee

The following text contains example paragraphs from an illustrative Relevant Trustee's report.

As [name of Relevant Trustee], we are responsible for:

- the identification of control objectives to be applied for the purpose of demonstrating "sound administrative and accounting procedures" relating to Relevant Trustee's own business operations for providing pensions trustee services **[for those Relevant Trustees who wish to apply/remain on the Trustee Register]** and in connection with its application to be on/to remain on the Pensions Regulator's Trustee Register (under section 23(4) of the Pensions Act 1995)];

- the design, implementation [and operation[13]] of the control procedures of [name of Relevant Trustee] to provide reasonable assurance that the control objectives identified in pages [ ] to [ ] are achieved.

The control objectives identified include/do not include all of those control objectives listed in Appendix 1 of the Relevant Trustee supplement. [*where applicable* We explain on pages [ ] to [ ] the reasons for not identifying all those control objectives listed in that appendix.]

In carrying out those responsibilities, we have regard to the requirements of the business and the general effectiveness and efficiency of the relevant operations.

We have evaluated the effectiveness of the [name of Relevant Trustee]'s control procedures having regard to ICAEW's Technical Release AAF 02/07 including its Relevant Trustee supplement and the criteria set out therein.

We set out on pages [ ] to [ ] in this report a description of the relevant control procedures together with the related control objectives which operated during the period [x] to [y] and confirm that:

(a) the report describes fairly the control procedures that relate to the control objectives referred to above which were in place [during the period [x] to [y]/[as at [date]];

(b) the control procedures described were suitably designed throughout the period [x] to [y] such that there is reasonable assurance that the specified control objectives would be achieved if the described control procedures were complied with satisfactorily; and

[*where applicable – see paragraph 4*

(c) the control procedures described were operating with sufficient effectiveness to provide reasonable assurance that the related control objectives were achieved during the specified period.]

Director

Date

Signed on behalf of [name of Relevant Trustee]

---

[13] *Applicable where operating effectiveness of control procedures are within the scope of assurance reporting.*

Appendix 3 – A pro forma practitioner's assurance report on the internal control procedures of Relevant Trustees

Practitioners issue an assurance report in a form suitable for the specific engagement. The report below is adapted from a pro forma assurance report (ii)(a) Appendix 2 of AAF 02/07 for the purpose of reporting in relation to the Relevant Trustee's control objectives related to their "sound administrative and accounting procedures" as set out in the Relevant Trustee's report in appendix 2 of this Supplement.

a. Assurance report that covers description, design and operating effectiveness of specified control procedures

Independent practitioners' assurance report on the internal control procedures of [name of Relevant Trustee]

To xxxxx (See AAF 02/07 for wording)

Use of Report

(Example wordings to describe applicable restrictions on the use of the report, together with supporting guidance on alternative forms of engagement and associated duties of care arising, are set out in AAF 02/07. However, restrictions should not exclude the Regulator's use of the report as support to the Relevant Trustee's application to be on, or remain on, the Trustee Register).

Scope

We have been engaged to report on the description and design, as at [date], and operating effectiveness of [name of Relevant Trustee]'s control procedures designed to achieve the control objectives throughout the period [date] to [date] as set out on pages [ ] to [ ] of your report.

Relevant Trustee's responsibilities

[Name of Relevant Trustee]'s responsibilities and assertions are set out on page [ ] of your report.

Our responsibilities

Our responsibility is to form an independent opinion, based on the work carried out in relation to the control procedures of [name of Relevant Trustee]'s as described in your report and report this to [name of Relevant Trustee].

We conducted our engagement in accordance with International Standard on Assurance Engagements (ISAE) 3000 and with ICAEW Technical Release AAF 02/07 including its Relevant Trustee Supplement. ISAE 3000 and AAF 02/07 require, among other things, that we comply with ethical and other professional requirements and plan and perform our procedures to obtain reasonable assurance about whether, in all material respects, [name of Relevant Trustee]'s report fairly describes the relevant control procedures and the control procedures are suitably designed and operating effectively. The criteria against which the control procedures were evaluated are the control objectives developed for Relevant Trustees as set out within the Relevant Trustee Supplement to AAF 02/07 and identified by the Relevant Trustee as control objectives to be applied for the purpose of demonstrating "sound administrative and accounting procedures".

Our work involved performing procedures to obtain evidence about the presentation of the Relevant Trustee's description of its Relevant Trustee services, and the design and operating effectiveness of the control procedures. Our procedures include assessing the risks that the description is not fairly presented, and that the control procedures were not suitably designed or operating effectively.

Our procedures included testing the operating effectiveness of those control procedures identified by [name of Relevant Trustee] as relevant, reasonable and proportionate in relation to its pensions trustee services and necessary to obtain reasonable assurance that the control objectives stated in the description were achieved. The nature, timing and extent of the tests we applied are detailed on pages [ ] to [ ] of the report.

An assurance engagement of this type also included evaluating the overall presentation of the description, and the suitability of the objectives stated therein.

Inherent limitations

[Control procedures designed to address specified control objectives are subject to inherent limitations and accordingly because of their nature, control procedures at [name of Relevant Trustee]'s may not prevent or detect and correct all errors or omissions in performing administrative and accounting procedures. Control procedures cannot guarantee protection against (among other things) fraudulent collusion especially on the part of those holding positions of authority or trust.

Our opinion is based on historical information. The projection of any evaluation of the fairness of the presentation of the description, or opinion about the suitability of the design or operating effectiveness of the control procedures to future periods would be inappropriate.

Opinion

In our opinion, in all material respects:

(i)   the accompanying Relevant Trustee's report describes fairly the control procedures that relate to the control objectives referred to above which were in place [during the period [x] to [y] on pages [ ] to [ ] The control objectives identified [include / do not include] all of those control objectives listed in Appendix 1 of the Relevant Trustee supplement to AAF 02/07;

(ii)   the control procedures described on pages [ ] to [ ] were suitably designed such that there is reasonable, but not absolute, assurance that the specified control objectives would have been achieved if the described control procedures were complied with satisfactorily; and

(iii) the control procedures that were tested, as set out in the attachment to this report, were operating with sufficient effectiveness for us to obtain reasonable, but not absolute, assurance that the related control objectives were achieved in the period [x] to [y].

[Name of firm]

Chartered accountants

[Location]

[Date]

b. Assurance report that covers description and design of specified control procedures

Independent practitioner's assurance report on the internal control procedures of [name of Relevant Trustee]

To xxxxx (See AAF 02/07 for wording)

Use of Report

(Example wordings to describe applicable restrictions on the use of the report, together with supporting guidance on alternative forms of engagement and associated duties of care arising, are set out in AAF 02/07. However, restrictions should not exclude the Regulator's use of the report as support to the Relevant Trustee's application to be on, or remain on, the Trustee Register).

Scope

We have been engaged to report on the description and design, as at [date], of [name of Relevant Trustee]'s control procedures designed to achieve the control objectives throughout the period [date] to [date] as set out on pages [ ] to [ ] of your report.

Relevant Trustee's responsibilities

[Name of Relevant Trustee]'s responsibilities and assertions are set out on page [ ] of your report.

Our responsibilities

Our responsibility is to form an independent opinion, based on the work carried out in relation to the control procedures of [name of Relevant Trustee]s as described in your report and report this to [name of Relevant Trustee].

We conducted our engagement in accordance with International Standard on Assurance Engagements (ISAE) 3000 and with ICAEW Technical Release AAF 02/07 including its Relevant Trustee Supplement. ISAE 3000 and AAF 02/07 require, among other things, that we comply with ethical and other professional requirements and plan and perform our procedures to obtain reasonable assurance about whether, in all material respects, the [name of Relevant Trustee]'s report fairly describes the relevant control procedures and the control procedures are suitably designed. The criteria against which the control procedures were evaluated are the control objectives developed for Relevant Trustees as set out within the Relevant Trustee Supplement to AAF 02/07 and identified by the Relevant Trustee as control objectives to be applied for the purpose of demonstrating "sound administrative and accounting procedures".

Our work involved performing procedures to obtain evidence about the presentation of the Relevant Trustee's description of its Relevant Trustee services, and the design of the control procedures. Our procedures include assessing the risks that the description is not fairly presented, and that the controls procedures were not suitably designed.

Inherent limitations

Control procedures designed to address specified control objectives are subject to inherent limitations and accordingly, because of their nature, control procedures at [name of Relevant Trustee]'s may not prevent or detect and correct all errors or omissions in performing administrative and accounting procedures. Control procedures cannot guarantee protection against (among other things) fraudulent collusion especially on the part of those holding positions of authority or trust.

Our opinion is based on historical information. The projection of any evaluation of the fairness of the presentation of the description, or opinion about the suitability of the design of the control procedures to future periods would be inappropriate.

Opinion

In our opinion, in all material respects:

(i) the accompanying Relevant Trustee's report describes fairly the control procedures that relate to the control objectives referred to above which were in place as at [date] on pages [ ] to [ ] The control objectives identified [include/do not include] all of those control objectives listed in Appendix 1 of the Relevant Trustee supplement to AAF 02/07;

(ii) the control procedures described on pages [ ] to [ ] were suitably designed such that there is reasonable, but not absolute, assurance that the specified control objectives would have been achieved if the described control procedures were complied with satisfactorily.

[Name of firm]

Chartered accountants

[Location]

[Date]

GLOSSARY

Term	Definition
Key Individuals	1. Individuals within the Relevant Trustee who have overall management responsibility for the pensions trustee services conducted by the applicant;
	2. director, member of the committee of management, chief executive, designated member in relation to a limited liability partnership, partner or controller who has significant influence over the management of the Relevant Trustee's work;
	3. any person whose signature may authorise, in part or in full, a transaction involving the assets of any scheme for which the applicant acts as trustee;
	4. Key Person; or
	5. Officer.
Key Persons	An individual as defined under regulation 1(2) of the Occupational Pension Schemes (Independent Trustee) Regulations 2005 (SI 2005703)
Officers	An individual as defined under regulation 1(2) of the Occupational Pension Schemes (Independent Trustee) Regulations 2005 (SI 2005703)
Regulator	The Pensions Regulator as established under section 1 of the Pensions Act 2004.

Relevant Trustee	An entity that, as part of its business, as a trustee offers pensions trustee services in relation to trust schemes and who either is on the Relevant Trustee Register or adopts this framework voluntarily.
Trustee Register	Register of trustees held by the Regulator.

TECH 07/13BL Exemption from Audit by Parent Guarantee

(June 2013)

Contents

Paragraphs

Introduction

Guidance

Q1 When does the new exemption become available? — 1.1 - 1.2
Q2 When do the formalities for obtaining the exemption need to be completed? — 2.1
Q3 Are any companies ineligible to use the exemption? — 3.1 - 3.4
Q4 What are the conditions for exemption? — 4.1
Q5 What are the formalities for members agreeing on use of the exemption? — 5.1 - 5.6
Q6 What are the requirements in relation to the parent? — 6.1 - 6.5
Q7 What are the requirements for filing the written notice of agreement? — 7.1
Q8 What does a subsidiary using the audit exemption need to disclose in its own accounts? — 8.1 - 8.2
Q9 How is the guarantee given? — 9.1
Q10 What are the requirements for the statement referred to in s479C? — 10.1 - 10.2
Q11 What is the effect of the guarantee? — 11.1 - 11.2
Q12 What is the scope of "outstanding liabilities" covered by the guarantee? — 12.1
Q13 Will the guarantee be enforceable against an overseas parent undertaking? — 13.1
Q14 What is the effect of a change of ownership of the company after a guarantee has been given? — 14.1 - 14.2
Q15 Does the guarantee fall away if the company later decides to have an audit for the year in question? — 15.1
Q16 Are there any special considerations for charities? — 16.1 - 16.4
Q17 Do the accounts of the subsidiary still have to be prepared and filed at Companies House? — 17.1 - 17.3
Q18 For a company with a premium listing in the UK, could entering into a guarantee require shareholder approval as a class 1 transaction? — 18.1 - 18.2

ABOUT ICAEW

ICAEW is a professional membership organisation, supporting over 140,000 chartered accountants around the world. Through our technical knowledge, skills and expertise, we provide insight and leadership to the global accountancy and finance profession.

Our members provide financial knowledge and guidance based on the highest professional, technical and ethical standards. We develop and support individuals, organisations and communities to help them achieve long-term, sustainable economic value.

This guidance has been prepared by the Company Law Subcommittee of the ICAEW Business Law Committee, which includes representatives from public practice and the business community. The Committee is responsible for ICAEW policy on business law issues and related submissions to legislators, regulators and other external bodies. The guidance reflects consultation with the Audit and Assurance Faculty, which is responsible for technical audit and assurance submissions on behalf of ICAEW as a whole.

ISBN 978-0-85760-927-4

Introduction

This Technical Release provides guidance on the exemption from audit under s479A-479C of the Companies Act 2006 (the Act) for companies. Equivalent provisions are in place for LLPs.

The guidance is concerned with the requirements for obtaining the exemption and its effect. The guidance provides no advice or recommendations as to the use of the exemption. Directors of parent undertakings should weigh up the benefits of using the exemption compared with the costs of giving that guarantee, in particular the risk that the guarantee may be called upon. They may wish to take their own legal advice based on the specific facts and circumstances. Some subsidiaries will require audits for contractual or regulatory reasons.

Counsel has confirmed that the guidance is consistent with English law at 1 June 2013. Counsel accepts no responsibility (other than to the Institute) in relation to this guidance.

Guidance

Q1 When does the new exemption become available?

The amendments to the Act which introduce the exemption are made by The Companies and Limited Liability Partnerships (Accounts and Audit Exemptions and Change of Accounting Framework) Regulations 2012 (SI 2012/2301). They apply to accounts for financial years ending on or after 1 October 2012. **1.1**

A company with an accounting reference period ending on 30 September 2012 can use the seven day flexibility in s390(3) so that its financial year ends on or after 1 October 2012. A company with an accounting reference period ending up to six months earlier may be able to extend its accounting reference period in accordance with s392 to qualify for the exemption. **1.2**

Q2 When do the formalities for obtaining the exemption need to be completed?

The formalities for obtaining the exemption do not need to be completed before the subsidiary's year end and need only be completed before the subsidiary's accounts are filed. However, the consolidated accounts of the parent providing the guarantee must refer to the guarantee being given and the name of the subsidiary and this may impose an earlier effective deadline. In practice, a decision would have to be made early enough to be taken into account when planning whether to carry out a statutory audit or only the work needed to support the audit of the parent's consolidated accounts. **2.1**

Q3 Are any companies ineligible to use the exemption?

In accordance with s479B, a company is not entitled to the exemption conferred by s479A if it was at any time within the financial year in question: **3.1**

● a quoted company as defined in s385(2) of the Act;

● a company that is an authorised insurance company as defined in s1165(2) of the Act;

● a banking company as defined in s1164(2) of the Act;

● an e-money issuer as defined in s474(1) of the Act

- a MiFID investment firm as defined in s474(1) of the Act;
- a UCITS management company as defined in s474(1); or
- a company that carries on insurance market activity as defined in s1165(7) of the Act; or is
- a special register body as defined in section 117(1) of the Trade Union and Labour Relations (Consolidation) Act 1992; or
- an employers' association as defined in section 122 of that Act or Article 4 of the Industrial Relations (Northern Ireland) Order 1992.

3.2   There is no limit on the size of a company for the purposes of the exemption. A subsidiary within a small group or a dormant subsidiary may qualify for exemption from audit under other provisions without the need for a parent guarantee.

3.3   The restrictions listed above refer to the status of the subsidiary company seeking to use the exemption. There is no concept of an "ineligible group" (ie the fact that the company's parent undertaking or fellow subsidiary is a quoted company or an authorised insurance company does not affect the company's own eligibility for the exemption).

3.4   A quoted company principally means one with equity share capital listed on the main market of the London Stock Exchange, officially listed in an EEA state or traded on the New York Stock Exchange or NASDAQ. It does not include a company traded on AIM although such a company would in practice require an audit to comply with AIM rule 19.

Q4 What are the conditions for exemption?

4.1   Under s479A, a company is exempt from the requirements of the Act relating to audit of its individual accounts (but not any group accounts) for a financial year if:

- it is itself a subsidiary undertaking;
- its parent undertaking is established under the law of an EEA state (see 6.1 below);
- all of the members of the company agree to the exemption in respect of the financial year in question (see 5.1 to 5.6 below);
- the parent undertaking gives a guarantee under section 479C in respect of that year (see 9.1 to 10.2 below);
- the company is included in the consolidated accounts drawn up for that year or to an earlier date in that year by the parent undertaking in accordance with the provisions of the Seventh EU Company Law Directive or EU-adopted IFRSs (see 6.2 and 6.3 below);
- the parent undertaking discloses in the notes to the consolidated accounts that the company is exempt from the requirements of the Act relating to the audit of individual accounts by virtue of s479A (see 6.4 and 6.5 below); and
- the directors of the company deliver to the registrar on or before the date that they file the accounts for that year:
  - a written notice of the agreement by members of the company in accordance with s479A(2)(a) (see 7.1 below);
  - the statement (of guarantee) referred to in s479C (see 10.1 and 10.2 below);

- a copy of the consolidated accounts of the parent which has provided the guarantee;
- a copy of the auditor's report on those accounts; and
- a copy of the consolidated annual report (ie directors' report) drawn up by the parent undertaking.

Q5 What are the formalities for members agreeing on use of the exemption?

The members of the subsidiary must consent unanimously. Members will include the immediate parent undertaking which may not be the company that is providing the guarantee. **5.1**

Separate consent will need to be given for each year the exemption is used. This is because, first, the Act is clear that consent must be specific to the financial year in question. Furthermore, it would not be advisable for members to consent in relation to future financial years. This is because the exemption is from an obligation (to have an audit) arising each financial year and so to give consent in advance of a financial year, on a prospective basis, might give rise to a claim of invalidity. **5.2**

There is no reason why a single document cannot evidence consent by a parent in relation to multiple subsidiaries. However, separate copies of the document should be filed at Companies House for each subsidiary claiming the exemption. **5.3**

The requirement for consent of all of the members of the company– being the legal holders of its shares (ie, those who have agreed to become a member and have been entered into the register of members, s112 Companies Act 2006) – and so this includes holders of preference shares or non-voting shares. It will also include any shares that are presented as liabilities for financial reporting purposes. What matters is the legal status of the shares and of their holders as members. **5.4**

There is no prescribed form in which consent must be given but the company will need evidence that consent was obtained. A written resolution signed by all the members would be satisfactory but is not the only way in which consent may be evidenced. **5.5**

There is no facility in the Act for a member to withdraw consent for a particular financial year once it has been given. However, the exemption is subject to the requirements of s476, which allows members holding 10 per cent of any class of shares to require an audit by giving notice to the company at least one month before the end of the financial year in question. This could be used by one or more members in effect to "withdraw their consent". **5.6**

Q6 What are the requirements in relation to the parent?

The parent undertaking providing the guarantee must be established under the law of an EEA state. The EEA comprises all Member States of the EU plus Norway, Iceland and Liechtenstein. The Channel Islands and the Isle of Man are not part of the EEA. The guarantee does not have to be provided by the ultimate parent undertaking and could be provided by an intermediate parent undertaking although that parent undertaking would have to prepare consolidated accounts. **6.1**

The consolidated accounts must be drawn up under EU-adopted IFRSs or in accordance with the provisions of the EU Seventh Company Law Directive. The national GAAP of any Member State would be acceptable for this purpose. **6.2**

6.3   If the parent's accounts are not in English (or Welsh for a non-traded Welsh company) a certified translation must be filed (see regulations issued under s1105(2)(d)).

6.4   The notes to the consolidated accounts of the parent undertaking must disclose that the company (ie the subsidiary) is exempt from the requirements of the Act relating to the audit of individual accounts. It is therefore necessary to state the name of each subsidiary for which a guarantee has been given even if the list would be very long. For a UK incorporated parent company, the concession granted by s410 where compliance with s409 would result in information of excessive length (which permits most disclosures about subsidiary undertakings to be restricted to "principal subsidiaries" and for full details to be attached to the annual return) does not apply for the purposes of s479A.

6.5   Companies House guidance booklet GP2 states that the parent's consolidated accounts should show the subsidiary companies' names and registered numbers in a prominent place. This could be done by adding a column for the registered number to the listing of subsidiary companies.

Q7 What are the requirements for filing the written notice of agreement?

7.1   There is no prescribed form for the written notice of agreement by the members of the company (see 5.1 to 5.6 above). Companies House guidance booklet GP2 states that the notice of agreement by members must show the subsidiary company's name and registered number in a prominent place.

Q8 What does a subsidiary using the audit exemption need to disclose in its own accounts?

8.1   The exemption has effect subject to s475(2) and (3) (requirements as to statements contained in balance sheet).

8.2   Companies House guidance booklet GP2 includes example wording for the subsidiary taking the exemption to include in its balance sheet which is as follows:

> For the year ending ....(dd/mm/yyyy) the company was entitled to exemption from audit under section 479A of the Companies Act 2006 relating to subsidiary companies.
>
> Directors' responsibilities:
>
> - the members have not required the company to obtain an audit of its accounts for the year in question in accordance with section 476;
>
> - the directors acknowledge their responsibilities for complying with the requirements of the Act with respect to accounting records and the preparation of accounts.

Q9 How is the guarantee given?

9.1   The guarantee is effected by delivering the s479C statement to Companies House. The guarantee is created by the operation of s479C rather than by contract. No contract is required between the parent giving the guarantee and the parties who benefit from the guarantee.

Q10 What are the requirements for the statement referred to in s479C?

10.1   A guarantee is given by a parent undertaking under s479C when the directors of the subsidiary company deliver to the registrar a statement by the parent undertaking that it guarantees the subsidiary company under s479C. The statement must be authenticated by the parent and must specify:

- the name of the parent undertaking
- if the parent undertaking is incorporated in the United Kingdom, its registered number (if any);
- if the parent undertaking is incorporated outside the United Kingdom and registered in the country in which it is incorporated, the identity of the register on which it is registered and the number with which it is so registered;
- the name and registered number of the subsidiary company in respect of which the guarantee is being given;
- the date of the statement; and
- the financial year to which the guarantee relates.

The requirement for a statement referred to in s479C will be met by filing a correctly completed Form AA06 with the registrar. Form AA06 indicates that it must be authenticated by being signed on behalf of the parent undertaking rather than merely indicating the name of the parent undertaking.   **10.2**

Q11 What is the effect of the guarantee?

A guarantee given under s479C has the effect that: **11.1**

- the parent undertaking guarantees all outstanding liabilities to which the subsidiary company is subject at the end of the financial year to which the guarantee relates, until they are satisfied in full; and
- the guarantee is enforceable against the parent undertaking by any person to whom the subsidiary is liable in respect of those liabilities.

Where the guaranteed liability is an amount outstanding on an account that may be partially repaid and redrawn several times after the year end ("churned"), such as a bank facility, there is case law[1] that the balance would be considered discharged when: **11.2**

- in the absence both of specific direction for appropriation by the debtor and of any contrary intention,
- monies repaid on the account are presumed to discharge the earliest debits on the account (ie first in, first out).

Q12 What is the scope of "outstanding liabilities" covered by the guarantee?

The question of scope is one of law and not accounting. Having sought legal advice, the position at law is uncertain. Whilst the obvious source of meaning for "liabilities" is insolvency law, which brings in all types of pecuniary obligation, including contingent and prospective liabilities (eg, respectively, a litigation and future rentals on a lease), it is uncertain whether and, if so, to what extent a court would restrict the set of guaranteed liabilities as a result of the reference to "*outstanding* liabilities". Ultimately these uncertainties would be resolved if one or more cases come before the courts. In the meantime, it would be prudent for companies that are contemplating the giving of such a guarantee to establish the population of the relevant subsidiaries' liabilities, including contingent and   **12.1**

---

[1] *Clayton's case [Devaynes v Noble **(1816)** 1 Mer 572]*

prospective liabilities since it is possible that they may be exposed to some or all of them.

Q13 Will the guarantee be enforceable against an overseas parent undertaking?

13.1   In a consultation on the proposed audit exemption in October 2011, BIS stated the following at paragraph 68:

> The Government is satisfied that guarantees will be enforceable. Where an elective parent is formed under the laws of another EU Member State, under the provisions of the European Convention on Jurisdiction and Enforcement of Judgements in Civil and Commercial Matters, an English or Scottish court has jurisdiction to hear a claim by a creditor of a British elective subsidiary against a parent incorporated elsewhere in the EU which has given a guarantee. If a creditor obtains a judgement in his favour in an English or Scottish court under the terms of the guarantee, then under the Convention, a court elsewhere in the EU should recognise that judgment.

Q14 What is the effect of a change of ownership of the company after a guarantee has been given?

14.1   The guarantee remains in force until the liabilities in question are settled in full. There is no provision to revoke the guarantee or novate it to another party. If a parent undertaking disposes of a subsidiary for which a guarantee has been given, it will remain liable under that guarantee until all the liabilities have been settled. It could seek an indemnity from the purchaser of the subsidiary but would remain liable to the creditors of the former subsidiary.

14.2   If the new parent also entered into a guarantee under s479C for a subsequent financial year and liabilities outstanding at a previous balance sheet date remained outstanding, it is possible that the same liabilities may have been guaranteed by more than one parent. A creditor might claim against either guarantor. The guarantor against which the claim is made is given no rights by the Act against the other guarantor but is likely to have an equitable right of contribution from other guarantors of the same outstanding liabilities.

Q15 Does the guarantee fall away if the company later decides to have an audit for the year in question?

15.1   No. Once the guarantee has been given by delivering the s479C statement to Companies House, there is no provision in the Act for the parent's liability to cease except on the full satisfaction of the subsidiary's liabilities that had been covered by the guarantee given previously. Therefore, reverting to an audit would not bring an end to those liabilities.

Q16 Are there any special considerations for charities?

16.1   Yes, the Charities Commission has issued guidance[2].

16.2   Charitable companies are required by the Charities Act to have an audit if they have income over £500,000. Those with income over £250,000 are also required to have an audit if their assets are greater than £3.26m. Those not required to have an audit are required to have an independent examination of their accounts if their income is over £25,000. These requirements apply irrespective of any guarantee.

---

[2] *http://www.charity-commission.gov.uk/faqs/sending_annual_returns/id247.aspx*

The Charity Commission guidance referred to above states that if a subsidiary is a charity, a guarantee under s479C can be given by a parent charity if it is in the parent charity's interest to do so but draws attention to the above requirements.   **16.3**

That guidance also states that a guarantee should not be given by a charity for a non-charitable subsidiary because it risks charitable funds being used for a non-charitable purpose if the guarantee were to be called upon. This would give rise to a breach of trust and so a guarantee for a non-charitable trading subsidiary should not be given.   **16.4**

Q17 Do the accounts of the subsidiary still have to be prepared and filed at Companies House?

In general, yes. However, dormant subsidiary companies fulfilling the conditions for exemption from audit by parent guarantee are also exempt from the requirement to prepare and/or file accounts at Companies House.   **17.1**

Most dormant companies were already exempt from audit under s480. However, for financial years ending on or after 1 October 2012, they can claim exemption from the requirements to prepare and file statutory accounts. The requirements to qualify for these exemptions are essentially the same as those set out in this guidance relating to audit exemption.   **17.2**

The exemption from preparing accounts for a dormant subsidiary is in s394A-C and the exemption from filing accounts for a dormant subsidiary is in s448A-C. Form AA06 should indicate which of the exemptions is being claimed.   **17.3**

Q18 For a company with a premium listing in the UK, could entering into a guarantee require shareholder approval as a class 1 transaction?

LR 10.2.4 requires certain indemnities and similar arrangements to be treated as class 1 transactions and therefore to require shareholder approval. However, this does not apply to an agreement or arrangement with a wholly-owned subsidiary undertaking of the listed company. It therefore appears that provided the subsidiary in question is wholly-owned, entering into a guarantee under s479A would not be a class 1 transaction. This is consistent with the draft guidance in TN/310.1[3], which was published for consultation by the UK Listing Authority (UKLA) in February 2013. The UKLA is considering the responses to that consultation.   **18.1**

Where the arrangements involve a subsidiary that is not wholly owned, it appears that the arrangements may be a class 1 transaction because the guarantee is unlimited. This is the position taken in the UKLA draft guidance in TN/310.1, but the UKLA is considering the responses to that consultation and has yet to reach a finalised position on this matter. Given the requirements in Listing Rule 10.2.4[4] apply only when the arrangements are "exceptional", pending clarification from the UKLA as to their finalised position in this regard, companies considering entering into guarantees in respect of non-wholly owned subsidiaries should obtain their own legal advice or consult their broker and/or the UKLA.   **18.2**

---

[3] *http://www.fsa.gov.uk/pubs/ukla/ukla_indemnities_guarantees_arrangements.pdf*

TECH 09/13AAF (Revised) – Assurance Review Engagements on Historical Financial Statements

(29 March 2019)

Contents

Paragraphs

Foreword
Why now?
What is an assurance review engagement?

Assurance review engagements
Introduction .... 1 - 4
The advantages of assurance review engagements .... 5 - 6

**Conduct of an assurance review engagement in
accordance with ISRE 2400 (revised)**
ISRE 2400.18–20 .... 7 - 12

Acceptance and continuance of client relationships
ISRE 2400.30 .... 13 - 24

Performing the engagement
ISRE 2400.52–54 .... 25 - 26

Evaluating evidence obtained from the procedures performed
ISRE 2400.66–85 .... 27 - 30

**Appendix 1: Illustrative contents and extracts of an
engagement letter**

Appendix 2: Illustrative management representation letter

Appendix 3: Illustrative directors' balance sheet statement

Appendix 4: Illustrative assurance review report

**Appendix 5: Illustrative material uncertainty related to going
concern paragraph**

Appendix 6: Illustrative directors' responsibilities statement

Appendix 7: Application to micro-entities regime

ICAEW connects over 150,000 chartered accountants worldwide, providing this community of professionals with the power to build and sustain strong economies. Our profession is right at the heart of the decisions that will define the future, and insight and we contribute by sharing our knowledge, insight and capabilities with others. That way, we can be sure that we are building robust, accountable and fair economies across the globe.

The ICAEW Audit and Assurance Faculty is the professional and public interest voice of audit and assurance matters for ICAEW and is a leading authority in its field. Internationally recognised as a source of expertise, the Faculty is responsible for submissions to regulators and standard setters and provides a range of resources to professionals, providing practical assistance in dealing with common audit and assurance problems.

Foreword

This technical release was issued by the Audit and Assurance Faculty of the Institute of Chartered Accountants in England and Wales in September 2013 and updated in September 2018 and March 2019. It provides guidance on the conduct of assurance reviews of financial statements.

Why now?

The absolute number and the proportion of audit exempt companies have been growing since audit exemption was introduced in 1993, due to a number of increases in the thresholds.

When all these companies are added to the large number of unincorporated businesses out there, there is a substantial potential market for chartered accountants to offer their assurance skills to businesses who are not required to have an audit.

The International Standard on Review Engagements (ISRE) 2400 (Revised) *Engagements to Review Historical Financial Statements* provides a framework for the conduct of reviews over historical financial information, so the client will know what it is getting and the accountant has access to guidance on the service they are providing.

What is an assurance review engagement?

ISRE 2400 (Revised) requires the chartered accountant to make enquiries of management, and others, and to carry out analytical procedures to gain a degree of assurance that:

- The financial statements comply with the chosen financial reporting framework and give a true and fair view; and

- Management is aware of its responsibilities for producing the financial statements.

In the UK, there are two financial reporting frameworks: EU-adopted International Financial Reporting Standards (IFRSs) and UK GAAP, and, within UK GAAP, there is a choice of the following Financial Reporting Standards (FRSs) subject to the relevant criteria being met:

- FRS 101 *Reduced Disclosure Framework*, for the individual accounts of qualifying entities;

- FRS 102 *The Financial Reporting Standard applicable in the UK and Republic of Ireland*. This includes reduced disclosures for the individual accounts of qualifying entities and for entities qualifying as small entities; and

- FRS 105 *The Financial Reporting Standard applicable to the Micro-entities Regime*, for entities qualifying as micro-entities and choosing to apply the micro-entities regime.

Further guidance on the application of this technical release to the micro-entities regime is provided in Appendix 7.

Further information on the UK financial reporting frameworks is available on the ICAEW website at icaew.com/financialreporting.

To be able to perform an assurance review engagement the chartered accountant will:

- Review all material items in the financial statements.

- Consider and make enquiries of management about factors which might lead to increased risk that the financial statements may contain material misstatements or be non-compliant such as:

  - The nature of the client's business and its organisational structures

  - The incidence of fraud

  - Non-compliance with laws and regulations

  - Undisclosed related party transactions

  - Going concern problems

  - Post balance sheet events

  - Accounting estimates

  - Suitability of accounting policies

  - Significant, unusual or complex transactions or events.

Assurance review engagements, like audits, may help the chartered accountant report weaknesses and other issues that come to their attention to the directors. In other words, such engagements can generate much more value for the directors than just the assurance report itself. This represents a substantial degree of understanding of the client's circumstances. Further substantive testing is not required unless the chartered accountant has reason to be concerned about some aspect of the business. An assurance review engagement is therefore a flexible and proportionate service which can be adapted to suit different clients.

Assurance review engagements

Introduction

1   This technical release provides guidance to assist with compliance with ISRE 2400 (Revised) *Engagements to Review Historical Financial Statements*, issued by the International Auditing and Assurance Standards Board (IAASB). It also provides, in the appendices, illustrative letters and reports to support these engagements. It should not be regarded as a substitute for reading and understanding ISRE 2400 (Revised) which remains the appropriate standard to support assurance review engagements and is available from IFAC.

2   An increasing number of companies are entitled to take advantage of exemption from audit.

3   Audit exemption has created an open market for services that add credibility to the financial statements of audit exempt companies. In summary, the options available are:

- A compilation engagement, where the chartered accountant is engaged to prepare the financial statements from accounting records provided by a company's directors but without carrying out any verification of those records. More information can be found in the International Standard on Related Services (ISRS) 4410 (Revised) *Compilation Engagements*, issued by the IAASB. ICAEW guidance can be found, for incorporated entities, in technical release TECH 07/16AAF *Chartered Accountants' reports on the compilation of financial information of incorporated entities*, and, for unincorporated entities, in technical release TECH 08/16AAF *Chartered Accountants' reports on the compilation of historical financial information of unincorporated entities*.

- Agreed-upon procedures, which result in a report of purely factual findings relating to tests carried out. The user is left to draw their own conclusions, but will have increased confidence as these conclusions will be based on facts that have been checked by a chartered accountant. More information can be found in the International Standard on Related Services (ISRS) 4400 *Engagements to Perform Agreed-Upon Procedures Regarding Financial Information*, issued by the IAASB, and in the ICAEW technical release TECH 10/12AAF *Reporting to third parties*. An agreed-upon procedures engagement does not lead to a conclusion over the information as a whole. Instead, factual procedures (sample tests of particular balances, for example) are agreed on between the business and its chartered accountant. The accountant then carries out those procedures and reports the results, so that the business and its stakeholders can make use of them.

- An assurance review engagement, providing limited assurance on financial statements in accordance with ISRE 2400 (Revised). Assurance review reports provide a conclusion on the basis of the work performed, which is limited in scope according to the judgement of the chartered accountant.

- A voluntary audit carried out under International Standards on Auditing (ISAs) (UK) issued by the Financial Reporting Council (FRC). Audit reports provide an opinion giving the highest reasonable level of assurance, and remain the gold standard.

Assurance services have also been successfully developed to cover a wide range **4** of other types of business information, for example an assurance engagement, providing limited or reasonable assurance, in accordance with the International Standard on Assurance Engagements (ISAE) 3000 (Revised) *Assurance Engagements Other Than Audits or Reviews of Historical Financial Information*, issued by the IAASB. ICAEW guidance can be found in technical release TECH 02/07AAF *A framework for assurance reports on third party operations*. It may be possible to develop a bespoke assurance engagement referencing this standard and guidance. Further information on assurance engagements is available on the ICAEW website at icaew.com/assurance.

The advantages of assurance review engagements

For the chartered accountant conducting an assurance review engagement instead **5** of an audit, the following benefits should result:

- Audit registration, and compliance with the Audit Regulations, is not required solely as a result of carrying out assurance reviews, although the work falls within the ambit of Practice Assurance Standards.

- Substantive testing and testing of controls are not mandated as part of the assurance review service. Any decision as to whether, and to what extent, these methods of assurance should be used is a matter of professional judgement.

- This guidance requires compliance with the ICAEW Code of Ethics on independence, but not necessarily the more restrictive requirements of the FRC Revised Ethical Standard.

6 There has been widespread use of this technical release and ISRE 2400 (Revised) to perform assurance review engagements. Some examples include:

- A sole practitioner found it particularly useful for some of their clients who were seeking finance from other institutions apart from the major banks.

- Investors and lenders without access to additional financial records are in a position to benefit from the extra confidence that an assurance review provides.

- Several clients have sold their businesses following assurance reporting, demonstrating that assurance reviews are particularly useful for companies considering an exit via a sale.

- Property investment companies may want an alternative to an audit.

- An assurance review could also be comforting for a company with outsourced bookkeeping, reassuring directors about this activity.

- Under any circumstances where the accounting function is independent from the owner/manager, or directors, there may be a need for assurance.

- Subsidiaries opting out of an audit may need some assurance for their parent company, particularly if there are bonus calculations or guarantees involved. An assurance review engagement could focus on the known risk areas.

- Overseas parent companies are likely to understand and appreciate a review carried out of their UK subsidiaries.

- A component auditor may be able to carry out an assurance review, rather than a full audit, on a component that is exempt from audit if that component is less significant to the group.

Conduct of an assurance review engagement in accordance with ISRE 2400 (revised)

ISRE 2400.18–20

Structure of this technical release

7 This and subsequent sections of this technical release are presented in the same order as the subsections of the requirements paragraphs of ISRE 2400 (Revised) and provide additional guidance for ICAEW members in applying the ISRE for the assurance review of a UK incorporated company.

8 References in the subsequent sections of this technical release are as follows:

X	Paragraph X of this technical release.
ISRE 2400.X	Paragraph X of the main body of ISRE 2400 (Revised)
ISRE 2400.AX	Paragraph AX of the Application and Other Explanatory Material of ISRE 2400 (Revised)

9 The general principles of this technical release may also be applied when engaged to carry out an assurance review under the ISRE of the financial statements of other types of entities, with suitable modifications.

Use of the terms "management" and "those charged with governance"

For the majority of small UK incorporated companies, management and those **10** charged with governance will normally be the directors. In other types of entity they will be equivalent persons, such as the partners, proprietors, committee of management or trustees.

Ethical requirements

ISRE 2400.21

Chartered accountants carrying out a review under the ISRE will comply with the **11** ICAEW Code of Ethics. In particular the independence requirements in Section 290 – Independence – Audit and Review Engagements will need to be applied. Paragraph 290.0c explains that accountants may, if more convenient, apply the independence requirements of the FRC's Ethical Standard (ES), and therefore make use of the Provisions Available for Audits of Small Entities (PAASE), as applicable.

Engagement level quality control

ISRE 2400.24–28

The engagement level quality control requirements of the ISRE are based on the **12** premise that the firm complies with the IAASB standard International Standard on Quality Control (ISQC) 1 *Quality Control for Firms that Perform Audits and Reviews of Financial Statements, and Other Assurance and Related Services Engagements*. In the UK, however, the applicable FRC standard on quality control is ISQC (UK) 1, which should be read in the context of the FRC's Scope and Authority of Audit and Assurance Pronouncements. ICAEW has published Quality control in the audit environment to provide guidance on compliance with ISQC (UK) 1, and further resources are available on the ICAEW website. This publication emphasises that ICAEW's Practice Assurance Standard 4 on quality control applies to these engagements.

Acceptance and continuance of client relationships

ISRE 2400.30

Financial reporting frameworks

ISRE 2400.30(a) requires the chartered accountant to determine whether the **13** applicable financial reporting framework is acceptable. The following frameworks will be acceptable:

- UK GAAP (including FRS 101, FRS 102 and FRS 105).

- IFRSs.

ISRE 2400.30(b) requires the chartered accountant to obtain acknowledgement **14** that management understands its responsibilities. For a UK company, some of these responsibilities overlap with the directors' statutory duties and it may be helpful to make reference to these responsibilities in the engagement letter. Example extracts to include in an engagement letter can be found in Appendix 1.

15   When taking audit exemption, the Companies Act 2006 s475(3) requires a statement by the directors on the balance sheet acknowledging their responsibilities for complying with the requirements of the Act with respect to accounting records and the preparation of accounts. An example of this statement is provided in Appendix 3.

16   This guidance requires the inclusion of a directors' responsibilities statement. An example of this statement is provided in Appendix 6.

17   It is possible to apply the principles of ISRE 2400 (Revised) to financial statements for entities which do not have to comply with a recognised GAAP but which do follow accepted accounting principles (eg, Trust accounts). The chartered accountant needs to be satisfied that the accounting policies provide sufficient detail as to the accounting basis and policies adopted and that there is sufficient information disclosed within the financial statements for purpose of the users of the financial statements. The report will need to be amended appropriately. See ISRE 2400.A40 for further information when assessing the appropriateness of the accounting framework.

Understanding the use of the financial statements and the proposed assurance review report, and managing the chartered accountant's risk

18   Chartered accountants need to be aware that third parties may seek to rely on the financial statements and, indeed, the whole purpose of the assurance review engagement is to enhance their credibility.

Seeking to limit liability to third parties by means of a contract

19   Under some circumstances (for example, special purpose financial statements) it may be possible to identify in advance all the third parties who will have access to the financial statements, and therefore to the assurance review report. When all the third parties can be identified, the accountant may seek to manage their risk with a tri-partite or multi-partite engagement contract with the client and the third parties. The contract would accept that they owe a duty of care not only to the client but also to those third parties, and could then include provisions limiting liability if appropriate.

20   It is important to note that ISRE 2400 (Revised) does not require any such contract, that this approach can only be effective if all the third parties are party to the contract, and that it may prove difficult and time-consuming to negotiate if there are numerous third parties.

Seeking to limit liability to third parties by means of a disclaimer

21   It is probable that in most cases assurance review reports will be obtained over general purpose financial statements. These are likely to be made widely available. For example, they may be filed at Companies House. This will make it impossible to restrict who has access to them, and it will therefore not be possible to avoid risk by means of a contract.

22   An assurance review report appended to general financial statements can, however, include a paragraph disclaiming liability to third parties. The illustrative report in Appendix 4 includes a paragraph to this effect, which is equivalent to the Bannerman paragraph used in audit reports, and relies on the same legal precedent.

Managing the chartered accountant's risk

Whether the chartered accountant seeks to limit liability by means of a contract or   **23**
a disclaimer, the chartered accountant's risk can be managed by good practice
throughout the engagement:

- Ensuring all members of the engagement team are familiar with the requirements of ISRE 2400 (Revised) and this technical release.

- Ensuring the required procedures are executed, documented and reviewed carefully.

- Setting out the scope of the engagement and the various responsibilities of management and the reviewing firm in the engagement letter.

- Wording the assurance review report appropriately (see Appendix 4).

For further guidance refer to the ICAEW technical release TECH 09/15BL   **24**
Managing the professional liability of accountants, and the ICAEW technical
release TECH 04/06AAF *Assurance engagements: Management of risk and
liability.*

Performing the engagement

ISRE 2400.52–54

In performing the engagement, the following additional sources of guidance and   **25**
standards may be helpful:

- ISRE 2400.52 covers fraud and non-compliance with laws and regulations. Chartered accountants remain subject to the Money Laundering, Terrorist Financing and Transfer of Funds Regulations 2017. More information can be found in the CCAB's *Anti-money laundering guidance for the accountancy sector.*

- ISRE 2400.53–54 cover going concern. The depth of work carried out by the chartered accountant will be less than that for an audit. However, the chartered accountant will need to consider the disclosures in this area in accordance with the applicable financial reporting framework and the FRC guidance for directors.

Written representations

ISRE 2400.61–65

Written representations are required from management by ISRE 2400.61–62.   **26**
Example wording is set out in Appendix 2.

Evaluating evidence obtained from the procedures performed

ISRE 2400.66–85

Modified conclusion

27 ISRE 2400.66–85 set out the requirement to evaluate the evidence obtained from the procedures performed and to consider the form of the chartered accountant's conclusion.

28 Where it is necessary to issue a modified conclusion, the illustrative assurance review report in Appendix 4 can be modified in the same way shown in Appendix 2 of the ISRE 2400 (Revised), where examples 2–5 can be applied to modify example 1 as follows:

- Example 2 contains a qualified conclusion due to apparent material misstatement of the financial statements;

- Example 3 contains a qualified conclusion due to inability to obtain sufficient appropriate evidence;

- Example 4 contains an adverse conclusion due to material misstatement of the financial statements; and

- Example 5 contains a disclaimer of conclusion due to inability to complete the review.

Going concern

29 ISRE 2400.87 requires an emphasis of matter paragraph where the chartered accountant considers a matter to be of such importance that it is fundamental to users' understanding of the financial statements. This will include where there is material uncertainty related to events or conditions that may cast significant doubt on the entity's ability to continue as a going concern. Example wording is set out in Appendix 5.

The assurance review report

ISRE 2400.86–92

30 Appendix 4 sets out an example unmodified assurance review report for a UK incorporated company.

Appendix 1: Illustrative contents and extracts of an engagement letter

> The words below have been designed for use as a schedule of work in conjunction with the ICAEW Helpsheet *Engagement letters*. Please note that the wording may be adapted, as appropriate.

1. Responsibilities and scope for review services

1.1 Your responsibilities as [directors] [members]

As [directors] [members] of the [company] [limited liability partnership], you are responsible for preparing financial statements which give a true and fair view and which have been prepared in accordance with the Companies Act 2006 (the Act). As [directors] [designated members] you must not approve the financial statements unless you are satisfied that they give a true and fair view of the assets, liabilities, financial position and profit or loss of the [company] [limited liability partnership]. **1.1.1**

In preparing the financial statements, you are required to: **1.1.2**

- select suitable accounting policies and apply them consistently;

- make judgements and estimates that are reasonable and prudent; and

- prepare the financial statements on the going-concern basis unless it is inappropriate to presume that the [company] [limited liability partnership] will continue in business.

You are responsible for keeping adequate accounting records that set out, with reasonable accuracy, at any time, the [company's] [limited liability partnership's] financial position and for ensuring that the financial statements comply with applicable accounting standards and with the Companies Act 2006 (the Act) and give a true and fair view. **1.1.3**

You are also responsible for such internal control as you determine is necessary to enable the preparation of financial statements that are free from material misstatement whether due to fraud or error. **1.1.4**

You are also responsible for safeguarding the assets of the [company] [limited liability partnership] and hence for taking reasonable steps to prevent and detect fraud and other irregularities. **1.1.5**

You are responsible for ensuring that the [company] [limited liability partnership] complies with the laws and regulations that apply to its activities, and for preventing non-compliance and detecting any that occurs. This is in addition to the general duties required by directors under s.170–177 of the Companies Act 2006. **1.1.6**

You have undertaken to make available to us, as and when required, all the [company's] [limited liability partnership's] accounting records and related **1.1.7**

financial information, including minutes of management and [shareholders']
[directors'] [members'] meetings, that we need to do our work.

1.2 Our responsibilities as reviewers

1.2.1   Our review will be conducted with the objective of expressing our conclusion on
the financial statements. Our conclusion, if unmodified, will be in the form:

> "Based on our review, nothing has come to our attention that causes us to
> believe that the financial statements have not been prepared:
>
> • so as to give a true and fair view of the state of the [company's]
>   [limited liability partnership's] affairs as at [date], and of its profit
>   [loss] for the year then ended;
>
> • in accordance with [applicable accounting standards]; and
>
> • in accordance with the requirements of the Companies Act 2006 (the
>   Act).".

1.2.2   Our report is made solely to the [company's] [limited liability partnership's]
[directors] [members], as a body, in accordance with the terms of this engagement
letter. Our review work will be undertaken so that we might state to the
[company's] [limited liability partnership's] [directors] [members] those matters
we have agreed to state to them in a reviewer's report and for no other purpose. To
the fullest extent permitted by law, we do not accept or assume responsibility to
anyone other than the [company] [limited liability partnership] and the
[company's] [limited liability partnership's] [directors] [members] as a body, for
our review work, for the review report, or for the conclusions we will form. The
review of the financial statements does not relieve you of your responsibilities.

1.3 Scope of review

1.3.1   We will conduct our review in accordance with International Standard on Review
Engagements (ISRE) 2400 (Revised) Engagements to Review Historical Financial
Statements and ICAEW technical release TECH 09/13AAF (Revised) *Assurance
Review Engagements on Historical Financial Information*. ISRE 2400 (Revised)
requires us to conclude whether anything has come to our attention that causes us
to believe that the financial statements, taken as a whole, are not prepared, in all
material respects, in accordance with the [applicable financial reporting
framework]. ISRE 2400 (Revised) also requires us to comply with the ICAEW
Code of Ethics [and the FRC's Ethical Standard, as applicable].

1.3.2   A review of financial statements in accordance with ISRE 2400 (Revised) is a
limited assurance engagement. We will perform procedures, primarily consisting
of making enquiries of management and others within the entity, as appropriate,
applying analytical procedures, and evaluating the evidence obtained. We will also
perform additional procedures if we become aware of matters that cause us to
believe the financial statements as a whole may be materially misstated. These
procedures are performed to enable us to express our conclusion on the financial
statements in accordance with ISRE 2400 (Revised). The procedures selected will
depend on what we consider necessary applying our professional judgement,
based on our understanding of the [company] [limited liability partnership] and its
environment, and our understanding of [applicable financial reporting framework]
and its application in the context of your [company] [limited liability partnership].

A review is not an audit of the financial statements, therefore: **1.3.3**

- There is a commensurate higher risk than there would be in an audit, that any material misstatements that exist in the financial statements reviewed may not be revealed by the review, even though the review is properly performed in accordance with ISRE 2400 (Revised).

- In expressing our conclusion from the review of the financial statements, our report on the financial statements will expressly disclaim any audit opinion on the financial statements.

As part of our normal review procedures, we may ask you to confirm in writing   **1.3.4**
representations you have made to us during the review.

In respect of the expected form and content of our report, we refer you to appendix 4   **1.3.5**
of TECH 09/13AAF (Revised) *Assurance Review Engagements on Historical Financial Information*. The form and content of our report may need to be amended in the light of our findings.

1.4 Claim limitation

Additional wording to be included in the letter of engagement if a practitioner wishes to limit their liability in respect of a claim. You should consider whether this is suitable and, if necessary, take legal advice.

We have discussed with you the extent of our liability to you in respect of the   **1.4.1**
professional services described in this engagement letter (the professional services). Having considered both your circumstances and our own, we have reached a mutual agreement that £.................... insert amount represents a fair maximum limit to our liability.

In reaching this agreement it is also agreed that: **1.4.2**

- in the event of any claim for loss or damage arising from the professional services, you have agreed that the sum of £.................... insert amount represents the maximum total liability to you in respect of the firm, [its] [principals] [directors] [members] [and staff]; this maximum total liability applies to any and all claims made on any basis and therefore includes any claims in respect of breaches of contract, tort (including negligence) or otherwise in respect of the professional services and shall also include interest;

- we confirm that the limit in respect of our total aggregate liability will not apply to any acts, omissions or representations that are in any way criminal, dishonest or fraudulent on the part of the firm, [its] [principals] [directors] [members] [or employees] or any other liabilities that cannot be lawfully limited or excluded; and

- you have agreed that you will not bring any claim of a kind that is included within the subject of the limit against any of our [principals] [directors] [members] [or employees] on a personal basis.

Appendix 2: Illustrative management representation letter

> The words below have been designed to be used in conjunction with the ICAEW Helpsheet *Letters of representation*. Please note that the wording may be adapted, as appropriate.

Entity letterhead

Date...........................

Dear Sir(s)

This representation letter is provided in connection with your review of the financial statements of...................... (name of company / business / trust, etc.) for the period / year ending........................ (date) for the purpose of .... (expressing a conclusion as to whether anything has come to our attention that causes us to believe that the financial statements, taken as a whole, are not prepared, in all material respects, in accordance with .... (The Companies Act 2006 / other applicable legislation / and United Kingdom Accounting Standards (United Kingdom Generally Accepted Accounting Practice) / International Financial Reporting Standards as adopted by the European Union).

Financial statements

1   I/We have fulfilled my/our responsibilities as .... (director(s) / owner(s) / proprietor(s) / trustees), as set out in the terms of your engagement dated...................... (date) [under the Companies Act 2006] for preparing financial statements .) in accordance with .... (The Companies Act 2006 / and United Kingdom Accounting Standards (United Kingdom Generally Accepted Accounting Practice) / International Financial Reporting Standards as adopted by the European Union) .... (, which you have drafted on my/our behalf,) which give a true and fair view of the financial position of .... (company / business / trust / charity, etc.) as of .... (date) and of the results of its operations [and its cash flows] for the year then ended and for making accurate representations to you.

Companies only

We confirm that the [company] was entitled to exemption under section [x] of the Companies Act 2006 from the requirement to have its financial statements for the financial year ended [date] audited. We also confirm that the members have not required the [company] to obtain an audit of its financial statements for the financial year in accordance with section 476 of the Act.

We acknowledge that the work performed by you is substantially less in scope than an audit performed in accordance with International Standards on Auditing (UK) and that you do not express an audit opinion.

2   Significant assumptions used by me/us in making accounting estimates, including those measured at fair value, are reasonable.

I/We have no plans or intentions that may materially alter the carrying value and where relevant the fair value measurements or classification of assets and liabilities reflected in the financial statements.   **3**

I/We have disclosed all known actual or possible litigation and claims whose effects should be considered when preparing the financial statements and these have been disclosed in accordance with the requirements of accounting standards.   **4**

Related party relationships and transactions have been appropriately accounted for and disclosed in accordance with the requirements of accounting standards.   **5**

All events since the balance sheet date which require disclosure or which would materially affect the amounts in the financial statements have been adjusted or disclosed in the financial statements.   **6**

I/We confirm the financial statements are free of material misstatements, including omissions. I/We believe that those uncorrected misstatements identified during the .... review are immaterial both individually and in aggregate to the financial statements as a whole. A list of these items is attached to this letter of representation, together with my/our reasons for not correcting them.   **7**

I/We confirm that, having considered my/our expectations and intentions for the next twelve months, and the availability of working capital, the .... (company / business / trust / charity, etc.) is a going concern. I/We confirm that the disclosures in the accounting policies are an accurate reflection of the reasons for my/our consideration that the financial statements should be drawn up on a going concern basis.   **8**

I/We confirm, in respect of the restatement made to correct a material misstatement in a prior period financial statements that affects the comparative information **9**

.... (Any other matters relevant to the financial statements that have been represented by management. For example stock or investment property valuations or bad debt or other provisions.)   **10**

Information provided

All accounting records and relevant information have been made available to you for the purpose of your .... review. We have provided to you all other information requested and given unrestricted access to persons within the entity from whom you have deemed it necessary to .... obtain review evidence. All other records and related information [including minutes of all management and shareholders meetings] have been made available to you.   **11**

All transactions undertaken by the .... (company / business / trust / charity, etc.) have been properly reflected in the accounting records and are reflected in the financial statements.   **12**

I/We acknowledge our responsibility for the design, implementation and maintenance of controls to prevent and detect fraud. I/We have disclosed to you the results of my/our assessment of the risk that the financial statements may be materially misstated as a result of fraud.   **13**

I/We have disclosed to you all information in relation to fraud or suspected fraud that we are aware of and that affects the entity and involves, management, employees who have significant roles in internal control, or others, where fraud could have a material effect on the financial statements.   **14**

15   I/We have disclosed to you all information in relation to allegations of fraud, or suspected fraud affecting the entity's financial statements communicated by employees, former employees, analysts, regulators or others.

16   I/We confirm that we are not aware of any possible or actual instance of non-compliance with those laws and regulations which provide a legal framework within which the .... (company / business / trust / charity, etc.) conducts its business and which could affect the financial statements. The .... (company / business / trust / charity, etc.) has complied with all aspects of contractual agreements that could have a material effect on the financial statements in the event of non-compliance.

17   I/We confirm that we have disclosed to you the identity of the entity's related parties and all related party relationships and transactions relevant to the .... (company / business / trust / charity, etc.) that we are aware of.

18   The .... (company / business / trust / charity, etc.) has satisfactory title to all assets, and there are no liens or encumbrances on the assets except for those disclosed in the financial statements.

19   There are no liabilities, contingent liabilities or guarantees to third parties other than those disclosed in the financial statements.

Companies only

20   The company has at no time during the year entered into any arrangement, transaction or agreement to provide credit facilities (including loans, quasi loans or credit transactions) for directors, nor to guarantee or provide security for such matters, except as disclosed in the financial statements.

21   .... (Any other information relevant to the financial statements that has been represented by management).

I/We confirm to the best of my/our knowledge and belief that the above representations are made on the basis of enquiries of management and staff with relevant knowledge and experience and, where appropriate, of inspection of supporting documentation sufficient to satisfy myself/ourselves that I/we can properly make each of the above representations to you.

Yours faithfully

Signed on behalf of the board of directors by:

....(Signature)

....(Director)

Date.......................................

Appendix 3: Illustrative directors' balance sheet statement

For the year ending [date] the company was entitled to exemption from audit under [section 477 of the Companies Act 2006 relating to small companies]/ [section 479A of the Companies Act 2006 relating to subsidiary companies]/ [section 480 of the Companies Act 2006 relating to dormant companies].

Directors' responsibilities:

- The members have not required the company to obtain an audit of its accounts for the year in question in accordance with section 476.
- The directors acknowledge their responsibilities for complying with the requirements of the Act with respect to accounting records and the preparation of accounts.
- [These accounts have been prepared in accordance with the provisions applicable to companies subject to the small companies' regime.]

Appendix 4: Illustrative assurance review report

Independent chartered accountants' review report to the directors of XYZ limited

We have reviewed the financial statements of XYZ Limited for the year ended [date], which comprise the [specify the titles of the primary statements] and notes to the financial statements, including a summary of significant accounting policies. The financial reporting framework that has been applied in their preparation is applicable law and United Kingdom Accounting Standards (United Kingdom Generally Accepted Accounting Practice) / International Financial Reporting Standards as adopted by the European Union.

Directors' Responsibility for the Financial Statements

As explained more fully in the Directors' Responsibilities Statement [set out on pages ...], the directors are responsible for the preparation of the financial statements and for being satisfied that they give a true and fair view.

Accountants' Responsibility

Our responsibility is to express a conclusion on the financial statements. We conducted our review in accordance with International Standard on Review Engagements (ISRE) 2400 (Revised) *Engagements to review historical financial statements* and ICAEW technical release TECH 09/13AAF (Revised) *Assurance review engagements on historical financial statements*. ISRE 2400 (Revised) requires us to conclude whether anything has come to our attention that causes us to believe that the financial statements, taken as a whole, are not prepared, in all material respects, in accordance with the [applicable financial reporting framework]. ISRE 2400 (Revised) also requires us to comply with the ICAEW Code of Ethics[and the FRC's Ethical Standard, as applicable].

Scope of the Assurance Review

A review of financial statements in accordance with ISRE 2400 (Revised) is a limited assurance engagement. We have performed procedures, primarily consisting of making enquiries of management and others within the entity, as appropriate, applying analytical procedures, and evaluating the evidence obtained. The procedures performed in a review are substantially less than those performed in an audit conducted in accordance with International Standards on Auditing (UK). Accordingly, we do not express an audit opinion on these financial statements.

Conclusion

Based on our review, nothing has come to our attention that causes us to believe that the financial statements have not been prepared:

- so as to give a true and fair view of the state of the [company's] affairs as at [date], and of its profit [loss] for the year then ended;
- in accordance with [applicable accounting standards]; and
- in accordance with the requirements of the Companies Act 2006.

Use of our report

This report is made solely to the company's directors, as a body, in accordance with the terms of our engagement letter dated [date]. Our review work has been undertaken so that we might state to the company's directors those matters we have agreed to state to them in a reviewer's report and for no other purpose. To the fullest extent permitted by law, we do not accept or assume responsibility to anyone other than the company and the company's directors as a body, for our review work, for this report, or for the conclusions we have formed.

[Accountant's signature – name of individual or firm]

[Firm name]

Chartered Accountants

[Address]

[Date]

Appendix 5: Illustrative material uncertainty related to going concern paragraph

We draw attention to note [X] in the financial statements, which indicates that [brief description of events or conditions identified that may cast significant doubt on the entity's ability to continue as a going concern]. As stated in note [X], these events or conditions, along with the other matters as set forth in note [X], indicate that a material uncertainty exists that may cast significant doubt on the company's ability to continue as a going concern. Our conclusion is not modified in respect of this matter.

Appendix 6: Illustrative directors' responsibilities statement

[The directors' responsibilities statement should be placed immediately before the assurance review report.]

The directors are responsible for preparing the [Strategic Report], Directors' Report and the financial statements in accordance with applicable law and regulations.

Company law requires the directors to prepare financial statements for each financial year. Under that law the directors have elected to prepare the financial statements in accordance with [United Kingdom Generally Accepted Accounting Practice (United Kingdom Accounting Standards and applicable law)]. Under company law the directors must not approve the financial statements unless they are satisfied that they give a true and fair view of the state of affairs of the company and the profit or loss of the company for that period.

In preparing these financial statements, the directors are required to:

- select suitable accounting policies and then apply them consistently;

- make judgments and accounting estimates that are reasonable and prudent;

- prepare the financial statements on the going concern basis unless it is inappropriate to presume that the company will continue in business.

The directors are responsible for keeping adequate accounting records that are sufficient to show and explain the company's transactions and disclose with reasonable accuracy at any time the financial position of the company and enable them to ensure that the financial statements comply with the Companies Act 2006. They are also responsible for safeguarding the assets of the company and hence for taking reasonable steps for the prevention and detection of fraud and other irregularities.

[Signature

Date]

Appendix 7: Application to micro-entities regime

This appendix is designed to support the application of this guidance to the micro-entities regime.

Further information on FRS 105 *The Financial Reporting Standard applicable to the Micro-entities Regime*, for entities qualifying as micro-entities and choosing to apply the micro-entities regime, is available on the ICAEW website at icaew.com/financialreporting.

An illustrative assurance review report for micro-entities is as follows:

Independent Chartered Accountants' Review Report to the Directors of XYZ Limited

We have reviewed the financial statements of XYZ Limited for the year ended [date], which comprise the [specify the titles of the primary statements] and notes to the financial statements. The financial reporting framework that has been applied in their preparation is applicable law and United Kingdom Accounting Standards, Financial Reporting Standard (FRS) 105 *The Financial Reporting Standard applicable to the Micro-entities Regime* (United Kingdom Generally Accepted Accounting Practice).

Directors' Responsibility for the Financial Statements

As explained more fully in the Directors' Responsibilities Statement [set out on pages ...], the directors are responsible for the preparation of the financial statements and for being satisfied that they give a true and fair view.

Accountants' Responsibility

Our responsibility is to express a conclusion on the financial statements. We conducted our review in accordance with International Standard on Review Engagements (ISRE) 2400 (Revised) *Engagements to review historical financial statements* and ICAEW technical release TECH 09/13AAF (Revised) *Assurance review engagements on historical financial statements*. ISRE 2400 (Revised) requires us to conclude whether anything has come to our attention that causes us to believe that the financial statements, taken as a whole, are not prepared, in all material respects, in accordance with United Kingdom Generally Accepted Accounting Practice, specifically FRS 105. ISRE 2400 (Revised) also requires us to comply with the ICAEW Code of Ethics and the FRC's Ethical Standard, as applicable.

Scope of the Assurance Review

A review of financial statements in accordance with ISRE 2400 (Revised) is a limited assurance engagement. We have performed procedures, primarily consisting of making enquiries of management and others within the entity, as appropriate, applying analytical procedures, and evaluating the evidence obtained. The procedures performed in a review are substantially less than those performed in an audit conducted in accordance with International Standards on Auditing (UK). Accordingly, we do not express an audit opinion on these financial statements.

Conclusion

Based on our review, nothing has come to our attention that causes us to believe that the financial statements have not been:

- properly prepared in accordance with United Kingdom Generally Accepted Accounting Practice, specifically FRS 105; and

- prepared in accordance with the requirements of the Companies Act 2006 as applied to micro-entities.

Use of our report

This report is made solely to the company's directors, as a body, in accordance with the terms of our engagement letter dated [date]. Our review work has been undertaken so that we might state to the company's directors those matters we have agreed to state to them in a reviewer's report and for no other purpose. To the fullest extent permitted by law, we do not accept or assume responsibility to anyone other than the company and the company's directors as a body, for our review work, for this report, or for the conclusions we have formed.

[Accountant's signature – name of individual or firm]

[Firm name]

Chartered Accountants

[Address] [Date]

TECH 09/14BL Accountants' Reports on Commercial Property Service Charge Accounts

(May 2014)

Contents

Paragraphs

Introduction

Glossary

Preparation of the statement of service charge expenditure
Background   1 - 5

Reporting on annual statements of service charge expenditure   6 - 53
Type of reporting engagement   6 - 14
Conduct of a review engagement in accordance with ISRE 2400 (Revised)   15 - 53

Appendix 1 – The accounting framework

**Appendix 2 – Example procedures for undertaking a review of annual
statement of service charge expenditure**

Appendix 3 – Example paragraphs for engagement letters

Appendix 4 – Example paragraphs for inclusion in a letter of representation

Appendix 5 – Example review engagement report

**Appendix 6 – Qualifications for conducting engagements to review statements
of service charge expenditure in accordance with ISRE 2400 (revised)**

ABOUT ICAEW

ICAEW is a professional membership organisation, supporting over 140,000 chartered accountants around the world. Through our technical knowledge, skills and expertise, we provide insight and leadership to the global accountancy and finance profession.

Our members provide financial knowledge and guidance based on the highest professional, technical and ethical standards. We develop and support individuals, organisations and communities to help them achieve long-term, sustainable economic value.

This guidance has been prepared by a working party of ICAEW commercial property specialist practitioners. The accounting framework applied in this guidance is that published by the Royal Institution of Chartered Surveyors (RICS) in the Third edition of its Code of Practice, Service Charges in Commercial Property (the Code) and has been developed by a working party of property industry bodies. Both working parties worked under the guidance of a steering group comprising representatives of ICAEW and RICS.

Laws and regulations referred to in this ICAEW Technical Release are stated as at April 2014. Every effort has been made to make sure the information it contains is accurate at the time of creation. ICAEW cannot guarantee the completeness or accuracy of the information in this ICAEW Technical Release and shall not be responsible for errors or inaccuracies. Under no circumstances shall ICAEW be liable for any reliance by you on any information in this ICAEW Technical Release.

ISBN 978-1-78363-147-6

Introduction

The Royal Institution of Chartered Surveyors (RICS) issued the Third edition of the Code of Practice, Service Charges in Commercial Property (the Code) that is designed to improve general standards and promote best practice, uniformity, fairness and transparency in the management and administration of service charges in commercial property. Section 4 of the Code is headed "Financial controls and competencies" and sets out key principles for the preparation of the annual statement of service charge expenditure. Appendix C to the Code provides example statements of service charge expenditure and accompanying notes. The Code represents best practice and so provides a clear accounting framework for the preparation of the annual statement of service charge expenditure against which the independent accountant can report.

Paragraph 4.2.5 of the Code states that annual statements of service charge expenditure should be reviewed by an independent accountant unless the cost of such a review would be disproportionate to the assurance obtained, for example in relation to smaller properties. The nature of the report would depend on the terms of the relevant lease or leases. The independent accountant reports the findings of their work to the party that has engaged them, usually the owner of the property or the owner's agent. The accountant's report is then issued with the annual statement of service charge expenditure as part of the service charge accounting report that is given to the occupiers of the property to communicate the nature, type and cost of services provided.

The Code outlines the differences between an audit and an independent accountant's report but does not prescribe the form of report to be given or the procedures to be undertaken in making the report. There are no statutory or regulatory provisions for the external review of annual statements of service charge expenditure for commercial property, so that the form of external review undertaken for a particular property will depend on the provisions of the lease.

There has been widespread inconsistency in the wording of independent accountants' reports so that occupiers of commercial properties may be confused as to what underlying procedures have been performed and may not understand what assurance they can take from an independent accountant's review of the annual statement of service charge expenditure.

Paragraphs 6 to 14 in this Technical Release describe the different types of reporting engagement that can be undertaken, depending on the terms of the relevant lease or leases. A review engagement carried out in accordance with International Standard on Review Engagements (ISRE) 2400 (Revised) is considered to be the most appropriate engagement where an audit is not required, because it provides a degree of assurance on the financial information under review, based on the professional judgment of an independent reporting accountant. The fact that this form of engagement is subject to an international standard also means that there will be consistency in reporting.

The purpose of this Technical Release is, therefore, to set out best practice in the conduct of a review engagement in the context of a report on the annual statement of service charge expenditure so that there is greater consistency in procedures and reporting. This should in turn lead to greater levels of occupier satisfaction.

Scope of guidance

This Technical Release applies to independent accountants' reports on the annual statement of service charge expenditure and supporting notes in relation to commercial properties. It is not intended to apply to engagements relating to properties containing residential accommodation (dwellings) because these are subject to Landlord and Tenant legislation, which governs the operation of service charges and protection of service charge monies. Guidance on the preparation of and reporting on residential service charge accounts is given in Technical Release 03/11 published by ICAEW in conjunction with ACCA, ICAS, RICS and ARMA. RICS has issued separate guidance on the issues of managing mixed use buildings and estates which at the date of publication of this Technical Release is under review. The nature of the reporting engagement to be undertaken in respect of a mixed use property is a matter for agreement with the property manager (who may be the owner or landlord, or managing agent acting for the owner or landlord – see Glossary.

Effective date

The effective date for implementation of this guidance is for reports on statements of service charge expenditure for periods starting on or after 1 April 2014. Earlier implementation is encouraged.

Glossary

Entity

There is no "entity" in the sense normally used in financial reporting standards. The reporting engagement concerns solely the service charge account that is prepared for a property in accordance with the terms of its lease The term "entity" is used in this Technical Release if the context and the requirements of ISRE 2400 (Revised) make such use necessary. For the purposes of considering independence on the part of the reporting accountant, those involved in the management, ownership or occupation of the property are related parties of the entity. For the purposes of obtaining an understanding of the entity as required by ISRE 2400 (Revised), the term includes the system for managing, administering and accounting for the property, whether instituted by the manager or the owner. Unlike residential property, the concept of a general accumulated reserve does not exist for commercial property and the term entity does not represent anything fixed or concrete.

ISRE 2400 (Revised)

International Standard on Review Engagements (ISRE) 2400 (Revised): *Engagements to review historical financial statements*, is issued by the International Auditing and Assurance Standards Board (IAASB) of the International Federation of Accountants (IFAC). The Association of Chartered Certified Accountants, the Institute of Chartered Accountants in England and Wales, the Institute of Chartered Accountants in Ireland and the Institute of Chartered Accountants of Scotland are members of IFAC and require their members to comply with Standards issued by IAASB that are applicable to the services they provide.

Landlord

Landlord is the term used in Landlord and Tenant legislation in respect of residential leases to denote the person or company which owns and rents or leases a flat or house. The person or company may own the freehold or may have a superior leasehold interest in the property themselves. The definitions in s30, of the LTA 1985 state that "in the provisions of this Act relating to service charges "landlord" includes any person who has a right to enforce payment of a service charge". To avoid confusion, this term is only used in this Technical Release where the context makes this necessary, for example in relation to mixed commercial/residential properties, or where the term is used in a source being quoted, for example the Code. In all other cases the reference is to "owner".

Manager

The term "manager" is used by the Code to denote the person or team that budgets, forecasts, procures, manages and accounts for the services that comprise the service charge on a commercial property, whether they are the owner, an in-house team, management company or a managing agent (including any wholly or partly related companies). The term manager is used in this sense throughout this Technical Release, except where the context or quotation from another source requires use of a more specific term, such as "owner".

Management

The term "management" is used in this Technical Release when the material is based on, or quotes, ISRE 2400 (Revised), and refers to staff or others carrying out and in control of the day-to-day operations of the manager.

Owner

The owner is the person who receives or is entitled to receive the rent on the property. This person is legally responsible for the provision of, or management of, and administration of the services and service charge. In practice the owner may appoint a third party manager to discharge the owner's obligations under the terms of the lease.

Occupier

The occupier is the person in possession or occupation of premises and usually responsible for payment of the service charge to the owner. The term "service charge payer" is used interchangeably with the term "occupier".

Statement of service charge expenditure

The statement of service charge expenditure is the account of service charge expenditure/ costs and related notes. Commercial leases usually provide for an annual statement of service charge expenditure to be issued to occupiers following the end of each service charge period. The statement may be issued to occupiers by the manager with other documents, such as an operational report, but these other documents are outside the scope of the reporting accountant's review. There are circumstances, for example if a property is sold or the manager changes, where the statement of service charge expenditure might be for a period other than a year.

Tenant

The term "tenant" is used in Landlord and Tenant legislation to describe any person (physical or legal) who owns the leasehold interest in a residential property (flat or house) and is liable to pay the service charge under the terms of the lease. As with "landlord", this term is only used when the context requires; references in the context of commercial property and service charges are to "occupier", see above.

Preparation of the Statement of Service Charge Expenditure

Background

1   The RICS Code states that "it is usual for leases to provide for an annual statement to be issued to occupiers following the end of each service charge period; this would normally include a summary of the costs and expenditure incurred in the provision of the services and a calculation of the service charge (paragraph 4.2.1)."

2   The Code recommends as best practice that this annual statement of service charge expenditure be certified by the Landlord's surveyor to confirm that it represents a true and accurate record of expenditure incurred in supplying the services to the building, and that the expenditure that is being recovered is in accordance with the terms of the occupational leases.

3   The Code sets out recommended best practice for the disclosures and information that managers should provide to the occupiers with the report by accountants appointed to carry out an independent review of the statement of service charge expenditure.

4   The Code includes guidance on information to be provided about the service charge allocation and apportionment and a comparison between budgeted and actual expenditure. The allocation and apportionment report and operational review and variance report are required to conform to best practice for meeting the core principles for communication and transparency, but will usually be outside the scope of the independent accountant's review.

5   The contents of the Manager's report on service charge expenditure set out in Appendix C to the Code are:

(1)   Introduction
(2)   The Management team
(3)   Service Charge Certificate (provided by the landlord's surveyor)
(4)   The independent accountant's report
(5)   Service Charge Expenditure report
(6)   Notes to the expenditure report
(7)   Service charge allocation and apportionment
(8)   Operational Review
(9)   General Notes.

Reporting on Annual Statements of Service Charge Expenditure

Type of reporting engagement

6   Commercial leases usually provide for an annual statement of service charge expenditure to be issued to occupiers following the end of each service charge period, giving a summary of the costs and expenditure incurred in the provision of

the services and of the calculation of the service charge. Paragraph 4.2.1 of the Code states that "many leases will set out the procedures regarding the preparation of the annual statement, and will often require that the annual statement be "certified" by the landlord's surveyor, managing agent and sometimes the landlord's accountant".

Some leases require the annual statement to be "audited". It is essential that **7** contractual requirements in the lease are followed. Compliance with the requirements and procedures set down in the lease may be a "condition precedent" and recent case law has determined that where a lease sets down specific requirements and procedures, failure to comply may adversely prejudice the owner's ability to recover such sums.

However, the terminology governing annual statements of service charge **8** expenditure, particularly in older leases, may be quite general, and auditing standards and practice have changed fundamentally since the Auditing Practices Committee was established by the Consultative Committee of Accountancy Bodies (CCAB) in 1976, leading to the publication of the first Auditing Standards and Guidelines in April 1980. The work effort required by the International Standards on Auditing (ISAs) (UK and Ireland) that are now in force is unlikely to be what was anticipated when some leases were drawn up, especially where the original lease dates back many years.

In practice, therefore, there is scope for the manager to consider whether the terms **9** in the lease may be construed according to the meaning given to those terms at the time when the lease was drawn up. Whereas the term "audit" in a lease made before 1980 would not have involved any particular procedures beyond those needed to assist in the preparation of the accounts, for an auditing professional or other qualified, practising accountant to state now that an audit has been undertaken requires the professional to conduct the work in accordance with ISAs (UK and Ireland).

Where a lease that has been drawn up since 1980 refers to an audit the manager **10** will need to consider whether an audit of the annual statement of service charge expenditure should be undertaken, or whether the occupiers will accept another type of examination, for example on the basis that the cost of an audit would be disproportionate to their need for assurance on the annual statement of service charge expenditure.

If the terms of the lease require, or are construed as requiring, an audit, or the **11** manager requires an audit to be carried out, International Standard on Auditing 800 (ISA 800) entitled Special Considerations – Audits of Financial Statements Prepared in Accordance with Special Purpose Frameworks, provides a framework for the audit of the annual statement of service charge expenditure. Guidance on the application of ISA 800 to the audit of residential service charge accounts is given in Technical Release 03/11 published by the professional accountancy bodies with RICS and the Association of Residential Managing Agents (ARMA): the same principles will apply in the audit of the annual statement of service charge expenditure for commercial properties.

In accordance with the Code, the manager will need to agree with the occupiers **12** that an audit is not required and, when engaging an accountant to carry out another form of reporting assignment, confirm that the manager does not consider an audit to be necessary.

Other forms of reporting engagement that may be undertaken in relation to annual **13** statements of service charge expenditure are:

- Review engagement in accordance with International Standard on Review Engagements (ISRE) 2400 (Revised) – Engagements to review historical financial statements;

- Engagement to perform agreed upon procedures resulting in a statement of factual findings; and

- Engagement to compile financial information.

14   Engagements to perform agreed upon procedures and engagements to compile financial information do not result in a report giving assurance to users. Further, the underlying work carried out by the practitioner will vary according to the terms of the engagement with the owner/manager of the property. A review engagement carried out in accordance with ISRE 2400 (Revised) is therefore considered to be the most appropriate engagement where an audit is not required, because it provides a degree of assurance on the financial information under review, based on the professional judgment of an independent reporting accountant. The fact that this form of engagement is subject to an international standard also means that there will be consistency in reporting.

Conduct of a review engagement in accordance with ISRE 2400 (Revised)

15   The engagement should be carried out in accordance with International Standard on Review Engagements (ISRE) 2400 (Revised), Engagements to Review Historical Financial Statements. ISRE 2400 (Revised) requires compliance with all of its requirements except those that are not relevant to the review engagement because the circumstances addressed by the requirement do not exist. The following paragraphs summarise the requirements of ISRE 2400 (Revised).

Ethical Requirements

16   ISRE 2400 (Revised) requires the reporting accountant to comply with relevant ethical requirements, including those pertaining to independence. The fundamental principles are:

(a)   Integrity;

(b)   Objectivity;

(c)   Professional competence and due care;

(d)   Confidentiality; and

(e)   Professional behaviour.

Independence

17   In the case of an engagement to review financial statements, the International Ethics Standards Board for Accountants (IESBA) Code requires that the practitioner be independent of the entity whose financial statements are reviewed. The IESBA Code (which is similar to ICAEW ethical standards) describes independence as comprising both independence of mind and independence in appearance. The practitioner's independence safeguards the practitioner's ability to form a conclusion without being affected by influences that might otherwise compromise that conclusion. Independence enhances the practitioner's ability to act with integrity, to be objective and to maintain an attitude of professional scepticism. In the context of a review of an annual statement of service charge expenditure, the reporting accountant should not be an employee or director or associate of the owner or manager of the property concerned or of any associate or agent of the owner or manager.

Professional Scepticism and Professional Judgment

ISRE 2400 (Revised) requires the reporting accountant to plan and perform the **18** engagement with professional scepticism recognising that circumstances may exist that cause the financial statements to be materially misstated, and to exercise professional judgment in conducting the engagement.

Quality control

Firm level quality control: relationship between ISRE 2400 (Revised) and ISQC1

ISRE 2400 (Revised) explains that its provisions regarding quality control at the **19** level of individual review engagements are premised on the basis that the firm is subject to International Standard on Quality Control (ISQC) 1, Quality Control for Firms that Perform Audits and Reviews of Financial Statements, and Other Assurance and Related Services Engagements or requirements that are at least as demanding.

ISQC 1 deals with the firm's responsibilities to establish and maintain a system of **20** quality control for assurance engagements, including review engagements. Those responsibilities are directed at establishing the firm's quality control system and related policies designed to achieve the objective of the quality control system and the firm's procedures to implement and monitor compliance with those policies. Further guidance on the application of ISQC1 is set out in paragraphs A3 to A5 of ISRE 2400 (Revised).

Engagement Level Quality Control

ISRE 2400 (Revised) requires the engagement partner to possess competence in **21** assurance skills and techniques, and competence in financial reporting, appropriate to the engagement circumstances and to take responsibility for:

(a)   the overall quality of each review engagement to which that partner is assigned;

(b)   the direction, supervision, planning and performance of the review engagement in compliance with professional standards and applicable legal and regulatory requirements;

(c)   the accountant's report being appropriate in the circumstances; and

(d)   the engagement being performed in accordance with the firm's quality control policies (which includes the maintenance of appropriate documentation).

Given the level of knowledge and competence required by ISRE 2400 (Revised), **22** it is likely that the reporting accountant will need to be a member of one of the five member bodies of the Consultative Committee of Accountancy Bodies, or possess equivalent qualifications. A list of eligible bodies is contained in Appendix 6. In accordance with the competence requirement of professional ethics (see paragraph 16(c) above), the reporting accountant should have knowledge and understanding of the commercial property sector appropriate to the size and complexity of the commercial property for which the annual statement of service charge expenditure has been prepared.

Acceptance and Continuance of Client Relationships and Review Engagements

23   ISRE 2400 (Revised) contains a number of requirements for the acceptance or continuation of a review engagement. The underlying principles are the same as for other reporting engagements and are therefore not covered in this guidance.

24   ISRE 2400 (Revised) requires the reporting accountant to agree the terms of the engagement with management or those charged with governance, as appropriate, prior to performing the engagement, and to record the agreed terms of engagement in an engagement letter or other suitable form of written agreement. In the case of an engagement to review an annual statement of service charge expenditure, the terms of engagement will therefore normally be agreed with the manager. The engagement letter should include:

(a)   The intended use and distribution of the annual statement of service charge expenditure, and any restrictions on use or distribution where applicable. Guidance on agreeing the terms of engagement is contained in ICAEW helpsheet PAS2/HS03 Managing professional liability risk, and Technical Release AAF 04/06 Assurance engagements: Management of risk and liability. In the context of an engagement to report on an annual statement of service charge expenditure, the engagement letter states that the purpose of the report is to enable the manager to attach the report to the annual statement of service charge expenditure that is provided to current occupiers of the property and that the report may not be distributed to or used by other parties;

(b)   Identification of the applicable financial reporting framework or accounting policies adopted. The RICS Code of Practice is a Guidance Note and is not mandatory. The Code does, however, represent professional best practice and if the manager decides not to follow the sample report in Appendix C, or be selective in what is included in their report, the reporting accountant will consider whether to qualify their opinion on the basis that the accounting framework has not been followed;

(c)   The objective and scope of the review engagement;

(d)   The responsibilities of the reporting accountant;

(e)   The responsibilities of the manager;

(f)   A statement that the engagement is not an audit, and that the practitioner will not express an audit opinion on the financial statements; and

(g)   Reference to the expected form and content of the report to be issued by the reporting accountant, and a statement that there may be circumstances in which the report may differ from its expected form and content.

25   Example paragraphs for use in an engagement letter for an engagement to review an annual statement of service charge expenditure are set out in Appendix 3.

Performing the Engagement

26   The following paragraphs include practical examples of how the requirements of ISRE 2400 (Revised) may be applied in the context of a review of an annual statement of service charge expenditure for commercial property. More detailed practical examples are contained in Appendix 2.

Materiality in a Review of Financial Statements

The reporting accountant is required to determine materiality for the annual   27
statement of service charge expenditure as a whole, and apply this materiality in
designing the procedures and in evaluating the results obtained from those
procedures. The materiality level should be revised if information becomes
available during the review that, if available at the outset, would have caused
the practitioner to have determined a different amount.

Obtaining an understanding of the management of the property and service charges

ISRE 2400 (Revised) requires the reporting accountant to obtain an understanding   28
of the entity for which the accounts have been prepared, and of the entity's
environment, and of the financial policies and principles applied in preparation of
the accounts. In the context of an annual statement of service charge expenditure
for a commercial property, the "entity" may be a single building or property, an
estate or a group of properties. The understanding should be sufficient to identify
areas in the annual statement of service charge expenditure where material
misstatements are likely to arise.

The terms of the leases that govern the charges in respect of which the annual   29
statement of service charge expenditure are clearly relevant to the reporting
accountant's understanding, but there may be many and complicated leases
covering the occupancy of even a single building. The accountant should
therefore use professional judgment about to the extent to which it is
appropriate to rely on any summary of key provisions of relevant leases
prepared by the manager or owner of the property.

Designing and Performing Procedures

The reporting accountant shall design and perform inquiry and analytical   30
procedures to address all material items in the annual statement of service
charge expenditure that are subject to review, including disclosures, and to
focus on addressing areas in the annual statement of service charge expenditure
where material misstatements are likely to arise.

Fraud and illegal acts

ISRE 2400 (Revised) requires specific consideration of the possibility that the   31
subject matter under review may have been affected by fraud or illegal acts or non-
compliance with provisions of laws and regulations that are generally recognised
to have a direct effect on the determination of material amounts and disclosures in
the financial statements. Fraud or illegal acts that may be of particular relevance in
the management of a commercial property include, but are not limited to, the
acceptance of inducements in return for awarding maintenance contracts, the
engagement of staff who are not entitled to work in the UK or the payment of
subcontractors without deduction of tax. The reporting accountant should
therefore consider and assess the risk that the annual statement of service
charge expenditure may have been affected by the occurrence of fraud, etc.

Related party transactions

ISRE 2400 (Revised) requires the reporting accountant to remain alert during the   32
review for arrangements or information that may indicate the existence of related
party relationships or transactions that management has not previously identified

or disclosed to the practitioner. However, there is no industry or legislative requirement for the disclosure or consideration of related party transactions, so this is not a standard requirement in a review of annual statements of service charge expenditure. If, however, the reporting accountant becomes aware of circumstances that indicate that the manager may have exploited the potential to profit from related party transactions the accountant should ask management for an explanation of the circumstances and consider whether, in the light of management's response, any modification is needed to the accountant's report.

Going concern

33   ISRE 2400 (Revised) also requires consideration of the entity's ability to continue as a going concern. However, annual statements of service charge expenditure are concerned with past expenditure and costs: they do not concern an entity as such. The obligation to provide future services lies with the owner. This means that the normal concept of going concern is not applicable to the review of annual statements of service charge expenditure.

Use of work performed by others

34   In performing the review, it may be necessary for the reporting accountant to use work performed by other practitioners, or the work of an individual or organisation possessing expertise in a field other than accounting or assurance. If the reporting accountant uses work performed by another practitioner or an expert in the course of performing the review, the reporting accountant should take appropriate steps to be satisfied that the work performed is adequate for the purposes of the review.

Reconciling the Financial Statements to the Underlying Accounting Records

35   The reporting accountant is required to obtain evidence that the annual statement of service charge expenditure agrees with, or reconciles to, the underlying accounting records maintained by the manager.

Additional Procedures When the Practitioner Becomes Aware that the Financial Statements May Be Materially Misstated

36   ISRE 2400 (Revised) states that, if the reporting accountant becomes aware of a matter(s) that causes them to believe that the annual statement of service charge expenditure may be materially misstated, they should design and perform additional procedures sufficient to enable them to conclude that the matter(s) is not likely to cause the statement to be materially misstated; or determine that the matter(s) does result in material misstatement. In the context of an annual statement of service charge expenditure, a material misstatement could arise if, for example, a major item of expenditure was included in respect of works carried out on another property. If such a misstatement is corrected no qualification is needed.

Written Representations

37   The reporting accountant is required by ISRE 2400 (Revised) to request management to provide a written representation that management has fulfilled its responsibilities described in the agreed terms of engagement. The reporting accountant should use professional judgment to decide at what level and by whom the representations should be made. This will depend on whether managing agents have been appointed, as well as the operational structure and accounting systems

established by the manager. For example, the representation letter may refer to a single property, or to an estate, or to a part of a managing agent's portfolio comprising properties all belonging to one owner and with the same accounting year end. The Standard specifies certain points to be included in the representation letter and these are set out below, adapted to the context of an annual statement of service charge expenditure for commercial property. Appendix 3 contains example paragraphs for inclusion in a letter of representation:

(a)　the manager has fulfilled its responsibility for the preparation of the annual statement of service charge expenditure in accordance with the Code, and has provided the reporting accountant with all relevant information and access to information as agreed in the terms of the engagement;

(b)　all transactions relating to the period have been recorded and are reflected in the annual statement of service charge expenditure;

(c)　the manager has disclosed to the reporting accountant:

(I)　the identity of the manager's related parties and details of all the related party relationships and transactions of which the manager is aware;

(II)　significant facts relating to any frauds or suspected frauds known to the manager that may have affected the annual service charge statement of expenditure;

(III)　known actual or possible non-compliance with laws and regulations for which the effects of non-compliance affect the annual statement of service charge expenditure;

(IV)　that all events occurring subsequent to the date of the service charge statements and for which the accounting policies adopted require adjustment or disclosure, have been adjusted or disclosed; and

(V)　whether there are any material commitments, contractual obligations or contingencies that have affected or may affect the annual statement of service charge expenditure, including disclosures.

If management does not provide the written representations, or if the reporting **38** accountant concludes that there is cause to doubt management's integrity such that the written representations provided are not reliable, the reporting accountant should discuss the matter with the manager, including the implications for the accountant's report. Further, if the manager does not provide the required representations the reporting accountant should disclaim a conclusion on the annual statement of service charge expenditure or, where appropriate, withdraw from the engagement.

Date of and Period(s) Covered by Written Representations

The date of the written representations shall be as near as practicable to, but not **39** after, the date of the accountant's report. The written representations shall be for all annual statements of service charge expenditure and period(s) referred to in the accountant's report.

Subsequent events

ISRE 2400 (Revised) states that, if the accountant becomes aware of events **40** occurring between the date of the annual service charge statements and the date of the accountant's report that require adjustment of, or disclosure in, the annual service charge statements, the accountant shall request management to correct those misstatements. An example in the context of an annual statement of service charge expenditure might be if an accrual for major works expenditure was materially overstated and was not corrected in the light of the actual invoice(s) received from the contractor after the year end.

41   ISRE 2400 (Revised) does not require the reporting accountant to perform any procedures regarding the annual statement of service charge expenditure after the date of the reporting accountant's report, but if something emerges that, had it been known to the reporting accountant at that date, may have caused the practitioner to amend the report, the reporting accountant should discuss the matter with the manager with a view to determining whether the annual statement of service charge expenditure needs to be amended.

Evaluating Evidence Obtained from the Procedures Performed

42   The reporting accountant is required to evaluate whether sufficient appropriate evidence has been obtained from the procedures performed and, if not, to perform other procedures as necessary in order to be able to form a conclusion on the annual statement of service charge expenditure.

43   If the reporting accountant is not able to obtain sufficient appropriate evidence to form a conclusion, the practitioner shall discuss with the owner/manager, as appropriate, the effects such limitations have on the scope of the review.

Forming the conclusion on the service charge statements

44   ISRE 2400 (Revised) requires the reporting accountant to evaluate whether the annual statement of service charge expenditure adequately refers to or describes the reporting framework. In addition, the reporting accountant is required to consider whether, in the context of the requirements of the applicable financial reporting framework and the results of the procedures performed:

● the terminology and disclosures are appropriate;

● the accounting policies selected and applied are consistent with the applicable financial reporting framework (that is, the provisions of the Code as amplified in the supplementary guidance) and are appropriate to the circumstances of the property;

● the accounting estimates made by management appear reasonable;

● the information presented in the annual statement of service charge expenditure appears relevant, reliable, comparable, and understandable; and

● the annual statement of service charge expenditure provides adequate disclosures to enable the intended users to understand the effects of material transactions and events on the information conveyed.

45   The report should be expressed as an unmodified or modified conclusion. An unmodified conclusion should be reported when the reporting accountant has obtained limited assurance to be able to conclude, based on the procedures performed and the evidence obtained, that nothing has come to the reporting accountant's attention that causes the reporting accountant to believe that the statement of service charge expenditure is not prepared, in all material respects, in accordance with the applicable financial reporting framework. A modified conclusion should be expressed where the reporting accountant concludes, based on the procedures performed and the evidence obtained, that the statement of service charge expenditure is materially misstated or where the reporting accountant has not been able to obtain the level of assurance required.

Very occasionally there may be circumstances in which ISRE 2400 (revised) requires the reporting accountant to withdraw from the engagement, for example if management does not provide the representations required by the reporting accountant (paragraph 60(ii)) or if management imposes a limitation of scope on the reporting accountant's review (paragraph 81(a)).

Contents of the report

ISRE 2400 (Revised) requires the reporting accountant's report for the review **46** engagement to be in writing, and to contain the following elements:

(a) a title, which shall clearly indicate that it is the report of an independent accountant for a review engagement;

(b) the addressee(s), as required by the circumstances of the engagement;

(c) an introductory paragraph that:

    (I) identifies the financial statements reviewed, (this will be the annual statement of service charge expenditure) and the date and period covered by the statement;

    (II) refers to the summary of significant accounting policies and other explanatory information; and

    (III) states that the annual statement of service charge expenditure has been reviewed;

(d) a description of the responsibility of the manager for the preparation of the annual statement of service charge expenditure, including an explanation that the manager is responsible for:

    (I) the preparation of the statement in accordance with the applicable financial reporting framework;

    (II) such internal control as the manager determines is necessary to enable the preparation of the statement of service charge expenditure that are free from material misstatement, whether due to fraud or error;

(e) (because the annual statement of service charge expenditure and notes are special purpose financial statements) a description of the purpose for which the statement is prepared and, if necessary, the intended users, or reference to a note in the special purpose financial statements that contains that information;

(f) a description of the reporting accountant's responsibility to express a conclusion on the annual statement of service charge expenditure based on the procedures performed and the evidence obtained, and of the scope of a review of the annual statement of service charge expenditure, including:

    (I) a reference to ISRE 2400 (Revised) and, where relevant, applicable law or regulation;

    (II) a description of a review of an annual statement of service charge expenditure in accordance with ISRE 2400 (Revised), as being a limited assurance engagement in which the procedures performed consist primarily of making inquiries of management and others within the entity as appropriate and applying analytical procedures, and evaluating the evidence obtained. The report should explain that the procedures performed in a review are substantially less than those performed in an audit conducted in accordance with ISAs, and, accordingly, the reporting accountant does not express an audit opinion on the statement of service charge expenditure;

(g)   a paragraph under the heading "Conclusion" that contains:

(I)   the reporting accountant's conclusion on the annual statement of service charge expenditure as a whole;

(II)   a reference to the applicable financial reporting framework used to prepare the annual statement of service charge expenditure;

(h)   [when the reporting accountant considers it necessary to draw users' attention to a matter presented or disclosed in the statement of service charge expenditure that they consider to be of such importance that it is fundamental to users' understanding of the statement] an Emphasis of Matter paragraph, immediately after the paragraph that contains the reporting accountant's conclusion on the annual statement of service charge expenditure, under the heading "Emphasis of Matter", or other appropriate heading;

(i)   [when the reporting accountant's conclusion on the annual statement of service charge expenditure is modified]:

(I)   a paragraph under the appropriate heading that contains the practitioner's modified conclusion; and

(II)   a paragraph, under an appropriate heading, that provides a description of the matter(s) giving rise to the modification;

(j)   a reference to the reporting accountant's obligation under ISRE 2400 (Revised) to comply with relevant ethical requirements;

(k)   the date of the reporting accountant's report. This should not be earlier than the date on which the reporting accountant has obtained sufficient appropriate evidence as the basis for the conclusion on the annual statement of service charge expenditure, which means not earlier than the date on which the manager has approved the statement;

(l)   the reporting accountant's signature (this will be in the name of the reporting accountant's firm, unless the appointment is personal); and

(m)   the location in the jurisdiction where the reporting accountant practices.

Basis of Accounting, and Restriction on Distribution and Use

47   ISRE 2400 (Revised) states that, if the reporting accountant considers it necessary to communicate a matter other than those that are presented or disclosed in the financial statements under review that, in the reporting accountant's judgment, is relevant to users' understanding of the review, the reporting accountant's responsibilities or the report itself and this is not prohibited by law or regulation, the reporting accountant shall do so in a paragraph in the report with the heading "Other Matter" or other appropriate heading. Such a paragraph is appropriate in the context of the report on the annual statement of service charge expenditure, because the statement is prepared in accordance with the Code.

48   As explained in paragraph 24(a) above, the engagement letter will have set out the purpose of the report and its agreed use, with accompanying disclosure restrictions setting out the extent to which, the context in which, and the basis on which, the report may be made available by the manager to third parties.

In accordance with the illustrative example in the Appendix to ISRE 2400 **49** (revised), the explanation of this arrangement and statement that the reporting accountant does not accept or assume responsibility to any third party are set out in the final paragraph of the report, after any emphasis of matter paragraph.

Appendix 4 contains an example accountant's report on the annual statement of **50** service charge expenditure for a commercial property, with illustrative example paragraphs for emphasis of matter, restrictions on distribution and use of the accountant's report and modified conclusions.

Documentation

ISRE 2400 (Revised) requires the review work performed as a basis for the **51** conclusion to be documented in a timely manner, sufficient to enable an experienced practitioner, having no previous connection with the engagement, to understand:

(a) the nature, timing, and extent of the procedures performed to comply with ISRE 2400 (Revised);

(b) the results obtained from the procedures, and the reporting accountant's conclusions formed on the basis of those results; and

(c) the significant matters arising during the engagement, the reporting accountant's conclusions reached thereon, and significant professional judgments made in reaching those conclusions.

In documenting the nature, timing and extent of procedures performed as required **52** in ISRE 2400 (revised), the reporting accountant is required to record:

(a) who performed the work and the date such work was completed; and

(b) who reviewed the work performed for the purpose of quality control for the engagement, and the date and extent of the review.

The reporting accountant is also required to document discussions with **53** management and others as relevant to the performance of the review of significant matters arising during the engagement, including the nature of those matters. If, in the course of the engagement, the reporting accountant identified information that is inconsistent with the reporting accountant's findings regarding significant matters affecting the annual statement of service charge expenditure, the reporting accountant shall document how the inconsistency was addressed.

APPENDIX 1 – The accounting framework

Appendix C to the Code, with Annexes A to E, provides a Service charge accounting sample report of which the annual statement of service charge expenditure and independent accountant's report thereon forms part. Only items 5 and 6 – the Service Charge Expenditure report and the Notes to the expenditure report – are covered by the reporting accountant's report.

The contents of the sample report are:

(1)   Introduction

(2)   The Management team

(3)   Service Charge Certificate (provided by the landlord's surveyor)

(4)   The independent accountant's report

(5)   Service Charge Expenditure report. Examples of summary and detailed statements are included as appendices to the supplementary guidance.

(6)   Notes to the expenditure report. The following notes are dealt with specifically:

- accounting principles including whether the accounts are prepared on an accruals basis or cash basis, best practice being an accruals basis

- waiver of exemption from VAT or not (and therefore whether expenditure is stated exclusive or inclusive of VAT);

- sinking fund/reserve fund – purpose of and movements on fund(s);

- banking – statement is to be provided as to whether service charge monies are held in one or more discrete bank accounts and whether interest earned is credited to the service charge account;

- accruals (large round sum provisions intended to spread the cost of significant works over a period of time are not accruals as they do not represent a liability at the end of the period. Accordingly, they should not be included as accruals but should be considered as contributions towards reserve or sinking funds and reported accordingly

- prepayments and security deposits;

- commercialisation (how and to where costs and income generated from services and activities in the property are allocated);

- marketing and promotions; and

- total cost of management.

This section may also be used to provide further details in respect of other accounting principles adopted in preparing the annual statement of service charge expenditure. For example, details of landlord contribution to the service charge or information regarding forward funding by the landlord.

(7)   Service charge allocation and apportionment. This section includes information about empty units and concessions granted to tenants. The information presented in this section is normally outside the scope of the independent accountant's review.

(8)   Operational Review. This information is considered to be best practice to meet the core principles for communication and transparency as set down in the Code as to the nature, type and cost of services provided to occupiers but is normally outside of the scope of the independent accountant's review.

(9)   General notes. This is any other information considered relevant to the tenants and is outside the scope of the accountant's report.

APPENDIX 2 – Example procedures for undertaking a review of annual statement of service charge expenditure

As stated in paragraph 15, the review engagement should be carried out in accordance with ISRE 2400 (Revised). The following paragraphs set out some of the practical considerations and provide examples of inquiry and analytical procedures in the context of a review of an annual statement of service charge expenditure for a commercial property.

General procedures

Accepting the engagement: form of engagement

ISRE 2400 (Revised) requires the reporting accountant to determine the acceptability of the financial reporting framework applied in the preparation of the financial statements. In a review of a statement of service charge expenditure, therefore, the reporting accountant is required to obtain an understanding of:

(a)   The purpose for which the statement of service charge expenditure is prepared;

(b)   The intended users of the statement; and

(c)   The steps taken by the manager (see definitions) to determine that the applicable financial reporting framework is acceptable, ie, the statement has been prepared on an appropriate basis (accruals or cash) that is clearly explained in the accompanying notes, and reflects the requirements of the lease and any additional accounting policies specified in the notes.

The purpose of the statement of service charge expenditure is to show occupiers how the service charges that they have paid have been spent.

The intended user of the report is the manager.

The purpose of a report made in accordance with ISRE 2400 (Revised) is to provide limited assurance to the manager that nothing has resulted from the accountant's work to indicate that the statement of service charge expenditure has not been prepared in all material respects in accordance with the stated accounting framework or accounting policies. The manager in turn attaches the report to the statement of service charge expenditure that is sent to all occupiers.

As explained in paragraph 24(b), best practice is for the statement of service charge expenditure to be prepared in accordance with the provisions of the Code of practice "*Service charges in commercial property*" issued by the RICS. If the manager has adopted a different accounting framework or policies, the accountant considers whether the report should be modified.

Engagement specific procedures

Obtaining an understanding

The reporting accountant is required to obtain an understanding of how the statement of service charge expenditure has been prepared, the property or group of properties to which it relates, and the applicable financial reporting framework, sufficient to identify areas in the financial statements where material misstatements are likely to arise.

Relevant information, which may be obtained by asking the manager's staff (or checking that existing information on file is up to date) includes:

- the nature of the property (eg, type and number of occupiers and size of individual units)

- the terms of the leases that govern the charges in respect of which the annual statement of service charge expenditure is prepared

- the extent and use of common areas

- the terms of relevant industry requirements, for example the preparation of service charge information in accordance with the RICS Code

- how the property is managed

- the accounting systems and accounting records including whether the data from the manager's accounting system and accounting records are adequate for the purpose of performing the analytical procedures

- the accounting policies in accordance with which the statement of service charge expenditure is prepared.

If there are many and complicated leases covering the occupancy of the property, the manager or owner of the property may be possible to obtain a summary of key provisions of relevant leases prepared by the manager or owner of the property.

Establishing a frame of reference based on understanding

Procedures include ascertaining how the stated accounting policies and any terms in the relevant leases that affect the amount or allocation of service charges are applied. Points to note if applicable are:

- whether the statement of service charge expenditure is prepared under the accruals or cash basis

- basis and operation of sinking/reserve funds

- the basis on which common parts expenditure is allocated between areas of the building

- the basis of owner contribution to common parts expenditure

- the treatment of non service charge receipts such as car parking fees and shopping mall revenues

- the basis for allocation of income and costs relating to commercialisation income

- other policies or terms.

Design and performance of analytical and other substantive procedures to

Procedures that may be performed to address all material items in the annual statement of service charge expenditure, including disclosures, and areas in the annual statement of service charge expenditure where material misstatements are likely to arise include:

- detailed review of material transactions (the review may consist of comparison to prior periods or budgeted amounts, estimates, and/or correspondence, as applicable)

- identification and review of items outside the date range of the service charge statement
- review of expenditure for completeness (reviewing for completeness may consist of comparison to prior periods and/or budget, or checking that the full number of periodic transactions due to take place in the course of the accounting period have been recorded)
- review of expenditure for duplicate transactions
- review of a random sample of transactions

Types of procedure that may be performed, depending on the circumstances, include inspection, re-calculation, re-performance, observation and confirmation.

Inquiries could include asking the manager or manager's staff whether there have been any significant, unusual or complex transactions or events that have affected or may affect the service charge expenditure in the period under review, for example:

- changes to any of the leases
- significant journals
- disproportionate changes in the amounts of commercialisation income or level of owner contributions to common parts expenditure
- significant transactions occurring or recognised near the end of the reporting period

Inquiry that should always be made of relevant staff and representatives of the manager or owner (if different) is to ask them to confirm whether they are aware of the existence of any actual, suspected or alleged:

- fraud or illegal acts affecting the statement of service charge expenditure
- non-compliance with provisions of the applicable lease or leases or applicable laws and regulations that could have a direct effect on the determination of material amounts and disclosures in the financial statements.

(Examples of fraud or illegal acts that may be of particular relevance in the management of a commercial property and affect the statement of service charge expenditure include, but are not limited to, the acceptance of inducements in return for awarding maintenance contracts, the engagement of staff who are not entitled to work in the UK or the payment of subcontractors without deduction of tax.)

APPENDIX 3 – Example paragraphs for engagement letters

General

In view of the importance of ensuring that there is no misunderstanding about the work to be undertaken, reporting accountants are advised to consider the following points when agreeing terms of engagement:

- engagement letters should indicate the reasons for, and objective of, the engagement;

- engagement letters should clearly indicate that the work to be undertaken is not an audit;

- engagement terms should specify to whom the report is to be made available, that it should not be made available to any other individual without the firm's consent; and

- the report should fully describe the scope of the work and, unless an audit is being carried out, it should avoid use of the word "audit" except to clarify that this word does not apply to the engagement undertaken.

The engagement letter will normally be addressed to the managing agent or the owner of the property, depending on which is party to the contract with the reporting accountant. The references to addressee in the letter should be adapted accordingly.

If the engagement is to be with the owner of the property, the engagement letter will need to be addressed to the managing agent as well as the owner, to acknowledge the role of the agent in arranging for the accountant's reporting service to be provided. The reporting framework and principles for tri-partite engagements are outlined in ICAEW Technical Release Audit 01/01, *Reporting to Third Parties* and AAF 04/06, *Assurance Engagements: Management of Risk and Liability*.

The following paragraphs are designed to be included in the standard letter of engagement used by the firm, in the client-specific section of the engagement letter that sets out the details the services to be provided. The terms and conditions of business attaching to an engagement governed by the engagement letter are a matter for individual firms and are not covered in this guidance.

To [Name of managing agent]/[Name of Owner] ("the Manager")

Re: [Property] ("the property")

Dear......................................

[In accordance with the terms of the lease(s) of the property a] [A] summary of the costs and expenditure incurred in the provision of the services and of the calculation of the service charge payable in each service charge year (statement of service charge expenditure) is to be provided to all occupiers. [You consider that the lease [does not require] / [is construed as not requiring] an audit of the statement of service charge expenditure.] [You have agreed with the occupiers that an audit of the statement of service charge expenditure is not required and do not consider an audit to be necessary.] Accordingly, this letter sets out the basis on which we are to review and report on the statement of service charge expenditure for (property) for the year ended [date], and the respective responsibilities of ourselves (the Accountant) and you (the Manager).

1 You are responsible for the preparation of the statement of service charge expenditure.

You are responsible for the proper application of the terms of all the leases that are relevant to [this statement of service charge expenditure]/[the statements of service charge expenditure included in this engagement]. You are responsible for the allocation and apportionment of expenditure to occupiers in accordance with the terms of their leases. You are also responsible for providing us with a summary of the service charge provisions of all leases relating to the property.   **1.1**

You have undertaken to make available to us, as and when required, all the accounting records and related financial information, including minutes of management meetings, which we need to do our work. You will provide us with all information and explanations relevant to the preparation of the statement of service charge expenditure, and you will disclose to us all relevant information in full.   **1.2**

You are responsible for ensuring that, to the best of your knowledge and belief, the information relating to the preparation of the statement of service charge expenditure is accurate and complete.   **1.3**

In accordance with the Code of Practice, Service Charges in Commercial Property issued by the RICS (the Code), you are responsible for the preparation of the statement of service charge expenditure and will approve and sign it in order to acknowledge responsibility for the statement.   **1.4**

2 Our responsibilities as reporting accountants

Our review will be conducted with the objective of expressing our conclusion on the statement of service charge expenditure. Our conclusion, if unmodified, will be in the form;   **2.1**

Based on the procedures we have performed and the evidence we have obtained, nothing has come to our attention that causes us to believe that the statement of service charge expenditure is not prepared, in all material respects, in accordance with the provisions of the Code.

We shall conduct our review in accordance with International Standard on Review Engagements (ISRE) 2400 (Revised), *Engagements to Review Historical Financial Statements* and ICAEW Technical Release TECH xx/13 *Accountants' reports on commercial property service charge accounts*. ISRE 2400 (Revised) requires us to conclude whether anything has come to our attention that causes us to believe that the statement of service charge expenditure is not prepared in all material respects in accordance with the provisions of the Code.   **2.2**

A review of financial statements in accordance with ISRE 2400 (Revised) is a limited assurance engagement. We shall perform procedures, primarily consisting of making enquiries of your management and staff, as appropriate, applying analytical procedures, and evaluating the evidence obtained. We shall also perform additional procedures if we become aware of matters that cause us to believe that the statement of service charge expenditure as a whole may be materially misstated. These procedures are performed to enable us to express our conclusion on the financial statements in accordance with ISRE 2400 (Revised). The procedures selected will depend on what we consider necessary applying our   **2.3** professional judgment, based on our understanding of the property, and our understanding of the Code and its application in the context of the property.

2.4   A review is not an audit of the financial statements, therefore:

(a)   There is a commensurate higher risk than there would be in an audit, that any material misstatements that exist in the statement of service charge expenditure reviewed may not be revealed by the review, even though the review is properly performed in accordance with ISRE 2400 (Revised).

(b)   In expressing our conclusion from the review of the statement of service charge expenditure, our report will expressly disclaim any audit opinion on the statement.

2.5   Because the work to be undertaken is not a statutory audit carried out under International Standards of Auditing (UK and Ireland) issued by the Auditing Practices Board (ISAs (UK and Ireland) we shall not evaluate the overall adequacy of the presentation of the information which would be required if we were to express an opinion under ISAs (UK and Ireland).

2.6   Whilst we shall perform our work with reasonable skill and care and will report any misstatement, frauds or errors that are revealed by enquiries within the scope of the engagement, our work should not be relied upon to disclose all misstatements, frauds or errors that might exist.

2.7   As part of our normal procedures we may ask you to confirm in writing any information or explanations given to us orally during our work in addition to written representations of matters that we shall require as a standard procedure on all engagements.

2.8   We are not responsible for reporting on the allocation and apportionment of expenditure or on the Manager's compliance with the terms of the lease(s) or on the value for money of services provided in accordance with the lease(s).

3 Form and use of report

Our Report will be made in accordance with the terms of our engagement and will be made solely to the Manager for issue to current occupiers [and the owner[1]] and for no other purpose. The report should not be distributed to or used by other parties. To the fullest extent permitted by law, we will not accept or assume responsibility or liability to anyone other than the Manager for our work, for our report or the conclusions we form.

4 Additional responsibilities

4.1   We have agreed to carry out the following accounting and other services on your behalf:

[details of any additional services, eg, assistance with preparation of statement of service charge expenditure.]

5 Limitation of liability

5.1   We will provide services as outlined in this letter with reasonable care and skill. Our liability to you is limited to losses, damages, costs and expenses caused by our negligence or wilful default. However, to the fullest extent permitted by law, we will not be responsible for any losses, [penalties, surcharges, interest or additional

---

[1] *Include if the owner is not the manager or addressee.*

tax liabilities] where you or others supply incorrect or incomplete information, or fail to supply any appropriate information or where you fail to act on our advice or respond promptly to communications from us [or the tax authorities].

You will not hold us [our] [principal][s] [director][s] [and staff], responsible, to the **5.2** fullest extent permitted by law, for any loss suffered by you arising from any misrepresentation (intentional or unintentional) supplied to us orally or in writing in connection with this agreement. You have agreed that you will not bring any claim in connection with services we provide to you against any of our partners or employees personally.

Our work is not, unless there is a legal or regulatory requirement, to be made **5.3** available to third parties without our written permission and we will accept no responsibility to third parties for any aspect of our professional services or work that is made available to them. [Additional wording where a practitioner wishes to limit their liability in respect of a claim. You should consider whether this is suitable and if necessary take legal advice.

We have discussed with you the extent of our liability to you in respect of the **5.4** professional services described within this engagement letter (the professional services). Having considered both your circumstances and our own, we have reached a mutual agreement that £..... represents a fair maximum limit to our liability.

In reaching this agreement it is also agreed that:

●   in the event of any claim for loss or damage arising from the professional services, you have agreed that the sum of £..... represents the maximum total liability to you in respect of the firm, [its] [principals] [directors] [members] [and staff]. This maximum total liability applies to any and all claims made on any basis and therefore includes any claims in respect of breaches of contract, tort (including negligence) or otherwise in respect of the professional services and shall also include interest;

●   we confirm that the limit in respect of our total aggregate liability will not apply to any acts, omissions or representations that are in any way criminal, dishonest or fraudulent on the part of the firm, [its] [principals] [directors] [members] [or employees]; and

●   you have agreed that you will not bring any claim of a kind that is included within the subject of the limit against any of our [principals] [directors] [members] [or employees]; on a personal basis.]

[Additional wording where the owner or manager of the property is a company and the reporting accountant is also the statutory auditor of that company:

This engagement is completely separate from, and unrelated to, the audit of the **5.5** Manager's/Owner's financial statements for the purposes of the Companies Act 2006 and performed in accordance with separate engagement terms. We do not, and will not, by virtue of providing a report under this letter or otherwise, assume any responsibility whether in contract, negligence or otherwise in relation to the audit of the Manager's/Owner's financial statements; we and our partners and employees shall have no liability whether in contract, negligence or otherwise to any other party, including the occupiers, in relation to the audit of the Manager's/ Owner's financial statements.]

The foregoing exclusions do not apply to any liability for fraud or other liability **5.6** that cannot lawfully be excluded under the laws of England and Wales.

5.7   No person who is not a party to this agreement other than us and our subcontractors, if any, shall have any rights under the Contracts (Rights of Third Parties) Act 1999 to enforce any of its terms. This agreement can be varied without any third party's consent.

6 Communicating with you

7 Agreement of terms: commencement and period of engagement and signatures of parties

APPENDIX 4 – Example paragraphs for inclusion in a letter of representation

Dear Sirs

[Property name] statement of service charge expenditure for the year ended (date)

We have determined that an audit of the statement of service charge expenditure in accordance with International Standards on Auditing is not required under the terms of the lease for (property).

In accordance with the Code of Practice, Service Charges in Commercial Property (Third edition) issued by the RICS (the Code), we are responsible [under the terms of the lease(s) for (property)] for preparing the statement of service charge expenditure for the year ended (date) and notes set out on pages to (the Statement). We are responsible for ensuring that the financial management of the service charges is sound and that there is an effective system of internal control which facilitates the proper use of the service charges and which includes arrangements for good management of the building [and (specify other areas/ aspects for which the manager is responsible)] for which we have responsibility in accordance with the terms of the lease(s). We are also responsible for the allocation and apportionment of expenditure to occupiers in accordance with the terms of their leases.

We confirm that all relevant costs included as expenditure in the Statement, [including payments to reserve funds,] are a proper charge to the property and are in accordance with the underlying lease(s). [The schedule that we have prepared, of service charge expenditure applicable to different leases within the property and the allocation of this expenditure to individual occupiers, is an accurate summary of all the lease agreements relevant to [property]][2].

All the accounting records have been made available to you for the purpose of your engagement and all the transactions relating to service charge expenditure and amounts received/receivable from occupiers in respect of the year have been properly reflected and recorded in the accounting records. Any significant matters of which we consider you ought to be aware have been brought to your attention.

We have given you details of all our related parties and all the related party relationships and transactions of which we are aware.

We know of no significant facts relating to any frauds or suspected frauds that may have affected the statement of service charge expenditure [apart from those already notified to you]. We know of no actual or possible non-compliance with laws and regulations for which the effects of non-compliance affect the statement of service charge expenditure [apart from those already notified to you].

Except as disclosed in the notes to the statement of service charge expenditure, there are no material commitments, contractual obligations or contingencies that have affected or may affect the statement of service charge expenditure.

---

[2] *For use where there is more than one lease governing the service charges applicable to the property.*

APPENDIX 5 – Example review engagement report

Independent accountant's review report

To the Manager, [Property] (address)

We have reviewed the statement of service charge expenditure for the above property and notes for the year/period ended (date), set out on pages x to y. The statement of service charge expenditure has been prepared by the Manager in accordance with guidance issued by the RICS in the Code of Practice, Service Charges in Commercial Property, Third edition.

Manager's Responsibility for the Statement of service charge expenditure

The Manager is responsible for the preparation of the statement of service charge expenditure and for such internal control as the Manager determines is necessary to enable the preparation of statements that are free from material misstatement, whether due to fraud or error.

Reporting Accountant's Responsibility

Our responsibility is to express a conclusion on the statement of service charge expenditure based on the procedures we have performed and the evidence we have obtained. We conducted our review in accordance with International Standard on Review Engagements (ISRE) 2400, *Engagements to Review Historical Financial Statements (Revised)*. ISRE 2400 (Revised) requires us to conclude whether anything has come to our attention that causes us to believe that the statement of service charge expenditure, taken as a whole, is not prepared in all material respects in accordance with the provisions of the Code of practice "*Service charges in commercial property*" issued by the RICS. ISRE 2400 (Revised) also requires us to comply with relevant ethical requirements.

A review of a statement of service charge expenditure in accordance with ISRE 2400 (Revised) is a limited assurance engagement. The reporting accountant performs procedures, primarily consisting of making inquiries of management and others responsible for the services that comprise the service charge on this property, as appropriate, and applying analytical procedures, and evaluates the evidence obtained. The procedures do not include review of the allocation or apportionment of service charge expenditure to occupiers.

The procedures performed in a review are substantially less than those performed in an audit conducted in accordance with International Standards on Auditing. Accordingly, we do not express an audit opinion on the statement of service charge expenditure.

Conclusion

Based on the procedures we have performed and the evidence we have obtained, nothing has come to our attention that causes us to believe that the statement of service charge expenditure is not prepared, in all material respects, in accordance with the provisions of the Code of practice "Service charges in commercial property" issued by the RICS.

Emphasis of matter – uncertain cost of replacing heating system

As explained in Note n, the main lifts for the property have become increasingly unreliable and an inspection by independent surveyors indicates that at least part of the fault is due to poor maintenance work on the part of the previous contractors. The manager has initiated a lawsuit against the contractors to recover £x towards the costs of repairs and the cost of £z in the statement of service charge expenditure is stated after deducting £x from the total estimated expenditure of £y. However, the ultimate outcome of the lawsuit cannot be determined.]

Basis of Accounting, and Restriction on Distribution and Use[3]

Without modifying our conclusion, we draw attention to Note X to the accounts, which describes the basis of accounting. The Statement of service charge expenditure and certificate are prepared by the Manager to show how the service charge costs charged to occupiers are made up. As a result, the Statement of service charge expenditure may not be suitable for another purpose.

Our report is made in accordance with the terms of our engagement and is intended solely for the Manager for issue to current occupiers [and the owner[4]]. This report should not be distributed to or used by other parties. Our work has been undertaken to enable us to make this report to the Manager and for no other purpose. To the fullest extent permitted by law, we do not accept or assume responsibility or liability to anyone other than the Manager in connection with the report or this engagement.

[Practitioner's signature], [Date of the practitioner's report],

[Practitioner's address]

Modified Conclusion

The reporting accountant should express a modified conclusion in the report on the statement of service charge expenditure as a whole when the accountant determines, based on the procedures performed and the evidence obtained, that the service charge statements are materially misstated; or the accountant is unable to obtain sufficient appropriate evidence in relation to one or more specific items in the statement and supporting notes that are material in relation to the statement as a whole (ISRE 2400 (Revised) paragraph 73).

When the reporting accountant modifies the conclusion expressed on the statement of service charge expenditure, the accountant is required to use the heading "Qualified Conclusion," "Adverse Conclusion" or "Disclaimer of Conclusion," as appropriate, for the conclusion paragraph in the practitioner's report. The report should then give a description of the matter giving rise to the modification, under an appropriate heading, (for example, "Basis for Qualified Conclusion," "Basis for Adverse Conclusion" or "Basis for Disclaimer of

---

[3] *The position and wording of this paragraph and sub-heading are based on Illustration 6 in the Appendix to ISRE 2400. The wording is not prescriptive so the text from the fourth sentence onwards may be adapted to wording used by the reporting accountant in other reports on similar engagements or based on that in square brackets.*

[4] *Include if the owner is not the manager or addressee.*

Conclusion," as appropriate) in a separate paragraph in the accountant's report immediately before the conclusion paragraph (referred to as the basis for conclusion paragraph) (ISRE 2400 (Revised) paragraph 74).

Illustrative paragraphs and headings for modified conclusion due to apparent material misstatement

Basis for Qualified Conclusion

As stated in note 1, the statement of service charge expenditure is prepared on the accruals basis. The statement includes an accrual of £x for electricity which appears to be overstated in the sum of £y.

Qualified Conclusion

Except for the effects of the matter described in the Basis for Qualified Conclusion paragraph, based on the procedures we have performed and the evidence we have obtained, nothing has come to our attention that causes us to believe that the statement of service charge expenditure for ABC property is not prepared, in all material respects, in accordance with the provisions of the Code of practice "Service charges in commercial property" issued by the RICS.

Illustrative paragraphs and headings for modified conclusion due to apparent fundamental/pervasive material misstatement

Basis for Adverse Conclusion

The findings of the procedures we undertook indicate that substantial elements of the statement of service charge expenditure are not prepared in accordance with the stated accounting policies, in that substantial accruals in the sum of £x have been made for costs that do not appear to have been incurred during the year.

Our adverse conclusion is given on the basis of the material misstatement(s) identified during our review, as described in this report. However we note that there may be other material misstatements in the statement of service charge expenditure that we have not identified, but that we might have identified had we performed an audit of the statement.

Adverse Conclusion

Based on our review due to the significance of the matter discussed in the Basis for Adverse Conclusion paragraph, the statement of service charge expenditure is not prepared in accordance with the provisions of the Code of practice "Service charges in commercial property" issued by the RICS.

Illustrative paragraphs and headings for modified conclusion due to inability to obtain sufficient appropriate evidence about multiple elements of the service charge statements, and the accountant believes the effect is material and pervasive to the financial statements

Basis for Disclaimer of Conclusion

[The managing agents for the property were replaced by (current managing agents) in (month (6 months or more before the end of the accounting period)). (Current managing agents) have not been able to provide all the information and explanations about the period before they took over the management of the property that we consider necessary for the purposes of our report[5].]

[There was a major failure in the accounting system operated by (managing agents) in (month) that resulted in a loss of data. We have not been able to agree the figures in the statement of service charge expenditure to entries in the underlying accounting records.]

Disclaimer of Conclusion

Due to the significance of the matters described in the Basis for Disclaimer of Conclusion paragraph, we were unable to form a conclusion on the accompanying statement of service charge expenditure. Accordingly, we do not express a conclusion on the statement of service charge expenditure.

---

[5] *In the circumstances where one managing agent has replaced another, it may be possible to cross-refer to an explanatory note. If the replacement of agents took place a relatively short space before the end of the year, it may be possible for the reporting accountant to obtain information and explanations from alternative sources so that a disclaimer is not needed.*

APPENDIX 6 – Qualifications for conducting engagements to review statements of service charge expenditure in accordance with ISRE 2400 (revised)

Accountants appointed to carry out a review engagement in accordance with this guidance should be members of one of the following bodies, who are entitled under the rules of the body to which they belong to engage in public practice:

Association of Authorised Public Accountants

Association of Chartered Certified Accountants

Chartered Institute of Management Accountants

Chartered Institute of Public Finance and Accountancy

Institute of Chartered Accountants in England and Wales

Institute of Chartered Accountants in Ireland

Institute of Chartered Accountants of Scotland

The accountant should be independent of the manager – see paragraph 17. The reporting accountant should not be an employee or director or associate of the owner or manager of the property or of any agent or associate of the owner or manager of the property.

TECH 10/14AAF Receipt of information in confidence by auditors

(May 2014)

Contents

	Paragraphs
Introduction	1 - 7
Investigation	8 - 15
Duty to informant	16 - 20

Guidance issued in May 2014 by ICAEW's Audit and Assurance Faculty. This guidance supersedes AUDIT 2/99/TECH 16/99 issued in December 1999 which is withdrawn.

About ICAEW

ICAEW is a world leading professional membership organisation that promotes, develops and supports over 142,000 chartered accountants worldwide. We provide qualifications and professional development, share our knowledge, insight and technical expertise, and protect the quality and integrity of the accountancy and finance professions.

As leaders in accountancy, finance and business our members have the knowledge, skills and commitment to maintain the highest professional standards and integrity. Together we contribute to the success of individuals, organisations, communities and economies around the world.

The ICAEW Audit and Assurance Faculty is a leading authority on external audit and other assurance activities and is recognised internationally as a source of expertise on audit issues. It is responsible for ICAEW technical audit and assurance leadership and provides a range of information sources to its members which give practical guidance in key audit and assurance areas.

ISBN: 978-1-78363-140-7

Introduction

1   It is in the interest of auditors and their clients as well as the entire financial community for accurate, timely and honest information to be available to auditors, from whatever source. It is therefore in the public interest for there to be a general business climate which encourages the open disclosure of financial and other information to auditors, whether in response to auditors' enquiries or on an unsolicited basis. ICAEW Chartered Accountants should encourage the development of such a climate, both by their reactions as auditors in the receipt of such information and as management, in setting the corporate tone of organisations.

2   Professional guidance on the ethics of the disclosure and use of confidential information is contained in Section 140 of the ICAEW Code of Ethics. This Technical Release provides additional assistance in the resolution of ethical problems that may arise where auditors receive information from a source other than their client, with a request or the implication that the information or its source should be kept confidential. Such circumstances may arise in relation to information received from regulators, from employees or from third parties such as trading partners. Auditors may show this guidance to clients' management or staff, where this would assist in clarifying the auditors' position, or to any person indicating that they wish to pass on sensitive information. This Technical Release does not cover the situation where auditors receive allegations about the direct conduct of the audit, or the behaviour or actions of members of the audit team, or their relationships with the client or with members of client staff.

3   There is a certain minimum standard of behaviour that should be adhered to by auditors at all times. This may be summarised as follows:

●   auditors should at all times act with integrity;

●   auditors should take into account relevant guidance and any obligations they have under the law;

●   auditors should use their best endeavours to protect the identity of informants;

●   auditors should assess the information received, taking into account any steps taken by the informant; and

●   auditors should consider significant issues raised by informants, in relation to their audit.

4   Auditors are not obliged to follow up matters if they are satisfied, on the basis of the information made available to them, that they are not relevant to their role as auditors. Relevant law and guidance may include that applying in the country where the client or informant is based, as well as in the UK. As stated in paragraph 15 below, no further action by the auditor is needed if the auditor judges information received to be unfounded or irrelevant to the audit.

5   Where information is given to the auditors by an employee of the client (including a director), this may be particularly sensitive since the informant's future employment prospects may be affected, though they may be protected by the Public Interest Disclosure Act 1998 as amended by the Enterprise and Regulatory Reform Act 2013. Employees should be advised to report their concerns through their firm's usual procedures, where they can do so without fear of victimisation or concealment of evidence and where they have not yet done so. They may also be advised as to the appropriate external authority to which a report might be made.

The legislation enables employees to claim unlimited compensation if they are **6** dismissed or otherwise disadvantaged following a disclosure which comes within certain defined categories, known as protected disclosures. Although the legislation does not specifically cover the case of disclosure to an external auditor, protected disclosures will include those made to auditors in accordance with the employer's laid down procedures and in those circumstances where disclosure to any appropriate third party is protected. These will cover most significant disclosures to auditors.

In the case of listed companies subject to the UK Corporate Governance Code, the **7** associated Guidance on Audit Committees states at paragraph 4.7:

> "The audit committee should review arrangements by which staff of the company may, in confidence, raise concerns about possible improprieties in matters of financial reporting or other matters. The audit committee's objective should be to ensure that arrangements are in place for the proportionate and independent investigation of such matters and for appropriate follow-up action."

Auditors of these companies should therefore normally expect a whistleblowing or similar system to be in place as part of the company's system of internal control.

Investigation

The receipt of any substantive information by auditors will put them on notice. As **8** a minimum, careful consideration will need to be given to the implications of the disclosure for the audit. For example, information may lead to the auditor needing to revisit their assessment of the risk of material misstatement (ISA (UK and Ireland) 315 (revised)) and hence their planned response (ISA (UK and Ireland) 330). In some cases, more specific ISA requirements may apply – for example, if information received in confidence suggests the existence of a previously unidentified or undisclosed related party or significant related party transactions, then ISA (UK and Ireland) 550 requires that the auditor carry out additional procedures[1].

If additional tests and enquiries are necessary, they should be carried out with **9** discretion. Auditors should, wherever possible, conduct their enquiries in a way that does not reveal the source of their information. Tests which do so should be used only as a last resort. This will not only help protect the informant, but will also increase the chances of auditors being able to perform their tests without action being taken to conceal or obscure the true position.

It should also be noted that: **10**

- auditors may also be required to report their findings or suspicions to third parties such as national regulators (for example under the duty to report matters of material significance to regulators in the financial sector,[2] or the duty to report matters to the Charity Commission or Office of the Scottish Charity Regulator,[3] or the duty to report certain matters to The Pensions Regulator[4]);

---

[1] *ISA (UK and Ireland) 550 Related parties, paragraphs 21-22.*

[2] *See ISA (UK and Ireland) 250 Section B The auditors right and duty to report to regulators in the financial sector.*

[3] *See FRC Practice Note 11 (Revised) The audit of charities in the United Kingdom.*

[4] *See FRC Practice Note 15 (Revised) The audit of occupational pension schemes in the United Kingdom.*

- suspicions of money laundering should normally be reported under the Anti Money Laundering legislation;[5] and

- in the case of engagements involving other countries, additional duties, rights, rules and restrictions may apply – for example those relating to the US Securities and Exchange Commission in relation to whistle-blowing and suspected unlawful acts.

11   International Standard on Auditing (UK and Ireland) 260 (revised) lays down requirements for the communication with an appropriate level of management and those charged with governance of a wide range of matters arising from the audit which may be relevant to information received in confidence. Many other ISAs (UK and Ireland) contain requirements in specific situations and the most relevant to information received in confidence are likely to be:

- actual or suspected fraud: ISA (UK and Ireland) 240 *The auditor's responsibilities relating to fraud in an audit of financial statements*;

- identified or suspected non-compliance with laws and regulations: ISA (UK and Ireland) 250 Section A *Consideration of laws and regulations in an audit of financial statements*;

- deficiencies in internal control: ISA (UK and Ireland) 265 *Communicating deficiencies in internal control to those charged with governance and management*; and

- related parties: ISA (UK and Ireland) 550 *Related parties*.

12   These requirements in the ISAs (UK and Ireland) do not indicate that the procedures used or information obtained by the auditors in forming their suspicions need be disclosed to management. Under the Data Protection Act 1998[6] if a report is received making an allegation against an individual, the individual has the right to be aware of the report against them and to respond where this is possible as part of the investigation. To avoid compromising audit procedures, it would be advisable if possible to have any conversation that is necessary after the auditor has undertaken the procedures.

13   In some cases, information given to auditors will be vague or imprecise, making it difficult to act upon. So far as is possible, the auditors should seek to persuade the informant to clarify the details of their concern. The fact that little practical benefit will result if the auditors are given inadequate information to enable them to follow up disclosures should be explained, and it should be made clear to informants that whatever their motives for making the disclosure, the desired outcome is unlikely to be achieved if details are withheld.

14   In the case of a disclosure made to an auditor by an employee, it must refer to an issue that is material to the financial statements, the control environment or risk profile of the organisation ie, from the auditor's perspective, to be acted upon it must be be of relevance to the audit.

15   Auditors should receive all disclosures in a proper spirit of professional scepticism. The previous paragraphs deal with matters that might be relevant to the audit but in some cases information may be received which the auditor judges to be clearly unfounded or irrelevant to the audit. No further action by the auditor is needed in such cases although for cases that are clearly relevant to the client the

---

[5] *See icaew.com/moneylaundering*

[6] *See icaew.com/en/technical/legal-and-regulatory/information-law-and-guidance/data-protection*

auditor might wish to consider how the matter should be escalated to the client's management.

Duty to informant

Auditors should use their best endeavours to protect the identity of informants. **16** They should also ensure, from the outset, that they do not mislead informants on the extent to which they can maintain confidentiality, or obscure the fact that the information will be used by the auditors in assessing the need for further investigations. Though these investigations should be carried out as discreetly as possible, in some cases management may be able to deduce that information has been given and occasionally its source. No unrealistic undertakings as to confidentiality should be given.

Many informants will find themselves in a difficult ethical and practical position, **17** and be making disclosure only after reaching a carefully considered decision as to the appropriate action and the balance of public interest. It will be appropriate for auditors to discuss with informants the implications of the disclosure, including internal actions or other reporting procedures that could be used by the informant. In addition to the guidance referred to in paragraph 10 above, ethical guidance on when disclosure of information to third parties in the public interest is appropriate is included in the ICAEW Council guidance on Professional Conduct in Relation to Defaults or Unlawful Acts.[7] Informants who are members may also be referred to ICAEW's ethical advisory service.[8]

In their dealings with informants, as in any other aspect of their professional lives, **18** members of ICAEW are bound by the fundamental principle of integrity. This principle would be breached where an auditor (or any other member) allowed or encouraged the disclosure of confidential information with an assurance or implication that confidentiality would be maintained and then disclosed the circumstances surrounding the disclosure to the client's management. Fair dealing applies to bona fide informants as well as to clients. Where information on the source of information has been withheld from management, a member of the client's staff may be erroneously assumed to be the provider of such information, to their disadvantage. Auditors should be aware of this possibility in designing their tests but cannot be expected to have a duty of care to such third parties.

Auditors need not consider that they have any responsibilities towards an **19** anonymous informant, whether of good or bad faith.

False information, given maliciously, might be subject to a report to management. **20** Where false and malicious information has been received from a member of ICAEW, consideration should be given to the need to make a report under Disciplinary Bye-Laws 9.1 and 9.2[9] and related guidance issued by the ICAEW Council on the Duty to report misconduct.[10]

---

[7] *icaew.com/en/members/regulations-standards-and-guidance/ethics/defaults-or-unlawful-acts-guidance*

[8] *icaew.com/en/members/advisory-helplines-and-services/ethic-faqs*

[9] *icaew.com/en/members/regulations-standards-and-guidance/bye-laws/disciplinary-bye-laws*

[10] *icaew.com/en/members/regulations-standards-and-guidance/complaints-and-regulation/duty-to-report-misconduct*

TECH 13/14AAF Auditing Implications of FRS 102 transition (Revised November 2017)

(November 2017)

Contents

Paragraphs

1 Introduction   1 - 9

2 Ethics and FRS 102   10 - 54
    Services   13 - 16
    Threats   17 - 21
    Non-audit services   22 - 23
    Accounting services   24 - 39
    Valuation services   40 - 49
    Tax services   50 - 53
    Other non-audit services   54

3 Issues for audited entities – what the auditor should expect management to be doing   55 - 64
    Questions that the auditor might wish to ask management   55 - 56
    Implementation of the project plan   57 - 62
    Small companies   63
    Ongoing considerations for management   64

4 What the auditor needs to consider   65 - 158
    Knowledge and training   65 - 68
    Engagement considerations   69 - 84
    Planning and project management   85
    Risk assessment   86 - 105
    Risks relating to transitional arrangements   106 - 146
    Communication with those charged with governance   147 - 151
    Documentation   152 - 154
    Reporting   155 - 156
    Ongoing issues post-transition   157 - 158

Appendix 1: Technical issues on compliance with specific ISAs (UK) and ISQC (UK) 1

**Appendix 2: Support from the ICAEW financial reporting faculty on
       FRS 102 Transition**

Appendix 3: Glossary of terms and abbreviations used

About ICAEW

ICAEW is a world leading professional membership organisation that promotes, develops and supports over 147,000 chartered accountants worldwide. We provide qualifications and professional development, share our knowledge, insight and technical expertise, and protect the quality and integrity of the accountancy and finance professions.

As leaders in accountancy, finance and business our members have the knowledge, skills and commitment to maintain the highest professional standards and integrity. Together we contribute to the success of individuals, organisations, communities and economies around the world.

The ICAEW Audit and Assurance Faculty is a leading authority on external audit and other assurance activities and is recognised internationally as a source of expertise on audit issues. It is responsible for ICAEW technical audit and assurance leadership and provides a range of information sources to its members which give practical guidance in key audit and assurance areas.

Laws and regulations referred to in this ICAEW Technical Release are stated as at November 2017. Every effort has been made to make sure the information it contains is accurate at the time of creation.

ICAEW cannot guarantee the completeness or accuracy of the information in this ICAEW Technical Release and shall not be responsible for errors or inaccuracies. ICAEW not be liable for any reliance you place on any information in this ICAEW Technical Release.

ISBN 978-1-78363-161-2

1. Introduction

FRS 102 The Financial Reporting Standard applicable in the UK and Republic of   **1**
Ireland is a single financial reporting standard which replaced almost all existing
UK accounting standards. It has been effective for accounting periods beginning
on or after 1 January 2015. For accounting periods beginning on or after 1 January
2016 Section 1A of FRS 102 has included the requirements for small companies,
which replaces the FRSSE.

While based on the IASB's IFRS for SMEs there were some significant changes   **2**
from that standard in the original version of FRS 102, and further differences have
been introduced subsequently. FRS 102 is also subject to an ongoing process of
triennial amendment.

This guidance is intended to assist auditors in making the transition to FRS 102. It   **3**
is an updated version of guidance that was originally issued in September 2014.
Many entities will already have made the move to FRS 102, but this guidance is
intended to reflect some changes in the audit environment that have taken place
since 2014 where these are relevant to entities still making the change. It is also
intended to deal with principles that apply to any change in accounting framework,
including changes in specific requirements of that framework or specific standards
within that framework. It does not, other than in passing, make reference to issues
that might arise when an entity is a public interest entity.

There are significant implications for the auditors of the entities that are changing   **4**
accounting framework and this guidance addresses the key issues of concern to
those auditors. It covers the technical and process challenges arising for them
and the risks that they will need to address. Auditors should consider at an early
stage both what they should expect the entities they are auditing to be doing (see
section 3) and also what they should be doing themselves (see section 4).

Many entities subject to changes of or in the accounting framework they apply are   **5**
likely to benefit from the support of their auditors in the transition process.
However, there are important ethical matters for auditors to consider if entities
request assistance from them (see section 2). Many of these entities will be owner-
managed businesses or other entities that may not have a clear and formal
distinction between management and those charged with governance. As a
result, this guidance normally refers to management, but this term should be
taken to include those charged with governance when the context requires.

This guidance has been informed by experience of FRS 102 implementation, as   **6**
well as IFRS implementation and previous guidance issued on this, including the
ICAEW Audit and Assurance Faculty Technical Release Audit 03/04 *Auditing
Implications of IFRS Transition*. Audit 03/04 remains in place. For those entities
applying FRS 101 *Reduced Disclosure Framework*, Audit 03/04 may be relevant.
These entities will need to consider whether they are qualifying entities as defined
by FRS 101 and have met the conditions for applying the standard.

Appendix 1 covers technical issues for the auditor on compliance with specific   **7**
ISAs (UK) and ISQC (UK) 1, and outlines what those issues are and what is
required of the auditor with respect to them. The auditing standards featured in
appendix 1 are key ones to consider as part of practical FRS 102 implementation,
but appendix 1 is not intended to provide a comprehensive guide – it is necessarily
limited in the standards it covers and in the way it describes the issues. Appendix 1
should therefore not be regarded as a substitute for reading the ISAs (UK) and
ISQC (UK) 1 themselves.

8   ICAEW is providing members with support in relation to FRS 102, and in particular, the Financial Reporting Faculty is providing a range of resources to help members deal with that standard as well as the UK's broader financial reporting framework.

9   A glossary of terms and abbreviations used is set out in appendix 3.

2. Ethics and FRS 102

10   In principle, the change to FRS 102 is no different from any other change in accounting framework, and many of the ethical issues that arise will be the same as those that have faced entities, and the auditors of those entities, that have moved from UK GAAP to IFRSs. However, the scope of the change to FRS 102 is far broader and, consequently, a much greater range of entities will be affected. While some of the entities transitioning to FRS 102 will have significant internal resources available to deal with the impact of change, many more will be relatively small, with limited accounting resources. For such entities, the prospect of moving to a different framework may appear daunting and many may look to their auditor for help in effecting the transition.

11   Both management and the auditor have a role to play in achieving successful implementation of FRS 102, but caution is required where the auditor is involved. Auditors need to remain independent of audited entities, and are bound by the FRC's Ethical Standard 2016 (the ES) that places limits on the services they can provide. There are further restrictions on the services that can be provided to audited entities that are listed and/or public interest entities (as defined in the ES).

12   For entities moving to FRS 102, the assistance that the auditor provides to facilitate the transition to FRS 102 with minimal disruption should be planned with care so as not to compromise the requirement for the auditor to retain their independence.

Services

13   For larger entities, the auditor may receive requests to provide a level of assurance, review, advance their audit work in a specific area or otherwise report on various forms of financial and non-financial information that has been prepared by management for the purposes of transition.

14   Smaller entities may be more likely to seek accounting advice or more direct assistance from their auditor on adoption of the new standard.

15   Whenever auditors are requested to provide non-audit services to audited entities, they are required to consider the potential for the provision of these services to create a threat to their objectivity or a perceived or actual loss of independence. More specifically, the ES requires that before any non-audit service is provided, the auditor has to identify and assess the significance of any threats to the auditor's objectivity, including any perceived loss of independence. The threats that need to be considered are:

(a)   self-interest

(b)   self-review

(c)   management

(d)   advocacy

(e)   familiarity or trust and

(f)   intimidation threats.

If any threats are identified, then the auditor is required to identify and assess the   **16**
effectiveness of any safeguards available to them that might eliminate or reduce
those threats to an acceptable level. If adequate safeguards cannot be applied, the
work cannot be performed.

Threats

While all of the threats listed above should be considered by the auditor when   **17**
asked for assistance on an entity's transition to FRS 102, the two key threats are
likely to be the self-review threat and the management threat.

Self-review threat

A self-review threat exists when the results of a non-audit service performed by   **18**
the engagement team or by others within the audit firm are reflected in the
amounts included or disclosed in the financial statements.

Management threat

A management decision-making threat exists when the audit firm undertakes work   **19**
that involves making judgements and taking decisions that are the responsibility of
management.

The ES provides further detail.   **20**

The following subsections deal with some of the services that may be requested,   **21**
how threats may arise and, where possible, how they can be mitigated.

Non-audit services

The following services are those likely to be of particular relevance to auditors of   **22**
entities transitioning to FRS 102:

(a)   accounting services

(b)   valuation services and

(c)   tax services.

The ES provides some specific requirements and guidance in relation to these   **23**
services.

Accounting services

The ES recognises that the audit process involves extensive dialogue between the   **24**
auditor and management.

As part of this process, management may request and receive significant input on   **25**
such matters as accounting principles and financial statements disclosures,
including on the impact of adopting accounting standards such as FRS 102.
Such advice to management may be seen as an appropriate part of the audit
process that promotes the fair presentation of financial statements.

However, in providing such accounting advice, the auditor should guard against   **26**
giving bookkeeping advice, initiating transactions, taking management decisions
and making specific accounting entries, where these go beyond the technical,
mechanical or informative nature mentioned in the ES, all of which could create

potential self-review and management threats to the auditor's independence. Accordingly, although such advice is important in many audits and will assist with any issues identified once entities have moved to FRS 102, it does not mean that the auditor is permitted to take decisions and apply judgement on behalf of management about the many policy and practice choices that might arise in the process of transitioning to FRS 102.

27   The ES (5.151) explicitly excludes advice on the implementation of current and proposed accounting standards from its definition of "accounting services", which is a very helpful starting point in considering the impact of objectivity with regards to the provision of accounting assistance in transitioning to FRS 102. The ES notes that it is usual for the auditor to provide advice to management on the accounting policies in use and on the application of current and proposed accounting standards, but this advice is expected to be a "by-product" of the audit service rather than the result of any specific engagement to provide non-audit services (5.157). Implementation advice that is a "by-product" should not give rise to a compromise of the auditor's independence, but consideration must be given in particular to self-review and management threats in such circumstances. The auditor should also be aware of the perception risk and consider whether the provision of accounting services would lead an objective, reasonable and informed third party to conclude that the auditor's independence had been compromised.

28   Some entities may opt to undertake their own impact assessments of the transition to FRS 102, select the accounting policies and transitional provisions to be applied on implementation and decide on the form of presentation to be adopted, without reference to the auditor. Having done so, they will often (and indeed should) ask the auditor for the auditor's views on the accounting policies and other matters that they have considered.

29   In such cases, when the auditor is asked to provide views, the communication should be restricted to a factual analysis of the entity's selected accounting policies and practices and whether they are consistent or otherwise with the requirements of FRS 102. It should avoid including any statement that could reasonably be mistaken for an element of an audit, review or any other assurance engagement. For example, it would not be appropriate for the communication to include commentary that appears to express a conclusion on the appropriateness and application of the selected accounting policies, because the auditor will not have obtained sufficient audit evidence regarding their application to actual transactions and events, nor will the entity have prepared a complete set of financial statements in which to assess the impact of the accounting policy and disclosure choices in context.

30   Other entities may lack the resources to undertake a full impact assessment in relation to FRS 102 and may therefore expect to make use of their auditor for this purpose. There are particular challenges for small entities adopting Section 1A of FRS 102, which will require smaller entities that will most likely have less sophisticated finance functions and resources at their disposal to apply significant judgement, for example when deciding which disclosures are required to give a true and fair view.

Example I – entity seeks advice from its auditor on disclosures required under Section 1A of FRS 102

An entity has requested advice from its auditor to assist with the preparation of its first FRS 102 Section 1A-compliant financial statements.

The risks to the independence of the auditor include:

- self-review: the auditor may get too involved in determining which disclosures are required to give a true & fair view during the period of preparation assistance, compromising the auditor's objectivity; and
- management decisions: the auditor is at risk of stepping into the shoes of management by taking decisions or applying judgement about which disclosures are required to give a true and fair view, which should be the preserve of management.

The safeguards employed by the auditor need to be sufficient to reduce the threats to an acceptable level and should include:

- assessing and documenting whether the entity has "informed management" so that management have the skill and expertise to apply properly their judgement and have the ability to take responsibility for decisions made about which disclosures will be included and those omitted;
- obtaining written representations from management about decisions taken and judgements applied by them in the preparation of the financial statements;
- avoiding misunderstanding about the auditor's and management's responsibility by agreeing with the client in writing the terms of engagement;
- ensuring that audit files demonstrate that the entity has taken all management decisions including determining the appropriateness of the level and nature of disclosures; and
- ensuring that if the smaller entity exemptions are taken, the requirements of ES 6.15 are met.

When considering the extent to which the auditor may provide advice on the **31** transition to FRS 102, it should be clearly established that management retain full responsibility for all financial information and the basis on which it is prepared and presented. That responsibility includes application of the judgement required for the preparation and presentation of the financial information, including the selection and application of appropriate accounting policies and, when needed, the development of reasonable accounting estimates.

Consequently, entities cannot simply subcontract the transition to FRS 102 to their **32** auditor and ask them to make decisions about the preparation and presentation of financial statements under the new standard. Management should retain overall control of the process at all stages and should make all of the relevant decisions.

In situations where entities do not employ a qualified accountant and management **33** does not have significant accounting experience, the auditor may not feel confident in undertaking an assessment alone. In such situations, the auditor should consider whether there is "informed management".

34   The ES states that in determining whether a non-audit service gives rise to a management threat, the auditor needs to consider whether there is informed management. Informed management is defined as follows:

Informed management

35   Informed management is defined as a member of management (or senior employee) of the entity relevant to the engagement who has the authority and capability to make independent management judgments and decisions in relation to non-audit / additional services on the basis of information provided by the firm.

36   For smaller entities the auditor is relieved from some of the prohibitions relating to undertaking part of the role of management as long as objectivity and independence is discussed with management and management accept their responsibility for any decisions taken. The auditor will need to disclose that the exemptions for smaller entities have been taken in accordance with ES 6.15.

37   For accounting services, informed management is generally a prerequisite and other safeguards, as mentioned below, will be necessary. Management must have the capability to make independent management judgements on the service, the authority to make any judgements and decisions required and receive an objective analysis of the issues the entity needs to consider, with reasonable alternatives, from which it can decide on an appropriate course of action.

38   In the context of the transition to FRS 102 this means that the auditor can assist in identifying the choices that need to be made and can discuss these with management. What they should not do is make any of these choices for management. It should be clear that management have made all of the important decisions and consequently that the financial statements reflect management's accounting policies, management's transitional choices and management's preferred methods of presentation.

39   Even when the auditor has not made decisions on behalf of the entity and has acted within the parameters set by the ES, this does not mean that the threats are eliminated entirely. The auditor should still consider any other safeguards that may be appropriate, depending on the auditor's level of involvement. The use of further safeguards will depend upon the extent of that involvement, but might include the use of different individuals to discuss the accounting policy choices from those involved in the audit, or the review of the financial statements on transition by a person of suitable experience not otherwise involved with the audit engagement.

Valuation services

40   The ES states that a valuation comprises the making of assumptions with regard to future developments, the application of appropriate methodologies and techniques, and the combination of both to compute a certain value, or range of values, for an asset, a liability or for a business as a whole.

41   On transition to FRS 102, many entities will be required to carry more items at a valuation than under their previous GAAP. For example, many financial instruments, including derivatives such as forward contracts or interest rates swaps, will need to be measured at fair value, and there may be more issues on valuation of intangible assets arising from an acquisition. This may mean that, when an entity is not familiar with the valuation techniques commonly used for such items, they may ask the auditor for assistance (see example IV in section 4).

42   There are strict prohibitions on provision of valuations by the auditor. The auditor shall not undertake an engagement to provide a valuation to either:

(a)   A listed audited entity that is a non-SME listed entity or a significant affiliate of such an entity, when the valuation would have a material effect on the listed entity's financial statements, either separately or in aggregate with other valuations provided; or

(b)   any other audited entity, when the valuation would both involve a significant degree of subjective judgement and have a material effect on the financial statements either separately or in aggregate with other valuations provided.

In addition, there are specific restrictions relating to auditors of public interest entities.

The main threats to the auditor's objectivity and independence arising from the   **43** provision of valuation services are self-review and management threats. In all cases, the self-review threat is considered too high to allow the provision of valuation services that involve the valuation of amounts with a significant degree of subjectivity and which have a material effect on the financial statements.

It is usual for the auditor to provide management with accounting advice in   **44** relation to valuation matters that have come to the auditor's attention during the course of the audit. Such matters might typically include providing:

(a)   comments on valuation assumptions and their appropriateness;

(b)   details of errors identified in a valuation calculation and suggestions for correcting them; and

(c)   advice on accounting policies and any valuation methodologies used in their application.

While providing advice on such matters does not constitute valuation services, it is   **45** important that auditors avoid taking a management decision by proposing audit adjustments that could result in the entity uncritically processing an adjustment and applying the auditor's judgement rather than management's.

Similarly, where the auditor is engaged to collect and verify the accuracy of data to   **46** be used in a valuation to be performed by others, such engagements do not constitute valuation services.

When valuations are largely objective, for example valuing investments in a listed   **47** company's shares as market prices are commonly available, the auditor can discuss potential sources of data with management. When valuations include more subjective elements, for example valuing investments in a private company's shares, the auditor can discuss the basis of valuation, but should not become involved in determining any of the assumptions that need to be made in arriving at the valuation. This may involve discussions with the entity on the mechanics of valuations, but allowing management to make its own assessments. In some situations the auditor may advise the entity to use the services of a third party with appropriate expertise in the area.

As with the provision of accounting services, the auditor should also consider   **48** whether the provision of valuation services would lead an objective, reasonable and informed third party to conclude that the auditor's independence had been compromised.

It should be noted that in some limited cases, FRS 102 does not currently require   **49** entities to obtain a valuation when one would normally be needed if doing so would involve undue cost or effort. For example, this exemption might be applied to certain investment properties and investments in associates and jointly controlled entities. In such circumstances the decision on whether the cost of obtaining valuations outweighs the benefit should be made, and supported, by management.

Tax services

50   The auditor is prohibited from providing tax services to a listed entity or a significant affiliate of a listed entity which would involve the preparation of current or deferred tax calculations that are, or may reasonably be expected to be, used when preparing accounting entries that are material to the financial statements of the audited entity. There are further prohibitions in the ES relating to auditors of public interest entities.

51   For entities other than listed companies or significant affiliates of listed companies, the auditor may prepare current or deferred tax calculations for the purpose of preparing accounting entries, provided that those services do not involve initiating transactions or taking management decisions and are of a technical, mechanical or an informative nature, and appropriate safeguards are applied.

52   This means that most entities now applying FRS 102, particularly those applying Section 1A, will not be subject to the more stringent requirements described above. Nonetheless, the auditor should take care to ensure that the services provided are limited to the technical, mechanical and informative nature mentioned in the ES and do not result in a management decision risk.

53   In many cases there will be tax implications of transitioning to FRS 102, in that accounting policy choices made, both on transition and thereafter, may have an effect on tax liabilities. The auditor should bear this in mind when discussing the policy choices made on transition and ensure that those policies, with their attendant tax implications, really are those of management.

Example II – providing tax services to an audited entity

The entity has requested the auditor provide advice on the tax consequences that might arise on adoption of FRS 102. The entity is an audited entity (but not a public interest and/or listed entity or a significant affiliate of such an entity) and the auditor is already engaged to audit the first financial statements prepared in accordance with FRS 102. The entity's activities are reasonably complex and there are a number of areas where there is a choice of accounting policy to be adopted. In some of these cases the choice of accounting policy adopted will affect the reported and/or taxable profits.

This situation creates primarily a management threat to the auditor's independence, but also a potential self-review threat. The management threat arises from the auditor taking management decisions in selecting accounting policies for the entity on the basis of their tax consequences. There is also a self-review threat, because if the auditor selected and applied accounting policies, they may not be objective to consider the appropriateness of those policies as part of the audit.

The auditor should therefore apply safeguards to reduce these threats to an acceptable level. Having separate individuals who are not part of the audit team provide the advice would be an obvious first step, but is unlikely to be considered sufficient. Of greater importance is ensuring that the nature of the advice provided is appropriate by, for example:

- documenting the auditor's assessment of informed management and the application of the smaller entity exemptions under 6.15 if applicable;
- setting out those areas where accounting policy choices are available and summarising for each policy the tax consequences on both transition and an ongoing basis;
- making clear that the accounting policy choices should be those of the entity's management, and that if a policy is not specifically addressed in FRS 102 then it should be developed in accordance with the criteria set out in Section 10 of that standard; and
- requesting that management provide a response detailing the accounting policy choices it has made including, where appropriate, the rationale for those choices.

Other non-audit services

The guidance in this section is not exhaustive and its addressing of non-audit **54** services is limited to those issues that are considered to be most relevant to an entity transitioning to FRS 102. The auditor will also need to consider any other non-audit services that could create a threat to the auditor's objectivity or a perceived loss of independence, for example providing information technology services to an audited entity to design, provide or implement systems relating to the production of financial statements as a result of the introduction of FRS 102. In all cases, careful consideration of all the potential threats to independence contained in the ES should be made, most notably self-review and management threats, as discussed above.

3. Issues for audited entities – what the auditor should expect management to be doing

Questions that the auditor might wish to ask management

The combination of complexity and potential lack of preparation for the transition **55** to FRS 102 can result in an increased challenge for auditors as they prepare to audit an entity's opening balance sheet as of its date of transition and its first financial statements that conform to the standard.

In order to assess the quality of the entity's transition process and readiness and **56** identify any key risk areas, the auditor may wish to ask the following questions of management at an early stage in the transition process:

(a) Have management laid out a realistic and achievable timetable for transition?

(b) Have management got commitment throughout the organisation as needed (eg, board, subsidiaries or other business units, IT)?

(c) Have management properly assessed the extent to which it has resource with the necessary skill and knowledge to manage the transition process?

(d) Does management have sufficient access to the specialist expertise that are often required in applying some of the new accounting policies required by FRS 102, such as valuations?

(e)   Have management rigorously evaluated the significance of the changes that will affect the entity on transition (eg, identification and classification of financial instruments)?

(f)   Is the entity undertaking a thorough exercise to understand the accounting policy changes necessary on transition?

(g)   Have the wider impacts of transition (eg, dividend planning, profit-related remuneration schemes) been identified and assessed?

(h)   Does management have records of their distributable reserves, separate to the financial statements?

(i)   Have management consulted with advisers, including considering possible tax elections which may need to be made?

(j)   Has consideration been given to whether or not systems and processes are able to capture sufficient, reliable data that will now be required in order to produce financial statements that comply with FRS 102?

(k)   Have management communicated details of the change to shareholders and other stakeholders?

(l)   Have management reviewed bank covenants whose terms are linked to the financial statements (eg, interest cover or gearing ratios) and contacted lenders to renegotiate the terms of such borrowings if necessary?

Implementation of the project plan

57   The following actions should be undertaken by management in planning for the transition:

(a)   establishing a timeline for transition in consultation with auditors and other impacted stakeholders, considering the needs of all external stakeholders and availability of staff and advisors;

(b)   timely and appropriate communication of any changes arising from the implementation that could impact key stakeholders;

(c)   assessing the number, skills and timing of staff required for a timely and effective transition and the extent to which support will be required from external advisors;

(d)   identifying additional training requirements for staff and appropriate approach to providing such training;

(e)   a comprehensive assessment of the differences between the current accounting policies applied under existing GAAP and those required from the new or revised accounting standard;

(f)   identifying the data needed to generate the adjustments that are required to the opening balance sheet under GAAP and to prepare the financial statements on an ongoing basis;

(g)   consideration of the impact on systems and processes, allowing any changes made to be implemented in a sustainable and structured way to allow for ongoing capture of the requisite data both for preparation of the primary statements and the disclosures required within the notes to the financial statements;

(h)   developing template or "pro forma" accounts for financial statements, budgets/forecasts and reporting packages;

(i)   identifying the impact on the entity's other business needs, as well as the financial statements, including:

    (I)   reviewing bank covenant arrangements and negotiating amendments as required;

    (II)   preparing forecasts and budgets under the accounting policies adopted going forward;

    (III)   establishing the impact on distributable reserves and reviewing dividend policy and plans;

    (IV)   considering the impact, where applicable, on the calculation of deferred consideration on recent acquisitions;

    (V)   assessing the impact of conversion and subsequent accounting on the entity's taxation;

    (VI)   reviewing remuneration and employee incentive schemes to understand the impact of transition on these and, if necessary, making any required adjustments (this may include liaison with trustees and/or union representatives as appropriate);

    (VII)   assessing the impact on regulated businesses; and

    (VIII) evaluating the need for assistance from external advisers; and

(j)   The auditor will need to gain appropriate understanding of each of the above actions, as well as provide clarification of the responsibilities of management. The auditor should remind management that it is responsible for the implementation of the new accounting standard and management should have considered carrying out an analysis of the impact on the business, including any requirements to train staff, update accounting systems, and implement changes in reporting encompassing all significant business units.

When considering the timely and appropriate communication of any changes arising from the implementation that could impact key stakeholders, management should consider the following stakeholders: **58**

(a)   shareholders;

(b)   other stakeholders, for example third party lenders, parties to contractual arrangement or grantors, all of who may have agreements in place that require financial statements are prepared under specific accounting standards.

(c)   the auditor:

    (I)   it is critical that management understand the extent to which the auditor can and cannot assist with transition (see section 2), as this will affect the extent to which management may need to seek input from other external advisers. Detailed discussions between management and the auditor should therefore take place at an early stage in proceedings to establish the degree of support that the auditor will be able to provide throughout the transition process.

    (II)   when management have identified significant areas of accounting judgement, these should be communicated to enable the auditor to plan appropriate procedures for those areas.

    (III)   management should agree an appropriate timeframe with the auditor for the audit to take place, taking into consideration the additional procedures that may be required as a result of the transition (see section 4).

(IV) management may seek consideration of the opening balance sheet and transitional adjustments prior to the audit of the first full financial statements under the new standard. When this is the case, the auditor will need to be notified at an early stage in order to plan the procedures to be undertaken for any such transitional adjustments. Depending upon the scope of the work to be undertaken, these procedures may form part of the audit or be a separate engagement. This will need to be agreed; and

(d)   tax advisors.

59   In performing a comprehensive assessment of the differences between the current accounting policies applied under existing GAAP and the requirements of the new standard, management may be faced with a choice in the selection of an accounting policy or there may be instances when the standard does not prescribe a particular accounting policy. In such cases, management will need to develop an appropriate policy. The differences identified allow management to make an informed decision and take responsibility for the accounting policies selected and applied. Other considerations for management will include:

(a)   assessing any transitional exemptions available on adoption and deciding which, if any, will be applied; and

(b)   discussing the selection of accounting policies with the auditor.

60   In undertaking its responsibilities management should consider the extent to which specialist expertise is required from either internal or external advisors. For example in the valuation of complex financial instruments management judgement is required in determining:

(a)   fair value hierarchy applicable;

(b)   valuation model used (if required); and

(c)   key inputs and assumptions used to derive the valuation.

61   Management would need to consider the extent to which it is appropriate, if at all, to rely on the valuations provided by counterparties to the contracts. Such valuations may not have been prepared for financial reporting requirements.

Example III – considerations for management on transition

When considering the effects of transition on other areas of the business, management may choose to revisit the existing reporting structure and consider whether the individual business units (subsidiaries or divisions) will report in accordance with FRS 102 or whether the business units will provide the information to a central team who will then convert this to FRS 102.

---

62   In implementing the changes, the actual transition process will include:

(a)   preparation of an opening balance sheet under FRS 102 with an explanation for each adjustment to opening equity;

(b) identification, to the extent practicable, of any adjustments to opening equity that are due to errors under previous GAAP and separation of these from transitional adjustments;

(c) preparation of the figures for the comparative balance sheet date under FRS 102;

(d) preparation of the figures for the comparative period under FRS 102; and

(e) preparing the first FRS 102 financial statements.

Small companies

In the case of small companies adopting Section 1A of FRS 102, management will **63** also need to consider whether there are any disclosures not generally required, but which will be necessary in the particular circumstances of the company, in order for the financial statements to give a true and fair view.

Ongoing considerations for management

It should be recognised that the transition is merely the start of reporting under the **64** revised GAAP and the auditor should expect management to continue to consider the accounting and disclosure requirements on an ongoing basis, including the impact on:

(a) structure and accounting for acquisitions;

(b) maintaining up-to-date valuations (eg, financial instruments);

(c) suitability of existing systems as the business expands;

(d) new transactions within the wider group in group situations;

(e) distributable reserves and dividend policies; and

(f) covenants and financing plans.

4. What the auditor needs to consider

Knowledge and training

a) Understanding the requirements of FRS 102 and any subsequent amendments to the standard introduced through triennial review or other amendment issued by the FRC from time to time.

The first set of financial statements prepared under FRS 102 will need to include **65** comparative information that is restated in accordance with the standard. Auditors will need to refer to ISA (UK) 710 *Comparative information – corresponding figures and comparative financial statements.* Auditors will need to plan and prepare for the transition of audited entities to FRS 102 in a timely manner, and it is likely that the auditor will need to dedicate more time and resources to the planning and project management of the audit. In particular, the auditor will need to consider carefully the timing of their involvement in the transition process of the audited entity and be familiar with their client's impact analysis and approach to transition.

To this end, the auditor will need to ensure that internal training plans for audit **66** staff capture the requirements of FRS 102 as well as any updates and amendments.

Application of FRS 102 will involve more subjectivity and judgement on the part **67** of the financial statement preparer and key areas of judgement and estimate are required by FRS 102 to be disclosed as part of the notes to the financial statements. Consequently a more significant level of auditor judgement in reaching the audit opinion will be necessary. The auditor needs to ensure that specific attention is given to related disclosures. For example, more subjectivity and judgement is likely to be involved in the recognition and measurement of intangibles acquired in a business combination, the fair value of investment property and the fair value of certain financial instruments that will be recognised in the financial statements. In each case the auditor also considers whether key judgements are adequately described in the notes to the financial statements.

b) Resource needs

68   The auditor will need to consider the availability of suitable resource (whether internal or external) in the following areas.

(a)   Technical expertise – following suitable training, does the auditor have staff with appropriate expertise in the framework? Is the expertise up-to-date with latest developments?

(b)   Training resource – does the auditor have access to suitable training resources, internally or externally, to ensure that staff have sufficient knowledge to undertake their role as part of the audit team?

(c)   Training resource to offer to the audited entity – does the audited entity require assistance with education for its own staff in relation to the preparation of financial statements? Is the auditor aware of the ethical limitations and implications?

(d)   Fair value accounting specialists or experts – does the auditor have access to staff within the audit firm who have a specialism or expertise in estimating, accounting for and auditing fair values? Does the auditor have access to external valuation expertise when the audit firm does not have adequate internal resource? Are those specialists and experts suitably trained on the changes arising in their area of specialism/expertise? Are specialists and experts independent?

(e)   Other experts – does the auditor have access to other expertise in areas that may be required eg, property valuation or deferred tax?

(f)   Valuation techniques – are all relevant staff familiar with appropriate valuation techniques permitted under the new financial reporting framework?

Example IV – involvement of fair value experts

If expertise other than in the field of accounting and auditing is necessary to obtain sufficient appropriate audit evidence, auditing standards require that the auditor considers whether there is a need to involve an auditor's internal or external expert in the audit process in order to obtain that evidence. The auditor determines whether an expert is needed to obtain audit evidence in relation to fair values. From the outset, the auditor is clear that the involvement of the expert in this respect is to provide the auditor with sufficient appropriate audit evidence concerning a fair value used by management in the preparation of the financial statements. The responsibility for determining an appropriate fair value rests with management and the involvement of an auditor's expert is not a substitute.

FRS 102 will require more extensive use of a "fair value" in certain circumstances when determining appropriate amounts to recognise in the financial statements eg, in the valuation of non-basic financial instruments, the valuation of intangible assets or the valuation of biological assets and agricultural produce when the fair value model is chosen.

Therefore, the incidence of situations in which it will be appropriate to involve an auditor's expert is likely to increase. The auditor needs to consider:

- whether appropriate resources are available within the audit firm or whether external experts would need to be engaged; and
- whether appropriate policies and procedures relating to the use of such experts are in place.

When the work of an auditor's expert is used to provide audit evidence, the auditor will need to ensure that they have complied with the requirements of ISA (UK) 620 *Using the work of an auditor's expert*, particularly in relation to evaluating the adequacy of the work performed for the auditor's purposes. The ISA also requires that any external fair value expert be independent from the entity. In the case of audits of public interest entities, the expert must confirm their independence to the auditor.

Engagement considerations

a) Nature of engagement and providing assistance with transition

As discussed in section 2, entities may ask their auditor to provide advice, **69** guidance and support during the transition period through to preparation of the first set of financial statements prepared for audit in accordance with FRS 102.

Entities may expect the auditor to provide assistance in determining whether FRS **70** 102 is appropriate in their circumstances (rather than adopting IFRSs, FRS 101 or the FRS 105) and what the impact on the financial statements will be following adoption of FRS 102.

The auditor will need to consider to what extent management's requests for "early **71** assurance" or private reports can be met through performance of enhanced, early or interim audit procedures, or whether an advisory engagement or a separate assurance or agreed-upon procedures engagement would be more appropriate in the circumstances.

Audit firms may also be called upon by management to offer early consideration **72** of an entity's state of readiness on FRS 102 information that is produced prior to the entity's first FRS 102 financial statements. Management may seek:

(a) views from the auditor on the appropriateness of accounting policies and interpretation of FRS 102;

(b) the auditor's considerations of key areas of judgement and estimation;

(c) the auditor's view of the implications of FRS 102 on other information (including statutory other information) presented alongside the financial statements;

(d) the auditor's consideration of the appropriateness of additional disclosures in the first published financial statements relating to transition to FRS 102;

(e)   a consideration of "parallel" or "dry-run", non-statutory financial information prepared in tandem with financial statements under existing GAAP;

(f)   agreement to, or opinion on, a proposed accounting treatment for a transaction proposed in the first reporting period under FRS 102; or

(g)   an assessment of the impact of the adoption of FRS 102 on existing banking covenants or profit-related contracts.

73   In considering the nature and timing of such peripheral engagements, the auditor should be conscious of the fact that there are inherent difficulties in undertaking such engagements and potential ethical concerns (see section 2). Where the auditor determines that such work can be accepted, respective responsibilities should be clarified in writing and the threats to independence and safeguards employed should be reported to, and discussed with, those charged with governance.

74   In addition, the auditor should remain aware of and alert to any changes in or clarifications as a result of emerging practice that may arise as a consequence of applying a framework for which "generally accepted" accounting practices are still evolving.

75   Particular concerns for the auditor to resolve when considering what additional services to provide and whether it will be appropriate to provide those additional services may include:

(a)   that the provision of certain non-audit services for audit clients that are public interest entities will be prohibited;

(b)   that the provision of certain non-audit services for public interest entities may have other implications on the audit (such as reporting in the auditor's report);

(c)   there may be uncertainty around the quality of the base data from which the FRS 102 information has been prepared, and whether this has been audited;

(d)   the scope, rigour and completeness of the entity's transition to FRS 102 at the time of the assignment;

(e)   that the absence of comparative data could limit the effectiveness of analytical procedures that the auditor is able to perform as part of their work; and

(f)   the possibility that the accompanying preliminary/initial balance sheet may have to be adjusted.

76   Management may also ask the auditor to provide staff on a secondment basis to help with certain aspects of the financial reporting process. In such circumstances there is a risk that the auditor's involvement in the financial reporting process and transition to a new standard may give rise to threats to the auditor's independence which may ultimately compromise the auditor's ability to provide the audit service.

77   Audit firms may need to consider whether there is a need to revisit and clarify partner and staff understanding of relevant ethical requirements, and may need to implement or refresh policies and procedures relating to the non- audit services that an auditor will and will not be able to provide to audited entities.

b) Agreeing the terms of engagement

78   In accordance with ISA (UK) 210 *Agreeing the terms of audit engagements*, the auditor should consider, for each audit to be conducted, whether the audited entity

needs to be reminded of the engagement terms and conditions or whether those terms and conditions need to be refreshed.

The auditor will need to consider the extent to which the audit engagement letter needs to be reissued either because the change in accounting framework has a significant impact on the contents of the existing terms of business or because respective responsibilities need to be clarified. **79**

The auditor should bear in mind that the standard(s) and related policy choices to be adopted under the accounting framework will be a policy choice made by management (see section 2). **80**

The auditor will need to ensure that they understand this policy choice and the implications of the choice of standard(s) to be applied. The auditor's work will involve ascertaining whether the entity has complied with all requirements and relevant conditions in relation to the use of a chosen framework. **81**

Before an auditor commences any entity-specific audit work relating to transition, they need to ensure that they have identified: **82**

(a)   any previous accounting framework applied by the entity and understand the legal and regulatory bases for any change to the framework; and

(b)   the framework to which the entity will be transitioning and understand the interrelationship with any existing accounting, legal and regulatory requirements including any relevant Accounting Directions or SORPs.

This is necessary to identify relevant reporting differences, any potential reporting conflicts, and reporting requirements that an entity should continue to comply with. **83**

Example V – unincorporated entities

Most entities not incorporated under the Companies Act 2006 will, under their current reporting framework, have historically had some flexibility in the presentation of the balance sheet and income statement as they are not required to apply the formats set out in the Accounting Regulations made under the Act. The auditor will need to be clear that should entities opt to apply FRS 102, Sections 4 and 5 of the standard require that primary statement formats laid out in the Accounting Regulations are followed unless prohibited by any statutory framework under which the entity reports.

There may also be some additional reporting requirements that apply as a consequence of the entity's legal or registration status. **84**

Example VI – special accounting requirements

Accounting requirements that have effect under existing law will continue to apply irrespective of the accounting standard the entity chooses to adopt. For example, a registered social housing provider should still ensure that it complies with, and applies the requirements of, the Accounting Direction made under relevant housing law. FRS 102 does not cross-refer to all possible sources of additional disclosure requirements.

Planning and project management

85   When planning their work, the auditor should:

(a)   agree with management the nature of, and timetable for, auditor involvement and reporting throughout the transition process;

(b)   determine the nature, extent and quality of audit evidence needed in relation to the judgements made and conclusions reached by management in the preparation of the financial statements that comply with FRS 102;

(c)   consider any changes to the audit plan that may be required as a result of a transition to FRS 102, such as those that make use of audited comparative numbers to set expectations, etc.;

(d)   communicate any information needs to management on a timely basis; and

(e)   explain to management the impact of a change of financial reporting framework and how it will affect the audit.

Risk assessment

86   In performing the risk assessment for the audit of the financial statements prepared in accordance with FRS 102, the auditor will need to consider carefully the specific circumstances of the entity and the sources of possible risks of material misstatement that may exist.

87   The auditor should aim to consider the following matters as early as possible in the audit process to determine the sources of significant risk of material misstatement on transition to FRS 102.

a) Materiality

88   The auditor should consider the extent to which unadjusted misstatements at the transition balance sheet date and for the comparative period, which were identified during prior audits, and that do not eliminate on transition to FRS 102, impact on the audit opinion on the first FRS 102 financial statements.

89   In so doing, the auditor will need to consider the level of audit materiality in respect of FRS 102 financial statements in accordance with ISA (UK) 320 *Materiality in planning and performing an audit*. The auditor may need to reconsider how materiality is determined, as the benchmark on which materiality was previously calculated may have moved eg, as a result of higher or lower reported profits.

90   The auditor may also need to consider whether the chosen materiality level suggests that additional work on opening balances is required compared with the work that may have been performed on comparative information under a previously assessed level of materiality. In addition, as FRS 102 also requires that more fair value movements are reported in the profit calculation, the auditor should consider whether adjustments are required to determine an appropriate level of "normalised" profits.

91   Depending on the circumstances, and as a consequence of the additional risks involved, the auditor may adjust the performance materiality levels or apply specific materiality thresholds to particular areas of the financial statements.

92   The auditor should also consider and conclude on whether it is appropriate to set specific materiality levels lower than the materiality for the financial statements as a whole.

Example VII – materiality levels for specific disclosures

Auditing standards require that the auditor consider whether specific materiality levels are necessary for specific classes of transactions, account balances or disclosures. ISAs (UK) place a particular emphasis on the possible need for specific materiality levels for disclosures within the financial statements.

There is a general increase in the level of disclosure required under FRS 102.

Many of these disclosures (such as details of directors loans, related parties, information about market, credit and liquidity risk, fair value hierarchy) may not have an obvious numerical benchmark because the information is likely to be important to users of the financial statements irrespective of the amounts involved. The auditor will need to consider the need for disclosures that may be material because of their qualitative features and ensure that the conclusions on materiality reflect these considerations.

b) Choice of accounting policies, management bias and fraud risk factors

As FRS 102 will result in a greater level of subjectivity and judgement on the part **93** of the financial statement preparer, the auditor should consider the increased risk of management bias and/or fraudulent financial reporting.

Adoption of a new accounting framework may introduce additional scope for **94** management to manipulate the financial statements through application of bias in their choice of accounting policies. Therefore, the auditor should consider whether the incentive, the motivation and the opportunity for such manipulation exists and tailor the nature, timing and extent of the work accordingly.

The auditor will need to identify the accounting policies to be adopted by **95** management in the preparation of the first FRS 102 financial statements and consider the appropriateness of those policy choices.

In particular, the auditor should be alert to changes to accounting policies that are **96** presented as a consequence of a change of financial reporting framework but in reality have changed for other reasons.

Equally the auditor should take the opportunity presented by the transition process to **97** challenge whether established and long-running practice continues to be appropriate.

Example VIII – the impact of management bias on the audit

NB This example refers to the specific scenario in which an organisation holds a defined benefit pension liability. Although many smaller organisations will not contribute to a defined benefit pension scheme, the principles dealing with the auditor's response to management bias will be relevant. This example has been used less because this is considered to be a new issue, but more because it is considered to be an issue which an auditor may find challenging.

As part of the auditor's work on a defined benefit pension deficit recognised within the financial statements, the auditor engages an external expert to provide the auditor with evidence about the suitability of assumptions used in determining the value of scheme liabilities.

> The expert reports to the auditor that the assumptions used in relation to RPI, the discount rate and mortality rates are all at the "aggressive" end of what they would consider to be an acceptable range. The outcome is that the pension scheme deficit is presented at what the actuary would consider to be the lowest possible value.
>
> In reaching conclusions, the auditor should consider such factors as:
>
> - The sensitivity of the resulting liability to changes in these assumptions. For example, if the assumptions were moved to a more "average" position whether would this have a material effect on the amounts presented?
> - The extent to which the position is described in the notes to the accounts (including accounting policies, disclosure of key judgements and estimates and the notes on the pension deficit) and whether the auditor agrees that the disclosures aid a user's understanding of the impact of the assumptions applied.
> - Whether items affected are of particular interest to users (eg, they have implications for loan covenants).
> - Management's rationale for the assumptions used and their consideration of alternatives (including why alternatives were rejected).
>
> In some cases, the auditor may conclude that the assumptions used are too aggressive even though, in isolation, they are within an acceptable range.

c) Accounting estimates and use of fair values

98   The requirements of ISA (UK) 540 *Auditing accounting estimates, including fair value accounting estimates, and related disclosures* will be of particular importance to entities with material items recognised in the financial statements at fair value. This is particularly the case because FRS 102 will require more extensive use of fair values in determining amounts to be recognised in the financial statements. Determining what is a "fair" value is subjective and likely to be subject to estimation uncertainty (although FRS 102 provides some guidance).

99   For accounting estimates that give rise to significant risks, the auditor is required under ISA (UK) 540 to evaluate how management have considered alternative assumptions or outcomes, and why it has rejected them, or how management have otherwise addressed measurement uncertainty in making the accounting estimate.

100   As a subjective, judgemental area the auditor may wish to explain the responsibilities for determining an appropriate fair value to management of audited entities.

101   When the audited entity is a public interest entity, the auditor has responsibilities for reporting management's approaches to valuations to those charged with governance.

d) Changes to the entity's system of internal control

102   As a consequence of applying FRS 102 for the first time, management may have (or may need to have) established new systems or implemented new controls relevant to the financial reporting process. The auditor will therefore need to:

(a)   update any existing systems notes;

(b)   assess the design and implementation of controls relevant to the audit (particularly those that relate to significant risks);

(c)   reconsider the consequences for the extent of assurance derived from tests of operating effectiveness of controls, particularly those that may have been tested on a cyclical basis or those that may not have operated throughout the entire period under review;

(d)   give consideration to whether or not to plan to derive assurance from any new controls over the preparation of financial statements under FRS 102; and

(e)   report to management and those charged with governance as appropriate, on a timely basis, any weaknesses that are identified.

e) Changes to the entity's IT environment

In determining where risks of material misstatements might arise, the auditor **103** should consider the continuing appropriateness of an entity's existing IT-related information systems (including choice of accounting software) and the possibility that material misstatement could arise from continuing to use such information systems that have not been suitably updated to reflect the requirements of a new accounting framework. The risk of misstatement could also be exacerbated through any amendments made to information systems.

The risk is likely to be increased when the IT systems and controls are: **104**

(a)   bespoke systems, designed specifically for the entity being audited;

(b)   complex, involving multiple applications and interfaces;

(c)   networked or involve connectivity across multiple sites;

(d)   part-manual or require manual intervention; or

(e)   easily overridden by management.

The auditor will need to consider how management have controlled changes to the **105** IT systems and how management have ensured that any upgrades or updates have been properly performed.

Risks relating to transitional arrangements

The audit of financial statements prepared under FRS 102 for the first time will **106** create additional risks when management is inexperienced in preparing financial statements under FRS 102 and/or the auditor is unfamiliar with the new challenges of auditing such financial statements.

The auditor should be mindful of the need to give greater consideration to any **107** new, first-time and/or non-recurring accounting adjustments that arise on transition, which may be more susceptible to material misstatement.

The following examples provide guidance on some of the areas that may give rise **108** to risks of material misstatement on transition and the auditor's related considerations.

a) Transitional requirements

The auditor will need to ascertain whether the entity has applied the transitional **109** requirements, set out in Section 35 of FRS 102, appropriately and has only taken advantage of any elections or exemptions on transition to FRS 102, if the standard permits. For any updates to the financial reporting framework made through triennial review and other amendment issued by the standard setters, the auditor will need to ascertain whether the amendments have effect and if so, whether they retrospectively apply.

b) Previously unidentified misstatements

110   In performing their work on opening balances and comparative information, the auditor may identify errors in the financial statements that have not previously been reported. The auditor should be mindful that such prior- year misstatements should be dealt with as such and may not be presented as adjustments required as a result of transition to the new framework.

c) Restatement of comparative information

111   The auditor will need to perform additional procedures to determine whether comparative information has been appropriately presented within the financial statements. This is likely to involve the performance of additional audit procedures to assess whether the comparative information has been accounted for and presented in accordance with FRS 102 in all material respects.

d) Disclosure of reconciliation from old to new framework

112   In the first set of financial statements prepared under FRS 102, preparers are required to make a number of disclosures explaining the effect of the transition to FRS 102, including a reconciliation of its equity determined under previous GAAP to equity under FRS 102 as at the transition date and the comparative period end. As a non-standard disclosure item, there may be a risk that misstatements exist within the reconciliation.

e) Classification of financial instruments

113   FRS 102 requires that most financial instruments that meet the definition of basic financial instruments are accounted for at amortised cost. Most financial instruments that are not basic (and certain equity instruments) are measured at fair value through profit or loss. In many cases, the determination of whether a financial instrument is basic or non-basic will be straightforward. However, certain financial instruments will be difficult to categorise and judgement may be needed in reaching a conclusion.

114   The auditor should consider whether the nature of the financial instruments held by the entity is such that an inappropriate categorisation will result in material misstatement in the carrying value of the instrument in the financial statements. In making this assessment, the auditor should consider the information needs of users and how users might be influenced by a different categorisation.

f) Financing transactions

115   FRS 102 requires that an entity should measure a financial asset or financial liability that constitutes a financing transaction at the present value of the future payments discounted at a market rate of interest for a similar debt instrument.

116   It will therefore be necessary for both the lender and the borrower separately to determine the market rate of interest for a similar debt instrument.

117   In such circumstances, and particularly in group situations when there may be more opportunity for the introduction of bias or for manipulation of amounts to be reported in the financial statements, the auditor should seek to understand whether the terms and conditions of the financing transaction are sufficiently formalised so

as to be clear on whether any resultant financial instrument is repayable on demand or not and, when relevant:

- determine the materiality of any discounting to be applied;

- ascertain how management will determine a market rate of interest for a similar debt instrument and the availability of such information;

- ascertain how management will determine such a market rate at the transition date; and

- consider the extent to which the auditor intends to use the work of a third party as audit evidence and whether the auditor needs to involve an internal or external expert.

g) Financial instruments measured at amortised cost

Key considerations for the auditor in this respect are likely to centre on management's ability to calculate the effective interest rate and the use of certain assumptions within the calculation. **118**

The auditor will need to ascertain whether they are satisfied with the validity of the information included within the calculation. **119**

h) Financial instruments measured at fair value

Key considerations for the auditor in assessing the risk of material misstatement in this area may include the following. **120**

How material are such financial instruments to the financial statements?

The source of the valuation, including, when relevant, asking who has conducted the valuation.

What qualifies that valuer to do so and is that valuer independent and objective?

How has the valuation been carried out and how will the auditor obtain this information directly from the valuer eg, an issuing banker?

Does the auditor need to involve their own internal or external expert to determine whether the valuation (or the underlying model or technique) is appropriate?

Obtaining sufficient appropriate audit evidence relating to the fair value of financial instruments is likely to be a particular concern to the auditor when management have been provided with a valuation of financial instruments by the same institution which issued the financial instruments to the entity (usually the entity's banker). **121**

It is unlikely that the auditor will be able to rely solely on a counterparty valuation report, although the decision of the extent to which to do so is influenced somewhat by materiality and/or risk and whether the entity maintains its own independent record of valuation. **122**

In situations where the issuer provides the entity with a year-end valuation for an instrument that it has issued to the entity and management use that information as the basis for the measurement of the instrument in the financial statements, that issuer is, in effect, acting as management's expert. **123**

This means that the auditor, when they choose to use the work of the management's expert as audit evidence, will need to ensure that they comply with the requirements of ISA 500 (UK) *Audit Evidence*. In particular, the auditor should understand how the valuation has been determined (ie, the technique **124** applied), the competence and capabilities of the issuer in forming such valuations and the assumptions that were involved.

125   The auditor should also consider whether information around key judgements and sensitivity in valuation is adequately disclosed in the financial statements, when relevant.

i) Use of fair values for the first time

126   As part of the responses to the requirements of ISA (UK) 540, the auditor will need to consider how management have determined the amounts to include where FRS 102 requires the use of fair values.

127   When the auditor considers that a particular fair value accounting estimate involves high estimation uncertainty, this will often be identified as a significant risk of material misstatement.

128   When a valuation technique is used by management, the auditor should understand that valuation technique (involving an auditor's expert, when appropriate) and aim to conclude on the appropriateness of the use of that technique in providing a valuation that accords with FRS 102. In subsequent accounting periods, the auditor should pay specific attention to the outcomes of prior-period estimates and valuations and whether there is any indication that the entity's technique is producing values that are later found not to approximate the actual values at the reporting date.

129   As part of the auditor's response to risk in this area and the requirements of ISA (UK) 540, the auditor may develop a range of possible appropriate outcomes against which they will assess the value provided by management. In forming this range, the auditor should not accept or assume responsibility for determining the appropriate fair value and should be clear that responsibility for this rests with management. However, in the transitional period the auditor can expect that entities may require additional support in this area and may need to consider the extent to which they can become involved (see section 2).

j) Residual values

130   Under FRS 102, preparers of financial statements should consider depreciable amount through comparison of cost to a residual value which is based on the estimated amount that an entity would currently obtain from the disposal of an asset, after deducting the estimated costs of disposal, if the asset were already in the age and condition expected at the end of its useful life. The auditor should therefore assess both whether the residual value used in calculating the annual depreciation charge is appropriate at transition and the risk that current prices at each reporting date will have changed such that depreciation is materially misstated. The auditor will also need to consider how best to obtain evidence that establishes what a current price for an asset at the reporting date should be.

k) Intangibles and goodwill

131   FRS 102 requires that intangible assets and goodwill are amortised over the useful economic life of the asset. The useful economic life of intangible non-current assets and goodwill is not more than 10 years unless a reliable estimate of their useful economic lives can be made.

132   Under the existing financial reporting framework, many entities have opted for significantly longer useful economic lives for intangibles and goodwill and may wish to continue to amortise intangibles and goodwill over the previously determined useful economic lives because they do not believe there is any new evidence to justify making a change. Provided that management can justify a longer useful economic life, there is no need to accelerate the period over which goodwill is written off. However, indefinite lives are not permitted.

The auditor should ensure that they understand the rationale for management's 133 decision either to continue amortisation under the previously assessed useful economic life or to reconsider the useful economic life on transition to FRS 102.

The auditor should also remain alert to the possibility that investigations into the 134 appropriateness of the useful economic lives of goodwill and intangibles may give rise to evidence that the useful economic life, as previously assessed, was not appropriate.

l) Defined benefit schemes

Under FRS 102, entities are no longer required to involve an actuary when 135 determining net liabilities arising from an entity's obligations under defined benefit schemes.

The auditor should conclude on whether the figures included in the accounts and/ 136 or the disclosures are materially misstated. Not involving an actuary in obtaining those figures may increase the audit risk if management are not suitably competent to prepare a valuation.

When an actuary is not involved, the auditor would need to form a particularly 137 robust assessment of:

- how the value of the assets and liabilities involved has been determined and the assumptions used in making that determination;

- the evidence available to be able to determine whether the amounts included within the financial statements and the related disclosures are appropriate; and

- whether the auditor will need to involve their own expert and ultimately charge that cost to the entity.

Based on this assessment, the auditor would reach a conclusion on whether it is 138 appropriate that management has not involved an actuary.

When management does not involve an actuary in such circumstances and the 139 auditor is unable to obtain sufficient appropriate audit evidence through alternative means, the auditor will need to consider modification of the auditor's report in relation to this limitation of scope.

m) Going concern

Applying FRS 102 can result in volatility in reported profits presented within a 140 statement of comprehensive income as many fair value adjustments and revaluation movements will be presented in determining profit for the year. Such volatility could have implications for loan covenants and other agreements with an entity's stakeholders. The auditor needs to establish whether and how an entity's agreements and contracts with third parties have been reconsidered and renegotiated, when necessary.

When possible breaches of terms and conditions of such agreements have been 141 identified, the auditor should perform procedures designed to check whether the possible implications for the going concern status have been appropriately considered by management in their assessment of going concern and adequately disclosed in the financial statements. The auditor may also need to consider any implications for the audit report.

n) Hedge accounting documentation

142   To qualify for hedge accounting an entity must fulfil certain conditions specified within FRS 102. One of the criteria specifies that certain information needs to be documented by management.

143   When an entity is to apply hedge accounting, the auditor needs to establish that management have put in place the appropriate documentation as required by FRS 102 and reach a conclusion on whether the documentation in place specifically addresses the requirements of FRS 102 and has been approved by appropriate individuals within the organisation.

o) Disclosures

144   The auditor should either have access to a suitable financial statements disclosure checklist or establish policies and procedures to determine how they will assess whether the disclosures are complete.

145   In addition to completeness of disclosures, the auditor will need to design audit procedures that address the quality of the disclosures including the understandability and accuracy of the information reported.

146   Auditors are always required to assess whether financial statements give a true and fair view by considering whether additional disclosure is required, over and above any disclosures specifically required by the framework. This is sometimes referred to as a "stand back" requirement. This issue may be of particular relevance where a company adopts Section 1A of FRS 102, as the specific disclosure requirements are quite limited.

Communication with those charged with governance

a) Clarification of respective responsibilities of transition to new framework

147   In establishing respective responsibilities the auditor should consider whether it is necessary to communicate responsibilities in relation to the FRS 102 transition to those charged with governance, and whether those charged with governance need to acknowledge that they understand those responsibilities, particularly in relation to:

(a)   preparation of the financial statements;

(b)   establishing an adequate system of internal control;

(c)   determination of appropriate accounting policies to be applied;

(d)   framework decisions (eg, that management or those charged with governance are not aware of any objections to application of the reduced disclosure framework);

(e)   forming judgements, estimates and fair values; and

(f)   any assertion of undue cost or effort.

148   The auditor may also wish to obtain specific representations from management and/or those charged with governance in relation to certain matters (including for policy choices adopted in relation to a new accounting framework) in order to ensure that all involved acknowledge and have understood certain specific responsibilities (see matters raised in appendix 1 on ISA (UK) 580 *Written representations*.

b) Communication of deficiencies in internal control

Aspects of an entity's system of internal control that have been updated or developed in response to the adoption of a new financial reporting framework are more likely to be deficient by virtue of the fact that they are more likely to be untried, untested and carried out by members of staff who are building experience with unfamiliar processes. When, as part of the auditor's work, deficiencies in internal control are identified, such deficiencies should be communicated to those charged with governance. If the deficiencies are considered to be significant, the auditor should communicate them in writing as soon as is practicable. **149**

c) Reporting misstatements

All factual, judgemental and projected misstatements (except for those that are clearly trivial) identified as part of the auditor's work in relation to transition to FRS 102 should be communicated to management and those charged with governance with a request that those misstatements be corrected. This should include disclosure misstatements and omissions and any inconsistencies identified between the financial statements and other information presented along with the financial statements that indicate a misstatement of the financial statements or the other information. **150**

Where misstatements are not corrected, the auditor should consider the implications for the audit opinion with reference to the materiality of uncorrected misstatements. In forming this conclusion, the auditor should be taking into account the effect of any apparent misstatements that exist within the comparative information and the consequences on the current year financial information. **151**

Documentation

The auditor will need to consider whether the audit approach and any audit work programmes need to be amended and updated for FRS 102, dealing particularly with the transitional issues, accounting policy selection and the audit of disclosure items. This will be particularly relevant where an auditor's work programmes provide details of the requirements of accounting standards. **152**

Audit documentation needs to provide a clear audit trail of the judgements and conclusions reached in relation to the transition to FRS 102. **153**

When the auditor has challenged management and/or those charged with governance in relation to judgements and estimates made, evidence of that challenge should be documented in the audit file. **154**

Reporting

The auditor will need to consider the possible effects on the audit opinion and audit report, including any qualifications or modifications, that may result from: **155**

(a)   the framework to be applied – the auditor should consider whether specific reference needs to be made to the relevant accounting standard(s) applied;

(b)   non-compliance with the financial reporting framework – including inappropriate application of particular standards;

(c)   implications for the auditors reporting on other information (including statutory other information) and going concern that may result from applying a new framework;

(d)   inappropriate application of transitional arrangements; and

(e)   insufficiently robust transition processes and procedures implemented by those charged with governance.

156   When the auditor's opinion is ultimately modified, the auditor should consider how they will describe the basis for that modification with reference to the requirements of the financial reporting framework.

Ongoing issues post-transition

157   In periods subsequent to the initial transition period, many of the ongoing requirements of FRS 102 will continue to provide challenges for auditors in practice.

158   A feature of the environment in which auditors will operate will be the establishment of accumulated familiarity with FRS 102. It will take time before there is an instinctive understanding of FRS 102. Auditors should expect interpretation, common practice and application of the requirements of the standard to evolve in the accounting periods that follow transition and should take measures to ensure awareness of new developments and emerging practice. Areas that are expected to be of particular interest include, but are not limited to:

(a)   undue cost or effort – and circumstances in which it may be appropriate to claim undue cost or effort;

(b)   fair values – and, in particular, the application of techniques for determining fair values of particular assets and liabilities;

(c)   hedge accounting – and, in particular, whether the entity has the required documentation in place at the time required;

(d)   financial instruments – and, in particular, common practice in terms of instruments identified as basic and those that are not;

(e)   the need to involve experts and/or specialists in the audit process and how the auditor will determine the appropriateness of their work for audit purposes;

(f)   business combinations – identification and valuation of intangibles, useful economic life of intangible assets, useful economic life of goodwill; and

(g)   establishing the recoverable amount in an impairment review.

Appendix 1: Technical issues on compliance with specific ISAs (UK) and ISQC (UK) 1

This appendix highlights some of the specific issues raised in this Technical Release/by the implementation of FRS 102 in the application of ISAs (UK) and ISQC (UK) 1. As stated in paragraph 7 of the Technical Release, this appendix should not be regarded as a substitute for reading the ISAs (UK) and ISQC (UK) 1 themselves. The issues selected, as well as their possible responses, are indicative examples only and users of this guidance should give careful consideration to any other requirements that might apply in the particular circumstances of the engagement.

Subject dealt with	FRS 102 implementation issues	Application/Action required
ISQC 1 *Quality control for firms that perform audits and reviews of financial statements, and other assurance and related services engagements*		
Competence and capabilities of engagement partner and engagement teams.	• Detection of improper or incorrect reconciling items on transition such as changes in previous estimates, policies or correction of errors. • Identification of items that have been incorrectly included within other reconciliation amounts and should be in reconciling items. • Identification of incorrect FRS 102 figures (where previous GAAP figures are unchanged).	• Audit staff require knowledge and understanding of FRS 102. • In the year of transition, audit staff require sufficient knowledge of both previous GAAP and FRS 102 to audit the completeness and accuracy of reconciliations between the two, as required by FRS 102. • Firm policies and procedures should ensure sufficient understanding is obtained by all levels of audit staff including engagement partners.
Engagement quality control review.	• Increased likelihood of requiring an engagement quality control review.	• Consider the need for engagement quality control review in accordance with the firm's policy. • Other ISQC 1 matters are addressed in other topics within this appendix eg, acceptance, ethics, consultation.

Subject dealt with	FRS 102 implementation issues	Application/Action required
ISA 200 *Overall objectives of the independent auditor and the conduct of an audit in accordance with ISAs and* **ISA 220** *Quality control for an audit of financial statements*		
Compliance with relevant ethical requirements.	• Increased likelihood of threats arising from the provision of non-audit services (Section 5 of ES) relating to transition eg: – valuation services – accountancy services – tax advisory services and – secondment of staff.	• Assessment of implications for auditor independence and objectivity prior to undertaking non-audit services, and documentation of this. • Documentation, assessment and communication of threats and safeguards prior to acceptance of appointment as auditor. • Ensure final decisions on the appropriateness of accounting policies to be adopted are those of the directors. • See section 2 of this Technical Release.
Plan and perform an audit with professional scepticism, recognising that circumstances may exist that cause the financial statements to be materially misstated.	• Increased focus on management judgement and risk of bias. • Undue cost and effort assessments may be used inappropriately. • Accounting policy and estimate choices on implementation of FRS 102. • Application of transition options and exemptions.	• Gain an understanding of the motives of management on implementation. • Assessment of accounting estimates (see ISA 540) and appropriate challenge. • Ensure the team is competent and capable of identifying items requiring critical assessment (see ISQC 1). • Clear documentation of significant professional judgements and demonstration of scepticism. • See also ISA 240.

Subject dealt with	FRS 102 implementation issues	Application/Action required
Consultation within engagement team and others.	• Increased likelihood of internal consultation with those responsible for technical financial reporting issues or externally where technical expertise not available.	• Assessment of need for consultation on critical transition matters. • Documentation of nature, scope and conclusions resulting from consultations. • Firm policies and procedures adhered to where differences of opinion exist.

ISA 210 *Agreeing the terms of audit engagements*

Obtain agreement from management that they acknowledge and understand their responsibility.	• Clarification of directors' responsibilities.	• Early communication to clarify expectation that management will be properly prepared and will have an appropriate plan in place.
		• Engagement letter may clarify that the directors are responsible for:
		  – analysing the impact of the introduction of FRS 102 on the business;
		  – developing plans to mitigate the effects identified;
		  – assessing any impact on the going concern assessment; and
		  – preparation of financial statements under FRS 102, including comparative figures, and the disclosures needed to give a fair presentation and true and fair view.

Subject dealt with	FRS 102 implementation issues	Application/Action required
ISA 230 *Audit documentation*		
Audit documentation outlines nature, timing and extent of the audit procedures performed; the results and audit evidence obtained; and significant matters, the conclusions reached thereon, and significant professional judgements made in reaching those conclusions.	• Areas where significant professional judgements are more prevalent in the year of transition.	• Ensure there is clear documentation of procedures undertaken and rationale for conclusions when assessing transition and accounting under FRS 102. • See also other areas where documentation is appropriate – essentially there needs to be clear documentation for all the matters highlighted in this appendix where applicable.
ISA 240 *The auditor's responsibilities relating to fraud in an audit of financial statements*		

Fraud risk assessment and discussion.	• Changes to accounting systems may provide increased opportunity for aggressive earnings management/fraud.
	
	• Opportunity for manipulation of transition accounts regarding:
	  – restatement of opening balances;
	  – increased choices under FRS 102; and
	  – increased use of fair values.
		• Ensure the assessment of risk related to fraud includes relevant consideration of application of new accounting standards.
		
		• Make teams aware of new areas of financial statements which are susceptible to manipulation.
		  – Discussion among the engagement team, with emphasis on how and where the financial statements are susceptible to material misstatement due to fraud, may include increased risk of fraud and non-detection arising from transition to FRS 102.
		
		• See also ISA 200 and ISA 450.

Subject dealt with	FRS 102 implementation issues	Application/Action required
Audit procedures responsive to risks related to management override of controls.	• Potentially increased incentive and opportunities to manipulate financial information by overriding controls.	• Test of appropriateness of journal entries may include specific enquiries of individuals and testing of journals related to FRS 102 adjustments. • Review of accounting estimates for bias includes: – clear evaluation of judgements and decisions made on implementation; – retrospective review of prior year judgements and assumptions for significant accounting estimates in light of management decisions in transition period. • Clear documentation of the above.

ISA 250A *Consideration of laws and regulations in an audit of financial statements*

Obtain sufficient appropriate audit evidence regarding compliance with the provisions of those laws and regulations generally recognised to have a direct effect on the determination of material amounts and disclosures in the financial statements.	• Increased potential for non-compliance with some laws and regulations, for example: – the requirement to keep adequate accounting records may be impacted by lack of familiarity with financial reporting framework; – the FRS 102 transition may affect distributable profits and the basis of assessment of distributable reserves; and – impact on tax payable and compliance with tax laws.	• Documentation of consideration/impact of specific laws and regulations that may be impacted by FRS 102 implementation, for example: – whether changes in accounting systems and controls made are sufficient to maintain adequate accounting records; – confirmation with directors of understanding of legal/fiduciary duties relating to distributions; and – consideration of whether a separate tax review is required.

Subject dealt with	FRS 102 implementation issues	Application/Action required
		• The team should have sufficient understanding of affected laws and regulations in order to consider them when auditing assertions related to the determination of amounts to be recorded and disclosures made.
		• Consideration of the impact of non-compliance on the audit report.

ISA 260 *Communication with those charged with governance and*
ISA 265 *Communicating deficiencies in internal control to those charged with governance and management*

Communicate views about significant qualitative aspects of the entity's accounting practices, including accounting policies, accounting estimates and financial statement disclosures.	• Management may not have fully considered the potential impact of FRS 102. • Changes of accounting policy driven by FRS 102-related matters may lead to specific communication requirements.	• Communication with those charged with governance prior to implementation of areas where FRS 102 may impact on accounts and the need for an appropriate action plan. • Communication of significant accounting practice, that is acceptable under FRS 102, though not considered to be most appropriate to the particular circumstances of the entity. • Communication when an entity has applied different accounting policies to those applied under old standards but old policies are acceptable under FRS 102. • Consider whether the approach to disclosure provides clear information, given the relative complexity of the transition exercise, and communicate findings as appropriate.

Subject dealt with	FRS 102 implementation issues	Application/Action required
Communication of deficiencies and significant deficiencies in internal control to management and those charged with governance (orally or in writing, as required).	• Resultant changes to accounting systems and controls may give rise to deficiencies in internal control that require communication.	• Written communication to those charged with governance is required where significant deficiencies are identified. (See ISA 265, paragraphs 9–10 for specific communication requirements.)

ISA 315 *Identifying and assessing the risks of material misstatement through understanding the entity and its environment and* **ISA 330** *The auditor's responses to assessed risks*

Risk assessment procedures, related activities and the required understanding of the entity and its environment, including the entity's internal control.	• Implementation of FRS 102 may increase risk of material misstatement at the financial statement and assertion level due to: – limited practical experience of application; – insufficient assessment of completeness of transition adjustments and ongoing accounting differences; – opportunities for aggressive earnings management; – incorrect disclosure regarding adjustments arising from historical errors; and – impact on going concern (see also ISA 570). • Changes may be required to accounting systems and controls to produce necessary FRS 102-compliant information.	• As part of planning, enquiries of management regarding: – major changes to financial statements due to implementation of FRS 102; – the impact of FRS 102 on key systems which generate specific accounting information; – the extent of fair value accounting; – whether the risk of error is increased; – the potential impact on going concern basis; and – other relevant areas of enquiry, as included within section 3 of this Technical Release. • Information on understanding of the entity and its environment, including internal control, may require a more comprehensive update than in GAAP-consistent periods.

Subject dealt with	FRS 102 implementation issues	Application/Action required
		• Assessment of design and implementation of controls relevant to the audit may include specific controls designed in response to FRS 102 implementation.
		• Analytical procedures as part of risk assessment may be based on incomplete or inconsistent data on the year of transition.
Design and implement responses to address the assessed risks of material misstatement at the financial statement and assertion level.	• The audit approach should be responsive to risks identified, including those due to change in financial reporting framework.	• The auditor will need to tailor planned approaches to the entity's circumstances, taking into account risks relating to FRS 102 implementation arising on risk assessment.
		• Clear documentation of all of the above.

ISA 320 *Materiality in planning and performing an audit and*
ISA 450 *Evaluation of misstatements identified during the audit*

Determine level of materiality for financial statements as a whole; levels to be applied to particular classes of transactions, account balances or disclosures; and performance materiality for purposes of assessing the risks of material misstatement and determining the nature, timing and extent of further audit procedures.	• Increased risk of material misstatement in areas subject to significant FRS 102 impact. • Increased sensitivity over certain accounts disclosures including reconciliation of transitional adjustments. • Items on which the attention of the users of the particular entity's financial statements tend to be focused (for example, for the purpose of evaluating financial performance, users may tend to focus on profit, revenue or net assets) may be impacted by implementation of FRS 102.	• The level of performance materiality may need adjustment in areas where there is significant FRS 102 impact. • The auditor should be mindful of sensitivity of transition or additional accounts disclosures when assessing materiality level or levels for particular classes of transactions, account balances or disclosures.

Subject dealt with	FRS 102 implementation issues	Application/Action required
		• Where a percentage is applied to a chosen benchmark as a starting point for determining materiality, consideration of normalisation where appropriate.
Determine whether uncorrected misstatements are material, individually or in aggregate.	• Consideration includes: – the effect of uncorrected misstatements related to prior periods; – FRS 102 requirements to perform prior period adjustment where there is a "material" error compared to FRS 3 and FRSSE "fundamental" error; and the size and nature of misstatements.	• Consider whether uncorrected misstatements of prior periods are impacted by FRS 102 implementation. • Consider whether errors discovered during the audit of the first FRS 102 accounts, which relate to prior periods, should result in a prior period adjustment. • Consider whether errors identified in certain transactions, account balances or disclosures are material by nature. • Clear documentation of all of the above.
ISA 500 *Audit evidence and* **ISA 620** *Using the work of an auditor's expert*		
Determine adequacy/ appropriateness of the work of the expert.	• There are likely to be more circumstances giving rise to the use of management's or auditor's experts due to increased prevalence of fair value measurements.	• Evaluate the expert, understand their work and evaluate its appropriateness in line with requirements of ISA 500/620 and document accordingly. • Consider the need to engage the auditor's expert prior to engagement.

Subject dealt with	FRS 102 implementation issues	Application/Action required
ISA 505 *External confirmations*		
Evaluate whether the results of the external confirmation procedures provide relevant and reliable audit evidence, or whether further audit evidence is necessary.	• Increased instances of recognition and measurement of financial instruments.	• Consider the need for direct confirmation from third parties where the reply is sent direct to the auditor for evidence over completeness and accuracy of financial instruments amounts and disclosures.
ISA 510 *Initial audit engagements – opening balances and* **ISA 710** *Comparative information – corresponding figures and comparative financial statements*		
Obtain sufficient appropriate audit evidence about whether the opening balances contain misstatements that materially affect the current period's financial statements.	• Transitional adjustments are likely to render usual levels of audit work on continuing engagements insufficient to ensure that opening balances on year of transition to FRS 102 are not materially misstated to the extent that they affect and determine the amounts in the current period's financial statements.	• Consider the availability of transition information and adjustments. Retain relevant information on preceding audits. • Encourage completion of transition calculations prior to the first application of FRS 102. • Encourage the entity to consider the need for a separate assurance engagement on transitional adjustments prior to first application.
Determine whether financial statements include the comparative information required and whether this is appropriately classified.		• Consider the completeness and accuracy of disclosure of exemptions and options on transition, and consequential implications on opening balance sheet position (and current period financial statements). • Consider whether errors are included in the reconciliation between opening FRS 102 and historic GAAP, and conclude accordingly.

Subject dealt with	FRS 102 implementation issues	Application/Action required
ISA 520 *Analytical procedures*		
Evaluate the reliability of data from which expectations are developed.	• Additional care is needed when using analytical techniques where significant change is driven by FRS 102 or when there is a lack of comparable information.	• Consider whether the effectiveness of analytical procedures is reduced and the consequential effect on the audit approach.
Design and perform analytical procedures near the end of the audit to assist in forming an overall conclusion.	• Effectiveness of final analytical procedures may be inhibited.	• Consider the design of final analytical procedures and whether additional alternative procedures are necessary. • Clearly document justification for the approach and procedures undertaken.
ISA 540 *Auditing accounting estimates, including fair value accounting estimates, and related disclosures*		
Obtain an understanding to provide a basis for the identification and assessment of risk for accounting estimates.	• Increased incidence of accounting estimates and fair value measurements under FRS 102. • Lack of management experience in making new estimates required under FRS 102. • Assessment of prior period estimate outcomes may be inhibited.	• Ensure consideration of the impact that FRS 102 has on understanding and update documentation as required. Relevant issues include: – awareness of requirements of FRS 102 relative to accounting estimates relevant to the entity; – enquiries of management about the impact of FRS 102; and – the method/model used in calculation of amounts and underlying assumptions.
Evaluate the degree of estimation uncertainty associated with the accounting estimate.	• Some new accounting estimates may implicitly have a high degree of estimation uncertainty attached.	• Consider whether a lack of track record or management experience increases risk.

Subject dealt with	FRS 102 implementation issues	Application/Action required
		• Where estimation uncertainty gives rise to significant risk, evaluate alternative assumptions or outcomes, reasonableness of significant assumptions and, where appropriate, develop a range with which to evaluate the estimate.
Determine whether requirements of the financial reporting framework are appropriately applied and whether changes in estimates or methods would be appropriate.	• Potential motivation to restate comparative accounting estimates on the basis that the initial estimates were in error. • Enhanced disclosure requirements related to judgements and key assumptions concerning the future and other sources of estimation uncertainty. • A number of other issues may also arise resulting in changes to treatment and options unavailable prior to FRS 102, for example: – application of options to use fair value as deemed cost; – recognition and measurement of intangible assets on business combinations; – recognition of deferred tax in an increased range of circumstances; – valuation of investments; and – accounting for basic financial instruments that represent financing transactions.	• Ensure estimates prohibited from restatement are only amended where there is objective evidence of error. • Evaluation of additional financial statement disclosure in year of transition and on an ongoing basis. • Review judgements and decisions for indicators of management bias. • Consideration of audit approach for previously unaudited information included within the financial statements. • Consideration of approach to intangible valuation in response to the subjectivity of valuation and techniques used. Assessment of the basis for determining useful economic life. • Consider availability and reliability of information required to assess appropriateness of estimates.

Subject dealt with	FRS 102 implementation issues	Application/Action required
		• Consider whether the audit team has the requisite skill set to assess the accounting estimate and fair value application and whether the auditor's expert is required (see ISA 620).
		• Ensure that recognition and measurement of financial instruments is appropriate and in line with requirements of Sections 11 and 12 of FRS 102.
		• See also ISA 500 relating to using the work of management's experts and ISA 505 on external confirmations.
		• Clear documentation of all of the above.

ISA 550 *Related parties*

Evaluate whether related party relationships and transactions are appropriately accounted for and disclosed.	• FRS 102 includes a similar definition of related parties, though disclosures differ in some areas, for example: – aggregation of related party transactions; and – disclosure of key management personnel remuneration.	• Consider the appropriateness of aggregation of transactions and whether separate disclosure is necessary for an understanding of the effects on the financial statements.
		• Assess the completeness of remuneration disclosures in light of the overlap with company law requirements.
		• Clear documentation of the above and conclusions.

Subject dealt with	FRS 102 implementation issues	Application/Action required
ISA 570 *Going concern*		

Consider whether events or conditions may cast significant doubt over the ability to continue as a going concern and evaluate management's assessment.	• FRS 102-related adjustments may have an effect on the underlying information used to form a conclusion on going concern.
	
	• Increases in the type and extent of liabilities recognised, changes in net assets and amounts reported through profit or loss may impact on items including:
	  – loan covenant calculations
	  – distributable reserves
	  – reported profits and
	  – bonus arrangements.
		• Communication to affected entities of specific terms in need of amendment prior to implementation.
		
		• Consider whether clauses exist that allow the use of GAAP that was being applied when the agreement was signed to assess compliance with financial covenants.
		
		• Consider whether it is necessary to renegotiate the terms that are effective and applicable.
		
		• Where a breach of terms is apparent, consider the implications on presentation and disclosure in financial statements.
		
		• Ensure forecasts used in assessment of going concern are prepared on an FRS 102 basis.
		
		• Documentation of the above.

ISA 580 *Written representations*		
Written representations about responsibilities for preparation of financial statements.	• Clarification of responsibilities relating to the implementation of FRS 102 may be sought.	• Consider the need to obtain representations on the potential impact of implementation of FRS 102 in the periods prior to implementation. • Use of a representation letter to clarify responsibilities regarding the first application of FRS 102 in the year of transition. See also ISA 210, paragraph 6 for reference to representations sought.

Subject dealt with	FRS 102 implementation issues	Application/Action required
ISA 600 *Special considerations – audits of group financial statements (including the work of component auditors)*		
Communicate the scope and timing of work with component auditors and obtain sufficient, appropriate evidence regarding financial information of components and consolidation, to express an opinion on group accounts.	• Potential for staggered first-time adoption of FRS 102 across entities within the same group and impact on consolidation. • Inconsistent application of treatment options across group companies. • Classifications and measurement in individual entity financial statements may be inconsistent with that required in group accounts.	• Confirmation of the basis of preparation of component financial statements prior to planning the approach to engagement and communication of key changes, as appropriate. • Consider the extent to which instructions to component auditors are required regarding the need to perform additional procedures and to provide information relevant to transition. • Consider the extent to which changes impact on the evaluation of component auditors and sufficiency of their work. • Consider the need to perform additional procedures on the work of component auditors related to transition or consolidation adjustments. • Documentation of conclusions related to the above.
ISA 610 *Using the work of internal auditors*		
Determine the nature and extent of work of the internal audit function that can be used.	• The internal audit function may have performed work on processes for preparation of FRS 102 accounts and related adjustments.	• Assess the work of internal audit to identify whether FRS 102-specific work can be used and to what extent for the purposes of the audit.

Subject dealt with	FRS 102 implementation issues	Application/Action required
		• Draw appropriate conclusions from this assessment and from the internal audit work as applicable, and document accordingly.

ISA 700 *The independent auditor's report on financial statements,*
ISA 705 *Modifications to the opinion in the independent auditor's report and*
ISA 706 *Emphasis of matter paragraphs and other matter paragraphs in the independent auditor's report*

An unqualified opinion on the financial statements shall be expressed only when the auditor concludes that they have been prepared in accordance with the identified financial reporting framework.	• Clarity over the financial reporting framework, in particular where there is early adoption of FRS 102.	• To make clear which accounting standards have been used (in particular where adopting FRS 102 prior to the mandatory implementation date) the Opinion section of the auditor's report may read: "The financial reporting framework that has been applied in their preparation is applicable law and United Kingdom Accounting Standards (United Kingdom Generally Accepted Accounting Practice), including FRS 102 "The Financial Reporting Standard applicable in the UK and Republic of Ireland"".
	• Differences in terminology between company law, auditing standards and FRS 102. • Departures identified from FRS 102 in the preparation and presentation of financial statements.	• FRS 102's use of the term "presented fairly" should be read as having the same meaning as "true and fair view". • Consider implications of departures on the audit report, for example:

Subject dealt with	FRS 102 implementation issues	Application/Action required
		– where a material departure results in a disagreement regarding application of accounting policy selection or application or disclosure, consider whether this is so misleading that an adverse, rather than qualified, opinion is required; and
		– assessment of the approach to transition to FRS 102 may lead to the conclusion that a limitation of scope has been imposed where the entity has failed to record information with the necessary level of detail or accuracy to obtain sufficient audit evidence.

Appendix 2: Support from the ICAEW Financial Reporting Faculty on FRS 102 Transition

The Financial Reporting Faculty provides a range of resources to help you keep abreast of the changes with practical tips on first-time application, including:

- factsheets
- frequently asked questions
- webinars
- UK standards tracker
- UK GAAP roadshows and
- the faculty's journal *By All Accounts*.

You can find out more at icaew.com/newukgaap Guidance for small and micro-entities is available at icaew.com/smallcompanyreporting

Appendix 3: Glossary of terms and abbreviations used

Accounting Regulations	The Small Companies and Groups (Accounts and Directors' Report) Regulations 2008
	The Large and Medium-sized Companies and Groups (Accounts and Reports) Regulations 2008
Management	This term is used to include those charged with governance over an entity when the context requires it
ES	FRC's Revised Ethical Standard 2016
IASB	International Accounting Standards Board
IFRS	International Financial Reporting Standard
ISA (UK)	International Standard on Auditing (UK)
ISQC (UK) 1	International Standard on Quality Control (UK) 1
UK GAAP	UK Generally Accepted Accounting Practice

TECH 16/15AAF Solicitors Regulation Authority (SRA) Accounts Rules: interim guidance for reporting accountants following changes to the accountant's report requirements

(December 2015)

Contents

	Paragraphs
Introduction	1 - 5
Background	6 - 11
Changes to the accountant's report requirements	12 - 24
Requirement to submit only qualified reports	14 - 15
Changes to the accountant's report and removal of SRA accounts rule 39	16 - 21
New accountant's report form and guidance notes	22 - 24
The role of the reporting accountant	25 - 43
What is the reporting accountant's role?	27 - 28
Fulfilling the reporting accountant's role in accordance with the SRA requirements	29 - 43
Practical implications for reporting accountants and law firms	44 - 77
Developing risk assessment procedures	44 - 45
Changes to the programme of work	46 - 51
Control systems	52 - 55
Reduced areas of work	56 - 61
New areas of work	62 - 63
Material breaches and significant weaknesses	64 - 67
Whistleblowing	68 - 74
Terms of engagement	75 - 77
Evolving guidance for reporting accountants	78 - 81
SRA guidance	78 - 80
Future ICAEW guidance	81

APPENDIX 1: Material breaches and significant weaknesses

APPENDIX 2: Examples of potential conclusions on the qualification of an accountant's report

About this Guidance

This guidance has been prepared by a working group of ICAEW Solicitors Special Interest Group Committee Members who have detailed knowledge and practical experience of the SRA Accounts Rules. The Solicitors Group Committee is made up of experts in solicitors' accounts from accountancy practices and those working in industry. The committee benefits from working relationships with other bodies and interested parties in the legal environment. This working group has worked under the guidance of a steering group comprising representatives of relevant ICAEW Committees and the ICAEW Audit and Assurance Faculty.

The ICAEW Audit and Assurance Faculty is a leading authority on external audit and other assurance activities and is recognised internationally as a source of expertise on audit issues. It is responsible for ICAEW technical audit and assurance leadership and provides a range of information sources to its members which gives practical assurance in key audit and assurance areas.

Laws and regulations referred to in this ICAEW Technical Release are stated as at 1 December 2015. Every effort has been made to make sure the information it contains is accurate at the time of creation. ICAEW cannot guarantee the completeness or accuracy of the information in this ICAEW Technical Release and shall not be responsible for errors or inaccuracies. Under no circumstances shall ICAEW be liable for any reliance by you on any information in this ICAEW Technical Release.

ISBN 978-1-78363-440-8

Introduction

This interim guidance (referred to as "guidance" throughout this Technical   **1**
Release) has been prepared in December 2015 for ICAEW members where
they are involved in the preparation of an Accountant's Report on behalf of law
firms in respect of the Solicitors Regulation Authority (SRA) Accounts Rules
requirements.

The guidance has been prepared following an announcement by the SRA of   **2**
changes to the form of the Accountant's Report and the background under which
Reporting Accountants are undertaking their role.

These changes affect Accountant's Reports being prepared for law firms whose   **3**
accounting period ends on or after 1 November 2015.

This guidance explains the background to and summary of the changes in the   **4**
Accountant's Report, considers the SRA objectives for these changes, and
provides additional guidance to members on the impact the changes might have
on their day to day work in this area.

In developing this guidance ICAEW has worked with, and taken on board   **5**
comments from, the SRA and the SRA is supportive of the guidance contained
in this ICAEW Technical Release.

Background

Up to 31 October 2014 the Accountant's Report prepared by a Reporting   **6**
Accountant was required to be filed with the SRA by the law firm on an annual
basis irrespective of whether the report was "qualified" or "unqualified".

The SRA, and previously the Law Society have from time to time shared data with   **7**
ICAEW and our understanding is that annually in the region of 50% to 55% of the
reports that were filed were qualified by the Reporting Accountant.

The SRA's and previously the Law Society's policy was for all qualified reports to   **8**
be reviewed in some form upon receipt in order to determine whether the
information provided in the report (namely the breaches noted by the
accountant) were sufficiently serious to warrant further review – ie, whether or
not the SRA considered them to be "material breaches". ICAEW understands that
these reports were considered as part of the sum of intelligence from various
sources available to the SRA.

The detailed nature of the SRA Accounts Rules themselves, the prescriptive nature   **9**
of rule 39 (test procedures) and the lack of framework around the concept of
material breaches left Reporting Accountants exposed to risk if they failed to
report all breaches that were found as a result of the tests, regardless of their
nature. As a result, for many years, the Accountant's Report was often qualified as
a result of breaches that, were a more risk-based approach taken to these
engagements, with only material breaches reportable, would not be reportable.

The SRA's forensic investigations team has previously indicated to ICAEW that   **10**
while information received from the Accountant's Report forms part of its wider
intelligence on law firms it is only one of the elements it considers. Furthermore,
ICAEW understands that frequently law firms investigated by the SRA have not
previously received a qualified Accountant's Report. This is not necessarily to say
that the Accountant's Report should have been qualified, more that the items
sample checked by the Reporting Accountant may not have contained the issues
identified and being investigated by the SRA.

11   Nonetheless, the SRA's experience combined with feedback from its consultation processes in recent years has confirmed that the Accountant's Report has an important role in upholding the quality of management and protection of client funds in law firms. This has a longer term impact of safeguarding the integrity and reputation of the legal sector and regulation by the SRA.

Changes to the Accountant's Report Requirements

12   There have been a number of significant changes introduced by the SRA; the two key changes covered by this guidance are:

- A requirement for law firms to submit only qualified Accountant's Reports; and

- Changes to the Accountant's Report and removal of SRA Accounts Rule 39.

13   Information and guidance on changes to exemptions from preparing Accountant's Reports and to the overseas provisions, neither of which are covered in this guidance, is available at: www.sra.org.uk/AR1 and http://www.sra.org.uk/solicitors/handbook/introoverseasrules/content.page

Requirement to submit only qualified reports

14   Since 1 November 2014 SRA Regulated Bodies (law firms undertaking reserved legal services) have only been required to submit Accountant's Reports to the SRA if they contain qualifications. While the obligation to submit the Accountant's Report rests with the law firm in practice Reporting Accountants will often undertake the process of formal submission. A clean Accountant's Report is retained by the law firm for inspection on request by the SRA.

15   ICAEW's understanding is that part of the drive by the SRA for this initial change was simply to reduce the burden and costs of administration resulting from receiving unqualified reports. The change was also consistent with the Outcomes Focused Regulation (OFR) regime being implemented by the SRA; that is law firms take responsibility for complying with the need for the Accountant's Report to be prepared without the requirement for formal submission to the SRA in the case where there were no non-compliance matters to report.

Changes to the Accountant's Report and removal of SRA Accounts Rule 39

16   These changes are primarily a further step by the SRA to reinforce the OFR regime for law firms in respect of client money and from a practical viewpoint to further reduce the level of resource it invests in reviewing the Accountant's Reports.

17   These changes took effect for Accountant's Reports being prepared for reporting periods ending on or after 1 November 2015.

18   The SRA has made significant changes to the format of the Accountant's Report and to the Rules under which it is prepared; specifically the SRA has:

(a)   Removed SRA Accounts Rule 39 which previously included a wide range of prescriptive testing that a Reporting Accountant was required to undertake in order to provide the Accountant's Report.

(b)   Introduced a requirement for the Reporting Accountant to:

(i)   Determine for themselves what is the correct type and level of work to be performed for each particular law firm - based on their professional assessment of risk, the size of the law firm and the range of services provided; and

(ii) Qualify the report only in respect of *"material breaches of the Accounts Rules ......, and/or significant weaknesses in the firm's systems and controls for compliance with the Accounts Rules" (wording from the revised AR1 form).*

To replace SRA Accounts Rule 39 a new Rule 43A.1 has been issued which states: **19**

"43A.1 The accountant should exercise his or her professional judgement in determining the work required for the firm they are instructed to obtain the report on in order to assess risks to client money arising from compliance with these rules. This should cover the work that the accountant considers is appropriate to enable completion of the report required by the SRA at the date the report is commissioned.

(Rule 43A.1) Guidance notes

(i) *The purpose of the accountant's report is to enable a proportionate degree of oversight by the SRA over risks to clients' funds. It may also help the firm to identify any improvements in its control systems that are required. The form of the report ...... is intended to provide assurance that client funds are properly safeguarded. If the accountant forms the judgement that these Rules have not been complied with such that the safety of client money is at risk, then the accountant is required to "qualify" the report and set out in the report details of the areas where risks have been identified. Rule 32A.1 sets out which firms are required to obtain a report but only qualified reports have to be delivered to the SRA within the time frame set out.'*

(ii) *The types of work that the accountant is required to undertake will depend on a number of factors including the size and complexity of the firm, the nature of the work undertaken, the number of transactions and amount of client funds held. The accountant may also want to consider the firm's existing systems and for example, the numbers and types of breaches of these Rules that the firm's COFA has recorded under his/her reporting obligations. Separate guidance as to the work that might be considered as part of a work programme has been issued by the SRA and will be updated from time to time; see the SRA's "Guidance to Reporting Accountants and firms on planning and completion of the annual Accountants' Reports, under Rule 32A of the SRA Accounts Rules 2011".*

ICAEW understands that the SRA's primary objectives for these changes are to **20** promote an OFR approach among its Regulated Bodies as well as ensuring the best use of its internal resources as a Regulator of law firms.

In effect the objective is to ensure that client funds are protected and safeguarded **21** but reduce significantly the volume of Accountant's Reports it receives and needs to review where there is no significant risk to client funds identified from the work Reporting Accountants have undertaken in their role.

New Accountant's Report form and guidance notes

22   The new Accountant's Report form (AR1) together with guidance notes prepared by the SRA can be located at www.sra.org.uk/AR1.

23   ICAEW members should closely consider both the contents of the new form and the guidance notes and examples of what are considered likely to be qualifications contained therein prior to completing SRA Accounts Rules engagements for periods ending on or after 1 November 2015. The SRA has emphasised that the examples in the guidance are intended to be helpful but are not definitive nor prescriptive, and the Reporting Accountant is expected to exercise professional judgement in completing the AR1 Accountant's Report form, whether qualified or not.

24   The SRA recorded a webinar in October 2015, *Exemptions and changing arrangements for the Reporting Accountant requirements – 15 October 2015* which provides further information and the SRA's views on the changes as well as a Q&A session: http://www.sra.org.uk/sra/news/events/webinar-2015-10-15-reporting-accountant-requirements.page

The Role of the Reporting Accountant

25   The SRA guidance notes make it clear that there is no expectation that the new regime will increase the scope of the role for the Reporting Accountant or indeed increase any actual or perceived risk exposure for the Reporting Accountant.

26   There is however an expectation from the SRA (and law firms) of the following impacts:-

- It might change the nature of the work the Reporting Accountant undertakes; and

- There will be fewer qualified reports submitted to the SRA.

What is the Reporting Accountant's role?

27   This ICAEW Technical Release only considers the role of the Reporting Accountant to prepare an Accountant's Report in accordance with the SRA's regulatory requirements.

28   However, some law firms may also engage Reporting Accountants to carry out an independent review of compliance generally, to help the client improve standards within its own legal practice(s). This will impact on the work the Reporting Accountant undertakes and the Reporting Accountant will need to be clear about its responsibilities here. The requirements may not be the same for each law firm client a Reporting Accountant is engaged with and will depend on the requirements of the individual practice and COFA.

Fulfilling the Reporting Accountant's role in accordance with the SRA requirements

29   Fundamentally if Reporting Accountants have been carrying out the SAR review work diligently and professionally up until now, in the vast majority of cases these Reporting Accountants will, when they carry out the work in future, find the same sort of issues they have found in the past. There is no reason to believe that Reporting Accountants will, under the new regime, start to identify different types of risks to client money or serious breaches. If the Reporting Accountant had uncovered serious breaches previously they would have been deemed reportable.

So the majority of issues found by Reporting Accountants in the future will most likely be the same as have been found in the past – the key difference is that there is now guidance from the SRA to help Reporting Accountants conclude on which of the breaches/weaknesses they identify are material/significant and reportable to the SRA on revised AR1 Accountant's Report form under the new regime, and which are reportable only to the law firm by way of management letter or discussions with the COFA and/or COLP.

The most notable impact from the new regime is that it does fall to the Reporting **30** Accountant, under Rule 38, to decide on the actual work and to report based explicitly on risk assessment and judgement. Previously this was determined (to a large extent) by the prescriptive requirements under Rule 39.

The requirement of the role of the Reporting Accountant within the new SRA **31** Accounts Rules has a number of risk factors most of which are not new. The risks are that the Reporting Accountant:

- Lacks detailed knowledge of the SRA Accounts Rules themselves;

- Does not understand or identify where the underlying risks lie in respect of the handling and holding of client money both generally, and more specifically with regard to the particular law firm;

- Does not gain a sufficient understanding of the law firm's systems of controls to perform enough work/testing or enough of the "right" work, for example, coverage of the high risk areas, work on areas of regular or common breaches;

- Does not actually identify the breaches and come to a reasoned judgement as to their severity and requirement for reporting on AR1 Accountant's Report form report or simply to the COFA/COLP; and

- Fails to report to the SRA in circumstances where the breaches or weaknesses are "material" or "significant" respectively, and directly affect the SRA's role in regulating the protection of client money.

The questions for the Reporting Accountant are: **32**

- How do I assess the risks within each individual reporting engagement – what are the key factors, such as system procedures and controls, sign off authorities, management approach to compliance, types of work undertaken including value and regularity of transactions, day to day protection of client money?

- How do I carry out the work to ensure that I have addressed those risks, as well as checking the law firm's compliance with the detailed SRA Accounts Rules?

- If I do find non-compliance with the SRA Accounts Rules, how much additional work should I do to ascertain how material or significant the issue is and risk to protection of client money?

- What would constitute "material breaches of the Accounts Rules, ... and/or significant weaknesses in the firm's systems and controls for compliance with the SRA Accounts Rules?"

- What are the implications for me/the law firm if I don't report non-compliance because I have judged it not to be reportable or putting protection of client money at risk but which the SRA later consider to have been reportable as material/significant?

33   Many Reporting Accountants have been working with this risk based approach for a number of years and so will not be doing anything very different, other than making a decision as to the items of non-compliance to include on the AR1 Accountant's Report form, and those which are for management and/or the COFA/COLP.

34   A fundamental challenge for Reporting Accountants is that on the face of it their perceived risk and exposure to the SRA will be deemed to be reduced if they qualify the Accountant's Report under the new regime. On the other hand, the Reporting Accountant may also come under pressure from law firms not to qualify the Accountant's Report and may not come to the same conclusion as the law firm about whether a breach/weakness is considered material/significant or not (see paragraph 68).

35   ICAEW understands that the SRA carefully considers the information received in the Accountant's Report and this forms an important element of their wider intelligence gathering processes.

36   The SRA considers that the role the Reporting Accountant undertakes provides an important incentive to law firms to have proper systems and procedures in place to safeguard client funds.

37   The SRA acknowledges the challenges and risks for Reporting Accountants under the new regime and that it is not possible to replicate an equivalent framework to that which surrounds the statutory audit under the Companies Act 2006 so that there is an equivalent for Reporting Accountants reporting under the SRA Accounts Rules. This is because the SRA wants Reporting Accountants to exercise professional judgement in the work they do and the qualifications reported in the AR1 Accountant's Report form, thus following the principles in the Solicitors Rule Book which is based on Outcomes Focused Regulation rather than being prescriptive.

38   The SRA has re-iterated that it is not seeking any change in the responsibility or risk to Reporting Accountants in performing this SRA Accounts Rules work. The SRA has pointed to the historical evidence which shows that it is rare for the SRA to take action against Reporting Accountants unless there have been blatant or deliberate deficiencies in their work or they have been complicit in fraud.

39   The SRA has offered further assurance in this area by explaining that typically on average less than ten events a year arise where the SRA would contact the Reporting Accountant and question the quality and nature of the work they have undertaken. The outcome of these discussions in the most extreme cases might lead to the SRA approaching the Reporting Accountant's professional body to prevent the Reporting Accountant completing future Accountant's Reports, where for example, the Reporting Accountant failed to report to the SRA any of the following:

   ● A lack of existence of any reconciliations of client funds;
   ● Unresolved shortages on client funds;
   ● Un-cleared lodgements on the client account reconciliations; or
   ● Evidence of fraud.

40   While not an exhaustive list the main point is that these are instances that simply indicate the Reporting Accountant had not actually properly undertaken the work they were expected to complete as opposed to questioning a judgement decision.

We believe that the SRA would give strong consideration to the factors listed **41** below in the event that there was an adverse client funds issue with a law firm where no qualification had been issued in the Accountant's Report by the Reporting Accountant.

Reporting Accountants should be able to demonstrate:– **42**

- **The breadth of experience of the team undertaking the work** – e.g. degree of experience in undertaking SRA Accounts Rules engagements and general statutory audit experience in the team as a measure of ability to form professional judgements of this nature.

- **The strength of the planning process** – Evidence that the work undertaken by the Reporting Accountant had been planned, was relevant to the law firm and type of work undertaken, proportionate and that there had been appropriate, documented consideration as to the risk assessment of the law firm in question prior to work commencing.

- **Training** – The extent to which key engagement team members are receiving training in the SRA Accounts Rules, Accountant's Report requirements and with auditing techniques more generally.

- **Work programme** – The existence of a formal programme of work which is relevant both in nature and tailoring to the law firm concerned.

- **Review process** – The existence of a robust internal review process by the Reporting Accountant with an appropriate level of senior resource in the engagement team and a methodology for review by more experienced team members and assessment of conclusions.

- **The quality of conclusions** – With the evidence available and provided to the Reporting Accountant there is a logical and supported conclusion reached on all matters of concern. This is set in the context of the Reporting Accountant completing a commercially reasonable level of investigation and without relying on specialist legal knowledge. The whole process should involve a level of professional scepticism in the judgement process being applied.

Clearly the above is not exhaustive; the broad direction of these comments and **43** discussion with the SRA in this area has been to reach a position where if a Reporting Accountant can demonstrate:

- A reasonable understanding of the systems, procedures, transactions and control systems that the law firm has in place and were operative in the relevant period;

- That they have planned and undertaken an appropriate level of work in completing the Accountant's Report; and

- That they have formed reasonable and well supported conclusions based upon the information received and matters of concern identified,

the SRA would not take the view that the work they have performed nor conclusions reached were inadequate in the event that the law firm or the SRA subsequently identifies a risk to or actual loss of client funds in the law firm concerned.

Practical Implications for Reporting Accountants and Law Firms

Developing risk assessment procedures

44   It is assumed that Reporting Accountants providing Accountant's Reports at present will already have formal systems in place to support the work they undertake e.g. system and controls checking and sample sizes. Moving forwards we believe that Reporting Accountants will need to be more focused on this area and documenting their methodology to support both the type of work they are undertaking and the volume in the context of the risk profile of their client.

45   Example risk factors here might include:

- History of significant breaches (and areas in which the breaches arose);
- History of client money frauds or Solicitors Disciplinary Tribunal (SDT) findings against fee earners / partners;
- The nature and volume of current year breaches on the law firm's own register of breaches (maintained by the COFA);
- Types of fee earning work the law firm undertakes, for example, probate and conveyancing are likely to be high risk;
- The nature and volume of complaints and PII claims against the law firm;
- The existence and effectiveness of control systems in the law firm;
- The law firm's attitude to compliance and ethical standards;
- The volume and complexity of the financial transactions undertaken by the law firm's clients;
- Experience and qualifications of the law firm's accounts team;
- Training provided for the law firm's accounts team and fee earners;
- Financial performance of the law firm; and
- Any known financial or personal circumstances of the law firm fee earners or partners.

Changes to the programme of work

46   Perhaps the most notable area of focus in the short term for Reporting Accountants will be the revisions needed to their internal work programmes; many of which are in electronic form.

47   Under the new Rule 38 more time will be required at the planning stage in tailoring the work programmes to match the specific law firm involved. This will be important to ensure that the work of the Reporting Accountant is directed in the most appropriate areas for the law firm concerned and its specific risk profile. It will also be important for the Reporting Accountant in terms of being able to justify to the SRA the sufficiency of the work undertaken.

48   Planning processes including planning memorandums and planning meetings for the engagement team and client will be an important feature for such engagements.

49   Control systems and their evaluation, which are considered below, will be an important feature for Reporting Accountants' work. For all engagements there will now be more work involved in this area than previously required and some

Reporting Accountants may wish to consider a more radical shift in their work programme overall to place far greater reliance upon law firm's control systems where they can be successfully evaluated and tested.

The requirements of the new Rule 38 may well result in more or less work being undertaken for a particular law firm and this may vary over time as the Reporting Accountants assessment of the risk profile of that law firm changes from year to year.   50

There will be some client management issues for Reporting Accountants as well; most law firms are used to the Reporting Accountant undertaking the same type of work and asking for the same types of information each year. Under the new regime the work of a Reporting Accountant could vary with both the nature and volume of such work changing notably between successive years.   51

Control systems

Under the new regime there is a specific requirement to consider the control systems and procedures that a law firm has in place. This involves some consideration and work being directed to: 52

● Documenting the control systems (both IT and non IT controls);

● Assessing their adequacy/effectiveness for their intended purpose; and

● Testing the application of the control systems.

For some engagements, there is likely to be a higher time cost to this process in the first year under the new regime and on an annual basis there will be a need to revisit this area and consider changes that have taken place (or perhaps that should have been implemented) as well as testing areas for continued effectiveness in accordance with the risk assessments undertaken at the planning stage.   53

The SRA has confirmed that there is no intention within the new guidance to drive the work of the Reporting Accountant towards a controls-based approach. The SRA expects the Reporting Accountant to undertake a risk-based approach towards planning the work and expects substantive testing to form a significant element of the Reporting Accountants work. The SRA has also confirmed that there is not an expectation that the work of the Reporting Accountant will be increased overall as a result of the need to consider the control systems that exist within a law firm.   54

The practical implications for Reporting Accountants here include the evolution of work programme systems, sufficiently trained and experienced staff to undertake the work, time scheduled within the overall work scheme, and law firm engagement in the process which for some will present a different approach that will need to be explained to the law firm.   55

Reduced areas of work

For Reporting Accountants currently working with a standard commercially available work programme for SRA Accounts Rules work it is possible that some work they were required to undertake as a result of the old Rule 39 could now be reduced or removed under the new Rule 43A.1 regime.   56

In order to be efficient and effective under the new regime the work that is carried out by the Reporting Accountant should be tailored for each engagement. Reporting Accountants may need to tailor any standardised work programmes that they are using. This may mean carrying out some additional work in some areas and allow for reductions in others, depending on both the overall risk   57 assessment performed by the Reporting Accountant and the risk areas identified within that particular law firm.

58   Some possible areas where less work may be required by the Reporting Accountant and some suggestions of areas where more focus might be needed are detailed at paragraphs 60 and 63 respectively. This cannot be prescriptive. For Reporting Accountants to reach a decision on work reductions and the key focus for their work, it may be constructive for them to undertake their work in the following order, allowing their work to evolve during the course of the engagement:

(a)   Document and test the control systems for client money;

(b)   Detailed checks on the three way client account reconciliations:

- Properly reconciled, reviewed and signed off client account reconciliations help provide evidence of the completeness and accuracy of the system;

- Reconciliations with unresolved, unexplained or uncorrected errors, numerous reconciling items and many going back several months, unsigned (or signed where differences are not corrected or explained) will point the Reporting Accountant to the areas where they are likely to need to focus their efforts; and

(c)   Detailed client file review work:

- The results of this work would help inform suitable sample sizes for the work on transactions and whether efficiencies can be considered by combining testing areas.

59   It is difficult to be prescriptive here simply because it will be for the Reporting Accountant to assess the nature and amount of work they should perform given the risk profile of their law firm client. However, in broad terms, it seems likely that areas of work where historically few breaches have arisen would be considered low risk and therefore not reviewed in as much detail or depth as a high risk area.

60   Examples ICAEW believes may fall into this risk based category, and where less work might be undertaken by the Reporting Accountant in future might include:

- Checking transactions from the bank statements to transaction records or nominal ledger;

- Detailed testing of bills of costs to transaction records;

- Paid cheque testing;

- Detailed transactional testing work at reconciliation dates; and

- Reliance on bank audit letters.

61   Equally in the above list it may well be that in some cases the Reporting Accountant may have a core work programme tailored to the law firm and then sporadically undertake other tests e.g. in the absence of any breaches being identified and strong control systems in place a paid cheque audit every three years might be appropriate.

New areas of work

62   This is subjective. The most pertinent point here is that it is clear under the new regime that work will be required to be undertaken in the area of control systems, and this has been considered above. This is likely to represent the greatest area of focus for most Reporting Accountants in conjunction with the risk profile and planning elements mentioned elsewhere in this guidance.

Outside the area of internal controls; example areas that ICAEW considers may involve additional work under the new regime include: **63**

- Review of monthly client funds three way reconciliations across the year;

- Greater focus on the office account and office account reconciliations as a source of breaches;

- Review of client funds reconciliation to look for shortfalls / differences compared to the bank balances and how these are managed and dealt with (as opposed to the current regime of examining two specific dates in detail);

- Reviewing instances of suspense accounts being used and compliance of their use with the SRA Accounts Rules; and

- Testing treatment of old residual balances – specifically for sweeping up, acting as banker and charging of inappropriate expenses.

Material Breaches and significant weaknesses

The SRA guidance gives examples in this area and we anticipate the extent and nature of this guidance may evolve over time. Clearly this guidance runs hand in hand with the perceived more onerous requirement for Reporting Accountants to exercise their professional judgement over the inclusion of qualifications when completing the Accountant's Report. **64**

Appendix 1 includes information from the SRA guidance notes (with the permission of the SRA) which set out when the SRA would expect a qualification and situations when the SRA might (rather than would) expect a qualification in the Accountants Report. It will be important for the Reporting Accountant to clearly document and be able to support their conclusion on whether or not an identified breach or control weakness (or combination of breaches and weaknesses) should result in a qualified opinion. **65**

ICAEW has prepared a more comprehensive list of practical examples that Reporting Accountants may also find themselves facing. The examples are included in Appendix 2 of this guidance. These examples give a base scenario and then provide further information that may change the view of the Reporting Accountant as to whether they represent a qualification. **66**

Clearly examples of this nature cannot be definitive and are an over simplification of what may be seen in real situations. Nevertheless the collective input of ICAEW volunteers and committees and review of these scenarios by the SRA during the process of the ICAEW developing this guidance is intended to provide some assurance to members in the process they may adopt in reaching conclusions in practice. **67**

Whistleblowing

As noted in paragraph 34, the reduction in the number of Accountant's Reports being submitted to the SRA and the backdrop to these regime changes may place increased pressure upon Reporting Accountants not to add a qualification to their report. This pressure may come directly from law firms who will perceive a higher risk of investigation from the SRA arising from the submission of a qualified report in future. **68**

69   The SRA guidance notes to Reporting Accountants (which are available to law firms as well) have been very strong in reminding the profession that Reporting Accountants would be expected to use the whistleblowing provisions in appropriate circumstances such as where it was considered that client money was at risk and where commercial pressure is exerted by the law firm surrounding the potential qualification of the report resulting in the appointment of an alternative Reporting Accountant. The SRA has also confirmed that there have been no changes under the rights and obligations of the Reporting Accountant in this area.

70   Clearly the Reporting Accountant also needs to consider their own professional integrity and position in such circumstances. If there is undue commercial pressure surrounding the completion of the Accountant's Report should the Reporting Accountant continue with the appointment? This is a matter on which the Reporting Accountant will need to make a professional judgement.

71   In any event the Reporting Accountant must report according to the findings from the work undertaken and on the basis of its professional view as to whether a qualification in the Accountant's Report is appropriate or not. The key point here is that the Accountant's Report is prepared by the Reporting Accountant and not by the law firm.

72   There is also an education process here for COFAs and law firms; primarily that an Accountant's Report with no qualification does not necessarily mean the Reporting Accountant has not been in contact with the SRA surrounding the report.

73   The SRA has re-iterated that safeguards are in place to ensure the confidential disclosure of information received from Reporting Accountants under the whistleblowing procedures.

74   Overall both the SRA and Reporting Accountants have an important role to play in the whistleblowing framework by continuing to exercise the rights and obligations of the Reporting Accountant in this respect.

Terms of engagement

75   The SRA does not contract with individual Reporting Accountants and, therefore, does not sign up to any terms of engagement. The Accountant's Report is, however, addressed to the SRA and the SRA expects that it will be owed a duty of care in respect of the Accountant's Report.

76   Terms of engagement will need to be agreed with the law firm to include:

- The scope of services to be provided by the Reporting Accountant;

- The identity of the law firm for whose benefit the services are to be provided;

- The fees to be paid by the law firm for the services;

- The purpose for which the Reporting Accountant is to provide the services;

- Any responsibilities of the law firm in relation to the services;

- The rights and obligations on Reporting Accountants to report directly to the Solicitors Regulation Authority;

- Following any direct report made to the Solicitors Regulation Authority under the above, to provide to the Solicitors Regulation Authority on request any further relevant information in the Reporting Accountant's possession or in the possession of the law firm; and

- Any limitations on the Reporting Accountant's liability to the law firm.

Refer to ICAEW Technical Release 09/15BL Managing the professional liability of accountants for further details.

Reporting Accountants will need to review and most likely revise the wording of any existing engagement terms for reporting periods ending on or after 1 November 2015 for example to address the requirement to keep a copy of the report for six years (increased from three years) and the requirement to report to the SRA if the Reporting Accountant discovers that an Accountant's Report has not been prepared previously, of if qualified has not been filed with the SRA when it should have been. Alongside any specific agreements between the law firm and the reporting accountants regarding work outside the scope of the SRA Accounts Rules engagement, the engagement letter should also include all the issues referred to in Rule 35 Reporting accountant's rights and duties – letter of engagement.   **77**

Evolving Guidance for Reporting Accountants

SRA guidance

We understand that the SRA envisages that its guidance to Reporting Accountants surrounding the completion of Accountants' Reports and, specifically, the circumstances in which the SRA might expect the Accountant's Report to be qualified will evolve over time.   **78**

This approach would be consistent with that adopted by the SRA in respect of law firms themselves under OFR and the reporting of material breaches by the COFA. Here the SRA has given initial guidance and then added to it with additional examples over time.   **79**

We are therefore anticipating the same will arise for the Reporting Accountant such that over time the initial examples the SRA has given in their guidance notes to Reporting Accountants will be developed and fine-tuned to better ensure that Reporting Accountants are reporting at a level to meet SRA expectations. This evolution is particularly important to the Reporting Accountant given the absence of any specific framework for this work which is in stark contrast to the position applicable to an auditor in a statutory Companies Act audit environment.   **80**

Future ICAEW guidance

This interim guidance is prepared in December 2015 at the commencement of the new regime for Reporting Accountants; consequently ICAEW guidance to members and views on this subject is likely to evolve over time in conjunction with the SRA and practical implementation of the new requirements from the SRA, including the future planned revisions to the Accounts Rules as part three of the SRA review.   **81**

Appendix 1: Material Breaches and Significant Weaknesses

The following information has been reproduced with the permission of the SRA from its guidance notes that seek to inform Reporting Accountants of key examples where the SRA would expect a report to receive a qualification (serious factors) or where there is ambiguity and the SRA might, depending on the Reporting Accountants assessment expect to receive a qualification (moderate factors).

It is also worth noting that in our view many if not all of these marked below as either * or ** would also fall under the Reporting Accountants whistle blowing duties (and hence a requirement to report to the SRA immediately outside of the AR1 regime). Those marked ** under Accounts Rule 35.1(a)(i) and those marked * under Accounts Rule 35.1(a)(ii).

Serious factors – Likely to be deemed reportable:

(1)   Significant and/or un-replaced shortfall on client account, unless caused by bank error and remedied in a timely manner;*

(2)   Evidence of wilful disregard for the safety of client money such as deliberately overriding the rules;*

(3)   Actual or suspected fraud or dishonesty by the managers or employees of the firm (if they may impact on client funds);**

(4)   Material breaches or serious failure to comply with the rules not being reported by the COFA to the SRA (where Reporting Accountant becomes aware of it as a result of carrying out work in respect of client money);*

(5)   No or wholly inadequate accounting records or records not retained;*

(6)   Significant failure to provide documents to Reporting Accountant;

(7)   Three way client account reconciliations not carried out; and

(8)   Banking facilities through client account.

Moderate factors – one of which or more may be material and/or represent a significant weakness in the firm's systems and controls, and lead to a potential qualification:

(1)   Significant fully replaced shortfall unless caused by bank error and remedied in a timely manner;

(2)   Actual or suspected fraud or dishonesty by third party that may impact client funds;

(3)   Material breaches not reported by COFA within a month;

(4)   Insufficient or unreliable accounting records or not retained for 6 years;

(5)   Three way client account reconciliations not regularly performed at least every 5 weeks;

(6)   Poor control environment;

(7)   Performance or review of three way client account reconciliations not adequate;

(8)   Long standing residual balances due to clients; and

(9)   Improper use of suspense accounts.

The full guidance issued by the SRA is available at www.sra.org.uk/ar1.

Appendix 2: Examples of Potential Conclusions on the Qualification of an Accountant's Report

Whether or not the rule breaches and weaknesses in the control systems identified by the Reporting Accountant should be included in the report to the SRA is of course a judgement to be made by the Reporting Accountant. The purpose of this Appendix is to provide the Reporting Accountant with some guidance when considering some of the most common and in some cases potentially more serious breaches of the Rules. These examples are neither definitive nor exhaustive. The Reporting Accountant may be making the judgement on whether or not to report the issues by considering a particular breach/weakness in systems and controls or as a result of the collective impact of several breaches/weaknesses in systems and controls. Any examples provided cannot, therefore, address the full breadth of situations that Reporting Accountants might be dealing with.

	Relevant SRA Accounts Rule	What is the risk to client money and what considerations are required by the Reporting Accountant to assess whether the breaches/weaknesses in systems and controls are material and or significant?	Is it likely the Reporting Accountant would qualify on this information alone?	Is it likely that the additional information would point the Reporting Accountant towards a potential qualification?
EXAMPLE 1 – OVERDRAWN CLIENT LEDGER BALANCES				
A number of overdrawn client ledger balances have been identified during the engagement.	Rule 20.9	That there are insufficient controls in place to ensure that one client's money cannot be used for another client's matter or be inappropriately taken from the client account. Do the breaches noted indicate to the Reporting Accountant an ongoing risk to client money?	No	
EXAMPLE ADDITIONAL INFORMATION (viewing each in isolation)				
9% of the client ledgers viewed during the RA's work identified overdrawn ledgers.		Potential ongoing risk?		Yes

Relevant SRA Accounts Rule	What is the risk to client money and what considerations are required by the Reporting Accountant to assess whether the breaches/weaknesses in systems and controls are material and or significant?	Is it likely the Reporting Accountant would qualify on this information alone?	Is it likely that the additional information would point the Reporting Accountant towards a potential qualification?
A number of breaches identified took in excess of 14 days to be rectified.	Potential ongoing risk as procedures not sufficient to recognise and rectify promptly?		Yes
The breaches were spread across a wide range of fee earners in the law firm.	Systemic and therefore increased risk?		Yes
The breaches were focused on a couple of fee earners who were not following the law firm's procedures correctly.	If law firm takes corrective action likely to be material or any ongoing risk?		No
The vast majority of the breaches were of a small nature (less than £100) and were identified by the law firm's weekly control procedures and corrected promptly.	Do amounts of breaches and correction procedures indicate significant risk?		No
The vast majority of the breaches were in excess of £1,000, and were not identified by the law firm's control procedures and were not corrected at all.		Yes	

	Relevant SRA Accounts Rule	What is the risk to client money and what considerations are required by the Reporting Accountant to assess whether the breaches/weaknesses in systems and controls are material and or significant?	Is it likely the Reporting Accountant would qualify on this information alone?	Is it likely that the additional information would point the Reporting Accountant towards a potential qualification?
EXAMPLE 2 – COSTS NOT TRANSFERRED WITHIN 14 DAYS				
A number of instances were identified where client funds earmarked for the settlement of costs notified to clients were not transferred from the client to office account within 14 days.	Rule 17.1 (c.)	The risk that client monies that are not properly transferred in respect of work done on one matter could either deliberately or inadvertently be covering up shortfalls elsewhere. Risk of teeming and lading?	No	
EXAMPLE ADDITIONAL INFORMATION (viewing each in isolation)				
2% of client ledgers viewed during the RA's work identified such instances where Rule 17.1(c) had been breached.		Material breaches or risk to client money?		No
The breaches were primarily identified by the Reporting Accountant and had not been corrected by the law firm indicating a lack of control over fee transfers.		Nature of the ongoing risk (how the breaches arose and why they hadn't been corrected) significant?		Yes

Relevant SRA Accounts Rule	What is the risk to client money and what considerations are required by the Reporting Accountant to assess whether the breaches/weaknesses in systems and controls are material and or significant?	Is it likely the Reporting Accountant would qualify on this information alone?	Is it likely that the additional information would point the Reporting Accountant towards a potential qualification?
	The law firm has control systems to identify costs that should be transferred but they failed to work in 8% of the cases reviewed during the work of the RA. Significant ongoing risk?		No
	The breaches were focused on a small number of fee earners who were not following the law firms procedures correctly Significant ongoing risk? Corrective action taken e.g. retraining, supervision?		No

EXAMPLE 3 – DEFICIENCY IN 3 WAY RECONCILIATION PROCEDURES

Relevant SRA Accounts Rule	What is the risk to client money and what considerations are required by the Reporting Accountant to assess whether the breaches/weaknesses in systems and controls are material and or significant?	Is it likely the Reporting Accountant would qualify on this information alone?	Is it likely that the additional information would point the Reporting Accountant towards a potential qualification?
Rule 29.12	The law firm prepares 3 way client fund reconciliations but Reporting Accountant work identified deficiencies in the accuracy of 2 out of 12 monthly reconciliations The risk that a key control over client monies is not properly undertaken and as a result, client money is at ongoing risk	No	

	Relevant SRA Accounts Rule	What is the risk to client money and what considerations are required by the Reporting Accountant to assess whether the breaches/weaknesses in systems and controls are material and or significant?	Is it likely the Reporting Accountant would qualify on this information alone?	Is it likely that the additional information would point the Reporting Accountant towards a potential qualification?
EXAMPLE ADDITIONAL INFORMATION (viewing each in isolation)				
The two reconciliations included differences in client funds of £50,000 and £4.12 on total client balances of £3,400,000 and £3,900,000 and they were subsequently rectified on a timely basis.		Fully explained differences, promptly corrected, one-off? Material breaches or indications of ongoing risk to client money?		No
The differences arose from cut off issues - receipts posted late to the ledger system. They were resolved within 2 working days of the month end.		Fully explained differences promptly corrected, one-off? Material breaches or indications of ongoing risk to client money?		No
There was evidence that the individual reviewing the reconciliation did not fully understand the process or what to consider on their review.		Significant weakness in the law firm's control systems for dealing with client money?		Yes
Two further reconciliations showed no evidence of review by the COFA or a partner.		Weakness in the law firm's control systems that leads to		Yes

	Relevant SRA Accounts Rule	What is the risk to client money and what considerations are required by the Reporting Accountant to assess whether the breaches/weaknesses in systems and controls are material and or significant?	Is it likely the Reporting Accountant would qualify on this information alone?	Is it likely that the additional information would point the Reporting Accountant towards a potential qualification?
		an ongoing risk to client money?		
The differences remain unresolved.			Yes	
The differences identified a shortfall of client monies as a result of misappropriation of funds which had been replenished by the law firm.		Replenishment does not mitigate the original breach	Yes	
The differences identified a shortfall of client monies as a result of misappropriation of funds which had not been replenished by the law firm.			Yes	
EXAMPLE 4 – INSTANCES OF PARTNERS MONEY BEING INCORRECTLY TREATED AS OFFICE MONEY				
During the engagement for a law firm (an LLP) 3 instances were identified where residential conveyance transactions were completed on behalf of members of the LLP. All the transactions were completed on the office ledger only.	Rule 12.8	Risk that all client money is not held correctly, and therefore protected, in a client bank account?	No	

	Relevant SRA Accounts Rule	What is the risk to client money and what considerations are required by the Reporting Accountant to assess whether the breaches/weaknesses in systems and controls are material and or significant?	Is it likely the Reporting Accountant would qualify on this information alone?	Is it likely that the additional information would point the Reporting Accountant towards a potential qualification?
EXAMPLE ADDITIONAL INFORMATION (viewing each in isolation)				
The matters all involved the receipt of money from third party lenders.				Yes
The law firm did not have a system for appropriately engaging members of the law firm and clients of the law firm.		Material as an ongoing risk that these will typically be treated incorrectly?		Yes
The 3 instances were matters for the same member. The law firm has 75 members and of the client ledgers reviewed during the RA's work only 1% of ledgers identified such a breach.		Breaches but is their materiality or significance affected by the "clients" being members?		No
The 3 instances were matters for different members. The law firm has 5 members and the instances identified reflected a breach rate of 6% given the number of client ledgers reviewed during the RA's work.				Yes

	Relevant SRA Accounts Rule	What is the risk to client money and what considerations are required by the Reporting Accountant to assess whether the breaches/weaknesses in systems and controls are material and or significant?	Is it likely the Reporting Accountant would qualify on this information alone?	Is it likely that the additional information would point the Reporting Accountant towards a potential qualification?
EXAMPLE 5 – CLIENT MONEY NOT HELD ON INSTANT ACCESS				
Engagement work identifies client money held in a client account which is a term deposit account which indicates it is not a breakable deposit and no evidence was provided to the contrary by the bank.	Rule 13.8	The risk that client money is not properly protected under the Rules and the Solicitors Act 1974 by being held in an account that is not a proper client account	Yes	
EXAMPLE ADDITIONAL INFORMATION (viewing each in isolation)				
Further evidence of the account type rules suggests that the underlying bank account is not actually breakable on demand but the law firm has a formal bank letter stating it is breakable.		Material breach?		No

	Relevant SRA Accounts Rule	What is the risk to client money and what considerations are required by the Reporting Accountant to assess whether the breaches/weaknesses in systems and controls are material and or significant?	Is it likely the Reporting Accountant would qualify on this information alone?	Is it likely that the additional information would point the Reporting Accountant towards a potential qualification?
EXAMPLE 6 – CLIENT MONEY HELD ON THE OFFICE ACCOUNT – BANK ERROR				
Engagement work identifies a bank error where client money has been paid into the office account.	Rule 14.1	The risk that client money is not afforded the protection of the Rules or the 1974 Solicitors Act by being held in a non-client account? The risk that client money will be used inappropriately as it is not separated from office monies?	No	
EXAMPLE ADDITIONAL INFORMATION (viewing each in isolation)				
The amount involved is £150,000 and relates to completion monies on a mortgage transaction; information provided to the bank from the firm was correct and the error was on the bank's behalf. It was rectified 1 working day later.		Law firm's own systems and controls indicating any significant ongoing risk?		No

	Relevant SRA Accounts Rule	What is the risk to client money and what considerations are required by the Reporting Accountant to assess whether the breaches/weaknesses in systems and controls are material and or significant?	Is it likely the Reporting Accountant would qualify on this information alone?	Is it likely that the additional information would point the Reporting Accountant towards a potential qualification?
The amount involved is £150,000 and relates to closure of a client designated deposit account. The error was not corrected but identified by the Reporting Accountant.		Law firm's own systems and controls indicating significant ongoing risk?		Yes
The £150,000 had been sitting in office account for over 3 months when the Reporting Accountant identified it, at a time when the practice was trading near to its overdraft limit and was short of funds to pay its creditors as they fell due.			Yes	
EXAMPLE 7 – NARRATIVE ON CLIENT LEDGERS IS INCORRECT				
Engagement work identifies a number of apparent administrative errors on client ledgers.	Rule 29.1		No	

	Relevant SRA Accounts Rule	What is the risk to client money and what considerations are required by the Reporting Accountant to assess whether the breaches/weaknesses in systems and controls are material and or significant?	Is it likely the Reporting Accountant would qualify on this information alone?	Is it likely that the additional information would point the Reporting Accountant towards a potential qualification?
EXAMPLE ADDITIONAL INFORMATION (viewing each in isolation)				
In 35% of the ledgers viewed during the RA's work instances were noted when the cheque numbers on client ledger payments were incorrect.		Material? Number of breaches indicating a significant weakness in the reliability of the accounting records? Risk to client funds?		Yes
In 6% of the ledgers viewed during the RA's work instances were noted where the law firm acted for a third party lender in a conveyance transaction which did not clearly identify on the ledger that the monies were a mortgage advances.		Material? Number of breaches?		No
In 50% of the ledgers viewed during the RA's work instances were noted where the law firm acted for a third party lender in a conveyance transaction which did not clearly identify on the ledger that the monies were mortgage advances.		Material? Number of breaches? System for properly separately identifying these funds effective?		Yes

	Relevant SRA Accounts Rule	What is the risk to client money and what considerations are required by the Reporting Accountant to assess whether the breaches/weaknesses in systems and controls are material and or significant?	Is it likely the Reporting Accountant would qualify on this information alone?	Is it likely that the additional information would point the Reporting Accountant towards a potential qualification?
An office to client transfer to remedy overdrawn client ledgers was backdated to the date the ledgers became overdrawn even though the transfer was at a later date. The amount of the transfer involved was £348. This breach arose on less than 0.5% of the ledgers viewed by the RA during their work.		Material? One-off breach?		No
An office to client transfer to remedy overdrawn client ledgers was backdated to the date the ledgers became overdrawn even though the transfer was at a later date. This breach arose in 5% of the ledgers viewed by the RA during their work. The chronological order of transactions on the client ledgers and office ledgers in a number of matters were not correct.		Material? Systemic problem with incorrect recording misrepresenting the financial transactions and "covering up" of breaches? Risk that breaches are a rising but that transactions are deliberately dated so as to "cover up" the breach? Risk that the law firm/COFA is unaware of the level of breaches and therefore weaknesses in controls?		Yes Yes

	Relevant SRA Accounts Rule	What is the risk to client money and what considerations are required by the Reporting Accountant to assess whether the breaches/weaknesses in systems and controls are material and or significant?	Is it likely the Reporting Accountant would qualify on this information alone?	Is it likely that the additional information would point the Reporting Accountant towards a potential qualification?
EXAMPLE 8 – OFFICE PAYMENTS MADE FROM CLIENT ACCOUNT BY MISTAKE				
Engagement work identifies a payment from the client account which is settlement of a liability of the law firm.	Rule 20.1	The risk that client money is either by accident or design being used to fund the payments of the business?	No	
EXAMPLE ADDITIONAL INFORMATION (viewing each in isolation)				
The payment represents the quarterly VAT payment. The law firm is running an overdraft on the office account and close to its limit. There is no evidence of a bank error involved. Corrected 4 working days later.		Material? Deliberate misuse of client money due to specific financial difficulties? Client money at ongoing risk?		Yes
The payment represents quarterly bank charges from the newly appointed bankers to the law firm. The amount is £2,500 and is corrected 3 working days after on discovery by the law firm.		Significant risk to client money? Accidental misuse by the law firm? (Changes to arrangements to be confirmed to ensure no ongoing problem that would be reportable?)		No

	Relevant SRA Accounts Rule	What is the risk to client money and what considerations are required by the Reporting Accountant to assess whether the breaches/weaknesses in systems and controls are material and or significant?	Is it likely the Reporting Accountant would qualify on this information alone?	Is it likely that the additional information would point the Reporting Accountant towards a potential qualification?
The amount represents the quarterly VAT payment. The law firm is running an overdraft on the office account and is near to its limit. There is no evidence of a bank error involved. It is not corrected after many months, and is identified by the Reporting Accountant.			Yes	

EXAMPLE 9 – SWEEPING UP

	Relevant SRA Accounts Rule	What is the risk to client money and what considerations are required by the Reporting Accountant to assess whether the breaches/weaknesses in systems and controls are material and or significant?	Is it likely the Reporting Accountant would qualify on this information alone?	Is it likely that the additional information would point the Reporting Accountant towards a potential qualification?
Engagement work identifies a write off on a small balance of client funds on a client matter.	Rule 20	There is lack of information here to form a view at this point. The risk that the law firm does not comply with its obligations to return money due back to clients at the end of matters and instead takes the money to the benefit of the office account?	No	

	Relevant SRA Accounts Rule	What is the risk to client money and what considerations are required by the Reporting Accountant to assess whether the breaches/weaknesses in systems and controls are material and or significant?	Is it likely the Reporting Accountant would qualify on this information alone?	Is it likely that the additional information would point the Reporting Accountant towards a potential qualification?
EXAMPLE ADDITIONAL INFORMATION (viewing each in isolation)				
1 instance was identified where a fee earner wrote off a residual balance of £1.35 by raising a "photocopying disbursement" to clear the balance without notifying the client. It was identified and rectified on notification by the Reporting Accountant. This breach arose in less than 1% of the total ledgers viewed by the RA during their work.		Material? Significant weakness in system/law firm allowing the "taking" of client money, however small? Risk to client money?		Yes
1 instance was identified where a fee earner wrote off a residual balance of £1.35. Contact details were available for the client but the amount was donated to charity. This breach arose in less than 1% of the total ledgers viewed by the RA during their work.		Material? Number of incidents arising? (Rules allow law firms to self-certify up to certain levels and the payment is made to charity). Significant risk to client money?		No

	Relevant SRA Accounts Rule	What is the risk to client money and what considerations are required by the Reporting Accountant to assess whether the breaches/weaknesses in systems and controls are material and or significant?	Is it likely the Reporting Accountant would qualify on this information alone?	Is it likely that the additional information would point the Reporting Accountant towards a potential qualification?
		7 instances were identified where various fee earners wrote off a residual balance ranging from £1.35 to £18.50 by donating the balances to charity. Contact details for the clients were available. This breach arose in around 4% of the total ledgers viewed by the RA during their work.		Yes
		Material? Incidents arising? (Rules allow law firms to self-certify up to certain levels and the payment is made to charity). Significant risk to client money?		
		7 instances were identified where various fee earners wrote off a residual balance ranging from £1.35 to £18.50 by donating the balances to charity. Contact details for the clients were NOT available and costs to trace would be excessive. This breach arose in around 4% of the total ledgers viewed by the RA during their work.		No
		Material? Incidents a rising? (Rules allow law firms to self-certify up to certain levels and the payment is made to charity). Significant risk to client money?		
		7 instances were identified where various fee earners wrote off a residual balance ranging from £1.35 to £18.50 by raising a "photocopying disbursement" to clear the balance without notifying the client. This breach arose in around 4% of the total ledgers viewed by the RA during their work.		Yes
		Material? Significant weakness in system/law firm allowing the "taking" of client money, however small? Risk to client money?		

	Relevant SRA Accounts Rule	What is the risk to client money and what considerations are required by the Reporting Accountant to assess whether the breaches/weaknesses in systems and controls are material and or significant?	Is it likely the Reporting Accountant would qualify on this information alone?	Is it likely that the additional information would point the Reporting Accountant towards a potential qualification?
15 instances were identified where various fee earners wrote off a residual balance that was generally £250 each by raising a "travelling disbursement" to clear the balance without notifying the client. This breach arose in around 8% of the total ledgers viewed by the RA during their work.			Yes	

EXAMPLE 10 – SUSPENSE ACCOUNTS

	Relevant SRA Accounts Rule	What is the risk to client money and what considerations are required by the Reporting Accountant to assess whether the breaches/weaknesses in systems and controls are material and or significant?	Is it likely the Reporting Accountant would qualify on this information alone?	Is it likely that the additional information would point the Reporting Accountant towards a potential qualification?
Engagement work identifies the incorrect use of a suspense account.	Rule 29.2(b) & Rule 29.25	The risk that client money will be held or used inappropriately as it is not properly identified and/or separated in the accounting system from other client's money? The risk that the law firm will not be able to identify the money held for every individual client?	No	

	Relevant SRA Accounts Rule	What is the risk to client money and what considerations are required by the Reporting Accountant to assess whether the breaches/weaknesses in systems and controls are material and or significant?	Is it likely the Reporting Accountant would qualify on this information alone?	Is it likely that the additional information would point the Reporting Accountant towards a potential qualification?
EXAMPLE ADDITIONAL INFORMATION (viewing each in isolation)				
1 suspense ledger was identified and it had been used for billing Will preparation fees of £100 plus VAT per Will. There were 5 such transactions on the suspense ledger. The law firm operated 7,000 client matters, with 150 fee earners.		Material? Posing significant risk to client money due? Number of breaches of this nature?		No
3 suspense ledgers were identified and in each case they had been used for billing Will preparation fees of £200 plus VAT per Will. There were 5 such transactions on each suspense ledger. The suspense accounts were operated by the same fee earner. The law firm operated 1,000 client matters, with 10 fee earners.		Material? Does number of breaches indicate a lack of appropriate separation of clients' money and/or lack of clear understanding of reason for the Rule? Does the breach indicate risk to client funds or administrative breaches?		No
The law firm uses a suspense account to hold unidentified client bank receipts. The balance held on the ledger was £1,467 and was in relation to a single bank receipt which is 14 months old. Efforts are still being made with the bankers to identify the source of the receipt.		Material? Posing significant risk to client money due? Number of breaches of this nature? Justified use of ledger?		No

Relevant SRA Accounts Rule	What is the risk to client money and what considerations are required by the Reporting Accountant to assess whether the breaches/weaknesses in systems and controls are material and or significant?	Is it likely the Reporting Accountant would qualify on this information alone?	Is it likely that the additional information would point the Reporting Accountant towards a potential qualification?
	Material? Significant risk that client money will be held or used inappropriately as it is not properly identified and/or separated in the accounting system from other client's money? Risk that the law firm will not be able to identify the money held for every individual client?		Yes

The law firm uses a suspense account to hold unidentified client bank receipts. The balance held on the ledger was £7,435 and was in relation to multiple receipts which range from 1 month to 38 months old.

EXAMPLE 11 – LAA MONIES HELD ON OFFICE ACCOUNT FOR IN EXCESS OF 14 DAYS

Relevant SRA Accounts Rule		Is it likely the Reporting Accountant would qualify on this information alone?	
Rule 19.1(b)		No	

Engagement work has identified LAA money received and banked in the office account which relates to money on account of future fees or unbilled disbursements (certificated matter).

	Relevant SRA Accounts Rule	What is the risk to client money and what considerations are required by the Reporting Accountant to assess whether the breaches/weaknesses in systems and controls are material and or significant?	Is it likely the Reporting Accountant would qualify on this information alone?	Is it likely that the additional information would point the Reporting Accountant towards a potential qualification?
EXAMPLE ADDITIONAL INFORMATION (viewing each in isolation)				
The breach arose in around 3% of the ledgers viewed by the RA during their work. The maximum value was £350 and in all instances they had been rectified on discovery by the law firm.				No
The breach arose in around 12% of the ledgers viewed by the RA during their work. The maximum value was £2,350 and in some instances they had been rectified on discovery by the law firm.				Yes
EXAMPLE 12 – PROVIDING BANKING FACILITIES				
At the completion of a residential conveyancing Rule 14.5 matter the law firm used the proceeds, under instruction from the client, to pay school fees, purchase a new motor vehicle and pay off a long standing credit card.			Yes	

	Relevant SRA Accounts Rule	What is the risk to client money and what considerations are required by the Reporting Accountant to assess whether the breaches/weaknesses in systems and controls are material and or significant?	Is it likely the Reporting Accountant would qualify on this information alone?	Is it likely that the additional information would point the Reporting Accountant towards a potential qualification?
EXAMPLE ADDITIONAL INFORMATION (viewing each in isolation)				
The matter identified represented an isolated event; the law firm had identified the breach and included it in its own breach register.				Yes
The breach arose in around 4% of the ledgers viewed by the RA during their work. They were predominately for a single fee earner in the law firm who had not appreciated the significance of the transactions. Systems and training have now been provided to the fee earner concerned.				Yes
The breach arose in around 13% of the ledgers viewed by the RA during their work. They were across a range of fee earners in the law firm.				Yes
Additional ledgers were identified where the fee earner had also banked cheques on behalf of a client in the law firm's client account because the client did not have a bank account of their own.				Yes

	Relevant SRA Accounts Rule	What is the risk to client money and what considerations are required by the Reporting Accountant to assess whether the breaches/weaknesses in systems and controls are material and or significant?	Is it likely the Reporting Accountant would qualify on this information alone?	Is it likely that the additional information would point the Reporting Accountant towards a potential qualification?
EXAMPLE 13 – SECRET PROFITS	Rule 17		No	
An instance is identified where the telegraphic transfer (TT) fee is shown as a disbursement on the fee to the client at £25 plus VAT. In this case the cost to the law firm from the bank for the TT was £5.				
The breach arose in around 5% of the ledgers viewed by the RA during their work.				Yes
The breach arose in around 38% of the ledgers viewed by the RA during their work. The law firm had identified the issue and had returned £20 plus VAT to each of the breaches identified.				No
EXAMPLE 14 – ACTING UNDER POWER OF ATTORNEY	Rule 10/Rule 14		Yes	
A matter is identified where the solicitor is acting under a general power of attorney and the solicitor transfers money from the client's own account into the law firm's general client account where no underlying legal transaction is involved.				

EXAMPLE ADDITIONAL INFORMATION (viewing each in isolation)	Relevant SRA Accounts Rule	What is the risk to client money and what considerations are required by the Reporting Accountant to assess whether the breaches/weaknesses in systems and controls are material and or significant?	Is it likely the Reporting Accountant would qualify on this information alone?	Is it likely that the additional information would point the Reporting Accountant towards a potential qualification?
It is identified that the matter involved is actually a Lasting (Enduring) Power of Attorney and the client has become mentally incapacitated. The monies being transferred from their own account are to meet medical costs and the reason for the transfer via the client account is to maintain better control over the matter.				No
It is identified that the matter involved is actually a Lasting (Enduring) Power of Attorney and the client has not at this point become mentally incapacitated. There is no evidence to conclude that the client does not have sufficient capacity at this point to manage their financial affairs.				Yes

TECH 02/16AAF Reporting to regulators on regulatory accounts – Update to AUDIT 05/03

(January 2016)

Contents

Paragraphs

Glossary of terms

Section 1: Introduction   1 - 8
  Background   6 - 8

Section 2: Duty of care and engagement contracts   9 - 21
  Who might rely on the accountants' work   10 - 15
  Guidance on the content of engagement contracts   16
  Tri-partite engagement contracts   17 - 18
  Bi-partite engagement contracts supplemented by a written notice   19 - 20
  Bi-partite engagement contracts not supplemented by a written notice   21

Section 3: Form of report   22 - 34
  The regulatory licence   23 - 25
  Regulatory accounts   26 - 33
  Other regulatory information/regulatory returns   34

Section 4: Materiality   35 - 43
  General guidance   36 - 37
  Regulatory accounts   38 - 42
  Other regulatory information/regulatory returns   43

Section 5: Working with independent experts   44 - 52
  Background   45
  Independent accountants rely on other independent experts   46 - 49
  Independent experts rely on work performed by the independent accountants   50 - 52

Appendix A: Regulatory accounts

Appendix B: Example of an unmodified audit report for regulatory accounts

Appendix C: Example tri-partite engagement contract

Appendix D: Example bi-partite engagement contract

Appendix E: Example written notice from the independent accountants to the regulator for bipartite engagement arrangements

ABOUT THE AUDIT AND ASSUANCE FACULTY

The ICAEW Audit and Assurance Faculty is a leading authority on external audit and other assurance activities and is recognised internationally as a source of expertise on audit issues. It is responsible for ICAEW technical audit and assurance leadership and provides a range of information sources to its members which gives practical assurance in key audit and assurance areas.

Glossary of Terms

Terms	Meaning
Independent Account	The accountant that is required to report on the Regulatory Accounts. The independent account may also be the auditor of the regulated entity's statutory accounts.
IFRS	International Financial Reporting Standards, as adopted by the European Union.
RAGs	Regulatory Accounting Guidelines (RAGs) issued by, or agreed with individual Regulators. RAGs specify how Regulatory Accounts are to be prepared by the Regulated Entities. In certain industries, RAGs may be supplemented by more detailed framework documentation which is not prepared by, nor agreed with, the Regulator.
Regulated Activities	Those activities of the Regulated Entities covered by the powers of the Regulators, usually defined in the Regulated Entities' regulatory licence.
Regulated Entities	Those entities whose activities are covered by the powers of the Regulators (as defined above) and who are required to provide Regulatory Accounts and/or Regulatory Information that is required to be reported upon by Independent Accountants.
Regulators/ Regulatory Bodies	Government appointed regulatory bodies that oversee the activities of Regulated Entities. For the purposes of this document, these are: • Ofgem (Office of Gas and Electricity Markets) • Ofwat (The Water Services Regulation Authority) • CAA (Civil Aviation Authority) • ORR (Office of Rail and Road) • URegNI (Utility Regulator, Northern Ireland) • Ofcom (Office of Communications).
Regulatory Accounts	Accounts prepared under bases and principles and incorporating information specified by, or agreed with, the Regulators.
Regulatory Information	Information provided to the Regulators by the Regulated Entities in connection with their regulated operations.
Regulatory Licence	The instrument of appointment of the Regulated Entity.
Regulatory reports/ Reporting	Reports made by Regulated Entities and/or accountants to Regulators.
Regulatory Return	A return of Regulatory Information (which can include Regulatory Accounts) provided to the Regulator by the Regulated Entities. Certain items within the Return are required to be reported upon by Independent Accountants as part of their regulatory reporting.
Third Party	Any party, other than the Regulator, who has access to Regulatory Accounts, Regulatory Returns or Regulatory Information.
UK GAAP	United Kingdom Generally Accepted Accounting Practice.

Section 1: Introduction

1   This guidance, ICAEW Technical Release TECH 02/16AAF is issued by the Audit and Assurance Faculty of ICAEW in January 2016 to assist Independent Accountants when asked to provide reports to Regulators of Regulated Entities and in applying ICAEW Technical Release TECH 10/12AAF *Reporting to third parties* to this reporting. ICAEW Technical Release TECH 02/16AAF updates ICAEW Technical Release Audit 05/03 *Reporting to regulators of regulated entities*, originally issued in 2003.

2   This technical release specifically excludes reporting to other regulatory bodies, for example the Financial Conduct Authority and the Prudential Regulation Authority.

3   Changes to the original Audit 05/03 comprise:

- updated references to the Companies Act 2006, International Standards on Auditing (UK and Ireland), TECH 10/12AAF and the names of the regulators;

- the addition of references to International Financial Reporting Standards; and

- revisions to the report on the Regulatory Accounts to align with International Standards on Auditing (UK and Ireland).

4   Audit 05/03 was originally issued following the formation of a working group comprising of representatives from the accountancy profession and ICAEW, and consultation with the Regulators. The Regulated Entities were included in the consultation process.

5   This guidance aims to promote consistency in the practices adopted in respect of Regulatory Reporting by Independent Accountants, taking into consideration the requirements of Regulators.

Background

6   Regulated Entities are required to submit a large volume of information to Regulators, much of which is financial in nature.

7   The exact reporting requirements can vary significantly between industries and are determined and set out in regulatory licences and in related guidance and instructions issued by the Regulators. In some cases, elements of this information are required to be reported upon by Independent Accountants, often being the Regulated Entities' statutory auditors.

8   This guidance is for the use of Independent Accountants to assist them where they are conducting work which involves reporting on Regulatory Information which is addressed to Regulators and is required to be produced by the Regulated Entity under its Licence or otherwise by the Regulator. However, this guidance should not be regarded as a substitute for the specific legal and professional advice which firms may need to take on particular matters or engagements.

Section 2: Duty of Care and Engagement Contracts

This section considers the issue of reliance by the Regulators on the work of **9** Independent Accountants reporting on Regulatory Information and provides guidance on this matter. It also considers the question of the potential for reliance by others on Regulatory Reports, and the steps which may be taken to clarify the scope of the Independent Accountants' work and responsibility to such third parties.

Who might rely on the accountants' work

ICAEW Technical Release TECH 10/12AAF *Reporting to third parties* provides **10** the following guidance:

Extract from ICAEW Technical Release TECH 10/12AAF

- When professional accountants know that their report has been requested by a third party and that the third party will rely on the report, there is a risk, in the absence of an effective disclaimer, that the professional accountants owe the third party a duty to take reasonable care in preparing and providing the report. If the professional accountants do owe the third party such a duty, they could be liable to that third party if they were negligent and the third party suffered loss in reliance on the report.

- It is vital, therefore, for professional accountants to understand who the third party is, why it requires the report and the extent of loss which the third party could suffer in reliance on the report. If, for example, the third party runs a scheme for compensating the client's customers in the event of the client's insolvency, the professional accountants' risk is much greater than if, for example, the third party's only role is to perform marketing for a particular service sector.

- The professional accountants' understanding of the risks involved in providing a report underpins the decisions they make about whether to accept the engagement and on what terms. Depending upon the circumstances professional accountants either:

  (a) accept that they owe a duty of care to the third party and enter into an engagement contract with the third party, including provisions limiting liability if appropriate; or

  (b) proceed with an engagement for their client but before allowing the third party access to their report, require the third party to acknowledge in writing that the professional accountants owe the third party no duty of care; or

  (c) proceed with an engagement for their client but disclaim or limit any liability or duty to the third party by notice in their report; or

  (d) do not accept the engagement.

- If professional accountants regard a report as high risk, they agree to provide the report only if the third party is a party to the engagement contract or the third party has acknowledged in writing that the professional accountants owe no duty of care to the third party. If professional accountants regard a report as low risk, typically because the third party could suffer little or no loss in reliance on the report, then they may decide to provide the report without contracting with the third party. In this case a notice can be included in the report disclaiming or limiting the accountants' liability to the third party. In addition to that notice, it may be appropriate for the professional accountants to write to the third party, in advance of the third party receiving the report, notifying the third party of the basis on which the report will be provided. Also, if a third party writes to the professional accountants in an attempt to indicate reliance on a report, the professional accountants consider whether it is reasonable to accept such reliance. Where it is not, a disclaimer is given in writing.

- Professional accountants are advised not to allow their reports to be provided to a third party unless the basis and extent of their liability to the third party is clear and agreed. Accountants refer to the guidance in ICAEW Technical Releases AAF 04/06 *Assurance engagements: management of risk and liability* and TECH 09/15BL *Managing the professional liability of accountants* [formerly TECH 02/11] and consider the consequences of The Contracts (Rights of Third Parties) Act 1999 – see the guidance in ICAEW Technical Release Audit 4/00.

11   There are a number of parties who might be interested in the contents of information published or otherwise supplied by Regulated Entities to their Regulatory Bodies. As well as the Regulatory Body itself, these might include others in the same industry, potential entrants to the market, academics, journalists, analysts, consumer bodies and consumers/members of the public at large. Independent Accountants do not accept that they owe a duty of care or have any other legal responsibility to any person in respect of their report on Regulatory Information except those who have engaged the Independent Accountants to perform services under a written engagement contract or with whom the Independent Accountants have otherwise agreed in writing to accept such a responsibility.

12   Regulatory Accounts and Regulatory Returns are required by an individual Regulator, who specifies or agrees what they should contain and who uses that information as part of its overall role in regulating the regulated entity. In these circumstances, Independent Accountants only accept that they owe a responsibility/duty of care to the Regulated Entity and the Regulator if either:

(i)   both the Regulated Entity and the Regulator are parties to the written engagement contract with the Independent Accountants ("a tri-partite engagement contract"). The tripartite engagement contract contains appropriate terms clarifying and limiting the scope and extent of the Independent Accountants' responsibilities and liability; or

(ii)   the Regulated Entity alone is a party to a written engagement contract with the Independent Accountants ("a bi-partite engagement contract") which makes provision for the Independent Accountants to accept separately a responsibility also to the Regulator, provided that the Regulator and the Independent Accountants can agree in writing the basis of this responsibility ("written notice") AND the Regulator and the Independent Accountants actually agree, in writing, the basis on which this responsibility/duty of care is extended to the Regulator.

The bi-partite engagement contract contains appropriate terms clarifying and limiting the scope and extent of the Independent Accountants' responsibilities and liability, and includes a mechanism enabling Independent Accountants to extend their responsibilities to the Regulator through the written notice on the basis that the Independent Accountants' liability is capped, in aggregate, at a level no greater than the amount which would have been payable by them to the Regulated Entity under the bi-partite engagement contract. It will be a matter for the Regulator and the Regulated Entity to agree how the aggregate liability will be shared and recorded in the bi-partite engagement contract and the written notice. Should such an agreement not be reached, the Independent Accountants will consider capping their liability in aggregate.

The written notice between the Independent Accountants and the Regulator will confirm that the Independent Accountants accept a responsibility to the Regulator for the Independent Accountants' report (even though the Regulator is a not an addressee of the bi-partite engagement contract) provided that the Regulator agrees, in writing, that this will be on the same terms as the bi-partite engagement contract, a copy of which will be attached to the written notice, as if the Regulator had been an original addressee of the bi-partite engagement contract. An example of a written notice between the Independent Accountants and the Regulator is set out as Appendix E.

If the Regulator will not agree the basis on which the Independent Accountants are   13
willing to accept a duty of care to the Regulator, either through (a) a tri-partite engagement contract, or (b) a bi-partite engagement contract supplemented by the written notice, the Independent Accountants do not accept a duty of care to the Regulator and will make that clear in their report. In these circumstances the Independent Accountants disapply in their bi-partite engagement letter any rights that the Regulator might otherwise have acquired under the Contracts (Rights of Third Parties) Act 1999 and send a copy of the bi-partite engagement contract to the Regulator.

Independent Accountants do not accept a responsibility/duty of care to other   14
parties who may have an interest in, or who may ultimately use, the Regulatory Accounts, Regulatory Returns or other Regulatory Information reported upon by the Independent Accountants unless the Independent Accountants have identified the other party and agreed with the other party, in writing, the basis on which they accept this duty of care. Where a report is made by Independent Accountants to a Regulated Entity and a Regulator under a tri-partite engagement contract, that report will include a specific disclaimer of any liability or duty to any Third Party. Where a report is made by the Independent Accountants to a Regulated Entity and/ or a Regulator under a bi-partite engagement contract, whether or not supplemented by written notice, that report will include a specific disclaimer of any liability or duty to any other person other than those to whom the Independent Accountants have addressed their report. The report is addressed to the Regulator as well as to the Company without any disclaimer of responsibility to the Regulator only where the Regulator has signed a tri-partite engagement contract or there is a bi-partite engagement contract supplemented by written notice signed by the Regulator. In other cases the report may be addressed to the Company and the Regulator (to meet the requirements of the Regulatory Licence) but includes a disclaimer under which responsibility is accepted to the Company only and co-addressing to the Regulator is expressed to be only to meet the requirements of the Regulatory Licence.

Where the Regulator has indicated to the Independent Accountants that they   15
would like a Third Party to be able to rely on the Independent Accountants' report and the Independent Accountants are in agreement with this, the Independent Accountants include in their report a clear statement that the Third Party can only rely on the report after becoming a party to the engagement contract for that report or agree with the Third Party a written notice specifying the basis on which the Independent Accountants extend their duty of care to the Third Party.

Guidance on the content of engagement contracts

16   ICAEW Technical Release TECH 10/12AAF includes the following guidance on engagement contracts:

Extract from ICAEW Technical Release TECH 10/12AAF

Engagement contracts include the following:

- a clear unambiguous description of the scope of work to be performed and the form of report to be provided using defined terms where appropriate to avoid misunderstandings;

- a description of the client's obligations and the client's responsibility for the information on which the professional accountants report;

- clarification that the engagement is separate from the statutory audit and that the professional accountants have no duty of care to the third party in relation to the statutory audit;

- an appropriate liability cap[1], agreed having regard to the nature of the work being performed, the level of fee charged and other relevant factors. Any limitation of liability must be negotiated and agreed with the client, and must be fair and reasonable in compliance with the Unfair Contract Terms Act 1977[2]; and

- details of the addressee for the report, limitations as to the purpose for which the report is prepared and restrictions on who is entitled to see and rely upon the report and on the distribution of it;

- a copy of the form of report to be provided.

Tri-partite engagement contracts

17   The above guidance from ICAEW Technical Release TECH 10/12AAF is incorporated into the tri-partite engagement contract, and is applied to both the Regulator and the Regulated Entity. In addition, in the circumstances covered by this guidance, engagement contracts signed by the Regulator, the Regulated Entity and the Independent Accountants include the following:

(i)   an acknowledgement of a duty of care by the Independent Accountants both to the Regulated Entity and to the Regulator;

(ii)   an explicit denial of liability by the Independent Accountants to any other party other than the Regulator and the Regulated Entity whose information is being reported on. This denial should also be incorporated into the Independent Accountants' report (see paragraph 30(i));

(iii)   an acknowledgement from the Regulator and the Regulated Entity that;

(a)   wherever the complete Regulatory Accounts or other Regulatory Information covered by the Independent Accountants' report is published or otherwise made available, the Independent Accountants' report will also be published or otherwise made available; and

---

[1] *Professional accountants consider whether the liability cap is reasonable given the specific circumstances of the engagement.*

[2] *See the guidance in ICAEW Technical Release TECH 09/15BL Managing the professional liability of accountants*

(b) wherever substantial extracts[3] from the Regulatory Accounts or other Regulatory Information covered by the Independent Accountants' report are published or otherwise made available, and reference is made to the fact that they are audited or otherwise examined by Independent Accountants, there will be explicit statements: a) that the information published is only an extract; and b) about the limitation of scope of the Independent Accountants' report and the duty of care owed by the Independent Accountants; and c) referring to where the full set of Regulatory Accounts or Regulatory Information can be found or otherwise obtained;

(c) wherever any other information is referenced from the Regulatory Accounts or other Regulatory Information covered by the Independent Accountants' report, there will be an explicit reference by the Regulator to the source of that information and the limitation of scope of the Independent Accountants' report and the duty of care owed by the Independent Accountants;

(iv) clarification that the Independent Accountants' opinion on the Regulatory Accounts is separate from their opinion on the statutory accounts of the Company, which are prepared for a different purpose;

(v) clarification, where relevant, that the Regulatory Accounts are/other Regulatory Information is prepared by disaggregating balances recorded in the general ledgers and other accounting records of the Company maintained in accordance with the Companies Act 2006 and used, in accordance with that Act, for the preparation of the Company's statutory financial statements;

(vi) a statement, where appropriate, that no additional tests will be performed of the transactions and balances which are recorded in the general ledgers of the Regulated Entity other than those carried out in performing the audit of the statutory financial statements that include the Regulated Entity;

(vii) a statement, where appropriate, clarifying what work is done in respect of any other information accompanying the Regulatory Accounts or other Regulatory Information, and confirmation if no audit opinion is expressed on this;

(viii) clarification about the obligations, if any, of the Independent Accountants to attend tripartite meetings with the Regulator, including frequency and timing, subject matter, arrangements for minutes and if appropriate the form of hold harmless letters to precede such meetings;

(ix) clarification of how any liability cap will be split between the Regulated Entity and the Regulator;

(x) a statement that the nature and format of the Regulatory Accounts or other Regulatory Information, RAGs and Regulatory Returns are determined by the individual Regulators, and that it is not appropriate for the Independent Accountants to assess whether the information being reported upon is suitable or appropriate for the Regulator's purpose. Independent Accountants do not agree to provide any implicit or explicit affirmation that the information being reported upon is suitable for the Regulator's purpose;

---

[3] *For example, reproduction of primary statements as a whole.*

(xi)   confirmation that there are differences between IFRS or UK GAAP and the basis of any information supplied to the Regulators. The engagement contract and the Independent Accountants' report will include a statement that financial information other than that prepared on the basis of IFRS or UK GAAP does not necessarily represent a true and fair view of the financial performance or financial position of a company as shown in financial statements prepared in accordance with the Companies Act 2006;

(xii) an example of the type of audit report/opinion that the Independent Accountants would expect to provide if the results of the audit work are satisfactory. This will be based on the example report set out in Appendix B, amended as appropriate for the particular circumstances of the engagement; and

(xiii) a statement that nothing in the tri-partite engagement contract is intended to, nor should it, affect or in any way alter the relationship or the rights and obligations between the Regulated Entity and the Regulator as set out in the Regulatory Licence.

18   An example of a tri-partite engagement contract is shown at Appendix C. This should be tailored as necessary for the circumstances of each particular engagement.

Bi-partite engagement contracts supplemented by a written notice

19   The guidance from ICAEW Technical Release TECH 10/12AAF is also incorporated into bipartite engagement contracts where the Regulator has agreed to sign a written notice, and is applied to both the Regulator and the Regulated Entity. In addition, in the circumstances covered by this guidance, bi-partite engagement contracts signed by the Regulated Entity and the Independent Accountants include the following:

(i)   an acknowledgement of a duty of care by the Independent Accountants to the Regulated Entity and an agreement to extend the duty of care to the Regulator provided that it agrees appropriate terms with the Independent Accountants in the form of a written notice;

(ii)   an explicit denial of liability by the Independent Accountants to any persons to whom they have not agreed, in writing, to accept responsibility. This denial should also be incorporated into the Independent Accountants' report (see paragraph 30(i));

(iii) an acknowledgement from the Regulated Entity (and from the Regulator where the Regulator has agreed to sign a written notice[4]) that;

(a)   wherever the complete Regulatory Information covered by the Independent Accountants' report is published or otherwise made available, the Independent Accountant's report will also be published or otherwise made available; and

(b)   wherever substantial extracts[5] from the Regulatory Accounts or other Regulatory Information covered by the Independent Accountants' report are published or otherwise made available, and reference is made to the fact that they are audited or otherwise examined by Independent Accountants, there will be explicit statements: a) that the

---

[4] *See Appendix E, example of a written notice.*

[5] *For example, reproduction of primary statements as a whole.*

information published is only an extract; and b) about the limitation of scope of the Independent Accountants' report and the duty of care owed by the Independent Accountants; and c) referring to where the full set of Regulatory Accounts or Regulatory Information can be found or otherwise obtained;

(c) wherever any other information is referenced from the Regulatory Accounts or other Regulatory Information covered by the Independent Accountants' report, there will be an explicit reference by the Regulator to the source of that information and the limitation of scope of the Independent Accountants' report and the duty of care owed by the Independent Accountants';

(iv) clarification that the Independent Accountants' opinion on the Regulatory Accounts is separate from their opinion on the statutory accounts of the Company, which are prepared for a different purpose;

(v) clarification, where relevant, that the Regulatory Accounts are/other Regulatory Information is prepared by disaggregating balances recorded in the general ledgers and other accounting records of the Company maintained in accordance with the Companies Act 2006 and used, in accordance with that Act, for the preparation of the Company's statutory financial statements;

(vi) a statement, where appropriate, that no additional tests will be performed of the transactions and balances which are recorded in the general ledgers of the Regulated Entity other than those carried out in performing the audit of the statutory financial statements that include the Regulated Entity;

(vii) a statement, where appropriate, clarifying what work is done in respect of any other information accompanying the Regulatory Accounts or other Regulatory Information, and confirmation if no audit opinion is expressed on this;

(viii) clarification about the obligations, if any, of the Independent Accountants to attend tri-partite meetings with the Regulator, including frequency and timing, subject matter, arrangements for minutes and if appropriate the form of hold harmless letters to precede such meetings;

(ix) clarification of how any liability cap will be split between the Regulated Entity and the Regulator;

(x) a statement that the nature and format of the Regulatory Accounts or other Regulatory Information, RAGs and Regulatory Returns are determined by the individual Regulators, and that it is not appropriate for the Independent Accountants to assess whether the information being reported upon is suitable or appropriate for the Regulator's purpose. Independent Accountants do not agree to provide any implicit or explicit affirmation that the information being reported upon is suitable for the Regulator's purpose;

(xi) confirmation that there are differences between IFRS or UK GAAP and the basis of any information supplied to the Regulators. The engagement contract and the Independent Accountants' report will include a statement that financial information other than that prepared on the basis of IFRS or UK GAAP does not necessarily represent a true and fair view of the financial performance or financial position of a company as shown in financial statements prepared in accordance with the Companies Act 2006;

(xii) an example of the type of audit report/opinion that the Independent Accountants would expect to provide if the results of the audit work are satisfactory. This will be based on the example report set out in Appendix B, amended as appropriate for the particular circumstances of the engagement; and

(xiii) a statement that nothing in the bi-partite engagement contract is intended to, nor should it, affect or in any way alter the relationship or the rights and obligations between the Regulated Entity and the Regulator as set out in the Regulatory Licence.

20 An example of a bi-partite engagement contract is shown at Appendix D. This should be tailored as necessary for the circumstances of each particular engagement.

Bi-partite engagement contracts not supplemented by a written notice

21 If the Regulator will not agree engagement terms, either on a tri-partite basis or on a bi-partite basis supplemented by written notice, the Independent Accountants will agree a bi-partite engagement contract with the Regulated Entity incorporating the relevant aspects of paragraph 19 (that is excluding irrelevant aspects, such as items (viii), (ix) and (x), and will expressly deny any duty of care to the Regulator in the engagement contract and their report.

Section 3: Form of Report

22 This section provides guidance on the form of report that is issued by Independent Accountants reporting on Regulatory Accounts and other Regulatory Information.

The Regulatory Licence

23 As noted in Section 1 of this guidance, the Regulatory Licence prescribes the Regulatory Information that it requires the Regulated Entity to report to the Regulator.

24 The Regulated Entity is usually required, under the terms of its Regulatory Licence, to procure an Independent Accountants' report, addressed to the Regulated Entity and/or the Regulator, supporting certain of the Regulatory Information submitted by the Regulated Entity to the Regulator.

25 Where a report on Regulatory Information is to be addressed to the Regulator and a duty of care is acknowledged to the Regulator, Independent Accountants agree either a tri-partite engagement contract with the Regulator and the Regulated Entity or a bi-partite engagement contract with the Regulated Entity supplemented by written notice with the Regulator, in accordance with the guidance set out in Section 2 (Duty of care and engagement contracts) of this paper.

Regulatory Accounts

26 ISA (UK and Ireland) 700 (The Auditor's Report on Financial Statements) is written to address both "true and fair frameworks", such as the statutory financial statements, and "compliance frameworks", such as Regulatory Accounts which are not prepared in accordance with the Companies Act 2006 nor necessarily in accordance with IFRS or UK GAAP. Therefore, the guidance contained in ISA (UK and Ireland) 700 can be applied equally to opinions expressed by Independent Accountants on Regulatory Accounts.

Applying ISA (UK and Ireland) 700 to reports issued by Independent **27**
Accountants:

- Independent Accountants' reports on financial statements should include the following matters:

    (a) an appropriate title

    (b) appropriately addressed as required by the circumstances of the engagement;

    (c) identify the financial statements of the entity that have been audited, including the date of, and period covered by, the financial statements;

    (d) a statement that those charged with governance are responsible for the preparation of the financial statements;

    (e) a statement that the responsibility of the auditor is to audit and express an opinion on the financial statements in accordance with applicable legal requirements and International Standards on Auditing (UK and Ireland);

    (f) the description of the scope of the audit;

    (g) the auditor's opinion as required by the relevant financial reporting framework used to prepare the financial statements, including applicable law;

    (h) the name of the location of the office where the auditor is based; and

    (i) the name of the auditor and be signed and dated.

- The use of a standard format for Independent Accountants' reports on financial statements assists the reader to follow the report's contents. The section headings indicate to the reader the nature of the matters contained in the section concerned: for example, where a modified opinion is expressed, a new section entitled "Basis for qualified/adverse/disclaimer of opinion" and the appropriate heading "Qualified opinion/adverse opinion/disclaimer of opinion" is used.

- Independent Accountants draft each section of their report on financial statements to reflect the requirements which apply to the particular engagement. However, the use of common language in Independent Accountants' reports assists the reader's understanding.

Where the entity is required by its regulatory licence, or voluntarily chooses, to **28**
adopt the UK Corporate Governance Code, Independent Accountants would also refer to ISA (UK and Ireland) 700[6] which would also require that the Independent Accountants' reports:

(a) Describe those assessed risks of material misstatement that were identified by the Independent Accountant and which had the greatest effect on: the overall audit strategy; the allocation of resources in the audit; and directing the efforts of the engagement team;

(b) Provide an explanation of how the Independent Accountant applied the concept of materiality in planning and performing the audit. Such explanation shall specify the threshold used by the Independent Accountant as being materiality for the financial statements as a whole; and

---

[6] *ISA (UK and Ireland) 700.19A and 19B*

(c)   Provide an overview of the scope of the audit including an explanation of how such scope addressed the assessed risks of material misstatement disclosed in accordance with (a) and was influenced by the Independent Accountant's application of materiality disclosed in accordance with (b).

In addition, the Independent Accountant reports by exception if, when reading the other financial and non-financial information included in the document containing the regulatory accounts, they identified information that is materially inconsistent with the information in the audited financial statements or is apparently materially incorrect based on, or materially inconsistent with, the knowledge acquired by the Independent Accountant in the course of performing the audit or that is otherwise misleading. Paragraph 22B of ISA (UK and Ireland) 700 gives examples of such matters.

29   Independent Accountants will also refer to ISA (UK and Ireland) 706 (Emphasis of matter paragraphs and other matter paragraphs in the independent auditor's report).

30   The guidance drawn from ISAs (UK and Ireland) 700 and 706 is incorporated into the form of report issued by Independent Accountants. In addition, opinions expressed by Independent Accountants on Regulatory Accounts include the following:

(i)   a statement clarifying to whom the Independent Accountants accept a responsibility, and to whom they do not[7];

(ii)   Within the basis of audit opinion paragraph, a statement that the audit of the Regulatory Accounts has been conducted in accordance with International Standards on Auditing (UK and Ireland) except that, as the nature, form and content of Regulatory Accounts are determined by the Regulator, the Independent Accountants' did not evaluate the overall adequacy of the presentation of the information, which would have been required if they were to express an audit opinion under International Standards on Auditing (UK and Ireland);

(iii)   an emphasis of matter paragraph:

- setting out the basis of the preparation of the Regulatory Accounts, for example in accordance with the RAGs and stating that the nature, form and content of Regulatory Accounts are determined by the Regulator, and that it is not appropriate for the auditors/ Independent Accountants or the directors to assess whether the nature of the information being reported upon is suitable or appropriate for the Regulator's purposes; and

- containing a statement that the Regulatory Accounts are separate from the statutory financial statements of the Company and have not been prepared on the basis of IFRS or UK GAAP, and that financial information other than that prepared on the basis of IFRS or UK GAAP does not necessarily represent a true and fair view of the financial position of a company.

31   Independent Accountants make clear, in their report, the Regulatory Information on which they are providing assurance, and that on which they are not. Where the Regulatory Information is part of a wider report or Regulatory Return, those additional matters being considered in connection with the Independent Accountants' report are clearly identified.

---

[7] *The Working Group has taken the advice of Leading Counsel in respect of appropriate wording to do this. The suggested wording is that in the second paragraph of the example Independent Accountants' report in Appendix B.*

The Independent Accountants' report on Regulatory Accounts will be based on **32** the example unmodified report set out at Appendix B, changed as appropriate for the particular circumstances of the engagement. Where changes are made, Independent Accountants will use existing guidance (for example ICAEW Technical Release TECH 10/12AAF and ISA (UK and Ireland) 700) in making those changes. Where such changes result in a departure from ISAs (UK and Ireland), the Independent Accountant will follow the guidance in ISA (UK and Ireland) 705 which will be reflected in the Independent Accountants' Report on the Regulatory Accounts.

An example of such a departure would arise if the Regulatory Accounts are an **33** integral part of a broader Regulatory Return. If the Independent Accountants did not read the other information contained in the Regulatory Return for apparent misstatements therein, or any material inconsistency with the audited Regulatory Accounts (as required under ISA (UK and Ireland) 720 Section A (The auditor's responsibilities related to other information in documents containing audited financial statements), then non-compliance with ISA (UK & Ireland) 720 Section A will be referred to in the "basis for qualified/adverse/disclaimer of opinion" and "opinion on regularity accounts" paragraphs of the report.

Other Regulatory Information/Regulatory Returns

When reporting on other Regulatory Information, Independent Accountants **34** follow the guidance set out in ICAEW Technical Release TECH 10/12AAF, ISAs (UK and Ireland) 700, 706 and, where applicable, 705 and this paper.

Section 4: Materiality

This section considers the assessment of materiality in respect of work performed, **35** and reports issued, by Independent Accountants reporting on Regulatory Accounts and other Regulatory Information, and provides guidance on this matter.

General guidance

Materiality is considered in ISA (UK and Ireland) 320 (Materiality in planning and **36** performing an audit) and ISA (UK and Ireland) 450 (Evaluation of misstatements identified during the audit). ISA 320 explains that although there is no definition of materiality:

- Misstatements, including omissions, are considered to be material if they, individually or in the aggregate, could reasonably be expected to influence the economic decisions of users taken on the basis of the financial statements;

- Judgments about materiality are made in light of surrounding circumstances, and are affected by the size or nature of a misstatement, or a combination of both; and

- Judgments about matters that are material to users of the financial statements are based on a consideration of the common financial information needs of users as a group. The possible effect of misstatements on specific individual users, whose needs may vary widely, is not considered.

Materiality is a matter of professional judgement for the Independent **37** Accountants/auditors, based on their understanding of the circumstances of the engagement and communications with the addressees of their report.

Regulatory Accounts

38   There is a growing trend, amongst Regulators, to draft licence conditions that require the Regulated Entity to include a number of different analyses of their business segments and/or operations within the Regulatory Accounts. In providing their report, Independent Accountants assess materiality in the context of the Regulatory Accounts as a whole, taking together the component analyses/disclosures in the Regulatory Accounts, rather than each component analysis/disclosure separately.

39   Where the Regulator is an addressee to the Independent Accountants' report, the Regulator may specify, with supporting reasons, particular factors that it considers to be material in the context of the Regulatory Accounts and the Independent Accountants' report. These factors are specified in the engagement contract, discussed in Section 2 of this guidance, and incorporated into the Independent Accountants' assessment of materiality. Independent Accountants plan their work to gain reasonable assurance that the Regulatory Accounts are free from material misstatement, whether caused by fraud or other error. Where, as a consequence of considering the Regulator's specified matters/factors, the Independent Accountants are required to perform additional procedures to provide the level of assurance required, they assess and agree with the parties to the engagement contract the scope of their work and the likely impact on audit fees for performing this work.

40   Although Independent Accountants consider the individual factors that the Regulator has asked them to consider in assessing materiality for the Regulatory Accounts, they only express an opinion on the Regulatory Accounts as a whole, and not on those individual factors.

41   Where the Regulator requires specific factors to be reported upon by the Independent Accountants, the Independent Accountants agree a list of procedures ("Agreed Upon Procedures") that they will perform for the Regulator. These procedures are specified within the engagement contract with the Regulator. The Independent Accountants report the findings of the procedures separately from the Regulatory Accounts opinion, by way of a factual report to the Regulator. The Independent Accountants do not express an opinion on the results of the Agreed Upon Procedures, nor the appropriateness of these procedures for the purposes of the Regulator. The engagement contract and report for the "Agreed Upon Procedures" include a statement that the Regulator needs to make its own assessment of the appropriateness of the Agreed Upon Procedures and the reported findings.

42   Where Agreed Upon Procedures are required in addition to an opinion on the Regulatory Accounts, Independent Accountants may choose not to complete their work nor express their opinion on the Regulatory Accounts until:

(i)   the Agreed Upon Procedures that have been specified by the Regulator have been completed and reported upon; and

(ii)   the Regulator has provided assurance to the Independent Accountants that nothing has come to the attention of the Regulator from that report (or otherwise) that indicates that there are any matters that the Regulator believes the Independent Accountants should take into account in arriving at their opinion on the Regulatory Accounts. If such matters do exist, the Independent Accountants will consider, in arriving at their opinion on the Regulatory Accounts, the matters noted by the Regulator and/or agree additional Agreed Upon Procedures with the Regulator.

Other Regulatory Information/Regulatory Returns

When reporting on Regulatory Information, the Independent Accountants follow   **43**
the principles set out in ISAs (UK and Ireland) 320 and 450, as appropriate.

Section 5: Working with independent experts

This section considers the use of other experts in respect of work performed, and   **44**
reports issued, by Independent Accountants reporting on Regulatory Accounts
and other Regulatory Information, and provides guidance on this matter.

Background

The provision of opinions on Regulatory Information may involve work with, or   **45**
reliance upon, other independent experts, for example there may be reliance upon
technical/engineering experts to determine whether the cost of projects should be
capitalised or expensed. In addition, other independent experts may work with, or
place reliance upon the Independent Accountants' work or report in discharging
their own reporting responsibilities.

Independent Accountants rely on other independent experts

Guidance in respect of the use of auditor's experts is contained within ISA (UK   **46**
and Ireland) 620 (Using the work of an auditor's expert), which states that "The
auditor has sole responsibility for the audit opinion expressed, and that
responsibility is not reduced by the auditor's use of the work of an auditor's
expert" [para 3] and "If using the work of an auditor's expert, [the auditor shall]
determine whether that work is adequate for the auditor's purposes" [para 5(b)].

Where the Independent Accountants have performed audit procedures and   **47**
expressed an unmodified audit opinion, auditors are required not to refer to the
work of an auditor's expert in an auditor's report unless required by law or
regulation to do so. Where such a reference is required because such reference is
relevant to an understanding of the reason for the modification, the auditor is
required to indicate that such reference does not reduce the auditor's responsibility
for that opinion.

Where the Independent Accountants have performed Agreed Upon Procedures   **48**
and the report provided does not include an audit opinion, it is expected that the
use and/or findings of the expert would be referred to in that report, unless such
reference is clearly not required. Such Agreed Upon Procedures and report would
include, for example, Agreed Upon Procedures that the Independent Accountants
may agree with the Regulator in relation to the Regulated Entity's compliance with
Regulatory Accounting Guidelines which may include steps such as obtaining the
opinion of the Regulated Entity's appointed technical consultants (sometimes
referred to as the reporter) for example, as to the appropriateness of capital
expenditure outlay and tendering procedures.

The Independent Accountants would need the consent of the expert prior to   **49**
making reference to, and/or including extracts from the expert's report in the
Independent Accountants' report.

Independent experts rely on work performed by the Independent Accountants

The Independent Accountants may be requested by a Third Party to perform   **50**
certain procedures in connection with that Third Party's own regulatory reporting.

For example, the Third Party (who may itself be an independent expert) may ask the Independent Accountants to verify that certain financial information is correctly extracted from a company's accounting records when reporting on information to be included in Regulatory Returns.

51   In such circumstances, the Independent Accountants obtain permission from the Regulated Entity prior to agreeing to do the work, and agree a tri-partite engagement contract with the Regulated Entity and the independent expert in accordance with the guidance set out in ICAEW Technical Release TECH 10/12AAF and Section 2 of this paper.

52   The form of report issued to the independent expert should be prepared in accordance with the guidance set out in ISA (UK and Ireland) 700 and Section 3 of this guidance.

Appendix A: Regulatory Accounts

There is no precise definition of Regulatory Accounts, either in law or in practice, although they are commonly referred to by Regulatory Bodies, Regulated Entities and accountants and within RAGs and the Regulated Entities' licence arrangements.

Regulatory Accounts are analogous to financial statements prepared under the Companies Act, but are usually prepared under some variation of, or other basis to, IFRS or UK GAAP[8] and therefore a "properly prepared in accordance with" opinion is more appropriate in the circumstances of Regulatory Accounts. Financial information other than that prepared on the basis of IFRS or UK GAAP does not necessarily represent a true and fair view of the financial performance or financial position of a company as shown in financial statements prepared in accordance with the Companies Act 2006.

Regulatory Accounts typically include:

- a profit and loss account or income statement;
- a balance sheet or statement of financial position;
- detailed/segmental analyses of operations, costs and income, as defined in the Regulatory licence; and
- a reconciliation between the results and net assets reported within the Regulatory Accounts and those reported within the statutory financial statements prepared in accordance with the Companies Act 2006.

Regulatory Returns usually incorporate Regulatory Accounts but may also include other financial information required by the Regulator. Independent Accountants are usually expected to report upon certain identified elements of the additional information contained within the Regulatory Return only.

Regulatory Accounts do not include other items included within Regulatory Returns, such as:

- the reports of other experts;
- management commentary on the accounting information; or
- other types of Regulatory Information required to comply with the Regulatory Licence.

---

[8] *Except as specified in the RAGs.*

Appendix B: Example of an Unmodified Audit Report for Regulatory accounts

(to be tailored as appropriate for the particular circumstances of each engagement)

Independent Auditor's report to the Director General, [Regulator] ("the Regulator") and the directors of ABC limited[9]

We have audited the Regulatory Accounts of ABC Limited ("the company") for the year ended [date] which comprise the profit and loss account, the statement of total recognised gains and losses, the balance sheet, [the cash flow statement] and the related notes to the Regulatory Accounts. The financial reporting framework that has been applied in their preparation is conditions [], [] and [] of the Company's Regulatory Licence, Regulatory Accounting Guidelines [], [] and [], and the accounting policies set out in note X.

This report is made, on terms that have been agreed[10], solely to the company and the Regulator in order to meet [the requirements of the Regulatory Licence[11]]. Our audit work has been undertaken so that we might state to the company and the Regulator those matters that we have agreed to state to them in our report, in order (a) to assist the Company to [meet its obligation under the Regulatory Licence to procure such a report] and (b) to facilitate the carrying out by the Regulator of its regulatory functions, and for no other purpose. To the fullest extent permitted by law, we do not accept or assume responsibility to anyone other than the company and the Regulator, for our audit work, for this report or for the opinions we have formed.

Respective responsibilities of the Directors and Auditor

As explained more fully in the Directors' Responsibility Statement [set out on page x], the directors are responsible for the preparation of the Regulatory Accounts.

Our responsibility is to audit and express an opinion on the Regulatory Accounts in accordance with International Standards on Auditing (UK and Ireland), except as stated in the "Scope of the audit of the Regulatory Accounts" section below and having regard to the guidance contained in ICAEW Technical Release TECH 02/16AAF *Reporting to regulators on regulatory accounts*. Those standards require us to comply with the Auditing Practices Board's Ethical Standards for Auditors.

---

[9] *Any changes to this form of report should be made in accordance with ISA (UK and Ireland) 700 – see Section 3. The report is addressed to the Regulator as well as to the Company without any disclaimer of responsibility to the Regulator only where the Regulator has signed a tri-partite engagement contract or there is a bi-partite engagement contract supplemented by written notice signed by the Regulator. In other cases the report may be addressed to the Company and the Regulator (to meet the requirements of the Regulatory Licence) but includes a disclaimer under which responsibility is accepted to the Company only and co-addressing to the Regulator is expressed to be only to meet the requirements of the Regulatory Licence. Refer to paragraph 14 for further guidance.*

[10] *This requires an engagement letter in a satisfactory form to be in place.*

[11] *Or other reference. If the appropriate reference is to a Regulatory Licence that licence will require to be defined appropriately in the reference or in some other suitable place.*

Scope of the audit of the Regulatory Accounts

An audit involves obtaining evidence about the amounts and disclosures in the Regulatory Accounts sufficient to give reasonable assurance that the Regulatory Accounts are free from material misstatement, whether caused by fraud or error. This includes an assessment of: whether the accounting policies are appropriate to the company's circumstances and have been consistently applied and adequately disclosed and the reasonableness of significant accounting estimates made by the directors. In addition, we read all the financial and non-financial information in the Regulatory Accounts to identify material inconsistencies with the audited Regulatory Accounts and to identify any information that is apparently materially incorrect based on, or materially inconsistent with, the knowledge acquired by us in the course of performing the audit. If we become aware of any apparent misstatements or inconsistencies we consider the implications for our report.

We have not assessed whether the accounting policies are appropriate to the circumstances of the company where these are laid down by condition []. Where condition [] does not give specific guidance on the accounting policies to be followed, our audit includes an assessment of whether the accounting policies adopted in respect of the transactions and balances required to be included in the Regulatory Accounts are consistent with those used in the preparation of the statutory financial statements of the company. Furthermore, as the nature, form and content of Regulatory Accounts are determined by the Regulator, we did not evaluate the overall adequacy of the presentation of the information, which would have been required if we were to express an audit opinion under International Standards on Auditing (UK and Ireland).

Opinion on Regulatory Accounts

In our opinion the Regulatory Accounts have been properly prepared in accordance with conditions [], [] and [] of the Company's Regulatory Licence, Regulatory Accounting Guidelines [], [] and [], and the accounting policies set out in note x.

Emphasis of matter – basis of preparation

Without modifying our opinion, we draw attention to the fact that the Regulatory Accounts have been prepared in accordance with conditions [], [] and [] of the Company's Regulatory Licence, Regulatory Accounting Guidelines [], [] and [] ("the RAGs") issued by the Regulator, the accounting policies set out in the statement of accounting policies [and in the case of the regulatory historical cost accounting statements, under the historical cost convention]. The nature, form and content of Regulatory Accounts are determined by the Regulator. It is not appropriate for us to assess whether the nature of the information being reported upon is suitable or appropriate for the Regulator's purposes. Accordingly we make no such assessment.

The Regulatory Accounts are separate from the statutory financial statements of the Company and have not been prepared under the basis of [International Financial Reporting Standards as adopted by the European Union ("IFRS")/ United Kingdom Generally Accepted Accounting Practice ("UK GAAP")]. Financial information other than that prepared on the basis of [IFRS/UK GAAP] does not necessarily represent a true and fair view of the financial performance or financial position of a company as shown in statutory financial statements prepared in accordance with the Companies Act 2006. [Where required, insert further matters to emphasise, for example: Furthermore, the regulatory historical cost accounting statements on pages [xx] and [xx] have been drawn up in accordance with Regulatory Accounting Guideline [] in that infrastructure renewals accounting as applied in previous years should continue to be applied and accordingly, that the relevant sections of FRS 102 The Financial Reporting Standard applicable in the UK and Republic of Ireland be disapplied. The effect of this departure from UK GAAP and a reconciliation of the balance sheet drawn up on this basis to the balance sheet drawn up under the Companies Act 2006 is given on page [xx].]

[Include the following three headings where the entity is either required by its regulatory licence or has chosen to follow the UK Corporate Governance Code:

Our assessment of risks of material misstatement

Insert a description of those specific assessed risks of material misstatement that were identified by the auditor and which had the greatest effect on the audit strategy; the allocation of resources in the audit; and directing the efforts of the engagement team.

Our application of materiality

Insert an explanation of how the auditor applied the concept of materiality in planning and performing the audit. Such explanation shall specify the threshold used by the auditor as being materiality for the financial statements as a whole.

An overview of the scope of our audit

Insert an overview of the scope of the audit, including an explanation of how the scope addressed the assessed risks of material misstatement and was influenced by the auditor's application of materiality.]

[Opinion on other matters prescribed by condition [x]

Under the terms of our contract we have assumed responsibility to provide those additional opinions required by condition [] in relation to the accounting records. In our opinion:

- proper accounting records have been kept by the company as required by paragraph x of condition [ ]; and
- the Regulatory Accounts are in agreement with the accounting records and returns retained for the purpose of preparing the Regulatory Accounts.]

[Include the following where the entity is either required by its regulatory licence or has chosen to follow the UK Corporate Governance Code:

Matters on which we are required to report by exception

We have nothing to report in respect of the following matters where under ISAs (UK and Ireland), we are required to report to you if, in our opinion, information in the [describe the document containing the regulatory accounts] is:

- materially inconsistent with the information in the audited financial statements; or
- apparently materially incorrect based on, or materially inconsistent with, our knowledge of the Group acquired in the course of performing our audit; or
- otherwise misleading.

In particular, we are required to consider whether we have identified any inconsistencies between our knowledge acquired during the audit and the directors' statement that they consider the [describe the document containing the regulatory accounts] is fair, balanced and understandable and whether the [describe the document containing the regulatory accounts] appropriately discloses those matters that we communicated to the audit committee which we consider should have been disclosed.]

Other matters

Our opinion on the Regulatory Accounts is separate from our opinion on the statutory financial statements of the Company for the year ended [] on which we reported on [], which are prepared for a different purpose. Our audit report in relation to the statutory financial statements of the Company (our "Statutory audit") was made solely to the Company's members, as a body, in accordance with Chapter 3 of Part 16 of the Companies Act 2006. Our Statutory audit work was undertaken so that we might state to the Company's members those matters we are required to state to them in a statutory audit report and for no other purpose. In these circumstances, to the fullest extent permitted by law, we do not accept or assume responsibility for any other purpose or to any other person to whom our Statutory audit report is shown or into whose hands it may come save where expressly agreed by our prior consent in writing.

[Name of auditor]

[Chartered Accountants and Statutory Auditor]

[Address]

[Date]

Appendix C: Example Tri-Partite Engagement Contract

(to be tailored as appropriate for the particular circumstances of each engagement)

Private and Confidential

The Directors

[Name and address of Regulated Entity]

For the attention of [ ]

The Director General

[Name and address of Regulator]

For the attention of [ ]

[Date]

[Name of Regulated Entity] ("the Company")

Audit of the regulatory financial statements for the year ended [DATE]

Dear Sirs,

Introduction

This letter (including the attached Appendices and the Terms and Conditions) sets out our understanding of the basis on which we act as auditors reporting on the regulatory financial statements ("the Regulatory Accounts") as specified in [LICENCE CONDITION OR OTHER REFERENCE] of the Instrument of Appointment of the Company as a [TYPE OF BUSINESS] under the [APPLICABLE LEGISLATION] ("the Regulatory Licence") and the Regulatory Accounting Guidelines ("RAGs") [agreed with/] issued by the Director General of [IDENTITY OF REGULATOR], [NAME OF REGULATOR] ("the Regulator"). We also set out the respective areas of responsibility of the directors of the Company ("the Directors"), the Regulator and ourselves, in respect of the audit of the Regulatory Accounts (the "Services"). This letter (with all its attachments) applies only to the audit report on the Regulatory Accounts and the scope of our work will be limited accordingly. If any additional work or report is required, separate engagement terms and conditions will need to be agreed.

This letter and the attached terms and conditions together comprise the entire contract ("the Contract") for the provision of the Services [to the exclusion of any other express or implied terms, whether expressed orally or in writing, including any conditions, warranties and representations unless made fraudulently] and shall supersede all previous contracts, letters of engagement, undertakings, agreements and correspondence regarding the Services.

Responsibilities of the Directors and the Auditors

The Directors are required to ensure that the Company complies with all of the terms of its Regulatory Licence [or other reference].

The Directors are required to prepare Regulatory Accounts in accordance with the Company's Regulatory Licence [or other reference] and the RAGs [agreed with/] issued by the Regulator, a copy of which are attached as Appendix []. The Directors are also required to:

- [OTHER LICENCE CONDITIONS ON WHICH THE DIRECTORS ARE REQUIRED TO GIVE A FINANCE-BASED REPORT PER THE REGULATORY LICENCE, for example]:

- [Confirm that, in their opinion, the Company has sufficient financial and management resources for the next twelve months];
- [Confirm that, in their opinion, the Company has sufficient rights and assets which would enable a special administrator to manage the affairs, business and property of the Company];
- [Report to the Director General of [NAME OF REGULATOR] changes in the Company's activities which may be material in relation to the Company's ability to finance its regulated activities];
- [Undertake the transactions entered into by the business consisting of the carrying out of the regulated activity ("the appointed business"), with or for the benefit of any group companies or related companies ("associated companies") or activities of the appointed business, at arm's length]; and
- [Keep proper accounting records which comply with [LICENCE CONDITION OR OTHER REFERENCE].

We refer to the above as "the Specific Obligations".

Other than reporting on whether or not proper accounting records have been kept by the Company as required by Condition [] of the Regulatory Licence [or other reference], it is not our responsibility in providing the Services to report on the Specific Obligations or on any other obligations of the Company or the Directors under the Regulatory Licence [or other reference].

The Directors are also responsible for ensuring that the Company maintains accounting records which disclose with reasonable accuracy, at any time, the financial position of the Company, and for preparing Regulatory Accounts which are properly prepared in accordance with the Regulatory Licence. The Directors are responsible for such internal control as they determine necessary to enable the preparation of financial statements that are free from material misstatement, whether due to fraud or error. They are also responsible for making available to us, as and when required, all of the Company's accounting records, all other relevant records, including minutes of all directors', management and shareholders' meetings, and such information and explanations which we consider necessary for the performance of our duties as auditors.

It is our responsibility to form an independent opinion, based on our audit, on the Regulatory Accounts and to report our opinion to the Company and the Regulator.

Our report will be addressed to the Company and the Regulator and will state whether, in our opinion, the Regulatory Accounts have been properly prepared in accordance with conditions [], [] and [] of that Licence [or other reference].

Our report will be made in accordance with the Contract, solely to the Company and the Regulator in order to meet the requirements of the Regulatory Licence [or other reference]. Our audit work will be undertaken so that we might state to the Company and the Regulator those matters we have agreed in the Contract to state to them in our report in order to (a) assist the Company to [meet its obligations under the Regulatory Licence to procure such a report] and (b) to facilitate the carrying out by the Regulator of its regulatory functions, and for no other purpose. To the fullest extent permitted by law, we will not accept or assume responsibility to anyone other than the Company and the Regulator for our audit work, for our report, or for the opinions we will form. Our report will contain a disclaimer of liability to other parties to this effect.

The Contract does not confer benefits on any parties who are not parties to it and the application of the Contracts (Rights of Third Parties) Act 1999 is excluded.

In arriving at our opinion, and in accordance with the Regulatory Licence (condition [REFERENCE]) [or other reference], we will consider the following matters, and report on any in respect of which we are not satisfied:

- whether appropriate accounting records have been kept by the Company and proper returns adequate for our audit have been received from operating locations not visited by us;

- whether the Regulatory Accounts are in agreement with the accounting records and returns retained for the purpose of preparing the Regulatory Accounts; and

- whether we have obtained all the information and explanations which we consider necessary for the purposes of our audit.

Our responsibilities also include considering whether other information in documents containing the Regulatory Accounts is consistent with those Regulatory Accounts.

The Regulator and the Company acknowledge and agree that:

- wherever the Regulatory Accounts or other Regulatory Information covered by the Independent Accountants' report are published or otherwise made available in full, our audit report will also be published or otherwise made available in full as part of that communication;

- wherever substantial extracts[12] from the Regulatory Accounts or other Regulatory Information covered by the Independent Accountants' report are published or otherwise made available, and reference is made to the fact that they are audited or otherwise examined by an Independent Accountants, there will be explicit statements by the Regulator: a) that the information published is only an extract; and b) about the limitation of scope of the Independent Accountants' report and the duty of care owed by the Independent Accountants; and c) referring to where the full set of Regulatory Accounts can be found or otherwise obtained; and

- wherever any other information is referenced from the Regulatory Accounts or other Regulatory Information covered by the Independent Accountants' report, there will be an explicit reference by the Regulator to the source of that information and the limitation of scope of the Independent Accountants' report and the duty of care owed by the Independent Accountant.

Relationship between the Regulator and the Company

For the avoidance of doubt, nothing in this Contract is intended to nor does it affect or in any way alter the relationship or the rights and obligations between the Company and the Regulator as set out in the Regulatory Licence [and all relevant legislation].

Scope of our audit

Our audit will be performed with regard to the guidance contained in ICAEW Technical Release TECH 02/16AAF *Reporting to regulators on regulatory accounts*.

Our audit will be conducted in accordance with International Standards on Auditing (UK and Ireland) issued by the Financial Reporting Council except that, as the nature, form and content of Regulatory Accounts are determined by the Regulator, we will not evaluate the overall adequacy of the presentation of the

---

[12] *For example, reproduction of primary statements as a whole.*

information, which would have been required if we were to express an audit opinion under International Standards on Auditing (UK and Ireland). Our audit will include such tests of transactions and of the existence, ownership and valuation of assets and liabilities as we consider necessary. We shall obtain an understanding of the accounting and internal financial control systems to the extent necessary in order to assess their adequacy as a basis for the preparation of the Regulatory Accounts and to establish whether appropriate accounting records have been maintained by the Company.

We shall expect to obtain such appropriate evidence as we consider sufficient to enable us to draw reasonable conclusions therefrom. The nature and extent of our procedures will vary according to our assessment of the Company's accounting system and, where we wish to place reliance on it, the internal financial control system and may cover any aspect of the business operations.

[The Regulatory Accounts are prepared by disaggregating balances recorded in the general ledgers and other accounting records of the [NAME OF STATUTORY ENTITY] maintained in accordance with the Companies Act 2006 and used, in accordance with that Act, for the preparation of [NAME OF STATUTORY ENTITY]'s statutory financial statements.]

[No additional tests will be performed of the transactions and balances which are recorded in the general ledgers of [NAME OF STATUTORY ENTITY] other than those carried out in performing the audit of the statutory financial statements that include the Company.]

Our audit includes assessing the significant estimates and judgements made by the Directors in the preparation of the Regulatory Accounts and whether the accounting policies are appropriate to the Company's circumstances, consistently applied and adequately disclosed.

[We will read the [SPECIFY INFORMATION] ("Other Information") contained within the Regulatory Accounts, including any supplementary schedules on which we do not express an audit opinion, and consider the implications for our report if we become aware of any apparent misstatements or material inconsistencies with the Regulatory Accounts. We will not perform any audit procedures nor provide any other assurance on the Other Information.]

We will plan our work to gain reasonable assurance that the Regulatory Accounts are free from material error, whether caused by fraud or other misstatement.

The concept of materiality affects our audit planning and our consideration of matters arising from our audit. We take into account both qualitative and quantitative factors when assessing materiality. We will only express an opinion on the Regulatory Accounts as a whole and not on individual factors/components within Regulatory Accounts.

Where the Regulator requires specific factors to be reported upon by us, this should be addressed through the powers vested in the Regulator through the Regulatory Licence [or other reference]. For such reporting, we will agree a list of procedures ("Agreed Upon Procedures") that we will perform for the Regulator. These procedures will be specified in a separate engagement contract between us and the Regulator [and will be shown to the Company]. We will report the findings of the Agreed Upon Procedures separately from the Regulatory Accounts opinion, by way of a factual report to the Regulator, in which we will not express an opinion on the results of the Agreed Upon Procedures, nor the appropriateness of those procedures for the purposes of the Regulator. As with the form and content of Regulatory Accounts, the Regulator will need to make its own assessment of the appropriateness of the Agreed Upon Procedures and the reported findings.

Where Agreed Upon Procedures are required in addition to an opinion on the Regulatory Accounts, we may choose not to complete our work nor express an opinion on the Regulatory Accounts until:

(i)   the Agreed Upon Procedures that have been specified by the Regulator have been completed and reported upon; and

(ii)   the Regulator has provided a written notice to us confirming that nothing has come to the attention of the Regulator from that report (or otherwise) that indicates that there are any matters which the Regulator believes that we should take into account in arriving at our opinion on the Regulatory Accounts. If such matters do exist we will consider, in arriving at our opinion on the Regulatory Accounts, the matters noted by the Regulator and/or agree additional Agreed Upon Procedures with the Regulator.

The Services are separate from our audit work on the statutory financial statements of the Company which is carried out in accordance with our statutory obligations under the Companies Act 2006. Our audit report on those statutory financial statements is intended for the sole benefit of the Company's shareholders as a group, to whom it is addressed, and not for any other purpose. Our audit of the Company's statutory financial statements are not planned or conducted in contemplation of the requirements of anyone other than such shareholders and, consequently, our audit work is not intended to address or reflect matters in which anyone other than such shareholders may be interested.

We do not and will not, by virtue of this report or otherwise in connection with this engagement, assume any responsibility whether in contract, negligence or otherwise in relation to our audits of the Company's statutory financial statements required by the Companies Act 2006; we and our employees shall have no liability whether in contract, tort (including negligence) or otherwise to any parties other than the Company and its members in relation to our audit of the Company's statutory financial statements.

The nature and format of the Regulatory Accounts are determined by the requirements of the Regulator. It is not appropriate for us to assess, and accordingly we will not make any assessment on, whether the nature of the information being reported upon is suitable or appropriate for the Regulator's purpose. It is a matter for the Regulator to consider whether the information being reported upon is appropriate for its own purposes and we will not give any implicit or explicit affirmation that the information being reported upon is suitable for the Regulator's purpose.

The Regulator and the Company accept that there [may be/are] differences between International Financial Reporting Standards ("IFRS") or United Kingdom Generally Accepted Accounting Principles ("UK GAAP") and the basis of information provided in the Regulatory Accounts. Financial information, other than that prepared on the basis of IFRS or UK GAAP, does not necessarily represent a true and fair view of the financial performance or financial position of a Company.

[Include the following where the entity is required by its regulatory licence, or voluntarily chooses, to comply with the UK Corporate Governance Code:

UK Corporate Governance Code

In addition to the matters described in the section "Responsibilities of directors and the auditors" above, our Independent Accountant's report will:

(a)   describe those assessed risks of material misstatement that were identified by us and which had the greatest effect on: the overall audit strategy; the allocation of resources in the audit; and directing the efforts of the engagement team;

(b)   provide an explanation of how we applied the concept of materiality in planning and performing our audit. This explanation will, as a minimum, specify the threshold used by us as being materiality for the financial statements as a whole; and

(c)   provide an overview of the scope of the audit, including an explanation of how such scope addressed the assessed risks of material misstatement disclosed in accordance with (a) and was influenced by the our application of materiality disclosed in accordance with (b).

We are required to report to you if, in our opinion, information in the [describe the document containing the regulatory accounts] is:

●   materially inconsistent with the information in the audited regulatory accounts; or

●   apparently materially incorrect based on, or materially inconsistent with, our knowledge of the Company acquired in the course of performing our audit; or

●   otherwise misleading.

In particular, we are required to consider whether we have identified any inconsistencies between our knowledge acquired during the audit and the directors' statement that they consider the [describe the document containing the regulatory accounts] is fair, balanced and understandable and whether the [describe the document containing the regulatory accounts] appropriately discloses those matters that we communicated to the audit committee which we consider should have been disclosed.

If we have nothing to report, we will report that fact.]

Internal audit

In developing our audit plan, we will liaise with the Company's internal auditors to ensure that our work is properly co-ordinated with theirs. It is our policy to rely upon internal audit work whenever possible, whilst ensuring that adequate audit coverage is achieved of all significant areas.

Meetings with the Regulator

We are willing to attend meetings with the Regulator to discuss the Services, if requested to do so, provided that we can agree appropriate terms on which such meetings are held. For the avoidance of doubt appropriate terms will include meeting only on a tri-partite basis in the absence of specific consent of the Company allowing us to meet with the Regulator [and its advisors].

Management representations

The information used by the Directors in preparing the Regulatory Accounts will invariably include facts or judgements which are not themselves recorded in the accounting records. As part of our normal audit procedures, we shall request appropriate directors or senior officials/management of the Company to provide written confirmation each year of such facts or judgements and any other oral representations which we have received during the course of the audit on matters having a material effect on the Regulatory Accounts. We will also ask the Directors to confirm in that letter that all important and relevant information has been brought to our attention. In connection with representations and the supply of information to us generally, we draw your attention to section 501 of the Companies Act 2006 under which it is an offence for an officer of the company to mislead the auditors.

Detection of fraud, error and non-compliance with laws and regulations

The responsibility for safeguarding the assets of the Company and for the prevention and detection of fraud, error and non-compliance with law or regulations rests with the Directors. However, we shall endeavour to plan our audit so that we have a reasonable expectation of detecting material misstatements in the Regulatory Accounts or accounting records (including any material misstatements resulting from fraud, error or non-compliance with law or regulations), but our examination should not be relied upon to disclose all such material misstatements or frauds, errors or instances of non-compliance as may exist.

Timetable

We expect to commence our work on [DATE] and would normally expect to issue our report by [DATE].

Completion of our work will depend upon receiving, without undue delay, full co-operation from all relevant officials of the Company and their disclosure to us of all the accounting records of the Company and all other records and related information (including certain representation s) that we may need for the purpose of our work.

Other requirements

In order to assist us with the examination of the Regulatory Accounts, we shall request early sight of all documents or statements which are due to be issued with those Regulatory Accounts.

Once we have issued our report we have no further direct responsibility in relation to the Regulatory Accounts for that financial year.

Preparation of Regulatory Accounts

Assistance with the preparation of Regulatory Accounts does not form a part of the audit function, but we shall discuss the Company's accounting principles with the management and/or the Directors and we may propose adjusting entries for their consideration.

Other services

We shall not be treated as having notice, for the purposes of our regulatory audit responsibilities, of information provided to members of our firm other than those engaged on the audit (for example information provided in connection with accounting, taxation and other services).

Fiduciary responsibilities

Because our audit work under the terms of this engagement is directed at forming an opinion on the Company's Regulatory Accounts our audit procedures will not normally extend to assets or documents of title in respect of assets that are in the Company's possession but owned by others.

Terms and conditions

The attached Terms and Conditions set out the duties of all parties in respect of the Services. The Terms and Conditions amongst other things:

(i)   limit our liability to a maximum aggregate amount of £[X]. This limitation shall be allocated between the Company and the Regulator. [It is agreed that such allocation will be entirely a matter for the addressees of this letter, who shall be under no obligation to inform [Name of Auditor] of it, provided always that if (for whatever reason) no such allocation is agreed, neither the Company nor the Regulator shall dispute the validity, enforceability or operation of the limit of liability on the grounds that no such allocation was agreed][13]; and

(ii)   limit the period within which a claim may be brought.

[NAME OF AUDITOR] alone will be responsible for the performance of the engagement contract formed by this letter. You therefore agree that you will not bring any claim in respect of or in connection with this engagement whether in contract, tort (including negligence), breach of statutory duty or otherwise against any partner or employee of [NAME OF AUDITOR]. The foregoing exclusion does not apply to any liability that cannot be excluded under the laws of England and Wales.

Fees [Detail]

The fee for the work covered by this engagement letter will be agreed with, and paid by, the Company.

Safeguarding service

It is our desire to provide you at all times with a high quality service to meet your needs. If at any time you would like to discuss with us how our service to you could be improved or if you are dissatisfied with any aspect of our services, please raise the matter immediately with the partner responsible for that aspect of our services to you. If, for any reason, you would prefer to discuss these matters with someone other than that partner, please contact [] at []. In this way we are able to ensure that your concerns are dealt with carefully and promptly. We undertake to look into any complaint carefully and promptly and to do all we can to explain the position to you. This will not affect your right to complain to ICAEW.

---

[13] *This paragraph may be replaced by a specific allocation of the aggregate liability between the Company and the Regulator where the Company and the Regulator have reached such agreement, independently of the Independent Accountants, and wish to incorporate this into the engagement contract.*

Acknowledgement and acceptance

Please acknowledge your acceptance of the terms of our engagement under the Contract by signing the confirmation below and returning a copy of this letter and the attached Terms and Conditions to us at the above address, whereupon the Contract will take effect from the date of the commencement by us of the Services.

Once it has been agreed, this letter will remain effective, from one audit appointment to another, until it is replaced.

If you have any questions regarding this Contract, please do not hesitate to contact us.

Yours faithfully,

[Name of Auditor]

I have read the above letter and accept the terms and conditions set out therein.

Signed:

_____   _____

(Name and position)   (Date)

for and on behalf of [Name of Company]

_____   _____

(Name and position)   (Date)

for and on behalf of [Name of Regulator]

Appendix D: Example Bi-Partite Engagement Contract

(to be tailored for the particular circumstances of each engagement)

Private and Confidential

The Directors

[Name and address of Regulated Entity]

For the attention of [ ]

[Date]

[Name of Regulated Entity] ("the Company")

Audit of the regulatory financial statements for the year ended [DATE]

Dear Sirs,

Introduction

This letter (including the attached Appendices and the Terms and Conditions) sets out our understanding of the basis on which we act as auditors reporting on the regulatory financial statements ("the Regulatory Accounts") as specified in [LICENCE CONDITION OR OTHER REFERENCE] of the Instrument of Appointment of the Company as a [TYPE OF BUSINESS] under the [APPLICABLE LEGISLATION] ("the Regulatory Licence") and the Regulatory Accounting Guidelines ("RAGs") [agreed with/] issued by the Director General of [IDENTITY OF REGULATOR], [NAME OF REGULATOR] ("the Regulator"). We also set out the respective areas of responsibility of the directors of the Company ("the Directors") and ourselves, in respect of the audit of the Regulatory Accounts (the "Services"). This letter (with all its attachments) applies only to the audit report on the Regulatory Accounts and the scope of our work will be limited accordingly. If any additional work or report is required, separate engagement terms and conditions will need to be agreed.

This letter and the attached Terms and Conditions together comprise the entire contract ("the Contract") for the provision of the Services [to the exclusion of any other express or implied terms, whether expressed orally or in writing, including any conditions, warranties and representations unless made fraudulently] and shall supersede all previous contracts, letters of engagement, undertakings, agreements and correspondence regarding the Services.

The Regulator is not a party to the Contract. On condition that the Regulator accepts in writing a notice in the form appended ("the Regulator's Contract"), we will accept duties and responsibilities to the Regulator in respect of our audit work, our audit report and our audit opinion on the Regulatory Accounts. Any such agreement will be on the basis that, amongst other things, the Company and the Regulator agree that our aggregate liability to the Company and the Regulator is limited to the maximum amount which would have been payable to the Company alone in respect of any breach of our obligations to the Company. References to rights and obligations between the Regulator and the auditors in relation to the Services and the Agreed upon Procedures are included in the Contract for the purpose only of the Regulator's Contract and are not intended to create rights or obligations between the Regulator and the Company.

Responsibilities of the Directors and the Auditors

The Directors are required to ensure that the Company complies with all of the terms of its Regulatory Licence [or other reference].

The Directors are required to prepare Regulatory Accounts in accordance with the Company's Regulatory Licence [or other reference] and the RAGs [agreed with/] issued by the Regulator, a copy of which are attached as Appendix []. The Directors are also required to:

- [OTHER LICENCE CONDITIONS ON WHICH THE DIRECTORS ARE REQUIRED TO GIVE A FINANCE-BASED REPORT PER THE REGULATORY LICENCE, for example];

- [Confirm that, in their opinion, the Company has sufficient financial and management resources for the next twelve months];

- [Confirm that, in their opinion, the Company has sufficient rights and assets which would enable a special administrator to manage the affairs, business and property of the Company];

- [Report to the Director General of [NAME OF REGULATOR] changes in the Company's activities which may be material in relation to the Company's ability to finance its regulated activities];

- [Undertake the transactions entered into by the business consisting of the carrying out of the regulated activity ("the appointed business"), with or for the benefit of any group companies or related companies ("associated companies") or activities of the appointed business, at arm's length]; and

- [Keep proper accounting records which comply with [LICENCE CONDITION OR OTHER REFERENCE].

We refer to the above as "the Specific Obligations".

Other than reporting on whether or not proper accounting records have been kept by the Company as required by Condition [] of the Regulatory Licence [or other reference], it is not our responsibility in providing the Services to report on the Specific Obligations or on any other obligations of the Company or the Directors under the Regulatory Licence [or other reference].

The Directors are also responsible for ensuring that the Company maintains accounting records which disclose with reasonable accuracy, at any time, the financial position of the Company, and for preparing Regulatory Accounts which have been properly prepared in accordance with the Regulatory Licence. The Directors are responsible for such internal control as they determine necessary to enable the preparation of financial statements that are free from material misstatement, whether due to fraud or error. They are also responsible for making available to us, as and when required, all of the Company's accounting records, all other relevant records, including minutes of all directors', management and shareholders' meetings, and such information and explanations which we consider necessary for the performance of our duties as auditors.

It is our responsibility to form an independent opinion, based on our audit, on the Regulatory Accounts and to report our opinion to the Company and (in order to meet the requirements of the Regulatory Licence) to the Regulator.

Our report will be made in accordance with the Contract, solely to the Company and the Regulator in accordance with the Regulatory Licence [or other reference]. Our audit work will be undertaken so that we might state to the Company and the Regulator those matters we have agreed in the Contract to state to them in our report in order to (a) assist the Company to [meet its obligations under the Regulatory Licence to procure such a report] and (b) to facilitate the carrying out by the Regulator of its regulatory functions, and for no other purpose. To the fullest extent permitted by law, we will not accept or assume responsibility to anyone other than the Company for our audit work, for our report, or for the opinions we will form. Our report will contain a disclaimer of liability to all other parties but we will confirm acceptance in our report of responsibility in respect of our audit work to the Regulator also if the Regulator has agreed to the Regulator's Contract by signing the written notice appended.

Our report will be addressed to the Company and the Regulator to meet the requirements of the Regulatory Licence and will state whether, in our opinion, the Regulatory Accounts have been properly prepared in accordance with conditions [], [] and [] of that licence [or other reference]. The Contract does not confer benefits on any parties who are not parties to it and the application of the Contracts (Rights of Third Parties) Act 1999 is excluded.

In arriving at our opinion, and in accordance with the Regulatory Licence (condition [REFERENCE]) [or other reference], we will consider the following matters, and report on any in respect of which we are not satisfied:

- whether appropriate accounting records have been kept by the Company and proper returns adequate for our audit have been received from operating locations not visited by us;

- whether the Regulatory Accounts are in agreement with the accounting records and returns retained for the purpose of preparing the Regulatory Accounts; and

- whether we have obtained all the information and explanations which we consider necessary for the purposes of our audit.

Our responsibilities also include:

- providing in our report a description of the Directors' responsibilities for the Regulatory Accounts where the Regulatory Accounts or accompanying information do not include such a description; and

- considering whether other information in documents containing the Regulatory Accounts is consistent with those Regulatory Accounts.

The Company and (where the Regulator signs the written notice appended) the Regulator acknowledge and agree that:

- wherever the Regulatory Accounts or other Regulatory Information covered by the Independent Accountants' report are published or otherwise made available in full, our audit report will also be published or otherwise made available in full as part of that communication;

- wherever substantial extracts from the Regulatory Accounts or other Regulatory Information covered by the Independent Accountants' report are published or otherwise made available, and reference is made to the fact that they are audited or otherwise examined by an Independent Accountant, there will be explicit statements by the Regulator: a) that the information published is only an extract; and b) about the limitation of scope of the Independent Accountants' report and the duty of care owed by the Independent Accountants; and c) referring to where the full set of Regulatory Accounts can be found or otherwise obtained; and

- wherever any other information is referenced from the Regulatory Accounts or other Regulatory Information covered by the Independent Accountants' report, there will be an explicit reference by the Regulator to the source of that information and the limitation of scope of the Independent Accountants' report and the duty of care owed by the Independent Accountant.

Where the Regulator does not sign a written notice in the form appended, the Company will procure that these events take place in the circumstances identified.

Relationship between the Regulator and the Company

For the avoidance of doubt, nothing in this Contract is intended to nor does it affect or in any way alter the relationship or the rights and obligations between the Company and the Regulator as set out in the Regulatory Licence [and all relevant legislation].

Scope of our audit

Our audit will be performed with regard to the guidance contained in ICAEW Technical Release TECH 02/16AAF *Reporting to regulators on regulatory accounts*.

Our audit will be conducted in accordance with International Standards on Auditing (UK and Ireland) issued by the Financial Reporting Council except that, as the nature, form and content of Regulatory Accounts are determined by the Regulator, we will not evaluate the overall adequacy of the presentation of the information, which would have been required if we were to express an audit opinion under International Standards on Auditing (UK and Ireland). Our audit will include such tests of transactions and of the existence, ownership and valuation of assets and liabilities as we consider necessary. We shall obtain an understanding of the accounting and internal financial control systems to the extent necessary in order to assess their adequacy as a basis for the preparation of the Regulatory Accounts and to establish whether appropriate accounting records have been maintained by the Company.

We shall expect to obtain such appropriate evidence as we consider sufficient to enable us to draw reasonable conclusions therefrom. The nature and extent of our procedures will vary according to our assessment of the Company's accounting system and, where we wish to place reliance on it, the internal financial control system and may cover any aspect of the business operations.

[The Regulatory Accounts are prepared by disaggregating balances recorded in the general ledgers and other accounting records of the [NAME OF STATUTORY ENTITY] maintained in accordance with the Companies Act 2006 and used, in accordance with that Act, for the preparation of [NAME OF STATUTORY ENTITY]'s statutory financial statements.]

[No additional tests will be performed of the transactions and balances which are recorded in the general ledgers of [NAME OF STATUTORY ENTITY] other than those carried out in performing the audit of the statutory financial statements that include the Company.]

Our audit includes assessing the significant estimates and judgements made by the Directors in the preparation of the Regulatory Accounts and whether the accounting policies are appropriate to the Company's circumstances, consistently applied and adequately disclosed.

[We will read the [SPECIFY INFORMATION] ("Other Information") contained within the Regulatory Accounts, including any supplementary schedules on which we do not express an audit opinion, and consider the implications for our report if we become aware of any apparent misstatements or material inconsistencies with the Regulatory Accounts. We will not perform any audit procedures nor provide any other assurance on the Other Information.]

We will plan our work to gain reasonable assurance that the Regulatory Accounts are free from material error, whether caused by fraud or other misstatement.

The concept of materiality affects our audit planning and our consideration of matters arising from our audit. We take into account both qualitative and quantitative factors when assessing materiality. We will only express an opinion on the Regulatory Accounts as a whole and not on individual factors within Regulatory Accounts.

Where the Regulator requires specific factors to be reported upon by us, this should be addressed through the powers vested in the Regulator through the Regulatory Licence [or other reference]. For such reporting, we will agree a list of procedures ("Agreed Upon Procedures") that we will perform for the Regulator. These procedures will be specified in a separate engagement contract between us [and] the Regulator and [will be shown to] the Company. We will report the findings of the Agreed Upon Procedures separately from the Regulatory Accounts opinion, by way of a factual report to the Regulator, in which we will not express an opinion on the results of the Agreed Upon Procedures, nor the appropriateness of those procedures for the purposes of the Regulator. As with the form and content of Regulatory Accounts, the Regulator will need to make its own assessment of the appropriateness of the Agreed Upon Procedures and the reported findings.

Where Agreed Upon Procedures are required in addition to an opinion on the Regulatory Accounts, we may choose not to complete our work nor express an opinion on the Regulatory Accounts until:

(i)   the Agreed Upon Procedures that have been specified by the Regulator have been completed and reported upon; and

(ii)   the Regulator has provided a written notice to us confirming that nothing has come to the attention of the Regulator from that report (or otherwise) that indicates that there are any matters which the Regulator believes that we should take into account in arriving at our opinion on the Regulatory Accounts. If such matters do exist we will consider, in arriving at our opinion on the Regulatory Accounts, the matters noted by the Regulator and/or agree additional Agreed Upon Procedures with the Regulator.]

The Services are separate from our audit work on the statutory financial statements of the Company which is carried out in accordance with our statutory obligations under the Companies Act 2006. Our audit report on those statutory financial statements is intended for the sole benefit of the Company's shareholders as a group, to whom it is addressed, and not for any other purpose. Our audits of the Company's statutory financial statements are not planned or conducted in contemplation of the requirements of anyone other than such shareholders and, consequently, our audit work is not intended to address or reflect matters in which anyone other than such shareholders may be interested.

We do not and will not, by virtue of this report or otherwise in connection with this engagement, assume any responsibility whether in contract, tort (including negligence) or otherwise in relation to our audits of the Company's statutory financial statements required by the Companies Act 2006; we and our employees shall have no liability whether in contract, tort (including negligence) or otherwise to any parties other than the Company and its members in relation to our audits of the Company's statutory financial statements.

The nature and format of the Regulatory Accounts are determined by the requirements of the Regulator. It is not appropriate for us to assess, and accordingly we will not make any assessment on, whether the nature of the information being reported upon is suitable or appropriate for the Regulator's purpose, whether or not the Regulator signs the written notice in the form appended. It is a matter for the Regulator to consider whether the information being reported upon is appropriate for its own purposes and we will not give any implicit or explicit affirmation that the information being reported upon is suitable for the Regulator's purpose.

There [may be/are] differences between International Financial Reporting Standards as adopted in the European Union ("IFRS") or United Kingdom Generally Accepted Accounting Principles ("UK GAAP") and the basis of information provided in the Regulatory Accounts. Financial information, other than that prepared on the basis of IFRS or UK GAAP, does not necessarily represent a true and fair view of the financial performance or financial position of a Company.

[Include the following where the entity is required by its regulatory licence, or voluntarily chooses, to comply with the UK Corporate Governance Code:

UK Corporate Governance Code

In addition to the matters described in the section "Responsibilities of directors and the auditors" above, our Independent Accountant's report will:

(a) describe those assessed risks of material misstatement that were identified by us and which had the greatest effect on: the overall audit strategy; the allocation of resources in the audit; and directing the efforts of the engagement team;

(b) provide an explanation of how we applied the concept of materiality in planning and performing our audit. This explanation will, as a minimum, specify the threshold used by us as being materiality for the financial statements as a whole; and

(c) provide an overview of the scope of the audit, including an explanation of how such scope addressed the assessed risks of material misstatement disclosed in accordance with (a) and was influenced by the our application of materiality disclosed in accordance with (b).

We are required to report to you if, in our opinion, information in the [describe the document containing the regulatory accounts] is:

● materially in consistent with the information in the audited regulatory accounts; or

● apparently materially incorrect based on, or materially inconsistent with, our knowledge of the Company acquired in the course of performing our audit; or

● otherwise misleading.

In particular, we are required to consider whether we have identified any inconsistencies between our knowledge acquired during the audit and the directors' statement that they consider the [describe the document containing the regulatory accounts] is fair, balanced and understandable and whether the [describe the document containing the regulatory accounts] appropriately discloses those matters that we communicated to the audit committee which we consider should have been disclosed.

If we have nothing to report, we will report that fact.]

Internal audit

In developing our audit plan, we will liaise with the Company's internal auditors to ensure that our work is properly co-ordinated with theirs. It is our policy to rely upon internal audit work whenever possible, whilst ensuring that adequate audit coverage is achieved of all significant areas.

Meetings with the Regulator

We are willing to attend meetings with the Regulator to discuss the Services, if requested to do so, provided that we can agree appropriate terms on which such meetings are held. For the avoidance of doubt appropriate terms will include meeting only on a tri-partite basis in the absence of specific consent of the Company allowing us to meet with the Regulator [and its advisors].

Management representations

The information used by the Directors in preparing the Regulatory Accounts will invariably include facts or judgements which are not themselves recorded in the accounting records. As part of our normal audit procedures, we shall request appropriate directors or senior officials/management of the Company to provide written confirmation each year of such facts or judgements and any other oral representations which we have received during the course of the audit on matters having a material effect on the Regulatory Accounts. We will also ask the Directors to confirm in that letter that all important and relevant information has been brought to our attention. In connection with representations and the supply of information to us generally, we draw your attention to section 501 of the Companies Act 2006 under which it is an offence for an officer of the Company to mislead the auditors.

Detection of fraud, error and non-compliance with laws and regulations

The responsibility for safeguarding the assets of the Company and for the prevention and detection of fraud, error and non-compliance with law or regulations rests with the Directors. However, we shall endeavour to plan our audit so that we have a reasonable expectation of detecting material misstatements in the Regulatory Accounts or accounting records (including any material misstatements resulting from fraud, error or non-compliance with law or regulations), but our examination should not be relied upon to disclose all such material misstatements or frauds, errors or in stances of non-compliance as may exist.

Timetable

We expect to commence our work on [DATE] and would normally expect to issue our report by [DATE].

Completion of our work will depend upon receiving, without undue delay, full co-operation from all relevant officials of the Company and their disclosure to us of all the accounting records of the Company and all other records and related information (including certain representations) that we may need for the purpose of our work.

Other requirements

In order to assist us with the examination of the Regulatory Accounts, we shall request early sight of all documents or statements which are due to be issued with those Regulatory Accounts.

Once we have issued our report we have no further direct responsibility in relation to the Regulatory Accounts for that financial year.

Preparation of Regulatory Accounts

Assistance with the preparation of Regulatory Accounts does not form a part of the audit function, but we shall discuss the Company's accounting principles with the management and/or the Directors and we may propose adjusting entries for their consideration.

Other services

We shall not be treated as having notice, for the purposes of our regulatory audit responsibilities, of information provided to members of our firm other than those engaged on the audit (for example information provided in connection with accounting, taxation and other services).

Fiduciary responsibilities

Because our audit work under the terms of this engagement is directed at forming an opinion on the Company's Regulatory Accounts our audit procedures will not normally extend to assets or documents of title in respect of assets that are in the Company's possession but owned by others.

Terms and conditions

The attached Terms and Conditions set out the duties of all parties in respect of the Services. The Terms and Conditions amongst other things:

(i)   limit our liability to a maximum aggregate amount of £[X]. Where the Regulator accepts in writing a notice in the form appended (and on that basis we accept duties and responsibilities to the Regulator), this limitation shall be allocated between the Company and the Regulator. [In such circumstances such allocation will be entirely a matter for the Company and the Regulator, who shall be under no obligation to inform [Name of Auditor] of it, provided always that if (for whatever reason) no such allocation is agreed, neither the Company nor the Regulator shall dispute the validity, enforceability or operation of the limit of liability on the grounds that no such allocation was agreed][14]; and

(ii)   limit the period within which a claim may be brought.

[NAME OF AUDITOR] alone will be responsible for the performance of the engagement contract formed by this letter. You therefore agree that you will not bring any claim in respect of or in connection with this engagement whether in contract, tort (including negligence), breach of statutory duty or otherwise against any partner or employee of [NAME OF AUDITOR]. The foregoing exclusion does not apply to any liability that cannot be excluded under the laws of England and Wales.

---

[14] *This paragraph may be replaced by a specific allocation of the aggregate liability between the Company and the Regulator where the Company and the Regulator have reached such agreement, independently of the Independent Accountants, and wish to incorporate this into the engagement contract.*

Fees

[Details]

The fee for the work covered by this engagement letter will be agreed with, and paid by, the Company.

Safeguarding service

It is our desire to provide you at all times with a high quality service to meet your needs. If at any time you would like to discuss with us how our service to you could be improved or if you are dissatisfied with any aspect of our services, please raise the matter immediately with the partner responsible for that aspect of our services to you. If, for any reason, you would prefer to discuss these matters with someone other than that partner, please contact [] at []. In this way we are able to ensure that your concerns are dealt with carefully and promptly. We undertake to look into any complaint carefully and promptly and to do all we can to explain the position to you. This will not affect your right to complain to ICAEW.

Acknowledgement and acceptance

Please acknowledge your acceptance of the terms of our engagement under the Contract by signing the confirmation below and returning a copy of this letter and the attached Terms and Conditions to us at the above address, whereupon the Contract will take effect from the date of the commencement by us of the Services.

Once it has been agreed, this letter will remain effective, from one audit appointment to another, until it is replaced.

If you have any questions regarding this Contract, please do not hesitate to contact us.

Yours faithfully,

[Name of Auditor]

I have read the above letter and accept the terms and conditions set out therein.

_____   _____

(Name and position)   (Date)

for and on behalf of [Name of Company]

Appendix E: Example Written Notice from the Independent Accountants to the Regulator for Bipartite Engagement Arrangements

(to be tailored for the particular circumstances of each engagement)

Private and Confidential

The Director General

[Name and address of Regulator]

For the attention of [ ]

[Date]

[Name of Regulated Entity] ("the Company")

Audit of the regulatory financial statements for the year ended [DATE]

Dear Sirs,

We refer to our engagement letter with the Company dated [DATE] ("the Contract") relating to our audit of the Company's regulatory financial statements for the year ended [DATE] ("the Regulatory Accounts"). A copy of the Contract is attached as Appendix 1 to this letter.

In the Contract we set out the basis on which we will act as auditors reporting on the Regulatory Accounts of the Company, together with the respective areas of responsibility of the directors of the Company and ourselves in respect of that audit and the scope of our audit. We also set out in the Contract the agreed extent of our liability to the Company in respect of our work. We confirm in the Contract that we will address our report on the Regulatory Accounts to the Company and, in order to meet the requirements of the Regulatory Licence, to you as well but we clarify that in our report we will deny liability in respect of our audit work and our report to any party other than the Company.

You have confirmed your interest in our audit of the Regulatory Accounts in your capacity as the Company's Regulator and your interest in the scope of our engagement agreed with the Company. You have asked us to accept responsibility for our audit work and our report to you as well as to the Company so that there is no denial of responsibility to you in our report. This letter ("the Regulator's Contract") sets out the basis on which we are willing to accept such a responsibility, in return for your agreement to the terms of this letter including the following:

(1)   Our duties and responsibilities to you and your obligations to us will be those set out in the Contract as if incorporated into this letter. This sets out, amongst other things, terms relating to the disclosure of the Regulatory Accounts and other Regulatory Information covered by the Independent Accountants' Report.

(2)   Our aggregate liability to you will be strictly limited to £[ ][15] in the event of any breach of our obligations to you under the Regulator's Contract.

(3)   You do not wish to acquire rights against us in respect of use of the audit report for any purposes other than as the Company's Regulator and accept

---

[15] *Independent Accountants will agree a figure by which their maximum aggregate liability to the Company and the Regulator is no greater than the amount which would have been payable by them to the Company under the Contract. For further guidance, see paragraph 12(ii).*

the disclaimer of liability to any Third Party (being a person other than the Company or the Regulator) as set out in the Contract.

(4)   You accept that the nature and format of the Regulatory Accounts are determined by your requirements and that it will be for you to consider whether the information on which we report as auditors is suitable or appropriate for your needs and purposes.

(5)   You will not be bound by any amendment to the Contract, whether written, oral or arising from the Contract, which is not formally accepted by you in writing.

Please acknowledge your acceptance of the terms and conditions of this letter by signing the confirmation below and returning a copy of it and the Contract to us at the above address.

Yours faithfully,

[Independent Accountants]

I have read the above letter and confirm acceptance of its terms and conditions on behalf of [NAME OF REGULATOR]

Signed   _____

Name and position   _____

[Cc: The Directors, [Name of Company]] Enclosure: Copy of the Contract.

TECH 07/16AAF Chartered Accountants' reports on the Compilation of Financial Information of Incorporated Entities (revised update of AAF 02/10)

(March 2016)

Contents

	Paragraphs
Scope	1 - 3
Professional ethics	4 - 8
Quality control	9
Terms of engagement	10 - 13
Content of financial statements	14
Responsibilities of directors	15 - 18
Planning	19
Procedures	20 - 22
Documentation	23
Management representations	24
Misleading financial statements	25 - 35
Approval of financial statements	36
Professional accountants' compilation reports	37 - 40
Filing the financial statements	41
applicable financial framework	42
Appendix: Example report	

ABOUT THE AUDIT AND ASSURANCE FACULTY

The ICAEW Audit and Assurance Faculty is a leading authority on external audit and other assurance activities and is recognised internationally as a source of expertise on audit issues. It is responsible for ICAEW technical audit and assurance leadership and provides a range of information sources to its members which gives practical assurance in key audit and assurance areas.

Scope

1 This Technical Release is intended to give general guidance to members of ICAEW in practice[1] when they compile financial statements for their clients. The guidance applies to the compilation of financial statements of incorporated entities ie, financial statements prepared in accordance with the Companies Act 2006. Limited Liability Partnerships (LLP) are included in the scope of this guidance[2]. This Technical Release replaces AUDIT 02/04 Chartered Accountants' Reports on the Compilation of Financial Statements of Incorporated Entities.

2 The principles included in this guidance may also be applied, in appropriate circumstances, to entities that prepare financial statements in accordance with legislation other than the Companies Act 2006. Where, however, professional accountants are compiling historical financial information of unincorporated entities for a specific purpose or purposes, for example financial information compiled for tax purposes, partnership accounts or the compilation of financial information (without providing any form of assurance) for grant claims, then professional accountants should follow the principles in Technical Release 08/16 AAF Chartered Accountants' Reports on the Compilation of Historical Information of Unincorporated Entities.

3 Professional accountants are encouraged to apply this guidance as soon as is practicable as best practice. The 2016 update has been carried out to reflect changes such as new UK GAAP but is not intended to change current best practice.

Professional Ethics

4 In carrying out financial statements compilation engagements, members of ICAEW are subject to the ethical and other guidance laid down by ICAEW, including the Fundamental Principles of ICAEW's Code of Ethics (the Code), as set out in section 100 and other relevant sections of the Code that deal with objectivity in relation to preparation of financial statements.

5 The Fundamental Principles are:

Fundamental Principle 1 – Integrity: A professional accountant shall be straightforward and honest in all professional and business relationships. Integrity also implies fair dealing and truthfulness.

Fundamental Principle 2 – Objectivity: A professional accountant shall not allow bias, conflict of interest or undue influence of others to compromise their professional or business judgements.

Fundamental Principle 3 – Professional Competence and Due Care: A professional accountant has a continuing duty to maintain professional knowledge and skill at the level required to ensure that a client or employer receives competent professional service based on current developments in practice, legislation and techniques. A professional accountant should act diligently and in accordance with applicable technical and professional standards when providing professional services.

---

[1] *Referred to in the remainder of this guidance as professional accountants*

[2] *When applying the guidance in this Technical Release to an LLP, the terms "company" and "directors" should be substituted with the words "Limited Liability Partnership" and "members" respectively, except where otherwise marked.*

Fundamental Principle 4 – Confidentiality: A professional accountant shall respect the confidentiality of information acquired as a result of professional and business relationships and may not disclose any such information to third parties without proper and specific authority unless there is a legal or professional right or duty to disclose. Confidential information acquired as a result of professional and business relationships should not be used for the personal advantage of the professional accountant or third parties.

Fundamental Principle 5 – Professional behaviour: A professional accountant should comply with relevant laws and regulations and should avoid any action that may discredit the profession.

Members shall not, therefore, knowingly be associated with financial information **6**
where the professional accountant believes that the information:

- Contains a materially false or misleading statement;

- Contains statements or information furnished recklessly; or

- Omits or obscures information required to be included where such omission or obscurity would be misleading.

When a professional accountant becomes aware that the accountant has been associated with such information, the accountant shall take steps to be disassociated from that information.

The independence requirements that apply to audit and other assurance **7**
engagements contained within the APB Ethical Standards for Auditors and the Code are not applicable to compilation of financial statements. However, the fundamental principles apply to all professional and business activities. The part of the Code dealing with objectivity highlights that there are certain factors, which by their nature are a threat to objectivity in any professional role and considers appropriate safeguards. These areas of risk include:

- family and other personal or business relationships;

- loans;

- beneficial interests in shares and other investment; and

- gifts and hospitality.

See sections 260 and 280 of the Code for further explanations.

The Code also makes reference to conflicts of interest. The relevant section, 220, **8**
considers possible safeguards, including disclosure of conflicts of interests to all relevant parties. Further discussion on this and other ethical dilemmas is available at icaew.com/ethics.

Quality Control

Practice Assurance standards apply to compilation engagements. Practitioners **9**
may wish to be aware of the guidance issued as a result of the work done by the Quality Assurance Department on unaudited financial statements prepared by ICAEW members[3].

---

[3] *The latest version of this guidance "Accounts filed at Companies House – Avoid a Difficult Conversation" is available at http://www.icaew.com/members/practice-resources/practice-regulation/practice-assurance-standards-and-regulations/practice-assurance-guidance*

Terms of Engagement

10   There needs to be a clear understanding between the client and the professional accountants regarding the terms of the engagement. The client needs to understand from the outset the responsibility which the professional accountants accept in relation to the financial statements. This is best dealt with by a discussion followed by an engagement letter. The engagement letter includes matters such as:

- the board of Directors as addressees;

- the directors' responsibilities with regard to the adequacy of accounting records and the truth and fairness of the financial statements as specified in the Companies Act 2006;

- the information to be supplied by the client to the professional accountants and a confirmation that any other information that the professional accountants consider necessary for the performance of the engagement will be supplied[4];

- the nature of the engagement;

- the professional accountants will make enquiries of management and undertake any procedures that they judge appropriate but are under no obligation to perform procedures that may be required for assurance engagements such as audits or any other type of assurance engagement;

- the engagement cannot be relied on to disclose errors, fraud, weaknesses in internal controls or other irregularities;

- an audit or any other type of assurance engagement will not be carried out and so no opinion will be given and no assurance either implied or expressed;

- the financial reporting framework based on which the financial statements will be prepared and the fact that any known departures will be disclosed;

- professional accountants' ethical and other professional obligations;

- written management representations may be required prior to the completion of the engagement and the issuing of the compilation report;

- the form of report to be issued.

12   In addition, after discussions with the client, it may be appropriate to include a section on the limitation of the professional accountants' liability.

13   ICAEW Helpsheet Engagement letters explains the importance of engagement letters and provides sample wordings to help professional accountants draft effective engagement letters for typical engagements including compilation. It is available from http://www.icaew.com/members/advisory-helplines-and-services/practice-helpsheets/engagement-letters

Content of Financial Statements

14   The directors must not approve financial statements unless they are satisfied that the financial statements give a true and fair view of the state of affairs of the

---

[4] *Section 210 of the Code requires that on appointment, professional accountants should assess threats to compliance with the fundamental principles. This implies, amongst other things, that where a member is engaged to prepare or audit accounts, he should always make it clear that he can only do so on the basis of full disclosure of all information relevant to the work in question. If the client will not agree, the members should not act for him.*

company and of the profit or loss of the company for that period[5]. The accounts of micro-entities, where the exemptions available are taken advantage of and the legal disclosure requirements are met, are presumed to give a true and fair view. Other company accounts are subject to the accounting and disclosure requirements of the Companies Act 2006 and must be prepared in accordance with the applicable financial reporting framework (relevant GAAP – see paragraph 37).

Responsibilities of Directors with Regard to Financial Statements

The directors are responsible for ensuring that the company keeps adequate **15** accounting records that are sufficient to show and explain the company's transactions and disclose with reasonable accuracy at any time the financial position of the company and enable them to ensure that the financial statements comply with the Companies Act 2006.

In preparing UK GAAP financial statements, the directors are required to[6]: **16**

- select suitable accounting policies and then apply them consistently;

- make judgements and estimates that are reasonable and prudent;

- state whether applicable UK accounting standards have been followed, subject to any material departures disclosed and explained in the financial statements[7]; and

- prepare financial statements on a going concern basis unless it is inappropriate to presume that the company will continue in business.

Similar duties apply in respect of IFRS financial statements.

The directors are also responsible for safeguarding the assets of the company and **17** for taking steps for the prevention and detection of fraud and other irregularities. An engagement to compile the financial statements cannot be regarded as providing assurance on the adequacy of the company's systems or on the incidence of fraud, non-compliance with laws and regulations or weaknesses in internal controls. Engaging professional accountants to compile the financial statements does not relieve the directors of their responsibilities in this respect.

The directors are required[8] to satisfy themselves that it is reasonable for them to **18** conclude whether it is appropriate to prepare financial statements on a going concern basis, considering all available information about the future of the entity at the date they authorise the financial statements for issue. The assessment carried out by the directors should be proportionate in nature and depth depending on the size, level of financial risk and complexity of the company and its operations. Their review should usually cover a period of at least twelve months from the date of approval of annual financial statements. Furthermore, in order for the financial statements to give a true and fair view, the directors are also required to provide

---

[5] *Section 393 Companies Act 2006.*

[6] *Companies Act 2006 and other relevant regulations. For guidance on directors' responsibilities see http://www. icaew.com/en/members/regulations-standards-and-guidance/members-in-business/financial-and-accounting-duties-of-directors.*

[7] *This duty does not apply to small and medium sized companies.*

[8] *Required by UK GAAP, including FRSSE, and IFRS. For further information on directors' responsibilities regarding going concern and example disclosure wordings, see Going concern and liquidity risk: Guidance for Directors of UK Companies 2009 from the Financial Reporting Council http://www.frc.org.uk/FRC-Documents/ FRC/Going-Concern-and-Liquidity-Risk-Guidance-for-Dire.aspx.*

balanced, proportionate and clear disclosures, including any material uncertainties of which they are aware arising from their assessment that may cast significant doubt on the company's ability to continue as a going concern.

Planning

19 Professional accountants plan engagements to compile financial statements. The level of planning may vary according to the complexity of the company's accounting records and the professional accountants' experience of the business.

Procedures

20 Professional accountants obtain a general understanding of the business and operations of the company. They need to be familiar with the accounting principles and practices of the sector in which the company operates and with the form and content of the accounting information that is appropriate in the circumstances. The professional accountants' understanding of the business is usually obtained through experience of the company or enquiry of the company's management and staff.

21 Professional accountants consider whether the financial statements are consistent with their understanding of the business and whether the financial statements are misleading. In so doing, professional accountants make such enquiries of management and undertake such procedures as they judge appropriate but are under no obligation to perform procedures that may be required for assurance engagements such as audits or any other type of assurance engagement.

22 Professional accountants consider methods available, such as disclosure checklists or software packages, to check that relevant disclosures have been made based on the information available to them.

Documentation

23 While there is no requirement to document the work that has been carried out, documentation may help the professional accountants demonstrate the adequacy of the work performed and that the engagement was carried out in accordance with the terms of engagement where the quality of the professional accountants' work is subsequently challenged. The level of documentation may vary according to the complexity of the company's accounting records and accounting procedures, according to the professional accountants' experience with the business and whether any matters have arisen during the course of the engagement.

Management Representations

24 In compiling financial statements, professional accountants are normally reliant on representations by management, particularly in relation to estimates and the reliability, accuracy and completeness of information provided. Professional accountants therefore consider obtaining written management representations on these matters.

Misleading Financial Statements

Financial statements prepared under the Companies Act 2006 are required to give **25** a true and fair view[9]. As explained in paragraph 14 above the accounts of micro-entity companies where the exemptions available are taken advantage of and the minimal legal disclosure requirements are met, are presumed to give a true and fair view. All other company accounts should, amongst other things, comply with the requirements of the applicable financial reporting framework including, where necessary, any disclosures required in relation to the use of the true and fair override.

Without carrying out an assurance service, professional accountants cannot form **26** an opinion as to the truth and fairness of the view given by financial statements. During the course of the engagement, however, matters may come to light which appear to indicate that the financial statements may be misleading including the inappropriate use of the going concern basis or inadequate disclosure relating to going concern (see paragraph 18). In other situations, the professional accountant may feel that they have not been provided with all the information required in order to compile the financial statements. The directors of a company are required by law to maintain adequate accounting records, and so in such circumstances they will request the directors to provide the missing information.

Similarly, if the professional accountants form a view that disclosures necessary **27** for the accounts to give a true and fair view (including those encouraged within Accounting Standards) have not been made, the professional accountants will request the directors to include the relevant disclosures.

Where a company's accounts have been prepared using the micro-entity option **28** there is no requirement for the disclosure of a going concern note or a note of accounting policies. If the accounts have been properly prepared so as to include the minimum accounting items required under the micro-entities regime they will be presumed to give a true and fair view[10]. However, should a micro-entity choose to include an item in addition to the minimum accounting items, the professional accountants must, in respect of that item, consider the provisions in the relevant accounting standard and decide if proper disclosure has been made.

In addition, professional accountants are bound by paragraph 110.2 of the Code of **29** Ethics (A) not to be knowingly associated with information that they consider misleading, including instances where the information may be misleading because of omissions. There may be rare occasions when professional accountants consider that the information disclosed in accordance with the micro-entity regime is misleading.

Small companies applying Section 1A Small Entities of FRS 102 The Financial **30** Reporting Standard applicable in the UK and the Republic of Ireland are also not required to provide disclosures on the going concern basis of accounting, although their directors are encouraged to provide such disclosures, where appropriate, in meeting their responsibility to prepare financial statements that give a true and fair view. However, as explained above, professional accountants may not knowingly be associated with misleading information. If professional accountants have any reason to believe that the company is not a going concern they should consider

---

[9] *s393 CA 2006 provides that the directors of a Company must not approve accounts unless they give a true and fair view of the assets, liabilities, financial position and profit or loss of the company and, where applicable, group.*

[10] *Companies Act 2006 s393(1A) as amended by SI 2013/3008 reg 5.*

whether the accounts could be misleading and, if so, should discuss the matter with the directors and take legal advice.

31   In cases such as outlined in 26) above, the professional accountants discuss the matter with the client with a view to agreeing appropriate adjustments or disclosures to be made in the financial statements or to provide the missing information. If, despite such a request, the directors refuse to permit the professional accountant to make appropriate adjustments or disclosures in the financial statements or to provide the missing information, the professional accountants may consider that the financial statements are misleading. If they do consider the financial statements to be misleading then they should withdraw from the engagement and should not permit their name to be associated with the financial statements.

32   In considering whether financial statements are misleading, professional accountants consider whether the financial statements appear to be appropriate in form and free from material misstatements that appear obvious to them as a result of, for example:

- misclassifications in the financial statements;

- mistakes in the application of, or non-disclosure of known departures from, any relevant statutory, regulatory or other reporting requirements, including applicable financial reporting framework and non-disclosure of significant changes in accounting policies;

- other significant matters of which the professional accountants are aware, such as non-disclosure of a going concern issue or any statements made in the accounts which the professional accountants believe not to be consistent with the accounts themselves.

33   When professional accountants withdraw from an engagement, they should normally explain to their clients their reasons for withdrawing, unless this would constitute a breach of legal or other regulatory requirement (such as the "tipping off" provisions of the money laundering legislation)[11].

34   In rare situations, the accountant may conclude that it remains appropriate for them to be associated with the financial statements despite the fact that they depart from an applicable standard or the fact that incomplete information is available (for example, if stock take records have been lost in a fire).

35   In such situations, the professional accountant will check that appropriate disclosures are made in the financial statements (for example, those required by paragraphs 3.4 to 3.6 of FRS 102 when the true and fair override is invoked and the accountant believes that the override is appropriate). They may further wish to highlight these disclosures in their report by way of an explanatory paragraph. For example, where the true and fair override has been used, there will already be extensive disclosure; however, if there is a lack of accounting records, there may not be. The Appendix contains an example wording for such a paragraph.

---

[11] *For further information, see the ICAEW anti-money laundering guidance http://www.icaew.com/en/members/regulations-standards-and-guidance/practice-management/anti-money-laundering-guidance*

Approval of Financial Statements

Financial statements should be approved and signed by the directors[12] before the   **36**
professional accountant signs the compilation report. The directors are statutorily
responsible for the financial statements. The Companies Act 2006 requires that
directors approve the financial statements and that the balance sheet states the
name of the director signing the financial statements on behalf of the board. The
directors of companies that are audit exempt are required to acknowledge, on the
face of the balance sheet, their responsibilities for complying with the
requirements of the Act with respect to accounting records and the preparation
of accounts in accordance with the provisions applicable to companies as well as
entitlement of the company to exemption from audit.

Professional Accountants' Compilation Reports

The professional accountants' report helps users derive comfort from the   **37**
involvement of Chartered Accountants who are subject to the ethical and other
guidance issued by ICAEW in relation to the preparation of the financial
statements. It also helps prevent users from deriving unwarranted assurance
from the financial statements where no audit has been performed and no
opinion is being expressed by the professional accountants.

The professional accountants' report on the financial statements of a company   **38**
may include the following elements. The text in [brackets] indicates that the
wording is optional:

- a title identifying the persons to whom the report is addressed (usually the
  board of directors) and including the words "Chartered Accountant's/
  Accountants' Report to …"[13];

- a statement that the professional accountants have prepared the financial
  statements [which comprise – state which – the primary financial statements
  such as the Profit and Loss Account, the balance Sheet, the Cash Flow
  Statement and the related notes] from the company's accounting records and
  from information and explanations given by the client;

- [a statement that the report is made to the Company's board of Directors as a
  body in accordance with the terms of engagement.]

- an explanation as to the work carried out being in accordance with the
  requirements of ICAEW guidance [and the purpose of the work and that, to
  the fullest extent permitted by law, no responsibility will be accepted for the
  work or the report to anyone other than the Company and the Company's
  board of Directors, as a body].

- a reference to the accounting framework according to which the accounts
  have been prepared. A similar reference should also be included as part of
  the directors' approval of the accounts.

---

[12] *In the case of an LLP, by a designated member on behalf of the members.*

[13] *A firm may only use the description Chartered Accountant(s) if it complies with the relevant regulations
governing the use of the description Chartered Accountant(s). Where a firm is not permitted to use the term
Chartered Accountant(s), the title "Accountants' Report to …" should be used, rather than "Chartered Accountant
(s) Report to …".*

- [a statement that it is the directors' duty to ensure that the entity has kept adequate accounting records and to prepare statutory financial statements that give a true and fair view of the assets, liabilities, financial position and profit[/loss] of the entity and that they consider that the entity is exempt from the statutory audit requirement for the year [/period].]

- [a statement that the professional accountants have not been instructed to carry out an audit or any other type of assurance engagement of the financial statements, verified the accuracy or completeness of the accounting records or information and explanations supplied, and that the professional accountants do not express any opinion on the financial statements];

- the name and signature of the professional accountant and any appropriate designation (but not "Statutory auditor");

- the date of the report.

39   The financial statements contain a reference to the fact that they are unaudited either on the front cover or on each page of the financial statements, or both.

40   An example professional accountants' report is set out in the Appendix. The appendix also provides an example explanatory paragraph to be used in the circumstances set out in paragraph 34 above.

Filing the Financial Statements

41   The Professional Oversight Board recommended that users of financial statements are given a clear explanation of the extent and relevance of the involvement of professional accountants in the preparation of those financial statements. In the light of this, provided the company is exempt from audit, the filing of the compilation report alongside the copy of the financial statements with the Registrar may help increase the credibility of the financial information placed on public record and differentiate the financial statements from those prepared by firms and individuals who are not members of one of the CCAB bodies. However, this consideration does not apply when financial statements contain an audit report, or abbreviated accounts[14] derived from audited accounts contain a special auditors' report under s449 Companies Act 2006, as inclusion of two different reports by professional accountants could be confusing.

Applicable Financial Framework

42   Prior to the adoption of UK's new financial reporting regime this framework would be chosen from:

- The small entities regime available to eligible entities under FRSSE 2008, including the amendments made in April 2014 to allow micro-entities to comply with both the micro-entities regulations and the applicable accounting standard

- FRSs and SSAPs

- IFRS as adopted by the EU

---

[14] *This Technical Release does not cover situations where abridged accounts are prepared. The abbreviated accounts regime is withdrawn for accounting periods starting on or after 1 January 2016.*

After the adoption of the UK's new financial reporting regime the framework would be chosen from:

- FRS 102 The Financial Reporting Standard applicable in the UK and Republic of Ireland

- The small entities regime available to eligible entities under Section 1A Small Entities of FRS 102[15]

- The micro entities regime available to eligible entities under FRS 105 The Financial Reporting Standard applicable to the Micro-entities Regime[16]

- FRS 101 Reduced Disclosure Framework

- FRSSE 2015 (withdrawn for accounting periods starting on or after 1 January 2016)

- IFRS as adopted by the EU

---

[15] *This is required for f accounting periods starting on or after 1 January 2016 and permitted for accounting periods starting on or after 1 January 2015.*

[16] *This is required for accounting periods starting on or after 1 January 2016 with early adoption permitted.*

Appendix

Example reports

Chartered Accountant's/Accountants'[17] report to the board of directors on the preparation of the unaudited statutory accounts of XYZ Limited for the year [/period] ended dd/mm/20yy[18]

In order to assist you to fulfil your duties under the Companies Act 2006, we[19] have prepared for your approval the accounts of XYZ Limited for the year [/period] ended dd/mm/20yy [as set out on pages x–x/ which comprise [insert statements]] from the company's accounting records and from information and explanations you have given us.

As a practising member [/member firm of] of the Institute of Chartered Accountants in England and Wales (ICAEW), we are subject to its ethical and other professional requirements which are detailed at http://www.icaew.com/en/members/regulations-standards-and-guidance/.

[This report is made solely to the board of Directors of XYZ Limited, as a body, in accordance with the terms of our engagement letter dated dd/mm/20yy.] Our work has been undertaken [solely to prepare for your approval the accounts of XYZ Limited and state those matters that we have agreed to state to them/ the board of Directors of XYZ Limited, as a body, in this report] in accordance with ICAEW Technical Release 07/16 AAF. [To the fullest extent permitted by law, we do not accept or assume responsibility to anyone other than XYZ Limited and its board of Directors as a body for our work or for this report.]

[It is your duty to ensure that XYZ Limited has kept adequate accounting records and to prepare statutory accounts that give a true and fair view of the assets, liabilities, financial position and profits[/loss] of XYZ Limited. you consider that XYZ Limited is exempt from the statutory audit requirement for the year [/period].]

[We have not been instructed to carry out an audit or a review of the accounts of XYZ Limited. For this reason, we have not verified the accuracy or completeness of the accounting records or information and explanations you have given to us and we do not, therefore, express any opinion on the statutory accounts.]

[Explanatory paragraph: eg, records destroyed by fire.][20]

Signature...................

Typed name of professional accountant[21]

Chartered Accountants

Addresss

Date ....

---

[17] *See footnote 12.*

[18] *© Consultative Committee Accountancy bodies (CCAB) 2009. All rights reserved.*

[19] *Professional accountants use "I" in place of "we," "my" in place of "our" etc, as appropriate.*

[20] *Explanatory paragraph may be positioned in other places in the report depending on the nature of the matter described.*

[21] *This report is signed in the name of the professional accountant or, where appropriate, in the name of the accounting firm.*

Explanatory paragraph to deal with information not being available

We draw your attention to note x in the financial statements which discloses and explains the year-end stock balance is an estimate derived from management accounts. Following a fire in the warehouse, the records of the year-end stock count were not available.

TECH 08/16AAF Chartered Accountants' reports on the Compilation of historical Financial Information of Unincorporated Entities (revised update of AAF 03/10)

(March 2016)

Contents

	Paragraphs
Scope	1 - 4
Professional ethics	5 - 8
Quality control	9
Compilation of financial information	10
Financial reporting framework and format	11 - 12
Terms of engagement	13 - 15
Content of financial information	16
Client responsibilities	17 - 19
Planning	20
Procedures	21 - 23
Documentation	24
Management representations	25
Misleading financial information	26 - 32
Approval of financial information	33
Professional accountants' compilation reports	34 - 38
APPENDIX A: Example wording for approval of financial information	
APPENDIX B: Example report	

ABOUT THE AUDIT AND ASSURANCE FACULTY

The ICAEW Audit and Assurance Faculty is a leading authority on external audit and other assurance activities and is recognised internationally as a source of expertise on audit issues. It is responsible for ICAEW technical audit and assurance leadership and provides a range of information sources to its members which gives practical assurance in key audit and assurance areas.

Scope

1   This Technical Release is intended to give general guidance to members when they compile historical financial information for their clients. This guidance covers the compilation of historical financial information of unincorporated entities for a specific purpose or purposes, for example financial information compiled for tax purposes, partnership accounts or the compilation of financial information (without providing any form of assurance) for grant claims. This Technical Release replaces AUDIT 03/10 Chartered Accountants' Reports on the Compilation of Financial Statements of Unincorporated Entities.

2   Financial information on unincorporated entities may be compiled by accountants for a number of different purposes. Depending on the purpose, unincorporated entities may not require full financial statements which give a true and fair view and comply with all applicable accounting standards. This guidance is designed to reflect this circumstance and to help professional accountants to provide compilation services where there is an appropriate framework established for the compilation and presentation of the financial information, including relevant and appropriate disclosures of the financial reporting framework adopted. The guidance in this release is consistent with that in ICAEW Technical Release TECH07/16AAF Chartered Accountants' Reports on the Compilation of Financial Statements of Incorporated Entities, but does not deal with compliance with aspects of company law required for such entities.

3   This guidance may also be relevant to the compilation of financial information for incorporated entities other than financial statements[1].

4   Professional accountants are encouraged to apply this guidance as soon as is practicable as best practice. The 2015 update has been carried out to reflect changes such as new UK GAAP but is not intended to change current best practice.

Professional Ethics

5   The Fundamental Principles are:

Fundamental Principle 1 – Integrity: A professional accountant shall be straightforward and honest in all professional and business relationships. Integrity also implies fair dealing and truthfulness.

Fundamental Principle 2 – Objectivity: A professional accountant shall not allow bias, conflict of interest or undue influence of others to compromise their professional or business judgements.

Fundamental Principle 3 – Professional Competence and Due Care: A professional accountant has a continuing duty to maintain professional knowledge and skill at the level required to ensure that a client or employer receives competent professional service based on current developments in practice, legislation and techniques. A professional accountant should act diligently and in accordance with applicable technical and professional standards when providing professional services.

---

[1] *Attention is drawn to s435 of the Companies Act 2006. Where a company publishes non-statutory accounts (any balance sheet or profit and loss account relating to or purporting to deal with a financial year of the company) it needs to publish a statement with them that they are not the statutory accounts, together with additional details about the status of the statutory accounts for the year in question.*

Fundamental Principle 4 – Confidentiality: A professional accountants shall respect the confidentiality of information acquired as a result of professional and business relationships and may not disclose any such information to third parties without proper and specific authority unless there is a legal or professional right or duty to disclose. Confidential information acquired as a result of professional and business relationships should not be used for the personal advantage of the professional accountant or third parties.

Fundamental Principle 5 – Professional behaviour: A professional accountants should comply with relevant laws and regulations and should avoid any action that may discredit the profession.

Members shall not, therefore, knowingly be associated with financial information **6** where the professional accountant believes that the information:

- contains a materially false or misleading statement;

- contains statements or information furnished recklessly; or

- omits or obscures information required to be included where such omission or obscurity would be misleading.

When a professional accountant becomes aware that the accountant has been associated with such information, the accountant shall take steps to be disassociated from that information.

The independence requirements that apply to audit and other assurance **7** engagements contained within the APB Ethical Standards for Auditors and the Code are not applicable to compilation of financial statements. However, the fundamental principles apply to all professional and business activities. The part of the Code dealing with objectivity highlights that there are certain factors, which by their nature are a threat to objectivity in any professional role and considers appropriate safeguards. These areas of risk include:

- family and other personal or business relationships;

- loans;

- beneficial interests in shares and other investments; and

- gifts and hospitality.

See sections 260 and 280 of the Code for further explanations.

The Code also makes reference to conflicts of interest. The relevant section, 220, **8** considers possible safeguards, including disclosure of conflicts of interest to all relevant parties. Further discussion on this and other ethical dilemmas is available at icaew.com/ethics.

Quality Control

Practice Assurance standards apply to compilation engagements. Practitioners **9** may wish to be aware of the guidance issued as a result of the work done by the Quality Assurance Department on unaudited financial statements prepared by ICAEW members[2].

---

[2] *The latest version of this guidance "Accounts filed at Companies House – Avoid a Difficult Conversation" is available at http://www.icaew.com/members/practice-resources/practice-regulation/practice-assurance-standards-and-regulations/practice-assurance-guidance.*

Compilation of Financial Information

10   When compiling financial information, professional accountants use their accounting expertise to collect, classify and present accounting information from the sources made available to them. This normally entails summarising detailed data into a manageable and understandable form. There is no requirement for the professional accountants to test the assertions underlying the information provided to them. This guidance is not designed and does not enable the professional accountants to express any assurance on the financial information being compiled. Nevertheless, users of the financial information compiled derive benefit because professional accountants are required to carry out work with professional competence and due care and are subject to the ethical and other guidance as stated in paragraph 5.

Financial Reporting Framework and Format

11   Unlike the statutory financial statements of companies, there is no statutory requirement for the financial information of unincorporated entities to give a true and fair view, nor to comply with any recognised financial reporting framework (eg, UK GAAP). Depending on the purpose of the financial information, it may be appropriate to prepare it on another basis. For example, an agreed financial reporting framework may be one that meets the requirements for calculating and reporting profits under s25 of Income Tax (Trading and Other Income) Act 2005 but which omits the disclosures required by accounting standards and the Companies Act, or where the taxpayer has elected to use the cash basis under s17, Finance Act 2013 rather than s25 referred to above.

12   Where an appropriate financial reporting framework or format cannot be agreed then the professional accountants should not accept the engagement.

Terms of Engagement

13   There needs to be a clear understanding between the client and the professional accountants of the terms of the engagement. The client needs to understand from the outset the responsibility which the professional accountants accept in relation to the financial information being compiled. This is best dealt with by a discussion followed by an engagement letter. The engagement letter includes matters such as:

- the client as addressee;

- the client's responsibility for the reliability, accuracy and completeness of the accounting records;

- the information to be supplied by the client to the professional accountants and a confirmation that any other information that the professional accountants consider necessary for the purpose of the engagement will be supplied[3];

- the nature of the engagement, including the purpose for which the financial information is being prepared;

---

[3] *Section 210 of the Code of Ethics requires that on appointment, professional accountants should assess threats to compliance with the fundamental principles. This implies, amongst other things, that where a member is engaged to prepare or audit accounts, he should always make it clear that he can only do so on the basis of full disclosure of all information relevant to the work in question. If the client will not agree, the member should not act for him.*

- the professional accountants will make enquiries of management and undertake any procedures that they judge appropriate but are under no obligation to perform procedures that may be required for assurance engagements such as audits or any other types of assurance engagement;

- the engagement cannot be relied on to disclose errors, fraud, weaknesses in internal controls or other irregularities;

- neither an audit nor any other type of assurance engagement will be carried out and so no opinion will be given and no assurance either implied or expressed;

- the financial reporting framework on which the financial information will be compiled and the fact that the purpose of the financial information and, where not in accordance with a recognised financial reporting framework such as UK GAAP (including, where relevant, the FRSSE) or IFRS as adopted by the European Union, any limitations of the basis adopted, will be disclosed in an accounting policy note to the financial information and referred to in the professional accountants' report;

- a professional accountants' obligation not be associated with reports, returns, communications or other information where they believe that the information:

  - contains a materially false or misleading statement;

  - contains statements or information furnished recklessly; or

  - omits or obscures information required to be included where such omission or obscurity would be misleading;

- written management representations may be required prior to the completion of the engagement and the issuing of the compilation report;

- the client will approve and sign the financial information which includes a statement acknowledging responsibility for the financial information, including the appropriateness of the financial reporting framework adopted, and for having provided all information and explanations necessary to the professional accountants of its compilation.

- the form of report to be issued.

In addition, after discussions with the client, it may be appropriate to include a section on the limitation of the professional accountants' liability. **14**

ICAEW Helpsheet Engagement letters explains the importance of engagement letters and provides sample wordings to help professional accountants draft effective engagement letters for typical engagements including compilation. It is available from http://www.icaew.com/en/members/advisory-helplines-and-services/practice-helpsheets/engagement-letters. **15**

Content of Financial Information

As described in paragraphs 11–12 above, financial information is compiled based on an appropriate financial reporting framework. This need not necessarily be a recognised financial reporting framework. The financial reporting framework adopted, purpose and limitations of the information presented should be fully disclosed in an accounting policy note to the financial information and referred to in the professional accountants' report that accompanies it, so that the financial information is not misleading. **16**

Client Responsibilities

17   Under the terms of the engagement the client is responsible for the reliability, accuracy and completeness of the accounting records of the entity and for the provision and disclosure to the professional accountants of all information relevant to the purpose and compilation of the financial information.

18   The client is also responsible for safeguarding the assets of the entity and for taking steps for the prevention and detection of fraud and other irregularities. An engagement to compile financial information cannot be regarded as providing assurance on the adequacy of the entity's systems or on the incidence of fraud, non-compliance with laws and regulations or weaknesses in internal controls. Engaging professional accountants to compile financial information does not relieve the client of their responsibilities in this respect.

19   Where required by the applicable financial reporting framework, for example UK GAAP or IFRS as adopted by the EU, the client is required[4] to satisfy themselves that it is reasonable for them to conclude whether it is appropriate to prepare financial statements on a going concern basis, considering all available information about the future of the entity at the date they authorise the financial statements for issue. The process carried out by the client should be proportionate in nature and depth depending on the size, level of financial risk and complexity of the company and its operations. The client's review should usually cover a period of at least twelve months from the date of approval of annual financial statements. Furthermore, in order for the financial statements to give a true and fair view, the directors are also required to provide balanced, proportionate and clear disclosures, including any material uncertainties of which they are aware arising from their assessment of going concern that may cast significant doubt on the entity's ability to continue as a going concern.

Planning

20   Professional accountants plan engagements to compile financial information. The level of planning will vary according to the complexity and completeness of the entity's accounting records and system and the professional accountants' experience of the business.

Procedures

21   Professional accountants obtain a general understanding of the business and operations of the entity. They need to be familiar with the accounting principles and practices of the sector in which the entity operates and with the form and content of the accounting information that is appropriate in the circumstances and is appropriate for the purpose for which the information is being compiled. The professional accountants' understanding of the business is usually obtained through experience of the entity or enquiry of the entity's management and staff.

22   Professional accountants consider whether the financial statements are consistent with their understanding of the business and whether the financial statements are

---

[4] *Required by UK GAAP including the FRSSE and IFRS. For further information on directors' responsibilities regarding going concern and example disclosure wordings, see Going concern and liquidity risk: Guidance for Directors of UK Companies 2009 from the Financial Reporting Council at https://www.frc.org.uk/FRC-Documents/FRC/Going-Concern-and-Liquidity-Risk-Guidance-for-Dire.aspx.*

misleading. In so doing, the professional accountants make such enquiries of management and undertake such procedures as they judge are appropriate but are under no obligation to perform procedures that may be required for assurance engagements such as audits or any other type of assurance engagement.

Where appropriate, for example because the financial reporting framework 23 adopted is a recognised accounting framework, the professional accountants consider using checklists or software packages to check that relevant disclosures have been made based on the information available to them.

Documentation

Documentation may help the professional accountants demonstrate the adequacy 24 of the work performed and that the engagement was carried out in accordance with the terms of engagement where the quality of the professional accountants' work is subsequently challenged. The level of documentation may vary according to the complexity of the entity's accounting records and accounting procedures, according to the professional accountants' experience with the entity and whether any matters have arisen during the course of the engagement.

Management Representations

In compiling financial information, professional accountants are normally reliant 25 on representations by management, particularly in relation to estimates and the reliability, accuracy and completeness of information provided. They therefore consider obtaining written management representations on these matters.

Misleading Financial Information

Without carrying out an assurance service, the professional accountants cannot 26 form an opinion as to whether the financial statements comply with the financial reporting framework adopted. During the course of the engagement, however, matters may come to light which appear to indicate that the financial information may be misleading. In other situations, the professional accountant may feel that they have not been provided with all the information required in order to compile the financial statements.

In such cases, the professional accountants discuss the matter with the client with a 27 view to agreeing appropriate adjustments or disclosures to be made in the financial information, or to provide the missing information. If, despite such a request, the directors refuse to permit the professional accountant to make appropriate adjustments or disclosures in the financial information or to provide the missing information, the professional accountants may consider that the financial information is misleading. If they do consider the financial information to be misleading then they should withdraw from the engagement and should not permit their name to be associated with the financial statements.

Where an entity's accounts have been prepared using the Micro-entity option there 28 is no requirement for the disclosure of a going concern note. Reporting accountants should use their professional judgement in considering whether the figures could be misleading.

A micro-entity is an entity that meets all of the following conditions: 29

- It is a company established under company law;
- It qualifies as a micro-entity in accordance with section 384A of the Act; and
- It is not excluded from being treated as a micro-entity under section 384B of the Act.

Micro-entities are a subset of small companies as defined in the Act.

30 In considering whether financial information is misleading, the professional accountants consider whether the financial information appears to be appropriate for the purpose for which it is compiled, appropriate in respect of the financial reporting framework agreed and free from material misstatements that appear obvious to them as a result of, for example:

- misclassifications in the financial information;
- mistakes in the application of the adopted financial reporting framework. Where the financial reporting framework adopted is a recognised accounting framework such as UK GAAP, this would include departures from applicable accounting standards and guidance;
- other significant matters of which the professional accountants are aware. For example, if a professional accountant is engaged to prepare a balance sheet without notes to support a lending application, they may nevertheless conclude that this would be misleading if it does not disclose a significant going concern problem.

31 When professional accountants withdraw from an engagement, they should normally explain to their clients their reasons for withdrawing, unless this would constitute a breach of legal or other regulatory requirement (such as the "tipping off" provisions of the money laundering legislation)[5].

32 In rare situations, the accountant may conclude that it remains appropriate for them to be associated with the financial statements despite the fact that they depart from an applicable standard or the fact that incomplete information is available (for example, if stock take records have been lost in a fire). In such situations, the professional accountant will check that appropriate disclosures are made in the financial statements (for example, those required by paragraphs 3.4 to 3.6 in FRS 102 when the true and fair override is invoked and the accountant believes that the override is appropriate). They may further wish to highlight these disclosures in their report by way of an explanatory paragraph. For example, where the true and fair override has been used, there will already be extensive disclosure; however, if there is a lack of accounting records, there may not be. Appendix B contains an example wording for such a paragraph.

Approval of Financial Information

33 Although there is no statutory requirement for the financial information of unincorporated entities to be signed or approved by the client it is recommended that the client does approve and sign the financial information. In so doing, the client acknowledges responsibility for the financial information, including the appropriateness of the financial reporting framework on which it has been compiled, and for having provided all information and explanations

---

[5] *For further information, see the CCAB anti-money laundering guidance.*

necessary to the professional accountants for its compilation. Example wording is included at Appendix A.

Professional Accountants' Compilation Reports

The professional accountants' report helps users derive comfort from the involvement of professional Accountants who are subject to the ethical and other guidance issued by ICAEW in relation to the preparation of the financial information. It also helps prevent users from deriving unwarranted assurance from the financial information compiled where no audit has been performed and no opinion is being expressed by the professional accountants.   **34**

The professional accountants' report on the financial information of an unincorporated entity may include following elements. The text in [brackets] indicates that the wording is optional: **35**

- a title identifying the persons to whom the report is addressed and including the words "Chartered Accountants'/Accountants' Report to …"[6];

- a statement that the professional accountants have prepared the financial information [which comprises [state the primary financial statements that have been compiled, such as the Profit and Loss Account, the Balance Sheet and the Cash Flow Statement and, where relevant, related notes] from the client's accounting records and from information and explanations given by the client;

- [a statement that the report is made to the Company's Board of Directors as a body in accordance with the terms of engagement.]

- a reference to the accounting policy note which sets out the financial reporting framework adopted for compilation and the purpose and limitations of the financial information;

- a statement that the report is made to the client in accordance with the terms of engagement.

- An explanation as to the work involved and the purpose of the work and that, to the fullest extent permitted by law, no responsibility will be accepted for the work or the report to anyone other than the client;

- a statement that the professional accountants have carried out the engagement in accordance with technical guidance issued by the Institute and that they have complied with the ethical guidance laid down by the Institute;

- a statement that the client has acknowledged his responsibility for the financial information;

- a statement that the professional accountants have not verified the accuracy or completeness of the accounting records or information and explanations supplied, and that the professional accountants do not express any opinion on the financial information;

---

[6] *A firm may only use the description Chartered Accountant(s) if it complies with the relevant regulations governing the use of the description Chartered Accountant(s). Where a firm is not permitted to use the term Chartered Accountant(s), the title "Accountants' Report to…" should be used, rather than "Chartered Accountant(s) Report to …".*

- the name and signature of the professional accountant and any appropriate designation (but not "Registered Auditor");

- the date of the report.

37   The financial information contains a reference to the fact that it is unaudited either on the front cover or on each page of the financial information, or both.

38   An example of a professional accountants' report is set out in Appendix B.

APPENDIX A

Example wording for approval of financial information

In accordance with the engagement letter dated [date], I/we approve the financial information which comprises [state the financial information compiled]. I/we acknowledge my/our responsibility for the financial information, including the appropriateness of the applicable financial reporting framework as set out in note x, and for providing [the accountants] with all information and explanations necessary for its compilation.

Signatures

[XYZ & Co] Date

APPENDIX B

Example report

Chartered Accountants'/Accountants' Report to [Entity] on the Unaudited Financial Information of XYZ& Co[7].

In accordance with the engagement letter dated [date], we[8] have prepared for your approval the financial information of [the entity] for the year [/period] which comprises of [insert statements]] from the entity's accounting records and from information and explanations you have given us.

As a practising member [/member firm of] of the Institute of Chartered Accountants in England and Wales (ICAEW), we are subject to its ethical and other professional requirements which are detailed at icaew.com/members handbook.

[This report is made solely to you, in accordance with the terms of our engagement letter dated dd/mm/20yy.] Our work has been undertaken [solely to prepare for your approval the financial information of [entity] and state those matters that we have agreed to state to you in this report] in accordance with ICAEW Technical release TECH08/16AAF. [To the fullest extent permitted by law, we do not accept or assume responsibility to anyone other than [addressee of this report] for our work or for this report.]

[you have approved the [financial information] [for the year/period] and have acknowledged your responsibility for it, for the appropriateness of the financial reporting framework adopted and for providing all information and explanations necessary for its compilation.

We have not verified the accuracy or completeness of the accounting records or information and explanations you have given to us and we do not, therefore, express any opinion on the financial information.]

Signature ....

Typed name of professional accountant[9]

Chartered Accountants

Address

Date ....

Explanatory paragraph to deal with information not being available

We draw your attention to note x in the financial statements which discloses and explains the year-end stock balance is an estimate derived from management accounts. Following a fire in the warehouse, the records of the year-end stock count were not available.

---

[7] *This report is based on CCAB accounts compilation report, © Consultative Committee of Accountancy Bodies (CCAB) 2009. All rights reserved.*

[8] *Professional accountants use "I" in place of "we," "my" in place of "our" etc. as appropriate.*

[9] *The report is signed in the name of the professional accountant or, where appropriate, in the name of the accounting firm.*

TECH 12/16AAF Assurance reporting on Master Trusts (Master Trust Supplement to ICAEW AAF 02/07)

(TECH 08/16AAF Amended 30 November 2016)

Contents

	Paragraphs
Foreword	1 - 11
About this supplement	12 - 24
Effective date and transitional arrangements	25 - 27

Assurance reporting on governance control procedures established by trustees of master trusts

The responsibility of trustees of the Master Trust	28
Assurance reporting on the trustees governance control procedures	29 - 30
A three party relationship	31
Responsible party	32 - 35
Intended users	36 - 38
Practitioner	39 - 40
An appropriate subject matter	41 - 43
Suitable criteria	44 - 49
Where the trustees of the Master Trust apply additional control objectives	50
Other information provided by trustees of Master Trusts	51 - 52
Sufficient appropriate evidence	53

Assurance report

Guidance for practitioners	54 - 56
Assurance report	57 - 59
Assurance reporting limitations	60 - 61
Reporting on description misstatements, design deficiencies or when governance control procedures are not operating effectively	62 - 68

Appendix 1: Control objectives addressing governance arrangements established by trustees of master trusts

Appendix 2: Example paragraphs from the report by the trustees of the master trust

Appendix 3: A pro forma practitioner's assurance report on governance control procedures established by the trustees of master trusts

ABOUT THE AUDIT AND ASSURANCE FACULTY

The ICAEW Audit and Assurance Faculty is a leading authority on external audit and other assurance activities and is recognised internationally as a source of expertise on audit issues. It is responsible for ICAEW technical audit and assurance leadership and provides a range of information sources to its members which gives practical assurance in key audit and assurance areas.

ISBN 978 2 78363 916 8

FOREWORD

This updated Master Trust Supplement to ICAEW AAF 02/07 (the 1
"Supplement"), produced in association with the Pensions Regulator (the
Regulator), addresses assurance reporting on governance control procedures
established by trustees of Relevant Multi-employer Schemes (referred to as
Master Trusts throughout this Supplement) and takes into account changes
made by the Regulator in response to new legalisation and regulatory
developments.

While this Supplement refers to specific sections of AAF 02/07, this does not 2
replace the need to read the guidance AAF 02/07 in its entirety and apply it as
appropriate.

References to trustees throughout this document includes individually appointed 3
trustees and Independent Trustee companies as well as corporate trustees.

The Regulator's original DC Code of Practice and DC regulatory Guidance 4
(published in November 2013 and April 2014 respectively) formed the basis of the
control objectives referred to in the previous Supplement published in May 2014.
These regulatory documents were designed around a number of DC quality
features that described those activities, behaviours and control processes that were
considered to be more likely to deliver good member outcomes. It was with these
DC quality features in mind, that the control objectives in the original Supplement
were drafted.

Since this date new legislation addressing minimum quality standards has enabled 5
the Regulator to strengthen its approach to scheme governance and administration
through the development of standards of conduct and practice as set out in its
revised DC code and relevant DC Guides published by the Regulator which came
into effect in July 2016. The Regulator expects both the DC Code and DC guides
to be read in conjunction with each other.

In response to these legal reforms, the revised DC Code and related DC Guides are 6
no longer structured specifically around quality features. It is the Regulator's view
that these should now be well established features and "principles" of governance
which should be present in all DC schemes, including Master Trusts, and therefore
remain firm aspects of good governance.

As a direct consequence of this, presentational changes have been made to this 7
Supplement and references and alignment with DC quality features previously
included in the original Supplement have been removed. A number of control
objectives have also been refined, although the impact on the nature of control
procedures needed to fulfil these objectives is not significant.

This Supplement is effective for Type 2 reports produced for reporting periods 8
commencing after 31 December 2016 and Type 1 reports (see paragraph 23)
that fall after the same date. Arrangements for Master Trusts transitioning from
the original Supplement to the updated Supplement are considered in
paragraphs 25 to 27.

To help employers select suitable qualifying schemes for automatic enrolment, the 9
Regulator now maintains a list of master trusts that have appropriately obtained
master trust assurance and have met other eligibility criteria, as outlined on their
website. Completion of the master trust assurance report in accordance with
requirements set out in this Supplement within timeframes set out by the Regulator
is just one of requirements to be met in order to be added and remain the of the
master trust list maintained by the Regulator.

10   Reporting Accountants should be aware of, and understand, their clients aspirations is respect of obtaining a master trust assurance report and carefully consider who the report may be made available to. Intended users of the report are considered further in paragraphs 36 to 38.

11   This Supplement will continue to be kept under review in light of any other regulatory or legislative changes.

ABOUT THIS SUPPLEMENT

12   This Supplement consists of:

- assurance reporting on governance control procedures established by trustees of Master Trusts;

- guidance for practitioners;

- Appendix 1: Control objectives on the governance of Master Trusts;

- Appendix 2: Example paragraphs from the assertion by the trustees of the Master Trust; and

- Appendix 3: A pro forma practitioner's assurance report on the governance control procedures of the Master Trust.

13   This Supplement has been produced in association with the Regulator. The focus of the assurance framework is specifically in relation to governance control procedures established and operated by the trustees of the Master Trust in relation to each of the control objectives set out in Appendix 1.

14   The assurance framework used for this Supplement is AAF 02/07 entitled "A Framework for assurance reports on third party operations". AAF 02/07 provides a framework for performing assurance engagements on various aspects of operations provided by external organisations (third-party operations) and which may be subject to external independent examination. AAF 02/07 sets out principal matters relevant to the determination of suitable criteria and hence control objectives to be used as evaluation criteria.

15   The assurance framework helps trustees demonstrate their accountabilities and help evidence the presence of standards of governance that the Regulator believes are attributable to a well-run scheme and are more likely to result in better outcomes for pension scheme members.

16   The trustees engage independent practitioners to issue an independent assurance report whereby:

- the trustee's report on the description, design, and operating effectiveness of the governance control procedures established by the trustees of the Master Trust related to the control objectives set out in Appendix 1; and

- practitioners undertake procedures in order to issue a reasonable assurance report on the description, design and operating effectiveness of the relevant governance control procedures related to those control objectives established by the trustees of the Master Trust.

17   The report therefore comprises a trustees' report on the governance control procedures and arrangements established by the trustees of the Master Trust supported by an independent assurance report over the description, design and effective operation of governance control procedures established by the trustees of the Master Trust in accordance with a defined set of control objectives.

This Supplement sets out what is expected from reports provided on specified **18** control procedures based on co ntrol objectives which are aligned with legal requirements and standards of governance expected by the Regulator, as set out in the revised DC code and related DC Guides published by the Regulator in July 2016. The governance control procedures established by the trustees of the Master Trust are assessed in the light of all the control objectives that are set out in Appendix 1.

For the purpose of this exercise, it remains the responsibility of trustees to ensure **19** that the control objectives that are described are sufficient to satisfy the Regulator's DC Code and related DC Guides and to add further objectives and supporting control procedures if appropriate.

It is expected that trustees of Master Trusts will report on all the control objectives **20** set out in Appendix 1 of this Supplement. If certain control objectives are not relevant to the master trust and are therefore omitted, this is explained in the report by the trustees of the Master Trust (see Appendix 2) and highlighted in the independent practitioners' assurance report where disclosure of the omission together with an explanation has not been provided in the report by the trustees of the Master Trust (see paragraphs 63 to 65). Suitable governance control procedures established by trustees will vary from Master Trust to Master Trust

Practical guidelines in the Regulator's DC code and related DC Guides should **21** form the primary basis of guidance for trustees when establishing governance control procedures, as well as reference material for independent practitioners when undertaking Master Trust assurance engagements.

The subject matter of the assurance reporting envisaged by this guidance may be **22** either: (a) the description and design of the governance control procedures established by the trustees of the Master Trust and their operating effectiveness over a period of time (Type 2 report); or (b) the description and design of governance control procedures established by the trustees of the Master Trust only at the point in time specified (Type 1 report).

The guidance that follows assumes that the report will cover a period of time. **23** However a report on governance control procedures at a point in time is an option, for example when preparing a report for the first time. This transitional provision recognises the fact that trustees may need time to establish and formalise governance control procedures to enable them to be evidenced. In some cases the governance control procedures may take time to develop and implement so a point in time engagement provides an interim assurance solution.

Trustees may wish to provide a report that covers a period of time that aligns **24** Master Trust assurance reporting with their financial accounting period and statutory audit.

EFFECTIVE DATE AND TRANSITIONAL ARRANGEMENTS

This revised Supplement is effective for all Type 2 reporting periods commencing **25** after 31 December 2016 and Type 1 reports that fall after this date. The Regulator expects Master Trusts to adopt this revised Supplement in accordance with these timescales.

26   Where possible, early adoption of this revised Supplement is encouraged. However, for Master Trusts that are in the process of or have already reported under the previous Supplement, the following transitional arrangements apply:

(a)   Type 1 reports dated after 31 December 2016 applicable to Master Trusts newly adopting the framework should adopt this revised Supplement. However, if significant work has already commenced at the date this revised Supplement was published it may be justifiable to prepare the report using the previous Supplement, although a note to this effect should be included in the report by the trustees. All subsequent Type 2 reports should adopt the revised Supplement.

(b)   Type 2 reports whose reporting periods straddle the 31 December 2016, for example 31 March 2017 reporting year ends, are encouraged to adopt this revised Supplement, although if a significant level of work has already been undertaken, trustees may decide to prepare the report under the previous Supplement. In this example, subsequent Type 2 reports should be prepared in accordance with this revised Supplement.

27   It is important to note that the revised DC code and related DC Guides came into effect in July 2016, superseding the previous DC code and DC regulatory guidance. Trustees adopting this revised Supplement and control objectives, and independent practitioners, should be familiar with the requirements in the new regulatory material underpinning this Supplement.

ASSURANCE REPORTING ON GOVERNANCE CONTROL PROCEDURES ESTABLISHED BY TRUSTEES OF MASTER TRUSTS

The responsibility of trustees of the Master Trust

28   Trustees of the Master Trust evaluate their governance control procedures, and related scheme operations, at all stages of the pension life-cycle by reference to all the control objectives set out in Appendix 1 and relevant legal requirements and standards of governance as set out in the Regulator's DC code and related DC Guides.

Assurance reporting on the trustees governance control procedures

29   The IAASB Assurance Framework, on whose principles ISAE 3000 and AAF 02/07 are based, sets out five elements of an assurance engagement. These five elements are:

- three party relationship;
- an appropriate subject matter;
- suitable criteria;
- sufficient appropriate evidence; and
- a written assurance report in the form appropriate to the type of assurance engagement.

30   Certain aspects of these elements are likely to require specific consideration in the context of this Supplement. These are a three party relationship, an appropriate subject matter, suitable criteria and sufficient appropriate evidence and are discussed below.

A three party relationship

Assurance engagements involve three parties: a responsible party, intended users, and a practitioner.   **31**

Responsible party

The responsible party performs operations or provides information for the benefit of the intended user and hence is responsible for the subject matter over which assurance is sought. The responsible party in the context of this Supplement are the trustees of the Master Trust. Trustees are responsible for the governance of the Master Trust.   **32**

The trustees of the Master Trust prepare a written report setting out their responsibilities and describing the governance control procedures established by the trustees of the Master Trust to support the control objectives set out in this Supplement. The report also includes the trustees' assertion on the description, design and operating effectiveness of those governance control procedures established by the trustees. When making this assertion in their report, the trustees state that it is referring to all the control objectives in this Supplement. Where this is not the case the trustees should explain this and the reason why a control objective has been omitted or a new control objective included in their assertion.   **33**

Example paragraphs from an illustrative trustees' statement are set out in Appendix 2.   **34**

The trustees of the Master Trust communicate to the practitioner the purpose of their report and the associated assurance reporting needed.   **35**

Intended users

The intended users of an AAF 02/07 report are typically expected to be employers who have entrusted their employees' contributions to the Master Trust, or are considering doing so (i.e. actual or potential customers of the Master Trust). It should also be recognised that the Regulator is likely to be an intended user where the master trust is seeking to go on, and remain on, the Regulator's master trust list (see paragraph 9). Depending on the purpose of reporting by the trustees of a Master Trust, the intended users would vary, and Reporting Accountants should determine who the intended users are likely to be at the outset.   **36**

It is also acknowledged that scheme members may also want to read the report, but are not generally expected to be a typical intended user.   **37**

One of the purposes of seeking independent assurance over trustee reporting on control objectives and supporting control procedures will be to enhance the confidence of the trustees over their procedures related to governance. Assurance reporting should also help increase the confidence of current and prospective users.   **38**

Practitioner

The practitioner performs the assurance engagement on the Master Trust's governance control procedures established by the trustees of the Master Trust. Relevant, generic guidance for the practitioner is set out in AAF 02/07 in the section entitled (a) Engagement with the responsible party within Third party operations (paragraphs 13–15) and where the responsible party is the client in AAF 02/07 (paragraphs 58–61).   **39**

40   When requested to provide an assurance report, the practitioner needs to clarify the purpose for which the assurance report is being sought, the party (or parties) seeking to benefit from the assurance report, and the use that will be made of the assurance report.

An appropriate subject matter

41   The subject matter in assurance reporting envisaged in this Supplement is the governance control procedures established by the trustees of the Master Trust. The trustees prepare a written report describing the governance control procedures that have been designed and implemented to deliver their Master Trust operations at a given date or for a given period having regard to all the control objectives as set out in this Supplement and further control objectives deemed relevant to the governance of the Master Trust, see paragraph 50 below.

42   Where aspects of governance (including certain administrative activities) of the Master Trust are outsourced (including those where the outsourced provider is a related party of the Master Trust), the trustees describe how they monitor those outsourced activities, including relevant control objectives, and may obtain an appropriate assurance report from the service organisation to which the trustees of the Master Trust has outsourced these operations as part of their evidence of monitoring those outsourced activities. Further generic guidance on outsourcing can be found in AAF 02/07 in the section entitled Responsible parties that use other organisations (paragraphs 78–82).

43   This assurance report would form part of the evidence of the trustees' monitoring of those outsourced activities when determining standards of governance established by the trustees of the Master Trust.

Suitable criteria

44   All the control objectives in Appendix 1 are considered to be suitable criteria for the evaluation of the governance control procedures established by the trustees of the Master Trust in so far as they:

- address key risks to members in DC schemes; and
- are complete and appropriate to the functions and provision of Master Trust services.

45   Control objectives:

- need to be relevant, complete, reliable, neutral and understandable so as to communicate the basis of the evaluation;
- are not intended to be exhaustive. The control objectives specified in Appendix 1 are intended to be a minimum set of control objectives for inclusion in the Master Trust report prepared by the trustees. However, it remains the responsibility of the trustees of the Master Trust to ensure that the control objectives that it describes are sufficient and to add further objectives and supporting governance control procedures where appropriate.

46   The trustees of the Master Trust describe their governance control procedures for a set of associated control objectives. The trustees explain in their report how the governance control procedures relate to the control objectives.

47   If there are omissions or misstatements with regard to the control objectives, in particular in the report by the trustees of the Master Trust, the practitioner asks the trustees to amend the description. This would include any new control objectives introduced by the trustees of the Master Trust. If it is not amended the practitioner considers the need to state that fact in their report.

Exceptionally, the trustees may determine that a control objective is not relevant to **48** their particular Master Trust's circumstances. Where this is the case, the trustees should explain why the control objective is not relevant in order to give users an understanding of the omission, and this should be included in their statement. An example where this could occur is where governance control procedures related to a particular control objective were still under development, but the trustees wanted to still seek assurance over the operational effectiveness of control procedures related to other control objectives. Any other omissions should be accompanied with a reasonable justification.

Suitable governance control procedures will vary from Master Trust to Master **49** Trust therefore disclosure of how each objective is addressed by trustees of a particular Master Trust is likely to be specific to each Master Trust.

Where the trustees of the Master Trust apply additional control objectives

Relevant control objectives that trustees need to have regard to are detailed in **50** Appendix 1. However, the trustees may include additional objectives if they consider them to be relevant and appropriate. If this is the case the trustee should report this fact in their trustee statement.

Other information provided by trustees of Master Trusts

The trustees of a Master Trust may include in their report information that is not a **51** part of the description of control objectives and associated governance control procedures.

If trustees of a Master Trust include other information in their report, they should **52** make it clear that this information would be outside the scope of assurance reporting unless there is a specific agreement with the practitioners in the engagement letter that it should be included.

Sufficient appropriate evidence

The trustees of the Master Trust are responsible for providing information to **53** practitioners on specific governance control procedures in place to meet the control objectives, to help the practitioner obtain sufficient evidence. Where the practitioners are unable to test a described governance control procedure because, for example, it has not operated during the year, they state the fact that no tests have been carried out and the reason in their description of tests.

ASSURANCE REPORT

A written assurance report in the form appropriate to the type of assurance engagement

Guidance for practitioners

Practitioners refer to the principles set out in AAF 02/07 which includes the role of **54** practitioners in the assurance reporting framework envisaged in AAF 02/07 (paragraphs 29–32).

Practitioners refer to the section entitled Guidance for practitioners (paragraphs **55** 46–105) and apply them as appropriate to the engagement. This includes guidance on accepting an engagement, planning and performing an engagement, the nature, timing and extent of tests and assurance reporting. In particular, practitioners understand and agree the scope and the purpose of the assurance engagement between the parties to the engagement as set out in the sub-section entitled agreeing the terms of engagement, as set out in AAF 02/07 (paragraphs 57–65) and in doing so refer to AAF 04/06 Assurance engagements: Management of risk and liability.

56   Practitioners note that they are governed by ethical and quality control requirements as set out AAF 02/07 (paragraphs 51–56) and ISAE 3000.

Assurance report

57   Practitioners conclude on the fairness of the description and the design and operating effectiveness of governance control procedures in relation to a specified reporting period. The practitioners' conclusion is expressed in a written assurance report attached to the trustees' report.

58   The assurance report reflects the agreement set out in the engagement letter. The report makes it clear for whom it is prepared and who is entitled to rely upon it and for what purpose as established in accordance with AAF 04/06.

59   A pro-forma practitioners' assurance report on the governance control procedures established by the trustees of the Master Trust is available in Appendix 3.

Assurance reporting limitations

60   Governance control procedures have inherent limitations and accordingly errors and irregularities may occur and not be detected. Also governance control procedures cannot guarantee protection against fraudulent collusion especially on the part of those holding positions of authority or trust. Practitioners refer to such inherent limitations in their report. Conclusions reached by the Reporting Accountant are based on historical information and the projection of any information or conclusions in the report to any future periods would be inappropriate.

61   The Master Trust assurance framework is designed to provide reasonable assurance over the design, description and operational effectiveness of specific governance control procedures established by the trustees. The scope of engagement terms and work undertaken by the Reporting Accountant will be set out in the terms of engagement which should be appended to the report.

Reporting on description misstatements, design deficiencies or when governance control procedures are not operating effectively

62   Practitioners discuss with the trustees when they become aware that the control objectives in place are not in accordance with all those set out in Appendix 1 so that the trustees can amend the description to include the specified control objective(s). If the trustees do not do so the practitioners add an explanation in the assurance report identifying the omitted or inappropriate control objective(s) to draw the attention of the relevant users. In addition, the wording of the conclusion paragraph may also be modified.

63   Where specified control objectives are omitted, trustees should give an explanation. The trustees should adopt the same approach if control objectives additional to those in Appendix 1 are included. If the trustees do not do so the practitioners add an explanation in the assurance report identifying additional or inappropriate control objective(s) to draw the attention of the intended users.

Practitioners note that it is the responsibility of the trustees and not the practitioners to ensure the completeness and the reasonableness of governance control procedures. Although practitioners may qualify their conclusion on the fairness of the description of control procedures, for example where governance control procedures are not clearly described or are misstated, this does not necessarily affect the suitability of design or operating effectiveness of the governance control procedures. **64**

Where governance control procedures associated with stated control objectives are incomplete or inappropriate, practitioners also discuss this with the trustees of the Master Trust so that they may amend the description to include the associated governance control procedures. If the trustees do not amend the description, the practitioners add an explanatory paragraph preceding the conclusion to the report identifying the omitted or inappropriate control procedures to draw the attention of the users of the report. In addition, the wording of the conclusion paragraph may be modified. **65**

Where practitioners conclude that a set of governance control procedures are not suitably designed in relation to a specified control objective, this is reported after the description of the test and they consider the design deficiencies in their overall assessment of the governance control procedures. If the practitioners determine that governance control procedures are not suitably designed to achieve a specified control objective, they add an explanatory paragraph preceding the conclusion to the report identifying the design deficiencies and modify their conclusion. **66**

Where practitioners' tests identify exceptions to the operating effectiveness of the governance control procedures, they consider whether this exception means that a control objective has not been achieved. In some cases deficiencies may be so pervasive that the practitioners modify their conclusion on the achievement of one or more control objectives or issue an adverse opinion. **67**

Where significant changes are introduced during the period covered by the report, the trustees of the Master Trust report this fact. If practitioners become aware that the description on changes is missing, they request the trustees to amend the description. **68**

APPENDIX 1: CONTROL OBJECTIVES ADDRESSING GOVERNANCE ARRANGEMENTS ESTABLISHED BY TRUSTEES OF MASTER TRUSTS

This Appendix sets out those control objectives that should be adopted by trustees of Master Trusts (Table 1) for the purposes of reporting under this Supplement which were developed in association with the Regulator.

The control objectives in Table 1 are not intended to be exhaustive. However, they represent the minimum set of control objectives for Master Trust assurance reporting purposes. It remains the responsibility of the trustees to ensure that the described control objectives are sufficient to meet standards of governance the Regulator would expect, as described in the Regulator's DC code of practice[1] and related DC Guides[2] published in July 2016.

Practical guidelines in each of these documents should form the primary basis of guidance for trustees when implementing governance control procedures applicable to the control objectives, as well as reference material for independent practitioners when undertaking Master Trust assurance engagements.

The governance control procedures established by the trustees of the Master Trust should be evaluated against all the control objectives to the extent that the trustees consider that they are relevant to their Master Trust activities.

Trustees may decide not to include a particular control objective, perhaps because (i) control procedures that underpin the control objective are not fully established or (ii) the trustees determine that the control objective is not relevant to their Master Trust.

Where control objectives set out in Table 1 are not included, the trustees of the Master Trust should in all cases explain in their report the fact and reasons for the omission.

For the purpose of being added to the Regulator's list of Master Trusts that have obtained Master Trust assurance services, among other things the trustees should ensure that, where relevant, in the introductory section of the report there is a summary of any exceptions, and in more serious cases any modifications, to the Reporting Accountant's assurance report (see paragraph 9).

Table 1 – The Master Trust assurance framework minimum set of control objectives

Value for members

Assessing value for members

1. A value for money assessment is undertaken annually and the process followed is documented and approved. The assessment should include value to members derived from scheme management and governance, administration, investment governance and communications.

Management of costs and charges

2. Disclosure of information to members of costs and charges (rates (%) and amounts (£)) are complete and accurate.

---

[1] http://www.thepensionsregulator.gov.uk/codes/code-governance-administration-occupational-dc-trust-based-schemes.aspx

[2] http://www.thepensionsregulator.gov.uk/guidance/guidance-dc-schemes.aspx

Investment governance

Protection of assets

3. Scheme and member assets or entitlements are safeguarded from loss, misappropriation and unauthorised use. Financial protection and compensation available to members in the event of a default is assessed and documented.

4. The design and on-going suitability of the default arrangement and range and risk profile of other investment options are regularly reviewed and monitored. This review is documented and the investment aims and objectives for the arrangement and investment policies for all investment options are included in an approved Statement of Investment Principles.

5. The performance of each investment option including the default arrangement(s) in which member funds are invested are regularly reviewed and monitored against objectives in the Statement of Investment Principles. This review is documented and approved.

The trustee board

6. Fitness and propriety requirements for trustees are recorded and managed in accordance with a policy which is regularly reviewed and approved. The fitness and propriety of trustees is reviewed prior to appointment and annually thereafter. This review is documented and approved.

Scheme management skills

7. Conflicts of interest are subject to ongoing monitoring and are identified, recorded and managed in accordance with a defined policy which is regularly reviewed and approved.

8. Trustee levels of knowledge and understanding are managed and maintained in accordance with an approved training and development plan. This plan is regularly reviewed and updated.

9. A business/resource plan is maintained, that sets out when scheme related activities are due to take place or be completed, and regularly reviewed to ensure that resources are available and allocated.

10. Roles, responsibilities and duties of all trustees, advsiers and service providers are documented and the performance and quality of their service is subject to regular documented reviews. The suitability of advisers and service providers is reviewed against criteria before appointment and this review is documented.

11. Discontinuance plans, which address how member assets or entitlements are safeguarded in the event of the Master Trust or any key service provider failing, defaulting or transferring ownership, are documented, approved and maintained.

12. A risk management framework is established to identify, evaluate and treat scheme risks. Risks are recorded in a risk register which is reviewed at least annually.

Administration

Core financial transactions

13. Core financial transactions are processed promptly and accurately.

14. Contributions are invested and allocated in accordance with member instructions or the requirements of the default arrangement.

15. Transaction errors are identified and rectified.

16. Cash is safeguarded and all payments are suitably authorised and controlled.

17. Late and inaccurate contributions are pursued and resolved. Core financial transactions are processed promptly and accurately.

Business and disaster recovery

18. Data and systems are backed up regularly, retained offsite and regularly tested for recoverability. Business and information systems recovery plans are documented, approved, tested and maintained.

19. The capacity of an administration system to take on new business is assessed, approved and regularly monitored.

20. New business take-ons are properly established in accordance with Master Trust's rules and contractual arrangements.

Data quality and security

21. Member data is complete and accurate and is subject to regular data evaluation.

22. Monitoring of operations implemented to support the security of data transmissions and measures implemented to mitigate the threat of malicious electronic attack are regularly reviewed and documented.

23. Physical and logical access to computer systems, and member and Master Trust records and data, is restricted to authorised persons.

24. IT equipment is maintained in a controlled environment and the maintenance and development of systems, applications and software is authorised, tested approved and implemented.

Communication and reporting

25. Retirements are managed in accordance with a documented process which is regularly reviewed and approved.

26. Member communications are accurate, clear and understandable and are produced in accordance with a communications plan. The plan is regularly reviewed and monitored.

27. Member communications contain information to support the decisions members need to make at retirement.

APPENDIX 2: EXAMPLE PARAGRAPHS FROM THE REPORT BY THE TRUSTEES OF THE MASTER TRUST

The following text contains example paragraphs from an illustrative trustees' statement.

As trustees of [name of Master Trust], we are responsible for the identification of control objectives relating to the governance of the Master Trust and for establishing governance control procedures that provide reasonable assurance that the control objectives are achieved. Those control objectives are derived from standards of governance set out in the Regulators DC code of practice and DC guides.

In carrying out those responsibilities, we have regard not only to the interest of employers (who have entrusted their employees' DC contributions to the Master Trust, or are considering doing so) and members of the Master Trust but also to the needs of the trust business and the general effectiveness and efficiency of the relevant operations.

We have evaluated the effectiveness of the [name of Master Trust]'s governance control procedures having regard to ICAEW's Technical Release AAF 02/07 including its Master Trusts Supplement and the control objectives set out therein. [Details of any omissions of control objectives included in this Supplement to be referred to here along with control objectives that are additional to those included in Table 1 above.]

We set out in this report a description of the relevant governance control procedures established by the trustees of [name of Master Trust] together with the related control objectives which operated during the period [x] to [y] and confirm that:

(a) the report describes fairly the governance control procedures established by the trustees that relate to the control objectives referred to above which were in place throughout the period [date] to [date];

(b) the governance control procedures described were suitably designed throughout the period [x] to [y] such that there is reasonable assurance that the specified control objectives would be achieved if the described governance control procedures were complied with satisfactorily; and

(c) the governance control procedures described were operating with sufficient effectiveness to provide reasonable assurance that the related control objectives were achieved throughout the specified period.

Trustee

Date

Signed on behalf of the trustees of [name of Master Trustee]

APPENDIX 3: A PRO FORMA PRACTITIONER'S ASSURANCE REPORT ON GOVERNANCE CONTROL PROCEDURES ESTABLISHED BY THE TRUSTEES OF MASTER TRUSTS

Practitioners issue an assurance report in a form suitable for the specific engagement. The report below is adapted from a pro forma assurance report (ii) (a) Appendix 2 of AAF 02/07 for the purpose of reporting in relation to the Master Trust's control objectives related to its governance as set out in the trustees report.

Independent practitioner's assurance report on the governance control procedures established by trustees of Master Trusts

To xxxxx (See AAF 02/07 for wording)

Use of report

Example wordings to describe applicable restrictions on the use of the report, together with supporting guidance on alternative forms of engagement and associated duties of care arising, are set out in AAF 02/07, Appendix 2 (ii).

However, restrictions should not exclude the use of the report by customers of the Master Trust who wish to obtain a better understanding of the governance arrangements established by the trustees of the Master Trust.

Scope

We have been engaged to report on the description of governance control procedures established by the trustees of the [name of Master Trust] throughout the period [date] to [date] and on the suitability of the design and operating effectiveness of those governance control procedures stated in the description.

Trustees' responsibilities

The trustees' responsibilities and statement are set out on page [] of your report. The control objectives stated in the description include those control objectives set out in the Master Trusts Supplement to AAF 02/07 that are considered relevant by the trustees.

Our responsibilities

Our responsibility is to form an independent opinion, based on the work carried out in relation to the governance control procedures established by the trustees of [name of Master Trust] as described in your report and report this to you. We conducted our engagement in accordance with International Standard on Assurance Engagements (ISAE) 3000 and with ICAEW Technical Release AAF 02/07 including its Master Trusts Supplement. ISAE 3000 and AAF 02/07 require, among other things, that we comply with ethical and other professional requirements.

We plan and perform our procedures to obtain reasonable assurance about whether, in all material respects, the description is fairly presented and the governance control procedures were suitably designed and operating effectively. The criteria against which the control procedures were evaluated are the control objectives developed for Master Trusts as set out within the Master Trust Supplement to AAF 02/07 and identified by the trustees as control objectives to be applied for the purpose of governance.

Our work involved performing procedures to obtain evidence about the presentation of the trustees' description of the governance control procedures and the design and operating effectiveness of those governance control procedures. Our procedures include assessing the risks that the description is not fairly presented, and that the governance control procedures were not suitably designed or operating effectively. Our procedures also included testing the operating effectiveness of those governance control procedures that we considered necessary to obtain reasonable assurance that the control objectives stated in the description were achieved. An assurance engagement of this type also included evaluating the overall presentation of the description and the suitability of the control objectives stated therein.

Our independence and quality control

We have complied with the independence and other ethical requirements of the "Code of Ethics for Professional Accountants" issued by the International Ethics Standards Board for Accountants which is founded on fundamental principles of integrity, objectivity, professional competence and due care, confidentiality and professional behaviour.

The firm applies International Standard on Quality Contrail and accordingly maintains a comprehensive system of quality control, including documented policies and procedures regarding compliance with ethical requirements, professional standards and applicable legal and regulatory requirements.

Inherent limitations

The trustees' description of governance control procedures was prepared to meet the common needs of a broad range of users and may not, therefore, include every aspect of the governance control procedures that may be relevant to each participating employer or member of the Master Trust. Also, because of their nature, governance control procedures may not prevent or detect and correct all errors or omissions in performing governance activities. Our opinion is based on historical information. The projection of any evaluation of the fairness of the presentation of the description, or opinion about the suitability of the design or operating effectiveness of the governance control procedures to future periods would be inappropriate.

Opinion

In our opinion, in all material respects:

(i)   the accompanying Master Trust's report fairly presents the governance control procedures established by the trustees that relate to the control objectives referred to above which were in place throughout the period [date] to [date];

(ii)   the governance control procedures established by the trustees described on pages [] to [] were suitably designed to provide reasonable, but not absolute, assurance that the specified control objectives would have been achieved if the described governance control procedures operated effectively throughout the period; and

(iii)   the governance control procedures established by the trustees that were tested were operating with sufficient effectiveness to provide reasonable, but not absolute, assurance that the related control objectives were achieved throughout the period [date] to [date].

[Name of firm]

Chartered accountants

[Location]

[Date]

ICAEW is a world leading professional membership organisation that promotes, develops and supports over 147,000 chartered accountants worldwide. We provide qualifications and professional development, share our knowledge, insight and technical expertise, and protect the quality and integrity of the accountancy and finance profession.

As leaders in accountancy, finance and business our members have the knowledge, skills and commitment to maintain the highest professional standards and integrity. Together we contribute to the success of individual, organisations, communities and economies around the world.

Because of us, people can do business with confidence.

We are a founder member of Chartered Accountants Worldwide and the Global Accounting Alliance.

www.charteredaccountantsworldwide.com

www.globalaccountingalliance.com

Part Eight

Standards for Investment Reporting (SIRs)

SIR 1000: Investment Reporting Standards applicable to all engagements in connection with an Investment Circular

(July 2005)

Contents

	Paragraphs
Introduction	1 - 5
Engagement acceptance and continuance	6 - 9
Agreeing the terms of the engagement	10 - 17
Ethical requirements	18 - 19
Legal and regulatory requirements	20 - 21
Quality control	22 - 27
Planning and performing the engagement	28 - 45
Documentation	46 - 49
Professional scepticism	50 - 52
Reporting	53 - 61
Modified opinions	62 - 64
Pre-existing financial information	65
Consent	66 - 74
Events occurring between the date of the reporting accountant's report and the completion date of the transaction	75 - 77
Effective date	78

Appendices
1. Summary of possible reporting accountant's public reporting engagements under the Prospectus Rules
2. Principal legal and regulatory requirements
3. Example of a content letter
4. Glossary of terms

Cross-reference – see also ISA (UK And Ireland) 720 (Revised)

The Auditing Practices Board Limited, which is part of the Financial Reporting Council, prepares for use within the United Kingdom and the Republic of Ireland:

- Standards and guidance for auditing;

- Standards and guidance for the work of reporting accountants in connection with investment circulars; and

- Standards and guidance for auditors' and reporting accountants' integrity, objectivity and independence

with the objective of enhancing public confidence in the audit process and the quality and relevance of audit services in the public interest.

The Auditing Practices Board Limited discharges its responsibilities through a Board ("the APB") comprising individuals who are eligible for appointment as company auditors, and those who are not so eligible. Those who are eligible for appointment as company auditors may not exceed 40% of the APB by number.

Neither the Auditing Practices Board Limited nor the APB accepts any liability to any party for any loss, damage or costs howsoever arising, whether directly or indirectly, whether in contract, tort or otherwise from any action or decision taken (or not taken) as a result of any person relying on or otherwise using this document or arising from any omission from it.

Investment Reporting Standards applicable to all engagements in connection with an investment circular

SIR 1000 contains basic principles and essential procedures ("Investment Reporting Standards"), indicated by paragraphs in bold type, with which a reporting accountant is required to comply in the conduct of all engagements in connection with an investment circular prepared for issue in connection with a securities transaction governed wholly or in part by the laws and regulations of the United Kingdom.

SIR 1000 also includes explanatory and other material, including appendices, in the context of which the basic principles and essential procedures are to be understood and applied. It is necessary to consider the whole text of the SIR to understand and apply the basic principles and essential procedures.

The definitions in the glossary of terms set out in Appendix 4 are to be applied in the interpretation of this and all other SIRs. Terms defined in the glossary are underlined the first time that they occur in the text.

This SIR replaces SIR 100 "Investment circulars and reporting accountants" issued in December 1997.

To assist readers, SIRs contain references to, and extracts from, certain legislation and chapters of the Rules of the UK Listing Authority. Readers are cautioned that these references may change subsequent to publication.

Introduction

The application of Standards for Investment Reporting (SIRs) is best understood by reference to the following four defined terms used throughout the SIRs:

1

(a) **investment circular** is a generic term defined as *"Any document issued by an entity pursuant to statutory or regulatory requirements relating to securities on which it is intended that a third party should make an investment decision, including a prospectus, listing particulars, a circular to shareholders or similar document"*;

(b) **reporting accountant** is defined as *"An accountant engaged to prepare a report for inclusion in, or in connection with, an investment circular." The reporting accountant may or may not be the auditor of the entity issuing the investment circular. The term "reporting accountant" is used to describe either the engagement partner or the engagement partner's firm[1]. The reporting accountant could be a limited company or an engagement principal employed by the company;*

(c) **public reporting engagement** is defined as *"An engagement in which a reporting accountant expresses a conclusion that is published in an investment circular, and which is designed to enhance the degree of confidence of the intended users of the report about the "outcome[2]" of the directors' evaluation or measurement of "subject matter" against "suitable criteria""*; and

---

[1] *Where the term applies to the engagement partner, it describes the responsibilities or obligations of the engagement partner. Such obligations or responsibilities may be fulfilled by either the engagement partner or a member of the engagement partner's team.*

[2] *The "outcome" is sometimes described as "subject matter information."*

(d) **private reporting engagement** is defined as *"An engagement, in connection with an investment circular, in which a reporting accountant does not express a conclusion that is published in an investment circular"*. Private reporting engagements are likely to involve the reporting accountant reporting privately to one or more of an issuer, sponsor or regulator.

2   In order to provide flexibility to develop SIRs for a wide range of possible public reporting engagements, the description of public reporting engagement includes three generic terms. Their meanings are as follows:

(a) the "**subject matter**" of the engagement is that which is being evaluated or measured against suitable criteria. Examples of subject matter are the entity's financial position and the directors' expectation of the issuer's profit for the period covered by a profit forecast;

(b) criteria are the benchmarks used to evaluate or measure the subject matter. "**Suitable criteria**" are usually derived from laws and regulations and are required by directors to enable them to make reasonably consistent evaluations or measurements of the subject matter. With respect to public reporting engagements the suitable criteria for specific types of engagement are described in the individual SIR dealing with such engagements. Where the reporting accountant's engagement requires it to consider only certain criteria, such criteria are described as "reporting accountant's criteria". Reporting accountant's criteria are set out in the SIRs. Where a SIR has not been issued with respect to a particular type of reporting engagement, the reporting accountant uses those criteria that are specified by legislation or regulation. The evaluation or measurement of a subject matter solely on the basis of the reporting accountant's own expectations, judgments and individual experience would not constitute suitable criteria; and

(c) the "**outcome**" of the evaluation or measurement of a subject matter is the information that results from the directors applying the suitable criteria to the subject matter. Examples of outcomes are historical financial information and a directors' profit forecast and related disclosures that are included in an investment circular.

3   Not all engagements performed by a reporting accountant are public reporting engagements. Examples of engagements that are not public reporting engagements include:

● Engagements involving the preparation of a comfort letter;

● Engagements involving the preparation of a long form report.

Such engagements are private reporting engagements.

4   This SIR establishes basic principles and essential procedures for the work of reporting accountants that are common to all reporting engagements (both public and private) relating to investment circulars. Other SIRs set out basic principles and essential procedures to address the particular issues and requirements arising on specific public reporting engagements. These comprise:

(a) SIR 2000 "Investment reporting standards applicable to public reporting engagements on historical financial information";

(b) SIR 3000 "Investment reporting standards applicable to public reporting engagements on profit forecasts"; and

(c) SIR 4000 "Investment reporting standards applicable to public reporting engagements on pro forma financial information".

Appendix 1 summarises public reporting engagements that reporting accountants   **5**
may be required to undertake under the <u>Prospectus Rules</u>.

Engagement acceptance and continuance

The reporting accountant should accept (or continue where applicable) a   **6**
reporting engagement only if, on the basis of a preliminary knowledge of the
engagement circumstances, nothing comes to the attention of the reporting
accountant to indicate that the requirements of relevant ethical standards
and guidance, issued by the Auditing Practices Board and the professional
bodies of which the reporting accountant is a member, will not be satisfied.
(SIR 1000.1)

The reporting accountant should accept (or continue where applicable) a   **7**
reporting engagement only if:

(a)   the scope of the engagement is expected to be sufficient to support the
required report;

(b)   the reporting accountant expects to be able to carry out the procedures
required by the SIRs; and

(c)   those persons who are to perform the engagement collectively possess
the necessary professional competencies. (SIR 1000.2)

In determining whether the scope of the engagement is expected to be sufficient to   **8**
support the required report, the reporting accountant considers whether there
appear to be any significant limitations on the scope of the reporting accountant's
work.

A reporting accountant may be requested to perform reporting engagements on a   **9**
wide range of matters. Some engagements may require specialised skills and
knowledge. In these circumstances the reporting accountant considers using
internal or external specialists having the appropriate skills.

Agreeing the terms of the engagement

The reporting accountant should agree the terms of the engagement with   **10**
those from whom they accept instructions. All the terms of the engagement
should be recorded in writing. (SIR 1000.3)

Generally, a letter is prepared by the reporting accountant, covering all aspects of   **11**
the engagement, and accepted in writing by the directors of the issuer and, where
relevant, the sponsor. With respect to a public reporting engagement the letter will
record the reporting accountant's understanding of what constitutes the subject
matter of the engagement, the suitable criteria, and the information that constitutes
the outcome of the evaluation or measurement of the subject matter against the
suitable criteria.

As an alternative to a letter drafted by the reporting accountant, an instruction   **12**
letter may be issued by the directors and, where relevant, the sponsor. In these
circumstances, its terms are formally acknowledged by the reporting accountant in
writing, clarifying particular aspects of the instructions and covering any matters
that may not have been addressed.

This letter, or exchange of letters (together referred to as "the engagement letter"),   **13**
provides evidence of the contractual relationship between the reporting

accountant, the entity and, where relevant, the sponsor. It sets out clearly the scope and limitations of the work to be performed by the reporting accountant. It also confirms the reporting accountant's acceptance of the engagement and includes a summary of the reporting accountant's responsibilities and those of the directors and, where relevant, the sponsor as they relate to the reporting accountant's role.

14   The engagement letter establishes a direct responsibility to the other parties from the reporting accountant. It is also the mechanism by which the scope of the reporting accountant's contribution is defined and agreed. If in the course of the engagement the terms of the engagement are changed, such changes are similarly agreed, and recorded in writing.

15   The engagement letter will usually set out the form of any reports (public or private) required (including, in each case, the nature of any opinion to be expressed by the reporting accountant). Accordingly, it is important to clarify those from whom the reporting accountant has agreed to accept instructions including, where relevant, sponsors, and determine their requirements and the scope of such reports, at an early stage.

16   **The engagement letter should specify those reports that are intended for publication in the investment circular and any other reports that are required. The engagement letter should specify, in respect of each report, to whom it is to be addressed. (SIR 1000.4)**

17   The engagement letter sets out the express terms governing the reporting accountant's contractual responsibilities in connection with the transaction to those instructing them. Reporting accountants do not accept responsibility beyond the matters or entities in respect of which they are specifically instructed. Nor are they expected to comment or report on matters which more properly fall within the skill and experience of other experts or advisers. They understand, however, the need to apply their own professional skill and experience in interpreting and carrying out their instructions. The reporting accountant may find information outside the defined scope of the engagement that it believes should be disclosed, because, in its view such information is material to the purpose of the investment circular or to the proposed transaction. The reporting accountant discusses such matters with the directors of the issuer and the sponsor, where relevant, and agrees a course of action.

Ethical requirements

18   **In the conduct of an engagement involving an investment circular, the reporting accountant should comply with the applicable ethical standards issued by the Auditing Practices Board. The reporting accountant should also adhere to the relevant ethical guidance of the professional bodies of which the reporting accountant is a member. (SIR 1000.5)**

19   While it is not the responsibility of the reporting accountant to judge the appropriateness, or otherwise, of a proposed transaction, in respect of which they have been engaged, there may be rare circumstances where a reporting accountant considers the proposed transaction, or their proposed association with the transaction, to be so inappropriate that the reporting accountant cannot properly commence work or continue to act.

Legal and regulatory requirements

The reporting accountant should be familiar with the applicable laws and   **20**
regulations governing the report which is to be given. (SIR 1000.6)

The principal legal and regulatory requirements applicable to reporting   **21**
accountants in the United Kingdom are summarised in Appendix 2. Readers are
cautioned that these references may change subsequent to publication of this SIR.

Quality control

The reporting accountant should comply with the applicable standards and   **22**
guidance set out in International Standard on Quality Control (UK and
Ireland) 1 and ISA (UK and Ireland) 220. (SIR 1000.7)

International Standard on Quality Control (UK and Ireland) 1"Quality control for   **23**
firms that perform audits and reviews of historical financial information, and other
assurance and related services engagements" provides standards and guidance on
the system of quality control that a firm establishes.

The quality control procedures that an engagement partner applies are those set out   **24**
in ISA (UK and Ireland) 220 *Quality control for audits of historical financial*
information. In applying ISA (UK and Ireland) 220, the terms "audit" and "audit
engagement" are read as "reporting accountant's engagement" and the term
"auditor's report" is read as "reporting accountant's report".

When undertaking any engagement involving an investment circular a   **25**
partner with appropriate experience should be involved in the conduct of
the work. (SIR 1000.8)

Reporting accountants are frequently from a firm that is also the auditor of the   **26**
entity. The audit partner, although having knowledge of the entity, may not have
the necessary experience to take responsibility for all aspects of an engagement
involving an investment circular. The extent of involvement of a partner with the
requisite experience of dealing with investment circulars is determined, for
example, by the expertise required to make the reports that the reporting
accountant has agreed to provide and the experience of the audit partner.

In some cases it may be appropriate for the partner with the requisite experience of   **27**
dealing with investment circulars to act as a second partner. In other cases it may
be appropriate for such a partner to be the lead engagement partner.

Planning and performing the engagement

The reporting accountant should develop and document a plan for the work   **28**
so as to perform the engagement in an effective manner. (SIR 1000.9)

Planning is an essential component of all reporting accountant's engagements.   **29**
Examples of the main matters to be considered include:

● The terms of the engagement;

● Ethical considerations;

● Whether the timetable is realistic;

● The reporting accountant's understanding of the entity and its environment;

- Identifying potential problems that could impact the performance of the engagement;
- The need for the involvement of specialists.

30   Planning is not a discrete phase, but rather an iterative process throughout the engagement. As a result of unexpected events, changes in conditions or the evidence obtained from the results of evidence-gathering procedures, the reporting accountant may need to revise the overall strategy and engagement plan, and thereby the resulting planned nature, timing and extent of further procedures.

31   A preliminary review of the available information may provide an indication of potential issues that might need to be addressed in carrying out the engagement. If the preliminary review indicates that there are factors which may give rise to a qualification or other modification of any report, then such factors are reported immediately to the directors and, where relevant, the sponsor.

32   Changes in circumstances, or unexpected results of work carried out, may require the plan to be amended as work progresses. Any such amendments are documented. Where the changes affect the work set out in the engagement letter, the engagement letter is also amended as necessary following agreement with the directors, and where relevant, the sponsor.

33   **The reporting accountant should consider materiality in planning its work in accordance with its instructions and in determining the effect of its findings on the report to be issued. (SIR 1000.10)**

34   Matters are material if their omission or misstatement could, individually or collectively, influence the economic decisions of users of the outcome. Materiality depends on the size and nature of the omission or misstatement judged in light of the surrounding circumstances. The size or nature of the matter, or a combination of both, could be the determining factor.

35   In certain circumstances, such as private reporting engagements to report the results of agreed-upon procedures, materiality may have been determined for the reporting accountant within the scope of the engagement.

36   **The reporting accountant should obtain sufficient appropriate evidence on which to base the report provided. (SIR 1000.11)**

37   The reporting accountant, either directly or indirectly, will seek to obtain evidence derived from one or more of the following procedures: inspection, observation, enquiry, confirmation, computation and analytical procedures. The choice of which of these, or which combination, is appropriate will depend on the circumstances of each engagement and on the form of opinion (if any) to be given. Guidance on considerations applicable in particular circumstances is given in other SIRs which address the particular issues and requirements arising on specific engagements.

38   The evidence gathered in support of an individual report takes account of the information gathered and conclusions drawn in support of other reporting engagements in connection with the transaction.

39   **If the reporting accountant becomes aware of any withholding, concealment or misrepresentation of information, it should take steps, as soon as practicable, to consider its obligation to report such findings and, if necessary, take legal advice to determine the appropriate response. (SIR 1000.12)**

In preparing any report the reporting accountant relies on information supplied to **40** it by the directors, employees or agents of the entity that is the subject of the reporting accountant's enquiries. The engagement letter may limit the extent of the reporting accountant's responsibility where information which is material to the report has been withheld from, concealed from or misrepresented to the reporting accountant. Notwithstanding any such limitation, the reporting accountant does not accept such information without further inquiry where, applying its professional skill and experience to the engagement, the information provided, prima facie, gives rise to doubts about its validity.

The reporting accountant normally informs the directors of the issuer and the **41** sponsor, where relevant, as soon as practicable, of any withholding, concealment or misrepresentation of information. The reporting accountant's duty of confidentiality would ordinarily preclude reporting to a third party. However, in certain circumstances, that duty of confidentiality is overridden by law, for example, in the case of suspected money laundering it may be appropriate to report the matter direct to the appropriate authority. The reporting accountant may need to seek legal advice in such circumstances, giving due consideration to any public interest considerations.

The reporting accountant should obtain appropriate written confirmation of **42** **representations from the directors of the entity. (SIR 1000.13)**

Written confirmation of representations made by the directors on matters material **43** to the reporting accountant's report is ordinarily obtained. These representations also encompass statements or opinions attributed to directors, management, employees or agents of an entity, which are relied upon by the reporting accountant.

This may be achieved by the directors confirming that they have read a final draft **44** of the report and that to the best of their knowledge and belief:

(a)   they have made available to the reporting accountant all significant information, relevant to the report, of which they have knowledge;

(b)   the report is factually accurate, no material facts have been omitted and the report is not otherwise misleading; and

(c)   the report accurately reflects any opinion or statements attributed therein to the directors, management, employees or agents of the entity.

Representations by the directors of the entity cannot replace the evidence that the **45** reporting accountant could reasonably expect to be available to support any opinion given, if any. An inability to obtain sufficient appropriate evidence regarding a matter could represent a limitation of scope even if a representation has been received on the matter.

Documentation

The reporting accountant should document matters that are significant in **46** **providing evidence that supports the report provided and in providing evidence that the engagement was performed in accordance with SIRs. (SIR 1000.14)**

The reporting accountant should record in the working papers (or, if **47** **applicable, the report) the reporting accountant's reasoning on all significant matters that require the exercise of judgment, and related conclusions. (SIR 1000.15)**

48   The information to be recorded in working papers is a matter of professional judgment since it is neither necessary nor practical to document every matter considered by the reporting accountant. When applying professional judgment in assessing the extent of documentation to be prepared and retained, the reporting accountant may consider what is necessary to provide an understanding of the work performed and the basis of the principal decisions taken to another person, such as a reporting accountant, who has no previous experience with the engagement. That other person may, however, only be able to obtain an understanding of detailed aspects of the engagement by discussing them with the reporting accountant who prepared the documentation.

49   The form and content of working papers are affected by matters such as:

- The nature and scope of the engagement;
- The form of the report and the opinion, if any, to be given;
- The nature and complexity of the entity's business;
- The nature and condition of the entity's accounting and internal control systems;
- The needs in the particular circumstances for direction, supervision and review of the work of members of the reporting accountant's team;
- The specific methodology and technology that the reporting accountant uses.

Professional scepticism

50   **The reporting accountant should plan and perform an engagement with an attitude of professional scepticism. (SIR 1000.16)**

51   An attitude of professional scepticism is essential to ensure that the reporting accountant makes a critical assessment, with a questioning mind, of the validity of evidence obtained and is alert to evidence that contradicts or brings into question the reliability of documents or representations.

52   Whilst the reporting accountant may proceed on the basis that information and explanations provided by the directors and management of the issuer are reliable, it assesses them critically and considers them in the context of its knowledge and findings derived from other areas of its work. The reporting accountant is alert for, and, where appropriate reports, on a timely basis, to the directors and sponsors, where relevant, any inconsistencies it considers to be significant. The extent to which the reporting accountant is required to perform further procedures on the information and explanations received will depend upon the reporting accountant's specific instructions, and the level of assurance, if any, it is to provide and the requirements of relevant SIRs.

Reporting

53   **In all reports the reporting accountant should:**

   (a)   **address reports only to those parties who are party to the engagement letter (and on the basis agreed in the engagement letter) or to a relevant regulatory body;**

   (b)   **identify the matters to which the report relates;**

(c)   **address all matters that are required by the engagement letter;**

(d)   **explain the basis of the reporting accountant's work;**

(e)   **give, where applicable, a clear expression of opinion;**

(f)   **include the reporting accountant's manuscript or printed signature;**

(g)   **include the reporting accountant's address; and**

(h)   **date the report. (SIR 1000.17)**

In all public reporting engagements the reporting accountant should explain the basis of the reporting accountant's opinion by including in its report: **54**

(a)   **a statement as to the reporting accountant's compliance, or otherwise, with applicable Standards for Investment Reporting; and**

(b)   **a summary description of the work performed by the reporting accountant. (SIR 1000.18)**

Certain of the reports prepared in connection with investment circulars are public reporting engagements and, therefore, intended for publication in the investment circular. Examples of such reports are accountant's reports, reports on profit forecasts and reports on pro forma financial information. Additional basic principles and essential procedures on the expression of opinions or conclusions relating to these example public reporting engagements are provided as follows: **55**

(a)   accountant's reports on historical financial information, in SIR 2000;

(b)   reports on profit forecasts, in SIR 3000; and

(c)   reports on pro forma financial information, in SIR 4000.

In private reporting engagements the reporting accountant would ordinarily include in its report: **56**

(a)   a statement of compliance with this SIR; and

(b)   either a summary description of the work performed or a cross reference to the description of work to be performed in the engagement letter.

In some private reporting engagements those engaging the reporting accountant agree with the reporting accountant the procedures to be performed[3]. In such cases it may be unnecessary for the report of the reporting accountant to repeat the description of the procedures that is set out in the engagement letter.

Before signing the report, the reporting accountant should consider whether it is appropriate to make the required report, having regard to the scope of the work performed and the evidence obtained. (SIR 1000.19)   **57**

The date of a report is the date on which the reporting accountant signs the report as being suitable for release. However, the reporting accountant should not sign the report (whether modified or not) unless sufficient appropriate evidence has been obtained and all relevant procedures have been finalised. Such procedures include the review procedures of both the engagement partner and the engagement quality control reviewer.   **58**

As noted in paragraph 15 above, the engagement letter usually sets out the form of the report to be issued, including, where applicable, the form of opinion to be expressed. The reporting accountant ensures that the form of report or opinion is consistent with the terms of the engagement letter.   **59**

---

[3] *These are often referred to as "agreed-upon procedures engagements".*

60   The level of assurance, if any, provided by the reporting accountant may vary from engagement to engagement. This reflects the wide range of characteristics of the matters to which the engagements undertaken by reporting accountants relate. To avoid any misunderstanding by the user of the report as to the scope of the opinion or the level of assurance provided, it is important that the matters to which the engagements undertaken by reporting accountants relate are clearly identified and that the reporting accountant's opinion or other assurance is expressed in terms that are appropriate to the particular engagement. Standards and guidance on the form and scope of reports appropriate in particular circumstances is given in other SIRs which address particular issues and requirements relevant to individual reports.

61   In certain circumstances the Prospectus Rules require, "a declaration by those responsible for certain parts of the registration document that, having taken all reasonable care to ensure that such is the case, the information contained in the part of the registration document for which they are responsible is, to the best of their knowledge, in accordance with the facts and contains no omission likely to affect its import". The reporting accountant is responsible for its reports included in investment circulars and ordinarily includes this declaration (when satisfied it is able to do so) at the end of each public report included in an investment circular to which the Prospectus Rules apply.

Modified opinions

62   **The reporting accountant should not express an unmodified opinion when the following circumstances exist and, in the reporting accountant's judgment, the effect of the matter is or may be material:**

(a)   **there is a limitation on the scope of the reporting accountant's work, that is, circumstances prevent, or there are restrictions imposed that prevent, the reporting accountant from obtaining evidence required to reduce engagement risk to the appropriate level; or**

(b)   **the outcome is materially misstated. (SIR 1000.20)**

63   Where not precluded by regulation, the reporting accountant expresses a qualified opinion when the effect of a matter described in paragraph 62 is not so material or pervasive as to require an adverse opinion or a disclaimer of opinion. When giving a qualified opinion, the opinion is expressed "except for" the matter to which the qualification relates.

64   Some regulations require a positive and unmodified opinion. Consequently, in the event that the reporting accountant is unable to report in the manner prescribed it considers, with the parties to whom it is to report, whether the outcome can be amended to alleviate its concerns, or whether the outcome should be omitted from the investment circular.

Pre-existing financial information

65   With respect to historical financial information, where the issuer already has available:

(a)   audited annual <u>financial statements</u>; or

(b)   audited or reviewed financial information, which meet the requirements of the applicable rules in respect of the preparation and presentation of historical financial information to be included in the investment circular,

it may choose to include these financial statements, or financial information, in the investment circular together with the pre-existing reports of the auditor. In these circumstances the audit firm is not required by the Prospectus Rules to consent to the inclusion of its reports in the investment circular.

Consent

Where the reporting accountant is required to give consent to the inclusion of   66 its public report, or references to its name, in an investment circular the reporting accountant should, before doing so, consider its public report in the form and context in which it appears, or is referred to, in the investment circular as a whole by:

(a)   comparing its public report together with the information being reported on to the other information in the rest of the investment circular and assessing whether the reporting accountant has any cause to believe that such other information is inconsistent with the information being reported on; and

(b)   assessing whether the reporting accountant has any cause to believe that any information in the investment circular is misleading.

When the reporting accountant believes information in the investment circular is either inconsistent with its public report, together with the information being reported on, or misleading, the reporting accountant should withhold its consent until the reporting accountant is satisfied that its concerns are unwarranted or until the investment circular has been appropriately amended. (SIR 1000.21)

The reporting accountant should give consent to the inclusion of any report in   67 an investment circular only when all relevant reports that it has agreed to make, in that investment circular, have been finalised. (SIR 1000.22)

In order to comply with the relevant legislation or regulations, the issuer of an   68 investment circular may ask a reporting accountant to provide a consent letter, consenting to the inclusion of public reports in investment circulars in a number of different circumstances. An example consent letter is set out in Appendix 3. The various circumstances include:

(a)   under the Prospectus Rules. These relate to a prospectus issued by an issuer (other than under the Listing Rules). No consent is required to the inclusion of previously issued reports. Where a reporting accountant prepares an accountant's report on a financial information table for the purposes of the prospectus, the reporting accountant's consent must be obtained. A statement referring to the reporting accountant's consent to the inclusion of such report in the prospectus is required, by item 23.1 of Annex I of the Prospectus Rules, to be included in the Prospectus;

(b)   under the Listing Rules. Where these relate to listing particulars prepared in connection with an application for admission of securities to listing, the same consent requirements, that is item 23.1 of Annex I of the Prospectus Rules, apply;

    (c)   under the Listing Rules. Where these relate to a <u>Class 1 circular</u>, paragraph 13.4.1(6) of the Listing Rules sets out similar consent requirements;

    (d)   under the <u>City Code</u>. In connection with a takeover, Rule 28.4 requires a similar consent requirement in respect of a public report on a profit forecast. Rule 28.5 requires a similar consent in connection with a subsequent document issued in connection with the offer; and

    (e)   under the <u>AIM Rules</u>. The consent requirements of item 23.1 of Annex I of the Prospectus Rules apply.

69   Whilst the reporting accountant's reporting responsibilities do not extend beyond its report, the process of giving consent involves an awareness of the overall process whereby the investment circular is prepared, and may entail discussions with those responsible for the document as a whole in relation to its contents.

70   In deciding whether to give its consent, a reporting accountant reads the final version of the investment circular with a view to assessing the overall impression given by the document, having regard to the purposes for which it has been prepared, as well as considering whether there are any inconsistencies between its report and the information in the rest of the document. As part of this process the reporting accountant considers whether it has any cause to believe that any information in the investment circular may be misleading such that the reporting accountant would not wish to be associated with it.

71   For this purpose the engagement partner uses the knowledge of the partners and professional staff working on the engagement. If particular issues are identified the engagement partner may make enquiries of partners and professional staff previously engaged on the audit of financial statements that are the basis of financial information in the investment circular, and any other partners and professional staff who may have been previously consulted regarding such issues, including the engagement quality review partner who is independent of the engagement. The engagement partner is not expected to make enquiries more widely within the reporting accountant's firm.

72   Because of the degree of knowledge required and the increased responsibility that may be assumed, it is inappropriate for a reporting accountant to provide consent unless the reporting accountant has been commissioned to undertake work specifically in connection with the relevant document in relation to the matter for which consent is sought. Hence, if an investment circular includes a reference to a report or opinion, previously provided by the reporting accountant, which is already in the public domain, the reporting accountant is not expected to provide consent to the inclusion of that information and does not generally do so. As discussed in paragraph 65, an example would be the inclusion or incorporation by reference in a prospectus of a previously published audit report or interim review report.

73   An exception to this general rule would be where the reporting accountant has previously consented to the inclusion in an investment circular of that earlier report or opinion and it is being repeated or referred to in connection with the same transaction in respect of which it was originally issued. For example, as noted in paragraph 68 above, Rule 28.5 of the City Code requires a profit forecast made and reported on in one document to be confirmed in any subsequent document in connection with the same offer, and for the reporting accountant to indicate that it has no objection to its report continuing to apply. In such a case, before issuing its consent the reporting accountant makes enquiries as to whether there have been any material events subsequent to the date of its original report which might require modification of or disclosure in that report.

Letters of consent are dated the same date as the relevant document. The City Code requires the letter of consent to be available for public inspection. The letter of consent may be made available for public inspection in other cases.   **74**

Events occurring between the date of the reporting accountant's report and the completion date of the transaction

If, in the period between the date of the reporting accountant's report and the completion date of the transaction, the reporting accountant becomes aware of events and other matters which, had they occurred and been known at the date of the report, might have caused it to issue a different report or withhold consent, the reporting accountant should discuss the implications of them with those responsible for the investment circular and take additional action as appropriate. (SIR 1000.23)   **75**

If, as a result of discussion with those responsible for the investment circular concerning an event that occurred prior to the completion date of the transaction, the reporting accountant is either uncertain about or disagrees with the course of action proposed, it may consider it necessary to take legal advice with respect to its responsibilities in the particular circumstances.   **76**

After the date of its report, the reporting accountant has no obligation to perform procedures or make enquiries regarding the investment circular.   **77**

Effective date

A reporting accountant is required to comply with the Investment Reporting Standards contained in this SIR for reports signed after 31 August 2005. Earlier adoption is encouraged.   **78**

Appendix 1 – Summary of possible reporting accountant's public reporting engagements under the Prospectus Rules

In the following table possible reporting accountant's responsibilities, as set out in the Prospectus Rules, are shaded.

	Shares	Debt, units <50k	Debt, units 50k	Derivatives, units <50k	Derivatives, units 50K	Asset backed securities, units <50k	Asset backed securities, units 50k	Depository receipts, units <50k	Depository receipts, units 50k	Banks issuing anything other than equity securities
Applicable annex:										
Registration document	I, II	IV	IX	IV	IX	VII	VII	X	X	XI
Securities note	III	V	XIII	XII	XII	VIII	VIII	X	X	As relevant instrument type
Historical financial information	I, 20.1	IV, 13.1	IX, 11.1	IV, 13.1	IX, 11.1	VII, 8.2	VII, 8.2 bis	X, 20.1	X, 20.1 bis	XI, 11.1
Number of years	3 years with latest 2 years on new GAAP	2 years with latest year on new GAAP	2 years with latest year on new GAAP	2 years with latest year on new GAAP	2 years with latest year on new GAAP	2 years with latest year on new GAAP	2 years with latest year on new GAAP	3 years with latest 2 years on new GAAP	3 years with latest 2 years on new GAAP	2 years with latest year on new GAAP
GAAP	National GAAP or IFRS[1] as applicable to EU issuer. IFRS or GAAP equivalent to IFRS for non-EU issuers	National GAAP or IFRS[1] as applicable to EU issuer. IFRS or GAAP equivalent to IFRS for non-EU issuers	National GAAP or IFRS[1] as applicable to EU issuer. Non-EU issuers may use local GAAP with a narrative description of differences	National GAAP or IFRS[1] as applicable to EU issuer. IFRS or GAAP equivalent to IFRS for non-EU issuers	National GAAP or IFRS[1] as applicable to EU issuer. Non-EU issuers may use local GAAP with a narrative description of differences	National GAAP or IFRS[1] as applicable to EU issuer. IFRS or GAAP equivalent to IFRS for non-EU issuers	National GAAP or IFRS[1] as applicable to EU issuer. Non-EU issuers may use local GAAP with a narrative description of differences	National GAAP or IFRS[1] as applicable to EU issuer. IFRS or GAAP equivalent to IFRS for non-EU issuers	National GAAP or IFRS[1] as applicable to EU issuer. Non-EU issuers may use local GAAP with a narrative description of differences	National GAAP or IFRS[1] as applicable to EU issuer. IFRS or GAAP equivalent to IFRS for non-EU issuers

	Shares	Debt, units <50k	Debt, units 50k	Derivatives, units <50k	Derivatives, units 50K	Asset backed securities, units <50k	Asset backed securities, units 50k	Depository receipts, units <50k	Depository receipts, units 50k	Banks issuing anything other than equity securities
Issuers operating less than one year	Special purpose financial information must be included	Special purpose financial information must be included	No additional requirements	Special purpose financial information must be included	No additional requirements	Special purpose financial information must be included	No additional requirements	Special purpose financial information must be included	No additional requirements	Special purpose financial information must be included
Report on financial information	Auditor's report or accountant's report as applicable	Auditor's report or accountant's report as applicable	Auditor's report or accountant's report as applicable	Auditor's report or accountant's report as applicable	Auditor's report or accountant's report as applicable	Auditor's report or accountant's report as applicable	Auditor's report or accountant's report as applicable	Auditor's report or accountant's report as applicable	Auditor's report or accountant's report as applicable	Auditor's report or accountant's report as applicable
Age of latest financial information	I, 20.5	IV, 13.4	IX, 11.4	IV, 13.4	IX, 11.4	–	–	X, 20.4	X, 20.4	XI, 11.4
Age of audited information	No more than 15 months if unaudited interims or 18 months if audited interims	No more than 18 months	No more than 18 months	No more than 18 months	No more than 18 months	No requirements	No requirements	No more than 15 months if unaudited interims or 18 months if audited interims	No more than 15 months if unaudited interims or 18 months if audited interims	No more than 18 months
Pro forma financial information	I, 20.2 & II	–	–	–	–	–	–	–	–	–
Information	Required to show effect of significant gross changes	No requirements	No requirements	No requirements	No requirements	No requirements	No requirements	No requirements	No requirements	No requirements

	Shares	Debt, units <50k	Debt, units 50k	Derivatives, units <50k	Derivatives, units 50k	Asset backed securities, units <50k	Asset backed securities, units 50k	Depository receipts, units <50k	Depository receipts, units 50k	Banks issuing anything other than equity securities
Report on proper compilation	Required, where pro forma included	No requirements	No requirements	No requirements	No requirements	No requirements	No requirements	No requirements	No requirements	No requirements
Profit forecasts and estimates	I, 13	IV, 9	IX, 8	IV, 9	IX, 8	–	–	X, 13	X, 13	XI, 8
Disclosure of assumptions	Required	Required	Required	Required	Required	No requirements	No requirements	Required	Required	Required
Report on proper compilation	Required	Required	No requirements	Required	No requirements	No requirements	No requirements	Required	Required	Required
Outstanding forecasts	Update statement required	No requirements	No requirements	No requirements	No requirements	No requirements	No requirements	Update statement required	Update statement required	No requirements

[1] *In this table the expression IFRS is intended to refer to "those IFRSs as adopted for use in the European Union".*

Appendix 2 – Principal legal and regulatory requirements

The description of legal and regulatory requirements provided in this appendix is intended to be a guide and not intended to be a definitive interpretation of such requirements.

The FSA Handbook

In July 2005 the then existing listing rules were modified to take account of the implementation of the Prospectus Directive in the United Kingdom. At the same time the opportunity was taken to revise the rules applying to the continuing obligations of listed companies.   **1**

The FSA Handbook now includes three parts relevant to securities and their issuers, namely: the "Prospectus Rules", the "Listing Rules" and the "Disclosure Rules".   **2**

The Prospectus Rules effect the practical implementation of the Prospectus Directive. They apply to all prospectuses required to be issued by UK companies either offering securities to the public or seeking admission of securities to a regulated market. The annexes to the PD Regulation provide detailed rules on prospectuses and, in particular, the content requirements of prospectuses. In respect of prospectus content requirements, the Prospectus Rules reproduce the Annexes to the PD Regulation. Accordingly, references to the contents requirements in Annexes to the Prospectus Rules are also references to the Annexes to the PD Regulation.   **3**

The Prospectus Rules also make it clear that the FSA expect "CESR's recommendations for the consistent implementation of the European Commission's Regulation on Prospectuses no. 809/2004"[1] to be followed by issuers when preparing a prospectus.   **4**

The Listing Rules provide the rules and guidance applicable to issuers of securities both seeking admission to, and once admitted to, the Official List. They include the conditions for admission to listing, the requirements concerning Sponsors under the Listing Rules, Class 1 and related party transactions and the requirements for listing particulars when a prospectus is not required to be prepared.   **5**

The Disclosure Rules contain rules and guidance in relation to the publication and control of "inside information" and the disclosure of transactions by persons discharging managerial responsibilities and their connected persons.   **6**

The annexes to the Prospectus Rules provide that historical financial information for the last three completed financial years, where it exists, is to be included in a prospectus. This information can either be extracted or incorporated by reference from the issuer's annual financial statements or presented in the prospectus specifically for that purpose. The Prospectus Rules provide that where the accounting framework to be applied in an issuer's next annual financial statements is different from that previously applied, at least some of the historical financial information must be represented on the basis of those new policies. The historical financial information must either be accompanied by the auditor's report on the statutory financial statements or by a new opinion by reporting accountants where the information has been presented for the purpose of the prospectus.   **7**

---

[1] *"CESR" is the Committee of European Securities Regulators. Its recommendations were issued in February 2005 and are sometimes referred to as the "Level 3 Guidance of the Lamfalussy Process". This guidance can be accessed on the CESR website www.cesr-eu.org.*

8   Where an issuer with listed equity securities proposes to undertake a Class 1 acquisition, Listing Rule 13.5 requires that certain historical financial information is presented in relation to the target and, where relevant, the target's subsidiary undertakings. The last three years historical financial information must be presented in a financial information table on a basis consistent with accounting policies of the issuer. Unless the target is itself admitted to trading on an EU regulated market or on an overseas regulated market or listed on an overseas investment exchange, the financial information table must be reported on by a reporting accountant. However, if there is no report by reporting accountants on the financial information table itself, it is necessary for the issuer to consider whether any material adjustment is required to achieve consistency between the target's historical financial information and the accounting policies of the issuer, in which event a reconciliation of key financial statement components must be presented and the reconciliation reported on by reporting accountants.

9   If an issuer chooses to include a profit forecast or profit estimate in a prospectus the registration document may be required to contain the following information:

(a)   a statement setting out the principal assumptions upon which the issuer has based its forecast or estimate. See item 13.1 of Annex I to the Prospectus Rules for more detailed requirements regarding assumptions; and

(b)   a report prepared by independent accountants or auditors stating that in the opinion of the independent accountants or auditors the forecast or estimate has been properly compiled on the basis stated and that the basis of accounting used for the profit forecast or estimate is consistent with the accounting policies of the issuer.

The profit forecast or estimate must be prepared on a basis comparable with the historical financial information.

10   If a profit forecast in a prospectus has been published which is still outstanding, the issuer must provide a statement setting out whether or not that forecast is still correct as at the time of the registration document, and an explanation of why such forecast is no longer valid if that is the case.

11   Where an issuer includes pro forma financial information in a prospectus, (relating to shares, transferable securities equivalent to shares and certain other securities convertible into shares), Annex I item 20.2 and Annex II of the Prospectus Rules require any such information to be reported on by the reporting accountants. The Listing Rules also require a reporting accountant's report on any pro forma financial information that an issuer chooses to include in a Class 1 circular.

12   Where a statement or report attributed to an expert (including reporting accountants) is included in a prospectus at the issuer's request, the Prospectus Rules require a statement of consent from the expert. This is discussed in more detail in paragraphs 66 to 74 in the body of this SIR. The consent of the auditor is not required where reports (audit or review) previously issued by the auditor are included in a prospectus.

13   Other rules apply in particular circumstances. By replication of the Prospectus Rules requirements an expert is required, by the Listing Rules, to consent to the inclusion of any report in any listing particulars. However, the consent of the auditor is not required where reports (audit or review) previously issued by the auditor are included in the listing particulars.

The Listing Rules also require pro forma financial information in a Class 1 circular to be reported on by an issuer's reporting accountants and to contain provisions requiring an expert's consent to any report included in a Class 1 circular. **14**

Admission to the Main Market of the London Stock Exchange

A two-stage admission process applies to companies who want to have their securities admitted to the Main Market for listed securities of the London Stock Exchange. The securities need to be admitted to the Official List by the UK Listing Authority (UKLA), a division of the Financial Services Authority, and also admitted to trading by the London Stock Exchange. To be admitted to trading the Admission and Disclosure Standards need to be met. Once both processes are complete the securities are officially listed on the Exchange. **15**

AIM requirements

Under the AIM Rules of the London Stock Exchange, companies seeking admission to AIM must publish an AIM admission document. This is the case whether or not they are required by the Prospectus Rules to prepare a prospectus (because they are also making an offer of securities to the public which is not exempt from the requirement to produce a prospectus). **16**

The AIM Rules provide that the content of an admission document should be based on the share disclosure requirements in the Prospectus Rules, modified to allow issuers to elect not to include certain financial information where no prospectus is required, notably profit forecasts and pro forma financial information. However, if such information is included the Prospectus Rules requirements must be followed. **17**

The Professional Securities Market

From 1 July 2005, issuers listing debt, convertibles or depository receipts in London will have a choice of being admitted to a regulated market or the Professional Securities Market, which is a market operated and regulated by the London Stock Exchange. Issuers listing on the Professional Securities Market will not be required to report historical financial information under IFRSs or an EU approved equivalent standard either in listing documents or as a continuing obligation requirement. **18**

The City Code

Where a document sent to shareholders in connection with an offer falling within the scope of the City Code contains a profit forecast or estimate, with certain exceptions, Rule 28.3 of the City Code requires that forecast or estimate to be reported on by reporting accountants and by the financial advisers. The City Code's requirements for such reports are similar to those under the Prospectus Rules. In certain circumstances, the City Code also provides for a reporting accountant to report on merger benefit statements (Rule 19.1) and interim financial information (Rule 28.6(c)). **19**

Companies legislation

20   In the United Kingdom, financial information presented in an investment circular may constitute "non statutory accounts" within the meaning of section 240 of the Companies Act 1985. The document in which the financial information is presented will usually, therefore, contain a statement complying with section 240(3) of the Companies Act 1985. However, this statement is only appropriate where the financial information comprises non-statutory accounts of the company issuing the document. No statement is needed in respect of financial information on a target company in an acquisition circular, for example, unless the directors of the target company explicitly accept responsibility for that part of the document. The statement is also the responsibility of the directors of the company publishing the document, not the reporting accountants.

Financial Services and Markets Act 2000

21   Upon implementation of the Prospectus Directive into UK law with effect from 1 July 2005, the existing regime regarding the issue of prospectuses in the UK whether in connection with an official listing of securities or a <u>public offer</u> was repealed.

22   Under Part VI, the FSA's function is a statutory one. Part VI covers not only the whole process by which securities are admitted to official listing but also the obligations to which companies are subject once they have obtained listing. The Listing Rules represent listing rules for the purposes of Part VI.

23   Prospectus Rule 5.5 (in relation to prospectuses), and regulation 6 of The Financial Services and Markets Act 2000 (Official Listing of Securities) Regulations 2001 (in relation to listing particulars, i.e. not prospectuses within the meaning of the Prospectus Directive) provide that each person:

(a)   who accepts, and is stated in the particulars as accepting, responsibility for the particulars or for any part of the particulars; or

(b)   who has authorised the contents of, or any part of, the particulars;

is deemed to accept responsibility for the particulars (or that part of them).

24   This raises potential issues for reporting accountants, for example:

- If they are involved in advising on an investment circular but are not named in it;

- If they issue a report or letter which is included in the investment circular.

25   In the first example the Prospectus Rules and The Financial Services and Markets Act 2000 (Official Listing of Securities) Regulations 2001 relieve professional advisers from responsibility for the circular where they are solely giving advice as to the contents of the listing particulars in a professional capacity.

26   In the second example the Prospectus Rules and The Financial Services and Markets Act 2000 (Official Listing of Securities) Regulations 2001 limit the responsibility of experts, including reporting accountants, to the part for which they accept responsibility and only if the part for which they accept responsibility is included in (or substantially in) the form and context to which they have agreed.

Appendix 3 – Example of a consent letter

The Directors

ABC plc

Dear Sirs

We hereby give our consent to the inclusion in the [describe Investment Circular] dated [ ] issued by ABC plc of [our accountant's report]/[our report relating to the profit estimate for the year ended 20 ,]/[our report relating to the profit forecast for the year ending 20 ,]/[our report relating to the pro forma financial information for the year ended 20] dated [ ] [[and] the references to our name[2]] in the form and context in which [it]/[they] are included, as shown in the enclosed proof of the [describe Investment Circular] which we have signed for identification.

[We also hereby authorise the contents of the [report[s]] referred to above which [is/are] included in the Prospectus for the purposes of Prospectus Rule [5.5.3R (2) (f)] [5.5.4R (2)(f)] **OR** [We also hereby authorise the contents of the [report[s]] referred to above which [is/are] included in the Listing Particulars for the purposes of Regulation 6(1)(e) of The Financial Services and Markets Act 2000(Official Listing of Securities) Regulations 2001.] **OR** [We also hereby authorise the contents of the report[s] referred to above which [is/are] included in the Admission Document for the purposes of the Schedule Two to the AIM Rules][3]

Yours faithfully

Reporting accountant

---

[2] *This is required only when a statement is attributed to a reporting accountant as an expert outside the context of a report from the reporting accountant included in the investment circular.*

[3] *This paragraph is not required in respect of a Class 1 Circular.*

Appendix 4 – Glossary of terms

Accountant's report – A report by a reporting accountant included in an investment circular, in which the reporting accountant normally expresses a "true and fair, for the purposes of the investment circular" opinion on historical financial information relating to the issuer and its subsidiaries in accordance with SIR 2000 "Investment Reporting Standards applicable to public reporting engagements on historical financial information".

Admission and Disclosure Standards – The Admission and Disclosure Standards published by the London Stock Exchange, for companies admitted or seeking to be admitted to trading by the Exchange.

Agreed-upon procedures [engagements] – An engagement where the reporting accountant is engaged to carry out procedures of an audit or assurance nature, that the reporting accountant, the entity and any appropriate third parties have agreed, and to report on factual findings. The recipients of the report must form their own conclusions from the report by the reporting accountant. The report is restricted to those parties that have agreed to the procedures to be performed, since others, unaware of the reasons for the procedures, may misinterpret the results.

AIM – The Alternative Investment Market operated by the London Stock Exchange plc. The market is for smaller growing companies. Securities admitted to AIM are unlisted.

AIM Admission Document – The document prepared in connection with an application for admission of an issuer's securities to trading on AIM. If upon admission a prospectus is required in accordance with the Prospectus Rules, such prospectus may serve as the AIM Admission Document.

AIM Rules – The Rules of the Alternative Investment Market.

CESR – The Committee of European Securities Regulators.

Circular – A circular issued by any company to its shareholders and/or holders of its debt securities in connection with a transaction, which does not constitute a prospectus, listing particulars or AIM admission document.

City Code – The City Code on Takeovers and Mergers, published by the Panel on Takeovers and Mergers.

Class 1 circular – A circular relating to a Class 1 transaction.

Class 1 transaction – A transaction where one or more of a number of specified percentage ratios exceed a predetermined level as specified in Chapter 10 of the Listing Rules.

Comfort letter – A private letter from the reporting accountant, usually prepared at the request of the issuer and/or the sponsor, where relevant. It is intended to provide the addressees with comfort (in the form of an opinion or a report on the results of specific procedures carried out by the reporting accountants) regarding matters relevant to the addressees' responsibilities.

Completion date of the transaction – The date by which any offer contained in the circular must have been accepted or application made for shares or other securities to be issued, or the date on which shareholders vote to approve the transaction.

Consent letter – A letter whereby the reporting accountant consents to the inclusion in an investment circular of references to its name or the inclusion of any of its reports or letters which are to be published therein.

Due diligence – The process whereby the directors of the issuer and other parties, whether as principal or in an advisory capacity, satisfy themselves that the transaction is entered into after due and careful enquiry and that all relevant regulatory and/or legal requirements have been properly complied with. There is no generally accepted definition of required procedures for this purpose and where others (such as reporting accountants) are engaged to carry out work that will form part of the process, it is for the instructing parties to make clear what is required of those others in the particular circumstances.

Engagement partner – The partner or other person in the firm who is responsible for the engagement and its performance, and for reports that are issued on behalf of the firm, and who, where required, has the appropriate authority from a professional, legal or regulatory body.

Financial information – The term is used to signify the specific information presented in the form of a table upon which a reporting accountant reports. Typically, this information encompasses a number of accounting periods.

Financial statements – A balance sheet, profit and loss account (or other form of income statement), statement of cash flow, and statement of total recognised gains and losses (or statement of changes in equity), notes and other statements and explanatory material. In order to avoid confusion the term financial information is used throughout the SIRs to refer to the information upon which the reporting accountant reports. When the term financial statements is used within the SIRs this refers to financial statements from which the financial information has been derived by the issuer.

FSA – Financial Services Authority.

FSMA – Financial Services and Markets Act 2000.

IFRSs – International Financial Reporting Standards issued by the International Accounting Standards Board. This term incorporates all International Financial Reporting Standards, International Accounting Standards (IASs) and Interpretations originated by the International Financial Reporting Interpretations Committee (IFRIC) or the former Standards Interpretation Committee of the IASC.

Investment circular – A generic term describing any document issued by an entity pursuant to statutory or regulatory requirements relating to securities on which it is intended that a third party should make an investment decision, including a prospectus, listing particulars, circular to shareholders or similar document.

ISAs (UK and Ireland) – International Standards on Auditing (UK and Ireland) issued by the Auditing Practices Board.

Issuer – For the purposes of the Prospectus Rules "A legal person who issues or proposes to issue securities". For the purposes of the Listing Rules "Any company or other legal person or undertaking (including a public sector issuer), any class of whose securities has been admitted to listing, or is the subject of an application for admission to listing".

Listing particulars – A document not being a Prospectus prepared in connection with an admission of securities to the Official List.

Listing Rules – The part of the FSA's Handbook entitled "Listing Rules" governing the conduct of companies whose securities are admitted to the Official List.

London Stock Exchange – The London Stock Exchange plc.

Long form report – A private report with a restricted circulation, normally prepared by the reporting accountants on the instructions of, and addressed to, the sponsor, where relevant, and the directors of the issuer as part of their due diligence, dealing with agreed matters including commentary on financial and other information in an orderly and relevant form for a specific purpose.

Main Market – The London Stock Exchange's market for larger and established companies. Securities admitted to the Main Market are listed.

Nominated adviser – A corporate broker, investment banker or other professional adviser approved by the London Stock Exchange to act as a nominated adviser to an AIM company under the AIM Rules.

Ofex – An independent, self regulated, UK market for smaller companies.

Official List – The Official List maintained by the FSA.

Outcome – The outcome of the evaluation or measurement of a subject matter is the information that results from the directors applying the suitable criteria to the subject matter. Examples of outcomes are historical financial information and a directors' profit forecast and related disclosures that are included in an investment circular.

Partner – Any individual with authority to bind a firm of reporting accountants with respect to the performance of any engagement in connection with an investment circular.

PD Regulation – the implementing EU Regulation 809/2004 that provides the detailed rules concerning Prospectuses and their contents. Much of the text of this regulation is included within the Prospectus Rules.

Private reporting engagement – An engagement in which a reporting accountant does not express a conclusion that is published in an investment circular.

Professional Securities Market – A market for debt, convertibles and depository receipts, which is operated and regulated by the London Stock Exchange. This is not a regulated market as defined by the Prospectus and Transparency Directives.

Profit estimate – Historical financial information for a financial period which has expired but for which the results have not yet been published.

Profit forecast – The PD Regulation defines a profit forecast as "a form of words which expressly states or by implication indicates a figure or a minimum or maximum figure for the likely level of profits or losses for the current financial period and/or financial periods subsequent to that period, or contains data from which calculation of such a figure for future profits or losses may be made, even if no particular figure is mentioned and the word "profit" is not used". Where a profit forecast relates to an extended period and/or is subject to significant uncertainty it is sometimes referred to as a projection.

Pro forma financial information – Financial information such as net assets, profit or cash flow statements that demonstrate the impact of a transaction on previously published financial information together with the explanatory notes thereto.

Projection – See "Profit forecast".

Prospectus – The document issued in accordance with the Prospectus Rules in connection with either a public offer or an admission of securities to trading on a regulated market.

Prospectus Regulations – The UK statutory instrument which makes amendments to Part VI of FSMA and to certain secondary legislation.

Prospectus Rules – The FSA's Handbook part "Prospectus Rules" which together with the PD Regulation and the changes to FSMA Part VI made by the Prospectus Regulations, implement the Prospectus Directive into UK law. In respect of Prospectus content requirements, the Prospectus Rules reproduce the Annexes to the PD Regulation. Accordingly, references to the contents requirements in Annexes to the Prospectus Rules are also references to the Annexes to the PD Regulation.

Public offer – An offer to the public in any form to subscribe for securities in an issuer.

Public reporting engagement – An engagement in which a reporting accountant expresses a conclusion that is published in an investment circular and which is designed to enhance the degree of confidence of the intended users of the report about the "outcome" of the directors' evaluation or measurement of "subject matter" (usually financial information) against "suitable criteria".

Report – This term encompasses letters that the reporting accountant may be required to send by regulation or arising from the terms of the engagement.

Reporting accountant – An accountant engaged to prepare a report for inclusion in, or in connection with, an investment circular. The reporting accountant may or may not be the auditor of the entity issuing the investment circular. The term "reporting accountant" is used to describe either the engagement partner or the engagement partner's firm. The reporting accountant could be a limited company or an engagement principal employed by the company.

Reporting accountant's criteria – A subset of suitable criteria which the reporting accountant's engagement requires the reporting accountant to consider. Reporting accountant's criteria are set out in appendices to the SIRs.

Securities – Are as defined by Article 4 of the EU's Markets in Financial Instruments Directive with the exception of money-market instruments having a maturity of less than twelve months.

Sponsor – For the purposes of SIRs, "sponsor" is a generic term which includes any one or more of the following to whom the reporting accountant has agreed, in its engagement letter, to address a relevant report:

(a) a person approved, under section 88 of FSMA, by the FSA as a sponsor. The FSA's sponsor regime applies to applications for admission to listing and major transactions. The sponsor regime is designed to ensure that effective due diligence is undertaken on issuers and transactions to ensure that issuers are eligible for listing, that major transactions are properly evaluated and that all relevant information has been included in the investment circular. Listing Rule 8.2.1 sets out the circumstances when an issuer must appoint a sponsor;

(b) a nominated adviser approved by the London Stock Exchange in connection with an application for admission to AIM and subsequent transactions by a company with securities traded on AIM; and

(c) in connection with any transaction, any party, other than the issuer, who may have specific responsibility for the preparation and/or contents of an investment circular.

Subject matter – The subject matter of an engagement is that which is being evaluated or measured against "suitable criteria". Examples of subject matter are the entity's financial position and the directors' expectation of the issuer's profit for the period covered by a profit forecast.

Suitable criteria – Criteria are the benchmarks used to evaluate or measure the subject matter. Suitable criteria are usually derived from laws and regulations and are required by directors to enable them to make reasonably consistent evaluations or measurements of the subject matter. With respect to public reporting engagements the suitable criteria for specific types of engagement are described in the individual SIR dealing with such engagements.

SIR 2000 (Revised) – Investment Reporting Standards applicable to public reporting engagements on historical financial information

(March 2011)

Contents

	Paragraphs
Introduction	1 - 14
Pre-existing financial information	15 - 16
True and fair view, for the purposes of the investment circular	17 - 22
General professional considerations	23 - 26
Planning	27 - 30
Understanding of the entity, its environment and risk assessment	31 - 37
Materiality	38
The reporting accountant's procedures	39 - 45
Evidence	46 - 53
Obtaining access to information in audit documentation	54 - 57
Events occurring up to the date of the accountant's report	58
Events occurring between the date of the accountant's report and the completion date of the transaction	59 - 62
Going concern	63 - 64
Representations	65 - 68
Joint reporting accountants	69
Reporting	70 - 76
Other information – references to previous audit opinions	77
Comparatives	78
Consent in the context of investment circulars containing a report by a reporting accountant	79

Effective date   80

Appendix 1: Examples of engagement letter clauses

Appendix 2: Example of an accountant's report on historical financial
             information prepared in accordance with International Financial
             Reporting Standards as adopted by the European Union

Appendix 3: Example of an accountant's report on historical financial
             information prepared in accordance with the basis described
             in a basis of preparation note

Annexure

Accounting conventions commonly used in the preparation of historical financial information in
investment circulars

THE AUDITING PRACTICES BOARD

The Auditing Practices Board (APB), which is part of the Financial
Reporting Council (FRC), prepares for use within the United Kingdom
and the Republic of Ireland:

- Standards and guidance for auditing;
- Standards and guidance for reviews of interim financial information
  performed by the auditor of the entity;
- Standards and guidance for the work of reporting accountants in
  connection with investment circulars; and
- Standards and guidance for auditor's and reporting accountant's
  integrity, objectivity and independence

with the objective of enhancing public confidence in the audit process and
the quality and relevance of audit services in the public interest.

The APB comprises individuals who are not eligible for appointment as
company auditors, as well as those who are so eligible. Those who are
eligible for appointment as company auditors may not exceed 40% of the
APB by number.

Neither the APB nor the FRC accepts any liability to any party for any loss,
damage or costs howsoever arising, whether directly or indirectly, whether
in contract, tort or otherwise from any action or decision taken (or not taken)
as a result of any person relying on or otherwise using this document or
arising from any omission from it.

Investment Reporting Standards applicable to public reporting engagements on historical financial information

SIR 1000 "Investment reporting standards applicable to all engagements in connection with an investment circular" contains basic principles and essential procedures ("Investment Reporting Standards") that are applicable to all engagements involving an investment circular. The definitions in the glossary of terms set out in Appendix 4 of SIR 1000 are to be applied in the interpretation of this and all other SIRs. Terms defined in the glossary are underlined the first time that they occur in the text.

SIR 2000 contains additional Investment Reporting Standards, indicated by paragraphs in bold type, with which a reporting accountant is required to comply in the conduct of an engagement involving the examination of historical financial information which is intended to give a true and fair view, for the purposes of the relevant investment circular, included within an investment circular prepared for issue in connection with a securities transaction governed wholly or in part by the laws and regulations of the United Kingdom or the Republic of Ireland.

SIR 2000 also includes explanatory and other material, including appendices, in the context of which the Investment Reporting Standards are to be understood and applied. It is necessary to consider the whole text of the SIR to understand and apply the basic principles and essential procedures.

To assist readers, SIRs contain references to, and extracts from, certain legislation and chapters of the Rules of the UK Listing Authority (UKLA) and the Listing Rules of the Irish Stock Exchange Limited (ISE) (together "the Listing Rules"). Readers are cautioned that these references may change subsequent to publication.

This version of SIR 2000 replaces the version issued in July 2005.

Introduction

The purpose of this Standard for Investment Reporting (SIR) is to establish **1** standards and provide guidance on the reporting accountant's responsibilities and procedures when preparing an "accountant's report" on historical financial information. The work required to prepare an "accountant's report" is referred to in this SIR as the "reporting accountant's exercise". The objective of the reporting accountant's exercise is to enable the reporting accountant to express an opinion as to whether, for the purposes of the relevant investment circular, the financial information gives a true and fair view of the state of affairs and profits, cash flows and statements of changes in equity of the issuer, or where applicable the target.

When the reporting accountant is engaged to prepare an accountant's report, 2 the reporting accountant should obtain sufficient appropriate evidence to express an opinion as to whether the financial information presents a true and fair view, for the purposes of the investment circular. (SIR 2000.1)

An engagement to prepare an accountant's report is a public reporting engagement **3** as described in SIR 1000. The description of a public reporting engagement includes three generic terms having the following meanings in the context of an engagement to report on historical financial information:

(a)   With respect to historical financial information the "**subject matter**" is the entity's financial position for the periods being reported on;

(b)   The "**suitable criteria**" are the requirements of the applicable financial reporting framework, the PD Regulation, and Listing Rules together with any "accepted conventions", as set out in the Annexure, that are applicable; and

(c)   With respect to historical financial information the "**outcome**" is the directors' historical financial information that is included in the investment circular and which has resulted from the directors applying the suitable criteria to the subject matter. The reporting accountant expresses an opinion (in the "**accountant's report**") as to whether the historical financial information gives, for the purposes of the investment circular, a true and fair view.

4   The Prospectus Rules set out certain requirements, derived from the PD Regulation, relating to the presentation of historical financial information in a prospectus. Annex I of the PD Regulation (and there are equivalent requirements in a number of the other annexes) requires that historical financial information is either audited or "reported on as to whether or not, for the purposes of the registration document, it gives a true and fair view, in accordance with auditing standards applicable in a Member State or an equivalent standard."[2].

5   With respect to Class 1 acquisitions, Chapter 13 of the Listing Rules sets out requirements for a financial information table relating to a target company and the accountant's opinion on that table. The accountant's opinion is required to state whether, for the purposes of the Class 1 circular, the financial information table gives a true and fair view of the financial matters set out in it, and whether the financial information table has been prepared in a form that is consistent with the accounting policies adopted in the listed company's latest annual accounts.

6   In this SIR, accountant's opinions on such financial information tables are described as "accountant's reports".

7   An accountant's report is likely to be used where the issuer's audited annual financial statements do not meet the standards of preparation and presentation prescribed in the applicable rules and need, therefore, to be adjusted in order that historical financial information which complies with the applicable rules can be presented. For example, where the entity is seeking a listing, the financial information for the last two years is required to be prepared and presented in a form consistent with that which will be adopted in the issuer's next published annual financial statements, having regard to accounting standards and policies and legislation applicable to such annual financial statements. In the context of Class 1 circulars, the objective may be to present the financial information of the target for all periods in a form which is consistent and comparable with the accounting policies adopted by the listed company in its latest annual accounts.

8   In addition, an accountant's report is used where the issuer has a complex financial history and there are no underlying financial statements that have been audited. Conventions for accounting where there are complex financial histories are described in the Annexure to this SIR.

---

[2]   *In respect of prospectus content requirements, the Prospectus Rules reproduce the Annexes to the PD Regulation. Accordingly, references to the contents requirements in the Annexes to the Prospectus Rules are also references to the Annexes to the PD Regulation.*

The nature of the accountant's report is such that the objective of the reporting **9** accountant's exercise does not differ in essence from that of an auditor. The underlying requirement of this SIR is that the reporting accountant will, in conducting the work necessary to provide the accountant's report, perform its own procedures, and/or use the work of the auditor(s), that meet those requirements of ISAs (UK and Ireland) that are relevant to the reporting accountant's exercise. The reporting accountant applies ISAs (UK and Ireland) on the basis set out in this SIR in the context of the following:

(a) The reporting accountant is often reporting on financial information that has been included in, or formed part of, financial statements which have themselves already been subject to audit by an independent auditor. In consequence, there may be available to the reporting accountant a body of independent evidence relating to the historical financial information which would not be available to an auditor examining the financial information for the first time;

(b) The financial information being examined may relate to accounting periods in circumstances where financial statements for one, and possibly two, subsequent periods have been prepared and audited. These circumstances mean that in assessing risks that may affect the historical financial information in relation to earlier periods the reporting accountant has the benefit of information relating to uncertainties affecting the financial information which would not have been available to an auditor auditing the information for the first time; and

(c) The reporting accountant does not have the statutory reporting responsibilities of an auditor.

This SIR provides standards that address those aspects of the reporting **10** accountant's exercise that require the reporting accountant to perform procedures directly, for example risk assessment procedures. It also provides guidance on the application of ISAs (UK and Ireland) to the reporting accountant's exercise.

This SIR recognises that the reporting accountant may wish to use evidence **11** previously obtained by the auditor who audited the historical financial statements for the relevant period covered by the reporting accountant's exercise. Guidance is provided on the steps that the reporting accountant undertakes, including initial planning considerations, in order to assess the suitability of the audit evidence for this purpose.

Subject to the considerations set out in this SIR, references in the ISAs (UK and **12** Ireland) to the auditor performing audit procedures or obtaining audit evidence may be read as references to the reporting accountant being satisfied that the procedures have been performed, or the evidence has been obtained, either by the reporting accountant or an auditor.

Certain requirements of ISAs (UK and Ireland) will not be relevant to the reporting **13** accountant's exercise, for example, when a requirement of an ISA (UK and Ireland) is predicated on a continuing relationship between an auditor and the entity being audited, or because of the specific nature of the reporting accountant's responsibilities, under applicable regulations, as discussed in this SIR.

This SIR also provides guidance to the reporting accountant in the context of **14** assessing whether the financial information shows a true and fair view, for the purposes of the investment circular. In situations where the issuer has a historical record of audited financial statements, the true and fair view for the purposes of the investment circular may be a financial reporting framework such as International Financial Reporting Standards as adopted by the European Union. In situations where the issuer has a complex financial history the conventions to support the true and fair view for the purposes of the investment circular are set out in the Annexure to this SIR.

Pre-existing financial information

15   With respect to historical financial information, where the issuer already has available:

(a)   Audited annual financial statements; or

(b)   Audited or reviewed interim financial information,

which meet the requirements of the applicable rules in respect of the preparation and presentation of historical financial information to be included in the investment circular, it may choose to include these financial statements, or financial information, in the investment circular together with the pre-existing reports of the auditor. In these circumstances an accountant's report is not prepared and this SIR does not apply to such circumstances. Furthermore, in these circumstances the audit firm is not required by the Prospectus Rules to consent to the inclusion of its reports in the investment circular.

16   Notwithstanding that the audit firm is not required to give consent, a reporting accountant that is also the auditor of the company may become aware that the financial statements are defective. For example, a material error may have been detected in the original financial statements. If the reporting accountant does become aware that the financial statements are defective and that the directors have not revised them as permitted by section 454 of the Companies Act 2006, it discusses the matter with those charged with governance. If the directors do not decide to revise the financial statements the reporting accountant considers the need to take legal advice[3].

True and fair view, for the purposes of the investment circular

17   **The reporting accountant should:**

(a)   **Obtain an understanding of the purpose of the investment circular;**

(b)   **Ascertain which financial reporting framework is required to be used by the applicable regulations and which, if any, accepted conventions as to the preparation and presentation of historical financial information for inclusion in investment circulars are to be applied[4]; and**

(c)   **Review the appropriateness of the accounting policies**

in order to determine whether the proposed historical financial information prepared by the issuer is capable of giving a true and fair view, for the purposes of the investment circular. (SIR 2000.2)

---

[3] *See also Bulletin 2008/5 "Auditor's Reports on Revised Accounts and Reports, in the United Kingdom".*

[4] *See Annexure.*

Where historical financial information is presented in a prospectus the Prospectus **18**
Rules generally determine the applicable financial reporting framework. The
Prospectus Rules require the most recent year's financial information to be
presented in a form consistent with that which will be adopted in the issuer's
next published annual financial statements, having regard to the accounting
standards, policies and legislation applicable to such annual financial statements.

The reporting accountant satisfies itself that the directors have performed a **19**
thorough review of the accounting policies used in preparing the historical
financial information in determining the accounting policies appropriate for the
business following the transaction that is the subject of the prospectus. The
reporting accountant also considers whether the policies are consistent with
the applicable financial reporting framework, and accounting policies used in
the relevant industry. Where the reporting accountant does not agree with the
directors' final proposed accounting policies they refer to the guidance on
reporting set out in paragraphs 70 to 76 of this SIR.

Where information is presented in a Class 1 circular, the suitable criteria regarding **20**
its presentation are those set out in the Listing Rules. These rules require financial
information to be presented in a form consistent with the accounting policies
adopted in the issuer's latest annual consolidated accounts.

The directors have regard to, and make appropriate disclosure of, accepted **21**
conventions which have been developed for the preparation and presentation of
historical financial information in investment circulars (including those relating
to additional disclosures). These conventions have been developed to assist the
directors, to the extent consistent with established accounting principles, to fulfil
the criteria set out in the relevant regulations, present the information in an easily
analysable form, and give a true and fair view for the purposes of the applicable
investment circular.

The Annexure provides a summary of these conventions including, among others, **22**
conventions that address:

●   Making adjustments to previously published financial statements and
     dealing with entities which have not previously prepared consolidated
     accounts.

●   Carve outs.

●   Acquisitions.

●   Newly-formed issuers.

In certain circumstances applying the conventions may result in combined or
aggregated, rather than consolidated, financial information being presented in
order to meet the requirement to present financial information that gives a true and
fair view, for the purposes of the investment circular.

General professional considerations

SIR 1000.3 and SIR 1000.4 set out basic principles and essential procedures **23**
applicable to agreeing the terms of the engagement. Paragraphs 11 to 15 and
paragraph 17 of SIR 1000 provide guidance with respect to these basic principles
and essential procedures. Illustrative examples of engagement letter clauses are
set out in Appendix 1. SIR 1000.5 sets out the basic principles and essential
procedures with respect to the ethical requirements that apply to a reporting
accountant.

24   Where the evidence used by the reporting accountant includes that contained within the audit documentation of an auditor, the reporting accountant's documentation identifies the working papers reviewed and the nature of the work performed. Whilst it is not necessary for the reporting accountant's documentation to replicate all of the detailed findings contained in the audit documentation reporting accountants do document the basis on which the auditor addressed the particular risks identified in the reporting accountant's risk assessment procedures.

25   In considering the requirements of ISA (UK and Ireland) 240 "The auditor's responsibilities relating to fraud in an audit of financial statements", ISA (UK and Ireland) 250 "Section A – Consideration of laws and regulations in an audit of financial statements and Section B – The auditor's right and duty to report to regulators in the financial sector" for the auditor to report any matters arising to certain authorities, the reporting accountant will need to assess the effect of these requirements when reporting in terms of the true and fair view, for the purposes of the investment circular. Where matters arise which may potentially require disclosure by the reporting accountant and the reporting accountant is unsure how to proceed, the reporting accountant takes legal advice.

26   In applying ISAs (UK and Ireland) 240, 250, 260 "Communication with those charged with governance", 265 "Communicating deficiencies in internal control to those charged with governance and management" and 450 "Evaluation of misstatements identified during the audit", the reporting accountant considers who, in relation to the investment circular, should be regarded as a person charged with governance. Where the issuer has already formed an audit committee, the reporting accountant communicates with the audit committee in accordance with the guidance set out in this SIR. In the absence of an audit committee those responsible for governance will usually be the directors of the issuer.

Planning

27   **The reporting accountant should perform and document risk assessment procedures to support the reporting accountant's exercise. (SIR 2000.3)**

28   In addition to those matters that a reporting accountant considers when applying SIR 1000, a reporting accountant may consider:

- Any previous modifications to the opinion in the auditor's report on underlying financial statements or emphasis of matter or other matters paragraphs and their potential impact on the approach to the reporting accountant's exercise.

- The nature of adjustments to previously published historical financial information which may be proposed by the preparer of the historical financial information (for example as a result of changing the applicable accounting framework) and the sources of evidence to support an examination of the adjustments.

- The interaction with other roles undertaken by the reporting accountant in connection with the transaction, for example preparing a long form report.

- Staffing, including relevant experience and skills linked to investment circular reporting, and sources of consultation.

- Liaison with the auditor and arrangements for terms of access to the audit documentation, or equivalent evidence if maintained in machine readable form.

- The nature and timing of procedures to support any decision to rely on audit evidence obtained by the auditor.

- Whether the financial reporting framework applicable to the audited financial statements is the same as that applicable to the financial information contained in the investment circular.

- Whether there are any special circumstances concerning the appointment, resignation or reporting responsibilities of the auditor.

- Whether there is evidence of any limitation having been placed on the work of the auditor.

- Whether corrections or adjustments to subsequent financial statements indicate possible inadequacies in the audits of earlier periods.

Where the reporting accountant is considering using audit evidence obtained by an auditor as part of the evidence for the reporting accountant's exercise, the reporting accountant should consider the professional qualification, independence and professional competence of the auditor and the quality control systems applied by the audit firm to that engagement. (SIR 2000.4) 29

Matters that the reporting accountant considers include: 30

- The integrity and experience of the auditor.

- Whether the auditor was required to comply with the APB's Ethical Standards for Auditors, International Standard on Quality Control (UK and Ireland) 1, ISAs (UK and Ireland) or equivalent standards.

Understanding of the entity, its environment and risk assessment

The reporting accountant should obtain an understanding of the entity and its environment, including its internal control, sufficient to identify and assess the risks of material misstatement of the historical financial information covered by the accountant's report whether due to fraud or error, and sufficient to design and perform further procedures. As part of this risk assessment the reporting accountant should determine whether any of the risks identified are, in the reporting accountant's judgment, significant risks. (SIR 2000.5) 31

Such an understanding is ordinarily obtained by: 32

(a) Meeting the directors and management of the entity;

(b) Visiting the entity's premises;

(c) Discussing the financial information and recent results with management;

(d) Applying analytical procedures to the financial information; and

(e) Obtaining from management an understanding of the principal transaction flows, internal controls and reporting arrangements of the business.

If this process indicates that there are factors which may give rise to a modification of the accountant's opinion or an emphasis of matter and other matter paragraphs 33 then such factors are reported immediately to those responsible for the investment circular, usually the directors, and any other responsible parties.

34   In considering areas of risk in relation to the periods for which historical financial information is presented, the reporting accountant has regard to the probability that misstatements in earlier periods, if they exist, are likely to have been detected in subsequent periods. Account is also taken of the fact that other uncertainties, particularly those affecting subjective matters in the historical financial information, may have been resolved with the passage of time.

35   **When performing the risk assessment, the reporting accountant should take into account the evidence obtained from all other relevant work performed in connection with the investment circular. (SIR 2000.6)**

36   The reporting accountant may be undertaking other relevant work related to the transaction giving rise to the accountant's report. For example, the reporting accountant may have been commissioned to prepare a long form report, or a comfort letter on a statement of sufficiency of working capital.

37   If other relevant work has been performed by another firm the reporting accountant requests the issuer to provide access to the documentation of such work. If the reporting accountant is not allowed access to such documentation it considers the implications for its report.

Materiality

38   The reporting accountant determines both materiality and performance materiality for the purposes of the reporting accountant's work independently from the auditor, if any, who audited the underlying financial statements, and accordingly the reporting accountant's determination of materiality and performance materiality may differ from that of the auditor. In determining materiality and performance materiality for the purposes of reporting on historical financial information, regard is had to the context in which the opinion is to be given (which includes the fact that the information may relate to a trend of results over a three year period).

The reporting accountant's procedures

39   **The reporting accountant should perform procedures to obtain sufficient appropriate evidence as to whether the work of an auditor, which the reporting accountant plans to use, is adequate for the reporting accountant's purposes. Where the reporting accountant, concludes that the auditor's work is not adequate, does not have access to the auditor's audit documentation, or an audit has not previously been performed, the reporting accountant should perform procedures that compensate for this. The procedures of the auditor and the reporting accountant, taken together, should comply with the requirements of ISAs (UK and Ireland) unless:**

   (a)   **An entire ISA (UK and Ireland) is not relevant to the reporting accountant's engagement; or**

   (b)   **A particular requirement is:**

      (i)   **Conditional and the condition does not exist; or**

      (ii)   **Less relevant than an equivalent requirement of a SIR; or**

(iii) **Predicated on the concept of a recurring engagement or an ongoing relationship with a client which is usually not relevant to engagements to report on an investment circular; or**

(c) **It is not practicable for the reporting accountant to undertake such procedures.**

If the reporting accountant decides not to comply with a requirement of ISAs (UK and Ireland) because it is not practicable for it to undertake such procedures, it should document the reason for not complying with the requirement and why its omission does not have an impact on its opinion. (SIR 2000.7)

In approaching the procedures to be performed in response to the assessed risk of material misstatement at the assertion level, the reporting accountant considers the extent to which the procedures that the reporting accountant wishes to perform have previously been performed by an auditor. Where such procedures have been performed by an auditor, the reporting accountant may, subject to the considerations discussed in this SIR, use the evidence obtained by the auditor from those procedures as part of the reporting accountant's own evidence. **40**

In exceptional circumstances a reporting accountant may judge it necessary to depart from a relevant requirement in an ISA (UK and Ireland) to achieve the aim of that requirement. In such circumstances the reporting accountant performs alternative procedures to achieve the aim of that requirement. When such a situation arises the reporting accountant documents the reason for the departure. **41**

Where applicable auditing standards have changed during the period covered by the historical financial information, or it is not practicable for the reporting accountant to undertake procedures that meet the requirements of ISAs (UK and Ireland), the reporting accountant considers the implications for the reporting accountant's exercise, having regard to its risk assessment. The reporting accountant may be able to conclude that it is unnecessary to apply certain requirements of the ISAs (UK and Ireland) throughout the three year period covered by the accountant's report because: **42**

(a) It is sufficient to apply them with respect to the latest period only, because sufficient appropriate evidence relating to earlier periods can be obtained from the latest period; or

(b) The auditing standards that were applicable at the time met the same objectives as the requirements of ISAs (UK and Ireland).

In such cases the reporting accountant documents the reason or justification for not meeting the requirement and why omitting it does not have an impact on its opinion.

When the reporting accountant intends to use audit evidence obtained by the auditor, it should evaluate whether the audit procedures performed by the auditor adequately respond to the reporting accountant's assessment of the risks (including significant risks) of material misstatement of the financial information to be included in the investment circular. (SIR 2000.8) **43**

The reporting accountant's procedures should include: **44**

(a) **Examining material adjustments from previously published historical financial statements made during the course of preparing the historical financial information and considering the responsible party's basis for satisfying itself that the adjustments are necessary and whether they have been correctly determined;**

(b)   **Evaluating whether all necessary adjustments to previously published historical financial statements have been made; and**

(c)   **Where the information is based on previously published financial statements, comparing the historical financial information to those financial statements and assessing whether the information has been accurately extracted therefrom. (SIR 2000.9)**

45   In certain areas, use of the work of the auditor may be the only practicable means of obtaining the evidence necessary to support the reporting accountant's opinion[5]. The timing of the reporting accountant's own work will inevitably be dictated by the timing of the preparation of the historical financial information and the related investment circular and this may be some time after the end of the periods to which the report relates.

Evidence

46   The reporting accountant reconsiders the matters considered at the planning stage as described in paragraphs 28 and 30.

47   Where the financial information to be reported on has previously been subject to audit, the audit documentation will be a useful source for the evidence which the reporting accountant may need to support its opinion on the financial information.

48   If planning to use the work of the auditor, the reporting accountant considers whether:

(a)   The work of the auditor was conducted to an appropriate materiality level; and

(b)   The auditor appears to have complied with the auditing standards that were applicable to the auditor's work.

49   The reporting accountant accepts evidence in audit documentation as being prima facie truthful and genuine, but in considering that evidence adopts an attitude of professional scepticism, whether the documentation was produced by an auditor from the reporting accountant's own firm or by another auditor. However, with respect to audit documentation from the reporting accountant's own firm, the reporting accountant is more familiar with the detailed quality control procedures that will have been applied in the conduct of the audit. The application of professional scepticism will include considering the evidence contained in the audit documentation in the light of the understanding of the entity and its environment, including its internal control and such other evidence as the reporting accountant obtains directly.

50   The extent to which independent testing of the evidence obtained by the auditor (for example, reperformance of tests performed by the auditor) will be necessary is a matter for the reporting accountant's judgment on the basis of the information available at the time, including the reporting accountant's evaluation of the auditor's work.

51   **The reporting accountant should evaluate the quality of the audit evidence obtained by the auditor that the reporting accountant intends to rely on. Where the reporting accountant concludes that such audit evidence is either not sufficient or is inappropriate for the purposes of the reporting**

---

[5] *Procedures which require the reporting accountant to be physically present at a relevant date (for example attendance at physical inventory counting) will clearly be impossible to perform.*

accountant's exercise the reporting accountant should obtain evidence directly. Where the evidence is not available, the reporting accountant should consider the implications for its report. (SIR 2000.10)

Where the reporting accountant intends to rely on internal controls the reporting   **52** accountant performs tests of control when unable to rely on the auditor's tests of such internal controls. This is likely to arise when the auditor:

(a) Has not performed tests of those internal controls; or

(b) Has performed tests of internal controls but the internal controls have subsequently changed.

Where relevant information is not available from the audit documentation, the   **53** reporting accountant will need to obtain the relevant evidence directly. The audit documentation is unlikely, for example, to contain information concerning post balance sheet events up to the date of signing the accountant's report or to contain evidence relating to any adjustments made to the financial statements in preparing the historical financial information.

Obtaining access to information in audit documentation

When the company's auditor, or former auditor, is not appointed as the reporting   **54** accountant, the auditor will be aware that the reporting accountant may need access to information contained in the audit documentation. The auditor or former auditor is normally prepared, in accordance with relevant professional guidance, to make the audit documentation available to reporting accountants for the purpose of work under this SIR.

Access may be granted only on the basis that the auditor accepts no responsibility   **55** or liability to the reporting accountant in connection with the use of the audit documentation by the reporting accountant. This has no effect on the reporting accountant's judgment regarding the extent to which reliance is placed on such audit documentation.

In cases where the reporting accountant is not able to obtain access to information   **56** in audit documentation, the reporting accountant will have no option other than to obtain the relevant evidence directly.

Irrespective of whether the reporting accountant has access to the auditor's   **57** documentation, the reporting accountant seeks to obtain, either from the directors or from the auditor, copies of all relevant communications sent by the auditor to those charged with governance of the entity, including those required to be sent by auditing standards applicable at the time, and copies of any responses to such communications made by management. A relevant communication would, for example, be one that discussed internal control and other weaknesses.

Events occurring up to the date of the accountant's report

Unless a post balance sheet event indicates that there has been an error in the   **58** preparation of the historical financial information in an earlier period, the reporting accountant will, having regard to the convention for treating post balance sheet events for the purposes of historical financial information in an investment circular (as referred to in the Annexure), only consider the impact of post balance sheet events occurring up to the date of the accountant's report on the final period presented.

Events occurring between the date of the accountant's report and the completion date of the transaction

59   **If, in the period between the date of the accountant's report and the completion date of the transaction, the reporting accountant becomes aware of events and other matters which, had they occurred and been known at the date of the report, might have caused it to issue a different report or to withhold consent, the reporting accountant should discuss the implications of them with those responsible for the investment circular and take additional action as appropriate. (SIR 2000.11)**

60   After the date of the accountant's report, the reporting accountant has no obligation to perform procedures or make enquiries regarding the investment circular.

61   Under Chapter 3 of the Prospectus Rules, a supplementary prospectus must be prepared if, after the date the prospectus has been formally approved by the FSA and before the final closing of the offer of securities to the public or the commencement of trading in the relevant securities, there is a significant change affecting any matter contained in the document or a significant new matter has arisen (or a material mistake or inaccuracy is noted).

62   If, as a result of discussions with those responsible for the investment circular concerning a subsequent event that occurred prior to the completion date of the transaction, the reporting accountant is either uncertain about or disagrees with the course of action proposed, the reporting accountant may consider it necessary to take legal advice with respect to an appropriate course of action.

Going concern

63   References to an emphasis of matter of a material uncertainty related to events or conditions that may cast significant doubt about the ability of the entity to continue as a going concern that is relevant at the time the accountant's report is signed, and which will not be resolved by a satisfactory outcome to the transaction to which the investment circular relates, will be included in the reporting accountants' report immediately after the reporting accountant's opinion on the financial information.

64   Where the material uncertainty, related to events or conditions that may cast significant doubt about the ability of the entity to continue as a going concern, will be resolved if the outcome of transactions to which the investment circular containing the report relates is satisfactory (for example the successful raising of money through a share issue or shareholder approval of a transaction), the reporting accountant will consider whether adequate disclosure of that matter or uncertainty is made in a basis of preparation note to the historical financial information. If adequate disclosure is made in the historical financial information it is unlikely to be necessary for the reporting accountant to include an emphasis of matter paragraph in its report.

Representations

65   SIR 1000.13 sets out the basic principles and essential procedures with respect to obtaining written confirmation of representations from the directors of the entity.

A number of specific representations are required by ISAs (UK and Ireland). **66**
Where representations have been obtained by the auditor, subject to the
considerations set out in this SIR, it may not be necessary for the reporting
accountant to seek further representations covering the same matters, other than in
relation to the period since the audit opinion relating to the final period included in
the historical financial information was given.

Representations additional to those pursuant to ISAs (UK and Ireland) that a **67**
reporting accountant may consider for incorporation in the letter of representation
or board minute include:

●   Confirmation from the directors or management of the entity that they are
    responsible for the preparation of the historical financial information.

●   Confirmation that any adjustments made to historical financial statements
    for the purposes of preparing the historical financial information are
    necessary, have been correctly determined and that there are no other
    adjustments that are necessary.

In relation to a Class 1 acquisition, the acquirer may not be in a position to make **68**
representations in relation to the historical financial information of the target entity
on matters such as fraud, non-compliance with laws and regulation and related
parties. In such circumstances representations may be sought from the
management of the target entity.

Joint reporting accountants

When joint reporting accountants are appointed, the division of work as between **69**
them is a matter for agreement. The arrangements between the joint reporting
accountants may form part of the engagement letter. Irrespective of any such
arrangement, the joint reporting accountants are jointly and severally responsible
for the report to be given. Each of the joint reporting accountants participates in
the planning of the engagement and they agree upon the scope of work and any
changes subsequently found to be necessary thereto. Each of the joint reporting
accountants has regard to the considerations set out in this SIR in respect of using
the work of an auditor in determining the extent to which it is appropriate to rely
on the evidence obtained by the other reporting accountants or the extent to which
they consider it necessary to carry out their own work. Each of the joint reporting
accountants reviews the work of the other to the extent considered necessary and
records the results of that review. A common record of documentation, in
accordance with paragraphs 46-48 of SIR 1000, is normally maintained.

Reporting

SIRs 1000.17, 1000.18, 1000.19 and 1000.20 set out the basic principles **70**
and essential procedures with respect to reporting. Appendices 2 and 3 set out
illustrative examples of accountant's reports on historical financial information.

The reporting accountant's opinion is usually expressed in terms of whether, for **71**
the purpose of the relevant investment circular, the financial information gives a
true and fair view of the state of affairs and profits, cash flows and statement of
changes in equity.

When there is a limitation on the scope of the reporting accountant's work, the **72**
reporting accountant considers whether the limitation results in a lack of sufficient

appropriate evidence necessary to form an opinion. When the possible effect is, in the opinion of the reporting accountant, material to the financial information, there will be insufficient evidence to support an unqualified opinion. The nature of the work of reporting accountants is such that in the absence of reliable contemporary evidence relating to significant accounts and balances it may not be possible to form an opinion on the financial information. This might be the case where there has been no audit of the underlying financial information in the past or where the auditor has given a qualified opinion because of a limitation in the scope of work.

73   As a consequence of the purpose for which financial information is presented and the importance which may be attached to it by readers of the document, a reporting accountant does not normally agree to be associated with financial information where a disclaimer of opinion needs to be given on the information for the entire period.

74   The reporting accountant needs to be satisfied that the financial information adequately describes both the applicable financial reporting framework used in the preparation of the financial information and any of the accounting conventions from the Annexure that have been used. Usually these are referred to within the financial information in a basis of preparation note.

75   Where the financial information has been prepared fully in accordance with a recognised financial reporting framework such as "International Financial Reporting Standards as adopted by the European Union" the accountant's opinion is expressed in terms of the financial information giving a true and fair view in accordance with that framework (see Appendix 2 for an illustration).

76   Where the financial information has not been prepared fully in accordance with a recognised financial reporting framework but, for example, in accordance with a financial reporting framework modified by applying a convention described in the Annexure to this SIR, the accountant's opinion is expressed in terms of the financial information being prepared in accordance with the basis of preparation described in note x to the financial information, rather than in accordance with the financial reporting framework. The basis of preparation note states which accounting convention has been applied and how it departs from the requirements of the recognised financial reporting framework. A statement is made in the note that in all other respects the recognised financial reporting framework has been applied (see Appendix 3 for an illustration of the accountant's report).

Other information – references to previous audit opinions

77   The reporting accountant's opinion is arrived at independently of any audit opinion previously given on the financial statements which form the basis for the financial information to be reported on. It is not part of the reporting accountant's role to explain (where this is the case) why the reporting accountant's opinion differs from the opinion of the auditor. In some cases, however, there may be an obligation on an issuer to disclose details of modified opinions contained in auditor's reports prepared by the statutory auditor. In such cases, the reporting accountant considers the disclosures made by the issuer relating to such modified opinions and whether any matters disclosed might give rise to questions as to how the reporting accountant has dealt with matters giving rise to the modified opinions. If the reporting accountant is not satisfied with the disclosures, the reporting accountant discusses the matter with those responsible for the investment circular and ensures that the appropriate information is included

by the issuer or is included in the accountant's report. Where the audit has been undertaken by another firm, the reporting accountant does not normally refer to the name of the auditor in the accountant's report.

Comparatives

The reporting accountant is required to provide a report on each period included in **78** the historical financial information to which the reporting requirement relates. In consequence the financial information does not constitute either "comparative information", "corresponding figures" or "comparative financial statements" as contemplated by ISA (UK and Ireland) 710 "Comparative information – corresponding figures and comparative financial statements". Accordingly ISA (UK and Ireland) 710 is not relevant to the work of the reporting accountant.

Consent in the context of investment circulars containing a report by a reporting accountant

Paragraphs 66 to 74 of SIR 1000 deal with consent in relation to the inclusion of **79** an accountant's report in an investment circular.

Effective date

A reporting accountant is required to comply with the Investment Reporting **80** Standards contained in this SIR for reports on financial information for periods ending on or after 15 December 2010.

Appendix 1

Examples of engagement letter clauses

These examples of engagement letter clauses are intended for consideration in the context of an accountant's report. They should be tailored to the specific circumstances and supplemented by such other clauses as are relevant and appropriate. Suitably adapted, this example may be used for reporting accountant's engagements with respect to <u>AIM admission documents</u>.

For a prospectus

Financial information upon which the report is to be given

We understand that the directors of ABC plc will include in the Prospectus historical financial information for the [three] years ended [ ] in relation to ABC plc, the last [two years] of which will be presented and prepared in a form consistent with that which will be adopted in ABC plc's next published annual financial statements, having regard to accounting standards and policies and legislation applicable to such annual financial statements in accordance with the requirements of Annex I item 20.1 of the Prospectus Rules.

Responsibilities

The directors of ABC plc are responsible for the historical financial information.

It is our responsibility to form an opinion as to whether the financial information gives a true and fair view for the purposes of the Prospectus and to report our opinion to the directors of ABC plc.

Scope of work

We shall expect to obtain such evidence as we consider sufficient and appropriate to enable us to draw reasonable conclusions therefrom. The nature and extent of our procedures will vary according to our assessment of the appropriate sources of evidence. Our work will be directed to those matters which in our view materially affect the overall financial information upon which our opinion is to be given, and will not be directed to the discovery of errors or misstatements which we consider to be immaterial.

It is expected that a substantial part of the evidence which we may require will be contained in the audit files of LMN Accountants. ABC plc has agreed that it will use its best endeavours to ensure that the relevant files are made available to us.

Our work may also depend upon receiving without undue delay full co-operation from all relevant officials of ABC plc and their disclosure to us of all the accounting records of ABC plc and all other records and related information (including certain representations) as we may need for the purposes of our examination.

For a Class 1 circular

Financial information upon which the report is to be given

We understand that the directors of ABC plc will include in the Class 1 Circular a historical financial information table for the [three] years ended [ ] in relation to XYZ Limited which will be presented and prepared in a form consistent with the accounting policies adopted in ABC plc's latest annual consolidated accounts in accordance with the requirements of chapter 13 of the Listing Rules.

Responsibilities

The directors of ABC plc are responsible for the historical financial information table.

It is our responsibility to form an opinion as to whether the financial information gives a true and fair view for the purposes of the Class 1 circular and whether the financial information table has been prepared in a form that is consistent with the accounting policies adopted in ABC plc's latest annual accounts and to report our opinion to the directors of ABC plc.

Scope of work

We shall expect to obtain such evidence as we consider sufficient and appropriate to enable us to draw reasonable conclusions therefrom. The nature and extent of our procedures will vary according to our assessment of the appropriate sources of evidence. Our work will be directed to those matters which in our view materially affect the overall financial information upon which our opinion is to be given, and will not be directed to the discovery of errors or misstatements which we consider to be immaterial.

It is expected that a substantial part of the evidence which we may require will be contained in the audit files of LMN Accountants. ABC plc has agreed that it will use its best endeavours to ensure that the relevant files are made available to us.

Our work may also depend upon receiving without undue delay full co-operation from all relevant officials of ABC plc and XYZ Limited and their disclosure to us of all the accounting records of XYZ Limited and all other records and related information (including certain representations) as we may need for the purposes of our examination.

Appendix 2

Example of an accountant's report on historical financial information prepared in accordance with International Financial Reporting Standards as adopted by the European Union

Date

Reporting accountant's address

Addressees, as agreed between the parties in the engagement letter

Dear Sirs

[ABC plc]/[XYZ Limited]

We report on the financial information [set out in paragraphs .... to ....] [which comprises[6]], for the *[specify periods]*. This financial information has been prepared for inclusion in the *[describe Document[7]]* dated of ABC plc on the basis of the accounting policies set out in paragraph [ ]. This report is required by *[Relevant Regulation]* and is given for the purpose of complying with that [paragraph] and for no other purpose. [We have not audited or reviewed the financial information for the *[26 weeks ended ...]* [which has been included for comparative purposes only,] and accordingly do not express an opinion thereon.[8]]

Responsibilities

The Directors of ABC plc are responsible for preparing the financial information in accordance with International Financial Reporting Standards as adopted by the European Union.

It is our responsibility to form an opinion on the financial information and to report our opinion to you.

Basis of opinion

We conducted our work in accordance with Standards for Investment Reporting issued by the Auditing Practices Board in the United Kingdom. Our work included an assessment of evidence relevant to the amounts and disclosures in the financial information. It also included an assessment of significant estimates and judgments made by those responsible for the preparation of the financial information and whether the accounting policies are appropriate to the entity's circumstances, consistently applied and adequately disclosed.

We planned and performed our work so as to obtain all the information and explanations which we considered necessary in order to provide us with sufficient

---

[6] *Where paragraph numbers are not referred to specify the titles of the primary statements on which the opinion is being expressed and refer to the notes to those primary statements.*

[7] *For example, "prospectus", "listing particulars", "Class 1 circular" and "AIM admission document."*

[8] *This wording is relevant where financial information for an interim period is required to be reported on in circumstances where comparative information for the same interim period in the prior financial period is also to be presented, but not reported on.*

evidence to give reasonable assurance that the financial information is free from material misstatement whether caused by fraud or other irregularity or error.

Opinion on financial information

In our opinion, the financial information gives, for the purposes of the [*describe Document*] dated, a true and fair view of the state of affairs of [ABC plc]/[XYZ Limited] as at [*specifydates*] and of its profits, cash flows and [recognised gains and losses] [changes in equity] for the [*specify periods*] in accordance with International Financial Reporting Standards as adopted by the European Union [and has been prepared in a form that is consistent with the accounting policies adopted in [ABC plc's] latest annual accounts[9]].

Declaration[10]

For the purposes of [Prospectus Rule [5.5.3R(2)(f)] [5.5.4R(2)(f)]] [Paragraph a of Schedule Two of the AIM Rules] we are responsible for [this report as part] [the following part(s)] of the [prospectus] [registration document] [AIM admission document] and declare that we have taken all reasonable care to ensure that the information contained in [this report] [those parts] is, to the best of our knowledge, in accordance with the facts and contains no omission likely to affect its import. This declaration is included in the [prospectus] [registration document] [AIM admission document] in compliance with [item 1.2 of annex 1 of the Prospectus Regulation] [item 1.2 of annex 3 of the Prospectus Regulation] [Schedule Two of the AIM Rules].

Yours faithfully

Reporting accountant

---

[9] *The wording in these square brackets is appropriate for inclusion where the report relates to historical financial information included in a Class 1 circular.*

[10] *This declaration is a requirement of the Prospectus Rules and is appropriate for inclusion when the report is included in a Prospectus, see Appendix 2 of SIR 1000. It is also appropriate for inclusion in an AIM admission document under Schedule Two of the AIM Rules.*

Appendix 3

Example of an accountant's report on historical financial information prepared in accordance with the basis described in a basis of preparation note

Date

Reporting accountant's address

Addressees, as agreed between the parties in the engagement letter

Dear Sirs

[ABC plc]/[XYZ Limited]

We report on the financial information [set out in paragraphs .... to ....] [which comprises[11]], for the *[specify periods]*. This financial information has been prepared for inclusion in the *[describe Document[12]]* dated..........of ABC plc on the basis of the accounting policies set out in paragraph [ ]. This report is required by *[Relevant Regulation]* and is given for the purpose of complying with that [paragraph] and for no other purpose. We have not audited or reviewed the financial information for the *[26 weeks ended ...]* [which has been included for comparative purposes only,] and accordingly do not express an opinion thereon.[13]

Responsibilities

As described in paragraph [ ] the Directors of ABC plc are responsible for preparing the financial information on the basis of preparation set out in note x to the financial information.

It is our responsibility to form an opinion on the financial information and to report our opinion to you.

Basis of opinion

We conducted our work in accordance with Standards for Investment Reporting issued by the Auditing Practices Board in the United Kingdom. Our work included an assessment of evidence relevant to the amounts and disclosures in the financial information. It also included an assessment of significant estimates and judgments made by those responsible for the preparation of the financial information and whether the accounting policies are appropriate to the entity's circumstances, consistently applied and adequately disclosed.

We planned and performed our work so as to obtain all the information and explanations which we considered necessary in order to provide us with sufficient

---

[11] *Where paragraph numbers are not referred to specify the titles of the primary statements on which the opinion is being expressed and refer to the notes to those primary statements.*

[12] *For example, "prospectus", "listing particulars", "Class 1 circular" and "AIM admission document."*

[13] *This wording is relevant where financial information for an interim period is required to be reported on in circumstances where comparative information for the same interim period in the prior financial period is also to be presented, but not reported on.*

evidence to give reasonable assurance that the financial information is free from material misstatement whether caused by fraud or other irregularity or error.

Opinion on financial information

In our opinion, the financial information gives, for the purposes of the [describe Document] dated ....., a true and fair view of the state of affairs of [ABC plc]/ [XYZ Limited] as at *[specify dates]* and of its profits, cash flows and [recognised gains and losses] [changes in equity] for the *[specify periods]* in accordance with the basis of preparation set out in note x[14] [and has been prepared in a form that is consistent with the accounting policies adopted in [ABC plc's] latest annual accounts[15]].

Declaration[16]

For the purposes of [Prospectus Rule [5.5.3R(2)(f)] [5.5.4R(2)(f)]] [Paragraph a of Schedule Two of the AIM Rules] we are responsible for [this report as part] [the following part(s)] of the [prospectus] [registration document] [AIM admission document] and declare that we have taken all reasonable care to ensure that the information contained in [this report] [those parts] is, to the best of our knowledge, in accordance with the facts and contains no omission likely to affect its import. This declaration is included in the [prospectus] [registration document] [AIM admission document] in compliance with [item 1.2 of annex 1 of the Prospectus Regulation] [item 1.2 of annex 3 of the Prospectus Regulation] [Schedule Two of the AIM Rules].

Yours faithfully

Reporting accountant

---

[14] *Where the financial information has not been prepared fully in accordance with a recognised financial reporting framework but, for example, in accordance with a financial reporting framework modified by applying a convention described in the Annexure to this SIR, the accountant's opinion is expressed in terms of the financial information being prepared in accordance with the basis of preparation described in note x to the financial information, rather than in accordance with the financial reporting framework. The basis of preparation note states which accounting convention has been applied and how it departs from the requirements of the recognised financial reporting framework. A statement is made in the note that in all other respects the recognised financial reporting framework has been applied.*

[15] *The wording in these square brackets is appropriate for inclusion where the report relates to historical financial information included in a Class 1 circular.*

[16] *This declaration is a requirement of the Prospectus Rules and is appropriate for inclusion when the report is included in a Prospectus, see Appendix 2 of SIR 1000. It is also appropriate for inclusion in an AIM admission document under Schedule Two of the AIM Rules.*

Annexure

Accounting conventions commonly used in the preparation of historical financial information in investment circulars

This Annexure has been compiled by the APB from a number of sources to describe conventions commonly used for the preparation of historical financial information intended to show a true and fair view for the purposes of an investment circular. It does not include basic principles, essential procedures, or guidance promulgated by the APB.

Introduction

1   Preparers[1] have regard to accepted conventions which have been developed for the preparation and presentation of historical financial information in investment circulars. They seek to assist preparers, to the extent consistent with established accounting principles, to meet the obligation that the historical financial information should give a true and fair view for the purposes of the relevant investment circular. These conventions also take into account the requirement contained in the Prospectus Directive that the information should be presented in an easily analysable and comprehensible form. The conventions are described in the material presented below.

Disclosure of the financial reporting framework adopted

2   Preparers summarise the applicable financial reporting framework within the notes to the financial information. Where one of the conventions described in this Annexure is applied and its application has a material effect on the financial information or is necessary for an understanding of the basis of preparation of the financial information, it is appropriate to describe the treatment adopted in the basis of preparation note in the historical financial information.

Adjustments to the financial information

3   Preparers make adjustments, only in respect of material items, in order to:

(a)   Present the financial information for all relevant years on the basis of consistent, acceptable and appropriately applied accounting policies, in accordance with the applicable requirements;

(b)   Correct errors; and

(c)   Record adjusting post balance sheet events where appropriate (see paragraph 13 below).

4   The historical financial information presented will be based on the records of the entity whose historical financial information is presented in the investment circular (referred to as "the entity" throughout this Annexure), for the periods reported on. These records reflect the representations and intentions of the entity's management at the time the underlying financial information was

---

[1]   *The directors and management of an entity are responsible for the preparation and presentation of the financial statements of an entity. In this Annexure they are collectively referred to as "the preparers".*

drawn up. Matters such as the selection of accounting policies, accounting estimates and valuation judgments form part of the responsibilities of management in compiling a record of their stewardship.

In presenting historical financial information in an investment circular, except insofar as necessary to achieve the objectives set out above, preparers do not seek to replace accounting policies, accounting estimates or valuation judgments with alternatives subsequently selected by themselves. They consider whether the specific application of the basis of accounting originally adopted by management falls within an acceptable range of alternatives (if not, the conclusion will usually be that an error has occurred, which may need to be adjusted). Furthermore, it is not normally appropriate for adjustments to be made to eliminate items of earned income or expenses incurred, nor, in any circumstances, to recognise notional items of income or expense. The historical financial information presented in the investment circular is thus a version of the historical record as presented by the entity's management and adjustments are introduced only to achieve those specific objectives set out in paragraph 3 of this Annexure. **5**

Trend of results

The historical financial information included in an investment circular presents a trend of results for the relevant period. In this respect the financial information may be distinguished from the financial information contained in statutory accounts. **6**

Notional, or other, adjustments that impact net profits or net assets are not introduced in order to make the "track record" more consistent with the entity's expected operations or structure following the transaction. Such adjustments would anticipate future events and are not consistent with the principle that the historical financial information should record the events which actually occurred during the period of the historical financial information. **7**

Adjustments for change in basis of accounting

Adjustments are made to ensure that, wherever practicable, the financial information is stated on the basis of consistent accounting policies. Under the PD Regulation (subject to certain transitional provisions in Article 35 of the PD Regulation), the financial information for the most recent year (where audited historical financial information is required for the latest 2 financial years) or most recent 2 years (where audited historical financial information is required for the latest 3 financial years) is required to be prepared and presented in a form consistent with that which will be adopted in the issuer's next published annual financial statements (having regard to accounting standards and policies and legislation applicable to such annual financial statements). The requirements do not prevent entities from presenting the financial information for all periods in a form which is consistent with that which will be adopted in the next published financial statements if they so choose. In other contexts such as in a Class 1 transaction, the objective may be for the financial information for all periods to be presented in a form consistent with the accounting policies adopted by the acquirer in its latest annual consolidated accounts. **8**

When considering the adjustments that may be necessary where a new International Financial Reporting Standard or other relevant accounting standard has been introduced during, or (where applicable under the regulations) subsequent to, the period to which the regulations apply, a **9** relevant factor will be whether the requirements for implementing the new accounting standard provide that it should be applied retroactively once adopted. Where adoption of a new accounting standard leads to the inclusion of a prior year adjustment in the accounts, adjustments are made, to the extent practicable, to reflect the effect of the policy in any relevant earlier period. Where the adoption of a new accounting standard does not lead to the inclusion of a prior year adjustment, for example where the accounting standard is stated to apply to transactions first accounted for after a certain date; no such adjustment is made to the financial information. Where an entity chooses to adopt a new accounting standard early and this is permitted or encouraged, although not required, by that standard, the financial information reflects the same treatment as adopted by the entity.

10   Although adjustments may be made for changes in accounting policies, adjustments are not normally made for changes in the methods of applying an accounting policy (whether a one-off change or a series of gradual refinements) or otherwise to correct the entity's accounting estimates, provided that there were no errors. The effect of correcting an estimate in a later period is normally reflected in the result of that period. Consideration may be given to whether an understanding of the trend of results would be assisted by separate or additional disclosure in relation to changes in the methods of applying accounting policies or the impact of a correction of an accounting estimate.

11   Occasionally, an accounting policy may have been applied on the basis of considerations other than relevant economic ones (for example where financial statements measure the carrying amount of depreciable fixed assets in accordance with depreciation policies which are influenced by taxation considerations – as is the case in certain jurisdictions). Those presenting historical financial information in an investment circular may determine that an adjustment is necessary in order for the financial information to present a true and fair view, for the purposes of the relevant investment circular.

Audit qualifications relating to non-compliance with accounting standards

12   Where the auditor's report(s) on the underlying financial statements was qualified on grounds for example of failure to comply with an applicable accounting standard or disagreement over an accounting treatment, it may be possible to make adjustments so as to remove the need for a similar qualification in a report on the adjusted historical financial information.

Post balance sheet events

13   In determining whether adjustment is to be made for post balance sheet events, subject to the guidance set out above, it is normal practice to consider events only up to the date on which the audit report on the relevant underlying financial statements was originally signed by the auditors except in relation to the final period presented. In respect of this final period, it will be necessary for post balance sheet events to be reflected up to the date on which the historical financial information to be presented in the investment circular is approved by the responsible party. Where the financial information is based upon financial records which were not audited, the relevant date for post balance sheet event considerations in the earlier periods is normally taken to be the date at which the underlying balance sheet was finalised.

Presentation of the financial information

Subject to the requirements of any applicable regulation, the financial information is presented on a consistent and comparable basis from period to period and includes such presentational changes to the financial information as are necessary in order to achieve this. **14**

Presentational changes might be made to: **15**

(a)   Present the financial information in a comparable way; and

(b)   Give due prominence to matters of particular importance in the context of the document in which the financial information is included.

The financial information contained in the entity's records may not have been presented on a comparable basis from period to period because the convention for presenting financial information adopted in earlier periods may have been different from that adopted in later periods. **16**

Whenever practicable, financial information is presented in such a way that information which a user of the investment circular might wish to compare, is in fact comparable. Presentational changes of this nature may be categorised as follows: **17**

(a)   Reclassifications (for example, cost of sales reclassified as distribution costs);

(b)   Re-analyses (for example, restatements of analyses between continuing and discontinued activities);

(c)   Grossing up of items netted off in earlier periods (for example, matched assets and liabilities previously left off balance sheet);

(d)   Derivation or computation of information undisclosed in earlier periods (for example, profit and loss account subtotals or cash flow statements); and

(e)   Harmonisation of note disclosures (for example the editing of notes for earlier periods to integrate them with notes for later periods).

For example, a business classed as a continuing operation in one year may have been designated a discontinued activity in financial statements drawn up for a later period. It will be desirable for the relevant information within continuing operations in the earlier periods to be reclassified as discontinued. Where separate disclosure of information relating to entities acquired during the period has been presented in the financial statements, it is customary to reclassify such information for the purposes of the historical financial information as continuing activities, other than in respect of acquisitions made in the final period of the track record. **18**

Changes are not, however, made to the presentation adopted in the financial statements on which the financial information is based, unless such changes are consistent with the requirement to give a true and fair view for the purposes of the investment circular. **19**

Where it is considered that the significance of certain items to an understanding of the financial information may be obscured by the presentation adopted in the financial statements, it is usually appropriate for that presentation to be changed, relevant disclosures to be made or relevant explanations to be introduced to highlight their significance. This approach may be adopted for example to highlight certain categories of expense, such as proprietors' **20** remuneration, in the trading record of a company seeking flotation. It may also be adopted to highlight the results of different classes of business, particularly in cases where there are proposals that a class of business is to be discontinued.

21   However, in all cases, changes in presentation would be inappropriate if they are in conflict with applicable accounting standards.

22   As noted above, in certain cases regulatory requirements stipulate that information for the most recent two of the three years is to be presented on a basis comparable with that which would be adopted in an issuer's next annual financial statements. In such cases, in order that the reader is able to relate the first year's information to the final two years, preparers may present financial information for the second year on the basis originally reported (and thus comparable with the first year) as well as on the adjusted basis required by the regulation.

Issues connected with underlying financial statements

23   Where the entity has prepared accounts consolidating all its subsidiaries during the period, the financial information will, subject to any adjustments made, be the information set out in the consolidated accounts.

24   There may be cases where historical financial information is to be prepared for an entity in circumstances where consolidated financial statements do not exist. This may arise for example where the business is a sub-group, the parent company of which was exempt from the requirement to prepare consolidated accounts, or where the business comprises companies under common ownership but which were not constituted as a legal sub-group.

Unconsolidated accounts

25   Where there has been a legal sub-group it will usually be appropriate, for ease of analysis and comprehension, for the accounts of the subsidiaries to be consolidated into the accounts of the parent company. For this purpose, specially prepared consolidated accounts may be compiled by the relevant entity, applying the normal conventions for consolidation.

Entities under common management and control

26   Where the entities have been under common management and control but do not form a legal group, the historical financial information will normally be presented on a combined or aggregated basis. Under this method, the results and net assets of the relevant entities are aggregated (with eliminations for intercompany transactions and balances), as are the related share capital balances and reserves. If the information is not presented on a combined or aggregated basis then separate historical financial information for entities accounting for substantially the whole of the historical revenue earning record is likely to be required.

Carve outs

27   Where a business has formed part of a larger group ("overall group") during the three year period, but has not been accounted for separately, it may be desirable to present a separate track record (a "carve out") for that business ("carve out business"), derived from the records of the overall group. This approach may be preferable to the alternative approach of presenting the track record of the overall group, with appropriate disclosures of operations discontinuing or not

acquired. Circumstances where a carve out approach might be followed include flotations of businesses in a demerger and Class 1 acquisitions of divisions of a selling group.

When considering whether it is appropriate to present carve out financial information, the following factors will be relevant: **28**

(a)   The extent to which the carve out business has been separately managed and financially controlled within the overall group; and

(b)   The extent to which it is practicable to identify the historical financial information attributable to the carve out business.

Where the omission of the results and assets of those operations not the subject of the transaction concerned would be misleading in the context of the circumstances in which the historical financial information is to be presented, it will generally be appropriate to adopt the approach of presenting financial information on the overall group. Disclosures are made to assist the user to understand the contribution made by the operations not the subject of the transaction concerned. However, each case will need to be assessed on its own facts and circumstances. **29**

In preparing the track record for the carve out business, the guidance in paragraph 5 of this Annexure will be relevant. The objective will be, so far as possible, to present a historical record reflecting the events which actually occurred in the reporting period. Whilst it may be possible to identify certain transactions and balances which clearly relate to the carve out business, there will often be cases where the accounting records do not differentiate between items which relate to the carve out business and items which relate to the remainder of the overall group's business. Examples include management overheads, funding arrangements and shared assets. The guidance below discusses some of the elements typically encountered in preparing a carve out track record. **30**

Clear and comprehensive disclosure in the notes to the historical financial information will normally be needed in the basis of preparation in order for the nature of the historical financial information to be clearly understood. The description would be expected to give a general indication of the process adopted for the preparation of the historical financial information, and describe any factors which are particularly important to an understanding of the manner in which the information has been prepared. **31**

The accounting policies to be adopted in the carve out accounts will need to reflect the requirements relating to the presentation of historical financial information and may differ from those previously adopted. The question of functional currency should also be considered having regard to the economic environment of the carve out business, which may lead to the adoption of a different functional currency from that of the overall group. **32**

Allocations

Where transactions or balances are not accounted for within the overall group in a manner which clearly attributes them to the carve out business, it will generally be desirable for a method for allocating the relevant amounts to the carve out business to be identified with a view to providing the fairest approximation to the amounts actually attributable to the carve out business. Any method should be adopted and applied on a rational and consistent basis. It **33** will not, however, be appropriate to make allocations where there is no rational or consistent basis for doing so.

Bases for allocating transactions and balances

34　The appropriate basis for allocating group income and expenditure to a carve out business will vary according to the circumstances. It may, for example, be appropriate to allocate centrally accounted-for human resources costs on the basis of headcount (but account might be taken also of relative levels of staff turnover or other factors which indicate greater or less than average use in deciding whether the approach was in fact appropriate). The costs of a head office accounts department might be allocated by reference to the relevant sizes of the carve out business and remaining group. Again if other factors suggest that size is not a good indicator – if for example a disproportionate number of the accounting team is engaged in work for one part of the business and not the other – refinements to the approach might be considered appropriate.

35　It is important to recognise that the purpose of the allocation is to attribute an appropriate element of the overall group record to the carve out business. As a consequence, the position shown will frequently not be that which might have existed if the carve out business had been a stand-alone business. The position will be affected by the arrangements which apply to the group as a whole, which are a matter of historical fact and which it is not the purpose of the carve out financial information to alter. Frequently, disclosure will be made accompanying the financial information highlighting that the information presented may not be representative of the position which may prevail after the transaction.

36　Where an element of overall group third party debt is to be assumed by the carve out business, it may be appropriate to allocate an appropriate element of such debt to the carve out business during the historical track record period. The basis for such an allocation may be by reference to the terms of the separation agreement. In other cases, the debt may be treated as part of the carve out business' balance with the overall group. Finance lease borrowings would be expected to be allocated in line with the allocation of the related asset. The allocation of interest income/costs would follow the way in which the related debt and debt instruments have been apportioned.

Relationship with the remaining group

37　In addition to transactions with "third parties", the results of the business will also include transactions with the part of the overall group which is not part of the carve out business (the "remaining group"). Hence, for example, sales which were previously regarded as "intra group" will need to be re-examined to determine whether they relate to entities within the carve out business or outside it.

38　The remaining group will normally also be regarded as a related party for the purposes of disclosing related party transactions, and it will normally be necessary to identify the extent of the relationships between the carve out business and the remaining group. Balances with the remaining group may have comprised elements of trading balances and short term or long term funding balances, which may or may not have been interest bearing. Balances of a trading nature will normally be presented as an element of debtors or creditors. Balances which are considered to be funding in nature (having regard inter alia to the use made of the balances, the period for which they remain outstanding and the level of other capital) will normally be classified according to their general nature. Where the balance is interest bearing and has other characteristics of debt, it will be presented in the manner of debt financing. Where the balance does not have the characteristics of debt, it will be re-classified from creditors into capital and be presented in the manner of equity, typically aggregated with the share capital and reserves of companies comprising carve out business, as "parent company net investment" in the carve out business.

Balances with the remaining group may also contain elements of third party **39** debtors or creditors which have been accounted for on behalf of the carve out business by the remaining group. Examples might be VAT costs, payroll taxes, certain customers or suppliers common to the carve out business and the remaining group, and external funding balances. Such elements of the balance with the remaining group would be expected to be reallocated to the appropriate third party captions.

Consolidation journals within the overall group accounting records will need to **40** be analysed and, if appropriate, allocated to the carve out business.

Pension costs

Where employees of the carve out business participate in a pension scheme **41** relating to the overall group, the track record of the carve out business would reflect the apportioned costs applicable to the carve out business. The accounting implications of any pension surplus/deficit attributable to the carve out business would also normally be expected to be reflected in the track record.

Acquisitions

Acquisitions will be treated in accordance with the guidance in paragraphs 50 **42** to 52 of this Annexure. It should be noted that acquisitions previously regarded as too small for separate disclosure in the overall group accounts may become sufficiently material to require separate disclosure in the context of the carve out business.

Disposals, non recurring and exceptional items

Non recurring and exceptional items are generally allocated to the carve out **43** business and accounted for in accordance with the applicable accounting standard. The treatment of disposals follows that described in paragraph 53 of this Annexure.

Taxation

Tax charges are generally allocated to the carve out business to reflect the **44** proportion of the overall group charge attributable to the carve out business. The approach will typically involve the aggregation of the tax charges actually incurred by the companies within the carve out business (and will therefore reflect the benefits, reliefs and charges arising as a result of membership of the overall group), after taking account of the tax effects of any adjustments. Where the information relating to the tax charges actually incurred is not available, the tax charge may be recomputed on the basis of the results of the carve out business. The tax rate applied is selected having regard to the tax position of the overall group and might thus include the impact of benefits, reliefs and charges arising as a result of membership of the overall group, to the extent that they would have been available to or imposed upon the carve out business.

Cash flow statements

45   A cash flow statement is prepared for the carve out business based on the carve out information. Where the overall group operates a central cash account, cash flows relating to centrally settled costs are allocated to the carve out business to the extent that the related balances are allocated to the carve out business.

Investments in subsidiaries, joint ventures and associates

46   The status of an entity in the overall group's accounts (that is, whether it is recorded as a subsidiary, joint venture or associate) may be the result of investments in the relevant entity by more than one group company. If not all the investing companies are to be part of the carve out business, this may mean that the status of the entity in the track record of the carve out business is different from that within the overall group. Additional or new disclosures may therefore be required.

Treatment of other items

47   Dividends are expected to be reflected in the track record of the carve out business where companies within the carve out business have paid dividends to members of the remaining group.

48   In relation to the disclosure of directors' remuneration, it is normal to present information for those individuals who are to be directors of the carve out business or who were employed by the overall group in a capacity equivalent to that of a director of the carve out business. The information disclosed will reflect the salaries and benefits paid in respect of services to the carve out business by any member of the overall group to those individuals (irrespective of whether the individuals were directors or not) during the period covered by the track record. No information is presented for proposed directors of the carve out business who were not employed by the overall group, or for individuals who served as directors of companies within the carve out group but who are not to be directors of the carve out group's holding company following the transaction.

49   A segmental analysis is prepared for the carve out business to reflect the segments which the carve out business has decided to adopt.

Acquisitions

50   Entities acquired during the period covered by the historical financial information will typically be accounted for, in the records of the acquiring entity, in accordance with the accounting treatment applicable, having regard to the set of accounting standards adopted. Hence, for example, if the accounting standards require acquisition accounting, the acquired subsidiary will be accounted for from the date of acquisition by the acquiring entity.

51   Chapter 13 of the Listing Rules states that, in the case of a Class 1 acquisition when, during the three year period to be covered by the historical financial information (or in the lesser period up to the date of the acquisition if the target's business has been in operation for less than 3 years), the target has acquired or has agreed to acquire an undertaking which would have been classified, at the date of the acquisition, as a Class 1 acquisition, financial information on that undertaking must be given, which covers as a minimum the period from the beginning of the three year period to the date of acquisition.

Generally (and typically where the acquisition has been or will be accounted for under the acquisition method), the requirement outlined in paragraph 50 of this Annexure leads to a separate table of historical financial information covering the results of the acquired subsidiary undertaking during the period prior to acquisition. The Listing Rules contain no express contents requirements for acquisitions which would have been classified as smaller than Class 1 (ie a Class 2 or Class 3 transaction), although Listing Rule 13.3 contains contents requirements applicable to all circulars. Additional financial information may be required where the financial information presented in the entity's own track record does not account for substantially all of the track record of the business during the three year period.

Disposals

Disposals of subsidiaries or a discontinuation of a material section of the business are reflected by separate analysis between the continuing business and the disposed or discontinued business, either under the relevant headings in the profit and loss table or in the notes to the historical financial information. It is not normally appropriate to make adjustments to eliminate the results of subsidiaries that have been disposed of or discontinued operations from the trading record. However, it may not be necessary to introduce the results of a subsidiary that has been disposed of or a discontinued operation into specially prepared consolidated accounts or combined accounts prepared having regard to the considerations set out in paragraphs 25 to 49 of this Annexure, unless the inclusion of such information is relevant to an understanding of the business to which the historical financial information relates.

Financial information on newly formed issuers

In many cases, investment circulars are prepared in relation to newly formed companies (for example start up businesses, investment trusts, newly formed holding companies etc). Generally such companies will not have prepared accounts for a financial year at the time the investment circular is to be issued and consequently financial statements will need to be prepared for the purposes of the investment circular.

Unincorporated entities and entities producing limited accounting information

Acquisitions may involve entities which do not prepare financial information which meets the standards required for statutory accounts in the UK (and additionally may not have been subject to the disciplines of an external audit). The accounting conventions adopted may be devised for internal management accounting purposes rather than to meet more generally applicable accounting standards. In such cases, it may not be possible to present financial information meeting the requirements of the relevant regulations. The decision as to what information to present will depend upon the degree to which the information can be regarded as sufficiently relevant and reliable having regard to the purpose for which it is presented. Frequently the purpose will be to assist shareholders in a decision; it is for those responsible for the investment circular to weigh up the balance between depriving shareholders of information which may be relevant to a decision and being satisfied that the information presented is of sufficient quality to be properly used as the basis for a decision. Where

52

53

54

55

there is significant doubt about the quality of the financial information available, those responsible for the investment circular would be advised not to present it in the investment circular. This may lead to very limited financial information appearing in the relevant investment circular. In the case of an investment circular regulated by the UK Listing Authority, the position should be discussed in advance with the UK Listing Authority.

Changes in the legal form of entities

56   There may be circumstances where businesses have been carried on during the period covered by the report by different legal entities with the consequence that the relevant financial information may be found in the accounts of different legal entities. A typical example is a management buy-out, where prior to the buy-out, the business might have been accounted for in the financial statements of a subsidiary undertaking of the vendor, but, following the buy-out, the financial information may be that of the entity formed to effect the acquisition.

57   In cases where the legal entity accounting for the business has changed (for example where a business has been transferred from one entity to another – typically a newly formed company) but where there is no essential change in the underlying business, it is normal for the financial information to be presented as part of a single table, with the results of the predecessor entity shown next to those of the successor entity (generally on a combined basis in the period during which the transaction took place).

58   A consequence of the change in legal entity may be a change in the capital structure. Frequently, where there is a management buy-out, debt becomes a significant part of the capitalisation of the business. In order to highlight for the reader the potential lack of comparability between periods, a statement is often included within the introduction or beneath the profit and loss account (and in the relevant notes) referring to the change in capital structure and alerting the reader to the fact that the information relating to financing costs may not be comparable throughout the period. In certain cases, where the effect is material to an appreciation of the figures, it may also be necessary to draw attention to a discontinuity in values attributed to balance sheet items. In circumstances where, as in the case of a management buy-out, fair value adjustments have been made during the period covered by the historical financial information, it is inappropriate to attempt to show the impact of such adjustments on the results prior to the acquisition. However, the impact of the fair value adjustments is, where practicable, highlighted in respect of the post-acquisition results.

Earnings per share

59   In cases where there has been a capital reorganisation since the date at which the last balance sheet was drawn up, it will usually be appropriate for the earnings per share figures disclosed to be adjusted to reflect the reorganisation (to the extent that it involves issues of shares for no consideration, issues containing a bonus element, share splits etc). In such cases, the number of shares used in the earnings per share calculation is adjusted so that the shares originally in issue are replaced by the number of new shares, representing the shares originally in issue, following the reorganisation. Where shares have been issued during the period, this is taken into account in calculating the equivalent weighted average number of post-reorganisation shares. Where the reconstruction involves conversions, for example of preference shares or loan stock, the earnings figures used in the calculation of earnings per share may also need to be adjusted to eliminate the effect of any related preference dividends or interest.

Difficulties may also arise over the relevance of the earnings per share figure in certain cases, for example where prior to flotation a new holding company has been created. In such cases an earnings per share figure based on the share capital of the subsidiary may be of limited significance to investors. Accordingly, it is usually appropriate to include a supplementary earnings per share figure, in addition to the historical earnings per share figure, based on the relevant number of shares in the new parent company (before the issue of shares to raise new funds). This approach is also generally adopted in the case of a carve out business which did not have share capital during the reporting period. Where the effect is material and where practicable, the number of shares used for the purposes of the calculation is adjusted to reflect variations in the levels of capital funding the operations arising, for example, from issues of equity for cash during the period under review. In some circumstances, such as where there has been a management buy out during the period reported on, the differences in the capital structure may be such that a comparison of the earnings per share figures is not meaningful. Where this is the case, the statement to be included beneath the profit and loss table mentioned above generally refers also to the lack of comparability of the earnings per share information.

Reporting currency

Where historical financial information is to be presented on a target entity, and that target has reported historically in a currency other than that of the acquiring entity, it is normal to present the financial information in the target's original reporting currency.

Extraction without material adjustment

In a Class 1 circular, the listed company must (in addition to citing the source of the information) state whether the financial information that has been extracted from audited accounts was extracted without material adjustment. It is not possible to prescribe conditions for determining whether an adjustment will be a material adjustment in any given case, although presentational changes which do not have the effect of altering net assets, are normally permitted to be made. The UK Listing Authority will need to agree the approach in individual cases.

SIR 3000: Investment Reporting Standards applicable to public reporting engagements on profit forecasts

(January 2006)

Contents

Paragraphs

Introduction — 1 - 5

The nature of profit forecasts — 6 - 17
Reliability — 13 - 14
Understandability — 15
Comparability — 16
Compilation process — 17

Engagement acceptance and continuance — 18 - 19

Agreeing the terms of the engagement — 20

Ethical requirements — 21

Legal and regulatory requirements — 22 - 24

Quality control — 25

Planning and performing the engagement — 26 - 61
Materiality — 34 - 38
Public reporting engagement risk — 39 - 45
Historical financial information — 46 - 50
Consistent accounting policies — 51 - 53
Presentation of the profit forecast — 54 - 59
Representation letter — 60 - 61

Documentation — 62

Professional scepticism — 63

Reporting — 64 - 73
Responsibilities — 65
Basis of preparation of the profit forecast — 66 - 67
Basis of opinion — 68 - 70
Expression of opinion — 71 - 73

Modified opinions — 74 - 77

Consent — 78 - 79

Events occurring between the date of the reporting accountant's report and the completion date of the transaction — 80 - 83

Effective date   84

Appendix 1 – The regulatory background

Appendix 2 – Reporting accountant's criteria

Appendix 3 – Other regulatory provisions relevant to the preparers of profit forecasts

Appendix 4 – Examples of engagement letter clauses

Appendix 5 – Examples of management representation letter clauses

Appendix 6 – Example of a report on a profit forecast

Appendix 7 – Example of a report on a profit estimate that is not subject to assumptions

Investment Reporting Standards applicable to public reporting engagements on profit forecasts

SIR 3000 contains basic principles and essential procedures ("Investment Reporting Standards"), indicated by paragraphs in bold type, with which a reporting accountant is required to comply in the conduct of an engagement to report on a profit forecast which is included within an investment circular prepared for issue in connection with a securities transaction governed wholly or in part by the law and regulations of the United Kingdom.

SIR 3000 also includes explanatory and other material, including appendices, in the context of which the basic principles and essential procedures are to be understood and applied. It is necessary to consider the whole text of the SIR to understand and apply the basic principles and essential procedures.

For the purposes of SIRs, an investment circular is defined as: "any document issued by an entity pursuant to statutory or regulatory requirements relating to listed or unlisted securities on which it is intended that a third party should make an investment decision, including a prospectus, listing particulars, circular to shareholders or similar document".

SIR 1000 "Investment reporting standards applicable to all engagements involving an investment circular" contains basic principles and essential procedures that are applicable to all engagements involving an investment circular. The definitions in the Glossary of terms set out in Appendix 4 of SIR 1000 are to be applied in the interpretation of this and all other SIRs. Terms defined in the glossary are underlined the first time that they occur in the text.

To assist readers, SIRs contain references to, and extracts from, certain legislation and chapters of the Rules of the UK Listing Authority. Readers are cautioned that these references may change subsequent to publication.

Introduction

Standard for Investment Reporting (SIR) 1000 "Investment Reporting Standards **1** applicable to all engagements in connection with an investment circular" establishes the Investment Reporting Standards applicable to all engagements involving investment circulars. The purpose of this SIR is to establish specific additional Investment Reporting Standards and provide guidance for a reporting accountant engaged to report publicly on profit forecasts to be included in an investment circular under the PD Regulation, other regulations with similar requirements[1], the City Code, or if required by the London Stock Exchange in respect of an AIM Admission Document.

An engagement to report publicly on the proper compilation of a profit forecast is **2** a public reporting engagement as described in SIR 1000. The description of a public reporting engagement includes three generic terms having the following meanings in the context of an engagement to report on the proper compilation of a profit forecast:

(a)   with respect to a profit forecast the "**subject matter**" is the directors' expectation of the issuer's profit for the period of the forecast;

---

[1] *In the UK the Prospectus Directive is implemented into law through amendments to Part VI of FSMA and to certain secondary legislation. The Annexes to the PD Regulation have been incorporated into the Prospectus Rules issued by the FSA.*

(b) "<u>**suitable criteria**</u>" to be used by directors in the preparation of the profit forecast are provided by the requirements of the PD Regulation and the guidance[2] issued by <u>CESR</u> (CESR Recommendations). In forming its opinion as to whether the profit forecast has been properly compiled the reporting accountant considers whether certain of those criteria ("<u>**reporting accountant's criteria**</u>") have been properly applied. Reporting accountant's criteria are set out in Appendix 2 of this SIR; and

(c) with respect to a profit forecast the "<u>**outcome**</u>"[3] is the directors' profit forecast and related disclosures, that is included in the investment circular, and on which the reporting accountant expresses an opinion (in the "**reporting accountant's report**") as to whether that forecast is properly compiled on the basis stated and the basis of accounting used is consistent with the accounting policies of the issuer.

3   The PD Regulation defines a profit forecast as "a form of words which expressly states or by implication indicates a figure or a minimum or maximum figure for the likely level of profits or losses for the current financial period and/or financial periods subsequent to that period, or contains data from which a calculation of such a figure for future profits or losses may be made, even if no particular figure is mentioned and the word "profit" is not used"[4]. Where a profit forecast relates to an extended period and/or is subject to significant uncertainty it is sometimes referred to as a <u>projection</u>.

4   A profit forecast may include historical financial information relating to a past period. For example, a forecast made on 15 October 20xx for the profit for the year ended 31 December 20xx may include the profit for the six months ended 30 June 20xx included in the issuer's half yearly report and amounts extracted from management accounts for July and August. A <u>profit estimate</u> is historical financial information for a financial period which has expired but for which the results have not yet been published.

5   In this SIR requirements relating to "profit forecasts" also apply to statements typically referred to as "profit estimates" or "projections". The Investment Circular Reporting Standards in this SIR are applied to the whole period of the profit forecast including historical financial information included therein.

The nature of profit forecasts

6   A profit forecast is, by definition, uncertain because events and circumstances may not occur as expected or may not be predicted at all, or because the directors may take actions different to those previously intended. A profit forecast will usually include disclosures which provide information to assist the intended users understand the uncertainties involved.

7   A profit forecast is usually based on assumptions, relating to the expected outcome of future events and possible actions by the entity. As assumptions on which any forward-looking element of a profit forecast is based are a critical element of the profit forecast, the various regulations require, among other things, the disclosure of the principal assumptions which could have a material effect on the

---

[2] *CESR issued "CESR's Recommendations for the Consistent Implementation of the European Commission's Regulation on Prospectuses No. 809/2004" in February 2005.*

[3] *The "outcome" is sometimes described as "subject matter information".*

[4] *The definition of a profit forecast in the City Code is similar to that used by the PD Regulation.*

achievement of the profit forecast including those within the influence and control of the directors.

The extent to which a profit forecast will differ materially from the actual out-turn will depend on a profit forecast's particular circumstances. The length of the period into the future to which the profit forecast relates is only one, and not necessarily the most significant, factor. For example, an established business may be able to predict with greater certainty its results for the following year, particularly if it operates in a very stable environment, than a start-up business or an established business entering a new field. **8**

Profit forecasts are inherently uncertain and the probability that a profit forecast will correctly predict the actual out-turn is dependent upon the many factors which determine that uncertainty. The fact that a profit forecast does not correctly predict the actual out-turn does not mean that the profit forecast was not properly compiled. **9**

The Institute of Chartered Accountants in England and Wales issued guidance entitled "Prospective Financial Information – Guidance for UK directors" in September 2003 ("ICAEW Guidance") to assist directors in meeting the needs of the intended users of such information and of regulators and to promote the production of high quality prospective financial information, including profit forecasts. **10**

As explained in Appendix 1 of this SIR the CESR Recommendations state that profit forecasts should be: **11**

(a)   reliable;

(b)   understandable;

(c)   comparable; and

(d)   relevant.

Directors are required to form a judgment as to whether the profit forecast is relevant to the purpose of the investment circular[5] and, therefore, whether or not it is appropriate for the profit forecast to be included in the investment circular. The directors' judgment in this regard will be influenced by the applicable regulatory requirements. The role of the reporting accountant is to report on whether a profit forecast, that the directors have decided to include in an investment circular, has been properly compiled. The role of the reporting accountant does not include questioning the directors' decision to include a profit forecast in an investment circular.

In order to provide an opinion on the proper compilation of a profit forecast the reporting accountant carries out the procedures required by this SIR and SIR 1000, and any others it considers necessary, to satisfy itself that the profit forecast is: **12**

(a)   reliable[6];

(b)   understandable[7]; and

(c)   comparable[8].

---

[5] *The ICAEW Guidance considers that a profit forecast will only be "relevant" if it:*

(a)   *has the ability to influence economic decisions of investors;*

(b)   *is provided in time to influence the economic decisions of investors; and*

(c)   *has predictive value or, by helping to confirm or correct past evaluations or assessments, it has confirmatory value.*

[6] *The business analysis principle in the ICAEW Guidance.*

[7] *The reasonable disclosure principle in the ICAEW Guidance.*

[8] *The subsequent validation principle in the ICAEW Guidance.*

Consequently, these three principles are considered to be suitable criteria for the evaluation of profit forecasts by the reporting accountant (see Appendix 2 of this SIR).

Reliability

13   The ICAEW Guidance explains that to be *reliable* a profit forecast will possess the following attributes:

(a)   it can be depended upon by the intended users as a faithful representation of what it either purports to represent or could reasonably be expected to represent;

(b)   it is neutral because it is free from deliberate or systematic bias intended to influence a decision or judgment to achieve a predetermined result;

(c)   it is free from material error;

(d)   it is complete within the bounds of what is material; and

(e)   it is prudent in that a degree of caution is applied in making judgments under conditions of uncertainty.

The ICAEW Guidance explains that a profit forecast will be a faithful representation where it reflects an entity's strategies, plans and risk analysis in a way that is appropriate for the purpose for which the profit forecast is being prepared. The fact that a profit forecast does not correctly predict the actual out-turn once reported, does not necessarily mean that it was not reliable when made.

14   A profit forecast, including the assumptions used, is more likely to possess the above attributes when the issuer has undertaken an analysis of the underlying business and its strategies, plans and risks (the directors' business analysis) and when the forecast is prepared as a faithful representation of that business analysis, taking prudent account of the risk analysis. The reliability of a profit forecast is, therefore, a function of:

(a)   the quality of the analysis undertaken; and

(b)   the degree to which that analysis is reflected in the profit forecast.

Understandability

15   To be *understandable* a profit forecast contains the information necessary for intended users to appreciate the degree of uncertainty attaching to the information and how that uncertainty might impact it. This requires the disclosure of assumptions and other matters relevant to the basis of preparation of the profit forecast which are of importance in assisting the intended users' understanding of the profit forecast. The omission of important information may prevent a profit forecast from being understandable and equally, if the disclosure is too complex or too extensive the understandability of the profit forecast may be also impaired. What constitutes reasonable disclosure will therefore depend upon the particular circumstances of each profit forecast but will need to take into consideration:

(a)   sources of uncertainty and the related assumptions made relating to uncertainties;

(b)   the factors that will affect whether assumptions will be borne out in practice; and

(c) alternative outcomes, being the consequences of assumptions not being borne out.

Comparability

The usefulness of a profit forecast is derived partly from its *comparability*, **16** namely the expectation that it will be possible to compare it to the actual results and that it can be compared to equivalent information for other reporting periods. For this to be the case profit forecasts need to be prepared and presented on a basis comparable with the actual financial information for that period and will involve the application of the accounting policies used by the entity in preparing the historical financial information included in the investment circular.

Compilation process

The compilation of a profit forecast is the gathering, classification and **17** summarisation of relevant financial information. The process followed by the preparer would be expected to include:

(a) an appropriate analysis of the business (what is appropriate will depend on a number of factors including the complexity and predictability of the business and the length of the period being forecast and accordingly the content, degree of detail and presentation of such analyses may vary significantly);

(b) identification of material uncertainties;

(c) selection of appropriate assumptions;

(d) where relevant, identification of and reference to, appropriate third party information (eg. market research reports);

(e) arithmetic computation of the profit forecast;

(f) appropriate sensitivity analysis;

(g) appropriate disclosures to enable the intended users to understand the profit forecast; and

(h) appropriate consideration of the profit forecast and approval of it by the directors of the entity.

Engagement acceptance and continuance

SIR 1000.1 and SIR 1000.2 set out the basic principles and essential procedures, **18** with respect to engagement acceptance and continuance, which are applicable to all engagements involving an investment circular.

When accepting or continuing an engagement to report publicly on a profit **19** forecast, the reporting accountant ascertains whether the directors intend to comply with all relevant regulatory requirements, in particular those that are the basis of the reporting accountant's criteria set out in Appendix 2 of this SIR.

Agreeing the terms of the engagement

SIR 1000.3 and SIR 1000.4 set out the basic principles and essential procedures **20** with respect to agreeing the terms of the engagement. Examples of engagement letter clauses are set out in Appendix 4 of this SIR.

Ethical requirements

21   SIR 1000.5 sets out the basic principles and essential procedures with respect to the ethical requirements that apply to a reporting accountant[9].

Legal and regulatory requirements

22   The PD Regulation requires any profit forecast or estimate included in a prospectus to be reported on by independent accountants or auditors (referred to in this SIR as "a reporting accountant") and specifies the form of opinion to be given[10]. The City Code contains provisions in relation to profit forecasts included in offer documents and requires reports from the auditors or reporting accountants in certain circumstances.

23   SIR 1000.6 sets out the basic principles with respect to the legal and regulatory requirements applicable to a reporting accountant.

24   Appendices 1, 2 and 3 to this SIR set out those provisions of the PD Regulation, the CESR Recommendations relating to the implementation of the PD Regulation, and the City Code, that provide the suitable criteria for directors. Those provisions that are the basis of criteria for a reporting accountant expressing an opinion on whether the profit forecast has been properly compiled are set out in Appendix 2 of this SIR.

Quality control

25   SIR 1000.7 and SIR 1000.8 set out the basic principles and essential procedures with respect to the quality control of engagements to report on profit forecasts.

Planning and performing the engagement

26   SIR 1000.9 and SIR 1000.10 set out the basic principles and essential procedures with respect to the planning of all reporting engagements. Additional essential procedures and guidance are set out below.

27   **The reporting accountant should obtain an understanding of the key factors affecting the subject matter sufficient to identify and assess the risk of the profit forecast not being properly compiled and sufficient to design and perform evidence gathering procedures including:**

   (a)   **the background to and nature of the circumstances in which the profit forecast, which is included in the investment circular, was made;**

   (b)   **the entity's business; and**

   (c)   **the procedures adopted, or planned to be adopted, by the directors for the preparation of the profit forecast. (SIR 3000.1)**

28   The reporting accountant gains an understanding of the background to and nature of the circumstances in which the profit forecast is being prepared, by discussion with the directors or management of the issuer and by reading relevant supporting documentation. In particular, the reporting accountant ascertains whether the

---

[9]   *In January 2006 the APB issued an Exposure Draft of an Ethical Standard for Reporting Accountants (ESRA).*

[10]   *The PD Regulation requirements are reproduced verbatim in the Prospectus Rules issued by the FSA.*

profit forecast is being made for the first time or whether it is a forecast that has previously been made by the issuer that may be required to be updated by the directors.

The reporting accountant uses professional judgment to determine the extent of **29** the understanding required of the entity's business. In a start-up situation or where an established business is entering a new field the reporting accountant's understanding of the prospective business is necessarily limited to general knowledge of the field being entered and an understanding of the business analysis undertaken by the entity.

Reporting on the proper compilation of a profit forecast generally requires an **30** understanding of the entity's management accounting, budgeting and forecasting systems and procedures beyond that normally considered necessary for an audit of historical financial statements.

Discussion with the preparers of a profit forecast will identify the process by **31** which the profit forecast has been, or will be prepared, the extent to which the ICAEW guidance has been followed, the sources of information used, areas of significant uncertainty where assumptions have been made and the basis for those assumptions and how those assumptions have been documented. Specific matters for consideration include:

- The organisational structure of the entity and the extent to which subsidiaries or local operating units have been involved in the preparation of the profit forecast;

- Whether the profit forecast is prepared on a basis comparable with the most recent historical financial information in the investment circular;

- The extent to which the period of the forecast includes historical financial information;

- Whether the profit forecast will be capable of comparison to subsequently published historical financial information.

Where profit forecasts are regularly prepared by the entity either for internal **32** management purposes or for publication, the reporting accountant considers the closeness to actual out-turns achieved in previous forecasts and the analysis of any variances. As well as helping to provide an understanding of the entity's business this may be helpful in identifying those aspects of the business which are subject to significant uncertainty.

The reporting accountant should consider materiality and public reporting **33** **engagement risk in planning its work in accordance with its instructions and in determining the effect of its findings on the report to be issued. (SIR 3000.2)**

Materiality

The ICAEW Guidance states that in order for a profit forecast to be *reliable* it will, **34** amongst other things, be free of material error. An error in the context of the proper compilation of a profit forecast includes:

- Assumptions that are not consistent with the analysis of the business;

- Mathematical or clerical mistakes in the compilation of the profit forecast;

- Misapplication of accounting policies;

- Misapplication of a stated assumption;

- Known misstatements in historical financial information embodied in the forecast without adjustment.

35   Additionally, there may be deficiencies in the presentation of a profit forecast which may impair the understandability or comparability of the forecast in a way that is material. An error could, therefore, also include:

(a)   failure to disclose an assumption or other explanation which is necessary for an understanding of the forecast; or

(b)   presenting the forecast in a way that it is not capable of being compared with subsequent published results.

36   Matters are material if their omission or misstatement could, individually or collectively, influence the economic decisions of the intended users of the profit forecast. Materiality depends on the size and nature of the omission or misstatement judged in light of the surrounding circumstances. The size or nature of the matter, or a combination of both, could be the determining factor.

37   Evaluating whether an omission or misstatement could influence economic decisions of the intended users of the profit forecast, and so be material, requires consideration of the characteristics of those intended users. The intended users are assumed to:

(a)   have a reasonable knowledge of business and economic activities and accounting and a willingness to study the profit forecast with reasonable diligence; and

(b)   make reasonable economic decisions on the basis of the profit forecast.

The determination of materiality, therefore, takes into account how intended users with such characteristics could reasonably be expected to be influenced in making economic decisions.

38   The fact that the out-turn differs from the forecast does not necessarily mean that the forecast was not properly compiled as, for example, actual economic conditions may have differed from those reasonably assumed in the preparation of the profit forecast.

Public reporting engagement risk

39   "Public reporting engagement risk" is the risk that the reporting accountant expresses the positive and unmodified opinion required by the PD Regulation or the City Code when the profit forecast has not been properly compiled on the basis stated or the basis of accounting used for the profit forecast is not consistent with the accounting policies of the issuer.

40   SIR 1000.11 and SIR 1000.12 set out the basic principles and essential procedures, with respect to obtaining evidence, that are applicable to all engagements involving an investment circular. Additional basic principles, essential procedures and guidance relating to engagements to report on profit forecasts are set out below.

41   **To form an opinion that the profit forecast has been properly compiled, the reporting accountant should obtain sufficient appropriate evidence that the forecast is free from material error in its compilation by:**

(a)   **obtaining evidence that the directors have applied the criteria set out in Appendix 2 of this SIR;**

(b)   **checking that the profit forecast has been accurately computed based upon the disclosed assumptions and the preparer's accounting policies;**

(c)   **considering whether the assumptions used are consistent with the directors' business analysis and the reporting accountant's own knowledge of the business; and**

(d)   **where applicable, evaluating the basis on which any historical financial information included in the profit forecast has been prepared. (SIR 3000.3)**

The reporting accountant considers the business analysis carried out by the   **42** preparer of the profit forecast and whether there is prima facie evidence that it has been used by the directors in compiling the profit forecast. The extent and nature of the analysis that is necessary to support a forecast, and therefore the extent of the reporting accountant's consideration of such analysis, will be dependent upon the specific circumstances in which the forecast is being prepared. The reporting accountant discusses the preparer's plans, strategies and risk analysis with the preparer of the profit forecast, considers documentary support for them and assesses whether they are consistent with the analysis of the business. Where the outcome is dependent upon the intent of the directors and management the reporting accountant will ordinarily obtain representations from the directors concerning such matters.

The preparer can be expected to document the assumptions that have been made   **43** relating to matters significant to the profit forecast. The reporting accountant will, therefore, obtain from preparers of the profit forecast details of those assumptions identified as being relevant to the compilation of the profit forecast. It will usually be the case that not all of the assumptions made in support of the profit forecast will be published. This is because only those that are material to an understanding of the profit forecast are required to be disclosed.

There may be a range of appropriate assumptions which can be used as the basis   **44** for a profit forecast and the resulting forecast may differ significantly depending on which assumptions are adopted. The reporting accountant is not required to express an opinion on the appropriateness of the assumptions used or the achievability of the results reflected in a profit forecast. The reporting accountant does however:

(a)   consider if any of the assumptions adopted by the directors which, in the opinion of the reporting accountant are necessary for a proper understanding of the profit forecast, have not been adequately disclosed; and

(b)   consider whether any material assumption made by the directors appears to be unrealistic.

When checking whether the profit forecast has been accurately computed the   **45** reporting accountant considers whether cash flow statements and balance sheets have been prepared to act as checks against omissions and inconsistencies. If cash flow statements and balance sheets have not been prepared, in circumstances where the reporting accountant considers this to be necessary, the reporting accountant discusses with the directors whether their preparation is necessary in order to properly compile the profit forecast.

Historical financial information

46 **When evaluating the basis on which any historical financial information included in the profit forecast has been prepared the reporting accountant should:**

    (a) **consider whether any element of that historical financial information has been audited or reviewed by the auditors and, if so, the results of that audit or review;**

    (b) **evaluate the suitability of unaudited historical financial information included in the profit forecast;**

    (c) **evaluate how the historical financial information has been embodied into the profit forecast; and**

    (d) **if adjustments have been made to previously published historical financial information evaluate whether the adjustments appear appropriate in the circumstances. (SIR 3000.4)**

47 If historical financial information has been audited or reviewed the reporting accountant evaluates the scope of the audit or review procedures performed. In performing such an evaluation the reporting accountant ordinarily seeks access to the working papers of the auditor or reviewer and considers whether the results of those procedures indicate that the historical financial information may be unreliable or reveal uncertainties that ought to require the directors to make and disclose assumptions in the forecast.

48 In order to evaluate the suitability of unaudited historical financial information included in the profit forecast the reporting accountant[11]:

    (a) understands the internal control environment of the entity relevant to the historical financial information;

    (b) discusses with the management of the issuer the accounting policies applied and any differences from the method of preparing the entity's published financial statements;

    (c) enquires of management, including internal audit, whether there have been any changes in the financial reporting systems or internal controls, or any breakdowns in systems and controls, which might affect the reliability of the financial information;

    (d) enquires about changes in the entity's procedures for recording, classifying and summarising transactions, accumulating information for disclosure, and preparing the financial information;

    (e) considers the accuracy of unaudited historical financial information by comparing it to audited financial statements for the same period;

    (f) compares the historical financial information to previous budgets or forecasts prepared by the entity in respect of the period covered by the historical financial information and gains an understanding of the reasons for any significant differences; and

    (g) checks the historical financial information used in the profit forecast agrees to, or reconciles with, the underlying accounting records of the entity.

49 Where the reporting accountant determines that it is not able to obtain sufficient appropriate evidence from the above procedures to indicate that the financial

---

[11] *Some of these procedures may already have been performed as part of a review.*

information for the expired part of the forecast period forms a suitable basis for inclusion in the profit forecast the reporting accountant discusses the matter with the directors of the issuer and, if appropriate, the issuer's advisers.

In considering historical financial information included in a profit forecast, it is **50** important that the reporting accountant understands the manner in which such information has been included in the profit forecast. Where different systems or processes have been used to produce prospective financial information and the historical information, there is a risk that there may be inconsistencies in the cut-off between these two sources of information which could lead to a material error in the compilation of the profit forecast.

Consistent accounting policies

The reporting accountant should compare the accounting policies used in **51**
connection with the profit forecast with those used by the entity in preparing
the most recent historical financial information in the investment circular,
and evaluate whether they are consistent with each other and continue to be
appropriate so far as concerns the profit forecast. (SIR 3000.5)

Where the profit forecast relates to the expansion of an existing business the **52** reporting accountant's primary consideration is the consistency of the accounting policies used. However, the reporting accountant also considers the ongoing appropriateness of the accounting policies in the light of the business plans underlying the profit forecast.

Where the profit forecast relates to a start-up situation the reporting accountant **53** considers the appropriateness of the accounting policies chosen.

Presentation of the profit forecast

The reporting accountant should consider whether it has become aware of **54**
anything to cause it to believe that:

(a)   the profit forecast is presented in a way that is not understandable;

(b)   a material assumption is unrealistic;

(c)   an assumption or other information which appears to it to be material
to a proper understanding of the profit forecast has not been disclosed;
or

(d)   the profit forecast is not capable of subsequently being compared with
historical financial information.

If the reporting accountant is aware of such matters it should discuss them
with the parties responsible for the profit forecast and with those persons to
whom its report is to be addressed and consider whether it is able to issue its
opinion. (SIR 3000.6)

The ICAEW Guidance provides guidance to directors with regard to the matters **55** that should be disclosed in connection with a profit forecast. This covers both the manner in which the profit forecast is presented and the use of disclosure to deal with uncertainty. It is important that useful information is not obscured through the inclusion of immaterial items or the use of headings or financial measures which are not meaningful to, or may be misunderstood by, the intended users.

When evaluating the presentation of a profit forecast the reporting accountant **56** considers whether the components of the profit forecast are clearly described and whether the descriptions are adequate to allow an intended user to understand the profit forecast. For example, if a profit forecast is presented as a single figure for profit before tax, and this was to be achieved by the inclusion of a significant non-recurring profit from the sale of a fixed asset, consideration is given as to whether additional disclosure is necessary to make the profit forecast understandable.

57   When evaluating whether the disclosures made in respect of a profit forecast are sufficient to make it understandable, the reporting accountant considers whether the degree of uncertainty inherent in the information is clearly disclosed. Disclosure of an assumption may not make the profit forecast understandable if the significance of that assumption is not apparent from the disclosure made.

58   Where a profit forecast is subject to significant uncertainty it is common practice for the preparers to perform a sensitivity analysis in respect of those assumptions which are either believed to be subject to the greatest uncertainty and/or where the profit forecast is most sensitive to variations in such assumptions. The reporting accountant considers such sensitivity analysis, as it may assist in the identification of material assumptions or other aspects of the profit forecast where the uncertainty requires additional disclosure to enable it to be understood.

59   The manner in which the profit forecast is presented in the investment circular will also be considered in respect of whether the profit forecast is capable of being compared with subsequent historical financial information. The choice of captions and disclosure or emphasis of particular numbers or attributes may determine how the profit forecast will be interpreted and consideration is given as to whether this is consistent with the purpose for which the profit forecast has been prepared.

Representation letter

60   SIR 1000.13 sets out the basic principles and essential procedures, with respect to representation letters, that are applicable to all engagements involving an investment circular. Examples of representation letter clauses are set out in Appendix 5 of this SIR.

61   Some of the assumptions used in the compilation of a profit forecast will be dependent on the intent of the directors and management. Consequently the representations of directors and management as to their intent are a particularly important source of evidence for the reporting accountant.

Documentation

62   SIR 1000.14 and SIR 1000.15 set out the basic principles and essential procedures with respect to the reporting accountant's working papers.

Professional scepticism

63   SIR 1000.16 sets out the basic principle with respect to the attitude of professional scepticism adopted by the reporting accountant in planning and performing an engagement.

Reporting

64   SIR 1000.17, SIR 1000.18 and SIR 1000.19 set out the basic principles and essential procedures, with respect to reporting, that are applicable to all engagements involving an investment circular. Additional basic principles and

essential procedures relating to engagements to report on profit forecasts are set out below.

Responsibilities

In all reports on profit forecasts in investment circulars the reporting   **65**
accountant should explain the extent of its responsibility in respect of the
profit forecast by including in its report:

(a)   a statement that the reporting accountant's responsibility is to form an
opinion (as required by the relevant regulatory requirement) on the
compilation of the profit forecast and to report its opinion to the
addressees of the report; and

(b)   a statement that the profit forecast and the assumptions on which it is
based are the responsibility of the directors. (SIR 3000.7)

Basis of preparation of the profit forecast

The reporting accountant should include a basis of preparation section of its   **66**
report that cross refers to disclosures that explain the basis of preparation of
the profit forecast including:

(a)   assumptions made;

(b)   the accounting policies applied; and

(c)   where appropriate, the source of historical financial information
embodied in the profit forecast. (SIR 3000.8)

Where the entity is reporting on the expansion of an established business it is usual   **67**
for it to report that the basis of accounting is consistent with the existing
accounting policies. Where the accounting policies used in the profit forecast
differ from those previously published a more detailed explanation of the
accounting policies used in the preparation of the profit forecast will be
appropriate.

Basis of opinion

SIR 1000.18 sets out the basic principles and essential procedures, with respect to   **68**
the basis of the reporting accountant's opinion, that are applicable to all
engagements involving an investment circular. Additional basic principles and
essential procedures relating to engagements to report on profit forecasts are set
out below.

The reporting accountant should explain the basis of its opinion by including   **69**
in its report a statement that where the profit forecast and any assumptions
on which it is based relate to the future and may, therefore, be affected by
unforeseen events, the reporting accountant does not express any opinion as
to whether the actual results achieved will correspond to those shown in the
profit forecast. (SIR 3000.9)

By its nature financial information relating to the future is inherently uncertain.   **70**
For a profit forecast to be understandable sufficient information must be disclosed
to allow an intended user to understand this uncertainty. As the reporting
accountant is not required to form or express an opinion on the achievability of
the result shown in the profit forecast, it is inappropriate for the reporting
accountant to include in the basis of preparation section of its report cautionary
language relating to uncertainty beyond that referred to above.

Expression of opinion

71　**The report should contain a clear expression of opinion that complies with applicable regulatory requirements. (SIR 3000.10)**

72　In forming its opinion the reporting accountant takes account of those events or information which the reporting accountant becomes aware of occurring up to the date on which the reporting accountant signs the report, that affect the opinion expressed in the report.

73　The investment circular in which the reporting accountant's report is included may be made available in other countries, such as the United States of America, which have their own standards for accountants when reporting on profit forecasts. In such circumstances, the reporting accountant considers whether to include a reference to the fact that a report issued in accordance with the SIRs should not be relied upon as if it had been issued in accordance with the standards applicable in that other country. An example of such a reference is included in the example reports set out in Appendices 6 and 7 of this SIR.

Modified opinions

74　SIR 1000.20 sets out the basic principles and essential procedures, with respect to modified opinions, that are applicable to all engagements involving an investment circular. Additional basic principles and essential procedures relating to engagements to report on profit forecasts are set out below.

75　**The reporting accountant should not express an unmodified opinion when the directors have not applied the criteria set out in Appendix 2 of this SIR and in the reporting accountant's judgment the effect of not doing so is, or may be, material. (SIR 3000.11)**

76　The PD and other regulations, such as the City Code, usually require a positive and unmodified opinion. Consequently, in the event that the reporting accountant concludes that it is unable to report in the manner prescribed it invites those responsible for the profit forecast to consider whether the profit forecast can be amended to alleviate its concerns or whether the profit forecast should be omitted from the investment circular.

77　Examples of reports on a profit forecast and a profit estimate expressing such positive and unmodified opinions are set out in Appendices 6 and 7 of this SIR.

Consent

78　SIR 1000.21 and SIR 1000.22 set out the basic principles and essential procedures with respect to the giving of consent by the reporting accountant.

79　The reporting accountant considers whether disclosures in the investment circular, such as those in the "Risk Factors" section, are consistent with the assumptions and other disclosures made in connection with the profit forecast before consent is given by the reporting accountant to its report on the profit forecast being included in the investment circular.

Events occurring between the date of the reporting accountant's report and the completion date of the transaction

SIR 1000.23 sets out the basic principles and essential procedures with respect to **80** events occurring between the date of the reporting accountant's report and the completion date of the transaction.

Under Sections 81 and 87G of the FSMA, Prospectus Rule 3.4, and Listing Rule **81** 4.4.1, a supplementary investment circular must be prepared if, after the date the investment circular has been formally approved by a regulator and before dealings in the relevant securities commence, the issuer becomes aware that there has been a significant change affecting any matter contained in the document or a significant new matter has arisen, the inclusion of information in respect of which would have been required if it had arisen at the time of its preparation. A similar obligation arises under Article 16 of the Prospectus Directive in respect of the period following registration of the investment circular during which an agreement in respect of the securities can be entered into in pursuance of the offer contained in the investment circular.

If, as a result of discussion with those responsible for the investment circular **82** concerning an event that occurred prior to the completion date of the transaction, the reporting accountant is either uncertain about or disagrees with the course of action proposed the reporting accountant may consider it necessary to take legal advice with respect to its responsibilities in the particular circumstances.

After the date of its report, the reporting accountant has no obligation to perform **83** procedures or make enquiries regarding the investment circular.

Effective date

A reporting accountant is required to comply with the Investment Reporting **84** Standards contained in this SIR for reports signed after 31 March 2006. Earlier adoption is encouraged.

Appendix 1 – The regulatory background

Prospectus Directive Requirements

The **Prospectus Directive** and **PD Regulation** determine the requirements for the content of a prospectus. In determining whether the PD Regulation has been complied with, the FSA will take into account whether a person has complied with the CESR Recommendations.

The PD Regulation requires that where an issuer chooses to include a profit forecast (including a profit estimate) in a prospectus it must:

(a) be prepared on a basis comparable with the historical financial information in the prospectus;

(b) include a statement setting out the principal assumptions upon which the issuer has based its forecast or estimate. There must be a clear distinction between assumptions about factors which the members of the administrative, management or supervisory bodies can influence and assumptions about factors which are exclusively outside the influence of the members of the administrative, management or supervisory bodies; the assumptions must be readily understandable by investors, be specific and precise and not relate to the general accuracy of the estimates underlying the forecast; and

(c) other than for issuers of high denomination debt and derivative securities, include a report prepared by independent accountants or auditors stating that in their opinion the forecast or estimate has been properly compiled on the basis stated and that the basis of accounting used for the profit forecast or estimate is consistent with the accounting policies of the issuer.

The CESR Recommendations provide further guidance concerning the principles that should be applied in preparing a profit forecast in a prospectus. In addition to due care and diligence being taken to ensure that profit forecasts or estimates are not misleading to investors, the following principles should be taken into consideration when profit forecasts are being compiled. Profit forecasts and estimates should be:

(a) *reliable* – they should be supported by a thorough analysis of the issuer's business and should represent factual and not hypothetical strategies, plans and risk analysis; (a criterion for a reporting accountant see Appendix 2 of this SIR);

(b) *understandable* – they should contain disclosure that is not too complex or extensive for investors to understand; (a criterion for a reporting accountant see Appendix 2 of this SIR);

(c) *comparable* – they should be capable of justification by comparison with outcomes in the form of historical financial information (a criterion for a reporting accountant see Appendix 2 of this SIR); and

(d) *relevant* – they must have an ability to influence economic decisions of investors and provided on a timely basis so as to influence such decisions and assist in confirming or correcting past evaluations or assessments. (Not a criterion for a reporting accountant see paragraph 11 of this SIR).

The City Code

The City Code requires that:

(a) all communications to shareholders in an offer, including forecasts, must maintain the highest standard of accuracy and fair presentation;

(b) assumptions should be drafted in a way that allows shareholders to understand their implications; and

(c) the forecast is compiled with due care and consideration by the directors and the disclosure of assumptions should provide useful information to assist shareholders to help them to form a view as to the reasonableness and reliability of the forecast.

Notes 1(c) and (d) to Rule 28.2 of the City Code state:

> *"The forecast and the assumptions on which it is based are the sole responsibility of the directors. However, a duty is placed on the financial advisers to discuss the assumptions with their client and to satisfy themselves that the forecast has been made with due care and consideration. Auditors or consultant accountants must satisfy themselves that the forecast, so far as the accounting policies and calculations are concerned, has been properly compiled on the basis of the assumptions made.*
>
> *Although the accountants have no responsibility for the assumptions, they will as a result of their review be in a position to advise the company on what assumptions should be listed in the circular and the way in which they should be described. The financial advisers and accountants obviously have substantial influence on the information about assumptions to be given in the circular; neither should allow an assumption to be published which appears to be unrealistic, or one to be omitted which appears to be important, without commenting appropriately in its report."*

Whilst the City Code does not explicitly identify the principles contained in the CESR Recommendations those principles are consistent with the requirement of the Code.

Appendix 2 – Reporting accountant's criteria

	PD Regulation	Annex I[1] of PD Regulation	CESR Recommendations
A statement setting out the principal assumptions upon which the issuer has based its forecast or estimate.		13.1	
There must be a clear distinction between assumptions about factors which the members of the administrative, management or supervisory bodies can influence and assumptions about factors which are exclusively outside the influence of the members of the administrative, management or supervisory bodies; the assumptions must be readily understandable by investors, be specific and precise and not relate to the general accuracy of the estimates underlying the forecast.		13.1	
The profit forecast or estimate must be prepared on a basis comparable with the historical financial information.		13.3	
The following principles should be taken into consideration when profit forecasts or estimates are being compiled. Profit forecasts or estimates should be • **Understandable**, ie Profit forecasts or estimates should contain disclosure that is not too complex or extensive for investors to understand; • **Reliable,** ie Profit forecasts should be supported by a thorough analysis of the issuer's business and should represent factual and not hypothetical strategies, plans and risk analysis; • **Comparable,** ie Profit forecasts or estimates should be capable of justification by comparison with outcomes in the form of historical financial information;			para 41

[1] *The column illustrates Annex I as an example. Other annexes to the PD Regulation contain identical requirements with respect to profit forecasts. See Appendix 1 of SIR 1000.*

Appendix 3 – Other regulatory provisions relevant to the preparers of profit forecasts

	PD Regulation	Annex I of PD Regulation	CESR Recommendations
(8) Voluntary disclosure of profit forecasts in a share registration document should be presented in a consistent and comparable manner and accompanied by a statement prepared by independent accountants or auditors. This information should not be confused with the disclosure of known trends or other factual data with material impact on the issuer's prospects. Moreover, they should provide an explanation of any changes in disclosure policy relating to profit forecasts when supplementing a prospectus or drafting a new prospectus.	**Recital 8**		
Profit forecast means a form of words which expressly states or by implication indicates a figure or a minimum or maximum figure for the likely level of profits or losses for the current financial period and/or financial periods subsequent to that period, or contains data from which a calculation of such a figure for future profits or losses may be made, even if no particular figure is mentioned and the word "profit" is not used.	**Article 2**		
Profit estimate means a profit forecast for a financial period which has expired and for which results have not yet been published.	**Article 2**		
If an issuer chooses to include a profit forecast or profit estimate the registration document must contain the information set out in items 13.1 and 13.2.		13	

	PD Regulation	Annex I of PD Regulation	CESR Recommendations
A report prepared by independent accountants or auditors stating that in the opinion of the independent accountants or auditors the forecast or estimate has been properly compiled on the basis stated and that the basis of accounting used for the profit forecast or estimate is consistent with the accounting policies of the issuer.		13.2	
If a profit forecast in a prospectus has been published which is still outstanding, then provide a statement setting out whether or not that forecast is still correct as at the time of the registration document, and an explanation of why such forecast is no longer valid if that is the case.		13.4	
The inclusion of a profit forecast or estimate in a prospectus is the responsibility of the issuer and persons responsible for the prospectus and due care and diligence must be taken to ensure that profit forecasts or estimates are not misleading to investors.			para 40
The following principles should be taken into consideration when profit forecasts or estimates are being compiled. Profit forecasts or estimates should be • **Relevant,** ie profit forecasts and estimates must have an ability to influence economic decisions of investors and provided on a timely basis so as to influence such decisions and assist in confirming or correcting past evaluations or assessments.			para 41

	PD Regulation	Annex I of PD Regulation	CESR Recommendations
Where an issuer provides a profit forecast or estimate in a registration document, if the related schedules so requires, it must be reported on by independent accountants or auditors in the registration document (as described in item 13.2 of Annex I of the Regulation). Where the issuer does not produce a single prospectus, upon the issuance of the securities note and summary at a later time, the issuer should either: • Confirm the profit forecasts or estimates; or • State that the profit forecasts or estimates are no longer valid or correct; or • Make appropriate alteration of profit forecasts or estimates. In this case they must be reported upon as described in item 13.2 of Annex I of the Regulation.			para 42
If an issuer has made a statement other than in a previous prospectus that would constitute a profit forecast or estimate if made in a prospectus, for instance, in a regulatory announcement, and that statement is still outstanding at the time of publication of the prospectus, the issuer should consider whether the forecasts or estimates are still material and valid and choose whether or not to include them in the prospectus. CESR considers that there is a presumption that an outstanding forecast made other than in a previous prospectus will be material in the case of share issues (especially in the context of an IPO). This is not necessarily the presumption in case of non-equity securities.			paras 43 & 44

	PD Regulation	Annex I of PD Regulation	CESR Recommendations
When there is an outstanding profit forecast or estimate in relation to a material undertaking which the issuer has acquired, the issuer should consider whether it is appropriate to make a statement as to whether or not the profit forecast or estimate is still valid or correct. The issuer should also evaluate the effects of the acquisition and the profit forecast made by that undertaking on its own financial position and report on it as it would have done if the profit forecast or estimate had been made by the issuer.			paras 45 & 46
The forecast or estimate should normally be of profit before tax (disclosing separately any non-recurrent items and tax charges if they are expected to be abnormally high or low). If the forecast or estimate is not of profit before tax, the reasons for presenting another figure from the profit and loss account must be disclosed and clearly explained. Furthermore the tax effect should be clearly explained. When the results are published relating to a period covered by a forecast or estimate, the published financial statements must disclose the relevant figure so as to enable the forecast and actual results to be directly compared.			paras 47 & 48

	PD Regulation	Annex I of PD Regulation	CESR Recommendations
CESR recognises that often in practice, there is a fine line between what constitutes a profit forecast and what constitutes trend information as detailed in item 12 of Annex I of the Regulation. A general discussion about the future or prospects of the issuer under trend information will not normally constitute a profit forecast or estimate as defined in Articles 2.10 and 2.11 of the Regulation. Whether or not a statement constitutes profit forecasts or estimates is a question of fact and will depend upon the circumstances of the particular issuer.			para 49
This is a non-exhaustive list of factors that an issuer is expected to take into consideration when preparing forecasts: • Past results, market analysis, strategic evolutions, market share and position of the issuer • Financial position and possible changes therein • Description of the impact of an acquisition or disposal, change in strategy or any major change in environmental matters and technology • Changes in legal and tax environment • Commitments towards third parties.			para 50

Appendix 4 – Examples of engagement letter clauses

The examples of engagement letter clauses are intended for consideration in the context of a public reporting engagement on a profit forecast. They should be tailored to the specific circumstances and supplemented by such other clauses as are relevant and appropriate.

Financial information upon which the report is to be given

The [investment circular] will contain a profit [forecast] [estimate] for the company for the period [ending] [ended] [date] (the "PFI") prepared and presented in accordance with [item 13 of Annex I of the PD Regulation] [the requirements of the City Code] [other applicable regulation]. We will prepare a report on the profit [forecast] [estimate] addressed to […] expressing our opinion on the profit [forecast] [estimate], in the form described below, to be included in the [investment circular].

We will ask the Directors to make certain representations to us regarding the PFI. If the PFI is intended only to be a hypothetical illustration, or the Directors are unable to make such representations to us, we will not wish to be associated with the PFI and accordingly, will be unable to report publicly on it.

Responsibilities

The preparation and presentation of the profit forecast will be the responsibility solely of the Directors. [This responsibility includes the identification and disclosure of the assumptions underlying the profit forecast. (omit if no assumptions)] The Directors are also responsible for ensuring that the PFI is prepared and presented in accordance with [item 13 of Annex I of the PD Regulation] [the requirements of the City Code] [other applicable regulation].

We will require the Directors to formally adopt the PFI before we report on it. We understand that the Directors will have regard to the guidance issued by The Institute of Chartered Accountants in England & Wales entitled "Prospective Financial Information – Guidance for UK directors" in preparing the PFI.

It is our responsibility to form an opinion as to whether the profit [forecast] [estimate] has been properly compiled on the basis stated and whether such basis is consistent with the accounting policies normally adopted by ABC plc.

If the results of our work are satisfactory, and having regard to the requirements of [item 13.2 of Annex I of the PD Regulation] [the City Code] [other applicable regulation], we shall prepare a report on the profit [forecast] [estimate] for inclusion in the [investment circular]. An illustration of the form of our report is attached.

Scope of work

Our work will be undertaken in accordance with Standard for Investment Reporting (SIR) 3000 "Investment Reporting Standards Applicable to Public Reporting Engagements on Profit Forecasts" issued by the Auditing Practices Board and will be subject to the limitations described therein.

We draw your attention in particular to paragraph 75 of SIR 3000 which would preclude us from expressing any opinion if the Directors have not complied with the regulatory requirements set out in Appendix 2 of that SIR.

As the purpose of our engagement is restricted as described above and since the PFI and the assumptions on which it is based relate to the future and may be affected by unforeseen events, we will not provide any opinion as to how closely the actual result achieved will correspond to the profit [forecast] [estimate]. Accordingly we neither confirm nor otherwise accept responsibility for the ultimate accuracy and achievability of the PFI.

Assumptions

We will discuss the assumptions with the persons responsible for preparing the PFI together with the evidence they have to support the assumptions, but we will not seek to independently verify or audit those assumptions. We are not responsible for identifying the assumptions.

In the event that anything comes to our attention to indicate that any of the assumptions adopted by the Directors which, in our opinion, are necessary for a proper understanding of the PFI have not been disclosed or if any material assumption made by the Directors appears to us to be unrealistic we will inform the directors so that steps can be taken to resolve the matter. However, we are required to comment in our report if an assumption is published which appears to us to be unrealistic or an assumption is omitted which appears to us to be important to an understanding of the PFI.

Appendix 5 – Examples of management representation letter clauses

Similar clauses to those below could be amended to be used in connection with a report on a profit estimate.

Introduction

We refer to the forecast of *[insert description of items forecast]*, profit for the financial year and earnings per share of ABC plc ("the Company") and its subsidiaries together ("the ABC Group") for the year ending *[date]* ("the profit forecast") set out on page [-] of the [Prospectus]/[Circular]/[Offer Document] to be issued on *[date]*. We acknowledge that we are solely responsible for the profit forecast and the assumptions on which it is based as set out on page [-] and confirm on behalf of the Directors [and Proposed Directors] of the Company to the best of our knowledge and belief, having made appropriate enquiries of officials of the Company, the following representations made to you in the course of your work:

Specific representations

- The profit forecast is based on our assessment of the financial position and results of operations and cash flow for the period and is presented on a basis consistent with the accounting policies [normally] [to be] adopted by the ABC Group and has been prepared in accordance with relevant legislative requirements.[1]

- We believe the forecast results are likely to be achieved although achievement of the forecast may be favourably or unfavourably affected by unforeseeable and uncontrollable events.

- We have made available to you all significant information relevant to the profit forecast of which we have knowledge.

- All significant assumptions have been disclosed and the assumptions underlying the profit forecast are reasonable and appropriate.

- The results shown in the [audited/unaudited] financial results for the six months ended *[date]* and the unaudited management accounts for the [-] months ended *[date]* which are included in the profit forecast have been prepared in accordance with the accounting policies [normally] [to be] adopted by the ABC Group and are free from material misstatement.

- There are no contingencies, (other than those which have been taken into account in making the forecast), that are material in the context of the profit forecast which should be disclosed or taken into account in the profit forecast.

- The profit forecast is presented in a manner which is balanced and fair and not misleading and contains all information necessary for a proper understanding of the profit forecast.

[1] *The reporting accountant may also wish to obtain a representation that the profit forecast has been prepared in accordance with "Prospective Financial Information – Guidance for UK directors" published by the Institute of Chartered Accountants in England and Wales.*

- The profit forecast together with the assumptions and the representations in this letter have been approved by the board of directors.

Representations in respect of specific assumptions such as;

- The assumed like for like increase in sales of 5% in the last quarter of 200X incorporates expected price increases of 2% based on preliminary discussions with three of our major customers.

- The assumed increase in gross margin of 2 percentage points from 1 July 200X is based on manufacturing cost savings as a result of the realisation of efficiencies resulting from the factory reorganisation which we expect to be completed by the end of May 200X.

- The assumed increase in sales prices by 2% more than the general level of inflation in 200Y is based upon the expectation that our major competitor will announce a price increase of at least that amount in November 200X. Our expectation takes account of similar timing of increases in previous years and information derived from conversations with mutual customers.

- The opening of two new sales outlets in the current financial year assumes that negotiations to agree a lease on one out of the three potential units in Guildford will be completed and that refitting and pre-opening will be completed within 10 weeks which is 25% longer than the historical average due to additional building works being required in one of the potential sites.

- The profit forecast assumes that a forward sale of $x million will be designated as a hedge against expected US$ income.

Appendix 6 – Example of a report on a profit forecast

Date

Reporting accountant's address

Addressees, as agreed between the parties in the engagement letter

Dear Sirs

[ABC plc]

We report on the profit forecast comprising [*insert description of items comprising the prospective financial information, e.g. [forecast of turnover, operating profit, profit before tax and earnings per share]//[projected profit and loss account]*] of ABC plc ("the Company") and its subsidiaries (together "the ABC Group") for the [*specify period*] ending [*date*] (the "Profit Forecast"). The Profit Forecast, and the material assumptions upon which it is based, are set out on pages [-] to [-] of the [*describe document*] ("the [Document]") issued by the Company dated [*date*]. This report is required by [Relevant Regulation] [guidance issued by the London Stock Exchange with respect to the AIM market] and is given for the purpose of complying with that [Relevant Regulation] [guidance issued by the London Stock Exchange] and for no other purpose.

[*Substitute the following text for the last sentence of the immediately preceding paragraph, where a profit forecast is made by an offeree in the context of a takeover.* This report is required by Rule 28.3(b) of the City Code and is given for the purpose of complying with that rule and for no other purpose. Accordingly, we assume no responsibility in respect of this report to the Offeror or any person connected to, or acting in concert with, the Offeror or to any other person who is seeking or may in future seek to acquire control of the Company (an "Alternative Offeror") or to any other person connected to, or acting in concert with, an Alternative Offeror.]

Responsibilities

It is the responsibility of the Directors of ABC plc to prepare the Profit Forecast in accordance with the requirements of the [PD Regulation]/[Listing Rules]/[City Code] [guidance issued by the London Stock Exchange].

It is our responsibility to form an opinion as required by the [PD Regulation]/ [Listing Rules]/ [City Code] [guidance issued by the London Stock Exchange] as to the proper compilation of the Profit Forecast and to report that opinion to you.

Basis of preparation of the Profit Forecast

The Profit Forecast has been prepared on the basis stated on page [ ] of the [Document][1] and is based on the [audited/unaudited] interim financial results for the [six] months ended [date], the unaudited management accounts for the [x] months ended [date] and a forecast to [date]. The Profit Forecast is required to be presented on a basis consistent with the accounting policies of the ABC Group.

Basis of opinion

We conducted our work in accordance with the Standards for Investment Reporting issued by the Auditing Practices Board in the United Kingdom. Our

---

[1] *The disclosures presented with the profit forecast should explain the basis on which the forecast has been prepared. This will include identification of the accounting policies used and the financial information used in compiling the forecast. Typically this may include reference to audited/unaudited financial statements of the entity for an interim period, unaudited management accounts and management's forecast for the period for which no management accounts are available.*

work included [evaluating the basis on which the historical financial information included in the Profit Forecast has been prepared and] considering whether the Profit Forecast has been accurately computed based upon the disclosed assumptions and the accounting policies of the ABC Group. Whilst the assumptions upon which the Profit Forecast are based are solely the responsibility of the Directors, we considered whether anything came to our attention to indicate that any of the assumptions adopted by the Directors which, in our opinion, are necessary for a proper understanding of the Profit Forecast have not been disclosed and whether any material assumption made by the Directors appears to us to be unrealistic.

We planned and performed our work so as to obtain the information and explanations we considered necessary in order to provide us with reasonable assurance that the Profit Forecast has been properly compiled on the basis stated.

Since the Profit Forecast and the assumptions on which it is based relate to the future and may therefore be affected by unforeseen events, we can express no opinion as to whether the actual results reported will correspond to those shown in the Profit Forecast and differences may be material.

[*This paragraph may be omitted if the document is not to be distributed outside the UK* – Our work has not been carried out in accordance with auditing or other standards and practices generally accepted in the United States of America [or other jurisdictions] and accordingly should not be relied upon as if it had been carried out in accordance with those standards and practices.]

Opinion

In our opinion, the Profit Forecast has been properly compiled on the basis [stated] [of the assumptions made by the Directors/][2] and the basis of accounting used is consistent with the accounting policies of the ABC Group[3].

Declaration[4]

For the purposes of [Prospectus Rule [5.5.3R(2)(f)] [5.5.4R(2)(f)] [guidance issued by the London Stock Exchange] we are responsible for [this report as part] [the following part(s) of the [prospectus] [registration document] [AIM admission document] and declare that we have taken all reasonable care to ensure that the information contained [in this report] [those parts] is, to the best of our knowledge, in accordance with the facts and contains no omission likely to affect its import. This declaration is included in the [prospectus] [registration document] [AIM admission document] in compliance with [item 1.2 of annex I of the PD Regulation] [item 1.2 of annex III of the PD Regulation] [guidance issued by the London Stock Exchange].

Yours faithfully

Reporting Accountant

---

[2] *The City Code requires "on the basis of the assumptions made by the Directors" but the PD Regulation requires "on the basis stated".*

[3] *Where the accounting policies used in the profit forecast either differ from those used by the company in its latest published financial statements or where the company has never published financial statements reference should be made to the accounting policies which have been used.*

[4] *This declaration is a requirement of the PD Regulation and is appropriate for inclusion when the report is included in a Prospectus, see Appendix 2 of SIR 1000.*

Appendix 7 – Example of a report on a profit estimate that is not subject to assumptions

Date

Reporting accountant's address

Addressees, as agreed between the parties in the engagement letter

Dear Sirs

[ABC plc]

We report on the profit estimate comprising [*insert description of items comprising the prospective financial information, e.g.* [estimate of turnover, operating profit, profit before tax and earnings per share]/[estimated profit and loss account]] of ABC plc ("the Company") and its subsidiaries (together "the ABC Group") for the [*specify period*] ended [*date*] (the "Profit Estimate"). The Profit Estimate and the basis on which it is prepared is set out on pages [-] to [-] of the [*describe document*] ("the [Document]") issued by the Company dated [*date*]. This report is required by [Relevant Regulation] [guidance issued by the London Stock Exchange with respect to the AIM market] and is given for the purpose of complying with that [Relevant Regulation] [guidance issued by the London Stock Exchange] and for no other purpose.

[*Substitute the following text for the last sentence of the immediately preceding paragraph, where a profit estimate is made by an offeree in the context of a takeover.* This report is required by Rule 28.3(b) of the City Code and is given for the purpose of complying with that rule and for no other purpose. Accordingly, we assume no responsibility in respect of this report to the Offeror or any person connected to, or acting in concert with, the Offeror or to any other person who is seeking or may in future seek to acquire control of the Company (an "Alternative Offeror") or to any other person connected to, or acting in concert with, an Alternative Offeror.]

Responsibilities

It is the responsibility of the directors of ABC plc to prepare the Profit Estimate in accordance with the requirements of the [PD Regulation]/[Listing Rules]/[City Code]. In preparing the Profit Estimate the directors of ABC plc are responsible for correcting errors that they have identified which may have arisen in unaudited financial results and unaudited management accounts used as the basis of preparation for the Profit Estimate.

It is our responsibility to form an opinion as required by the [PD Regulation]/ [Listing Rules]/ [City Code] as to the proper compilation of the Profit Estimate and to report that opinion to you.

Basis of preparation of the Profit Estimate

The Profit Estimate has been prepared on the basis stated on page [ ] of the [Document][1] and is based on the [audited/unaudited] interim financial results for the [six] months ended [date], the unaudited management accounts for the [x] months ended [date] and an estimate for the [month] to [date]. The Profit Estimate

---

[1] *The disclosures presented with the profit estimate should explain the basis on which the estimate has been prepared. This will include identification of the accounting policies used and the financial information used in compiling the estimate. Typically this may include reference to audited/unaudited financial statements of the entity for an interim period, unaudited management accounts and management's estimate (which may itself be based on other forms of management information for the period for which no management accounts are available.*

is required to be presented on a basis consistent with the accounting policies of the ABC Group.

Basis of opinion

We conducted our work in accordance with the Standards for Investment Reporting issued by the Auditing Practices Board in the United Kingdom. Our work included evaluating the basis on which the historical financial information for the [x] months to [date] included in the Profit Estimate has been prepared and considering whether the Profit Estimate has been accurately computed using that information and whether the basis of accounting used is consistent with the accounting policies of the ABC Group.

We planned and performed our work so as to obtain the information and explanations we considered necessary in order to provide us with reasonable assurance that the Profit Estimate has been properly compiled on the basis stated.

However, the Profit Estimate has not been audited. The actual results reported, therefore, may be affected by revisions required to accounting estimates due to changes in circumstances, the impact of unforeseen events and the correction of errors in the [interim financial results] [management accounts]. Consequently we can express no opinion as to whether the actual results achieved will correspond to those shown in the Profit Estimate and the difference may be material.

[This paragraph may be omitted if the document is not to be distributed outside the UK Our work has not been carried out in accordance with auditing or other standards and practices generally accepted in the United States of America [or other jurisdictions] and accordingly should not be relied upon as if it had been carried out in accordance with those standards and practices.]

Opinion

In our opinion, the Profit Estimate has been properly compiled on the basis stated and the basis of accounting used is consistent with the accounting policies of the ABC Group[2].

Declaration[3]

For the purposes of [Prospectus Rule [5.5.3R(2)(f)] [5.5.4R(2)(f)] [guidance issued by the London Stock Exchange] we are responsible for [this report as part] [the following part(s) of the [prospectus] [registration document] [AIM admission document] and declare that we have taken all reasonable care to ensure that the information contained [in this report] [those parts] is, to the best of our knowledge, in accordance with the facts and contains no omission likely to affect its import. This declaration is included in the [prospectus] [registration document] [AIM admission document] in compliance with [item 1.2 of annex I of the PD Regulation] [item 1.2 of annex III of the PD Regulation] [guidance issued by the London Stock Exchange].

Yours faithfully

Reporting Accountant

---

[2] *Where the accounting policies used in the profit estimate either differ from those used by the company in its latest published financial statements or where the company has never published financial statements reference should be made to the accounting policies which have been used.*

[3] *This declaration is a requirement of the PD Regulation and is appropriate for inclusion when the report is included in a Prospectus, see Appendix 2 of SIR 1000.*

SIR 4000: Investment Reporting Standards applicable to public reporting engagements on pro forma financial information

(January 2006)

Contents

Paragraphs

Introduction   1 - 2

The nature of pro forma financial information   3 - 5
     Compilation process   5

Engagement acceptance and continuance   6 - 7

Agreeing the terms of the engagement   8

Ethical requirements   9

Legal and regulatory requirements   10 - 12

Quality control   13

Planning and performing the engagement   14 - 48
     Materiality   20 - 22
     Public reporting engagement risk   23 - 26
     Unadjusted financial information of the issuer   27 - 29
     Adjustments   30 - 38
     Omitted adjustments   39 - 41
     Checking the calculations   42
     Consistent accounting policies   43 - 45
     Presentation of pro forma financial information   46 - 47
     Representation letter   48

Documentation   49

Professional scepticism   50

Reporting   51 - 59
     Responsibilities   52 - 53
     Basis of preparation of the pro forma financial information   54 - 55
     Expression of opinion   56 - 59

Modified opinions   60 - 63

Consent   64

**Events occurring between the date of the reporting accountant's report and
the completion date of the transaction**   65 - 68

Effective date   69

Appendix 1 – Reporting accountant's criteria

Appendix 2 – Other regulatory provisions relevant to the preparers of
              pro forma financial information

Appendix 3 – Examples of engagement letter clauses

Appendix 4 – Examples of management representation letter clauses

Appendix 5 – Example report on pro forma financial information in accordance
              with the PD regulation or the listing rules

Annexure – Sections of TECH 18/98 "Pro forma financial information – Guidance for preparers
under the Listing Rules" (published by the Institute of Chartered Accountants in England &
Wales) that remain relevant

Investment Reporting Standards applicable to public reporting engagements on pro forma financial information

SIR 4000 contains basic principles and essential procedures ("Investment Reporting Standards"), indicated by paragraphs in bold type, with which a reporting accountant is required to comply in the conduct of an engagement to report on pro forma financial information, which is included within an investment circular prepared for issue in connection with a securities transaction governed wholly or in part by the laws and regulations of the United Kingdom.

SIR 4000 also includes explanatory and other material, including appendices, in the context of which the basic principles and essential procedures are to be understood and applied. It is necessary to consider the whole text of the SIR to understand and apply the basic principles and essential procedures.

For the purposes of the SIRs, an investment circular is defined as: "any document issued by an entity pursuant to statutory or regulatory requirements relating to listed or unlisted securities on which it is intended that a third party should make an investment decision, including a prospectus, listing particulars, circular to shareholders or similar document".

SIR 1000 "Investment reporting standards applicable to all engagements involving an investment circular" contains basic principles and essential procedures that are applicable to all engagements involving an investment circular. The definitions in the glossary of terms set out in Appendix 4 of SIR 1000 are to be applied in the interpretation of this and all other SIRs. Terms defined in the glossary are underlined the first time that they occur in the text.

To assist readers, SIRs contain references to, and extracts from, certain legislation and chapters of the Rules of the UK Listing Authority. Readers are cautioned that these references may change subsequent to publication.

Introduction

Standard for Investment Reporting (SIR) 1000 "Investment Reporting Standards **1** applicable to all engagements in connection with an investment circular" establishes the Investment Reporting Standards applicable to all engagements involving investment circulars. The purpose of this SIR is to establish specific additional Investment Reporting Standards and provide guidance for a reporting accountant engaged to report publicly on pro forma financial information to be included in an investment circular under the PD Regulation, the Listing Rules[1], or if required by the London Stock Exchange in respect of an AIM Admission Document.

An engagement to report publicly on the proper compilation of pro forma financial **2** information is a public reporting engagement as described in SIR 1000. The description of a public reporting engagement includes three generic terms having the following meanings in the context of an engagement to report on the proper compilation of pro forma financial information:

(a) with respect to pro forma financial information the "**subject matter**" is the impact that the transaction, that is the subject of the investment circular, would have had on the earnings of the issuer (assuming that the transaction

---

[1] *In the UK the Prospectus Directive is implemented into law through amendments to Part VI of FSMA and to certain secondary legislation. The Annexes to the PD Regulation have been incorporated into the Prospectus Rules issued by the FSA.*

had been undertaken at the commencement of the financial period used for the illustration) or on the assets and liabilities of the issuer (assuming that the transaction had been undertaken at the end of the financial period used for the illustration);

(b)   "**suitable criteria**" to be used by directors in the preparation of the pro forma financial information are provided by the requirements of the PD Regulation and the guidance issued by CESR[2] (CESR Recommendations). In forming its opinion as to whether the pro forma financial information has been properly compiled the reporting accountant considers whether certain of those criteria ("**reporting accountant's criteria**") have been properly applied. Reporting accountant's criteria are set out in Appendix 1 of this SIR; and

(c)   with respect to pro forma financial information the "**outcome**"[3] is the pro forma financial information and related disclosures that are included in the investment circular and on which the reporting accountant expresses an opinion (in the "**reporting accountant's report**") as to whether that information is properly compiled on the basis stated and whether such basis is consistent with the accounting policies of the issuer.

The nature of pro forma financial information

3   For the purpose of this SIR "pro forma financial information" is defined to include financial information such as net assets, profit or cash flow statements that demonstrate the impact of a transaction on previously published financial information together with the explanatory notes thereto. Under item 1 of Annex II of the PD Regulation the pro forma financial information must be accompanied by introductory text describing the transaction, the businesses or entities involved, the period to which it refers and its purpose and limitations.

4   The Institute of Chartered Accountants in England and Wales (ICAEW) issued guidance entitled "Pro forma financial information – Guidance for preparers under the Listing Rules"[4] in September 1998 (the "ICAEW Guidance") to assist directors when preparing pro forma financial information for inclusion in documents subject to approval by the FSA prior to their issue. While aspects of this guidance remain of assistance to directors there are differences between the requirements of the PD Regulation, the CESR Recommendations and the requirements on which the ICAEW guidance was based. The Annexure has been prepared to assist in determining which parts of the ICAEW guidance continue to be relevant.

Compilation process

5   The compilation of pro forma information is the gathering, classification and summarisation of relevant financial information. The process followed by the preparer would be expected to include the following:

(a)   the accurate extraction of information from sources permitted under the PD Regulation;

---

[2] CESR issued "CESR's Recommendations for the Consistent Implementation of the European Commission's Regulation on Prospectuses No. 809/2004" in February 2005.

[3] The "outcome" is sometimes described as "subject matter information".

[4] TECH 18/98

(b)   the making of adjustments to the source information that are arithmetically correct, appropriate and complete for the purpose for which the pro forma financial information is presented;

(c)   arithmetic computation of the pro forma information;

(d)   consideration of accounting policies;

(e)   appropriate disclosure to enable the intended users to understand the pro forma financial information; and

(f)   appropriate consideration of the pro forma financial information and approval by the directors of the entity.

Engagement acceptance and continuance

SIR 1000.1 and SIR 1000.2 set out the basic principles and essential procedures, with respect to engagement acceptance and continuance, that are applicable to all engagements involving an investment circular.   **6**

When accepting or continuing an engagement to report publicly on pro forma information, the reporting accountant ascertains whether the directors intend to comply with all relevant regulatory requirements, in particular those that constitute the reporting accountant's criteria set out in Appendix 1 of this SIR.   **7**

Agreeing the terms of the engagement

SIR 1000.3 and SIR 1000.4 set out the basic principles and essential procedures with respect to agreeing the terms of the engagement. Examples of engagement letter clauses are set out in Appendix 3 of this SIR.   **8**

Ethical requirements

SIR 1000.5 sets out the basic principles and essential procedures with respect to the ethical requirements that apply to a reporting accountant[5].   **9**

Legal and regulatory requirements

The PD Regulation requires any pro forma financial information included in a prospectus to be reported on by independent accountants or auditors (referred to in this SIR as the "reporting accountant") and specifies the form of opinion to be given. The Listing Rules require any pro forma financial information included in a Class 1 circular to be reported on in the same way. References in the SIR to the PD Regulation apply equally to the Listing Rules where those Rules apply.   **10**

SIR 1000.6 sets out the basic principles with respect to the legal and regulatory requirements applicable to a reporting accountant.   **11**

Appendices 1 and 2 to this SIR set out those provisions of the PD Regulation and the CESR Recommendations, relating to the implementation of the Regulation, that provide the suitable criteria for directors. Those provisions that constitute   **12**

---

[5] *In January 2006 the APB issued an Exposure Draft of an Ethical Standard for Reporting Accountants (ESRA).*

criteria for a reporting accountant expressing an opinion on whether the pro forma information has been properly compiled are set out in Appendix 1 of this SIR.

Quality control

13   SIR 1000.7 and SIR 1000.8 set out the basic principles and essential procedures with respect to the quality control of engagements to report on pro forma financial information.

Planning and performing the engagement

14   SIR 1000.9 and SIR 1000.10 set out the basic principles and essential procedures with respect to the planning of all reporting engagements. Additional basic principles, essential procedures and guidance are set out below.

15   **The reporting accountant should obtain an understanding of the key factors affecting the subject matter sufficient to identify and assess the risk of the pro forma financial information not being properly compiled and sufficient to design and perform evidence gathering procedures including:**

(a)   **the nature of the transaction being undertaken by the issuer;**

(b)   **the entity's business; and**

(c)   **the procedures adopted, or planned to be adopted, by the directors for the preparation of the pro forma financial information. (SIR 4000.1)**

16   The reporting accountant gains an understanding of the transaction, in respect of which the pro forma financial information is being prepared, by discussion with the directors or management of the issuer and by reading relevant supporting documentation.

17   The reporting accountant uses professional judgment to determine the extent of the understanding required of the entity's business.

18   Other matters for consideration by the reporting accountant include the availability of evidence to provide factual support for the proposed adjustments and the accounting policies that will form the basis of the adjustments to the pro forma financial information.

19   **The reporting accountant should consider materiality and public reporting engagement risk in planning its work in accordance with its instructions and in determining the effect of its findings on the report to be issued. (SIR 4000.2)**

Materiality

20   Matters are material if their omission or misstatement could, individually or collectively, influence the economic decisions of the intended users of the pro forma financial information. Materiality depends on the size and nature of the omission or misstatement judged in light of the surrounding circumstances. The size or nature of the matter, or a combination of both, could be the determining factor.

21   A misstatement in the context of the compilation of pro forma financial information includes, for example:

●   Use of an inappropriate source for the unadjusted financial information;

- Incorrect extraction of the unadjusted financial information from an appropriate source;
- In relation to adjustments, the misapplication of accounting policies or failure to use the accounting policies adopted in the last, or to be adopted in the next, financial statements;
- Failure to make an adjustment required by the PD regulation;
- Making an adjustment that does not comply with the PD regulation;
- A mathematical or clerical mistake;
- Inadequate, or incorrect, disclosures.

Evaluating whether an omission or misstatement could influence economic **22** decisions of the intended users of the pro forma financial information, and so be material, requires consideration of the characteristics of those intended users. The intended users are assumed to:

(a) have a reasonable knowledge of business and economic activities and accounting and a willingness to study the pro forma financial information with reasonable diligence; and

(b) make reasonable economic decisions on the basis of the pro forma financial information.

The determination of materiality, therefore, takes into account how intended users with such characteristics could reasonably be expected to be influenced in making economic decisions.

Public reporting engagement risk

"Public reporting engagement risk" is the risk that the reporting accountant **23** expresses an inappropriate opinion when the pro forma financial information has not been properly compiled on the basis stated or that basis is not consistent with the accounting policies of the issuer[6].

SIR 1000.11 and SIR 1000.12 set out the basic principles and essential **24** procedures, with respect to obtaining evidence, that are applicable to all engagements involving an investment circular. Additional basic principles, essential procedures and guidance relating to engagements to report on pro forma financial information are set out below.

The reporting accountant should obtain sufficient appropriate evidence that **25** **the pro forma financial information is free from material error in its compilation by:**

(a) checking that the unadjusted financial information of the issuer has been accurately extracted from a source that is both appropriate and in accordance with the relevant regulation;

(b) obtaining evidence that the directors have applied the criteria set out in Appendix 1 of this SIR and, therefore, that the adjustments are appropriate and complete for the purpose for which the pro forma financial information is presented; and

(c) checking that the calculations within the pro forma financial information are arithmetically correct. (SIR 4000.3)

---

[6] *The PD Regulation requires a positive and unmodified opinion – for this reason there is no risk that the reporting accountant will inappropriately modify its opinion.*

26   Item 5 of Annex II of the PD Regulation permits pro forma financial information to be published only in respect of:

    (a)   the current financial period;

    (b)   the most recently completed financial period; and

    (c)   the most recent interim period for which relevant unadjusted information has been or will be published or is being published in the same investment circular.

Unadjusted financial information of the issuer

27   The reporting accountant considers whether the period in respect of which the pro forma financial information is proposed to be published is permitted under the PD Regulation. The reporting accountant also considers whether the source of the unadjusted financial information for the issuer is appropriate and whether the source of the unadjusted financial information is clearly stated.

28   The reporting accountant is not required to perform specific procedures on the unadjusted financial information of the issuer other than as described in paragraph 27. However, if the reporting accountant has reason to believe that the unadjusted financial information is, or may be, unreliable, or if a report thereon has identified any uncertainties or disagreements, the reporting accountant considers the effect on the pro forma financial information.

29   The reporting accountant checks the extraction of the unadjusted financial information from the source concerned.

Adjustments

30   Item 6 of Annex II to the PD Regulation requires pro forma adjustments to be:

    (a)   clearly shown and explained;

    (b)   directly attributable to the transaction; and

    (c)   factually supportable.

31   In addition, in respect of a pro forma profit and loss or cash flow statement, they must be clearly identified as to those adjustments which are expected to have a continuing impact on the issuer and those which are not.

32   More detailed guidance for directors concerning the implementation of these requirements is provided by the CESR Recommendations and those parts of the ICAEW Guidance that remain relevant (see Annexure).

33   The reporting accountant considers the way in which the directors have fulfilled their responsibilities. With its understanding of the transaction and the entity's business as background the reporting accountant discusses with the directors the steps the directors have taken to identify relevant adjustments and whether such adjustments are permitted to be made.

34   If, as a result of these enquiries, the reporting accountant becomes aware of a significant adjustment which, in its opinion, ought to be made for the purposes of the pro forma financial information it discusses the position with the directors of the issuer and, if necessary, the issuer's advisers. If the reporting accountant is not able to agree with the directors and the issuer's advisers as to how the matter is to be resolved it considers the consequences for its report.

35   The reporting accountant considers the adjustments to assess whether they are "directly attributable" to the transaction whose impact is being illustrated by the pro forma financial information, that is, they are an integral part of the transaction concerned. If a potential adjustment is not directly attributable to the transaction or transactions described in the investment circular, it cannot be made (although it may be appropriate to disclose by way of note to the pro forma financial information the nature of a prohibited potential adjustment and the effect it would have had if it had been permissible to include it).

In assessing whether adjustments are directly attributable to the transaction the reporting accountant considers whether the adjustments relate to future events and/or decisions. This is because adjustments that are related to the transaction being illustrated but which are dependent on actions to be taken once the transaction has been completed, cannot be said to be "directly attributable". **36**

The reporting accountant considers whether the adjustments have been clearly shown and explained and, in respect of a pro forma profit and loss or cash flow statement, whether they have been clearly identified as to those which are expected to have a continuing impact on the issuer (that is, relate to events or circumstances that are expected to recur) and to those which are not. **37**

The reporting accountant obtains appropriate evidence that the directors of the issuer have factual support for each adjustment. Sources of such evidence would include published financial statements, other financial information or valuations disclosed elsewhere in the investment circular, purchase and sale agreements and other agreements relating to the transaction. **38**

Omitted adjustments

In view of the specific restrictions on the nature of the adjustments permitted to be made under item 6 of Annex II of the PD Regulation, the directors may not be permitted to make all the adjustments that they would otherwise wish to. For example, an adjustment which is directly attributable but which is not factually supportable could not be included in pro forma financial information. **39**

If any adjustments are excluded because of the requirement in item 6 of Annex II of the PD Regulation for adjustments to be factually supportable, the reporting accountant considers the effect on the pro forma financial information and in particular whether the exclusion renders the pro forma financial information misleading. In such circumstances, the reporting accountant may consider that disclosure in the notes to the pro forma financial information of the fact that such an adjustment has not been made is sufficient in the context of the overall purpose of the pro forma financial information. **40**

However, if the reporting accountant concludes that an omitted adjustment is so fundamental as to render the pro forma statement misleading in the context of the investment circular, it discusses the matter with the directors and, if necessary, the issuer's advisers and in the event that acceptable changes to the disclosures are not made, considers whether it is able to issue its report. **41**

Checking the calculations

The reporting accountant ascertains whether the adjustments made in the pro forma financial information are included under the appropriate financial statement caption as well as the arithmetical accuracy of the calculations within the pro forma financial information itself. **42**

Consistent accounting policies

43   The reporting accountant should evaluate whether the adjustments made to the unadjusted financial information are consistent with the accounting policies adopted in the last, or to be adopted in the next, financial statements of the entity presenting the pro forma financial information. (SIR 4000.4)

44   It is the responsibility of the directors of the issuer to ensure that in accordance with item 4 of Annex II of the PD Regulation the pro forma financial information is prepared in a manner consistent with either the accounting policies adopted in the last, or to be adopted in the next, financial statements of the issuer.

45   Where the reporting accountant is not the auditor of the issuer or has not otherwise reported on the financial information relating to the subject of the transaction, it evaluates the steps taken to ensure that the pro forma financial information has been prepared in a manner consistent with the accounting policies of the issuer. Guidance for directors with respect to the consistency of accounting policies is provided by the ICAEW Guidance.

Presentation of pro forma financial information

46   The reporting accountant should consider whether it has become aware of anything to cause it to believe that the pro forma financial information is presented in a way that is not understandable or is misleading in the context in which it is provided. If the reporting accountant is aware of such matters it should discuss them with the parties responsible for the pro forma financial information and with those persons to whom its report is to be addressed, and consider whether it is able to issue its report. (SIR 4000.5)

47   The reporting accountant reads the pro forma financial information to assess whether:

(a)   as required by item 1 of Annex II of the PD Regulation, the pro forma financial information includes a description of the transaction, the businesses or entities involved and the period to which it refers and clearly states the purpose for which it has been prepared, that it has been prepared for illustrative purposes only and that, because of its nature, it addresses a hypothetical situation and, therefore, does not represent the company's actual financial position or results;

(b)   in accordance with the normal form of presentation under item 3 of Annex II of the PD Regulation, the pro forma financial information is presented in columnar format composed of (a) the historical unadjusted information, (b) the pro forma adjustments and (c) the resulting pro forma financial information in the final column; and

(c)   disclosures, in the notes to the pro forma financial information, concerning omitted adjustments are satisfactory (see paragraphs 40 and 41 above).

Representation letter

48   SIR 1000.13 sets out the basic principles and essential procedures, with respect to representation letters, that are applicable to all engagements involving an investment circular. Examples of management representation letter clauses are set out in Appendix 4 of this SIR.

Documentation

SIR 1000.14 and SIR 1000.15 set out the basic principles and essential procedures **49** with respect to the reporting accountant's working papers.

Professional scepticism

SIR 1000.16 sets out the basic principle with respect to the attitude of professional **50** scepticism adopted by the reporting accountant in planning and performing an engagement.

Reporting

SIRs 1000.17, SIR 1000.18 and SIR 1000.19 set out the basic principles and **51** essential procedures, with respect to reporting, that are applicable to all engagements involving an investment circular. Additional basic principles and essential procedures relating to engagements to report on pro forma financial information are set out below.

Responsibilities

In all reports on pro forma financial information in investment circulars the **52** **reporting accountant should explain the extent of its responsibility in respect of the pro forma financial information by including in its report:**

(a) a statement that the reporting accountant's responsibility is to form an opinion (as required by the applicable regulatory requirements) on the proper compilation of the pro forma financial information and to report its opinion to the addressees of the report; and

(b) a statement that the pro forma financial information is the responsibility of the directors. (SIR 4000.6)

The reporting accountant's responsibility in relation to the opinion required by the **53** PD Regulation is limited to the provision of the report and the opinion expressed.

Basis of preparation of the pro forma financial information

The reporting accountant should include a basis of preparation section of its **54** **report that cross refers to disclosures that explain the basis of preparation of the pro forma financial information. (SIR 4000.7)**

The basis of preparation section of the report will make clear whether the **55** accounting policies applied in the preparation of the pro forma information are those adopted by the entity in preparing the last published financial statements or those that it plans to adopt in the next published financial statements.

Expression of opinion

The report on the pro forma financial information should contain a clear **56** **expression of opinion that complies with applicable regulatory requirements. (SIR 4000.8)**

In forming its opinion the reporting accountant takes account of those events **57** which the reporting accountant becomes aware of occurring up to the date on which the reporting accountant signs the report, that affect the opinion expressed in the report.

58 In providing the opinion required by the PD Regulation the reporting accountant is not providing any assurance in relation to any source financial information on which the pro forma financial information is based beyond that opinion. In particular, the reporting accountant is not refreshing or updating any opinion that it may have given in any other capacity on that source financial information.

59 The investment circular in which the reporting accountant's report is included may be made available in other countries, such as the United States of America, which have their own standards for accountants when reporting on pro forma financial information. In such circumstances, the reporting accountant considers whether to include a reference to the fact that a report issued in accordance with the SIRs should not be relied upon as if it had been issued in accordance with the standards applicable in that other country. An example of such a reference is included in the example report set out in Appendix 5 of this SIR.

Modified opinions

60 SIR 1000.20 sets out the basic principles and essential procedures, with respect to modified opinions, that are applicable to all engagements involving an investment circular. Additional basic principles and essential procedures relating to engagements to report on pro forma financial information are set out below.

61 In the event that the reporting accountant concludes that it is unable to report in the manner prescribed it considers, with the parties to whom it is to report, whether the pro forma financial information can be amended to alleviate its concerns or whether the pro forma information should be omitted from the investment circular and the requirement for information to be given on the effect of the transaction satisfied in some other way.

62 **As the PD Regulation requires a positive and unmodified opinion, the reporting accountant should not express an opinion when the directors have not applied the criteria set out in Appendix 1 of this SIR and, in the reporting accountant's judgment the effect of not doing so is, or may be, material. (SIR 4000.9)**

63 An example of a report on pro forma financial information expressing a positive and unmodified opinion, pursuant to the PD Regulation, is set out in Appendix 5 of this SIR.

Consent

64 SIR 1000.21 and SIR 1000.22 set out the basic principles and essential procedures with respect to the giving of consent by the reporting accountant.

Events occurring between the date of the reporting accountant's report and the completion date of the transaction

65 SIR 1000.23 sets out the basic principles and essential procedures with respect to events occurring between the date of the reporting accountant's report and the completion date of the transaction.

Under Section 81 and 87G of the FSMA, Prospectus Rule 3.4 and Listing Rule   **66**
4.4.1, a supplementary investment circular must be prepared if, after the date the
investment circular has been formally approved by a regulator and before dealings
in the relevant securities commence, the issuer becomes aware that there has been
a significant change affecting any matter contained in the document or a
significant new matter has arisen, the inclusion of information in respect of
which would have been required if it had arisen at the time of its preparation. A
similar obligation arises, under Article 16 of the Prospectus Directive, in respect of
the period following registration of the investment circular during which an
agreement in respect of the securities can be entered into in pursuance of the offer
contained in the investment circular.

If, as a result of discussions with those responsible for the investment circular   **67**
concerning an event that occurred prior to the completion date of the transaction,
the reporting accountant is either uncertain about or disagrees with the course of
action proposed it may consider it necessary to take legal advice with respect to its
responsibilities in the particular circumstances.

After the date of its report, the reporting accountant has no obligation to perform   **68**
procedures or make enquiries regarding the investment circular.

Effective date

A reporting accountant is required to comply with the Investment Reporting   **69**
Standards contained in this SIR for reports signed after 31 March 2006. Earlier
adoption is encouraged.

Appendix 1 – Reporting accountant's criteria

	Annex I of PD Regulation	Annex II of PD Regulation	CESR Recommendations
In the case of a significant gross change, a description of how the transaction might have affected the assets and liabilities and earnings of the issuer, had the transaction been undertaken at the commencement of the period being reported on or at the date reported. This requirement will normally be satisfied by the inclusion of pro forma financial information.	20.2		
The pro forma information must normally be presented in columnar format composed of: (a) the historical unadjusted information; (b) the pro forma adjustments; and (c) the resulting pro forma financial information in the final column		3	
The sources of the pro forma financial information have to be stated.		3	
The pro forma information must be prepared in a manner consistent with the accounting policies adopted by the issuer in its last or next financial statements and shall identify the following: (a) the basis upon which it is prepared; (b) the source of each item of information and adjustment.		4	
Pro forma adjustments related to the pro forma financial information must be: (a) clearly shown and explained.		6	
Pro forma adjustments related to the pro forma financial information must be: (b) directly attributable to the transaction.		6	
"Directly attributable to transactions". Pro forma information should only reflect matters that are an integral part of the transactions which are described in the prospectus. In particular, pro forma financial information should not include adjustments which are dependent on actions to be taken once the current transactions have been completed, even where such actions are central to the issuer's purpose in entering into the transactions.			Para 88
Pro forma adjustments related to the pro forma financial information must be: (c) factually supportable.		6	

	Annex I of PD Regulation	Annex II of PD Regulation	CESR Recommendations
"Factually supportable". The nature of the facts supporting an adjustment will vary according to the circumstances. Nevertheless, facts are expected to be capable of some reasonable degree of objective determination. Support might typically be provided by published accounts, management accounts, other financial information and valuations contained in the document, purchase and sale agreements and other agreements to the transaction covered by the prospectus. For instance in relation to management accounts, the interim figures for an undertaking being acquired may be derived from the consolidation schedules underlying that undertaking's interim statements.			Para 87
In respect of a pro forma profit and loss or cash flow statement, the adjustments must be clearly identified as to those expected to have a continuing impact on the issuer and those which are not.		6	
The accounting treatment applied to adjustments should be presented and prepared in a form consistent with the policy the issuer would adopt in its last or next published financial statements.			Para 89[1]

---

[1] *Paragraph 89 of the CESR guidance also makes recommendations that do not constitute criteria but provide useful guidance with respect to this criterion.*

Appendix 2 – Other regulatory provisions relevant to the preparers of pro forma financial information

	PD Regulation	Annex I of PD Regulation	Annex II of PD Regulation	CESR Recommendations
(9) Pro forma financial information is needed in case of significant gross change, i.e. a variation of more than 25% relative to one or more indicators of the size of the issuer's business, in the situation of an issuer due to a particular transaction, with the exception of those situations where merger accounting is required.	Recital 9			
For these purposes, "Significant gross change" is described in recital 9 of the PD Regulation.				Paras 90 to 94
Thus, in order to assess whether the variation to an issuer's business as a result of a transaction is more than 25%, the size of the transaction should be assessed relative to the size of the issuer by using appropriate indicators of size prior to the relevant transaction. A transaction will constitute a significant gross change where at least one of the indicators of size is more than 25%.				
A non-exhaustive list of indicators of size is provided below: – Total assets – Revenue – Profit or loss				
Other indicators of size can be applied by the issuer especially where the stated indicators of size produce an anomalous result or are inappropriate to the specific industry of the issuer, in these cases the issuers should address these anomalies by agreement of the competent authority.				
The appropriate indicators of size should refer to figures from the issuer's last or next published annual financial statements.				
Pro forma financial information should be preceded by an introductory explanatory paragraph that states in clear terms the purpose of including this information in the prospectus	Article 5			
This pro forma financial information is to be presented as set out in Annex II and must include the information indicated therein.		20.2		
Pro forma financial information must be accompanied by a report prepared by independent accountants or auditors.				

	PD Regulation	Annex I of PD Regulation	Annex II of PD Regulation	CESR Recommendations
The pro forma information must include a description of the transaction, the businesses or entities involved and the period to which it refers.			1	
The pro forma information must clearly state the purpose to which it has been prepared			1	
The pro forma information must clearly state that it has been prepared for illustrative purposes only			1	
The pro forma information must clearly state that, because of its nature, it addresses a hypothetical situation and, therefore, does not represent the company's actual financial position or results.			1	
In order to present pro forma financial information, a balance sheet and profit and loss account, and accompanying explanatory notes, depending on the circumstances may be included			2	
Where applicable the financial statements of the acquired businesses or entities must be included in the prospectus.			3	
Pro forma information may only be published in respect of: (a) the current financial period; (b) the most recently completed financial period; and/or (c) the most recent interim period for which relevant unadjusted information has been or will be published or is being published in the same document			5	

Appendix 3 – Examples of engagement letter clauses

The examples of engagement letter clauses are intended for consideration in the context of a public reporting engagement on pro forma financial information. They should be tailored to the specific circumstances and supplemented by such other clauses as are relevant and appropriate.

Financial information upon which the report is to be given

The [investment circular] will include a pro forma [balance sheet/profit and loss account] together with a description of the basis of presentation (including the accounting policies used) and supporting notes to illustrate how the transaction might have affected the financial information of the company had the transaction been undertaken at the beginning of the period[s] concerned or as at the date[s] stated (the "pro forma financial information").

Responsibilities

The pro forma financial information, which will be the responsibility solely of the directors, will be prepared for illustrative purposes only. This is required to be prepared in accordance with items 1 to 6 of Annex II of the PD Regulation.

It is our responsibility to form an opinion as to whether the pro forma financial information has been properly compiled on the basis stated and that such basis is consistent with the accounting policies of ABC plc.

If the results of our work are satisfactory, and having regard to the requirements of item 7 of Annex II of the PD Regulation, we shall prepare a report on the pro forma financial information for inclusion in the [*describe document*]. An illustration of the form of our report is attached.

Scope of work

Our work will be undertaken in accordance with Standard for Investment Reporting (SIR) 4000 "Investment Reporting Standards Applicable to Public Reporting Engagements on Pro Forma Financial Information" issued by the Auditing Practices Board and will be subject to the limitations described therein.

We draw your attention in particular to paragraph 62 of SIR 4000 which would preclude us from expressing any opinion if the directors have not complied with the regulatory requirements set out in Appendix 1 of that SIR.

Appendix 4 – Examples of management representation letter clauses

The following are examples of management representation letter clauses relating to a report on pro forma financial information, issued pursuant to the PD Regulation or Listing Rules, which may be obtained from the issuer. Alternatively they may form the basis for a board minute.

Introduction

We refer to the pro forma financial information set out in Part [...] of the [investment circular] dated...to be issued in connection with [...] dated. We acknowledge that we are solely responsible for the pro forma financial information and confirm on behalf of the Directors of the Company to the best of our knowledge and belief, having made appropriate enquiries of officials of the Company [and the directors and officials of the target company], the following representations made to you in the course of your work.

Specific representations

- We acknowledge as duly appointed officials of the Company our responsibility for the pro forma financial information (which has been prepared in accordance with [CESR's Recommendations for the Consistent Implementation of the European Commission's Regulation on Prospectuses No. 809/2004"] [and, to the extent applicable, with Technical Release TECH 18/98 published by the Institute of Chartered Accountants in England and Wales].

- We have considered the pro forma financial information and we confirm that, in our opinion, as required by item 20.2 of Annex I of the PD Regulation, the pro forma financial information provides investors with information about the impact of the transaction by illustrating how that transaction might have affected the [assets and liabilities] [and] [earnings] of the issuer, had the transaction been undertaken at the commencement of the period being reported on or at the date reported. Furthermore, we confirm that, in our opinion, the pro forma financial information is not misleading.

- We have considered the adjustments included in the pro forma financial information. We confirm that, in our opinion, the pro forma financial information includes all appropriate adjustments permitted by item 6 of Annex II of the PD Regulation, of which we are aware, necessary to give effect to the transaction as if the transaction had been undertaken [at the date reported on} [at the commencement of the period being reported on].

- [We have considered those adjustments which have been omitted by virtue of not being permitted to be included by item 6 of Annex II of the PD Regulation and the disclosures made in respect thereof. In our opinion the omission of these adjustments does not render the pro forma financial information misleading.]

- [*Where the accounting policies in the issuer's next financial statements are used.* The accounting policies used in compiling the pro forma financial information are those to be adopted in the Company's next financial statements, and all changes necessary to reflect those policies have been made.]

- [*Any specific representations relating to information included in the pro forma financial information.*]

Appendix 5 – Example report on pro forma financial information in accordance with the PD regulation or the listing rules

Date

Reporting accountant's address

Addressees, as agreed between the parties in the engagement letter

Dear Sirs,

[ABC plc]

We report on the pro forma [financial information] (the "Pro forma financial information") set out in Part [...] of the [investment circular] dated......., which has been prepared on the basis described [in note x], for illustrative purposes only, to provide information about how the [transaction] might have affected the financial information presented on the basis of the accounting policies [adopted/ to be adopted[1]] by ABC plc in preparing the financial statements for the period [ended/ending] [*date*]. This report is required by [Relevant Regulation] [guidance issued by the London Stock Exchange with respect to the AIM market] and is given for the purpose of complying with that [Relevant Regulation] [guidance issued by the London Stock Exchange] and for no other purpose.

Responsibilities

It is the responsibility of the directors of ABC plc to prepare the Pro forma financial information in accordance with [item 20.2 of Annex I of the PD Regulation] [guidance issued by the London Stock Exchange].

It is our responsibility to form an opinion, as required by [item 7 of Annex II of the PD Regulation] [guidance issued by the London Stock Exchange], as to the proper compilation of the Pro forma financial information and to report that opinion to you.

In providing this opinion we are not updating or refreshing any reports or opinions previously made by us on any financial information used in the compilation of the Pro forma financial information, nor do we accept responsibility for such reports or opinions beyond that owed to those to whom those reports or opinions were addressed by us at the dates of their issue.

Basis of Opinion

We conducted our work in accordance with the Standards for Investment Reporting issued by the Auditing Practices Board in the United Kingdom. The work that we performed for the purpose of making this report, which involved no independent examination of any of the underlying financial information, consisted primarily of comparing the unadjusted financial information with the source documents, considering the evidence supporting the adjustments and discussing the Pro forma financial information with the directors of ABC plc.

We planned and performed our work so as to obtain the information and explanations we considered necessary in order to provide us with reasonable assurance that the Pro forma financial information has been properly compiled on the basis stated and that such basis is consistent with the accounting policies of ABC plc.

---

[1] *See paragraph 44 of SIR 4000*

[*This paragraph may be omitted if the document is not to be distributed outside the UK* - Our work has not been carried out in accordance with auditing or other standards and practices generally accepted in the United States of America [or other jurisdictions] and accordingly should not be relied upon as if it had been carried out in accordance with those standards and practices.]

Opinion

In our opinion:

(a)   the Pro forma financial information has been properly compiled on the basis stated; and

(b)   such basis is consistent with the accounting policies of ABC plc.

Declaration[2]

For the purposes of [Prospectus Rule [5.5.3R(2)(f)] [5.5.4R(2)(f)]] [guidance issued by the London Stock Exchange] we are responsible for [this report as part] [the following part(s)] of the [prospectus] [registration document] [AIM Admission Document] and declare that we have taken all reasonable care to ensure that the information contained [in this report] [those parts] is, to the best of our knowledge, in accordance with the facts and contains no omission likely to affect its import. This declaration is included in the [prospectus] [registration document] [AIM Admission Document] in compliance with [item 1.2 of Annex I of the PD Regulation] [item 1.2 of Annex III of the Prospectus Regulation] [guidance issued by the London Stock Exchange].

Yours faithfully

Reporting accountant

---

[2] *This declaration is a requirement of the Prospectus Rules and is appropriate for inclusion when the report is included in a Prospectus, see Appendix 2 of SIR 1000. It is also appropriate for inclusion in an AIM admission document under Schedule Two of the AIM Rules.*

Annexure – Sections of TECH 18/98 "Pro forma financial information – Guidance for preparers under the Listing Rules"[1] (published by the Institute of Chartered Accountants in England & Wales) that remain relevant

This Annexure has been compiled by the APB to indicate those paragraphs of TECH 18/98 that continue to be relevant. (There are differences between the requirements of the PD Regulation and the CESR Recommendations compared to the requirements on which TECH 18/98 was based.) The Annexure does not include either basic principles, essential procedures, or guidance promulgated by the APB.

Paragraphs in TECH 18/98	Application under the PD Regulation
1 to 5	*Not applicable*
6	Principles still applicable, save that under Item 20.2 of Annex I of the PD Regulation inclusion of pro forma information is now normally included where there has been a "significant gross change" (as defined in Recital (9))
7 and 8	Principles still applicable
9	*Not applicable – replaced by the following:*
	Item 20.2 of Annex 1 of the PD Regulation. In the case of a significant gross change, a description of how the transaction might have affected the assets and liabilities and earnings of the issuer, had the transaction been undertaken at the commencement of the period being reported on or at the date reported.
	This requirement will normally be satisfied by the inclusion of pro forma financial information.
	This pro forma financial information is to be presented as set out in Annex II and must include the information indicated therein.
	Pro forma financial information must be accompanied by a report prepared by independent accountants or auditors.
10 and 11	Principles still applicable
12 to 19	Principles still applicable save that there is no express requirement under the PD Regulation for all appropriate adjustments to be included, nor for the pro forma financial information not to be misleading
20	*Not applicable – replaced by the following (the words <u>emphasised</u> are additional to the original Listing Rule and certain other words have been deleted):*
	Item 1 of Annex II of the PD Regulation. The pro forma information <u>must include a description of the transaction, the businesses or entities involved and the period to which it refers</u>, and must clearly state the following:

---

[1] *In the UK the Prospectus Directive is implemented into law through amendments to Part VI of FSMA and to certain secondary legislation. The Annexes to the PD Regulation have been incorporated into the <u>Prospectus Rules</u> issued by the FSA.*

Paragraphs in TECH 18/98	Application under the PD Regulation
	(a) the purpose to which it has been prepared;
	(b) the fact that it has been prepared for illustrative purposes only;
	(c) the fact that because of its nature, the pro forma financial information addresses a hypothetical situation and, therefore, does not represent the company's actual financial position or results.
	Item 2 of Annex II of the PD Regulation In order to present pro forma financial information, a balance sheet and profit and loss account, and accompanying explanatory notes, depending on the circumstances may be included.
21 to 24	Principles still applicable
25	*Not applicable – replaced by the following:*
	Item 3 of Annex II of the PD Regulation. Pro forma financial information must normally *be presented in columnar format,* composed of*:*
	(a) the historical *unadjusted information;*
	(b) the pro forma adjustments; and
	(c) the resulting *pro forma financial information* in the final column*.*
	The sources of the pro forma financial information have to be stated and, if applicable, the financial statements of the acquired businesses or entities must be included in the prospectus
	Item 4 of Annex II of the PD Regulation. The pro forma information must be prepared in a manner consistent with the accounting policies adopted by the issuer in its last or next *financial statements and shall identify the following:*
	(a) the basis upon which it is prepared;
	(b) the source of each item of information and adjustment.
26	Principles still applicable
27	Principles still applicable, save that the accounting policies to be used in the next financial statements may also be applied
28 to 29	Principles still applicable
30	*Not applicable*
31 and 32	Principles still applicable
33	*Not applicable*
34	Applicable, save that the words *"and, in the case of a pro forma balance sheet or net asset statement, as at the date on which such periods end or ended"* are omitted
35 to 43	Principles still applicable
44 and 45	*Not applicable*
46 to 71	Principles still applicable
72 to 74	*Not applicable*

SIR 5000: Investment Reporting Standards applicable to Public Reporting Engagements on financial information reconciliations under the Listing Rules

(February 2008)

Contents

	Paragraphs
Introduction	1 - 4
The nature of financial information reconciliations	5 - 9
Engagement acceptance and continuance	10 - 14
Agreeing the terms of the engagement	15
Ethical requirements	16
Legal and regulatory requirements	17 - 19
Quality control	20
Planning and performing the engagement	21 - 51
Materiality	28 - 32
Public reporting engagement risk	33 - 35
Consideration of directors' procedures and controls	36 - 38
Unadjusted financial information of the target	39 - 41
Completeness of adjustments and consistency of accounting policies	42 - 46
Checking the calculations	47 - 48
Presentation of the financial information reconciliation	49 - 50
Representation letter	51
Documentation	52
Professional scepticism	53
Reporting	54 - 60
Responsibilities	55 - 57
Basis of preparation of the financial information reconciliation	58
Expression of opinion	59 - 60
Modified opinions	61 - 63
Consent	64
Events occurring between the date of the reporting accountant's report and the completion date of the transaction	65

Effective date   66

Appendix 1 – Regulatory provisions applicable to Class 1 circulars

Appendix 2 – Examples of engagement letter clauses

Appendix 3 – Examples of management representation letter clauses

**Appendix 4 – Example report on a financial information reconciliation in accordance
with the Listing Rules**

**Annexure – Accounting conventions and processes used in preparing financial
information reconciliations for inclusion in Class 1 circulars**

Investment Reporting Standards applicable to public reporting engagements on financial information reconciliations under the Listing Rules

SIR 1000 "Investment reporting standards applicable to all engagements in connection with an investment circular" contains basic principles and essential procedures ("Investment Reporting Standards") that are applicable to all engagements involving an investment circular. The definitions in the glossary of terms set out in Appendix 4 of SIR 1000 are to be applied in the interpretation of this and all other SIRs. Terms defined in the glossary are underlined the first time that they occur in the text.

SIR 5000 contains additional Investment Reporting Standards, indicated by paragraphs in bold type, with which a reporting accountant is required to comply in the conduct of an engagement to report on financial information reconciliations which are included within a Class 1 circular prepared for issue in connection with a securities transaction governed wholly or in part by the laws and regulations of the United Kingdom or the Republic of Ireland.

SIR 5000 also includes explanatory and other material, including appendices, in the context of which the Investment Reporting Standards are to be understood and applied. It is necessary to consider the whole text of the SIR to understand and apply the basic principles and essential procedures.

To assist readers, SIRs contain references to, and extracts from, certain legislation and chapters of the Rules of the UK Listing Authority (UKLA) and the Listing Rules of the Irish Stock Exchange Limited (ISE) (together "the Listing Rules"). Readers are cautioned that these references may change subsequent to publication.

Introduction

Standard for Investment Reporting (SIR) 1000 "Investment Reporting Standards   **1** applicable to all engagements in connection with an Investment Circular" establishes the Investment Reporting Standards applicable to all engagements involving investment circulars. The purpose of SIR 5000 is to establish specific additional Investment Reporting Standards and provide guidance for a reporting accountant engaged to report publicly on reconciliations of the financial information of a target[1] to the accounting policies of an issuer (financial information reconciliations) to be included in a Class 1 circular under the Listing Rules.

Financial information reconciliations (sometimes referred to as GAAP   **2** reconciliations) may be included in investment circulars other than Class 1 circulars. If the reporting accountant is requested to report in similar terms to those for a Class 1 circular in such a context, and agrees to do so, the guidance in this SIR may be helpful. However, this SIR is not intended to be used in connection with GAAP reconciliations that are included within a note to financial statements included in an investment circular.

An engagement to report on the proper compilation of financial information   **3** reconciliations is a public reporting engagement as described in SIR 1000. The

---

[1] *Under UKLA LR 13.5.1R(1): ISE LR 10.5.1(1) where a listed company is seeking to acquire an interest in another company, that company is described as a "target".*

description of a public reporting engagement includes three generic terms having the following meanings in the context of an engagement to report on the proper compilation of financial information reconciliations:

(a) the "**subject matter**" is the target's financial information for the periods being reported on, presented in accordance with the target's accounting policies (ie the target's unadjusted financial information);

(b) the "**suitable criteria**" are the requirements of the financial reporting framework adopted by the issuer, the accounting policies of the issuer and any "accepted conventions", as set out in the Annexure, that have been applied; and

(c) the "**outcome**[2]" is the financial information of the target, as adjusted, together with the adjustments, that is included in the Class 1 circular and which has resulted from the directors applying the suitable criteria to the subject matter. The reporting accountant expresses an opinion as to whether that financial information (as adjusted) is properly compiled on the basis stated and whether the adjustments are appropriate for presenting the financial information (as adjusted) on a basis consistent in all material respects with the issuer's accounting policies.

4 In order to express an opinion on the reconciliation the reporting accountant is not required to re-assess any judgments or estimates underlying the subject matter or provide an opinion on the subject matter.

The nature of financial information reconciliations

5 Paragraph 5 of SIR 2000 *Investment Reporting Standards Applicable to Public Reporting Engagements on Historical Financial Information* describes, with respect to Class 1 acquisitions, the requirements of the Listing Rules for a Class 1 circular to include a financial information table relating to the target and an accountant's opinion on that table.

6 However, under the Listing Rules, when an issuer seeks to acquire a publicly traded company (a target) a financial information table is not required to be presented on the basis of the issuer's accounting policies but is presented on the basis of the target's accounting policies. Consequently the accountant's opinion described in SIR 2000 is not required and there are additional Listing Rules that apply[3].

7 Under these additional rules (see Appendix 1), where a material adjustment needs to be made to the financial information presented in respect of the target in the Class 1 circular to achieve consistency with the issuer's accounting policies, the issuer is required to include the following in the Class 1 circular[4]:

(a) a reconciliation of financial information on the target, for all periods covered by the financial information table, normally on the basis of the accounting policies used in the issuer's last published accounts[5];

---

[2] *The "outcome" is sometimes described as "subject matter information".*

[3] *These rules are UKLA LR 13.5.27R and 13.5.28R; ISE LR 10.5.27 and 10.5.28.*

[4] *Under UKLA LR 13.5.30R(2) and ISE LR 10.5.30(2) similar requirements apply where the target has published half yearly or quarterly financial information subsequent to the end of its last financial year and a material adjustment needs to be made to the financial information presented in respect of the relevant interim period of the target in the Class 1 circular to achieve consistency with the issuer's accounting policies.*

[5] *The UKLA's publication "List!" 16 at paragraph 2.5 discusses certain circumstances where accounting policies other than those used in the issuer's last published accounts are used.*

(b)   an accountant's opinion that sets out:

(i)   whether the reconciliation of financial information in the financial information table has been properly compiled on the basis stated; and

(ii) whether the adjustments are appropriate for the purpose of presenting the financial information (as adjusted) on a basis consistent in all material respects with the issuer's accounting policies.

If no material adjustment needs to be made to the target's financial information, in order to achieve consistency with the issuer's accounting policies, then the Class 1 circular is not required to include a financial information reconciliation.

The need for a financial information reconciliation usually arises because the   **8** target and the issuer prepare their respective financial statements in accordance with different financial reporting frameworks (for example, the issuer may prepare its financial statements in accordance with International Financial Reporting Standards as adopted by the European Union and the target may prepare its financial statements in accordance with United States Generally Accepted Accounting Principles) but may also arise through different choices made within the same financial reporting framework.

Other than the need for the financial information to be presented on a basis   **9** consistent in all material respects with the listed company's accounting policies, the Listing Rules contain no further requirements regarding the proper compilation of the financial information reconciliation, or the appropriateness of adjustments. In particular, the Listing Rules do not specify the individual financial statements or financial statement components that should comprise "financial information" for this purpose. Consequently the directors have regard to accepted conventions which have developed for the preparation and presentation of financial information reconciliations in Class 1 circulars. The Annexure provides a summary of these accepted conventions.

Engagement acceptance and continuance

SIR 1000.1 and SIR 1000.2 set out the Investment Reporting Standards with   **10** respect to engagement acceptance and continuance that are applicable to all engagements involving an investment circular. Additional Investment Reporting Standards and guidance are set out below.

When accepting or continuing an engagement to report publicly on financial   **11** information reconciliations, the reporting accountant ascertains whether the directors intend to comply with the relevant regulatory requirements.

In determining whether the persons who are to perform the engagement   **12** **collectively possess the necessary professional competence the reporting accountant should:**

(a)   assess whether the engagement team[6], or those with whom the engagement team intend to consult, have sufficient knowledge and experience of the issuer's financial reporting framework; and

---

[6] *The "engagement team" is any person within the reporting accountant's firm who is directly involved in the engagement including:*

(a)   the partners, managers and staff from assurance and other disciplines involved in the engagement (for example, taxation specialists, IT specialists, treasury management specialists, lawyers, actuaries), and

(b)   those who provide quality control or direct oversight of the engagement

(b)   **consider the extent to which the engagement team requires knowledge of the target's financial reporting framework or are able to consult with those having such knowledge having regard to management's processes. (SIR 5000.1)**

13   Where the target's or the issuer's financial information has been prepared in accordance with a financial reporting framework other than that of the country in which the reporting accountant practises[7], the reporting accountant determines whether it has, or can obtain, the necessary professional competence to evaluate whether the financial information reconciliation has been prepared in accordance with the requirements of the Listing Rules.

14   The successful completion of the reporting accountant's engagement will depend on receiving, on a timely basis, the co-operation of the management and directors both of the issuer and of the target including their disclosure to the reporting accountant of all the pertinent accounting records and any other relevant records and related information. In a hostile bid, or other limited access situation, the reporting accountant is unlikely to obtain the necessary access to the officials and records of the target and, therefore, is unlikely to be in a position to report on a financial information reconciliation. In such situations the circumstances are discussed with the UK Listing Authority[8] (UKLA) or the Irish Stock Exchange (ISE).

Agreeing the terms of the engagement

15   SIR 1000.3 and SIR 1000.4 set out the Investment Reporting Standards with respect to agreeing the terms of the engagement. Examples of engagement letter clauses are set out in Appendix 2 of this SIR.

Ethical requirements

16   SIR 1000.5 sets out the Investment Reporting Standard with respect to the ethical requirements that apply to a reporting accountant[9].

Legal and regulatory requirements

17   The legal and regulatory requirements relating to financial information reconciliations in Class 1 circulars are set out in Chapter 13 of the UKLA Listing Rules and Chapter 10 of the ISE Listing Rules. These chapters also set out the requirements for the inclusion of financial information tables in Class 1 circulars.

18   SIR 1000.6 sets out the Investment Reporting Standards with respect to the legal and regulatory requirements applicable to a reporting accountant.

---

[7] *UKLA LR 13.5.23R and ISE LR 10.5.23 require that the accountant's opinion must be given by an independent accountant who is qualified to act as an auditor. With the exception of paragraph 56, this SIR is drafted on the presumption that the opinion is provided by the issuer's reporting accountant or auditor. However, this need not be the case.*

[8] *The UKLA generally encourages advisers or issuers preparing an investment circular in a limited access situation to contact them as soon as possible to discuss the exact disclosure requirements. In certain circumstances it may be appropriate for a financial information reconciliation to be published in a supplementary circular within 28 days of a contested offer becoming unconditional.*

[9] *In October 2006 the APB issued the Ethical Standard for Reporting Accountants (ESRA).*

Appendix 1 summarises the relevant requirements of the Listing Rules and   **19**
illustrates those requirements that are dealt with by SIR 2000 and those dealt
with by SIR 5000.

Quality control

SIR 1000.7 and SIR 1000.8 set out the Investment Reporting Standards with   **20**
respect to the quality control of engagements to report on financial information
reconciliations.

Planning and performing the engagement

SIR 1000.9 and SIR 1000.10 set out the Investment Reporting Standards with   **21**
respect to the planning of all reporting engagements. Additional Investment
Reporting Standards and guidance are set out below.

The reporting accountant should obtain an understanding of those factors   **22**
affecting the subject matter sufficient to identify and assess the risk of the
financial information reconciliation not being properly compiled and the
adjustments being inappropriate for the purpose of presenting the financial
information (as adjusted) on a basis consistent in all material respects with
the issuer's accounting policies. The reporting accountant's understanding
should be sufficient to design and perform evidence gathering procedures
and in particular should include:

(a)   the nature of the target's and the issuer's businesses;

(b)   the accounting policies of the target and of the issuer and the
application of those policies;

(c)   the requirements of the issuer's financial reporting framework;

(d)   the extent to which the issuer has employees with the requisite
knowledge of the financial reporting framework used by the target,
or the ability to consult with those having such knowledge; and

(e)   the procedures and controls adopted, or planned to be adopted, by the
directors for the preparation of the financial information reconciliation.
(SIR 5000.2)

The reporting accountant may gain an understanding of the nature of the target's   **23**
business in a number of ways, for example:

● Reviewing publicly available information on the target;

● Through discussion with the issuer's directors or management;

● Through discussion with the target's directors or management;

● Through discussion with the target's auditor, where that auditor is prepared
to assist the reporting accountant to gain a wider understanding of the target,
its financial reporting procedures and the way in which its accounting
policies are applied.

In obtaining an understanding of the target's and the issuer's businesses the   **24**
reporting accountant may consider the following, for example:

● Business operations:

–   Conduct of operations and nature of revenue sources;

- – Products or services and markets.
- Financing and Investments:
  - – Group structure;
  - – Finance structure;
  - – Investments in non-consolidated entities, including partnerships, joint ventures and special purpose entities.
- Financial reporting:
  - – Industry specific practices;
  - – Revenue recognition practices;
  - – Accounting for unusual or complex transactions including those in emerging areas.

25   Under the Listing Rules the financial information reconciliation on the target is required to be prepared on the basis of the accounting policies of the issuer[10]. Guidance in the Listing Rules indicates that "accounting policies" includes accounting standards and accounting disclosures[11]. A financial information reconciliation, therefore, is not confined to a reconciliation to the published accounting policies of an issuer but also to those accounting standards comprising the issuer's financial reporting framework, regardless of whether they are articulated within the issuer's statement of accounting policies, even if they have not previously been relevant to the issuer. Accordingly, both the issuer and the reporting accountant consider the extent to which they will need access to expertise in the target's financial reporting framework. However financial information reconciliations do not normally extend to reconciling note disclosures.

26   Other matters for consideration by the reporting accountant include the availability of evidence to support the proposed adjustments and the accounting policies that will form the basis of the adjustments to the target's financial information.

27   **The reporting accountant should consider materiality and public reporting engagement risk in planning its work in accordance with its instructions and in determining the effect of its findings on the report to be issued. (SIR 5000.3)**

Materiality

28   The Listing Rules require a financial information reconciliation to be included in a Class 1 circular only when a material adjustment needs to be made to the target's financial information to achieve consistency with the listed company's accounting policies[12]. The judgment concerning materiality to comply with the Listing Rules is the responsibility of the issuer. The reporting accountant is not required to evaluate this determination of materiality made by the issuer. However, if the reporting accountant becomes aware that a material adjustment may need to be made to the target's financial statements to achieve consistency with the listed company's accounting policies, and the issuer has not prepared a financial information reconciliation, it discusses the matter with the directors of the issuer.

---

[10] *UKLA LR 13.5.4R and ISE LR10.5.4.*

[11] *UKLA LR 13.5.5G and ISE LR 10.5.5.*

[12] *UKLA LRs 13.5.27R and 13.5.28R and ISE LRs 10.5.27 and 10.5.28.*

The following guidance on materiality addresses the reporting accountant's **29** responsibilities with respect to a financial information reconciliation once the issuer is satisfied that the preparation of a financial information reconciliation is required under the Listing Rules.

Matters are material if their omission or misstatement could, individually or **30** collectively, influence the economic decisions of the intended users of the financial information reconciliation. Materiality depends on the size and nature of the omission or misstatement judged in the light of the surrounding circumstances. Materiality is determined by reference to the financial information of the target, as adjusted in the financial information reconciliation.

A misstatement in the context of the compilation of a financial information **31** reconciliation includes, for example:

● Use of an inappropriate source for the target's financial information;

● Incorrect extraction of the target's financial information from an appropriate source;

● In relation to adjustments, the misapplication of accounting policies or failure to use the issuer's accounting policies;

● Failure to make an adjustment necessary for the purpose of presenting the financial information (as adjusted) on a basis consistent in all material respects with the issuer's accounting policies;

● Disclosing as an adjustment the rectification of an error in the underlying financial information of the target[13].

● A mathematical or clerical mistake.

If the reporting accountant becomes aware of a material misstatement in the **32** financial information reconciliation it discusses the matter with the directors of the issuer. If the reporting accountant is not able to agree with the directors as to how the matter is to be resolved it considers the consequences for its opinion.

Public reporting engagement risk

"Public reporting engagement risk" is the risk that the reporting accountant **33** expresses an inappropriate opinion when the financial information reconciliation has not been properly compiled on the basis stated or when the adjustments are not appropriate for the purpose of presenting the financial information (as adjusted) on a basis consistent, in all material respects, with the accounting policies of the issuer.

SIR 1000.11 and SIR 1000.12 set out the Investment Reporting Standards with **34** respect to obtaining evidence that are applicable to all engagements involving an investment circular. Additional Investment Reporting Standards and guidance relating to engagements to report on financial information reconciliations are set out below.

The reporting accountant should assess whether the reconciliation of **35** **financial information in the financial information table has been properly compiled on the basis stated and whether the adjustments are appropriate for the purpose of presenting the financial information (as adjusted) on a basis consistent in all material respects with the issuer's accounting policies. In**

---

[13] *See discussion in paragraph 12 of Annexure concerning the manner in which a rectification of a misstatement in the underlying financial information may be disclosed;*

making these assessments the reporting accountant should, having regard to the procedures and controls adopted by the directors:

(a)   check whether the financial information of the target has been accurately extracted from an appropriate source;

(b)   assess whether all adjustments necessary for the purpose of presenting the financial information (as adjusted) on a basis consistent in all material respects with the issuer's accounting policies have been made; and

(c)   check the arithmetical accuracy of the calculations within the financial information reconciliation. (SIR 5000.4)

Consideration of directors' procedures and controls

36   In assessing whether the financial information reconciliation has been properly compiled on the basis stated and whether the adjustments are appropriate the reporting accountant has regard to the procedures and controls adopted by the issuer. Such procedures and controls may encompass both high-level internal controls over the reconciliation process and lower level accounting control activities.

37   High-level internal controls over the reconciliation process that the reporting accountant may wish to assess include, whether:

● Employees (or outside experts utilised by the issuer), have the requisite knowledge and experience to prepare and monitor the preparation of the reconciliation;

● The directors of the issuer have been involved to an appropriate extent in the preparation of the financial information reconciliation;

● Where applicable, management has compared the reconciliation to any that may have been made before.

38   Examples of accounting control activities that the reporting accountant may wish to assess include, whether:

● When making adjustments management sought to ensure that the principles of double-entry bookkeeping were followed such that "one-sided" entries were not made;

● Management considered the tax effects of the adjustments and assessed whether the resultant effective tax rate is understandable and meaningful;

● Management analysed the differences between the opening and closing equity account balances, as adjusted. (This is sometimes referred to as an equity roll forward reconciliation.) Such an analysis would have assisted management in seeking to ensure that the principles of double-entry bookkeeping have been followed where the other side of an adjustment is to an equity account;

● Management considered whether the cash and cash equivalent position, as adjusted, is (and should be) the same as that shown by the unadjusted financial statements. If there is a difference between the cash position reported on the two bases management should be able to explain how the difference arises and, in particular, to have considered whether the difference may reflect an error in the double-entry bookkeeping applied to the reconciliation process.

Unadjusted financial information of the target

The reporting accountant assesses whether the unadjusted financial information   **39** has been extracted from an appropriate source: namely the financial information table of the target included in the Class 1 circular or such published half yearly or quarterly financial information that is required, by the Listing Rules[14], to be reproduced in the Class 1 circular.

The reporting accountant is not required to perform specific procedures on the   **40** unadjusted financial information of the target other than as described in paragraph 39, and in particular is not required to audit the unadjusted financial information. However, if the reporting accountant has reason to believe that the unadjusted financial information is, or may be, unreliable, or if a report thereon has identified any uncertainties or disagreements, the reporting accountant considers the effect on the financial information reconciliation.

When the directors have identified an error in the underlying financial information   **41** that does not reflect a genuine difference between the accounting policies of the target and the issuer it is not rectified by being presented as an adjustment. The issuer would discuss the proposed presentation of the rectification of the error with the UKLA or the ISE. The reporting accountant would wish to see evidence, based on such discussions, of the agreement of the UKLA or the ISE to the proposed presentation of the rectification of the error.

Completeness of adjustments and consistency of accounting policies

In assessing the completeness of the adjustments and whether the adjustments are   **42** appropriate for the purpose of presenting the financial information (as adjusted) on a basis consistent, in all material respects, with the issuer's accounting policies, the reporting accountant utilises its expertise, and the expertise of those with whom they have consulted, in the issuer's financial reporting framework.

The reporting accountant assesses the thoroughness with which the directors have   **43** fulfilled their responsibility for ensuring the completeness of adjustments. In view of the importance of the accuracy of a financial reconciliation to potential investors the directors will be expected to have carefully analysed the target's accounting policies and prepared an "impact analysis" of the effect of applying the issuer's accounting policies to the target's financial information. With its understanding of the target and the issuer's business as background (see paragraph 24) the reporting accountant discusses with the directors the steps the directors have taken to identify relevant adjustments.

As described in paragraph 25 the definition of accounting policies in the Listing   **44** Rules encompasses the accounting standards of the applicable financial reporting framework. The reporting accountant's assessment of the completeness of adjustments is likely to include gaining an understanding of the differences between the financial reporting frameworks of the target and the issuer and, in particular:

(a) identifying those accounting standards in the issuer's or the target's financial reporting framework that may have a particular impact on the target's or issuer's industries;

(b) assessing the adequacy of the directors' impact analysis;

---

[14] *UKLA LR13.5.30R(1) and ISE LR10.5.30(1).*

(c)   considering the adequacy of the process followed by the issuer in ensuring the completeness of the adjustments, in particular the depth of involvement of senior management in the preparation of the reconciliation. Paragraphs 23 to 33 of the Annexure describe in more detail the processes that management may use when preparing a financial information reconciliation; and

(d)   assessing whether the reconciliation, taken as a whole, appears to have any material omissions.

45   The reporting accountant should obtain sufficient appropriate evidence that the issuer can support each adjustment (including the detailed calculation of the adjustment) and that, where appropriate, such support has been obtained from the appropriate level of management of the target. (SIR 5000.5)

46   If the reporting accountant becomes aware of an adjustment which:

(a)   in its opinion, ought to be made for the purposes of the financial information reconciliation; or

(b)   in its opinion, ought not to have been made for the purposes of the financial information reconciliation; or

(c)   the directors of the issuer cannot support (either in principle or in matters of detail and computation),

it discusses the position with the directors of the issuer and, if necessary, the issuer's advisers. If the reporting accountant is not able to agree with the directors of the issuer and the issuer's advisers as to how the matter is to be resolved it considers the consequences for its report.

Checking the calculations

47   The reporting accountant ascertains whether the adjustments made in the financial information reconciliation are included under the appropriate financial statement captions as well as the arithmetical accuracy of the calculations within the financial information reconciliation itself.

48   In respect of the adjustments the reporting accountant checks the calculation of the effect on the target's financial information of applying the accounting policy of the issuer rather than the accounting policies of the target.

Presentation of the financial information reconciliation

49   The reporting accountant should consider whether it has become aware of anything to cause it to believe that the financial information reconciliation is presented in a way that is not understandable or is misleading in the context in which it is provided. If the reporting accountant is aware of such matters it should discuss them with the directors of the issuer and any other persons to whom its report is to be addressed, and consider whether it is able to issue its opinion. (SIR 5000.6)

50   The underlying principle is that a reader of the Class 1 circular will be able to understand how the adjustments that have been made affect the underlying financial information. The reporting accountant may wish to assess whether, for example, there is adequate disclosure of the specific line items of the income statement or balance sheet that give rise to an adjustment.

Representation letter

SIR 1000.13 sets out the Investment Reporting Standard with respect to   **51**
representation letters that is applicable to all engagements involving an
investment circular. Examples of representation letter clauses applicable to
financial information reconciliations are set out in Appendix 3.

Documentation

SIR 1000.14 and SIR 1000.15 set out the Investment Reporting Standards with   **52**
respect to the reporting accountant's working papers.

Professional scepticism

SIR 1000.16 sets out the Investment Reporting Standard with respect to the   **53**
attitude of professional scepticism adopted by the reporting accountant in planning
and performing an engagement.

Reporting

SIR 1000.17, SIR 1000.18 and SIR 1000.19 set out the Investment Reporting   **54**
Standards with respect to reporting that are applicable to all engagements
involving an investment circular. Additional Investment Reporting Standards
relating to engagements to report on financial information reconciliations are set
out below. An example report on a financial information reconciliation prepared in
accordance with the Listing Rules is set out in Appendix 4.

Responsibilities

In all reports on financial information reconciliations in Class 1 circulars the   **55**
reporting accountant should explain the extent of its responsibility in respect
of the reconciliations by including in its report:

(a)   **a statement that the reporting accountant's responsibility is to form an**
      opinion as to whether the reconciliations have been properly compiled
      on the basis stated and the adjustments are appropriate for the purpose
      of presenting the financial information (as adjusted) on a basis
      consistent in all material respects with the accounting policies of the
      issuer and to report its opinion to the addressees of the report; and

(b)   **a statement that the financial information reconciliation is the**
      responsibility of the directors. (SIR 5000.7)

The reporting accountant's responsibility in relation to the opinion required by the   **56**
Listing Rules is limited to the provision of the report and the opinion expressed.
Where an audit or other opinion has been expressed on the financial information of
the target by a firm other than the reporting accountant, the reporting accountant
may state in the responsibilities section that it does not accept any responsibility
for any of the historical financial statements of the target and that it expresses no
opinion on those financial statements. An example of such a reference is included
in the example report in Appendix 4.

57   Where the reporting accountant has provided an audit or other opinion on the financial information of the target the reporting accountant may state in the responsibilities section that:

(a)   it is not updating or refreshing any reports or opinions previously made by it on any financial information used in the compilation of the reconciliations; and

(b)   it accepts no responsibility for such reports or opinions beyond that owed to those to whom those reports or opinions were addressed at the date of their issue.

An example of such a reference is included in the example report in Appendix 4.

Basis of preparation of the financial information reconciliation

58   **The reporting accountant should, in its report, cross refer to disclosures that explain the basis of preparation of the financial information reconciliation (SIR 5000.8).**

Expression of opinion

59   **The report on the financial information reconciliation should contain a clear expression of opinion that complies with the requirements of the Listing Rules. (SIR 5000.9)**

60   The Class 1 circular in which the reporting accountant's report is included may be made available in other countries, such as the United States of America, which have their own standards for accountants when reporting on financial information reconciliations. In such circumstances, the reporting accountant considers whether to include a reference to the fact that a report issued in accordance with the SIRs should not be relied upon as if it had been issued in accordance with the standards applicable in that other country. An example of such a reference is included in the example report in Appendix 4.

Modified opinions

61   SIR 1000.20 sets out the Investment Reporting Standard, with respect to modified opinions, that is applicable to all engagements involving an investment circular.

62   With respect to the compilation of a financial information reconciliation, the reporting accountant may conclude that the outcome is materially misstated, (for example, in the circumstances described in paragraph 31 above), and in such circumstances considers the impact of such misstatements on its opinion.

63   In the event that the reporting accountant concludes that it is necessary to express a modified opinion it explains the circumstances to the directors of the issuer and any other parties to whom it is to report so that the issuer has an opportunity to amend the financial information reconciliation to alleviate the reporting accountant's concerns.

Consent

64   SIR 1000.21 and SIR 1000.22 set out the Investment Reporting Standards with respect to the giving of consent by the reporting accountant.

Events occurring between the date of the reporting accountant's report and the completion date of the transaction

After the date of its report, the reporting accountant has no obligation to perform 65
procedures or make enquiries regarding the Class 1 circular. However, the
reporting accountant may become aware of events and other matters which, had
they occurred and been known at the date of the report, might have caused it to
issue a different report or to withhold consent. SIR 1000.23 sets out the Investment
Reporting Standards with respect to such events occurring between the date of the
reporting accountant's report and the completion date of the transaction.

Effective date

A reporting accountant is required to comply with the Investment Reporting 66
Standards contained in this SIR for reports signed after 31 May 2008. Earlier
adoption is encouraged.

Appendix 1 – Regulatory provisions applicable to Class 1 circulars

Type of Class 1 Transaction	SIR 2000			SIR 5000		
	Requirement for a financial information table	Requirement for an accountant's opinion in true and fair terms	Possibility of a modified opinion	Requirement for a financial information reconciliation	Requirement for an accountant's opinion in properly compiled terms	Possibility of a modified opinion
Class 1 Acquisition of a target that is neither admitted to trading, listed on an overseas investment exchange, nor admitted to trading on an overseas regulated market.	✓ UKLA 13.5.12R UKLA 13.5.14R ISE 10.5.12 ISE 10.5.14	✓ UKLA 13.5.21R UKLA 13.5.22R ISE 10.5.21 ISE 10.5.22	✓ UKLA 13.5.25R ISE 10.5.25			n/a
Class 1 Acquisition of a target that is admitted to trading ...and a material adjustment needs to be made.	✓ UKLA 13.5.12R UKLA 13.5.14R ISE 10.5.12 ISE 10.5.14	UKLA 13.5.21R ISE 10.5.21	n/a	✓ UKLA 13.5.27R(2)(a) UKLA 13.5.30R(2) ISE 10.5.27(2)(a) ISE 10.5.30(2)	✓ UKLA 13.5.27R(2)(b) UKLA 13.5.30R(2) ISE 10.5.27(2)(b) ISE 10.5.30(2)	✓ UKLA 13.5.27R(2)(b) UKLA 13.5.30R ISE 10.5.27(2)(b) ISE 10.5.30
Class 1 Acquisition of a target that is admitted to trading ... and NO material adjustment needs to be made	✓ UKLA 13.5.12R UKLA 13.5.14R ISE 10.5.12 ISE 10.5.14	UKLA 13.5.21R ISE 10.5.21	n/a	If no material adjustment required then not in scope of UKLA 13.5.27R: ISE 10.5.27	UKLA 13.5.28R ISE 10.5.28	n/a
Class 1 disposal	✓ UKLA 13.5.12R UKLA 13.5.19R ISE 10.5.12 ISE 10.5.19	UKLA 13.5.21R UKLA 13.5.29G ISE 10.5.21 ISE 10.5.29	n/a			

Note 1: Within Chapter 13 of the UKLA Listing Rules and Chapter 10 of the ISE Listing Rules the terms "financial information" and "financial information table" are used. The terms have different meanings in that the requirements for a financial information table are set out in UKLA LR 13.5.18R and ISE 10.5.18 whereas the term financial information is not defined.

Note 2: Within Chapter 13 of the UKLA Listing Rules and Chapter 10 of the ISE Listing Rules two different types of accountant's opinion are discussed. The opinion relevant to financial information reconciliations is set out in UKLA 13.5.27R (2)(b) and ISE 10.5.27(2)(b) and is dealt with in this SIR. The other opinion which is relevant to opinions on financial information tables is set out in UKLA LR 13.5.22R and ISE 10.5.22 and dealt with in SIR 2000.

Note 3: UKLA LR13.5.30R(2) and ISE 10.5.30(2) require a financial information reconciliation of a target to be produced with respect to subsequent half yearly or quarterly financial information

Appendix 2 – Examples of engagement letter clauses

The examples of engagement letter clauses are intended for consideration in the context of a public reporting engagement on a financial information reconciliation in a Class 1 circular. They should be tailored to the specific circumstances and supplemented by such other clauses as are relevant and appropriate.

Financial information upon which the report is to be given

The Class 1 circular will include a financial information table relating to ABC Inc. prepared in accordance with the requirements of Listing Rule [13.5.18R] [10.5.18] [and interim financial information relating to ABC Inc. reproduced in accordance with Listing Rule [13.5.30R(2)] [10.5.30(2)]].

We understand that the Class 1 circular will also include a financial information reconciliation of ABC Inc. for the three years ended [31 December 200X] [and the interim period ended [*date*]] (the "Reconciliation"). The Reconciliation will comprise [the income statements] and [balance sheets] of ABC Inc. showing the adjustments necessary to restate them to conform to XYZ plc's stated accounting policies. The Reconciliation will include supporting notes to explain the adjustments made.

Responsibilities

The preparation of the Reconciliation in accordance with the requirements of the Listing Rules will be the responsibility solely of the directors.

It is our responsibility to form an opinion as to whether the Reconciliation has been properly compiled on the basis stated and the adjustments are appropriate for the purpose of presenting the financial information (as adjusted) on a basis consistent in all material respects with the accounting policies of XYZ plc.

If the results of our work are satisfactory, and having regard to the requirements of Listing Rule [13.5.27R(2)(b)] [10.5.27(2)(b)] [and Listing Rule [13.5.30(2)] [10.5.30(2)]], we shall prepare a report on the Reconciliation for inclusion in the Class 1 circular. An illustration of the form of our report if the results of our work are satisfactory is attached.

Scope of work

Our work will be undertaken in accordance with the Standards for Investment Reporting issued by the Auditing Practices Board and will be subject to the limitations described therein.

In performing this engagement we will expect to receive, without undue delay, such;

(a) co-operation from all relevant officials of XYZ plc and ABC Inc. [including its auditors];

(b) access to all the pertinent accounting records of XYZ plc and ABC Inc. and any other relevant records and related information; [and]

(c)   representations from XYZ plc[; and]

(d)   [access to the files of the auditors of ABC Inc.],

as we may need for the purposes of our examination.

Appendix 3 – Examples of management representation letter clauses

The following are examples of management representation letter clauses relating to reports on financial information reconciliations, issued pursuant to the Listing Rules, which may be obtained from the issuer. Alternatively they may form the basis for a board minute.

Introduction

We refer to the financial information reconciliation set out in Part [...] of the [Class 1 circular] dated...(the "Reconciliation"). We acknowledge that we are solely responsible for the Reconciliation and confirm on behalf of the directors of the company to the best of our knowledge and belief, having made appropriate enquiries of officials of the company [and the directors and officials of the [target]], the following representations made to you in the course of your work.

Specific representations

- We acknowledge as duly appointed officials of the company our responsibility for the Reconciliation which has been prepared in accordance with the requirements of the Listing Rules of [the United Kingdom Listing Authority] [the Irish Stock Exchange Limited].

- We have considered the adjustments included in the Reconciliation. We confirm that, in our opinion, the Reconciliation includes all adjustments that are appropriate for the purpose of presenting the financial information (as adjusted) on a basis consistent in all material respects with the accounting policies of XYZ plc.

- We have made available to you all significant information relevant to the Reconciliation of which we have knowledge.

- [...*Any specific representations relating to information included in the Reconciliations (for example representations concerning accounting policies in greater detail than that included in the published financial statements).*]

Appendix 4 – Example report on a financial information reconciliation in accordance with the Listing Rules

Date

Reporting accountant's address

Addressees, as agreed between the parties in the engagement letter

Dear Sirs,

XYZ plc (the "Company"): proposed acquisition of ABC Inc (the "Target")

We report on the reconciliation of [*describe items reconciled* the consolidated income statement for each of the years in the three-year period ended [*date*] [and the interim period ended [*date*]], and of *describe items reconciled* the consolidated balance sheet as at [*dates*]], together the "financial information", as previously reported in the financial statements of the Target prepared under [United States Generally Accepted Accounting Principles], showing the adjustments necessary to restate it on the basis of the Company's accounting policies [specify the accounting policies e.g. those used in preparing the Company's last set of annual financial statements] (the "Reconciliation"), set out in Part [ ] of the Class 1 circular of the Company dated [*date*]. This report is required by Listing Rule[s] [13.5.27R(2)(b) [and 13.5.30R(2)] of the United Kingdom Listing Authority] [10.5.27(2)(b) [and 10.5.30(2) of the Irish Stock Exchange Limited]] and is given for the purpose of complying with [that] [those] Listing Rule[s] and for no other purpose.

Responsibilities

It is the responsibility of the directors of the Company (the "Directors") to prepare the Reconciliation in accordance with Listing Rule[s] [13.5.27R(2)(a) [and 13.5.30R(2)]] [10.5.27(2)(a) [and 10.5.30(2)]].

It is our responsibility to form an opinion, as required by Listing Rule[s] [13.5.27R(2(b)] [and 13.5.30R(2)]] [10.5.27(2)(a) and 10.5.30(2)]], as to whether:

(a)   the Reconciliation has been properly compiled on the basis stated; and

(b)   the adjustments are appropriate for the purpose of presenting the financial information (as adjusted) on a basis consistent in all material respects with the Company's accounting policies,

and to report that opinion to you.

[*Insert where an audit or other opinion has been expressed on the financial statements of the Target upon which the Reconciliation is based by a firm other than the reporting accountant, or where such information is unaudited:* The Reconciliation is based on the [un]audited balance sheet[s] as at [*dates*] and income statement[s] for [each of] the [year[s]]/[period[s]] then ended of [the Target] which were the responsibility of the directors of [the Target] [and were audited by another firm of accountants]. We do not accept any responsibility for any of the historical financial statements of [the Target], nor do we express any opinion on those financial statements.]

[*Insert where the reporting accountant has provided an audit or other opinion on the financial statements of the Target upon which the Reconciliation is based:* In providing this opinion we are not updating or refreshing any reports or opinions previously made by us on any financial information used in the compilation of the Reconciliation, nor do we accept responsibility for such reports or opinions beyond that owed to those to whom those reports or opinions were addressed at the date of their issue.]

Basis of Opinion

We conducted our work in accordance with the Standards for Investment Reporting issued by the Auditing Practices Board in [the United Kingdom] [Ireland]. The work that we performed for the purpose of making this report, which involved no independent examination of any of the underlying financial information, consisted primarily of checking whether the unadjusted financial information of [the Target] has been accurately extracted from an appropriate source, assessing whether all adjustments necessary for the purpose of presenting the financial information on a basis consistent in all material respects with [the Company's] accounting policies have been made, examination of evidence supporting the adjustments in the Reconciliation and checking the arithmetical accuracy of the calculations within the Reconciliation.

We planned and performed our work so as to obtain the information and explanations we considered necessary in order to provide us with reasonable assurance that the Reconciliation has been properly compiled on the basis stated and that the adjustments are appropriate for the purpose of presenting the financial information (as adjusted) on a basis consistent in all material respects with the Company's accounting policies.

[*This paragraph may be omitted if the document is not to be distributed outside [the UK] [Ireland]* – Our work has not been carried out in accordance with auditing or other standards and practices generally accepted in the United States of America [or other jurisdictions] and accordingly should not be relied upon as if it had been carried out in accordance with those standards and practices.]

Opinion

In our opinion:

(a)   the Reconciliation has been properly compiled on the basis stated; and

(b)   the adjustments are appropriate for the purpose of presenting the financial information (as adjusted) on a basis consistent in all material respects with the Company's accounting policies.

Declaration

[This paragraph is only included if the investment circular is also a prospectus. For the purposes of [Prospectus Rule [5.5.3R(2)(f)] [5.5.4R(2)(f)]]/[Paragraph 2(2)(f) of Schedule 1 to "The Prospectus (Directive 2003/71/EC) Regulations 2005"] [Paragraph 3(2)(f) of Schedule 1 to "the Prospectus (Directive 2003/71/EC) Regulations 2005"] we are responsible for this report as part of the [prospectus] [registration document] and declare that we have taken all reasonable care to ensure that the information contained [in this report] [those parts] is, to the best of our knowledge, in accordance with the facts and contains no omission likely to affect its import. This declaration is included in the [prospectus] [registration document] in compliance with [item 1.2 of Annex I of the PD Regulation] [item 1.2 of Annex III of the PD Regulation].]

Yours faithfully

Reporting accountant

Annexure – Accounting conventions and processes used in preparing financial information reconciliations for inclusion in Class 1 circulars

This Annexure has been compiled by the APB from a number of sources to describe conventions and processes commonly used for the proper compilation of financial information reconciliations. It does not constitute basic principles, essential procedures, or guidance promulgated by the APB.

Introduction

Financial information tables

1   With respect to Class 1 acquisitions, Chapter 13 of the Listing Rules of the UK Listing Authority (UKLA) and Chapter 10 of the Listing Rules of the Irish Stock Exchange Limited (ISE) set out requirements for a financial information table relating to targets[1].

2   A financial information table is required to include, for each of the periods covered by the table:

(a)   a balance sheet and its explanatory notes;

(b)   an income statement and its explanatory notes;

(c)   a cash flow statement and its explanatory notes;

(d)   a statement showing either all changes in equity or changes in equity other than those arising from capital transactions with owners and distributions to owners;

(e)   the accounting policies; and

(f)   any additional explanatory notes.

3   When an issuer seeks to acquire a target that is not publicly traded[2], the financial information table is presented on the basis of the issuer's accounting policies. However, when an issuer seeks to acquire a publicly traded target the financial information table is presented on the basis of the target's accounting policies.

4   With respect to a target that is not publicly traded a reporting accountant's opinion is required as to whether, for the purposes of the Class 1 circular, the financial information table gives a true and fair view of the financial matters set out in it, and whether the financial information table has been prepared in a form that is consistent with the accounting policies adopted in the listed company's latest annual consolidated accounts.

Financial information of publicly traded targets

5   With respect to targets that are publicly traded a reporting accountant's opinion on the financial information table is not required. However, with respect to a publicly traded target, if a material adjustment needs to be made to the target's financial statements to achieve consistency with the issuer's accounting policies there are additional requirements.

---

[1] *Where a listed company is seeking to acquire an interest in another company, that company is described as a target.*

[2] *A target that is not publicly traded is one that is neither admitted to the Official List nor admitted to trading, listed on an overseas investment exchange nor admitted to trading on an overseas regulated market.*

Therefore, with respect to a publicly traded target, the issuer is required to make a determination as to whether material adjustments need to be made to the target's financial statements in order to achieve consistency with the issuer's accounting policies. Such a determination will need to be made by a staff member or outside expert having appropriate qualifications (see paragraph 23) and involve the identification of material differences (if any) between the accounting policies of the issuer and the accounting policies of the target (see paragraph 24). **6**

Where such a material adjustment does need to be made the issuer is required to include the following in the Class 1 circular in addition to the financial information table referred to above[3]: **7**

(a) a reconciliation of "financial information" on the target, for all periods covered by the financial information table, normally on the basis of the accounting policies used in the issuer's last published accounts[4];

(b) a reporting accountant's opinion on that reconciliation that sets out:

   (i) whether the reconciliation of financial information in the financial information table has been properly compiled on the basis stated; and

   (ii) whether the adjustments are appropriate for the purpose of presenting the financial information (as adjusted) on a basis consistent in all material respects with the issuer's accounting policies.

The need for accounting conventions

The term "financial information" is not defined by the Listing Rules nor are there any detailed rules regarding the "proper compilation" of a financial information reconciliation. The directors, therefore, have regard to accepted conventions which have developed for the preparation and presentation of financial information reconciliation tables in Class 1 circulars. These conventions are summarised in paragraphs 9 to 22 that follow. In paragraphs 23 to 33 there is a discussion of processes that the issuer may adopt when preparing financial information reconciliations. **8**

Conventions

Format of financial information reconciliations

The overriding principle regarding the format of the presentation of a financial information reconciliation is that the presentation discloses all the material adjustments that are required to be made in order to present the financial information (as adjusted) on a basis consistent with the issuer's accounting policies. The relevant accounting policies of the issuer are normally those adopted by the issuer in its last published accounts. **9**

---

[3] *Under UKLA LR 13.5.30R(2) and ISE LR 10.5.30(2) similar requirements apply where the target has published half yearly or quarterly financial information subsequent to the end of its last financial year and a material adjustment needs to be made to the financial information presented in respect of the relevant interim period of the target in the Class 1 circular to achieve consistency with the issuer's accounting policies.*

[4] *The UKLA's publication "List!" 16 at paragraph 2.5 discusses certain circumstances where accounting policies other than those used in the issuer's last published accounts are used.*

10   Financial information reconciliations typically address the balance sheet and income statement or extracts of the balance sheet and income statement. However, if there is a material adjustment required, for example, to the cash flow statement or the Statement of Changes in Equity then relevant financial information from the relevant statement may also be presented. A material adjustment may arise to the cash flow statement where the target and the issuer use different definitions of the composition of cash and cash equivalents.

11   There is no prescribed format for the presentation of the reconciliation. Sometimes they are presented in columnar form using as a basis the descriptions of financial statement items in the target's financial information. However, alternative presentations are commonly used and the underlying principle is that the reader of the Class 1 circular should be able to understand how the adjustments affect the underlying financial information.

Errors in the underlying financial information

12   Where an error in the underlying financial information is identified that does not reflect a genuine difference between the accounting policies of the target and the issuer it is not rectified by being presented as an adjustment. The issuer discusses the proposed presentation of the rectification of the error with the UKLA or the ISE.

13   What constitutes an error will be defined by the financial reporting framework used by the issuer. In the case of International Financial Reporting Standards (IFRSs) as adopted by the EU, for example, an error is defined as: "omissions from, and misstatements in, the target's financial statements, for one or more prior periods arising from a failure to use, or misuse of, reliable information that:

    (a)   was available when financial statements for those periods were authorised for issue; and

    (b)   could reasonably be expected to have been obtained and taken into account in the preparation and presentation of those financial statements.

    Such errors include the effects of mathematical mistakes, mistakes in applying accounting policies, oversights or misinterpretations of fact and fraud".

Accounting policies

14   Guidance in UKLA Listing Rule 13.5.5G and ISE Listing Rule 10.5.5 indicates that "accounting policies include accounting standards and accounting disclosures". A financial information reconciliation, therefore, is not confined to a reconciliation to the stated accounting policies of an issuer but to those policies and the accounting standards comprising the financial reporting framework of the issuer regardless of whether they are articulated within the issuer's statement of accounting policies. However, reconciliations do not normally extend to reconciling note disclosures.

Under many financial reporting frameworks, such as IFRSs as adopted by the   **15**
EU, the application of different measurement bases to financial statement items
is evidence that different accounting policies have been applied. IAS 8 states
"A change in the measurement basis applied is a change in an accounting
policy and is not a change in an accounting estimate"[5]. Examples of
measurement bases, described in IFRSs as adopted by the EU are: historical
cost, current cost, net realisable value, fair value or recoverable amount[6].

In the process of applying the entity's accounting policies, management makes   **16**
various judgments, apart from those involving estimations (see paragraph 19)
that can have a significant effect on the amounts recognised in the financial
statements. Under IFRSs as adopted by the EU the entity is required to disclose
those judgments that have the most significant effect on the amounts
recognised in the financial statements[7].

Examples of such judgments are: **17**

● Whether financial assets are held-to-maturity investments.

● When substantially all the significant risks and rewards of ownership of
    financial assets and lease assets are transferred to other entities.

● Whether, in substance, particular sales of goods are financing
    arrangements and therefore do not give rise to revenue.

● Whether the substance of the relationship between the entity and a special
    purpose entity indicates that the special purpose entity is controlled by
    the entity.

Where the target and the issuer have made, or would make, different judgments
in similar circumstances this gives rise to the need for an adjustment.

Accounting estimates

Although adjustments are made for differences in accounting policies (as   **18**
defined), adjustments are not made to replace the target's accounting estimates
with new estimates made by the issuer. However, in rare circumstances the effect
of a difference from applying an accounting estimate may be material to the
adjusted financial information and the issuer may consider that it is necessary to
explain this through supplemental disclosure to allow the financial information
reconciliation to be considered in context. An example of such a circumstance is
where the issuer and the target both have a policy of depreciating a particular class
of property, plant and equipment on a straight line basis over its expected useful
life. However, the target's estimate of the expected useful life differs significantly
from the issuer's estimated useful life and the effect of the difference in estimate is
material to the financial information reconciliation.

Distinguishing between accounting policies and accounting estimates

Many financial reporting frameworks recognise that it can be difficult to   **19**
distinguish changes in accounting policies from changes in accounting
estimates and that in such instances of uncertainty the change is treated as a

---

[5] *IAS 8 Accounting Policies, Changes in Accounting Estimates and Errors, paragraph 35*

[6] *IAS 1 Presentation of financial statements, paragraph 109*

[7] *IAS 1 paragraphs 113 and 114*

change in accounting estimate[8]. A similar principle applies when determining whether a target uses different accounting policies to those used by the issuer.

Explanation of adjustments

20   The overriding principle that the issuer follows is to ensure that the adjustments are clearly shown and explained.

21   The convention is that material adjustments are presented on a disaggregated basis (that is offsetting adjustments are not netted off) as such presentation enhances the understanding of the users of the reconciliation.

Material adjustments

22   The requirement for a reconciliation arises where a material adjustment needs to be made to the target's financial statements to achieve consistency with the listed company's accounting policies. It is not possible to prescribe conditions for determining whether an adjustment will be a material adjustment in any given case, although presentational accounting policy differences, which do not have the effect of altering net assets, net income or cash flows are not normally treated as material. The UKLA or the ISE will usually wish to agree the approach in individual cases.

Processes for preparing a financial information reconciliation

Identification of all material differences

23   In order to identify all material differences between the accounting policies of the issuer and the accounting policies of the target the issuer's staff responsible for preparation of the reconciliation will need to have (or acquire) a requisite degree of expertise with respect to both financial reporting frameworks. Such expertise may be augmented by the use of appropriate reference material and technical guides. In complex cases the issuer may have to employ an outside expert having appropriate qualifications.

Preparing a financial information reconciliation

24   There are four basic steps involved in preparing a financial information reconciliation. These are:

(a)   identification of all material differences between the accounting policies of the issuer and the accounting policies of the target (See paragraph 6);

(b)   performing an "impact analysis" by performing a detailed analysis of the application of those policies and gathering the relevant data to enable either:

(i)   the adjustments to be calculated; or

(ii)   a determination to be made that no adjustments are required.

---

[8] *IAS 8 paragraph 35*

(c)   in respect of each material difference calculating the effect on the target's financial information of applying the accounting policies of the issuer rather than the accounting policies of the target; and

(d)   ensuring that the bookkeeping underpinning the financial information reconciliation is complete and accurate.

In practice these steps will need to be undertaken by the issuer's staff responsible for preparation of the reconciliation in consultation with, and with the cooperation of, the relevant finance staff of the target. It is unlikely that the issuer's staff will be able to achieve the necessary understanding of the target's financial information without a high degree of involvement of the target's finance staff in the process. In a hostile bid, or other limited access situation, the issuer is unlikely to be in a position to prepare a financial information reconciliation. In such situations the circumstances are discussed with the UKLA or the ISE.   **25**

The UKLA generally encourages issuers preparing an investment circular in a limited access situation to contact them as soon as possible to discuss the exact disclosure requirements. In certain circumstances it may be appropriate for a financial information reconciliation to be published in a supplementary circular within 28 days of a contested offer becoming unconditional.   **26**

Identification of all material differences between the accounting policies of the issuer and the target

As explained in paragraph 14 the identification is not confined to the stated accounting policies of the issuer or the target but also encompasses differences between those accounting standards that affect the financial statements of the issuer or the target regardless of whether the application of the accounting standards has been articulated in the statement of accounting policies.   **27**

Impact analysis

The issuer, therefore, gains an understanding of the differences between the financial reporting frameworks of the target and the issuer and may prepare an "impact analysis". Such an impact analysis may be prepared in conjunction with, or as a development of, the initial determination prepared by the issuer referred to in paragraph 6.   **28**

The impact analysis should in particular identify those accounting standards in the issuer's or target's financial reporting frameworks that may have a particular impact on the target's or issuer's industries.   **29**

Using proprietary checklists or synopses of the requirements of accounting standards may assist issuers in preparing an impact analysis.   **30**

Calculating the effect on the target's financial information of applying the issuer's accounting policies

In order to calculate the adjustments required to be made in respect of each identified difference, between the accounting policies of the target and the issuer, the issuer is likely to require access to the accounting records and related information of the target. To provide support for the calculation of each adjustment the issuer retains appropriate documented evidence.   **31**

Ensuring that the bookkeeping is complete and accurate

32   When preparing a financial information reconciliation there are a number of accounting controls that an issuer may apply, for example:

- Ensuring, when making adjustments, that the principles of double-entry bookkeeping are followed. The risk of making one-sided adjustments is mitigated to a great extent if working papers are prepared covering an adjusted income statement, an adjusted balance sheet and an adjusted statement of equity, even if not all of these are to be published.

- Considering the income, and other, tax effects of the adjustments and assessing whether the resultant effective tax rate is understandable and meaningful.

- Analysing the differences between the (adjusted) opening and closing equity account balances. (This is sometimes referred to as an equity roll forward reconciliation.) Such an analysis will be of assistance in checking that the principles of double-entry bookkeeping have been followed where the other side of an adjustment is to an equity account.

- Proving that the cash and cash equivalent position, as adjusted, is the same as that shown by the unadjusted financial statements (unless there is a reason for there being a difference). If there is a difference between the cash position reported on the two bases the issuer should understand how this difference arises and consider whether it may reflect an error in the double-entry bookkeeping applied to the reconciliation process[9].

Internal controls over the reconciliation

33   The following high level internal controls should typically be in place:

- The issuer should have employees (or access to outside experts), and other technical resources, with requisite knowledge and experience to prepare and monitor the preparation of the financial information reconciliation.

- The directors of the issuer should be committed to the proper preparation of financial information reconciliations as evidenced by a careful review of the financial information reconciliations being performed.

- Where applicable, comparing the reconciliation to those made in earlier periods. This may be applicable where the listed company has made an unsuccessful bid for the target in a previous period or a bid for other targets that use the same financial reporting framework.

---

[9] *Cash flow statements are usually not published as part of a financial information reconciliation. Nevertheless, comparing the resultant cash position from moving from the target's financial reporting framework to that of the issuer may be a useful accounting control.*

Part Nine

Statement of Standards for reporting accountants

International Standard on Review Engagements (UK and Ireland) 2410 – Review of interim financial information performed by the Independent Auditor of the Entity

(July 2007)

Contents

	Paragraphs
Introduction	1 - 3-1
General principles of a review of interim financial information	4 - 6
Objective of an engagement to review interim financial information	7 - 9
Agreeing the terms of the engagement	10 - 11
Procedures for a review of interim financial information	12 - 29-1
Evaluation of misstatements	30 - 33-1
Management representations	34 - 35
Auditor's responsibility for accompanying information	36 - 37
Communication	38 - 42
Reporting the nature, extent and results of the review of interim financial information	43 - 63
Documentation	64
Effective date	65

Appendix 1: Example of an engagement letter for a review of interim financial information

Appendix 2: Analytical procedures the auditor may consider when performing a review of interim financial information

Appendix 3: Example of a management representation letter

Appendix 4: Examples of review reports on interim financial information

Appendix 5: Examples of review reports with a qualified conclusion for a departure from the applicable Financial Reporting Framework

Appendix 6: Examples of review reports with a qualified conclusion for a limitation on scope not imposed by management

Appendix 7: Examples of review reports with an adverse conclusion for a departure from the applicable Financial Reporting Framework

Appendix 8: Example review report for a UK or Irish company listed in the UK or Ireland preparing a half-yearly financial report in compliance with IAS 34 as adopted by the European Union

Appendix 9: Summary of particular requirements of half-yearly reports prepared by listed companies in the UK and Ireland

The Auditing Practices Board Limited, which is part of the Financial Reporting Council, prepares for use within the United Kingdom and the Republic of Ireland:

- Standards and guidance for auditing;
- Standards and guidance for reviews of interim financial information performed by auditors of the entity;
- Standards and guidance for the work of reporting accountants in connection with investment circulars; and
- Standards and guidance for auditors' integrity, objectivity and independence

with the objective of enhancing public confidence in the audit process and the quality and relevance of audit services in the public interest.

The Auditing Practices Board Limited discharges its responsibilities through a Board ("the APB") comprising individuals who are eligible for appointment as company auditors, and those who are not so eligible. Those who are eligible for appointment as company auditors may not exceed 40% of the APB by number.

Neither the Auditing Practices Board Limited nor the APB accepts any liability to any party for any loss, damage or costs howsoever arising, whether directly or indirectly, whether in contract, tort or otherwise from any action or decision taken (or not taken) as a result of any person relying or otherwise using this document or arising from any omission from it.

For reviews of interim financial information for periods ending on or after 20 September 2007, this ISRE (UK and Ireland) supersedes APB Bulletin 1999/4. Early adoption is permitted.

© The Auditing Practices Board Limited 2007

Introduction

The purpose of this International Standard on Review Engagements (UK and **1**
(Ireland) (ISRE (UK and Ireland)) is to establish standards and provide guidance
on the auditor's professional responsibilities when the auditor undertakes an
engagement to review interim financial information of an audit client, and on the
form and content of the report. The term "auditor" is used throughout this ISRE
(UK and Ireland), not because the auditor is performing an audit function but
because the scope of this ISRE (UK and Ireland) is limited to a review of interim
financial information performed by the independent auditor of the financial
statements of the entity.

This ISRE (UK and Ireland) uses the terms "those charged with governance" **1-1**
and "management". The term "governance" describes the role of persons
entrusted with the supervision, control and direction of an entity. Ordinarily,
those charged with governance are accountable for ensuring that the entity
achieves its objectives, and for the quality of its financial reporting and
reporting to interested parties. Those charged with governance include
management only when they perform such functions.

In the UK and Ireland, those charged with governance include the directors **1-2**
(executive and non-executive) of a company or other body, the members of an
audit committee where one exists, the partners, proprietors, committee of
management or trustees of other forms of entity, or equivalent persons
responsible for directing the entity's affairs and preparing its financial statements.

"Management" comprises those persons who perform senior managerial **1-3**
functions.

In the UK and Ireland, depending on the nature and circumstances of the entity, **1-4**
management may include some or all of those charged with governance (e.g.
executive directors). Management will not normally include non-executive
directors.

For purposes of this ISRE (UK and Ireland), interim financial information is **2**
financial information that is prepared and presented in accordance with an
applicable financial reporting framework[1] and comprises either a complete or a
condensed set of financial statements for a period that is shorter than the entity's
financial year.

In the UK and Ireland, interim financial information usually comprises **2-1**
condensed financial information prepared for the first six months of the
financial year. For entities listed on the London Stock Exchange the
applicable financial reporting framework is established by the Disclosure and
Transparency Rules of the Financial Services Authority (FSA)[1a]. For entities
listed on the Irish Stock Exchange the applicable financial reporting framework
is established by the Transparency (Directive 2004/109/EC) Regulations 2007
and the Transparency Rules of the Financial Regulator[1b].

---

[1] *For example, International Financial Reporting Standards as issued by the International Accounting Standards Board.*

[1a] *Disclosure and Transparency Rule (DTR) 4.2 "Half-yearly financial reports" applies to all issuers whose shares or debt securities are admitted to trading and whose home state is the UK, subject to the exemptions set out in DTR 4.4.*

[1b] *Requirements for half yearly financial reports are set out in regulations 6 to 8 of Part 2 of the Transparency (Directive 2004/109/EC) Regulations 2007, subject to the exemptions set out in Part 3. Further requirements applicable to half-yearly financial reports are set out in the Transparency Rules issued by The Financial Regulator in Ireland.*

2-2   For entities listed on the London or Irish Stock Exchanges, issuers that are required to prepare consolidated annual accounts using International Financial Reporting Standards (IFRS) are required to prepare half-yearly financial reports that include a condensed set of financial statements that comply with International Accounting Standard (IAS) 34, *Interim Financial Reporting*, as adopted by the European Union. The relatively few issuers that do not prepare consolidated accounts are required to comply with the minimum disclosure requirements set out in the relevant rules of the UK FSA and the Irish Transparency Regulations and rules of the Irish Financial Regulator as applicable. These rules and regulations also make clear that the persons making the required responsibility statements can satisfy the requirement to confirm that the condensed set of financial statements give a true and fair view by giving a statement that they have been prepared in accordance with IAS 34 as adopted by the European Union or, for UK or Irish issuers not using IFRS, pronouncements on interim reporting issued by the Accounting Standards Board[1c], provided always that such persons have reasonable grounds to be satisfied that the condensed set of financial statements is not misleading. Further information on the rules and regulations applicable to issuers is given in Appendix 9.

2-3   In the context of a review of consolidated interim financial information "the entity," as referred to in this ISRE (UK and Ireland), is the group.

3   **The auditor who is engaged to perform a review of interim financial information should perform the review in accordance with this ISRE (UK and Ireland).** Through performing the audit of the annual financial statements, the auditor obtains an understanding of the entity and its environment, including its internal control. When the auditor is engaged to review the interim financial information, this understanding is updated through inquiries made in the course of the review, and assists the auditor in focusing the inquiries to be made and the analytical and other review procedures to be applied. A practitioner who is engaged to perform a review of interim financial information, and who is not the auditor of the entity, performs the review in accordance with ISRE 2400, *Engagements to Review Financial Statements*.[1d] As the practitioner does not ordinarily have the same understanding of the entity and its environment, including its internal control, as the auditor of the entity, the practitioner needs to carry out different inquiries and procedures to meet the objective of the review.

3-1   In some cases the auditor may be asked to carry out specific agreed-upon procedures as an alternative to a review, or the auditor may be approached for advice and guidance on specific accounting and financial reporting issues such as the policies relating to asset impairment or the useful life of an intangible asset. In such circumstances the auditor first agrees the procedures to be carried out, and then reports within that context. Such engagements are outside the scope of this ISRE (UK and Ireland) and, in such circumstances, the auditor requests the entity to describe interim financial information as "neither audited nor reviewed"[1e]

[1c] *For half-yearly periods ending on or after 20 September 2007, the relevant ASB pronouncement is the Statement "Half-Yearly Financial Reports".*

[1d] *ISRE 2400 has not been promulgated by the APB for application in the UK and Ireland.*

[1e] *The FSA's Disclosure and Transparency Rule 4.2.9(1), and the Irish Regulation 8(4)(a), requires that if the half-yearly financial report has been audited or reviewed by auditors pursuant to the Auditing Practices Board guidance on Review of Interim Financial Information, the audit report or review report must be reproduced in full.*
The FSA's Disclosure and Transparency Rule 4.2.9(2), and the Irish Regulation 8(4)(b), requires that if the half-yearly financial report has not been audited or reviewed by auditors pursuant to the Auditing Practices Board guidance on Review of Interim Financial Information, an issuer must make a statement to this effect in its report.

General principles of a review of interim financial information

The auditor should comply with the ethical requirements relevant to the audit of the annual financial statements of the entity[f].These ethical requirements govern the auditor's professional responsibilities in the following areas: independence, integrity, objectivity, professional competence and due care, confidentiality, professional behavior, and technical standards. **4**

The auditor should implement quality control procedures that are applicable to the individual engagement. The elements of quality control that are relevant to an individual engagement include leadership responsibilities for quality on the engagement, ethical requirements, acceptance and continuance of client relationships and specific engagements, assignment of engagement teams, engagement performance, and monitoring. **5**

The auditor should plan and perform the review with an attitude of professional skepticism, recognizing that circumstances may exist that cause the interim financial information to require a material adjustment for it to be prepared, in all material respects, in accordance with the applicable financial reporting framework. An attitude of professional skepticism means that the auditor makes a critical assessment, with a questioning mind, of the validity of evidence obtained and is alert to evidence that contradicts or brings into question the reliability of documents or representations by management of the entity. **6**

Objective of an engagement to review interim financial information

The objective of an engagement to review interim financial information is to enable the auditor to express a conclusion whether, on the basis of the review, anything has come to the auditor's attention that causes the auditor to believe that the interim financial information is not prepared, in all material respects, in accordance with an applicable financial reporting framework. The auditor makes inquiries, and performs analytical and other review procedures in order to reduce to a moderate level the risk of expressing an inappropriate conclusion when the interim financial information is materially misstated. **7**

The objective of a review of interim financial information differs significantly from that of an audit conducted in accordance with International Standards on Auditing (UK and Ireland) (ISAs (UK and Ireland)). A review of interim financial information does not provide a basis for expressing an opinion whether the financial information gives a true and fair view, or is presented fairly, in all material respects, in accordance with an applicable financial reporting framework. **8**

A review, in contrast to an audit, is not designed to obtain reasonable assurance that the interim financial information is free from material misstatement. A review consists of making inquiries, primarily of persons responsible for financial and accounting matters, and applying analytical and other review procedures. A review may bring significant matters affecting the interim financial information **9**

---

[f] *In the UK and Ireland the relevant ethical pronouncements with which the auditor complies are the APB's Ethical Standards for Auditors and the ethical pronouncements relating to the work of auditors issued by the auditor's relevant professional body.*

to the auditor's attention, but it does not provide all of the evidence that would be required in an audit.

Agreeing the terms of the engagement

10   **The auditor and the client should agree on the terms of the engagement.**

11   The agreed terms of the engagement are ordinarily recorded in an engagement letter. Such a communication helps to avoid misunderstandings regarding the nature of the engagement and, in particular, the objective and scope of the review, management's responsibilities, the extent of the auditor's responsibilities, the assurance obtained, and the nature and form of the report. The communication ordinarily covers the following matters:

- The objective of a review of interim financial information.

- The scope of the review.

- Management's responsibility for the interim financial information.

- The applicable financial reporting framework (e.g. IAS 34 as adopted by the European Union and/or, where applicable, rules and regulations of a listing/regulatory authority relating to the form and content of interim financial information).

- Management's responsibility for establishing and maintaining effective internal control relevant to the preparation of interim financial information.

- Management's responsibility for making all financial records and related information available to the auditor.

- Management's agreement to provide written representations to the auditor to confirm representations made orally during the review, as well as representations that are implicit in the entity's records.

- The anticipated form and content of the report to be issued, including the identity of the addressee of the report.

- Management's agreement that where any document containing interim financial information indicates that the interim financial information has been reviewed by the entity's auditor, the review report will also be included in the document.

An illustrative engagement letter is set out in Appendix 1 to this ISRE (UK and Ireland). The terms of engagement to review interim financial information can also be combined with the terms of engagement to audit the annual financial statements.

Procedures for a review of interim financial information

Understanding the entity and its environment, including its internal control

12   **The auditor should have an understanding of the entity and its environment, including its internal control, as it relates to the preparation of both annual and interim financial information, sufficient to plan and conduct the engagement so as to be able to:**

(a)   **Identify the types of potential material misstatement and consider the likelihood of their occurrence; and**

(b)   **Select the inquiries, analytical and other review procedures that will provide the auditor with a basis for reporting whether anything has come to the auditor's attention that causes the auditor to believe that the interim financial information is not prepared, in all material respects, in accordance with the applicable financial reporting framework.**

As required by ISA (UK and Ireland) 315, *Understanding the Entity and its*   **13**
Environment and Assessing the Risks of Material Misstatement, the auditor who has audited the entity's financial statements for one or more annual periods has obtained an understanding of the entity and its environment, including its internal control, as it relates to the preparation of annual financial information that was sufficient to conduct the audit. In planning a review of interim financial information, the auditor updates this understanding. The auditor also obtains a sufficient understanding of internal control as it relates to the preparation of interim financial information as it may differ from internal control as it relates to annual financial information.

The auditor uses the understanding of the entity and its environment, including its   **14**
internal control, to determine the inquiries to be made and the analytical and other review procedures to be applied, and to identify the particular events, transactions or assertions to which inquiries may be directed or analytical or other review procedures applied.

The procedures performed by the auditor to update the understanding of the entity   **15**
and its environment, including its internal control, ordinarily include the following:

●   Reading the documentation, to the extent necessary, of the preceding year's audit and reviews of prior interim period(s) of the current year and corresponding interim period(s) of the prior year, to enable the auditor to identify matters that may affect the current-period interim financial information.

●   Considering any significant risks, including the risk of management override of controls, that were identified in the audit of the prior year's financial statements.

●   Reading the most recent annual and comparable prior period interim financial information.

●   Considering materiality with reference to the applicable financial reporting framework as it relates to interim financial information to assist in determining the nature and extent of the procedures to be performed and evaluating the effect of misstatements.

●   Considering the nature of any corrected material misstatements and any identified uncorrected immaterial misstatements in the prior year's financial statements.

●   Considering significant financial accounting and reporting matters that may be of continuing significance such as material weaknesses in internal control.

●   Considering the results of any audit procedures performed with respect to the current year's financial statements.

- Considering the results of any internal audit performed and the subsequent actions taken by management.

- Reading management accounts and commentaries for the period.

- Considering any findings from prior periods relating to the quality and reliability of management accounts.

- Inquiring of management about the results of management's assessment of the risk that the interim financial information may be materially misstated as a result of fraud.

- Inquiring of management about the effect of changes in the entity's business activities.

- Inquiring of management about any significant changes in internal control and the potential effect of any such changes on the preparation of interim financial information.

- Inquiring of management of the process by which the interim financial information has been prepared and the reliability of the underlying accounting records to which the interim financial information is agreed or reconciled.

16   The auditor determines the nature of the review procedures, if any, to be performed for components and, where applicable, communicates these matters to other auditors involved in the review. Factors to be considered include the materiality of, and risk of misstatement in, the interim financial information of components, and the auditor's understanding of the extent to which internal control over the preparation of such information is centralized or decentralized.

17   **In order to plan and conduct a review of interim financial information, a recently appointed auditor, who has not yet performed an audit of the annual financial statements in accordance with ISAs (UK and Ireland), should obtain an understanding of the entity and its environment, including its internal control, as it relates to the preparation of both annual and interim financial information.**

18   This understanding enables the auditor to focus the inquiries made, and the analytical and other review procedures applied in performing a review of interim financial information in accordance with this ISRE (UK and Ireland). As part of obtaining this understanding, the auditor ordinarily makes inquiries of the predecessor auditor and, where practicable, reviews the predecessor auditor's documentation for the preceding annual audit, and for any prior interim periods in the current year that have been reviewed by the predecessor auditor. In doing so, the auditor considers the nature of any corrected misstatements, and any uncorrected misstatements aggregated by the predecessor auditor, any significant risks, including the risk of management override of controls, and significant accounting and any reporting matters that may be of continuing significance, such as material weaknesses in internal control.

Inquiries, analytical and other review procedures

19   **The auditor should make inquiries, primarily of persons responsible for financial and accounting matters, and perform analytical and other review procedures to enable the auditor to conclude whether, on the basis of the procedures performed, anything has come to the auditor's attention that causes the auditor to believe that the interim financial information is not**

prepared, in all material respects, in accordance with the applicable financial reporting framework.

A review ordinarily does not require tests of the accounting records through 20 inspection, observation or confirmation. Procedures for performing a review of interim financial information are ordinarily limited to making inquiries, primarily of persons responsible for financial and accounting matters, and applying analytical and other review procedures, rather than corroborating information obtained concerning significant accounting matters relating to the interim financial information. The auditor's understanding of the entity and its environment, including its internal control, the results of the risk assessments relating to the preceding audit and the auditor's consideration of materiality as it relates to the interim financial information, affects the nature and extent of the inquiries made, and analytical and other review procedures applied.

The auditor ordinarily performs the following procedures: 21

● Reading the minutes of the meetings of shareholders, those charged with governance, and other appropriate committees to identify matters that may affect the interim financial information, and inquiring about matters dealt with at meetings for which minutes are not available that may affect the interim financial information.

● Considering the effect, if any, of matters giving rise to a modification of the audit or review report, accounting adjustments or unadjusted misstatements, at the time of the previous audit or reviews.

● Communicating, where appropriate, with other auditors who are performing a review of the interim financial information of the reporting entity's significant components.

● Inquiring of members of management responsible for financial and accounting matters, and others as appropriate about the following:

    – Whether the interim financial information has been prepared and presented in accordance with the applicable financial reporting framework.

    – Whether there have been any changes in accounting principles or in the methods of applying them.

    – Whether any new transactions have necessitated the application of a new accounting principle.

    – Whether the interim financial information contains any known uncorrected misstatements.

    – Unusual or complex situations that may have affected the interim financial information, such as a business combination or disposal of a segment of the business.

    – Significant assumptions that are relevant to the fair value measurement or disclosures and management's intention and ability to carry out specific courses of action on behalf of the entity.

    – Whether related party transactions have been appropriately accounted for and disclosed in the interim financial information.

    – Significant changes in commitments and contractual obligations.

    – Significant changes in contingent liabilities including litigation or claims.

- Compliance with debt covenants.

- Matters about which questions have arisen in the course of applying the review procedures.

- Significant transactions occurring in the last several days of the interim period or the first several days of the next interim period.

- Knowledge of any fraud or suspected fraud affecting the entity involving:

  - Management;
  - Employees who have significant roles in internal control; or
  - Others where the fraud could have a material effect on the interim financial information.

- Knowledge of any allegations of fraud, or suspected fraud, affecting the entity's interim financial information communicated by employees, former employees, analysts, regulators, or others.

- Knowledge of any actual or possible noncompliance with laws and regulations that could have a material effect on the interim financial information.

- For group interim financial information, reviewing consolidation adjustments for consistency with the preceding annual financial statements and enquiring into large or unusual adjustments, and into adjustments made in the preceding annual financial statements but not made in the financial information in the interim report.

- Reviewing correspondence with regulators where applicable.

- Applying analytical procedures to the interim financial information designed to identify relationships and individual items that appear to be unusual and that may reflect a material misstatement in the interim financial information. Analytical procedures may include ratio analysis and statistical techniques such as trend analysis or regression analysis and may be performed manually or with the use of computer-assisted techniques. Appendix 2 to this ISRE (UK and Ireland) contains examples of analytical procedures the auditor may consider when performing a review of interim financial information.

- Reading the interim financial information, and considering whether anything has come to the auditor's attention that causes the auditor to believe that the interim financial information is not prepared, in all material respects, in accordance with the applicable financial reporting framework.

22   The auditor may perform many of the review procedures before or simultaneously with the entity's preparation of the interim financial information. For example, it may be practicable to update the understanding of the entity and its environment, including its internal control, and begin reading applicable minutes before the end of the interim period. Performing some of the review procedures earlier in the interim period also permits early identification and consideration of significant accounting matters affecting the interim financial information.

23   The auditor performing the review of interim financial information is also engaged to perform an audit of the annual financial statements of the entity. For convenience and efficiency, the auditor may decide to perform certain audit procedures concurrently with the review of interim financial information. For example, information gained from reading the minutes of meetings of the board of

directors in connection with the review of the interim financial information also may be used for the annual audit. The auditor may also decide to perform, at the time of the interim review, auditing procedures that would need to be performed for the purpose of the audit of the annual financial statements, for example, performing audit procedures on significant or unusual transactions that occurred during the period, such as business combinations, restructurings, or significant revenue transactions.

A review of interim financial information ordinarily does not require corroborating the inquiries about litigation or claims. It is, therefore, ordinarily not necessary to send an inquiry letter to the entity's lawyer. Direct communication with the entity's lawyer with respect to litigation or claims may, however, be appropriate if a matter comes to the auditor's attention that causes the auditor to question whether the interim financial information is not prepared, in all material respects, in accordance with the applicable financial reporting framework, and the auditor believes the entity's lawyer may have pertinent information. **24**

The auditor should obtain evidence that the interim financial information agrees or reconciles with the underlying accounting records. The auditor may obtain evidence that the interim financial information agrees or reconciles with the underlying accounting records by tracing the interim financial information to: **25**

(a)   The accounting records, such as the general ledger, or a consolidating schedule that agrees or reconciles with the accounting records; and

(b)   Other supporting data in the entity's records as necessary.

For a review of consolidated group interim financial information, the auditor traces the financial information of group components to the consolidation schedules and records of significant consolidation journals and adjustments. The auditor is not required to check the financial information back to the accounting records of individual group components. **25-1**

The auditor should inquire whether management has identified all events up to the date of the review report that may require adjustment to or disclosure in the interim financial information. It is not necessary for the auditor to perform other procedures to identify events occurring after the date of the review report. **26**

The auditor should inquire whether management has changed its assessment of the entity's ability to continue as a going concern. When, as a result of this inquiry or other review procedures, the auditor becomes aware of events or conditions that may cast significant doubt on the entity's ability to continue as a going concern, the auditor should: **27**

(a)   **Inquire of management as to its plans for future actions based on its going concern assessment, the feasibility of these plans, and whether management believes that the outcome of these plans will improve the situation; and**

(b)   **Consider the adequacy of the disclosure about such matters in the interim financial information.**

The guidance in *Going concern and financial reporting – guidance for directors of listed companies registered in the UK* issued in 1994 states "Directors cannot be expected to consider going concern as fully at the interim, but they should undertake a review of their previous work." Paragraph 57 of that guidance also states: "They should look at the position at the previous year-end to see whether any of the significant factors which they **27-1** had identified at that time have changed in the interim to such an extent as to affect the appropriateness of the going concern assumption."

28   Events or conditions which may cast significant doubt on the entity's ability to continue as a going concern may have existed at the date of the annual financial statements or may be identified as a result of inquiries of management or in the course of performing other review procedures. When such events or conditions come to the auditor's attention, the auditor inquires of management as to its plans for future action, such as its plans to liquidate assets, borrow money or restructure debt, reduce or delay expenditures, or increase capital. The auditor also inquires as to the feasibility of management's plans and whether management believes that the outcome of these plans will improve the situation. However, it is not ordinarily necessary for the auditor to corroborate the feasibility of management's plans and whether the outcome of these plans will improve the situation.

29   **When a matter comes to the auditor's attention that leads the auditor to question whether a material adjustment should be made for the interim financial information to be prepared, in all material respects, in accordance with the applicable financial reporting framework, the auditor should make additional inquiries or perform other procedures to enable the auditor to express a conclusion in the review report.** For example, if the auditor's review procedures lead the auditor to question whether a significant sales transaction is recorded in accordance with the applicable financial reporting framework, the auditor performs additional procedures sufficient to resolve the auditor's questions, such as discussing the terms of the transaction with senior marketing and accounting personnel, or reading the sales contract.

Comparative interim financial information

29-1   **When comparative interim financial information is presented, the auditor should consider whether:**

   (a)   The accounting policies used for the comparative financial information are consistent with those of the current period and appropriate adjustments and disclosures have been made where this is not the case; and

   (b)   The comparative amounts agree with the amounts and other disclosures presented in the preceding interim financial report for the corresponding period or whether appropriate disclosures and adjustments have been made where this is not the case.

Evaluation of misstatements

30   **The auditor should evaluate, individually and in the aggregate, whether uncorrected misstatements that have come to the auditor's attention are material to the interim financial information.**

31   A review of interim financial information, in contrast to an audit engagement, is not designed to obtain reasonable assurance that the interim financial information is free from material misstatement. However, misstatements which come to the auditor's attention, including inadequate disclosures, are evaluated individually and in the aggregate to determine whether a material adjustment is required to be made to the interim financial information for it to be prepared, in all material respects, in accordance with the applicable financial reporting framework.

32   The auditor exercises professional judgment in evaluating the materiality of any misstatements that the entity has not corrected. The auditor considers matters such

as the nature, cause and amount of the misstatements, whether the misstatements originated in the preceding year or interim period of the current year, and the potential effect of the misstatements on future interim or annual periods.

The auditor may designate an amount below which misstatements need not be aggregated, because the auditor expects that the aggregation of such amounts clearly would not have a material effect on the interim financial information. In so doing, the auditor considers the fact that the determination of materiality involves quantitative as well as qualitative considerations, and that misstatements of a relatively small amount could nevertheless have a material effect on the interim financial information. **33**

The amount designated by the auditor, below which misstatements that have come to the auditors attention need not be aggregated, is the amount below which the auditor believes misstatements are clearly trivial[1g]. **33-1**

Management representations

The auditor should obtain written representation from management that: **34**

(a) **It acknowledges its responsibility for the design and implementation of internal control to prevent and detect fraud and error;**

(b) **The interim financial information is prepared and presented in accordance with the applicable financial reporting framework;**

(c) **It believes the effect of those uncorrected misstatements aggregated by the auditor during the review are immaterial, both individually and in the aggregate, to the interim financial information taken as a whole. A summary of such items is included in or attached to the written representations;**

(d) **It has disclosed to the auditor all significant facts relating to any frauds or suspected frauds known to management that may have affected the entity;**

(e) **It has disclosed to the auditor the results of its assessment of the risks that the interim financial information may be materially misstated as a result of fraud;[2]**

(f) **It has disclosed to the auditor all known actual or possible noncompliance with laws and regulations whose effects are to be considered when preparing the interim financial information; and**

(g) **It has disclosed to the auditor all significant events that have occurred subsequent to the balance sheet date and through to the date of the review report that may require adjustment to or disclosure in the interim financial information.**

[1g] *This is not another expression for "immaterial". Matters which are "clearly trivial" will be of an wholly different (smaller) order of magnitude than the materiality thresholds used in the review, and will be matters that are clearly inconsequential, whether taken individually or in aggregate and whether judged by any quantitative and/or qualitative criteria. Further, whenever there is any uncertainty about whether one or more items are "clearly trivial" (in accordance with this definition), the presumption should be that the matter is not "clearly trivial".*

[2] *Paragraph 35 of ISA (UK and Ireland) 240, The Auditor's Responsibility to Consider Fraud in an Audit of Financial Statements explains that the nature, extent and frequency of such an assessment vary from entity to entity and that management may make a detailed assessment on an annual basis or as part of continuous monitoring. Accordingly, this representation, insofar as it relates to the interim financial information, is tailored to the entity's specific circumstances.*

35   The auditor obtains additional representations as are appropriate related to matters specific to the entity's business or industry. An illustrative management representation letter is set out in Appendix 3 to this ISRE (UK and Ireland).

Auditor's responsibility for accompanying information[2a]

36   **The auditor should read the other information that accompanies the interim financial information to consider whether any such information is materially inconsistent with the interim financial information.** If the auditor identifies a material inconsistency, the auditor considers whether the interim financial information or the other information needs to be amended. If an amendment is necessary in the interim financial information and management refuses to make the amendment, the auditor considers the implications for the review report. If an amendment is necessary in the other information and management refuses to make the amendment, the auditor considers including in the review report an additional paragraph describing the material inconsistency, or taking other actions, such as withholding the issuance of the review report or withdrawing from the engagement. For example, management may present alternative measures of earnings that more positively portray financial performance than the interim financial information, and such alternative measures are given excessive prominence, are not clearly defined, or not clearly reconciled to the interim financial information such that they are confusing and potentially misleading[2b].

37   **If a matter comes to the auditor's attention that causes the auditor to believe that the other information appears to include a material misstatement of fact, the auditor should discuss the matter with the entity's management.** While reading the other information for the purpose of identifying material inconsistencies, an apparent material misstatement of fact may come to the auditor's attention (i.e., information, not related to matters appearing in the interim financial information, that is incorrectly stated or presented). When discussing the matter with the entity's management, the auditor considers the validity of the other information and management's responses to the auditor's inquiries, whether valid differences of judgment or opinion exist and whether to request management to consult with a qualified third party to resolve the apparent misstatement of fact. If an amendment is necessary to correct a material

---

[2a] *Other information in the half-yearly financial report of a listed entity includes the interim management report and the responsibility statements required by the rules and regulations of the listing/regulatory authorities. It may also include, for example, performance summaries, prospective information and a chairman's statement.*

[2b] *The APB recognises that in some circumstances the presentation of alternative performance measures and associated narrative explanations may help shareholders understand better the financial performance of a company. However, the APB is concerned that in other circumstances such alternative performance measures have the potential to be misleading and shareholders may sometimes be misinformed by the manner in which alternative performance measures are presented. The APB believes that the potential for alternative performance measures to be misleading is considerable when they are given undue and inappropriate prominence, when there is no description of the basis on which the information was produced and, where appropriate, the adjusted numbers are not reconciled to the financial information that is presented in accordance with the applicable financial reporting framework.*
The APB's concerns are shared by the UK Listing Authority (UKLA). In its September 2005 newsletter, List!, the UKLA reminded issuers that they were free to disclose additional non-GAAP numbers in their interim accounts but, where they did, the UKLA said they should make clear the basis on which the numbers are calculated in order to avoid misleading investors. The UKLA also explained that it would not expect non-GAAP figures to be given greater prominence in interim announcements than any GAAP numbers. On 3 November 2005, the Committee of European Securities Regulators (CESR) published a recommendation on the use of alternative performance measures. In the February 2006 edition of List! the UKLA indicated that in its view the CESR recommendation represents best practice for the disclosure of alternative performance measures and encouraged issuers to follow the recommendation.

misstatement of fact and management refuses to make the amendment, the auditor considers taking further action as appropriate, such as notifying those charged with governance and obtaining legal advice.

Communication

When, as a result of performing the review of interim financial information, a matter comes to the auditor's attention that causes the auditor to believe that it is necessary to make a material adjustment to the interim financial information for it to be prepared, in all material respects, in accordance with the applicable financial reporting framework, the auditor should communicate this matter as soon as practicable to the appropriate level of management.   **38**

When, in the auditor's judgment, management does not respond appropriately within a reasonable period of time, the auditor should inform those charged with governance. The communication is made as soon as practicable, either orally or in writing. The auditor's decision whether to communicate orally or in writing is affected by factors such as the nature, sensitivity and significance of the matter to be communicated and the timing of such communications. If the information is communicated orally, the auditor documents the communication.   **39**

When, in the auditor's judgment, those charged with governance do not respond appropriately within a reasonable period of time, the auditor should consider: **40**

(a)   **Whether to modify the report; or**

(b)   **The possibility of withdrawing from the engagement; and**

(c)   **The possibility of resigning from the appointment to audit the annual financial statements.**

When, as a result of performing the review of interim financial information, a matter comes to the auditor's attention that causes the auditor to believe in the existence of fraud or noncompliance by the entity with laws and regulations the auditor should communicate the matter as soon as practicable to the appropriate level of management. The determination of which level of management is the appropriate one is affected by the likelihood of collusion or the involvement of a member of management. The auditor also considers the need to report such matters to those charged with governance and considers the implication for the review.   **41**

The auditor should communicate relevant matters of governance interest arising from the review of interim financial information to those charged with governance. As a result of performing the review of the interim financial information, the auditor may become aware of matters that in the opinion of the auditor are both important and relevant to those charged with governance in overseeing the financial reporting and disclosure process. The auditor communicates such matters to those charged with governance.   **42**

Reporting the nature, extent and results of the review of interim financial information

43   The auditor should issue a written report that contains the following:

(a)   An appropriate title.

(b)   An addressee, as required by the circumstances of the engagement.

(c)   Identification of the interim financial information reviewed, including identification of the title of each of the statements contained in the complete or condensed set of financial statements and the date and period covered by the interim financial information.

(d)   If the interim financial information comprises a complete set of general purpose financial statements prepared in accordance with a financial reporting framework designed to achieve fair presentation, a statement that management is responsible for the preparation and fair presentation of the interim financial information in accordance with the applicable financial reporting framework.

(e)   In other circumstances, a statement that management is responsible for the preparation and presentation of the interim financial information in accordance with the applicable financial reporting framework.

(f)   A statement that the auditor is responsible for expressing a conclusion on the interim financial information based on the review.

(g)   A statement that the review of the interim financial information was conducted in accordance with International Standard on Review Engagements (UK and Ireland) (ISRE (UK and Ireland)) 2410, *Review of Interim Financial Information Performed by the Independent Auditor of the Entity,* and a statement that that such a review consists of making inquiries, primarily of persons responsible for financial and accounting matters, and applying analytical and other review procedures.

(h)   A statement that a review is substantially less in scope than an audit conducted in accordance with International Standards on Auditing (UK and Ireland) and consequently does not enable the auditor to obtain assurance that the auditor would become aware of all significant matters that might be identified in an audit and that accordingly no audit opinion is expressed.

(i)   If the interim financial information comprises a complete set of general purpose financial statements prepared in accordance with a financial reporting framework designed to achieve fair presentation, a conclusion as to whether anything has come to the auditor's attention that causes the auditor to believe that the interim financial information does not give a true and fair view, or does not present fairly, in all material respects, in accordance with the applicable financial reporting framework (including a reference to the jurisdiction or country of origin of the financial reporting framework when the financial reporting framework used is not International Financial Reporting Standards); or

(j)   In other circumstances, a conclusion as to whether anything has come to the auditor's attention that causes the auditor to believe that the interim financial information is not prepared, in all material respects, in accordance with the applicable financial reporting framework (including a reference to the jurisdiction or country of origin of the financial reporting framework when the financial reporting framework used is not International Financial Reporting Standards).

(k)   The date of the report.

(l)   The location in the country or jurisdiction where the auditor practices.

(m)   The auditor's signature.

Illustrative review reports are set out in Appendix 4 to this ISRE (UK and Ireland).

An illustrative review report for a UK or Irish Company listed in the UK or Ireland and complying with IAS 34 as adopted by the European Union is set out in Appendix 8 to this ISRE (UK and Ireland).   **43-1**

In some jurisdictions, law or regulation governing the review of interim financial information may prescribe wording for the auditor's conclusion that is different from the wording described in paragraph 43(i) or (j). Although the auditor may be obliged to use the prescribed wording, the auditor's responsibilities as described in this ISRE (UK and Ireland) for coming to the conclusion remain the same.   **44**

Date of the review report

The date of the review report on an entity's financial information is the date on which the auditor signs the review report. The auditor should not date the review report earlier than the date on which the financial information is approved by management and those charged with governance.   **44-1**

Departure from the applicable financial reporting framework

The auditor should express a qualified or adverse conclusion when a matter has come to the auditor's attention that causes the auditor to believe that a material adjustment should be made to the interim financial information for it to be prepared, in all material respects, in accordance with the applicable financial reporting framework.   **45**

If matters have come to the auditor's attention that cause the auditor to believe that the interim financial information is or may be materially affected by a departure from the applicable financial reporting framework, and management does not correct the interim financial information, the auditor modifies the review report. The modification describes the nature of the departure and, if practicable, states the effects on the interim financial information. If the information that the auditor believes is necessary for adequate disclosure is not included in the interim financial information, the auditor modifies the review report and, if practicable, includes the necessary information in the review report. The modification to the review report is ordinarily accomplished by adding an explanatory paragraph to the review report, and qualifying the conclusion. Illustrative review reports with a qualified conclusion are set out in Appendix 5 to this ISRE (UK and Ireland).   **46**

When the effect of the departure is so material and pervasive to the interim financial information that the auditor concludes a qualified conclusion is not adequate to disclose the misleading or incomplete nature of the interim financial information, the auditor expresses an adverse conclusion. Illustrative review reports with an adverse conclusion are set out in Appendix 7 to this ISRE (UK and Ireland).   **47**

Limitation on scope

48   A limitation on scope ordinarily prevents the auditor from completing the review.

49   **When the auditor is unable to complete the review, the auditor should communicate, in writing, to the appropriate level of management and to those charged with governance the reason why the review cannot be completed, and consider whether it is appropriate to issue a report.**

Limitation on scope imposed by management

50   The auditor does not accept an engagement to review the interim financial information if the auditor's preliminary knowledge of the engagement circumstances indicates that the auditor would be unable to complete the review because there will be a limitation on the scope of the auditor's review imposed by management of the entity.

51   If, after accepting the engagement, management imposes a limitation on the scope of the review, the auditor requests the removal of that limitation. If management refuses to do so, the auditor is unable to complete the review and express a conclusion. In such cases, the auditor communicates, in writing, to the appropriate level of management and those charged with governance the reason why the review cannot be completed. Nevertheless, if a matter comes to the auditor's attention that causes the auditor to believe that a material adjustment to the interim financial information is necessary for it to be prepared, in all material respects, in accordance with the applicable financial reporting framework, the auditor communicates such matters in accordance with the guidance in paragraphs 38-40.

52   The auditor also considers the legal and regulatory responsibilities, including whether there is a requirement for the auditor to issue a report. If there is such a requirement, the auditor disclaims a conclusion, and provides in the review report the reason why the review cannot be completed. However, if a matter comes to the auditor's attention that causes the auditor to believe that a material adjustment to the interim financial information is necessary for it to be prepared, in all material respects, in accordance with the applicable financial reporting framework, the auditor also communicates such a matter in the report.

Other limitations on scope

53   A limitation on scope may occur due to circumstances other than a limitation on scope imposed by management. In such circumstances, the auditor is ordinarily unable to complete the review and express a conclusion and is guided by paragraphs 51-52. There may be, however, some rare circumstances where the limitation on the scope of the auditor's work is clearly confined to one or more specific matters that, while material, are not in the auditor's judgment pervasive to the interim financial information. In such circumstances, the auditor modifies the review report by indicating that, except for the matter which is described in an explanatory paragraph to the review report, the review was conducted in accordance with this ISRE (UK and Ireland), and by qualifying the conclusion. Illustrative review reports with a qualified conclusion are set out in Appendix 6 to this ISRE (UK and Ireland).

54   The auditor may have expressed a qualified opinion on the audit of the latest annual financial statements because of a limitation on the scope of that audit. The auditor considers whether that limitation on scope still exists and, if so, the implications for the review report.

Going concern and significant uncertainties

In certain circumstances, an emphasis of matter paragraph may be added to a   **55**
review report, without affecting the auditor's conclusion, to highlight a matter that
is included in a note to the interim financial information that more extensively
discusses the matter. The paragraph would preferably be included after the
conclusion paragraph and ordinarily refers to the fact that the conclusion is not
qualified in this respect.

If adequate disclosure is made in the interim financial information, the   **56**
auditor should add an emphasis of matter paragraph to the review report
to highlight a material uncertainty relating to an event or condition that may
cast significant doubt on the entity's ability to continue as a going concern.

The auditor may have modified a prior audit or review report by adding an   **57**
emphasis of matter paragraph to highlight a material uncertainty relating to an
event or condition that may cast significant doubt on the entity's ability to continue
as a going concern. If the material uncertainty still exists and adequate disclosure
is made in the interim financial information, the auditor modifies the review report
on the current interim financial information by adding a paragraph to highlight the
continued material uncertainty.

If, as a result of inquiries or other review procedures, a material uncertainty   **58**
relating to an event or condition comes to the auditor's attention that may cast
significant doubt on the entity's ability to continue as a going concern, and
adequate disclosure is made in the interim financial information the auditor
modifies the review report by adding an emphasis of matter paragraph.

If a material uncertainty that casts significant doubt about the entity's ability   **59**
to continue as a going concern is not adequately disclosed in the interim
financial information, the auditor should express a qualified or adverse
conclusion, as appropriate. The report should include specific reference to
the fact that there is such a material uncertainty.

The auditor should consider modifying the review report by adding a   **60**
paragraph to highlight a significant uncertainty (other than a going
concern problem) that came to the auditor's attention, the resolution of
which is dependent upon future events and which may affect the interim
financial information.

Requests to discontinue an interim review engagement

There may be rare circumstances in which the auditor indicates in advance to   **60-1**
those charged with governance that the review report may be modified for one
or more of the reasons set out in paragraphs 45 to 60 above. In these cases those
charged with governance may choose to request the auditor to discontinue the
review engagement rather than include a modified review report with the
interim financial information.

The auditor informs the audit committee, where one exists, of this situation as   **60-2**
soon as practicable. If information is communicated orally, the auditor
subsequently documents the communication as appropriate. For a listed
entity, if, in the auditor's judgment, the entity does not take appropriate
action to address the auditor's concerns regarding the financial information
to be published, the auditor considers requesting those charged with
governance to discuss the matter with the entity's brokers, including whether
the matter should be reported to the relevant regulatory authority. The auditor
also evaluates whether to resign as the entity's auditor and include the auditor's

reasons for resigning in a statement of circumstances as required by the Companies Act. The auditor may wish to take legal advice when considering resignation.

Other considerations

61   The terms of the engagement include management's agreement that where any document containing interim financial information indicates that such information has been reviewed by the entity's auditor, the review report will also be included in the document. If management has not included the review report in the document, the auditor considers seeking legal advice to assist in determining the appropriate course of action in the circumstances.

62   If the auditor has issued a modified review report and management issues the interim financial information without including the modified review report in the document containing the interim financial information, the auditor considers seeking legal advice to assist in determining the appropriate course of action in the circumstances, and the possibility of resigning from the appointment to audit the annual financial statements.

63   Interim financial information consisting of a condensed set of financial statements does not necessarily include all the information that would be included in a complete set of financial statements, but may rather present an explanation of the events and changes that are significant to an understanding of the changes in the financial position and performance of the entity since the annual reporting date. This is because it is presumed that the users of the interim financial information will have access to the latest audited financial statements, such as is the case with listed entities. In other circumstances, the auditor discusses with management the need for such interim financial information to include a statement that it is to be read in conjunction with the latest audited financial statements. In the absence of such a statement, the auditor considers whether, without a reference to the latest audited financial statements, the interim financial information is misleading in the circumstances, and the implications for the review report.

Documentation

64   **The auditor should prepare review documentation that is sufficient and appropriate to provide a basis for the auditor's conclusion and to provide evidence that the review was performed in accordance with this ISRE (UK and Ireland) and applicable legal and regulatory requirements.** The documentation enables an experienced auditor having no previous connection with the engagement to understand the nature, timing and extent of the inquiries made, and analytical and other review procedures applied, information obtained, and any significant matters considered during the performance of the review, including the disposition of such matters.

Effective date

65   This ISRE (UK and Ireland) is effective for reviews of interim financial information for periods ending on or after 20 September 2007. Early adoption is permitted.

Public sector perspective

Paragraph 10 requires that the auditor and the client agree on the terms of **1**
*engagement. Paragraph 11 explains that an engagement letter helps to avoid
misunderstandings regarding the nature of the engagement and, in particular, the
objective and scope of the review, management's responsibilities, the extent of the
auditor's responsibilities, the assurance obtained, and the nature and form of the
report. Law or regulation governing review engagements in the public sector
ordinarily mandates the appointment of the auditor. Consequently, engagement
letters may not be a widespread practice in the public sector. Nevertheless, an
engagement letter setting out the matters referred to in paragraph 11 may be
useful to both the public sector auditor and the client. Public sector auditors,
therefore, consider agreeing with the client the terms of a review engagement by
way of an engagement letter.*

In the public sector, the auditor's statutory audit obligation may extend to other **2**
*work, such as a review of interim financial information. Where this is the case, the
public sector auditor cannot avoid such an obligation and, consequently, may not
be in a position not to accept (see paragraph 50) or to withdraw from a review
engagement (see paragraphs 36 and 40(b)). The public sector auditor also may
not be in the position to resign from the appointment to audit the annual financial
statements (see paragraphs 40(c)) and 62).*

Paragraph 41 discusses the auditor's responsibility when a matter comes to the **3**
*auditor's attention that causes the auditor to believe in the existence of fraud or
noncompliance by the entity with laws and regulations. In the public sector, the
auditor may be subject to statutory or other regulatory requirements to report
such a matter to regulatory or other public authorities.*

Appendix 1

Example of an engagement letter for a review of interim financial information

The following letter is to be used as a guide in conjunction with the consideration outlined in paragraph 10 of this ISRE (UK and Ireland) and will need to be adapted according to individual requirements and circumstances.

> For an engagement to review interim financial information prepared by a listed company in the UK or Ireland, the letter would ordinarily include paragraphs such as:
>
>> "As directors of XYZ PLC you are responsible under the [Companies Act 1985] [Companies Act 1990] for keeping proper accounting records. You are also responsible for presenting the half-yearly financial report in accordance with [International Accounting Standard 34, "Interim Financial Reporting," as adopted by the European Union] [the Accounting Standards Board Statement "Half-Yearly Financial Reports"] and the requirements of the [Disclosure and Transparency Rules of the Financial Services Authority] [Transparency (Directive 2004/109/EC) Regulations 2007 and the Transparency Rules of the Financial Regulator]." [*The second sentence identifies the applicable financial reporting framework for the entity and should be amended as necessary.*]
>>
>> "For the purpose of our review you will make available to us all of the company's accounting records and all other related information, including minutes of directors' shareholders', and audit committee meetings and of all relevant management meetings, that we consider necessary."

To the Board of Directors (or the appropriate representative of senior management)

We are providing this letter to confirm our understanding of the terms and objectives of our engagement to review the entity's interim balance sheet as at June 30, 20X1 and the related statements of income, changes in equity and cash flows for the six-month period then ended.

Our review will be conducted in accordance with International Standard on Review Engagements (UK and Ireland) 2410, "Review of Interim Financial Information Performed by the Independent Auditor of the Entity" issued by the Auditing Practices Board with the objective of providing us with a basis for reporting whether anything has come to our attention that causes us to believe that the interim financial information is not prepared, in all material respects, in accordance with the [indicate applicable financial reporting framework, including a reference to the jurisdiction or country of origin of the financial reporting when the financial reporting framework used is not International Financial Reporting Standards]. Such a review consists of making inquiries, primarily of persons responsible for financial and accounting matters, and applying analytical and other review procedures and does not, ordinarily, require corroboration of the information obtained. The scope of a review of interim financial information is substantially less than the scope of an audit conducted in accordance with International Standards on Auditing (UK and Ireland) whose objective is the expression of an opinion regarding the financial statements and, accordingly, we shall express no such opinion.

We expect to report on the interim financial information as follows:

[Include text of sample report]

Responsibility for the interim financial information, including adequate disclosure, is that of management of the entity. This includes designing, implementing and maintaining internal control relevant to the preparation and presentation of interim financial information that is free from material misstatement, whether due to fraud or error; selecting and applying appropriate accounting policies; and making accounting estimates that are reasonable in the circumstances. As part of our review, we will request written representations from management concerning assertions made in connection with the review. We will also request that where any document containing interim financial information indicates that the interim financial information has been reviewed, our report will also be included in the document.

A review of interim financial information does not provide assurance that we will become aware of all significant matters that might be identified in an audit. Further, our engagement cannot be relied upon to disclose whether fraud or errors, or illegal acts exist. However, we will inform you of any material matters that come to our attention.

We look forward to full cooperation with your staff ~~and we trust that they will make available to us whatever records, documentation and other information are requested in connection with our review.~~[2c]

[Insert additional information here regarding fee arrangements and billings, as appropriate.]

This letter will be effective for future years unless it is terminated, amended or superseded (if applicable).

Please sign and return the attached copy of this letter to indicate that it is in accordance with your understanding of the arrangements for our review of the financial statements.

Acknowledged on behalf of ABC Entity by

(signed)

Name and Title

Date

[2c] *Rendered unnecessary by the alternative text presented in the shaded note immediately before this example letter.*

Appendix 2

Analytical procedures the auditor may consider when performing a review of interim financial information

Examples of analytical procedures the auditor may consider when performing a review of interim financial information include the following:

- Comparing the interim financial information with the interim financial information of the immediately preceding interim period, with the interim financial information of the corresponding interim period of the preceding financial year, with the interim financial information that was expected by management for the current period, and with the most recent audited annual financial statements.

- Comparing current interim financial information with anticipated results, such as budgets or forecasts (for example, comparing tax balances and the relationship between the provision for income taxes to pretax income in the current interim financial information with corresponding information in (a) budgets, using expected rates, and (b) financial information for prior periods).

- Comparing current interim financial information with relevant non-financial information.

- Comparing the recorded amounts, or ratios developed from recorded amounts, to expectations developed by the auditor. The auditor develops such expectations by identifying and applying relationships that are reasonably expected to exist based on the auditor's understanding of the entity and of the industry in which the entity operates.

- Comparing ratios and indicators for the current interim period with those of entities in the same industry.

- Comparing relationships among elements in the current interim financial information with corresponding relationships in the interim financial information of prior periods, for example, expense by type as a percentage of sales, assets by type as a percentage of total assets, and percentage of change in sales to percentage of change in receivables.

- Comparing disaggregated data. The following are examples of how data may be disaggregated:

  - By period, for example, revenue or expense items disaggregated into quarterly, monthly, or weekly amounts.

  - By product line or source of revenue.

  - By location, for example, by component.

  - By attributes of the transaction, for example, revenue generated by designers, architects, or craftsmen.

  - By several attributes of the transaction, for example, sales by product and month.

Appendix 3

Example of a management representation letter

The following letter is not intended to be a standard letter. Representations by management will vary from entity to entity and from one interim period to the next.

(Entity Letterhead)

(To Auditor)   (Date)

Opening paragraphs if interim financial information comprises condensed financial statements:

This representation letter is provided in connection with your review of the condensed balance sheet of ABC Entity as of March 31, 20X1 and the related condensed statements of income, changes in equity and cash flows for the three-month period then ended for the purposes of expressing a conclusion whether anything has come to your attention that causes you to believe that the interim financial information is not prepared, in all material respects, in accordance with [indicate applicable financial reporting framework, including a reference to the jurisdiction or country of origin of the financial reporting framework when the financial reporting framework used is not International Financial Reporting Standards].

We acknowledge our responsibility for the preparation and presentation of the interim financial information in accordance with [indicate applicable financial reporting framework].

Opening paragraphs if interim financial information comprises a complete set of general purpose financial statements prepared in accordance with a financial reporting framework designed to achieve fair presentation

This representation letter is provided in connection with your review of the balance sheet of ABC Entity as of March 31, 20X1 and the related statements of income, changes in equity and cash flows for the three-month period then ended and a summary of the significant accounting policies and other explanatory notes for the purposes of expressing a conclusion whether anything has come to your attention that causes you to believe that the interim financial information does not give a true and fair view of *(or "does not present fairly, in all material respects,")* the financial position of ABC Entity as at March 31, 20X1, and of its financial performance and its cash flows in accordance with [indicate applicable financial reporting framework, including a reference to the jurisdiction or country of origin of the financial reporting framework when the financial reporting framework used is not International Financial Reporting Standards].

We acknowledge our responsibility for the fair presentation of the interim financial information in accordance with [indicate applicable financial reporting framework].

We confirm, to the best of our knowledge and belief, the following representations:

- The interim financial information referred to above has been prepared and presented in accordance with [indicate applicable financial reporting framework].

- We have made available to you all books of account and supporting documentation, and all minutes of meetings of shareholders and the board of directors (namely those held on [insert applicable dates]).

- There are no material transactions that have not been properly recorded in the accounting records underlying the interim financial information.

- There has been no known actual or possible noncompliance with laws and regulations that could have a material effect on the interim financial information in the event of noncompliance.

- We acknowledge responsibility for the design and implementation of internal control to prevent and detect fraud and error.

- We have disclosed to you all significant facts relating to any known frauds or suspected frauds that may have affected the entity.

- We have disclosed to you the results of our assessment of the risk that the interim financial information may be materially misstated as the result of fraud.

- We believe the effects of uncorrected misstatements summarized in the accompanying schedule are immaterial, both individually and in the aggregate, to the interim financial information taken as a whole.

- We confirm the completeness of the information provided to you regarding the identification of related parties.

- The following have been properly recorded and, when appropriate, adequately disclosed in the interim financial information:

    – Related party transactions, including sales, purchases, loans, transfers, leasing arrangements and guarantees, and amounts receivable from or payable to related parties;

    – Guarantees, whether written or oral, under which the entity is contingently liable; and

    – Agreements and options to buy back assets previously sold.

- The presentation and disclosure of the fair value measurements of assets and liabilities are in accordance with [indicate applicable financial reporting framework]. The assumptions used reflect our intent and ability to carry specific courses of action on behalf of the entity, where relevant to the fair value measurements or disclosure.

- We have no plans or intentions that may materially affect the carrying value or classification of assets and liabilities reflected in the interim financial information.

- We have no plans to abandon lines of product or other plans or intentions that will result in any excess or obsolete inventory, and no inventory is stated at an amount in excess of realizable value.

- The entity has satisfactory title to all assets and there are no liens or encumbrances on the entity's assets.

- We have recorded or disclosed, as appropriate, all liabilities, both actual and contingent.

- [Add any additional representations related to new accounting standards that are being implemented for the first time and consider any additional representations required by a new International Standard on Auditing (UK and Ireland) that are relevant to interim financial information.]

To the best of our knowledge and belief, no events have occurred subsequent to the balance sheet date and through the date of this letter that may require adjustment to or disclosure in the aforementioned interim financial information.

(Senior Executive Officer)

(Senior Financial Officer)

Appendix 4

Examples of review reports on interim financial information

An example review report for a UK or Irish company listed in the UK or Ireland is set out in Appendix 8.

Complete set of General Purpose Financial Statements prepared in accordance with a Financial Reporting Framework designed to achieve fair presentation (see paragraph 43(i))

Report on review of interim financial information

(Appropriate addressee)

Introduction

We have reviewed the accompanying balance sheet of ABC Entity as of March 31, 20X1 and the related statements of income, changes in equity and cash flows for the threemonth period then ended, and a summary of significant accounting policies and other explanatory notes.[3] Management is responsible for the preparation and fair presentation of this interim financial information in accordance with [indicate applicable financial reporting framework]. Our responsibility is to express a conclusion on this interim financial information based on our review.

Scope of review

We conducted our review in accordance with International Standard on Review Engagements 2410, "Review of Interim Financial Information Performed by the Independent Auditor of the Entity." A review of interim financial information consists of making inquiries, primarily of persons responsible for financial and accounting matters, and applying analytical and other review procedures. A review is substantially less in scope than an audit conducted in accordance with International Standards on Auditing and consequently does not enable us to obtain assurance that we would become aware of all significant matters that might be identified in an audit. Accordingly, we do not express an audit opinion.

Conclusion

Based on our review, nothing has come to our attention that causes us to believe that the accompanying interim financial information does not give a true and fair view of (or "does not present fairly, in all material respects,") the financial position of the entity as at March 31, 20X1, and of its financial performance and its cash flows for the threemonth period then ended in accordance with [applicable financial reporting framework, including a reference to the jurisdiction or country of origin of the financial reporting framework when the financial reporting framework used is not International Financial Reporting Standards].

---

[3] *The auditor may wish to specify the regulatory authority or equivalent with whom the interim financial information is filed.*

AUDITOR

Date

Address

Other interim financial information (see paragraph 43(j))

Report on review of interim financial information

(Appropriate addressee)

Introduction

We have reviewed the accompanying [condensed] balance sheet of ABC Entity as of March 31, 20X1 and the related [condensed] statements of income, changes in equity and cash flows for the three-month period then ended.[4] Management is responsible for the preparation and presentation of this interim financial information in accordance with [indicate applicable financial reporting framework]. Our responsibility is to express a conclusion on this interim financial information based on our review.

Scope of review

We conducted our review in accordance with International Standard on Review Engagements 2410, "Review of Interim Financial Information Performed by the Independent Auditor of the Entity." A review of interim financial information consists of making inquiries, primarily of persons responsible for financial and accounting matters, and applying analytical and other review procedures. A review is substantially less in scope than an audit conducted in accordance with International Standards on Auditing and consequently does not enable us to obtain assurance that we would become aware of all significant matters that might be identified in an audit. Accordingly, we do not express an audit opinion.

Conclusion

Based on our review, nothing has come to our attention that causes us to believe that the accompanying interim financial information is not prepared, in all material respects, in accordance with [applicable financial reporting framework, including a reference to the jurisdiction or country of origin of the financial reporting framework when the financial reporting framework used is not International Financial Reporting Standards].

AUDITOR

Date

Address

---

[4] *The auditor may wish to specify the regulatory authority or equivalent with whom the interim financial information is filed.*

Appendix 5

Examples of review reports with a qualified conclusion for a departure from the applicable Financial Reporting Framework

An example unqualified review report for a UK or Irish company listed in the UK or Ireland is set out in Appendix 8 and can be tailored to give a report with a qualified conclusion when appropriate.

Complete set of General Purpose Financial Statements prepared in accordance with a Financial Reporting Framework designed to achieve fair presentation (see paragraph 43(i))

Report on review of interim financial information

(Appropriate addressee)

Introduction

We have reviewed the accompanying balance sheet of ABC Entity as of March 31, 20X1 and the related statements of income, changes in equity and cash flows for the threemonth period then ended, and a summary of significant accounting policies and other explanatory notes.[5] Management is responsible for the preparation and fair presentation of this interim financial information in accordance with [indicate applicable financial reporting framework]. Our responsibility is to express a conclusion on this interim financial information based on our review.

Scope of review

We conducted our review in accordance with International Standard on Review Engagements 2410, "Review of Interim Financial Information Performed by the Independent Auditor of the Entity." A review of interim financial information consists of making inquiries, primarily of persons responsible for financial and accounting matters, and applying analytical and other review procedures. A review is substantially less in scope than an audit conducted in accordance with International Standards on Auditing and consequently does not enable us to obtain assurance that we would become aware of all significant matters that might be identified in an audit. Accordingly, we do not express an audit opinion.

Basis for qualified conclusion

Based on information provided to us by management, ABC Entity has excluded from property and long-term debt certain lease obligations that we believe should be capitalized to conform with [indicate applicable financial reporting framework]. This information indicates that if these lease obligations were capitalized at March 31, 20X1, property would be increased by \$_____, long-term debt by \$_____, and net income and earnings per share would be increased (decreased) by \$_____, \$_____, \$_____, and \$_____, respectively for the three-month period then ended.

---

[5] *The auditor may wish to specify the regulatory authority or equivalent with whom the interim financial information is filed.*

Qualified conclusion

Based on our review, with the exception of the matter described in the preceding paragraph, nothing has come to our attention that causes us to believe that the accompanying interim financial information does not give a true and fair view of (or "does not present fairly, in all material respects,") the financial position of the entity as at March 31, 20X1, and of its financial performance and its cash flows for the threemonth period then ended in accordance with [indicate applicable financial reporting framework, including the reference to the jurisdiction or country of origin of the financial reporting framework when the financial reporting framework used is not International Financial Reporting Standards].

AUDITOR

Date

Address

Other interim financial information (see paragraph 43(j))

Report on review of interim financial information

(Appropriate addressee)

Introduction

We have reviewed the accompanying [condensed] balance sheet of ABC Entity as of March 31, 20X1 and the related [condensed] statements of income, changes in equity and cash flows for the three-month period then ended.[6] Management is responsible for the preparation and presentation of this interim financial information in accordance with [indicate applicable financial reporting framework]. Our responsibility is to express a conclusion on this interim financial information based on our review.

Scope of review

We conducted our review in accordance with International Standard on Review Engagements 2410, "Review of Interim Financial Information Performed by the Independent Auditor of the Entity." A review of interim financial information consists of making inquiries, primarily of persons responsible for financial and accounting matters, and applying analytical and other review procedures. A review is substantially less in scope than an audit conducted in accordance with International Standards on Auditing and consequently does not enable us to obtain assurance that we would become aware of all significant matters that might be identified in an audit. Accordingly, we do not express an audit opinion.

Basis for qualified conclusion

Based on information provided to us by management, ABC Entity has excluded from property and long-term debt certain lease obligations that we believe should

---

[6] *The auditor may wish to specify the regulatory authority or equivalent with whom the interim financial information is filed.*

be capitalized to conform with [indicate applicable financial reporting framework]. This information indicates that if these lease obligations were capitalized at March 31, 20X1, property would be increased by $_____, long-term debt by $_____, and net income and earnings per share would be increased (decreased) by $_____, $_____, $_____, and $_____, respectively for the three-month period then ended.

Qualified conclusion

Based on our review, with the exception of the matter described in the preceding paragraph, nothing has come to our attention that causes us to believe that the accompanying interim financial information is not prepared, in all material respects, in accordance with [indicate applicable financial reporting framework, including a reference to the jurisdiction or country of origin of the financial reporting framework when the financial reporting framework used is not International Financial Reporting Standards].

AUDITOR

Date

Address

Appendix 6

Examples of review reports with a qualified conclusion for a limitation on scope not imposed by management

An example unqualified review report for a UK or Irish company listed in the UK or Ireland is set out in Appendix 8 and can be tailored to give a report with a qualified conclusion when appropriate.

Complete set of General Purpose Financial Statements prepared in accordance with a Financial Reporting Framework designed to achieve fair presentation (see paragraph 43(i))

Report on review of interim financial information

(Appropriate addressee)

Introduction

We have reviewed the accompanying balance sheet of ABC Entity as of March 31, 20X1 and the related statements of income, changes in equity and cash flows for the threemonth period then ended, and a summary of significant accounting policies and other explanatory notes.[7] Management is responsible for the preparation and fair presentation of this interim financial information in accordance with [indicate applicable financial reporting framework]. Our responsibility is to express a conclusion on this interim financial information based on our review.

Scope of review

Except as explained in the following paragraph, we conducted our review in accordance with International Standard on Review Engagements 2410, "Review of Interim Financial Information Performed by the Independent Auditor of the Entity." A review of interim financial information consists of making inquiries, primarily of persons responsible for financial and accounting matters, and applying analytical and other review procedures. A review is substantially less in scope than an audit conducted in accordance with International Standards on Auditing and consequently does not enable us to obtain assurance that we would become aware of all significant matters that might be identified in an audit. Accordingly, we do not express an audit opinion.

Basis for qualified conclusion

As a result of a fire in a branch office on (date) that destroyed its accounts receivable records, we were unable to complete our review of accounts receivable totaling $_____ included in the interim financial information. The entity is in the process of reconstructing these records and is uncertain as to whether these records will support the amount shown above and the related allowance for uncollectible accounts. Had we been able to complete our review of accounts receivable, matters might have come to our attention indicating that adjustments might be necessary to the interim financial information.

---

[7] *The auditor may wish to specify the regulatory authority or equivalent with whom the interim financial information is filed.*

Qualified conclusion

Except for the adjustments to the interim financial information that we might have become aware of had it not been for the situation described above, based on our review, nothing has come to our attention that causes us to believe that the accompanying interim financial information does not give a true and fair view of (or "does not present fairly, in all material respects,") the financial position of the entity as at March 31, 20X1, and of its financial performance and its cash flows for the three-month period then ended in accordance with [indicate applicable financial reporting framework, including a reference to the jurisdiction or country of origin of the financial reporting framework when the financial reporting framework used is not International Financial Reporting Standards].

AUDITOR

Date

Address

Other interim financial information (see paragraph 43(j))

Report on review of interim financial information

(Appropriate addressee)

Introduction

We have reviewed the accompanying [condensed] balance sheet of ABC Entity as of March 31, 20X1 and the related [condensed] statements of income, changes in equity and cash flows for the three-month period then ended.[8] Management is responsible for the preparation and presentation of this interim financial information in accordance with [indicate applicable financial reporting framework]. Our responsibility is to express a conclusion on this interim financial information based on our review.

Scope of review

Except as explained in the following paragraph, we conducted our review in accordance with International Standards on Review Engagements 2410, "Review of Interim Financial Information Performed by the Auditor of the Entity." A review of interim financial information consists of making inquiries, primarily of persons responsible for financial and accounting matters, and applying analytical and other review procedures. A review is substantially less in scope than an audit conducted in accordance with International Standards on Auditing and consequently does not enable us to obtain assurance that we would become aware of all significant matters that might be identified in an audit. Accordingly, we do not express an audit opinion.

---

[8] *The auditor may wish to specify the regulatory authority or equivalent with whom the interim financial information is filed.*

Basis for qualified conclusion

As a result of a fire in a branch office on (date) that destroyed its accounts receivable records, we were unable to complete our review of accounts receivable totaling $_____ included in the interim financial information. The entity is in the process of reconstructing these records and is uncertain as to whether these records will support the amount shown above and the related allowance for uncollectible accounts. Had we been able to complete our review of accounts receivable, matters might have come to our attention indicating that adjustments might be necessary to the interim financial information.

Qualified conclusion

Except for the adjustments to the interim financial information that we might have become aware of had it not been for the situation described above, based on our review, nothing has come to our attention that causes us to believe that the accompanying interim financial information is not prepared, in all material respects, in accordance with [indicate applicable financial reporting framework, including a reference to the jurisdiction or country of origin of the financial reporting framework when the financial reporting framework used is not International Financial Reporting Standards].

AUDITOR

Date

Address

Appendix 7

Examples of review reports with an adverse conclusion for a departure from the applicable Financial Reporting Framework

An example unqualified review report for a UK or Irish company listed in the UK or Ireland is set out in Appendix 8 and can be tailored to give a report with an adverse conclusion when appropriate.

Complete set of General Purpose Financial Statements prepared in accordance with a Financial Reporting Framework designed to achieve fair presentation (see paragraph 43(i))

Report on review of interim financial information

(Appropriate addressee)

Introduction

We have reviewed the accompanying balance sheet of ABC Entity as of March 31, 20X1 and the related statements of income, changes in equity and cash flows for the three-month period then ended, and a summary of significant accounting policies and other explanatory notes.[9] Management is responsible for the preparation and fair presentation of this interim financial information in accordance with [indicate applicable financial reporting framework]. Our responsibility is to express a conclusion on this interim financial information based on our review.

Scope of review

We conducted our review in accordance with International Standard on Review Engagements 2410, "Review of Interim Financial Information Performed by the Auditor of the Entity." A review of interim financial information consists of making inquiries, primarily of persons responsible for financial and accounting matters, and applying analytical and other review procedures. A review is substantially less in scope than an audit conducted in accordance with International Standards on Auditing and consequently does not enable us to obtain assurance that we would become aware of all significant matters that might be identified in an audit. Accordingly, we do not express an audit opinion.

Basis for adverse conclusion

Commencing this period, management of the entity ceased to consolidate the financial statements of its subsidiary companies since management considers consolidation to be inappropriate because of the existence of new substantial non-controlling interests. This is not in accordance with [indicate applicable financial reporting framework, including a reference to the jurisdiction or country of origin of the financial reporting framework when the financial reporting framework used is not International Financial Reporting Standards]. Had consolidated financial

---

[9] *The auditor may wish to specify the regulatory authority or equivalent with whom the interim financial information is filed.*

statements been prepared, virtually every account in the interim financial information would have been materially different.

Adverse conclusion

Our review indicates that, because the entity's investment in subsidiary companies is not accounted for on a consolidated basis, as described in the preceding paragraph, this interim financial information does not give a true and fair view of (or "does not present fairly, in all material respects,") the financial position of the entity as at March 31, 20X1, and of its financial performance and its cash flows for the three-month period then ended in accordance with [indicate applicable financial reporting framework, including a reference to the jurisdiction or country of origin of the financial reporting framework when the financial reporting framework used is not International Financial Reporting Standards].

AUDITOR

Date

Address

Other interim financial information (see paragraph 43(j))

Report on review of interim financial information

(Appropriate addressee)

Introduction

We have reviewed the accompanying [condensed] balance sheet of ABC Entity as of March 31, 20X1 and the related [condensed] statements of income, changes in equity and cash flows for the three-month period then ended.[10] Management is responsible for the preparation and presentation of this interim financial information in accordance with [indicate applicable financial reporting framework]. Our responsibility is to express a conclusion on this interim financial information based on our review.

Scope of review

We conducted our review in accordance with International Standard on Review Engagements 2410, "Review of Interim Financial Information Performed by the Independence Auditor of the Entity." A review of interim financial information consists of making inquiries, primarily of persons responsible for financial and accounting matters, and applying analytical and other review procedures. A review is substantially less in scope than an audit conducted in accordance with International Standards on Auditing and consequently does not enable us to obtain assurance that we would become aware of all significant matters that might be identified in an audit. Accordingly, we do not express an audit opinion.

---

[10] *The auditor may wish to specify the regulatory authority or equivalent with whom the interim financial information is filed.*

Basis for adverse conclusion

Commencing this period, management of the entity ceased to consolidate the financial statements of its subsidiary companies since management considers consolidation to be inappropriate because of the existence of new substantial non-controlling interests. This is not in accordance with *[indicate applicable financial reporting framework, including the reference to the jurisdiction or country of origin of the financial reporting framework when the financial reporting framework used is not International Financial Reporting Standards]*. Had consolidated financial statements been prepared, virtually every account in the interim financial information would have been materially different.

Adverse conclusion

Our review indicates that, because the entity's investment in subsidiary companies is not accounted for on a consolidated basis, as described in the preceding paragraph, this interim financial information is not prepared, in all material respects, in accordance with *[indicate applicable financial reporting framework, including a reference to the jurisdiction or country of origin of the financial reporting framework when the financial reporting framework used is not International Financial Reporting Standards]*.

AUDITOR

Date

Address

Appendix 8

Example review report for a UK or Irish company listed in the UK or Ireland preparing a half-yearly financial report in compliance with IAS 34 as adopted by the European Union

INDEPENDENT REVIEW REPORT TO XYZ PLC

Introduction

We have been engaged by the company to review the condensed set of financial statements in the half-yearly financial report for the six months ended ... which comprises [specify the primary financial statements and the related explanatory notes that have been reviewed].[10a] We have read the other information contained in the halfyearly financial report and considered whether it contains any apparent misstatements or material inconsistencies with the information in the condensed set of financial statements.

Directors' responsibilities

The half-yearly financial report is the responsibility of, and has been approved by, the directors. The directors are responsible for preparing the half-yearly financial report in accordance with the [Disclosure and Transparency Rules of the United Kingdom's Financial Services Authority] [Transparency (Directive 2004/109/EC) Regulations 2007 and the Transparency Rules of the Republic of Ireland's Financial Regulator].

As disclosed in note X, the annual financial statements of the [group/company] are prepared in accordance with IFRSs as adopted by the European Union. The condensed set of financial statements included in this half-yearly financial report has been prepared in accordance with International Accounting Standard 34, "Interim Financial Reporting," as adopted by the European Union.

Our responsibility

Our responsibility is to express to the Company a conclusion on the condensed set of financial statements in the half-yearly financial report based on our review.

Scope of review

We conducted our review in accordance with International Standard on Review Engagements (UK and Ireland) 2410, Review of Interim Financial Information Performed by the Independent Auditor of the Entity *issued by the Auditing Practices Board for use in [the United Kingdom] [Ireland]. A review of interim financial information consists of making enquiries, primarily of persons responsible for financial and accounting matters, and applying analytical and other review procedures. A review is substantially less in scope than an*

[10a] *Review reports of entities that do not publish their half-yearly reports on a web site or publish them using "PDF" format may continue to refer to the pages of the half-yearly report.*

audit conducted in accordance with International Standards on Auditing (UK and Ireland) and consequently does not enable us to obtain assurance that we would become aware of all significant matters that might be identified in an audit. Accordingly, we do not express an audit opinion.

Conclusion

Based on our review, nothing has come to our attention that causes us to believe that the condensed set of financial statements in the half-yearly financial report for the six months ended ... is not prepared, in all material respects, in accordance with International Accounting Standard 34 as adopted by the European Union and [the Disclosure and Transparency Rules of the United Kingdom's Financial Services Authority] [the Transparency (Directive 2004/109/EC) Regulations 2007 and the Transparency Rules of the Republic of Ireland's Financial Regulator].

AUDITOR

Date

Address

Appendix 9

Summary of particular requirements of half-yearly reports prepared by listed companies in the UK and Ireland

This Appendix sets out a summary of particular requirements of the FSA's Disclosure and Transparency Rules (DTRs) applicable to half-yearly financial reports prepared by an "issuer" whose shares or debt securities are admitted to trading and whose home state is the United Kingdom, subject to the exemptions in DTR 4.4. Equivalent requirements are included in the Irish Transparency (Directive 2004/109/EC) Regulations 2007 (specifically Regulations 6 – 8 in Part 2, subject to the exemptions in Part 3) and Transparency Rules of the Financial Regulator in the Republic of Ireland (specifically Rule 6.2). It also gives a summary of Companies Act requirements relevant to the publication of non-statutory accounts. It does not set out in full all the applicable requirements and, therefore, is not intended to provide a substitute for the auditor reading the applicable Rules, Regulations and legislation to obtain an understanding of them.

FSA Disclosure and Transparency Rules

Rule 4.2.3 requires that an issuer publish a half-yearly financial report, containing:

(1)   a condensed set of financial statements;

(2)   an interim management report; and

(3)   responsibility statements.

Rule 4.2.4 requires that if an issuer is required to prepare consolidated accounts, the condensed set of financial statements must be prepared in accordance with International Accounting Standard 34 *Interim Financial Reporting*. (Under the FSA's definitions of "International Accounting Standards" this will be IAS 34 as adopted by the European Union.)

If an issuer is not required to prepare consolidated accounts, the condensed set of financial information must contain, as a minimum, the following:

(a)   a condensed balance sheet;

(b)   a condensed profit and loss account; and

(c)   explanatory notes on these accounts.

Rule 4.2.5 requires that the condensed balance sheet and condensed profit and loss account referred to in (a) and (b) above must:

- follow the same principles for recognising and measuring as when preparing annual financial reports,

- show each of the headings and subtotals included in the most recent annual financial statements of the issuer. Additional line items must be included if, as a result of their omission, the half-yearly financial statements would give a misleading view of the assets, liabilities, financial position and profit or loss of the issuer.

For issuers not required to prepare consolidated accounts the Rules also set out further specific requirements in relation to comparative information and the content of the explanatory notes.

Rule 4.2.6 requires that the accounting policies and presentation applied to the halfyearly figures must be consistent with those applied in the latest published annual accounts except where:

(1)   the accounting policies and presentation are to be changed in the subsequent annual financial statements, in which case the new accounting policies and presentation should be followed, and the changes and the reasons for the changes should be disclosed in the half-yearly report; or

(2)   the FSA otherwise agrees.

Companies may choose to have the half-yearly financial report reviewed or audited by an auditor. Rule 4.2.9 requires that "if the half-yearly financial report has been audited or reviewed by auditors pursuant to the Auditing Practices Board guidance on Review of Interim Financial Information, the audit report or review report must be reproduced in full."

Responsibility statements

Rule 4.2.10 requires that for each person making a responsibility statement, the statement must confirm that to the best of his or her knowledge, inter alia:

"the condensed set of financial statements, which has been prepared in accordance with the applicable set of accounting standards, gives a true and fair view of the assets, liabilities, financial position and profit or loss of the issuer, or the undertakings included in the consolidation as a whole ..."

However, Rule 4.2.10 also provides that:

"A person making a responsibility statement will satisfy the requirement ... to confirm that the condensed set of financial statements gives a true and fair view ... by including a statement that the condensed set of financial statements have been prepared in accordance with:

(a)   IAS 34; or

(b)   for UK issuers not using IFRS, pronouncements on interim reporting issued by the Accounting Standards Board[10b]; or

(c)   for all other issuers not using IFRS, a national accounting standard relating to interim reporting,

provided always that a person making such a statement has reasonable grounds to be satisfied that the condensed set of financial statements prepared in accordance with such a standard is not misleading."

[10b] *For half-yearly periods ending on or after 20 September 2007, the relevant ASB pronouncement is the Statement "Half-Yearly Financial Reports".*

Companies Act requirements

United Kingdom

Financial statements included in half-yearly financial reports constitute non-statutory accounts under the provisions of the Companies Act[10c] and therefore must include a statement indicating:

(a)   that they are not the statutory accounts;

(b)   whether statutory accounts for any relevant financial year have been delivered to the registrar of companies;

(c)   whether the auditors reported on the statutory accounts for any such year; and

(d)   if so, whether it was qualified or unqualified, or included an emphasis of matter, or contained a statement by the auditor required under the Companies Act[10d] (accounting records or returns inadequate or accounts or directors' remuneration report not agreeing with records and returns, or failure to obtain necessary information and explanations).

Republic of Ireland

In the Republic of Ireland, financial statements included in a half-yearly report made by a single entity constitute abbreviated accounts under section 19 of the Companies (Amendment) Act, 1986. Financial statements included in a half-yearly report made by a group constitute abbreviated group accounts under regulation 40 of the European Communities (Companies: Group Accounts) Regulations, 1992. This states that where a parent undertaking publishes abbreviated group accounts relating to any financial year, it shall also publish a statement indicating:

(a)   that the abbreviated group accounts are not the group accounts, copies of which are required by law to be annexed to the annual return,

(b)   whether the copies of the group accounts so required to be annexed have in fact been so annexed,

(c)   whether the auditors have made a report under section 193 of the Companies Act, 1990 in respect of the group accounts which relate to any financial year with which the abbreviated group accounts purport to deal, and

(d)   whether the report of the auditors contained any qualifications.

The statement required for a single entity is similar.

[10c] *Relevant references are: for the Companies Act 1985 – section 240 (the equivalent legislation in Northern Ireland is Article 243(3) of the Companies (Northern Ireland) Order, 1986); for the Companies Act 2006 – section 435 (this also applies in Northern Ireland).*

[10d] *Relevant references are: for the Companies Act 1985 – section 237(2) and (3); for the Companies Act 2006 – section 498(2) and (3).*